I0814855
PRESENTED
TO:
BY:
ON:

NKJV

STUDY BIBLE

FOR KIDS

FOR KIDS

THE PREMIER NKJV
STUDY BIBLE FOR KIDS

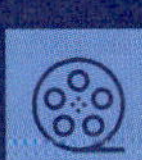

NKJV Study Bible for Kids

Published by Thomas Nelson, 2024. Thomas Nelson is a registered trademark of HarperCollins Christian Publishing, Inc.

Library of Congress Control Number: 2023947128

Printed in China

24 25 26 27 28 29 30 31 /DSC/ 18 17 16 15 14 13 12 11 10

PREFACE TO THE New King James Version®

Purpose

In the preface to the 1611 edition, the translators of the Authorized Version, known popularly as the King James Bible, state that it was not their purpose "to make a new translation ... but to make a good one better." Indebted to the earlier work of William Tyndale and others, they saw their best contribution to consist in revising and enhancing the excellence of the English versions which had sprung from the Reformation of the sixteenth century. In harmony with the purpose of the King James scholars, the translators and editors of the present work have not pursued a goal of innovation. They have perceived the Holy Bible, New King James Version, as a continuation of the labors of the earlier translators, thus unlocking for today's readers the spiritual treasures found especially in the Authorized Version of the Holy Scriptures.

A Living Legacy

For nearly four hundred years, and throughout several revisions of its English form, the King James Bible has been deeply revered among the English-speaking peoples of the world. The precision of translation for which it is historically renowned, and its majesty of style, have enabled that monumental version of the word of God to become the mainspring of the religion, language, and legal foundations of our civilization.

Although the Elizabethan period and our own era share in zeal for technical advance, the former period was more aggressively devoted to classical learning. Along with this awakened concern for the classics came a flourishing companion interest in the Scriptures, an interest that was enlivened by the conviction that the manuscripts were providentially handed down and were a trustworthy record of the inspired Word of God. The King James translators were committed to producing an English Bible that would be a precise translation, and by no means a paraphrase or a broadly approximate rendering. On the one hand, the scholars were almost as familiar with the original languages of the Bible as with their native English. On the other hand, their reverence for the divine Author and His Word assured a translation of the Scriptures in which only a principle of utmost accuracy could be accepted.

In 1786 Catholic scholar Alexander Geddes said of the King James Bible, "If accuracy and strictest attention to the letter of the text be supposed to constitute an excellent version, this is of all versions the most excellent." George Bernard Shaw became a literary legend in the twentieth century because of his severe and often humorous criticisms of our most cherished values. Surprisingly, however, Shaw pays the following tribute to the scholars commissioned by King James: "The translation was extraordinarily well done because to the translators what they were translating was not merely a curious collection of ancient books written by different authors in different stages of culture, but the Word of God divinely revealed through His chosen and expressly inspired scribes. In this conviction they carried out their work with boundless reverence and care and achieved a beautifully artistic result." History agrees with these estimates. Therefore, while seeking to unveil the excellent *form* of the traditional English Bible, special care has also been taken in the present edition to preserve the work of *precision* which is the legacy of the 1611 translators.

Complete Equivalence in Translation

Where new translation has been necessary in the New King James Version, the most complete representation of the original has been rendered by considering the history of usage and etymology of words in their contexts. This principle of complete equivalence seeks to preserve *all* of the information in the text, while presenting it in good literary form. Dynamic equivalence, a recent procedure in Bible translation, commonly results in paraphrasing where a more literal rendering is needed to reflect a specific and vital sense. For example, complete equivalence truly renders the original text in expressions such as "lifted her voice and wept" (Gen. 21:16); "I gave you cleanness of teeth" (Amos 4:6); "Jesus met them, saying, 'Rejoice!'" (Matt. 28:9); and "Woman, what does your concern have to do with Me?" (John 2:4). Complete equivalence translates fully, in order to provide an English text that is both accurate and readable.

In keeping with the principle of complete equivalence, it is the policy to translate interjections which are commonly omitted in modern language renderings of the Bible. As an example, the interjection *behold,* in the older King James editions, continues to have a place in English usage, especially in dramatically calling attention to a spectacular

scene, or an event of profound importance such as the Immanuel prophecy of Isaiah 7:14. Consequently, *behold* is retained for these occasions in the present edition. However, the Hebrew and Greek originals for this word can be translated variously, depending on the circumstances in the passage. Therefore, in addition to *behold,* words such as *indeed, look, see,* and *surely* are also rendered to convey the appropriate sense suggested by the context in each case.

In faithfulness to God and to our readers, it was deemed appropriate that all participating scholars sign a statement affirming their belief in the verbal and plenary inspiration of Scripture, and in the inerrancy of the original autographs.

Devotional Quality

The King James scholars readily appreciated the intrinsic beauty of divine revelation. They accordingly disciplined their talents to render well-chosen English words of their time, as well as a graceful, often musical arrangement of language, which has stirred the hearts of Bible readers through the years. The translators, the committees, and the editors of the present edition, while sensitive to the late-twentieth-century English idiom, and while adhering faithfully to the Hebrew, Aramaic, and Greek texts, have sought to maintain those lyrical and devotional qualities that are so highly regarded in the Authorized Version. This devotional quality is especially apparent in the poetic and prophetic books, although even the relatively plain style of the Gospels and Epistles cannot strictly be likened, as sometimes suggested, to modern newspaper style. The Koine Greek of the New Testament is influenced by the Hebrew background of the writers, for whom even the gospel narratives were not merely flat utterance, but often song in various degrees of rhythm.

The Style

Students of the Bible applaud the timeless devotional character of our historic Bible. Yet it is also universally understood that our language, like all living languages, has undergone profound change since 1611. Subsequent revisions of the King James Bible have sought to keep abreast of changes in English speech. The present work is a further step toward this objective. Where obsolescence and other reading difficulties exist, present-day vocabulary, punctuation, and grammar have been carefully integrated. Words representing ancient objects, such as *chariot* and *phylactery,* have no modern substitutes and are therefore retained.

A special feature of the New King James Version is its conformity to the thought flow of the 1611 Bible. The reader discovers that the sequence and selection of words, phrases, and clauses of the new edition, while much clearer, are so close to the traditional that there is remarkable ease in listening to the reading of either edition while following with the other.

In the discipline of translating biblical and other ancient languages, a standard method of transliteration, that is, the English spelling of untranslated words, such as names of persons and places, has never been commonly adopted. In keeping with the design of the present work, the King James spelling of untranslated words is retained, although made uniform throughout. For example, instead of the spellings *Isaiah* and *Elijah* in the Old Testament, and *Esaias* and *Elias* in the New Testament, *Isaiah* and *Elijah* now appear in both Testaments.

King James doctrinal and theological terms, for example, *propitiation, justification,* and *sanctification,* are generally familiar to English-speaking peoples. Such terms have been retained except where the original language indicates need for a more precise translation.

Readers of the Authorized Version will immediately be struck by the absence of several pronouns: *thee, thou,* and *ye* are replaced by the simple *you,* while *your* and *yours* are substituted for *thy* and *thine* as applicable. *Thee, thou, thy* and *thine* were once forms of address to express a special relationship to human as well as divine persons. These pronouns are no longer part of our language. However, reverence for God in the present work is preserved by capitalizing pronouns, including *You, Your,* and *Yours,* which refer to Him. Additionally, capitalization of these pronouns benefits the reader by clearly distinguishing divine and human persons referred to in a passage. Without such capitalization the distinction is often obscure, because the antecedent of a pronoun is not always clear in the English translation.

In addition to the pronoun usages of the seventeenth century, the *-eth* and *-est* verb endings, so familiar in the earlier King James editions, are now obsolete. Unless a speaker is schooled in these verb endings, there is common difficulty in selecting the correct form to be used with a given subject of the verb in vocal prayer. That is, should we use *love, loveth,* or *lovest? do, doeth, doest,* or *dost? have, hath,* or *hast?* Because these forms are obsolete, contemporary English usage has been substituted for the previous verb endings.

In older editions of the King James Version, the frequency of the connective *and* far exceeded the limits of present English usage. Also, biblical linguists agree that the Hebrew and Greek original words for this conjunction may commonly be translated otherwise, depending on the immediate context. Therefore, instead of *and,* alternatives such as *also, but, however, now, so, then,*

and *thus* are accordingly rendered in the present edition, when the original language permits.

The real character of the Authorized Version does not reside in its archaic pronouns or verbs or other grammatical forms of the seventeenth century, but rather in the care taken by its scholars to impart the letter and spirit of the original text in a majestic and reverent style.

The Format

The format of the New King James Version is designed to enhance the vividness and devotional quality of the Holy Scriptures:

- Subject headings assist the reader to identify topics and transitions in the biblical content.
- Words or phrases in *italics* indicate expressions in the original language which require clarification by additional English words, as also done throughout the history of the King James Bible.
- Prose is divided into paragraphs to indicate the structure of thought.
- Poetry is structured as contemporary verse to reflect the poetic form and beauty of the passage in the original language.
- The covenant name of God was usually translated from the Hebrew as LORD or GOD (using capital letters as shown) in the King James Old Testament. This tradition is maintained. In the present edition the name is so capitalized whenever the covenant name is quoted in the New Testament from a passage in the Old Testament.

The Old Testament Text

The Hebrew Bible has come down to us through the scrupulous care of ancient scribes who copied the original text in successive generations. By the sixth century A.D. the scribes were succeeded by a group known as the Masoretes, who continued to preserve the sacred Scriptures for another five hundred years in a form known as the Masoretic Text. Babylonia, Palestine, and Tiberias were the main centers of Masoretic activity; but by the tenth century A.D. the Masoretes of Tiberias, led by the family of ben Asher, gained the ascendancy. Through subsequent editions, the ben Asher text became in the twelfth century the only recognized form of the Hebrew Scriptures.

Daniel Bomberg printed the first Rabbinic Bible in 1516–17; that work was followed in 1524–25 by a second edition prepared by Jacob ben Chayyim and also published by Bomberg. The text of ben Chayyim was adopted in most subsequent Hebrew Bibles, including those used by the King James translators. The ben Chayyim text was also used for the first two editions of Rudolph Kittel's *Biblia Hebraica* of 1906 and 1912. In 1937 Paul Kahle published a third edition of *Biblia Hebraica*. This edition was based on the oldest dated manuscript of the ben Asher text, the Leningrad Manuscript B19a (A.D. 1008), which Kahle regarded as superior to that used by ben Chayyim.

For the New King James Version the text used was the 1967/1977 Stuttgart edition of the *Biblia Hebraica,* with frequent comparisons being made with the Bomberg edition of 1524–25. The Septuagint (Greek) Version of the Old Testament and the Latin Vulgate also were consulted. In addition to referring to a variety of ancient versions of the Hebrew Scriptures, the New King James Version draws on the resources of relevant manuscripts from the Dead Sea caves. In the few places where the Hebrew was so obscure that the 1611 King James was compelled to follow one of the versions, but where information is now available to resolve the problems, the New King James Version follows the Hebrew text. Significant variations are recorded in the New King James translators' notes.

The New Testament Text

There is more manuscript support for the New Testament than for any other body of ancient literature. Over five thousand Greek, eight thousand Latin, and many more manuscripts in other languages attest the integrity of the New Testament. There is only one basic New Testament used by Protestants, Roman Catholics, and Orthodox, by conservatives and liberals. Minor variations in hand copying have appeared through the centuries, before mechanical printing began about A.D. 1450.

Some variations exist in the spelling of Greek words, in word order, and in similar details. These ordinarily do not show up in translation and do not affect the sense of the text in any way.

Other manuscript differences such as omission or inclusion of a word or a clause, and two paragraphs in the Gospels, should not overshadow the overwhelming degree of *agreement* which exists among the ancient records. Bible readers may be assured that the most important differences in English New Testaments of today are due, not to manuscript divergence, but to the way in which translators view the task of translation: How literally should the text be rendered? How does the translator view the matter of biblical inspiration? Does the translator adopt a paraphrase when a literal rendering would be quite clear and more to the point? The New King James Version follows the historic precedent of the Authorized Version in maintaining a literal approach to translation, except where the idiom of the original language cannot be translated directly into our tongue.

The King James New Testament was based on the traditional text of the Greek-speaking churches, first published in 1516, and later called the Textus Receptus or Received Text. Although based on the relatively few available

manuscripts, these were representative of many more which existed at the time but only became known later. In the late nineteenth century, B. Westcott and F. Hort taught that this text had been officially edited by the fourth-century church, but a total lack of historical evidence for this event has forced a revision of the theory. It is now widely held that the Byzantine Text that largely supports the Textus Receptus has as much right as the Alexandrian or any other tradition to be weighed in determining the text of the New Testament.

Since the 1880s most contemporary translations of the New Testament have relied upon a relatively few manuscripts discovered chiefly in the late nineteenth and early twentieth centuries. Such translations depend primarily on two manuscripts, Codex Vaticanus and Codex Sinaiticus, because of their greater age. The Greek text obtained by using these sources and the related papyri (our most ancient manuscripts) is known as the Alexandrian Text. However, some scholars have grounds for doubting the faithfulness of Vaticanus and Sinaiticus, since they often disagree with one another, and Sinaiticus exhibits excessive omission.

A third viewpoint of New Testament scholarship holds that the best text is based on the consensus of the majority of existing Greek manuscripts. This text is called the Majority Text. Most of these manuscripts are in substantial agreement. Even though many are late, and none is earlier than the fifth century, usually their readings are verified by papyri, ancient versions, quotations from the early church fathers, or a combination of these. The Majority Text is similar to the Textus Receptus, but it corrects those readings which have little or no support in the Greek manuscript tradition.

Today, scholars agree that the science of New Testament textual criticism is in a state of flux. Very few scholars still favor the Textus Receptus as such, and then often for its historical prestige as the text of Luther, Calvin, Tyndale, and the King James Version. For about a century most have followed a Critical Text (so called because it is edited according to specific principles of textual criticism) which depends heavily upon the Alexandrian type of text. More recently many have abandoned this Critical Text (which is quite similar to the one edited by Westcott and Hort) for one that is more eclectic. Finally, a small but growing number of scholars prefer the Majority Text, which is close to the traditional text except in the Revelation.

In light of these facts, and also because the New King James Version is the fifth revision of a historic document translated from specific Greek texts, the editors decided to retain the traditional text in the body of the New Testament and to indicate major Critical and Majority Text variant readings in the translators' notes. Although these variations are duly indicated in the translators' notes of the present edition, it is most important to emphasize that fully eighty-five percent of the New Testament text is the same in the Textus Receptus, the Alexandrian Text, and the Majority Text.

New King James Translators' Notes

Significant textual explanations, alternate translations, and New Testament citations of Old Testament passages are supplied in the New King James translators' notes.

Important textual variants in the Old Testament are identified in a standard form.

The textual notes in the present edition of the New Testament make no evaluation of readings, but do clearly indicate the manuscript sources of readings. They objectively present the facts without such tendentious remarks as "the best manuscripts omit" or "the most reliable manuscripts read." Such notes are value judgments that differ according to varying viewpoints on the text. By giving a clearly defined set of variants the New King James Version benefits readers of all textual persuasions.

Where significant variations occur in the New Testament Greek manuscripts, textual notes are classified as follows:

1. NU-Text
   These variations from the traditional text generally represent the Alexandrian or Egyptian type of text described previously in "The New Testament Text." They are found in the Critical Text published in the twenty-seventh edition of the Nestle-Aland Greek New Testament (N) and in the United Bible Societies' fourth edition (U), hence the acronym, "NU-Text."
2. M-Text
   This symbol indicates points of variation in the Majority Text from the traditional text, as also previously discussed in "The New Testament Text." It should be noted that M stands for whatever reading is printed in the published *Greek New Testament According to the Majority Text*, whether supported by overwhelming, strong, or only a divided majority textual tradition.

The textual notes reflect the scholarship of the past two centuries and will assist the reader to observe the variations between the different manuscript traditions of the New Testament. Such information is generally not available in English translations of the New Testament.

TABLE OF Contents

NKJV STUDY BIBLE FOR KIDS

Features

The NKJV Study Bible for Kids is the premier study Bible for kids in the trustworthy New King James Version®. This Bible has been created and designed especially for you! Now studying the Bible can be easy and fun. There are many themed articles placed within the Bible text to help make it easier for you to read, understand, and learn about God's Word. By studying this Bible you can experience the big picture of the incredible Bible story, God's love for you, and how to use it in your daily life.

BOOK INTRODUCTIONS: Basic information about what each book is about, who wrote it, highlights, and more.

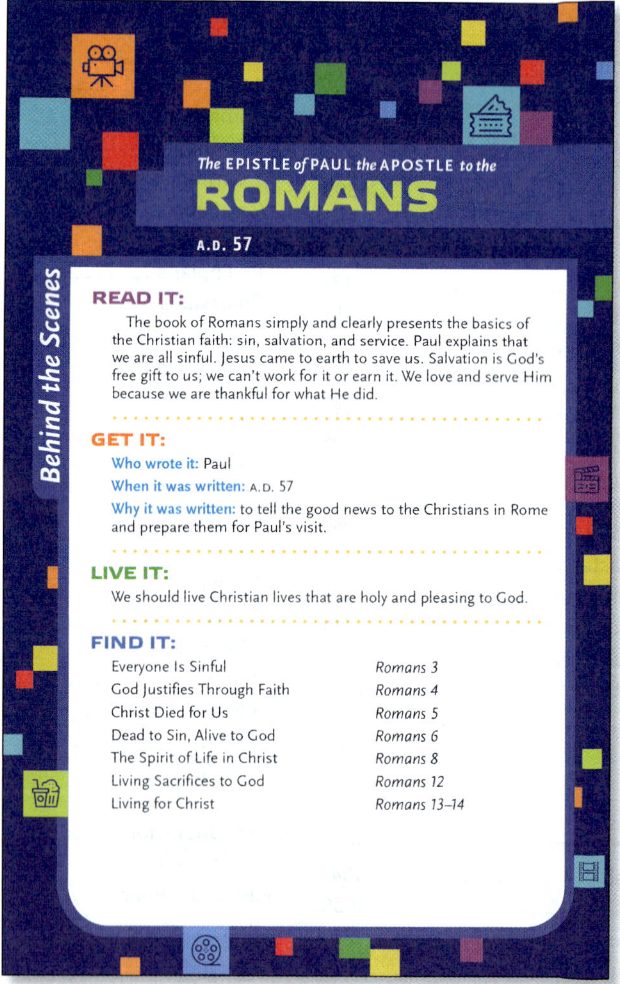

DATES ARE APPROXIMATE

BIBLE EVENTS
- King Josiah begins 31-year reign 640 B.C.
- Zephaniah delivers his prophecy 630 B.C.
- Jerusalem destroyed by Babylonians 586 B.C.

650 B.C. — 600 B.C. — 550 B.C.

WORLD EVENTS
- Japan founded, says a legend 660 B.C.
- Assyrian Empire begins to crumble when King Ashurbanipal dies 630 B.C.
- Horse racing becomes Olympic event 624 B.C.

TIMELINES

On Location

Churches of Revelation

John writes from fifty miles offshore of western Turkey, on the rocky island of Patmos, about ten miles long and five miles wide. He begins the book with letters addressed to churches in seven cities near the coast of western Turkey. The futuristic visions that John writes about involve the entire planet. He says the last battle between good and evil will take place in the Valley of Armageddon, known today as Megiddo, and that God will make a new Jerusalem. Since the genre of the book is apocalyptic, characterized by extreme symbolism, scholars debate whether John had any of these actual sites in mind.

ON LOCATION: Maps

Spotlight

GOD IS PRESENT WITH HIS PEOPLE

READ IT: NUMBERS 9:15–23

GET IT:

God first appeared to His people "face-to-face" on Mount Sinai. When Moses finished constructing the tabernacle, God's presence came down off the mountain and moved into the tabernacle in a cloud filled with His glory. Now God lived in the middle of His people. They saw God's presence during the day when they looked at the tabernacle and saw the cloud hanging over it. They saw His presence at night when the cloud glowed with fire. When the cloud rose up and moved, the people packed up their stuff and moved to another campsite. They stopped when the cloud stopped. This was their training to obey God and follow Him.

LIVE IT:

This cloud and fire thing sounds pretty cool, doesn't it? Well, we don't have clouds or fires hanging over our churches to visually see God's presence. But we have something better. We have God's presence living inside of us. Christians have God's Spirit living inside their hearts and minds. God isn't outside hanging around someplace. God is with us! He's with us every moment, in every step.

SPOTLIGHT:

Stories of the Bible to help kids learn about God and His people, and how the Bible connects to them and their lives.

STARRING ROLES:

Personality profiles of major people from the Bible.

Starring Roles

DEBORAH was a prophetess in Israel when Barak was ordered to defend the people of Israel against the king of Canaan (pronounced *KAY-nun*). The Lord showed Deborah that Barak should take ten thousand men to fight against the army of General Sisera of Canaan.

Although Deborah didn't take part in the battle, she kept her promise to go to the battlefield with Barak and his troops. Barak was encouraged by her advice, and that day he and his army defeated the army of the king of Canaan. So Deborah and Barak celebrated by singing their victory duet together (see Judges 5).

Barak won the victory that day because he was willing to listen to good advice and because Deborah was willing to take her place beside him as encourager.

Learn to respect one another's God-given abilities while you are growing up. Respect, or honor, is the basis of the love God commands you to have for others.

IN FOCUS:

Definitions for words in the Bible

In Focus

1:1 Genealogy The history of a family listing the most famous ancestors from the beginning. This genealogy of Jesus begins with Abraham and ends with Joseph, husband of Mary

1:16 Christ The divine title of the Man Jesus. The word means "the Anointed" (by the Holy Spirit). Christos is a Greek word translated from the Hebrew *Messiah*.

Action!

ANGELS

WHERE ANGELS GO

READ IT: JUDGES 13:1–25

GET IT:

Were you ever an angel in a Christmas pageant? Did you wear cardboard wings and a tinsel halo? It's a cute image for Sunday school, but God's angels are so much more. The Bible says some angels bring comfort. Some bring a sword. They are above us to protect us, next to us to walk with us, in front of us to lead us, and beneath us to support us.

God created angels to be His messengers to us. The angel who appeared to Samson's mother let her know a couple of things. First, nothing is impossible with God. And second, she was supposed to raise Samson according to the faith. That way he would be able to accomplish wonderful things with God's help.

After giving the message, the angel "ascended in the flame" (v. 20) up into heaven. (Sounds like the end of a crazy concert, doesn't it?) Until that moment Samson's family had no idea they were talking to an angel of God. Angels can appear to us in many ways, and sometimes we may not even know it.

It's been said that intelligence is learning your lessons, and wisdom is knowing your lessons can come from anywhere. If that's true, then faith is understanding that God's message will come to us, and we have to decide whether to listen. God sends us messengers with good news. He chooses ordinary people leading ordinary lives to do extraordinary things!

LIVE IT:

Even if you don't see angels, they are around you all the time, protecting you, guiding you, and maybe even whispering in your ear. They are not only God's messengers; they are also His examples. Have you ever had an experience with someone or something that may have been an angel?

ACTION!:

Helpful articles on day-to-day topics, some that show how a person from the Bible experienced the same things that kids encounter today.

EPIC IDEAS:

Key articles that give kids information about must-know topics, things that help them learn important themes to live the Christian life.

Epic Ideas

45:6 GOD IS FOREVER AND EVER

Have you thought about *eternity*? Eternity means forever and ever—no beginning and no ending. You had a beginning, and someday your life in this world will end. Even the world itself will come to an end. In fact, we're so used to everything we know having a beginning and an end, we can hardly think of anything that doesn't end.

God is forever and ever. He is different from everything He made because He never had a beginning and He will never end. He has eternal life in Himself. Then He shares His life with the people He made in His image. So, even if we die in this world, we will go on living somewhere. God wants you to share eternal life with Him. You can live with Him forever if you give your life to Him now. Later may be too late.

DICTIONARY/ CONCORDANCE

DICTIONARY-CONCORDANCE–U • 1572

Passover celebration and the priestly rituals, recalling the Exodus, when the Hebrews left Egypt so quickly that they had no time to wait for the bread to rise (Ex. 12:8, 15–20, 34, 39; 13:6, 7).

Ur An ancient city on the Euphrates, called "Ur of the Chaldees"; home of Abraham (Gen. 11:28).

Uzziah (uh-ZIGH-uh) The name of three persons in the OT, one of them a king of Judah (c. 783–742 B.C.).

vanity Futility; emptiness.
V. of v., all is v. Eccl. 1:2

viper A poisonous snake.
stings like a v. Prov. 23:32

vision Something seen other than by ordinary sight, as in a dream. God's revelations to the prophets were usually by visions.
They err in v. Is. 28:7
revealed to Daniel in a night v. Dan. 2:19
Tell the v. to no one Matt. 17:9

voice A sound uttered through the mouth as in speaking.
a still small v. 1 Kin. 19:12
v. of the turtledove is heard Song 2:12
v. of one crying Is. 40:3; Matt. 3:3; Mark 1:3; Luke 3:4; John 1:23

wadi (WAH-dih) A valley, ravine, or riverbed that usually remains dry except during the rainy season; similar to an ar-

w. and rumors of w. Matt. 24:6; M
Luke 21:9

wash To clean with water or othe
w. His feet with her tears Luke 7:3
w. the disciples' feet John 13:5

water The colorless fluid that fal
over the face of the w. Gen. 1:2
the flood of w. was on Gen. 7:6
Planted by the rivers of w. Ps. 1:3
me beside the still w. Ps. 23:2
Cast your bread upon the w. Eccl.
baptized you with w. Mark 1:8; L
John 1:26

way The direction; path; man's r
living.
the w. of the righteous Ps. 1:6
Train up a child in the w. Prov. 22
Prepare the w. of the LORD Is. 40
3:3; Mark 1:3; Luke 3:4; John 1:2
I am the w., the truth John 14:6

Weeks
Passo
Also
See P

will De
Your w.
good w.

wine T
W. is a
new w.
Mark

wise H
tree des
man w.
w. men

ARTICLES INDEX:

A great study help to find the location of articles within the Bible text.

BEHIND THE SCENES & ACTION! • 1574

ARTICLES INDEX

Behind the Scenes

Action!

NKJV STUDY BIBLE FOR KIDS
Introduction

God's world is full of color. Colors of the seasons, your school and community, your friends and family...just look at the world around you. God created the rainbow...He took white light, and broke it down into something beautiful for His people to enjoy, and more importantly to understand what He was trying to communicate to them. Instead of just saying it, or writing it, He also showed it through a colorful visual lesson.

Your world is vibrant, colorful, exciting, busy, active, and full of life. Sometimes learning, especially the Bible, can be a bit of a challenge. Understanding what is being said is difficult in black and white. But adding color and excitement helps to engage your curiosity, your desire to learn, and your ability to grasp the lesson! Look at the video games, apps, TV shows, movies, and media you are exposed to every day! Color, action, and fun make for a better learning experience.

You are holding in your hands a true study Bible in full-color, created just for you. The pages of the *NKJV Study Bible for Kids* are packed with articles that apply to your world. We have included features that are academic and relational, historical and modern. With over 800 features to inspire and teach, you will enjoy the brightly colored articles and easy fan-tabs to navigate through the pages.

We have worked diligently to prepare one of the finest Bibles for young people like you, in the trustworthy and reliable New King James Version®. We have also earnestly prayed that, through this incredible Bible, you will learn to love God and live a life of faith and happiness. We hope you will use these lessons to inspire others to know Him.

—*The Publishers*

Old Testament

The FIRST BOOK of MOSES CALLED

GENESIS

1445 B.C.–1400 B.C.

Behind the Scenes

READ IT:

The book of Genesis tells the story of God and His relationship with His creation from the beginning of time. It's all about beginnings: the beginning of the universe, the beginning of humans, the beginning of sin, the beginning of God's promises and plans for salvation, and the beginning of a special relationship between Abraham and God.

GET IT:

Who wrote it: Most people think Moses wrote it.

When it was written: 1445 B.C.–1400 B.C.

Why it was written: to explain the beginning of all things — how God created the world, how sin entered the world, and how and why God created humans. It also explains how God chose one family to become a great nation.

LIVE IT:

God created all things.

We are created in God's image.

God wants a relationship with us.

FIND IT:

The History of Creation	*Genesis 1–2*
The Temptation and Fall of Man	*Genesis 3*
Noah and the Great Flood	*Genesis 6–9*
Abraham's Life and Story	*Genesis 12–24*
The Stories of Isaac, Jacob, and Esau	*Genesis 25–36*
The Stories of Joseph in Egypt	*Genesis 37–50*

The History of Creation

1 In the beginning God created the heavens and the earth. 2 The earth was without form, and void; and darkness *was*[a] on
the face of the deep. And the Spirit of God
was hovering over the face of the waters.
3 Then God said, "Let there be light"; and
there was light. 4 And God saw the light, that
it was good; and God divided the light from
the darkness. 5 God called the light Day, and
the darkness He called Night. So the evening and the morning were the first day.
6 Then God said, "Let there be a firmament in the midst of the waters, and let it
divide the waters from the waters." 7 Thus
God made the firmament, and divided the
waters which *were* under the firmament
from the waters which *were* above the firmament; and it was so. 8 And God called the
firmament Heaven. So the evening and the
morning were the second day.
9 Then God said, "Let the waters under
the heavens be gathered together into one
place, and let the dry *land* appear"; and it
was so. 10 And God called the dry *land* Earth,
and the gathering together of the waters He
called Seas. And God saw that *it was* good.
11 Then God said, "Let the earth bring
forth grass, the herb *that* yields seed, *and*
the fruit tree *that* yields fruit according to its
kind, whose seed *is* in itself, on the earth";
and it was so. 12 And the earth brought forth
grass, the herb *that* yields seed according to
its kind, and the tree *that* yields fruit, whose
seed *is* in itself according to its kind. And
God saw that *it was* good. 13 So the evening
and the morning were the third day.
14 Then God said, "Let there be lights in
the firmament of the heavens to divide the

1:2 [a] Words in italic type have been added for clarity. They are not found in the original Hebrew or Aramaic.

Starring Roles

The first man's name was ADAM, which means "Ground," because God formed Adam out of the very elements of the earth. His wife was called Eve, meaning "Life-Giver," because she was the mother of all people.

Adam and Eve were very happy in the garden God made for them. Their world was like an immense park in which only the most elegant things lived and grew. The perfume of lilies and roses filled the air continually. Even the mighty lions played gently with them, and the lion cubs ate from Eve's hand.

Best of all, God Himself often visited in the evening to walk and talk with Adam and Eve in the garden. He taught them how to live in His world.

But one day everything went wrong. You can read about it in Genesis, chapter 3.

Timeline

DATES ARE APPROXIMATE

BIBLE EVENTS

- God creates the universe Before 4500 B.C.
- Flood destroys the world Before 4500 B.C.

4500 B.C. — 4000 B.C. — 3500 B.C. — 3000 B.C.

WORLD EVENTS

- First known Egyptian calendar 4230 B.C.
- Floods devastate river basin of Iraq 3400 B.C.
- Chinese develop acupuncture 2700 B.C.

day from the night; and let them be for signs
and seasons, and for days and years; 15and
let them be for lights in the firmament of
the heavens to give light on the earth"; and
it was so. 16Then God made two great lights:
the greater light to rule the day, and the lesser light to rule the night. *He made* the stars
also. 17God set them in the firmament of the
heavens to give light on the earth, 18and to
rule over the day and over the night, and to
divide the light from the darkness. And God
saw that *it was* good. 19So the evening and the
morning were the fourth day.
20Then God said, "Let the waters abound
with an abundance of living creatures, and
let birds fly above the earth across the face
of the firmament of the heavens." 21So God
created great sea creatures and every living
thing that moves, with which the waters
abounded, according to their kind, and every winged bird according to its kind. And
God saw that *it was* good. 22And God blessed
them, saying, "Be fruitful and multiply, and
fill the waters in the seas, and let birds multiply on the earth." 23So the evening and the
morning were the fifth day.
24Then God said, "Let the earth bring
forth the living creature according to its
kind: cattle and creeping thing and beast
of the earth, *each* according to its kind"; and
it was so. 25And God made the beast of the
earth according to its kind, cattle according
to its kind, and everything that creeps on the
earth according to its kind. And God saw
that *it was* good.
26Then God said, "Let Us make man in
Our image, according to Our likeness; let
them have dominion over the fish of the sea,
over the birds of the air, and over the cattle,
over all[a] the earth and over every creeping
thing that creeps on the earth." 27So God created man in His *own* image; in the image of
God He created him; male and female He
created them. 28Then God blessed them, and

In Focus

1:1 Created As used here, it means that God made the heavens and the earth from nothing. Compare with Genesis 2:7 where God only "formed" Adam from the dust of the ground.

God said to them, "Be fruitful and multiply;
fill the earth and subdue it; have dominion
over the fish of the sea, over the birds of the
air, and over every living thing that moves
on the earth."
29And God said, "See, I have given you every herb *that* yields seed which *is* on the face
of all the earth, and every tree whose fruit
yields seed; to you it shall be for food. 30Also,
to every beast of the earth, to every bird of
the air, and to everything that creeps on the
earth, in which *there is* life, *I have given* every
green herb for food"; and it was so. 31Then
God saw everything that He had made, and
indeed *it was* very good. So the evening and
the morning were the sixth day.

2 Thus the heavens and the earth, and all
the host of them, were finished. 2And
on the seventh day God ended His work
which He had done, and He rested on the
seventh day from all His work which He
had done. 3Then God blessed the seventh
day and sanctified it, because in it He rested
from all His work which God had created
and made.
4This *is* the history[a] of the heavens and
the earth when they were created, in the day

1:26 [a] Syriac reads *all the wild animals of.* 2:4 [a] Hebrew *toledoth,* literally *generations*

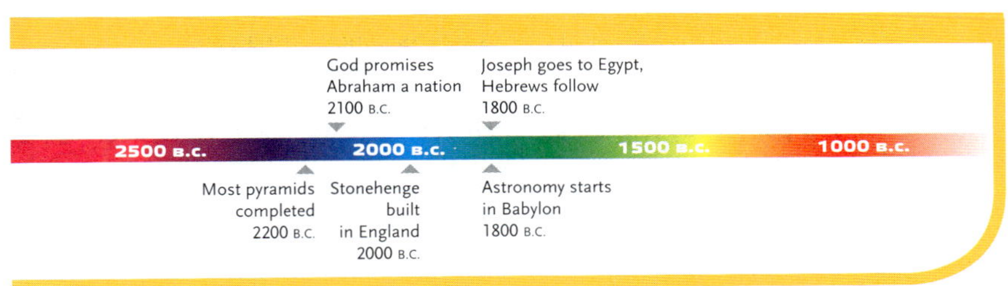

In Focus

2:7 Formed As used here, it means that God formed Adam from the dust of the ground. Compare with Genesis 1:1 where God made the heavens and the earth *from nothing*.

2:9 Tree of Life The tree God planted whose fruit Adam and Eve could have eaten and lived forever. We read about this tree again in Revelation 22:2.

that the LORD God made the earth and the
heavens, 5before any plant of the field was in
the earth and before any herb of the field had
grown. For the LORD God had not caused it
to rain on the earth, and *there was* no man
to till the ground; 6but a mist went up from
the earth and watered the whole face of the
ground.
7And the LORD God formed man *of* the
dust of the ground, and breathed into his
nostrils the breath of life; and man became
a living being.

Life in God's Garden

8The LORD God planted a garden eastward in Eden, and there He put the man
whom He had formed. 9And out of the
ground the LORD God made every tree grow

Spotlight

GOD CREATES THE WORLD

READ IT: GENESIS 1:1—2:3

GET IT:

The first story in the Bible is about God and what He did—He created! Only God can create something out of nothing. From nothingness came light and darkness, then heavens and land, then all sorts of plants, planets, and creatures. And because God is good, what He created was good. After He made a place for humans to live, He created a man and a woman to take care of and rule over His creation. He made humans in His own image because He wanted people around to talk to and have fun with. They were the crowning achievement of His creation. God made people so they could have a relationship with Him. He planned to walk and talk with them in a special garden. It all was going to be perfect!

God looked at everything He'd created and said, "This is good." God did all His work in six days, then He rested.

LIVE IT:

God created the earth and humans. He assigned humans to "subdue" and "have dominion over" (1:28) all the earth. This was their purpose—to take care of God's world. God still expects us to take care of His creation. When you pull weeds to grow a garden, recycle newspapers, cans, and bottles, take a shorter shower, and turn off lights in the house, you are doing what God has asked humans to do since the beginning of time. You are taking care of God's world.

that is pleasant to the sight and good for
food. The tree of life *was* also in the midst of
the garden, and the tree of the knowledge of
good and evil.
10Now a river went out of Eden to water
the garden, and from there it parted and
became four riverheads. 11The name of the
first *is* Pishon; it *is* the one which skirts the
whole land of Havilah, where *there is* gold.
12And the gold of that land *is* good. Bdellium
and the onyx stone *are* there. 13The name of
the second river *is* Gihon; it *is* the one which
goes around the whole land of Cush. 14The
name of the third river *is* Hiddekel;[a] it *is* the
one which goes toward the east of Assyria.
The fourth river *is* the Euphrates.
15Then the LORD God took the man and
put him in the garden of Eden to tend and
keep it. 16And the LORD God commanded
the man, saying, "Of every tree of the garden you may freely eat; 17but of the tree of
the knowledge of good and evil you shall not
eat, for in the day that you eat of it you shall
surely die."
18And the LORD God said, "*It is* not good
that man should be alone; I will make him
a helper comparable to him." 19Out of the
ground the LORD God formed every beast
of the field and every bird of the air, and

2:14 [a] Or *Tigris*

WHO IS GOD? VERY GOOD!

READ IT: GENESIS 1:1, 26, 31

GET IT:

In the beginning: before there was anything at all, when there was nothing, God created everything—out of nothing. Think of the creativity, the imagination, the vision, and the power. If you want to know something about God, just look at the natural created world around you: the big things—mountains, oceans, and galaxies; the smaller things—trees, animals, plants, and cells. Then look at people—cells, DNA, skin, muscles, babies. It's amazing. Unthinkable. Only God can create life from nothing. Only He has that power. And only He has the heart to love His creation unconditionally.

God isn't just some out-there, unseen, unknowable, impersonal being. He makes things that are interesting and unique, wonderful and creative. And He makes living, breathing human beings that are, in some unimaginable way, an image of God Himself. You—yes, you—are a creation of God, just as much as the oceans, mountains, stars, and sun. Out of all those amazing things, God made you in His image. And He loves and treasures *you* the most.

LIVE IT:

Look carefully at God's creation. What does it tell you about Him? What kind of God is He, based on what He's made? Spend time getting to know God—the creative Creator—by learning about the world He made. Make a commitment to honor, respect, and care for His creation—both nature and people.

brought *them* to Adam to see what he would
call them. And whatever Adam called each
living creature, that *was* its name. 20 So Adam
gave names to all cattle, to the birds of the
air, and to every beast of the field. But for
Adam there was not found a helper comparable to him.

21 And the LORD God caused a deep sleep
to fall on Adam, and he slept; and He took
one of his ribs, and closed up the flesh in its
place. 22 Then the rib which the LORD God
had taken from man He made into a woman, and He brought her to the man.

23 And Adam said:

"This *is* now bone of my bones
And flesh of my flesh;
She shall be called Woman,
Because she was taken out of Man."

24 Therefore a man shall leave his father and
mother and be joined to his wife, and they
shall become one flesh.

25 And they were both naked, the man and
his wife, and were not ashamed.

The Temptation and Fall of Man

3 Now the serpent was more cunning
than any beast of the field which the
LORD God had made. And he said to the

RELATIONSHIPS

GOD'S DESIGN FOR RELATIONSHIPS

READ IT: GENESIS 2:18

GET IT:

Think about it: God created the world and said it was good. That almost seems like an understatement in the midst of perfect weather, no sin, beauty and peace everywhere. But even in that perfect world, God said it wasn't good for man to be alone. What was the big deal about Adam being alone?

God is the creator of relationships. They are of top importance to Him—even more significant than God's other creations. So God made a helper comparable to Adam. He created Eve—a partner for Adam, someone who was like him. He created them to be a team and work together, to love each other and to care for the world He'd made.

Why does God value relationships so much? God Himself lives in relationship with Jesus and the Holy Spirit. If He exists in community, then it makes sense that He'd want us to experience the same blessing and rewards of relationships.

LIVE IT:

Think about the kinds of relationships you have. Do you live in a way that brings reward and blessing to the people in your life?

If you want better relationships, take some time to think about what *you're* bringing to them. Do you value relationships by investing time in them? By being a source of encouragement and hope? By seeing how every person has great worth and is a gift from God?

woman, "Has God indeed said, 'You shall
not eat of every tree of the garden'?"
2And the woman said to the serpent, "We
may eat the fruit of the trees of the garden;
3but of the fruit of the tree which *is* in the
midst of the garden, God has said, 'You
shall not eat it, nor shall you touch it, lest
you die.'"
4Then the serpent said to the woman,
"You will not surely die. 5For God knows
that in the day you eat of it your eyes will be
opened, and you will be like God, knowing
good and evil."
6So when the woman saw that the tree
was good for food, that it *was* pleasant to the
eyes, and a tree desirable to make *one* wise,
she took of its fruit and ate. She also gave to
her husband with her, and he ate. 7Then the

In Focus

2:17 Tree of the Knowledge of Good and Evil The tree God planted, but whose fruit Adam and Eve were forbidden to eat. By eating the fruit, they first experienced sin.

eyes of both of them were opened, and they
knew that they *were* naked; and they sewed
fig leaves together and made themselves
coverings.
8And they heard the sound of the LORD
God walking in the garden in the cool of the

Spotlight

GOD GIVES HUMANS A CHOICE

READ IT: GENESIS 3:1–24

GET IT:

God's relationship with humans was going well. He put Adam in a perfect garden, then created Eve to be his helper and companion. They had free run of the place with only one—yes, just *one*—rule. That rule was they couldn't eat the fruit of a special tree—the Tree of the Knowledge of Good and Evil. That sounds simple enough—there were tons of fruits on other trees to eat, so they weren't hungry. But a sneaky snake made a big deal about the one rule. He bugged Eve about it, and suddenly she couldn't resist. She made a choice—a very, very bad choice. She liked the looks of the fruit and really, really liked the idea of being as wise as God. So she disobeyed God's command. She picked a piece of fruit, ate it, and shared it with Adam, who took a bite, too. Suddenly everything changed. The brilliance on God's good creation was dimmer. Their perfect, casual, and comfortable relationship with God was badly broken. A new something had entered the world—sin.

LIVE IT:

God didn't let one bad choice ruin everything. He promised to conquer sin and Satan someday (Genesis 3:15). The good news for us is that "someday" has come! Jesus came to earth to be that Conqueror. Sin is still around, but we are free from its deadly effects because of Jesus. And He makes it easier for us to have a relationship with God.

day, and Adam and his wife hid themselves
from the presence of the LORD God among
the trees of the garden.
9 Then the LORD God called to Adam and
said to him, "Where *are* you?"
10 So he said, "I heard Your voice in the
garden, and I was afraid because I was naked; and I hid myself."
11 And He said, "Who told you that you
were naked? Have you eaten from the tree
of which I commanded you that you should
not eat?"
12 Then the man said, "The woman whom
You gave *to be* with me, she gave me of the
tree, and I ate."
13 And the LORD God said to the woman,
"What *is* this you have done?"
The woman said, "The serpent deceived
me, and I ate."
14 So the LORD God said to the serpent:

"Because you have done this,
You *are* cursed more than all cattle,
And more than every beast of the field;
On your belly you shall go,
And you shall eat dust
All the days of your life.
15 And I will put enmity
Between you and the woman,
And between your seed and her Seed;
He shall bruise your head,
And you shall bruise His heel."

16 To the woman He said:

"I will greatly multiply your sorrow and
your conception;
In pain you shall bring forth children;
Your desire *shall be* for your husband,
And he shall rule over you."

17 Then to Adam He said, "Because you
have heeded the voice of your wife, and have
eaten from the tree of which I commanded
you, saying, 'You shall not eat of it':

"Cursed *is* the ground for your sake;

On Location

The Ancient Near East 3000 B.C.

During the 3rd millenium Lower and Upper Egypt were united. Egypt's Old Kingdom (2700–2160 B.C.) produced the great pyramids, such as those at Giza. In Mesopotamia, the land of Sumer developed a system of independent city-states. Toward the end of the millennium this city-state rule was replaced by a more extensive territorial rule centered in Accad.

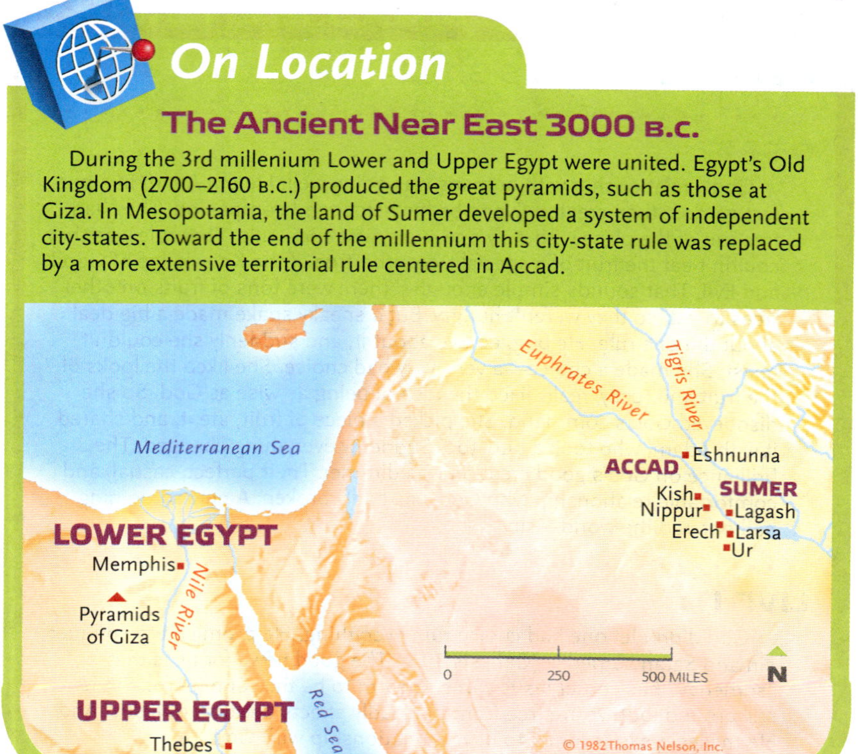

In toil you shall eat *of* it
All the days of your life.
18 Both thorns and thistles it shall bring
forth for you,
And you shall eat the herb of the field.
19 In the sweat of your face you shall eat
bread
Till you return to the ground,
For out of it you were taken;
For dust you *are*,
And to dust you shall return."

20 And Adam called his wife's name Eve,
because she was the mother of all living.
21 Also for Adam and his wife the LORD
God made tunics of skin, and clothed them.
22 Then the LORD God said, "Behold, the
man has become like one of Us, to know
good and evil. And now, lest he put out his
hand and take also of the tree of life, and eat,
and live forever"— 23 therefore the LORD God
sent him out of the garden of Eden to till the
ground from which he was taken. 24 So He
drove out the man; and He placed cherubim
at the east of the garden of Eden, and a flaming sword which turned every way, to guard
the way to the tree of life.

Cain Murders Abel

4 Now Adam knew Eve his wife, and
she conceived and bore Cain, and said,
"I have acquired a man from the LORD."
2 Then she bore again, this time his brother Abel. Now Abel was a keeper of sheep,
but Cain was a tiller of the ground. 3 And
in the process of time it came to pass that
Cain brought an offering of the fruit of the
ground to the LORD. 4 Abel also brought of
the firstborn of his flock and of their fat.
And the LORD respected Abel and his offering, 5 but He did not respect Cain and his
offering. And Cain was very angry, and his
countenance fell.
6 So the LORD said to Cain, "Why are you
angry? And why has your countenance fall-
en? 7 If you do well, will you not be accepted?
And if you do not do well, sin lies at the door.
And its desire *is* for you, but you should rule
over it."
8 Now Cain talked with Abel his brother;[a] and it came to pass, when they were in
the field, that Cain rose up against Abel his
brother and killed him.
9 Then the LORD said to Cain, "Where *is*
Abel your brother?"

In Focus

3:24 Cherubim Pronounced *CHER-uh-bim*. Plural of cherub. These are special angels who are always in the presence of God and continually praise Him.

He said, "I do not know. *Am* I my brother's keeper?"
10 And He said, "What have you done?
The voice of your brother's blood cries out to
Me from the ground. 11 So now you *are* cursed
from the earth, which has opened its mouth
to receive your brother's blood from your
hand. 12 When you till the ground, it shall no
longer yield its strength to you. A fugitive
and a vagabond you shall be on the earth."
13 And Cain said to the LORD, "My punishment *is* greater than I can bear! 14 Surely You
have driven me out this day from the face
of the ground; I shall be hidden from Your
face; I shall be a fugitive and a vagabond on
the earth, and it will happen *that* anyone
who finds me will kill me."
15 And the LORD said to him, "Therefore,[a]
whoever kills Cain, vengeance shall be taken
on him sevenfold." And the LORD set a mark on
Cain, lest anyone finding him should kill him.

The Family of Cain

16 Then Cain went out from the presence
of the LORD and dwelt in the land of Nod on
the east of Eden. 17 And Cain knew his wife,
and she conceived and bore Enoch. And
he built a city, and called the name of the
city after the name of his son—Enoch. 18 To
Enoch was born Irad; and Irad begot Mehujael, and Mehujael begot Methushael, and
Methushael begot Lamech.
19 Then Lamech took for himself two
wives: the name of one *was* Adah, and the
name of the second *was* Zillah. 20 And Adah
bore Jabal. He was the father of those who
dwell in tents and have livestock. 21 His brother's name *was* Jubal. He was the father of all

---

4:8 [a] Samaritan Pentateuch, Septuagint, Syriac, and Vulgate add *"Let us go out to the field."* **4:15** [a] Following Masoretic Text and Targum; Septuagint, Syriac, and Vulgate read *Not so.*

those who play the harp and flute. 22And
as for Zillah, she also bore Tubal-Cain, an instructor of every craftsman in bronze and iron. And the sister of Tubal-Cain *was* Naamah.

23Then Lamech said to his wives:

"Adah and Zillah, hear my voice;
Wives of Lamech, listen to my speech!
For I have killed a man for wounding me,
Even a young man for hurting me.
24 If Cain shall be avenged sevenfold,
Then Lamech seventy-sevenfold."

A New Son

25And Adam knew his wife again, and she bore a son and named him Seth, "For God has appointed another seed for me instead of Abel, whom Cain killed."
26And as for Seth, to him also a son was born; and he named him Enosh.[a] Then *men* began to call on the name of the LORD.

The Family of Adam

5 This is the book of the genealogy of Adam. In the day that God created man, He made him in the likeness of God.
2He created them male and female, and blessed them and called them Mankind in the day they were created.
3And Adam lived one hundred and thirty years, and begot *a son* in his own likeness, after his image, and named him Seth.
4After he begot Seth, the days of Adam were eight hundred years; and he had sons and daughters.
5So all the days

4:26 [a] Greek *Enos*

SIN HIS BROTHER'S KEEPER

READ IT: GENESIS 4:1–26

GET IT:

Nothing was really wrong with Cain's offering. It was okay to give "the fruit of the ground" (v. 3). But Cain's attitude was all wrong. He didn't give God the best; he just gave some. And then he chose to remain in his anger and rebellion. He walked away from his conversation with God and killed his brother out of jealousy and pride.

After that Cain's sin took a famous turn when he answered God's question with a lie: "I do not know. Am I my brother's keeper?" (v. 9). If you've ever given your parents a smart-aleck response to an important question, you probably can imagine God's response to Cain's disrespect. The Lord's righteous anger burned against the sin that Cain committed and the sin that was still hiding in his calloused—hard—heart.

LIVE IT:

We've all had opportunities like Cain to please God or to disobey Him.

First of all, obey. Do what God says, because it's the right thing to do. But if you don't, and you have to face your sin—you have a choice. You can walk away and continue in sin, as Cain did, or you can turn away from *sin. You know what you* need to do. Either apologize and make things right, or head in another direction. But whatever you do, never try to lie your way out.

that Adam lived were nine hundred and thirty years; and he died.
6Seth lived one hundred and five years,
and begot Enosh. 7After he begot Enosh,
Seth lived eight hundred and seven years,
and had sons and daughters. 8So all the days
of Seth were nine hundred and twelve years;
and he died.
9Enosh lived ninety years, and begot
Cainan.[a] 10After he begot Cainan, Enosh
lived eight hundred and fifteen years, and
had sons and daughters. 11So all the days of
Enosh were nine hundred and five years;
and he died.
12Cainan lived seventy years, and begot
Mahalalel. 13After he begot Mahalalel, Cainan lived eight hundred and forty years, and
had sons and daughters. 14So all the days of
Cainan were nine hundred and ten years;
and he died.
15Mahalalel lived sixty-five years, and begot Jared. 16After he begot Jared, Mahalalel
lived eight hundred and thirty years, and
had sons and daughters. 17So all the days of
Mahalalel were eight hundred and ninety-
five years; and he died.
18Jared lived one hundred and sixty-two
years, and begot Enoch. 19After he begot
Enoch, Jared lived eight hundred years, and
had sons and daughters. 20So all the days
of Jared were nine hundred and sixty-two
years; and he died.
21Enoch lived sixty-five years, and begot
Methuselah. 22After he begot Methuselah,
Enoch walked with God three hundred
years, and had sons and daughters. 23So all
the days of Enoch were three hundred and
sixty-five years. 24And Enoch walked with
God; and he *was* not, for God took him.
25Methuselah lived one hundred and
eighty-seven years, and begot Lamech.
26After he begot Lamech, Methuselah lived
seven hundred and eighty-two years, and
had sons and daughters. 27So all the days of
Methuselah were nine hundred and sixty-
nine years; and he died.
28Lamech lived one hundred and eighty-
two years, and had a son. 29And he called his
name Noah, saying, "This *one* will comfort
us concerning our work and the toil of our
hands, because of the ground which the
LORD has cursed." 30After he begot Noah,
Lamech lived five hundred and ninety-five
years, and had sons and daughters. 31So all
the days of Lamech were seven hundred and
seventy-seven years; and he died.
32And Noah was five hundred years old,
and Noah begot Shem, Ham, and Japheth.

The Wickedness and Judgment of Man

6 Now it came to pass, when men began
to multiply on the face of the earth,
and daughters were born to them, 2that the
sons of God saw the daughters of men, that
they *were* beautiful; and they took wives for
themselves of all whom they chose.
3And the LORD said, "My Spirit shall not
strive[a] with man forever, for he *is* indeed
flesh; yet his days shall be one hundred
and twenty years." 4There were giants on
the earth in those days, and also afterward,
when the sons of God came in to the daughters of men and they bore *children* to them.
Those *were* the mighty men who *were* of old,
men of renown.
5Then the LORD[a] saw that the wickedness
of man *was* great in the earth, and *that* every
intent of the thoughts of his heart *was* only
evil continually. 6And the LORD was sorry
that He had made man on the earth, and
He was grieved in His heart. 7So the LORD
said, "I will destroy man whom I have created from the face of the earth, both man and
beast, creeping thing and birds of the air,
for I am sorry that I have made them." 8But
Noah found grace in the eyes of the LORD.

Noah Pleases God

9This is the genealogy of Noah. Noah was
a just man, perfect in his generations. Noah
walked with God. 10And Noah begot three
sons: Shem, Ham, and Japheth.
11The earth also was corrupt before God,
and the earth was filled with violence. 12So
God looked upon the earth, and indeed it
was corrupt; for all flesh had corrupted their
way on the earth.

The Ark Prepared

13And God said to Noah, "The end of all
flesh has come before Me, for the earth is
filled with violence through them; and behold, I will destroy them with the earth.
14Make yourself an ark of gopherwood;
make rooms in the ark, and cover it inside

5:9 [a] Hebrew *Qenan* **6:3** [a] Septuagint, Syriac, Targum, and Vulgate read *abide.* **6:5** [a] Following Masoretic Text and Targum; Vulgate reads *God;* Septuagint reads *LORD God.*

and outside with pitch. 15 And this is how you
shall make it: The length of the ark *shall be*
three hundred cubits, its width fifty cubits,
and its height thirty cubits. 16 You shall make
a window for the ark, and you shall finish
it to a cubit from above; and set the door of
the ark in its side. You shall make it *with*
lower, second, and third *decks*. 17 And behold,
I Myself am bringing floodwaters on the
earth, to destroy from under heaven all flesh
in which *is* the breath of life; everything that
is on the earth shall die. 18 But I will establish
My covenant with you; and you shall go into
the ark—you, your sons, your wife, and your
sons' wives with you. 19 And of every living
thing of all flesh you shall bring two of every
sort into the ark, to keep *them* alive with you;
they shall be male and female. 20 Of the birds
after their kind, of animals after their kind,
and of every creeping thing of the earth after its kind, two of every *kind* will come to
you to keep *them* alive. 21 And you shall take
for yourself of all food that is eaten, and you
shall gather *it* to yourself; and it shall be food
for you and for them."

22 Thus Noah did; according to all that
God commanded him, so he did.

The Great Flood

7 Then the LORD said to Noah, "Come
into the ark, you and all your household, because I have seen *that* you *are* righteous before Me in this generation. 2 You
shall take with you seven each of every clean
animal, a male and his female; two each of
animals that *are* unclean, a male and his
female; 3 also seven each of birds of the air,
male and female, to keep the species alive
on the face of all the earth. 4 For after seven
more days I will cause it to rain on the earth
forty days and forty nights, and I will destroy
from the face of the earth all living things
that I have made." 5 And Noah did according
to all that the LORD commanded him. 6 Noah
was six hundred years old when the floodwaters were on the earth.

7 So Noah, with his sons, his wife, and
his sons' wives, went into the ark because of
the waters of the flood. 8 Of clean animals,
of animals that *are* unclean, of birds, and
of everything that creeps on the earth, 9 two
by two they went into the ark to Noah, male
and female, as God had commanded Noah.
10 And it came to pass after seven days that
the waters of the flood were on the earth. 11 In
the six hundredth year of Noah's life, in the
second month, the seventeenth day of the
month, on that day all the fountains of the
great deep were broken up, and the windows
of heaven were opened. 12 And the rain was
on the earth forty days and forty nights.

13 On the very same day Noah and Noah's
sons, Shem, Ham, and Japheth, and Noah's
wife and the three wives of his sons with
them, entered the ark— 14 they and every
beast after its kind, all cattle after their kind,
every creeping thing that creeps on the earth
after its kind, and every bird after its kind,

Starring Roles

You've seen those funny pictures of NOAH and the ark. Well, Noah didn't think it was very funny at all! He tried to tell everybody that God was going to send a big flood, but they only laughed and said that Noah was out of his mind.

So Noah built the ark just as God told him, and one day every kind of animal came pouring into it. After Noah and his family went in, it all started to happen—the frightening rain that fell and the underground springs that burst upward. You should have heard the pounding of the wind, the swirling waters—and Noah would never forget the horrible cries of the drowning people!

But Noah's family was saved, and the ark settled on Mount Ararat in Turkey. Then they began again to enjoy the life they had in the world before the Flood.

every bird of every sort. 15And they went into
the ark to Noah, two by two, of all flesh in
which *is* the breath of life. 16So those that entered, male and female of all flesh, went in
as God had commanded him; and the LORD
shut him in.

17Now the flood was on the earth forty
days. The waters increased and lifted up the
ark, and it rose high above the earth. 18The
waters prevailed and greatly increased on the
earth, and the ark moved about on the surface of the waters. 19And the waters prevailed
exceedingly on the earth, and all the high
hills under the whole heaven were covered.
20The waters prevailed fifteen cubits upward,
and the mountains were covered. 21And all
flesh died that moved on the earth: birds and
cattle and beasts and every creeping thing
that creeps on the earth, and every man. 22All
in whose nostrils *was* the breath of the spirit[a]
of life, all that *was* on the dry *land,* died. 23So

7:22 [a] Septuagint and Vulgate omit *of the spirit.*

GOD SENDS A GREAT FLOOD

READ IT: GENESIS 7:1–24

GET IT:

This new thing called sin lived in every person born. As more and more people populated the earth, sin had more places to live and grow. Soon the world and its people were very, very wicked. God couldn't stand it anymore. He decided to destroy all living things with a flood. But He wouldn't destroy everybody. One man, Noah, was a really good guy (Genesis 6:9). God selected him to build a big boat and save himself, his family, and a huge assortment of animals.

Noah obeyed God, built the boat, gathered the animals, called together his family, and entered the ark. The rain came. The ocean waters surged. Soon water covered the earth. Everything died. Everything except the people and animals in God's big boat. They sat there, bobbing on the water for five months. Waiting.

LIVE IT:

Little kids love this story—the boat, the animals, the water. It all sounds like fun. But you know differently now. This was serious stuff. Sad, too. Everything died except a handful of people and a boatful of animals. But that's not the end of the story. God promised a happy ending.

Maybe you've experienced a rough time, a flood, or a devastating storm. Did you wonder where God was? Did you feel His presence with you? God doesn't abandon His people in rough times. He stays with them through it all. You'll find safety. The disaster will pass. Eventually things will seem more normal. God never promised we wouldn't face some tough times in life. Even Noah had to ride out the storm. But He does promise to see us through the rough experiences and give us hope for a wonderful future.

He destroyed all living things which were on
the face of the ground: both man and cattle,
creeping thing and bird of the air. They were
destroyed from the earth. Only Noah and
those who *were* with him in the ark remained
alive. 24And the waters prevailed on the earth
one hundred and fifty days.

Noah's Deliverance

8 Then God remembered Noah, and
every living thing, and all the animals
that *were* with him in the ark. And God made
a wind to pass over the earth, and the waters
subsided. 2The fountains of the deep and
the windows of heaven were also stopped,
and the rain from heaven was restrained.
3And the waters receded continually from
the earth. At the end of the hundred and
fifty days the waters decreased. 4Then the
ark rested in the seventh month, the seventeenth day of the month, on the mountains
of Ararat. 5And the waters decreased continually until the tenth month. In the tenth
month, on the first *day* of the month, the tops
of the mountains were seen.

6So it came to pass, at the end of forty
days, that Noah opened the window of the
ark which he had made. 7Then he sent out
a raven, which kept going to and fro until
the waters had dried up from the earth. 8He
also sent out from himself a dove, to see if
the waters had receded from the face of the
ground. 9But the dove found no resting place
for the sole of her foot, and she returned into
the ark to him, for the waters *were* on the face
of the whole earth. So he put out his hand
and took her, and drew her into the ark to
himself. 10And he waited yet another seven
days, and again he sent the dove out from
the ark. 11Then the dove came to him in the
evening, and behold, a freshly plucked olive
leaf *was* in her mouth; and Noah knew that
the waters had receded from the earth. 12So
he waited yet another seven days and sent
out the dove, which did not return again to
him anymore.

GOD MAKES A PROMISE TO THE WORLD

READ IT: GENESIS 8:1–22

GET IT:

Noah and his family were safe in the boat with the animals for more than a month. The rain stopped. The water started to go down. Finally the water went back into the oceans and rivers where it belonged. The land dried up enough for Noah and his family (a total of eight people) to walk off the ark. They were alive, but the land was a mess with the aftereffects of the Flood.

LIVE IT:

We don't have to be concerned about a humongous flood swamping the world. Spring floods or floods from hurricanes will still happen, but those are in one area, not the whole world. God promised He would never *destroy the earth* again this way. He won't. He promised. Every time you see a rainbow in the sky, you'll know it's a sign that God made a promise to the earth and everybody who lives here.

13 And it came to pass in the six hundred
and first year, in the first *month,* the first *day*
of the month, that the waters were dried up
from the earth; and Noah removed the covering of the ark and looked, and indeed the
surface of the ground was dry. 14 And in the
second month, on the twenty-seventh day of
the month, the earth was dried.

15 Then God spoke to Noah, saying, 16 "Go
out of the ark, you and your wife, and your
sons and your sons' wives with you. 17 Bring
out with you every living thing of all flesh
that *is* with you: birds and cattle and every
creeping thing that creeps on the earth,
so that they may abound on the earth, and
be fruitful and multiply on the earth." 18 So
Noah went out, and his sons and his wife
and his sons' wives with him. 19 Every animal, every creeping thing, every bird, *and*
whatever creeps on the earth, according to
their families, went out of the ark.

God's Covenant with Creation

20 Then Noah built an altar to the LORD,
and took of every clean animal and of every
clean bird, and offered burnt offerings on
the altar. 21 And the LORD smelled a soothing
aroma. Then the LORD said in His heart, "I
will never again curse the ground for man's
sake, although the imagination of man's
heart *is* evil from his youth; nor will I again
destroy every living thing as I have done.

22 "While the earth remains,
Seedtime and harvest,
Cold and heat,
Winter and summer,
And day and night
Shall not cease."

9 So God blessed Noah and his sons, and
said to them: "Be fruitful and multiply,
and fill the earth.[a] 2 And the fear of you and
the dread of you shall be on every beast of
the earth, on every bird of the air, on all that
move *on* the earth, and on all the fish of the
sea. They are given into your hand. 3 Every
moving thing that lives shall be food for you.
I have given you all things, even as the green
herbs. 4 But you shall not eat flesh with its
life, *that is,* its blood. 5 Surely for your life-
blood I will demand *a reckoning;* from the
hand of every beast I will require it, and from
the hand of man. From the hand of every
man's brother I will require the life of man.

6 "Whoever sheds man's blood,
By man his blood shall be shed;
For in the image of God
He made man.
7 And as for you, be fruitful and multiply;
Bring forth abundantly in the earth
And multiply in it."

8 Then God spoke to Noah and to his sons
with him, saying: 9 "And as for Me, behold,
I establish My covenant with you and with
your descendants[a] after you, 10 and with every

9:1 [a] Compare Genesis 1:28 **9:9** [a] Literally *seed*

CREATION CARE

READ IT: GENESIS 9:2–7

Being vegetarian is popular and may be healthier for a lot of people. Some would also say that it's environmentally friendly and economical since supplying the world with meat takes up resources. However, it would be a mistake for a Christian to believe that killing an animal in order to eat is a sin. There may be good reasons not to eat meat, but worries that you're "murdering" isn't one of them. God intended for people to use animals as food, even though whether or not you eat meat is up to you. No matter what you decide, eat responsibly.

living creature that *is* with you: the birds, the
cattle, and every beast of the earth with you,
of all that go out of the ark, every beast of the
earth. 11 Thus I establish My covenant with
you: Never again shall all flesh be cut off
by the waters of the flood; never again shall
there be a flood to destroy the earth."

12 And God said: "This *is* the sign of the
covenant which I make between Me and you,
and every living creature that *is* with you, for
perpetual generations: 13 I set My rainbow
in the cloud, and it shall be for the sign of
the covenant between Me and the earth. 14 It
shall be, when I bring a cloud over the earth,
that the rainbow shall be seen in the cloud;
15 and I will remember My covenant which *is*
between Me and you and every living creature of all flesh; the waters shall never again
become a flood to destroy all flesh. 16 The
rainbow shall be in the cloud, and I will look
on it to remember the everlasting covenant
between God and every living creature of all
flesh that *is* on the earth." 17 And God said
to Noah, "This *is* the sign of the covenant
which I have established between Me and
all flesh that *is* on the earth."

Noah and His Sons

18 Now the sons of Noah who went out of
the ark were Shem, Ham, and Japheth. And
Ham *was* the father of Canaan. 19 These three
were the sons of Noah, and from these the
whole earth was populated.

20 And Noah began *to be* a farmer, and he
planted a vineyard. 21 Then he drank of the
wine and was drunk, and became uncovered
in his tent. 22 And Ham, the father of Canaan,
saw the nakedness of his father, and told
his two brothers outside. 23 But Shem and
Japheth took a garment, laid *it* on both their
shoulders, and went backward and covered
the nakedness of their father. Their faces
were turned away, and they did not see their
father's nakedness.

24 So Noah awoke from his wine, and
knew what his younger son had done to him.
25 Then he said:

"Cursed *be* Canaan;
A servant of servants
He shall be to his brethren."

26 And he said:

"Blessed *be* the LORD,
The God of Shem,
And may Canaan be his servant.

27 May God enlarge Japheth,
And may he dwell in the tents of Shem;
And may Canaan be his servant."

28 And Noah lived after the flood three
hundred and fifty years. 29 So all the days of
Noah were nine hundred and fifty years; and
he died.

Nations Descended from Noah

10 Now this *is* the genealogy of the
sons of Noah: Shem, Ham, and
Japheth. And sons were born to them after
the flood.

2 The sons of Japheth *were* Gomer, Magog,
Madai, Javan, Tubal, Meshech, and Tiras. 3 The
sons of Gomer *were* Ashkenaz, Riphath,[a] and
Togarmah. 4 The sons of Javan *were* Elishah,
Tarshish, Kittim, and Dodanim.[a] 5 From these
the coastland *peoples* of the Gentiles were separated into their lands, everyone according to
his language, according to their families, into
their nations.

6 The sons of Ham *were* Cush, Mizraim, Put,[a] and Canaan. 7 The sons of Cush
were Seba, Havilah, Sabtah, Raamah, and
Sabtechah; and the sons of Raamah *were*
Sheba and Dedan.

8 Cush begot Nimrod; he began to be a
mighty one on the earth. 9 He was a mighty
hunter before the LORD; therefore it is said,
"Like Nimrod the mighty hunter before the
LORD." 10 And the beginning of his kingdom
was Babel, Erech, Accad, and Calneh, in the
land of Shinar. 11 From that land he went to
Assyria and built Nineveh, Rehoboth Ir,
Calah, 12 and Resen between Nineveh and
Calah (that *is* the principal city).

13 Mizraim begot Ludim, Anamim,
Lehabim, Naphtuhim, 14 Pathrusim, and
Casluhim (from whom came the Philistines
and Caphtorim).

15 Canaan begot Sidon his firstborn,
and Heth; 16 the Jebusite, the Amorite, and
the Girgashite; 17 the Hivite, the Arkite,
and the Sinite; 18 the Arvadite, the Zemarite,
and the Hamathite. Afterward the families
of the Canaanites were dispersed. 19 And the
border of the Canaanites was from Sidon as
you go toward Gerar, as far as Gaza; then as
you go toward Sodom, Gomorrah, Admah,
and Zeboiim, as far as Lasha. 20 These *were*

10:3 [a] Spelled *Diphath* in 1 Chronicles 1:6 **10:4** [a] Spelled *Rodanim* in Samaritan Pentateuch and 1 Chronicles 1:7
10:6 [a] Or *Phut*

the sons of Ham, according to their families, according to their languages, in their
lands *and* in their nations.

21And *children* were born also to Shem,
the father of all the children of Eber, the
brother of Japheth the elder. 22The sons of
Shem *were* Elam, Asshur, Arphaxad, Lud,
and Aram. 23The sons of Aram *were* Uz,
Hul, Gether, and Mash.[a] 24Arphaxad begot
Salah,[a] and Salah begot Eber. 25To Eber were
born two sons: the name of one *was* Peleg,
for in his days the earth was divided; and his
brother's name *was* Joktan. 26Joktan begot
Almodad, Sheleph, Hazarmaveth, Jerah,
27Hadoram, Uzal, Diklah, 28Obal,[a] Abimael,
Sheba, 29Ophir, Havilah, and Jobab. All these
were the sons of Joktan. 30And their dwelling place was from Mesha as you go toward
Sephar, the mountain of the east. 31These
were the sons of Shem, according to their
families, according to their languages, in
their lands, according to their nations.

32These *were* the families of the sons of
Noah, according to their generations, in
their nations; and from these the nations
were divided on the earth after the flood.

The Tower of Babel

11 Now the whole earth had one language and one speech. 2And it came
to pass, as they journeyed from the east, that
they found a plain in the land of Shinar, and
they dwelt there. 3Then they said to one another, "Come, let us make bricks and bake
them thoroughly." They had brick for stone,
and they had asphalt for mortar. 4And they
said, "Come, let us build ourselves a city, and
a tower whose top *is* in the heavens; let us
make a name for ourselves, lest we be scattered abroad over the face of the whole earth."

5But the LORD came down to see the city
and the tower which the sons of men had
built. 6And the LORD said, "Indeed the people *are* one and they all have one language,
and this is what they begin to do; now nothing that they propose to do will be withheld
from them. 7Come, let Us go down and
there confuse their language, that they may
not understand one another's speech." 8So
the LORD scattered them abroad from there
over the face of all the earth, and they ceased
building the city. 9Therefore its name is
called Babel, because there the LORD confused the language of all the earth; and from

In Focus

10:18 Canaanites Pronounced *KAY-nuh-nights*. Descendants of Noah's grandson, Canaan. Canaanites settled in Palestine long before God told Abraham to move there. Then Palestine was called Canaan.

there the LORD scattered them abroad over
the face of all the earth.

Shem's Descendants

10This *is* the genealogy of Shem: Shem
was one hundred years old, and begot Arphaxad two years after the flood. 11After he
begot Arphaxad, Shem lived five hundred
years, and begot sons and daughters.

12Arphaxad lived thirty-five years, and begot Salah. 13After he begot Salah, Arphaxad
lived four hundred and three years, and begot sons and daughters.

14Salah lived thirty years, and begot Eber.
15After he begot Eber, Salah lived four hundred and three years, and begot sons and
daughters.

16Eber lived thirty-four years, and begot
Peleg. 17After he begot Peleg, Eber lived four
hundred and thirty years, and begot sons
and daughters.

18Peleg lived thirty years, and begot Reu.
19After he begot Reu, Peleg lived two hundred and nine years, and begot sons and
daughters.

20Reu lived thirty-two years, and begot
Serug. 21After he begot Serug, Reu lived two
hundred and seven years, and begot sons
and daughters.

22Serug lived thirty years, and begot Nahor. 23After he begot Nahor, Serug lived two
hundred years, and begot sons and daughters.

24Nahor lived twenty-nine years, and
begot Terah. 25After he begot Terah, Nahor
lived one hundred and nineteen years, and
begot sons and daughters.

10:23 [a] Called *Meshech* in Septuagint and 1 Chronicles 1:17
10:24 [a] Following Masoretic Text, Vulgate, and Targum; Septuagint reads *Arphaxad begot Cainan, and Cainan begot Salah* (compare Luke 3:35, 36). **10:28** [a] Spelled *Ebal* in 1 Chronicles 1:22

In Focus

11:28 Chaldeans The people who lived in Chaldea (pronounced *kal-DEE-uh*), a land found in the region of modern Iran and Iraq. Chaldea later included nearly all of Babylonia (pronounced *bab-ih-LOW-nih-uh*).

26Now Terah lived seventy years, and begot Abram, Nahor, and Haran.

Terah's Descendants

27This *is* the genealogy of Terah: Terah
begot Abram, Nahor, and Haran. Haran begot Lot. 28And Haran died before his father
Terah in his native land, in Ur of the Chaldeans. 29Then Abram and Nahor took wives:
the name of Abram's wife *was* Sarai, and the
name of Nahor's wife, Milcah, the daughter
of Haran the father of Milcah and the father
of Iscah. 30But Sarai was barren; she had no
child.

31And Terah took his son Abram and his
grandson Lot, the son of Haran, and his
daughter-in-law Sarai, his son Abram's wife,
and they went out with them from Ur of the
Chaldeans to go to the land of Canaan; and
they came to Haran and dwelt there. 32So the
days of Terah were two hundred and five
years, and Terah died in Haran.

Promises to Abram

12 Now the LORD had said to Abram:

"Get out of your country,
From your family
And from your father's house,
To a land that I will show you.
2 I will make you a great nation;
I will bless you
And make your name great;
And you shall be a blessing.
3 I will bless those who bless you,
And I will curse him who curses you;
And in you all the families of the earth
shall be blessed."

4So Abram departed as the LORD had
spoken to him, and Lot went with him. And
Abram *was* seventy-five years old when he
departed from Haran. 5Then Abram took
Sarai his wife and Lot his brother's son, and
all their possessions that they had gathered,
and the people whom they had acquired in
Haran, and they departed to go to the land
of Canaan. So they came to the land of Canaan. 6Abram passed through the land to the
place of Shechem, as far as the terebinth tree

Starring Roles

You are going to read a lot about **ABRAM** in the Bible. God changed his name from Abram (pronounced *AY-brum*), meaning "Great Father," to Abraham (pronounced *AY-bruh-ham*), meaning "Father of Many People." He lived two thousand years before Jesus was born.

The most important thing to remember is that God made some of His greatest promises to Abraham. Those promises are just as good today as they were in Abraham's own time.

God promised to lead Abraham to a new country that would belong to his people forever—and God did just that! Abraham's people, the Hebrews, still live in Palestine today.

Not only that, but God also promised Abraham a very great Grandson who would someday save us from our sins. You have probably heard of Him. His name is Jesus.

of Moreh.[a] And the Canaanites *were* then in
the land.
[7]Then the LORD appeared to Abram and
said, "To your descendants I will give this
land." And there he built an altar to the
LORD, who had appeared to him. [8]And he
moved from there to the mountain east of
Bethel, and he pitched his tent *with* Bethel
on the west and Ai on the east; there he built
an altar to the LORD and called on the name
of the LORD. [9]So Abram journeyed, going on
still toward the South.[a]

Abram in Egypt

[10]Now there was a famine in the land,
and Abram went down to Egypt to dwell
there, for the famine *was* severe in the land.
[11]And it came to pass, when he was close
to entering Egypt, that he said to Sarai his
wife, "Indeed I know that you *are* a woman
of beautiful countenance. [12]Therefore it will
happen, when the Egyptians see you, that
they will say, 'This *is* his wife'; and they will
kill me, but they will let you live. [13]Please say
you *are* my sister, that it may be well with me
for your sake, and that I[a] may live because
of you."
[14]So it was, when Abram came into
Egypt, that the Egyptians saw the woman,

12:6 [a] Hebrew *Alon Moreh* 12:9 [a] Hebrew *Negev*
12:13 [a] Literally *my soul*

GOD'S PROMISE FOR A NATION

READ IT: GENESIS 12:1–9; 13:1–18

GET IT:

After the Flood, the world got back to normal. Babies were born and grew up and had more babies. Time passed. Eventually the earth was full of people again.

God selected one person out of all the people in the world. He selected a man named Abram. God wanted to have a special relationship again with His people. So He chose Abram and his wife, Sarai, and told them what to do: "Leave the life you know and go where I show you. I'll bless you and make you into a great nation. Now go."

Can you imagine listening to someone who said, "Get in the car and start driving. I'll tell you when to stop"? That would seem crazy. But basically, that's what Abram and Sarai did. They packed up and headed into the desert to follow God. Later we find out that Abram did this because "he believed in the LORD" (Genesis 15:6). It sounded nuts, but Abram believed God had a really good plan for him.

LIVE IT:

God doesn't talk as directly to us as He did to Abram. But He still speaks. You can hear Him through the voices of wise people: parents, grandparents, leaders, teachers, or coaches. You can find this out through what you're good at doing and what you love to do. God is calling you to follow Him now, while you are young. Believe in Him. He's got a great plan for your life.

that she *was* very beautiful. 15The princes of
Pharaoh also saw her and commended her
to Pharaoh. And the woman was taken to
Pharaoh's house. 16He treated Abram well for
her sake. He had sheep, oxen, male donkeys,
male and female servants, female donkeys,
and camels.

17But the LORD plagued Pharaoh and his
house with great plagues because of Sarai,
Abram's wife. 18And Pharaoh called Abram
and said, "What *is* this you have done to me?
Why did you not tell me that she *was* your
wife? 19Why did you say, 'She *is* my sister'? I
might have taken her as my wife. Now therefore, here is your wife; take *her* and go your
way." 20So Pharaoh commanded *his* men concerning him; and they sent him away, with
his wife and all that he had.

Abram Inherits Canaan

13 Then Abram went up from Egypt,
he and his wife and all that he had,
and Lot with him, to the South.[a] 2Abram *was*
very rich in livestock, in silver, and in gold.
3And he went on his journey from the South
as far as Bethel, to the place where his tent
had been at the beginning, between Bethel
and Ai, 4to the place of the altar which he had
made there at first. And there Abram called
on the name of the LORD.

5Lot also, who went with Abram, had
flocks and herds and tents. 6Now the land
was not able to support them, that they
might dwell together, for their possessions
were so great that they could not dwell together. 7And there was strife between the
herdsmen of Abram's livestock and the
herdsmen of Lot's livestock. The Canaanites
and the Perizzites then dwelt in the land.

8So Abram said to Lot, "Please let there
be no strife between you and me, and between my herdsmen and your herdsmen; for
we *are* brethren. 9*Is* not the whole land before
you? Please separate from me. If *you take* the
left, then I will go to the right; or, if *you go* to
the right, then I will go to the left."

10And Lot lifted his eyes and saw all the
plain of Jordan, that it *was* well watered everywhere (before the LORD destroyed Sodom
and Gomorrah) like the garden of the LORD,
like the land of Egypt as you go toward Zoar.
11Then Lot chose for himself all the plain of
Jordan, and Lot journeyed east. And they
separated from each other. 12Abram dwelt
in the land of Canaan, and Lot dwelt in the
cities of the plain and pitched *his* tent even
as far as Sodom. 13But the men of Sodom
were exceedingly wicked and sinful against
the LORD.

14And the LORD said to Abram, after Lot
had separated from him: "Lift your eyes now
and look from the place where you are—
northward, southward, eastward, and westward; 15for all the land which you see I give
to you and your descendants[a] forever. 16And

13:1 [a] Hebrew *Negev* 13:15 [a] Literally *seed,* and so throughout the book

Starring Roles

SARAH'S name means "Princess." She was Abraham's first wife and the mother of Isaac.

She is a lesson to all boys that they should promise to be fair to their wives when they marry. Abraham wasn't always fair to Sarah. Twice he pretended she was only his sister, and both the Pharaoh (pronounced *FAY-row*) of Egypt and the king of Gerar (pronounced *GHEE-rar*) nearly got into a lot of trouble because of Abraham's lie.

Sometimes Sarah did what was wrong, too, like when she sent poor Hagar and her son Ishmael (pronounced *HAY-gar* and *ISH-may-el*) away. Although God forgave her, she was always sorry for what she had done. The Lord cared for Hagar and Ishmael in spite of Sarah's lack of love (see Genesis 17:20).

I will make your descendants as the dust of
the earth; so that if a man could number the
dust of the earth, *then* your descendants also
could be numbered. 17Arise, walk in the land
through its length and its width, for I give
it to you."

18Then Abram moved *his* tent, and went
and dwelt by the terebinth trees of Mamre,[a]
which *are* in Hebron, and built an altar there
to the LORD.

Lot's Captivity and Rescue

14 And it came to pass in the days of
Amraphel king of Shinar, Arioch
king of Ellasar, Chedorlaomer king of Elam,
and Tidal king of nations,[a] 2*that* they made
war with Bera king of Sodom, Birsha king of
Gomorrah, Shinab king of Admah, Sheme-
ber king of Zeboiim, and the king of Bela
(that is, Zoar). 3All these joined together in
the Valley of Siddim (that is, the Salt Sea).
4Twelve years they served Chedorlaomer,
and in the thirteenth year they rebelled.

5In the fourteenth year Chedorlaomer
and the kings that *were* with him came and
attacked the Rephaim in Ashteroth Karnaim, the Zuzim in Ham, the Emim in
Shaveh Kiriathaim, 6and the Horites in their
mountain of Seir, as far as El Paran, which
is by the wilderness. 7Then they turned back
and came to En Mishpat (that *is,* Kadesh),
and attacked all the country of the Amalekites, and also the Amorites who dwelt in
Hazezon Tamar.

8And the king of Sodom, the king of
Gomorrah, the king of Admah, the king
of Zeboiim, and the king of Bela (that *is,*
Zoar) went out and joined together in battle
in the Valley of Siddim 9against Chedorlaomer king of Elam, Tidal king of nations,[a]
Amraphel king of Shinar, and Arioch king
of Ellasar—four kings against five. 10Now
the Valley of Siddim *was full of* asphalt pits;
and the kings of Sodom and Gomorrah fled;
some fell there, and the remainder fled to the
mountains. 11Then they took all the goods of
Sodom and Gomorrah, and all their provisions, and went their way. 12They also took
Lot, Abram's brother's son who dwelt in
Sodom, and his goods, and departed.

13Then one who had escaped came and
told Abram the Hebrew, for he dwelt by
the terebinth trees of Mamre[a] the Amorite,
brother of Eshcol and brother of Aner; and
they *were* allies with Abram. 14Now when
Abram heard that his brother was taken
captive, he armed his three hundred and
eighteen trained *servants* who were born in
his own house, and went in pursuit as far as
Dan. 15He divided his forces against them by
night, and he and his servants attacked them
and pursued them as far as Hobah, which *is*
north of Damascus. 16So he brought back all
the goods, and also brought back his brother
Lot and his goods, as well as the women and
the people.

17And the king of Sodom went out to
meet him at the Valley of Shaveh (that *is,*
the King's Valley), after his return from the
defeat of Chedorlaomer and the kings who
were with him.

Abram and Melchizedek

18Then Melchizedek king of Salem
brought out bread and wine; he *was* the
priest of God Most High. 19And he blessed
him and said:

"Blessed be Abram of God Most High,
Possessor of heaven and earth;
20 And blessed be God Most High,
Who has delivered your enemies into
your hand."

And he gave him a tithe of all.

21Now the king of Sodom said to Abram,
"Give me the persons, and take the goods for
yourself."

22But Abram said to the king of Sodom, "I
have raised my hand to the LORD, God Most
High, the Possessor of heaven and earth,
23that I *will take* nothing, from a thread to
a sandal strap, and that I will not take anything that *is* yours, lest you should say, 'I
have made Abram rich'— 24except only what
the young men have eaten, and the portion
of the men who went with me: Aner, Eshcol,
and Mamre; let them take their portion."

God's Covenant with Abram

15 After these things the word of the
LORD came to Abram in a vision,
saying, "Do not be afraid, Abram. I *am* your
shield, your exceedingly great reward."

2But Abram said, "Lord GOD, what will
You give me, seeing I go childless, and the
heir of my house *is* Eliezer of Damascus?"
3Then Abram said, "Look, You have given
me no offspring; indeed one born in my
house is my heir!"

13:18 [a] Hebrew *Alon Mamre* 14:1 [a] Hebrew *goyim*
14:9 [a] Hebrew *goyim* 14:13 [a] Hebrew *Alon Mamre*

4And behold, the word of the LORD *came* to him, saying, "This one shall not be your heir, but one who will come from your own body shall be your heir." 5Then He brought him outside and said, "Look now toward heaven, and count the stars if you are able to number them." And He said to him, "So shall your descendants be."

6And he believed in the LORD, and He accounted it to him for righteousness.

7Then He said to him, "I *am* the LORD, who brought you out of Ur of the Chaldeans, to give you this land to inherit it."

8And he said, "Lord GOD, how shall I know that I will inherit it?"

9So He said to him, "Bring Me a three-year-old heifer, a three-year-old female goat, a three-year-old ram, a turtledove, and a young pigeon." 10Then he brought all these to Him and cut them in two, down the middle, and placed each piece opposite the other; but he did not cut the birds in two. 11And when the vultures came down on the carcasses, Abram drove them away.

12Now when the sun was going down, a deep sleep fell upon Abram; and behold, horror *and* great darkness fell upon him. 13Then He said to Abram: "Know certainly that your descendants will be strangers in a land *that is* not theirs, and will serve them, and they will afflict them four hundred years. 14And also the nation whom they serve I will judge; afterward they shall come out with great possessions. 15Now as for you, you shall go to your fathers in peace; you shall be buried at a good old age. 16But in the fourth generation they shall return here, for the iniquity of the Amorites *is* not yet complete."

17And it came to pass, when the sun went down and it was dark, that behold, there appeared a smoking oven and a burning torch that passed between those pieces. 18On the same day the LORD made a covenant with Abram, saying:

"To your descendants I have given this land, from the river of Egypt to the great river, the River Euphrates— 19the Kenites, the Kenezzites, the Kadmonites, 20the Hittites, the Perizzites, the Rephaim, 21the Amorites, the Canaanites, the Girgashites, and the Jebusites."

Hagar and Ishmael

16 Now Sarai, Abram's wife, had borne him no *children*. And she had an Egyptian maidservant whose name was Hagar. 2So Sarai said to Abram, "See now, the LORD has restrained me from bearing *children*. Please, go in to my maid; perhaps I shall obtain children by her." And Abram heeded the voice of Sarai. 3Then Sarai, Abram's wife, took Hagar her maid, the Egyptian, and gave her to her husband Abram to be his wife, after Abram had dwelt ten years in the land of Canaan. 4So he went in to Hagar, and she conceived. And when she saw that she had conceived, her mistress became despised in her eyes.

5Then Sarai said to Abram, "My wrong *be* upon you! I gave my maid into your embrace; and when she saw that she had conceived, I became despised in her eyes. The LORD judge between you and me."

6So Abram said to Sarai, "Indeed your maid *is* in your hand; do to her as you please." And when Sarai dealt harshly with her, she fled from her presence.

7Now the Angel of the LORD found her by a spring of water in the wilderness, by the spring on the way to Shur. 8And He said, "Hagar, Sarai's maid, where have you come from, and where are you going?"

She said, "I am fleeing from the presence of my mistress Sarai."

9The Angel of the LORD said to her, "Return to your mistress, and submit yourself under her hand." 10Then the Angel of the LORD said to her, "I will multiply your descendants exceedingly, so that they shall not be counted for multitude." 11And the Angel of the LORD said to her:

"Behold, you *are* with child,
And you shall bear a son.
You shall call his name Ishmael,
Because the LORD has heard your
affliction.
12 He shall be a wild man;
His hand *shall be* against every man,
And every man's hand against him.
And he shall dwell in the presence of all
his brethren."

13Then she called the name of the LORD who spoke to her, You-Are-the-God-Who-Sees; for she said, "Have I also here seen Him who sees me?" 14Therefore the well was called Beer Lahai Roi;[a] observe, *it is* between Kadesh and Bered.

16:14 [a] Literally *Well of the One Who Lives and Sees Me*

15So Hagar bore Abram a son; and Abram named his son, whom Hagar bore, Ishmael. 16Abram *was* eighty-six years old when Hagar bore Ishmael to Abram.

The Sign of the Covenant

17 When Abram was ninety-nine years old, the LORD appeared to Abram and said to him, "I *am* Almighty God; walk before Me and be blameless. 2And I will make My covenant between Me and you, and will multiply you exceedingly." 3Then Abram fell on his face, and God talked with him, saying: 4"As for Me, behold, My covenant is with you, and you shall be a father of many nations. 5No longer shall your name be called Abram, but your name shall be Abraham; for I have made you a father of many nations. 6I will make you exceedingly fruitful; and I will make nations of you, and kings shall come from you. 7And I will establish My covenant between Me and you and your descendants after you in their generations, for an everlasting covenant, to be God to you and your descendants after you. 8Also I give to you and your descendants after you the land in which you are a stranger, all the land of Canaan, as an everlasting possession; and I will be their God."

9And God said to Abraham: "As for you, you shall keep My covenant, you and your descendants after you throughout their generations. 10This *is* My covenant which you shall keep, between Me and you and your descendants after you: Every male child among you shall be circumcised; 11and you shall be circumcised in the flesh of your foreskins, and it shall be a sign of the covenant between Me and you. 12He who is eight days old among you shall be circumcised, every male child in your generations, he who is born in your house or bought with money from any foreigner who is not your descendant. 13He who is born in your house and he who is bought with your money must be circumcised, and My covenant shall be in your flesh for an everlasting covenant. 14And the uncircumcised male child, who is not circumcised in the flesh of his foreskin, that person shall be cut off from his people; he has broken My covenant."

15Then God said to Abraham, "As for Sarai your wife, you shall not call her name Sarai, but Sarah *shall be* her name. 16And I will bless her and also give you a son by her; then I will bless her, and she shall be *a mother of* nations; kings of peoples shall be from her."

17Then Abraham fell on his face and laughed, and said in his heart, "Shall *a child* be born to a man who is one hundred years old? And shall Sarah, who is ninety years old, bear *a child?*" 18And Abraham said to God, "Oh, that Ishmael might live before You!"

19Then God said: "No, Sarah your wife shall bear you a son, and you shall call his name Isaac; I will establish My covenant with him for an everlasting covenant, *and* with his descendants after him. 20And as for Ishmael, I have heard you. Behold, I have blessed him, and will make him fruitful, and will multiply him exceedingly. He shall beget twelve princes, and I will make him a great nation. 21But My covenant I will establish with Isaac, whom Sarah shall bear to you at this set time next year." 22Then He finished talking with him, and God went up from Abraham.

23So Abraham took Ishmael his son, all who were born in his house and all who were bought with his money, every male among the men of Abraham's house, and circumcised the flesh of their foreskins that very same day, as God had said to him. 24Abraham *was* ninety-nine years old when he was circumcised in the flesh of his foreskin. 25And Ishmael his son *was* thirteen years old when he was circumcised in the flesh of his foreskin. 26That very same day Abraham was circumcised, and his son Ishmael; 27and all the men of his house, born in the house or

In Focus

16:7 Angel of the Lord Sometimes called the Angel of the Presence. This Angel was really a way in which the Lord Himself was revealed to people.

17:2 Covenant A legal agreement. God made a covenant with Abraham to give the land of Canaan to his descendants and to make Abraham a blessing to the whole world.

bought with money from a foreigner, were circumcised with him.

The Son of Promise

18 Then the LORD appeared to him by
the terebinth trees of Mamre,[a] as
he was sitting in the tent door in the heat
of the day. 2So he lifted his eyes and looked,
and behold, three men were standing by
him; and when he saw *them,* he ran from the
tent door to meet them, and bowed himself
to the ground, 3and said, "My Lord, if I have
now found favor in Your sight, do not pass
on by Your servant. 4Please let a little water
be brought, and wash your feet, and rest
yourselves under the tree. 5And I will bring
a morsel of bread, that you may refresh your
hearts. After that you may pass by, inasmuch
as you have come to your servant."

They said, "Do as you have said."

6So Abraham hurried into the tent to
Sarah and said, "Quickly, make ready three
measures of fine meal; knead *it* and make
cakes." 7And Abraham ran to the herd, took
a tender and good calf, gave *it* to a young
man, and he hastened to prepare it. 8So he

18:1 [a] Hebrew *Alon Mamre*

Spotlight

GOD'S PROMISE TO ABRAHAM

READ IT: GENESIS 18:1–15

GET IT:

Abram and Sarai believed God. They followed Him to a new country. Abram heard God's promise that he would be the father of a great nation. He would be the father of so many people they would be as many as the stars in the sky! What a promise! God even changed Abram's name to Abraham to seal the deal. Abraham means "father of many."

One problem: Abraham and Sarah were getting old and they still didn't have any kids. They had one son, whose name was Ishmael, by their slave, Hagar. But God said, "No, he's not the heir of this great nation. You and Sarah will have your own son."

More years passed. No baby. Then visitors showed up and told Abraham he was going to be a father. What a joke. Abraham was one hundred years old and Sarah was ninety-nine. Old people don't have new babies! It's just not possible. But it was possible because anything is possible for God. Nothing's too hard for Him.

LIVE IT:

At one time or another you've probably given up on something and said, "I can't do it. It's just too hard." Maybe you couldn't find success in a class, or you felt like a failure in a skill you were trying to develop, or you couldn't seem to fix a problem with a friend. We're human. We have limits on physical and mental strength. Sometimes we can keep trying, *keep practicing, and get there.* Sometimes not. With God it's different. Nothing—absolutely, positively nothing—is too hard for God. He's God. He can do anything.

took butter and milk and the calf which he
had prepared, and set *it* before them; and he
stood by them under the tree as they ate.
9 Then they said to him, "Where *is* Sarah
your wife?"

So he said, "Here, in the tent."
10 And He said, "I will certainly return to
you according to the time of life, and behold,
Sarah your wife shall have a son."

(Sarah was listening in the tent door
which *was* behind him.) 11 Now Abraham and
Sarah were old, well advanced in age; *and*
Sarah had passed the age of childbearing.[a]
12 Therefore Sarah laughed within herself,
saying, "After I have grown old, shall I have
pleasure, my lord being old also?"
13 And the LORD said to Abraham, "Why
did Sarah laugh, saying, 'Shall I surely bear
a child, since I am old?' 14 Is anything too
hard for the LORD? At the appointed time I
will return to you, according to the time of
life, and Sarah shall have a son."
15 But Sarah denied *it,* saying, "I did not
laugh," for she was afraid.

And He said, "No, but you did laugh!"

Abraham Intercedes for Sodom

16 Then the men rose from there and
looked toward Sodom, and Abraham went
with them to send them on the way. 17 And
the LORD said, "Shall I hide from Abraham
what I am doing, 18 since Abraham shall surely become a great and mighty nation, and
all the nations of the earth shall be blessed
in him? 19 For I have known him, in order
that he may command his children and his
household after him, that they keep the way
of the LORD, to do righteousness and justice,
that the LORD may bring to Abraham what
He has spoken to him." 20 And the LORD said,
"Because the outcry against Sodom and Gomorrah is great, and because their sin is very
grave, 21 I will go down now and see whether
they have done altogether according to the
outcry against it that has come to Me; and if
not, I will know."
22 Then the men turned away from there
and went toward Sodom, but Abraham still
stood before the LORD. 23 And Abraham came
near and said, "Would You also destroy the
righteous with the wicked? 24 Suppose there
were fifty righteous within the city; would
You also destroy the place and not spare *it*
for the fifty righteous that were in it? 25 Far
be it from You to do such a thing as this, to
slay the righteous with the wicked, so that
the righteous should be as the wicked; far
be it from You! Shall not the Judge of all the
earth do right?"
26 So the LORD said, "If I find in Sodom
fifty righteous within the city, then I will
spare all the place for their sakes."
27 Then Abraham answered and said, "Indeed now, I who *am but* dust and ashes have
taken it upon myself to speak to the Lord:
28 Suppose there were five less than the fifty
righteous; would You destroy all of the city
for *lack of* five?"

So He said, "If I find there forty-five, I
will not destroy *it.*"
29 And he spoke to Him yet again and
said, "Suppose there should be forty found
there?"

So He said, "I will not do *it* for the sake
of forty."
30 Then he said, "Let not the Lord be angry, and I will speak: Suppose thirty should
be found there?"

So He said, "I will not do *it* if I find thirty
there."
31 And he said, "Indeed now, I have taken
it upon myself to speak to the Lord: Suppose
twenty should be found there?"

So He said, "I will not destroy *it* for the
sake of twenty."
32 Then he said, "Let not the Lord be angry, and I will speak but once more: Suppose
ten should be found there?"

And He said, "I will not destroy *it* for the
sake of ten." 33 So the LORD went His way
as soon as He had finished speaking with
Abraham; and Abraham returned to his
place.

Sodom's Depravity

19 Now the two angels came to Sodom
in the evening, and Lot was sitting
in the gate of Sodom. When Lot saw *them,*
he rose to meet them, and he bowed himself with his face toward the ground. 2 And
he said, "Here now, my lords, please turn in
to your servant's house and spend the night,
and wash your feet; then you may rise early
and go on your way."

And they said, "No, but we will spend the
night in the open square."

18:11 [a] Literally *the manner of women had ceased to be with Sarah*

3But he insisted strongly; so they turned
in to him and entered his house. Then he
made them a feast, and baked unleavened
bread, and they ate.
4Now before they lay down, the men of
the city, the men of Sodom, both old and
young, all the people from every quarter,
surrounded the house. 5And they called to
Lot and said to him, "Where are the men
who came to you tonight? Bring them out to
us that we may know them *carnally.*"
6So Lot went out to them through the
doorway, shut the door behind him, 7and
said, "Please, my brethren, do not do so
wickedly! 8See now, I have two daughters
who have not known a man; please, let me
bring them out to you, and you may do to
them as you wish; only do nothing to these
men, since this is the reason they have come
under the shadow of my roof."
9And they said, "Stand back!" Then they
said, "This one came in to stay *here,* and he
keeps acting as a judge; now we will deal
worse with you than with them." So they
pressed hard against the man Lot, and came
near to break down the door. 10But the men
reached out their hands and pulled Lot into
the house with them, and shut the door.
11And they struck the men who *were* at the
doorway of the house with blindness, both
small and great, so that they became weary
trying to find the door.

Sodom and Gomorrah Destroyed

12Then the men said to Lot, "Have you
anyone else here? Son-in-law, your sons,
your daughters, and whomever you have in
the city—take *them* out of this place! 13For
we will destroy this place, because the outcry against them has grown great before the
face of the LORD, and the LORD has sent us
to destroy it."
14So Lot went out and spoke to his sons-
in-law, who had married his daughters, and
said, "Get up, get out of this place; for the
LORD will destroy this city!" But to his sons-
in-law he seemed to be joking.
15When the morning dawned, the angels
urged Lot to hurry, saying, "Arise, take your
wife and your two daughters who are here,
lest you be consumed *in the punishment* of
the city." 16And while he lingered, the men
took hold of his hand, his wife's hand, and
the hands of his two daughters, the LORD
being merciful to him, and they brought
him out and set him outside the city. 17So it
came to pass, when they had brought them
outside, that he[a] said, "Escape for your life!
Do not look behind you nor stay anywhere in
the plain. Escape to the mountains, lest you
be destroyed."
18Then Lot said to them, "Please, no, my
lords! 19Indeed now, your servant has found
favor in your sight, and you have increased
your mercy which you have shown me by
saving my life; but I cannot escape to the
mountains, lest some evil overtake me and I
die. 20See now, this city *is* near *enough* to flee
to, and it *is* a little one; please let me escape
there (*is* it not a little one?) and my soul shall
live."
21And he said to him, "See, I have favored
you concerning this thing also, in that I will
not overthrow this city for which you have
spoken. 22Hurry, escape there. For I cannot
do anything until you arrive there."
Therefore the name of the city was called
Zoar.
23The sun had risen upon the earth when
Lot entered Zoar. 24Then the LORD rained
brimstone and fire on Sodom and Gomorrah, from the LORD out of the heavens. 25So
He overthrew those cities, all the plain, all
the inhabitants of the cities, and what grew
on the ground.
26But his wife looked back behind him,
and she became a pillar of salt.
27And Abraham went early in the morning to the place where he had stood before
the LORD. 28Then he looked toward Sodom
and Gomorrah, and toward all the land of
the plain; and he saw, and behold, the smoke
of the land which went up like the smoke of
a furnace. 29And it came to pass, when God
destroyed the cities of the plain, that God remembered Abraham, and sent Lot out of the
midst of the overthrow, when He overthrew
the cities in which Lot had dwelt.

The Descendants of Lot

30Then Lot went up out of Zoar and dwelt
in the mountains, and his two daughters
were with him; for he was afraid to dwell in
Zoar. And he and his two daughters dwelt in a
cave. 31Now the firstborn said to the younger,
"Our father *is* old, and *there is* no man on the
earth to come in to us as is the custom of
all the earth. 32Come, let us make our father

19:17 [a] Septuagint, Syriac, and Vulgate read *they.*

drink wine, and we will lie with him, that
we may preserve the lineage of our father."
33So they made their father drink wine that
night. And the firstborn went in and lay with
her father, and he did not know when she lay
down or when she arose.

34It happened on the next day that the
firstborn said to the younger, "Indeed I lay
with my father last night; let us make him
drink wine tonight also, and you go in *and*
lie with him, that we may preserve the lineage of our father." 35Then they made their
father drink wine that night also. And the
younger arose and lay with him, and he did
not know when she lay down or when she
arose.

36Thus both the daughters of Lot were
with child by their father. 37The firstborn
bore a son and called his name Moab; he *is*
the father of the Moabites to this day. 38And
the younger, she also bore a son and called
his name Ben-Ammi; he *is* the father of the
people of Ammon to this day.

Abraham and Abimelech

20 And Abraham journeyed from
there to the South, and dwelt
between Kadesh and Shur, and stayed in
Gerar. 2Now Abraham said of Sarah his wife,
"She *is* my sister." And Abimelech king of
Gerar sent and took Sarah.

3But God came to Abimelech in a dream
by night, and said to him, "Indeed you *are* a
dead man because of the woman whom you
have taken, for she *is* a man's wife."

4But Abimelech had not come near her;
and he said, "Lord, will You slay a righteous
nation also? 5Did he not say to me, 'She *is* my
sister'? And she, even she herself said, 'He *is*
my brother.' In the integrity of my heart and
innocence of my hands I have done this."

6And God said to him in a dream, "Yes,
I know that you did this in the integrity of
your heart. For I also withheld you from sinning against Me; therefore I did not let you
touch her. 7Now therefore, restore the man's
wife; for he *is* a prophet, and he will pray for
you and you shall live. But if you do not restore *her,* know that you shall surely die, you
and all who *are* yours."

8So Abimelech rose early in the morning, called all his servants, and told all these
things in their hearing; and the men were
very much afraid. 9And Abimelech called

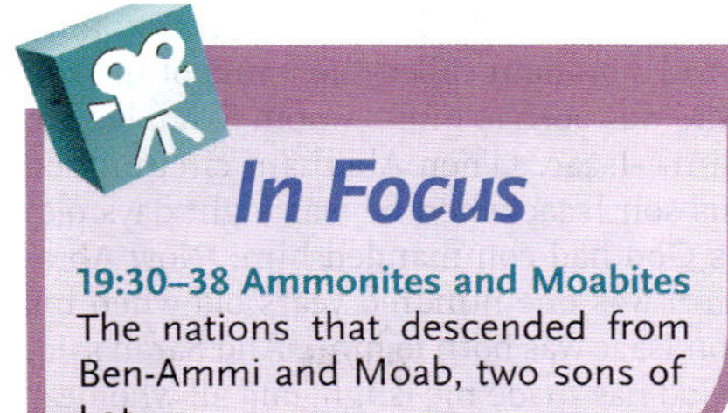

19:30–38 Ammonites and Moabites
The nations that descended from Ben-Ammi and Moab, two sons of Lot.

Abraham and said to him, "What have you
done to us? How have I offended you, that
you have brought on me and on my kingdom a great sin? You have done deeds to me
that ought not to be done." 10Then Abimelech said to Abraham, "What did you have in
view, that you have done this thing?"

11And Abraham said, "Because I thought,
surely the fear of God *is* not in this place;
and they will kill me on account of my wife.
12But indeed *she is* truly my sister. She *is* the
daughter of my father, but not the daughter
of my mother; and she became my wife.
13And it came to pass, when God caused me
to wander from my father's house, that I said
to her, 'This *is* your kindness that you should
do for me: in every place, wherever we go, say
of me, "He *is* my brother." ' "

14Then Abimelech took sheep, oxen, and
male and female servants, and gave *them* to
Abraham; and he restored Sarah his wife to
him. 15And Abimelech said, "See, my land
is before you; dwell where it pleases you."
16Then to Sarah he said, "Behold, I have giv-
en your brother a thousand *pieces* of silver;
indeed this vindicates you[a] before all who
are with you and before everybody." Thus
she was rebuked.

17So Abraham prayed to God; and God
healed Abimelech, his wife, and his female
servants. Then they bore *children;* 18for the
LORD had closed up all the wombs of the
house of Abimelech because of Sarah, Abraham's wife.

Isaac Is Born

21 And the LORD visited Sarah as He
had said, and the LORD did for Sarah as He had spoken. 2For Sarah conceived
and bore Abraham a son in his old age, at the

20:16 [a] Literally *it is a covering of the eyes for you*

set time of which God had spoken to him.
3And Abraham called the name of his son
who was born to him—whom Sarah bore to
him—Isaac. 4Then Abraham circumcised
his son Isaac when he was eight days old,
as God had commanded him. 5Now Abraham was one hundred years old when his
son Isaac was born to him. 6And Sarah said,
"God has made me laugh, *and* all who hear
will laugh with me." 7She also said, "Who
would have said to Abraham that Sarah
would nurse children? For I have borne *him*
a son in his old age."

Hagar and Ishmael Depart

8So the child grew and was weaned. And
Abraham made a great feast on the same day
that Isaac was weaned.

9And Sarah saw the son of Hagar the
Egyptian, whom she had borne to Abraham,
scoffing. 10Therefore she said to Abraham,
"Cast out this bondwoman and her son; for
the son of this bondwoman shall not be heir
with my son, *namely* with Isaac." 11And the
matter was very displeasing in Abraham's
sight because of his son.

12But God said to Abraham, "Do not let it
be displeasing in your sight because of the
lad or because of your bondwoman. Whatever Sarah has said to you, listen to her voice;
for in Isaac your seed shall be called. 13Yet
I will also make a nation of the son of the
bondwoman, because he *is* your seed."

14So Abraham rose early in the morning,
and took bread and a skin of water; and putting *it* on her shoulder, he gave *it* and the
boy to Hagar, and sent her away. Then she
departed and wandered in the Wilderness of
Beersheba. 15And the water in the skin was
used up, and she placed the boy under one
of the shrubs. 16Then she went and sat down
across from *him* at a distance of about a bow-
shot; for she said to herself, "Let me not see
the death of the boy." So she sat opposite
him, and lifted her voice and wept.

17And God heard the voice of the lad.
Then the angel of God called to Hagar out
of heaven, and said to her, "What ails you,
Hagar? Fear not, for God has heard the voice
of the lad where he *is.* 18Arise, lift up the
lad and hold him with your hand, for I will
make him a great nation."

19Then God opened her eyes, and she saw
a well of water. And she went and filled the
skin with water, and gave the lad a drink.
20So God was with the lad; and he grew and
dwelt in the wilderness, and became an archer. 21He dwelt in the Wilderness of Paran;
and his mother took a wife for him from the
land of Egypt.

A Covenant with Abimelech

22And it came to pass at that time that
Abimelech and Phichol, the commander of
his army, spoke to Abraham, saying, "God *is*
with you in all that you do. 23Now therefore,

Starring Roles

ISAAC'S name is pronounced *EYE-zik* and means "Laughter." As Isaac and his father Abraham climbed the mountain together, Abraham told Isaac that they were going to make a sacrifice to God. Making sacrifices was the custom in those days. But Isaac was puzzled because they had no animal to sacrifice. When Isaac asked his father about it, Abraham only looked sad and said that God would provide His own sacrifice.

Suddenly Abraham picked Isaac up and tied him to the altar. While Isaac was still trying to understand what was happening, he heard the voice of God shouting, "Don't harm the boy, Abraham!"

Years later Isaac found out that what happened that day was to show that God Himself would sacrifice His very own Son for our sins two thousand years later.

swear to me by God that you will not deal falsely with me, with my offspring, or with my posterity; but that according to the kindness that I have done to you, you will do to me and to the land in which you have dwelt."
24 And Abraham said, "I will swear."
25 Then Abraham rebuked Abimelech because of a well of water which Abimelech's
servants had seized. 26 And Abimelech said,
"I do not know who has done this thing; you did not tell me, nor had I heard *of it* until
today." 27 So Abraham took sheep and oxen and gave them to Abimelech, and the two of
them made a covenant. 28 And Abraham set
seven ewe lambs of the flock by themselves.
29 Then Abimelech asked Abraham, "What *is the meaning of* these seven ewe lambs which you have set by themselves?"
30 And he said, "You will take *these* seven ewe lambs from my hand, that they may be my witness that I have dug this well."
31 Therefore he called that place Beersheba,[a] because the two of them swore an oath there.
32 Thus they made a covenant at Beersheba. So Abimelech rose with Phichol, the commander of his army, and they returned

21:31 [a] Literally *Well of the Oath* or *Well of the Seven*

GOD KEEPS HIS PROMISE

READ IT: GENESIS 21:1–21

GET IT:

Abraham was seventy-five years old when God told him to leave his hometown and move. He was eighty-six years old when Sarah got tired of waiting for a child and told him to have a son by a slave. Now he was one hundred years old, and God came through! Just like God said, Sarah got pregnant, and Isaac was born. Abraham had waited twenty-five years for God to keep this promise.

But now Abraham had a problem. Ishmael, unofficial son number one, didn't get along with Isaac, the official son. And their mothers weren't happy either. This was sibling rivalry at its worst. Abraham and Sarah didn't handle the situation very well, but God made it all work out in the end. God was with Ishmael, and he became a great man.

LIVE IT:

You've probably found it impossible to wait a few hours for supper, or a few days until the big game, or a few weeks for school to end and vacation to start. Can you even imagine waiting twenty-five years for anything? Probably not.

Sometimes God takes His time to do something. It may seem like a long time to us, but it's not a long time for God. In fact, it's always just the right amount of time. He does what He does when it's the right time. The next time you have to wait for something, think about Abraham and how he waited because he believed that God would do it. Sure enough—God did.

to the land of the Philistines. 33 Then *Abra-*
ham planted a tamarisk tree in Beersheba,
and there called on the name of the LORD,
the Everlasting God. 34 And Abraham stayed
in the land of the Philistines many days.

Abraham's Faith Confirmed

22 Now it came to pass after these
things that God tested Abraham,
and said to him, "Abraham!"

And he said, "Here I am."

2 Then He said, "Take now your son, your
only *son* Isaac, whom you love, and go to the
land of Moriah, and offer him there as a
burnt offering on one of the mountains of
which I shall tell you."

3 So Abraham rose early in the morning
and saddled his donkey, and took two of his
young men with him, and Isaac his son; and
he split the wood for the burnt offering, and
arose and went to the place of which God
had told him. 4 Then on the third day Abraham lifted his eyes and saw the place afar
off. 5 And Abraham said to his young men,
"Stay here with the donkey; the lad[a] and I
will go yonder and worship, and we will
come back to you."

6 So Abraham took the wood of the burnt
offering and laid *it* on Isaac his son; and he
took the fire in his hand, and a knife, and the
two of them went together. 7 But Isaac spoke

22:5 [a] Or *young man*

Spotlight

GOD GIVES ABRAHAM A TEST

READ IT: GENESIS 22:1–19

GET IT:

Abraham was older than old, about one hundred sixteen years old by now. He believed in God and in God's promises. God had come through on the baby—but the nation thing was off to a very slow start. Now God wanted him to do what? It was all very mysterious, but Abraham believed that God would make it all work out, even this unbelievable request. So he did what God asked.

Abraham's faith in God was huge. In all the years he had been alive, Abraham heard from God only three times. Do the math—that leaves a lot of silent years. But still, God and Abraham were close. God didn't tell Abraham all the details of His plan; He just told him the highlights and expected Abraham to follow in faith. Abraham did what God said and things turned out way, way better than Abraham ever dreamed.

LIVE IT:

You know what a test is: a test at school, the test of tornado sirens, or tests of the Emergency Alert System that interrupts the TV show. All those come with warnings: "This is a test." When you hear, "The math test is on Thursday," you know what's going to happen. Abraham, however, didn't get the heads-up. He had to take the test without warning or any announcement. He did it without asking questions and without complaining. He believed God knew best. That's called faith.

to Abraham his father and said, "My father!"
And he said, "Here I am, my son."
Then he said, "Look, the fire and the
wood, but where *is* the lamb for a burnt
offering?"
8And Abraham said, "My son, God will
provide for Himself the lamb for a burnt offering." So the two of them went together.
9Then they came to the place of which
God had told him. And Abraham built an
altar there and placed the wood in order;
and he bound Isaac his son and laid him on
the altar, upon the wood. 10And Abraham
stretched out his hand and took the knife to
slay his son.
11But the Angel of the LORD called to
him from heaven and said, "Abraham,
Abraham!"
So he said, "Here I am."
12And He said, "Do not lay your hand
on the lad, or do anything to him; for now I
know that you fear God, since you have not
withheld your son, your only *son,* from Me."
13Then Abraham lifted his eyes and
looked, and there behind *him was* a ram
caught in a thicket by its horns. So Abraham went and took the ram, and offered it
up for a burnt offering instead of his son.
14And Abraham called the name of the place,
The-LORD-Will-Provide;[a] as it is said *to* this
day, "In the Mount of the LORD it shall be
provided."
15Then the Angel of the LORD called to
Abraham a second time out of heaven, 16and
said: "By Myself I have sworn, says the LORD,
because you have done this thing, and have
not withheld your son, your only *son*—
17blessing I will bless you, and multiplying
I will multiply your descendants as the stars
of the heaven and as the sand which *is* on
the seashore; and your descendants shall
possess the gate of their enemies. 18In your
seed all the nations of the earth shall be
blessed, because you have obeyed My voice."
19So Abraham returned to his young men,
and they rose and went together to Beersheba; and Abraham dwelt at Beersheba.

The Family of Nahor

20Now it came to pass after these things
that it was told Abraham, saying, "Indeed
Milcah also has borne children to your brother Nahor: 21Huz his firstborn, Buz his brother, Kemuel the father of Aram, 22Chesed,
Hazo, Pildash, Jidlaph, and Bethuel." 23And
Bethuel begot Rebekah.[a] These eight Milcah
bore to Nahor, Abraham's brother. 24His concubine, whose name was Reumah, also bore
Tebah, Gaham, Thahash, and Maachah.

Sarah's Death and Burial

23 Sarah lived one hundred and
twenty-seven years; *these were* the
years of the life of Sarah. 2So Sarah died in
Kirjath Arba (that *is,* Hebron) in the land of
Canaan, and Abraham came to mourn for
Sarah and to weep for her.
3Then Abraham stood up from before his
dead, and spoke to the sons of Heth, saying,
4"I *am* a foreigner and a visitor among you.
Give me property for a burial place among
you, that I may bury my dead out of my
sight."
5And the sons of Heth answered Abraham, saying to him, 6"Hear us, my lord: You
are a mighty prince among us; bury your
dead in the choicest of our burial places.
None of us will withhold from you his burial
place, that you may bury your dead."
7Then Abraham stood up and bowed
himself to the people of the land, the sons of
Heth. 8And he spoke with them, saying, "If
it is your wish that I bury my dead out of my
sight, hear me, and meet with Ephron the
son of Zohar for me, 9that he may give me
the cave of Machpelah which he has, which
is at the end of his field. Let him give it to me
at the full price, as property for a burial place
among you."
10Now Ephron dwelt among the sons
of Heth; and Ephron the Hittite answered
Abraham in the presence of the sons of
Heth, all who entered at the gate of his city,
saying, 11"No, my lord, hear me: I give you
the field and the cave that *is* in it; I give it to
you in the presence of the sons of my people.
I give it to you. Bury your dead!"
12Then Abraham bowed himself down
before the people of the land; 13and he spoke
to Ephron in the hearing of the people of the
land, saying, "If you *will give it,* please hear
me. I will give you money for the field; take
it from me and I will bury my dead there."
14And Ephron answered Abraham, saying to him, 15"My lord, listen to me; the land
is worth four hundred shekels of silver. What

22:14 [a] Hebrew *YHWH Yireh* **22:23** [a] Spelled *Rebecca* in Romans 9:10

is that between you and me? So bury your
dead." 16And Abraham listened to Ephron;
and Abraham weighed out the silver for
Ephron which he had named in the hearing
of the sons of Heth, four hundred shekels of
silver, currency of the merchants.

17So the field of Ephron which *was* in
Machpelah, which *was* before Mamre, the
field and the cave which *was* in it, and all the
trees that *were* in the field, which *were* within all the surrounding borders, were deeded
18to Abraham as a possession in the presence
of the sons of Heth, before all who went in at
the gate of his city.

19And after this, Abraham buried Sarah
his wife in the cave of the field of Machpelah, before Mamre (that *is,* Hebron) in the
land of Canaan. 20So the field and the cave
that *is* in it were deeded to Abraham by the
sons of Heth as property for a burial place.

A Bride for Isaac

24 Now Abraham was old, well advanced in age; and the LORD had
blessed Abraham in all things. 2So Abraham
said to the oldest servant of his house, who
ruled over all that he had, "Please, put your
hand under my thigh, 3and I will make you
swear by the LORD, the God of heaven and
the God of the earth, that you will not take
a wife for my son from the daughters of the
Canaanites, among whom I dwell; 4but you
shall go to my country and to my family, and
take a wife for my son Isaac."

5And the servant said to him, "Perhaps
the woman will not be willing to follow me
to this land. Must I take your son back to the
land from which you came?"

6But Abraham said to him, "Beware that
you do not take my son back there. 7The
LORD God of heaven, who took me from
my father's house and from the land of my
family, and who spoke to me and swore to
me, saying, 'To your descendants[a] I give this
land,' He will send His angel before you, and
you shall take a wife for my son from there.
8And if the woman is not willing to follow
you, then you will be released from this
oath; only do not take my son back there."
9So the servant put his hand under the thigh
of Abraham his master, and swore to him
concerning this matter.

10Then the servant took ten of his master's camels and departed, for all his master's goods *were in* his hand. And he arose
and went to Mesopotamia, to the city of Nahor. 11And he made his camels kneel down
outside the city by a well of water at evening
time, the time when women go out to draw
water. 12Then he said, "O LORD God of my
master Abraham, please give me success
this day, and show kindness to my master
Abraham. 13Behold, *here* I stand by the well
of water, and the daughters of the men of
the city are coming out to draw water. 14Now

24:7 [a] Literally *seed*

Starring Roles

REBEKAH'S name is pronounced *ree-BECK-uh*. Rebekah's father Bethuel and brother Laban had told her about her Uncle Abraham who went to live in Palestine. Abraham and his wife Sarah had a son named Isaac.

One day Abraham's hired man went to visit Rebekah's family in Mesopotamia (pronounced *mess-uh-puh-TAY-mee-uh*) where Abraham also had grown up. Rebekah was going to the well, and the hired man was standing there with his camels. When he asked Rebekah for a drink from the well, she offered to water his camels, too. Then the hired man did a strange thing—he gave Rebekah jewelry and thanked God that he had found a wife for Isaac. *Rebekah* was speechless!

Later Bethuel and Laban both agreed that the hired man's actions were directed by the Lord, so Rebekah became Isaac's bride.

let it be that the young woman to whom I
say, 'Please let down your pitcher that I may
drink,' and she says, 'Drink, and I will also
give your camels a drink'—*let* her *be the one*
You have appointed for Your servant Isaac.
And by this I will know that You have shown
kindness to my master."

15And it happened, before he had finished speaking, that behold, Rebekah, who
was born to Bethuel, son of Milcah, the
wife of Nahor, Abraham's brother, came out
with her pitcher on her shoulder. 16Now the
young woman *was* very beautiful to behold,
a virgin; no man had known her. And she
went down to the well, filled her pitcher, and
came up. 17And the servant ran to meet her
and said, "Please let me drink a little water
from your pitcher."

18So she said, "Drink, my lord." Then she
quickly let her pitcher down to her hand,
and gave him a drink. 19And when she had
finished giving him a drink, she said, "I will
draw *water* for your camels also, until they
have finished drinking." 20Then she quickly emptied her pitcher into the trough, ran
back to the well to draw *water,* and drew for
all his camels. 21And the man, wondering at
her, remained silent so as to know whether
the Lord had made his journey prosperous
or not.

22So it was, when the camels had finished
drinking, that the man took a golden nose
ring weighing half a shekel, and two bracelets for her wrists weighing ten *shekels* of
gold, 23and said, "Whose daughter *are* you?
Tell me, please, is there room *in* your father's
house for us to lodge?"

24So she said to him, "I *am* the daughter

GOD PROVIDES A BRIDE FOR ISAAC

READ IT: GENESIS 24:1–67

GET IT:

Abraham and God had a close relationship. God promised Abraham a baby and it happened. God tested Abraham's loyalty by asking him to sacrifice his son. Abraham passed the test, and Isaac lived. So now Abraham wanted to be sure to get the right girl to marry Isaac. This girl needed to be God's choice from the right family who also recognized God as the only God. So Abraham made a plan. He gave instructions to a responsible servant. Then he trusted his servant and God to follow through.

LIVE IT:

A lot of trust is going on in this story. Abraham trusted the servant with an important family mission. Laban trusted the servant's story. And Rebekah trusted the servant to take her to her new husband (a two-month journey across the desert). This all required huge trust! But the basis for their trust was God. They all believed the true God, so they trusted one another. Every day you have to trust people. Sometimes they deserve your trust and come through for you. Sometimes they don't. With God, it's different. You can trust God all the time. He only wants the very best for you.

of Bethuel, Milcah's son, whom she bore to
Nahor." 25Moreover she said to him, "We
have both straw and feed enough, and room
to lodge."

26Then the man bowed down his head
and worshiped the LORD. 27And he said,
"Blessed *be* the LORD God of my master
Abraham, who has not forsaken His mercy and His truth toward my master. As for
me, being on the way, the LORD led me to
the house of my master's brethren." 28So the
young woman ran and told her mother's
household these things.

29Now Rebekah had a brother whose
name *was* Laban, and Laban ran out to the
man by the well. 30So it came to pass, when
he saw the nose ring, and the bracelets on
his sister's wrists, and when he heard the
words of his sister Rebekah, saying, "Thus
the man spoke to me," that he went to the
man. And there he stood by the camels at
the well. 31And he said, "Come in, O blessed
of the LORD! Why do you stand outside? For
I have prepared the house, and a place for
the camels."

32Then the man came to the house. And
he unloaded the camels, and provided straw
and feed for the camels, and water to wash
his feet and the feet of the men who *were*
with him. 33*Food* was set before him to eat,
but he said, "I will not eat until I have told
about my errand."

And he said, "Speak on."

34So he said, "I *am* Abraham's servant.
35The LORD has blessed my master greatly,
and he has become great; and He has given
him flocks and herds, silver and gold, male
and female servants, and camels and donkeys. 36And Sarah my master's wife bore a
son to my master when she was old; and to
him he has given all that he has. 37Now my
master made me swear, saying, 'You shall
not take a wife for my son from the daughters of the Canaanites, in whose land I dwell;
38but you shall go to my father's house and to
my family, and take a wife for my son.' 39And
I said to my master, 'Perhaps the woman
will not follow me.' 40But he said to me, 'The
LORD, before whom I walk, will send His angel with you and prosper your way; and you
shall take a wife for my son from my family
and from my father's house. 41You will be
clear from this oath when you arrive among
my family; for if they will not give *her* to you,
then you will be released from my oath.'

42"And this day I came to the well and
said, 'O LORD God of my master Abraham,
if You will now prosper the way in which
I go, 43behold, I stand by the well of water;
and it shall come to pass that when the
virgin comes out to draw *water,* and I say
to her, "Please give me a little water from
your pitcher to drink," 44and she says to me,
"Drink, and I will draw for your camels
also,"—*let* her *be* the woman whom the LORD
has appointed for my master's son.'

45"But before I had finished speaking in
my heart, there was Rebekah, coming out
with her pitcher on her shoulder; and she
went down to the well and drew *water.* And
I said to her, 'Please let me drink.' 46And she
made haste and let her pitcher down from
her *shoulder,* and said, 'Drink, and I will give
your camels a drink also.' So I drank, and
she gave the camels a drink also. 47Then
I asked her, and said, 'Whose daughter
are you?' And she said, 'The daughter of
Bethuel, Nahor's son, whom Milcah bore to
him.' So I put the nose ring on her nose and
the bracelets on her wrists. 48And I bowed
my head and worshiped the LORD, and
blessed the LORD God of my master Abraham, who had led me in the way of truth to
take the daughter of my master's brother for
his son. 49Now if you will deal kindly and truly with my master, tell me. And if not, tell
me, that I may turn to the right hand or to
the left."

50Then Laban and Bethuel answered
and said, "The thing comes from the LORD;
we cannot speak to you either bad or good.
51Here *is* Rebekah before you; take *her* and
go, and let her be your master's son's wife,
as the LORD has spoken."

52And it came to pass, when Abraham's
servant heard their words, that he worshiped
the LORD, *bowing himself* to the earth. 53Then
the servant brought out jewelry of silver,
jewelry of gold, and clothing, and gave *them*
to Rebekah. He also gave precious things to
her brother and to her mother.

54And he and the men who *were* with him
ate and drank and stayed all night. Then they
arose in the morning, and he said, "Send me
away to my master."

55But her brother and her mother said,

"Let the young woman stay with us *a few*
days, at least ten; after that she may go."
56And he said to them, "Do not hinder
me, since the LORD has prospered my way;
send me away so that I may go to my master."
57So they said, "We will call the young
woman and ask her personally." 58Then they
called Rebekah and said to her, "Will you go
with this man?"

And she said, "I will go."
59So they sent away Rebekah their sister
and her nurse, and Abraham's servant and
his men. 60And they blessed Rebekah and
said to her:

"Our sister, *may* you *become*
The mother of thousands of ten
thousands;
And may your descendants possess
The gates of those who hate them."

61Then Rebekah and her maids arose,
and they rode on the camels and followed
the man. So the servant took Rebekah and
departed.
62Now Isaac came from the way of Beer
Lahai Roi, for he dwelt in the South. 63And
Isaac went out to meditate in the field in the
evening; and he lifted his eyes and looked,
and there, the camels *were* coming. 64Then
Rebekah lifted her eyes, and when she saw
Isaac she dismounted from her camel; 65for
she had said to the servant, "Who *is* this man
walking in the field to meet us?"

The servant said, "It *is* my master." So
she took a veil and covered herself.

Epic Ideas

LOVE MATCHMAKER

READ IT: GENESIS 24:61–66

GET IT:

God promised Abraham a son, and miraculously in his old age, Abraham got his son Isaac (thanks to God and Sarah). When it was time to find Isaac a wife, Abraham sent his servant to play divine matchmaker. The servant asked God for guidance. Along the way, the servant stopped to get water and met Rebekah. Rebekah was beautiful and humble. She offered to get Abraham's servant and all his camels a drink. The servant knew he had stumbled on a special girl.

Rebekah's family agreed for her to marry Isaac, and Rebekah went back to Canaan with the servant. On meeting Isaac, Rebekah humbled herself by covering her face with a veil. This showed Isaac she respected him. Then Rebekah became his wife, and he loved her. This entire story is put together with themes of love. Human love is a powerful thing, but the big picture here shows God's love in how He provides for and guides His people.

LIVE IT:

Think of an early memory you have of experiencing love and write it down or draw a picture of it. From that experience, draw a timeline to the present. For each year of your life, put down other times you've received love from God and others. Keep this in a special place and look at it when you need to feel loved.

66And the servant told Isaac all the things
that he had done. 67Then Isaac brought her
into his mother Sarah's tent; and he took
Rebekah and she became his wife, and he
loved her. So Isaac was comforted after his
mother's *death*.

Abraham and Keturah

25 Abraham again took a wife, and
her name *was* Keturah. 2And she
bore him Zimran, Jokshan, Medan, Midian,
Ishbak, and Shuah. 3Jokshan begot Sheba
and Dedan. And the sons of Dedan were As-
shurim, Letushim, and Leummim. 4And the
sons of Midian *were* Ephah, Epher, Hanoch,
Abidah, and Eldaah. All these *were* the children of Keturah.

5And Abraham gave all that he had to
Isaac. 6But Abraham gave gifts to the sons
of the concubines which Abraham had;
and while he was still living he sent them
eastward, away from Isaac his son, to the
country of the east.

Abraham's Death and Burial

7This *is* the sum of the years of Abraham's life which he lived: one hundred and
seventy-five years. 8Then Abraham breathed
his last and died in a good old age, an old
man and full *of years,* and was gathered to
his people. 9And his sons Isaac and Ishmael
buried him in the cave of Machpelah, which
is before Mamre, in the field of Ephron the
son of Zohar the Hittite, 10the field which
Abraham purchased from the sons of Heth.
There Abraham was buried, and Sarah his
wife. 11And it came to pass, after the death
of Abraham, that God blessed his son Isaac.
And Isaac dwelt at Beer Lahai Roi.

The Families of Ishmael and Isaac

12Now this *is* the genealogy of Ishmael,
Abraham's son, whom Hagar the Egyptian,

GOD BLESSES REBEKAH WITH TWINS

READ IT: GENESIS 25:19–34

GET IT:

Jacob and Esau, the twin boys born to Rebekah and Isaac, were complete opposites. Jacob, the younger twin, was a homebody and mom's favorite. Esau, the older twin, was a strong hunter and dad's favorite. The way things worked in those days was that the oldest son got the "birthright"—the most land, animals, blessings, and leadership of the family—and the youngest got less. But God sometimes works outside the usual way things are done. Esau didn't care much about his birthright when he was starving. He carelessly made a deal with Jacob.

LIVE IT:

Have you ever heard someone say, "Never go grocery shopping on an empty stomach"? That's good advice because if you're hungry you'll make bad decisions and buy too much snack food and forget about buying stuff *that's good for you*. Too bad Esau didn't know that. He made a careless decision because his stomach was growling. The only good part is that God used his foolish decision to work things out for everybody's good.

Sarah's maidservant, bore to Abraham.
13And these *were* the names of the sons of
Ishmael, by their names, according to their
generations: The firstborn of Ishmael, Nebajoth; then Kedar, Adbeel, Mibsam, 14Mish-
ma, Dumah, Massa, 15Hadar,[a] Tema, Jetur,
Naphish, and Kedemah. 16These *were* the
sons of Ishmael and these *were* their names,
by their towns and their settlements, twelve
princes according to their nations. 17These
were the years of the life of Ishmael: one hundred and thirty-seven years; and he breathed
his last and died, and was gathered to his
people. 18(They dwelt from Havilah as far as
Shur, which *is* east of Egypt as you go toward
Assyria.) He died in the presence of all his
brethren.

19This *is* the genealogy of Isaac, Abraham's son. Abraham begot Isaac. 20Isaac
was forty years old when he took Rebekah as
wife, the daughter of Bethuel the Syrian of
Padan Aram, the sister of Laban the Syrian.
21Now Isaac pleaded with the LORD for his
wife, because she *was* barren; and the LORD
granted his plea, and Rebekah his wife conceived. 22But the children struggled together
within her; and she said, "If *all is* well, why
am I like this?" So she went to inquire of the
LORD.

23And the LORD said to her:

"Two nations *are* in your womb,
Two peoples shall be separated from
your body;
One people shall be stronger than the
other,
And the older shall serve the younger."

24So when her days were fulfilled *for her*
to give birth, indeed *there were* twins in her
womb. 25And the first came out red. *He was*
like a hairy garment all over; so they called
his name Esau.[a] 26Afterward his brother
came out, and his hand took hold of Esau's
heel; so his name was called Jacob.[a] Isaac
was sixty years old when she bore them.

27So the boys grew. And Esau was a skillful hunter, a man of the field; but Jacob was
a mild man, dwelling in tents. 28And Isaac
loved Esau because he ate *of his* game, but
Rebekah loved Jacob.

Esau Sells His Birthright

29Now Jacob cooked a stew; and Esau
came in from the field, and he *was* weary.
30And Esau said to Jacob, "Please feed me

In Focus

25:11 Blessed An adjective that means a person is favored by God and His kindness. Sometimes the word means the "happiness that God gives."

with that same red *stew*, for I *am* weary."
Therefore his name was called Edom.[a]

31But Jacob said, "Sell me your birthright
as of this day."

32And Esau said, "Look, I *am* about to die;
so what *is* this birthright to me?"

33Then Jacob said, "Swear to me as of this
day."

So he swore to him, and sold his birthright to Jacob. 34And Jacob gave Esau bread
and stew of lentils; then he ate and drank,
arose, and went his way. Thus Esau despised
his birthright.

Isaac and Abimelech

26 There was a famine in the land,
besides the first famine that was
in the days of Abraham. And Isaac went to
Abimelech king of the Philistines, in Gerar.

2Then the LORD appeared to him and said:
"Do not go down to Egypt; live in the land of
which I shall tell you. 3Dwell in this land, and
I will be with you and bless you; for to you
and your descendants I give all these lands,
and I will perform the oath which I swore to
Abraham your father. 4And I will make your
descendants multiply as the stars of heaven; I
will give to your descendants all these lands;
and in your seed all the nations of the earth
shall be blessed; 5because Abraham obeyed
My voice and kept My charge, My commandments, My statutes, and My laws."

6So Isaac dwelt in Gerar. 7And the men
of the place asked about his wife. And he
said, "She *is* my sister"; for he was afraid to
say, "*She is* my wife," *because he thought,* "lest
the men of the place kill me for Rebekah,
because she *is* beautiful to behold." 8Now it
came to pass, when he had been there a long

25:15 [a] Masoretic Text reads *Hadad.* 25:25 [a] Literally *Hairy* 25:26 [a] Literally *Supplanter* 25:30 [a] Literally *Red*

time, that Abimelech king of the Philistines
looked through a window, and saw, and there
was Isaac, showing endearment to Rebekah
his wife. 9 Then Abimelech called Isaac and
said, "Quite obviously she *is* your wife; so
how could you say, 'She *is* my sister'?"

Isaac said to him, "Because I said, 'Lest I
die on account of her.'"

10 And Abimelech said, "What *is* this you
have done to us? One of the people might
soon have lain with your wife, and you
would have brought guilt on us." 11 So Abimelech charged all *his* people, saying, "He who
touches this man or his wife shall surely be
put to death."

12 Then Isaac sowed in that land, and
reaped in the same year a hundredfold; and
the LORD blessed him. 13 The man began to
prosper, and continued prospering until he
became very prosperous; 14 for he had possessions of flocks and possessions of herds and
a great number of servants. So the Philistines envied him. 15 Now the Philistines had
stopped up all the wells which his father's
servants had dug in the days of Abraham his
father, and they had filled them with earth.
16 And Abimelech said to Isaac, "Go away
from us, for you are much mightier than we."

17 Then Isaac departed from there and
pitched his tent in the Valley of Gerar, and
dwelt there. 18 And Isaac dug again the wells
of water which they had dug in the days of
Abraham his father, for the Philistines had
stopped them up after the death of Abraham. He called them by the names which
his father had called them.

19 Also Isaac's servants dug in the valley,
and found a well of running water there.
20 But the herdsmen of Gerar quarreled
with Isaac's herdsmen, saying, "The water
is ours." So he called the name of the well
Esek,[a] because they quarreled with him.
21 Then they dug another well, and they quarreled over that *one* also. So he called its name
Sitnah.[a] 22 And he moved from there and dug
another well, and they did not quarrel over
it. So he called its name Rehoboth,[a] because
he said, "For now the LORD has made room
for us, and we shall be fruitful in the land."

23 Then he went up from there to Beersheba. 24 And the LORD appeared to him the
same night and said, "I *am* the God of your
father Abraham; do not fear, for I *am* with
you. I will bless you and multiply your descendants for My servant Abraham's sake."
25 So he built an altar there and called on the
name of the LORD, and he pitched his tent
there; and there Isaac's servants dug a well.

26 Then Abimelech came to him from
Gerar with Ahuzzath, one of his friends, and

26:20 [a] Literally *Quarrel* **26:21** [a] Literally *Enmity*
26:22 [a] Literally *Spaciousness*

Starring Roles

JACOB'S name is pronounced *JAY-kob* and means "Usurper." A usurper is someone who steals another person's position in the world.

Because Jacob's brother Esau was the oldest son, he was the legal heir to Isaac's property. But when Isaac was old and blind, Jacob tricked him into believing he was Esau. So Isaac gave Jacob what belonged to his brother.

Later Jacob wrestled with an Angel all night long. That Angel was really the Lord who appeared to Jacob in the form of a man. The Angel gave Jacob a new name and a new heart. His new name, Israel (pronounced *IZ-ray-el*), means "Prince with God." Unworthy as Jacob was, God kindly gave him the honor of being the father of the great nation of Israel.

The Lord is ready to give you a new heart, too, so you can begin right now to learn more about Him. As you do this, you will become a prince or princess of God.

Phichol the commander of his army. 27And
Isaac said to them, "Why have you come to
me, since you hate me and have sent me
away from you?"

28But they said, "We have certainly seen
that the LORD is with you. So we said, 'Let
there now be an oath between us, between
you and us; and let us make a covenant with
you, 29that you will do us no harm, since we
have not touched you, and since we have
done nothing to you but good and have sent
you away in peace. You *are* now the blessed
of the LORD.'"

30So he made them a feast, and they ate
and drank. 31Then they arose early in the
morning and swore an oath with one another; and Isaac sent them away, and they departed from him in peace.

32It came to pass the same day that Isaac's
servants came and told him about the well
which they had dug, and said to him, "We
have found water." 33So he called it Shebah.[a]
Therefore the name of the city *is* Beersheba[b]
to this day.

34When Esau was forty years old, he took
as wives Judith the daughter of Beeri the
Hittite, and Basemath the daughter of Elon
the Hittite. 35And they were a grief of mind
to Isaac and Rebekah.

Isaac Blesses Jacob

27 Now it came to pass, when Isaac
was old and his eyes were so dim
that he could not see, that he called Esau his
older son and said to him, "My son."

And he answered him, "Here I am."

2Then he said, "Behold now, I am old.
I do not know the day of my death. 3Now
therefore, please take your weapons, your
quiver and your bow, and go out to the field
and hunt game for me. 4And make me savory food, such as I love, and bring *it* to me
that I may eat, that my soul may bless you
before I die."

5Now Rebekah was listening when Isaac
spoke to Esau his son. And Esau went to the
field to hunt game and to bring *it.* 6So Rebekah spoke to Jacob her son, saying, "Indeed I heard your father speak to Esau your
brother, saying, 7'Bring me game and make
savory food for me, that I may eat it and bless
you in the presence of the LORD before my
death.' 8Now therefore, my son, obey my
voice according to what I command you. 9Go
now to the flock and bring me from there
two choice kids of the goats, and I will make
savory food from them for your father, such
as he loves. 10Then you shall take *it* to your
father, that he may eat *it,* and that he may
bless you before his death."

11And Jacob said to Rebekah his mother,
"Look, Esau my brother *is* a hairy man, and
I *am* a smooth-*skinned* man. 12Perhaps my
father will feel me, and I shall seem to be a
deceiver to him; and I shall bring a curse on
myself and not a blessing."

13But his mother said to him, "*Let* your
curse *be* on me, my son; only obey my voice,
and go, get *them* for me." 14And he went and
got *them* and brought *them* to his mother,
and his mother made savory food, such as
his father loved. 15Then Rebekah took the
choice clothes of her elder son Esau, which
were with her in the house, and put them
on Jacob her younger son. 16And she put the
skins of the kids of the goats on his hands
and on the smooth part of his neck. 17Then
she gave the savory food and the bread,
which she had prepared, into the hand of
her son Jacob.

18So he went to his father and said, "My
father."

And he said, "Here I am. Who *are* you,
my son?"

19Jacob said to his father, "I *am* Esau your
firstborn; I have done just as you told me;
please arise, sit and eat of my game, that
your soul may bless me."

20But Isaac said to his son, "How *is it* that
you have found *it* so quickly, my son?"

And he said, "Because the LORD your
God brought *it* to me."

21Isaac said to Jacob, "Please come near,
that I may feel you, my son, whether you *are*
really my son Esau or not." 22So Jacob went
near to Isaac his father, and he felt him
and said, "The voice *is* Jacob's voice, but the
hands *are* the hands of Esau." 23And he did
not recognize him, because his hands were
hairy like his brother Esau's hands; so he
blessed him.

24Then he said, "*Are* you really my son
Esau?"

He said, "I *am.*"

25He said, "Bring *it* near to me, and I
will eat of my son's game, so that my soul

26:33 [a] Literally *Oath* or *Seven* [b] Literally *Well of the Oath* or *Well of the Seven*

may bless you." So he brought *it* near to
him, and he ate; and he brought him wine,
and he drank. 26Then his father Isaac said
to him, "Come near now and kiss me, my
son." 27And he came near and kissed him;
and he smelled the smell of his clothing, and
blessed him and said:

"Surely, the smell of my son
Is like the smell of a field
Which the LORD has blessed.
28 Therefore may God give you
Of the dew of heaven,
Of the fatness of the earth,
And plenty of grain and wine.
29 Let peoples serve you,
And nations bow down to you.
Be master over your brethren,
And let your mother's sons bow down
to you.
Cursed *be* everyone who curses you,
And blessed *be* those who bless you!"

Esau's Lost Hope

30Now it happened, as soon as Isaac
had finished blessing Jacob, and Jacob had
scarcely gone out from the presence of Isaac
his father, that Esau his brother came in
from his hunting. 31He also had made savory
food, and brought it to his father, and said to
his father, "Let my father arise and eat of his
son's game, that your soul may bless me."
32And his father Isaac said to him, "Who
are you?"

So he said, "I *am* your son, your first-born, Esau."

JACOB RECEIVES ISAAC'S BLESSING

READ IT: GENESIS 27:1–46

GET IT:

What a mess. It's just so wrong to deceive your father. It's even worse to trick an old, blind man. Isaac was all of these things, and yet Jacob and his mother took advantage of the poor guy. Even though God told Rebekah before the boys were born that "the older shall serve the younger" (Genesis 25:23), Rebekah thought God needed her help to make sure it happened. She got all involved and created drama in the family. It almost sounds like reality TV. In the end, she didn't win. Her favorite son had to leave the country.

LIVE IT:

You can almost hear Esau screaming, "That's not fair!" Well, according to the social rules of that day, it sure wasn't fair. But it happened, and God made it all work out in the end for everybody. This, of course, took many, many years. In the end, both Esau and Jacob were wealthy and the ancestors of entire nations. Jacob became the head of the nation of Israel. *Esau was the head of the* nation of Edom. So the next time you want to scream about fairness, remember God's got a plan—it'll be far better than you could ever make.

33 Then Isaac trembled exceedingly, and
said, "Who? Where *is* the one who hunted
game and brought *it* to me? I ate all *of it* before you came, and I have blessed him—*and*
indeed he shall be blessed."

34 When Esau heard the words of his father, he cried with an exceedingly great and
bitter cry, and said to his father, "Bless me—
me also, O my father!"

35 But he said, "Your brother came with
deceit and has taken away your blessing."

36 And *Esau* said, "Is he not rightly named
Jacob? For he has supplanted me these two
times. He took away my birthright, and now
look, he has taken away my blessing!" And
he said, "Have you not reserved a blessing
for me?"

37 Then Isaac answered and said to Esau,
"Indeed I have made him your master, and
all his brethren I have given to him as servants; with grain and wine I have sustained
him. What shall I do now for you, my son?"

38 And Esau said to his father, "Have you
only one blessing, my father? Bless me—me
also, O my father!" And Esau lifted up his
voice and wept.

39 Then Isaac his father answered and
said to him:

"Behold, your dwelling shall be of the
    fatness of the earth,
And of the dew of heaven from above.
40 By your sword you shall live,
And you shall serve your brother;
And it shall come to pass, when you
    become restless,
That you shall break his yoke from your
    neck."

Jacob Escapes from Esau

41 So Esau hated Jacob because of the
blessing with which his father blessed him,
and Esau said in his heart, "The days of
mourning for my father are at hand; then I
will kill my brother Jacob."

42 *And* the words of Esau her older son
were told to Rebekah. So she sent and
called Jacob her younger son, and said to
him, "Surely your brother Esau comforts
himself concerning you *by intending* to
kill you. 43 Now therefore, my son, obey my
voice: arise, flee to my brother Laban in Haran. 44 And stay with him a few days, until
your brother's fury turns away, 45 until your
brother's anger turns away from you, and
he forgets what you have done to him; then
I will send and bring you from there. Why
should I be bereaved also of you both in one
day?"

46 And Rebekah said to Isaac, "I am weary of my life because of the daughters of
Heth; if Jacob takes a wife of the daughters
of Heth, like these *who are* the daughters of
the land, what good will my life be to me?"

28 Then Isaac called Jacob and
blessed him, and charged him,
and said to him: "You shall not take a wife
from the daughters of Canaan. 2 Arise, go to
Padan Aram, to the house of Bethuel your
mother's father; and take yourself a wife
from there of the daughters of Laban your
mother's brother.

3 "May God Almighty bless you,
And make you fruitful and multiply
    you,
That you may be an assembly of
    peoples;
4 And give you the blessing of Abraham,
To you and your descendants with you,
That you may inherit the land
In which you are a stranger,
Which God gave to Abraham."

5 So Isaac sent Jacob away, and he went to
Padan Aram, to Laban the son of Bethuel the
Syrian, the brother of Rebekah, the mother
of Jacob and Esau.

Esau Marries Mahalath

6 Esau saw that Isaac had blessed Jacob
and sent him away to Padan Aram to take
himself a wife from there, *and that* as he
blessed him he gave him a charge, saying,
"You shall not take a wife from the daughters of Canaan," 7 and that Jacob had obeyed
his father and his mother and had gone to
Padan Aram. 8 Also Esau saw that the daughters of Canaan did not please his father Isaac.
9 So Esau went to Ishmael and took Mahalath
the daughter of Ishmael, Abraham's son, the
sister of Nebajoth, to be his wife in addition
to the wives he had.

Jacob's Vow at Bethel

10 Now Jacob went out from Beersheba
and went toward Haran. 11 So he came to a
certain place and stayed there all night, because the sun had set. And he took one of
the stones of that place and put it at his head,
and he lay down in that place to sleep. 12 Then

he dreamed, and behold, a ladder *was* set up
on the earth, and its top reached to heaven;
and there the angels of God were ascending
and descending on it.
13 And behold, the LORD stood above it
and said: "I *am* the LORD God of Abraham
your father and the God of Isaac; the land
on which you lie I will give to you and your
descendants. 14 Also your descendants shall
be as the dust of the earth; you shall spread
abroad to the west and the east, to the north
and the south; and in you and in your seed
all the families of the earth shall be blessed.
15 Behold, I *am* with you and will keep you
wherever you go, and will bring you back to
this land; for I will not leave you until I have
done what I have spoken to you."
16 Then Jacob awoke from his sleep and
said, "Surely the LORD is in this place, and
I did not know *it*." 17 And he was afraid and
said, "How awesome *is* this place! This *is*
none other than the house of God, and this
is the gate of heaven!"
18 Then Jacob rose early in the morning,
and took the stone that he had put at his
head, set it up as a pillar, and poured oil on
top of it. 19 And he called the name of that
place Bethel;[a] but the name of that city had
been Luz previously. 20 Then Jacob made a
vow, saying, "If God will be with me, and
keep me in this way that I am going, and
give me bread to eat and clothing to put on,
21 so that I come back to my father's house in
peace, then the LORD shall be my God. 22 And
this stone which I have set as a pillar shall
be God's house, and of all that You give me I
will surely give a tenth to You."

Jacob Meets Rachel

29 So Jacob went on his journey and
came to the land of the people of
the East. 2 And he looked, and saw a well in
the field; and behold, there *were* three flocks
of sheep lying by it; for out of that well they
watered the flocks. A large stone *was* on the
well's mouth. 3 Now all the flocks would be
gathered there; and they would roll the stone
from the well's mouth, water the sheep, and
put the stone back in its place on the well's
mouth.
4 And Jacob said to them, "My brethren,
where *are* you from?"
And they said, "We *are* from Haran."
5 Then he said to them, "Do you know
Laban the son of Nahor?"
And they said, "We know him."
6 So he said to them, "Is he well?"
And they said, "*He is* well. And look, his
daughter Rachel is coming with the sheep."
7 Then he said, "Look, *it is* still high day;
it is not time for the cattle to be gathered
together. Water the sheep, and go and feed
them."
8 But they said, "We cannot until all the
flocks are gathered together, and they have
rolled the stone from the well's mouth; then
we water the sheep."
9 Now while he was still speaking with
them, Rachel came with her father's sheep,
for she was a shepherdess. 10 And it came to
pass, when Jacob saw Rachel the daughter of
Laban his mother's brother, and the sheep of
Laban his mother's brother, that Jacob went
near and rolled the stone from the well's
mouth, and watered the flock of Laban his
mother's brother. 11 Then Jacob kissed Rachel, and lifted up his voice and wept. 12 And
Jacob told Rachel that he *was* her father's relative and that he *was* Rebekah's son. So she
ran and told her father.
13 Then it came to pass, when Laban heard
the report about Jacob his sister's son, that
he ran to meet him, and embraced him and
kissed him, and brought him to his house.
So he told Laban all these things. 14 And Laban said to him, "Surely you *are* my bone
and my flesh." And he stayed with him for
a month.

Jacob Marries Leah and Rachel

15 Then Laban said to Jacob, "Because you
are my relative, should you therefore serve
me for nothing? Tell me, what *should* your
wages *be*?" 16 Now Laban had two daughters:
the name of the elder *was* Leah, and the
name of the younger *was* Rachel. 17 Leah's
eyes *were* delicate, but Rachel was beautiful
of form and appearance.
18 Now Jacob loved Rachel; so he said, "I
will serve you seven years for Rachel your
younger daughter."
19 And Laban said, "*It is* better that I give
her to you than that I should give her to another man. Stay with me." 20 So Jacob served
seven years for Rachel, and they seemed *only*
a few days to him because of the love he had
for her.
21 Then Jacob said to Laban, "Give *me* my

28:19 [a] Literally *House of God*

wife, for my days are fulfilled, that I may go
in to her." 22 And Laban gathered together all
the men of the place and made a feast. 23 Now
it came to pass in the evening, that he took
Leah his daughter and brought her to Jacob;
and he went in to her. 24 And Laban gave his
maid Zilpah to his daughter Leah *as* a maid.
25 So it came to pass in the morning, that
behold, it *was* Leah. And he said to Laban,
"What is this you have done to me? Was it
not for Rachel that I served you? Why then
have you deceived me?"

26 And Laban said, "It must not be done
so in our country, to give the younger before
the firstborn. 27 Fulfill her week, and we will
give you this one also for the service which
you will serve with me still another seven
years."

28 Then Jacob did so and fulfilled her
week. So he gave him his daughter Rachel as
wife also. 29 And Laban gave his maid Bilhah
to his daughter Rachel as a maid. 30 Then *Jacob* also went in to Rachel, and he also loved
Rachel more than Leah. And he served with
Laban still another seven years.

The Children of Jacob

31 When the LORD saw that Leah *was* unloved, He opened her womb; but Rachel *was*
barren. 32 So Leah conceived and bore a son,
and she called his name Reuben;[a] for she
said, "The LORD has surely looked on my
affliction. Now therefore, my husband will
love me." 33 Then she conceived again and
bore a son, and said, "Because the LORD has
heard that I *am* unloved, He has therefore
given me this *son* also." And she called his
name Simeon.[a] 34 She conceived again and
bore a son, and said, "Now this time my husband will become attached to me, because I
have borne him three sons." Therefore his
name was called Levi.[a] 35 And she conceived
again and bore a son, and said, "Now I will
praise the LORD." Therefore she called his
name Judah.[a] Then she stopped bearing.

30 Now when Rachel saw that she
bore Jacob no children, Rachel envied her sister, and said to Jacob, "Give me
children, or else I die!"

2 And Jacob's anger was aroused against
Rachel, and he said, "*Am* I in the place of
God, who has withheld from you the fruit
of the womb?"

3 So she said, "Here is my maid Bilhah;
go in to her, and she will bear *a child* on my
knees, that I also may have children by her."
4 Then she gave him Bilhah her maid as wife,
and Jacob went in to her. 5 And Bilhah conceived and bore Jacob a son. 6 Then Rachel
said, "God has judged my case; and He has
also heard my voice and given me a son."
Therefore she called his name Dan.[a] 7 And
Rachel's maid Bilhah conceived again and
bore Jacob a second son. 8 Then Rachel said,
"With great wrestlings I have wrestled with
my sister, *and* indeed I have prevailed." So
she called his name Naphtali.[a]

9 When Leah saw that she had stopped
bearing, she took Zilpah her maid and
gave her to Jacob as wife. 10 And Leah's maid
Zilpah bore Jacob a son. 11 Then Leah said, "A
troop comes!"[a] So she called his name Gad.[b]
12 And Leah's maid Zilpah bore Jacob a second son. 13 Then Leah said, "I am happy, for
the daughters will call me blessed." So she
called his name Asher.[a]

14 Now Reuben went in the days of wheat
harvest and found mandrakes in the field,
and brought them to his mother Leah. Then
Rachel said to Leah, "Please give me *some* of
your son's mandrakes."

15 But she said to her, "*Is it* a small matter that you have taken away my husband?
Would you take away my son's mandrakes
also?"

And Rachel said, "Therefore he will lie
with you tonight for your son's mandrakes."

16 When Jacob came out of the field in
the evening, Leah went out to meet him and
said, "You must come in to me, for I have
surely hired you with my son's mandrakes."
And he lay with her that night.

17 And God listened to Leah, and she
conceived and bore Jacob a fifth son. 18 Leah
said, "God has given me my wages, because
I have given my maid to my husband." So
she called his name Issachar.[a] 19 Then Leah
conceived again and bore Jacob a sixth son.
20 And Leah said, "God has endowed me *with*
a good endowment; now my husband will
dwell with me, because I have borne him
six sons." So she called his name Zebulun.[a]

29:32 [a] Literally *See, a Son* **29:33** [a] Literally *Heard*
29:34 [a] Literally *Attached* **29:35** [a] Literally *Praise*
30:6 [a] Literally *Judge* **30:8** [a] Literally *My Wrestling*
30:11 [a] Following Qere, Syriac, and Targum; Kethib, Septuagint, and Vulgate read *in fortune.* [b] Literally *Troop* or *Fortune* **30:13** [a] Literally *Happy* **30:18** [a] Literally *Wages* **30:20** [a] Literally *Dwelling*

21Afterward she bore a daughter, and called
her name Dinah.
22Then God remembered Rachel, and
God listened to her and opened her womb.
23And she conceived and bore a son, and
said, "God has taken away my reproach."
24So she called his name Joseph,[a] and said,
"The LORD shall add to me another son."

Jacob's Agreement with Laban

25And it came to pass, when Rachel had
borne Joseph, that Jacob said to Laban, "Send
me away, that I may go to my own place and
to my country. 26Give *me* my wives and my
children for whom I have served you, and let
me go; for you know my service which I have
done for you."
27And Laban said to him, "Please *stay,* if
I have found favor in your eyes, *for* I have
learned by experience that the LORD has
blessed me for your sake." 28Then he said,
"Name me your wages, and I will give *it.*"
29So *Jacob* said to him, "You know how I
have served you and how your livestock has
been with me. 30For what you had before I
came was little, and it has increased to a great
amount; the LORD has blessed you since my
coming. And now, when shall I also provide
for my own house?"
31So he said, "What shall I give you?"
And Jacob said, "You shall not give me
anything. If you will do this thing for me,
I will again feed and keep your flocks: 32Let
me pass through all your flock today, remov-
ing from there all the speckled and spotted
sheep, and all the brown ones among the
lambs, and the spotted and speckled among
the goats; and *these* shall be my wages. 33So
my righteousness will answer for me in
time to come, when the subject of my wages comes before you: every one that *is* not
speckled and spotted among the goats, and
brown among the lambs, will be considered
stolen, if *it is* with me."
34And Laban said, "Oh, that it were according to your word!" 35So he removed that
day the male goats that were speckled and
spotted, all the female goats that were speckled and spotted, every one that had *some*
white in it, and all the brown ones among
the lambs, and gave *them* into the hand of
his sons. 36Then he put three days' journey
between himself and Jacob, and Jacob fed
the rest of Laban's flocks.
37Now Jacob took for himself rods of
green poplar and of the almond and chestnut trees, peeled white strips in them, and
exposed the white which *was* in the rods.
38And the rods which he had peeled, he set
before the flocks in the gutters, in the watering troughs where the flocks came to drink,
so that they should conceive when they came
to drink. 39So the flocks conceived before the
rods, and the flocks brought forth streaked,
speckled, and spotted. 40Then Jacob separated the lambs, and made the flocks face
toward the streaked and all the brown in the

30:24 [a] Literally *He Will Add*

LEARNING

READ IT: GENESIS 30:25–43

Jacob and Laban have a unique story. And Laban is not a role model in lots of ways. But one thing about Laban is particularly interesting: Laban learned by experience (he said so in v. 27) that when Jacob was around, God seemed to be there also.

Are there people in your life who cause you to feel closer to God just by being around them? If so, that's a learning experience worth pursuing more often!

flock of Laban; but he put his own flocks
by themselves and did not put them with
Laban's flock.

41 And it came to pass, whenever the stronger livestock conceived, that Jacob placed the
rods before the eyes of the livestock in the
gutters, that they might conceive among
the rods. 42 But when the flocks were feeble,
he did not put *them* in; so the feebler were
Laban's and the stronger Jacob's. 43 Thus the
man became exceedingly prosperous, and
had large flocks, female and male servants,
and camels and donkeys.

Jacob Flees from Laban

31 Now *Jacob* heard the words of Laban's sons, saying, "Jacob has tak-
en away all that was our father's, and from
what was our father's he has acquired all this
wealth." 2 And Jacob saw the countenance of
Laban, and indeed it *was* not *favorable* toward
him as before. 3 Then the LORD said to Jacob,
"Return to the land of your fathers and to
your family, and I will be with you."

4 So Jacob sent and called Rachel and Leah
to the field, to his flock, 5 and said to them, "I
see your father's countenance, that it *is* not
favorable toward me as before; but the God of
my father has been with me. 6 And you know
that with all my might I have served your
father. 7 Yet your father has deceived me and
changed my wages ten times, but God did
not allow him to hurt me. 8 If he said thus:
'The speckled shall be your wages,' then all
the flocks bore speckled. And if he said thus:
'The streaked shall be your wages,' then all
the flocks bore streaked. 9 So God has taken
away the livestock of your father and given
them to me.

10 "And it happened, at the time when the
flocks conceived, that I lifted my eyes and
saw in a dream, and behold, the rams which
leaped upon the flocks *were* streaked, speckled, and gray-spotted. 11 Then the Angel of
God spoke to me in a dream, saying, 'Jacob.'
And I said, 'Here I am.' 12 And He said, 'Lift
your eyes now and see, all the rams which
leap on the flocks *are* streaked, speckled,
and gray-spotted; for I have seen all that Laban is doing to you. 13 I *am* the God of Bethel,
where you anointed the pillar *and* where you
made a vow to Me. Now arise, get out of this
land, and return to the land of your family.'"

14 Then Rachel and Leah answered and
said to him, "Is there still any portion or
inheritance for us in our father's house?
15 Are we not considered strangers by him?
For he has sold us, and also completely
consumed our money. 16 For all these riches
which God has taken from our father are
really ours and our children's; now then,
whatever God has said to you, do it."

17 Then Jacob rose and set his sons and his
wives on camels. 18 And he carried away all
his livestock and all his possessions which he
had gained, his acquired livestock which
he had gained in Padan Aram, to go to his
father Isaac in the land of Canaan. 19 Now Laban had gone to shear his sheep, and Rachel
had stolen the household idols that were her
father's. 20 And Jacob stole away, unknown to
Laban the Syrian, in that he did not tell him
that he intended to flee. 21 So he fled with
all that he had. He arose and crossed the river,
and headed toward the mountains of Gilead.

Laban Pursues Jacob

22 And Laban was told on the third day
that Jacob had fled. 23 Then he took his brethren with him and pursued him for seven
days' journey, and he overtook him in the
mountains of Gilead. 24 But God had come to
Laban the Syrian in a dream by night, and
said to him, "Be careful that you speak to Jacob neither good nor bad."

25 So Laban overtook Jacob. Now Jacob had
pitched his tent in the mountains, and Laban with his brethren pitched in the mountains of Gilead.

26 And Laban said to Jacob: "What have
you done, that you have stolen away unknown to me, and carried away my daughters like captives *taken* with the sword?
27 Why did you flee away secretly, and steal
away from me, and not tell me; for I might
have sent you away with joy and songs, with
timbrel and harp? 28 And you did not allow
me to kiss my sons and my daughters. Now
you have done foolishly in *so* doing. 29 It is in
my power to do you harm, but the God of
your father spoke to me last night, saying,
'Be careful that you speak to Jacob neither
good nor bad.' 30 And now you have surely
gone because you greatly long for your father's house, *but* why did you steal my gods?"

31 Then Jacob answered and said to Laban,
"Because I was afraid, for I said, 'Perhaps
you would take your daughters from me by
force.' 32 With whomever you find your gods,
do not let him live. In the presence of our

brethren, identify what I have of yours and
take *it* with you." For Jacob did not know that
Rachel had stolen them.

33 And Laban went into Jacob's tent, into
Leah's tent, and into the two maids' tents,
but he did not find *them*. Then he went out
of Leah's tent and entered Rachel's tent.
34 Now Rachel had taken the household idols,
put them in the camel's saddle, and sat on
them. And Laban searched all about the
tent but did not find *them*. 35 And she said to
her father, "Let it not displease my lord that
I cannot rise before you, for the manner of
women *is* with me." And he searched but did
not find the household idols.

36 Then Jacob was angry and rebuked Laban, and Jacob answered and said to Laban:
"What *is* my trespass? What *is* my sin, that
you have so hotly pursued me? 37 Although
you have searched all my things, what part of
your household things have you found? Set
it here before my brethren and your brethren, that they may judge between us both!
38 These twenty years I *have been* with you;
your ewes and your female goats have not
miscarried their young, and I have not eat-
en the rams of your flock. 39 That which was
torn *by beasts* I did not bring to you; I bore
the loss of it. You required it from my hand,
whether stolen by day or stolen by night.
40 *There* I was! In the day the drought consumed me, and the frost by night, and my
sleep departed from my eyes. 41 Thus I have
been in your house twenty years; I served
you fourteen years for your two daughters,
and six years for your flock, and you have
changed my wages ten times. 42 Unless the
God of my father, the God of Abraham and
the Fear of Isaac, had been with me, surely
now you would have sent me away empty-
handed. God has seen my affliction and
the labor of my hands, and rebuked *you* last
night."

Laban's Covenant with Jacob

43 And Laban answered and said to Jacob,
"*These* daughters *are* my daughters, and *these*
children *are* my children, and *this* flock *is*
my flock; all that you see *is* mine. But what
can I do this day to these my daughters or to
their children whom they have borne? 44 Now
therefore, come, let us make a covenant, you
and I, and let it be a witness between you
and me."

45 So Jacob took a stone and set it up *as*
a pillar. 46 Then Jacob said to his brethren,
"Gather stones." And they took stones and
made a heap, and they ate there on the heap.
47 Laban called it Jegar Sahadutha,[a] but Jacob
called it Galeed.[b] 48 And Laban said, "This
heap *is* a witness between you and me this
day." Therefore its name was called Galeed,
49 also Mizpah,[a] because he said, "May the
LORD watch between you and me when we
are absent one from another. 50 If you afflict
my daughters, or if you take *other* wives besides my daughters, *although* no man *is* with
us—see, God *is* witness between you and
me!"

51 Then Laban said to Jacob, "Here is this
heap and here is *this* pillar, which I have
placed between you and me. 52 This heap *is* a
witness, and *this* pillar *is* a witness, that I will
not pass beyond this heap to you, and you
will not pass beyond this heap and this pillar
to me, for harm. 53 The God of Abraham, the
God of Nahor, and the God of their father
judge between us." And Jacob swore by the
Fear of his father Isaac. 54 Then Jacob offered
a sacrifice on the mountain, and called his
brethren to eat bread. And they ate bread and
stayed all night on the mountain. 55 And early
in the morning Laban arose, and kissed his
sons and daughters and blessed them. Then
Laban departed and returned to his place.

Esau Comes to Meet Jacob

32 So Jacob went on his way, and the
angels of God met him. 2 When
Jacob saw them, he said, "This *is* God's
camp." And he called the name of that place
Mahanaim.[a]

3 Then Jacob sent messengers before
him to Esau his brother in the land of Seir,
the country of Edom. 4 And he commanded
them, saying, "Speak thus to my lord Esau,
'Thus your servant Jacob says: "I have dwelt
with Laban and stayed there until now. 5 I
have oxen, donkeys, flocks, and male and
female servants; and I have sent to tell my
lord, that I may find favor in your sight." ' "

6 Then the messengers returned to Jacob, saying, "We came to your brother Esau,
and he also is coming to meet you, and four
hundred men *are* with him." 7 So Jacob was
greatly afraid and distressed; and he divided

31:47 [a] Literally, in Aramaic, *Heap of Witness* [b] Literally, in Hebrew, *Heap of Witness* 31:49 [a] Literally *Watch*
32:2 [a] Literally *Double Camp*

the people that *were* with him, and the flocks
and herds and camels, into two companies.
8And he said, "If Esau comes to the one company and attacks it, then the other company
which is left will escape."

9Then Jacob said, "O God of my father
Abraham and God of my father Isaac, the
LORD who said to me, 'Return to your country and to your family, and I will deal well
with you': 10I am not worthy of the least of all
the mercies and of all the truth which You
have shown Your servant; for I crossed over
this Jordan with my staff, and now I have
become two companies. 11Deliver me, I pray,
from the hand of my brother, from the hand
of Esau; for I fear him, lest he come and attack me *and* the mother with the children.
12For You said, 'I will surely treat you well,
and make your descendants as the sand
of the sea, which cannot be numbered for
multitude.'"

13So he lodged there that same night, and
took what came to his hand as a present for
Esau his brother: 14two hundred female goats
and twenty male goats, two hundred ewes
and twenty rams, 15thirty milk camels with
their colts, forty cows and ten bulls, twenty
female donkeys and ten foals. 16Then he delivered *them* to the hand of his servants, every drove by itself, and said to his servants,
"Pass over before me, and put some distance
between successive droves." 17And he commanded the first one, saying, "When Esau
my brother meets you and asks you, saying,
'To whom do you belong, and where are you
going? Whose *are* these in front of you?'
18then you shall say, 'They *are* your servant Jacob's. It is a present sent to my lord Esau; and
behold, he also *is* behind us.'" 19So he commanded the second, the third, and all who
followed the droves, saying, "In this manner
you shall speak to Esau when you find him;
20and also say, 'Behold, your servant Jacob *is*
behind us.'" For he said, "I will appease him
with the present that goes before me, and
afterward I will see his face; perhaps he will
accept me." 21So the present went on over before him, but he himself lodged that night in
the camp.

Wrestling with God

22And he arose that night and took his
two wives, his two female servants, and his
eleven sons, and crossed over the ford of
Jabbok. 23He took them, sent them over the

In Focus

31:54 Sacrifice Pronounced *SACK-rih-fyce*. An offering to God. In the Old Testament, the people sacrificed the blood of animals for sin. In the New Testament, Christ is our only sacrifice for sin.

brook, and sent over what he had. 24Then Jacob was left alone; and a Man wrestled with
him until the breaking of day. 25Now when
He saw that He did not prevail against him,
He touched the socket of his hip; and the
socket of Jacob's hip was out of joint as He
wrestled with him. 26And He said, "Let Me
go, for the day breaks."

But he said, "I will not let You go unless
You bless me!"

27So He said to him, "What *is* your
name?"

He said, "Jacob."

28And He said, "Your name shall no longer be called Jacob, but Israel;[a] for you have
struggled with God and with men, and have
prevailed."

29Then Jacob asked, saying, "Tell *me* Your
name, I pray."

And He said, "Why *is* it *that* you ask
about My name?" And He blessed him there.

30So Jacob called the name of the place
Peniel:[a] "For I have seen God face to face,
and my life is preserved." 31Just as he crossed
over Penuel[a] the sun rose on him, and he
limped on his hip. 32Therefore to this day the
children of Israel do not eat the muscle that
shrank, which *is* on the hip socket, because
He touched the socket of Jacob's hip in the
muscle that shrank.

Jacob and Esau Meet

33 Now Jacob lifted his eyes and
looked, and there, Esau was coming, and with him were four hundred men.
So he divided the children among Leah,
Rachel, and the two maidservants. 2And he
put the maidservants and their children in

32:28 [a] Literally *Prince with God* **32:30** [a] Literally *Face of God* **32:31** [a] Same as *Peniel*, verse 30

front, Leah and her children behind, and
Rachel and Joseph last. 3 Then he crossed
over before them and bowed himself to the
ground seven times, until he came near to
his brother.

4 But Esau ran to meet him, and embraced him, and fell on his neck and kissed
him, and they wept. 5 And he lifted his eyes
and saw the women and children, and said,
“Who *are* these with you?”

So he said, “The children whom God
has graciously given your servant.” 6 Then
the maidservants came near, they and their
children, and bowed down. 7 And Leah also
came near with her children, and they
bowed down. Afterward Joseph and Rachel
came near, and they bowed down.

8 Then Esau said, “What *do* you *mean by*
all this company which I met?”

And he said, “*These are* to find favor in
the sight of my lord.”

9 But Esau said, “I have enough, my
brother; keep what you have for yourself.”

10 And Jacob said, “No, please, if I have
now found favor in your sight, then receive
my present from my hand, inasmuch as I
have seen your face as though I had seen the
face of God, and you were pleased with me.
11 Please, take my blessing that is brought to
you, because God has dealt graciously with
me, and because I have enough.” So he
urged him, and he took *it*.

12 Then Esau said, “Let us take our journey; let us go, and I will go before you.”

13 But Jacob said to him, “My lord knows
that the children *are* weak, and the flocks
and herds which are nursing *are* with me.
And if the men should drive them hard one

GOD WRESTLES WITH JACOB

READ IT: GENESIS 32:22–32

GET IT:

Jacob, the guy who got dad’s blessing, had to run away from his brother, Esau, who wanted to kill him. While gone, Jacob married two women, Leah and Rachel, and had twelve kids. On his way back to Canaan (the land he inherited), Jacob was challenged to a wrestling match. He wrestled with a guy all night. At dawn, when it was finally over, Jacob realized it was God who fought with him all night. This fight changed Jacob’s life . . . and his name. God changed his name to Israel. This would be the name of God’s great nation forever.

LIVE IT:

You’ve probably heard of people who had life-changing moments: an accident, winning the lottery, moving to a new city, or making the team. Maybe you’ve had such an experience yourself, maybe not. Jacob’s moment came late in his life. He wasn’t a kid anymore; he was old with lots of responsibilities: big family, herds of animals, lots of servants. His life-changing moment was directly with God. Your life-changing moment might not be this dramatic, but God will still be part of it. God speaks through big moments and little ones in life. Watch and listen carefully. God will speak to you, too.

day, all the flock will die. [14]Please let my lord go on ahead before his servant. I will lead on slowly at a pace which the livestock that go before me, and the children, are able to endure, until I come to my lord in Seir."

[15]And Esau said, "Now let me leave with you *some* of the people who *are* with me."

But he said, "What need is there? Let me find favor in the sight of my lord." [16]So Esau returned that day on his way to Seir. [17]And Jacob journeyed to Succoth, built himself a house, and made booths for his livestock. Therefore the name of the place is called Succoth.[a]

Jacob Comes to Canaan

[18]Then Jacob came safely to the city of Shechem, which *is* in the land of Canaan, when he came from Padan Aram; and he pitched his tent before the city. [19]And he bought the parcel of land, where he had pitched his tent, from the children of Hamor, Shechem's father, for one hundred pieces of money. [20]Then he erected an altar there and called it El Elohe Israel.[a]

The Dinah Incident

34 Now Dinah the daughter of Leah, whom she had borne to Jacob, went out to see the daughters of the land. [2]And when Shechem the son of Hamor the Hivite, prince of the country, saw her, he took her and lay with her, and violated her. [3]His soul was strongly attracted to Dinah the daughter of Jacob, and he loved the young woman and spoke kindly to the young woman. [4]So Shechem spoke to his father Hamor, saying, "Get me this young woman as a wife."

[5]And Jacob heard that he had defiled Dinah his daughter. Now his sons were with his livestock in the field; so Jacob held his peace until they came. [6]Then Hamor the father of Shechem went out to Jacob to speak with him. [7]And the sons of Jacob came in from the field when they heard *it;* and the men were grieved and very angry, because he had done a disgraceful thing in Israel by lying with Jacob's daughter, a thing which ought not to be done. [8]But Hamor spoke with them, saying, "The soul of my son Shechem longs for your daughter. Please give her to him as a wife. [9]And make marriages with us; give your daughters to us, and take our daughters to yourselves. [10]So you shall dwell with us, and the land shall be before you. Dwell and trade in it, and acquire possessions for yourselves in it."

[11]Then Shechem said to her father and her brothers, "Let me find favor in your eyes, and whatever you say to me I will give. [12]Ask me ever so much dowry and gift, and I will give according to what you say to me; but give me the young woman as a wife."

[13]But the sons of Jacob answered Shechem and Hamor his father, and spoke deceitfully, because he had defiled Dinah their sister. [14]And they said to them, "We cannot do this thing, to give our sister to one who is uncircumcised, for that *would be* a reproach to us. [15]But on this *condition* we will consent to you: If you will become as we *are,* if every male of you is circumcised, [16]then we will give our daughters to you, and we will take your daughters to us; and we will dwell with you, and we will become one people. [17]But if you will not heed us and be circumcised, then we will take our daughter and be gone."

[18]And their words pleased Hamor and Shechem, Hamor's son. [19]So the young man did not delay to do the thing, because he delighted in Jacob's daughter. He *was* more honorable than all the household of his father.

[20]And Hamor and Shechem his son came to the gate of their city, and spoke with the men of their city, saying: [21]"These men *are* at peace with us. Therefore let them dwell in the land and trade in it. For indeed the land *is* large enough for them. Let us take their daughters to us as wives, and let us give them our daughters. [22]Only on this *condition* will the men consent to dwell with us, to be one people: if every male among us is circumcised as they *are* circumcised. [23]*Will* not their livestock, their property, and every animal of theirs *be* ours? Only let us consent to them, and they will dwell with us." [24]And all who went out of the gate of his city heeded Hamor and Shechem his son; every male was circumcised, all who went out of the gate of his city.

[25]Now it came to pass on the third day, when they were in pain, that two of the sons of Jacob, Simeon and Levi, Dinah's brothers, each took his sword and came boldly upon

---

33:17 [a] Literally *Booths* 33:20 [a] Literally *God, the God of Israel*

the city and killed all the males. 26And they
killed Hamor and Shechem his son with
the edge of the sword, and took Dinah from
Shechem's house, and went out. 27The sons
of Jacob came upon the slain, and plundered
the city, because their sister had been defiled. 28They took their sheep, their oxen,
and their donkeys, what *was* in the city and
what *was* in the field, 29and all their wealth.
All their little ones and their wives they took
captive; and they plundered even all that *was*
in the houses.

30Then Jacob said to Simeon and Levi,
"You have troubled me by making me ob-
noxious among the inhabitants of the land,
among the Canaanites and the Perizzites;
and since I *am* few in number, they will
gather themselves together against me and
kill me. I shall be destroyed, my household
and I."

31But they said, "Should he treat our sister
like a harlot?"

Jacob's Return to Bethel

35 Then God said to Jacob, "Arise, go
up to Bethel and dwell there; and
make an altar there to God, who appeared
to you when you fled from the face of Esau
your brother."

2And Jacob said to his household and to
all who *were* with him, "Put away the foreign
gods that *are* among you, purify yourselves,
and change your garments. 3Then let us
arise and go up to Bethel; and I will make
an altar there to God, who answered me in
the day of my distress and has been with me
in the way which I have gone." 4So they gave
Jacob all the foreign gods which *were* in their
hands, and the earrings which *were* in their
ears; and Jacob hid them under the terebinth
tree which *was* by Shechem.

5And they journeyed, and the terror of
God was upon the cities that *were* all around
them, and they did not pursue the sons of
Jacob. 6So Jacob came to Luz (that *is,* Bethel),
which *is* in the land of Canaan, he and all
the people who *were* with him. 7And he built
an altar there and called the place El Bethel,[a]
because there God appeared to him when he
fled from the face of his brother.

8Now Deborah, Rebekah's nurse, died,
and she was buried below Bethel under the
terebinth tree. So the name of it was called
Allon Bachuth.[a]

9Then God appeared to Jacob again,
when he came from Padan Aram, and
blessed him. 10And God said to him, "Your
name *is* Jacob; your name shall not be called
Jacob anymore, but Israel shall be your
name." So He called his name Israel. 11Also
God said to him: "I *am* God Almighty. Be
fruitful and multiply; a nation and a company of nations shall proceed from you,
and kings shall come from your body. 12The
land which I gave Abraham and Isaac I give
to you; and to your descendants after you I
give this land." 13Then God went up from
him in the place where He talked with him.
14So Jacob set up a pillar in the place where
He talked with him, a pillar of stone; and he
poured a drink offering on it, and he poured
oil on it. 15And Jacob called the name of the
place where God spoke with him, Bethel.

Death of Rachel

16Then they journeyed from Bethel. And
when there was but a little distance to go to
Ephrath, Rachel labored *in childbirth,* and
she had hard labor. 17Now it came to pass,
when she was in hard labor, that the midwife
said to her, "Do not fear; you will have this
son also." 18And so it was, as her soul was
departing (for she died), that she called his
name Ben-Oni;[a] but his father called him
Benjamin.[b] 19So Rachel died and was buried
on the way to Ephrath (that *is,* Bethlehem).
20And Jacob set a pillar on her grave, which *is*
the pillar of Rachel's grave to this day.

21Then Israel journeyed and pitched his
tent beyond the tower of Eder. 22And it happened, when Israel dwelt in that land, that
Reuben went and lay with Bilhah his father's
concubine; and Israel heard *about it.*

Jacob's Twelve Sons

Now the sons of Jacob were twelve: 23the
sons of Leah *were* Reuben, Jacob's firstborn,
and Simeon, Levi, Judah, Issachar, and Zebulun; 24the sons of Rachel *were* Joseph and
Benjamin; 25the sons of Bilhah, Rachel's
maidservant, *were* Dan and Naphtali; 26and
the sons of Zilpah, Leah's maidservant, *were*
Gad and Asher. These *were* the sons of Jacob
who were born to him in Padan Aram.

Death of Isaac

27Then Jacob came to his father Isaac at
Mamre, or Kirjath Arba[a] (that *is,* Hebron),

35:7 [a] Literally *God of the House of God* **35:8** [a] Literally *Terebinth of Weeping* **35:18** [a] Literally *Son of My Sorrow* [b] Literally *Son of the Right Hand* **35:27** [a] Literally *Town of Arba*

where Abraham and Isaac had dwelt. 28Now
the days of Isaac were one hundred and
eighty years. 29So Isaac breathed his last and
died, and was gathered to his people, *being*
old and full of days. And his sons Esau and
Jacob buried him.

The Family of Esau

36 Now this *is* the genealogy of Esau,
who is Edom. 2Esau took his wives
from the daughters of Canaan: Adah the
daughter of Elon the Hittite; Aholibamah
the daughter of Anah, the daughter of Zibeon the Hivite; 3and Basemath, Ishmael's
daughter, sister of Nebajoth. 4Now Adah
bore Eliphaz to Esau, and Basemath bore
Reuel. 5And Aholibamah bore Jeush, Jaalam, and Korah. These *were* the sons of Esau
who were born to him in the land of Canaan.

6Then Esau took his wives, his sons, his
daughters, and all the persons of his household, his cattle and all his animals, and all
his goods which he had gained in the land
of Canaan, and went to a country away from
the presence of his brother Jacob. 7For their
possessions were too great for them to dwell
together, and the land where they were
strangers could not support them because
of their livestock. 8So Esau dwelt in Mount
Seir. Esau *is* Edom.

9And this *is* the genealogy of Esau the
father of the Edomites in Mount Seir. 10These
were the names of Esau's sons: Eliphaz the
son of Adah the wife of Esau, and Reuel
the son of Basemath the wife of Esau. 11And
the sons of Eliphaz were Teman, Omar, Zepho,[a] Gatam, and Kenaz.

12Now Timna was the concubine of Eliphaz, Esau's son, and she bore Amalek to
Eliphaz. These *were* the sons of Adah, Esau's
wife.

13These *were* the sons of Reuel: Nahath,
Zerah, Shammah, and Mizzah. These were
the sons of Basemath, Esau's wife.

14These were the sons of Aholibamah,
Esau's wife, the daughter of Anah, the
daughter of Zibeon. And she bore to Esau:
Jeush, Jaalam, and Korah.

The Chiefs of Edom

15These *were* the chiefs of the sons of Esau.
The sons of Eliphaz, the firstborn *son* of Esau,
were Chief Teman, Chief Omar, Chief Zepho,
Chief Kenaz, 16Chief Korah,[a] Chief Gatam,
and Chief Amalek. These *were* the chiefs
of Eliphaz in the land of Edom. They *were*
the sons of Adah.

17These *were* the sons of Reuel, Esau's
son: Chief Nahath, Chief Zerah, Chief
Shammah, and Chief Mizzah. These *were*
the chiefs of Reuel in the land of Edom.
These *were* the sons of Basemath, Esau's
wife.

18And these *were* the sons of Aholibamah,
Esau's wife: Chief Jeush, Chief Jaalam, and
Chief Korah. These *were* the chiefs *who descended* from Aholibamah, Esau's wife, the
daughter of Anah. 19These *were* the sons of
Esau, who is Edom, and these *were* their
chiefs.

The Sons of Seir

20These *were* the sons of Seir the Horite
who inhabited the land: Lotan, Shobal, Zibeon, Anah, 21Dishon, Ezer, and Dishan.
These *were* the chiefs of the Horites, the sons
of Seir, in the land of Edom.

22And the sons of Lotan were Hori and
Hemam.[a] Lotan's sister *was* Timna.

23These *were* the sons of Shobal: Alvan,[a]
Manahath, Ebal, Shepho,[b] and Onam.

24These *were* the sons of Zibeon: both
Ajah and Anah. This *was the* Anah who
found the water[a] in the wilderness as he
pastured the donkeys of his father Zibeon.
25These *were* the children of Anah: Dishon
and Aholibamah the daughter of Anah.

26These *were* the sons of Dishon:[a] Hemdan,[b] Eshban, Ithran, and Cheran. 27These
were the sons of Ezer: Bilhan, Zaavan, and
Akan.[a] 28These *were* the sons of Dishan: Uz
and Aran.

29These *were* the chiefs of the Horites:
Chief Lotan, Chief Shobal, Chief Zibeon,
Chief Anah, 30Chief Dishon, Chief Ezer,
and Chief Dishan. These *were* the chiefs of
the Horites, according to their chiefs in the
land of Seir.

The Kings of Edom

31Now these *were* the kings who reigned
in the land of Edom before any king reigned

36:11 [a] Spelled *Zephi* in 1 Chronicles 1:36
36:16 [a] Samaritan Pentateuch omits *Chief Korah.*
36:22 [a] Spelled *Homam* in 1 Chronicles 1:39
36:23 [a] Spelled *Alian* in 1 Chronicles 1:40 [b] Spelled *Shephi* in 1 Chronicles 1:40 **36:24** [a] Following Masoretic Text and Vulgate (*hot springs*); Septuagint reads *Jamin;* Targum reads *mighty men;* Talmud interprets as *mules.*
36:26 [a] Hebrew *Dishan* [b] Spelled *Hamran* in 1 Chronicles 1:41 **36:27** [a] Spelled *Jaakan* in 1 Chronicles 1:42

over the children of Israel: 32 Bela the son of
Beor reigned in Edom, and the name of his
city *was* Dinhabah. 33 And when Bela died,
Jobab the son of Zerah of Bozrah reigned in
his place. 34 When Jobab died, Husham of the
land of the Temanites reigned in his place.
35 And when Husham died, Hadad the son of
Bedad, who attacked Midian in the field of
Moab, reigned in his place. And the name
of his city *was* Avith. 36 When Hadad died,
Samlah of Masrekah reigned in his place.
37 And when Samlah died, Saul of Rehoboth-
by-the-River reigned in his place. 38 When
Saul died, Baal-Hanan the son of Achbor
reigned in his place. 39 And when Baal-Hanan
the son of Achbor died, Hadar[a] reigned in
his place; and the name of his city *was* Pau.[b]
His wife's name *was* Mehetabel, the daughter of Matred, the daughter of Mezahab.

The Chiefs of Esau

40 And these *were* the names of the chiefs
of Esau, according to their families and their
places, by their names: Chief Timnah, Chief
Alvah,[a] Chief Jetheth, 41 Chief Aholibamah,
Chief Elah, Chief Pinon, 42 Chief Kenaz,
Chief Teman, Chief Mibzar, 43 Chief Magdiel, and Chief Iram. These *were* the chiefs
of Edom, according to their dwelling places
in the land of their possession. Esau *was* the
father of the Edomites.

Joseph Dreams of Greatness

37 Now Jacob dwelt in the land where
his father was a stranger, in the
land of Canaan. 2 This *is* the history of Jacob.
Joseph, *being* seventeen years old, was
feeding the flock with his brothers. And
the lad *was* with the sons of Bilhah and the

36:39 [a] Spelled *Hadad* in Samaritan Pentateuch, Syriac, and 1 Chronicles 1:50 [b] Spelled *Pai* in 1 Chronicles 1:50
36:40 [a] Spelled *Aliah* in 1 Chronicles 1:51

GOD'S GIFT TO JOSEPH

READ IT: GENESIS 37:1–36

GET IT:

In ancient times, dreams had significant meaning. The dreams of people in the Bible weren't the usual, ordinary dreams. These were dreams sent by God for a specific reason. God gave Joseph an amazing talent that, unfortunately, was not considered very useful when he was a teenager. In fact, his dreams (and his bragging about them) got him in trouble with his brothers. And it caused a lot of misery for him and his father.

LIVE IT:

People don't always understand or appreciate someone else who has a great talent. If someone can run a fast mile, play an instrument, ace every test she takes, or balance a marshmallow on his nose, other people may be jealous. And if the talented person brags too much about it, everyone groans. Talents are good things. They come from God, and we should use them. But we shouldn't draw attention to what we can do, but what God can do through us. Enjoy your talent, no matter what it is. Thank God for it. But be careful to use it for His glory, not your own.

sons of Zilpah, his father's wives; and Joseph
brought a bad report of them to his father.
3Now Israel loved Joseph more than all
his children, because he *was* the son of his
old age. Also he made him a tunic of *many*
colors. 4But when his brothers saw that their
father loved him more than all his brothers,
they hated him and could not speak peaceably to him.
5Now Joseph had a dream, and he told
it to his brothers; and they hated him even
more. 6So he said to them, "Please hear this
dream which I have dreamed: 7There we
were, binding sheaves in the field. Then behold, my sheaf arose and also stood upright;
and indeed your sheaves stood all around
and bowed down to my sheaf."
8And his brothers said to him, "Shall you
indeed reign over us? Or shall you indeed
have dominion over us?" So they hated him
even more for his dreams and for his words.
9Then he dreamed still another dream
and told it to his brothers, and said, "Look,
I have dreamed another dream. And this
time, the sun, the moon, and the eleven
stars bowed down to me."
10So he told *it* to his father and his brothers; and his father rebuked him and said
to him, "What *is* this dream that you have
dreamed? Shall your mother and I and your
brothers indeed come to bow down to the
earth before you?" 11And his brothers envied
him, but his father kept the matter *in mind.*

Joseph Sold by His Brothers

12Then his brothers went to feed their father's flock in Shechem. 13And Israel said to
Joseph, "Are not your brothers feeding *the*
flock in Shechem? Come, I will send you to
them."
So he said to him, "Here I am."
14Then he said to him, "Please go and see
if it is well with your brothers and well with
the flocks, and bring back word to me." So
he sent him out of the Valley of Hebron, and
he went to Shechem.
15Now a certain man found him, and
there he was, wandering in the field. And
the man asked him, saying, "What are you
seeking?"
16So he said, "I am seeking my brothers.
Please tell me where they are feeding *their*
flocks."
17And the man said, "They have departed
from here, for I heard them say, 'Let us go to
Dothan.'" So Joseph went after his brothers
and found them in Dothan.
18Now when they saw him afar off, even
before he came near them, they conspired
against him to kill him. 19Then they said to
one another, "Look, this dreamer is coming!
20Come therefore, let us now kill him and
cast him into some pit; and we shall say,
'Some wild beast has devoured him.' We
shall see what will become of his dreams!"
21But Reuben heard *it,* and he delivered
him out of their hands, and said, "Let us not
kill him." 22And Reuben said to them, "Shed
no blood, *but* cast him into this pit which *is*
in the wilderness, and do not lay a hand on
him"—that he might deliver him out of their
hands, and bring him back to his father.
23So it came to pass, when Joseph had
come to his brothers, that they stripped Joseph *of* his tunic, the tunic of *many* colors
that *was* on him. 24Then they took him and
cast him into a pit. And the pit *was* empty;
there was no water in it.
25And they sat down to eat a meal. Then
they lifted their eyes and looked, and there
was a company of Ishmaelites, coming from
Gilead with their camels, bearing spices,
balm, and myrrh, on their way to carry
them down to Egypt. 26So Judah said to his
brothers, "What profit *is there* if we kill our
brother and conceal his blood? 27Come and
let us sell him to the Ishmaelites, and let not
our hand be upon him, for he *is* our brother
and our flesh." And his brothers listened.
28Then Midianite traders passed by; so *the*
brothers pulled Joseph up and lifted him out
of the pit, and sold him to the Ishmaelites for
twenty *shekels* of silver. And they took Joseph
to Egypt.
29Then Reuben returned to the pit, and
indeed Joseph *was* not in the pit; and he
tore his clothes. 30And he returned to his
brothers and said, "The lad *is* no *more;* and
I, where shall I go?"
31So they took Joseph's tunic, killed a
kid of the goats, and dipped the tunic in the
blood. 32Then they sent the tunic of *many*
colors, and they brought *it* to their father
and said, "We have found this. Do you know
whether it *is* your son's tunic or not?"
33And he recognized it and said, "*It is*
my son's tunic. A wild beast has devoured
him. Without doubt Joseph is torn to pieces."
34Then Jacob tore his clothes, put sackcloth
on his waist, and mourned for his son many

days. 35 And all his sons and all his daughters
arose to comfort him; but he refused to be
comforted, and he said, "For I shall go down
into the grave to my son in mourning." Thus
his father wept for him.
36 Now the Midianites[a] had sold him in
Egypt to Potiphar, an officer of Pharaoh *and*
captain of the guard.

Judah and Tamar

38 It came to pass at that time that
Judah departed from his broth-
ers, and visited a certain Adullamite whose
name *was* Hirah. 2 And Judah saw there a
daughter of a certain Canaanite whose name
was Shua, and he married her and went in to
her. 3 So she conceived and bore a son, and he
called his name Er. 4 She conceived again and
bore a son, and she called his name Onan.
5 And she conceived yet again and bore a
son, and called his name Shelah. He was at
Chezib when she bore him.
6 Then Judah took a wife for Er his firstborn, and her name *was* Tamar. 7 But Er, Judah's firstborn, was wicked in the sight of
the LORD, and the LORD killed him. 8 And
Judah said to Onan, "Go in to your brother's
wife and marry her, and raise up an heir to
your brother." 9 But Onan knew that the heir
would not be his; and it came to pass, when
he went in to his brother's wife, that he emit-
ted on the ground, lest he should give an heir
to his brother. 10 And the thing which he did
displeased the LORD; therefore He killed him
also.
11 Then Judah said to Tamar his daughter-
in-law, "Remain a widow in your father's
house till my son Shelah is grown." For he
said, "Lest he also die like his brothers." And
Tamar went and dwelt in her father's house.
12 Now in the process of time the daughter
of Shua, Judah's wife, died; and Judah was
comforted, and went up to his sheepshear-
ers at Timnah, he and his friend Hirah the
Adullamite. 13 And it was told Tamar, saying,
"Look, your father-in-law is going up to Timnah to shear his sheep." 14 So she took off her
widow's garments, covered *herself* with a
veil and wrapped herself, and sat in an open
place which *was* on the way to Timnah; for
she saw that Shelah was grown, and she was
not given to him as a wife. 15 When Judah saw
her, he thought she *was* a harlot, because she
had covered her face. 16 Then he turned to her
by the way, and said, "Please let me come in
to you"; for he did not know that she *was* his
daughter-in-law.
So she said, "What will you give me, that
you may come in to me?"
17 And he said, "I will send a young goat
from the flock."
So she said, "Will you give *me* a pledge
till you send *it*?"
18 Then he said, "What pledge shall I give
you?"
So she said, "Your signet and cord, and
your staff that *is* in your hand." Then he
gave *them* to her, and went in to her, and she
conceived by him. 19 So she arose and went
away, and laid aside her veil and put on the
garments of her widowhood.
20 And Judah sent the young goat by the
hand of his friend the Adullamite, to receive
his pledge from the woman's hand, but he
did not find her. 21 Then he asked the men of
that place, saying, "Where is the harlot who
was openly by the roadside?"
And they said, "There was no harlot in
this *place*."
22 So he returned to Judah and said, "I
cannot find her. Also, the men of the place
said there was no harlot in this *place*."
23 Then Judah said, "Let her take *them* for
herself, lest we be shamed; for I sent this
young goat and you have not found her."
24 And it came to pass, about three months
after, that Judah was told, saying, "Tamar
your daughter-in-law has played the harlot;
furthermore she *is* with child by harlotry."
So Judah said, "Bring her out and let her
be burned!"
25 When she *was* brought out, she sent
to her father-in-law, saying, "By the man to
whom these belong, I *am* with child." And
she said, "Please determine whose these
are—the signet and cord, and staff."
26 So Judah acknowledged *them* and said,
"She has been more righteous than I, because I did not give her to Shelah my son."
And he never knew her again.
27 Now it came to pass, at the time for
giving birth, that behold, twins *were* in her
womb. 28 And so it was, when she was giving birth, that *the one* put out *his* hand; and
the midwife took a scarlet *thread* and bound
it on his hand, saying, "This one came out
first." 29 Then it happened, as he drew back

37:36 [a] Masoretic Text reads *Medanites*.

his hand, that his brother came out unexpectedly; and she said, "How did you break
through? *This* breach *be* upon you!" Therefore his name was called Perez.[a] 30Afterward
his brother came out who had the scarlet
thread on his hand. And his name was called
Zerah.

Joseph a Slave in Egypt

39 Now Joseph had been taken down
to Egypt. And Potiphar, an officer
of Pharaoh, captain of the guard, an Egyptian, bought him from the Ishmaelites who
had taken him down there. 2The LORD was
with Joseph, and he was a successful man;
and he was in the house of his master the
Egyptian. 3And his master saw that the LORD
was with him and that the LORD made all he
did to prosper in his hand. 4So Joseph found
favor in his sight, and served him. Then he
made him overseer of his house, and all *that*
he had he put under his authority. 5So it was,
from the time *that* he had made him overseer of his house and all that he had, that
the LORD blessed the Egyptian's house for
Joseph's sake; and the blessing of the LORD
was on all that he had in the house and in
the field. 6Thus he left all that he had in Joseph's hand, and he did not know what he
had except for the bread which he ate.

Now Joseph was handsome in form and appearance.

7And it came to pass after these things
that his master's wife cast longing eyes on
Joseph, and she said, "Lie with me."

8But he refused and said to his master's
wife, "Look, my master does not know what
is with me in the house, and he has committed all that he has to my hand. 9*There is* no
one greater in this house than I, nor has he
kept back anything from me but you, because you *are* his wife. How then can I do
this great wickedness, and sin against God?"

10So it was, as she spoke to Joseph day by
day, that he did not heed her, to lie with her
or to be with her.

11But it happened about this time, when
Joseph went into the house to do his work,
and none of the men of the house *was* inside,
12that she caught him by his garment, saying, "Lie with me." But he left his garment
in her hand, and fled and ran outside. 13And
so it was, when she saw that he had left his
garment in her hand and fled outside, 14that
she called to the men of her house and spoke
to them, saying, "See, he has brought in to
us a Hebrew to mock us. He came in to me
to lie with me, and I cried out with a loud
voice. 15And it happened, when he heard that
I lifted my voice and cried out, that he left
his garment with me, and fled and went
outside."

16So she kept his garment with her until
his master came home. 17Then she spoke to
him with words like these, saying, "The Hebrew servant whom you brought to us came
in to me to mock me; 18so it happened, as I

38:29 [a] Literally *Breach* or *Breakthrough*

LIFE'S NOT FAIR

READ IT: GENESIS 39:1–23

Doing the right thing doesn't always "pay off" the way we'd like. While we can be sure that God's pleased when we do what's right, it's not a guarantee of immediate rewards like popularity, success, or money.

Do right things because they're right—not for a pat on the back or cosmic bonus points to help you "win" the game. And don't assume you see God's plan as well as He can. It's bigger than you could imagine! What seems unfair to you might lead to something amazing, so don't waste time keeping score.

lifted my voice and cried out, that he left his garment with me and fled outside."

19 So it was, when his master heard the words which his wife spoke to him, saying, "Your servant did to me after this manner," that his anger was aroused. 20 Then Joseph's master took him and put him into the prison, a place where the king's prisoners *were* confined. And he was there in the prison. 21 But the LORD was with Joseph and showed him mercy, and He gave him favor in the sight of the keeper of the prison. 22 And the keeper of the prison committed to Joseph's hand all the prisoners who *were* in the prison; whatever they did there, it was his doing. 23 The keeper of the prison did not look into anything *that was* under *Joseph's* authority,[a] because the LORD was with him; and whatever he did, the LORD made *it* prosper.

The Prisoners' Dreams

40 It came to pass after these things *that* the butler and the baker of the king of Egypt offended their lord, the king of Egypt. 2 And Pharaoh was angry with his two officers, the chief butler and the chief baker. 3 So he put them in custody in the house of the captain of the guard, in the prison, the place where Joseph *was* confined. 4 And the captain of the guard charged Joseph with them, and he served them; so they were in custody for a while.

5 Then the butler and the baker of the king of Egypt, who *were* confined in the prison, had a dream, both of them, each man's dream in one night *and* each man's dream with its *own* interpretation. 6 And Joseph came in to them in the morning and looked at them, and saw that they *were* sad. 7 So he asked Pharaoh's officers who *were* with him in the custody of his lord's house, saying, "Why do you look *so* sad today?"

8 And they said to him, "We each have had a dream, and *there is* no interpreter of it."

So Joseph said to them, "Do not interpretations belong to God? Tell *them* to me, please."

9 Then the chief butler told his dream to Joseph, and said to him, "Behold, in my dream a vine *was* before me, 10 and in the vine *were* three branches; it *was* as though it budded, its blossoms *shot forth, and its clusters* brought forth ripe grapes. 11 Then Pharaoh's cup *was* in my hand; and I took the grapes and pressed them into Pharaoh's cup, and placed the cup in Pharaoh's hand."

12 And Joseph said to him, "This *is* the interpretation of it: The three branches *are* three days. 13 Now within three days Pharaoh will lift up your head and restore you to your place, and you will put Pharaoh's cup in his hand according to the former manner, when you were his butler. 14 But remember me when it is well with you, and please show kindness to me; make mention of me to Pharaoh, and get me out of this house. 15 For indeed I was stolen away from the land of the Hebrews; and also I have done nothing here that they should put me into the dungeon."

16 When the chief baker saw that the interpretation was good, he said to Joseph, "I also *was* in my dream, and there *were* three white baskets on my head. 17 In the uppermost basket *were* all kinds of baked goods for Pharaoh, and the birds ate them out of the basket on my head."

18 So Joseph answered and said, "This *is* the interpretation of it: The three baskets *are* three days. 19 Within three days Pharaoh will lift off your head from you and hang you on a tree; and the birds will eat your flesh from you."

20 Now it came to pass on the third day, *which was* Pharaoh's birthday, that he made a feast for all his servants; and he lifted up the head of the chief butler and of the chief baker among his servants. 21 Then he restored the chief butler to his butlership again, and he placed the cup in Pharaoh's hand. 22 But he hanged the chief baker, as Joseph had interpreted to them. 23 Yet the chief butler did not remember Joseph, but forgot him.

Pharaoh's Dreams

41 Then it came to pass, at the end of two full years, that Pharaoh had a dream; and behold, he stood by the river. 2 Suddenly there came up out of the river seven cows, fine looking and fat; and they fed in the meadow. 3 Then behold, seven other cows came up after them out of the river, ugly and gaunt, and stood by the *other* cows on the bank of the river. 4 And the ugly and gaunt cows ate up the seven fine looking and fat cows. So Pharaoh awoke. 5 He slept and dreamed a second time; and suddenly seven heads of grain came up on one stalk, plump and good. 6 Then behold, seven thin heads, blighted by the east wind, sprang up after

39:23 [a] Literally *his hand*

them. 7And the seven thin heads devoured
the seven plump and full heads. So Pharaoh
awoke, and indeed, *it was* a dream. 8Now it
came to pass in the morning that his spirit
was troubled, and he sent and called for all
the magicians of Egypt and all its wise men.
And Pharaoh told them his dreams, but
there was no one who could interpret them
for Pharaoh.

9Then the chief butler spoke to Pharaoh,
saying: "I remember my faults this day.
10When Pharaoh was angry with his servants, and put me in custody in the house
of the captain of the guard, *both* me and the
chief baker, 11we each had a dream in one
night, he and I. Each of us dreamed according to the interpretation of his *own* dream.
12Now there *was* a young Hebrew man with
us there, a servant of the captain of the
guard. And we told him, and he interpreted our dreams for us; to each man he interpreted according to his *own* dream. 13And it
came to pass, just as he interpreted for us,
so it happened. He restored me to my office,
and he hanged him."

14Then Pharaoh sent and called Joseph,
and they brought him quickly out of the dungeon; and he shaved, changed his clothing,
and came to Pharaoh. 15And Pharaoh said to
Joseph, "I have had a dream, and *there is* no
one who can interpret it. But I have heard it
said of you *that* you can understand a dream,
to interpret it."

16So Joseph answered Pharaoh, saying,

Spotlight

GOD SENDS A GREAT FAMINE

READ IT: GENESIS 41:1–57

GET IT:

Food shortages (famine) were common in the ancient world. People struggled against nature to grow crops and have enough to eat. The people in Egypt, however, rarely suffered because of the fertile Nile River that brought water and rich soil to the area. Egypt was kind of like the breadbasket of the ancient world. But God had a plan for this world famine. He planned for it and sent Joseph to Egypt to warn the Egyptians that it was coming. Joseph's preparation also helped his own family back in Canaan. Everything was ready for the good of God's people. They didn't starve even though the famine lasted seven years.

LIVE IT:

Very few of us have ever experienced a nationwide famine. From time to time our area might suffer from a poor harvest due to a late spring frost or too much or too little rain. But most of us don't go hungry. Our food comes from all over the world.

Famine in the ancient world was a death sentence unless you could get food from another country (a difficult and expensive thing to do back then). But God used this famine for good. The widespread famine forced Jacob to move his family from Canaan to Egypt. God worked in and through the circumstances. He was in control at all times. He still is in control, even when we don't understand what's going on.

"*It is* not in me; God will give Pharaoh an
answer of peace."
17Then Pharaoh said to Joseph: "Behold,
in my dream I stood on the bank of the river. 18Suddenly seven cows came up out of
the river, fine looking and fat; and they fed
in the meadow. 19Then behold, seven other
cows came up after them, poor and very
ugly and gaunt, such ugliness as I have never seen in all the land of Egypt. 20And the
gaunt and ugly cows ate up the first seven,
the fat cows. 21When they had eaten them up,
no one would have known that they had eat-
en them, for they *were* just as ugly as at the
beginning. So I awoke. 22Also I saw in my
dream, and suddenly seven heads came up
on one stalk, full and good. 23Then behold,
seven heads, withered, thin, *and* blighted by
the east wind, sprang up after them. 24And
the thin heads devoured the seven good
heads. So I told *this* to the magicians, but
there was no one who could explain *it* to me."
25Then Joseph said to Pharaoh, "The
dreams of Pharaoh *are* one; God has shown
Pharaoh what He *is* about to do: 26The sev-
en good cows *are* seven years, and the sev-
en good heads *are* seven years; the dreams
are one. 27And the seven thin and ugly cows
which came up after them *are* seven years,
and the seven empty heads blighted by the
east wind are seven years of famine. 28This
is the thing which I have spoken to Pharaoh.
God has shown Pharaoh what He *is* about to
do. 29Indeed seven years of great plenty will
come throughout all the land of Egypt; 30but
after them seven years of famine will arise,
and all the plenty will be forgotten in the
land of Egypt; and the famine will deplete
the land. 31So the plenty will not be known
in the land because of the famine following,
for it *will be* very severe. 32And the dream was
repeated to Pharaoh twice because the thing
is established by God, and God will shortly
bring it to pass.
33"Now therefore, let Pharaoh select a discerning and wise man, and set him over the
land of Egypt. 34Let Pharaoh do *this,* and let
him appoint officers over the land, to collect
one-fifth *of the produce* of the land of Egypt
in the seven plentiful years. 35And let them
gather all the food of *those good years that*
are coming, and store up grain under the authority of Pharaoh, and let them keep food
in the cities. 36Then that food shall be as a
reserve for the land for the seven years of
famine which shall be in the land of Egypt,
that the land may not perish during the
famine."

Joseph's Rise to Power

37So the advice was good in the eyes of
Pharaoh and in the eyes of all his servants.
38And Pharaoh said to his servants, "Can we
find *such a one* as this, a man in whom *is* the
Spirit of God?"
39Then Pharaoh said to Joseph, "Inasmuch as God has shown you all this, *there is*
no one as discerning and wise as you. 40You
shall be over my house, and all my people
shall be ruled according to your word; only
in regard to the throne will I be greater than
you." 41And Pharaoh said to Joseph, "See, I
have set you over all the land of Egypt."
42Then Pharaoh took his signet ring off
his hand and put it on Joseph's hand; and he
clothed him in garments of fine linen and
put a gold chain around his neck. 43And he
had him ride in the second chariot which he
had; and they cried out before him, "Bow
the knee!" So he set him over all the land of
Egypt. 44Pharaoh also said to Joseph, "I *am*
Pharaoh, and without your consent no man
may lift his hand or foot in all the land of
Egypt." 45And Pharaoh called Joseph's name
Zaphnath-Paaneah. And he gave him as a
wife Asenath, the daughter of Poti-Pherah
priest of On. So Joseph went out over *all* the
land of Egypt.
46Joseph was thirty years old when he
stood before Pharaoh king of Egypt. And Joseph went out from the presence of Pharaoh,
and went throughout all the land of Egypt.
47Now in the seven plentiful years the ground
brought forth abundantly. 48So he gathered
up all the food of the seven years which were
in the land of Egypt, and laid up the food in
the cities; he laid up in every city the food of
the fields which surrounded them. 49Joseph
gathered very much grain, as the sand of
the sea, until he stopped counting, for *it was*
immeasurable.
50And to Joseph were born two sons
before the years of famine came, whom
Asenath, the daughter of Poti-Pherah priest
of On, bore to him. 51Joseph called the name
of the firstborn Manasseh:[a] "For God has
made me forget all my toil and all my father's

41:51 [a] Literally *Making Forgetful*

house." 52And the name of the second he called Ephraim:[a] "For God has caused me to be fruitful in the land of my affliction."

53Then the seven years of plenty which were in the land of Egypt ended, 54and the seven years of famine began to come, as Joseph had said. The famine was in all lands, but in all the land of Egypt there was bread. 55So when all the land of Egypt was famished, the people cried to Pharaoh for bread. Then Pharaoh said to all the Egyptians, "Go to Joseph; whatever he says to you, do." 56The famine was over all the face of the earth, and Joseph opened all the storehouses[a] and sold to the Egyptians. And the famine became severe in the land of Egypt. 57So all countries came to Joseph in Egypt to buy *grain,* because the famine was severe in all lands.

Joseph's Brothers Go to Egypt

42 When Jacob saw that there was grain in Egypt, Jacob said to his sons, "Why do you look at one another?" 2And he said, "Indeed I have heard that there is grain in Egypt; go down to that place and buy for us there, that we may live and not die."

3So Joseph's ten brothers went down to buy grain in Egypt. 4But Jacob did not send Joseph's brother Benjamin with his brothers, for he said, "Lest some calamity befall him." 5And the sons of Israel went to buy *grain* among those who journeyed, for the famine was in the land of Canaan.

6Now Joseph *was* governor over the land; and it was he who sold to all the people of the land. And Joseph's brothers came and bowed down before him with *their* faces to the earth. 7Joseph saw his brothers and recognized them, but he acted as a stranger to them and spoke roughly to them. Then he said to them, "Where do you come from?"

And they said, "From the land of Canaan to buy food."

8So Joseph recognized his brothers, but they did not recognize him. 9Then Joseph remembered the dreams which he had dreamed about them, and said to them, "You *are* spies! You have come to see the nakedness of the land!"

10And they said to him, "No, my lord, but your servants have come to buy food. 11We *are* all one man's sons; we *are* honest *men;* your servants are not spies."

12But he said to them, "No, but you have come to see the nakedness of the land."

13And they said, "Your servants *are* twelve brothers, the sons of one man in the land of Canaan; and in fact, the youngest *is* with our father today, and one *is* no more."

14But Joseph said to them, "It *is* as I spoke to you, saying, 'You *are* spies!' 15In this *manner* you shall be tested: By the life of Pharaoh, you shall not leave this place unless your youngest brother comes here. 16Send one of you, and let him bring your brother; and you shall be kept in prison, that your words may be tested to see whether *there is* any truth in you; or else, by the life of Pharaoh, surely you *are* spies!" 17So he put them all together in prison three days.

18Then Joseph said to them the third day, "Do this and live, *for* I fear God: 19If you *are* honest *men,* let one of your brothers be confined to your prison house; but you, go and carry grain for the famine of your houses. 20And bring your youngest brother to me; so your words will be verified, and you shall not die."

And they did so. 21Then they said to one another, "We *are* truly guilty concerning our brother, for we saw the anguish of his soul when he pleaded with us, and we would not hear; therefore this distress has come upon us."

22And Reuben answered them, saying, "Did I not speak to you, saying, 'Do not sin against the boy'; and you would not listen? Therefore behold, his blood is now required of us." 23But they did not know that Joseph understood *them,* for he spoke to them through an interpreter. 24And he turned himself away from them and wept. Then he returned to them again, and talked with them. And he took Simeon from them and bound him before their eyes.

The Brothers Return to Canaan

25Then Joseph gave a command to fill their sacks with grain, to restore every man's money to his sack, and to give them provisions for the journey. Thus he did for them. 26So they loaded their donkeys with the grain and departed from there. 27But as one *of them* opened his sack to give his donkey feed at

41:52 [a] Literally *Fruitfulness* 41:56 [a] Literally *all that was in them*

the encampment, he saw his money; and
there it was, in the mouth of his sack. 28So
he said to his brothers, "My money has been
restored, and there it is, in my sack!" Then
their hearts failed *them* and they were afraid,
saying to one another, "What *is* this *that* God
has done to us?"

29Then they went to Jacob their father in
the land of Canaan and told him all that had
happened to them, saying: 30"The man *who*
is lord of the land spoke roughly to us, and
took us for spies of the country. 31But we said
to him, 'We *are* honest *men;* we are not spies.
32We *are* twelve brothers, sons of our father;
one *is* no *more,* and the youngest *is* with our
father this day in the land of Canaan.' 33Then
the man, the lord of the country, said to us,
'By this I will know that you *are* honest *men:*
Leave one of your brothers *here* with me, take
food for the famine of your households, and
be gone. 34And bring your youngest brother
to me; so I shall know that you *are* not spies,
but *that* you *are* honest *men.* I will grant
your brother to you, and you may trade in
the land.'"

35Then it happened as they emptied their
sacks, that surprisingly each man's bundle
of money *was* in his sack; and when they and
their father saw the bundles of money, they
were afraid. 36And Jacob their father said to
them, "You have bereaved me: Joseph is no
more, Simeon is no *more,* and you want to
take Benjamin. All these things are against
me."

37Then Reuben spoke to his father, saying, "Kill my two sons if I do not bring him
back to you; put him in my hands, and I will
bring him back to you."

38But he said, "My son shall not go down
with you, for his brother is dead, and he is
left alone. If any calamity should befall him
along the way in which you go, then you
would bring down my gray hair with sorrow
to the grave."

Joseph's Brothers Return with Benjamin

43 Now the famine *was* severe in the
land. 2And it came to pass, when
they had eaten up the grain which they had
brought from Egypt, that their father said to
them, "Go back, buy us a little food."

3But Judah spoke to him, saying, "The
man solemnly warned us, saying, 'You shall
not see my face unless your brother *is* with
you.' 4If you send our brother with us, we
will go down and buy you food. 5But if you
will not send *him,* we will not go down; for
the man said to us, 'You shall not see my
face unless your brother *is* with you.'"

6And Israel said, "Why did you deal *so*
wrongfully with me *as* to tell the man whether you had still *another* brother?"

7But they said, "The man asked us point-
edly about ourselves and our family, saying,
'*Is* your father still alive? Have you *another*
brother?' And we told him according to these
words. Could we possibly have known that
he would say, 'Bring your brother down'?"

8Then Judah said to Israel his father,
"Send the lad with me, and we will arise and
go, that we may live and not die, both we and
you *and* also our little ones. 9I myself will be
surety for him; from my hand you shall require him. If I do not bring him *back* to you
and set him before you, then let me bear the
blame forever. 10For if we had not lingered,
surely by now we would have returned this
second time."

11And their father Israel said to them, "If
it must be so, then do this: Take some of the
best fruits of the land in your vessels and
carry down a present for the man—a little
balm and a little honey, spices and myrrh,
pistachio nuts and almonds. 12Take double
money in your hand, and take back in your
hand the money that was returned in the
mouth of your sacks; perhaps it was an oversight. 13Take your brother also, and arise, go
back to the man. 14And may God Almighty
give you mercy before the man, that he may
release your other brother and Benjamin. If
I am bereaved, I am bereaved!"

15So the men took that present and Benjamin, and they took double money in their
hand, and arose and went down to Egypt;
and they stood before Joseph. 16When Joseph saw Benjamin with them, he said to
the steward of his house, "Take *these* men
to my home, and slaughter an animal and
make ready; for *these* men will dine with me
at noon." 17Then the man did as Joseph ordered, and the man brought the men into
Joseph's house.

18Now the men were afraid because they
were brought into Joseph's house; and they
said, "*It is* because of the money, which was
returned in our sacks the first time, that we
are brought in, so that he may make a case

against us and seize us, to take us as slaves
with our donkeys."
¹⁹When they drew near to the steward of
Joseph's house, they talked with him at the
door of the house, ²⁰and said, "O sir, we indeed came down the first time to buy food;
²¹but it happened, when we came to the encampment, that we opened our sacks, and
there, *each* man's money *was* in the mouth
of his sack, our money in full weight; so
we have brought it back in our hand. ²²And
we have brought down other money in our
hands to buy food. We do not know who put
our money in our sacks."
²³But he said, "Peace *be* with you, do not
be afraid. Your God and the God of your father has given you treasure in your sacks; I
had your money." Then he brought Simeon
out to them.
²⁴So the man brought the men into Joseph's house and gave *them* water, and they
washed their feet; and he gave their donkeys
feed. ²⁵Then they made the present ready for
Joseph's coming at noon, for they heard that
they would eat bread there.
²⁶And when Joseph came home, they
brought him the present which *was* in their
hand into the house, and bowed down before him to the earth. ²⁷Then he asked them
about *their* well-being, and said, "*Is* your father well, the old man of whom you spoke?
Is he still alive?"
²⁸And they answered, "Your servant our
father *is* in good health; he *is* still alive." And
they bowed their heads down and prostrated
themselves.
²⁹Then he lifted his eyes and saw his
brother Benjamin, his mother's son, and
said, "*Is* this your younger brother of whom
you spoke to me?" And he said, "God be
gracious to you, my son." ³⁰Now his heart
yearned for his brother; so Joseph made
haste and sought *somewhere* to weep. And
he went into *his* chamber and wept there.
³¹Then he washed his face and came out;
and he restrained himself, and said, "Serve
the bread."
³²So they set him a place by himself, and
them by themselves, and the Egyptians
who ate with him by themselves; because
the Egyptians could not eat food with the
Hebrews, for that *is* an abomination to the
Egyptians. ³³And they sat before him, the
firstborn according to his birthright and
the youngest according to his youth; and the
men looked in astonishment at one another.
³⁴Then he took servings to them from before
him, but Benjamin's serving was five times
as much as any of theirs. So they drank and
were merry with him.

Joseph's Cup

44 And he commanded the steward of his house, saying, "Fill
the men's sacks with food, as much as they
can carry, and put each man's money in the
mouth of his sack. ²Also put my cup, the
silver cup, in the mouth of the sack of the
youngest, and his grain money." So he did
according to the word that Joseph had spoken. ³As soon as the morning dawned, the
men were sent away, they and their donkeys.
⁴When they had gone out of the city, *and*
were not *yet* far off, Joseph said to his steward, "Get up, follow the men; and when you
overtake them, say to them, 'Why have you
repaid evil for good? ⁵*Is* not this *the one* from
which my lord drinks, and with which he
indeed practices divination? You have done
evil in so doing.'"
⁶So he overtook them, and he spoke to
them these same words. ⁷And they said to
him, "Why does my lord say these words?
Far be it from us that your servants should
do such a thing. ⁸Look, we brought back
to you from the land of Canaan the money
which we found in the mouth of our sacks.
How then could we steal silver or gold from
your lord's house? ⁹With whomever of your
servants it is found, let him die, and we also
will be my lord's slaves."
¹⁰And he said, "Now also *let* it *be* according to your words; he with whom it is found
shall be my slave, and you shall be blameless." ¹¹Then each man speedily let down
his sack to the ground, and each opened his
sack. ¹²So he searched. He began with the
oldest and left off with the youngest; and the
cup was found in Benjamin's sack. ¹³Then
they tore their clothes, and each man loaded
his donkey and returned to the city.
¹⁴So Judah and his brothers came to Joseph's house, and he *was* still there; and they
fell before him on the ground. ¹⁵And Joseph
said to them, "What deed *is* this you have
done? Did you not know that such a man as
I can certainly practice divination?"
¹⁶Then Judah said, "What shall we say to
my lord? What shall we speak? Or how shall

we clear ourselves? God has found out the
iniquity of your servants; here we are, my
lord's slaves, both we and *he* also with whom
the cup was found."

17But he said, "Far be it from me that I
should do so; the man in whose hand the
cup was found, he shall be my slave. And as
for you, go up in peace to your father."

Judah Intercedes for Benjamin

18Then Judah came near to him and said:
"O my lord, please let your servant speak a
word in my lord's hearing, and do not let
your anger burn against your servant; for
you *are* even like Pharaoh. 19My lord asked
his servants, saying, 'Have you a father or
a brother?' 20And we said to my lord, 'We
have a father, an old man, and a child of *his*
old age, *who is* young; his brother is dead,
and he alone is left of his mother's children,
and his father loves him.' 21Then you said to
your servants, 'Bring him down to me, that
I may set my eyes on him.' 22And we said to
my lord, 'The lad cannot leave his father, for
if he should leave his father, *his father* would
die.' 23But you said to your servants, 'Unless
your youngest brother comes down with
you, you shall see my face no more.'

24"So it was, when we went up to your servant my father, that we told him the words of
my lord. 25And our father said, 'Go back *and*
buy us a little food.' 26But we said, 'We cannot go down; if our youngest brother is with
us, then we will go down; for we may not see
the man's face unless our youngest brother
is with us.' 27Then your servant my father
said to us, 'You know that my wife bore me
two sons; 28and the one went out from me,
and I said, "Surely he is torn to pieces"; and
I have not seen him since. 29But if you take
this one also from me, and calamity befalls
him, you shall bring down my gray hair with
sorrow to the grave.'

30"Now therefore, when I come to your
servant my father, and the lad *is* not with us,
since his life is bound up in the lad's life,
31it will happen, when he sees that the lad
is not *with us,* that he will die. So your servants will bring down the gray hair of your
servant our father with sorrow to the grave.
32For your servant became surety for the
lad to my father, saying, 'If I do not bring
him *back* to you, then I shall bear the blame
before my father forever.' 33Now therefore,
please let your servant remain instead of the
lad as a slave to my lord, and let the lad go
up with his brothers. 34For how shall I go up
to my father if the lad *is* not with me, lest
perhaps I see the evil that would come upon
my father?"

Joseph Revealed to His Brothers

45 Then Joseph could not restrain
himself before all those who stood
by him, and he cried out, "Make everyone
go out from me!" So no one stood with him

Starring Roles

You should have seen JOSEPH'S brothers when he told them who he really was. He said, "I am Joseph, your brother, whom you sold into Egypt" (Genesis 45:4). For a long time they didn't recognize Joseph in his official Egyptian robes.

Years before, the brothers had even told their father Jacob that Joseph was dead. But all the time Joseph was in Egypt, God gave him higher and higher positions in Pharaoh's government. Joseph had stored enough grain for seven years of famine, and when his father and brothers were hungry, Joseph was able to feed them. Then Pharaoh allowed Joseph's family to come and live in Egypt.

Wasn't it a beautiful thing God did for Joseph's brothers? They meant to hurt him, but God used Joseph to help them. That is how Jesus loves us. Our sins put Him to death, but He gives us life that never ends.

while Joseph made himself known to his
brothers. 2And he wept aloud, and the Egyptians and the house of Pharaoh heard *it*.
3Then Joseph said to his brothers, "I *am*
Joseph; does my father still live?" But his
brothers could not answer him, for they
were dismayed in his presence. 4And Joseph
said to his brothers, "Please come near to
me." So they came near. Then he said: "I
am Joseph your brother, whom you sold into
Egypt. 5But now, do not therefore be grieved
or angry with yourselves because you sold
me here; for God sent me before you to preserve life. 6For these two years the famine
has been in the land, and *there are* still five
years in which *there will be* neither plowing
nor harvesting. 7And God sent me before
you to preserve a posterity for you in the
earth, and to save your lives by a great deliverance. 8So now *it was* not you *who* sent me
here, but God; and He has made me a father
to Pharaoh, and lord of all his house, and a
ruler throughout all the land of Egypt.
9"Hurry and go up to my father, and say
to him, 'Thus says your son Joseph: "God
has made me lord of all Egypt; come down to
me, do not tarry. 10You shall dwell in the land
of Goshen, and you shall be near to me, you
and your children, your children's children,
your flocks and your herds, and all that you
have. 11There I will provide for you, lest you
and your household, and all that you have,
come to poverty; for *there are* still five years
of famine."'
12"And behold, your eyes and the eyes
of my brother Benjamin see that *it is* my

GOD MEANT IT FOR GOOD

READ IT: GENESIS 45:1–28

GET IT:

Joseph's brothers traveled from Canaan to Egypt several times to buy grain to feed their families. They came face-to-face with their long-lost brother but didn't have a clue it was him. Joseph immediately knew who they were and tested them out. Joseph had the position, power, and authority to get revenge on his brothers. He could have easily had them killed. Instead, he told them who he was. In his speech he said that he saw what God was doing through his life and realized that it was all in God's good plan for him and his family. Eventually Joseph forgave his brothers for the past hurts.

LIVE IT:

When someone hurts us, our first reaction is to get even. Getting back at someone for what he or she did is a common reaction. Too many people, however, carry a grudge forever, and the hatred and bitterness never ends. Joseph is a good example for all of us. He had a rough life. It was downright terrible. And when he could have been ruthless, he wasn't. He did the right thing. He examined everything that had happened and saw that it all worked out. And he forgave his brothers. The next time someone hurts you, remember Joseph and the hurt he experienced. He suffered for years, but he forgave. You can, too.

mouth that speaks to you. 13 So you shall tell
my father of all my glory in Egypt, and of all
that you have seen; and you shall hurry and
bring my father down here."

14 Then he fell on his brother Benjamin's
neck and wept, and Benjamin wept on his
neck. 15 Moreover he kissed all his brothers
and wept over them, and after that his brothers talked with him.

16 Now the report of it was heard in Pharaoh's house, saying, "Joseph's brothers have
come." So it pleased Pharaoh and his servants well. 17 And Pharaoh said to Joseph,
"Say to your brothers, 'Do this: Load your animals and depart; go to the land of Canaan.
18 Bring your father and your households and
come to me; I will give you the best of the
land of Egypt, and you will eat the fat of the
land. 19 Now you are commanded—do this:
Take carts out of the land of Egypt for your
little ones and your wives; bring your father
and come. 20 Also do not be concerned about
your goods, for the best of all the land of
Egypt *is* yours.'"

21 Then the sons of Israel did so; and
Joseph gave them carts, according to the
command of Pharaoh, and he gave them
provisions for the journey. 22 He gave to all
of them, to each man, changes of garments;
but to Benjamin he gave three hundred *pieces* of silver and five changes of garments.
23 And he sent to his father these *things:* ten
donkeys loaded with the good things of
Egypt, and ten female donkeys loaded with
grain, bread, and food for his father for the
journey. 24 So he sent his brothers away, and
they departed; and he said to them, "See that
you do not become troubled along the way."

25 Then they went up out of Egypt, and
came to the land of Canaan to Jacob their
father. 26 And they told him, saying, "Joseph
is still alive, and he *is* governor over all the
land of Egypt." And Jacob's heart stood still,
because he did not believe them. 27 But when
they told him all the words which Joseph
had said to them, and when he saw the carts
which Joseph had sent to carry him, the
spirit of Jacob their father revived. 28 Then
Israel said, "*It is* enough. Joseph my son *is*
still alive. I will go and see him before I die."

Jacob's Journey to Egypt

46 So Israel took his journey with
all that he had, and came to Beersheba, and offered sacrifices to the God of
his father Isaac. 2 Then God spoke to Israel
in the visions of the night, and said, "Jacob,
Jacob!"

And he said, "Here I am."

3 So He said, "I *am* God, the God of your
father; do not fear to go down to Egypt, for I
will make of you a great nation there. 4 I will
go down with you to Egypt, and I will also
surely bring you up *again;* and Joseph will
put his hand on your eyes."

5 Then Jacob arose from Beersheba; and
the sons of Israel carried their father Jacob,
their little ones, and their wives, in the carts
which Pharaoh had sent to carry him. 6 So
they took their livestock and their goods,
which they had acquired in the land of Canaan, and went to Egypt, Jacob and all his descendants with him. 7 His sons and his sons'
sons, his daughters and his sons' daughters,
and all his descendants he brought with him
to Egypt.

8 Now these *were* the names of the children of Israel, Jacob and his sons, who went
to Egypt: Reuben *was* Jacob's firstborn. 9 The
sons of Reuben *were* Hanoch, Pallu, Hezron, and Carmi. 10 The sons of Simeon *were*
Jemuel,[a] Jamin, Ohad, Jachin,[b] Zohar,[c] and
Shaul, the son of a Canaanite woman. 11 The
sons of Levi *were* Gershon, Kohath, and
Merari. 12 The sons of Judah *were* Er, Onan,
Shelah, Perez, and Zerah (but Er and Onan
died in the land of Canaan). The sons of Perez were Hezron and Hamul. 13 The sons of
Issachar *were* Tola, Puvah,[a] Job,[b] and Shimron. 14 The sons of Zebulun *were* Sered, Elon,
and Jahleel. 15 These *were* the sons of Leah,
whom she bore to Jacob in Padan Aram,
with his daughter Dinah. All the persons,
his sons and his daughters, *were* thirty-three.

16 The sons of Gad *were* Ziphion,[a] Haggi,
Shuni, Ezbon,[b] Eri, Arodi,[c] and Areli. 17 The
sons of Asher *were* Jimnah, Ishuah, Isui, Beriah, and Serah, their sister. And the sons
of Beriah *were* Heber and Malchiel. 18 These
were the sons of Zilpah, whom Laban gave
to Leah his daughter; and these she bore to
Jacob: sixteen persons.

19 The sons of Rachel, Jacob's wife, *were*
Joseph and Benjamin. 20 And to Joseph in

46:10 [a] Spelled *Nemuel* in 1 Chronicles 4:24 [b] Called *Jarib* in 1 Chronicles 4:24 [c] Called *Zerah* in 1 Chronicles 4:24 **46:13** [a] Spelled *Puah* in 1 Chronicles 7:1 [b] Same as *Jashub* in Numbers 26:24 and 1 Chronicles 7:1 **46:16** [a] Spelled *Zephon* in Samaritan Pentateuch, Septuagint, and Numbers 26:15 [b] Called *Ozni* in Numbers 26:16 [c] Spelled *Arod* in Numbers 26:17

the land of Egypt were born Manasseh and
Ephraim, whom Asenath, the daughter of
Poti-Pherah priest of On, bore to him. 21 The
sons of Benjamin *were* Belah, Becher, Ashbel, Gera, Naaman, Ehi, Rosh, Muppim,
Huppim,[a] and Ard. 22 These *were* the sons
of Rachel, who were born to Jacob: fourteen
persons in all.
23 The son of Dan *was* Hushim.[a] 24 The
sons of Naphtali *were* Jahzeel,[a] Guni,
Jezer, and Shillem.[b] 25 These *were* the sons
of Bilhah, whom Laban gave to Rachel his
daughter, and she bore these to Jacob: seven
persons in all.
26 All the persons who went with Jacob
to Egypt, who came from his body, besides
Jacob's sons' wives, *were* sixty-six persons in

46:21 [a] Called *Hupham* in Numbers 26:39 **46:23** [a] Called *Shuham* in Numbers 26:42 **46:24** [a] Spelled *Jahziel* in 1 Chronicles 7:13 [b] Spelled *Shallum* in 1 Chronicles 7:13

FAMILY

FAMILY BUSINESS

READ IT: GENESIS 46:1–7, 28–34; 47:1–12

GET IT:

The story of Joseph and his family reads like the script of a cliffhanger movie. For a long time, it looks like evil will triumph, but in the end God brings good. As you read through these chapters in Genesis, you get a snapshot of how messy, complicated, and unbelievably painful family life can be. Most of us have had at least a taste of it. Some have had a lot.

Joseph's brothers hated him and sold him into slavery. Then the brothers lied to their father, Jacob, about what happened. At this point, all seemed lost for Joseph, who became a slave in Egypt. At the same time, his father, Jacob, grieved for the son he thought was dead. The evil plan of Joseph's brothers appeared to succeed. What a horrible situation!

But God had another plan. From the hurt and sadness, God brought a chance for forgiveness and healing in Joseph's family. God allowed Joseph to save the lives of his family and bring blessing where there was no hope. Joseph was not only willing to forgive his brothers but also to provide for them, ultimately saving their lives.

LIVE IT:

When someone in your family hurts you, it's really difficult to not strike back. And the thought of forgiveness can seem impossible. But Joseph's example shows that it *is* possible to turn a bad situation around with God's help.

God isn't asking you to put yourself in harm's way. Sometimes you need a hand when you're working through problems in a family. Don't be afraid to ask for help from a trusted adult. And ask God for help. He wants to bring good out of even the worst situations.

all. [27]And the sons of Joseph who were born
to him in Egypt *were* two persons. All the
persons of the house of Jacob who went to
Egypt were seventy.

Jacob Settles in Goshen

[28]Then he sent Judah before him to Joseph, to point out before him *the way* to Goshen. And they came to the land of Goshen.
[29]So Joseph made ready his chariot and went
up to Goshen to meet his father Israel; and
he presented himself to him, and fell on his
neck and wept on his neck a good while.

[30]And Israel said to Joseph, "Now let me
die, since I have seen your face, because you
are still alive."

[31]Then Joseph said to his brothers and to
his father's household, "I will go up and tell
Pharaoh, and say to him, 'My brothers and
those of my father's house, who *were* in the
land of Canaan, have come to me. [32]And the
men *are* shepherds, for their occupation has
been to feed livestock; and they have brought
their flocks, their herds, and all that they
have.' [33]So it shall be, when Pharaoh calls
you and says, 'What is your occupation?'
[34]that you shall say, 'Your servants' occupation has been with livestock from our youth
even till now, both we *and* also our fathers,'
that you may dwell in the land of Goshen;
for every shepherd *is* an abomination to the
Egyptians."

47 Then Joseph went and told Pharaoh,
and said, "My father and my broth-
ers, their flocks and their herds and all that
they possess, have come from the land of
Canaan; and indeed they *are* in the land
of Goshen." [2]And he took five men from
among his brothers and presented them to
Pharaoh. [3]Then Pharaoh said to his brothers, "What *is* your occupation?"

And they said to Pharaoh, "Your servants
are shepherds, both we *and* also our fathers."
[4]And they said to Pharaoh, "We have come
to dwell in the land, because your servants
have no pasture for their flocks, for the
famine *is* severe in the land of Canaan. Now
therefore, please let your servants dwell in
the land of Goshen."

[5]Then Pharaoh spoke to Joseph, saying,
"Your father and your brothers have come to
you. [6]The land of Egypt is before you. Have
your father and brothers dwell in the best of
the land; let them dwell in the land of Goshen. And if you know *any* competent men
among them, then make them chief herdsmen over my livestock."

[7]Then Joseph brought in his father Jacob and set him before Pharaoh; and Jacob
blessed Pharaoh. [8]Pharaoh said to Jacob,
"How old *are* you?"

[9]And Jacob said to Pharaoh, "The days of
the years of my pilgrimage *are* one hundred
and thirty years; few and evil have been the
days of the years of my life, and they have not
attained to the days of the years of the life of
my fathers in the days of their pilgrimage."
[10]So Jacob blessed Pharaoh, and went out
from before Pharaoh.

[11]And Joseph situated his father and his
brothers, and gave them a possession in
the land of Egypt, in the best of the land, in
the land of Rameses, as Pharaoh had commanded. [12]Then Joseph provided his father,
his brothers, and all his father's household
with bread, according to the number in *their*
families.

Joseph Deals with the Famine

[13]Now *there was* no bread in all the land;
for the famine *was* very severe, so that the
land of Egypt and the land of Canaan languished because of the famine. [14]And Joseph
gathered up all the money that was found in
the land of Egypt and in the land of Canaan,
for the grain which they bought; and Joseph
brought the money into Pharaoh's house.

[15]So when the money failed in the land
of Egypt and in the land of Canaan, all the
Egyptians came to Joseph and said, "Give us
bread, for why should we die in your presence? For the money has failed."

[16]Then Joseph said, "Give your livestock,
and I will give you *bread* for your livestock,
if the money is gone." [17]So they brought their
livestock to Joseph, and Joseph gave them
bread *in exchange* for the horses, the flocks,
the cattle of the herds, and for the donkeys.
Thus he fed them with bread *in exchange* for
all their livestock that year.

[18]When that year had ended, they came
to him the next year and said to him, "We
will not hide from my lord that our money
is gone; my lord also has our herds of livestock. There is nothing left in the sight of
my lord but our bodies and our lands. [19]Why
should we die before your eyes, both we and
our land? Buy us and our land for bread, and
we and our land will be servants of Pharaoh;

give *us* seed, that we may live and not die,
that the land may not be desolate."
20 Then Joseph bought all the land of
Egypt for Pharaoh; for every man of the
Egyptians sold his field, because the famine
was severe upon them. So the land became
Pharaoh's. 21 And as for the people, he moved
them into the cities,[a] from *one* end of the
borders of Egypt to the *other* end. 22 Only
the land of the priests he did not buy; for
the priests had rations *allotted to them* by
Pharaoh, and they ate their rations which
Pharaoh gave them; therefore they did not
sell their lands.
23 Then Joseph said to the people, "Indeed
I have bought you and your land this day for
Pharaoh. Look, *here is* seed for you, and you
shall sow the land. 24 And it shall come to
pass in the harvest that you shall give one-
fifth to Pharaoh. Four-fifths shall be your
own, as seed for the field and for your food,
for those of your households and as food for
your little ones."
25 So they said, "You have saved our lives;
let us find favor in the sight of my lord, and
we will be Pharaoh's servants." 26 And Joseph
made it a law over the land of Egypt to this
day, *that* Pharaoh should have one-fifth, except for the land of the priests only, *which* did
not become Pharaoh's.

Joseph's Vow to Jacob

27 So Israel dwelt in the land of Egypt,
in the country of Goshen; and they had
possessions there and grew and multiplied
exceedingly. 28 And Jacob lived in the land of
Egypt seventeen years. So the length of Jacob's life was one hundred and forty-seven
years. 29 When the time drew near that Israel
must die, he called his son Joseph and said
to him, "Now if I have found favor in your
sight, please put your hand under my thigh,
and deal kindly and truly with me. Please do
not bury me in Egypt, 30 but let me lie with
my fathers; you shall carry me out of Egypt
and bury me in their burial place."
And he said, "I will do as you have said."
31 Then he said, "Swear to me." And he
swore to him. So Israel bowed himself on
the head of the bed.

Jacob Blesses Joseph's Sons

48 Now it came to pass after these
things that Joseph was told, "Indeed your father *is* sick"; and he took with
him his two sons, Manasseh and Ephraim.
2 And Jacob was told, "Look, your son Joseph
is coming to you"; and Israel strengthened
himself and sat up on the bed. 3 Then Jacob
said to Joseph: "God Almighty appeared to
me at Luz in the land of Canaan and blessed
me, 4 and said to me, 'Behold, I will make you
fruitful and multiply you, and I will make of
you a multitude of people, and give this land
to your descendants after you *as* an everlasting possession.' 5 And now your two sons,
Ephraim and Manasseh, who were born to
you in the land of Egypt before I came to you
in Egypt, *are* mine; as Reuben and Simeon,
they shall be mine. 6 Your offspring whom
you beget after them shall be yours; they
will be called by the name of their brothers
in their inheritance. 7 But as for me, when I
came from Padan, Rachel died beside me in
the land of Canaan on the way, when *there*
was but a little distance to go to Ephrath;
and I buried her there on the way to Ephrath
(that is, Bethlehem)."
8 Then Israel saw Joseph's sons, and said,
"Who *are* these?"
9 Joseph said to his father, "They *are* my
sons, whom God has given me in this *place*."
And he said, "Please bring them to me,
and I will bless them." 10 Now the eyes of
Israel were dim with age, *so that* he could
not see. Then Joseph brought them near
him, and he kissed them and embraced
them. 11 And Israel said to Joseph, "I had not
thought to see your face; but in fact, God has
also shown me your offspring!"
12 So Joseph brought them from beside
his knees, and he bowed down with his face
to the earth. 13 And Joseph took them both,
Ephraim with his right hand toward Israel's
left hand, and Manasseh with his left hand
toward Israel's right hand, and brought
them near him. 14 Then Israel stretched out
his right hand and laid *it* on Ephraim's head,
who *was* the younger, and his left hand on
Manasseh's head, guiding his hands know-
ingly, for Manasseh *was* the firstborn. 15 And
he blessed Joseph, and said:

"God, before whom my fathers Abraham
  and Isaac walked,
The God who has fed me all my life long
  to this day,

47:21 [a] Following Masoretic Text and Targum; Samaritan Pentateuch, Septuagint, and Vulgate read *made the people virtual slaves.*

16 The Angel who has redeemed me from all evil,
Bless the lads;
Let my name be named upon them,
And the name of my fathers Abraham and Isaac;
And let them grow into a multitude in the midst of the earth."

17Now when Joseph saw that his father
laid his right hand on the head of Ephraim,
it displeased him; so he took hold of his father's hand to remove it from Ephraim's
head to Manasseh's head. 18And Joseph said
to his father, "Not so, my father, for this *one*
is the firstborn; put your right hand on his
head."

19But his father refused and said, "I know,
my son, I know. He also shall become a people, and he also shall be great; but truly his
younger brother shall be greater than he,
and his descendants shall become a multitude of nations."

20So he blessed them that day, saying,
"By you Israel will bless, saying, 'May God
make you as Ephraim and as Manasseh!'"
And thus he set Ephraim before Manasseh.

21Then Israel said to Joseph, "Behold,
I am dying, but God will be with you and
bring you back to the land of your fathers.
22Moreover I have given to you one portion
above your brothers, which I took from the
hand of the Amorite with my sword and my
bow."

Jacob's Last Words to His Sons

49 And Jacob called his sons and said, "Gather together, that I may tell you what shall befall you in the last days:

2 "Gather together and hear, you sons of Jacob,
And listen to Israel your father.

3 "Reuben, you are my firstborn,
My might and the beginning of my strength,
The excellency of dignity and the excellency of power.
4 Unstable as water, you shall not excel,
Because you went up to your father's bed;
Then you defiled *it*—
He went up to my couch.

5 "Simeon and Levi *are* brothers;
Instruments of cruelty *are in* their dwelling place.
6 Let not my soul enter their council;
Let not my honor be united to their assembly;
For in their anger they slew a man,
And in their self-will they hamstrung an ox.
7 Cursed *be* their anger, for *it is* fierce;
And their wrath, for it is cruel!
I will divide them in Jacob
And scatter them in Israel.

8 "Judah, you *are he* whom your brothers shall praise;
Your hand *shall be* on the neck of your enemies;
Your father's children shall bow down before you.
9 Judah *is* a lion's whelp;
From the prey, my son, you have gone up.
He bows down, he lies down as a lion;
And as a lion, who shall rouse him?
10 The scepter shall not depart from Judah,
Nor a lawgiver from between his feet,
Until Shiloh comes;
And to Him *shall be* the obedience of the people.
11 Binding his donkey to the vine,
And his donkey's colt to the choice vine,
He washed his garments in wine,
And his clothes in the blood of grapes.
12 His eyes *are* darker than wine,
And his teeth whiter than milk.

13 "Zebulun shall dwell by the haven of the sea;
He *shall become* a haven for ships,
And his border shall adjoin Sidon.

14 "Issachar is a strong donkey,
Lying down between two burdens;
15 He saw that rest *was* good,
And that the land *was* pleasant;
He bowed his shoulder to bear *a burden,*
And became a band of slaves.

16 "Dan shall judge his people
As one of the tribes of Israel.
17 Dan shall be a serpent by the way,
A viper by the path,
That bites the horse's heels
So that its rider shall fall backward.
18 I have waited for your salvation, O LORD!

19 "Gad, a troop shall tramp upon him,
But he shall triumph at last.

20 "Bread from Asher *shall be* rich,

And he shall yield royal dainties.

21 "Naphtali *is* a deer let loose;
He uses beautiful words.

22 "Joseph *is* a fruitful bough,
A fruitful bough by a well;
His branches run over the wall.
23 The archers have bitterly grieved him,
Shot at *him* and hated him.
24 But his bow remained in strength,
And the arms of his hands were made
strong
By the hands of the Mighty *God* of Jacob
(From there *is* the Shepherd, the Stone
of Israel),
25 By the God of your father who will help
you,
And by the Almighty who will bless you
With blessings of heaven above,
Blessings of the deep that lies beneath,
Blessings of the breasts and of the
womb.
26 The blessings of your father
Have excelled the blessings of my
ancestors,
Up to the utmost bound of the
everlasting hills.
They shall be on the head of Joseph,
And on the crown of the head of him
who was separate from his brothers.

27 "Benjamin is a ravenous wolf;
In the morning he shall devour the prey,
And at night he shall divide the spoil."

28All these *are* the twelve tribes of Israel,
and this *is* what their father spoke to them.
And he blessed them; he blessed each one
according to his own blessing.

Jacob's Death and Burial

29Then he charged them and said to
them: "I am to be gathered to my people;
bury me with my fathers in the cave that *is* in
the field of Ephron the Hittite, 30in the cave
that *is* in the field of Machpelah, which *is*
before Mamre in the land of Canaan, which
Abraham bought with the field of Ephron
the Hittite as a possession for a burial place.
31There they buried Abraham and Sarah his
wife, there they buried Isaac and Rebekah
his wife, and there I buried Leah. 32The field
and the cave that *is* there *were* purchased
from the sons of Heth." 33And when Jacob
had finished commanding his sons, he drew
his feet up into the bed and breathed his last,
and was gathered to his people.

50 Then Joseph fell on his father's
face and wept over him, and
kissed him. 2And Joseph commanded his
servants the physicians to embalm his father. So the physicians embalmed Israel.
3Forty days were required for him, for such
are the days required for those who are embalmed; and the Egyptians mourned for
him seventy days.

4Now when the days of his mourning
were past, Joseph spoke to the household of
Pharaoh, saying, "If now I have found favor
in your eyes, please speak in the hearing
of Pharaoh, saying, 5'My father made me
swear, saying, "Behold, I am dying; in my
grave which I dug for myself in the land
of Canaan, there you shall bury me." Now
therefore, please let me go up and bury my
father, and I will come back.'"

6And Pharaoh said, "Go up and bury your
father, as he made you swear."

7So Joseph went up to bury his father;
and with him went up all the servants of
Pharaoh, the elders of his house, and all
the elders of the land of Egypt, 8as well as
all the house of Joseph, his brothers, and his
father's house. Only their little ones, their
flocks, and their herds they left in the land of
Goshen. 9And there went up with him both
chariots and horsemen, and it was a very
great gathering.

10Then they came to the threshing floor
of Atad, which *is* beyond the Jordan, and they
mourned there with a great and very solemn lamentation. He observed seven days
of mourning for his father. 11And when the
inhabitants of the land, the Canaanites, saw
the mourning at the threshing floor of Atad,
they said, "This *is* a deep mourning of the
Egyptians." Therefore its name was called
Abel Mizraim,[a] which *is* beyond the Jordan.

12So his sons did for him just as he had
commanded them. 13For his sons carried
him to the land of Canaan, and buried him
in the cave of the field of Machpelah, before
Mamre, which Abraham bought with the
field from Ephron the Hittite as property for
a burial place. 14And after he had buried his
father, Joseph returned to Egypt, he and his

50:11 [a] Literally *Mourning of Egypt*

brothers and all who went up with him to
bury his father.

Joseph Reassures His Brothers

15 When Joseph's brothers saw that their
father was dead, they said, "Perhaps Joseph
will hate us, and may actually repay us for
all the evil which we did to him." 16 So they
sent *messengers* to Joseph, saying, "Before
your father died he commanded, saying,
17 'Thus you shall say to Joseph: "I beg you,
please forgive the trespass of your brothers
and their sin; for they did evil to you."' Now,
please, forgive the trespass of the servants
of the God of your father." And Joseph wept
when they spoke to him.

18 Then his brothers also went and fell
down before his face, and they said, "Behold,
we *are* your servants."

19 Joseph said to them, "Do not be afraid,
for *am* I in the place of God? 20 But as for you,
you meant evil against me; *but* God meant
it for good, in order to bring it about as *it is*
this day, to save many people alive. 21 Now
therefore, do not be afraid; I will provide for
you and your little ones." And he comforted
them and spoke kindly to them.

Death of Joseph

22 So Joseph dwelt in Egypt, he and his father's household. And Joseph lived one hundred and ten years. 23 Joseph saw Ephraim's
children to the third *generation*. The children of Machir, the son of Manasseh, were
also brought up on Joseph's knees.

24 And Joseph said to his brethren, "I am
dying; but God will surely visit you, and
bring you out of this land to the land of
which He swore to Abraham, to Isaac, and to
Jacob." 25 Then Joseph took an oath from the
children of Israel, saying, "God will surely
visit you, and you shall carry up my bones
from here." 26 So Joseph died, *being* one hundred and ten years old; and they embalmed
him, and he was put in a coffin in Egypt.

The SECOND BOOK of MOSES CALLED

EXODUS

1445 B.C.–1400 B.C.

Behind the Scenes

READ IT:

The book of Exodus continues the story of God's people, now called Israelites. They were in Egypt for hundreds of years. Then God selected Moses to lead His people out from slavery in Egypt. God showed Pharaoh how powerful He was by sending a series of plagues on Egypt. Once the people were free, God stayed with them and led them on a journey through the wilderness. The Israelites were traveling to the land God promised them.

GET IT:

Who wrote it: Most people think Moses wrote it.

When it was written: 1445 B.C.–1400 B.C.

Why it was written: to record the story of how God saved His people from slavery in Egypt and what happened when the people came into God's presence at Mount Sinai.

LIVE IT:

God saves us from sin as He saved His people from slavery.

The Ten Commandments are God's instructions for living well.

We must remember all the things God has done for us.

FIND IT:

Moses Is Born	*Exodus 2*
Moses at the Burning Bush	*Exodus 4*
The Ten Plagues	*Exodus 7–12*
The Red Sea Crossing	*Exodus 14*
Bread from Heaven	*Exodus 16*
The Ten Commandments	*Exodus 20*
The Golden Calf	*Exodus 32*
Building the Tabernacle	*Exodus 36–40*

Israel's Suffering in Egypt

1 Now these *are* the names of the children
of Israel who came to Egypt; each man
and his household came with Jacob: 2Reu-
ben, Simeon, Levi, and Judah; 3Issachar,
Zebulun, and Benjamin; 4Dan, Naphtali, Gad, and Asher. 5All those who were
descendants[a] of Jacob were seventy[b] persons (for Joseph was in Egypt *already*). 6And
Joseph died, all his brothers, and all that
generation. 7But the children of Israel were
fruitful and increased abundantly, multiplied and grew exceedingly mighty; and the
land was filled with them.

8Now there arose a new king over Egypt,
who did not know Joseph. 9And he said to
his people, "Look, the people of the children of Israel *are* more and mightier than
we; 10come, let us deal shrewdly with them,
lest they multiply, and it happen, in the
event of war, that they also join our enemies
and fight against us, and *so* go up out of the
land." 11Therefore they set taskmasters over
them to afflict them with their burdens. And
they built for Pharaoh supply cities, Pithom
and Raamses. 12But the more they afflicted
them, the more they multiplied and grew.
And they were in dread of the children of Israel. 13So the Egyptians made the children of
Israel serve with rigor. 14And they made their
lives bitter with hard bondage—in mortar,
in brick, and in all manner of service in the
field. All their service in which they made
them serve *was* with rigor.

15Then the king of Egypt spoke to the
Hebrew midwives, of whom the name of
one *was* Shiphrah and the name of the other
Puah; 16and he said, "When you do the duties
of a midwife for the Hebrew women, and see
them on the birthstools, if it *is* a son, then
you shall kill him; but if it *is* a daughter, then
she shall live." 17But the midwives feared
God, and did not do as the king of Egypt
commanded them, but saved the male children alive. 18So the king of Egypt called for
the midwives and said to them, "Why have
you done this thing, and saved the male children alive?"

19And the midwives said to Pharaoh, "Because the Hebrew women *are* not like the
Egyptian women; for they *are* lively and give
birth before the midwives come to them."

20Therefore God dealt well with the
midwives, and the people multiplied and
grew very mighty. 21And so it was, because
the midwives feared God, that He provided
households for them.

22So Pharaoh commanded all his people,
saying, "Every son who is born[a] you shall
cast into the river, and every daughter you
shall save alive."

Moses Is Born

2 And a man of the house of Levi went
and took *as wife* a daughter of Levi. 2So
the woman conceived and bore a son. And
when she saw that he *was* a beautiful *child,*
she hid him three months. 3But when she
could no longer hide him, she took an ark
of bulrushes for him, daubed it with asphalt
and pitch, put the child in it, and laid *it* in
the reeds by the river's bank. 4And his sister

1:5 [a] Literally *who came from the loins of* [b] Dead Sea Scrolls and Septuagint read *seventy-five* (compare Acts 7:14).
1:22 [a] Samaritan Pentateuch, Septuagint, and Targum add *to the Hebrews.*

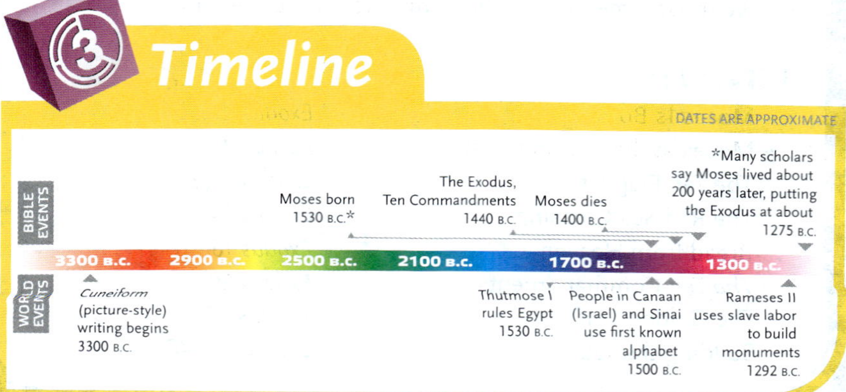

stood afar off, to know what would be done
to him.
⁵Then the daughter of Pharaoh came
down to bathe at the river. And her maidens
walked along the riverside; and when she
saw the ark among the reeds, she sent her
maid to get it. ⁶And when she opened *it,* she
saw the child, and behold, the baby wept. So
she had compassion on him, and said, "This
is one of the Hebrews' children."
⁷Then his sister said to Pharaoh's daughter, "Shall I go and call a nurse for you from
the Hebrew women, that she may nurse the
child for you?"
⁸And Pharaoh's daughter said to her,
"Go." So the maiden went and called the
child's mother. ⁹Then Pharaoh's daughter
said to her, "Take this child away and nurse
him for me, and I will give *you* your wages."
So the woman took the child and nursed
him. ¹⁰And the child grew, and she brought
him to Pharaoh's daughter, and he became
her son. So she called his name Moses,[a] saying, "Because I drew him out of the water."

Moses Flees to Midian

¹¹Now it came to pass in those days, when
Moses was grown, that he went out to his
brethren and looked at their burdens. And
he saw an Egyptian beating a Hebrew, one
of his brethren. ¹²So he looked this way and
that way, and when he saw no one, he killed
the Egyptian and hid him in the sand. ¹³And
when he went out the second day, behold,
two Hebrew men were fighting, and he said
to the one who did the wrong, "Why are you
striking your companion?"
¹⁴Then he said, "Who made you a prince
and a judge over us? Do you intend to kill me
as you killed the Egyptian?"
So Moses feared and said, "Surely this
thing is known!" ¹⁵When Pharaoh heard of

2:10 [a] Literally *Drawn Out*

GOD'S PEOPLE LIVE IN EGYPT

READ IT: EXODUS 1:8—2:10

GET IT:

Jacob's family settled in Egypt. Over the next four hundred years they had many, many children. Generations passed, the nation grew, and the new pharaohs didn't remember that Joseph had saved Egypt from starving to death. God's people became Pharaoh's slaves, and the boy babies were killed. But God had a plan to save His people. A clever woman saved her son by hiding him in a basket and floating it on the river. Pharaoh's daughter found the baby floating on the river, brought him back to the palace, and raised him as her son. This was Moses, who grew up in the royal palace. Many years later he led his people out of Egypt.

LIVE IT:

God's people suffered as slaves in Egypt for hundreds of years. But they didn't forget God, and God didn't forget them. God had a plan to free them and make their lives better. When you are facing a difficult or unhappy time, you may think that God is far away. He's not. He's there with you and He has a plan. He will strengthen you through this situation and give you a great life.

this matter, he sought to kill Moses. But Moses fled from the face of Pharaoh and dwelt
in the land of Midian; and he sat down by
a well.

16 Now the priest of Midian had seven
daughters. And they came and drew water,
and they filled the troughs to water their father's flock. 17 Then the shepherds came and
drove them away; but Moses stood up and
helped them, and watered their flock.

18 When they came to Reuel their father,
he said, "How *is it that* you have come so
soon today?"

19 And they said, "An Egyptian delivered
us from the hand of the shepherds, and he
also drew enough water for us and watered
the flock."

20 So he said to his daughters, "And where
is he? Why *is* it *that* you have left the man?
Call him, that he may eat bread."

21 Then Moses was content to live with the
man, and he gave Zipporah his daughter to
Moses. 22 And she bore *him* a son. He called
his name Gershom,[a] for he said, "I have
been a stranger in a foreign land."

23 Now it happened in the process of time
that the king of Egypt died. Then the children of Israel groaned because of the bondage, and they cried out; and their cry came
up to God because of the bondage. 24 So God
heard their groaning, and God remembered
His covenant with Abraham, with Isaac, and
with Jacob. 25 And God looked upon the children of Israel, and God acknowledged *them*.

Moses at the Burning Bush

3 Now Moses was tending the flock of
Jethro his father-in-law, the priest
of Midian. And he led the flock to the
back of the desert, and came to Horeb,
the mountain of God. 2 And the Angel of
the LORD appeared to him in a flame of fire
from the midst of a bush. So he looked, and
behold, the bush was burning with fire,
but the bush *was* not consumed. 3 Then
Moses said, "I will now turn aside and see
this great sight, why the bush does not
burn."

2:22 [a] Literally *Stranger There*

Starring Roles

The name **MOSES** (pronounced *MO-zez*) is connected with a Hebrew word meaning "Drawn Out," because Moses was drawn out of the Nile River.

Moses wrote Genesis, Exodus, Leviticus, Numbers, and Deuteronomy, but you don't meet him until the Book of Exodus where you read that he was born in Egypt (Exodus 2:2).

Although Moses was really a Hebrew, he grew up as an Egyptian prince (Exodus 2:1–10). Because he was a Hebrew, he became angry when he saw an Egyptian slave driver beating one of his people. He killed the Egyptian, and he had to run away into the desert where he became a hired shepherd (Exodus 2:11–25).

One day God spoke to Moses from a bush that seemed to be burning but didn't actually burn up (Exodus 3:1–6). He commanded Moses to go back to Egypt and lead the Hebrew people out of slavery and back to the land that God promised them.

In the end, the Lord didn't let Moses go into the Promised Land because he lost his temper with the people in a way that displeased the Lord (Numbers 20:7–12).

Always remember that you must ask for self-control if you are going to be a leader for God.

4So when the LORD saw that he turned
aside to look, God called to him from the
midst of the bush and said, "Moses, Moses!"
And he said, "Here I am."
5Then He said, "Do not draw near this
place. Take your sandals off your feet, for
the place where you stand *is* holy ground."
6Moreover He said, "I *am* the God of your
father—the God of Abraham, the God of
Isaac, and the God of Jacob." And Moses hid
his face, for he was afraid to look upon God.
7And the LORD said: "I have surely seen
the oppression of My people who *are* in
Egypt, and have heard their cry because of
their taskmasters, for I know their sorrows.
8So I have come down to deliver them out of
the hand of the Egyptians, and to bring them
up from that land to a good and large land,
to a land flowing with milk and honey, to
the place of the Canaanites and the Hittites
and the Amorites and the Perizzites and the
Hivites and the Jebusites. 9Now therefore,
behold, the cry of the children of Israel has
come to Me, and I have also seen the oppression with which the Egyptians oppress
them. 10Come now, therefore, and I will send
you to Pharaoh that you may bring My people, the children of Israel, out of Egypt."

KNOWING AND FINDING GOD

MEETING GOD

READ IT: EXODUS 3:1–22

GET IT:

Moses was just a normal guy, taking care of his family's sheep, doing his job, minding his own business. But he was also keeping his eyes open to what was going on around him. When he saw something out of the ordinary—a burning bush—he paid attention. And because he paid attention, he met God in a plain old, ordinary bush!

When Moses met God, it wasn't what you might expect. It wasn't earth-shattering. It didn't draw huge crowds. There were no fireworks or drumrolls or angel choirs singing in the background. It was just Moses and God and a bush in the middle of a desert.

God told Moses who He was. He told Moses who Moses was. He told Moses what He wanted Moses to do. He let Moses ask questions, lots of questions. He didn't tell Moses to be quiet. He listened and responded.

Moses wasn't looking for God, but he found Him anyway because he kept his eyes and ears open and noticed the world around him.

LIVE IT:

Most people will never have a conversation with God like Moses did, but we can still get to know Him. Keep your eyes and ears open for the ordinary but amazing things that happen around you. What do those things tell you about God? Don't be afraid to ask God questions and then listen for His answers in the Bible or from people who know Him well. God wants you to know Him, so if you look for Him, you'll find Him.

11But Moses said to God, "Who *am* I that
I should go to Pharaoh, and that I should
bring the children of Israel out of Egypt?"
12So He said, "I will certainly be with you.
And this *shall be* a sign to you that I have
sent you: When you have brought the people out of Egypt, you shall serve God on this
mountain."
13Then Moses said to God, "Indeed, *when*
I come to the children of Israel and say to
them, 'The God of your fathers has sent
me to you,' and they say to me, 'What *is* His
name?' what shall I say to them?"
14And God said to Moses, "I AM WHO
I AM." And He said, "Thus you shall say to
the children of Israel, 'I AM has sent me to
you.'" 15Moreover God said to Moses, "Thus
you shall say to the children of Israel: 'The
LORD God of your fathers, the God of Abraham, the God of Isaac, and the God of Jacob,
has sent me to you. This *is* My name forever,
and this *is* My memorial to all generations.'
16Go and gather the elders of Israel together,
and say to them, 'The LORD God of your fathers, the God of Abraham, of Isaac, and of
Jacob, appeared to me, saying, "I have surely
visited you and *seen* what is done to you in

In Focus

3:14 I AM WHO I AM The name God gave Himself. The name means that He always existed, even before time, and He always will exist. He depends on nothing outside Himself for His existence.

On Location

Exodus from Egypt

The Hebrew captivity and the confrontation between Moses and Pharaoh take place in the Nile Delta of northern Egypt. The Exodus and 40 years of wandering in the wilderness take place in the Sinai Peninsula, a barren expanse between Egypt and Canaan, just north of the Red Sea. The map shows possible routes of the Exodus.

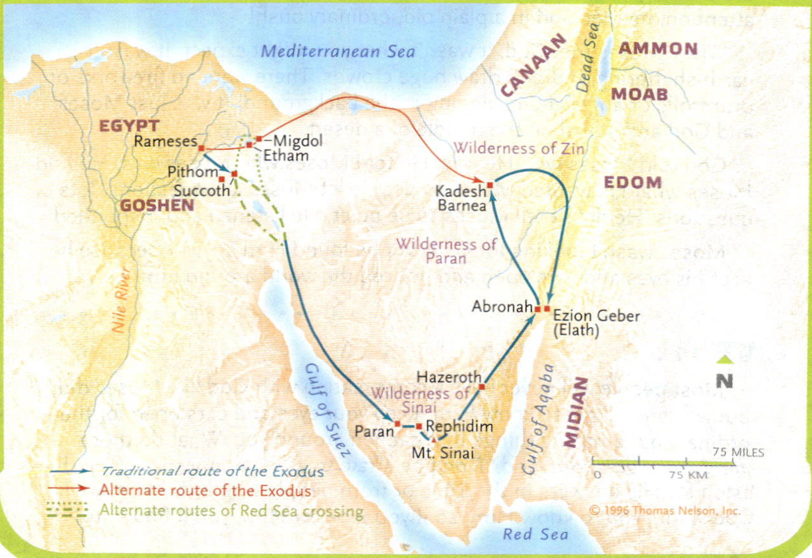

Egypt; [17]and I have said I will bring you up
out of the affliction of Egypt to the land of
the Canaanites and the Hittites and the Amorites and the Perizzites and the Hivites and
the Jebusites, to a land flowing with milk
and honey."' [18]Then they will heed your
voice; and you shall come, you and the elders
of Israel, to the king of Egypt; and you shall
say to him, 'The LORD God of the Hebrews
has met with us; and now, please, let us go
three days' journey into the wilderness, that
we may sacrifice to the LORD our God.' [19]But
I am sure that the king of Egypt will not let
you go, no, not even by a mighty hand. [20]So
I will stretch out My hand and strike Egypt
with all My wonders which I will do in its
midst; and after that he will let you go. [21]And
I will give this people favor in the sight of
the Egyptians; and it shall be, when you go,
that you shall not go empty-handed. [22]But
every woman shall ask of her neighbor,
namely, of her who dwells near her house,
articles of silver, articles of gold, and clothing; and you shall put *them* on your sons and
on your daughters. So you shall plunder the
Egyptians."

Miraculous Signs for Pharaoh

4 Then Moses answered and said, "But
suppose they will not believe me or listen to my voice; suppose they say, 'The LORD
has not appeared to you.'"

[2]So the LORD said to him, "What *is* that
in your hand?"

He said, "A rod."

[3]And He said, "Cast it on the ground."
So he cast it on the ground, and it became a
serpent; and Moses fled from it. [4]Then the
LORD said to Moses, "Reach out your hand
and take *it* by the tail" (and he reached out

GOD CALLS MOSES FROM A BUSH

READ IT: EXODUS 3:1–22

GET IT:

Moses left Egypt in a hurry after he killed an Egyptian who was beating a Hebrew slave. He wandered through the desert to Midian and became a shepherd. One day while out with the sheep, he saw a burning bush and ended up talking to God. God told Moses the plan He had to get His people out of Egypt. Moses wasn't excited about the job God wanted him to do. God assured Moses, "I will be with you." But that didn't convince Moses. In fact, he came up with lots of excuses that God didn't accept. God gave him some special signs to use in front of Pharaoh. That didn't convince Moses either. Eventually Moses agreed to face Pharaoh and be the leader of God's people.

LIVE IT:

God told Moses what He wanted him to do. It was a big job, and Moses didn't think he was the right person. He argued with God, but God wouldn't take no for an answer. Many times we think we aren't good enough, talented enough, or smart enough to handle what God wants us to do. But we shouldn't make excuses. We need to accept the challenge and trust God to help us face it and finish the task. God puts experiences in front of us to prepare us for bigger things to come.

his hand and caught it, and it became a rod
in his hand), 5"that they may believe that the
LORD God of their fathers, the God of Abraham, the God of Isaac, and the God of Jacob,
has appeared to you."

6Furthermore the LORD said to him,
"Now put your hand in your bosom." And
he put his hand in his bosom, and when he
took it out, behold, his hand *was* leprous,
like snow. 7And He said, "Put your hand
in your bosom again." So he put his hand
in his bosom again, and drew it out of his
bosom, and behold, it was restored like his
other flesh. 8"Then it will be, if they do not
believe you, nor heed the message of the
first sign, that they may believe the message
of the latter sign. 9And it shall be, if they do
not believe even these two signs, or listen to
your voice, that you shall take water from the
river[a] and pour *it* on the dry *land*. The water
which you take from the river will become
blood on the dry *land*."

10Then Moses said to the LORD, "O my
Lord, I *am* not eloquent, neither before nor

4:9 [a] That is, the Nile

COMMUNICATION

SPEAK UP!

READ IT: EXODUS 4

GET IT:

Moses is one of the most influential figures in the Bible. In Exodus, we learn all about him, and his legacy continues into the New Testament, where he's described as one of the most faithful people in Scripture.

Though God used Moses in big ways, he wasn't perfect. In fact, when God called him to be the voice of the Israelites, Moses freaked out. Even after God gave him some very clear signs, Moses was worried the people wouldn't listen to him—or if they did listen, they wouldn't believe him. He tried to back out, telling God he wasn't a good speaker, that he was "slow of speech" (v. 10). God responded by asking, "Who has made man's mouth?" (v. 11). Once again God commanded Moses to go and speak.

Still, Moses hesitated. The Bible says that God got angry at Moses. Finally, He offered Moses a compromise—God would use Moses' brother, Aaron, to speak, but the words would still have to come from Moses first.

LIVE IT:

When God asks us to do something, it might seem scary. We might not think we're good enough or have the right skills. It's normal to feel afraid. If you feel like God is leading you into a new adventure, talk to some friends about it. Share what you think God is asking you to do with a pastor or your parents. They can help you make a plan and encourage you when you're afraid. Try keeping a journal of the journey. Over time, you can look back and see how God has put everything you need into place for you to step out and speak up!

since You have spoken to Your servant; but I *am* slow of speech and slow of tongue."

11So the LORD said to him, "Who has made man's mouth? Or who makes the mute, the deaf, the seeing, or the blind? *Have* not I, the LORD? 12Now therefore, go, and I will be with your mouth and teach you what you shall say."

13But he said, "O my Lord, please send by the hand of whomever *else* You may send."

14So the anger of the LORD was kindled against Moses, and He said: "Is not Aaron the Levite your brother? I know that he can speak well. And look, he is also coming out to meet you. When he sees you, he will be glad in his heart. 15Now you shall speak to him and put the words in his mouth. And I will be with your mouth and with his mouth, and I will teach you what you shall do. 16So he shall be your spokesman to the people. And he himself shall be as a mouth for you, and you shall be to him as God. 17And you shall take this rod in your hand, with which you shall do the signs."

Moses Goes to Egypt

18So Moses went and returned to Jethro his father-in-law, and said to him, "Please let me go and return to my brethren who *are* in Egypt, and see whether they are still alive."

And Jethro said to Moses, "Go in peace."

19Now the LORD said to Moses in Midian, "Go, return to Egypt; for all the men who sought your life are dead." 20Then Moses took his wife and his sons and set them on a donkey, and he returned to the land of Egypt. And Moses took the rod of God in his hand.

21And the LORD said to Moses, "When you go back to Egypt, see that you do all those wonders before Pharaoh which I have put in your hand. But I will harden his heart, so that he will not let the people go. 22Then you shall say to Pharaoh, 'Thus says the LORD: "Israel *is* My son, My firstborn. 23So I say to you, let My son go that he may serve Me. But if you refuse to let him go, indeed I will kill your son, your firstborn." ' "

24And it came to pass on the way, at the encampment, that the LORD met him and sought to kill him. 25Then Zipporah took a sharp stone and cut off the foreskin of her son and cast *it* at *Moses'*[a] feet, and said, "Surely you *are* a husband of blood to me!" 26So He let him go. Then she said, "*You are* a husband of blood!"—because of the circumcision.

27And the LORD said to Aaron, "Go into the wilderness to meet Moses." So he went and met him on the mountain of God, and kissed him. 28So Moses told Aaron all the words of the LORD who had sent him, and all the signs which He had commanded him. 29Then Moses and Aaron went and gathered together all the elders of the children of Israel. 30And Aaron spoke all the words which the LORD had spoken to Moses. Then he did the signs in the sight of the people. 31So the people believed; and when they heard that the LORD had visited the children of Israel and that He had looked on their affliction, then they bowed their heads and worshiped.

First Encounter with Pharaoh

5 Afterward Moses and Aaron went in and told Pharaoh, "Thus says the LORD God of Israel: 'Let My people go, that they may hold a feast to Me in the wilderness.' "

2And Pharaoh said, "Who *is* the LORD, that I should obey His voice to let Israel go? I do not know the LORD, nor will I let Israel go."

3So they said, "The God of the Hebrews has met with us. Please, let us go three days' journey into the desert and sacrifice to the LORD our God, lest He fall upon us with pestilence or with the sword."

4Then the king of Egypt said to them, "Moses and Aaron, why do you take the people from their work? Get *back* to your labor." 5And Pharaoh said, "Look, the people of the land *are* many now, and you make them rest from their labor!"

6So the same day Pharaoh commanded the taskmasters of the people and their officers, saying, 7"You shall no longer give the people straw to make brick as before. Let them go and gather straw for themselves. 8And you shall lay on them the quota of bricks which they made before. You shall not reduce it. For they are idle; therefore they cry out, saying, 'Let us go and sacrifice to our God.' 9Let more work be laid on the men, that they may labor in it, and let them not regard false words."

10And the taskmasters of the people and their officers went out and spoke to the people, saying, "Thus says Pharaoh: 'I will not

4:25 [a] Literally *his*

give you straw. 11Go, get yourselves straw
where you can find it; yet none of your work
will be reduced.'" 12So the people were scattered abroad throughout all the land of Egypt
to gather stubble instead of straw. 13And the
taskmasters forced *them* to hurry, saying,
"Fulfill your work, *your* daily quota, as when
there was straw." 14Also the officers of the
children of Israel, whom Pharaoh's taskmasters had set over them, were beaten *and* were
asked, "Why have you not fulfilled your task
in making brick both yesterday and today,
as before?"

15Then the officers of the children of Israel came and cried out to Pharaoh, saying,
"Why are you dealing thus with your servants? 16There is no straw given to your servants, and they say to us, 'Make brick!' And
indeed your servants *are* beaten, but the fault
is in your *own* people."

17But he said, "You *are* idle! Idle! Therefore you say, 'Let us go *and* sacrifice to the
LORD.' 18Therefore go now *and* work; for no
straw shall be given you, yet you shall deliver
the quota of bricks." 19And the officers of the
children of Israel saw *that* they *were* in trouble after it was said, "You shall not reduce
any bricks from your daily quota."

20Then, as they came out from Pharaoh,
they met Moses and Aaron who stood there
to meet them. 21And they said to them, "Let
the LORD look on you and judge, because
you have made us abhorrent in the sight of
Pharaoh and in the sight of his servants, to
put a sword in their hand to kill us."

GOD SPEAKS TO PHARAOH THROUGH MOSES AND AARON

READ IT: EXODUS 5:1–23; 6:28—7:13

GET IT:

God allowed Moses to bring along his brother, Aaron, who was better at making speeches than Moses was. But the job was still difficult. Pharaoh was stubborn. He wasn't impressed with Moses' rod turning into a snake. And he didn't want to lose his slaves. After all, they did all the work building the cities of Egypt. Moses' job seemed impossible because of this stubborn ruler. But God was in control all the time. He had a plan to show Pharaoh that He was the ruler of everything. Even nature would listen and obey His commands.

LIVE IT:

Giving a speech in front of class is hard enough. Can you imagine having to give a speech in front of a mighty and powerful ruler? You can understand why Moses wasn't eager for that job. But Moses wasn't in this alone. God was with him. God was working through Moses the entire time. God had a plan to show all of Egypt and Pharaoh that He was the God of all gods, the one true God in control of everything. Whatever you find scary—giving a speech, performing on a stage, walking the halls in school, entering an empty house, going someplace new—remember that God goes with you. He's working with you and in you to prepare you for bigger things.

Israel's Deliverance Assured

22So Moses returned to the LORD and
said, "Lord, why have You brought trouble on
this people? Why *is* it You have sent me? 23For
since I came to Pharaoh to speak in Your
name, he has done evil to this people; neither
have You delivered Your people at all."

6 Then the LORD said to Moses, "Now
you shall see what I will do to Pharaoh.
For with a strong hand he will let them go,
and with a strong hand he will drive them
out of his land."

2And God spoke to Moses and said to
him: "I *am* the LORD. 3I appeared to Abraham, to Isaac, and to Jacob, as God Almighty, but *by* My name LORD[a] I was not
known to them. 4I have also established My
covenant with them, to give them the land
of Canaan, the land of their pilgrimage, in
which they were strangers. 5And I have also
heard the groaning of the children of Israel
whom the Egyptians keep in bondage, and I
have remembered My covenant. 6Therefore
say to the children of Israel: 'I *am* the LORD;
I will bring you out from under the burdens
of the Egyptians, I will rescue you from their
bondage, and I will redeem you with an outstretched arm and with great judgments.
7I will take you as My people, and I will be
your God. Then you shall know that I *am*
the LORD your God who brings you out from
under the burdens of the Egyptians. 8And I
will bring you into the land which I swore to
give to Abraham, Isaac, and Jacob; and I will
give it to you *as* a heritage: I *am* the LORD.'"
9So Moses spoke thus to the children of Israel; but they did not heed Moses, because of
anguish of spirit and cruel bondage.

10And the LORD spoke to Moses, saying,
11"Go in, tell Pharaoh king of Egypt to let the
children of Israel go out of his land."

12And Moses spoke before the LORD, saying, "The children of Israel have not heeded
me. How then shall Pharaoh heed me, for I
am of uncircumcised lips?"

13Then the LORD spoke to Moses and
Aaron, and gave them a command for the
children of Israel and for Pharaoh king of
Egypt, to bring the children of Israel out of
the land of Egypt.

The Family of Moses and Aaron

14These *are* the heads of their fathers'
houses: The sons of Reuben, the firstborn of

In Focus

6:6 Redeem To buy something back
from someone. Jesus bought back
believers from the slavery of sin.

Israel, *were* Hanoch, Pallu, Hezron, and Carmi. These are the families of Reuben. 15And
the sons of Simeon *were* Jemuel,[a] Jamin,
Ohad, Jachin, Zohar, and Shaul the son of a
Canaanite woman. These *are* the families of
Simeon. 16These *are* the names of the sons
of Levi according to their generations: Gershon, Kohath, and Merari. And the years of
the life of Levi *were* one hundred and thirty-
seven. 17The sons of Gershon *were* Libni and
Shimi according to their families. 18And the
sons of Kohath *were* Amram, Izhar, Hebron,
and Uzziel. And the years of the life of Kohath *were* one hundred and thirty-three.
19The sons of Merari *were* Mahli and Mushi.
These *are* the families of Levi according to
their generations.

20Now Amram took for himself Jochebed,
his father's sister, as wife; and she bore him
Aaron and Moses. And the years of the life of
Amram *were* one hundred and thirty-seven.
21The sons of Izhar *were* Korah, Nepheg,
and Zichri. 22And the sons of Uzziel *were*
Mishael, Elzaphan, and Zithri. 23Aaron took
to himself Elisheba, daughter of Amminadab, sister of Nahshon, as wife; and she bore
him Nadab, Abihu, Eleazar, and Ithamar.
24And the sons of Korah *were* Assir, Elkanah,
and Abiasaph. These are the families of the
Korahites. 25Eleazar, Aaron's son, took for
himself one of the daughters of Putiel as
wife; and she bore him Phinehas. These *are*
the heads of the fathers' houses of the Levites according to their families.

26These *are the same* Aaron and Moses to
whom the LORD said, "Bring out the children
of Israel from the land of Egypt according
to their armies." 27These *are* the ones who
spoke to Pharaoh king of Egypt, to bring out
the children of Israel from Egypt. These *are
the same* Moses and Aaron.

6:3 [a] Hebrew *YHWH,* traditionally *Jehovah* **6:15** [a] Spelled *Nemuel* in Numbers 26:12

Aaron Is Moses' Spokesman

28And it came to pass, on the day the
LORD spoke to Moses in the land of Egypt,
29that the LORD spoke to Moses, saying, "I *am*
the LORD. Speak to Pharaoh king of Egypt all
that I say to you."

30But Moses said before the LORD, "Behold, I *am* of uncircumcised lips, and how
shall Pharaoh heed me?"

7 So the LORD said to Moses: "See, I have
made you *as* God to Pharaoh, and Aaron your brother shall be your prophet. 2You
shall speak all that I command you. And
Aaron your brother shall tell Pharaoh to
send the children of Israel out of his land.
3And I will harden Pharaoh's heart, and multiply My signs and My wonders in the land
of Egypt. 4But Pharaoh will not heed you, so
that I may lay My hand on Egypt and bring
My armies *and* My people, the children of
Israel, out of the land of Egypt by great judgments. 5And the Egyptians shall know that
I *am* the LORD, when I stretch out My hand
on Egypt and bring out the children of Israel
from among them."

6Then Moses and Aaron did *so;* just as
the LORD commanded them, so they did.
7And Moses *was* eighty years old and Aaron
eighty-three years old when they spoke to
Pharaoh.

Aaron's Miraculous Rod

8Then the LORD spoke to Moses and Aaron, saying, 9"When Pharaoh speaks to you,
saying, 'Show a miracle for yourselves,' then
you shall say to Aaron, 'Take your rod and
cast *it* before Pharaoh, *and* let it become a
serpent.'" 10So Moses and Aaron went in to
Pharaoh, and they did so, just as the LORD
commanded. And Aaron cast down his rod
before Pharaoh and before his servants, and
it became a serpent.

11But Pharaoh also called the wise men
and the sorcerers; so the magicians of Egypt,
they also did in like manner with their enchantments. 12For every man threw down his
rod, and they became serpents. But Aaron's
rod swallowed up their rods. 13And Pharaoh's
heart grew hard, and he did not heed them,
as the LORD had said.

The First Plague: Waters Become Blood

14So the LORD said to Moses: "Pharaoh's
heart *is* hard; he refuses to let the people go.
15Go to Pharaoh in the morning, when he
goes out to the water, and you shall stand
by the river's bank to meet him; and the rod
which was turned to a serpent you shall take
in your hand. 16And you shall say to him,
'The LORD God of the Hebrews has sent me
to you, saying, "Let My people go, that they
may serve Me in the wilderness"; but indeed,
until now you would not hear! 17Thus says
the LORD: "By this you shall know that I *am*
the LORD. Behold, I will strike the waters
which *are* in the river with the rod that *is* in
my hand, and they shall be turned to blood.
18And the fish that *are* in the river shall die,
the river shall stink, and the Egyptians will
loathe to drink the water of the river."'"

19Then the LORD spoke to Moses, "Say to
Aaron, 'Take your rod and stretch out your
hand over the waters of Egypt, over their
streams, over their rivers, over their ponds,
and over all their pools of water, that they
may become blood. And there shall be blood
throughout all the land of Egypt, both in
buckets of wood and *pitchers of* stone.'" 20And
Moses and Aaron did so, just as the LORD
commanded. So he lifted up the rod and
struck the waters that *were* in the river, in
the sight of Pharaoh and in the sight of his
servants. And all the waters that *were* in the
river were turned to blood. 21The fish that
were in the river died, the river stank, and
the Egyptians could not drink the water of
the river. So there was blood throughout all
the land of Egypt.

22Then the magicians of Egypt did so
with their enchantments; and Pharaoh's
heart grew hard, and he did not heed them,
as the LORD had said. 23And Pharaoh turned
and went into his house. Neither was his
heart moved by this. 24So all the Egyptians
dug all around the river for water to drink,
because they could not drink the water of the
river. 25And seven days passed after the LORD
had struck the river.

The Second Plague: Frogs

8 And the LORD spoke to Moses, "Go to
Pharaoh and say to him, 'Thus says the
LORD: "Let My people go, that they may serve
Me. 2But if you refuse to let *them* go, behold,
I will smite all your territory with frogs. 3So
the river shall bring forth frogs abundantly,
which shall go up and come into your house,
into your bedroom, on your bed, into the
houses of your servants, on your people, into

your ovens, and into your kneading bowls.
4And the frogs shall come up on you, on your
people, and on all your servants."'"

5Then the LORD spoke to Moses, "Say to
Aaron, 'Stretch out your hand with your rod
over the streams, over the rivers, and over
the ponds, and cause frogs to come up on
the land of Egypt.'" 6So Aaron stretched
out his hand over the waters of Egypt, and
the frogs came up and covered the land of
Egypt. 7And the magicians did so with their
enchantments, and brought up frogs on the
land of Egypt.

8Then Pharaoh called for Moses and Aaron, and said, "Entreat the LORD that He may
take away the frogs from me and from my
people; and I will let the people go, that they
may sacrifice to the LORD."

9And Moses said to Pharaoh, "Accept the
honor of saying when I shall intercede for
you, for your servants, and for your people,
to destroy the frogs from you and your houses, *that* they may remain in the river only."

10So he said, "Tomorrow." And he said,
"*Let it be* according to your word, that you
may know that *there is* no one like the LORD
our God. 11And the frogs shall depart from
you, from your houses, from your servants,
and from your people. They shall remain in
the river only."

12Then Moses and Aaron went out from
Pharaoh. And Moses cried out to the LORD
concerning the frogs which He had brought
against Pharaoh. 13So the LORD did according
to the word of Moses. And the frogs died out
of the houses, out of the courtyards, and out
of the fields. 14They gathered them together in heaps, and the land stank. 15But when
Pharaoh saw that there was relief, he hardened his heart and did not heed them, as the
LORD had said.

The Third Plague: Lice

16So the LORD said to Moses, "Say to
Aaron, 'Stretch out your rod, and strike the
dust of the land, so that it may become lice
throughout all the land of Egypt.'" 17And
they did so. For Aaron stretched out his hand
with his rod and struck the dust of the earth,
and it became lice on man and beast. All the
dust of the land became lice throughout all
the land of Egypt.

18Now the magicians so worked with
their enchantments to bring forth lice, but
they could not. So there were lice on man
and beast. 19Then the magicians said to
Pharaoh, "This *is* the finger of God." But
Pharaoh's heart grew hard, and he did not
heed them, just as the LORD had said.

The Fourth Plague: Flies

20And the LORD said to Moses, "Rise early
in the morning and stand before Pharaoh as
he comes out to the water. Then say to him,
'Thus says the LORD: "Let My people go, that
they may serve Me. 21Or else, if you will not
let My people go, behold, I will send swarms
of flies on you and your servants, on your
people and into your houses. The houses of
the Egyptians shall be full of swarms *of flies*,
and also the ground on which they *stand*.
22And in that day I will set apart the land of
Goshen, in which My people dwell, that no
swarms *of flies* shall be there, in order that
you may know that I *am* the LORD in the
midst of the land. 23I will make a difference[a]
between My people and your people. Tomorrow this sign shall be."'" 24And the LORD
did so. Thick swarms *of flies* came into the
house of Pharaoh, *into* his servants' houses,
and into all the land of Egypt. The land was
corrupted because of the swarms *of flies*.

25Then Pharaoh called for Moses and
Aaron, and said, "Go, sacrifice to your God
in the land."

26And Moses said, "It is not right to do so,
for we would be sacrificing the abomination
of the Egyptians to the LORD our God. If we
sacrifice the abomination of the Egyptians
before their eyes, then will they not stone us?
27We will go three days' journey into the wilderness and sacrifice to the LORD our God as
He will command us."

28So Pharaoh said, "I will let you go, that
you may sacrifice to the LORD your God in
the wilderness; only you shall not go very far
away. Intercede for me."

29Then Moses said, "Indeed I am going
out from you, and I will entreat the LORD,
that the swarms *of flies* may depart tomorrow from Pharaoh, from his servants, and
from his people. But let Pharaoh not deal deceitfully anymore in not letting the people go
to sacrifice to the LORD."

30So Moses went out from Pharaoh and
entreated the LORD. 31And the LORD did according to the word of Moses; He removed
the swarms *of flies* from Pharaoh, from his

8:23 [a] Literally *set a ransom* (compare Exodus 9:4 and 11:7)

servants, and from his people. Not one remained. 32But Pharaoh hardened his heart at this time also; neither would he let the people go.

The Fifth Plague: Livestock Diseased

9 Then the LORD said to Moses, "Go in to Pharaoh and tell him, 'Thus says the LORD God of the Hebrews: "Let My people go, that they may serve Me. 2For if you refuse to let *them* go, and still hold them, 3behold, the hand of the LORD will be on your cattle in the field, on the horses, on the donkeys, on the camels, on the oxen, and on the sheep—a very severe pestilence. 4And the LORD will make a difference between the livestock of Israel and the livestock of Egypt. So nothing shall die of all *that* belongs to the children of Israel." ' " 5Then the LORD appointed a set time, saying, "Tomorrow the LORD will do this thing in the land."

6So the LORD did this thing on the next day, and all the livestock of Egypt died; but of the livestock of the children of Israel, not one died. 7Then Pharaoh sent, and indeed, not even one of the livestock of the Israelites was dead. But the heart of Pharaoh became hard, and he did not let the people go.

The Sixth Plague: Boils

8So the LORD said to Moses and Aaron, "Take for yourselves handfuls of ashes from a furnace, and let Moses scatter it toward the heavens in the sight of Pharaoh. 9And it will become fine dust in all the land of Egypt, and it will cause boils that break out in sores on man and beast throughout all the land of Egypt." 10Then they took ashes from the furnace and stood before Pharaoh, and Moses scattered *them* toward heaven. And *they* caused boils that break out in sores on man and beast. 11And the magicians could not stand before Moses because of the boils, for the boils were on the magicians and on all the Egyptians. 12But the LORD hardened the heart of Pharaoh; and he did not heed them, just as the LORD had spoken to Moses.

The Seventh Plague: Hail

13Then the LORD said to Moses, "Rise early in the morning and stand before Pharaoh, and say to him, 'Thus says the LORD God of the Hebrews: "Let My people go, that they may serve Me, 14for at this time I will send all My plagues to your very heart, and on your servants and on your people, that you may know that *there is* none like Me in all the earth. 15Now if I had stretched out My hand and struck you and your people with pestilence, then you would have been cut off from the earth. 16But indeed for this *purpose* I have raised you up, that I may show My power *in* you, and that My name may be declared in all the earth. 17As yet you exalt yourself against My people in that you will not let them go. 18Behold, tomorrow about this time I will cause very heavy hail to rain down, such as has not been in Egypt since its founding until now. 19Therefore send now *and* gather your livestock and all that you have in the field, for the hail shall come down on every man and every animal which is found in the field and is not brought home; and they shall die." ' "

20He who feared the word of the LORD among the servants of Pharaoh made his servants and his livestock flee to the houses. 21But he who did not regard the word of the LORD left his servants and his livestock in the field.

22Then the LORD said to Moses, "Stretch out your hand toward heaven, that there may be hail in all the land of Egypt—on man, on beast, and on every herb of the field, throughout the land of Egypt." 23And Moses stretched out his rod toward heaven; and the LORD sent thunder and hail, and fire darted to the ground. And the LORD rained hail on the land of Egypt. 24So there was hail, and fire mingled with the hail, so very heavy that there was none like it in all the land of Egypt since it became a nation. 25And the hail struck throughout the whole land of Egypt, all that *was* in the field, both man and beast; and the hail struck every herb of the field and broke every tree of the field. 26Only in the land of Goshen, where the children of Israel *were,* there was no hail.

27And Pharaoh sent and called for Moses and Aaron, and said to them, "I have sinned this time. The LORD *is* righteous, and my people and I *are* wicked. 28Entreat the LORD, that there may be no *more* mighty thundering and hail, for *it is* enough. I will let you go, *and you shall* stay no longer."

29So Moses said to him, "As soon as I have gone out of the city, I will spread out my hands to the LORD; the thunder will cease, and there will be no more hail, that you may

know that the earth *is* the LORD's. 30 But as for
you and your servants, I know that you will
not yet fear the LORD God."
31 Now the flax and the barley were struck,
for the barley *was* in the head and the flax
was in bud. 32 But the wheat and the spelt
were not struck, for they *are* late crops.
33 So Moses went out of the city from
Pharaoh and spread out his hands to the
LORD; then the thunder and the hail ceased,
and the rain was not poured on the earth.
34 And when Pharaoh saw that the rain, the
hail, and the thunder had ceased, he sinned
yet more; and he hardened his heart, he and
his servants. 35 So the heart of Pharaoh was
hard; neither would he let the children of Israel go, as the LORD had spoken by Moses.

The Eighth Plague: Locusts

10 Now the LORD said to Moses, "Go
in to Pharaoh; for I have hardened
his heart and the hearts of his servants, that
I may show these signs of Mine before him,
2 and that you may tell in the hearing of your
son and your son's son the mighty things I
have done in Egypt, and My signs which I
have done among them, that you may know
that I *am* the LORD."
3 So Moses and Aaron came in to Pharaoh
and said to him, "Thus says the LORD God of
the Hebrews: 'How long will you refuse to
humble yourself before Me? Let My people
go, that they may serve Me. 4 Or else, if you
refuse to let My people go, behold, tomorrow
I will bring locusts into your territory. 5 And
they shall cover the face of the earth, so that
no one will be able to see the earth; and they
shall eat the residue of what is left, which remains to you from the hail, and they shall
eat every tree which grows up for you out of
the field. 6 They shall fill your houses, the
houses of all your servants, and the houses
of all the Egyptians—which neither your
fathers nor your fathers' fathers have seen,
since the day that they were on the earth to
this day.'" And he turned and went out from
Pharaoh.
7 Then Pharaoh's servants said to him,
"How long shall this man be a snare to us?
Let the men go, that they may serve the
LORD their God. Do you not yet know that
Egypt is destroyed?"
8 So Moses and Aaron were brought again
to Pharaoh, and he said to them, "Go, serve
the LORD your God. Who *are* the ones that
are going?"
9 And Moses said, "We will go with our
young and our old; with our sons and our
daughters, with our flocks and our herds we
will go, for we must hold a feast to the LORD."
10 Then he said to them, "The LORD had
better be with you when I let you and your
little ones go! Beware, for evil is ahead of
you. 11 Not so! Go now, you *who are* men, and
serve the LORD, for that is what you desired."
And they were driven out from Pharaoh's
presence.
12 Then the LORD said to Moses, "Stretch
out your hand over the land of Egypt for the
locusts, that they may come upon the land
of Egypt, and eat every herb of the land—all
that the hail has left." 13 So Moses stretched
out his rod over the land of Egypt, and the
LORD brought an east wind on the land all
that day and all *that* night. When it was
morning, the east wind brought the locusts.
14 And the locusts went up over all the land of
Egypt and rested on all the territory of Egypt.
They were very severe; previously there had
been no such locusts as they, nor shall there
be such after them. 15 For they covered the
face of the whole earth, so that the land was
darkened; and they ate every herb of the land
and all the fruit of the trees which the hail
had left. So there remained nothing green
on the trees or on the plants of the field
throughout all the land of Egypt.
16 Then Pharaoh called for Moses and
Aaron in haste, and said, "I have sinned
against the LORD your God and against you.
17 Now therefore, please forgive my sin only
this once, and entreat the LORD your God,
that He may take away from me this death
only." 18 So he went out from Pharaoh and
entreated the LORD. 19 And the LORD turned
a very strong west wind, which took the locusts away and blew them into the Red Sea.
There remained not one locust in all the
territory of Egypt. 20 But the LORD hardened
Pharaoh's heart, and he did not let the children of Israel go.

The Ninth Plague: Darkness

21 Then the LORD said to Moses, "Stretch
out your hand toward heaven, that there may
be darkness over the land of Egypt, darkness *which* may even be felt." 22 So Moses
stretched out his hand toward heaven, and
there was thick darkness in all the land of

Egypt three days. 23 They did not see one another; nor did anyone rise from his place for
three days. But all the children of Israel had
light in their dwellings.

24 Then Pharaoh called to Moses and said,
"Go, serve the LORD; only let your flocks and
your herds be kept back. Let your little ones
also go with you."

25 But Moses said, "You must also give us
sacrifices and burnt offerings, that we may
sacrifice to the LORD our God. 26 Our livestock also shall go with us; not a hoof shall
be left behind. For we must take some of
them to serve the LORD our God, and even
we do not know with what we must serve the
LORD until we arrive there."

27 But the LORD hardened Pharaoh's heart,
and he would not let them go. 28 Then Pharaoh
said to him, "Get away from me! Take heed to
yourself and see my face no more! For in the
day you see my face you shall die!"

29 So Moses said, "You have spoken well. I
will never see your face again."

Death of the Firstborn Announced

11 And the LORD said to Moses, "I will
bring one more plague on Pharaoh
and on Egypt. Afterward he will let you go
from here. When he lets *you* go, he will surely drive you out of here altogether. 2 Speak
now in the hearing of the people, and let
every man ask from his neighbor and every
woman from her neighbor, articles of silver

GOD SAVES HIS PEOPLE FROM THE DEATH PLAGUE

READ IT: EXODUS 12:21–42

GET IT:

God sent nine different plagues on Egypt to try to convince Pharaoh to release the Hebrew people from slavery. Each time Pharaoh begged Moses to end the plague and promised to let the people leave. When Moses asked God to end the plague, it stopped. Then Pharaoh changed his mind. This happened nine times. Then God sent the tenth plague. It was the very worst one of all. The plague of death killed the oldest child in every family and the oldest animal in every flock in Egypt. God's people and their animals weren't touched at all. The angel of death passed over them (that's why there's a celebration called Passover). God used this extreme action to show Pharaoh who was in charge and make Pharaoh release His people. It worked.

LIVE IT:

Most of us are not familiar with someone dying. Maybe you've had a grandparent die, or another close relative. But none of us knows what it's like to have a dead person in every house at the same time. That's what was going on for the Egyptians, but not for God's people. They were safe. So while all the other people were grieving, God's people packed up and left Egypt. God was working through a horrible situation to save His people. God told them what to do while everyone else was confused. Even when all we see is chaos, God is in control. Trust Him.

and articles of gold." 3And the LORD gave the
people favor in the sight of the Egyptians.
Moreover the man Moses *was* very great in
the land of Egypt, in the sight of Pharaoh's
servants and in the sight of the people.

4Then Moses said, "Thus says the LORD:
'About midnight I will go out into the midst
of Egypt; 5and all the firstborn in the land
of Egypt shall die, from the firstborn of
Pharaoh who sits on his throne, even to the
firstborn of the female servant who *is* behind the handmill, and all the firstborn of
the animals. 6Then there shall be a great cry
throughout all the land of Egypt, such as was
not like it *before,* nor shall be like it again.
7But against none of the children of Israel
shall a dog move its tongue, against man or
beast, that you may know that the LORD does
make a difference between the Egyptians
and Israel.' 8And all these your servants shall
come down to me and bow down to me, saying, 'Get out, and all the people who follow
you!' After that I will go out." Then he went
out from Pharaoh in great anger.

9But the LORD said to Moses, "Pharaoh
will not heed you, so that My wonders may
be multiplied in the land of Egypt." 10So Moses and Aaron did all these wonders before
Pharaoh; and the LORD hardened Pharaoh's
heart, and he did not let the children of Israel go out of his land.

The Passover Instituted

12 Now the LORD spoke to Moses and
Aaron in the land of Egypt, say-
ing, 2"This month *shall be* your beginning
of months; it *shall be* the first month of the
year to you. 3Speak to all the congregation of
Israel, saying: 'On the tenth of this month
every man shall take for himself a lamb,
according to the house of *his* father, a lamb
for a household. 4And if the household is too
small for the lamb, let him and his neighbor next to his house take *it* according to the
number of the persons; according to each
man's need you shall make your count for
the lamb. 5Your lamb shall be without blemish, a male of the first year. You may take *it*
from the sheep or from the goats. 6Now you
shall keep it until the fourteenth day of the
same month. Then the whole assembly of
the congregation of Israel shall kill it at twilight. 7And they shall take *some* of the blood
and put *it* on the two doorposts and on the
lintel of the houses where they eat it. 8Then

In Focus

12:11 Passover The greatest Hebrew celebration. The people remember that the Lord "passed over" their homes in Egypt because a lamb's blood was applied to their doorways (see Exodus 12). After the death of the firstborn in Egypt, Pharaoh freed God's people.

they shall eat the flesh on that night; roasted
in fire, with unleavened bread *and* with bitter *herbs* they shall eat it. 9Do not eat it raw,
nor boiled at all with water, but roasted in
fire—its head with its legs and its entrails.
10You shall let none of it remain until morning, and what remains of it until morning
you shall burn with fire. 11And thus you shall
eat it: *with* a belt on your waist, your sandals
on your feet, and your staff in your hand.
So you shall eat it in haste. It *is* the LORD's
Passover.

12'For I will pass through the land of
Egypt on that night, and will strike all the
firstborn in the land of Egypt, both man and
beast; and against all the gods of Egypt I will
execute judgment: I *am* the LORD. 13Now the
blood shall be a sign for you on the houses
where you *are.* And when I see the blood, I
will pass over you; and the plague shall not
be on you to destroy *you* when I strike the
land of Egypt.

14'So this day shall be to you a memorial;
and you shall keep it as a feast to the LORD
throughout your generations. You shall keep
it as a feast by an everlasting ordinance.
15Seven days you shall eat unleavened bread.
On the first day you shall remove leaven
from your houses. For whoever eats leavened
bread from the first day until the seventh
day, that person shall be cut off from Israel.
16On the first day *there shall be* a holy convocation, and on the seventh day there shall
be a holy convocation for you. No manner of
work shall be done on them; but *that* which
everyone must eat—that only may be prepared by you. 17So you shall observe *the Feast
of* Unleavened Bread, for on this same day
I will have brought your armies out of the

land of Egypt. Therefore you shall observe
this day throughout your generations as an
everlasting ordinance. 18In the first *month,*
on the fourteenth day of the month at evening, you shall eat unleavened bread, until
the twenty-first day of the month at evening.
19For seven days no leaven shall be found in
your houses, since whoever eats what is leavened, that same person shall be cut off from
the congregation of Israel, whether *he is* a
stranger or a native of the land. 20You shall
eat nothing leavened; in all your dwellings
you shall eat unleavened bread.' "

21Then Moses called for all the elders of
Israel and said to them, "Pick out and take
lambs for yourselves according to your families, and kill the Passover *lamb.* 22And you
shall take a bunch of hyssop, dip *it* in the
blood that *is* in the basin, and strike the lintel
and the two doorposts with the blood that *is*
in the basin. And none of you shall go out of
the door of his house until morning. 23For the
LORD will pass through to strike the Egyptians; and when He sees the blood on the lintel and on the two doorposts, the LORD will
pass over the door and not allow the destroyer
to come into your houses to strike *you.* 24And
you shall observe this thing as an ordinance
for you and your sons forever. 25It will come
to pass when you come to the land which the
LORD will give you, just as He promised, that
you shall keep this service. 26And it shall be,
when your children say to you, 'What do you
mean by this service?' 27that you shall say,
'It *is* the Passover sacrifice of the LORD, who
passed over the houses of the children of Israel in Egypt when He struck the Egyptians
and delivered our households.'" So the people bowed their heads and worshiped. 28Then
the children of Israel went away and did *so;*
just as the LORD had commanded Moses and
Aaron, so they did.

The Tenth Plague: Death of the Firstborn

29And it came to pass at midnight that the
LORD struck all the firstborn in the land of
Egypt, from the firstborn of Pharaoh who sat
on his throne to the firstborn of the captive
who *was in the dungeon, and all the firstborn*
of livestock. 30So Pharaoh rose in the night,
he, all his servants, and all the Egyptians;
and there was a great cry in Egypt, for *there*
was not a house where *there was* not one dead.

The Exodus

31Then he called for Moses and Aaron by
night, and said, "Rise, go out from among
my people, both you and the children of
Israel. And go, serve the LORD as you have
said. 32Also take your flocks and your herds,
as you have said, and be gone; and bless me
also."

33And the Egyptians urged the people,
that they might send them out of the land in
haste. For they said, "We *shall* all *be* dead."
34So the people took their dough before it
was leavened, having their kneading bowls
bound up in their clothes on their shoulders. 35Now the children of Israel had done
according to the word of Moses, and they
had asked from the Egyptians articles of silver, articles of gold, and clothing. 36And the
LORD had given the people favor in the sight
of the Egyptians, so that they granted them
what they requested. Thus they plundered the
Egyptians.

37Then the children of Israel journeyed
from Rameses to Succoth, about six hundred
thousand men on foot, besides children. 38A
mixed multitude went up with them also,
and flocks and herds—a great deal of livestock. 39And they baked unleavened cakes
of the dough which they had brought out
of Egypt; for it was not leavened, because
they were driven out of Egypt and could not
wait, nor had they prepared provisions for
themselves.

40Now the sojourn of the children of Israel who lived in Egypt[a] *was* four hundred
and thirty years. 41And it came to pass at the
end of the four hundred and thirty years—
on that very same day—it came to pass that
all the armies of the LORD went out from the
land of Egypt. 42It *is* a night of solemn observance to the LORD for bringing them out of
the land of Egypt. This *is* that night of the
LORD, a solemn observance for all the children of Israel throughout their generations.

Passover Regulations

43And the LORD said to Moses and Aaron, "This *is* the ordinance of the Passover:
No foreigner shall eat it. 44But every man's
servant who is bought for money, when you
have circumcised him, then he may eat it.
45A sojourner and a hired servant shall not

12:40 [a] Samaritan Pentateuch and Septuagint read *Egypt and Canaan.*

eat it. 46In one house it shall be eaten; you
shall not carry any of the flesh outside the
house, nor shall you break one of its bones.
47All the congregation of Israel shall keep it.
48And when a stranger dwells with you *and*
wants to keep the Passover to the LORD, let
all his males be circumcised, and then let
him come near and keep it; and he shall be
as a native of the land. For no uncircumcised
person shall eat it. 49One law shall be for the
native-born and for the stranger who dwells
among you."

50Thus all the children of Israel did; as
the LORD commanded Moses and Aaron,
so they did. 51And it came to pass, on that
very same day, that the LORD brought the
children of Israel out of the land of Egypt
according to their armies.

The Firstborn Consecrated

13 Then the LORD spoke to Moses,
saying, 2"Consecrate to Me all the
firstborn, whatever opens the womb among
the children of Israel, *both* of man and beast;
it is Mine."

The Feast of Unleavened Bread

3And Moses said to the people: "Remember this day in which you went out of Egypt,
out of the house of bondage; for by strength
of hand the LORD brought you out of this
place. No leavened bread shall be eaten. 4On
this day you are going out, in the month
Abib. 5And it shall be, when the LORD brings
you into the land of the Canaanites and the
Hittites and the Amorites and the Hivites
and the Jebusites, which He swore to your
fathers to give you, a land flowing with milk
and honey, that you shall keep this service
in this month. 6Seven days you shall eat
unleavened bread, and on the seventh day
there shall be a feast to the LORD. 7Unleav-
ened bread shall be eaten seven days. And
no leavened bread shall be seen among you,
nor shall leaven be seen among you in all
your quarters. 8And you shall tell your son
in that day, saying, '*This is done* because of
what the LORD did for me when I came up
from Egypt.' 9It shall be as a sign to you on
your hand and as a memorial between your
eyes, that the LORD's law may be in your
mouth; for with a strong hand the LORD has
brought you out of Egypt. 10You shall therefore keep this ordinance in its season from
year to year.

The Law of the Firstborn

11"And it shall be, when the LORD brings
you into the land of the Canaanites, as He
swore to you and your fathers, and gives it to
you, 12that you shall set apart to the LORD all
that open the womb, that is, every firstborn
that comes from an animal which you have;
the males *shall be* the LORD's. 13But every
firstborn of a donkey you shall redeem with a
lamb; and if you will not redeem *it,* then you
shall break its neck. And all the firstborn of
man among your sons you shall redeem. 14So
it shall be, when your son asks you in time to
come, saying, 'What *is* this?' that you shall
say to him, 'By strength of hand the LORD
brought us out of Egypt, out of the house
of bondage. 15And it came to pass, when
Pharaoh was stubborn about letting us go,
that the LORD killed all the firstborn in the
land of Egypt, both the firstborn of man and
the firstborn of beast. Therefore I sacrifice
to the LORD all males that open the womb,
but all the firstborn of my sons I redeem.'
16It shall be as a sign on your hand and as
frontlets between your eyes, for by strength
of hand the LORD brought us out of Egypt."

The Wilderness Way

17Then it came to pass, when Pharaoh
had let the people go, that God did not lead
them *by* way of the land of the Philistines,
although that *was* near; for God said, "Lest
perhaps the people change their minds
when they see war, and return to Egypt."
18So God led the people around *by* way of the
wilderness of the Red Sea. And the children
of Israel went up in orderly ranks out of the
land of Egypt.

19And Moses took the bones of Joseph
with him, for he had placed the children of
Israel under solemn oath, saying, "God will
surely visit you, and you shall carry up my
bones from here with you."[a]

20So they took their journey from Succoth
and camped in Etham at the edge of the wilderness. 21And the LORD went before them
by day in a pillar of cloud to lead the way, and
by night in a pillar of fire to give them light,
so as to go by day and night. 22He did not take
away the pillar of cloud by day or the pillar of
fire by night *from* before the people.

13:19 [a] Genesis 50:25

The Red Sea Crossing

14 Now the LORD spoke to Moses,
saying: 2"Speak to the children of
Israel, that they turn and camp before Pi
Hahiroth, between Migdol and the sea, opposite Baal Zephon; you shall camp before
it by the sea. 3For Pharaoh will say of the
children of Israel, 'They *are* bewildered by
the land; the wilderness has closed them in.'
4Then I will harden Pharaoh's heart, so that
he will pursue them; and I will gain honor
over Pharaoh and over all his army, that the
Egyptians may know that I *am* the LORD."
And they did so.

5Now it was told the king of Egypt that
the people had fled, and the heart of Pharaoh
and his servants was turned against the
people; and they said, "Why have we done
this, that we have let Israel go from serving us?"
6So he made ready his chariot and
took his people with him. 7Also, he took six
hundred choice chariots, and all the chariots of Egypt with captains over every one of
them. 8And the LORD hardened the heart of
Pharaoh king of Egypt, and he pursued the
children of Israel; and the children of Israel
went out with boldness. 9So the Egyptians
pursued them, all the horses *and* chariots of
Pharaoh, his horsemen and his army, and
overtook them camping by the sea beside Pi
Hahiroth, before Baal Zephon.

10And when Pharaoh drew near, the children of Israel lifted their eyes, and behold,
the Egyptians marched after them. So they

GOD DIVIDES THE RED SEA

READ IT: EXODUS 13:17—14:31

GET IT:

The people were on their way to freedom. But God had one more lesson to teach Pharaoh about who was really in charge of heaven and earth. So Moses and the mass of people made a U-turn and camped near the Red Sea. Everything was fine until someone spotted the Egyptian army in the distance. Then—panic! The people were stuck between a sea of water and a sea of soldiers. Pharaoh's army was closing in on them, and they had no way out! But God was there all the time, guarding His people in the pillar of cloud during the day and a pillar of fire at night. Next, God showed His power. He opened up the sea to allow His people to cross on dry ground. He closed it up again when Pharaoh's entire army was in the middle and couldn't escape. Nothing and nobody was going to stop God's plan to save His people.

LIVE IT:

Every once in a while we face obstacles or problems that seem to be totally impossible. All we want to do is scream, "I can't do that!" If that happens, don't panic. Ask God to help. He might work through other people you ask for help. He might clear your head and help you figure it out. He can handle anything. Nothing is impossible for Him—not even *dividing a huge sea so His people could* walk across it and not even get their feet wet! Trust your God—He's the Ruler and Creator of everything in heaven and on earth. He can do it.

were very afraid, and the children of Israel
cried out to the LORD. 11 Then they said to
Moses, "Because *there were* no graves in
Egypt, have you taken us away to die in the
wilderness? Why have you so dealt with us,
to bring us up out of Egypt? 12 *Is* this not the
word that we told you in Egypt, saying, 'Let
us alone that we may serve the Egyptians'?
For *it would have been* better for us to serve
the Egyptians than that we should die in the
wilderness."

13 And Moses said to the people, "Do not
be afraid. Stand still, and see the salvation
of the LORD, which He will accomplish for
you today. For the Egyptians whom you see
today, you shall see again no more forever.
14 The LORD will fight for you, and you shall
hold your peace."

15 And the LORD said to Moses, "Why do
you cry to Me? Tell the children of Israel to
go forward. 16 But lift up your rod, and stretch
out your hand over the sea and divide it. And
the children of Israel shall go on dry *ground*
through the midst of the sea. 17 And I indeed
will harden the hearts of the Egyptians, and
they shall follow them. So I will gain honor
over Pharaoh and over all his army, his chariots, and his horsemen. 18 Then the Egyptians shall know that I *am* the LORD, when I
have gained honor for Myself over Pharaoh,
his chariots, and his horsemen."

19 And the Angel of God, who went before
the camp of Israel, moved and went behind
them; and the pillar of cloud went from before them and stood behind them. 20 So it
came between the camp of the Egyptians
and the camp of Israel. Thus it was a cloud
and darkness *to the one,* and it gave light by
night *to the other,* so that the one did not
come near the other all that night.

21 Then Moses stretched out his hand over
the sea; and the LORD caused the sea to go
back by a strong east wind all that night, and
made the sea into dry *land,* and the waters
were divided. 22 So the children of Israel went
into the midst of the sea on the dry *ground,*
and the waters *were* a wall to them on their
right hand and on their left. 23 And the Egyptians pursued and went after them into the
midst of the sea, all Pharaoh's horses, his
chariots, and his horsemen.

24 Now it came to pass, in the morning
watch, that the LORD looked down upon the
army of the Egyptians through the pillar of

In Focus

14:24 Pillar of Fire and Cloud A special appearance of God. This was one of the ways the invisible God once showed Himself to human eyes.

fire and cloud, and He troubled the army of
the Egyptians. 25 And He took off[a] their chariot wheels, so that they drove them with difficulty; and the Egyptians said, "Let us flee
from the face of Israel, for the LORD fights
for them against the Egyptians."

26 Then the LORD said to Moses, "Stretch
out your hand over the sea, that the waters
may come back upon the Egyptians, on their
chariots, and on their horsemen." 27 And
Moses stretched out his hand over the sea;
and when the morning appeared, the sea
returned to its full depth, while the Egyptians were fleeing into it. So the LORD overthrew the Egyptians in the midst of the sea.
28 Then the waters returned and covered the
chariots, the horsemen, *and* all the army of
Pharaoh that came into the sea after them.
Not so much as one of them remained. 29 But
the children of Israel had walked on dry *land*
in the midst of the sea, and the waters *were*
a wall to them on their right hand and on
their left.

30 So the LORD saved Israel that day out
of the hand of the Egyptians, and Israel saw
the Egyptians dead on the seashore. 31 Thus
Israel saw the great work which the LORD
had done in Egypt; so the people feared the
LORD, and believed the LORD and His servant Moses.

The Song of Moses

15 Then Moses and the children of Israel sang this song to the LORD, and
spoke, saying:

"I will sing to the LORD,
For He has triumphed gloriously!
The horse and its rider
He has thrown into the sea!
2 The LORD *is* my strength and song,

14:25 [a] Samaritan Pentateuch, Septuagint, and Syriac read *bound.*

And He has become my salvation;
He *is* my God, and I will praise Him;
My father's God, and I will exalt Him.
3 The LORD *is* a man of war;
The LORD *is* His name.
4 Pharaoh's chariots and his army He has cast into the sea;
His chosen captains also are drowned in the Red Sea.
5 The depths have covered them;
They sank to the bottom like a stone.

6 "Your right hand, O LORD, has become glorious in power;
Your right hand, O LORD, has dashed the enemy in pieces.
7 And in the greatness of Your excellence
You have overthrown those who rose against You;
You sent forth Your wrath;
It consumed them like stubble.
8 And with the blast of Your nostrils
The waters were gathered together;
The floods stood upright like a heap;
The depths congealed in the heart of the sea.
9 The enemy said, 'I will pursue,
I will overtake,
I will divide the spoil;
My desire shall be satisfied on them.
I will draw my sword,
My hand shall destroy them.'
10 You blew with Your wind,
The sea covered them;
They sank like lead in the mighty waters.

11 "Who *is* like You, O LORD, among the gods?
Who *is* like You, glorious in holiness,
Fearful in praises, doing wonders?
12 You stretched out Your right hand;
The earth swallowed them.
13 You in Your mercy have led forth
The people whom You have redeemed;
You have guided *them* in Your strength
To Your holy habitation.

14 "The people will hear *and* be afraid;
Sorrow will take hold of the inhabitants of Philistia.
15 Then the chiefs of Edom will be dismayed;
The mighty men of Moab,
Trembling will take hold of them;
All the inhabitants of Canaan will melt away.
16 Fear and dread will fall on them;
By the greatness of Your arm
They will be *as* still as a stone,
Till Your people pass over, O LORD,
Till the people pass over
Whom You have purchased.
17 You will bring them in and plant them
In the mountain of Your inheritance,
In the place, O LORD, *which* You have made
For Your own dwelling,
The sanctuary, O Lord, *which* Your hands have established.

18 "The LORD shall reign forever and ever."

19 For the horses of Pharaoh went with his
chariots and his horsemen into the sea, and
the LORD brought back the waters of the sea
upon them. But the children of Israel went
on dry *land* in the midst of the sea.

The Song of Miriam

20 Then Miriam the prophetess, the sister of Aaron, took the timbrel in her hand;
and all the women went out after her with
timbrels and with dances. 21 And Miriam answered them:

"Sing to the LORD,
For He has triumphed gloriously!
The horse and its rider
He has thrown into the sea!"

Bitter Waters Made Sweet

22 So Moses brought Israel from the Red
Sea; then they went out into the Wilderness
of Shur. And they went three days in the
wilderness and found no water. 23 Now when
they came to Marah, they could not drink
the waters of Marah, for they *were* bitter.
Therefore the name of it was called Marah.[a]
24 And the people complained against Moses,
saying, "What shall we drink?" 25 So he cried
out to the LORD, and the LORD showed him
a tree. When he cast *it* into the waters, the
waters were made sweet.

There He made a statute and an ordinance for them, and there He tested them,
26 and said, "If you diligently heed the voice
of the LORD your God and do what is right in
His sight, give ear to His commandments
and keep all His statutes, I will put none of

15:23 [a] Literally *Bitter*

the diseases on you which I have brought on
the Egyptians. For I *am* the LORD who heals
you."
27 Then they came to Elim, where there
were twelve wells of water and seventy palm
trees; so they camped there by the waters.

Bread from Heaven

16 And they journeyed from Elim, and
all the congregation of the children
of Israel came to the Wilderness of Sin,
which is between Elim and Sinai, on the fifteenth day of the second month after they
departed from the land of Egypt. 2 Then the
whole congregation of the children of Israel
complained against Moses and Aaron in the
wilderness. 3 And the children of Israel said
to them, "Oh, that we had died by the hand
of the LORD in the land of Egypt, when we sat
by the pots of meat *and* when we ate bread
to the full! For you have brought us out into
this wilderness to kill this whole assembly
with hunger."
4 Then the LORD said to Moses, "Behold, I
will rain bread from heaven for you. And the
people shall go out and gather a certain quota every day, that I may test them, whether
they will walk in My law or not. 5 And it shall
be on the sixth day that they shall prepare
what they bring in, and it shall be twice as
much as they gather daily."
6 Then Moses and Aaron said to all the
children of Israel, "At evening you shall
know that the LORD has brought you out of
the land of Egypt. 7 And in the morning you
shall see the glory of the LORD; for He hears
your complaints against the LORD. But what

GOD PROVIDES FOOD FROM HEAVEN

READ IT: EXODUS 16:1–35

GET IT:

Only one month after God's people were freed from Egypt, they started complaining. The supplies they had brought with them were gone. Two million people were getting hungry, and there was nothing in the desert to eat. So, like all people, they whined that there wasn't anything good to eat and blamed the person in charge—Moses. Moses didn't even need to ask God for help. God knew the problem and had a solution. He sent food from heaven—bread and quail. But there was one catch. The people could only take what they needed for the day. No hoarding allowed! They needed to learn to rely on God. He would supply what they needed for each day until the day they entered the Promised Land.

LIVE IT:

Most of us don't worry about where our next meal will come from. We have cabinets full of snack food and supplies. We have freezers that hold more meat than we can use in a week. We are super blessed. But in the Lord's Prayer we pray, "Give us this day our daily bread." We ask God to supply food for the day (as He did in the desert). Remember the Israelites in the desert the next time you say those words. God gives us so much more than we deserve or even ask for!

are we, that you complain against us?" 8Also
Moses said, "*This shall be seen* when the
LORD gives you meat to eat in the evening,
and in the morning bread to the full; for
the LORD hears your complaints which you
make against Him. And what *are* we? Your
complaints *are* not against us but against the
LORD."

9Then Moses spoke to Aaron, "Say to all
the congregation of the children of Israel,
'Come near before the LORD, for He has
heard your complaints.'" 10Now it came to
pass, as Aaron spoke to the whole congregation of the children of Israel, that they looked
toward the wilderness, and behold, the glory
of the LORD appeared in the cloud.

11And the LORD spoke to Moses, saying,
12"I have heard the complaints of the children of Israel. Speak to them, saying, 'At twilight you shall eat meat, and in the morning
you shall be filled with bread. And you shall
know that I *am* the LORD your God.'"

13So it was that quail came up at evening
and covered the camp, and in the morning
the dew lay all around the camp. 14And when
the layer of dew lifted, there, on the surface
of the wilderness, was a small round substance, *as* fine as frost on the ground. 15So
when the children of Israel saw *it,* they said
to one another, "What is it?" For they did not
know what it *was.*

And Moses said to them, "This *is* the
bread which the LORD has given you to eat.
16This is the thing which the LORD has commanded: 'Let every man gather it according
to each one's need, one omer for each person, *according to the* number of persons; let
every man take for *those* who *are* in his tent.'"

17Then the children of Israel did so and
gathered, some more, some less. 18So when
they measured *it* by omers, he who gathered much had nothing left over, and he
who gathered little had no lack. Every man
had gathered according to each one's need.
19And Moses said, "Let no one leave any of
it till morning." 20Notwithstanding they did
not heed Moses. But some of them left part
of it until morning, and it bred worms and
stank. And Moses was angry with them. 21So
they gathered it every morning, every man
according to his need. And when the sun became hot, it melted.

22And so it was, on the sixth day, *that* they
gathered twice as much bread, two omers for
each one. And all the rulers of the congregation came and told Moses. 23Then he said
to them, "This *is what* the LORD has said:
'Tomorrow *is* a Sabbath rest, a holy Sabbath
to the LORD. Bake what you will bake *today,*
and boil what you will boil; and lay up for
yourselves all that remains, to be kept until
morning.'" 24So they laid it up till morning,
as Moses commanded; and it did not stink,
nor were there any worms in it. 25Then Moses said, "Eat that today, for today *is* a Sabbath to the LORD; today you will not find it
in the field. 26Six days you shall gather it, but
on the seventh day, the Sabbath, there will
be none."

27Now it happened *that some* of the people went out on the seventh day to gather,
but they found none. 28And the LORD said to
Moses, "How long do you refuse to keep My
commandments and My laws? 29See! For the
LORD has given you the Sabbath; therefore He
gives you on the sixth day bread for two days.
Let every man remain in his place; let no man
go out of his place on the seventh day." 30So
the people rested on the seventh day.

31And the house of Israel called its name
Manna.[a] And it *was* like white coriander
seed, and the taste of it *was* like wafers *made*
with honey.

32Then Moses said, "This *is* the thing
which the LORD has commanded: 'Fill an
omer with it, to be kept for your generations,
that they may see the bread with which I fed
you in the wilderness, when I brought you
out of the land of Egypt.'" 33And Moses said
to Aaron, "Take a pot and put an omer of
manna in it, and lay it up before the LORD,
to be kept for your generations." 34As the
LORD commanded Moses, so Aaron laid it
up before the Testimony, to be kept. 35And
the children of Israel ate manna forty years,
until they came to an inhabited land; they
ate manna until they came to the border of
the land of Canaan. 36Now an omer *is* one-
tenth of an ephah.

Water from the Rock

17 Then all the congregation of the
children of Israel set out on their
journey from the Wilderness of Sin, according to the commandment of the LORD,
and camped in Rephidim; but *there was* no
water for the people to drink. 2Therefore

16:31 [a] Literally *What?* (compare Exodus 16:15)

the people contended with Moses, and said,
"Give us water, that we may drink."
So Moses said to them, "Why do you contend with me? Why do you tempt the LORD?"
3And the people thirsted there for water,
and the people complained against Moses,
and said, "Why *is* it you have brought us up
out of Egypt, to kill us and our children and
our livestock with thirst?"
4So Moses cried out to the LORD, saying,
"What shall I do with this people? They are
almost ready to stone me!"
5And the LORD said to Moses, "Go on before the people, and take with you some of
the elders of Israel. Also take in your hand
your rod with which you struck the river,
and go. 6Behold, I will stand before you there
on the rock in Horeb; and you shall strike
the rock, and water will come out of it, that
the people may drink."
And Moses did so in the sight of the elders of Israel. 7So he called the name of the
place Massah[a] and Meribah,[b] because of the
contention of the children of Israel, and because they tempted the LORD, saying, "Is the
LORD among us or not?"

Victory over the Amalekites

8Now Amalek came and fought with Israel in Rephidim. 9And Moses said to Joshua, "Choose us some men and go out, fight
with Amalek. Tomorrow I will stand on the
top of the hill with the rod of God in my
hand." 10So Joshua did as Moses said to him,
and fought with Amalek. And Moses, Aaron,
and Hur went up to the top of the hill. 11And
so it was, when Moses held up his hand, that
Israel prevailed; and when he let down his
hand, Amalek prevailed. 12But Moses' hands
became heavy; so they took a stone and put
it under him, and he sat on it. And Aaron
and Hur supported his hands, one on one
side, and the other on the other side; and his
hands were steady until the going down of
the sun. 13So Joshua defeated Amalek and
his people with the edge of the sword.
14Then the LORD said to Moses, "Write
this *for* a memorial in the book and recount
it in the hearing of Joshua, that I will utterly blot out the remembrance of Amalek
from under heaven." 15And Moses built an
altar and called its name, The-LORD-Is-My-
Banner;[a] 16for he said, "Because the LORD
has sworn: the LORD *will have* war with Amalek from generation to generation."

Jethro's Advice

18 And Jethro, the priest of Midian,
Moses' father-in-law, heard of all
that God had done for Moses and for Israel
His people—that the LORD had brought
Israel out of Egypt. 2Then Jethro, Moses'
father-in-law, took Zipporah, Moses' wife,
after he had sent her back, 3with her two
sons, of whom the name of one *was* Gershom (for he said, "I have been a stranger in
a foreign land")[a] 4and the name of the other *was* Eliezer[a] (for *he said,* "The God of my
father *was* my help, and delivered me from
the sword of Pharaoh"); 5and Jethro, Moses' father-in-law, came with his sons and
his wife to Moses in the wilderness, where
he was encamped at the mountain of God.
6Now he had said to Moses, "I, your father-
in-law Jethro, am coming to you with your
wife and her two sons with her."
7So Moses went out to meet his father-
in-law, bowed down, and kissed him. And
they asked each other about *their* well-being,
and they went into the tent. 8And Moses told
his father-in-law all that the LORD had done
to Pharaoh and to the Egyptians for Israel's
sake, all the hardship that had come upon
them on the way, and *how* the LORD had delivered them. 9Then Jethro rejoiced for all
the good which the LORD had done for Israel, whom He had delivered out of the hand
of the Egyptians. 10And Jethro said, "Blessed
be the LORD, who has delivered you out of the
hand of the Egyptians and out of the hand
of Pharaoh, *and* who has delivered the people from under the hand of the Egyptians.
11Now I know that the LORD *is* greater than
all the gods; for in the very thing in which
they behaved proudly, *He was* above them."
12Then Jethro, Moses' father-in-law, took[a] a
burnt offering and *other* sacrifices *to offer* to
God. And Aaron came with all the elders of
Israel to eat bread with Moses' father-in-law
before God.
13And so it was, on the next day, that Moses sat to judge the people; and the people
stood before Moses from morning until
evening. 14So when Moses' father-in-law
saw all that he did for the people, he said,

17:7 [a] Literally *Tempted* [b] Literally *Contention*
17:15 [a] Hebrew *YHWH Nissi* 18:3 [a] Compare Exodus 2:22
18:4 [a] Literally *My God Is Help* 18:12 [a] Following Masoretic Text and Septuagint; Syriac, Targum, and Vulgate read *offered.*

"What *is* this thing that you are doing for
the people? Why do you alone sit, and all the
people stand before you from morning until
evening?"
15And Moses said to his father-in-law,
"Because the people come to me to inquire
of God. 16When they have a difficulty, they
come to me, and I judge between one and
another; and I make known the statutes of
God and His laws."
17So Moses' father-in-law said to him,
"The thing that you do *is* not good. 18Both
you and these people who *are* with you will
surely wear yourselves out. For this thing *is*
too much for you; you are not able to perform
it by yourself. 19Listen now to my voice; I will

WISDOM

WISE GUY

READ IT: EXODUS 18:1–27

GET IT:

Moses' father-in-law was named Jethro (isn't that an awesome name?). In this story Jethro shows great wisdom two times.

There's a difference between being smart and having wisdom. Being smart is about intelligence. That's nice to have, but it's not necessary for wisdom. Wisdom is all about knowing how to live; it's about making great choices based on what you know to be true.

First, Jethro hears about the fantastic rescue of the Hebrew slaves from the horrible treatment of Pharaoh, and his wise response is to give God all the credit. He doesn't look for other explanations, and he doesn't assume it's because Moses is "smart." Instead, Jethro worships God. In fact, it seems that, at this point, Jethro fully turns to God, rejecting other gods.

Then Jethro gives some super-wise advice to Moses, after seeing Moses try to be the only person helping the people make good choices and resolve differences. Jethro can tell that Moses is going to get worn out—there are too many people, and the job is too big. So Jethro recommends that Moses appoint some other leaders to share the work.

Jethro's wisdom is a great example to us. He shows us the wisdom of giving God credit and the wisdom of making decisions that are good for other people.

LIVE IT:

We can't make ourselves wiser, unfortunately. Sure, we are capable of good decisions (and bad decisions). But God gives wisdom.

So if you want to live the best life—a wise life—ask God to give you *wisdom. Make it a regular prayer.* This would be a great prayer to pray every morning: "God, give me wisdom today, so I can give You the credit and make great choices that help other people."

give you counsel, and God will be with you:
Stand before God for the people, so that you
may bring the difficulties to God. 20And you
shall teach them the statutes and the laws,
and show them the way in which they must
walk and the work they must do. 21Moreover
you shall select from all the people able men,
such as fear God, men of truth, hating covetousness; and place *such* over them *to be* rulers of thousands, rulers of hundreds, rulers
of fifties and rulers of tens. 22And let them
judge the people at all times. Then it will be
that every great matter they shall bring to
you, but every small matter they themselves
shall judge. So it will be easier for you, for
they will bear *the burden* with you. 23If you do
this thing, and God *so* commands you, then
you will be able to endure, and all this people
will also go to their place in peace."

24So Moses heeded the voice of his father-
in-law and did all that he had said. 25And
Moses chose able men out of all Israel, and
made them heads over the people: rulers
of thousands, rulers of hundreds, rulers of
fifties, and rulers of tens. 26So they judged
the people at all times; the hard cases they
brought to Moses, but they judged every
small case themselves.

27Then Moses let his father-in-law depart,
and he went his way to his own land.

Israel at Mount Sinai

19 In the third month after the children of Israel had gone out of the
land of Egypt, on the same day, they came
to the Wilderness of Sinai. 2For they had
departed from Rephidim, had come *to* the
Wilderness of Sinai, and camped in the wilderness. So Israel camped there before the
mountain.

3And Moses went up to God, and the
LORD called to him from the mountain, saying, "Thus you shall say to the house of Jacob, and tell the children of Israel: 4'You have
seen what I did to the Egyptians, and *how* I
bore you on eagles' wings and brought you
to Myself. 5Now therefore, if you will indeed
obey My voice and keep My covenant, then
you shall be a special treasure to Me above
all people; for all the earth *is* Mine. 6And you
shall be to Me a kingdom of priests and a
holy nation.' These *are* the words which you
shall speak to the children of Israel."

7So Moses came and called for the elders
of the people, and laid before them all these
words which the LORD commanded him.
8Then all the people answered together and
said, "All that the LORD has spoken we will
do." So Moses brought back the words of the
people to the LORD. 9And the LORD said to
Moses, "Behold, I come to you in the thick
cloud, that the people may hear when I
speak with you, and believe you forever."

So Moses told the words of the people to
the LORD.

10Then the LORD said to Moses, "Go to
the people and consecrate them today and
tomorrow, and let them wash their clothes.
11And let them be ready for the third day. For
on the third day the LORD will come down
upon Mount Sinai in the sight of all the people. 12You shall set bounds for the people all
around, saying, 'Take heed to yourselves *that*
you do *not* go up to the mountain or touch its
base. Whoever touches the mountain shall
surely be put to death. 13Not a hand shall
touch him, but he shall surely be stoned or
shot *with an arrow;* whether man or beast,
he shall not live.' When the trumpet sounds
long, they shall come near the mountain."

14So Moses went down from the mountain to the people and sanctified the people,
and they washed their clothes. 15And he said
to the people, "Be ready for the third day; do
not come near *your* wives."

16Then it came to pass on the third day,
in the morning, that there were thunderings and lightnings, and a thick cloud on
the mountain; and the sound of the trumpet
was very loud, so that all the people who *were*
in the camp trembled. 17And Moses brought
the people out of the camp to meet with
God, and they stood at the foot of the mountain. 18Now Mount Sinai *was* completely in
smoke, because the LORD descended upon it
in fire. Its smoke ascended like the smoke of
a furnace, and the whole mountain[a] quaked
greatly. 19And when the blast of the trumpet
sounded long and became louder and louder, Moses spoke, and God answered him by
voice. 20Then the LORD came down upon
Mount Sinai, on the top of the mountain.
And the LORD called Moses to the top of the
mountain, and Moses went up.

21And the LORD said to Moses, "Go down
and warn the people, lest they break through
to gaze at the LORD, and many of them perish. 22Also let the priests who come near the

19:18 [a] Septuagint reads *all the people.*

LORD consecrate themselves, lest the LORD
break out against them."
23But Moses said to the LORD, "The people cannot come up to Mount Sinai; for You
warned us, saying, 'Set bounds around the
mountain and consecrate it.'"
24Then the LORD said to him, "Away! Get
down and then come up, you and Aaron with
you. But do not let the priests and the people
break through to come up to the LORD, lest
He break out against them." 25So Moses went
down to the people and spoke to them.

The Ten Commandments

20 And God spoke all these words, saying:

2 "I *am* the LORD your God, who brought
you out of the land of Egypt, out of the
house of bondage.
3 "You shall have no other gods before Me.
4 "You shall not make for yourself a carved
image—any likeness *of anything* that
is in heaven above, or that *is* in the
earth beneath, or that *is* in the water
under the earth; 5you shall not bow
down to them nor serve them. For
I, the LORD your God, *am* a jealous
God, visiting the iniquity of the fathers upon the children to the third
and fourth *generations* of those who
hate Me, 6but showing mercy to thousands, to those who love Me and keep
My commandments.
7 "You shall not take the name of the LORD
your God in vain, for the LORD will

RULES FOR HOLY LIVING

READ IT: EXODUS 19:16—20:21

GET IT:

"Get ready, everybody. God's coming to talk to us!" Yikes! Scary thought. God would speak once He got everyone's attention. He made it very, very clear to the people through their senses that this was serious stuff. They saw it (smoke and fire on the mountain), they felt it (the mountain shook), and they heard it (loud trumpet blaring). Then God gave them ten rules for living for their own good (Deuteronomy 6:24). The rules would keep them close to God and far from sin. The rules would give them happy and long lives, peace, and freedom.

LIVE IT:

Most of the time we don't like rules. They all sound like "the don'ts" in life. And we just don't like limits. But God's rules—the Ten Commandments—are clearly stated for our good. They apply to us today as much as they applied to the Israelites long ago. God wants His people to live holy, happy lives. He wants to be with them and have a relationship with them. But God is a holy God, and His people need to be holy, too.

The rules may sound strange to you. They are different from how we talk today. Some are very clear; some aren't. So you might want to study *them and then rewrite them for your life.* Try rewriting them positively—state what you *should do* to get a new view of these best rules for living a happy life.

not hold *him* guiltless who takes His
name in vain.
8 "Remember the Sabbath day, to keep it
holy. [9]Six days you shall labor and do
all your work, [10]but the seventh day *is*
the Sabbath of the LORD your God. *In*
it you shall do no work: you, nor your
son, nor your daughter, nor your male
servant, nor your female servant, nor
your cattle, nor your stranger who *is*
within your gates. [11]For *in* six days
the LORD made the heavens and the

Action!

FAMILY

READ IT: EXODUS 20:12

What does *honor* mean? One way to think of it is showing someone respect simply because of the position he or she has in your life—like a parent. This can be really hard when you're frustrated or angry with your mom or dad, stepmom or stepdad. But God doesn't give a list of exceptions for honoring parents—He simply says to do it.

It can be difficult to honor your parents without God's help. And depending on your parents' relationship with God, what they do and say might be different from what you believe. God still says to honor them. But God doesn't ask you to disobey Him as you honor your parents. If what your parents are asking you to do seems to go against God's Word, try talking to a trusted adult or pastor to get his or her counsel.

Action!

STEALING IS A SIN

READ IT: EXODUS 20:15

It's an unhappy fact that some people steal the things that belong to others. Sin breaks God's loving arrangements for our lives, and the sin of stealing causes special suffering. If you love someone, you care about everything in that person's life, including his belongings.

God has given us the privilege of having property, whether it is a little or a lot. If you love your next-door neighbor, you are careful not to dump trash on the lawn or do other things that take away the privilege of your neighbor enjoying that home. To do such things is a kind of stealing. The less people love God, the less they love their neighbors, and the less they care about their neighbors' property.

Wouldn't it be a wonderful world if we all cared as much about our neighbors' things as we care about our own things? That's what God really means when He says, "You shall not steal."

earth, the sea, and all that *is* in them, and rested the seventh day. Therefore the LORD blessed the Sabbath day and hallowed it.

12 "Honor your father and your mother, that your days may be long upon the land which the LORD your God is giving you.

13 "You shall not murder.

14 "You shall not commit adultery.

15 "You shall not steal.

16 "You shall not bear false witness against your neighbor.

17 "You shall not covet your neighbor's house; you shall not covet your neighbor's wife, nor his male servant, nor his female servant, nor his ox, nor his donkey, nor anything that *is* your neighbor's."

The People Afraid of God's Presence

18Now all the people witnessed the thunderings, the lightning flashes, the sound of
the trumpet, and the mountain smoking;
and when the people saw *it,* they trembled
and stood afar off. 19Then they said to Moses,
"You speak with us, and we will hear; but let
not God speak with us, lest we die."

20And Moses said to the people, "Do not
fear; for God has come to test you, and that
His fear may be before you, so that you may
not sin." 21So the people stood afar off, but
Moses drew near the thick darkness where
God *was.*

The Law of the Altar

22Then the LORD said to Moses, "Thus
you shall say to the children of Israel: 'You
have seen that I have talked with you from
heaven. 23You shall not make *anything to be*
with Me—gods of silver or gods of gold you
shall not make for yourselves. 24An altar of
earth you shall make for Me, and you shall
sacrifice on it your burnt offerings and your
peace offerings, your sheep and your oxen.
In every place where I record My name I will
come to you, and I will bless you. 25And if
you make Me an altar of stone, you shall not
build it of hewn stone; for if you use your
tool on it, you have profaned it. 26Nor shall
you go up by steps to My altar, that your nakedness may not be exposed on it.'

The Law Concerning Servants

21 "Now these *are* the judgments
which you shall set before them: 2If
you buy a Hebrew servant, he shall serve six
years; and in the seventh he shall go out free
and pay nothing. 3If he comes in by himself,
he shall go out by himself; if he *comes in*
married, then his wife shall go out with him.
4If his master has given him a wife, and she
has borne him sons or daughters, the wife
and her children shall be her master's, and
he shall go out by himself. 5But if the servant
plainly says, 'I love my master, my wife, and
my children; I will not go out free,' 6then his
master shall bring him to the judges. He
shall also bring him to the door, or to the
doorpost, and his master shall pierce his ear
with an awl; and he shall serve him forever.

HONESTY

READ IT: EXODUS 20:16

You know God means business when He puts something smack-dab in the Ten Commandments. The Ten Commandments are like the CliffsNotes to living life. Simply put, "You shall not bear false witness against your neighbor" means this: don't lie to people. Don't tell anyone anything that isn't true, whether it's about yourself, your circumstances, your stuff, or anything else. And even if you think something is true, check again, especially if it's about someone else. Gossip is no good either.

[7]"And if a man sells his daughter to be a
female slave, she shall not go out as the male
slaves do. [8]If she does not please her master,
who has betrothed her to himself, then he
shall let her be redeemed. He shall have no
right to sell her to a foreign people, since he
has dealt deceitfully with her. [9]And if he has
betrothed her to his son, he shall deal with
her according to the custom of daughters. [10]If
he takes another *wife,* he shall not diminish
her food, her clothing, and her marriage
rights. [11]And if he does not do these three
for her, then she shall go out free, without
paying money.

The Law Concerning Violence

[12]"He who strikes a man so that he dies
shall surely be put to death. [13]However, if he
did not lie in wait, but God delivered *him*
into his hand, then I will appoint for you a
place where he may flee.

[14]"But if a man acts with premeditation
against his neighbor, to kill him by treachery, you shall take him from My altar, that
he may die.

[15]"And he who strikes his father or his
mother shall surely be put to death.

[16]"He who kidnaps a man and sells him,
or if he is found in his hand, shall surely be
put to death.

[17]"And he who curses his father or his
mother shall surely be put to death.

[18]"If men contend with each other, and
one strikes the other with a stone or with *his*
fist, and he does not die but is confined to
his bed, [19]if he rises again and walks about
outside with his staff, then he who struck
him shall be acquitted. He shall only pay *for*
the loss of his time, and shall provide *for him*
to be thoroughly healed.

[20]"And if a man beats his male or female
servant with a rod, so that he dies under his
hand, he shall surely be punished. [21]Not-
withstanding, if he remains alive a day or
two, he shall not be punished; for he *is* his
property.

[22]"If men fight, and hurt a woman with
child, so that she gives birth prematurely, yet
no harm follows, he shall surely be punished
accordingly as the woman's husband imposes on him; and he shall pay as the judges
determine. [23]But if *any* harm follows, then
you shall give life for life, [24]eye for eye, tooth

LYING IS A SIN

READ IT: EXODUS 20:16

God Himself is the greatest Truth. So God also loves the truth.

Lies bring confusion and pain. When people no longer care about the truth, they stop being like God, and they make God's world an unhappy place to live in.

Lying about a neighbor is especially wrong. Such lies can ruin one's good name, and no one will trust that person anymore. Think what happens when someone accuses an innocent person of murder or some other crime. Even though that person is innocent, he may suffer just as much as if he is guilty. Lies have great power to destroy people. The old saying, "Sticks and stones may break my bones, but names can never hurt me," just isn't true!

The greatest guard against lying is to love the truth and to tell the truth as often as we can. Be quick to praise someone when he or she does something good. Always be ready to tell people the truth about Jesus. In fact, Jesus said, "I am . . . the truth" (John 14:6).

for tooth, hand for hand, foot for foot, [25]burn
for burn, wound for wound, stripe for stripe.
[26]"If a man strikes the eye of his male or
female servant, and destroys it, he shall let
him go free for the sake of his eye. [27]And if
he knocks out the tooth of his male or female servant, he shall let him go free for the
sake of his tooth.

Animal Control Laws

[28]"If an ox gores a man or a woman to
death, then the ox shall surely be stoned,
and its flesh shall not be eaten; but the owner of the ox *shall be* acquitted. [29]But if the ox
tended to thrust with its horn in times past,
and it has been made known to his owner,
and he has not kept it confined, so that it
has killed a man or a woman, the ox shall
be stoned and its owner also shall be put to
death. [30]If there is imposed on him a sum of
money, then he shall pay to redeem his life,
whatever is imposed on him. [31]Whether it
has gored a son or gored a daughter, according to this judgment it shall be done to him.
[32]If the ox gores a male or female servant, he
shall give to their master thirty shekels of
silver, and the ox shall be stoned.
[33]"And if a man opens a pit, or if a man
digs a pit and does not cover it, and an ox or a
donkey falls in it, [34]the owner of the pit shall
make *it* good; he shall give money to their
owner, but the dead *animal* shall be his.
[35]"If one man's ox hurts another's, so that
it dies, then they shall sell the live ox and divide the money from it; and the dead *ox* they
shall also divide. [36]Or if it was known that
the ox tended to thrust in time past, and its
owner has not kept it confined, he shall surely pay ox for ox, and the dead animal shall
be his own.

Responsibility for Property

22 "If a man steals an ox or a sheep,
and slaughters it or sells it, he
shall restore five oxen for an ox and four
sheep for a sheep. [2]If the thief is found
breaking in, and he is struck so that he dies,
there shall be no guilt for his bloodshed. [3]If
the sun has risen on him, *there shall be* guilt
for his bloodshed. He should make full restitution; if he has nothing, then he shall be
sold for his theft. [4]If the theft is certainly
found alive in his hand, whether it is an ox
or donkey or sheep, he shall restore double.
[5]"If a man causes a field or vineyard to
be grazed, and lets loose his animal, and it
feeds in another man's field, he shall make
restitution from the best of his own field and
the best of his own vineyard.
[6]"If fire breaks out and catches in thorns,
so that stacked grain, standing grain, or the
field is consumed, he who kindled the fire
shall surely make restitution.
[7]"If a man delivers to his neighbor money
or articles to keep, and it is stolen out of the
man's house, if the thief is found, he shall
pay double. [8]If the thief is not found, then
the master of the house shall be brought to
the judges *to see* whether he has put his hand
into his neighbor's goods.
[9]"For any kind of trespass, *whether it concerns* an ox, a donkey, a sheep, or clothing,
or for any kind of lost thing which *another*
claims to be his, the cause of both parties
shall come before the judges; *and* whomever
the judges condemn shall pay double to his
neighbor. [10]If a man delivers to his neighbor
a donkey, an ox, a sheep, or any animal to
keep, and it dies, is hurt, or driven away, no
one seeing *it,* [11]*then* an oath of the LORD shall
be between them both, that he has not put
his hand into his neighbor's goods; and the
owner of it shall accept *that,* and he shall not
make *it* good. [12]But if, in fact, it is stolen from
him, he shall make restitution to the owner
of it. [13]If it is torn to pieces *by a beast, then* he
shall bring it as evidence, *and* he shall not
make good what was torn.
[14]"And if a man borrows *anything* from
his neighbor, and it becomes injured or
dies, the owner of it not *being* with it, he shall
surely make *it* good. [15]If its owner *was* with
it, he shall not make *it* good; if it *was* hired, it
came for its hire.

Moral and Ceremonial Principles

[16]"If a man entices a virgin who is not betrothed, and lies with her, he shall surely pay
the bride-price for her *to be* his wife. [17]If her
father utterly refuses to give her to him, he
shall pay money according to the bride-price
of virgins.
[18]"You shall not permit a sorceress to live.
[19]"Whoever lies with an animal shall
surely be put to death.
[20]"He who sacrifices to any god, except to
the LORD only, he shall be utterly destroyed.
[21]"You shall neither mistreat a stranger
nor oppress him, for you were strangers in
the land of Egypt.

22“You shall not afflict any widow or fatherless child. 23If you afflict them in any
way, *and* they cry at all to Me, I will surely
hear their cry; 24and My wrath will become
hot, and I will kill you with the sword; your
wives shall be widows, and your children
fatherless.
25“If you lend money to *any of* My people
who are poor among you, you shall not be
like a moneylender to him; you shall not
charge him interest. 26If you ever take your
neighbor's garment as a pledge, you shall
return it to him before the sun goes down.
27For that *is* his only covering, it *is* his garment for his skin. What will he sleep in?
And it will be that when he cries to Me, I
will hear, for I *am* gracious.
28“You shall not revile God, nor curse a
ruler of your people.
29“You shall not delay *to offer* the first
of your ripe produce and your juices. The
firstborn of your sons you shall give to Me.
30Likewise you shall do with your oxen *and*
your sheep. It shall be with its mother sev-
en days; on the eighth day you shall give it
to Me.
31“And you shall be holy men to Me: you
shall not eat meat torn *by beasts* in the field;
you shall throw it to the dogs.

Justice for All

23 “You shall not circulate a false report. Do not put your hand with
the wicked to be an unrighteous witness.
2You shall not follow a crowd to do evil; nor
shall you testify in a dispute so as to turn
aside after many to pervert *justice*. 3You
shall not show partiality to a poor man in
his dispute.
4“If you meet your enemy's ox or his
donkey going astray, you shall surely bring
it back to him again. 5If you see the donkey
of one who hates you lying under its burden,
and you would refrain from helping it, you
shall surely help him with it.
6“You shall not pervert the judgment of
your poor in his dispute. 7Keep yourself far
from a false matter; do not kill the innocent
and righteous. For I will not justify the wicked. 8And you shall take no bribe, for a bribe
blinds the discerning and perverts the words
of the righteous.
9“Also you shall not oppress a stranger,
for you know the heart of a stranger, because
you were strangers in the land of Egypt.

In Focus

23:16 Firstfruits Israel's offering to God at the Feast of Harvest. They gave God the first and best of their work. Our first and best also belong to God.

The Law of Sabbaths

10“Six years you shall sow your land and
gather in its produce, 11but the seventh *year*
you shall let it rest and lie fallow, that the
poor of your people may eat; and what they
leave, the beasts of the field may eat. In like
manner you shall do with your vineyard
and your olive grove. 12Six days you shall do
your work, and on the seventh day you shall
rest, that your ox and your donkey may rest,
and the son of your female servant and the
stranger may be refreshed.
13“And in all that I have said to you, be
circumspect and make no mention of the
name of other gods, nor let it be heard from
your mouth.

Three Annual Feasts

14“Three times you shall keep a feast to
Me in the year: 15You shall keep the Feast of
Unleavened Bread (you shall eat unleavened
bread seven days, as I commanded you, at
the time appointed in the month of Abib,
for in it you came out of Egypt; none shall
appear before Me empty); 16and the Feast of
Harvest, the firstfruits of your labors which
you have sown in the field; and the Feast of
Ingathering at the end of the year, when you
have gathered in *the fruit of* your labors from
the field.
17“Three times in the year all your males
shall appear before the Lord GOD.[a]
18“You shall not offer the blood of My sacrifice with leavened bread; nor shall the fat
of My sacrifice remain until morning. 19The
first of the firstfruits of your land you shall
bring into the house of the LORD your God.
You shall not boil a young goat in its mother's milk.

23:17 [a] Hebrew *YHWH*, usually translated *LORD*

In Focus

24:12 Law The words of God that we must live by. Sometimes the law refers to the Ten Commandments. At other times it includes all things that God says in the Scriptures.

25:17 Mercy Seat A flat gold lid that covered the top of the ark of the covenant. God revealed Himself in a cloud and fire over the mercy seat.

The Angel and the Promises

20“Behold, I send an Angel before you to
keep you in the way and to bring you into
the place which I have prepared. 21Beware
of Him and obey His voice; do not provoke
Him, for He will not pardon your transgressions; for My name *is* in Him. 22But if you
indeed obey His voice and do all that I speak,
then I will be an enemy to your enemies and
an adversary to your adversaries. 23For My
Angel will go before you and bring you in to
the Amorites and the Hittites and the Perizzites and the Canaanites and the Hivites and
the Jebusites; and I will cut them off. 24You
shall not bow down to their gods, nor serve
them, nor do according to their works; but
you shall utterly overthrow them and completely break down their *sacred* pillars.
25“So you shall serve the LORD your God,
and He will bless your bread and your water.
And I will take sickness away from the midst
of you. 26No one shall suffer miscarriage or
be barren in your land; I will fulfill the number of your days.
27“I will send My fear before you, I will
cause confusion among all the people to
whom you come, and will make all your enemies turn *their* backs to you. 28And I will send
hornets before you, which shall drive out the
Hivite, the Canaanite, and the Hittite from
before you. 29I will not drive them out from
before you in one year, lest the land become
desolate and the beasts of the field become
too numerous for you. 30Little by little I will
drive them out from before you, until you
have increased, and you inherit the land.
31And I will set your bounds from the Red Sea
to the sea, Philistia, and from the desert to
the River.[a] For I will deliver the inhabitants of
the land into your hand, and you shall drive
them out before you. 32You shall make no covenant with them, nor with their gods. 33They
shall not dwell in your land, lest they make
you sin against Me. For *if* you serve their
gods, it will surely be a snare to you.”

Israel Affirms the Covenant

24 Now He said to Moses, “Come up
to the LORD, you and Aaron, Na-
dab and Abihu, and seventy of the elders of
Israel, and worship from afar. 2And Moses
alone shall come near the LORD, but they
shall not come near; nor shall the people go
up with him.”
3So Moses came and told the people all
the words of the LORD and all the judgments.
And all the people answered with one voice
and said, “All the words which the LORD has
said we will do.” 4And Moses wrote all the
words of the LORD. And he rose early in the
morning, and built an altar at the foot of
the mountain, and twelve pillars according
to the twelve tribes of Israel. 5Then he sent
young men of the children of Israel, who
offered burnt offerings and sacrificed peace
offerings of oxen to the LORD. 6And Moses
took half the blood and put *it* in basins,
and half the blood he sprinkled on the altar. 7Then he took the Book of the Covenant
and read in the hearing of the people. And
they said, “All that the LORD has said we will
do, and be obedient.” 8And Moses took the
blood, sprinkled *it* on the people, and said,
“This is the blood of the covenant which the
LORD has made with you according to all
these words.”

On the Mountain with God

9Then Moses went up, also Aaron, Nadab, and Abihu, and seventy of the elders of
Israel, 10and they saw the God of Israel. And
there was under His feet as it were a paved
work of sapphire stone, and it was like the
very heavens in *its* clarity. 11But on the nobles of the children of Israel He did not lay
His hand. So they saw God, and they ate and
drank.
12Then the LORD said to Moses, “Come
up to Me on the mountain and be there; and

23:31 [a] Hebrew *Nahar,* the Euphrates

I will give you tablets of stone, and the law
and commandments which I have written,
that you may teach them."
[13]So Moses arose with his assistant Joshua, and Moses went up to the mountain of
God. [14]And he said to the elders, "Wait here
for us until we come back to you. Indeed,
Aaron and Hur *are* with you. If any man has
a difficulty, let him go to them." [15]Then Moses went up into the mountain, and a cloud
covered the mountain.
[16]Now the glory of the LORD rested on
Mount Sinai, and the cloud covered it six
days. And on the seventh day He called to
Moses out of the midst of the cloud. [17]The
sight of the glory of the LORD *was* like a consuming fire on the top of the mountain in
the eyes of the children of Israel. [18]So Moses
went into the midst of the cloud and went up
into the mountain. And Moses was on the
mountain forty days and forty nights.

Offerings for the Sanctuary

25 Then the LORD spoke to Moses,
saying: [2]"Speak to the children
of Israel, that they bring Me an offering.
From everyone who gives it willingly with
his heart you shall take My offering. [3]And
this *is* the offering which you shall take
from them: gold, silver, and bronze; [4]blue,
purple, and scarlet *thread,* fine linen, and
goats' *hair;* [5]ram skins dyed red, badger
skins, and acacia wood; [6]oil for the light, and
spices for the anointing oil and for the sweet
incense; [7]onyx stones, and stones to be set
in the ephod and in the breastplate. [8]And let
them make Me a sanctuary, that I may dwell
among them. [9]According to all that I show
you, *that is,* the pattern of the tabernacle and
the pattern of all its furnishings, just so you
shall make *it.*

The Ark of the Testimony

[10]"And they shall make an ark of acacia wood; two and a half cubits *shall be* its
length, a cubit and a half its width, and a cubit and a half its height. [11]And you shall overlay it with pure gold, inside and out you shall
overlay it, and shall make on it a molding of
gold all around. [12]You shall cast four rings
of gold for it, and put *them* in its four corners; two rings *shall be* on one side, and two
rings on the other side. [13]And you shall make
poles *of* acacia wood, and overlay them with
gold. [14]You shall put the poles into the rings

In Focus

25:22 Ark of the Testimony A gold-covered wooden chest about 45 inches long by 27 inches wide by 27 inches high. The chest first contained the Ten Commandments, but later also contained some manna and Aaron's wooden staff (see Exodus 16:33 and Numbers 17:10).

25:23 Table of Showbread A table about 36 inches long by 18 inches wide by 27 inches high. Every Sabbath 12 loaves of bread were arranged on the table. They were a symbol of God's presence and supply.

25:31 Lampstand An ornate, gold lamp of seven branches. It was a symbol of God's presence in what was called the Holy Place of Israel's place of worship.

on the sides of the ark, that the ark may be
carried by them. [15]The poles shall be in the
rings of the ark; they shall not be taken from
it. [16]And you shall put into the ark the Testimony which I will give you.
[17]"You shall make a mercy seat of pure
gold; two and a half cubits *shall be* its length
and a cubit and a half its width. [18]And you
shall make two cherubim of gold; of hammered work you shall make them at the two
ends of the mercy seat. [19]Make one cherub at
one end, and the other cherub at the other
end; you shall make the cherubim at the two
ends of it *of one piece* with the mercy seat.
[20]And the cherubim shall stretch out *their*
wings above, covering the mercy seat with
their wings, and they shall face one another;
the faces of the cherubim *shall be* toward the
mercy seat. [21]You shall put the mercy seat
on top of the ark, and in the ark you shall
put the Testimony that I will give you. [22]And
there I will meet with you, and I will speak
with you from above the mercy seat, from
between the two cherubim which *are* on
the ark of the Testimony, about everything

which I will give you in commandment to
the children of Israel.

The Table for the Showbread

23“You shall also make a table of acacia
wood; two cubits *shall be* its length, a cubit
its width, and a cubit and a half its height.
24And you shall overlay it with pure gold, and
make a molding of gold all around. 25You
shall make for it a frame of a handbreadth
all around, and you shall make a gold molding for the frame all around. 26And you shall
make for it four rings of gold, and put the
rings on the four corners that *are* at its four
legs. 27The rings shall be close to the frame,
as holders for the poles to bear the table.
28And you shall make the poles of acacia
wood, and overlay them with gold, that the
table may be carried with them. 29You shall
make its dishes, its pans, its pitchers, and its
bowls for pouring. You shall make them of
pure gold. 30And you shall set the showbread
on the table before Me always.

The Gold Lampstand

31“You shall also make a lampstand of
pure gold; the lampstand shall be of hammered work. Its shaft, its branches, its bowls,
its *ornamental* knobs, and flowers shall be
of one piece. 32And six branches shall come
out of its sides: three branches of the lampstand out of one side, and three branches of
the lampstand out of the other side. 33Three
bowls *shall be* made like almond *blossoms* on
one branch, *with* an *ornamental* knob and a
flower, and three bowls made like almond
blossoms on the other branch, *with* an *ornamental* knob and a flower—and so for the six
branches that come out of the lampstand.
34On the lampstand itself four bowls *shall be*
made like almond *blossoms, each with* its *ornamental* knob and flower. 35And *there shall
be* a knob under the *first* two branches of the
same, a knob under the *second* two branches
of the same, and a knob under the *third* two
branches of the same, according to the six
branches that extend from the lampstand.
36Their knobs and their branches *shall be
of one piece;* all of it *shall be* one hammered
piece of pure gold. 37You shall make seven
lamps for it, and they shall *arrange its lamps*
so that they give light in front of it. 38And
its wick-trimmers and their trays *shall be*
of pure gold. 39It shall be made of a talent of
pure gold, with all these utensils. 40And see
to it that you make *them* according to the pattern which was shown you on the mountain.

The Tabernacle

26 “Moreover you shall make the tabernacle *with* ten curtains *of* fine
woven linen and blue, purple, and scarlet
thread; with artistic designs of cherubim
you shall weave them. 2The length of each
curtain *shall be* twenty-eight cubits, and the
width of each curtain four cubits. And every
one of the curtains shall have the same measurements. 3Five curtains shall be coupled
to one another, and *the other* five curtains
shall be coupled to one another. 4And you
shall make loops of blue *yarn* on the edge of
the curtain on the selvedge of *one* set, and
likewise you shall do on the outer edge of *the
other* curtain of the second set. 5Fifty loops
you shall make in the one curtain, and fifty loops you shall make on the edge of the
curtain that *is* on the end of the second set,
that the loops may be clasped to one another.
6And you shall make fifty clasps of gold, and
couple the curtains together with the clasps,
so that it may be one tabernacle.

7“You shall also make curtains of goats'
hair, to be a tent over the tabernacle. You
shall make eleven curtains. 8The length
of each curtain *shall be* thirty cubits, and
the width of each curtain four cubits; and
the eleven curtains shall all have the same
measurements. 9And you shall couple five
curtains by themselves and six curtains by
themselves, and you shall double over the
sixth curtain at the forefront of the tent.
10You shall make fifty loops on the edge of
the curtain that is outermost in *one* set, and
fifty loops on the edge of the curtain of the
second set. 11And you shall make fifty bronze
clasps, put the clasps into the loops, and
couple the tent together, that it may be one.
12The remnant that remains of the curtains
of the tent, the half curtain that remains,
shall hang over the back of the tabernacle.
13And a cubit on one side and a cubit on the
other side, of what remains of the length of
the curtains of the tent, shall hang over the
sides of the tabernacle, on this side and on
that side, to cover it.

14“You shall also make a covering of ram
skins dyed red for the tent, and a covering of
badger skins above that.

15“And for the tabernacle you shall make
the boards of acacia wood, standing upright.

In Focus

27:1 Altar of Burnt Offering An altar about 90 inches long by 90 inches wide by 54 inches high, used for burnt offerings. The people brought animals to the altar. The animals were killed, then sacrificed by fire to pay for the people's sins.

16 Ten cubits *shall be* the length of a board,
and a cubit and a half *shall be* the width of
each board. 17 Two tenons *shall be* in each
board for binding one to another. Thus you
shall make for all the boards of the tabernacle. 18 And you shall make the boards for the
tabernacle, twenty boards for the south side.
19 You shall make forty sockets of silver under
the twenty boards: two sockets under each of
the boards for its two tenons. 20 And for the
second side of the tabernacle, the north side,
there shall be twenty boards 21 and their forty
sockets of silver: two sockets under each of
the boards. 22 For the far side of the tabernacle, westward, you shall make six boards.
23 And you shall also make two boards for the
two back corners of the tabernacle. 24 They
shall be coupled together at the bottom and
they shall be coupled together at the top by
one ring. Thus it shall be for both of them.
They shall be for the two corners. 25 So there
shall be eight boards with their sockets of
silver—sixteen sockets—two sockets under
each of the boards.

26 "And you shall make bars of acacia
wood: five for the boards on one side of the
tabernacle, 27 five bars for the boards on the
other side of the tabernacle, and five bars for
the boards of the side of the tabernacle, for
the far side westward. 28 The middle bar shall
pass through the midst of the boards from
end to end. 29 You shall overlay the boards
with gold, make their rings of gold *as* holders
for the bars, and overlay the bars with gold.
30 And you shall raise up the tabernacle according to its pattern which you were shown
on the mountain.

31 "You shall make a veil woven of blue,
purple, and scarlet *thread,* and fine woven
linen. It shall be woven with an artistic design of cherubim. 32 You shall hang it upon
the four pillars of acacia *wood* overlaid with
gold. Their hooks *shall be* gold, upon four
sockets of silver. 33 And you shall hang the
veil from the clasps. Then you shall bring
the ark of the Testimony in there, behind
the veil. The veil shall be a divider for you
between the holy *place* and the Most Holy.
34 You shall put the mercy seat upon the ark
of the Testimony in the Most Holy. 35 You
shall set the table outside the veil, and the
lampstand across from the table on the side
of the tabernacle toward the south; and you
shall put the table on the north side.

36 "You shall make a screen for the door
of the tabernacle, *woven of* blue, purple, and
scarlet *thread,* and fine woven linen, made by
a weaver. 37 And you shall make for the screen
five pillars of acacia *wood,* and overlay them
with gold; their hooks *shall be* gold, and you
shall cast five sockets of bronze for them.

The Altar of Burnt Offering

27 "You shall make an altar of acacia
wood, five cubits long and five cubits wide—the altar shall be square—and its
height *shall be* three cubits. 2 You shall make
its horns on its four corners; its horns shall
be of one piece with it. And you shall overlay
it with bronze. 3 Also you shall make its pans
to receive its ashes, and its shovels and its basins and its forks and its firepans; you shall
make all its utensils of bronze. 4 You shall
make a grate for it, a network of bronze; and
on the network you shall make four bronze
rings at its four corners. 5 You shall put it under the rim of the altar beneath, that the network may be midway up the altar. 6 And you
shall make poles for the altar, poles of acacia
wood, and overlay them with bronze. 7 The
poles shall be put in the rings, and the poles
shall be on the two sides of the altar to bear
it. 8 You shall make it hollow with boards; as
it was shown you on the mountain, so shall
they make *it.*

The Court of the Tabernacle

9 "You shall also make the court of the
tabernacle. For the south side *there shall be*
hangings for the court *made of* fine woven
linen, one hundred cubits long for one side.
10 And its twenty pillars and their twenty
sockets *shall be* bronze. The hooks of the pillars and their bands *shall be* silver. 11 Likewise
along the length of the north side *there shall*

be hangings one hundred *cubits* long, with
its twenty pillars and their twenty sockets of
bronze, and the hooks of the pillars and their
bands of silver.

12“And along the width of the court on the
west side *shall be* hangings of fifty cubits,
with their ten pillars and their ten sockets.
13The width of the court on the east side *shall*
be fifty cubits. 14The hangings on *one* side
of the gate shall be fifteen cubits, *with* their
three pillars and their three sockets. 15And
on the other side *shall be* hangings of fifteen
cubits, with their three pillars and their three
sockets.

16“For the gate of the court *there shall be*
a screen twenty cubits long, *woven of* blue,
purple, and scarlet *thread,* and fine woven
linen, made by a weaver. It *shall have* four pillars and four sockets. 17All the pillars around
the court shall have bands of silver; their
hooks *shall be* of silver and their sockets of
bronze. 18The length of the court *shall be* one
hundred cubits, the width fifty throughout,
and the height five cubits, *made of* fine woven linen, and its sockets of bronze. 19All the
utensils of the tabernacle for all its service,
all its pegs, and all the pegs of the court, *shall*
be of bronze.

The Care of the Lampstand

20“And you shall command the children of Israel that they bring you pure oil
of pressed olives for the light, to cause the
lamp to burn continually. 21In the tabernacle
of meeting, outside the veil which *is* before
the Testimony, Aaron and his sons shall tend
it from evening until morning before the
LORD. *It shall be* a statute forever to their generations on behalf of the children of Israel.

Garments for the Priesthood

28 “Now take Aaron your brother, and his sons with him, from
among the children of Israel, that he may
minister to Me as priest, Aaron *and* Aaron’s
sons: Nadab, Abihu, Eleazar, and Ithamar.
2And you shall make holy garments for Aaron your brother, for glory and for beauty. 3So
you shall speak to all *who are* gifted artisans,
whom I have filled with the spirit of wisdom,
that they may make Aaron’s garments, to
consecrate him, that he may minister to Me
as priest. 4And these *are* the garments which
they shall make: a breastplate, an ephod,[a] a
robe, a skillfully woven tunic, a turban, and
a sash. So they shall make holy garments
for Aaron your brother and his sons, that he
may minister to Me as priest.

The Ephod

5“They shall take the gold, blue, purple,
and scarlet *thread,* and the fine linen, 6and
they shall make the ephod of gold, blue,
purple, *and* scarlet *thread,* and fine woven
linen, artistically worked. 7It shall have two
shoulder straps joined at its two edges, and
so it shall be joined together. 8And the intricately woven band of the ephod, which *is* on
it, shall be of the same workmanship, *made*
of gold, blue, purple, and scarlet *thread,* and
fine woven linen.

9“Then you shall take two onyx stones
and engrave on them the names of the sons
of Israel: 10six of their names on one stone
and six names on the other stone, in order
of their birth. 11With the work of an engraver
in stone, *like* the engravings of a signet, you
shall engrave the two stones with the names
of the sons of Israel. You shall set them in
settings of gold. 12And you shall put the two
stones on the shoulders of the ephod *as* memorial stones for the sons of Israel. So Aaron
shall bear their names before the LORD on
his two shoulders as a memorial. 13You shall
also make settings of gold, 14and you shall
make two chains of pure gold like braided
cords, and fasten the braided chains to the
settings.

The Breastplate

15“You shall make the breastplate of judgment. Artistically woven according to the
workmanship of the ephod you shall make
it: of gold, blue, purple, and scarlet *thread,*
and fine woven linen, you shall make it. 16It
shall be doubled into a square: a span *shall*
be its length, and a span *shall be* its width.
17And you shall put settings of stones in it,
four rows of stones: *The first* row *shall be* a
sardius, a topaz, and an emerald; *this shall*
be the first row; 18the second row *shall be* a
turquoise, a sapphire, and a diamond; 19the
third row, a jacinth, an agate, and an amethyst; 20and the fourth row, a beryl, an onyx,
and a jasper. They shall be set in gold settings. 21And the stones shall have the names
of the sons of Israel, twelve according to
their names, *like* the engravings of a signet,

28:4 [a] That is, an ornamented vest

each one with its own name; they shall be according to the twelve tribes.

22"You shall make chains for the breastplate at the end, like braided cords of pure gold. 23And you shall make two rings of gold for the breastplate, and put the two rings on the two ends of the breastplate. 24Then you shall put the two braided *chains* of gold in the two rings which are on the ends of the breastplate; 25and the *other* two ends of the two braided *chains* you shall fasten to the two settings, and put them on the shoulder straps of the ephod in the front.

26"You shall make two rings of gold, and put them on the two ends of the breastplate, on the edge of it, which is on the inner side of the ephod. 27And two *other* rings of gold you shall make, and put them on the two shoulder straps, underneath the ephod toward its front, right at the seam above the intricately woven band of the ephod. 28They shall bind the breastplate by means of its rings to the rings of the ephod, using a blue cord, so that it is above the intricately woven band of the ephod, and so that the breastplate does not come loose from the ephod.

29"So Aaron shall bear the names of the sons of Israel on the breastplate of judgment over his heart, when he goes into the holy *place,* as a memorial before the LORD continually. 30And you shall put in the breastplate of judgment the Urim and the Thummim,[a] and they shall be over Aaron's heart when he goes in before the LORD. So Aaron shall bear the judgment of the children of Israel over his heart before the LORD continually.

Other Priestly Garments

31"You shall make the robe of the ephod all of blue. 32There shall be an opening for his head in the middle of it; it shall have a woven binding all around its opening, like the opening in a coat of mail, so that it does not tear. 33And upon its hem you shall make pomegranates of blue, purple, and scarlet, all around its hem, and bells of gold between them all around: 34a golden bell and a pomegranate, a golden bell and a pomegranate, upon the hem of the robe all around. 35And it shall be upon Aaron when he ministers, and its sound will be heard when he goes into the holy *place* before the LORD and when he comes out, that he may not die.

36"You shall also make a plate of pure gold and engrave on it, *like* the engraving of a signet:

In Focus

28:41 Consecrate Pronounced *KON-see-krate.* A verb meaning "set apart" for God's use. Holy places and holy objects are consecrated, but people also must be consecrated.

HOLINESS TO THE LORD.

37And you shall put it on a blue cord, that it may be on the turban; it shall be on the front of the turban. 38So it shall be on Aaron's forehead, that Aaron may bear the iniquity of the holy things which the children of Israel hallow in all their holy gifts; and it shall always be on his forehead, that they may be accepted before the LORD.

39"You shall skillfully weave the tunic of fine linen *thread,* you shall make the turban of fine linen, and you shall make the sash of woven work.

40"For Aaron's sons you shall make tunics, and you shall make sashes for them. And you shall make hats for them, for glory and beauty. 41So you shall put them on Aaron your brother and on his sons with him. You shall anoint them, consecrate them, and sanctify them, that they may minister to Me as priests. 42And you shall make for them linen trousers to cover their nakedness; they shall reach from the waist to the thighs. 43They shall be on Aaron and on his sons when they come into the tabernacle of meeting, or when they come near the altar to minister in the holy *place,* that they do not incur iniquity and die. *It shall be* a statute forever to him and his descendants after him.

Aaron and His Sons Consecrated

29 "And this is what you shall do to them to hallow them for ministering to Me as priests: Take one young bull and two rams without blemish, 2and unleavened bread, unleavened cakes mixed with oil, and

28:30 [a] Literally *the Lights and the Perfections* (compare Leviticus 8:8)

In Focus

29:36 Atonement The act of paying God what we owe for our sins. In the Old Testament, the sacrificed animal was a symbol of atonement, but Christ is now our true Atonement.

unleavened wafers anointed with oil (you
shall make them of wheat flour). 3You shall
put them in one basket and bring them in
the basket, with the bull and the two rams.
4"And Aaron and his sons you shall bring
to the door of the tabernacle of meeting, and
you shall wash them with water. 5Then you
shall take the garments, put the tunic on
Aaron, and the robe of the ephod, the ephod,
and the breastplate, and gird him with the
intricately woven band of the ephod. 6You
shall put the turban on his head, and put the
holy crown on the turban. 7And you shall
take the anointing oil, pour *it* on his head,
and anoint him. 8Then you shall bring his
sons and put tunics on them. 9And you shall
gird them with sashes, Aaron and his sons,
and put the hats on them. The priesthood
shall be theirs for a perpetual statute. So you
shall consecrate Aaron and his sons.
10"You shall also have the bull brought
before the tabernacle of meeting, and Aaron and his sons shall put their hands on the
head of the bull. 11Then you shall kill the bull
before the LORD, *by* the door of the tabernacle of meeting. 12You shall take *some* of the
blood of the bull and put *it* on the horns of
the altar with your finger, and pour all the
blood beside the base of the altar. 13And you
shall take all the fat that covers the entrails,
the fatty lobe *attached* to the liver, and the
two kidneys and the fat that *is* on them, and
burn *them* on the altar. 14But the flesh of the
bull, with its skin and its offal, you shall
burn with fire outside the camp. It *is* a sin
offering.
15"You shall also take one ram, and Aaron and his sons shall put their hands on the
head of the ram; 16and you shall kill the ram,
and you shall take its blood and sprinkle *it*
all around on the altar. 17Then you shall cut
the ram in pieces, wash its entrails and its
legs, and put *them* with its pieces and with
its head. 18And you shall burn the whole
ram on the altar. It *is* a burnt offering to the
LORD; it *is* a sweet aroma, an offering made
by fire to the LORD.
19"You shall also take the other ram, and
Aaron and his sons shall put their hands on
the head of the ram. 20Then you shall kill the
ram, and take some of its blood and put *it* on
the tip of the right ear of Aaron and on the
tip of the right ear of his sons, on the thumb
of their right hand and on the big toe of their
right foot, and sprinkle the blood all around
on the altar. 21And you shall take some of
the blood that is on the altar, and some of
the anointing oil, and sprinkle *it* on Aaron
and on his garments, on his sons and on the
garments of his sons with him; and he and
his garments shall be hallowed, and his sons
and his sons' garments with him.
22"Also you shall take the fat of the ram,
the fat tail, the fat that covers the entrails,
the fatty lobe *attached to* the liver, the two
kidneys and the fat on them, the right thigh
(for it *is* a ram of consecration), 23one loaf of
bread, one cake *made with* oil, and one wafer from the basket of the unleavened bread
that *is* before the LORD; 24and you shall put
all these in the hands of Aaron and in the
hands of his sons, and you shall wave them
as a wave offering before the LORD. 25You
shall receive them back from their hands
and burn *them* on the altar as a burnt offering, as a sweet aroma before the LORD. It *is*
an offering made by fire to the LORD.
26"Then you shall take the breast of the
ram of Aaron's consecration and wave it *as*
a wave offering before the LORD; and it shall
be your portion. 27And from the ram of the
consecration you shall consecrate the breast
of the wave offering which is waved, and the
thigh of the heave offering which is raised,
of *that* which *is* for Aaron and of *that* which
is for his sons. 28It shall be from the children
of Israel *for* Aaron and his sons by a statute
forever. For it is a heave offering; it shall be
a heave offering from the children of Israel
from the sacrifices of their peace offerings,
that is, their heave offering to the LORD.
29"And the holy garments of Aaron shall
be his sons' after him, to be anointed in
them and to be consecrated in them. 30That
son who becomes priest in his place shall
put them on for seven days, when he enters

the tabernacle of meeting to minister in the
holy *place.*
31 “And you shall take the ram of the consecration and boil its flesh in the holy place.
32 Then Aaron and his sons shall eat the flesh
of the ram, and the bread that *is* in the basket, *by* the door of the tabernacle of meeting.
33 They shall eat those things with which the
atonement was made, to consecrate *and* to
sanctify them; but an outsider shall not eat
them, because they *are* holy. 34 And if any of
the flesh of the consecration offerings, or of
the bread, remains until the morning, then
you shall burn the remainder with fire. It
shall not be eaten, because it *is* holy.
35 “Thus you shall do to Aaron and his
sons, according to all that I have commanded
you. Seven days you shall consecrate them.
36 And you shall offer a bull every day *as* a sin
offering for atonement. You shall cleanse the
altar when you make atonement for it, and
you shall anoint it to sanctify it. 37 Seven days
you shall make atonement for the altar and
sanctify it. And the altar shall be most holy.
Whatever touches the altar must be holy.[a]

The Daily Offerings

38 “Now this *is* what you shall offer on the
altar: two lambs of the first year, day by day
continually. 39 One lamb you shall offer in the
morning, and the other lamb you shall offer
at twilight. 40 With the one lamb shall be one-
tenth *of an ephah* of flour mixed with one-
fourth of a hin of pressed oil, and one-fourth
of a hin of wine *as* a drink offering. 41 And the
other lamb you shall offer at twilight; and
you shall offer with it the grain offering and
the drink offering, as in the morning, for
a sweet aroma, an offering made by fire to
the LORD. 42 *This shall be* a continual burnt
offering throughout your generations *at* the
door of the tabernacle of meeting before
the LORD, where I will meet you to speak
with you. 43 And there I will meet with the
children of Israel, and *the tabernacle* shall
be sanctified by My glory. 44 So I will consecrate the tabernacle of meeting and the
altar. I will also consecrate both Aaron and
his sons to minister to Me as priests. 45 I will
dwell among the children of Israel and will
be their God. 46 And they shall know that I
am the LORD their God, who brought them
up out of the land of Egypt, that I may dwell
among them. I *am* the LORD their God.

The Altar of Incense

30 “You shall make an altar to burn
incense on; you shall make it of
acacia wood. 2 A cubit *shall be* its length and
a cubit its width—it shall be square—and
two cubits *shall be* its height. Its horns *shall
be* of one piece with it. 3 And you shall overlay its top, its sides all around, and its horns
with pure gold; and you shall make for it a
molding of gold all around. 4 Two gold rings
you shall make for it, under the molding on

29:37 [a] Compare Numbers 4:15 and Haggai 2:11–13

RELATIONSHIPS

READ IT: EXODUS 29:45

God wanted to have a good relationship with His people, the Israelites. He'd rescued them from slavery and delivered them to the Promised Land. However, God's people then—like us today—sinned and often forgot about God, His protection, and His great gifts. Throughout the Old Testament, God created traditions and practices to help the Israelites remember to not take their relationship with Him for granted. In the New Testament, Jesus provided the bridge for relationship with God. Do you ever take your relationship with God for granted? God constantly desires a relationship with you and wants to live every day with you!

In Focus

30:18 Laver Pronounced *LAY-ver.* A special washstand made of bronze. The laver stood between the altar of burnt offering and the door of the Old Testament worship place. The priests washed their hands there as an act of purifying themselves.

30:27 Altar of Incense A gold-covered altar about 18 inches long by 18 inches wide by 36 inches high. Every morning the high priest burned incense on the altar as a symbol of the prayers of the people.

both its sides. You shall place *them* on its two
sides, and they will be holders for the poles
with which to bear it. 5 You shall make the
poles of acacia wood, and overlay them with
gold. 6 And you shall put it before the veil that
is before the ark of the Testimony, before the
mercy seat that *is* over the Testimony, where
I will meet with you.

7 "Aaron shall burn on it sweet incense every morning; when he tends the lamps, he
shall burn incense on it. 8 And when Aaron
lights the lamps at twilight, he shall burn
incense on it, a perpetual incense before the
LORD throughout your generations. 9 You
shall not offer strange incense on it, or a
burnt offering, or a grain offering; nor shall
you pour a drink offering on it. 10 And Aaron
shall make atonement upon its horns once
a year with the blood of the sin offering of
atonement; once a year he shall make atonement upon it throughout your generations.
It *is* most holy to the LORD."

The Ransom Money

11 Then the LORD spoke to Moses, saying:
12 "When you take the census of the children
of Israel for their number, then every man
shall give a ransom for himself to the LORD,
when you number them, that there may be
no plague among them when *you* number
them. 13 This is what everyone among those
who are numbered shall give: half a shekel
according to the shekel of the sanctuary (a
shekel *is* twenty gerahs). The half-shekel
shall be an offering to the LORD. 14 Everyone
included among those who are numbered,
from twenty years old and above, shall give
an offering to the LORD. 15 The rich shall not
give more and the poor shall not give less
than half a shekel, when *you* give an offering to the LORD, to make atonement for yourselves. 16 And you shall take the atonement
money of the children of Israel, and shall
appoint it for the service of the tabernacle of
meeting, that it may be a memorial for the
children of Israel before the LORD, to make
atonement for yourselves."

The Bronze Laver

17 Then the LORD spoke to Moses, saying:
18 "You shall also make a laver of bronze, with
its base also of bronze, for washing. You
shall put it between the tabernacle of meeting and the altar. And you shall put water in
it, 19 for Aaron and his sons shall wash their
hands and their feet in water from it. 20 When
they go into the tabernacle of meeting, or
when they come near the altar to minister,
to burn an offering made by fire to the LORD,
they shall wash with water, lest they die. 21 So
they shall wash their hands and their feet,
lest they die. And it shall be a statute forever to them—to him and his descendants
throughout their generations."

The Holy Anointing Oil

22 Moreover the LORD spoke to Moses, saying: 23 "Also take for yourself quality spices—
five hundred *shekels* of liquid myrrh, half
as much sweet-smelling cinnamon (two
hundred and fifty *shekels*), two hundred and
fifty *shekels* of sweet-smelling cane, 24 five
hundred *shekels* of cassia, according to the
shekel of the sanctuary, and a hin of olive
oil. 25 And you shall make from these a holy
anointing oil, an ointment compounded according to the art of the perfumer. It shall
be a holy anointing oil. 26 With it you shall
anoint the tabernacle of meeting and the
ark of the Testimony; 27 the table and all its
utensils, the lampstand and its utensils, and
the altar of incense; 28 the altar of burnt offering with all its utensils, and the laver and its
base. 29 You shall consecrate them, that they
may be most holy; whatever touches them
must be holy.[a] 30 And you shall anoint Aaron

30:29 [a] Compare Numbers 4:15 and Haggai 2:11–13

and his sons, and consecrate them, that *they*
may minister to Me as priests.
31“And you shall speak to the children of
Israel, saying: ‘This shall be a holy anointing
oil to Me throughout your generations. 32It
shall not be poured on man’s flesh; nor shall
you make *any other* like it, according to its
composition. It *is* holy, *and* it shall be holy
to you. 33Whoever compounds *any* like it, or
whoever puts *any* of it on an outsider, shall
be cut off from his people.’ ”

The Incense

34And the LORD said to Moses: “Take
sweet spices, stacte and onycha and gal-
banum, and pure frankincense with *these*
sweet spices; there shall be equal amounts of
each. 35You shall make of these an incense,
a compound according to the art of the perfumer, salted, pure, *and* holy. 36And you shall
beat *some* of it very fine, and put some of it
before the Testimony in the tabernacle of
meeting where I will meet with you. It shall
be most holy to you. 37But *as for* the incense
which you shall make, you shall not make
any for yourselves, according to its composition. It shall be to you holy for the LORD.
38Whoever makes *any* like it, to smell it, he
shall be cut off from his people.”

Artisans for Building the Tabernacle

31 Then the LORD spoke to Moses,
saying: 2“See, I have called by name
Bezalel the son of Uri, the son of Hur, of
the tribe of Judah. 3And I have filled him
with the Spirit of God, in wisdom, in understanding, in knowledge, and in all *manner*
of workmanship, 4to design artistic works, to
work in gold, in silver, in bronze, 5in cutting
jewels for setting, in carving wood, and to
work in all *manner of* workmanship.
6“And I, indeed I, have appointed with
him Aholiab the son of Ahisamach, of the
tribe of Dan; and I have put wisdom in the

GOD’S PEOPLE MAKE A GOLD CALF

READ IT: EXODUS 32:1–21

GET IT:

In a few weeks, the people forgot all about their awesome experience at the mountain with God. Moses wasn’t around, so they let loose. They went wild! P-A-R-T-Y! But this wasn’t a good party; this was all wrong. They said they would worship only God, no idols. Instead, without Moses around, they blew it. They threw away the new rules and went back to their old Egyptian way of thinking and living. They even built a big gold cow to worship! God and Moses were furious.

LIVE IT:

Don’t point your finger at these folks. It’s easy for us to see how bad they were. After all, they forgot all about God shortly after that awesome experience. But don’t we sometimes do the same thing? How often have you said you’d do better next week as you sat in church on Sunday? Then Monday came and you blew it. The Israelites blew it, and so do we. But thankfully we have a God who forgives us through Jesus and even forgets about the wrong that we do.

hearts of all the gifted artisans, that they
may make all that I have commanded you:
7the tabernacle of meeting, the ark of the
Testimony and the mercy seat that *is* on it,
and all the furniture of the tabernacle—
8the table and its utensils, the pure *gold*
lampstand with all its utensils, the altar of
incense, 9the altar of burnt offering with all
its utensils, and the laver and its base— 10the
garments of ministry,[a] the holy garments
for Aaron the priest and the garments of his
sons, to minister as priests, 11and the anointing oil and sweet incense for the holy *place*.
According to all that I have commanded you
they shall do."

The Sabbath Law

12And the LORD spoke to Moses, saying,
13"Speak also to the children of Israel, saying: 'Surely My Sabbaths you shall keep, for
it *is* a sign between Me and you throughout
your generations, that *you* may know that I
am the LORD who sanctifies you. 14You shall
keep the Sabbath, therefore, for *it is* holy to
you. Everyone who profanes it shall surely be
put to death; for whoever does *any* work on
it, that person shall be cut off from among
his people. 15Work shall be done for six days,
but the seventh *is* the Sabbath of rest, holy
to the LORD. Whoever does *any* work on the
Sabbath day, he shall surely be put to death.
16Therefore the children of Israel shall
keep the Sabbath, to observe the Sabbath
throughout their generations *as* a perpetual covenant. 17It *is* a sign between Me and
the children of Israel forever; for *in* six days
the LORD made the heavens and the earth,
and on the seventh day He rested and was
refreshed.'"

18And when He had made an end of
speaking with him on Mount Sinai, He gave
Moses two tablets of the Testimony, tablets
of stone, written with the finger of God.

The Gold Calf

32 Now when the people saw that
Moses delayed coming down from
the mountain, the people gathered together
to Aaron, and said to him, "Come, make us
gods that shall go before us; for *as for* this
Moses, the man who brought us up out of
the land of Egypt, we do not know what has
become of him."

2And Aaron said to them, "Break off the
golden earrings which *are* in the ears of your
wives, your sons, and your daughters, and
bring *them* to me." 3So all the people broke
off the golden earrings which *were* in their
ears, and brought *them* to Aaron. 4And he received *the gold* from their hand, and he fashioned it with an engraving tool, and made a
molded calf.

Then they said, "This *is* your god, O Israel, that brought you out of the land of
Egypt!"

5So when Aaron saw *it,* he built an altar
before it. And Aaron made a proclamation
and said, "Tomorrow *is* a feast to the LORD."
6Then they rose early on the next day, offered burnt offerings, and brought peace
offerings; and the people sat down to eat and
drink, and rose up to play.

7And the LORD said to Moses, "Go, get
down! For your people whom you brought
out of the land of Egypt have corrupted *themselves.* 8They have turned aside quickly out
of the way which I commanded them. They
have made themselves a molded calf, and
worshiped it and sacrificed to it, and said,
'This *is* your god, O Israel, that brought you
out of the land of Egypt!'" 9And the LORD
said to Moses, "I have seen this people,
and indeed it *is* a stiff-necked people! 10Now
therefore, let Me alone, that My wrath may
burn hot against them and I may consume
them. And I will make of you a great nation."

11Then Moses pleaded with the LORD
his God, and said: "LORD, why does Your
wrath burn hot against Your people whom
You have brought out of the land of Egypt
with great power and with a mighty hand?
12Why should the Egyptians speak, and say,
'He brought them out to harm them, to kill
them in the mountains, and to consume
them from the face of the earth'? Turn from
Your fierce wrath, and relent from this harm
to Your people. 13Remember Abraham, Isaac,
and Israel, Your servants, to whom You
swore by Your own self, and said to them,
'I will multiply your descendants as the
stars of heaven; and all this land that I have
spoken of I give to your descendants, and
they shall inherit *it* forever.'"[a] 14So the LORD
relented from the harm which He said He
would do to His people.

15And Moses turned and went down from
the mountain, and the two tablets of the
Testimony *were* in his hand. The tablets *were*

31:10 [a] Or *woven garments* **32:13** [a] Genesis 13:15 and 22:17

written on both sides; on the one *side* and on
the other they were written. 16Now the tablets
were the work of God, and the writing *was*
the writing of God engraved on the tablets.
17And when Joshua heard the noise of the
people as they shouted, he said to Moses,
"*There is* a noise of war in the camp."
18But he said:

"*It is* not the noise of the shout of victory,
Nor the noise of the cry of defeat,
But the sound of singing I hear."

19So it was, as soon as he came near the
camp, that he saw the calf *and* the dancing.
So Moses' anger became hot, and he cast the
tablets out of his hands and broke them at
the foot of the mountain. 20Then he took the
calf which they had made, burned *it* in the
fire, and ground *it* to powder; and he scattered *it* on the water and made the children
of Israel drink *it*. 21And Moses said to Aaron,
"What did this people do to you that you have
brought *so* great a sin upon them?"

PEER PRESSURE

DECEIVED

READ IT: EXODUS 32:1–35

GET IT:

There's good pressure, and there's bad pressure. For example, when you put a piece of coal under an extreme amount of pressure, it produces a diamond. That's good pressure!

But there's bad pressure that can lead you to be deceived. Peer pressure happens when you let friends and other people your age influence you to make unwise decisions.

While Moses met with God on the mountain, he left Aaron in charge. Aaron faced some really bad peer pressure from the Israelites. They were afraid God had bailed on them. They took matters into their own hands. They begged Aaron to let them build a gold statue that they called a god. Then they prayed and worshiped it. Instead of trusting the real God, they created a fake god that they could control.

Aaron gave in to them and had to face some pretty terrible consequences. Aaron allowed the pressure of the people around him to deceive him.

LIVE IT:

When you face peer pressure, you can choose either to shine like a diamond or be deceived.

If you want to shine under pressure, try this:

- Speak the truth. (Explain to your friends the consequences of an unwise choice.)
- Stand up for yourself. (Decide that no one will be in charge of you but God.)
- Stand up for God. (God's choice is the best choice.)

In Focus

34:7 Sin Disobedience of God's law or rebellion against His will. All people sin, but Christ died to take sin away.

22So Aaron said, "Do not let the anger of my lord become hot. You know the people, that they *are set* on evil. 23For they said to me, 'Make us gods that shall go before us; *as for* this Moses, the man who brought us out of the land of Egypt, we do not know what has become of him.' 24And I said to them, 'Whoever has any gold, let them break *it* off.' So they gave *it* to me, and I cast it into the fire, and this calf came out."

25Now when Moses saw that the people *were* unrestrained (for Aaron had not restrained them, to *their* shame among their enemies), 26then Moses stood in the entrance of the camp, and said, "Whoever *is* on the LORD's side—*come* to me!" And all the sons of Levi gathered themselves together to him. 27And he said to them, "Thus says the LORD God of Israel: 'Let every man put his sword on his side, and go in and out from entrance to entrance throughout the camp, and let every man kill his brother, every man his companion, and every man his neighbor.'" 28So the sons of Levi did according to the word of Moses. And about three thousand men of the people fell that day. 29Then Moses said, "Consecrate yourselves today to the LORD, that He may bestow on you a blessing this day, for every man has opposed his son and his brother."

30Now it came to pass on the next day that Moses said to the people, "You have committed a great sin. So now I will go up to the LORD; perhaps I can make atonement for your sin." 31Then Moses returned to the LORD and said, "Oh, these people have committed a great sin, and have made for themselves a god of gold! 32Yet now, if You will *forgive their sin—but if not*, I pray, blot me out of Your book which You have written."

33And the LORD said to Moses, "Whoever has sinned against Me, I will blot him out of My book. 34Now therefore, go, lead the people to *the place* of which I have spoken to you. Behold, My Angel shall go before you. Nevertheless, in the day when I visit for punishment, I will visit punishment upon them for their sin."

35So the LORD plagued the people because of what they did with the calf which Aaron made.

The Command to Leave Sinai

33 Then the LORD said to Moses, "Depart *and* go up from here, you and the people whom you have brought out of the land of Egypt, to the land of which I swore to Abraham, Isaac, and Jacob, saying, 'To your descendants I will give it.' 2And I will send *My* Angel before you, and I will drive out the Canaanite and the Amorite and the Hittite and the Perizzite and the Hivite and the Jebusite. 3*Go up* to a land flowing with milk and honey; for I will not go up in your midst, lest I consume you on the way, for you *are* a stiff-necked people."

4And when the people heard this bad news, they mourned, and no one put on his ornaments. 5For the LORD had said to Moses, "Say to the children of Israel, 'You *are* a stiff-necked people. I could come up into your midst in one moment and consume you. Now therefore, take off your ornaments, that I may know what to do to you.'" 6So the children of Israel stripped themselves of their ornaments by Mount Horeb.

Moses Meets with the LORD

7Moses took his tent and pitched it outside the camp, far from the camp, and called it the tabernacle of meeting. And it came to pass *that* everyone who sought the LORD went out to the tabernacle of meeting which *was* outside the camp. 8So it was, whenever Moses went out to the tabernacle, *that* all the people rose, and each man stood *at* his tent door and watched Moses until he had gone into the tabernacle. 9And it came to pass, when Moses entered the tabernacle, that the pillar of cloud descended and stood *at* the door of the tabernacle, and *the LORD* talked with Moses. 10All the people saw the pillar of cloud standing at the tabernacle door, and all the people rose and worshiped, each man *in* his tent door. 11So the LORD spoke to Moses face to face, as a man speaks to his friend. And he would return to the camp, but his

servant Joshua the son of Nun, a young man,
did not depart from the tabernacle.

The Promise of God's Presence

12 Then Moses said to the LORD, "See, You
say to me, 'Bring up this people.' But You
have not let me know whom You will send
with me. Yet You have said, 'I know you by
name, and you have also found grace in My
sight.' 13 Now therefore, I pray, if I have found
grace in Your sight, show me now Your way,
that I may know You and that I may find
grace in Your sight. And consider that this
nation *is* Your people."
14 And He said, "My Presence will go *with
you,* and I will give you rest."
15 Then he said to Him, "If Your Presence
does not go *with us,* do not bring us up from
here. 16 For how then will it be known that
Your people and I have found grace in Your
sight, except You go with us? So we shall be
separate, Your people and I, from all the people who *are* upon the face of the earth."
17 So the LORD said to Moses, "I will also
do this thing that you have spoken; for you
have found grace in My sight, and I know
you by name."
18 And he said, "Please, show me Your
glory."
19 Then He said, "I will make all My goodness pass before you, and I will proclaim
the name of the LORD before you. I will be
gracious to whom I will be gracious, and I
will have compassion on whom I will have
compassion." 20 But He said, "You cannot see
My face; for no man shall see Me, and live."
21 And the LORD said, "Here is a place by Me,
and you shall stand on the rock. 22 So it shall
be, while My glory passes by, that I will put
you in the cleft of the rock, and will cover
you with My hand while I pass by. 23 Then
I will take away My hand, and you shall see
My back; but My face shall not be seen."

Moses Makes New Tablets

34 And the LORD said to Moses, "Cut
two tablets of stone like the first
ones, and I will write on *these* tablets the
words that were on the first tablets which
you broke. 2 So be ready in the morning, and
come up in the morning to Mount Sinai, and
present yourself to Me there on the top of the
mountain. 3 And no man shall come up with
you, and let no man be seen throughout all
the mountain; let neither flocks nor herds
feed before that mountain."
4 So he cut two tablets of stone like the
first *ones.* Then Moses rose early in the
morning and went up Mount Sinai, as the
LORD had commanded him; and he took in
his hand the two tablets of stone.
5 Now the LORD descended in the cloud
and stood with him there, and proclaimed
the name of the LORD. 6 And the LORD passed
before him and proclaimed, "The LORD, the
LORD God, merciful and gracious, longsuffering, and abounding in goodness and
truth, 7 keeping mercy for thousands, forgiving iniquity and transgression and sin,
by no means clearing *the guilty,* visiting the
iniquity of the fathers upon the children and
the children's children to the third and the
fourth generation."
8 So Moses made haste and bowed his
head toward the earth, and worshiped.
9 Then he said, "If now I have found grace
in Your sight, O Lord, let my Lord, I pray, go
among us, even though we *are* a stiff-necked
people; and pardon our iniquity and our sin,
and take us as Your inheritance."

The Covenant Renewed

10 And He said: "Behold, I make a covenant. Before all your people I will do mar-
vels such as have not been done in all the
earth, nor in any nation; and all the people
among whom you *are* shall see the work of
the LORD. For it *is* an awesome thing that I
will do with you. 11 Observe what I command
you this day. Behold, I am driving out from
before you the Amorite and the Canaanite
and the Hittite and the Perizzite and the Hivite and the Jebusite. 12 Take heed to yourself,
lest you make a covenant with the inhabitants of the land where you are going, lest
it be a snare in your midst. 13 But you shall
destroy their altars, break their *sacred* pillars,
and cut down their wooden images 14 (for you
shall worship no other god, for the LORD,
whose name *is* Jealous, *is* a jealous God),
15 lest you make a covenant with the inhabitants of the land, and they play the harlot
with their gods and make sacrifice to their
gods, and *one of them* invites you and you eat
of his sacrifice, 16 and you take of his daughters for your sons, and his daughters play the
harlot with their gods and make your sons
play the harlot with their gods.

17“You shall make no molded gods for
yourselves.

18“The Feast of Unleavened Bread you
shall keep. Seven days you shall eat unleavened bread, as I commanded you, in the appointed time of the month of Abib; for in the
month of Abib you came out from Egypt.

19“All that open the womb *are* Mine, and
every male firstborn among your livestock,
whether ox or sheep. 20But the firstborn of a
donkey you shall redeem with a lamb. And
if you will not redeem *him*, then you shall
break his neck. All the firstborn of your sons
you shall redeem.

“And none shall appear before Me
empty-handed.

21“Six days you shall work, but on the seventh day you shall rest; in plowing time and
in harvest you shall rest.

22“And you shall observe the Feast of
Weeks, of the firstfruits of wheat harvest,
and the Feast of Ingathering at the year's
end.

23“Three times in the year all your men
shall appear before the Lord, the LORD God
of Israel. 24For I will cast out the nations before you and enlarge your borders; neither
will any man covet your land when you go
up to appear before the LORD your God three
times in the year.

25“You shall not offer the blood of My
sacrifice with leaven, nor shall the sacrifice of the Feast of the Passover be left until
morning.

26“The first of the firstfruits of your land
you shall bring to the house of the LORD your
God. You shall not boil a young goat in its
mother's milk.”

27Then the LORD said to Moses, “Write
these words, for according to the tenor of
these words I have made a covenant with you
and with Israel.” 28So he was there with the
LORD forty days and forty nights; he neither
ate bread nor drank water. And He wrote on
the tablets the words of the covenant, the Ten
Commandments.[a]

The Shining Face of Moses

29Now it was so, when Moses came down
from Mount Sinai (and the two tablets of
the Testimony were in Moses' hand when he
came down from the mountain), that Moses
did not know that the skin of his face shone
while he talked with Him. 30So when Aaron and all the children of Israel saw Moses,
behold, the skin of his face shone, and they
were afraid to come near him. 31Then Moses
called to them, and Aaron and all the rulers
of the congregation returned to him; and
Moses talked with them. 32Afterward all the
children of Israel came near, and he gave
them as commandments all that the LORD
had spoken with him on Mount Sinai. 33And
when Moses had finished speaking with
them, he put a veil on his face. 34But whenever Moses went in before the LORD to speak
with Him, he would take the veil off until
he came out; and he would come out and
speak to the children of Israel whatever he
had been commanded. 35And whenever the
children of Israel saw the face of Moses, that
the skin of Moses' face shone, then Moses
would put the veil on his face again, until he
went in to speak with Him.

Sabbath Regulations

35 Then Moses gathered all the congregation of the children of Israel
together, and said to them, “These *are* the
words which the LORD has commanded *you*
to do: 2Work shall be done for six days, but
the seventh day shall be a holy day for you,
a Sabbath of rest to the LORD. Whoever does
any work on it shall be put to death. 3You
shall kindle no fire throughout your dwellings on the Sabbath day.”

Offerings for the Tabernacle

4And Moses spoke to all the congregation of the children of Israel, saying, “This
is the thing which the LORD commanded,
saying: 5‘Take from among you an offering
to the LORD. Whoever *is* of a willing heart, let
him bring it as an offering to the LORD: gold,
silver, and bronze; 6blue, purple, and scarlet
thread, fine linen, and goats' *hair*; 7ram skins
dyed red, badger skins, and acacia wood; 8oil
for the light, and spices for the anointing
oil and for the sweet incense; 9onyx stones,
and stones to be set in the ephod and in the
breastplate.

Articles of the Tabernacle

10‘All *who are* gifted artisans among you
shall come and make all that the LORD has
commanded: 11the tabernacle, its tent, its
covering, its clasps, its boards, its bars, its
pillars, and its sockets; 12the ark and its poles,

34:28 [a] Literally *Ten Words*

with the mercy seat, and the veil of the covering; 13the table and its poles, all its utensils,
and the showbread; 14also the lampstand for
the light, its utensils, its lamps, and the oil
for the light; 15the incense altar, its poles, the
anointing oil, the sweet incense, and the
screen for the door at the entrance of the
tabernacle; 16the altar of burnt offering with
its bronze grating, its poles, all its utensils,
and the laver and its base; 17the hangings of
the court, its pillars, their sockets, and the
screen for the gate of the court; 18the pegs
of the tabernacle, the pegs of the court, and
their cords; 19the garments of ministry,[a] for
ministering in the holy *place*—the holy garments for Aaron the priest and the garments
of his sons, to minister as priests.'"

The Tabernacle Offerings Presented

20And all the congregation of the children
of Israel departed from the presence of Moses. 21Then everyone came whose heart was
stirred, and everyone whose spirit was willing, *and* they brought the LORD's offering for
the work of the tabernacle of meeting, for all
its service, and for the holy garments. 22They
came, both men and women, as many as had
a willing heart, *and* brought earrings and
nose rings, rings and necklaces, all jewelry
of gold, that is, every man who *made* an offering of gold to the LORD. 23And every man,
with whom was found blue, purple, and
scarlet *thread,* fine linen, and goats' *hair,* red
skins of rams, and badger skins, brought
them. 24Everyone who offered an offering of
silver or bronze brought the LORD's offering.
And everyone with whom was found acacia
wood for any work of the service, brought
it. 25All the women *who were* gifted artisans
spun yarn with their hands, and brought
what they had spun, of blue, purple, *and*
scarlet, and fine linen. 26And all the wom-
en whose hearts stirred with wisdom spun
yarn of goats' *hair.* 27The rulers brought onyx
stones, and the stones to be set in the ephod
and in the breastplate, 28and spices and oil
for the light, for the anointing oil, and for
the sweet incense. 29The children of Israel
brought a freewill offering to the LORD, all
the men and women whose hearts were willing to bring *material* for all kinds of work
which the LORD, by the hand of Moses, had
commanded to be done.

The Artisans Called by God

30And Moses said to the children of Israel,
"See, the LORD has called by name Bezalel
the son of Uri, the son of Hur, of the tribe of
Judah; 31and He has filled him with the Spirit of God, in wisdom and understanding, in
knowledge and all manner of workmanship,
32to design artistic works, to work in gold
and silver and bronze, 33in cutting jewels for
setting, in carving wood, and to work in all
manner of artistic workmanship.

34"And He has put in his heart the ability
to teach, *in* him and Aholiab the son of Ahisamach, of the tribe of Dan. 35He has filled
them with skill to do all manner of work of
the engraver and the designer and the tapestry maker, in blue, purple, and scarlet *thread,*
and fine linen, and of the weaver—those
who do every work and those who design
artistic works.

36 "And Bezalel and Aholiab, and
every gifted artisan in whom the
LORD has put wisdom and understanding,
to know how to do all manner of work for the
service of the sanctuary, shall do according
to all that the LORD has commanded."

The People Give More than Enough

2Then Moses called Bezalel and Aholiab,
and every gifted artisan in whose heart the
LORD had put wisdom, everyone whose heart
was stirred, to come and do the work. 3And
they received from Moses all the offering
which the children of Israel had brought for
the work of the service of making the sanctuary. So they continued bringing to him
freewill offerings every morning. 4Then all
the craftsmen who were doing all the work
of the sanctuary came, each from the work
he was doing, 5and they spoke to Moses,
saying, "The people bring much more than
enough for the service of the work which the
LORD commanded *us* to do."

6So Moses gave a commandment, and
they caused it to be proclaimed throughout the camp, saying, "Let neither man nor
woman do any more work for the offering
of the sanctuary." And the people were restrained from bringing, 7for the material
they had was sufficient for all the work to be
done—indeed too much.

35:19 [a] Or *woven garments*

Building the Tabernacle

8Then all the gifted artisans among
them who worked on the tabernacle made
ten curtains woven of fine linen, and of
blue, purple, and scarlet *thread; with* artistic
designs of cherubim they made them. 9The
length of each curtain *was* twenty-eight
cubits, and the width of each curtain four
cubits; the curtains *were* all the same size.
10And he coupled five curtains to one another, and *the other* five curtains he coupled to
one another. 11He made loops of blue *yarn*
on the edge of the curtain on the selvedge
of one set; likewise he did on the outer edge
of *the other* curtain of the second set. 12Fif-
ty loops he made on one curtain, and fifty
loops he made on the edge of the curtain
on the end of the second set; the loops held
one *curtain* to another. 13And he made fifty
clasps of gold, and coupled the curtains to
one another with the clasps, that it might be
one tabernacle.

14He made curtains of goats' *hair* for the
tent over the tabernacle; he made eleven curtains. 15The length of each curtain *was* thirty
cubits, and the width of each curtain four cubits; the eleven curtains *were* the same size.
16He coupled five curtains by themselves and
six curtains by themselves. 17And he made
fifty loops on the edge of the curtain that
is outermost in one set, and fifty loops he
made on the edge of the curtain of the second set. 18He also made fifty bronze clasps
to couple the tent together, that it might be
one. 19Then he made a covering for the tent
of ram skins dyed red, and a covering of badger skins above *that.*

20For the tabernacle he made boards of
acacia wood, standing upright. 21The length
of each board *was* ten cubits, and the width
of each board a cubit and a half. 22Each board
had two tenons for binding one to another.
Thus he made for all the boards of the tabernacle. 23And he made boards for the tabernacle, twenty boards for the south side.
24Forty sockets of silver he made to go under
the twenty boards: two sockets under each
of the boards for its two tenons. 25And for
the other side of the tabernacle, the north
side, he made twenty boards 26and their forty sockets of silver: two sockets under each
of the boards. 27For the west side of the tabernacle he made six boards. 28He also made
two boards for the two back corners of the
tabernacle. 29And they were coupled at the
bottom and coupled together at the top by
one ring. Thus he made both of them for the
two corners. 30So there were eight boards and
their sockets—sixteen sockets of silver—
two sockets under each of the boards.

31And he made bars of acacia wood: five
for the boards on one side of the tabernacle, 32five bars for the boards on the other
side of the tabernacle, and five bars for the
boards of the tabernacle on the far side westward. 33And he made the middle bar to pass
through the boards from one end to the other. 34He overlaid the boards with gold, made
their rings of gold *to be* holders for the bars,
and overlaid the bars with gold.

35And he made a veil of blue, purple, and
scarlet *thread,* and fine woven linen; it was
worked *with* an artistic design of cherubim.
36He made for it four pillars of acacia *wood,*
and overlaid them with gold, with their
hooks of gold; and he cast four sockets of
silver for them.

37He also made a screen for the tabernacle door, of blue, purple, and scarlet *thread,*
and fine woven linen, made by a weaver,
38and its five pillars with their hooks. And he
overlaid their capitals and their rings with
gold, but their five sockets *were* bronze.

Making the Ark of the Testimony

37 Then Bezalel made the ark of acacia wood; two and a half cubits *was*
its length, a cubit and a half its width, and
a cubit and a half its height. 2He overlaid it
with pure gold inside and outside, and made
a molding of gold all around it. 3And he cast
for it four rings of gold *to be set* in its four corners: two rings on one side, and two rings on
the other side of it. 4He made poles of acacia
wood, and overlaid them with gold. 5And he
put the poles into the rings at the sides of the
ark, to bear the ark. 6He also made the mercy
seat of pure gold; two and a half cubits *was*
its length and a cubit and a half its width.
7He made two cherubim of beaten gold; he
made them of one piece at the two ends of
the mercy seat: 8one cherub at one end on
this side, and the other cherub at the *other*
end on that side. He made the cherubim
at the two ends of one piece with the mercy
seat. 9The cherubim spread out *their* wings
above, *and* covered the mercy seat with their
wings. They faced one another; the faces of
the cherubim were toward the mercy seat.

Making the Table for the Showbread

10 He made the table of acacia wood; two
cubits *was* its length, a cubit its width, and
a cubit and a half its height. 11 And he overlaid it with pure gold, and made a molding
of gold all around it. 12 Also he made a frame
of a handbreadth all around it, and made a
molding of gold for the frame all around it.
13 And he cast for it four rings of gold, and
put the rings on the four corners that *were*
at its four legs. 14 The rings were close to the
frame, as holders for the poles to bear the
table. 15 And he made the poles of acacia wood
to bear the table, and overlaid them with
gold. 16 He made of pure gold the utensils
which were on the table: its dishes, its cups,
its bowls, and its pitchers for pouring.

Making the Gold Lampstand

17 He also made the lampstand of pure
gold; of hammered work he made the lampstand. Its shaft, its branches, its bowls, its
ornamental knobs, and its flowers were of
the same piece. 18 And six branches came out
of its sides: three branches of the lampstand
out of one side, and three branches of the
lampstand out of the other side. 19 There were
three bowls made like almond *blossoms* on
one branch, with an *ornamental* knob and a
flower, and three bowls made like almond
blossoms on the other branch, with an *ornamental* knob and a flower—and so for the
six branches coming out of the lampstand.
20 And on the lampstand itself *were* four
bowls made like almond *blossoms, each with*
its *ornamental* knob and flower. 21 *There was*
a knob under the *first* two branches of the
same, a knob under the *second* two branches
of the same, and a knob under the *third* two
branches of the same, according to the six
branches extending from it. 22 Their knobs
and their branches were of one piece; all of it
was one hammered piece of pure gold. 23 And
he made its seven lamps, its wick-trimmers,
and its trays of pure gold. 24 Of a talent of
pure gold he made it, with all its utensils.

Making the Altar of Incense

25 He made the incense altar of acacia
wood. Its length *was* a cubit and its width
a cubit—*it was* square—and two cubits *was*
its height. Its horns were *of one piece* with it.
26 And he overlaid it with pure gold: its top,
its sides all around, and its horns. He also
made for it a molding of gold all around it.

In Focus

38:8 Tabernacle of Meeting Israel's worship place in the desert. It was a special tent divided into two rooms—a Holy Place and a Most Holy Place. Only the priests were allowed in the tabernacle.

27 He made two rings of gold for it under its
molding, by its two corners on both sides, as
holders for the poles with which to bear it.
28 And he made the poles of acacia wood, and
overlaid them with gold.

Making the Anointing Oil and the Incense

29 He also made the holy anointing oil and
the pure incense of sweet spices, according
to the work of the perfumer.

Making the Altar of Burnt Offering

38 He made the altar of burnt offering of acacia wood; five cubits *was*
its length and five cubits its width—*it was*
square—and its height *was* three cubits. 2 He
made its horns on its four corners; the horns
were *of one piece* with it. And he overlaid it
with bronze. 3 He made all the utensils for
the altar: the pans, the shovels, the basins,
the forks, and the firepans; all its utensils
he made of bronze. 4 And he made a grate of
bronze network for the altar, under its rim,
midway from the bottom. 5 He cast four rings
for the four corners of the bronze grating,
as holders for the poles. 6 And he made the
poles of acacia wood, and overlaid them with
bronze. 7 Then he put the poles into the rings
on the sides of the altar, with which to bear
it. He made the altar hollow with boards.

Making the Bronze Laver

8 He made the laver of bronze and its base
of bronze, from the bronze mirrors of the
serving women who assembled at the door
of the tabernacle of meeting.

Making the Court of the Tabernacle

9 Then he made the court on the south
side; the hangings of the court *were of* fine
woven linen, one hundred cubits long.

10There *were* twenty pillars for them, with
twenty bronze sockets. The hooks of the
pillars and their bands *were* silver. 11On the
north side *the hangings were* one hundred
cubits *long,* with twenty pillars and their
twenty bronze sockets. The hooks of the pillars and their bands *were* silver. 12And on the
west side *there were* hangings of fifty cubits,
with ten pillars and their ten sockets. The
hooks of the pillars and their bands *were* silver. 13For the east side *the hangings were* fifty
cubits. 14The hangings of one side *of the gate
were* fifteen cubits *long, with* their three pillars and their three sockets, 15and the same
for the other side of the court gate; on this
side and that *were* hangings of fifteen cubits, *with* their three pillars and their three
sockets. 16All the hangings of the court all
around *were of* fine woven linen. 17The sockets for the pillars *were* bronze, the hooks of
the pillars and their bands *were* silver, and
the overlay of their capitals *was* silver; and
all the pillars of the court had bands of silver. 18The screen for the gate of the court *was*
woven of blue, purple, and scarlet *thread,* and
of fine woven linen. The length *was* twenty
cubits, and the height along its width *was*
five cubits, corresponding to the hangings
of the court. 19And *there were* four pillars *with*
their four sockets of bronze; their hooks *were*
silver, and the overlay of their capitals and
their bands *was* silver. 20All the pegs of the
tabernacle, and of the court all around, *were*
bronze.

Materials of the Tabernacle

21This is the inventory of the tabernacle,
the tabernacle of the Testimony, which was
counted according to the commandment of
Moses, for the service of the Levites, by the
hand of Ithamar, son of Aaron the priest.

22Bezalel the son of Uri, the son of Hur,
of the tribe of Judah, made all that the LORD
had commanded Moses. 23And with him *was*
Aholiab the son of Ahisamach, of the tribe of
Dan, an engraver and designer, a weaver of
blue, purple, and scarlet *thread,* and of fine
linen.

24All the gold that was used in all the
work of the holy *place,* that is, the gold of the
offering, was twenty-nine talents and seven
hundred and thirty shekels, according to
the shekel of the sanctuary. 25And the silver
from those who were numbered of the congregation *was* one hundred talents and one
thousand seven hundred and seventy-five
shekels, according to the shekel of the sanctuary: 26a bekah for each man (*that is,* half a
shekel, according to the shekel of the sanctuary), for everyone included in the num-
bering from twenty years old and above, for
six hundred and three thousand, five hundred and fifty *men.* 27And from the hundred
talents of silver were cast the sockets of the
sanctuary and the bases of the veil: one hundred sockets from the hundred talents, one
talent for each socket. 28Then from the one
thousand seven hundred and seventy-five
shekels he made hooks for the pillars, overlaid their capitals, and made bands for them.

29The offering of bronze *was* seventy talents and two thousand four hundred shekels. 30And with it he made the sockets for
the door of the tabernacle of meeting, the
bronze altar, the bronze grating for it, and
all the utensils for the altar, 31the sockets for
the court all around, the bases for the court
gate, all the pegs for the tabernacle, and all
the pegs for the court all around.

Making the Garments of the Priesthood

39 Of the blue, purple, and scarlet
thread they made garments of
ministry,[a] for ministering in the holy *place,*
and made the holy garments for Aaron, as
the LORD had commanded Moses.

Making the Ephod

2He made the ephod of gold, blue, purple,
and scarlet *thread,* and of fine woven linen.
3And they beat the gold into thin sheets and
cut *it into* threads, to work *it* in *with* the blue,
purple, and scarlet *thread,* and the fine lin-
en, *into* artistic designs. 4They made shoulder straps for it to couple *it* together; it was
coupled together at its two edges. 5And the
intricately woven band of his ephod that *was*
on it *was* of the same workmanship, *woven
of* gold, blue, purple, and scarlet *thread,* and
of fine woven linen, as the LORD had commanded Moses.

6And they set onyx stones, enclosed in settings of gold; they were engraved, as signets
are engraved, with the names of the sons of
Israel. 7He put them on the shoulders of the
ephod *as* memorial stones for the sons of
Israel, as the LORD had commanded Moses.

39:1 [a] Or *woven garments*

Making the Breastplate

8 And he made the breastplate, artistically
woven like the workmanship of the ephod,
of gold, blue, purple, and scarlet *thread,* and
of fine woven linen. 9 They made the breastplate square by doubling it; a span *was* its
length and a span its width when doubled.
10 And they set in it four rows of stones: a row
with a sardius, a topaz, and an emerald was
the first row; 11 the second row, a turquoise,
a sapphire, and a diamond; 12 the third row,
a jacinth, an agate, and an amethyst; 13 the
fourth row, a beryl, an onyx, and a jasper.
They were enclosed in settings of gold in
their mountings. 14 *There were* twelve stones
according to the names of the sons of Israel:
according to their names, *engraved like* a signet, each one with its own name according
to the twelve tribes. 15 And they made chains
for the breastplate at the ends, like braided
cords of pure gold. 16 They also made two settings of gold and two gold rings, and put the
two rings on the two ends of the breastplate.
17 And they put the two braided *chains* of gold
in the two rings on the ends of the breastplate. 18 The two ends of the two braided
chains they fastened in the two settings, and
put them on the shoulder straps of the ephod
in the front. 19 And they made two rings of
gold and put *them* on the two ends of the
breastplate, on the edge of it, which *was* on
the inward side of the ephod. 20 They made
two *other* gold rings and put them on the
two shoulder straps, underneath the ephod
toward its front, right at the seam above the
intricately woven band of the ephod. 21 And
they bound the breastplate by means of its
rings to the rings of the ephod with a blue
cord, so that it would be above the intricately woven band of the ephod, and that the
breastplate would not come loose from the
ephod, as the LORD had commanded Moses.

Making the Other Priestly Garments

22 He made the robe of the ephod of woven work, all of blue. 23 And *there was* an
opening in the middle of the robe, like the
opening in a coat of mail, *with* a woven
binding all around the opening, so that it
would not tear. 24 They made on the hem of
the robe pomegranates of blue, purple, and
scarlet, and of fine woven *linen.* 25 And they
made bells of pure gold, and put the bells
between the pomegranates on the hem of
the robe all around between the pomegranates: 26 a bell and a pomegranate, a bell and a
pomegranate, all around the hem of the robe
to minister in, as the LORD had commanded
Moses.

27 They made tunics, artistically woven of
fine linen, for Aaron and his sons, 28 a turban of fine linen, exquisite hats of fine linen,
short trousers of fine woven linen, 29 and a
sash of fine woven linen with blue, purple,
and scarlet *thread,* made by a weaver, as the
LORD had commanded Moses.

30 Then they made the plate of the holy
crown of pure gold, and wrote on it an inscription *like* the engraving of a signet:

HOLINESS TO THE LORD.

31 And they tied to it a blue cord, to fasten *it*
above on the turban, as the LORD had commanded Moses.

The Work Completed

32 Thus all the work of the tabernacle of
the tent of meeting was finished. And the
children of Israel did according to all that the
LORD had commanded Moses; so they did.
33 And they brought the tabernacle to Moses,
the tent and all its furnishings: its clasps, its
boards, its bars, its pillars, and its sockets;
34 the covering of ram skins dyed red, the
covering of badger skins, and the veil of the
covering; 35 the ark of the Testimony with its
poles, and the mercy seat; 36 the table, all its
utensils, and the showbread; 37 the pure *gold*
lampstand with its lamps (the lamps set in
order), all its utensils, and the oil for light;
38 the gold altar, the anointing oil, and the
sweet incense; the screen for the tabernacle
door; 39 the bronze altar, its grate of bronze,
its poles, and all its utensils; the laver with its
base; 40 the hangings of the court, its pillars
and its sockets, the screen for the court gate,
its cords, and its pegs; all the utensils for
the service of the tabernacle, for the tent of
meeting; 41 and the garments of ministry,[a] to
minister in the holy place: the holy garments
for Aaron the priest, and his sons' garments,
to minister as priests.

42 According to all that the LORD had commanded Moses, so the children of Israel did
all the work. 43 Then Moses looked over all
the work, and indeed they had done it; as the

39:41 [a] Or *woven garments*

LORD had commanded, just so they had done
it. And Moses blessed them.

The Tabernacle Erected and Arranged

40 Then the LORD spoke to Moses,
saying: 2"On the first day of the
first month you shall set up the tabernacle
of the tent of meeting. 3You shall put in it
the ark of the Testimony, and partition off
the ark with the veil. 4You shall bring in
the table and arrange the things that are
to be set in order on it; and you shall bring
in the lampstand and light its lamps. 5You
shall also set the altar of gold for the incense
before the ark of the Testimony, and put up
the screen for the door of the tabernacle.
6Then you shall set the altar of the burnt offering before the door of the tabernacle of
the tent of meeting. 7And you shall set the
laver between the tabernacle of meeting and
the altar, and put water in it. 8You shall set
up the court all around, and hang up the
screen at the court gate.

9"And you shall take the anointing oil,
and anoint the tabernacle and all that *is* in
it; and you shall hallow it and all its utensils,
and it shall be holy. 10You shall anoint the
altar of the burnt offering and all its utensils, and consecrate the altar. The altar shall
be most holy. 11And you shall anoint the laver
and its base, and consecrate it.

12"Then you shall bring Aaron and his
sons to the door of the tabernacle of meeting
and wash them with water. 13You shall put
the holy garments on Aaron, and anoint him
and consecrate him, that he may minister to
Me as priest. 14And you shall bring his sons
and clothe them with tunics. 15You shall
anoint them, as you anointed their father,
that they may minister to Me as priests; for
their anointing shall surely be an everlasting
priesthood throughout their generations."

16Thus Moses did; according to all that
the LORD had commanded him, so he did.

17And it came to pass in the first month
of the second year, on the first *day* of the
month, *that* the tabernacle was raised up.
18So Moses raised up the tabernacle, fastened its sockets, set up its boards, put in
its bars, and raised up its pillars. 19And he
spread out the tent over the tabernacle and
put the covering of the tent on top of it, as the
LORD had commanded Moses. 20He took the
Testimony and put *it* into the ark, inserted
the poles through the rings of the ark, and
put the mercy seat on top of the ark. 21And
he brought the ark into the tabernacle, hung
up the veil of the covering, and partitioned
off the ark of the Testimony, as the LORD had
commanded Moses.

22He put the table in the tabernacle of
meeting, on the north side of the tabernacle,
outside the veil; 23and he set the bread in order upon it before the LORD, as the LORD had
commanded Moses. 24He put the lampstand
in the tabernacle of meeting, across from
the table, on the south side of the tabernacle; 25and he lit the lamps before the LORD, as
the LORD had commanded Moses. 26He put
the gold altar in the tabernacle of meeting
in front of the veil; 27and he burned sweet
incense on it, as the LORD had commanded
Moses. 28He hung up the screen *at* the door
of the tabernacle. 29And he put the altar of
burnt offering *before* the door of the tabernacle of the tent of meeting, and offered upon
it the burnt offering and the grain offering,
as the LORD had commanded Moses. 30He
set the laver between the tabernacle of meeting and the altar, and put water there for
washing; 31and Moses, Aaron, and his sons
would wash their hands and their feet *with
water* from it. 32Whenever they went into the
tabernacle of meeting, and when they came
near the altar, they washed, as the LORD had
commanded Moses. 33And he raised up the
court all around the tabernacle and the altar,
and hung up the screen of the court gate. So
Moses finished the work.

The Cloud and the Glory

34Then the cloud covered the tabernacle
of meeting, and the glory of the LORD filled
the tabernacle. 35And Moses was not able to
enter the tabernacle of meeting, because the
cloud rested above it, and the glory of the
LORD filled the tabernacle. 36Whenever the
cloud was taken up from above the tabernacle, the children of Israel would go onward
in all their journeys. 37But if the cloud was
not taken up, then they did not journey till
the day that it was taken up. 38For the cloud
of the LORD *was* above the tabernacle by day,
and fire was over it by night, in the sight of
all the house of Israel, throughout all their
journeys.

The THIRD BOOK of MOSES CALLED

LEVITICUS

1445 B.C.–1400 B.C.

Behind the Scenes

READ IT:

Leviticus contains lots of rules. Many of the rules were for the Levites, who included the priests who worked in the tabernacle of God. There were rules about what food to eat and not eat, rules about offerings and feast days, and even rules about how to take care of mildew.

GET IT:

Who wrote it: Most people think Moses wrote it.

When it was written: 1445 B.C.–1400 B.C.

Why it was written: to help the Israelites worship and live as God's holy people. They needed to be holy to live in the presence of a holy God.

LIVE IT:

We need to live holy lives because we love and worship a holy God.

FIND IT:

Aaron and His Sons Consecrated as Priests — *Leviticus 8*

Foods Permitted and Forbidden — *Leviticus 11*

Feasts of the Lord — *Leviticus 23*

The Burnt Offering

1 Now the LORD called to Moses, and
spoke to him from the tabernacle of
meeting, saying, 2"Speak to the children of
Israel, and say to them: 'When any one of
you brings an offering to the LORD, you shall
bring your offering of the livestock—of the
herd and of the flock.

3'If his offering *is* a burnt sacrifice of the
herd, let him offer a male without blemish;
he shall offer it of his own free will at the
door of the tabernacle of meeting before the
LORD. 4Then he shall put his hand on the
head of the burnt offering, and it will be accepted on his behalf to make atonement for
him. 5He shall kill the bull before the LORD;
and the priests, Aaron's sons, shall bring the
blood and sprinkle the blood all around on
the altar that *is by* the door of the tabernacle
of meeting. 6And he shall skin the burnt offering and cut it into its pieces. 7The sons of
Aaron the priest shall put fire on the altar,
and lay the wood in order on the fire. 8Then
the priests, Aaron's sons, shall lay the parts,
the head, and the fat in order on the wood
that *is* on the fire upon the altar; 9but he shall
wash its entrails and its legs with water. And
the priest shall burn all on the altar as a
burnt sacrifice, an offering made by fire, a
sweet aroma to the LORD.

10'If his offering *is* of the flocks—of the
sheep or of the goats—as a burnt sacrifice,
he shall bring a male without blemish. 11He
shall kill it on the north side of the altar
before the LORD; and the priests, Aaron's
sons, shall sprinkle its blood all around on
the altar. 12And he shall cut it into its pieces,
with its head and its fat; and the priest shall
lay them in order on the wood that *is* on the
fire upon the altar; 13but he shall wash the
entrails and the legs with water. Then the
priest shall bring *it* all and burn *it* on the altar; it *is* a burnt sacrifice, an offering made
by fire, a sweet aroma to the LORD.

14'And if the burnt sacrifice of his offering to the LORD *is* of birds, then he shall
bring his offering of turtledoves or young pigeons. 15The priest shall bring it to the altar,
wring off its head, and burn *it* on the altar;
its blood shall be drained out at the side of
the altar. 16And he shall remove its crop with
its feathers and cast it beside the altar on the
east side, into the place for ashes. 17Then he
shall split it at its wings, *but* shall not divide
it completely; and the priest shall burn it on
the altar, on the wood that *is* on the fire. It *is*
a burnt sacrifice, an offering made by fire, a
sweet aroma to the LORD.

The Grain Offering

2 'When anyone offers a grain offering
to the LORD, his offering shall be *of*
fine flour. And he shall pour oil on it, and
put frankincense on it. 2He shall bring it to
Aaron's sons, the priests, one of whom shall
take from it his handful of fine flour and
oil with all the frankincense. And the priest
shall burn *it as* a memorial on the altar, an

Starring Roles

AARON'S name is pronounced *AIR-un*. He was the brother of Moses. He was honored when the Lord ordered him to speak for Moses to the king of Egypt. His brother Moses was never a good public speaker, so he was afraid to speak face to face with the king (see Exodus 4).

Aaron was always sorry for one thing though. One day he gave in to the sinful wills of the people and made a golden idol (Exodus 32:1–4). This nearly caused the end of the Hebrews' great dream of living in the new land that God had promised them. But Moses prayed for the people, and God forgave them and Aaron.

After that, Aaron became the high priest of Israel. In addition to offering the regular sacrifice to God, Aaron came before the Lord in the Most Holy Place once a year.

offering made by fire, a sweet aroma to the
LORD. 3The rest of the grain offering *shall be*
Aaron's and his sons'. *It is* most holy of the
offerings to the LORD made by fire.
4'And if you bring as an offering a grain
offering baked in the oven, *it shall be* unleavened cakes of fine flour mixed with oil, or
unleavened wafers anointed with oil. 5But
if your offering *is* a grain offering *baked* in
a pan, *it shall be of* fine flour, unleavened,
mixed with oil. 6You shall break it in pieces
and pour oil on it; it *is* a grain offering.
7'If your offering *is* a grain offering *baked*
in a covered pan, it shall be made *of* fine
flour with oil. 8You shall bring the grain
offering that is made of these things to the
LORD. And when it is presented to the priest,
he shall bring it to the altar. 9Then the priest
shall take from the grain offering a memorial portion, and burn *it* on the altar. *It is* an
offering made by fire, a sweet aroma to the
LORD. 10And what is left of the grain offering
shall be Aaron's and his sons'. *It is* most holy
of the offerings to the LORD made by fire.
11'No grain offering which you bring to
the LORD shall be made with leaven, for you
shall burn no leaven nor any honey in any
offering to the LORD made by fire. 12As for
the offering of the firstfruits, you shall offer them to the LORD, but they shall not be
burned on the altar for a sweet aroma. 13And
every offering of your grain offering you
shall season with salt; you shall not allow the
salt of the covenant of your God to be lacking
from your grain offering. With all your offerings you shall offer salt.
14'If you offer a grain offering of your
firstfruits to the LORD, you shall offer for
the grain offering of your firstfruits green
heads of grain roasted on the fire, grain beat-
en from full heads. 15And you shall put oil on
it, and lay frankincense on it. It *is* a grain offering. 16Then the priest shall burn the memorial portion: *part* of its beaten grain and
part of its oil, with all the frankincense, as an
offering made by fire to the LORD.

The Peace Offering

3 'When his offering *is* a sacrifice of
a peace offering, if he offers *it* of the
herd, whether male or female, he shall offer
it without blemish before the LORD. 2And he
shall lay his hand on the head of his offering, and kill it *at* the door of the tabernacle of
meeting and Aaron's sons, the priests, shall

In Focus

1:4 Atonement In Old Testament times, people brought animal sacrifices to the priest. This was to make "atonement" for their sins (pronounced *ah-TONE-ment*). An atonement is a price paid for a person's sins. We put people in jail to "atone" for crimes. Only Jesus could pay the price we owe to God for our sins.

2:11 Leaven Pronounced *LEV-in.* A substance used in ancient times to make bread dough rise. Today bakers use yeast to do this. Jesus compared the growth of God's kingdom to the slow work of making bread with leaven (Matthew 13:33).

sprinkle the blood all around on the altar.
3Then he shall offer from the sacrifice of
the peace offering an offering made by fire
to the LORD. The fat that covers the entrails
and all the fat that *is* on the entrails, 4the two
kidneys and the fat that *is* on them by the
flanks, and the fatty lobe *attached* to the liver above the kidneys, he shall remove; 5and
Aaron's sons shall burn it on the altar upon
the burnt sacrifice, which *is* on the wood that
is on the fire, *as* an offering made by fire, a
sweet aroma to the LORD.
6'If his offering as a sacrifice of a peace
offering to the LORD *is* of the flock, *whether* male or female, he shall offer it without
blemish. 7If he offers a lamb as his offering,
then he shall offer it before the LORD. 8And
he shall lay his hand on the head of his offering, and kill it before the tabernacle of meeting; and Aaron's sons shall sprinkle its blood
all around on the altar.
9'Then he shall offer from the sacrifice
of the peace offering, as an offering made
by fire to the LORD, its fat *and* the whole fat
tail which he shall remove close to the back-
bone. And the fat that covers the entrails and
all the fat that *is* on the entrails, 10the two
kidneys and the fat that *is* on them by the
flanks, and the fatty lobe *attached* to the liver

above the kidneys, he shall remove; 11and the
priest shall burn *them* on the altar *as* food,
an offering made by fire to the LORD.

12'And if his offering *is* a goat, then he
shall offer it before the LORD. 13He shall lay
his hand on its head and kill it before the
tabernacle of meeting; and the sons of Aaron shall sprinkle its blood all around on the
altar. 14Then he shall offer from it his offering, as an offering made by fire to the LORD.
The fat that covers the entrails and all the fat
that *is* on the entrails, 15the two kidneys and
the fat that *is* on them by the flanks, and the
fatty lobe *attached* to the liver above the kidneys, he shall remove; 16and the priest shall
burn them on the altar *as* food, an offering
made by fire for a sweet aroma; all the fat *is*
the LORD's.

17'*This shall be* a perpetual statute
throughout your generations in all your
dwellings: you shall eat neither fat nor
blood.'"

The Sin Offering

4 Now the LORD spoke to Moses, saying,
2"Speak to the children of Israel, saying: 'If a person sins unintentionally against
any of the commandments of the LORD *in
anything* which ought not to be done, and
does any of them, 3if the anointed priest
sins, bringing guilt on the people, then let
him offer to the LORD for his sin which he
has sinned a young bull without blemish
as a sin offering. 4He shall bring the bull to
the door of the tabernacle of meeting before
the LORD, lay his hand on the bull's head,
and kill the bull before the LORD. 5Then the
anointed priest shall take some of the bull's
blood and bring it to the tabernacle of meeting. 6The priest shall dip his finger in the
blood and sprinkle some of the blood seven
times before the LORD, in front of the veil
of the sanctuary. 7And the priest shall put
some of the blood on the horns of the altar
of sweet incense before the LORD, which is
in the tabernacle of meeting; and he shall
pour the remaining blood of the bull at the
base of the altar of the burnt offering, which
is at the door of the tabernacle of meeting.
8He shall take from it all the fat of the bull as
the sin offering. The fat that covers the entrails and all the fat which *is* on the entrails,
9the two kidneys and the fat that *is* on them
by the flanks, and the fatty lobe *attached* to
the liver above the kidneys, he shall remove,
10as it was taken from the bull of the sacrifice of the peace offering; and the priest shall
burn them on the altar of the burnt offering.
11But the bull's hide and all its flesh, with its
head and legs, its entrails and offal— 12the
whole bull he shall carry outside the camp
to a clean place, where the ashes are poured
out, and burn it on wood with fire; where the
ashes are poured out it shall be burned.

13'Now if the whole congregation of Israel
sins unintentionally, and the thing is hidden from the eyes of the assembly, and they
have done *something against* any of the commandments of the LORD *in anything* which
should not be done, and are guilty; 14when
the sin which they have committed becomes
known, then the assembly shall offer a
young bull for the sin, and bring it before
the tabernacle of meeting. 15And the elders
of the congregation shall lay their hands on
the head of the bull before the LORD. Then
the bull shall be killed before the LORD.
16The anointed priest shall bring some of
the bull's blood to the tabernacle of meeting. 17Then the priest shall dip his finger in
the blood and sprinkle *it* seven times before
the LORD, in front of the veil. 18And he shall
put *some* of the blood on the horns of the altar which *is* before the LORD, which *is* in the
tabernacle of meeting; and he shall pour the
remaining blood at the base of the altar of
burnt offering, which is at the door of the
tabernacle of meeting. 19He shall take all the
fat from it and burn *it* on the altar. 20And he
shall do with the bull as he did with the bull
as a sin offering; thus he shall do with it. So
the priest shall make atonement for them,
and it shall be forgiven them. 21Then he shall
carry the bull outside the camp, and burn it
as he burned the first bull. It *is* a sin offering
for the assembly.

22'When a ruler has sinned, and done
something unintentionally *against* any of
the commandments of the LORD his God *in
anything* which should not be done, and is
guilty, 23or if his sin which he has committed
comes to his knowledge, he shall bring as
his offering a kid of the goats, a male without blemish. 24And he shall lay his hand on
the head of the goat, and kill it at the place
where they kill the burnt offering before the
LORD. It *is* a sin offering. 25The priest shall
take some of the blood of the sin offering
with his finger, put *it* on the horns of the

altar of burnt offering, and pour its blood at
the base of the altar of burnt offering. 26And
he shall burn all its fat on the altar, like the
fat of the sacrifice of the peace offering. So
the priest shall make atonement for him
concerning his sin, and it shall be forgiven
him.

27'If anyone of the common people sins
unintentionally by doing *something against*
any of the commandments of the LORD *in*
anything which ought not to be done, and is
guilty, 28or if his sin which he has committed
comes to his knowledge, then he shall bring
as his offering a kid of the goats, a female
without blemish, for his sin which he has
committed. 29And he shall lay his hand on
the head of the sin offering, and kill the sin
offering at the place of the burnt offering.
30Then the priest shall take *some* of its blood
with his finger, put *it* on the horns of the altar of burnt offering, and pour all *the remain-*
ing blood at the base of the altar. 31He shall
remove all its fat, as fat is removed from the
sacrifice of the peace offering; and the priest
shall burn it on the altar for a sweet aroma
to the LORD. So the priest shall make atonement for him, and it shall be forgiven him.

32'If he brings a lamb as his sin offering,
he shall bring a female without blemish.
33Then he shall lay his hand on the head of
the sin offering, and kill it as a sin offering
at the place where they kill the burnt offering. 34The priest shall take *some* of the blood
of the sin offering with his finger, put *it* on
the horns of the altar of burnt offering, and
pour all *the remaining* blood at the base of the
altar. 35He shall remove all its fat, as the fat of
the lamb is removed from the sacrifice of the
peace offering. Then the priest shall burn it
on the altar, according to the offerings made
by fire to the LORD. So the priest shall make
atonement for his sin that he has committed,
and it shall be forgiven him.

The Trespass Offering

5 'If a person sins in hearing the utterance of an oath, and *is* a witness,
whether he has seen or known *of the*
matter—if he does not tell *it*, he bears guilt.

2'Or if a person touches any unclean
thing, whether *it is* the carcass of an unclean
beast, or the carcass of unclean livestock,
or the carcass of unclean creeping things,
and he is unaware of it, he also shall be unclean and guilty. 3Or if he touches human
uncleanness—whatever uncleanness with
which a man may be defiled, and he is unaware of it—when he realizes *it*, then he
shall be guilty.

4'Or if a person swears, speaking
thoughtlessly with *his* lips to do evil or to
do good, whatever *it is* that a man may pronounce by an oath, and he is unaware of it—
when he realizes *it*, then he shall be guilty in
any of these *matters*.

5'And it shall be, when he is guilty in any
of these *matters*, that he shall confess that he
has sinned in that *thing*; 6and he shall bring
his trespass offering to the LORD for his sin
which he has committed, a female from the
flock, a lamb or a kid of the goats as a sin
offering. So the priest shall make atonement
for him concerning his sin.

7'If he is not able to bring a lamb, then

THE VALUE OF WORDS

READ IT: LEVITICUS 5:4

Has someone ever asked you to pray for him or her, and you immediately said yes because that's the "right" thing to do? When we make a promise, we should keep it. Leviticus 5:4 shows us how important this is. Sometimes we may quickly answer and not follow through. Whether what we say is for good—like promising someone we'll pray—or not for good, we're held responsible for our words.

he shall bring to the LORD, for his trespass
which he has committed, two turtledoves or
two young pigeons: one as a sin offering and
the other as a burnt offering. 8And he shall
bring them to the priest, who shall offer *that*
which *is* for the sin offering first, and wring
off its head from its neck, but shall not divide
it completely. 9Then he shall sprinkle *some*
of the blood of the sin offering on the side
of the altar, and the rest of the blood shall be
drained out at the base of the altar. It *is* a sin
offering. 10And he shall offer the second *as*
a burnt offering according to the prescribed
manner. So the priest shall make atonement
on his behalf for his sin which he has committed, and it shall be forgiven him.

11'But if he is not able to bring two turtledoves or two young pigeons, then he who
sinned shall bring for his offering one-tenth
of an ephah of fine flour as a sin offering.
He shall put no oil on it, nor shall he put
frankincense on it, for it *is* a sin offering.
12Then he shall bring it to the priest, and
the priest shall take his handful of it as a
memorial portion, and burn *it* on the altar
according to the offerings made by fire to the
LORD. It *is* a sin offering. 13The priest shall
make atonement for him, for his sin that he
has committed in any of these matters; and
it shall be forgiven him. *The rest* shall be the
priest's as a grain offering.'"

Offerings with Restitution

14Then the LORD spoke to Moses, saying:
15"If a person commits a trespass, and sins
unintentionally in regard to the holy things
of the LORD, then he shall bring to the LORD
as his trespass offering a ram without blemish from the flocks, with your valuation in
shekels of silver according to the shekel of
the sanctuary, as a trespass offering. 16And
he shall make restitution for the harm that
he has done in regard to the holy thing, and
shall add one-fifth to it and give it to the
priest. So the priest shall make atonement
for him with the ram of the trespass offering, and it shall be forgiven him.

17"If a person sins, and commits any of
these things which are forbidden to be done
by the commandments of the LORD, though
he does not know *it*, yet he is guilty and shall
bear his iniquity. 18And he shall bring to the
priest a ram without blemish from the flock,
with your valuation, as a trespass offering.
So the priest shall make atonement for him
regarding his ignorance in which he erred
and did not know *it*, and it shall be forgiven
him. 19It is a trespass offering; he has certainly trespassed against the LORD."

6 And the LORD spoke to Moses, saying: 2"If a person sins and commits
a trespass against the LORD by lying to his
neighbor about what was delivered to him
for safekeeping, or about a pledge, or about a
robbery, or if he has extorted from his neighbor, 3or if he has found what was lost and
lies concerning it, and swears falsely—in
any one of these things that a man may do
in which he sins: 4then it shall be, because he
has sinned and is guilty, that he shall restore
what he has stolen, or the thing which he
has extorted, or what was delivered to him
for safekeeping, or the lost thing which he
found, 5or all that about which he has sworn
falsely. He shall restore its full value, add
one-fifth more to it, *and* give it to whomever
it belongs, on the day of his trespass offering. 6And he shall bring his trespass offering to the LORD, a ram without blemish from
the flock, with your valuation, as a trespass
offering, to the priest. 7So the priest shall
make atonement for him before the LORD,
and he shall be forgiven for any one of these
things that he may have done in which he
trespasses."

The Law of the Burnt Offering

8Then the LORD spoke to Moses, saying,
9"Command Aaron and his sons, saying,
'This *is* the law of the burnt offering: The
burnt offering *shall be* on the hearth upon
the altar all night until morning, and the
fire of the altar shall be kept burning on it.
10And the priest shall put on his linen garment, and his linen trousers he shall put on
his body, and take up the ashes of the burnt
offering which the fire has consumed on
the altar, and he shall put them beside the
altar. 11Then he shall take off his garments,
put on other garments, and carry the ashes
outside the camp to a clean place. 12And the
fire on the altar shall be kept burning on it;
it shall not be put out. And the priest shall
burn wood on it every morning, and lay the
burnt offering in order on it; and he shall
burn on it the fat of the peace offerings. 13A
fire shall always be burning on the altar; it
shall never go out.

The Law of the Grain Offering

[14]'This *is* the law of the grain offering:
The sons of Aaron shall offer it on the altar
before the LORD. [15]He shall take from it his
handful of the fine flour of the grain offering, with its oil, and all the frankincense
which *is* on the grain offering, and shall
burn *it* on the altar *for* a sweet aroma, as a
memorial to the LORD. [16]And the remainder of it Aaron and his sons shall eat; with
unleavened bread it shall be eaten in a holy
place; in the court of the tabernacle of meeting they shall eat it. [17]It shall not be baked
with leaven. I have given it *as* their portion
of My offerings made by fire; it *is* most holy,
like the sin offering and the trespass offering. [18]All the males among the children of
Aaron may eat it. *It shall be* a statute forever
in your generations concerning the offerings made by fire to the LORD. Everyone who
touches them must be holy.'"[a]

[19]And the LORD spoke to Moses, saying,
[20]"This *is* the offering of Aaron and his sons,
which they shall offer to the LORD, *beginning*
on the day when he is anointed: one-tenth of
an ephah of fine flour as a daily grain offering, half of it in the morning and half of it
at night. [21]It shall be made in a pan with oil.
When it is mixed, you shall bring it in. The
baked pieces of the grain offering you shall
offer *for* a sweet aroma to the LORD. [22]The
priest from among his sons, who is anointed
in his place, shall offer it. *It is* a statute forever to the LORD. It shall be wholly burned.
[23]For every grain offering for the priest shall
be wholly burned. It shall not be eaten."

The Law of the Sin Offering

[24]Also the LORD spoke to Moses, saying,
[25]"Speak to Aaron and to his sons, saying,
'This *is* the law of the sin offering: In the
place where the burnt offering is killed, the
sin offering shall be killed before the LORD.
It *is* most holy. [26]The priest who offers it for
sin shall eat it. In a holy place it shall be eat-
en, in the court of the tabernacle of meeting. [27]Everyone who touches its flesh must
be holy.[a] And when its blood is sprinkled on
any garment, you shall wash that on which
it was sprinkled, in a holy place. [28]But the
earthen vessel in which it is boiled shall be
broken. And if it is boiled in a bronze pot, it
shall be both scoured and rinsed in water.
[29]All the males among the priests may eat
it. It *is* most holy. [30]But no sin offering from
which *any* of the blood is brought into the
tabernacle of meeting, to make atonement
in the holy *place*,[a] shall be eaten. It shall be
burned in the fire.

The Law of the Trespass Offering

7 'Likewise this *is* the law of the trespass
offering (it *is* most holy): [2]In the place
where they kill the burnt offering they shall
kill the trespass offering. And its blood he
shall sprinkle all around on the altar. [3]And
he shall offer from it all its fat. The fat tail
and the fat that covers the entrails, [4]the two
kidneys and the fat that *is* on them by the
flanks, and the fatty lobe *attached* to the liver above the kidneys, he shall remove; [5]and
the priest shall burn them on the altar *as* an
offering made by fire to the LORD. It *is* a trespass offering. [6]Every male among the priests
may eat it. It shall be eaten in a holy place. It
is most holy. [7]The trespass offering *is* like the
sin offering; *there is* one law for them both:
the priest who makes atonement with it shall
have *it*. [8]And the priest who offers anyone's
burnt offering, that priest shall have for himself the skin of the burnt offering which he
has offered. [9]Also every grain offering that
is baked in the oven and all that is prepared
in the covered pan, or in a pan, shall be the
priest's who offers it. [10]Every grain offering,
whether mixed with oil or dry, shall belong
to all the sons of Aaron, to one *as much* as
the other.

The Law of Peace Offerings

[11]'This *is* the law of the sacrifice of peace
offerings which he shall offer to the LORD:
[12]If he offers it for a thanksgiving, then he
shall offer, with the sacrifice of thanksgiving, unleavened cakes mixed with oil, unleavened wafers anointed with oil, or cakes
of blended flour mixed with oil. [13]Besides the
cakes, *as* his offering he shall offer leavened
bread with the sacrifice of thanksgiving of
his peace offering. [14]And from it he shall offer one cake from each offering as a heave
offering to the LORD. It shall belong to the
priest who sprinkles the blood of the peace
offering.

[15]'The flesh of the sacrifice of his peace
offering for thanksgiving shall be eaten the

6:18 [a] Compare Numbers 4:15 and Haggai 2:11–13
6:27 [a] Compare Numbers 4:15 and Haggai 2:11–13
6:30 [a] The Most Holy Place when capitalized

same day it is offered. He shall not leave any
of it until morning. 16But if the sacrifice of
his offering *is* a vow or a voluntary offering,
it shall be eaten the same day that he offers
his sacrifice; but on the next day the remainder of it also may be eaten; 17the remainder
of the flesh of the sacrifice on the third day
must be burned with fire. 18And if *any* of the
flesh of the sacrifice of his peace offering is
eaten at all on the third day, it shall not be
accepted, nor shall it be imputed to him; it
shall be an abomination *to* him who offers it,
and the person who eats of it shall bear guilt.

19'The flesh that touches any unclean
thing shall not be eaten. It shall be burned
with fire. And as for the *clean* flesh, all who
are clean may eat of it. 20But the person who
eats the flesh of the sacrifice of the peace offering that *belongs* to the LORD, while he is
unclean, that person shall be cut off from his
people. 21Moreover the person who touches
any unclean thing, *such as* human uncleanness, *an* unclean animal, or any abominable
unclean thing,[a] and who eats the flesh of the
sacrifice of the peace offering that *belongs* to
the LORD, that person shall be cut off from
his people.'"

Fat and Blood May Not Be Eaten

22And the LORD spoke to Moses, saying,
23"Speak to the children of Israel, saying:
'You shall not eat any fat, of ox or sheep or
goat. 24And the fat of an animal that dies
naturally, and the fat of what is torn by wild
beasts, may be used in any other way; but
you shall by no means eat it. 25For whoever eats the fat of the animal of which men
offer an offering made by fire to the LORD,
the person who eats *it* shall be cut off from
his people. 26Moreover you shall not eat any
blood in any of your dwellings, *whether* of
bird or beast. 27Whoever eats any blood, that
person shall be cut off from his people.'"

The Portion of Aaron and His Sons

28Then the LORD spoke to Moses, saying,
29"Speak to the children of Israel, saying:
'He who offers the sacrifice of his peace offering to the LORD shall bring his offering
to the LORD from the sacrifice of his peace
offering. 30His own hands shall bring the
offerings made by fire to the LORD. The fat
with the breast he shall bring, that the breast
may be waved *as* a wave offering before the
LORD. 31And the priest shall burn the fat on
the altar, but the breast shall be Aaron's and
his sons'. 32Also the right thigh you shall give
to the priest *as* a heave offering from the sacrifices of your peace offerings. 33He among
the sons of Aaron, who offers the blood of
the peace offering and the fat, shall have the
right thigh for *his* part. 34For the breast of
the wave offering and the thigh of the heave
offering I have taken from the children of
Israel, from the sacrifices of their peace offerings, and I have given them to Aaron the
priest and to his sons from the children of
Israel by a statute forever.'"

35This *is* the consecrated portion for Aaron and his sons, from the offerings made
by fire to the LORD, on the day when *Moses*
presented them to minister to the LORD as
priests. 36The LORD commanded this to be
given to them by the children of Israel, on
the day that He anointed them, *by* a statute
forever throughout their generations.

37This *is* the law of the burnt offering, the
grain offering, the sin offering, the trespass
offering, the consecrations, and the sacrifice
of the peace offering, 38which the LORD commanded Moses on Mount Sinai, on the day
when He commanded the children of Israel
to offer their offerings to the LORD in the
Wilderness of Sinai.

Aaron and His Sons Consecrated

8 And the LORD spoke to Moses, saying:
2"Take Aaron and his sons with him,
and the garments, the anointing oil, a bull
as the sin offering, two rams, and a basket
of unleavened bread; 3and gather all the congregation together at the door of the tabernacle of meeting."

4So Moses did as the LORD commanded
him. And the congregation was gathered together at the door of the tabernacle of meeting. 5And Moses said to the congregation,
"This *is* what the LORD commanded to be
done."

6Then Moses brought Aaron and his
sons and washed them with water. 7And he
put the tunic on him, girded him with the
sash, clothed him with the robe, and put the
ephod on him; and he girded him with the
intricately woven band of the ephod, and
with it tied *the ephod* on him. 8Then he put
the breastplate on him, and he put the Urim

7:21 [a] Following Masoretic Text, Septuagint, and Vulgate; Samaritan Pentateuch, Syriac, and Targum read *swarming thing* (compare 5:2).

and the Thummim[a] in the breastplate. 9 And he put the turban on his head. Also on the turban, on its front, he put the golden plate, the holy crown, as the LORD had commanded Moses.

10 Also Moses took the anointing oil, and anointed the tabernacle and all that *was* in it, and consecrated them. 11 He sprinkled some of it on the altar seven times, anointed the altar and all its utensils, and the laver and its base, to consecrate them. 12 And he poured some of the anointing oil on Aaron's head and anointed him, to consecrate him.

13 Then Moses brought Aaron's sons and put tunics on them, girded them with sashes, and put hats on them, as the LORD had commanded Moses.

14 And he brought the bull for the sin offering. Then Aaron and his sons laid their hands on the head of the bull for the sin offering, 15 and Moses killed *it*. Then he took the blood, and put *some* on the horns of the altar all around with his finger, and purified the altar. And he poured the blood at the base of the altar, and consecrated it, to make atonement for it. 16 Then he took all the fat that *was* on the entrails, the fatty lobe *attached to* the liver, and the two kidneys with their fat, and Moses burned *them* on the altar. 17 But the bull, its hide, its flesh, and its offal, he burned with fire outside the camp, as the LORD had commanded Moses.

18 Then he brought the ram as the burnt offering. And Aaron and his sons laid their hands on the head of the ram, 19 and Moses killed *it*. Then he sprinkled the blood all around on the altar. 20 And he cut the ram into pieces; and Moses burned the head, the pieces, and the fat. 21 Then he washed the entrails and the legs in water. And Moses burned the whole ram on the altar. It *was* a burnt sacrifice for a sweet aroma, an offering made by fire to the LORD, as the LORD had commanded Moses.

22 And he brought the second ram, the ram of consecration. Then Aaron and his sons laid their hands on the head of the ram, 23 and Moses killed *it*. Also he took *some* of its blood and put it on the tip of Aaron's right ear, on the thumb of his right hand, and on the big toe of his right foot. 24 Then he brought Aaron's sons. And Moses put *some* of the blood on the tips of their right ears, on the thumbs of their right hands, and on the big toes of their right feet. And Moses sprinkled the blood all around on the altar. 25 Then he took the fat and the fat tail, all the fat that *was* on the entrails, the fatty lobe *attached to* the liver, the two kidneys and their fat, and the right thigh; 26 and from the basket of unleavened bread that was before the LORD he took one unleavened cake, a cake of bread *anointed with* oil, and one wafer, and put *them* on the fat and on the right thigh; 27 and he put all *these* in Aaron's hands and in his sons' hands, and waved them *as* a wave offering before the LORD. 28 Then Moses took them from their hands and burned *them* on the altar, on the burnt offering. They *were* consecration offerings for a sweet aroma. That *was* an offering made by fire to the LORD. 29 And Moses took the breast and waved it *as* a wave offering before the LORD. It was Moses' part of the ram of consecration, as the LORD had commanded Moses.

30 Then Moses took some of the anointing oil and some of the blood which *was* on the altar, and sprinkled *it* on Aaron, on his garments, on his sons, and on the garments of his sons with him; and he consecrated Aaron, his garments, his sons, and the garments of his sons with him.

31 And Moses said to Aaron and his sons, "Boil the flesh *at* the door of the tabernacle of meeting, and eat it there with the bread that *is* in the basket of consecration offerings, as I commanded, saying, 'Aaron and his sons shall eat it.' 32 What remains of the flesh and of the bread you shall burn with fire. 33 And you shall not go outside the door of the tabernacle of meeting *for* seven days, until the days of your consecration are ended. For seven days he shall consecrate you. 34 As he has done this day, *so* the LORD has commanded to do, to make atonement for you. 35 Therefore you shall stay *at* the door of the tabernacle of meeting day and night for seven days, and keep the charge of the LORD, so that you may not die; for so I have been commanded." 36 So Aaron and his sons did all the things that the LORD had commanded by the hand of Moses.

The Priestly Ministry Begins

It came to pass on the eighth day that Moses called Aaron and his sons and

8:8 [a] Literally *the Lights and the Perfections* (compare Exodus 28:30)

the elders of Israel. 2And he said to Aaron, "Take for yourself a young bull as a sin offering and a ram as a burnt offering, without blemish, and offer *them* before the LORD. 3And to the children of Israel you shall speak, saying, 'Take a kid of the goats as a sin offering, and a calf and a lamb, *both* of the first year, without blemish, as a burnt offering, 4also a bull and a ram as peace offerings, to sacrifice before the LORD, and a grain offering mixed with oil; for today the LORD will appear to you.' "

5So they brought what Moses commanded before the tabernacle of meeting. And all the congregation drew near and stood before the LORD. 6Then Moses said, "This *is* the thing which the LORD commanded you to do, and the glory of the LORD will appear to you." 7And Moses said to Aaron, "Go to the altar, offer your sin offering and your burnt offering, and make atonement for yourself and for the people. Offer the offering of the people, and make atonement for them, as the LORD commanded."

8Aaron therefore went to the altar and killed the calf of the sin offering, which *was* for himself. 9Then the sons of Aaron brought the blood to him. And he dipped his finger in the blood, put *it* on the horns of the altar, and poured the blood at the base of the altar. 10But the fat, the kidneys, and the fatty lobe from the liver of the sin offering he burned on the altar, as the LORD had commanded Moses. 11The flesh and the hide he burned with fire outside the camp.

12And he killed the burnt offering; and Aaron's sons presented to him the blood, which he sprinkled all around on the altar. 13Then they presented the burnt offering to him, with its pieces and head, and he burned *them* on the altar. 14And he washed the entrails and the legs, and burned *them* with the burnt offering on the altar.

15Then he brought the people's offering, and took the goat, which *was* the sin offering for the people, and killed it and offered it for sin, like the first one. 16And he brought the burnt offering and offered it according to the prescribed manner. 17Then he brought *the* grain offering, took a handful of it, and burned *it* on the altar, besides the burnt sacrifice of the morning.

18He also killed the bull and the ram *as* sacrifices of peace offerings, which *were* for the people. And Aaron's sons presented to him the blood, which he sprinkled all around on the altar, 19and the fat from the bull and the ram—the fatty tail, what covers *the entrails* and the kidneys, and the fatty lobe *attached to* the liver; 20and they put the fat on the breasts. Then he burned the fat on the altar; 21but the breasts and the right thigh Aaron waved *as* a wave offering before the LORD, as Moses had commanded.

22Then Aaron lifted his hand toward the people, blessed them, and came down from offering the sin offering, the burnt offering, and peace offerings. 23And Moses and Aaron went into the tabernacle of meeting, and came out and blessed the people. Then the glory of the LORD appeared to all the people, 24and fire came out from before the LORD and consumed the burnt offering and the fat on the altar. When all the people saw *it*, they shouted and fell on their faces.

The Profane Fire of Nadab and Abihu

10 Then Nadab and Abihu, the sons of Aaron, each took his censer and put fire in it, put incense on it, and offered profane fire before the LORD, which He had not commanded them. 2So fire went out from the LORD and devoured them, and they died before the LORD. 3And Moses said to Aaron, "This is what the LORD spoke, saying:

'By those who come near Me
I must be regarded as holy;
And before all the people
I must be glorified.' "

So Aaron held his peace.

4Then Moses called Mishael and Elzaphan, the sons of Uzziel the uncle of Aaron, and said to them, "Come near, carry your brethren from before the sanctuary out of the camp." 5So they went near and carried them by their tunics out of the camp, as Moses had said.

6And Moses said to Aaron, and to Eleazar and Ithamar, his sons, "Do not uncover your heads nor tear your clothes, lest you die, and *wrath come upon all* the people. But let your brethren, the whole house of Israel, bewail the burning which the LORD has kindled. 7You shall not go out from the door of the tabernacle of meeting, lest you die, for the

anointing oil of the LORD *is* upon you." And
they did according to the word of Moses.

Conduct Prescribed for Priests

8Then the LORD spoke to Aaron, saying:
9"Do not drink wine or intoxicating drink,
you, nor your sons with you, when you go
into the tabernacle of meeting, lest you die.
It shall be a statute forever throughout your
generations, 10that you may distinguish between holy and unholy, and between unclean and clean, 11and that you may teach
the children of Israel all the statutes which
the LORD has spoken to them by the hand
of Moses."

12And Moses spoke to Aaron, and to Eleazar and Ithamar, his sons who were left:
"Take the grain offering that remains of
the offerings made by fire to the LORD, and
eat it without leaven beside the altar; for it *is*
most holy. 13You shall eat it in a holy place,
because it *is* your due and your sons' due, of
the sacrifices made by fire to the LORD; for
so I have been commanded. 14The breast of
the wave offering and the thigh of the heave
offering you shall eat in a clean place, you,
your sons, and your daughters with you; for
they are your due and your sons' due, *which*
are given from the sacrifices of peace offerings of the children of Israel. 15The thigh of
the heave offering and the breast of the wave
offering they shall bring with the offerings
of fat made by fire, to offer *as* a wave offering
before the LORD. And it shall be yours and
your sons' with you, by a statute forever, as
the LORD has commanded."

16Then Moses made careful inquiry
about the goat of the sin offering, and there
it was—burned up. And he was angry with
Eleazar and Ithamar, the sons of Aaron *who*
were left, saying, 17"Why have you not eat-
en the sin offering in a holy place, since it
is most holy, and *God* has given it to you to
bear the guilt of the congregation, to make
atonement for them before the LORD? 18See!
Its blood was not brought inside the holy
place;[a] indeed you should have eaten it in a
holy *place*, as I commanded."

19And Aaron said to Moses, "Look, this
day they have offered their sin offering
and their burnt offering before the LORD,
and such things have befallen me! *If* I had
eaten the sin offering today, would it have
been accepted in the sight of the LORD?" 20So
when Moses heard *that*, he was content.

Foods Permitted and Forbidden

11 Now the LORD spoke to Moses and
Aaron, saying to them, 2"Speak to
the children of Israel, saying, 'These *are* the
animals which you may eat among all the animals that *are* on the earth: 3Among the
animals, whatever divides the hoof, having cloven hooves *and* chewing the cud—
that you may eat. 4Nevertheless these you
shall not eat among those that chew the
cud or those that have cloven hooves: the
camel, because it chews the cud but does
not have cloven hooves, is unclean to you;
5the rock hyrax, because it chews the cud but
does not have cloven hooves, *is* unclean to you;
6the hare, because it chews the cud but does
not have cloven hooves, *is* unclean to you;
7and the swine, though it divides the hoof,
having cloven hooves, yet does not chew
the cud, *is* unclean to you. 8Their flesh you
shall not eat, and their carcasses you shall
not touch. They *are* unclean to you.

9'These you may eat of all that *are* in the
water: whatever in the water has fins and
scales, whether in the seas or in the rivers—
that you may eat. 10But all in the seas or in
the rivers that do not have fins and scales,
all that move in the water or any living thing
which *is* in the water, they *are* an abomination to you. 11They shall be an abomination
to you; you shall not eat their flesh, but you
shall regard their carcasses as an abomination. 12Whatever in the water does not have
fins or scales—that *shall be* an abomination
to you.

13'And these you shall regard as an abomination among the birds; they shall not be
eaten, they *are* an abomination: the eagle,
the vulture, the buzzard, 14the kite, and the
falcon after its kind; 15every raven after its
kind, 16the ostrich, the short-eared owl, the
sea gull, and the hawk after its kind; 17the little owl, the fisher owl, and the screech owl;
18the white owl, the jackdaw, and the carrion
vulture; 19the stork, the heron after its kind,
the hoopoe, and the bat.

20'All flying insects that creep on *all*
fours *shall be* an abomination to you. 21Yet

10:18 [a] The Most Holy Place when capitalized

these you may eat of every flying insect that
creeps on *all* fours: those which have jointed
legs above their feet with which to leap on
the earth. 22 These you may eat: the locust
after its kind, the destroying locust after
its kind, the cricket after its kind, and the
grasshopper after its kind. 23 But all *other* flying insects which have four feet *shall be* an
abomination to you.

Unclean Animals

24 'By these you shall become unclean;
whoever touches the carcass of any of them
shall be unclean until evening; 25 whoever
carries part of the carcass of any of them
shall wash his clothes and be unclean until
evening: 26 *The carcass* of any animal which
divides the foot, but is not cloven-hoofed or
does not chew the cud, *is* unclean to you.
Everyone who touches it shall be unclean.
27 And whatever goes on its paws, among all
kinds of animals that go on *all* fours, those
are unclean to you. Whoever touches any
such carcass shall be unclean until evening.
28 Whoever carries *any such* carcass shall
wash his clothes and be unclean until evening. It *is* unclean to you.

29 'These also *shall be* unclean to you
among the creeping things that creep on
the earth: the mole, the mouse, and the large
lizard after its kind; 30 the gecko, the monitor
lizard, the sand reptile, the sand lizard, and
the chameleon. 31 These *are* unclean to you
among all that creep. Whoever touches them
when they are dead shall be unclean until
evening. 32 Anything on which *any* of them
falls, when they are dead shall be unclean,
whether *it is* any item of wood or clothing
or skin or sack, whatever item *it is*, in which
any work is done, it must be put in water.
And it shall be unclean until evening; then
it shall be clean. 33 Any earthen vessel into
which *any* of them falls you shall break; and
whatever *is* in it shall be unclean: 34 in such
a vessel, any edible food upon which water
falls becomes unclean, and any drink that
may be drunk from it becomes unclean.
35 And everything on which *a part* of *any such*
carcass falls shall be unclean; *whether it is*
an oven or cooking stove, it shall be broken
down; *for* they *are* unclean, and shall be unclean to you. 36 Nevertheless a spring or a cistern, *in which there is* plenty of water, shall be
clean, but whatever touches any such carcass
becomes unclean. 37 And if a part of *any such*
carcass falls on any planting seed which is to
be sown, it *remains* clean. 38 But if water is put
on the seed, and if *a part* of *any such* carcass
falls on it, it *becomes* unclean to you.

39 'And if any animal which you may eat
dies, he who touches its carcass shall be unclean until evening. 40 He who eats of its carcass shall wash his clothes and be unclean
until evening. He also who carries its carcass shall wash his clothes and be unclean
until evening.

41 'And every creeping thing that creeps
on the earth *shall be* an abomination. It shall
not be eaten. 42 Whatever crawls on its belly, whatever goes on *all* fours, or whatever
has many feet among all creeping things
that creep on the earth—these you shall
not eat, for they *are* an abomination. 43 You
shall not make yourselves abominable with
any creeping thing that creeps; nor shall you
make yourselves unclean with them, lest
you be defiled by them. 44 For I *am* the LORD
your God. You shall therefore consecrate
yourselves, and you shall be holy; for I *am*
holy. Neither shall you defile yourselves with
any creeping thing that creeps on the earth.
45 For I *am* the LORD who brings you up out of
the land of Egypt, to be your God. You shall
therefore be holy, for I *am* holy.

46 'This *is* the law of the animals and the
birds and every living creature that moves in
the waters, and of every creature that creeps
on the earth, 47 to distinguish between the
unclean and the clean, and between the animal that may be eaten and the animal that
may not be eaten.' "

The Ritual After Childbirth

12 Then the LORD spoke to Moses,
saying, 2 "Speak to the children of
Israel, saying: 'If a woman has conceived,
and borne a male child, then she shall be
unclean seven days; as in the days of her customary impurity she shall be unclean. 3 And
on the eighth day the flesh of his foreskin
shall be circumcised. 4 She shall then continue in the blood of *her* purification thirty-
three days. She shall not touch any hallowed
thing, nor come into the sanctuary until the
days of her purification are fulfilled.

5 'But if she bears a female child, then she
shall be unclean two weeks, as in her customary impurity, and she shall continue in
the blood of *her* purification sixty-six days.

6'When the days of her purification are
fulfilled, whether for a son or a daughter,
she shall bring to the priest a lamb of the
first year as a burnt offering, and a young
pigeon or a turtledove as a sin offering, to
the door of the tabernacle of meeting. 7Then
he shall offer it before the LORD, and make
atonement for her. And she shall be clean
from the flow of her blood. This *is* the law
for her who has borne a male or a female.

8'And if she is not able to bring a lamb,
then she may bring two turtledoves or two
young pigeons—one as a burnt offering
and the other as a sin offering. So the priest
shall make atonement for her, and she will
be clean.'"

The Law Concerning Leprosy

13 And the LORD spoke to Moses and
Aaron, saying: 2"When a man has
on the skin of his body a swelling, a scab, or
a bright spot, and it becomes on the skin of
his body *like* a leprous[a] sore, then he shall be
brought to Aaron the priest or to one of his
sons the priests. 3The priest shall examine
the sore on the skin of the body; and if the
hair on the sore has turned white, and the
sore appears *to be* deeper than the skin of his
body, it *is* a leprous sore. Then the priest shall
examine him, and pronounce him unclean.
4But if the bright spot *is* white on the skin of
his body, and does not appear *to be* deeper
than the skin, and its hair has not turned
white, then the priest shall isolate *the one*
who has the sore seven days. 5And the priest
shall examine him on the seventh day; and
indeed if the sore appears to be as it was, *and*
the sore has not spread on the skin, then the
priest shall isolate him another seven days.
6Then the priest shall examine him again
on the seventh day; and indeed *if* the sore
has faded, *and* the sore has not spread on the
skin, then the priest shall pronounce him
clean; it *is only* a scab, and he shall wash his
clothes and be clean. 7But if the scab should
at all spread over the skin, after he has been
seen by the priest for his cleansing, he shall
be seen by the priest again. 8And *if* the priest
sees that the scab has indeed spread on the
skin, then the priest shall pronounce him
unclean. It *is* leprosy.

9"When the leprous sore is on a person,
then he shall be brought to the priest. 10And
the priest shall examine *him;* and indeed *if*
the swelling on the skin *is* white, and it has
turned the hair white, and *there is* a spot of
raw flesh in the swelling, 11it *is* an old leprosy
on the skin of his body. The priest shall pronounce him unclean, and shall not isolate
him, for he *is* unclean.

12"And if leprosy breaks out all over the
skin, and the leprosy covers all the skin of
the one who has the sore, from his head to
his foot, wherever the priest looks, 13then
the priest shall consider; and indeed *if* the
leprosy has covered all his body, he shall
pronounce *him* clean *who has* the sore. It
has all turned white. He *is* clean. 14But when
raw flesh appears on him, he shall be unclean. 15And the priest shall examine the raw
flesh and pronounce him to be unclean; *for*
the raw flesh *is* unclean. It *is* leprosy. 16Or
if the raw flesh changes and turns white
again, he shall come to the priest. 17And the
priest shall examine him; and indeed *if* the
sore has turned white, then the priest shall
pronounce *him* clean *who has* the sore. He
is clean.

18"If the body develops a boil in the skin,
and it is healed, 19and in the place of the boil
there comes a white swelling or a bright
spot, reddish-white, then it shall be shown
to the priest; 20and *if,* when the priest sees it,
it indeed appears deeper than the skin, and
its hair has turned white, the priest shall
pronounce him unclean. It *is* a leprous sore
which has broken out of the boil. 21But if the
priest examines it, and indeed *there are* no
white hairs in it, and it *is* not deeper than
the skin, but has faded, then the priest shall
isolate him seven days; 22and if it should at
all spread over the skin, then the priest shall
pronounce him unclean. It *is* a leprous sore.
23But if the bright spot stays in one place, *and*
has not spread, it *is* the scar of the boil; and
the priest shall pronounce him clean.

24"Or if the body receives a burn on its
skin by fire, and the raw *flesh* of the burn becomes a bright spot, reddish-white or white,
25then the priest shall examine it; and indeed *if* the hair of the bright spot has turned
white, and it appears deeper than the skin, it
is leprosy broken out in the burn. Therefore
the priest shall pronounce him unclean. It
is a leprous sore. 26But if the priest examines it, and indeed *there are* no white hairs
in the bright spot, and it *is* not deeper than

13:2 [a] Hebrew *saraath,* disfiguring skin diseases, including leprosy, and so in verses 2–46 and 14:1–32

the skin, but has faded, then the priest shall
isolate him seven days. 27And the priest shall
examine him on the seventh day. If it has at
all spread over the skin, then the priest shall
pronounce him unclean. It *is* a leprous sore.
28But if the bright spot stays in one place, *and*
has not spread on the skin, but has faded, it
is a swelling from the burn. The priest shall
pronounce him clean, for it *is* the scar from
the burn.

29"If a man or woman has a sore on the
head or the beard, 30then the priest shall
examine the sore; and indeed if it appears
deeper than the skin, *and there is* in it thin
yellow hair, then the priest shall pronounce
him unclean. It *is* a scaly leprosy of the head
or beard. 31But if the priest examines the
scaly sore, and indeed it does not appear
deeper than the skin, and *there is* no black
hair in it, then the priest shall isolate *the
one who has* the scale seven days. 32And on
the seventh day the priest shall examine the
sore; and indeed *if* the scale has not spread,
and there is no yellow hair in it, and the scale
does not appear deeper than the skin, 33he
shall shave himself, but the scale he shall
not shave. And the priest shall isolate *the
one who has* the scale another seven days.
34On the seventh day the priest shall examine the scale; and indeed *if* the scale has not
spread over the skin, and does not appear
deeper than the skin, then the priest shall
pronounce him clean. He shall wash his
clothes and be clean. 35But if the scale should
at all spread over the skin after his cleansing, 36then the priest shall examine him; and
indeed *if* the scale has spread over the skin,
the priest need not seek for yellow hair. He
is unclean. 37But if the scale appears to be at
a standstill, and there is black hair grown up
in it, the scale has healed. He *is* clean, and
the priest shall pronounce him clean.

38"If a man or a woman has bright spots
on the skin of the body, *specifically* white
bright spots, 39then the priest shall look; and
indeed *if* the bright spots on the skin of the
body *are* dull white, it *is* a white spot *that*
grows on the skin. He *is* clean.

40"As for the man whose hair has fallen
from his head, he *is* bald, *but* he *is* clean. 41He
whose hair has fallen from his forehead, he
is bald on the forehead, *but* he *is* clean. 42And
if there is on the bald head or bald forehead a
reddish-white sore, it *is* leprosy breaking out
on his bald head or his bald forehead. 43Then
the priest shall examine it; and indeed *if* the
swelling of the sore *is* reddish-white on his
bald head or on his bald forehead, as the appearance of leprosy on the skin of the body,
44he is a leprous man. He *is* unclean. The
priest shall surely pronounce him unclean;
his sore *is* on his head.

45"Now the leper on whom the sore *is*, his
clothes shall be torn and his head bare; and
he shall cover his mustache, and cry, 'Unclean! Unclean!' 46He shall be unclean. All
the days he has the sore he shall be unclean.
He *is* unclean, and he shall dwell alone; his
dwelling *shall be* outside the camp.

The Law Concerning Leprous Garments

47"Also, if a garment has a leprous plague[a]
in it, *whether it is* a woolen garment or a lin-
en garment, 48whether *it is* in the warp or
woof of linen or wool, whether in leather
or in anything made of leather, 49and if the
plague is greenish or reddish in the garment
or in the leather, whether in the warp or in
the woof, or in anything made of leather, it
is a leprous plague and shall be shown to the
priest. 50The priest shall examine the plague
and isolate *that which has* the plague seven
days. 51And he shall examine the plague on
the seventh day. If the plague has spread in
the garment, either in the warp or in the
woof, in the leather *or* in anything made of
leather, the plague *is* an active leprosy. It *is*
unclean. 52He shall therefore burn that garment in which is the plague, whether warp
or woof, in wool or in linen, or anything of
leather, for it *is* an active leprosy; *the garment*
shall be burned in the fire.

53"But if the priest examines *it*, and indeed the plague has not spread in the garment, either in the warp or in the woof, or in
anything made of leather, 54then the priest
shall command that they wash *the thing* in
which *is* the plague; and he shall isolate it another seven days. 55Then the priest shall examine the plague after it has been washed;
and indeed *if* the plague has not changed its
color, though the plague has not spread, it *is*
unclean, and you shall burn it in the fire; it
continues eating away, *whether* the damage
is outside or inside. 56If the priest examines
it, and indeed the plague has faded after

13:47 [a] A mold, fungus, or similar infestation, and so in verses 47–59

washing it, then he shall tear it out of the
garment, whether out of the warp or out
of the woof, or out of the leather. [57]But if it
appears again in the garment, either in the
warp or in the woof, or in anything made
of leather, it *is* a spreading *plague*; you shall
burn with fire that in which is the plague.
[58]And if you wash the garment, either warp
or woof, or whatever is made of leather, if the
plague has disappeared from it, then it shall
be washed a second time, and shall be clean.

[59]"This *is* the law of the leprous plague
in a garment of wool or linen, either in the
warp or woof, or in anything made of leather, to pronounce it clean or to pronounce it
unclean."

The Ritual for Cleansing Healed Lepers

14 Then the LORD spoke to Moses, saying, [2]"This shall be the law of the
leper for the day of his cleansing: He shall be
brought to the priest. [3]And the priest shall go
out of the camp, and the priest shall examine *him;* and indeed, *if* the leprosy is healed
in the leper, [4]then the priest shall command
to take for him who is to be cleansed two
living *and* clean birds, cedar wood, scarlet,
and hyssop. [5]And the priest shall command
that one of the birds be killed in an earthen
vessel over running water. [6]As for the living
bird, he shall take it, the cedar wood and the
scarlet and the hyssop, and dip them and the
living bird in the blood of the bird *that was*
killed over the running water. [7]And he shall
sprinkle it seven times on him who is to be
cleansed from the leprosy, and shall pronounce him clean, and shall let the living
bird loose in the open field. [8]He who is to
be cleansed shall wash his clothes, shave off
all his hair, and wash himself in water, that
he may be clean. After that he shall come
into the camp, and shall stay outside his tent
seven days. [9]But on the seventh day he shall
shave all the hair off his head and his beard
and his eyebrows—all his hair he shall shave
off. He shall wash his clothes and wash his
body in water, and he shall be clean.

[10]"And on the eighth day he shall take
two male lambs without blemish, one ewe
lamb of the first year without blemish, three-tenths *of an ephah* of fine flour mixed with
oil as a grain offering, and one log of oil.
[11]Then the priest who makes *him* clean shall
present the man who is to be made clean,
and those things, before the LORD, *at* the
door of the tabernacle of meeting. [12]And the
priest shall take one male lamb and offer
it as a trespass offering, and the log of oil,
and wave them *as* a wave offering before the
LORD. [13]Then he shall kill the lamb in the
place where he kills the sin offering and the
burnt offering, in a holy place; for as the sin
offering *is* the priest's, so *is* the trespass offering. It *is* most holy. [14]The priest shall take
some of the blood of the trespass offering,
and the priest shall put *it* on the tip of the
right ear of him who is to be cleansed, on
the thumb of his right hand, and on the big
toe of his right foot. [15]And the priest shall
take *some* of the log of oil, and pour *it* into
the palm of his own left hand. [16]Then the
priest shall dip his right finger in the oil that
is in his left hand, and shall sprinkle some
of the oil with his finger seven times before
the LORD. [17]And of the rest of the oil in his
hand, the priest shall put *some* on the tip of
the right ear of him who is to be cleansed, on
the thumb of his right hand, and on the big
toe of his right foot, on the blood of the trespass offering. [18]The rest of the oil that *is* in
the priest's hand he shall put on the head of
him who is to be cleansed. So the priest shall
make atonement for him before the LORD.

[19]"Then the priest shall offer the sin offering, and make atonement for him who is
to be cleansed from his uncleanness. Afterward he shall kill the burnt offering. [20]And
the priest shall offer the burnt offering and
the grain offering on the altar. So the priest
shall make atonement for him, and he shall
be clean.

[21]"But if he *is* poor and cannot afford it,
then he shall take one male lamb *as* a trespass offering to be waved, to make atonement for him, one-tenth *of an ephah* of fine
flour mixed with oil as a grain offering, a
log of oil, [22]and two turtledoves or two young
pigeons, such as he is able to afford: one
shall be a sin offering and the other a burnt
offering. [23]He shall bring them to the priest
on the eighth day for his cleansing, to the
door of the tabernacle of meeting, before the
LORD. [24]And the priest shall take the lamb of
the trespass offering and the log of oil, and
the priest shall wave them *as* a wave offering before the LORD. [25]Then he shall kill the
lamb of the trespass offering, and the priest
shall take *some* of the blood of the trespass

offering and put *it* on the tip of the right ear of him who is to be cleansed, on the thumb of his right hand, and on the big toe of his right foot. 26 And the priest shall pour some of the oil into the palm of his own left hand. 27 Then the priest shall sprinkle with his right finger *some* of the oil that *is* in his left hand seven times before the LORD. 28 And the priest shall put *some* of the oil that *is* in his hand on the tip of the right ear of him who is to be cleansed, on the thumb of the right hand, and on the big toe of his right foot, on the place of the blood of the trespass offering. 29 The rest of the oil that *is* in the priest's hand he shall put on the head of him who is to be cleansed, to make atonement for him before the LORD. 30 And he shall offer one of the turtledoves or young pigeons, such as he can afford— 31 such as he is able to afford, the one *as* a sin offering and the other *as* a burnt offering, with the grain offering. So the priest shall make atonement for him who is to be cleansed before the LORD. 32 This *is* the law *for one* who had a leprous sore, who cannot afford the usual cleansing."

The Law Concerning Leprous Houses

33 And the LORD spoke to Moses and Aaron, saying: 34 "When you have come into the land of Canaan, which I give you as a possession, and I put the leprous plague[a] in a house in the land of your possession, 35 and he who owns the house comes and tells the priest, saying, 'It seems to me that *there is* some plague in the house,' 36 then the priest shall command that they empty the house, before the priest goes *into it* to examine the plague, that all that *is* in the house may not be made unclean; and afterward the priest shall go in to examine the house. 37 And he shall examine the plague; and indeed *if* the plague *is* on the walls of the house with ingrained streaks, greenish or reddish, which appear to be deep in the wall, 38 then the priest shall go out of the house, to the door of the house, and shut up the house seven days. 39 And the priest shall come again on the seventh day and look; and indeed *if* the plague has spread on the walls of the house, 40 then the priest shall command that they take away the *stones in which is the plague*, and they shall cast them into an unclean place outside the city. 41 And he shall cause the house to be scraped inside, all around, and the dust that they scrape off they shall pour out in an unclean place outside the city. 42 Then they shall take other stones and put *them* in the place of *those* stones, and he shall take other mortar and plaster the house.

43 "Now if the plague comes back and breaks out in the house, after he has taken away the stones, after he has scraped the house, and after it is plastered, 44 then the priest shall come and look; and indeed *if* the plague has spread in the house, it *is* an active leprosy in the house. It *is* unclean. 45 And he shall break down the house, its stones, its timber, and all the plaster of the house, and he shall carry *them* outside the city to an unclean place. 46 Moreover he who goes into the house at all while it is shut up shall be unclean until evening. 47 And he who lies down in the house shall wash his clothes, and he who eats in the house shall wash his clothes.

48 "But if the priest comes in and examines *it*, and indeed the plague has not spread in the house after the house was plastered, then the priest shall pronounce the house clean, because the plague is healed. 49 And he shall take, to cleanse the house, two birds, cedar wood, scarlet, and hyssop. 50 Then he shall kill one of the birds in an earthen vessel over running water; 51 and he shall take the cedar wood, the hyssop, the scarlet, and the living bird, and dip them in the blood of the slain bird and in the running water, and sprinkle the house seven times. 52 And he shall cleanse the house with the blood of the bird and the running water and the living bird, with the cedar wood, the hyssop, and the scarlet. 53 Then he shall let the living bird loose outside the city in the open field, and make atonement for the house, and it shall be clean.

54 "This *is* the law for any leprous sore and scale, 55 for the leprosy of a garment and of a house, 56 for a swelling and a scab and a bright spot, 57 to teach when *it is* unclean and when *it is* clean. This *is* the law of leprosy."

The Law Concerning Bodily Discharges

15 And the LORD spoke to Moses and Aaron, saying, 2 "Speak to the children of Israel, and say to them: 'When any man has a discharge from his body, his discharge *is* unclean. 3 And this shall be his

14:34 [a] Decomposition by mildew, mold, dry rot, etc., and so in verses 34–53

uncleanness in regard to his discharge—
whether his body runs with his discharge,
or his body is stopped up by his discharge,
it *is* his uncleanness. 4Every bed is unclean
on which he who has the discharge lies, and
everything on which he sits shall be unclean. 5And whoever touches his bed shall
wash his clothes and bathe in water, and
be unclean until evening. 6He who sits on
anything on which he who has the discharge
sat shall wash his clothes and bathe in water, and be unclean until evening. 7And he
who touches the body of him who has the
discharge shall wash his clothes and bathe
in water, and be unclean until evening. 8If
he who has the discharge spits on him who
is clean, then he shall wash his clothes and
bathe in water, and be unclean until evening. 9Any saddle on which he who has the
discharge rides shall be unclean. 10Whoever
touches anything that was under him shall
be unclean until evening. He who carries
any of those things shall wash his clothes
and bathe in water, and be unclean until
evening. 11And whomever the one who has
the discharge touches, and has not rinsed
his hands in water, he shall wash his clothes
and bathe in water, and be unclean until evening. 12The vessel of earth that he who has
the discharge touches shall be broken, and
every vessel of wood shall be rinsed in water.

13'And when he who has a discharge is
cleansed of his discharge, then he shall
count for himself seven days for his cleansing, wash his clothes, and bathe his body in
running water; then he shall be clean. 14On
the eighth day he shall take for himself two
turtledoves or two young pigeons, and come
before the LORD, to the door of the tabernacle of meeting, and give them to the priest.
15Then the priest shall offer them, the one
as a sin offering and the other *as* a burnt offering. So the priest shall make atonement
for him before the LORD because of his
discharge.

16'If *any* man has an emission of semen,
then he shall wash all his body in water, and
be unclean until evening. 17And any garment
and any leather on which there is semen, it
shall be washed with water, and be unclean
until evening. 18Also, when a woman lies
with a man, and *there is* an emission of semen, they shall bathe in water, and be unclean until evening.

19'If a woman has a discharge, *and* the
discharge from her body is blood, she shall
be set apart seven days; and whoever touches
her shall be unclean until evening. 20Every-
thing that she lies on during her impurity
shall be unclean; also everything that she
sits on shall be unclean. 21Whoever touches
her bed shall wash his clothes and bathe in
water, and be unclean until evening. 22And
whoever touches anything that she sat on
shall wash his clothes and bathe in water,
and be unclean until evening. 23If *anything* is
on *her* bed or on anything on which she sits,
when he touches it, he shall be unclean until
evening. 24And if any man lies with her at all,
so that her impurity is on him, he shall be
unclean seven days; and every bed on which
he lies shall be unclean.

25'If a woman has a discharge of blood
for many days, other than at the time of her
customary impurity, or if it runs beyond her
usual time of impurity, all the days of her unclean discharge shall be as the days of her
customary impurity. She *shall be* unclean.
26Every bed on which she lies all the days of
her discharge shall be to her as the bed of
her impurity; and whatever she sits on shall
be unclean, as the uncleanness of her impurity. 27Whoever touches those things shall be
unclean; he shall wash his clothes and bathe
in water, and be unclean until evening.

28'But if she is cleansed of her discharge,
then she shall count for herself seven days,
and after that she shall be clean. 29And on
the eighth day she shall take for herself two
turtledoves or two young pigeons, and bring
them to the priest, to the door of the tabernacle of meeting. 30Then the priest shall offer
the one *as* a sin offering and the other *as* a
burnt offering, and the priest shall make
atonement for her before the LORD for the
discharge of her uncleanness.

31'Thus you shall separate the children of
Israel from their uncleanness, lest they die
in their uncleanness when they defile My
tabernacle that *is* among them. 32This *is* the
law for one who has a discharge, and *for him*
who emits semen and is unclean thereby,
33and for her who is indisposed because of
her *customary* impurity, and for one who has
a discharge, either man or woman, and for
him who lies with her who is unclean.' "

The Day of Atonement

16 Now the LORD spoke to Moses after
the death of the two sons of Aaron,

when they offered *profane fire* before the
LORD, and died; 2and the LORD said to Moses: "Tell Aaron your brother not to come at
just any time into the Holy *Place* inside the
veil, before the mercy seat which *is* on the
ark, lest he die; for I will appear in the cloud
above the mercy seat.

3"Thus Aaron shall come into the Holy
Place: with *the blood of* a young bull as a sin
offering, and *of* a ram as a burnt offering.
4He shall put the holy linen tunic and the
linen trousers on his body; he shall be girded
with a linen sash, and with the linen turban
he shall be attired. These *are* holy garments.
Therefore he shall wash his body in water,
and put them on. 5And he shall take from
the congregation of the children of Israel two
kids of the goats as a sin offering, and one
ram as a burnt offering.

6"Aaron shall offer the bull as a sin offering, which *is* for himself, and make atonement for himself and for his house. 7He
shall take the two goats and present them
before the LORD *at* the door of the tabernacle of meeting. 8Then Aaron shall cast lots
for the two goats: one lot for the LORD and
the other lot for the scapegoat. 9And Aaron
shall bring the goat on which the LORD's lot
fell, and offer it *as* a sin offering. 10But the
goat on which the lot fell to be the scapegoat
shall be presented alive before the LORD, to
make atonement upon it, *and* to let it go as
the scapegoat into the wilderness.

11"And Aaron shall bring the bull of the
sin offering, which is for himself, and make
atonement for himself and for his house,
and shall kill the bull as the sin offering
which *is* for himself. 12Then he shall take a
censer full of burning coals of fire from the
altar before the LORD, with his hands full of
sweet incense beaten fine, and bring *it* inside the veil. 13And he shall put the incense
on the fire before the LORD, that the cloud
of incense may cover the mercy seat that *is*
on the Testimony, lest he die. 14He shall take
some of the blood of the bull and sprinkle
it with his finger on the mercy seat on the
east *side;* and before the mercy seat he shall
sprinkle some of the blood with his finger
seven times.

15"Then he shall kill the goat of the sin
offering, which *is* for the people, bring its
blood inside the veil, do with that blood as
he did with the blood of the bull, and sprinkle it on the mercy seat and before the mercy
seat. 16So he shall make atonement for the
Holy *Place,* because of the uncleanness of
the children of Israel, and because of their
transgressions, for all their sins; and so he
shall do for the tabernacle of meeting which
remains among them in the midst of their
uncleanness. 17There shall be no man in

16:1–34 THE DAY OF ATONEMENT

Because God loves you, He takes away your sins. God taught the Old Testament people this truth in a special ceremony called the Day of Atonement. On this day, which came only once a year, the high priest would take the blood of the sacrifice and sprinkle it in the Most Holy Place of the tabernacle. The sacrifice was a bull and a goat. Then the high priest would lay his hands on another goat and send it away into the desert. By laying his hands on this goat, the high priest showed that the sins of the people were being carried away.

This Old Testament ceremony is just a picture of what Jesus has done for you. He is your real High Priest, and He has carried the blood of His sacrifice into heaven for you. He also has carried away your sins forever if you have trusted Him as your Savior.

the tabernacle of meeting when he goes in to make atonement in the Holy *Place,* until he comes out, that he may make atonement for himself, for his household, and for all the assembly of Israel. 18 And he shall go out to the altar that *is* before the LORD, and make atonement for it, and shall take some of the blood of the bull and some of the blood of the goat, and put it on the horns of the altar all around. 19 Then he shall sprinkle some of the blood on it with his finger seven times, cleanse it, and consecrate it from the uncleanness of the children of Israel.

20 "And when he has made an end of atoning for the Holy *Place,* the tabernacle of meeting, and the altar, he shall bring the live goat. 21 Aaron shall lay both his hands on the head of the live goat, confess over it all the iniquities of the children of Israel, and all their transgressions, concerning all their sins, putting them on the head of the goat, and shall send *it* away into the wilderness by the hand of a suitable man. 22 The goat shall bear on itself all their iniquities to an uninhabited land; and he shall release the goat in the wilderness.

23 "Then Aaron shall come into the tabernacle of meeting, shall take off the linen garments which he put on when he went into the Holy *Place,* and shall leave them there. 24 And he shall wash his body with water in a holy place, put on his garments, come out and offer his burnt offering and the burnt offering of the people, and make atonement for himself and for the people. 25 The fat of the sin offering he shall burn on the altar. 26 And he who released the goat as the scapegoat shall wash his clothes and bathe his body in water, and afterward he may come into the camp. 27 The bull *for* the sin offering and the goat *for* the sin offering, whose blood was brought in to make atonement in the Holy *Place,* shall be carried outside the camp. And they shall burn in the fire their *skins,* their flesh, and their offal. 28 Then he who burns them shall wash his clothes and bathe his body in water, and afterward he may come into the camp.

29 "*This* shall be a statute forever for you: In the seventh month, on the tenth *day* of the month, you shall afflict your souls, and do no work at all, *whether* a native of your own country or a stranger who dwells among you. 30 For on that day *the priest* shall make

In Focus

16:8 Scapegoat A goat over whose head the high priest confessed the people's sins on the Day of Atonement. The goat then symbolically carried the sins away from the people into the desert.

atonement for you, to cleanse you, *that* you may be clean from all your sins before the LORD. 31 It *is* a sabbath of solemn rest for you, and you shall afflict your souls. *It is* a statute forever. 32 And the priest, who is anointed and consecrated to minister as priest in his father's place, shall make atonement, and put on the linen clothes, the holy garments; 33 then he shall make atonement for the Holy Sanctuary,[a] and he shall make atonement for the tabernacle of meeting and for the altar, and he shall make atonement for the priests and for all the people of the assembly. 34 This shall be an everlasting statute for you, to make atonement for the children of Israel, for all their sins, once a year." And he did as the LORD commanded Moses.

The Sanctity of Blood

17 And the LORD spoke to Moses, saying, 2 "Speak to Aaron, to his sons, and to all the children of Israel, and say to them, 'This *is* the thing which the LORD has commanded, saying: 3 "Whatever man of the house of Israel who kills an ox or lamb or goat in the camp, or who kills *it* outside the camp, 4 and does not bring it to the door of the tabernacle of meeting to offer an offering to the LORD before the tabernacle of the LORD, the guilt of bloodshed shall be imputed to that man. He has shed blood; and that man shall be cut off from among his people, 5 to the end that the children of Israel may bring their sacrifices which they offer in the open field, that they may bring them to the LORD at the door of the tabernacle of meeting, to the priest, and offer them *as* peace offerings to the LORD. 6 And the priest shall sprinkle the blood on the altar of the LORD *at* the door of the tabernacle of meeting, and

16:33 [a] That is, *the Most Holy Place*

burn the fat for a sweet aroma to the LORD.
7They shall no more offer their sacrifices to
demons, after whom they have played the
harlot. This shall be a statute forever for
them throughout their generations."'
8"Also you shall say to them: 'Whatever
man of the house of Israel, or of the strangers
who dwell among you, who offers a burnt
offering or sacrifice, 9and does not bring it
to the door of the tabernacle of meeting, to
offer it to the LORD, that man shall be cut off
from among his people.
10'And whatever man of the house of Israel,
or of the strangers who dwell among
you, who eats any blood, I will set My face
against that person who eats blood, and will
cut him off from among his people. 11For the
life of the flesh *is* in the blood, and I have
given it to you upon the altar to make atonement
for your souls; for it *is* the blood *that*
makes atonement for the soul.' 12Therefore I
said to the children of Israel, 'No one among
you shall eat blood, nor shall any stranger
who dwells among you eat blood.'
13"Whatever man of the children of Israel,
or of the strangers who dwell among you,
who hunts and catches any animal or bird
that may be eaten, he shall pour out its blood
and cover it with dust; 14for *it is* the life of all
flesh. Its blood sustains its life. Therefore I
said to the children of Israel, 'You shall not
eat the blood of any flesh, for the life of all
flesh is its blood. Whoever eats it shall be
cut off.'
15"And every person who eats what died
naturally or what was torn *by beasts, whether
he is* a native of your own country or a stranger,
he shall both wash his clothes and bathe
in water, and be unclean until evening. Then
he shall be clean. 16But if he does not wash
them or bathe his body, then he shall bear
his guilt."

Laws of Sexual Morality

18 Then the LORD spoke to Moses,
saying, 2"Speak to the children of
Israel, and say to them: 'I am the LORD your
God. 3According to the doings of the land
of Egypt, where you dwelt, you shall not
do; and according to the doings of the land
of Canaan, where I am bringing you, you
shall not do; nor shall you walk in their ordinances.
4You shall observe My judgments
and keep My ordinances, to walk in them: I
am the LORD your God. 5You shall therefore
keep My statutes and My judgments, which
if a man does, he shall live by them: I *am*
the LORD.
6'None of you shall approach anyone who
is near of kin to him, to uncover his nakedness:
I *am* the LORD. 7The nakedness of your
father or the nakedness of your mother you
shall not uncover. She *is* your mother; you
shall not uncover her nakedness. 8The nakedness
of your father's wife you shall not
uncover; it *is* your father's nakedness. 9The
nakedness of your sister, the daughter of
your father, or the daughter of your mother,
whether born at home or elsewhere, their
nakedness you shall not uncover. 10The
nakedness of your son's daughter or your
daughter's daughter, their nakedness you

Action!

THE VALUE OF WORDS

READ IT: LEVITICUS 19:12

What's your most valuable possession, the object you care about the most? You probably do what you can to take care of it because it's important to you. Because God is holy, even His name is sacred. Some people carelessly use God's name profanely, meaning they use it in a disrespectful way or as a curse word, and some people swear by God's name. However, God clearly tells us in this passage that doing those things is not allowed.

shall not uncover; for theirs *is* your own nakedness. [11]The nakedness of your father's
wife's daughter, begotten by your father—
she *is* your sister—you shall not uncover
her nakedness. [12]You shall not uncover the
nakedness of your father's sister; she *is* near
of kin to your father. [13]You shall not uncover
the nakedness of your mother's sister, for
she *is* near of kin to your mother. [14]You shall
not uncover the nakedness of your father's
brother. You shall not approach his wife;
she *is* your aunt. [15]You shall not uncover the
nakedness of your daughter-in-law—she
is your son's wife—you shall not uncover
her nakedness. [16]You shall not uncover the
nakedness of your brother's wife; it *is* your
brother's nakedness. [17]You shall not uncover
the nakedness of a woman and her daughter,
nor shall you take her son's daughter or her
daughter's daughter, to uncover her nakedness. They *are* near of kin to her. It *is* wickedness. [18]Nor shall you take a woman as a rival
to her sister, to uncover her nakedness while
the other is alive.

[19]'Also you shall not approach a woman
to uncover her nakedness as long as she is in
her *customary* impurity. [20]Moreover you shall
not lie carnally with your neighbor's wife, to
defile yourself with her. [21]And you shall not
let any of your descendants pass through
the fire to Molech, nor shall you profane the
name of your God: I *am* the LORD. [22]You
shall not lie with a male as with a woman. It
is an abomination. [23]Nor shall you mate with
any animal, to defile yourself with it. Nor
shall any woman stand before an animal to
mate with it. It *is* perversion.

[24]'Do not defile yourselves with any of
these things; for by all these the nations are
defiled, which I am casting out before you.
[25]For the land is defiled; therefore I visit the
punishment of its iniquity upon it, and the
land vomits out its inhabitants. [26]You shall
therefore keep My statutes and My judgments, and shall not commit *any* of these
abominations, either any of your own nation
or any stranger who dwells among you [27](for
all these abominations the men of the land
have done, who *were* before you, and thus the
land is defiled), [28]lest the land vomit you out
also when you defile it, as it vomited out the
nations that *were* before you. [29]For whoever
commits any of these abominations, the persons who commit *them* shall be cut off from
among their people.

In Focus

19:2 Holy An adjective meaning "separate," but includes the idea of moral purity and being like God.

[30]'Therefore you shall keep My ordinance,
so that *you* do not commit *any* of these
abominable customs which were committed
before you, and that you do not defile yourselves by them: I *am* the LORD your God.'"

Moral and Ceremonial Laws

19 And the LORD spoke to Moses, saying, [2]"Speak to all the congregation
of the children of Israel, and say to them:
'You shall be holy, for I the LORD your God
am holy.

[3]'Every one of you shall revere his mother
and his father, and keep My Sabbaths: I *am*
the LORD your God.

[4]'Do not turn to idols, nor make for yourselves molded gods: I *am* the LORD your God.

[5]'And if you offer a sacrifice of a peace offering to the LORD, you shall offer it of your
own free will. [6]It shall be eaten the same
day you offer *it,* and on the next day. And
if any remains until the third day, it shall
be burned in the fire. [7]And if it is eaten at
all on the third day, it *is* an abomination. It
shall not be accepted. [8]Therefore *everyone*
who eats it shall bear his iniquity, because
he has profaned the hallowed *offering* of the
LORD; and that person shall be cut off from
his people.

[9]'When you reap the harvest of your land,
you shall not wholly reap the corners of your
field, nor shall you gather the gleanings of
your harvest. [10]And you shall not glean your
vineyard, nor shall you gather *every* grape of
your vineyard; you shall leave them for the
poor and the stranger: I *am* the LORD your
God.

[11]'You shall not steal, nor deal falsely, nor
lie to one another. [12]And you shall not swear
by My name falsely, nor shall you profane
the name of your God: I *am* the LORD.

[13]'You shall not cheat your neighbor, nor
rob *him.* The wages of him who is hired shall
not remain with you all night until morning.

In Focus

19:30 Reverence Pronounced *REV-er-ents.* An attitude of respect and awe. Reverence is an attitude we should have for God in worship and in serving Him.

14You shall not curse the deaf, nor put a
stumbling block before the blind, but shall
fear your God: I *am* the LORD.

15'You shall do no injustice in judgment.
You shall not be partial to the poor, nor hon-
or the person of the mighty. In righteousness you shall judge your neighbor. 16You
shall not go about *as* a talebearer among your
people; nor shall you take a stand against the
life of your neighbor: I *am* the LORD.

17'You shall not hate your brother in
your heart. You shall surely rebuke your
neighbor, and not bear sin because of him.
18You shall not take vengeance, nor bear any
grudge against the children of your people,
but you shall love your neighbor as yourself:
I *am* the LORD.

19'You shall keep My statutes. You shall
not let your livestock breed with another kind. You shall not sow your field with
mixed seed. Nor shall a garment of mixed
linen and wool come upon you.

20'Whoever lies carnally with a woman
who *is* betrothed to a man as a concubine,
and who has not at all been redeemed nor
given her freedom, for this there shall be
scourging; *but* they shall not be put to death,
because she was not free. 21And he shall
bring his trespass offering to the LORD,
to the door of the tabernacle of meeting, a
ram as a trespass offering. 22The priest shall
make atonement for him with the ram of the
trespass offering before the LORD for his sin
which he has committed. And the sin which
he has committed shall be forgiven him.

23'When you come into the land, and have
planted all kinds of trees for food, then you
shall count their fruit as uncircumcised.
Three years it shall be as uncircumcised to
you. *It* shall not be eaten. 24But in the fourth
year all its fruit shall be holy, a praise to the
LORD. 25And in the fifth year you may eat its
fruit, that it may yield to you its increase: I
am the LORD your God.

26'You shall not eat *anything* with the
blood, nor shall you practice divination or
soothsaying. 27You shall not shave around
the sides of your head, nor shall you disfigure the edges of your beard. 28You shall not
make any cuttings in your flesh for the dead,
nor tattoo any marks on you: I *am* the LORD.

29'Do not prostitute your daughter, to
cause her to be a harlot, lest the land fall
into harlotry, and the land become full of
wickedness.

30'You shall keep My Sabbaths and reverence My sanctuary: I *am* the LORD.

31'Give no regard to mediums and familiar spirits; do not seek after them, to be defiled by them: I *am* the LORD your God.

32'You shall rise before the gray headed
and honor the presence of an old man, and
fear your God: I *am* the LORD.

33'And if a stranger dwells with you in
your land, you shall not mistreat him. 34The
stranger who dwells among you shall be to
you as one born among you, and you shall
love him as yourself; for you were strangers
in the land of Egypt: I *am* the LORD your God.

35'You shall do no injustice in judgment,
in measurement of length, weight, or volume. 36You shall have honest scales, honest
weights, an honest ephah, and an honest
hin: I *am* the LORD your God, who brought
you out of the land of Egypt.

37'Therefore you shall observe all My
statutes and all My judgments, and perform
them: I *am* the LORD.'"

Penalties for Breaking the Law

20 Then the LORD spoke to Moses,
saying, 2"Again, you shall say to
the children of Israel: 'Whoever of the children of Israel, or of the strangers who dwell
in Israel, who gives *any* of his descendants
to Molech, he shall surely be put to death.
The people of the land shall stone him with
stones. 3I will set My face against that man,
and will cut him off from his people, because he has given *some* of his descendants
to Molech, to defile My sanctuary and profane My holy name. 4And if the people of the
land should in any way hide their eyes from
the man, when he gives *some* of his descendants to Molech, and they do not kill him,
5then I will set My face against that man
and against his family; and I will cut him

off from his people, and all who prostitute
themselves with him to commit harlotry
with Molech.

6'And the person who turns to mediums
and familiar spirits, to prostitute himself
with them, I will set My face against that
person and cut him off from his people.
7Consecrate yourselves therefore, and be
holy, for I *am* the LORD your God. 8And you
shall keep My statutes, and perform them: I
am the LORD who sanctifies you.

9'For everyone who curses his father or
his mother shall surely be put to death. He
has cursed his father or his mother. His
blood *shall be* upon him.

10'The man who commits adultery with
another man's wife, *he* who commits adultery with his neighbor's wife, the adulterer
and the adulteress, shall surely be put to
death. 11The man who lies with his father's
wife has uncovered his father's nakedness;
both of them shall surely be put to death.
Their blood *shall be* upon them. 12If a man
lies with his daughter-in-law, both of them
shall surely be put to death. They have committed perversion. Their blood *shall be* upon
them. 13If a man lies with a male as he lies
with a woman, both of them have committed an abomination. They shall surely be put
to death. Their blood *shall be* upon them. 14If
a man marries a woman and her mother, it *is*
wickedness. They shall be burned with fire,
both he and they, that there may be no wickedness among you. 15If a man mates with an
animal, he shall surely be put to death, and
you shall kill the animal. 16If a woman approaches any animal and mates with it, you
shall kill the woman and the animal. They
shall surely be put to death. Their blood *is*
upon them.

17'If a man takes his sister, his father's
daughter or his mother's daughter, and sees
her nakedness and she sees his nakedness,
it *is* a wicked thing. And they shall be cut off
in the sight of their people. He has uncovered his sister's nakedness. He shall bear his
guilt. 18If a man lies with a woman during
her sickness and uncovers her nakedness, he
has exposed her flow, and she has uncovered
the flow of her blood. Both of them shall be
cut off from their people.

19'You shall not uncover the nakedness
of your mother's sister nor of your father's
sister, for that would uncover his near of kin.
They shall bear their guilt. 20If a man lies
with his uncle's wife, he has uncovered his
uncle's nakedness. They shall bear their sin;
they shall die childless. 21If a man takes his
brother's wife, it *is* an unclean thing. He has
uncovered his brother's nakedness. They
shall be childless.

22'You shall therefore keep all My statutes
and all My judgments, and perform them,
that the land where I am bringing you to
dwell may not vomit you out. 23And you shall
not walk in the statutes of the nation which
I am casting out before you; for they commit
all these things, and therefore I abhor them.
24But I have said to you, "You shall inherit
their land, and I will give it to you to possess, a land flowing with milk and honey."
I *am* the LORD your God, who has separated
you from the peoples. 25You shall therefore
distinguish between clean animals and unclean, between unclean birds and clean, and
you shall not make yourselves abominable
by beast or by bird, or by any kind of living
thing that creeps on the ground, which I
have separated from you as unclean. 26And
you shall be holy to Me, for I the LORD *am*
holy, and have separated you from the peoples, that you should be Mine.

27'A man or a woman who is a medium,
or who has familiar spirits, shall surely be
put to death; they shall stone them with
stones. Their blood *shall be* upon them.'"

Regulations for Conduct of Priests

21 And the LORD said to Moses,
"Speak to the priests, the sons of
Aaron, and say to them: 'None shall defile
himself for the dead among his people, 2ex-
cept for his relatives who are nearest to him:
his mother, his father, his son, his daughter,
and his brother; 3also his virgin sister who
is near to him, who has had no husband,
for her he may defile himself. 4*Otherwise* he
shall not defile himself, *being* a chief man
among his people, to profane himself.

5'They shall not make any bald *place* on
their heads, nor shall they shave the edges of
their beards nor make any cuttings in their
flesh. 6They shall be holy to their God and
not profane the name of their God, for they
offer the offerings of the LORD made by fire,
and the bread of their God; therefore they
shall be holy. 7They shall not take a wife *who*
is a harlot or a defiled woman, nor shall they
take a woman divorced from her husband;

for *the priest*[a] is holy to his God. 8Therefore
you shall consecrate him, for he offers the
bread of your God. He shall be holy to you,
for I the LORD, who sanctify you, *am* holy.
9The daughter of any priest, if she profanes
herself by playing the harlot, she profanes
her father. She shall be burned with fire.

10'*He who is* the high priest among his
brethren, on whose head the anointing oil
was poured and who is consecrated to wear
the garments, shall not uncover his head nor
tear his clothes; 11nor shall he go near any
dead body, nor defile himself for his father
or his mother; 12nor shall he go out of the
sanctuary, nor profane the sanctuary of his
God; for the consecration of the anointing oil
of his God *is* upon him: I *am* the LORD. 13And
he shall take a wife in her virginity. 14A widow or a divorced woman or a defiled woman
or a harlot—these he shall not marry; but he
shall take a virgin of his own people as wife.
15Nor shall he profane his posterity among
his people, for I the LORD sanctify him.' "

16And the LORD spoke to Moses, saying,
17"Speak to Aaron, saying: 'No man of your
descendants in *succeeding* generations, who
has *any* defect, may approach to offer the
bread of his God. 18For any man who has a
defect shall not approach: a man blind or
lame, who has a marred *face* or any *limb* too
long, 19a man who has a broken foot or broken hand, 20or is a hunchback or a dwarf, or
a man who has a defect in his eye, or ecze-
ma or scab, or is a eunuch. 21No man of the
descendants of Aaron the priest, who has a
defect, shall come near to offer the offerings
made by fire to the LORD. He has a defect; he
shall not come near to offer the bread of his
God. 22He may eat the bread of his God, *both*
the most holy and the holy; 23only he shall
not go near the veil or approach the altar,
because he has a defect, lest he profane My
sanctuaries; for I the LORD sanctify them.' "

24And Moses told *it* to Aaron and his
sons, and to all the children of Israel.

22 Then the LORD spoke to Moses,
saying, 2"Speak to Aaron and his
sons, that they separate themselves from the
holy things of the children of Israel, and that
they do not profane My holy name *by* what
they dedicate to Me: I *am* the LORD. 3Say
to them: 'Whoever of all your descendants
throughout your generations, who goes
near the holy things which the children of
Israel dedicate to the LORD, while he has
uncleanness upon him, that person shall be
cut off from My presence: I *am* the LORD.

4'Whatever man of the descendants of
Aaron, who *is* a leper or has a discharge,
shall not eat the holy offerings until he is
clean. And whoever touches anything made
unclean *by* a corpse, or a man who has had
an emission of semen, 5or whoever touches
any creeping thing by which he would be
made unclean, or any person by whom he
would become unclean, whatever his uncleanness may be— 6the person who has
touched any such thing shall be unclean
until evening, and shall not eat the holy *offerings* unless he washes his body with water.
7And when the sun goes down he shall be
clean; and afterward he may eat the holy *offerings,* because it *is* his food. 8Whatever dies
naturally or is torn *by beasts* he shall not eat,
to defile himself with it: I *am* the LORD.

9'They shall therefore keep My ordinance,
lest they bear sin for it and die thereby, if
they profane it: I the LORD sanctify them.

10'No outsider shall eat the holy *offering;*
one who dwells with the priest, or a hired
servant, shall not eat the holy thing. 11But if
the priest buys a person with his money, he
may eat it; and one who is born in his house
may eat his food. 12If the priest's daughter is
married to an outsider, she may not eat of
the holy offerings. 13But if the priest's daughter is a widow or divorced, and has no child,
and has returned to her father's house as in
her youth, she may eat her father's food; but
no outsider shall eat it.

14'And if a man eats the holy *offering* unintentionally, then he shall restore a holy *offering* to the priest, and add one-fifth to it.
15They shall not profane the holy *offerings*
of the children of Israel, which they offer to
the LORD, 16or allow them to bear the guilt
of trespass when they eat their holy *offerings;*
for I the LORD sanctify them.' "

Offerings Accepted and Not Accepted

17And the LORD spoke to Moses, saying,
18"Speak to Aaron and his sons, and to all the
children of Israel, and say to them: 'Whatever man of the house of Israel, or of the
strangers in Israel, who offers his sacrifice
for any of his vows or for any of his freewill

21:7 [a] Literally *he*

offerings, which they offer to the LORD as a
burnt offering— 19*you shall offer* of your own
free will a male without blemish from the
cattle, from the sheep, or from the goats.
20Whatever has a defect, you shall not offer,
for it shall not be acceptable on your behalf.
21And whoever offers a sacrifice of a peace
offering to the LORD, to fulfill *his* vow, or a
freewill offering from the cattle or the sheep,
it must be perfect to be accepted; there shall
be no defect in it. 22Those *that are* blind or
broken or maimed, or have an ulcer or ecze-
ma or scabs, you shall not offer to the LORD,
nor make an offering by fire of them on the
altar to the LORD. 23Either a bull or a lamb
that has any limb too long or too short you
may offer *as* a freewill offering, but for a vow
it shall not be accepted.

24'You shall not offer to the LORD what is
bruised or crushed, or torn or cut; nor shall
you make *any offering of them* in your land.
25Nor from a foreigner's hand shall you offer any of these as the bread of your God,
because their corruption *is* in them, *and* defects *are* in them. They shall not be accepted
on your behalf.'"

26And the LORD spoke to Moses, saying:
27"When a bull or a sheep or a goat is born,
it shall be seven days with its mother; and
from the eighth day and thereafter it shall be
accepted as an offering made by fire to the
LORD. 28 *Whether it is* a cow or ewe, do not kill
both her and her young on the same day.
29And when you offer a sacrifice of thanksgiving to the LORD, offer *it* of your own free will.
30On the same day it shall be eaten; you shall
leave none of it until morning: I *am* the LORD.

31"Therefore you shall keep My commandments, and perform them: I *am* the LORD.
32You shall not profane My holy name, but I
will be hallowed among the children of Israel. I *am* the LORD who sanctifies you, 33who
brought you out of the land of Egypt, to be
your God: I *am* the LORD."

Feasts of the LORD

23 And the LORD spoke to Moses,
saying, 2"Speak to the children
of Israel, and say to them: 'The feasts of the
LORD, which you shall proclaim *to be* holy
convocations, these *are* My feasts.

The Sabbath

3'Six days shall work be done, but the
seventh day *is* a Sabbath of solemn rest, a
holy convocation. You shall do no work *on
it; it is* the Sabbath of the LORD in all your
dwellings.

The Passover and Unleavened Bread

4'These *are* the feasts of the LORD, holy
convocations which you shall proclaim at
their appointed times. 5On the fourteenth
day of the first month at twilight *is* the
LORD's Passover. 6And on the fifteenth day
of the same month *is* the Feast of Unleavened Bread to the LORD; seven days you must
eat unleavened bread. 7On the first day you
shall have a holy convocation; you shall do
no customary work on it. 8But you shall offer
an offering made by fire to the LORD for
seven days. The seventh day *shall be* a holy

COMMUNITY

READ IT: LEVITICUS 23:1–44

In the Old Testament, a lot of feasts and assemblies were part of the Jewish calendar. Christian churches still acknowledge and celebrate many of these today. These feasts were intentional—a time of celebration with family and friends as well as a time of honoring the Lord through sacrifice. Do you and your Christian friends eat together? Consider this the next time you do!

convocation; you shall do no customary work
on it.'"

The Feast of Firstfruits

9And the LORD spoke to Moses, saying,
10"Speak to the children of Israel, and say to
them: 'When you come into the land which
I give to you, and reap its harvest, then you
shall bring a sheaf of the firstfruits of your
harvest to the priest. 11He shall wave the
sheaf before the LORD, to be accepted on
your behalf; on the day after the Sabbath the
priest shall wave it. 12And you shall offer on
that day, when you wave the sheaf, a male
lamb of the first year, without blemish, as
a burnt offering to the LORD. 13Its grain offering *shall be* two-tenths *of an ephah* of fine
flour mixed with oil, an offering made by
fire to the LORD, for a sweet aroma; and its
drink offering *shall be* of wine, one-fourth
of a hin. 14You shall eat neither bread nor
parched grain nor fresh grain until the same
day that you have brought an offering to your
God; *it shall be* a statute forever throughout
your generations in all your dwellings.

The Feast of Weeks

15'And you shall count for yourselves from
the day after the Sabbath, from the day that
you brought the sheaf of the wave offering:
seven Sabbaths shall be completed. 16Count
fifty days to the day after the seventh Sabbath; then you shall offer a new grain offering to the LORD. 17You shall bring from your
dwellings two wave *loaves* of two-tenths *of an
ephah*. They shall be of fine flour; they shall
be baked with leaven. *They are* the firstfruits
to the LORD. 18And you shall offer with the
bread seven lambs of the first year, without
blemish, one young bull, and two rams.
They shall be *as* a burnt offering to the LORD,
with their grain offering and their drink offerings, an offering made by fire for a sweet
aroma to the LORD. 19Then you shall sacrifice
one kid of the goats as a sin offering, and
two male lambs of the first year as a sacrifice
of a peace offering. 20The priest shall wave
them with the bread of the firstfruits *as* a
wave offering before the LORD, with the two
lambs. They shall be holy to the LORD for the
priest. 21And you shall proclaim on the same
day *that* it is a holy convocation to you. You
shall do no customary work *on it*. *It shall be* a
statute forever in all your dwellings throughout your generations.

22'When you reap the harvest of your
land, you shall not wholly reap the corners of
your field when you reap, nor shall you gather any gleaning from your harvest. You shall
leave them for the poor and for the stranger:
I *am* the LORD your God.'"

The Feast of Trumpets

23Then the LORD spoke to Moses, saying,
24"Speak to the children of Israel, saying: 'In
the seventh month, on the first *day* of the
month, you shall have a sabbath-*rest*, a memorial of blowing of trumpets, a holy convocation. 25You shall do no customary work
on it; and you shall offer an offering made by
fire to the LORD.'"

The Day of Atonement

26And the LORD spoke to Moses, saying:
27"Also the tenth *day* of this seventh month
shall be the Day of Atonement. It shall be a
holy convocation for you; you shall afflict
your souls, and offer an offering made by
fire to the LORD. 28And you shall do no work
on that same day, for it *is* the Day of Atonement, to make atonement for you before the
LORD your God. 29For any person who is not
afflicted *in soul* on that same day shall be cut
off from his people. 30And any person who
does any work on that same day, that person I will destroy from among his people.
31You shall do no manner of work; *it shall be* a
statute forever throughout your generations
in all your dwellings. 32It *shall be* to you a
sabbath of *solemn* rest, and you shall afflict
your souls; on the ninth *day* of the month at
evening, from evening to evening, you shall
celebrate your sabbath."

The Feast of Tabernacles

33Then the LORD spoke to Moses, saying,
34"Speak to the children of Israel, saying:
'The fifteenth day of this seventh month
shall be the Feast of Tabernacles *for* seven
days to the LORD. 35On the first day *there
shall be* a holy convocation. You shall do no
customary work *on it*. 36*For* seven days you
shall offer an offering made by fire to the
LORD. On the eighth day you shall have a
holy convocation, and you shall offer an offering made by fire to the LORD. It is a sacred
assembly, *and* you shall do no customary
work *on it*.

37'These *are* the feasts of the LORD which
you shall proclaim *to be* holy convocations, to

offer an offering made by fire to the LORD, a
burnt offering and a grain offering, a sacrifice and drink offerings, everything on its
day— 38besides the Sabbaths of the LORD,
besides your gifts, besides all your vows, and
besides all your freewill offerings which you
give to the LORD.
39'Also on the fifteenth day of the seventh
month, when you have gathered in the fruit
of the land, you shall keep the feast of the
LORD *for* seven days; on the first day *there*
shall be a sabbath-*rest*, and on the eighth day
a sabbath-*rest*. 40And you shall take for yourselves on the first day the fruit of beautiful
trees, branches of palm trees, the boughs
of leafy trees, and willows of the brook; and
you shall rejoice before the LORD your God
for seven days. 41You shall keep it as a feast
to the LORD for seven days in the year. *It*
shall be a statute forever in your generations.
You shall celebrate it in the seventh month.
42You shall dwell in booths for seven days.
All who are native Israelites shall dwell in
booths, 43that your generations may know
that I made the children of Israel dwell in
booths when I brought them out of the land
of Egypt: I *am* the LORD your God.'"
44So Moses declared to the children of Israel the feasts of the LORD.

Care of the Tabernacle Lamps

24 Then the LORD spoke to Moses,
saying: 2"Command the children
of Israel that they bring to you pure oil of
pressed olives for the light, to make the
lamps burn continually. 3Outside the veil of
the Testimony, in the tabernacle of meeting,
Aaron shall be in charge of it from evening
until morning before the LORD continually;
it shall be a statute forever in your generations. 4He shall be in charge of the lamps
on the pure *gold* lampstand before the LORD
continually.

The Bread of the Tabernacle

5"And you shall take fine flour and bake
twelve cakes with it. Two-tenths *of an ephah*
shall be in each cake. 6You shall set them in
two rows, six in a row, on the pure *gold* table before the LORD. 7And you shall put pure
frankincense on *each* row, that it may be on
the bread for a memorial, an offering made
by fire to the LORD. 8Every Sabbath he shall
set it in order before the LORD continually,
being taken from the children of Israel by
an everlasting covenant. 9And it shall be for
Aaron and his sons, and they shall eat it in
a holy place; for it *is* most holy to him from
the offerings of the LORD made by fire, by a
perpetual statute."

The Penalty for Blasphemy

10Now the son of an Israelite woman,
whose father *was* an Egyptian, went out
among the children of Israel; and this Israelite *woman's* son and a man of Israel fought
each other in the camp. 11And the Israelite
woman's son blasphemed the name *of the*
LORD and cursed; and so they brought him
to Moses. (His mother's name *was* Shelomith the daughter of Dibri, of the tribe of
Dan.) 12Then they put him in custody, that
the mind of the LORD might be shown to
them.
13And the LORD spoke to Moses, saying, 14"Take outside the camp him who has
cursed; then let all who heard *him* lay their
hands on his head, and let all the congregation stone him.
15"Then you shall speak to the children of
Israel, saying: 'Whoever curses his God shall
bear his sin. 16And whoever blasphemes the
name of the LORD shall surely be put to
death. All the congregation shall certainly
stone him, the stranger as well as him who
is born in the land. When he blasphemes the
name *of the LORD*, he shall be put to death.
17'Whoever kills any man shall surely be
put to death. 18Whoever kills an animal shall
make it good, animal for animal.
19'If a man causes disfigurement of his
neighbor, as he has done, so shall it be done
to him— 20fracture for fracture, eye for eye,
tooth for tooth; as he has caused disfigurement of a man, so shall it be done to him.
21And whoever kills an animal shall restore
it; but whoever kills a man shall be put to
death. 22You shall have the same law for the
stranger and for one from your own country;
for I *am* the LORD your God.'"
23Then Moses spoke to the children
of Israel; and they took outside the camp
him who had cursed, and stoned him with
stones. So the children of Israel did as the
LORD commanded Moses.

The Sabbath of the Seventh Year

25 And the LORD spoke to Moses
on Mount Sinai, saying, 2"Speak
to the children of Israel, and say to them:

'When you come into the land which I give
you, then the land shall keep a sabbath to the
LORD. 3Six years you shall sow your field, and
six years you shall prune your vineyard, and
gather its fruit; 4but in the seventh year there
shall be a sabbath of solemn rest for the land,
a sabbath to the LORD. You shall neither sow
your field nor prune your vineyard. 5What
grows of its own accord of your harvest you
shall not reap, nor gather the grapes of your
untended vine, *for* it is a year of rest for the
land. 6And the sabbath *produce* of the land
shall be food for you: for you, your male and
female servants, your hired man, and the
stranger who dwells with you, 7for your livestock and the beasts that *are* in your land—
all its produce shall be for food.

The Year of Jubilee

8'And you shall count seven sabbaths of
years for yourself, seven times seven years;
and the time of the seven sabbaths of years
shall be to you forty-nine years. 9Then
you shall cause the trumpet of the Jubilee
to sound on the tenth *day* of the seventh
month; on the Day of Atonement you shall
make the trumpet to sound throughout all
your land. 10And you shall consecrate the fiftieth year, and proclaim liberty throughout
all the land to all its inhabitants. It shall be
a Jubilee for you; and each of you shall return to his possession, and each of you shall
return to his family. 11That fiftieth year shall
be a Jubilee to you; in it you shall neither sow
nor reap what grows of its own accord, nor
gather *the grapes* of your untended vine. 12For
it *is* the Jubilee; it shall be holy to you; you
shall eat its produce from the field.

13'In this Year of Jubilee, each of you
shall return to his possession. 14And if you
sell anything to your neighbor or buy from
your neighbor's hand, you shall not oppress
one another. 15According to the number of
years after the Jubilee you shall buy from
your neighbor, and according to the number
of years of crops he shall sell to you. 16Ac-
cording to the multitude of years you shall
increase its price, and according to the fewer
number of years you shall diminish its price;
for he sells to you *according* to the number *of
the years* of the crops. 17Therefore you shall
not oppress one another, but you shall fear
your God; for I *am* the LORD your God.

Provisions for the Seventh Year

18'So you shall observe My statutes and
keep My judgments, and perform them; and
you will dwell in the land in safety. 19Then
the land will yield its fruit, and you will eat
your fill, and dwell there in safety.

20'And if you say, "What shall we eat in
the seventh year, since we shall not sow
nor gather in our produce?" 21Then I will
command My blessing on you in the sixth

CREATION CARE

READ IT: LEVITICUS 25:1–7

God wanted the Hebrews to give the earth a twelve-month break (Sabbath) from farming every seventh year. Some have suggested that if Christians simply made our weekly Sabbath (a day of rest) an environmentally friendly day, it would have a huge impact on the world. Imagine if we paid that much attention every day. Try the following:

- Walking instead of being driven
- Conserving electricity and water
- Using as little paper (and paper products) as possible
- Recycling
- Drinking purified tap water instead of bottled

year, and it will bring forth produce enough
for three years. 22And you shall sow in the
eighth year, and eat old produce until the
ninth year; until its produce comes in, you
shall eat *of* the old *harvest*.

Redemption of Property

23'The land shall not be sold permanently, for the land *is* Mine; for you *are* strangers
and sojourners with Me. 24And in all the land
of your possession you shall grant redemption of the land.

25'If one of your brethren becomes poor,
and has sold *some* of his possession, and if
his redeeming relative comes to redeem it,
then he may redeem what his brother sold.
26Or if the man has no one to redeem it, but
he himself becomes able to redeem it, 27then
let him count the years since its sale, and restore the remainder to the man to whom he
sold it, that he may return to his possession.
28But if he is not able to have *it* restored to
himself, then what was sold shall remain in
the hand of him who bought it until the Year
of Jubilee; and in the Jubilee it shall be released, and he shall return to his possession.

29'If a man sells a house in a walled city,
then he may redeem it within a whole year
after it is sold; *within* a full year he may redeem it. 30But if it is not redeemed within
the space of a full year, then the house in
the walled city shall belong permanently to
him who bought it, throughout his generations. It shall not be released in the Jubilee.
31However the houses of villages which have
no wall around them shall be counted as
the fields of the country. They may be redeemed, and they shall be released in the
Jubilee. 32Nevertheless the cities of the Levites, *and* the houses in the cities of their
possession, the Levites may redeem at any
time. 33And if a man purchases a house from
the Levites, then the house that was sold in
the city of his possession shall be released in
the Jubilee; for the houses in the cities of the
Levites *are* their possession among the children of Israel. 34But the field of the common-
land of their cities may not be sold, for it *is*
their perpetual possession.

Lending to the Poor

35'If one of your brethren becomes poor,
and falls into poverty among you, then you
shall help him, like a stranger or a sojourner,
that he may live with you. 36Take no usury or
interest from him; but fear your God, that
your brother may live with you. 37You shall
not lend him your money for usury, nor lend
him your food at a profit. 38I *am* the LORD
your God, who brought you out of the land
of Egypt, to give you the land of Canaan *and*
to be your God.

The Law Concerning Slavery

39'And if *one of* your brethren *who dwells*
by you becomes poor, and sells himself to
you, you shall not compel him to serve as a
slave. 40As a hired servant *and* a sojourner he
shall be with you, *and* shall serve you until
the Year of Jubilee. 41And *then* he shall depart
from you—he and his children with him—
and shall return to his own family. He shall
return to the possession of his fathers. 42For
they *are* My servants, whom I brought out of
the land of Egypt; they shall not be sold as
slaves. 43You shall not rule over him with rig-
or, but you shall fear your God. 44And as for
your male and female slaves whom you may
have—from the nations that are around you,
from them you may buy male and female
slaves. 45Moreover you may buy the children
of the strangers who dwell among you, and
their families who are with you, which they
beget in your land; and they shall become
your property. 46And you may take them as
an inheritance for your children after you,
to inherit *them as* a possession; they shall be
your permanent slaves. But regarding your
brethren, the children of Israel, you shall not
rule over one another with rigor.

47'Now if a sojourner or stranger close to
you becomes rich, and *one of* your brethren
who dwells by him becomes poor, and sells
himself to the stranger *or* sojourner close to
you, or to a member of the stranger's family,
48after he is sold he may be redeemed again.
One of his brothers may redeem him; 49or
his uncle or his uncle's son may redeem
him; or *anyone* who is near of kin to him
in his family may redeem him; or if he is
able he may redeem himself. 50Thus he shall
reckon with him who bought him: The price
of his release shall be according to the number of years, from the year that he was sold
to him until the Year of Jubilee; *it shall be*
according to the time of a hired servant for
him. 51If *there are* still many years *remaining*,
according to them he shall repay the price of
his redemption from the money with which
he was bought. 52And if there remain but a

few years until the Year of Jubilee, then he
shall reckon with him, *and* according to his
years he shall repay him the price of his redemption. 53He shall be with him as a yearly hired servant, and he shall not rule with
rigor over him in your sight. 54And if he is
not redeemed in these *years,* then he shall be
released in the Year of Jubilee—he and his
children with him. 55For the children of Israel *are* servants to Me; they *are* My servants
whom I brought out of the land of Egypt: I
am the LORD your God.

Promise of Blessing and Retribution

26 'You shall not make idols for yourselves;
neither a carved image nor a *sacred* pillar shall you rear up for yourselves;
nor shall you set up an engraved stone in your land, to bow down to it;
for I *am* the LORD your God.
2 You shall keep My Sabbaths and reverence My sanctuary:
I *am* the LORD.

3 'If you walk in My statutes and keep My commandments, and perform them,
4 then I will give you rain in its season, the land shall yield its produce, and the trees of the field shall yield their fruit.
5 Your threshing shall last till the time of vintage, and the vintage shall last till the time of sowing;
you shall eat your bread to the full, and dwell in your land safely.
6 I will give peace in the land, and you shall lie down, and none will make *you* afraid;
I will rid the land of evil beasts,
and the sword will not go through your land.
7 You will chase your enemies, and they shall fall by the sword before you.
8 Five of you shall chase a hundred, and a hundred of you shall put ten thousand to flight;
your enemies shall fall by the sword before you.

9 'For I will look on you favorably and make you fruitful, multiply you and confirm My covenant with you.
10 You shall eat the old harvest, and clear out the old because of the new.
11 I will set My tabernacle among you, and My soul shall not abhor you.
12 I will walk among you and be your God, and you shall be My people.
13 I *am* the LORD your God, who brought you out of the land of Egypt, that *you* should not be their slaves;
I have broken the bands of your yoke and made you walk upright.

14 'But if you do not obey Me, and do not observe all these commandments,
15 and if you despise My statutes, or if your soul abhors My judgments, so that you do not perform all My commandments, *but* break My covenant,
16 I also will do this to you:
I will even appoint terror over you, wasting disease and fever which shall consume the eyes and cause sorrow of heart.
And you shall sow your seed in vain, for your enemies shall eat it.
17 I will set My face against you, and you shall be defeated by your enemies.
Those who hate you shall reign over you, and you shall flee when no one pursues you.

18 'And after all this, if you do not obey Me, then I will punish you seven times more for your sins.
19 I will break the pride of your power;
I will make your heavens like iron and your earth like bronze.
20 And your strength shall be spent in vain;
for your land shall not yield its produce, nor shall the trees of the land yield their fruit.

21 'Then, if you walk contrary to Me, and are not willing to obey Me, I will bring on you seven times more plagues, according to your sins.
22 I will also send wild beasts among you, which shall rob you of your children, destroy your livestock, and make you few in number;
and your highways shall be desolate.

23 'And if by these things you are not reformed by Me, but walk contrary to Me,
24 then I also will walk contrary to you, and I will punish you yet seven times for your sins.
25 And I will bring a sword against you that will execute the vengeance of the covenant;

when you are gathered together within your cities I will send pestilence among you;
and you shall be delivered into the hand of the enemy.
26 When I have cut off your supply of bread, ten women shall bake your bread in one oven, and they shall bring back your bread by weight, and you shall eat and not be satisfied.

27 'And after all this, if you do not obey Me, but walk contrary to Me,
28 then I also will walk contrary to you in fury;
and I, even I, will chastise you seven times for your sins.
29 You shall eat the flesh of your sons, and you shall eat the flesh of your daughters.
30 I will destroy your high places, cut down your incense altars, and cast your carcasses on the lifeless forms of your idols;
and My soul shall abhor you.
31 I will lay your cities waste and bring your sanctuaries to desolation, and I will not smell the fragrance of your sweet aromas.
32 I will bring the land to desolation, and your enemies who dwell in it shall be astonished at it.
33 I will scatter you among the nations and draw out a sword after you;
your land shall be desolate and your cities waste.
34 Then the land shall enjoy its sabbaths as long as it lies desolate and you *are* in your enemies' land;
then the land shall rest and enjoy its sabbaths.
35 As long as *it* lies desolate it shall rest—
for the time it did not rest on your sabbaths when you dwelt in it.

36 'And as for those of you who are left, I will send faintness into their hearts in the lands of their enemies;
the sound of a shaken leaf shall cause them to flee;
they shall flee as though fleeing from a sword, and they shall fall when no one pursues.
37 They shall stumble over one another, as it were before a sword, when no one pursues;
and you shall have no *power* to stand before your enemies.
38 You shall perish among the nations, and the land of your enemies shall eat you up.
39 And those of you who are left shall waste away in their iniquity in your enemies' lands;
also in their fathers' iniquities, which are with them, they shall waste away.

40 '*But* if they confess their iniquity and the iniquity of their fathers, with their unfaithfulness in which they were unfaithful to Me, and that they also have walked contrary to Me,
41 and *that* I also have walked contrary to them and have brought them into the land of their enemies;
if their uncircumcised hearts are humbled, and they accept their guilt—
42 then I will remember My covenant with Jacob, and My covenant with Isaac and My covenant with Abraham I will remember;
I will remember the land.
43 The land also shall be left empty by them, and will enjoy its sabbaths while it lies desolate without them;
they will accept their guilt, because they despised My judgments and because their soul abhorred My statutes.
44 Yet for all that, when they are in the land of their enemies, I will not cast them away, nor shall I abhor them, to utterly destroy them and break My covenant with them;
for I *am* the LORD their God.
45 But for their sake I will remember the covenant of their ancestors, whom I brought out of the land of Egypt in the sight of the nations, that I might be their God:
I *am* the LORD.'"

46 These *are* the statutes and judgments and laws which the LORD made between Himself and the children of Israel on Mount Sinai by the hand of Moses.

Redeeming Persons and Property Dedicated to God

27 Now the LORD spoke to Moses,
saying, 2 "Speak to the children of
Israel, and say to them: 'When a man consecrates by a vow certain persons to the LORD,

according to your valuation, 3if your valuation is of a male from twenty years old up to sixty years old, then your valuation shall be fifty shekels of silver, according to the shekel of the sanctuary. 4If it *is* a female, then your valuation shall be thirty shekels; 5and if from five years old up to twenty years old, then your valuation for a male shall be twenty shekels, and for a female ten shekels; 6and if from a month old up to five years old, then your valuation for a male shall be five shekels of silver, and for a female your valuation shall be three shekels of silver; 7and if from sixty years old and above, if *it is* a male, then your valuation shall be fifteen shekels, and for a female ten shekels.

8'But if he is too poor to pay your valuation, then he shall present himself before the priest, and the priest shall set a value for him; according to the ability of him who vowed, the priest shall value him.

9'If *it is* an animal that men may bring as an offering to the LORD, all that *anyone* gives to the LORD shall be holy. 10He shall not substitute it or exchange it, good for bad or bad for good; and if he at all exchanges animal for animal, then both it and the one exchanged for it shall be holy. 11If *it is* an unclean animal which they do not offer as a sacrifice to the LORD, then he shall present the animal before the priest; 12and the priest shall set a value for it, whether it is good or bad; as you, the priest, value it, so it shall be. 13But if he *wants* at all *to* redeem it, then he must add one-fifth to your valuation.

14'And when a man dedicates his house *to be* holy to the LORD, then the priest shall set a value for it, whether it is good or bad; as the priest values it, so it shall stand. 15If he who dedicated it *wants to* redeem his house, then he must add one-fifth of the money of your valuation to it, and it shall be his.

16'If a man dedicates to the LORD *part* of a field of his possession, then your valuation shall be according to the seed for it. A homer of barley seed *shall be valued* at fifty shekels of silver. 17If he dedicates his field from the Year of Jubilee, according to your valuation it shall stand. 18But if he dedicates his field after the Jubilee, then the priest shall reckon *to him the money due according to* the years that remain till the Year of Jubilee, and it shall be deducted from your valuation. 19And if he who dedicates the field ever wishes to redeem it, then he must add one-fifth of the money of your valuation to it, and it shall belong to him. 20But if he does not want to redeem the field, or if he has sold the field to another man, it shall not be redeemed anymore; 21but the field, when it is released in the Jubilee, shall be holy to the LORD, as a devoted field; it shall be the possession of the priest.

22'And if a man dedicates to the LORD a field which he has bought, which is not the field of his possession, 23then the priest shall reckon to him the worth of your valuation, up to the Year of Jubilee, and he shall give your valuation on that day *as* a holy *offering* to the LORD. 24In the Year of Jubilee the field shall return to him from whom it was bought, to the one who *owned* the land as a possession. 25And all your valuations shall be according to the shekel of the sanctuary: twenty gerahs to the shekel.

26'But the firstborn of the animals, which should be the LORD's firstborn, no man shall dedicate; whether *it is* an ox or sheep, it *is* the LORD's. 27And if *it is* an unclean animal, then he shall redeem *it* according to your valuation, and shall add one-fifth to it; or if it is not redeemed, then it shall be sold according to your valuation.

28'Nevertheless no devoted *offering* that a man may devote to the LORD of all that he has, *both* man and beast, or the field of his possession, shall be sold or redeemed; every devoted *offering is* most holy to the LORD. 29No person under the ban, who may become doomed to destruction among men, shall be redeemed, *but* shall surely be put to death. 30And all the tithe of the land, *whether* of the seed of the land *or* of the fruit of the tree, *is* the LORD's. It *is* holy to the LORD. 31If a man wants at all to redeem *any* of his tithes, he shall add one-fifth to it. 32And concerning the tithe of the herd or the flock, of whatever passes under the rod, the tenth one shall be holy to the LORD. 33He shall not inquire whether it is good or bad, nor shall he exchange it; and if he exchanges it at all, then both it and the one exchanged for it shall be holy; it shall not be redeemed.'"

34These *are* the commandments which the LORD commanded Moses for the children of Israel on Mount Sinai.

The FOURTH BOOK of MOSES CALLED

NUMBERS

1445 B.C.–1400 B.C.

Behind the Scenes

READ IT:

Numbers is a book of stories about Israel's thirty-eight years of wandering in the wilderness: camping at Mount Sinai, traveling across the desert to the east side of the Dead Sea, and getting ready to enter the Promised Land. Almost every story tells about God's constant care for His people. He miraculously supplied the basics to stay alive: manna, water, and quail. He continued to love and forgive His people even when they rebelled against Him and their leaders.

GET IT:

Who wrote it: Most people think Moses wrote it.

When it was written: 1445 B.C.–1400 B.C.

Why it was written: to continue the history of God's people. Moses wants the people to know how faithful, caring, and protective God was through the years they traveled to Canaan.

LIVE IT:

God will forgive us, but we probably will suffer the consequences of our sin.

FIND IT:

The Cloud and the Fire	*Numbers 9*
The Departure from Sinai	*Numbers 10*
The People Complain	*Numbers 11*
Spies Sent into Canaan	*Numbers 13–14*
The Rebellion Against Moses and Aaron	*Numbers 16–17*
Balaam, the Donkey, and the Angel	*Numbers 22–24*
Vengeance on the Midianites	*Numbers 31*

The First Census of Israel

1 Now the LORD spoke to Moses in the
Wilderness of Sinai, in the tabernacle of meeting, on the first *day* of the second month, in the second year after they
had come out of the land of Egypt, saying:
2“Take a census of all the congregation of
the children of Israel, by their families, by
their fathers’ houses, according to the number of names, every male individually, 3from
twenty years old and above—all who *are able
to* go to war in Israel. You and Aaron shall
number them by their armies. 4And with
you there shall be a man from every tribe,
each one the head of his father’s house.

5“These are the names of the men who
shall stand with you: from Reuben, Elizur
the son of Shedeur; 6from Simeon, Shelumiel the son of Zurishaddai; 7from Judah,
Nahshon the son of Amminadab; 8from Issachar, Nethanel the son of Zuar; 9from Zebulun, Eliab the son of Helon; 10from the sons
of Joseph: from Ephraim, Elishama the son
of Ammihud; from Manasseh, Gamaliel the
son of Pedahzur; 11from Benjamin, Abidan
the son of Gideoni; 12from Dan, Ahiezer the
son of Ammishaddai; 13from Asher, Pagiel
the son of Ocran; 14from Gad, Eliasaph the
son of Deuel;[a] 15from Naphtali, Ahira the
son of Enan.” 16These *were* chosen from the
congregation, leaders of their fathers’ tribes,
heads of the divisions in Israel.

17Then Moses and Aaron took these men
who had been mentioned by name, 18and
they assembled all the congregation together
on the first *day* of the second month; and
they recited their ancestry by families, by
their fathers’ houses, according to the number of names, from twenty years old and
above, each one individually. 19As the LORD
commanded Moses, so he numbered them
in the Wilderness of Sinai.

20Now the children of Reuben, Israel’s
oldest son, their genealogies by their families, by their fathers’ house, according to the
number of names, every male individually,
from twenty years old and above, all who
were able to go to war: 21those who were numbered of the tribe of Reuben *were* forty-six
thousand five hundred.

22From the children of Simeon, their
genealogies by their families, by their fathers’ house, of those who were numbered,
according to the number of names, every
male individually, from twenty years old and
above, all who *were able to* go to war: 23those
who were numbered of the tribe of Simeon
were fifty-nine thousand three hundred.

24From the children of Gad, their genealogies by their families, by their fathers’
house, according to the number of names,
from twenty years old and above, all who
were able to go to war: 25those who were numbered of the tribe of Gad *were* forty-five thousand six hundred and fifty.

26From the children of Judah, their genealogies by their families, by their fathers’
house, according to the number of names,
from twenty years old and above, all who
were able to go to war: 27those who were numbered of the tribe of Judah *were* seventy-four
thousand six hundred.

28From the children of Issachar, their genealogies by their families, by their fathers’
house, according to the number of names,
from twenty years old and above, all who
were able to go to war: 29those who were numbered of the tribe of Issachar *were* fifty-four
thousand four hundred.

30From the children of Zebulun, their genealogies by their families, by their fathers’
house, according to the number of names,
from twenty years old and above, all who
were able to go to war: 31those who were numbered of the tribe of Zebulun *were* fifty-seven
thousand four hundred.

32From the sons of Joseph, the children
of Ephraim, their genealogies by their families, by their fathers’ house, according to the
number of names, from twenty years old and
above, all who *were able to* go to war: 33those
who were numbered of the tribe of Ephraim
were forty thousand five hundred.

34From the children of Manasseh, their
genealogies by their families, by their fathers’ house, according to the number of
names, from twenty years old and above, all
who *were able to* go to war: 35those who were
numbered of the tribe of Manasseh *were*
thirty-two thousand two hundred.

36From the children of Benjamin, their
genealogies by their families, by their fathers’ house, according to the number of
names, from twenty years old and above, all
who *were able to* go to war: 37those who were
numbered of the tribe of Benjamin *were*
thirty-five thousand four hundred.

1:14 [a] Spelled *Reuel* in 2:14

38From the children of Dan, their genealogies by their families, by their fathers'
house, according to the number of names,
from twenty years old and above, all who
were able to go to war: 39those who were numbered of the tribe of Dan *were* sixty-two thousand seven hundred.

40From the children of Asher, their genealogies by their families, by their fathers'
house, according to the number of names,
from twenty years old and above, all who
were able to go to war: 41those who were numbered of the tribe of Asher *were* forty-one
thousand five hundred.

42From the children of Naphtali, their genealogies by their families, by their fathers'
house, according to the number of names,
from twenty years old and above, all who
were able to go to war: 43those who were numbered of the tribe of Naphtali *were* fifty-three
thousand four hundred.

44These are the ones who were numbered, whom Moses and Aaron numbered,
with the leaders of Israel, twelve men, each
one representing his father's house. 45So all
who were numbered of the children of Israel, by their fathers' houses, from twenty
years old and above, all who *were able to* go
to war in Israel— 46all who were numbered
were six hundred and three thousand five
hundred and fifty.

47But the Levites were not numbered
among them by their fathers' tribe; 48for the
LORD had spoken to Moses, saying: 49"Only
the tribe of Levi you shall not number, nor
take a census of them among the children
of Israel; 50but you shall appoint the Levites
over the tabernacle of the Testimony, over all
its furnishings, and over all things that belong to it; they shall carry the tabernacle and
all its furnishings; they shall attend to it and
camp around the tabernacle. 51And when
the tabernacle is to go forward, the Levites
shall take it down; and when the tabernacle is to be set up, the Levites shall set it up.
The outsider who comes near shall be put
to death. 52The children of Israel shall pitch
their tents, everyone by his own camp, everyone by his own standard, according to their
armies; 53but the Levites shall camp around
the tabernacle of the Testimony, that there
may be no wrath on the congregation of the
children of Israel; and the Levites shall keep
charge of the tabernacle of the Testimony."

54Thus the children of Israel did; according to all that the LORD commanded Moses,
so they did.

The Tribes and Leaders by Armies

2 And the LORD spoke to Moses and Aaron, saying: 2"Everyone of the children
of Israel shall camp by his own standard,
beside the emblems of his father's house;
they shall camp some distance from the tabernacle of meeting. 3On the east side, toward
the rising of the sun, those of the standard
of the forces with Judah shall camp according to their armies; and Nahshon the son of
Amminadab *shall be* the leader of the children of Judah." 4And his army was numbered at seventy-four thousand six hundred.

5"Those who camp next to him *shall be*
the tribe of Issachar, and Nethanel the son
of Zuar *shall be* the leader of the children of
Issachar." 6And his army was numbered at
fifty-four thousand four hundred.

7"Then *comes* the tribe of Zebulun, and
Eliab the son of Helon *shall be* the leader of
the children of Zebulun." 8And his army
was numbered at fifty-seven thousand four
hundred. 9"All who were numbered according to their armies of the forces with Judah,
one hundred and eighty-six thousand four
hundred—these shall break camp first.

10"On the south side *shall be* the standard
of the forces with Reuben according to their
armies, and the leader of the children of
Reuben *shall be* Elizur the son of Shedeur."
11And his army was numbered at forty-six
thousand five hundred.

12"Those who camp next to him *shall be*
the tribe of Simeon, and the leader of the
children of Simeon *shall be* Shelumiel the
son of Zurishaddai." 13And his army was
numbered at fifty-nine thousand three
hundred.

14"Then *comes* the tribe of Gad, and the
leader of the children of Gad *shall be* Eliasaph
the son of Reuel."[a] 15And his army was numbered at forty-five thousand six hundred and
fifty. 16"All who were numbered according to
their armies of the forces with Reuben, one
hundred and fifty-one thousand four hundred and fifty—they shall be the second to
break camp.

17"And the tabernacle of meeting shall
move out with the camp of the Levites in the
middle of the camps; as they camp, so they

2:14 [a] Spelled *Deuel* in 1:14 and 7:42

shall move out, everyone in his place, by
their standards.
18"On the west side *shall be* the standard
of the forces with Ephraim according to
their armies, and the leader of the children
of Ephraim *shall be* Elishama the son of
Ammihud." 19And his army was numbered
at forty thousand five hundred.
20"Next to him *comes* the tribe of Manasseh, and the leader of the children of
Manasseh *shall be* Gamaliel the son of Pedahzur." 21And his army was numbered at
thirty-two thousand two hundred.
22"Then *comes* the tribe of Benjamin,
and the leader of the children of Benjamin *shall be* Abidan the son of Gideoni."
23And his army was numbered at thirty-five
thousand four hundred. 24"All who were
numbered according to their armies of
the forces with Ephraim, one hundred and
eight thousand one hundred—they shall
be the third to break camp.
25"The standard of the forces with Dan
shall be on the north side according to their
armies, and the leader of the children of
Dan *shall be* Ahiezer the son of Ammishaddai." 26And his army was numbered at
sixty-two thousand seven hundred.
27"Those who camp next to him *shall
be* the tribe of Asher, and the leader of the
children of Asher *shall be* Pagiel the son of
Ocran." 28And his army was numbered at
forty-one thousand five hundred.
29"Then *comes* the tribe of Naphtali, and
the leader of the children of Naphtali *shall
be* Ahira the son of Enan." 30And his army
was numbered at fifty-three thousand four
hundred. 31"All who were numbered of the
forces with Dan, one hundred and fifty-
seven thousand six hundred—they shall
break camp last, with their standards."
32These *are* the ones who were numbered of the children of Israel by their
fathers' houses. All who were numbered
according to their armies of the forces *were*
six hundred and three thousand five hundred and fifty. 33But the Levites were not
numbered among the children of Israel,
just as the LORD commanded Moses.
34Thus the children of Israel did according to all that the LORD commanded Moses; so they camped by their standards and
so they broke camp, each one by his family,
according to their fathers' houses.

The Sons of Aaron

3 Now these *are* the records of Aaron
and Moses when the LORD spoke with
Moses on Mount Sinai. 2And these *are* the
names of the sons of Aaron: Nadab, the
firstborn, and Abihu, Eleazar, and Ithamar.
3These *are* the names of the sons of Aaron,
the anointed priests, whom he consecrated
to minister as priests. 4Nadab and Abihu had
died before the LORD when they offered profane fire before the LORD in the Wilderness
of Sinai; and they had no children. So Eleazar and Ithamar ministered as priests in the
presence of Aaron their father.

The Levites Serve in the Tabernacle

5And the LORD spoke to Moses, saying:
6"Bring the tribe of Levi near, and present
them before Aaron the priest, that they
may serve him. 7And they shall attend to
his needs and the needs of the whole congregation before the tabernacle of meeting,
to do the work of the tabernacle. 8Also they
shall attend to all the furnishings of the
tabernacle of meeting, and to the needs of
the children of Israel, to do the work of the
tabernacle. 9And you shall give the Levites to
Aaron and his sons; they *are* given entirely
to him[a] from among the children of Israel.
10So you shall appoint Aaron and his sons,
and they shall attend to their priesthood; but
the outsider who comes near shall be put to
death."
11Then the LORD spoke to Moses, saying:
12"Now behold, I Myself have taken the Levites from among the children of Israel instead of every firstborn who opens the womb
among the children of Israel. Therefore the
Levites shall be Mine, 13because all the firstborn *are* Mine. On the day that I struck all
the firstborn in the land of Egypt, I sanctified to Myself all the firstborn in Israel, both
man and beast. They shall be Mine: I *am* the
LORD."

Census of the Levites Commanded

14Then the LORD spoke to Moses in the
Wilderness of Sinai, saying: 15"Number the
children of Levi by their fathers' houses, by
their families; you shall number every male
from a month old and above."
16So Moses numbered them according to the word of the LORD, as he was

3:9 [a] Samaritan Pentateuch and Septuagint read *Me*.

commanded. 17These were the sons of Levi
by their names: Gershon, Kohath, and Merari. 18And these *are* the names of the sons of
Gershon by their families: Libni and Shimei.
19And the sons of Kohath by their families:
Amram, Izehar, Hebron, and Uzziel. 20And
the sons of Merari by their families: Mahli
and Mushi. These *are* the families of the Levites by their fathers' houses.

21From Gershon *came* the family of the
Libnites and the family of the Shimites;
these *were* the families of the Gershonites.
22Those who were numbered, according to
the number of all the males from a month
old and above—of those who were numbered *there were* seven thousand five hundred. 23The families of the Gershonites were
to camp behind the tabernacle westward.
24And the leader of the father's house of the
Gershonites *was* Eliasaph the son of Lael.
25The duties of the children of Gershon in
the tabernacle of meeting *included* the tabernacle, the tent with its covering, the screen
for the door of the tabernacle of meeting,
26the screen for the door of the court, the
hangings of the court which *are* around the
tabernacle and the altar, and their cords, according to all the work relating to them.

27From Kohath *came* the family of the
Amramites, the family of the Izharites, the
family of the Hebronites, and the family of
the Uzzielites; these *were* the families of the
Kohathites. 28According to the number of
all the males, from a month old and above,
there were eight thousand six[a] hundred keeping charge of the sanctuary. 29The families
of the children of Kohath were to camp on
the south side of the tabernacle. 30And the
leader of the fathers' house of the families
of the Kohathites *was* Elizaphan the son of
Uzziel. 31Their duty *included* the ark, the table, the lampstand, the altars, the utensils of
the sanctuary with which they ministered,
the screen, and all the work relating to them.

32And Eleazar the son of Aaron the priest
was to be chief over the leaders of the Levites,
with oversight of those who kept charge of
the sanctuary.

33From Merari *came* the family of the
Mahlites and the family of the Mushites;
these *were* the families of Merari. 34And
those who were numbered, according to the
number of all the males from a month old
and above, *were* six thousand two hundred.
35The leader of the fathers' house of the families of Merari *was* Zuriel the son of Abihail.
These *were* to camp on the north side of the
tabernacle. 36And the appointed duty of the
children of Merari *included* the boards of the
tabernacle, its bars, its pillars, its sockets, its
utensils, all the work relating to them, 37and
the pillars of the court all around, with their
sockets, their pegs, and their cords.

38Moreover those who were to camp before the tabernacle on the east, before the
tabernacle of meeting, *were* Moses, Aaron,
and his sons, keeping charge of the sanctuary, to meet the needs of the children of Israel; but the outsider who came near was to
be put to death. 39All who were numbered of
the Levites, whom Moses and Aaron numbered at the commandment of the LORD, by
their families, all the males from a month
old and above, *were* twenty-two thousand.

Levites Dedicated Instead of the Firstborn

40Then the LORD said to Moses: "Number
all the firstborn males of the children of Israel from a month old and above, and take
the number of their names. 41And you shall
take the Levites for Me—I *am* the LORD—
instead of all the firstborn among the children of Israel, and the livestock of the Levites
instead of all the firstborn among the livestock of the children of Israel." 42So Moses
numbered all the firstborn among the children of Israel, as the LORD commanded him.
43And all the firstborn males, according to
the number of names from a month old and
above, of those who were numbered of them,
were twenty-two thousand two hundred and
seventy-three.

44Then the LORD spoke to Moses, saying:
45"Take the Levites instead of all the firstborn
among the children of Israel, and the livestock of the Levites instead of their livestock.
The Levites shall be Mine: I *am* the LORD.
46And for the redemption of the two hundred and seventy-three of the firstborn of
the children of Israel, who are more than the
number of the Levites, 47you shall take five
shekels for each one individually; you shall
take *them* in the currency of the shekel of
the sanctuary, the shekel of twenty gerahs.
48And you shall give the money, with which
the excess number of them is redeemed, to
Aaron and his sons."

3:28 [a] Some manuscripts of the Septuagint read *three*.

49So Moses took the redemption money
from those who were over and above those
who were redeemed by the Levites. 50From
the firstborn of the children of Israel he took
the money, one thousand three hundred and
sixty-five *shekels,* according to the shekel of
the sanctuary. 51And Moses gave their redemption money to Aaron and his sons, according to the word of the LORD, as the LORD
commanded Moses.

Duties of the Sons of Kohath

4 Then the LORD spoke to Moses and
Aaron, saying: 2"Take a census of the
sons of Kohath from among the children
of Levi, by their families, by their fathers'
house, 3from thirty years old and above, even
to fifty years old, all who enter the service
to do the work in the tabernacle of meeting.
4"This *is* the service of the sons of Kohath
in the tabernacle of meeting, *relating to* the
most holy things: 5When the camp prepares
to journey, Aaron and his sons shall come,
and they shall take down the covering veil
and cover the ark of the Testimony with it.
6Then they shall put on it a covering of badger skins, and spread over *that* a cloth entirely of blue; and they shall insert its poles.
7"On the table of showbread they shall
spread a blue cloth, and put on it the dishes, the pans, the bowls, and the pitchers for
pouring; and the showbread[a] shall be on it.
8They shall spread over them a scarlet cloth,
and cover the same with a covering of badger
skins; and they shall insert its poles. 9And
they shall take a blue cloth and cover the
lampstand of the light, with its lamps, its
wick-trimmers, its trays, and all its oil vessels, with which they service it. 10Then they
shall put it with all its utensils in a covering of badger skins, and put *it* on a carrying
beam.
11"Over the golden altar they shall spread
a blue cloth, and cover it with a covering
of badger skins; and they shall insert its
poles. 12Then they shall take all the utensils
of service with which they minister in the
sanctuary, put *them* in a blue cloth, cover
them with a covering of badger skins, and
put *them* on a carrying beam. 13Also they
shall take away the ashes from the altar, and
spread a purple cloth over it. 14They shall
put on it all its implements with which they
minister there—the firepans, the forks, the
shovels, the basins, and all the utensils of the
altar—and they shall spread on it a covering
of badger skins, and insert its poles. 15And
when Aaron and his sons have finished covering the sanctuary and all the furnishings
of the sanctuary, when the camp is set to go,
then the sons of Kohath shall come to carry
them; but they shall not touch any holy thing,
lest they die.
"These *are* the things in the tabernacle
of meeting which the sons of Kohath are to
carry.
16"The appointed duty of Eleazar the son
of Aaron the priest *is* the oil for the light, the
sweet incense, the daily grain offering, the
anointing oil, the oversight of all the tabernacle, of all that *is* in it, with the sanctuary
and its furnishings."
17Then the LORD spoke to Moses and
Aaron, saying: 18"Do not cut off the tribe of
the families of the Kohathites from among
the Levites; 19but do this in regard to them,
that they may live and not die when they approach the most holy things: Aaron and his
sons shall go in and appoint each of them
to his service and his task. 20But they shall
not go in to watch while the holy things are
being covered, lest they die."

Duties of the Sons of Gershon

21Then the LORD spoke to Moses, saying:
22"Also take a census of the sons of Gershon,
by their fathers' house, by their families.
23From thirty years old and above, even to fifty years old, you shall number them, all who
enter to perform the service, to do the work
in the tabernacle of meeting. 24This *is* the
service of the families of the Gershonites, in
serving and carrying: 25They shall carry the
curtains of the tabernacle and the tabernacle of meeting *with* its covering, the covering
of badger skins that *is* on it, the screen for
the door of the tabernacle of meeting, 26the
screen for the door of the gate of the court,
the hangings of the court which *are* around
the tabernacle and altar, and their cords, all
the furnishings for their service and all that
is made for these things: so shall they serve.
27"Aaron and his sons shall assign all
the service of the sons of the Gershonites,
all their tasks and all their service. And you
shall appoint to them all their tasks as their
duty. 28This *is* the service of the families of
the sons of Gershon in the tabernacle of

4:7 [a] Literally *the continual bread*

meeting. And their duties *shall be* under the
authority[a] of Ithamar the son of Aaron the
priest.

Duties of the Sons of Merari

29 “*As for* the sons of Merari, you shall
number them by their families and by their
fathers’ house. 30 From thirty years old and
above, even to fifty years old, you shall number them, everyone who enters the service
to do the work of the tabernacle of meeting.
31 And this is what they must carry as all their
service for the tabernacle of meeting: the
boards of the tabernacle, its bars, its pillars,
its sockets, 32 and the pillars around the court
with their sockets, pegs, and cords, with all
their furnishings and all their service; and
you shall assign *to each man* by name the
items he must carry. 33 This *is* the service of
the families of the sons of Merari, as all their
service for the tabernacle of meeting, under
the authority[a] of Ithamar the son of Aaron
the priest.”

Census of the Levites

34 And Moses, Aaron, and the leaders of
the congregation numbered the sons of the
Kohathites by their families and by their
fathers’ house, 35 from thirty years old and
above, even to fifty years old, everyone who
entered the service for work in the tabernacle
of meeting; 36 and those who were numbered
by their families were two thousand seven
hundred and fifty. 37 These *were* the ones
who were numbered of the families of the
Kohathites, all who might serve in the tabernacle of meeting, whom Moses and Aaron
numbered according to the commandment
of the LORD by the hand of Moses.

38 And those who were numbered of the
sons of Gershon, by their families and by
their fathers’ house, 39 from thirty years old
and above, even to fifty years old, everyone who entered the service for work in the
tabernacle of meeting— 40 those who were
numbered by their families, by their fathers’
house, were two thousand six hundred and
thirty. 41 These *are* the ones who were numbered of the families of the sons of Gershon,
of all who might serve in the tabernacle of
meeting, whom Moses and Aaron numbered according to the commandment of
the LORD.

42 Those of the families of the sons of Merari who were numbered, by their families,
by their fathers’ house, 43 from thirty years
old and above, even to fifty years old, everyone who entered the service for work in the
tabernacle of meeting— 44 those who were
numbered by their families were three thousand two hundred. 45 These *are* the ones who
were numbered of the families of the sons of
Merari, whom Moses and Aaron numbered
according to the word of the LORD by the
hand of Moses.

46 All who were numbered of the Levites,
whom Moses, Aaron, and the leaders of Israel numbered, by their families and by
their fathers’ houses, 47 from thirty years old
and above, even to fifty years old, everyone
who came to do the work of service and the
work of bearing burdens in the tabernacle of
meeting— 48 those who were numbered were
eight thousand five hundred and eighty.

49 According to the commandment of
the LORD they were numbered by the hand
of Moses, each according to his service and
according to his task; thus were they numbered by him, as the LORD commanded
Moses.

Ceremonially Unclean Persons Isolated

5 And the LORD spoke to Moses, saying:
2 “Command the children of Israel that
they put out of the camp every leper, everyone who has a discharge, and whoever becomes defiled by a corpse. 3 You shall put out
both male and female; you shall put them
outside the camp, that they may not defile
their camps in the midst of which I dwell.”
4 And the children of Israel did so, and put
them outside the camp; as the LORD spoke to
Moses, so the children of Israel did.

Confession and Restitution

5 Then the LORD spoke to Moses, saying,
6 “Speak to the children of Israel: ‘When a
man or woman commits any sin that men
commit in unfaithfulness against the LORD,
and that person is guilty, 7 then he shall confess the sin which he has committed. He
shall make restitution for his trespass in full,
plus one-fifth of it, and give *it* to the one he
has wronged. 8 But if the man has no relative
to whom restitution may be made for the
wrong, the restitution for the wrong *must go*
to the LORD for the priest, in addition to the

4:28 [a] Literally *hand* 4:33 [a] Literally *hand*

ram of the atonement with which atonement
is made for him. 9Every offering of all the
holy things of the children of Israel, which
they bring to the priest, shall be his. 10And
every man's holy things shall be his; whatever any man gives the priest shall be his.'"

Concerning Unfaithful Wives

11And the LORD spoke to Moses, saying,
12"Speak to the children of Israel, and say to
them: 'If any man's wife goes astray and be-
haves unfaithfully toward him, 13and a man
lies with her carnally, and it is hidden from
the eyes of her husband, and it is concealed
that she has defiled herself, and *there was* no
witness against her, nor was she caught— 14if
the spirit of jealousy comes upon him and he
becomes jealous of his wife, who has defiled
herself; or if the spirit of jealousy comes
upon him and he becomes jealous of his
wife, although she has not defiled herself—
15then the man shall bring his wife to the
priest. He shall bring the offering required
for her, one-tenth of an ephah of barley meal;
he shall pour no oil on it and put no frankincense on it, because it *is* a grain offering of
jealousy, an offering for remembering, for
bringing iniquity to remembrance.

16'And the priest shall bring her near, and
set her before the LORD. 17The priest shall
take holy water in an earthen vessel, and
take some of the dust that is on the floor
of the tabernacle and put *it* into the water.
18Then the priest shall stand the woman before the LORD, uncover the woman's head,
and put the offering for remembering in her
hands, which *is* the grain offering of jealousy. And the priest shall have in his hand the
bitter water that brings a curse. 19And the
priest shall put her under oath, and say to
the woman, "If no man has lain with you,
and if you have not gone astray to uncleanness *while* under your husband's *authority,*
be free from this bitter water that brings
a curse. 20But if you have gone astray *while*
under your husband's *authority,* and if you
have defiled yourself and some man other
than your husband has lain with you"—
21then the priest shall put the woman under
the oath of the curse, and he shall say to the
woman—"the LORD make you a curse and
an oath among your people, when the LORD
makes your thigh rot and your belly swell;
22and may this water that causes the curse go
into your stomach, and make *your* belly swell
and *your* thigh rot."

'Then the woman shall say, "Amen, so
be it."

23'Then the priest shall write these curses in a book, and he shall scrape *them* off
into the bitter water. 24And he shall make the
woman drink the bitter water that brings a
curse, and the water that brings the curse
shall enter her *to become* bitter. 25Then the
priest shall take the grain offering of jealousy from the woman's hand, shall wave the
offering before the LORD, and bring it to the
altar; 26and the priest shall take a handful of
the offering, as its memorial portion, burn
it on the altar, and afterward make the woman drink the water. 27When he has made her
drink the water, then it shall be, if she has
defiled herself and behaved unfaithfully toward her husband, that the water that brings
a curse will enter her *and become* bitter, and
her belly will swell, her thigh will rot, and
the woman will become a curse among her
people. 28But if the woman has not defiled
herself, and is clean, then she shall be free
and may conceive children.

29'This *is* the law of jealousy, when a wife,
while under her husband's *authority,* goes
astray and defiles herself, 30or when the
spirit of jealousy comes upon a man, and he
becomes jealous of his wife; then he shall
stand the woman before the LORD, and the
priest shall execute all this law upon her.
31Then the man shall be free from iniquity,
but that woman shall bear her guilt.'"

The Law of the Nazirite

6 Then the LORD spoke to Moses, saying,
2"Speak to the children of Israel, and
say to them: 'When either a man or woman
consecrates an offering to take the vow of a
Nazirite, to separate himself to the LORD,
3he shall separate himself from wine and
similar drink; he shall drink neither vinegar
made from wine nor vinegar made from *similar* drink; neither shall he drink any grape
juice, nor eat fresh grapes or raisins. 4All the
days of his separation he shall eat nothing
that is produced by the grapevine, from seed
to skin.

5'All the days of the vow of his separation
no razor shall come upon his head; until
the days are fulfilled for which he separated
himself to the LORD, he shall be holy. *Then*
he shall let the locks of the hair of his head

grow. 6All the days that he separates himself
to the LORD he shall not go near a dead body.
7He shall not make himself unclean even for
his father or his mother, for his brother or
his sister, when they die, because his separation to God *is* on his head. 8All the days of
his separation he shall be holy to the LORD.

9'And if anyone dies very suddenly beside
him, and he defiles his consecrated head,
then he shall shave his head on the day of
his cleansing; on the seventh day he shall
shave it. 10Then on the eighth day he shall
bring two turtledoves or two young pigeons
to the priest, to the door of the tabernacle of
meeting; 11and the priest shall offer one as a
sin offering and *the* other as a burnt offering, and make atonement for him, because
he sinned in regard to the corpse; and he
shall sanctify his head that same day. 12He
shall consecrate to the LORD the days of his
separation, and bring a male lamb in its first
year as a trespass offering; but the former
days shall be lost, because his separation
was defiled.

13'Now this *is* the law of the Nazirite:
When the days of his separation are fulfilled,
he shall be brought to the door of the tabernacle of meeting. 14And he shall present his
offering to the LORD: one male lamb in its
first year without blemish as a burnt offering, one ewe lamb in its first year without
blemish as a sin offering, one ram without
blemish as a peace offering, 15a basket of
unleavened bread, cakes of fine flour mixed
with oil, unleavened wafers anointed with
oil, and their grain offering with their drink
offerings.

16'Then the priest shall bring *them* before the LORD and offer his sin offering and
his burnt offering; 17and he shall offer the
ram as a sacrifice of a peace offering to the
LORD, with the basket of unleavened bread;
the priest shall also offer its grain offering
and its drink offering. 18Then the Nazirite
shall shave his consecrated head *at* the door
of the tabernacle of meeting, and shall take
the hair from his consecrated head and put
it on the fire which is under the sacrifice of
the peace offering.

19'And the priest shall take the boiled
shoulder of the ram, one unleavened cake
from the basket, and one unleavened wafer,
and put *them* upon the hands of the Nazirite
after he has shaved his consecrated *hair,*
20and the priest shall wave them as a wave offering before the LORD; they *are* holy for the
priest, together with the breast of the wave
offering and the thigh of the heave offering.
After that the Nazirite may drink wine.'

21"This is the law of the Nazirite who
vows to the LORD the offering for his separation, and besides that, whatever else his
hand is able to provide; according to the vow
which he takes, so he must do according to
the law of his separation."

The Priestly Blessing

22And the LORD spoke to Moses, saying:
23"Speak to Aaron and his sons, saying, 'This
is the way you shall bless the children of Israel. Say to them:

24 "The LORD bless you and keep you;
25 The LORD make His face shine upon
you,
And be gracious to you;
26 The LORD lift up His countenance upon
you,
And give you peace."'

27"So they shall put My name on the children of Israel, and I will bless them."

Offerings of the Leaders

7 Now it came to pass, when Moses had
finished setting up the tabernacle, that
he anointed it and consecrated it and all its
furnishings, and the altar and all its utensils;
so he anointed them and consecrated them.
2Then the leaders of Israel, the heads of their
fathers' houses, who *were* the leaders of the
tribes and over those who were numbered,
made an offering. 3And they brought their
offering before the LORD, six covered carts
and twelve oxen, a cart for *every* two of the
leaders, and for each one an ox; and they presented them before the tabernacle.

4Then the LORD spoke to Moses, saying,
5"Accept *these* from them, that they may be
used in doing the work of the tabernacle of
meeting; and you shall give them to the Levites, *to* every man according to his service."
6So Moses took the carts and the oxen, and
gave them to the Levites. 7Two carts and four
oxen he gave to the sons of Gershon, according to their service; 8and four carts and eight
oxen he gave to the sons of Merari, according to their service, under the authority[a] of

7:8 [a] Literally *hand*

Ithamar the son of Aaron the priest. 9But to the sons of Kohath he gave none, because theirs *was* the service of the holy things, *which* they carried on their shoulders.

10Now the leaders offered the dedication *offering* for the altar when it was anointed; so the leaders offered their offering before the altar. 11For the LORD said to Moses, "They shall offer their offering, one leader each day, for the dedication of the altar."

12And the one who offered his offering on the first day *was* Nahshon the son of Amminadab, from the tribe of Judah. 13His offering *was* one silver platter, the weight of which *was* one hundred and thirty *shekels,* and one silver bowl of seventy shekels, according to the shekel of the sanctuary, both of them full of fine flour mixed with oil as a grain offering; 14one gold pan of ten *shekels,* full of incense; 15one young bull, one ram, and one male lamb in its first year, as a burnt offering; 16one kid of the goats as a sin offering; 17and for the sacrifice of peace offerings: two oxen, five rams, five male goats, and five male lambs in their first year. This *was* the offering of Nahshon the son of Amminadab.

18On the second day Nethanel the son of Zuar, leader of Issachar, presented *an offering.* 19*For* his offering he offered one silver platter, the weight of which *was* one hundred and thirty *shekels,* and one silver bowl of seventy shekels, according to the shekel of the sanctuary, both of them full of fine flour mixed with oil as a grain offering; 20one gold pan of ten *shekels,* full of incense; 21one young bull, one ram, and one male lamb in its first year, as a burnt offering; 22one kid of the goats as a sin offering; 23and as the sacrifice of peace offerings: two oxen, five rams, five male goats, and five male lambs in their first year. This *was* the offering of Nethanel the son of Zuar.

24On the third day Eliab the son of Helon, leader of the children of Zebulun, *presented an offering.* 25His offering *was* one silver platter, the weight of which *was* one hundred and thirty *shekels,* and one silver bowl of seventy shekels, according to the shekel of the sanctuary, both of them full of fine flour mixed with oil as a grain offering; 26one gold pan of ten *shekels,* full of incense; 27one young bull, one ram, and one male lamb in its first year, as a burnt offering; 28one kid of the goats as a sin offering; 29and for the sacrifice of peace offerings: two oxen, five rams, five male goats, and five male lambs in their first year. This *was* the offering of Eliab the son of Helon.

30On the fourth day Elizur the son of Shedeur, leader of the children of Reuben, *presented an offering.* 31His offering *was* one silver platter, the weight of which *was* one hundred and thirty *shekels,* and one silver bowl of seventy shekels, according to the shekel of the sanctuary, both of them full of fine flour mixed with oil as a grain offering; 32one gold pan of ten *shekels,* full of incense; 33one young bull, one ram, and one male lamb in its first year, as a burnt offering; 34one kid of the goats as a sin offering; 35and as the sacrifice of peace offerings: two oxen, five rams, five male goats, and five male lambs in their first year. This *was* the offering of Elizur the son of Shedeur.

36On the fifth day Shelumiel the son of Zurishaddai, leader of the children of Simeon, *presented an offering.* 37His offering *was* one silver platter, the weight of which *was* one hundred and thirty *shekels,* and one silver bowl of seventy shekels, according to the shekel of the sanctuary, both of them full of fine flour mixed with oil as a grain offering; 38one gold pan of ten *shekels,* full of incense; 39one young bull, one ram, and one male lamb in its first year, as a burnt offering; 40one kid of the goats as a sin offering; 41and as the sacrifice of peace offerings: two oxen, five rams, five male goats, and five male lambs in their first year. This *was* the offering of Shelumiel the son of Zurishaddai.

42On the sixth day Eliasaph the son of Deuel,[a] leader of the children of Gad, *presented an offering.* 43His offering *was* one silver platter, the weight of which *was* one hundred and thirty *shekels,* and one silver bowl of seventy shekels, according to the shekel of the sanctuary, both of them full of fine flour mixed with oil as a grain offering; 44one gold pan of ten *shekels,* full of incense; 45one young bull, one ram, and one male lamb in its first year, as a burnt offering; 46one kid of the goats as a sin offering; 47and as the sacrifice of peace offerings: two oxen, five rams, five male goats, and five male lambs in their

7:42 [a] Spelled *Reuel* in 2:14

first year. This *was* the offering of Eliasaph
the son of Deuel.

48On the seventh day Elishama the son
of Ammihud, leader of the children of
Ephraim, *presented an offering.* 49His offering
was one silver platter, the weight of which
was one hundred and thirty *shekels,* and one
silver bowl of seventy shekels, according to
the shekel of the sanctuary, both of them
full of fine flour mixed with oil as a grain
offering; 50one gold pan of ten *shekels,* full
of incense; 51one young bull, one ram, and
one male lamb in its first year, as a burnt
offering; 52one kid of the goats as a sin offering; 53and as the sacrifice of peace offerings:
two oxen, five rams, five male goats, and five
male lambs in their first year. This *was* the
offering of Elishama the son of Ammihud.

54On the eighth day Gamaliel the son
of Pedahzur, leader of the children of Manasseh, *presented an offering.* 55His offering
was one silver platter, the weight of which
was one hundred and thirty *shekels,* and one
silver bowl of seventy shekels, according to
the shekel of the sanctuary, both of them
full of fine flour mixed with oil as a grain
offering; 56one gold pan of ten *shekels,* full
of incense; 57one young bull, one ram, and
one male lamb in its first year, as a burnt
offering; 58one kid of the goats as a sin offering; 59and as the sacrifice of peace offerings:
two oxen, five rams, five male goats, and five
male lambs in their first year. This *was* the
offering of Gamaliel the son of Pedahzur.

60On the ninth day Abidan the son of
Gideoni, leader of the children of Benjamin,
presented an offering. 61His offering *was* one
silver platter, the weight of which *was* one
hundred and thirty *shekels,* and one silver
bowl of seventy shekels, according to the
shekel of the sanctuary, both of them full of
fine flour mixed with oil as a grain offering;
62one gold pan of ten *shekels,* full of incense;
63one young bull, one ram, and one male
lamb in its first year, as a burnt offering;
64one kid of the goats as a sin offering; 65and
as the sacrifice of peace offerings: two oxen,
five rams, five male goats, and five male
lambs in their first year. This *was* the offering of Abidan the son of Gideoni.

66On the tenth day Ahiezer the son of
Ammishaddai, leader of the children of
Dan, *presented an offering.* 67His offering *was*
one silver platter, the weight of which *was*
one hundred and thirty *shekels,* and one silver bowl of seventy shekels, according to the
shekel of the sanctuary, both of them full of
fine flour mixed with oil as a grain offering;
68one gold pan of ten *shekels,* full of incense;
69one young bull, one ram, and one male
lamb in its first year, as a burnt offering;
70one kid of the goats as a sin offering; 71and
as the sacrifice of peace offerings: two oxen,
five rams, five male goats, and five male
lambs in their first year. This *was* the offering of Ahiezer the son of Ammishaddai.

72On the eleventh day Pagiel the son of
Ocran, leader of the children of Asher, *presented an offering.* 73His offering *was* one
silver platter, the weight of which *was* one
hundred and thirty *shekels,* and one silver
bowl of seventy shekels, according to the
shekel of the sanctuary, both of them full
of fine flour mixed with oil as a grain offering; 74one gold pan of ten *shekels,* full of
incense; 75one young bull, one ram, and one
male lamb in its first year, as a burnt offering; 76one kid of the goats as a sin offering;
77and as the sacrifice of peace offerings: two
oxen, five rams, five male goats, and five
male lambs in their first year. This *was* the
offering of Pagiel the son of Ocran.

78On the twelfth day Ahira the son of
Enan, leader of the children of Naphtali,
presented an offering. 79His offering *was* one
silver platter, the weight of which *was* one
hundred and thirty *shekels,* and one silver
bowl of seventy shekels, according to the
shekel of the sanctuary, both of them full
of fine flour mixed with oil as a grain offering; 80one gold pan of ten *shekels,* full of
incense; 81one young bull, one ram, and one
male lamb in its first year, as a burnt offering; 82one kid of the goats as a sin offering;
83and as the sacrifice of peace offerings: two
oxen, five rams, five male goats, and five
male lambs in their first year. This *was* the
offering of Ahira the son of Enan.

84This *was* the dedication *offering* for the
altar from the leaders of Israel, when it was
anointed: twelve silver platters, twelve silver
bowls, and twelve gold pans. 85Each silver
platter *weighed* one hundred and thirty *shekels* and each bowl seventy *shekels.* All the silver of the vessels *weighed* two thousand four
hundred *shekels,* according to the shekel of
the sanctuary. 86The twelve gold pans full of
incense *weighed* ten *shekels* apiece, according

to the shekel of the sanctuary; all the gold of
the pans *weighed* one hundred and twenty
shekels. 87All the oxen for the burnt offering
were twelve young bulls, the rams twelve,
the male lambs in their first year twelve,
with their grain offering, and the kids of the
goats as a sin offering twelve. 88And all the
oxen for the sacrifice of peace offerings were
twenty-four bulls, the rams sixty, the male
goats sixty, and the lambs in their first year
sixty. This *was* the dedication *offering* for the
altar after it was anointed.

89Now when Moses went into the tabernacle of meeting to speak with Him, he heard
the voice of One speaking to him from above
the mercy seat that *was* on the ark of the Testimony, from between the two cherubim;
thus He spoke to him.

Arrangement of the Lamps

8 And the LORD spoke to Moses, saying: 2"Speak to Aaron, and say to him,
'When you arrange the lamps, the seven
lamps shall give light in front of the lampstand.'" 3And Aaron did so; he arranged the
lamps to face toward the front of the lampstand, as the LORD commanded Moses.
4Now this workmanship of the lampstand
was hammered gold; from its shaft to its
flowers it *was* hammered work. According
to the pattern which the LORD had shown
Moses, so he made the lampstand.

Cleansing and Dedication of the Levites

5Then the LORD spoke to Moses, saying:
6"Take the Levites from among the children
of Israel and cleanse them *ceremonially*.
7Thus you shall do to them to cleanse them:
Sprinkle water of purification on them, and
let them shave all their body, and let them
wash their clothes, and *so* make themselves
clean. 8Then let them take a young bull with
its grain offering of fine flour mixed with
oil, and you shall take another young bull as
a sin offering. 9And you shall bring the Levites before the tabernacle of meeting, and
you shall gather together the whole congregation of the children of Israel. 10So you shall
bring the Levites before the LORD, and the
children of Israel shall lay their hands on the
Levites; 11and Aaron shall offer the Levites
before the LORD *like* a wave offering from the
children of Israel, that they may perform the
work of the LORD. 12Then the Levites shall lay
their hands on the heads of the young bulls,
and you shall offer one as a sin offering and
the other as a burnt offering to the LORD, to
make atonement for the Levites.

13"And you shall stand the Levites before
Aaron and his sons, and then offer them
like a wave offering to the LORD. 14Thus you
shall separate the Levites from among the
children of Israel, and the Levites shall be
Mine. 15After that the Levites shall go in to
service the tabernacle of meeting. So you
shall cleanse them and offer them *like* a
wave offering. 16For they *are* wholly given to
Me from among the children of Israel; I have
taken them for Myself instead of all who
open the womb, the firstborn of all the children of Israel. 17For all the firstborn among
the children of Israel *are* Mine, *both* man and
beast; on the day that I struck all the firstborn in the land of Egypt I sanctified them
to Myself. 18I have taken the Levites instead
of all the firstborn of the children of Israel.
19And I have given the Levites as a gift to Aaron and his sons from among the children
of Israel, to do the work for the children of
Israel in the tabernacle of meeting, and to
make atonement for the children of Israel,
that there be no plague among the children
of Israel when the children of Israel come
near the sanctuary."

20Thus Moses and Aaron and all the
congregation of the children of Israel did to
the Levites; according to all that the LORD
commanded Moses concerning the Levites,
so the children of Israel did to them. 21And
the Levites purified themselves and washed
their clothes; then Aaron presented them
like a wave offering before the LORD, and
Aaron made atonement for them to cleanse
them. 22After that the Levites went in to do
their work in the tabernacle of meeting before Aaron and his sons; as the LORD commanded Moses concerning the Levites, so
they did to them.

23Then the LORD spoke to Moses, saying,
24"This *is* what *pertains* to the Levites: From
twenty-five years old and above one may enter to perform service in the work of the tabernacle of meeting; 25and at the age of fifty
years they must cease performing this work,
and shall work no more. 26They may minister with their brethren in the tabernacle of
meeting, to attend to needs, but they *themselves* shall do no work. Thus you shall do to
the Levites regarding their duties."

The Second Passover

9 Now the LORD spoke to Moses in the
Wilderness of Sinai, in the first month
of the second year after they had come out of
the land of Egypt, saying: 2"Let the children
of Israel keep the Passover at its appointed
time. 3On the fourteenth day of this month,
at twilight, you shall keep it at its appointed
time. According to all its rites and ceremonies you shall keep it." 4So Moses told the
children of Israel that they should keep the
Passover. 5And they kept the Passover on the
fourteenth day of the first month, at twilight, in the Wilderness of Sinai; according
to all that the LORD commanded Moses, so
the children of Israel did.

6Now there were *certain* men who were
defiled by a human corpse, so that they
could not keep the Passover on that day; and
they came before Moses and Aaron that day.
7And those men said to him, "We *became* defiled by a human corpse. Why are we kept
from presenting the offering of the LORD
at its appointed time among the children of
Israel?"

8And Moses said to them, "Stand still,
that I may hear what the LORD will command concerning you."

9Then the LORD spoke to Moses, saying,
10"Speak to the children of Israel, saying: 'If
anyone of you or your posterity is unclean
because of a corpse, or *is* far away on a journey, he may still keep the LORD's Passover.
11On the fourteenth day of the second month,
at twilight, they may keep it. They shall eat
it with unleavened bread and bitter herbs.
12They shall leave none of it until morning,
nor break one of its bones. According to all
the ordinances of the Passover they shall
keep it. 13But the man who *is* clean and is not

GOD IS PRESENT WITH HIS PEOPLE

READ IT: NUMBERS 9:15–23

GET IT:

God first appeared to His people "face-to-face" on Mount Sinai. When Moses finished constructing the tabernacle, God's presence came down off the mountain and moved into the tabernacle in a cloud filled with His glory. Now God lived in the middle of His people. They saw God's presence during the day when they looked at the tabernacle and saw the cloud hanging over it. They saw His presence at night when the cloud glowed with fire. When the cloud rose up and moved, the people packed up their stuff and moved to another campsite. They stopped when the cloud stopped. This was their training to obey God and follow Him.

LIVE IT:

This cloud and fire thing sounds pretty cool, doesn't it? Well, we don't have clouds or fires hanging over our churches to visually see God's presence. But we have something better. We have God's presence living inside of us. Christians have God's Spirit living inside their hearts and minds. God isn't outside hanging around someplace. God is with us! He's with us every moment, in every step.

on a journey, and ceases to keep the Passover, that same person shall be cut off from among his people, because he did not bring the offering of the LORD at its appointed time; that man shall bear his sin.

14‘And if a stranger dwells among you, and would keep the LORD’s Passover, he must do so according to the rite of the Passover and according to its ceremony; you shall have one ordinance, both for the stranger and the native of the land.’ ”

The Cloud and the Fire

15Now on the day that the tabernacle was raised up, the cloud covered the tabernacle, the tent of the Testimony; from evening until morning it was above the tabernacle like the appearance of fire. 16So it was always: the cloud covered it *by day,* and the appearance of fire by night. 17Whenever the cloud was taken up from above the tabernacle, after that the children of Israel would journey; and in the place where the cloud settled, there the children of Israel would pitch their tents. 18At the command of the LORD the children of Israel would journey, and at the command of the LORD they would camp; as long as the cloud stayed above the tabernacle they remained encamped. 19Even when the cloud continued long, many days above the tabernacle, the children of Israel kept the charge of the LORD and did not journey. 20So it was, when the cloud was above the tabernacle a few days: according to the command of the LORD they would remain encamped, and according to the command of the LORD they would journey. 21So it was, when the cloud remained only from evening until morning: when the cloud was taken up in the morning, then they would journey; whether by day or by night, whenever the cloud was taken up, they would journey. 22 *Whether it was* two days, a month, or a year that the cloud remained above the tabernacle, the children of Israel would remain encamped and not journey; but when it was taken up, they would journey. 23At the command of the LORD they remained encamped, and at the command of the LORD they journeyed; they kept the charge of the LORD, at the command *of the LORD by the hand of Moses.*

Two Silver Trumpets

10 And the LORD spoke to Moses, saying: 2“Make two silver trumpets for yourself; you shall make them of hammered work; you shall use them for calling the congregation and for directing the movement of the camps. 3When they blow both of them, all the congregation shall gather before you at the door of the tabernacle of meeting. 4But if they blow *only* one, then the leaders, the heads of the divisions of Israel, shall gather to you. 5When you sound the advance, the camps that lie on the east side shall then begin their journey. 6When you sound the advance the second time, then the camps that lie on the south side shall begin their journey; they shall sound the call for them to begin their journeys. 7And when the assembly is to be gathered together, you shall blow, but not sound the advance. 8The sons of Aaron, the priests, shall blow the trumpets; and these shall be to you as an ordinance forever throughout your generations.

9“When you go to war in your land against the enemy who oppresses you, then you shall sound an alarm with the trumpets, and you will be remembered before the LORD your God, and you will be saved from your enemies. 10Also in the day of your gladness, in your appointed feasts, and at the beginning of your months, you shall blow the trumpets over your burnt offerings and over the sacrifices of your peace offerings; and they shall be a memorial for you before your God: I *am* the LORD your God.”

Departure from Sinai

11Now it came to pass on the twentieth *day* of the second month, in the second year, that the cloud was taken up from above the tabernacle of the Testimony. 12And the children of Israel set out from the Wilderness of Sinai on their journeys; then the cloud settled down in the Wilderness of Paran. 13So they started out for the first time according to the command of the LORD by the hand of Moses.

14The standard of the camp of the children of Judah set out first according to their armies; over their army was Nahshon the son of Amminadab. 15Over the army of the tribe of the children of Issachar *was* Nethanel the son of Zuar. 16And over the army of the tribe of the children of Zebulun *was* Eliab the son of Helon.

17Then the tabernacle was taken down; and the sons of Gershon and the sons of Merari set out, carrying the tabernacle.

18And the standard of the camp of Reuben set out according to their armies; over
their army *was* Elizur the son of Shedeur.
19Over the army of the tribe of the children
of Simeon *was* Shelumiel the son of Zurishaddai. 20And over the army of the tribe of
the children of Gad *was* Eliasaph the son of
Deuel.

21Then the Kohathites set out, carrying
the holy things. (The tabernacle would be
prepared for their arrival.)

22And the standard of the camp of the
children of Ephraim set out according to
their armies; over their army *was* Elishama
the son of Ammihud. 23Over the army of the
tribe of the children of Manasseh *was* Gamaliel the son of Pedahzur. 24And over the army
of the tribe of the children of Benjamin *was*
Abidan the son of Gideoni.

25Then the standard of the camp of the
children of Dan (the rear guard of all the
camps) set out according to their armies;
over their army *was* Ahiezer the son of
Ammishaddai. 26Over the army of the tribe
of the children of Asher *was* Pagiel the son
of Ocran. 27And over the army of the tribe of
the children of Naphtali *was* Ahira the son
of Enan.

28Thus *was* the order of march of the
children of Israel, according to their armies,
when they began their journey.

29Now Moses said to Hobab the son of
Reuel[a] the Midianite, Moses' father-in-law,
"We are setting out for the place of which the
LORD said, 'I will give it to you.' Come with
us, and we will treat you well; for the LORD
has promised good things to Israel."

30And he said to him, "I will not go,
but I will depart to my *own* land and to my
relatives."

31So *Moses* said, "Please do not leave, inasmuch as you know how we are to camp
in the wilderness, and you can be our eyes.
32And it shall be, if you go with us—indeed it
shall be—that whatever good the LORD will
do to us, the same we will do to you."

33So they departed from the mountain of
the LORD on a journey of three days; and the
ark of the covenant of the LORD went before
them for the three days' journey, to search
out a resting place for them. 34And the cloud
of the LORD *was* above them by day when
they went out from the camp.

35So it was, whenever the ark set out, that
Moses said:

"Rise up, O LORD!
Let Your enemies be scattered,
And let those who hate You flee before
You."

36And when it rested, he said:

"Return, O LORD,
To the many thousands of Israel."

The People Complain

11 Now *when* the people complained,
it displeased the LORD; for the LORD
heard *it,* and His anger was aroused. So
the fire of the LORD burned among them,
and consumed *some* in the outskirts of the
camp. 2Then the people cried out to Moses,
and when Moses prayed to the LORD, the fire
was quenched. 3So he called the name of the
place Taberah,[a] because the fire of the LORD
had burned among them.

4Now the mixed multitude who were
among them yielded to intense craving; so
the children of Israel also wept again and
said: "Who will give us meat to eat? 5We
remember the fish which we ate freely in
Egypt, the cucumbers, the melons, the
leeks, the onions, and the garlic; 6but now
our whole being *is* dried up; *there is* nothing
at all except this manna *before* our eyes!"

7Now the manna *was* like coriander seed,
and its color like the color of bdellium. 8The
people went about and gathered *it,* ground *it*
on millstones or beat *it* in the mortar, cooked
it in pans, and made cakes of it; and its taste
was like the taste of pastry prepared with oil.
9And when the dew fell on the camp in the
night, the manna fell on it.

10Then Moses heard the people weeping
throughout their families, everyone at the
door of his tent; and the anger of the LORD
was greatly aroused; Moses also was displeased. 11So Moses said to the LORD, "Why
have You afflicted Your servant? And why
have I not found favor in Your sight, that
You have laid the burden of all these people
on me? 12Did I conceive all these people? Did
I beget them, that You should say to me,
'Carry them in your bosom, as a guardian
carries a nursing child,' to the land which
You swore to their fathers? 13Where am I

10:29 [a] Septuagint reads *Raguel* (compare Exodus 2:18).
11:3 [a] Literally *Burning*

to get meat to give to all these people? For
they weep all over me, saying, 'Give us meat,
that we may eat.' 14I am not able to bear all
these people alone, because the burden *is*
too heavy for me. 15If You treat me like this,
please kill me here and now—if I have found
favor in Your sight—and do not let me see
my wretchedness!"

The Seventy Elders

16So the LORD said to Moses: "Gather
to Me seventy men of the elders of Israel,
whom you know to be the elders of the people and officers over them; bring them to the
tabernacle of meeting, that they may stand
there with you. 17Then I will come down and
talk with you there. I will take of the Spirit
that *is* upon you and will put *the same* upon
them; and they shall bear the burden of the
people with you, that you may not bear *it*
yourself alone. 18Then you shall say to the
people, 'Consecrate yourselves for tomorrow,
and you shall eat meat; for you have wept in
the hearing of the LORD, saying, "Who will
give us meat to eat? For *it was* well with us
in Egypt." Therefore the LORD will give you
meat, and you shall eat. 19You shall eat, not
one day, nor two days, nor five days, nor
ten days, nor twenty days, 20but *for* a whole
month, until it comes out of your nostrils
and becomes loathsome to you, because you
have despised the LORD who is among you,
and have wept before Him, saying, "Why did
we ever come up out of Egypt?"'"

21And Moses said, "The people whom I
am among *are* six hundred thousand men
on foot; yet You have said, 'I will give them
meat, that they may eat *for* a whole month.'
22Shall flocks and herds be slaughtered for
them, to provide enough for them? Or shall
all the fish of the sea be gathered together
for them, to provide enough for them?"

23And the LORD said to Moses, "Has the
LORD's arm been shortened? Now you shall
see whether what I say will happen to you
or not."

24So Moses went out and told the people
the words of the LORD, and he gathered the
seventy men of the elders of the people and
placed them around the tabernacle. 25Then
the LORD came down in the cloud, and spoke
to him, and took of the Spirit that *was* upon
him, and placed *the same* upon the seventy elders; and it happened, when the Spirit
rested upon them, that they prophesied, although they never did *so* again.[a]

26But two men had remained in the
camp: the name of one *was* Eldad, and the
name of the other Medad. And the Spirit
rested upon them. Now they *were* among
those listed, but who had not gone out to the
tabernacle; yet they prophesied in the camp.
27And a young man ran and told Moses, and
said, "Eldad and Medad are prophesying in
the camp."

28So Joshua the son of Nun, Moses' assistant, *one* of his choice men, answered and
said, "Moses my lord, forbid them!"

29Then Moses said to him, "Are you zealous for my sake? Oh, that all the LORD's people were prophets *and* that the LORD would
put His Spirit upon them!" 30And Moses
returned to the camp, he and the elders of
Israel.

The LORD Sends Quail

31Now a wind went out from the LORD,
and it brought quail from the sea and left
them fluttering near the camp, about a day's
journey on this side and about a day's journey on the other side, all around the camp,
and about two cubits above the surface of
the ground. 32And the people stayed up all
that day, all night, and all the next day, and
gathered the quail (he who gathered least
gathered ten homers); and they spread *them*
out for themselves all around the camp.
33But while the meat *was* still between their
teeth, before it was chewed, the wrath of the
LORD was aroused against the people, and
the LORD struck the people with a very great
plague. 34So he called the name of that place
Kibroth Hattaavah,[a] because there they buried the people who had yielded to craving.

35From Kibroth Hattaavah the people moved to Hazeroth, and camped at
Hazeroth.

Dissension of Aaron and Miriam

12 Then Miriam and Aaron spoke
against Moses because of the Ethiopian woman whom he had married; for he
had married an Ethiopian woman. 2So they
said, "Has the LORD indeed spoken only
through Moses? Has He not spoken through
us also?" And the LORD heard *it*. 3(Now the

11:25 [a] Targum and Vulgate read *did not cease*. 11:34 [a] Literally *Graves of Craving*

man Moses *was* very humble, more than all
men who *were* on the face of the earth.)
4 Suddenly the LORD said to Moses, Aaron, and Miriam, "Come out, you three, to the
tabernacle of meeting!" So the three came
out. 5 Then the LORD came down in the pillar
of cloud and stood *in* the door of the tabernacle, and called Aaron and Miriam. And they
both went forward. 6 Then He said,

"Hear now My words:
If there is a prophet among you,
I, the LORD, make Myself known to him
in a vision;
I speak to him in a dream.
7 Not so with My servant Moses;
He *is* faithful in all My house.
8 I speak with him face to face,
Even plainly, and not in dark sayings;
And he sees the form of the LORD.
Why then were you not afraid
To speak against My servant Moses?"

9 So the anger of the LORD was aroused
against them, and He departed. 10 And when
the cloud departed from above the tabernacle, suddenly Miriam *became* leprous, as
white as snow. Then Aaron turned toward
Miriam, and there she was, a leper. 11 So
Aaron said to Moses, "Oh, my lord! Please
do not lay *this* sin on us, in which we have
done foolishly and in which we have sinned.
12 Please do not let her be as one dead, whose
flesh is half consumed when he comes out
of his mother's womb!"
13 So Moses cried out to the LORD, saying,
"Please heal her, O God, I pray!"
14 Then the LORD said to Moses, "If her
father had but spit in her face, would she not
be shamed seven days? Let her be shut out of
the camp seven days, and afterward she may
be received *again*." 15 So Miriam was shut
out of the camp seven days, and the people
did not journey till Miriam was brought in
again. 16 And afterward the people moved
from Hazeroth and camped in the Wilderness of Paran.

Spies Sent into Canaan

13 And the LORD spoke to Moses, saying, 2 "Send men to spy out the land
of Canaan, which I am giving to the children
of Israel; from each tribe of their fathers you
shall send a man, every one a leader among
them."
3 So Moses sent them from the Wilderness
of Paran according to the command of the
LORD, all of them men who *were* heads of
the children of Israel. 4 Now these *were* their
names: from the tribe of Reuben, Shammua
the son of Zaccur; 5 from the tribe of Simeon,
Shaphat the son of Hori; 6 from the tribe of
Judah, Caleb the son of Jephunneh; 7 from
the tribe of Issachar, Igal the son of Joseph;
8 from the tribe of Ephraim, Hoshea[a] the son
of Nun; 9 from the tribe of Benjamin, Palti
the son of Raphu; 10 from the tribe of Zebulun, Gaddiel the son of Sodi; 11 from the tribe
of Joseph, *that is*, from the tribe of Manasseh, Gaddi the son of Susi; 12 from the tribe
of Dan, Ammiel the son of Gemalli; 13 from
the tribe of Asher, Sethur the son of Michael;
14 from the tribe of Naphtali, Nahbi the son
of Vophsi; 15 from the tribe of Gad, Geuel the
son of Machi.
16 These *are* the names of the men whom
Moses sent to spy out the land. And Moses
called Hoshea[a] the son of Nun, Joshua.
17 Then Moses sent them to spy out the
land of Canaan, and said to them, "Go up
this *way* into the South, and go up to the
mountains, 18 and see what the land is like:
whether the people who dwell in it *are* strong
or weak, few or many; 19 whether the land
they dwell in *is* good or bad; whether the
cities they inhabit *are* like camps or strongholds; 20 whether the land *is* rich or poor; and
whether there are forests there or not. Be of
good courage. And bring some of the fruit
of the land." Now the time *was* the season of
the first ripe grapes.
21 So they went up and spied out the land
from the Wilderness of Zin as far as Rehob,
near the entrance of Hamath. 22 And they
went up through the South and came to Hebron; Ahiman, Sheshai, and Talmai, the descendants of Anak, *were* there. (Now Hebron
was built seven years before Zoan in Egypt.)
23 Then they came to the Valley of Eshcol,
and there cut down a branch with one cluster of grapes; they carried it between two of
them on a pole. *They* also *brought* some of
the pomegranates and figs. 24 The place was
called the Valley of Eshcol,[a] because of the
cluster which the men of Israel cut down
there. 25 And they returned from spying out
the land after forty days.
26 Now they departed and came back to

13:8 [a] Septuagint and Vulgate read *Oshea*. 13:16 [a] Septuagint and Vulgate read *Oshea*. 13:24 [a] Literally *Cluster*

Moses and Aaron and all the congregation
of the children of Israel in the Wilderness
of Paran, at Kadesh; they brought back word
to them and to all the congregation, and
showed them the fruit of the land. 27 Then
they told him, and said: "We went to the
land where you sent us. It truly flows with
milk and honey, and this *is* its fruit. 28 Nevertheless the people who dwell in the land *are*
strong; the cities *are* fortified *and* very large;
moreover we saw the descendants of Anak
there. 29 The Amalekites dwell in the land of
the South; the Hittites, the Jebusites, and the
Amorites dwell in the mountains; and the
Canaanites dwell by the sea and along the
banks of the Jordan."
30 Then Caleb quieted the people before
Moses, and said, "Let us go up at once and
take possession, for we are well able to overcome it."
31 But the men who had gone up with him
said, "We are not able to go up against the
people, for they *are* stronger than we." 32 And
they gave the children of Israel a bad report
of the land which they had spied out, saying,
"The land through which we have gone as
spies *is* a land that devours its inhabitants,
and all the people whom we saw in it *are* men
of *great* stature. 33 There we saw the giants[a]
(the descendants of Anak came from the giants); and we were like grasshoppers in our
own sight, and so we were in their sight."

13:33 [a] Hebrew *nephilim*

SPIES SENT INTO CANAAN

READ IT: NUMBERS 13:17—14:25

GET IT:

God moved His people to the Wilderness of Paran, close to the Promised Land. He told Moses to pick twelve men to play spy and check out the land. Everything went fine until the men returned with their report. Ten of the spies were panicky. They were scared and advised God's people not to go into the land. Two guys, Caleb and Joshua, saw things completely differently, but no one really wanted to listen after hearing about giants and cities with high walls. Why the difference in the two viewpoints? Well, Caleb and Joshua believed that if God wanted them to have this land, He would help them conquer it. The others only thought about doing the work on their own.

LIVE IT:

Any new challenge in our lives can at first seem impossible. The first day in a new school, giving a speech, entering the lunch room all alone, asking someone for a donation, trying out for the school play, or auditioning for first chair in the orchestra can be downright scary. In fact, you might want to skip it and say, "I can't do this." But you've forgotten about something. You've forgotten that you don't have to do this alone. Just like the ten spies who forgot about God and said, "Don't go, it's too tough," you've forgotten that God can help. You don't do things on your own. God is there beside you to give you the strength and the courage you need. You and God together can do it!

Israel Refuses to Enter Canaan

14 So all the congregation lifted up
their voices and cried, and the people wept that night. 2And all the children of
Israel complained against Moses and Aaron,
and the whole congregation said to them, "If
only we had died in the land of Egypt! Or if
only we had died in this wilderness! 3Why
has the LORD brought us to this land to fall
by the sword, that our wives and children
should become victims? Would it not be better for us to return to Egypt?" 4So they said
to one another, "Let us select a leader and
return to Egypt."
5Then Moses and Aaron fell on their faces before all the assembly of the congregation of the children of Israel.
6But Joshua the son of Nun and Caleb
the son of Jephunneh, *who were* among
those who had spied out the land, tore their
clothes; 7and they spoke to all the congregation of the children of Israel, saying: "The
land we passed through to spy out *is* an exceedingly good land. 8If the LORD delights
in us, then He will bring us into this land
and give it to us, 'a land which flows with
milk and honey.'[a] 9Only do not rebel against
the LORD, nor fear the people of the land, for
they *are* our bread; their protection has departed from them, and the LORD *is* with us.
Do not fear them."
10And all the congregation said to stone
them with stones. Now the glory of the LORD
appeared in the tabernacle of meeting before
all the children of Israel.

Moses Intercedes for the People

11Then the LORD said to Moses: "How
long will these people reject Me? And how
long will they not believe Me, with all the
signs which I have performed among them?
12I will strike them with the pestilence and
disinherit them, and I will make of you a nation greater and mightier than they."
13And Moses said to the LORD: "Then the
Egyptians will hear *it,* for by Your might You
brought these people up from among them,
14and they will tell *it* to the inhabitants of
this land. They have heard that You, LORD,
are among these people; that You, LORD,
are seen face to face and Your cloud stands
above them, and You go before them in a
pillar of cloud by day and in a pillar of fire
by night. 15Now *if* You kill these people as
one man, then the nations which have heard
of Your fame will speak, saying, 16'Because
the LORD was not able to bring this people
to the land which He swore to give them,
therefore He killed them in the wilderness.'
17And now, I pray, let the power of my Lord be
great, just as You have spoken, saying, 18'The
LORD is longsuffering and abundant in mercy, forgiving iniquity and transgression; but
He by no means clears *the guilty,* visiting the
iniquity of the fathers on the children to the
third and fourth *generation.*'[a] 19Pardon the
iniquity of this people, I pray, according to
the greatness of Your mercy, just as You have
forgiven this people, from Egypt even until
now."
20Then the LORD said: "I have pardoned,
according to your word; 21but truly, as I live,
all the earth shall be filled with the glory of
the LORD— 22because all these men who
have seen My glory and the signs which I did
in Egypt and in the wilderness, and have put
Me to the test now these ten times, and have
not heeded My voice, 23they certainly shall
not see the land of which I swore to their
fathers, nor shall any of those who rejected
Me see it. 24But My servant Caleb, because he
has a different spirit in him and has followed
Me fully, I will bring into the land where he
went, and his descendants shall inherit it.
25Now the Amalekites and the Canaanites
dwell in the valley; tomorrow turn and move
out into the wilderness by the Way of the
Red Sea."

Death Sentence on the Rebels

26And the LORD spoke to Moses and Aaron, saying, 27"How long *shall I bear with* this
evil congregation who complain against
Me? I have heard the complaints which the
children of Israel make against Me. 28Say
to them, 'As I live,' says the LORD, 'just as
you have spoken in My hearing, so I will
do to you: 29The carcasses of you who have
complained against Me shall fall in this wilderness, all of you who were numbered, according to your entire number, from twenty
years old and above. 30Except for Caleb the
son of Jephunneh and Joshua the son of
Nun, you shall by no means enter the land
which I swore I would make you dwell in.
31But your little ones, whom you said would
be victims, I will bring in, and they shall

14:8 [a] Exodus 3:8 **14:18** [a] Exodus 34:6, 7

know the land which you have despised. 32But *as for* you, your carcasses shall fall in this wilderness. 33And your sons shall be shepherds in the wilderness forty years, and bear the brunt of your infidelity, until your carcasses are consumed in the wilderness. 34According to the number of the days in which you spied out the land, forty days, for each day you shall bear your guilt one year, *namely* forty years, and you shall know My rejection. 35I the LORD have spoken this. I will surely do so to all this evil congregation who are gathered together against Me. In this wilderness they shall be consumed, and there they shall die.' "

36Now the men whom Moses sent to spy out the land, who returned and made all the congregation complain against him by bringing a bad report of the land, 37those very men who brought the evil report about the land, died by the plague before the LORD. 38But Joshua the son of Nun and Caleb the son of Jephunneh remained alive, of the men who went to spy out the land.

A Futile Invasion Attempt

39Then Moses told these words to all the children of Israel, and the people mourned greatly. 40And they rose early in the morning and went up to the top of the mountain, saying, "Here we are, and we will go up to the place which the LORD has promised, for we have sinned!"

41And Moses said, "Now why do you transgress the command of the LORD? For this will not succeed. 42Do not go up, lest you be defeated by your enemies, for the LORD *is* not among you. 43For the Amalekites and the Canaanites *are* there before you, and you shall fall by the sword; because you have turned away from the LORD, the LORD will not be with you."

44But they presumed to go up to the mountaintop. Nevertheless, neither the ark of the covenant of the LORD nor Moses departed from the camp. 45Then the Amalekites and the Canaanites who dwelt in that mountain came down and attacked them, and drove them back as far as Hormah.

Laws of Grain and Drink Offerings

15 And the LORD spoke to Moses, saying, 2"Speak to the children of Israel, and say to them: 'When you have come into the land you are to inhabit, which I am giving to you, 3and you make an offering by fire to the LORD, a burnt offering or a sacrifice, to fulfill a vow or as a freewill offering or in your appointed feasts, to make a sweet aroma to the LORD, from the herd or the flock, 4then he who presents his offering to the LORD shall bring a grain offering of one-tenth *of an ephah* of fine flour mixed with one-fourth of a hin of oil; 5and one-fourth of a hin of wine as a drink offering you shall prepare with the burnt offering or the sacrifice, for each lamb. 6Or for a ram you shall prepare as a grain offering two-tenths *of an ephah* of fine flour mixed with one-third of a hin of oil; 7and as a drink offering you shall offer one-third of a hin of wine as a sweet aroma to the LORD. 8And when you prepare a young bull as a burnt offering, or as a sacrifice to fulfill a vow, or as a peace offering to the LORD, 9then shall be offered with the young bull a grain offering of three-tenths *of an ephah* of fine flour mixed with half a hin of oil; 10and you shall bring as the drink offering half a hin of wine as an offering made by fire, a sweet aroma to the LORD.

11'Thus it shall be done for each young bull, for each ram, or for each lamb or young goat. 12According to the number that you prepare, so you shall do with everyone according to their number. 13All who are native-born shall do these things in this manner, in presenting an offering made by fire, a sweet aroma to the LORD. 14And if a stranger dwells with you, or whoever *is* among you throughout your generations, and would present an offering made by fire, a sweet aroma to the LORD, just as you do, so shall he do. 15One ordinance *shall be* for you of the assembly and for the stranger who dwells *with you,* an ordinance forever throughout your generations; as you are, so shall the stranger be before the LORD. 16One law and one custom shall be for you and for the stranger who dwells with you.' "[a]

17Again the LORD spoke to Moses, saying, 18"Speak to the children of Israel, and say to them: 'When you come into the land to which I bring you, 19then it will be, when you eat of the bread of the land, that you shall offer up a heave offering to the LORD. 20You shall offer up a cake of the first of your ground meal *as* a heave offering; as a heave offering of the threshing floor, so shall you

---

15:16 [a] Compare Exodus 12:49

offer it up. 21Of the first of your ground meal
you shall give to the LORD a heave offering
throughout your generations.

Laws Concerning Unintentional Sin

22'If you sin unintentionally, and do not
observe all these commandments which
the LORD has spoken to Moses— 23all
that the LORD has commanded you by the
hand of Moses, from the day the LORD gave
commandment and onward throughout
your generations— 24then it will be, if it is
unintentionally committed, without the
knowledge of the congregation, that the
whole congregation shall offer one young
bull as a burnt offering, as a sweet aroma
to the LORD, with its grain offering and its
drink offering, according to the ordinance,
and one kid of the goats as a sin offering.
25So the priest shall make atonement for the
whole congregation of the children of Israel,
and it shall be forgiven them, for it was un-
intentional; they shall bring their offering,
an offering made by fire to the LORD, and
their sin offering before the LORD, for their
unintended sin. 26It shall be forgiven the
whole congregation of the children of Israel
and the stranger who dwells among them,
because all the people *did it* unintentionally.

27'And if a person sins unintentionally,
then he shall bring a female goat in its first
year as a sin offering. 28So the priest shall
make atonement for the person who sins
unintentionally, when he sins unintentionally before the LORD, to make atonement for
him; and it shall be forgiven him. 29You shall
have one law for him who sins unintentionally, *for* him who is native-born among the
children of Israel and for the stranger who
dwells among them.

Law Concerning Presumptuous Sin

30'But the person who does *anything* presumptuously, *whether he is* native-born or a
stranger, that one brings reproach on the
LORD, and he shall be cut off from among
his people. 31Because he has despised the
word of the LORD, and has broken His commandment, that person shall be completely
cut off; his guilt *shall be* upon him.'"

Penalty for Violating the Sabbath

32Now while the children of Israel were in
the wilderness, they found a man gathering
sticks on the Sabbath day. 33And those who
found him gathering sticks brought him to
Moses and Aaron, and to all the congregation. 34They put him under guard, because it
had not been explained what should be done
to him.

35Then the LORD said to Moses, "The
man must surely be put to death; all the
congregation shall stone him with stones
outside the camp." 36So, as the LORD commanded Moses, all the congregation brought
him outside the camp and stoned him with
stones, and he died.

Tassels on Garments

37Again the LORD spoke to Moses, saying,
38"Speak to the children of Israel: Tell them
to make tassels on the corners of their garments throughout their generations, and to
put a blue thread in the tassels of the corners. 39And you shall have the tassel, that
you may look upon it and remember all the
commandments of the LORD and do them,
and that you *may* not follow the harlotry to
which your own heart and your own eyes are
inclined, 40and that you may remember and
do all My commandments, and be holy for
your God. 41I *am* the LORD your God, who
brought you out of the land of Egypt, to be
your God: I *am* the LORD your God."

Rebellion Against Moses and Aaron

16 Now Korah the son of Izhar, the
son of Kohath, the son of Levi, with
Dathan and Abiram the sons of Eliab, and
On the son of Peleth, sons of Reuben, took
men; 2and they rose up before Moses with
some of the children of Israel, two hundred and fifty leaders of the congregation,
representatives of the congregation, men of
renown. 3They gathered together against
Moses and Aaron, and said to them, "*You
take* too much upon yourselves, for all the
congregation *is* holy, every one of them, and
the LORD *is* among them. Why then do you
exalt yourselves above the assembly of the
LORD?"

4So when Moses heard *it,* he fell on his
face; 5and he spoke to Korah and all his
company, saying, "Tomorrow morning the
LORD will show who *is* His and *who is* holy,
and will cause *him* to come near to Him.
That one whom He chooses He will cause
to come near to Him. 6Do this: Take censers, Korah and all your company; 7put fire
in them and put incense in them before the

LORD tomorrow, and it shall be *that* the man
whom the LORD chooses *is* the holy one. *You
take* too much upon yourselves, you sons of
Levi!"

8Then Moses said to Korah, "Hear now,
you sons of Levi: 9*Is it* a small thing to you
that the God of Israel has separated you from
the congregation of Israel, to bring you near
to Himself, to do the work of the tabernacle
of the LORD, and to stand before the congregation to serve them; 10and that He has
brought you near *to Himself*, you and all your
brethren, the sons of Levi, with you? And are
you seeking the priesthood also? 11Therefore
you and all your company *are* gathered together against the LORD. And what *is* Aaron
that you complain against him?"

12And Moses sent to call Dathan and
Abiram the sons of Eliab, but they said, "We
will not come up! 13*Is it* a small thing that
you have brought us up out of a land flowing with milk and honey, to kill us in the
wilderness, that you should keep acting like
a prince over us? 14Moreover you have not
brought us into a land flowing with milk
and honey, nor given us inheritance of fields
and vineyards. Will you put out the eyes of
these men? We will not come up!"

15Then Moses was very angry, and said
to the LORD, "Do not respect their offering.
I have not taken one donkey from them, nor
have I hurt one of them."

16And Moses said to Korah, "Tomorrow,
you and all your company be present before
the LORD—you and they, as well as Aaron.
17Let each take his censer and put incense in
it, and each of you bring his censer before
the LORD, two hundred and fifty censers;
both you and Aaron, each *with* his censer."
18So every man took his censer, put fire in
it, laid incense on it, and stood at the door of
the tabernacle of meeting with Moses and
Aaron. 19And Korah gathered all the congregation against them at the door of the tabernacle of meeting. Then the glory of the LORD
appeared to all the congregation.

20And the LORD spoke to Moses and
Aaron, saying, 21"Separate yourselves from
among this congregation, that I may con-
sume them in a moment."

22Then they fell on their faces, and said,
"O God, the God of the spirits of all flesh,
shall one man sin, and You be angry with all
the congregation?"

23So the LORD spoke to Moses, saying,
24"Speak to the congregation, saying, 'Get
away from the tents of Korah, Dathan, and
Abiram.'"

25Then Moses rose and went to Dathan
and Abiram, and the elders of Israel followed
him. 26And he spoke to the congregation,
saying, "Depart now from the tents of these
wicked men! Touch nothing of theirs, lest
you be consumed in all their sins." 27So they
got away from around the tents of Korah,
Dathan, and Abiram; and Dathan and Abiram came out and stood at the door of their
tents, with their wives, their sons, and their
little children.

28And Moses said: "By this you shall
know that the LORD has sent me to do all
these works, for *I have* not *done them* of my
own will. 29If these men die naturally like all
men, or if they are visited by the common
fate of all men, *then* the LORD has not sent
me. 30But if the LORD creates a new thing,
and the earth opens its mouth and swallows
them up with all that belongs to them, and
they go down alive into the pit, then you will
understand that these men have rejected the
LORD."

31Now it came to pass, as he finished
speaking all these words, that the ground
split apart under them, 32and the earth
opened its mouth and swallowed them up,
with their households and all the men with
Korah, with all *their* goods. 33So they and all
those with them went down alive into the
pit; the earth closed over them, and they
perished from among the assembly. 34Then
all Israel who *were* around them fled at their
cry, for they said, "Lest the earth swallow us
up *also!*"

35And a fire came out from the LORD and
consumed the two hundred and fifty men
who were offering incense.

36Then the LORD spoke to Moses, saying:
37"Tell Eleazar, the son of Aaron the priest,
to pick up the censers out of the blaze, for
they are holy, and scatter the fire some distance away. 38The censers of these men who
sinned against their own souls, let them be
made into hammered plates as a covering
for the altar. Because they presented them
before the LORD, therefore they are holy; and
they shall be a sign to the children of Israel."
39So Eleazar the priest took the bronze censers, which those who were burned up had
presented, and they were hammered out as

a covering on the altar, 40*to be* a memorial to
the children of Israel that no outsider, who
is not a descendant of Aaron, should come
near to offer incense before the LORD, that he
might not become like Korah and his companions, just as the LORD had said to him
through Moses.

Complaints of the People

41On the next day all the congregation of
the children of Israel complained against
Moses and Aaron, saying, "You have killed
the people of the LORD." 42Now it happened,
when the congregation had gathered against
Moses and Aaron, that they turned toward
the tabernacle of meeting; and suddenly the
cloud covered it, and the glory of the LORD
appeared. 43Then Moses and Aaron came
before the tabernacle of meeting.

44And the LORD spoke to Moses, saying,
45"Get away from among this congregation,
that I may consume them in a moment."

HONESTY

LIES DON'T PAY

READ IT: NUMBERS 16:1–50

GET IT:

Lying might be one of the easiest sins to commit because it's often an instinctive reaction. We lie to avoid getting in trouble, lie about the grade we received on a test, lie about what time we'll be home, lie about what friends we're hanging out with, lie about why we were late to class. But unfortunately, lying to avoid getting in trouble almost always results in even more trouble after getting caught.

Have you ever told a lie so big it changed your life?

In this chapter, Korah accused Moses and Aaron of pride and selfishness. Korah thought Moses had appointed himself to be the people's leader, not that God called him to it. He believed Moses thought he was better than everyone else.

But Korah didn't just think these things. He accused Moses in front of hundreds of people, causing them to believe the lies and to rebel. The accusation, as we know, was tremendously bold and downright false.

That lie cost many people their lives when God judged Korah and his followers. While we don't hear about God striking people down for being dishonest and deceitful these days, there are still major consequences when we lie.

LIVE IT:

Whether you call them white lies, half-truths, or exaggerations, lying is lying. When you are caught in a lie, your character and integrity are questioned, and it can take a really long time to earn trust back. The consequences of lying just aren't worth it. So no matter how difficult the situation is or who you think you're helping, always tell the truth.

And they fell on their faces.
46 So Moses said to Aaron, "Take a censer
and put fire in it from the altar, put incense
on it, and take it quickly to the congregation
and make atonement for them; for wrath
has gone out from the LORD. The plague
has begun." 47 Then Aaron took *it* as Moses
commanded, and ran into the midst of the
assembly; and already the plague had begun
among the people. So he put in the incense
and made atonement for the people. 48 And
he stood between the dead and the living;
so the plague was stopped. 49 Now those who
died in the plague were fourteen thousand
seven hundred, besides those who died in
the Korah incident. 50 So Aaron returned to
Moses at the door of the tabernacle of meeting, for the plague had stopped.

The Budding of Aaron's Rod

17 And the LORD spoke to Moses, saying: 2 "Speak to the children of Israel,
and get from them a rod from each father's
house, all their leaders according to their
fathers' houses—twelve rods. Write each
man's name on his rod. 3 And you shall write
Aaron's name on the rod of Levi. For there
shall be one rod for the head of *each* father's
house. 4 Then you shall place them in the
tabernacle of meeting before the Testimony,
where I meet with you. 5 And it shall be *that*
the rod of the man whom I choose will blossom; thus I will rid Myself of the complaints
of the children of Israel, which they make
against you."
6 So Moses spoke to the children of Israel, and each of their leaders gave him a
rod apiece, for each leader according to their
fathers' houses, twelve rods; and the rod of
Aaron *was* among their rods. 7 And Moses
placed the rods before the LORD in the tabernacle of witness.
8 Now it came to pass on the next day that
Moses went into the tabernacle of witness,
and behold, the rod of Aaron, of the house
of Levi, had sprouted and put forth buds,
had produced blossoms and yielded ripe
almonds. 9 Then Moses brought out all the
rods from before the LORD to all the children
of Israel; and they looked, and each man
took his rod.
10 And the LORD said to Moses, "Bring
Aaron's rod back before the Testimony, to
be kept as a sign against the rebels, that you
may put their complaints away from Me, lest
they die." 11 Thus did Moses; just as the LORD
had commanded him, so he did.
12 So the children of Israel spoke to Moses, saying, "Surely we die, we perish, we
all perish! 13 Whoever even comes near the
tabernacle of the LORD must die. Shall we
all utterly die?"

Duties of Priests and Levites

18 Then the LORD said to Aaron: "You
and your sons and your father's
house with you shall bear the iniquity *related to* the sanctuary, and you and your sons
with you shall bear the iniquity *associated
with* your priesthood. 2 Also bring with you
your brethren of the tribe of Levi, the tribe
of your father, that they may be joined with
you and serve you while you and your sons
are with you before the tabernacle of witness.
3 They shall attend to your needs and all the
needs of the tabernacle; but they shall not
come near the articles of the sanctuary and
the altar, lest they die—they and you also.
4 They shall be joined with you and attend to
the needs of the tabernacle of meeting, for
all the work of the tabernacle; but an outsider shall not come near you. 5 And you shall
attend to the duties of the sanctuary and the
duties of the altar, that there *may* be no more
wrath on the children of Israel. 6 Behold, I
Myself have taken your brethren the Levites
from among the children of Israel; *they are* a
gift to you, given by the LORD, to do the work
of the tabernacle of meeting. 7 Therefore you
and your sons with you shall attend to your
priesthood for everything at the altar and
behind the veil; and you shall serve. I give
your priesthood *to you* as a gift for service,
but the outsider who comes near shall be put
to death."

Offerings for Support of the Priests

8 And the LORD spoke to Aaron: "Here,
I Myself have also given you charge of My
heave offerings, all the holy gifts of the children of Israel; I have given them as a portion
to you and your sons, as an ordinance forever. 9 This shall be yours of the most holy
things *reserved* from the fire: every offering
of theirs, every grain offering and every sin
offering and every trespass offering which
they render to Me, *shall be* most holy for you
and your sons. 10 In a most holy *place* you
shall eat it; every male shall eat it. It shall be
holy to you.

11"This also *is* yours: the heave offering of
their gift, with all the wave offerings of the
children of Israel; I have given them to you,
and your sons and daughters with you, as an
ordinance forever. Everyone who is clean in
your house may eat it.
12"All the best of the oil, all the best of
the new wine and the grain, their firstfruits
which they offer to the LORD, I have given
them to you. 13Whatever first ripe fruit is in
their land, which they bring to the LORD,
shall be yours. Everyone who is clean in your
house may eat it.
14"Every devoted thing in Israel shall be
yours.
15"Everything that first opens the womb
of all flesh, which they bring to the LORD,
whether man or beast, shall be yours; nevertheless the firstborn of man you shall
surely redeem, and the firstborn of unclean
animals you shall redeem. 16And those redeemed of the devoted things you shall
redeem when one month old, according to
your valuation, for five shekels of silver, according to the shekel of the sanctuary, which
is twenty gerahs. 17But the firstborn of a cow,
the firstborn of a sheep, or the firstborn of a
goat you shall not redeem; they *are* holy. You
shall sprinkle their blood on the altar, and
burn their fat *as* an offering made by fire for
a sweet aroma to the LORD. 18And their flesh
shall be yours, just as the wave breast and
the right thigh are yours.
19"All the heave offerings of the holy
things, which the children of Israel offer to
the LORD, I have given to you and your sons
and daughters with you as an ordinance forever; it *is* a covenant of salt forever before the
LORD with you and your descendants with
you."
20Then the LORD said to Aaron: "You
shall have no inheritance in their land, nor
shall you have any portion among them;
I *am* your portion and your inheritance
among the children of Israel.

Tithes for Support of the Levites

21"Behold, I have given the children
of Levi all the tithes in Israel as an inheritance in return for the work which they
perform, the work of the tabernacle of meeting. 22Hereafter the children of Israel shall
not come near the tabernacle of meeting,
lest they bear sin and die. 23But the Levites
shall perform the work of the tabernacle of
meeting, and they shall bear their iniquity;
it shall be a statute forever, throughout your
generations, that among the children of Israel they shall have no inheritance. 24For the
tithes of the children of Israel, which they
offer up *as* a heave offering to the LORD, I
have given to the Levites as an inheritance;
therefore I have said to them, 'Among
the children of Israel they shall have no
inheritance.'"

The Tithe of the Levites

25Then the LORD spoke to Moses, saying,
26"Speak thus to the Levites, and say to them:
'When you take from the children of Israel
the tithes which I have given you from them
as your inheritance, then you shall offer up
a heave offering of it to the LORD, a tenth of
the tithe. 27And your heave offering shall be
reckoned to you as though *it were* the grain
of the threshing floor and as the fullness of
the winepress. 28Thus you shall also offer
a heave offering to the LORD from all your
tithes which you receive from the children
of Israel, and you shall give the LORD's heave
offering from it to Aaron the priest. 29Of all
your gifts you shall offer up every heave offering due to the LORD, from all the best of
them, the consecrated part of them.' 30There-
fore you shall say to them: 'When you have
lifted up the best of it, then *the rest* shall be
accounted to the Levites as the produce of
the threshing floor and as the produce of the
winepress. 31You may eat it in any place, you
and your households, for it *is* your reward
for your work in the tabernacle of meeting.
32And you shall bear no sin because of it,
when you have lifted up the best of it. But
you shall not profane the holy gifts of the
children of Israel, lest you die.'"

Laws of Purification

19 Now the LORD spoke to Moses
and Aaron, saying, 2"This *is* the
ordinance of the law which the LORD has
commanded, saying: 'Speak to the children
of Israel, that they bring you a red heifer
without blemish, in which there *is* no defect *and* on which a yoke has never come.
3You shall give it to Eleazar the priest, that
he may take it outside the camp, and it shall
be slaughtered before him; 4and Eleazar the
priest shall take some of its blood with his
finger, and sprinkle some of its blood seven
times directly in front of the tabernacle of

meeting. 5Then the heifer shall be burned in his sight: its hide, its flesh, its blood, and its offal shall be burned. 6And the priest shall take cedar wood and hyssop and scarlet, and cast *them* into the midst of the fire burning the heifer. 7Then the priest shall wash his clothes, he shall bathe in water, and afterward he shall come into the camp; the priest shall be unclean until evening. 8And the one who burns it shall wash his clothes in water, bathe in water, and shall be unclean until evening. 9Then a man *who is* clean shall gather up the ashes of the heifer, and store *them* outside the camp in a clean place; and they shall be kept for the congregation of the children of Israel for the water of purification;[a] it *is* for purifying from sin. 10And the one who gathers the ashes of the heifer shall wash his clothes, and be unclean until evening. It shall be a statute forever to the children of Israel and to the stranger who dwells among them.

11'He who touches the dead body of anyone shall be unclean seven days. 12He shall purify himself with the water on the third day and on the seventh day; *then* he will be clean. But if he does not purify himself on the third day and on the seventh day, he will not be clean. 13Whoever touches the body of anyone who has died, and does not purify himself, defiles the tabernacle of the LORD. That person shall be cut off from Israel. He shall be unclean, because the water of purification was not sprinkled on him; his uncleanness *is* still on him.

14'This *is* the law when a man dies in a tent: All who come into the tent and all who *are* in the tent shall be unclean seven days; 15and every open vessel, which has no cover fastened on it, *is* unclean. 16Whoever in the open field touches one who is slain by a sword or who has died, or a bone of a man, or a grave, shall be unclean seven days.

17'And for an unclean *person* they shall take some of the ashes of the heifer burnt for purification from sin, and running water shall be put on them in a vessel. 18A clean person shall take hyssop and dip *it* in the water, sprinkle *it* on the tent, on all the vessels, on the persons who were there, or on the one who touched a bone, the slain, the dead, or a grave. 19The clean *person* shall sprinkle the unclean on the third day and on the seventh day; and on the seventh day he shall purify himself, wash his clothes, and bathe in water; and at evening he shall be clean.

20'But the man who is unclean and does not purify himself, that person shall be cut off from among the assembly, because he has defiled the sanctuary of the LORD. The water of purification has not been sprinkled on him; he *is* unclean. 21It shall be a perpetual statute for them. He who sprinkles the water of purification shall wash his clothes; and he who touches the water of purification shall be unclean until evening. 22Whatever the unclean *person* touches shall be unclean; and the person who touches *it* shall be unclean until evening.'"

Moses' Error at Kadesh

20 Then the children of Israel, the whole congregation, came into the Wilderness of Zin in the first month, and the people stayed in Kadesh; and Miriam died there and was buried there.

2Now there was no water for the congregation; so they gathered together against Moses and Aaron. 3And the people contended with Moses and spoke, saying: "If only we had died when our brethren died before the LORD! 4Why have you brought up the assembly of the LORD into this wilderness, that we and our animals should die here? 5And why have you made us come up out of Egypt, to bring us to this evil place? It *is* not a place of grain or figs or vines or pomegranates; nor *is* there any water to drink." 6So Moses and Aaron went from the presence of the assembly to the door of the tabernacle of meeting, and they fell on their faces. And the glory of the LORD appeared to them.

7Then the LORD spoke to Moses, saying, 8"Take the rod; you and your brother Aaron gather the congregation together. Speak to the rock before their eyes, and it will yield its water; thus you shall bring water for them out of the rock, and give drink to the congregation and their animals." 9So Moses took the rod from before the LORD as He commanded him.

10And Moses and Aaron gathered the assembly together before the rock; and he said to them, "Hear now, you rebels! Must we bring water for you out of this rock?"

19:9 [a] Literally *impurity*

[11]Then Moses lifted his hand and struck the
rock twice with his rod; and water came out abundantly, and the congregation and their animals drank.
[12]Then the LORD spoke to Moses and Aaron, "Because you did not believe Me, to hallow Me in the eyes of the children of Israel, therefore you shall not bring this assembly into the land which I have given them."
[13]This was the water of Meribah,[a] because the children of Israel contended with the LORD, and He was hallowed among them.

Passage Through Edom Refused

[14]Now Moses sent messengers from Kadesh to the king of Edom. "Thus says your brother Israel: 'You know all the hardship that has befallen us,
[15]how our fathers went down to Egypt, and we dwelt in Egypt a long

20:13 [a] Literally *Contention*

ANGER
TEMPER TANTRUM

READ IT: NUMBERS 20:7–13

GET IT:

It's easy to read this passage and miss Moses' mistake—his big, big mistake. If you examine the story carefully, you'll see that God wanted Moses to *speak* to the rock in order to get the miracle water for the Hebrew people and their animals, but Moses didn't just speak. He was angry, maybe impatient, maybe even a little self-righteous and full of his own authority. So when the time came, he didn't speak to the rock like God asked. Instead, he hit it.

Only God knows exactly what was in Moses' heart at that moment, but whatever it was wasn't pretty. Because Moses didn't do as God asked, he was not allowed to enter the Promised Land with his people.

LIVE IT:

Not everything can be undone, and not everything can be taken back. Sometimes we say things in anger that people we love will never be able to forget, even if they forgive us. We won't get a free pass for temper tantrums just because we were emotional.

So control that temper. Be careful about the things you say and do, especially if you're angry. Actions have consequences. Disobeying God in our anger—no matter where that anger is directed—has consequences.

Learn how to walk away. Sometimes it's too hard to interact with someone else when you are mad. Learn how to say calmly, "I need a few minutes." Then take a walk until you have a cooler head.

Finally, reach for God's forgiveness when you cross a line in anger. Did God forgive Moses for his outburst? Yes. Moses is mentioned later many times in Scripture for his faithfulness.

time, and the Egyptians afflicted us and our
fathers. 16When we cried out to the LORD,
He heard our voice and sent the Angel and
brought us up out of Egypt; now here we are
in Kadesh, a city on the edge of your border.
17Please let us pass through your country. We
will not pass through fields or vineyards, nor
will we drink water from wells; we will go
along the King's Highway; we will not turn
aside to the right hand or to the left until we
have passed through your territory.'"

18Then Edom said to him, "You shall
not pass through my *land*, lest I come out
against you with the sword."

19So the children of Israel said to him,
"We will go by the Highway, and if I or my
livestock drink any of your water, then I will
pay for it; let me only pass through on foot,
nothing *more*."

20Then he said, "You shall not pass
through." So Edom came out against them
with many men and with a strong hand.
21Thus Edom refused to give Israel passage
through his territory; so Israel turned away
from him.

Death of Aaron

22Now the children of Israel, the whole
congregation, journeyed from Kadesh and
came to Mount Hor. 23And the LORD spoke
to Moses and Aaron in Mount Hor by the
border of the land of Edom, saying: 24"Aaron
shall be gathered to his people, for he shall
not enter the land which I have given to
the children of Israel, because you rebelled
against My word at the water of Meribah.
25Take Aaron and Eleazar his son, and bring
them up to Mount Hor; 26and strip Aaron
of his garments and put them on Eleazar
his son; for Aaron shall be gathered *to his
people* and die there." 27So Moses did just as
the LORD commanded, and they went up to
Mount Hor in the sight of all the congregation. 28Moses stripped Aaron of his garments
and put them on Eleazar his son; and Aaron
died there on the top of the mountain. Then
Moses and Eleazar came down from the
mountain. 29Now when all the congregation
saw that Aaron was dead, all the house of Israel mourned for Aaron thirty days.

Canaanites Defeated at Hormah

21 The king of Arad, the Canaanite,
who dwelt in the South, heard that
Israel was coming on the road to Atharim.
Then he fought against Israel and took *some*
of them prisoners. 2So Israel made a vow to
the LORD, and said, "If You will indeed deliver this people into my hand, then I will
utterly destroy their cities." 3And the LORD
listened to the voice of Israel and delivered
up the Canaanites, and they utterly destroyed them and their cities. So the name
of that place was called Hormah.[a]

The Bronze Serpent

4Then they journeyed from Mount Hor
by the Way of the Red Sea, to go around the
land of Edom; and the soul of the people
became very discouraged on the way. 5And
the people spoke against God and against
Moses: "Why have you brought us up out of
Egypt to die in the wilderness? For *there is*
no food and no water, and our soul loathes
this worthless bread." 6So the LORD sent fiery
serpents among the people, and they bit the
people; and many of the people of Israel died.

7Therefore the people came to Moses,
and said, "We have sinned, for we have spoken against the LORD and against you; pray
to the LORD that He take away the serpents
from us." So Moses prayed for the people.

8Then the LORD said to Moses, "Make
a fiery *serpent*, and set it on a pole; and it
shall be that everyone who is bitten, when
he looks at it, shall live." 9So Moses made a
bronze serpent, and put it on a pole; and so it
was, if a serpent had bitten anyone, when he
looked at the bronze serpent, he lived.

From Mount Hor to Moab

10Now the children of Israel moved on
and camped in Oboth. 11And they journeyed
from Oboth and camped at Ije Abarim, in
the wilderness which *is* east of Moab, toward
the sunrise. 12From there they moved and
camped in the Valley of Zered. 13From there
they moved and camped on the other side of
the Arnon, which *is* in the wilderness that
extends from the border of the Amorites; for
the Arnon *is* the border of Moab, between
Moab and the Amorites. 14Therefore it is said
in the Book of the Wars of the LORD:

"Waheb in Suphah,[a]
The brooks of the Arnon,
15 And the slope of the brooks
That reaches to the dwelling of Ar,
And lies on the border of Moab."

21:3 [a] Literally *Utter Destruction* 21:14 [a] Ancient unknown places; Vulgate reads *What He did in the Red Sea.*

[16]From there *they went* to Beer, which
is the well where the LORD said to Moses,
"Gather the people together, and I will give
them water." [17]Then Israel sang this song:

"Spring up, O well!
All of you sing to it—
18 The well the leaders sank,
Dug by the nation's nobles,
By the lawgiver, with their staves."

And from the wilderness *they went* to
Mattanah, [19]from Mattanah to Nahaliel,
from Nahaliel to Bamoth, [20]and from Ba-
moth, *in* the valley that *is* in the country of Moab, to the top of Pisgah which looks down on the wasteland.[a]

King Sihon Defeated

[21]Then Israel sent messengers to Sihon
king of the Amorites, saying, [22]"Let me pass
through your land. We will not turn aside into fields or vineyards; we will not drink water from wells. We will go by the King's Highway until we have passed through
your territory." [23]But Sihon would not al-
low Israel to pass through his territory. So Sihon gathered all his people together and went out against Israel in the wilderness, and he came to Jahaz and fought against
Israel. [24]Then Israel defeated him with the edge of the sword, and took possession of his land from the Arnon to the Jabbok, as far as the people of Ammon; for the border
of the people of Ammon *was* fortified. [25]So
Israel took all these cities, and Israel dwelt in all the cities of the Amorites, in Heshbon
and in all its villages. [26]For Heshbon *was* the
city of Sihon king of the Amorites, who had fought against the former king of Moab, and had taken all his land from his hand as far
as the Arnon. [27]Therefore those who speak
in proverbs say:

"Come to Heshbon, let it be built;
Let the city of Sihon be repaired.

28 "For fire went out from Heshbon,
A flame from the city of Sihon;
It consumed Ar of Moab,
The lords of the heights of the Arnon.
29 Woe to you, Moab!
You have perished, O people of
Chemosh!
He has given his sons as fugitives,
And his daughters into captivity,
To Sihon king of the Amorites.

30 "But we have shot at them;
Heshbon has perished as far as Dibon.
Then we laid waste as far as Nophah,
Which *reaches* to Medeba."

[31]Thus Israel dwelt in the land of the Amorites. [32]Then Moses sent to spy out Jazer;
and they took its villages and drove out the Amorites who *were* there.

21:20 [a] Hebrew *Jeshimon*

ATTITUDES

READ IT: NUMBERS 21:4, 5

God was with the Israelites starting with their freedom from slavery and continuing throughout their journey to the Promised Land. He answered their prayers and provided for them in many ways. You'd expect them to be grateful, but instead they were grumpy and they complained. They quickly forgot all that God had done. God was sad and appropriately angry about their bitter attitudes. He responded with harsh consequences to help them see where they had gone off track. Ever been there? When you face discouragement, have a conversation with a trusted friend and with God to help you find healthy ways to walk through it.

King Og Defeated

33 And they turned and went up by the
way to Bashan. So Og king of Bashan went
out against them, he and all his people, to
battle at Edrei. 34 Then the LORD said to Moses, "Do not fear him, for I have delivered
him into your hand, with all his people and
his land; and you shall do to him as you did
to Sihon king of the Amorites, who dwelt at
Heshbon." 35 So they defeated him, his sons,
and all his people, until there was no survivor left him; and they took possession of
his land.

Balak Sends for Balaam

22 Then the children of Israel moved,
and camped in the plains of Moab
on the side of the Jordan *across from* Jericho.
2 Now Balak the son of Zippor saw all
that Israel had done to the Amorites. 3 And
Moab was exceedingly afraid of the people
because they *were* many, and Moab was sick
with dread because of the children of Israel. 4 So Moab said to the elders of Midian,
"Now this company will lick up everything
around us, as an ox licks up the grass of the
field." And Balak the son of Zippor *was* king
of the Moabites at that time. 5 Then he sent
messengers to Balaam the son of Beor at Pethor, which *is* near the River[a] in the land of
the sons of his people,[b] to call him, saying:
"Look, a people has come from Egypt. See,
they cover the face of the earth, and are set-
tling next to me! 6 Therefore please come at
once, curse this people for me, for they *are*
too mighty for me. Perhaps I shall be able to
defeat them and drive them out of the land,
for I know that he whom you bless *is* blessed,
and he whom you curse is cursed."
7 So the elders of Moab and the elders of
Midian departed with the diviner's fee in
their hand, and they came to Balaam and
spoke to him the words of Balak. 8 And he
said to them, "Lodge here tonight, and I will
bring back word to you, as the LORD speaks
to me." So the princes of Moab stayed with
Balaam.
9 Then God came to Balaam and said,
"Who *are* these men with you?"
10 So Balaam said to God, "Balak the son
of Zippor, king of Moab, has sent to me, *saying,* 11 'Look, a people has come out of Egypt,
and they cover the face of the earth. Come
now, curse them for me; perhaps I shall
be able to overpower them and drive them
out.'"
12 And God said to Balaam, "You shall not
go with them; you shall not curse the people,
for they *are* blessed."
13 So Balaam rose in the morning and
said to the princes of Balak, "Go back to
your land, for the LORD has refused to give
me permission to go with you."
14 And the princes of Moab rose and went
to Balak, and said, "Balaam refuses to come
with us."
15 Then Balak again sent princes, more
numerous and more honorable than they.
16 And they came to Balaam and said to him,
"Thus says Balak the son of Zippor: 'Please
let nothing hinder you from coming to me;
17 for I will certainly honor you greatly, and
I will do whatever you say to me. Therefore
please come, curse this people for me.'"
18 Then Balaam answered and said to the
servants of Balak, "Though Balak were to
give me his house full of silver and gold, I
could not go beyond the word of the LORD
my God, to do less or more. 19 Now therefore,
please, you also stay here tonight, that I may
know what more the LORD will say to me."
20 And God came to Balaam at night and
said to him, "If the men come to call you,
rise *and* go with them; but only the word
which I speak to you—that you shall do."
21 So Balaam rose in the morning, saddled
his donkey, and went with the princes of
Moab.

Balaam, the Donkey, and the Angel

22 Then God's anger was aroused because
he went, and the Angel of the LORD took
His stand in the way as an adversary against
him. And he was riding on his donkey, and
his two servants *were* with him. 23 Now the
donkey saw the Angel of the LORD standing
in the way with His drawn sword in His
hand, and the donkey turned aside out of
the way and went into the field. So Balaam
struck the donkey to turn her back onto the
road. 24 Then the Angel of the LORD stood in
a narrow path between the vineyards, *with*
a wall on this side and a wall on that side.
25 And when the donkey saw the Angel of the
LORD, she pushed herself against the wall
and crushed Balaam's foot against the wall;
so he struck her again. 26 Then the Angel of

22:5 [a] That is, the Euphrates [b] Or *the people of Amau*

the LORD went further, and stood in a narrow place where there *was* no way to turn
either to the right hand or to the left. 27And
when the donkey saw the Angel of the LORD,
she lay down under Balaam; so Balaam's anger was aroused, and he struck the donkey
with his staff.

28Then the LORD opened the mouth of
the donkey, and she said to Balaam, "What
have I done to you, that you have struck me
these three times?"

29And Balaam said to the donkey, "Because you have abused me. I wish there
were a sword in my hand, for now I would
kill you!"

30So the donkey said to Balaam, "*Am* I not
your donkey on which you have ridden, ever
since *I became* yours, to this day? Was I ever
disposed to do this to you?"

And he said, "No."

31Then the LORD opened Balaam's eyes,
and he saw the Angel of the LORD standing
in the way with His drawn sword in His
hand; and he bowed his head and fell flat on
his face. 32And the Angel of the LORD said
to him, "Why have you struck your donkey
these three times? Behold, I have come out
to stand against you, because *your* way is
perverse before Me. 33The donkey saw Me
and turned aside from Me these three times.
If she had not turned aside from Me, surely
I would also have killed you by now, and let
her live."

34And Balaam said to the Angel of the
LORD "I have sinned, for I did not know You
stood in the way against me. Now therefore,
if it displeases You, I will turn back."

35Then the Angel of the LORD said to Balaam, "Go with the men, but only the word
that I speak to you, that you shall speak." So
Balaam went with the princes of Balak.

36Now when Balak heard that Balaam
was coming, he went out to meet him at the
city of Moab, which *is* on the border at the
Arnon, the boundary of the territory. 37Then
Balak said to Balaam, "Did I not earnestly
send to you, calling for you? Why did you not
come to me? Am I not able to honor you?"

38And Balaam said to Balak, "Look, I have
come to you! Now, have I any power at all
to say anything? The word that God puts in
my mouth, that I must speak." 39So Balaam
went with Balak, and they came to Kirjath
Huzoth. 40Then Balak offered oxen and
sheep, and he sent *some* to Balaam and to
the princes who *were* with him.

Balaam's First Prophecy

41So it was, the next day, that Balak took
Balaam and brought him up to the high places of Baal, that from there he might observe
the extent of the people.

23 Then Balaam said to Balak, "Build
seven altars for me here, and prepare for me here seven bulls and seven
rams."

2And Balak did just as Balaam had spoken, and Balak and Balaam offered a bull
and a ram on *each* altar. 3Then Balaam said
to Balak, "Stand by your burnt offering,
and I will go; perhaps the LORD will come
to meet me, and whatever He shows me I
will tell you." So he went to a desolate height.
4And God met Balaam, and he said to Him,
"I have prepared the seven altars, and I have
offered on *each* altar a bull and a ram."

5Then the LORD put a word in Balaam's
mouth, and said, "Return to Balak, and thus
you shall speak." 6So he returned to him,
and there he was, standing by his burnt offering, he and all the princes of Moab.

7And he took up his oracle and said:

"Balak the king of Moab has brought me
from Aram,
From the mountains of the east.
'Come, curse Jacob for me,
And come, denounce Israel!'

8 "How shall I curse whom God has not
cursed?
And how shall I denounce *whom* the
LORD has not denounced?
9 For from the top of the rocks I see him,
And from the hills I behold him;
There! A people dwelling alone,
Not reckoning itself among the nations.

10 "Who can count the dust[a] of Jacob,
Or number one-fourth of Israel?
Let me die the death of the righteous,
And let my end be like his!"

11Then Balak said to Balaam, "What
have you done to me? I took you to curse my
enemies, and look, you have blessed *them*
bountifully!"

12So he answered and said, "Must I not
take heed to speak what the LORD has put in
my mouth?"

23:10 [a] Or *dust cloud*

Balaam's Second Prophecy

13 Then Balak said to him, "Please come
with me to another place from which you
may see them; you shall see only the outer part of them, and shall not see them
all; curse them for me from there." 14 So he
brought him to the field of Zophim, to the
top of Pisgah, and built seven altars, and offered a bull and a ram on *each* altar.

15 And he said to Balak, "Stand here by
your burnt offering while I meet[a] *the* LORD
over there."

16 Then the LORD met Balaam, and put a
word in his mouth, and said, "Go back to Balak, and thus you shall speak." 17 So he came
to him, and there he was, standing by his
burnt offering, and the princes of Moab were
with him. And Balak said to him, "What has
the LORD spoken?"

18 Then he took up his oracle and said:

"Rise up, Balak, and hear!
Listen to me, son of Zippor!

19 "God *is* not a man, that He should lie,
Nor a son of man, that He should
repent.
Has He said, and will He not do?
Or has He spoken, and will He not
make it good?
20 Behold, I have received *a command* to
bless;
He has blessed, and I cannot reverse it.

21 "He has not observed iniquity in Jacob,
Nor has He seen wickedness in Israel.
The LORD his God *is* with him,
And the shout of a King *is* among them.
22 God brings them out of Egypt;
He has strength like a wild ox.

23 "For *there is* no sorcery against Jacob,
Nor any divination against Israel.
It now must be said of Jacob
And of Israel, 'Oh, what God has done!'
24 Look, a people rises like a lioness,
And lifts itself up like a lion;
It shall not lie down until it devours the
prey,
And drinks the blood of the slain."

25 Then Balak said to Balaam, "Neither
curse them at all, nor bless them at all!"
26 So Balaam answered and said to Balak,
"Did I not tell you, saying, 'All that the LORD
speaks, that I must do'?"

Balaam's Third Prophecy

27 Then Balak said to Balaam, "Please
come, I will take you to another place; perhaps it will please God that you may curse
them for me from there." 28 So Balak took
Balaam to the top of Peor, that overlooks the
wasteland.[a] 29 Then Balaam said to Balak,
"Build for me here seven altars, and prepare
for me here seven bulls and seven rams."
30 And Balak did as Balaam had said, and offered a bull and a ram on *every* altar.

24

Now when Balaam saw that it
pleased the LORD to bless Israel,
he did not go as at other times, to seek to
use sorcery, but he set his face toward the
wilderness. 2 And Balaam raised his eyes,
and saw Israel encamped according to their
tribes; and the Spirit of God came upon him.

3 Then he took up his oracle and said:

"The utterance of Balaam the son of
Beor,
The utterance of the man whose eyes
are opened,
4 The utterance of him who hears the
words of God,
Who sees the vision of the Almighty,
Who falls down, with eyes wide open:

5 "How lovely are your tents, O Jacob!
Your dwellings, O Israel!
6 Like valleys that stretch out,
Like gardens by the riverside,
Like aloes planted by the LORD,
Like cedars beside the waters.
7 He shall pour water from his buckets,
And his seed *shall be* in many waters.

"His king shall be higher than Agag,
And his kingdom shall be exalted.

8 "God brings him out of Egypt;
He has strength like a wild ox;
He shall consume the nations, his
enemies;
He shall break their bones
And pierce *them* with his arrows.
9 'He bows down, he lies down as a lion;
And as a lion, who shall rouse him?'[a]

"Blessed *is* he who blesses you,
And cursed *is* he who curses you."

10 Then Balak's anger was aroused against
Balaam, and he struck his hands together;

23:15 [a] Following Masoretic Text, Targum, and Vulgate; Syriac reads *call;* Septuagint reads *go and ask God.*
23:28 [a] Hebrew *Jeshimon* **24:9** [a] Genesis 49:9

and Balak said to Balaam, "I called you to
curse my enemies, and look, you have bountifully blessed *them* these three times! 11 Now
therefore, flee to your place. I said I would
greatly honor you, but in fact, the LORD has
kept you back from honor."
12 So Balaam said to Balak, "Did I not also
speak to your messengers whom you sent to
me, saying, 13 'If Balak were to give me his
house full of silver and gold, I could not go
beyond the word of the LORD, to do good or
bad of my own will. What the LORD says,
that I must speak'? 14 And now, indeed, I am
going to my people. Come, I will advise you
what this people will do to your people in the
latter days."

Balaam's Fourth Prophecy

15 So he took up his oracle and said:

"The utterance of Balaam the son of
Beor,
And the utterance of the man whose
eyes are opened;
16 The utterance of him who hears the
words of God,
And has the knowledge of the Most
High,
Who sees the vision of the Almighty,
Who falls down, with eyes wide open:

17 "I see Him, but not now;
I behold Him, but not near;
A Star shall come out of Jacob;
A Scepter shall rise out of Israel,
And batter the brow of Moab,
And destroy all the sons of tumult.[a]

18 "And Edom shall be a possession;
Seir also, his enemies, shall be a
possession,
While Israel does valiantly.
19 Out of Jacob One shall have dominion,
And destroy the remains of the city."

20 Then he looked on Amalek, and he took
up his oracle and said:

"Amalek *was* first among the nations,
But *shall be* last until he perishes."

21 Then he looked on the Kenites, and he
took up his oracle and said:

"Firm is your dwelling place,
And your nest is set in the rock;
22 Nevertheless Kain shall be burned.
How long until Asshur carries you away
captive?"

23 Then he took up his oracle and said:

"Alas! Who shall live when God does
this?
24 But ships *shall come* from the coasts of
Cyprus,[a]
And they shall afflict Asshur and afflict
Eber,
And so shall *Amalek*,[b] until he
perishes."

25 So Balaam rose and departed and returned to his place; Balak also went his way.

Israel's Harlotry in Moab

25 Now Israel remained in Acacia
Grove,[a] and the people began to
commit harlotry with the women of Moab.
2 They invited the people to the sacrifices of
their gods, and the people ate and bowed
down to their gods. 3 So Israel was joined to
Baal of Peor, and the anger of the LORD was
aroused against Israel.
4 Then the LORD said to Moses, "Take all
the leaders of the people and hang the offenders before the LORD, out in the sun, that
the fierce anger of the LORD may turn away
from Israel."
5 So Moses said to the judges of Israel,
"Every one of you kill his men who were
joined to Baal of Peor."
6 And indeed, one of the children of Israel
came and presented to his brethren a Midianite woman in the sight of Moses and in
the sight of all the congregation of the children of Israel, who *were* weeping at the door
of the tabernacle of meeting. 7 Now when
Phinehas the son of Eleazar, the son of Aaron the priest, saw *it*, he rose from among the
congregation and took a javelin in his hand;
8 and he went after the man of Israel into the
tent and thrust both of them through, the
man of Israel, and the woman through her
body. So the plague was stopped among the
children of Israel. 9 And those who died in
the plague were twenty-four thousand.
10 Then the LORD spoke to Moses, saying:
11 "Phinehas the son of Eleazar, the son of
Aaron the priest, has turned back My wrath
from the children of Israel, because he was
zealous with My zeal among them, so that I
did not consume the children of Israel in My

24:17 [a] Hebrew *Sheth* (compare Jeremiah 48:45)
24:24 [a] Hebrew *Kittim* [b] Literally *he* or *that one*
25:1 [a] Hebrew *Shittim*

zeal. 12 Therefore say, 'Behold, I give to him
My covenant of peace; 13 and it shall be to him
and his descendants after him a covenant of
an everlasting priesthood, because he was
zealous for his God, and made atonement
for the children of Israel.'"

14 Now the name of the Israelite who was
killed, who was killed with the Midianite
woman, *was* Zimri the son of Salu, a leader
of a father's house among the Simeonites.
15 And the name of the Midianite woman who
was killed *was* Cozbi the daughter of Zur; he
was head of the people of a father's house in
Midian.

16 Then the LORD spoke to Moses, saying:
17 "Harass the Midianites, and attack them;
18 for they harassed you with their schemes by
which they seduced you in the matter of Peor
and in the matter of Cozbi, the daughter of a
leader of Midian, their sister, who was killed
in the day of the plague because of Peor."

The Second Census of Israel

26 And it came to pass, after the
plague, that the LORD spoke to
Moses and Eleazar the son of Aaron the
priest, saying: 2 "Take a census of all the
congregation of the children of Israel from
twenty years old and above, by their fathers'
houses, all who are able to go to war in Israel." 3 So Moses and Eleazar the priest spoke
with them in the plains of Moab by the Jordan, *across from* Jericho, saying: 4 "*Take a census of the people* from twenty years old and
above, just as the LORD commanded Moses
and the children of Israel who came out of
the land of Egypt."

5 Reuben *was* the firstborn of Israel. The
children of Reuben *were: of* Hanoch, the
family of the Hanochites; *of* Pallu, the family of the Palluites; 6 *of* Hezron, the family of
the Hezronites; *of* Carmi, the family of the
Carmites. 7 These *are* the families of the Reubenites: those who were numbered of them
were forty-three thousand seven hundred
and thirty. 8 And the son of Pallu *was* Eliab.
9 The sons of Eliab *were* Nemuel, Dathan,
and Abiram. These *are* the Dathan and Abiram, representatives of the congregation,
who contended against Moses and Aaron in
the company of Korah, when they contended against the LORD; 10 and the earth opened
its mouth and swallowed them up together
with Korah when that company died, when
the fire devoured two hundred and fifty
men; and they became a sign. 11 Nevertheless
the children of Korah did not die.

12 The sons of Simeon according to their
families *were: of* Nemuel,[a] the family of the
Nemuelites; *of* Jamin, the family of the Ja-
minites; *of* Jachin,[b] the family of the Jachi-
nites; 13 *of* Zerah,[a] the family of the Zarhites;
of Shaul, the family of the Shaulites. 14 These
are the families of the Simeonites: twenty-
two thousand two hundred.

15 The sons of Gad according to their
families *were: of* Zephon,[a] the family of the
Zephonites; *of* Haggi, the family of the Hag-
gites; *of* Shuni, the family of the Shunites;
16 *of* Ozni,[a] the family of the Oznites; *of* Eri,
the family of the Erites; 17 *of* Arod,[a] the family of the Arodites; *of* Areli, the family of the
Arelites. 18 These *are* the families of the sons
of Gad according to those who were numbered of them: forty thousand five hundred.

19 The sons of Judah *were* Er and Onan;
and Er and Onan died in the land of Canaan.
20 And the sons of Judah according to their
families were: *of* Shelah, the family of the
Shelanites; *of* Perez, the family of the Par-
zites; *of* Zerah, the family of the Zarhites.
21 And the sons of Perez were: *of* Hezron, the
family of the Hezronites; *of* Hamul, the family of the Hamulites. 22 These *are* the families
of Judah according to those who were numbered of them: seventy-six thousand five
hundred.

23 The sons of Issachar according to their
families *were: of* Tola, the family of the To-
laites; of Puah,[a] the family of the Punites;[b]
24 of Jashub, the family of the Jashubites; of
Shimron, the family of the Shimronites.
25 These *are* the families of Issachar according to those who were numbered of them:
sixty-four thousand three hundred.

26 The sons of Zebulun according to their
families *were:* of Sered, the family of the Sar-
dites; of Elon, the family of the Elonites; of
Jahleel, the family of the Jahleelites. 27 These
are the families of the Zebulunites according
to those who were numbered of them: sixty
thousand five hundred.

26:12 [a] Spelled *Jemuel* in Genesis 46:10 and Exodus 6:15 [b] Called *Jarib* in 1 Chronicles 4:24 **26:13** [a] Called *Zohar* in Genesis 46:10 **26:15** [a] Called *Ziphion* in Genesis 46:16 **26:16** [a] Called *Ezbon* in Genesis 46:16 **26:17** [a] Spelled *Arodi* in Samaritan Pentateuch, Syriac, and Genesis 46:16 **26:23** [a] Hebrew *Puvah* (compare Genesis 46:13 and 1 Chronicles 7:1); Samaritan Pentateuch, Septuagint, Syriac, and Vulgate read *Puah.* [b] Samaritan Pentateuch, Septuagint, Syriac, and Vulgate read *Puaites.*

28The sons of Joseph according to their
families, by Manasseh and Ephraim, *were:*
29The sons of Manasseh: of Machir, the family of the Machirites; and Machir begot Gilead; of Gilead, the family of the Gileadites.
30These *are* the sons of Gilead: *of* Jeezer,[a] the
family of the Jeezerites; of Helek, the family of the Helekites; 31*of* Asriel, the family of
the Asrielites; *of* Shechem, the family of the
Shechemites; 32*of* Shemida, the family of the
Shemidaites; *of* Hepher, the family of the
Hepherites. 33Now Zelophehad the son of
Hepher had no sons, but daughters; and the
names of the daughters of Zelophehad *were*
Mahlah, Noah, Hoglah, Milcah, and Tirzah. 34These *are* the families of Manasseh;
and those who were numbered of them *were*
fifty-two thousand seven hundred.

35These *are* the sons of Ephraim according to their families: of Shuthelah, the
family of the Shuthalhites; of Becher,[a] the
family of the Bachrites; of Tahan, the family
of the Tahanites. 36And these *are* the sons of
Shuthelah: of Eran, the family of the Eran-
ites. 37These *are* the families of the sons of
Ephraim according to those who were numbered of them: thirty-two thousand five
hundred.

These *are* the sons of Joseph according to
their families.

38The sons of Benjamin according to
their families were: of Bela, the family of
the Belaites; of Ashbel, the family of the
Ashbelites; of Ahiram, the family of the
Ahiramites; 39of Shupham,[a] the family of
the Shuphamites; of Hupham,[b] the family
of the Huphamites. 40And the sons of Bela
were Ard[a] and Naaman: *of Ard,* the family
of the Ardites; of Naaman, the family of the
Naamites. 41These *are* the sons of Benjamin
according to their families; and those who
were numbered of them *were* forty-five thousand six hundred.

42These *are* the sons of Dan according to
their families: of Shuham,[a] the family of the
Shuhamites. These *are* the families of Dan
according to their families. 43All the families
of the Shuhamites, according to those who
were numbered of them, *were* sixty-four
thousand four hundred.

44The sons of Asher according to their
families *were:* of Jimna, the family of the
Jimnites; of Jesui, the family of the Jesuites;
of Beriah, the family of the Beriites. 45Of the
sons of Beriah: of Heber, the family of the
Heberites; of Malchiel, the family of the Mal-
chielites. 46And the name of the daughter of
Asher *was* Serah. 47These *are* the families of
the sons of Asher according to those who
were numbered of them: fifty-three thousand four hundred.

48The sons of Naphtali according to
their families *were:* of Jahzeel,[a] the family of the Jahzeelites; of Guni, the family
of the Gunites; 49of Jezer, the family of the
Jezerites; of Shillem, the family of the Shil-
lemites. 50These *are* the families of Naphtali
according to their families; and those who
were numbered of them *were* forty-five thousand four hundred.

51These *are* those who were numbered of
the children of Israel: six hundred and one
thousand seven hundred and thirty.

52Then the LORD spoke to Moses, saying: 53"To these the land shall be divided as
an inheritance, according to the number
of names. 54To a large *tribe* you shall give a
larger inheritance, and to a small *tribe* you
shall give a smaller inheritance. Each shall
be given its inheritance according to those
who were numbered of them. 55But the land
shall be divided by lot; they shall inherit according to the names of the tribes of their fathers. 56According to the lot their inheritance
shall be divided between the larger and the
smaller."

57And these *are* those who were numbered
of the Levites according to their families: of
Gershon, the family of the Gershonites; of
Kohath, the family of the Kohathites; of Merari, the family of the Merarites. 58These *are* the
families of the Levites: the family of the Libnites, the family of the Hebronites, the family
of the Mahlites, the family of the Mushites,
and the family of the Korathites. And Kohath
begot Amram. 59The name of Amram's wife
was Jochebed the daughter of Levi, who was
born to Levi in Egypt; and to Amram she
bore Aaron and Moses and their sister Miriam. 60To Aaron were born Nadab and Abihu, Eleazar and Ithamar. 61And Nadab and
Abihu died when they offered profane fire
before the LORD.

26:30 [a] Called *Abiezer* in Joshua 17:2 **26:35** [a] Called *Bered* in 1 Chronicles 7:20 **26:39** [a] Masoretic Text reads *Shephupham,* spelled *Shephuphan* in 1 Chronicles 8:5. [b] Called *Huppim* in Genesis 46:21 **26:40** [a] Called *Addar* in 1 Chronicles 8:3 **26:42** [a] Called *Hushim* in Genesis 46:23 **26:48** [a] Spelled *Jahziel* in 1 Chronicles 7:13

62 Now those who were numbered of them
were twenty-three thousand, every male
from a month old and above; for they were
not numbered among the other children
of Israel, because there was no inheritance
given to them among the children of Israel.
63 These *are* those who were numbered
by Moses and Eleazar the priest, who numbered the children of Israel in the plains
of Moab by the Jordan, *across from* Jericho.
64 But among these there was not a man of
those who were numbered by Moses and
Aaron the priest when they numbered the
children of Israel in the Wilderness of Sinai.
65 For the LORD had said of them, "They shall
surely die in the wilderness." So there was
not left a man of them, except Caleb the son
of Jephunneh and Joshua the son of Nun.

Inheritance Laws

27 Then came the daughters of Zelophehad the son of Hepher, the
son of Gilead, the son of Machir, the son of
Manasseh, from the families of Manasseh
the son of Joseph; and these *were* the names
of his daughters: Mahlah, Noah, Hoglah,
Milcah, and Tirzah. 2 And they stood before
Moses, before Eleazar the priest, and before
the leaders and all the congregation, *by* the
doorway of the tabernacle of meeting, saying: 3 "Our father died in the wilderness;
but he was not in the company of those who
gathered together against the LORD, in company with Korah, but he died in his own
sin; and he had no sons. 4 Why should the
name of our father be removed from among
his family because he had no son? Give us
a possession among our father's brothers."
5 So Moses brought their case before the
LORD.
6 And the LORD spoke to Moses, saying:
7 "The daughters of Zelophehad speak *what
is* right; you shall surely give them a possession of inheritance among their father's
brothers, and cause the inheritance of their
father to pass to them. 8 And you shall speak
to the children of Israel, saying: 'If a man
dies and has no son, then you shall cause his
inheritance to pass to his daughter. 9 If he has
no daughter, then you shall give his inheritance to his brothers. 10 If he has no brothers,
then you shall give his inheritance to his
father's brothers. 11 And if his father has no
brothers, then you shall give his inheritance
to the relative closest to him in his family,
and he shall possess it.'" And it shall be to
the children of Israel a statute of judgment,
just as the LORD commanded Moses.

Joshua the Next Leader of Israel

12 Now the LORD said to Moses: "Go up
into this Mount Abarim, and see the land
which I have given to the children of Israel.
13 And when you have seen it, you also shall
be gathered to your people, as Aaron your
brother was gathered. 14 For in the Wilderness of Zin, during the strife of the congregation, you rebelled against My command to
hallow Me at the waters before their eyes."
(These *are* the waters of Meribah, at Kadesh
in the Wilderness of Zin.)
15 Then Moses spoke to the LORD, saying: 16 "Let the LORD, the God of the spirits
of all flesh, set a man over the congregation, 17 who may go out before them and go
in before them, who may lead them out and
bring them in, that the congregation of the
LORD may not be like sheep which have no
shepherd."
18 And the LORD said to Moses: "Take
Joshua the son of Nun with you, a man in
whom *is* the Spirit, and lay your hand on
him; 19 set him before Eleazar the priest and
before all the congregation, and inaugu-
rate him in their sight. 20 And you shall give
some of your authority to him, that all the
congregation of the children of Israel may
be obedient. 21 He shall stand before Eleazar
the priest, who shall inquire before the LORD
for him by the judgment of the Urim. At his
word they shall go out, and at his word they
shall come in, he and all the children of Israel with him—all the congregation."
22 So Moses did as the LORD commanded him. He took Joshua and set him before
Eleazar the priest and before all the congregation. 23 And he laid his hands on him and
inaugurated him, just as the LORD commanded by the hand of Moses.

Daily Offerings

28 Now the LORD spoke to Moses,
saying, 2 "Command the children
of Israel, and say to them, 'My offering, My
food for My offerings made by fire as a sweet
aroma to Me, you shall be careful to offer to
Me at their appointed time.'
3 "And you shall say to them, 'This *is* the
offering made by fire which you shall offer
to the LORD: two male lambs in their first

year without blemish, day by day, as a regular burnt offering. 4The one lamb you shall
offer in the morning, the other lamb you
shall offer in the evening, 5and one-tenth
of an ephah of fine flour as a grain offering
mixed with one-fourth of a hin of pressed
oil. 6*It is* a regular burnt offering which was
ordained at Mount Sinai for a sweet aroma,
an offering made by fire to the LORD. 7And
its drink offering *shall be* one-fourth of a hin
for each lamb; in a holy *place* you shall pour
out the drink to the LORD as an offering.
8The other lamb you shall offer in the evening; as the morning grain offering and its
drink offering, you shall offer *it* as an offering made by fire, a sweet aroma to the LORD.

Sabbath Offerings

9'And on the Sabbath day two lambs in
their first year, without blemish, and two-
tenths *of an ephah* of fine flour as a grain
offering, mixed with oil, with its drink offering— 10*this is* the burnt offering for every
Sabbath, besides the regular burnt offering
with its drink offering.

Monthly Offerings

11'At the beginnings of your months you
shall present a burnt offering to the LORD:
two young bulls, one ram, and seven lambs
in their first year, without blemish; 12three-
tenths *of an ephah* of fine flour as a grain
offering, mixed with oil, for each bull; two-
tenths *of an ephah* of fine flour as a grain offering, mixed with oil, for the one ram; 13and
one-tenth *of an ephah* of fine flour, mixed
with oil, as a grain offering for each lamb,
as a burnt offering of sweet aroma, an offering made by fire to the LORD. 14Their drink
offering shall be half a hin of wine for a bull,
one-third of a hin for a ram, and one-fourth
of a hin for a lamb; this *is* the burnt offering for each month throughout the months
of the year. 15Also one kid of the goats as a
sin offering to the LORD shall be offered,
besides the regular burnt offering and its
drink offering.

Offerings at Passover

16'On the fourteenth day of the first
month *is* the Passover of the LORD. 17And on
the fifteenth day of this month *is* the feast;
unleavened bread shall be eaten for seven
days. 18On the first day *you shall have* a holy
convocation. You shall do no customary
work. 19And you shall present an offering
made by fire as a burnt offering to the LORD:
two young bulls, one ram, and seven lambs
in their first year. Be sure they are without
blemish. 20Their grain offering shall be of
fine flour mixed with oil: three-tenths *of
an ephah* you shall offer for a bull, and two-
tenths for a ram; 21you shall offer one-tenth
of an ephah for each of the seven lambs; 22also
one goat *as* a sin offering, to make atonement for you. 23You shall offer these besides
the burnt offering of the morning, which *is*
for a regular burnt offering. 24In this manner
you shall offer the food of the offering made
by fire daily for seven days, as a sweet aroma
to the LORD; it shall be offered besides the
regular burnt offering and its drink offering. 25And on the seventh day you shall have
a holy convocation. You shall do no customary work.

Offerings at the Feast of Weeks

26'Also on the day of the firstfruits, when
you bring a new grain offering to the LORD
at your *Feast of* Weeks, you shall have a holy
convocation. You shall do no customary
work. 27You shall present a burnt offering
as a sweet aroma to the LORD: two young
bulls, one ram, and seven lambs in their first
year, 28with their grain offering of fine flour
mixed with oil: three-tenths *of an ephah* for
each bull, two-tenths for the one ram, 29and
one-tenth for each of the seven lambs; 30*also*
one kid of the goats, to make atonement for
you. 31Be sure they are without blemish. You
shall present *them* with their drink offerings, besides the regular burnt offering with
its grain offering.

Offerings at the Feast of Trumpets

29 'And in the seventh month, on the
first *day* of the month, you shall
have a holy convocation. You shall do no customary work. For you it is a day of blowing
the trumpets. 2You shall offer a burnt offering as a sweet aroma to the LORD: one young
bull, one ram, *and* seven lambs in their first
year, without blemish. 3Their grain offering
shall be fine flour mixed with oil: three-
tenths *of an ephah* for the bull, two-tenths for
the ram, 4and one-tenth for each of the seven
lambs; 5also one kid of the goats *as* a sin offering, to make atonement for you; 6besides
the burnt offering with its grain offering for
the New Moon, the regular burnt offering

with its grain offering, and their drink offerings, according to their ordinance, as a sweet
aroma, an offering made by fire to the LORD.

Offerings on the Day of Atonement

7 'On the tenth *day* of this seventh month
you shall have a holy convocation. You shall
afflict your souls; you shall not do any work.
8 You shall present a burnt offering to the
LORD *as* a sweet aroma: one young bull, one
ram, *and* seven lambs in their first year. Be
sure they are without blemish. 9 Their grain
offering *shall be of* fine flour mixed with oil:
three-tenths *of an ephah* for the bull, two-
tenths for the one ram, 10 and one-tenth for
each of the seven lambs; 11 also one kid of the
goats *as* a sin offering, besides the sin offering for atonement, the regular burnt offering with its grain offering, and their drink
offerings.

Offerings at the Feast of Tabernacles

12 'On the fifteenth day of the seventh
month you shall have a holy convocation.
You shall do no customary work, and you
shall keep a feast to the LORD seven days.
13 You shall present a burnt offering, an offering made by fire as a sweet aroma to the
LORD: thirteen young bulls, two rams, *and*
fourteen lambs in their first year. They shall
be without blemish. 14 Their grain offering
shall be of fine flour mixed with oil: three-
tenths *of an ephah* for each of the thirteen
bulls, two-tenths for each of the two rams,
15 and one-tenth for each of the fourteen
lambs; 16 also one kid of the goats *as* a sin offering, besides the regular burnt offering, its
grain offering, and its drink offering.

17 'On the second day *present* twelve young
bulls, two rams, fourteen lambs in their first
year without blemish, 18 and their grain offering and their drink offerings for the bulls,
for the rams, and for the lambs, by their
number, according to the ordinance; 19 also
one kid of the goats *as* a sin offering, besides
the regular burnt offering with its grain offering, and their drink offerings.

20 'On the third day *present* eleven bulls,
two rams, fourteen lambs in their first year
without blemish, 21 and their grain offering
and their drink offerings for the bulls, for
the rams, and for the lambs, by their number, according to the ordinance; 22 also one
goat *as* a sin offering, besides the regular
burnt offering, its grain offering, and its
drink offering.

23 'On the fourth day *present* ten bulls, two
rams, *and* fourteen lambs in their first year,
without blemish, 24 and their grain offering
and their drink offerings for the bulls, for
the rams, and for the lambs, by their number, according to the ordinance; 25 also one
kid of the goats *as* a sin offering, besides the
regular burnt offering, its grain offering,
and its drink offering.

26 'On the fifth day *present* nine bulls, two
rams, *and* fourteen lambs in their first year
without blemish, 27 and their grain offering
and their drink offerings for the bulls, for
the rams, and for the lambs, by their number, according to the ordinance; 28 also one
goat *as* a sin offering, besides the regular
burnt offering, its grain offering, and its
drink offering.

29 'On the sixth day *present* eight bulls, two
rams, *and* fourteen lambs in their first year
without blemish, 30 and their grain offering
and their drink offerings for the bulls, for
the rams, and for the lambs, by their number, according to the ordinance; 31 also one
goat *as* a sin offering, besides the regular
burnt offering, its grain offering, and its
drink offering.

32 'On the seventh day *present* seven bulls,
two rams, *and* fourteen lambs in their first
year without blemish, 33 and their grain offering and their drink offerings for the bulls,
for the rams, and for the lambs, by their
number, according to the ordinance; 34 also
one goat *as* a sin offering, besides the regular burnt offering, its grain offering, and its
drink offering.

35 'On the eighth day you shall have a sacred assembly. You shall do no customary
work. 36 You shall present a burnt offering,
an offering made by fire as a sweet aroma to
the LORD: one bull, one ram, seven lambs in
their first year without blemish, 37 and their
grain offering and their drink offerings for
the bull, for the ram, and for the lambs, by
their number, according to the ordinance;
38 also one goat *as* a sin offering, besides the
regular burnt offering, its grain offering,
and its drink offering.

39 'These you shall present to the LORD at
your appointed feasts (besides your vowed
offerings and your freewill offerings) as your
burnt offerings and your grain offerings,

as your drink offerings and your peace offerings.'"

40So Moses told the children of Israel everything, just as the LORD commanded Moses.

The Law Concerning Vows

30 Then Moses spoke to the heads of the tribes concerning the children of Israel, saying, "This *is* the thing which the LORD has commanded: 2If a man makes a
vow to the LORD, or swears an oath to bind himself by some agreement, he shall not break his word; he shall do according to all that proceeds out of his mouth.

3"Or if a woman makes a vow to the LORD, and binds *herself* by some agreement
while in her father's house in her youth, 4and
her father hears her vow and the agreement by which she has bound herself, and her father holds his peace, then all her vows shall stand, and every agreement with which she
has bound herself shall stand. 5But if her father overrules her on the day that he hears, then none of her vows nor her agreements by which she has bound herself shall stand; and the LORD will release her, because her father overruled her.

6"If indeed she takes a husband, while bound by her vows or by a rash utterance from her lips by which she bound herself,
7and her husband hears *it*, and makes no response to her on the day that he hears, then her vows shall stand, and her agreements by
which she bound herself shall stand. 8But if
her husband overrules her on the day that he hears *it*, he shall make void her vow which she took and what she uttered with her lips, by which she bound herself, and the LORD will release her.

9"Also any vow of a widow or a divorced woman, by which she has bound herself, shall stand against her.

10"If she vowed in her husband's house, or bound herself by an agreement with an
oath, 11and her husband heard *it*, and made no response to her *and* did not overrule her, then all her vows shall stand, and every agreement by which she bound herself shall
stand. 12But if her husband truly made them void on the day he heard *them*, then whatever proceeded from her lips concerning her vows or concerning the agreement binding her, it shall not stand; her husband has made them void, and the LORD will release
her. 13Every vow and every binding oath to afflict her soul, her husband may confirm
it, or her husband may make it void. 14Now
if her husband makes no response whatever to her from day to day, then he confirms all her vows or all the agreements that bind her; he confirms them, because he made no response to her on the day that he heard *them*.
15But if he does make them void after he has heard *them*, then he shall bear her guilt."

16These *are* the statutes which the LORD commanded Moses, between a man and his wife, and between a father and his daughter in her youth in her father's house.

Vengeance on the Midianites

31 And the LORD spoke to Moses, say-
ing: 2"Take vengeance on the Midianites for the children of Israel. Afterward you shall be gathered to your people."

3So Moses spoke to the people, saying, "Arm some of yourselves for war, and let them go against the Midianites to take vengeance for the LORD on Midian. 4A thousand
from each tribe of all the tribes of Israel you shall send to the war."

5So there were recruited from the divisions of Israel one thousand from *each*
tribe, twelve thousand armed for war. 6Then
Moses sent them to the war, one thousand from *each* tribe; he sent them to the war with Phinehas the son of Eleazar the priest, with the holy articles and the signal trumpets in
his hand. 7And they warred against the Midianites, just as the LORD commanded Moses,
and they killed all the males. 8They killed
the kings of Midian with *the rest of* those who were killed—Evi, Rekem, Zur, Hur, and Reba, the five kings of Midian. Balaam the son of Beor they also killed with the sword.

9And the children of Israel took the women of Midian captive, with their little ones, and took as spoil all their cattle, all
their flocks, and all their goods. 10They also burned with fire all the cities where they
dwelt, and all their forts. 11And they took all the spoil and all the booty—of man and beast.

Return from the War

12Then they brought the captives, the booty, and the spoil to Moses, to Eleazar the priest, and to the congregation of the children of Israel, to the camp in the plains of Moab by the Jordan, *across from* Jericho.

13 And Moses, Eleazar the priest, and all the
leaders of the congregation, went to meet
them outside the camp. 14 But Moses was angry with the officers of the army, *with* the
captains over thousands and captains over
hundreds, who had come from the battle.

15 And Moses said to them: "Have you
kept all the women alive? 16 Look, these *wom-*
en caused the children of Israel, through the
counsel of Balaam, to trespass against the
LORD in the incident of Peor, and there was a
plague among the congregation of the LORD.
17 Now therefore, kill every male among the
little ones, and kill every woman who has
known a man intimately. 18 But keep alive
for yourselves all the young girls who have
not known a man intimately. 19 And as for
you, remain outside the camp seven days;
whoever has killed any person, and whoever
has touched any slain, purify yourselves and
your captives on the third day and on the seventh day. 20 Purify every garment, everything
made of leather, everything woven of goats'
hair, and everything made of wood."

21 Then Eleazar the priest said to the men
of war who had gone to the battle, "This *is*
the ordinance of the law which the LORD
commanded Moses: 22 Only the gold, the
silver, the bronze, the iron, the tin, and the
lead, 23 everything that can endure fire, you
shall put through the fire, and it shall be
clean; and it shall be purified with the water
of purification. But all that cannot endure
fire you shall put through water. 24 And you
shall wash your clothes on the seventh day
and be clean, and afterward you may come
into the camp."

Division of the Plunder

25 Now the LORD spoke to Moses, saying:
26 "Count up the plunder that was taken—of
man and beast—you and Eleazar the priest
and the chief fathers of the congregation;
27 and divide the plunder into two parts, between those who took part in the war, who
went out to battle, and all the congregation.
28 And levy a tribute for the LORD on the men
of war who went out to battle: one of every
five hundred of the persons, the cattle, the
donkeys, and the sheep; 29 take *it* from their
half, and give *it* to Eleazar the priest as a
heave offering to the LORD. 30 And from the
children of Israel's half you shall take one of
every fifty, drawn from the persons, the cattle, the donkeys, and the sheep, from all the
livestock, and give them to the Levites who
keep charge of the tabernacle of the LORD."
31 So Moses and Eleazar the priest did as the
LORD commanded Moses.

32 The booty remaining from the plunder,
which the men of war had taken, was six
hundred and seventy-five thousand sheep,
33 seventy-two thousand cattle, 34 sixty-one
thousand donkeys, 35 and thirty-two thousand persons in all, of women who had not
known a man intimately. 36 And the half,
the portion for those who had gone out to
war, was in number three hundred and
thirty-seven thousand five hundred sheep;
37 and the LORD's tribute of the sheep was six
hundred and seventy-five. 38 The cattle *were*
thirty-six thousand, of which the LORD's
tribute *was* seventy-two. 39 The donkeys *were*
thirty thousand five hundred, of which the
LORD's tribute *was* sixty-one. 40 The persons
were sixteen thousand, of which the LORD's
tribute *was* thirty-two persons. 41 So Moses
gave the tribute *which was* the LORD's heave
offering to Eleazar the priest, as the LORD
commanded Moses.

42 And from the children of Israel's half,
which Moses separated from the men who
fought— 43 now the half belonging to the
congregation was three hundred and thirty-
seven thousand five hundred sheep, 44 thirty-
six thousand cattle, 45 thirty thousand five
hundred donkeys, 46 and sixteen thousand
persons— 47 and from the children of Israel's
half Moses took one of every fifty, drawn
from man and beast, and gave them to the
Levites, who kept charge of the tabernacle of
the LORD, as the LORD commanded Moses.

48 Then the officers who *were* over thousands of the army, the captains of thousands
and captains of hundreds, came near to Moses; 49 and they said to Moses, "Your servants
have taken a count of the men of war who *are*
under our command, and not a man of us
is missing. 50 Therefore we have brought an
offering for the LORD, what every man found
of ornaments of gold: armlets and bracelets
and signet rings and earrings and necklaces,
to make atonement for ourselves before the
LORD." 51 So Moses and Eleazar the priest received the gold from them, all the fashioned
ornaments. 52 And all the gold of the offering that they offered to the LORD, from the
captains of thousands and captains of hundreds, was sixteen thousand seven hundred

and fifty shekels. 53(The men of war had
taken spoil, every man for himself.) 54And
Moses and Eleazar the priest received the
gold from the captains of thousands and of
hundreds, and brought it into the tabernacle
of meeting as a memorial for the children of
Israel before the LORD.

The Tribes Settling East of the Jordan

32 Now the children of Reuben and
the children of Gad had a very
great multitude of livestock; and when they
saw the land of Jazer and the land of Gilead, that indeed the region *was* a place for
livestock, 2the children of Gad and the children of Reuben came and spoke to Moses,
to Eleazar the priest, and to the leaders of
the congregation, saying, 3"Ataroth, Dibon,
Jazer, Nimrah, Heshbon, Elealeh, Shebam,
Nebo, and Beon, 4the country which the
LORD defeated before the congregation of Israel, *is* a land for livestock, and your servants
have livestock." 5Therefore they said, "If we
have found favor in your sight, let this land
be given to your servants as a possession. Do
not take us over the Jordan."

6And Moses said to the children of Gad
and to the children of Reuben: "Shall your
brethren go to war while you sit here? 7Now
why will you discourage the heart of the
children of Israel from going over into the
land which the LORD has given them? 8Thus
your fathers did when I sent them away
from Kadesh Barnea to see the land. 9For
when they went up to the Valley of Eshcol
and saw the land, they discouraged the heart
of the children of Israel, so that they did not
go into the land which the LORD had given
them. 10So the LORD's anger was aroused
on that day, and He swore an oath, saying,
11'Surely none of the men who came up from
Egypt, from twenty years old and above,
shall see the land of which I swore to Abraham, Isaac, and Jacob, because they have
not wholly followed Me, 12except Caleb the
son of Jephunneh, the Kenizzite, and Joshua the son of Nun, for they have wholly followed the LORD.' 13So the LORD's anger was
aroused against Israel, and He made them
wander in the wilderness forty years, until
all the generation that had done evil in the
sight of the LORD was gone. 14And look! You
have risen in your fathers' place, a brood of
sinful men, to increase still more the fierce
anger of the LORD against Israel. 15For if you
turn away from following Him, He will once
again leave them in the wilderness, and you
will destroy all these people."

16Then they came near to him and said:
"We will build sheepfolds here for our livestock, and cities for our little ones, 17but we
ourselves will be armed, ready *to go* before
the children of Israel until we have brought
them to their place; and our little ones will
dwell in the fortified cities because of the
inhabitants of the land. 18We will not return
to our homes until every one of the children
of Israel has received his inheritance. 19For
we will not inherit with them on the other
side of the Jordan and beyond, because our
inheritance has fallen to us on this eastern
side of the Jordan."

20Then Moses said to them: "If you do
this thing, if you arm yourselves before the
LORD for the war, 21and all your armed men
cross over the Jordan before the LORD until
He has driven out His enemies from before
Him, 22and the land is subdued before the
LORD, then afterward you may return and
be blameless before the LORD and before Israel; and this land shall be your possession
before the LORD. 23But if you do not do so,
then take note, you have sinned against the
LORD; and be sure your sin will find you out.
24Build cities for your little ones and folds for
your sheep, and do what has proceeded out
of your mouth."

25And the children of Gad and the children of Reuben spoke to Moses, saying:
"Your servants will do as my lord commands. 26Our little ones, our wives, our
flocks, and all our livestock will be there in
the cities of Gilead; 27but your servants will
cross over, every man armed for war, before
the LORD to battle, just as my lord says."

28So Moses gave command concerning
them to Eleazar the priest, to Joshua the son
of Nun, and to the chief fathers of the tribes
of the children of Israel. 29And Moses said to
them: "If the children of Gad and the children of Reuben cross over the Jordan with
you, every man armed for battle before the
LORD, and the land is subdued before you,
then you shall give them the land of Gilead as a possession. 30But if they do not cross
over armed with you, they shall have possessions among you in the land of Canaan."

31Then the children of Gad and the children of Reuben answered, saying: "As the

LORD has said to your servants, so we will do.
32 We will cross over armed before the LORD
into the land of Canaan, but the possession
of our inheritance *shall remain* with us on
this side of the Jordan."

33 So Moses gave to the children of Gad,
to the children of Reuben, and to half the
tribe of Manasseh the son of Joseph, the
kingdom of Sihon king of the Amorites and
the kingdom of Og king of Bashan, the land
with its cities within the borders, the cities
of the surrounding country. 34 And the children of Gad built Dibon and Ataroth and
Aroer, 35 Atroth and Shophan and Jazer and
Jogbehah, 36 Beth Nimrah and Beth Haran,
fortified cities, and folds for sheep. 37 And the
children of Reuben built Heshbon and Elealeh and Kirjathaim, 38 Nebo and Baal Meon
(*their* names being changed) and Shibmah;
and they gave *other* names to the cities which
they built.

39 And the children of Machir the son of
Manasseh went to Gilead and took it, and
dispossessed the Amorites who *were* in it.
40 So Moses gave Gilead to Machir the son
of Manasseh, and he dwelt in it. 41 Also Jair
the son of Manasseh went and took its small
towns, and called them Havoth Jair.[a] 42 Then
Nobah went and took Kenath and its villages,
and he called it Nobah, after his own name.

Israel's Journey from Egypt Reviewed

33 These *are* the journeys of the
children of Israel, who went out
of the land of Egypt by their armies under
the hand of Moses and Aaron. 2 Now Moses
wrote down the starting points of their journeys at the command of the LORD. And these
are their journeys according to their starting
points:

3 They departed from Rameses in the
first month, on the fifteenth day of the first
month; on the day after the Passover the
children of Israel went out with boldness
in the sight of all the Egyptians. 4 For the
Egyptians were burying all *their* firstborn,
whom the LORD had killed among them.
Also on their gods the LORD had executed
judgments.

5 Then the children of Israel moved from
Rameses and camped at Succoth. 6 They departed from Succoth and camped at Etham,
which *is* on the edge of the wilderness. 7 They
moved from Etham and turned back to Pi
Hahiroth, which *is* east of Baal Zephon; and
they camped near Migdol. 8 They departed
from before Hahiroth[a] and passed through
the midst of the sea into the wilderness,
went three days' journey in the Wilderness
of Etham, and camped at Marah. 9 They
moved from Marah and came to Elim. At
Elim *were* twelve springs of water and seventy palm trees; so they camped there.

10 They moved from Elim and camped
by the Red Sea. 11 They moved from the
Red Sea and camped in the Wilderness of
Sin. 12 They journeyed from the Wilderness
of Sin and camped at Dophkah. 13 They departed from Dophkah and camped at Alush.
14 They moved from Alush and camped at
Rephidim, where there was no water for the
people to drink.

15 They departed from Rephidim and
camped in the Wilderness of Sinai. 16 They
moved from the Wilderness of Sinai and
camped at Kibroth Hattaavah. 17 They departed from Kibroth Hattaavah and camped
at Hazeroth. 18 They departed from Hazeroth
and camped at Rithmah. 19 They departed
from Rithmah and camped at Rimmon
Perez. 20 They departed from Rimmon Perez and camped at Libnah. 21 They moved
from Libnah and camped at Rissah. 22 They
journeyed from Rissah and camped at Kehelathah. 23 They went from Kehelathah and
camped at Mount Shepher. 24 They moved
from Mount Shepher and camped at Haradah. 25 They moved from Haradah and
camped at Makheloth. 26 They moved from
Makheloth and camped at Tahath. 27 They
departed from Tahath and camped at Terah. 28 They moved from Terah and camped
at Mithkah. 29 They went from Mithkah and
camped at Hashmonah. 30 They departed
from Hashmonah and camped at Moseroth.
31 They departed from Moseroth and camped
at Bene Jaakan. 32 They moved from Bene
Jaakan and camped at Hor Hagidgad. 33 They
went from Hor Hagidgad and camped at Jotbathah. 34 They moved from Jotbathah and
camped at Abronah. 35 They departed from
Abronah and camped at Ezion Geber. 36 They
moved from Ezion Geber and camped in the
Wilderness of Zin, which *is* Kadesh. 37 They
moved from Kadesh and camped at Mount
Hor, on the boundary of the land of Edom.

32:41 [a] Literally *Towns of Jair* 33:8 [a] Many Hebrew manuscripts, Samaritan Pentateuch, Syriac, Targum, and Vulgate read *from Pi Hahiroth* (compare verse 7).

38 Then Aaron the priest went up to
Mount Hor at the command of the LORD,
and died there in the fortieth year after the
children of Israel had come out of the land
of Egypt, on the first *day* of the fifth month.
39 Aaron *was* one hundred and twenty-three
years old when he died on Mount Hor.

40 Now the king of Arad, the Canaanite,
who dwelt in the South in the land of Canaan, heard of the coming of the children
of Israel.

41 So they departed from Mount Hor and
camped at Zalmonah. 42 They departed from
Zalmonah and camped at Punon. 43 They departed from Punon and camped at Oboth.
44 They departed from Oboth and camped
at Ije Abarim, at the border of Moab. 45 They
departed from Ijim[a] and camped at Dibon
Gad. 46 They moved from Dibon Gad and
camped at Almon Diblathaim. 47 They moved
from Almon Diblathaim and camped in the
mountains of Abarim, before Nebo. 48 They
departed from the mountains of Abarim and
camped in the plains of Moab by the Jordan,
across from Jericho. 49 They camped by the
Jordan, from Beth Jesimoth as far as the
Abel Acacia Grove[a] in the plains of Moab.

Instructions for the Conquest of Canaan

50 Now the LORD spoke to Moses in the
plains of Moab by the Jordan, *across from*
Jericho, saying, 51 "Speak to the children of
Israel, and say to them: 'When you have
crossed the Jordan into the land of Canaan,
52 then you shall drive out all the inhabitants
of the land from before you, destroy all their
engraved stones, destroy all their molded
images, and demolish all their high places;
53 you shall dispossess *the inhabitants of* the
land and dwell in it, for I have given you the
land to possess. 54 And you shall divide the
land by lot as an inheritance among your
families; to the larger you shall give a larger
inheritance, and to the smaller you shall give
a smaller inheritance; there everyone's *inheritance* shall be whatever falls to him by lot.
You shall inherit according to the tribes of
your fathers. 55 But if you do not drive out the
inhabitants of the land from before you, then
it shall be that those whom you let remain
shall be irritants in your eyes and thorns in
your sides, and they shall harass you in the
land where you dwell. 56 Moreover it shall
be *that* I will do to you as I thought to do to
them.'"

The Appointed Boundaries of Canaan

34 Then the LORD spoke to Moses,
saying, 2 "Command the children
of Israel, and say to them: 'When you come
into the land of Canaan, this *is* the land that
shall fall to you as an inheritance—the land
of Canaan to its boundaries. 3 Your southern
border shall be from the Wilderness of Zin
along the border of Edom; then your southern border shall extend eastward to the end
of the Salt Sea; 4 your border shall turn from
the southern side of the Ascent of Akrabbim, continue to Zin, and be on the south of
Kadesh Barnea; then it shall go on to Hazar
Addar, and continue to Azmon; 5 the border shall turn from Azmon to the Brook of
Egypt, and it shall end at the Sea.

6 'As for the western border, you shall
have the Great Sea for a border; this shall be
your western border.

7 'And this shall be your northern border:
From the Great Sea you shall mark out your
border line to Mount Hor; 8 from Mount Hor
you shall mark out *your border* to the entrance of Hamath; then the direction of the
border shall be toward Zedad; 9 the border
shall proceed to Ziphron, and it shall end
at Hazar Enan. This shall be your northern
border.

10 'You shall mark out your eastern border
from Hazar Enan to Shepham; 11 the border
shall go down from Shepham to Riblah on
the east side of Ain; the border shall go down
and reach to the eastern side of the Sea of
Chinnereth; 12 the border shall go down along
the Jordan, and it shall end at the Salt Sea.
This shall be your land with its surrounding
boundaries.'"

13 Then Moses commanded the children
of Israel, saying: "This *is* the land which you
shall inherit by lot, which the LORD has commanded to give to the nine tribes and to the
half-tribe. 14 For the tribe of the children of
Reuben according to the house of their fathers, and the tribe of the children of Gad
according to the house of their fathers, have
received *their inheritance;* and the half-tribe
of Manasseh has received its inheritance.
15 The two tribes and the half-tribe have received their inheritance on this side of the

---

33:45 [a] Same as *Ije Abarim,* verse 44 33:49 [a] Hebrew *Abel Shittim*

Jordan, *across from* Jericho eastward, toward
the sunrise."

The Leaders Appointed to Divide the Land

16 And the LORD spoke to Moses, saying,
17 "These *are* the names of the men who shall
divide the land among you as an inheritance:
Eleazar the priest and Joshua the son of
Nun. 18 And you shall take one leader of every
tribe to divide the land for the inheritance.
19 These *are* the names of the men: from the
tribe of Judah, Caleb the son of Jephunneh;
20 from the tribe of the children of Simeon,
Shemuel the son of Ammihud; 21 from the
tribe of Benjamin, Elidad the son of Chis-
lon; 22 a leader from the tribe of the children of Dan, Bukki the son of Jogli; 23 from
the sons of Joseph: a leader from the tribe
of the children of Manasseh, Hanniel the
son of Ephod, 24 and a leader from the tribe
of the children of Ephraim, Kemuel the son
of Shiphtan; 25 a leader from the tribe of the
children of Zebulun, Elizaphan the son of
Parnach; 26 a leader from the tribe of the children of Issachar, Paltiel the son of Azzan; 27 a
leader from the tribe of the children of Asher, Ahihud the son of Shelomi; 28 and a leader
from the tribe of the children of Naphtali,
Pedahel the son of Ammihud."

29 These *are* the ones the LORD commanded to divide the inheritance among the children of Israel in the land of Canaan.

Cities for the Levites

35 And the LORD spoke to Moses in
the plains of Moab by the Jordan
across from Jericho, saying: 2 "Command
the children of Israel that they give the Levites cities to dwell in from the inheritance
of their possession, and you shall *also* give
the Levites common-land around the cities.
3 They shall have the cities to dwell in; and
their common-land shall be for their cattle,
for their herds, and for all their animals.
4 The common-land of the cities which you
will give the Levites *shall extend* from the
wall of the city outward a thousand cubits all
around. 5 And you shall measure outside the
city on the east side two thousand cubits, on
the south side two thousand cubits, on the
west side two thousand cubits, and on the
north side two thousand cubits. The city *shall
be* in the middle. This shall belong to them
as common-land for the cities.

6 "Now among the cities which you will
give to the Levites *you shall appoint* six cities
of refuge, to which a manslayer may flee.
And to these you shall add forty-two cities.
7 So all the cities you will give to the Levites
shall be forty-eight; these *you shall give* with
their common-land. 8 And the cities which
you will give *shall be* from the possession of
the children of Israel; from the larger *tribe*
you shall give many, from the smaller you
shall give few. Each shall give some of its
cities to the Levites, in proportion to the inheritance that each receives."

Cities of Refuge

9 Then the LORD spoke to Moses, saying,
10 "Speak to the children of Israel, and say to
them: 'When you cross the Jordan into the
land of Canaan, 11 then you shall appoint
cities to be cities of refuge for you, that the
manslayer who kills any person accidentally
may flee there. 12 They shall be cities of refuge for you from the avenger, that the manslayer may not die until he stands before the
congregation in judgment. 13 And of the cities
which you give, you shall have six cities of
refuge. 14 You shall appoint three cities on
this side of the Jordan, and three cities you
shall appoint in the land of Canaan, *which*
will be cities of refuge. 15 These six cities
shall be for refuge for the children of Israel, for the stranger, and for the sojourner
among them, that anyone who kills a person
accidentally may flee there.

16 'But if he strikes him with an iron implement, so that he dies, he *is* a murderer;
the murderer shall surely be put to death.
17 And if he strikes him with a stone in the
hand, by which one could die, and he does
die, he *is* a murderer; the murderer shall
surely be put to death. 18 Or *if* he strikes him
with a wooden hand weapon, by which one
could die, and he does die, he *is* a murderer;
the murderer shall surely be put to death.
19 The avenger of blood himself shall put the
murderer to death; when he meets him, he
shall put him to death. 20 If he pushes him
out of hatred or, while lying in wait, hurls
something at him so that he dies, 21 or in enmity he strikes him with his hand so that he
dies, the one who struck *him* shall surely be
put to death. He *is* a murderer. The avenger of blood shall put the murderer to death
when he meets him.

22 'However, if he pushes him suddenly

The Previous Command to Enter Canaan

1 These *are* the words which Moses spoke
to all Israel on this side of the Jordan in
the wilderness, in the plain[a] opposite Suph,[b]
between Paran, Tophel, Laban, Hazeroth,
and Dizahab. 2*It is* eleven days' *journey* from
Horeb by way of Mount Seir to Kadesh Barnea. 3Now it came to pass in the fortieth year,
in the eleventh month, on the first *day* of the
month, *that* Moses spoke to the children of
Israel according to all that the LORD had giv-
en him as commandments to them, 4after he
had killed Sihon king of the Amorites, who
dwelt in Heshbon, and Og king of Bashan,
who dwelt at Ashtaroth in[a] Edrei.

5On this side of the Jordan in the land
of Moab, Moses began to explain this law,
saying, 6"The LORD our God spoke to us in
Horeb, saying: 'You have dwelt long enough
at this mountain. 7Turn and take your journey, and go to the mountains of the Amorites,
to all the neighboring *places* in the plain,[a] in
the mountains and in the lowland, in the
South and on the seacoast, to the land of the
Canaanites and to Lebanon, as far as the great
river, the River Euphrates. 8See, I have set the
land before you; go in and possess the land
which the LORD swore to your fathers—to
Abraham, Isaac, and Jacob—to give to them
and their descendants after them.'

Tribal Leaders Appointed

9"And I spoke to you at that time, saying:
'I alone am not able to bear you. 10The LORD
your God has multiplied you, and here you *are*
today, as the stars of heaven in multitude. 11May
the LORD God of your fathers make you a thousand times more numerous than you are, and
bless you as He has promised you! 12How can
I alone bear your problems and your burdens
and your complaints? 13Choose wise, understanding, and knowledgeable men from
among your tribes, and I will make them
heads over you.' 14And you answered me and
said, 'The thing which you have told *us* to do
is good.' 15So I took the heads of your tribes,
wise and knowledgeable men, and made
them heads over you, leaders of thousands,
leaders of hundreds, leaders of fifties, leaders of tens, and officers for your tribes.

16"Then I commanded your judges at that
time, saying, 'Hear *the cases* between your
brethren, and judge righteously between a
man and his brother or the stranger who is
with him. 17You shall not show partiality in
judgment; you shall hear the small as well
as the great; you shall not be afraid in any
man's presence, for the judgment *is* God's.
The case that is too hard for you, bring to
me, and I will hear it.' 18And I commanded
you at that time all the things which you
should do.

Israel's Refusal to Enter the Land

19"So we departed from Horeb, and went
through all that great and terrible wilderness
which you saw on the way to the mountains
of the Amorites, as the LORD our God had
commanded us. Then we came to Kadesh
Barnea. 20And I said to you, 'You have come
to the mountains of the Amorites, which the
LORD our God is giving us. 21Look, the LORD
your God has set the land before you; go up
and possess *it*, as the LORD God of your fathers has spoken to you; do not fear or be
discouraged.'

22"And every one of you came near to me
and said, 'Let us send men before us, and

1:1 [a] Hebrew *arabah* [b] One manuscript of the Septuagint, also Targum and Vulgate, read *Red Sea*. 1:4 [a] Septuagint, Syriac, and Vulgate read *and* (compare Joshua 12:4).
1:7 [a] Hebrew *arabah*

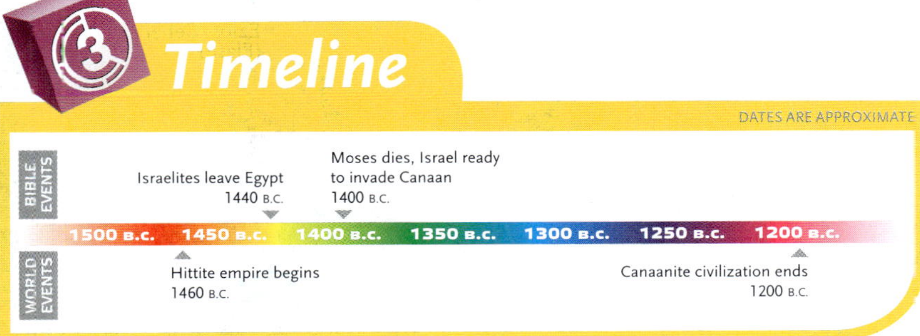

let them search out the land for us, and
bring back word to us of the way by which
we should go up, and of the cities into which
we shall come.'

23"The plan pleased me well; so I took
twelve of your men, one man from *each*
tribe. 24And they departed and went up into
the mountains, and came to the Valley of
Eshcol, and spied it out. 25They also took
some of the fruit of the land in their hands
and brought *it* down to us; and they brought
back word to us, saying, '*It is* a good land
which the LORD our God is giving us.'

26"Nevertheless you would not go up, but
rebelled against the command of the LORD
your God; 27and you complained in your
tents, and said, 'Because the LORD hates us,
He has brought us out of the land of Egypt
to deliver us into the hand of the Amorites,
to destroy us. 28Where can we go up? Our
brethren have discouraged our hearts, saying,
"The people *are* greater and taller than
we; the cities *are* great and fortified up to
heaven; moreover we have seen the sons of
the Anakim there."'

29"Then I said to you, 'Do not be terrified,
or afraid of them. 30The LORD your God, who
goes before you, He will fight for you, according
to all He did for you in Egypt before
your eyes, 31and in the wilderness where you
saw how the LORD your God carried you, as
a man carries his son, in all the way that you
went until you came to this place.' 32Yet, for
all that, you did not believe the LORD your

On Location

From Canaan to Egypt

The Israelites move out of the wilderness and are camped in what is now Jordan, near where the Jordan River empties into the Dead Sea. Soon they will march west and cross the river into Canaan, the land God has promised them. From Mt. Nebo, Moses gets a view of the land.

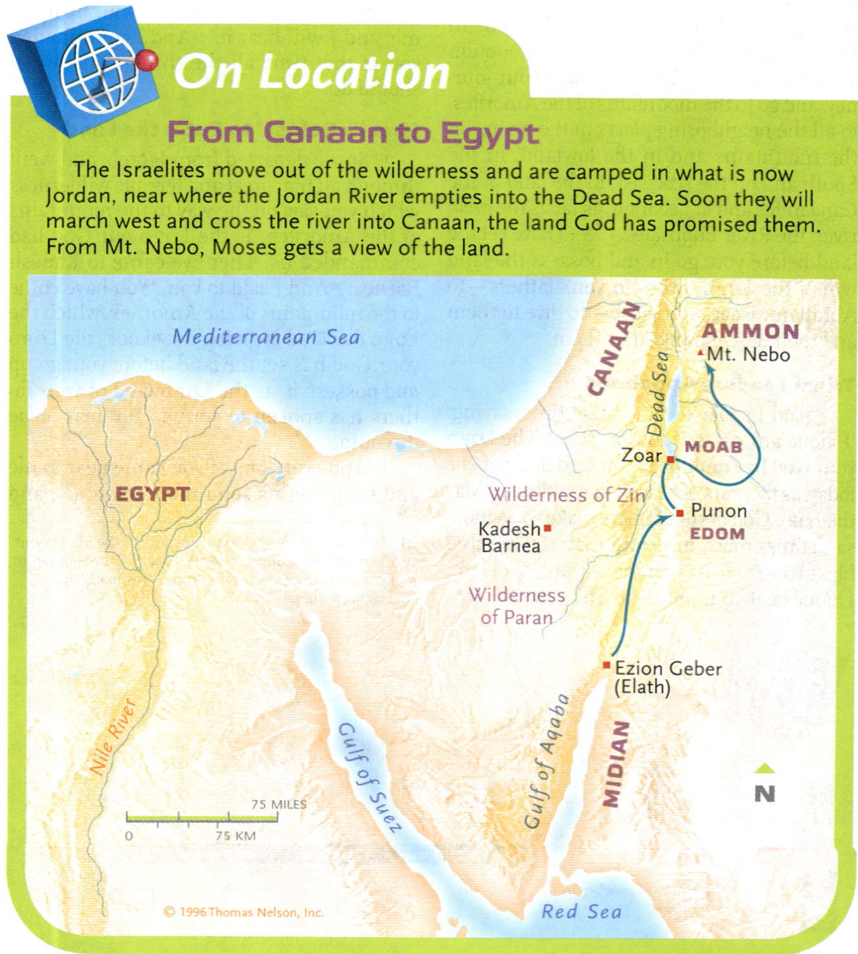

God, 33who went in the way before you to
search out a place for you to pitch your tents,
to show you the way you should go, in the
fire by night and in the cloud by day.

The Penalty for Israel's Rebellion

34"And the LORD heard the sound of your
words, and was angry, and took an oath, saying, 35'Surely not one of these men of this
evil generation shall see that good land of
which I swore to give to your fathers, 36except
Caleb the son of Jephunneh; he shall see it,
and to him and his children I am giving the
land on which he walked, because he wholly followed the LORD.' 37The LORD was also
angry with me for your sakes, saying, 'Even
you shall not go in there. 38Joshua the son of
Nun, who stands before you, he shall go in
there. Encourage him, for he shall cause Israel to inherit it.

39'Moreover your little ones and your children, who you say will be victims, who today
have no knowledge of good and evil, they
shall go in there; to them I will give it, and
they shall possess it. 40But *as for* you, turn
and take your journey into the wilderness by
the Way of the Red Sea.'

41"Then you answered and said to me,
'We have sinned against the LORD; we will
go up and fight, just as the LORD our God
commanded us.' And when everyone of you
had girded on his weapons of war, you were
ready to go up into the mountain.

42"And the LORD said to me, 'Tell them,
"Do not go up nor fight, for I *am* not among
you; lest you be defeated before your enemies."' 43So I spoke to you; yet you would not
listen, but rebelled against the command
of the LORD, and presumptuously went up
into the mountain. 44And the Amorites who
dwelt in that mountain came out against
you and chased you as bees do, and drove
you back from Seir to Hormah. 45Then you
returned and wept before the LORD, but the
LORD would not listen to your voice nor give
ear to you.

46"So you remained in Kadesh many days,
according to the days that you spent *there.*

The Desert Years

2 "Then we turned and journeyed into
the wilderness of the Way of the Red
Sea, as the LORD spoke to me, and we skirted
Mount Seir for many days.

2"And the LORD spoke to me, saying:
3'You have skirted this mountain long
enough; turn northward. 4And command
the people, saying, "You *are about to* pass
through the territory of your brethren, the
descendants of Esau, who live in Seir; and
they will be afraid of you. Therefore watch
yourselves carefully. 5Do not meddle with
them, for I will not give you *any* of their
land, no, not so much as one footstep, because I have given Mount Seir to Esau *as* a
possession. 6You shall buy food from them
with money, that you may eat; and you shall
also buy water from them with money, that
you may drink.

7"For the LORD your God has blessed you
in all the work of your hand. He knows your
trudging through this great wilderness.
These forty years the LORD your God *has
been* with you; you have lacked nothing."'

8"And when we passed beyond our brethren, the descendants of Esau who dwell in
Seir, away from the road of the plain, away
from Elath and Ezion Geber, we turned and
passed by way of the Wilderness of Moab.
9Then the LORD said to me, 'Do not harass
Moab, nor contend with them in battle, for I
will not give you *any* of their land *as* a possession, because I have given Ar to the descendants of Lot *as* a possession.'"

10(The Emim had dwelt there in times
past, a people as great and numerous and tall
as the Anakim. 11They were also regarded as
giants,[a] like the Anakim, but the Moabites
call them Emim. 12The Horites formerly
dwelt in Seir, but the descendants of Esau
dispossessed them and destroyed them from
before them, and dwelt in their place, just
as Israel did to the land of their possession
which the LORD gave them.)

13"'Now rise and cross over the Valley of
the Zered.' So we crossed over the Valley of
the Zered. 14And the time we took to come
from Kadesh Barnea until we crossed over
the Valley of the Zered *was* thirty-eight years,
until all the generation of the men of war
was consumed from the midst of the camp,
just as the LORD had sworn to them. 15For
indeed the hand of the LORD was against
them, to destroy them from the midst of the
camp until they were consumed.

16"So it was, when all the men of war had
finally perished from among the people,
17that the LORD spoke to me, saying: 18'This

2:11 [a] Hebrew *rephaim*

day you are to cross over at Ar, the boundary of Moab. 19And *when* you come near the
people of Ammon, do not harass them or
meddle with them, for I will not give you
any of the land of the people of Ammon *as*
a possession, because I have given it to the
descendants of Lot *as* a possession.'"

20(That was also regarded as a land of
giants;[a] giants formerly dwelt there. But the
Ammonites call them Zamzummim, 21a
people as great and numerous and tall as the
Anakim. But the LORD destroyed them before them, and they dispossessed them and
dwelt in their place, 22just as He had done for
the descendants of Esau, who dwelt in Seir,
when He destroyed the Horites from before
them. They dispossessed them and dwelt in
their place, even to this day. 23And the Avim,
who dwelt in villages as far as Gaza—the
Caphtorim, who came from Caphtor, destroyed them and dwelt in their place.)

24"'Rise, take your journey, and cross over
the River Arnon. Look, I have given into your
hand Sihon the Amorite, king of Heshbon,
and his land. Begin to possess *it*, and engage
him in battle. 25This day I will begin to put
the dread and fear of you upon the nations
under the whole heaven, who shall hear the
report of you, and shall tremble and be in
anguish because of you.'

King Sihon Defeated

26"And I sent messengers from the Wilderness of Kedemoth to Sihon king of Heshbon, with words of peace, saying, 27'Let me
pass through your land; I will keep strictly to
the road, and I will turn neither to the right
nor to the left. 28You shall sell me food for
money, that I may eat, and give me water for
money, that I may drink; only let me pass
through on foot, 29just as the descendants
of Esau who dwell in Seir and the Moabites
who dwell in Ar did for me, until I cross the
Jordan to the land which the LORD our God
is giving us.'

30"But Sihon king of Heshbon would not
let us pass through, for the LORD your God
hardened his spirit and made his heart obstinate, that He might deliver him into your
hand, as *it is* this day.

31"And the LORD said to me, 'See, I have
begun to give Sihon and his land over to you.
Begin to possess *it*, that you may inherit his
land.' 32Then Sihon and all his people came
out against us to fight at Jahaz. 33And the
LORD our God delivered him over to us; so
we defeated him, his sons, and all his people.
34We took all his cities at that time, and we
utterly destroyed the men, women, and little
ones of every city; we left none remaining.
35We took only the livestock as plunder for
ourselves, with the spoil of the cities which
we took. 36From Aroer, which *is* on the bank
of the River Arnon, and *from* the city that
is in the ravine, as far as Gilead, there was
not one city too strong for us; the LORD our
God delivered all to us. 37Only you did not
go near the land of the people of Ammon—
anywhere along the River Jabbok, or to the
cities of the mountains, or wherever the
LORD our God had forbidden us.

King Og Defeated

3 "Then we turned and went up the road
to Bashan; and Og king of Bashan
came out against us, he and all his people, to
battle at Edrei. 2And the LORD said to me, 'Do
not fear him, for I have delivered him and all
his people and his land into your hand; you
shall do to him as you did to Sihon king of
the Amorites, who dwelt at Heshbon.'

3"So the LORD our God also delivered into
our hands Og king of Bashan, with all his
people, and we attacked him until he had no
survivors remaining. 4And we took all his
cities at that time; there was not a city which
we did not take from them: sixty cities, all
the region of Argob, the kingdom of Og in
Bashan. 5All these cities *were* fortified with
high walls, gates, and bars, besides a great
many rural towns. 6And we utterly destroyed
them, as we did to Sihon king of Heshbon,
utterly destroying the men, women, and
children of every city. 7But all the livestock
and the spoil of the cities we took as booty
for ourselves.

8"And at that time we took the land from
the hand of the two kings of the Amorites
who *were* on this side of the Jordan, from the
River Arnon to Mount Hermon 9(the Sidonians call Hermon Sirion, and the Amorites
call it Senir), 10all the cities of the plain, all
Gilead, and all Bashan, as far as Salcah and
Edrei, cities of the kingdom of Og in Bashan.

11"For only Og king of Bashan remained
of the remnant of the giants.[a] Indeed his
bedstead *was* an iron bedstead. (*Is* it not in
Rabbah of the people of Ammon?) Nine

2:20 [a] Hebrew *rephaim*   3:11 [a] Hebrew *rephaim*

cubits *is* its length and four cubits its width,
according to the standard cubit.

The Land East of the Jordan Divided

12“And this land, *which* we possessed at
that time, from Aroer, which *is* by the River Arnon, and half the mountains of Gilead
and its cities, I gave to the Reubenites and
the Gadites. 13The rest of Gilead, and all
Bashan, the kingdom of Og, I gave to half
the tribe of Manasseh. (All the region of Argob, with all Bashan, was called the land of
the giants.[a] 14Jair the son of Manasseh took
all the region of Argob, as far as the border
of the Geshurites and the Maachathites, and
called Bashan after his own name, Havoth
Jair,[a] to this day.)
15“Also I gave Gilead to Machir. 16And to
the Reubenites and the Gadites I gave from
Gilead as far as the River Arnon, the middle
of the river as *the* border, as far as the River
Jabbok, the border of the people of Ammon;
17the plain also, with the Jordan as *the* border,
from Chinnereth as far as the east side of the
Sea of the Arabah (the Salt Sea), below the
slopes of Pisgah.
18“Then I commanded you at that time,
saying: ‘The LORD your God has given you
this land to possess. All you men of valor
shall cross over armed before your brethren, the children of Israel. 19But your wives,
your little ones, and your livestock (I know
that you have much livestock) shall stay in
your cities which I have given you, 20until the
LORD has given rest to your brethren as to
you, and they also possess the land which
the LORD your God is giving them beyond
the Jordan. Then each of you may return to
his possession which I have given you.’
21“And I commanded Joshua at that
time, saying, ‘Your eyes have seen all that
the LORD your God has done to these two
kings; so will the LORD do to all the kingdoms through which you pass. 22You must
not fear them, for the LORD your God Himself *fights for you.*’

Moses Forbidden to Enter the Land

23“Then I pleaded with the LORD at that
time, saying: 24‘O Lord GOD, You have begun to show Your servant Your greatness
and Your mighty hand, for what god *is there*
in heaven or on earth who can do *anything*
like Your works and Your mighty *deeds?* 25I
pray, let me cross over and see the good land
beyond the Jordan, those pleasant mountains, and Lebanon.’
26“But the LORD was angry with me on
your account, and would not listen to me. So
the LORD said to me: ‘Enough of that! Speak
no more to Me of this matter. 27Go up to the
top of Pisgah, and lift your eyes toward the
west, the north, the south, and the east; behold *it* with your eyes, for you shall not cross
over this Jordan. 28But command Joshua, and
encourage him and strengthen him; for he
shall go over before this people, and he shall
cause them to inherit the land which you
will see.’
29“So we stayed in the valley opposite
Beth Peor.

Moses Commands Obedience

4 “Now, O Israel, listen to the statutes
and the judgments which I teach you
to observe, that you may live, and go in and
possess the land which the LORD God of
your fathers is giving you. 2You shall not
add to the word which I command you, nor
take from it, that you may keep the commandments of the LORD your God which I
command you. 3Your eyes have seen what
the LORD did at Baal Peor; for the LORD your
God has destroyed from among you all the
men who followed Baal of Peor. 4But you
who held fast to the LORD your God *are* alive
today, every one of you.
5“Surely I have taught you statutes and
judgments, just as the LORD my God commanded me, that you should act according
to them in the land which you go to possess.
6Therefore be careful to observe *them;* for
this *is* your wisdom and your understanding in the sight of the peoples who will hear
all these statutes, and say, ‘Surely this great
nation *is* a wise and understanding people.’
7“For what great nation *is there* that has
God *so* near to it, as the LORD our God *is* to
us, for whatever *reason* we may call upon
Him? 8And what great nation *is there* that
has *such* statutes and righteous judgments
as are in all this law which I set before you
this day? 9Only take heed to yourself, and
diligently keep yourself, lest you forget the
things your eyes have seen, and lest they depart from your heart all the days of your life.
And teach them to your children and your
grandchildren, 10*especially concerning* the

3:13 [a] Hebrew *rephaim* 3:14 [a] Literally *Towns of Jair*

day you stood before the LORD your God in
Horeb, when the LORD said to me, 'Gather
the people to Me, and I will let them hear My
words, that they may learn to fear Me all the
days they live on the earth, and *that* they may
teach their children.'

11"Then you came near and stood at the
foot of the mountain, and the mountain
burned with fire to the midst of heaven, with
darkness, cloud, and thick darkness. 12And
the LORD spoke to you out of the midst of
the fire. You heard the sound of the words,
but saw no form; *you* only *heard* a voice. 13So
He declared to you His covenant which He
commanded you to perform, the Ten Commandments; and He wrote them on two
tablets of stone. 14And the LORD commanded me at that time to teach you statutes and
judgments, that you might observe them in
the land which you cross over to possess.

Beware of Idolatry

15"Take careful heed to yourselves, for you
saw no form when the LORD spoke to you
at Horeb out of the midst of the fire, 16lest
you act corruptly and make for yourselves a
carved image in the form of any figure: the
likeness of male or female, 17the likeness of
any animal that *is* on the earth or the likeness of any winged bird that flies in the air,
18the likeness of anything that creeps on the
ground or the likeness of any fish that *is* in
the water beneath the earth. 19And *take heed,*
lest you lift your eyes to heaven, and *when*
you see the sun, the moon, and the stars, all
the host of heaven, you feel driven to worship them and serve them, which the LORD
your God has given to all the peoples under
the whole heaven as a heritage. 20But the
LORD has taken you and brought you out of
the iron furnace, out of Egypt, to be His people, an inheritance, as you are this day. 21Fur-
thermore the LORD was angry with me for
your sakes, and swore that I would not cross
over the Jordan, and that I would not enter
the good land which the LORD your God is
giving you as an inheritance. 22But I must
die in this land, I must not cross over the
Jordan; but you shall cross over and possess
that good land. 23Take heed to yourselves,
lest you forget the covenant of the LORD your
God which He made with you, and make
for yourselves a carved image in the form
of anything which the LORD your God has
forbidden you. 24For the LORD your God *is* a
consuming fire, a jealous God.

25"When you beget children and grandchildren and have grown old in the land, and
act corruptly and make a carved image in the
form of anything, and do evil in the sight of
the LORD your God to provoke Him to anger,
26I call heaven and earth to witness against
you this day, that you will soon utterly perish from the land which you cross over the
Jordan to possess; you will not prolong *your*
days in it, but will be utterly destroyed. 27And
the LORD will scatter you among the peoples,
and you will be left few in number among
the nations where the LORD will drive you.
28And there you will serve gods, the work of
men's hands, wood and stone, which neither
see nor hear nor eat nor smell. 29But from
there you will seek the LORD your God, and
you will find *Him* if you seek Him with all
your heart and with all your soul. 30When
you are in distress, and all these things come
upon you in the latter days, when you turn to
the LORD your God and obey His voice 31(for
the LORD your God *is* a merciful God), He
will not forsake you nor destroy you, nor forget the covenant of your fathers which He
swore to them.

32"For ask now concerning the days that
are past, which were before you, since the
day that God created man on the earth, and
ask from one end of heaven to the other,
whether *any* great *thing* like this has happened, or *anything* like it has been heard.
33Did *any* people *ever* hear the voice of God
speaking out of the midst of the fire, as you
have heard, and live? 34Or did God *ever* try to
go *and* take for Himself a nation from the
midst of *another* nation, by trials, by signs,
by wonders, by war, by a mighty hand and
an outstretched arm, and by great terrors, according to all that the LORD your God did for
you in Egypt before your eyes? 35To you it was
shown, that you might know that the LORD
Himself *is* God; *there is* none other besides
Him. 36Out of heaven He let you hear His
voice, that He might instruct you; on earth
He showed you His great fire, and you heard
His words out of the midst of the fire. 37And
because He loved your fathers, therefore He
chose their descendants after them; and He
brought you out of Egypt with His Presence,
with His mighty power, 38driving out from
before you nations greater and mightier than

you, to bring you in, to give you their land *as*
an inheritance, as *it is* this day. 39Therefore
know this day, and consider *it* in your heart,
that the LORD Himself *is* God in heaven
above and on the earth beneath; *there is* no
other. 40You shall therefore keep His statutes
and His commandments which I command
you today, that it may go well with you and
with your children after you, and that you
may prolong *your* days in the land which the
LORD your God is giving you for all time."

Cities of Refuge East of the Jordan

41Then Moses set apart three cities on
this side of the Jordan, toward the rising
of the sun, 42that the manslayer might flee
there, who kills his neighbor unintentionally, without having hated him in time past,
and that by fleeing to one of these cities he
might live: 43Bezer in the wilderness on the
plateau for the Reubenites, Ramoth in Gilead for the Gadites, and Golan in Bashan for
the Manassites.

Introduction to God's Law

44Now this *is* the law which Moses set
before the children of Israel. 45These *are* the
testimonies, the statutes, and the judgments
which Moses spoke to the children of Israel
after they came out of Egypt, 46on this side of
the Jordan, in the valley opposite Beth Peor,
in the land of Sihon king of the Amorites,
who dwelt at Heshbon, whom Moses and the
children of Israel defeated after they came
out of Egypt. 47And they took possession of
his land and the land of Og king of Bashan,
two kings of the Amorites, who *were* on this
side of the Jordan, toward the rising of the
sun, 48from Aroer, which *is* on the bank of
the River Arnon, even to Mount Sion[a] (that
is, Hermon), 49and all the plain on the east
side of the Jordan as far as the Sea of the Arabah, below the slopes of Pisgah.

The Ten Commandments Reviewed

5 And Moses called all Israel, and said to
them: "Hear, O Israel, the statutes and
judgments which I speak in your hearing today, that you may learn them and be careful
to observe them. 2The LORD our God made
a covenant with us in Horeb. 3The LORD did
not make this covenant with our fathers, but
with us, those who *are* here today, all of us
who *are* alive. 4The LORD talked with you
face to face on the mountain from the midst
of the fire. 5I stood between the LORD and
you at that time, to declare to you the word
of the LORD; for you were afraid because of
the fire, and you did not go up the mountain.
He said:

6 'I *am* the LORD your God who brought
you out of the land of Egypt, out of the
house of bondage.

7 'You shall have no other gods before Me.

8 'You shall not make for yourself a carved
image—any likeness *of anything* that
is in heaven above, or that *is* in the
earth beneath, or that *is* in the water
under the earth; 9you shall not bow
down to them nor serve them. For I,
the LORD your God, *am* a jealous God,
visiting the iniquity of the fathers
upon the children to the third and
fourth *generations* of those who hate
Me, 10but showing mercy to thousands,

4:48 [a] Syriac reads *Sirion* (compare 3:9).

THE VALUE OF WORDS

READ IT: DEUTERONOMY 5:11

When something is done "in vain," it means it's pointless. Because God's name carries so much power, we should use it freely but carefully. Deuteronomy 5:11 makes this clear. God hears each time His name is used, and if we use it carelessly or for evil, He hears, and we are responsible.

to those who love Me and keep My commandments.
11 'You shall not take the name of the LORD your God in vain, for the LORD will not hold *him* guiltless who takes His name in vain.
12 'Observe the Sabbath day, to keep it holy, as the LORD your God commanded
you. 13Six days you shall labor and do
all your work, 14but the seventh day *is*
the Sabbath of the LORD your God. *In it* you shall do no work: you, nor your son, nor your daughter, nor your male servant, nor your female servant, nor your ox, nor your donkey, nor any of your cattle, nor your stranger who *is* within your gates, that your male servant and your female servant may rest
as well as you. 15And remember that
you were a slave in the land of Egypt, and the LORD your God brought you out from there by a mighty hand and by an outstretched arm; therefore the LORD your God commanded you to keep the Sabbath day.
16 'Honor your father and your mother, as the LORD your God has commanded you, that your days may be long, and that it may be well with you in the land which the LORD your God is giving you.
17 'You shall not murder.
18 'You shall not commit adultery.
19 'You shall not steal.
20 'You shall not bear false witness against your neighbor.
21 'You shall not covet your neighbor's wife; and you shall not desire your neighbor's house, his field, his male servant, his female servant, his ox, his donkey, or anything that *is* your neighbor's.'

22"These words the LORD spoke to all your assembly, in the mountain from the midst of the fire, the cloud, and the thick darkness, with a loud voice; and He added no more. And He wrote them on two tablets of stone and gave them to me.

The People Afraid of God's Presence

23"So it was, when you heard the voice from the midst of the darkness, while the mountain was burning with fire, that you came near to me, all the heads of your tribes
and your elders. 24And you said: 'Surely the
LORD our God has shown us His glory and

Epic Ideas

5:32, 33 WHY GOD GAVE US THE TEN COMMANDMENTS

RED LIGHT AHEAD! says the sign. Without good warning signs, our lives can be ruined. Good rules of the road show us the way around the places we can be hurt.

As you study God's Ten Rules (or Commandments) you will see that they aren't just ten separate rules. They are all linked together by one goal—that we may enjoy God and the world that God made. If you think carefully, you can see that people who break God's laws get into a lot of trouble.

When you make something with your hands you know that you made it to bring you joy. God also made you so you could bring Him joy, and since He is our Creator, He knows what is best for us and what will do *us harm.* He made rules so that we could be the best we can possibly be. When you keep God's commands, you are being the person God planned for you to be. That pleases Him, and then you are happy, too.

His greatness, and we have heard His voice
from the midst of the fire. We have seen
this day that God speaks with man; yet he
still lives. 25 Now therefore, why should we
die? For this great fire will consume us; if
we hear the voice of the LORD our God anymore, then we shall die. 26 For who *is there* of
all flesh who has heard the voice of the living
God speaking from the midst of the fire, as
we *have,* and lived? 27 You go near and hear all
that the LORD our God may say, and tell us
all that the LORD our God says to you, and we
will hear and do *it.*'

28 "Then the LORD heard the voice of your
words when you spoke to me, and the LORD
said to me: 'I have heard the voice of the
words of this people which they have spoken
to you. They are right *in* all that they have
spoken. 29 Oh, that they had such a heart in
them that they would fear Me and always
keep all My commandments, that it might
be well with them and with their children
forever! 30 Go and say to them, "Return to
your tents." 31 But as for you, stand here by
Me, and I will speak to you all the commandments, the statutes, and the judgments
which you shall teach them, that they may
observe *them* in the land which I am giving
them to possess.'

32 "Therefore you shall be careful to do as
the LORD your God has commanded you;
you shall not turn aside to the right hand or
to the left. 33 You shall walk in all the ways
which the LORD your God has commanded
you, that you may live and *that it may be* well
with you, and *that* you may prolong *your* days
in the land which you shall possess.

The Greatest Commandment

6 "Now this *is* the commandment, *and
these are* the statutes and judgments
which the LORD your God has commanded
to teach you, that you may observe *them* in
the land which you are crossing over to possess, 2 that you may fear the LORD your God,
to keep all His statutes and His commandments which I command you, you and your
son and your grandson, all the days of your
life, and that your days may be prolonged.
3 Therefore hear, O Israel, and be careful to
observe *it,* that it may be well with you, and
that you may multiply greatly as the LORD
God of your fathers has promised you—'a
land flowing with milk and honey.'[a]

4 "Hear, O Israel: The LORD our God, the
LORD *is* one![a] 5 You shall love the LORD your
God with all your heart, with all your soul,
and with all your strength.

6:3 [a] Exodus 3:8 6:4 [a] Or *The LORD is our God, the LORD alone* (that is, the only one)

THE GREAT COMMANDMENT

READ IT: DEUTERONOMY 6:5

When Jesus was asked about the greatest commandment, He used the words of Deuteronomy 6:5: "You shall love the LORD your God with all your heart, with all your soul, and with all your strength."

Don't miss the best in life. You will miss the best if you don't obey this great commandment. Knowing and loving God is worth more than the greatest treasure you can think of. Why is this true? Because God Himself is the Author and Giver of everything you now have or ever will have. Nothing you own can bring you happiness if you do not love God.

Decide now to love God "with all your heart"—that is, with all your mind, feelings, and decisions. Also, love Him with all your life—that is, with all your actions. Finally, love God with all your might—that is, with all the strength you have.

In Focus

6:5 Love An attitude that leads to the behavior Paul describes in 1 Corinthians 13. Christian love is not selfish, but always seeks the best for everybody. Such love is the greatest gift of God.

6"And these words which I command you
today shall be in your heart. 7You shall teach
them diligently to your children, and shall
talk of them when you sit in your house,
when you walk by the way, when you lie
down, and when you rise up. 8You shall bind
them as a sign on your hand, and they shall
be as frontlets between your eyes. 9You shall
write them on the doorposts of your house
and on your gates.

Caution Against Disobedience

10"So it shall be, when the LORD your
God brings you into the land of which He
swore to your fathers, to Abraham, Isaac,
and Jacob, to give you large and beautiful
cities which you did not build, 11houses
full of all good things, which you did not
fill, hewn-out wells which you did not dig,
vineyards and olive trees which you did not
plant—when you have eaten and are full—
12*then* beware, lest you forget the LORD who
brought you out of the land of Egypt, from
the house of bondage. 13You shall fear the
LORD your God and serve Him, and shall
take oaths in His name. 14You shall not go
after other gods, the gods of the peoples who
are all around you 15(for the LORD your God *is*
a jealous God among you), lest the anger of
the LORD your God be aroused against you
and destroy you from the face of the earth.

16"You shall not tempt the LORD your God
as you tempted *Him* in Massah. 17You shall
diligently keep the commandments of the
LORD your God, His testimonies, and His
statutes which He has commanded you.
18And you shall do *what is* right and good
in the sight of the LORD, that it may be well
with you, and that you may go in and possess
the good land of which the LORD swore to
your fathers, 19to cast out all your enemies
from before you, as the LORD has spoken.

20"When your son asks you in time to
come, saying, 'What *is the meaning of* the testimonies, the statutes, and the judgments
which the LORD our God has commanded
you?' 21then you shall say to your son: 'We
were slaves of Pharaoh in Egypt, and the
LORD brought us out of Egypt with a mighty
hand; 22and the LORD showed signs and
wonders before our eyes, great and severe,
against Egypt, Pharaoh, and all his household. 23Then He brought us out from there,
that He might bring us in, to give us the land
of which He swore to our fathers. 24And the
LORD commanded us to observe all these
statutes, to fear the LORD our God, for our
good always, that He might preserve us
alive, as *it is* this day. 25Then it will be righteousness for us, if we are careful to observe
all these commandments before the LORD
our God, as He has commanded us.'

A Chosen People

7 "When the LORD your God brings you
into the land which you go to possess,
and has cast out many nations before you,
the Hittites and the Girgashites and the Amorites and the Canaanites and the Perizzites
and the Hivites and the Jebusites, seven nations greater and mightier than you, 2and
when the LORD your God delivers them over
to you, you shall conquer them *and* utterly
destroy them. You shall make no covenant
with them nor show mercy to them. 3Nor
shall you make marriages with them. You
shall not give your daughter to their son, nor
take their daughter for your son. 4For they
will turn your sons away from following
Me, to serve other gods; so the anger of the
LORD will be aroused against you and destroy you suddenly. 5But thus you shall deal
with them: you shall destroy their altars,
and break down their *sacred* pillars, and cut
down their wooden images,[a] and burn their
carved images with fire.

6"For you *are* a holy people to the LORD
your God; the LORD your God has chosen
you to be a people for Himself, a special
treasure above all the peoples on the face of
the earth. 7The LORD did not set His love on
you nor choose you because you were more
in number than any other people, for you

7:5 [a] Hebrew *Asherim*, Canaanite deities

were the least of all peoples; 8but because the LORD loves you, and because He would keep the oath which He swore to your fathers, the LORD has brought you out with a mighty hand, and redeemed you from the house of bondage, from the hand of Pharaoh king of Egypt.

9"Therefore know that the LORD your God, He *is* God, the faithful God who keeps covenant and mercy for a thousand generations with those who love Him and keep His commandments; 10and He repays those who hate Him to their face, to destroy them. He will not be slack with him who hates Him; He will repay him to his face. 11Therefore you shall keep the commandment, the statutes, and the judgments which I command you today, to observe them.

Blessings of Obedience

12"Then it shall come to pass, because you listen to these judgments, and keep and do them, that the LORD your God will keep with you the covenant and the mercy which He swore to your fathers. 13And He will love you and bless you and multiply you; He will also bless the fruit of your womb and the fruit of your land, your grain and your new wine and your oil, the increase of your cattle and the offspring of your flock, in the land of which He swore to your fathers to give you. 14You shall be blessed above all peoples; there shall not be a male or female barren among you or among your livestock. 15And the LORD will take away from you all sickness, and will afflict you with none of the terrible diseases of Egypt which you have known, but will lay *them* on all those who hate you. 16Also you shall destroy all the peoples whom the LORD your God delivers over to you; your eye shall have no pity on them; nor shall you serve their gods, for that *will be* a snare to you.

17"If you should say in your heart, 'These nations are greater than I; how can I dispossess them?'— 18you shall not be afraid of them, *but* you shall remember well what the LORD your God did to Pharaoh and to all Egypt: 19the great trials which your eyes saw, the signs and the wonders, the mighty hand and the outstretched arm, by which the LORD your God brought you out. So shall the LORD your God do to all the peoples of whom you are afraid. 20Moreover the LORD your God will send the hornet among them until those who are left, who hide themselves from you, are destroyed. 21You shall not be terrified of them; for the LORD your God, the great and awesome God, *is* among you. 22And the LORD your God will drive out those nations before you little by little; you will be unable to destroy them at once, lest the beasts of the field become *too* numerous for you. 23But the LORD your God will deliver them over to you, and will inflict defeat upon them until they are destroyed. 24And He will deliver their kings into your hand, and you will destroy their name from under heaven; no one shall be able to stand against you until you have destroyed them. 25You shall burn the carved images of their gods with fire; you shall not covet the silver or gold *that is* on them, nor take *it* for yourselves, lest you be snared by it; for it *is* an abomination to the LORD your God. 26Nor shall you bring an abomination into your house, lest you be doomed to destruction like it. You shall utterly detest it and utterly abhor it, for it *is* an accursed thing.

Remember the LORD Your God

8 "Every commandment which I command you today you must be careful to observe, that you may live and multiply, and go in and possess the land of which the LORD swore to your fathers. 2And you shall remember that the LORD your God led you all the way these forty years in the wilderness, to humble you *and* test you, to know what *was* in your heart, whether you would keep His commandments or not. 3So He humbled you, allowed you to hunger, and fed you with manna which you did not know nor did your fathers know, that He might make you know that man shall not live by bread alone; but man lives by every *word* that proceeds from the mouth of the LORD. 4Your garments did not wear out on you, nor did your foot swell these forty years. 5You should know in your heart that as a man chastens his son, *so* the LORD your God chastens you.

6"Therefore you shall keep the commandments of the LORD your God, to walk in His ways and to fear Him. 7For the LORD your God is bringing you into a good land, a land of brooks of water, of fountains and springs, that flow out of valleys and hills; 8a land of wheat and barley, of vines and fig trees and pomegranates, a land of olive oil and honey; 9a land in which you will eat bread without scarcity, in which you will lack nothing; a

land whose stones *are* iron and out of whose
hills you can dig copper. 10When you have
eaten and are full, then you shall bless the
LORD your God for the good land which He
has given you.

11"Beware that you do not forget the LORD
your God by not keeping His commandments,
His judgments, and His statutes
which I command you today, 12lest—*when*
you have eaten and are full, and have built
beautiful houses and dwell *in them;* 13and
when your herds and your flocks multiply,
and your silver and your gold are multiplied,
and all that you have is multiplied; 14when
your heart is lifted up, and you forget the
LORD your God who brought you out of the
land of Egypt, from the house of bondage;
15who led you through that great and terrible
wilderness, *in which were* fiery serpents and
scorpions and thirsty land where there was
no water; who brought water for you out of
the flinty rock; 16who fed you in the wilderness
with manna, which your fathers did
not know, that He might humble you and
that He might test you, to do you good in the
end— 17then you say in your heart, 'My power
and the might of my hand have gained me
this wealth.'

18"And you shall remember the LORD
your God, for *it is* He who gives you power
to get wealth, that He may establish His covenant
which He swore to your fathers, as *it
is* this day. 19Then it shall be, if you by any
means forget the LORD your God, and follow
other gods, and serve them and worship
them, I testify against you this day that you
shall surely perish. 20As the nations which
the LORD destroys before you, so you shall
perish, because you would not be obedient
to the voice of the LORD your God.

Israel's Rebellions Reviewed

9 "Hear, O Israel: You *are* to cross over
the Jordan today, and go in to dispossess
nations greater and mightier than yourself,
cities great and fortified up to heaven, 2a
people great and tall, the descendants of the
Anakim, whom you know, and *of whom* you
heard *it said,* 'Who can stand before the descendants
of Anak?' 3Therefore understand
today that the LORD your God *is* He who goes
over before you *as* a consuming fire. He will
destroy them and bring them down before
you; so you shall drive them out and destroy
them quickly, as the LORD has said to you.

4"Do not think in your heart, after the
LORD your God has cast them out before
you, saying, 'Because of my righteousness
the LORD has brought me in to possess this
land'; but *it is* because of the wickedness of
these nations *that* the LORD is driving them
out from before you. 5*It is* not because of your
righteousness or the uprightness of your
heart *that* you go in to possess their land, but
because of the wickedness of these nations
that the LORD your God drives them out
from before you, and that He may fulfill the
word which the LORD swore to your fathers,
to Abraham, Isaac, and Jacob. 6Therefore

ATTITUDES

READ IT: DEUTERONOMY 8:6–20

Ever raise your hand in class and then forget what you were going to say? No big deal, right? Maybe you got a little embarrassed. Check out God's thoughts about remembering the important stuff. Moses reminded the Israelites about what God had done for them and what waited just around the corner in the Promised Land. Moses emphasized their need *to remember* God's gifts and to avoid pride. Whether it's your skill on the court or the field, your ability in the classroom, or your talent in music or art, those gifts are all truly given by God. He deserves our thanks!

understand that the LORD your God is not
giving you this good land to possess because
of your righteousness, for you *are* a stiff-
necked people.

7"Remember! Do not forget how you provoked the LORD your God to wrath in the
wilderness. From the day that you departed
from the land of Egypt until you came to this
place, you have been rebellious against the
LORD. 8Also in Horeb you provoked the LORD
to wrath, so that the LORD was angry *enough*
with you to have destroyed you. 9When I
went up into the mountain to receive the
tablets of stone, the tablets of the covenant
which the LORD made with you, then I stayed
on the mountain forty days and forty nights.
I neither ate bread nor drank water. 10Then
the LORD delivered to me two tablets of stone
written with the finger of God, and on them
were all the words which the LORD had spoken to you on the mountain from the midst
of the fire in the day of the assembly. 11And
it came to pass, at the end of forty days and
forty nights, *that* the LORD gave me the two
tablets of stone, the tablets of the covenant.

12"Then the LORD said to me, 'Arise,
go down quickly from here, for your people whom you brought out of Egypt have
acted corruptly; they have quickly turned
aside from the way which I commanded
them; they have made themselves a molded image.'

13"Furthermore the LORD spoke to me,
saying, 'I have seen this people, and indeed
they are a stiff-necked people. 14Let Me
alone, that I may destroy them and blot out
their name from under heaven; and I will
make of you a nation mightier and greater
than they.'

15"So I turned and came down from the
mountain, and the mountain burned with
fire; and the two tablets of the covenant
were in my two hands. 16And I looked, and
behold, you had sinned against the LORD
your God—had made for yourselves a
molded calf! You had turned aside quickly
from the way which the LORD had commanded you. 17Then I took the two tablets
and threw them out of my two hands and
broke them before your eyes. 18And I fell
down before the LORD, as at the first, forty
days and forty nights; I neither ate bread
nor drank water, because of all your sin
which you committed in doing wickedly
in the sight of the LORD, to provoke Him
to anger. 19For I was afraid of the anger
and hot displeasure with which the LORD
was angry with you, to destroy you. But
the LORD listened to me at that time also.
20And the LORD was very angry with Aaron
and would have destroyed him; so I prayed
for Aaron also at the same time. 21Then I
took your sin, the calf which you had made,
and burned it with fire and crushed it *and*
ground *it* very small, until it was as fine
as dust; and I threw its dust into the brook
that descended from the mountain.

22"Also at Taberah and Massah and
Kibroth Hattaavah you provoked the LORD
to wrath. 23Likewise, when the LORD sent
you from Kadesh Barnea, saying, 'Go up
and possess the land which I have given
you,' then you rebelled against the commandment of the LORD your God, and you
did not believe Him nor obey His voice.
24You have been rebellious against the
LORD from the day that I knew you.

25"Thus I prostrated myself before the
LORD; forty days and forty nights I kept pros-
trating myself, because the LORD had said He
would destroy you. 26Therefore I prayed to the
LORD, and said: 'O Lord GOD, do not destroy
Your people and Your inheritance whom
You have redeemed through Your greatness,
whom You have brought out of Egypt with
a mighty hand. 27Remember Your servants,
Abraham, Isaac, and Jacob; do not look on
the stubbornness of this people, or on their
wickedness or their sin, 28lest the land from
which You brought us should say, "Because
the LORD was not able to bring them to the
land which He promised them, and because
He hated them, He has brought them out to
kill them in the wilderness." 29Yet they *are*
Your people and Your inheritance, whom
You brought out by Your mighty power and
by Your outstretched arm.'

The Second Pair of Tablets

10 "At that time the LORD said to me,
'Hew for yourself two tablets of
stone like the first, and come up to Me on
the mountain and make yourself an ark of
wood. 2And I will write on the tablets the
words that were on the first tablets, which
you broke; and you shall put them in the ark.'

3"So I made an ark of acacia wood, hewed
two tablets of stone like the first, and went
up the mountain, having the two tablets in

my hand. 4And He wrote on the tablets according to the first writing, the Ten Commandments, which the LORD had spoken to you in the mountain from the midst of the fire in the day of the assembly; and the LORD gave them to me. 5Then I turned and came down from the mountain, and put the tablets in the ark which I had made; and there they are, just as the LORD commanded me."

6(Now the children of Israel journeyed from the wells of Bene Jaakan to Moserah, where Aaron died, and where he was buried; and Eleazar his son ministered as priest in his stead. 7From there they journeyed to Gudgodah, and from Gudgodah to Jotbathah, a land of rivers of water. 8At that time the LORD separated the tribe of Levi to bear the ark of the covenant of the LORD, to stand before the LORD to minister to Him and to bless in His name, to this day. 9Therefore Levi has no portion nor inheritance with his brethren; the LORD *is* his inheritance, just as the LORD your God promised him.)

10"As at the first time, I stayed in the mountain forty days and forty nights; the LORD also heard me at that time, *and* the LORD chose not to destroy you. 11Then the LORD said to me, 'Arise, begin *your* journey before the people, that they may go in and possess the land which I swore to their fathers to give them.'

The Essence of the Law

12"And now, Israel, what does the LORD your God require of you, but to fear the LORD your God, to walk in all His ways and to love Him, to serve the LORD your God with all your heart and with all your soul, 13*and* to keep the commandments of the LORD and His statutes which I command you today for your good? 14Indeed heaven and the highest heavens belong to the LORD your God, *also* the earth with all that *is* in it. 15The LORD delighted only in your fathers, to love them; and He chose their descendants after them, you above all peoples, as *it is* this day. 16Therefore circumcise the foreskin of your heart, and be stiff-necked no longer. 17For the LORD your God *is* God of gods and Lord of lords, the great God, mighty and awesome, who shows no partiality nor takes a bribe. 18He administers justice for the fatherless and the widow, and loves the stranger, giving him food and clothing. 19Therefore love the stranger, for you were strangers in the land of Egypt. 20You shall fear the LORD your God; you shall serve Him, and to Him you shall hold fast, and take oaths in His name. 21He *is* your praise, and He *is* your God, who has done for you these great and awesome things which your eyes have seen. 22Your fathers went down to Egypt with seventy persons, and now the LORD your God has made you as the stars of heaven in multitude.

Love and Obedience Rewarded

11 "Therefore you shall love the LORD your God, and keep His charge, His statutes, His judgments, and His commandments always. 2Know today that *I do*

OBEDIENCE

READ IT: DEUTERONOMY 10:12, 13

God had requirements for His people on how they should live. He made them clear and simple in this summary right here. Basically the people needed to obey God. If they did all that the Lord commanded, things would be super good. God didn't make up these commands just because. He gave His people rules as a gift so that they could live the very *best lives possible*. He gives us this gift, too. The best life possible comes from obeying Him and following the rules He has given us in the Bible. Obey and live magnificently!

not *speak* with your children, who have not
known and who have not seen the chastening of the LORD your God, His greatness
and His mighty hand and His outstretched
arm— 3His signs and His acts which He
did in the midst of Egypt, to Pharaoh king
of Egypt, and to all his land; 4what He did to
the army of Egypt, to their horses and their
chariots: how He made the waters of the Red
Sea overflow them as they pursued you, and
how the LORD has destroyed them to this
day; 5what He did for you in the wilderness
until you came to this place; 6and what He
did to Dathan and Abiram the sons of Eliab,
the son of Reuben: how the earth opened its
mouth and swallowed them up, their households, their tents, and all the substance that
was in their possession, in the midst of all
Israel— 7but your eyes have seen every great
act of the LORD which He did.

8"Therefore you shall keep every commandment which I command you today, that
you may be strong, and go in and possess the
land which you cross over to possess, 9and
that you may prolong *your* days in the land
which the LORD swore to give your fathers, to
them and their descendants, 'a land flowing
with milk and honey.'[a] 10For the land which
you go to possess *is* not like the land of Egypt
from which you have come, where you sowed
your seed and watered *it* by foot, as a vege-
table garden; 11but the land which you cross
over to possess *is* a land of hills and valleys,
which drinks water from the rain of heaven,
12a land for which the LORD your God cares;
the eyes of the LORD your God *are* always on
it, from the beginning of the year to the very
end of the year.

13'And it shall be that if you earnestly obey
My commandments which I command you
today, to love the LORD your God and serve
Him with all your heart and with all your
soul, 14then I[a] will give *you* the rain for your
land in its season, the early rain and the latter rain, that you may gather in your grain,
your new wine, and your oil. 15And I will
send grass in your fields for your livestock,
that you may eat and be filled.' 16Take heed to
yourselves, lest your heart be deceived, and
you turn aside and serve other gods and worship them, 17lest the LORD's anger be aroused
against you, and He shut up the heavens so
that there be no rain, and the land yield no
produce, and you perish quickly from the
good land which the LORD is giving you.

18"Therefore you shall lay up these words
of mine in your heart and in your soul, and
bind them as a sign on your hand, and they
shall be as frontlets between your eyes. 19You
shall teach them to your children, speaking
of them when you sit in your house, when
you walk by the way, when you lie down,
and when you rise up. 20And you shall write
them on the doorposts of your house and on
your gates, 21that your days and the days of
your children may be multiplied in the land
of which the LORD swore to your fathers to
give them, like the days of the heavens above
the earth.

22"For if you carefully keep all these commandments which I command you to do—
to love the LORD your God, to walk in all His
ways, and to hold fast to Him— 23then the
LORD will drive out all these nations from
before you, and you will dispossess greater and mightier nations than yourselves.
24Every place on which the sole of your foot
treads shall be yours: from the wilderness
and Lebanon, from the river, the River Euphrates, even to the Western Sea,[a] shall
be your territory. 25No man shall be able to
stand against you; the LORD your God will
put the dread of you and the fear of you upon
all the land where you tread, just as He has
said to you.

26"Behold, I set before you today a blessing and a curse: 27the blessing, if you obey
the commandments of the LORD your God
which I command you today; 28and the curse,
if you do not obey the commandments of
the LORD your God, but turn aside from the
way which I command you today, to go after other gods which you have not known.
29Now it shall be, when the LORD your God
has brought you into the land which you go
to possess, that you shall put the blessing
on Mount Gerizim and the curse on Mount
Ebal. 30*Are* they not on the other side of the
Jordan, toward the setting sun, in the land
of the Canaanites who dwell in the plain
opposite Gilgal, beside the terebinth trees of
Moreh? 31For you will cross over the Jordan
and go in to possess the land which the LORD
your God is giving you, and you will possess

11:9 [a] Exodus 3:8 **11:14** [a] Following Masoretic Text and Targum; Samaritan Pentateuch, Septuagint, and Vulgate read *He*. **11:24** [a] That is, the Mediterranean

it and dwell in it. 32 And you shall be careful
to observe all the statutes and judgments
which I set before you today.

A Prescribed Place of Worship

12 "These *are* the statutes and judgments which you shall be careful to
observe in the land which the LORD God of
your fathers is giving you to possess, all the
days that you live on the earth. 2 You shall utterly destroy all the places where the nations
which you shall dispossess served their
gods, on the high mountains and on the
hills and under every green tree. 3 And you
shall destroy their altars, break their *sacred*
pillars, and burn their wooden images with
fire; you shall cut down the carved images of
their gods and destroy their names from that
place. 4 You shall not worship the LORD your
God *with* such *things*.

5 "But you shall seek the place where
the LORD your God chooses, out of all your
tribes, to put His name for His dwelling
place; and there you shall go. 6 There you
shall take your burnt offerings, your sacrifices, your tithes, the heave offerings of your
hand, your vowed offerings, your freewill
offerings, and the firstborn of your herds
and flocks. 7 And there you shall eat before
the LORD your God, and you shall rejoice in
all to which you have put your hand, you and
your households, in which the LORD your
God has blessed you.

8 "You shall not at all do as we are doing
here today—every man doing whatever *is*
right in his own eyes— 9 for as yet you have
not come to the rest and the inheritance
which the LORD your God is giving you. 10 But
when you cross over the Jordan and dwell in
the land which the LORD your God is giving
you to inherit, and He gives you rest from all
your enemies round about, so that you dwell
in safety, 11 then there will be the place where
the LORD your God chooses to make His
name abide. There you shall bring all that
I command you: your burnt offerings, your
sacrifices, your tithes, the heave offerings
of your hand, and all your choice offerings
which you vow to the LORD. 12 And you shall
rejoice before the LORD your God, you and
your sons and your daughters, your male
and female servants, and the Levite who *is*
within your gates, since he has no portion
nor inheritance with you. 13 Take heed to
yourself that you do not offer your burnt offerings in every place that you see; 14 but in
the place which the LORD chooses, in one of
your tribes, there you shall offer your burnt
offerings, and there you shall do all that I
command you.

GIVING TO GOD

READ IT: DEUTERONOMY 12:11

Some churches teach that Christians should tithe like Israel did. A tithe is one-tenth of one's possessions.

Of course everything you are and everything you have comes from God. You may say, "Yes, but I worked for it!" But you couldn't work at all if God didn't give you the strength and the chance to work. So you really owe God everything.

God knows what we need to live, and He is very generous to ask us for only a tenth of our money. Doing His work—feeding the poor, ministering to the sick, reaching out to unbelievers—can cost a lot of money!

If your church teaches tithing (pronounced TIE-*thing*), the time to start is *now*. Then, as you grow up, tithing will be a habit of life. People who tithe say, "It seems like the more I give to God, the more He gives back to me."

15“However, you may slaughter and eat
meat within all your gates, whatever your
heart desires, according to the blessing of
the LORD your God which He has given you;
the unclean and the clean may eat of it, of
the gazelle and the deer alike. 16Only you
shall not eat the blood; you shall pour it on
the earth like water. 17You may not eat within your gates the tithe of your grain or your
new wine or your oil, of the firstborn of your
herd or your flock, of any of your offerings
which you vow, of your freewill offerings, or
of the heave offering of your hand. 18But you
must eat them before the LORD your God in
the place which the LORD your God chooses,
you and your son and your daughter, your
male servant and your female servant, and
the Levite who *is* within your gates; and you
shall rejoice before the LORD your God in all
to which you put your hands. 19Take heed to
yourself that you do not forsake the Levite as
long as you live in your land.

20“When the LORD your God enlarges
your border as He has promised you, and
you say, ‘Let me eat meat,’ because you long
to eat meat, you may eat as much meat as
your heart desires. 21If the place where the
LORD your God chooses to put His name is
too far from you, then you may slaughter
from your herd and from your flock which
the LORD has given you, just as I have commanded you, and you may eat within your
gates as much as your heart desires. 22Just
as the gazelle and the deer are eaten, so you
may eat them; the unclean and the clean
alike may eat them. 23Only be sure that you
do not eat the blood, for the blood *is* the life;
you may not eat the life with the meat. 24You
shall not eat it; you shall pour it on the earth
like water. 25You shall not eat it, that it may
go well with you and your children after you,
when you do *what is* right in the sight of the
LORD. 26Only the holy things which you have,
and your vowed offerings, you shall take
and go to the place which the LORD chooses.
27And you shall offer your burnt offerings,
the meat and the blood, on the altar of the
LORD your God; and the blood of your sacrifices shall be poured out on the altar of the
LORD your God, and you shall eat the meat.
28Observe and obey all these words which I
command you, that it may go well with you
and your children after you forever, when
you do *what is* good and right in the sight of
the LORD your God.

Beware of False Gods

29“When the LORD your God cuts off from
before you the nations which you go to dispossess, and you displace them and dwell in
their land, 30take heed to yourself that you
are not ensnared to follow them, after they
are destroyed from before you, and that you
do not inquire after their gods, saying, ‘How
did these nations serve their gods? I also
will do likewise.’ 31You shall not worship the
LORD your God in that way; for every abomination to the LORD which He hates they have
done to their gods; for they burn even their
sons and daughters in the fire to their gods.

32“Whatever I command you, be careful
to observe it; you shall not add to it nor take
away from it.

Punishment of Apostates

13 “If there arises among you a prophet or a dreamer of dreams, and he
gives you a sign or a wonder, 2and the sign or
the wonder comes to pass, of which he spoke
to you, saying, ‘Let us go after other gods’—
which you have not known—‘and let us
serve them,’ 3you shall not listen to the words
of that prophet or that dreamer of dreams,
for the LORD your God is testing you to know
whether you love the LORD your God with all
your heart and with all your soul. 4You shall
walk after the LORD your God and fear Him,
and keep His commandments and obey His
voice; you shall serve Him and hold fast to
Him. 5But that prophet or that dreamer of
dreams shall be put to death, because he has
spoken in order to turn *you* away from the
LORD your God, who brought you out of the
land of Egypt and redeemed you from the
house of bondage, to entice you from the way
in which the LORD your God commanded
you to walk. So you shall put away the evil
from your midst.

6“If your brother, the son of your mother,
your son or your daughter, the wife of your
bosom, or your friend who is as your own
soul, secretly entices you, saying, ‘Let us go
and serve other gods,’ which you have not
known, neither you nor your fathers, 7of the
gods of the people which *are* all around you,
near to you or far off from you, from *one* end
of the earth to the *other* end of the earth, 8you
shall not consent to him or listen to him, nor

shall your eye pity him, nor shall you spare
him or conceal him; 9but you shall surely kill
him; your hand shall be first against him to
put him to death, and afterward the hand
of all the people. 10And you shall stone him
with stones until he dies, because he sought
to entice you away from the LORD your God,
who brought you out of the land of Egypt,
from the house of bondage. 11So all Israel
shall hear and fear, and not again do such
wickedness as this among you.

12"If you hear someone in one of your
cities, which the LORD your God gives you
to dwell in, saying, 13'Corrupt men have
gone out from among you and enticed the
inhabitants of their city, saying, "Let us go
and serve other gods"'—which you have not
known— 14then you shall inquire, search
out, and ask diligently. And *if it is* indeed
true *and* certain *that* such an abomination
was committed among you, 15you shall surely strike the inhabitants of that city with the
edge of the sword, utterly destroying it, all
that is in it and its livestock—with the edge
of the sword. 16And you shall gather all its
plunder into the middle of the street, and
completely burn with fire the city and all its
plunder, for the LORD your God. It shall be a
heap forever; it shall not be built again. 17So
none of the accursed things shall remain in
your hand, that the LORD may turn from the
fierceness of His anger and show you mercy,
have compassion on you and multiply you,
just as He swore to your fathers, 18because
you have listened to the voice of the LORD
your God, to keep all His commandments
which I command you today, to do *what is*
right in the eyes of the LORD your God.

Improper Mourning

14 "You *are* the children of the LORD
your God; you shall not cut yourselves nor shave the front of your head for
the dead. 2For you *are* a holy people to the
LORD your God, and the LORD has chosen
you to be a people for Himself, a special treasure above all the peoples who *are* on the face
of the earth.

Clean and Unclean Meat

3"You shall not eat any detestable thing.
4These *are* the animals which you may eat:
the ox, the sheep, the goat, 5the deer, the gazelle, the roe deer, the wild goat, the mountain goat,[a] the antelope, and the mountain
sheep. 6And you may eat every animal with
cloven hooves, having the hoof split into two
parts, *and that* chews the cud, among the animals. 7Nevertheless, of those that chew the
cud or have cloven hooves, you shall not eat,
such as these: the camel, the hare, and the
rock hyrax; for they chew the cud but do not
have cloven hooves; they *are* unclean for you.
8Also the swine is unclean for you, because it
has cloven hooves, yet *does* not *chew* the cud;
you shall not eat their flesh or touch their
dead carcasses.

9"These you may eat of all that *are* in the
waters: you may eat all that have fins and
scales. 10And whatever does not have fins and
scales you shall not eat; it *is* unclean for you.

11"All clean birds you may eat. 12But these
you shall not eat: the eagle, the vulture, the
buzzard, 13the red kite, the falcon, and the
kite after their kinds; 14every raven after its
kind; 15the ostrich, the short-eared owl, the
sea gull, and the hawk after their kinds; 16the
little owl, the screech owl, the white owl, 17the
jackdaw, the carrion vulture, the fisher owl,
18the stork, the heron after its kind, and the
hoopoe and the bat.

19"Also every creeping thing that flies is
unclean for you; they shall not be eaten.

20"You may eat all clean birds.

21"You shall not eat anything that dies *of
itself;* you may give it to the alien who *is* within your gates, that he may eat it, or you may
sell it to a foreigner; for you *are* a holy people
to the LORD your God.

"You shall not boil a young goat in its
mother's milk.

Tithing Principles

22"You shall truly tithe all the increase
of your grain that the field produces year
by year. 23And you shall eat before the LORD
your God, in the place where He chooses to
make His name abide, the tithe of your grain
and your new wine and your oil, of the firstborn of your herds and your flocks, that you
may learn to fear the LORD your God always.
24But if the journey is too long for you, so that
you are not able to carry *the tithe, or* if the
place where the LORD your God chooses to
put His name is too far from you, when the
LORD your God has blessed you, 25then you
shall exchange *it* for money, take the money in your hand, and go to the place which

14:5 [a] Or *addax*

the LORD your God chooses. 26And you shall
spend that money for whatever your heart
desires: for oxen or sheep, for wine or similar
drink, for whatever your heart desires; you
shall eat there before the LORD your God,
and you shall rejoice, you and your household. 27You shall not forsake the Levite who
is within your gates, for he has no part nor
inheritance with you.

28"At the end of *every* third year you shall
bring out the tithe of your produce of that
year and store *it* up within your gates. 29And
the Levite, because he has no portion nor
inheritance with you, and the stranger and
the fatherless and the widow who *are* within
your gates, may come and eat and be satisfied, that the LORD your God may bless you
in all the work of your hand which you do.

Debts Canceled Every Seven Years

15 "At the end of *every* seven years you
shall grant a release *of debts.* 2And
this *is* the form of the release: Every creditor who has lent *anything* to his neighbor
shall release *it;* he shall not require *it* of his
neighbor or his brother, because it is called
the LORD's release. 3Of a foreigner you may
require *it;* but you shall give up your claim to
what is owed by your brother, 4except when
there may be no poor among you; for the
LORD will greatly bless you in the land which
the LORD your God is giving you to possess
as an inheritance— 5only if you carefully obey the voice of the LORD your God, to
observe with care all these commandments
which I command you today. 6For the LORD
your God will bless you just as He promised
you; you shall lend to many nations, but you
shall not borrow; you shall reign over many
nations, but they shall not reign over you.

Generosity to the Poor

7"If there is among you a poor man of
your brethren, within any of the gates in
your land which the LORD your God is giving you, you shall not harden your heart nor
shut your hand from your poor brother, 8but
you shall open your hand wide to him and
willingly lend him sufficient for his need,
whatever he needs. 9Beware lest there be a
wicked thought in your heart, saying, 'The
seventh year, the year of release, is at hand,'
and your eye be evil against your poor brother and you give him nothing, and he cry out
to the LORD against you, and it become sin
among you. 10You shall surely give to him,
and your heart should not be grieved when
you give to him, because for this thing the
LORD your God will bless you in all your
works and in all to which you put your hand.

BE GENEROUS TO YOUR NEIGHBORS

READ IT: DEUTERONOMY 15:1–6

The real proof that someone loves God is that he loves others, too. Love is not just a warm fuzzy, or a kind feeling. Love *works.*

Being kind to nice people is easy. But you may know some people who are not always nice. That fact doesn't allow you to act in an unkind way. You aren't expected to give away everything you own, but sharing with others in need is a mark of love.

A little boy lived across the fence from a little girl. The boy had a tricycle, but the girl didn't have one. So the little boy took apart his tricycle and gave half of it to the little girl! Of course, neither the boy nor the girl had much to play with. But the idea in the boy's heart was right.

Generous actions send a message to hopeless people that God still lives.

11 For the poor will never cease from the land;
therefore I command you, saying, 'You shall
open your hand wide to your brother, to your
poor and your needy, in your land.'

The Law Concerning Bondservants

12 "If your brother, a Hebrew man, or a
Hebrew woman, is sold to you and serves
you six years, then in the seventh year you
shall let him go free from you. 13 And when
you send him away free from you, you shall
not let him go away empty-handed; 14 you
shall supply him liberally from your flock,
from your threshing floor, and from your
winepress. *From what* the LORD your God
has blessed you with, you shall give to him.
15 You shall remember that you were a slave
in the land of Egypt, and the LORD your God
redeemed you; therefore I command you
this thing today. 16 And if it happens that he
says to you, 'I will not go away from you,' because he loves you and your house, since he
prospers with you, 17 then you shall take an
awl and thrust *it* through his ear to the door,
and he shall be your servant forever. Also to
your female servant you shall do likewise. 18 It
shall not seem hard to you when you send
him away free from you; for he has been
worth a double hired servant in serving you
six years. Then the LORD your God will bless
you in all that you do.

The Law Concerning Firstborn Animals

19 "All the firstborn males that come from
your herd and your flock you shall sanctify
to the LORD your God; you shall do no work
with the firstborn of your herd, nor shear
the firstborn of your flock. 20 You and your
household shall eat *it* before the LORD your
God year by year in the place which the LORD
chooses. 21 But if there is a defect in it, *if it is*
lame or blind *or has* any serious defect, you
shall not sacrifice it to the LORD your God.
22 You may eat it within your gates; the unclean and the clean *person* alike *may eat it,*
as *if it were* a gazelle or a deer. 23 Only you
shall not eat its blood; you shall pour it on
the ground like water.

The Passover Reviewed

16 "Observe the month of Abib, and
keep the Passover to the LORD your
God, for in the month of Abib the LORD
your God brought you out of Egypt by night.

In Focus

15:19 Sanctify Pronounced *SANK-tih-fy*. Means "set apart" for God's use. The Scriptures teach you to be useful to God when you have trusted Him.

2 Therefore you shall sacrifice the Passover
to the LORD your God, from the flock and
the herd, in the place where the LORD chooses to put His name. 3 You shall eat no leavened bread with it; seven days you shall eat
unleavened bread with it, *that is,* the bread
of affliction (for you came out of the land
of Egypt in haste), that you may remember
the day in which you came out of the land of
Egypt all the days of your life. 4 And no leaven
shall be seen among you in all your territory for seven days, nor shall *any* of the meat
which you sacrifice the first day at twilight
remain overnight until morning.

5 "You may not sacrifice the Passover
within any of your gates which the LORD
your God gives you; 6 but at the place where
the LORD your God chooses to make His
name abide, there you shall sacrifice the
Passover at twilight, at the going down of
the sun, at the time you came out of Egypt.
7 And you shall roast and eat *it* in the place
which the LORD your God chooses, and in
the morning you shall turn and go to your
tents. 8 Six days you shall eat unleavened
bread, and on the seventh day there *shall be* a
sacred assembly to the LORD your God. You
shall do no work *on it.*

The Feast of Weeks Reviewed

9 "You shall count seven weeks for yourself; begin to count the seven weeks from *the
time* you begin *to put* the sickle to the grain.
10 Then you shall keep the Feast of Weeks
to the LORD your God with the tribute of a
freewill offering from your hand, which you
shall give as the LORD your God blesses you.
11 You shall rejoice before the LORD your God,
you and your son and your daughter, your
male servant and your female servant, the
Levite who *is* within your gates, the stranger and the fatherless and the widow who *are*

among you, at the place where the LORD your
God chooses to make His name abide. 12And
you shall remember that you were a slave in
Egypt, and you shall be careful to observe
these statutes.

The Feast of Tabernacles Reviewed

13“You shall observe the Feast of Tabernacles seven days, when you have gathered
from your threshing floor and from your
winepress. 14And you shall rejoice in your
feast, you and your son and your daughter,
your male servant and your female servant
and the Levite, the stranger and the fatherless and the widow, who *are* within your
gates. 15Seven days you shall keep a sacred
feast to the LORD your God in the place
which the LORD chooses, because the LORD
your God will bless you in all your produce
and in all the work of your hands, so that you
surely rejoice.
16“Three times a year all your males shall
appear before the LORD your God in the
place which He chooses: at the Feast of Unleavened Bread, at the Feast of Weeks, and
at the Feast of Tabernacles; and they shall
not appear before the LORD empty-handed.
17Every man *shall give* as he is able, according
to the blessing of the LORD your God which
He has given you.

Justice Must Be Administered

18“You shall appoint judges and officers
in all your gates, which the LORD your God
gives you, according to your tribes, and they
shall judge the people with just judgment.
19You shall not pervert justice; you shall not
show partiality, nor take a bribe, for a bribe
blinds the eyes of the wise and twists the
words of the righteous. 20You shall follow
what is altogether just, that you may live and
inherit the land which the LORD your God
is giving you.
21“You shall not plant for yourself any
tree, as a wooden image, near the altar which
you build for yourself to the LORD your God.
22You shall not set up a *sacred* pillar, which
the LORD your God hates.

17 “You shall not sacrifice to the LORD
your God a bull or sheep which has
any blemish *or* defect, for that *is* an abomination to the LORD your God.
2“If there is found among you, within
any of your gates which the LORD your God
gives you, a man or a woman who has been
wicked in the sight of the LORD your God, in
transgressing His covenant, 3who has gone
and served other gods and worshiped them,
either the sun or moon or any of the host
of heaven, which I have not commanded,
4and it is told you, and you hear *of it,* then
you shall inquire diligently. And if *it is* indeed true *and* certain that such an abomination has been committed in Israel, 5then
you shall bring out to your gates that man
or woman who has committed that wicked
thing, and shall stone to death that man or
woman with stones. 6Whoever is deserving
of death shall be put to death on the testimony of two or three witnesses; he shall not be
put to death on the testimony of one witness.
7The hands of the witnesses shall be the first
against him to put him to death, and afterward the hands of all the people. So you shall
put away the evil from among you.
8“If a matter arises which is too hard for
you to judge, between degrees of guilt for
bloodshed, between one judgment or another, or between one punishment or another,
matters of controversy within your gates,
then you shall arise and go up to the place
which the LORD your God chooses. 9And you
shall come to the priests, the Levites, and to
the judge *there* in those days, and inquire
of them; they shall pronounce upon you the
sentence of judgment. 10You shall do according to the sentence which they pronounce
upon you in that place which the LORD
chooses. And you shall be careful to do according to all that they order you. 11According
to the sentence of the law in which they instruct you, according to the judgment which
they tell you, you shall do; you shall not turn
aside *to* the right hand or *to* the left from the
sentence which they pronounce upon you.
12Now the man who acts presumptuously
and will not heed the priest who stands to
minister there before the LORD your God, or
the judge, that man shall die. So you shall
put away the evil from Israel. 13And all the
people shall hear and fear, and no longer act
presumptuously.

Principles Governing Kings

14“When you come to the land which the
LORD your God is giving you, and possess it
and dwell in it, and say, ‘I will set a king over
me like all the nations that *are* around me,’
15you shall surely set a king over you whom
the LORD your God chooses; *one* from among
your brethren you shall set as king over you;

you may not set a foreigner over you, who *is*
not your brother. 16But he shall not multiply
horses for himself, nor cause the people to
return to Egypt to multiply horses, for the
LORD has said to you, 'You shall not return
that way again.' 17Neither shall he multiply
wives for himself, lest his heart turn away;
nor shall he greatly multiply silver and gold
for himself.

18"Also it shall be, when he sits on the
throne of his kingdom, that he shall write
for himself a copy of this law in a book, from
the one before the priests, the Levites. 19And
it shall be with him, and he shall read it all
the days of his life, that he may learn to fear
the LORD his God and be careful to observe
all the words of this law and these statutes,
20that his heart may not be lifted above his
brethren, that he may not turn aside from
the commandment *to* the right hand or *to*
the left, and that he may prolong *his* days
in his kingdom, he and his children in the
midst of Israel.

The Portion of the Priests and Levites

18 "The priests, the Levites—all the
tribe of Levi—shall have no part
nor inheritance with Israel; they shall eat
the offerings of the LORD made by fire, and
His portion. 2Therefore they shall have no
inheritance among their brethren; the LORD
is their inheritance, as He said to them.

3"And this shall be the priest's due from
the people, from those who offer a sacrifice,
whether *it is* bull or sheep: they shall give to
the priest the shoulder, the cheeks, and the
stomach. 4The firstfruits of your grain and
your new wine and your oil, and the first of
the fleece of your sheep, you shall give him.
5For the LORD your God has chosen him out
of all your tribes to stand to minister in the
name of the LORD, him and his sons forever.

6"So if a Levite comes from any of your
gates, from where he dwells among all Israel, and comes with all the desire of his
mind to the place which the LORD chooses,
7then he may serve in the name of the LORD
his God as all his brethren the Levites *do,*
who stand there before the LORD. 8They
shall have equal portions to eat, besides what
comes from the sale of his inheritance.

Avoid Wicked Customs

9"When you come into the land which the
LORD your God is giving you, you shall not
learn to follow the abominations of those
nations. 10There shall not be found among
you *anyone* who makes his son or his daughter pass through the fire, *or one* who practices witchcraft, *or* a soothsayer, or one who
interprets omens, or a sorcerer, 11or one who
conjures spells, or a medium, or a spiritist,
or one who calls up the dead. 12For all who
do these things *are* an abomination to the
LORD, and because of these abominations
the LORD your God drives them out from before you. 13You shall be blameless before the
LORD your God. 14For these nations which
you will dispossess listened to soothsayers
and diviners; but as for you, the LORD your
God has not appointed such for you.

A New Prophet Like Moses

15"The LORD your God will raise up for
you a Prophet like me from your midst, from
your brethren. Him you shall hear, 16accord-
ing to all you desired of the LORD your God
in Horeb in the day of the assembly, saying,
'Let me not hear again the voice of the LORD
my God, nor let me see this great fire anymore, lest I die.'

17"And the LORD said to me: 'What they
have spoken is good. 18I will raise up for
them a Prophet like you from among their
brethren, and will put My words in His
mouth, and He shall speak to them all that I
command Him. 19And it shall be *that* whoever will not hear My words, which He speaks
in My name, I will require *it* of him. 20But
the prophet who presumes to speak a word
in My name, which I have not commanded
him to speak, or who speaks in the name of
other gods, that prophet shall die.' 21And if
you say in your heart, 'How shall we know
the word which the LORD has not spoken?'—
22when a prophet speaks in the name of the
LORD, if the thing does not happen or come
to pass, that *is* the thing which the LORD has
not spoken; the prophet has spoken it presumptuously; you shall not be afraid of him.

Three Cities of Refuge

19 "When the LORD your God has cut
off the nations whose land the LORD
your God is giving you, and you dispossess
them and dwell in their cities and in their
houses, 2you shall separate three cities for
yourself in the midst of your land which
the LORD your God is giving you to possess.
3You shall prepare roads for yourself, and
divide into three parts the territory of your

land which the LORD your God is giving you
to inherit, that any manslayer may flee there.
4“And this *is* the case of the manslayer
who flees there, that he may live: Whoever
kills his neighbor unintentionally, not having hated him in time past— 5as when *a
man* goes to the woods with his neighbor
to cut timber, and his hand swings a stroke
with the ax to cut down the tree, and the
head slips from the handle and strikes his
neighbor so that he dies—he shall flee to
one of these cities and live; 6lest the avenger
of blood, while his anger is hot, pursue the
manslayer and overtake him, because the
way is long, and kill him, though he *was* not
deserving of death, since he had not hated
the victim in time past. 7Therefore I command you, saying, ‘You shall separate three
cities for yourself.’
8“Now if the LORD your God enlarges
your territory, as He swore to your fathers,
and gives you the land which He promised
to give to your fathers, 9and if you keep all
these commandments and do them, which
I command you today, to love the LORD your
God and to walk always in His ways, then
you shall add three more cities for yourself
besides these three, 10lest innocent blood be
shed in the midst of your land which the
LORD your God is giving you *as* an inheritance, and *thus* guilt of bloodshed be upon
you.
11“But if anyone hates his neighbor,
lies in wait for him, rises against him and
strikes him mortally, so that he dies, and he
flees to one of these cities, 12then the elders
of his city shall send and bring him from
there, and deliver him over to the hand of
the avenger of blood, that he may die. 13Your
eye shall not pity him, but you shall put away
the guilt of innocent blood from Israel, that it
may go well with you.

Property Boundaries

14“You shall not remove your neighbor’s
landmark, *which the men of old have set*, in
your inheritance which you will inherit in
the land that the LORD your God is giving
you to possess.

The Law Concerning Witnesses

15“One witness shall not rise against a
man concerning any iniquity or any sin that
he commits; by the mouth of two or three
witnesses the matter shall be established. 16If
a false witness rises against any man to testify against him of wrongdoing, 17then both
men in the controversy shall stand before
the LORD, before the priests and the judges
who serve in those days. 18And the judges
shall make careful inquiry, and indeed, *if* the
witness *is* a false witness, who has testified
falsely against his brother, 19then you shall
do to him as he thought to have done to his
brother; so you shall put away the evil from
among you. 20And those who remain shall
hear and fear, and hereafter they shall not
again commit such evil among you. 21Your
eye shall not pity: life *shall be* for life, eye for
eye, tooth for tooth, hand for hand, foot for
foot.

Principles Governing Warfare

20 “When you go out to battle against
your enemies, and see horses and
chariots *and* people more numerous than
you, do not be afraid of them; for the LORD
your God *is* with you, who brought you up
from the land of Egypt. 2So it shall be, when
you are on the verge of battle, that the priest
shall approach and speak to the people. 3And
he shall say to them, ‘Hear, O Israel: Today
you are on the verge of battle with your enemies. Do not let your heart faint, do not be
afraid, and do not tremble or be terrified because of them; 4for the LORD your God *is* He
who goes with you, to fight for you against
your enemies, to save you.’
5“Then the officers shall speak to the
people, saying: ‘What man *is there* who has
built a new house and has not dedicated it?
Let him go and return to his house, lest he
die in the battle and another man dedicate
it. 6Also what man *is there* who has planted
a vineyard and has not eaten of it? Let him
go and return to his house, lest he die in the
battle and another man eat of it. 7And what
man *is there* who is betrothed to a woman
and has not married her? Let him go and return to his house, lest he die in the battle and
another man marry her.’
8“The officers shall speak further to the
people, and say, ‘What man *is there who is*
fearful and fainthearted? Let him go and return to his house, lest the heart of his brethren faint[a] like his heart.’ 9And so it shall be,

20:8 [a] Following Masoretic Text and Targum; Samaritan Pentateuch, Septuagint, Syriac, and Vulgate read *lest he make his brother’s heart faint.*

when the officers have finished speaking to
the people, that they shall make captains of
the armies to lead the people.
10“When you go near a city to fight
against it, then proclaim an offer of peace
to it. 11And it shall be that if they accept your
offer of peace, and open to you, then all the
people *who are* found in it shall be placed under tribute to you, and serve you. 12Now if *the*
city will not make peace with you, but war
against you, then you shall besiege it. 13And
when the LORD your God delivers it into your
hands, you shall strike every male in it with
the edge of the sword. 14But the women, the
little ones, the livestock, and all that is in the
city, all its spoil, you shall plunder for yourself; and you shall eat the enemies' plunder
which the LORD your God gives you. 15Thus
you shall do to all the cities *which are* very
far from you, which *are* not of the cities of
these nations.
16“But of the cities of these peoples which
the LORD your God gives you *as* an inheritance, you shall let nothing that breathes
remain alive, 17but you shall utterly destroy
them: the Hittite and the Amorite and the
Canaanite and the Perizzite and the Hivite
and the Jebusite, just as the LORD your God
has commanded you, 18lest they teach you to
do according to all their abominations which
they have done for their gods, and you sin
against the LORD your God.
19“When you besiege a city for a long
time, while making war against it to take
it, you shall not destroy its trees by wielding
an ax against them; if you can eat of them,
do not cut them down to use in the siege,
for the tree of the field *is* man's *food*. 20Only
the trees which you know *are* not trees for
food you may destroy and cut down, to build
siegeworks against the city that makes war
with you, until it is subdued.

The Law Concerning Unsolved Murder

21 “If *anyone* is found slain, lying
in the field in the land which the
LORD your God is giving you to possess,
and it is not known who killed him, 2then
your elders and your judges shall go out and
measure *the distance* from the slain man to
the surrounding cities. 3And it shall be *that*
the elders of the city nearest to the slain man
will take a heifer which has not been worked
and which has not pulled with a yoke. 4The
elders of that city shall bring the heifer down
to a valley with flowing water, which is neither plowed nor sown, and they shall break
the heifer's neck there in the valley. 5Then
the priests, the sons of Levi, shall come near,
for the LORD your God has chosen them to
minister to Him and to bless in the name

20:1–4 ARE YOU A SOLDIER FOR JESUS?

The fact of war should tell us that we still live in a sinful world. If God could have given Israel the Promised Land of Canaan without war, He would have done so. God sent His armies into Canaan to judge that nation for its horrible sins (see Deuteronomy 7).

Now Jesus calls us to a new kind of war. It is not a war of physical combat and bloodshed. Jesus is leading His people in a *spiritual* war against the unseen kingdom of Satan. Our main weapon in this war is the Word of God. The Holy Spirit gives us power to fight and win the Christian war.

Christ's method or strategy is to send His army of people into all the world to proclaim the gospel of free salvation to all who will trust Jesus.

You, too, may have a part in Christ's war. Ask the Lord to show you how He wants you to serve in His army.

of the LORD; by their word every controversy
and every assault shall be *settled.* 6And all the
elders of that city nearest to the slain *man*
shall wash their hands over the heifer whose
neck was broken in the valley. 7Then they
shall answer and say, 'Our hands have not
shed this blood, nor have our eyes seen *it.*
8Provide atonement, O LORD, for Your people Israel, whom You have redeemed, and
do not lay innocent blood to the charge of
Your people Israel.' And atonement shall be
provided on their behalf for the blood. 9So
you shall put away the *guilt of* innocent blood
from among you when you do *what is* right
in the sight of the LORD.

Female Captives

10"When you go out to war against your
enemies, and the LORD your God delivers
them into your hand, and you take them
captive, 11and you see among the captives a
beautiful woman, and desire her and would
take her for your wife, 12then you shall bring
her home to your house, and she shall shave
her head and trim her nails. 13She shall put
off the clothes of her captivity, remain in
your house, and mourn her father and her
mother a full month; after that you may go
in to her and be her husband, and she shall
be your wife. 14And it shall be, if you have
no delight in her, then you shall set her free,
but you certainly shall not sell her for money; you shall not treat her brutally, because
you have humbled her.

Firstborn Inheritance Rights

15"If a man has two wives, one loved and
the other unloved, and they have borne him
children, *both* the loved and the unloved, and
if the firstborn son is of her who is unloved,
16then it shall be, on the day he bequeaths his
possessions to his sons, *that* he must not bestow firstborn status on the son of the loved
wife in preference to the son of the unloved,
the *true* firstborn. 17But he shall acknowledge
the son of the unloved wife *as* the firstborn
by giving him a double portion of all that he
has, for he *is* the beginning of his strength;
the right of the firstborn *is* his.

The Rebellious Son

18"If a man has a stubborn and rebellious
son who will not obey the voice of his father
or the voice of his mother, and *who,* when
they have chastened him, will not heed
them, 19then his father and his mother shall
take hold of him and bring him out to the
elders of his city, to the gate of his city. 20And
they shall say to the elders of his city, 'This
son of ours is stubborn and rebellious; he
will not obey our voice; he is a glutton and
a drunkard.' 21Then all the men of his city
shall stone him to death with stones; so you
shall put away the evil from among you, and
all Israel shall hear and fear.

Miscellaneous Laws

22"If a man has committed a sin deserving of death, and he is put to death, and you
hang him on a tree, 23his body shall not remain overnight on the tree, but you shall
surely bury him that day, so that you do not
defile the land which the LORD your God is
giving you *as* an inheritance; for he who is
hanged *is* accursed of God.

22

"You shall not see your brother's
ox or his sheep going astray, and
hide yourself from them; you shall certainly bring them back to your brother. 2And if
your brother *is* not near you, or if you do not
know him, then you shall bring it to your
own house, and it shall remain with you
until your brother seeks it; then you shall restore it to him. 3You shall do the same with
his donkey, and so shall you do with his garment; with any lost thing of your brother's,
which he has lost and you have found, you
shall do likewise; you must not hide yourself.
4"You shall not see your brother's donkey
or his ox fall down along the road, and hide
yourself from them; you shall surely help
him lift *them* up again.
5"A woman shall not wear anything that
pertains to a man, nor shall a man put on a
woman's garment, for all who do so *are* an
abomination to the LORD your God.
6"If a bird's nest happens to be before you
along the way, in any tree or on the ground,
with young ones or eggs, with the mother
sitting on the young or on the eggs, you shall
not take the mother with the young; 7you
shall surely let the mother go, and take the
young for yourself, that it may be well with
you and *that* you may prolong *your* days.
8"When you build a new house, then you
shall make a parapet for your roof, that you
may not bring guilt of bloodshed on your
household if anyone falls from it.
9"You shall not sow your vineyard with
different kinds of seed, lest the yield of the

seed which you have sown and the fruit of
your vineyard be defiled.
10“You shall not plow with an ox and a
donkey together.
11“You shall not wear a garment of different sorts, *such as* wool and linen mixed
together.
12“You shall make tassels on the four corners of the clothing with which you cover
yourself.

Laws of Sexual Morality

13“If any man takes a wife, and goes in to
her, and detests her, 14and charges her with
shameful conduct, and brings a bad name
on her, and says, ‘I took this woman, and
when I came to her I found she *was* not a
virgin,’ 15then the father and mother of the
young woman shall take and bring out *the*
evidence of the young woman’s virginity to
the elders of the city at the gate. 16And the
young woman’s father shall say to the elders,
‘I gave my daughter to this man as wife, and
he detests her. 17Now he has charged her with
shameful conduct, saying, “I found your
daughter *was* not a virgin,” and yet these *are*
the evidences of my daughter’s virginity.’ And
they shall spread the cloth before the elders
of the city. 18Then the elders of that city shall
take that man and punish him; 19and they
shall fine him one hundred *shekels* of silver and give *them* to the father of the young
woman, because he has brought a bad name
on a virgin of Israel. And she shall be his
wife; he cannot divorce her all his days.
20“But if the thing is true, *and evidences of*
virginity are not found for the young woman, 21then they shall bring out the young
woman to the door of her father’s house,
and the men of her city shall stone her to
death with stones, because she has done a
disgraceful thing in Israel, to play the harlot
in her father’s house. So you shall put away
the evil from among you.
22“If a man is found lying with a woman
married to a husband, then both of them
shall die—the man that lay with the woman, and the woman; so you shall put away
the evil from Israel.
23“If a young woman *who is* a virgin is
betrothed to a husband, and a man finds
her in the city and lies with her, 24then you
shall bring them both out to the gate of that
city, and you shall stone them to death with
stones, the young woman because she did
not cry out in the city, and the man because
he humbled his neighbor’s wife; so you shall
put away the evil from among you.
25“But if a man finds a betrothed young
woman in the countryside, and the man
forces her and lies with her, then only the
man who lay with her shall die. 26But you
shall do nothing to the young woman; *there*
is in the young woman no sin *deserving* of
death, for just as when a man rises against
his neighbor and kills him, even so *is* this
matter. 27For he found her in the countryside, *and* the betrothed young woman cried
out, but *there was* no one to save her.
28“If a man finds a young woman *who is*
a virgin, who is not betrothed, and he seizes
her and lies with her, and they are found out,
29then the man who lay with her shall give
to the young woman’s father fifty *shekels* of
silver, and she shall be his wife because he
has humbled her; he shall not be permitted
to divorce her all his days.
30“A man shall not take his father’s wife,
nor uncover his father’s bed.

Those Excluded from the Congregation

23 “He who is emasculated by crushing or mutilation shall not enter
the assembly of the LORD.
2“One of illegitimate birth shall not enter
the assembly of the LORD; even to the tenth
generation none of his *descendants* shall enter the assembly of the LORD.
3“An Ammonite or Moabite shall not
enter the assembly of the LORD; even to the
tenth generation none of his *descendants*
shall enter the assembly of the LORD forever,
4because they did not meet you with bread
and water on the road when you came out
of Egypt, and because they hired against
you Balaam the son of Beor from Pethor of
Mesopotamia,[a] to curse you. 5Nevertheless
the LORD your God would not listen to Balaam, but the LORD your God turned the
curse into a blessing for you, because the
LORD your God loves you. 6You shall not
seek their peace nor their prosperity all your
days forever.
7“You shall not abhor an Edomite, for he
is your brother. You shall not abhor an Egyptian, because you were an alien in his land.

23:4 [a] Hebrew *Aram Naharaim*

8 The children of the third generation born
to them may enter the assembly of the LORD.

Cleanliness of the Campsite

9 "When the army goes out against your
enemies, then keep yourself from every
wicked thing. 10 If there is any man among
you who becomes unclean by some occurrence in the night, then he shall go outside
the camp; he shall not come inside the camp.
11 But it shall be, when evening comes, that
he shall wash with water; and when the sun
sets, he may come into the camp.

12 "Also you shall have a place outside the
camp, where you may go out; 13 and you shall
have an implement among your equipment,
and when you sit down outside, you shall
dig with it and turn and cover your refuse.
14 For the LORD your God walks in the midst
of your camp, to deliver you and give your
enemies over to you; therefore your camp
shall be holy, that He may see no unclean
thing among you, and turn away from you.

Miscellaneous Laws

15 "You shall not give back to his master
the slave who has escaped from his master to
you. 16 He may dwell with you in your midst,
in the place which he chooses within one of
your gates, where it seems best to him; you
shall not oppress him.

17 "There shall be no *ritual* harlot[a] of the
daughters of Israel, or a perverted[b] one of
the sons of Israel. 18 You shall not bring the
wages of a harlot or the price of a dog to the
house of the LORD your God for any vowed
offering, for both of these *are* an abomination to the LORD your God.

19 "You shall not charge interest to your
brother—interest on money *or* food *or* anything that is lent out at interest. 20 To a foreigner you may charge interest, but to your
brother you shall not charge interest, that
the LORD your God may bless you in all to
which you set your hand in the land which
you are entering to possess.

21 "When you make a vow to the LORD
your God, you shall not delay to pay it; for
the LORD your God will surely require it of
you, and it would be sin to you. 22 But if you
abstain from vowing, it shall not be sin to
you. 23 That which has gone from your lips
you shall keep and perform, for you volun-
tarily vowed to the LORD your God what you
have promised with your mouth.

24 "When you come into your neighbor's
vineyard, you may eat your fill of grapes at
your pleasure, but you shall not put *any* in
your container. 25 When you come into your
neighbor's standing grain, you may pluck the
heads with your hand, but you shall not use
a sickle on your neighbor's standing grain.

Law Concerning Divorce

24 "When a man takes a wife and
marries her, and it happens that
she finds no favor in his eyes because he
has found some uncleanness in her, and he
writes her a certificate of divorce, puts *it* in
her hand, and sends her out of his house,
2 when she has departed from his house, and
goes and becomes another man's *wife,* 3 *if* the
latter husband detests her and writes her a
certificate of divorce, puts *it* in her hand, and
sends her out of his house, or if the latter
husband dies who took her as his wife, 4 *then*
her former husband who divorced her must
not take her back to be his wife after she has
been defiled; for that *is* an abomination before the LORD, and you shall not bring sin on
the land which the LORD your God is giving
you *as* an inheritance.

Miscellaneous Laws

5 "When a man has taken a new wife, he
shall not go out to war or be charged with
any business; he shall be free at home one
year, and bring happiness to his wife whom
he has taken.

6 "No man shall take the lower or the upper millstone in pledge, for he takes *one's*
living in pledge.

7 "If a man is found kidnapping any of his
brethren of the children of Israel, and mistreats him or sells him, then that kidnapper
shall die; and you shall put away the evil
from among you.

8 "Take heed in an outbreak of leprosy,
that you carefully observe and do according
to all that the priests, the Levites, shall teach
you; just as I commanded them, *so* you shall
be careful to do. 9 Remember what the LORD
your God did to Miriam on the way when
you came out of Egypt!

10 "When you lend your brother anything, you shall not go into his house to get
his pledge. 11 You shall stand outside, and

23:17 [a] Hebrew *qedeshah,* feminine of *qadesh* (see note *b*)
[b] Hebrew *qadesh,* that is, one practicing sodomy and
prostitution in religious rituals

the man to whom you lend shall bring the
pledge out to you. 12And if the man *is* poor,
you shall not keep his pledge overnight.
13You shall in any case return the pledge to
him again when the sun goes down, that he
may sleep in his own garment and bless you;
and it shall be righteousness to you before
the LORD your God.

14"You shall not oppress a hired servant
who is poor and needy, *whether* one of your
brethren or one of the aliens who *is* in your
land within your gates. 15Each day you shall
give *him* his wages, and not let the sun go
down on it, for he *is* poor and has set his
heart on it; lest he cry out against you to the
LORD, and it be sin to you.

16"Fathers shall not be put to death for
their children, nor shall children be put to
death for *their* fathers; a person shall be put
to death for his own sin.

17"You shall not pervert justice due the
stranger or the fatherless, nor take a widow's
garment as a pledge. 18But you shall remember that you were a slave in Egypt, and the
LORD your God redeemed you from there;
therefore I command you to do this thing.

19"When you reap your harvest in your
field, and forget a sheaf in the field, you
shall not go back to get it; it shall be for the
stranger, the fatherless, and the widow, that
the LORD your God may bless you in all the
work of your hands. 20When you beat your
olive trees, you shall not go over the boughs
again; it shall be for the stranger, the fatherless, and the widow. 21When you gather the
grapes of your vineyard, you shall not glean
it afterward; it shall be for the stranger, the
fatherless, and the widow. 22And you shall
remember that you were a slave in the land
of Egypt; therefore I command you to do this
thing.

25 "If there is a dispute between
men, and they come to court, that
the judges may judge them, and they justify the righteous and condemn the wicked,
2then it shall be, if the wicked man deserves
to be beaten, that the judge will cause him
to lie down and be beaten in his presence,
according to his guilt, with a certain number
of blows. 3Forty blows he may give him *and
no more, lest he should* exceed this and beat
him with many blows above these, and your
brother be humiliated in your sight.

4"You shall not muzzle an ox while it
treads out *the grain.*

Marriage Duty of the Surviving Brother

5"If brothers dwell together, and one of
them dies and has no son, the widow of the
dead man shall not be *married* to a stranger outside *the family;* her husband's brother
shall go in to her, take her as his wife, and
perform the duty of a husband's brother to
her. 6And it shall be *that* the firstborn son
which she bears will succeed to the name of
his dead brother, that his name may not be
blotted out of Israel. 7But if the man does not
want to take his brother's wife, then let his
brother's wife go up to the gate to the elders,
and say, 'My husband's brother refuses to
raise up a name to his brother in Israel; he
will not perform the duty of my husband's
brother.' 8Then the elders of his city shall
call him and speak to him. But *if* he stands
firm and says, 'I do not want to take her,'
9then his brother's wife shall come to him
in the presence of the elders, remove his
sandal from his foot, spit in his face, and answer and say, 'So shall it be done to the man
who will not build up his brother's house.'
10And his name shall be called in Israel, 'The
house of him who had his sandal removed.'

Miscellaneous Laws

11"If *two* men fight together, and the wife
of one draws near to rescue her husband
from the hand of the one attacking him, and
puts out her hand and seizes him by the gen-
itals, 12then you shall cut off her hand; your
eye shall not pity *her.*

13"You shall not have in your bag differing weights, a heavy and a light. 14You shall
not have in your house differing measures,
a large and a small. 15You shall have a perfect
and just weight, a perfect and just measure,
that your days may be lengthened in the land
which the LORD your God is giving you. 16For
all who do such things, all who behave un-
righteously, *are* an abomination to the LORD
your God.

Destroy the Amalekites

17"Remember what Amalek did to you on
the way as you were coming out of Egypt,
18how he met you on the way and attacked
your rear ranks, all the stragglers at your
rear, when you *were* tired and weary; and
he did not fear God. 19Therefore it shall be,
when the LORD your God has given you rest
from your enemies all around, in the land

which the LORD your God is giving you to
possess *as* an inheritance, *that* you will blot
out the remembrance of Amalek from under
heaven. You shall not forget.

Offerings of Firstfruits and Tithes

26 "And it shall be, when you come
into the land which the LORD
your God is giving you *as* an inheritance,
and you possess it and dwell in it, 2that you
shall take some of the first of all the produce
of the ground, which you shall bring from
your land that the LORD your God is giving
you, and put *it* in a basket and go to the place
where the LORD your God chooses to make
His name abide. 3And you shall go to the one
who is priest in those days, and say to him,
'I declare today to the LORD your[a] God that
I have come to the country which the LORD
swore to our fathers to give us.'

4"Then the priest shall take the basket
out of your hand and set it down before the
altar of the LORD your God. 5And you shall
answer and say before the LORD your God:
'My father *was* a Syrian,[a] about to perish,
and he went down to Egypt and dwelt there,
few in number; and there he became a nation, great, mighty, and populous. 6But the
Egyptians mistreated us, afflicted us, and
laid hard bondage on us. 7Then we cried
out to the LORD God of our fathers, and the
LORD heard our voice and looked on our affliction and our labor and our oppression.
8So the LORD brought us out of Egypt with a
mighty hand and with an outstretched arm,
with great terror and with signs and wonders. 9He has brought us to this place and
has given us this land, "a land flowing with
milk and honey";[a] 10and now, behold, I have
brought the firstfruits of the land which you,
O LORD, have given me.'

"Then you shall set it before the LORD
your God, and worship before the LORD your
God. 11So you shall rejoice in every good *thing*
which the LORD your God has given to you
and your house, you and the Levite and the
stranger who *is* among you.

12"When you have finished laying aside
all the tithe of your increase in the third
year—the year of tithing—and have given
it to the Levite, the stranger, the fatherless,
and the widow, so that they may eat within
your gates and be filled, 13then you shall say
before the LORD your God: 'I have removed
the holy *tithe* from *my* house, and also have
given them to the Levite, the stranger, the
fatherless, and the widow, according to all
Your commandments which You have commanded me; I have not transgressed Your
commandments, nor have I forgotten *them.*
14I have not eaten any of it when in mourning, nor have I removed *any* of it for an unclean *use,* nor given *any* of it for the dead. I
have obeyed the voice of the LORD my God,
and have done according to all that You have
commanded me. 15Look down from Your
holy habitation, from heaven, and bless Your
people Israel and the land which You have
given us, just as You swore to our fathers, "a
land flowing with milk and honey." '[a]

A Special People of God

16"This day the LORD your God commands you to observe these statutes and
judgments; therefore you shall be careful to
observe them with all your heart and with
all your soul. 17Today you have proclaimed
the LORD to be your God, and that you will
walk in His ways and keep His statutes, His
commandments, and His judgments, and
that you will obey His voice. 18Also today the
LORD has proclaimed you to be His special
people, just as He promised you, that *you*
should keep all His commandments, 19and
that He will set you high above all nations
which He has made, in praise, in name, and
in honor, and that you may be a holy people to the LORD your God, just as He has
spoken."

The Law Inscribed on Stones

27 Now Moses, with the elders of Israel, commanded the people, saying: "Keep all the commandments which
I command you today. 2And it shall be, on
the day when you cross over the Jordan to
the land which the LORD your God is giving
you, that you shall set up for yourselves large
stones, and whitewash them with lime. 3You
shall write on them all the words of this law,
when you have crossed over, that you may
enter the land which the LORD your God is
giving you, 'a land flowing with milk and
honey,'[a] just as the LORD God of your fathers
promised you. 4Therefore it shall be, when
you have crossed over the Jordan, *that* on
Mount Ebal you shall set up these stones,
which I command you today, and you shall

26:3 [a] Septuagint reads *my.* 26:5 [a] Or *Aramean*
26:9 [a] Exodus 3:8 26:15 [a] Exodus 3:8 27:3 [a] Exodus 3:8

whitewash them with lime. 5And there you
shall build an altar to the LORD your God, an
altar of stones; you shall not use an iron *tool*
on them. 6You shall build with whole stones
the altar of the LORD your God, and offer
burnt offerings on it to the LORD your God.
7You shall offer peace offerings, and shall
eat there, and rejoice before the LORD your
God. 8And you shall write very plainly on the
stones all the words of this law."
9Then Moses and the priests, the Levites,
spoke to all Israel, saying, "Take heed and
listen, O Israel: This day you have become
the people of the LORD your God. 10There-
fore you shall obey the voice of the LORD your
God, and observe His commandments and
His statutes which I command you today."

Curses Pronounced from Mount Ebal

11And Moses commanded the people on
the same day, saying, 12"These shall stand
on Mount Gerizim to bless the people, when
you have crossed over the Jordan: Simeon,
Levi, Judah, Issachar, Joseph, and Benjamin;
13and these shall stand on Mount Ebal to
curse: Reuben, Gad, Asher, Zebulun, Dan,
and Naphtali.
14"And the Levites shall speak with a
loud voice and say to all the men of Israel:
15'Cursed *is* the one who makes a carved or
molded image, an abomination to the LORD,
the work of the hands of the craftsman, and
sets *it* up in secret.'
"And all the people shall answer and say,
'Amen!'
16'Cursed *is* the one who treats his father
or his mother with contempt.'
"And all the people shall say, 'Amen!'
17'Cursed *is* the one who moves his neighbor's landmark.'
"And all the people shall say, 'Amen!'
18'Cursed *is* the one who makes the blind
to wander off the road.'
"And all the people shall say, 'Amen!'
19'Cursed *is* the one who perverts the
justice due the stranger, the fatherless, and
widow.'
"And all the people shall say, 'Amen!'
20'Cursed *is* the one who lies with his father's wife, because he has uncovered his
father's bed.'
"And all the people shall say, 'Amen!'
21'Cursed *is* the one who lies with any
kind of animal.'
"And all the people shall say, 'Amen!'
22'Cursed *is* the one who lies with his sister, the daughter of his father or the daughter of his mother.'
"And all the people shall say, 'Amen!'
23'Cursed *is* the one who lies with his
mother-in-law.'
"And all the people shall say, 'Amen!'
24'Cursed *is* the one who attacks his
neighbor secretly.'
"And all the people shall say, 'Amen!'
25'Cursed *is* the one who takes a bribe to
slay an innocent person.'
"And all the people shall say, 'Amen!'
26'Cursed *is* the one who does not confirm
all the words of this law by observing them.'
"And all the people shall say, 'Amen!'"

Blessings on Obedience

28 "Now it shall come to pass, if you
diligently obey the voice of the
LORD your God, to observe carefully all His
commandments which I command you today, that the LORD your God will set you high
above all nations of the earth. 2And all these
blessings shall come upon you and overtake
you, because you obey the voice of the LORD
your God:
3"Blessed *shall* you *be* in the city, and
blessed *shall* you *be* in the country.
4"Blessed *shall be* the fruit of your body,
the produce of your ground and the increase
of your herds, the increase of your cattle and
the offspring of your flocks.
5"Blessed *shall be* your basket and your
kneading bowl.
6"Blessed *shall* you *be* when you come in,
and blessed *shall* you *be* when you go out.
7"The LORD will cause your enemies who
rise against you to be defeated before your
face; they shall come out against you one way
and flee before you seven ways.
8"The LORD will command the blessing
on you in your storehouses and in all to
which you set your hand, and He will bless
you in the land which the LORD your God is
giving you.
9"The LORD will establish you as a holy
people to Himself, just as He has sworn to
you, if you keep the commandments of the
LORD your God and walk in His ways. 10Then
all peoples of the earth shall see that you are
called by the name of the LORD, and they
shall be afraid of you. 11And the LORD will
grant you plenty of goods, in the fruit of your
body, in the increase of your livestock, and

in the produce of your ground, in the land of
which the LORD swore to your fathers to give
you. 12The LORD will open to you His good
treasure, the heavens, to give the rain to your
land in its season, and to bless all the work of
your hand. You shall lend to many nations,
but you shall not borrow. 13And the LORD
will make you the head and not the tail; you
shall be above only, and not be beneath, if
you heed the commandments of the LORD
your God, which I command you today, and
are careful to observe *them.* 14So you shall
not turn aside from any of the words which
I command you this day, *to* the right or the
left, to go after other gods to serve them.

Curses on Disobedience

15"But it shall come to pass, if you do not
obey the voice of the LORD your God, to observe carefully all His commandments and
His statutes which I command you today,
that all these curses will come upon you and
overtake you:

16"Cursed *shall* you *be* in the city, and
cursed *shall* you *be* in the country.

17"Cursed *shall be* your basket and your
kneading bowl.

18"Cursed *shall be* the fruit of your body
and the produce of your land, the increase of
your cattle and the offspring of your flocks.

19"Cursed *shall* you *be* when you come in,
and cursed *shall* you *be* when you go out.

20"The LORD will send on you cursing,
confusion, and rebuke in all that you set
your hand to do, until you are destroyed
and until you perish quickly, because of the
wickedness of your doings in which you
have forsaken Me. 21The LORD will make the
plague cling to you until He has consumed
you from the land which you are going to
possess. 22The LORD will strike you with
consumption, with fever, with inflammation, with severe burning fever, with the
sword, with scorching, and with mildew;
they shall pursue you until you perish. 23And
your heavens which *are* over your head shall
be bronze, and the earth which is under you
shall be iron. 24The LORD will change the rain
of your land to powder and dust; from the
heaven it shall come down on you until you
are destroyed.

25"The LORD will cause you to be defeated before your enemies; you shall go out one
way against them and flee seven ways before
them; and you shall become troublesome to
all the kingdoms of the earth. 26Your carcasses shall be food for all the birds of the
air and the beasts of the earth, and no one
shall frighten *them* away. 27The LORD will
strike you with the boils of Egypt, with tumors, with the scab, and with the itch, from
which you cannot be healed. 28The LORD will
strike you with madness and blindness and
confusion of heart. 29And you shall grope at
noonday, as a blind man gropes in darkness;
you shall not prosper in your ways; you shall
be only oppressed and plundered continually, and no one shall save *you.*

30"You shall betroth a wife, but another man shall lie with her; you shall build
a house, but you shall not dwell in it; you
shall plant a vineyard, but shall not gather its grapes. 31Your ox *shall be* slaughtered
before your eyes, but you shall not eat of it;
your donkey *shall be* violently taken away
from before you, and shall not be restored
to you; your sheep *shall be* given to your enemies, and you shall have no one to rescue
them. 32Your sons and your daughters *shall*
be given to another people, and your eyes
shall look and fail *with longing* for them all
day long; and *there shall be* no strength in
your hand. 33A nation whom you have not
known shall eat the fruit of your land and
the produce of your labor, and you shall be
only oppressed and crushed continually. 34So
you shall be driven mad because of the sight
which your eyes see. 35The LORD will strike
you in the knees and on the legs with severe
boils which cannot be healed, and from the
sole of your foot to the top of your head.

36"The LORD will bring you and the king
whom you set over you to a nation which
neither you nor your fathers have known,
and there you shall serve other gods—wood
and stone. 37And you shall become an astonishment, a proverb, and a byword among all
nations where the LORD will drive you.

38"You shall carry much seed out to the
field but gather little in, for the locust shall
consume it. 39You shall plant vineyards and
tend *them,* but you shall neither drink *of* the
wine nor gather the *grapes;* for the worms
shall eat them. 40You shall have olive trees
throughout all your territory, but you shall
not anoint *yourself* with the oil; for your olives shall drop off. 41You shall beget sons and
daughters, but they shall not be yours; for
they shall go into captivity. 42Locusts shall

consume all your trees and the produce of
your land.

43 "The alien who *is* among you shall rise
higher and higher above you, and you shall
come down lower and lower. 44 He shall lend
to you, but you shall not lend to him; he shall
be the head, and you shall be the tail.

45 "Moreover all these curses shall come
upon you and pursue and overtake you, until
you are destroyed, because you did not obey
the voice of the LORD your God, to keep His
commandments and His statutes which He
commanded you. 46 And they shall be upon
you for a sign and a wonder, and on your descendants forever.

47 "Because you did not serve the LORD
your God with joy and gladness of heart, for
the abundance of everything, 48 therefore you
shall serve your enemies, whom the LORD
will send against you, in hunger, in thirst,
in nakedness, and in need of everything;
and He will put a yoke of iron on your neck
until He has destroyed you. 49 The LORD will
bring a nation against you from afar, from
the end of the earth, *as swift* as the eagle
flies, a nation whose language you will not
understand, 50 a nation of fierce countenance,
which does not respect the elderly nor show
favor to the young. 51 And they shall eat the
increase of your livestock and the produce
of your land, until you are destroyed; they
shall not leave you grain or new wine or oil,
or the increase of your cattle or the offspring
of your flocks, until they have destroyed you.

52 "They shall besiege you at all your gates
until your high and fortified walls, in which
you trust, come down throughout all your
land; and they shall besiege you at all your
gates throughout all your land which the
LORD your God has given you. 53 You shall eat
the fruit of your own body, the flesh of your
sons and your daughters whom the LORD
your God has given you, in the siege and
desperate straits in which your enemy shall
distress you. 54 The sensitive and very refined
man among you will be hostile toward his
brother, toward the wife of his bosom, and
toward the rest of his children whom he
leaves behind, 55 so that he will not give any
of them the flesh of his children whom he
will eat, because he has nothing left in the
siege and desperate straits in which your enemy shall distress you at all your gates. 56 The
tender and delicate woman among you, who
would not venture to set the sole of her foot
on the ground because of her delicateness
and sensitivity, will refuse[a] to the husband
of her bosom, and to her son and her daughter, 57 her placenta which comes out from
between her feet and her children whom
she bears; for she will eat them secretly for
lack of everything in the siege and desperate
straits in which your enemy shall distress
you at all your gates.

58 "If you do not carefully observe all the
words of this law that are written in this
book, that you may fear this glorious and
awesome name, THE LORD YOUR GOD,
59 then the LORD will bring upon you and
your descendants extraordinary plagues—
great and prolonged plagues—and serious
and prolonged sicknesses. 60 Moreover He
will bring back on you all the diseases of
Egypt, of which you were afraid, and they
shall cling to you. 61 Also every sickness and
every plague, which *is* not written in this
Book of the Law, will the LORD bring upon
you until you are destroyed. 62 You shall be
left few in number, whereas you were as the
stars of heaven in multitude, because you
would not obey the voice of the LORD your
God. 63 And it shall be, *that* just as the LORD
rejoiced over you to do you good and multiply you, so the LORD will rejoice over you to
destroy you and bring you to nothing; and
you shall be plucked from off the land which
you go to possess.

64 "Then the LORD will scatter you among
all peoples, from one end of the earth to the
other, and there you shall serve other gods,
which neither you nor your fathers have
known—wood and stone. 65 And among
those nations you shall find no rest, nor
shall the sole of your foot have a resting
place; but there the LORD will give you a
trembling heart, failing eyes, and anguish
of soul. 66 Your life shall hang in doubt before
you; you shall fear day and night, and have
no assurance of life. 67 In the morning you
shall say, 'Oh, that it were evening!' And at
evening you shall say, 'Oh, that it were morning!' because of the fear which terrifies your
heart, and because of the sight which your
eyes see.

68 "And the LORD will take you back to
Egypt in ships, by the way of which I said to
you, 'You shall never see it again.' And there

28:56 [a] Literally *her eye shall be evil toward*

you shall be offered for sale to your enemies
as male and female slaves, but no one will
buy *you*."

The Covenant Renewed in Moab

29 These *are* the words of the covenant which the LORD command-
ed Moses to make with the children of
Israel in the land of Moab, besides the covenant which He made with them in Horeb.
2Now Moses called all Israel and said
to them: "You have seen all that the LORD
did before your eyes in the land of Egypt,
to Pharaoh and to all his servants and to
all his land— 3the great trials which your
eyes have seen, the signs, and those great
wonders. 4Yet the LORD has not given you
a heart to perceive and eyes to see and ears
to hear, to this *very* day. 5And I have led you
forty years in the wilderness. Your clothes
have not worn out on you, and your sandals
have not worn out on your feet. 6You have
not eaten bread, nor have you drunk wine or
similar drink, that you may know that I *am*
the LORD your God. 7And when you came to
this place, Sihon king of Heshbon and Og
king of Bashan came out against us to battle, and we conquered them. 8We took their
land and gave it as an inheritance to the Reubenites, to the Gadites, and to half the tribe
of Manasseh. 9Therefore keep the words of
this covenant, and do them, that you may
prosper in all that you do.
10"All of you stand today before the LORD
your God: your leaders and your tribes and
your elders and your officers, all the men
of Israel, 11your little ones and your wives—
also the stranger who *is* in your camp, from
the one who cuts your wood to the one who
draws your water— 12that you may enter into
covenant with the LORD your God, and into
His oath, which the LORD your God makes
with you today, 13that He may establish you
today as a people for Himself, and *that* He
may be God to you, just as He has spoken
to you, and just as He has sworn to your fathers, to Abraham, Isaac, and Jacob.
14"I make this covenant and this oath, not
with you alone, 15but with *him* who stands
here with us today before the LORD our God,
as well as with *him* who *is* not here with us
today 16(for you know that we dwelt in the
land of Egypt and that we came through the
nations which you passed by, 17and you saw
their abominations and their idols which
were among them—wood and stone and
silver and gold); 18so that there may not be
among you man or woman or family or tribe,
whose heart turns away today from the LORD
our God, to go *and* serve the gods of these
nations, and that there may not be among
you a root bearing bitterness or wormwood;
19and so it may not happen, when he hears
the words of this curse, that he blesses himself in his heart, saying, 'I shall have peace,
even though I follow the dictates[a] of my
heart'—as though the drunkard could be
included with the sober.
20"The LORD would not spare him; for
then the anger of the LORD and His jealousy would burn against that man, and every
curse that is written in this book would settle on him, and the LORD would blot out his
name from under heaven. 21And the LORD
would separate him from all the tribes of Israel for adversity, according to all the curses
of the covenant that are written in this Book
of the Law, 22so that the coming generation
of your children who rise up after you, and
the foreigner who comes from a far land,
would say, when they see the plagues of that
land and the sicknesses which the LORD has
laid on it:
23'The whole land *is* brimstone, salt, and
burning; it is not sown, nor does it bear, nor
does any grass grow there, like the overthrow of Sodom and Gomorrah, Admah,
and Zeboiim, which the LORD overthrew
in His anger and His wrath.' 24All nations
would say, 'Why has the LORD done so to this
land? What does the heat of this great anger
mean?' 25Then *people* would say: 'Because
they have forsaken the covenant of the LORD
God of their fathers, which He made with
them when He brought them out of the land
of Egypt; 26for they went and served other
gods and worshiped them, gods that they did
not know and that He had not given to them.
27Then the anger of the LORD was aroused
against this land, to bring on it every curse
that is written in this book. 28And the LORD
uprooted them from their land in anger, in
wrath, and in great indignation, and cast
them into another land, as *it is* this day.'
29"The secret *things belong* to the LORD
our God, but those *things which are* revealed
belong to us and to our children forever, that
we may do all the words of this law.

29:19 [a] Or *stubbornness*

The Blessing of Returning to God

30 "Now it shall come to pass, when
all these things come upon you,
the blessing and the curse which I have
set before you, and you call *them* to mind
among all the nations where the LORD your
God drives you, 2and you return to the LORD
your God and obey His voice, according
to all that I command you today, you and
your children, with all your heart and with
all your soul, 3that the LORD your God will
bring you back from captivity, and have compassion on you, and gather you again from
all the nations where the LORD your God
has scattered you. 4If *any* of you are driven
out to the farthest *parts* under heaven, from
there the LORD your God will gather you,
and from there He will bring you. 5Then the
LORD your God will bring you to the land
which your fathers possessed, and you shall
possess it. He will prosper you and multiply
you more than your fathers. 6And the LORD
your God will circumcise your heart and the
heart of your descendants, to love the LORD
your God with all your heart and with all
your soul, that you may live.

7"Also the LORD your God will put all
these curses on your enemies and on those
who hate you, who persecuted you. 8And you
will again obey the voice of the LORD and do
all His commandments which I command
you today. 9The LORD your God will make
you abound in all the work of your hand, in
the fruit of your body, in the increase of your
livestock, and in the produce of your land for
good. For the LORD will again rejoice over
you for good as He rejoiced over your fathers,
10if you obey the voice of the LORD your God,
to keep His commandments and His statutes which are written in this Book of the
Law, *and* if you turn to the LORD your God
with all your heart and with all your soul.

The Choice of Life or Death

11"For this commandment which I com-
mand you today *is* not *too* mysterious for you,
nor *is* it far off. 12It *is* not in heaven, that you
should say, 'Who will ascend into heaven
for us and bring it to us, that we may hear it
and do it?' 13Nor *is* it beyond the sea, that you
should say, 'Who will go over the sea for us
and bring it to us, that we may hear it and do
it?' 14But the word *is* very near you, in your
mouth and in your heart, that you may do it.

15"See, I have set before you today life and
good, death and evil, 16in that I command you
today to love the LORD your God, to walk in
His ways, and to keep His commandments,
His statutes, and His judgments, that you
may live and multiply; and the LORD your
God will bless you in the land which you go
to possess. 17But if your heart turns away so

30:18–20 CHOOSE LIFE

Moses had to say some tough things to Israel before they crossed the Jordan River into the Promised Land of Canaan. Israel still had a lot of hard lessons to learn. Their biggest lesson: "Choose life, that both you and your descendants may live."

This is a very simple lesson, but it's very hard for people to learn. Many say they want to live, but they act like they want to die. On busy streets and highways, you see this every day. People drive as if they want to die. Alcohol and drugs have ruined their wish to live. But God is always there, even if we can't see Him. He keeps saying, "Choose life!"

You have to make that choice for yourself. You must say to God, "I'm turning my back on the ways of death, and I'm going to live because Jesus gives me His power to live."

sight of the LORD, to provoke Him to anger through the work of your hands."

The Song of Moses

30 Then Moses spoke in the hearing of all the assembly of Israel the words of this song until they were ended:

32 "Give ear, O heavens, and I will speak;
And hear, O earth, the words of my mouth.
2 Let my teaching drop as the rain,
My speech distill as the dew,
As raindrops on the tender herb,
And as showers on the grass.
3 For I proclaim the name of the LORD:
Ascribe greatness to our God.
4 *He is* the Rock, His work *is* perfect;
For all His ways *are* justice,
A God of truth and without injustice;
Righteous and upright *is* He.

5 "They have corrupted themselves;
They are not His children,
Because of their blemish:
A perverse and crooked generation.
6 Do you thus deal with the LORD,
O foolish and unwise people?
Is He not your Father, *who* bought you?
Has He not made you and established you?

7 "Remember the days of old,
Consider the years of many generations.
Ask your father, and he will show you;
Your elders, and they will tell you:
8 When the Most High divided their inheritance to the nations,
When He separated the sons of Adam,
He set the boundaries of the peoples
According to the number of the children of Israel.
9 For the LORD's portion *is* His people;
Jacob *is* the place of His inheritance.

10 "He found him in a desert land
And in the wasteland, a howling wilderness;
He encircled him, He instructed him,
He kept him as the apple of His eye.
11 As an eagle stirs up its nest,
Hovers over its young,
Spreading out its wings, taking them up,
Carrying them on its wings,
12 *So* the LORD alone led him,
And *there was* no foreign god with him.

13 "He made him ride in the heights of the earth,
That he might eat the produce of the fields;
He made him draw honey from the rock,
And oil from the flinty rock;
14 Curds from the cattle, and milk of the flock,
With fat of lambs;
And rams of the breed of Bashan, and goats,
With the choicest wheat;
And you drank wine, the blood of the grapes.

15 "But Jeshurun grew fat and kicked;
You grew fat, you grew thick,
You are obese!
Then he forsook God *who* made him,
And scornfully esteemed the Rock of his salvation.
16 They provoked Him to jealousy with foreign *gods;*
With abominations they provoked Him to anger.
17 They sacrificed to demons, not to God,
To gods they did not know,
To new *gods,* new arrivals
That your fathers did not fear.
18 Of the Rock *who* begot you, you are unmindful,
And have forgotten the God who fathered you.

19 "And when the LORD saw *it,* He spurned *them,*
Because of the provocation of His sons and His daughters.
20 And He said: 'I will hide My face from them,
I will see what their end *will be,*
For they *are* a perverse generation,
Children in whom *is* no faith.
21 They have provoked Me to jealousy by *what* is not God;
They have moved Me to anger by their foolish idols.
But I will provoke them to jealousy by *those who are* not a nation;
I will move them to anger by a foolish nation.
22 For a fire is kindled in My anger,
And shall burn to the lowest hell;

It shall consume the earth with her increase,
And set on fire the foundations of the mountains.

23 'I will heap disasters on them;
I will spend My arrows on them.
24 *They shall be* wasted with hunger,
Devoured by pestilence and bitter destruction;
I will also send against them the teeth of beasts,
With the poison of serpents of the dust.
25 The sword shall destroy outside;
There shall be terror within
For the young man and virgin,
The nursing child with the man of gray hairs.
26 I would have said, "I will dash them in pieces,
I will make the memory of them to cease from among men,"
27 Had I not feared the wrath of the enemy,
Lest their adversaries should misunderstand,
Lest they should say, "Our hand *is* high;
And it is not the LORD who has done all this."'

28 "For they *are* a nation void of counsel,
Nor *is there any* understanding in them.
29 Oh, that they were wise, *that* they understood this,
That they would consider their latter end!
30 How could one chase a thousand,
And two put ten thousand to flight,
Unless their Rock had sold them,
And the LORD had surrendered them?
31 For their rock *is* not like our Rock,
Even our enemies themselves *being* judges.
32 For their vine *is* of the vine of Sodom
And of the fields of Gomorrah;
Their grapes *are* grapes of gall,
Their clusters *are* bitter.
33 Their wine *is* the poison of serpents,
And the cruel venom of cobras.

34 '*Is* this not laid up in store with Me,
Sealed up among My treasures?
35 Vengeance is Mine, and recompense;
Their foot shall slip in *due* time;
For the day of their calamity *is* at hand,
And the things to come hasten upon them.'

36 "For the LORD will judge His people
And have compassion on His servants,
When He sees that *their* power is gone,
And *there is* no one *remaining*, bond or free.
37 He will say: 'Where *are* their gods,
The rock in which they sought refuge?
38 Who ate the fat of their sacrifices,
And drank the wine of their drink offering?
Let them rise and help you,
And be your refuge.

39 'Now see that I, *even* I, *am* He,
And *there is* no God besides Me;
I kill and I make alive;
I wound and I heal;
Nor *is there any* who can deliver from My hand.
40 For I raise My hand to heaven,
And say, "*As* I live forever,
41 If I whet My glittering sword,
And My hand takes hold on judgment,
I will render vengeance to My enemies,
And repay those who hate Me.
42 I will make My arrows drunk with blood,
And My sword shall devour flesh,
With the blood of the slain and the captives,
From the heads of the leaders of the enemy."'

43 "Rejoice, O Gentiles, *with* His people;[a]
For He will avenge the blood of His servants,
And render vengeance to His adversaries;
He will provide atonement for His land *and* His people."

44So Moses came with Joshua[a] the son of
Nun and spoke all the words of this song in
the hearing of the people. 45Moses finished
speaking all these words to all Israel, 46and
he said to them: "Set your hearts on all the
words which I testify among you today,
which you shall command your children
to be careful to observe—all the words of
this law. 47For it *is* not a futile thing for you,
because it *is* your life, and by this word you
shall prolong *your* days in the land which you
cross over the Jordan to possess."

32:43 [a] A Dead Sea Scroll fragment adds *And let all the gods (angels) worship Him* (compare Septuagint and Hebrews 1:6). **32:44** [a] Hebrew *Hoshea* (compare Numbers 13:8, 16)

Moses to Die on Mount Nebo

48 Then the LORD spoke to Moses that very same day, saying: 49 "Go up this mountain of the Abarim, Mount Nebo, which *is* in the land of Moab, across from Jericho; view the land of Canaan, which I give to the children of Israel as a possession; 50 and die on the mountain which you ascend, and be gathered to your people, just as Aaron your brother died on Mount Hor and was gathered to his people; 51 because you trespassed against Me among the children of Israel at the waters of Meribah Kadesh, in the Wilderness of Zin, because you did not hallow Me in the midst of the children of Israel. 52 Yet you shall see the land before *you*, though you shall not go there, into the land which I am giving to the children of Israel."

Moses' Final Blessing on Israel

33 Now this *is* the blessing with which Moses the man of God blessed the children of Israel before his death. 2 And he said:

"The LORD came from Sinai,
And dawned on them from Seir;
He shone forth from Mount Paran,
And He came with ten thousands of saints;
From His right hand
Came a fiery law for them.
3 Yes, He loves the people;
All His saints *are* in Your hand;
They sit down at Your feet;
Everyone receives Your words.
4 Moses commanded a law for us,
A heritage of the congregation of Jacob.
5 And He was King in Jeshurun,
When the leaders of the people were gathered,
All the tribes of Israel together.

6 "Let Reuben live, and not die,
Nor let his men be few."

7 And this he said of Judah:

"Hear, LORD, the voice of Judah,
And bring him to his people;
Let his hands be sufficient for him,
And may You be a help against his enemies."

8 And of Levi he said:

"*Let* Your Thummim and Your Urim *be* with Your holy one,
Whom You tested at Massah,
And with whom You contended at the waters of Meribah,
9 Who says of his father and mother,
'I have not seen them';
Nor did he acknowledge his brothers,
Or know his own children;
For they have observed Your word
And kept Your covenant.
10 They shall teach Jacob Your judgments,
And Israel Your law.
They shall put incense before You,
And a whole burnt sacrifice on Your altar.
11 Bless his substance, LORD,
And accept the work of his hands;
Strike the loins of those who rise against him,
And of those who hate him, that they rise not again."

12 Of Benjamin he said:

"The beloved of the LORD shall dwell in safety by Him,
Who shelters him all the day long;
And he shall dwell between His shoulders."

13 And of Joseph he said:

"Blessed of the LORD *is* his land,
With the precious things of heaven, with the dew,
And the deep lying beneath,
14 With the precious fruits of the sun,
With the precious produce of the months,
15 With the best things of the ancient mountains,
With the precious things of the everlasting hills,
16 With the precious things of the earth and its fullness,
And the favor of Him who dwelt in the bush.
Let *the blessing* come 'on the head of Joseph,
And on the crown of the head of him *who was* separate from his brothers.'[a]
17 His glory *is like* a firstborn bull,
And his horns *like* the horns of the wild ox;
Together with them
He shall push the peoples
To the ends of the earth;
They *are* the ten thousands of Ephraim,
And they *are* the thousands of Manasseh."

18 And of Zebulun he said:

33:16 [a] Genesis 49:26

"Rejoice, Zebulun, in your going out,
And Issachar in your tents!
19 They shall call the peoples *to* the mountain;
There they shall offer sacrifices of righteousness;
For they shall partake *of* the abundance of the seas
And *of* treasures hidden in the sand."

20And of Gad he said:

"Blessed *is* he who enlarges Gad;
He dwells as a lion,
And tears the arm and the crown of his head.
21 He provided the first *part* for himself,
Because a lawgiver's portion was reserved there.
He came *with* the heads of the people;
He administered the justice of the LORD,
And His judgments with Israel."

22And of Dan he said:

"Dan *is* a lion's whelp;
He shall leap from Bashan."

23And of Naphtali he said:

"O Naphtali, satisfied with favor,
And full of the blessing of the LORD,
Possess the west and the south."

24And of Asher he said:

"Asher *is* most blessed of sons;
Let him be favored by his brothers,
And let him dip his foot in oil.
25 Your sandals *shall be* iron and bronze;
As your days, *so shall* your strength *be*.

26 "*There is* no one like the God of Jeshurun,
Who rides the heavens to help you,
And in His excellency on the clouds.
27 The eternal God *is your* refuge,
And underneath *are* the everlasting arms;
He will thrust out the enemy from before you,
And will say, 'Destroy!'
28 Then Israel shall dwell in safety,
The fountain of Jacob alone,
In a land of grain and new wine;
His heavens shall also drop dew.
29 Happy *are* you, O Israel!
Who *is* like you, a people saved by the LORD,
The shield of your help
And the sword of your majesty!
Your enemies shall submit to you,
And you shall tread down their high places."

Moses Dies on Mount Nebo

34 Then Moses went up from the
plains of Moab to Mount Nebo, to
the top of Pisgah, which is across from Jericho. And the LORD showed him all the land
of Gilead as far as Dan, 2all Naphtali and
the land of Ephraim and Manasseh, all the
land of Judah as far as the Western Sea,[a] 3the
South, and the plain of the Valley of Jericho,
the city of palm trees, as far as Zoar. 4Then
the LORD said to him, "This *is* the land of
which I swore to give Abraham, Isaac, and
Jacob, saying, 'I will give it to your descendants.' I have caused you to see *it* with your
eyes, but you shall not cross over there."
5So Moses the servant of the LORD died
there in the land of Moab, according to the
word of the LORD. 6And He buried him in
a valley in the land of Moab, opposite Beth
Peor; but no one knows his grave to this day.
7Moses *was* one hundred and twenty years
old when he died. His eyes were not dim nor
his natural vigor diminished. 8And the children of Israel wept for Moses in the plains
of Moab thirty days. So the days of weeping
and mourning for Moses ended.
9Now Joshua the son of Nun was full
of the spirit of wisdom, for Moses had laid
his hands on him; so the children of Israel
heeded him, and did as the LORD had commanded Moses.
10But since then there has not arisen in
Israel a prophet like Moses, whom the LORD
knew face to face, 11in all the signs and wonders which the LORD sent him to do in the
land of Egypt, before Pharaoh, before all his
servants, and in all his land, 12and by all that
mighty power and all the great terror which
Moses performed in the sight of all Israel.

34:2 [a] That is, the Mediterranean

The BOOK of JOSHUA

1405 B.C.–1390 B.C.

Behind the Scenes

READ IT:

The book of Joshua is the story of Joshua, the leader of God's people. It's also the history of the people of Israel. With God's help, the people conquered the Promised Land—Canaan. They miraculously crossed the Jordan River and captured the town of Jericho. Then, with God's help again, they quickly took over all the main areas of Canaan.

GET IT:

Who wrote it: Joshua probably wrote it.

When it was written: 1405 B.C.–1390 B.C.

Why it was written: to tell the history of God's people as they enter the Promised Land.

LIVE IT:

Don't be afraid. God goes with you wherever you go.

You have to choose for yourself whom or what you'll love and serve: God or something else.

FIND IT:

God's Commission to Joshua	*Joshua 1*
Rahab Hides the Spies	*Joshua 2*
Israel Crosses the Jordan	*Joshua 3–4*
The Destruction of Jericho	*Joshua 6*
The Treaty with the Gibeonites	*Joshua 9*
The Sun Stands Still	*Joshua 10*
The Cities of Refuge	*Joshua 20*
The Covenant at Shechem	*Joshua 24*

God's Commission to Joshua

1 After the death of Moses the servant of
the LORD, it came to pass that the LORD
spoke to Joshua the son of Nun, Moses' assistant, saying: 2"Moses My servant is dead.
Now therefore, arise, go over this Jordan, you
and all this people, to the land which I am
giving to them—the children of Israel. 3Ev-
ery place that the sole of your foot will tread
upon I have given you, as I said to Moses.
4From the wilderness and this Lebanon as
far as the great river, the River Euphrates, all
the land of the Hittites, and to the Great Sea
toward the going down of the sun, shall be
your territory. 5No man shall *be able to* stand
before you all the days of your life; as I was
with Moses, *so* I will be with you. I will not
leave you nor forsake you. 6Be strong and of
good courage, for to this people you shall
divide as an inheritance the land which I
swore to their fathers to give them. 7Only be
strong and very courageous, that you may
observe to do according to all the law which
Moses My servant commanded you; do not
turn from it to the right hand or to the left,
that you may prosper wherever you go. 8This
Book of the Law shall not depart from your
mouth, but you shall meditate in it day and
night, that you may observe to do according
to all that is written in it. For then you will
make your way prosperous, and then you
will have good success. 9Have I not commanded you? Be strong and of good courage;
do not be afraid, nor be dismayed, for the
LORD your God *is* with you wherever you go."

The Order to Cross the Jordan

10Then Joshua commanded the officers
of the people, saying, 11"Pass through the
camp and command the people, saying,
'Prepare provisions for yourselves, for within three days you will cross over this Jordan,
to go in to possess the land which the LORD
your God is giving you to possess.'"

12And to the Reubenites, the Gadites, and
half the tribe of Manasseh Joshua spoke,
saying, 13"Remember the word which Moses the servant of the LORD commanded
you, saying, 'The LORD your God is giving
you rest and is giving you this land.' 14Your
wives, your little ones, and your livestock
shall remain in the land which Moses gave
you on this side of the Jordan. But you shall
pass before your brethren armed, all your
mighty men of valor, and help them, 15until
the LORD has given your brethren rest, as He
gave you, and they also have taken possession of the land which the LORD your God
is giving them. Then you shall return to the
land of your possession and enjoy it, which
Moses the LORD's servant gave you on this
side of the Jordan toward the sunrise."

16So they answered Joshua, saying, "All
that you command us we will do, and wherever you send us we will go. 17Just as we
heeded Moses in all things, so we will heed
you. Only the LORD your God be with you,
as He was with Moses. 18Whoever rebels
against your command and does not heed
your words, in all that you command him,
shall be put to death. Only be strong and of
good courage."

Rahab Hides the Spies

2 Now Joshua the son of Nun sent out
two men from Acacia Grove[a] to spy secretly, saying, "Go, view the land, especially
Jericho."

2:1 [a] Hebrew *Shittim*

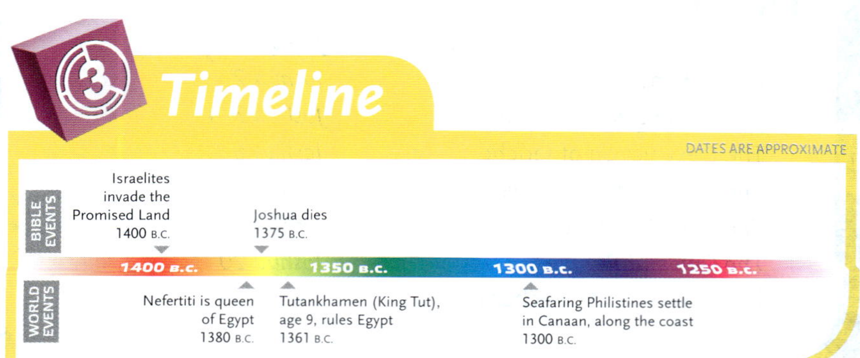

So they went, and came to the house of a
harlot named Rahab, and lodged there. 2And
it was told the king of Jericho, saying, "Behold,
men have come here tonight from the
children of Israel to search out the country."
3So the king of Jericho sent to Rahab, saying,
"Bring out the men who have come to
you, who have entered your house, for they
have come to search out all the country."
4Then the woman took the two men and
hid them. So she said, "Yes, the men came to
me, but I did not know where they *were* from.
5And it happened as the gate was being shut,
when it was dark, that the men went out.
Where the men went I do not know; pursue
them quickly, for you may overtake them."
6(But she had brought them up to the roof
and hidden them with the stalks of flax,
which she had laid in order on the roof.)
7Then the men pursued them by the road
to the Jordan, to the fords. And as soon as
those who pursued them had gone out, they
shut the gate.
8Now before they lay down, she came up

Starring Roles

JOSHUA'S name is pronounced *JOSH-you-uh* and means "Savior." God really did lead him to save his people from their enemies.

Joshua brought God's people across the Jordan River into the land of Canaan, which God long before had promised to Abraham. There the Commander of the Army of the Lord—who was really God Himself—led them in battle.

Since Abraham's time, the land of Canaan was filled with evil people who even sacrificed little children to their false gods. So the Lord decided to clear the land of such people and give the land back to the Hebrews for as long as they obeyed His laws.

You also live in a country where God has blessed you because your ancestors have obeyed His laws. The Lord will bless people with a good land when they honor Him.

Joshua's name means the same as the name of the great Savior from heaven—Jesus.

Action!

SUCCESS

READ IT: JOSHUA 1:7, 8

The Bible tells us not to turn to the left or the right from God's Word. That means don't deviate from what God says. And don't try to take detours either, avoiding the ways God wants you to live—with love and mercy, kindness and goodness. Keeping God's Word in front of you, constantly referring to it, and making it a part of your everyday life will make it easier to experience success as a follower of Jesus. Eventually God's Word will become a guide rather than a burden.

to them on the roof, 9and said to the men: "I
know that the LORD has given you the land,
that the terror of you has fallen on us, and
that all the inhabitants of the land are fainthearted because of you. 10For we have heard
how the LORD dried up the water of the Red
Sea for you when you came out of Egypt,
and what you did to the two kings of the
Amorites who *were* on the other side of the
Jordan, Sihon and Og, whom you utterly
destroyed. 11And as soon as we heard *these
things,* our hearts melted; neither did there
remain any more courage in anyone because
of you, for the LORD your God, He *is* God in
heaven above and on earth beneath. 12Now
therefore, I beg you, swear to me by the
LORD, since I have shown you kindness, that
you also will show kindness to my father's
house, and give me a true token, 13and spare
my father, my mother, my brothers, my sisters, and all that they have, and deliver our
lives from death."

14So the men answered her, "Our lives
for yours, if none of you tell this business
of ours. And it shall be, when the LORD has
given us the land, that we will deal kindly
and truly with you."

15Then she let them down by a rope
through the window, for her house *was* on
the city wall; she dwelt on the wall. 16And she
said to them, "Get to the mountain, lest the
pursuers meet you. Hide there three days,

COURAGE

READ IT: JOSHUA 1:9

It's in our nature to be afraid when we're faced with uncertain situations. A new school, a new church, or a class presentation can bring us fear. God promises to be near us wherever we may go, so we can press on. When we take a step into the unknown, we're being obedient to Him because we're being strong and courageous. Courage doesn't mean being fearless. Courage is having the guts to act even when we're afraid.

Starring Roles

RAHAB was terrified when the Hebrew spies went to her home. She was a very wicked person living in Jericho (pronounced *JERRY-ko*), and she had heard that Joshua's Hebrew army was going to destroy her city.

When she realized what was going to happen, she agreed that God was right to judge her sinful country. She confessed her sins and became a new person. God saved her that day not because she was a good woman (she wasn't), but because she was sorry and gave her life to Him. You might say she joined God's army. When the Hebrew troops came into Jericho, they didn't harm her. She left a scarlet cord in her window to remind them that she had hidden their spies.

Someday God is going to destroy the whole world for its wickedness. If you receive Jesus as your Savior, the scarlet sign of His blood will save you from that awful judgment.

until the pursuers have returned. Afterward
you may go your way."

17So the men said to her: "We *will be*
blameless of this oath of yours which you
have made us swear, 18unless, *when* we come
into the land, you bind this line of scarlet
cord in the window through which you let
us down, and unless you bring your father,
your mother, your brothers, and all your father's household to your own home. 19So it
shall be *that* whoever goes outside the doors
of your house into the street, his blood *shall
be* on his own head, and we *will be* guiltless.
And whoever is with you in the house, his
blood *shall be* on our head if a hand is laid on
him. 20And if you tell this business of ours,
then we will be free from your oath which
you made us swear."

21Then she said, "According to your
words, so *be* it." And she sent them away,
and they departed. And she bound the scarlet cord in the window.

22They departed and went to the mountain, and stayed there three days until the
pursuers returned. The pursuers sought
them all along the way, but did not find *them*.
23So the two men returned, descended from
the mountain, and crossed over; and they
came to Joshua the son of Nun, and told him
all that had befallen them. 24And they said
to Joshua, "Truly the LORD has delivered all
the land into our hands, for indeed all the
inhabitants of the country are fainthearted
because of us."

Israel Crosses the Jordan

3 Then Joshua rose early in the morning;
and they set out from Acacia Grove[a]
and came to the Jordan, he and all the children of Israel, and lodged there before they
crossed over. 2So it was, after three days, that
the officers went through the camp; 3and
they commanded the people, saying, "When
you see the ark of the covenant of the LORD
your God, and the priests, the Levites, bearing it, then you shall set out from your place
and go after it. 4Yet there shall be a space between you and it, about two thousand cubits
by measure. Do not come near it, that you
may know the way by which you must go, for
you have not passed *this* way before."

5And Joshua said to the people, "Sanctify
yourselves, for tomorrow the LORD will do
wonders among you." 6Then Joshua spoke
to the priests, saying, "Take up the ark of the
covenant and cross over before the people."

3:1 [a] Hebrew *Shittim*

2:17, 18 THE SCARLET CORD

You have seen how Rahab helped Joshua's spies in Joshua 2. The sign that saved Rahab when the army of Israel came was the sign of the scarlet cord in her window. The scarlet cord was easy to see, but isn't it interesting that the cord was also the color of blood?

On the night of Passover in Egypt (see Exodus 12), God "passed over" the Hebrew homes when He saw the scarlet blood of the Passover lamb on their doors. So they were saved from death.

As time passed, God taught His Old Testament people that their sins had to be paid for by the life of someone else. At first He taught them to sacrifice sheep, goats, cattle, and birds. But their beloved animals couldn't pay the awful cost of sin. That was only a way of teaching the people that *sin costs death*.

But this *scarlet line* of death points to the beloved Son of God whose blood takes away the sin of the world.

So they took up the ark of the covenant
and went before the people.
7And the LORD said to Joshua, "This day
I will begin to exalt you in the sight of all
Israel, that they may know that, as I was
with Moses, *so* I will be with you. 8You shall
command the priests who bear the ark of the
covenant, saying, 'When you have come to
the edge of the water of the Jordan, you shall
stand in the Jordan.'"
9So Joshua said to the children of Israel,
"Come here, and hear the words of the LORD
your God." 10And Joshua said, "By this you
shall know that the living God *is* among
you, and *that* He will without fail drive out
from before you the Canaanites and the Hittites and the Hivites and the Perizzites and
the Girgashites and the Amorites and the
Jebusites: 11Behold, the ark of the covenant
of the Lord of all the earth is crossing over
before you into the Jordan. 12Now therefore,
take for yourselves twelve men from the
tribes of Israel, one man from every tribe.
13And it shall come to pass, as soon as the
soles of the feet of the priests who bear the
ark of the LORD, the Lord of all the earth,
shall rest in the waters of the Jordan, *that*
the waters of the Jordan shall be cut off, the
waters that come down from upstream, and
they shall stand as a heap."
14So it was, when the people set out from
their camp to cross over the Jordan, with the
priests bearing the ark of the covenant before the people, 15and as those who bore the
ark came to the Jordan, and the feet of the
priests who bore the ark dipped in the edge

GOD LEADS ISRAEL'S ARMY INTO THE PROMISED LAND

READ IT: JOSHUA 3:1–17

GET IT:

Joshua got ready to move all the people into the Promised Land. But first they had to cross the Jordan River. The river was flooded. The water was high and dangerous. But God had a plan. Just as He had divided the Red Sea long ago to get His people across, He now divided the Jordan River. The water stopped flowing and the ground became dry so the people could cross the river without getting wet. And as promised, God led the way. His presence was in the ark of the covenant that the priests carried into the river. God was in charge. He would claim the land for His people.

LIVE IT:

Just like the Israelites, we often face obstacles in our lives. And when there's a delay in getting what we want, we get cranky and impatient. When that happens, we obviously don't trust that God can move us through, over, or around the obstacle, or even take the entire obstacle out of our way. What kinds of obstacles or impossible problems are you facing? Are you trying to do it all alone? Trust God to help. Or better yet, trust Him to take care of it. Ask Him. He can do anything (even stop a flooded river from flowing downstream).

of the water (for the Jordan overflows all its
banks during the whole time of harvest),
16that the waters which came down from upstream stood *still, and* rose in a heap very far
away at Adam, the city that *is* beside Zaretan.
So the waters that went down into the Sea
of the Arabah, the Salt Sea, failed, *and* were
cut off; and the people crossed over opposite
Jericho. 17Then the priests who bore the ark
of the covenant of the LORD stood firm on
dry ground in the midst of the Jordan; and
all Israel crossed over on dry ground, until
all the people had crossed completely over
the Jordan.

The Memorial Stones

4 And it came to pass, when all the people had completely crossed over the Jordan, that the LORD spoke to Joshua, saying:
2"Take for yourselves twelve men from the
people, one man from every tribe, 3and command them, saying, 'Take for yourselves
twelve stones from here, out of the midst of
the Jordan, from the place where the priests'
feet stood firm. You shall carry them over
with you and leave them in the lodging place
where you lodge tonight.'"
4Then Joshua called the twelve men
whom he had appointed from the children of
Israel, one man from every tribe; 5and Joshua said to them: "Cross over before the ark
of the LORD your God into the midst of the
Jordan, and each one of you take up a stone
on his shoulder, according to the number of
the tribes of the children of Israel, 6that this
may be a sign among you when your children ask in time to come, saying, 'What do
these stones *mean* to you?' 7Then you shall

On Location

Conquest of Canaan

Most of the story is set in what is now Israel. But the Israelites also conquered and claimed surrounding territory in what is now parts of Jordan, Syria, and Lebanon. After Jericho they moved west, then south (map at left). Only then did they attack the northern area, pressing past the Sea of Galilee (Chinnereth).

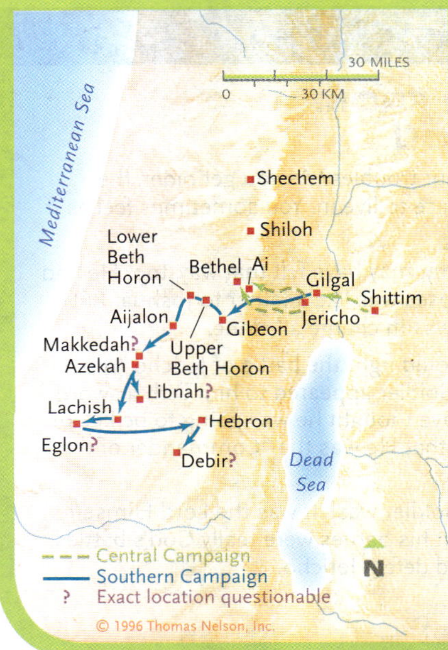

Central & Southern Campaign

Northern Campaign

answer them that the waters of the Jordan
were cut off before the ark of the covenant of
the LORD; when it crossed over the Jordan,
the waters of the Jordan were cut off. And
these stones shall be for a memorial to the
children of Israel forever."

8 And the children of Israel did so, just
as Joshua commanded, and took up twelve
stones from the midst of the Jordan, as the
LORD had spoken to Joshua, according to
the number of the tribes of the children of
Israel, and carried them over with them to
the place where they lodged, and laid them
down there. 9 Then Joshua set up twelve
stones in the midst of the Jordan, in the
place where the feet of the priests who bore
the ark of the covenant stood; and they are
there to this day.

10 So the priests who bore the ark stood
in the midst of the Jordan until everything
was finished that the LORD had commanded
Joshua to speak to the people, according to
all that Moses had commanded Joshua; and
the people hurried and crossed over. 11 Then
it came to pass, when all the people had completely crossed over, that the ark of the LORD
and the priests crossed over in the presence
of the people. 12 And the men of Reuben, the
men of Gad, and half the tribe of Manasseh
crossed over armed before the children of Israel, as Moses had spoken to them. 13 About
forty thousand prepared for war crossed over
before the LORD for battle, to the plains of
Jericho. 14 On that day the LORD exalted Joshua in the sight of all Israel; and they feared
him, as they had feared Moses, all the days
of his life.

15 Then the LORD spoke to Joshua, saying,
16 "Command the priests who bear the ark of
the Testimony to come up from the Jordan."
17 Joshua therefore commanded the priests,
saying, "Come up from the Jordan." 18 And it
came to pass, when the priests who bore the
ark of the covenant of the LORD had come
from the midst of the Jordan, *and* the soles
of the priests' feet touched the dry land, that
the waters of the Jordan returned to their
place and overflowed all its banks as before.

19 Now the people came up from the Jordan on the tenth *day* of the first month, and
they camped in Gilgal on the east border of
Jericho. 20 And those twelve stones which

5:13–15 THE SOLDIER FROM HEAVEN WILL HELP YOU

Do you ever feel all alone with your troubles? As you get older, the world seems to become a harder place to live in. You sometimes feel as if you have to get along by yourself.

Joshua, the general of Israel's army, may have felt that way, too. He had always had Moses to guide him. Moses was like a father to Joshua. But then Moses was gone, and Joshua was in charge all alone.

Joshua was wondering how he would fight the battle of Jericho (pronounced *JERRY-ko*) when a mighty Soldier appeared to him with a sword in His hand. At first Joshua must have thought he was going to be killed! But the strange Soldier told Joshua that He was the "Commander of the army of the LORD."

Can you guess who this mighty Soldier was? It was the Lord Himself who appeared to remind Joshua that his battles were really God's battles. As you will see, the Lord Himself did defeat Jericho.

You are *never* alone.

they took out of the Jordan, Joshua set up in
Gilgal. 21 Then he spoke to the children of Israel, saying: "When your children ask their
fathers in time to come, saying, 'What *are*
these stones?' 22 then you shall let your children know, saying, 'Israel crossed over this
Jordan on dry land'; 23 for the LORD your God
dried up the waters of the Jordan before you
until you had crossed over, as the LORD your
God did to the Red Sea, which He dried up
before us until we had crossed over, 24 that all
the peoples of the earth may know the hand
of the LORD, that it *is* mighty, that you may
fear the LORD your God forever."

The Second Generation Circumcised

5 So it was, when all the kings of the Amorites who *were* on the west side of the
Jordan, and all the kings of the Canaanites
who *were* by the sea, heard that the LORD had
dried up the waters of the Jordan from before
the children of Israel until we[a] had crossed
over, that their heart melted; and there was
no spirit in them any longer because of the
children of Israel.

2 At that time the LORD said to Joshua,
"Make flint knives for yourself, and circumcise the sons of Israel again the second
time." 3 So Joshua made flint knives for himself, and circumcised the sons of Israel at the
hill of the foreskins.[a] 4 And this *is* the reason
why Joshua circumcised them: All the people who came out of Egypt *who were* males,
all the men of war, had died in the wilderness on the way, after they had come out of
Egypt. 5 For all the people who came out had
been circumcised, but all the people born in
the wilderness, on the way as they came out
of Egypt, had not been circumcised. 6 For the
children of Israel walked forty years in the
wilderness, till all the people *who were* men
of war, who came out of Egypt, were consumed, because they did not obey the voice
of the LORD—to whom the LORD swore that
He would not show them the land which
the LORD had sworn to their fathers that He
would give us, "a land flowing with milk and
honey."[a] 7 Then Joshua circumcised their
sons *whom* He raised up in their place; for
they were uncircumcised, because they had
not been circumcised on the way.

8 So it was, when they had finished cir-
cumcising all the people, that they stayed
in their places in the camp till they were
healed. 9 Then the LORD said to Joshua, "This
day I have rolled away the reproach of Egypt
from you." Therefore the name of the place
is called Gilgal[a] to this day.

10 Now the children of Israel camped in
Gilgal, and kept the Passover on the fourteenth day of the month at twilight on the
plains of Jericho. 11 And they ate of the produce of the land on the day after the Passover, unleavened bread and parched grain,
on the very same day. 12 Then the manna
ceased on the day after they had eaten the
produce of the land; and the children of Israel no longer had manna, but they ate the
food of the land of Canaan that year.

The Commander of the Army of the LORD

13 And it came to pass, when Joshua was
by Jericho, that he lifted his eyes and looked,
and behold, a Man stood opposite him with
His sword drawn in His hand. And Joshua
went to Him and said to Him, "*Are* You for
us or for our adversaries?"

14 So He said, "No, but *as* Commander of
the army of the LORD I have now come."

And Joshua fell on his face to the earth
and worshiped, and said to Him, "What does
my Lord say to His servant?"

15 Then the Commander of the LORD's
army said to Joshua, "Take your sandal off
your foot, for the place where you stand *is*
holy." And Joshua did so.

The Destruction of Jericho

6 Now Jericho was securely shut up because of the children of Israel; none
went out, and none came in. 2 And the LORD
said to Joshua: "See! I have given Jericho into
your hand, its king, *and* the mighty men of
valor. 3 You shall march around the city, all
you men of war; you shall go all around the
city once. This you shall do six days. 4 And
seven priests shall bear seven trumpets
of rams' horns before the ark. But the seventh day you shall march around the city
seven times, and the priests shall blow the
trumpets. 5 It shall come to pass, when they
make a long *blast* with the ram's horn, *and*
when you hear the sound of the trumpet,
that all the people shall shout with a great
shout; then the wall of the city will fall down

5:1 [a] Following Kethib; Qere, some Hebrew manuscripts and editions, Septuagint, Syriac, Targum, and Vulgate read *they*. 5:3 [a] Hebrew *Gibeath Haaraloth* 5:6 [a] Exodus 3:8 5:9 [a] Literally *Rolling*

flat. And the people shall go up every man
straight before him."
6Then Joshua the son of Nun called the
priests and said to them, "Take up the ark
of the covenant, and let seven priests bear
seven trumpets of rams' horns before the
ark of the LORD." 7And he said to the people,
"Proceed, and march around the city, and let
him who is armed advance before the ark of
the LORD."
8So it was, when Joshua had spoken to
the people, that the seven priests bearing
the seven trumpets of rams' horns before
the LORD advanced and blew the trumpets,
and the ark of the covenant of the LORD followed them. 9The armed men went before
the priests who blew the trumpets, and the
rear guard came after the ark, while *the
priests* continued blowing the trumpets.
10Now Joshua had commanded the people,
saying, "You shall not shout or make any
noise with your voice, nor shall a word proceed out of your mouth, until the day I say
to you, 'Shout!' Then you shall shout." 11So
he had the ark of the LORD circle the city, going around *it* once. Then they came into the
camp and lodged in the camp.
12And Joshua rose early in the morning,
and the priests took up the ark of the LORD.
13Then seven priests bearing seven trumpets
of rams' horns before the ark of the LORD
went on continually and blew with the trumpets. And the armed men went before them.
But the rear guard came after the ark of the
LORD, while *the priests* continued blowing
the trumpets. 14And the second day they
marched around the city once and returned
to the camp. So they did six days.
15But it came to pass on the seventh day
that they rose early, about the dawning of
the day, and marched around the city seven
times in the same manner. On that day only
they marched around the city seven times.
16And the seventh time it happened, when
the priests blew the trumpets, that Joshua said to the people: "Shout, for the LORD
has given you the city! 17Now the city shall
be doomed by the LORD to destruction, it
and all who *are* in it. Only Rahab the har-
lot shall live, she and all who *are* with her in
the house, because she hid the messengers
that we sent. 18And you, by all means abstain
from the accursed things, lest you become
accursed when you take of the accursed
things, and make the camp of Israel a curse,
and trouble it. 19But all the silver and gold,
and vessels of bronze and iron, *are* consecrated to the LORD; they shall come into the
treasury of the LORD."
20So the people shouted when *the priests*
blew the trumpets. And it happened when
the people heard the sound of the trumpet,
and the people shouted with a great shout,
that the wall fell down flat. Then the people went up into the city, every man straight
before him, and they took the city. 21And
they utterly destroyed all that *was* in the city,
both man and woman, young and old, ox
and sheep and donkey, with the edge of the
sword.
22But Joshua had said to the two men
who had spied out the country, "Go into
the harlot's house, and from there bring
out the woman and all that she has, as you
swore to her." 23And the young men who had
been spies went in and brought out Rahab,
her father, her mother, her brothers, and
all that she had. So they brought out all her
relatives and left them outside the camp of
Israel. 24But they burned the city and all that
was in it with fire. Only the silver and gold,
and the vessels of bronze and iron, they put
into the treasury of the house of the LORD.
25And Joshua spared Rahab the harlot, her
father's household, and all that she had. So
she dwells in Israel to this day, because she
hid the messengers whom Joshua sent to spy
out Jericho.
26Then Joshua charged *them* at that time,
saying, "Cursed *be* the man before the LORD
who rises up and builds this city Jericho; he
shall lay its foundation with his firstborn,
and with his youngest he shall set up its
gates."
27So the LORD was with Joshua, and his
fame spread throughout all the country.

Defeat at Ai

7 But the children of Israel committed a
trespass regarding the accursed things,
for Achan the son of Carmi, the son of Zabdi,[a] the son of Zerah, of the tribe of Judah,
took of the accursed things; so the anger of
the LORD burned against the children of
Israel.
2Now Joshua sent men from Jericho to
Ai, which *is* beside Beth Aven, on the east

7:1 [a] Called *Zimri* in 1 Chronicles 2:6

side of Bethel, and spoke to them, saying,
"Go up and spy out the country." So the
men went up and spied out Ai. 3And they
returned to Joshua and said to him, "Do not
let all the people go up, but let about two or
three thousand men go up and attack Ai. Do
not weary all the people there, for *the people
of Ai are* few." 4So about three thousand men
went up there from the people, but they fled
before the men of Ai. 5And the men of Ai
struck down about thirty-six men, for they
chased them *from* before the gate as far as
Shebarim, and struck them down on the
descent; therefore the hearts of the people
melted and became like water.

6Then Joshua tore his clothes, and fell to
the earth on his face before the ark of the
LORD until evening, he and the elders of Israel; and they put dust on their heads. 7And
Joshua said, "Alas, Lord GOD, why have You
brought this people over the Jordan at all—
to deliver us into the hand of the Amorites,
to destroy us? Oh, that we had been content,
and dwelt on the other side of the Jordan! 8O
Lord, what shall I say when Israel turns its
back before its enemies? 9For the Canaanites
and all the inhabitants of the land will hear
it, and surround us, and cut off our name
from the earth. Then what will You do for
Your great name?"

The Sin of Achan

10So the LORD said to Joshua: "Get up!
Why do you lie thus on your face? 11Israel
has sinned, and they have also transgressed
My covenant which I commanded them. For
they have even taken some of the accursed
things, and have both stolen and deceived;
and they have also put *it* among their own
stuff. 12Therefore the children of Israel could
not stand before their enemies, *but* turned
their backs before their enemies, because
they have become doomed to destruction.
Neither will I be with you anymore, unless
you destroy the accursed from among you.
13Get up, sanctify the people, and say, 'Sanctify yourselves for tomorrow, because thus
says the LORD God of Israel: "*There is* an
accursed thing in your midst, O Israel; you
cannot stand before your enemies until you
take away the accursed thing from among
you." 14In the morning therefore you shall be
brought according to your tribes. And it shall
be *that* the tribe which the LORD takes shall
come according to families; and the family
which the LORD takes shall come by households; and the household which the LORD
takes shall come man by man. 15Then it shall
be *that* he who is taken with the accursed
thing shall be burned with fire, he and all
that he has, because he has transgressed the
covenant of the LORD, and because he has
done a disgraceful thing in Israel.'"

16So Joshua rose early in the morning
and brought Israel by their tribes, and the
tribe of Judah was taken. 17He brought
the clan of Judah, and he took the family of
the Zarhites; and he brought the family of the
Zarhites man by man, and Zabdi was taken.
18Then he brought his household man by
man, and Achan the son of Carmi, the son
of Zabdi, the son of Zerah, of the tribe of Judah, was taken.

19Now Joshua said to Achan, "My son, I
beg you, give glory to the LORD God of Israel, and make confession to Him, and tell
me now what you have done; do not hide *it*
from me."

20And Achan answered Joshua and said,
"Indeed I have sinned against the LORD
God of Israel, and this is what I have done:
21When I saw among the spoils a beautiful
Babylonian garment, two hundred shekels
of silver, and a wedge of gold weighing fifty
shekels, I coveted them and took them. And
there they are, hidden in the earth in the
midst of my tent, with the silver under it."

22So Joshua sent messengers, and they
ran to the tent; and there it was, hidden
in his tent, with the silver under it. 23And
they took them from the midst of the tent,
brought them to Joshua and to all the children of Israel, and laid them out before the
LORD. 24Then Joshua, and all Israel with
him, took Achan the son of Zerah, the silver, the garment, the wedge of gold, his
sons, his daughters, his oxen, his donkeys,
his sheep, his tent, and all that he had, and
they brought them to the Valley of Achor.
25And Joshua said, "Why have you troubled
us? The LORD will trouble you this day." So
all Israel stoned him with stones; and they
burned them with fire after they had stoned
them with stones.

26Then they raised over him a great heap
of stones, still there to this day. So the LORD
turned from the fierceness of His anger.

Therefore the name of that place has been
called the Valley of Achor[a] to this day.

The Fall of Ai

8 Now the LORD said to Joshua: "Do not
be afraid, nor be dismayed; take all the
people of war with you, and arise, go up to
Ai. See, I have given into your hand the king
of Ai, his people, his city, and his land. 2And
you shall do to Ai and its king as you did to
Jericho and its king. Only its spoil and its
cattle you shall take as booty for yourselves.
Lay an ambush for the city behind it."

3So Joshua arose, and all the people of
war, to go up against Ai; and Joshua chose
thirty thousand mighty men of valor and
sent them away by night. 4And he commanded them, saying: "Behold, you shall lie
in ambush against the city, behind the city.
Do not go very far from the city, but all of you
be ready. 5Then I and all the people who *are*
with me will approach the city; and it will
come about, when they come out against us
as at the first, that we shall flee before them.
6For they will come out after us till we have
drawn them from the city, for they will say,
'*They are* fleeing before us as at the first.'
Therefore we will flee before them. 7Then
you shall rise from the ambush and seize the
city, for the LORD your God will deliver it into
your hand. 8And it will be, when you have
taken the city, *that* you shall set the city on
fire. According to the commandment of the
LORD you shall do. See, I have commanded
you."

9Joshua therefore sent them out; and they
went to lie in ambush, and stayed between
Bethel and Ai, on the west side of Ai; but
Joshua lodged that night among the people.
10Then Joshua rose up early in the morning
and mustered the people, and went up, he
and the elders of Israel, before the people to
Ai. 11And all the people of war who *were* with
him went up and drew near; and they came
before the city and camped on the north side
of Ai. Now a valley *lay* between them and Ai.
12So he took about five thousand men and set
them in ambush between Bethel and Ai, on
the west side of the city. 13And when they had
set the people, all the army that *was* on the
north of the city, and its rear guard on the
west of the city, Joshua went that night into
the midst of the valley.

14Now it happened, when the king of
Ai saw *it,* that the men of the city hurried
and rose early and went out against Israel to
battle, he and all his people, at an appointed place before the plain. But he did not
know that *there was* an ambush against him
behind the city. 15And Joshua and all Israel
made as if they were beaten before them,
and fled by the way of the wilderness. 16So all
the people who *were* in Ai were called together to pursue them. And they pursued Joshua
and were drawn away from the city. 17There
was not a man left in Ai or Bethel who did
not go out after Israel. So they left the city
open and pursued Israel.

18Then the LORD said to Joshua, "Stretch
out the spear that *is* in your hand toward Ai,
for I will give it into your hand." And Joshua
stretched out the spear that *was* in his hand
toward the city. 19So *those in* ambush arose
quickly out of their place; they ran as soon
as he had stretched out his hand, and they
entered the city and took it, and hurried to
set the city on fire. 20And when the men of Ai
looked behind them, they saw, and behold,
the smoke of the city ascended to heaven. So
they had no power to flee this way or that
way, and the people who had fled to the wilderness turned back on the pursuers.

21Now when Joshua and all Israel saw that
the ambush had taken the city and that the
smoke of the city ascended, they turned back
and struck down the men of Ai. 22Then the
others came out of the city against them; so
they were *caught* in the midst of Israel, some
on this side and some on that side. And they
struck them down, so that they let none of
them remain or escape. 23But the king of Ai
they took alive, and brought him to Joshua.

24And it came to pass when Israel had
made an end of slaying all the inhabitants of
Ai in the field, in the wilderness where they
pursued them, and when they all had fallen
by the edge of the sword until they were consumed, that all the Israelites returned to Ai
and struck it with the edge of the sword. 25So
it was *that* all who fell that day, both men
and women, *were* twelve thousand—all the
people of Ai. 26For Joshua did not draw back
his hand, with which he stretched out the
spear, until he had utterly destroyed all the
inhabitants of Ai. 27Only the livestock and
the spoil of that city Israel took as booty for
themselves, according to the word of the
LORD which He had commanded Joshua.

7:26 [a] Literally *Trouble*

28So Joshua burned Ai and made it a heap forever, a desolation to this day. 29And the king of Ai he hanged on a tree until evening. And as soon as the sun was down, Joshua commanded that they should take his corpse down from the tree, cast it at the entrance of the gate of the city, and raise over it a great heap of stones *that remains* to this day.

Joshua Renews the Covenant

30Now Joshua built an altar to the LORD God of Israel in Mount Ebal, 31as Moses the servant of the LORD had commanded the children of Israel, as it is written in the Book of the Law of Moses: "an altar of whole stones over which no man has wielded an iron *tool*."[a] And they offered on it burnt offerings to the LORD, and sacrificed peace offerings. 32And there, in the presence of the children of Israel, he wrote on the stones a copy of the law of Moses, which he had written. 33Then all Israel, with their elders and officers and judges, stood on either side of the ark before the priests, the Levites, who bore the ark of the covenant of the LORD, the stranger as well as he who was born among them. Half of them *were* in front of Mount Gerizim and half of them in front of Mount Ebal, as Moses the servant of the LORD had commanded before, that they should bless the people of Israel. 34And afterward he read all the words of the law, the blessings and the cursings, according to all that is written in the Book of the Law. 35There was not a word of all that Moses had commanded which Joshua did not read before all the assembly of Israel, with the women, the little ones, and the strangers who were living among them.

The Treaty with the Gibeonites

9 And it came to pass when all the kings who *were* on this side of the Jordan, in the hills and in the lowland and in all the coasts of the Great Sea toward Lebanon—the Hittite, the Amorite, the Canaanite, the Perizzite, the Hivite, and the Jebusite—heard *about it,* 2that they gathered together to fight with Joshua and Israel with one accord.

3But when the inhabitants of Gibeon heard what Joshua had done to Jericho and Ai, 4they worked craftily, and went and pretended to be ambassadors. And they took old sacks on their donkeys, old wineskins torn and mended, 5old and patched sandals on their feet, and old garments on themselves; and all the bread of their provision was dry *and* moldy. 6And they went to Joshua, to the camp at Gilgal, and said to him and to the men of Israel, "We have come from a far country; now therefore, make a covenant with us."

7Then the men of Israel said to the Hivites, "Perhaps you dwell among us; so how can we make a covenant with you?"

8But they said to Joshua, "We *are* your servants."

And Joshua said to them, "Who *are* you, and where do you come from?"

9So they said to him: "From a very far country your servants have come, because of the name of the LORD your God; for we have heard of His fame, and all that He did in Egypt, 10and all that He did to the two kings of the Amorites who *were* beyond the Jordan—to Sihon king of Heshbon, and Og king of Bashan, who was at Ashtaroth. 11Therefore our elders and all the inhabitants of our country spoke to us, saying, 'Take provisions with you for the journey, and go to meet them, and say to them, "We *are* your servants; now therefore, make a covenant with us."' 12This bread of ours we took hot *for* our provision from our houses on the day we departed to come to you. But now look, it is dry and moldy. 13And these wineskins which we filled *were* new, and see, they are torn; and these our garments and our sandals have become old because of the very long journey."

14Then the men of Israel took some of their provisions; but they did not ask counsel of the LORD. 15So Joshua made peace with them, and made a covenant with them to let them live; and the rulers of the congregation swore to them.

16And it happened at the end of three days, after they had made a covenant with them, that they heard that they *were* their neighbors who dwelt near them. 17Then the children of Israel journeyed and came to their cities on the third day. Now their cities *were* Gibeon, Chephirah, Beeroth, and Kirjath Jearim. 18But the children of Israel did not attack them, because the rulers of the congregation had sworn to them by the LORD God of Israel. And all the congregation complained against the rulers.

19Then all the rulers said to all the

8:31 [a] Deuteronomy 27:5, 6

congregation, "We have sworn to them by the LORD God of Israel; now therefore, we may not touch them. 20This we will do to them: We will let them live, lest wrath be upon us because of the oath which we swore to them." 21And the rulers said to them, "Let them live, but let them be woodcutters and water carriers for all the congregation, as the rulers had promised them."

22Then Joshua called for them, and he spoke to them, saying, "Why have you deceived us, saying, 'We *are* very far from you,' when you dwell near us? 23Now therefore, you *are* cursed, and none of you shall be freed from being slaves—woodcutters and water carriers for the house of my God."

24So they answered Joshua and said, "Because your servants were clearly told that the LORD your God commanded His servant Moses to give you all the land, and to destroy all the inhabitants of the land from before you; therefore we were very much afraid for our lives because of you, and have done this thing. 25And now, here we are, in your hands; do with us as it seems good and right to do to us." 26So he did to them, and delivered them out of the hand of the children of Israel, so that they did not kill them. 27And that day Joshua made them woodcutters and water carriers for the congregation and for the altar of the LORD, in the place which He would choose, even to this day.

The Sun Stands Still

10 Now it came to pass when Adoni-Zedek king of Jerusalem heard how Joshua had taken Ai and had utterly destroyed it—as he had done to Jericho and its king, so he had done to Ai and its king—and how the inhabitants of Gibeon had made peace with Israel and were among them, 2that they feared greatly, because Gibeon *was* a great city, like one of the royal cities, and because it *was* greater than Ai, and all its men *were* mighty. 3Therefore Adoni-Zedek king of Jerusalem sent to Hoham king of Hebron, Piram king of Jarmuth, Japhia king of Lachish, and Debir king of Eglon, saying, 4"Come up to me and help me, that we may attack Gibeon, for it has made peace with Joshua and with the children of Israel." 5Therefore the five kings of the Amorites, the king of Jerusalem, the king of Hebron, the king of Jarmuth, the king of Lachish, *and* the king of Eglon, gathered together and went up, they and all their armies, and camped before Gibeon and made war against it.

6And the men of Gibeon sent to Joshua at the camp at Gilgal, saying, "Do not forsake your servants; come up to us quickly, save us and help us, for all the kings of the Amorites who dwell in the mountains have gathered together against us."

7So Joshua ascended from Gilgal, he and all the people of war with him, and all the mighty men of valor. 8And the LORD said to Joshua, "Do not fear them, for I have delivered them into your hand; not a man of them shall stand before you." 9Joshua therefore came upon them suddenly, having marched all night from Gilgal. 10So the LORD routed them before Israel, killed them with a great slaughter at Gibeon, chased them along the road that goes to Beth Horon, and struck them down as far as Azekah and Makkedah. 11And it happened, as they fled before Israel *and* were on the descent of Beth Horon, that the LORD cast down large hailstones from heaven on them as far as Azekah, and they died. *There were* more who died from the hailstones than the children of Israel killed with the sword.

12Then Joshua spoke to the LORD in the day when the LORD delivered up the Amorites before the children of Israel, and he said in the sight of Israel:

"Sun, stand still over Gibeon;
And Moon, in the Valley of Aijalon."
13 So the sun stood still,
And the moon stopped,
Till the people had revenge
Upon their enemies.

Is this not written in the Book of Jasher? So the sun stood still in the midst of heaven, and did not hasten to go *down* for about a whole day. 14And there has been no day like that, before it or after it, that the LORD heeded the voice of a man; for the LORD fought for Israel.

15Then Joshua returned, and all Israel with him, to the camp at Gilgal.

The Amorite Kings Executed

16But these five kings had fled and hidden themselves in a cave at Makkedah. 17And it was told Joshua, saying, "The five kings have been found hidden in the cave at Makkedah."

18So Joshua said, "Roll large stones against the mouth of the cave, and set men by it to guard them. 19And do not stay *there* yourselves, *but* pursue your enemies, and attack their rear *guard*. Do not allow them to enter their cities, for the LORD your God has delivered them into your hand." 20Then it happened, while Joshua and the children of Israel made an end of slaying them with a very great slaughter, till they had finished, that those who escaped entered fortified cities. 21And all the people returned to the camp, to Joshua at Makkedah, in peace.

No one moved his tongue against any of the children of Israel.

22Then Joshua said, "Open the mouth of the cave, and bring out those five kings to me from the cave." 23And they did so, and brought out those five kings to him from the cave: the king of Jerusalem, the king of Hebron, the king of Jarmuth, the king of Lachish, *and* the king of Eglon.

24So it was, when they brought out those kings to Joshua, that Joshua called for all the men of Israel, and said to the captains of the men of war who went with him, "Come near, put your feet on the necks of these kings." And they drew near and put their feet on their necks. 25Then Joshua said to them, "Do not be afraid, nor be dismayed; be strong and of good courage, for thus the LORD will do to all your enemies against whom you fight." 26And afterward Joshua struck them and killed them, and hanged them on five trees; and they were hanging on the trees until evening. 27So it was at the time of the going down of the sun *that* Joshua commanded, and they took them down from the trees, cast them into the cave where they had been hidden, and laid large stones against the cave's mouth, *which remain* until this very day.

Conquest of the Southland

28On that day Joshua took Makkedah, and struck it and its king with the edge of the sword. He utterly destroyed them[a]—all the people who *were* in it. He let none remain. He also did to the king of Makkedah as he had done to the king of Jericho.

29Then Joshua passed from Makkedah, and all Israel with him, to Libnah; and they fought against Libnah. 30And the LORD also delivered it and its king into the hand of Israel; he struck it and all the people who *were* in it with the edge of the sword. He let none remain in it, but did to its king as he had done to the king of Jericho.

31Then Joshua passed from Libnah, and all Israel with him, to Lachish; and they encamped against it and fought against it. 32And the LORD delivered Lachish into the hand of Israel, who took it on the second day, and struck it and all the people who *were* in it with the edge of the sword, according to all that he had done to Libnah. 33Then Horam king of Gezer came up to help Lachish; and Joshua struck him and his people, until he left him none remaining.

34From Lachish Joshua passed to Eglon, and all Israel with him; and they encamped against it and fought against it. 35They took it on that day and struck it with the edge of the sword; all the people who *were* in it he utterly destroyed that day, according to all that he had done to Lachish.

36So Joshua went up from Eglon, and all Israel with him, to Hebron; and they fought against it. 37And they took it and struck it with the edge of the sword—its king, all its cities, and all the people who *were* in it; he left none remaining, according to all that he had done to Eglon, but utterly destroyed it and all the people who *were* in it.

38Then Joshua returned, and all Israel with him, to Debir; and they fought against it. 39And he took it and its king and all its cities; they struck them with the edge of the sword and utterly destroyed all the people who *were* in it. He left none remaining; as he had done to Hebron, so he did to Debir and its king, as he had done also to Libnah and its king.

40So Joshua conquered all the land: the mountain country and the South[a] and the lowland and the wilderness slopes, and all their kings; he left none remaining, but utterly destroyed all that breathed, as the LORD God of Israel had commanded. 41And Joshua conquered them from Kadesh Barnea as far as Gaza, and all the country of Goshen, even as far as Gibeon. 42All these kings and their land Joshua took at one time, because the LORD God of Israel fought for Israel. 43Then

10:28 [a] Following Masoretic Text and most authorities; many Hebrew manuscripts, some manuscripts of the Septuagint, and some manuscripts of the Targum read *it*.
10:40 [a] Hebrew *Negev*, and so throughout this book

Joshua returned, and all Israel with him, to the camp at Gilgal.

The Northern Conquest

11 And it came to pass, when Jabin king of Hazor heard *these things,* that he sent to Jobab king of Madon, to the king of Shimron, to the king of Achshaph, 2and to the kings who *were* from the north, in the mountains, in the plain south of Chinneroth, in the lowland, and in the heights of Dor on the west, 3to the Canaanites in the east and in the west, the Amorite, the Hittite, the Perizzite, the Jebusite in the mountains, and the Hivite below Hermon in the land of Mizpah. 4So they went out, they and all their armies with them, *as* many people *as* the sand that *is* on the seashore in multitude, with very many horses and chariots. 5And when all these kings had met together, they came and camped together at the waters of Merom to fight against Israel.

6But the LORD said to Joshua, "Do not be afraid because of them, for tomorrow about this time I will deliver all of them slain before Israel. You shall hamstring their horses and burn their chariots with fire." 7So Joshua and all the people of war with him came against them suddenly by the waters of Merom, and they attacked them. 8And the LORD delivered them into the hand of Israel, who defeated them and chased them to Greater Sidon, to the Brook Misrephoth,[a] and to the Valley of Mizpah eastward; they attacked them until they left none of them remaining. 9So Joshua did to them as the LORD had told him: he hamstrung their horses and burned their chariots with fire.

10Joshua turned back at that time and took Hazor, and struck its king with the sword; for Hazor was formerly the head of all those kingdoms. 11And they struck all the people who *were* in it with the edge of the sword, utterly destroying *them.* There was none left breathing. Then he burned Hazor with fire.

12So all the cities of those kings, and all their kings, Joshua took and struck with the edge of the sword. He utterly destroyed them, as Moses the servant of the LORD *had commanded.* 13*But as for* the cities that stood on their mounds,[a] Israel burned none of them, except Hazor only, *which* Joshua burned. 14And all the spoil of these cities and the livestock, the children of Israel took as booty for themselves; but they struck every man with the edge of the sword until they had destroyed them, and they left none breathing. 15As the LORD had commanded Moses His servant, so Moses commanded Joshua, and so Joshua did. He left nothing undone of all that the LORD had commanded Moses.

Summary of Joshua's Conquests

16Thus Joshua took all this land: the mountain country, all the South, all the land of Goshen, the lowland, and the Jordan plain[a]—the mountains of Israel and its lowlands, 17from Mount Halak and the ascent to Seir, even as far as Baal Gad in the Valley of Lebanon below Mount Hermon. He captured all their kings, and struck them down and killed them. 18Joshua made war a long time with all those kings. 19There was not a city that made peace with the children of Israel, except the Hivites, the inhabitants of Gibeon. All *the others* they took in battle. 20For it was of the LORD to harden their hearts, that they should come against Israel in battle, that He might utterly destroy them, *and* that they might receive no mercy, but that He might destroy them, as the LORD had commanded Moses.

21And at that time Joshua came and cut off the Anakim from the mountains: from Hebron, from Debir, from Anab, from all the mountains of Judah, and from all the mountains of Israel; Joshua utterly destroyed them with their cities. 22None of the Anakim were left in the land of the children of Israel; they remained only in Gaza, in Gath, and in Ashdod.

23So Joshua took the whole land, according to all that the LORD had said to Moses; and Joshua gave it as an inheritance to Israel according to their divisions by their tribes. Then the land rested from war.

The Kings Conquered by Moses

12 These *are* the kings of the land whom the children of Israel defeated, and whose land they possessed on the other side of the Jordan toward the rising of the sun, from the River Arnon to Mount Hermon, and all the eastern Jordan plain: 2*One king was* Sihon king of the Amorites, who dwelt in Heshbon *and* ruled half of

---

11:8 [a] Hebrew *Misrephoth Maim* **11:13** [a] Hebrew *tel,* a heap of successive city ruins **11:16** [a] Hebrew *arabah*

Gilead, from Aroer, which is on the bank
of the River Arnon, from the middle of that
river, even as far as the River Jabbok, *which*
is the border of the Ammonites, 3 and the
eastern Jordan plain from the Sea of Chinneroth as far as the Sea of the Arabah (the
Salt Sea), the road to Beth Jeshimoth, and
southward below the slopes of Pisgah. 4 *The*
other king was Og king of Bashan and his territory, *who was* of the remnant of the giants,
who dwelt at Ashtaroth and at Edrei, 5 and
reigned over Mount Hermon, over Salcah,
over all Bashan, as far as the border of the
Geshurites and the Maachathites, and over
half of Gilead *to* the border of Sihon king of
Heshbon.

6 These Moses the servant of the LORD
and the children of Israel had conquered;
and Moses the servant of the LORD had giv-
en it *as* a possession to the Reubenites, the
Gadites, and half the tribe of Manasseh.

The Kings Conquered by Joshua

7 And these *are* the kings of the country
which Joshua and the children of Israel
conquered on this side of the Jordan, on the
west, from Baal Gad in the Valley of Lebanon as far as Mount Halak and the ascent to
Seir, which Joshua gave to the tribes of Israel
as a possession according to their divisions,
8 in the mountain country, in the lowlands,
in the *Jordan* plain, in the slopes, in the wilderness, and in the South—the Hittites, the
Amorites, the Canaanites, the Perizzites,
the Hivites, and the Jebusites: 9 the king of
Jericho, one; the king of Ai, which *is* beside
Bethel, one; 10 the king of Jerusalem, one; the
king of Hebron, one; 11 the king of Jarmuth,
one; the king of Lachish, one; 12 the king of
Eglon, one; the king of Gezer, one; 13 the king
of Debir, one; the king of Geder, one; 14 the
king of Hormah, one; the king of Arad, one;
15 the king of Libnah, one; the king of Adullam, one; 16 the king of Makkedah, one; the
king of Bethel, one; 17 the king of Tappuah,
one; the king of Hepher, one; 18 the king of
Aphek, one; the king of Lasharon, one; 19 the
king of Madon, one; the king of Hazor, one;
20 the king of Shimron Meron, one; the king
of Achshaph, one; 21 the king of Taanach,
one; the king of Megiddo, one; 22 the king of
Kedesh, one; the king of Jokneam in Carmel, one; 23 the king of Dor in the heights of
Dor, one; the king of the people of Gilgal,
one; 24 the king of Tirzah, one—all the kings,
thirty-one.

Remaining Land to Be Conquered

13 Now Joshua was old, advanced in
years. And the LORD said to him:
"You are old, advanced in years, and there
remains very much land yet to be possessed. 2 This is the land that yet remains:
all the territory of the Philistines and all
that of the Geshurites, 3 from Sihor, which *is*
east of Egypt, as far as the border of Ekron
northward (*which* is counted as Canaanite); the five lords of the Philistines—the
Gazites, the Ashdodites, the Ashkelonites,
the Gittites, and the Ekronites; also the
Avites; 4 from the south, all the land of the
Canaanites, and Mearah that belongs to the
Sidonians as far as Aphek, to the border of
the Amorites; 5 the land of the Gebalites,[a]
and all Lebanon, toward the sunrise, from
Baal Gad below Mount Hermon as far as the
entrance to Hamath; 6 all the inhabitants of
the mountains from Lebanon as far as the
Brook Misrephoth,[a] *and* all the Sidonians—
them I will drive out from before the children of Israel; only divide it by lot to Israel as
an inheritance, as I have commanded you.
7 Now therefore, divide this land as an inheritance to the nine tribes and half the tribe of
Manasseh."

The Land Divided East of the Jordan

8 With the other half-tribe the Reubenites
and the Gadites received their inheritance,
which Moses had given them, beyond the
Jordan eastward, as Moses the servant of the
LORD had given them: 9 from Aroer which
is on the bank of the River Arnon, and the
town that *is* in the midst of the ravine, and
all the plain of Medeba as far as Dibon; 10 all
the cities of Sihon king of the Amorites, who
reigned in Heshbon, as far as the border of
the children of Ammon; 11 Gilead, and the
border of the Geshurites and Maachathites,
all Mount Hermon, and all Bashan as far as
Salcah; 12 all the kingdom of Og in Bashan,
who reigned in Ashtaroth and Edrei, who
remained of the remnant of the giants; for
Moses had defeated and cast out these.

13 Nevertheless the children of Israel
did not drive out the Geshurites or the
Maachathites, but the Geshurites and the

13:5 [a] Or *Giblites* **13:6** [a] Hebrew *Misrephoth Maim*

Maachathites dwell among the Israelites
until this day.
14Only to the tribe of Levi he had given no
inheritance; the sacrifices of the LORD God
of Israel made by fire *are* their inheritance,
as He said to them.

The Land of Reuben

15And Moses had given to the tribe of the
children of Reuben *an inheritance* according
to their families. 16Their territory was from
Aroer, which *is* on the bank of the River Arnon, and the city that *is* in the midst of the
ravine, and all the plain by Medeba; 17Hesh-
bon and all its cities that *are* in the plain:
Dibon, Bamoth Baal, Beth Baal Meon, 18Ja-
haza, Kedemoth, Mephaath, 19Kirjathaim,
Sibmah, Zereth Shahar on the mountain
of the valley, 20Beth Peor, the slopes of Pisgah, and Beth Jeshimoth— 21all the cities of
the plain and all the kingdom of Sihon king
of the Amorites, who reigned in Heshbon,
whom Moses had struck with the princes
of Midian: Evi, Rekem, Zur, Hur, and Reba,
who *were* princes of Sihon dwelling in the
country. 22The children of Israel also killed
with the sword Balaam the son of Beor, the
soothsayer, among those who were killed by
them. 23And the border of the children of
Reuben was the bank of the Jordan. This *was*
the inheritance of the children of Reuben according to their families, the cities and their
villages.

The Land of Gad

24Moses also had given *an inheritance*
to the tribe of Gad, to the children of Gad
according to their families. 25Their territory
was Jazer, and all the cities of Gilead, and
half the land of the Ammonites as far as
Aroer, which *is* before Rabbah, 26and from
Heshbon to Ramath Mizpah and Betonim,
and from Mahanaim to the border of Debir,
27and in the valley Beth Haram, Beth Nimrah,
Succoth, and Zaphon, the rest of the kingdom
of Sihon king of Heshbon, with the Jordan
as *its* border, as far as the edge of the Sea
of Chinnereth, on the other side of the Jordan eastward. 28This *is* the inheritance of the
children of Gad according to their families,
the cities and their villages.

Half the Tribe of Manasseh (East)

29Moses also had given *an inheritance* to
half the tribe of Manasseh; it was for half the
tribe of the children of Manasseh according
to their families: 30Their territory was from
Mahanaim, all Bashan, all the kingdom of
Og king of Bashan, and all the towns of Jair
which are in Bashan, sixty cities; 31half of
Gilead, and Ashtaroth and Edrei, cities of
the kingdom of Og in Bashan, *were* for the
children of Machir the son of Manasseh, for
half of the children of Machir according to
their families.
32These *are the areas* which Moses had
distributed as an inheritance in the plains
of Moab on the other side of the Jordan, by
Jericho eastward. 33But to the tribe of Levi
Moses had given no inheritance; the LORD
God of Israel *was* their inheritance, as He
had said to them.

The Land Divided West of the Jordan

14 These *are the areas* which the children of Israel inherited in the land
of Canaan, which Eleazar the priest, Joshua
the son of Nun, and the heads of the fathers
of the tribes of the children of Israel distributed as an inheritance to them. 2Their
inheritance *was* by lot, as the LORD had commanded by the hand of Moses, for the nine
tribes and the half-tribe. 3For Moses had giv-
en the inheritance of the two tribes and the
half-tribe on the other side of the Jordan; but
to the Levites he had given no inheritance
among them. 4For the children of Joseph
were two tribes: Manasseh and Ephraim.
And they gave no part to the Levites in the
land, except cities to dwell *in,* with their
common-lands for their livestock and their
property. 5As the LORD had commanded Moses, so the children of Israel did; and they
divided the land.

Caleb Inherits Hebron

6Then the children of Judah came to
Joshua in Gilgal. And Caleb the son of Jephunneh the Kenizzite said to him: "You
know the word which the LORD said to Moses the man of God concerning you and
me in Kadesh Barnea. 7I *was* forty years
old when Moses the servant of the LORD
sent me from Kadesh Barnea to spy out the
land, and I brought back word to him as *it*
was in my heart. 8Nevertheless my brethren who went up with me made the heart
of the people melt, but I wholly followed the
LORD my God. 9So Moses swore on that day,
saying, 'Surely the land where your foot has
trodden shall be your inheritance and your

children's forever, because you have wholly
followed the LORD my God.' 10And now, behold, the LORD has kept me alive, as He said,
these forty-five years, ever since the LORD
spoke this word to Moses while Israel wandered in the wilderness; and now, here I am
this day, eighty-five years old. 11As yet I *am*
as strong this day as on the day that Moses
sent me; just as my strength *was* then, so
now *is* my strength for war, both for going
out and for coming in. 12Now therefore, give
me this mountain of which the LORD spoke
in that day; for you heard in that day how the
Anakim *were* there, and *that* the cities *were*
great *and* fortified. It may be that the LORD
will be with me, and I shall be able to drive
them out as the LORD said."

13And Joshua blessed him, and gave Hebron to Caleb the son of Jephunneh as an
inheritance. 14Hebron therefore became the
inheritance of Caleb the son of Jephunneh
the Kenizzite to this day, because he wholly followed the LORD God of Israel. 15And
the name of Hebron formerly was Kirjath
Arba (*Arba was* the greatest man among the
Anakim).

Then the land had rest from war.

The Land of Judah

15 So *this* was the lot of the tribe of the
children of Judah according to their
families:

The border of Edom at the Wilderness
of Zin southward *was* the extreme southern
boundary. 2And their southern border began
at the shore of the Salt Sea, from the bay that
faces southward. 3Then it went out to the
southern side of the Ascent of Akrabbim,
passed along to Zin, ascended on the south
side of Kadesh Barnea, passed along to Hezron, went up to Adar, and went around to
Karkaa. 4*From there* it passed toward Azmon
and went out to the Brook of Egypt; and the
border ended at the sea. This shall be your
southern border.

5*The east border was* the Salt Sea as far as
the mouth of the Jordan.

And the border on the northern quarter
began at the bay of the sea at the mouth of the
Jordan. 6The border went up to Beth Hoglah
and passed north of Beth Arabah; and the
border went up to the stone of Bohan the
son of Reuben. 7Then the border went up
toward Debir from the Valley of Achor, and
it turned northward toward Gilgal, which *is*
before the Ascent of Adummim, which *is*
on the south side of the valley. The border
continued toward the waters of En Shemesh
and ended at En Rogel. 8And the border went
up by the Valley of the Son of Hinnom to the
southern slope of the Jebusite *city* (which *is*
Jerusalem). The border went up to the top
of the mountain that *lies* before the Valley
of Hinnom westward, which *is* at the end of
the Valley of Rephaim[a] northward. 9Then
the border went around from the top of the
hill to the fountain of the water of Nephtoah,
and extended to the cities of Mount Ephron.
And the border went around to Baalah
(which *is* Kirjath Jearim). 10Then the border
turned westward from Baalah to Mount Seir,
passed along to the side of Mount Jearim on
the north (which *is* Chesalon), went down
to Beth Shemesh, and passed on to Timnah. 11And the border went out to the side
of Ekron northward. Then the border went
around to Shicron, passed along to Mount
Baalah, and extended to Jabneel; and the
border ended at the sea.

12The west border *was* the coastline of the
Great Sea. This *is* the boundary of the children of Judah all around according to their
families.

Caleb Occupies Hebron and Debir

13Now to Caleb the son of Jephunneh he
gave a share among the children of Judah,
according to the commandment of the LORD
to Joshua, *namely*, Kirjath Arba, which *is* Hebron (*Arba was* the father of Anak). 14Caleb
drove out the three sons of Anak from there:
Sheshai, Ahiman, and Talmai, the children
of Anak. 15Then he went up from there to the
inhabitants of Debir (formerly the name of
Debir *was* Kirjath Sepher).

16And Caleb said, "He who attacks Kirjath Sepher and takes it, to him I will give
Achsah my daughter as wife." 17So Othniel
the son of Kenaz, the brother of Caleb, took
it; and he gave him Achsah his daughter as
wife. 18Now it was so, when she came *to him*,
that she persuaded him to ask her father for
a field. So she dismounted from *her* donkey,
and Caleb said to her, "What do you wish?"
19She answered, "Give me a blessing; since
you have given me land in the South, give
me also springs of water." So he gave her the
upper springs and the lower springs.

15:8 [a] Literally *Giants*

The Cities of Judah

20 This *was* the inheritance of the tribe
of the children of Judah according to their
families:

21 The cities at the limits of the tribe of
the children of Judah, toward the border of
Edom in the South, were Kabzeel, Eder, Ja-
gur, 22 Kinah, Dimonah, Adadah, 23 Kedesh,
Hazor, Ithnan, 24 Ziph, Telem, Bealoth,
25 Hazor, Hadattah, Kerioth, Hezron (which
is Hazor), 26 Amam, Shema, Moladah, 27 Hazar Gaddah, Heshmon, Beth Pelet, 28 Hazar
Shual, Beersheba, Bizjothjah, 29 Baalah, Ijim,
Ezem, 30 Eltolad, Chesil, Hormah, 31 Ziklag,
Madmannah, Sansannah, 32 Lebaoth, Shil-
him, Ain, and Rimmon: all the cities *are*
twenty-nine, with their villages.

33 In the lowland: Eshtaol, Zorah, Ashnah,
34 Zanoah, En Gannim, Tappuah, Enam,
35 Jarmuth, Adullam, Socoh, Azekah, 36 Shara-
im, Adithaim, Gederah, and Gederothaim:
fourteen cities with their villages; 37 Zenan,
Hadashah, Migdal Gad, 38 Dilean, Mizpah,
Joktheel, 39 Lachish, Bozkath, Eglon, 40 Cab-
bon, Lahmas,[a] Kithlish, 41 Gederoth, Beth
Dagon, Naamah, and Makkedah: sixteen
cities with their villages; 42 Libnah, Ether,
Ashan, 43 Jiphtah, Ashnah, Nezib, 44 Keilah,
Achzib, and Mareshah: nine cities with their
villages; 45 Ekron, with its towns and villages; 46 from Ekron to the sea, all that *lay* near
Ashdod, with their villages; 47 Ashdod with
its towns and villages, Gaza with its towns
and villages—as far as the Brook of Egypt
and the Great Sea with *its* coastline.

48 And in the mountain country: Shamir,
Jattir, Sochoh, 49 Dannah, Kirjath Sannah
(which *is* Debir), 50 Anab, Eshtemoh, Anim,
51 Goshen, Holon, and Giloh: eleven cities
with their villages; 52 Arab, Dumah, Eshean,
53 Janum, Beth Tappuah, Aphekah, 54 Hum-
tah, Kirjath Arba (which *is* Hebron), and
Zior: nine cities with their villages; 55 Maon,
Carmel, Ziph, Juttah, 56 Jezreel, Jokdeam,
Zanoah, 57 Kain, Gibeah, and Timnah: ten
cities with their villages; 58 Halhul, Beth Zur,
Gedor, 59 Maarath, Beth Anoth, and Eltekon:
six cities with their villages; 60 Kirjath Baal
(which *is* Kirjath Jearim) and Rabbah: two
cities with their villages.

61 *In the wilderness:* Beth Arabah, Mid-
din, Secacah, 62 Nibshan, the City of Salt, and
En Gedi: six cities with their villages.

63 As for the Jebusites, the inhabitants of
Jerusalem, the children of Judah could not
drive them out; but the Jebusites dwell with
the children of Judah at Jerusalem to this day.

Ephraim and West Manasseh

16 The lot fell to the children of Joseph
from the Jordan, by Jericho, to the
waters of Jericho on the east, to the wilderness that goes up from Jericho through the
mountains to Bethel, 2 then went out from
Bethel to Luz,[a] passed along to the border
of the Archites at Ataroth, 3 and went down
westward to the boundary of the Japhletites,
as far as the boundary of Lower Beth Horon
to Gezer; and it ended at the sea.

4 So the children of Joseph, Manasseh
and Ephraim, took their inheritance.

The Land of Ephraim

5 The border of the children of Ephraim,
according to their families, was *thus:* The
border of their inheritance on the east side
was Ataroth Addar as far as Upper Beth
Horon.

6 And the border went out toward the sea
on the north side of Michmethath; then the
border went around eastward to Taanath
Shiloh, and passed by it on the east of Janohah. 7 Then it went down from Janohah to
Ataroth and Naarah,[a] reached to Jericho, and
came out at the Jordan.

8 The border went out from Tappuah
westward to the Brook Kanah, and it ended
at the sea. This *was* the inheritance of the
tribe of the children of Ephraim according
to their families. 9 The separate cities for the
children of Ephraim *were* among the inheritance of the children of Manasseh, all the
cities with their villages.

10 And they did not drive out the Canaanites who dwelt in Gezer; but the Canaanites
dwell among the Ephraimites to this day and
have become forced laborers.

The Other Half-Tribe of Manasseh (West)

17 There was also a lot for the tribe of
Manasseh, for he *was* the firstborn
of Joseph: *namely* for Machir the firstborn of
Manasseh, the father of Gilead, because he
was a man of war; therefore he was given Gilead and Bashan. 2 And there was *a lot* for the
rest of the children of Manasseh according

15:40 [a] Or *Lahmam* **16:2** [a] Septuagint reads Bethel (that is, Luz). **16:7** [a] Or *Naaran* (compare 1 Chronicles 7:28)

to their families: for the children of Abiezer,[a]
the children of Helek, the children of Asriel, the children of Shechem, the children of
Hepher, and the children of Shemida; these
were the male children of Manasseh the son
of Joseph according to their families.
3But Zelophehad the son of Hepher, the
son of Gilead, the son of Machir, the son of
Manasseh, had no sons, but only daughters.
And these *are* the names of his daughters:
Mahlah, Noah, Hoglah, Milcah, and Tirzah. 4And they came near before Eleazar the
priest, before Joshua the son of Nun, and
before the rulers, saying, "The LORD commanded Moses to give us an inheritance
among our brothers." Therefore, according
to the commandment of the LORD, he gave
them an inheritance among their father's
brothers. 5Ten shares fell to Manasseh, besides the land of Gilead and Bashan, which
were on the other side of the Jordan, 6because
the daughters of Manasseh received an inheritance among his sons; and the rest of
Manasseh's sons had the land of Gilead.
7And the territory of Manasseh was
from Asher to Michmethath, that *lies* east of
Shechem; and the border went along south
to the inhabitants of En Tappuah. 8Manasseh
had the land of Tappuah, but Tappuah on the
border of Manasseh *belonged* to the children
of Ephraim. 9And the border descended to
the Brook Kanah, southward to the brook.
These cities of Ephraim *are* among the cities
of Manasseh. The border of Manasseh *was*
on the north side of the brook; and it ended
at the sea.
10Southward *it was* Ephraim's, northward
it was Manasseh's, and the sea was its border.
Manasseh's territory was adjoining Asher on
the north and Issachar on the east. 11And in
Issachar and in Asher, Manasseh had Beth
Shean and its towns, Ibleam and its towns,
the inhabitants of Dor and its towns, the
inhabitants of En Dor and its towns, the inhabitants of Taanach and its towns, and the
inhabitants of Megiddo and its towns—three
hilly regions. 12Yet the children of Manasseh
could not drive out *the inhabitants of* those
cities, but the Canaanites were determined
to dwell in that land. 13And it happened,
when the children of Israel grew strong, that
they put the Canaanites to forced labor, but
did not utterly drive them out.

More Land for Ephraim and Manasseh

14Then the children of Joseph spoke to
Joshua, saying, "Why have you given us *only*
one lot and one share to inherit, since we *are*
a great people, inasmuch as the LORD has
blessed us until now?"
15So Joshua answered them, "If you *are*
a great people, *then* go up to the forest *coun-*
try and clear a place for yourself there in the
land of the Perizzites and the giants, since
the mountains of Ephraim are too confined
for you."
16But the children of Joseph said, "The
mountain country is not enough for us; and
all the Canaanites who dwell in the land of
the valley have chariots of iron, *both those*
who *are* of Beth Shean and its towns and
those who *are* of the Valley of Jezreel."
17And Joshua spoke to the house of
Joseph—to Ephraim and Manasseh—
saying, "You *are* a great people and have
great power; you shall not have *only* one lot,
18but the mountain country shall be yours.
Although it *is* wooded, you shall cut it down,
and its farthest extent shall be yours; for you
shall drive out the Canaanites, though they
have iron chariots *and* are strong."

The Remainder of the Land Divided

18 Now the whole congregation of the
children of Israel assembled together at Shiloh, and set up the tabernacle
of meeting there. And the land was subdued
before them. 2But there remained among the
children of Israel seven tribes which had not
yet received their inheritance.
3Then Joshua said to the children of Israel: "How long will you neglect to go and
possess the land which the LORD God of your
fathers has given you? 4Pick out from among
you three men for *each* tribe, and I will send
them; they shall rise and go through the
land, survey it according to their inheritance,
and come *back* to me. 5And they shall divide
it into seven parts. Judah shall remain in
their territory on the south, and the house of
Joseph shall remain in their territory on the
north. 6You shall therefore survey the land
in seven parts and bring *the survey* here to
me, that I may cast lots for you here before
the LORD our God. 7But the Levites have no
part among you, for the priesthood of the

17:2 [a] Called *Jeezer* in Numbers 26:30

Lord *is* their inheritance. And Gad, Reuben,
and half the tribe of Manasseh have received
their inheritance beyond the Jordan on the
east, which Moses the servant of the Lord
gave them."

8 Then the men arose to go away; and
Joshua charged those who went to survey
the land, saying, "Go, walk through the
land, survey it, and come back to me, that I
may cast lots for you here before the Lord in
Shiloh." 9 So the men went, passed through
the land, and wrote the survey in a book in
seven parts by cities; and they came to Joshua at the camp in Shiloh. 10 Then Joshua cast
lots for them in Shiloh before the Lord, and
there Joshua divided the land to the children
of Israel according to their divisions.

The Land of Benjamin

11 Now the lot of the tribe of the children of
Benjamin came up according to their families, and the territory of their lot came out between the children of Judah and the children
of Joseph. 12 Their border on the north side
began at the Jordan, and the border went up
to the side of Jericho on the north, and went
up through the mountains westward; it ended at the Wilderness of Beth Aven. 13 The border went over from there toward Luz, to the
side of Luz (which *is* Bethel) southward; and
the border descended to Ataroth Addar, near
the hill that *lies* on the south side of Lower
Beth Horon.

14 Then the border extended around the
west side to the south, from the hill that *lies*
before Beth Horon southward; and it ended
at Kirjath Baal (which *is* Kirjath Jearim), a
city of the children of Judah. This *was* the
west side.

15 The south side *began* at the end of Kirjath Jearim, and the border extended on the
west and went out to the spring of the waters
of Nephtoah. 16 Then the border came down
to the end of the mountain that *lies* before
the Valley of the Son of Hinnom, which *is*
in the Valley of the Rephaim[a] on the north,
descended to the Valley of Hinnom, to the
side of the Jebusite *city* on the south, and descended to En Rogel. 17 And it went around
from the north, went out to En Shemesh,
and extended toward Geliloth, which is before the Ascent of Adummim, and descended to the stone of Bohan the son of Reuben.
18 Then it passed along toward the north side
of Arabah,[a] and went down to Arabah. 19 And
the border passed along to the north side of
Beth Hoglah; then the border ended at the
north bay at the Salt Sea, at the south end of
the Jordan. This *was* the southern boundary.

20 The Jordan was its border on the east
side. This *was* the inheritance of the children
of Benjamin, according to its boundaries all
around, according to their families.

21 Now the cities of the tribe of the children of Benjamin, according to their families, were Jericho, Beth Hoglah, Emek
Keziz, 22 Beth Arabah, Zemaraim, Bethel,
23 Avim, Parah, Ophrah, 24 Chephar Haam-
moni, Ophni, and Gaba: twelve cities with
their villages; 25 Gibeon, Ramah, Beeroth,
26 Mizpah, Chephirah, Mozah, 27 Rekem,
Irpeel, Taralah, 28 Zelah, Eleph, Jebus (which
is Jerusalem), Gibeath, *and* Kirjath: fourteen
cities with their villages. This was the inheritance of the children of Benjamin according
to their families.

Simeon's Inheritance with Judah

19 The second lot came out for Simeon, for the tribe of the children of
Simeon according to their families. And
their inheritance was within the inheritance
of the children of Judah. 2 They had in their
inheritance Beersheba (Sheba), Moladah,
3 Hazar Shual, Balah, Ezem, 4 Eltolad, Bethul,
Hormah, 5 Ziklag, Beth Marcaboth, Hazar
Susah, 6 Beth Lebaoth, and Sharuhen: thirteen cities and their villages; 7 Ain, Rimmon,
Ether, and Ashan: four cities and their villages; 8 and all the villages that *were* all around
these cities as far as Baalath Beer, Ramah of
the South. This *was* the inheritance of the
tribe of the children of Simeon according to
their families.

9 The inheritance of the children of Simeon *was included* in the share of the children
of Judah, for the share of the children of Judah was too much for them. Therefore the
children of Simeon had *their* inheritance
within the inheritance of that people.

The Land of Zebulun

10 The third lot came out for the children
of Zebulun according to their families, and
the border of their inheritance was as far as
Sarid. 11 Their border went toward the west
and to Maralah, went to Dabbasheth, and

18:16 [a] Literally *Giants* 18:18 [a] Or *Beth Arabah* (compare 15:6 and 18:22)

extended along the brook that is east of Jokneam. 12 Then from Sarid it went eastward
toward the sunrise along the border of Chis-
loth Tabor, and went out toward Daberath,
bypassing Japhia. 13 And from there it passed
along on the east of Gath Hepher, toward
Eth Kazin, and extended to Rimmon, which
borders on Neah. 14 Then the border went
around it on the north side of Hannathon,
and it ended in the Valley of Jiphthah El.
15 Included were Kattath, Nahallal, Shimron,
Idalah, and Bethlehem: twelve cities with
their villages. 16 This *was* the inheritance of
the children of Zebulun according to their
families, these cities with their villages.

The Land of Issachar

17 The fourth lot came out to Issachar,
for the children of Issachar according to
their families. 18 And their territory went to
Jezreel, and *included* Chesulloth, Shunem,
19 Haphraim, Shion, Anaharath, 20 Rabbith,
Kishion, Abez, 21 Remeth, En Gannim, En
Haddah, and Beth Pazzez. 22 And the border
reached to Tabor, Shahazimah, and Beth
Shemesh; their border ended at the Jordan:
sixteen cities with their villages. 23 This *was*
the inheritance of the tribe of the children
of Issachar according to their families, the
cities and their villages.

The Land of Asher

24 The fifth lot came out for the tribe of
the children of Asher according to their families. 25 And their territory included Helkath,
Hali, Beten, Achshaph, 26 Alammelech,
Amad, and Mishal; it reached to Mount Carmel westward, along *the Brook* Shihor Lib-
nath. 27 It turned toward the sunrise to Beth
Dagon; and it reached to Zebulun and to the
Valley of Jiphthah El, then northward beyond Beth Emek and Neiel, bypassing Cabul
which was on the left, 28 including Ebron,[a] Rehob, Hammon, and Kanah, as far as Greater
Sidon. 29 And the border turned to Ramah
and to the fortified city of Tyre; then the border turned to Hosah, and ended at the sea by
the region of Achzib. 30 Also Ummah, Aphek,
and Rehob *were included:* twenty-two cities
with their villages. 31 This *was* the inheritance of the tribe of the children of Asher
according to their families, these cities with
their villages.

The Land of Naphtali

32 The sixth lot came out to the children
of Naphtali, for the children of Naphtali according to their families. 33 And their border
began at Heleph, enclosing the territory
from the terebinth tree in Zaanannim, Ada-
mi Nekeb, and Jabneel, as far as Lakkum;
it ended at the Jordan. 34 From Heleph the
border extended westward to Aznoth Tabor,
and went out from there toward Hukkok;
it adjoined Zebulun on the south side and
Asher on the west side, and ended at Judah
by the Jordan toward the sunrise. 35 And the
fortified cities *are* Ziddim, Zer, Hammath,
Rakkath, Chinnereth, 36 Adamah, Ramah,
Hazor, 37 Kedesh, Edrei, En Hazor, 38 Iron,
Migdal El, Horem, Beth Anath, and Beth
Shemesh: nineteen cities with their villages. 39 This *was* the inheritance of the tribe of
the children of Naphtali according to their
families, the cities and their villages.

The Land of Dan

40 The seventh lot came out for the tribe of
the children of Dan according to their families. 41 And the territory of their inheritance
was Zorah, Eshtaol, Ir Shemesh, 42 Shaalabbin, Aijalon, Jethlah, 43 Elon, Timnah, Ekron,
44 Eltekeh, Gibbethon, Baalath, 45 Jehud, Bene
Berak, Gath Rimmon, 46 Me Jarkon, and Rak-
kon, with the region near Joppa. 47 And the
border of the children of Dan went beyond
these, because the children of Dan went up
to fight against Leshem and took it; and they
struck it with the edge of the sword, took
possession of it, and dwelt in it. They called
Leshem, Dan, after the name of Dan their
father. 48 This *is* the inheritance of the tribe of
the children of Dan according to their families, these cities with their villages.

Joshua's Inheritance

49 When they had made an end of dividing the land as an inheritance according
to their borders, the children of Israel gave
an inheritance among them to Joshua the
son of Nun. 50 According to the word of the
LORD they gave him the city which he asked
for, Timnath Serah in the mountains of
Ephraim; and he built the city and dwelt
in it.

19:28 [a] Following Masoretic Text, Targum, and Vulgate; a few Hebrew manuscripts read *Abdon* (compare 21:30 and 1 Chronicles 6:74).

51 These *were* the inheritances which Eleazar the priest, Joshua the son of Nun, and
the heads of the fathers of the tribes of the
children of Israel divided as an inheritance
by lot in Shiloh before the LORD, at the door
of the tabernacle of meeting. So they made
an end of dividing the country.

The Cities of Refuge

20 The LORD also spoke to Joshua,
saying, 2 "Speak to the children of
Israel, saying: 'Appoint for yourselves cities
of refuge, of which I spoke to you through
Moses, 3 that the slayer who kills a person
accidentally *or* unintentionally may flee
there; and they shall be your refuge from
the avenger of blood. 4 And when he flees
to one of those cities, and stands at the entrance of the gate of the city, and declares
his case in the hearing of the elders of that
city, they shall take him into the city as one
of them, and give him a place, that he may
dwell among them. 5 Then if the avenger of
blood pursues him, they shall not deliver the
slayer into his hand, because he struck his
neighbor unintentionally, but did not hate
him beforehand. 6 And he shall dwell in that
city until he stands before the congregation
for judgment, *and* until the death of the one
who is high priest in those days. Then the
slayer may return and come to his own city
and his own house, to the city from which
he fled.'"

7 So they appointed Kedesh in Galilee, in
the mountains of Naphtali, Shechem in the
mountains of Ephraim, and Kirjath Arba
(which *is* Hebron) in the mountains of Judah. 8 And on the other side of the Jordan,
by Jericho eastward, they assigned Bezer in
the wilderness on the plain, from the tribe
of Reuben, Ramoth in Gilead, from the
tribe of Gad, and Golan in Bashan, from the
tribe of Manasseh. 9 These were the cities
appointed for all the children of Israel and
for the stranger who dwelt among them, that
whoever killed a person accidentally might
flee there, and not die by the hand of the
avenger of blood until he stood before the
congregation.

Cities of the Levites

21 Then the heads of the fathers'
houses of the Levites came near
to Eleazar the priest, to Joshua the son of
Nun, and to the heads of the fathers' *houses*
of the tribes of the children of Israel. 2 And
they spoke to them at Shiloh in the land of
Canaan, saying, "The LORD commanded
through Moses to give us cities to dwell in,
with their common-lands for our livestock."
3 So the children of Israel gave to the Levites
from their inheritance, at the commandment of the LORD, these cities and their
common-lands:

4 Now the lot came out for the families
of the Kohathites. And the children of Aaron the priest, *who were* of the Levites, had
thirteen cities by lot from the tribe of Judah,
from the tribe of Simeon, and from the tribe
of Benjamin. 5 The rest of the children of Kohath had ten cities by lot from the families of
the tribe of Ephraim, from the tribe of Dan,
and from the half-tribe of Manasseh.

6 And the children of Gershon had thirteen cities by lot from the families of the
tribe of Issachar, from the tribe of Asher,
from the tribe of Naphtali, and from the half-
tribe of Manasseh in Bashan.

7 The children of Merari according to
their families had twelve cities from the
tribe of Reuben, from the tribe of Gad, and
from the tribe of Zebulun.

8 And the children of Israel gave these
cities with their common-lands by lot to the
Levites, as the LORD had commanded by the
hand of Moses.

9 So they gave from the tribe of the children of Judah and from the tribe of the
children of Simeon these cities which are
designated by name, 10 which were for the
children of Aaron, one of the families of the
Kohathites, *who were* of the children of Levi;
for the lot was theirs first. 11 And they gave
them Kirjath Arba (*Arba was* the father of
Anak), which *is* Hebron, in the mountains of
Judah, with the common-land surrounding
it. 12 But the fields of the city and its villages
they gave to Caleb the son of Jephunneh as
his possession.

13 Thus to the children of Aaron the priest
they gave Hebron with its common-land (a
city of refuge for the slayer), Libnah with
its common-land, 14 Jattir with its common-
land, Eshtemoa with its common-land,
15 Holon with its common-land, Debir with
its common-land, 16 Ain with its common-
land, Juttah with its common-land, and Beth
Shemesh with its common-land: nine cities
from those two tribes; 17 and from the tribe
of Benjamin, Gibeon with its common-land,

Geba with its common-land, 18Anathoth
with its common-land, and Almon with its
common-land: four cities. 19All the cities of
the children of Aaron, the priests, *were* thirteen cities with their common-lands.

20And the families of the children of Kohath, the Levites, the rest of the children of
Kohath, even they had the cities of their lot
from the tribe of Ephraim. 21For they gave
them Shechem with its common-land in the
mountains of Ephraim (a city of refuge for
the slayer), Gezer with its common-land,
22Kibzaim with its common-land, and Beth
Horon with its common-land: four cities;
23and from the tribe of Dan, Eltekeh with its
common-land, Gibbethon with its common-
land, 24Aijalon with its common-land, *and*
Gath Rimmon with its common-land: four
cities; 25and from the half-tribe of Manasseh, Tanach with its common-land and Gath
Rimmon with its common-land: two cities.
26All the ten cities with their common-lands
were for the rest of the families of the children of Kohath.

27Also to the children of Gershon, of the
families of the Levites, from the *other* half-
tribe of Manasseh, *they gave* Golan in Bashan
with its common-land (a city of refuge for the
slayer), and Be Eshterah with its common-
land: two cities; 28and from the tribe of Issachar, Kishion with its common-land,
Daberath with its common-land, 29Jarmuth
with its common-land, *and* En Gannim with
its common-land: four cities; 30and from the
tribe of Asher, Mishal with its common-
land, Abdon with its common-land, 31Hel-
kath with its common-land, and Rehob with
its common-land: four cities; 32and from the
tribe of Naphtali, Kedesh in Galilee with its
common-land (a city of refuge for the slayer),
Hammoth Dor with its common-land, and
Kartan with its common-land: three cities.
33All the cities of the Gershonites according
to their families *were* thirteen cities with
their common-lands.

34And to the families of the children
of Merari, the rest of the Levites from
the tribe of Zebulun, Jokneam with its
common-land, Kartah with its common-
land, 35Dimnah with its common-land, *and*
Nahalal with its common-land: four cities;
36and from the tribe of Reuben, Bezer with
its common-land, Jahaz with its common-
land, 37Kedemoth with its common-land,
and Mephaath with its common-land: four
cities;[a] 38and from the tribe of Gad, Ramoth
in Gilead with its common-land (a city of
refuge for the slayer), Mahanaim with its

21:37 [a] Following Septuagint and Vulgate (compare 1 Chronicles 6:78, 79); Masoretic Text, Bomberg, and Targum omit verses 36 and 37.

Epic Ideas

21:43–45 GOD IS TRUE TO HIS PROMISES

Take time to talk to older people who have known God for a long time. It can save you a lot of learning from hard knocks. It is wise to learn from experience, but it's even wiser to learn from the experience of others.

There's another great reason for asking older believers to share with you. They have proven what Joshua found out at the end of his battles in Canaan. God doesn't just keep His promises—He keeps all of His promises to the letter.

It's really neat as you get a little older to look back in memory and see how good God has been. There will be times when your faith almost failed, and you were scared because you thought God would not come through. But He always did!

The more times you see God working like that, the more you trust Him.

common-land, 39 Heshbon with its common-land, *and* Jazer with its common-land: four cities in all. 40 So all the cities for the children of Merari according to their families, the rest of the families of the Levites, were *by* their lot twelve cities.

41 All the cities of the Levites within the possession of the children of Israel *were* forty-eight cities with their common-lands. 42 Every one of these cities had its common-land surrounding it; thus *were* all these cities.

The Promise Fulfilled

43 So the LORD gave to Israel all the land of which He had sworn to give to their fathers, and they took possession of it and dwelt in it. 44 The LORD gave them rest all around, according to all that He had sworn to their fathers. And not a man of all their enemies stood against them; the LORD delivered all their enemies into their hand. 45 Not a word failed of any good thing which the LORD had spoken to the house of Israel. All came to pass.

Eastern Tribes Return to Their Lands

22 Then Joshua called the Reubenites, the Gadites, and half the tribe of Manasseh, 2 and said to them: "You have kept all that Moses the servant of the LORD commanded you, and have obeyed my voice in all that I commanded you. 3 You have not left your brethren these many days, up to this day, but have kept the charge of the commandment of the LORD your God. 4 And now the LORD your God has given rest to your brethren, as He promised them; now therefore, return and go to your tents *and* to the land of your possession, which Moses the servant of the LORD gave you on the other side of the Jordan. 5 But take careful heed to do the commandment and the law which Moses the servant of the LORD commanded you, to love the LORD your God, to walk in all His ways, to keep His commandments, to hold fast to Him, and to serve Him with all your heart and with all your soul." 6 So Joshua blessed them and sent them away, and they went to their tents.

7 Now to half the tribe of Manasseh Moses had given a possession in Bashan, but to the *other* half of it Joshua gave *a possession* among their brethren on this side of the Jordan, westward. And indeed, when Joshua sent them away to their tents, he blessed them, 8 and spoke to them, saying, "Return with much riches to your tents, with very much livestock, with silver, with gold, with bronze, with iron, and with very much clothing. Divide the spoil of your enemies with your brethren."

9 So the children of Reuben, the children of Gad, and half the tribe of Manasseh returned, and departed from the children of Israel at Shiloh, which *is* in the land of Canaan, to go to the country of Gilead, to the land of their possession, which they had obtained according to the word of the LORD by the hand of Moses.

An Altar by the Jordan

10 And when they came to the region of the Jordan which *is* in the land of Canaan, the children of Reuben, the children of Gad, and half the tribe of Manasseh built an altar there by the Jordan—a great, impressive altar. 11 Now the children of Israel heard *someone* say, "Behold, the children of Reuben, the children of Gad, and half the tribe of Manasseh have built an altar on the frontier of the land of Canaan, in the region of the Jordan—on the children of Israel's side." 12 And when the children of Israel heard *of it*, the whole congregation of the children of Israel gathered together at Shiloh to go to war against them.

13 Then the children of Israel sent Phinehas the son of Eleazar the priest to the children of Reuben, to the children of Gad, and to half the tribe of Manasseh, into the land of Gilead, 14 and with him ten rulers, one ruler each from the chief house of every tribe of Israel; and each one *was* the head of the house of his father among the divisions[a] of Israel. 15 Then they came to the children of Reuben, to the children of Gad, and to half the tribe of Manasseh, to the land of Gilead, and they spoke with them, saying, 16 "Thus says the whole congregation of the LORD: 'What treachery *is* this that you have committed against the God of Israel, to turn away this day from following the LORD, in that you have built for yourselves an altar, that you might rebel this day against the LORD? 17 *Is* the iniquity of Peor not enough for us, from which we are not cleansed till this day, although there was a plague in

22:14 [a] Literally *thousands*

the congregation of the LORD, 18but that
you must turn away this day from following the LORD? And it shall be, if you rebel
today against the LORD, that tomorrow He
will be angry with the whole congregation
of Israel. 19Nevertheless, if the land of your
possession *is* unclean, *then* cross over to the
land of the possession of the LORD, where
the LORD's tabernacle stands, and take possession among us; but do not rebel against
the LORD, nor rebel against us, by building
yourselves an altar besides the altar of the
LORD our God. 20Did not Achan the son of
Zerah commit a trespass in the accursed
thing, and wrath fell on all the congregation
of Israel? And that man did not perish alone
in his iniquity.'"

21Then the children of Reuben, the children of Gad, and half the tribe of Manasseh
answered and said to the heads of the divisions[a] of Israel: 22"The LORD God of gods,
the LORD God of gods, He knows, and let Israel itself know—if *it is* in rebellion, or if in
treachery against the LORD, do not save us
this day. 23If we have built ourselves an altar
to turn from following the LORD, or if to offer
on it burnt offerings or grain offerings, or if
to offer peace offerings on it, let the LORD
Himself require *an account*. 24But in fact we
have done it for fear, for a reason, saying, 'In
time to come your descendants may speak
to our descendants, saying, "What have you
to do with the LORD God of Israel? 25For the
LORD has made the Jordan a border between
you and us, *you* children of Reuben and children of Gad. You have no part in the LORD."
So your descendants would make our descendants cease fearing the LORD.' 26There-
fore we said, 'Let us now prepare to build
ourselves an altar, not for burnt offering nor
for sacrifice, 27but *that* it *may be* a witness between you and us and our generations after
us, that we may perform the service of the
LORD before Him with our burnt offerings,
with our sacrifices, and with our peace offerings; that your descendants may not say
to our descendants in time to come, "You
have no part in the LORD."' 28Therefore we
said that it will be, when they say *this* to us
or to our generations in time to come, that
we may say, 'Here is the replica of the altar
of the LORD which our fathers made, though
not for burnt offerings nor for sacrifices; but
it *is* a witness between you and us.' 29Far be
it from us that we should rebel against the
LORD, and turn from following the LORD this
day, to build an altar for burnt offerings, for
grain offerings, or for sacrifices, besides the
altar of the LORD our God which *is* before
His tabernacle."

30Now when Phinehas the priest and the
rulers of the congregation, the heads of the
divisions[a] of Israel who *were* with him, heard
the words that the children of Reuben, the
children of Gad, and the children of Manasseh spoke, it pleased them. 31Then Phinehas
the son of Eleazar the priest said to the children of Reuben, the children of Gad, and the
children of Manasseh, "This day we perceive
that the LORD *is* among us, because you have
not committed this treachery against the
LORD. Now you have delivered the children
of Israel out of the hand of the LORD."

32And Phinehas the son of Eleazar the
priest, and the rulers, returned from the
children of Reuben and the children of Gad,
from the land of Gilead to the land of Canaan, to the children of Israel, and brought
back word to them. 33So the thing pleased
the children of Israel, and the children of
Israel blessed God; they spoke no more of
going against them in battle, to destroy the
land where the children of Reuben and Gad
dwelt.

34The children of Reuben and the children of Gad[a] called the altar, *Witness*, "For
it is a witness between us that the LORD *is*
God."

Joshua's Farewell Address

23 Now it came to pass, a long time
after the LORD had given rest to
Israel from all their enemies round about,
that Joshua was old, advanced in age. 2And
Joshua called for all Israel, for their elders,
for their heads, for their judges, and for their
officers, and said to them:

"I am old, advanced in age. 3You have
seen all that the LORD your God has done
to all these nations because of you, for the
LORD your God *is* He who has fought for
you. 4See, I have divided to you by lot these
nations that remain, to be an inheritance for
your tribes, from the Jordan, with all the nations that I have cut off, as far as the Great
Sea westward. 5And the LORD your God will

22:21 [a] Literally *thousands* 22:30 [a] Literally *thousands*
22:34 [a] Septuagint adds *and half the tribe of Manasseh.*

expel them from before you and drive them
out of your sight. So you shall possess their
land, as the LORD your God promised you.
6 Therefore be very courageous to keep and
to do all that is written in the Book of the
Law of Moses, lest you turn aside from it to
the right hand or to the left, 7 *and* lest you
go among these nations, these who remain
among you. You shall not make mention of
the name of their gods, nor cause *anyone* to
swear *by them;* you shall not serve them nor
bow down to them, 8 but you shall hold fast
to the LORD your God, as you have done to
this day. 9 For the LORD has driven out from
before you great and strong nations; but *as
for* you, no one has been able to stand against
you to this day. 10 One man of you shall chase
a thousand, for the LORD your God *is* He who
fights for you, as He promised you. 11 Therefore take careful heed to yourselves, that you
love the LORD your God. 12 Or else, if indeed
you do go back, and cling to the remnant of
these nations—these that remain among
you—and make marriages with them, and
go in to them and they to you, 13 know for certain that the LORD your God will no longer
drive out these nations from before you. But
they shall be snares and traps to you, and
scourges on your sides and thorns in your
eyes, until you perish from this good land
which the LORD your God has given you.

14 "Behold, this day I *am* going the way of

GOD GIVES HIS PEOPLE THE LAND

READ IT: JOSHUA 23:1–16

GET IT:

After entering the Promised Land, the Israelite army successfully captured cities and regions (with God's help, of course). Finally they had the land God promised, and they divided it up among the twelve tribes. Everybody settled down. The battles were over (for now), and God let the people rest. Joshua had done what God had called him to do—he brought His people into the Promised Land, took over the land, and divided it up. Joshua commanded the people to obey God's commandments and to force the last of the original people out of the land (by God's instructions). He warned the Israelites not to worship the gods of the local people and told them what would happen if they did.

LIVE IT:

We have a hard time keeping a promise for even a short time. And we've all experienced the disappointment that happens when someone breaks a promise or never comes through on it. God is completely different. He is always true to His promise, even if a long time passes before He comes through on it. Hundreds of years before, God promised Abraham that he would be the father of a huge nation of people who would settle down in a great land. God was faithful to His promise, and He did it. Finally that promise came true. God takes His promises to His people very seriously. He keeps them. You should keep any promise you make, too.

all the earth. And you know in all your hearts
and in all your souls that not one thing has
failed of all the good things which the LORD
your God spoke concerning you. All have
come to pass for you; not one word of them
has failed. 15 Therefore it shall come to pass,
that as all the good things have come upon
you which the LORD your God promised you,
so the LORD will bring upon you all harmful things, until He has destroyed you from
this good land which the LORD your God has
given you. 16 When you have transgressed the
covenant of the LORD your God, which He
commanded you, and have gone and served
other gods, and bowed down to them, then
the anger of the LORD will burn against you,
and you shall perish quickly from the good
land which He has given you."

The Covenant at Shechem

24 Then Joshua gathered all the
tribes of Israel to Shechem and
called for the elders of Israel, for their heads,
for their judges, and for their officers; and
they presented themselves before God. 2 And
Joshua said to all the people, "Thus says the
LORD God of Israel: 'Your fathers, *including*
Terah, the father of Abraham and the father
of Nahor, dwelt on the other side of the River[a] in old times; and they served other gods.
3 Then I took your father Abraham from the
other side of the River, led him throughout
all the land of Canaan, and multiplied his
descendants and gave him Isaac. 4 To Isaac
I gave Jacob and Esau. To Esau I gave the
mountains of Seir to possess, but Jacob and
his children went down to Egypt. 5 Also I
sent Moses and Aaron, and I plagued Egypt,
according to what I did among them. Afterward I brought you out.

6 'Then I brought your fathers out of
Egypt, and you came to the sea; and the
Egyptians pursued your fathers with chariots and horsemen to the Red Sea. 7 So they
cried out to the LORD; and He put darkness
between you and the Egyptians, brought
the sea upon them, and covered them. And
your eyes saw what I did in Egypt. Then you
dwelt in the wilderness a long time. 8 And I
brought you into the land of the Amorites,
who dwelt on the other side of the Jordan,
and they fought with you. But I gave them
into your hand, that you might possess their
land, and I destroyed them from before
you. 9 Then Balak the son of Zippor, king of
Moab, arose to make war against Israel, and
sent and called Balaam the son of Beor to
curse you. 10 But I would not listen to Balaam;
therefore he continued to bless you. So I delivered you out of his hand. 11 Then you went
over the Jordan and came to Jericho. And the
men of Jericho fought against you—*also* the
Amorites, the Perizzites, the Canaanites,
the Hittites, the Girgashites, the Hivites,
and the Jebusites. But I delivered them into
your hand. 12 I sent the hornet before you
which drove them out from before you, *also*
the two kings of the Amorites, *but* not with
your sword or with your bow. 13 I have given
you a land for which you did not labor, and
cities which you did not build, and you dwell
in them; you eat of the vineyards and olive
groves which you did not plant.'

14 "Now therefore, fear the LORD, serve
Him in sincerity and in truth, and put away
the gods which your fathers served on the
other side of the River and in Egypt. Serve
the LORD! 15 And if it seems evil to you to
serve the LORD, choose for yourselves this
day whom you will serve, whether the gods
which your fathers served that *were* on the
other side of the River, or the gods of the
Amorites, in whose land you dwell. But
as for me and my house, we will serve the
LORD."

16 So the people answered and said: "Far
be it from us that we should forsake the
LORD to serve other gods; 17 for the LORD our
God *is* He who brought us and our fathers
up out of the land of Egypt, from the house
of bondage, who did those great signs in our
sight, and preserved us in all the way that
we went and among all the people through
whom we passed. 18 And the LORD drove out
from before us all the people, including the
Amorites who dwelt in the land. We also will
serve the LORD, for He *is* our God."

19 But Joshua said to the people, "You
cannot serve the LORD, for He *is* a holy God.
He *is* a jealous God; He will not forgive your
transgressions nor your sins. 20 If you forsake
the LORD and serve foreign gods, then He
will turn and do you harm and consume
you, after He has done you good."

21 And the people said to Joshua, "No, but
we will serve the LORD!"

24:2 [a] Hebrew *Nahar,* the Euphrates, and so in verses
3, 14, and 15

MAKING YOUR FAITH YOUR OWN

READ IT: JOSHUA 24:14, 15

Part of making your faith your own is deciding that God is the only one you believe in and serve. Saying yes to God means saying no to anything else that you worship or serve. (This doesn't mean giving up everything you love or enjoy—just the things that take the place of God.) Only God can give your life its ultimate meaning, purpose, and identity.

22So Joshua said to the people, "You *are*
witnesses against yourselves that you have
chosen the LORD for yourselves, to serve
Him."

And they said, "*We are* witnesses!"

23"Now therefore," *he said,* "put away the
foreign gods which *are* among you, and incline your heart to the LORD God of Israel."

24And the people said to Joshua, "The
LORD our God we will serve, and His voice
we will obey!"

25So Joshua made a covenant with the
people that day, and made for them a statute
and an ordinance in Shechem.

26Then Joshua wrote these words in the
Book of the Law of God. And he took a large
stone, and set it up there under the oak that
was by the sanctuary of the LORD. 27And Joshua said to all the people, "Behold, this stone
shall be a witness to us, for it has heard all
the words of the LORD which He spoke to us.
It shall therefore be a witness to you, lest you
deny your God." 28So Joshua let the people
depart, each to his own inheritance.

Death of Joshua and Eleazar

29Now it came to pass after these things
that Joshua the son of Nun, the servant of
the LORD, died, *being* one hundred and ten
years old. 30And they buried him within the
border of his inheritance at Timnath Serah,
which *is* in the mountains of Ephraim, on
the north side of Mount Gaash.

31Israel served the LORD all the days of
Joshua, and all the days of the elders who
outlived Joshua, who had known all the
works of the LORD which He had done for
Israel.

32The bones of Joseph, which the children of Israel had brought up out of Egypt,
they buried at Shechem, in the plot of
ground which Jacob had bought from the
sons of Hamor the father of Shechem for
one hundred pieces of silver, and which had
become an inheritance of the children of
Joseph.

33And Eleazar the son of Aaron died.
They buried him in a hill *belonging to* Phinehas his son, which was given to him in the
mountains of Ephraim.

The BOOK of

JUDGES

1043 B.C.–1004 B.C.

Behind the Scenes

READ IT:

The book of Judges tells the stories of the leaders of Israel after Joshua died. This block of time (325 years) was known for its heroes—called judges—who ruled the tribes of Israel. These leaders took care of the problems Israel had with their enemies. They were unusual characters, but God chose them and they helped their people.

GET IT:

Who wrote it: Most people think Samuel wrote it.

When it was written: 1043 B.C.–1004 B.C.

Why it was written: to tell Israel's history and the stories of the heroes who helped the nation. It also reminded the people of the problems that occurred when they forgot about God and didn't worship Him or follow His rules.

LIVE IT:

God can use all types of people to do what He needs to have done.

Chaos happens when we forget God and do our own thing.

FIND IT:

Israel's Disobedience	*Judges 2*
Deborah	*Judges 4–5*
Gideon	*Judges 6–8*
Jephthah	*Judges 11–12*
Samson	*Judges 13–16*
Israel's War with the Benjamites	*Judges 20*

The Continuing Conquest of Canaan

1 Now after the death of Joshua it came to
pass that the children of Israel asked the
LORD, saying, "Who shall be first to go up
for us against the Canaanites to fight against
them?"
2And the LORD said, "Judah shall go up.
Indeed I have delivered the land into his
hand."
3So Judah said to Simeon his brother,
"Come up with me to my allotted territory,
that we may fight against the Canaanites;
and I will likewise go with you to your allotted territory." And Simeon went with him.
4Then Judah went up, and the LORD delivered the Canaanites and the Perizzites into
their hand; and they killed ten thousand
men at Bezek. 5And they found Adoni-Bezek
in Bezek, and fought against him; and they
defeated the Canaanites and the Perizzites.
6Then Adoni-Bezek fled, and they pursued
him and caught him and cut off his thumbs
and big toes. 7And Adoni-Bezek said, "Seventy kings with their thumbs and big toes
cut off used to gather *scraps* under my table;
as I have done, so God has repaid me." Then
they brought him to Jerusalem, and there he
died.
8Now the children of Judah fought
against Jerusalem and took it; they struck it
with the edge of the sword and set the city
on fire. 9And afterward the children of Judah
went down to fight against the Canaanites
who dwelt in the mountains, in the South,[a]
and in the lowland. 10Then Judah went
against the Canaanites who dwelt in Hebron.
(Now the name of Hebron *was* formerly Kirjath Arba.) And they killed Sheshai, Ahiman, and Talmai.
11From there they went against the
inhabitants of Debir. (The name of Debir
was formerly Kirjath Sepher.)
12Then Caleb said, "Whoever attacks Kirjath Sepher and takes it, to him I will give
my daughter Achsah as wife." 13And Othniel
the son of Kenaz, Caleb's younger brother,
took it; so he gave him his daughter Achsah
as wife. 14Now it happened, when she came
to him, that she urged him[a] to ask her father for a field. And she dismounted from
her donkey, and Caleb said to her, "What do
you wish?" 15So she said to him, "Give me a
blessing; since you have given me land in the
South, give me also springs of water."
And Caleb gave her the upper springs
and the lower springs.
16Now the children of the Kenite, Moses'
father-in-law, went up from the City of Palms
with the children of Judah into the Wilderness of Judah, which *lies* in the South *near*
Arad; and they went and dwelt among the
people. 17And Judah went with his brother
Simeon, and they attacked the Canaanites
who inhabited Zephath, and utterly destroyed it. So the name of the city was called
Hormah. 18Also Judah took Gaza with its
territory, Ashkelon with its territory, and
Ekron with its territory. 19So the LORD was
with Judah. And they drove out the moun-
taineers, but they could not drive out the inhabitants of the lowland, because they had
chariots of iron. 20And they gave Hebron to
Caleb, as Moses had said. Then he expelled
from there the three sons of Anak. 21But the
children of Benjamin did not drive out the
Jebusites who inhabited Jerusalem; so the

1:9 [a] Hebrew *Negev,* and so throughout this book
1:14 [a] Septuagint and Vulgate read *he urged her.*

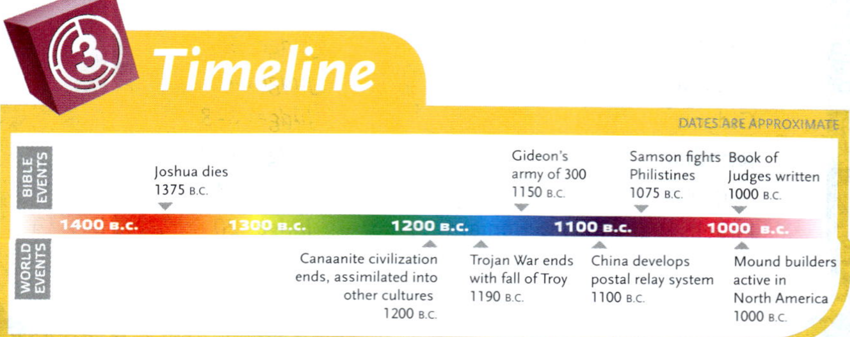

Jebusites dwell with the children of Benjamin in Jerusalem to this day.
22And the house of Joseph also went up
against Bethel, and the LORD *was* with them.
23So the house of Joseph sent men to spy out
Bethel. (The name of the city *was* formerly
Luz.) 24And when the spies saw a man coming out of the city, they said to him, "Please
show us the entrance to the city, and we will
show you mercy." 25So he showed them the
entrance to the city, and they struck the city
with the edge of the sword; but they let the
man and all his family go. 26And the man
went to the land of the Hittites, built a city,
and called its name Luz, which *is* its name
to this day.

Incomplete Conquest of the Land

27However, Manasseh did not drive
out *the inhabitants of* Beth Shean and its
villages, or Taanach and its villages, or the
inhabitants of Dor and its villages, or the inhabitants of Ibleam and its villages, or the
inhabitants of Megiddo and its villages; for
the Canaanites were determined to dwell
in that land. 28And it came to pass, when Israel was strong, that they put the Canaanites
under tribute, but did not completely drive
them out.
29Nor did Ephraim drive out the Canaanites who dwelt in Gezer; so the Canaanites
dwelt in Gezer among them.
30Nor did Zebulun drive out the inhabitants of Kitron or the inhabitants of Nahalol;
so the Canaanites dwelt among them, and
were put under tribute.
31Nor did Asher drive out the inhabitants
of Acco or the inhabitants of Sidon, or of
Ahlab, Achzib, Helbah, Aphik, or Rehob.
32So the Asherites dwelt among the Canaanites, the inhabitants of the land; for they did
not drive them out.
33Nor did Naphtali drive out the inhabitants of Beth Shemesh or the inhabitants of
Beth Anath; but they dwelt among the Canaanites, the inhabitants of the land. Nevertheless the inhabitants of Beth Shemesh and
Beth Anath were put under tribute to them.
34And the Amorites forced the children of
Dan into the mountains, for they would not
allow them to come down to the valley; 35and
the Amorites were determined to dwell in
Mount Heres, in Aijalon, and in Shaalbim;[a]
yet when the strength of the house of Joseph
became greater, they were put under tribute.
36Now the boundary of the Amorites *was*
from the Ascent of Akrabbim, from Sela,
and upward.

Israel's Disobedience

2 Then the Angel of the LORD came up
from Gilgal to Bochim, and said: "I
led you up from Egypt and brought you to
the land of which I swore to your fathers;
and I said, 'I will never break My covenant
with you. 2And you shall make no covenant
with the inhabitants of this land; you shall
tear down their altars.' But you have not
obeyed My voice. Why have you done this?
3Therefore I also said, 'I will not drive them
out before you; but they shall be *thorns* in
your side,[a] and their gods shall be a snare
to you.'" 4So it was, when the Angel of the
LORD spoke these words to all the children
of Israel, that the people lifted up their voices
and wept.
5Then they called the name of that place
Bochim;[a] and they sacrificed there to the
LORD. 6And when Joshua had dismissed the
people, the children of Israel went each to
his own inheritance to possess the land.

Death of Joshua

7So the people served the LORD all the
days of Joshua, and all the days of the elders who outlived Joshua, who had seen all
the great works of the LORD which He had
done for Israel. 8Now Joshua the son of Nun,
the servant of the LORD, died *when he was*
one hundred and ten years old. 9And they
buried him within the border of his inheritance at Timnath Heres, in the mountains
of Ephraim, on the north side of Mount
Gaash. 10When all that generation had been
gathered to their fathers, another generation
arose after them who did not know the LORD
nor the work which He had done for Israel.

Israel's Unfaithfulness

11Then the children of Israel did evil in
the sight of the LORD, and served the Baals;
12and they forsook the LORD God of their
fathers, who had brought them out of the
land of Egypt; and they followed other gods
from *among* the gods of the people who *were*
all around them, and they bowed down to
them; and they provoked the LORD to anger.

1:35 [a] Spelled *Shaalabbin* in Joshua 19:42 2:3 [a] Septuagint, Targum, and Vulgate read *enemies to you.* 2:5 [a] Literally *Weeping*

13 They forsook the LORD and served Baal and the Ashtoreths.[a] 14 And the anger of the LORD was hot against Israel. So He delivered them into the hands of plunderers who despoiled them; and He sold them into the hands of their enemies all around, so that they could no longer stand before their enemies. 15 Wherever they went out, the hand of the LORD was against them for calamity, as the LORD had said, and as the LORD had sworn to them. And they were greatly distressed.

16 Nevertheless, the LORD raised up judges who delivered them out of the hand of those who plundered them. 17 Yet they would not listen to their judges, but they played the harlot with other gods, and bowed down to them. They turned quickly from the way in which their fathers walked, in obeying the commandments of the LORD; they did not do so. 18 And when the LORD raised up judges for them, the LORD was with the judge and delivered them out of the hand of their enemies all the days of the judge; for the LORD was moved to pity by their groaning because of those who oppressed them and harassed them. 19 And it came to pass, when the judge was dead, that they reverted and behaved more corruptly than their fathers, by following other gods, to serve them and bow down to them. They did not cease from their own doings nor from their stubborn way.

20 Then the anger of the LORD was hot against Israel; and He said, "Because this nation has transgressed My covenant which I commanded their fathers, and has not heeded My voice, 21 I also will no longer drive out before them any of the nations which Joshua left when he died, 22 so that through them I may test Israel, whether they will keep the ways of the LORD, to walk in them as their fathers kept *them,* or not." 23 Therefore the LORD left those nations, without driving them out immediately; nor did He deliver them into the hand of Joshua.

The Nations Remaining in the Land

3 Now these *are* the nations which the LORD left, that He might test Israel by them, *that is,* all who had not known any of the wars in Canaan 2 (*this was* only so that the generations of the children of Israel might be taught to know war, at least those who had not formerly known it), 3 *namely,* five lords of the Philistines, all the Canaanites, the Sidonians, and the Hivites who dwelt in Mount Lebanon, from Mount Baal Hermon to the entrance of Hamath. 4 And they were *left, that He might* test Israel by them, to know whether they would obey the commandments of the LORD, which He had commanded their fathers by the hand of Moses.

5 Thus the children of Israel dwelt among the Canaanites, the Hittites, the Amorites, the Perizzites, the Hivites, and the Jebusites. 6 And they took their daughters to be their wives, and gave their daughters to their sons; and they served their gods.

Othniel

7 So the children of Israel did evil in the sight of the LORD. They forgot the LORD their God, and served the Baals and Asherahs.[a] 8 Therefore the anger of the LORD was hot against Israel, and He sold them into the hand of Cushan-Rishathaim king of Mesopotamia; and the children of Israel served Cushan-Rishathaim eight years. 9 When the children of Israel cried out to the LORD, the LORD raised up a deliverer for the children of Israel, who delivered them: Othniel the son of Kenaz, Caleb's younger brother. 10 The Spirit of the LORD came upon him, and he judged Israel. He went out to war, and the LORD delivered Cushan-Rishathaim king of Mesopotamia into his hand; and his hand prevailed over Cushan-Rishathaim. 11 So the land had rest for forty years. Then Othniel the son of Kenaz died.

Ehud

12 And the children of Israel again did evil in the sight of the LORD. So the LORD strengthened Eglon king of Moab against Israel, because they had done evil in the sight of the LORD. 13 Then he gathered to himself the people of Ammon and Amalek, went and defeated Israel, and took possession of the City of Palms. 14 So the children of Israel served Eglon king of Moab eighteen years.

15 But when the children of Israel cried out to the LORD, the LORD raised up a deliverer for them: Ehud the son of Gera, the Benjamite, a left-handed man. By him the children of Israel sent tribute to Eglon king of Moab. 16 Now Ehud made himself a dagger (it was double-edged and a cubit in

---

2:13 [a] Canaanite goddesses **3:7** [a] Name or symbol for Canaanite goddesses

length) and fastened it under his clothes on
his right thigh. 17So he brought the tribute to
Eglon king of Moab. (Now Eglon *was* a very
fat man.) 18And when he had finished presenting the tribute, he sent away the people
who had carried the tribute. 19But he himself
turned back from the stone images that *were*
at Gilgal, and said, "I have a secret message
for you, O king."

He said, "Keep silence!" And all who attended him went out from him.

20So Ehud came to him (now he was sitting upstairs in his cool private chamber).
Then Ehud said, "I have a message from
God for you." So he arose from *his* seat.
21Then Ehud reached with his left hand,
took the dagger from his right thigh, and
thrust it into his belly. 22Even the hilt went
in after the blade, and the fat closed over the
blade, for he did not draw the dagger out of
his belly; and his entrails came out. 23Then
Ehud went out through the porch and shut
the doors of the upper room behind him and
locked them.

24When he had gone out, *Eglon's*[a] servants
came to look, and *to their* surprise, the doors
of the upper room were locked. So they said,
"He is probably attending to his needs in the
cool chamber." 25So they waited till they were
embarrassed, and still he had not opened the
doors of the upper room. Therefore they took
the key and opened *them*. And there was
their master, fallen dead on the floor.

26But Ehud had escaped while they delayed, and passed beyond the stone images
and escaped to Seirah. 27And it happened,
when he arrived, that he blew the trumpet
in the mountains of Ephraim, and the children of Israel went down with him from the
mountains; and he led them. 28Then he said
to them, "Follow *me,* for the LORD has delivered your enemies the Moabites into your
hand." So they went down after him, seized
the fords of the Jordan leading to Moab, and
did not allow anyone to cross over. 29And
at that time they killed about ten thousand
men of Moab, all stout men of valor; not a
man escaped. 30So Moab was subdued that
day under the hand of Israel. And the land
had rest for eighty years.

Shamgar

31After him was Shamgar the son of
Anath, who killed six hundred men of the
Philistines with an ox goad; and he also de-
livered Israel.

Deborah

4 When Ehud was dead, the children
of Israel again did evil in the sight of

3:24 [a] Literally *his*

Starring Roles

DEBORAH was a prophetess in Israel when Barak was ordered to defend the people of Israel against the king of Canaan (pronounced *KAY-nun*). The Lord showed Deborah that Barak should take ten thousand men to fight against the army of General Sisera of Canaan.

Although Deborah didn't take part in the battle, she kept her promise to go to the battlefield with Barak and his troops. Barak was encouraged by her advice, and that day he and his army defeated the army of the king of Canaan. So Deborah and Barak celebrated by singing their victory duet together (see Judges 5).

Barak won the victory that day because he was willing to listen to good advice and because Deborah was willing to take her place beside him as encourager.

Learn to respect one another's God-given abilities while you are growing up. Respect, or honor, is the basis of the love God commands you to have for others.

the Lord. 2So the Lord sold them into the
hand of Jabin king of Canaan, who reigned
in Hazor. The commander of his army *was*
Sisera, who dwelt in Harosheth Hagoyim.
3And the children of Israel cried out to the
Lord; for Jabin had nine hundred chariots
of iron, and for twenty years he had harshly
oppressed the children of Israel.

4Now Deborah, a prophetess, the wife of
Lapidoth, was judging Israel at that time.
5And she would sit under the palm tree of
Deborah between Ramah and Bethel in
the mountains of Ephraim. And the children of Israel came up to her for judgment.
6Then she sent and called for Barak the son
of Abinoam from Kedesh in Naphtali, and
said to him, "Has not the Lord God of Israel
commanded, 'Go and deploy *troops* at Mount
Tabor; take with you ten thousand men of
the sons of Naphtali and of the sons of Zebulun; 7and against you I will deploy Sisera, the
commander of Jabin's army, with his chariots and his multitude at the River Kishon;
and I will deliver him into your hand'?"

8And Barak said to her, "If you will go
with me, then I will go; but if you will not go
with me, I will not go!"

9So she said, "I will surely go with you;
nevertheless there will be no glory for you
in the journey you are taking, for the Lord
will sell Sisera into the hand of a woman."
Then Deborah arose and went with Barak
to Kedesh. 10And Barak called Zebulun and
Naphtali to Kedesh; he went up with ten

GOD GIVES DEBORAH AND BARAK VICTORY

READ IT: JUDGES 4:1–24

GET IT:

Time passed. The Israelites didn't clear out the local people as God had told them to do. After Joshua died, the people forgot about God and worshiped the local god Baal. And what God warned would happen—"the Lord will bring upon you all harmful things" (Joshua 23:15)—did happen. The local people became Israel's enemies and attacked them.

God then sent judges to guide the people in battle and back to Him. Deborah was one of those judges. It was very unusual in ancient times for a woman to have any kind of leadership role. But Deborah was very wise, and people came to her for advice. She also encouraged Barak to fight a Canaanite king. That day God gave the Israelites a great victory!

LIVE IT:

We have to look closely at this story to understand what God is telling us. Look for the words "the Lord" as you read. You'll find a chain of events that show God was leading and directing all the action in this story. The Israelites learned that God had to direct their battles. If they did it on their own, they were defeated. If they attacked the enemy at God's command, they won. God no longer directs us into war like He did back then, but He still leads. Let God lead the way in your life. Listen for His advice and direction.

thousand men under his command,[a] and
Deborah went up with him.
11 Now Heber the Kenite, of the children
of Hobab the father-in-law of Moses, had
separated himself from the Kenites and
pitched his tent near the terebinth tree at
Zaanaim, which *is* beside Kedesh.
12 And they reported to Sisera that Barak
the son of Abinoam had gone up to Mount
Tabor. 13 So Sisera gathered together all his
chariots, nine hundred chariots of iron, and
all the people who *were* with him, from Harosheth Hagoyim to the River Kishon.
14 Then Deborah said to Barak, "Up! For
this *is* the day in which the LORD has delivered Sisera into your hand. Has not the LORD
gone out before you?" So Barak went down
from Mount Tabor with ten thousand men
following him. 15 And the LORD routed Sisera
and all *his* chariots and all *his* army with the
edge of the sword before Barak; and Sisera
alighted from *his* chariot and fled away on
foot. 16 But Barak pursued the chariots and
the army as far as Harosheth Hagoyim, and
all the army of Sisera fell by the edge of the
sword; not a man was left.
17 However, Sisera had fled away on foot to
the tent of Jael, the wife of Heber the Kenite;
for *there was* peace between Jabin king of
Hazor and the house of Heber the Kenite.
18 And Jael went out to meet Sisera, and said
to him, "Turn aside, my lord, turn aside to
me; do not fear." And when he had turned
aside with her into the tent, she covered him
with a blanket.
19 Then he said to her, "Please give me a
little water to drink, for I am thirsty." So she
opened a jug of milk, gave him a drink, and
covered him. 20 And he said to her, "Stand at
the door of the tent, and if any man comes
and inquires of you, and says, 'Is there any
man here?' you shall say, 'No.'"
21 Then Jael, Heber's wife, took a tent peg
and took a hammer in her hand, and went
softly to him and drove the peg into his tem-
ple, and it went down into the ground; for he
was fast asleep and weary. So he died. 22 And
then, as Barak pursued Sisera, Jael came out
to meet him, and said to him, "Come, I will
show you the man whom you seek." And
when he went into her *tent,* there lay Sisera,
dead with the peg in his temple.
23 So on that day God subdued Jabin king
of Canaan in the presence of the children
of Israel. 24 And the hand of the children of
Israel grew stronger and stronger against
Jabin king of Canaan, until they had destroyed Jabin king of Canaan.

The Song of Deborah

5 Then Deborah and Barak the son of
Abinoam sang on that day, saying:

2 "When leaders lead in Israel,
When the people willingly offer
themselves,
Bless the LORD!

3 "Hear, O kings! Give ear, O princes!
I, *even* I, will sing to the LORD;
I will sing praise to the LORD God of
Israel.

4 "LORD, when You went out from Seir,
When You marched from the field of
Edom,
The earth trembled and the heavens
poured,
The clouds also poured water;
5 The mountains gushed before the LORD,
This Sinai, before the LORD God of
Israel.

6 "In the days of Shamgar, son of Anath,
In the days of Jael,
The highways were deserted,
And the travelers walked along the
byways.
7 Village life ceased, it ceased in Israel,
Until I, Deborah, arose,
Arose a mother in Israel.
8 They chose new gods;
Then *there was* war in the gates;
Not a shield or spear was seen among
forty thousand in Israel.
9 My heart *is* with the rulers of Israel
Who offered themselves willingly with
the people.
Bless the LORD!

10 "Speak, you who ride on white donkeys,
Who sit in judges' attire,
And who walk along the road.
11 Far from the noise of the archers,
among the watering places,
There they shall recount the righteous
acts of the LORD,
The righteous acts *for* His villagers in
Israel;
Then the people of the LORD shall go
down to the gates.

4:10 [a] Literally *at his feet*

12 "Awake, awake, Deborah!
Awake, awake, sing a song!
Arise, Barak, and lead your captives
away,
O son of Abinoam!

13 "Then the survivors came down, the
people against the nobles;
The LORD came down for me against
the mighty.
14 From Ephraim *were* those whose roots
were in Amalek.
After you, Benjamin, with your peoples,
From Machir rulers came down,
And from Zebulun those who bear the
recruiter's staff.
15 And the princes of Issachar[a] *were* with
Deborah;
As Issachar, so *was* Barak
Sent into the valley under his
command;[b]
Among the divisions of Reuben
There were great resolves of heart.
16 Why did you sit among the sheepfolds,
To hear the pipings for the flocks?
The divisions of Reuben have great
searchings of heart.
17 Gilead stayed beyond the Jordan,
And why did Dan remain on ships?[a]
Asher continued at the seashore,
And stayed by his inlets.
18 Zebulun *is* a people *who* jeopardized
their lives to the point of death,
Naphtali also, on the heights of the
battlefield.

19 "The kings came *and* fought,
Then the kings of Canaan fought
In Taanach, by the waters of Megiddo;
They took no spoils of silver.
20 They fought from the heavens;
The stars from their courses fought
against Sisera.
21 The torrent of Kishon swept them away,
That ancient torrent, the torrent of
Kishon.
O my soul, march on in strength!
22 Then the horses' hooves pounded,
The galloping, galloping of his steeds.
23 'Curse Meroz,' said the angel[a] of the
LORD,
'*Curse its inhabitants bitterly,*
Because they did not come to the help of
the LORD,
To the help of the LORD against the
mighty.'

24 "Most blessed among women is Jael,
The wife of Heber the Kenite;
Blessed is she among women in tents.
25 He asked for water, she gave milk;
She brought out cream in a lordly bowl.
26 She stretched her hand to the tent peg,
Her right hand to the workmen's
hammer;
She pounded Sisera, she pierced his
head,
She split and struck through his temple.
27 At her feet he sank, he fell, he lay still;
At her feet he sank, he fell;
Where he sank, there he fell dead.

28 "The mother of Sisera looked through
the window,
And cried out through the lattice,
'Why is his chariot *so* long in coming?
Why tarries the clatter of his chariots?'
29 Her wisest ladies answered her,
Yes, she answered herself,
30 'Are they not finding and dividing the
spoil:
To every man a girl *or* two;
For Sisera, plunder of dyed garments,
Plunder of garments embroidered and
dyed,
Two pieces of dyed embroidery for the
neck of the looter?'

31 "Thus let all Your enemies perish,
O LORD!
But *let* those who love Him *be* like the
sun
When it comes out in full strength."

So the land had rest for forty years.

Midianites Oppress Israel

6 Then the children of Israel did evil in
the sight of the LORD. So the LORD delivered them into the hand of Midian for sev-
en years, 2and the hand of Midian prevailed
against Israel. Because of the Midianites, the
children of Israel made for themselves the
dens, the caves, and the strongholds which
are in the mountains. 3So it was, whenever
Israel had sown, Midianites would come up;
also Amalekites and the people of the East
would come up against them. 4Then they
would encamp against them and destroy
the produce of the earth as far as Gaza, and

5:15 [a] Following Septuagint, Syriac, Targum, and Vulgate; Masoretic Text reads *And my princes in Issachar.* [b] Literally *at his feet* 5:17 [a] Or *at ease* 5:23 [a] Or *Angel*

leave no sustenance for Israel, neither sheep
nor ox nor donkey. 5For they would come up
with their livestock and their tents, coming
in as numerous as locusts; both they and
their camels were without number; and they
would enter the land to destroy it. 6So Israel
was greatly impoverished because of the
Midianites, and the children of Israel cried
out to the LORD.

7And it came to pass, when the children
of Israel cried out to the LORD because
of the Midianites, 8that the LORD sent a
prophet to the children of Israel, who said
to them, "Thus says the LORD God of Israel:
'I brought you up from Egypt and brought
you out of the house of bondage; 9and I delivered you out of the hand of the Egyptians
and out of the hand of all who oppressed
you, and drove them out before you and gave
you their land. 10Also I said to you, "I *am* the
LORD your God; do not fear the gods of the
Amorites, in whose land you dwell." But you
have not obeyed My voice.'"

Gideon

11Now the Angel of the LORD came and
sat under the terebinth tree which *was* in
Ophrah, which *belonged* to Joash the Abiez-
rite, while his son Gideon threshed wheat in
the winepress, in order to hide *it* from the

IDENTITY
THE COMPARISON GAME

READ IT: JUDGES 6

GET IT:

Gideon experienced something unique—he had a conversation with the Angel of the Lord. Most of us will never have that happen. But Gideon's reaction was pretty normal. In fact, it was an awful lot like our reaction to many challenges—panic. "Pick the other guy, God. He's better at it than I am."

In Gideon's case, God didn't take no for an answer. He promised to stay with Gideon and give him victory over the Midianites, Israel's enemy. After God performed a series of miracles, Gideon obeyed God and did everything He asked. Eventually he received all that the Angel of the Lord promised. Gideon was wrong about what he could and couldn't do. He had everything he needed right in front of him.

LIVE IT:

We tend to look at others the way Gideon looked at himself and assume they have something we don't. This kind of comparison game can rob you of amazing opportunities and take away your happiness.

We shouldn't make assumptions about ourselves or others 'cause they're usually wrong. Assumptions can blind us from knowing our strengths and potential to do great things.

Remember: all Gideon had to do was take his eyes off others and put them on God. He was able to do hard things with God's help, and we can, too.

Midianites. 12And the Angel of the LORD appeared to him, and said to him, "The LORD *is*
with you, you mighty man of valor!"
13Gideon said to Him, "O my lord,[a] if the
LORD is with us, why then has all this happened to us? And where *are* all His miracles
which our fathers told us about, saying, 'Did
not the LORD bring us up from Egypt?' But
now the LORD has forsaken us and delivered
us into the hands of the Midianites."
14Then the LORD turned to him and said,
"Go in this might of yours, and you shall
save Israel from the hand of the Midianites.
Have I not sent you?"
15So he said to Him, "O my Lord,[a] how
can I save Israel? Indeed my clan *is* the
weakest in Manasseh, and I *am* the least in
my father's house."
16And the LORD said to him, "Surely I will
be with you, and you shall defeat the Midianites as one man."
17Then he said to Him, "If now I have
found favor in Your sight, then show me a
sign that it is You who talk with me. 18Do not
depart from here, I pray, until I come to You
and bring out my offering and set *it* before
You."

And He said, "I will wait until you come back."

6:13 [a] Hebrew *adoni,* used of man 6:15 [a] Hebrew *Adonai,* used of God

GOD CALLS GIDEON

READ IT: JUDGES 6:11–40

GET IT:

The Midianites were another enemy of Israel. These people were raiders. They would invade Israel's land and destroy the crops so there was nothing left to eat. Big problem. So Gideon had to hide to process the wheat—something that's usually done out in the field. Then one day God (in angel form) showed up to talk to Gideon. He called him "a mighty man" (v. 12), but Gideon saw himself as weak and "the least" (v. 15). Basically he told God, "Don't pick me—get someone else." Next he said, "Okay, I'll do it, but prove to me You are who You say You are." God did. Later, when the Midianites invaded, Gideon was still not quite ready, so twice he gave God a test. In the end, in spite of Gideon's doubt, God gave Gideon victory over the Midianites, and the people lived in peace for forty years.

LIVE IT:

If God calls you, don't make excuses. Gideon made several excuses for why he couldn't lead God's people. But God didn't see it that way. God evaluates and looks at people differently than people look at each other. His standards are very different from the standards of the world. God uses all types of people to get His work done here on earth. He doesn't always pick the strongest or the most qualified person for the job. He *picks who He wants*. Then He gives that person (like Gideon) the wisdom or power to do the job. Really, it's not about you; it's about God working in and through you.

19 So Gideon went in and prepared a
young goat, and unleavened bread from an
ephah of flour. The meat he put in a basket,
and he put the broth in a pot; and he brought
them out to Him under the terebinth tree
and presented *them*. 20 The Angel of God said
to him, "Take the meat and the unleavened
bread and lay *them* on this rock, and pour out
the broth." And he did so.

21 Then the Angel of the LORD put out the
end of the staff that *was* in His hand, and
touched the meat and the unleavened bread;
and fire rose out of the rock and consumed
the meat and the unleavened bread. And the
Angel of the LORD departed out of his sight.

22 Now Gideon perceived that He *was* the
Angel of the LORD. So Gideon said, "Alas, O
Lord GOD! For I have seen the Angel of the
LORD face to face."

23 Then the LORD said to him, "Peace *be*
with you; do not fear, you shall not die." 24 So
Gideon built an altar there to the LORD, and
called it The-LORD-*Is*-Peace.[a] To this day it *is*
still in Ophrah of the Abiezrites.

25 Now it came to pass the same night that
the LORD said to him, "Take your father's
young bull, the second bull of seven years
old, and tear down the altar of Baal that your
father has, and cut down the wooden image[a]
that *is* beside it; 26 and build an altar to the
LORD your God on top of this rock in the
proper arrangement, and take the second
bull and offer a burnt sacrifice with the wood
of the image which you shall cut down." 27 So
Gideon took ten men from among his servants and did as the LORD had said to him.
But because he feared his father's household
and the men of the city too much to do *it* by
day, he did *it* by night.

Gideon Destroys the Altar of Baal

28 And when the men of the city arose
early in the morning, there was the altar of
Baal, torn down; and the wooden image that
was beside it was cut down, and the second
bull was being offered on the altar *which*
had been built. 29 So they said to one another,
"Who has done this thing?" And when they
had inquired and asked, they said, "Gideon
the son of Joash has done this thing." 30 Then
the men of the city said to Joash, "Bring out
your son, that he may die, because he has
torn down the altar of Baal, and because he
has cut down the wooden image that *was*
beside it."

31 But Joash said to all who stood against
him, "Would you plead for Baal? Would you
save him? Let the one who would plead for
him be put to death by morning! If he *is* a
god, let him plead for himself, because his
altar has been torn down!" 32 Therefore on
that day he called him Jerubbaal,[a] saying,
"Let Baal plead against him, because he has
torn down his altar."

33 Then all the Midianites and Amalekites, the people of the East, gathered together; and they crossed over and encamped in
the Valley of Jezreel. 34 But the Spirit of the
LORD came upon Gideon; then he blew the
trumpet, and the Abiezrites gathered behind
him. 35 And he sent messengers throughout
all Manasseh, who also gathered behind
him. He also sent messengers to Asher,
Zebulun, and Naphtali; and they came up to
meet them.

The Sign of the Fleece

36 So Gideon said to God, "If You will save
Israel by my hand as You have said— 37 look,
I shall put a fleece of wool on the threshing
floor; if there is dew on the fleece only, and
it is dry on all the ground, then I shall know
that You will save Israel by my hand, as You
have said." 38 And it was so. When he rose early the next morning and squeezed the fleece
together, he wrung the dew out of the fleece,
a bowlful of water. 39 Then Gideon said to
God, "Do not be angry with me, but let me
speak just once more: Let me test, I pray, just
once more with the fleece; let it now be dry
only on the fleece, but on all the ground let
there be dew." 40 And God did so that night. It
was dry on the fleece only, but there was dew
on all the ground.

Gideon's Valiant Three Hundred

7 Then Jerubbaal (that *is*, Gideon) and all
the people who *were* with him rose early
and encamped beside the well of Harod, so
that the camp of the Midianites was on the
north side of them by the hill of Moreh in
the valley.

2 And the LORD said to Gideon, "The
people who *are* with you *are* too many for
Me to give the Midianites into their hands,
lest Israel claim glory for itself against Me,
saying, 'My own hand has saved me.' 3 Now
therefore, proclaim in the hearing of the

6:24 [a] Hebrew *YHWH Shalom* 6:25 [a] Hebrew *Asherah*, a
Canaanite goddess 6:32 [a] Literally *Let Baal Plead*

people, saying, 'Whoever *is* fearful and
afraid, let him turn and depart at once from
Mount Gilead.'" And twenty-two thousand
of the people returned, and ten thousand
remained.

4But the LORD said to Gideon, "The people *are* still *too* many; bring them down to
the water, and I will test them for you there.
Then it will be, *that* of whom I say to you,
'This one shall go with you,' the same shall
go with you; and of whomever I say to you,
'This one shall not go with you,' the same
shall not go." 5So he brought the people
down to the water. And the LORD said to
Gideon, "Everyone who laps from the water
with his tongue, as a dog laps, you shall set
apart by himself; likewise everyone who gets
down on his knees to drink." 6And the number of those who lapped, *putting* their hand
to their mouth, was three hundred men; but
all the rest of the people got down on their
knees to drink water. 7Then the LORD said
to Gideon, "By the three hundred men who
lapped I will save you, and deliver the Midianites into your hand. Let all the *other* people
go, every man to his place." 8So the people
took provisions and their trumpets in their
hands. And he sent away all *the rest of* Israel,
every man to his tent, and retained those
three hundred men. Now the camp of Midian was below him in the valley.

9It happened on the same night that the
LORD said to him, "Arise, go down against
the camp, for I have delivered it into your
hand. 10But if you are afraid to go down, go
down to the camp with Purah your servant,
11and you shall hear what they say; and afterward your hands shall be strengthened to
go down against the camp." Then he went
down with Purah his servant to the outpost
of the armed men who *were* in the camp.
12Now the Midianites and Amalekites, all the
people of the East, were lying in the valley as
numerous as locusts; and their camels *were*
without number, as the sand by the seashore
in multitude.

13And when Gideon had come, there was
a man telling a dream to his companion. He
said, "I have had a dream: *To my* surprise, a
loaf of barley bread tumbled into the camp
of Midian; it came to a tent and struck it
so that it fell and overturned, and the tent
collapsed."

14Then his companion answered and
said, "This *is* nothing else but the sword of
Gideon the son of Joash, a man of Israel! Into
his hand God has delivered Midian and the
whole camp."

15And so it was, when Gideon heard
the telling of the dream and its interpretation, that he worshiped. He returned to
the camp of Israel, and said, "Arise, for the
LORD has delivered the camp of Midian into
your hand." 16Then he divided the three
hundred men *into* three companies, and
he put a trumpet into every man's hand,
with empty pitchers, and torches inside the
pitchers. 17And he said to them, "Look at me
and do likewise; watch, and when I come to
the edge of the camp you shall do as I do:
18When I blow the trumpet, I and all who *are*
with me, then you also blow the trumpets on
every side of the whole camp, and say, '*The
sword of* the LORD and of Gideon!'"

19So Gideon and the hundred men who
were with him came to the outpost of the
camp at the beginning of the middle watch,
just as they had posted the watch; and they
blew the trumpets and broke the pitchers
that *were* in their hands. 20Then the three
companies blew the trumpets and broke the
pitchers—they held the torches in their left
hands and the trumpets in their right hands
for blowing—and they cried, "The sword of
the LORD and of Gideon!" 21And every man
stood in his place all around the camp; and
the whole army ran and cried out and fled.
22When the three hundred blew the trumpets, the LORD set every man's sword against
his companion throughout the whole camp;
and the army fled to Beth Acacia,[a] toward
Zererah, as far as the border of Abel Meholah, by Tabbath.

23And the men of Israel gathered together
from Naphtali, Asher, and all Manasseh, and
pursued the Midianites.

24Then Gideon sent messengers
throughout all the mountains of Ephraim,
saying, "Come down against the Midianites,
and seize from them the watering places as
far as Beth Barah and the Jordan." Then all
the men of Ephraim gathered together and
seized the watering places as far as Beth Barah and the Jordan. 25And they captured two
princes of the Midianites, Oreb and Zeeb.
They killed Oreb at the rock of Oreb, and

7:22 [a] Hebrew *Beth Shittah*

Zeeb they killed at the winepress of Zeeb. They pursued Midian and brought the heads of Oreb and Zeeb to Gideon on the other side of the Jordan.

Gideon Subdues the Midianites

8 Now the men of Ephraim said to him, "Why have you done this to us by not calling us when you went to fight with the Midianites?" And they reprimanded him sharply.

2So he said to them, "What have I done now in comparison with you? *Is* not the gleaning *of the grapes* of Ephraim better than the vintage of Abiezer? 3God has delivered into your hands the princes of Midian, Oreb and Zeeb. And what was I able to do in comparison with you?" Then their anger toward him subsided when he said that.

4When Gideon came to the Jordan, he and the three hundred men who *were* with him crossed over, exhausted but still in pursuit. 5Then he said to the men of Succoth, "Please give loaves of bread to the people who follow me, for they are exhausted, and I am pursuing Zebah and Zalmunna, kings of Midian."

6And the leaders of Succoth said, "*Are* the hands of Zebah and Zalmunna now in your hand, that we should give bread to your army?"

7So Gideon said, "For this cause, when the LORD has delivered Zebah and Zalmunna into my hand, then I will tear your flesh with the thorns of the wilderness and with briers!" 8Then he went up from there to Penuel and spoke to them in the same way. And the men of Penuel answered him as the men of Succoth had answered. 9So he also spoke to the men of Penuel, saying, "When I come back in peace, I will tear down this tower!"

10Now Zebah and Zalmunna *were* at Karkor, and their armies with them, about fifteen thousand, all who were left of all the army of the people of the East; for one hundred and twenty thousand men who drew the sword had fallen. 11Then Gideon went up by the road of those who dwell in tents on the east of Nobah and Jogbehah; and he attacked the army while the camp felt secure. 12When Zebah and Zalmunna fled, he pursued them; and he took the two kings of Midian, Zebah and Zalmunna, and routed the whole army.

13Then Gideon the son of Joash returned from battle, from the Ascent of Heres. 14And he caught a young man of the men of Succoth and interrogated him; and he wrote down for him the leaders of Succoth and its elders, seventy-seven men. 15Then he came to the men of Succoth and said, "Here are Zebah and Zalmunna, about whom you ridiculed me, saying, '*Are* the hands of Zebah and Zalmunna now in your hand, that we should give bread to your weary men?'" 16And he took the elders of the city, and thorns of the wilderness and briers, and with them he taught the men of Succoth. 17Then he tore down the tower of Penuel and killed the men of the city.

18And he said to Zebah and Zalmunna, "What kind of men *were they* whom you killed at Tabor?"

So they answered, "As you *are,* so *were* they; each one resembled the son of a king."

19Then he said, "They *were* my brothers, the sons of my mother. *As* the LORD lives, if you had let them live, I would not kill you." 20And he said to Jether his firstborn, "Rise, kill them!" But the youth would not draw his sword; for he was afraid, because he *was* still a youth.

21So Zebah and Zalmunna said, "Rise yourself, and kill us; for as a man *is, so is* his strength." So Gideon arose and killed Zebah and Zalmunna, and took the crescent ornaments that *were* on their camels' necks.

Gideon's Ephod

22Then the men of Israel said to Gideon, "Rule over us, both you and your son, and your grandson also; for you have delivered us from the hand of Midian."

23But Gideon said to them, "I will not rule over you, nor shall my son rule over you; the LORD shall rule over you." 24Then Gideon said to them, "I would like to make a request of you, that each of you would give me the earrings from his plunder." For they had golden earrings, because they *were* Ishmaelites.

25So they answered, "We will gladly give *them.*" And they spread out a garment, and each man threw into it the earrings from his plunder. 26Now the weight of the gold earrings that he requested was one thousand seven hundred *shekels* of gold, besides the crescent ornaments, pendants, and purple robes which *were* on the kings of Midian,

and besides the chains that *were* around
their camels' necks. [27]Then Gideon made
it into an ephod and set it up in his city,
Ophrah. And all Israel played the harlot with
it there. It became a snare to Gideon and to
his house.
[28]Thus Midian was subdued before the
children of Israel, so that they lifted their
heads no more. And the country was quiet
for forty years in the days of Gideon.

Death of Gideon

[29]Then Jerubbaal the son of Joash went
and dwelt in his own house. [30]Gideon had
seventy sons who were his own offspring,
for he had many wives. [31]And his concubine
who *was* in Shechem also bore him a son,
whose name he called Abimelech. [32]Now
Gideon the son of Joash died at a good old
age, and was buried in the tomb of Joash his
father, in Ophrah of the Abiezrites.
[33]So it was, as soon as Gideon was dead,
that the children of Israel again played the
harlot with the Baals, and made Baal-Berith
their god. [34]Thus the children of Israel did
not remember the LORD their God, who had
delivered them from the hands of all their
enemies on every side; [35]nor did they show
kindness to the house of Jerubbaal (Gideon)
in accordance with the good he had done for
Israel.

Abimelech's Conspiracy

9 Then Abimelech the son of Jerubbaal
went to Shechem, to his mother's
brothers, and spoke with them and with all
the family of the house of his mother's father, saying, [2]"Please speak in the hearing
of all the men of Shechem: 'Which is better
for you, that all seventy of the sons of Jerubbaal reign over you, or that one reign over
you?' Remember that I *am* your own flesh
and bone."
[3]And his mother's brothers spoke all
these words concerning him in the hearing
of all the men of Shechem; and their heart
was inclined to follow Abimelech, for they
said, "He is our brother." [4]So they gave him
seventy *shekels* of silver from the temple of
Baal-Berith, with which Abimelech hired
worthless and reckless men; and they followed him. [5]Then he went to his father's
house at Ophrah and killed his brothers, the
seventy sons of Jerubbaal, on one stone. But
Jotham the youngest son of Jerubbaal was
left, because he hid himself. [6]And all the
men of Shechem gathered together, all of
Beth Millo, and they went and made Abimelech king beside the terebinth tree at the
pillar that *was* in Shechem.

The Parable of the Trees

[7]Now when they told Jotham, he went
and stood on top of Mount Gerizim, and
lifted his voice and cried out. And he said
to them:

"Listen to me, you men of Shechem,
That God may listen to you!

8 "The trees once went forth to anoint a
king over them.
And they said to the olive tree,
'Reign over us!'
9 But the olive tree said to them,
'Should I cease giving my oil,
With which they honor God and men,
And go to sway over trees?'

10 "Then the trees said to the fig tree,
'You come *and* reign over us!'
11 But the fig tree said to them,
'Should I cease my sweetness and my
good fruit,
And go to sway over trees?'

12 "Then the trees said to the vine,
'You come *and* reign over us!'
13 But the vine said to them,
'Should I cease my new wine,
Which cheers *both* God and men,
And go to sway over trees?'

14 "Then all the trees said to the bramble,
'You come *and* reign over us!'
15 And the bramble said to the trees,
'If in truth you anoint me as king over
you,
Then come *and* take shelter in my shade;
But if not, let fire come out of the
bramble
And devour the cedars of Lebanon!'

[16]"Now therefore, if you have acted in
truth and sincerity in making Abimelech
king, and if you have dealt well with Jerubbaal and his house, and have done to him
as he deserves— [17]for my father fought for
you, risked his life, and delivered you out of
the hand of Midian; [18]but you have risen up
against my father's house this day, and killed
his seventy sons on one stone, and made
Abimelech, the son of his female servant,

king over the men of Shechem, because he
is your brother— 19if then you have acted in
truth and sincerity with Jerubbaal and with
his house this day, *then* rejoice in Abimelech,
and let him also rejoice in you. 20But if not,
let fire come from Abimelech and devour the
men of Shechem and Beth Millo; and let fire
come from the men of Shechem and from
Beth Millo and devour Abimelech!" 21And
Jotham ran away and fled; and he went to
Beer and dwelt there, for fear of Abimelech
his brother.

Downfall of Abimelech

22After Abimelech had reigned over Israel
three years, 23God sent a spirit of ill will between Abimelech and the men of Shechem;
and the men of Shechem dealt treacherously
with Abimelech, 24that the crime *done* to the
seventy sons of Jerubbaal might be settled
and their blood be laid on Abimelech their
brother, who killed them, and on the men
of Shechem, who aided him in the killing
of his brothers. 25And the men of Shechem
set men in ambush against him on the tops
of the mountains, and they robbed all who
passed by them along that way; and it was
told Abimelech.

26Now Gaal the son of Ebed came with
his brothers and went over to Shechem; and
the men of Shechem put their confidence
in him. 27So they went out into the fields,
and gathered *grapes* from their vineyards
and trod *them*, and made merry. And they
went into the house of their god, and ate and
drank, and cursed Abimelech. 28Then Gaal
the son of Ebed said, "Who *is* Abimelech,
and who *is* Shechem, that we should serve
him? *Is he* not the son of Jerubbaal, and *is not*
Zebul his officer? Serve the men of Hamor
the father of Shechem; but why should we
serve him? 29If only this people were under
my authority![a] Then I would remove Abimelech." So he[b] said to Abimelech, "Increase
your army and come out!"

30When Zebul, the ruler of the city, heard
the words of Gaal the son of Ebed, his anger
was aroused. 31And he sent messengers to
Abimelech secretly, saying, "Take note! Gaal
the son of Ebed and his brothers have come
to Shechem; and here they are, fortifying the
city against you. 32Now therefore, get up by
night, you and the people who *are* with you,
and lie in wait in the field. 33And it shall be,
as soon as the sun is up in the morning, *that*
you shall rise early and rush upon the city;
and *when* he and the people who are with
him come out against you, you may then do
to them as you find opportunity."

34So Abimelech and all the people who
were with him rose by night, and lay in wait
against Shechem in four companies. 35When
Gaal the son of Ebed went out and stood in
the entrance to the city gate, Abimelech and
the people who *were* with him rose from lying in wait. 36And when Gaal saw the people,
he said to Zebul, "Look, people are coming
down from the tops of the mountains!"

But Zebul said to him, "You see the shadows of the mountains as *if they were* men."

37So Gaal spoke again and said, "See, people are coming down from the center of the
land, and another company is coming from
the Diviners'[a] Terebinth Tree."

38Then Zebul said to him, "Where indeed
is your mouth now, with which you said,
'Who is Abimelech, that we should serve
him?' *Are* not these the people whom you
despised? Go out, if you will, and fight with
them now."

39So Gaal went out, leading the men of
Shechem, and fought with Abimelech. 40And
Abimelech chased him, and he fled from
him; and many fell wounded, to the *very* entrance of the gate. 41Then Abimelech dwelt
at Arumah, and Zebul drove out Gaal and
his brothers, so that they would not dwell in
Shechem.

42And it came about on the next day that
the people went out into the field, and they
told Abimelech. 43So he took his people, divided them into three companies, and lay in
wait in the field. And he looked, and there
were the people, coming out of the city; and
he rose against them and attacked them.
44Then Abimelech and the company that
was with him rushed forward and stood at
the entrance of the gate of the city; and the
other two companies rushed upon all who
were in the fields and killed them. 45So Abimelech fought against the city all that day; he
took the city and killed the people who *were*
in it; and he demolished the city and sowed
it with salt.

46Now when all the men of the tower of
Shechem had heard *that*, they entered the

9:29 [a] Literally *hand* [b] Following Masoretic Text and Targum; Dead Sea Scrolls read *they*; Septuagint reads *I*.
9:37 [a] Hebrew *Meonenim*

stronghold of the temple of the god Berith.
47And it was told Abimelech that all the men
of the tower of Shechem were gathered together. 48Then Abimelech went up to Mount
Zalmon, he and all the people who *were* with
him. And Abimelech took an ax in his hand
and cut down a bough from the trees, and
took it and laid *it* on his shoulder; then he
said to the people who were with him, "What
you have seen me do, make haste *and* do as
I *have done*." 49So each of the people likewise cut down his own bough and followed
Abimelech, put *them* against the stronghold,
and set the stronghold on fire above them, so
that all the people of the tower of Shechem
died, about a thousand men and women.

50Then Abimelech went to Thebez, and
he encamped against Thebez and took it.
51But there was a strong tower in the city,
and all the men and women—all the people
of the city—fled there and shut themselves
in; then they went up to the top of the tower. 52So Abimelech came as far as the tower
and fought against it; and he drew near the
door of the tower to burn it with fire. 53But a
certain woman dropped an upper millstone
on Abimelech's head and crushed his skull.
54Then he called quickly to the young man,
his armorbearer, and said to him, "Draw
your sword and kill me, lest men say of me,
'A woman killed him.'" So his young man
thrust him through, and he died. 55And
when the men of Israel saw that Abimelech
was dead, they departed, every man to his
place.

56Thus God repaid the wickedness of
Abimelech, which he had done to his father
by killing his seventy brothers. 57And all the
evil of the men of Shechem God returned
on their own heads, and on them came the
curse of Jotham the son of Jerubbaal.

Tola

10 After Abimelech there arose to save
Israel Tola the son of Puah, the son
of Dodo, a man of Issachar; and he dwelt in
Shamir in the mountains of Ephraim. 2He
judged Israel twenty-three years; and he died
and was buried in Shamir.

Jair

3After him arose Jair, a Gileadite; and
he judged Israel twenty-two years. 4Now he
had thirty sons who rode on thirty donkeys;
they also had thirty towns, which are called
"Havoth Jair"[a] to this day, which *are* in the
land of Gilead. 5And Jair died and was buried
in Camon.

Israel Oppressed Again

6Then the children of Israel again did
evil in the sight of the LORD, and served
the Baals and the Ashtoreths, the gods of
Syria, the gods of Sidon, the gods of Moab,
the gods of the people of Ammon, and the
gods of the Philistines; and they forsook the
LORD and did not serve Him. 7So the anger
of the LORD was hot against Israel; and He
sold them into the hands of the Philistines
and into the hands of the people of Ammon.
8From that year they harassed and oppressed
the children of Israel for eighteen years—all
the children of Israel who *were* on the other
side of the Jordan in the land of the Amorites, in Gilead. 9Moreover the people of Ammon crossed over the Jordan to fight against
Judah also, against Benjamin, and against
the house of Ephraim, so that Israel was severely distressed.

10And the children of Israel cried out to
the LORD, saying, "We have sinned against
You, because we have both forsaken our God
and served the Baals!"

11So the LORD said to the children of Israel, "*Did I* not *deliver you* from the Egyptians and from the Amorites and from the
people of Ammon and from the Philistines?
12Also the Sidonians and Amalekites and
Maonites[a] oppressed you; and you cried out
to Me, and I delivered you from their hand.
13Yet you have forsaken Me and served other
gods. Therefore I will deliver you no more.
14"Go and cry out to the gods which you have
chosen; let them deliver you in your time of
distress."

15And the children of Israel said to the
LORD, "We have sinned! Do to us whatever
seems best to You; only deliver us this day,
we pray." 16So they put away the foreign gods
from among them and served the LORD. And
His soul could no longer endure the misery
of Israel.

17Then the people of Ammon gathered
together and encamped in Gilead. And the
children of Israel assembled together and
encamped in Mizpah. 18And the people, the

10:4 [a] Literally *Towns of Jair* (compare Numbers 32:41 and Deuteronomy 3:14) **10:12** [a] Some Septuagint manuscripts read *Midianites*.

leaders of Gilead, said to one another, "Who
is the man who will begin the fight against
the people of Ammon? He shall be head over
all the inhabitants of Gilead."

Jephthah

11 Now Jephthah the Gileadite was a
mighty man of valor, but he *was* the
son of a harlot; and Gilead begot Jephthah.
2Gilead's wife bore sons; and when his wife's
sons grew up, they drove Jephthah out, and
said to him, "You shall have no inheritance
in our father's house, for you *are* the son of
another woman." 3Then Jephthah fled from
his brothers and dwelt in the land of Tob;
and worthless men banded together with
Jephthah and went out *raiding* with him.
4It came to pass after a time that the
people of Ammon made war against Israel.
5And so it was, when the people of Ammon
made war against Israel, that the elders of
Gilead went to get Jephthah from the land
of Tob. 6Then they said to Jephthah, "Come
and be our commander, that we may fight
against the people of Ammon."
7So Jephthah said to the elders of Gilead,
"Did you not hate me, and expel me from my
father's house? Why have you come to me
now when you are in distress?"
8And the elders of Gilead said to
Jephthah, "That is why we have turned again
to you now, that you may go with us and
fight against the people of Ammon, and be
our head over all the inhabitants of Gilead."
9So Jephthah said to the elders of Gilead,
"If you take me back home to fight against
the people of Ammon, and the LORD delivers
them to me, shall I be your head?"
10And the elders of Gilead said to
Jephthah, "The LORD will be a witness
between us, if we do not do according to
your words." 11Then Jephthah went with
the elders of Gilead, and the people made
him head and commander over them; and
Jephthah spoke all his words before the
LORD in Mizpah.
12Now Jephthah sent messengers to the
king of the people of Ammon, saying, "What
do you have against me, that you have come
to fight against me in my land?"
13And the king of the people of Ammon
answered the messengers of Jephthah, "Because Israel took away my land when they
came up out of Egypt, from the Arnon as far
as the Jabbok, and to the Jordan. Now therefore, restore those *lands* peaceably."
14So Jephthah again sent messengers to
the king of the people of Ammon, 15and said
to him, "Thus says Jephthah: 'Israel did not
take away the land of Moab, nor the land
of the people of Ammon; 16for when Israel
came up from Egypt, they walked through
the wilderness as far as the Red Sea and
came to Kadesh. 17Then Israel sent messengers to the king of Edom, saying, "Please let
me pass through your land." But the king of
Edom would not heed. And in like manner
they sent to the king of Moab, but he would
not *consent*. So Israel remained in Kadesh.
18And they went along through the wilderness and bypassed the land of Edom and the
land of Moab, came to the east side of the
land of Moab, and encamped on the other
side of the Arnon. But they did not enter the
border of Moab, for the Arnon *was* the border
of Moab. 19Then Israel sent messengers to
Sihon king of the Amorites, king of Heshbon; and Israel said to him, "Please let us
pass through your land into our place." 20But
Sihon did not trust Israel to pass through
his territory. So Sihon gathered all his people together, encamped in Jahaz, and fought
against Israel. 21And the LORD God of Israel delivered Sihon and all his people into
the hand of Israel, and they defeated them.
Thus Israel gained possession of all the land
of the Amorites, who inhabited that country.
22They took possession of all the territory of
the Amorites, from the Arnon to the Jabbok
and from the wilderness to the Jordan.
23'And now the LORD God of Israel has
dispossessed the Amorites from before His
people Israel; should you then possess it?
24Will you not possess whatever Chemosh
your god gives you to possess? So whatever
the LORD our God takes possession of before
us, we will possess. 25And now, *are* you any
better than Balak the son of Zippor, king of
Moab? Did he ever strive against Israel? Did
he ever fight against them? 26While Israel
dwelt in Heshbon and its villages, in Aroer
and its villages, and in all the cities along the
banks of the Arnon, for three hundred years,
why did you not recover *them* within that
time? 27Therefore I have not sinned against
you, but you wronged me by fighting against
me. May the LORD, the Judge, render judgment this day between the children of Israel
and the people of Ammon.'" 28However, the

king of the people of Ammon did not heed the words which Jephthah sent him.

Jephthah's Vow and Victory

29Then the Spirit of the LORD came upon Jephthah, and he passed through Gilead and Manasseh, and passed through Mizpah of Gilead; and from Mizpah of Gilead he advanced *toward* the people of Ammon. 30And Jephthah made a vow to the LORD, and said, "If You will indeed deliver the people of Ammon into my hands, 31then it will be that whatever comes out of the doors of my house to meet me, when I return in peace from the people of Ammon, shall surely be the LORD's, and I will offer it up as a burnt offering."

32So Jephthah advanced toward the people of Ammon to fight against them, and the LORD delivered them into his hands. 33And he defeated them from Aroer as far as Minnith—twenty cities—and to Abel Keramim,[a] with a very great slaughter. Thus the people of Ammon were subdued before the children of Israel.

Jephthah's Daughter

34When Jephthah came to his house at Mizpah, there was his daughter, coming out to meet him with timbrels and dancing; and she *was his* only child. Besides her he had neither son nor daughter. 35And it came to pass, when he saw her, that he tore his clothes, and said, "Alas, my daughter! You have brought me very low! You are among those who trouble me! For I have given my word to the LORD, and I cannot go back on it."

36So she said to him, "My father, *if* you have given your word to the LORD, do to me according to what has gone out of your mouth, because the LORD has avenged you of your enemies, the people of Ammon." 37Then she said to her father, "Let this thing be done for me: let me alone for two months, that I may go and wander on the mountains and bewail my virginity, my friends and I."

38So he said, "Go." And he sent her away *for* two months; and she went with her friends, and bewailed her virginity on the mountains. 39And it was so at the end of two months that she returned to her father, and he carried out his vow with her which he had vowed. She knew no man.

And it became a custom in Israel 40*that* the daughters of Israel went four days each year to lament the daughter of Jephthah the Gileadite.

Jephthah's Conflict with Ephraim

12 Then the men of Ephraim gathered together, crossed over toward Zaphon, and said to Jephthah, "Why did you cross over to fight against the people of Ammon, and did not call us to go with you? We will burn your house down on you with fire!"

2And Jephthah said to them, "My people and I were in a great struggle with the people of Ammon; and when I called you, you did not deliver me out of their hands. 3So when I saw that you would not deliver *me,* I took my life in my hands and crossed over against the people of Ammon; and the LORD delivered them into my hand. Why then have you come up to me this day to fight against me?" 4Now Jephthah gathered together all the men of Gilead and fought against Ephraim. And the men of Gilead defeated Ephraim, because they said, "You Gileadites *are* fugitives of Ephraim among the Ephraimites *and* among the Manassites." 5The Gileadites seized the fords of the Jordan before the Ephraimites *arrived.* And when *any* Ephraimite who escaped said, "Let me cross over," the men of Gilead would say to him, "*Are* you an Ephraimite?" If he said, "No," 6then they would say to him, "Then say, 'Shibboleth'!" And he would say, "Sibboleth," for he could not pronounce *it* right. Then they would take him and kill him at the fords of the Jordan. There fell at that time forty-two thousand Ephraimites.

7And Jephthah judged Israel six years. Then Jephthah the Gileadite died and was buried among the cities of Gilead.

Ibzan, Elon, and Abdon

8After him, Ibzan of Bethlehem judged Israel. 9He had thirty sons. And he gave away thirty daughters in marriage, and brought in thirty daughters from elsewhere for his sons. He judged Israel seven years. 10Then Ibzan died and was buried at Bethlehem.

11After him, Elon the Zebulunite judged Israel. He judged Israel ten years. 12And Elon the Zebulunite died and was buried at Aijalon in the country of Zebulun.

13After him, Abdon the son of Hillel the Pirathonite judged Israel. 14He had forty

---

11:33 [a] Literally *Plain of Vineyards*

sons and thirty grandsons, who rode on seventy young donkeys. He judged Israel eight
years. 15 Then Abdon the son of Hillel the
Pirathonite died and was buried in Pirathon
in the land of Ephraim, in the mountains of
the Amalekites.

The Birth of Samson

13 Again the children of Israel did evil
in the sight of the LORD, and the
LORD delivered them into the hand of the
Philistines for forty years.

2 Now there was a certain man from
Zorah, of the family of the Danites, whose
name *was* Manoah; and his wife *was* barren
and had no children. 3 And the Angel of the
LORD appeared to the woman and said to
her, "Indeed now, you are barren and have
borne no children, but you shall conceive
and bear a son. 4 Now therefore, please be

ANGELS

WHERE ANGELS GO

READ IT: JUDGES 13:1–25

GET IT:

Were you ever an angel in a Christmas pageant? Did you wear cardboard wings and a tinsel halo? It's a cute image for Sunday school, but God's angels are so much more. The Bible says some angels bring comfort. Some bring a sword. They are above us to protect us, next to us to walk with us, in front of us to lead us, and beneath us to support us.

God created angels to be His messengers to us. The angel who appeared to Samson's mother let her know a couple of things. First, nothing is impossible with God. And second, she was supposed to raise Samson according to the faith. That way he would be able to accomplish wonderful things with God's help.

After giving the message, the angel "ascended in the flame" (v. 20) up into heaven. (Sounds like the end of a crazy concert, doesn't it?) Until that moment Samson's family had no idea they were talking to an angel of God. Angels can appear to us in many ways, and sometimes we may not even know it.

It's been said that intelligence is learning your lessons, and wisdom is knowing your lessons can come from anywhere. If that's true, then faith is understanding that God's message will come to us, and we have to decide whether to listen. God sends us messengers with good news. He chooses ordinary people leading ordinary lives to do extraordinary things!

LIVE IT:

Even if you don't see angels, they are around you all the time, protecting you, guiding you, and maybe even whispering in your ear. They are not only God's messengers; they are also His examples. Have you ever had an experience with someone or something that may have been an angel?

careful not to drink wine or *similar* drink,
and not to eat anything unclean. 5For behold,
you shall conceive and bear a son. And no
razor shall come upon his head, for the child
shall be a Nazirite to God from the womb;
and he shall begin to deliver Israel out of the
hand of the Philistines."

6So the woman came and told her husband, saying, "A Man of God came to me,
and His countenance *was* like the countenance of the Angel of God, very awesome;
but I did not ask Him where He *was* from,
and He did not tell me His name. 7And He
said to me, 'Behold, you shall conceive and
bear a son. Now drink no wine or *similar*
drink, nor eat anything unclean, for the
child shall be a Nazirite to God from the
womb to the day of his death.'"

8Then Manoah prayed to the LORD, and
said, "O my Lord, please let the Man of God
whom You sent come to us again and teach
us what we shall do for the child who will
be born."

9And God listened to the voice of Manoah, and the Angel of God came to the
woman again as she was sitting in the field;
but Manoah her husband *was* not with her.
10Then the woman ran in haste and told her
husband, and said to him, "Look, the Man
who came to me the *other* day has just now
appeared to me!"

11So Manoah arose and followed his
wife. When he came to the Man, he said to
Him, "Are You the Man who spoke to this
woman?"

And He said, "I *am*."

12Manoah said, "Now let Your words
come *to pass*! What will be the boy's rule of
life, and his work?"

13So the Angel of the LORD said to Manoah, "Of all that I said to the woman let
her be careful. 14She may not eat anything
that comes from the vine, nor may she drink
wine or *similar* drink, nor eat anything
unclean. All that I commanded her let her
observe."

15Then Manoah said to the Angel of the
LORD, "Please let us detain You, and we will
prepare a young goat for You."

16And the Angel of the LORD said to Manoah, "Though you detain Me, I will not eat
your food. But if you offer a burnt offering,
you must offer it to the LORD." (For Manoah
did not know He *was* the Angel of the LORD.)

17Then Manoah said to the Angel of the
LORD, "What *is* Your name, that when Your
words come *to pass* we may honor You?"

18And the Angel of the LORD said to
him, "Why do you ask My name, seeing it
is wonderful?"

19So Manoah took the young goat with
the grain offering, and offered it upon the
rock to the LORD. And He did a wondrous
thing while Manoah and his wife looked
on— 20it happened as the flame went up
toward heaven from the altar—the Angel of
the LORD ascended in the flame of the altar!
When Manoah and his wife saw *this*, they
fell on their faces to the ground. 21When the
Angel of the LORD appeared no more to Manoah and his wife, then Manoah knew that
He *was* the Angel of the LORD.

22And Manoah said to his wife, "We shall
surely die, because we have seen God!"

23But his wife said to him, "If the LORD
had desired to kill us, He would not have accepted a burnt offering and a grain offering
from our hands, nor would He have shown
us all these *things*, nor would He have told us
such things as these at this time."

24So the woman bore a son and called his
name Samson; and the child grew, and the
LORD blessed him. 25And the Spirit of the
LORD began to move upon him at Mahaneh
Dan[a] between Zorah and Eshtaol.

Samson's Philistine Wife

14 Now Samson went down to Timnah, and saw a woman in Timnah
of the daughters of the Philistines. 2So he
went up and told his father and mother, saying, "I have seen a woman in Timnah of the
daughters of the Philistines; now therefore,
get her for me as a wife."

3Then his father and mother said to him,
"*Is there* no woman among the daughters of
your brethren, or among all my people, that
you must go and get a wife from the uncircumcised Philistines?"

And Samson said to his father, "Get her
for me, for she pleases me well."

4But his father and mother did not know
that it was of the LORD—that He was seeking an occasion to move against the Philistines. For at that time the Philistines had
dominion over Israel.

5So Samson went down to Timnah with

13:25 [a] Literally *Camp of Dan* (compare 18:12)

his father and mother, and came to the vineyards of Timnah.
Now *to his* surprise, a young lion *came*
roaring against him. 6And the Spirit of the
LORD came mightily upon him, and he tore
the lion apart as one would have torn apart
a young goat, though *he had* nothing in his
hand. But he did not tell his father or his
mother what he had done.
7Then he went down and talked with the
woman; and she pleased Samson well. 8After
some time, when he returned to get her, he
turned aside to see the carcass of the lion.
And behold, a swarm of bees and honey *were*
in the carcass of the lion. 9He took some of it
in his hands and went along, eating. When
he came to his father and mother, he gave
some to them, and they also ate. But he did
not tell them that he had taken the honey out
of the carcass of the lion.
10So his father went down to the woman.
And Samson gave a feast there, for young
men used to do so. 11And it happened, when
they saw him, that they brought thirty companions to be with him.
12Then Samson said to them, "Let me
pose a riddle to you. If you can correctly
solve and explain it to me within the seven
days of the feast, then I will give you thirty
linen garments and thirty changes of clothing. 13But if you cannot explain *it* to me, then
you shall give me thirty linen garments and
thirty changes of clothing."
And they said to him, "Pose your riddle,
that we may hear it."
14So he said to them:

"Out of the eater came something to eat,
And out of the strong came something
sweet."

Now for three days they could not explain
the riddle.
15But it came to pass on the seventh[a] day
that they said to Samson's wife, "Entice your
husband, that he may explain the riddle to
us, or else we will burn you and your father's
house with fire. Have you invited us in order
to take what is ours? *Is that* not *so*?"
16Then Samson's wife wept on him, and
said, "You only hate me! You do not love me!
You have posed a riddle to the sons of my
people, but you have not explained *it* to me."
And he said to her, "Look, I have not
explained *it* to my father or my mother; so
should I explain *it* to you?" 17Now she had
wept on him the seven days while their feast
lasted. And it happened on the seventh day
that he told her, because she pressed him so
much. Then she explained the riddle to the
sons of her people. 18So the men of the city

14:15 [a] Following Masoretic Text, Targum, and Vulgate; Septuagint and Syriac read *fourth*.

Starring Roles

SAMSON'S birth was a miracle because everybody thought his mother could not have children. But the Angel of God told his mother and father, Manoah that they would have a son.

God also told Manoah that Samson would be a Nazirite (pronounced *NAZ-uh-right*). A Nazirite was someone whose life was especially given to God. One of the signs of a Nazirite was that he didn't cut his hair.

When Samson was born, the Holy Spirit gave him unusual physical strength. At that time, the Philistines (pronounced *fih-LIS-teens*) were Israel's enemies. When Samson fought against them, they went to arrest him. But he broke the ropes they tied him with and killed a thousand of their troops with only the jawbone of a donkey!

This is just one of the miracles of strength Samson performed against Israel's enemies. The truth to remember is that you and God are a winning team in all the tests of life.

said to him on the seventh day before the
sun went down:

"What *is* sweeter than honey?
And what *is* stronger than a lion?"

And he said to them:

"If you had not plowed with my heifer,
You would not have solved my riddle!"

19 Then the Spirit of the LORD came upon
him mightily, and he went down to Ashkelon and killed thirty of their men, took
their apparel, and gave the changes *of clothing* to those who had explained the riddle. So
his anger was aroused, and he went back up
to his father's house. 20 And Samson's wife
was *given* to his companion, who had been
his best man.

Samson Defeats the Philistines

15 After a while, in the time of wheat
harvest, it happened that Samson
visited his wife with a young goat. And
he said, "Let me go in to my wife, into *her*
room." But her father would not permit him
to go in.

2 Her father said, "I really thought that
you thoroughly hated her; therefore I gave
her to your companion. *Is* not her younger sister better than she? Please, take her
instead."

3 And Samson said to them, "This time I
shall be blameless regarding the Philistines
if I harm them!" 4 Then Samson went and
caught three hundred foxes; and he took
torches, turned *the foxes* tail to tail, and put
a torch between each pair of tails. 5 When he
had set the torches on fire, he let *the foxes*
go into the standing grain of the Philistines,
and burned up both the shocks and the
standing grain, as well as the vineyards *and*
olive groves.

6 Then the Philistines said, "Who has
done this?"

And they answered, "Samson, the son-
in-law of the Timnite, because he has taken
his wife and given her to his companion." So
the Philistines came up and burned her and
her father with fire.

7 Samson said to them, "Since you would
do a thing like this, I will surely take revenge
on you, and after that I will cease." 8 So he
attacked them hip and thigh with a great
slaughter; then he went down and dwelt in
the cleft of the rock of Etam.

9 Now the Philistines went up, encamped
in Judah, and deployed themselves against
Lehi. 10 And the men of Judah said, "Why
have you come up against us?"

So they answered, "We have come up to
arrest Samson, to do to him as he has done
to us."

11 Then three thousand men of Judah
went down to the cleft of the rock of Etam,
and said to Samson, "Do you not know that
the Philistines rule over us? What *is* this you
have done to us?"

And he said to them, "As they did to me,
so I have done to them."

12 But they said to him, "We have come
down to arrest you, that we may deliver you
into the hand of the Philistines."

Then Samson said to them, "Swear to me
that you will not kill me yourselves."

13 So they spoke to him, saying, "No, but
we will tie you securely and deliver you into
their hand; but we will surely not kill you."
And they bound him with two new ropes
and brought him up from the rock.

14 When he came to Lehi, the Philistines
came shouting against him. Then the Spirit
of the LORD came mightily upon him; and
the ropes that *were* on his arms became like
flax that is burned with fire, and his bonds
broke loose from his hands. 15 He found a
fresh jawbone of a donkey, reached out his
hand and took it, and killed a thousand men
with it. 16 Then Samson said:

"With the jawbone of a donkey,
Heaps upon heaps,
With the jawbone of a donkey
I have slain a thousand men!"

17 And so it was, when he had finished speaking, that he threw the jawbone from his
hand, and called that place Ramath Lehi.[a]

18 Then he became very thirsty; so he
cried out to the LORD and said, "You have giv-
en this great deliverance by the hand of Your
servant; and now shall I die of thirst and fall
into the hand of the uncircumcised?" 19 So
God split the hollow place that *is* in Lehi,[a]
and water came out, and he drank; and his
spirit returned, and he revived. Therefore
he called its name En Hakkore,[b] which is in
Lehi to this day. 20 And he judged Israel twenty years in the days of the Philistines.

15:17 [a] Literally *Jawbone Height* 15:19 [a] Literally *Jawbone* (compare verse 14) [b] Literally *Spring of the Caller*

Samson and Delilah

16 Now Samson went to Gaza and saw
a harlot there, and went in to her.
2 *When* the Gazites *were told,* "Samson has
come here!" they surrounded *the place* and
lay in wait for him all night at the gate of the
city. They were quiet all night, saying, "In
the morning, when it is daylight, we will kill
him." 3 And Samson lay *low* till midnight;
then he arose at midnight, took hold of the
doors of the gate of the city and the two gateposts, pulled them up, bar and all, put *them*
on his shoulders, and carried them to the top
of the hill that faces Hebron.
4 Afterward it happened that he loved a
woman in the Valley of Sorek, whose name
was Delilah. 5 And the lords of the Philistines
came up to her and said to her, "Entice him,
and find out where his great strength *lies,*
and by what *means* we may overpower him,
that we may bind him to afflict him; and
every one of us will give you eleven hundred
pieces of silver."
6 So Delilah said to Samson, "Please tell

Action!

REVENGE

BLIND REVENGE

READ IT: JUDGES 15:1–20

GET IT:

Samson was in a feud with the Philistines. They hated each other. Samson burned the grain fields of the Philistines and destroyed their harvest. The Philistines responded by killing people. Samson responded by killing more people, and the killing just went on and on. What fueled all this hatred? Samson said that he wanted to get his revenge on the Philistines.

Because both sides sought revenge, a lot of people suffered and died. Getting revenge won't solve a problem. When someone hurts you and you hurt that person back, you're only causing more pain.

If you read Samson's entire story, you'll see the results of revenge. Samson found himself imprisoned, blind, powerless, alone, and afraid. But as soon as Samson stopped trying to get his revenge, God took over and did the work of punishing the Philistines for him.

LIVE IT:

When someone hurts you and you want to take revenge, try this:

- Ask God to help you forgive the person who hurt you.
- Give up your right to take revenge on him or her.
- Remember that God has forgiven you of so much, so you can forgive others.
- Trust that God will deal with the person who hurt you the way He chooses to.

me where your great strength *lies,* and with
what you may be bound to afflict you."

7And Samson said to her, "If they bind
me with seven fresh bowstrings, not yet
dried, then I shall become weak, and be like
any *other* man."

8So the lords of the Philistines brought
up to her seven fresh bowstrings, not yet
dried, and she bound him with them. 9Now
men were lying in wait, staying with her in
the room. And she said to him, "The Philistines *are* upon you, Samson!" But he broke
the bowstrings as a strand of yarn breaks
when it touches fire. So the secret of his
strength was not known.

10Then Delilah said to Samson, "Look,
you have mocked me and told me lies. Now,
please tell me what you may be bound with."

11So he said to her, "If they bind me securely with new ropes that have never been
used, then I shall become weak, and be like
any *other* man."

12Therefore Delilah took new ropes and
bound him with them, and said to him,
"The Philistines *are* upon you, Samson!"
And *men were* lying in wait, staying in the
room. But he broke them off his arms like
a thread.

13Delilah said to Samson, "Until now you
have mocked me and told me lies. Tell me
what you may be bound with."

And he said to her, "If you weave the
seven locks of my head into the web of the
loom"—

14So she wove *it* tightly with the batten of
the loom, and said to him, "The Philistines
are upon you, Samson!" But he awoke from
his sleep, and pulled out the batten and the
web from the loom.

15Then she said to him, "How can you
say, 'I love you,' when your heart *is* not
with me? You have mocked me these three
times, and have not told me where your great
strength *lies.*" 16And it came to pass, when
she pestered him daily with her words and
pressed him, *so* that his soul was vexed to
death, 17that he told her all his heart, and said
to her, "No razor has ever come upon my
head, for I *have been* a Nazirite to God from
my mother's womb. If I am shaven, then my
strength will leave me, and I shall become
weak, and be like any *other* man."

18When Delilah saw that he had told her
all his heart, she sent and called for the lords
of the Philistines, saying, "Come up once
more, for he has told me all his heart." So the
lords of the Philistines came up to her and
brought the money in their hand. 19Then she
lulled him to sleep on her knees, and called
for a man and had him shave off the seven
locks of his head. Then she began to torment
him,[a] and his strength left him. 20And she
said, "The Philistines *are* upon you, Samson!" So he awoke from his sleep, and said,
"I will go out as before, at other times, and
shake myself free!" But he did not know that
the LORD had departed from him.

21Then the Philistines took him and put
out his eyes, and brought him down to Gaza.
They bound him with bronze fetters, and he
became a grinder in the prison. 22However,
the hair of his head began to grow again
after it had been shaven.

Samson Dies with the Philistines

23Now the lords of the Philistines gathered together to offer a great sacrifice to
Dagon their god, and to rejoice. And they
said:

"Our god has delivered into our hands
Samson our enemy!"

24When the people saw him, they praised
their god; for they said:

"Our god has delivered into our hands
our enemy,
The destroyer of our land,
And the one who multiplied our dead."

25So it happened, when their hearts were
merry, that they said, "Call for Samson, that
he may perform for us." So they called for
Samson from the prison, and he performed
for them. And they stationed him between
the pillars. 26Then Samson said to the lad
who held him by the hand, "Let me feel the
pillars which support the temple, so that I
can lean on them." 27Now the temple was full
of men and women. All the lords of the Philistines *were* there—about three thousand
men and women on the roof watching while
Samson performed.

28Then Samson called to the LORD, saying, "O Lord GOD, remember me, I pray!
Strengthen me, I pray, just this once, O God,
that I may with one *blow* take vengeance on

16:19 [a] Following Masoretic Text, Targum, and Vulgate; Septuagint reads *he began to be weak.*

the Philistines for my two eyes!" 29And Samson took hold of the two middle pillars which
supported the temple, and he braced himself
against them, one on his right and the other
on his left. 30Then Samson said, "Let me die
with the Philistines!" And he pushed with
all his might, and the temple fell on the lords
and all the people who *were* in it. So the dead
that he killed at his death were more than he
had killed in his life.

31And his brothers and all his father's
household came down and took him, and
brought *him* up and buried him between
Zorah and Eshtaol in the tomb of his father
Manoah. He had judged Israel twenty years.

Micah's Idolatry

17 Now there was a man from the
mountains of Ephraim, whose
name *was* Micah. 2And he said to his mother, "The eleven hundred *shekels* of silver that
were taken from you, and on which you put a
curse, even saying it in my ears—here *is* the
silver with me; I took it."

And his mother said, "*May you be* blessed
by the LORD, my son!" 3So when he had returned the eleven hundred *shekels* of silver
to his mother, his mother said, "I had wholly dedicated the silver from my hand to the
LORD for my son, to make a carved image
and a molded image; now therefore, I will
return it to you." 4Thus he returned the silver to his mother. Then his mother took two
hundred *shekels* of silver and gave them to
the silversmith, and he made it into a carved
image and a molded image; and they were in
the house of Micah.

5The man Micah had a shrine, and made
an ephod and household idols;[a] and he consecrated one of his sons, who became his
priest. 6In those days *there was* no king in
Israel; everyone did *what was* right in his
own eyes.

7Now there was a young man from Bethlehem in Judah, of the family of Judah; he
was a Levite, and was staying there. 8The
man departed from the city of Bethlehem in
Judah to stay wherever he could find *a place.*
Then he came to the mountains of Ephraim,
to the house of Micah, as he journeyed. 9And
Micah said to him, "Where do you come
from?"

So he said to him, "I *am* a Levite from
Bethlehem in Judah, and I am on my way to
find *a place* to stay."

10Micah said to him, "Dwell with me,
and be a father and a priest to me, and I will
give you ten *shekels* of silver per year, a suit
of clothes, and your sustenance." So the Levite went in. 11Then the Levite was content to
dwell with the man; and the young man became like one of his sons to him. 12So Micah
consecrated the Levite, and the young man
became his priest, and lived in the house of
Micah. 13Then Micah said, "Now I know that
the LORD will be good to me, since I have a
Levite as priest!"

The Danites Adopt Micah's Idolatry

18 In those days *there was* no king in
Israel. And in those days the tribe
of the Danites was seeking an inheritance
for itself to dwell in; for until that day *their*
inheritance among the tribes of Israel had
not fallen to them. 2So the children of Dan
sent five men of their family from their territory, men of valor from Zorah and Eshtaol,
to spy out the land and search it. They said
to them, "Go, search the land." So they went
to the mountains of Ephraim, to the house
of Micah, and lodged there. 3While they *were*
at the house of Micah, they recognized the
voice of the young Levite. They turned aside
and said to him, "Who brought you here?
What are you doing in this *place?* What do
you have here?"

4He said to them, "Thus and so Micah
did for me. He has hired me, and I have become his priest."

5So they said to him, "Please inquire of
God, that we may know whether the journey
on which we go will be prosperous."

6And the priest said to them, "Go in
peace. The presence of the LORD *be* with you
on your way."

7So the five men departed and went to
Laish. They saw the people who *were* there,
how they dwelt safely, in the manner of the
Sidonians, quiet and secure. *There were*
no rulers in the land who might put *them*
to shame for anything. They *were* far from
the Sidonians, and they had no ties with
anyone.[a]

8Then *the spies* came back to their brethren at Zorah and Eshtaol, and their brethren
said to them, "What *is* your *report?*"

9So they said, "Arise, let us go up against

17:5 [a] Hebrew *teraphim* 18:7 [a] Following Masoretic Text,
Targum, and Vulgate; Septuagint reads *with Syria.*

them. For we have seen the land, and indeed
it *is* very good. *Would* you *do* nothing? Do not
hesitate to go, *and* enter to possess the land.
10 When you go, you will come to a secure
people and a large land. For God has given
it into your hands, a place where *there is* no
lack of anything that *is* on the earth."

11 And six hundred men of the family of
the Danites went from there, from Zorah
and Eshtaol, armed with weapons of war.
12 Then they went up and encamped in
Kirjath Jearim in Judah. (Therefore they
call that place Mahaneh Dan[a] to this day.
There *it is,* west of Kirjath Jearim.) 13 And
they passed from there to the mountains of
Ephraim, and came to the house of Micah.

14 Then the five men who had gone to spy
out the country of Laish answered and said
to their brethren, "Do you know that there
are in these houses an ephod, household
idols, a carved image, and a molded image?
Now therefore, consider what you should
do." 15 So they turned aside there, and came
to the house of the young Levite man—to
the house of Micah—and greeted him. 16 The
six hundred men armed with their weapons
of war, who *were* of the children of Dan,
stood by the entrance of the gate. 17 Then the
five men who had gone to spy out the land
went up. Entering there, they took the carved
image, the ephod, the household idols, and
the molded image. The priest stood at the
entrance of the gate with the six hundred
men *who were* armed with weapons of war.

18 When these went into Micah's house
and took the carved image, the ephod, the
household idols, and the molded image, the
priest said to them, "What are you doing?"

19 And they said to him, "Be quiet, put
your hand over your mouth, and come with
us; be a father and a priest to us. *Is it* better
for you to be a priest to the household of one
man, or that you be a priest to a tribe and a
family in Israel?" 20 So the priest's heart was
glad; and he took the ephod, the household
idols, and the carved image, and took his
place among the people.

21 Then they turned and departed, and
put the little ones, the livestock, and the
goods in front of them. 22 When they were a
good way from the house of Micah, the men
who *were* in the houses near Micah's house
gathered together and overtook the children of Dan. 23 And they called out to the
children of Dan. So they turned around
and said to Micah, "What ails you, that you
have gathered such a company?"

24 So he said, "You have taken away my
gods which I made, and the priest, and you
have gone away. Now what more do I have?
How can you say to me, 'What ails you?' "

25 And the children of Dan said to him,
"Do not let your voice be heard among us,
lest angry men fall upon you, and you lose
your life, with the lives of your household!"
26 Then the children of Dan went their way.
And when Micah saw that they *were* too
strong for him, he turned and went back to
his house.

Danites Settle in Laish

27 So they took *the things* Micah had made,
and the priest who had belonged to him, and
went to Laish, to a people quiet and secure;
and they struck them with the edge of the
sword and burned the city with fire. 28 *There
was* no deliverer, because it *was* far from
Sidon, and they had no ties with anyone. It
was in the valley that belongs to Beth Rehob. So they rebuilt the city and dwelt there.
29 And they called the name of the city Dan,
after the name of Dan their father, who was
born to Israel. However, the name of the city
formerly *was* Laish.

30 Then the children of Dan set up for
themselves the carved image; and Jonathan
the son of Gershom, the son of Manasseh,[a]
and his sons were priests to the tribe of Dan
until the day of the captivity of the land. 31 So
they set up for themselves Micah's carved
image which he made, all the time that the
house of God was in Shiloh.

The Levite's Concubine

19 And it came to pass in those days,
when *there was* no king in Israel,
that there was a certain Levite staying in
the remote mountains of Ephraim. He took
for himself a concubine from Bethlehem in
Judah. 2 But his concubine played the harlot
against him, and went away from him to her
father's house at Bethlehem in Judah, and
was there four whole months. 3 Then her
husband arose and went after her, to speak
kindly to her *and* bring her back, having his
servant and a couple of donkeys with him.

18:12 [a] Literally *Camp of Dan* 18:30 [a] Septuagint and Vulgate read *Moses.*

So she brought him into her father's house;
and when the father of the young woman
saw him, he was glad to meet him. 4Now his
father-in-law, the young woman's father, detained him; and he stayed with him three
days. So they ate and drank and lodged there.
5Then it came to pass on the fourth day
that they arose early in the morning, and
he stood to depart; but the young woman's
father said to his son-in-law, "Refresh your
heart with a morsel of bread, and afterward
go your way."
6So they sat down, and the two of them
ate and drank together. Then the young
woman's father said to the man, "Please be
content to stay all night, and let your heart be
merry." 7And when the man stood to depart,
his father-in-law urged him; so he lodged
there again. 8Then he arose early in the
morning on the fifth day to depart, but the
young woman's father said, "Please refresh
your heart." So they delayed until afternoon;
and both of them ate.
9And when the man stood to depart—
he and his concubine and his servant—his
father-in-law, the young woman's father, said
to him, "Look, the day is now drawing toward evening; please spend the night. See,
the day is coming to an end; lodge here, that
your heart may be merry. Tomorrow go your
way early, so that you may get home."
10However, the man was not willing to
spend that night; so he rose and departed,
and came opposite Jebus (that *is,* Jerusalem).
With him were the two saddled donkeys;
his concubine *was* also with him. 11They
were near Jebus, and the day was far spent;
and the servant said to his master, "Come,
please, and let us turn aside into this city of
the Jebusites and lodge in it."
12But his master said to him, "We will
not turn aside here into a city of foreigners,
who *are* not of the children of Israel; we will
go on to Gibeah." 13So he said to his servant,
"Come, let us draw near to one of these places, and spend the night in Gibeah or in Ramah." 14And they passed by and went their
way; and the sun went down on them near
Gibeah, which belongs to Benjamin. 15They
turned aside there to go in to lodge in Gibeah. And when he went in, he sat down in the
open square of the city, for no one would
take them into *his* house to spend the night.
16Just then an old man came in from his
work in the field at evening, who also *was*
from the mountains of Ephraim; he was
staying in Gibeah, whereas the men of the
place *were* Benjamites. 17And when he raised
his eyes, he saw the traveler in the open
square of the city; and the old man said,
"Where are you going, and where do you
come from?"
18So he said to him, "We *are* passing from
Bethlehem in Judah toward the remote
mountains of Ephraim; I *am* from there. I
went to Bethlehem in Judah; *now* I am going
to the house of the LORD. But there *is* no one
who will take me into his house, 19although
we have both straw and fodder for our donkeys, and bread and wine for myself, for
your female servant, and for the young man
who is with your servant; *there is* no lack of
anything."
20And the old man said, "Peace *be* with
you! However, *let* all your needs *be* my responsibility; only do not spend the night in
the open square." 21So he brought him into
his house, and gave fodder to the donkeys.
And they washed their feet, and ate and
drank.

Gibeah's Crime

22As they were enjoying themselves,
suddenly certain men of the city, perverted
men,[a] surrounded the house *and* beat on the
door. They spoke to the master of the house,
the old man, saying, "Bring out the man
who came to your house, that we may know
him *carnally!*"
23But the man, the master of the house,
went out to them and said to them, "No, my
brethren! I beg you, do not act *so* wickedly!
Seeing this man has come into my house, do
not commit this outrage. 24Look, *here is* my
virgin daughter and *the man's*[a] concubine;
let me bring them out now. Humble them,
and do with them as you please; but to this
man do not do such a vile thing!" 25But the
men would not heed him. So the man took
his concubine and brought *her* out to them.
And they knew her and abused her all night
until morning; and when the day began to
break, they let her go.
26Then the woman came as the day was
dawning, and fell down at the door of the
man's house where her master *was,* till it
was light.
27When her master arose in the morning,

19:22 [a] Literally *sons of Belial* **19:24** [a] Literally *his*

and opened the doors of the house and went out to go his way, there was his concubine, fallen *at* the door of the house with her hands on the threshold. 28And he said to her, "Get up and let us be going." But there was no answer. So the man lifted her onto the donkey; and the man got up and went to his place.

29When he entered his house he took a knife, laid hold of his concubine, and divided her into twelve pieces, limb by limb,[a] and sent her throughout all the territory of Israel. 30And so it was that all who saw it said, "No such deed has been done or seen from the day that the children of Israel came up from the land of Egypt until this day. Consider it, confer, and speak up!"

Israel's War with the Benjamites

20 So all the children of Israel came out, from Dan to Beersheba, as well as from the land of Gilead, and the congregation gathered together as one man before the LORD at Mizpah. 2And the leaders of all the people, all the tribes of Israel, presented themselves in the assembly of the people of God, four hundred thousand foot soldiers who drew the sword. 3(Now the children of Benjamin heard that the children of Israel had gone up to Mizpah.)

Then the children of Israel said, "Tell *us,* how did this wicked deed happen?"

4So the Levite, the husband of the woman who was murdered, answered and said, "My concubine and I went into Gibeah, which belongs to Benjamin, to spend the night. 5And the men of Gibeah rose against me, and surrounded the house at night because of me. They intended to kill me, but instead they ravished my concubine so that she died. 6So I took hold of my concubine, cut her in pieces, and sent her throughout all the territory of the inheritance of Israel, because they committed lewdness and outrage in Israel. 7Look! All of you *are* children of Israel; give your advice and counsel here and now!"

8So all the people arose as one man, saying, "None *of us* will go to his tent, nor will any turn back to his house; 9but now this *is* the thing which we will do to Gibeah: *We will go up* against it by lot. 10We will take ten men out of *every* hundred throughout all the tribes of Israel, a hundred out of *every* thousand, and a thousand out of *every* ten thousand, to make provisions for the people, that when they come to Gibeah in Benjamin, they may repay all the vileness that they have done in Israel." 11So all the men of Israel were gathered against the city, united together as one man.

12Then the tribes of Israel sent men through all the tribe of Benjamin, saying, "What *is* this wickedness that has occurred among you? 13Now therefore, deliver up the men, the perverted men[a] who *are* in Gibeah, that we may put them to death and remove the evil from Israel!" But the children of Benjamin would not listen to the voice of their brethren, the children of Israel. 14Instead, the children of Benjamin gathered together from their cities to Gibeah, to go to battle against the children of Israel. 15And from their cities at that time the children of Benjamin numbered twenty-six thousand men who drew the sword, besides the inhabitants of Gibeah, who numbered seven hundred select men. 16Among all this people *were* seven hundred select men *who were* left-handed; every one could sling a stone at a hair's *breadth* and not miss. 17Now besides Benjamin, the men of Israel numbered four hundred thousand men who drew the sword; all of these *were* men of war.

18Then the children of Israel arose and went up to the house of God[a] to inquire of God. They said, "Which of us shall go up first to battle against the children of Benjamin?"

The LORD said, "Judah first!"

19So the children of Israel rose in the morning and encamped against Gibeah. 20And the men of Israel went out to battle against Benjamin, and the men of Israel put themselves in battle array to fight against them at Gibeah. 21Then the children of Benjamin came out of Gibeah, and on that day cut down to the ground twenty-two thousand men of the Israelites. 22And the people, that is, the men of Israel, encouraged themselves and again formed the battle line at the place where they had put themselves in array on the first day. 23Then the children of Israel went up and wept before the LORD until evening, and asked counsel of the LORD, saying, "Shall I again draw near for battle against the children of my brother Benjamin?"

And the LORD said, "Go up against him."

19:29 [a] Literally *with her bones* **20:13** [a] Literally *sons of Belial* **20:18** [a] Or *Bethel*

24So the children of Israel approached
the children of Benjamin on the second day.
25And Benjamin went out against them from
Gibeah on the second day, and cut down to
the ground eighteen thousand more of the
children of Israel; all these drew the sword.

26Then all the children of Israel, that
is, all the people, went up and came to the
house of God[a] and wept. They sat there before the LORD and fasted that day until evening; and they offered burnt offerings and
peace offerings before the LORD. 27So the
children of Israel inquired of the LORD (the
ark of the covenant of God *was* there in those
days, 28and Phinehas the son of Eleazar, the
son of Aaron, stood before it in those days),
saying, "Shall I yet again go out to battle
against the children of my brother Benjamin, or shall I cease?"

And the LORD said, "Go up, for tomorrow
I will deliver them into your hand."

29Then Israel set men in ambush all
around Gibeah. 30And the children of Israel
went up against the children of Benjamin on
the third day, and put themselves in battle
array against Gibeah as at the other times.
31So the children of Benjamin went out
against the people, *and* were drawn away
from the city. They began to strike down
and kill some of the people, as at the other
times, in the highways (one of which goes
up to Bethel and the other to Gibeah) and in
the field, about thirty men of Israel. 32And
the children of Benjamin said, "They *are* defeated before us, as at first."

But the children of Israel said, "Let us
flee and draw them away from the city to
the highways." 33So all the men of Israel rose
from their place and put themselves in battle array at Baal Tamar. Then Israel's men in
ambush burst forth from their position in
the plain of Geba. 34And ten thousand select
men from all Israel came against Gibeah,
and the battle was fierce. But *the Benjamites*[a]
did not know that disaster *was* upon them.
35The LORD defeated Benjamin before Israel. And the children of Israel destroyed
that day twenty-five thousand one hundred
Benjamites; all these drew the sword.

36So the children of Benjamin saw that
they were defeated. The men of Israel had
given ground to the Benjamites, because
they relied on the men in ambush whom
they had set against Gibeah. 37And the men
in ambush quickly rushed upon Gibeah; the
men in ambush spread out and struck the
whole city with the edge of the sword. 38Now
the appointed signal between the men of Israel and the men in ambush was that they
would make a great cloud of smoke rise up
from the city, 39whereupon the men of Israel
would turn in battle. Now Benjamin had begun to strike *and* kill about thirty of the men
of Israel. For they said, "Surely they are defeated before us, as *in* the first battle." 40But
when the cloud began to rise from the city in
a column of smoke, the Benjamites looked
behind them, and there was the whole city
going up *in smoke* to heaven. 41And when
the men of Israel turned back, the men of
Benjamin panicked, for they saw that disaster had come upon them. 42Therefore they
turned *their backs* before the men of Israel
in the direction of the wilderness; but the
battle overtook them, and whoever *came* out
of the cities they destroyed in their midst.
43They surrounded the Benjamites, chased
them, *and* easily trampled them down as far
as the front of Gibeah toward the east. 44And
eighteen thousand men of Benjamin fell; all
these *were* men of valor. 45Then they[a] turned
and fled toward the wilderness to the rock
of Rimmon; and they cut down five thousand of them on the highways. Then they
pursued them relentlessly up to Gidom, and
killed two thousand of them. 46So all who fell
of Benjamin that day were twenty-five thousand men who drew the sword; all these *were*
men of valor.

47But six hundred men turned and fled
toward the wilderness to the rock of Rimmon, and they stayed at the rock of Rimmon
for four months. 48And the men of Israel
turned back against the children of Benjamin, and struck them down with the edge of
the sword—from *every* city, men and beasts,
all who were found. They also set fire to all
the cities they came to.

Wives Provided for the Benjamites

21 Now the men of Israel had sworn
an oath at Mizpah, saying, "None
of us shall give his daughter to Benjamin
as a wife." 2Then the people came to the
house of God,[a] and remained there before
God till evening. They lifted up their voices
and wept bitterly, 3and said, "O LORD God of

20:26 [a] Or *Bethel* 20:34 [a] Literally *they* 20:45 [a] Septuagint reads *the rest.* 21:2 [a] Or *Bethel*

Israel, why has this come to pass in Israel,
that today there should be one tribe *missing*
in Israel?"
4 So it was, on the next morning, that the
people rose early and built an altar there, and
offered burnt offerings and peace offerings.
5 The children of Israel said, "Who *is there*
among all the tribes of Israel who did not
come up with the assembly to the LORD?"
For they had made a great oath concerning
anyone who had not come up to the LORD at
Mizpah, saying, "He shall surely be put to
death." 6 And the children of Israel grieved
for Benjamin their brother, and said, "One
tribe is cut off from Israel today. 7 What shall
we do for wives for those who remain, seeing
we have sworn by the LORD that we will not
give them our daughters as wives?"
8 And they said, "What one *is there* from
the tribes of Israel who did not come up to
Mizpah to the LORD?" And, in fact, no one
had come to the camp from Jabesh Gilead
to the assembly. 9 For when the people were
counted, indeed, not one of the inhabitants
of Jabesh Gilead *was* there. 10 So the congregation sent out there twelve thousand of their
most valiant men, and commanded them,
saying, "Go and strike the inhabitants of
Jabesh Gilead with the edge of the sword,
including the women and children. 11 And
this *is* the thing that you shall do: You shall
utterly destroy every male, and every woman
who has known a man intimately." 12 So they
found among the inhabitants of Jabesh Gilead four hundred young virgins who had not
known a man intimately; and they brought
them to the camp at Shiloh, which is in the
land of Canaan.
13 Then the whole congregation sent *word*
to the children of Benjamin who *were* at the
rock of Rimmon, and announced peace to
them. 14 So Benjamin came back at that time,
and they gave them the women whom they
had saved alive of the women of Jabesh Gilead;
and yet they had not found enough for them.
15 And the people grieved for Benjamin,
because the LORD had made a void in the
tribes of Israel.
16 Then the elders of the congregation
said, "What shall we do for wives for those
who remain, since the women of Benjamin
have been destroyed?" 17 And they said, "*There
must be* an inheritance for the survivors of
Benjamin, that a tribe may not be destroyed
from Israel. 18 However, we cannot give them
wives from our daughters, for the children
of Israel have sworn an oath, saying, 'Cursed
be the one who gives a wife to Benjamin.'"
19 Then they said, "In fact, *there is* a yearly
feast of the LORD in Shiloh, which *is* north of
Bethel, on the east side of the highway that
goes up from Bethel to Shechem, and south
of Lebonah."
20 Therefore they instructed the children
of Benjamin, saying, "Go, lie in wait in the
vineyards, 21 and watch; and just when the
daughters of Shiloh come out to perform
their dances, then come out from the vineyards, and every man catch a wife for himself from the daughters of Shiloh; then go
to the land of Benjamin. 22 Then it shall be,
when their fathers or their brothers come to
us to complain, that we will say to them, 'Be
kind to them for our sakes, because we did
not take a wife for any of them in the war; for
it is not *as though* you have given the *wom-
en* to them at this time, making yourselves
guilty of your oath.'"
23 And the children of Benjamin did so;
they took enough wives for their number
from those who danced, whom they caught.
Then they went and returned to their inheritance, and they rebuilt the cities and dwelt
in them. 24 So the children of Israel departed
from there at that time, every man to his
tribe and family; they went out from there,
every man to his inheritance.
25 In those days *there was* no king in Israel;
everyone did *what was* right in his own eyes.

The BOOK of

RUTH

Date Written Unknown

Behind the Scenes

READ IT:

This book is the story about two women—Ruth and Naomi—who return to Bethlehem in Judah after living in another country. The women don't have husbands or sons to take care of them so they worry about how they'll take care of themselves. God takes care of everything and the story has a happy ending.

GET IT:

Who wrote it: No one really knows.

When it was written: No one really knows.

Why it was written: to teach us about human love and commitment, and that God cares about our everyday needs. It also shows us that long ago God was working on His plan for salvation.

LIVE IT:

God wants us to live a rich and full life, but it only comes through Him.

FIND IT:

Naomi Returns with Ruth	*Ruth 1*
Ruth Meets Boaz	*Ruth 2*
A Happy Ending for Everyone	*Ruth 4*

Elimelech's Family Goes to Moab

1 Now it came to pass, in the days when
the judges ruled, that there was a famine in the land. And a certain man of Bethlehem, Judah, went to dwell in the country
of Moab, he and his wife and his two sons.
2 The name of the man *was* Elimelech, the
name of his wife *was* Naomi, and the names
of his two sons *were* Mahlon and Chilion—
Ephrathites of Bethlehem, Judah. And they
went to the country of Moab and remained
there. 3 Then Elimelech, Naomi's husband,
died; and she was left, and her two sons.
4 Now they took wives of the women of Moab:
the name of the one *was* Orpah, and the
name of the other Ruth. And they dwelt
there about ten years. 5 Then both Mahlon
and Chilion also died; so the woman survived her two sons and her husband.

Naomi Returns with Ruth

6 Then she arose with her daughters-in-
law that she might return from the country
of Moab, for she had heard in the country of
Moab that the LORD had visited His people
by giving them bread. 7 Therefore she went
out from the place where she was, and her
two daughters-in-law with her; and they
went on the way to return to the land of Judah. 8 And Naomi said to her two daughters-
in-law, "Go, return each to her mother's
house. The LORD deal kindly with you, as
you have dealt with the dead and with me.
9 The LORD grant that you may find rest, each
in the house of her husband."

So she kissed them, and they lifted up
their voices and wept. 10 And they said to
her, "Surely we will return with you to your
people."

11 But Naomi said, "Turn back, my daughters; why will you go with me? *Are* there
still sons in my womb, that they may be
your husbands? 12 Turn back, my daughters,
go—for I am too old to have a husband. If
I should say I have hope, *if* I should have a
husband tonight and should also bear sons,
13 would you wait for them till they were
grown? Would you restrain yourselves from
having husbands? No, my daughters; for it
grieves me very much for your sakes that the
hand of the LORD has gone out against me!"

14 Then they lifted up their voices and
wept again; and Orpah kissed her mother-
in-law, but Ruth clung to her.

15 And she said, "Look, your sister-in-law
has gone back to her people and to her gods;
return after your sister-in-law."

16 But Ruth said:

"Entreat me not to leave you,
Or to turn back from following after
you;
For wherever you go, I will go;
And wherever you lodge, I will lodge;
Your people *shall be* my people,
And your God, my God.
17 Where you die, I will die,
And there will I be buried.
The LORD do so to me, and more also,
If *anything but* death parts you and me."

18 When she saw that she was determined to
go with her, she stopped speaking to her.

19 Now the two of them went until they
came to Bethlehem. And it happened, when
they had come to Bethlehem, that all the city
was excited because of them; and the women
said, "*Is* this Naomi?"

20 But she said to them, "Do not call me
Naomi;[a] call me Mara,[b] for the Almighty has
dealt very bitterly with me. 21 I went out full,

1:20 [a] Literally *Pleasant* [b] Literally *Bitter*

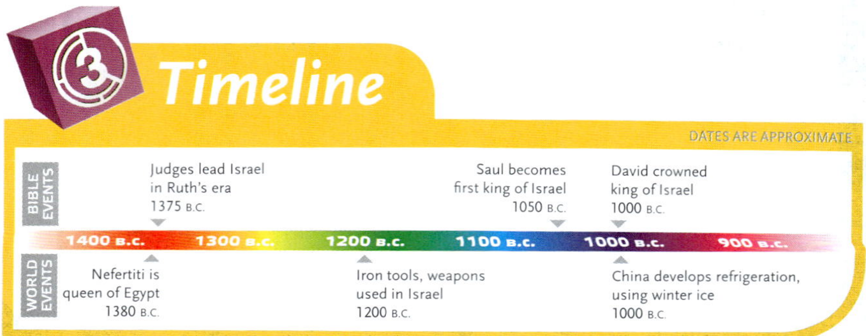

and the LORD has brought me home again
empty. Why do you call me Naomi, since the
LORD has testified against me, and the Almighty has afflicted me?"
22So Naomi returned, and Ruth the Moabitess her daughter-in-law with her, who
returned from the country of Moab. Now
they came to Bethlehem at the beginning of
barley harvest.

Ruth Meets Boaz

2 There was a relative of Naomi's husband, a man of great wealth, of the
family of Elimelech. His name *was* Boaz. 2So
Ruth the Moabitess said to Naomi, "Please
let me go to the field, and glean heads of
grain after *him* in whose sight I may find
favor."

And she said to her, "Go, my daughter."
3Then she left, and went and gleaned in
the field after the reapers. And she happened
to come to the part of the field *belonging* to
Boaz, who *was* of the family of Elimelech.
4Now behold, Boaz came from Bethlehem, and said to the reapers, "The LORD *be*
with you!"

And they answered him, "The LORD
bless you!"
5Then Boaz said to his servant who was
in charge of the reapers, "Whose young
woman *is* this?"
6So the servant who was in charge of the

GOD CHOOSES RUTH, A FOREIGNER

READ IT: RUTH 1:1—2:23

GET IT:

During the time of the judges, the land of Israel had a terrible famine. Lack of food made people move to other countries. That's how Naomi got to Moab and met Ruth. Time passed. Naomi decided to go back to Judah. Ruth insisted on going with her, but neither of them knew how they would support themselves (men usually took care of the women back then). They knew they could get some food by picking up the leftovers in the field, but they needed the help of a close relative—that's where Boaz came in. They came back to Judah with nothing. But thanks to God and His goodness, they soon had a lot: security, a family, and a baby who brought hope for the future.

LIVE IT:

This is another story of God using unlikely people to do His work on earth. Ruth was an outsider, a woman from an enemy country, Moab. But God chose her to marry into His family, the chosen people of Israel, and have a son. This son was a very special son because he was the grandfather of David, the great king. And David was the ancestor of Jesus. God uses all kinds of people to do His work, even an outsider from enemy territory. It doesn't matter who they are, where they're from, or what they've done in the past—God welcomes all kinds of people who love and follow Him. Because God loves these "outsiders," we should, too.

reapers answered and said, "It *is* the young
Moabite woman who came back with Naomi from the country of Moab. 7And she said,
'Please let me glean and gather after the
reapers among the sheaves.' So she came
and has continued from morning until now,
though she rested a little in the house."
8Then Boaz said to Ruth, "You will listen, my daughter, will you not? Do not go
to glean in another field, nor go from here,
but stay close by my young women. 9*Let* your
eyes *be* on the field which they reap, and
go after them. Have I not commanded the
young men not to touch you? And when you
are thirsty, go to the vessels and drink from
what the young men have drawn."
10So she fell on her face, bowed down to
the ground, and said to him, "Why have I
found favor in your eyes, that you should
take notice of me, since I *am* a foreigner?"
11And Boaz answered and said to her, "It
has been fully reported to me, all that you
have done for your mother-in-law since the
death of your husband, and *how* you have left
your father and your mother and the land of
your birth, and have come to a people whom
you did not know before. 12The LORD repay
your work, and a full reward be given you by
the LORD God of Israel, under whose wings
you have come for refuge."
13Then she said, "Let me find favor in
your sight, my lord; for you have comforted
me, and have spoken kindly to your maidservant, though I am not like one of your
maidservants."
14Now Boaz said to her at mealtime,
"Come here, and eat of the bread, and dip
your piece of bread in the vinegar." So she sat
beside the reapers, and he passed parched
grain to her; and she ate and was satisfied,
and kept some back. 15And when she rose
up to glean, Boaz commanded his young
men, saying, "Let her glean even among the
sheaves, and do not reproach her. 16Also let
grain from the bundles fall purposely for
her; leave *it* that she may glean, and do not
rebuke her."
17So she gleaned in the field until evening, and beat out what she had gleaned,
and it was about an ephah of barley. 18Then
she took *it* up and went into the city, and her
mother-in-law saw what she had gleaned. So
she brought out and gave to her what she had
kept back after she had been satisfied.
19And her mother-in-law said to her,
"Where have you gleaned today? And where
did you work? Blessed be the one who took
notice of you."
So she told her mother-in-law with whom

Starring Roles

NAOMI'S name means "Pleasant," but at one time she wanted to be called "Mara," which is a Hebrew word meaning "Bitter."

When Naomi's family moved to Moab, they were filled with hope. In their own land of Israel there was only famine and hunger, but in Moab there was plenty.

Then everything went wrong. First Naomi's husband died, then her two sons. Her sons had married two of the girls from Moab—Ruth and Orpah.

When Naomi decided to go back to Israel, the girls wanted to go with her. But Naomi thought they would be happier in their own land with their own families.

Orpah did go back home, but Ruth was determined to go with Naomi. Ruth's faith was strong, for she said, "Your God shall be my God."

To Naomi's surprise, God did supply a wonderful new husband to care for Ruth, so Naomi's life became truly pleasant again—just like her name means.

she had worked, and said, "The man's name
with whom I worked today *is* Boaz."
20Then Naomi said to her daughter-in-
law, "Blessed *be* he of the LORD, who has not
forsaken His kindness to the living and the
dead!" And Naomi said to her, "This man *is*
a relation of ours, one of our close relatives."
21Ruth the Moabitess said, "He also said
to me, 'You shall stay close by my young men
until they have finished all my harvest.'"
22And Naomi said to Ruth her daughter-
in-law, "*It is* good, my daughter, that you go
out with his young women, and that people
do not meet you in any other field." 23So she
stayed close by the young women of Boaz,
to glean until the end of barley harvest
and wheat harvest; and she dwelt with her
mother-in-law.

Ruth's Redemption Assured

3 Then Naomi her mother-in-law said to
her, "My daughter, shall I not seek security for you, that it may be well with you?
2Now Boaz, whose young women you were
with, *is he* not our relative? In fact, he is winnowing barley tonight at the threshing floor.
3Therefore wash yourself and anoint yourself, put on your *best* garment and go down
to the threshing floor; *but* do not make yourself known to the man until he has finished
eating and drinking. 4Then it shall be, when
he lies down, that you shall notice the place
where he lies; and you shall go in, uncover
his feet, and lie down; and he will tell you
what you should do."
5And she said to her, "All that you say to
me I will do."
6So she went down to the threshing floor
and did according to all that her mother-in-
law instructed her. 7And after Boaz had eat-
en and drunk, and his heart was cheerful,
he went to lie down at the end of the heap
of grain; and she came softly, uncovered his
feet, and lay down.
8Now it happened at midnight that the
man was startled, and turned himself; and
there, a woman was lying at his feet. 9And he
said, "Who *are* you?"

So she answered, "I *am* Ruth, your maidservant. Take your maidservant under your
wing,[a] for you are a close relative."
10Then he said, "Blessed *are* you of the
LORD, my daughter! For you have shown
more kindness at the end than at the beginning, in that you did not go after young men,
whether poor or rich. 11And now, my daughter, do not fear. I will do for you all that you
request, for all the people of my town know
that you *are* a virtuous woman. 12Now it is
true that I *am* a close relative; however, there
is a relative closer than I. 13Stay this night,
and in the morning it shall be *that* if he will

3:9 [a] Or *Spread the corner of your garment over your maidservant*

Action!

FAMILY

READ IT: RUTH 1:6–22

Ruth and Naomi were from different generations. Ruth was young and Naomi was old. And they grew up in different cultures with different beliefs. Ruth didn't worship God—she grew up worshiping her family's gods. Yet, because of the family ties created through her marriage to Naomi's son, Ruth chose to honor her mother-in-law. Ruth cared for and loved Naomi, even in a most painful situation. Ruth was loyal to Naomi, and God honored this. Ruth came to love God, and she eventually became the great-grandmother of David and an ancestor of Jesus! What a legacy—all because she chose to love even in an extremely tough situation.

perform the duty of a close relative for you—
good; let him do it. But if he does not want
to perform the duty for you, then I will perform the duty for you, *as* the LORD lives! Lie
down until morning."

14 So she lay at his feet until morning, and
she arose before one could recognize another. Then he said, "Do not let it be known that
the woman came to the threshing floor."
15 Also he said, "Bring the shawl that *is* on
you and hold it." And when she held it, he
measured six *ephahs* of barley, and laid *it* on
her. Then she[a] went into the city.

16 When she came to her mother-in-law,
she said, "*Is* that you, my daughter?"

Then she told her all that the man had
done for her. 17 And she said, "These six
ephahs of barley he gave me; for he said
to me, 'Do not go empty-handed to your
mother-in-law.'"

18 Then she said, "Sit still, my daughter,
until you know how the matter will turn out;
for the man will not rest until he has concluded the matter this day."

Boaz Redeems Ruth

4 Now Boaz went up to the gate and sat
down there; and behold, the close relative of whom Boaz had spoken came by. So
Boaz said, "Come aside, friend,[a] sit down
here." So he came aside and sat down. 2 And
he took ten men of the elders of the city,
and said, "Sit down here." So they sat down.
3 Then he said to the close relative, "Naomi,
who has come back from the country of
Moab, sold the piece of land which *belonged*
to our brother Elimelech. 4 And I thought to
inform you, saying, 'Buy *it* back in the presence of the inhabitants and the elders of my
people. If you will redeem *it,* redeem *it;* but
if you[a] will not redeem *it, then* tell me, that
I may know; for *there is* no one but you to
redeem *it,* and I *am* next after you.'"

And he said, "I will redeem *it.*"

5 Then Boaz said, "On the day you buy
the field from the hand of Naomi, you must
also buy *it* from Ruth the Moabitess, the wife
of the dead, to perpetuate[a] the name of the
dead through his inheritance."

6 And the close relative said, "I cannot redeem *it* for myself, lest I ruin my own inheritance. You redeem my right of redemption
for yourself, for I cannot redeem *it.*"

7 Now this *was the custom* in former
times in Israel concerning redeeming and
exchanging, to confirm anything: one man
took off his sandal and gave *it* to the other,
and this *was* a confirmation in Israel.

8 Therefore the close relative said to Boaz,
"Buy *it* for yourself." So he took off his sandal. 9 And Boaz said to the elders and all the
people, "You *are* witnesses this day that I
have bought all that was Elimelech's, and all
that *was* Chilion's and Mahlon's, from the
hand of Naomi. 10 Moreover, Ruth the Moabitess, the widow of Mahlon, I have acquired
as my wife, to perpetuate the name of the
dead through his inheritance, that the name
of the dead may not be cut off from among
his brethren and from his position at the
gate.[a] You *are* witnesses this day."

11 And all the people who *were* at the gate,
and the elders, said, "*We are* witnesses. The
LORD make the woman who is coming to
your house like Rachel and Leah, the two
who built the house of Israel; and may you
prosper in Ephrathah and be famous in
Bethlehem. 12 May your house be like the
house of Perez, whom Tamar bore to Judah,
because of the offspring which the LORD will
give you from this young woman."

Descendants of Boaz and Ruth

13 So Boaz took Ruth and she became his
wife; and when he went in to her, the LORD
gave her conception, and she bore a son.
14 Then the women said to Naomi, "Blessed
be the LORD, who has not left you this day
without a close relative; and may his name
be famous in Israel! 15 And may he be to you
a restorer of life and a nourisher of your old
age; for your daughter-in-law, who loves you,
who is better to you than seven sons, has
borne him." 16 Then Naomi took the child
and laid him on her bosom, and became a
nurse to him. 17 Also the neighbor women
gave him a name, saying, "There is a son
born to Naomi." And they called his name
Obed. He *is* the father of Jesse, the father of
David.

18 Now this *is* the genealogy of Perez: Perez begot Hezron; 19 Hezron begot Ram, and
Ram begot Amminadab; 20 Amminadab begot Nahshon, and Nahshon begot Salmon;[a]
21 Salmon begot Boaz, and Boaz begot Obed;
22 Obed begot Jesse, and Jesse begot David.

3:15 [a] Many Hebrew manuscripts, Syriac, and Vulgate read *she;* Masoretic Text, Septuagint, and Targum read *he.* **4:1** [a] Hebrew *peloni almoni;* literally *so and so* **4:4** [a] Following many Hebrew manuscripts, Septuagint, Syriac, Targum, and Vulgate; Masoretic Text reads *he.* **4:5** [a] Literally *raise up* **4:10** [a] Probably his civic office **4:20** [a] Hebrew *Salmah*

The BOOK *of*

1 SAMUEL

1050 B.C.–750 B.C.

Behind the Scenes

READ IT:

The book of 1 Samuel contains the events that happened as Israel went from God as their only leader to a human king. Samuel was a prophet, priest, and judge who had a lot of influence on the people during this time. The book contains the stories of Samuel's life, the selection of the first king, Saul, and the early years of David's life.

GET IT:

Who wrote it: Most people think Samuel wrote it.

When it was written: 1050 B.C.–750 B.C.

Why it was written: to record Israel's transition from being led by judges to being led by a king.

LIVE IT:

God has a plan for the world and His people.

God sees people differently than people do.

FIND IT:

Hannah's Vow	*1 Samuel 1–2*
Samuel's First Prophecy	*1 Samuel 3*
The Philistines and the Ark	*1 Samuel 5*
Saul, the First King	*1 Samuel 9–10*
Saul's Unlawful Sacrifice	*1 Samuel 13*
David Anointed King	*1 Samuel 16*
David and Goliath	*1 Samuel 17*
Jonathan's Loyalty to David	*1 Samuel 20*
The Tragic End of Saul and His Sons	*1 Samuel 31*

The Family of Elkanah

1 Now there was a certain man of Ra-
mathaim Zophim, of the mountains
of Ephraim, and his name *was* Elkanah the
son of Jeroham, the son of Elihu,[a] the son
of Tohu,[b] the son of Zuph, an Ephraimite.
2And he had two wives: the name of one *was*
Hannah, and the name of the other Peninnah. Peninnah had children, but Hannah
had no children. 3This man went up from
his city yearly to worship and sacrifice to the
LORD of hosts in Shiloh. Also the two sons of
Eli, Hophni and Phinehas, the priests of the
LORD, *were* there. 4And whenever the time
came for Elkanah to make an offering, he
would give portions to Peninnah his wife
and to all her sons and daughters. 5But to
Hannah he would give a double portion, for
he loved Hannah, although the LORD had
closed her womb. 6And her rival also provoked her severely, to make her miserable,
because the LORD had closed her womb. 7So
it was, year by year, when she went up to the
house of the LORD, that she provoked her;
therefore she wept and did not eat.

Hannah's Vow

8Then Elkanah her husband said to her,
"Hannah, why do you weep? Why do you not
eat? And why is your heart grieved? *Am* I not
better to you than ten sons?"

9So Hannah arose after they had finished
eating and drinking in Shiloh. Now Eli the
priest was sitting on the seat by the doorpost
of the tabernacle[a] of the LORD. 10And she
was in bitterness of soul, and prayed to the
LORD and wept in anguish. 11Then she made
a vow and said, "O LORD of hosts, if You will
indeed look on the affliction of Your maidservant and remember me, and not forget

In Focus

1:3 LORD of Hosts A name for God as the leader of His heavenly armies. Lord Sabaoth (pronounced *SAB-ay-oth*), from the Hebrew, means the same.

Your maidservant, but will give Your maidservant a male child, then I will give him to
the LORD all the days of his life, and no razor
shall come upon his head."

12And it happened, as she continued praying before the LORD, that Eli watched her
mouth. 13Now Hannah spoke in her heart;
only her lips moved, but her voice was not
heard. Therefore Eli thought she was drunk.
14So Eli said to her, "How long will you be
drunk? Put your wine away from you!"

15But Hannah answered and said, "No,
my lord, I *am* a woman of sorrowful spirit.
I have drunk neither wine nor intoxicating
drink, but have poured out my soul before
the LORD. 16Do not consider your maidservant a wicked woman,[a] for out of the abundance of my complaint and grief I have
spoken until now."

17Then Eli answered and said, "Go in
peace, and the God of Israel grant your petition which you have asked of Him."

18And she said, "Let your maidservant find
favor in your sight." So the woman went her
way and ate, and her face was no longer *sad*.

1:1 [a] Spelled *Eliel* in 1 Chronicles 6:34 [b] Spelled *Toah* in 1 Chronicles 6:34 1:9 [a] Hebrew *heykal,* palace or temple 1:16 [a] Literally *daughter of Belial*

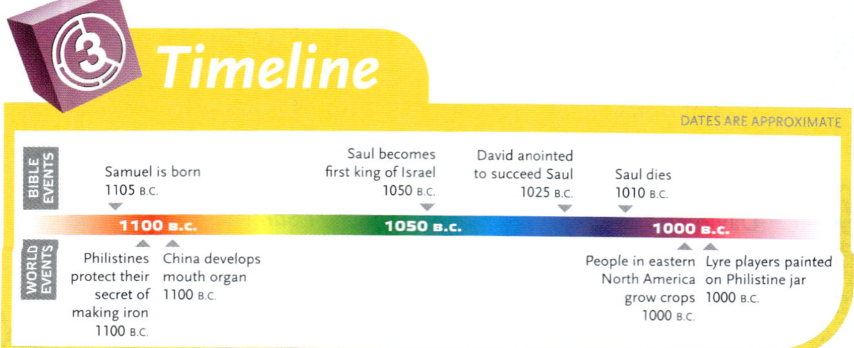

Samuel Is Born and Dedicated

19Then they rose early in the morning
and worshiped before the LORD, and returned and came to their house at Ramah.
And Elkanah knew Hannah his wife, and
the LORD remembered her. 20So it came to
pass in the process of time that Hannah conceived and bore a son, and called his name
Samuel,[a] *saying,* "Because I have asked for
him from the LORD."

21Now the man Elkanah and all his house
went up to offer to the LORD the yearly sacrifice and his vow. 22But Hannah did not go up,
for she said to her husband, "*Not* until the

1:20 [a] Literally *Heard by God*

PRAYER

HANNAH'S PRAYER

READ IT: 1 SAMUEL 1:1–28

GET IT:

Have you ever wanted something so much it made you sick? Or been so sad about something you couldn't eat? That's how Hannah felt. She wanted a child so much she was physically suffering. To make matters worse, Hannah's husband had two wives, and the other wife, Peninnah, had kids of her own and loved nothing more than teasing and upsetting Hannah about not having a baby. Hannah was trapped in a miserable situation, and she literally begged God to answer her prayers for a child. She even promised God that if He would give her a son, she would give her son to the Lord's service. When God answered her prayers, she did just that.

LIVE IT:

It would have been easy for Hannah to keep Samuel for herself and not take him to live at the temple. It's natural for a mother to want to be with her child—especially one she has been wanting for so long. But Hannah kept her promise to God. Could you do the same?

Ask God to take care of your needs. He knows the good things you long for, whether it's happy parents or a healthy sibling. Trust these desires to God.

Use the good gifts He has given you for His glory—just like Hannah taking Samuel to the temple. If your gifts are material (money, possessions), share them and be generous with others. If you have the gift of influence (like popularity), use it to tell others about God. (Hint: If you are having a hard time knowing what your gifts are and how to use them, ask a friend or a youth leader from church to help you figure it out.)

Always, always pray—especially when you are hurting. Hannah continued to seek God, no matter how much it hurt. You can, too!

child is weaned; then I will take him, that
he may appear before the LORD and remain
there forever."

23 So Elkanah her husband said to her,
"Do what seems best to you; wait until you
have weaned him. Only let the LORD establish His[a] word." Then the woman stayed and
nursed her son until she had weaned him.

24 Now when she had weaned him, she
took him up with her, with three bulls,[a]
one ephah of flour, and a skin of wine, and
brought him to the house of the LORD in Shiloh. And the child *was* young. 25 Then they
slaughtered a bull, and brought the child to
Eli. 26 And she said, "O my lord! As your soul
lives, my lord, I *am* the woman who stood
by you here, praying to the LORD. 27 For this
child I prayed, and the LORD has granted me
my petition which I asked of Him. 28 Therefore I also have lent him to the LORD; as long
as he lives he shall be lent to the LORD." So
they worshiped the LORD there.

Hannah's Prayer

2 And Hannah prayed and said:

"My heart rejoices in the LORD;
My horn[a] is exalted in the LORD.
I smile at my enemies,
Because I rejoice in Your salvation.

2 "No one is holy like the LORD,
For *there is* none besides You,
Nor *is there* any rock like our God.

3 "Talk no more so very proudly;
Let no arrogance come from your
mouth,
For the LORD *is* the God of knowledge;
And by Him actions are weighed.

4 "The bows of the mighty men *are*
broken,
And those who stumbled are girded
with strength.
5 *Those who were* full have hired
themselves out for bread,
And the hungry have ceased *to hunger.*
Even the barren has borne seven,
And she who has many children has
become feeble.

6 "The LORD kills and makes alive;
He brings down to the grave and
brings up.
7 The LORD makes poor and makes rich;
He brings low and lifts up.
8 He raises the poor from the dust
And lifts the beggar from the ash heap,
To set *them* among princes
And make them inherit the throne of
glory.

"For the pillars of the earth *are* the
LORD's,
And He has set the world upon them.
9 He will guard the feet of His saints,
But the wicked shall be silent in
darkness.

"For by strength no man shall prevail.
10 The adversaries of the LORD shall be
broken in pieces;
From heaven He will thunder against
them.
The LORD will judge the ends of the
earth.

"He will give strength to His king,
And exalt the horn of His anointed."

11 Then Elkanah went to his house at Ramah.
But the child ministered to the LORD before
Eli the priest.

The Wicked Sons of Eli

12 Now the sons of Eli *were* corrupt;[a] they
did not know the LORD. 13 And the priests'
custom with the people *was that* when any
man offered a sacrifice, the priest's servant
would come with a three-pronged fleshhook in his hand while the meat was boiling. 14 Then he would thrust *it* into the pan,
or kettle, or caldron, or pot; and the priest
would take for himself all that the fleshhook
brought up. So they did in Shiloh to all the
Israelites who came there. 15 Also, before they
burned the fat, the priest's servant would
come and say to the man who sacrificed,
"Give meat for roasting to the priest, for he
will not take boiled meat from you, but raw."

16 And *if* the man said to him, "They
should really burn the fat first; *then* you may
take *as much* as your heart desires," he would
then answer him, "*No,* but you must give *it*
now; and if not, I will take *it* by force."

17 Therefore the sin of the young men was
very great before the LORD, for men abhorred
the offering of the LORD.

Samuel's Childhood Ministry

18 But Samuel ministered before the

1:23 [a] Following Masoretic Text, Targum, and Vulgate; Dead Sea Scrolls, Septuagint, and Syriac read *your.*
1:24 [a] Dead Sea Scrolls, Septuagint, and Syriac read *a three-year-old bull.* **2:1** [a] That is, strength **2:12** [a] Literally *sons of Belial*

LORD, *even as* a child, wearing a linen ephod.
19Moreover his mother used to make him a
little robe, and bring *it* to him year by year
when she came up with her husband to offer the yearly sacrifice. 20And Eli would bless
Elkanah and his wife, and say, "The LORD
give you descendants from this woman for
the loan that was given to the LORD." Then
they would go to their own home.

21And the LORD visited Hannah, so that
she conceived and bore three sons and two
daughters. Meanwhile the child Samuel
grew before the LORD.

Prophecy Against Eli's Household

22Now Eli was very old; and he heard
everything his sons did to all Israel,[a] and
how they lay with the women who assembled at the door of the tabernacle of meeting.
23So he said to them, "Why do you do such
things? For I hear of your evil dealings from
all the people. 24No, my sons! For *it is* not a
good report that I hear. You make the LORD's
people transgress. 25If one man sins against
another, God will judge him. But if a man
sins against the LORD, who will intercede for
him?" Nevertheless they did not heed the
voice of their father, because the LORD desired to kill them.

26And the child Samuel grew in stature,
and in favor both with the LORD and men.

27Then a man of God came to Eli and
said to him, "Thus says the LORD: 'Did I not
clearly reveal Myself to the house of your father when they were in Egypt in Pharaoh's
house? 28Did I not choose him out of all
the tribes of Israel *to be* My priest, to offer
upon My altar, to burn incense, and to wear
an ephod before Me? And did I not give to
the house of your father all the offerings of
the children of Israel made by fire? 29Why
do you kick at My sacrifice and My offering
which I have commanded *in My* dwelling
place, and honor your sons more than Me, to
make yourselves fat with the best of all the
offerings of Israel My people?' 30Therefore
the LORD God of Israel says: 'I said indeed
that your house and the house of your father
would walk before Me forever.' But now the
LORD says: 'Far be it from Me; for those who
honor Me I will honor, and those who despise Me shall be lightly esteemed. 31Behold,
the days are coming that I will cut off your
arm and the arm of your father's house, so
that there will not be an old man in your
house. 32And you will see an enemy *in My*
dwelling place, *despite* all the good which
God does for Israel. And there shall not be
an old man in your house forever. 33But any
of your men *whom* I do not cut off from My
altar shall consume your eyes and grieve
your heart. And all the descendants of your
house shall die in the flower of their age.
34Now this *shall be* a sign to you that will
come upon your two sons, on Hophni and
Phinehas: in one day they shall die, both
of them. 35Then I will raise up for Myself a
faithful priest *who* shall do according to what
is in My heart and in My mind. I will build
him a sure house, and he shall walk before
My anointed forever. 36And it shall come to
pass that everyone who is left in your house
will come *and* bow down to him for a piece of

2:22 [a] Following Masoretic Text, Targum, and Vulgate; Dead Sea Scrolls and Septuagint omit the rest of this verse.

Starring Roles

Some people think God calls only older people to serve Him. That isn't true *because* ***SAMUEL*** *was helping Eli the* priest in his ministry when he was even younger than you.

One night after Samuel went to bed, God spoke to him. He told Samuel He was angry with Eli because his sons were priests who did not respect God or God's house. When Eli asked him, Samuel told him what God said to him, and Eli believed that what Samuel told him was God's message. As he was growing up, the Lord revealed Himself to Samuel, and Samuel spoke God's words to Israel, His people.

silver and a morsel of bread, and say, "Please, put me in one of the priestly positions, that I may eat a piece of bread."'"

Samuel's First Prophecy

3 Now the boy Samuel ministered to
the LORD before Eli. And the word of
the LORD was rare in those days; *there was*
no widespread revelation. 2And it came to
pass at that time, while Eli *was* lying down
in his place, and when his eyes had begun
to grow so dim that he could not see, 3and
before the lamp of God went out in the tabernacle[a] of the LORD where the ark of God
was, and while Samuel was lying down, 4that
the LORD called Samuel. And he answered,
"Here I am!" 5So he ran to Eli and said,
"Here I am, for you called me."
And he said, "I did not call; lie down
again." And he went and lay down.
6Then the LORD called yet again,
"Samuel!"
So Samuel arose and went to Eli, and
said, "Here I am, for you called me." He
answered, "I did not call, my son; lie down
again." 7(Now Samuel did not yet know the
LORD, nor was the word of the LORD yet revealed to him.)
8And the LORD called Samuel again the
third time. So he arose and went to Eli, and
said, "Here I am, for you did call me."
Then Eli perceived that the LORD had
called the boy. 9Therefore Eli said to Samuel, "Go, lie down; and it shall be, if He calls
you, that you must say, 'Speak, LORD, for

3:3 [a] Hebrew *heykal,* palace or temple

GOD SPEAKS TO SAMUEL

READ IT: 1 SAMUEL 3:1–21

GET IT:

Years before, Hannah, Samuel's mother, had come to the tabernacle to worship God. She prayed that God would give her a child. He did. So when Samuel was three or four years old, Hannah brought him to the tabernacle to serve God. He lived in the tabernacle with Eli, the priest. One night God called Samuel in the middle of the night. Samuel ran to Eli, assuming that Eli had called him. He wasn't afraid at all; he just obeyed. Three times God called Samuel's name. Three times Samuel got up and ran to Eli, thinking he had called him. Finally it dawned on Eli that this young boy did not know that God was calling. So Eli told Samuel what to do. Samuel obeyed. After that, Samuel grew up serving God. He stayed in God's service all his life as a great prophet and leader of Israel.

LIVE IT:

God calls and uses people of all ages to do His work. In this story there's a very old man and a very young boy who served God. You don't have to be an adult or an old person to serve God. You can serve Him right now. He's calling you to do special things for Him now, right at your age, *right where you* live. Serving God is not a "sometime later" thing. It's a "right now, right where you live" thing. Look around. Listen to others. Find opportunities in which you can serve God now, while you're young.

Your servant hears.'" So Samuel went and
lay down in his place.
10Now the LORD came and stood and
called as at other times, "Samuel! Samuel!"
And Samuel answered, "Speak, for Your
servant hears."
11Then the LORD said to Samuel: "Behold,
I will do something in Israel at which both
ears of everyone who hears it will tingle. 12In
that day I will perform against Eli all that
I have spoken concerning his house, from
beginning to end. 13For I have told him that
I will judge his house forever for the iniquity which he knows, because his sons made
themselves vile, and he did not restrain
them. 14And therefore I have sworn to the
house of Eli that the iniquity of Eli's house
shall not be atoned for by sacrifice or offering forever."
15So Samuel lay down until morning,[a]
and opened the doors of the house of the
LORD. And Samuel was afraid to tell Eli the

3:15 [a] Following Masoretic Text, Targum, and Vulgate; Septuagint adds *and he arose in the morning.*

MATURITY

GROW WITH THE FLOW

READ IT: 1 SAMUEL 3:1–21

GET IT:

Samuel had been raised by Eli, a priest, since the time he was very young. He probably knew a lot about all the traditions and responsibilities of tabernacle life. But he didn't know the Lord yet. Samuel was still a kid with a lot of growing up to do, not just physically and emotionally and mentally, but also spiritually.

If you've ever tried to make yourself grow taller, you know it doesn't work. You can't force it. On the other hand, if you eat good food, exercise regularly, and get enough rest, over time you will grow. Same thing with wisdom. Over time, the lessons you learn from life's experiences will make you wiser (if you pay attention to them). It's like that with everything in life. Growth and maturity take time. Small changes and steps aren't always noticeable, but they add up over time. "Samuel grew, and the LORD was with him" (v. 19) could also be said this way: "The Lord was with Samuel, and so he grew." Maturity—growing into a person of honor and character and depth and wisdom and goodness—starts right now. But it only moves forward the way it's supposed to when God is part of the story.

LIVE IT:

Being young is no excuse for being childish. Even if there's a lot of growing and maturing still ahead of you, you should live now with that goal in mind. Do what Samuel did: He listened for God's voice. He sought guidance and advice from an older, wiser mentor. He pursued the kind of life that pleased God. Everyone can do that, no matter his or her age.

vision. 16Then Eli called Samuel and said,
"Samuel, my son!"
He answered, "Here I am."
17And he said, "What *is* the word that *the*
Lord spoke to you? Please do not hide *it*
from me. God do so to you, and more also, if
you hide anything from me of all the things
that He said to you." 18Then Samuel told him
everything, and hid nothing from him. And
he said, "It *is* the Lord. Let Him do what
seems good to Him."
19So Samuel grew, and the Lord was
with him and let none of his words fall to
the ground. 20And all Israel from Dan to
Beersheba knew that Samuel *had been* established as a prophet of the Lord. 21Then
the Lord appeared again in Shiloh. For the
Lord revealed Himself to Samuel in Shiloh
by the word of the Lord.

4 And the word of Samuel came to all
Israel.[a]

The Ark of God Captured

Now Israel went out to battle against the
Philistines, and encamped beside Ebenezer;
and the Philistines encamped in Aphek.
2Then the Philistines put themselves in
battle array against Israel. And when they
joined battle, Israel was defeated by the
Philistines, who killed about four thousand
men of the army in the field. 3And when the
people had come into the camp, the elders of
Israel said, "Why has the Lord defeated us
today before the Philistines? Let us bring the
ark of the covenant of the Lord from Shiloh
to us, that when it comes among us it may
save us from the hand of our enemies." 4So
the people sent to Shiloh, that they might
bring from there the ark of the covenant of
the Lord of hosts, who dwells *between* the
cherubim. And the two sons of Eli, Hophni
and Phinehas, *were* there with the ark of the
covenant of God.
5And when the ark of the covenant of the
Lord came into the camp, all Israel shouted
so loudly that the earth shook. 6Now when
the Philistines heard the noise of the shout,
they said, "What *does* the sound of this great
shout in the camp of the Hebrews *mean?*"
Then they understood that the ark of the
Lord had come into the camp. 7So the Philistines were afraid, for they said, "God has
come into the camp!" And they said, "Woe
to us! For such a thing has never happened
before. 8Woe to us! Who will deliver us from
the hand of these mighty gods? These *are*
the gods who struck the Egyptians with all
the plagues in the wilderness. 9Be strong
and conduct yourselves like men, you Philistines, that you do not become servants of the
Hebrews, as they have been to you. Conduct
yourselves like men, and fight!"
10So the Philistines fought, and Israel
was defeated, and every man fled to his tent.
There was a very great slaughter, and there
fell of Israel thirty thousand foot soldiers.
11Also the ark of God was captured; and the
two sons of Eli, Hophni and Phinehas, died.

Death of Eli

12Then a man of Benjamin ran from the
battle line the same day, and came to Shiloh
with his clothes torn and dirt on his head.
13Now when he came, there was Eli, sitting
on a seat by the wayside watching,[a] for his
heart trembled for the ark of God. And when
the man came into the city and told *it,* all
the city cried out. 14When Eli heard the noise
of the outcry, he said, "What *does* the sound
of this tumult *mean?*" And the man came
quickly and told Eli. 15Eli was ninety-eight
years old, and his eyes were so dim that he
could not see.
16Then the man said to Eli, "I *am* he who
came from the battle. And I fled today from
the battle line."
And he said, "What happened, my son?"
17So the messenger answered and said,
"Israel has fled before the Philistines, and
there has been a great slaughter among the
people. Also your two sons, Hophni and
Phinehas, are dead; and the ark of God has
been captured."
18Then it happened, when he made mention of the ark of God, that Eli fell off the
seat backward by the side of the gate; and his
neck was broken and he died, for the man
was old and heavy. And he had judged Israel
forty years.

Ichabod

19Now his daughter-in-law, Phinehas'
wife, was with child, *due* to be delivered; and
when she heard the news that the ark of God
was captured, and that her father-in-law and

4:1 [a] Following Masoretic Text and Targum; Septuagint and Vulgate add *And it came to pass in those days that the Philistines gathered themselves together to fight;* Septuagint adds further *against Israel.* **4:13** [a] Following Masoretic Text and Vulgate; Septuagint reads *beside the gate watching the road.*

her husband were dead, she bowed herself
and gave birth, for her labor pains came
upon her. 20And about the time of her death
the women who stood by her said to her, "Do
not fear, for you have borne a son." But she
did not answer, nor did she regard *it*. 21Then
she named the child Ichabod,[a] saying, "The
glory has departed from Israel!" because the
ark of God had been captured and because of
her father-in-law and her husband. 22And she
said, "The glory has departed from Israel, for
the ark of God has been captured."

The Philistines and the Ark

5 Then the Philistines took the ark of
God and brought it from Ebenezer
to Ashdod. 2When the Philistines took the
ark of God, they brought it into the house
of Dagon[a] and set it by Dagon. 3And when
the people of Ashdod arose early in the
morning, there was Dagon, fallen on its face
to the earth before the ark of the LORD. So
they took Dagon and set it in its place again.
4And when they arose early the next morning, there was Dagon, fallen on its face to the
ground before the ark of the LORD. The head
of Dagon and both the palms of its hands
were broken off on the threshold; only Dagon's *torso*[a] was left of it. 5Therefore neither
the priests of Dagon nor any who come into
Dagon's house tread on the threshold of Dagon in Ashdod to this day.

6But the hand of the LORD was heavy on
the people of Ashdod, and He ravaged them
and struck them with tumors,[a] *both* Ashdod
and its territory. 7And when the men of Ashdod saw how *it was,* they said, "The ark of
the God of Israel must not remain with us,
for His hand is harsh toward us and Dagon
our god." 8Therefore they sent and gathered
to themselves all the lords of the Philistines,
and said, "What shall we do with the ark of
the God of Israel?"

And they answered, "Let the ark of the
God of Israel be carried away to Gath." So
they carried the ark of the God of Israel
away. 9So it was, after they had carried it
away, that the hand of the LORD was against
the city with a very great destruction; and He
struck the men of the city, both small and
great, and tumors broke out on them.

10Therefore they sent the ark of God to
Ekron. So it was, as the ark of God came to
Ekron, that the Ekronites cried out, saying,
"They have brought the ark of the God of
Israel to us, to kill us and our people!" 11So
they sent and gathered together all the lords
of the Philistines, and said, "Send away the
ark of the God of Israel, and let it go back to
its own place, so that it does not kill us and
our people." For there was a deadly destruction throughout all the city; the hand of God
was very heavy there. 12And the men who did
not die were stricken with the tumors, and
the cry of the city went up to heaven.

The Ark Returned to Israel

6 Now the ark of the LORD was in the
country of the Philistines seven
months. 2And the Philistines called for the
priests and the diviners, saying, "What shall
we do with the ark of the LORD? Tell us how
we should send it to its place."

3So they said, "If you send away the ark
of the God of Israel, do not send it empty;
but by all means return *it* to Him *with* a trespass offering. Then you will be healed, and
it will be known to you why His hand is not
removed from you."

4Then they said, "What *is* the trespass offering which we shall return to Him?"

They answered, "Five golden tumors and
five golden rats, *according to* the number of
the lords of the Philistines. For the same
plague *was* on all of you and on your lords.
5Therefore you shall make images of your
tumors and images of your rats that ravage
the land, and you shall give glory to the God
of Israel; perhaps He will lighten His hand
from you, from your gods, and from your
land. 6Why then do you harden your hearts
as the Egyptians and Pharaoh hardened
their hearts? When He did mighty things
among them, did they not let the people
go, that they might depart? 7Now therefore,
make a new cart, take two milk cows which
have never been yoked, and hitch the cows
to the cart; and take their calves home, away
from them. 8Then take the ark of the LORD
and set it on the cart; and put the articles of
gold which you are returning to Him *as* a
trespass offering in a chest by its side. Then
send it away, and let it go. 9And watch: if it
goes up the road to its own territory, to Beth

4:21 [a] Literally *Inglorious* 5:2 [a] A Philistine idol
5:4 [a] Following Septuagint, Syriac, Targum, and Vulgate; Masoretic Text reads *Dagon*. 5:6 [a] Probably bubonic plague. Septuagint and Vulgate add here *And in the midst of their land rats sprang up, and there was a great death panic in the city.*

Shemesh, *then* He has done us this great evil. But if not, then we shall know that *it is* not His hand *that* struck us—it happened to us by chance."

10 Then the men did so; they took two milk cows and hitched them to the cart, and shut up their calves at home. 11 And they set the ark of the LORD on the cart, and the chest with the gold rats and the images of their tumors. 12 Then the cows headed straight for the road to Beth Shemesh, *and* went along the highway, lowing as they went, and did not turn aside to the right hand or the left. And the lords of the Philistines went after them to the border of Beth Shemesh.

13 Now *the people of* Beth Shemesh *were* reaping their wheat harvest in the valley; and they lifted their eyes and saw the ark, and rejoiced to see *it*. 14 Then the cart came into the field of Joshua of Beth Shemesh, and stood there; a large stone *was* there. So they split the wood of the cart and offered the cows as a burnt offering to the LORD. 15 The Levites took down the ark of the LORD and the chest that *was* with it, in which *were* the articles of gold, and put *them* on the large stone. Then the men of Beth Shemesh offered burnt offerings and made sacrifices the same day to the LORD. 16 So when the five lords of the Philistines had seen *it*, they returned to Ekron the same day.

17 These *are* the golden tumors which the Philistines returned *as* a trespass offering to the LORD: one for Ashdod, one for Gaza, one for Ashkelon, one for Gath, one for Ekron; 18 and the golden rats, *according to* the number of all the cities of the Philistines *belonging* to the five lords, *both* fortified cities and country villages, even as far as the large *stone of* Abel on which they set the ark of the LORD, *which stone remains* to this day in the field of Joshua of Beth Shemesh.

19 Then He struck the men of Beth Shemesh, because they had looked into the ark of the LORD. He struck fifty thousand and seventy men[a] of the people, and the people lamented because the LORD had struck the people with a great slaughter.

The Ark at Kirjath Jearim

20 And the men of Beth Shemesh said, "Who is able to stand before this holy LORD God? And to whom shall it go up from us?" 21 So they sent messengers to the inhabitants of Kirjath Jearim, saying, "The Philistines have brought back the ark of the LORD; come down *and* take it up with you."

7 Then the men of Kirjath Jearim came and took the ark of the LORD, and brought it into the house of Abinadab on the hill, and consecrated Eleazar his son to keep the ark of the LORD.

Samuel Judges Israel

2 So it was that the ark remained in Kirjath Jearim a long time; it was there twenty years. And all the house of Israel lamented after the LORD.

3 Then Samuel spoke to all the house of Israel, saying, "If you return to the LORD with all your hearts, *then* put away the foreign gods and the Ashtoreths[a] from among you, and prepare your hearts for the LORD, and serve Him only; and He will deliver you from the hand of the Philistines." 4 So the children of Israel put away the Baals and the Ashtoreths,[a] and served the LORD only.

5 And Samuel said, "Gather all Israel to Mizpah, and I will pray to the LORD for you." 6 So they gathered together at Mizpah, drew water, and poured *it* out before the LORD. And they fasted that day, and said there, "We have sinned against the LORD." And Samuel judged the children of Israel at Mizpah.

7 Now when the Philistines heard that the children of Israel had gathered together at Mizpah, the lords of the Philistines went up against Israel. And when the children of Israel heard *of it*, they were afraid of the Philistines. 8 So the children of Israel said to Samuel, "Do not cease to cry out to the LORD our God for us, that He may save us from the hand of the Philistines."

9 And Samuel took a suckling lamb and offered *it as* a whole burnt offering to the LORD. Then Samuel cried out to the LORD for Israel, and the LORD answered him. 10 Now as Samuel was offering up the burnt offering, the Philistines drew near to battle against Israel. But the LORD thundered with a loud thunder upon the Philistines that day, and so confused them that they were overcome before Israel. 11 And the men of Israel went out of Mizpah and pursued the Philistines, and drove them back as far as below Beth Car. 12 Then Samuel took a stone and set *it* up between Mizpah and Shen, and called its

---

6:19 [a] Or *He struck seventy men of the people and fifty oxen of a man* 7:3 [a] Canaanite goddesses 7:4 [a] Canaanite goddesses

name Ebenezer,[a] saying, "Thus far the LORD
has helped us."
13 So the Philistines were subdued, and
they did not come anymore into the territory of Israel. And the hand of the LORD was
against the Philistines all the days of Samuel. 14 Then the cities which the Philistines
had taken from Israel were restored to Israel,
from Ekron to Gath; and Israel recovered its
territory from the hands of the Philistines.
Also there was peace between Israel and the
Amorites.
15 And Samuel judged Israel all the days
of his life. 16 He went from year to year on a
circuit to Bethel, Gilgal, and Mizpah, and
judged Israel in all those places. 17 But he always returned to Ramah, for his home *was*
there. There he judged Israel, and there he
built an altar to the LORD.

Israel Demands a King

8 Now it came to pass when Samuel was
old that he made his sons judges over Israel. 2 The name of his firstborn was Joel, and
the name of his second, Abijah; *they were* judges in Beersheba. 3 But his sons did not walk in
his ways; they turned aside after dishonest
gain, took bribes, and perverted justice.

7:12 [a] Literally *Stone of Help*

GOD ALLOWS ISRAEL TO HAVE A KING

READ IT: 1 SAMUEL 8:1–22

GET IT:

Samuel led God's people all his life. Eventually, like everybody, he got old. That's when the people of Israel said, "We don't like your sons; they don't do things the way you did. We want a king, like all the nations around us." Actually, Israel already had a king—God. God had been their ruler for hundreds of years. But now the people wanted a human king. They wanted an important person whom they could look up to, a strong man who could lead them into battle. They wanted a person decked out in robes with a crown on his head and a sword at his side! This didn't make Samuel (or God) happy. But God allowed it. After a long process, Samuel chose Saul to be the first king of Israel.

LIVE IT:

Sometimes we don't recognize when we have it good. We always want something else, something different, or something like everyone else has. Like the people of Israel, too often we want to look like, be like, and act like everybody else. *That's what Israel wanted.* They wanted to be more like a "real" nation, with a real king. What they had wasn't good enough. Samuel knew this wasn't the best thing for them. He told them that and told them why, but they still wanted a king. Having a king didn't solve all their problems. It just made things a little different. Remember this the next time you want to "be like everybody else" and your parents tell you it's not the best thing for you. You might get what you want (like Israel), but it might not be the best thing for you.

4 Then all the elders of Israel gathered together and came to Samuel at Ramah, 5 and said to him, "Look, you are old, and your sons do not walk in your ways. Now make us a king to judge us like all the nations."

6 But the thing displeased Samuel when they said, "Give us a king to judge us." So Samuel prayed to the LORD. 7 And the LORD said to Samuel, "Heed the voice of the people in all that they say to you; for they have not rejected you, but they have rejected Me, that I should not reign over them. 8 According to all the works which they have done since the day that I brought them up out of Egypt, even to this day—with which they have forsaken Me and served other gods—so they are doing to you also. 9 Now therefore, heed their voice. However, you shall solemnly forewarn them, and show them the behavior of the king who will reign over them."

10 So Samuel told all the words of the LORD to the people who asked him for a king. 11 And he said, "This will be the behavior of the king who will reign over you: He will take your sons and appoint *them* for his own chariots and *to be* his horsemen, and *some* will run before his chariots. 12 He will appoint captains over his thousands and captains over his fifties, *will set some* to plow his ground and reap his harvest, and *some* to make his weapons of war and equipment for his chariots. 13 He will take your daughters *to be* perfumers, cooks, and bakers. 14 And he will take the best of your fields, your vineyards, and your olive groves, and give *them* to his servants. 15 He will take a tenth of your grain and your vintage, and give it to his officers and servants. 16 And he will take your male servants, your female servants, your finest young men,[a] and your donkeys, and put *them* to his work. 17 He will take a tenth of your sheep. And you will be his servants. 18 And you will cry out in that day because of your king whom you have chosen for yourselves, and the LORD will not hear you in that day."

19 Nevertheless the people refused to obey the voice of Samuel; and they said, "No, but we will have a king over us, 20 that we also may be like all the nations, and that our king may judge us and go out before us and fight *our battles.*"

21 And Samuel heard all the words of the people, and he repeated them in the hearing of the LORD. 22 So the LORD said to Samuel, "Heed their voice, and make them a king."

And Samuel said to the men of Israel, "Every man go to his city."

Saul Chosen to Be King

9 There was a man of Benjamin whose name *was* Kish the son of Abiel, the son of Zeror, the son of Bechorath, the son of Aphiah, a Benjamite, a mighty man of power. 2 And he had a choice and handsome son whose name *was* Saul. *There was* not a more handsome person than he among the children of Israel. From his shoulders upward *he was* taller than any of the people.

3 Now the donkeys of Kish, Saul's father, were lost. And Kish said to his son Saul, "Please take one of the servants with you, and arise, go and look for the donkeys." 4 So he passed through the mountains of Ephraim and through the land of Shalisha, but they did not find *them.* Then they passed through the land of Shaalim, and *they were* not *there.* Then he passed through the land of the Benjamites, but they did not find *them.*

5 When they had come to the land of Zuph, Saul said to his servant who *was* with him, "Come, let us return, lest my father cease *caring* about the donkeys and become worried about us."

6 And he said to him, "Look now, *there is* in this city a man of God, and *he is* an honorable man; all that he says surely comes to pass. So let us go there; perhaps he can show us the way that we should go."

7 Then Saul said to his servant, "But look, *if* we go, what shall we bring the man? For the bread in our vessels is all gone, and *there is* no present to bring to the man of God. What do we have?"

8 And the servant answered Saul again and said, "Look, I have here at hand one-fourth of a shekel of silver. I will give *that* to the man of God, to tell us our way." 9 (Formerly in Israel, when a man went to inquire of God, he spoke thus: "Come, let us go to the seer"; for *he who is* now *called* a prophet was formerly called a seer.)

10 Then Saul said to his servant, "Well said; come, let us go." So they went to the city where the man of God *was.*

11 As they went up the hill to the city, they met some young women going out to draw water, and said to them, "Is the seer here?"

8:16 [a] Septuagint reads *cattle.*

[12]And they answered them and said, "Yes, there he is, just ahead of you. Hurry now; for today he came to this city, because there is a sacrifice of the people today on the high place. [13]As soon as you come into the city, you will surely find him before he goes up to the high place to eat. For the people will not eat until he comes, because he must bless the sacrifice; afterward those who are invited will eat. Now therefore, go up, for about this time you will find him." [14]So they went up to the city. As they were coming into the city, there was Samuel, coming out toward them on his way up to the high place.

[15]Now the LORD had told Samuel in his ear the day before Saul came, saying, [16]"Tomorrow about this time I will send you a man from the land of Benjamin, and you shall anoint him commander over My people Israel, that he may save My people from the hand of the Philistines; for I have looked upon My people, because their cry has come to Me."

[17]So when Samuel saw Saul, the LORD said to him, "There he is, the man of whom I spoke to you. This one shall reign over My people." [18]Then Saul drew near to Samuel in the gate, and said, "Please tell me, where *is* the seer's house?"

[19]Samuel answered Saul and said, "I *am* the seer. Go up before me to the high place, for you shall eat with me today; and tomorrow I will let you go and will tell you all that *is* in your heart. [20]But as for your donkeys that were lost three days ago, do not be anxious about them, for they have been found. And on whom *is* all the desire of Israel? *Is it* not on you and on all your father's house?"

[21]And Saul answered and said, "*Am* I not a Benjamite, of the smallest of the tribes of Israel, and my family the least of all the families of the tribe[a] of Benjamin? Why then do you speak like this to me?"

[22]Now Samuel took Saul and his servant and brought them into the hall, and had *them* sit in the place of honor among those who were invited; there *were* about thirty persons. [23]And Samuel said to the cook, "Bring the portion which I gave you, of which I said to you, 'Set it apart.'" [24]So the cook took up the thigh with its upper part and set *it* before Saul. And *Samuel* said, "Here it is, what was kept back. *It* was set apart for you. Eat; for until this time it has been kept for you, since I said I invited the people." So Saul ate with Samuel that day.

[25]When they had come down from the high place into the city, *Samuel* spoke with Saul on the top of the house.[a] [26]They arose early; and it was about the dawning of the day that Samuel called to Saul on the top of the house, saying, "Get up, that I may send you on your way." And Saul arose, and both of them went outside, he and Samuel.

Saul Anointed King

[27]As they were going down to the outskirts of the city, Samuel said to Saul, "Tell the servant to go on ahead of us." And he went on. "But you stand here awhile, that I may announce to you the word of God."

10 Then Samuel took a flask of oil and poured *it* on his head, and kissed him and said: "*Is it* not because the LORD has anointed you commander over His inheritance?[a] [2]When you have departed from me today, you will find two men by Rachel's tomb in the territory of Benjamin at Zelzah; and they will say to you, 'The donkeys which you went to look for have been found. And now your father has ceased caring about the donkeys and is worrying about you, saying, "What shall I do about my son?"' [3]Then you shall go on forward from there and come to the terebinth tree of Tabor. There three men going up to God at Bethel will meet you, one carrying three young goats, another carrying three loaves of bread, and another carrying a skin of wine. [4]And they will greet you and give you two *loaves* of bread, which you shall receive from their hands. [5]After that you shall come to the hill of God where the Philistine garrison *is*. And it will happen, when you have come there to the city, that you will meet a group of prophets coming down from the high place with a stringed instrument, a tambourine, a flute, and a harp before them; and they will be prophesying. [6]Then the Spirit of the LORD will come upon you, and you will prophesy with them and

---

9:21 [a] Literally *tribes* **9:25** [a] Following Masoretic Text and Targum; Septuagint omits *He spoke with Saul on the top of the house;* Septuagint and Vulgate add *And he prepared a bed for Saul on the top of the house, and he slept.* **10:1** [a] Following Masoretic Text, Targum, and Vulgate; Septuagint reads *His people Israel; and you shall rule the people of the Lord;* Septuagint and Vulgate add *And you shall deliver His people from the hands of their enemies all around them. And this shall be a sign to you, that God has anointed you to be a prince.*

be turned into another man. 7And let it be,
when these signs come to you, *that* you do as
the occasion demands; for God *is* with you.
8You shall go down before me to Gilgal; and
surely I will come down to you to offer burnt
offerings *and* make sacrifices of peace offerings. Seven days you shall wait, till I come to
you and show you what you should do."

9So it was, when he had turned his back
to go from Samuel, that God gave him another heart; and all those signs came to pass
that day. 10When they came there to the hill,
there was a group of prophets to meet him;
then the Spirit of God came upon him, and
he prophesied among them. 11And it happened, when all who knew him formerly
saw that he indeed prophesied among the
prophets, that the people said to one another, "What *is* this *that* has come upon the son
of Kish? *Is* Saul also among the prophets?"
12Then a man from there answered and
said, "But who *is* their father?" Therefore
it became a proverb: "*Is* Saul also among
the prophets?" 13And when he had finished
prophesying, he went to the high place.

14Then Saul's uncle said to him and his
servant, "Where did you go?"

So he said, "To look for the donkeys.
When we saw that *they were* nowhere *to be
found,* we went to Samuel."

15And Saul's uncle said, "Tell me, please,
what Samuel said to you."

16So Saul said to his uncle, "He told us
plainly that the donkeys had been found."
But about the matter of the kingdom, he did
not tell him what Samuel had said.

Saul Proclaimed King

17Then Samuel called the people together to the LORD at Mizpah, 18and said to the
children of Israel, "Thus says the LORD God
of Israel: 'I brought up Israel out of Egypt,
and delivered you from the hand of the
Egyptians *and* from the hand of all kingdoms and from those who oppressed you.'
19But you have today rejected your God, who
Himself saved you from all your adversities
and your tribulations; and you have said to
Him, 'No, set a king over us!' Now therefore,
present yourselves before the LORD by your
tribes and by your clans."[a]

20And when Samuel had caused all
the tribes of Israel to come near, the tribe
of Benjamin was chosen. 21When he had
caused the tribe of Benjamin to come near
by their families, the family of Matri was
chosen. And Saul the son of Kish was chosen. But when they sought him, he could not
be found. 22Therefore they inquired of the
LORD further, "Has the man come here yet?"

And the LORD answered, "There he is,
hidden among the equipment."

10:19 [a] Literally *thousands*

Starring Roles

Israel had grown tired of having only God as their King. Since other nations had kings who dressed up and strutted like peacocks and wore crowns on their heads, Israel wanted a king, too. When SAUL looked back, he wished he had never been king of Israel.

Saul's father Kish was a leading citizen, and people said Saul was the tallest and most handsome young man in Israel. They wanted Saul to be their king because they thought he *looked* like a king and because of his good name.

At first everything seemed to go well. Israel won a great battle against the nation of Ammon. Then Samuel the prophet made a fine speech when Saul was crowned king of Israel. Samuel also reminded Israel that they could still be a *happy and prosperous* nation.

Saul realized he should have never let Israel make him a king. There is a lot more to being a leader than looks and family connections.

23So they ran and brought him from
there; and when he stood among the people,
he was taller than any of the people from
his shoulders upward. 24And Samuel said to
all the people, "Do you see him whom the
LORD has chosen, that *there is* no one like
him among all the people?"
So all the people shouted and said, "Long
live the king!"
25Then Samuel explained to the people
the behavior of royalty, and wrote *it* in a book
and laid *it* up before the LORD. And Samuel
sent all the people away, every man to his
house. 26And Saul also went home to Gibeah; and valiant *men* went with him, whose
hearts God had touched. 27But some rebels
said, "How can this man save us?" So they
despised him, and brought him no presents.
But he held his peace.

Saul Saves Jabesh Gilead

11 Then Nahash the Ammonite came
up and encamped against Jabesh
Gilead; and all the men of Jabesh said to Nahash, "Make a covenant with us, and we will
serve you."
2And Nahash the Ammonite answered
them, "On this *condition* I will make *a covenant* with you, that I may put out all your
right eyes, and bring reproach on all Israel."
3Then the elders of Jabesh said to him,
"Hold off for seven days, that we may send
messengers to all the territory of Israel. And
then, if *there is* no one to save us, we will
come out to you."
4So the messengers came to Gibeah of
Saul and told the news in the hearing of the
people. And all the people lifted up their
voices and wept. 5Now there was Saul, coming behind the herd from the field; and Saul
said, "What *troubles* the people, that they
weep?" And they told him the words of the
men of Jabesh. 6Then the Spirit of God came
upon Saul when he heard this news, and his
anger was greatly aroused. 7So he took a yoke
of oxen and cut them in pieces, and sent
them throughout all the territory of Israel by
the hands of messengers, saying, "Whoever
does not go out with Saul and Samuel to battle, so it shall be done to his oxen."
And the fear of the LORD fell on the people, and they came out with one consent.
8When he numbered them in Bezek, the
children of Israel were three hundred thousand, and the men of Judah thirty thousand.
9And they said to the messengers who came,
"Thus you shall say to the men of Jabesh Gilead: 'Tomorrow, by *the time* the sun is hot,
you shall have help.'" Then the messengers
came and reported *it* to the men of Jabesh,
and they were glad. 10Therefore the men of
Jabesh said, "Tomorrow we will come out to
you, and you may do with us whatever seems
good to you."
11So it was, on the next day, that Saul put
the people in three companies; and they
came into the midst of the camp in the
morning watch, and killed Ammonites until the heat of the day. And it happened that
those who survived were scattered, so that
no two of them were left together.
12Then the people said to Samuel, "Who
is he who said, 'Shall Saul reign over us?'
Bring the men, that we may put them to
death."
13But Saul said, "Not a man shall be put to
death this day, for today the LORD has accomplished salvation in Israel."
14Then Samuel said to the people,
"Come, let us go to Gilgal and renew the
kingdom there." 15So all the people went to
Gilgal, and there they made Saul king before
the LORD in Gilgal. There they made sacrifices of peace offerings before the LORD, and
there Saul and all the men of Israel rejoiced
greatly.

Samuel's Address at Saul's Coronation

12 Now Samuel said to all Israel: "Indeed I have heeded your voice in all
that you said to me, and have made a king
over you. 2And now here is the king, walking before you; and I am old and grayheaded, and look, my sons *are* with you. I have
walked before you from my childhood to this
day. 3Here I am. Witness against me before
the LORD and before His anointed: Whose ox
have I taken, or whose donkey have I taken,
or whom have I cheated? Whom have I oppressed, or from whose hand have I received
any bribe with which to blind my eyes? I will
restore *it* to you."
4And they said, "You have not cheated
us or oppressed us, nor have you taken anything from any man's hand."
5Then he said to them, "The LORD *is*
witness against you, and His anointed *is*
witness this day, that you have not found
anything in my hand."

And they answered, "*He is* witness."
[6]Then Samuel said to the people, "*It is*
the LORD who raised up Moses and Aaron,
and who brought your fathers up from the
land of Egypt. [7]Now therefore, stand still,
that I may reason with you before the LORD
concerning all the righteous acts of the
LORD which He did to you and your fathers:
[8]When Jacob had gone into Egypt,[a] and your
fathers cried out to the LORD, then the LORD
sent Moses and Aaron, who brought your fathers out of Egypt and made them dwell in
this place. [9]And when they forgot the LORD
their God, He sold them into the hand of
Sisera, commander of the army of Hazor,
into the hand of the Philistines, and into the
hand of the king of Moab; and they fought
against them. [10]Then they cried out to the
LORD, and said, 'We have sinned, because
we have forsaken the LORD and served the
Baals and Ashtoreths;[a] but now deliver us
from the hand of our enemies, and we will
serve You.' [11]And the LORD sent Jerubbaal,[a]
Bedan,[b] Jephthah, and Samuel,[c] and delivered you out of the hand of your enemies
on every side; and you dwelt in safety. [12]And
when you saw that Nahash king of the Ammonites came against you, you said to me,
'No, but a king shall reign over us,' when the
LORD your God *was* your king.

[13]"Now therefore, here is the king whom
you have chosen *and* whom you have desired. And take note, the LORD has set a king
over you. [14]If you fear the LORD and serve
Him and obey His voice, and do not rebel
against the commandment of the LORD, then
both you and the king who reigns over you
will continue following the LORD your God.
[15]However, if you do not obey the voice of the
LORD, but rebel against the commandment
of the LORD, then the hand of the LORD will
be against you, as *it was* against your fathers.

[16]"Now therefore, stand and see this great
thing which the LORD will do before your
eyes: [17]*Is* today not the wheat harvest? I will
call to the LORD, and He will send thunder
and rain, that you may perceive and see that
your wickedness *is* great, which you have
done in the sight of the LORD, in asking a
king for yourselves."

[18]*So Samuel called to the* LORD, and the
LORD sent thunder and rain that day; and
all the people greatly feared the LORD and
Samuel.

[19]And all the people said to Samuel, "Pray
for your servants to the LORD your God, that
we may not die; for we have added to all our
sins the evil of asking a king for ourselves."

[20]Then Samuel said to the people, "Do
not fear. You have done all this wickedness; yet do not turn aside from following
the LORD, but serve the LORD with all your
heart. [21]And do not turn aside; for *then you
would go* after empty things which cannot
profit or deliver, for they *are* nothing. [22]For
the LORD will not forsake His people, for His
great name's sake, because it has pleased the
LORD to make you His people. [23]Moreover,
as for me, far be it from me that I should sin
against the LORD in ceasing to pray for you;
but I will teach you the good and the right
way. [24]Only fear the LORD, and serve Him in
truth with all your heart; for consider what
great things He has done for you. [25]But if you
still do wickedly, you shall be swept away,
both you and your king."

Saul's Unlawful Sacrifice

13 Saul reigned one year; and when he
had reigned two years over Israel,[a]
[2]Saul chose for himself three thousand *men*
of Israel. Two thousand were with Saul in
Michmash and in the mountains of Bethel,
and a thousand were with Jonathan in Gibeah of Benjamin. The rest of the people he
sent away, every man to his tent.

[3]And Jonathan attacked the garrison of
the Philistines that *was* in Geba, and the Philistines heard *of it*. Then Saul blew the trumpet throughout all the land, saying, "Let
the Hebrews hear!" [4]Now all Israel heard it
said *that* Saul had attacked a garrison of the
Philistines, and *that* Israel had also become
an abomination to the Philistines. And the
people were called together to Saul at Gilgal.

[5]Then the Philistines gathered together
to fight with Israel, thirty[a] thousand chariots and six thousand horsemen, and people as the sand which *is* on the seashore in
multitude. And they came up and encamped
in Michmash, to the east of Beth Aven.
[6]When the men of Israel saw that they were

12:8 [a] Following Masoretic Text, Targum, and Vulgate; Septuagint adds *and the Egyptians afflicted them.*
12:10 [a] Canaanite goddesses **12:11** [a] Syriac reads *Deborah;* Targum reads *Gideon.* [b] Septuagint and Syriac read *Barak;* Targum reads *Simson.* [c] Syriac reads *Simson.*
13:1 [a] The Hebrew is difficult (compare 2 Samuel 5:4; 2 Kings 14:2; see also 2 Samuel 2:10; Acts 13:21). **13:5** [a] Following Masoretic Text, Septuagint, Targum, and Vulgate; Syriac and some manuscripts of the Septuagint read *three.*

in danger (for the people were distressed),
then the people hid in caves, in thickets, in
rocks, in holes, and in pits. 7And *some of* the
Hebrews crossed over the Jordan to the land
of Gad and Gilead.

As for Saul, he *was* still in Gilgal, and all
the people followed him trembling. 8Then he
waited seven days, according to the time set
by Samuel. But Samuel did not come to Gilgal; and the people were scattered from him.
9So Saul said, "Bring a burnt offering and
peace offerings here to me." And he offered
the burnt offering. 10Now it happened, as
soon as he had finished presenting the burnt
offering, that Samuel came; and Saul went
out to meet him, that he might greet him.

11And Samuel said, "What have you
done?"

Saul said, "When I saw that the people
were scattered from me, and *that* you did not
come within the days appointed, and *that* the
Philistines gathered together at Michmash,
12then I said, 'The Philistines will now come
down on me at Gilgal, and I have not made
supplication to the LORD.' Therefore I felt
compelled, and offered a burnt offering."

13And Samuel said to Saul, "You have
done foolishly. You have not kept the commandment of the LORD your God, which He
commanded you. For now the LORD would
have established your kingdom over Israel
forever. 14But now your kingdom shall not
continue. The LORD has sought for Himself
a man after His own heart, and the LORD has
commanded him *to be* commander over His
people, because you have not kept what the
LORD commanded you."

15Then Samuel arose and went up from
Gilgal to Gibeah of Benjamin.[a] And Saul
numbered the people present with him,
about six hundred men.

No Weapons for the Army

16Saul, Jonathan his son, and the people
present with them remained in Gibeah of
Benjamin. But the Philistines encamped
in Michmash. 17Then raiders came out of
the camp of the Philistines in three companies. One company turned onto the road to
Ophrah, to the land of Shual, 18another company turned to the road *to* Beth Horon, and
another company turned *to* the road of the
border that overlooks the Valley of Zeboim
toward the wilderness.

19Now there was no blacksmith to be
found throughout all the land of Israel, for
the Philistines said, "Lest the Hebrews make
swords or spears." 20But all the Israelites
would go down to the Philistines to sharpen
each man's plowshare, his mattock, his ax,
and his sickle; 21and the charge for a sharp-
ening was a pim[a] for the plowshares, the
mattocks, the forks, and the axes, and to set
the points of the goads. 22So it came about,
on the day of battle, that there was neither
sword nor spear found in the hand of any of
the people who *were* with Saul and Jonathan.
But they were found with Saul and Jonathan
his son.

23And the garrison of the Philistines went
out to the pass of Michmash.

Jonathan Defeats the Philistines

14 Now it happened one day that Jonathan the son of Saul said to the
young man who bore his armor, "Come, let
us go over to the Philistines' garrison that
is on the other side." But he did not tell his
father. 2And Saul was sitting in the outskirts
of Gibeah under a pomegranate tree which
is in Migron. The people who *were* with him
were about six hundred men. 3Ahijah the
son of Ahitub, Ichabod's brother, the son of
Phinehas, the son of Eli, the LORD's priest
in Shiloh, was wearing an ephod. But the
people did not know that Jonathan had gone.

4Between the passes, by which Jonathan
sought to go over to the Philistines' garrison, *there was* a sharp rock on one side and a
sharp rock on the other side. And the name
of one *was* Bozez, and the name of the other
Seneh. 5The front of one faced northward
opposite Michmash, and the other southward opposite Gibeah.

6Then Jonathan said to the young man
who bore his armor, "Come, let us go over
to the garrison of these uncircumcised; it
may be that the LORD will work for us. For
nothing restrains the LORD from saving by
many or by few."

7So his armorbearer said to him, "Do all
that is in your heart. Go then; here I am with
you, according to your heart."

8Then Jonathan said, "Very well, let us
cross over to *these* men, and we will show

13:15 [a] Following Masoretic Text and Targum; Septuagint and Vulgate add *And the rest of the people went up after Saul to meet the people who fought against them, going from Gilgal to Gibeah in the hill of Benjamin.* 13:21 [a] About two-thirds shekel weight

ourselves to them. 9If they say thus to us,
'Wait until we come to you,' then we will
stand still in our place and not go up to
them. 10But if they say thus, 'Come up to us,'
then we will go up. For the LORD has delivered them into our hand, and this *will be* a
sign to us."
11So both of them showed themselves
to the garrison of the Philistines. And the
Philistines said, "Look, the Hebrews are
coming out of the holes where they have
hidden." 12Then the men of the garrison
called to Jonathan and his armorbearer, and
said, "Come up to us, and we will show you
something."

Jonathan said to his armorbearer, "Come
up after me, for the LORD has delivered them
into the hand of Israel." 13And Jonathan
climbed up on his hands and knees with his
armorbearer after him; and they fell before
Jonathan. And as he came after him, his armorbearer killed them. 14That first slaughter
which Jonathan and his armorbearer made
was about twenty men within about half an
acre of land.[a]

15And there was trembling in the camp,
in the field, and among all the people. The
garrison and the raiders also trembled; and
the earth quaked, so that it was a very great
trembling. 16Now the watchmen of Saul in
Gibeah of Benjamin looked, and *there* was
the multitude, melting away; and they went
here and there. 17Then Saul said to the people
who *were* with him, "Now call the roll and see
who has gone from us." And when they had
called the roll, surprisingly, Jonathan and
his armorbearer *were* not *there*. 18And Saul
said to Ahijah, "Bring the ark[a] of God here"
(for at that time the ark[b] of God was with the
children of Israel). 19Now it happened, while
Saul talked to the priest, that the noise which
was in the camp of the Philistines continued
to increase; so Saul said to the priest, "Withdraw your hand." 20Then Saul and all the
people who *were* with him assembled, and
they went to the battle; and indeed every
man's sword was against his neighbor, *and
there was* very great confusion. 21Moreover
the Hebrews *who* were with the Philistines
before that time, who went up with them
into the camp *from the* surrounding *country*, they also joined the Israelites who *were*
with Saul and Jonathan. 22Likewise all the
men of Israel who had hidden in the mountains of Ephraim, *when* they heard that the
Philistines fled, they also followed hard after
them in the battle. 23So the LORD saved Israel
that day, and the battle shifted to Beth Aven.

Saul's Rash Oath

24And the men of Israel were distressed
that day, for Saul had placed the people under oath, saying, "Cursed *is* the man who
eats *any* food until evening, before I have
taken vengeance on my enemies." So none
of the people tasted food. 25Now all *the people*
of the land came to a forest; and there was
honey on the ground. 26And when the people
had come into the woods, there was the honey, dripping; but no one put his hand to his
mouth, for the people feared the oath. 27But
Jonathan had not heard his father charge the
people with the oath; therefore he stretched
out the end of the rod that *was* in his hand
and dipped it in a honeycomb, and put his
hand to his mouth; and his countenance
brightened. 28Then one of the people said,
"Your father strictly charged the people with
an oath, saying, 'Cursed *is* the man who eats
food this day.'" And the people were faint.
29But Jonathan said, "My father has
troubled the land. Look now, how my countenance has brightened because I tasted a
little of this honey. 30How much better if the
people had eaten freely today of the spoil of
their enemies which they found! For now
would there not have been a much greater
slaughter among the Philistines?"
31Now they had driven back the Philistines that day from Michmash to Aijalon. So
the people were very faint. 32And the people
rushed on the spoil, and took sheep, oxen,
and calves, and slaughtered *them* on the
ground; and the people ate *them* with the
blood. 33Then they told Saul, saying, "Look,
the people are sinning against the LORD by
eating with the blood!"

So he said, "You have dealt treacherously;
roll a large stone to me this day." 34Then Saul
said, "Disperse yourselves among the people, and say to them, 'Bring me here every
man's ox and every man's sheep, slaughter
them here, and eat; and do not sin against
the LORD by eating with the blood.'" So every
one of the people brought his ox with him
that night, and slaughtered *it* there. 35Then

14:14 [a] Literally *half the area plowed by a yoke* (of oxen in a day) **14:18** [a] Following Masoretic Text, Targum, and Vulgate; Septuagint reads *ephod*. [b] Following Masoretic Text, Targum, and Vulgate; Septuagint reads *ephod*.

Saul built an altar to the LORD. This was the first altar that he built to the LORD.

36 Now Saul said, "Let us go down after the Philistines by night, and plunder them until the morning light; and let us not leave a man of them."

And they said, "Do whatever seems good to you."

Then the priest said, "Let us draw near to God here."

37 So Saul asked counsel of God, "Shall I go down after the Philistines? Will You deliver them into the hand of Israel?" But He did not answer him that day. 38 And Saul said, "Come over here, all you chiefs of the people, and know and see what this sin was today. 39 For *as* the LORD lives, who saves Israel, though it be in Jonathan my son, he shall surely die." But not a man among all the people answered him. 40 Then he said to all Israel, "You be on one side, and my son Jonathan and I will be on the other side."

And the people said to Saul, "Do what seems good to you."

41 Therefore Saul said to the LORD God of Israel, "Give a perfect *lot*."[a] So Saul and Jonathan were taken, but the people escaped. 42 And Saul said, "Cast *lots* between my son Jonathan and me." So Jonathan was taken. 43 Then Saul said to Jonathan, "Tell me what you have done."

And Jonathan told him, and said, "I only tasted a little honey with the end of the rod that *was* in my hand. So now I must die!"

44 Saul answered, "God do so and more also; for you shall surely die, Jonathan."

45 But the people said to Saul, "Shall Jonathan die, who has accomplished this great deliverance in Israel? Certainly not! *As* the LORD lives, not one hair of his head shall fall to the ground, for he has worked with God this day." So the people rescued Jonathan, and he did not die.

46 Then Saul returned from pursuing the Philistines, and the Philistines went to their own place.

Saul's Continuing Wars

47 So Saul established his sovereignty over Israel, and fought against all his enemies on every side, against Moab, against the people of Ammon, against Edom, against the kings of Zobah, and against the Philistines. Wherever he turned, he harassed *them*.[a] 48 And he gathered an army and attacked the Amalekites, and delivered Israel from the hands of those who plundered them.

49 The sons of Saul were Jonathan, Jishui,[a] and Malchishua. And the names of his two daughters *were these:* the name of the firstborn Merab, and the name of the younger Michal. 50 The name of Saul's wife *was* Ahinoam the daughter of Ahimaaz. And the name of the commander of his army *was* Abner the son of Ner, Saul's uncle. 51 Kish *was* the father of Saul, and Ner the father of Abner *was* the son of Abiel.

52 Now there was fierce war with the Philistines all the days of Saul. And when Saul saw any strong man or any valiant man, he took him for himself.

Saul Spares King Agag

15 Samuel also said to Saul, "The LORD sent me to anoint you king over His people, over Israel. Now therefore, heed the voice of the words of the LORD. 2 Thus says the LORD of hosts: 'I will punish Amalek *for* what he did to Israel, how he ambushed him on the way when he came up from Egypt. 3 Now go and attack Amalek, and utterly destroy all that they have, and do not spare them. But kill both man and woman, infant and nursing child, ox and sheep, camel and donkey.'"

4 So Saul gathered the people together and numbered them in Telaim, two hundred thousand foot soldiers and ten thousand men of Judah. 5 And Saul came to a city of Amalek, and lay in wait in the valley.

6 Then Saul said to the Kenites, "Go, depart, get down from among the Amalekites, lest I destroy you with them. For you showed kindness to all the children of Israel when they came up out of Egypt." So the Kenites departed from among the Amalekites. 7 And Saul attacked the Amalekites, from Havilah all the way to Shur, which is east of Egypt. 8 He also took Agag king of the Amalekites alive, and utterly destroyed all the people with the edge of the sword. 9 But Saul and the people spared Agag and the best of the sheep, the oxen, the fatlings, the lambs, and all *that was* good, and were unwilling

---

14:41 [a] Following Masoretic Text and Targum; Septuagint and Vulgate read *Why do You not answer Your servant today? If the injustice is with me or Jonathan my son, O LORD God of Israel, give proof; and if You say it is with Your people Israel, give holiness.* **14:47** [a] Septuagint and Vulgate read *prospered.* **14:49** [a] Called *Abinadab* in 1 Chronicles 8:33 and 9:39

to utterly destroy them. But everything
despised and worthless, that they utterly
destroyed.

Saul Rejected as King

10 Now the word of the LORD came to Samuel, saying, 11 "I greatly regret that I have set
up Saul *as* king, for he has turned back from
following Me, and has not performed My
commandments." And it grieved Samuel,
and he cried out to the LORD all night. 12 So
when Samuel rose early in the morning to
meet Saul, it was told Samuel, saying, "Saul
went to Carmel, and indeed, he set up a
monument for himself; and he has gone on
around, passed by, and gone down to Gilgal."
13 Then Samuel went to Saul, and Saul said
to him, "Blessed *are* you of the LORD! I have
performed the commandment of the LORD."

14 But Samuel said, "What then *is* this
bleating of the sheep in my ears, and the
lowing of the oxen which I hear?"

15 And Saul said, "They have brought
them from the Amalekites; for the people
spared the best of the sheep and the oxen, to
sacrifice to the LORD your God; and the rest
we have utterly destroyed."

16 Then Samuel said to Saul, "Be quiet!
And I will tell you what the LORD said to me
last night."

And he said to him, "Speak on."

17 So Samuel said, "When you *were* little
in your own eyes, *were* you not head of the
tribes of Israel? And did not the LORD anoint
you king over Israel? 18 Now the LORD sent
you on a mission, and said, 'Go, and utterly destroy the sinners, the Amalekites, and
fight against them until they are consumed.'
19 Why then did you not obey the voice of the
LORD? Why did you swoop down on the
spoil, and do evil in the sight of the LORD?"

20 And Saul said to Samuel, "But I have
obeyed the voice of the LORD, and gone on
the mission on which the LORD sent me, and
brought back Agag king of Amalek; I have
utterly destroyed the Amalekites. 21 But the
people took of the plunder, sheep and oxen,
the best of the things which should have
been utterly destroyed, to sacrifice to the
LORD your God in Gilgal."

22 So Samuel said:

"Has the LORD *as great* delight in burnt
offerings and sacrifices,
As in obeying the voice of the LORD?
Behold, to obey is better than sacrifice,
And to heed than the fat of rams.
23 For rebellion *is as* the sin of witchcraft,

In Focus

15:23 Idolatry Pronounced *eye-DOLL-uh-tree.* The worship of idols and false gods. Unless you serve God, you will serve something or someone less than God.

Action!

REBELLION

READ IT: 1 SAMUEL 15:22–24

This is a difficult passage to interpret. Transgression (breaking the rules) comes when we think we have a better plan than God's rules. Deviation (leaving the path God set) comes from following false gods like money and power. Rebellion comes from demanding our own way all the time.

Saul wanted nothing more than to be king, but because he rebelled against God, God essentially rebelled against Saul.

And stubbornness *is as* iniquity and
idolatry.
Because you have rejected the word of
the LORD,
He also has rejected you from *being*
king."

24Then Saul said to Samuel, "I have
sinned, for I have transgressed the commandment of the LORD and your words, because I feared the people and obeyed their
voice. 25Now therefore, please pardon my sin,
and return with me, that I may worship the
LORD."

26But Samuel said to Saul, "I will not return with you, for you have rejected the word
of the LORD, and the LORD has rejected you
from being king over Israel."

27And as Samuel turned around to go
away, *Saul* seized the edge of his robe, and it
tore. 28So Samuel said to him, "The LORD has
torn the kingdom of Israel from you today,
and has given it to a neighbor of yours, *who
is* better than you. 29And also the Strength of
Israel will not lie nor relent. For He *is* not a
man, that He should relent."

30Then he said, "I have sinned; *yet* hon-
or me now, please, before the elders of my
people and before Israel, and return with
me, that I may worship the LORD your God."
31So Samuel turned back after Saul, and Saul
worshiped the LORD.

32Then Samuel said, "Bring Agag king of
the Amalekites here to me." So Agag came
to him cautiously.

And Agag said, "Surely the bitterness of
death is past."

33But Samuel said, "As your sword has
made women childless, so shall your mother be childless among women." And Samuel hacked Agag in pieces before the LORD
in Gilgal.

34Then Samuel went to Ramah, and
Saul went up to his house at Gibeah of Saul.
35And Samuel went no more to see Saul until the day of his death. Nevertheless Samuel
mourned for Saul, and the LORD regretted
that He had made Saul king over Israel.

David Anointed King

16 Now the LORD said to Samuel,
"How long will you mourn for Saul,
seeing I have rejected him from reigning
over Israel? Fill your horn with oil, and go;
I am sending you to Jesse the Bethlehemite.
For I have provided Myself a king among his
sons."

2And Samuel said, "How can I go? If Saul
hears *it*, he will kill me."

But the LORD said, "Take a heifer with
you, and say, 'I have come to sacrifice to the
LORD.' 3Then invite Jesse to the sacrifice,
and I will show you what you shall do; you
shall anoint for Me the one I name to you."

4So Samuel did what the LORD said, and
went to Bethlehem. And the elders of the

DAVID was very happy as a shepherd, but one day the prophet Samuel went to David's family home and called David out of the fields from tending his sheep. Next thing David knew, Samuel had poured oil on David's head and said he was going to be king of Israel. It was the custom to pour holy oil on a new priest or king in those times. Right away the Spirit of God filled David, and he knew he would really be king one day.

But David was always sad for King Saul. Saul seemed to fail at everything he tried, while everything David did turned out well. Because David killed the Philistine giant Goliath with just a sling, he became a national hero overnight.

One day poor Saul killed himself when he was losing a battle with the Philistines. So David wrote a song about him and Jonathan, Saul's son. (See 2 Samuel 1:19–27.)

town trembled at his coming, and said, "Do
you come peaceably?"
5And he said, "Peaceably; I have come to
sacrifice to the LORD. Sanctify yourselves,
and come with me to the sacrifice." Then he
consecrated Jesse and his sons, and invited
them to the sacrifice.
6So it was, when they came, that he
looked at Eliab and said, "Surely the LORD's
anointed *is* before Him!"
7But the LORD said to Samuel, "Do not
look at his appearance or at his physical
stature, because I have refused him. For
the LORD does not *see* as man sees;[a] for man
looks at the outward appearance, but the
LORD looks at the heart."
8So Jesse called Abinadab, and made him
pass before Samuel. And he said, "Neither
has the LORD chosen this one." 9Then Jesse
made Shammah pass by. And he said, "Neither has the LORD chosen this one." 10Thus
Jesse made seven of his sons pass before
Samuel. And Samuel said to Jesse, "The
LORD has not chosen these." 11And Samuel
said to Jesse, "Are all the young men here?"
Then he said, "There remains yet the youngest, and there he is, keeping the sheep."
And Samuel said to Jesse, "Send and
bring him. For we will not sit down[a] till he
comes here." 12So he sent and brought him
in. Now he *was* ruddy, with bright eyes, and
good-looking. And the LORD said, "Arise,
anoint him; for this *is* the one!" 13Then Samuel took the horn of oil and anointed him
in the midst of his brothers; and the Spirit of the LORD came upon David from that
day forward. So Samuel arose and went to
Ramah.

A Distressing Spirit Troubles Saul

14But the Spirit of the LORD departed from
Saul, and a distressing spirit from the LORD
troubled him. 15And Saul's servants said to
him, "Surely, a distressing spirit from God
is troubling you. 16Let our master now command your servants, *who are* before you, to
seek out a man *who is* a skillful player on the
harp. And it shall be that he will play it with
his hand when the distressing spirit from
God is upon you, and you shall be well."
17So Saul said to his servants, "Provide
me now a man who can play well, and bring
him to me."
18Then one of the servants answered and
said, "Look, I have seen a son of Jesse the
Bethlehemite, *who is* skillful in playing, a
mighty man of valor, a man of war, prudent
in speech, and a handsome person; and the
LORD *is* with him."
19Therefore Saul sent messengers to Jesse, and said, "Send me your son David, who
is with the sheep." 20And Jesse took a donkey *loaded with* bread, a skin of wine, and a

16:7 [a] Septuagint reads *For God does not see as man sees;* Targum reads *It is not by the appearance of a man;* Vulgate reads *Nor do I judge according to the looks of a man.*
16:11 [a] Following Septuagint and Vulgate; Masoretic Text reads *turn around;* Targum and Syriac read *turn away.*

IDOL AND HERO WORSHIP

READ IT: 1 SAMUEL 16:7

David was a young teenager who had lots of brothers. When his family received a surprise visit from a prophet of God to pick out the next king, they were shocked that David was chosen. The biggest shock of all was that God didn't choose one of David's older and stronger brothers. God chose the smallest, youngest, and weakest brother to represent Him. God valued David's character rather than what he looked like. In God's eyes, looks don't matter as much as what's inside a person's heart. Keep that in mind when you idolize someone.

young goat, and sent *them* by his son David
to Saul. 21So David came to Saul and stood
before him. And he loved him greatly, and he
became his armorbearer. 22Then Saul sent
to Jesse, saying, "Please let David stand before me, for he has found favor in my sight."
23And so it was, whenever the spirit from
God was upon Saul, that David would take
a harp and play *it* with his hand. Then Saul
would become refreshed and well, and the
distressing spirit would depart from him.

David and Goliath

17 Now the Philistines gathered their
armies together to battle, and were
gathered at Sochoh, which *belongs* to Judah;
they encamped between Sochoh and Azekah,
in Ephes Dammim. 2And Saul and the men
of Israel were gathered together, and they encamped in the Valley of Elah, and drew up
in battle array against the Philistines. 3The
Philistines stood on a mountain on one side,
and Israel stood on a mountain on the other
side, with a valley between them.

4And a champion went out from the
camp of the Philistines, named Goliath,
from Gath, whose height *was* six cubits and
a span. 5*He had* a bronze helmet on his head,
and he *was* armed with a coat of mail, and
the weight of the coat *was* five thousand

DAVID FACES GOLIATH

READ IT: 1 SAMUEL 17:1–50

GET IT:

Israel had their king—King Saul. But their problems didn't stop. They had an ongoing war with the Philistines. The army was on full alert, ready to do battle, but they didn't dare attack. The Philistines had a secret weapon—a nine-foot giant, Goliath, who terrorized everyone with threats, twice a day for over a month. Goliath wanted one man to take him on. Nobody in the army wanted to do that. Then David, a young boy who took care of his father's sheep, came to the battlefield to bring his older brothers some food. He heard what Goliath said against God and decided to take Goliath down himself. David knew God had trained him to defend himself. He knew God would do it again against this giant. David relied on God for his courage and skill to do what trained warriors were afraid to do—take out Goliath.

LIVE IT:

Almost everyone knows the story of David and Goliath. News reporters will use "David vs. Goliath" in headlines or lead-ins to a news story to tell about a small community college football team winning over a university team, or a small business winning a legal battle against a huge corporation. When they talk that way, this is the story they are talking about. But there's a more important lesson here. It's that God can use people whom others dismiss as young, inexperienced, naive, small, weak, or whatever to do the impossible. The person succeeds because God is working in and through him or her. You can do great things—you can take on a huge problem or challenge if you let God work through you.

shekels of bronze. 6And *he had* bronze armor
on his legs and a bronze javelin between his
shoulders. 7Now the staff of his spear *was*
like a weaver's beam, and his iron spearhead
weighed six hundred shekels; and a shield-
bearer went before him. 8Then he stood and
cried out to the armies of Israel, and said to
them, "Why have you come out to line up for
battle? *Am* I not a Philistine, and you the servants of Saul? Choose a man for yourselves,
and let him come down to me. 9If he is able
to fight with me and kill me, then we will be
your servants. But if I prevail against him
and kill him, then you shall be our servants
and serve us." 10And the Philistine said, "I
defy the armies of Israel this day; give me
a man, that we may fight together." 11When
Saul and all Israel heard these words of the
Philistine, they were dismayed and greatly
afraid.

12Now David *was* the son of that Eph-
rathite of Bethlehem Judah, whose name
was Jesse, and who had eight sons. And the
man was old, advanced *in years,* in the days
of Saul. 13The three oldest sons of Jesse had
gone to follow Saul to the battle. The names
of his three sons who went to the battle
were Eliab the firstborn, next to him Abinadab, and the third Shammah. 14David *was*
the youngest. And the three oldest followed
Saul. 15But David occasionally went and returned from Saul to feed his father's sheep
at Bethlehem.

16And the Philistine drew near and presented himself forty days, morning and
evening.

17Then Jesse said to his son David, "Take
now for your brothers an ephah of this dried
grain and these ten loaves, and run to your
brothers at the camp. 18And carry these ten
cheeses to the captain of *their* thousand, and
see how your brothers fare, and bring back
news of them." 19Now Saul and they and all
the men of Israel *were* in the Valley of Elah,
fighting with the Philistines.

20So David rose early in the morning, left
the sheep with a keeper, and took *the things*
and went as Jesse had commanded him.
And he came to the camp as the army was
going out to the fight and shouting for the
battle. 21For Israel and the Philistines had
drawn up in battle array, army against army.
22And David left his supplies in the hand of
the supply keeper, ran to the army, and came
and greeted his brothers. 23Then as he talked
with them, there was the champion, the Philistine of Gath, Goliath by name, coming up
from the armies of the Philistines; and he
spoke according to the same words. So David
heard *them.* 24And all the men of Israel, when
they saw the man, fled from him and were
dreadfully afraid. 25So the men of Israel said,
"Have you seen this man who has come up?
Surely he has come up to defy Israel; and it
shall be *that* the man who kills him the king
will enrich with great riches, will give him
his daughter, and give his father's house ex-
emption *from taxes* in Israel."

26Then David spoke to the men who
stood by him, saying, "What shall be done
for the man who kills this Philistine and
takes away the reproach from Israel? For
who *is* this uncircumcised Philistine, that he
should defy the armies of the living God?"

27And the people answered him in this
manner, saying, "So shall it be done for the
man who kills him."

28Now Eliab his oldest brother heard
when he spoke to the men; and Eliab's anger was aroused against David, and he said,
"Why did you come down here? And with
whom have you left those few sheep in the
wilderness? I know your pride and the insolence of your heart, for you have come down
to see the battle."

29And David said, "What have I done
now? *Is there* not a cause?" 30Then he turned
from him toward another and said the same
thing; and these people answered him as the
first ones *did.*

31Now when the words which David
spoke were heard, they reported *them* to
Saul; and he sent for him. 32Then David said
to Saul, "Let no man's heart fail because of
him; your servant will go and fight with this
Philistine."

33And Saul said to David, "You are not
able to go against this Philistine to fight with
him; for you *are* a youth, and he a man of war
from his youth."

34But David said to Saul, "Your servant
used to keep his father's sheep, and when a
lion or a bear came and took a lamb out of
the flock, 35I went out after it and struck it,
and delivered *the lamb* from its mouth; and
when it arose against me, I caught *it* by its
beard, and struck and killed it. 36Your servant has killed both lion and bear; and this
uncircumcised Philistine will be like one

of them, seeing he has defied the armies of
the living God." 37Moreover David said, "The
LORD, who delivered me from the paw of the
lion and from the paw of the bear, He will
deliver me from the hand of this Philistine."

And Saul said to David, "Go, and the
LORD be with you!"

38So Saul clothed David with his armor,
and he put a bronze helmet on his head; he
also clothed him with a coat of mail. 39David
fastened his sword to his armor and tried to
walk, for he had not tested *them*. And David
said to Saul, "I cannot walk with these, for I
have not tested *them*." So David took them off.

40Then he took his staff in his hand; and
he chose for himself five smooth stones
from the brook, and put them in a shepherd's bag, in a pouch which he had, and his
sling was in his hand. And he drew near to
the Philistine. 41So the Philistine came, and
began drawing near to David, and the man
who bore the shield *went* before him. 42And
when the Philistine looked about and saw
David, he disdained him; for he was *only* a
youth, ruddy and good-looking. 43So the Philistine said to David, "*Am* I a dog, that you
come to me with sticks?" And the Philistine
cursed David by his gods. 44And the Philistine said to David, "Come to me, and I will
give your flesh to the birds of the air and the
beasts of the field!"

45Then David said to the Philistine, "You
come to me with a sword, with a spear, and
with a javelin. But I come to you in the name
of the LORD of hosts, the God of the armies
of Israel, whom you have defied. 46This day
the LORD will deliver you into my hand, and
I will strike you and take your head from
you. And this day I will give the carcasses
of the camp of the Philistines to the birds
of the air and the wild beasts of the earth,
that all the earth may know that there is a
God in Israel. 47Then all this assembly shall
know that the LORD does not save with sword
and spear; for the battle *is* the LORD's, and
He will give you into our hands."

48So it was, when the Philistine arose and
came and drew near to meet David, that David hurried and ran toward the army to meet
the Philistine. 49Then David put his hand in
his bag and took out a stone; and he slung
it and struck the Philistine in his forehead,
so that the stone sank into his forehead, and
he fell on his face to the earth. 50So David
prevailed over the Philistine with a sling and
a stone, and struck the Philistine and killed
him. But *there was* no sword in the hand of
David. 51Therefore David ran and stood over
the Philistine, took his sword and drew it out
of its sheath and killed him, and cut off his
head with it.

And when the Philistines saw that their
champion was dead, they fled. 52Now the
men of Israel and Judah arose and shouted,
and pursued the Philistines as far as the
entrance of the valley[a] and to the gates of
Ekron. And the wounded of the Philistines

17:52 [a] Following Masoretic Text, Syriac, Targum, and Vulgate; Septuagint reads *Gath*.

BULLYING

READ IT: 1 SAMUEL 17:43, 44

Goliath taunted and bullied the Israelite army, not just with his size and strength, but also with his words. He did the same thing to David, a young shepherd who wasn't too afraid to challenge the giant. Goliath bullied because he was overconfident and cocky. In the end, all that confidence and cockiness was destroyed by one brave boy who trusted God. Don't go after bullies with a slingshot. But do ask God for patience and strength and wisdom when dealing with them.

fell along the road to Shaaraim, even as far as
Gath and Ekron. 53 Then the children of Israel
returned from chasing the Philistines, and
they plundered their tents. 54 And David took
the head of the Philistine and brought it to
Jerusalem, but he put his armor in his tent.

55 When Saul saw David going out against
the Philistine, he said to Abner, the commander of the army, "Abner, whose son *is*
this youth?"

And Abner said, "As your soul lives, O king, I do not know."

56 So the king said, "Inquire whose son
this young man *is*."

57 Then, as David returned from the
slaughter of the Philistine, Abner took him
and brought him before Saul with the head
of the Philistine in his hand. 58 And Saul said
to him, "Whose son *are* you, young man?"

So David answered, "*I am* the son of your servant Jesse the Bethlehemite."

Saul Resents David

18 Now when he had finished speaking to Saul, the soul of Jonathan
was knit to the soul of David, and Jonathan
loved him as his own soul. 2 Saul took him
that day, and would not let him go home to
his father's house anymore. 3 Then Jonathan
and David made a covenant, because he
loved him as his own soul. 4 And Jonathan
took off the robe that *was* on him and gave it
to David, with his armor, even to his sword
and his bow and his belt.

5 So David went out wherever Saul sent
him, *and* behaved wisely. And Saul set him
over the men of war, and he was accepted
in the sight of all the people and also in the
sight of Saul's servants. 6 Now it had happened as they were coming *home,* when David was returning from the slaughter of the
Philistine, that the women had come out of
all the cities of Israel, singing and dancing,
to meet King Saul, with tambourines, with
joy, and with musical instruments. 7 So the
women sang as they danced, and said:

"Saul has slain his thousands,
And David his ten thousands."

8 Then Saul was very angry, and the saying
displeased him; and he said, "They have
ascribed to David ten thousands, and to me
they have ascribed *only* thousands. Now
what more can he have but the kingdom?"
9 So Saul eyed David from that day forward.

10 And it happened on the next day that
the distressing spirit from God came upon
Saul, and he prophesied inside the house. So
David played *music* with his hand, as at other
times; but *there was* a spear in Saul's hand.
11 And Saul cast the spear, for he said, "I will
pin David to the wall!" But David escaped his
presence twice.

12 Now Saul was afraid of David, because
the LORD was with him, but had departed
from Saul. 13 Therefore Saul removed him
from his presence, and made him his captain over a thousand; and he went out and
came in before the people. 14 And David behaved wisely in all his ways, and the LORD

IDOL AND HERO WORSHIP

READ IT: 1 SAMUEL 18:5–9

When King Saul met David for the first time, he didn't feel threatened by him at all. King Saul just saw a little shepherd boy. But when David killed Goliath, everything changed. David became famous. The people cheered David. They loved having a strong, brave hero who won battles and returned in victory. But being a hero created problems for David. *David fought in order to honor God.* Saul wanted the battles to bring honor to *him* as the king, not to David. Saul's anger and jealousy made David's life very difficult.

was with him. 15Therefore, when Saul saw
that he behaved very wisely, he was afraid
of him. 16But all Israel and Judah loved David, because he went out and came in before
them.

David Marries Michal

17Then Saul said to David, "Here is my
older daughter Merab; I will give her to you
as a wife. Only be valiant for me, and fight
the LORD's battles." For Saul thought, "Let
my hand not be against him, but let the hand
of the Philistines be against him."

18So David said to Saul, "Who *am* I, and
what *is* my life *or* my father's family in Israel, that I should be son-in-law to the king?"
19But it happened at the time when Merab,
Saul's daughter, should have been given to
David, that she was given to Adriel the Meholathite as a wife.

20Now Michal, Saul's daughter, loved
David. And they told Saul, and the thing
pleased him. 21So Saul said, "I will give her
to him, that she may be a snare to him,
and that the hand of the Philistines may be
against him." Therefore Saul said to David
a second time, "You shall be my son-in-law
today."

22And Saul commanded his servants,
"Communicate with David secretly, and say,
'Look, the king has delight in you, and all his
servants love you. Now therefore, become
the king's son-in-law.'"

23So Saul's servants spoke those words in
the hearing of David. And David said, "Does
it seem to you *a* light *thing* to be a king's
son-in-law, seeing I *am* a poor and lightly
esteemed man?" 24And the servants of Saul
told him, saying, "In this manner David
spoke."

25Then Saul said, "Thus you shall say to
David: 'The king does not desire any dowry
but one hundred foreskins of the Philistines,
to take vengeance on the king's enemies.'"
But Saul thought to make David fall by the
hand of the Philistines. 26So when his servants told David these words, it pleased
David well to become the king's son-in-law.
Now the days had not expired; 27therefore
David arose and went, he and his men, and
killed two hundred men of the Philistines.
And David brought their foreskins, and they
gave them in full count to the king, that he
might become the king's son-in-law. Then
Saul gave him Michal his daughter as a wife.

28Thus Saul saw and knew that the LORD
was with David, and *that* Michal, Saul's
daughter, loved him; 29and Saul was still
more afraid of David. So Saul became David's enemy continually. 30Then the princes
of the Philistines went out *to war*. And so
it was, whenever they went out, *that* David
behaved more wisely than all the servants
of Saul, so that his name became highly
esteemed.

Saul Persecutes David

19 Now Saul spoke to Jonathan his
son and to all his servants, that they
should kill David; but Jonathan, Saul's son,
delighted greatly in David. 2So Jonathan told
David, saying, "My father Saul seeks to kill
you. Therefore please be on your guard until morning, and stay in a secret *place* and

SUCCESS

READ IT: 1 SAMUEL 18:14

Whatever God wants to happen is going to happen. If we ask to be part of His plan and accept that, we will have success. You might say, "I want to fly," and then take a leap off the roof. But it's almost certainly not part of God's plan, and you're not going to experience success! Ask God if you can be His servant, and you will not lose.

hide. 3And I will go out and stand beside my
father in the field where you *are,* and I will
speak with my father about you. Then what
I observe, I will tell you."

4Thus Jonathan spoke well of David to
Saul his father, and said to him, "Let not the
king sin against his servant, against David,
because he has not sinned against you, and
because his works *have been* very good toward you. 5For he took his life in his hands
and killed the Philistine, and the LORD
brought about a great deliverance for all Israel. You saw *it* and rejoiced. Why then will
you sin against innocent blood, to kill David
without a cause?"

6So Saul heeded the voice of Jonathan,
and Saul swore, "*As* the LORD lives, he shall
not be killed." 7Then Jonathan called David,
and Jonathan told him all these things. So
Jonathan brought David to Saul, and he was
in his presence as in times past.

8And there was war again; and David
went out and fought with the Philistines,
and struck them with a mighty blow, and
they fled from him.

9Now the distressing spirit from the
LORD came upon Saul as he sat in his house
with his spear in his hand. And David was
playing *music* with *his* hand. 10Then Saul
sought to pin David to the wall with the
spear, but he slipped away from Saul's presence; and he drove the spear into the wall. So
David fled and escaped that night.

11Saul also sent messengers to David's
house to watch him and to kill him in the
morning. And Michal, David's wife, told
him, saying, "If you do not save your life tonight, tomorrow you will be killed." 12So Michal let David down through a window. And
he went and fled and escaped. 13And Michal
took an image and laid *it* in the bed, put a
cover of goats' *hair* for his head, and covered
it with clothes. 14So when Saul sent messengers to take David, she said, "He *is* sick."

15Then Saul sent the messengers *back* to
see David, saying, "Bring him up to me in
the bed, that I may kill him." 16And when the
messengers had come in, there was the image in the bed, with a cover of goats' *hair* for
his head. 17Then Saul said to Michal, "Why
have you deceived me like this, and sent my
enemy away, so that he has escaped?"

And Michal answered Saul, "He said to
me, 'Let me go! Why should I kill you?'"

18So David fled and escaped, and went
to Samuel at Ramah, and told him all that
Saul had done to him. And he and Samuel
went and stayed in Naioth. 19Now it was told
Saul, saying, "Take note, David *is* at Naioth
in Ramah!" 20Then Saul sent messengers to
take David. And when they saw the group of
prophets prophesying, and Samuel standing
as leader over them, the Spirit of God came
upon the messengers of Saul, and they also
prophesied. 21And when Saul was told, he
sent other messengers, and they prophesied
likewise. Then Saul sent messengers again
the third time, and they prophesied also.
22Then he also went to Ramah, and came to
the great well that *is* at Sechu. So he asked,
and said, "Where *are* Samuel and David?"

And *someone* said, "Indeed *they are* at
Naioth in Ramah." 23So he went there to
Naioth in Ramah. Then the Spirit of God
was upon him also, and he went on and
prophesied until he came to Naioth in Ramah. 24And he also stripped off his clothes
and prophesied before Samuel in like manner, and lay down naked all that day and all
that night. Therefore they say, "*Is* Saul also
among the prophets?"[a]

Jonathan's Loyalty to David

20 Then David fled from Naioth in
Ramah, and went and said to Jonathan, "What have I done? What *is* my iniquity, and what *is* my sin before your father, that
he seeks my life?"

2So Jonathan said to him, "By no means!
You shall not die! Indeed, my father will do
nothing either great or small without first
telling me. And why should my father hide
this thing from me? It *is* not *so!*"

3Then David took an oath again, and
said, "Your father certainly knows that I
have found favor in your eyes, and he has
said, 'Do not let Jonathan know this, lest he
be grieved.' But truly, *as* the LORD lives and
as your soul lives, *there is* but a step between
me and death."

4So Jonathan said to David, "Whatever
you yourself desire, I will do *it* for you."

5And David said to Jonathan, "Indeed tomorrow *is* the New Moon, and I should not
fail to sit with the king to eat. But let me go,
that I may hide in the field until the third

19:24 [a] Compare 1 Samuel 10:12

day at evening. 6If your father misses me at
all, then say, 'David earnestly asked *permis-*
sion of me that he might run over to Bethlehem, his city, for *there is* a yearly sacrifice
there for all the family.' 7If he says thus: '*It is*
well,' your servant will be safe. But if he is
very angry, be sure that evil is determined
by him. 8Therefore you shall deal kindly
with your servant, for you have brought your
servant into a covenant of the LORD with you.
Nevertheless, if there is iniquity in me, kill
me yourself, for why should you bring me to
your father?"

9But Jonathan said, "Far be it from you!
For if I knew certainly that evil was determined by my father to come upon you, then
would I not tell you?"

10Then David said to Jonathan, "Who will

FRIENDSHIP

TRUE FRIENDSHIP

READ IT: 1 SAMUEL 20:1–42

GET IT:

Best friends forever! That's how you could describe the relationship between David and Jonathan. The Bible says that their souls were knit together (1 Samuel 18:1). That's an amazing picture of friendship!

The Bible doesn't give us a simple formula for creating a "BFF" kind of friendship. But Scripture does help us identify the qualities that need to exist for a deep and meaningful friendship. Look at David and Jonathan:

- They both loved God more than anyone or anything else.
- They truly trusted each other.
- They didn't let their situation change how they felt about each other.
- When tough times hit, they stayed true to each other.
- They weren't afraid to be real with each other.
- They believed the best about each other.

The friendship between David and Jonathan meant that they were willing to put each other first. Jonathan even stood up to his own father, Saul, when Saul felt threatened by David and wanted to kill him. There was something very special about David and Jonathan's commitment to each other. That's probably why God chose to include their story in Scripture—so we could have a model of what true friendship can look like.

LIVE IT:

A "David and Jonathan" kind of friendship is not guaranteed for any of us. But you can definitely do your part to be that kind of friend. Take some time to reflect on your current friendship skills compared to the "David and Jonathan" qualities listed above. What area might God be prompting you to grow in?

tell me, or what *if* your father answers you
roughly?"
11And Jonathan said to David, "Come,
let us go out into the field." So both of them
went out into the field. 12Then Jonathan said
to David: "The LORD God of Israel *is witness!*
When I have sounded out my father sometime tomorrow, *or* the third *day,* and indeed
there is good toward David, and I do not send
to you and tell you, 13may the LORD do so and
much more to Jonathan. But if it pleases my
father *to do* you evil, then I will report it to
you and send you away, that you may go in
safety. And the LORD be with you as He has
been with my father. 14And you shall not only
show me the kindness of the LORD while I
still live, that I may not die; 15but you shall
not cut off your kindness from my house
forever, no, not when the LORD has cut off
every one of the enemies of David from the
face of the earth." 16So Jonathan made *a covenant* with the house of David, *saying,* "Let
the LORD require *it* at the hand of David's
enemies."
17Now Jonathan again caused David to
vow, because he loved him; for he loved him
as he loved his own soul. 18Then Jonathan
said to David, "Tomorrow *is* the New Moon;
and you will be missed, because your seat
will be empty. 19And *when* you have stayed
three days, go down quickly and come to the
place where you hid on the day of the deed;
and remain by the stone Ezel. 20Then I will
shoot three arrows to the side, as though I
shot at a target; 21and there I will send a lad,
saying, 'Go, find the arrows.' If I expressly
say to the lad, 'Look, the arrows *are* on this
side of you; get them and come'—then, as
the LORD lives, *there is* safety for you and no
harm. 22But if I say thus to the young man,
'Look, the arrows *are* beyond you'—go your
way, for the LORD has sent you away. 23And as
for the matter which you and I have spoken
of, indeed the LORD *be* between you and me
forever."
24Then David hid in the field. And when
the New Moon had come, the king sat down
to eat the feast. 25Now the king sat on his
seat, as at other times, on a seat by the wall.
And Jonathan arose,[a] and Abner sat by Saul's
side, but David's place was empty. 26Never-
theless Saul did not say anything that day,
for he thought, "Something has happened
to him; he *is* unclean, surely he *is* unclean."
27And it happened the next day, the second
day of the month, that David's place was
empty. And Saul said to Jonathan his son,
"Why has the son of Jesse not come to eat,
either yesterday or today?"
28So Jonathan answered Saul, "David earnestly asked *permission* of me *to go* to Bethlehem. 29And he said, 'Please let me go, for
our family has a sacrifice in the city, and my
brother has commanded me *to be there.* And
now, if I have found favor in your eyes, please
let me get away and see my brothers.' Therefore he has not come to the king's table."
30Then Saul's anger was aroused against
Jonathan, and he said to him, "You son of a
perverse, rebellious *woman!* Do I not know
that you have chosen the son of Jesse to your
own shame and to the shame of your mother's
nakedness? 31For as long as the son of Jesse
lives on the earth, you shall not be established,
nor your kingdom. Now therefore, send and
bring him to me, for he shall surely die."
32And Jonathan answered Saul his father,
and said to him, "Why should he be killed?
What has he done?" 33Then Saul cast a spear
at him to kill him, by which Jonathan knew
that it was determined by his father to kill
David.
34So Jonathan arose from the table in
fierce anger, and ate no food the second
day of the month, for he was grieved for
David, because his father had treated him
shamefully.
35And so it was, in the morning, that
Jonathan went out into the field at the time
appointed with David, and a little lad *was*
with him. 36Then he said to his lad, "Now
run, find the arrows which I shoot." As
the lad ran, he shot an arrow beyond him.
37When the lad had come to the place where
the arrow was which Jonathan had shot,
Jonathan cried out after the lad and said, "*Is*
not the arrow beyond you?" 38And Jonathan
cried out after the lad, "Make haste, hurry,
do not delay!" So Jonathan's lad gathered
up the arrows and came back to his master.
39But the lad did not know anything. Only
Jonathan and David knew of the matter.
40Then Jonathan gave his weapons to his lad,
and said to him, "Go, carry *them* to the city."
41As soon as the lad had gone, David arose
from *a place* toward the south, fell on his face
to the ground, and bowed down three times.

20:25 [a] Following Masoretic Text, Syriac, Targum, and Vulgate; Septuagint reads *he sat across from Jonathan.*

And they kissed one another; and they wept
together, but David more so. 42Then Jonathan said to David, "Go in peace, since we
have both sworn in the name of the LORD,
saying, 'May the LORD be between you and
me, and between your descendants and my
descendants, forever.'" So he arose and departed, and Jonathan went into the city.

David and the Holy Bread

21 Now David came to Nob, to Ahimelech the priest. And Ahimelech was
afraid when he met David, and said to him,
"Why *are* you alone, and no one is with you?"
2So David said to Ahimelech the priest,
"The king has ordered me on some business, and said to me, 'Do not let anyone
know anything about the business on which
I send you, or what I have commanded you.'
And I have directed *my* young men to such
and such a place. 3Now therefore, what have
you on hand? Give *me* five *loaves of* bread in
my hand, or whatever can be found."
4And the priest answered David and said,
"*There is* no common bread on hand; but
there is holy bread, if the young men have at
least kept themselves from women."
5Then David answered the priest, and
said to him, "Truly, women *have been* kept
from us about three days since I came out.
And the vessels of the young men are holy,
and *the bread is* in effect common, even
though it was consecrated in the vessel this
day."
6So the priest gave him holy *bread;* for
there was no bread there but the showbread
which had been taken from before the LORD,
in order to put hot bread *in its place* on the
day when it was taken away.
7Now a certain man of the servants of
Saul *was* there that day, detained before the
LORD. And his name *was* Doeg, an Edomite,
the chief of the herdsmen who *belonged* to
Saul.
8And David said to Ahimelech, "Is there
not here on hand a spear or a sword? For
I have brought neither my sword nor my
weapons with me, because the king's business required haste."
9So the priest said, "The sword of Goliath
the Philistine, whom you killed in the Valley
of Elah, there it is, wrapped in a cloth behind
the ephod. If you will take that, take *it.* For
there is no other except that one here."
And David said, "*There is* none like it;
give it to me."

David Flees to Gath

10Then David arose and fled that day
from before Saul, and went to Achish the
king of Gath. 11And the servants of Achish
said to him, "*Is* this not David the king of
the land? Did they not sing of him to one
another in dances, saying:

'Saul has slain his thousands,
And David his ten thousands'?"[a]

12Now David took these words to heart,
and was very much afraid of Achish the king
of Gath. 13So he changed his behavior before
them, pretended madness in their hands,
scratched on the doors of the gate, and let
his saliva fall down on his beard. 14Then
Achish said to his servants, "Look, you see
the man is insane. Why have you brought
him to me? 15Have I need of madmen, that
you have brought this *fellow* to play the madman in my presence? Shall this *fellow* come
into my house?"

David's Four Hundred Men

22 David therefore departed from
there and escaped to the cave of
Adullam. So when his brothers and all his
father's house heard *it,* they went down there
to him. 2And everyone *who was* in distress,
everyone who *was* in debt, and everyone *who*
was discontented gathered to him. So he
became captain over them. And there were
about four hundred men with him.
3Then David went from there to Mizpah
of Moab; and he said to the king of Moab,
"Please let my father and mother come here
with you, till I know what God will do for
me." 4So he brought them before the king of
Moab, and they dwelt with him all the time
that David was in the stronghold.
5Now the prophet Gad said to David, "Do
not stay in the stronghold; depart, and go to
the land of Judah." So David departed and
went into the forest of Hereth.

Saul Murders the Priests

6When Saul heard that David and
the men who *were* with him had been
discovered—now Saul was staying in Gibeah under a tamarisk tree in Ramah, with his

21:11 [a] Compare 1 Samuel 18:7

spear in his hand, and all his servants standing about him— 7then Saul said to his servants who stood about him, "Hear now, you
Benjamites! Will the son of Jesse give every
one of you fields and vineyards, *and* make
you all captains of thousands and captains of
hundreds? 8All of you have conspired against
me, and *there is* no one who reveals to me
that my son has made a covenant with the
son of Jesse; and *there is* not one of you who
is sorry for me or reveals to me that my son
has stirred up my servant against me, to lie
in wait, as *it is* this day."

9Then answered Doeg the Edomite, who
was set over the servants of Saul, and said, "I
saw the son of Jesse going to Nob, to Ahimelech the son of Ahitub. 10And he inquired
of the LORD for him, gave him provisions,
and gave him the sword of Goliath the
Philistine."

11So the king sent to call Ahimelech the
priest, the son of Ahitub, and all his father's
house, the priests who *were* in Nob. And they
all came to the king. 12And Saul said, "Hear
now, son of Ahitub!"

He answered, "Here I am, my lord."

13Then Saul said to him, "Why have you
conspired against me, you and the son of
Jesse, in that you have given him bread and
a sword, and have inquired of God for him,
that he should rise against me, to lie in wait,
as it is this day?"

14So Ahimelech answered the king and
said, "And who among all your servants *is*
as faithful as David, who is the king's son-
in-law, who goes at your bidding, and is honorable in your house? 15Did I then begin to
inquire of God for him? Far be it from me!
Let not the king impute anything to his servant, *or* to any in the house of my father. For
your servant knew nothing of all this, little
or much."

16And the king said, "You shall surely die,
Ahimelech, you and all your father's house!"
17Then the king said to the guards who stood
about him, "Turn and kill the priests of the
LORD, because their hand also *is* with David,
and because they knew when he fled and
did not tell it to me." But the servants of the
king would not lift their hands to strike the
priests of the LORD. 18And the king said to
Doeg, "You turn and kill the priests!" So
Doeg the Edomite turned and struck the
priests, and killed on that day eighty-five

22:15 Impute Pronounced *im-PYOOT*. To consider a person guilty or not guilty. God *imputes* the goodness of Christ to people who believe the gospel. He no longer *imputes* sin to them (no longer considers them guilty).

men who wore a linen ephod. 19Also Nob, the
city of the priests, he struck with the edge of
the sword, both men and women, children
and nursing infants, oxen and donkeys and
sheep—with the edge of the sword.

20Now one of the sons of Ahimelech the
son of Ahitub, named Abiathar, escaped and
fled after David. 21And Abiathar told David
that Saul had killed the LORD's priests. 22So
David said to Abiathar, "I knew that day,
when Doeg the Edomite *was* there, that
he would surely tell Saul. I have caused
the death of all the persons of your father's
house. 23Stay with me; do not fear. For he
who seeks my life seeks your life, but with
me you *shall be* safe."

David Saves the City of Keilah

23 Then they told David, saying,
"Look, the Philistines are fight-
ing against Keilah, and they are robbing the
threshing floors."

2Therefore David inquired of the
LORD, saying, "Shall I go and attack these
Philistines?"

And the LORD said to David, "Go and attack the Philistines, and save Keilah."

3But David's men said to him, "Look, we
are afraid here in Judah. How much more
then if we go to Keilah against the armies
of the Philistines?" 4Then David inquired of
the LORD once again.

And the LORD answered him and said,
"Arise, go down to Keilah. For I will deliver
the Philistines into your hand." 5And David
and his men went to Keilah and fought with
the Philistines, struck them with a mighty
blow, and took away their livestock. So David
saved the inhabitants of Keilah.

6Now it happened, when Abiathar the son

of Ahimelech fled to David at Keilah, *that* he
went down *with* an ephod in his hand.
7 And Saul was told that David had gone
to Keilah. So Saul said, "God has delivered
him into my hand, for he has shut himself in
by entering a town that has gates and bars."
8 Then Saul called all the people together for
war, to go down to Keilah to besiege David
and his men.
9 When David knew that Saul plotted evil
against him, he said to Abiathar the priest,
"Bring the ephod here." 10 Then David said,
"O LORD God of Israel, Your servant has
certainly heard that Saul seeks to come to
Keilah to destroy the city for my sake. 11 Will
the men of Keilah deliver me into his hand?
Will Saul come down, as Your servant has
heard? O LORD God of Israel, I pray, tell Your
servant."
And the LORD said, "He will come down."
12 Then David said, "Will the men of Keilah deliver me and my men into the hand
of Saul?"
And the LORD said, "They will deliver
you."
13 So David and his men, about six hundred, arose and departed from Keilah and
went wherever they could go. Then it was
told Saul that David had escaped from Keilah; so he halted the expedition.

David in Wilderness Strongholds

14 And David stayed in strongholds in
the wilderness, and remained in the mountains in the Wilderness of Ziph. Saul sought
him every day, but God did not deliver him
into his hand. 15 So David saw that Saul had
come out to seek his life. And David *was* in
the Wilderness of Ziph in a forest.[a] 16 Then
Jonathan, Saul's son, arose and went to David in the woods and strengthened his hand
in God. 17 And he said to him, "Do not fear,
for the hand of Saul my father shall not find
you. You shall be king over Israel, and I shall
be next to you. Even my father Saul knows
that." 18 So the two of them made a covenant
before the LORD. And David stayed in the
woods, and Jonathan went to his own house.
19 Then the Ziphites came up to Saul at
Gibeah, saying, "Is David not hiding with
us in strongholds in the woods, in the hill
of Hachilah, which *is* on the south of Jeshimon? 20 Now therefore, O king, come down
according to all the desire of your soul to
come down; and our part *shall be* to deliver
him into the king's hand."
21 And Saul said, "Blessed *are* you of the
LORD, for you have compassion on me.
22 Please go and find out for sure, and see the
place where his hideout is, *and* who has seen
him there. For I am told he is very crafty.
23 See therefore, and take knowledge of all
the lurking places where he hides; and come
back to me with certainty, and I will go with
you. And it shall be, if he is in the land, that I
will search for him throughout all the clans[a]
of Judah."
24 So they arose and went to Ziph before
Saul. But David and his men *were* in the Wilderness of Maon, in the plain on the south
of Jeshimon. 25 When Saul and his men went
to seek *him,* they told David. Therefore he
went down to the rock, and stayed in the
Wilderness of Maon. And when Saul heard
that, he pursued David in the Wilderness of
Maon. 26 Then Saul went on one side of the
mountain, and David and his men on the
other side of the mountain. So David made
haste to get away from Saul, for Saul and his
men were encircling David and his men to
take them.
27 But a messenger came to Saul, saying,
"Hurry and come, for the Philistines have invaded the land!" 28 Therefore Saul returned
from pursuing David, and went against the
Philistines; so they called that place the Rock
of Escape.[a] 29 Then David went up from there
and dwelt in strongholds at En Gedi.

David Spares Saul

24 Now it happened, when Saul had
returned from following the Philistines, that it was told him, saying, "Take
note! David *is* in the Wilderness of En Gedi."
2 Then Saul took three thousand chosen men
from all Israel, and went to seek David and
his men on the Rocks of the Wild Goats.
3 So he came to the sheepfolds by the road,
where there *was* a cave; and Saul went in to
attend to his needs. (David and his men were
staying in the recesses of the cave.) 4 Then
the men of David said to him, "This is the
day of which the LORD said to you, 'Behold, I
will deliver your enemy into your hand, that
you may do to him as it seems good to you.' "
And David arose and secretly cut off a corner

23:15 [a] Or *in Horesh* 23:23 [a] Literally *thousands*
23:28 [a] Hebrew *Sela Hammahlekoth*

of Saul's robe. 5Now it happened afterward
that David's heart troubled him because he
had cut Saul's robe. 6And he said to his men,
"The LORD forbid that I should do this thing
to my master, the LORD's anointed, to stretch
out my hand against him, seeing he *is* the
anointed of the LORD." 7So David restrained
his servants with *these* words, and did not allow them to rise against Saul. And Saul got
up from the cave and went on *his* way.

8David also arose afterward, went out
of the cave, and called out to Saul, saying,
"My lord the king!" And when Saul looked
behind him, David stooped with his face
to the earth, and bowed down. 9And David
said to Saul: "Why do you listen to the words
of men who say, 'Indeed David seeks your
harm'? 10Look, this day your eyes have seen
that the LORD delivered you today into my
hand in the cave, and *someone* urged *me* to
kill you. But *my eye* spared you, and I said, 'I
will not stretch out my hand against my lord,
for he *is* the LORD's anointed.' 11Moreover, my
father, see! Yes, see the corner of your robe
in my hand! For in that I cut off the corner
of your robe, and did not kill you, know and
see that *there is* neither evil nor rebellion
in my hand, and I have not sinned against
you. Yet you hunt my life to take it. 12Let the
LORD judge between you and me, and let
the LORD avenge me on you. But my hand
shall not be against you. 13As the proverb
of the ancients says, 'Wickedness proceeds
from the wicked.' But my hand shall not be
against you. 14After whom has the king of
Israel come out? Whom do you pursue? A
dead dog? A flea? 15Therefore let the LORD be
judge, and judge between you and me, and
see and plead my case, and deliver me out of
your hand."

16So it was, when David had finished
speaking these words to Saul, that Saul said,
"*Is* this your voice, my son David?" And Saul
lifted up his voice and wept. 17Then he said
to David: "You *are* more righteous than I; for
you have rewarded me with good, whereas
I have rewarded you with evil. 18And you
have shown this day how you have dealt well
with me; for when the LORD delivered me
into your hand, you did not kill me. 19For if
a man finds his enemy, will he let him get
away safely? Therefore may the LORD reward
you with good for what you have done to me
this day. 20And now I know indeed that you
shall surely be king, and that the kingdom
of Israel shall be established in your hand.
21Therefore swear now to me by the LORD
that you will not cut off my descendants after
me, and that you will not destroy my name
from my father's house."

22So David swore to Saul. And Saul went
home, but David and his men went up to the
stronghold.

Death of Samuel

25 Then Samuel died; and the
Israelites gathered together and

PERSEVERANCE

READ IT: 1 SAMUEL 24:1–22

David messed up—a lot. But God looked into David's heart and saw goodness. David tried to do the right thing. He failed frequently, but he always kept trying. Here David had the opportunity to end Saul's persecution of him. Saul was alone. Saul was, well . . . relieving himself. David had the chance to slip in and cut his throat. Instead, David sliced off a piece of Saul's robe, gave it to Saul, and said, "I could have killed you, but *I didn't*. Now will you believe I'm not out to get you?" Sometimes the easy way out is right in front of us, and yet we have to keep trying to live the way God wants us to. The right way is seldom the easy way.

lamented for him, and buried him at his
home in Ramah. And David arose and went
down to the Wilderness of Paran.[a]

David and the Wife of Nabal

2Now *there was* a man in Maon whose
business *was* in Carmel, and the man *was*
very rich. He had three thousand sheep and
a thousand goats. And he was shearing his
sheep in Carmel. 3The name of the man *was*
Nabal, and the name of his wife Abigail. And
she was a woman of good understanding and
beautiful appearance; but the man *was* harsh
and evil in *his* doings. He *was of the house
of* Caleb.

4When David heard in the wilderness
that Nabal was shearing his sheep, 5David
sent ten young men; and David said to the
young men, "Go up to Carmel, go to Nabal, and greet him in my name. 6And thus
you shall say to him who lives *in prosperity:*
'Peace *be* to you, peace to your house, and
peace to all that you have! 7Now I have heard

25:1 [a] Following Masoretic Text, Syriac, Targum, and Vulgate; Septuagint reads *Maon.*

HEARING GOD'S VOICE

ABBY'S TACT

READ IT: 1 SAMUEL 25:1–44

GET IT:

Abigail was married to Nabal, a scoundrel of a businessman who refused to help David. When Abigail found out David was ready to attack Nabal's armies, she made some calculated choices borne out of wisdom and a discerning spirit.

If Abigail told her husband, no one could predict his reaction. If she did nothing, her entire household would probably be killed. Knowing her husband was a bad guy, she used her creativity and tact, which means dealing with others in a way that does not offend them, to navigate through a complex situation.

Abigail acted quickly. She didn't wait for the situation to get worse but responded right away.

She was resourceful, using the things within her reach. She offered gifts and spoke with humility. She was thankful for the protection they had received. She had a servant's heart. She waited until the right time to speak to her husband. She trusted in God to provide.

When Abigail told her husband what had happened, he didn't care, and he died soon after that. However, her wise choices led her to safety and helped everyone around her.

LIVE IT:

Think about a situation that is tough for you right now. How can you, like Abigail, use tact to work through it?

that you have shearers. Your shepherds were with us, and we did not hurt them, nor was there anything missing from them all the while they were in Carmel. 8Ask your young men, and they will tell you. Therefore let *my* young men find favor in your eyes, for we come on a feast day. Please give whatever comes to your hand to your servants and to your son David.'"

9So when David's young men came, they spoke to Nabal according to all these words in the name of David, and waited.

10Then Nabal answered David's servants, and said, "Who *is* David, and who *is* the son of Jesse? There are many servants nowadays who break away each one from his master. 11Shall I then take my bread and my water and my meat that I have killed for my shearers, and give *it* to men when I do not know where they *are* from?"

12So David's young men turned on their heels and went back; and they came and told him all these words. 13Then David said to his men, "Every man gird on his sword." So every man girded on his sword, and David also girded on his sword. And about four hundred men went with David, and two hundred stayed with the supplies.

14Now one of the young men told Abigail, Nabal's wife, saying, "Look, David sent messengers from the wilderness to greet our master; and he reviled them. 15But the men *were* very good to us, and we were not hurt, nor did we miss anything as long as we accompanied them, when we were in the fields. 16They were a wall to us both by night and day, all the time we were with them keeping the sheep. 17Now therefore, know and consider what you will do, for harm is determined against our master and against all his household. For he *is such* a scoundrel[a] that *one* cannot speak to him."

18Then Abigail made haste and took two hundred *loaves* of bread, two skins of wine, five sheep already dressed, five seahs of roasted *grain,* one hundred clusters of raisins, and two hundred cakes of figs, and loaded *them* on donkeys. 19And she said to her servants, "Go on before me; see, I am coming after you." But she did not tell her husband Nabal.

20So it was, *as* she rode on the donkey, that she went down under cover of the hill; and there were David and his men, coming down toward her, and she met them. 21Now David had said, "Surely in vain I have protected all that this *fellow* has in the wilderness, so that nothing was missed of all that *belongs* to him. And he has repaid me evil for good. 22May God do so, and more also, to the enemies of David, if I leave one male of all who *belong* to him by morning light."

23Now when Abigail saw David, she dismounted quickly from the donkey, fell on her face before David, and bowed down to the ground. 24So she fell at his feet and said: "On me, my lord, *on* me *let* this iniquity *be!* And please let your maidservant speak in your ears, and hear the words of your maidservant. 25Please, let not my lord regard this scoundrel Nabal. For as his name *is,* so *is* he: Nabal[a] *is* his name, and folly *is* with him! But I, your maidservant, did not see the young men of my lord whom you sent. 26Now therefore, my lord, *as* the LORD lives and *as* your soul lives, since the LORD has held you back from coming to bloodshed and from avenging yourself with your own hand, now then, let your enemies and those who seek harm for my lord be as Nabal. 27And now this present which your maidservant has brought to my lord, let it be given to the young men who follow my lord. 28Please forgive the trespass of your maidservant. For the LORD will certainly make for my lord an enduring house, because my lord fights the battles of the LORD, and evil is not found in you throughout your days. 29Yet a man has risen to pursue you and seek your life, but the life of my lord shall be bound in the bundle of the living with the LORD your God; and the lives of your enemies He shall sling out, *as from* the pocket of a sling. 30And it shall come to pass, when the LORD has done for my lord according to all the good that He has spoken concerning you, and has appointed you ruler over Israel, 31that this will be no grief to you, nor offense of heart to my lord, either that you have shed blood without cause, or that my lord has avenged himself. But when the LORD has dealt well with my lord, then remember your maidservant."

32Then David said to Abigail: "Blessed *is* the LORD God of Israel, who sent you this day to meet me! 33And blessed *is* your advice and blessed *are* you, because you have kept me this day from coming to bloodshed and from avenging myself with my own hand.

25:17 [a] Literally *son of Belial* 25:25 [a] Literally *Fool*

34For indeed, *as* the LORD God of Israel lives,
who has kept me back from hurting you,
unless you had hurried and come to meet
me, surely by morning light no males would
have been left to Nabal!" 35So David received
from her hand what she had brought him,
and said to her, "Go up in peace to your
house. See, I have heeded your voice and respected your person."

36Now Abigail went to Nabal, and there
he was, holding a feast in his house, like the
feast of a king. And Nabal's heart *was* merry
within him, for he *was* very drunk; therefore
she told him nothing, little or much, until
morning light. 37So it was, in the morning,
when the wine had gone from Nabal, and his
wife had told him these things, that his heart
died within him, and he became *like* a stone.
38Then it happened, *after* about ten days, that
the LORD struck Nabal, and he died.

39So when David heard that Nabal was
dead, he said, "Blessed *be* the LORD, who
has pleaded the cause of my reproach from
the hand of Nabal, and has kept His servant
from evil! For the LORD has returned the
wickedness of Nabal on his own head."

And David sent and proposed to Abigail,
to take her as his wife. 40When the servants
of David had come to Abigail at Carmel, they
spoke to her saying, "David sent us to you, to
ask you to become his wife."

41Then she arose, bowed her face to the
earth, and said, "Here is your maidservant,
a servant to wash the feet of the servants of
my lord." 42So Abigail rose in haste and rode
on a donkey, attended by five of her maidens;
and she followed the messengers of David,
and became his wife. 43David also took Ahinoam of Jezreel, and so both of them were his
wives.

44But Saul had given Michal his daughter,
David's wife, to Palti[a] the son of Laish, who
was from Gallim.

David Spares Saul a Second Time

26 *Now the Ziphites came to Saul at*
Gibeah, saying, "Is David not hiding in the hill of Hachilah, opposite Jeshimon?" 2Then Saul arose and went down to
the Wilderness of Ziph, having three thousand chosen men of Israel with him, to seek
David in the Wilderness of Ziph. 3And Saul
encamped in the hill of Hachilah, which *is*
opposite Jeshimon, by the road. But David
stayed in the wilderness, and he saw that
Saul came after him into the wilderness.
4David therefore sent out spies, and understood that Saul had indeed come.

5So David arose and came to the place
where Saul had encamped. And David saw
the place where Saul lay, and Abner the son
of Ner, the commander of his army. Now
Saul lay within the camp, with the people
encamped all around him. 6Then David answered, and said to Ahimelech the Hittite
and to Abishai the son of Zeruiah, brother
of Joab, saying, "Who will go down with me
to Saul in the camp?"

And Abishai said, "I will go down with
you."

7So David and Abishai came to the people
by night; and there Saul lay sleeping within
the camp, with his spear stuck in the ground
by his head. And Abner and the people lay
all around him. 8Then Abishai said to David,
"God has delivered your enemy into your
hand this day. Now therefore, please, let me
strike him at once with the spear, right to
the earth; and I will not *have to strike* him a
second time!"

9But David said to Abishai, "Do not destroy him; for who can stretch out his hand
against the LORD's anointed, and be guiltless?" 10David said furthermore, "*As* the LORD
lives, the LORD shall strike him, or his day
shall come to die, or he shall go out to battle
and perish. 11The LORD forbid that I should
stretch out my hand against the LORD's
anointed. But please, take now the spear and
the jug of water that *are* by his head, and let
us go." 12So David took the spear and the jug
of water *by* Saul's head, and they got away;
and no man saw or knew *it* or awoke. For
they *were* all asleep, because a deep sleep
from the LORD had fallen on them.

13Now David went over to the other side,
and stood on the top of a hill afar off, a great
distance *being* between them. 14And David
called out to the people and to Abner the son
of Ner, saying, "Do you not answer, Abner?"

Then Abner answered and said, "Who
are you, calling out to the king?"

15So David said to Abner, "*Are* you not a
man? And who *is* like you in Israel? Why
then have you not guarded your lord the
king? For one of the people came in to destroy your lord the king. 16This thing that
you have done *is* not good. *As* the LORD lives,

25:44 [a] Spelled *Paltiel* in 2 Samuel 3:15

you deserve to die, because you have not
guarded your master, the LORD's anointed.
And now see where the king's spear *is,* and
the jug of water that *was* by his head."
17 Then Saul knew David's voice, and said,
"*Is* that your voice, my son David?"
David said, "*It is* my voice, my lord, O
king." 18 And he said, "Why does my lord thus
pursue his servant? For what have I done,
or what evil *is* in my hand? 19 Now therefore,
please, let my lord the king hear the words
of his servant: If the LORD has stirred you
up against me, let Him accept an offering.
But if *it is* the children of men, *may* they *be*
cursed before the LORD, for they have driven
me out this day from sharing in the inheritance of the LORD, saying, 'Go, serve other
gods.' 20 So now, do not let my blood fall to
the earth before the face of the LORD. For
the king of Israel has come out to seek a
flea, as when one hunts a partridge in the
mountains."
21 Then Saul said, "I have sinned. Return,
my son David. For I will harm you no more,
because my life was precious in your eyes
this day. Indeed I have played the fool and
erred exceedingly."
22 And David answered and said, "Here
is the king's spear. Let one of the young
men come over and get it. 23 May the LORD
repay every man *for* his righteousness and
his faithfulness; for the LORD delivered you
into *my* hand today, but I would not stretch
out my hand against the LORD's anointed.
24 And indeed, as your life was valued much
this day in my eyes, so let my life be valued
much in the eyes of the LORD, and let Him
deliver me out of all tribulation."
25 Then Saul said to David, "*May* you *be*
blessed, my son David! You shall both do
great things and also still prevail."
So David went on his way, and Saul returned to his place.

David Allied with the Philistines

27 And David said in his heart, "Now
I shall perish someday by the hand
of Saul. *There is* nothing better for me than
that I should speedily escape to the land of
the Philistines; and Saul will despair of me,
to seek me anymore in any part of Israel. So
I shall escape out of his hand." 2 Then David
arose and went over with the six hundred
men who *were* with him to Achish the son of
Maoch, king of Gath. 3 So David dwelt with
Achish at Gath, he and his men, each man
with his household, *and* David with his two
wives, Ahinoam the Jezreelitess, and Abigail
the Carmelitess, Nabal's widow. 4 And it was
told Saul that David had fled to Gath; so he
sought him no more.
5 Then David said to Achish, "If I have
now found favor in your eyes, let them give
me a place in some town in the country, that
I may dwell there. For why should your servant dwell in the royal city with you?" 6 So
Achish gave him Ziklag that day. Therefore
Ziklag has belonged to the kings of Judah to
this day. 7 Now the time that David dwelt in
the country of the Philistines was one full
year and four months.
8 And David and his men went up and
raided the Geshurites, the Girzites,[a] and
the Amalekites. For those *nations* were the
inhabitants of the land from of old, as you
go to Shur, even as far as the land of Egypt.
9 Whenever David attacked the land, he left
neither man nor woman alive, but took
away the sheep, the oxen, the donkeys, the
camels, and the apparel, and returned and
came to Achish. 10 Then Achish would say,
"Where have you made a raid today?" And
David would say, "Against the southern *area*
of Judah, or against the southern *area* of the
Jerahmeelites, or against the southern *area*
of the Kenites." 11 David would save neither
man nor woman alive, to bring *news* to Gath,
saying, "Lest they should inform on us, saying, 'Thus David did.'" And thus *was* his behavior all the time he dwelt in the country of
the Philistines. 12 So Achish believed David,
saying, "He has made his people Israel utterly abhor him; therefore he will be my servant
forever."

28 Now it happened in those days
that the Philistines gathered their
armies together for war, to fight with Israel.
And Achish said to David, "You assuredly
know that you will go out with me to battle,
you and your men."
2 So David said to Achish, "Surely you
know what your servant can do."
And Achish said to David, "Therefore
I will make you one of my chief guardians
forever."

Saul Consults a Medium

3 Now Samuel had died, and all Israel had
lamented for him and buried him in Ramah,

27:8 [a] Or *Gezrites*

in his own city. And Saul had put the mediums and the spiritists out of the land.
4 Then the Philistines gathered together, and came and encamped at Shunem. So
Saul gathered all Israel together, and they
encamped at Gilboa. 5 When Saul saw the
army of the Philistines, he was afraid, and
his heart trembled greatly. 6 And when Saul
inquired of the LORD, the LORD did not answer him, either by dreams or by Urim or by
the prophets.
7 Then Saul said to his servants, "Find me
a woman who is a medium, that I may go to
her and inquire of her."
And his servants said to him, "In fact,
there is a woman who is a medium at En
Dor."
8 So Saul disguised himself and put on
other clothes, and he went, and two men
with him; and they came to the woman by
night. And he said, "Please conduct a séance
for me, and bring up for me the one I shall
name to you."
9 Then the woman said to him, "Look,
you know what Saul has done, how he has
cut off the mediums and the spiritists from
the land. Why then do you lay a snare for my
life, to cause me to die?"
10 And Saul swore to her by the LORD, saying, "*As* the LORD lives, no punishment shall
come upon you for this thing."
11 Then the woman said, "Whom shall I
bring up for you?"
And he said, "Bring up Samuel for me."
12 When the woman saw Samuel, she
cried out with a loud voice. And the woman
spoke to Saul, saying, "Why have you deceived me? For you *are* Saul!"
13 And the king said to her, "Do not be
afraid. What did you see?"
And the woman said to Saul, "I saw a
spirit[a] ascending out of the earth."
14 So he said to her, "What *is* his form?"
And she said, "An old man is coming up,
and he *is* covered with a mantle." And Saul
perceived that it *was* Samuel, and he stooped
with *his* face to the ground and bowed down.
15 Now Samuel said to Saul, "Why have
you disturbed me by bringing me up?"
And Saul answered, "I am deeply distressed; for the Philistines make war against
me, and God has departed from me and does
not answer me anymore, neither by prophets
nor by dreams. Therefore I have called you,
that you may reveal to me what I should do."
16 Then Samuel said: "So why do you ask
me, seeing the LORD has departed from
you and has become your enemy? 17 And the
LORD has done for Himself[a] as He spoke by
me. For the LORD has torn the kingdom out
of your hand and given it to your neighbor,
David. 18 Because you did not obey the voice
of the LORD nor execute His fierce wrath
upon Amalek, therefore the LORD has done
this thing to you this day. 19 Moreover the
LORD will also deliver Israel with you into
the hand of the Philistines. And tomorrow
you and your sons *will be* with me. The LORD
will also deliver the army of Israel into the
hand of the Philistines."
20 Immediately Saul fell full length on the
ground, and was dreadfully afraid because
of the words of Samuel. And there was no
strength in him, for he had eaten no food all
day or all night.
21 And the woman came to Saul and saw
that he was severely troubled, and said to
him, "Look, your maidservant has obeyed
your voice, and I have put my life in my
hands and heeded the words which you
spoke to me. 22 Now therefore, please, heed
also the voice of your maidservant, and let
me set a piece of bread before you; and eat,
that you may have strength when you go on
your way."
23 But he refused and said, "I will not eat."
So his servants, together with the woman, urged him; and he heeded their voice.
Then he arose from the ground and sat on
the bed. 24 Now the woman had a fatted calf
in the house, and she hastened to kill it. And
she took flour and kneaded *it*, and baked
unleavened bread from it. 25 So she brought
it before Saul and his servants, and they ate.
Then they rose and went away that night.

The Philistines Reject David

29 Then the Philistines gathered together all their armies at Aphek,
and the Israelites encamped by a fountain
which *is* in Jezreel. 2 And the lords of the Philistines passed in review by hundreds and
by thousands, but David and his men passed
in review at the rear with Achish. 3 Then the
princes of the Philistines said, "What *are*
these Hebrews *doing here?*"
And Achish said to the princes of the
Philistines, "*Is* this not David, the servant of
Saul king of Israel, who has been with me

28:13 [a] Hebrew *elohim* 28:17 [a] Or *him*, that is, David

these days, or these years? And to this day I have found no fault in him since he defected *to me*."

4But the princes of the Philistines were angry with him; so the princes of the Philistines said to him, "Make this fellow return, that he may go back to the place which you have appointed for him, and do not let him go down with us to battle, lest in the battle he become our adversary. For with what could he reconcile himself to his master, if not with the heads of these men? 5*Is* this not David, of whom they sang to one another in dances, saying:

'Saul has slain his thousands,
And David his ten thousands'?"[a]

6Then Achish called David and said to him, "Surely, *as* the LORD lives, you have been upright, and your going out and your coming in with me in the army *is* good in my sight. For to this day I have not found evil in you since the day of your coming to me. Nevertheless the lords do not favor you. 7Therefore return now, and go in peace, that you may not displease the lords of the Philistines."

8So David said to Achish, "But what have I done? And to this day what have you found in your servant as long as I have been with you, that I may not go and fight against the enemies of my lord the king?"

9Then Achish answered and said to David, "I know that you *are* as good in my sight as an angel of God; nevertheless the princes of the Philistines have said, 'He shall not go up with us to the battle.' 10Now therefore, rise early in the morning with your master's servants who have come with you.[a] And as soon as you are up early in the morning and have light, depart."

11So David and his men rose early to depart in the morning, to return to the land of the Philistines. And the Philistines went up to Jezreel.

David's Conflict with the Amalekites

30 Now it happened, when David and his men came to Ziklag, on the third day, that the Amalekites had invaded the South and Ziklag, attacked Ziklag and burned it with fire, 2and had taken captive the women and those who *were* there, from small to great; they did not kill anyone, but carried *them* away and went their way. 3So David and his men came to the city, and there it was, burned with fire; and their wives, their sons, and their daughters had been taken captive. 4Then David and the people who *were* with him lifted up their voices and wept, until they had no more power to weep. 5And David's two wives, Ahinoam the Jezreelitess, and Abigail the widow of Nabal the Carmelite, had been taken captive. 6Now David was greatly distressed, for the people spoke of stoning him, because the soul of all the people was grieved, every man for his sons and his daughters. But David strengthened himself in the LORD his God.

7Then David said to Abiathar the priest, Ahimelech's son, "Please bring the ephod here to me." And Abiathar brought the ephod to David. 8So David inquired of the LORD, saying, "Shall I pursue this troop? Shall I overtake them?"

And He answered him, "Pursue, for you shall surely overtake *them* and without fail recover *all*."

9So David went, he and the six hundred men who *were* with him, and came to the Brook Besor, where those stayed who were left behind. 10But David pursued, he and four hundred men; for two hundred stayed *behind*, who were so weary that they could not cross the Brook Besor.

11Then they found an Egyptian in the field, and brought him to David; and they gave him bread and he ate, and they let him drink water. 12And they gave him a piece of a cake of figs and two clusters of raisins. So when he had eaten, his strength came back to him; for he had eaten no bread nor drunk water for three days and three nights. 13Then David said to him, "To whom do you *belong*, and where *are* you from?"

And he said, "I *am* a young man from Egypt, servant of an Amalekite; and my master left me behind, because three days ago I fell sick. 14We made an invasion of the southern *area* of the Cherethites, in the *territory* which *belongs* to Judah, and of the southern *area* of Caleb; and we burned Ziklag with fire."

15And David said to him, "Can you take me down to this troop?"

So he said, "Swear to me by God that

29:5 [a] Compare 1 Samuel 18:7 **29:10** [a] Following Masoretic Text, Targum, and Vulgate; Septuagint adds *and go to the place which I have selected for you there; and set no bothersome word in your heart, for you are good before me. And rise on your way.*

you will neither kill me nor deliver me into
the hands of my master, and I will take you
down to this troop."

16And when he had brought him down,
there they were, spread out over all the land,
eating and drinking and dancing, because
of all the great spoil which they had taken
from the land of the Philistines and from the
land of Judah. 17Then David attacked them
from twilight until the evening of the next
day. Not a man of them escaped, except four
hundred young men who rode on camels
and fled. 18So David recovered all that the
Amalekites had carried away, and David rescued his two wives. 19And nothing of theirs
was lacking, either small or great, sons or
daughters, spoil or anything which they
had taken from them; David recovered all.
20Then David took all the flocks and herds
they had driven before those *other* livestock,
and said, "This *is* David's spoil."

21Now David came to the two hundred
men who had been so weary that they could
not follow David, whom they also had made
to stay at the Brook Besor. So they went out
to meet David and to meet the people who
were with him. And when David came near
the people, he greeted them. 22Then all the
wicked and worthless men[a] of those who
went with David answered and said, "Because they did not go with us, we will not
give them *any* of the spoil that we have recovered, except for every man's wife and
children, that they may lead *them* away and
depart."

23But David said, "My brethren, you shall
not do so with what the LORD has given us,
who has preserved us and delivered into our
hand the troop that came against us. 24For
who will heed you in this matter? But as his
part *is* who goes down to the battle, so *shall*
his part *be* who stays by the supplies; they
shall share alike." 25So it was, from that day
forward; he made it a statute and an ordinance for Israel to this day.

26Now when David came to Ziklag, he
sent *some* of the spoil to the elders of Judah,
to his friends, saying, "Here is a present for
you from the spoil of the enemies of the
LORD"— 27to *those* who *were* in Bethel, *those*
who *were* in Ramoth of the South, *those* who
were in Jattir, 28*those* who *were* in Aroer, *those*
who *were* in Siphmoth, *those* who *were* in
Eshtemoa, 29*those* who *were* in Rachal, *those*
who *were* in the cities of the Jerahmeelites,
those who *were* in the cities of the Kenites,
30*those* who *were* in Hormah, *those* who *were*
in Chorashan,[a] *those* who *were* in Athach,
31*those* who *were* in Hebron, and to all the
places where David himself and his men
were accustomed to rove.

The Tragic End of Saul and His Sons

31 Now the Philistines fought against
Israel; and the men of Israel fled
from before the Philistines, and fell slain
on Mount Gilboa. 2Then the Philistines followed hard after Saul and his sons. And the
Philistines killed Jonathan, Abinadab, and
Malchishua, Saul's sons. 3The battle became
fierce against Saul. The archers hit him, and
he was severely wounded by the archers.

4Then Saul said to his armorbearer,
"Draw your sword, and thrust me through
with it, lest these uncircumcised men come
and thrust me through and abuse me."

But his armorbearer would not, for he
was greatly afraid. Therefore Saul took a
sword and fell on it. 5And when his armorbearer saw that Saul was dead, he also fell on
his sword, and died with him. 6So Saul, his
three sons, his armorbearer, and all his men
died together that same day.

7And when the men of Israel who *were*
on the other side of the valley, and *those* who
were on the other side of the Jordan, saw that
the men of Israel had fled and that Saul and
his sons were dead, they forsook the cities
and fled; and the Philistines came and dwelt
in them. 8So it happened the next day, when
the Philistines came to strip the slain, that
they found Saul and his three sons fallen on
Mount Gilboa. 9And they cut off his head
and stripped off his armor, and sent *word*
throughout the land of the Philistines, to
proclaim *it in* the temple of their idols and
among the people. 10Then they put his armor
in the temple of the Ashtoreths, and they fastened his body to the wall of Beth Shan.[a]

11Now when the inhabitants of Jabesh
Gilead heard what the Philistines had done
to Saul, 12all the valiant men arose and traveled all night, and took the body of Saul and
the bodies of his sons from the wall of Beth
Shan; and they came to Jabesh and burned
them there. 13Then they took their bones
and buried *them* under the tamarisk tree at
Jabesh, and fasted seven days.

30:22 [a] Literally *men of Belial* **30:30** [a] Or *Borashan*
31:10 [a] Spelled *Beth Shean* in Joshua 17:11 and elsewhere

The BOOK of 2 SAMUEL

1050 B.C.–750 B.C.

Behind the Scenes

READ IT:

Second Samuel continues the story of the kingdom of Israel. It begins with King Saul's death and David's struggle to become king. Then it describes David's forty-year reign: what he conquered, what he accomplished, and what happened in his family life.

GET IT:

Who wrote it: Possibly the prophets Nathan and Gad wrote it.

When it was written: 1050 B.C.–750 B.C.

Why it was written: to tell Israel's history and to show what happens when people obey God, and what happens when they disobey Him.

LIVE IT:

God works through sinful people to accomplish what needs to get done on earth.

God loves His people even when they sin.

FIND IT:

David Reigns over All Israel	*2 Samuel 5*
David's Kindness to Mephibosheth	*2 Samuel 9*
David, Bathsheba, and Uriah	*2 Samuel 11–12*
Absalom's Treason	*2 Samuel 15*
David's Census of Israel and Judah	*2 Samuel 24*

The Report of Saul's Death

1 Now it came to pass after the death of
Saul, when David had returned from the
slaughter of the Amalekites, and David had
stayed two days in Ziklag, 2on the third day,
behold, it happened that a man came from
Saul's camp with his clothes torn and dust
on his head. So it was, when he came to David, that he fell to the ground and prostrated
himself.
3And David said to him, "Where have you
come from?"
So he said to him, "I have escaped from
the camp of Israel."
4Then David said to him, "How did the
matter go? Please tell me."
And he answered, "The people have fled
from the battle, many of the people are fallen
and dead, and Saul and Jonathan his son are
dead also."
5So David said to the young man who told
him, "How do you know that Saul and Jonathan his son are dead?"
6Then the young man who told him said,
"As I happened by chance *to be* on Mount
Gilboa, there was Saul, leaning on his spear;
and indeed the chariots and horsemen followed hard after him. 7Now when he looked
behind him, he saw me and called to me.
And I answered, 'Here I am.' 8And he said to
me, 'Who *are* you?' So I answered him, 'I *am*
an Amalekite.' 9He said to me again, 'Please
stand over me and kill me, for anguish has
come upon me, but my life still *remains* in
me.' 10So I stood over him and killed him, because I was sure that he could not live after he
had fallen. And I took the crown that *was* on
his head and the bracelet that *was* on his arm,
and have brought them here to my lord."
11Therefore David took hold of his own
clothes and tore them, and *so did* all the men
who *were* with him. 12And they mourned and
wept and fasted until evening for Saul and
for Jonathan his son, for the people of the
LORD and for the house of Israel, because
they had fallen by the sword.
13Then David said to the young man who
told him, "Where *are* you from?"
And he answered, "I *am* the son of an
alien, an Amalekite."
14So David said to him, "How was it you
were not afraid to put forth your hand to
destroy the LORD's anointed?" 15Then David called one of the young men and said,
"Go near, *and* execute him!" And he struck
him so that he died. 16So David said to him,
"Your blood *is* on your own head, for your
own mouth has testified against you, saying,
'I have killed the LORD's anointed.'"

The Song of the Bow

17Then David lamented with this lamentation over Saul and over Jonathan his son,
18and he told *them* to teach the children of Judah *the Song of* the Bow; indeed *it is* written
in the Book of Jasher:

19 "The beauty of Israel is slain on your
high places!
How the mighty have fallen!
20 Tell *it* not in Gath,
Proclaim *it* not in the streets of
Ashkelon—
Lest the daughters of the Philistines
rejoice,
Lest the daughters of the uncircumcised
triumph.

21 "O mountains of Gilboa,
Let there be no dew nor rain upon you,

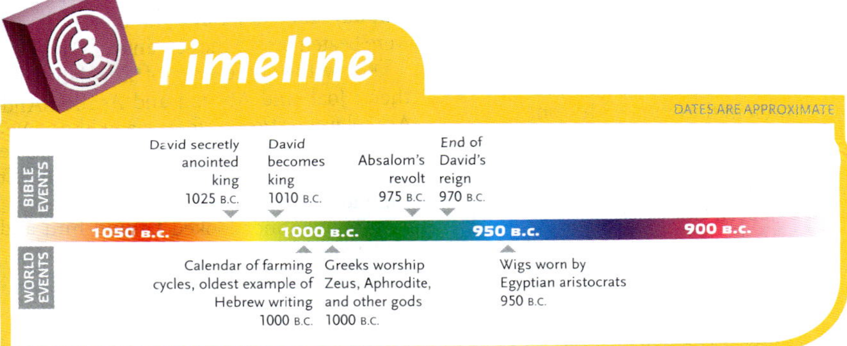

Nor fields of offerings.
For the shield of the mighty is cast away
there!
The shield of Saul, not anointed with
oil.
22 From the blood of the slain,
From the fat of the mighty,
The bow of Jonathan did not turn back,
And the sword of Saul did not return
empty.

23 "Saul and Jonathan *were* beloved and
pleasant in their lives,
And in their death they were not
divided;
They were swifter than eagles,
They were stronger than lions.

24 "O daughters of Israel, weep over Saul,
Who clothed you in scarlet, with luxury;
Who put ornaments of gold on your
apparel.

25 "How the mighty have fallen in the
midst of the battle!
Jonathan *was* slain in your high places.
26 I am distressed for you, my brother
Jonathan;
You have been very pleasant to me;
Your love to me was wonderful,
Surpassing the love of women.

27 "How the mighty have fallen,
And the weapons of war perished!"

David Anointed King of Judah

2 It happened after this that David inquired of the LORD, saying, "Shall I go
up to any of the cities of Judah?"
And the LORD said to him, "Go up."
David said, "Where shall I go up?"
And He said, "To Hebron."
2 So David went up there, and his two
wives also, Ahinoam the Jezreelitess, and
Abigail the widow of Nabal the Carmelite.
3 And David brought up the men who *were*
with him, every man with his household. So
they dwelt in the cities of Hebron.
4 Then the men of Judah came, and there
they anointed David king over the house of
Judah. And they told David, saying, "The
men of Jabesh Gilead *were the ones* who buried Saul." 5 So David sent messengers to the
men of Jabesh Gilead, and said to them, "You
are blessed of the LORD, for you have shown
this kindness to your lord, to Saul, and have
buried him. 6 And now may the LORD show
kindness and truth to you. I also will repay
you this kindness, because you have done
this thing. 7 Now therefore, let your hands be
strengthened, and be valiant; for your master Saul is dead, and also the house of Judah
has anointed me king over them."

Ishbosheth Made King of Israel

8 But Abner the son of Ner, commander
of Saul's army, took Ishbosheth[a] the son of
Saul and brought him over to Mahanaim;
9 and he made him king over Gilead, over the
Ashurites, over Jezreel, over Ephraim, over
Benjamin, and over all Israel. 10 Ishbosheth,
Saul's son, *was* forty years old when he began to reign over Israel, and he reigned two
years. Only the house of Judah followed David. 11 And the time that David was king in
Hebron over the house of Judah was seven
years and six months.

Israel and Judah at War

12 Now Abner the son of Ner, and the servants of Ishbosheth the son of Saul, went out
from Mahanaim to Gibeon. 13 And Joab the
son of Zeruiah, and the servants of David,
went out and met them by the pool of Gibeon.
So they sat down, one on one side of the pool
and the other on the other side of the pool.
14 Then Abner said to Joab, "Let the young
men now arise and compete before us."
And Joab said, "Let them arise."
15 So they arose and went over by number, twelve from Benjamin, *followers* of Ishbosheth the son of Saul, and twelve from the
servants of David. 16 And each one grasped
his opponent by the head and *thrust* his
sword in his opponent's side; so they fell
down together. Therefore that place was
called the Field of Sharp Swords,[a] which *is*
in Gibeon. 17 So there was a very fierce battle
that day, and Abner and the men of Israel
were beaten before the servants of David.
18 Now the three sons of Zeruiah were
there: Joab and Abishai and Asahel. And
Asahel *was as* fleet of foot as a wild gazelle.
19 So Asahel pursued Abner, and in going he
did not turn to the right hand or to the left
from following Abner.
20 Then Abner looked behind him and
said, "*Are* you Asahel?"
He answered, "I *am*."

2:8 [a] Called *Esh-Baal* in 1 Chronicles 8:33 and 9:39
2:16 [a] Hebrew *Helkath Hazzurim*

21And Abner said to him, "Turn aside to
your right hand or to your left, and lay hold
on one of the young men and take his armor for yourself." But Asahel would not turn
aside from following him. 22So Abner said
again to Asahel, "Turn aside from following
me. Why should I strike you to the ground?
How then could I face your brother Joab?"
23However, he refused to turn aside. Therefore Abner struck him in the stomach with
the blunt end of the spear, so that the spear
came out of his back; and he fell down there
and died on the spot. So it was *that* as many
as came to the place where Asahel fell down
and died, stood still.

24Joab and Abishai also pursued Abner. And the sun was going down when
they came to the hill of Ammah, which *is*
before Giah by the road to the Wilderness
of Gibeon. 25Now the children of Benjamin
gathered together behind Abner and became
a unit, and took their stand on top of a hill.
26Then Abner called to Joab and said, "Shall
the sword devour forever? Do you not know
that it will be bitter in the latter end? How
long will it be then until you tell the people
to return from pursuing their brethren?"

27And Joab said, "*As* God lives, unless you
had spoken, surely then by morning all the
people would have given up pursuing their
brethren." 28So Joab blew a trumpet; and all
the people stood still and did not pursue Israel anymore, nor did they fight anymore.
29Then Abner and his men went on all that
night through the plain, crossed over the Jordan, and went through all Bithron; and they
came to Mahanaim.

30So Joab returned from pursuing Abner. And when he had gathered all the people together, there were missing of David's
servants nineteen men and Asahel. 31But
the servants of David had struck down, of
Benjamin and Abner's men, three hundred
and sixty men who died. 32Then they took up
Asahel and buried him in his father's tomb,
which was in Bethlehem. And Joab and his
men went all night, and they came to Hebron at daybreak.

3 Now there was a long war between the
house of Saul and the house of David.
But David grew stronger and stronger, and
the house of Saul grew weaker and weaker.

Sons of David

2Sons were born to David in Hebron:
His firstborn was Amnon by Ahinoam the
Jezreelitess; 3his second, Chileab, by Abigail
the widow of Nabal the Carmelite; the third,
Absalom the son of Maacah, the daughter of
Talmai, king of Geshur; 4the fourth, Adoni-
jah the son of Haggith; the fifth, Shephatiah
the son of Abital; 5and the sixth, Ithream,
by David's wife Eglah. These were born to
David in Hebron.

Abner Joins Forces with David

6Now it was so, while there was war between the house of Saul and the house of David, that Abner was strengthening *his hold*
on the house of Saul.

7And Saul had a concubine, whose name
was Rizpah, the daughter of Aiah. So *Ishbosheth* said to Abner, "Why have you gone
in to my father's concubine?"

8Then Abner became very angry at the
words of Ishbosheth, and said, "*Am* I a dog's
head that belongs to Judah? Today I show
loyalty to the house of Saul your father, to
his brothers, and to his friends, and have not
delivered you into the hand of David; and
you charge me today with a fault concerning this woman? 9May God do so to Abner,
and more also, if I do not do for David as the
LORD has sworn to him— 10to transfer the
kingdom from the house of Saul, and set up
the throne of David over Israel and over Judah, from Dan to Beersheba." 11And he could
not answer Abner another word, because he
feared him.

12Then Abner sent messengers on his behalf to David, saying, "Whose *is* the land?"
saying *also*, "Make your covenant with me,
and indeed my hand *shall be* with you to
bring all Israel to you."

13And *David* said, "Good, I will make a
covenant with you. But one thing I require
of you: you shall not see my face unless you
first bring Michal, Saul's daughter, when
you come to see my face." 14So David sent
messengers to Ishbosheth, Saul's son, saying, "Give *me* my wife Michal, whom I betrothed to myself for a hundred foreskins of
the Philistines." 15And Ishbosheth sent and
took her from *her* husband, from Paltiel[a] the
son of Laish. 16Then her husband went along
with her to Bahurim, weeping behind her.

3:15 [a] Spelled *Palti* in 1 Samuel 25:44

So Abner said to him, "Go, return!" And he
returned.

17 Now Abner had communicated with
the elders of Israel, saying, "In time past you
were seeking for David *to be* king over you.
18 Now then, do *it!* For the LORD has spoken
of David, saying, 'By the hand of My servant
David, I[a] will save My people Israel from the
hand of the Philistines and the hand of all
their enemies.'" 19 And Abner also spoke in
the hearing of Benjamin. Then Abner also
went to speak in the hearing of David in Hebron all that seemed good to Israel and the
whole house of Benjamin.

20 So Abner and twenty men with him
came to David at Hebron. And David made
a feast for Abner and the men who *were*
with him. 21 Then Abner said to David, "I
will arise and go, and gather all Israel to
my lord the king, that they may make a covenant with you, and that you may reign over
all that your heart desires." So David sent
Abner away, and he went in peace.

Joab Murders Abner

22 At that moment the servants of David
and Joab came from a raid and brought
much spoil with them. But Abner *was* not
with David in Hebron, for he had sent him
away, and he had gone in peace. 23 When
Joab and all the troops that *were* with him
had come, they told Joab, saying, "Abner the
son of Ner came to the king, and he sent him
away, and he has gone in peace." 24 Then Joab
came to the king and said, "What have you
done? Look, Abner came to you; why *is* it *that*
you sent him away, and he has already gone?
25 Surely you realize that Abner the son of Ner
came to deceive you, to know your going out
and your coming in, and to know all that you
are doing."

26 And when Joab had gone from David's
presence, he sent messengers after Abner,
who brought him back from the well of
Sirah. But David did not know *it.* 27 Now
when Abner had returned to Hebron, Joab
took him aside in the gate to speak with him
privately, and there stabbed him in the stomach, so that he died for the blood of Asahel
his brother.

28 Afterward, when David heard *it,* he
said, "My kingdom and I *are* guiltless before
the LORD forever of the blood of Abner the
son of Ner. 29 Let it rest on the head of Joab
and on all his father's house; and let there
never fail to be in the house of Joab one who
has a discharge or is a leper, who leans on
a staff or falls by the sword, or who lacks
bread." 30 So Joab and Abishai his brother
killed Abner, because he had killed their
brother Asahel at Gibeon in the battle.

David's Mourning for Abner

31 Then David said to Joab and to all
the people who were with him, "Tear your
clothes, gird yourselves with sackcloth, and
mourn for Abner." And King David followed
the coffin. 32 So they buried Abner in Hebron; and the king lifted up his voice and
wept at the grave of Abner, and all the people wept. 33 And the king sang *a lament* over
Abner and said:

"Should Abner die as a fool dies?
34 Your hands were not bound
Nor your feet put into fetters;
As a man falls before wicked men, *so*
you fell."

Then all the people wept over him again.

35 And when all the people came to persuade David to eat food while it was still day,
David took an oath, saying, "God do so to
me, and more also, if I taste bread or anything else till the sun goes down!" 36 Now
all the people took note *of it,* and it pleased
them, since whatever the king did pleased
all the people. 37 For all the people and all Israel understood that day that it had not been
the king's *intent* to kill Abner the son of Ner.
38 Then the king said to his servants, "Do you
not know that a prince and a great man has
fallen this day in Israel? 39 And I *am* weak today, though anointed king; and these men,
the sons of Zeruiah, *are* too harsh for me.
The LORD shall repay the evildoer according
to his wickedness."

Ishbosheth Is Murdered

4 When Saul's son[a] heard that Abner had
died in Hebron, he lost heart, and all
Israel was troubled. 2 Now Saul's son *had* two
men *who were* captains of troops. The name
of one *was* Baanah and the name of the other
Rechab, the sons of Rimmon the Beerothite,
of the children of Benjamin. (For Beeroth
also was *part* of Benjamin, 3 because the
Beerothites fled to Gittaim and have been
sojourners there until this day.)

3:18 [a] Following many Hebrew manuscripts, Septuagint, Syriac, and Targum; Masoretic Text reads *he.* 4:1 [a] That is, Ishbosheth

4Jonathan, Saul's son, had a son *who was*
lame in *his* feet. He was five years old when
the news about Saul and Jonathan came
from Jezreel; and his nurse took him up and
fled. And it happened, as she made haste to
flee, that he fell and became lame. His name
was Mephibosheth.[a]
5Then the sons of Rimmon the Beerothite, Rechab and Baanah, set out and came
at about the heat of the day to the house of
Ishbosheth, who was lying on his bed at
noon. 6And they came there, all the way into
the house, *as though* to get wheat, and they
stabbed him in the stomach. Then Rechab
and Baanah his brother escaped. 7For when
they came into the house, he was lying on
his bed in his bedroom; then they struck
him and killed him, beheaded him and
took his head, and were all night escaping
through the plain. 8And they brought the
head of Ishbosheth to David at Hebron, and
said to the king, "Here is the head of Ishbosheth, the son of Saul your enemy, who
sought your life; and the LORD has avenged
my lord the king this day of Saul and his
descendants."
9But David answered Rechab and Baanah
his brother, the sons of Rimmon the Beerothite, and said to them, "*As* the LORD lives,
who has redeemed my life from all adversity, 10when someone told me, saying, 'Look,
Saul is dead,' thinking to have brought
good news, I arrested him and had him
executed in Ziklag—the one who *thought* I
would give him a reward for *his* news. 11How
much more, when wicked men have killed
a righteous person in his own house on his
bed? Therefore, shall I not now require his
blood at your hand and remove you from the
earth?" 12So David commanded his young
men, and they executed them, cut off their
hands and feet, and hanged *them* by the
pool in Hebron. But they took the head of
Ishbosheth and buried *it* in the tomb of Abner in Hebron.

David Reigns over All Israel

5 Then all the tribes of Israel came to
David at Hebron and spoke, saying,
"Indeed we *are* your bone and your flesh.
2Also, in time past, when Saul was king over
us, you were the one who led Israel out and
brought them in; and the LORD said to you,
'You shall shepherd My people Israel, and be
ruler over Israel.'" 3Therefore all the elders
of Israel came to the king at Hebron, and
King David made a covenant with them at
Hebron before the LORD. And they anointed David king over Israel. 4David *was* thirty
years old when he began to reign, *and* he
reigned forty years. 5In Hebron he reigned
over Judah seven years and six months, and
in Jerusalem he reigned thirty-three years
over all Israel and Judah.

4:4 [a] Called *Merib-Baal* in 1 Chronicles 8:34 and 9:40

5:5 DAVID RULES OVER ALL ISRAEL

There were 12 tribes, or nations, in the greater nation of Israel. David came from the tribe of Judah, and for seven years, he ruled over that tribe. Then there was a long war between David and the rest of Israel, which was led by the tribe of Benjamin.

At last the other tribes of Israel came and asked David to be their king, too. So David ruled over all 12 tribes of Israel for 33 years. David was a king for 40 years, beginning about a thousand years before Jesus was born. God called David the man with a heart like His.

As you go through life, you also can have a heart like God's. You can still please Him, even though sometimes you fail as David did.

The Conquest of Jerusalem

6And the king and his men went to Jerusalem against the Jebusites, the inhabitants
of the land, who spoke to David, saying, "You
shall not come in here; but the blind and the
lame will repel you," thinking, "David cannot come in here." 7Nevertheless David took
the stronghold of Zion (that *is*, the City of
David).

8Now David said on that day, "Whoever
climbs up by way of the water shaft and de-
feats the Jebusites (the lame and the blind,
who are hated by David's soul), *he shall be
chief and captain*."[a] Therefore they say, "The
blind and the lame shall not come into the
house."

9Then David dwelt in the stronghold, and
called it the City of David. And David built
all around from the Millo[a] and inward. 10So
David went on and became great, and the
LORD God of hosts *was* with him.

11Then Hiram king of Tyre sent messengers to David, and cedar trees, and carpenters and masons. And they built David
a house. 12So David knew that the LORD had
established him as king over Israel, and that
He had exalted His kingdom for the sake of
His people Israel.

13And David took more concubines and
wives from Jerusalem, after he had come
from Hebron. Also more sons and daughters were born to David. 14Now these *are*
the names of those who were born to him

5:8 [a] Compare 1 Chronicles 11:6 5:9 [a] Literally *The Landfill*

GOD MAKES DAVID KING

READ IT: 2 SAMUEL 5:1–25

GET IT:

God had a special plan for David, the young boy who trusted Him to help him kill Goliath. He planned to make him the second king of Israel. David was in training for this position for a long time. He served King Saul in the palace and led armies in battle for years. David trusted God when Saul became jealous of David's success and tried to kill him. David was on the run for years. He had opportunities to kill his enemy, Saul, but he would not hurt the person God had chosen as king. Finally, after Saul was killed in a battle, David became the new king of Israel. He was only thirty years old!

LIVE IT:

David had to work hard before he got to the position of king. When he was a boy he was a shepherd who slept outside, fought wild animals to protect the sheep, and killed a giant. When he was a teenager he served the king in the palace (and almost got killed by a spear thrown at him) and fought in many wars. As a young man he was on the run from the king who wanted to kill him. Once again he lived outside or in caves. Not a pretty life for a future king. But God had a plan. All of this was training David to be a great king. God has a plan for your life, too. You may not understand exactly what He's doing. You may suffer through some rough stuff. But trust Him. He's preparing you to serve Him in bigger ways.

in Jerusalem: Shammua,[a] Shobab, Nathan,
Solomon, 15Ibhar, Elishua,[a] Nepheg, Japhia,
16Elishama, Eliada, and Eliphelet.

The Philistines Defeated

17Now when the Philistines heard that
they had anointed David king over Israel, all
the Philistines went up to search for David.
And David heard *of it* and went down to the
stronghold. 18The Philistines also went and
deployed themselves in the Valley of Rephaim. 19So David inquired of the LORD, saying,
"Shall I go up against the Philistines? Will
You deliver them into my hand?"

And the LORD said to David, "Go up, for
I will doubtless deliver the Philistines into
your hand."

20So David went to Baal Perazim, and
David defeated them there; and he said,
"The LORD has broken through my enemies
before me, like a breakthrough of water."
Therefore he called the name of that place
Baal Perazim.[a] 21And they left their images
there, and David and his men carried them
away.

22Then the Philistines went up once
again and deployed themselves in the Valley
of Rephaim. 23Therefore David inquired of
the LORD, and He said, "You shall not go up;
circle around behind them, and come upon
them in front of the mulberry trees. 24And it
shall be, when you hear the sound of marching in the tops of the mulberry trees, then
you shall advance quickly. For then the LORD
will go out before you to strike the camp of
the Philistines." 25And David did so, as the
LORD commanded him; and he drove back
the Philistines from Geba[a] as far as Gezer.

The Ark Brought to Jerusalem

6 Again David gathered all *the* choice
men of Israel, thirty thousand. 2And
David arose and went with all the people
who *were* with him from Baale Judah to
bring up from there the ark of God, whose
name is called by the Name,[a] the LORD of
Hosts, who dwells *between* the cherubim.
3So they set the ark of God on a new cart,
and brought it out of the house of Abinadab, which *was* on the hill; and Uzzah and
Ahio, the sons of Abinadab, drove the new
cart.[a] 4And they brought it out of the house
of Abinadab, which *was* on the hill, accompanying the ark of God; and Ahio went before the ark. 5Then David and all the house
of Israel played *music* before the LORD on all
kinds of *instruments of* fir wood, on harps,
on stringed instruments, on tambourines,
on sistrums, and on cymbals.

6And when they came to Nachon's
threshing floor, Uzzah put out *his hand* to
the ark of God and took hold of it, for the
oxen stumbled. 7Then the anger of the LORD
was aroused against Uzzah, and God struck
him there for *his* error; and he died there by

5:14 [a] Spelled *Shimea* in 1 Chronicles 3:5 5:15 [a] Spelled *Elishama* in 1 Chronicles 3:6 5:20 [a] Literally *Master of Breakthroughs* 5:25 [a] Following Masoretic Text, Targum, and Vulgate; Septuagint reads *Gibeon*. 6:2 [a] Septuagint, Targum, and Vulgate omit *by the Name;* many Hebrew manuscripts and Syriac read *there*. 6:3 [a] Septuagint adds *with the ark*.

BEING YOURSELF

READ IT: 2 SAMUEL 6:1–23

David was happy. Life was good! The ark of the Lord was brought to his hometown, and with it came a party. People were feasting and dancing in the streets, including King David. One of Saul's daughters, who was also David's wife, saw him dancing so freely and thought he was being foolish. She even confronted him about it later, saying he should be ashamed of himself. David's reply? No way! God was with him, and he was going to celebrate.

the ark of God. [8]And David became angry
because of the LORD's outbreak against Uzzah; and he called the name of the place Perez Uzzah[a] to this day.

[9]David was afraid of the LORD that day;
and he said, "How can the ark of the LORD
come to me?" [10]So David would not move
the ark of the LORD with him into the City of
David; but David took it aside into the house
of Obed-Edom the Gittite. [11]The ark of the
LORD remained in the house of Obed-Edom
the Gittite three months. And the LORD
blessed Obed-Edom and all his household.

[12]Now it was told King David, saying,
"The LORD has blessed the house of Obed-
Edom and all that *belongs* to him, because of
the ark of God." So David went and brought
up the ark of God from the house of Obed-
Edom to the City of David with gladness.
[13]And so it was, when those bearing the ark
of the LORD had gone six paces, that he sacrificed oxen and fatted sheep. [14]Then David
danced before the LORD with all *his* might;
and David *was* wearing a linen ephod. [15]So
David and all the house of Israel brought up
the ark of the LORD with shouting and with
the sound of the trumpet.

[16]Now as the ark of the LORD came into
the City of David, Michal, Saul's daughter,
looked through a window and saw King David leaping and whirling before the LORD;
and she despised him in her heart. [17]So they
brought the ark of the LORD, and set it in
its place in the midst of the tabernacle that
David had erected for it. Then David offered
burnt offerings and peace offerings before
the LORD. [18]And when David had finished offering burnt offerings and peace offerings,
he blessed the people in the name of the
LORD of hosts. [19]Then he distributed among
all the people, among the whole multitude
of Israel, both the women and the men, to
everyone a loaf of bread, a piece *of meat,* and
a cake of raisins. So all the people departed,
everyone to his house.

[20]Then David returned to bless his
household. And Michal the daughter of Saul
came out to meet David, and said, "How glorious was the king of Israel today, uncovering himself today in the eyes of the maids
of his servants, as one of the base fellows
shamelessly uncovers himself!"

[21]So David said to Michal, "*It was* before
the LORD, who chose me instead of your
father and all his house, to appoint me
ruler over the people of the LORD, over Israel. Therefore I will play *music* before the
LORD. [22]And I will be even more undignified
than this, and will be humble in my own
sight. But as for the maidservants of whom
you have spoken, by them I will be held in
honor."

[23]Therefore Michal the daughter of Saul
had no children to the day of her death.

6:8 [a] Literally *Outburst Against Uzzah*

RELATIONSHIPS

READ IT: 2 SAMUEL 7:1–17

In 2 Samuel 6, David was so joyful toward God that he danced to express his emotion. In chapter 7, David's gratefulness caused him to want to do more: to build a permanent home for the ark of God. God's response was beautiful. He was honored by David's desire, but He didn't ask him to build it. Instead, He told David how He would bless him and his descendants, which eventually included Jesus' earthly parents, Mary and Joseph. David's desire to do more to express his love and gratitude to God is a great, simple model for your relationship with God. He wants this kind of relationship with you!

God's Covenant with David

7 Now it came to pass when the king was
dwelling in his house, and the LORD
had given him rest from all his enemies
all around, 2that the king said to Nathan
the prophet, "See now, I dwell in a house of
cedar, but the ark of God dwells inside tent
curtains."

3Then Nathan said to the king, "Go, do
all that *is* in your heart, for the LORD *is* with
you."

4But it happened that night that the word
of the LORD came to Nathan, saying, 5"Go
and tell My servant David, 'Thus says the
LORD: "Would you build a house for Me to
dwell in? 6For I have not dwelt in a house
since the time that I brought the children of
Israel up from Egypt, even to this day, but
have moved about in a tent and in a tabernacle. 7Wherever I have moved about with
all the children of Israel, have I ever spoken
a word to anyone from the tribes of Israel,
whom I commanded to shepherd My people
Israel, saying, 'Why have you not built Me a
house of cedar?' "' 8Now therefore, thus shall
you say to My servant David, 'Thus says the
LORD of hosts: "I took you from the sheepfold, from following the sheep, to be ruler
over My people, over Israel. 9And I have been
with you wherever you have gone, and have
cut off all your enemies from before you,
and have made you a great name, like the
name of the great men who *are* on the earth.
10Moreover I will appoint a place for My people Israel, and will plant them, that they may
dwell in a place of their own and move no
more; nor shall the sons of wickedness oppress them anymore, as previously, 11since
the time that I commanded judges *to be* over
My people Israel, and have caused you to rest
from all your enemies. Also the LORD tells
you that He will make you a house.[a]

12"When your days are fulfilled and you
rest with your fathers, I will set up your seed
after you, who will come from your body,
and I will establish his kingdom. 13He shall
build a house for My name, and I will establish the throne of his kingdom forever. 14I
will be his Father, and he shall be My son.
If he commits iniquity, I will chasten him
with the rod of men and with the blows of
the sons of men. 15But My mercy shall not depart from him, as I took *it* from Saul, whom
I removed from before you. 16And your house
and your kingdom shall be established forever before you.[a] Your throne shall be established forever." ' "

17According to all these words and according to all this vision, so Nathan spoke
to David.

David's Thanksgiving to God

18Then King David went in and sat before the LORD; and he said: "Who *am* I, O
Lord GOD? And what is my house, that You
have brought me this far? 19And yet this was
a small thing in Your sight, O Lord GOD; and
You have also spoken of Your servant's house
for a great while to come. *Is* this the manner
of man, O Lord GOD? 20Now what more can
David say to You? For You, Lord GOD, know
Your servant. 21For Your word's sake, and according to Your own heart, You have done
all these great things, to make Your servant
know *them*. 22Therefore You are great, O
Lord GOD.[a] For *there is* none like You, nor *is*
there any God besides You, according to all
that we have heard with our ears. 23And who
is like Your people, like Israel, the one nation
on the earth whom God went to redeem for
Himself as a people, to make for Himself a
name—and to do for Yourself great and awesome deeds for Your land—before Your people whom You redeemed for Yourself from
Egypt, the nations, and their gods? 24For You
have made Your people Israel Your very own
people forever; and You, LORD, have become
their God.

25"Now, O LORD God, the word which You
have spoken concerning Your servant and
concerning his house, establish *it* forever
and do as You have said. 26So let Your name
be magnified forever, saying, 'The LORD
of hosts *is* the God over Israel.' And let the
house of Your servant David be established
before You. 27For You, O LORD of hosts, God
of Israel, have revealed *this* to Your servant,
saying, 'I will build you a house.' Therefore
Your servant has found it in his heart to pray
this prayer to You.

28"And now, O Lord GOD, You are God,
and Your words are true, and You have
promised this goodness to Your servant.
29Now therefore, let it please You to bless
the house of Your servant, that it may continue before You forever; for You, O Lord

7:11 [a] That is, a royal dynasty 7:16 [a] Septuagint reads *Me.*
7:22 [a] Targum and Syriac read *O LORD God.*

God, have spoken *it,* and with Your blessing let the house of Your servant be blessed
forever."

David's Further Conquests

8 After this it came to pass that David
attacked the Philistines and subdued
them. And David took Metheg Ammah from
the hand of the Philistines.
2Then he defeated Moab. Forcing them
down to the ground, he measured them off
with a line. With two lines he measured off
those to be put to death, and with one full
line those to be kept alive. So the Moabites
became David's servants, *and* brought
tribute.
3David also defeated Hadadezer the son
of Rehob, king of Zobah, as he went to recover his territory at the River Euphrates. 4David
took from him one thousand *chariots,* seven
hundred[a] horsemen, and twenty thousand
foot soldiers. Also David hamstrung all the
chariot *horses,* except that he spared *enough*
of them for one hundred chariots.
5When the Syrians of Damascus came to
help Hadadezer king of Zobah, David killed
twenty-two thousand of the Syrians. 6Then
David put garrisons in Syria of Damascus;
and the Syrians became David's servants,
and brought tribute. So the Lord preserved
David wherever he went. 7And David took
the shields of gold that had belonged to the
servants of Hadadezer, and brought them
to Jerusalem. 8Also from Betah[a] and from
Berothai, cities of Hadadezer, King David
took a large amount of bronze.
9When Toi[a] king of Hamath heard
that David had defeated all the army of
Hadadezer, 10then Toi sent Joram[a] his son to
King David, to greet him and bless him, because he had fought against Hadadezer and
defeated him (for Hadadezer had been at war
with Toi); and *Joram* brought with him articles of silver, articles of gold, and articles of
bronze. 11King David also dedicated these to
the Lord, along with the silver and gold that
he had dedicated from all the nations which
he had subdued— 12from Syria,[a] from Moab,
from the people of Ammon, from the Philistines, from Amalek, and from the spoil of
Hadadezer the son of Rehob, king of Zobah.
13And David made *himself* a name when
he returned from killing eighteen thousand
Syrians[a] in the Valley of Salt. 14He also put
garrisons in Edom; throughout all Edom he
put garrisons, and all the Edomites became
David's servants. And the Lord preserved
David wherever he went.

David's Administration

15So David reigned over all Israel; and
David administered judgment and justice
to all his people. 16Joab the son of Zeruiah
was over the army; Jehoshaphat the son of
Ahilud *was* recorder; 17Zadok the son of
Ahitub and Ahimelech the son of Abiathar
were the priests; Seraiah[a] *was* the scribe; 18Be-
naiah the son of Jehoiada *was over* both the

8:4 [a] Or *seven thousand* (compare 1 Chronicles 18:4)
8:8 [a] Spelled *Tibhath* in 1 Chronicles 18:8 8:9 [a] Spelled *Tou* in 1 Chronicles 18:9 8:10 [a] Spelled *Hadoram* in 1 Chronicles 18:10 8:12 [a] Septuagint, Syriac, and some Hebrew manuscripts read *Edom.* 8:13 [a] Septuagint, Syriac, and some Hebrew manuscripts read *Edomites* (compare 1 Chronicles 18:12). 8:17 [a] Spelled *Shavsha* in 1 Chronicles 18:16

KINDNESS

READ IT: 2 SAMUEL 9:1–13

Think of the person in your life who least expects you to be kind—maybe it's a step-parent or a former friend or a teacher no one likes. Start *praying and asking God* how you can show this person kindness. It may not be easy, and this person may not respond like you hope. But you can be sure that your kindness will not be overlooked by God.

Cherethites and the Pelethites; and David's
sons were chief ministers.

David's Kindness to Mephibosheth

9 Now David said, "Is there still anyone
who is left of the house of Saul, that
I may show him kindness for Jonathan's
sake?"
2 And *there was* a servant of the house of
Saul whose name *was* Ziba. So when they
had called him to David, the king said to
him, "*Are* you Ziba?"
He said, "At your service!"
3 Then the king said, "*Is* there not still
someone of the house of Saul, to whom I
may show the kindness of God?"
And Ziba said to the king, "There is still
a son of Jonathan *who is* lame in *his* feet."
4 So the king said to him, "Where *is* he?"
And Ziba said to the king, "Indeed he *is*
in the house of Machir the son of Ammiel,
in Lo Debar."
5 Then King David sent and brought him
out of the house of Machir the son of Ammiel,
from Lo Debar.
6 Now when Mephibosheth the son of
Jonathan, the son of Saul, had come to David,
he fell on his face and prostrated himself.
Then David said, "Mephibosheth?"
And he answered, "Here is your servant!"
7 So David said to him, "Do not fear, for I
will surely show you kindness for Jonathan
your father's sake, and will restore to you all
the land of Saul your grandfather; and you
shall eat bread at my table continually."
8 Then he bowed himself, and said,
"What *is* your servant, that you should look
upon such a dead dog as I?"
9 And the king called to Ziba, Saul's servant,
and said to him, "I have given to your
master's son all that belonged to Saul and
to all his house. 10 You therefore, and your
sons and your servants, shall work the land
for him, and you shall bring in *the harvest,*
that your master's son may have food to eat.
But Mephibosheth your master's son shall
eat bread at my table always." Now Ziba had
fifteen sons and twenty servants.
11 Then Ziba said to the king, "According
to all that my lord the king has commanded
his servant, so will your servant do."
"As for Mephibosheth," *said the king,* "he
shall eat at my table[a] like one of the king's
sons." 12 Mephibosheth had a young son
whose name *was* Micha. And all who dwelt
in the house of Ziba *were* servants of Mephibosheth.
13 So Mephibosheth dwelt in Jerusalem,
for he ate continually at the king's
table. And he was lame in both his feet.

9:11 [a] Septuagint reads *David's table.*

Starring Roles

MEPHIBOSHETH (pronounced *meh-FIB-oh-sheth*) was five years old when his father Jonathan and his grandfather Saul were killed in battle. When Mephibosheth's nurse was trying to save him, he fell and became lame for the rest of his life.

Long before this, King David had promised he would always take care of Jonathan's family. (See 1 Samuel 20:14, 15.) David and Jonathan had loved each other like brothers.

David kept his promise. He gave Mephibosheth all of his grandfather's property. Saul's servants would then farm the family's land for Mephibosheth while he lived at King David's palace like one of his own sons.

King David was not always right in what he did, but he truly loved God. Sometimes you can see that he was like his greater Son, Jesus. Like Jesus, David forgave his enemies and was kind to them. (See Luke 23:34.) David was kind to Mephibosheth, too.

The Ammonites and Syrians Defeated

10 It happened after this that the king of the people of Ammon died, and Hanun his son reigned in his place. 2 Then David said, "I will show kindness to Hanun the son of Nahash, as his father showed kindness to me."

So David sent by the hand of his servants to comfort him concerning his father. And David's servants came into the land of the people of Ammon. 3 And the princes of the people of Ammon said to Hanun their lord, "Do you think that David really honors your father because he has sent comforters to you? Has David not *rather* sent his servants to you to search the city, to spy it out, and to overthrow it?"

4 Therefore Hanun took David's servants, shaved off half of their beards, cut off their garments in the middle, at their buttocks, and sent them away. 5 When they told David, he sent to meet them, because the men were greatly ashamed. And the king said, "Wait at Jericho until your beards have grown, and *then* return."

6 When the people of Ammon saw that they had made themselves repulsive to David, the people of Ammon sent and hired the Syrians of Beth Rehob and the Syrians of Zoba, twenty thousand foot soldiers; and from the king of Maacah one thousand men, and from Ish-Tob twelve thousand men. 7 Now when David heard *of it,* he sent Joab and all the army of the mighty men. 8 Then the people of Ammon came out and put themselves in battle array at the entrance of the gate. And the Syrians of Zoba, Beth Rehob, Ish-Tob, and Maacah *were* by themselves in the field.

9 When Joab saw that the battle line was against him before and behind, he chose some of Israel's best and put *them* in battle array against the Syrians. 10 And the rest of the people he put under the command of Abishai his brother, that he might set *them* in battle array against the people of Ammon. 11 Then he said, "If the Syrians are too strong for me, then you shall help me; but if the people of Ammon are too strong for you, then I will come and help you. 12 Be of good courage, and let us be strong for our people and for the cities of our God. And may the LORD do *what is* good in His sight."

13 So Joab and the people who *were* with him drew near for the battle against the Syrians, and they fled before him. 14 When the people of Ammon saw that the Syrians were fleeing, they also fled before Abishai, and entered the city. So Joab returned from the people of Ammon and went to Jerusalem.

15 When the Syrians saw that they had been defeated by Israel, they gathered together. 16 Then Hadadezer[a] sent and brought out the Syrians who *were* beyond the River,[b] and they came to Helam. And Shobach the commander of Hadadezer's army *went* before them. 17 When it was told David, he gathered all Israel, crossed over the Jordan, and came to Helam. And the Syrians set themselves in battle array against David and fought with him. 18 Then the Syrians fled before Israel; and David killed seven hundred charioteers and forty thousand horsemen of the Syrians, and struck Shobach the commander of their army, who died there. 19 And when all the kings *who were* servants to Hadadezer[a] saw that they were defeated by Israel, they made peace with Israel and served them. So the Syrians were afraid to help the people of Ammon anymore.

David, Bathsheba, and Uriah

11 It happened in the spring of the year, at the time when kings go out *to battle,* that David sent Joab and his servants with him, and all Israel; and they destroyed the people of Ammon and besieged Rabbah. But David remained at Jerusalem.

2 Then it happened one evening that David arose from his bed and walked on the roof of the king's house. And from the roof he saw a woman bathing, and the woman *was* very beautiful to behold. 3 So David sent and inquired about the woman. And *someone* said, "*Is* this not Bathsheba, the daughter of Eliam, the wife of Uriah the Hittite?" 4 Then David sent messengers, and took her; and she came to him, and he lay with her, for she was cleansed from her impurity; and she returned to her house. 5 And the woman conceived; so she sent and told David, and said, "I *am* with child."

6 Then David sent to Joab, *saying,* "Send me Uriah the Hittite." And Joab sent Uriah to David. 7 When Uriah had come to him, David asked how Joab was doing, and how the

---

10:16 [a] Hebrew *Hadarezer* [b] That is, the *Euphrates*
10:19 [a] Hebrew *Hadarezer*

people were doing, and how the war prospered. 8And David said to Uriah, "Go down
to your house and wash your feet." So Uriah
departed from the king's house, and a gift *of*
food from the king followed him. 9But Uriah
slept at the door of the king's house with all
the servants of his lord, and did not go down
to his house. 10So when they told David, saying, "Uriah did not go down to his house,"
David said to Uriah, "Did you not come from
a journey? Why did you not go down to your
house?"

11And Uriah said to David, "The ark and
Israel and Judah are dwelling in tents, and
my lord Joab and the servants of my lord are
encamped in the open fields. Shall I then go
to my house to eat and drink, and to lie with
my wife? *As* you live, and *as* your soul lives, I
will not do this thing."

12Then David said to Uriah, "Wait here
today also, and tomorrow I will let you depart." So Uriah remained in Jerusalem that
day and the next. 13Now when David called
him, he ate and drank before him; and he
made him drunk. And at evening he went
out to lie on his bed with the servants of his
lord, but he did not go down to his house.

14In the morning it happened that David
wrote a letter to Joab and sent *it* by the hand
of Uriah. 15And he wrote in the letter, saying, "Set Uriah in the forefront of the hottest
battle, and retreat from him, that he may be
struck down and die." 16So it was, while Joab
besieged the city, that he assigned Uriah to
a place where he knew there *were* valiant
men. 17Then the men of the city came out
and fought with Joab. And *some* of the people
of the servants of David fell; and Uriah the
Hittite died also.

18Then Joab sent and told David all the
things concerning the war, 19and charged the
messenger, saying, "When you have finished
telling the matters of the war to the king, 20if
it happens that the king's wrath rises, and he
says to you: 'Why did you approach so near to
the city when you fought? Did you not know
that they would shoot from the wall? 21Who
struck Abimelech the son of Jerubbesheth?[a]
Was it not a woman who cast a piece of a millstone on him from the wall, so that he died
in Thebez? Why did you go near the wall?'—
then you shall say, 'Your servant Uriah the
Hittite is dead also.'"

22So the messenger went, and came and
told David all that Joab had sent by him.
23And the messenger said to David, "Surely
the men prevailed against us and came out
to us in the field; then we drove them back as
far as the entrance of the gate. 24The archers
shot from the wall at your servants; and *some*
of the king's servants are dead, and your servant Uriah the Hittite is dead also."

11:21 [a] Same as *Jerubbaal* (Gideon), Judges 6:32ff

Starring Roles

BATHSHEBA'S name is pronounced *bath-SHE-bah*. She was the wife of Uriah (pronounced *you-RIGH-uh*), a soldier in King David's army. Bathsheba was all that poor Uriah had, but David stole her from him. David also arranged to have Uriah killed in battle, so that he could feel free to take Bathsheba as his own wife.

The prophet Nathan (pronounced *NAY-thun*) finally accused David of his *great sin* (see 2 Samuel 12), and David had to confess, "I have sinned." David and Bathsheba's innocent infant son died because of what David had done. A thousand years later, David's greater Son, Jesus, would die for the sins of the whole world.

David was sorry for his sins. Then God gave him and Bathsheba another son, whose name was Solomon, meaning "Peaceful." Yes, the Lord did make peace with David. Solomon grew up to be king of Israel, the greatest country in the world of that day.

25Then David said to the messenger,
"Thus you shall say to Joab: 'Do not let this
thing displease you, for the sword devours
one as well as another. Strengthen your attack against the city, and overthrow it.' So
encourage him."
26When the wife of Uriah heard that
Uriah her husband was dead, she mourned
for her husband. 27And when her mourning
was over, David sent and brought her to his
house, and she became his wife and bore
him a son. But the thing that David had done
displeased the LORD.

Nathan's Parable and David's Confession

12 Then the LORD sent Nathan to David. And he came to him, and said
to him: "There were two men in one city, one
rich and the other poor. 2The rich *man* had
exceedingly many flocks and herds. 3But the
poor *man* had nothing, except one little ewe
lamb which he had bought and nourished;
and it grew up together with him and with
his children. It ate of his own food and drank
from his own cup and lay in his bosom; and
it was like a daughter to him. 4And a traveler
came to the rich man, who refused to take
from his own flock and from his own herd
to prepare one for the wayfaring man who
had come to him; but he took the poor man's
lamb and prepared it for the man who had
come to him."
5So David's anger was greatly aroused
against the man, and he said to Nathan, "*As*
the LORD lives, the man who has done this
shall surely die! 6And he shall restore fourfold for the lamb, because he did this thing
and because he had no pity."
7Then Nathan said to David, "You *are* the
man! Thus says the LORD God of Israel: 'I
anointed you king over Israel, and I delivered you from the hand of Saul. 8I gave you
your master's house and your master's wives
into your keeping, and gave you the house of
Israel and Judah. And if *that had been* too little, I also would have given you much more!
9Why have you despised the commandment
of the LORD, to do evil in His sight? You have
killed Uriah the Hittite with the sword; you
have taken his wife *to be* your wife, and have
killed him with the sword of the people of
Ammon. 10Now therefore, the sword shall
never depart from your house, because you
have despised Me, and have taken the wife of
Uriah the Hittite to be your wife.' 11Thus says
the LORD: 'Behold, I will raise up adversity
against you from your own house; and I will
take your wives before your eyes and give
them to your neighbor, and he shall lie with
your wives in the sight of this sun. 12For you
did *it* secretly, but I will do this thing before
all Israel, before the sun.'"
13So David said to Nathan, "I have sinned
against the LORD."
And Nathan said to David, "The LORD
also has put away your sin; you shall not die.
14However, because by this deed you have
given great occasion to the enemies of the
LORD to blaspheme, the child also *who is*
born to you shall surely die." 15Then Nathan
departed to his house.

GUILT

READ IT: 2 SAMUEL 12:1–15

David is referred to in the Bible as a man after God's own heart. However, he wasn't perfect. He made some sinful choices and had a man killed to cover up his mistakes. But David couldn't escape this sin. God sent the prophet Nathan to confront David, and eventually David owned up. Next time you're feeling guilty because you're trying to keep a sin a secret, take courage in knowing God will forgive you when you confess your sin to Him.

wept. Also the king and all his servants wept
very bitterly.
37But Absalom fled and went to Talmai
the son of Ammihud, king of Geshur. And
David mourned for his son every day. 38So
Absalom fled and went to Geshur, and was
there three years. 39And King David[a] longed
to go to[b] Absalom. For he had been comforted concerning Amnon, because he was
dead.

Absalom Returns to Jerusalem

14 So Joab the son of Zeruiah perceived that the king's heart *was*
concerned about Absalom. 2And Joab sent to
Tekoa and brought from there a wise woman, and said to her, "Please pretend to be a
mourner, and put on mourning apparel; do
not anoint yourself with oil, but act like a
woman who has been mourning a long time
for the dead. 3Go to the king and speak to
him in this manner." So Joab put the words
in her mouth.
4And when the woman of Tekoa spoke[a]
to the king, she fell on her face to the ground
and prostrated herself, and said, "Help, O
king!"
5Then the king said to her, "What troubles you?"
And she answered, "Indeed I *am* a widow, my husband is dead. 6Now your maidservant had two sons; and the two fought with
each other in the field, and *there was* no one
to part them, but the one struck the other
and killed him. 7And now the whole family
has risen up against your maidservant, and
they said, 'Deliver him who struck his brother, that we may execute him for the life of his
brother whom he killed; and we will destroy
the heir also.' So they would extinguish my
ember that is left, and leave to my husband
neither name nor remnant on the earth."
8Then the king said to the woman, "Go
to your house, and I will give orders concerning you."
9And the woman of Tekoa said to the
king, "My lord, O king, *let* the iniquity *be* on
me and on my father's house, and the king
and his throne *be* guiltless."
10So the king said, "Whoever says *anything* to you, bring him to me, and he shall
not touch you anymore."
11Then she said, "Please let the king remember the LORD your God, and do not
permit the avenger of blood to destroy anymore, lest they destroy my son."
And he said, "*As* the LORD lives, not one
hair of your son shall fall to the ground."
12Therefore the woman said, "Please, let
your maidservant speak *another* word to my
lord the king."
And he said, "Say on."
13So the woman said: "Why then have
you schemed such a thing against the people of God? For the king speaks this thing
as one who is guilty, *in that* the king does
not bring his banished one home again.
14For we will surely die and *become* like water
spilled on the ground, which cannot be gathered up again. Yet God does not take away
a life; but He devises means, so that His
banished ones are not expelled from Him.
15Now therefore, I have come to speak of this
thing to my lord the king because the people
have made me afraid. And your maidservant
said, 'I will now speak to the king; it may
be that the king will perform the request of
his maidservant. 16For the king will hear and
deliver his maidservant from the hand of the
man *who would* destroy me and my son together from the inheritance of God.' 17Your
maidservant said, 'The word of my lord the
king will now be comforting; for as the angel
of God, so *is* my lord the king in discerning
good and evil. And may the LORD your God
be with you.'"
18Then the king answered and said to the
woman, "Please do not hide from me anything that I ask you."
And the woman said, "Please, let my lord
the king speak."
19So the king said, "*Is* the hand of Joab
with you in all this?" And the woman answered and said, "*As* you live, my lord the
king, no one can turn to the right hand or
to the left from anything that my lord the
king has spoken. For your servant Joab commanded me, and he put all these words in
the mouth of your maidservant. 20To bring
about this change of affairs your servant
Joab has done this thing; but my lord *is* wise,

13:39 [a] Following Masoretic Text, Syriac, and Vulgate; Septuagint reads *the spirit of the king;* Targum reads *the soul of King David.* [b] Following Masoretic Text and Targum; Septuagint and Vulgate read *ceased to pursue after.*
14:4 [a] Many Hebrew manuscripts, Septuagint, Syriac, and Vulgate read *came.*

according to the wisdom of the angel of God,
to know everything that *is* in the earth."
21And the king said to Joab, "All right, I
have granted this thing. Go therefore, bring
back the young man Absalom."
22Then Joab fell to the ground on his face
and bowed himself, and thanked the king.
And Joab said, "Today your servant knows
that I have found favor in your sight, my
lord, O king, in that the king has fulfilled
the request of his servant." 23So Joab arose
and went to Geshur, and brought Absalom
to Jerusalem. 24And the king said, "Let him
return to his own house, but do not let him
see my face." So Absalom returned to his
own house, but did not see the king's face.

David Forgives Absalom

25Now in all Israel there was no one
who was praised as much as Absalom for
his good looks. From the sole of his foot to
the crown of his head there was no blemish
in him. 26And when he cut the hair of his
head—at the end of every year he cut *it* because it was heavy on him—when he cut it,
he weighed the hair of his head at two hundred shekels according to the king's standard. 27To Absalom were born three sons,
and one daughter whose name *was* Tamar.
She was a woman of beautiful appearance.
28And Absalom dwelt two full years in
Jerusalem, but did not see the king's face.
29Therefore Absalom sent for Joab, to send
him to the king, but he would not come to
him. And when he sent again the second
time, he would not come. 30So he said to his
servants, "See, Joab's field is near mine, and
he has barley there; go and set it on fire."
And Absalom's servants set the field on fire.
31Then Joab arose and came to Absalom's
house, and said to him, "Why have your servants set my field on fire?"
32And Absalom answered Joab, "Look,
I sent to you, saying, 'Come here, so that I
may send you to the king, to say, "Why have I
come from Geshur? *It would be* better for me
to be there still."' Now therefore, let me see
the king's face; but if there is iniquity in me,
let him execute me."
33So Joab went to the king and told him.
And when he had called for Absalom, he
came to the king and bowed himself on his
face to the ground before the king. Then the
king kissed Absalom.

Absalom's Treason

15 After this it happened that Absalom
provided himself with chariots and
horses, and fifty men to run before him.
2Now Absalom would rise early and stand beside the way to the gate. *So* it was, whenever
anyone who had a lawsuit came to the king
for a decision, that Absalom would call to
him and say, "What city *are* you from?" And
he would say, "Your servant *is* from such
and such a tribe of Israel." 3Then Absalom
would say to him, "Look, your case *is* good
and right; but *there is* no deputy of the king
to hear you." 4Moreover Absalom would say,
"Oh, that I were made judge in the land, and
everyone who has any suit or cause would
come to me; then I would give him justice."
5And *so* it was, whenever anyone came near
to bow down to him, that he would put out
his hand and take him and kiss him. 6In this
manner Absalom acted toward all Israel who
came to the king for judgment. So Absalom
stole the hearts of the men of Israel.
7Now it came to pass after forty[a] years
that Absalom said to the king, "Please, let
me go to Hebron and pay the vow which I
made to the LORD. 8For your servant took a
vow while I dwelt at Geshur in Syria, saying,
'If the LORD indeed brings me back to Jerusalem, then I will serve the LORD.'"
9And the king said to him, "Go in peace."
So he arose and went to Hebron.
10Then Absalom sent spies throughout
all the tribes of Israel, saying, "As soon as
you hear the sound of the trumpet, then you
shall say, 'Absalom reigns in Hebron!'" 11And
with Absalom went two hundred men invited from Jerusalem, and they went along innocently and did not know anything. 12Then
Absalom sent for Ahithophel the Gilonite,
David's counselor, from his city—from
Giloh—while he offered sacrifices. And the
conspiracy grew strong, for the people with
Absalom continually increased in number.

David Escapes from Jerusalem

13Now a messenger came to David, saying, "The hearts of the men of Israel are with
Absalom."
14So David said to all his servants who
were with him at Jerusalem, "Arise, and let
us flee, or we shall not escape from Absalom. Make haste to depart, lest he overtake

---

15:7 [a] Septuagint manuscripts, Syriac, and Josephus read *four*.

us suddenly and bring disaster upon us, and
strike the city with the edge of the sword."
15And the king's servants said to the king,
"We *are* your servants, *ready to do* whatever
my lord the king commands." 16Then the
king went out with all his household after
him. But the king left ten women, concubines, to keep the house. 17And the king
went out with all the people after him, and
stopped at the outskirts. 18Then all his servants passed before him; and all the Cherethites, all the Pelethites, and all the Gittites,
six hundred men who had followed him
from Gath, passed before the king.
19Then the king said to Ittai the Gittite,
"Why are you also going with us? Return
and remain with the king. For you *are* a
foreigner and also an exile from your own
place. 20In fact, you came *only* yesterday.
Should I make you wander up and down
with us today, since I go I know not where?
Return, and take your brethren back. Mercy
and truth *be* with you."
21But Ittai answered the king and said,
"*As* the LORD lives, and *as* my lord the king
lives, surely in whatever place my lord the
king shall be, whether in death or life, even
there also your servant will be."
22So David said to Ittai, "Go, and cross
over." Then Ittai the Gittite and all his men
and all the little ones who *were* with him
crossed over. 23And all the country wept
with a loud voice, and all the people crossed
over. The king himself also crossed over the
Brook Kidron, and all the people crossed
over toward the way of the wilderness.
24There was Zadok also, and all the Levites with him, bearing the ark of the covenant of God. And they set down the ark
of God, and Abiathar went up until all the
people had finished crossing over from the
city. 25Then the king said to Zadok, "Carry
the ark of God back into the city. If I find
favor in the eyes of the LORD, He will bring
me back and show me *both* it and His dwelling place. 26But if He says thus: 'I have no
delight in you,' here I am, let Him do to me
as seems good to Him." 27The king also said
to Zadok the priest, "*Are* you *not* a seer? Return to the city in peace, and your two sons
with you, Ahimaaz your son, and Jonathan
the son of Abiathar. 28See, I will wait in the
plains of the wilderness until word comes
from you to inform me." 29Therefore Zadok
and Abiathar carried the ark of God back to
Jerusalem. And they remained there.
30So David went up by the Ascent of the
Mount of Olives, and wept as he went up; and
he had his head covered and went barefoot.
And all the people who *were* with him covered their heads and went up, weeping as
they went up. 31Then *someone* told David,
saying, "Ahithophel *is* among the conspir-
ators with Absalom." And David said, "O
LORD, I pray, turn the counsel of Ahithophel
into foolishness!"
32Now it happened when David had come
to the top *of the mountain,* where he worshiped God—there was Hushai the Archite
coming to meet him with his robe torn and
dust on his head. 33David said to him, "If
you go on with me, then you will become a
burden to me. 34But if you return to the city,
and say to Absalom, 'I will be your servant,
O king; *as* I *was* your father's servant previously, so I *will* now also *be* your servant,'
then you may defeat the counsel of Ahithophel for me. 35And *do* you not *have* Zadok
and Abiathar the priests with you there?
Therefore it will be *that* whatever you hear
from the king's house, you shall tell to Zadok
and Abiathar the priests. 36Indeed *they have*
there with them their two sons, Ahimaaz,
Zadok's *son,* and Jonathan, Abiathar's *son;*
and by them you shall send me everything
you hear."
37So Hushai, David's friend, went into the
city. And Absalom came into Jerusalem.

Mephibosheth's Servant

16 When David was a little past the top
of the mountain, there was Ziba the
servant of Mephibosheth, who met him with
a couple of saddled donkeys, and on them
two hundred *loaves* of bread, one hundred
clusters of raisins, one hundred summer
fruits, and a skin of wine. 2And the king
said to Ziba, "What do you mean to do with
these?"

So Ziba said, "The donkeys *are* for the
king's household to ride on, the bread and
summer fruit for the young men to eat, and
the wine for those who are faint in the wilderness to drink."
3Then the king said, "And where *is* your
master's son?"

And Ziba said to the king, "Indeed he is
staying in Jerusalem, for he said, 'Today the

house of Israel will restore the kingdom of
my father to me.'"
4So the king said to Ziba, "Here, all that
belongs to Mephibosheth *is* yours."
And Ziba said, "I humbly bow before
you, *that* I may find favor in your sight, my
lord, O king!"

Shimei Curses David

5Now when King David came to Bahurim, there was a man from the family of
the house of Saul, whose name *was* Shimei
the son of Gera, coming from there. He
came out, cursing continuously as he came.
6And he threw stones at David and at all the
servants of King David. And all the people
and all the mighty men *were* on his right
hand and on his left. 7Also Shimei said thus
when he cursed: "Come out! Come out! You
bloodthirsty man, you rogue! 8The LORD has
brought upon you all the blood of the house
of Saul, in whose place you have reigned;
and the LORD has delivered the kingdom
into the hand of Absalom your son. So now
you *are caught* in your own evil, because you
are a bloodthirsty man!"
9Then Abishai the son of Zeruiah said to
the king, "Why should this dead dog curse
my lord the king? Please, let me go over and
take off his head!"
10But the king said, "What have I to do
with you, you sons of Zeruiah? So let him
curse, because the LORD has said to him,
'Curse David.' Who then shall say, 'Why
have you done so?'"
11And David said to Abishai and all his
servants, "See how my son who came from
my own body seeks my life. How much more
now *may this* Benjamite? Let him alone, and
let him curse; for so the LORD has ordered
him. 12It may be that the LORD will look on
my affliction,[a] and that the LORD will repay
me with good for his cursing this day." 13And
as David and his men went along the road,
Shimei went along the hillside opposite him
and cursed as he went, threw stones at him
and kicked up dust. 14Now the king and all
the people who *were* with him became weary; so they refreshed themselves there.

The Advice of Ahithophel

15Meanwhile Absalom and all the people,
the men of Israel, came to Jerusalem; and
Ahithophel *was* with him. 16And so it was,
when Hushai the Archite, David's friend,
came to Absalom, that Hushai said to Absalom, "*Long* live the king! *Long* live the king!"
17So Absalom said to Hushai, "*Is* this your
loyalty to your friend? Why did you not go
with your friend?"
18And Hushai said to Absalom, "No,
but whom the LORD and this people and
all the men of Israel choose, his I will be,
and with him I will remain. 19Furthermore,
whom should I serve? *Should I* not *serve* in
the presence of his son? As I have served in
your father's presence, so will I be in your
presence."
20Then Absalom said to Ahithophel,
"Give advice as to what we should do."
21And Ahithophel said to Absalom, "Go
in to your father's concubines, whom he has
left to keep the house; and all Israel will hear
that you are abhorred by your father. Then
the hands of all who are with you will be
strong." 22So they pitched a tent for Absalom
on the top of the house, and Absalom went
in to his father's concubines in the sight of
all Israel.
23Now the advice of Ahithophel, which
he gave in those days, *was* as if one had inquired at the oracle of God. So *was* all the
advice of Ahithophel both with David and
with Absalom.

17 Moreover Ahithophel said to Absalom, "Now let me choose twelve
thousand men, and I will arise and pursue
David tonight. 2I will come upon him while
he *is* weary and weak, and make him afraid.
And all the people who *are* with him will
flee, and I will strike only the king. 3Then I
will bring back all the people to you. When
all return except the man whom you seek, all
the people will be at peace." 4And the saying
pleased Absalom and all the elders of Israel.

The Advice of Hushai

5Then Absalom said, "Now call Hushai
the Archite also, and let us hear what he says
too." 6And when Hushai came to Absalom,
Absalom spoke to him, saying, "Ahithophel
has spoken in this manner. Shall we do as he
says? If not, speak up."
7So Hushai said to Absalom: "The advice
that Ahithophel has given *is* not good at this
time. 8For," said Hushai, "you know your
father and his men, that they *are* mighty

16:12 [a] Following Kethib, Septuagint, Syriac, and Vulgate; Qere reads *my eyes;* Targum reads *tears of my eyes.*

men, and they *are* enraged in their minds,
like a bear robbed of her cubs in the field;
and your father *is* a man of war, and will
not camp with the people. 9Surely by now
he is hidden in some pit, or in some *other*
place. And it will be, when some of them are
overthrown at the first, that whoever hears
it will say, 'There is a slaughter among the
people who follow Absalom.' 10And even he
who is valiant, whose heart *is* like the heart
of a lion, will melt completely. For all Israel
knows that your father *is* a mighty man,
and *those* who *are* with him *are* valiant men.
11Therefore I advise that all Israel be fully
gathered to you, from Dan to Beersheba,
like the sand that *is* by the sea for multitude,
and that you go to battle in person. 12So we
will come upon him in some place where he
may be found, and we will fall on him as the
dew falls on the ground. And of him and all
the men who *are* with him there shall not
be left so much as one. 13Moreover, if he has
withdrawn into a city, then all Israel shall
bring ropes to that city; and we will pull it
into the river, until there is not one small
stone found there."

14So Absalom and all the men of Israel
said, "The advice of Hushai the Archite *is*
better than the advice of Ahithophel." For
the LORD had purposed to defeat the good
advice of Ahithophel, to the intent that the
LORD might bring disaster on Absalom.

Hushai Warns David to Escape

15Then Hushai said to Zadok and Abiathar the priests, "Thus and so Ahithophel
advised Absalom and the elders of Israel,
and thus and so I have advised. 16Now therefore, send quickly and tell David, saying,
'Do not spend this night in the plains of the
wilderness, but speedily cross over, lest the
king and all the people who *are* with him be
swallowed up.'" 17Now Jonathan and Ahimaaz stayed at En Rogel, for they dared not
be seen coming into the city; so a female
servant would come and tell them, and they
would go and tell King David. 18Nevertheless
a lad saw them, and told Absalom. But both
of them went away quickly and came to a
man's house in Bahurim, who had a well in
his court; and they went down into it. 19Then
the woman took and spread a covering
over the well's mouth, and spread ground
grain on it; and the thing was not known.
20And when Absalom's servants came to the
woman at the house, they said, "Where *are*
Ahimaaz and Jonathan?"

So the woman said to them, "They have
gone over the water brook."

And when they had searched and could
not find *them,* they returned to Jerusalem.
21Now it came to pass, after they had departed, that they came up out of the well and
went and told King David, and said to David,
"Arise and cross over the water quickly. For
thus has Ahithophel advised against you."
22So David and all the people who *were* with
him arose and crossed over the Jordan. By
morning light not one of them was left who
had not gone over the Jordan.

23Now when Ahithophel saw that his advice was not followed, he saddled a donkey,
and arose and went home to his house, to
his city. Then he put his household in order,
and hanged himself, and died; and he was
buried in his father's tomb.

24Then David went to Mahanaim. And
Absalom crossed over the Jordan, he and all
the men of Israel with him. 25And Absalom
made Amasa captain of the army instead
of Joab. This Amasa *was* the son of a man
whose name *was* Jithra,[a] an Israelite,[b] who
had gone in to Abigail the daughter of Nahash, sister of Zeruiah, Joab's mother. 26So
Israel and Absalom encamped in the land of
Gilead.

27Now it happened, when David had come
to Mahanaim, that Shobi the son of Nahash
from Rabbah of the people of Ammon,
Machir the son of Ammiel from Lo Debar,
and Barzillai the Gileadite from Rogelim,
28brought beds and basins, earthen vessels
and wheat, barley and flour, parched *grain*
and beans, lentils and parched *seeds,* 29honey
and curds, sheep and cheese of the herd, for
David and the people who *were* with him to
eat. For they said, "The people are hungry
and weary and thirsty in the wilderness."

Absalom's Defeat and Death

18 And David numbered the people
who *were* with him, and set captains
of thousands and captains of hundreds over
them. 2Then David sent out one third of the

17:25 [a] Spelled *Jether* in 1 Chronicles 2:17 and elsewhere [b] Following Masoretic Text, some manuscripts of the Septuagint, and Targum; some manuscripts of the Septuagint read *Ishmaelite* (compare 1 Chronicles 2:17); Vulgate reads *of Jezrael.*

people under the hand of Joab, one third under the hand of Abishai the son of Zeruiah,
Joab's brother, and one third under the hand
of Ittai the Gittite. And the king said to the
people, "I also will surely go out with you
myself."
3But the people answered, "You shall not
go out! For if we flee away, they will not care
about us; nor if half of us die, will they care
about us. But *you are* worth ten thousand of
us now. For you are now more help to us in
the city."
4Then the king said to them, "Whatever seems best to you I will do." So the king
stood beside the gate, and all the people went
out by hundreds and by thousands. 5Now the
king had commanded Joab, Abishai, and Ittai, saying, "*Deal* gently for my sake with the
young man Absalom." And all the people
heard when the king gave all the captains
orders concerning Absalom.
6So the people went out into the field of
battle against Israel. And the battle was in
the woods of Ephraim. 7The people of Israel
were overthrown there before the servants of
David, and a great slaughter of twenty thousand took place there that day. 8For the battle
there was scattered over the face of the whole
countryside, and the woods devoured more
people that day than the sword devoured.
9Then Absalom met the servants of David. Absalom rode on a mule. The mule went
under the thick boughs of a great terebinth
tree, and his head caught in the terebinth;
so he was left hanging between heaven and
earth. And the mule which *was* under him
went on. 10Now a certain man saw *it* and told
Joab, and said, "I just saw Absalom hanging
in a terebinth tree!"
11So Joab said to the man who told him,
"You just saw *him!* And why did you not
strike him there to the ground? I would have
given you ten *shekels* of silver and a belt."
12But the man said to Joab, "Though I
were to receive a thousand *shekels* of silver in
my hand, I would not raise my hand against
the king's son. For in our hearing the king
commanded you and Abishai and Ittai, saying, 'Beware lest anyone *touch* the young
man Absalom!'[a] 13Otherwise I would have
dealt falsely against my own life. For there
is nothing hidden from the king, and you
yourself would have set yourself against *me*."
14Then Joab said, "I cannot linger with
you." And he took three spears in his hand
and thrust them through Absalom's heart,
while he was *still* alive in the midst of the
terebinth tree. 15And ten young men who
bore Joab's armor surrounded Absalom, and
struck and killed him.
16So Joab blew the trumpet, and the
people returned from pursuing Israel. For
Joab held back the people. 17And they took
Absalom and cast him into a large pit in the
woods, and laid a very large heap of stones

18:12 [a] The ancient versions read *'Protect the young man Absalom for me!'*

REBELLION

READ IT: 2 SAMUEL 18:1–33

Absalom led a rebellion against his own father, King David. It was a long, bloody rebellion that eventually ended badly for everyone. Rebellion in a kingdom is bad enough. Rebellion in a family—a son against his father—is even worse. This rebellion was everything all at once.

Absalom's rebellion takes up four long chapters in the Old Testament. It's full of violence and betrayal and death (a nasty one for Absalom), a *king on the run*, and finally a kingdom restored, but at a great price. This rebellion ended with a father weeping and calling out his son's name over and over.

over him. Then all Israel fled, everyone to
his tent.
18 Now Absalom in his lifetime had taken
and set up a pillar for himself, which *is* in the
King's Valley. For he said, "I have no son to
keep my name in remembrance." He called
the pillar after his own name. And to this
day it is called Absalom's Monument.

David Hears of Absalom's Death

19 Then Ahimaaz the son of Zadok said,
"Let me run now and take the news to the
king, how the LORD has avenged him of his
enemies."
20 And Joab said to him, "You shall not
take the news this day, for you shall take the
news another day. But today you shall take
no news, because the king's son is dead."
21 Then Joab said to the Cushite, "Go, tell the
king what you have seen." So the Cushite
bowed himself to Joab and ran.
22 And Ahimaaz the son of Zadok said
again to Joab, "But whatever happens, please
let me also run after the Cushite."
So Joab said, "Why will you run, my son,
since you have no news ready?"
23 "But whatever happens," *he said,* "let me
run."
So he said to him, "Run." Then Ahimaaz ran by way of the plain, and outran the
Cushite.
24 Now David was sitting between the two
gates. And the watchman went up to the roof
over the gate, to the wall, lifted his eyes and
looked, and there was a man, running alone.
25 Then the watchman cried out and told the
king. And the king said, "If he *is* alone, *there*
is news in his mouth." And he came rapidly
and drew near.
26 Then the watchman saw *another* man
running, and the watchman called to the
gatekeeper and said, "There is *another* man,
running alone!"
And the king said, "He also brings
news."
27 So the watchman said, "I think the run-
ning of the first is like the running of Ahimaaz the son of Zadok."
And the king said, "He *is* a good man,
and comes with good news."
28 So Ahimaaz called out and said to the
king, "All is well!" Then he bowed down
with his face to the earth before the king,
and said, "Blessed *be* the LORD your God,
who has delivered up the men who raised
their hand against my lord the king!"
29 The king said, "Is the young man Absalom safe?"
Ahimaaz answered, "When Joab sent the
king's servant and *me* your servant, I saw a
great tumult, but I did not know what *it was*
about."
30 And the king said, "Turn aside *and*
stand here." So he turned aside and stood
still.
31 Just then the Cushite came, and the
Cushite said, "There is good news, my lord
the king! For the LORD has avenged you this
day of all those who rose against you."
32 And the king said to the Cushite, "Is the
young man Absalom safe?"
So the Cushite answered, "May the enemies of my lord the king, and all who rise
against you to do harm, be like *that* young
man!"

David's Mourning for Absalom

33 Then the king was deeply moved, and
went up to the chamber over the gate, and
wept. And as he went, he said thus: "O my
son Absalom—my son, my son Absalom—if
only I had died in your place! O Absalom my
son, my son!"

19 And Joab was told, "Behold, the
king is weeping and mourning
for Absalom." 2 So the victory that day was
turned into mourning for all the people. For
the people heard it said that day, "The king
is grieved for his son." 3 And the people stole
back into the city that day, as people who are
ashamed steal away when they flee in battle.
4 But the king covered his face, and the king
cried out with a loud voice, "O my son Absalom! O Absalom, my son, my son!"
5 Then Joab came into the house to the
king, and said, "Today you have disgraced
all your servants who today have saved your
life, the lives of your sons and daughters,
the lives of your wives and the lives of your
concubines, 6 in that you love your enemies
and hate your friends. For you have declared
today that you regard neither princes nor
servants; for today I perceive that if Absalom
had lived and all of us had died today, then it
would have pleased you well. 7 Now therefore,
arise, go out and speak comfort to your servants. For I swear by the LORD, if you do not
go out, not one will stay with you this night.
And that will be worse for you than all the
evil that has befallen you from your youth
until now." 8 Then the king arose and sat in

the gate. And they told all the people, saying,
"There is the king, sitting in the gate." So all
the people came before the king.

For everyone of Israel had fled to his tent.

David Returns to Jerusalem

9Now all the people were in a dispute
throughout all the tribes of Israel, saying,
"The king saved us from the hand of our
enemies, he delivered us from the hand of
the Philistines, and now he has fled from
the land because of Absalom. 10But Absalom,
whom we anointed over us, has died in battle. Now therefore, why do you say nothing
about bringing back the king?"

11So King David sent to Zadok and Abiathar the priests, saying, "Speak to the elders
of Judah, saying, 'Why are you the last to
bring the king back to his house, since the
words of all Israel have come to the king, to
his *very* house? 12You *are* my brethren, you
are my bone and my flesh. Why then are
you the last to bring back the king?' 13And
say to Amasa, '*Are* you not my bone and my
flesh? God do so to me, and more also, if you
are not commander of the army before me
continually in place of Joab.'" 14So he swayed
the hearts of all the men of Judah, just as
the heart of one man, so that they sent *this
word* to the king: "Return, you and all your
servants!"

15Then the king returned and came to the
Jordan. And Judah came to Gilgal, to go to
meet the king, to escort the king across the
Jordan. 16And Shimei the son of Gera, a Benjamite, who *was* from Bahurim, hurried and
came down with the men of Judah to meet
King David. 17*There were* a thousand men of
Benjamin with him, and Ziba the servant of
the house of Saul, and his fifteen sons and
his twenty servants with him; and they went
over the Jordan before the king. 18Then a fer-
ryboat went across to carry over the king's
household, and to do what he thought good.

David's Mercy to Shimei

Now Shimei the son of Gera fell down
before the king when he had crossed the Jordan. 19Then he said to the king, "Do not let
my lord impute iniquity to me, or remember what wrong your servant did on the day
that my lord the king left Jerusalem, that
the king should take *it* to heart. 20For I, your
servant, know that I have sinned. Therefore
here I am, the first to come today of all the
house of Joseph to go down to meet my lord
the king."

21But Abishai the son of Zeruiah answered and said, "Shall not Shimei be put to
death for this, because he cursed the LORD's
anointed?"

22And David said, "What have I to do
with you, you sons of Zeruiah, that you
should be adversaries to me today? Shall any
man be put to death today in Israel? For do I
not know that today I *am* king over Israel?"
23Therefore the king said to Shimei, "You
shall not die." And the king swore to him.

David and Mephibosheth Meet

24Now Mephibosheth the son of Saul
came down to meet the king. And he had
not cared for his feet, nor trimmed his mustache, nor washed his clothes, from the day
the king departed until the day he returned
in peace. 25So it was, when he had come to
Jerusalem to meet the king, that the king
said to him, "Why did you not go with me,
Mephibosheth?"

26And he answered, "My lord, O king, my
servant deceived me. For your servant said,
'I will saddle a donkey for myself, that I may
ride on it and go to the king,' because your
servant *is* lame. 27And he has slandered your
servant to my lord the king, but my lord the
king *is* like the angel of God. Therefore do
what is good in your eyes. 28For all my father's
house were but dead men before my lord the
king. Yet you set your servant among those
who eat at your own table. Therefore what
right have I still to cry out anymore to the
king?"

29So the king said to him, "Why do you
speak anymore of your matters? I have said,
'You and Ziba divide the land.'"

30Then Mephibosheth said to the king,
"Rather, let him take it all, inasmuch as my
lord the king has come back in peace to his
own house."

David's Kindness to Barzillai

31And Barzillai the Gileadite came down
from Rogelim and went across the Jordan
with the king, to escort him across the Jordan. 32Now Barzillai was a very aged man,
eighty years old. And he had provided the
king with supplies while he stayed at Mahanaim, for he *was* a very rich man. 33And
the king said to Barzillai, "Come across with

me, and I will provide for you while you are with me in Jerusalem."

34 But Barzillai said to the king, "How long have I to live, that I should go up with the king to Jerusalem? 35 I *am* today eighty years old. Can I discern between the good and bad? Can your servant taste what I eat or what I drink? Can I hear any longer the voice of singing men and singing women? Why then should your servant be a further burden to my lord the king? 36 Your servant will go a little way across the Jordan with the king. And why should the king repay me *with* such a reward? 37 Please let your servant turn back again, that I may die in my own city, near the grave of my father and mother. But here is your servant Chimham; let him cross over with my lord the king, and do for him what seems good to you."

38 And the king answered, "Chimham shall cross over with me, and I will do for him what seems good to you. Now whatever you request of me, I will do for you." 39 Then all the people went over the Jordan. And when the king had crossed over, the king kissed Barzillai and blessed him, and he returned to his own place.

The Quarrel About the King

40 Now the king went on to Gilgal, and Chimham[a] went on with him. And all the people of Judah escorted the king, and also half the people of Israel. 41 Just then all the men of Israel came to the king, and said to the king, "Why have our brethren, the men of Judah, stolen you away and brought the king, his household, and all David's men with him across the Jordan?"

42 So all the men of Judah answered the men of Israel, "Because the king *is* a close relative of ours. Why then are you angry over this matter? Have we ever eaten at the king's *expense*? Or has he given us any gift?"

43 And the men of Israel answered the men of Judah, and said, "We have ten shares *in the king; therefore we also have more right* to David than you. Why then do you despise us—were we not the first to advise bringing back our king?"

Yet the words of the men of Judah were fiercer than the words of the men of Israel.

The Rebellion of Sheba

20 And there happened to be there a rebel,[a] whose name *was* Sheba the son of Bichri, a Benjamite. And he blew a trumpet, and said:

"We have no share in David,
Nor do we have inheritance in the son of Jesse;
Every man to his tents, O Israel!"

2 So every man of Israel deserted David, *and* followed Sheba the son of Bichri. But the men of Judah, from the Jordan as far as Jerusalem, remained loyal to their king.

3 Now David came to his house at Jerusalem. And the king took the ten women, his concubines whom he had left to keep the house, and put them in seclusion and supported them, but did not go in to them. So they were shut up to the day of their death, living in widowhood.

4 And the king said to Amasa, "Assemble the men of Judah for me within three days, and be present here yourself." 5 So Amasa went to assemble *the men of* Judah. But he delayed longer than the set time which David had appointed him. 6 And David said to Abishai, "Now Sheba the son of Bichri will do us more harm than Absalom. Take your lord's servants and pursue him, lest he find for himself fortified cities, and escape us." 7 So Joab's men, with the Cherethites, the Pelethites, and all the mighty men, went out after him. And they went out of Jerusalem to pursue Sheba the son of Bichri. 8 When they *were* at the large stone which *is* in Gibeon, Amasa came before them. Now Joab was dressed in battle armor; on it was a belt *with* a sword fastened in its sheath at his hips; and as he was going forward, it fell out. 9 Then Joab said to Amasa, "*Are* you in health, my brother?" And Joab took Amasa by the beard with his right hand to kiss him. 10 But Amasa did not notice the sword that *was* in Joab's hand. And he struck him with it in the stomach, and his entrails poured out on the ground; and he did not *strike* him again. Thus he died.

Then Joab and Abishai his brother pursued Sheba the son of Bichri. 11 Meanwhile one of Joab's men stood near Amasa, and said, "Whoever favors Joab and whoever *is* for David—follow Joab!" 12 But Amasa wallowed in *his* blood in the middle of the highway. And when the man saw that all the

---

19:40 [a] Masoretic Text reads *Chimhan.* 20:1 [a] Literally *man of Belial*

people stood still, he moved Amasa from the highway to the field and threw a garment over him, when he saw that everyone who came upon him halted. 13When he was removed from the highway, all the people went on after Joab to pursue Sheba the son of Bichri.

14And he went through all the tribes of Israel to Abel and Beth Maachah and all the Berites. So they were gathered together and also went after *Sheba*.[a] 15Then they came and besieged him in Abel of Beth Maachah; and they cast up a siege mound against the city, and it stood by the rampart. And all the people who *were* with Joab battered the wall to throw it down.

16Then a wise woman cried out from the city, "Hear, hear! Please say to Joab, 'Come nearby, that I may speak with you.'" 17When he had come near to her, the woman said, "*Are* you Joab?"

He answered, "I *am*."

Then she said to him, "Hear the words of your maidservant."

And he answered, "I am listening."

18So she spoke, saying, "They used to talk in former times, saying, 'They shall surely seek *guidance* at Abel,' and so they would end *disputes*. 19I *am among the* peaceable *and* faithful in Israel. You seek to destroy a city and a mother in Israel. Why would you swallow up the inheritance of the LORD?"

20And Joab answered and said, "Far be it, far be it from me, that I should swallow up or destroy! 21That *is* not so. But a man from the mountains of Ephraim, Sheba the son of Bichri by name, has raised his hand against the king, against David. Deliver him only, and I will depart from the city."

So the woman said to Joab, "Watch, his head will be thrown to you over the wall." 22Then the woman in her wisdom went to all the people. And they cut off the head of Sheba the son of Bichri, and threw *it* out to Joab. Then he blew a trumpet, and they withdrew from the city, every man to his tent. So Joab returned to the king at Jerusalem.

David's Government Officers

23And Joab *was* over all the army of Israel; Benaiah the son of Jehoiada *was* over the Cherethites and the Pelethites; 24Adoram *was* in charge of revenue; Jehoshaphat the son of Ahilud *was* recorder; 25Sheva *was* scribe; Zadok and Abiathar *were* the priests; 26and Ira the Jairite was a chief minister under David.

David Avenges the Gibeonites

21 Now there was a famine in the days of David for three years, year after year; and David inquired of the LORD. And the LORD answered, "*It is* because of Saul and *his* bloodthirsty house, because he killed the Gibeonites." 2So the king called the Gibeonites and spoke to them. Now the Gibeonites *were* not of the children of Israel, but of the remnant of the Amorites; the children of Israel had sworn protection to them, but Saul had sought to kill them in his zeal for the children of Israel and Judah.

3Therefore David said to the Gibeonites, "What shall I do for you? And with what shall I make atonement, that you may bless the inheritance of the LORD?"

4And the Gibeonites said to him, "We will have no silver or gold from Saul or from his house, nor shall you kill any man in Israel for us."

So he said, "Whatever you say, I will do for you."

5Then they answered the king, "As for the man who consumed us and plotted against us, *that* we should be destroyed from remaining in any of the territories of Israel, 6let seven men of his descendants be delivered to us, and we will hang them before the LORD in Gibeah of Saul, *whom* the LORD chose."

And the king said, "I will give *them*."

7But the king spared Mephibosheth the son of Jonathan, the son of Saul, because of the LORD's oath that *was* between them, between David and Jonathan the son of Saul. 8So the king took Armoni and Mephibosheth, the two sons of Rizpah the daughter of Aiah, whom she bore to Saul, and the five sons of Michal[a] the daughter of Saul, whom she brought up for Adriel the son of Barzillai the Meholathite; 9and he delivered them into the hands of the Gibeonites, and they hanged them on the hill before the LORD. So they fell, *all* seven together, and were put to death in the days of harvest, in the first *days*, in the beginning of barley harvest.

10Now Rizpah the daughter of Aiah took

20:14 [a] Literally *him* 21:8 [a] Or *Merab* (compare 1 Samuel 18:19 and 25:44; 2 Samuel 3:14 and 6:23)

sackcloth and spread it for herself on the
rock, from the beginning of harvest until the
late rains poured on them from heaven. And
she did not allow the birds of the air to rest
on them by day nor the beasts of the field
by night.
11 And David was told what Rizpah the
daughter of Aiah, the concubine of Saul,
had done. 12 Then David went and took the
bones of Saul, and the bones of Jonathan his
son, from the men of Jabesh Gilead who had
stolen them from the street of Beth Shan,[a]
where the Philistines had hung them up,
after the Philistines had struck down Saul
in Gilboa. 13 So he brought up the bones of
Saul and the bones of Jonathan his son from
there; and they gathered the bones of those
who had been hanged. 14 They buried the
bones of Saul and Jonathan his son in the
country of Benjamin in Zelah, in the tomb
of Kish his father. So they performed all that
the king commanded. And after that God
heeded the prayer for the land.

Philistine Giants Destroyed

15 When the Philistines were at war again
with Israel, David and his servants with
him went down and fought against the
Philistines; and David grew faint. 16 Then
Ishbi-Benob, who *was* one of the sons of the
giant, the weight of whose bronze spear *was*
three hundred *shekels,* who was bearing a
new *sword,* thought he could kill David. 17 But
Abishai the son of Zeruiah came to his aid,
and struck the Philistine and killed him.
Then the men of David swore to him, saying, "You shall go out no more with us to
battle, lest you quench the lamp of Israel."
18 Now it happened afterward that there
was again a battle with the Philistines at
Gob. Then Sibbechai the Hushathite killed
Saph,[a] who *was* one of the sons of the giant. 19 Again there was war at Gob with
the Philistines, where Elhanan the son of
Jaare-Oregim[a] the Bethlehemite killed *the
brother of* Goliath the Gittite, the shaft of
whose spear *was* like a weaver's beam.
20 Yet again there was war at Gath, where
there was a man of *great* stature, who had six
fingers on each hand and six toes on each
foot, twenty-four in number; and he also was
born to the giant. 21 So when he defied Israel,
Jonathan the son of Shimea,[a] David's brother, killed him.
22 These four were born to the giant in
Gath, and fell by the hand of David and by
the hand of his servants.

Praise for God's Deliverance

22 Then David spoke to the LORD
the words of this song, on the day
when the LORD had delivered him from the
hand of all his enemies, and from the hand
of Saul. 2 And he said:[a]

"The LORD *is* my rock and my fortress
and my deliverer;
3 The God of my strength, in whom I will
trust;
My shield and the horn of my salvation,
My stronghold and my refuge;
My Savior, You save me from violence.
4 I will call upon the LORD, *who is worthy*
to be praised;
So shall I be saved from my enemies.

5 "When the waves of death surrounded
me,
The floods of ungodliness made me
afraid.
6 The sorrows of Sheol surrounded me;
The snares of death confronted me.
7 In my distress I called upon the LORD,
And cried out to my God;
He heard my voice from His temple,
And my cry *entered* His ears.

8 "Then the earth shook and trembled;
The foundations of heaven[a] quaked and
were shaken,
Because He was angry.
9 Smoke went up from His nostrils,
And devouring fire from His mouth;
Coals were kindled by it.
10 He bowed the heavens also, and came
down
With darkness under His feet.
11 He rode upon a cherub, and flew;
And He was seen[a] upon the wings of
the wind.
12 He made darkness canopies around
Him,
Dark waters *and* thick clouds of the
skies.

21:12 [a] Spelled *Beth Shean* in Joshua 17:11 and elsewhere **21:18** [a] Spelled *Sippai* in 1 Chronicles 20:4 **21:19** [a] Spelled *Jair* in 1 Chronicles 20:5 **21:21** [a] Spelled *Shammah* in 1 Samuel 16:9 and elsewhere **22:2** [a] Compare Psalm 18 **22:8** [a] Following Masoretic Text, Septuagint, and Targum; Syriac and Vulgate read *hills* (compare Psalm 18:7). **22:11** [a] Following Masoretic Text and Septuagint; many Hebrew manuscripts, Syriac, and Vulgate read *He flew* (compare Psalm 18:10); Targum reads *He spoke with power.*

13 From the brightness before Him
Coals of fire were kindled.

14 "The LORD thundered from heaven,
And the Most High uttered His voice.
15 He sent out arrows and scattered them;
Lightning bolts, and He vanquished
them.
16 Then the channels of the sea were seen,
The foundations of the world were
uncovered,
At the rebuke of the LORD,
At the blast of the breath of His nostrils.

17 "He sent from above, He took me,
He drew me out of many waters.
18 He delivered me from my strong enemy,
From those who hated me;
For they were too strong for me.
19 They confronted me in the day of my
calamity,
But the LORD was my support.
20 He also brought me out into a broad
place;
He delivered me because He delighted
in me.

21 "The LORD rewarded me according to my
righteousness;
According to the cleanness of my hands
He has recompensed me.
22 For I have kept the ways of the LORD,
And have not wickedly departed from
my God.
23 For all His judgments *were* before me;
And *as for* His statutes, I did not depart
from them.
24 I was also blameless before Him,
And I kept myself from my iniquity.
25 Therefore the LORD has recompensed
me according to my righteousness,
According to my cleanness in His eyes.[a]

26 "With the merciful You will show
Yourself merciful;
With a blameless man You will show
Yourself blameless;
27 With the pure You will show Yourself
pure;
And with the devious You will show
Yourself shrewd.
28 You will save the humble people;
But Your eyes *are* on the haughty, *that*
You may bring *them* down.

29 "For You *are* my lamp, O LORD;
The LORD shall enlighten my darkness.
30 For by You I can run against a troop;
By my God I can leap over a wall.
31 *As for* God, His way *is* perfect;

22:25 [a] Septuagint, Syriac, and Vulgate read *the cleanness of my hands in His sight* (compare Psalm 18:24); Targum reads *my cleanness before His word.*

DEPRESSION

READ IT: 2 SAMUEL 22:29, 30

No one can turn a situation around like God. No matter how dark your circumstances seem, the Lord can bring light, changing how you see things. Here's how you can help flip the switch:

- Believe that God can help, and don't underestimate His ways.
- Ask God to light up your darkness. Ask Him every single day.
- Tell a trusted adult that you need help seeing the light. You might be surprised how much better you feel, just knowing that someone else gets it!
- Be patient. Healing takes time.

The word of the LORD *is* proven;
He *is* a shield to all who trust in Him.

32 "For who *is* God, except the LORD?
And who *is* a rock, except our God?
33 God *is* my strength *and* power,[a]
And He makes my[b] way perfect.
34 He makes my[a] feet like the *feet* of deer,
And sets me on my high places.
35 He teaches my hands to make war,
So that my arms can bend a bow of bronze.

36 "You have also given me the shield of Your salvation;
Your gentleness has made me great.
37 You enlarged my path under me;
So my feet did not slip.

38 "I have pursued my enemies and destroyed them;
Neither did I turn back again till they were destroyed.
39 And I have destroyed them and wounded them,
So that they could not rise;
They have fallen under my feet.
40 For You have armed me with strength for the battle;
You have subdued under me those who rose against me.
41 You have also given me the necks of my enemies,
So that I destroyed those who hated me.
42 They looked, but *there was* none to save;
Even to the LORD, but He did not answer them.
43 Then I beat them as fine as the dust of the earth;
I trod them like dirt in the streets,
And I spread them out.

44 "You have also delivered me from the strivings of my people;
You have kept me as the head of the nations.
A people I have not known shall serve me.
45 The foreigners submit to me;
As soon as they hear, they obey me.
46 The foreigners fade away,
And come frightened[a] from their hideouts.

47 "The LORD lives!
Blessed *be* my Rock!
Let God be exalted,
The Rock of my salvation!
48 *It is* God who avenges me,
And subdues the peoples under me;
49 He delivers me from my enemies.
You also lift me up above those who rise against me;
You have delivered me from the violent man.
50 Therefore I will give thanks to You, O LORD, among the Gentiles,
And sing praises to Your name.

51 "*He is* the tower of salvation to His king,
And shows mercy to His anointed,
To David and his descendants forevermore."

David's Last Words

23 Now these *are* the last words of David.

Thus says David the son of Jesse;
Thus says the man raised up on high,
The anointed of the God of Jacob,
And the sweet psalmist of Israel:

2 "The Spirit of the LORD spoke by me,
And His word *was* on my tongue.
3 The God of Israel said,
The Rock of Israel spoke to me:
'He who rules over men *must be* just,
Ruling in the fear of God.
4 And *he shall be* like the light of the morning *when* the sun rises,
A morning without clouds,
Like the tender grass *springing* out of the earth,
By clear shining after rain.'

5 "Although my house *is* not so with God,
Yet He has made with me an everlasting covenant,
Ordered in all *things* and secure.
For *this is* all my salvation and all *my* desire;
Will He not make *it* increase?
6 But *the sons* of rebellion *shall* all *be* as thorns thrust away,
Because they cannot be taken with hands.
7 But the man *who* touches them

22:33 [a] Dead Sea Scrolls, Septuagint, Syriac, and Vulgate read *It is God who arms me with strength* (compare Psalm 18:32); Targum reads *It is God who sustains me with strength.* [b] Following Qere, Septuagint, Syriac, Targum, and Vulgate (compare Psalm 18:32); Kethib reads *His.* 22:34 [a] Following Qere, Septuagint, Syriac, Targum, and Vulgate (compare Psalm 18:33); Kethib reads *His.* 22:46 [a] Following Septuagint, Targum, and Vulgate (compare Psalm 18:45); Masoretic Text reads *gird themselves.*

Must be armed with iron and the shaft
of a spear,
And they shall be utterly burned with
fire in *their* place."

David's Mighty Men

8These *are* the names of the mighty men
whom David had: Josheb-Basshebeth[a] the
Tachmonite, chief among the captains.[b] He
was called Adino the Eznite, because he had
killed eight hundred men at one time. 9And
after him *was* Eleazar the son of Dodo,[a] the
Ahohite, *one* of the three mighty men with
David when they defied the Philistines
who were gathered there for battle, and the
men of Israel had retreated. 10He arose and
attacked the Philistines until his hand was
weary, and his hand stuck to the sword. The
LORD brought about a great victory that day;
and the people returned after him only to
plunder. 11And after him *was* Shammah the
son of Agee the Hararite. The Philistines
had gathered together into a troop where
there was a piece of ground full of lentils. So
the people fled from the Philistines. 12But he
stationed himself in the middle of the field,
defended it, and killed the Philistines. So the
LORD brought about a great victory.

13Then three of the thirty chief men went
down at harvest time and came to David at
the cave of Adullam. And the troop of Philistines encamped in the Valley of Rephaim.
14David *was* then in the stronghold, and the
garrison of the Philistines *was* then *in* Bethlehem. 15And David said with longing, "Oh,
that someone would give me a drink of the
water from the well of Bethlehem, which
is by the gate!" 16So the three mighty men
broke through the camp of the Philistines,
drew water from the well of Bethlehem that
was by the gate, and took it and brought *it* to
David. Nevertheless he would not drink it,
but poured it out to the LORD. 17And he said,
"Far be it from me, O LORD, that I should
do this! Is *this not* the blood of the men who
went in *jeopardy of* their lives?" Therefore he
would not drink it.

These things were done by the three
mighty men.

18Now Abishai the brother of Joab, the
son of Zeruiah, was chief of *another* three.[a]
He lifted his spear against three hundred
men, killed *them,* and won a name among
these three. 19Was he not the most honored
of three? Therefore he became their captain.
However, he did not attain to the *first* three.

20Benaiah *was* the son of Jehoiada, the
son of a valiant man from Kabzeel, who had
done many deeds. He had killed two lion-
like heroes of Moab. He also had gone down
and killed a lion in the midst of a pit on a
snowy day. 21And he killed an Egyptian, a
spectacular man. The Egyptian *had* a spear
in his hand; so he went down to him with a
staff, wrested the spear out of the Egyptian's
hand, and killed him with his own spear.
22These *things* Benaiah the son of Jehoiada
did, and won a name among three mighty
men. 23He was more honored than the thirty,
but he did not attain to the *first* three. And
David appointed him over his guard.

24Asahel the brother of Joab *was* one of
the thirty; Elhanan the son of Dodo of Bethlehem, 25Shammah the Harodite, Elika the
Harodite, 26Helez the Paltite, Ira the son
of Ikkesh the Tekoite, 27Abiezer the Anathothite, Mebunnai the Hushathite, 28Zal-
mon the Ahohite, Maharai the Netophathite,
29Heleb the son of Baanah (the Netophathite), Ittai the son of Ribai from Gibeah of
the children of Benjamin, 30Benaiah a Pirathonite, Hiddai from the brooks of Gaash,
31Abi-Albon the Arbathite, Azmaveth the
Barhumite, 32Eliahba the Shaalbonite (of the
sons of Jashen), Jonathan, 33Shammah the
Hararite, Ahiam the son of Sharar the Hararite, 34Eliphelet the son of Ahasbai, the son
of the Maachathite, Eliam the son of Ahithophel the Gilonite, 35Hezrai[a] the Carmelite,
Paarai the Arbite, 36Igal the son of Nathan of
Zobah, Bani the Gadite, 37Zelek the Ammonite, Naharai the Beerothite (armorbearer of
Joab the son of Zeruiah), 38Ira the Ithrite,
Gareb the Ithrite, 39*and* Uriah the Hittite:
thirty-seven in all.

David's Census of Israel and Judah

24 Again the anger of the LORD was
aroused against Israel, and He
moved David against them to say, "Go, number Israel and Judah."

23:8 [a] Literally *One Who Sits in the Seat* (compare 1 Chronicles 11:11) [b] Following Masoretic Text and Targum; Septuagint and Vulgate read *the three.* 23:9 [a] Spelled *Dodai* in 1 Chronicles 27:4 23:18 [a] Following Masoretic Text, Septuagint, and Vulgate; some Hebrew manuscripts and Syriac read *thirty;* Targum reads *the mighty men.*
23:35 [a] Spelled *Hezro* in 1 Chronicles 11:37

The BOOK of

1 KINGS

590 B.C.–570 B.C.

READ IT:

This book records one hundred years of Israel's history. The first stories are about King David and his son Solomon, who ruled over a united kingdom. Then Israel split into two kingdoms: Israel and Judah. The rest of the book is about the kings of those two kingdoms. Some of the kings were good and worshiped God. Some were bad and worshiped idols. First Kings also includes the stories of the prophet Elijah who believed in God even when the king, the queen, and most of the people worshiped the idol Baal.

GET IT:

Who wrote it: Possibly the prophet Jeremiah, but nobody knows for sure.

When it was written: 590 B.C.–570 B.C.

Why it was written: to record Israel's history and to tell the people what happens when the king and the people obey or disobey God.

LIVE IT:

If you believe in God and obey Him, He'll be present in your life.

Spiritual wisdom is the most important thing you can have.

God is in control no matter what.

FIND IT:

Solomon Requests Wisdom	*1 Kings 3*
The Ark Brought into the Temple	*1 Kings 8*
The Queen of Sheba's Praise of Solomon	*1 Kings 10*
The Revolt Against Rehoboam	*1 Kings 12*
Elijah Proclaims a Drought	*1 Kings 17*
Elijah's Mount Carmel Victory	*1 Kings 18*
Elijah Escapes from Jezebel	*1 Kings 19*
Naboth Is Murdered for His Vineyard	*1 Kings 21*
Ahab Dies in Battle	*1 Kings 22*

Adonijah Presumes to Be King

1 Now King David was old, advanced in
years; and they put covers on him, but
he could not get warm. 2Therefore his servants said to him, "Let a young woman, a virgin, be sought for our lord the king, and let
her stand before the king, and let her care for
him; and let her lie in your bosom, that our
lord the king may be warm." 3So they sought
for a lovely young woman throughout all the
territory of Israel, and found Abishag the
Shunammite, and brought her to the king.
4The young woman *was* very lovely; and she
cared for the king, and served him; but the
king did not know her.

5Then Adonijah the son of Haggith exalted himself, saying, "I will be king"; and
he prepared for himself chariots and horsemen, and fifty men to run before him. 6(And
his father had not rebuked him at any time
by saying, "Why have you done so?" He
was also very good-looking. *His mother* had
borne him after Absalom.) 7Then he conferred with Joab the son of Zeruiah and with
Abiathar the priest, and they followed and
helped Adonijah. 8But Zadok the priest, Benaiah the son of Jehoiada, Nathan the prophet, Shimei, Rei, and the mighty men who
belonged to David were not with Adonijah.

9And Adonijah sacrificed sheep and oxen
and fattened cattle by the stone of Zoheleth,
which *is* by En Rogel; he also invited all his
brothers, the king's sons, and all the men
of Judah, the king's servants. 10But he did
not invite Nathan the prophet, Benaiah, the
mighty men, or Solomon his brother.

11So Nathan spoke to Bathsheba the
mother of Solomon, saying, "Have you not
heard that Adonijah the son of Haggith has
become king, and David our lord does not
know *it*? 12Come, please, let me now give you
advice, that you may save your own life and
the life of your son Solomon. 13Go immediately to King David and say to him, 'Did you
not, my lord, O king, swear to your maidservant, saying, "Assuredly your son Solomon
shall reign after me, and he shall sit on my
throne"? Why then has Adonijah become
king?' 14Then, while you are still talking
there with the king, I also will come in after
you and confirm your words."

15So Bathsheba went into the chamber to
the king. (Now the king was very old, and
Abishag the Shunammite was serving the
king.) 16And Bathsheba bowed and did homage to the king. Then the king said, "What
is your wish?"

17Then she said to him, "My lord, you
swore by the LORD your God to your maidservant, *saying*, 'Assuredly Solomon your
son shall reign after me, and he shall sit on
my throne.' 18So now, look! Adonijah has
become king; and now, my lord the king,
you do not know about *it*. 19He has sacrificed oxen and fattened cattle and sheep in
abundance, and has invited all the sons of
the king, Abiathar the priest, and Joab the
commander of the army; but Solomon your
servant he has not invited. 20And as for you,
my lord, O king, the eyes of all Israel *are* on
you, that you should tell them who will sit
on the throne of my lord the king after him.
21Otherwise it will happen, when my lord the
king rests with his fathers, that I and my son
Solomon will be counted as offenders."

22And just then, while she was still
talking with the king, Nathan the prophet
also came in. 23So they told the king, saying,
"Here is Nathan the prophet." And when he
came in before the king, he bowed down

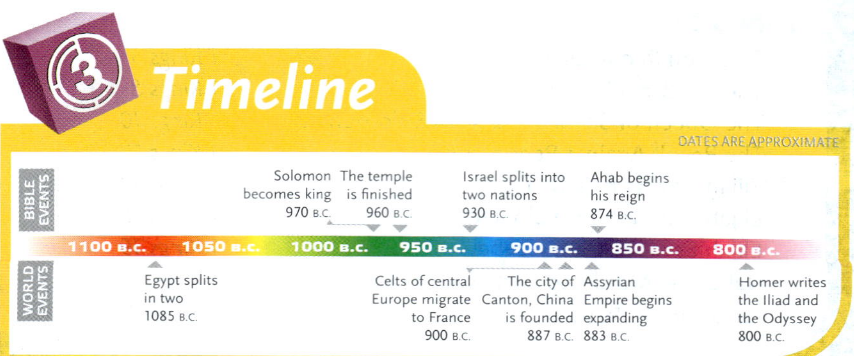

before the king with his face to the ground.
24And Nathan said, "My lord, O king, have
you said, 'Adonijah shall reign after me,
and he shall sit on my throne'? 25For he has
gone down today, and has sacrificed oxen
and fattened cattle and sheep in abundance,
and has invited all the king's sons, and the
commanders of the army, and Abiathar the
priest; and look! They are eating and drinking before him; and they say, '*Long* live King
Adonijah!' 26But he has not invited me—me
your servant—nor Zadok the priest, nor Benaiah the son of Jehoiada, nor your servant
Solomon. 27Has this thing been done by my
lord the king, and you have not told your servant who should sit on the throne of my lord
the king after him?"

David Proclaims Solomon King

28Then King David answered and said,
"Call Bathsheba to me." So she came into the
king's presence and stood before the king.
29And the king took an oath and said, "*As* the
LORD lives, who has redeemed my life from
every distress, 30just as I swore to you by the
LORD God of Israel, saying, 'Assuredly Solomon your son shall be king after me, and
he shall sit on my throne in my place,' so I
certainly will do this day."
31Then Bathsheba bowed with *her* face to
the earth, and paid homage to the king, and
said, "Let my lord King David live forever!"
32And King David said, "Call to me Zadok
the priest, Nathan the prophet, and Benaiah
the son of Jehoiada." So they came before
the king. 33The king also said to them, "Take
with you the servants of your lord, and have
Solomon my son ride on my own mule, and
take him down to Gihon. 34There let Zadok

On Location

Solomon's Economic Influence

Israel is the center of the action. But other areas in the Middle East add to the setting. To build the temple in Jerusalem, Solomon sends loggers to cut cedar from the forests of Lebanon (Phoenicia on this map). Visiting Solomon, to investigate rumors of his incredible wisdom, is the queen of Sheba, coming from what may have been southern Arabia. The shaded area shows Solomon's kingdom. Trade and transportation routes through the kingdom added to Solomon's influence.

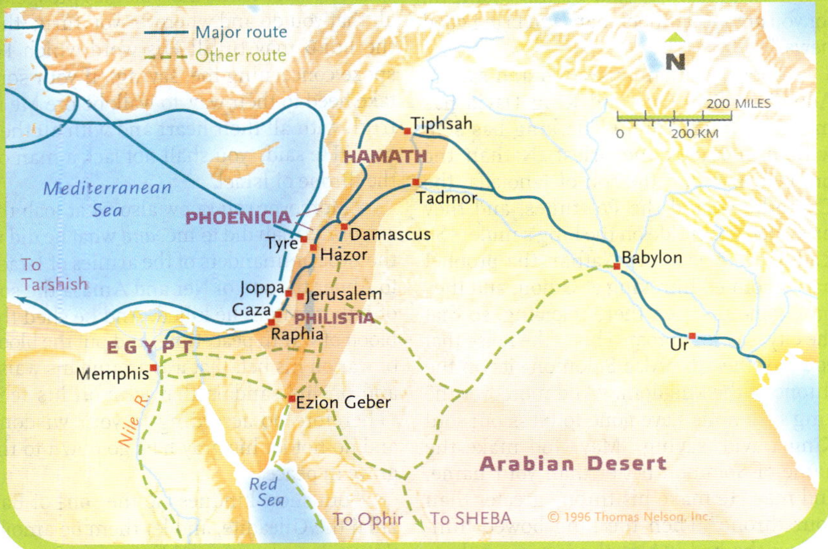

the priest and Nathan the prophet anoint
him king over Israel; and blow the horn, and
say, '*Long* live King Solomon!' 35Then you
shall come up after him, and he shall come
and sit on my throne, and he shall be king
in my place. For I have appointed him to be
ruler over Israel and Judah."
36Benaiah the son of Jehoiada answered
the king and said, "Amen! May the LORD
God of my lord the king say so *too.* 37As the
LORD has been with my lord the king, even
so may He be with Solomon, and make his
throne greater than the throne of my lord
King David."
38So Zadok the priest, Nathan the prophet, Benaiah the son of Jehoiada, the Cherethites, and the Pelethites went down and
had Solomon ride on King David's mule,
and took him to Gihon. 39Then Zadok the
priest took a horn of oil from the tabernacle
and anointed Solomon. And they blew the
horn, and all the people said, "*Long* live King
Solomon!" 40And all the people went up after
him; and the people played the flutes and rejoiced with great joy, so that the earth *seemed*
to split with their sound.
41Now Adonijah and all the guests who
were with him heard *it* as they finished
eating. And when Joab heard the sound of
the horn, he said, "Why *is* the city in such a
noisy uproar?" 42While he was still speaking,
there came Jonathan, the son of Abiathar the
priest. And Adonijah said to him, "Come in,
for you *are* a prominent man, and bring good
news."
43Then Jonathan answered and said to
Adonijah, "No! Our lord King David has
made Solomon king. 44The king has sent
with him Zadok the priest, Nathan the
prophet, Benaiah the son of Jehoiada, the
Cherethites, and the Pelethites; and they
have made him ride on the king's mule. 45So
Zadok the priest and Nathan the prophet
have anointed him king at Gihon; and they
have gone up from there rejoicing, so that
the city is in an uproar. This *is* the noise that
you have heard. 46Also Solomon sits on the
throne of the kingdom. 47And moreover the
king's servants have gone to bless our lord
King David, saying, 'May God make the
name of Solomon better than your name,
and may He make his throne greater than
your throne.' Then the king bowed himself on the bed. 48Also the king said thus,
'Blessed *be* the LORD God of Israel, who has
given *one* to sit on my throne this day, while
my eyes see *it!*'"
49So all the guests who were with Adonijah were afraid, and arose, and each one
went his way.
50Now Adonijah was afraid of Solomon;
so he arose, and went and took hold of the
horns of the altar. 51And it was told Solomon,
saying, "Indeed Adonijah is afraid of King
Solomon; for look, he has taken hold of the
horns of the altar, saying, 'Let King Solomon
swear to me today that he will not put his
servant to death with the sword.'"
52Then Solomon said, "If he proves himself a worthy man, not one hair of him shall
fall to the earth; but if wickedness is found
in him, he shall die." 53So King Solomon
sent them to bring him down from the altar. And he came and fell down before King
Solomon; and Solomon said to him, "Go to
your house."

David's Instructions to Solomon

2 Now the days of David drew near that
he should die, and he charged Solomon his son, saying: 2"I go the way of all
the earth; be strong, therefore, and prove
yourself a man. 3And keep the charge of the
LORD your God: to walk in His ways, to keep
His statutes, His commandments, His judgments, and His testimonies, as it is written
in the Law of Moses, that you may prosper in
all that you do and wherever you turn; 4that
the LORD may fulfill His word which He
spoke concerning me, saying, 'If your sons
take heed to their way, to walk before Me in
truth with all their heart and with all their
soul,' He said, 'you shall not lack a man on
the throne of Israel.'
5"Moreover you know also what Joab the
son of Zeruiah did to me, *and* what he did to
the two commanders of the armies of Israel,
to Abner the son of Ner and Amasa the son
of Jether, whom he killed. And he shed the
blood of war in peacetime, and put the blood
of war on his belt that *was* around his waist,
and on his sandals that *were* on his feet.
6Therefore do according to your wisdom,
and do not let his gray hair go down to the
grave in peace.
7"But show kindness to the sons of Barzillai the Gileadite, and let them be among
those who eat at your table, for so they came

to me when I fled from Absalom your
brother.
8“And see, *you have* with you Shimei the
son of Gera, a Benjamite from Bahurim,
who cursed me with a malicious curse in
the day when I went to Mahanaim. But he
came down to meet me at the Jordan, and
I swore to him by the LORD, saying, ‘I will
not put you to death with the sword.’ 9Now
therefore, do not hold him guiltless, for you
are a wise man and know what you ought to
do to him; but bring his gray hair down to
the grave with blood.”

Death of David

10So David rested with his fathers, and
was buried in the City of David. 11The period that David reigned over Israel *was* forty
years; seven years he reigned in Hebron, and
in Jerusalem he reigned thirty-three years.
12Then Solomon sat on the throne of his
father David; and his kingdom was firmly
established.

Solomon Executes Adonijah

13Now Adonijah the son of Haggith came
to Bathsheba the mother of Solomon. So she
said, “Do you come peaceably?”
And he said, “Peaceably.” 14Moreover he
said, “I have something *to say* to you.”
And she said, “Say it.”
15Then he said, “You know that the kingdom was mine, and all Israel had set their
expectations on me, that I should reign.
However, the kingdom has been turned
over, and has become my brother’s; for it was
his from the LORD. 16Now I ask one petition
of you; do not deny me.”
And she said to him, “Say it.”
17Then he said, “Please speak to King Solomon, for he will not refuse you, that he may
give me Abishag the Shunammite as wife.”
18So Bathsheba said, “Very well, I will
speak for you to the king.”
19Bathsheba therefore went to King Solomon, to speak to him for Adonijah. And the
king rose up to meet her and bowed down to
her, and sat down on his throne and had a
throne set for the king’s mother; so she sat
at his right hand. 20Then she said, “I desire
one small petition of you; do not refuse me.”
And the king said to her, “Ask it, my
mother, for I will not refuse you.”
21So she said, “Let Abishag the Shunammite be given to Adonijah your brother
as wife.”
22And King Solomon answered and said
to his mother, “Now why do you ask Abishag
the Shunammite for Adonijah? Ask for
him the kingdom also—for he *is* my older brother—for him, and for Abiathar the
priest, and for Joab the son of Zeruiah.”
23Then King Solomon swore by the LORD,
saying, “May God do so to me, and more
also, if Adonijah has not spoken this word
against his own life! 24Now therefore, *as* the
LORD lives, who has confirmed me and set
me on the throne of David my father, and
who has established a house[a] for me, as He
promised, Adonijah shall be put to death
today!”
25So King Solomon sent by the hand of
Benaiah the son of Jehoiada; and he struck
him down, and he died.

Abiathar Exiled, Joab Executed

26And to Abiathar the priest the king
said, “Go to Anathoth, to your own fields,
for you *are* deserving of death; but I will not
put you to death at this time, because you
carried the ark of the Lord GOD before my
father David, and because you were afflicted
every time my father was afflicted.” 27So Solomon removed Abiathar from being priest
to the LORD, that he might fulfill the word
of the LORD which He spoke concerning the
house of Eli at Shiloh.
28Then news came to Joab, for Joab had
defected to Adonijah, though he had not defected to Absalom. So Joab fled to the tabernacle of the LORD, and took hold of the horns
of the altar. 29And King Solomon was told,
“Joab has fled to the tabernacle of the LORD;
there *he is,* by the altar.” Then Solomon sent
Benaiah the son of Jehoiada, saying, “Go,
strike him down.” 30So Benaiah went to the
tabernacle of the LORD, and said to him,
“Thus says the king, ‘Come out!’ ”
And he said, “No, but I will die here.”
And Benaiah brought back word to the king,
saying, “Thus said Joab, and thus he answered me.”
31Then the king said to him, “Do as he
has said, and strike him down and bury him,
that you may take away from me and from
the house of my father the innocent blood
which Joab shed. 32So the LORD will return

2:24 [a] That is, a royal dynasty

his blood on his head, because he struck down two men more righteous and better than he, and killed them with the sword—Abner the son of Ner, the commander of the army of Israel, and Amasa the son of Jether, the commander of the army of Judah—though my father David did not know *it*. 33 Their blood shall therefore return upon the head of Joab and upon the head of his descendants forever. But upon David and his descendants, upon his house and his throne, there shall be peace forever from the LORD."

34 So Benaiah the son of Jehoiada went up and struck and killed him; and he was buried in his own house in the wilderness. 35 The king put Benaiah the son of Jehoiada in his place over the army, and the king put Zadok the priest in the place of Abiathar.

Shimei Executed

36 Then the king sent and called for Shimei, and said to him, "Build yourself a house in Jerusalem and dwell there, and do not go out from there anywhere. 37 For it shall be, on the day you go out and cross the Brook Kidron, know for certain you shall surely die; your blood shall be on your own head."

38 And Shimei said to the king, "The saying *is* good. As my lord the king has said, so your servant will do." So Shimei dwelt in Jerusalem many days.

39 Now it happened at the end of three years, that two slaves of Shimei ran away to Achish the son of Maachah, king of Gath. And they told Shimei, saying, "Look, your slaves *are* in Gath!" 40 So Shimei arose, saddled his donkey, and went to Achish at Gath to seek his slaves. And Shimei went and brought his slaves from Gath. 41 And Solomon was told that Shimei had gone from Jerusalem to Gath and had come back. 42 Then the king sent and called for Shimei, and said to him, "Did I not make you swear by the LORD, and warn you, saying, 'Know for certain that on the day you go out and travel anywhere, you shall surely die'? And you said to me, 'The word I have heard *is* good.' 43 Why then have you not kept the oath of the LORD and the commandment that I gave you?" 44 The king said moreover to Shimei, "You know, as your heart acknowledges, all the wickedness that you did to my father David; therefore the LORD will return your wickedness on your own head. 45 But King Solomon *shall be* blessed, and the throne of David shall be established before the LORD forever."

46 So the king commanded Benaiah the son of Jehoiada; and he went out and struck him down, and he died. Thus the kingdom was established in the hand of Solomon.

Solomon Requests Wisdom

3 Now Solomon made a treaty with Pharaoh king of Egypt, and married Pharaoh's daughter; then he brought her to the City of David until he had finished building his own house, and the house of the LORD, and the wall all around Jerusalem. 2 Meanwhile the people sacrificed at the high places, because there was no house built for the name of the LORD until those days. 3 And Solomon loved the LORD, walking in the statutes of his father David, except that he sacrificed and burned incense at the high places.

4 Now the king went to Gibeon to sacrifice there, for that *was* the great high place: Solomon offered a thousand burnt offerings on that altar. 5 At Gibeon the LORD appeared to Solomon in a dream by night; and God said, "Ask! What shall I give you?"

6 And Solomon said: "You have shown great mercy to Your servant David my father, because he walked before You in truth, in righteousness, and in uprightness of heart with You; You have continued this great kindness for him, and You have given him a son to sit on his throne, as *it is* this day. 7 Now, O LORD my God, You have made Your servant king instead of my father David, but I *am* a little child; I do not know *how* to go out or come in. 8 And Your servant *is* in the midst of Your people whom You have chosen, a great people, too numerous to be numbered or counted. 9 Therefore give to Your servant an understanding heart to judge Your people, that I may discern between good and evil. For who is able to judge this great people of Yours?"

10 The speech pleased the Lord, that Solomon had asked this thing. 11 Then God said to him: "Because you have asked this thing, and have not asked long life for yourself, nor have asked riches for yourself, nor have asked the life of your enemies, but have asked for yourself understanding to discern justice, 12 behold, I have done according to your words; see, I have given you a wise and understanding heart, so that there has not

been anyone like you before you, nor shall
any like you arise after you. 13And I have also
given you what you have not asked: both
riches and honor, so that there shall not be
anyone like you among the kings all your
days. 14So if you walk in My ways, to keep My
statutes and My commandments, as your
father David walked, then I will lengthen
your days."

15Then Solomon awoke; and indeed it had
been a dream. And he came to Jerusalem
and stood before the ark of the covenant of
the LORD, offered up burnt offerings, offered
peace offerings, and made a feast for all his
servants.

Solomon's Wise Judgment

16Now two women *who were* harlots came
to the king, and stood before him. 17And one
woman said, "O my lord, this woman and
I dwell in the same house; and I gave birth
while she *was* in the house. 18Then it happened, the third day after I had given birth,
that this woman also gave birth. And we *were*
together; no one *was* with us in the house,
except the two of us in the house. 19And this
woman's son died in the night, because she
lay on him. 20So she arose in the middle of
the night and took my son from my side,
while your maidservant slept, and laid him
in her bosom, and laid her dead child in my

GOD GIVES SOLOMON WISDOM AND RICHES

READ IT: 1 KINGS 3:4–28

GET IT:

David grew old and died. His son Solomon became the next king of Israel. He loved the Lord and brought special sacrifices to worship God. At night he had a dream, and God asked him a fantastic question—"What shall I give you?" (v. 5). What an opportunity! Solomon could have asked for anything, but he asked for "an understanding heart" (v. 9). This quality would make him wise and give him patience to listen carefully to others. Solomon was only twenty years old when he became king, so he knew he needed help to rule God's people.

God liked Solomon's request so much that He gave him what he asked for and threw in a bonus. God gave Solomon wisdom, wealth, and power. Solomon was the wisest and richest king in the ancient world. Rulers of other nations were wowed by how he ruled, what he built, and how wealthy he was.

LIVE IT:

If someone asked you that same question—"Ask! What shall I give you?"—what would you answer? Would you want to have lots of money? Lots of friends? To be happy? To know God better? Many of us would think of money first, but money doesn't guarantee anything else. Money can even cause a lot of problems in life. This is a good question to think about and discuss with your parents or youth leader. How you answer may be what motivates you in life.

bosom. 21And when I rose in the morning to
nurse my son, there he was, dead. But when
I had examined him in the morning, indeed,
he was not my son whom I had borne."
22Then the other woman said, "No! But
the living one *is* my son, and the dead one
is your son."

And the first woman said, "No! But the
dead one *is* your son, and the living one *is*
my son."

Thus they spoke before the king.
23And the king said, "The one says, 'This
is my son, who lives, and your son *is* the dead
one'; and the other says, 'No! But your son *is*
the dead one, and my son *is* the living one.'"
24Then the king said, "Bring me a sword." So
they brought a sword before the king. 25And
the king said, "Divide the living child in two,
and give half to one, and half to the other."
26Then the woman whose son *was* living
spoke to the king, for she yearned with compassion for her son; and she said, "O my lord,
give her the living child, and by no means
kill him!"

But the other said, "Let him be neither
mine nor yours, *but* divide *him*."
27So the king answered and said, "Give
the first woman the living child, and by no
means kill him; she *is* his mother."
28And all Israel heard of the judgment
which the king had rendered; and they
feared the king, for they saw that the wisdom
of God *was* in him to administer justice.

Solomon's Administration

4 So King Solomon was king over all
Israel. 2And these *were* his officials:

3:28 Wisdom The ability to use facts to bring about good results. The so-called wisdom of this world could not do this. Jesus Christ is the source of true wisdom.

Azariah the son of Zadok, the priest; 3Eli-
horeph and Ahijah, the sons of Shisha,
scribes; Jehoshaphat the son of Ahilud, the
recorder; 4Benaiah the son of Jehoiada, over
the army; Zadok and Abiathar, the priests;
5Azariah the son of Nathan, over the officers;
Zabud the son of Nathan, a priest *and* the
king's friend; 6Ahishar, over the household;
and Adoniram the son of Abda, over the labor force.
7And Solomon had twelve governors
over all Israel, who provided food for the
king and his household; each one made
provision for one month of the year. 8These
are their names: Ben-Hur,[a] in the mountains of Ephraim; 9Ben-Deker,[a] in Makaz,
Shaalbim, Beth Shemesh, and Elon Beth
Hanan; 10Ben-Hesed,[a] in Arubboth; to him
belonged Sochoh and all the land of Hepher;
11Ben-Abinadab,[a] *in* all the regions of Dor;
he had Taphath the daughter of Solomon as

4:8 [a] Literally *Son of Hur* 4:9 [a] Literally *Son of Deker*
4:10 [a] Literally *Son of Hesed* 4:11 [a] Literally *Son of Abinadab*

HEARING GOD'S VOICE

READ IT: 1 KINGS 3:16–28

Solomon was quick and creative. In just minutes he solved the baby tug-of-war by appealing to the compassion of the real mother. You may be thinking, *I wish I could be that smart.* Wisdom like this comes from God. *Solomon asked for it, and* God gave it. When you read 1 Kings 3:7–9, you can hear Solomon asking the Lord for a discerning heart when he was a young man. It's never too early to ask God for wisdom beyond your years.

wife; [12]Baana the son of Ahilud, *in* Taanach, Megiddo, and all Beth Shean, which *is* beside Zaretan below Jezreel, from Beth Shean to Abel Meholah, as far as the other side of Jokneam; [13]Ben-Geber,[a] in Ramoth Gilead; to him *belonged* the towns of Jair the son of Manasseh, in Gilead; to him *also belonged* the region of Argob in Bashan—sixty large cities with walls and bronze gate-bars; [14]Ahinadab the son of Iddo, *in* Mahanaim; [15]Ahimaaz, in Naphtali; he also took Basemath the daughter of Solomon as wife; [16]Baanah the son of Hushai, in Asher and Aloth; [17]Jehoshaphat the son of Paruah, in Issachar; [18]Shimei the son of Elah, in Benjamin; [19]Geber the son of Uri, in the land of Gilead, *in* the country of Sihon king of the Amorites, and of Og king of Bashan. *He was* the only governor who *was* in the land.

Prosperity and Wisdom of Solomon's Reign

[20]Judah and Israel *were* as numerous as the sand by the sea in multitude, eating and drinking and rejoicing. [21]So Solomon reigned over all kingdoms from the River[a] *to* the land of the Philistines, as far as the border of Egypt. *They* brought tribute and served Solomon all the days of his life.

[22]Now Solomon's provision for one day was thirty kors of fine flour, sixty kors of meal, [23]ten fatted oxen, twenty oxen from the pastures, and one hundred sheep, besides deer, gazelles, roebucks, and fatted fowl.

[24]For he had dominion over all *the region* on this side of the River[a] from Tiphsah even to Gaza, namely over all the kings on this side of the River; and he had peace on every side all around him. [25]And Judah and Israel dwelt safely, each man under his vine and his fig tree, from Dan as far as Beersheba, all the days of Solomon.

[26]Solomon had forty[a] thousand stalls of horses for his chariots, and twelve thousand horsemen. [27]And these governors, each man in his month, provided food for King Solomon and for all who came to King Solomon's table. There was no lack in their supply. [28]They also brought barley and straw to the proper place, for the horses and steeds, each man according to his charge.

[29]And God gave Solomon wisdom and exceedingly great understanding, and largeness of heart like the sand on the seashore. [30]Thus Solomon's wisdom excelled the wisdom of all the men of the East and all the wisdom of Egypt. [31]For he was wiser than all men—than Ethan the Ezrahite, and Heman, Chalcol, and Darda, the sons of Mahol; and his fame was in all the surrounding nations. [32]He spoke three thousand proverbs, and his songs were one thousand and five. [33]Also he spoke of trees, from the cedar tree of Lebanon even to the hyssop that springs out of the wall; he spoke also of animals, of birds, of creeping things, and of fish. [34]And men of all nations, from all the kings of the earth who had heard of his wisdom, came to hear the wisdom of Solomon.

Solomon Prepares to Build the Temple

5 Now Hiram king of Tyre sent his servants to Solomon, because he heard that they had anointed him king in place of his father, for Hiram had always loved David. [2]Then Solomon sent to Hiram, saying:

3 You know how my father David could
not build a house for the name of the
LORD his God because of the wars
which were fought against him on every
side, until the LORD put *his foes*[a] under
the soles of his feet.
4 But now the LORD my God has given me
rest on every side; *there is* neither adversary
nor evil occurrence.
5 And behold, I propose to build a house
for the name of the LORD my God, as
the LORD spoke to my father David, saying,
"Your son, whom I will set on your
throne in your place, he shall build the
house for My name."
6 Now therefore, command that they cut
down cedars for me from Lebanon;
and my servants will be with your
servants, and I will pay you wages for
your servants according to whatever you
say. For you know *there is* none among
us who has skill to cut timber like the
Sidonians.

[7]So it was, when Hiram heard the words of Solomon, that he rejoiced greatly and said,

Blessed *be* the LORD this day, for He has

4:13 [a] Literally *Son of Geber* 4:21 [a] That is, the Euphrates 4:24 [a] That is, the Euphrates 4:26 [a] Following Masoretic Text and most other authorities; some manuscripts of the Septuagint read *four* (compare 2 Chronicles 9:25).
5:3 [a] Literally *them*

given David a wise son over this great people!

8 Then Hiram sent to Solomon, saying:

I have considered *the message* which you sent me, *and* I will do all you desire concerning the cedar and cypress logs.
9 My servants shall bring *them* down from Lebanon to the sea; I will float them in rafts by sea to the place you indicate to me, and will have them broken apart there; then you can take *them* away. And you shall fulfill my desire by giving food for my household.

10 Then Hiram gave Solomon cedar and
cypress logs *according to* all his desire. 11 And
Solomon gave Hiram twenty thousand kors of wheat *as* food for his household, and twenty[a] kors of pressed oil. Thus Solomon gave to Hiram year by year.
12 So the LORD gave Solomon wisdom, as He had promised him; and there was peace between Hiram and Solomon, and the two of them made a treaty together.
13 Then King Solomon raised up a labor force out of all Israel; and the labor force was
thirty thousand men. 14 And he sent them to
Lebanon, ten thousand a month in shifts: they were one month in Lebanon *and* two months at home; Adoniram *was* in charge of
the labor force. 15 Solomon had seventy thou-
sand who carried burdens, and eighty thousand who quarried *stone* in the mountains,
16 besides three thousand three hundred[a] from the chiefs of Solomon's deputies, who supervised the people who labored in the
work. 17 And the king commanded them to quarry large stones, costly stones, *and* hewn stones, to lay the foundation of the temple.[a]
18 So Solomon's builders, Hiram's builders, and the Gebalites quarried *them;* and they prepared timber and stones to build the temple.

Solomon Builds the Temple

6 And it came to pass in the four hundred and eightieth[a] year after the children of Israel had come out of the land of Egypt, in the fourth year of Solomon's reign over Israel, in the month of Ziv, which *is* the second month, that he began to build the
house of the LORD. 2 Now the house which
King Solomon built for the LORD, its length *was* sixty cubits, its width twenty, and its
height thirty cubits. 3 The vestibule in front

In Focus

5:17 Temple Israel's place of worship after they settled in Canaan. It was a building of finished stone. Worship in the temple was the same as it had been in the tabernacle.

of the sanctuary[a] of the house *was* twenty cubits long across the width of the house, *and* the width of *the vestibule*[b] *extended* ten cubits
from the front of the house. 4 And he made for the house windows with beveled frames.
5 Against the wall of the temple he built chambers all around, *against* the walls of the temple, all around the sanctuary and the inner sanctuary.[a] Thus he made side cham-
bers all around it. 6 The lowest chamber *was* five cubits wide, the middle *was* six cubits wide, and the third *was* seven cubits wide; for he made narrow ledges around the outside of the temple, so that *the support beams* would not be fastened into the walls of the
temple. 7 And the temple, when it was being built, was built with stone finished at the quarry, so that no hammer or chisel *or* any iron tool was heard in the temple while it was
being built. 8 The doorway for the middle story[a] *was* on the right side of the temple. They went up by stairs to the middle *story,* and from the middle to the third.
9 So he built the temple and finished it, and he paneled the temple with beams and
boards of cedar. 10 And he built side chambers against the entire temple, each five cubits high; they were attached to the temple with cedar beams.
11 Then the word of the LORD came to
Solomon, saying: 12 "*Concerning* this temple which you are building, if you walk in My

5:11 [a] Following Masoretic Text, Targum, and Vulgate; Septuagint and Syriac read *twenty thousand.* 5:16 [a] Following Masoretic Text, Targum, and Vulgate; Septuagint reads *three thousand six hundred.* 5:17 [a] Literally *house,* and so frequently throughout this book 6:1 [a] Following Masoretic Text, Targum, and Vulgate; Septuagint reads *fortieth.* 6:3 [a] Hebrew *heykal;* here the main room of the temple, elsewhere called the holy place (compare Exodus 26:33 and Ezekiel 41:1) [b] Literally *it* 6:5 [a] Hebrew *debir;* here the inner room of the temple, elsewhere called the Most Holy Place (compare verse 16) 6:8 [a] Following Masoretic Text and Vulgate; Septuagint reads *upper story;* Targum reads *ground story.*

statutes, execute My judgments, keep all My
commandments, and walk in them, then
I will perform My word with you, which I
spoke to your father David. 13And I will dwell
among the children of Israel, and will not
forsake My people Israel."

14So Solomon built the temple and finished it. 15And he built the inside walls of
the temple with cedar boards; from the floor
of the temple to the ceiling he paneled the
inside with wood; and he covered the floor
of the temple with planks of cypress. 16Then
he built the twenty-cubit room at the rear of
the temple, from floor to ceiling, with cedar
boards; he built *it* inside as the inner sanctuary, as the Most Holy *Place*. 17And in front of
it the temple sanctuary was forty cubits *long*.
18The inside of the temple was cedar, carved
with ornamental buds and open flowers. All
was cedar; there was no stone *to be* seen.

19And he prepared the inner sanctuary
inside the temple, to set the ark of the covenant of the LORD there. 20The inner sanctuary *was* twenty cubits long, twenty cubits
wide, and twenty cubits high. He overlaid it
with pure gold, and overlaid the altar of cedar.
21So Solomon overlaid the inside of the temple with pure gold. He stretched gold chains
across the front of the inner sanctuary, and
overlaid it with gold. 22The whole temple he
overlaid with gold, until he had finished all
the temple; also he overlaid with gold the entire altar that *was* by the inner sanctuary.

23Inside the inner sanctuary he made two
cherubim *of* olive wood, *each* ten cubits high.
24One wing of the cherub *was* five cubits,
and the other wing of the cherub five cubits:
ten cubits from the tip of one wing to the
tip of the other. 25And the other cherub *was*
ten cubits; both cherubim *were* of the same
size and shape. 26The height of one cherub
was ten cubits, and so *was* the other cherub.
27Then he set the cherubim inside the inner
room;[a] and they stretched out the wings of
the cherubim so that the wing of the one
touched *one* wall, and the wing of the other cherub touched the other wall. And their
wings touched each other in the middle of
the room. 28Also he overlaid the cherubim
with gold.

29Then he carved all the walls of the
temple all around, both the inner and outer *sanctuaries*, with carved figures of cherubim, palm trees, and open flowers. 30And
the floor of the temple he overlaid with gold,
both the inner and outer *sanctuaries*.

31For the entrance of the inner sanctuary
he made doors *of* olive wood; the lintel *and*
doorposts *were* one-fifth *of the wall*. 32The
two doors *were of* olive wood; and he carved
on them figures of cherubim, palm trees,
and open flowers, and overlaid *them* with
gold; and he spread gold on the cherubim
and on the palm trees. 33So for the door of
the sanctuary he also made doorposts *of* olive wood, one-fourth *of the wall*. 34And the
two doors *were of* cypress wood; two panels
comprised one folding door, and two panels
comprised the other folding door. 35Then
he carved cherubim, palm trees, and open
flowers *on them*, and overlaid *them* with gold
applied evenly on the carved work.

36And he built the inner court with three
rows of hewn stone and a row of cedar
beams.

37In the fourth year the foundation of the
house of the LORD was laid, in the month of
Ziv. 38And in the eleventh year, in the month
of Bul, which is the eighth month, the house
was finished in all its details and according
to all its plans. So he was seven years in
building it.

Solomon's Other Buildings

7 But Solomon took thirteen years to
build his own house; so he finished all
his house.

2He also built the House of the Forest of
Lebanon; its length *was* one hundred cubits,
its width fifty cubits, and its height thirty
cubits, with four rows of cedar pillars, and
cedar beams on the pillars. 3And *it was* paneled with cedar above the beams that *were* on
forty-five pillars, fifteen *to* a row. 4*There were*
windows *with beveled frames in* three rows,
and window *was* opposite window *in* three
tiers. 5And all the doorways and doorposts
had rectangular frames; and window *was*
opposite window *in* three tiers.

6He also made the Hall of Pillars: its
length *was* fifty cubits, and its width thirty
cubits; and in front of them *was* a portico
with pillars, and a canopy *was* in front of
them.

7Then he made a hall for the throne, the
Hall of Judgment, where he might judge;

6:27 [a] Literally *house*

and *it was* paneled with cedar from floor to
ceiling.[a]
8And the house where he dwelt *had* another court inside the hall, of like workmanship. Solomon also made a house like this
hall for Pharaoh's daughter, whom he had
taken *as wife*.
9All these *were of* costly stones cut to size,
trimmed with saws, inside and out, from
the foundation to the eaves, and also on the
outside to the great court. 10The foundation
was of costly stones, large stones, some ten
cubits and some eight cubits. 11And above
were costly stones, hewn to size, and cedar
wood. 12The great court *was* enclosed with
three rows of hewn stones and a row of cedar
beams. So were the inner court of the house
of the LORD and the vestibule of the temple.

Hiram the Craftsman

13Now King Solomon sent and brought
Huram[a] from Tyre. 14He *was* the son of a
widow from the tribe of Naphtali, and his father *was* a man of Tyre, a bronze worker; he
was filled with wisdom and understanding
and skill in working with all kinds of bronze
work. So he came to King Solomon and did
all his work.

The Bronze Pillars for the Temple

15And he cast two pillars of bronze, each
one eighteen cubits high, and a line of twelve
cubits measured the circumference of each.
16Then he made two capitals *of* cast bronze,
to set on the tops of the pillars. The height of
one capital *was* five cubits, and the height of
the other capital *was* five cubits. 17*He made* a
lattice network, with wreaths of chainwork,
for the capitals which *were* on top of the pillars: seven chains for one capital and seven
for the other capital. 18So he made the pillars, and two rows of pomegranates above
the network all around to cover the capitals
that *were* on top; and thus he did for the other capital.
19The capitals which *were* on top of the
pillars in the hall *were* in the shape of lilies,
four cubits. 20The capitals on the two pillars
also *had pomegranates* above, by the convex
surface which *was* next to the network; and
there *were* two hundred such pomegranates
in rows on each of the capitals all around.
21Then he set up the pillars by the vestibule of the temple; he set up the pillar on the
right and called its name Jachin, and he set
up the pillar on the left and called its name
Boaz. 22The tops of the pillars were in the
shape of lilies. So the work of the pillars was
finished.

The Sea and the Oxen

23And he made the Sea of cast bronze,
ten cubits from one brim to the other; *it was*
completely round. Its height *was* five cubits, and a line of thirty cubits measured its
circumference.
24Below its brim *were* ornamental buds
encircling it all around, ten to a cubit, all the
way around the Sea. The ornamental buds
were cast in two rows when it was cast. 25It
stood on twelve oxen: three looking toward
the north, three looking toward the west,
three looking toward the south, and three
looking toward the east; the Sea *was set* upon
them, and all their back parts *pointed* inward. 26It *was* a handbreadth thick; and its
brim was shaped like the brim of a cup, *like*
a lily blossom. It contained two thousand[a]
baths.

The Carts and the Lavers

27He also made ten carts of bronze; four
cubits *was* the length of each cart, four cubits its width, and three cubits its height.
28And this *was* the design of the carts: They
had panels, and the panels *were* between
frames; 29on the panels that *were* between
the frames *were* lions, oxen, and cherubim.
And on the frames *was* a pedestal on top.
Below the lions and oxen *were* wreaths of
plaited work. 30Every cart had four bronze
wheels and axles of bronze, and its four feet
had supports. Under the laver *were* supports
of cast *bronze* beside each wreath. 31Its opening inside the crown at the top *was* one cubit
in diameter; and the opening *was* round,
shaped *like* a pedestal, one and a half cubits
in outside diameter; and also on the opening
were engravings, but the panels were square,
not round. 32Under the panels *were* the four
wheels, and the axles of the wheels *were*
joined to the cart. The height of a wheel *was*
one and a half cubits. 33The workmanship
of the wheels *was* like the workmanship of
a chariot wheel; their axle pins, their rims,
their spokes, and their hubs *were* all of cast
bronze. 34And *there were* four supports at the

7:7 [a] Literally *floor*, that is, of the upper level   7:13 [a] Hebrew *Hiram* (compare 2 Chronicles 2:13, 14)   7:26 [a] Or *three thousand* (compare 2 Chronicles 4:5)

four corners of each cart; its supports *were* part of the cart itself. 35On the top of the cart, at the height of half a cubit, *it was* perfectly round. And on the top of the cart, its flanges and its panels *were* of the same casting. 36On the plates of its flanges and on its panels he engraved cherubim, lions, and palm trees, wherever there was a clear space on each, with wreaths all around. 37Thus he made the ten carts. All of them were of the same mold, one measure, *and* one shape.

38Then he made ten lavers of bronze; each laver contained forty baths, *and* each laver *was* four cubits. On each of the ten carts *was* a laver. 39And he put five carts on the right side of the house, and five on the left side of the house. He set the Sea on the right side of the house, toward the southeast.

Furnishings of the Temple

40Huram[a] made the lavers and the shovels and the bowls. So Huram finished doing all the work that he was to do for King Solomon *for* the house of the LORD: 41the two pillars, the *two* bowl-shaped capitals that *were* on top of the two pillars; the two networks covering the two bowl-shaped capitals which *were* on top of the pillars; 42four hundred pomegranates for the two networks (two rows of pomegranates for each network, to cover the two bowl-shaped capitals that *were* on top of the pillars); 43the ten carts, and ten lavers on the carts; 44one Sea, and twelve oxen under the Sea; 45the pots, the shovels, and the bowls.

All these articles which Huram[a] made for King Solomon *for* the house of the LORD *were of* burnished bronze. 46In the plain of Jordan the king had them cast in clay molds, between Succoth and Zaretan. 47And Solomon did not weigh all the articles, because *there were* so many; the weight of the bronze was not determined.

48Thus Solomon had all the furnishings made for the house of the LORD: the altar of gold, and the table of gold on which *was* the showbread; 49the lampstands of pure gold, five on the right *side* and five on the left in front of the inner sanctuary, with the flowers and the lamps and the wick-trimmers of gold; 50the basins, the trimmers, the bowls, the ladles, and the censers of pure gold; and the hinges of gold, *both* for the doors of the inner room (the Most Holy *Place*) *and* for the doors of the main hall of the temple.

51So all the work that King Solomon had done for the house of the LORD was finished; and Solomon brought in the things which his father David had dedicated: the silver and the gold and the furnishings. He put them in the treasuries of the house of the LORD.

The Ark Brought into the Temple

8 Now Solomon assembled the elders of Israel and all the heads of the tribes, the chief fathers of the children of Israel, to King Solomon in Jerusalem, that they might bring up the ark of the covenant of the LORD from the City of David, which *is* Zion. 2Therefore all the men of Israel assembled with King Solomon at the feast in the month of Ethanim, which *is* the seventh month. 3So all the elders of Israel came, and the priests took up the ark. 4Then they brought up the ark of the LORD, the tabernacle of meeting, and all the holy furnishings that *were* in the tabernacle. The priests and the Levites brought them up. 5Also King Solomon, and all the congregation of Israel who were assembled with him, *were* with him before the ark, sacrificing sheep and oxen that could not be counted or numbered for multitude. 6Then the priests brought in the ark of the covenant of the LORD to its place, into the inner sanctuary of the temple, to the Most Holy *Place,* under the wings of the cherubim. 7For the cherubim spread *their* two wings over the place of the ark, and the cherubim overshadowed the ark and its poles. 8The poles extended so that the ends of the poles could be seen from the holy *place,* in front of the inner sanctuary; but they could not be seen from outside. And they are there to this day. 9Nothing *was* in the ark except the two tablets of stone which Moses put there at Horeb, when the LORD made *a covenant* with the children of Israel, when they came out of the land of Egypt.

10And it came to pass, when the priests came out of the holy *place,* that the cloud filled the house of the LORD, 11so that the priests could not continue ministering because of the cloud; for the glory of the LORD filled the house of the LORD.

12Then Solomon spoke:

7:40 [a] Hebrew *Hiram* (compare 2 Chronicles 2:13, 14)
7:45 [a] Hebrew *Hiram* (compare 2 Chronicles 2:13, 14)

"The LORD said He would dwell in the
dark cloud.
13 I have surely built You an exalted house,
And a place for You to dwell in forever."

Solomon's Speech at Completion of the Work

14 Then the king turned around and
blessed the whole assembly of Israel, while
all the assembly of Israel was standing.
15 And he said: "Blessed *be* the LORD God of
Israel, who spoke with His mouth to my father David, and with His hand has fulfilled
it, saying, 16 'Since the day that I brought My
people Israel out of Egypt, I have chosen no
city from any tribe of Israel *in which* to build
a house, that My name might be there; but
I chose David to be over My people Israel.'
17 Now it was in the heart of my father David
to build a temple[a] for the name of the LORD
God of Israel. 18 But the LORD said to my father David, 'Whereas it was in your heart to
build a temple for My name, you did well
that it was in your heart. 19 Nevertheless you
shall not build the temple, but your son who
will come from your body, he shall build the
temple for My name.' 20 So the LORD has fulfilled His word which He spoke; and I have
filled the position of my father David, and sit
on the throne of Israel, as the LORD promised; and I have built a temple for the name
of the LORD God of Israel. 21 And there I have
made a place for the ark, in which *is* the covenant of the LORD which He made with our
fathers, when He brought them out of the
land of Egypt."

8:17 [a] Literally *house,* and so in verses 18–20

GOD'S GLORY FILLS THE TEMPLE

READ IT: 1 KINGS 8:1–21

GET IT:

David made all the plans for a temple for God. He even lined up the building supplies and the workers. But his son Solomon was the one who actually built the huge and magnificent temple in Jerusalem. The building project was so big that it took several years just to get the area ready where the temple would stand. Then it took another seven years to build it. Finally, all the people were ready to celebrate the completed project. At last God had an official house to live in. Solomon and the people celebrated the event with a feast that lasted more than a week. But the best part of the event was that God's glory filled the temple in a cloud. This was an important moment. God's presence could be seen in His temple!

LIVE IT:

In Solomon's time, God lived in the magnificent temple in Jerusalem that Solomon had built just for Him. Today God doesn't live in just one specific building in one specific city. He lives inside every believer. That means our bodies are God's temple. The body you have is where God lives 24/7. When you become a Christian, God moves into your life and makes your heart His home. Solomon threw a huge party, a grand celebration for God's temple. How can you celebrate the fact that God lives in you?

Solomon's Prayer of Dedication

[22]Then Solomon stood before the altar
of the LORD in the presence of all the assembly of Israel, and spread out his hands
toward heaven; [23]and he said: "LORD God
of Israel, *there is* no God in heaven above
or on earth below like You, who keep *Your*
covenant and mercy with Your servants who
walk before You with all their hearts. [24]You
have kept what You promised Your servant
David my father; You have both spoken with
Your mouth and fulfilled *it* with Your hand,
as *it is* this day. [25]Therefore, LORD God of
Israel, now keep what You promised Your
servant David my father, saying, 'You shall
not fail to have a man sit before Me on the
throne of Israel, only if your sons take heed
to their way, that they walk before Me as you
have walked before Me.' [26]And now I pray,
O God of Israel, let Your word come true,
which You have spoken to Your servant
David my father.

[27]"But will God indeed dwell on the
earth? Behold, heaven and the heaven of
heavens cannot contain You. How much less
this temple which I have built! [28]Yet regard
the prayer of Your servant and his supplication, O LORD my God, and listen to the cry
and the prayer which Your servant is praying before You today: [29]that Your eyes may
be open toward this temple night and day, toward the place of which You said, 'My name
shall be there,' that You may hear the prayer
which Your servant makes toward this place.
[30]And may You hear the supplication of Your
servant and of Your people Israel, when they
pray toward this place. Hear in heaven Your
dwelling place; and when You hear, forgive.

[31]"When anyone sins against his neighbor, and is forced to take an oath, and comes
and takes an oath before Your altar in this
temple, [32]then hear in heaven, and act, and
judge Your servants, condemning the wicked, bringing his way on his head, and justifying the righteous by giving him according
to his righteousness.

[33]"When Your people Israel are defeated
before an enemy because they have sinned
against You, and when they turn back to You
and confess Your name, and pray and make
supplication to You in this temple, [34]then
hear in heaven, and forgive the sin of Your
people Israel, and bring them back to the
land which You gave to their fathers.

[35]"When the heavens are shut up and
there is no rain because they have sinned
against You, when they pray toward this
place and confess Your name, and turn
from their sin because You afflict them,
[36]then hear in heaven, and forgive the sin of
Your servants, Your people Israel, that You
may teach them the good way in which they
should walk; and send rain on Your land
which You have given to Your people as an
inheritance.

[37]"When there is famine in the land, pestilence *or* blight *or* mildew, locusts *or* grasshoppers; when their enemy besieges them
in the land of their cities; whatever plague or
whatever sickness *there is;* [38]whatever prayer,
whatever supplication is made by anyone,
or by all Your people Israel, when each one
knows the plague of his own heart, and
spreads out his hands toward this temple:
[39]then hear in heaven Your dwelling place,
and forgive, and act, and give to everyone
according to all his ways, whose heart You
know (for You alone know the hearts of all
the sons of men), [40]that they may fear You all
the days that they live in the land which You
gave to our fathers.

[41]"Moreover, concerning a foreigner, who
is not of Your people Israel, but has come
from a far country for Your name's sake
[42](for they will hear of Your great name and
Your strong hand and Your outstretched
arm), when he comes and prays toward this
temple, [43]hear in heaven Your dwelling place,
and do according to all for which the foreigner calls to You, that all peoples of the earth
may know Your name and fear You, as *do*
Your people Israel, and that they may know
that this temple which I have built is called
by Your name.

[44]"When Your people go out to battle
against their enemy, wherever You send
them, and when they pray to the LORD toward the city which You have chosen and
the temple which I have built for Your name,
[45]then hear in heaven their prayer and their
supplication, and maintain their cause.

[46]"When they sin against You (for *there is*
no one who does not sin), and You become
angry with them and deliver them to the enemy, and they take them captive to the land
of the enemy, far or near; [47]*yet* when they
come to themselves in the land where they
were carried captive, and repent, and make

supplication to You in the land of those who took them captive, saying, 'We have sinned and done wrong, we have committed wickedness'; 48 and *when* they return to You with all their heart and with all their soul in the land of their enemies who led them away captive, and pray to You toward their land which You gave to their fathers, the city which You have chosen and the temple which I have built for Your name: 49 then hear in heaven Your dwelling place their prayer and their supplication, and maintain their cause, 50 and forgive Your people who have sinned against You, and all their transgressions which they have transgressed against You; and grant them compassion before those who took them captive, that they may have compassion on them 51 (for they *are* Your people and Your inheritance, whom You brought out of Egypt, out of the iron furnace), 52 that Your eyes may be open to the supplication of Your servant and the supplication of Your people Israel, to listen to them whenever they call to You. 53 For You separated them from among all the peoples of the earth *to be* Your inheritance, as You spoke by Your servant Moses, when You brought our fathers out of Egypt, O Lord GOD."

Solomon Blesses the Assembly

54 And so it was, when Solomon had finished praying all this prayer and supplication to the LORD, that he arose from before the altar of the LORD, from kneeling on his knees with his hands spread up to heaven. 55 Then he stood and blessed all the assembly of Israel with a loud voice, saying: 56 "Blessed *be* the LORD, who has given rest to His people Israel, according to all that He promised. There has not failed one word of all His good promise, which He promised through His servant Moses. 57 May the LORD our God be with us, as He was with our fathers. May He not leave us nor forsake us, 58 that He may incline our hearts to Himself, to walk in all His ways, and to keep His commandments and His statutes and His judgments, which He commanded our fathers. 59 And may these words of mine, with which I have made supplication before the LORD, be near the LORD our God day and night, that He may maintain the cause of His servant and the cause of His people Israel, as each day may require, 60 that all the peoples of the earth may know that the LORD *is* God; *there is* no other. 61 Let your heart therefore be loyal to the LORD our God, to walk in His statutes and keep His commandments, as at this day."

Solomon Dedicates the Temple

62 Then the king and all Israel with him offered sacrifices before the LORD. 63 And Solomon offered a sacrifice of peace offerings, which he offered to the LORD, twenty-two thousand bulls and one hundred and twenty thousand sheep. So the king and all the children of Israel dedicated the house of the LORD. 64 On the same day the king consecrated the middle of the court that *was* in front of the house of the LORD; for there he offered burnt offerings, grain offerings, and the fat of the peace offerings, because the bronze altar that *was* before the LORD *was* too small to receive the burnt offerings, the grain offerings, and the fat of the peace offerings.

65 At that time Solomon held a feast, and all Israel with him, a great assembly from the entrance of Hamath to the Brook of Egypt, before the LORD our God, seven days and seven *more* days—fourteen days. 66 On the eighth day he sent the people away; and they blessed the king, and went to their tents joyful and glad of heart for all the good that the LORD had done for His servant David, and for Israel His people.

God's Second Appearance to Solomon

9 And it came to pass, when Solomon had finished building the house of the LORD and the king's house, and all Solomon's desire which he wanted to do, 2 that the LORD appeared to Solomon the second time, as He had appeared to him at Gibeon. 3 And the LORD said to him: "I have heard your prayer and your supplication that you have made before Me; I have consecrated this house which you have built to put My name there forever, and My eyes and My heart will be there perpetually. 4 Now if you walk before Me as your father David walked, in integrity of heart and in uprightness, to do according to all that I have commanded you, *and* if you keep My statutes and My judgments, 5 then I will establish the throne of your kingdom over Israel forever, as I promised David your father, saying, 'You shall not fail to have a man on the throne of Israel.' 6 *But* if you or your sons at all turn from following Me, and do not keep My commandments *and*

My statutes which I have set before you, but
go and serve other gods and worship them,
7then I will cut off Israel from the land which
I have given them; and this house which I
have consecrated for My name I will cast out
of My sight. Israel will be a proverb and a
byword among all peoples. 8And *as for* this
house, *which* is exalted, everyone who passes
by it will be astonished and will hiss, and say,
'Why has the LORD done thus to this land
and to this house?' 9Then they will answer,
'Because they forsook the LORD their God,
who brought their fathers out of the land of
Egypt, and have embraced other gods, and
worshiped them and served them; therefore
the LORD has brought all this calamity on
them.'"

Solomon and Hiram Exchange Gifts

10Now it happened at the end of twenty years, when Solomon had built the two
houses, the house of the LORD and the king's
house 11(Hiram the king of Tyre had supplied
Solomon with cedar and cypress and gold,
as much as he desired), *that* King Solomon
then gave Hiram twenty cities in the land of
Galilee. 12Then Hiram went from Tyre to see
the cities which Solomon had given him, but
they did not please him. 13So he said, "What
kind of cities *are* these which you have given
me, my brother?" And he called them the
land of Cabul,[a] as they are to this day. 14Then
Hiram sent the king one hundred and twenty talents of gold.

Solomon's Additional Achievements

15And this *is* the reason for the labor
force which King Solomon raised: to build
the house of the LORD, his own house, the
Millo,[a] the wall of Jerusalem, Hazor, Megiddo, and Gezer. 16(Pharaoh king of Egypt had
gone up and taken Gezer and burned it with
fire, had killed the Canaanites who dwelt in
the city, and had given it *as* a dowry to his
daughter, Solomon's wife.) 17And Solomon
built Gezer, Lower Beth Horon, 18Baalath,
and Tadmor in the wilderness, in the land
of Judah, 19all the storage cities that Solomon
had, cities for his chariots and cities for his
cavalry, and whatever Solomon desired to
build in Jerusalem, in Lebanon, and in all
the land of his dominion.

20All the people *who were* left of the Amorites, Hittites, Perizzites, Hivites, and
Jebusites, who *were* not of the children of
Israel— 21that is, their descendants who were
left in the land after them, whom the children of Israel had not been able to destroy
completely—from these Solomon raised
forced labor, as it is to this day. 22But of the
children of Israel Solomon made no forced laborers, because they *were* men of war and his
servants: his officers, his captains, commanders of his chariots, and his cavalry.

23Others *were* chiefs of the officials who
were over Solomon's work: five hundred and
fifty, who ruled over the people who did the
work.

24But Pharaoh's daughter came up from
the City of David to her house which *Solomon*[a]
had built for her. Then he built the Millo.

25Now three times a year Solomon offered
burnt offerings and peace offerings on the
altar which he had built for the LORD, and
he burned incense with them *on the altar*
that *was* before the LORD. So he finished the
temple.

26King Solomon also built a fleet of ships
at Ezion Geber, which *is* near Elath[a] on the
shore of the Red Sea, in the land of Edom.
27Then Hiram sent his servants with the
fleet, seamen who knew the sea, to work
with the servants of Solomon. 28And they
went to Ophir, and acquired four hundred
and twenty talents of gold from there, and
brought *it* to King Solomon.

The Queen of Sheba's Praise of Solomon

10 Now when the queen of Sheba
heard of the fame of Solomon concerning the name of the LORD, she came to
test him with hard questions. 2She came to
Jerusalem with a very great retinue, with
camels that bore spices, very much gold, and
precious stones; and when she came to Solomon, she spoke with him about all that was
in her heart. 3So Solomon answered all her
questions; there was nothing so difficult for
the king that he could not explain *it* to her.
4And when the queen of Sheba had seen all
the wisdom of Solomon, the house that he
had built, 5the food on his table, the seating
of his servants, the service of his waiters and
their apparel, his cupbearers, and his entryway by which he went up to the house of the

9:13 [a] Literally *Good for Nothing* 9:15 [a] Literally *The Landfill* 9:24 [a] Literally *he* (compare 2 Chronicles 8:11) 9:26 [a] Hebrew *Eloth* (compare 2 Kings 14:22)

LORD, there was no more spirit in her. 6 Then
she said to the king: "It was a true report
which I heard in my own land about your
words and your wisdom. 7 However I did not
believe the words until I came and saw with
my own eyes; and indeed the half was not
told me. Your wisdom and prosperity exceed
the fame of which I heard. 8 Happy *are* your
men and happy *are* these your servants, who
stand continually before you *and* hear your
wisdom! 9 Blessed be the LORD your God,
who delighted in you, setting you on the
throne of Israel! Because the LORD has loved
Israel forever, therefore He made you king,
to do justice and righteousness."

10 Then she gave the king one hundred
and twenty talents of gold, spices in great
quantity, and precious stones. There never
again came such abundance of spices as
the queen of Sheba gave to King Solomon.
11 Also, the ships of Hiram, which brought
gold from Ophir, brought great quantities
of almug[a] wood and precious stones from
Ophir. 12 And the king made steps of the almug wood for the house of the LORD and for
the king's house, also harps and stringed
instruments for singers. There never again
came such almug wood, nor has the like
been seen to this day.

13 Now King Solomon gave the queen of
Sheba all she desired, whatever she asked,
besides what Solomon had given her according to the royal generosity. So she turned
and went to her own country, she and her
servants.

Solomon's Great Wealth

14 The weight of gold that came to Solomon yearly was six hundred and sixty-six
talents of gold, 15 besides *that* from the traveling merchants, from the income of traders,
from all the kings of Arabia, and from the
governors of the country.

16 And King Solomon made two hundred
large shields *of* hammered gold; six hundred
shekels of gold went into each shield. 17 He
also *made* three hundred shields *of* hammered gold; three minas of gold went into
each shield. The king put them in the House
of the Forest of Lebanon.

18 Moreover the king made a great throne
of ivory, and overlaid it with pure gold. 19 The
throne had six steps, and the top of the
throne *was* round at the back; *there were* armrests on either side of the place of the seat,
and two lions stood beside the armrests.
20 Twelve lions stood there, one on each side
of the six steps; nothing like *this* had been
made for any *other* kingdom.

21 All King Solomon's drinking vessels
were gold, and all the vessels of the House
of the Forest of Lebanon *were* pure gold.
Not *one was* silver, for this was accounted
as nothing in the days of Solomon. 22 For the
king had merchant ships[a] at sea with the
fleet of Hiram. Once every three years the
merchant ships came bringing gold, silver,
ivory, apes, and monkeys.[b] 23 So King Solomon surpassed all the kings of the earth in
riches and wisdom.

24 Now all the earth sought the presence
of Solomon to hear his wisdom, which God
had put in his heart. 25 Each man brought his
present: articles of silver and gold, garments,
armor, spices, horses, and mules, at a set rate
year by year.

26 And Solomon gathered chariots and
horsemen; he had one thousand four hundred chariots and twelve thousand horsemen, whom he stationed[a] in the chariot
cities and with the king at Jerusalem. 27 The
king made silver *as common* in Jerusalem as
stones, and he made cedar trees as abundant
as the sycamores which *are* in the lowland.

28 Also Solomon had horses imported
from Egypt and Keveh; the king's merchants
bought them in Keveh at the *current* price.
29 Now a chariot that was imported from
Egypt cost six hundred *shekels* of silver, and
a horse one hundred and fifty; and thus,
through their agents,[a] they exported *them*
to all the kings of the Hittites and the kings
of Syria.

10:11 [a] Or *algum* (compare 2 Chronicles 9:10, 11)
10:22 [a] Literally *ships of Tarshish,* deep-sea vessels [b] Or *peacocks* **10:26** [a] Following Septuagint, Syriac, Targum, and Vulgate (compare 2 Chronicles 9:25); Masoretic Text reads *led.* **10:29** [a] Literally *by their hands*

Solomon's Heart Turns from the LORD

11 But King Solomon loved many foreign women, as well as the daughter
of Pharaoh: women of the Moabites, Ammonites, Edomites, Sidonians, *and* Hittites— 2from the nations of whom the LORD
had said to the children of Israel, "You shall
not intermarry with them, nor they with
you. Surely they will turn away your hearts
after their gods." Solomon clung to these
in love. 3And he had seven hundred wives,
princesses, and three hundred concubines;
and his wives turned away his heart. 4For
it was so, when Solomon was old, that his
wives turned his heart after other gods; and
his heart was not loyal to the LORD his God,
as *was* the heart of his father David. 5For Solomon went after Ashtoreth the goddess of
the Sidonians, and after Milcom the abomination of the Ammonites. 6Solomon did evil
in the sight of the LORD, and did not fully
follow the LORD, as *did* his father David.
7Then Solomon built a high place for Chemosh the abomination of Moab, on the hill
that *is* east of Jerusalem, and for Molech the
abomination of the people of Ammon. 8And
he did likewise for all his foreign wives, who
burned incense and sacrificed to their gods.

9So the LORD became angry with Solomon, because his heart had turned from
the LORD God of Israel, who had appeared
to him twice, 10and had commanded him
concerning this thing, that he should not go
after other gods; but he did not keep what
the LORD had commanded. 11Therefore the
LORD said to Solomon, "Because you have
done this, and have not kept My covenant
and My statutes, which I have commanded you, I will surely tear the kingdom away
from you and give it to your servant. 12Never-
theless I will not do it in your days, for the
sake of your father David; I will tear it out
of the hand of your son. 13However I will not
tear away the whole kingdom; I will give one
tribe to your son for the sake of My servant
David, and for the sake of Jerusalem which
I have chosen."

Adversaries of Solomon

14Now the LORD raised up an adversary
against Solomon, Hadad the Edomite; he
was a descendant of the king in Edom. 15For
it happened, when David was in Edom, and
Joab the commander of the army had gone
up to bury the slain, after he had killed every
male in Edom 16(because for six months Joab
remained there with all Israel, until he had
cut down every male in Edom), 17that Hadad
fled to go to Egypt, he and certain Edomites
of his father's servants with him. Hadad *was*
still a little child. 18Then they arose from
Midian and came to Paran; and they took
men with them from Paran and came to
Egypt, to Pharaoh king of Egypt, who gave
him a house, apportioned food for him, and
gave him land. 19And Hadad found great favor in the sight of Pharaoh, so that he gave
him as wife the sister of his own wife, that is,
the sister of Queen Tahpenes. 20Then the sister of Tahpenes bore him Genubath his son,
whom Tahpenes weaned in Pharaoh's house.
And Genubath was in Pharaoh's household
among the sons of Pharaoh.

21So when Hadad heard in Egypt that David rested with his fathers, and that Joab the
commander of the army was dead, Hadad
said to Pharaoh, "Let me depart, that I may
go to my own country."

22Then Pharaoh said to him, "But what
have you lacked with me, that suddenly you
seek to go to your own country?"

So he answered, "Nothing, but do let me
go anyway."

23And God raised up *another* adversary
against him, Rezon the son of Eliadah, who
had fled from his lord, Hadadezer king of
Zobah. 24So he gathered men to him and
became captain over a band *of raiders,* when
David killed those *of Zobah.* And they went
to Damascus and dwelt there, and reigned in
Damascus. 25He was an adversary of Israel
all the days of Solomon (besides the trouble
that Hadad *caused*); and he abhorred Israel,
and reigned over Syria.

Jeroboam's Rebellion

26Then Solomon's servant, Jeroboam the
son of Nebat, an Ephraimite from Zereda,
whose mother's name *was* Zeruah, a widow,
also rebelled against the king.

27And this *is* what caused him to rebel
against the king: Solomon had built the Millo *and* repaired the damages to the City of
David his father. 28The man Jeroboam *was* a
mighty man of valor; and Solomon, seeing
that the young man was industrious, made
him the officer over all the labor force of the
house of Joseph.

29Now it happened at that time, when

Jeroboam went out of Jerusalem, that the
prophet Ahijah the Shilonite met him on
the way; and he had clothed himself with
a new garment, and the two *were* alone in
the field. 30Then Ahijah took hold of the new
garment that *was* on him, and tore it *into*
twelve pieces. 31And he said to Jeroboam,
"Take for yourself ten pieces, for thus says
the LORD, the God of Israel: 'Behold, I will
tear the kingdom out of the hand of Solomon
and will give ten tribes to you 32(but he shall
have one tribe for the sake of My servant
David, and for the sake of Jerusalem, the
city which I have chosen out of all the tribes
of Israel), 33because they have[a] forsaken
Me, and worshiped Ashtoreth the goddess
of the Sidonians, Chemosh the god of the
Moabites, and Milcom the god of the people
of Ammon, and have not walked in My ways
to do *what is* right in My eyes and *keep* My
statutes and My judgments, as *did* his father
David. 34However I will not take the whole
kingdom out of his hand, because I have
made him ruler all the days of his life for
the sake of My servant David, whom I chose
because he kept My commandments and My
statutes. 35But I will take the kingdom out of
his son's hand and give it to you—ten tribes.
36And to his son I will give one tribe, that My
servant David may always have a lamp before Me in Jerusalem, the city which I have
chosen for Myself, to put My name there.
37So I will take you, and you shall reign over
all your heart desires, and you shall be king
over Israel. 38Then it shall be, if you heed all
that I command you, walk in My ways, and
do *what is* right in My sight, to keep My statutes and My commandments, as My servant
David did, then I will be with you and build
for you an enduring house, as I built for David, and will give Israel to you. 39And I will
afflict the descendants of David because of
this, but not forever.'"

40Solomon therefore sought to kill Jeroboam. But Jeroboam arose and fled to Egypt,
to Shishak king of Egypt, and was in Egypt
until the death of Solomon.

Death of Solomon

41Now the rest of the acts of Solomon, all
that he did, and his wisdom, *are* they not
written in the book of the acts of Solomon?
42And the period that Solomon reigned in
Jerusalem over all Israel *was* forty years.
43Then Solomon rested with his fathers, and
was buried in the City of David his father.
And Rehoboam his son reigned in his place.

The Revolt Against Rehoboam

12 And Rehoboam went to Shechem,
for all Israel had gone to Shechem
to make him king. 2So it happened, when
Jeroboam the son of Nebat heard *it* (he was
still in Egypt, for he had fled from the presence of King Solomon and had been dwelling in Egypt), 3that they sent and called him.
Then Jeroboam and the whole assembly of
Israel came and spoke to Rehoboam, saying, 4"Your father made our yoke heavy; now
therefore, lighten the burdensome service of
your father, and his heavy yoke which he put
on us, and we will serve you."

5So he said to them, "Depart *for* three
days, then come back to me." And the people departed.

6Then King Rehoboam consulted the
elders who stood before his father Solomon
while he still lived, and he said, "How do you
advise *me* to answer these people?"

7And they spoke to him, saying, "If you
will be a servant to these people today, and
serve them, and answer them, and speak
good words to them, then they will be your
servants forever."

8But he rejected the advice which the
elders had given him, and consulted the
young men who had grown up with him,
who stood before him. 9And he said to them,
"What advice do you give? How should we
answer this people who have spoken to me,
saying, 'Lighten the yoke which your father
put on us'?"

10Then the young men who had grown
up with him spoke to him, saying, "Thus
you should speak to this people who have
spoken to you, saying, 'Your father made our
yoke heavy, but you make *it* lighter on us'—
thus you shall say to them: 'My little *finger*
shall be thicker than my father's waist! 11And
now, whereas my father put a heavy yoke on
you, I will add to your yoke; my father chastised you with whips, but I will chastise you
with scourges!'"[a]

12So Jeroboam and all the people came
to Rehoboam the third day, as the king had

11:33 [a] Following Masoretic Text and Targum; Septuagint, Syriac, and Vulgate read *he has.* 12:11 [a] Literally *scorpions*

directed, saying, "Come back to me the third
day." 13 Then the king answered the people
roughly, and rejected the advice which the
elders had given him; 14 and he spoke to them
according to the advice of the young men,
saying, "My father made your yoke heavy,
but I will add to your yoke; my father chastised you with whips, but I will chastise you
with scourges!"[a] 15 So the king did not listen
to the people; for the turn *of events* was from
the LORD, that He might fulfill His word,
which the LORD had spoken by Ahijah the
Shilonite to Jeroboam the son of Nebat.

16 Now when all Israel saw that the king
did not listen to them, the people answered
the king, saying:

"What share have we in David?
We have no inheritance in the son of
Jesse.
To your tents, O Israel!
Now, see to your own house, O David!"

So Israel departed to their tents. 17 But Rehoboam reigned over the children of Israel
who dwelt in the cities of Judah.

18 Then King Rehoboam sent Adoram,
who *was* in charge of the revenue; but all
Israel stoned him with stones, and he died.
Therefore King Rehoboam mounted his
chariot in haste to flee to Jerusalem. 19 So

12:14 [a] Literally *scorpions*

GOD'S KINGDOM DIVIDES IN TWO

READ IT: 1 KINGS 12:1–33

GET IT:

For 120 years, Israel was one big nation made up of twelve different groups called tribes. Three kings had ruled Israel: Saul, David, and Solomon. Things were really good in the kingdom while it was united under one ruler. But that suddenly changed. Solomon's son, Rehoboam, was supposed to be the only king. But when the people heard that he was going to raise taxes and make their lives worse than before, they wanted out of the kingdom. They made Jeroboam king over ten of the tribes—called Israel. Rehoboam was now the king of only two tribes—called Judah. It certainly didn't seem to be a very good idea, but God told them it was His plan, so they shouldn't start a civil war over it.

In order to be sure he would stay king, Jeroboam did something really dumb. He built two big gold cows and told the people to worship them instead of going to Jerusalem to worship God. This was the beginning of a long line of bad kings in Israel.

LIVE IT:

The people had their priorities all mixed up. God should have been more important to them than the possibility that their taxes would go up. They followed the wrong leader. Leaders today are important to us. But we have to be responsible for judging what kind of leader a person is—whether he or she is the leader of a group of friends, the leader of a club, or the leader of a nation. You have the right, the freedom, and the responsibility to decide what kind of leader you want to follow.

Israel has been in rebellion against the
house of David to this day.

20Now it came to pass when all Israel
heard that Jeroboam had come back, they
sent for him and called him to the congregation, and made him king over all Israel.
There was none who followed the house of
David, but the tribe of Judah only.

21And when Rehoboam came to Jerusalem, he assembled all the house of Judah
with the tribe of Benjamin, one hundred and
eighty thousand chosen *men* who were warriors, to fight against the house of Israel, that
he might restore the kingdom to Rehoboam
the son of Solomon. 22But the word of God
came to Shemaiah the man of God, saying,
23"Speak to Rehoboam the son of Solomon,
king of Judah, to all the house of Judah and
Benjamin, and to the rest of the people,
saying, 24'Thus says the LORD: "You shall
not go up nor fight against your brethren
the children of Israel. Let every man return
to his house, for this thing is from Me."'"
Therefore they obeyed the word of the LORD,
and turned back, according to the word of
the LORD.

Jeroboam's Gold Calves

25Then Jeroboam built Shechem in the
mountains of Ephraim, and dwelt there.
Also he went out from there and built Penuel. 26And Jeroboam said in his heart, "Now
the kingdom may return to the house of
David: 27If these people go up to offer sacrifices in the house of the LORD at Jerusalem,
then the heart of this people will turn back
to their lord, Rehoboam king of Judah, and
they will kill me and go back to Rehoboam
king of Judah."

28Therefore the king asked advice, made
two calves of gold, and said to the people, "It
is too much for you to go up to Jerusalem.
Here are your gods, O Israel, which brought
you up from the land of Egypt!" 29And he
set up one in Bethel, and the other he put
in Dan. 30Now this thing became a sin, for
the people went *to worship* before the one as
far as Dan. 31He made shrines[a] on the high
places, and made priests from every class of
people, who were not of the sons of Levi.

32Jeroboam ordained a feast on the fifteenth day of the eighth month, like the feast
that *was* in Judah, and offered sacrifices on
the altar. So he did at Bethel, sacrificing to
the calves that he had made. And at Bethel
he installed the priests of the high places
which he had made. 33So he made offerings
on the altar which he had made at Bethel
on the fifteenth day of the eighth month, in
the month which he had devised in his own
heart. And he ordained a feast for the children of Israel, and offered sacrifices on the
altar and burned incense.

The Message of the Man of God

13 And behold, a man of God went
from Judah to Bethel by the word of
the LORD, and Jeroboam stood by the altar
to burn incense. 2Then he cried out against
the altar by the word of the LORD, and said,
"O altar, altar! Thus says the LORD: 'Behold,
a child, Josiah by name, shall be born to the
house of David; and on you he shall sacrifice the priests of the high places who burn
incense on you, and men's bones shall be
burned on you.'" 3And he gave a sign the
same day, saying, "This *is* the sign which the
LORD has spoken: Surely the altar shall split
apart, and the ashes on it shall be poured
out."

4So it came to pass when King Jeroboam
heard the saying of the man of God, who
cried out against the altar in Bethel, that he
stretched out his hand from the altar, saying, "Arrest him!" Then his hand, which
he stretched out toward him, withered, so
that he could not pull it back to himself.
5The altar also was split apart, and the ashes
poured out from the altar, according to the
sign which the man of God had given by the
word of the LORD. 6Then the king answered
and said to the man of God, "Please entreat
the favor of the LORD your God, and pray for
me, that my hand may be restored to me."

So the man of God entreated the LORD,
and the king's hand was restored to him, and
became as before. 7Then the king said to the
man of God, "Come home with me and refresh yourself, and I will give you a reward."

8But the man of God said to the king, "If
you were to give me half your house, I would
not go in with you; nor would I eat bread nor
drink water in this place. 9For so it was commanded me by the word of the LORD, saying,
'You shall not eat bread, nor drink water, nor
return by the same way you came.'" 10So he
went another way and did not return by the
way he came to Bethel.

12:31 [a] Literally *a house*

Death of the Man of God

11Now an old prophet dwelt in Bethel, and
his sons came and told him all the works
that the man of God had done that day in
Bethel; they also told their father the words
which he had spoken to the king. 12And their
father said to them, "Which way did he go?"
For his sons had seen[a] which way the man of
God went who came from Judah. 13Then he
said to his sons, "Saddle the donkey for me."
So they saddled the donkey for him; and he
rode on it, 14and went after the man of God,
and found him sitting under an oak. Then
he said to him, "*Are* you the man of God who
came from Judah?"

And he said, "I *am*."

15Then he said to him, "Come home with
me and eat bread."

16And he said, "I cannot return with you
nor go in with you; neither can I eat bread
nor drink water with you in this place. 17For I
have been told by the word of the LORD, 'You
shall not eat bread nor drink water there, nor
return by going the way you came.'"

18He said to him, "I too *am* a prophet as
you *are,* and an angel spoke to me by the
word of the LORD, saying, 'Bring him back
with you to your house, that he may eat bread
and drink water.'" (He was lying to him.)

19So he went back with him, and ate bread
in his house, and drank water.

20Now it happened, as they sat at the table, that the word of the LORD came to the
prophet who had brought him back; 21and
he cried out to the man of God who came
from Judah, saying, "Thus says the LORD:
'Because you have disobeyed the word of the
LORD, and have not kept the commandment
which the LORD your God commanded you,
22but you came back, ate bread, and drank
water in the place of which *the LORD* said to
you, "Eat no bread and drink no water," your
corpse shall not come to the tomb of your
fathers.'"

23So it was, after he had eaten bread and
after he had drunk, that he saddled the
donkey for him, the prophet whom he had
brought back. 24When he was gone, a lion
met him on the road and killed him. And
his corpse was thrown on the road, and the
donkey stood by it. The lion also stood by the
corpse. 25And there, men passed by and saw
the corpse thrown on the road, and the lion
standing by the corpse. Then they went and
told *it* in the city where the old prophet dwelt.

26Now when the prophet who had brought
him back from the way heard *it,* he said, "It
is the man of God who was disobedient to
the word of the LORD. Therefore the LORD
has delivered him to the lion, which has torn
him and killed him, according to the word
of the LORD which He spoke to him." 27And
he spoke to his sons, saying, "Saddle the
donkey for me." So they saddled *it.* 28Then
he went and found his corpse thrown on the
road, and the donkey and the lion standing
by the corpse. The lion had not eaten the
corpse nor torn the donkey. 29And the prophet took up the corpse of the man of God, laid
it on the donkey, and brought it back. So the
old prophet came to the city to mourn, and
to bury him. 30Then he laid the corpse in his
own tomb; and they mourned over him, *saying,* "Alas, my brother!" 31So it was, after he
had buried him, that he spoke to his sons,
saying, "When I am dead, then bury me in
the tomb where the man of God *is* buried; lay
my bones beside his bones. 32For the saying
which he cried out by the word of the LORD
against the altar in Bethel, and against all
the shrines[a] on the high places which *are*
in the cities of Samaria, will surely come to
pass."

33After this event Jeroboam did not turn
from his evil way, but again he made priests
from every class of people for the high places; whoever wished, he consecrated him,
and he became *one* of the priests of the high
places. 34And this thing was the sin of the
house of Jeroboam, so as to exterminate and
destroy *it* from the face of the earth.

Judgment on the House of Jeroboam

14 At that time Abijah the son of Jeroboam became sick. 2And Jeroboam
said to his wife, "Please arise, and disguise
yourself, that they may not recognize you as
the wife of Jeroboam, and go to Shiloh. Indeed, Ahijah the prophet *is* there, who told
me that *I would be* king over this people.
3Also take with you ten loaves, *some* cakes,
and a jar of honey, and go to him; he will
tell you what will become of the child." 4And
Jeroboam's wife did so; she arose and went
to Shiloh, and came to the house of Ahijah.
But Ahijah could not see, for his eyes were
glazed by reason of his age.

13:12 [a] Septuagint, Syriac, Targum, and Vulgate read *showed him.* 13:32 [a] Literally *houses*

5 Now the LORD had said to Ahijah, "Here is the wife of Jeroboam, coming to ask you something about her son, for he *is* sick. Thus and thus you shall say to her; for it will be, when she comes in, that she will pretend *to be* another *woman.*"

6 And so it was, when Ahijah heard the sound of her footsteps as she came through the door, he said, "Come in, wife of Jeroboam. Why do you pretend *to be* another *person?* For I *have been* sent to you *with* bad *news.* 7 Go, tell Jeroboam, 'Thus says the LORD God of Israel: "Because I exalted you from among the people, and made you ruler over My people Israel, 8 and tore the kingdom away from the house of David, and gave it to you; and *yet* you have not been as My servant David, who kept My commandments and who followed Me with all his heart, to do only *what was* right in My eyes; 9 but you have done more evil than all who were before you, for you have gone and made for yourself other gods and molded images to provoke Me to anger, and have cast Me behind your back— 10 therefore behold! I will bring disaster on the house of Jeroboam, and will cut off from Jeroboam every male in Israel, bond and free; I will take away the remnant of the house of Jeroboam, as one takes away refuse until it is all gone. 11 The dogs shall eat whoever belongs to Jeroboam and dies in the city, and the birds of the air shall eat whoever dies in the field; for the LORD has spoken!"' 12 Arise therefore, go to your own house. When your feet enter the city, the child shall die. 13 And all Israel shall mourn for him and bury him, for he is the only one of Jeroboam who shall come to the grave, because in him there is found something good toward the LORD God of Israel in the house of Jeroboam.

14 "Moreover the LORD will raise up for Himself a king over Israel who shall cut off the house of Jeroboam; this is the day. What? Even now! 15 For the LORD will strike Israel, as a reed is shaken in the water. He will uproot Israel from this good land which He gave to their fathers, and will scatter them beyond the River,[a] because they have made their wooden images,[b] provoking the LORD to anger. 16 And He will give Israel up because of the sins of Jeroboam, who sinned and who made Israel sin."

17 Then Jeroboam's wife arose and departed, and came to Tirzah. When she came to the threshold of the house, the child died. 18 And they buried him; and all Israel mourned for him, according to the word of the LORD which He spoke through His servant Ahijah the prophet.

Death of Jeroboam

19 Now the rest of the acts of Jeroboam, how he made war and how he reigned, indeed they *are* written in the book of the chronicles of the kings of Israel. 20 The period that Jeroboam reigned *was* twenty-two years. So he rested with his fathers. Then Nadab his son reigned in his place.

Rehoboam Reigns in Judah

21 And Rehoboam the son of Solomon reigned in Judah. Rehoboam *was* forty-one years old when he became king. He reigned seventeen years in Jerusalem, the city which the LORD had chosen out of all the tribes of Israel, to put His name there. His mother's name *was* Naamah, an Ammonitess. 22 Now Judah did evil in the sight of the LORD, and they provoked Him to jealousy with their sins which they committed, more than all that their fathers had done. 23 For they also built for themselves high places, *sacred* pillars, and wooden images on every high hill and under every green tree. 24 And there were also perverted persons[a] in the land. They did according to all the abominations of the nations which the LORD had cast out before the children of Israel.

25 It happened in the fifth year of King Rehoboam *that* Shishak king of Egypt came up against Jerusalem. 26 And he took away the treasures of the house of the LORD and the treasures of the king's house; he took away everything. He also took away all the gold shields which Solomon had made. 27 Then King Rehoboam made bronze shields in their place, and committed *them* to the hands of the captains of the guard, who guarded the doorway of the king's house. 28 And whenever the king entered the house of the LORD, the guards carried them, then brought them back into the guardroom.

29 Now the rest of the acts of Rehoboam, and all that he did, *are* they not written in the book of the chronicles of the kings of Judah? 30 And there was war between Rehoboam

14:15 [a] That is, the Euphrates [b] Hebrew *Asherim,* Canaanite deities 14:24 [a] Hebrew *qadesh,* that is, one practicing sodomy and prostitution in religious rituals

and Jeroboam all *their* days. 31So Rehoboam
rested with his fathers, and was buried with
his fathers in the City of David. His mother's
name *was* Naamah, an Ammonitess. Then
Abijam[a] his son reigned in his place.

Abijam Reigns in Judah

15 In the eighteenth year of King Jeroboam the son of Nebat, Abijam
became king over Judah. 2He reigned three
years in Jerusalem. His mother's name *was*
Maachah the granddaughter of Abishalom.
3And he walked in all the sins of his father,
which he had done before him; his heart
was not loyal to the LORD his God, as was
the heart of his father David. 4Nevertheless
for David's sake the LORD his God gave him
a lamp in Jerusalem, by setting up his son
after him and by establishing Jerusalem;
5because David did *what was* right in the eyes
of the LORD, and had not turned aside from
anything that He commanded him all the
days of his life, except in the matter of Uriah the Hittite. 6And there was war between
Rehoboam[a] and Jeroboam all the days of
his life. 7Now the rest of the acts of Abijam,
and all that he did, *are* they not written in
the book of the chronicles of the kings of
Judah? And there was war between Abijam
and Jeroboam.

8So Abijam rested with his fathers, and
they buried him in the City of David. Then
Asa his son reigned in his place.

Asa Reigns in Judah

9In the twentieth year of Jeroboam king
of Israel, Asa became king over Judah. 10And
he reigned forty-one years in Jerusalem.
His grandmother's name *was* Maachah the
granddaughter of Abishalom. 11Asa did *what
was* right in the eyes of the LORD, as *did* his
father David. 12And he banished the perverted persons[a] from the land, and removed all
the idols that his fathers had made. 13Also he
removed Maachah his grandmother from
being queen mother, because she had made
an obscene image of Asherah.[a] And Asa
cut down her obscene image and burned *it*
by the Brook Kidron. 14But the high places
were not removed. Nevertheless Asa's heart
was loyal to the LORD all his days. 15He also
brought into the house of the LORD the
things which his father had dedicated, and
the things which he himself had dedicated:
silver and gold and utensils.

16Now there was war between Asa and
Baasha king of Israel all their days. 17And
Baasha king of Israel came up against Judah,
and built Ramah, that he might let none go
out or come in to Asa king of Judah. 18Then
Asa took all the silver and gold *that was* left
in the treasuries of the house of the LORD
and the treasuries of the king's house, and
delivered them into the hand of his servants.
And King Asa sent them to Ben-Hadad the
son of Tabrimmon, the son of Hezion, king
of Syria, who dwelt in Damascus, saying,
19"*Let there be* a treaty between you and me,
as there was between my father and your father. See, I have sent you a present of silver
and gold. Come and break your treaty with
Baasha king of Israel, so that he will withdraw from me."

20So Ben-Hadad heeded King Asa, and
sent the captains of his armies against the
cities of Israel. He attacked Ijon, Dan, Abel
Beth Maachah, and all Chinneroth, with
all the land of Naphtali. 21Now it happened,
when Baasha heard *it*, that he stopped building Ramah, and remained in Tirzah.

22Then King Asa made a proclamation
throughout all Judah; none *was* exempted.
And they took away the stones and timber
of Ramah, which Baasha had used for building; and with them King Asa built Geba of
Benjamin, and Mizpah.

23The rest of all the acts of Asa, all his
might, all that he did, and the cities which
he built, *are* they not written in the book of
the chronicles of the kings of Judah? But in
the time of his old age he was diseased in
his feet. 24So Asa rested with his fathers, and
was buried with his fathers in the City of
David his father. Then Jehoshaphat his son
reigned in his place.

Nadab Reigns in Israel

25Now Nadab the son of Jeroboam became king over Israel in the second year of
Asa king of Judah, and he reigned over Israel two years. 26And he did evil in the sight
of the LORD, and walked in the way of his
father, and in his sin by which he had made
Israel sin.

27Then Baasha the son of Ahijah, of the
house of Issachar, conspired against him.

14:31 [a] Spelled *Abijah* in 2 Chronicles 12:16ff **15:6** [a] Following Masoretic Text, Septuagint, Targum, and Vulgate; some Hebrew manuscripts and Syriac read *Abijam*. **15:12** [a] Hebrew *qedeshim*, that is, those practicing sodomy and prostitution in religious rituals **15:13** [a] A Canaanite goddess

And Baasha killed him at Gibbethon, which
belonged to the Philistines, while Nadab and
all Israel laid siege to Gibbethon. 28 Baasha
killed him in the third year of Asa king of
Judah, and reigned in his place. 29 And it was
so, when he became king, *that* he killed all
the house of Jeroboam. He did not leave to
Jeroboam anyone that breathed, until he had
destroyed him, according to the word of the
LORD which He had spoken by His servant
Ahijah the Shilonite, 30 because of the sins
of Jeroboam, which he had sinned and by
which he had made Israel sin, because of his
provocation with which he had provoked the
LORD God of Israel to anger.

31 Now the rest of the acts of Nadab, and all
that he did, *are* they not written in the book
of the chronicles of the kings of Israel? 32 And
there was war between Asa and Baasha king
of Israel all their days.

Baasha Reigns in Israel

33 In the third year of Asa king of Judah,
Baasha the son of Ahijah became king over
all Israel in Tirzah, and *reigned* twenty-four
years. 34 He did evil in the sight of the LORD,
and walked in the way of Jeroboam, and in
his sin by which he had made Israel sin.

16 Then the word of the LORD came
to Jehu the son of Hanani, against
Baasha, saying: 2 "Inasmuch as I lifted you
out of the dust and made you ruler over My
people Israel, and you have walked in the
way of Jeroboam, and have made My people
Israel sin, to provoke Me to anger with their
sins, 3 surely I will take away the posterity of
Baasha and the posterity of his house, and I
will make your house like the house of Jeroboam the son of Nebat. 4 The dogs shall eat
whoever belongs to Baasha and dies in the
city, and the birds of the air shall eat whoever
dies in the fields."

5 Now the rest of the acts of Baasha, what
he did, and his might, *are* they not written
in the book of the chronicles of the kings of
Israel? 6 So Baasha rested with his fathers
and was buried in Tirzah. Then Elah his son
reigned in his place.

7 And also the word of the LORD came by
the prophet Jehu the son of Hanani against
Baasha and his house, because of all the evil
that he did in the sight of the LORD in provoking Him to anger with the work of his
hands, in being like the house of Jeroboam,
and because he killed them.

Elah Reigns in Israel

8 In the twenty-sixth year of Asa king of
Judah, Elah the son of Baasha became king
over Israel, *and reigned* two years in Tirzah.
9 Now his servant Zimri, commander of half
his chariots, conspired against him as he
was in Tirzah drinking himself drunk in
the house of Arza, steward of *his* house in
Tirzah. 10 And Zimri went in and struck him
and killed him in the twenty-seventh year of
Asa king of Judah, and reigned in his place.

11 Then it came to pass, when he began
to reign, as soon as he was seated on his
throne, *that* he killed all the household of
Baasha; he did not leave him one male, neither of his relatives nor of his friends. 12 Thus
Zimri destroyed all the household of Baasha,
according to the word of the LORD, which He
spoke against Baasha by Jehu the prophet,
13 for all the sins of Baasha and the sins of
Elah his son, by which they had sinned and
by which they had made Israel sin, in provoking the LORD God of Israel to anger with
their idols.

14 Now the rest of the acts of Elah, and all
that he did, *are* they not written in the book
of the chronicles of the kings of Israel?

Zimri Reigns in Israel

15 In the twenty-seventh year of Asa king
of Judah, Zimri had reigned in Tirzah seven
days. And the people *were* encamped against
Gibbethon, which *belonged* to the Philistines.
16 Now the people *who were* encamped heard
it said, "Zimri has conspired and also has
killed the king." So all Israel made Omri,
the commander of the army, king over Israel that day in the camp. 17 Then Omri and
all Israel with him went up from Gibbethon,
and they besieged Tirzah. 18 And it happened,
when Zimri saw that the city was taken, that
he went into the citadel of the king's house
and burned the king's house down upon
himself with fire, and died, 19 because of the
sins which he had committed in doing evil
in the sight of the LORD, in walking in the
way of Jeroboam, and in his sin which he
had committed to make Israel sin.

20 Now the rest of the acts of Zimri, and
the treason he committed, *are* they not written in the book of the chronicles of the kings
of Israel?

Omri Reigns in Israel

21 Then the people of Israel were divided
into two parts: half of the people followed

Tibni the son of Ginath, to make him king, and half followed Omri. 22But the people who followed Omri prevailed over the people who followed Tibni the son of Ginath. So Tibni died and Omri reigned. 23In the thirty-first year of Asa king of Judah, Omri became king over Israel, *and reigned* twelve years. Six years he reigned in Tirzah. 24And he bought the hill of Samaria from Shemer for two talents of silver; then he built on the hill, and called the name of the city which he built, Samaria, after the name of Shemer, owner of the hill. 25Omri did evil in the eyes of the LORD, and did worse than all who *were* before him. 26For he walked in all the ways of Jeroboam the son of Nebat, and in his sin by which he had made Israel sin, provoking the LORD God of Israel to anger with their idols.

27Now the rest of the acts of Omri which he did, and the might that he showed, *are* they not written in the book of the chronicles of the kings of Israel?

28So Omri rested with his fathers and was buried in Samaria. Then Ahab his son reigned in his place.

Ahab Reigns in Israel

29In the thirty-eighth year of Asa king of Judah, Ahab the son of Omri became king over Israel; and Ahab the son of Omri reigned over Israel in Samaria twenty-two years. 30Now Ahab the son of Omri did evil in the sight of the LORD, more than all who *were* before him. 31And it came to pass, as though it had been a trivial thing for him to walk in the sins of Jeroboam the son of Nebat, that he took as wife Jezebel the daughter of Ethbaal, king of the Sidonians; and he went and served Baal and worshiped him. 32Then he set up an altar for Baal in the temple of Baal, which he had built in Samaria.

GOD PROVIDES FOR THE PROPHET ELIJAH

READ IT: 1 KINGS 16:29—17:24

GET IT:

The kings in Israel were evil. They forgot about God and worshiped a fake god named Baal. The people followed their leader and worshiped Baal, too. God wasn't going to stand by and watch this happen, so He sent Elijah, a prophet, to tell King Ahab (the most evil king ever) and the people they were wrong. God spoke through Elijah and gave him the power to perform miracles. Elijah did some amazing things. He helped people in a big way and showed them the way to God. But Elijah was an outcast because he was different from the crowd. He had to rely on God to provide him with food and water.

LIVE IT:

Sometimes it's easy to live for God and follow Him. Sometimes it's not. But we live in a country that lets us choose our religion. Even if our nation's leaders have a different religion from ours, we can still worship God. If we can freely live for God, why do you think we sometimes choose not to?

[33]And Ahab made a wooden image.[a] Ahab
did more to provoke the LORD God of Israel
to anger than all the kings of Israel who
were before him. [34]In his days Hiel of Bethel built Jericho. He laid its foundation with
Abiram his firstborn, and with his youngest
son Segub he set up its gates, according to
the word of the LORD, which He had spoken
through Joshua the son of Nun.[a]

Elijah Proclaims a Drought

17 And Elijah the Tishbite, of the inhabitants of Gilead, said to Ahab, *"As*
the LORD God of Israel lives, before whom I
stand, there shall not be dew nor rain these
years, except at my word."

[2]Then the word of the LORD came to him,
saying, [3]"Get away from here and turn eastward, and hide by the Brook Cherith, which
flows into the Jordan. [4]And it will be *that* you
shall drink from the brook, and I have commanded the ravens to feed you there."

[5]So he went and did according to the
word of the LORD, for he went and stayed
by the Brook Cherith, which flows into the
Jordan. [6]The ravens brought him bread and
meat in the morning, and bread and meat in
the evening; and he drank from the brook.
[7]And it happened after a while that the brook
dried up, because there had been no rain in
the land.

Elijah and the Widow

[8]Then the word of the LORD came to him,
saying, [9]"Arise, go to Zarephath, which *belongs* to Sidon, and dwell there. See, I have
commanded a widow there to provide for
you." [10]So he arose and went to Zarephath.
And when he came to the gate of the city,
indeed a widow *was* there gathering sticks.
And he called to her and said, "Please bring
me a little water in a cup, that I may drink."
[11]And as she was going to get *it,* he called to
her and said, "Please bring me a morsel of
bread in your hand."

[12]So she said, "As the LORD your God
lives, I do not have bread, only a handful of
flour in a bin, and a little oil in a jar; and see,
I *am* gathering a couple of sticks that I may
go in and prepare it for myself and my son,
that we may eat it, and die."

[13]And Elijah said to her, "Do not fear;
go *and* do as you have said, but make me a
small cake from it first, and bring *it* to me;
and afterward make *some* for yourself and
your son. [14]For thus says the LORD God of
Israel: 'The bin of flour shall not be used up,
nor shall the jar of oil run dry, until the day
the LORD sends rain on the earth.'"

[15]So she went away and did according to
the word of Elijah; and she and he and her
household ate for *many* days. [16]The bin of

16:33 [a] Hebrew *Asherah,* a Canaanite goddess
16:34 [a] Compare Joshua 6:26

Starring Roles

ELIJAH (pronounced *ih-LIE-jah*) means "The Lord Is My God." God began to send prophets to warn Israel about the suffering that sin brings. Then God called Elijah to announce a drought (pronounced *drowt*) in the land. There would be no rain for a long, long time.

Elijah challenged the prophets of the false god Baal (pronounced *BAYL*) to a contest on Mount Carmel. If Baal could send fire, then he would be their god. But if Elijah's Lord sent fire, then He would be God.

Elijah laughed to see those Baal-worshipers screaming and shouting all day at their god. But Baal couldn't answer them, because he was really nothing at all!

Finally Elijah built a simple altar, offered a sacrifice, and made a short prayer to the Lord. God's fire came from heaven and ate up Elijah's sacrifice, and the rain came at last.

flour was not used up, nor did the jar of oil
run dry, according to the word of the LORD
which He spoke by Elijah.

Elijah Revives the Widow's Son

17Now it happened after these things *that*
the son of the woman who owned the house
became sick. And his sickness was so serious that there was no breath left in him. 18So
she said to Elijah, "What have I to do with
you, O man of God? Have you come to me
to bring my sin to remembrance, and to kill
my son?"
19And he said to her, "Give me your son."
So he took him out of her arms and carried
him to the upper room where he was staying, and laid him on his own bed. 20Then
he cried out to the LORD and said, "O LORD
my God, have You also brought tragedy on
the widow with whom I lodge, by killing
her son?" 21And he stretched himself out on
the child three times, and cried out to the
LORD and said, "O LORD my God, I pray, let
this child's soul come back to him." 22Then
the LORD heard the voice of Elijah; and the
soul of the child came back to him, and he
revived.
23And Elijah took the child and brought
him down from the upper room into the
house, and gave him to his mother. And Elijah said, "See, your son lives!"
24Then the woman said to Elijah, "Now
by this I know that you *are* a man of God,
and that the word of the LORD in your mouth
is the truth."

Elijah's Message to Ahab

18 And it came to pass *after* many days
that the word of the LORD came to
Elijah, in the third year, saying, "Go, present
yourself to Ahab, and I will send rain on the
earth."
2So Elijah went to present himself to
Ahab; and *there was* a severe famine in Samaria. 3And Ahab had called Obadiah, who
was in charge of *his* house. (Now Obadiah
feared the LORD *greatly.* 4For so it was, while
Jezebel massacred the prophets of the LORD,
that Obadiah had taken one hundred prophets and hidden them, fifty to a cave, and had
fed them with bread and water.) 5And Ahab
had said to Obadiah, "Go into the land to all
the springs of water and to all the brooks;
perhaps we may find grass to keep the horses and mules alive, so that we will not have to
kill any livestock." 6So they divided the land
between them to explore it; Ahab went one
way by himself, and Obadiah went another
way by himself.
7Now as Obadiah was on his way, suddenly Elijah met him; and he recognized him,
and fell on his face, and said, "*Is* that you,
my lord Elijah?"
8And he answered him, "*It is* I. Go, tell
your master, 'Elijah *is here.*'"
9So he said, "How have I sinned, that you
are delivering your servant into the hand of
Ahab, to kill me? 10*As* the LORD your God
lives, there is no nation or kingdom where
my master has not sent someone to hunt for
you; and when they said, '*He is* not *here,*' he
took an oath from the kingdom or nation
that they could not find you. 11And now you
say, 'Go, tell your master, "Elijah *is here*"'!
12And it shall come to pass, *as soon as* I am
gone from you, that the Spirit of the LORD
will carry you to a place I do not know; so
when I go and tell Ahab, and he cannot find
you, he will kill me. But I your servant have
feared the LORD from my youth. 13Was it not
reported to my lord what I did when Jezebel
killed the prophets of the LORD, how I hid
one hundred men of the LORD's prophets,
fifty to a cave, and fed them with bread and
water? 14And now you say, 'Go, tell your master, "Elijah *is here.*"' He will kill me!"
15Then Elijah said, "*As* the LORD of hosts
lives, before whom I stand, I will surely present myself to him today."
16So Obadiah went to meet Ahab, and told
him; and Ahab went to meet Elijah.
17Then it happened, when Ahab saw Elijah, that Ahab said to him, "*Is that* you, O
troubler of Israel?"
18And he answered, "I have not troubled
Israel, but you and your father's house *have,*
in that you have forsaken the commandments of the LORD and have followed the
Baals. 19Now therefore, send *and* gather all
Israel to me on Mount Carmel, the four hundred and fifty prophets of Baal, and the four
hundred prophets of Asherah,[a] who eat at
Jezebel's table."

Elijah's Mount Carmel Victory

20So Ahab sent for all the children of Israel, and gathered the prophets together on
Mount Carmel. 21And Elijah came to all the
people, and said, "How long will you falter

18:19 [a] A Canaanite goddess

between two opinions? If the LORD *is* God,
follow Him; but if Baal, follow him." But the
people answered him not a word. 22Then
Elijah said to the people, "I alone am left a
prophet of the LORD; but Baal's prophets *are*
four hundred and fifty men. 23Therefore let
them give us two bulls; and let them choose
one bull for themselves, cut it in pieces, and
lay *it* on the wood, but put no fire *under it;*
and I will prepare the other bull, and lay *it*
on the wood, but put no fire *under it.* 24Then
you call on the name of your gods, and I will
call on the name of the LORD; and the God
who answers by fire, He is God."

So all the people answered and said, "It
is well spoken."

25Now Elijah said to the prophets of Baal,
"Choose one bull for yourselves and prepare
it first, for you *are* many; and call on the
name of your god, but put no fire *under it.*"

26So they took the bull which was given
them, and they prepared *it,* and called on the
name of Baal from morning even till noon,
saying, "O Baal, hear us!" But *there was* no
voice; no one answered. Then they leaped
about the altar which they had made.

27And so it was, at noon, that Elijah
mocked them and said, "Cry aloud, for he *is*
a god; either he is meditating, or he is busy,
or he is on a journey, *or* perhaps he is sleeping and must be awakened." 28So they cried
aloud, and cut themselves, as was their custom, with knives and lances, until the blood
gushed out on them. 29And when midday
was past, they prophesied until the *time* of
the offering of the *evening* sacrifice. But *there*
was no voice; no one answered, no one paid
attention.

30Then Elijah said to all the people,
"Come near to me." So all the people came
near to him. And he repaired the altar of the
LORD *that was* broken down. 31And Elijah
took twelve stones, according to the number
of the tribes of the sons of Jacob, to whom
the word of the LORD had come, saying, "Israel shall be your name."[a] 32Then with the
stones he built an altar in the name of the
LORD; and he made a trench around the altar large enough to hold two seahs of seed.
33And he put the wood in order, cut the bull
in pieces, and laid *it* on the wood, and said,
"Fill four waterpots with water, and pour
it on the burnt sacrifice and on the wood."
34Then he said, "Do *it* a second time," and
they did *it* a second time; and he said, "Do

In Focus

18:19 Baal The chief false god of the Canaanites (pronounced *KAY-nuh-nights*) and Phoenicians (pronounced *fe-NISH-she-uns*). He was a nature god and was worshiped in immoral ceremonies forbidden to Israel.

it a third time," and they did *it* a third time.
35So the water ran all around the altar; and he
also filled the trench with water.

36And it came to pass, at *the time of* the offering of the *evening* sacrifice, that Elijah the
prophet came near and said, "LORD God of
Abraham, Isaac, and Israel, let it be known
this day that You *are* God in Israel and I *am*
Your servant, and *that* I have done all these
things at Your word. 37Hear me, O LORD,
hear me, that this people may know that You
are the LORD God, and *that* You have turned
their hearts back *to You* again."

38Then the fire of the LORD fell and consumed the burnt sacrifice, and the wood and
the stones and the dust, and it licked up the
water that *was* in the trench. 39Now when all
the people saw *it,* they fell on their faces; and
they said, "The LORD, He *is* God! The LORD,
He *is* God!"

40And Elijah said to them, "Seize the
prophets of Baal! Do not let one of them
escape!" So they seized them; and Elijah
brought them down to the Brook Kishon and
executed them there.

The Drought Ends

41Then Elijah said to Ahab, "Go up, eat
and drink; for *there is* the sound of abundance of rain." 42So Ahab went up to eat and
drink. And Elijah went up to the top of Carmel; then he bowed down on the ground,
and put his face between his knees, 43and
said to his servant, "Go up now, look toward
the sea."

So he went up and looked, and said,
"*There is* nothing." And seven times he said,
"Go again."

18:31 [a] Genesis 32:28

44Then it came to pass the seventh *time,*
that he said, "There is a cloud, as small as
a man's hand, rising out of the sea!" So he
said, "Go up, say to Ahab, 'Prepare *your chariot,* and go down before the rain stops you.'"
45Now it happened in the meantime that
the sky became black with clouds and wind,
and there was a heavy rain. So Ahab rode
away and went to Jezreel. 46Then the hand of
the LORD came upon Elijah; and he girded
up his loins and ran ahead of Ahab to the
entrance of Jezreel.

Elijah Escapes from Jezebel

19 And Ahab told Jezebel all that Elijah
had done, also how he had executed all the prophets with the sword. 2Then
Jezebel sent a messenger to Elijah, saying,
"So let the gods do *to me,* and more also, if
I do not make your life as the life of one of
them by tomorrow about this time." 3And
when he saw *that,* he arose and ran for his
life, and went to Beersheba, which *belongs* to
Judah, and left his servant there.
4But he himself went a day's journey
into the wilderness, and came and sat down
under a broom tree. And he prayed that he
might die, and said, "It is enough! Now,
LORD, take my life, for I *am* no better than
my fathers!"
5Then as he lay and slept under a broom
tree, suddenly an angel[a] touched him,

19:5 [a] Or *Angel*

Spotlight

GOD AND ELIJAH WIN THE CONTEST

READ IT: 1 KINGS 18:17–40

GET IT:

Everybody climbed to the top of Mount Carmel for the battle of the gods: the true God versus Baal. The sides were very lopsided. One person, Elijah, was on God's side. A huge crowd of people and 450 supporters of Baal were on Baal's side. Baal was very popular because the people believed that Baal controlled the rain, the harvest, and life in general. But he really was just a statue carved from wood who couldn't talk or even hear (that's because he wasn't a real god!). He was nothing compared to the real God. And that's exactly what Elijah wanted to prove. Only the real God, the Creator of heaven and earth and the ruler of all things, would hear and answer prayer. Elijah knew God would win the contest, but he also wanted the people to believe in God again.

LIVE IT:

Have you watched your parents ever try to light a fire in the rain? Or even tried to get wet wood to burn? You know how impossible it is. But Elijah knew that a ton of water and wet, soggy wood couldn't keep God from making fire. Elijah did everything to create what seemed like an impossible situation, but this wasn't an obstacle for God. Elijah had great faith, and God answered his prayer. What seems impossible for you right now? Ask God to handle it for you. He can handle anything.

and said to him, "Arise *and* eat." 6Then he
looked, and there by his head *was* a cake
baked on coals, and a jar of water. So he ate
and drank, and lay down again. 7And the angel[a] of the LORD came back the second time,
and touched him, and said, "Arise *and* eat,
because the journey *is* too great for you." 8So
he arose, and ate and drank; and he went in
the strength of that food forty days and forty
nights as far as Horeb, the mountain of God.
9And there he went into a cave, and spent
the night in that place; and behold, the word
of the LORD *came* to him, and He said to
him, "What are you doing here, Elijah?"
10So he said, "I have been very zealous for
the LORD God of hosts; for the children of Israel have forsaken Your covenant, torn down
Your altars, and killed Your prophets with
the sword. I alone am left; and they seek to
take my life."

God's Revelation to Elijah

11Then He said, "Go out, and stand on
the mountain before the LORD." And behold,
the LORD passed by, and a great and strong
wind tore into the mountains and broke
the rocks in pieces before the LORD, *but* the
LORD *was* not in the wind; and after the wind
an earthquake, *but* the LORD *was* not in the
earthquake; 12and after the earthquake a fire,
but the LORD *was* not in the fire; and after the
fire a still small voice.
13So it was, when Elijah heard *it,* that he
wrapped his face in his mantle and went out
and stood in the entrance of the cave. Suddenly a voice *came* to him, and said, "What
are you doing here, Elijah?"
14And he said, "I have been very zealous
for the LORD God of hosts; because the children of Israel have forsaken Your covenant,
torn down Your altars, and killed Your prophets with the sword. I alone am left; and they
seek to take my life."
15Then the LORD said to him: "Go, return
on your way to the Wilderness of Damascus; and when you arrive, anoint Hazael *as*
king over Syria. 16Also you shall anoint Jehu
the son of Nimshi *as* king over Israel. And
Elisha the son of Shaphat of Abel Meholah
you shall anoint *as* prophet in your place. 17It
shall be *that* whoever escapes the sword of
Hazael, Jehu will kill; and whoever escapes
the sword of Jehu, Elisha will kill. 18Yet I
have reserved seven thousand in Israel, all
whose knees have not bowed to Baal, and every mouth that has not kissed him."

Elisha Follows Elijah

19So he departed from there, and found
Elisha the son of Shaphat, who *was* plowing
with twelve yoke *of oxen* before him, and he
was with the twelfth. Then Elijah passed by
him and threw his mantle on him. 20And he
left the oxen and ran after Elijah, and said,
"Please let me kiss my father and my mother, and *then* I will follow you."
And he said to him, "Go back again, for
what have I done to you?"
21So *Elisha* turned back from him, and
took a yoke of oxen and slaughtered them
and boiled their flesh, using the oxen's
equipment, and gave it to the people, and

19:7 [a] Or *Angel*

KNOWING AND FINDING GOD

READ IT: 1 KINGS 19:9–18

Elijah had just out-dueled hundreds of the queen's powerful false priests with prayer, a stack of soaking wet wood, and a powerful God who sent fire from heaven. After this victory Elijah might have been looking for God in thunder and lightning and earthquakes and fire. Instead, God showed up in a still, small voice. God does that sometimes, surprising us, not just with His power and majesty, but with His quiet love and patience. Don't miss it.

they ate. Then he arose and followed Elijah,
and became his servant.

Ahab Defeats the Syrians

20 Now Ben-Hadad the king of Syria
gathered all his forces together;
thirty-two kings *were* with him, with horses
and chariots. And he went up and besieged
Samaria, and made war against it. 2 Then he
sent messengers into the city to Ahab king
of Israel, and said to him, "Thus says Ben-
Hadad: 3 'Your silver and your gold *are* mine;
your loveliest wives and children are mine.'"
4 And the king of Israel answered and
said, "My lord, O king, just as you say, I and
all that I have *are* yours."
5 Then the messengers came back and
said, "Thus speaks Ben-Hadad, saying, 'Indeed I have sent to you, saying, "You shall
deliver to me your silver and your gold, your
wives and your children"; 6 but I will send my
servants to you tomorrow about this time,
and they shall search your house and the
houses of your servants. And it shall be, *that*
whatever is pleasant in your eyes, they will
put *it* in their hands and take *it*.'"
7 So the king of Israel called all the elders
of the land, and said, "Notice, please, and see
how this *man* seeks trouble, for he sent to me
for my wives, my children, my silver, and my
gold; and I did not deny him."
8 And all the elders and all the people said
to him, "Do not listen or consent."
9 Therefore he said to the messengers of
Ben-Hadad, "Tell my lord the king, 'All that
you sent for to your servant the first time I
will do, but this thing I cannot do.'"
And the messengers departed and
brought back word to him.
10 Then Ben-Hadad sent to him and said,
"The gods do so to me, and more also, if
enough dust is left of Samaria for a handful
for each of the people who follow me."
11 So the king of Israel answered and said,
"Tell *him*, 'Let not the one who puts on *his
armor* boast like the one who takes *it off*.'"
12 And it happened when *Ben-Hadad*
heard this message, as he and the kings *were*
drinking at the command post, that he said
to his servants, "Get ready." And they got
ready to attack the city.
13 Suddenly a prophet approached Ahab
king of Israel, saying, "Thus says the LORD:
'Have you seen all this great multitude? Behold, I will deliver it into your hand today,
and you shall know that I *am* the LORD.'"
14 So Ahab said, "By whom?"
And he said, "Thus says the LORD: 'By
the young leaders of the provinces.'"
Then he said, "Who will set the battle in
order?"
And he answered, "You."
15 Then he mustered the young leaders of
the provinces, and there were two hundred
and thirty-two; and after them he mustered
all the people, all the children of Israel—
seven thousand.
16 So they went out at noon. Meanwhile
Ben-Hadad and the thirty-two kings helping him were getting drunk at the command
post. 17 The young leaders of the provinces
went out first. And Ben-Hadad sent out *a
patrol*, and they told him, saying, "Men are
coming out of Samaria!" 18 So he said, "If they
have come out for peace, take them alive;
and if they have come out for war, take them
alive."
19 Then these young leaders of the provinces went out of the city with the army
which followed them. 20 And each one killed
his man; so the Syrians fled, and Israel pursued them; and Ben-Hadad the king of Syria
escaped on a horse with the cavalry. 21 Then
the king of Israel went out and attacked the
horses and chariots, and killed the Syrians
with a great slaughter.
22 And the prophet came to the king of Israel and said to him, "Go, strengthen yourself; take note, and see what you should do,
for in the spring of the year the king of Syria
will come up against you."

The Syrians Again Defeated

23 Then the servants of the king of Syria
said to him, "Their gods *are* gods of the hills.
Therefore they were stronger than we; but
if we fight against them in the plain, surely
we will be stronger than they. 24 So do this
thing: Dismiss the kings, each from his position, and put captains in their places; 25 and
you shall muster an army like the army that
you have lost, horse for horse and chariot for
chariot. Then we will fight against them in
the plain; surely we will be stronger than
they."
And he listened to their voice and did so.
26 So it was, in the spring of the year, that
Ben-Hadad mustered the Syrians and went
up to Aphek to fight against Israel. 27 And the
children of Israel were mustered and given
provisions, and they went against them.
Now the children of Israel encamped before

them like two little flocks of goats, while the
Syrians filled the countryside.

28 Then a man of God came and spoke
to the king of Israel, and said, "Thus says
the LORD: 'Because the Syrians have said,
"The LORD *is* God of the hills, but He *is* not
God of the valleys," therefore I will deliver
all this great multitude into your hand, and
you shall know that I *am* the LORD.'" 29 And
they encamped opposite each other for seven
days. So it was that on the seventh day the
battle was joined; and the children of Israel
killed one hundred thousand foot soldiers
of the Syrians in one day. 30 But the rest fled
to Aphek, into the city; then a wall fell on
twenty-seven thousand of the men *who were*
left.

And Ben-Hadad fled and went into the
city, into an inner chamber.

Ahab's Treaty with Ben-Hadad

31 Then his servants said to him, "Look
now, we have heard that the kings of the
house of Israel *are* merciful kings. Please,
let us put sackcloth around our waists and
ropes around our heads, and go out to the
king of Israel; perhaps he will spare your
life." 32 So they wore sackcloth around their
waists and *put* ropes around their heads, and
came to the king of Israel and said, "Your
servant Ben-Hadad says, 'Please let me live.'"

And he said, "*Is* he still alive? He *is* my
brother."

33 Now the men were watching closely to
see whether *any sign of mercy would come*
from him; and they quickly grasped *at this*
word and said, "Your brother Ben-Hadad."

So he said, "Go, bring him." Then Ben-
Hadad came out to him; and he had him
come up into the chariot.

34 So *Ben-Hadad* said to him, "The cities
which my father took from your father I will
restore; and you may set up marketplaces for
yourself in Damascus, as my father did in
Samaria."

Then *Ahab said,* "I will send you away
with this treaty." So he made a treaty with
him and sent him away.

Ahab Condemned

35 Now a certain man of the sons of the
prophets said to his neighbor by the word of
the LORD, "Strike me, please." And the man
refused to strike him. 36 Then he said to him,
"Because you have not obeyed the voice of
the LORD, surely, as soon as you depart from
me, a lion shall kill you." And as soon as he
left him, a lion found him and killed him.

37 And he found another man, and said,
"Strike me, please." So the man struck him,
inflicting a wound. 38 Then the prophet departed and waited for the king by the road,
and disguised himself with a bandage over
his eyes. 39 Now as the king passed by, he
cried out to the king and said, "Your servant
went out into the midst of the battle; and
there, a man came over and brought a man
to me, and said, 'Guard this man; if by any
means he is missing, your life shall be for
his life, or else you shall pay a talent of silver.' 40 While your servant was busy here and
there, he was gone."

Then the king of Israel said to him, "So
shall your judgment *be;* you yourself have
decided *it.*"

41 And he hastened to take the bandage
away from his eyes; and the king of Israel
recognized him as one of the prophets.
42 Then he said to him, "Thus says the LORD:
'Because you have let slip out of *your* hand a
man whom I appointed to utter destruction,
therefore your life shall go for his life, and
your people for his people.'"

43 So the king of Israel went to his house
sullen and displeased, and came to Samaria.

Naboth Is Murdered for His Vineyard

21 And it came to pass after these
things *that* Naboth the Jezreelite
had a vineyard which *was* in Jezreel, next
to the palace of Ahab king of Samaria. 2 So
Ahab spoke to Naboth, saying, "Give me
your vineyard, that I may have it for a veg-
etable garden, because it *is* near, next to my
house; and for it I will give you a vineyard
better than it. *Or,* if it seems good to you, I
will give you its worth in money."

3 But Naboth said to Ahab, "The LORD forbid that I should give the inheritance of my
fathers to you!"

4 So Ahab went into his house sullen
and displeased because of the word which
Naboth the Jezreelite had spoken to him; for
he had said, "I will not give you the inheritance of my fathers." And he lay down on his
bed, and turned away his face, and would eat
no food. 5 But Jezebel his wife came to him,
and said to him, "Why is your spirit so sullen
that you eat no food?"

6 He said to her, "Because I spoke to
Naboth the Jezreelite, and said to him, 'Give
me your vineyard for money; or else, if it

pleases you, I will give you *another* vineyard for it.' And he answered, 'I will not give you my vineyard.'"

7Then Jezebel his wife said to him, "You now exercise authority over Israel! Arise, eat food, and let your heart be cheerful; I will give you the vineyard of Naboth the Jezreelite."

8And she wrote letters in Ahab's name, sealed *them* with his seal, and sent the letters to the elders and the nobles who *were*
dwelling in the city with Naboth. 9She wrote
in the letters, saying,

> Proclaim a fast, and seat Naboth with
> high honor among the people; 10and seat
> two men, scoundrels, before him to bear witness against him, saying, "You have blasphemed God and the king." *Then* take him out, and stone him, that he may die.

11So the men of his city, the elders and

GREED
I WANT MORE!

READ IT: 1 KINGS 21:1–29

GET IT:

Ahab wanted something that wasn't his, and he didn't care what it cost to get it. He wanted a vineyard so much that he stopped eating and moped around in the dumps. His wife responded to his pouting by coming up with a plan. The evil plan was to have the innocent owner of the vineyard blamed for a crime he didn't commit and have him stoned to death.

But God knew what was going on in the hearts of Ahab and Jezebel so He spoke to the prophet Elijah. He gave Elijah a message for the wicked pair. The message wasn't pretty. It spoke of a gruesome death for both of them as punishment for their selfishness.

When Ahab heard the news of what would happen to him and his wife, he tore his clothes and fasted, this time for good reason. He mourned the loss of goodness in his life, and he mourned for those he had hurt and stolen from.

God saw his heart and spared him from the consequences of his choices, but his descendants would pay the price for his behavior.

LIVE IT:

Even when we correct our wrongs, there can still be fallout for days, *months, years,* and generations. Our choices don't just hurt us; they can hurt other people in our lives. Ahab let his jealous heart take the lead in his life. Instead of letting the Lord lead him, he allowed greed to rule. It led to wickedness, pain, and sorrow.

Most people find themselves wanting things they don't have, but not everyone responds like Ahab. It's possible to choose good ways over wicked ways. That means relying on God, not on ourselves. It means believing that God will give us what is best for us. God always knows best!

nobles who were inhabitants of his city, did
as Jezebel had sent to them, as it *was* written
in the letters which she had sent to them.
12They proclaimed a fast, and seated Naboth
with high honor among the people. 13And
two men, scoundrels, came in and sat before
him; and the scoundrels witnessed against
him, against Naboth, in the presence of the
people, saying, "Naboth has blasphemed
God and the king!" Then they took him outside the city and stoned him with stones, so
that he died. 14Then they sent to Jezebel, saying, "Naboth has been stoned and is dead."

15And it came to pass, when Jezebel
heard that Naboth had been stoned and was
dead, that Jezebel said to Ahab, "Arise, take
possession of the vineyard of Naboth the
Jezreelite, which he refused to give you for
money; for Naboth is not alive, but dead."
16So it was, when Ahab heard that Naboth
was dead, that Ahab got up and went down
to take possession of the vineyard of Naboth
the Jezreelite.

The LORD Condemns Ahab

17Then the word of the LORD came to Elijah the Tishbite, saying, 18"Arise, go down
to meet Ahab king of Israel, who *lives* in Samaria. There *he is,* in the vineyard of Naboth,
where he has gone down to take possession
of it. 19You shall speak to him, saying, 'Thus
says the LORD: "Have you murdered and also
taken possession?"' And you shall speak to
him, saying, 'Thus says the LORD: "In the
place where dogs licked the blood of Naboth,
dogs shall lick your blood, even yours."'"

20So Ahab said to Elijah, "Have you found
me, O my enemy?"

And he answered, "I have found *you,*
because you have sold yourself to do evil in
the sight of the LORD: 21'Behold, I will bring
calamity on you. I will take away your posterity, and will cut off from Ahab every male in
Israel, both bond and free. 22I will make your
house like the house of Jeroboam the son of
Nebat, and like the house of Baasha the son
of Ahijah, because of the provocation with
which you have provoked *Me* to anger, and
made Israel sin.' 23And concerning Jezebel
the LORD also spoke, saying, 'The dogs shall
eat Jezebel by the wall[a] of Jezreel.' 24The dogs
shall eat whoever belongs to Ahab and dies
in the city, and the birds of the air shall eat
whoever dies in the field."

25But there was no one like Ahab who
sold himself to do wickedness in the sight
of the LORD, because Jezebel his wife stirred
him up. 26And he behaved very abominably
in following idols, according to all *that* the
Amorites had done, whom the LORD had cast
out before the children of Israel.

27So it was, when Ahab heard those
words, that he tore his clothes and put sackcloth on his body, and fasted and lay in sackcloth, and went about mourning.

28And the word of the LORD came to Elijah the Tishbite, saying, 29"See how Ahab has
humbled himself before Me? Because he has
humbled himself before Me, I will not bring
the calamity in his days. In the days of his
son I will bring the calamity on his house."

Micaiah Warns Ahab

22 Now three years passed without
war between Syria and Israel.
2Then it came to pass, in the third year, that
Jehoshaphat the king of Judah went down to
visit the king of Israel.

3And the king of Israel said to his servants, "Do you know that Ramoth in Gilead
is ours, but we hesitate to take it out of the
hand of the king of Syria?" 4So he said to Jehoshaphat, "Will you go with me to fight at
Ramoth Gilead?"

Jehoshaphat said to the king of Israel, "I
am as you *are,* my people as your people, my
horses as your horses." 5Also Jehoshaphat
said to the king of Israel, "Please inquire for
the word of the LORD today."

6Then the king of Israel gathered the
prophets together, about four hundred men,
and said to them, "Shall I go against Ramoth
Gilead to fight, or shall I refrain?"

So they said, "Go up, for the Lord will deliver *it* into the hand of the king."

7And Jehoshaphat said, "*Is there* not still
a prophet of the LORD here, that we may inquire of Him?"[a]

8So the king of Israel said to Jehoshaphat,
"*There is* still one man, Micaiah the son of
Imlah, by whom we may inquire of the
LORD; but I hate him, because he does not
prophesy good concerning me, but evil."

And Jehoshaphat said, "Let not the king
say such things!"

9Then the king of Israel called an officer

21:23 [a] Following Masoretic Text and Septuagint; some Hebrew manuscripts, Syriac, Targum, and Vulgate read *plot of ground* (compare 2 Kings 9:36). **22:7** [a] Or *him*

and said, "Bring Micaiah the son of Imlah
quickly!"
10 The king of Israel and Jehoshaphat the
king of Judah, having put on *their* robes, sat
each on his throne, at a threshing floor at
the entrance of the gate of Samaria; and all
the prophets prophesied before them. 11 Now
Zedekiah the son of Chenaanah had made
horns of iron for himself; and he said, "Thus
says the LORD: 'With these you shall gore the
Syrians until they are destroyed.'" 12 And all
the prophets prophesied so, saying, "Go up
to Ramoth Gilead and prosper, for the LORD
will deliver *it* into the king's hand."
13 Then the messenger who had gone to
call Micaiah spoke to him, saying, "Now
listen, the words of the prophets with one
accord encourage the king. Please, let your
word be like the word of one of them, and
speak encouragement."
14 And Micaiah said, "*As* the LORD lives,
whatever the LORD says to me, that I will
speak."
15 Then he came to the king; and the king
said to him, "Micaiah, shall we go to war
against Ramoth Gilead, or shall we refrain?"
And he answered him, "Go and prosper,
for the LORD will deliver *it* into the hand of
the king!"
16 So the king said to him, "How many
times shall I make you swear that you tell
me nothing but the truth in the name of the
LORD?"
17 Then he said, "I saw all Israel scattered
on the mountains, as sheep that have no
shepherd. And the LORD said, 'These have
no master. Let each return to his house in
peace.'"
18 And the king of Israel said to Jehoshaphat, "Did I not tell you he would not
prophesy good concerning me, but evil?"
19 Then *Micaiah* said, "Therefore hear the
word of the LORD: I saw the LORD sitting on
His throne, and all the host of heaven standing by, on His right hand and on His left.
20 And the LORD said, 'Who will persuade
Ahab to go up, that he may fall at Ramoth
Gilead?' So one spoke in this manner, and
another spoke in that manner. 21 Then a spirit came forward and stood before the LORD,
and said, 'I will persuade him.' 22 The LORD
said to him, 'In what way?' So he said, 'I will
go out and be a lying spirit in the mouth of
all his prophets.' And the LORD said, 'You
shall persuade *him*, and also prevail. Go out
and do so.' 23 Therefore look! The LORD has
put a lying spirit in the mouth of all these
prophets of yours, and the LORD has declared disaster against you."
24 Now Zedekiah the son of Chenaanah
went near and struck Micaiah on the cheek,
and said, "Which way did the spirit from the
LORD go from me to speak to you?"
25 And Micaiah said, "Indeed, you shall
see on that day when you go into an inner
chamber to hide!"
26 So the king of Israel said, "Take Micaiah, and return him to Amon the governor of
the city and to Joash the king's son; 27 and say,
'Thus says the king: "Put this *fellow* in prison, and feed him with bread of affliction and
water of affliction, until I come in peace."'"
28 But Micaiah said, "If you ever return in
peace, the LORD has not spoken by me." And
he said, "Take heed, all you people!"

Ahab Dies in Battle

29 So the king of Israel and Jehoshaphat
the king of Judah went up to Ramoth Gilead.
30 And the king of Israel said to Jehoshaphat,
"I will disguise myself and go into battle; but
you put on your robes." So the king of Israel
disguised himself and went into battle.
31 Now the king of Syria had commanded the thirty-two captains of his chariots,
saying, "Fight with no one small or great,
but only with the king of Israel." 32 So it was,
when the captains of the chariots saw Jehoshaphat, that they said, "Surely it *is* the
king of Israel!" Therefore they turned aside
to fight against him, and Jehoshaphat cried
out. 33 And it happened, when the captains of
the chariots saw that it *was* not the king of
Israel, that they turned back from pursuing
him. 34 Now a *certain* man drew a bow at random, and struck the king of Israel between
the joints of his armor. So he said to the driver of his chariot, "Turn around and take me
out of the battle, for I am wounded."
35 The battle increased that day; and the
king was propped up in his chariot, facing
the Syrians, and died at evening. The blood
ran out from the wound onto the floor of the
chariot. 36 Then, as the sun was going down,
a shout went throughout the army, saying,
"Every man to his city, and every man to his
own country!"
37 So the king died, and was brought to Samaria. And they buried the king in Samaria.

38 Then *someone* washed the chariot at a pool
in Samaria, and the dogs licked up his blood
while the harlots bathed,[a] according to the
word of the LORD which He had spoken.

39 Now the rest of the acts of Ahab, and all
that he did, the ivory house which he built and
all the cities that he built, *are* they not written
in the book of the chronicles of the kings of
Israel? 40 So Ahab rested with his fathers. Then
Ahaziah his son reigned in his place.

Jehoshaphat Reigns in Judah

41 Jehoshaphat the son of Asa had become
king over Judah in the fourth year of Ahab
king of Israel. 42 Jehoshaphat *was* thirty-five
years old when he became king, and he
reigned twenty-five years in Jerusalem. His
mother's name *was* Azubah the daughter of
Shilhi. 43 And he walked in all the ways of his
father Asa. He did not turn aside from them,
doing *what was* right in the eyes of the LORD.
Nevertheless the high places were not taken
away, *for* the people offered sacrifices and
burned incense on the high places. 44 Also Jehoshaphat made peace with the king of Israel.

45 Now the rest of the acts of Jehoshaphat,
the might that he showed, and how he made
war, *are* they not written in the book of the
chronicles of the kings of Judah? 46 And the
rest of the perverted persons,[a] who remained
in the days of his father Asa, he banished
from the land. 47 *There was* then no king in
Edom, only a deputy of the king.

48 Jehoshaphat made merchant ships[a] to
go to Ophir for gold; but they never sailed,
for the ships were wrecked at Ezion Geber.
49 Then Ahaziah the son of Ahab said to Jehoshaphat, "Let my servants go with your
servants in the ships." But Jehoshaphat
would not.

50 And Jehoshaphat rested with his fathers, and was buried with his fathers in the
City of David his father. Then Jehoram his
son reigned in his place.

Ahaziah Reigns in Israel

51 Ahaziah the son of Ahab became king
over Israel in Samaria in the seventeenth
year of Jehoshaphat king of Judah, and
reigned two years over Israel. 52 He did evil in
the sight of the LORD, and walked in the way
of his father and in the way of his mother
and in the way of Jeroboam the son of Nebat,
who had made Israel sin; 53 for he served Baal
and worshiped him, and provoked the LORD
God of Israel to anger, according to all that
his father had done.

22:38 [a] Syriac and Targum read *they washed his armor.*
22:46 [a] Hebrew *qadesh,* that is, one practicing sodomy and prostitution in religious rituals 22:48 [a] Or *ships of Tarshish*

22:53 THE KINGS OF THE NORTH AND SOUTH

All twenty of northern Israel's kings were wicked, and most of Judah's twenty kings were also wicked. Only a few, like Asa, Hezekiah, and Josiah, were good kings.

About two hundred years after Israel split into two kingdoms, the northern kingdom was destroyed by the nation of Assyria (pronounced *ah-SEER-ih-uh*). The southern kingdom of Judah was conquered by the army of Babylon (pronounced *BAB-ih-lun*) about two hundred years after that. The destruction of Israel and Judah was the result of the people disobeying God's laws.

Keep in mind that the gradual fall of Israel began with David. God told him that, because of his sins, "the sword shall never depart from your house" (2 Samuel 12:10).

The BOOK of

2 KINGS

590 B.C.–550 B.C.

Behind the Scenes

READ IT:

Second Kings contains the stories of the kings of Israel and Judah, and the great prophets Elijah and Elisha. It tells the history of the northern kingdom of Israel and the southern kingdom of Judah until they were conquered by two different empires. God's prophets warned the people that God would punish them if they didn't repent from their sins. God sent many prophets, but the people continued to sin, so He used other nations to punish His people.

GET IT:

Who wrote it: Possibly the prophet Jeremiah, but nobody knows for sure.

When it was written: 590 B.C.–550 B.C.

Why it was written: to remind the people what happens when they do not obey God, do not listen to the prophets, and do not follow God's rules.

LIVE IT:

We must stay faithful to God even if everybody else is doing something wrong.

God is the true God. He is the Creator and controller of everything.

FIND IT:

Elijah Ascends to Heaven	*2 Kings 2*
Elisha's Miracles	*2 Kings 4–5*
Jehu Anointed King of Israel	*2 Kings 9–10*
Jehoash Repairs the Temple	*2 Kings 12*
Israel Carried Captive to Assyria	*2 Kings 17*
Hezekiah Reigns in Judah	*2 Kings 18–20*
Josiah Reigns in Judah	*2 Kings 22*
The Fall and Captivity of Judah	*2 Kings 25*

God Judges Ahaziah

1 Moab rebelled against Israel after the
death of Ahab.
2 Now Ahaziah fell through the lattice
of his upper room in Samaria, and was injured; so he sent messengers and said to
them, "Go, inquire of Baal-Zebub, the god
of Ekron, whether I shall recover from this
injury." 3 But the angel[a] of the LORD said to
Elijah the Tishbite, "Arise, go up to meet the
messengers of the king of Samaria, and say
to them, '*Is it* because *there is* no God in Israel
that you are going to inquire of Baal-Zebub,
the god of Ekron?' 4 Now therefore, thus says
the LORD: 'You shall not come down from
the bed to which you have gone up, but you
shall surely die.'" So Elijah departed.
5 And when the messengers returned to
him, he said to them, "Why have you come
back?"
6 So they said to him, "A man came up to
meet us, and said to us, 'Go, return to the
king who sent you, and say to him, "Thus
says the LORD: '*Is it* because *there is* no God
in Israel *that* you are sending to inquire of
Baal-Zebub, the god of Ekron? Therefore
you shall not come down from the bed to
which you have gone up, but you shall surely
die.'"'"
7 Then he said to them, "What kind of
man *was it* who came up to meet you and
told you these words?"
8 So they answered him, "A hairy man
wearing a leather belt around his waist."
And he said, "It *is* Elijah the Tishbite."
9 Then the king sent to him a captain of
fifty with his fifty men. So he went up to
him; and there he was, sitting on the top of a
hill. And he spoke to him: "Man of God, the
king has said, 'Come down!'"
10 So Elijah answered and said to the captain of fifty, "If I *am* a man of God, then let
fire come down from heaven and consume
you and your fifty men." And fire came
down from heaven and consumed him and
his fifty. 11 Then he sent to him another captain of fifty with his fifty men.
And he answered and said to him: "Man
of God, thus has the king said, 'Come down
quickly!'"
12 So Elijah answered and said to them,
"If I *am* a man of God, let fire come down
from heaven and consume you and your fifty
men." And the fire of God came down from
heaven and consumed him and his fifty.
13 Again, he sent a third captain of fifty
with his fifty men. And the third captain of
fifty went up, and came and fell on his knees
before Elijah, and pleaded with him, and
said to him: "Man of God, please let my life
and the life of these fifty servants of yours be
precious in your sight. 14 Look, fire has come
down from heaven and burned up the first
two captains of fifties with their fifties. But
let my life now be precious in your sight."
15 And the angel[a] of the LORD said to Elijah, "Go down with him; do not be afraid of
him." So he arose and went down with him
to the king. 16 Then he said to him, "Thus
says the LORD: 'Because you have sent messengers to inquire of Baal-Zebub, the god of
Ekron, *is it* because *there is* no God in Israel
to inquire of His word? Therefore you shall
not come down from the bed to which you
have gone up, but you shall surely die.'"
17 So *Ahaziah* died according to the
word of the LORD which Elijah had spoken.

1:3 [a] Or *Angel* 1:15 [a] Or *Angel*

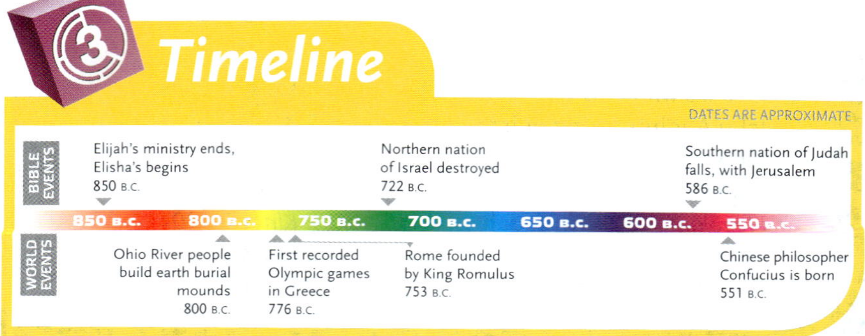

Because he had no son, Jehoram[a] became king in his place, in the second year of Jehoram the son of Jehoshaphat, king of Judah.
18 Now the rest of the acts of Ahaziah which he did, *are* they not written in the book of the chronicles of the kings of Israel?

Elijah Ascends to Heaven

2 And it came to pass, when the LORD was about to take up Elijah into heaven by a whirlwind, that Elijah went with Elisha from Gilgal.
2 Then Elijah said to Elisha, "Stay here, please, for the LORD has sent me on to Bethel."

But Elisha said, "*As* the LORD lives, and *as* your soul lives, I will not leave you!" So they went down to Bethel.

3 Now the sons of the prophets who *were* at Bethel came out to Elisha, and said to him, "Do you know that the LORD will take away your master from over you today?"

And he said, "Yes, I know; keep silent!"

4 Then Elijah said to him, "Elisha, stay here, please, for the LORD has sent me on to Jericho."

But he said, "*As* the LORD lives, and *as* your soul lives, I will not leave you!" So they came to Jericho.

5 Now the sons of the prophets who *were* at Jericho came to Elisha and said to him, "Do you know that the LORD will take away your master from over you today?"

So he answered, "Yes, I know; keep silent!"

6 Then Elijah said to him, "Stay here, please, for the LORD has sent me on to the Jordan."

But he said, "*As* the LORD lives, and *as* your soul lives, I will not leave you!" So the
two of them went on.
7 And fifty men of the sons of the prophets went and stood facing *them* at a distance, while the two of them
stood by the Jordan.
8 Now Elijah took his mantle, rolled *it* up, and struck the water; and it was divided this way and that, so that the two of them crossed over on dry ground.

9 And so it was, when they had crossed over, that Elijah said to Elisha, "Ask! What may I do for you, before I am taken away from you?"

Elisha said, "Please let a double portion of your spirit be upon me."

10 So he said, "You have asked a hard thing. *Nevertheless,* if you see me *when I am* taken from you, it shall be so for you; but if
not, it shall not be *so.*"
11 Then it happened, as they continued on and talked, that suddenly a chariot of fire *appeared* with horses of fire, and separated the two of them; and Elijah went up by a whirlwind into heaven.

12 And Elisha saw *it,* and he cried out, "My father, my father, the chariot of Israel and its horsemen!" So he saw him no more. And he took hold of his own clothes and tore them

1:17 [a] The son of Ahab king of Israel (compare 3:1)

Starring Roles

ELISHA (pronounced *ih-LIE-shuh*) means "His God Is the Lord."

You should have been there! Horses and chariots of fire roared down from the skies, and Elisha saw the prophet Elijah go up to heaven in a whirlwind!

But Elijah's outer covering, called a mantle, fell on Elisha. This was a sign that he would follow Elijah in his work as a prophet. Elisha also had twice as much power as Elijah did to perform miracles.

Elisha's best miracle was probably at the town of Shunem, where he told a childless couple that they would have a baby boy.

When their little son became sick and died, the mother was sorry that she had ever had a child. But God restored the boy's life, and the family was reunited and happy again, thankful to God for His gift.

into two pieces. 13He also took up the mantle
of Elijah that had fallen from him, and went
back and stood by the bank of the Jordan.
14Then he took the mantle of Elijah that had
fallen from him, and struck the water, and
said, "Where *is* the LORD God of Elijah?"
And when he also had struck the water, it
was divided this way and that; and Elisha
crossed over.

15Now when the sons of the prophets
who *were* from Jericho saw him, they said,
"The spirit of Elijah rests on Elisha." And
they came to meet him, and bowed to the
ground before him. 16Then they said to him,
"Look now, there are fifty strong men with
your servants. Please let them go and search
for your master, lest perhaps the Spirit of the
LORD has taken him up and cast him upon
some mountain or into some valley."

And he said, "You shall not send anyone."

17But when they urged him till he was
ashamed, he said, "Send *them!*" Therefore
they sent fifty men, and they searched for
three days but did not find him. 18And when
they came back to him, for he had stayed in
Jericho, he said to them, "Did I not say to
you, 'Do not go'?"

Elisha Performs Miracles

19Then the men of the city said to Elisha, "Please notice, the situation of this city
is pleasant, as my lord sees; but the water *is*
bad, and the ground barren."

20And he said, "Bring me a new bowl,
and put salt in it." So they brought *it* to him.
21Then he went out to the source of the water,
and cast in the salt there, and said, "Thus
says the LORD: 'I have healed this water;
from it there shall be no more death or barrenness.'" 22So the water remains healed
to this day, according to the word of Elisha
which he spoke.

23Then he went up from there to Bethel; and as he was going up the road, some
youths came from the city and mocked him,
and said to him, "Go up, you baldhead! Go
up, you baldhead!"

24So he turned around and looked at
them, and pronounced a curse on them in
the name of the LORD. And two female bears
came out of the woods and mauled forty-two
of the youths.

25Then he went from there to Mount Carmel, and from there he returned to Samaria.

Moab Rebels Against Israel

3 Now Jehoram the son of Ahab became
king over Israel at Samaria in the eighteenth year of Jehoshaphat king of Judah,
and reigned twelve years. 2And he did evil in
the sight of the LORD, but not like his father
and mother; for he put away the *sacred* pillar
of Baal that his father had made. 3Nevertheless he persisted in the sins of Jeroboam the
son of Nebat, who had made Israel sin; he
did not depart from them.

4Now Mesha king of Moab was a sheepbreeder, and he regularly paid the king of
Israel one hundred thousand lambs and the
wool of one hundred thousand rams. 5But it
happened, when Ahab died, that the king of
Moab rebelled against the king of Israel.

6So King Jehoram went out of Samaria
at that time and mustered all Israel. 7Then
he went and sent to Jehoshaphat king of Judah, saying, "The king of Moab has rebelled

BULLYING

READ IT: 2 KINGS 2:23–25

People often bully, or get bullied, simply because of differences in outer appearance—height, weight, complexion, skin color, you name it. But none of these things matter. None of these things make a person who he or she really is. To judge someone—and then bully him or her—based on outer appearance is hurtful, spiteful, and wrong. Don't do it. Ever.

against me. Will you go with me to fight
against Moab?"

And he said, "I will go up; I *am* as you *are,*
my people as your people, my horses as your
horses." 8 Then he said, "Which way shall we
go up?"

And he answered, "By way of the Wilderness of Edom."

9 So the king of Israel went with the king
of Judah and the king of Edom, and they
marched on that roundabout route seven
days; and there was no water for the army,
nor for the animals that followed them.
10 And the king of Israel said, "Alas! For the
LORD has called these three kings together
to deliver them into the hand of Moab."

11 But Jehoshaphat said, "*Is there* no prophet of the LORD here, that we may inquire of
the LORD by him?"

So one of the servants of the king of Israel answered and said, "Elisha the son of
Shaphat *is* here, who poured water on the
hands of Elijah."

12 And Jehoshaphat said, "The word of
the LORD is with him." So the king of Israel
and Jehoshaphat and the king of Edom went
down to him.

13 Then Elisha said to the king of Israel,
"What have I to do with you? Go to the
prophets of your father and the prophets of
your mother."

But the king of Israel said to him, "No,
for the LORD has called these three kings
together to deliver them into the hand of
Moab."

14 And Elisha said, "*As* the LORD of hosts
lives, before whom I stand, surely were it not
that I regard the presence of Jehoshaphat
king of Judah, I would not look at you, nor
see you. 15 But now bring me a musician."

Then it happened, when the musician
played, that the hand of the LORD came upon
him. 16 And he said, "Thus says the LORD:
'Make this valley full of ditches.' 17 For thus
says the LORD: 'You shall not see wind, nor
shall you see rain; yet that valley shall be filled
with water, so that you, your cattle, and your
animals may drink.' 18 And this is a simple
matter in the sight of the LORD; He will also
deliver the Moabites into your hand. 19 Also
you shall attack every fortified city and every
choice city, and shall cut down every good
tree, and stop up every spring of water, and
ruin every good piece of land with stones."

20 Now it happened in the morning, when
the grain offering was offered, that suddenly
water came by way of Edom, and the land
was filled with water.

21 And when all the Moabites heard that
the kings had come up to fight against them,
all who were able to bear arms and older
were gathered; and they stood at the border.
22 Then they rose up early in the morning,
and the sun was shining on the water; and
the Moabites saw the water on the other side
as red as blood. 23 And they said, "This is
blood; the kings have surely struck swords
and have killed one another; now therefore,
Moab, to the spoil!"

24 So when they came to the camp of
Israel, Israel rose up and attacked the
Moabites, so that they fled before them; and
they entered *their* land, killing the Moabites.
25 Then they destroyed the cities, and each
man threw a stone on every good piece of
land and filled it; and they stopped up all the
springs of water and cut down all the good
trees. But they left the stones of Kir Haraseth
intact. However the slingers surrounded and
attacked it.

26 And when the king of Moab saw that
the battle was too fierce for him, he took
with him seven hundred men who drew
swords, to break through to the king of
Edom, but they could not. 27 Then he took his
eldest son who would have reigned in his
place, and offered him *as* a burnt offering
upon the wall; and there was great indignation against Israel. So they departed from
him and returned to *their own* land.

Elisha and the Widow's Oil

4 A certain woman of the wives of the
sons of the prophets cried out to Elisha, saying, "Your servant my husband is
dead, and you know that your servant feared
the LORD. And the creditor is coming to take
my two sons to be his slaves."

2 So Elisha said to her, "What shall I do
for you? Tell me, what do you have in the
house?" And she said, "Your maidservant
has nothing in the house but a jar of oil."

3 Then he said, "Go, borrow vessels from
everywhere, from all your neighbors—empty
vessels; do not gather just a few. 4 And when
you have come in, you shall shut the door behind you and your sons; then pour it into all
those vessels, and set aside the full ones."

5 So she went from him and shut the door
behind her and her sons, who brought *the*

vessels to her; and she poured *it* out. [6]Now it came to pass, when the vessels were full, that she said to her son, "Bring me another vessel."

And he said to her, "*There is* not another vessel." So the oil ceased. [7]Then she came and told the man of God. And he said, "Go, sell the oil and pay your debt; and you *and* your sons live on the rest."

Elisha Raises the Shunammite's Son

[8]Now it happened one day that Elisha went to Shunem, where there *was* a notable woman, and she persuaded him to eat some food. So it was, as often as he passed by, he would turn in there to eat some food. [9]And she said to her husband, "Look now, I know that this *is* a holy man of God, who passes by us regularly. [10]Please, let us make a small upper room on the wall; and let us put a bed for him there, and a table and a chair and a lampstand; so it will be, whenever he comes to us, he can turn in there."

[11]And it happened one day that he came there, and he turned in to the upper room and lay down there. [12]Then he said to Gehazi his servant, "Call this Shunammite woman." When he had called her, she stood before him. [13]And he said to him, "Say now to her, 'Look, you have been concerned for us with all this care. What *can I* do for you? Do you want me to speak on your behalf to the king or to the commander of the army?'"

She answered, "I dwell among my own people."

[14]So he said, "What then *is* to be done for her?"

And Gehazi answered, "Actually, she has no son, and her husband is old."

[15]So he said, "Call her." When he had called her, she stood in the doorway. [16]Then he said, "About this time next year you shall embrace a son."

And she said, "No, my lord. Man of God, do not lie to your maidservant!"

[17]But the woman conceived, and bore a son when the appointed time had come, of which Elisha had told her.

[18]And the child grew. Now it happened one day that he went out to his father, to the reapers. [19]And he said to his father, "My head, my head!"

So he said to a servant, "Carry him to his mother." [20]When he had taken him and brought him to his mother, he sat on her knees till noon, and *then* died. [21]And she went up and laid him on the bed of the man of God, shut *the door* upon him, and went out. [22]Then she called to her husband, and said, "Please send me one of the young men and one of the donkeys, that I may run to the man of God and come back."

[23]So he said, "Why are you going to him today? *It is* neither the New Moon nor the Sabbath."

And she said, "*It is* well." [24]Then she saddled a donkey, and said to her servant, "Drive, and go forward; do not slacken the pace for me unless I tell you." [25]And so she departed, and went to the man of God at Mount Carmel.

So it was, when the man of God saw her afar off, that he said to his servant Gehazi, "Look, the Shunammite woman! [26]Please run now to meet her, and say to her, '*Is it* well with you? *Is it* well with your husband? *Is it* well with the child?'"

And she answered, "*It is* well." [27]Now when she came to the man of God at the hill, she caught him by the feet, but Gehazi came near to push her away. But the man of God said, "Let her alone; for her soul *is* in deep distress, and the LORD has hidden *it* from me, and has not told me."

[28]So she said, "Did I ask a son of my lord? Did I not say, 'Do not deceive me'?"

[29]Then he said to Gehazi, "Get yourself ready, and take my staff in your hand, and be on your way. If you meet anyone, do not greet him; and if anyone greets you, do not answer him; but lay my staff on the face of the child."

[30]And the mother of the child said, "*As* the LORD lives, and *as* your soul lives, I will not leave you." So he arose and followed her. [31]Now Gehazi went on ahead of them, and laid the staff on the face of the child; but *there was* neither voice nor hearing. Therefore he went back to meet him, and told him, saying, "The child has not awakened."

[32]When Elisha came into the house, there was the child, lying dead on his bed. [33]He went in therefore, shut the door behind the two of them, and prayed to the LORD. [34]And he went up and lay on the child, and put his mouth on his mouth, his eyes on his eyes, and his hands on his hands; and he stretched himself out on the child, and the flesh of the child became warm. [35]He returned and walked back and forth in the

house, and again went up and stretched
himself out on him; then the child sneezed
seven times, and the child opened his eyes.
36And he called Gehazi and said, "Call this
Shunammite woman." So he called her. And
when she came in to him, he said, "Pick up
your son." 37So she went in, fell at his feet,
and bowed to the ground; then she picked up
her son and went out.

Elisha Purifies the Pot of Stew

38And Elisha returned to Gilgal, and *there*
was a famine in the land. Now the sons of
the prophets *were* sitting before him; and he
said to his servant, "Put on the large pot, and
boil stew for the sons of the prophets." 39So
one went out into the field to gather herbs,
and found a wild vine, and gathered from it
a lapful of wild gourds, and came and sliced
them into the pot of stew, though they did
not know *what they were*. 40Then they served
it to the men to eat. Now it happened, as they
were eating the stew, that they cried out and
said, "Man of God, *there is* death in the pot!"
And they could not eat *it*.

41So he said, "Then bring some flour."
And he put *it* into the pot, and said, "Serve *it*
to the people, that they may eat." And there
was nothing harmful in the pot.

Elisha Feeds One Hundred Men

42Then a man came from Baal Shalisha,
and brought the man of God bread of the
firstfruits, twenty loaves of barley bread,
and newly ripened grain in his knapsack.
And he said, "Give *it* to the people, that they
may eat."

43But his servant said, "What? Shall I set
this before one hundred men?"

He said again, "Give it to the people, that
they may eat; for thus says the LORD: 'They
shall eat and have *some* left over.'" 44So he set
it before them; and they ate and had *some* left
over, according to the word of the LORD.

Naaman's Leprosy Healed

5 Now Naaman, commander of the
army of the king of Syria, was a great
and honorable man in the eyes of his master,
because by him the LORD had given victory
to Syria. He was also a mighty man of valor, *but* a leper. 2And the Syrians had gone
out on raids, and had brought back captive a
young girl from the land of Israel. She waited on Naaman's wife. 3Then she said to her
mistress, "If only my master *were* with the
prophet who *is* in Samaria! For he would
heal him of his leprosy." 4And *Naaman* went
in and told his master, saying, "Thus and
thus said the girl who *is* from the land of
Israel."

5Then the king of Syria said, "Go now,
and I will send a letter to the king of Israel."

So he departed and took with him ten
talents of silver, six thousand *shekels* of
gold, and ten changes of clothing. 6Then he
brought the letter to the king of Israel, which
said,

> Now be advised, when this letter comes to you, that I have sent Naaman my servant to you, that you may heal him of his leprosy.

7And it happened, when the king of Israel
read the letter, that he tore his clothes and
said, "*Am* I God, to kill and make alive, that
this man sends a man to me to heal him of
his leprosy? Therefore please consider, and
see how he seeks a quarrel with me."

8So it was, when Elisha the man of God
heard that the king of Israel had torn his
clothes, that he sent to the king, saying,
"Why have you torn your clothes? Please
let him come to me, and he shall know that
there is a prophet in Israel."

9Then Naaman went with his horses and
chariot, and he stood at the door of Elisha's
house. 10And Elisha sent a messenger to
him, saying, "Go and wash in the Jordan
seven times, and your flesh shall be restored
to you, and *you shall* be clean." 11But Naaman
became furious, and went away and said,
"Indeed, I said to myself, 'He will surely
come out *to me*, and stand and call on the
name of the LORD his God, and wave his
hand over the place, and heal the leprosy.'
12*Are* not the Abanah[a] and the Pharpar, the
rivers of Damascus, better than all the waters of Israel? Could I not wash in them and
be clean?" So he turned and went away in a
rage. 13And his servants came near and spoke
to him, and said, "My father, *if* the prophet
had told you *to do* something great, would
you not have done *it*? How much more then,
when he says to you, 'Wash, and be clean'?"
14So he went down and dipped seven times
in the Jordan, according to the saying of the

5:12 [a] Following Kethib, Septuagint, and Vulgate; Qere, Syriac, and Targum read *Amanah*.

man of God; and his flesh was restored like
the flesh of a little child, and he was clean.
15 And he returned to the man of God, he
and all his aides, and came and stood before
him; and he said, "Indeed, now I know that
there is no God in all the earth, except in Israel; now therefore, please take a gift from
your servant."
16 But he said, "*As* the LORD lives, before
whom I stand, I will receive nothing." And
he urged him to take *it*, but he refused.
17 So Naaman said, "Then, if not, please
let your servant be given two mule-loads of
earth; for your servant will no longer offer either burnt offering or sacrifice to other gods,
but to the LORD. 18 Yet in this thing may the
LORD pardon your servant: when my master goes into the temple of Rimmon to worship there, and he leans on my hand, and I bow down in the temple of Rimmon—when I bow down in the temple of Rimmon, may the LORD please pardon your servant in this thing."
19 Then he said to him, "Go in peace." So
he departed from him a short distance.

Gehazi's Greed

20 But Gehazi, the servant of Elisha the man of God, said, "Look, my master has spared Naaman this Syrian, while not receiving from his hands what he brought; but *as* the LORD lives, I will run after him and take

KINDNESS

HEALING WITH KINDNESS

READ IT: 2 KINGS 5:1–19

GET IT:

It was remarkable for a young Israelite servant girl to demonstrate kindness and compassion to her Syrian master because their nations were at odds. The Syrians were aggressive invaders, and the Israelites struggled against them for centuries. What's more, this girl was a slave, not a paid worker, and she was acquired by Naaman's soldiers during a raid against Israel. Nowadays we'd call her a victim of human trafficking, the slave trade. But despite all she had been through, she still had kindness in her heart. Her compassion in the midst of that difficult situation—compassion for a Syrian warrior, no less—completely changed Naaman's life.

Naaman received dramatic healing from a devastating disease that had no cure, and he came to faith in God, turning his back on the idols of Syria. All this because a young girl spoke with kindness in his dark hour.

LIVE IT:

No matter how difficult your life has been, God has given you the ability to be kind to others. If bitterness about your circumstances or what you've been through is keeping you from showing kindness to others, it's *time to let it go*.

Ask God to soften the hardness that has built up inside you so that His love and His kindness can change you and the lives of those around you.

something from him." 21So Gehazi pursued
Naaman. When Naaman saw *him* running
after him, he got down from the chariot to
meet him, and said, "*Is* all well?"
22And he said, "All *is* well. My master
has sent me, saying, 'Indeed, just now two
young men of the sons of the prophets have
come to me from the mountains of Ephraim.
Please give them a talent of silver and two
changes of garments.'"
23So Naaman said, "Please, take two talents." And he urged him, and bound two
talents of silver in two bags, with two changes of garments, and handed *them* to two of
his servants; and they carried *them* on ahead
of him. 24When he came to the citadel, he
took *them* from their hand, and stored *them*
away in the house; then he let the men go,
and they departed. 25Now he went in and
stood before his master. Elisha said to him,
"Where *did you go,* Gehazi?"
And he said, "Your servant did not go
anywhere."
26Then he said to him, "Did not my heart
go *with you* when the man turned back from
his chariot to meet you? *Is it* time to receive
money and to receive clothing, olive groves
and vineyards, sheep and oxen, male and
female servants? 27Therefore the leprosy of
Naaman shall cling to you and your descendants forever." And he went out from his
presence leprous, *as white* as snow.

The Floating Ax Head

6 And the sons of the prophets said to
Elisha, "See now, the place where we
dwell with you is too small for us. 2Please, let
us go to the Jordan, and let every man take
a beam from there, and let us make there a
place where we may dwell."
So he answered, "Go."
3Then one said, "Please consent to go
with your servants."
And he answered, "I will go." 4So he went
with them. And when they came to the Jordan, they cut down trees. 5But as one was
cutting down a tree, the iron *ax head* fell into
the water; and he cried out and said, "Alas,
master! For it was borrowed."
6So the man of God said, "Where did it
fall?" And he showed him the place. So he
cut off a stick, and threw *it* in there; and
he made the iron float. 7Therefore he said,
"Pick *it* up for yourself." So he reached out
his hand and took it.

The Blinded Syrians Captured

8Now the king of Syria was making war
against Israel; and he consulted with his
servants, saying, "My camp *will be* in such
and such a place." 9And the man of God sent
to the king of Israel, saying, "Beware that
you do not pass this place, for the Syrians
are coming down there." 10Then the king of
Israel sent *someone* to the place of which the
man of God had told him. Thus he warned
him, and he was watchful there, not just
once or twice.
11Therefore the heart of the king of Syria
was greatly troubled by this thing; and he
called his servants and said to them, "Will

GREED

READ IT: 2 KINGS 5:20–27

Naaman offered Elisha a reward for curing him, but Elisha refused, knowing the credit belonged to God. Gehazi, Elisha's servant, was greedy; he wanted the stuff. He thought Elisha would never find out anyway. And besides being greedy, Gehazi lied—twice! First to Naaman to get the stuff, then to Elisha to keep the stuff. But he didn't get away with any of it. Elisha knew what he had done and punished him. Avoid being greedy, 'cause it might make you do more wrong to cover it up.

you not show me which of us *is* for the king
of Israel?"
12 And one of his servants said, "None, my
lord, O king; but Elisha, the prophet who *is*
in Israel, tells the king of Israel the words
that you speak in your bedroom."
13 So he said, "Go and see where he *is*, that
I may send and get him."
And it was told him, saying, "Surely *he*
is in Dothan."
14 Therefore he sent horses and chariots
and a great army there, and they came by
night and surrounded the city. 15 And when
the servant of the man of God arose early
and went out, there was an army, surrounding the city with horses and chariots. And
his servant said to him, "Alas, my master!
What shall we do?"
16 So he answered, "Do not fear, for those
who *are* with us *are* more than those who *are*
with them." 17 And Elisha prayed, and said,
"LORD, I pray, open his eyes that he may see."
Then the LORD opened the eyes of the young
man, and he saw. And behold, the mountain
was full of horses and chariots of fire all
around Elisha. 18 So when *the Syrians* came
down to him, Elisha prayed to the LORD, and
said, "Strike this people, I pray, with blindness." And He struck them with blindness
according to the word of Elisha.
19 Now Elisha said to them, "This *is* not
the way, nor *is* this the city. Follow me, and I
will bring you to the man whom you seek."
But he led them to Samaria.
20 So it was, when they had come to Samaria, that Elisha said, "LORD, open the eyes
of these *men*, that they may see." And the
LORD opened their eyes, and they saw; and
there *they were*, inside Samaria!
21 Now when the king of Israel saw them,
he said to Elisha, "My father, shall I kill
them? Shall I kill *them*?"
22 But he answered, "You shall not kill
them. Would you kill those whom you have
taken captive with your sword and your bow?
Set food and water before them, that they
may eat and drink and go to their master."
23 Then he prepared a great feast for them;
and after they ate and drank, he sent them
away and they went to their master. So the
bands of Syrian *raiders* came no more into
the land of Israel.

Syria Besieges Samaria in Famine

24 And it happened after this that Ben-
Hadad king of Syria gathered all his army,
and went up and besieged Samaria. 25 And
there was a great famine in Samaria; and
indeed they besieged it until a donkey's
head was *sold* for eighty *shekels* of silver, and

6:8–17 GOD AND YOU ARE ENOUGH

When Syria was making war against Israel, Elisha's servant went out one morning and saw the army of Syria surrounding the city of Dothan (pronounced *DOH-thun*). He was terrified. But the prophet Elisha asked God to open his servant's eyes. Then the servant could see horses and chariots of fire all around Elisha.

What can you learn from what Elisha's servant saw? Sometimes you think you are alone with all your problems. That is when you should remember Elisha. God's army was all around even though Elisha's servant couldn't see it.

God's army is always there to help His people. Like Elisha's servant, sometimes you need to ask God to open your eyes to see that you aren't really alone. Don't believe only what you see with your eyes. God is invisible, but you and He are enough to make you a winner over all your trials.

one-fourth of a kab of dove droppings for five
shekels of silver.
[26]Then, as the king of Israel was passing
by on the wall, a woman cried out to him,
saying, "Help, my lord, O king!"
[27]And he said, "If the LORD does not help
you, where can I find help for you? From
the threshing floor or from the winepress?"
[28]Then the king said to her, "What is troubling you?"
And she answered, "This woman said to
me, 'Give your son, that we may eat him today, and we will eat my son tomorrow.' [29]So
we boiled my son, and ate him. And I said to
her on the next day, 'Give your son, that we
may eat him'; but she has hidden her son."
[30]Now it happened, when the king heard
the words of the woman, that he tore his
clothes; and as he passed by on the wall, the
people looked, and there underneath *he had*
sackcloth on his body. [31]Then he said, "God
do so to me and more also, if the head of
Elisha the son of Shaphat remains on him
today!"
[32]But Elisha was sitting in his house, and
the elders were sitting with him. And *the*
king sent a man ahead of him, but before the
messenger came to him, he said to the elders, "Do you see how this son of a murderer has sent someone to take away my head?
Look, when the messenger comes, shut the
door, and hold him fast at the door. *Is* not
the sound of his master's feet behind him?"
[33]And while he was still talking with them,
there was the messenger, coming down to
him; and then *the king* said, "Surely this calamity *is* from the LORD; why should I wait
for the LORD any longer?"
7 Then Elisha said, "Hear the word of the
LORD. Thus says the LORD: 'Tomorrow
about this time a seah of fine flour *shall be*
sold for a shekel, and two seahs of barley for
a shekel, at the gate of Samaria.'"
[2]So an officer on whose hand the king
leaned answered the man of God and said,
"*Look, if the* LORD *would* make windows in
heaven, could this thing be?"
And he said, "In fact, you shall see *it* with
your eyes, but you shall not eat of it."

The Syrians Flee

[3]Now there were four leprous men at the
entrance of the gate; and they said to one another, "Why are we sitting here until we die?
[4]If we say, 'We will enter the city,' the famine
is in the city, and we shall die there. And if
we sit here, we die also. Now therefore, come,
let us surrender to the army of the Syrians. If
they keep us alive, we shall live; and if they
kill us, we shall only die." [5]And they rose at
twilight to go to the camp of the Syrians; and
when they had come to the outskirts of the
Syrian camp, to their surprise no one *was*
there. [6]For the Lord had caused the army
of the Syrians to hear the noise of chariots
and the noise of horses—the noise of a great
army; so they said to one another, "Look, the
king of Israel has hired against us the kings
of the Hittites and the kings of the Egyptians
to attack us!" [7]Therefore they arose and fled
at twilight, and left the camp intact—their
tents, their horses, and their donkeys—and
they fled for their lives. [8]And when these lepers came to the outskirts of the camp, they
went into one tent and ate and drank, and
carried from it silver and gold and clothing,
and went and hid *them;* then they came back
and entered another tent, and carried *some*
from there *also,* and went and hid *it.*
[9]Then they said to one another, "We are
not doing right. This day *is* a day of good
news, and we remain silent. If we wait until
morning light, some punishment will come
upon us. Now therefore, come, let us go and
tell the king's household." [10]So they went and
called to the gatekeepers of the city, and told
them, saying, "We went to the Syrian camp,
and surprisingly no one *was* there, not a human sound—only horses and donkeys tied,
and the tents intact." [11]And the gatekeepers called out, and they told *it* to the king's
household inside.
[12]So the king arose in the night and said
to his servants, "Let me now tell you what
the Syrians have done to us. They know that
we *are* hungry; therefore they have gone out
of the camp to hide themselves in the field,
saying, 'When they come out of the city, we
shall catch them alive, and get into the city.'"
[13]And one of his servants answered and
said, "Please, let several *men* take five of the
remaining horses which are left in the city.
Look, they *may either become* like all the multitude of Israel that are left in it; or indeed,
I say, they *may become* like all the multitude
of Israel left from those who are consumed;
so let us send them and see." [14]Therefore
they took two chariots with horses; and the
king sent them in the direction of the Syrian

army, saying, "Go and see." 15And they went
after them to the Jordan; and indeed all
the road *was* full of garments and weapons
which the Syrians had thrown away in their
haste. So the messengers returned and told
the king. 16Then the people went out and
plundered the tents of the Syrians. So a seah
of fine flour was *sold* for a shekel, and two
seahs of barley for a shekel, according to the
word of the LORD.

17Now the king had appointed the officer
on whose hand he leaned to have charge of
the gate. But the people trampled him in the
gate, and he died, just as the man of God had
said, who spoke when the king came down
to him. 18So it happened just as the man of
God had spoken to the king, saying, "Two
seahs of barley for a shekel, and a seah of
fine flour for a shekel, shall be *sold* tomorrow about this time in the gate of Samaria."

19Then that officer had answered the
man of God, and said, "Now look, *if* the
LORD would make windows in heaven, could
such a thing be?"

And he had said, "In fact, you shall see
it with your eyes, but you shall not eat of it."
20And so it happened to him, for the people
trampled him in the gate, and he died.

The King Restores the Shunammite's Land

8 Then Elisha spoke to the woman
whose son he had restored to life, saying, "Arise and go, you and your household,
and stay wherever you can; for the LORD has
called for a famine, and furthermore, it will
come upon the land for seven years." 2So the
woman arose and did according to the saying of the man of God, and she went with
her household and dwelt in the land of the
Philistines seven years.

3It came to pass, at the end of seven years,
that the woman returned from the land of
the Philistines; and she went to make an appeal to the king for her house and for her
land. 4Then the king talked with Gehazi,
the servant of the man of God, saying, "Tell
me, please, all the great things Elisha has
done." 5Now it happened, as he was telling
the king how he had restored the dead to
life, that there was the woman whose son
he had restored to life, appealing to the king
for her house and for her land. And Gehazi
said, "My lord, O king, this *is* the woman,
and this *is* her son whom Elisha restored to
life." 6And when the king asked the woman,
she told him.

So the king appointed a certain officer
for her, saying, "Restore all that *was* hers,
and all the proceeds of the field from the day
that she left the land until now."

Death of Ben-Hadad

7Then Elisha went to Damascus, and
Ben-Hadad king of Syria was sick; and
it was told him, saying, "The man of God
has come here." 8And the king said to Hazael, "Take a present in your hand, and go to
meet the man of God, and inquire of the
LORD by him, saying, 'Shall I recover from
this disease?'" 9So Hazael went to meet him
and took a present with him, of every good
thing of Damascus, forty camel-loads; and
he came and stood before him, and said,
"Your son Ben-Hadad king of Syria has sent
me to you, saying, 'Shall I recover from this
disease?'"

10And Elisha said to him, "Go, say to
him, 'You shall certainly recover.' However
the LORD has shown me that he will really
die." 11Then he set his countenance in a stare
until he was ashamed; and the man of God
wept. 12And Hazael said, "Why is my lord
weeping?"

He answered, "Because I know the
evil that you will do to the children of Israel: Their strongholds you will set on fire,
and their young men you will kill with the
sword; and you will dash their children, and
rip open their women with child."

13So Hazael said, "But what *is* your servant—a dog, that he should do this gross
thing?"

And Elisha answered, "The LORD has
shown me that you *will become* king over
Syria."

14Then he departed from Elisha, and
came to his master, who said to him, "What
did Elisha say to you?" And he answered,
"He told me you would surely recover." 15But
it happened on the next day that he took a
thick cloth and dipped *it* in water, and spread
it over his face so that he died; and Hazael
reigned in his place.

Jehoram Reigns in Judah

16Now in the fifth year of Joram the son
of Ahab, king of Israel, Jehoshaphat *having
been* king of Judah, Jehoram the son of Jehoshaphat began to reign as king of Judah.

17He was thirty-two years old when he became king, and he reigned eight years in
Jerusalem. 18And he walked in the way of
the kings of Israel, just as the house of Ahab
had done, for the daughter of Ahab was his
wife; and he did evil in the sight of the LORD.
19Yet the LORD would not destroy Judah, for
the sake of His servant David, as He promised him to give a lamp to him *and* his sons
forever.
20In his days Edom revolted against
Judah's authority, and made a king over
themselves. 21So Joram[a] went to Zair, and
all his chariots with him. Then he rose by
night and attacked the Edomites who had
surrounded him and the captains of the
chariots; and the troops fled to their tents.
22Thus Edom has been in revolt against Judah's authority to this day. And Libnah revolted at that time.
23Now the rest of the acts of Joram, and
all that he did, *are* they not written in the

8:21 [a] Spelled *Jehoram* in verse 16

GOD'S JUSTICE

GOOD PAYBACK

READ IT: 2 KINGS 8:1–6

GET IT:

Our God is a God of justice. He will always restore—or make right—what has been lost when that loss is unfair in His eyes. Elisha had brought back to life the son of a Shunammite woman. He told the woman to take her family out of the land for seven years because there was going to be a famine. Because she knew Elisha was a man of God, she listened. For seven years her family lived as foreigners with the Philistines. Talk about a culture shock. Everything she had was gone, including her farm and her friends. How would she ever make it?

After seven years passed, the woman went back. She decided to ask the king for her land and her farm. Guess who was talking to the king at the same time the woman and her son showed up? Gehazi, who was Elisha's servant. The king wanted to know all about Elisha and what he had done. Gehazi said, "My lord, O king, this is the woman, and this is her son whom Elisha restored to life" (v. 5). The king asked the woman if it was true, and she confirmed it. The king gave her the farm and her land back; he also appointed an officer to keep her safe and gave her all of the profits from her farm for the seven years she was gone.

LIVE IT:

Sometimes things happen to us that don't make sense or don't seem fair. One of God's characteristics is that He restores what was lost. Most of the time we have no idea how that will happen. The Shunammite woman didn't know what would happen when she returned, and look at God's justice! Next time you feel loss, make a note of it. God will restore it, maybe in an unexpected way.

book of the chronicles of the kings of Judah?
24 So Joram rested with his fathers, and was
buried with his fathers in the City of David.
Then Ahaziah his son reigned in his place.

Ahaziah Reigns in Judah

25 In the twelfth year of Joram the son
of Ahab, king of Israel, Ahaziah the son
of Jehoram, king of Judah, began to reign.
26 Ahaziah *was* twenty-two years old when he
became king, and he reigned one year in Jerusalem. His mother's name *was* Athaliah
the granddaughter of Omri, king of Israel.
27 And he walked in the way of the house of
Ahab, and did evil in the sight of the LORD,
like the house of Ahab, for he *was* the son-in-
law of the house of Ahab.

28 Now he went with Joram the son of
Ahab to war against Hazael king of Syria
at Ramoth Gilead; and the Syrians wounded Joram. 29 Then King Joram went back to
Jezreel to recover from the wounds which
the Syrians had inflicted on him at Ramah,
when he fought against Hazael king of Syria. And Ahaziah the son of Jehoram, king of
Judah, went down to see Joram the son of
Ahab in Jezreel, because he was sick.

Jehu Anointed King of Israel

9 And Elisha the prophet called one of
the sons of the prophets, and said to
him, "Get yourself ready, take this flask of
oil in your hand, and go to Ramoth Gilead.
2 Now when you arrive at that place, look
there for Jehu the son of Jehoshaphat, the
son of Nimshi, and go in and make him rise
up from among his associates, and take him
to an inner room. 3 Then take the flask of oil,
and pour *it* on his head, and say, 'Thus says
the LORD: "I have anointed you king over Israel."' Then open the door and flee, and do
not delay."

4 So the young man, the servant of the
prophet, went to Ramoth Gilead. 5 And when
he arrived, there *were* the captains of the
army sitting; and he said, "I have a message
for you, Commander."

Jehu said, "For which *one* of us?"

And he said, "For you, Commander."
6 Then he arose and went into the house.
And he poured the oil on his head, and said
to him, "Thus says the LORD God of Israel:
'I have anointed you king over the people of
the LORD, over Israel. 7 You shall strike down
the house of Ahab your master, that I may
avenge the blood of My servants the prophets, and the blood of all the servants of the
LORD, at the hand of Jezebel. 8 For the whole
house of Ahab shall perish; and I will cut off
from Ahab all the males in Israel, both bond
and free. 9 So I will make the house of Ahab
like the house of Jeroboam the son of Nebat,
and like the house of Baasha the son of Ahijah. 10 The dogs shall eat Jezebel on the plot
of ground at Jezreel, and *there shall be* none to
bury *her*.'" And he opened the door and fled.

11 Then Jehu came out to the servants of
his master, and *one* said to him, "*Is* all well?
Why did this madman come to you?"

And he said to them, "You know the man
and his babble."

12 And they said, "A lie! Tell us now."

So he said, "Thus and thus he spoke to
me, saying, 'Thus says the LORD: "I have
anointed you king over Israel."'"

13 Then each man hastened to take his
garment and put *it* under him on the top of
the steps; and they blew trumpets, saying,
"Jehu is king!"

Joram of Israel Killed

14 So Jehu the son of Jehoshaphat, the son
of Nimshi, conspired against Joram. (Now
Joram had been defending Ramoth Gilead, he and all Israel, against Hazael king
of Syria. 15 But King Joram had returned to
Jezreel to recover from the wounds which
the Syrians had inflicted on him when he
fought with Hazael king of Syria.) And Jehu
said, "If you are so minded, let no one leave
or escape from the city to go and tell *it* in Jezreel." 16 So Jehu rode in a chariot and went
to Jezreel, for Joram was laid up there; and
Ahaziah king of Judah had come down to
see Joram.

17 Now a watchman stood on the tower in
Jezreel, and he saw the company of Jehu as
he came, and said, "I see a company of men."

And Joram said, "Get a horseman and
send him to meet them, and let him say, '*Is*
it peace?'"

18 So the horseman went to meet him, and
said, "Thus says the king: '*Is it* peace?'"

And Jehu said, "What have you to do with
peace? Turn around and follow me."

So the watchman reported, saying, "The
messenger went to them, but is not coming
back."

19 Then he sent out a second horseman

who came to them, and said, "Thus says the
king: '*Is it* peace?'"
And Jehu answered, "What have you to
do with peace? Turn around and follow me."
20 So the watchman reported, saying, "He
went up to them and is not coming back; and
the driving *is* like the driving of Jehu the son
of Nimshi, for he drives furiously!"
21 Then Joram said, "Make ready." And
his chariot was made ready. Then Joram
king of Israel and Ahaziah king of Judah
went out, each in his chariot; and they went
out to meet Jehu, and met him on the property of Naboth the Jezreelite. 22 Now it happened, when Joram saw Jehu, that he said,
"*Is it* peace, Jehu?"
So he answered, "What peace, as long as
the harlotries of your mother Jezebel and her
witchcraft *are so* many?"
23 Then Joram turned around and fled,
and said to Ahaziah, "Treachery, Ahaziah!"
24 Now Jehu drew his bow with full strength
and shot Jehoram between his arms; and
the arrow came out at his heart, and he sank
down in his chariot. 25 Then *Jehu* said to Bid-
kar his captain, "Pick *him* up, *and* throw him
into the tract of the field of Naboth the Jezreelite; for remember, when you and I were
riding together behind Ahab his father, that
the LORD laid this burden upon him: 26 'Surely I saw yesterday the blood of Naboth and
the blood of his sons,' says the LORD, 'and
I will repay you in this plot,' says the LORD.
Now therefore, take *and* throw him on the
plot *of ground,* according to the word of the
LORD."

Ahaziah of Judah Killed

27 But when Ahaziah king of Judah saw
this, he fled by the road to Beth Haggan.[a]
So Jehu pursued him, and said, "Shoot him
also in the chariot." *And they shot him* at the
Ascent of Gur, which is by Ibleam. Then he
fled to Megiddo, and died there. 28 And his
servants carried him in the chariot to Jerusalem, and buried him in his tomb with his
fathers in the City of David. 29 In the eleventh
year of Joram the son of Ahab, Ahaziah had
become king over Judah.

Jezebel's Violent Death

30 Now when Jehu had come to Jezreel,
Jezebel heard *of it;* and she put paint on
her eyes and adorned her head, and looked
through a window. 31 Then, as Jehu entered
at the gate, she said, "*Is it* peace, Zimri, murderer of your master?"
32 And he looked up at the window, and
said, "Who *is* on my side? Who?" So two *or*
three eunuchs looked out at him. 33 Then he
said, "Throw her down." So they threw her
down, and *some* of her blood spattered on the
wall and on the horses; and he trampled her
underfoot. 34 And when he had gone in, he
ate and drank. Then he said, "Go now, see
to this accursed *woman,* and bury her, for
she was a king's daughter." 35 So they went to
bury her, but they found no more of her than
the skull and the feet and the palms of *her*
hands. 36 Therefore they came back and told
him. And he said, "This *is* the word of the
LORD, which He spoke by His servant Elijah
the Tishbite, saying, 'On the plot *of ground*
at Jezreel dogs shall eat the flesh of Jezebel;[a] 37 and the corpse of Jezebel shall be as
refuse on the surface of the field, in the plot
at Jezreel, so that they shall not say, "Here
lies Jezebel."'"

Ahab's Seventy Sons Killed

10 Now Ahab had seventy sons in Samaria. And Jehu wrote and sent let-
ters to Samaria, to the rulers of Jezreel,[a] to
the elders, and to those who reared Ahab's
sons, saying:

2 Now as soon as this letter comes to you,
since your master's sons *are* with you,
and you have chariots and horses, a
fortified city also, and weapons, 3 choose
the best qualified of your master's sons,
set *him* on his father's throne, and fight
for your master's house.

4 But they were exceedingly afraid, and
said, "Look, two kings could not stand up
to him; how then can we stand?" 5 And he
who *was* in charge of the house, and he who
was in charge of the city, the elders also, and
those who reared *the sons,* sent to Jehu, saying, "We *are* your servants, we will do all you
tell us; but we will not make anyone king. Do
what is good in your sight." 6 Then he wrote a
second letter to them, saying:

If you *are* for me and will obey my voice,
take the heads of the men, your master's
sons, and come to me at Jezreel by this
time tomorrow.

9:27 [a] Literally *The Garden House* **9:36** [a] 1 Kings 21:23
10:1 [a] Following Masoretic Text, Syriac, and Targum; Septuagint reads *Samaria;* Vulgate reads *city.*

Now the king's sons, seventy persons, *were* with the great men of the city, *who* were rearing them. 7So it was, when the letter came to them, that they took the king's sons and slaughtered seventy persons, put their heads in baskets and sent *them* to him at Jezreel.

8Then a messenger came and told him, saying, "They have brought the heads of the king's sons."

And he said, "Lay them in two heaps at the entrance of the gate until morning."

9So it was, in the morning, that he went out and stood, and said to all the people, "You *are* righteous. Indeed I conspired against my master and killed him; but who killed all these? 10Know now that nothing shall fall to the earth of the word of the LORD which the LORD spoke concerning the house of Ahab; for the LORD has done what He spoke by His servant Elijah." 11So Jehu killed all who remained of the house of Ahab in Jezreel, and all his great men and his close acquaintances and his priests, until he left him none remaining.

Ahaziah's Forty-two Brothers Killed

12And he arose and departed and went to Samaria. On the way, at Beth Eked[a] of the Shepherds, 13Jehu met with the brothers of Ahaziah king of Judah, and said, "Who *are* you?"

So they answered, "We *are* the brothers of Ahaziah; we have come down to greet the sons of the king and the sons of the queen mother."

14And he said, "Take them alive!" So they took them alive, and killed them at the well of Beth Eked, forty-two men; and he left none of them.

The Rest of Ahab's Family Killed

15Now when he departed from there, he met Jehonadab the son of Rechab, *coming* to meet him; and he greeted him and said to him, "Is your heart right, as my heart *is* toward your heart?"

And Jehonadab answered, "It is."

Jehu said, "If it is, give *me* your hand." So he gave *him* his hand, and he took him up to *him into the chariot.* 16*Then* he said, "Come with me, and see my zeal for the LORD." So they had him ride in his chariot. 17And when he came to Samaria, he killed all who remained to Ahab in Samaria, till he had destroyed them, according to the word of the LORD which He spoke to Elijah.

Worshipers of Baal Killed

18Then Jehu gathered all the people together, and said to them, "Ahab served Baal a little, Jehu will serve him much. 19Now therefore, call to me all the prophets of Baal, all his servants, and all his priests. Let no one be missing, for I have a great sacrifice for Baal. Whoever is missing shall not live." But Jehu acted deceptively, with the intent of destroying the worshipers of Baal. 20And Jehu said, "Proclaim a solemn assembly for Baal." So they proclaimed *it.* 21Then Jehu sent throughout all Israel; and all the worshipers of Baal came, so that there was not a man left who did not come. So they came into the temple[a] of Baal, and the temple of Baal was full from one end to the other. 22And he said to the one in charge of the wardrobe, "Bring out vestments for all the worshipers of Baal." So he brought out vestments for them. 23Then Jehu and Jehonadab the son of Rechab went into the temple of Baal, and said to the worshipers of Baal, "Search and see that no servants of the LORD are here with you, but only the worshipers of Baal." 24So they went in to offer sacrifices and burnt offerings. Now Jehu had appointed for himself eighty men on the outside, and had said, "*If* any of the men whom I have brought into your hands escapes, *whoever lets him escape, it shall be* his life for the life of the other."

25Now it happened, as soon as he had made an end of offering the burnt offering, that Jehu said to the guard and to the captains, "Go in *and* kill them; let no one come out!" And they killed them with the edge of the sword; then the guards and the officers threw *them* out, and went into the inner room of the temple of Baal. 26And they brought the *sacred* pillars out of the temple of Baal and burned them. 27Then they broke down the *sacred* pillar of Baal, and tore down the temple of Baal and made it a refuse dump to this day. 28Thus Jehu destroyed Baal from Israel.

29However Jehu did not turn away from the sins of Jeroboam the son of Nebat, who had made Israel sin, *that is,* from the golden

---

10:12 [a] Or *The Shearing House* 10:21 [a] Literally *house,* and so elsewhere in this chapter

calves that *were* at Bethel and Dan. 30And the
LORD said to Jehu, "Because you have done
well in doing *what is* right in My sight, *and*
have done to the house of Ahab all that *was*
in My heart, your sons shall sit on the throne
of Israel to the fourth *generation*." 31But Jehu
took no heed to walk in the law of the LORD
God of Israel with all his heart; for he did not
depart from the sins of Jeroboam, who had
made Israel sin.

Death of Jehu

32In those days the LORD began to cut off
parts of Israel; and Hazael conquered them
in all the territory of Israel 33from the Jordan
eastward: all the land of Gilead—Gad, Reuben, and Manasseh—from Aroer, which *is*
by the River Arnon, including Gilead and
Bashan.

34Now the rest of the acts of Jehu, all that
he did, and all his might, *are* they not written
in the book of the chronicles of the kings of
Israel? 35So Jehu rested with his fathers, and
they buried him in Samaria. Then Jehoahaz
his son reigned in his place. 36And the period
that Jehu reigned over Israel in Samaria *was*
twenty-eight years.

Athaliah Reigns in Judah

11 When Athaliah the mother of Ahaziah saw that her son was dead, she
arose and destroyed all the royal heirs. 2But
Jehosheba, the daughter of King Joram, sister of Ahaziah, took Joash the son of Ahaziah, and stole him away from among the
king's sons *who were* being murdered; and
they hid him and his nurse in the bedroom,
from Athaliah, so that he was not killed. 3So
he was hidden with her in the house of the
LORD for six years, while Athaliah reigned
over the land.

Joash Crowned King of Judah

4In the seventh year Jehoiada sent and
brought the captains of hundreds—of the
bodyguards and the escorts—and brought
them into the house of the LORD to him. And
he made a covenant with them and took an
oath from them in the house of the LORD,
and showed them the king's son. 5Then he
commanded them, saying, "This *is* what you
shall do: One-third of you who come on duty
on the Sabbath shall be keeping watch over
the king's house, 6one-third *shall be* at the
gate of Sur, and one-third at the gate behind
the escorts. You shall keep the watch of the
house, lest it be broken down. 7The two con-
tingents of you who go off duty on the Sabbath shall keep the watch of the house of the
LORD for the king. 8But you shall surround
the king on all sides, every man with his
weapons in his hand; and whoever comes
within range, let him be put to death. You
are to be with the king as he goes out and as
he comes in."

9So the captains of the hundreds did according to all that Jehoiada the priest commanded. Each of them took his men who
were to be on duty on the Sabbath, with
those who were going off duty on the Sabbath, and came to Jehoiada the priest. 10And
the priest gave the captains of hundreds the
spears and shields which *had belonged* to
King David, that were in the temple of the
LORD. 11Then the escorts stood, every man
with his weapons in his hand, all around the
king, from the right side of the temple to the
left side of the temple, by the altar and the
house. 12And he brought out the king's son,
put the crown on him, and *gave him* the Testimony;[a] they made him king and anointed
him, and they clapped their hands and said,
"Long live the king!"

Death of Athaliah

13Now when Athaliah heard the noise of
the escorts *and* the people, she came to the
people *in* the temple of the LORD. 14When
she looked, there was the king standing by
a pillar according to custom; and the leaders
and the trumpeters were by the king. All the
people of the land were rejoicing and blowing trumpets. So Athaliah tore her clothes
and cried out, "Treason! Treason!"

15And Jehoiada the priest commanded
the captains of the hundreds, the officers of
the army, and said to them, "Take her outside under guard, and slay with the sword
whoever follows her." For the priest had said,
"Do not let her be killed in the house of the
LORD." 16So they seized her; and she went by
way of the horses' entrance *into* the king's
house, and there she was killed.

17Then Jehoiada made a covenant between the LORD, the king, and the people,
that they should be the LORD's people, and
also between the king and the people. 18And

11:12 [a] That is, the Law (compare Exodus 25:16, 21 and Deuteronomy 31:9)

all the people of the land went to the temple
of Baal, and tore it down. They thoroughly
broke in pieces its altars and images, and
killed Mattan the priest of Baal before the
altars. And the priest appointed officers over
the house of the LORD. 19Then he took the
captains of hundreds, the bodyguards, the
escorts, and all the people of the land; and
they brought the king down from the house
of the LORD, and went by way of the gate of
the escorts to the king's house. Then he sat
on the throne of the kings. 20So all the people
of the land rejoiced; and the city was quiet,
for they had slain Athaliah with the sword *in*
the king's house. 21Jehoash *was* seven years
old when he became king.

Jehoash Repairs the Temple

12 In the seventh year of Jehu, Jehoash[a] became king, and he reigned
forty years in Jerusalem. His mother's name
was Zibiah of Beersheba. 2Jehoash did *what*
was right in the sight of the LORD all the days
in which Jehoiada the priest instructed him.
3But the high places were not taken away; the
people still sacrificed and burned incense on
the high places.

4And Jehoash said to the priests, "All the
money of the dedicated gifts that are brought
into the house of the LORD—each man's
census money, each man's assessment money[a]—*and* all the money that a man purposes
in his heart to bring into the house of the
LORD, 5let the priests take *it* themselves, each
from his constituency; and let them repair
the damages of the temple, wherever any di-
lapidation is found."

6Now it was so, by the twenty-third year
of King Jehoash, *that* the priests had not repaired the damages of the temple. 7So King
Jehoash called Jehoiada the priest and the
other priests, and said to them, "Why have
you not repaired the damages of the temple?
Now therefore, do not take *more* money from
your constituency, but deliver it for repairing
the damages of the temple." 8And the priests
agreed that they would neither receive *more*
money from the people, nor repair the damages of the temple.

9Then Jehoiada the priest took a chest,
bored a hole in its lid, and set it beside the
altar, on the right side as one comes into
the house of the LORD; and the priests
who kept the door put there all the money
brought into the house of the LORD. 10So it
was, whenever they saw that *there was* much
money in the chest, that the king's scribe
and the high priest came up and put it in
bags, and counted the money that was found
in the house of the LORD. 11Then they gave
the money, which had been apportioned,
into the hands of those who did the work,
who had the oversight of the house of the
LORD; and they paid it out to the carpenters
and builders who worked on the house of
the LORD, 12and to masons and stonecutters,
and for buying timber and hewn stone, to
repair the damage of the house of the LORD,
and for all that was paid out to repair the
temple. 13However there were not made
for the house of the LORD basins of silver,
trimmers, sprinkling-bowls, trumpets, any
articles of gold or articles of silver, from the
money brought into the house of the LORD.
14But they gave that to the workmen, and
they repaired the house of the LORD with it.
15Moreover they did not require an account
from the men into whose hand they delivered the money to be paid to workmen, for
they dealt faithfully. 16The money from the
trespass offerings and the money from the
sin offerings was not brought into the house
of the LORD. It belonged to the priests.

Hazael Threatens Jerusalem

17Hazael king of Syria went up and fought
against Gath, and took it; then Hazael set
his face to go up to Jerusalem. 18And Jehoash king of Judah took all the sacred things
that his fathers, Jehoshaphat and Jehoram
and Ahaziah, kings of Judah, had dedicated,
and his own sacred things, and all the gold
found in the treasuries of the house of the
LORD and in the king's house, and sent *them*
to Hazael king of Syria. Then he went away
from Jerusalem.

Death of Joash

19Now the rest of the acts of Joash,[a] and
all that he did, *are* they not written in the
book of the chronicles of the kings of Judah?

20And his servants arose and formed a
conspiracy, and killed Joash in the house of
the Millo,[a] which goes down to Silla. 21For
Jozachar[a] the son of Shimeath and Jehozabad the son of Shomer,[b] his servants, struck

12:1 [a] Spelled *Joash* in 11:2ff 12:4 [a] Compare Leviticus 27:2ff 12:19 [a] Spelled *Jehoash* in 12:1ff 12:20 [a] Literally *The Landfill* 12:21 [a] Called *Zabad* in 2 Chronicles 24:26 [b] Called *Shimrith* in 2 Chronicles 24:26

him. So he died, and they buried him with
his fathers in the City of David. Then Amaziah his son reigned in his place.

Jehoahaz Reigns in Israel

13 In the twenty-third year of Joash[a]
the son of Ahaziah, king of Judah,
Jehoahaz the son of Jehu became king over
Israel in Samaria, *and reigned* seventeen
years. 2And he did evil in the sight of the
LORD, and followed the sins of Jeroboam the
son of Nebat, who had made Israel sin. He
did not depart from them.
3Then the anger of the LORD was aroused
against Israel, and He delivered them into
the hand of Hazael king of Syria, and into
the hand of Ben-Hadad the son of Hazael,
all *their* days. 4So Jehoahaz pleaded with the
LORD, and the LORD listened to him; for He
saw the oppression of Israel, because the
king of Syria oppressed them. 5Then the
LORD gave Israel a deliverer, so that they escaped from under the hand of the Syrians;
and the children of Israel dwelt in their tents
as before. 6Nevertheless they did not depart
from the sins of the house of Jeroboam, who
had made Israel sin, *but* walked in them;
and the wooden image[a] also remained in Samaria. 7For He left of the army of Jehoahaz
only fifty horsemen, ten chariots, and ten
thousand foot soldiers; for the king of Syria
had destroyed them and made them like the
dust at threshing.
8Now the rest of the acts of Jehoahaz,
all that he did, and his might, *are* they not
written in the book of the chronicles of the
kings of Israel? 9So Jehoahaz rested with his
fathers, and they buried him in Samaria.
Then Joash his son reigned in his place.

Jehoash Reigns in Israel

10In the thirty-seventh year of Joash
king of Judah, Jehoash[a] the son of Jehoahaz
became king over Israel in Samaria, *and
reigned* sixteen years. 11And he did evil in the
sight of the LORD. He did not depart from all
the sins of Jeroboam the son of Nebat, who
made Israel sin, *but* walked in them.
12Now the rest of the acts of Joash, all that
he did, and his might with which he fought
against Amaziah king of Judah, *are* they not
written in the book of the chronicles of the
kings of Israel? 13So Joash rested with his fathers. Then Jeroboam sat on his throne. And
Joash was buried in Samaria with the kings
of Israel.

Death of Elisha

14Elisha had become sick with the illness
of which he would die. Then Joash the king
of Israel came down to him, and wept over
his face, and said, "O my father, my father,
the chariots of Israel and their horsemen!"
15And Elisha said to him, "Take a bow
and some arrows." So he took himself a bow
and some arrows. 16Then he said to the king
of Israel, "Put your hand on the bow." So he
put his hand *on it,* and Elisha put his hands
on the king's hands. 17And he said, "Open
the east window"; and he opened *it*. Then
Elisha said, "Shoot"; and he shot. And he
said, "The arrow of the LORD's deliverance
and the arrow of deliverance from Syria; for
you must strike the Syrians at Aphek till you
have destroyed *them*." 18Then he said, "Take
the arrows"; so he took *them*. And he said to
the king of Israel, "Strike the ground"; so he
struck three times, and stopped. 19And the
man of God was angry with him, and said,
"You should have struck five or six times;
then you would have struck Syria till you had
destroyed *it!* But now you will strike Syria
only three times."
20Then Elisha died, and they buried him.
And the *raiding* bands from Moab invaded
the land in the spring of the year. 21So it was,
as they were burying a man, that suddenly they spied a band *of raiders;* and they put
the man in the tomb of Elisha; and when the
man was let down and touched the bones of
Elisha, he revived and stood on his feet.

Israel Recaptures Cities from Syria

22And Hazael king of Syria oppressed Israel all the days of Jehoahaz. 23But the LORD
was gracious to them, had compassion on
them, and regarded them, because of His
covenant with Abraham, Isaac, and Jacob,
and would not yet destroy them or cast them
from His presence.
24Now Hazael king of Syria died. Then
Ben-Hadad his son reigned in his place.
25And Jehoash[a] the son of Jehoahaz recaptured from the hand of Ben-Hadad, the son
of Hazael, the cities which he had taken out

13:1 [a] Spelled *Jehoash* in 12:1ff 13:6 [a] Hebrew *Asherah,* a Canaanite goddess 13:10 [a] Spelled *Joash* in verse 9 13:25 [a] Spelled *Joash* in verses 12–14, 25

of the hand of Jehoahaz his father by war.
Three times Joash defeated him and recaptured the cities of Israel.

Amaziah Reigns in Judah

14 In the second year of Joash the son
of Jehoahaz, king of Israel, Amaziah the son of Joash, king of Judah, became
king. 2He was twenty-five years old when he
became king, and he reigned twenty-nine
years in Jerusalem. His mother's name was
Jehoaddan of Jerusalem. 3And he did *what
was* right in the sight of the LORD, yet not like
his father David; he did everything as his
father Joash had done. 4However the high
places were not taken away, and the people
still sacrificed and burned incense on the
high places.

5Now it happened, as soon as the kingdom was established in his hand, that he
executed his servants who had murdered
his father the king. 6But the children of the
murderers he did not execute, according to
what is written in the Book of the Law of Moses, in which the LORD commanded, saying,
"Fathers shall not be put to death for their
children, nor shall children be put to death
for their fathers; but a person shall be put to
death for his own sin."[a]

7He killed ten thousand Edomites in
the Valley of Salt, and took Sela by war, and
called its name Joktheel to this day.

8Then Amaziah sent messengers to Jehoash[a] the son of Jehoahaz, the son of Jehu,
king of Israel, saying, "Come, let us face
one another *in battle.*" 9And Jehoash king of
Israel sent to Amaziah king of Judah, saying, "The thistle that *was* in Lebanon sent
to the cedar that *was* in Lebanon, saying,
'Give your daughter to my son as wife'; and
a wild beast that *was* in Lebanon passed by
and trampled the thistle. 10You have indeed
defeated Edom, and your heart has lifted you
up. Glory *in that,* and stay at home; for why
should you meddle with trouble so that you
fall—you and Judah with you?"

11But Amaziah would not heed. Therefore
Jehoash king of Israel went out; so he and
Amaziah king of Judah faced one another
at Beth Shemesh, which *belongs* to Judah.
12*And Judah was defeated* by Israel, and every man fled to his tent. 13Then Jehoash king
of Israel captured Amaziah king of Judah,
the son of Jehoash, the son of Ahaziah, at
Beth Shemesh; and he went to Jerusalem,
and broke down the wall of Jerusalem from
the Gate of Ephraim to the Corner Gate—
four hundred cubits. 14And he took all the
gold and silver, all the articles that were
found in the house of the LORD and in the
treasuries of the king's house, and hostages,
and returned to Samaria.

15Now the rest of the acts of Jehoash
which he did—his might, and how he fought
with Amaziah king of Judah—*are* they not
written in the book of the chronicles of the
kings of Israel? 16So Jehoash rested with his
fathers, and was buried in Samaria with
the kings of Israel. Then Jeroboam his son
reigned in his place.

17Amaziah the son of Joash, king of Judah, lived fifteen years after the death of
Jehoash the son of Jehoahaz, king of Israel.
18Now the rest of the acts of Amaziah, *are*
they not written in the book of the chronicles
of the kings of Judah? 19And they formed a
conspiracy against him in Jerusalem, and
he fled to Lachish; but they sent after him
to Lachish and killed him there. 20Then they
brought him on horses, and he was buried
at Jerusalem with his fathers in the City of
David.

21And all the people of Judah took Azariah,[a] who *was* sixteen years old, and made
him king instead of his father Amaziah.
22He built Elath and restored it to Judah, after the king rested with his fathers.

Jeroboam II Reigns in Israel

23In the fifteenth year of Amaziah the
son of Joash, king of Judah, Jeroboam the
son of Joash, king of Israel, became king in
Samaria, *and reigned* forty-one years. 24And
he did evil in the sight of the LORD; he did
not depart from all the sins of Jeroboam the
son of Nebat, who had made Israel sin. 25He
restored the territory of Israel from the entrance of Hamath to the Sea of the Arabah,
according to the word of the LORD God of Israel, which He had spoken through His servant Jonah the son of Amittai, the prophet
who *was* from Gath Hepher. 26For the LORD
saw *that* the affliction of Israel *was* very bitter; and whether bond or free, there was no
helper for Israel. 27And the LORD did not say
that He would blot out the name of Israel

14:6 [a] Deuteronomy 24:16 **14:8** [a] Spelled *Joash* in 13:12ff and 2 Chronicles 25:17ff **14:21** [a] Called *Uzziah* in 2 Chronicles 26:1ff, Isaiah 6:1, and elsewhere

from under heaven; but He saved them by
the hand of Jeroboam the son of Joash.
[28]Now the rest of the acts of Jeroboam,
and all that he did—his might, how he made
war, and how he recaptured for Israel, from
Damascus and Hamath, *what had belonged*
to Judah—*are* they not written in the book
of the chronicles of the kings of Israel? [29]So
Jeroboam rested with his fathers, the kings
of Israel. Then Zechariah his son reigned in
his place.

Azariah Reigns in Judah

15 In the twenty-seventh year of Jeroboam king of Israel, Azariah the
son of Amaziah, king of Judah, became
king. [2]He was sixteen years old when he became king, and he reigned fifty-two years in
Jerusalem. His mother's name *was* Jecholiah
of Jerusalem. [3]And he did *what was* right in
the sight of the LORD, according to all that
his father Amaziah had done, [4]except that
the high places were not removed; the people still sacrificed and burned incense on
the high places. [5]Then the LORD struck the
king, so that he was a leper until the day of
his death; so he dwelt in an isolated house.
And Jotham the king's son *was* over the *royal*
house, judging the people of the land.
[6]Now the rest of the acts of Azariah, and
all that he did, *are* they not written in the
book of the chronicles of the kings of Judah?
[7]So Azariah rested with his fathers, and they
buried him with his fathers in the City of
David. Then Jotham his son reigned in his
place.

Zechariah Reigns in Israel

[8]In the thirty-eighth year of Azariah king
of Judah, Zechariah the son of Jeroboam
reigned over Israel in Samaria six months.
[9]And he did evil in the sight of the LORD, as
his fathers had done; he did not depart from
the sins of Jeroboam the son of Nebat, who
had made Israel sin. [10]Then Shallum the son
of Jabesh conspired against him, and struck
and killed him in front of the people; and he
reigned in his place.
[11]Now the rest of the acts of Zechariah,
indeed they *are* written in the book of the
chronicles of the kings of Israel.
[12]This *was* the word of the LORD which
He spoke to Jehu, saying, "Your sons shall
sit on the throne of Israel to the fourth *generation.*"[a] And so it was.

Shallum Reigns in Israel

[13]Shallum the son of Jabesh became king
in the thirty-ninth year of Uzziah[a] king of
Judah; and he reigned a full month in Samaria. [14]For Menahem the son of Gadi
went up from Tirzah, came to Samaria, and
struck Shallum the son of Jabesh in Samaria
and killed him; and he reigned in his place.
[15]Now the rest of the acts of Shallum, and
the conspiracy which he led, indeed they
are written in the book of the chronicles
of the kings of Israel. [16]Then from Tirzah,
Menahem attacked Tiphsah, all who *were*
there, and its territory. Because they did not
surrender, therefore he attacked *it*. All the
women there who were with child he ripped
open.

Menahem Reigns in Israel

[17]In the thirty-ninth year of Azariah king
of Judah, Menahem the son of Gadi became
king over Israel, *and reigned* ten years in Samaria. [18]And he did evil in the sight of the
LORD; he did not depart all his days from
the sins of Jeroboam the son of Nebat, who
had made Israel sin. [19]Pul[a] king of Assyria
came against the land; and Menahem gave
Pul a thousand talents of silver, that his
hand might be with him to strengthen the
kingdom under his control. [20]And Menahem
exacted the money from Israel, from all the
very wealthy, from each man fifty shekels of
silver, to give to the king of Assyria. So the
king of Assyria turned back, and did not stay
there in the land.
[21]Now the rest of the acts of Menahem,
and all that he did, *are* they not written in the
book of the chronicles of the kings of Israel?
[22]So Menahem rested with his fathers. Then
Pekahiah his son reigned in his place.

Pekahiah Reigns in Israel

[23]In the fiftieth year of Azariah king of Judah, Pekahiah the son of Menahem became
king over Israel in Samaria, *and reigned* two
years. [24]And he did evil in the sight of the
LORD; he did not depart from the sins of Jeroboam the son of Nebat, who had made Israel sin. [25]Then Pekah the son of Remaliah,
an officer of his, conspired against him and
killed him in Samaria, in the citadel of the
king's house, along with Argob and Arieh;

15:12 [a] 2 Kings 10:30 **15:13** [a] Called *Azariah* in 14:21ff and 15:1ff **15:19** [a] That is, Tiglath-Pileser III (compare verse 29)

and with him were fifty men of Gilead. He
killed him and reigned in his place.
26Now the rest of the acts of Pekahiah,
and all that he did, indeed they *are* written
in the book of the chronicles of the kings of
Israel.

Pekah Reigns in Israel

27In the fifty-second year of Azariah
king of Judah, Pekah the son of Remaliah
became king over Israel in Samaria, *and*
reigned twenty years. 28And he did evil in the
sight of the LORD; he did not depart from
the sins of Jeroboam the son of Nebat, who
had made Israel sin. 29In the days of Pekah
king of Israel, Tiglath-Pileser king of Assyria came and took Ijon, Abel Beth Maachah,
Janoah, Kedesh, Hazor, Gilead, and Galilee,
all the land of Naphtali; and he carried them
captive to Assyria. 30Then Hoshea the son of
Elah led a conspiracy against Pekah the son
of Remaliah, and struck and killed him; so
he reigned in his place in the twentieth year
of Jotham the son of Uzziah.
31Now the rest of the acts of Pekah, and
all that he did, indeed they *are* written in the
book of the chronicles of the kings of Israel.

Jotham Reigns in Judah

32In the second year of Pekah the son of
Remaliah, king of Israel, Jotham the son of
Uzziah, king of Judah, began to reign. 33He
was twenty-five years old when he became
king, and he reigned sixteen years in Jerusalem. His mother's name *was* Jerusha[a] the
daughter of Zadok. 34And he did *what was*
right in the sight of the LORD; he did according to all that his father Uzziah had done.
35However the high places were not removed;
the people still sacrificed and burned incense on the high places. He built the Upper
Gate of the house of the LORD.
36Now the rest of the acts of Jotham, and
all that he did, *are* they not written in the
book of the chronicles of the kings of Judah?
37In those days the LORD began to send Rezin
king of Syria and Pekah the son of Remaliah
against Judah. 38So Jotham rested with his
fathers, and was buried with his fathers in
the City of David his father. Then Ahaz his
son reigned in his place.

Ahaz Reigns in Judah

16 In the seventeenth year of Pekah
the son of Remaliah, Ahaz the son
of Jotham, king of Judah, began to reign.
2Ahaz *was* twenty years old when he became
king, and he reigned sixteen years in Jerusalem; and he did not do *what was* right in
the sight of the LORD his God, as his father
David *had done*. 3But he walked in the way
of the kings of Israel; indeed he made his
son pass through the fire, according to the
abominations of the nations whom the LORD
had cast out from before the children of Israel. 4And he sacrificed and burned incense
on the high places, on the hills, and under
every green tree.
5Then Rezin king of Syria and Pekah the
son of Remaliah, king of Israel, came up to
Jerusalem to *make* war; and they besieged
Ahaz but could not overcome *him*. 6At that
time Rezin king of Syria captured Elath
for Syria, and drove the men of Judah from
Elath. Then the Edomites[a] went to Elath, and
dwell there to this day.
7So Ahaz sent messengers to Tiglath-
Pileser king of Assyria, saying, "I *am* your
servant and your son. Come up and save
me from the hand of the king of Syria and
from the hand of the king of Israel, who rise
up against me." 8And Ahaz took the silver
and gold that was found in the house of the
LORD, and in the treasuries of the king's
house, and sent *it as* a present to the king of
Assyria. 9So the king of Assyria heeded him;
for the king of Assyria went up against Damascus and took it, carried *its people* captive
to Kir, and killed Rezin.
10Now King Ahaz went to Damascus to
meet Tiglath-Pileser king of Assyria, and
saw an altar that *was* at Damascus; and King
Ahaz sent to Urijah the priest the design
of the altar and its pattern, according to all
its workmanship. 11Then Urijah the priest
built an altar according to all that King
Ahaz had sent from Damascus. So Urijah
the priest made *it* before King Ahaz came
back from Damascus. 12And when the king
came back from Damascus, the king saw
the altar; and the king approached the altar
and made offerings on it. 13So he burned his
burnt offering and his grain offering; and
he poured his drink offering and sprinkled
the blood of his peace offerings on the altar. 14He also brought the bronze altar which
was before the LORD, from the front of the

15:33 [a] Spelled *Jerushah* in 2 Chronicles 27:1 16:6 [a] Some ancient authorities read *Syrians*.

temple—from between the *new* altar and the
house of the LORD—and put it on the north
side of the *new* altar. 15Then King Ahaz commanded Urijah the priest, saying, "On the
great *new* altar burn the morning burnt offering, the evening grain offering, the king's
burnt sacrifice, and his grain offering, with
the burnt offering of all the people of the
land, their grain offering, and their drink offerings; and sprinkle on it all the blood of the
burnt offering and all the blood of the sacrifice. And the bronze altar shall be for me
to inquire *by*." 16Thus did Urijah the priest,
according to all that King Ahaz commanded.
17And King Ahaz cut off the panels of
the carts, and removed the lavers from
them; and he took down the Sea from the
bronze oxen that *were* under it, and put it
on a pavement of stones. 18Also he removed
the Sabbath pavilion which they had built in
the temple, and he removed the king's outer
entrance from the house of the LORD, on account of the king of Assyria.
19Now the rest of the acts of Ahaz which
he did, *are* they not written in the book of the
chronicles of the kings of Judah? 20So Ahaz
rested with his fathers, and was buried with
his fathers in the City of David. Then Hezekiah his son reigned in his place.

Hoshea Reigns in Israel

17 In the twelfth year of Ahaz king
of Judah, Hoshea the son of Elah
became king of Israel in Samaria, *and he
reigned* nine years. 2And he did evil in the
sight of the LORD, but not as the kings of
Israel who were before him. 3Shalmaneser
king of Assyria came up against him; and
Hoshea became his vassal, and paid him
tribute money. 4And the king of Assyria uncovered a conspiracy by Hoshea; for he had
sent messengers to So, king of Egypt, and
brought no tribute to the king of Assyria, as
he had done year by year. Therefore the king
of Assyria shut him up, and bound him in
prison.

Israel Carried Captive to Assyria

5Now the king of Assyria went throughout all the land, and went up to Samaria
and besieged it for three years. 6In the ninth
year of Hoshea, the king of Assyria took Samaria and carried Israel away to Assyria,
and placed them in Halah and by the Habor,
the River of Gozan, and in the cities of the
Medes.
7For so it was that the children of Israel
had sinned against the LORD their God,
who had brought them up out of the land of
Egypt, from under the hand of Pharaoh king
of Egypt; and they had feared other gods,
8and had walked in the statutes of the nations
whom the LORD had cast out from before the
children of Israel, and of the kings of Israel,
which they had made. 9Also the children of
Israel secretly did against the LORD their
God things that *were* not right, and they built
for themselves high places in all their cities,
from watchtower to fortified city. 10They set
up for themselves *sacred* pillars and wooden
images[a] on every high hill and under every
green tree. 11There they burned incense on
all the high places, like the nations whom
the LORD had carried away before them; and
they did wicked things to provoke the LORD
to anger, 12for they served idols, of which the
LORD had said to them, "You shall not do
this thing."
13Yet the LORD testified against Israel
and against Judah, by all of His prophets,
every seer, saying, "Turn from your evil
ways, and keep My commandments *and*
My statutes, according to all the law which I
commanded your fathers, and which I sent
to you by My servants the prophets." 14Nev-
ertheless they would not hear, but stiffened
their necks, like the necks of their fathers,
who did not believe in the LORD their God.
15And they rejected His statutes and His covenant that He had made with their fathers,
and His testimonies which He had testified
against them; they followed idols, became
idolaters, and *went* after the nations who
were all around them, *concerning* whom the
LORD had charged them that they should
not do like them. 16So they left all the commandments of the LORD their God, made for
themselves a molded image *and* two calves,
made a wooden image and worshiped all
the host of heaven, and served Baal. 17And
they caused their sons and daughters to
pass through the fire, practiced witchcraft
and soothsaying, and sold themselves to
do evil in the sight of the LORD, to provoke
Him to anger. 18Therefore the LORD was very
angry with Israel, and removed them from

17:10 [a] Hebrew *Asherim,* Canaanite deities

His sight; there was none left but the tribe
of Judah alone.

19 Also Judah did not keep the commandments of the LORD their God, but walked
in the statutes of Israel which they made.
20 And the LORD rejected all the descendants
of Israel, afflicted them, and delivered them
into the hand of plunderers, until He had
cast them from His sight. 21 For He tore Israel from the house of David, and they made
Jeroboam the son of Nebat king. Then Jeroboam drove Israel from following the LORD,
and made them commit a great sin. 22 For the
children of Israel walked in all the sins of
Jeroboam which he did; they did not depart
from them, 23 until the LORD removed Israel
out of His sight, as He had said by all His
servants the prophets. So Israel was carried
away from their own land to Assyria, *as it is*
to this day.

Assyria Resettles Samaria

24 Then the king of Assyria brought *people* from Babylon, Cuthah, Ava, Hamath,
and from Sepharvaim, and placed *them* in
the cities of Samaria instead of the children of Israel; and they took possession of
Samaria and dwelt in its cities. 25 And it was

GOD BRINGS AN END TO ISRAEL

READ IT: 2 KINGS 17:5–23

GET IT:

Maybe you've wondered what an entire nation could do so wrong that God would destroy them. Well, here it is: every sin that Israel had committed against God for the last two hundred years is listed here. Basically they did everything that God had told them *not* to do. They broke every rule. They acted like they had never heard of God or known that they were His people. They copied the local customs; worshiped idols and the stars; and practiced child sacrifice, witchcraft, and fortune-telling. And besides that, they were stubborn (that's what "stiffened their necks" [v. 14] means). They refused to listen to the prophets who warned them that God wouldn't tolerate their disobedience. God had put up with their evil long enough. The Assyrians swept in from the north and destroyed the kingdom of Israel.

LIVE IT:

Israel's problem started long, long before this time. When they had first come into Canaan, God had told them over and over and over again, "Remember the rules. Worship Me only. Stay away from the locals. Don't pick up their bad habits." God promised that if they followed those simple rules, they would live happy, peaceful, and good lives. Rules from God and rules in school and society are there to protect us, to make us safe, and to keep us happy. Not having any rules or breaking the rules leads to chaos and unhappiness, and usually somebody gets hurt. When Israel broke the rules, their lives weren't as good as they were supposed to be. God told them to follow the rules and live abundantly. He says that to you, too.

so, at the beginning of their dwelling there,
that they did not fear the LORD; therefore the
LORD sent lions among them, which killed
some of them. 26 So they spoke to the king
of Assyria, saying, "The nations whom you
have removed and placed in the cities of Samaria do not know the rituals of the God of
the land; therefore He has sent lions among
them, and indeed, they are killing them
because they do not know the rituals of the
God of the land." 27 Then the king of Assyria
commanded, saying, "Send there one of the
priests whom you brought from there; let
him go and dwell there, and let him teach
them the rituals of the God of the land."
28 Then one of the priests whom they had
carried away from Samaria came and dwelt
in Bethel, and taught them how they should
fear the LORD.

29 However every nation continued to
make gods of its own, and put *them* in the
shrines on the high places which the Samaritans had made, *every* nation in the
cities where they dwelt. 30 The men of Babylon made Succoth Benoth, the men of Cuth
made Nergal, the men of Hamath made
Ashima, 31 and the Avites made Nibhaz
and Tartak; and the Sepharvites burned
their children in fire to Adrammelech and
Anammelech, the gods of Sepharvaim. 32 So
they feared the LORD, and from every class
they appointed for themselves priests of the
high places, who sacrificed for them in the
shrines of the high places. 33 They feared the
LORD, yet served their own gods—according
to the rituals of the nations from among
whom they were carried away.

34 To this day they continue practicing the
former rituals; they do not fear the LORD,
nor do they follow their statutes or their
ordinances, or the law and commandment
which the LORD had commanded the children of Jacob, whom He named Israel, 35 with
whom the LORD had made a covenant and
charged them, saying: "You shall not fear
other gods, nor bow down to them nor serve
them nor sacrifice to them; 36 but the LORD,
who brought you up from the land of Egypt
with great power and an outstretched arm,
Him you shall fear, Him you shall worship,
and to Him you shall offer sacrifice. 37 And
the statutes, the ordinances, the law, and the
commandment which He wrote for you, you
shall be careful to observe forever; you shall
not fear other gods. 38 And the covenant
that I have made with you, you shall not
forget, nor shall you fear other gods. 39 But
the LORD your God you shall fear; and He
will deliver you from the hand of all your
enemies." 40 However they did not obey,
but they followed their former rituals. 41 So
these nations feared the LORD, yet served
their carved images; also their children and
their children's children have continued doing as their fathers did, even to this day.

Hezekiah Reigns in Judah

18 Now it came to pass in the third year
of Hoshea the son of Elah, king of
Israel, *that* Hezekiah the son of Ahaz, king
of Judah, began to reign. 2 He was twenty-
five years old when he became king, and
he reigned twenty-nine years in Jerusalem.
His mother's name *was* Abi[a] the daughter of
Zechariah. 3 And he did *what was* right in the
sight of the LORD, according to all that his
father David had done.

4 He removed the high places and broke
the *sacred* pillars, cut down the wooden image[a] and broke in pieces the bronze serpent
that Moses had made; for until those days
the children of Israel burned incense to it,
and called it Nehushtan.[b] 5 He trusted in the
LORD God of Israel, so that after him was
none like him among all the kings of Judah,
nor who were before him. 6 For he held fast to
the LORD; he did not depart from following
Him, but kept His commandments, which
the LORD had commanded Moses. 7 The
LORD was with him; he prospered wherever
he went. And he rebelled against the king of
Assyria and did not serve him. 8 He subdued
the Philistines, as far as Gaza and its territory, from watchtower to fortified city.

9 Now it came to pass in the fourth year
of King Hezekiah, which *was* the seventh
year of Hoshea the son of Elah, king of Israel, *that* Shalmaneser king of Assyria came
up against Samaria and besieged it. 10 And
at the end of three years they took it. In the
sixth year of Hezekiah, that *is,* the ninth
year of Hoshea king of Israel, Samaria was
taken. 11 Then the king of Assyria carried Israel away captive to Assyria, and put them
in Halah and by the Habor, the River of Gozan, and in the cities of the Medes, 12 because

---

18:2 [a] Called *Abijah* in 2 Chronicles 29:1ff 18:4 [a] Hebrew *Asherah,* a Canaanite goddess [b] Literally *Bronze Thing*

they did not obey the voice of the LORD their
God, but transgressed His covenant *and* all
that Moses the servant of the LORD had commanded; and they would neither hear nor do
them.
13And in the fourteenth year of King
Hezekiah, Sennacherib king of Assyria
came up against all the fortified cities of Judah and took them. 14Then Hezekiah king of
Judah sent to the king of Assyria at Lachish,
saying, "I have done wrong; turn away from
me; whatever you impose on me I will pay."
And the king of Assyria assessed Hezekiah
king of Judah three hundred talents of silver and thirty talents of gold. 15So Hezekiah
gave *him* all the silver that was found in the
house of the LORD and in the treasuries of
the king's house. 16At that time Hezekiah
stripped *the gold from* the doors of the temple of the LORD, and *from* the pillars which
Hezekiah king of Judah had overlaid, and
gave it to the king of Assyria.

Sennacherib Boasts Against the LORD

17Then the king of Assyria sent *the* Tartan,[a] *the* Rabsaris,[b] *and the* Rabshakeh[c]
from Lachish, with a great army against
Jerusalem, to King Hezekiah. And they
went up and came to Jerusalem. When they
had come up, they went and stood by the
aqueduct from the upper pool, which *was*
on the highway to the Fuller's Field. 18And
when they had called to the king, Eliakim
the son of Hilkiah, who *was* over the household, Shebna the scribe, and Joah the son
of Asaph, the recorder, came out to them.
19Then *the* Rabshakeh said to them, "Say
now to Hezekiah, 'Thus says the great king,
the king of Assyria: "What confidence *is* this
in which you trust? 20You speak of *having*
plans and power for war; but *they are* mere
words. And in whom do you trust, that you
rebel against me? 21Now look! You are trusting in the staff of this broken reed, Egypt, on
which if a man leans, it will go into his hand
and pierce it. So *is* Pharaoh king of Egypt to
all who trust in him. 22But if you say to me,
'We trust in the LORD our God,' *is* it not He
whose high places and whose altars Hezekiah has taken away, and said to Judah and Je-
rusalem, 'You shall worship before this altar
in Jerusalem'?"' 23Now therefore, I urge you,
give a pledge to my master the king of Assyria, and I will give you two thousand horses—
if you are able on your part to put riders on
them! 24How then will you repel one captain
of the least of my master's servants, and put
your trust in Egypt for chariots and horsemen? 25Have I now come up without the
LORD against this place to destroy it? The
LORD said to me, 'Go up against this land,
and destroy it.'"
26Then Eliakim the son of Hilkiah, Shebna, and Joah said to *the* Rabshakeh, "Please
speak to your servants in Aramaic, for we
understand *it;* and do not speak to us in Hebrew[a] in the hearing of the people who *are*
on the wall."
27But *the* Rabshakeh said to them, "Has
my master sent me to your master and to
you to speak these words, and not to the men
who sit on the wall, who will eat and drink
their own waste with you?"
28Then *the* Rabshakeh stood and called
out with a loud voice in Hebrew, and spoke,
saying, "Hear the word of the great king, the
king of Assyria! 29Thus says the king: 'Do
not let Hezekiah deceive you, for he shall not
be able to deliver you from his hand; 30nor let
Hezekiah make you trust in the LORD, saying, "The LORD will surely deliver us; this
city shall not be given into the hand of the
king of Assyria."' 31Do not listen to Hezekiah; for thus says the king of Assyria: 'Make
peace with me by a present and come out to
me; and every one of you eat from his own
vine and every one from his own fig tree, and
every one of you drink the waters of his own
cistern; 32until I come and take you away to a
land like your own land, a land of grain and
new wine, a land of bread and vineyards, a
land of olive groves and honey, that you may
live and not die. But do not listen to Hezekiah, lest he persuade you, saying, "The
LORD will deliver us." 33Has any of the gods
of the nations at all delivered its land from
the hand of the king of Assyria? 34Where
are the gods of Hamath and Arpad? Where
are the gods of Sepharvaim and Hena and
Ivah? Indeed, have they delivered Samaria
from my hand? 35Who among all the gods
of the lands have delivered their countries
from my hand, that the LORD should deliver
Jerusalem from my hand?'"
36But the people held their peace and
answered him not a word; for the king's
commandment was, "Do not answer him."

18:17 [a] A title, probably *Commander in Chief* [b] A title, probably *Chief Officer* [c] A title, probably *Chief of Staff* or *Governor* 18:26 [a] Literally *Judean*

37Then Eliakim the son of Hilkiah, who *was*
over the household, Shebna the scribe, and
Joah the son of Asaph, the recorder, came to
Hezekiah with *their* clothes torn, and told
him the words of *the* Rabshakeh.

Isaiah Assures Deliverance

19 And so it was, when King Hezekiah heard *it,* that he tore his clothes,
covered himself with sackcloth, and went
into the house of the LORD. 2Then he sent
Eliakim, who *was* over the household, Shebna the scribe, and the elders of the priests,
covered with sackcloth, to Isaiah the prophet, the son of Amoz. 3And they said to him,
"Thus says Hezekiah: 'This day *is* a day of
trouble, and rebuke, and blasphemy; for the
children have come to birth, but *there is* no
strength to bring them forth. 4It may be that
the LORD your God will hear all the words of
the Rabshakeh, whom his master the king of
Assyria has sent to reproach the living God,
and will rebuke the words which the LORD
your God has heard. Therefore lift up *your*
prayer for the remnant that is left.' "
5So the servants of King Hezekiah came
to Isaiah. 6And Isaiah said to them, "Thus
you shall say to your master, 'Thus says the
LORD: "Do not be afraid of the words which
you have heard, with which the servants of
the king of Assyria have blasphemed Me.
7Surely I will send a spirit upon him, and
he shall hear a rumor and return to his
own land; and I will cause him to fall by the
sword in his own land." ' "

Sennacherib's Threat and Hezekiah's Prayer

8Then *the* Rabshakeh returned and
found the king of Assyria warring against
Libnah, for he heard that he had departed
from Lachish. 9And the king heard concerning Tirhakah king of Ethiopia, "Look,
he has come out to make war with you."
So he again sent messengers to Hezekiah,
saying, 10"Thus you shall speak to Hezekiah
king of Judah, saying: 'Do not let your God
in whom you trust deceive you, saying, "Jerusalem shall not be given into the hand of
the king of Assyria." 11Look! You have heard
what the kings of Assyria have done to all
lands by utterly destroying them; and shall
you be delivered? 12Have the gods of the nations delivered those whom my fathers have
destroyed, Gozan and Haran and Rezeph,
and the people of Eden who *were* in Telassar?

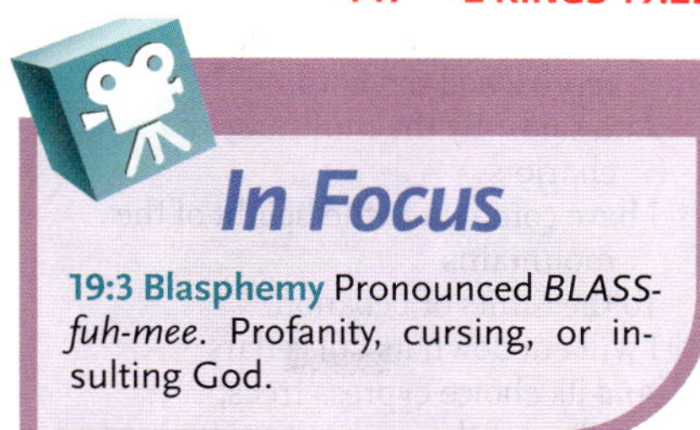

19:3 Blasphemy Pronounced *BLASS-fuh-mee.* Profanity, cursing, or insulting God.

13Where *is* the king of Hamath, the king of
Arpad, and the king of the city of Sepharvaim, Hena, and Ivah?' "
14And Hezekiah received the letter from
the hand of the messengers, and read it;
and Hezekiah went up to the house of the
LORD, and spread it before the LORD. 15Then
Hezekiah prayed before the LORD, and said:
"O LORD God of Israel, *the One* who dwells
between the cherubim, You are God, You
alone, of all the kingdoms of the earth. You
have made heaven and earth. 16Incline Your
ear, O LORD, and hear; open Your eyes, O
LORD, and see; and hear the words of Sennacherib, which he has sent to reproach the
living God. 17Truly, LORD, the kings of Assyria have laid waste the nations and their
lands, 18and have cast their gods into the fire;
for they *were* not gods, but the work of men's
hands—wood and stone. Therefore they destroyed them. 19Now therefore, O LORD our
God, I pray, save us from his hand, that all
the kingdoms of the earth may know that
You *are* the LORD God, You alone."

The Word of the LORD Concerning Sennacherib

20Then Isaiah the son of Amoz sent to
Hezekiah, saying, "Thus says the LORD God
of Israel: 'Because you have prayed to Me
against Sennacherib king of Assyria, I have
heard.' 21This *is* the word which the LORD has
spoken concerning him:

'The virgin, the daughter of Zion,
Has despised you, laughed you to scorn;
The daughter of Jerusalem
Has shaken *her* head behind your back!

22 'Whom have you reproached and
blasphemed?
Against whom have you raised *your*
voice,
And lifted up your eyes on high?
Against the Holy *One* of Israel.

23 By your messengers you have
reproached the Lord,
And said: "By the multitude of my
chariots
I have come up to the height of the
mountains,
To the limits of Lebanon;
I will cut down its tall cedars
And its choice cypress trees;
I will enter the extremity of its borders,
To its fruitful forest.
24 I have dug and drunk strange water,
And with the soles of my feet I have
dried up
All the brooks of defense."

25 'Did you not hear long ago
How I made it,
From ancient times that I formed it?
Now I have brought it to pass,
That you should be
For crushing fortified cities *into* heaps
of ruins.
26 Therefore their inhabitants had little
power;
They were dismayed and confounded;
They were *as* the grass of the field
And the green herb,
As the grass on the housetops
And *grain* blighted before it is grown.

27 'But I know your dwelling place,
Your going out and your coming in,
And your rage against Me.
28 Because your rage against Me and your
tumult
Have come up to My ears,
Therefore I will put My hook in your
nose
And My bridle in your lips,
And I will turn you back
By the way which you came.

29 'This *shall be* a sign to you:

'You shall eat this year such as grows of
itself,
And in the second year what springs
from the same;
Also in the third year sow and reap,
Plant vineyards and eat the fruit of
them.
30 *And the remnant who have* escaped of
the house of Judah
Shall again take root downward,
And bear fruit upward.
31 For out of Jerusalem shall go a remnant,
And those who escape from Mount
Zion.
The zeal of the LORD of hosts[a] will do
this.'

32 "Therefore thus says the LORD concerning the king of Assyria:

'He shall not come into this city,
Nor shoot an arrow there,
Nor come before it with shield,
Nor build a siege mound against it.
33 By the way that he came,
By the same shall he return;
And he shall not come into this city,'
Says the LORD.
34 'For I will defend this city, to save it
For My own sake and for My servant
David's sake.'"

Sennacherib's Defeat and Death

35 And it came to pass on a certain night
that the angel[a] of the LORD went out, and
killed in the camp of the Assyrians one hundred and eighty-five thousand; and when
people arose early in the morning, there
were the corpses—all dead. 36 So Sennacherib king of Assyria departed and went away,
returned *home,* and remained at Nineveh.
37 Now it came to pass, as he was worshiping
in the temple of Nisroch his god, that his
sons Adrammelech and Sharezer struck
him down with the sword; and they escaped
into the land of Ararat. Then Esarhaddon his
son reigned in his place.

Hezekiah's Life Extended

20 In those days Hezekiah was sick
and near death. And Isaiah the
prophet, the son of Amoz, went to him and
said to him, "Thus says the LORD: 'Set your
house in order, for you shall die, and not
live.'"

2 Then he turned his face toward the wall,
and prayed to the LORD, saying, 3 "Remember
now, O LORD, I pray, how I have walked before You in truth and with a loyal heart, and
have done *what was* good in Your sight." And
Hezekiah wept bitterly.

4 And it happened, before Isaiah had gone
out into the middle court, that the word of
the LORD came to him, saying, 5 "Return and
tell Hezekiah the leader of My people, 'Thus

19:31 [a] Following many Hebrew manuscripts and ancient versions (compare Isaiah 37:32); Masoretic Text omits *of hosts.* **19:35** [a] Or *Angel*

says the LORD, the God of David your father:
"I have heard your prayer, I have seen your
tears; surely I will heal you. On the third day
you shall go up to the house of the LORD.
6And I will add to your days fifteen years. I
will deliver you and this city from the hand
of the king of Assyria; and I will defend this
city for My own sake, and for the sake of My
servant David."'"

7Then Isaiah said, "Take a lump of figs."
So they took and laid *it* on the boil, and he
recovered.

8And Hezekiah said to Isaiah, "What *is*
the sign that the LORD will heal me, and that
I shall go up to the house of the LORD the
third day?"

9Then Isaiah said, "This is the sign to
you from the LORD, that the LORD will do the
thing which He has spoken: *shall* the shadow go forward ten degrees or go backward
ten degrees?"

10And Hezekiah answered, "It is an easy
thing for the shadow to go down ten degrees; no, but let the shadow go backward
ten degrees."

11So Isaiah the prophet cried out to the
LORD, and He brought the shadow ten degrees backward, by which it had gone down
on the sundial of Ahaz.

The Babylonian Envoys

12At that time Berodach-Baladan[a] the
son of Baladan, king of Babylon, sent letters
and a present to Hezekiah, for he heard that
Hezekiah had been sick. 13And Hezekiah
was attentive to them, and showed them all
the house of his treasures—the silver and
gold, the spices and precious ointment, and
all[a] his armory—all that was found among
his treasures. There was nothing in his
house or in all his dominion that Hezekiah
did not show them.

14Then Isaiah the prophet went to King
Hezekiah, and said to him, "What did these
men say, and from where did they come to
you?"

So Hezekiah said, "They came from a far
country, from Babylon."

15And he said, "What have they seen in
your house?"

So Hezekiah answered, "They have seen
all that *is* in my house; there is nothing
among my treasures that I have not shown
them."

16Then Isaiah said to Hezekiah, "Hear

20:12 [a] Spelled *Merodach-Baladan* in Isaiah 39:1
20:13 [a] Following many Hebrew manuscripts, Syriac, and Targum; Masoretic Text omits *all.*

PRAYER

READ IT: 2 KINGS 20:1–11

Our prayers won't always be answered with miraculous signs and fifteen more years of life, but God hears our prayers just as He heard Hezekiah's.

- *Turn to God when you're hurting.* He hears you.
- *Believe that God can answer your prayers.* You are talking to *the giver of life.*
- *Understand that God's answer isn't always yes.* He knows what's best; trust Him to do it.
- *Share your prayers with others.* Ask friends and family to pray for the same things.
- *Write down prayers.* Keeping a prayer journal can be life-changing—try it!

the word of the LORD: 17'Behold, the days are
coming when all that *is* in your house, and
what your fathers have accumulated until
this day, shall be carried to Babylon; nothing shall be left,' says the LORD. 18'And they
shall take away some of your sons who will
descend from you, whom you will beget; and
they shall be eunuchs in the palace of the
king of Babylon.'"

19So Hezekiah said to Isaiah, "The word
of the LORD which you have spoken *is* good!"
For he said, "Will there not be peace and
truth at least in my days?"

Death of Hezekiah

20Now the rest of the acts of Hezekiah—
all his might, and how he made a pool and a
tunnel and brought water into the city—*are*
they not written in the book of the chronicles
of the kings of Judah? 21So Hezekiah rested
with his fathers. Then Manasseh his son
reigned in his place.

Manasseh Reigns in Judah

21 Manasseh *was* twelve years old
when he became king, and he
reigned fifty-five years in Jerusalem. His
mother's name *was* Hephzibah. 2And he did
evil in the sight of the LORD, according to
the abominations of the nations whom the
LORD had cast out before the children of Israel. 3For he rebuilt the high places which
Hezekiah his father had destroyed; he raised
up altars for Baal, and made a wooden image,[a] as Ahab king of Israel had done; and he
worshiped all the host of heaven[b] and served
them. 4He also built altars in the house of
the LORD, of which the LORD had said, "In
Jerusalem I will put My name." 5And he
built altars for all the host of heaven in the
two courts of the house of the LORD. 6Also
he made his son pass through the fire, practiced soothsaying, used witchcraft, and consulted spiritists and mediums. He did much
evil in the sight of the LORD, to provoke *Him*
to anger. 7He even set a carved image of
Asherah[a] that he had made, in the house
of which the LORD had said to David and to
Solomon his son, "In this house and in Jerusalem, which I have chosen out of all the
tribes of Israel, I will put My name forever;
8and I will not make the feet of Israel wander
anymore from the land which I gave their
fathers—only if they are careful to do according to all that I have commanded them,
and according to all the law that My servant
Moses commanded them." 9But they paid no
attention, and Manasseh seduced them to do
more evil than the nations whom the LORD
had destroyed before the children of Israel.

10And the LORD spoke by His servants the
prophets, saying, 11"Because Manasseh king
of Judah has done these abominations (he
has acted more wickedly than all the Amorites who *were* before him, and has also
made Judah sin with his idols), 12therefore
thus says the LORD God of Israel: 'Behold, *I*
am bringing *such* calamity upon Jerusalem
and Judah, that whoever hears of it, both his
ears will tingle. 13And I will stretch over Jerusalem the measuring line of Samaria and
the plummet of the house of Ahab; I will
wipe Jerusalem as *one* wipes a dish, wiping
it and turning *it* upside down. 14So I will
forsake the remnant of My inheritance and
deliver them into the hand of their enemies;
and they shall become victims of plunder to
all their enemies, 15because they have done
evil in My sight, and have provoked Me to
anger since the day their fathers came out of
Egypt, even to this day.'"

16Moreover Manasseh shed very much
innocent blood, till he had filled Jerusalem
from one end to another, besides his sin by
which he made Judah sin, in doing evil in
the sight of the LORD.

17Now the rest of the acts of Manasseh—
all that he did, and the sin that he
committed—*are* they not written in the book
of the chronicles of the kings of Judah? 18So
Manasseh rested with his fathers, and was
buried in the garden of his own house, in the
garden of Uzza. Then his son Amon reigned
in his place.

Amon's Reign and Death

19Amon *was* twenty-two years old when
he became king, and he reigned two years
in Jerusalem. His mother's name *was* Me-
shullemeth the daughter of Haruz of Jotbah.
20And he did evil in the sight of the LORD,
as his father Manasseh had done. 21So he
walked in all the ways that his father had
walked; and he served the idols that his father had served, and worshiped them. 22He
forsook the LORD God of his fathers, and did
not walk in the way of the LORD.

21:3 [a] Hebrew *Asherah,* a Canaanite goddess [b] The gods of the Assyrians 21:7 [a] A Canaanite goddess

23Then the servants of Amon conspired
against him, and killed the king in his own
house. 24But the people of the land executed
all those who had conspired against King
Amon. Then the people of the land made
his son Josiah king in his place.
25Now the rest of the acts of Amon which
he did, *are* they not written in the book of
the chronicles of the kings of Judah? 26And
he was buried in his tomb in the garden of
Uzza. Then Josiah his son reigned in his
place.

Josiah Reigns in Judah

22 Josiah *was* eight years old when
he became king, and he reigned
thirty-one years in Jerusalem. His mother's
name *was* Jedidah the daughter of Adaiah of
Bozkath. 2And he did *what was* right in the
sight of the LORD, and walked in all the ways
of his father David; he did not turn aside to
the right hand or to the left.

Hilkiah Finds the Book of the Law

3Now it came to pass, in the eighteenth
year of King Josiah, *that* the king sent
Shaphan the scribe, the son of Azaliah,
the son of Meshullam, to the house of the
LORD, saying: 4"Go up to Hilkiah the high
priest, that he may count the money which
has been brought into the house of the LORD,
which the doorkeepers have gathered from

SUCCESS

BURYING SUCCESS

READ IT: 2 KINGS 22:1–20

GET IT:

The temple was falling apart because the kings of Judah had neglected it when they worshiped other gods for over fifty years. King Josiah was a young man, probably around twenty-six years old, when he decided to have the temple rebuilt. While the workers were starting their repair work, in the ruins of the temple they found a book. It was the Book of the Law, written by Moses himself. The book had probably been buried under a paving stone in the temple to hide it from people who wanted to destroy all copies of the Law. But it had long since been forgotten, even by the priests who were supposed to be teaching from it! Now that God's Word was in King Josiah's hands, he realized the Law was the foundation for the people's relationship with God. Josiah uncovered the truth and brought it out into the light of day.

LIVE IT:

We're not all that different from those temple priests who forgot about the truth buried somewhere deep in the temple. How often do we know the words and lessons of the Bible but bury them down deep? We hide them. We don't want them to be a part of our lives, and then we wonder where God went. Unearth that wisdom. Take it out of that dark place and read it again. This is the foundation for your life. This is wisdom and the secret of success.

the people. 5And let them deliver it into the
hand of those doing the work, who are the
overseers in the house of the LORD; let them
give it to those who *are* in the house of the
LORD doing the work, to repair the damages
of the house— 6to carpenters and builders
and masons—and to buy timber and hewn
stone to repair the house. 7However there
need be no accounting made with them of
the money delivered into their hand, because they deal faithfully."

8Then Hilkiah the high priest said to
Shaphan the scribe, "I have found the Book
of the Law in the house of the LORD." And
Hilkiah gave the book to Shaphan, and he
read it. 9So Shaphan the scribe went to the
king, bringing the king word, saying, "Your
servants have gathered the money that was
found in the house, and have delivered it
into the hand of those who do the work,
who oversee the house of the LORD." 10Then
Shaphan the scribe showed the king, saying,
"Hilkiah the priest has given me a book."
And Shaphan read it before the king.

11Now it happened, when the king heard
the words of the Book of the Law, that he
tore his clothes. 12Then the king commanded Hilkiah the priest, Ahikam the son of
Shaphan, Achbor[a] the son of Michaiah,
Shaphan the scribe, and Asaiah a servant of
the king, saying, 13"Go, inquire of the LORD
for me, for the people and for all Judah, concerning the words of this book that has been
found; for great *is* the wrath of the LORD that
is aroused against us, because our fathers
have not obeyed the words of this book, to
do according to all that is written concerning us."

14So Hilkiah the priest, Ahikam, Achbor, Shaphan, and Asaiah went to Huldah
the prophetess, the wife of Shallum the son
of Tikvah, the son of Harhas, keeper of the
wardrobe. (She dwelt in Jerusalem in the
Second Quarter.) And they spoke with her.
15Then she said to them, "Thus says the
LORD God of Israel, 'Tell the man who sent
you to Me, 16"Thus says the LORD: 'Behold, I
will bring calamity on this place and on its
inhabitants—all the words of the book which
the king of Judah has read— 17because they
have forsaken Me and burned incense to
other gods, that they might provoke Me
to anger with all the works of their hands.
Therefore My wrath shall be aroused against
this place and shall not be quenched.'"' 18But
as for the king of Judah, who sent you to inquire of the LORD, in this manner you shall
speak to him, 'Thus says the LORD God of
Israel: "*Concerning* the words which you have
heard— 19because your heart was tender,
and you humbled yourself before the LORD
when you heard what I spoke against this
place and against its inhabitants, that they
would become a desolation and a curse, and
you tore your clothes and wept before Me, I
also have heard *you*," says the LORD. 20"Surely, therefore, I will gather you to your fathers,
and you shall be gathered to your grave in
peace; and your eyes shall not see all the calamity which I will bring on this place."'" So
they brought back word to the king.

Josiah Restores True Worship

23 Now the king sent them to gather
all the elders of Judah and Jerusalem to him. 2The king went up to the house
of the LORD with all the men of Judah, and
with him all the inhabitants of Jerusalem—
the priests and the prophets and all the
people, both small and great. And he read
in their hearing all the words of the Book of
the Covenant which had been found in the
house of the LORD.

3Then the king stood by a pillar and
made a covenant before the LORD, to follow
the LORD and to keep His commandments
and His testimonies and His statutes, with
all *his* heart and all *his* soul, to perform the
words of this covenant that were written in
this book. And all the people took a stand
for the covenant. 4And the king commanded Hilkiah the high priest, the priests of
the second order, and the doorkeepers, to
bring out of the temple of the LORD all the
articles that were made for Baal, for Asherah,[a] and for all the host of heaven;[b] and he
burned them outside Jerusalem in the fields
of Kidron, and carried their ashes to Bethel. 5Then he removed the idolatrous priests
whom the kings of Judah had ordained to
burn incense on the high places in the cities of Judah and in the places all around Jerusalem, and those who burned incense to
Baal, to the sun, to the moon, to the constellations, and to all the host of heaven. 6And
he brought out the wooden image[a] from
the house of the LORD, to the Brook Kidron

22:12 [a] *Abdon the son of Micah* in 2 Chronicles 34:20
23:4 [a] A Canaanite goddess [b] The gods of the Assyrians
23:6 [a] Hebrew *Asherah,* a Canaanite goddess

outside Jerusalem, burned it at the Brook
Kidron and ground *it* to ashes, and threw its
ashes on the graves of the common people.
7Then he tore down the *ritual* booths of the
perverted persons[a] that *were* in the house of
the LORD, where the women wove hangings
for the wooden image. 8And he brought all
the priests from the cities of Judah, and defiled the high places where the priests had
burned incense, from Geba to Beersheba;
also he broke down the high places at the
gates which *were* at the entrance of the Gate
of Joshua the governor of the city, which *were*
to the left of the city gate. 9Nevertheless the
priests of the high places did not come up to
the altar of the LORD in Jerusalem, but they
ate unleavened bread among their brethren.
10And he defiled Topheth, which *is* in
the Valley of the Son[a] of Hinnom, that no
man might make his son or his daughter
pass through the fire to Molech. 11Then he
removed the horses that the kings of Judah
had dedicated to the sun, at the entrance to
the house of the LORD, by the chamber of
Nathan-Melech, the officer who *was* in the
court; and he burned the chariots of the sun
with fire. 12The altars that *were* on the roof,
the upper chamber of Ahaz, which the kings
of Judah had made, and the altars which Manasseh had made in the two courts of the
house of the LORD, the king broke down and
pulverized there, and threw their dust into
the Brook Kidron. 13Then the king defiled
the high places that *were* east of Jerusalem,
which *were* on the south of the Mount of Corruption, which Solomon king of Israel had
built for Ashtoreth the abomination of the
Sidonians, for Chemosh the abomination of
the Moabites, and for Milcom the abomination of the people of Ammon. 14And he broke
in pieces the *sacred* pillars and cut down the
wooden images, and filled their places with
the bones of men.
15Moreover the altar that *was* at Bethel,
and the high place which Jeroboam the son
of Nebat, who made Israel sin, had made,
both that altar and the high place he broke
down; and he burned the high place *and*
crushed *it* to powder, and burned the wood-
en image. 16As Josiah turned, he saw the
tombs that *were* there on the mountain. And
he sent and took the bones out of the tombs
and burned *them* on the altar, and defiled it
according to the word of the LORD which the
man of God proclaimed, who proclaimed
these words. 17Then he said, "What grave-
stone *is* this that I see?"

So the men of the city told him, "*It is* the
tomb of the man of God who came from Judah and proclaimed these things which you
have done against the altar of Bethel."
18And he said, "Let him alone; let no one
move his bones." So they let his bones alone,
with the bones of the prophet who came
from Samaria.
19Now Josiah also took away all the
shrines of the high places that *were* in the
cities of Samaria, which the kings of Israel
had made to provoke the LORD[a] to anger; and
he did to them according to all the deeds he
had done in Bethel. 20He executed all the
priests of the high places who *were* there, on
the altars, and burned men's bones on them;
and he returned to Jerusalem.
21Then the king commanded all the people, saying, "Keep the Passover to the LORD
your God, as *it is* written in this Book of the
Covenant." 22Such a Passover surely had never been held since the days of the judges who
judged Israel, nor in all the days of the kings
of Israel and the kings of Judah. 23But in the
eighteenth year of King Josiah this Passover
was held before the LORD in Jerusalem.
24Moreover Josiah put away those who consulted mediums and spiritists, the household gods and idols, all the abominations
that were seen in the land of Judah and in
Jerusalem, that he might perform the words
of the law which were written in the book
that Hilkiah the priest found in the house
of the LORD. 25Now before him there was no
king like him, who turned to the LORD with
all his heart, with all his soul, and with all
his might, according to all the Law of Moses;
nor after him did *any* arise like him.

Impending Judgment on Judah

26Nevertheless the LORD did not turn
from the fierceness of His great wrath, with
which His anger was aroused against Judah,
because of all the provocations with which
Manasseh had provoked Him. 27And the
LORD said, "I will also remove Judah from
My sight, as I have removed Israel, and will
cast off this city Jerusalem which I have

23:7 [a] Hebrew *qedeshim,* that is, those practicing sodomy and prostitution in religious rituals **23:10** [a] Kethib reads *Sons.* **23:19** [a] Following Septuagint, Syriac, and Vulgate; Masoretic Text and Targum omit *the LORD.*

chosen, and the house of which I said, 'My
name shall be there.'"[a]

Josiah Dies in Battle

28Now the rest of the acts of Josiah, and
all that he did, *are* they not written in the
book of the chronicles of the kings of Judah?
29In his days Pharaoh Necho king of Egypt
went to the aid of the king of Assyria, to
the River Euphrates; and King Josiah went
against him. And *Pharaoh Necho* killed him
at Megiddo when he confronted him. 30Then
his servants moved his body in a chariot
from Megiddo, brought him to Jerusalem,
and buried him in his own tomb. And the
people of the land took Jehoahaz the son of
Josiah, anointed him, and made him king in
his father's place.

The Reign and Captivity of Jehoahaz

31Jehoahaz *was* twenty-three years old
when he became king, and he reigned three
months in Jerusalem. His mother's name
was Hamutal the daughter of Jeremiah of
Libnah. 32And he did evil in the sight of the
LORD, according to all that his fathers had
done. 33Now Pharaoh Necho put him in prison at Riblah in the land of Hamath, that he
might not reign in Jerusalem; and he imposed on the land a tribute of one hundred
talents of silver and a talent of gold. 34Then
Pharaoh Necho made Eliakim the son of
Josiah king in place of his father Josiah,
and changed his name to Jehoiakim. And
Pharaoh took Jehoahaz and went to Egypt,
and he[a] died there.

Jehoiakim Reigns in Judah

35So Jehoiakim gave the silver and gold to
Pharaoh; but he taxed the land to give money according to the command of Pharaoh; he
exacted the silver and gold from the people
of the land, from every one according to his
assessment, to give *it* to Pharaoh Necho. 36Je-
hoiakim *was* twenty-five years old when he
became king, and he reigned eleven years in
Jerusalem. His mother's name *was* Zebudah
the daughter of Pedaiah of Rumah. 37And he
did evil in the sight of the LORD, according to
all that his fathers had done.

Judah Overrun by Enemies

24 In his days Nebuchadnezzar
king of Babylon came up, and Jehoiakim became his vassal *for* three years.
Then he turned and rebelled against him.
2And the LORD sent against him *raiding*
bands of Chaldeans, bands of Syrians,
bands of Moabites, and bands of the people
of Ammon; He sent them against Judah to
destroy it, according to the word of the LORD
which He had spoken by His servants the
prophets. 3Surely at the commandment of
the LORD *this* came upon Judah, to remove
them from His sight because of the sins of
Manasseh, according to all that he had done,
4and also because of the innocent blood that
he had shed; for he had filled Jerusalem with
innocent blood, which the LORD would not
pardon.

5Now the rest of the acts of Jehoiakim,
and all that he did, *are* they not written in the
book of the chronicles of the kings of Judah?
6So Jehoiakim rested with his fathers. Then
Jehoiachin his son reigned in his place.

7And the king of Egypt did not come out
of his land anymore, for the king of Babylon
had taken all that belonged to the king of
Egypt from the Brook of Egypt to the River
Euphrates.

The Reign and Captivity of Jehoiachin

8Jehoiachin *was* eighteen years old when
he became king, and he reigned in Jerusalem three months. His mother's name *was*
Nehushta the daughter of Elnathan of Jerusalem. 9And he did evil in the sight of the
LORD, according to all that his father had
done.

10At that time the servants of Nebuchadnezzar king of Babylon came up against
Jerusalem, and the city was besieged. 11And
Nebuchadnezzar king of Babylon came
against the city, as his servants were besieging it. 12Then Jehoiachin king of Judah, his
mother, his servants, his princes, and his
officers went out to the king of Babylon; and
the king of Babylon, in the eighth year of his
reign, took him prisoner.

The Captivity of Jerusalem

13And he carried out from there all the
treasures of the house of the LORD and the
treasures of the king's house, and he cut
in pieces all the articles of gold which Solomon king of Israel had made in the temple
of the LORD, as the LORD had said. 14Also he
carried into captivity all Jerusalem: all the

23:27 [a] 1 Kings 8:29 **23:34** [a] That is, Jehoahaz

captains and all the mighty men of valor, ten
thousand captives, and all the craftsmen and
smiths. None remained except the poorest
people of the land. 15 And he carried Jehoiachin captive to Babylon. The king's mother,
the king's wives, his officers, and the mighty
of the land he carried into captivity from Jerusalem to Babylon. 16 All the valiant men,
seven thousand, and craftsmen and smiths,
one thousand, all *who were* strong *and* fit for
war, these the king of Babylon brought captive to Babylon.

Zedekiah Reigns in Judah

17 Then the king of Babylon made Mattaniah, *Jehoiachin's*[a] uncle, king in his place,
and changed his name to Zedekiah.

18 Zedekiah *was* twenty-one years old
when he became king, and he reigned elev-
en years in Jerusalem. His mother's name
was Hamutal the daughter of Jeremiah of
Libnah. 19 He also did evil in the sight of the
LORD, according to all that Jehoiakim had
done. 20 For because of the anger of the LORD
this happened in Jerusalem and Judah, that
He finally cast them out from His presence.
Then Zedekiah rebelled against the king of
Babylon.

The Fall and Captivity of Judah

25 Now it came to pass in the ninth
year of his reign, in the tenth
month, on the tenth *day* of the month, *that*
Nebuchadnezzar king of Babylon and all
his army came against Jerusalem and encamped against it; and they built a siege
wall against it all around. 2 So the city was
besieged until the eleventh year of King Zedekiah. 3 By the ninth *day* of the *fourth* month
the famine had become so severe in the city
that there was no food for the people of the
land.

4 Then the city wall was broken through,
and all the men of war *fled* at night by way of
the gate between two walls, which was by the
king's garden, even though the Chaldeans
were still encamped all around against the
city. And *the king*[a] went by way of the plain.[b]
5 But the army of the Chaldeans pursued the
king, and they overtook him in the plains
of Jericho. All his army was scattered from
him. 6 So they took the king and brought
him up to the king of Babylon at Riblah, and
they pronounced judgment on him. 7 Then
they killed the sons of Zedekiah before his
eyes, put out the eyes of Zedekiah, bound
him with bronze fetters, and took him to
Babylon.

8 And in the fifth month, on the seventh
day of the month (which *was* the nineteenth
year of King Nebuchadnezzar king of Babylon), Nebuzaradan the captain of the guard,
a servant of the king of Babylon, came to Jerusalem. 9 He burned the house of the LORD
and the king's house; all the houses of Jerusalem, that is, all the houses of the great, he
burned with fire. 10 And all the army of the
Chaldeans who *were with* the captain of the
guard broke down the walls of Jerusalem all
around.

11 Then Nebuzaradan the captain of the
guard carried away captive the rest of the
people *who* remained in the city and the defectors who had deserted to the king of Babylon, with the rest of the multitude. 12 But the
captain of the guard left *some* of the poor of
the land as vinedressers and farmers. 13 The
bronze pillars that *were* in the house of the
LORD, and the carts and the bronze Sea that
were in the house of the LORD, the Chaldeans
broke in pieces, and carried their bronze to
Babylon. 14 They also took away the pots, the
shovels, the trimmers, the spoons, and all
the bronze utensils with which the priests
ministered. 15 The firepans and the basins,
the things of solid gold and solid silver, the
captain of the guard took away. 16 The two
pillars, one Sea, and the carts, which Solomon had made for the house of the LORD,
the bronze of all these articles was beyond
measure. 17 The height of one pillar *was*
eighteen cubits, and the capital on it *was* of
bronze. The height of the capital was three
cubits, and the network and pomegranates
all around the capital were all of bronze. The
second pillar was the same, with a network.

18 And the captain of the guard took Seraiah the chief priest, Zephaniah the second
priest, and the three doorkeepers. 19 He also
took out of the city an officer who had charge
of the men of war, five men of the king's
close associates who were found in the city,
the chief recruiting officer of the army, who
mustered the people of the land, and sixty
men of the people of the land *who were* found
in the city. 20 So Nebuzaradan, captain of the
guard, took these and brought them to the

24:17 [a] Literally *his* 25:4 [a] Literally *he* [b] Or *Arabah*, that is, the Jordan Valley

king of Babylon at Riblah. 21Then the king of
Babylon struck them and put them to death
at Riblah in the land of Hamath. Thus Judah
was carried away captive from its own land.

Gedaliah Made Governor of Judah

22Then he made Gedaliah the son of
Ahikam, the son of Shaphan, governor over
the people who remained in the land of Judah, whom Nebuchadnezzar king of Babylon had left. 23Now when all the captains of
the armies, they and *their* men, heard that
the king of Babylon had made Gedaliah governor, they came to Gedaliah at Mizpah—
Ishmael the son of Nethaniah, Johanan the
son of Careah, Seraiah the son of Tanhumeth the Netophathite, and Jaazaniah[a] the
son of a Maachathite, they and their men.
24And Gedaliah took an oath before them
and their men, and said to them, "Do not
be afraid of the servants of the Chaldeans.
Dwell in the land and serve the king of Babylon, and it shall be well with you."
25But it happened in the seventh month
that Ishmael the son of Nethaniah, the son
of Elishama, of the royal family, came with
ten men and struck and killed Gedaliah,
the Jews, as well as the Chaldeans who were
with him at Mizpah. 26And all the people,
small and great, and the captains of the
armies, arose and went to Egypt; for they
were afraid of the Chaldeans.

Jehoiachin Released from Prison

27Now it came to pass in the thirty-
seventh year of the captivity of Jehoiachin
king of Judah, in the twelfth month, on the
twenty-seventh *day* of the month, *that* Evil-
Merodach[a] king of Babylon, in the year that
he began to reign, released Jehoiachin king
of Judah from prison. 28He spoke kindly to
him, and gave him a more prominent seat
than those of the kings who *were* with him in
Babylon. 29So Jehoiachin changed from his
prison garments, and he ate bread regularly
before the king all the days of his life. 30And
as for his provisions, *there was* a regular
ration given him by the king, a portion for
each day, all the days of his life.

25:23 [a] Spelled *Jezaniah* in Jeremiah 40:8 25:27 [a] Literally *Man of Marduk*

Epic Ideas

25:21 THE EMPIRE OF BABYLONIA

You must remember that Abraham, the father of the Jews, came from Babylonia, sometimes called Chaldea (pronounced *kal-DEE-uh*) in the Bible.

The empires of Assyria and Babylonia were at war for a long time. First, the Assyrians conquered the Babylonians 1,270 years before Jesus was born. About 600 years later, the Babylonians defeated the Assyrians. Babylonia spread its empire as far west as Israel on the Mediterranean Sea about 600 years before Jesus. About 20 years after that, the Babylonians burned Jerusalem and took many prisoners to Babylon for a total of 70 years. The Persians came and set the Jews free 536 years before Christ.

The main fact you should remember is that, although God's people of Israel have suffered, they have continued to exist all this time. The nation of Israel still exists today, but Assyria and Babylonia have long ago passed away. God remembers His promise to Abraham, the father of Israel. (See Genesis 12:1–3.)

The BOOK of

1 CHRONICLES

430 B.C.–425 B.C.

Behind the Scenes

READ IT:

This history of Judah was written after God punished His people for disobeying Him. The people were living in their own country again and were being reminded of the good times before their nation was defeated. The main theme is that God is always faithful to His promise.

GET IT:

Who wrote it: Possibly Ezra wrote it.

When it was written: 430 B.C.–425 B.C.

Why it was written: to remind the people who had come back home that they were from the royal line of David and were God's chosen people.

LIVE IT:

God blesses people who worship and love Him.

FIND IT:

The Tragic End of Saul and His Sons	*1 Chronicles 10*
The Ark Brought to Jerusalem	*1 Chronicles 15*
God's Covenant with David	*1 Chronicles 17*
The Census of Israel and Judah	*1 Chronicles 21*
Solomon Instructed to Build the Temple	*1 Chronicles 22*

The Family of Adam— Seth to Abraham

1 Adam, Seth, Enosh, 2Cainan,[a] Mahalalel, Jared, 3Enoch, Methuselah, Lamech, 4Noah,[a] Shem, Ham, and Japheth.

5The sons of Japheth *were* Gomer, Magog, Madai, Javan, Tubal, Meshech, and Tiras. 6The sons of Gomer *were* Ashkenaz, Diphath,[a] and Togarmah. 7The sons of Javan *were* Elishah, Tarshishah,[a] Kittim, and Rodanim.[b]

8The sons of Ham *were* Cush, Mizraim, Put, and Canaan. 9The sons of Cush *were* Seba, Havilah, Sabta,[a] Raama,[b] and Sabtecha. The sons of Raama *were* Sheba and Dedan. 10Cush begot Nimrod; he began to be a mighty one on the earth. 11Mizraim begot Ludim, Anamim, Lehabim, Naphtuhim, 12Pathrusim, Casluhim (from whom came the Philistines and the Caphtorim). 13Canaan begot Sidon, his firstborn, and Heth; 14the Jebusite, the Amorite, and the Girgashite; 15the Hivite, the Arkite, and the Sinite; 16the Arvadite, the Zemarite, and the Hamathite.

17The sons of Shem *were* Elam, Asshur, Arphaxad, Lud, Aram, Uz, Hul, Gether, and Meshech.[a] 18Arphaxad begot Shelah, and Shelah begot Eber. 19To Eber were born two sons: the name of one *was* Peleg,[a] for in his days the earth was divided; and his brother's name *was* Joktan. 20Joktan begot Almodad, Sheleph, Hazarmaveth, Jerah, 21Hadoram, Uzal, Diklah, 22Ebal,[a] Abimael, Sheba, 23Ophir, Havilah, and Jobab. All these *were* the sons of Joktan.

24Shem, Arphaxad, Shelah, 25Eber, Peleg, Reu, 26Serug, Nahor, Terah, 27and Abram, who *is* Abraham. 28The sons of Abraham *were* Isaac and Ishmael.

The Family of Ishmael

29These *are* their genealogies: The firstborn of Ishmael *was* Nebajoth; then Kedar, Adbeel, Mibsam, 30Mishma, Dumah, Massa, Hadad,[a] Tema, 31Jetur, Naphish, and Kedemah. These *were* the sons of Ishmael.

The Family of Keturah

32Now the sons born to Keturah, Abraham's concubine, *were* Zimran, Jokshan, Medan, Midian, Ishbak, and Shuah. The sons of Jokshan *were* Sheba and Dedan. 33The sons of Midian *were* Ephah, Epher, Hanoch, Abida, and Eldaah. All these were the children of Keturah.

1:2 [a] Hebrew *Qenan* 1:4 [a] Following Masoretic Text and Vulgate; Septuagint adds *the sons of Noah.* 1:6 [a] Spelled *Riphath* in Genesis 10:3 1:7 [a] Spelled *Tarshish* in Genesis 10:4 [b] Spelled *Dodanim* in Genesis 10:4 1:9 [a] Spelled *Sabtah* in Genesis 10:7 [b] Spelled *Raamah* in Genesis 10:7 1:17 [a] Spelled *Mash* in Genesis 10:23 1:19 [a] Literally *Division* 1:22 [a] Spelled *Obal* in Genesis 10:28 1:30 [a] Spelled *Hadar* in Genesis 25:15

1:1 GOD CREATED THE FAMILY

The first eight chapters of 1 Chronicles may seem very boring. They just list some of the descendants of Adam, leading to the nation of Israel. Right now most of these names don't mean very much to you. But they are really a wonderful book of memories, showing God's faithfulness to some ordinary people who lived during those early times.

The first thing you should notice is that God thinks the family is very important. In fact, God created the family to be the way in which young people would learn the plan of salvation through Jesus. God meant us to have parents who would teach us the Bible and lead us to Christ.

You may not have a mother and father, or you may have only one parent. But God cares for all children in a special way. He knows how to send people who will love you and help you understand God's ways.

The Family of Isaac

34 And Abraham begot Isaac. The sons
of Isaac *were* Esau and Israel. 35 The sons of
Esau *were* Eliphaz, Reuel, Jeush, Jaalam,
and Korah. 36 And the sons of Eliphaz *were*
Teman, Omar, Zephi,[a] Gatam, *and* Kenaz;
and *by* Timna,[b] Amalek. 37 The sons of Reuel
were Nahath, Zerah, Shammah, and Mizzah.

The Family of Seir

38 The sons of Seir *were* Lotan, Shobal,
Zibeon, Anah, Dishon, Ezer, and Dishan.
39 And the sons of Lotan *were* Hori and
Homam; Lotan's sister *was* Timna. 40 The
sons of Shobal *were* Alian,[a] Manahath, Ebal,
Shephi,[b] and Onam. The sons of Zibeon
were Ajah and Anah. 41 The son of Anah *was*
Dishon. The sons of Dishon *were* Hamran,[a]
Eshban, Ithran, and Cheran. 42 The sons of
Ezer *were* Bilhan, Zaavan, *and* Jaakan.[a] The
sons of Dishan *were* Uz and Aran.

The Kings of Edom

43 Now these *were* the kings who reigned
in the land of Edom before a king reigned
over the children of Israel: Bela the son of
Beor, and the name of his city was Dinhabah. 44 And when Bela died, Jobab the son
of Zerah of Bozrah reigned in his place.
45 When Jobab died, Husham of the land of
the Temanites reigned in his place. 46 And
when Husham died, Hadad the son of Bedad, who attacked Midian in the field of
Moab, reigned in his place. The name of his
city *was* Avith. 47 When Hadad died, Samlah of Masrekah reigned in his place. 48 And
when Samlah died, Saul of Rehoboth-by-the-
River reigned in his place. 49 When Saul died,
Baal-Hanan the son of Achbor reigned in his
place. 50 And when Baal-Hanan died, Hadad[a]
reigned in his place; and the name of his
city was Pai.[b] His wife's name was Mehetabel the daughter of Matred, the daughter of
Mezahab. 51 Hadad died also. And the chiefs
of Edom were Chief Timnah, Chief Aliah,[a]
Chief Jetheth, 52 Chief Aholibamah, Chief
Elah, Chief Pinon, 53 Chief Kenaz, Chief
Teman, Chief Mibzar, 54 Chief Magdiel, and
Chief Iram. These *were* the chiefs of Edom.

The Family of Israel

2 These *were* the sons of Israel: Reuben,
Simeon, Levi, Judah, Issachar, Zebulun, 2 Dan, Joseph, Benjamin, Naphtali, Gad,
and Asher.

From Judah to David

3 The sons of Judah *were* Er, Onan, and
Shelah. *These* three were born to him by the
daughter of Shua, the Canaanitess. Er, the
firstborn of Judah, was wicked in the sight of
the LORD; so He killed him. 4 And Tamar, his
daughter-in-law, bore him Perez and Zerah.
All the sons of Judah *were* five.

5 The sons of Perez *were* Hezron and Hamul. 6 The sons of Zerah *were* Zimri, Ethan,
Heman, Calcol, and Dara—five of them in all.

7 The son of Carmi *was* Achar,[a] the troubler of Israel, who transgressed in the accursed thing.

8 The son of Ethan *was* Azariah.

9 Also the sons of Hezron who were born
to him *were* Jerahmeel, Ram, and Chelubai.[a]
10 Ram begot Amminadab, and Amminadab
begot Nahshon, leader of the children of Judah; 11 Nahshon begot Salma,[a] and Salma begot Boaz; 12 Boaz begot Obed, and Obed begot
Jesse; 13 Jesse begot Eliab his firstborn, Abinadab the second, Shimea[a] the third, 14 Nethanel the fourth, Raddai the fifth, 15 Ozem
the sixth, *and* David the seventh.

16 Now their sisters *were* Zeruiah and Abigail. And the sons of Zeruiah *were* Abishai,
Joab, and Asahel—three. 17 Abigail bore
Amasa; and the father of Amasa *was* Jether
the Ishmaelite.[a]

The Family of Hezron

18 Caleb the son of Hezron had children by
Azubah, *his* wife, and by Jerioth. Now these
were her sons: Jesher, Shobab, and Ardon.
19 When Azubah died, Caleb took Ephrath[a]
as his wife, who bore him Hur. 20 And Hur
begot Uri, and Uri begot Bezalel.

21 Now afterward Hezron went in to the
daughter of Machir the father of Gilead,
whom he married when he *was* sixty years
old; and she bore him Segub. 22 Segub begot
Jair, who had twenty-three cities in the land
of Gilead. 23 (Geshur and Syria took from
them the towns of Jair, with Kenath and

1:36 [a] Spelled *Zepho* in Genesis 36:11 [b] Compare Genesis 36:12 **1:40** [a] Spelled *Alvan* in Genesis 36:23 [b] Spelled *Shepho* in Genesis 36:23 **1:41** [a] Spelled *Hemdan* in Genesis 36:26 **1:42** [a] Spelled *Akan* in Genesis 36:27 **1:50** [a] Spelled *Hadar* in Genesis 36:39 [b] Spelled *Pau* in Genesis 36:39 **1:51** [a] Spelled *Alvah* in Genesis 36:40 **2:7** [a] Spelled *Achan* in Joshua 7:1 and elsewhere **2:9** [a] Spelled *Caleb* in 2:18, 42 **2:11** [a] Spelled *Salmon* in Ruth 4:21 and Luke 3:32 **2:13** [a] Spelled *Shammah* in 1 Samuel 16:9 and elsewhere **2:17** [a] Compare 2 Samuel 17:25 **2:19** [a] Spelled *Ephrathah* elsewhere

its towns—sixty towns.) All these *belonged*
to the sons of Machir the father of Gilead.
24After Hezron died in Caleb Ephrathah,
Hezron's wife Abijah bore him Ashhur the
father of Tekoa.

The Family of Jerahmeel

25The sons of Jerahmeel, the firstborn of
Hezron, *were* Ram, the firstborn, and Bu-
nah, Oren, Ozem, *and* Ahijah. 26Jerahmeel
had another wife, whose name was Atarah;
she was the mother of Onam. 27The sons of
Ram, the firstborn of Jerahmeel, were Maaz,
Jamin, and Eker. 28The sons of Onam were
Shammai and Jada. The sons of Shammai
were Nadab and Abishur.

29And the name of the wife of Abishur
was Abihail, and she bore him Ahban and
Molid. 30The sons of Nadab *were* Seled and
Appaim; Seled died without children. 31The
son of Appaim *was* Ishi, the son of Ishi *was*
Sheshan, and Sheshan's son *was* Ahlai. 32The
sons of Jada, the brother of Shammai, *were*
Jether and Jonathan; Jether died without
children. 33The sons of Jonathan *were* Peleth
and Zaza. These were the sons of Jerahmeel.

34Now Sheshan had no sons, only daughters. And Sheshan had an Egyptian servant
whose name *was* Jarha. 35Sheshan gave his
daughter to Jarha his servant as wife, and
she bore him Attai. 36Attai begot Nathan, and
Nathan begot Zabad; 37Zabad begot Ephlal,
and Ephlal begot Obed; 38Obed begot Jehu,
and Jehu begot Azariah; 39Azariah begot
Helez, and Helez begot Eleasah; 40Eleasah
begot Sismai, and Sismai begot Shallum;
41Shallum begot Jekamiah, and Jekamiah
begot Elishama.

The Family of Caleb

42The descendants of Caleb the brother of Jerahmeel *were* Mesha, his firstborn,
who was the father of Ziph, and the sons of
Mareshah the father of Hebron. 43The sons
of Hebron *were* Korah, Tappuah, Rekem, and
Shema. 44Shema begot Raham the father of
Jorkoam, and Rekem begot Shammai. 45And
the son of Shammai *was* Maon, and Maon
was the father of Beth Zur.

46Ephah, Caleb's concubine, bore Haran, Moza, and Gazez; and Haran begot
Gazez. 47And the sons of Jahdai *were* Regem,
Jotham, Geshan, Pelet, Ephah, and Shaaph.
48Maachah, Caleb's concubine, bore
Sheber and Tirhanah. 49She also bore Shaaph
the father of Madmannah, Sheva the father
of Machbenah and the father of Gibea. And
the daughter of Caleb *was* Achsah.

50These were the descendants of Caleb:
The sons of Hur, the firstborn of Ephra-
thah, *were* Shobal the father of Kirjath
Jearim, 51Salma the father of Bethlehem, *and*
Hareph the father of Beth Gader.

52And Shobal the father of Kirjath Jearim
had descendants: Haroeh, *and* half of the
families of Manuhoth.[a] 53The families of
Kirjath Jearim *were* the Ithrites, the Pu-
thites, the Shumathites, and the Mishraites.
From these came the Zorathites and the
Eshtaolites.

54The sons of Salma *were* Bethlehem, the
Netophathites, Atroth Beth Joab, half of the
Manahethites, and the Zorites.

55And the families of the scribes who
dwelt at Jabez *were* the Tirathites, the
Shimeathites, *and* the Suchathites. These
were the Kenites who came from Hammath,
the father of the house of Rechab.

The Family of David

3 Now these were the sons of David
who were born to him in Hebron:
The firstborn *was* Amnon, by Ahinoam the
Jezreelitess; the second, Daniel,[a] by Abigail
the Carmelitess; 2the third, Absalom the son
of Maacah, the daughter of Talmai, king
of Geshur; the fourth, Adonijah the son of
Haggith; 3the fifth, Shephatiah, by Abital;
the sixth, Ithream, by his wife Eglah.

4*These* six were born to him in Hebron.
There he reigned seven years and six
months, and in Jerusalem he reigned thirty-
three years. 5And these were born to him in
Jerusalem: Shimea,[a] Shobab, Nathan, and
Solomon—four by Bathshua[b] the daugh-
ter of Ammiel.[c] 6Also *there* were Ibhar,
Elishama,[a] Eliphelet,[b] 7Nogah, Nepheg,
Japhia, 8Elishama, Eliada,[a] and Eliphelet—
nine *in all.* 9*These were* all the sons of David,
besides the sons of the concubines, and
Tamar their sister.

2:52 [a] Same as *the Manahethites,* verse 54 3:1 [a] Called *Chileab* in 2 Samuel 3:3 3:5 [a] Spelled *Shammua* in 14:4 and 2 Samuel 5:14 [b] Spelled *Bathsheba* in 2 Samuel 11:3 [c] Called *Eliam* in 2 Samuel 11:3 3:6 [a] Spelled *Elishua* in 14:5 and 2 Samuel 5:15 [b] Spelled *Elpelet* in 14:5 3:8 [a] Spelled *Beeliada* in 14:7

The Family of Solomon

10 Solomon's son *was* Rehoboam; Abijah[a] *was* his son, Asa his son, Jehoshaphat
his son, 11 Joram[a] his son, Ahaziah his son,
Joash[b] his son, 12 Amaziah his son, Azariah[a] his son, Jotham his son, 13 Ahaz his
son, Hezekiah his son, Manasseh his son,
14 Amon his son, *and* Josiah his son. 15 The
sons of Josiah *were* Johanan the firstborn,
the second Jehoiakim, the third Zedekiah,
and the fourth Shallum.[a] 16 The sons of Jehoiakim *were* Jeconiah his son *and* Zedekiah[a] his son.

The Family of Jeconiah

17 And the sons of Jeconiah[a] *were* Assir,[b]
Shealtiel his son, 18 *and* Malchiram, Pedaiah,
Shenazzar, Jecamiah, Hoshama, and Neda-
biah. 19 The sons of Pedaiah *were* Zerubbabel
and Shimei. The sons of Zerubbabel *were*
Meshullam, Hananiah, Shelomith their sister, 20 and Hashubah, Ohel, Berechiah, Hasa-
diah, and Jushab-Hesed—five *in all.*
21 The sons of Hananiah *were* Pelatiah
and Jeshaiah, the sons of Rephaiah, the
sons of Arnan, the sons of Obadiah, and the
sons of Shechaniah. 22 The son of Shechaniah was Shemaiah. The sons of Shemaiah
were Hattush, Igal, Bariah, Neariah, and
Shaphat—six *in all.* 23 The sons of Neariah
were Elioenai, Hezekiah, and Azrikam—
three *in all.* 24 The sons of Elioenai *were* Hodaviah, Eliashib, Pelaiah, Akkub, Johanan,
Delaiah, and Anani—seven *in all.*

The Family of Judah

4 The sons of Judah *were* Perez, Hezron,
Carmi, Hur, and Shobal. 2 And Reaiah
the son of Shobal begot Jahath, and Jahath
begot Ahumai and Lahad. These *were* the
families of the Zorathites. 3 These *were the
sons of* the father of Etam: Jezreel, Ishma,
and Idbash; and the name of their sister *was*
Hazelelponi; 4 and Penuel *was* the father of
Gedor, and Ezer *was the* father of Hushah.
These were the sons of Hur, the firstborn
of Ephrathah the father of Bethlehem.
5 And Ashhur the father of Tekoa had
two wives, Helah and Naarah. 6 Naarah bore
him Ahuzzam, Hepher, Temeni, and Haa-
hashtari. These *were* the sons of Naarah.
7 The sons of Helah *were* Zereth, Zohar, and
Ethnan; 8 and Koz begot Anub, Zobebah, and
the families of Aharhel the son of Harum.
9 Now Jabez was more honorable than his
brothers, and his mother called his name
Jabez,[a] saying, "Because I bore *him* in pain."
10 And Jabez called on the God of Israel saying, "Oh, that You would bless me indeed,
and enlarge my territory, that Your hand
would be with me, and that You would keep
me from evil, that I may not cause pain!" So
God granted him what he requested.
11 Chelub the brother of Shuhah begot
Mehir, who *was* the father of Eshton. 12 And
Eshton begot Beth-Rapha, Paseah, and Te-
hinnah the father of Ir-Nahash. These *were*
the men of Rechah.
13 The sons of Kenaz *were* Othniel and
Seraiah. The sons of Othniel *were* Hathath,[a]
14 and Meonothai *who* begot Ophrah. Seraiah
begot Joab the father of Ge Harashim,[a] for
they were craftsmen. 15 The sons of Caleb
the son of Jephunneh *were* Iru, Elah, and
Naam. The son of Elah *was* Kenaz. 16 The
sons of Jehallelel *were* Ziph, Ziphah, Tiria,
and Asarel. 17 The sons of Ezrah *were* Jether,
Mered, Epher, and Jalon. And *Mered's wife*[a]
bore Miriam, Shammai, and Ishbah the father of Eshtemoa. 18 (His wife Jehudijah[a] bore
Jered the father of Gedor, Heber the father
of Sochoh, and Jekuthiel the father of Zanoah.) And these were the sons of Bithiah the
daughter of Pharaoh, whom Mered took.
19 The sons of Hodiah's wife, the sister
of Naham, *were* the fathers of Keilah the
Garmite and of Eshtemoa the Maachathite.
20 And the sons of Shimon *were* Amnon, Rin-
nah, Ben-Hanan, and Tilon. And the sons of
Ishi *were* Zoheth and Ben-Zoheth.
21 The sons of Shelah the son of Judah
were Er the father of Lecah, Laadah the father of Mareshah, and the families of the
house of the linen workers of the house of
Ashbea; 22 also Jokim, the men of Chozeba,
and Joash; Saraph, who ruled in Moab, and
Jashubi-Lehem. Now the records are ancient.
23 These *were* the potters and those who dwell
at Netaim[a] and Gederah;[b] there they dwelt
with the king for his work.

3:10 [a] Spelled *Abijam* in 1 Kings 15:1 **3:11** [a] Spelled *Jehoram* in 2 Kings 1:17 and 8:16 [b] Spelled *Jehoash* in 2 Kings 12:1 **3:12** [a] Called *Uzziah* in Isaiah 6:1 **3:15** [a] Called *Jehoahaz* in 2 Kings 23:31 **3:16** [a] Compare 2 Kings 24:17 **3:17** [a] Also called *Coniah* in Jeremiah 22:24 and *Jehoiachin* in 2 Kings 24:8 [b] Or *Jeconiah the captive were* **4:9** [a] Literally *He Will Cause Pain* **4:13** [a] Septuagint and Vulgate add *and Meonothai.* **4:14** [a] Literally *Valley of Craftsmen* **4:17** [a] Literally *she* **4:18** [a] Or *His Judean wife* **4:23** [a] Literally *Plants* [b] Literally *Hedges*

The Family of Simeon

24The sons of Simeon *were* Nemuel, Jamin, Jarib,[a] Zerah,[b] *and* Shaul, 25Shallum his
son, Mibsam his son, and Mishma his son.
26And the sons of Mishma *were* Hamuel his
son, Zacchur his son, and Shimei his son.
27Shimei had sixteen sons and six daughters;
but his brothers did not have many children,
nor did any of their families multiply as
much as the children of Judah.

28They dwelt at Beersheba, Moladah, Hazar Shual, 29Bilhah, Ezem, Tolad, 30Bethuel,
Hormah, Ziklag, 31Beth Marcaboth, Hazar Susim, Beth Biri, and at Shaaraim.
These *were* their cities until the reign of
David. 32And their villages *were* Etam, Ain,
Rimmon, Tochen, and Ashan—five cities— 33and all the villages that *were* around
these cities as far as Baal.[a] These *were* their
dwelling places, and they maintained their
genealogy: 34Meshobab, Jamlech, and Joshah
the son of Amaziah; 35Joel, and Jehu the son
of Joshibiah, the son of Seraiah, the son of
Asiel; 36Elioenai, Jaakobah, Jeshohaiah, Asaiah, Adiel, Jesimiel, and Benaiah; 37Ziza the
son of Shiphi, the son of Allon, the son of
Jedaiah, the son of Shimri, the son of Shemaiah— 38these mentioned by name *were*
leaders in their families, and their father's
house increased greatly.

39So they went to the entrance of Gedor,
as far as the east side of the valley, to seek
pasture for their flocks. 40And they found
rich, good pasture, and the land *was* broad,
quiet, and peaceful; for some Hamites formerly lived there.

41These recorded by name came in the
days of Hezekiah king of Judah; and they
attacked their tents and the Meunites who
were found there, and utterly destroyed
them, as it is to this day. So they dwelt in
their place, because *there was* pasture for
their flocks there. 42Now *some* of them, five
hundred men of the sons of Simeon, went
to Mount Seir, having as their captains
Pelatiah, Neariah, Rephaiah, and Uzziel, the
sons of Ishi. 43And they defeated the rest of
the Amalekites who had escaped. They have
dwelt there to this day.

The Family of Reuben

5 Now the sons of Reuben the firstborn
of Israel—he *was* indeed the firstborn,
but because he defiled his father's bed, his
birthright was given to the sons of Joseph,
the son of Israel, so that the genealogy is not
listed according to the birthright; 2yet Judah
prevailed over his brothers, and from him
came a ruler, although the birthright was Joseph's— 3the sons of Reuben the firstborn
of Israel were Hanoch, Pallu, Hezron, and
Carmi.

4The sons of Joel *were* Shemaiah his son,
Gog his son, Shimei his son, 5Micah his son,
Reaiah his son, Baal his son, 6and Beerah
his son, whom Tiglath-Pileser[a] king of Assyria carried into captivity. He *was* leader of
the Reubenites. 7And his brethren by their
families, when the genealogy of their generations was registered: the chief, Jeiel, and
Zechariah, 8and Bela the son of Azaz, the
son of Shema, the son of Joel, who dwelt in
Aroer, as far as Nebo and Baal Meon. 9East-
ward they settled as far as the entrance of the
wilderness this side of the River Euphrates,
because their cattle had multiplied in the
land of Gilead.

10Now in the days of Saul they made war
with the Hagrites, who fell by their hand;
and they dwelt in their tents throughout the
entire *area* east of Gilead.

The Family of Gad

11And the children of Gad dwelt next to
them in the land of Bashan as far as Salcah:
12Joel *was* the chief, Shapham the next, then
Jaanai and Shaphat in Bashan, 13and their
brethren of their father's house: Michael,
Meshullam, Sheba, Jorai, Jachan, Zia, and
Eber—seven *in all*. 14These *were* the children
of Abihail the son of Huri, the son of Jaroah,
the son of Gilead, the son of Michael, the
son of Jeshishai, the son of Jahdo, the son
of Buz; 15Ahi the son of Abdiel, the son of
Guni, *was* chief of their father's house. 16And
the Gadites dwelt in Gilead, in Bashan and
in its villages, and in all the common-lands
of Sharon within their borders. 17All these
were registered by genealogies in the days
of Jotham king of Judah, and in the days of
Jeroboam king of Israel.

18The sons of Reuben, the Gadites, and
half the tribe of Manasseh *had* forty-four
thousand seven hundred and sixty valiant
men, men able to bear shield and sword, to
shoot with the bow, and skillful in war, who

4:24 [a] Called *Jachin* in Genesis 46:10 [b] Called *Zohar* in Genesis 46:10 **4:33** [a] Or *Baalath Beer* (compare Joshua 19:8) **5:6** [a] Hebrew *Tilgath-Pilneser*

went to war. 19They made war with the Hagrites, Jetur, Naphish, and Nodab. 20And they
were helped against them, and the Hagrites
were delivered into their hand, and all who
were with them, for they cried out to God in
the battle. He heeded their prayer, because
they put their trust in Him. 21Then they took
away their livestock—fifty thousand of their
camels, two hundred and fifty thousand
of their sheep, and two thousand of their
donkeys—also one hundred thousand of
their men; 22for many fell dead, because the
war *was* God's. And they dwelt in their place
until the captivity.

The Family of Manasseh (East)

23So the children of the half-tribe of Manasseh dwelt in the land. Their *numbers* increased from Bashan to Baal Hermon, that
is, to Senir, or Mount Hermon. 24These *were*
the heads of their fathers' houses: Epher,
Ishi, Eliel, Azriel, Jeremiah, Hodaviah,
and Jahdiel. They were mighty men of val-
or, famous men, *and* heads of their fathers'
houses.

25And they were unfaithful to the God of
their fathers, and played the harlot after the
gods of the peoples of the land, whom God
had destroyed before them. 26So the God of
Israel stirred up the spirit of Pul king of Assyria, that is, Tiglath-Pileser[a] king of Assyria. He carried the Reubenites, the Gadites,
and the half-tribe of Manasseh into captivity.
He took them to Halah, Habor, Hara, and
the river of Gozan to this day.

The Family of Levi

6 The sons of Levi *were* Gershon, Kohath, and Merari. 2The sons of Kohath
were Amram, Izhar, Hebron, and Uzziel.
3The children of Amram *were* Aaron, Moses, and Miriam. And the sons of Aaron
were Nadab Abihu, Eleazar, and Ithamar.
4Eleazar begot Phinehas, *and* Phinehas begot
Abishua; 5Abishua begot Bukki, and Bukki
begot Uzzi; 6Uzzi begot Zerahiah, and Zerahiah begot Meraioth; 7Meraioth begot Amariah, and Amariah begot Ahitub; 8Ahitub
begot Zadok, and Zadok begot Ahimaaz;
9Ahimaaz begot Azariah, and Azariah begot
Johanan; 10Johanan begot Azariah (it was
he who ministered as priest in the temple
that Solomon built in Jerusalem); 11Aza-
riah begot Amariah, and Amariah begot
Ahitub; 12Ahitub begot Zadok, and Zadok
begot Shallum; 13Shallum begot Hilkiah,
and Hilkiah begot Azariah; 14Azariah begot
Seraiah, and Seraiah begot Jehozadak. 15Je-
hozadak went *into captivity* when the LORD
carried Judah and Jerusalem into captivity
by the hand of Nebuchadnezzar.

16The sons of Levi *were* Gershon,[a] Kohath, and Merari. 17These are the names
of the sons of Gershon: Libni and Shimei.
18The sons of Kohath *were* Amram, Izhar,
Hebron, and Uzziel. 19The sons of Merari
were Mahli and Mushi. Now these *are* the
families of the Levites according to their
fathers: 20Of Gershon *were* Libni his son,
Jahath his son, Zimmah his son, 21Joah his
son, Iddo his son, Zerah his son, *and* Jeath-
erai his son. 22The sons of Kohath *were* Amminadab his son, Korah his son, Assir his
son, 23Elkanah his son, Ebiasaph his son, Assir his son, 24Tahath his son, Uriel his son,
Uzziah his son, and Shaul his son. 25The
sons of Elkanah *were* Amasai and Ahimoth.
26*As for* Elkanah,[a] the sons of Elkanah *were*
Zophai[b] his son, Nahath[c] his son, 27Eliab[a] his
son, Jeroham his son, *and* Elkanah his son.
28The sons of Samuel *were Joel*[a] the firstborn,
and Abijah the second.[b] 29The sons of Merari
were Mahli, Libni his son, Shimei his son,
Uzzah his son, 30Shimea his son, Haggiah
his son, *and* Asaiah his son.

Musicians in the House of the LORD

31Now these are the men whom David
appointed over the service of song in the
house of the LORD, after the ark came to rest.
32They were ministering with music before
the dwelling place of the tabernacle of meeting, until Solomon had built the house of the
LORD in Jerusalem, and they served in their
office according to their order.

33And these *are* the ones who ministered
with their sons: Of the sons of the Kohathites *were* Heman the singer, the son of Joel,
the son of Samuel, 34the son of Elkanah, the
son of Jeroham, the son of Eliel,[a] the son of
Toah,[b] 35the son of Zuph, the son of Elkanah,
the son of Mahath, the son of Amasai, 36the

5:26 [a] Hebrew *Tilgath-Pilneser* **6:16** [a] Hebrew *Gershom* (alternate spelling of *Gershon*, as in verses 1, 17, 20, 43, 62, and 71) **6:26** [a] Compare verse 35 [b] Spelled *Zuph* in verse 35 and 1 Samuel 1:1 [c] Compare verse 34 **6:27** [a] Compare verse 34 **6:28** [a] Following Septuagint, Syriac, and Arabic (compare verse 33 and 1 Samuel 8:2) [b] Hebrew *Vasheni* **6:34** [a] Spelled *Elihu* in 1 Samuel 1:1 [b] Spelled *Tohu* in 1 Samuel 1:1

son of Elkanah, the son of Joel, the son of
Azariah, the son of Zephaniah, 37the son of
Tahath, the son of Assir, the son of Ebiasaph,
the son of Korah, 38the son of Izhar, the son
of Kohath, the son of Levi, the son of Israel.
39And his brother Asaph, who stood at his
right hand, *was* Asaph the son of Berachiah,
the son of Shimea, 40the son of Michael, the
son of Baaseiah, the son of Malchijah, 41the
son of Ethni, the son of Zerah, the son of
Adaiah, 42the son of Ethan, the son of Zimmah, the son of Shimei, 43the son of Jahath,
the son of Gershon, the son of Levi.

44Their brethren, the sons of Merari, on
the left hand, *were* Ethan the son of Kishi,
the son of Abdi, the son of Malluch, 45the
son of Hashabiah, the son of Amaziah, the
son of Hilkiah, 46the son of Amzi, the son of
Bani, the son of Shamer, 47the son of Mahli,
the son of Mushi, the son of Merari, the son
of Levi.

48And their brethren, the Levites, *were*
appointed to every kind of service of the tabernacle of the house of God.

The Family of Aaron

49But Aaron and his sons offered sacrifices on the altar of burnt offering and on the
altar of incense, for all the work of the Most
Holy *Place,* and to make atonement for Israel, according to all that Moses the servant
of God had commanded. 50Now these *are* the
sons of Aaron: Eleazar his son, Phinehas his
son, Abishua his son, 51Bukki his son, Uzzi
his son, Zerahiah his son, 52Meraioth his
son, Amariah his son, Ahitub his son, 53Za-
dok his son, *and* Ahimaaz his son.

Dwelling Places of the Levites

54Now these *are* their dwelling places
throughout their settlements in their territory, for they were *given* by lot to the sons
of Aaron, of the family of the Kohathites:
55They gave them Hebron in the land of Judah, with its surrounding common-lands.
56But the fields of the city and its villages
they gave to Caleb the son of Jephunneh.
57And to the sons of Aaron they gave *one of*
the cities of refuge, Hebron; also Libnah
with its common-lands, Jattir, Eshtemoa
with its common-lands, 58Hilen[a] with its
common-lands, Debir with its common-
lands, 59Ashan[a] with its common-lands,
and Beth Shemesh with its common-lands.
60And from the tribe of Benjamin: Geba
with its common-lands, Alemeth[a] with
its common-lands, and Anathoth with its
common-lands. All their cities among their
families *were* thirteen.

61To the rest of the family of the tribe
of the Kohathites *they gave* by lot ten cities
from half the tribe of Manasseh. 62And to
the sons of Gershon, throughout their families, *they gave* thirteen cities from the tribe
of Issachar, from the tribe of Asher, from the
tribe of Naphtali, and from the tribe of Manasseh in Bashan. 63To the sons of Merari,
throughout their families, *they gave* twelve
cities from the tribe of Reuben, from the
tribe of Gad, and from the tribe of Zebulun.
64So the children of Israel gave *these* cities
with their common-lands to the Levites.
65And they gave by lot from the tribe of the
children of Judah, from the tribe of the children of Simeon, and from the tribe of the
children of Benjamin these cities which are
called by *their* names.

66Now some of the families of the sons
of Kohath *were given* cities as their territory
from the tribe of Ephraim. 67And they gave
them *one of* the cities of refuge, Shechem
with its common-lands, in the mountains of
Ephraim, also Gezer with its common-lands,
68Jokmeam with its common-lands, Beth
Horon with its common-lands, 69Aijalon with
its common-lands, and Gath Rimmon with
its common-lands. 70And from the half-tribe
of Manasseh: Aner with its common-lands
and Bileam with its common-lands, for the
rest of the family of the sons of Kohath.

71From the family of the half-tribe of Manasseh the sons of Gershon *were given* Golan in Bashan with its common-lands and
Ashtaroth with its common-lands. 72And
from the tribe of Issachar: Kedesh with its
common-lands, Daberath with its common-
lands, 73Ramoth with its common-lands,
and Anem with its common-lands. 74And
from the tribe of Asher: Mashal with its
common-lands, Abdon with its common-
lands, 75Hukok with its common-lands,
and Rehob with its common-lands. 76And
from the tribe of Naphtali: Kedesh in Galilee with its common-lands, Hammon with
its common-lands, and Kirjathaim with its
common-lands.

6:58 [a] Spelled *Holon* in Joshua 21:15 **6:59** [a] Spelled *Ain* in Joshua 21:16 **6:60** [a] Spelled *Almon* in Joshua 21:18

77 From the tribe of Zebulun the rest
of the children of Merari *were given* Rimmon[a] with its common-lands and Tabor
with its common-lands. 78 And on the other
side of the Jordan, across from Jericho, on
the east side of the Jordan, *they were given*
from the tribe of Reuben: Bezer in the wilderness with its common-lands, Jahzah
with its common-lands, 79 Kedemoth with
its common-lands, and Mephaath with its
common-lands. 80 And from the tribe of Gad:
Ramoth in Gilead with its common-lands,
Mahanaim with its common-lands, 81 Heshbon with its common-lands, and Jazer with
its common-lands.

The Family of Issachar

7 The sons of Issachar *were* Tola, Puah,[a]
Jashub, and Shimron—four *in all.* 2 The
sons of Tola *were* Uzzi, Rephaiah, Jeriel, Jah-
mai, Jibsam, and Shemuel, heads of their
father's house. *The sons* of Tola *were* mighty
men of valor in their generations; their
number in the days of David *was* twenty-
two thousand six hundred. 3 The son of Uzzi
was Izrahiah, and the sons of Izrahiah *were*
Michael, Obadiah, Joel, and Ishiah. All five
of them *were* chief men. 4 And with them, by
their generations, according to their fathers'
houses, *were* thirty-six thousand troops ready
for war; for they had many wives and sons.
5 Now their brethren among all the families of Issachar *were* mighty men of valor,
listed by their genealogies, eighty-seven
thousand in all.

The Family of Benjamin

6 *The sons* of Benjamin *were* Bela, Becher, and Jediael—three *in all.* 7 The sons
of Bela were Ezbon, Uzzi, Uzziel, Jerimoth, and Iri—five *in all.* They *were* heads of
their fathers' houses, and they were listed by
their genealogies, twenty-two thousand and
thirty-four mighty men of valor.
8 The sons of Becher *were* Zemirah,
Joash, Eliezer, Elioenai, Omri, Jerimoth,
Abijah, Anathoth, and Alemeth. All these
are the sons of Becher. 9 And they were recorded by genealogy according to their
generations, heads of their fathers' houses,
twenty thousand two hundred mighty men
of valor. 10 The son of Jediael *was* Bilhan, and
the sons of Bilhan *were* Jeush, Benjamin,
Ehud, Chenaanah, Zethan, Tharshish, and
Ahishahar.
11 All these sons of Jediael *were* heads of
their fathers' houses; *there were* seventeen
thousand two hundred mighty men of val-
or fit to go out for war *and* battle. 12 Shuppim and Huppim[a] *were* the sons of Ir, *and*
Hushim *was* the son of Aher.

The Family of Naphtali

13 The sons of Naphtali *were* Jahziel,[a]
Guni, Jezer, and Shallum,[b] the sons of
Bilhah.

The Family of Manasseh (West)

14 The descendants of Manasseh: his Syrian concubine bore him Machir the father of
Gilead, the father of Asriel.[a] 15 Machir took as
his wife *the sister* of Huppim and Shuppim,[a]
whose name *was* Maachah. The name of *Gil-*
ead's grandson[b] *was* Zelophehad,[c] but Zelophehad begot only daughters. 16 (Maachah
the wife of Machir bore a son, and she called
his name Peresh. The name of his brother
was Sheresh, and his sons *were* Ulam and
Rakem. 17 The son of Ulam *was* Bedan.)
These *were* the descendants of Gilead the son
of Machir, the son of Manasseh.
18 His sister Hammoleketh bore Ishhod,
Abiezer, and Mahlah.
19 And the sons of Shemida were Ahian,
Shechem, Likhi, and Aniam.

The Family of Ephraim

20 The sons of Ephraim *were* Shuthelah,
Bered his son, Tahath his son, Eladah
his son, Tahath his son, 21 Zabad his son,
Shuthelah his son, and Ezer and Elead. The
men of Gath who were born in *that* land
killed *them* because they came down to take
away their cattle. 22 Then Ephraim their father mourned many days, and his brethren
came to comfort him.
23 And when he went in to his wife, she
conceived and bore a son; and he called his
name Beriah,[a] because tragedy had come
upon his house. 24 Now his daughter *was*
Sheerah, who built Lower and Upper Beth
Horon and Uzzen Sheerah; 25 and Rephah
was his son, *as well* as Resheph, and Telah

6:77 [a] Hebrew *Rimmono,* alternate spelling of *Rimmon;* see 4:32 7:1 [a] Spelled *Puvah* in Genesis 46:13
7:12 [a] Called *Hupham* in Numbers 26:39 7:13 [a] Spelled *Jahzeel* in Genesis 46:24 [b] Spelled *Shillem* in Genesis 46:24
7:14 [a] The son of Gilead (compare Numbers 26:30, 31)
7:15 [a] Compare verse 12 [b] Literally *the second* [c] Compare Numbers 26:30–33 7:23 [a] Literally *In Tragedy*

his son, Tahan his son, 26Laadan his son,
Ammihud his son, Elishama his son, 27Nun[a]
his son, and Joshua his son.

28Now their possessions and dwelling
places *were* Bethel and its towns: to the east
Naaran, to the west Gezer and its towns, and
Shechem and its towns, as far as Ayyah[a] and
its towns; 29and by the borders of the children of Manasseh *were* Beth Shean and its
towns, Taanach and its towns, Megiddo and
its towns, Dor and its towns. In these dwelt
the children of Joseph, the son of Israel.

The Family of Asher

30The sons of Asher *were* Imnah, Ishvah,
Ishvi, Beriah, and their sister Serah. 31The
sons of Beriah *were* Heber and Malchiel,
who was the father of Birzaith.[a] 32And Heber begot Japhlet, Shomer,[a] Hotham,[b] and
their sister Shua. 33The sons of Japhlet *were*
Pasach, Bimhal, and Ashvath. These *were*
the children of Japhlet. 34The sons of Shemer *were* Ahi, Rohgah, Jehubbah, and Aram.
35And the sons of his brother Helem *were*
Zophah, Imna, Shelesh, and Amal. 36The
sons of Zophah *were* Suah, Harnepher,
Shual, Beri, Imrah, 37Bezer, Hod, Shamma,
Shilshah, Jithran,[a] and Beera. 38The sons
of Jether *were* Jephunneh, Pispah, and Ara.
39The sons of Ulla *were* Arah, Haniel, and
Rizia.

40All these *were* the children of Asher,
heads of *their* fathers' houses, choice men,
mighty men of valor, chief leaders. And they
were recorded by genealogies among the
army fit for battle; their number *was* twenty-
six thousand.

The Family Tree of King Saul of Benjamin

8 Now Benjamin begot Bela his firstborn, Ashbel the second, Aharah[a] the
third, 2Nohah the fourth, and Rapha the
fifth. 3The sons of Bela *were* Addar,[a] Gera,
Abihud, 4Abishua, Naaman, Ahoah, 5Gera,
Shephuphan, and Huram.

6These *are* the sons of Ehud, who were
the heads of the fathers' *houses* of the inhabitants of Geba, and who forced them to move
to Manahath: 7Naaman, Ahijah, and Gera
who forced them to move. He begot Uzza
and Ahihud.

8Also Shaharaim had children in the
country of Moab, after he had sent away
Hushim and Baara his wives. 9By Hodesh
his wife he begot Jobab, Zibia, Mesha, Malcam, 10Jeuz, Sachiah, and Mirmah. These
were his sons, heads of their fathers' *houses*.

11And by Hushim he begot Abitub and
Elpaal. 12The sons of Elpaal *were* Eber, Mi-
sham, and Shemed, who built Ono and Lod
with its towns; 13and Beriah and Shema,
who *were* heads of their fathers' *houses* of
the inhabitants of Aijalon, who drove out
the inhabitants of Gath. 14Ahio, Shashak,
Jeremoth, 15Zebadiah, Arad, Eder, 16Mi-
chael, Ispah, and Joha *were* the sons of Beriah. 17Zebadiah, Meshullam, Hizki, Heber,
18Ishmerai, Jizliah, and Jobab *were* the sons
of Elpaal. 19Jakim, Zichri, Zabdi, 20Elienai,
Zillethai, Eliel, 21Adaiah, Beraiah, and Shim-
rath *were* the sons of Shimei. 22Ishpan, Eber,
Eliel, 23Abdon, Zichri, Hanan, 24Hananiah,
Elam, Antothijah, 25Iphdeiah, and Penuel
were the sons of Shashak. 26Shamsherai,
Shehariah, Athaliah, 27Jaareshiah, Elijah,
and Zichri *were* the sons of Jeroham.

28These *were* heads of the fathers' *houses*
by their generations, chief men. These dwelt
in Jerusalem.

29Now the father of Gibeon, whose wife's
name *was* Maacah, dwelt at Gibeon. 30And
his firstborn son *was* Abdon, then Zur, Kish,
Baal, Nadab, 31Gedor, Ahio, Zecher, 32and
Mikloth, *who* begot Shimeah.[a] They also
dwelt alongside their relatives in Jerusalem,
with their brethren. 33Ner[a] begot Kish, Kish
begot Saul, and Saul begot Jonathan, Malchishua, Abinadab,[b] and Esh-Baal.[c] 34The
son of Jonathan *was* Merib-Baal,[a] and Merib-
Baal begot Micah. 35The sons of Micah *were*
Pithon, Melech, Tarea, and Ahaz. 36And
Ahaz begot Jehoaddah;[a] Jehoaddah begot
Alemeth, Azmaveth, and Zimri; and Zimri
begot Moza. 37Moza begot Binea, Raphah[a]
his son, Eleasah his son, *and* Azel his son.

38Azel had six sons whose names
were these: Azrikam, Bocheru, Ishmael,
Sheariah, Obadiah, and Hanan. All these
were the sons of Azel. 39And the sons of

7:27 [a] Hebrew *Non* **7:28** [a] Many Hebrew manuscripts, Bomberg, Septuagint, Targum, and Vulgate read *Gazza.* **7:31** [a] Or *Birzavith* or *Birzoth* **7:32** [a] Spelled *Shemer* in verse 34 [b] Spelled *Helem* in verse 35 **7:37** [a] Spelled *Jether* in verse 38 **8:1** [a] Spelled *Ahiram* in Numbers 26:38 **8:3** [a] Called *Ard* in Numbers 26:40 **8:32** [a] Spelled *Shimeam* in 9:38 **8:33** [a] Also the son of Gibeon (compare 9:36, 39) [b] Called *Jishui* in 1 Samuel 14:49 [c] Called *Ishbosheth* in 2 Samuel 2:8 and elsewhere **8:34** [a] Called *Mephibosheth* in 2 Samuel 4:4 **8:36** [a] Spelled *Jarah* in 9:42 **8:37** [a] Spelled *Rephaiah* in 9:43

Eshek his brother *were* Ulam his firstborn,
Jeush the second, and Eliphelet the third.
40The sons of Ulam were mighty men
of valor—archers. *They* had many sons and
grandsons, one hundred and fifty *in all.*
These *were* all sons of Benjamin.

9 So all Israel was recorded by genealogies, and indeed, they *were* inscribed
in the book of the kings of Israel. But Judah
was carried away captive to Babylon because
of their unfaithfulness. 2And the first inhabitants who *dwelt* in their possessions in their
cities *were* Israelites, priests, Levites, and the
Nethinim.

Dwellers in Jerusalem

3Now in Jerusalem the children of Judah
dwelt, and some of the children of Benjamin,
and of the children of Ephraim and Manasseh: 4Uthai the son of Ammihud, the son of
Omri, the son of Imri, the son of Bani, of the
descendants of Perez, the son of Judah. 5Of
the Shilonites: Asaiah the firstborn and his
sons. 6Of the sons of Zerah: Jeuel, and their
brethren—six hundred and ninety. 7Of the
sons of Benjamin: Sallu the son of Meshullam, the son of Hodaviah, the son of Hassenuah; 8Ibneiah the son of Jeroham; Elah the
son of Uzzi, the son of Michri; Meshullam
the son of Shephatiah, the son of Reuel, the
son of Ibnijah; 9and their brethren, according to their generations—nine hundred and
fifty-six. All these men *were* heads of a father's *house* in their fathers' houses.

The Priests at Jerusalem

10Of the priests: Jedaiah, Jehoiarib, and
Jachin; 11Azariah the son of Hilkiah, the son
of Meshullam, the son of Zadok, the son
of Meraioth, the son of Ahitub, the officer
over the house of God; 12Adaiah the son of
Jeroham, the son of Pashur, the son of Malchijah; Maasai the son of Adiel, the son of
Jahzerah, the son of Meshullam, the son of
Meshillemith, the son of Immer; 13and their
brethren, heads of their fathers' houses—
one thousand seven hundred and sixty. *They
were* very able men for the work of the service
of the house of God.

The Levites at Jerusalem

14Of the Levites: Shemaiah the son of
Hasshub, the son of Azrikam, the son of
Hashabiah, of the sons of Merari; 15Bakbak-
kar, Heresh, Galal, and Mattaniah the son of
Micah, the son of Zichri, the son of Asaph;
16Obadiah the son of Shemaiah, the son of
Galal, the son of Jeduthun; and Berechiah
the son of Asa, the son of Elkanah, who lived
in the villages of the Netophathites.

The Levite Gatekeepers

17And the gatekeepers *were* Shallum, Akkub, Talmon, Ahiman, and their brethren.
Shallum *was* the chief. 18Until then *they had
been* gatekeepers for the camps of the children of Levi at the King's Gate on the east.
19Shallum the son of Kore, the son of
Ebiasaph, the son of Korah, and his brethren, from his father's house, the Korahites,
were in charge of the work of the service,
gatekeepers of the tabernacle. Their fathers
had been keepers of the entrance to the
camp of the LORD. 20And Phinehas the son
of Eleazar had been the officer over them in
time past; the LORD *was* with him. 21Zechari-
ah the son of Meshelemiah *was* keeper of the
door of the tabernacle of meeting.
22All those chosen as gatekeepers *were*
two hundred and twelve. They were recorded by their genealogy, in their villages. David
and Samuel the seer had appointed them to
their trusted office. 23So they and their children *were* in charge of the gates of the house
of the LORD, the house of the tabernacle,
by assignment. 24The gatekeepers were assigned to the four directions: the east, west,
north, and south. 25And their brethren in
their villages *had* to come with them from
time to time for seven days. 26For in this
trusted office *were* four chief gatekeepers;
they were Levites. And they had charge over
the chambers and treasuries of the house of
God. 27And they lodged *all* around the house
of God because they *had* the responsibility,
and they *were* in charge of opening *it* every
morning.

Other Levite Responsibilities

28Now *some* of them were in charge of
the serving vessels, for they brought them
in and took them out by count. 29*Some* of
them *were* appointed over the furnishings
and over all the implements of the sanctuary, and over the fine flour and the wine and
the oil and the incense and the spices. 30And
some of the sons of the priests made the ointment of the spices.
31Mattithiah of the Levites, the firstborn
of Shallum the Korahite, had the trusted

office over the things that were baked in
the pans. 32And some of their brethren of
the sons of the Kohathites *were* in charge of
preparing the showbread for every Sabbath.
33These are the singers, heads of the fathers' *houses* of the Levites, *who lodged* in the
chambers, *and were* free *from other duties;*
for they were employed in *that* work day and
night. 34These heads of the fathers' *houses* of
the Levites *were* heads throughout their generations. They dwelt at Jerusalem.

The Family of King Saul

35Jeiel the father of Gibeon, whose wife's
name *was* Maacah, dwelt at Gibeon. 36His
firstborn son *was* Abdon, then Zur, Kish,
Baal, Ner, Nadab, 37Gedor, Ahio, Zechariah,[a] and Mikloth. 38And Mikloth begot
Shimeam.[a] They also dwelt alongside their
relatives in Jerusalem, with their brethren.
39Ner begot Kish, Kish begot Saul, and Saul
begot Jonathan, Malchishua, Abinadab, and
Esh-Baal. 40The son of Jonathan *was* Merib-
Baal, and Merib-Baal begot Micah. 41The
sons of Micah *were* Pithon, Melech, Tahrea,[a]
and Ahaz.[b] 42And Ahaz begot Jarah;[a] Jarah
begot Alemeth, Azmaveth, and Zimri; and
Zimri begot Moza; 43Moza begot Binea, Rephaiah[a] his son, Eleasah his son, and Azel
his son.
44And Azel had six sons whose names
were these: Azrikam, Bocheru, Ishmael,
Sheariah, Obadiah, and Hanan; these *were*
the sons of Azel.

Tragic End of Saul and His Sons

10 Now the Philistines fought against
Israel; and the men of Israel fled
from before the Philistines, and fell slain
on Mount Gilboa. 2Then the Philistines followed hard after Saul and his sons. And the
Philistines killed Jonathan, Abinadab, and
Malchishua, Saul's sons. 3The battle became
fierce against Saul. The archers hit him, and
he was wounded by the archers. 4Then Saul
said to his armorbearer, "Draw your sword,
and thrust me through with it, lest these
uncircumcised men come and abuse me."
But his armorbearer would not, for he was
greatly afraid. Therefore Saul took a sword
and fell on it. 5And when his armorbearer
saw that Saul was dead, he also fell on his
sword and died. 6So Saul and his three sons
died, and all his house died together. 7And
when all the men of Israel who *were* in the

9:37 [a] Called *Zecher* in 8:31 **9:38** [a] Spelled *Shimeah* in 8:32 **9:41** [a] Spelled *Tarea* in 8:35 [b] Following Arabic, Syriac, Targum, and Vulgate (compare 8:35); Masoretic Text and Septuagint omit *and Ahaz.* **9:42** [a] Spelled *Jehoaddah* in 8:36 **9:43** [a] Spelled *Raphah* in 8:37

9:44 GOD KEEPS PERFECT LISTS

In 1 Chronicles 1, we saw how God uses the family in His plan of salvation.

Another fact we learn from the story of Israel is that God keeps perfect lists of His people and everything they do—and everything they *don't* do. We forget things, but God can remember everything!

Sometimes we do things that we like to hide. Then we imagine nobody knows, but we are only fooling ourselves. God sees all, He knows all, and He never forgets. We should think hard about that.

But wait a minute! God also said, "Their sin I will remember no more" (Jeremiah 31:34). Can God remember and forget at the same time? Yes! *When we remember* our sins and tell Him we hate them, He forgives us. "The blood of Jesus Christ His Son cleanses us from all sin" (1 John 1:7). Then God doesn't remember our sins anymore.

valley saw that they had fled and that Saul and his sons were dead, they forsook their cities and fled; then the Philistines came and dwelt in them.

8So it happened the next day, when the Philistines came to strip the slain, that they found Saul and his sons fallen on Mount Gilboa. 9And they stripped him and took his head and his armor, and sent word throughout the land of the Philistines to proclaim the news *in the temple* of their idols and among the people. 10Then they put his armor in the temple of their gods, and fastened his head in the temple of Dagon.

11And when all Jabesh Gilead heard all that the Philistines had done to Saul, 12all the valiant men arose and took the body of Saul and the bodies of his sons; and they brought them to Jabesh, and buried their bones under the tamarisk tree at Jabesh, and fasted seven days.

13So Saul died for his unfaithfulness which he had committed against the LORD, because he did not keep the word of the LORD, and also because he consulted a medium for guidance. 14But *he* did not inquire of the LORD; therefore He killed him, and turned the kingdom over to David the son of Jesse.

David Made King over All Israel

11 Then all Israel came together to David at Hebron, saying, "Indeed we *are* your bone and your flesh. 2Also, in time past, even when Saul was king, you *were* the one who led Israel out and brought them in; and the LORD your God said to you, 'You shall shepherd My people Israel, and be ruler over My people Israel.'" 3Therefore all the elders of Israel came to the king at Hebron, and David made a covenant with them at Hebron before the LORD. And they anointed David king over Israel, according to the word of the LORD by Samuel.

The City of David

4And David and all Israel went to Jerusalem, which is Jebus, where the Jebusites *were*, the inhabitants of the land. 5But the inhabitants of Jebus said to David, "You shall not come in here!" Nevertheless David took the stronghold of Zion (that is, the City of David). 6Now David said, "Whoever attacks the Jebusites first shall be chief and captain." And Joab the son of Zeruiah went up first, and became chief. 7Then David dwelt in the stronghold; therefore they called it the City of David. 8And he built the city around it, from the Millo[a] to the surrounding area. Joab repaired the rest of the city. 9So David went on and became great, and the LORD of hosts *was* with him.

The Mighty Men of David

10Now these *were* the heads of the mighty men whom David had, who strengthened themselves with him in his kingdom, with all Israel, to make him king, according to the word of the LORD concerning Israel.

11And this *is* the number of the mighty men whom David had: Jashobeam the son of a Hachmonite, chief of the captains;[a] he had lifted up his spear against three hundred, killed *by him* at one time.

12After him *was* Eleazar the son of Dodo, the Ahohite, who *was one* of the three mighty men. 13He was with David at Pasdammim. Now there the Philistines were gathered for battle, and there was a piece of ground full of barley. So the people fled from the Philistines. 14But they stationed themselves in the middle of *that* field, defended it, and killed the Philistines. So the LORD brought about a great victory.

15Now three of the thirty chief men went down to the rock to David, into the cave of Adullam; and the army of the Philistines encamped in the Valley of Rephaim. 16David *was* then in the stronghold, and the garrison of the Philistines *was* then in Bethlehem. 17And David said with longing, "Oh, that someone would give me a drink of water from the well of Bethlehem, which is by the gate!" 18So the three broke through the camp of the Philistines, drew water from the well of Bethlehem that *was* by the gate, and took *it* and brought *it* to David. Nevertheless David would not drink it, but poured it out to the LORD. 19And he said, "Far be it from me, O my God, that I should do this! Shall I drink the blood of these men *who have put* their lives *in jeopardy*? For at the risk of their lives they brought it." Therefore he would not drink it. These things were done by the three mighty men.

20Abishai the brother of Joab was chief of *another* three.[a] He had lifted up his spear against three hundred *men*, killed *them*,

---

11:8 [a] Literally *The Landfill* 11:11 [a] Following Qere; Kethib, Septuagint, and Vulgate read *the thirty* (compare 2 Samuel 23:8). 11:20 [a] Following Masoretic Text, Septuagint, and Vulgate; Syriac reads *thirty*.

and won a name among *these* three. 21Of the
three he was more honored than the other
two men. Therefore he became their captain. However he did not attain to the *first*
three.

22Benaiah was the son of Jehoiada, the
son of a valiant man from Kabzeel, who had
done many deeds. He had killed two lion-
like heroes of Moab. He also had gone down
and killed a lion in the midst of a pit on a
snowy day. 23And he killed an Egyptian, a
man of *great* height, five cubits tall. In the
Egyptian's hand *there was* a spear like a weaver's beam; and he went down to him with a
staff, wrested the spear out of the Egyptian's
hand, and killed him with his own spear.
24These *things* Benaiah the son of Jehoiada
did, and won a name among three mighty
men. 25Indeed he was more honored than
the thirty, but he did not attain to the *first*
three. And David appointed him over his
guard.

26Also the mighty warriors *were* Asahel
the brother of Joab, Elhanan the son of Dodo
of Bethlehem, 27Shammoth the Harorite,[a]
Helez the Pelonite,[b] 28Ira the son of Ikkesh
the Tekoite, Abiezer the Anathothite, 29Sib-
bechai the Hushathite, Ilai the Ahohite,
30Maharai the Netophathite, Heled[a] the
son of Baanah the Netophathite, 31Ithai[a] the
son of Ribai of Gibeah, of the sons of Benjamin, Benaiah the Pirathonite, 32Hurai[a] of
the brooks of Gaash, Abiel[b] the Arbathite,
33Azmaveth the Baharumite,[a] Eliahba the
Shaalbonite, 34the sons of Hashem the Gizo-
nite, Jonathan the son of Shageh the Hararite, 35Ahiam the son of Sacar the Hararite,
Eliphal the son of Ur, 36Hepher the Meche-
rathite, Ahijah the Pelonite, 37Hezro the
Carmelite, Naarai the son of Ezbai, 38Joel the
brother of Nathan, Mibhar the son of Hagri,
39Zelek the Ammonite, Naharai the Beroth-
ite[a] (the armorbearer of Joab the son of
Zeruiah), 40Ira the Ithrite, Gareb the Ithrite,
41Uriah the Hittite, Zabad the son of Ahlai,
42Adina the son of Shiza the Reubenite (a
chief of the Reubenites) and thirty with him,
43Hanan the son of Maachah, Joshaphat the
Mithnite, 44Uzzia the Ashterathite, Shama
and Jeiel the sons of Hotham the Aroerite,
45Jediael the son of Shimri, and Joha his
brother, the Tizite, 46Eliel the Mahavite, Jeri-
bai and Joshaviah the sons of Elnaam, Ith-
mah the Moabite, 47Eliel, Obed, and Jaasiel
the Mezobaite.

The Growth of David's Army

12 Now these *were* the men who came
to David at Ziklag while he was still
a fugitive from Saul the son of Kish; and
they *were* among the mighty men, helpers
in the war, 2armed with bows, using both the
right hand and the left in *hurling* stones and
shooting arrows with the bow. *They were* of
Benjamin, Saul's brethren.

3The chief *was* Ahiezer, then Joash, the
sons of Shemaah the Gibeathite; Jeziel and
Pelet the sons of Azmaveth; Berachah, and
Jehu the Anathothite; 4Ishmaiah the Gibeon-
ite, a mighty man among the thirty, and over
the thirty; Jeremiah, Jahaziel, Johanan, and
Jozabad the Gederathite; 5Eluzai, Jerimoth,
Bealiah, Shemariah, and Shephatiah the
Haruphite; 6Elkanah, Jisshiah, Azarel, Jo-
ezer, and Jashobeam, the Korahites; 7and
Joelah and Zebadiah the sons of Jeroham of
Gedor.

8*Some* Gadites joined David at the stronghold in the wilderness, mighty men of valor,
men trained for battle, who could handle
shield and spear, whose faces *were like* the
faces of lions, and *were* as swift as gazelles on
the mountains: 9Ezer the first, Obadiah the
second, Eliab the third, 10Mishmannah the
fourth, Jeremiah the fifth, 11Attai the sixth,
Eliel the seventh, 12Johanan the eighth, Elzabad the ninth, 13Jeremiah the tenth, and
Machbanai the eleventh. 14These *were* from
the sons of Gad, captains of the army; the
least was over a hundred, and the greatest
was over a thousand. 15These *are* the ones
who crossed the Jordan in the first month,
when it had overflowed all its banks; and
they put to flight all *those* in the valleys, to
the east and to the west.

16Then some of the sons of Benjamin
and Judah came to David at the stronghold.
17And David went out to meet them, and answered and said to them, "If you have come
peaceably to me to help me, my heart will be
united with you; but if to betray me to my enemies, since *there is* no wrong in my hands,
may the God of our fathers look and bring
judgment." 18Then the Spirit came upon
Amasai, chief of the captains, *and he said:*

11:27 [a] Spelled *Harodite* in 2 Samuel 23:25 [b] Called *Paltite* in 2 Samuel 23:26 **11:30** [a] Spelled *Heleb* in 2 Samuel 23:29 and *Heldai* in 1 Chronicles 27:15 **11:31** [a] Spelled *Ittai* in 2 Samuel 23:29 **11:32** [a] Spelled *Hiddai* in 2 Samuel 23:30 [b] Spelled *Abi-Albon* in 2 Samuel 23:31
11:33 [a] Spelled *Barhumite* in 2 Samuel 23:31
11:39 [a] Spelled *Beerothite* in 2 Samuel 23:37

"*We are* yours, O David;
We *are* on your side, O son of Jesse!
Peace, peace to you,
And peace to your helpers!
For your God helps you."

So David received them, and made them
captains of the troop.
19And *some* from Manasseh defected to
David when he was going with the Philistines to battle against Saul; but they did not
help them, for the lords of the Philistines
sent him away by agreement, saying, "He
may defect to his master Saul *and endanger*
our heads." 20When he went to Ziklag, those
of Manasseh who defected to him were Adnah, Jozabad, Jediael, Michael, Jozabad, Elihu, and Zillethai, captains of the thousands
who *were* from Manasseh. 21And they helped
David against the bands *of raiders*, for they
were all mighty men of valor, and they were
captains in the army. 22For at *that* time they
came to David day by day to help him, until *it*
was a great army, like the army of God.

David's Army at Hebron

23Now these *were* the numbers of the divisions *that were* equipped for war, *and* came
to David at Hebron to turn *over* the kingdom of Saul to him, according to the word
of the LORD: 24of the sons of Judah bearing
shield and spear, six thousand eight hundred armed for war; 25of the sons of Simeon, mighty men of valor fit for war, seven
thousand one hundred; 26of the sons of Levi
four thousand six hundred; 27Jehoiada, the
leader of the Aaronites, and with him three
thousand seven hundred; 28Zadok, a young
man, a valiant warrior, and from his father's
house twenty-two captains; 29of the sons of
Benjamin, relatives of Saul, three thousand
(until then the greatest part of them had remained loyal to the house of Saul); 30of the
sons of Ephraim twenty thousand eight
hundred, mighty men of valor, famous men
throughout their father's house; 31of the half-
tribe of Manasseh eighteen thousand, who
were designated by name to come and make
David king; 32of the sons of Issachar who
had understanding of the times, to know
what Israel ought to do, their chiefs were
two hundred; and all their brethren were
at their command; 33of Zebulun there were
fifty thousand who went out to battle, expert
in war with all weapons of war, stouthearted
men who could keep ranks; 34of Naphtali one
thousand captains, and with them thirty-
seven thousand with shield and spear; 35of
the Danites who could keep battle formation, twenty-eight thousand six hundred; 36of
Asher, those who could go out to war, able
to keep battle formation, forty thousand; 37of
the Reubenites and the Gadites and the half-
tribe of Manasseh, from the other side of the
Jordan, one hundred and twenty thousand
armed for battle with every *kind* of weapon
of war.

38All these men of war, who could keep
ranks, came to Hebron with a loyal heart,
to make David king over all Israel; and all
the rest of Israel *were* of one mind to make
David king. 39And they were there with David three days, eating and drinking, for their
brethren had prepared for them. 40Moreover
those who were near to them, from as far
away as Issachar and Zebulun and Naphtali,
were bringing food on donkeys and camels,
on mules and oxen—provisions of flour and
cakes of figs and cakes of raisins, wine and
oil and oxen and sheep abundantly, for *there*
was joy in Israel.

The Ark Brought from Kirjath Jearim

13 Then David consulted with the captains of thousands and hundreds,
and with every leader. 2And David said to all
the assembly of Israel, "If *it seems* good to
you, and if it is of the LORD our God, let us
send out to our brethren everywhere *who are*
left in all the land of Israel, and with them to
the priests and Levites *who are* in their cities *and* their common-lands, that they may
gather together to us; 3and let us bring the
ark of our God back to us, for we have not
inquired at it since the days of Saul." 4Then
all the assembly said that they would do so,
for the thing was right in the eyes of all the
people.

5So David gathered all Israel together,
from Shihor in Egypt to as far as the entrance of Hamath, to bring the ark of God
from Kirjath Jearim. 6And David and all Israel went up to Baalah,[a] to Kirjath Jearim,
which belonged to Judah, to bring up from
there the ark of God the LORD, who dwells
between the cherubim, where *His* name is
proclaimed. 7So they carried the ark of God
on a new cart from the house of Abinadab,
and Uzza and Ahio drove the cart. 8Then

13:6 [a] Called *Baale Judah* in 2 Samuel 6:2

David and all Israel played *music* before God
with all *their* might, with singing, on harps,
on stringed instruments, on tambourines,
on cymbals, and with trumpets.

9And when they came to Chidon's[a]
threshing floor, Uzza put out his hand to
hold the ark, for the oxen stumbled. 10Then
the anger of the LORD was aroused against
Uzza, and He struck him because he put
his hand to the ark; and he died there before
God. 11And David became angry because of
the LORD's outbreak against Uzza; therefore
that place is called Perez Uzza[a] to this day.
12David was afraid of God that day, saying,
"How can I bring the ark of God to me?"

13So David would not move the ark with
him into the City of David, but took it aside
into the house of Obed-Edom the Gittite.
14The ark of God remained with the family of
Obed-Edom in his house three months. And
the LORD blessed the house of Obed-Edom
and all that he had.

David Established at Jerusalem

14 Now Hiram king of Tyre sent messengers to David, and cedar trees,
with masons and carpenters, to build him
a house. 2So David knew that the LORD had
established him as king over Israel, for his
kingdom was highly exalted for the sake of
His people Israel.

3Then David took more wives in Jerusalem, and David begot more sons and
daughters. 4And these are the names of his
children whom he had in Jerusalem: Shammua,[a] Shobab, Nathan, Solomon, 5Ibhar,
Elishua,[a] Elpelet,[b] 6Nogah, Nepheg, Japhia,
7Elishama, Beeliada,[a] and Eliphelet.

The Philistines Defeated

8Now when the Philistines heard that David had been anointed king over all Israel, all
the Philistines went up to search for David.
And David heard *of it* and went out against
them. 9Then the Philistines went and made
a raid on the Valley of Rephaim. 10And David inquired of God, saying, "Shall I go up
against the Philistines? Will You deliver
them into my hand?"

The LORD said to him, "Go up, for I will
deliver them into your hand."

11So they went up to Baal Perazim, and
David defeated them there. Then David
said, "God has broken through my enemies
by my hand like a breakthrough of water."
Therefore they called the name of that place
Baal Perazim.[a] 12And when they left their
gods there, David gave a commandment,
and they were burned with fire.

13Then the Philistines once again made
a raid on the valley. 14Therefore David inquired again of God, and God said to him,
"You shall not go up after them; circle
around them, and come upon them in front
of the mulberry trees. 15And it shall be, when
you hear a sound of marching in the tops
of the mulberry trees, then you shall go out
to battle, for God has gone out before you to
strike the camp of the Philistines." 16So David did as God commanded him, and they
drove back the army of the Philistines from
Gibeon as far as Gezer. 17Then the fame of
David went out into all lands, and the LORD
brought the fear of him upon all nations.

The Ark Brought to Jerusalem

15 *David* built houses for himself in
the City of David; and he prepared
a place for the ark of God, and pitched a tent
for it. 2Then David said, "No one may carry
the ark of God but the Levites, for the LORD
has chosen them to carry the ark of God and
to minister before Him forever." 3And David
gathered all Israel together at Jerusalem,
to bring up the ark of the LORD to its place,
which he had prepared for it. 4Then David
assembled the children of Aaron and the Levites: 5of the sons of Kohath, Uriel the chief,
and one hundred and twenty of his brethren;
6of the sons of Merari, Asaiah the chief, and
two hundred and twenty of his brethren; 7of
the sons of Gershom, Joel the chief, and one
hundred and thirty of his brethren; 8of the
sons of Elizaphan, Shemaiah the chief, and
two hundred of his brethren; 9of the sons
of Hebron, Eliel the chief, and eighty of his
brethren; 10of the sons of Uzziel, Amminadab the chief, and one hundred and twelve
of his brethren.

11And David called for Zadok and Abiathar the priests, and for the Levites: for
Uriel, Asaiah, Joel, Shemaiah, Eliel, and
Amminadab. 12He said to them, "You *are* the
heads of the fathers' *houses* of the Levites;
sanctify yourselves, you and your brethren,

13:9 [a] Called *Nachon* in 2 Samuel 6:6 **13:11** [a] Literally *Outburst Against Uzza* **14:4** [a] Spelled *Shimea* in 3:5 **14:5** [a] Spelled *Elishama* in 3:6 [b] Spelled *Eliphelet* in 3:6 **14:7** [a] Spelled *Eliada* in 3:8 **14:11** [a] Literally *Master of Breakthroughs*

that you may bring up the ark of the LORD
God of Israel to *the place* I have prepared for
it. 13For because you *did* not *do it* the first
time, the LORD our God broke out against
us, because we did not consult Him about
the proper order."

14So the priests and the Levites sanctified
themselves to bring up the ark of the LORD
God of Israel. 15And the children of the Levites bore the ark of God on their shoulders,
by its poles, as Moses had commanded according to the word of the LORD.

16Then David spoke to the leaders of the
Levites to appoint their brethren *to be* the
singers accompanied by instruments of
music, stringed instruments, harps, and
cymbals, by raising the voice with resound-
ing joy. 17So the Levites appointed Heman
the son of Joel; and of his brethren, Asaph
the son of Berechiah; and of their brethren, the sons of Merari, Ethan the son of
Kushaiah; 18and with them their brethren
of the second *rank:* Zechariah, Ben,[a] Jaaziel,
Shemiramoth, Jehiel, Unni, Eliab, Benaiah,
Maaseiah, Mattithiah, Elipheleh, Mikneiah,
Obed-Edom, and Jeiel, the gatekeepers; 19the
singers, Heman, Asaph, and Ethan, *were* to

15:18 [a] Following Masoretic Text and Vulgate; Septuagint omits *Ben.*

Spotlight

GOD'S ARK COMES BACK TO JERUSALEM

READ IT: 1 CHRONICLES 15:1–29

GET IT:

The ark of the covenant was a big deal. It had been built by Moses hundreds of years before, when the people were in the wilderness. It was so important because it symbolized God's presence with His people. For a long time it wasn't where it was supposed to be. In fact, the enemy captured it and took it away. The Israelites got it back, but when they first tried to move it, they messed up and someone died. They forgot how important the ark was and that God had given detailed instructions about how to carry it. Only the priests could move it, but they had to do it without touching it.

King David got it right the second time. There was a big celebration as the ark came into the city. Everybody dressed up, joined the procession, and shouted out praise songs. The ark, the symbol of God's presence with His people, was finally in the right place. David placed it in a special tent in Jerusalem.

LIVE IT:

We no longer need a special gold box to know that God is with us. God's Spirit lives in each person who believes in Jesus. Our bodies are where God's Spirit lives. God gave special instructions for handling the ark of the covenant. He also gives us special instructions on how to treat and care for our bodies. Knowing that your body is God's dwelling place, what will you do to take better care of it?

sound the cymbals of bronze; 20Zechariah,
Aziel, Shemiramoth, Jehiel, Unni, Eliab,
Maaseiah, and Benaiah, with strings according to Alamoth; 21Mattithiah, Elipheleh,
Mikneiah, Obed-Edom, Jeiel, and Azaziah, to direct with harps on the Sheminith;
22Chenaniah, leader of the Levites, was instructor *in charge of* the music, because
he *was* skillful; 23Berechiah and Elkanah
were doorkeepers for the ark; 24Shebaniah,
Joshaphat, Nethanel, Amasai, Zechariah,
Benaiah, and Eliezer, the priests, were to
blow the trumpets before the ark of God;
and Obed-Edom and Jehiah, doorkeepers
for the ark.

25So David, the elders of Israel, and the
captains over thousands went to bring up
the ark of the covenant of the LORD from the
house of Obed-Edom with joy. 26And so it
was, when God helped the Levites who bore
the ark of the covenant of the LORD, that
they offered seven bulls and seven rams.
27David was clothed with a robe of fine linen,
as were all the Levites who bore the ark, the
singers, and Chenaniah the music master
with the singers. David also wore a linen
ephod. 28Thus all Israel brought up the ark
of the covenant of the LORD with shouting
and with the sound of the horn, with trumpets and with cymbals, making music with
stringed instruments and harps.

29And it happened, *as* the ark of the covenant of the LORD came to the City of David,
that Michal, Saul's daughter, looked through
a window and saw King David whirling and
playing music; and she despised him in her
heart.

The Ark Placed in the Tabernacle

16 So they brought the ark of God, and
set it in the midst of the tabernacle
that David had erected for it. Then they offered burnt offerings and peace offerings
before God. 2And when David had finished
offering the burnt offerings and the peace
offerings, he blessed the people in the name
of the LORD. 3Then he distributed to everyone of Israel, both man and woman, to
everyone a loaf of bread, a piece *of meat,* and
a cake of raisins.

4*And he appointed some* of the Levites to
minister before the ark of the LORD, to com-
memorate, to thank, and to praise the LORD
God of Israel: 5Asaph the chief, and next to
him Zechariah, *then* Jeiel, Shemiramoth,
Jehiel, Mattithiah, Eliab, Benaiah, and Obed-
Edom: Jeiel with stringed instruments and
harps, but Asaph made music with cymbals;
6Benaiah and Jahaziel the priests regularly
blew the trumpets before the ark of the covenant of God.

David's Song of Thanksgiving

7On that day David first delivered *this
psalm* into the hand of Asaph and his brethren, to thank the LORD:

8 Oh, give thanks to the LORD!
Call upon His name;
Make known His deeds among the
peoples!
9 Sing to Him, sing psalms to Him;
Talk of all His wondrous works!
10 Glory in His holy name;
Let the hearts of those rejoice who seek
the LORD!
11 Seek the LORD and His strength;
Seek His face evermore!
12 Remember His marvelous works which
He has done,
His wonders, and the judgments of His
mouth,
13 O seed of Israel His servant,
You children of Jacob, His chosen ones!

14 He *is* the LORD our God;
His judgments *are* in all the earth.
15 Remember His covenant forever,
The word which He commanded, for a
thousand generations,
16 *The covenant which* He made with
Abraham,
And His oath to Isaac,
17 And confirmed it to Jacob for a statute,
To Israel *for* an everlasting covenant,
18 Saying, "To you I will give the land of
Canaan
As the allotment of your inheritance,"
19 When you were few in number,
Indeed very few, and strangers in it.

20 When they went from one nation to
another,
And from *one* kingdom to another
people,
21 He permitted no man to do them
wrong;
Yes, He rebuked kings for their sakes,
22 *Saying,* "Do not touch My anointed ones,
And do My prophets no harm."[a]

16:22 [a] Compare verses 8–22 with Psalm 105:1–15

23 Sing to the LORD, all the earth;
Proclaim the good news of His salvation
from day to day.
24 Declare His glory among the nations,
His wonders among all peoples.

25 For the LORD *is* great and greatly to be
praised;
He *is* also to be feared above all gods.
26 For all the gods of the peoples *are* idols,
But the LORD made the heavens.
27 Honor and majesty *are* before Him;
Strength and gladness are in His place.

28 Give to the LORD, O families of the
peoples,
Give to the LORD glory and strength.
29 Give to the LORD the glory *due* His
name;
Bring an offering, and come before
Him.
Oh, worship the LORD in the beauty of
holiness!
30 Tremble before Him, all the earth.
The world also is firmly established,
It shall not be moved.

31 Let the heavens rejoice, and let the earth
be glad;
And let them say among the nations,
"The LORD reigns."
32 Let the sea roar, and all its fullness;
Let the field rejoice, and all that *is* in it.
33 Then the trees of the woods shall rejoice
before the LORD,
For He is coming to judge the earth.[a]

34 Oh, give thanks to the LORD, for *He is*
good!
For His mercy *endures* forever.[a]
35 And say, "Save us, O God of our
salvation;
Gather us together, and deliver us from
the Gentiles,
To give thanks to Your holy name,
To triumph in Your praise."

36 Blessed *be* the LORD God of Israel
From everlasting to everlasting![a]

And all the people said, "Amen!" and praised the LORD.

Regular Worship Maintained

37So he left Asaph and his brothers there
before the ark of the covenant of the LORD
to minister before the ark regularly, as every
day's work required; 38and Obed-Edom with

16:33 [a] Compare verses 23–33 with Psalm 96:1–13
16:34 [a] Compare verse 34 with Psalm 106:1
16:36 [a] Compare verses 35, 36 with Psalm 106:47, 48

Epic Ideas

16:5, 6 MUSIC IN OLD TESTAMENT TIMES

Music played a large part in Old Testament worship. You can read in Exodus 15 how Miriam and the other women sang before the Lord. The earliest song in the Bible is the song of Moses in the same chapter. Later, there was music at banquets, feasts, and at the crowning of kings. The Hebrew people were so musical that even the king of Assyria commanded Jewish musicians to play before him.

King David brought music into the Jewish temple service with a choir and orchestra of four thousand members. Asaph, Heman, and Jeduthun (pronounced *AY-saf, HE-man,* and *je-DEW-thun*) helped David set up this orchestra and choir. The psalms were written for singing.

At the end of Old Testament times a Greek scholar wrote that Hebrew female singers were the most musical in the world.

Some musical instruments used were bagpipes, trumpets, bells, flutes, harps, drums, and tambourines.

his sixty-eight brethren, including Obed-
Edom the son of Jeduthun, and Hosah, *to*
be gatekeepers; 39and Zadok the priest and
his brethren the priests, before the tabernacle of the LORD at the high place that *was*
at Gibeon, 40to offer burnt offerings to the
LORD on the altar of burnt offering regularly
morning and evening, and *to do* according
to all that is written in the Law of the LORD
which He commanded Israel; 41and with
them Heman and Jeduthun and the rest
who were chosen, who were designated by
name, to give thanks to the LORD, because
His mercy *endures* forever; 42and with them
Heman and Jeduthun, to sound aloud with
trumpets and cymbals and the musical instruments of God. Now the sons of Jeduthun
were gatekeepers.
43Then all the people departed, every
man to his house; and David returned to
bless his house.

God's Covenant with David

17 Now it came to pass, when David
was dwelling in his house, that David said to Nathan the prophet, "See now, I
dwell in a house of cedar, but the ark of the
covenant of the LORD *is* under tent curtains."
2Then Nathan said to David, "Do all that
is in your heart, for God *is* with you."
3But it happened that night that the word
of God came to Nathan, saying, 4"Go and
tell My servant David, 'Thus says the LORD:
"You shall not build Me a house to dwell in.
5For I have not dwelt in a house since the
time that I brought up Israel, even to this
day, but have gone from tent to tent, and
from *one* tabernacle *to another.* 6Wherever
I have moved about with all Israel, have I
ever spoken a word to any of the judges of
Israel, whom I commanded to shepherd My
people, saying, 'Why have you not built Me a
house of cedar?'"' 7Now therefore, thus shall
you say to My servant David, 'Thus says the
LORD of hosts: "I took you from the sheepfold, from following the sheep, to be ruler
over My people Israel. 8And I have been with
you wherever you have gone, and have cut
off all your enemies from before you, and
have made you a name like the name of the
great men who *are* on the earth. 9Moreover
I will appoint a place for My people Israel,
and will plant them, that they may dwell in
a place of their own and move no more; nor
shall the sons of wickedness oppress them
anymore, as previously, 10since the time that
I commanded judges *to be* over My people
Israel. Also I will subdue all your enemies.
Furthermore I tell you that the LORD will
build you a house.[a] 11And it shall be, when
your days are fulfilled, when you must go *to*
be with your fathers, that I will set up your
seed after you, who will be of your sons; and
I will establish his kingdom. 12He shall build
Me a house, and I will establish his throne
forever. 13I will be his Father, and he shall be
My son; and I will not take My mercy away
from him, as I took *it* from *him* who was
before you. 14And I will establish him in My
house and in My kingdom forever; and his
throne shall be established forever."'"
15According to all these words and according to all this vision, so Nathan spoke
to David.
16Then King David went in and sat before the LORD; and he said: "Who *am* I, O
LORD God? And what is my house, that You
have brought me this far? 17And *yet* this was
a small thing in Your sight, O God; and You
have *also* spoken of Your servant's house for
a great while to come, and have regarded me
according to the rank of a man of high degree, O LORD God. 18What more can David
say to You for the honor of Your servant? For
You know Your servant. 19O LORD, for Your
servant's sake, and according to Your own
heart, You have done all this greatness, in
making known all these great things. 20O
LORD, *there is* none like You, nor *is there*
any God besides You, according to all that
we have heard with our ears. 21And who *is*
like Your people Israel, the one nation on
the earth whom God went to redeem for
Himself *as* a people—to make for Yourself
a name by great and awesome deeds, by
driving out nations from before Your people
whom You redeemed from Egypt? 22For You
have made Your people Israel Your very own
people forever; and You, LORD, have become
their God.
23"And now, O LORD, the word which You
have spoken concerning Your servant and
concerning his house, *let it* be established
forever, and do as You have said. 24So let it
be established, that Your name may be magnified forever, saying, 'The LORD of hosts,
the God of Israel, *is* Israel's God.' And let the

17:10 [a] That is, a royal dynasty

house of Your servant David be established
before You. [25]For You, O my God, have revealed to Your servant that You will build
him a house. Therefore Your servant has
found it *in his heart* to pray before You. [26]And
now, LORD, You are God, and have promised
this goodness to Your servant. [27]Now You
have been pleased to bless the house of Your
servant, that it may continue before You forever; for You have blessed it, O LORD, and *it
shall be* blessed forever."

David's Further Conquests

18 After this it came to pass that David
attacked the Philistines, subdued
them, and took Gath and its towns from the
hand of the Philistines. [2]Then he defeated
Moab, and the Moabites became David's servants, *and* brought tribute.

[3]And David defeated Hadadezer[a] king of
Zobah *as far as* Hamath, as he went to establish his power by the River Euphrates. [4]David
took from him one thousand chariots, seven
thousand[a] horsemen, and twenty thousand
foot soldiers. Also David hamstrung all the
chariot *horses,* except that he spared enough
of them for one hundred chariots.

[5]When the Syrians of Damascus came to
help Hadadezer king of Zobah, David killed
twenty-two thousand of the Syrians. [6]Then
David put *garrisons* in Syria of Damascus;
and the Syrians became David's servants,
and brought tribute. So the LORD preserved
David wherever he went. [7]And David took
the shields of gold that were on the servants
of Hadadezer, and brought them to Jerusalem. [8]Also from Tibhath[a] and from Chun,
cities of Hadadezer, David brought a large
amount of bronze, with which Solomon
made the bronze Sea, the pillars, and the
articles of bronze.

[9]Now when Tou[a] king of Hamath heard
that David had defeated all the army of Hadadezer king of Zobah, [10]he sent Hadoram[a]
his son to King David, to greet him and
bless him, because he had fought against
Hadadezer and defeated him (for Hadadezer had been at war with Tou); and *Hadoram
brought with him* all kinds of articles of gold,
silver, and bronze. [11]King David also dedicated these to the LORD, along with the silver
and gold that he had brought from all *these*
nations—from Edom, from Moab, from the
people of Ammon, from the Philistines, and
from Amalek.

[12]Moreover Abishai the son of Zeruiah
killed eighteen thousand Edomites[a] in the
Valley of Salt. [13]He also put garrisons in
Edom, and all the Edomites became David's
servants. And the LORD preserved David
wherever he went.

David's Administration

[14]So David reigned over all Israel, and administered judgment and justice to all his
people. [15]Joab the son of Zeruiah *was* over the
army; Jehoshaphat the son of Ahilud *was* recorder; [16]Zadok the son of Ahitub and Abimelech the son of Abiathar *were* the priests;
Shavsha[a] *was* the scribe; [17]Benaiah the son
of Jehoiada *was* over the Cherethites and the
Pelethites; and David's sons *were* chief ministers at the king's side.

The Ammonites and Syrians Defeated

19 It happened after this that Nahash
the king of the people of Ammon
died, and his son reigned in his place. [2]Then
David said, "I will show kindness to Hanun the son of Nahash, because his father
showed kindness to me." So David sent
messengers to comfort him concerning his
father. And David's servants came to Hanun
in the land of the people of Ammon to comfort him.

[3]And the princes of the people of Ammon said to Hanun, "Do you think that David really honors your father because he has
sent comforters to you? Did his servants not
come to you to search and to overthrow and
to spy out the land?"

[4]Therefore Hanun took David's servants,
shaved them, and cut off their garments in
the middle, at their buttocks, and sent them
away. [5]Then *some* went and told David about
the men; and he sent to meet them, because
the men were greatly ashamed. And the king
said, "Wait at Jericho until your beards have
grown, and *then* return."

[6]When the people of Ammon saw that
they had made themselves repulsive to
David, Hanun and the people of Ammon
sent a thousand talents of silver to hire for
themselves chariots and horsemen from

18:3 [a] Hebrew *Hadarezer,* and so throughout chapters 18 and 19 **18:4** [a] Or *seven hundred* (compare 2 Samuel 8:4) **18:8** [a] Spelled *Betah* in 2 Samuel 8:8 **18:9** [a] Spelled *Toi* in 2 Samuel 8:9, 10 **18:10** [a] Spelled *Joram* in 2 Samuel 8:10 **18:12** [a] Or *Syrians* (compare 2 Samuel 8:13) **18:16** [a] Spelled *Seraiah* in 2 Samuel 8:17

Mesopotamia,[a] from Syrian Maacah, and
from Zobah.[b] 7So they hired for themselves
thirty-two thousand chariots, with the king
of Maacah and his people, who came and encamped before Medeba. Also the people of
Ammon gathered together from their cities,
and came to battle.

8Now when David heard *of it,* he sent Joab
and all the army of the mighty men. 9Then
the people of Ammon came out and put
themselves in battle array before the gate of
the city, and the kings who had come *were* by
themselves in the field.

10When Joab saw that the battle line was
against him before and behind, he chose
some of Israel's best and put *them* in battle
array against the Syrians. 11And the rest of
the people he put under the command of
Abishai his brother, and they set *themselves*
in battle array against the people of Ammon.
12Then he said, "If the Syrians are too strong
for me, then you shall help me; but if the
people of Ammon are too strong for you,
then I will help you. 13Be of good courage,
and let us be strong for our people and for
the cities of our God. And may the LORD do
what is good in His sight."

14So Joab and the people who *were* with
him drew near for the battle against the Syrians, and they fled before him. 15When the
people of Ammon saw that the Syrians were
fleeing, they also fled before Abishai his
brother, and entered the city. So Joab went
to Jerusalem.

16Now when the Syrians saw that they
had been defeated by Israel, they sent messengers and brought the Syrians who were
beyond the River,[a] and Shophach[b] the commander of Hadadezer's army *went* before
them. 17When it was told David, he gathered
all Israel, crossed over the Jordan and came
upon them, and set up in battle array against
them. So when David had set up in battle
array against the Syrians, they fought with
him. 18Then the Syrians fled before Israel;
and David killed seven thousand[a] charioteers and forty thousand foot soldiers[b] of the
Syrians, and killed Shophach the commander of the army. 19And when the servants of
Hadadezer saw that they were defeated by
Israel, they made peace with David and
became his servants. So the Syrians were
not willing to help the people of Ammon
anymore.

In Focus

21:1 Satan Pronounced *SAY-tun*. The personal name of the devil. The name means "Adversary" or "Enemy." Satan is the chief spiritual enemy of God. He is an angel who rebelled against the Lord.

Rabbah Is Conquered

20 It happened in the spring of the
year, at the time kings go out *to*
battle, that Joab led out the armed forces
and ravaged the country of the people of
Ammon, and came and besieged Rabbah.
But David stayed at Jerusalem. And Joab
defeated Rabbah and overthrew it. 2Then
David took their king's crown from his head,
and found it to weigh a talent of gold, and
there were precious stones in it. And it was
set on David's head. Also he brought out the
spoil of the city in great abundance. 3And he
brought out the people who *were* in it, and
put *them* to work[a] with saws, with iron picks,
and with axes. So David did to all the cities
of the people of Ammon. Then David and all
the people returned *to* Jerusalem.

Philistine Giants Destroyed

4Now it happened afterward that war
broke out at Gezer with the Philistines, at
which time Sibbechai the Hushathite killed
Sippai,[a] *who was one* of the sons of the giant.
And they were subdued.

5Again there was war with the Philistines, and Elhanan the son of Jair[a] killed
Lahmi the brother of Goliath the Gittite,
the shaft of whose spear *was* like a weaver's
beam.

6Yet again there was war at Gath, where
there was a man of *great* stature, with
twenty-four fingers and toes, six *on each*
hand and six *on each foot;* and he also was
born to the giant. 7So when he defied Israel,

19:6 [a] Hebrew *Aram Naharaim* [b] Spelled *Zoba* in 2 Samuel 10:6 **19:16** [a] That is, the Euphrates [b] Spelled *Shobach* in 2 Samuel 10:16 **19:18** [a] Or *seven hundred* (compare 2 Samuel 10:18) [b] Or *horsemen* (compare 2 Samuel 10:18) **20:3** [a] Septuagint reads *cut them.* **20:4** [a] Spelled *Saph* in 2 Samuel 21:18 **20:5** [a] Spelled *Jaare-Oregim* in 2 Samuel 21:19

Jonathan the son of Shimea,[a] David's brother, killed him.
8These were born to the giant in Gath,
and they fell by the hand of David and by the
hand of his servants.

The Census of Israel and Judah

21 Now Satan stood up against Israel,
and moved David to number Israel.
2So David said to Joab and to the leaders of
the people, "Go, number Israel from Beersheba to Dan, and bring the number of them
to me that I may know *it*."
3And Joab answered, "May the LORD
make His people a hundred times more
than they are. But, my lord the king, *are* they
not all my lord's servants? Why then does my
lord require this thing? Why should he be a
cause of guilt in Israel?"
4Nevertheless the king's word prevailed
against Joab. Therefore Joab departed and
went throughout all Israel and came to Jerusalem. 5Then Joab gave the sum of the
number of the people to David. All Israel
had one million one hundred thousand men
who drew the sword, and Judah *had* four
hundred and seventy thousand men who

20:7 [a] Spelled *Shimeah* in 2 Samuel 21:21 and *Shammah* in 1 Samuel 16:9

Spotlight

GOD PUNISHES THE NATION FOR DAVID'S SIN

READ IT: 1 CHRONICLES 21:1–15

GET IT:

What was so wrong with David counting the people? It's important for leaders to know how many people live in their countries or how many soldiers are in their armies. But God didn't want David to think his power came from the number of people or the size of the army. Instead, God wanted David to count on God's power and strength. It was all about David obeying and relying on God, not on his own power.

David took the blame for his mistake. He had three options for the punishment, and he decided to take the shortest punishment of three days. He also knew that God's punishments would be better than any other punishment. He knew God was a God of mercy and His anger wouldn't last long. Although God sent a plague that wiped out a lot of people, God did show mercy and said it was enough.

LIVE IT:

What do you do when you've done something wrong? Do you admit your mistake and face the consequences? Or do you act like nothing happened and hope everybody forgets about it? David knew he had done wrong. He admitted it and took the blame. He was in agony knowing his people would suffer because of what he did. We often disappoint others, break rules, or disobey our parents. When we do, we need to admit what we did wrong, ask for forgiveness from God and others, and accept the consequences.

drew the sword. 6But he did not count Levi
and Benjamin among them, for the king's
word was abominable to Joab.

7And God was displeased with this thing;
therefore He struck Israel. 8So David said to
God, "I have sinned greatly, because I have
done this thing; but now, I pray, take away
the iniquity of Your servant, for I have done
very foolishly."

9Then the LORD spoke to Gad, David's
seer, saying, 10"Go and tell David, saying,
'Thus says the LORD: "I offer you three
things; choose one of them for yourself, that
I may do *it* to you." ' "

11So Gad came to David and said to him,
"Thus says the LORD: 'Choose for yourself,
12either three[a] years of famine, or three
months to be defeated by your foes with the
sword of your enemies overtaking *you,* or
else for three days the sword of the LORD—
the plague in the land, with the angel[b] of the
LORD destroying throughout all the territory of Israel.' Now consider what answer I
should take back to Him who sent me."

13And David said to Gad, "I am in great
distress. Please let me fall into the hand of
the LORD, for His mercies *are* very great; but
do not let me fall into the hand of man."

14So the LORD sent a plague upon Israel,
and seventy thousand men of Israel fell.
15And God sent an angel to Jerusalem to
destroy it. As he[a] was destroying, the LORD
looked and relented of the disaster, and
said to the angel who was destroying, "It is
enough; now restrain your[b] hand." And the
angel of the LORD stood by the threshing
floor of Ornan[c] the Jebusite.

16Then David lifted his eyes and saw the
angel of the LORD standing between earth
and heaven, having in his hand a drawn
sword stretched out over Jerusalem. So
David and the elders, clothed in sackcloth,
fell on their faces. 17And David said to God,
"Was it not I who commanded the people to
be numbered? I am the one who has sinned
and done evil indeed; but these sheep, what
have they done? Let Your hand, I pray, O
LORD my God, be against me and my father's
house, but not against Your people that they
should be plagued."

18Therefore, the angel of the LORD commanded Gad to say to David that David
should go and erect an altar to the LORD
on the threshing floor of Ornan the Jebusite. 19So David went up at the word of Gad,

In Focus

21:15 Angel Means "messenger." The messenger is usually from heaven, but sometimes the messenger is human. For example, Malachi, the name of the Old Testament prophet, means "my angel" or "my messenger."

which he had spoken in the name of the
LORD. 20Now Ornan turned and saw the angel; and his four sons *who were* with him hid
themselves, but Ornan continued threshing
wheat. 21So David came to Ornan, and Ornan
looked and saw David. And he went out from
the threshing floor, and bowed before David
with *his* face to the ground. 22Then David
said to Ornan, "Grant me the place of *this*
threshing floor, that I may build an altar on
it to the LORD. You shall grant it to me at the
full price, that the plague may be withdrawn
from the people."

23But Ornan said to David, "Take *it* to
yourself, and let my lord the king do *what
is* good in his eyes. Look, I *also* give *you* the
oxen for burnt offerings, the threshing implements for wood, and the wheat for the
grain offering; I give *it* all."

24Then King David said to Ornan, "No,
but I will surely buy *it* for the full price, for
I will not take what is yours for the LORD,
nor offer burnt offerings with *that which*
costs *me* nothing." 25So David gave Ornan
six hundred shekels of gold by weight for the
place. 26And David built there an altar to the
LORD, and offered burnt offerings and peace
offerings, and called on the LORD; and He
answered him from heaven by fire on the
altar of burnt offering.

27So the LORD commanded the angel, and
he returned his sword to its sheath.

28At that time, when David saw that the
LORD had answered him on the threshing
floor of Ornan the Jebusite, he sacrificed
there. 29For the tabernacle of the LORD and

21:12 [a] Or *seven* (compare 2 Samuel 24:13) [b] Or *Angel,* and so elsewhere in this chapter **21:15** [a] Or *He* [b] Or *Your* [c] Spelled *Araunah* in 2 Samuel 24:16

the altar of the burnt offering, which Moses had made in the wilderness, *were* at that time at the high place in Gibeon. 30But David could not go before it to inquire of God, for he was afraid of the sword of the angel of the LORD.

David Prepares to Build the Temple

22 Then David said, "This *is* the house of the LORD God, and this *is* the altar of burnt offering for Israel." 2So David commanded to gather the aliens who *were* in the land of Israel; and he appointed masons to cut hewn stones to build the house of God. 3And David prepared iron in abundance for the nails of the doors of the gates and for the joints, and bronze in abundance beyond measure, 4and cedar trees in abundance; for the Sidonians and those from Tyre brought much cedar wood to David.

5Now David said, "Solomon my son *is* young and inexperienced, and the house to be built for the LORD *must be* exceedingly magnificent, famous and glorious throughout all countries. I will now make preparation for it." So David made abundant preparations before his death.

6Then he called for his son Solomon, and charged him to build a house for the LORD God of Israel. 7And David said to Solomon: "My son, as for me, it was in my mind to build a house to the name of the LORD my God; 8but the word of the LORD came to me, saying, 'You have shed much blood and have made great wars; you shall not build a house for My name, because you have shed much blood on the earth in My sight. 9Behold, a son shall be born to you, who shall be a man of rest; and I will give him rest from all his enemies all around. His name shall be Solomon,[a] for I will give peace and quietness to Israel in his days. 10He shall build a house for My name, and he shall be My son, and I *will be* his Father; and I will establish the throne of his kingdom over Israel forever.' 11Now, my son, may the LORD be with you; and may you prosper, and build the house of the LORD your God, as He has said to you. 12Only may the LORD give you wisdom and understanding, and give you charge concerning Israel, that you may keep the law of the LORD your God. 13Then you will prosper, if you take care to fulfill the statutes and judgments with which the LORD charged Moses concerning Israel. Be strong and of good courage; do not fear nor be dismayed. 14Indeed I have taken much trouble to prepare for the house of the LORD one hundred thousand talents of gold and one million talents of silver, and bronze and iron beyond measure, for it is so abundant. I have prepared timber and stone also, and you may add to them. 15Moreover *there are* workmen with you in abundance: woodsmen and stonecutters, and all types of skillful men for every kind of work. 16Of gold and silver and bronze and iron *there is* no limit. Arise and begin working, and the LORD be with you."

17David also commanded all the leaders of Israel to help Solomon his son, *saying*, 18"*Is* not the LORD your God with you? And has He *not* given you rest on every side? For He has given the inhabitants of the land into my hand, and the land is subdued before the LORD and before His people. 19Now set your heart and your soul to seek the LORD your God. Therefore arise and build the sanctuary of the LORD God, to bring the ark of the covenant of the LORD and the holy articles of God into the house that is to be built for the name of the LORD."

The Divisions of the Levites

23 So when David was old and full of days, he made his son Solomon king over Israel.

2And he gathered together all the leaders of Israel, with the priests and the Levites. 3Now the Levites were numbered from the age of thirty years and above; and the number of individual males was thirty-eight thousand. 4Of these, twenty-four thousand *were* to look after the work of the house of the LORD, six thousand *were* officers and judges, 5four thousand *were* gatekeepers, and four thousand praised the LORD with *musical* instruments, "which I made," *said David*, "for giving praise."

6Also David separated them into divisions among the sons of Levi: Gershon, Kohath, and Merari.

7Of the Gershonites: Laadan[a] and Shimei. 8The sons of Laadan: the first Jehiel, then Zetham and Joel—three *in all*. 9The sons of Shimei: Shelomith, Haziel, and Haran—three *in all*. These were the heads of the fathers' *houses* of Laadan. 10And the sons

22:9 [a] Literally *Peaceful* 23:7 [a] Spelled *Libni* in Exodus 6:17

of Shimei: Jahath, Zina,[a] Jeush, and Beriah.
These *were* the four sons of Shimei. 11Jahath
was the first and Zizah the second. But
Jeush and Beriah did not have many sons;
therefore they were assigned as one father's
house.

12The sons of Kohath: Amram, Izhar,
Hebron, and Uzziel—four *in all.* 13The sons
of Amram: Aaron and Moses; and Aaron
was set apart, he and his sons forever, that
he should sanctify the most holy things, to
burn incense before the LORD, to minister to
Him, and to give the blessing in His name
forever. 14Now the sons of Moses the man
of God were reckoned to the tribe of Levi.
15The sons of Moses *were* Gershon[a] and
Eliezer. 16Of the sons of Gershon, Shebuel[a]
was the first. 17Of the descendants of Eliezer,
Rehabiah was the first. And Eliezer had no
other sons, but the sons of Rehabiah were
very many. 18Of the sons of Izhar, Shelomith
was the first. 19Of the sons of Hebron, Jeriah
was the first, Amariah the second, Jahaziel
the third, and Jekameam the fourth. 20Of
the sons of Uzziel, Michah *was* the first and
Jesshiah the second.

21The sons of Merari *were* Mahli and
Mushi. The sons of Mahli *were* Eleazar and
Kish. 22And Eleazar died, and had no sons,
but only daughters; and their brethren, the
sons of Kish, took them *as wives.* 23The sons
of Mushi *were* Mahli, Eder, and Jeremoth—
three *in all.*

24These *were* the sons of Levi by their
fathers' houses—the heads of the fathers'
houses as they were counted individually
by the number of their names, who did the
work for the service of the house of the LORD,
from the age of twenty years and above.

25For David said, "The LORD God of Israel
has given rest to His people, that they may
dwell in Jerusalem forever"; 26and also to the
Levites, "They shall no longer carry the tabernacle, or any of the articles for its service."
27For by the last words of David the Levites
were numbered from twenty years old and
above; 28because their duty *was* to help the
sons of Aaron in the service of the house
of the LORD, in the courts and in the chambers, in the purifying of all holy things and
the work of the service of the house of God,
29both with the showbread and the fine flour
for the grain offering, with the unleavened
cakes and *what is baked in* the pan, with what
is mixed and with all kinds of measures and
sizes; 30to stand every morning to thank and
praise the LORD, and likewise at evening;
31and at every presentation of a burnt offering to the LORD on the Sabbaths and on the
New Moons and on the set feasts, by number
according to the ordinance governing them,
regularly before the LORD; 32and that they
should attend to the needs of the tabernacle
of meeting, the needs of the holy *place,* and
the needs of the sons of Aaron their brethren
in the work of the house of the LORD.

The Divisions of the Priests

24 Now *these are* the divisions of the
sons of Aaron. The sons of Aaron
were Nadab, Abihu, Eleazar, and Ithamar.
2And Nadab and Abihu died before their father, and had no children; therefore Eleazar
and Ithamar ministered as priests. 3Then
David with Zadok of the sons of Eleazar, and
Ahimelech of the sons of Ithamar, divided them according to the schedule of their
service.

4There were more leaders found of the
sons of Eleazar than of the sons of Ithamar,
and *thus* they were divided. Among the sons
of Eleazar *were* sixteen heads of *their* fathers'
houses, and eight heads of their fathers'
houses among the sons of Ithamar. 5Thus
they were divided by lot, one group as another, for there were officials of the sanctuary and officials *of the house* of God, from
the sons of Eleazar and from the sons of
Ithamar. 6And the scribe, Shemaiah the son
of Nethanel, *one of* the Levites, wrote them
down before the king, the leaders, Zadok
the priest, Ahimelech the son of Abiathar,
and the heads of the fathers' *houses* of the
priests and Levites, one father's house taken
for Eleazar and *one* for Ithamar.

7Now the first lot fell to Jehoiarib, the
second to Jedaiah, 8the third to Harim, the
fourth to Seorim, 9the fifth to Malchijah, the
sixth to Mijamin, 10the seventh to Hakkoz,
the eighth to Abijah, 11the ninth to Jeshua,
the tenth to Shecaniah, 12the eleventh to
Eliashib, the twelfth to Jakim, 13the thirteenth to Huppah, the fourteenth to Jesheb-
eab, 14the fifteenth to Bilgah, the sixteenth
to Immer, 15the seventeenth to Hezir, the

23:10 [a] Septuagint and Vulgate read *Zizah* (compare verse 11). 23:15 [a] Hebrew *Gershom* (compare 6:16)
23:16 [a] Spelled *Shubael* in 24:20

eighteenth to Happizzez,[a] 16the nineteenth
to Pethahiah, the twentieth to Jehezekel,[a]
17the twenty-first to Jachin, the twenty-
second to Gamul, 18the twenty-third to Delaiah, the twenty-fourth to Maaziah.

19This *was* the schedule of their service
for coming into the house of the LORD according to their ordinance by the hand of
Aaron their father, as the LORD God of Israel
had commanded him.

Other Levites

20And the rest of the sons of Levi: of the
sons of Amram, Shubael;[a] of the sons of
Shubael, Jehdeiah. 21Concerning Rehabiah,
of the sons of Rehabiah, the first *was* Isshiah. 22Of the Izharites, Shelomoth;[a] of the
sons of Shelomoth, Jahath. 23Of the sons *of*
Hebron,[a] Jeriah *was the first*,[b] Amariah the
second, Jahaziel the third, *and* Jekameam
the fourth. 24*Of* the sons of Uzziel, Michah;
of the sons of Michah, Shamir. 25The brother
of Michah, Isshiah; of the sons of Isshiah,
Zechariah. 26The sons of Merari *were* Mahli
and Mushi; the son of Jaaziah, Beno. 27The
sons of Merari by Jaaziah *were* Beno, Sho-
ham, Zaccur, and Ibri. 28Of Mahli: Eleazar,
who had no sons. 29Of Kish: the son of Kish,
Jerahmeel.

30Also the sons of Mushi *were* Mahli,
Eder, and Jerimoth. These *were* the sons
of the Levites according to their fathers'
houses.

31These also cast lots just as their brothers the sons of Aaron did, in the presence
of King David, Zadok, Ahimelech, and the
heads of the fathers' *houses* of the priests and
Levites. The chief fathers *did* just as their
younger brethren.

The Musicians

25 Moreover David and the captains
of the army separated for the service *some* of the sons of Asaph, of Heman,
and of Jeduthun, who *should* prophesy with
harps, stringed instruments, and cymbals.
And the number of the skilled men performing their service was: 2Of the sons of Asaph:
Zaccur, Joseph, Nethaniah, and Asharelah;[a]
the sons of Asaph *were* under the direction
of Asaph, who prophesied according to the
order of the king. 3Of Jeduthun, the sons of
Jeduthun: Gedaliah, Zeri,[a] Jeshaiah, *Shim-*
ei, Hashabiah, and Mattithiah, six,[b] under
the direction of their father Jeduthun, who
prophesied with a harp to give thanks and
to praise the LORD. 4Of Heman, the sons
of Heman: Bukkiah, Mattaniah, Uzziel,[a]
Shebuel,[b] Jerimoth,[c] Hananiah, Hanani,
Eliathah, Giddalti, Romamti-Ezer, Joshbekashah, Mallothi, Hothir, *and* Mahazioth.
5All these *were* the sons of Heman the king's
seer in the words of God, to exalt his horn.[a]
For God gave Heman fourteen sons and
three daughters.

6All these *were* under the direction of
their father for the music *in* the house of the
LORD, with cymbals, stringed instruments,
and harps, for the service of the house of
God. Asaph, Jeduthun, and Heman *were*
under the authority of the king. 7So the
number of them, with their brethren who
were instructed in the songs of the LORD,
all who were skillful, *was* two hundred and
eighty-eight.

8And they cast lots for their duty, the
small as well as the great, the teacher with
the student.

9Now the first lot for Asaph came out for
Joseph; the second for Gedaliah, him with
his brethren and sons, twelve; 10the third for
Zaccur, his sons and his brethren, twelve;
11the fourth for Jizri,[a] his sons and his brethren, twelve; 12the fifth for Nethaniah, his
sons and his brethren, twelve; 13the sixth for
Bukkiah, his sons and his brethren, twelve;
14the seventh for Jesharelah,[a] his sons and
his brethren, twelve; 15the eighth for Jeshaiah, his sons and his brethren, twelve; 16the
ninth for Mattaniah, his sons and his brethren, twelve; 17the tenth for Shimei, his sons
and his brethren, twelve; 18the eleventh for
Azarel,[a] his sons and his brethren, twelve;
19the twelfth for Hashabiah, his sons and
his brethren, twelve; 20the thirteenth for
Shubael,[a] his sons and his brethren, twelve;

24:15 [a] Septuagint and Vulgate read *Aphses*.
24:16 [a] Masoretic Text reads *Jehezkel*. **24:20** [a] Spelled *Shebuel* in 23:16 **24:22** [a] Spelled *Shelomith* in 23:18
24:23 [a] Supplied from 23:19 (following some Hebrew manuscripts and Septuagint manuscripts) [b] Supplied from 23:19 (following some Hebrew manuscripts and Septuagint manuscripts) **25:2** [a] Spelled *Jesharelah* in verse 14 **25:3** [a] Spelled *Jizri* in verse 11 [b] *Shimei*, appearing in one Hebrew and several Septuagint manuscripts, completes the total of six sons (compare verse 17). **25:4** [a] Spelled *Azarel* in verse 18 [b] Spelled *Shubael* in verse 20 [c] Spelled *Jeremoth* in verse 22
25:5 [a] That is, to increase his power or influence
25:11 [a] Spelled *Zeri* in verse 3 **25:14** [a] Spelled *Asharelah* in verse 2 **25:18** [a] Spelled *Uzziel* in verse 4
25:20 [a] Spelled *Shebuel* in verse 4

21the fourteenth for Mattithiah, his sons and
his brethren, twelve; 22the fifteenth for Jeremoth,[a] his sons and his brethren, twelve;
23the sixteenth for Hananiah, his sons and
his brethren, twelve; 24the seventeenth for
Joshbekashah, his sons and his brethren,
twelve; 25the eighteenth for Hanani, his sons
and his brethren, twelve; 26the nineteenth for
Mallothi, his sons and his brethren, twelve;
27the twentieth for Eliathah, his sons and
his brethren, twelve; 28the twenty-first for
Hothir, his sons and his brethren, twelve;
29the twenty-second for Giddalti, his sons
and his brethren, twelve; 30the twenty-third
for Mahazioth, his sons and his brethren,
twelve; 31the twenty-fourth for Romamti-
Ezer, his sons and his brethren, twelve.

The Gatekeepers

26 Concerning the divisions of the
gatekeepers: of the Korahites, Meshelemiah the son of Kore, of the sons of
Asaph. 2And the sons of Meshelemiah *were*
Zechariah the firstborn, Jediael the second,
Zebadiah the third, Jathniel the fourth,
3Elam the fifth, Jehohanan the sixth, Eliehoenai the seventh.

4Moreover the sons of Obed-Edom *were*
Shemaiah the firstborn, Jehozabad the second, Joah the third, Sacar the fourth, Nethanel the fifth, 5Ammiel the sixth, Issachar
the seventh, Peulthai the eighth; for God
blessed him.

6Also to Shemaiah his son were sons
born who governed their fathers' houses,
because they *were* men of great ability. 7The
sons of Shemaiah *were* Othni, Rephael,
Obed, and Elzabad, whose brothers Elihu
and Semachiah *were* able men.

8All these *were* of the sons of Obed-Edom,
they and their sons and their brethren, able
men with strength for the work: sixty-two of
Obed-Edom.

9And Meshelemiah had sons and brethren, eighteen able men.

10Also Hosah, of the children of Merari,
had sons: Shimri the first (for *though* he
was not the firstborn, his father made him
the first), 11Hilkiah the second, Tebaliah the
third, Zechariah the fourth; all the sons and
brethren of Hosah were thirteen.

12Among these *were* the divisions of the
gatekeepers, among the chief men, *having*
duties just like their brethren, to serve in
the house of the LORD. 13And they cast lots
for each gate, the small as well as the great,
according to their father's house. 14The lot
for the East *Gate* fell to Shelemiah. Then
they cast lots *for* his son Zechariah, a wise
counselor, and his lot came out for the North
Gate; 15to Obed-Edom the South Gate, and to
his sons the storehouse.[a] 16To Shuppim and
Hosah *the lot came out* for the West Gate,
with the Shallecheth Gate on the ascending
highway—watchman opposite watchman.
17On the east *were* six Levites, on the north
four each day, on the south four each day,
and for the storehouse[a] two by two. 18As for
the Parbar[a] on the west, *there were* four on
the highway *and* two at the Parbar. 19These
were the divisions of the gatekeepers among
the sons of Korah and among the sons of
Merari.

The Treasuries and Other Duties

20Of the Levites, Ahijah *was* over the treasuries of the house of God and over the treasuries of the dedicated things. 21The sons of
Laadan, the descendants of the Gershonites
of Laadan, heads of their fathers' *houses,* of
Laadan the Gershonite: Jehieli. 22The sons
of Jehieli, Zetham and Joel his brother, *were*
over the treasuries of the house of the LORD.
23Of the Amramites, the Izharites, the Hebronites, and the Uzzielites: 24Shebuel the
son of Gershom, the son of Moses, *was* overseer of the treasuries. 25And his brethren by
Eliezer *were* Rehabiah his son, Jeshaiah his
son, Joram his son, Zichri his son, and Shelomith his son.

26This Shelomith and his brethren *were*
over all the treasuries of the dedicated things
which King David and the heads of fathers'
houses, the captains over thousands and
hundreds, and the captains of the army, had
dedicated. 27Some of the spoils won in battles
they dedicated to maintain the house of the
LORD. 28And all that Samuel the seer, Saul
the son of Kish, Abner the son of Ner, and
Joab the son of Zeruiah had dedicated, every
dedicated *thing,* was under the hand of Shelomith and his brethren.

29Of the Izharites, Chenaniah and his
sons *performed* duties as officials and judges
over Israel outside Jerusalem.

30Of the Hebronites, Hashabiah and

25:22 [a] Spelled *Jerimoth* in verse 4 26:15 [a] Hebrew *asuppim* 26:17 [a] Hebrew *asuppim* 26:18 [a] Probably a court or colonnade extending west of the temple

his brethren, one thousand seven hundred
able men, had the oversight of Israel on the
west side of the Jordan for all the business
of the LORD, and in the service of the king.
31 Among the Hebronites, Jerijah *was* head
of the Hebronites according to his genealogy of the fathers. In the fortieth year of the
reign of David they were sought, and there
were found among them capable men at
Jazer of Gilead. 32 And his brethren *were* two
thousand seven hundred able men, heads of
fathers' *houses,* whom King David made officials over the Reubenites, the Gadites, and
the half-tribe of Manasseh, for every matter
pertaining to God and the affairs of the king.

The Military Divisions

27 And the children of Israel, according to their number, the heads of
fathers' *houses,* the captains of thousands
and hundreds and their officers, served the
king in every matter of the *military* divisions. *These divisions* came in and went out
month by month throughout all the months
of the year, each division *having* twenty-four
thousand.

2 Over the first division for the first
month *was* Jashobeam the son of Zabdiel,
and in his division *were* twenty-four thousand; 3 *he was* of the children of Perez, and
the chief of all the captains of the army for
the first month. 4 Over the division of the second month *was* Dodai[a] an Ahohite, and of
his division Mikloth also *was* the leader; in
his division *were* twenty-four thousand. 5 The
third captain of the army for the third month
was Benaiah, the son of Jehoiada the priest,
who was chief; in his division *were* twenty-
four thousand. 6 This was the Benaiah *who
was* mighty *among* the thirty, and was over
the thirty; in his division *was* Ammizabad
his son. 7 The fourth *captain* for the fourth
month *was* Asahel the brother of Joab, and
Zebadiah his son after him; in his division
were twenty-four thousand. 8 The fifth captain for the fifth month *was* Shamhuth[a] the
Izrahite; in his division were twenty-four
thousand. 9 The sixth *captain* for the sixth
month *was* Ira the son of Ikkesh the Tekoite;
in his division *were* twenty-four thousand.
10 The seventh *captain* for the seventh month
was Helez the Pelonite, of the children of
Ephraim; in his division *were* twenty-four
thousand. 11 The eighth *captain* for the eighth
month *was* Sibbechai the Hushathite, of the
Zarhites; in his division *were* twenty-four
thousand. 12 The ninth *captain* for the ninth
month *was* Abiezer the Anathothite, of the
Benjamites; in his division *were* twenty-four
thousand. 13 The tenth *captain* for the tenth
month *was* Maharai the Netophathite, of the
Zarhites; in his division *were* twenty-four
thousand. 14 The eleventh *captain* for the eleventh month *was* Benaiah the Pirathonite, of
the children of Ephraim; in his division *were*
twenty-four thousand. 15 The twelfth *captain*
for the twelfth month *was* Heldai[a] the Netophathite, of Othniel; in his division *were*
twenty-four thousand.

Leaders of Tribes

16 Furthermore, over the tribes of Israel:
the officer over the Reubenites *was* Eliezer
the son of Zichri; over the Simeonites,
Shephatiah the son of Maachah; 17 *over* the
Levites, Hashabiah the son of Kemuel; over
the Aaronites, Zadok; 18 *over* Judah, Elihu, *one*
of David's brothers; *over* Issachar, Omri the
son of Michael; 19 *over* Zebulun, Ishmaiah the
son of Obadiah; *over* Naphtali, Jerimoth the
son of Azriel; 20 *over* the children of Ephraim,
Hoshea the son of Azaziah; *over* the half-
tribe of Manasseh, Joel the son of Pedaiah;
21 *over* the half-*tribe* of Manasseh in Gilead,
Iddo the son of Zechariah; *over* Benjamin,
Jaasiel the son of Abner; 22 *over* Dan, Azarel
the son of Jeroham. These *were* the leaders
of the tribes of Israel.

23 But David did not take the number of
those twenty years old and under, because
the LORD had said He would multiply Israel
like the stars of the heavens. 24 Joab the son of
Zeruiah began a census, but he did not finish, for wrath came upon Israel because of
this census; nor was the number recorded in
the account of the chronicles of King David.

Other State Officials

25 And Azmaveth the son of Adiel *was*
over the king's treasuries; and Jehonathan
the son of Uzziah was over the storehouses
in the field, in the cities, in the villages, and
in the fortresses. 26 Ezri the son of Chelub
was over those who did the work of the
field for tilling the ground. 27 And Shimei
the Ramathite *was* over the vineyards, and

27:4 [a] Hebrew *Dodai,* usually spelled *Dodo* (compare 2 Samuel 23:9) **27:8** [a] Spelled *Shammoth* in 11:27 and *Shammah* in 2 Samuel 23:11 **27:15** [a] Spelled *Heled* in 11:30 and *Heleb* in 2 Samuel 23:29

Zabdi the Shiphmite was over the produce of the vineyards for the supply of wine. 28Baal-Hanan the Gederite was over the olive trees and the sycamore trees that *were* in the lowlands, and Joash *was* over the store of oil. 29And Shitrai the Sharonite *was* over the herds that fed in Sharon, and Shaphat the son of Adlai was over the herds *that were* in the valleys. 30Obil the Ishmaelite *was* over the camels, Jehdeiah the Meronothite *was* over the donkeys, 31and Jaziz the Hagrite *was* over the flocks. All these *were* the officials over King David's property.

32Also Jehonathan, David's uncle, *was* a counselor, a wise man, and a scribe; and Jehiel the son of Hachmoni *was* with the king's sons. 33Ahithophel *was* the king's counselor, and Hushai the Archite *was* the king's companion. 34After Ahithophel *was* Jehoiada the son of Benaiah, then Abiathar. And the general of the king's army *was* Joab.

Solomon Instructed to Build the Temple

28 Now David assembled at Jerusalem all the leaders of Israel: the officers of the tribes and the captains of the divisions who served the king, the captains over thousands and captains over hundreds, and the stewards over all the substance and possessions of the king and of his sons, with the officials, the valiant men, and all the mighty men of valor.

2Then King David rose to his feet and said, "Hear me, my brethren and my people: I *had* it in my heart to build a house of rest for the ark of the covenant of the LORD, and for the footstool of our God, and had made preparations to build it. 3But God said to me, 'You shall not build a house for My name, because you *have been* a man of war and have shed blood.' 4However the LORD God of Israel chose me above all the house of my father to be king over Israel forever, for He has chosen Judah *to be* the ruler. And of the house of Judah, the house of my father, and among the sons of my father, He was pleased with me to make *me* king over all Israel. 5And of all my sons (for the LORD has given me many sons) He has chosen my son *Solomon to sit on* the throne of the kingdom of the LORD over Israel. 6Now He said to me, 'It is your son Solomon *who* shall build My house and My courts; for I have chosen him *to be* My son, and I will be his Father.

In Focus

28:1 Stewards Those in charge of property or an area of work. The apostles of the New Testament were "stewards of the mysteries of God" (1 Corinthians 4:1). They were in charge of the work of preaching the gospel.

7Moreover I will establish his kingdom forever, if he is steadfast to observe My commandments and My judgments, as it is this day.' 8Now therefore, in the sight of all Israel, the assembly of the LORD, and in the hearing of our God, be careful to seek out all the commandments of the LORD your God, that you may possess this good land, and leave *it* as an inheritance for your children after you forever.

9"As for you, my son Solomon, know the God of your father, and serve Him with a loyal heart and with a willing mind; for the LORD searches all hearts and understands all the intent of the thoughts. If you seek Him, He will be found by you; but if you forsake Him, He will cast you off forever. 10Consider now, for the LORD has chosen you to build a house for the sanctuary; be strong, and do it."

11Then David gave his son Solomon the plans for the vestibule, its houses, its treasuries, its upper chambers, its inner chambers, and the place of the mercy seat; 12and the plans for all that he had by the Spirit, of the courts of the house of the LORD, of all the chambers all around, of the treasuries of the house of God, and of the treasuries for the dedicated things; 13also for the division of the priests and the Levites, for all the work of the service of the house of the LORD, and for all the articles of service in the house of the LORD. 14*He gave* gold by weight for *things* of gold, for all articles used in every kind of service; also *silver* for all articles of silver by weight, for all articles used in every kind of service; 15the weight for the lampstands of gold, and their lamps of gold, by weight for each lampstand and its lamps; for the lampstands of silver by weight, for the lampstand and its lamps, according to

the use of each lampstand. 16And by weight
he gave gold for the tables of the showbread,
for each table, and silver for the tables of silver; 17also pure gold for the forks, the basins,
the pitchers of pure gold, and the golden
bowls—*he gave gold* by weight for every bowl;
and for the silver bowls, *silver* by weight for
every bowl; 18and refined gold by weight for
the altar of incense, and for the construction
of the chariot, that is, the gold cherubim that
spread *their wings* and overshadowed the ark
of the covenant of the LORD. 19"All *this," said*
David, "the LORD made me understand in
writing, by *His* hand upon me, all the works
of these plans."
20And David said to his son Solomon,
"Be strong and of good courage, and do *it;*
do not fear nor be dismayed, for the LORD
God—my God—*will be* with you. He will
not leave you nor forsake you, until you have
finished all the work for the service of the
house of the LORD. 21*Here are* the divisions of
the priests and the Levites for all the service
of the house of God; and every willing craftsman *will be* with you for all manner of workmanship, for every kind of service; also the
leaders and all the people *will be* completely
at your command."

Offerings for Building the Temple

29 Furthermore King David said
to all the assembly: "My son

WHO IS GOD? HIDE OR SEEK

READ IT: 1 CHRONICLES 28:9

GET IT:

Do you imagine God as a policeman, waiting for you to break a law? Or a teacher, grading your mistakes with red checkmarks?

Sure, God sees and notices what you do. But He's not all about scorecards and penalties. He's interested in your heart: what goes on inside of you, who you are at your core, and what you think about and believe in.

That's good news since no one will ever live a perfect life. But it's also serious news because we have a lot in our hearts and minds that we'd rather keep secret from everyone, including God. God doesn't search our hearts and minds in order to keep a hidden-thoughts scorecard. He searches our hearts and minds because He loves us. He made us and knows us inside and out. If we search for Him in return, He will live life with us and help us know who we really are on the inside, both the good and the not-so-good. Then He will mold us into the person He made us to be.

LIVE IT:

Are you hiding from God and living life on your own? Or are you seeking God and living life with Him? You can seek God by reading the Bible, talking to Him in prayer, and learning from other people who know Him and follow Him. Make time for these activities. The Bible promises that "if you seek Him, He will be found by you."

Solomon, whom alone God has chosen, *is*
young and inexperienced; and the work *is*
great, because the temple[a] *is* not for man but
for the LORD God. 2Now for the house of my
God I have prepared with all my might: gold
for *things to be made of* gold, silver for *things*
of silver, bronze for *things of* bronze, iron for
things of iron, wood for *things of* wood, onyx
stones, *stones* to be set, glistening stones of
various colors, all kinds of precious stones,
and marble slabs in abundance. 3Moreover,
because I have set my affection on the house
of my God, I have given to the house of my
God, over and above all that I have prepared
for the holy house, my own special treasure
of gold and silver: 4three thousand talents of
gold, of the gold of Ophir, and seven thousand talents of refined silver, to overlay the
walls of the houses; 5the gold for *things of*
gold and the silver for *things of* silver, and for
all kinds of work *to be done* by the hands of
craftsmen. Who *then* is willing to consecrate
himself this day to the LORD?"

6Then the leaders of the fathers' *houses,*
leaders of the tribes of Israel, the captains
of thousands and of hundreds, with the officers over the king's work, offered willingly. 7They gave for the work of the house of
God five thousand talents and ten thousand
darics of gold, ten thousand talents of silver,
eighteen thousand talents of bronze, and
one hundred thousand talents of iron. 8And
whoever had *precious* stones gave *them* to the
treasury of the house of the LORD, into the
hand of Jehiel[a] the Gershonite. 9Then the
people rejoiced, for they had offered willingly, because with a loyal heart they had offered willingly to the LORD; and King David
also rejoiced greatly.

David's Praise to God

10Therefore David blessed the LORD before all the assembly; and David said:

"Blessed are You, LORD God of Israel, our
  Father, forever and ever.
11 Yours, O LORD, *is* the greatness,
The power and the glory,
The victory and the majesty;
For all *that is* in heaven and in earth *is*
  Yours;
Yours *is* the kingdom, O LORD,
And You are exalted as head over all.
12 Both riches and honor *come* from You,
And You reign over all.
In Your hand *is* power and might;
In Your hand *it is* to make great
And to give strength to all.

13 "Now therefore, our God,
We thank You
And praise Your glorious name.
14 But who *am* I, and who *are* my people,

29:1 [a] Literally *palace* 29:8 [a] Possibly the same as *Jehieli* (compare 26:21, 22)

MONEY

READ IT: 1 CHRONICLES 29:12

King David was growing old. He was obsessed—focused completely—with finishing the temple (a job he eventually left to his son). David spent his wealth on God's house of worship. He gave freely and hoped others would do the same. Why? Because David knew his wealth came from God. David didn't see his generosity as giving things *back* to God; the money never left God's ownership. Just a few verses later David asked, "But who am I?" (v. 14). He recognized God's greatness by humbling himself. In effect, David was saying, "I'm not rich. I'm not powerful. I'm not worthy of praise. Only God is. Everything that comes from God is His."

Solomon Requests Wisdom

1 Now Solomon the son of David was
strengthened in his kingdom, and the
LORD his God *was* with him and exalted him
exceedingly.
2And Solomon spoke to all Israel, to the
captains of thousands and of hundreds, to
the judges, and to every leader in all Israel,
the heads of the fathers' *houses.* 3Then Solomon, and all the assembly with him, went
to the high place that *was* at Gibeon; for the
tabernacle of meeting with God was there,
which Moses the servant of the LORD had
made in the wilderness. 4But David had
brought up the ark of God from Kirjath
Jearim to *the place* David had prepared for it,
for he had pitched a tent for it at Jerusalem.
5Now the bronze altar that Bezalel the son
of Uri, the son of Hur, had made, he put[a]
before the tabernacle of the LORD; Solomon
and the assembly sought Him *there.* 6And
Solomon went up there to the bronze altar
before the LORD, which *was* at the tabernacle
of meeting, and offered a thousand burnt
offerings on it.
7On that night God appeared to Solomon, and said to him, "Ask! What shall I
give you?"
8And Solomon said to God: "You have
shown great mercy to David my father, and
have made me king in his place. 9Now, O
LORD God, let Your promise to David my
father be established, for You have made
me king over a people like the dust of the
earth in multitude. 10Now give me wisdom
and knowledge, that I may go out and come
in before this people; for who can judge this
great people of Yours?"
11Then God said to Solomon: "Because
this was in your heart, and you have not
asked riches or wealth or honor or the life of
your enemies, nor have you asked long life—
but have asked wisdom and knowledge for
yourself, that you may judge My people over
whom I have made you king— 12wisdom and
knowledge *are* granted to you; and I will give
you riches and wealth and honor, such as
none of the kings have had who *were* before
you, nor shall any after you have the like."

Solomon's Military and Economic Power

13So Solomon came to Jerusalem from
the high place that *was* at Gibeon, from before the tabernacle of meeting, and reigned
over Israel. 14And Solomon gathered chariots and horsemen; he had one thousand
four hundred chariots and twelve thousand
horsemen, whom he stationed in the chariot
cities and with the king in Jerusalem. 15Also
the king made silver and gold as common
in Jerusalem as stones, and he made cedars
as abundant as the sycamores which *are*
in the lowland. 16And Solomon had horses
imported from Egypt and Keveh; the king's
merchants bought them in Keveh at the *current* price. 17They also acquired and imported
from Egypt a chariot for six hundred *shekels*
of silver, and a horse for one hundred and

1:5 [a] Some authorities read *it was there.*

WISDOM

READ IT: 2 CHRONICLES 1:7–12

King Solomon is considered one of the wisest people in the whole Bible (other than Jesus, of course). Sometimes he's even referred to as "wise King Solomon." But Solomon didn't get wise on his own. He wasn't wise because his parents taught him to be. He wasn't wise because he was super smart or because he just naturally made great decisions. Solomon was wise because God gave him wisdom in response to Solomon's request. You can ask God for wisdom, too!

fifty; thus, through their agents,[a] they exported them to all the kings of the Hittites
and the kings of Syria.

Solomon Prepares to Build the Temple

2 Then Solomon determined to build
a temple for the name of the LORD,
and a royal house for himself. 2Solomon
selected seventy thousand men to bear burdens, eighty thousand to quarry *stone* in the
mountains, and three thousand six hundred
to oversee them.
3Then Solomon sent to Hiram[a] king of
Tyre, saying:

As you have dealt with David my father,
and sent him cedars to build himself
a house to dwell in, *so deal with me.*
4Behold, I am building a temple for the
name of the LORD my God, to dedicate
it to Him, to burn before Him sweet
incense, for the continual showbread,
for the burnt offerings morning and
evening, on the Sabbaths, on the New
Moons, and on the set feasts of the LORD
our God. This *is an ordinance* forever to
Israel.

5 And the temple which I build *will be*
great, for our God is greater than all
gods. 6But who is able to build Him a
temple, since heaven and the heaven of
heavens cannot contain Him? Who *am* I
then, that I should build Him a temple,
except to burn sacrifice before Him?

7 Therefore send me at once a man skillful to work in gold and silver, in bronze
and iron, in purple and crimson and
blue, who has skill to engrave with the
skillful men who are with me in Judah
and Jerusalem, whom David my father
provided. 8Also send me cedar and cypress and algum logs from Lebanon, for
I know that your servants have skill to
cut timber in Lebanon; and indeed my
servants *will be* with your servants, 9to
prepare timber for me in abundance, for
the temple which I am about to build
shall be great and wonderful.

10 And indeed I will give to your servants,
the woodsmen who cut timber, twenty
thousand kors of ground wheat, twenty
thousand kors of barley, twenty thousand baths of wine, and twenty thousand baths of oil.

11Then Hiram king of Tyre answered in
writing, which he sent to Solomon:

Because the LORD loves His people, He
has made you king over them.

12Hiram[a] also said:

Blessed *be* the LORD God of Israel, who
made heaven and earth, for He has giv-
en King David a wise son, endowed with
prudence and understanding, who will
build a temple for the LORD and a royal
house for himself!

13 And now I have sent a skillful man, endowed with understanding, Huram[a] my
master[b] *craftsman* 14(the son of a woman
of the daughters of Dan, and his father
was a man of Tyre), skilled to work in
gold and silver, bronze and iron, stone
and wood, purple and blue, fine linen
and crimson, and to make any engraving and to accomplish any plan which
may be given to him, with your skillful
men and with the skillful men of my
lord David your father.

15 Now therefore, the wheat, the barley,
the oil, and the wine which my lord has
spoken of, let him send to his servants.
16And we will cut wood from Lebanon,
as much as you need; we will bring it to
you in rafts by sea to Joppa, and you will
carry it up to Jerusalem.

17Then Solomon numbered all the aliens
who *were* in the land of Israel, after the census in which David his father had numbered
them; and there were found to be one hundred and fifty-three thousand six hundred.
18And he made seventy thousand of them
bearers of burdens, eighty thousand stonecutters in the mountain, and three thousand six
hundred overseers to make the people work.

Solomon Builds the Temple

3 Now Solomon began to build the house
of the LORD at Jerusalem on Mount
Moriah, where *the LORD*[a] had appeared to his
father David, at the place that David had prepared on the threshing floor of Ornan[b] the

---

1:17 [a] Literally *by their hands* 2:3 [a] Hebrew *Huram* (compare 1 Kings 5:1) 2:12 [a] Hebrew *Huram* (compare 1 Kings 5:1) 2:13 [a] Spelled *Hiram* in 1 Kings 7:13 [b] Literally *father* (compare 1 Kings 7:13, 14) 3:1 [a] Literally *He,* following Masoretic Text and Vulgate; Septuagint reads *the LORD;* Targum reads *the Angel of the LORD.* [b] Spelled *Araunah* in 2 Samuel 24:16ff

Jebusite. 2And he began to build on the second day of the second month in the fourth
year of his reign.

3This is the foundation which Solomon
laid for building the house of God: The
length *was* sixty cubits (by cubits according
to the former measure) and the width twenty
cubits. 4And the vestibule that *was* in front *of*
the sanctuary[a] was twenty cubits long across
the width of the house, and the height *was*
one hundred and[b] twenty. He overlaid the
inside with pure gold. 5The larger room[a]
he paneled with cypress which he overlaid
with fine gold, and he carved palm trees
and chainwork on it. 6And he decorated the
house with precious stones for beauty, and
the gold *was* gold from Parvaim. 7He also
overlaid the house—the beams and doorposts, its walls and doors—with gold; and
he carved cherubim on the walls.

8And he made the Most Holy Place. Its
length was according to the width of the
house, twenty cubits, and its width twenty
cubits. He overlaid it with six hundred talents of fine gold. 9The weight of the nails
was fifty shekels of gold; and he overlaid
the upper area with gold. 10In the Most Holy
Place he made two cherubim, fashioned by
carving, and overlaid them with gold. 11The
wings of the cherubim *were* twenty cubits
in *overall* length: one wing *of the one cher-*
ub was five cubits, touching the wall of the
room, and the other wing *was* five cubits,
touching the wing of the other cherub;
12*one* wing of the other cherub *was* five cubits, touching the wall of the room, and the
other wing *also was* five cubits, touching
the wing of the other cherub. 13The wings
of these cherubim spanned twenty cubits
overall. They stood on their feet, and they
faced inward. 14And he made the veil of blue,
purple, crimson, and fine linen, and wove
cherubim into it.

15Also he made in front of the temple[a]
two pillars thirty-five[b] cubits high, and the
capital that *was* on the top of each of *them*
was five cubits. 16He made wreaths of chainwork, as in the inner sanctuary, and put
them on top of the pillars; and he made one
hundred pomegranates, and put *them* on the
wreaths of chainwork. 17Then he set up the
pillars before the temple, one on the right

3:4 [a] The main room of the temple; elsewhere called the holy place (compare 1 Kings 6:3) [b] Following Masoretic Text, Septuagint, and Vulgate; Arabic, some manuscripts of the Septuagint, and Syriac omit *one hundred and.*
3:5 [a] Literally *house* 3:15 [a] Literally *house* [b] Or *eighteen* (compare 1 Kings 7:15; 2 Kings 25:17; and Jeremiah 52:21)

3:1 THE TEMPLE IN GOD'S PLAN

The earliest place of worship was a special tent called a tabernacle (pronounced *TAB-er-nak-kel*). Later, God commanded Solomon to build the temple that was meant to be the permanent place of worship at Jerusalem. Both the tabernacle and the temple were the places where God revealed Himself to His people. Here also was the place where the people brought their offerings for sin and thanksgiving.

The stone temple didn't last forever. It was destroyed twice—first by the Babylonians and finally by the Romans. Each time God allowed the temple to be destroyed because the people were not worshiping Him in their hearts. The heart is the real temple where God must be worshiped. Any other place of worship means nothing without the true worship of our hearts. Those who now truly worship God are themselves the real temple of God.

hand and the other on the left; he called the
name of the one on the right hand Jachin,
and the name of the one on the left Boaz.

Furnishings of the Temple

4 Moreover he made a bronze altar:
twenty cubits was its length, twenty
cubits its width, and ten cubits its height.

2 Then he made the Sea of cast *bronze,*
ten cubits from one brim to the other; *it was*
completely round. Its height *was* five cubits,
and a line of thirty cubits measured its circumference. 3 And under it *was* the likeness
of oxen encircling it all around, ten to a cubit, all the way around the Sea. The oxen *were*
cast in two rows, when it was cast. 4 It stood
on twelve oxen: three looking toward the
north, three looking toward the west, three
looking toward the south, and three looking
toward the east; the Sea *was set* upon them,
and all their back parts *pointed* inward. 5 It
was a handbreadth thick; and its brim was
shaped like the brim of a cup, *like* a lily blossom. It contained three thousand[a] baths.

6 He also made ten lavers, and put five on
the right side and five on the left, to wash
in them; such things as they offered for the
burnt offering they would wash in them, but
the Sea *was* for the priests to wash in. 7 And
he made ten lampstands of gold according to
their design, and set *them* in the temple, five
on the right side and five on the left. 8 He also
made ten tables, and placed *them* in the temple, five on the right side and five on the left.
And he made one hundred bowls of gold.

9 Furthermore he made the court of the
priests, and the great court and doors for
the court; and he overlaid these doors with
bronze. 10 He set the Sea on the right side, toward the southeast.

11 Then Huram made the pots and the
shovels and the bowls. So Huram finished
doing the work that he was to do for King
Solomon for the house of God: 12 the two pillars and the bowl-shaped capitals *that were*
on top of the two pillars; the two networks
covering the two bowl-shaped capitals which
were on top of the pillars; 13 four hundred
pomegranates for the two networks (two
rows of pomegranates for each network,
to cover the two bowl-shaped capitals that
were on the pillars); 14 he also made carts and
the lavers on the carts; 15 one Sea and twelve
oxen under it; 16 also the pots, the shovels,
the forks—and all their articles Huram
his master[a] *craftsman* made of burnished
bronze for King Solomon for the house of
the LORD.

17 In the plain of Jordan the king had them
cast in clay molds, between Succoth and
Zeredah.[a] 18 And Solomon had all these articles made in such great abundance that the
weight of the bronze was not determined.

19 Thus Solomon had all the furnishings
made for the house of God: the altar of gold
and the tables on which *was* the showbread;
20 the lampstands with their lamps of pure
gold, to burn in the prescribed manner in
front of the inner sanctuary, 21 with the flowers and the lamps and the wick-trimmers of
gold, of purest gold; 22 the trimmers, the bowls,
the ladles, and the censers of pure gold. As for
the entry of the sanctuary, its inner doors to
the Most Holy *Place,* and the doors of the main
hall of the temple, *were* gold.

5 So all the work that Solomon had done
for the house of the LORD was finished;
and Solomon brought in the things which
his father David had dedicated: the silver and
the gold and all the furnishings. And he put
them in the treasuries of the house of God.

The Ark Brought into the Temple

2 Now Solomon assembled the elders of
Israel and all the heads of the tribes, the
chief fathers of the children of Israel, in Jerusalem, that they might bring the ark of the
covenant of the LORD up from the City of David, which *is* Zion. 3 Therefore all the men of
Israel assembled with the king at the feast,
which *was* in the seventh month. 4 So all the
elders of Israel came, and the Levites took
up the ark. 5 Then they brought up the ark,
the tabernacle of meeting, and all the holy
furnishings that *were* in the tabernacle. The
priests and the Levites brought them up.
6 Also King Solomon, and all the congregation of Israel who were assembled with him
before the ark, were sacrificing sheep and
oxen that could not be counted or numbered
for multitude. 7 Then the priests brought in
the ark of the covenant of the LORD to its
place, into the inner sanctuary of the temple,[a] to the Most Holy *Place,* under the wings
of the cherubim. 8 For the cherubim spread
their wings over the place of the ark, and

4:5 [a] Or *two thousand* (compare 1 Kings 7:26) 4:16 [a] Literally *father* 4:17 [a] Spelled *Zaretan* in 1 Kings 7:46
5:7 [a] Literally *house*

the cherubim overshadowed the ark and its poles. 9The poles extended so that the ends of the poles of the ark could be seen from *the holy place,* in front of the inner sanctuary; but they could not be seen from outside. And they are there to this day. 10Nothing was in the ark except the two tablets which Moses put *there* at Horeb, when the LORD made *a covenant* with the children of Israel, when they had come out of Egypt.

11And it came to pass when the priests came out of the *Most* Holy *Place* (for all the priests who *were* present had sanctified themselves, without keeping to their divisions), 12and the Levites *who were* the singers, all those of Asaph and Heman and Jeduthun, with their sons and their brethren, stood at the east end of the altar, clothed in white linen, having cymbals, stringed instruments and harps, and with them one hundred and twenty priests sounding with trumpets— 13indeed it came to pass, when the trumpeters and singers *were* as one, to make one sound to be heard in praising and thanking the LORD, and when they lifted up their voice with the trumpets and cymbals and instruments of music, and praised the LORD, *saying:*

"For He is good,
For His mercy *endures* forever,"[a]

that the house, the house of the LORD, was filled with a cloud, 14so that the priests could not continue ministering because of the cloud; for the glory of the LORD filled the house of God.

6 Then Solomon spoke:

"The LORD said He would dwell in the
dark cloud.
2 I have surely built You an exalted house,
And a place for You to dwell in forever."

Solomon's Speech upon Completion of the Work

3Then the king turned around and blessed the whole assembly of Israel, while all the assembly of Israel was standing. 4And he said: "Blessed *be* the LORD God of Israel, who has fulfilled with His hands *what* He spoke with His mouth to my father David, saying, 5'Since the day that I brought My people out of the land of Egypt, I have chosen no city from any tribe of Israel *in which* to build a house, that My name might be there, nor did I choose any man to be a ruler over My people Israel. 6Yet I have chosen Jerusalem, that My name may be there, and I have chosen David to be over My people Israel.' 7Now it was in the heart of my father David to build a temple[a] for the name of the LORD

5:13 [a] Compare Psalm 106:1 6:7 [a] Literally *house,* and so in verses 8–10

Epic Ideas

5:14 THE GLORY OF GOD IN THE TEMPLE

Sometimes God visited His people in the form of a bright cloud, called the "Shekinah" (pronounced *shi-KIGH-nuh*). We first read about this cloud in Exodus 14, when the cloud of God's presence protected Israel from the army of Egypt. This same cloud led the people in the desert (Exodus 13:21). This is the cloud that covered the mountain when God gave Moses the Ten Commandments (Exodus 19:18). Finally, the cloud of God's presence filled the tent of meeting (Exodus 40:34) and the temple (2 Chronicles 5:14).

In the New Testament, God's presence comes to us by the Holy Spirit. When you believe in Jesus, the Holy Spirit comes to live in your body. The Holy Spirit is God Himself. He is the same Spirit who visited the people in the cloud of the Old Testament.

God of Israel. [8]But the LORD said to my father David, 'Whereas it was in your heart to build a temple for My name, you did well in that it was in your heart. [9]Nevertheless you shall not build the temple, but your son who will come from your body, he shall build the temple for My name.' [10]So the LORD has fulfilled His word which He spoke, and I have filled the position of my father David, and sit on the throne of Israel, as the LORD promised; and I have built the temple for the name of the LORD God of Israel. [11]And there I have put the ark, in which *is* the covenant of the LORD which He made with the children of Israel."

Solomon's Prayer of Dedication

[12]Then *Solomon*[a] stood before the altar of the LORD in the presence of all the assembly of Israel, and spread out his hands [13](for Solomon had made a bronze platform five cubits long, five cubits wide, and three cubits high, and had set it in the midst of the court; and he stood on it, knelt down on his knees before all the assembly of Israel, and spread out his hands toward heaven); [14]and he said: "LORD God of Israel, *there is* no God in heaven or on earth like You, who keep *Your* covenant and mercy with Your servants who walk before You with all their hearts. [15]You have kept what You promised Your servant David my father; You have both spoken with Your mouth and fulfilled *it* with Your hand, as *it is* this day. [16]Therefore, LORD God of Israel, now keep what You promised Your servant David my father, saying, 'You shall not fail to have a man sit before Me on the throne of Israel, only if your sons take heed to their way, that they walk in My law as you have walked before Me.' [17]And now, O LORD God of Israel, let Your word come true, which You have spoken to Your servant David.

[18]"But will God indeed dwell with men on the earth? Behold, heaven and the heaven of heavens cannot contain You. How much less this temple[a] which I have built! [19]Yet regard the prayer of Your servant and his supplication, O LORD my God, and listen to the cry and the prayer which Your servant is praying before You: [20]that Your eyes may be open toward this temple day and night, toward the place where *You* said *You would* put Your name, that You may hear the prayer which Your servant makes toward this place. [21]And may You hear the supplications of Your servant and of Your people Israel, when they pray toward this place. Hear from heaven Your dwelling place, and when You hear, forgive.

[22]"If anyone sins against his neighbor, and is forced to take an oath, and comes *and* takes an oath before Your altar in this temple, [23]then hear from heaven, and act, and judge Your servants, bringing retribution on the wicked by bringing his way on his own head, and justifying the righteous by giving him according to his righteousness.

[24]"Or if Your people Israel are defeated before an enemy because they have sinned against You, and return and confess Your name, and pray and make supplication before You in this temple, [25]then hear from heaven and forgive the sin of Your people Israel, and bring them back to the land which You gave to them and their fathers.

[26]"When the heavens are shut up and there is no rain because they have sinned against You, when they pray toward this place and confess Your name, and turn from their sin because You afflict them, [27]then hear *in* heaven, and forgive the sin of Your servants, Your people Israel, that You may teach them the good way in which they should walk; and send rain on Your land which You have given to Your people as an inheritance.

[28]"When there is famine in the land, pestilence or blight or mildew, locusts or grasshoppers; when their enemies besiege them in the land of their cities; whatever plague or whatever sickness *there is;* [29]whatever prayer, whatever supplication is *made* by anyone, or by all Your people Israel, when each one knows his own burden and his own grief, and spreads out his hands to this temple: [30]then hear from heaven Your dwelling place, and forgive, and give to everyone according to all his ways, whose heart You know (for You alone know the hearts of the sons of men), [31]that they may fear You, to walk in Your ways as long as they live in the land which You gave to our fathers.

[32]"Moreover, concerning a foreigner, who is not of Your people Israel, but has come from a far country for the sake of Your great name and Your mighty hand and Your

6:12 [a] Literally *he* (compare 1 Kings 8:22) **6:18** [a] Literally *house*

outstretched arm, when they come and pray
in this temple; 33 then hear from heaven Your
dwelling place, and do according to all for
which the foreigner calls to You, that all peoples of the earth may know Your name and
fear You, as *do* Your people Israel, and that
they may know that this temple which I have
built is called by Your name.
34 "When Your people go out to battle
against their enemies, wherever You send
them, and when they pray to You toward this
city which You have chosen and the temple
which I have built for Your name, 35 then hear
from heaven their prayer and their supplication, and maintain their cause.
36 "When they sin against You (for *there is*
no one who does not sin), and You become
angry with them and deliver them to the enemy, and they take them captive to a land far
or near; 37 *yet* when they come to themselves
in the land where they were carried captive,
and repent, and make supplication to You in
the land of their captivity, saying, 'We have
sinned, we have done wrong, and have committed wickedness'; 38 and *when* they return
to You with all their heart and with all their
soul in the land of their captivity, where they
have been carried captive, and pray toward
their land which You gave to their fathers,
the city which You have chosen, and toward
the temple which I have built for Your name:
39 then hear from heaven Your dwelling place
their prayer and their supplications, and
maintain their cause, and forgive Your people who have sinned against You. 40 Now, my
God, I pray, let Your eyes be open and *let*
Your ears *be* attentive to the prayer *made* in
this place.

41 "Now therefore,
Arise, O LORD God, to Your resting
place,
You and the ark of Your strength.
Let Your priests, O LORD God, be
clothed with salvation,
And let Your saints rejoice in goodness.

42 "O LORD God, do not turn away the face
of Your Anointed;
Remember the mercies of Your servant
David."[a]

Solomon Dedicates the Temple

7 When Solomon had finished praying,
fire came down from heaven and consumed the burnt offering and the sacrifices;
and the glory of the LORD filled the temple.[a]
2 And the priests could not enter the house of
the LORD, because the glory of the LORD had
filled the LORD's house. 3 When all the children of Israel saw how the fire came down,
and the glory of the LORD on the temple, they
bowed their faces to the ground on the pavement, and worshiped and praised the LORD,
saying:

"For *He is* good,
For His mercy *endures* forever."[a]

4 Then the king and all the people offered
sacrifices before the LORD. 5 King Solomon
offered a sacrifice of twenty-two thousand
bulls and one hundred and twenty thousand
sheep. So the king and all the people dedicated the house of God. 6 And the priests
attended to their services; the Levites also
with instruments of the music of the LORD,
which King David had made to praise the
LORD, saying, "For His mercy *endures* forever,"[a] whenever David offered praise by their
ministry. The priests sounded trumpets opposite them, while all Israel stood.
7 Furthermore Solomon consecrated the
middle of the court that *was* in front of the
house of the LORD; for there he offered burnt
offerings and the fat of the peace offerings,
because the bronze altar which Solomon had
made was not able to receive the burnt offerings, the grain offerings, and the fat.
8 At that time Solomon kept the feast
seven days, and all Israel with him, a very
great assembly from the entrance of Hamath
to the Brook of Egypt.[a] 9 And on the eighth
day they held a sacred assembly, for they observed the dedication of the altar seven days,
and the feast seven days. 10 On the twenty-
third day of the seventh month he sent the
people away to their tents, joyful and glad of
heart for the good that the LORD had done
for David, for Solomon, and for His people
Israel. 11 Thus Solomon finished the house of
the LORD and the king's house; and Solomon
successfully accomplished all that came into
his heart to make in the house of the LORD
and in his own house.

God's Second Appearance to Solomon

12 Then the LORD appeared to Solomon by

6:42 [a] Compare Psalm 132:8–10 **7:1** [a] Literally *house*
7:3 [a] Compare Psalm 106:1 **7:6** [a] Compare Psalm 106:1
7:8 [a] That is, the Shihor (compare 1 Chronicles 13:5)

night, and said to him: "I have heard your prayer, and have chosen this place for Myself as a house of sacrifice. 13 When I shut up heaven and there is no rain, or command the locusts to devour the land, or send pestilence among My people, 14 if My people who are called by My name will humble themselves, and pray and seek My face, and turn from their wicked ways, then I will hear from heaven, and will forgive their sin and heal their land. 15 Now My eyes will be open and My ears attentive to prayer *made* in this place. 16 For now I have chosen and sanctified this house, that My name may be there forever; and My eyes and My heart will be there perpetually. 17 As for you, if you walk before Me as your father David walked, and do according to all that I have commanded you, and if you keep My statutes and My judgments, 18 then I will establish the throne of your kingdom, as I covenanted with David your father, saying, 'You shall not fail *to have* a man as ruler in Israel.'

19 "But if you turn away and forsake My statutes and My commandments which I have set before you, and go and serve other gods, and worship them, 20 then I will uproot them from My land which I have given them; and this house which I have sanctified for My name I will cast out of My sight, and will make it a proverb and a byword among all peoples.

21 "And *as for* this house, which is exalted, everyone who passes by it will be astonished and say, 'Why has the LORD done thus to this land and this house?' 22 Then they will answer, 'Because they forsook the LORD God of their fathers, who brought them out of the land of Egypt, and embraced other gods, and worshiped them and served them; therefore He has brought all this calamity on them.' "

Solomon's Additional Achievements

8 It came to pass at the end of twenty years, when Solomon had built the house of the LORD and his own house, 2 that the cities which Hiram[a] had given to Solomon, Solomon built them; and he settled the children of Israel there. 3 And Solomon went to Hamath Zobah and seized it. 4 He also built Tadmor in the wilderness, and all the storage cities which he built in Hamath. 5 He built Upper Beth Horon and Lower Beth Horon, fortified cities *with* walls, gates, and bars, 6 also Baalath and all the storage cities that Solomon had, and all the chariot cities and the cities of the cavalry, and all that Solomon desired to build in Jerusalem, in Lebanon, and in all the land of his dominion.

7 All the people *who were* left of the Hittites, Amorites, Perizzites, Hivites, and Jebusites, who *were* not of Israel— 8 that is, their descendants who were left in the land after them, whom the children of Israel did not destroy—from these Solomon raised forced labor, as it is to this day. 9 But Solomon did not make the children of Israel servants for his work. Some *were* men of war, captains

8:2 [a] Hebrew *Huram* (compare 2 Chronicles 2:3)

PRAYER

READ IT: 2 CHRONICLES 7:14

Have you ever been so embarrassed by how you behaved in class that you avoided the teacher all day? Sometimes we do that with God. We think if we stop talking to Him, maybe He won't see how we're behaving—or we won't have to see His face when He sees our hearts. But God is always ready to hear you—no matter how long it's been and no matter what you've done. He is waiting to hear from you right now, so don't wait a second longer to pray.

of his officers, captains of his chariots, and
his cavalry. 10And others *were* chiefs of the
officials of King Solomon: two hundred and
fifty, who ruled over the people.
11Now Solomon brought the daughter of
Pharaoh up from the City of David to the
house he had built for her, for he said, "My
wife shall not dwell in the house of David
king of Israel, because *the places* to which the
ark of the LORD has come are holy."
12Then Solomon offered burnt offerings
to the LORD on the altar of the LORD which
he had built before the vestibule, 13according
to the daily rate, offering according to the
commandment of Moses, for the Sabbaths,
the New Moons, and the three appointed yearly feasts—the Feast of Unleavened
Bread, the Feast of Weeks, and the Feast of
Tabernacles. 14And, according to the order of
David his father, he appointed the divisions
of the priests for their service, the Levites
for their duties (to praise and serve before
the priests) as the duty of each day required,
and the gatekeepers by their divisions at
each gate; for so David the man of God had
commanded. 15They did not depart from the
command of the king to the priests and Levites concerning any matter or concerning
the treasuries.
16Now all the work of Solomon was well-
ordered from[a] the day of the foundation of
the house of the LORD until it was finished.
So the house of the LORD was completed.
17Then Solomon went to Ezion Geber and
Elath[a] on the seacoast, in the land of Edom.
18And Hiram sent him ships by the hand of
his servants, and servants who knew the sea.
They went with the servants of Solomon to
Ophir, and acquired four hundred and fifty
talents of gold from there, and brought it to
King Solomon.

The Queen of Sheba's Praise of Solomon

9 Now when the queen of Sheba heard
of the fame of Solomon, she came to
Jerusalem to test Solomon with hard questions, *having* a very great retinue, camels
that bore spices, gold in abundance, and
precious stones; and when she came to Solomon, she spoke with him about all that was
in her heart. 2So Solomon answered all her
questions; there was nothing so difficult for
Solomon that he could not explain it to her.
3And when the queen of Sheba had seen the
wisdom of Solomon, the house that he had
built, 4the food on his table, the seating of
his servants, the service of his waiters and
their apparel, his cupbearers and their apparel, and his entryway by which he went up
to the house of the LORD, there was no more
spirit in her.
5Then she said to the king: "*It was* a true
report which I heard in my own land about
your words and your wisdom. 6However I
did not believe their words until I came and
saw with my own eyes; and indeed the half
of the greatness of your wisdom was not told
me. You exceed the fame of which I heard.
7Happy *are* your men and happy *are* these
your servants, who stand continually before you and hear your wisdom! 8Blessed be
the LORD your God, who delighted in you,
setting you on His throne *to be* king for the
LORD your God! Because your God has loved
Israel, to establish them forever, therefore
He made you king over them, to do justice
and righteousness."
9And she gave the king one hundred and
twenty talents of gold, spices in great abundance, and precious stones; there never were
any spices such as those the queen of Sheba
gave to King Solomon.
10Also, the servants of Hiram and the
servants of Solomon, who brought gold from
Ophir, brought algum[a] wood and precious
stones. 11And the king made walkways *of* the
algum[a] wood for the house of the LORD and
for the king's house, also harps and stringed
instruments for singers; and there were
none such *as these* seen before in the land
of Judah.
12Now King Solomon gave to the queen
of Sheba all she desired, whatever she asked,
much more than she had brought to the king.
So she turned and went to her own country,
she and her servants.

Solomon's Great Wealth

13The weight of gold that came to Solomon yearly was six hundred and sixty-six
talents of gold, 14besides *what* the traveling
merchants and traders brought. And all
the kings of Arabia and governors of the
country brought gold and silver to Solomon.
15And King Solomon made two hundred
large shields of hammered gold; six hundred

8:16 [a] Following Septuagint, Syriac, and Vulgate; Masoretic Text reads *as far as.* **8:17** [a] Hebrew *Eloth* (compare 2 Kings 14:22) **9:10** [a] Or *almug* (compare 1 Kings 10:11, 12) **9:11** [a] Or *almug* (compare 1 Kings 10:11, 12)

shekels of hammered gold went into each shield. 16*He* also *made* three hundred shields of hammered gold; three hundred *shekels*[a] of gold went into each shield. The king put them in the House of the Forest of Lebanon.

17Moreover the king made a great throne of ivory, and overlaid it with pure gold. 18The throne *had* six steps, with a footstool of gold, *which were* fastened to the throne; there were armrests on either side of the place of the seat, and two lions stood beside the armrests. 19Twelve lions stood there, one on each side of the six steps; nothing like *this* had been made for any *other* kingdom.

20All King Solomon's drinking vessels *were* gold, and all the vessels of the House of the Forest of Lebanon *were* pure gold. Not *one was* silver, for this was accounted as nothing in the days of Solomon. 21For the king's ships went to Tarshish with the servants of Hiram.[a] Once every three years the merchant ships[b] came, bringing gold, silver, ivory, apes, and monkeys.[c]

22So King Solomon surpassed all the kings of the earth in riches and wisdom. 23And all the kings of the earth sought the presence of Solomon to hear his wisdom, which God had put in his heart. 24Each man brought his present: articles of silver and gold, garments, armor, spices, horses, and mules, at a set rate year by year.

25Solomon had four thousand stalls for horses and chariots, and twelve thousand horsemen whom he stationed in the chariot cities and with the king at Jerusalem.

26So he reigned over all the kings from the River[a] to the land of the Philistines, as far as the border of Egypt. 27The king made silver *as common* in Jerusalem as stones, and he made cedar trees as abundant as the sycamores which *are* in the lowland. 28And they brought horses to Solomon from Egypt and from all lands.

Death of Solomon

29Now the rest of the acts of Solomon, first and last, *are* they not written in the book of Nathan the prophet, in the prophecy of Ahijah the Shilonite, and in the visions of Iddo the seer concerning Jeroboam the son of Nebat? 30Solomon reigned in Jerusalem over all Israel forty years. 31Then Solomon rested with his fathers, and was buried in the City of David his father. And Rehoboam his son reigned in his place.

The Revolt Against Rehoboam

10 And Rehoboam went to Shechem, for all Israel had gone to Shechem to make him king. 2So it happened, when Jeroboam the son of Nebat heard *it* (he was in Egypt, where he had fled from the presence of King Solomon), that Jeroboam returned from Egypt. 3Then they sent for him and called him. And Jeroboam and all Israel came and spoke to Rehoboam, saying, 4"Your father made our yoke heavy; now therefore, lighten the burdensome service of your father and his heavy yoke which he put on us, and we will serve you."

5So he said to them, "Come back to me after three days." And the people departed.

6Then King Rehoboam consulted the elders who stood before his father Solomon while he still lived, saying, "How do you advise *me* to answer these people?"

7And they spoke to him, saying, "If you are kind to these people, and please them, and speak good words to them, they will be your servants forever."

8But he rejected the advice which the elders had given him, and consulted the young men who had grown up with him, who stood before him. 9And he said to them, "What advice do you give? How should we answer this people who have spoken to me, saying, 'Lighten the yoke which your father put on us'?"

10Then the young men who had grown up with him spoke to him, saying, "Thus you should speak to the people who have spoken to you, saying, 'Your father made our yoke heavy, but you make *it* lighter on us'—thus you shall say to them: 'My little *finger* shall be thicker than my father's waist! 11And now, whereas my father put a heavy yoke on you, I will add to your yoke; my father chastised you with whips, but I *will chastise you* with scourges!' "[a]

12So Jeroboam and all the people came to Rehoboam on the third day, as the king had directed, saying, "Come back to me the third day." 13Then the king answered them roughly. King Rehoboam rejected the advice of the elders, 14and he spoke to them according to

---

9:16 [a] Or *three minas* (compare 1 Kings 10:17) **9:21** [a] Hebrew *Huram* (compare 1 Kings 10:22) [b] Literally *ships of Tarshish* (deep-sea vessels) [c] Or *peacocks* **9:26** [a] That is, the Euphrates **10:11** [a] Literally *scorpions*

the advice of the young men, saying, "My
father[a] made your yoke heavy, but I will add
to it; my father chastised you with whips, but
I *will chastise you* with scourges!"[b] 15So the
king did not listen to the people; for the turn
of events was from God, that the LORD might
fulfill His word, which He had spoken by
the hand of Ahijah the Shilonite to Jeroboam
the son of Nebat.

16Now when all Israel *saw* that the king
did not listen to them, the people answered
the king, saying:

"What share have we in David?
We have no inheritance in the son of
Jesse.
Every man to your tents, O Israel!
Now see to your own house, O David!"

So all Israel departed to their tents. 17But
Rehoboam reigned over the children of Israel who dwelt in the cities of Judah.

18Then King Rehoboam sent Hadoram,
who *was* in charge of revenue; but the children of Israel stoned him with stones, and
he died. Therefore King Rehoboam mounted *his* chariot in haste to flee to Jerusalem.
19So Israel has been in rebellion against the
house of David to this day.

11 Now when Rehoboam came to Jerusalem, he assembled from the house
of Judah and Benjamin one hundred and
eighty thousand chosen *men* who were warriors, to fight against Israel, that he might
restore the kingdom to Rehoboam.

2But the word of the LORD came to Shemaiah the man of God, saying, 3"Speak to
Rehoboam the son of Solomon, king of Judah, and to all Israel in Judah and Benjamin,
saying, 4'Thus says the LORD: "You shall not
go up or fight against your brethren! Let every man return to his house, for this thing
is from Me."'" Therefore they obeyed the
words of the LORD, and turned back from
attacking Jeroboam.

Rehoboam Fortifies the Cities

5So Rehoboam dwelt in Jerusalem, and
built cities for defense in Judah. 6And he
built Bethlehem, Etam, Tekoa, 7Beth Zur,
Sochoh, Adullam, 8Gath, Mareshah, Ziph,
9Adoraim, Lachish, Azekah, 10Zorah, Aijalon, and Hebron, which are in Judah and
Benjamin, fortified cities. 11And he fortified
the strongholds, and put captains in them,
and stores of food, oil, and wine. 12Also in
every city *he put* shields and spears, and
made them very strong, having Judah and
Benjamin on his side.

Priests and Levites Move to Judah

13And from all their territories the priests
and the Levites who *were* in all Israel took
their stand with him. 14For the Levites left
their common-lands and their possessions
and came to Judah and Jerusalem, for Jeroboam and his sons had rejected them from
serving as priests to the LORD. 15Then he appointed for himself priests for the high places, for the demons, and the calf idols which
he had made. 16And after *the* Levites *left*,[a]
those from all the tribes of Israel, such as set
their heart to seek the LORD God of Israel,
came to Jerusalem to sacrifice to the LORD
God of their fathers. 17So they strengthened
the kingdom of Judah, and made Rehoboam
the son of Solomon strong for three years,
because they walked in the way of David and
Solomon for three years.

The Family of Rehoboam

18Then Rehoboam took for himself as
wife Mahalath the daughter of Jerimoth the
son of David, *and of* Abihail the daughter of
Eliah the son of Jesse. 19And she bore him
children: Jeush, Shamariah, and Zaham.
20After her he took Maachah the granddaughter[a] of Absalom; and she bore him
Abijah, Attai, Ziza, and Shelomith. 21Now
Rehoboam loved Maachah the granddaughter of Absalom more than all his
wives and his concubines; for he took eighteen wives and sixty concubines, and begot twenty-eight sons and sixty daughters.
22And Rehoboam appointed Abijah the son
of Maachah as chief, *to be* leader among his
brothers; for he *intended* to make him king.
23He dealt wisely, and dispersed some of his
sons throughout all the territories of Judah
and Benjamin, to every fortified city; and he
gave them provisions in abundance. He also
sought many wives *for them*.

Egypt Attacks Judah

12 Now it came to pass, when Rehoboam had established the

10:14 [a] Following many Hebrew manuscripts, Septuagint, Syriac, and Vulgate (compare verse 10 and 1 Kings 12:14); Masoretic Text reads *I*. [b] Literally *scorpions* **11:16** [a] Literally *after them* **11:20** [a] Literally *daughter*, but in the broader sense of granddaughter (compare 2 Chronicles 13:2)

kingdom and had strengthened himself, that
he forsook the law of the LORD, and all Israel
along with him. 2And it happened in the fifth
year of King Rehoboam *that* Shishak king of
Egypt came up against Jerusalem, because
they had transgressed against the LORD, 3with
twelve hundred chariots, sixty thousand
horsemen, and people without number who
came with him out of Egypt—the Lubim and
the Sukkiim and the Ethiopians. 4And he
took the fortified cities of Judah and came to
Jerusalem.

5Then Shemaiah the prophet came to Re-
hoboam and the leaders of Judah, who were
gathered together in Jerusalem because of
Shishak, and said to them, "Thus says the
LORD: 'You have forsaken Me, and therefore
I also have left you in the hand of Shishak.'"

6So the leaders of Israel and the king
humbled themselves; and they said, "The
LORD *is* righteous."

7Now when the LORD saw that they humbled themselves, the word of the LORD came
to Shemaiah, saying, "They have humbled
themselves; *therefore* I will not destroy them,
but I will grant them some deliverance. My
wrath shall not be poured out on Jerusalem
by the hand of Shishak. 8Nevertheless they
will be his servants, that they may distinguish My service from the service of the
kingdoms of the nations."

9So Shishak king of Egypt came up
against Jerusalem, and took away the treasures of the house of the LORD and the
treasures of the king's house; he took everything. He also carried away the gold shields
which Solomon had made. 10Then King Rehoboam made bronze shields in their place,
and committed *them* to the hands of the captains of the guard, who guarded the doorway
of the king's house. 11And whenever the king
entered the house of the LORD, the guard
would go and bring them out; then they
would take them back into the guardroom.
12When he humbled himself, the wrath of
the LORD turned from him, so as not to destroy *him* completely; and things also went
well in Judah.

The End of Rehoboam's Reign

13*Thus* King Rehoboam strengthened
himself in Jerusalem and reigned. Now
Rehoboam *was* forty-one years old when
he became king; and he reigned seventeen
years in Jerusalem, the city which the LORD
had chosen out of all the tribes of Israel, to
put His name there. His mother's name *was*
Naamah, an Ammonitess. 14And he did evil,
because he did not prepare his heart to seek
the LORD.

15The acts of Rehoboam, first and last,
are they not written in the book of Shemaiah
the prophet, and of Iddo the seer concerning
genealogies? And *there were* wars between
Rehoboam and Jeroboam all their days. 16So
Rehoboam rested with his fathers, and was
buried in the City of David. Then Abijah[a] his
son reigned in his place.

Abijah Reigns in Judah

13 In the eighteenth year of King Jeroboam, Abijah became king over
Judah. 2He reigned three years in Jerusalem. His mother's name *was* Michaiah[a] the
daughter of Uriel of Gibeah.

And there was war between Abijah and
Jeroboam. 3Abijah set the battle in order
with an army of valiant warriors, four hundred thousand choice men. Jeroboam also
drew up in battle formation against him
with eight hundred thousand choice men,
mighty men of valor.

4Then Abijah stood on Mount Zemaraim, which *is* in the mountains of Ephraim,
and said, "Hear me, Jeroboam and all Israel:
5Should you not know that the LORD God of
Israel gave the dominion over Israel to David
forever, to him and his sons, by a covenant
of salt? 6Yet Jeroboam the son of Nebat, the
servant of Solomon the son of David, rose up
and rebelled against his lord. 7Then worthless rogues gathered to him, and strengthened themselves against Rehoboam the son
of Solomon, when Rehoboam was young
and inexperienced and could not withstand
them. 8And now you think to withstand the
kingdom of the LORD, which is in the hand
of the sons of David; and you *are* a great
multitude, and with you are the gold calves
which Jeroboam made for you as gods. 9Have
you not cast out the priests of the LORD, the
sons of Aaron, and the Levites, and made for
yourselves priests, like the peoples of *other*
lands, so that whoever comes to consecrate
himself with a young bull and seven rams
may be a priest of things that are not gods?
10But as for us, the LORD *is* our God, and we

12:16 [a] Spelled *Abijam* in 1 Kings 14:31 13:2 [a] Spelled *Maachah* in 11:20, 21 and 1 Kings 15:2

have not forsaken Him; and the priests who minister to the LORD *are* the sons of Aaron, and the Levites *attend* to *their* duties. 11And they burn to the LORD every morning and every evening burnt sacrifices and sweet incense; *they* also *set* the showbread *in order on* the pure *gold* table, and the lampstand of gold with its lamps to burn every evening; for we keep the command of the LORD our God, but you have forsaken Him. 12Now look, God Himself is with us as *our* head, and His priests with sounding trumpets to sound the alarm against you. O children of Israel, do not fight against the LORD God of your fathers, for you shall not prosper!"

13But Jeroboam caused an ambush to go around behind them; so they were in front of Judah, and the ambush *was* behind them. 14And when Judah looked around, to their surprise the battle line *was* at both front and rear; and they cried out to the LORD, and the priests sounded the trumpets. 15Then the men of Judah gave a shout; and as the men of Judah shouted, it happened that God struck Jeroboam and all Israel before Abijah and Judah. 16And the children of Israel fled before Judah, and God delivered them into their hand. 17Then Abijah and his people struck them with a great slaughter; so five hundred thousand choice men of Israel fell slain. 18Thus the children of Israel were subdued at that time; and the children of Judah prevailed, because they relied on the LORD God of their fathers.

19And Abijah pursued Jeroboam and took cities from him: Bethel with its villages, Jeshanah with its villages, and Ephraim[a] with its villages. 20So Jeroboam did not recover strength again in the days of Abijah; and the LORD struck him, and he died.

21But Abijah grew mighty, married fourteen wives, and begot twenty-two sons and sixteen daughters. 22Now the rest of the acts of Abijah, his ways, and his sayings *are* written in the annals of the prophet Iddo.

14 *So Abijah rested with his fathers,* and they buried him in the City of David. Then Asa his son reigned in his place. In his days the land was quiet for ten years.

Asa Reigns in Judah

2Asa did *what was* good and right in the eyes of the LORD his God, 3for he removed the altars of the foreign *gods* and the high places, and broke down the *sacred* pillars and cut down the wooden images. 4He commanded Judah to seek the LORD God of their fathers, and to observe the law and the commandment. 5He also removed the high places and the incense altars from all the cities of Judah, and the kingdom was quiet under him. 6And he built fortified cities in Judah, for the land had rest; he had no war in those years, because the LORD had given him rest. 7Therefore he said to Judah, "Let us build these cities and make walls around *them,* and towers, gates, and bars, *while* the land *is* yet before us, because we have sought the LORD our God; we have sought *Him,* and He has given us rest on every side." So they built and prospered. 8And Asa had an army of three hundred thousand from Judah who carried shields and spears, and from Benjamin two hundred and eighty thousand men who carried shields and drew bows; all these *were* mighty men of valor.

9Then Zerah the Ethiopian came out against them with an army of a million men and three hundred chariots, and he came to Mareshah. 10So Asa went out against him, and they set the troops in battle array in the Valley of Zephathah at Mareshah. 11And Asa cried out to the LORD his God, and said, "LORD, *it is* nothing for You to help, whether with many or with those who have no power; help us, O LORD our God, for we rest on You, and in Your name we go against this multitude. O LORD, You *are* our God; do not let man prevail against You!"

12So the LORD struck the Ethiopians before Asa and Judah, and the Ethiopians fled. 13And Asa and the people who *were* with him pursued them to Gerar. So the Ethiopians were overthrown, and they could not recover, for they were broken before the LORD and His army. And they carried away very much spoil. 14Then they defeated all the cities around Gerar, for the fear of the LORD came upon them; and they plundered all the cities, for there was exceedingly much spoil in them. 15They also attacked the livestock enclosures, and carried off sheep and camels in abundance, and returned to Jerusalem.

The Reforms of Asa

15 Now the Spirit of God came upon Azariah the son of Oded. 2And he

---

13:19 [a] Or *Ephron*

went out to meet Asa, and said to him: "Hear
me, Asa, and all Judah and Benjamin. The
LORD *is* with you while you are with Him. If
you seek Him, He will be found by you; but
if you forsake Him, He will forsake you. 3For
a long time Israel *has been* without the true
God, without a teaching priest, and without
law; 4but when in their trouble they turned
to the LORD God of Israel, and sought Him,
He was found by them. 5And in those times
there was no peace to the one who went out,
nor to the one who came in, but great turmoil *was* on all the inhabitants of the lands.
6So nation was destroyed by nation, and city
by city, for God troubled them with every
adversity. 7But you, be strong and do not let
your hands be weak, for your work shall be
rewarded!"

8And when Asa heard these words and
the prophecy of Oded[a] the prophet, he took
courage, and removed the abominable idols
from all the land of Judah and Benjamin
and from the cities which he had taken in
the mountains of Ephraim; and he restored
the altar of the LORD that *was* before the vestibule of the LORD. 9Then he gathered all
Judah and Benjamin, and those who dwelt
with them from Ephraim, Manasseh, and
Simeon, for they came over to him in great
numbers from Israel when they saw that the
LORD his God was with him.

10So they gathered together at Jerusalem
in the third month, in the fifteenth year of
the reign of Asa. 11And they offered to the
LORD at that time seven hundred bulls and
seven thousand sheep from the spoil they
had brought. 12Then they entered into a
covenant to seek the LORD God of their fathers with all their heart and with all their
soul; 13and whoever would not seek the
LORD God of Israel was to be put to death,
whether small or great, whether man or
woman. 14Then they took an oath before the
LORD with a loud voice, with shouting and
trumpets and rams' horns. 15And all Judah
rejoiced at the oath, for they had sworn with
all their heart and sought Him with all their
soul; and He was found by them, and the
LORD gave them rest all around.

16Also he removed Maachah, the mother
of Asa the king, from being queen mother,
because she had made an obscene image
of Asherah;[a] and Asa cut down her obscene
image, then crushed and burned *it* by the
Brook Kidron. 17But the high places were not
removed from Israel. Nevertheless the heart
of Asa was loyal all his days.

18He also brought into the house of God
the things that his father had dedicated and
that he himself had dedicated: silver and
gold and utensils. 19And there was no war
until the thirty-fifth year of the reign of Asa.

Asa's Treaty with Syria

16 In the thirty-sixth year of the reign
of Asa, Baasha king of Israel came
up against Judah and built Ramah, that he
might let none go out or come in to Asa king
of Judah. 2Then Asa brought silver and gold
from the treasuries of the house of the LORD
and of the king's house, and sent to Ben-
Hadad king of Syria, who dwelt in Damascus, saying, 3"*Let there be* a treaty between
you and me, as there was between my father
and your father. See, I have sent you silver
and gold; come, break your treaty with Baasha king of Israel, so that he will withdraw
from me."

4So Ben-Hadad heeded King Asa, and
sent the captains of his armies against the
cities of Israel. They attacked Ijon, Dan, Abel
Maim, and all the storage cities of Naphtali. 5Now it happened, when Baasha heard *it*,
that he stopped building Ramah and ceased
his work. 6Then King Asa took all Judah,
and they carried away the stones and timber of Ramah, which Baasha had used for
building; and with them he built Geba and
Mizpah.

Hanani's Message to Asa

7And at that time Hanani the seer came
to Asa king of Judah, and said to him: "Because you have relied on the king of Syria,
and have not relied on the LORD your God,
therefore the army of the king of Syria has
escaped from your hand. 8Were the Ethiopians and the Lubim not a huge army with
very many chariots and horsemen? Yet, because you relied on the LORD, He delivered
them into your hand. 9For the eyes of the
LORD run to and fro throughout the whole
earth, to show Himself strong on behalf of
those whose heart *is* loyal to Him. In this you
have done foolishly; therefore from now on
you shall have wars." 10Then Asa was angry
with the seer, and put him in prison, for *he*

15:8 [a] Following Masoretic Text and Septuagint; Syriac and Vulgate read *Azariah the son of Oded* (compare verse 1).
15:16 [a] A Canaanite deity

was enraged at him because of this. And Asa oppressed *some* of the people at that time.

Illness and Death of Asa

11 Note that the acts of Asa, first and last, are indeed written in the book of the kings of Judah and Israel. 12 And in the thirty-ninth year of his reign, Asa became diseased in his feet, and his malady was severe; yet in his disease he did not seek the LORD, but the physicians.

13 So Asa rested with his fathers; he died in the forty-first year of his reign. 14 They buried him in his own tomb, which he had made for himself in the City of David; and they laid him in the bed which was filled with spices and various ingredients prepared in a mixture of ointments. They made a very great burning for him.

Jehoshaphat Reigns in Judah

17 Then Jehoshaphat his son reigned in his place, and strengthened himself against Israel. 2 And he placed troops in all the fortified cities of Judah, and set garrisons in the land of Judah and in the cities of Ephraim which Asa his father had taken. 3 Now the LORD was with Jehoshaphat, because he walked in the former ways of his father David; he did not seek the Baals, 4 but sought the God[a] of his father, and walked in His commandments and not according to the acts of Israel. 5 Therefore the LORD established the kingdom in his hand; and all Judah gave presents to Jehoshaphat, and he had riches and honor in abundance. 6 And his heart took delight in the ways of the LORD; moreover he removed the high places and wooden images from Judah.

7 Also in the third year of his reign he sent his leaders, Ben-Hail, Obadiah, Zechariah, Nethanel, and Michaiah, to teach in the cities of Judah. 8 And with them *he sent* Levites: Shemaiah, Nethaniah, Zebadiah, Asahel, Shemiramoth, Jehonathan, Adonijah, Tobijah, and Tobadonijah—the Levites; and with *them* Elishama and Jehoram, the priests. 9 So they taught in Judah, and *had* the Book of the Law of the LORD with them; they went throughout all the cities of Judah and taught the people.

10 And the fear of the LORD fell on all the kingdoms of the lands that *were* around Judah, so that they did not make war against Jehoshaphat. 11 Also *some* of the Philistines brought Jehoshaphat presents and silver as tribute; and the Arabians brought him flocks, seven thousand seven hundred rams and seven thousand seven hundred male goats.

12 So Jehoshaphat became increasingly powerful, and he built fortresses and storage cities in Judah. 13 He had much property in the cities of Judah; and the men of war, mighty men of valor, *were* in Jerusalem.

14 These *are* their numbers, according to their fathers' houses. Of Judah, the captains of thousands: Adnah the captain, and with him three hundred thousand mighty men of valor; 15 and next to him *was* Jehohanan the captain, and with him two hundred and eighty thousand; 16 and next to him *was* Amasiah the son of Zichri, who willingly offered himself to the LORD, and with him two hundred thousand mighty men of valor. 17 Of Benjamin: Eliada a mighty man of valor, and with him two hundred thousand men armed with bow and shield; 18 and next to him *was* Jehozabad, and with him one hundred and eighty thousand prepared for war. 19 These served the king, besides those the king put in the fortified cities throughout all Judah.

Micaiah Warns Ahab

18 Jehoshaphat had riches and honor in abundance; and by marriage he allied himself with Ahab. 2 After some years he went down to *visit* Ahab in Samaria; and Ahab killed sheep and oxen in abundance for him and the people who were with him, and persuaded him to go up *with him* to Ramoth Gilead. 3 So Ahab king of Israel said to Jehoshaphat king of Judah, "Will you go with me *against* Ramoth Gilead?"

And he answered him, "I *am* as you *are,* and my people as your people; *we will be* with you in the war."

4 Also Jehoshaphat said to the king of Israel, "Please inquire for the word of the LORD today."

5 Then the king of Israel gathered the prophets together, four hundred men, and said to them, "Shall we go to war against Ramoth Gilead, or shall I refrain?"

So they said, "Go up, for God will deliver it into the king's hand."

6 But Jehoshaphat said, "*Is there* not still

17:4 [a] Septuagint reads *LORD God.*

a prophet of the LORD here, that we may inquire of Him?"[a]
7So the king of Israel said to Jehoshaphat,
"*There is* still one man by whom we may inquire of the LORD; but I hate him, because he
never prophesies good concerning me, but
always evil. He *is* Micaiah the son of Imla."
And Jehoshaphat said, "Let not the king
say such things!"
8Then the king of Israel called one *of his*
officers and said, "Bring Micaiah the son of
Imla quickly!"
9The king of Israel and Jehoshaphat king
of Judah, clothed in *their* robes, sat each on
his throne; and they sat at a threshing floor
at the entrance of the gate of Samaria; and all
the prophets prophesied before them. 10Now
Zedekiah the son of Chenaanah had made
horns of iron for himself; and he said, "Thus
says the LORD: 'With these you shall gore the
Syrians until they are destroyed.'"
11And all the prophets prophesied so, saying, "Go up to Ramoth Gilead and prosper,
for the LORD will deliver *it* into the king's
hand."
12Then the messenger who had gone to
call Micaiah spoke to him, saying, "Now
listen, the words of the prophets with one
accord encourage the king. Therefore please
let your word be like *the word of* one of them,
and speak encouragement."
13And Micaiah said, "*As* the LORD lives,
whatever my God says, that I will speak."
14Then he came to the king; and the king
said to him, "Micaiah, shall we go to war
against Ramoth Gilead, or shall I refrain?"
And he said, "Go and prosper, and they
shall be delivered into your hand!"
15So the king said to him, "How many
times shall I make you swear that you tell
me nothing but the truth in the name of the
LORD?"
16Then he said, "I saw all Israel scattered
on the mountains, as sheep that have no
shepherd. And the LORD said, 'These have
no master. Let each return to his house in
peace.'"
17And the king of Israel said to Jehoshaphat, "Did I not tell you he would not
prophesy good concerning me, but evil?"
18Then *Micaiah* said, "Therefore hear the
word of the LORD: I saw the LORD sitting on
His throne, and all the host of heaven standing on His right hand and His left. 19And the
LORD said, 'Who will persuade Ahab king of
Israel to go up, that he may fall at Ramoth
Gilead?' So one spoke in this manner, and
another spoke in that manner. 20Then a
spirit came forward and stood before the
LORD, and said, 'I will persuade him.' The
LORD said to him, 'In what way?' 21So he
said, 'I will go out and be a lying spirit in
the mouth of all his prophets.' And *the LORD*
said, 'You shall persuade *him* and also prevail; go out and do so.' 22Therefore look! The
LORD has put a lying spirit in the mouth of
these prophets of yours, and the LORD has
declared disaster against you."
23Then Zedekiah the son of Chenaanah
went near and struck Micaiah on the cheek,
and said, "Which way did the spirit from the
LORD go from me to speak to you?"
24And Micaiah said, "Indeed you shall
see on that day when you go into an inner
chamber to hide!"
25Then the king of Israel said, "Take Micaiah, and return him to Amon the governor
of the city and to Joash the king's son; 26and
say, 'Thus says the king: "Put this *fellow* in
prison, and feed him with bread of affliction and water of affliction, until I return in
peace."'"
27But Micaiah said, "If you ever return in
peace, the LORD has not spoken by me." And
he said, "Take heed, all you people!"

Ahab Dies in Battle

28So the king of Israel and Jehoshaphat
the king of Judah went up to Ramoth Gilead.
29And the king of Israel said to Jehoshaphat,
"I will disguise myself and go into battle; but
you put on your robes." So the king of Israel
disguised himself, and they went into battle.
30Now the king of Syria had commanded
the captains of the chariots who *were* with
him, saying, "Fight with no one small or
great, but only with the king of Israel."
31So it was, when the captains of the chariots saw Jehoshaphat, that they said, "It *is* the
king of Israel!" Therefore they surrounded
him to attack; but Jehoshaphat cried out,
and the LORD helped him, and God divert-
ed them from him. 32For so it was, when the
captains of the chariots saw that it was not
the king of Israel, that they turned back from
pursuing him. 33Now a certain man drew a
bow at random, and struck the king of Israel

18:6 [a] Or *him*

between the joints of his armor. So he said to the driver of his chariot, "Turn around and take me out of the battle, for I am wounded." 34The battle increased that day, and the king of Israel propped *himself* up in *his* chariot facing the Syrians until evening; and about the time of sunset he died.

19 Then Jehoshaphat the king of Judah returned safely to his house in Jerusalem. 2And Jehu the son of Hanani the seer went out to meet him, and said to King Jehoshaphat, "Should you help the wicked and love those who hate the LORD? Therefore the wrath of the LORD *is* upon you. 3Nevertheless good things are found in you, in that you have removed the wooden images from the land, and have prepared your heart to seek God."

The Reforms of Jehoshaphat

4So Jehoshaphat dwelt at Jerusalem; and he went out again among the people from Beersheba to the mountains of Ephraim, and brought them back to the LORD God of their fathers. 5Then he set judges in the land throughout all the fortified cities of Judah, city by city, 6and said to the judges, "Take heed to what you are doing, for you do not judge for man but for the LORD, who *is* with you in the judgment. 7Now therefore, let the fear of the LORD be upon you; take care and do *it,* for *there is* no iniquity with the LORD our God, no partiality, nor taking of bribes."

8Moreover in Jerusalem, for the judgment of the LORD and for controversies, Jehoshaphat appointed some of the Levites and priests, and some of the chief fathers of Israel, when they returned to Jerusalem.[a] 9And he commanded them, saying, "Thus you shall act in the fear of the LORD, faithfully and with a loyal heart: 10Whatever case comes to you from your brethren who dwell in their cities, whether of bloodshed or offenses against law or commandment, against statutes or ordinances, you shall warn them, lest they trespass against the LORD and wrath come upon you and your brethren. Do this, and you will not be guilty. 11And take notice: Amariah the chief priest *is* over you in all matters of the LORD; and Zebadiah the son of Ishmael, the ruler of the house of Judah, for all the king's matters; also the Levites *will be* officials before you. Behave courageously, and the LORD will be with the good."

Ammon, Moab, and Mount Seir Defeated

20 It happened after this *that* the people of Moab with the people of Ammon, and *others* with them besides the Ammonites,[a] came to battle against Jehoshaphat. 2Then some came and told Jehoshaphat, saying, "A great multitude is coming against you from beyond the sea, from Syria;[a] and they are in Hazazon Tamar" (which *is* En Gedi). 3And Jehoshaphat feared, and set himself to seek the LORD, and proclaimed a fast throughout all Judah. 4So Judah gathered together to ask *help* from the LORD; and from all the cities of Judah they came to seek the LORD.

5Then Jehoshaphat stood in the assembly of Judah and Jerusalem, in the house of the LORD, before the new court, 6and said: "O LORD God of our fathers, *are* You not God in heaven, and do You *not* rule over all the kingdoms of the nations, and in Your hand *is there not* power and might, so that no one is able to withstand You? 7*Are* You not our God, *who* drove out the inhabitants of this land before Your people Israel, and gave it to the descendants of Abraham Your friend forever? 8And they dwell in it, and have built You a sanctuary in it for Your name, saying, 9'If disaster comes upon us—sword, judgment, pestilence, or famine—we will stand before this temple and in Your presence (for Your name *is* in this temple), and cry out to You in our affliction, and You will hear and save.' 10And now, here are the people of Ammon, Moab, and Mount Seir—whom You would not let Israel invade when they came out of the land of Egypt, but they turned from them and did not destroy them— 11here they are, rewarding us by coming to throw us out of Your possession which You have given us to inherit. 12O our God, will You not judge them? For we have no power against this great multitude that is coming against us; nor do we know what to do, but our eyes *are* upon You."

13Now all Judah, with their little ones, their wives, and their children, stood before the LORD.

14Then the Spirit of the LORD came upon

19:8 [a] Septuagint and Vulgate read *for the inhabitants of Jerusalem.* 20:1 [a] Following Masoretic Text and Vulgate; Septuagint reads *Meunites* (compare 26:7). 20:2 [a] Following Masoretic Text, Septuagint, and Vulgate; some Hebrew manuscripts and Old Latin read *Edom.*

Jahaziel the son of Zechariah, the son of Benaiah, the son of Jeiel, the son of Mattaniah,
a Levite of the sons of Asaph, in the midst of
the assembly. 15And he said, "Listen, all you
of Judah and you inhabitants of Jerusalem,
and you, King Jehoshaphat! Thus says the
LORD to you: 'Do not be afraid nor dismayed
because of this great multitude, for the battle
is not yours, but God's. 16Tomorrow go down
against them. They will surely come up by
the Ascent of Ziz, and you will find them at
the end of the brook before the Wilderness
of Jeruel. 17You will not *need* to fight in this
battle. Position yourselves, stand still and see
the salvation of the LORD, who is with you,
O Judah and Jerusalem!' Do not fear or be
dismayed; tomorrow go out against them,
for the LORD *is* with you."

18And Jehoshaphat bowed his head with
his face to the ground, and all Judah and the
inhabitants of Jerusalem bowed before the
LORD, worshiping the LORD. 19Then the Levites of the children of the Kohathites and
of the children of the Korahites stood up to
praise the LORD God of Israel with voices
loud and high.

20So they rose early in the morning and
went out into the Wilderness of Tekoa; and
as they went out, Jehoshaphat stood and
said, "Hear me, O Judah and you inhabitants of Jerusalem: Believe in the LORD your
God, and you shall be established; believe
His prophets, and you shall prosper." 21And
when he had consulted with the people,
he appointed those who should sing to the
LORD, and who should praise the beauty of
holiness, as they went out before the army
and were saying:

"Praise the LORD,
For His mercy *endures* forever."[a]

22Now when they began to sing and to
praise, the LORD set ambushes against the
people of Ammon, Moab, and Mount Seir,
who had come against Judah; and they were
defeated. 23For the people of Ammon and
Moab stood up against the inhabitants of
Mount Seir to utterly kill and destroy *them.*
And when they had made an end of the inhabitants of Seir, they helped to destroy one
another.

24So when Judah came to a place overlooking the wilderness, they looked toward
the multitude; and there *were* their dead bodies, fallen on the earth. No one had escaped.

25When Jehoshaphat and his people came
to take away their spoil, they found among
them an abundance of valuables on the dead
bodies,[a] and precious jewelry, which they
stripped off for themselves, more than they
could carry away; and they were three days
gathering the spoil because there was so
much. 26And on the fourth day they assembled in the Valley of Berachah, for there they
blessed the LORD; therefore the name of that
place was called The Valley of Berachah[a] until this day. 27Then they returned, every man
of Judah and Jerusalem, with Jehoshaphat in
front of them, to go back to Jerusalem with
joy, for the LORD had made them rejoice over
their enemies. 28So they came to Jerusalem,
with stringed instruments and harps and
trumpets, to the house of the LORD. 29And
the fear of God was on all the kingdoms of
those countries when they heard that the
LORD had fought against the enemies of Israel. 30Then the realm of Jehoshaphat was
quiet, for his God gave him rest all around.

The End of Jehoshaphat's Reign

31So Jehoshaphat was king over Judah.
He was thirty-five years old when he became
king, and he reigned twenty-five years in
Jerusalem. His mother's name *was* Azubah
the daughter of Shilhi. 32And he walked in
the way of his father Asa, and did not turn
aside from it, doing *what was* right in the
sight of the LORD. 33Nevertheless the high
places were not taken away, for as yet the
people had not directed their hearts to the
God of their fathers.

34Now the rest of the acts of Jehoshaphat,
first and last, indeed they *are* written in the
book of Jehu the son of Hanani, which *is*
mentioned in the book of the kings of Israel.

35After this Jehoshaphat king of Judah
allied himself with Ahaziah king of Israel,
who acted very wickedly. 36And he allied
himself with him to make ships to go to
Tarshish, and they made the ships in Ezion
Geber. 37But Eliezer the son of Dodavah of
Mareshah prophesied against Jehoshaphat,
saying, "Because you have allied yourself
with Ahaziah, the LORD has destroyed your
works." Then the ships were wrecked, so
that they were not able to go to Tarshish.

20:21 [a] Compare Psalm 106:1 **20:25** [a] A few Hebrew manuscripts, Old Latin, and Vulgate read *garments;* Septuagint reads *armor.* **20:26** [a] Literally *Blessing*

Jehoram Reigns in Judah

21 And Jehoshaphat rested with his fathers, and was buried with his fathers in the City of David. Then Jehoram his son reigned in his place. 2He had brothers, the sons of Jehoshaphat: Azariah, Jehiel, Zechariah, Azaryahu, Michael, and Shephatiah; all these *were* the sons of Jehoshaphat king of Israel. 3Their father gave them great gifts of silver and gold and precious things, with fortified cities in Judah; but he gave the kingdom to Jehoram, because he *was* the firstborn.

4Now when Jehoram was established over the kingdom of his father, he strengthened himself and killed all his brothers with the sword, and also *others* of the princes of Israel.

5Jehoram *was* thirty-two years old when he became king, and he reigned eight years in Jerusalem. 6And he walked in the way of the kings of Israel, just as the house of Ahab had done, for he had the daughter of Ahab as a wife; and he did evil in the sight of the LORD. 7Yet the LORD would not destroy the house of David, because of the covenant that He had made with David, and since He had promised to give a lamp to him and to his sons forever.

8In his days Edom revolted against Judah's authority, and made a king over themselves. 9So Jehoram went out with his officers, and all his chariots with him. And he rose by night and attacked the Edomites who had surrounded him and the captains of the chariots. 10Thus Edom has been in revolt against Judah's authority to this day. At that time Libnah revolted against his rule, because he had forsaken the LORD God of his fathers. 11Moreover he made high places in the mountains of Judah, and caused the inhabitants of Jerusalem to commit harlotry, and led Judah astray.

12And a letter came to him from Elijah the prophet, saying,

> Thus says the LORD God of your father David:
> Because you have not walked in the ways of Jehoshaphat your father, or in the ways of Asa king of Judah, 13but have walked in the way of the kings of Israel, and have made Judah and the inhabitants of Jerusalem to play the harlot like the harlotry of the house of Ahab, and also have killed your brothers, those of your father's household, *who were* better than yourself, 14behold, the LORD will strike your people with a serious affliction—your children, your wives, and all your possessions; 15and you *will become* very sick with a disease of your intestines, until your intestines come out by reason of the sickness, day by day.

16Moreover the LORD stirred up against Jehoram the spirit of the Philistines and the Arabians who *were* near the Ethiopians. 17And they came up into Judah and invaded it, and carried away all the possessions that were found in the king's house, and also his sons and his wives, so that there was not a son left to him except Jehoahaz,[a] the youngest of his sons.

18After all this the LORD struck him in his intestines with an incurable disease. 19Then it happened in the course of time, after the end of two years, that his intestines came out because of his sickness; so he died in severe pain. And his people made no burning for him, like the burning for his fathers.

20He was thirty-two years old when he became king. He reigned in Jerusalem eight years and, to no one's sorrow, departed. However they buried him in the City of David, but not in the tombs of the kings.

Ahaziah Reigns in Judah

22 Then the inhabitants of Jerusalem made Ahaziah his youngest son king in his place, for the raiders who came with the Arabians into the camp had killed all the older *sons*. So Ahaziah the son of Jehoram, king of Judah, reigned. 2Ahaziah *was* forty-two[a] years old when he became king, and he reigned one year in Jerusalem. His mother's name *was* Athaliah the granddaughter of Omri. 3He also walked in the ways of the house of Ahab, for his mother advised him to do wickedly. 4Therefore he did evil in the sight of the LORD, like the house of Ahab; for they were his counselors after the death of his father, to his destruction. 5He also followed their advice, and went with Jehoram[a] the son of Ahab king of Israel to war against Hazael king of Syria at Ramoth Gilead; and the Syrians wounded

---

21:17 [a] Elsewhere called *Ahaziah* (compare 2 Chronicles 22:1) **22:2** [a] Or *twenty-two* (compare 2 Kings 8:26)
22:5 [a] Also spelled *Joram* (compare verses 5 and 7; 2 Kings 8:28; and elsewhere)

Joram. 6Then he returned to Jezreel to recover from the wounds which he had received at
Ramah, when he fought against Hazael king
of Syria. And Azariah[a] the son of Jehoram,
king of Judah, went down to see Jehoram the
son of Ahab in Jezreel, because he was sick.
7His going to Joram was God's occasion
for Ahaziah's downfall; for when he arrived,
he went out with Jehoram against Jehu the
son of Nimshi, whom the LORD had anointed to cut off the house of Ahab. 8And it happened, when Jehu was executing judgment
on the house of Ahab, and found the princes
of Judah and the sons of Ahaziah's brothers
who served Ahaziah, that he killed them.
9Then he searched for Ahaziah; and they
caught him (he was hiding in Samaria), and
brought him to Jehu. When they had killed
him, they buried him, "because," they said,
"he is the son of Jehoshaphat, who sought
the LORD with all his heart."

So the house of Ahaziah had no one to assume power over the kingdom.

Athaliah Reigns in Judah

10Now when Athaliah the mother of Ahaziah saw that her son was dead, she arose
and destroyed all the royal heirs of the house
of Judah. 11But Jehoshabeath,[a] the daughter
of the king, took Joash the son of Ahaziah,
and stole him away from among the king's
sons who were being murdered, and put
him and his nurse in a bedroom. So Jehoshabeath, the daughter of King Jehoram,
the wife of Jehoiada the priest (for she was
the sister of Ahaziah), hid him from Athaliah so that she did not kill him. 12And he
was hidden with them in the house of God
for six years, while Athaliah reigned over the
land.

Joash Crowned King of Judah

23 In the seventh year Jehoiada
strengthened himself, *and made
a* covenant with the captains of hundreds:
Azariah the son of Jeroham, Ishmael the
son of Jehohanan, Azariah the son of Obed,
Maaseiah the son of Adaiah, and Elishaphat
the son of Zichri. 2And they went throughout Judah and gathered the Levites from all
the cities of Judah, and the chief fathers of
Israel, and they came to Jerusalem.
3Then all the assembly made a covenant
with the king in the house of God. And he
said to them, "Behold, the king's son shall
reign, as the LORD has said of the sons of
David. 4This *is* what you shall do: One-third
of you entering on the Sabbath, of the priests
and the Levites, *shall be* keeping watch over
the doors; 5one-third *shall be* at the king's

22:6 [a] Some Hebrew manuscripts, Septuagint, Syriac, Vulgate, and 2 Kings 8:29 read *Ahaziah.* **22:11** [a] Spelled *Jehosheba* in 2 Kings 11:2

Starring Roles

KING JOASH'S (pronounced *JO-ash*) name means "The Lord Supports." Joash was only seven years old when he became king of Judah. Jehoiada (pronounced *jeh-HOY-uh-dah*) the priest was like a father to Joash while he lived. He was a very good man.

The temple of the Lord had fallen into ruin and its costly furniture had been stolen. So Jehoiada and Joash collected money to restore the beauty of the temple. All of its furniture and implements were replaced, and all was well for them as long as Jehoiada lived.

After Jehoiada died, the leaders of Judah made Joash agree to allow false worship of idols in the land. Jehoiada's son, Zechariah (pronounced *zek-uh-RIGH-uh*), warned Judah about their wicked plans, but they killed him.

Soon after that, the Syrian army attacked Judah, and Joash was wounded. Then his own servants killed him. So King Joash was at last punished for his great sin (see Numbers 32:23).

house; and one-third at the Gate of the Foundation. All the people *shall be* in the courts of the house of the LORD. [6]But let no one come into the house of the LORD except the priests and those of the Levites who serve. They may go in, for they *are* holy; but all the people shall keep the watch of the LORD.
[7]And the Levites shall surround the king on all sides, every man with his weapons in his hand; and whoever comes into the house, let him be put to death. You are to be with the king when he comes in and when he goes out."

[8]So the Levites and all Judah did according to all that Jehoiada the priest commanded. And each man took his men who were to be on duty on the Sabbath, with those who were going *off duty* on the Sabbath; for Jehoiada the priest had not dismissed the
divisions. [9]And Jehoiada the priest gave to the captains of hundreds the spears and the large and small shields which *had belonged* to King David, that *were* in the temple of
God. [10]Then he set all the people, every man with his weapon in his hand, from the right side of the temple to the left side of the temple, along by the altar and by the temple, all
around the king. [11]And they brought out the king's son, put the crown on him, *gave him* the Testimony,[a] and made him king. Then Jehoiada and his sons anointed him, and said, "*Long* live the king!"

Death of Athaliah

[12]Now when Athaliah heard the noise of the people running and praising the king, she came to the people *in* the temple of the
LORD. [13]*When* she looked, there was the king standing by his pillar at the entrance; and the leaders and the trumpeters *were* by the king. All the people of the land were rejoicing and blowing trumpets, also the singers with musical instruments, and those who led in praise. So Athaliah tore her clothes and said, "Treason! Treason!"

[14]And Jehoiada the priest brought out the captains of hundreds who were set over the army, and said to them, "Take her outside under guard, and slay with the sword whoever follows her." For the priest had said, "Do not kill her in the house of the LORD."

[15]So they seized her; and she went by way of the entrance of the Horse Gate *into* the king's house, and they killed her there.

[16]Then Jehoiada made a covenant between himself, the people, and the king, that they should be the LORD's people. [17]And all the people went to the temple[a] of Baal, and tore it down. They broke in pieces its altars and images, and killed Mattan the priest
of Baal before the altars. [18]Also Jehoiada appointed the oversight of the house of the LORD to the hand of the priests, the Levites, whom David had assigned in the house of the LORD, to offer the burnt offerings of the LORD, as *it is* written in the Law of Moses, with rejoicing and with singing, *as it was*
established by David. [19]And he set the gatekeepers at the gates of the house of the LORD, so that no one *who was* in any way unclean should enter.

[20]Then he took the captains of hundreds, the nobles, the governors of the people, and all the people of the land, and brought the king down from the house of the LORD; and they went through the Upper Gate to the king's house, and set the king on the throne
of the kingdom. [21]So all the people of the land rejoiced; and the city was quiet, for they had slain Athaliah with the sword.

Joash Repairs the Temple

24 Joash *was* seven years old when he became king, and he reigned forty years in Jerusalem. His mother's name
was Zibiah of Beersheba. [2]Joash did *what was* right in the sight of the LORD all the days
of Jehoiada the priest. [3]And Jehoiada took two wives for him, and he had sons and daughters.

[4]Now it happened after this *that* Joash set his heart on repairing the house of the LORD.
[5]Then he gathered the priests and the Levites, and said to them, "Go out to the cities of Judah, and gather from all Israel money to repair the house of your God from year to year, and see that you do it quickly."

However the Levites did not do it quickly.
[6]So the king called Jehoiada the chief *priest*, and said to him, "Why have you not required the Levites to bring in from Judah and from Jerusalem the collection, *according to the commandment* of Moses the servant of the LORD and of the assembly of Israel, for the
tabernacle of witness?" [7]For the sons of Athaliah, that wicked woman, had broken into the house of God, and had also presented

23:11 [a] That is, the Law (compare Exodus 25:16, 21; 31:18)
23:17 [a] Literally *house*

all the dedicated things of the house of the
LORD to the Baals.
8 Then at the king's command they made
a chest, and set it outside at the gate of the
house of the LORD. 9 And they made a proclamation throughout Judah and Jerusalem to
bring to the LORD the collection *that* Moses
the servant of God *had imposed* on Israel in
the wilderness. 10 Then all the leaders and all
the people rejoiced, brought their contribu-
tions, and put *them* into the chest until all
had given. 11 So it was, at that time, when the
chest was brought to the king's official by
the hand of the Levites, and when they saw
that *there was* much money, that the king's
scribe and the high priest's officer came and
emptied the chest, and took it and returned
it to its place. Thus they did day by day, and
gathered money in abundance.
12 The king and Jehoiada gave it to those
who did the work of the service of the house
of the LORD; and they hired masons and carpenters to repair the house of the LORD, and
also those who worked in iron and bronze to
restore the house of the LORD. 13 So the workmen labored, and the work was completed by
them; they restored the house of God to its
original condition and reinforced it. 14 When
they had finished, they brought the rest of
the money before the king and Jehoiada;
they made from it articles for the house of
the LORD, articles for serving and offering,

KING JOASH REPAIRS THE TEMPLE

READ IT: 2 CHRONICLES 24:1–14

GET IT:

The kingdom of Judah had a lot of good kings who loved and served God. Joash was one of them. He became king when he was just a kid—seven years old! A good priest, Jehoiada, helped him rule the kingdom. One of the positive things that Joash did was to clean and fix up the temple. Nobody had paid attention to the temple for a long, long time. The evil queen Athaliah had broken into the temple and stolen a lot of the important ceremonial gold dishes. That stuff needed to be collected and returned. But, of course, it would take time, money, and people to do the work. Once the people heard about the plan to fix up God's house, they were glad to help, and they put money in the box outside the temple.

LIVE IT:

Have you ever walked through an abandoned building or an old, deserted house? That would give you an idea of what kind of shape God's temple was in. Nobody had taken care of it for over ten years (think of how dirty and dusty your room gets in just ten days). Joash was young, but he knew that God's house was important and needed attention.

Every church and place of worship needs cleaning and repairs. And just like the people of Judah, we should gladly give money and time to keep God's house in good condition. What can you do to help keep your church in good shape?

spoons and vessels of gold and silver. And
they offered burnt offerings in the house of
the LORD continually all the days of Jehoiada.

Apostasy of Joash

15But Jehoiada grew old and was full of
days, and he died; *he was* one hundred and
thirty years old when he died. 16And they
buried him in the City of David among the
kings, because he had done good in Israel,
both toward God and His house.

17Now after the death of Jehoiada the leaders of Judah came and bowed down to the
king. And the king listened to them. 18There-
fore they left the house of the LORD God of
their fathers, and served wooden images and
idols; and wrath came upon Judah and Jerusalem because of their trespass. 19Yet He
sent prophets to them, to bring them back to
the LORD; and they testified against them,
but they would not listen.

20Then the Spirit of God came upon
Zechariah the son of Jehoiada the priest,
who stood above the people, and said to
them, "Thus says God: 'Why do you transgress the commandments of the LORD, so
that you cannot prosper? Because you have
forsaken the LORD, He also has forsaken
you.'" 21So they conspired against him, and
at the command of the king they stoned him
with stones in the court of the house of the
LORD. 22Thus Joash the king did not remember the kindness which Jehoiada his father
had done to him, but killed his son; and as
he died, he said, "The LORD look on *it,* and
repay!"

Death of Joash

23So it happened in the spring of the year
that the army of Syria came up against him;
and they came to Judah and Jerusalem, and
destroyed all the leaders of the people from
among the people, and sent all their spoil to
the king of Damascus. 24For the army of the
Syrians came with a small company of men;
but the LORD delivered a very great army
into their hand, because they had forsaken
the LORD God of their fathers. So they executed judgment against Joash. 25And when
they had withdrawn from him (for they left
him severely wounded), his own servants
conspired against him because of the blood
of the sons[c] of Jehoiada the priest, and killed
him on his bed. So he died. And they buried
him in the City of David, but they did not
bury him in the tombs of the kings.

26These are the ones who conspired
against him: Zabad[a] the son of Shimeath
the Ammonitess, and Jehozabad the son of
Shimrith[b] the Moabitess. 27Now *concerning*
his sons, and the many oracles about him,
and the repairing of the house of God, indeed they *are* written in the annals of the
book of the kings. Then Amaziah his son
reigned in his place.

Amaziah Reigns in Judah

25 Amaziah *was* twenty-five years
old *when* he became king, and he
reigned twenty-nine years in Jerusalem. His
mother's name *was* Jehoaddan of Jerusalem.
2And he did *what was* right in the sight of the
LORD, but not with a loyal heart.

3Now it happened, as soon as the kingdom was established for him, that he executed his servants who had murdered his father
the king. 4However he did not execute their
children, but *did* as *it is* written in the Law
in the Book of Moses, where the LORD commanded, saying, "The fathers shall not be
put to death for their children, nor shall the
children be put to death for their fathers; but
a person shall die for his own sin."[a]

The War Against Edom

5Moreover Amaziah gathered Judah together and set over them captains of thousands and captains of hundreds, according
to *their* fathers' houses, throughout all Judah
and Benjamin; and he numbered them from
twenty years old and above, and found them
to be three hundred thousand choice *men,*
able to go to war, who could handle spear
and shield. 6He also hired one hundred
thousand mighty men of valor from Israel
for one hundred talents of silver. 7But a man
of God came to him, saying, "O king, do not
let the army of Israel go with you, for the
LORD *is* not with Israel—*not with* any of the
children of Ephraim. 8But if you go, be gone!
Be strong in battle! *Even so,* God shall make
you fall before the enemy; for God has power
to help and to overthrow."

9Then Amaziah said to the man of God,
"But what *shall we* do about the hundred

24:25 [a] Septuagint and Vulgate read *son* (compare verses 20–22). **24:26** [a] Or *Jozachar* (compare 2 Kings 12:21) [b] Or *Shomer* (compare 2 Kings 12:21) **25:4** [a] Deuteronomy 24:16

talents which I have given to the troops of
Israel?"

And the man of God answered, "The
LORD is able to give you much more than
this." 10So Amaziah discharged the troops
that had come to him from Ephraim, to go
back home. Therefore their anger was greatly aroused against Judah, and they returned
home in great anger.

11Then Amaziah strengthened himself,
and leading his people, he went to the Valley
of Salt and killed ten thousand of the people
of Seir. 12Also the children of Judah took captive ten thousand alive, brought them to the
top of the rock, and cast them down from the
top of the rock, so that they all were dashed
in pieces.

13But as for the soldiers of the army which
Amaziah had discharged, so that they would
not go with him to battle, they raided the cities of Judah from Samaria to Beth Horon,
killed three thousand in them, and took
much spoil.

14Now it was so, after Amaziah came
from the slaughter of the Edomites, that he
brought the gods of the people of Seir, set
them up *to be* his gods, and bowed down
before them and burned incense to them.
15Therefore the anger of the LORD was
aroused against Amaziah, and He sent him
a prophet who said to him, "Why have you
sought the gods of the people, which could
not rescue their own people from your
hand?"

16So it was, as he talked with him, that
the king said to him, "Have we made you the
king's counselor? Cease! Why should you be
killed?"

Then the prophet ceased, and said, "I
know that God has determined to destroy
you, because you have done this and have
not heeded my advice."

Israel Defeats Judah

17Now Amaziah king of Judah asked
advice and sent to Joash[a] the son of Jehoahaz, the son of Jehu, king of Israel, saying,
"Come, let us face one another *in battle*."

18And Joash king of Israel sent to Amaziah king of Judah, saying, "The thistle that
was in Lebanon sent to the cedar that was
in Lebanon, saying, 'Give your daughter to
my son as wife'; and a wild beast that *was*
in Lebanon passed by and trampled the thistle. 19Indeed you say that you have defeated
the Edomites, and your heart is lifted up to
boast. Stay at home now; why should you
meddle with trouble, that you should fall—
you and Judah with you?"

20But Amaziah would not heed, for it
came from God, that He might give them
into the hand *of their enemies,* because they
sought the gods of Edom. 21So Joash king of
Israel went out; and he and Amaziah king of
Judah faced one another at Beth Shemesh,
which *belongs* to Judah. 22And Judah was defeated by Israel, and every man fled to his
tent. 23Then Joash the king of Israel captured
Amaziah king of Judah, the son of Joash,
the son of Jehoahaz, at Beth Shemesh; and
he brought him to Jerusalem, and broke
down the wall of Jerusalem from the Gate of
Ephraim to the Corner Gate—four hundred
cubits. 24And *he took* all the gold and silver,
all the articles that were found in the house
of God with Obed-Edom, the treasures of the
king's house, and hostages, and returned to
Samaria.

Death of Amaziah

25Amaziah the son of Joash, king of Judah, lived fifteen years after the death of
Joash the son of Jehoahaz, king of Israel.
26Now the rest of the acts of Amaziah, from
first to last, indeed *are* they not written in the
book of the kings of Judah and Israel? 27Af-
ter the time that Amaziah turned away from
following the LORD, they made a conspiracy
against him in Jerusalem, and he fled to Lachish; but they sent after him to Lachish and
killed him there. 28Then they brought him
on horses and buried him with his fathers
in the City of Judah.

Uzziah Reigns in Judah

26 Now all the people of Judah took
Uzziah,[a] who *was* sixteen years
old, and made him king instead of his father
Amaziah. 2He built Elath[a] and restored it to
Judah, after the king rested with his fathers.

3Uzziah *was* sixteen years old when he
became king, and he reigned fifty-two
years in Jerusalem. His mother's name was
Jecholiah of Jerusalem. 4And he did *what*
was right in the sight of the LORD, according to all that his father Amaziah had done.
5He sought God in the days of Zechariah,

25:17 [a] Spelled *Jehoash* in 2 Kings 14:8ff **26:1** [a] Called *Azariah* in 2 Kings 14:21ff **26:2** [a] Hebrew *Eloth*

who had understanding in the visions[a] of
God; and as long as he sought the LORD,
God made him prosper.
6Now he went out and made war against
the Philistines, and broke down the wall
of Gath, the wall of Jabneh, and the wall of
Ashdod; and he built cities *around* Ashdod
and among the Philistines. 7God helped him
against the Philistines, against the Arabians who lived in Gur Baal, and against the
Meunites. 8Also the Ammonites brought
tribute to Uzziah. His fame spread as far as
the entrance of Egypt, for he became exceedingly strong.
9And Uzziah built towers in Jerusalem
at the Corner Gate, at the Valley Gate, and
at the corner buttress of the wall; then he
fortified them. 10Also he built towers in the
desert. He dug many wells, for he had much
livestock, both in the lowlands and in the
plains; *he also had* farmers and vinedressers in the mountains and in Carmel, for he
loved the soil.
11Moreover Uzziah had an army of fighting men who went out to war by companies,
according to the number on their roll as
prepared by Jeiel the scribe and Maaseiah
the officer, under the hand of Hananiah,
one of the king's captains. 12The total number of chief officers[a] of the mighty men of
valor *was* two thousand six hundred. 13And
under their authority *was* an army of three
hundred and seven thousand five hundred,
that made war with mighty power, to help
the king against the enemy. 14Then Uzziah prepared for them, for the entire army,
shields, spears, helmets, body armor, bows,
and slings *to cast* stones. 15And he made devices in Jerusalem, invented by skillful men,
to be on the towers and the corners, to shoot
arrows and large stones. So his fame spread
far and wide, for he was marvelously helped
till he became strong.

The Penalty for Uzziah's Pride

16But when he was strong his heart was
lifted up, to *his* destruction, for he transgressed against the LORD his God by entering the temple of the LORD to burn incense
on the altar of incense. 17So Azariah the
priest went in after him, and with him were
eighty priests of the LORD—valiant men.
18And they withstood King Uzziah, and said
to him, "*It is* not for you, Uzziah, to burn
incense to the LORD, but for the priests, the
sons of Aaron, who are consecrated to burn
incense. Get out of the sanctuary, for you
have trespassed! You *shall have* no honor
from the LORD God."
19Then Uzziah became furious; and he
had a censer in his hand to burn incense.
And while he was angry with the priests,
leprosy broke out on his forehead, before the
priests in the house of the LORD, beside the
incense altar. 20And Azariah the chief priest
and all the priests looked at him, and there,
on his forehead, he *was* leprous; so they
thrust him out of that place. Indeed he also
hurried to get out, because the LORD had
struck him.

26:5 [a] Several Hebrew manuscripts, Septuagint, Syriac, Targum, and Arabic read *fear*. **26:12** [a] Literally *chief fathers*

IDOL AND HERO WORSHIP

READ IT: 2 CHRONICLES 26:8

Uzziah was only sixteen years old when he became king. He started out his reign as king by listening to what God told him to do. God blessed Uzziah for his obedience and gave him success. Uzziah's success led to his becoming quite famous throughout all the land. But as his fame grew, so did his pride. Uzziah ended his time as king by proudly rebelling against God and suffering the consequences.

21King Uzziah was a leper until the day
of his death. He dwelt in an isolated house,
because he was a leper; for he was cut off
from the house of the LORD. Then Jotham
his son *was* over the king's house, judging
the people of the land.

22Now the rest of the acts of Uzziah, from
first to last, the prophet Isaiah the son of
Amoz wrote. 23So Uzziah rested with his fathers, and they buried him with his fathers
in the field of burial which *belonged* to the
kings, for they said, "He is a leper." Then
Jotham his son reigned in his place.

Jotham Reigns in Judah

27 Jotham *was* twenty-five years old
when he became king, and he
reigned sixteen years in Jerusalem. His
mother's name *was* Jerushah[a] the daughter
of Zadok. 2And he did *what was* right in the
sight of the LORD, according to all that his
father Uzziah had done (although he did not
enter the temple of the LORD). But still the
people acted corruptly.

3He built the Upper Gate of the house
of the LORD, and he built extensively on
the wall of Ophel. 4Moreover he built cities
in the mountains of Judah, and in the forests he built fortresses and towers. 5He also
fought with the king of the Ammonites and
defeated them. And the people of Ammon
gave him in that year one hundred talents of
silver, ten thousand kors of wheat, and ten
thousand of barley. The people of Ammon
paid this to him in the second and third
years also. 6So Jotham became mighty, because he prepared his ways before the LORD
his God.

7Now the rest of the acts of Jotham, and
all his wars and his ways, indeed they *are*
written in the book of the kings of Israel and
Judah. 8He was twenty-five years old when
he became king, and he reigned sixteen
years in Jerusalem. 9So Jotham rested with
his fathers, and they buried him in the City
of David. Then Ahaz his son reigned in his
place.

Ahaz Reigns in Judah

28 Ahaz *was* twenty years old when
he became king, and he reigned
sixteen years in Jerusalem; and he did not
do *what was* right in the sight of the LORD,
as his father David *had done*. 2For he walked
in the ways of the kings of Israel, and made
molded images for the Baals. 3He burned
incense in the Valley of the Son of Hinnom,
and burned his children in the fire, according to the abominations of the nations
whom the LORD had cast out before the children of Israel. 4And he sacrificed and burned
incense on the high places, on the hills, and
under every green tree.

Syria and Israel Defeat Judah

5Therefore the LORD his God delivered
him into the hand of the king of Syria. They
defeated him, and carried away a great multitude of them as captives, and brought *them*
to Damascus. Then he was also delivered
into the hand of the king of Israel, who defeated him with a great slaughter. 6For Pekah the son of Remaliah killed one hundred
and twenty thousand in Judah in one day, all
valiant men, because they had forsaken the
LORD God of their fathers. 7Zichri, a mighty
man of Ephraim, killed Maaseiah the king's
son, Azrikam the officer over the house, and
Elkanah *who was* second to the king. 8And
the children of Israel carried away captive of
their brethren two hundred thousand wom-
en, sons, and daughters; and they also took
away much spoil from them, and brought
the spoil to Samaria.

Israel Returns the Captives

9But a prophet of the LORD was there,
whose name *was* Oded; and he went out before the army that came to Samaria, and said
to them: "Look, because the LORD God of
your fathers was angry with Judah, He has
delivered them into your hand; but you have
killed them in a rage *that* reaches up to heav-
en. 10And now you propose to force the children of Judah and Jerusalem to be your male
and female slaves; *but are* you not also guilty
before the LORD your God? 11Now hear me,
therefore, and return the captives, whom you
have taken captive from your brethren, for
the fierce wrath of the LORD *is* upon you."

12Then some of the heads of the children
of Ephraim, Azariah the son of Johanan,
Berechiah the son of Meshillemoth, Jehiz-
kiah the son of Shallum, and Amasa the son
of Hadlai, stood up against those who came
from the war, 13and said to them, "You shall
not bring the captives here, for we *already*

27:1 [a] Spelled *Jerusha* in 2 Kings 15:33

have offended the LORD. You intend to add
to our sins and to our guilt; for our guilt is
great, and *there is* fierce wrath against Israel." 14So the armed men left the captives
and the spoil before the leaders and all the
assembly. 15Then the men who were designated by name rose up and took the captives,
and from the spoil they clothed all who were
naked among them, dressed them and gave
them sandals, gave them food and drink,
and anointed them; and they let all the feeble
ones ride on donkeys. So they brought them
to their brethren at Jericho, the city of palm
trees. Then they returned to Samaria.

Assyria Refuses to Help Judah

16At the same time King Ahaz sent to the
kings[a] of Assyria to help him. 17For again
the Edomites had come, attacked Judah,
and carried away captives. 18The Philistines
also had invaded the cities of the lowland
and of the South of Judah, and had taken
Beth Shemesh, Aijalon, Gederoth, Sochoh
with its villages, Timnah with its villages,
and Gimzo with its villages; and they dwelt
there. 19For the LORD brought Judah low
because of Ahaz king of Israel, for he had
encouraged moral decline in Judah and had
been continually unfaithful to the LORD.
20Also Tiglath-Pileser[a] king of Assyria came
to him and distressed him, and did not assist him. 21For Ahaz took part *of the treasures*
from the house of the LORD, from the house
of the king, and from the leaders, and he
gave *it* to the king of Assyria; but he did not
help him.

Apostasy and Death of Ahaz

22Now in the time of his distress King
Ahaz became increasingly unfaithful to the
LORD. This *is that* King Ahaz. 23For he sacrificed to the gods of Damascus which had defeated him, saying, "Because the gods of the
kings of Syria help them, I will sacrifice to
them that they may help me." But they were
the ruin of him and of all Israel. 24So Ahaz
gathered the articles of the house of God, cut
in pieces the articles of the house of God,
shut up the doors of the house of the LORD,
and made for himself altars in every corner
of Jerusalem. 25And in every single city of Judah he made high places to burn incense to
other gods, and provoked to anger the LORD
God of his fathers.

26Now the rest of his acts and all his ways,
from first to last, indeed they *are* written in
the book of the kings of Judah and Israel.
27So Ahaz rested with his fathers, and they
buried him in the city, in Jerusalem; but
they did not bring him into the tombs of
the kings of Israel. Then Hezekiah his son
reigned in his place.

Hezekiah Reigns in Judah

29 Hezekiah became king *when he
was* twenty-five years old, and he
reigned twenty-nine years in Jerusalem. His
mother's name *was* Abijah[a] the daughter of
Zechariah. 2And he did *what was* right in the
sight of the LORD, according to all that his
father David had done.

Hezekiah Cleanses the Temple

3In the first year of his reign, in the first
month, he opened the doors of the house
of the LORD and repaired them. 4Then he
brought in the priests and the Levites, and
gathered them in the East Square, 5and said
to them: "Hear me, Levites! Now sanctify
yourselves, sanctify the house of the LORD
God of your fathers, and carry out the rubbish from the holy *place*. 6For our fathers
have trespassed and done evil in the eyes of
the LORD our God; they have forsaken Him,
have turned their faces away from the dwelling place of the LORD, and turned *their* backs
on Him. 7They have also shut up the doors
of the vestibule, put out the lamps, and have
not burned incense or offered burnt offerings in the holy *place* to the God of Israel.
8Therefore the wrath of the LORD fell upon
Judah and Jerusalem, and He has given
them up to trouble, to desolation, and to jeer-
ing, as you see with your eyes. 9For indeed,
because of this our fathers have fallen by the
sword; and our sons, our daughters, and our
wives *are* in captivity.

10"Now *it is* in my heart to make a covenant with the LORD God of Israel, that His
fierce wrath may turn away from us. 11My
sons, do not be negligent now, for the LORD
has chosen you to stand before Him, to serve
Him, and that you should minister to Him
and burn incense."

12Then these Levites arose: Mahath the
son of Amasai and Joel the son of Azariah, of

28:16 [a] Septuagint, Syriac, and Vulgate read *king* (compare verse 20). **28:20** [a] Hebrew *Tilgath-Pilneser*
29:1 [a] Spelled *Abi* in 2 Kings 18:2

the sons of the Kohathites; of the sons of Merari, Kish the son of Abdi and Azariah the son of Jehallelel; of the Gershonites, Joah the son of Zimmah and Eden the son of Joah;
13of the sons of Elizaphan, Shimri and Jeiel; of the sons of Asaph, Zechariah and Mattaniah;
14of the sons of Heman, Jehiel and Shimei; and of the sons of Jeduthun, Shemaiah and Uzziel.

15And they gathered their brethren, sanctified themselves, and went according to the commandment of the king, at the words of the LORD, to cleanse the house of the LORD.
16Then the priests went into the inner part of the house of the LORD to cleanse *it,* and brought out all the debris that they found in the temple of the LORD to the court of the house of the LORD. And the Levites took *it* out and carried *it* to the Brook Kidron.

17Now they began to sanctify on the first *day* of the first month, and on the eighth day of the month they came to the vestibule of the LORD. So they sanctified the house of the LORD in eight days, and on the sixteenth day of the first month they finished.

18Then they went in to King Hezekiah and said, "We have cleansed all the house of the LORD, the altar of burnt offerings with all its articles, and the table of the showbread with all its articles.
19Moreover all the articles which King Ahaz in his reign had cast aside in his transgression we have prepared and sanctified; and there they *are,* before the altar of the LORD."

Hezekiah Restores Temple Worship

20Then King Hezekiah rose early, gathered the rulers of the city, and went up to the house of the LORD.
21And they brought seven bulls, seven rams, seven lambs, and seven male goats for a sin offering for the kingdom, for the sanctuary, and for Judah. Then he commanded the priests, the sons of Aaron, to offer *them* on the altar of the LORD.
22So they killed the bulls, and the priests received the blood and sprinkled *it* on the altar. Likewise they killed the rams and sprinkled the blood on the altar. They also killed the lambs and sprinkled the blood on the altar.
23Then they brought out the male goats *for* the sin offering before the king and the assembly, and they laid their hands on them.
24And the priests killed them; and they presented their blood on the altar as a sin offering to make an atonement for all Israel, for the king commanded *that* the burnt offering and the sin offering *be made* for all Israel.

25And he stationed the Levites in the house of the LORD with cymbals, with stringed instruments, and with harps,

Starring Roles

KING HEZEKIAH'S (pronounced *hez-uh-KIGH-uh*) name means "The Lord Is Strength." He was one of the greatest kings of Judah. He reigned after his wicked father Ahaz, who had even sacrificed his children to false gods.

During Hezekiah's reign, he destroyed all the idols that his father worshiped, and he caused the people to return to the true worship of the Lord.

Then the army of Sennacherib (pronounced *suh-NAK-er-rib*), king of Assyria, attacked Judah and took some of their cities. He also boasted that he would destroy Jerusalem, but Hezekiah and Isaiah the prophet prayed to the Lord. Then one morning when they awoke, there was Sennacherib's army all lying dead on the ground!

At another time Hezekiah was sick and nearly died, but Isaiah helped him in prayer again, and he was saved.

The underground water tunnel Hezekiah built—so Jerusalem would be able to get water without going outside the city walls—lasted long after he was gone.

according to the commandment of David,
of Gad the king's seer, and of Nathan the
prophet; for thus *was* the commandment
of the LORD by His prophets. 26 The Levites
stood with the instruments of David, and
the priests with the trumpets. 27 Then Hezekiah commanded *them* to offer the burnt
offering on the altar. And when the burnt
offering began, the song of the LORD *also*
began, with the trumpets and with the instruments of David king of Israel. 28 So all the
assembly worshiped, the singers sang, and
the trumpeters sounded; all *this continued*
until the burnt offering was finished. 29 And
when they had finished offering, the king
and all who were present with him bowed
and worshiped. 30 Moreover King Hezekiah
and the leaders commanded the Levites to
sing praise to the LORD with the words of
David and of Asaph the seer. So they sang
praises with gladness, and they bowed their
heads and worshiped.

31 Then Hezekiah answered and said,
"Now *that* you have consecrated yourselves
to the LORD, come near, and bring sacrifices and thank offerings into the house of the
LORD." So the assembly brought in sacrifices
and thank offerings, and as many as were
of a willing heart *brought* burnt offerings.
32 And the number of the burnt offerings
which the assembly brought was seventy
bulls, one hundred rams, *and* two hundred
lambs; all these *were* for a burnt offering to
the LORD. 33 The consecrated things *were* six
hundred bulls and three thousand sheep.
34 But the priests were too few, so that they
could not skin all the burnt offerings; therefore their brethren the Levites helped them
until the work was ended and until the *other*
priests had sanctified themselves, for the
Levites were more diligent in sanctifying
themselves than the priests. 35 Also the burnt
offerings *were* in abundance, with the fat of
the peace offerings and *with* the drink offerings for *every* burnt offering.

So the service of the house of the LORD
was set in order. 36 Then Hezekiah and all
the people rejoiced that God had prepared
the people, since the events took place so
suddenly.

Hezekiah Keeps the Passover

30 And Hezekiah sent to all Israel
and Judah, and also wrote letters
to Ephraim and Manasseh, that they should
come to the house of the LORD at Jerusalem, to keep the Passover to the LORD God
of Israel. 2 For the king and his leaders and
all the assembly in Jerusalem had agreed to
keep the Passover in the second month. 3 For
they could not keep it at the regular time,[a]
because a sufficient number of priests had
not consecrated themselves, nor had the people gathered together at Jerusalem. 4 And the
matter pleased the king and all the assembly. 5 So they resolved to make a proclamation throughout all Israel, from Beersheba
to Dan, that they should come to keep the
Passover to the LORD God of Israel at Jerusalem, since they had not done *it* for a long *time*
in the *prescribed* manner.

6 Then the runners went throughout all
Israel and Judah with the letters from the
king and his leaders, and spoke according
to the command of the king: "Children of
Israel, return to the LORD God of Abraham,
Isaac, and Israel; then He will return to the
remnant of you who have escaped from the
hand of the kings of Assyria. 7 And do not
be like your fathers and your brethren, who
trespassed against the LORD God of their fathers, so that He gave them up to desolation,
as you see. 8 Now do not be stiff-necked, as
your fathers *were, but* yield yourselves to the
LORD; and enter His sanctuary, which He
has sanctified forever, and serve the LORD
your God, that the fierceness of His wrath
may turn away from you. 9 For if you return
to the LORD, your brethren and your children
will be treated with compassion by those who
lead them captive, so that they may come
back to this land; for the LORD your God *is*
gracious and merciful, and will not turn *His*
face from you if you return to Him."

10 So the runners passed from city to city
through the country of Ephraim and Manasseh, as far as Zebulun; but they laughed
at them and mocked them. 11 Nevertheless
some from Asher, Manasseh, and Zebulun
humbled themselves and came to Jerusalem. 12 Also the hand of God was on Judah
to give them singleness of heart to obey the
command of the king and the leaders, at the
word of the LORD.

13 Now many people, a very great assembly, gathered at Jerusalem to keep the Feast

---

30:3 [a] That is, the first month (compare Leviticus 23:5); literally *at that time*

of Unleavened Bread in the second month.
14They arose and took away the altars that
were in Jerusalem, and they took away all the
incense altars and cast *them* into the Brook
Kidron. 15Then they slaughtered the Passover *lambs* on the fourteenth *day* of the second month. The priests and the Levites were
ashamed, and sanctified themselves, and
brought the burnt offerings to the house of
the LORD. 16They stood in their place according to their custom, according to the Law of
Moses the man of God; the priests sprinkled
the blood *received* from the hand of the Levites. 17For *there were* many in the assembly
who had not sanctified themselves; therefore the Levites had charge of the slaughter of the Passover *lambs* for everyone *who*
was not clean, to sanctify *them* to the LORD.
18For a multitude of the people, many from
Ephraim, Manasseh, Issachar, and Zebulun,
had not cleansed themselves, yet they ate the
Passover contrary to what was written. But
Hezekiah prayed for them, saying, "May the
good LORD provide atonement for everyone
19*who* prepares his heart to seek God, the
LORD God of his fathers, though *he is* not
cleansed according to the purification of the
sanctuary." 20And the LORD listened to Hezekiah and healed the people.

21So the children of Israel who were present at Jerusalem kept the Feast of Unleavened Bread seven days with great gladness;
and the Levites and the priests praised the
LORD day by day, *singing* to the LORD, accompanied by loud instruments. 22And Hezekiah gave encouragement to all the Levites
who taught the good knowledge of the LORD;
and they ate throughout the feast seven days,
offering peace offerings and making confession to the LORD God of their fathers.

23Then the whole assembly agreed to
keep *the feast* another seven days, and they
kept it *another* seven days with gladness.
24For Hezekiah king of Judah gave to the
assembly a thousand bulls and seven thousand sheep, and the leaders gave to the assembly a thousand bulls and ten thousand
sheep; and a great number of priests sanctified themselves. 25The whole assembly of
Judah rejoiced, also the priests and Levites,
all the assembly that came from Israel, the
sojourners who came from the land of Israel,
and those who dwelt in Judah. 26So there was
great joy in Jerusalem, for since the time of
Solomon the son of David, king of Israel,
there had been nothing like this in Jerusalem. 27Then the priests, the Levites, arose
and blessed the people, and their voice was
heard; and their prayer came *up* to His holy
dwelling place, to heaven.

The Reforms of Hezekiah

31 Now when all this was finished, all
Israel who were present went out
to the cities of Judah and broke the *sacred*
pillars in pieces, cut down the wooden images, and threw down the high places and the
altars—from all Judah, Benjamin, Ephraim,
and Manasseh—until they had utterly destroyed them all. Then all the children of Israel returned to their own cities, every man
to his possession.

2And Hezekiah appointed the divisions
of the priests and the Levites according to
their divisions, each man according to his
service, the priests and Levites for burnt
offerings and peace offerings, to serve, to
give thanks, and to praise in the gates of the
camp[a] of the LORD. 3The king also *appointed*
a portion of his possessions for the burnt offerings: for the morning and evening burnt
offerings, the burnt offerings for the Sabbaths and the New Moons and the set feasts,
as *it is* written in the Law of the LORD.

4Moreover he commanded the people
who dwelt in Jerusalem to contribute support for the priests and the Levites, that they
might devote themselves to the Law of the
LORD.

5As soon as the commandment was cir-
culated, the children of Israel brought in
abundance the firstfruits of grain and wine,
oil and honey, and of all the produce of the
field; and they brought in abundantly the
tithe of everything. 6And the children of
Israel and Judah, who dwelt in the cities of
Judah, brought the tithe of oxen and sheep;
also the tithe of holy things which were consecrated to the LORD their God they laid in
heaps.

7In the third month they began laying
them in heaps, and they finished in the seventh month. 8And when Hezekiah and the
leaders came and saw the heaps, they blessed
the LORD and His people Israel. 9Then Hezekiah questioned the priests and the Levites
concerning the heaps. 10And Azariah the

31:2 [a] That is, the temple

chief priest, from the house of Zadok, answered him and said, "Since *the people* began
to bring the offerings into the house of the
LORD, we have had enough to eat and have
plenty left, for the LORD has blessed His people; and what is left *is* this great abundance."
11Now Hezekiah commanded *them* to prepare rooms in the house of the LORD, and
they prepared them. 12Then they faithfully brought in the offerings, the tithes, and
the dedicated things; Cononiah the Levite
had charge of them, and Shimei his brother *was* the next. 13Jehiel, Azaziah, Nahath,
Asahel, Jerimoth, Jozabad, Eliel, Ismachiah,
Mahath, and Benaiah *were* overseers under
the hand of Cononiah and Shimei his brother, at the commandment of Hezekiah the
king and Azariah the ruler of the house of
God. 14Kore the son of Imnah the Levite, the
keeper of the East Gate, *was* over the freewill
offerings to God, to distribute the offerings
of the LORD and the most holy things. 15And
under him *were* Eden, Miniamin, Jeshua,
Shemaiah, Amariah, and Shecaniah, *his*
faithful assistants in the cities of the priests,
to distribute allotments to their brethren by
divisions, to the great as well as the small.
16Besides those males from three years

KING HEZEKIAH REPAIRS GOD'S TEMPLE

READ IT: 2 CHRONICLES 31:1–21

GET IT:

Hezekiah ruled the kingdom of Judah about one hundred years after Joash did. Once again the temple was a mess. The people had forgotten about God and hadn't used the temple or offered sacrifices to God in a very long time. Hezekiah changed all that. He told the priests to clean the temple. Then he started following the rules for giving sacrifices to God. He also called the people together to celebrate the feast of Passover (to remember that God had brought them out of Egypt a long time ago). He got the people excited about following God again. So the people broke down their idols and the altars used for worshiping other gods. Hezekiah set the pace and followed all the rules that God had given His people long ago. "He did what was good and right and true before the LORD his God" (v. 20).

LIVE IT:

Every once in a while, someone in a group stops everybody and says, "*No, that's wrong. We can't do it that way.* The rules say we need to do it another way." Life without rules can be chaos. A team sport without rules can be frustrating. Nobody wants to play if the rules are changing all the time. Hezekiah was a king who said, "That's wrong. That's not what God's rules say." When was the last time you reviewed the rules for living God's way? Reread Jesus' summary of the two rules that are the most important (Mark 12:28–31), and make sure you're following these rules for living the best life ever.

old and up who were written in the genealogy, they distributed to everyone who entered the house of the LORD his daily portion
for the work of his service, by his division,
17 and to the priests who were written in the
genealogy according to their father's house,
and to the Levites from twenty years old and
up according to their work, by their divisions, 18 and to all who were written in the
genealogy—their little ones and their wives,
their sons and daughters, the whole company of them—for in their faithfulness they
sanctified themselves in holiness.

19 Also for the sons of Aaron the priests,
who were in the fields of the common-lands
of their cities, in every single city, *there were*
men who were designated by name to distribute portions to all the males among the
priests and to all who were listed by genealogies among the Levites.

20 Thus Hezekiah did throughout all Judah, and he did what *was* good and right
and true before the LORD his God. 21 And in
every work that he began in the service of
the house of God, in the law and in the commandment, to seek his God, he did *it* with all
his heart. So he prospered.

Sennacherib Boasts Against the LORD

32 After these deeds of faithfulness,
Sennacherib king of Assyria came
and entered Judah; he encamped against the
fortified cities, thinking to win them over to
himself. 2 And when Hezekiah saw that Sennacherib had come, and that his purpose
was to make war against Jerusalem, 3 he consulted with his leaders and commanders[a]
to stop the water from the springs which
were outside the city; and they helped him.
4 Thus many people gathered together who
stopped all the springs and the brook that
ran through the land, saying, "Why should
the kings[a] of Assyria come and find much
water?" 5 And he strengthened himself, built
up all the wall that was broken, raised *it* up
to the towers, and *built* another wall outside;
also he repaired the Millo[a] *in* the City of David, and made weapons and shields in abundance. 6 Then he set military captains over
the people, gathered them together to him
in the open square of the city gate, and gave
them encouragement, saying, 7 "Be strong
and courageous; do not be afraid nor dismayed before the king of Assyria, nor before
all the multitude that *is* with him; for *there
are* more with us than with him. 8 With him
is an arm of flesh; but with us *is* the LORD
our God, to help us and to fight our battles."
And the people were strengthened by the
words of Hezekiah king of Judah.

9 After this Sennacherib king of Assyria
sent his servants to Jerusalem (but he and
all the forces with him *laid siege* against Lachish), to Hezekiah king of Judah, and to
all Judah who *were* in Jerusalem, saying,
10 "Thus says Sennacherib king of Assyria:
'In what do you trust, that you remain under siege in Jerusalem? 11 Does not Hezekiah persuade you to give yourselves over to
die by famine and by thirst, saying, "The
LORD our God will deliver us from the hand
of the king of Assyria"? 12 Has not the same

32:3 [a] Literally *mighty men* 32:4 [a] Following Masoretic Text and Vulgate; Arabic, Septuagint, and Syriac read *king.*
32:5 [a] Literally *The Landfill*

OBEDIENCE

READ IT: 2 CHRONICLES 31:20, 21

If you're looking for a hero, Hezekiah would be a great candidate! This young man became king at age twenty-five. The first thing he did was repair the temple and announce to everyone that he was going to obey God and lead the country to honor God. In the end, Hezekiah sought God with all his heart, and he prospered. Hezekiah did not regret his obedience to God.

Hezekiah taken away His high places and
His altars, and commanded Judah and Jerusalem, saying, "You shall worship before
one altar and burn incense on it"? 13Do you
not know what I and my fathers have done to
all the peoples of *other* lands? Were the gods
of the nations of those lands in any way able
to deliver their lands out of my hand? 14Who
was there among all the gods of those nations
that my fathers utterly destroyed that could
deliver his people from my hand, that your
God should be able to deliver you from my
hand? 15Now therefore, do not let Hezekiah
deceive you or persuade you like this, and do
not believe him; for no god of any nation or
kingdom was able to deliver his people from

CONFIDENCE
WHEN GOD FIGHTS

READ IT: 2 CHRONICLES 32:1–23

GET IT:

King Hezekiah was a faithful man who showed his confidence in God when Jerusalem was under siege. The king of Assyria, Sennacherib, had taken over many countries before. He decided that Jerusalem would be his next conquest.

Although Hezekiah was confident that God would save Jerusalem, he didn't just sit back and let God do all the work. He used his abilities as a leader to protect his people. Hezekiah started by consulting with his advisors and military commanders. Together, they decided to cut off the water that went outside the city. They rebuilt the city walls, stockpiled weapons, and made sure the people in Jerusalem knew there were plans in place to protect them. Yes, Sennacherib had a perfect track record of winning. But the people of Jerusalem had God fighting for them.

Hezekiah never lost confidence in God's ability to save them. He prayed to God, and God sent an angel who killed all the Assyrian soldiers except Sennacherib. Sennacherib returned to Assyria ashamed of his loss, and his own family killed him because of his disgrace.

As for Hezekiah and Jerusalem, God continued to bless them, and people started coming to visit and bringing offerings to God. Hezekiah's confidence in God spread throughout the land, and God's glory was made known.

LIVE IT:

Whenever you're faced with a difficult situation, take your concerns to God. If you begin to feel like God has forgotten you, remember how God was faithful to Hezekiah. Write a story or draw a picture of a time that God was faithful when you were going through a tough situation. You'll have your own story about God's faithfulness that you can share with others to give them hope.

my hand or the hand of my fathers. How much less will your God deliver you from my hand?' "

16 Furthermore, his servants spoke against the LORD God and against His servant Hezekiah.

17 He also wrote letters to revile the LORD God of Israel, and to speak against Him, saying, "As the gods of the nations of *other* lands have not delivered their people from my hand, so the God of Hezekiah will not deliver His people from my hand." 18 Then they called out with a loud voice in Hebrew[a] to the people of Jerusalem who *were* on the wall, to frighten them and trouble them, that they might take the city. 19 And they spoke against the God of Jerusalem, as against the gods of the people of the earth—the work of men's hands.

Sennacherib's Defeat and Death

20 Now because of this King Hezekiah and the prophet Isaiah, the son of Amoz, prayed and cried out to heaven. 21 Then the LORD sent an angel who cut down every mighty man of valor, leader, and captain in the camp of the king of Assyria. So he returned shamefaced to his own land. And when he had gone into the temple of his god, some of his own offspring struck him down with the sword there.

22 Thus the LORD saved Hezekiah and the inhabitants of Jerusalem from the hand of Sennacherib the king of Assyria, and from the hand of all *others,* and guided them[a] on every side. 23 And many brought gifts to the LORD at Jerusalem, and presents to Hezekiah king of Judah, so that he was exalted in the sight of all nations thereafter.

Hezekiah Humbles Himself

24 In those days Hezekiah was sick and near death, and he prayed to the LORD; and He spoke to him and gave him a sign. 25 But Hezekiah did not repay according to the favor *shown* him, for his heart was lifted up; therefore wrath was looming over him and over Judah and Jerusalem. 26 Then Hezekiah humbled himself for the pride of his heart, he and the inhabitants of Jerusalem, so that the wrath of the LORD did not come upon them in the days of Hezekiah.

Hezekiah's Wealth and Honor

27 Hezekiah had very great riches and honor. And he made himself treasuries for silver, for gold, for precious stones, for spices, for shields, and for all kinds of desirable items; 28 storehouses for the harvest of grain, wine, and oil; and stalls for all kinds of livestock, and folds for flocks.[a] 29 Moreover he provided cities for himself, and possessions of flocks and herds in abundance; for God had given him very much property. 30 This same Hezekiah also stopped the water outlet of Upper Gihon, and brought the water by tunnel[a] to the west side of the City of David. Hezekiah prospered in all his works.

31 However, *regarding* the ambassadors of the princes of Babylon, whom they sent to him to inquire about the wonder that was *done* in the land, God withdrew from him, in order to test him, that He might know all *that was* in his heart.

Death of Hezekiah

32 Now the rest of the acts of Hezekiah, and his goodness, indeed they *are* written in the vision of Isaiah the prophet, the son of Amoz, *and* in the book of the kings of Judah and Israel. 33 So Hezekiah rested with his fathers, and they buried him in the upper tombs of the sons of David; and all Judah and the inhabitants of Jerusalem honored him at his death. Then Manasseh his son reigned in his place.

Manasseh Reigns in Judah

33 Manasseh *was* twelve years old when he became king, and he reigned fifty-five years in Jerusalem. 2 But he did evil in the sight of the LORD, according to the abominations of the nations whom the LORD had cast out before the children of Israel. 3 For he rebuilt the high places which Hezekiah his father had broken down; he raised up altars for the Baals, and made wooden images; and he worshiped all the host of heaven[a] and served them. 4 He also built altars in the house of the LORD, of which the LORD had said, "In Jerusalem shall My name be forever." 5 And he built altars for all the host of heaven in the two courts of the house of the LORD. 6 Also he caused his sons to pass through the fire in the Valley of the Son of Hinnom; he

---

32:18 [a] Literally *Judean* 32:22 [a] Septuagint reads *gave them rest;* Vulgate reads *gave them treasures.* 32:28 [a] Following Septuagint and Vulgate; Arabic and Syriac omit *folds for flocks;* Masoretic Text reads *flocks for sheepfolds.* 32:30 [a] Literally *brought it straight* (compare 2 Kings 20:20) 33:3 [a] The gods of the Assyrians

practiced soothsaying, used witchcraft and
sorcery, and consulted mediums and spiritists. He did much evil in the sight of the
LORD, to provoke Him to anger. 7He even
set a carved image, the idol which he had
made, in the house of God, of which God
had said to David and to Solomon his son,
"In this house and in Jerusalem, which I
have chosen out of all the tribes of Israel,
I will put My name forever; 8and I will not
again remove the foot of Israel from the land
which I have appointed for your fathers—
only if they are careful to do all that I have
commanded them, according to the whole
law and the statutes and the ordinances by
the hand of Moses." 9So Manasseh seduced
Judah and the inhabitants of Jerusalem to do
more evil than the nations whom the LORD
had destroyed before the children of Israel.

Manasseh Restored After Repentance

10And the LORD spoke to Manasseh
and his people, but they would not listen.
11Therefore the LORD brought upon them
the captains of the army of the king of Assyria, who took Manasseh with hooks,[a]
bound him with bronze *fetters,* and carried
him off to Babylon. 12Now when he was in
affliction, he implored the LORD his God,
and humbled himself greatly before the God
of his fathers, 13and prayed to Him; and He
received his entreaty, heard his supplication,
and brought him back to Jerusalem into his
kingdom. Then Manasseh knew that the
LORD *was* God.

14After this he built a wall outside the City
of David on the west side of Gihon, in the
valley, as far as the entrance of the Fish Gate;
and *it* enclosed Ophel, and he raised it to a
very great height. Then he put military captains in all the fortified cities of Judah. 15He
took away the foreign gods and the idol from
the house of the LORD, and all the altars that
he had built in the mount of the house of the
LORD and in Jerusalem; and he cast *them* out
of the city. 16He also repaired the altar of the
LORD, sacrificed peace offerings and thank
offerings on it, and commanded Judah to
serve the LORD God of Israel. 17Nevertheless
the people still sacrificed on the high places,
but only to the LORD their God.

Death of Manasseh

18Now the rest of the acts of Manasseh,
his prayer to his God, and the words of the
seers who spoke to him in the name of the
LORD God of Israel, indeed they *are written*
in the book[a] of the kings of Israel. 19Also his
prayer and *how God* received his entreaty,
and all his sin and trespass, and the sites
where he built high places and set up wood-
en images and carved images, before he was
humbled, indeed they *are* written among
the sayings of Hozai.[a] 20So Manasseh rested
with his fathers, and they buried him in his
own house. Then his son Amon reigned in
his place.

Amon's Reign and Death

21Amon *was* twenty-two years old when
he became king, and he reigned two years
in Jerusalem. 22But he did evil in the sight of
the LORD, as his father Manasseh had done;
for Amon sacrificed to all the carved images
which his father Manasseh had made, and
served them. 23And he did not humble himself before the LORD, as his father Manasseh
had humbled himself; but Amon trespassed
more and more.

24Then his servants conspired against
him, and killed him in his own house. 25But
the people of the land executed all those who
had conspired against King Amon. Then the
people of the land made his son Josiah king
in his place.

Josiah Reigns in Judah

34 Josiah *was* eight years old when
he became king, and he reigned
thirty-one years in Jerusalem. 2And he did
what was right in the sight of the LORD, and
walked in the ways of his father David; *he* did
not turn aside to the right hand or to the left.

3For in the eighth year of his reign, while
he was still young, he began to seek the God
of his father David; and in the twelfth year he
began to purge Judah and Jerusalem of the
high places, the wooden images, the carved
images, and the molded images. 4They
broke down the altars of the Baals in his
presence, and the incense altars which *were*
above them he cut down; and the wooden
images, the carved images, and the molded
images he broke in pieces, and made dust of
them and scattered *it* on the graves of those
who had sacrificed to them. 5He also burned
the bones of the priests on their altars, and
cleansed Judah and Jerusalem. 6And *so he*

33:11 [a] That is, nose hooks (compare 2 Kings 19:28)
33:18 [a] Literally *words* 33:19 [a] Septuagint reads *the seers.*

did in the cities of Manasseh, Ephraim, and
Simeon, as far as Naphtali and all around,
with axes.[a] 7When he had broken down the
altars and the wooden images, had beaten
the carved images into powder, and cut
down all the incense altars throughout all
the land of Israel, he returned to Jerusalem.

Hilkiah Finds the Book of the Law

8In the eighteenth year of his reign, when
he had purged the land and the temple,[a] he
sent Shaphan the son of Azaliah, Maaseiah
the governor of the city, and Joah the son
of Joahaz the recorder, to repair the house
of the LORD his God. 9When they came to
Hilkiah the high priest, they delivered the
money that was brought into the house of
God, which the Levites who kept the doors
had gathered from the hand of Manasseh
and Ephraim, from all the remnant of Israel, from all Judah and Benjamin, and
which they had brought back to Jerusalem.
10Then they put *it* in the hand of the foremen
who had the oversight of the house of the
LORD; and they gave it to the workmen who
worked in the house of the LORD, to repair
and restore the house. 11They gave *it* to the
craftsmen and builders to buy hewn stone
and timber for beams, and to floor the houses which the kings of Judah had destroyed.
12And the men did the work faithfully. Their
overseers *were* Jahath and Obadiah the Levites, of the sons of Merari, and Zechariah
and Meshullam, of the sons of the Kohathites, to supervise. *Others of* the Levites, all of

34:6 [a] Literally *swords* 34:8 [a] Literally *house*

KING JOSIAH FINDS GOD'S LAW

READ IT: 2 CHRONICLES 34:8–33

GET IT:

After Hezekiah died, his son and grandson ruled. But they undid all the good that Hezekiah had done. Then Josiah became king. Josiah was a good king like his great-grandfather Hezekiah. Once again the temple needed to be cleaned and repaired. During the cleanup, a priest found a book. It was part of God's law that had been lost and forgotten. When the scribe read it to the king, Josiah was very upset by what he heard because he knew nobody was doing what it said. But he didn't stop at the listening part. He immediately got back to work on the project. He listened to what God's rules required and then followed through on them.

LIVE IT:

Every once in a while, you have to clean your bedroom. You know—the big-time clean—drag the junk out from under the bed, sort through the drawers that no longer close, and pull out the stuff piled on the closet floor. Sometimes you'll find something you forgot about—a lesson from Sunday school or your Bible wedged in the corner, covered with dust. You remember doing the lesson or planning to read the Bible every night, but *you forgot about it*. Now you feel bad. Well, that's something like what happened to Josiah. But like Josiah, don't stop there. Move on. Change things. Get back on track. Keep the promises and try again.

whom were skillful with instruments of music, 13*were* over the burden bearers and *were*
overseers of all who did work in any kind of
service. And *some* of the Levites *were* scribes,
officers, and gatekeepers.
14Now when they brought out the money
that was brought into the house of the LORD,
Hilkiah the priest found the Book of the Law
of the LORD *given* by Moses. 15Then Hilkiah
answered and said to Shaphan the scribe, "I
have found the Book of the Law in the house
of the LORD." And Hilkiah gave the book to
Shaphan. 16So Shaphan carried the book to
the king, bringing the king word, saying,
"All that was committed to your servants
they are doing. 17And they have gathered the
money that was found in the house of the
LORD, and have delivered it into the hand
of the overseers and the workmen." 18Then
Shaphan the scribe told the king, saying,
"Hilkiah the priest has given me a book."
And Shaphan read it before the king.
19Thus it happened, when the king
heard the words of the Law, that he tore his
clothes. 20Then the king commanded Hilkiah, Ahikam the son of Shaphan, Abdon[a]
the son of Micah, Shaphan the scribe, and
Asaiah a servant of the king, saying, 21"Go,
inquire of the LORD for me, and for those
who are left in Israel and Judah, concerning
the words of the book that is found; for great
is the wrath of the LORD that is poured out
on us, because our fathers have not kept the
word of the LORD, to do according to all that
is written in this book."
22So Hilkiah and those the king *had appointed* went to Huldah the prophetess, the
wife of Shallum the son of Tokhath,[a] the son
of Hasrah,[b] keeper of the wardrobe. (She
dwelt in Jerusalem in the Second Quarter.)
And they spoke to her to that *effect.*
23Then she answered them, "Thus says
the LORD God of Israel, 'Tell the man who
sent you to Me, 24"Thus says the LORD: 'Behold, I will bring calamity on this place and
on its inhabitants, all the curses that are
written in the book which they have read before the king of Judah, 25because they have
forsaken Me and burned incense to other
gods, that they might provoke Me to anger
with all the works of their hands. Therefore My wrath will be poured out on this
place, and not be quenched.'"' 26But as for
the king of Judah, who sent you to inquire
of the LORD, in this manner you shall speak
to him, 'Thus says the LORD God of Israel:
"*Concerning* the words which you have
heard— 27because your heart was tender,
and you humbled yourself before God when
you heard His words against this place and
against its inhabitants, and you humbled
yourself before Me, and you tore your clothes
and wept before Me, I also have heard *you,*"
says the LORD. 28"Surely I will gather you
to your fathers, and you shall be gathered
to your grave in peace; and your eyes shall
not see all the calamity which I will bring
on this place and its inhabitants."'" So they
brought back word to the king.

Josiah Restores True Worship

29Then the king sent and gathered all the
elders of Judah and Jerusalem. 30The king
went up to the house of the LORD, with all
the men of Judah and the inhabitants of
Jerusalem—the priests and the Levites, and
all the people, great and small. And he read
in their hearing all the words of the Book of
the Covenant which had been found in the
house of the LORD. 31Then the king stood in
his place and made a covenant before the
LORD, to follow the LORD, and to keep His
commandments and His testimonies and
His statutes with all his heart and all his
soul, to perform the words of the covenant
that were written in this book. 32And he
made all who were present in Jerusalem and
Benjamin take a stand. So the inhabitants
of Jerusalem did according to the covenant
of God, the God of their fathers. 33Thus
Josiah removed all the abominations from
all the country that *belonged* to the children
of Israel, and made all who were present in
Israel diligently serve the LORD their God.
All his days they did not depart from following the LORD God of their fathers.

Josiah Keeps the Passover

35 Now Josiah kept a Passover to
the LORD in Jerusalem, and they
slaughtered the Passover *lambs* on the fourteenth *day* of the first month. 2And he set the
priests in their duties and encouraged them
for the service of the house of the LORD.
3Then he said to the Levites who taught

34:20 [a] *Achbor the son of Michaiah* in 2 Kings 22:12
34:22 [a] Spelled *Tikvah* in 2 Kings 22:14 [b] Spelled *Harhas* in 2 Kings 22:14

all Israel, who were holy to the LORD: "Put
the holy ark in the house which Solomon
the son of David, king of Israel, built. *It*
shall no longer *be* a burden on *your* shoulders. Now serve the LORD your God and His
people Israel. 4 Prepare *yourselves* according
to your fathers' houses, according to your
divisions, following the written instruction
of David king of Israel and the written instruction of Solomon his son. 5 And stand in
the holy *place* according to the divisions of
the fathers' houses of your brethren the *lay*
people, and *according to* the division of the
father's house of the Levites. 6 So slaughter
the Passover *offerings,* consecrate yourselves,
and prepare *them* for your brethren, that *they*
may do according to the word of the LORD by
the hand of Moses."

7 Then Josiah gave the *lay* people lambs
and young goats from the flock, all for Passover *offerings* for all who were present, to the
number of thirty thousand, as well as three
thousand cattle; these *were* from the king's
possessions. 8 And his leaders gave willingly
to the people, to the priests, and to the Levites. Hilkiah, Zechariah, and Jehiel, rulers
of the house of God, gave to the priests for
the Passover *offerings* two thousand six hundred *from the flock,* and three hundred cattle.
9 Also Conaniah, his brothers Shemaiah and
Nethanel, and Hashabiah and Jeiel and Jozabad, chief of the Levites, gave to the Levites
for Passover *offerings* five thousand *from the*
flock and five hundred cattle.

10 So the service was prepared, and the
priests stood in their places, and the Levites
in their divisions, according to the king's
command. 11 And they slaughtered the Passover *offerings;* and the priests sprinkled *the*
blood with their hands, while the Levites
skinned *the animals.* 12 Then they removed
the burnt offerings that *they* might give
them to the divisions of the fathers' houses
of the *lay* people, to offer to the LORD, as *it is*
written in the Book of Moses. And so *they*
did with the cattle. 13 Also they roasted the
Passover *offerings* with fire according to the
ordinance; but the *other* holy *offerings* they
boiled in pots, in caldrons, and in pans, and
divided *them* quickly among all the *lay* people. 14 Then afterward they prepared portions
for themselves and for the priests, because
the priests, the sons of Aaron, *were busy* in
offering burnt offerings and fat until night;
therefore the Levites prepared portions for
themselves and for the priests, the sons of
Aaron. 15 And the singers, the sons of Asaph,
were in their places, according to the command of David, Asaph, Heman, and Jeduthun the king's seer. Also the gatekeepers
were at each gate; they did not have to leave
their position, because their brethren the Levites prepared portions for them.

16 So all the service of the LORD was prepared the same day, to keep the Passover and
to offer burnt offerings on the altar of the
LORD, according to the command of King
Josiah. 17 And the children of Israel who were
present kept the Passover at that time, and
the Feast of Unleavened Bread for seven
days. 18 There had been no Passover kept in
Israel like that since the days of Samuel the
prophet; and none of the kings of Israel had
kept such a Passover as Josiah kept, with the
priests and the Levites, all Judah and Israel
who were present, and the inhabitants of Jerusalem. 19 In the eighteenth year of the reign
of Josiah this Passover was kept.

Josiah Dies in Battle

20 After all this, when Josiah had prepared
the temple, Necho king of Egypt came up to
fight against Carchemish by the Euphrates; and Josiah went out against him. 21 But
he sent messengers to him, saying, "What
have I to do with you, king of Judah? *I have*
not *come* against you this day, but against
the house with which I have war; for God
commanded me to make haste. Refrain *from*
meddling with God, who *is* with me, lest He
destroy you." 22 Nevertheless Josiah would
not turn his face from him, but disguised
himself so that he might fight with him, and
did not heed the words of Necho from the
mouth of God. So he came to fight in the
Valley of Megiddo.

23 And the archers shot King Josiah; and
the king said to his servants, "Take me away,
for I am severely wounded." 24 His servants
therefore took him out of that chariot and
put him in the second chariot that he had,
and they brought him to Jerusalem. So he
died, and was buried in *one of* the tombs of
his fathers. And all Judah and Jerusalem
mourned for Josiah.

25 Jeremiah also lamented for Josiah.
And to this day all the singing men and
the singing women speak of Josiah in their

lamentations. They made it a custom in
Israel; and indeed they *are* written in the
Laments.

[26]Now the rest of the acts of Josiah and
his goodness, according to *what was* written
in the Law of the LORD, [27]and his deeds from
first to last, indeed they *are* written in the
book of the kings of Israel and Judah.

The Reign and Captivity of Jehoahaz

36 Then the people of the land took
Jehoahaz the son of Josiah, and
made him king in his father's place in Jerusalem. [2]Jehoahaz[a] *was* twenty-three years
old when he became king, and he reigned
three months in Jerusalem. [3]Now the king
of Egypt deposed him at Jerusalem; and he
imposed on the land a tribute of one hundred talents of silver and a talent of gold.
[4]Then the king of Egypt made *Jehoahaz's*[a]
brother Eliakim king over Judah and Jerusalem, and changed his name to Jehoiakim.
And Necho took Jehoahaz[b] his brother and
carried him off to Egypt.

The Reign and Captivity of Jehoiakim

[5]Jehoiakim *was* twenty-five years old
when he became king, and he reigned elev-
en years in Jerusalem. And he did evil in the
sight of the LORD his God. [6]Nebuchadnezzar
king of Babylon came up against him, and

36:2 [a] Masoretic Text reads *Joahaz*. **36:4** [a] Literally *his* [b] Masoretic Text reads *Joahaz*.

GOD BRINGS AN END TO JERUSALEM

READ IT: 2 CHRONICLES 36:11–21

GET IT:

In 586 B.C. the kingdom of Judah came to an end. Nebuchadnezzar, king of Babylon, made his third and final attack on Jerusalem. Each time he captured people and took them back to Babylon. This time he killed a lot of people. Those who were captured were fortunate—they were still alive. Then the Babylonians destroyed and burned the palace, the temple, and the city. They broke down the city wall and left behind smashed buildings and piles of burning trash. The people's pride and identity were gone. Those who survived got swept up into the culture of a foreign country. They would live in Babylon for the next seventy years.

LIVE IT:

It's really hard for us to understand what these people were going through. Most of us don't know what being captured by an enemy and moved to another country is like. For most of us, just the idea of moving to a new city or state is upsetting enough. Change is hard, no matter what kind of change it is. But when God is in control, change can be really good. God had a plan for His people. He promised to bring His people back home again to live in the land they loved. God has a plan for your life, too. It's a wonderful, amazing plan. If you follow Him, He'll make it happen.

bound him in bronze *fetters* to carry him off
to Babylon. 7Nebuchadnezzar also carried
off *some* of the articles from the house of the
LORD to Babylon, and put them in his temple at Babylon. 8Now the rest of the acts of
Jehoiakim, the abominations which he did,
and what was found against him, indeed
they *are* written in the book of the kings of
Israel and Judah. Then Jehoiachin his son
reigned in his place.

The Reign and Captivity of Jehoiachin

9Jehoiachin *was* eight[a] years old when he
became king, and he reigned in Jerusalem
three months and ten days. And he did evil
in the sight of the LORD. 10At the turn of the
year King Nebuchadnezzar summoned *him*
and took him to Babylon, with the costly articles from the house of the LORD, and made
Zedekiah, *Jehoiakim's*[a] brother, king over Judah and Jerusalem.

Zedekiah Reigns in Judah

11Zedekiah *was* twenty-one years old
when he became king, and he reigned eleven
years in Jerusalem. 12He did evil in the sight
of the LORD his God, *and* did not humble
himself before Jeremiah the prophet, *who*
spoke from the mouth of the LORD. 13And he
also rebelled against King Nebuchadnezzar,
who had made him swear *an oath* by God;
but he stiffened his neck and hardened his
heart against turning to the LORD God of Israel. 14Moreover all the leaders of the priests
and the people transgressed more and more,
according to all the abominations of the nations, and defiled the house of the LORD
which He had consecrated in Jerusalem.

The Fall of Jerusalem

15And the LORD God of their fathers sent
warnings to them by His messengers, rising
up early and sending *them*, because He had
compassion on His people and on His dwelling place. 16But they mocked the messengers
of God, despised His words, and scoffed at His
prophets, until the wrath of the LORD arose
against His people, till *there was* no remedy.

17Therefore He brought against them
the king of the Chaldeans, who killed their
young men with the sword in the house of
their sanctuary, and had no compassion
on young man or virgin, on the aged or the
weak; He gave *them* all into his hand. 18And
all the articles from the house of God, great
and small, the treasures of the house of the
LORD, and the treasures of the king and
of his leaders, all *these* he took to Babylon.
19Then they burned the house of God, broke
down the wall of Jerusalem, burned all its
palaces with fire, and destroyed all its precious possessions. 20And those who escaped
from the sword he carried away to Babylon,
where they became servants to him and his
sons until the rule of the kingdom of Persia,
21to fulfill the word of the LORD by the mouth
of Jeremiah, until the land had enjoyed her
Sabbaths. As long as she lay desolate she
kept Sabbath, to fulfill seventy years.

The Proclamation of Cyrus

22Now in the first year of Cyrus king
of Persia, that the word of the LORD by the
mouth of Jeremiah might be fulfilled, the
LORD stirred up the spirit of Cyrus king
of Persia, so that he made a proclamation
throughout all his kingdom, and also *put it*
in writing, saying,

23 Thus says Cyrus king of Persia:
All the kingdoms of the earth the LORD
God of heaven has given me. And He
has commanded me to build Him a
house at Jerusalem which is in Judah.
Who *is* among you of all His people?
May the LORD his God *be* with him, and
let him go up!

36:9 [a] Some Hebrew manuscripts, Septuagint, Syriac, and 2 Kings 24:8 read *eighteen*. **36:10** [a] Literally *his* (compare 2 Kings 24:17)

Behind the Scenes

The BOOK of

EZRA

457 B.C.–444 B.C.

READ IT:

The book of Ezra tells the story of coming home. After living in a faraway country for seventy years, some of the Jews returned to Jerusalem. God had promised He would bring them home, and He did. This is the story of how they started over. They rebuilt God's altar and started rebuilding the temple. Their neighbors were angry and tried to stop them. Finally, after eighteen years, the people completed the temple.

GET IT:

Who wrote it: Probably Ezra wrote it.

When it was written: 457 B.C.–444 B.C.

Why it was written: to tell the story of God's people coming home. God had punished them, but He also kept His promise to bring them home again.

LIVE IT:

God keeps His promises.

FIND IT:

The End of the Babylonian Captivity	*Ezra 1*
Restoration of the Temple Begins	*Ezra 3–6*
The Arrival of Ezra in Jerusalem	*Ezra 7–8*
Judah Confesses Its Sins	*Ezra 10*

End of the Babylonian Captivity

1 Now in the first year of Cyrus king of
Persia, that the word of the LORD by
the mouth of Jeremiah might be fulfilled,
the LORD stirred up the spirit of Cyrus king
of Persia, so that he made a proclamation
throughout all his kingdom, and also *put it*
in writing, saying,

2 Thus says Cyrus king of Persia:
All the kingdoms of the earth the LORD
God of heaven has given me. And He
has commanded me to build Him a
house at Jerusalem which *is* in Judah.
3Who *is* among you of all His people?
May his God be with him, and let him
go up to Jerusalem which *is* in Judah,
and build the house of the LORD God of
Israel (He *is* God), which *is* in Jerusalem. 4And whoever is left in any place
where he dwells, let the men of his place
help him with silver and gold, with
goods and livestock, besides the freewill
offerings for the house of God which *is*
in Jerusalem.

5Then the heads of the fathers' *houses* of
Judah and Benjamin, and the priests and
the Levites, with all whose spirits God had
moved, arose to go up and build the house
of the LORD which *is* in Jerusalem. 6And all
those who *were* around them encouraged
them with articles of silver and gold, with
goods and livestock, and with precious
things, besides all *that* was willingly offered.
7King Cyrus also brought out the articles
of the house of the LORD, which Nebuchadnezzar had taken from Jerusalem and put
in the temple of his gods; 8and Cyrus king
of Persia brought them out by the hand of
Mithredath the treasurer, and counted them
out to Sheshbazzar the prince of Judah.
9This *is* the number of them: thirty gold
platters, one thousand silver platters, twenty-
nine knives, 10thirty gold basins, four hundred and ten silver basins of a similar *kind,*
and one thousand other articles. 11All the
articles of gold and silver *were* five thousand
four hundred. All *these* Sheshbazzar took
with the captives who were brought from
Babylon to Jerusalem.

The Captives Who Returned to Jerusalem

2 Now[a] these *are* the people of the province who came back from the captivity,
of those who had been carried away, whom
Nebuchadnezzar the king of Babylon had
carried away to Babylon, and who returned
to Jerusalem and Judah, everyone to his *own*
city.

2*Those* who came with Zerubbabel *were*
Jeshua, Nehemiah, Seraiah, Reelaiah, Mordecai, Bilshan, Mispar,[a] Bigvai, Rehum,[b]
and Baanah. The number of the men of the
people of Israel: 3the people of Parosh, two
thousand one hundred and seventy-two;
4the people of Shephatiah, three hundred
and seventy-two; 5the people of Arah, sev-
en hundred and seventy-five; 6the people
of Pahath-Moab, of the people of Jeshua
and Joab, two thousand eight hundred and
twelve; 7the people of Elam, one thousand
two hundred and fifty-four; 8the people of
Zattu, nine hundred and forty-five; 9the

2:1 [a] Compare this chapter with Nehemiah 7:6–73.
2:2 [a] Spelled *Mispereth* in Nehemiah 7:7 [b] Spelled *Nehum* in Nehemiah 7:7

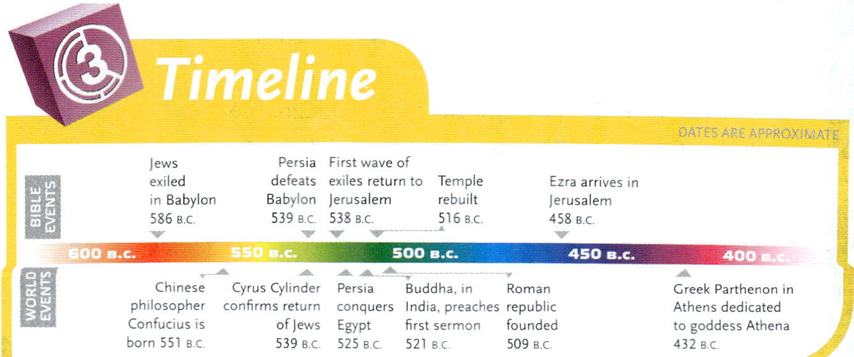

people of Zaccai, seven hundred and sixty;
10the people of Bani,[a] six hundred and forty-
two; 11the people of Bebai, six hundred and
twenty-three; 12the people of Azgad, one
thousand two hundred and twenty-two; 13the
people of Adonikam, six hundred and sixty-
six; 14the people of Bigvai, two thousand and
fifty-six; 15the people of Adin, four hundred
and fifty-four; 16the people of Ater of Hezekiah, ninety-eight; 17the people of Bezai, three
hundred and twenty-three; 18the people of
Jorah,[a] one hundred and twelve; 19the people
of Hashum, two hundred and twenty-three;
20the people of Gibbar,[a] ninety-five; 21the people of Bethlehem, one hundred and twenty-
three; 22the men of Netophah, fifty-six; 23the
men of Anathoth, one hundred and twenty-
eight; 24the people of Azmaveth,[a] forty-two;
25the people of Kirjath Arim,[a] Chephirah,
and Beeroth, seven hundred and forty-
three; 26the people of Ramah and Geba, six
hundred and twenty-one; 27the men of Michmas, one hundred and twenty-two; 28the
men of Bethel and Ai, two hundred and
twenty-three; 29the people of Nebo, fifty-two;
30the people of Magbish, one hundred and
fifty-six; 31the people of the other Elam, one
thousand two hundred and fifty-four; 32the
people of Harim, three hundred and twenty;
33the people of Lod, Hadid, and Ono, seven
hundred and twenty-five; 34the people of Jericho, three hundred and forty-five; 35the people of Senaah, three thousand six hundred
and thirty.

36The priests: the sons of Jedaiah, of the
house of Jeshua, nine hundred and seventy-
three; 37the sons of Immer, one thousand

2:10 [a] Spelled *Binnui* in Nehemiah 7:15 2:18 [a] Called *Hariph* in Nehemiah 7:24 2:20 [a] Called *Gibeon* in Nehemiah 7:25 2:24 [a] Called *Beth Azmaveth* in Nehemiah 7:28 2:25 [a] Called *Kirjath Jearim* in Nehemiah 7:29

On Location

The Return from Exile

The story takes place in two locations: first in Babylon (modern Iraq), where exiled Jews prepare to return home, then in Jerusalem, where they begin re-building the temple. Zerubbabel and the first group of exiles returned to Jerusalem in 538 B.C.–537 B.C. The city walls were not rebuilt until Ezra and Nehemiah led a second wave of Jews back eighty years later.

and fifty-two; 38the sons of Pashhur, one
thousand two hundred and forty-seven; 39the
sons of Harim, one thousand and seventeen.

40The Levites: the sons of Jeshua and Kadmiel, of the sons of Hodaviah,[a] seventy-four.

41The singers: the sons of Asaph, one hundred and twenty-eight.

42The sons of the gatekeepers: the sons of Shallum, the sons of Ater, the sons of Talmon, the sons of Akkub, the sons of Hatita, and the sons of Shobai, one hundred and thirty-nine *in* all.

43The Nethinim: the sons of Ziha, the
sons of Hasupha, the sons of Tabbaoth, 44the
sons of Keros, the sons of Siaha,[a] the sons
of Padon, 45the sons of Lebanah, the sons of
Hagabah, the sons of Akkub, 46the sons of
Hagab, the sons of Shalmai, the sons of Hanan, 47the sons of Giddel, the sons of Gahar,
the sons of Reaiah, 48the sons of Rezin, the
sons of Nekoda, the sons of Gazzam, 49the
sons of Uzza, the sons of Paseah, the sons
of Besai, 50the sons of Asnah, the sons of
Meunim, the sons of Nephusim,[a] 51the sons
of Bakbuk, the sons of Hakupha, the sons of
Harhur, 52the sons of Bazluth,[a] the sons of
Mehida, the sons of Harsha, 53the sons of Barkos, the sons of Sisera, the sons of Tamah,
54the sons of Neziah, and the sons of Hatipha.

55The sons of Solomon's servants: the

2:40 [a] Spelled *Hodevah* in Nehemiah 7:43 **2:44** [a] Spelled *Sia* in Nehemiah 7:47 **2:50** [a] Spelled *Nephishesim* in Nehemiah 7:52 **2:52** [a] Spelled *Bazlith* in Nehemiah 7:54

THE JEWS RETURN TO JUDAH

READ IT: EZRA 1:1–11

GET IT:

God's people lived in a foreign country for seventy years. Finally, King Cyrus became ruler of the Persian Empire (pretty much the entire world at that time). He believed it was best to have the foreigners living in Babylon return to their homelands if they wanted to. A large group of God's people wanted to go home to Judah. Cyrus gave the okay and even gave them all the things that King Nebuchadnezzar had stolen from the temple years before. The people who decided to stay in Babylon gave the group money and livestock to help them start over in Judah. So Sheshbazzar led about forty-two thousand people, including some priests, back to Judah to rebuild their towns, God's altar, and God's temple.

LIVE IT:

You know that feeling you get when you come home from vacation—back to your house, your room, your stuff? Feels good, doesn't it? It's comfortable and familiar. Sometimes we say, "This feels like home." That's what it felt like for the people who went back to the land of Judah. Some of them remembered it well. Some probably had only heard stories about this amazing place, but they were eager to see it for themselves. Going home felt good because it was a place where they belonged and felt comfortable. God had promised He would bring them back home again where they belonged. And His promise came true. God kept His promises to His people long ago, and He keeps His promises to us today.

sons of Sotai, the sons of Sophereth, the
sons of Peruda,[a] 56the sons of Jaala, the sons
of Darkon, the sons of Giddel, 57the sons of
Shephatiah, the sons of Hattil, the sons of
Pochereth of Zebaim, and the sons of Ami.[a]
58All the Nethinim and the children of Solomon's servants were three hundred and
ninety-two.

59And these *were* the ones who came up
from Tel Melah, Tel Harsha, Cherub, Addan,[a] and Immer; but they could not identify their father's house or their genealogy,[b]
whether they *were* of Israel: 60the sons of
Delaiah, the sons of Tobiah, and the sons of
Nekoda, six hundred and fifty-two; 61and of
the sons of the priests: the sons of Habaiah,
the sons of Koz,[a] and the sons of Barzillai,
who took a wife of the daughters of Barzillai
the Gileadite, and was called by their name.
62These sought their listing *among* those
who were registered by genealogy, but they
were not found; therefore they *were excluded* from the priesthood as defiled. 63And the
governor[a] said to them that they should not
eat of the most holy things till a priest could
consult with the Urim and Thummim.

64The whole assembly together *was* forty-
two thousand three hundred *and* sixty,
65besides their male and female servants,
of whom *there were* seven thousand three
hundred and thirty-seven; and they had two
hundred men and women singers. 66Their
horses *were* seven hundred and thirty-six,
their mules two hundred and forty-five,
67their camels four hundred and thirty-five,
and *their* donkeys six thousand seven hundred and twenty.

68*Some* of the heads of the fathers' *houses,*
when they came to the house of the LORD
which *is* in Jerusalem, offered freely for the
house of God, to erect it in its place: 69Accord-
ing to their ability, they gave to the treasury
for the work sixty-one thousand gold drachmas, five thousand minas of silver, and one
hundred priestly garments.

70So the priests and the Levites, *some* of
the people, the singers, the gatekeepers, and
the Nethinim, dwelt in their cities, and all
Israel in their cities.

Worship Restored at Jerusalem

3 And when the seventh month had
come, and the children of Israel *were*
in the cities, the people gathered together
as one man to Jerusalem. 2Then Jeshua the
son of Jozadak[a] and his brethren the priests,
and Zerubbabel the son of Shealtiel and his
brethren, arose and built the altar of the God
of Israel, to offer burnt offerings on it, as *it is*
written in the Law of Moses the man of God.
3Though fear *had come* upon them because
of the people of those countries, they set the
altar on its bases; and they offered burnt
offerings on it to the LORD, *both* the morning and evening burnt offerings. 4They also
kept the Feast of Tabernacles, as *it is* written,
and *offered* the daily burnt offerings in the
number required by ordinance for each day.
5Afterwards *they offered* the regular burnt offering, and *those* for New Moons and for all
the appointed feasts of the LORD that were
consecrated, and *those* of everyone who willingly offered a freewill offering to the LORD.
6From the first day of the seventh month
they began to offer burnt offerings to the
LORD, although the foundation of the temple of the LORD had not been laid. 7They also
gave money to the masons and the carpenters, and food, drink, and oil to the people
of Sidon and Tyre to bring cedar logs from
Lebanon to the sea, to Joppa, according to
the permission which they had from Cyrus
king of Persia.

Restoration of the Temple Begins

8Now in the second month of the second
year of their coming to the house of God at
Jerusalem, Zerubbabel the son of Shealtiel,
Jeshua the son of Jozadak,[a] and the rest of
their brethren the priests and the Levites,
and all those who had come out of the captivity to Jerusalem, began *work* and appointed the Levites from twenty years old and
above to oversee the work of the house of
the LORD. 9Then Jeshua *with* his sons and
brothers, Kadmiel *with* his sons, and the
sons of Judah,[a] arose as one to oversee those
working on the house of God: the sons of
Henadad *with* their sons and their brethren
the Levites.

10When the builders laid the foundation
of the temple of the LORD, the priests stood[a]
in their apparel with trumpets, and the

2:55 [a] Spelled *Perida* in Nehemiah 7:57 **2:57** [a] Spelled *Amon* in Nehemiah 7:59 **2:59** [a] Spelled *Addon* in Nehemiah 7:61 [b] Literally *seed* **2:61** [a] Or *Hakkoz* **2:63** [a] Hebrew *Tirshatha* **3:2** [a] Spelled *Jehozadak* in 1 Chronicles 6:14 **3:8** [a] Spelled *Jehozadak* in 1 Chronicles 6 14 **3:9** [a] Or *Hodaviah* (compare 2:40) **3:10** [a] Following Septuagint, Syriac, and Vulgate; Masoretic Text reads *they stationed the priests.*

Levites, the sons of Asaph, with cymbals, to
praise the LORD, according to the ordinance
of David king of Israel. 11And they sang re-
sponsively, praising and giving thanks to the
LORD:

"For *He is* good,
For His mercy *endures* forever toward
Israel."[a]

Then all the people shouted with a great
shout, when they praised the LORD, because
the foundation of the house of the LORD was
laid.

12But many of the priests and Levites and
heads of the fathers' *houses,* old men who
had seen the first temple, wept with a loud
voice when the foundation of this temple
was laid before their eyes. Yet many shouted
aloud for joy, 13so that the people could not
discern the noise of the shout of joy from the
noise of the weeping of the people, for the
people shouted with a loud shout, and the
sound was heard afar off.

Resistance to Rebuilding the Temple

4 Now when the adversaries of Judah
and Benjamin heard that the descendants of the captivity were building the temple of the LORD God of Israel, 2they came to
Zerubbabel and the heads of the fathers'
houses, and said to them, "Let us build with
you, for we seek your God as you *do;* and
we have sacrificed to Him since the days of
Esarhaddon king of Assyria, who brought
us here." 3But Zerubbabel and Jeshua and
the rest of the heads of the fathers' *houses*
of Israel said to them, "You may do nothing
with us to build a house for our God; but
we alone will build to the LORD God of Israel, as King Cyrus the king of Persia has
commanded us." 4Then the people of the
land tried to discourage the people of Judah.
They troubled them in building, 5and hired
counselors against them to frustrate their
purpose all the days of Cyrus king of Persia,
even until the reign of Darius king of Persia.

Rebuilding of Jerusalem Opposed

6In the reign of Ahasuerus, in the beginning of his reign, they wrote an accusation against the inhabitants of Judah and
Jerusalem.

7In the days of Artaxerxes also, Bishlam,
Mithredath, Tabel, and the rest of their companions wrote to Artaxerxes king of Persia;
and the letter *was* written in Aramaic script,
and translated into the Aramaic language.
8Rehum[a] the commander and Shimshai the
scribe wrote a letter against Jerusalem to
King Artaxerxes in this fashion:

9 From[a] Rehum the commander, Shimshai the scribe, and the rest of their
companions—*representatives* of the
Dinaites, the Apharsathchites, the
Tarpelites, the people of Persia and
Erech and Babylon and Shushan,[b] the
Dehavites, the Elamites, 10and the rest
of the nations whom the great and noble
Osnapper took captive and settled in
the cities of Samaria and the remainder
beyond the River[a]—and so forth.[b]

11(This *is* a copy of the letter that they sent
him.)

To King Artaxerxes from your servants,
the men *of the region* beyond the River,
and so forth:[a]

12 Let it be known to the king that the Jews
who came up from you have come to us
at Jerusalem, and are building the rebellious and evil city, and are finishing
its walls and repairing the foundations.
13Let it now be known to the king that,
if this city is built and the walls completed, they will not pay tax, tribute, or
custom, and the king's treasury will be
diminished. 14Now because we receive
support from the palace, it was not
proper for us to see the king's dishonor;
therefore we have sent and informed the
king, 15that search may be made in the
book of the records of your fathers. And
you will find in the book of the records
and know that this city *is* a rebellious
city, harmful to kings and provinces,
and that they have incited sedition within the city in former times, for which
cause this city was destroyed.

16 We inform the king that if this city is
rebuilt and its walls are completed, the
result will be that you will have no dominion beyond the River.

17The king sent an answer:

To Rehum the commander, *to* Shimshai

3:11 [a] Compare Psalm 136:1 **4:8** [a] The original language of Ezra 4:8 through 6:18 is Aramaic. **4:9** [a] Literally *Then* [b] Or *Susa* **4:10** [a] That is, the Euphrates [b] Literally *and now* **4:11** [a] Literally *and now*

the scribe, *to* the rest of their companions who dwell in Samaria, and *to* the
remainder beyond the River:

Peace, and so forth.[a]

18 The letter which you sent to us has been
clearly read before me. 19And I gave the
command, and a search has been made,
and it was found that this city in former
times has revolted against kings, and rebellion and sedition have been fostered
in it. 20There have also been mighty
kings over Jerusalem, who have ruled
over all *the region* beyond the River; and
tax, tribute, and custom were paid to
them. 21Now give the command to make
these men cease, that this city may not
be built until the command is given
by me.

22 Take heed now that you do not fail to do
this. Why should damage increase to
the hurt of the kings?

23Now when the copy of King Artaxerxes'
letter *was* read before Rehum, Shimshai the
scribe, and their companions, they went up
in haste to Jerusalem against the Jews, and
by force of arms made them cease. 24Thus
the work of the house of God which *is* at
Jerusalem ceased, and it was discontinued
until the second year of the reign of Darius
king of Persia.

Restoration of the Temple Resumed

5 Then the prophet Haggai and Zechariah the son of Iddo, prophets, prophesied to the Jews who *were* in Judah and
Jerusalem, in the name of the God of Israel,
who was over them. 2So Zerubbabel the son
of Shealtiel and Jeshua the son of Jozadak[a]
rose up and began to build the house of God
which *is* in Jerusalem; and the prophets of
God *were* with them, helping them.

3At the same time Tattenai the governor
of *the region* beyond the River[a] and Shethar-
Boznai and their companions came to them
and spoke thus to them: "Who has commanded you to build this temple and finish
this wall?" 4Then, accordingly, we told them
the names of the men who were constructing this building. 5But the eye of their God
was upon the elders of the Jews, so that they
could not make them cease till a report could
go to Darius. Then a written answer was
returned concerning this *matter.* 6This is a
copy of the letter that Tattenai sent:

The governor of *the region* beyond the
River, and Shethar-Boznai, and his
companions, the Persians who *were in
the region* beyond the River, to Darius
the king.

7(They sent a letter to him, in which was
written thus.)

To Darius the king:

All peace.

8 Let it be known to the king that we went
into the province of Judea, to the temple
of the great God, which is being built
with heavy stones, and timber is being
laid in the walls; and this work goes on
diligently and prospers in their hands.

9 Then we asked those elders, *and* spoke
thus to them: "Who commanded you
to build this temple and to finish these
walls?" 10We also asked them their
names to inform you, that we might
write the names of the men who *were*
chief among them.

11 And thus they returned us an answer,
saying: "We are the servants of the God
of heaven and earth, and we are rebuilding the temple that was built many
years ago, which a great king of Israel
built and completed. 12But because our
fathers provoked the God of heaven to
wrath, He gave them into the hand of
Nebuchadnezzar king of Babylon, the
Chaldean, *who* destroyed this temple
and carried the people away to Babylon.
13However, in the first year of Cyrus
king of Babylon, King Cyrus issued
a decree to build this house of God.
14Also, the gold and silver articles of the
house of God, which Nebuchadnezzar
had taken from the temple that *was* in
Jerusalem and carried into the temple of
Babylon—those King Cyrus took from
the temple of Babylon, and they were
given to one named Sheshbazzar, whom
he had made governor. 15And he said to
him, 'Take these articles; go, carry them
to the temple *site* that *is* in Jerusalem,
and let the house of God be rebuilt on
its former site.' 16Then the same Sheshbazzar came *and* laid the foundation of

4:17 [a] Literally *and now* **5:2** [a] Spelled *Jehozadak* in 1 Chronicles 6:14 **5:3** [a] That is, the Euphrates

the house of God which *is* in Jerusalem;
but from that time even until now it has
been under construction, and it is not
finished."

17 Now therefore, if *it seems* good to the
king, let a search be made in the king's
treasure house, which *is* there in Babylon, whether it is *so* that a decree was
issued by King Cyrus to build this
house of God at Jerusalem, and let the
king send us his pleasure concerning
this *matter.*

The Decree of Darius

6 Then King Darius issued a decree, and
a search was made in the archives,[a]
where the treasures were stored in Babylon.
2And at Achmetha,[a] in the palace that *is* in
the province of Media, a scroll was found,
and in it a record *was* written thus:

3 In the first year of King Cyrus, King
Cyrus issued a decree *concerning* the
house of God at Jerusalem: "Let the
house be rebuilt, the place where they
offered sacrifices; and let the foundations of it be firmly laid, its height sixty
cubits *and* its width sixty cubits, 4*with*
three rows of heavy stones and one row
of new timber. Let the expenses be paid
from the king's treasury. 5Also let the
gold and silver articles of the house of
God, which Nebuchadnezzar took from
the temple which *is* in Jerusalem and
brought to Babylon, be restored and
taken back to the temple which *is* in
Jerusalem, *each* to its place; and deposit
them in the house of God"—

6 Now *therefore,* Tattenai, governor of *the
region* beyond the River, and Shethar-
Boznai, and your companions the
Persians who *are* beyond the River, keep
yourselves far from there. 7Let the work
of this house of God alone; let the governor of the Jews and the elders of the
Jews build this house of God on its site.

8 Moreover I issue a decree *as to* what
you shall do for the elders of these
Jews, for the building of this house
of God: Let the cost be paid at the
king's expense from taxes *on the region*
beyond the River; this is to be given
immediately to these men, so that they
are not hindered. 9And whatever they
need—young bulls, rams, and lambs for
the burnt offerings of the God of heav-
en, wheat, salt, wine, and oil, according
to the request of the priests who *are* in
Jerusalem—let it be given them day by
day without fail, 10that they may offer
sacrifices of sweet aroma to the God of
heaven, and pray for the life of the king
and his sons.

11 Also I issue a decree that whoever alters
this edict, let a timber be pulled from
his house and erected, and let him be
hanged on it; and let his house be made
a refuse heap because of this. 12And may
the God who causes His name to dwell
there destroy any king or people who
put their hand to alter it, or to destroy
this house of God which is in Jerusalem. I Darius issue a decree; let it be
done diligently.

The Temple Completed and Dedicated

13Then Tattenai, governor of *the region*
beyond the River, Shethar-Boznai, and their
companions diligently did according to what
King Darius had sent. 14So the elders of the
Jews built, and they prospered through the
prophesying of Haggai the prophet and
Zechariah the son of Iddo. And they built
and finished *it,* according to the commandment of the God of Israel, and according to
the command of Cyrus, Darius, and Artaxerxes king of Persia. 15Now the temple was finished on the third day of the month of Adar,
which was in the sixth year of the reign of
King Darius. 16Then the children of Israel,
the priests and the Levites and the rest of
the descendants of the captivity, celebrated
the dedication of this house of God with joy.
17And they offered sacrifices at the dedication of this house of God, one hundred bulls,
two hundred rams, four hundred lambs, and
as a sin offering for all Israel twelve male
goats, according to the number of the tribes
of Israel. 18They assigned the priests to their
divisions and the Levites to their divisions,
over the service of God in Jerusalem, as it is
written in the Book of Moses.

The Passover Celebrated

19And the descendants of the captivity

6:1 [a] Literally *house of the scrolls* 6:2 [a] Probably *Ecbatana,* the ancient capital of Media

kept the Passover on the fourteenth *day* of the first month. 20For the priests and the Levites had purified themselves; all of them *were ritually* clean. And they slaughtered the Passover *lambs* for all the descendants of the captivity, for their brethren the priests, and for themselves. 21Then the children of Israel who had returned from the captivity ate together with all who had separated themselves from the filth of the nations of the land in order to seek the LORD God of Israel. 22And they kept the Feast of Unleavened Bread seven days with joy; for the LORD made them joyful, and turned the heart of the king of Assyria toward them, to strengthen their hands in the work of the house of God, the God of Israel.

The Arrival of Ezra

7 Now after these things, in the reign of Artaxerxes king of Persia, Ezra the son of Seraiah, the son of Azariah, the son of Hilkiah, 2the son of Shallum, the son of Zadok, the son of Ahitub, 3the son of Amariah, the son of Azariah, the son of Meraioth, 4the son of Zerahiah, the son of Uzzi, the son of Bukki, 5the son of Abishua, the son of Phinehas, the son of Eleazar, the son of Aaron the chief priest— 6this Ezra came up from Babylon; and he *was* a skilled scribe in the Law of Moses, which the LORD God of Israel had given. The king granted him all his request, according to the hand of the LORD his God upon him. 7*Some* of the children of Israel, the priests, the Levites, the singers, the gatekeepers, and the Nethinim came up to Jerusalem in the seventh year of King Artaxerxes. 8And Ezra came to Jerusalem in the fifth month, which *was* in the seventh year of the king. 9On the first *day* of the first month he began *his* journey from Babylon, and on the first *day* of the fifth month he came to Jerusalem, according to the good hand of his God upon him. 10For Ezra had prepared his heart to seek the Law of the LORD, and to do *it,* and to teach statutes and ordinances in Israel.

The Letter of Artaxerxes to Ezra

11This *is* a copy of the letter that King Artaxerxes gave Ezra the priest, the scribe, expert in the words of the commandments of the LORD, and of His statutes to Israel:

12 Artaxerxes,[a] king of kings,

To Ezra the priest, a scribe of the Law of the God of heaven:

Perfect *peace,* and so forth.[b]

13 I issue a decree that all those of the people of Israel and the priests and Levites in my realm, who volunteer to go up to Jerusalem, may go with you. 14And whereas you are being sent by the king and his seven counselors to inquire concerning Judah and Jerusalem, with regard to the Law of your God which *is* in your hand; 15and *whereas you are* to carry the silver and gold which the king and his counselors have freely offered to the God of Israel, whose dwelling *is* in Jerusalem; 16and *whereas* all the silver and gold that you may find in all the province of Babylon, along with the freewill offering of the people and the priests, *are to be* freely offered for the house of their God in Jerusalem— 17now therefore, be careful to buy with this money bulls, rams, and lambs, with their grain offerings and their drink offerings, and offer them on the altar of the house of your God in Jerusalem.

18 And whatever seems good to you and your brethren to do with the rest of the silver and the gold, do it according to the will of your God. 19Also the articles that are given to you for the service of the house of your God, deliver in full before the God of Jerusalem. 20And whatever more may be needed for the house of your God, which you may have occasion to provide, pay *for it* from the king's treasury.

21 And I, *even* I, Artaxerxes the king, issue a decree to all the treasurers who *are in the region* beyond the River, that whatever Ezra the priest, the scribe of the Law of the God of heaven, may require of you, let it be done diligently, 22up to one hundred talents of silver, one hundred kors of wheat, one hundred baths of wine, one hundred baths of oil and salt without prescribed limit. 23Whatever is commanded by the God of heaven, let it diligently be done for the house of the God of heaven. For why should there be

---

7:12 [a] The original language of Ezra 7:12–26 is Aramaic. [b] Literally *and now*

wrath against the realm of the king and
his sons?

24 Also we inform you that it shall not be
lawful to impose tax, tribute, or custom
on any of the priests, Levites, singers,
gatekeepers, Nethinim, or servants
of this house of God. [25]And you, Ezra,
according to your God-given wisdom,
set magistrates and judges who may
judge all the people who *are in the region*
beyond the River, all such as know the
laws of your God; and teach those who
do not know *them*. [26]Whoever will not
observe the law of your God and the law
of the king, let judgment be executed
speedily on him, whether *it be* death, or
banishment, or confiscation of goods, or
imprisonment.

[27]Blessed *be* the LORD God of our fathers,
who has put *such a thing* as this in the king's
heart, to beautify the house of the LORD
which *is* in Jerusalem, [28]and has extended
mercy to me before the king and his counselors, and before all the king's mighty princes.
So I was encouraged, as the hand of the
LORD my God *was* upon me; and I gathered
leading men of Israel to go up with me.

Heads of Families Who Returned with Ezra

8 These *are* the heads of their fathers'
houses, and *this is* the genealogy of
those who went up with me from Babylon, in
the reign of King Artaxerxes: [2]of the sons of
Phinehas, Gershom; of the sons of Ithamar,
Daniel; of the sons of David, Hattush; [3]of
the sons of Shecaniah, of the sons of Parosh, Zechariah; and registered with him
were one hundred and fifty males; [4]of the
sons of Pahath-Moab, Eliehoenai the son of
Zerahiah, and with him two hundred males;
[5]of the sons of Shechaniah,[a] Ben-Jahaziel,
and with him three hundred males; [6]of the
sons of Adin, Ebed the son of Jonathan, and
with him fifty males; [7]of the sons of Elam,
Jeshaiah the son of Athaliah, and with him
seventy males; [8]of the sons of Shephatiah,
Zebadiah the son of Michael, and with him
eighty males; [9]of the sons of Joab, Obadiah
the son of Jehiel, and with him two hundred and eighteen males; [10]of the sons of
Shelomith,[a] Ben-Josiphiah, and with him
one hundred and sixty males; [11]of the sons
of Bebai, Zechariah the son of Bebai, and
with him twenty-eight males; [12]of the sons
of Azgad, Johanan the son of Hakkatan, and
with him one hundred and ten males; [13]of
the last sons of Adonikam, whose names *are*
these—Eliphelet, Jeiel, and Shemaiah—and
with them sixty males; [14]also of the sons of
Bigvai, Uthai and Zabbud, and with them
seventy males.

Servants for the Temple

[15]Now I gathered them by the river that
flows to Ahava, and we camped there three
days. And I looked among the people and
the priests, and found none of the sons of
Levi there. [16]Then I sent for Eliezer, Ariel,
Shemaiah, Elnathan, Jarib, Elnathan, Nathan, Zechariah, and Meshullam, leaders;
also for Joiarib and Elnathan, men of understanding. [17]And I gave them a command
for Iddo the chief man at the place Casiphia,
and I told them what they should say to
Iddo *and* his brethren[a] the Nethinim at the
place Casiphia—that they should bring us
servants for the house of our God. [18]Then,
by the good hand of our God upon us, they
brought us a man of understanding, of the
sons of Mahli the son of Levi, the son of Israel, namely Sherebiah, with his sons and
brothers, eighteen men; [19]and Hashabiah,
and with him Jeshaiah of the sons of Merari,
his brothers and their sons, twenty men;
[20]also of the Nethinim, whom David and the
leaders had appointed for the service of the
Levites, two hundred and twenty Nethinim.
All of them were designated by name.

Fasting and Prayer for Protection

[21]Then I proclaimed a fast there at the river of Ahava, that we might humble ourselves
before our God, to seek from Him the right
way for us and our little ones and all our possessions. [22]For I was ashamed to request of
the king an escort of soldiers and horsemen
to help us against the enemy on the road,
because we had spoken to the king, saying,
"The hand of our God *is* upon all those for
good who seek Him, but His power and
His wrath *are* against all those who forsake

8:5 [a] Following Masoretic Text and Vulgate; Septuagint reads *the sons of Zatho, Shechaniah.* 8:10 [a] Following Masoretic Text and Vulgate; Septuagint reads *the sons of Banni, Shelomith.* 8:17 [a] Following Vulgate; Masoretic Text reads *to Iddo his brother;* Septuagint reads *to their brethren.*

Him." 23 So we fasted and entreated our God
for this, and He answered our prayer.

Gifts for the Temple

24 And I separated twelve of the leaders of
the priests—Sherebiah, Hashabiah, and ten
of their brethren with them— 25 and weighed
out to them the silver, the gold, and the articles, the offering for the house of our God
which the king and his counselors and his
princes, and all Israel *who were* present, had
offered. 26 I weighed into their hand six hundred and fifty talents of silver, silver articles
weighing one hundred talents, one hundred
talents of gold, 27 twenty gold basins *worth* a
thousand drachmas, and two vessels of fine
polished bronze, precious as gold. 28 And I
said to them, "You *are* holy to the LORD; the
articles *are* holy also; and the silver and the
gold *are* a freewill offering to the LORD God of
your fathers. 29 Watch and keep *them* until you
weigh *them* before the leaders of the priests
and the Levites and heads of the fathers' *houses* of Israel in Jerusalem, *in* the chambers of
the house of the LORD." 30 So the priests and
the Levites received the silver and the gold
and the articles by weight, to bring *them* to
Jerusalem to the house of our God.

The Return to Jerusalem

31 Then we departed from the river of
Ahava on the twelfth *day* of the first month,
to go to Jerusalem. And the hand of our God
was upon us, and He delivered us from the
hand of the enemy and from ambush along
the road. 32 So we came to Jerusalem, and
stayed there three days.

33 Now on the fourth day the silver and
the gold and the articles were weighed in the
house of our God by the hand of Meremoth
the son of Uriah the priest, and with him
was Eleazar the son of Phinehas; with them
were the Levites, Jozabad the son of Jeshua
and Noadiah the son of Binnui, 34 with the
number *and* weight of everything. All the
weight was written down at that time.

35 The children of those who had been
carried away captive, who had come from the
captivity, offered burnt offerings to the God
of Israel: twelve bulls for all Israel, ninety-six
rams, seventy-seven lambs, and twelve male
goats *as* a sin offering. All *this was* a burnt
offering to the LORD.

36 And they delivered the king's orders to
the king's satraps and the governors *in the region* beyond the River. So they gave support
to the people and the house of God.

Intermarriage with Pagans

9 When these things were done, the
leaders came to me, saying, "The people of Israel and the priests and the Levites
have not separated themselves from the peoples of the lands, with respect to the abominations of the Canaanites, the Hittites, the
Perizzites, the Jebusites, the Ammonites,
the Moabites, the Egyptians, and the Amorites. 2 For they have taken some of their
daughters *as wives* for themselves and their
sons, so that the holy seed is mixed with the

COMMUNITY

READ IT: EZRA 8:21–23

During the time of this passage, there were many good people who were considered Israel's outcasts and who had been thrown away. Ezra assembled these people to go on a journey with him back to Jerusalem from Babylon. As we see in the verses, Ezra did nothing without prayer and fasting, and he asked the people traveling with him to do the same. They also gave offerings to the Lord. They experienced the Lord's blessing and favor on the journey. They were protected by each other and the hand of God.

peoples of *those* lands. Indeed, the hand of
the leaders and rulers has been foremost in
this trespass." 3So when I heard this thing, I
tore my garment and my robe, and plucked
out some of the hair of my head and beard,
and sat down astonished. 4Then everyone
who trembled at the words of the God of Israel assembled to me, because of the transgression of those who had been carried away
captive, and I sat astonished until the evening sacrifice.
5At the evening sacrifice I arose from my
fasting; and having torn my garment and my
robe, I fell on my knees and spread out my
hands to the LORD my God. 6And I said: "O
my God, I am too ashamed and humiliated
to lift up my face to You, my God; for our
iniquities have risen higher than *our* heads,
and our guilt has grown up to the heavens.
7Since the days of our fathers to this day we
have been very guilty, and for our iniquities
we, our kings, *and* our priests have been
delivered into the hand of the kings of the
lands, to the sword, to captivity, to plunder,
and to humiliation, as *it is* this day. 8And
now for a little while grace has been *shown*

GUILT

CONFESSION IS GOOD FOR EVERYONE

READ IT: EZRA 9:1–6

GET IT:

Ezra was a respected priest who was known for being a man who loved God. He committed his life to understanding and following God's laws and teaching truth to those around him.

It was against God's law for people to marry outside of their tribe. When Ezra discovered this was happening, he grieved—not only for the people who were sinning, but also for himself since he was their leader. He prayed, "I am too ashamed and humiliated to lift up my face to You, my God; for our iniquities have risen higher than our heads, and our guilt has grown up to the heavens" (9:6).

Ezra recognized that when one person sins, it affects everyone. In the same way, when someone confesses, openly admits, his or her sin, that confession can help others. Ezra began to weep and confess before God, and the rest of his community saw it. He led by example, and others joined him in repenting. When the community owned up to their sin, they began to heal. God did great things through them. The temple was rebuilt. What could have been a roadblock in God's story turned into something beautiful because of one man's confession.

LIVE IT:

Is there something you need to confess? Start by confessing to God and asking for His forgiveness. Next, it's helpful to tell someone else (see James 5:16). Who would be a good person to talk to? A family member, a friend, a pastor?

from the LORD our God, to leave us a remnant to escape, and to give us a peg in His
holy place, that our God may enlighten our
eyes and give us a measure of revival in our
bondage. 9For we *were* slaves. Yet our God
did not forsake us in our bondage; but He extended mercy to us in the sight of the kings
of Persia, to revive us, to repair the house of
our God, to rebuild its ruins, and to give us
a wall in Judah and Jerusalem. 10And now,
O our God, what shall we say after this? For
we have forsaken Your commandments,
11which You commanded by Your servants
the prophets, saying, 'The land which you
are entering to possess is an unclean land,
with the uncleanness of the peoples of the
lands, with their abominations which have
filled it from one end to another with their
impurity. 12Now therefore, do not give your
daughters as wives for their sons, nor take
their daughters to your sons; and never seek
their peace or prosperity, that you may be
strong and eat the good of the land, and leave
it as an inheritance to your children forever.' 13And after all that has come upon us for
our evil deeds and for our great guilt, since
You our God have punished us less than our
iniquities *deserve,* and have given us *such*
deliverance as this, 14should we again break
Your commandments, and join in marriage
with the people *committing* these abominations? Would You not be angry with us until
You had consumed *us,* so that *there would be*
no remnant or survivor? 15O LORD God of Israel, You *are* righteous, for we are left as a
remnant, as *it is* this day. Here we *are* before
You, in our guilt, though no one can stand
before You because of this!"

Confession of Improper Marriages

10 Now while Ezra was praying, and
while he was confessing, weeping,
and bowing down before the house of God,
a very large assembly of men, women, and
children gathered to him from Israel; for the
people wept very bitterly. 2And Shechaniah
the son of Jehiel, *one* of the sons of Elam,
spoke up and said to Ezra, "We have trespassed against our God, and have taken
pagan wives from the peoples of the land;
yet now there is hope in Israel in spite of
this. 3Now therefore, let us make a covenant
with our God to put away all these wives and
those who have been born to them, according to the advice of my master and of those
who tremble at the commandment of our
God; and let it be done according to the law.
4Arise, for *this* matter *is* your *responsibility.*
We also *are* with you. Be of good courage,
and do *it.*"

5Then Ezra arose, and made the leaders of the priests, the Levites, and all Israel
swear an oath that they would do according
to this word. So they swore an oath. 6Then
Ezra rose up from before the house of God,
and went into the chamber of Jehohanan
the son of Eliashib; and *when* he came there,
he ate no bread and drank no water, for he
mourned because of the guilt of those from
the captivity.

7And they issued a proclamation
throughout Judah and Jerusalem to all the
descendants of the captivity, that they must
gather at Jerusalem, 8and that whoever
would not come within three days, according
to the instructions of the leaders and elders,
all his property would be confiscated, and he
himself would be separated from the assembly of those from the captivity.

9So all the men of Judah and Benjamin
gathered at Jerusalem within three days.
It *was* the ninth month, on the twentieth
of the month; and all the people sat in the
open square of the house of God, trembling
because of *this* matter and because of heavy
rain. 10Then Ezra the priest stood up and
said to them, "You have transgressed and
have taken pagan wives, adding to the guilt
of Israel. 11Now therefore, make confession
to the LORD God of your fathers, and do His
will; separate yourselves from the peoples of
the land, and from the pagan wives."

12Then all the assembly answered and
said with a loud voice, "Yes! As you have
said, so we must do. 13But *there are* many
people; *it is* the season for heavy rain, and we
are not able to stand outside. Nor *is this* the
work of one or two days, for *there are* many
of us who have transgressed in this matter.
14Please, let the leaders of our entire assembly stand; and let all those in our cities who
have taken pagan wives come at appointed
times, together with the elders and judges
of their cities, until the fierce wrath of our
God is turned away from us in this matter." 15Only Jonathan the son of Asahel and
Jahaziah the son of Tikvah opposed this, and
Meshullam and Shabbethai the Levite gave
them support.

16Then the descendants of the captivity did so. And Ezra the priest, *with* certain
heads of the fathers' *households,* were set
apart by the fathers' households, each of
them by name; and they sat down on the
first day of the tenth month to examine the
matter. 17By the first day of the first month
they finished *questioning* all the men who
had taken pagan wives.

Pagan Wives Put Away

18And among the sons of the priests who
had taken pagan wives *the following* were
found of the sons of Jeshua the son of Jozadak,[a] and his brothers: Maaseiah, Eliezer,
Jarib, and Gedaliah. 19And they gave their
promise that they would put away their
wives; and *being* guilty, *they presented* a ram
of the flock as their trespass offering.

20Also of the sons of Immer: Hanani and
Zebadiah; 21of the sons of Harim: Maaseiah,
Elijah, Shemaiah, Jehiel, and Uzziah; 22of
the sons of Pashhur: Elioenai, Maaseiah,
Ishmael, Nethanel, Jozabad, and Elasah.

23Also of the Levites: Jozabad, Shimei,
Kelaiah (the same *is* Kelita), Pethahiah, Judah, and Eliezer.

24Also of the singers: Eliashib; and of the
gatekeepers: Shallum, Telem, and Uri.

25And others of Israel: of the sons
of Parosh: Ramiah, Jeziah, Malchiah,
Mijamin, Eleazar, Malchijah, and Benaiah;
26of the sons of Elam: Mattaniah, Zechariah,
Jehiel, Abdi, Jeremoth, and Eliah; 27of
the sons of Zattu: Elioenai, Eliashib,
Mattaniah, Jeremoth, Zabad, and Aziza; 28of
the sons of Bebai: Jehohanan, Hananiah,
Zabbai, *and* Athlai; 29of the sons of Bani:
Meshullam, Malluch, Adaiah, Jashub,
Sheal, *and* Ramoth;[a] 30of the sons of Pahath-
Moab: Adna, Chelal, Benaiah, Maaseiah,
Mattaniah, Bezalel, Binnui, and Manasseh;
31*of* the sons of Harim: Eliezer, Ishijah,
Malchijah, Shemaiah, Shimeon, 32Benjamin,
Malluch, *and* Shemariah; 33of the sons
of Hashum: Mattenai, Mattattah, Zabad,
Eliphelet, Jeremai, Manasseh, *and* Shimei;
34of the sons of Bani: Maadai, Amram, Uel,
35Benaiah, Bedeiah, Cheluh,[a] 36Vaniah,
Meremoth, Eliashib, 37Mattaniah, Mattenai,
Jaasai,[a] 38Bani, Binnui, Shimei, 39Shelemiah,
Nathan, Adaiah, 40Machnadebai, Shashai,
Sharai, 41Azarel, Shelemiah, Shemariah,
42Shallum, Amariah, *and* Joseph; 43of the
sons of Nebo: Jeiel, Mattithiah, Zabad,
Zebina, Jaddai,[a] Joel, *and* Benaiah.

44All these had taken pagan wives, and
some of them had wives *by whom* they had
children.

10:18 [a] Spelled *Jehozadak* in 1 Chronicles 6:14 **10:29** [a] Or *Jeremoth* **10:35** [a] Or *Cheluhi,* or *Cheluhu* **10:37** [a] Or *Jaasu* **10:43** [a] Or *Jaddu*

The BOOK of
NEHEMIAH

457 B.C.–444 B.C.

Behind the Scenes

READ IT:

The book of Nehemiah continues the history of the Jews who returned to their homes from a foreign country, Babylon. Nehemiah led a second group of people back to Judah almost one hundred years after the first group went back. When they got back home, Nehemiah encouraged the people to rebuild the walls of the city of Jerusalem.

GET IT:

Who wrote it: Probably Nehemiah wrote it.

When it was written: 457 B.C.–444 B.C.

Why it was written: to record the history of God's people after they returned from Babylon to the city of Jerusalem.

LIVE IT:

If we love God, we should live in a way that is distinct and different from other people.

FIND IT:

Nehemiah Sent to Judah	*Nehemiah 2*
Rebuilding the Wall	*Nehemiah 3*
Nehemiah Helps the Poor	*Nehemiah 5*
Ezra Reads the Law	*Nehemiah 8*
The People Confess Their Sins	*Nehemiah 9*

Nehemiah Prays for His People

1 The words of Nehemiah the son of
Hachaliah.
It came to pass in the month of Chislev,
in the twentieth year, as I was in Shushan[a]
the citadel, 2 that Hanani one of my brethren
came with men from Judah; and I asked
them concerning the Jews who had escaped,
who had survived the captivity, and concerning Jerusalem. 3 And they said to me, "The
survivors who are left from the captivity in
the province *are* there in great distress and
reproach. The wall of Jerusalem *is* also broken down, and its gates are burned with
fire."
4 So it was, when I heard these words, that
I sat down and wept, and mourned *for many*
days; I was fasting and praying before the
God of heaven.
5 And I said: "I pray, LORD God of heav-
en, O great and awesome God, *You* who
keep *Your* covenant and mercy with those
who love You[a] and observe Your[b] commandments, 6 please let Your ear be attentive and
Your eyes open, that You may hear the prayer
of Your servant which I pray before You now,
day and night, for the children of Israel Your
servants, and confess the sins of the children
of Israel which we have sinned against You.
Both my father's house and I have sinned.
7 We have acted very corruptly against You,
and have not kept the commandments, the

1:1 [a] Or *Susa* 1:5 [a] Literally *Him* [b] Literally *His*

NEHEMIAH REBUILDS JERUSALEM'S WALLS

READ IT: NEHEMIAH 2:1–20

GET IT:

After the first group of Jews returned to Judah, a second and a third group returned to their homeland. Nehemiah led a group back to help rebuild the wall around the city of Jerusalem. A wall was a big deal in those days. It protected the people from their enemies, and it let everybody know that this was an important city. People were very proud of the size and strength of the city walls. So it was really important to work on the walls that were destroyed. Things didn't go smoothly. The local people challenged the newcomers and their right to build a wall. But Nehemiah stood firm because he had clear orders from God to do this.

LIVE IT:

Have you ever worked on a school project with other kids in your class? If you worked with a group of people, you know there's usually someone in the group who isn't as serious about the project as the others. Maybe this person doesn't do much to help or grumbles under his or her breath and acts miserable. That's what Nehemiah faced—people who wanted to cause trouble. God needs all kinds of workers in His kingdom. But the best kind of worker is a willing and eager one. The next time you're in a group doing something, remember to do your part. Give it all you've got—including your enthusiasm.

statutes, nor the ordinances which You commanded Your servant Moses. 8Remember,
I pray, the word that You commanded Your
servant Moses, saying, '*If* you are unfaithful,
I will scatter you among the nations;[a] 9but *if*
you return to Me, and keep My commandments and do them, though some of you
were cast out to the farthest part of the heavens, *yet* I will gather them from there, and
bring them to the place which I have chosen
as a dwelling for My name.'[a] 10Now these *are*
Your servants and Your people, whom You
have redeemed by Your great power, and by
Your strong hand. 11O Lord, I pray, please let
Your ear be attentive to the prayer of Your
servant, and to the prayer of Your servants
who desire to fear Your name; and let Your
servant prosper this day, I pray, and grant
him mercy in the sight of this man."

For I was the king's cupbearer.

Nehemiah Sent to Judah

2 And it came to pass in the month of
Nisan, in the twentieth year of King
Artaxerxes, *when* wine *was* before him, that
I took the wine and gave it to the king. Now
I had never been sad in his presence before.
2Therefore the king said to me, "Why *is* your
face sad, since you *are* not sick? This *is* noth-
ing but sorrow of heart."

So I became dreadfully afraid, 3and said
to the king, "May the king live forever! Why
should my face not be sad, when the city, the
place of my fathers' tombs, *lies* waste, and its
gates are burned with fire?"

4Then the king said to me, "What do you
request?"

So I prayed to the God of heaven. 5And I
said to the king, "If it pleases the king, and
if your servant has found favor in your sight,
I ask that you send me to Judah, to the city
of my fathers' tombs, that I may rebuild it."

6Then the king said to me (the queen
also sitting beside him), "How long will your
journey be? And when will you return?" So
it pleased the king to send me; and I set him
a time.

7Furthermore I said to the king, "If it
pleases the king, let letters be given to me for
the governors *of the region* beyond the River,[a]
that they must permit me to pass through
till I come to Judah, 8and a letter to Asaph
the keeper of the king's forest, that he must
give me timber to make beams for the gates
of the citadel which *pertains* to the temple,[a]
for the city wall, and for the house that I
will occupy." And the king granted *them* to
me according to the good hand of my God
upon me.

9Then I went to the governors *in the region* beyond the River, and gave them the
king's letters. Now the king had sent captains of the army and horsemen with me.
10When Sanballat the Horonite and Tobiah
the Ammonite official[a] heard *of it*, they were
deeply disturbed that a man had come to
seek the well-being of the children of Israel.

Nehemiah Views the Wall of Jerusalem

11So I came to Jerusalem and was there
three days. 12Then I arose in the night, I and
a few men with me; I told no one what my
God had put in my heart to do at Jerusalem;
nor was there any animal with me, except
the one on which I rode. 13And I went out by
night through the Valley Gate to the Serpent
Well and the Refuse Gate, and viewed the
walls of Jerusalem which were broken down
and its gates which were burned with fire.
14Then I went on to the Fountain Gate and to
the King's Pool, but *there was* no room for the
animal under me to pass. 15So I went up in
the night by the valley, and viewed the wall;
then I turned back and entered by the Valley Gate, and so returned. 16And the officials
did not know where I had gone or what I had
done; I had not yet told the Jews, the priests,
the nobles, the officials, or the others who
did the work.

17Then I said to them, "You see the distress that we *are* in, how Jerusalem *lies* waste,
and its gates are burned with fire. Come and
let us build the wall of Jerusalem, that we
may no longer be a reproach." 18And I told
them of the hand of my God which had been
good upon me, and also of the king's words
that he had spoken to me.

So they said, "Let us rise up and build."
Then they set their hands to *this* good *work*.

19But when Sanballat the Horonite, Tobiah the Ammonite official, and Geshem
the Arab heard *of it*, they laughed at us and
despised us, and said, "What *is* this thing
that you are doing? Will you rebel against
the king?"

1:8 [a] Leviticus 26:33 1:9 [a] Deuteronomy 30:2–5
2:7 [a] That is, the Euphrates, and so elsewhere in this book
2:8 [a] Literally *house* 2:10 [a] Literally *servant*, and so elsewhere in this book

20 So I answered them, and said to them,
"The God of heaven Himself will prosper
us; therefore we His servants will arise and
build, but you have no heritage or right or
memorial in Jerusalem."

Rebuilding the Wall

3 Then Eliashib the high priest rose
up with his brethren the priests and
built the Sheep Gate; they consecrated it
and hung its doors. They built as far as the
Tower of the Hundred,[a] *and* consecrated it,
then as far as the Tower of Hananel. 2 Next to
Eliashib[a] the men of Jericho built. And next
to them Zaccur the son of Imri built.
3 Also the sons of Hassenaah built the
Fish Gate; they laid its beams and hung its
doors with its bolts and bars. 4 And next to
them Meremoth the son of Urijah, the son
of Koz,[a] made repairs. Next to them Meshullam the son of Berechiah, the son of Meshezabel, made repairs. Next to them Zadok the
son of Baana made repairs. 5 Next to them
the Tekoites made repairs; but their nobles
did not put their shoulders[a] to the work of
their Lord.
6 Moreover Jehoiada the son of Paseah
and Meshullam the son of Besodeiah repaired the Old Gate; they laid its beams and
hung its doors, with its bolts and bars. 7 And
next to them Melatiah the Gibeonite, Jadon
the Meronothite, the men of Gibeon and
Mizpah, repaired the residence[a] of the governor *of the region* beyond the River. 8 Next to
him Uzziel the son of Harhaiah, one of the
goldsmiths, made repairs. Also next to him
Hananiah, one[a] of the perfumers, made repairs; and they fortified Jerusalem as far as
the Broad Wall. 9 And next to them Rephaiah
the son of Hur, leader of half the district of
Jerusalem, made repairs. 10 Next to them Jedaiah the son of Harumaph made repairs in
front of his house. And next to him Hattush
the son of Hashabniah made repairs.
11 Malchijah the son of Harim and
Hashub the son of Pahath-Moab repaired
another section, as well as the Tower of the
Ovens. 12 And next to him was Shallum the
son of Hallohesh, leader of half the district
of Jerusalem; he and his daughters made
repairs.
13 Hanun and the inhabitants of Zanoah
repaired the Valley Gate. They built it, hung
its doors with its bolts and bars, and *repaired*
a thousand cubits of the wall as far as the
Refuse Gate.
14 Malchijah the son of Rechab, leader of
the district of Beth Haccerem, repaired the
Refuse Gate; he built it and hung its doors
with its bolts and bars.
15 Shallun the son of Col-Hozeh, leader of
the district of Mizpah, repaired the Fountain
Gate; he built it, covered it, hung its doors
with its bolts and bars, and repaired the wall
of the Pool of Shelah by the King's Garden,
as far as the stairs that go down from the
City of David. 16 After him Nehemiah the son
of Azbuk, leader of half the district of Beth
Zur, made repairs as far as *the place* in front
of the tombs[a] of David, to the man-made
pool, and as far as the House of the Mighty.
17 After him the Levites, *under* Rehum
the son of Bani, made repairs. Next to him
Hashabiah, leader of half the district of
Keilah, made repairs for his district. 18 After
him their brethren, *under* Bavai[a] the son
of Henadad, leader of the *other* half of the
district of Keilah, made repairs. 19 And next
to him Ezer the son of Jeshua, the leader of
Mizpah, repaired another section in front
of the Ascent to the Armory at the buttress.
20 After him Baruch the son of Zabbai[a] carefully repaired the other section, from the
buttress to the door of the house of Eliashib
the high priest. 21 After him Meremoth the
son of Urijah, the son of Koz,[a] repaired another section, from the door of the house of
Eliashib to the end of the house of Eliashib.
22 And after him the priests, the men of
the plain, made repairs. 23 After him Benjamin and Hasshub made repairs opposite
their house. After them Azariah the son of
Maaseiah, the son of Ananiah, made repairs
by his house. 24 After him Binnui the son of
Henadad repaired another section, from the
house of Azariah to the buttress, even as far
as the corner. 25 Palal the son of Uzai *made repairs* opposite the buttress, and on the tower
which projects from the king's upper house
that *was* by the court of the prison. After him
Pedaiah the son of Parosh *made repairs.*

3:1 [a] Hebrew *Hammeah,* also at 12:39 3:2 [a] Literally *On his hand* 3:4 [a] Or *Hakkoz* 3:5 [a] Literally *necks* 3:7 [a] Literally *throne* 3:8 [a] Literally *the son* 3:16 [a] Septuagint, Syriac, and Vulgate read *tomb.* 3:18 [a] Following Masoretic Text and Vulgate; some Hebrew manuscripts, Septuagint, and Syriac read *Binnui* (compare verse 24). 3:20 [a] A few Hebrew manuscripts, Syriac, and Vulgate read *Zaccai.* 3:21 [a] Or *Hakkoz*

26Moreover the Nethinim who dwelt in
Ophel *made repairs* as far as *the place* in front
of the Water Gate toward the east, and on the
projecting tower. 27After them the Tekoites
repaired another section, next to the great
projecting tower, and as far as the wall of
Ophel.

28Beyond the Horse Gate the priests
made repairs, each in front of his *own* house.
29After them Zadok the son of Immer made
repairs in front of his *own* house. After him
Shemaiah the son of Shechaniah, the keeper of the East Gate, made repairs. 30After
him Hananiah the son of Shelemiah, and
Hanun, the sixth son of Zalaph, repaired
another section. After him Meshullam the
son of Berechiah made repairs in front of his
dwelling. 31After him Malchijah, one of the
goldsmiths, made repairs as far as the house
of the Nethinim and of the merchants, in
front of the Miphkad[a] Gate, and as far as the
upper room at the corner. 32And between the
upper room at the corner, as far as the Sheep
Gate, the goldsmiths and the merchants
made repairs.

The Wall Defended Against Enemies

4 But it so happened, when Sanballat
heard that we were rebuilding the wall,
that he was furious and very indignant, and
mocked the Jews. 2And he spoke before his
brethren and the army of Samaria, and said,
"What are these feeble Jews doing? Will they
fortify themselves? Will they offer sacrifices?
Will they complete it in a day? Will they revive the stones from the heaps of rubbish—
stones that are burned?"

3Now Tobiah the Ammonite *was* beside
him, and he said, "Whatever they build, if
even a fox goes up *on it,* he will break down
their stone wall."

4Hear, O our God, for we are despised;
turn their reproach on their own heads, and
give them as plunder to a land of captivity!
5Do not cover their iniquity, and do not let
their sin be blotted out from before You; for
they have provoked *You* to anger before the
builders.

6So we built the wall, and the entire wall
was joined together up to half its *height,* for
the people had a mind to work.

7Now it happened, when Sanballat, Tobiah, the Arabs, the Ammonites, and the
Ashdodites heard that the walls of Jerusalem
were being restored and the gaps were beginning to be closed, that they became very
angry, 8and all of them conspired together to
come *and* attack Jerusalem and create confusion. 9Nevertheless we made our prayer to
our God, and because of them we set a watch
against them day and night.

10Then Judah said, "The strength of the
laborers is failing, and *there is* so much rubbish that we are not able to build the wall."

11And our adversaries said, "They will

3:31 [a] Literally *Inspection* or *Recruiting*

COMPETITION

READ IT: NEHEMIAH 4:1–23

When Nehemiah and his people set out to rebuild the walls of Jerusalem, they faced resistance so strong that they started to feel defeated. Rumors spread that everyone was tired and would fail.

Nehemiah knew better. He knew it would take everyone's help and cooperation. Some would build while others would defend. Many would do both at the same time.

When we face hard times or harsh words, we can stand firm with other people who believe like we do and experience success together.

neither know nor see anything, till we come
into their midst and kill them and cause the
work to cease."
12So it was, when the Jews who dwelt
near them came, that they told us ten times,
"From whatever place you turn, *they will be*
upon us."
13Therefore I positioned *men* behind the
lower parts of the wall, at the openings; and
I set the people according to their families,
with their swords, their spears, and their
bows. 14And I looked, and arose and said to
the nobles, to the leaders, and to the rest of
the people, "Do not be afraid of them. Remember the Lord, great and awesome, and
fight for your brethren, your sons, your
daughters, your wives, and your houses."
15And it happened, when our enemies
heard that it was known to us, and *that* God
had brought their plot to nothing, that all of
us returned to the wall, everyone to his work.
16So it was, from that time on, *that* half of
my servants worked at construction, while
the other half held the spears, the shields,
the bows, and *wore* armor; and the leaders
were behind all the house of Judah. 17Those
who built on the wall, and those who carried
burdens, loaded themselves so that with one
hand they worked at construction, and with
the other held a weapon. 18Every one of the
builders had his sword girded at his side
as he built. And the one who sounded the
trumpet *was* beside me.
19Then I said to the nobles, the rulers,
and the rest of the people, "The work *is* great
and extensive, and we are separated far from
one another on the wall. 20Wherever you
hear the sound of the trumpet, rally to us
there. Our God will fight for us."
21So we labored in the work, and half of
the men[a] held the spears from daybreak until
the stars appeared. 22At the same time I also
said to the people, "Let each man and his
servant stay at night in Jerusalem, that they
may be our guard by night and a working
party by day." 23So neither I, my brethren,
my servants, nor the men of the guard who
followed me took off our clothes, *except* that
everyone took them off for washing.

Nehemiah Deals with Oppression

5 And there was a great outcry of the
people and their wives against their
Jewish brethren. 2For there were those who
said, "We, our sons, and our daughters *are*
many; therefore let us get grain, that we may
eat and live."
3There were also *some* who said, "We
have mortgaged our lands and vineyards and
houses, that we might buy grain because of
the famine."
4There were also those who said, "We
have borrowed money for the king's tax *on*
our lands and vineyards. 5Yet now our flesh
is as the flesh of our brethren, our children
as their children; and indeed we are forcing
our sons and our daughters to be slaves, and
some of our daughters have been brought
into slavery. *It is* not in our power *to redeem
them,* for other men have our lands and
vineyards."
6And I became very angry when I heard
their outcry and these words. 7After serious
thought, I rebuked the nobles and rulers,
and said to them, "Each of you is exacting
usury from his brother." So I called a great
assembly against them. 8And I said to them,
"According to our ability we have redeemed
our Jewish brethren who were sold to the
nations. Now indeed, will you even sell your
brethren? Or should they be sold to us?"
Then they were silenced and found nothing *to say.* 9Then I said, "What you are doing
is not good. Should you not walk in the fear
of our God because of the reproach of the
nations, our enemies? 10I also, *with* my brethren and my servants, am lending them money and grain. Please, let us stop this usury!
11Restore now to them, even this day, their
lands, their vineyards, their olive groves, and
their houses, also a hundredth of the money
and the grain, the new wine and the oil, that
you have charged them."
12So they said, "We will restore *it,* and
will require nothing from them; we will do
as you say."
Then I called the priests, and required an
oath from them that they would do according to this promise. 13Then I shook out the
fold of my garment[a] and said, "So may God
shake out each man from his house, and
from his property, who does not perform
this promise. Even thus may he be shaken
out and emptied."
And all the assembly said, "Amen!" and
praised the LORD. Then the people did according to this promise.

4:21 [a] Literally *them* 5:13 [a] Literally *my lap*

The Generosity of Nehemiah

14Moreover, from the time that I was
appointed to be their governor in the land
of Judah, from the twentieth year until
the thirty-second year of King Artaxerxes,
twelve years, neither I nor my brothers ate
the governor's provisions. 15But the former
governors who *were* before me laid burdens
on the people, and took from them bread
and wine, besides forty shekels of silver.
Yes, even their servants bore rule over the
people, but I did not do so, because of the
fear of God. 16Indeed, I also continued the
work on this wall, and we[a] did not buy any
land. All my servants *were* gathered there for
the work.

17And at my table *were* one hundred and
fifty Jews and rulers, besides those who
came to us from the nations around us.
18Now *that* which was prepared daily *was*
one ox *and* six choice sheep. Also fowl were
prepared for me, and once every ten days an
abundance of all kinds of wine. Yet in spite
of this I did not demand the governor's provisions, because the bondage was heavy on
this people.

19Remember me, my God, for good, *according to* all that I have done for this people.

Conspiracy Against Nehemiah

6 Now it happened when Sanballat, Tobiah, Geshem the Arab, and the rest
of our enemies heard that I had rebuilt the
wall, and *that* there were no breaks left in
it (though at that time I had not hung the
doors in the gates), 2that Sanballat and Geshem sent to me, saying, "Come, let us meet
together among the villages in the plain of
Ono." But they thought to do me harm.

3So I sent messengers to them, saying, "I
am doing a great work, so that I cannot come
down. Why should the work cease while I
leave it and go down to you?"

4But they sent me this message four
times, and I answered them in the same
manner.

5Then Sanballat sent his servant to me as
before, the fifth time, with an open letter in
his hand. 6In it *was* written:

> It is reported among the nations, and
> Geshem[a] says, *that* you and the Jews
> plan to rebel; therefore, according to
> these rumors, you are rebuilding the
> wall, that you may be their king. 7And
> you have also appointed prophets to
> proclaim concerning you at Jerusalem,
> saying, "*There is* a king in Judah!" Now
> these matters will be reported to the
> king. So come, therefore, and let us con-
> sult together.

In Focus

6:12 Prophecy Pronounced *PROFF-uh-see.* A message or messages from God. Such messages in the Bible often tell about God's plans for the future.

8Then I sent to him, saying, "No such
things as you say are being done, but you
invent them in your own heart."

9For they all *were trying to* make us afraid,
saying, "Their hands will be weakened in
the work, and it will not be done."

Now therefore, *O God,* strengthen my
hands.

10Afterward I came to the house of Shemaiah the son of Delaiah, the son of Mehetabel, who *was* a secret informer; and he said,
"Let us meet together in the house of God,
within the temple, and let us close the doors
of the temple, for they are coming to kill you;
indeed, at night they will come to kill you."

11And I said, "Should such a man as I
flee? And who *is there* such as I who would
go into the temple to save his life? I will not
go in!" 12Then I perceived that God had not
sent him at all, but that he pronounced *this*
prophecy against me because Tobiah and
Sanballat had hired him. 13For this reason he
was hired, that I should be afraid and act that
way and sin, so *that* they might have *cause* for
an evil report, that they might reproach me.

14My God, remember Tobiah and Sanballat, according to these their works, and
the prophetess Noadiah and the rest of the
prophets who would have made me afraid.

The Wall Completed

15So the wall was finished on the twenty-
fifth *day* of Elul, in fifty-two days. 16And it

5:16 [a] Following Masoretic Text; Septuagint, Syriac, and Vulgate read *I.* **6:6** [a] Hebrew *Gashmu*

happened, when all our enemies heard *of*
it, and all the nations around us saw *these*
things, that they were very disheartened in
their own eyes; for they perceived that this
work was done by our God.

17Also in those days the nobles of Judah
sent many letters to Tobiah, and *the letters*
of Tobiah came to them. 18For many in Judah were pledged to him, because he was
the son-in-law of Shechaniah the son of
Arah, and his son Jehohanan had married
the daughter of Meshullam the son of Berechiah. 19Also they reported his good deeds
before me, and reported my words to him.
Tobiah sent letters to frighten me.

7 Then it was, when the wall was built
and I had hung the doors, when the
gatekeepers, the singers, and the Levites
had been appointed, 2that I gave the charge
of Jerusalem to my brother Hanani, and
Hananiah the leader of the citadel, for he
was a faithful man and feared God more
than many.

3And I said to them, "Do not let the gates
of Jerusalem be opened until the sun is hot;
and while they stand *guard,* let them shut
and bar the doors; and appoint guards from
among the inhabitants of Jerusalem, one at
his watch station and another in front of his
own house."

The Captives Who Returned to Jerusalem

4Now the city *was* large and spacious,
but the people in it *were* few, and the houses
were not rebuilt. 5Then my God put it into
my heart to gather the nobles, the rulers, and
the people, that they might be registered by
genealogy. And I found a register of the genealogy of those who had come up in the
first *return,* and found written in it:

6 These[a] *are* the people of the province who came back from the captivity, of those who had been carried away, whom Nebuchadnezzar the king of Babylon had carried away, and who returned to Jerusalem and Judah, everyone to his city.

7 Those who came with Zerubbabel *were* Jeshua, Nehemiah, Azariah, Raamiah, Nahamani, Mordecai, Bilshan, Mispereth,[a] Bigvai, Nehum, and Baanah.

The number of the men of the people of Israel: 8the sons of Parosh, two thousand one hundred and seventy-two;
9the sons of Shephatiah, three hundred and seventy-two;
10the sons of Arah, six hundred and fifty-two;
11the sons of Pahath-Moab, of the sons of Jeshua and Joab, two thousand eight hundred and eighteen;
12the sons of Elam, one thousand two hundred and fifty-four;
13the sons of Zattu, eight hundred and forty-five;
14the sons of Zaccai, seven hundred and sixty;
15the sons of Binnui,[a] six hundred and forty-eight;
16the sons of Bebai, six hundred and twenty-eight;
17the sons of Azgad, two thousand three hundred and twenty-two;
18the sons of Adonikam, six hundred and sixty-seven;
19the sons of Bigvai, two thousand and sixty-seven;
20the sons of Adin, six hundred and fifty-five;
21the sons of Ater of Hezekiah, ninety-eight;
22the sons of Hashum, three hundred and twenty-eight;
23the sons of Bezai, three hundred and twenty-four;
24the sons of Hariph,[a] one hundred and twelve;
25the sons of Gibeon,[a] ninety-five;
26the men of Bethlehem and Netophah, one hundred and eighty-eight;
27the men of Anathoth, one hundred and twenty-eight;
28the men of Beth Azmaveth,[a] forty-two;
29the men of Kirjath Jearim, Chephirah, and Beeroth, seven hundred and forty-three;
30the men of Ramah and Geba, six hundred and twenty-one;
31the men of Michmas, one hundred and twenty-two;
32the men of Bethel and Ai, one hundred and twenty-three;

7:6 [a] Compare verses 6–72 with Ezra 2:1–70 7:7 [a] Spelled *Mispar* in Ezra 2:2 7:15 [a] Spelled *Bani* in Ezra 2:10 7:24 [a] Called *Jorah* in Ezra 2:18 7:25 [a] Called *Gibbar* in Ezra 2:20 7:28 [a] Called *Azmaveth* in Ezra 2:24

[33]the men of the other Nebo, fifty-two;
[34]the sons of the other Elam, one thousand two hundred and fifty-four;
[35]the sons of Harim, three hundred and twenty;
[36]the sons of Jericho, three hundred and forty-five;
[37]the sons of Lod, Hadid, and Ono, seven hundred and twenty-one;
[38]the sons of Senaah, three thousand nine hundred and thirty.

39 The priests: the sons of Jedaiah, of the house of Jeshua, nine hundred and seventy-three;
[40]the sons of Immer, one thousand and fifty-two;
[41]the sons of Pashhur, one thousand two hundred and forty-seven;
[42]the sons of Harim, one thousand and seventeen.

43 The Levites: the sons of Jeshua, of Kadmiel,
and of the sons of Hodevah,[a]
seventy-four.

44 The singers: the sons of Asaph, one hundred and forty-eight.

45 The gatekeepers: the sons of Shallum,
the sons of Ater,
the sons of Talmon,
the sons of Akkub,
the sons of Hatita,
the sons of Shobai, one hundred and thirty-eight.

46 The Nethinim: the sons of Ziha,
the sons of Hasupha,
the sons of Tabbaoth,
[47]the sons of Keros,
the sons of Sia,[a]
the sons of Padon,
[48]the sons of Lebana,[a]
the sons of Hagaba,[b]
the sons of Salmai,[c]
[49]the sons of Hanan,
the sons of Giddel,
the sons of Gahar,
[50]the sons of Reaiah,
the sons of Rezin,
the sons of Nekoda,
[51]the sons of Gazzam,
the sons of Uzza,
the sons of Paseah,
[52]the sons of Besai,

In Focus

7:64 Listing (Genealogy) The history of a family showing the family members of each generation from the beginning.

the sons of Meunim,
the sons of Nephishesim,[a]
[53]the sons of Bakbuk,
the sons of Hakupha,
the sons of Harhur,
[54]the sons of Bazlith,[a]
the sons of Mehida,
the sons of Harsha,
[55]the sons of Barkos,
the sons of Sisera,
the sons of Tamah,
[56]the sons of Neziah,
and the sons of Hatipha.

57 The sons of Solomon's servants: the sons of Sotai,
the sons of Sophereth,
the sons of Perida,[a]
[58]the sons of Jaala,
the sons of Darkon,
the sons of Giddel,
[59]the sons of Shephatiah,
the sons of Hattil,
the sons of Pochereth of Zebaim,
and the sons of Amon.[a]
[60]All the Nethinim, and the sons of Solomon's servants, *were* three hundred and ninety-two.

61 And these *were* the ones who came up from Tel Melah, Tel Harsha, Cherub, Addon,[a] and Immer, but they could not identify their father's house nor their lineage, whether they *were* of Israel:
[62]the sons of Delaiah,
the sons of Tobiah,
the sons of Nekoda, six hundred and forty-two;

7:43 [a] Spelled *Hodaviah* in Ezra 2:40 **7:47** [a] Spelled *Siaha* in Ezra 2:44 **7:48** [a] Masoretic Text reads *Lebanah.* [b] Masoretic Text reads *Hogabah.* [c] Or *Shalmai,* or *Shamlai* **7:52** [a] Spelled *Nephusim* in Ezra 2:50 **7:54** [a] Spelled *Bazluth* in Ezra 2:52 **7:57** [a] Spelled *Peruda* in Ezra 2:55 **7:59** [a] Spelled *Ami* in Ezra 2:57 **7:61** [a] Spelled *Addan* in Ezra 2:59

63 and of the priests: the sons of Habaiah,
the sons of Koz,[a]
the sons of Barzillai, who took a wife of
the daughters of Barzillai the Gileadite,
and was called by their name.
64 These sought their listing *among* those
who were registered by genealogy, but
it was not found; therefore they were
excluded from the priesthood as defiled.
65 And the governor[a] said to them that
they should not eat of the most holy
things till a priest could consult with
the Urim and Thummim.

66 Altogether the whole assembly *was*
forty-two thousand three hundred and
sixty, 67 besides their male and female
servants, of whom *there were* seven thousand three hundred and thirty-seven;
and they had two hundred and forty-five
men and women singers. 68 Their horses
were seven hundred and thirty-six, their
mules two hundred and forty-five, 69 *their*
camels four hundred and thirty-five,
and donkeys six thousand seven hundred and twenty.

70 And some of the heads of the fathers'
houses gave to the work. The governor[a]
gave to the treasury one thousand
gold drachmas, fifty basins, and five
hundred and thirty priestly garments.
71 Some of the heads of the fathers' *houses*
gave to the treasury of the work twenty
thousand gold drachmas, and two thousand two hundred silver minas. 72 And
that which the rest of the people gave
was twenty thousand gold drachmas,
two thousand silver minas, and sixty-
seven priestly garments.

73 So the priests, the Levites, the gatekeepers, the singers, *some* of the people, the Nethinim, and all Israel dwelt in their cities.

Ezra Reads the Law

When the seventh month came, the children of Israel *were* in their cities.

8 Now all the people gathered together as one man in the open square that *was* in front of the Water Gate; and they told Ezra the scribe to bring the Book of the Law of Moses, which the LORD had commanded Israel. 2 So Ezra the priest brought the Law before the assembly of men and women and all who *could* hear with understanding on the first day of the seventh month. 3 Then he read from it in the open square that *was* in front of the Water Gate from morning until midday, before the men and women and those who could understand; and the ears of all the people *were attentive* to the Book of the Law.

4 So Ezra the scribe stood on a platform of wood which they had made for the purpose; and beside him, at his right hand, stood Mattithiah, Shema, Anaiah, Urijah, Hilkiah, and Maaseiah; and at his left hand Pedaiah, Mishael, Malchijah, Hashum, Hashbadana, Zechariah, *and* Meshullam. 5 And Ezra opened the book in the sight of all the people, for he was *standing* above all the

7:63 [a] Or *Hakkoz* 7:65 [a] Hebrew *Tirshatha* 7:70 [a] Hebrew *Tirshatha*

JOY

READ IT: NEHEMIAH 8:10

The captives returning to Jerusalem were in bad shape. Thousands of families were coming home after King Nebuchadnezzar had carried them away. As they returned to the city, they had nothing left—or so they thought. *But they still had God.* The joy of the Lord was something no one could take from them, and it could be their strength. It was a help to them as they healed and rebuilt their lives.

people; and when he opened it, all the people
stood up. 6And Ezra blessed the LORD, the
great God.

Then all the people answered, "Amen,
Amen!" while lifting up their hands. And
they bowed their heads and worshiped the
LORD with *their* faces to the ground.

7Also Jeshua, Bani, Sherebiah, Jamin,
Akkub, Shabbethai, Hodijah, Maaseiah,
Kelita, Azariah, Jozabad, Hanan, Pelaiah,
and the Levites, helped the people to understand the Law; and the people *stood* in their
place. 8So they read distinctly from the book,
in the Law of God; and they gave the sense,
and helped *them* to understand the reading.

9And Nehemiah, who *was* the governor,[a]
Ezra the priest *and* scribe, and the Levites
who taught the people said to all the people,
"This day *is* holy to the LORD your God; do
not mourn nor weep." For all the people
wept, when they heard the words of the Law.

10Then he said to them, "Go your way, eat
the fat, drink the sweet, and send portions to
those for whom nothing is prepared; for *this*
day *is* holy to our Lord. Do not sorrow, for the
joy of the LORD is your strength."

11So the Levites quieted all the people,
saying, "Be still, for the day *is* holy; do not be
grieved." 12And all the people went their way
to eat and drink, to send portions and rejoice
greatly, because they understood the words
that were declared to them.

The Feast of Tabernacles

13Now on the second day the heads of the
fathers' *houses* of all the people, with the
priests and Levites, were gathered to Ezra
the scribe, in order to understand the words
of the Law. 14And they found written in the
Law, which the LORD had commanded by
Moses, that the children of Israel should
dwell in booths during the feast of the
seventh month, 15and that they should announce and proclaim in all their cities and
in Jerusalem, saying, "Go out to the mountain, and bring olive branches, branches of
oil trees, myrtle branches, palm branches,
and branches of leafy trees, to make booths,
as *it is* written."

16Then the people went out and brought
them and made themselves booths, each one
on the roof of his house, or in their courtyards or the courts of the house of God, and
in the open square of the Water Gate and
in the open square of the Gate of Ephraim.
17So the whole assembly of those who had
returned from the captivity made booths
and sat under the booths; for since the days
of Joshua the son of Nun until that day the
children of Israel had not done so. And there
was very great gladness. 18Also day by day,
from the first day until the last day, he read
from the Book of the Law of God. And they
kept the feast seven days; and on the eighth
day *there was* a sacred assembly, according to
the *prescribed* manner.

The People Confess Their Sins

9 Now on the twenty-fourth day of this
month the children of Israel were
assembled with fasting, in sackcloth, and
with dust on their heads.[a] 2Then those of
Israelite lineage separated themselves from
all foreigners; and they stood and confessed
their sins and the iniquities of their fathers.
3And they stood up in their place and read
from the Book of the Law of the LORD their
God *for one*-fourth of the day; and *for another* fourth they confessed and worshiped the
LORD their God.

4Then Jeshua, Bani, Kadmiel, Shebaniah, Bunni, Sherebiah, Bani, *and* Chenani
stood on the stairs of the Levites and cried
out with a loud voice to the LORD their God.
5And the Levites, Jeshua, Kadmiel, Bani,
Hashabniah, Sherebiah, Hodijah, Shebaniah, *and* Pethahiah, said:

"Stand up *and* bless the LORD your God
Forever and ever!

"Blessed be Your glorious name,
Which is exalted above all blessing and
praise!
6 You alone *are* the LORD;
You have made heaven,
The heaven of heavens, with all their
host,
The earth and everything on it,
The seas and all that is in them,
And You preserve them all.
The host of heaven worships You.

7 "You *are* the LORD God,
Who chose Abram,
And brought him out of Ur of the
Chaldeans,
And gave him the name Abraham;
8 You found his heart faithful before You,

8:9 [a] Hebrew *Tirshatha* 9:1 [a] Literally *earth on them*

And made a covenant with him
To give the land of the Canaanites,
The Hittites, the Amorites,
The Perizzites, the Jebusites,
And the Girgashites—
To give *it* to his descendants.
You have performed Your words,
For You *are* righteous.

9 "You saw the affliction of our fathers in Egypt,
And heard their cry by the Red Sea.
10 You showed signs and wonders against Pharaoh,
Against all his servants,
And against all the people of his land.
For You knew that they acted proudly against them.
So You made a name for Yourself, as *it is* this day.
11 And You divided the sea before them,
So that they went through the midst of the sea on the dry land;
And their persecutors You threw into the deep,
As a stone into the mighty waters.
12 Moreover You led them by day with a cloudy pillar,
And by night with a pillar of fire,
To give them light on the road
Which they should travel.

13 "You came down also on Mount Sinai,
And spoke with them from heaven,
And gave them just ordinances and true laws,
Good statutes and commandments.
14 You made known to them Your holy Sabbath,
And commanded them precepts, statutes and laws,
By the hand of Moses Your servant.
15 You gave them bread from heaven for their hunger,
And brought them water out of the rock for their thirst,
And told them to go in to possess the land
Which You had sworn to give them.

16 "But they and our fathers acted proudly,
Hardened their necks,
And did not heed Your commandments.
17 They refused to obey,
And they were not mindful of Your wonders
That You did among them.
But they hardened their necks,
And in their rebellion[a]
They appointed a leader
To return to their bondage.
But You *are* God,
Ready to pardon,
Gracious and merciful,
Slow to anger,
Abundant in kindness,
And did not forsake them.

18 "Even when they made a molded calf for themselves,

9:17 [a] Following Masoretic Text and Vulgate; Septuagint reads *in Egypt*.

COMPASSION

READ IT: NEHEMIAH 9:16, 17

The Israelites had turned away from God. The prophet Nehemiah wrote that they refused to obey and ignored everything God was showing them. They even found someone to lead a rebellion away from God. However, God still had love for them. He was ready to forgive them and offered them grace.

Even when we're rebellious, God doesn't lose hope in us. Just like He didn't forsake the Israelites, He will never leave us. He will always show us His compassion.

And said, 'This *is* your god
That brought you up out of Egypt,'
And worked great provocations,
19 Yet in Your manifold mercies
You did not forsake them in the wilderness.
The pillar of the cloud did not depart from them by day,
To lead them on the road;
Nor the pillar of fire by night,
To show them light,
And the way they should go.
20 You also gave Your good Spirit to instruct them,
And did not withhold Your manna from their mouth,
And gave them water for their thirst.
21 Forty years You sustained them in the wilderness;
They lacked nothing;
Their clothes did not wear out[a]
And their feet did not swell.

22 "Moreover You gave them kingdoms and nations,
And divided them into districts.[a]
So they took possession of the land of Sihon,
The land of [b] the king of Heshbon,
And the land of Og king of Bashan.
23 You also multiplied their children as the stars of heaven,
And brought them into the land
Which You had told their fathers
To go in and possess.
24 So the people went in
And possessed the land;
You subdued before them the inhabitants of the land,
The Canaanites,
And gave them into their hands,
With their kings
And the people of the land,
That they might do with them as they wished.
25 And they took strong cities and a rich *land*,
And possessed houses full of all goods,
Cisterns *already* dug, vineyards, olive groves,
And fruit trees in abundance.
So they ate and were filled and grew fat,
And delighted themselves in Your great goodness.

26 "Nevertheless they were disobedient
And rebelled against You,
Cast Your law behind their backs
And killed Your prophets, who testified against them
To turn them to Yourself;
And they worked great provocations.
27 Therefore You delivered them into the hand of their enemies,
Who oppressed them;
And in the time of their trouble,
When they cried to You,
You heard from heaven;
And according to Your abundant mercies
You gave them deliverers who saved them
From the hand of their enemies.

28 "But after they had rest,
They again did evil before You.
Therefore You left them in the hand of their enemies,
So that they had dominion over them;
Yet when they returned and cried out to You,
You heard from heaven;
And many times You delivered them according to Your mercies,
29 And testified against them,
That You might bring them back to Your law.
Yet they acted proudly,
And did not heed Your commandments,
But sinned against Your judgments,
'Which if a man does, he shall live by them.'[a]
And they shrugged their shoulders,
Stiffened their necks,
And would not hear.
30 Yet for many years You had patience with them,
And testified against them by Your Spirit in Your prophets.
Yet they would not listen;
Therefore You gave them into the hand of the peoples of the lands.
31 Nevertheless in Your great mercy
You did not utterly consume them nor forsake them;
For You *are* God, gracious and merciful.

9:21 [a] Compare Deuteronomy 29:5 **9:22** [a] Literally *corners* [b] Following Masoretic Text and Vulgate; Septuagint omits *The land of.* **9:29** [a] Leviticus 18:5

32 "Now therefore, our God,
The great, the mighty, and awesome God,
Who keeps covenant and mercy:
Do not let all the trouble seem small before You
That has come upon us,
Our kings and our princes,
Our priests and our prophets,
Our fathers and on all Your people,
From the days of the kings of Assyria until this day.
33 However You *are* just in all that has befallen us;
For You have dealt faithfully,
But we have done wickedly.
34 Neither our kings nor our princes,
Our priests nor our fathers,
Have kept Your law,
Nor heeded Your commandments and Your testimonies,
With which You testified against them.
35 For they have not served You in their kingdom,
Or in the many good *things* that You gave them,
Or in the large and rich land which You set before them;
Nor did they turn from their wicked works.

36 "Here we *are,* servants today!
And the land that You gave to our fathers,
To eat its fruit and its bounty,
Here we *are,* servants in it!
37 And it yields much increase to the kings
You have set over us,
Because of our sins;
Also they have dominion over our bodies and our cattle
At their pleasure;
And we *are* in great distress.

38 "And because of all this,
We make a sure *covenant* and write *it;*
Our leaders, our Levites, *and* our priests seal *it.*"

The People Who Sealed the Covenant

10 Now those who placed *their* seal on *the document were:*

Nehemiah the governor, the son of Hac-
aliah, and Zedekiah, 2Seraiah, Azariah,
Jeremiah, 3Pashhur, Amariah, Malchijah,
4Hattush, Shebaniah, Malluch, 5Harim,
Meremoth, Obadiah, 6Daniel, Ginnethon,

MAKE YOUR PROMISE TO GOD

READ IT: NEHEMIAH 10:28–31

God kept His promise to bring the people of Israel from Babylon back to their land in Palestine. Then Ezra read the Scriptures to them. When the people heard God's Word, they realized it was God who had set them free. They made a promise to live for Him.

When anyone does a great kindness for you, do you feel thankful? Do you want to show that person how grateful you are for that kindness? Unthankful people are usually very unhappy people, too.

You have heard often that God sent His Son Jesus to die for your sins and give you eternal life. If you believe this promise of God, then you know you have the gift of eternal life. This is God's great kindness to you. So it only makes sense to promise God your life. God wants to use your life to show His goodness and mercy to other people. Have you promised God your life?

Baruch, 7 Meshullam, Abijah, Mijamin,
8 Maaziah, Bilgai, *and* Shemaiah. These *were*
the priests.

9 The Levites: Jeshua the son of Aza-
niah, Binnui of the sons of Henadad, *and*
Kadmiel.

10 Their brethren: Shebaniah, Hodijah,
Kelita, Pelaiah, Hanan, 11 Micha, Rehob,
Hashabiah, 12 Zaccur, Sherebiah, Shebaniah,
13 Hodijah, Bani, *and* Beninu.

14 The leaders of the people: Parosh,
Pahath-Moab, Elam, Zattu, Bani, 15 Bunni, Azgad, Bebai, 16 Adonijah, Bigvai, Adin,
17 Ater, Hezekiah, Azzur, 18 Hodijah, Hashum,
Bezai, 19 Hariph, Anathoth, Nebai, 20 Mag-
piash, Meshullam, Hezir, 21 Meshezabel,
Zadok, Jaddua, 22 Pelatiah, Hanan, Anaiah,
23 Hoshea, Hananiah, Hasshub, 24 Hallohesh,
Pilha, Shobek, 25 Rehum, Hashabnah, Maaseiah, 26 Ahijah, Hanan, Anan, 27 Malluch,
Harim, *and* Baanah.

The Covenant That Was Sealed

28 Now the rest of the people—the priests,
the Levites, the gatekeepers, the singers, the
Nethinim, and all those who had separated
themselves from the peoples of the lands to
the Law of God, their wives, their sons, and
their daughters, everyone who had knowledge and understanding— 29 these joined
with their brethren, their nobles, and entered into a curse and an oath to walk in
God's Law, which was given by Moses the
servant of God, and to observe and do all the
commandments of the LORD our Lord, and
His ordinances and His statutes: 30 We would
not give our daughters as wives to the peoples of the land, nor take their daughters for
our sons; 31 *if* the peoples of the land brought
wares or any grain to sell on the Sabbath day,
we would not buy it from them on the Sabbath, or on a holy day; and we would forego
the seventh year's *produce* and the exacting
of every debt.

32 Also we made ordinances for ourselves,
to exact from ourselves yearly one-third of
a shekel for the service of the house of our
God: 33 for the showbread, for the regular
grain offering, for the regular burnt offering of the Sabbaths, the New Moons, and
the set feasts; for the holy things, for the sin
offerings to make atonement for Israel, and
all the work of the house of our God. 34 We
cast lots among the priests, the Levites, and
the people, for bringing the wood offering
into the house of our God, according to our
fathers' houses, at the appointed times year
by year, to burn on the altar of the LORD our
God as *it is* written in the Law.

35 And *we made ordinances* to bring the
firstfruits of our ground and the firstfruits
of all fruit of all trees, year by year, to the
house of the LORD; 36 to bring the firstborn of
our sons and our cattle, as *it is* written in the
Law, and the firstborn of our herds and our
flocks, to the house of our God, to the priests
who minister in the house of our God; 37 to
bring the firstfruits of our dough, our offerings, the fruit from all kinds of trees, *the*
new wine and oil, to the priests, to the storerooms of the house of our God; and to bring
the tithes of our land to the Levites, for the
Levites should receive the tithes in all our
farming communities. 38 And the priest, the
descendant of Aaron, shall be with the Levites when the Levites receive tithes; and the
Levites shall bring up a tenth of the tithes
to the house of our God, to the rooms of the
storehouse.

39 For the children of Israel and the children of Levi shall bring the offering of the
grain, of the new wine and the oil, to the
storerooms where the articles of the sanctuary *are, where* the priests who minister and
the gatekeepers and the singers *are;* and we
will not neglect the house of our God.

The People Dwelling in Jerusalem

11 Now the leaders of the people dwelt
at Jerusalem; the rest of the people
cast lots to bring one out of ten to dwell in
Jerusalem, the holy city, and nine-tenths
were to dwell in *other* cities. 2 And the people
blessed all the men who willingly offered
themselves to dwell at Jerusalem.

3 These *are* the heads of the province who
dwelt in Jerusalem. (But in the cities of Judah everyone dwelt in his own possession
in their cities—Israelites, priests, Levites,
Nethinim, and descendants of Solomon's
servants.) 4 Also in Jerusalem dwelt *some* of
the children of Judah and of the children of
Benjamin.

The children of Judah: Athaiah the son
of Uzziah, the son of Zechariah, the son
of Amariah, the son of Shephatiah, the
son of Mahalalel, of the children of Perez;
5 and Maaseiah the son of Baruch, the son

of Col-Hozeh, the son of Hazaiah, the son of Adaiah, the son of Joiarib, the son of Zechariah, the son of Shiloni. 6All the sons of Perez who dwelt at Jerusalem *were* four hundred and sixty-eight valiant men.

7And these are the sons of Benjamin: Sallu the son of Meshullam, the son of Joed, the son of Pedaiah, the son of Kolaiah, the son of Maaseiah, the son of Ithiel, the son of Jeshaiah; 8and after him Gabbai *and* Sallai, nine hundred and twenty-eight. 9Joel the son of Zichri *was* their overseer, and Judah the son of Senuah[a] *was* second over the city.

10Of the priests: Jedaiah the son of Joiarib, and Jachin; 11Seraiah the son of Hilkiah, the son of Meshullam, the son of Zadok, the son of Meraioth, the son of Ahitub, *was* the leader of the house of God. 12Their brethren who did the work of the house *were* eight hundred and twenty-two; and Adaiah the son of Jeroham, the son of Pelaliah, the son of Amzi, the son of Zechariah, the son of Pashhur, the son of Malchijah, 13and his brethren, heads of the fathers' *houses, were* two hundred and forty-two; and Amashai the son of Azarel, the son of Ahzai, the son of Meshillemoth, the son of Immer, 14and their brethren, mighty men of valor, *were* one hundred and twenty-eight. Their overseer *was* Zabdiel the son of *one of* the great men.[a]

15Also of the Levites: Shemaiah the son of Hasshub, the son of Azrikam, the son of Hashabiah, the son of Bunni; 16Shabbethai and Jozabad, of the heads of the Levites, *had* the oversight of the business outside of the house of God; 17Mattaniah the son of Micha,[a] the son of Zabdi, the son of Asaph, the leader *who* began the thanksgiving with prayer; Bakbukiah, the second among his brethren; and Abda the son of Shammua, the son of Galal, the son of Jeduthun. 18All the Levites in the holy city *were* two hundred and eighty-four.

19Moreover the gatekeepers, Akkub, Talmon, and their brethren who kept the gates, *were* one hundred and seventy-two.

20And the rest of Israel, of the priests *and* Levites, *were* in all the cities of Judah, everyone in his inheritance. 21But the Nethinim *dwelt in Ophel. And Ziha and Gishpa were* over the Nethinim.

22Also the overseer of the Levites at Jerusalem *was* Uzzi the son of Bani, the son of Hashabiah, the son of Mattaniah, the son of Micha, of the sons of Asaph, the singers in charge of the service of the house of God. 23For *it was* the king's command concerning them that a certain portion should be for the singers, a quota day by day. 24Pethahiah the son of Meshezabel, of the children of Zerah the son of Judah, *was* the king's deputy[a] in all matters concerning the people.

The People Dwelling Outside Jerusalem

25And as for the villages with their fields, *some* of the children of Judah dwelt in Kirjath Arba and its villages, Dibon and its villages, Jekabzeel and its villages; 26in Jeshua, Moladah, Beth Pelet, 27Hazar Shual, and Beersheba and its villages; 28in Ziklag and Meconah and its villages; 29in En Rimmon, Zorah, Jarmuth, 30Zanoah, Adullam, and their villages; in Lachish and its fields; in Azekah and its villages. They dwelt from Beersheba to the Valley of Hinnom.

31Also the children of Benjamin from Geba *dwelt* in Michmash, Aija, and Bethel, and their villages; 32in Anathoth, Nob, Ananiah; 33in Hazor, Ramah, Gittaim; 34in Hadid, Zeboim, Neballat; 35in Lod, Ono, *and* the Valley of Craftsmen. 36Some of the Judean divisions of Levites *were* in Benjamin.

The Priests and Levites

12 Now these *are* the priests and the Levites who came up with Zerubbabel the son of Shealtiel, and Jeshua: Seraiah, Jeremiah, Ezra, 2Amariah, Malluch, Hattush, 3Shechaniah, Rehum, Meremoth, 4Iddo, Ginnethoi,[a] Abijah, 5Mijamin, Maadiah, Bilgah, 6Shemaiah, Joiarib, Jedaiah, 7Sallu, Amok, Hilkiah, *and* Jedaiah.

These *were* the heads of the priests and their brethren in the days of Jeshua.

8Moreover the Levites *were* Jeshua, Binnui, Kadmiel, Sherebiah, Judah, *and* Mattaniah *who led* the thanksgiving *psalms,* he and his brethren. 9Also Bakbukiah and Unni, their brethren, *stood* across from them in *their* duties.

10Jeshua begot Joiakim, Joiakim begot Eliashib, Eliashib begot Joiada, 11Joiada begot Jonathan, and Jonathan begot Jaddua.

12Now in the days of Joiakim, the priests,

11:9 [a] Or *Hassenuah* 11:14 [a] Or *the son of Haggedolim*
11:17 [a] Or *Michah* 11:24 [a] Literally *at the king's hand*
12:4 [a] Or *Ginnethon* (compare verse 16)

the heads of the fathers' *houses were:* of Se-
raiah, Meraiah; of Jeremiah, Hananiah; 13of
Ezra, Meshullam; of Amariah, Jehohanan;
14of Melichu,[a] Jonathan; of Shebaniah,[b]
Joseph; 15of Harim,[a] Adna; of Meraioth,[b]
Helkai; 16of Iddo, Zechariah; of Ginnethon,
Meshullam; 17of Abijah, Zichri; *the son* of
Minjamin;[a] of Moadiah,[b] Piltai; 18of Bil-
gah, Shammua; of Shemaiah, Jehonathan;
19of Joiarib, Mattenai; of Jedaiah, Uzzi; 20of
Sallai,[a] Kallai; of Amok, Eber; 21of Hilkiah,
Hashabiah; *and* of Jedaiah, Nethanel.

22During the reign of Darius the Persian, a record *was also kept* of the Levites and
priests *who had been* heads of their fathers'
houses in the days of Eliashib, Joiada, Johanan, and Jaddua. 23The sons of Levi, the
heads of the fathers' *houses* until the days of
Johanan the son of Eliashib, *were* written in
the book of the chronicles.

24And the heads of the Levites *were* Hashabiah, Sherebiah, and Jeshua the son of Kadmiel, with their brothers across from them,
to praise *and* give thanks, group alternating
with group, according to the command of
David the man of God. 25Mattaniah, Bakbukiah, Obadiah, Meshullam, Talmon, and
Akkub *were* gatekeepers keeping the watch
at the storerooms of the gates. 26These *lived*
in the days of Joiakim the son of Jeshua, the
son of Jozadak,[a] and in the days of Nehemiah the governor, and of Ezra the priest, the
scribe.

Nehemiah Dedicates the Wall

27Now at the dedication of the wall of Jerusalem they sought out the Levites in all
their places, to bring them to Jerusalem to
celebrate the dedication with gladness, both
with thanksgivings and singing, *with* cymbals and stringed instruments and harps.
28And the sons of the singers gathered together from the countryside around Jerusalem, from the villages of the Netophathites,
29from the house of Gilgal, and from the
fields of Geba and Azmaveth; for the singers had built themselves villages all around
Jerusalem. 30Then the priests and Levites
purified themselves, and purified the people, the gates, and the wall.

31So I brought the leaders of Judah up on
the wall, and appointed two large thanksgiving choirs. *One* went to the right hand on the
wall toward the Refuse Gate. 32After them
went Hoshaiah and half of the leaders of
Judah, 33and Azariah, Ezra, Meshullam, 34Ju-
dah, Benjamin, Shemaiah, Jeremiah, 35and
some of the priests' sons with trumpets—
Zechariah the son of Jonathan, the son of
Shemaiah, the son of Mattaniah, the son
of Michaiah, the son of Zaccur, the son of
Asaph, 36and his brethren, Shemaiah, Azarel, Milalai, Gilalai, Maai, Nethanel, Judah,
and Hanani, with the musical instruments
of David the man of God. And Ezra the
scribe *went* before them. 37By the Fountain
Gate, in front of them, they went up the
stairs of the City of David, on the stairway of
the wall, beyond the house of David, as far as
the Water Gate eastward.

38The other thanksgiving choir went the
opposite *way,* and I *was* behind them with
half of the people on the wall, going past the
Tower of the Ovens as far as the Broad Wall,
39and above the Gate of Ephraim, above the
Old Gate, above the Fish Gate, the Tower of
Hananel, the Tower of the Hundred, as far
as the Sheep Gate; and they stopped by the
Gate of the Prison.

40So the two thanksgiving choirs stood
in the house of God, likewise I and the
half of the rulers with me; 41and the priests,
Eliakim, Maaseiah, Minjamin,[a] Michaiah,
Elioenai, Zechariah, *and* Hananiah, with
trumpets; 42also Maaseiah, Shemaiah, Eleazar, Uzzi, Jehohanan, Malchijah, Elam, and
Ezer. The singers sang loudly with Jezrahiah
the director.

43Also that day they offered great sacrifices, and rejoiced, for God had made them
rejoice with great joy; the women and the
children also rejoiced, so that the joy of Jerusalem was heard afar off.

Temple Responsibilities

44And at the same time some were appointed over the rooms of the storehouse for
the offerings, the firstfruits, and the tithes,
to gather into them from the fields of the
cities the portions specified by the Law for
the priests and Levites; for Judah rejoiced
over the priests and Levites who ministered.
45Both the singers and the gatekeepers kept

12:14 [a] Or *Malluch* (compare verse 2) [b] Or *Shechaniah* (compare verse 3) **12:15** [a] Or *Rehum* (compare verse 3) [b] Or *Meremoth* (compare verse 3) **12:17** [a] Or *Mijamin* (compare verse 5) [b] Or *Maadiah* (compare verse 5) **12:20** [a] Or *Sallu* (compare verse 7) **12:26** [a] Spelled *Jehozadak* in 1 Chronicles 6:14 **12:41** [a] Or *Mijamin* (compare verse 5)

the charge of their God and the charge of the
purification, according to the command of
David *and* Solomon his son. 46For in the days
of David and Asaph of old *there were* chiefs of
the singers, and songs of praise and thanksgiving to God. 47In the days of Zerubbabel
and in the days of Nehemiah all Israel gave
the portions for the singers and the gatekeepers, a portion for each day. They also
consecrated *holy things* for the Levites, and
the Levites consecrated *them* for the children
of Aaron.

Principles of Separation

13 On that day they read from the
Book of Moses in the hearing of the
people, and in it was found written that no
Ammonite or Moabite should ever come into
the assembly of God, 2because they had not
met the children of Israel with bread and
water, but hired Balaam against them to
curse them. However, our God turned the
curse into a blessing. 3So it was, when they
had heard the Law, that they separated all the
mixed multitude from Israel.

The Reforms of Nehemiah

4Now before this, Eliashib the priest,
having authority over the storerooms of the
house of our God, *was* allied with Tobiah.
5And he had prepared for him a large room,
where previously they had stored the grain
offerings, the frankincense, the articles, the
tithes of grain, the new wine and oil, which
were commanded *to be given* to the Levites
and singers and gatekeepers, and the offerings for the priests. 6But during all this I was
not in Jerusalem, for in the thirty-second
year of Artaxerxes king of Babylon I had returned to the king. Then after certain days
I obtained leave from the king, 7and I came
to Jerusalem and discovered the evil that
Eliashib had done for Tobiah, in preparing
a room for him in the courts of the house of
God. 8And it grieved me bitterly; therefore I
threw all the household goods of Tobiah out
of the room. 9Then I commanded them to
cleanse the rooms; and I brought back into
them the articles of the house of God, with
the grain offering and the frankincense.

10I also realized that the portions for the
Levites had not been given *them;* for each of
the Levites and the singers who did the work
had gone back to his field. 11So I contended
with the rulers, and said, "Why is the house
of God forsaken?" And I gathered them together and set them in their place. 12Then
all Judah brought the tithe of the grain and
the new wine and the oil to the storehouse.
13And I appointed as treasurers over the
storehouse Shelemiah the priest and Zadok
the scribe, and of the Levites, Pedaiah; and
next to them *was* Hanan the son of Zaccur,
the son of Mattaniah; for they were considered faithful, and their task *was* to distribute
to their brethren.

14Remember me, O my God, concerning
this, and do not wipe out my good deeds that
I have done for the house of my God, and for
its services!

15In those days I saw *people* in Judah
treading winepresses on the Sabbath, and
bringing in sheaves, and loading donkeys
with wine, grapes, figs, and all *kinds of* burdens, which they brought into Jerusalem on
the Sabbath day. And I warned *them* about
the day on which they were selling provisions. 16Men of Tyre dwelt there also, who
brought in fish and all kinds of goods, and
sold *them* on the Sabbath to the children of
Judah, and in Jerusalem.

17Then I contended with the nobles of
Judah, and said to them, "What evil thing
is this that you do, by which you profane the
Sabbath day? 18Did not your fathers do thus,
and did not our God bring all this disaster
on us and on this city? Yet you bring added
wrath on Israel by profaning the Sabbath."

19So it was, at the gates of Jerusalem,
as it began to be dark before the Sabbath,
that I commanded the gates to be shut, and
charged that they must not be opened till
after the Sabbath. Then I posted *some* of
my servants at the gates, *so that* no burdens
would be brought in on the Sabbath day.
20Now the merchants and sellers of all kinds
of wares lodged outside Jerusalem once or
twice.

21Then I warned them, and said to them,
"Why do you spend the night around the
wall? If you do *so* again, I will lay hands on
you!" From that time on they came no *more*
on the Sabbath. 22And I commanded the Levites that they should cleanse themselves,
and that they should go and guard the gates,
to sanctify the Sabbath day.

Remember me, O my God, *concerning*
this also, and spare me according to the
greatness of Your mercy!

23In those days I also saw Jews *who* had

The King Dethrones Queen Vashti

1 Now it came to pass in the days of Ahasuerus[a] (this *was* the Ahasuerus who
reigned over one hundred and twenty-seven
provinces, from India to Ethiopia), 2in those
days when King Ahasuerus sat on the throne
of his kingdom, which *was* in Shushan[a] the
citadel, 3*that* in the third year of his reign
he made a feast for all his officials and
servants—the powers of Persia and Media,
the nobles, and the princes of the provinces *being* before him— 4when he showed
the riches of his glorious kingdom and the
splendor of his excellent majesty for many
days, one hundred and eighty days *in all.*
5And when these days were completed,
the king made a feast lasting seven days for
all the people who were present in Shushan
the citadel, from great to small, in the court
of the garden of the king's palace. 6*There*
were white and blue linen *curtains* fastened
with cords of fine linen and purple on silver rods and marble pillars; *and the* couches
were of gold and silver on a *mosaic* pavement
of alabaster, turquoise, and white and black
marble. 7And they served drinks in golden
vessels, each vessel being different from
the other, with royal wine in abundance,
according to the generosity of the king. 8In
accordance with the law, the drinking was
not compulsory; for so the king had ordered
all the officers of his household, that they
should do according to each man's pleasure.
9Queen Vashti also made a feast for the
women *in* the royal palace which *belonged* to
King Ahasuerus.
10On the seventh day, when the heart
of the king was merry with wine, he commanded Mehuman, Biztha, Harbona,
Bigtha, Abagtha, Zethar, and Carcas, seven
eunuchs who served in the presence of King
Ahasuerus, 11to bring Queen Vashti before
the king, *wearing* her royal crown, in order
to show her beauty to the people and the officials, for she *was* beautiful to behold. 12But
Queen Vashti refused to come at the king's
command *brought* by *his* eunuchs; therefore
the king was furious, and his anger burned
within him.
13Then the king said to the wise men
who understood the times (for this *was* the
king's manner toward all who knew law and
justice, 14those closest to him *being* Carshe-
na, Shethar, Admatha, Tarshish, Meres,
Marsena, and Memucan, the seven princes
of Persia and Media, who had access to the
king's presence, *and* who ranked highest in
the kingdom): 15"What *shall we* do to Queen
Vashti, according to law, because she did
not obey the command of King Ahasuerus
brought to her by the eunuchs?"
16And Memucan answered before the
king and the princes: "Queen Vashti has not
only wronged the king, but also all the princes, and all the people who *are* in all the provinces of King Ahasuerus. 17For the queen's
behavior will become known to all women,
so that they will despise their husbands in
their eyes, when they report, 'King Ahasuerus commanded Queen Vashti to be brought
in before him, but she did not come.' 18This
very day the *noble* ladies of Persia and Media
will say to all the king's officials that they
have heard of the behavior of the queen.
Thus *there will be* excessive contempt and

1:1 [a] Generally identified with Xerxes I (485–464 BC)
1:2 [a] Or *Susa,* and so throughout this book

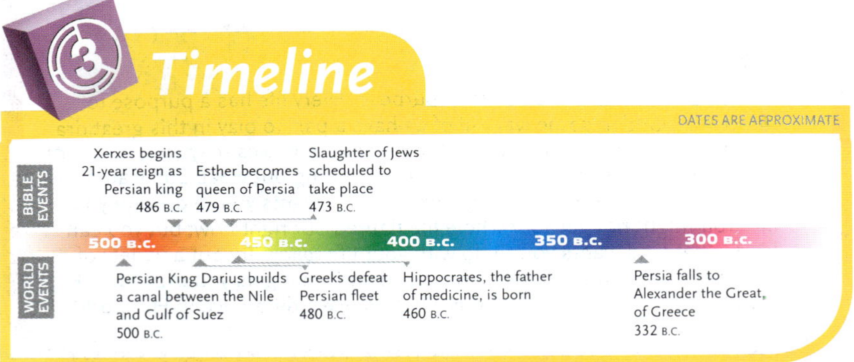

wrath. 19If it pleases the king, let a royal decree go out from him, and let it be recorded
in the laws of the Persians and the Medes,
so that it will not be altered, that Vashti shall
come no more before King Ahasuerus; and
let the king give her royal position to another who is better than she. 20When the king's
decree which he will make is proclaimed
throughout all his empire (for it is great), all
wives will honor their husbands, both great
and small."

21And the reply pleased the king and the
princes, and the king did according to the
word of Memucan. 22Then he sent letters to
all the king's provinces, to each province in
its own script, and to every people in their
own language, that each man should be
master in his own house, and speak in the
language of his own people.

Esther Becomes Queen

2 After these things, when the wrath
of King Ahasuerus subsided, he remembered Vashti, what she had done, and
what had been decreed against her. 2Then
the king's servants who attended him said:
"Let beautiful young virgins be sought for
the king; 3and let the king appoint officers
in all the provinces of his kingdom, that they
may gather all the beautiful young virgins to
Shushan the citadel, into the women's quarters, under the custody of Hegai[a] the king's

2:3 [a] Hebrew *Hege*

ESTHER BECOMES QUEEN OF PERSIA

READ IT: ESTHER 2:1–23

GET IT:

Like Daniel, Mordecai and Esther lived far away from the homeland of their ancestors. They lived in a foreign country ruled by the Persian king Ahasuerus. God had big plans for their lives. They were in the right place at just the right time to influence world events. God worked things out so that Esther became queen and was in a position of authority to help save the Jewish people from being wiped out by their enemies. Through her beauty, wisdom, and talents, she made a difference for the future of God's people.

LIVE IT:

God puts us on this earth for a purpose. Every life has a purpose to affect the world in some way. All of us have a part to play in this great drama called life. From our viewpoint the size of our roles may vary, but from God's viewpoint every role is important. Figuring out what God wants you to do can be tricky. Keep asking Him what He wants you to do with your life. You might not get your whole life figured out right now; but you can learn what God wants you to do with your life *today*. Try out a variety of activities to see what really interests you and what gets you excited. Ask God to show you what you should do to make a difference in His world.

eunuch, custodian of the women. And let
beauty preparations be given *them*. 4Then
let the young woman who pleases the king
be queen instead of Vashti."

This thing pleased the king, and he
did so.

5In Shushan the citadel there was a certain Jew whose name *was* Mordecai the son
of Jair, the son of Shimei, the son of Kish,
a Benjamite. 6*Kish*[a] had been carried away
from Jerusalem with the captives who had
been captured with Jeconiah[b] king of Judah,
whom Nebuchadnezzar the king of Babylon had carried away. 7And *Mordecai* had
brought up Hadassah, that *is*, Esther, his
uncle's daughter, for she had neither father
nor mother. The young woman *was* lovely

2:6 [a] Literally *Who* [b] Same as *Jehoiachin*, 2 Kings 24:6 and elsewhere

AUTHORITY

JUST WAIT!

READ IT: ESTHER 2:5–20

GET IT:

There are two important words that are implied if you read this entire passage: *for now*. They're not actually there, but they seem to be there. This is what must happen *for now*. God has a plan in place. Mordecai sees it or at least knows it's there. Esther is going to be a major part of that plan, but *for now* she must keep quiet. She must do what she is told.

This is big-picture thinking. Sometimes it's hard to see the whole puzzle when all your focus is on the one piece right in your hand. This is what it's like sometimes when we obey God. We often don't see the whole picture at the time when obedience is needed.

Keeping quiet can be the most difficult kind of obedience—even more so than speaking up. We might not always like what those in authority ask us to do. But, like Esther, we're still supposed to follow authority. Nowadays quietly obeying an authority—a parent, a teacher, an employer, a coach, a police officer—can go against the grain. But respecting authority is what God asks of us. Since God loves us perfectly, it must be what's best for us.

LIVE IT:

- Listen.
- Listen to those who have been there.
- Listen to those who see the bigger picture.
- Listen to those who know what they're talking about.
- Listen, because sometimes that's smarter than talking.
- Listen.

and beautiful. When her father and mother
died, Mordecai took her as his own daughter.
8So it was, when the king's command
and decree were heard, and when many
young women were gathered at Shushan the
citadel, *under* the custody of Hegai, that Esther also was taken to the king's palace, into
the care of Hegai the custodian of the wom-
en. 9Now the young woman pleased him,
and she obtained his favor; so he readily
gave beauty preparations to her, besides her
allowance. Then seven choice maidservants
were provided for her from the king's palace,
and he moved her and her maidservants to
the best *place* in the house of the women.
10Esther had not revealed her people or
family, for Mordecai had charged her not to
reveal *it.* 11And every day Mordecai paced in
front of the court of the women's quarters, to
learn of Esther's welfare and what was happening to her.
12Each young woman's turn came to go
in to King Ahasuerus after she had completed twelve months' preparation, according to
the regulations for the women, for thus were
the days of their preparation apportioned: six
months with oil of myrrh, and six months
with perfumes and preparations for beauti-
fying women. 13Thus *prepared, each* young
woman went to the king, and she was given
whatever she desired to take with her from
the women's quarters to the king's palace.
14In the evening she went, and in the morning she returned to the second house of the
women, to the custody of Shaashgaz, the
king's eunuch who kept the concubines.
She would not go in to the king again unless
the king delighted in her and called for her
by name.
15Now when the turn came for Esther the
daughter of Abihail the uncle of Mordecai,
who had taken her as his daughter, to go in
to the king, she requested nothing but what
Hegai the king's eunuch, the custodian of
the women, advised. And Esther obtained
favor in the sight of all who saw her. 16So Esther was taken to King Ahasuerus, into his
royal palace, in the tenth month, which *is* the
month of Tebeth, in the seventh year of his
reign. 17The king loved Esther more than all
the *other* women, and she obtained grace and
favor in his sight more than all the virgins;
so he set the royal crown upon her head and
made her queen instead of Vashti. 18Then the
king made a great feast, the Feast of Esther,
for all his officials and servants; and he proclaimed a holiday in the provinces and gave
gifts according to the generosity of a king.

In Focus

What Was The Feast Of Purim? The Hebrew word *purim* (pronounced *PEW-reem*) comes from the word *pur*, meaning "lot." To "cast lots" in helping to make a decision was like throwing dice nowadays. Haman had cast lots to decide the day when all Jews would be murdered (see Esther 3:7). The Feast of Purim celebrates Esther's work of saving the Jews.

Mordecai Discovers a Plot

19When virgins were gathered together a second time, Mordecai sat within the
king's gate. 20*Now* Esther had not revealed
her family and her people, just as Mordecai
had charged her, for Esther obeyed the command of Mordecai as when she was brought
up by him.
21In those days, while Mordecai sat within the king's gate, two of the king's eunuchs,
Bigthan and Teresh, doorkeepers, became
furious and sought to lay hands on King
Ahasuerus. 22So the matter became known
to Mordecai, who told Queen Esther, and Esther informed the king in Mordecai's name.
23And when an inquiry was made into the
matter, it was confirmed, and both were
hanged on a gallows; and it was written in
the book of the chronicles in the presence
of the king.

Haman's Conspiracy Against the Jews

3 After these things King Ahasuerus
promoted Haman, the son of Hammedatha the Agagite, and advanced him
and set his seat above all the princes who
were with him. 2And all the king's servants
who *were* within the king's gate bowed and
paid homage to Haman, for so the king had
commanded concerning him. But Mordecai
would not bow or pay homage. 3Then the

king's servants who *were* within the king's
gate said to Mordecai, "Why do you transgress the king's command?" [4]Now it happened, when they spoke to him daily and he
would not listen to them, that they told *it* to
Haman, to see whether Mordecai's words
would stand; for *Mordecai* had told them
that he *was* a Jew. [5]When Haman saw that
Mordecai did not bow or pay him homage,
Haman was filled with wrath. [6]But he disdained to lay hands on Mordecai alone, for
they had told him of the people of Mordecai.
Instead, Haman sought to destroy all the
Jews who *were* throughout the whole kingdom of Ahasuerus—the people of Mordecai.

[7]In the first month, which is the month
of Nisan, in the twelfth year of King Ahasuerus, they cast Pur (that *is,* the lot), before Haman to determine the day and the
month,[a] until *it fell on the* twelfth *month,*[b]
which *is* the month of Adar.

[8]Then Haman said to King Ahasuerus,
"There is a certain people scattered and dispersed among the people in all the provinces of your kingdom; their laws *are* different
from all *other* people's, and they do not keep

3:7 [a] Septuagint adds *to destroy the people of Mordecai in one day;* Vulgate adds *the nation of the Jews should be destroyed.* [b] Following Masoretic Text and Vulgate; Septuagint reads *and the lot fell on the fourteenth of the month.*

IDOL AND HERO WORSHIP

WORTHY OF WORSHIP

READ IT: ESTHER 3:1–16

GET IT:

Human beings are not meant to be worshiped. But for some reason, it still happens today. Think about sports stars, movie stars, music stars, or even the popular kids at your school. It's obvious that people still worship other people. The problem is that the only one worthy of worship is God.

King Ahasuerus wanted to honor one of the nobles in his court named Haman. The king ordered that everyone bow down and worship Haman. Imagine being Haman as he walked through town and saw everyone around him drop to a knee and sing his praises. This had to reinforce Haman's feeling that he was pretty important.

However, a man named Mordecai refused to bow down to Haman. Mordecai refused to worship another human being. This made Haman angry, and he wanted to kill Mordecai and all the other Jewish people in the kingdom.

LIVE IT:

God deserves your greatest respect. God deserves your worship. Are you giving too much of your respect and devotion to another human being? Ask God to always help you recognize when you have crossed the line between respecting someone's talent and giving another person your worship.

the king's laws. Therefore it *is* not fitting for
the king to let them remain. 9If it pleases the
king, let *a decree* be written that they be destroyed, and I will pay ten thousand talents
of silver into the hands of those who do the
work, to bring *it* into the king's treasuries."
10So the king took his signet ring from
his hand and gave it to Haman, the son of
Hammedatha the Agagite, the enemy of the
Jews. 11And the king said to Haman, "The
money and the people *are* given to you, to do
with them as seems good to you."
12Then the king's scribes were called on
the thirteenth day of the first month, and *a
decree* was written according to all that Haman commanded—to the king's satraps, to
the governors who *were* over each province,
to the officials of all people, to every province according to its script, and to every people in their language. In the name of King
Ahasuerus it was written, and sealed with
the king's signet ring. 13And the letters were
sent by couriers into all the king's provinces,
to destroy, to kill, and to annihilate all the
Jews, both young and old, little children and
women, in one day, on the thirteenth *day*
of the twelfth month, which *is* the month
of Adar, and to plunder their possessions.[a]
14A copy of the document was to be issued
as law in every province, being published
for all people, that they should be ready for
that day. 15The couriers went out, hastened
by the king's command; and the decree was
proclaimed in Shushan the citadel. So the
king and Haman sat down to drink, but the
city of Shushan was perplexed.

Esther Agrees to Help the Jews

4 When Mordecai learned all that had
happened, he tore his clothes and put
on sackcloth and ashes, and went out into
the midst of the city. He cried out with a loud
and bitter cry. 2He went as far as the front of
the king's gate, for no one *might* enter the
king's gate clothed with sackcloth. 3And in
every province where the king's command
and decree arrived, *there was* great mourning among the Jews, with fasting, weeping,
and wailing; and many lay in sackcloth and
ashes.
4So Esther's maids and eunuchs came
and told her, and the queen was deeply distressed. Then she sent garments to clothe
Mordecai and take his sackcloth away from
him, but he would not accept *them.* 5Then
Esther called Hathach, *one* of the king's eunuchs whom he had appointed to attend her,
and she gave him a command concerning
Mordecai, to learn what and why this *was.*
6So Hathach went out to Mordecai in the city
square that *was* in front of the king's gate.
7And Mordecai told him all that had happened to him, and the sum of money that
Haman had promised to pay into the king's
treasuries to destroy the Jews. 8He also gave
him a copy of the written decree for their
destruction, which was given at Shushan,
that he might show it to Esther and explain
it to her, and that he might command her
to go in to the king to make supplication to
him and plead before him for her people. 9So

3:13 [a] Septuagint adds the text of the letter here.

HEARING GOD'S VOICE

READ IT: ESTHER 4:1–17

Esther needed a clear head to make a big decision. She was going to risk her life for her people, so she asked them to fast and pray as she prepared to make a dangerous request in front of the king.

Like Esther, we often need help making decisions. We may have what it takes, but we can never have too many people praying when we face tough situations. Ask some friends and adults to pray for you today.

Hathach returned and told Esther the words
of Mordecai.
10Then Esther spoke to Hathach, and
gave him a command for Mordecai: 11"All the
king's servants and the people of the king's
provinces know that any man or woman who
goes into the inner court to the king, who
has not been called, *he has* but one law: put
all to death, except the one to whom the king
holds out the golden scepter, that he may
live. Yet I myself have not been called to go
in to the king these thirty days." 12So they
told Mordecai Esther's words.
13And Mordecai told *them* to answer Esther: "Do not think in your heart that you
will escape in the king's palace any more
than all the other Jews. 14For if you remain
completely silent at this time, relief and
deliverance will arise for the Jews from another place, but you and your father's house
will perish. Yet who knows whether you
have come to the kingdom for *such* a time
as this?"
15Then Esther told *them* to reply to Mordecai: 16"Go, gather all the Jews who are present in Shushan, and fast for me; neither eat
nor drink for three days, night or day. My
maids and I will fast likewise. And so I will
go to the king, which *is* against the law; and
if I perish, I perish!"
17So Mordecai went his way and did according to all that Esther commanded him.[a]

Esther's Banquet

5 Now it happened on the third day that
Esther put on *her* royal *robes* and stood
in the inner court of the king's palace, across
from the king's house, while the king sat on
his royal throne in the royal house, facing
the entrance of the house.[a] 2So it was, when
the king saw Queen Esther standing in the
court, *that* she found favor in his sight, and
the king held out to Esther the golden scepter that *was* in his hand. Then Esther went
near and touched the top of the scepter.
3And the king said to her, "What do you
wish, Queen Esther? What *is* your request?
It shall be given to you—up to half the
kingdom!"
4So Esther answered, "If it pleases the
king, let the king and Haman come today
to the banquet that I have prepared for him."
5Then the king said, "Bring Haman
quickly, that he may do as Esther has said."
So the king and Haman went to the banquet
that Esther had prepared.
6At the banquet of wine the king said to
Esther, "What *is* your petition? It shall be
granted you. What *is* your request, up to half
the kingdom? It shall be done!"
7Then Esther answered and said, "My
petition and request *is this:* 8If I have found
favor in the sight of the king, and if it pleases
the king to grant my petition and fulfill my
request, then let the king and Haman come
to the banquet which I will prepare for them,
and tomorrow I will do as the king has said."

Haman's Plot Against Mordecai

9So Haman went out that day joyful and
with a glad heart; but when Haman saw
Mordecai in the king's gate, and that he did
not stand or tremble before him, he was
filled with indignation against Mordecai.
10Nevertheless Haman restrained himself
and went home, and he sent and called for
his friends and his wife Zeresh. 11Then Haman told them of his great riches, the multitude of his children, everything in which the
king had promoted him, and how he had advanced him above the officials and servants
of the king.
12Moreover Haman said, "Besides, Queen
Esther invited no one but me to come in with
the king to the banquet that she prepared;
and tomorrow I am again invited by her,
along with the king. 13Yet all this avails me
nothing, so long as I see Mordecai the Jew
sitting at the king's gate."
14Then his wife Zeresh and all his friends
said to him, "Let a gallows be made, fifty cubits high, and in the morning suggest to the
king that Mordecai be hanged on it; then go
merrily with the king to the banquet."
And the thing pleased Haman; so he had
the gallows made.

The King Honors Mordecai

6 That night the king could not sleep. So
one was commanded to bring the book
of the records of the chronicles; and they
were read before the king. 2And it was found
written that Mordecai had told of Bigthana
and Teresh, two of the king's eunuchs, the
doorkeepers who had sought to lay hands
on King Ahasuerus. 3Then the king said,

4:17 [a] Septuagint adds a prayer of Mordecai here.
5:1 [a] Septuagint adds many extra details in verses 1 and 2.

"What honor or dignity has been bestowed
on Mordecai for this?"
And the king's servants who attended
him said, "Nothing has been done for him."
4 So the king said, "Who *is* in the court?"
Now Haman had *just* entered the outer court
of the king's palace to suggest that the king
hang Mordecai on the gallows that he had
prepared for him.
5 The king's servants said to him, "Haman is there, standing in the court."
And the king said, "Let him come in."
6 So Haman came in, and the king asked
him, "What shall be done for the man whom
the king delights to honor?"
Now Haman thought in his heart,
"Whom would the king delight to honor
more than me?" 7 And Haman answered the
king, "*For* the man whom the king delights
to honor, 8 let a royal robe be brought which
the king has worn, and a horse on which
the king has ridden, which has a royal crest
placed on its head. 9 Then let this robe and
horse be delivered to the hand of one of the
king's most noble princes, that he may array
the man whom the king delights to honor.
Then parade him on horseback through the
city square, and proclaim before him: 'Thus
shall it be done to the man whom the king
delights to honor!' "
10 Then the king said to Haman, "Hurry,
take the robe and the horse, as you have suggested, and do so for Mordecai the Jew who
sits within the king's gate! Leave nothing
undone of all that you have spoken."
11 So Haman took the robe and the horse,
arrayed Mordecai and led him on horseback
through the city square, and proclaimed before him, "Thus shall it be done to the man
whom the king delights to honor!"
12 Afterward Mordecai went back to
the king's gate. But Haman hurried to his
house, mourning and with his head covered.
13 When Haman told his wife Zeresh and all
his friends everything that had happened to
him, his wise men and his wife Zeresh said
to him, "If Mordecai, before whom you have
begun to fall, is of Jewish descent, you will
not prevail against him but will surely fall
before him."
14 While they *were* still talking with him,
the king's eunuchs came, and hastened to
bring Haman to the banquet which Esther
had prepared.

Haman Hanged Instead of Mordecai

7 So the king and Haman went to dine
with Queen Esther. 2 And on the second
day, at the banquet of wine, the king again
said to Esther, "What *is* your petition, Queen
Esther? It shall be granted you. And what
is your request, up to half the kingdom? It
shall be done!"
3 Then Queen Esther answered and said,
"If I have found favor in your sight, O king,
and if it pleases the king, let my life be giv-
en me at my petition, and my people at my
request. 4 For we have been sold, my people
and I, to be destroyed, to be killed, and to be
annihilated. Had we been sold as male and

BEING YOURSELF

READ IT: ESTHER 7:1–10

Esther is one of the most highly esteemed women in the Bible because of her awareness and confidence. She knew God wanted to use her to save the Jews from Haman. In order to do so, she had to approach the king and make her request—not an easy task. However, she knew God wouldn't leave her hanging. He gave her everything she needed to approach the king and win him over: confidence, wisdom, and opportunity. She answered God's call and accepted who He created her to be.

female slaves, I would have held my tongue,
although the enemy could never compensate
for the king's loss."

5So King Ahasuerus answered and said
to Queen Esther, "Who is he, and where is
he, who would dare presume in his heart to
do such a thing?"

6And Esther said, "The adversary and enemy *is* this wicked Haman!"

So Haman was terrified before the king
and queen.

7Then the king arose in his wrath from
the banquet of wine *and went* into the palace
garden; but Haman stood before Queen Esther, pleading for his life, for he saw that evil
was determined against him by the king.
8When the king returned from the palace
garden to the place of the banquet of wine,
Haman had fallen across the couch where
Esther *was*. Then the king said, "Will he also
assault the queen while I *am* in the house?"

As the word left the king's mouth, they
covered Haman's face. 9Now Harbonah, one
of the eunuchs, said to the king, "Look! The
gallows, fifty cubits high, which Haman
made for Mordecai, who spoke good on the
king's behalf, is standing at the house of
Haman."

Then the king said, "Hang him on it!"

10So they hanged Haman on the gallows
that he had prepared for Mordecai. Then the
king's wrath subsided.

Esther Saves the Jews

8 On that day King Ahasuerus gave
Queen Esther the house of Haman,
the enemy of the Jews. And Mordecai came
before the king, for Esther had told how he
was related to her. 2So the king took off his
signet ring, which he had taken from Haman, and gave it to Mordecai; and Esther appointed Mordecai over the house of Haman.

3Now Esther spoke again to the king, fell
down at his feet, and implored him with
tears to counteract the evil of Haman the
Agagite, and the scheme which he had devised against the Jews. 4And the king held
out the golden scepter toward Esther. So Esther arose and stood before the king, 5and
said, "If it pleases the king, and if I have
found favor in his sight and the thing *seems*
right to the king and I am pleasing in his
eyes, let it be written to revoke the letters devised by Haman, the son of Hammedatha
the Agagite, which he wrote to annihilate
the Jews who *are* in all the king's provinces.
6For how can I endure to see the evil that will
come to my people? Or how can I endure to
see the destruction of my countrymen?"

7Then King Ahasuerus said to Queen Esther and Mordecai the Jew, "Indeed, I have
given Esther the house of Haman, and they
have hanged him on the gallows because he
tried to lay his hand on the Jews. 8You yourselves write *a decree* concerning the Jews, as
you please, in the king's name, and seal *it*
with the king's signet ring; for whatever is
written in the king's name and sealed with
the king's signet ring no one can revoke."

9So the king's scribes were called at that
time, in the third month, which *is* the month
of Sivan, on the twenty-third *day;* and it was
written, according to all that Mordecai commanded, to the Jews, the satraps, the governors, and the princes of the provinces from
India to Ethiopia, one hundred and twenty-
seven provinces *in all,* to every province in
its own script, to every people in their own
language, and to the Jews in their own script
and language. 10And he wrote in the name
of King Ahasuerus, sealed *it* with the king's
signet ring, and sent letters by couriers on
horseback, riding on royal horses bred from
swift steeds.[a]

11By these letters the king permitted the
Jews who *were* in every city to gather together and protect their lives—to destroy, kill,
and annihilate all the forces of any people or
province that would assault them, *both* little
children and women, and to plunder their
possessions, 12on one day in all the provinces of King Ahasuerus, on the thirteenth *day*
of the twelfth month, which *is* the month of
Adar.[a] 13A copy of the document was to be
issued as a decree in every province and published for all people, so that the Jews would
be ready on that day to avenge themselves on
their enemies. 14The couriers who rode on
royal horses went out, hastened and pressed
on by the king's command. And the decree
was issued in Shushan the citadel.

15So Mordecai went out from the presence of the king in royal apparel of blue
and white, with a great crown of gold and a
garment of fine linen and purple; and the
city of Shushan rejoiced and was glad. 16The
Jews had light and gladness, joy and honor.

8:10 [a] Literally *sons of the swift horses* **8:12** [a] Septuagint adds the text of the letter here.

[17]And in every province and city, wherever
the king's command and decree came, the
Jews had joy and gladness, a feast and a holiday. Then many of the people of the land
became Jews, because fear of the Jews fell
upon them.

The Jews Destroy Their Tormentors

9 Now in the twelfth month, that *is,* the
month of Adar, on the thirteenth day,
the time came for the king's command and
his decree to be executed. On the day that
the enemies of the Jews had hoped to overpower them, the opposite occurred, in that
the Jews themselves overpowered those who
hated them. [2]The Jews gathered together
in their cities throughout all the provinces
of King Ahasuerus to lay hands on those
who sought their harm. And no one could
withstand them, because fear of them fell
upon all people. [3]And all the officials of
the provinces, the satraps, the governors,
and all those doing the king's work, helped
the Jews, because the fear of Mordecai fell
upon them. [4]For Mordecai *was* great in the
king's palace, and his fame spread throughout all the provinces; for this man Mordecai became increasingly prominent. [5]Thus
the Jews defeated all their enemies with
the stroke of the sword, with slaughter and

GOD SAVES HIS PEOPLE THROUGH ESTHER

READ IT: ESTHER 9:1–32

GET IT:

Haman, an important official, hated Mordecai (Esther's relative) because Mordecai wouldn't bow down to him. So Haman got the king to make an announcement that on a certain day the people could attack and kill all the Jews in the empire. Mordecai heard the plan and sent a message to Esther. He told her she had to do something to save her people. Esther daringly went to the king and invited him to a special dinner. At the dinner she told the king of Haman's plan to kill her people, the Jews. The king was furious at Haman. He had Haman killed and then made another law that let the Jews defend themselves. On the day that the people were going to wipe out the Jews, the Jews defended themselves and won. God worked through Esther to save His people from their enemies.

LIVE IT:

What's the most difficult, impossible, or daring situation you've ever had to face? What did you do about it? Did you talk about it with someone you trusted? Did you keep it to yourself? In this story, Esther faced a massive problem. She asked everybody to help her come up with a solution. In three days of searching and thinking, she came up with her plan. It was *risky, courageous,* and daring. She put her life on the line to approach the king without being asked to show up. She didn't think about herself; she thought about doing the right thing for the Jews. Her plan was successful.

destruction, and did what they pleased with those who hated them.

6And in Shushan the citadel the Jews killed and destroyed five hundred men. 7Also Parshandatha, Dalphon, Aspatha, 8Poratha, Adalia, Aridatha, 9Parmashta, Arisai, Aridai, and Vajezatha— 10the ten sons of Haman the son of Hammedatha, the enemy of the Jews—they killed; but they did not lay a hand on the plunder.

11On that day the number of those who were killed in Shushan the citadel was brought to the king. 12And the king said to Queen Esther, "The Jews have killed and destroyed five hundred men in Shushan the citadel, and the ten sons of Haman. What have they done in the rest of the king's provinces? Now what *is* your petition? It shall be granted to you. Or what *is* your further request? It shall be done."

13Then Esther said, "If it pleases the king, let it be granted to the Jews who *are* in Shushan to do again tomorrow according to today's decree, and let Haman's ten sons be hanged on the gallows."

14So the king commanded this to be done; the decree was issued in Shushan, and they hanged Haman's ten sons.

15And the Jews who *were* in Shushan gathered together again on the fourteenth day of the month of Adar and killed three hundred men at Shushan; but they did not lay a hand on the plunder.

16The remainder of the Jews in the king's provinces gathered together and protected their lives, had rest from their enemies, and killed seventy-five thousand of their enemies; but they did not lay a hand on the plunder. 17*This was* on the thirteenth day of the month of Adar. And on the fourteenth of *the month*[a] they rested and made it a day of feasting and gladness.

The Feast of Purim

18But the Jews who *were* at Shushan assembled together on the thirteenth *day,* as well as on the fourteenth; and on the fifteenth of *the month*[a] they rested, and made it a day of feasting and gladness. 19Therefore the Jews of the villages who dwelt in the unwalled towns celebrated the fourteenth day of the month of Adar *with* gladness and feasting, as a holiday, and for sending presents to one another.

20And Mordecai wrote these things and sent letters to all the Jews, near and far, who *were* in all the provinces of King Ahasuerus, 21to establish among them that they should celebrate yearly the fourteenth and fifteenth days of the month of Adar, 22as the days on which the Jews had rest from their enemies, as the month which was turned from sorrow to joy for them, and from mourning to a holiday; that they should make them days of feasting and joy, of sending presents to one another and gifts to the poor. 23So the Jews accepted the custom which they had begun, as Mordecai had written to them, 24because Haman, the son of Hammedatha the Agagite, the enemy of all the Jews, had plotted against the Jews to annihilate them, and had cast Pur (that *is,* the lot), to consume them and destroy them; 25but when *Esther*[a] came before the king, he commanded by letter that this[b] wicked plot which *Haman* had devised against the Jews should return on his own head, and that he and his sons should be hanged on the gallows.

26So they called these days Purim, after the name Pur. Therefore, because of all the words of this letter, what they had seen concerning this matter, and what had happened to them, 27the Jews established and imposed it upon themselves and their descendants and all who would join them, that without fail they should celebrate these two days every year, according to the written *instructions* and according to the *prescribed* time, 28*that* these days *should be* remembered and kept throughout every generation, every family, every province, and every city, that these days of Purim should not fail *to be observed* among the Jews, and *that* the memory of them should not perish among their descendants.

29Then Queen Esther, the daughter of Abihail, with Mordecai the Jew, wrote with full authority to confirm this second letter about Purim. 30And *Mordecai* sent letters to all the Jews, to the one hundred and twenty-seven provinces of the kingdom of Ahasuerus, *with* words of peace and truth, 31to confirm these days of Purim at their *appointed* time, as Mordecai the Jew and Queen Esther had prescribed for them, and as they had decreed for themselves and their descendants concerning matters of their

9:17 [a] Literally *it* 9:18 [a] Literally *it* 9:25 [a] Literally *she* or *it* [b] Literally *his*

fasting and lamenting. [32]So the decree of
Esther confirmed these matters of Purim,
and it was written in the book.

Mordecai's Advancement

10 And King Ahasuerus imposed tribute on the land and *on* the islands
of the sea. [2]Now all the acts of his power and
his might, and the account of the greatness
of Mordecai, to which the king advanced
him, *are* they not written in the book of the
chronicles of the kings of Media and Persia?
[3]For Mordecai the Jew *was* second to King
Ahasuerus, and was great among the Jews
and well received by the multitude of his
brethren, seeking the good of his people and
speaking peace to all his countrymen.[a]

10:3 [a] Literally *seed.* Septuagint and Vulgate add a dream of Mordecai here; Vulgate adds six more chapters.

The BOOK of

JOB

Date Written Unknown

Behind the Scenes

READ IT:

The book of Job is about a righteous man who was very rich. Even after losing everything he owned and all his children, Job still confessed his love for God. Job and his friends discussed his situation and came up with possible answers. When they finished talking, God spoke. Job finally admitted that God was too great and wonderful for anyone to understand.

GET IT:

Who wrote it: We don't know.

When it was written: We don't know.

Why it was written: The book asks and answers the question "Why do good people suffer?"

LIVE IT:

God allows bad things to happen to people, but it doesn't mean they have done something wrong.

We must trust God and believe He has a plan for our lives even when things go wrong.

FIND IT:

Satan Attacks Job	*Job 1–2*
Job Speaks	*Job 3*
Job Pleads with God	*Job 10, 12*
Job's Discourse on Wisdom	*Job 28*
God Answers Job	*Job 40–41*
Job's Repentance and Restoration	*Job 42*

Job and His Family in Uz

1 There was a man in the land of Uz, whose name *was* Job; and that man was blameless and upright, and one who feared God and shunned evil. 2 And seven sons and three daughters were born to him. 3 Also, his possessions were seven thousand sheep, three thousand camels, five hundred yoke of oxen, five hundred female donkeys, and a very large household, so that this man was the greatest of all the people of the East.

4 And his sons would go and feast *in their* houses, each on his *appointed* day, and would send and invite their three sisters to eat and drink with them. 5 So it was, when the days of feasting had run their course, that Job would send and sanctify them, and he would rise early in the morning and offer burnt offerings *according to* the number of them all. For Job said, "It may be that my sons have sinned and cursed[a] God in their hearts." Thus Job did regularly.

Satan Attacks Job's Character

6 Now there was a day when the sons of God came to present themselves before the LORD, and Satan[a] also came among them. 7 And the LORD said to Satan, "From where do you come?"

So Satan answered the LORD and said, "From going to and fro on the earth, and from walking back and forth on it."

8 Then the LORD said to Satan, "Have you considered My servant Job, that *there is* none like him on the earth, a blameless and upright man, one who fears God and shuns evil?"

9 So Satan answered the LORD and said, "Does Job fear God for nothing? 10 Have You not made a hedge around him, around his household, and around all that he has on every side? You have blessed the work of his hands, and his possessions have increased in the land. 11 But now, stretch out Your hand and touch all that he has, and he will surely curse You to Your face!"

12 And the LORD said to Satan, "Behold, all that he has *is* in your power; only do not lay a hand on his *person.*"

So Satan went out from the presence of the LORD.

Job Loses His Property and Children

13 Now there was a day when his sons and daughters *were* eating and drinking wine in their oldest brother's house; 14 and a messenger came to Job and said, "The oxen were plowing and the donkeys feeding beside them, 15 when the Sabeans[a] raided *them* and took them away—indeed they have killed the servants with the edge of the sword; and I alone have escaped to tell you!"

16 While he *was* still speaking, another also came and said, "The fire of God fell from heaven and burned up the sheep and the servants, and consumed them; and I alone have escaped to tell you!"

17 While he *was* still speaking, another also came and said, "The Chaldeans formed three bands, raided the camels and took them away, yes, and killed the servants with the edge of the sword; and I alone have escaped to tell you!"

18 While he *was* still speaking, another also came and said, "Your sons and daughters *were* eating and drinking wine in their oldest brother's house, 19 and suddenly a great wind came from across[a] the wilderness and struck the four corners of the house, and it fell on the young people, and they are dead; and I alone have escaped to tell you!"

20 Then Job arose, tore his robe, and shaved his head; and he fell to the ground and worshiped. 21 And he said:

"Naked I came from my mother's womb,
And naked shall I return there.
The LORD gave, and the LORD has taken away;
Blessed be the name of the LORD."

22 In all this Job did not sin nor charge God with wrong.

Satan Attacks Job's Health

2 Again there was a day when the sons of God came to present themselves before the LORD, and Satan came also among them to present himself before the LORD. 2 And the LORD said to Satan, "From where do you come?"

Satan answered the LORD and said, "From going to and fro on the earth, and from walking back and forth on it."

3 Then the LORD said to Satan, "Have you considered My servant Job, that *there is* none like him on the earth, a blameless and

---

1:5 [a] Literally *blessed,* but used here in the evil sense, and so in verse 11 and 2:5, 9 **1:6** [a] Literally *the Adversary,* and so throughout this book **1:15** [a] Literally *Sheba* (compare 6:19) **1:19** [a] Septuagint omits *across.*

upright man, one who fears God and shuns
evil? And still he holds fast to his integrity,
although you incited Me against him, to destroy him without cause."
4So Satan answered the LORD and said,
"Skin for skin! Yes, all that a man has he will
give for his life. 5But stretch out Your hand
now, and touch his bone and his flesh, and
he will surely curse You to Your face!"
6And the LORD said to Satan, "Behold, he
is in your hand, but spare his life."
7So Satan went out from the presence of
the LORD, and struck Job with painful boils
from the sole of his foot to the crown of his
head. 8And he took for himself a potsherd
with which to scrape himself while he sat in
the midst of the ashes.
9Then his wife said to him, "Do you still

LIFE'S NOT FAIR

POOR JOB

READ IT: JOB 1:1—2:13

GET IT:

Of all the people we learn about in the Bible, Job is the one most tied to suffering and misery, but he hadn't done anything that deserved punishment. Job loved God, and the most important thing to him was pleasing God. If anyone ever had the right to complain about the unfairness of life, it was this man. He lost people he loved, he lost property, and he suffered terrible physical pain—all at the same time.

We can learn a lot from Job's story, but one of the most important things is that bad things don't happen just to bad people. Bad things can happen to anyone, even you. Making good choices and following Jesus are no guarantee that life will be easy.

LIVE IT:

Another thing we can learn from Job is how to respond when life doesn't seem fair. Job's perspective—how he sees his life—is remarkable. He says, "I came into the world with nothing, and I'll leave with nothing. God gives, God takes, but He is always good."

The next time you go through something hard, try to learn from Job's example.

- Remember that whatever you've lost was a gift from God and was a blessing—something (or someone) to be thankful you *were able to enjoy* for a time.
- Know that life is full of both good things (blessings) and hard things (adversity).
- Acknowledge that God is still good: "Blessed be the name of the LORD" (1:21).
- Practice all these things with life's little frustrations, so that you're prepared for the bigger, harder disappointments.

hold fast to your integrity? Curse God and
die!"
10But he said to her, "You speak as one of
the foolish women speaks. Shall we indeed
accept good from God, and shall we not accept
adversity?" In all this Job did not sin
with his lips.

Job's Three Friends

11Now when Job's three friends heard of
all this adversity that had come upon him,
each one came from his own place—Eliphaz
the Temanite, Bildad the Shuhite, and Zophar
the Naamathite. For they had made an
appointment together to come and mourn
with him, and to comfort him. 12And when
they raised their eyes from afar, and did not
recognize him, they lifted their voices and
wept; and each one tore his robe and sprinkled
dust on his head toward heaven. 13So
they sat down with him on the ground seven
days and seven nights, and no one spoke a
word to him, for they saw that *his* grief was
very great.

Job Deplores His Birth

3 After this Job opened his mouth and
cursed the day of his *birth*. 2And Job
spoke, and said:

3 "May the day perish on which I was born,
And the night *in which* it was said,
'A male child is conceived.'
4 May that day be darkness;
May God above not seek it,
Nor the light shine upon it.
5 May darkness and the shadow of death claim it;
May a cloud settle on it;
May the blackness of the day terrify it.
6 *As for* that night, may darkness seize it;
May it not rejoice[a] among the days of the year,
May it not come into the number of the months.
7 Oh, may that night be barren!
May no joyful shout come into it!
8 May those curse it who curse the day,
Those who are ready to arouse Leviathan.
9 *May the stars of its morning* be dark;
May it look for light, but *have* none,
And not see the dawning of the day;
10 Because it did not shut up the doors of my *mother's* womb,
Nor hide sorrow from my eyes.

11 "Why did I not die at birth?
Why did I *not* perish when I came from the womb?
12 Why did the knees receive me?
Or why the breasts, that I should nurse?
13 For now I would have lain still and been quiet,
I would have been asleep;
Then I would have been at rest
14 With kings and counselors of the earth,
Who built ruins for themselves,
15 Or with princes who had gold,
Who filled their houses *with* silver;
16 Or *why* was I not hidden like a stillborn child,
Like infants who never saw light?
17 There the wicked cease *from* troubling,
And there the weary are at rest.
18 *There* the prisoners rest together;
They do not hear the voice of the oppressor.
19 The small and great are there,
And the servant *is* free from his master.

20 "Why is light given to him who is in misery,
And life to the bitter of soul,
21 Who long for death, but it does not *come*,
And search for it more than hidden treasures;
22 Who rejoice exceedingly,
And are glad when they can find the grave?
23 *Why is light given* to a man whose way is hidden,
And whom God has hedged in?
24 For my sighing comes before I eat,[a]
And my groanings pour out like water.
25 For the thing I greatly feared has come upon me,
And what I dreaded has happened to me.
26 I am not at ease, nor am I quiet;
I have no rest, for trouble comes."

Eliphaz: Job Has Sinned

4 Then Eliphaz the Temanite answered
and said:

2 "*If* one attempts a word with you, will you become weary?

3:6 [a] Septuagint, Syriac, Targum, and Vulgate read *be joined*. 3:24 [a] Literally *my bread*

But who can withhold himself from speaking?
3 Surely you have instructed many,
And you have strengthened weak hands.
4 Your words have upheld him who was stumbling,
And you have strengthened the feeble knees;
5 But now it comes upon you, and you are weary;
It touches you, and you are troubled.
6 *Is* not your reverence your confidence?
And the integrity of your ways your hope?

7 "Remember now, who *ever* perished being innocent?
Or where were the upright *ever* cut off?
8 Even as I have seen,
Those who plow iniquity
And sow trouble reap the same.
9 By the blast of God they perish,
And by the breath of His anger they are consumed.
10 The roaring of the lion,
The voice of the fierce lion,
And the teeth of the young lions are broken.
11 The old lion perishes for lack of prey,
And the cubs of the lioness are scattered.

12 "Now a word was secretly brought to me,
And my ear received a whisper of it.
13 In disquieting thoughts from the visions of the night,
When deep sleep falls on men,
14 Fear came upon me, and trembling,
Which made all my bones shake.
15 Then a spirit passed before my face;
The hair on my body stood up.
16 It stood still,
But I could not discern its appearance.
A form *was* before my eyes;
There was silence;
Then I heard a voice *saying:*
17 'Can a mortal be more righteous than God?
Can a man be more pure than his Maker?
18 If He puts no trust in His servants,
If He charges His angels with error,
19 How much more those who dwell in houses of clay,
Whose foundation is in the dust,
Who are crushed before a moth?

In Focus

4:17 Mortal The opposite of immortal (see definition at Romans 2:7). Your present body will die, but your soul is *immortal* (cannot die). Someday believers will receive immortal bodies like Christ's body.

20 They are broken in pieces from morning till evening;
They perish forever, with no one regarding.
21 Does not their own excellence go away?
They die, even without wisdom.'

Eliphaz: Job Is Chastened by God

5 "Call out now;
Is there anyone who will answer you?
And to which of the holy ones will you turn?
2 For wrath kills a foolish man,
And envy slays a simple one.
3 I have seen the foolish taking root,
But suddenly I cursed his dwelling place.
4 His sons are far from safety,
They are crushed in the gate,
And *there is* no deliverer.
5 Because the hungry eat up his harvest,
Taking it even from the thorns,[a]
And a snare snatches their substance.[b]
6 For affliction does not come from the dust,
Nor does trouble spring from the ground;
7 Yet man is born to trouble,
As the sparks fly upward.

8 "But as for me, I would seek God,
And to God I would commit my cause—
9 Who does great things, and unsearchable,
Marvelous things without number.
10 He gives rain on the earth,
And sends waters on the fields.
11 He sets on high those who are lowly,

5:5 [a] Septuagint reads *They shall not be taken from evil men;* Vulgate reads *And the armed man shall take him by violence.* [b] Septuagint reads *The might shall draw them off;* Vulgate reads *And the thirsty shall drink up their riches.*

And those who mourn are lifted to safety.
12 He frustrates the devices of the crafty,
So that their hands cannot carry out their plans.
13 He catches the wise in their own craftiness,
And the counsel of the cunning comes quickly upon them.
14 They meet with darkness in the daytime,
And grope at noontime as in the night.
15 But He saves the needy from the sword,
From the mouth of the mighty,
And from their hand.
16 So the poor have hope,
And injustice shuts her mouth.

17 "Behold, happy *is* the man whom God corrects;
Therefore do not despise the chastening of the Almighty.
18 For He bruises, but He binds up;
He wounds, but His hands make whole.
19 He shall deliver you in six troubles,
Yes, in seven no evil shall touch you.
20 In famine He shall redeem you from death,
And in war from the power of the sword.
21 You shall be hidden from the scourge of the tongue,
And you shall not be afraid of destruction when it comes.
22 You shall laugh at destruction and famine,
And you shall not be afraid of the beasts of the earth.
23 For you shall have a covenant with the stones of the field,
And the beasts of the field shall be at peace with you.
24 You shall know that your tent *is* in peace;
You shall visit your dwelling and find nothing amiss.
25 You shall also know that your descendants *shall be* many,
And your offspring like the grass of the earth.
26 You shall come to the grave at a full age,
As a sheaf of grain ripens in its season.
27 Behold, this we have searched out;
It *is* true.
Hear it, and know for yourself."

Job: My Complaint Is Just

6 Then Job answered and said:

2 "Oh, that my grief were fully weighed,
And my calamity laid with it on the scales!
3 For then it would be heavier than the sand of the sea—
Therefore my words have been rash.
4 For the arrows of the Almighty *are* within me;
My spirit drinks in their poison;
The terrors of God are arrayed against me.
5 Does the wild donkey bray when it has grass,
Or does the ox low over its fodder?

GRIEF

READ IT: JOB 5:11

If anyone had a reason to grieve, that person was Job. He lost everything, and the friends who stuck around gave him a hard time about it. *Through all his loss, Job continued to worship God.* When we worship God as we grieve, we show Him we trust Him beyond our pain. God promises to keep those who are mourning close to Him, "lifted to safety."

6 Can flavorless food be eaten without
salt?
Or is there *any* taste in the white of an
egg?
7 My soul refuses to touch them;
They *are* as loathsome food to me.

8 "Oh, that I might have my request,
That God would grant *me* the thing that
I long for!
9 That it would please God to crush me,
That He would loose His hand and cut
me off!
10 Then I would still have comfort;
Though in anguish I would exult,
He will not spare;
For I have not concealed the words of
the Holy One.

11 "What strength do I have, that I should
hope?
And what *is* my end, that I should
prolong my life?
12 *Is* my strength the strength of stones?
Or is my flesh bronze?
13 *Is* my help not within me?
And is success driven from me?

14 "To him who is afflicted, kindness *should
be shown* by his friend,
Even though he forsakes the fear of the
Almighty.
15 My brothers have dealt deceitfully like a
brook,
Like the streams of the brooks that pass
away,
16 Which are dark because of the ice,
And into which the snow vanishes.
17 When it is warm, they cease to flow;
When it is hot, they vanish from their
place.
18 The paths of their way turn aside,
They go nowhere and perish.
19 The caravans of Tema look,
The travelers of Sheba hope for them.
20 They are disappointed because they
were confident;
They come there and are confused.
21 For now you are nothing,
You see terror and are afraid.
22 Did I ever say, 'Bring *something* to me'?
Or, 'Offer a bribe for me from your
wealth'?
23 Or, 'Deliver me from the enemy's
hand'?
Or, 'Redeem me from the hand of
oppressors'?

24 "Teach me, and I will hold my tongue;
Cause me to understand wherein I have
erred.
25 How forceful are right words!
But what does your arguing prove?
26 Do you intend to rebuke *my* words,
And the speeches of a desperate one,
which are as wind?
27 Yes, you overwhelm the fatherless,
And you undermine your friend.
28 Now therefore, be pleased to look at me;
For I would never lie to your face.
29 Yield now, let there be no injustice!
Yes, concede, my righteousness still
stands!
30 Is there injustice on my tongue?
Cannot my taste discern the unsavory?

Job: My Suffering Is Comfortless

7 "*Is there* not a time of hard service for
man on earth?
Are not his days also like the days of a
hired man?
2 Like a servant who earnestly desires the
shade,
And like a hired man who eagerly looks
for his wages,
3 So I have been allotted months of
futility,
And wearisome nights have been
appointed to me.
4 When I lie down, I say, 'When shall I
arise,
And the night be ended?'
For I have had my fill of tossing till
dawn.
5 My flesh is caked with worms and dust,
My skin is cracked and breaks out
afresh.

6 "My days are swifter than a weaver's
shuttle,
And are spent without hope.
7 Oh, remember that my life *is* a breath!
My eye will never again see good.
8 The eye of him who sees me will see me
no *more;*
While your eyes *are* upon me, I shall no
longer *be.*
9 *As* the cloud disappears and vanishes
away,
So he who goes down to the grave does
not come up.

10 He shall never return to his house,
Nor shall his place know him anymore.

11 "Therefore I will not restrain my mouth;
I will speak in the anguish of my spirit;
I will complain in the bitterness of my soul.
12 *Am* I a sea, or a sea serpent,
That You set a guard over me?
13 When I say, 'My bed will comfort me,
My couch will ease my complaint,'
14 Then You scare me with dreams
And terrify me with visions,
15 So that my soul chooses strangling
And death rather than my body.[a]
16 I loathe *my life;*
I would not live forever.
Let me alone,
For my days *are but* a breath.

17 "What *is* man, that You should exalt him,
That You should set Your heart on him,
18 That You should visit him every morning,
And test him every moment?
19 How long?
Will You not look away from me,
And let me alone till I swallow my saliva?
20 Have I sinned?
What have I done to You, O watcher of men?
Why have You set me as Your target,
So that I am a burden to myself?[a]
21 Why then do You not pardon my transgression,
And take away my iniquity?
For now I will lie down in the dust,
And You will seek me diligently,
But I *will* no longer *be.*"

Bildad: Job Should Repent

8 Then Bildad the Shuhite answered and said:

2 "How long will you speak these *things,*
And the words of your mouth *be like* a strong wind?
3 Does God subvert judgment?
Or does the Almighty pervert justice?
4 If your sons have sinned against Him,
He has cast them away for their transgression.
5 If you would earnestly seek God
And make your supplication to the Almighty,
6 If you *were* pure and upright,
Surely now He would awake for you,
And prosper your rightful dwelling place.
7 Though your beginning was small,

7:15 [a] Literally *my bones* 7:20 [a] Following Masoretic Text, Targum, and Vulgate; Septuagint and Jewish tradition read *to You.*

Epic Ideas

6:29, 30 A SELF-SATISFIED MAN

Job was a good man. The Lord said so (see Job 1:8). Then Job made a mistake we all make too often. Job thought he had nothing more to learn: "My righteousness still stands," he said. Job's friends were wrong about Job, but Job still needed to learn that he was *nothing without God.* Can you learn that lesson?

Some of us are like Job. We do very well at everything we try. So we become self-satisfied. That's when God may have to remind us that we need Him. Perhaps you've been gifted with a sharp mind, or you're good at sports, or you can think or move faster than most of your friends. Does *that make you feel smug? Look out!* God may have to show you how weak you really are! But sometimes that's best. You can only be the kind of person God can use if you aren't self-satisfied.

Yet your latter end would increase
abundantly.

8 "For inquire, please, of the former age,
And consider the things discovered by
their fathers;
9 For we *were born* yesterday, and know
nothing,
Because our days on earth *are* a shadow.
10 Will they not teach you and tell you,
And utter words from their heart?

11 "Can the papyrus grow up without a
marsh?
Can the reeds flourish without water?
12 While it *is* yet green *and* not cut down,
It withers before any *other* plant.
13 So *are* the paths of all who forget God;
And the hope of the hypocrite shall
perish,
14 Whose confidence shall be cut off,
And whose trust *is* a spider's web.
15 He leans on his house, but it does not
stand.
He holds it fast, but it does not endure.
16 He grows green in the sun,
And his branches spread out in his
garden.
17 His roots wrap around the rock heap,
And look for a place in the stones.
18 If he is destroyed from his place,
Then *it* will deny him, *saying,* 'I have not
seen you.'

19 "Behold, this is the joy of His way,
And out of the earth others will grow.
20 Behold, God will not cast away the
blameless,
Nor will He uphold the evildoers.
21 He will yet fill your mouth with
laughing,
And your lips with rejoicing.
22 Those who hate you will be clothed with
shame,
And the dwelling place of the wicked
will come to nothing."[a]

Job: There Is No Mediator

9 Then Job answered and said:

2 "Truly I know *it is* so,
But how can a man be righteous before
God?
3 If one wished to contend with Him,
He could not answer Him one time out
of a thousand.

In Focus

8:11 Papyrus Pronounced *pun-PIE-rus.* A reed that grows in northern Africa and southern Europe. In ancient times, these reeds were cut and pressed chiefly to make a kind of writing paper.

4 *God is* wise in heart and mighty in
strength.
Who has hardened *himself* against Him
and prospered?
5 He removes the mountains, and they do
not know
When He overturns them in His anger;
6 He shakes the earth out of its place,
And its pillars tremble;
7 He commands the sun, and it does not
rise;
He seals off the stars;
8 He alone spreads out the heavens,
And treads on the waves of the sea;
9 He made the Bear, Orion, and the
Pleiades,
And the chambers of the south;
10 He does great things past finding out,
Yes, wonders without number.
11 If He goes by me, I do not see *Him;*
If He moves past, I do not perceive Him;
12 If He takes away, who can hinder Him?
Who can say to Him, 'What are You
doing?'
13 God will not withdraw His anger,
The allies of the proud[a] lie prostrate
beneath Him.

14 "How then can I answer Him,
And choose my words *to reason* with
Him?
15 For though I were righteous, I could not
answer Him;
I would beg mercy of my Judge.
16 If I called and He answered me,
I would not believe that He was
listening to my voice.
17 For He crushes me with a tempest,
And multiplies my wounds without
cause.

8:22 [a] Literally *will not be* 9:13 [a] Hebrew *rahab*

18 He will not allow me to catch my breath,
But fills me with bitterness.
19 If *it is a matter* of strength, indeed *He is* strong;
And if of justice, who will appoint my day *in court?*
20 Though I were righteous, my own mouth would condemn me;
Though I *were* blameless, it would prove me perverse.

21 "I am blameless, yet I do not know myself;
I despise my life.
22 It *is* all one *thing;*
Therefore I say, 'He destroys the blameless and the wicked.'
23 If the scourge slays suddenly,
He laughs at the plight of the innocent.
24 The earth is given into the hand of the wicked.
He covers the faces of its judges.
If it is not *He,* who else could it be?

25 "Now my days are swifter than a runner;
They flee away, they see no good.
26 They pass by like swift ships,
Like an eagle swooping on its prey.
27 If I say, 'I will forget my complaint,
I will put off my sad face and wear a smile,'
28 I am afraid of all my sufferings;
I know that You will not hold me innocent.
29 *If* I am condemned,
Why then do I labor in vain?
30 If I wash myself with snow water,
And cleanse my hands with soap,
31 Yet You will plunge me into the pit,
And my own clothes will abhor me.

32 "For *He is* not a man, as I *am,*
That I may answer Him,
And that we should go to court together.
33 Nor is there any mediator between us,
Who may lay his hand on us both.
34 Let Him take His rod away from me,
And do not let dread of Him terrify me.
35 *Then* I would speak and not fear Him,
But it is not so with me.

Job: I Would Plead with God

10 "My soul loathes *my* life;
I will give free course to my complaint,
I will speak in the bitterness of my soul.
2 I will say to God, 'Do not condemn me;
Show me why You contend with me.
3 *Does it* seem good to You that You should oppress,
That You should despise the work of Your hands,
And smile on the counsel of the wicked?
4 Do You have eyes of flesh?
Or do You see as man sees?
5 *Are* Your days like the days of a mortal man?
Are Your years like the days of a mighty man,
6 That You should seek for my iniquity
And search out my sin,
7 Although You know that I am not wicked,
And *there is* no one who can deliver from Your hand?

8 'Your hands have made me and fashioned me,
An intricate unity;
Yet You would destroy me.
9 Remember, I pray, that You have made me like clay.
And will You turn me into dust again?
10 Did You not pour me out like milk,
And curdle me like cheese,
11 Clothe me with skin and flesh,
And knit me together with bones and sinews?
12 You have granted me life and favor,
And Your care has preserved my spirit.

13 'And these *things* You have hidden in Your heart;
I know that this *was* with You:
14 If I sin, then You mark me,
And will not acquit me of my iniquity.
15 If I am wicked, woe to me;
Even *if* I am righteous, I cannot lift up my head.
I am full of disgrace;
See my misery!
16 If *my head* is exalted,
You hunt me like a fierce lion,
And again You show Yourself awesome against me.
17 You renew Your witnesses against me,
And increase Your indignation toward me;
Changes and war are *ever* with me.

18 'Why then have You brought me out of the womb?
Oh, that I had perished and no eye had seen me!

19 I would have been as though I had not
been.
I would have been carried from the
womb to the grave.
20 Are not my days few?
Cease! Leave me alone, that I may take a
little comfort,
21 Before I go *to the place from which* I shall
not return,
To the land of darkness and the shadow
of death,
22 A land as dark as darkness *itself,*
As the shadow of death, without any
order,
Where even the light *is* like darkness.'"

Zophar Urges Job to Repent

11 Then Zophar the Naamathite answered and said:

2 "Should not the multitude of words be
answered?
And should a man full of talk be
vindicated?
3 Should your empty talk make men hold
their peace?
And when you mock, should no one
rebuke you?
4 For you have said,
'My doctrine *is* pure,
And I am clean in your eyes.'
5 But oh, that God would speak,
And open His lips against you,
6 That He would show you the secrets of
wisdom!
For *they would* double *your* prudence.
Know therefore that God exacts from
you
Less than your iniquity *deserves.*

7 "Can you search out the deep things of
God?
Can you find out the limits of the
Almighty?
8 *They are* higher than heaven—what can
you do?
Deeper than Sheol—what can you
know?
9 Their measure *is* longer than the earth
And broader than the sea.

In Focus

11:4 Doctrine Pronounced *DOK-trin.* The truth taught in the Bible. Christians believe all of God's doctrine or teaching as their foundation for salvation and living in the world.

Epic Ideas

11:1–6 A MAN WITHOUT MERCY

Zophar (pronounced *ZO-far*) was supposed to be a friend to Job. But he was no true friend! Listen to his hard words to Job: "Know therefore that God exacts from you less than your iniquity deserves" (Job 11:6). What Zophar didn't know was that God wasn't really punishing Job at all! God was only making Job a *better* man than he was. When good people suffer, they become better people.

Poor Zophar is the one to be pitied. He doesn't even know how to say a kind word to his suffering friend. What a small soul Zophar must have had!

Jesus once said, "Blessed are the merciful, for they shall obtain mercy" (Matthew 5:7). You may not believe it, but some people really don't know how to show mercy. So it is important for you to be a merciful person. Then people will see Jesus in you.

10 "If He passes by, imprisons, and gathers *to judgment,*
Then who can hinder Him?
11 For He knows deceitful men;
He sees wickedness also.
Will He not then consider *it?*
12 For an empty-headed man will be wise,
When a wild donkey's colt is born a man.

13 "If you would prepare your heart,
And stretch out your hands toward Him;
14 If iniquity *were* in your hand, *and you* put it far away,
And would not let wickedness dwell in your tents;
15 Then surely you could lift up your face without spot;
Yes, you could be steadfast, and not fear;
16 Because you would forget *your* misery,
And remember *it* as waters *that have* passed away,
17 And *your* life would be brighter than noonday.
Though you were dark, you would be like the morning.
18 And you would be secure, because there is hope;
Yes, you would dig *around you, and* take your rest in safety.
19 You would also lie down, and no one would make *you* afraid;
Yes, many would court your favor.
20 But the eyes of the wicked will fail,
And they shall not escape,
And their hope—loss of life!"

Job Answers His Critics

12 Then Job answered and said:

2 "No doubt you *are* the people,
And wisdom will die with you!
3 But I have understanding as well as you;
I *am* not inferior to you.
Indeed, who does not *know* such things as these?

4 "I am one mocked by his friends,
Who called on God, and He answered him,
The just and blameless *who is* ridiculed.
5 A lamp[a] is despised in the thought of one who is at ease;
It is made ready for those whose feet slip.
6 The tents of robbers prosper,
And those who provoke God are secure—
In what God provides by His hand.

7 "But now ask the beasts, and they will teach you;
And the birds of the air, and they will tell you;
8 Or speak to the earth, and it will teach you;
And the fish of the sea will explain to you.
9 Who among all these does not know
That the hand of the LORD has done this,
10 In whose hand *is* the life of every living thing,
And the breath of all mankind?
11 Does not the ear test words
And the mouth taste its food?
12 Wisdom *is* with aged men,
And with length of days, understanding.

13 "With Him *are* wisdom and strength,
He has counsel and understanding.
14 If He breaks *a thing* down, it cannot be rebuilt;
If He imprisons a man, there can be no release.
15 If He withholds the waters, they dry up;
If He sends them out, they overwhelm the earth.
16 With Him *are* strength and prudence.
The deceived and the deceiver *are* His.
17 He leads counselors away plundered,
And makes fools of the judges.
18 He loosens the bonds of kings,
And binds their waist with a belt.
19 He leads princes[a] away plundered,
And overthrows the mighty.
20 He deprives the trusted ones of speech,
And takes away the discernment of the elders.
21 He pours contempt on princes,
And disarms the mighty.
22 He uncovers deep things out of darkness,
And brings the shadow of death to light.
23 He makes nations great, and destroys them;
He enlarges nations, and guides them.

12:5 [a] Or *disaster* 12:19 [a] Literally *priests,* but not in a technical sense

24 He takes away the understanding[a] of
the chiefs of the people of the earth,
And makes them wander in a pathless
wilderness.
25 They grope in the dark without light,
And He makes them stagger like a
drunken *man*.

13 "Behold, my eye has seen all *this*,
My ear has heard and
understood it.
2 What you know, I also know;
I *am* not inferior to you.
3 But I would speak to the Almighty,
And I desire to reason with God.
4 But you forgers of lies,
You *are* all worthless physicians.
5 Oh, that you would be silent,
And it would be your wisdom!
6 Now hear my reasoning,
And heed the pleadings of my lips.
7 Will you speak wickedly for God,
And talk deceitfully for Him?
8 Will you show partiality for Him?
Will you contend for God?
9 Will it be well when He searches you
out?
Or can you mock Him as one mocks a
man?
10 He will surely rebuke you
If you secretly show partiality.
11 Will not His excellence make you afraid,
And the dread of Him fall upon you?
12 Your platitudes *are* proverbs of ashes,
Your defenses are defenses of clay.

13 "Hold your peace with me, and let me
speak,
Then let come on me what *may!*
14 Why do I take my flesh in my teeth,
And put my life in my hands?
15 Though He slay me, yet will I trust
Him.
Even so, I will defend my own ways
before Him.
16 He also *shall* be my salvation,
For a hypocrite could not come before
Him.
17 Listen carefully to my speech,
And to my declaration with your ears.
18 See now, I have prepared *my* case,
I know that I shall be vindicated.
19 Who *is* he *who* will contend with me?
If now I hold my tongue, I perish.

Job's Despondent Prayer

20 "Only two *things* do not do to me,

In Focus

13:16 Hypocrite Pronounced *HIP-puh-krit*. A person who pretends to be good or godly, but who actually is not. Jesus condemned hypocrites most of all.

Then I will not hide myself from You:
21 Withdraw Your hand far from me,
And let not the dread of You make me
afraid.
22 Then call, and I will answer;
Or let me speak, then You respond
to me.
23 How many *are* my iniquities and sins?
Make me know my transgression and
my sin.
24 Why do You hide Your face,
And regard me as Your enemy?
25 Will You frighten a leaf driven to and
fro?
And will You pursue dry stubble?
26 For You write bitter things against me,
And make me inherit the iniquities of
my youth.
27 You put my feet in the stocks,
And watch closely all my paths.
You set a limit[a] for the soles of my feet.

28 "*Man*[a] decays like a rotten thing,
Like a garment that is moth-eaten.

14 "Man *who is* born of woman
Is of few days and full of trouble.
2 He comes forth like a flower and fades
away;
He flees like a shadow and does not
continue.
3 And do You open Your eyes on such a
one,
And bring me[a] to judgment with
Yourself?
4 Who can bring a clean *thing* out of an
unclean?
No one!
5 Since his days *are* determined,
The number of his months *is* with You;

12:24 [a] Literally *heart* 13:27 [a] Literally *inscribe a print*
13:28 [a] Literally *He* 14:3 [a] Septuagint, Syriac, and Vulgate read *him*.

You have appointed his limits, so that he cannot pass.
6 Look away from him that he may rest,
Till like a hired man he finishes his day.

7 "For there is hope for a tree,
If it is cut down, that it will sprout again,
And that its tender shoots will not cease.
8 Though its root may grow old in the earth,
And its stump may die in the ground,
9 *Yet* at the scent of water it will bud
And bring forth branches like a plant.
10 But man dies and is laid away;
Indeed he breathes his last
And where *is* he?
11 *As* water disappears from the sea,
And a river becomes parched and dries up,
12 So man lies down and does not rise.
Till the heavens *are* no more,
They will not awake
Nor be roused from their sleep.

13 "Oh, that You would hide me in the grave,
That You would conceal me until Your wrath is past,
That You would appoint me a set time, and remember me!
14 If a man dies, shall he live *again?*
All the days of my hard service I will wait,
Till my change comes.
15 You shall call, and I will answer You;
You shall desire the work of Your hands.
16 For now You number my steps,
But do not watch over my sin.
17 My transgression *is* sealed up in a bag,
And You cover[a] my iniquity.

18 "But *as* a mountain falls *and* crumbles away,
And *as* a rock is moved from its place;
19 *As* water wears away stones,
And as torrents wash away the soil of the earth;
So You destroy the hope of man.
20 You prevail forever against him, and he passes on;
You change his countenance and send him away.
21 His sons come to honor, and he does not know *it;*
They are brought low, and he does not perceive *it.*
22 But his flesh will be in pain over it,
And his soul will mourn over it."

Eliphaz Accuses Job of Folly

15 Then Eliphaz the Temanite answered and said:

2 "Should a wise man answer with empty knowledge,
And fill himself with the east wind?
3 Should he reason with unprofitable talk,
Or by speeches with which he can do no good?
4 Yes, you cast off fear,
And restrain prayer before God.
5 For your iniquity teaches your mouth,
And you choose the tongue of the crafty.
6 Your own mouth condemns you, and not I;
Yes, your own lips testify against you.

7 "*Are* you the first man *who* was born?
Or were you made before the hills?
8 Have you heard the counsel of God?
Do you limit wisdom to yourself?
9 What do you know that we do not know?
What do you understand that *is* not in us?
10 Both the gray-haired and the aged *are* among us,
Much older than your father.
11 *Are* the consolations of God too small for you,
And the word *spoken* gently[a] with you?
12 Why does your heart carry you away,
And what do your eyes wink at,
13 That you turn your spirit against God,
And let *such* words go out of your mouth?

14 "What *is* man, that he could be pure?
And *he who is* born of a woman, that he could be righteous?
15 If *God* puts no trust in His saints,
And the heavens are not pure in His sight,
16 How much less man, *who is* abominable and filthy,
Who drinks iniquity like water!

17 "I will tell you, hear me;
What I have seen I will declare,
18 What wise men have told,
Not hiding *anything received* from their fathers,

14:17 [a] Literally *plaster over* 15:11 [a] Septuagint reads *a secret thing.*

19 To whom alone the land was given,
And no alien passed among them:
20 The wicked man writhes with pain all *his* days,
And the number of years is hidden from the oppressor.
21 Dreadful sounds *are* in his ears;
In prosperity the destroyer comes upon him.
22 He does not believe that he will return from darkness,
For a sword is waiting for him.
23 He wanders about for bread, *saying,* 'Where *is it?'*
He knows that a day of darkness is ready at his hand.
24 Trouble and anguish make him afraid;
They overpower him, like a king ready for battle.
25 For he stretches out his hand against God,
And acts defiantly against the Almighty,
26 Running stubbornly against Him
With his strong, embossed shield.

27 "Though he has covered his face with his fatness,
And made *his* waist heavy with fat,
28 He dwells in desolate cities,
In houses which no one inhabits,
Which are destined to become ruins.
29 He will not be rich,
Nor will his wealth continue,
Nor will his possessions overspread the earth.
30 He will not depart from darkness;
The flame will dry out his branches,
And by the breath of His mouth he will go away.
31 Let him not trust in futile *things,* deceiving himself,
For futility will be his reward.
32 It will be accomplished before his time,
And his branch will not be green.
33 He will shake off his unripe grape like a vine,
And cast off his blossom like an olive tree.
34 For the company of hypocrites *will be* barren,
And fire will consume the tents of bribery.
35 They conceive trouble and bring forth futility;
Their womb prepares deceit."

Job Reproaches His Pitiless Friends

16 Then Job answered and said:

2 "I have heard many such things;
Miserable comforters *are* you all!
3 Shall words of wind have an end?
Or what provokes you that you answer?
4 I also could speak as you *do,*
If your soul were in my soul's place.
I could heap up words against you,
And shake my head at you;
5 *But* I would strengthen you with my mouth,
And the comfort of my lips would relieve *your grief.*

6 "Though I speak, my grief is not relieved;
And *if* I remain silent, how am I eased?
7 But now He has worn me out;
You have made desolate all my company.
8 You have shriveled me up,
And it is a witness *against me;*
My leanness rises up against me
And bears witness to my face.
9 He tears *me* in His wrath, and hates me;
He gnashes at me with His teeth;
My adversary sharpens His gaze on me.
10 They gape at me with their mouth,
They strike me reproachfully on the cheek,
They gather together against me.
11 God has delivered me to the ungodly,
And turned me over to the hands of the wicked.
12 I was at ease, but He has shattered me;
He also has taken *me* by my neck, and shaken me to pieces;
He has set me up for His target,
13 His archers surround me.
He pierces my heart[a] and does not pity;
He pours out my gall on the ground.
14 He breaks me with wound upon wound;
He runs at me like a warrior.[a]

15 "I have sewn sackcloth over my skin,
And laid my head[a] in the dust.
16 My face is flushed from weeping,
And on my eyelids *is* the shadow of death;
17 Although no violence *is* in my hands,
And my prayer *is* pure.

18 "O earth, do not cover my blood,

16:13 [a] Literally *kidneys* 16:14 [a] Vulgate reads *giant.*
16:15 [a] Literally *horn*

And let my cry have no *resting* place!
19 Surely even now my witness *is* in heaven,
And my evidence *is* on high.
20 My friends scorn me;
My eyes pour out *tears* to God.
21 Oh, that one might plead for a man with God,
As a man *pleads* for his neighbor!
22 For when a few years are finished,
I shall go the way of no return.

Job Prays for Relief

17 "My spirit is broken,
My days are extinguished,
The grave *is ready* for me.
2 *Are* not mockers with me?
And does not my eye dwell on their provocation?

3 "Now put down a pledge for me with Yourself.
Who *is* he *who* will shake hands with me?
4 For You have hidden their heart from understanding;
Therefore You will not exalt *them*.
5 He who speaks flattery to *his* friends,
Even the eyes of his children will fail.

6 "But He has made me a byword of the people,
And I have become one in whose face men spit.
7 My eye has also grown dim because of sorrow,
And all my members *are* like shadows.
8 Upright *men* are astonished at this,
And the innocent stirs himself up against the hypocrite.
9 Yet the righteous will hold to his way,
And he who has clean hands will be stronger and stronger.

10 "But please, come back again, all of you,[a]
For I shall not find *one* wise *man* among you.
11 My days are past,
My purposes are broken off,
Even the thoughts of my heart.
12 They change the night into day;
'The light *is* near,' *they say,* in the face of darkness.
13 If I wait *for* the grave *as* my house,
If I make my bed in the darkness,
14 If I say to corruption, 'You *are* my father,'
And to the worm, 'You *are* my mother and my sister,'
15 Where then *is* my hope?
As for my hope, who can see it?
16 *Will* they go down to the gates of Sheol?
Shall *we have* rest together in the dust?"

Bildad: The Wicked Are Punished

18 Then Bildad the Shuhite answered and said:

2 "How long *till* you put an end to words?
Gain understanding, and afterward we will speak.
3 Why are we counted as beasts,
And regarded as stupid in your sight?
4 You who tear yourself in anger,
Shall the earth be forsaken for you?
Or shall the rock be removed from its place?

5 "The light of the wicked indeed goes out,
And the flame of his fire does not shine.
6 The light is dark in his tent,
And his lamp beside him is put out.
7 The steps of his strength are shortened,
And his own counsel casts him down.
8 For he is cast into a net by his own feet,
And he walks into a snare.
9 The net takes *him* by the heel,
And a snare lays hold of him.
10 A noose *is* hidden for him on the ground,
And a trap for him in the road.
11 Terrors frighten him on every side,
And drive him to his feet.
12 His strength is starved,
And destruction *is* ready at his side.
13 It devours patches of his skin;
The firstborn of death devours his limbs.
14 He is uprooted from the shelter of his tent,
And they parade him before the king of terrors.
15 They dwell in his tent *who are* none of his;
Brimstone is scattered on his dwelling.
16 His roots are dried out below,
And his branch withers above.
17 The memory of him perishes from the earth,

17:10 [a] Following some Hebrew manuscripts, Septuagint, Syriac, and Vulgate; Masoretic Text and Targum read *all of them*.

And he has no name among the
renowned.[a]
18 He is driven from light into darkness,
And chased out of the world.
19 He has neither son nor posterity among
his people,
Nor any remaining in his dwellings.
20 Those in the west are astonished at his
day,
As those in the east are frightened.
21 Surely such *are* the dwellings of the
wicked,
And this *is* the place *of him who* does not
know God."

Job Trusts in His Redeemer

19 Then Job answered and said:

2 "How long will you torment my soul,
And break me in pieces with words?
3 These ten times you have reproached
me;
You are not ashamed *that* you have
wronged me.[a]
4 And if indeed I have erred,
My error remains with me.
5 If indeed you exalt *yourselves* against me,
And plead my disgrace against me,
6 Know then that God has wronged me,
And has surrounded me with His net.

7 "If I cry out concerning wrong, I am not
heard.
If I cry aloud, *there is* no justice.
8 He has fenced up my way, so that I
cannot pass;
And He has set darkness in my paths.
9 He has stripped me of my glory,
And taken the crown *from* my head.
10 He breaks me down on every side,
And I am gone;
My hope He has uprooted like a tree.
11 He has also kindled His wrath against
me,
And He counts me as *one of* His
enemies.
12 His troops come together
And build up their road against me;
They encamp all around my tent.

13 "He has removed my brothers far from
me,
And my acquaintances are completely
estranged from me.
14 My relatives have failed,
And my close friends have forgotten me.
15 Those who dwell in my house, and my
maidservants,
Count me as a stranger;
I am an alien in their sight.
16 I call my servant, but he gives no
answer;
I beg him with my mouth.
17 My breath is offensive to my wife,
And I am repulsive to the children of
my own body.
18 Even young children despise me;
I arise, and they speak against me.
19 All my close friends abhor me,
And those whom I love have turned
against me.
20 My bone clings to my skin and to my
flesh,
And I have escaped by the skin of my
teeth.

21 "Have pity on me, have pity on me, O you
my friends,
For the hand of God has struck me!
22 Why do you persecute me as God *does,*
And are not satisfied with my flesh?

23 "Oh, that my words were written!
Oh, that they were inscribed in a book!
24 That they were engraved on a rock
With an iron pen and lead, forever!
25 For I know *that* my Redeemer lives,
And He shall stand at last on the earth;
26 And after my skin is destroyed, this *I
know,*
That in my flesh I shall see God,
27 Whom I shall see for myself,
And my eyes shall behold, and not
another.
How my heart yearns within me!
28 If you should say, 'How shall we
persecute him?'—
Since the root of the matter is found in
me,
29 Be afraid of the sword for yourselves;
For wrath *brings* the punishment of the
sword,
That you may know *there is* a judgment."

Zophar's Sermon on the Wicked Man

20 Then Zophar the Naamathite answered and said:

2 "Therefore my anxious thoughts make
me answer,

18:17 [a] Literally *before the outside,* meaning distinguished, famous 19:3 [a] A Jewish tradition reads *make yourselves strange to me.*

Because of the turmoil within me.
3 I have heard the rebuke that reproaches me,
And the spirit of my understanding causes me to answer.

4 "Do you *not* know this of old,
Since man was placed on earth,
5 That the triumphing of the wicked is short,
And the joy of the hypocrite is *but* for a moment?
6 Though his haughtiness mounts up to the heavens,
And his head reaches to the clouds,
7 *Yet* he will perish forever like his own refuse;
Those who have seen him will say, 'Where is he?'
8 He will fly away like a dream, and not be found;
Yes, he will be chased away like a vision of the night.
9 The eye *that* saw him will *see him* no more,
Nor will his place behold him anymore.
10 His children will seek the favor of the poor,
And his hands will restore his wealth.
11 His bones are full of his youthful vigor,
But it will lie down with him in the dust.

12 "Though evil is sweet in his mouth,
And he hides it under his tongue,
13 *Though* he spares it and does not forsake it,
But still keeps it in his mouth,
14 *Yet* his food in his stomach turns sour;
It becomes cobra venom within him.
15 He swallows down riches
And vomits them up again;
God casts them out of his belly.
16 He will suck the poison of cobras;
The viper's tongue will slay him.
17 He will not see the streams,
The rivers flowing with honey and cream.
18 He will restore that for which he labored,
And will not swallow *it* down;
From the proceeds of business
He will get no enjoyment.
19 For he has oppressed *and* forsaken the poor,
He has violently seized a house which he did not build.

20 "Because he knows no quietness in his heart,[a]
He will not save anything he desires.
21 Nothing is left for him to eat;
Therefore his well-being will not last.
22 In his self-sufficiency he will be in distress;
Every hand of misery will come against him.
23 *When* he is about to fill his stomach,
God will cast on him the fury of His wrath,
And will rain *it* on him while he is eating.
24 He will flee from the iron weapon;
A bronze bow will pierce him through.
25 It is drawn, and comes out of the body;
Yes, the glittering *point comes* out of his gall.
Terrors *come* upon him;
26 Total darkness *is* reserved for his treasures.
An unfanned fire will consume him;
It shall go ill with him who is left in his tent.
27 The heavens will reveal his iniquity,
And the earth will rise up against him.
28 The increase of his house will depart,
And his goods will flow away in the day of His wrath.
29 This *is* the portion from God for a wicked man,
The heritage appointed to him by God."

Job's Discourse on the Wicked

21 Then Job answered and said:

2 "Listen carefully to my speech,
And let this be your consolation.
3 Bear with me that I may speak,
And after I have spoken, keep mocking.

4 "As for me, *is* my complaint against man?
And if *it were,* why should I not be impatient?
5 Look at me and be astonished;
Put *your* hand over *your* mouth.
6 Even when I remember I am terrified,
And trembling takes hold of my flesh.
7 Why do the wicked live *and* become old,

20:20 [a] Literally *belly*

Yes, become mighty in power?
8 Their descendants are established with them in their sight,
And their offspring before their eyes.
9 Their houses *are* safe from fear,
Neither *is* the rod of God upon them.
10 Their bull breeds without failure;
Their cow calves without miscarriage.
11 They send forth their little ones like a flock,
And their children dance.
12 They sing to the tambourine and harp,
And rejoice to the sound of the flute.
13 They spend their days in wealth,
And in a moment go down to the grave.[a]
14 Yet they say to God, 'Depart from us,
For we do not desire the knowledge of Your ways.
15 Who *is* the Almighty, that we should serve Him?
And what profit do we have if we pray to Him?'
16 Indeed their prosperity *is* not in their hand;
The counsel of the wicked is far from me.

17 "How often is the lamp of the wicked put out?
How often does their destruction come upon them,
The sorrows *God* distributes in His anger?
18 They are like straw before the wind,
And like chaff that a storm carries away.
19 *They say,* 'God lays up one's[a] iniquity for his children';
Let Him recompense him, that he may know *it*.
20 Let his eyes see his destruction,
And let him drink of the wrath of the Almighty.
21 For what does he care about his household after him,
When the number of his months is cut in half?

22 "Can *anyone* teach God knowledge,
Since He judges those on high?
23 One dies in his full strength,
Being wholly at ease and secure;
24 His pails[a] are full of milk,
And the marrow of his bones is moist.
25 Another man dies in the bitterness of his soul,
Never having eaten with pleasure.
26 They lie down alike in the dust,
And worms cover them.

27 "Look, I know your thoughts,
And the schemes *with which* you would wrong me.
28 For you say,
'Where *is* the house of the prince?
And where *is* the tent,[a]
The dwelling place of the wicked?'
29 Have you not asked those who travel the road?
And do you not know their signs?
30 For the wicked are reserved for the day of doom;
They shall be brought out on the day of wrath.
31 Who condemns his way to his face?
And who repays him *for what* he has done?
32 Yet he shall be brought to the grave,
And a vigil kept over the tomb.
33 The clods of the valley shall be sweet to him;
Everyone shall follow him,
As countless *have gone* before him.
34 How then can you comfort me with empty words,
Since falsehood remains in your answers?"

Eliphaz Accuses Job of Wickedness

22 Then Eliphaz the Temanite answered and said:

2 "Can a man be profitable to God,
Though he who is wise may be profitable to himself?
3 *Is it* any pleasure to the Almighty that you are righteous?
Or *is it* gain *to Him* that you make your ways blameless?

4 "Is it because of your fear of Him that He corrects you,
And enters into judgment with you?
5 *Is* not your wickedness great,
And your iniquity without end?
6 For you have taken pledges from your brother for no reason,
And stripped the naked of their clothing.
7 You have not given the weary water to drink,

21:13 [a] Or *Sheol* 21:19 [a] Literally *his* 21:24 [a] Septuagint and Vulgate read *bowels;* Syriac reads *sides;* Targum reads *breasts.* 21:28 [a] Vulgate omits *the tent.*

And you have withheld bread from the
hungry.
8 But the mighty man possessed the land,
And the honorable man dwelt in it.
9 You have sent widows away empty,
And the strength of the fatherless was
crushed.
10 Therefore snares *are* all around you,
And sudden fear troubles you,
11 Or darkness *so that* you cannot see;
And an abundance of water covers you.

12 "Is not God in the height of heaven?
And see the highest stars, how lofty
they are!
13 And you say, 'What does God know?
Can He judge through the deep
darkness?
14 Thick clouds cover Him, so that He
cannot see,
And He walks above the circle of
heaven.'
15 Will you keep to the old way
Which wicked men have trod,
16 Who were cut down before their time,
Whose foundations were swept away by
a flood?
17 They said to God, 'Depart from us!
What can the Almighty do to them?'[a]
18 Yet He filled their houses with good
things;
But the counsel of the wicked is far
from me.

19 "The righteous see *it* and are glad,
And the innocent laugh at them:
20 'Surely our adversaries[a] are cut down,
And the fire consumes their remnant.'

21 "Now acquaint yourself with Him, and
be at peace;
Thereby good will come to you.
22 Receive, please, instruction from His
mouth,
And lay up His words in your heart.
23 If you return to the Almighty, you will
be built up;
You will remove iniquity far from your
tents.
24 Then you will lay your gold in the dust,
And the *gold* of Ophir among the stones
of the brooks.
25 Yes, the Almighty will be your gold[a]
And your precious silver;
26 For then you will have your delight in
the Almighty,

In Focus

22:12 Heaven The dwelling place of God, angels, and souls of the dead who belong to God. Sometimes the word "heaven" is also used as another word for the sky (see Genesis 1:8).

And lift up your face to God.
27 You will make your prayer to Him,
He will hear you,
And you will pay your vows.
28 You will also declare a thing,
And it will be established for you;
So light will shine on your ways.
29 When they cast *you* down, and you say,
'Exaltation *will come!*'
Then He will save the humble *person.*
30 He will *even* deliver one who is not
innocent;
Yes, he will be delivered by the purity of
your hands."

Job Proclaims God's Righteous Judgments

23 Then Job answered and said:

2 "Even today my complaint is bitter;
My[a] hand is listless because of my
groaning.
3 Oh, that I knew where I might find
Him,
That I might come to His seat!
4 I would present *my* case before Him,
And fill my mouth with arguments.
5 I would know the words *which* He would
answer me,
And understand what He would say
to me.
6 Would He contend with me in His great
power?
No! But He would take *note* of me.
7 There the upright could reason with
Him,

22:17 [a] Septuagint and Syriac read *us.* 22:20 [a] Septuagint reads *substance.* 22:25 [a] The ancient versions suggest *defense;* Hebrew reads *gold* as in verse 24. 23:2 [a] Following Masoretic Text, Targum, and Vulgate; Septuagint and Syriac read *His.*

And I would be delivered forever from
my Judge.

8 "Look, I go forward, but He is not *there,*
And backward, but I cannot perceive
Him;
9 When He works on the left hand, I
cannot behold *Him;*
When He turns to the right hand, I
cannot see *Him.*
10 But He knows the way that I take;
When He has tested me, I shall come
forth as gold.
11 My foot has held fast to His steps;
I have kept His way and not turned
aside.
12 I have not departed from the
commandment of His lips;
I have treasured the words of His mouth
More than my necessary *food.*

13 "But He *is* unique, and who can make
Him change?
And *whatever* His soul desires, *that* He
does.
14 For He performs *what is* appointed for
me,
And many such *things are* with Him.
15 Therefore I am terrified at His presence;
When I consider *this,* I am afraid of
Him.
16 For God made my heart weak,
And the Almighty terrifies me;
17 Because I was not cut off from the
presence of darkness,
And He did *not* hide deep darkness
from my face.

Job Complains of Violence on the Earth

24 "*Since* times are not hidden from
the Almighty,
Why do those who know Him see not
His days?

2 "*Some* remove landmarks;
They seize flocks violently and feed *on
them;*
3 They drive away the donkey of the
fatherless;
They take the widow's ox as a pledge.
4 They push the needy off the road;
All the poor of the land are forced to
hide.
5 Indeed, *like* wild donkeys in the desert,
They go out to their work, searching for
food.
The wilderness *yields* food for them *and*
for *their* children.
6 They gather their fodder in the field
And glean in the vineyard of the wicked.
7 They spend the night naked, without
clothing,
And have no covering in the cold.
8 They are wet with the showers of the
mountains,
And huddle around the rock for want of
shelter.

9 "*Some* snatch the fatherless from the
breast,
And take a pledge from the poor.
10 They cause *the poor* to go naked, without
clothing;
And they take away the sheaves from
the hungry.
11 They press out oil within their walls,
And tread winepresses, yet suffer thirst.
12 The dying groan in the city,
And the souls of the wounded cry out;
Yet God does not charge *them* with
wrong.

13 "There are those who rebel against the
light;
They do not know its ways
Nor abide in its paths.
14 The murderer rises with the light;
He kills the poor and needy;
And in the night he is like a thief.
15 The eye of the adulterer waits for the
twilight,
Saying, 'No eye will see me';
And he disguises *his* face.
16 In the dark they break into houses
Which they marked for themselves in
the daytime;
They do not know the light.
17 For the morning is the same to them as
the shadow of death;
If *someone* recognizes *them,*
They are in the terrors of the shadow of
death.

18 "They *should be* swift on the face of the
waters,
Their portion *should be* cursed in the
earth,
So that no *one would* turn into the way of
their vineyards.
19 As drought and heat consume the snow
waters,

So the grave[a] *consumes those who* have
sinned.
20 The womb *should* forget him,
The worm *should* feed sweetly on him;
He *should* be remembered no more,
And wickedness *should* be broken like
a tree.
21 For he preys on the barren *who* do not
bear,
And does no good for the widow.

22 "But *God* draws the mighty away with
His power;
He rises up, but no *man* is sure of life.
23 He gives them security, and they rely
on it;
Yet His eyes *are* on their ways.
24 They are exalted for a little while,
Then they are gone.
They are brought low;
They are taken out of the way like all
others;
They dry out like the heads of grain.

25 "Now if *it is* not *so,* who will prove me a
liar,
And make my speech worth nothing?"

Bildad: How Can Man Be Righteous?

25 Then Bildad the Shuhite answered
and said:

2 "Dominion and fear *belong* to Him;
He makes peace in His high places.
3 Is there any number to His armies?
Upon whom does His light not rise?
4 How then can man be righteous before
God?
Or how can he be pure *who is* born of a
woman?
5 If even the moon does not shine,
And the stars are not pure in His sight,
6 How much less man, *who is* a maggot,
And a son of man, *who is* a worm?"

Job: Man's Frailty and God's Majesty

26 But Job answered and said:

2 "How have you helped *him who is* without
power?
How have you saved the arm *that has* no
strength?
3 How have you counseled *one who has* no
wisdom?
And *how* have you declared sound
advice to many?
4 To whom have you uttered words?

In Focus

27:2 Soul The inner life of a person that cannot die. The soul of a believing person who dies goes to be with God in heaven. But the unbelieving person's soul is cut off from God.

And whose spirit came from you?

5 "The dead tremble,
Those under the waters and those
inhabiting them.
6 Sheol *is* naked before Him,
And Destruction has no covering.
7 He stretches out the north over empty
space;
He hangs the earth on nothing.
8 He binds up the water in His thick
clouds,
Yet the clouds are not broken under it.
9 He covers the face of *His* throne,
And spreads His cloud over it.
10 He drew a circular horizon on the face
of the waters,
At the boundary of light and darkness.
11 The pillars of heaven tremble,
And are astonished at His rebuke.
12 He stirs up the sea with His power,
And by His understanding He breaks
up the storm.
13 By His Spirit He adorned the heavens;
His hand pierced the fleeing serpent.
14 Indeed these *are* the mere edges of His
ways,
And how small a whisper we hear of Him!
But the thunder of His power who can
understand?"

Job Maintains His Integrity

27 Moreover Job continued his discourse, and said:

2 "*As* God lives, *who* has taken away my
justice,
And the Almighty, *who* has made my
soul bitter,
3 As long as my breath *is* in me,
And the breath of God in my nostrils,

24:19 [a] Or *Sheol*

4 My lips will not speak wickedness,
Nor my tongue utter deceit.
5 Far be it from me
That I should say you are right;
Till I die I will not put away my integrity from me.
6 My righteousness I hold fast, and will not let it go;
My heart shall not reproach *me* as long as I live.

7 "May my enemy be like the wicked,
And he who rises up against me like the unrighteous.
8 For what is the hope of the hypocrite,
Though he may gain *much,*
If God takes away his life?
9 Will God hear his cry
When trouble comes upon him?
10 Will he delight himself in the Almighty?
Will he always call on God?

11 "I will teach you about the hand of God;
What *is* with the Almighty I will not conceal.
12 Surely all of you have seen *it;*
Why then do you behave with complete nonsense?

13 "This is the portion of a wicked man with God,
And the heritage of oppressors, received from the Almighty:
14 If his children are multiplied, *it is* for the sword;
And his offspring shall not be satisfied with bread.
15 Those who survive him shall be buried in death,
And their[a] widows shall not weep,
16 Though he heaps up silver like dust,
And piles up clothing like clay—
17 He may pile *it* up, but the just will wear *it,*
And the innocent will divide the silver.
18 He builds his house like a moth,[a]
Like a booth *which* a watchman makes.
19 The rich man will lie down,
But not be gathered *up;*[a]
He opens his eyes,
And he *is* no more.
20 Terrors overtake him like a flood;
A tempest steals him away in the night.
21 The east wind carries him away, and he is gone;
It sweeps him out of his place.
22 It hurls against him and does not spare;
He flees desperately from its power.
23 *Men* shall clap their hands at him,
And shall hiss him out of his place.

Job's Discourse on Wisdom

28 "Surely there is a mine for silver,
And a place *where* gold is refined.
2 Iron is taken from the earth,
And copper *is* smelted *from* ore.
3 *Man* puts an end to darkness,
And searches every recess
For ore in the darkness and the shadow of death.
4 He breaks open a shaft away from people;
In places forgotten by feet
They hang far away from men;
They swing to and fro.
5 *As for* the earth, from it comes bread,
But underneath it is turned up as by fire;
6 Its stones *are* the source of sapphires,
And it contains gold dust.
7 *That* path no bird knows,
Nor has the falcon's eye seen it.
8 The proud lions[a] have not trodden it,
Nor has the fierce lion passed over it.
9 He puts his hand on the flint;
He overturns the mountains at the roots.
10 He cuts out channels in the rocks,
And his eye sees every precious thing.
11 He dams up the streams from trickling;
What is hidden he brings forth to light.

12 "But where can wisdom be found?
And where *is* the place of understanding?
13 Man does not know its value,
Nor is it found in the land of the living.
14 The deep says, '*It is* not in me'
And the sea says, '*It is* not with me.'
15 It cannot be purchased for gold,
Nor can silver be weighed *for* its price.
16 It cannot be valued in the gold of Ophir,
In precious onyx or sapphire.
17 Neither gold nor crystal can equal it,

27:15 [a] Literally *his* 27:18 [a] Following Masoretic Text and Vulgate; Septuagint and Syriac read *spider* (compare 8:14); Targum reads *decay.* 27:19 [a] Following Masoretic Text and Targum; Septuagint and Syriac read *But shall not add* (that is, do it again); Vulgate reads *But take away nothing.* 28:8 [a] Literally *sons of pride,* figurative of the great lions

Nor can it be exchanged for jewelry of
fine gold.
18 No mention shall be made of coral or
quartz,
For the price of wisdom *is* above rubies.
19 The topaz of Ethiopia cannot equal it,
Nor can it be valued in pure gold.

20 "From where then does wisdom come?
And where *is* the place of
understanding?
21 It is hidden from the eyes of all living,
And concealed from the birds of the air.
22 Destruction and Death say,
'We have heard a report about it with
our ears.'
23 God understands its way,
And He knows its place.
24 For He looks to the ends of the earth,
And sees under the whole heavens,
25 To establish a weight for the wind,
And apportion the waters by measure.
26 When He made a law for the rain,
And a path for the thunderbolt,
27 Then He saw *wisdom*[a] and declared it;
He prepared it, indeed, He searched it
out.
28 And to man He said,
'Behold, the fear of the Lord, that *is*
wisdom,
And to depart from evil *is*
understanding.'"

Job's Summary Defense

29 Job further continued his discourse, and said:

2 "Oh, that I were as *in* months past,
As *in* the days *when* God watched over
me;
3 When His lamp shone upon my head,
And when by His light I walked *through*
darkness;
4 Just as I was in the days of my prime,
When the friendly counsel of God *was*
over my tent;
5 When the Almighty *was* yet with me,
When my children *were* around me;
6 When my steps were bathed with
cream,[a]
And the rock poured out rivers of oil
for me!

7 "When I went out to the gate by the city,
When I took my seat in the open square,
8 The young men saw me and hid,
And the aged arose *and* stood;
9 The princes refrained from talking,
And put *their* hand on their mouth;
10 The voice of nobles was hushed,
And their tongue stuck to the roof of
their mouth.
11 When the ear heard, then it blessed me,
And when the eye saw, then it approved
me;
12 Because I delivered the poor who cried
out,
The fatherless and *the one who* had no
helper.
13 The blessing of a perishing *man* came
upon me,
And I caused the widow's heart to sing
for joy.
14 I put on righteousness, and it clothed
me;
My justice *was* like a robe and a turban.
15 I *was* eyes to the blind,
And I *was* feet to the lame.
16 I *was* a father to the poor,
And I searched out the case *that* I did
not know.
17 I broke the fangs of the wicked,
And plucked the victim from his teeth.

18 "Then I said, 'I shall die in my nest,
And multiply *my* days as the sand.
19 My root *is* spread out to the waters,
And the dew lies all night on my
branch.
20 My glory *is* fresh within me,
And my bow is renewed in my hand.'

21 "*Men* listened to me and waited,
And kept silence for my counsel.
22 After my words they did not speak
again,
And my speech settled on them *as dew*.
23 They waited for me *as* for the rain,
And they opened their mouth wide *as*
for the spring rain.
24 *If* I mocked at them, they did not believe
it,
And the light of my countenance they
did not cast down.
25 I chose the way for them, and sat as
chief;
So I dwelt as a king in the army,
As one *who* comforts mourners.

30 "But now they mock at me, *men*
younger than I,

28:27 [a] Literally *it* 29:6 [a] Masoretic Text reads *wrath;* ancient versions and some Hebrew manuscripts read *cream* (compare 20:17).

Whose fathers I disdained to put with
the dogs of my flock.
2 Indeed, what *profit* is the strength of
their hands to me?
Their vigor has perished.
3 *They are* gaunt from want and famine,
Fleeing late to the wilderness, desolate
and waste,
4 Who pluck mallow by the bushes,
And broom tree roots *for* their food.
5 They were driven out from among *men,*
They shouted at them as *at* a thief.
6 *They had* to live in the clefts of the
valleys,
In caves of the earth and the rocks.
7 Among the bushes they brayed,
Under the nettles they nestled.
8 *They were* sons of fools,
Yes, sons of vile men;
They were scourged from the land.

9 "And now I am their taunting song;
Yes, I am their byword.
10 They abhor me, they keep far from me;
They do not hesitate to spit in my face.
11 Because He has loosed my[a] bowstring
and afflicted me,
They have cast off restraint before me.
12 At *my* right *hand* the rabble arises;
They push away my feet,
And they raise against me their ways of
destruction.
13 They break up my path,
They promote my calamity;
They have no helper.
14 They come as broad breakers;
Under the ruinous storm they roll
along.
15 Terrors are turned upon me;
They pursue my honor as the wind,
And my prosperity has passed like a
cloud.

16 "And now my soul is poured out because
of my *plight;*
The days of affliction take hold of me.
17 My bones are pierced in me at night,
And my gnawing pains take no rest.
18 By great force my garment is disfigured;
It binds me about as the collar of my
coat.
19 He has cast me into the mire,
And I have become like dust and ashes.

20 "I cry out to You, but You do not answer
me;
I stand up, and You regard me.
21 *But* You have become cruel to me;
With the strength of Your hand You
oppose me.
22 You lift me up to the wind and cause me
to ride *on it;*
You spoil my success.
23 For I know *that* You will bring me *to*
death,
And *to* the house appointed for all
living.

24 "Surely He would not stretch out *His*
hand against a heap of ruins,
If they cry out when He destroys *it.*
25 Have I not wept for him who was in
trouble?
Has *not* my soul grieved for the poor?
26 But when I looked for good, evil came *to*
me;
And when I waited for light, then came
darkness.
27 My heart is in turmoil and cannot rest;
Days of affliction confront me.
28 I go about mourning, but not in the
sun;
I stand up in the assembly *and* cry out
for help.
29 I am a brother of jackals,
And a companion of ostriches.
30 My skin grows black and falls from me;
My bones burn with fever.
31 My harp is *turned* to mourning,
And my flute to the voice of those who
weep.

31 "I have made a covenant with my
eyes;
Why then should I look upon a young
woman?
2 For what *is* the allotment of God from
above,
And the inheritance of the Almighty
from on high?
3 *Is* it not destruction for the wicked,
And disaster for the workers of iniquity?
4 Does He not see my ways,
And count all my steps?

5 "If I have walked with falsehood,
Or if my foot has hastened to deceit,
6 Let me be weighed on honest scales,
That God may know my integrity.
7 If my step has turned from the way,
Or my heart walked after my eyes,

30:11 [a] Following Masoretic Text, Syriac, and Targum; Septuagint and Vulgate read *His.*

Or if any spot adheres to my hands,
8 *Then* let me sow, and another eat;
Yes, let my harvest be rooted out.

9 "If my heart has been enticed by a woman,
Or *if* I have lurked at my neighbor's door,
10 *Then* let my wife grind for another,
And let others bow down over her.
11 For that *would be* wickedness;
Yes, it *would be* iniquity *deserving of* judgment.
12 For that *would be* a fire *that* consumes to destruction,
And would root out all my increase.

13 "If I have despised the cause of my male or female servant
When they complained against me,
14 What then shall I do when God rises up?
When He punishes, how shall I answer Him?
15 Did not He who made me in the womb make them?
Did not the same One fashion us in the womb?

16 "If I have kept the poor from *their* desire,
Or caused the eyes of the widow to fail,
17 Or eaten my morsel by myself,
So that the fatherless could not eat of it
18 (But from my youth I reared him as a father,
And from my mother's womb I guided *the widow*[a]);
19 If I have seen anyone perish for lack of clothing,
Or any poor *man* without covering;
20 If his heart[a] has not blessed me,
And *if* he was *not* warmed with the fleece of my sheep;
21 If I have raised my hand against the fatherless,
When I saw I had help in the gate;
22 *Then* let my arm fall from my shoulder,
Let my arm be torn from the socket.
23 For destruction *from* God *is* a terror to me,
And because of His magnificence I cannot endure.

24 "If I have made gold my hope,
Or said to fine gold, '*You are* my confidence';
25 If I have rejoiced because my wealth *was* great,
And because my hand had gained much;
26 If I have observed the sun[a] when it shines,
Or the moon moving *in* brightness,
27 So that my heart has been secretly enticed,
And my mouth has kissed my hand;
28 This also *would be* an iniquity *deserving of* judgment,
For I would have denied God *who is* above.

29 "If I have rejoiced at the destruction of him who hated me,
Or lifted myself up when evil found him
30 (Indeed I have not allowed my mouth to sin
By asking for a curse on his soul);
31 If the men of my tent have not said,
'Who is there that has not been satisfied with his meat?'
32 (*But* no sojourner had to lodge in the street,
For I have opened my doors to the traveler[a]);
33 If I have covered my transgressions as Adam,
By hiding my iniquity in my bosom,
34 Because I feared the great multitude,
And dreaded the contempt of families,
So that I kept silence
And did not go out of the door—
35 Oh, that I had one to hear me!
Here is my mark.
Oh, that the Almighty would answer me,
That my Prosecutor had written a book!
36 Surely I would carry it on my shoulder,
And bind it on me *like* a crown;
37 I would declare to Him the number of my steps;
Like a prince I would approach Him.

38 "If my land cries out against me,
And its furrows weep together;
39 If I have eaten its fruit[a] without money,
Or caused its owners to lose their lives;
40 *Then* let thistles grow instead of wheat,
And weeds instead of barley."

The words of Job are ended.

31:18 [a] Literally *her* (compare verse 16) **31:20** [a] Literally *loins* **31:26** [a] Literally *light* **31:32** [a] Following Septuagint, Syriac, Targum, and Vulgate; Masoretic Text reads *road*. **31:39** [a] Literally *its strength*

Elihu Contradicts Job's Friends

32 1So these three men ceased answering Job, because he *was* righteous in his own eyes. 2Then the wrath of
Elihu, the son of Barachel the Buzite, of the
family of Ram, was aroused against Job; his
wrath was aroused because he justified himself rather than God. 3Also against his three
friends his wrath was aroused, because
they had found no answer, and *yet* had condemned Job.

4Now because they *were* years older than
he, Elihu had waited to speak to Job.[a] 5When
Elihu saw that *there was* no answer in the
mouth of these three men, his wrath was
aroused.

6So Elihu, the son of Barachel the Buzite,
answered and said:

"I *am* young in years, and you *are* very old;
Therefore I was afraid,
And dared not declare my opinion to you.
7 I said, 'Age[a] should speak,
And multitude of years should teach wisdom.'
8 But *there is* a spirit in man,
And the breath of the Almighty gives him understanding.
9 Great men[a] are not *always* wise,
Nor do the aged *always* understand justice.

In Focus

32:2 Justified Pronounced *JUSS-tih-fyed.* In the New Testament, you are considered righteous by God because you trust in Jesus Chr st as your Savior from sin.

10 "Therefore I say, 'Listen to me,
I also will declare my opinion.'
11 Indeed I waited for your words,
I listened to your reasonings, while you searched out what to say.
12 I paid close attention to you;
And surely not one of you convinced Job,
Or answered his words—
13 Lest you say,
'We have found wisdom';
God will vanquish him, not man.
14 Now he has not directed *his* words against me;
So I will not answer him with your words.

32:4 [a] Vulgate reads *till Job had spoken.* 32:7 [a] Literally *Days,* that is, years 32:9 [a] Or *Men of many years*

Epic Ideas

32:1—37:24 A MAN OF TRUE WISDOM

After Job's so-called friends finished their foolish speeches, a young man named Elihu spoke up. (Pronounce his name *ih-LIE-hew.*) Elihu told Job's friends they had spoken foolishness. Actually, Job said, "It profits a man nothing that he should delight in God" (Job 34:9), so Job was not always right in everything he said to his friends either.

Elihu was wise because he didn't judge Job harshly. Instead, Elihu helped Job understand God's ways. He said, "Listen to this, O Job; stand still and consider the wondrous works of God" (Job 37:14).

We are thrilled as we read the wisdom of Elihu. Let us pray to be ike this young man who spoke such wonderful things to Job. Wisdom is the gift of God.

15 "They are dismayed and answer no more;
Words escape them.
16 And I have waited, because they did not speak,
Because they stood still *and* answered no more.
17 I also will answer my part,
I too will declare my opinion.
18 For I am full of words;
The spirit within me compels me.
19 Indeed my belly *is* like wine *that* has no vent;
It is ready to burst like new wineskins.
20 I will speak, that I may find relief;
I must open my lips and answer.
21 Let me not, I pray, show partiality to anyone;
Nor let me flatter any man.
22 For I do not know how to flatter,
Else my Maker would soon take me away.

Elihu Contradicts Job

33 "But please, Job, hear my speech,
And listen to all my words.
2 Now, I open my mouth;
My tongue speaks in my mouth.
3 My words *come* from my upright heart;
My lips utter pure knowledge.
4 The Spirit of God has made me,
And the breath of the Almighty gives me life.
5 If you can answer me,
Set *your words* in order before me;
Take your stand.
6 Truly I *am* as your spokesman[a] before God;
I also have been formed out of clay.
7 Surely no fear of me will terrify you,
Nor will my hand be heavy on you.

8 "Surely you have spoken in my hearing,
And I have heard the sound of *your* words, *saying,*
9 'I *am* pure, without transgression;
I *am* innocent, and *there is* no iniquity in me.
10 Yet He finds occasions against me,
He counts me as His enemy;
11 He puts my feet in the stocks,
He watches all my paths.'

12 "Look, *in* this you are not righteous.
I will answer you,
For God is greater than man.
13 Why do you contend with Him?
For He does not give an accounting of any of His words.
14 For God may speak in one way, or in another,
Yet man does not perceive it.
15 In a dream, in a vision of the night,
When deep sleep falls upon men,
While slumbering on their beds,
16 Then He opens the ears of men,
And seals their instruction.
17 In order to turn man *from his* deed,
And conceal pride from man,
18 He keeps back his soul from the Pit,
And his life from perishing by the sword.

19 "*Man* is also chastened with pain on his bed,
And with strong *pain* in many of his bones,
20 So that his life abhors bread,
And his soul succulent food.
21 His flesh wastes away from sight,
And his bones stick out *which once* were not seen.
22 Yes, his soul draws near the Pit,
And his life to the executioners.

23 "If there is a messenger for him,
A mediator, one among a thousand,
To show man His uprightness,
24 Then He is gracious to him, and says,
'Deliver him from going down to the Pit;
I have found a ransom';
25 His flesh shall be young like a child's,
He shall return to the days of his youth.
26 He shall pray to God, and He will delight in him,
He shall see His face with joy,
For He restores to man His righteousness.
27 Then he looks at men and says,
'I have sinned, and perverted *what was* right,
And it did not profit me.'
28 He will redeem his[a] soul from going down to the Pit,
And his[b] life shall see the light.

29 "Behold, God works all these *things,*
Twice, *in fact,* three *times* with a man,
30 To bring back his soul from the Pit,
That he may be enlightened with the light of life.

33:6 [a] Literally *as your mouth* 33:28 [a] Or *my* (Kethib) [b] Or *my* (Kethib)

31 "Give ear, Job, listen to me;
Hold your peace, and I will speak.
32 If you have anything to say, answer me;
Speak, for I desire to justify you.
33 If not, listen to me;
Hold your peace, and I will teach you wisdom."

Elihu Proclaims God's Justice

34 Elihu further answered and said:

2 "Hear my words, you wise *men;*
Give ear to me, you who have knowledge.
3 For the ear tests words
As the palate tastes food.
4 Let us choose justice for ourselves;
Let us know among ourselves what *is* good.

5 "For Job has said, 'I am righteous,
But God has taken away my justice;
6 Should I lie concerning my right?
My wound *is* incurable, *though I am* without transgression.'
7 What man *is* like Job,
Who drinks scorn like water,
8 Who goes in company with the workers of iniquity,
And walks with wicked men?
9 For he has said, 'It profits a man nothing
That he should delight in God.'

10 "Therefore listen to me, you men of understanding:
Far be it from God *to do* wickedness,
And *from* the Almighty to *commit* iniquity.
11 For He repays man *according to* his work,
And makes man to find a reward according to *his* way.
12 Surely God will never do wickedly,
Nor will the Almighty pervert justice.
13 Who gave Him charge over the earth?
Or who appointed *Him over* the whole world?
14 If He should set His heart on it,
If He should gather to Himself His Spirit and His breath,
15 All flesh would perish together,
And man would return to dust.

16 "If *you have* understanding, hear this;
Listen to the sound of my words:
17 Should one who hates justice govern?
Will you condemn *Him who is* most just?
18 *Is it fitting* to say to a king, '*You are* worthless,'
And to nobles, '*You are* wicked'?
19 Yet He is not partial to princes,
Nor does He regard the rich more than the poor;
For they *are* all the work of His hands.
20 In a moment they die, in the middle of the night;
The people are shaken and pass away;
The mighty are taken away without a hand.

21 "For His eyes *are* on the ways of man,
And He sees all his steps.
22 There is no darkness nor shadow of death
Where the workers of iniquity may hide themselves.
23 For He need not further consider a man,
That he should go before God in judgment.
24 He breaks in pieces mighty men without inquiry,
And sets others in their place.
25 Therefore He knows their works;
He overthrows *them* in the night,
And they are crushed.
26 He strikes them as wicked *men*
In the open sight of others,
27 Because they turned back from Him,
And would not consider any of His ways,
28 So that they caused the cry of the poor to come to Him;
For He hears the cry of the afflicted.
29 When He gives quietness, who then can make trouble?
And when He hides *His* face, who then can see Him,
Whether *it is* against a nation or a man alone?—
30 That the hypocrite should not reign,
Lest the people be ensnared.

31 "For has *anyone* said to God,
'I have borne *chastening;*
I will offend no more;
32 Teach me *what* I do not see;
If I have done iniquity, I will do no more'?

33 Should He repay *it* according to your
terms,
Just because you disavow it?
You must choose, and not I;
Therefore speak what you know.

34 "Men of understanding say to me,
Wise men who listen to me:
35 'Job speaks without knowledge,
His words *are* without wisdom.'
36 Oh, that Job were tried to the utmost,
Because *his* answers *are like* those of
wicked men!
37 For he adds rebellion to his sin;
He claps *his hands* among us,
And multiplies his words against God."

Elihu Condemns Self-Righteousness

35 Moreover Elihu answered and said:

2 "Do you think this is right?
Do you say,
'My righteousness is more than God's'?
3 For you say,
'What advantage will it be to You?
What profit shall I have, more than *if* I
had sinned?'

4 "I will answer you,
And your companions with you.
5 Look to the heavens and see;
And behold the clouds—
They are higher than you.
6 If you sin, what do you accomplish
against Him?
Or, *if* your transgressions are
multiplied, what do you do to Him?
7 If you are righteous, what do you give
Him?
Or what does He receive from your
hand?
8 Your wickedness affects a man such as
you,
And your righteousness a son of man.

9 "Because of the multitude of oppressions
they cry out;
They cry out for help because of the arm
of the mighty.
10 But no one says, 'Where *is* God my
Maker,
Who gives songs in the night,
11 Who teaches us more than the beasts of
the earth,
And makes us wiser than the birds of
heaven?'
12 There they cry out, but He does not
answer,
Because of the pride of evil men.
13 Surely God will not listen to empty *talk,*
Nor will the Almighty regard it.
14 Although you say you do not see Him,
Yet justice *is* before Him, and you must
wait for Him.
15 And now, because He has not punished
in His anger,
Nor taken much notice of folly,
16 Therefore Job opens his mouth in vain;
He multiplies words without
knowledge."

Elihu Proclaims God's Goodness

36 Elihu also proceeded and said:

2 "Bear with me a little, and I will show
you
That *there are* yet words to speak on
God's behalf.
3 I will fetch my knowledge from afar;
I will ascribe righteousness to my
Maker.
4 For truly my words *are* not false;
One who is perfect in knowledge *is* with
you.

5 "Behold, God *is* mighty, but despises *no
one;*
He is mighty in strength of
understanding.
6 He does not preserve the life of the
wicked,
But gives justice to the oppressed.
7 He does not withdraw His eyes from the
righteous;
But *they are* on the throne with kings,
For He has seated them forever,
And they are exalted.
8 And if *they are* bound in fetters,
Held in the cords of affliction,
9 Then He tells them their work and their
transgressions—
That they have acted defiantly.
10 He also opens their ear to instruction,
And commands that they turn from
iniquity.
11 If they obey and serve *Him,*
They shall spend their days in
prosperity,
And their years in pleasures.

12 But if they do not obey,
They shall perish by the sword,
And they shall die without knowledge.[a]

13 "But the hypocrites in heart store up wrath;
They do not cry for help when He binds them.
14 They die in youth,
And their life *ends* among the perverted persons.[a]
15 He delivers the poor in their affliction,
And opens their ears in oppression.

16 "Indeed He would have brought you out of dire distress,
Into a broad place where *there is* no restraint;
And what is set on your table *would be* full of richness.
17 But you are filled with the judgment due the wicked;
Judgment and justice take hold *of you.*
18 Because *there is* wrath, *beware* lest He take you away with *one* blow;
For a large ransom would not help you avoid *it.*
19 Will your riches,
Or all the mighty forces,
Keep you from distress?
20 Do not desire the night,
When people are cut off in their place.
21 Take heed, do not turn to iniquity,
For you have chosen this rather than affliction.

22 "Behold, God is exalted by His power;
Who teaches like Him?
23 Who has assigned Him His way,
Or who has said, 'You have done wrong'?

Elihu Proclaims God's Majesty

24 "Remember to magnify His work,
Of which men have sung.
25 Everyone has seen it;
Man looks on *it* from afar.

26 "Behold, God *is* great, and we do not know *Him;*
Nor can the number of His years *be* discovered.
27 For He draws up drops of water,
Which distill as rain from the mist,
28 Which the clouds drop down
And pour abundantly on man.
29 Indeed, can *anyone* understand the spreading of clouds,
The thunder from His canopy?
30 Look, He scatters His light upon it,
And covers the depths of the sea.
31 For by these He judges the peoples;
He gives food in abundance.
32 He covers *His* hands with lightning,
And commands it to strike.
33 His thunder declares it,
The cattle also, concerning the rising *storm.*

37 "At this also my heart trembles,
And leaps from its place.
2 Hear attentively the thunder of His voice,
And the rumbling *that* comes from His mouth.
3 He sends it forth under the whole heaven,
His lightning to the ends of the earth.
4 After it a voice roars;
He thunders with His majestic voice,
And He does not restrain them when His voice is heard.
5 God thunders marvelously with His voice;
He does great things which we cannot comprehend.
6 For He says to the snow, 'Fall on the earth';
Likewise to the gentle rain and the heavy rain of His strength.
7 He seals the hand of every man,
That all men may know His work.
8 The beasts go into dens,
And remain in their lairs.
9 From the chamber *of the south* comes the whirlwind,
And cold from the scattering winds *of the north.*
10 By the breath of God ice is given,
And the broad waters are frozen.
11 Also with moisture He saturates the thick clouds;
He scatters His bright clouds.
12 And they swirl about, being turned by His guidance,
That they may do whatever He commands them
On the face of the whole earth.[a]
13 He causes it to come,
Whether for correction,
Or for His land,
Or for mercy.

36:12 [a] Masoretic Text reads *as one without knowledge.*
36:14 [a] Hebrew *qedeshim,* that is, those practicing sodomy and prostitution in religious rituals 37:12 [a] Literally *the world of the earth*

14 "Listen to this, O Job;
Stand still and consider the wondrous works of God.
15 Do you know when God dispatches them,
And causes the light of His cloud to shine?
16 Do you know how the clouds are balanced,
Those wondrous works of Him who is perfect in knowledge?
17 Why *are* your garments hot,
When He quiets the earth by the south *wind?*
18 With Him, have you spread out the skies,
Strong as a cast metal mirror?

19 "Teach us what we should say to Him,
For we can prepare nothing because of the darkness.
20 Should He be told that I *wish to* speak?
If a man were to speak, surely he would be swallowed up.
21 Even now *men* cannot look at the light *when it is* bright in the skies,
When the wind has passed and cleared them.
22 He comes from the north *as* golden *splendor;*
With God *is* awesome majesty.
23 *As for* the Almighty, we cannot find Him;
He is excellent in power,
In judgment and abundant justice;
He does not oppress.
24 Therefore men fear Him;
He shows no partiality to any *who are* wise of heart."

The LORD Reveals His Omnipotence to Job

38 Then the LORD answered Job out of the whirlwind, and said:

2 "Who *is* this who darkens counsel
By words without knowledge?
3 Now prepare yourself like a man;
I will question you, and you shall answer Me.

4 "Where were you when I laid the foundations of the earth?
Tell *Me, if you have understanding.*
5 Who determined its measurements?
Surely you know!
Or who stretched the line upon it?
6 To what were its foundations fastened?
Or who laid its cornerstone,
7 When the morning stars sang together,
And all the sons of God shouted for joy?

8 "Or *who* shut in the sea with doors,
When it burst forth *and* issued from the womb;
9 When I made the clouds its garment,
And thick darkness its swaddling band;
10 When I fixed My limit for it,
And set bars and doors;
11 When I said,
'This far you may come, but no farther,
And here your proud waves must stop!'

12 "Have you commanded the morning since your days *began,*
And caused the dawn to know its place,
13 That it might take hold of the ends of the earth,
And the wicked be shaken out of it?
14 It takes on form like clay *under* a seal,
And stands out like a garment.
15 From the wicked their light is withheld,
And the upraised arm is broken.

16 "Have you entered the springs of the sea?
Or have you walked in search of the depths?
17 Have the gates of death been revealed to you?
Or have you seen the doors of the shadow of death?
18 Have you comprehended the breadth of the earth?
Tell *Me,* if you know all this.

19 "Where *is* the way *to* the dwelling of light?
And darkness, where *is* its place,
20 That you may take it to its territory,
That you may know the paths *to* its home?
21 Do you know *it,* because you were born then,
Or *because* the number of your days *is* great?

22 "Have you entered the treasury of snow,
Or have you seen the treasury of hail,
23 Which I have reserved for the time of trouble,
For the day of battle and war?
24 By what way is light diffused,
Or the east wind scattered over the earth?

25 "Who has divided a channel for the overflowing *water,*
Or a path for the thunderbolt,

26 To cause it to rain on a land *where there is* no one,
A wilderness in which *there is* no man;
27 To satisfy the desolate waste,
And cause to spring forth the growth of tender grass?
28 Has the rain a father?
Or who has begotten the drops of dew?
29 From whose womb comes the ice?
And the frost of heaven, who gives it birth?
30 The waters harden like stone,
And the surface of the deep is frozen.

31 "Can you bind the cluster of the Pleiades,
Or loose the belt of Orion?
32 Can you bring out Mazzaroth[a] in its season?
Or can you guide the Great Bear with its cubs?
33 Do you know the ordinances of the heavens?
Can you set their dominion over the earth?

34 "Can you lift up your voice to the clouds,
That an abundance of water may cover you?
35 Can you send out lightnings, that they may go,
And say to you, 'Here we *are!*'?
36 Who has put wisdom in the mind?[a]
Or who has given understanding to the heart?
37 Who can number the clouds by wisdom?
Or who can pour out the bottles of heaven,
38 When the dust hardens in clumps,
And the clods cling together?

39 "Can you hunt the prey for the lion,
Or satisfy the appetite of the young lions,
40 When they crouch in *their* dens,
Or lurk in their lairs to lie in wait?
41 Who provides food for the raven,
When its young ones cry to God,
And wander about for lack of food?

39 "Do you know the time when the wild mountain goats bear young?
Or can you mark when the deer gives birth?

38:32 [a] Literally *Constellations* 38:36 [a] Literally *inward parts*

Epic Ideas

38:1—41:34 CAN YOU ANSWER GOD'S QUESTIONS?

When Job and his friends and the young man Elihu had finished talking, God Himself spoke up and answered everybody. He asked Job a long list of questions, like, "Where were you when I laid the foundations of the earth?" This is God's way of telling Job he isn't as smart as he thinks he is!

As you get older, you will begin to notice that the experts in science are always changing their minds. Human theories constantly contradict one another. The medicine for an illness this year may be thought bad for your health five years from now.

We're learning more and more that we know less and less about the world. What this adds up to is that people should trust God more than they trust people, even "experts." We need to keep studying the world around us, but we need even more to understand God's ways in His world.

2 Can you number the months *that* they fulfill?
Or do you know the time when they bear young?
3 They bow down,
They bring forth their young,
They deliver their offspring.[a]
4 Their young ones are healthy,
They grow strong with grain;
They depart and do not return to them.

5 "Who set the wild donkey free?
Who loosed the bonds of the onager,
6 Whose home I have made the wilderness,
And the barren land his dwelling?
7 He scorns the tumult of the city;
He does not heed the shouts of the driver.
8 The range of the mountains *is* his pasture,
And he searches after every green thing.

9 "Will the wild ox be willing to serve you?
Will he bed by your manger?
10 Can you bind the wild ox in the furrow with ropes?
Or will he plow the valleys behind you?
11 Will you trust him because his strength *is* great?
Or will you leave your labor to him?
12 Will you trust him to bring home your grain,
And gather it to your threshing floor?

13 "The wings of the ostrich wave proudly,
But are her wings and pinions *like the* kindly stork's?
14 For she leaves her eggs on the ground,
And warms them in the dust;
15 She forgets that a foot may crush them,
Or that a wild beast may break them.
16 She treats her young harshly, as though *they were* not hers;
Her labor is in vain, without concern,
17 Because God deprived her of wisdom,
And did not endow her with understanding.
18 When she lifts herself on high,
She scorns the horse and its rider.

19 "Have you given the horse strength?
Have you clothed his neck with thunder?[a]
20 Can you frighten him like a locust?
His majestic snorting strikes terror.
21 He paws in the valley, and rejoices in *his* strength;
He gallops into the clash of arms.
22 He mocks at fear, and is not frightened;
Nor does he turn back from the sword.
23 The quiver rattles against him,
The glittering spear and javelin.
24 He devours the distance with fierceness and rage;
Nor does he come to a halt because the trumpet *has* sounded.
25 At *the blast of* the trumpet he says, 'Aha!'
He smells the battle from afar,
The thunder of captains and shouting.

26 "Does the hawk fly by your wisdom,
And spread its wings toward the south?
27 Does the eagle mount up at your command,
And make its nest on high?
28 On the rock it dwells and resides,
On the crag of the rock and the stronghold.
29 From there it spies out the prey;
Its eyes observe from afar.
30 Its young ones suck up blood;
And where the slain *are*, there it *is*."

40

Moreover the LORD answered Job, and said:

2 "Shall the one who contends with the Almighty correct *Him?*
He who rebukes God, let him answer it."

Job's Response to God

3 Then Job answered the LORD and said:

4 "Behold, I am vile;
What shall I answer You?
I lay my hand over my mouth.
5 Once I have spoken, but I will not answer;
Yes, twice, but I will proceed no further."

God's Challenge to Job

6 Then the LORD answered Job out of the whirlwind, and said:

7 "Now prepare yourself like a man;
I will question you, and you shall answer Me:

39:3 [a] Literally *pangs,* figurative of offspring **39:19** [a] Or *a mane*

8 "Would you indeed annul My judgment?
Would you condemn Me that you may
be justified?
9 Have you an arm like God?
Or can you thunder with a voice like
His?
10 Then adorn yourself *with* majesty and
splendor,
And array yourself with glory and
beauty.
11 Disperse the rage of your wrath;
Look on everyone *who is* proud, and
humble him.
12 Look on everyone *who is* proud, *and*
bring him low;
Tread down the wicked in their place.
13 Hide them in the dust together,
Bind their faces in hidden *darkness*.
14 Then I will also confess to you
That your own right hand can save you.

15 "Look now at the behemoth,[a] which I
made *along* with you;
He eats grass like an ox.
16 See now, his strength *is* in his hips,
And his power *is* in his stomach
muscles.
17 He moves his tail like a cedar;
The sinews of his thighs are tightly knit.
18 His bones *are like* beams of bronze,
His ribs like bars of iron.
19 He *is* the first of the ways of God;
Only He who made him can bring near
His sword.
20 Surely the mountains yield food for
him,
And all the beasts of the field play there.
21 He lies under the lotus trees,
In a covert of reeds and marsh.
22 The lotus trees cover him *with* their
shade;
The willows by the brook surround him.
23 Indeed the river may rage,
Yet he is not disturbed;
He is confident, though the Jordan
gushes into his mouth,
24 *Though* he takes it in his eyes,
Or one pierces *his* nose with a snare.

41 "Can you draw out Leviathan[a] with
a hook,
Or *snare* his tongue with a line *which*
you lower?
2 Can you put a reed through his nose,
Or pierce his jaw with a hook?
3 Will he make many supplications to you?
Will he speak softly to you?
4 Will he make a covenant with you?
Will you take him as a servant forever?
5 Will you play with him as *with* a bird,
Or will you leash him for your maidens?
6 Will *your* companions make a banquet[a]
of him?
Will they apportion him among the
merchants?
7 Can you fill his skin with harpoons,
Or his head with fishing spears?
8 Lay your hand on him;
Remember the battle—
Never do it again!
9 Indeed, *any* hope of *overcoming* him is
false;
Shall *one not* be overwhelmed at the
sight of him?
10 No one *is so* fierce that he would dare
stir him up.
Who then is able to stand against Me?
11 Who has preceded Me, that I should pay
him?
Everything under heaven is Mine.

12 "I will not conceal[a] his limbs,
His mighty power, or his graceful
proportions.
13 Who can remove his outer coat?
Who can approach *him* with a double
bridle?
14 Who can open the doors of his face,
With his terrible teeth all around?
15 *His* rows of scales are *his* pride,
Shut up tightly *as with* a seal;
16 One is so near another
That no air can come between them;
17 They are joined one to another,
They stick together and cannot be
parted.
18 His sneezings flash forth light,
And his eyes *are* like the eyelids of the
morning.
19 Out of his mouth go burning lights;
Sparks of fire shoot out.
20 Smoke goes out of his nostrils,
As *from* a boiling pot and burning
rushes.
21 His breath kindles coals,
And a flame goes out of his mouth.
22 Strength dwells in his neck,

40:15 [a] A large animal, exact identity unknown 41:1 [a] A large sea creature, exact identity unknown 41:6 [a] Or *bargain over him* 41:12 [a] Literally *keep silent about*

And sorrow dances before him.
23 The folds of his flesh are joined together;
They are firm on him and cannot be moved.
24 His heart is as hard as stone,
Even as hard as the lower *millstone.*
25 When he raises himself up, the mighty are afraid;
Because of his crashings they are beside[a] themselves.
26 *Though* the sword reaches him, it cannot avail;
Nor does spear, dart, or javelin.
27 He regards iron as straw,
And bronze as rotten wood.
28 The arrow cannot make him flee;
Slingstones become like stubble to him.
29 Darts are regarded as straw;
He laughs at the threat of javelins.
30 His undersides *are* like sharp potsherds;
He spreads pointed *marks* in the mire.
31 He makes the deep boil like a pot;
He makes the sea like a pot of ointment.
32 He leaves a shining wake behind him;
One would think the deep had white hair.
33 On earth there is nothing like him,
Which is made without fear.
34 He beholds every high *thing;*
He *is* king over all the children of pride."

Job's Repentance and Restoration

42 Then Job answered the LORD and said:
2 "I know that You can do everything,
And that no purpose *of Yours* can be withheld from You.
3 *You asked,* 'Who *is* this who hides counsel without knowledge?'
Therefore I have uttered what I did not understand,
Things too wonderful for me, which I did not know.
4 Listen, please, and let me speak;
You said, 'I will question you, and you shall answer Me.'

5 "I have heard of You by the hearing of the ear,
But now my eye sees You.
6 Therefore I abhor *myself,*
And repent in dust and ashes."

7And so it was, after the LORD had spoken these words to Job, that the LORD said to
Eliphaz the Temanite, "My wrath is aroused
against you and your two friends, for you
have not spoken of Me *what is* right, as My
servant Job *has.* 8Now therefore, take for
yourselves seven bulls and seven rams, go to
My servant Job, and offer up for yourselves
a burnt offering; and My servant Job shall
pray for you. For I will accept him, lest I deal
with you *according to your* folly; because you
have not spoken of Me *what is* right, as My
servant Job *has.*"
9So Eliphaz the Temanite and Bildad the
Shuhite *and* Zophar the Naamathite went

41:25 [a] Or *purify themselves*

LEARNING

READ IT: JOB 42:1–17

Early in this passage, Job admits to God that he was wrong. Admitting your mistakes is a massive part of learning and growing in wisdom. What's something you do differently now because you learned from a mistake in the past? What's a mistake you've made in the last week, and what can you learn from it? Pray that God will give you the insight, or understanding, to see what you can learn from your mistakes.

and did as the LORD commanded them; for
the LORD had accepted Job. 10And the LORD
restored Job's losses[a] when he prayed for his
friends. Indeed the LORD gave Job twice as
much as he had before. 11Then all his brothers, all his sisters, and all those who had
been his acquaintances before, came to him
and ate food with him in his house; and they
consoled him and comforted him for all the
adversity that the LORD had brought upon
him. Each one gave him a piece of silver and
each a ring of gold.

12Now the LORD blessed the latter *days*
of Job more than his beginning; for he had
fourteen thousand sheep, six thousand
camels, one thousand yoke of oxen, and one
thousand female donkeys. 13He also had sev-
en sons and three daughters. 14And he called
the name of the first Jemimah, the name of
the second Keziah, and the name of the third
Keren-Happuch. 15In all the land were found
no women *so* beautiful as the daughters of
Job; and their father gave them an inheritance among their brothers.

16After this Job lived one hundred and
forty years, and saw his children and grandchildren *for* four generations. 17So Job died,
old and full of days.

42:10 [a] Literally *Job's captivity,* that is, what was captured from Job

The BOOK of PSALMS

1410 B.C.–430 B.C.

Behind the Scenes

READ IT:

The book of Psalms is a collection of poems and songs used by God's people for many, many years. These songs were used for praise and worship, to show thanks, and to ask God for forgiveness. They also show a variety of feelings, attitudes, and interests.

GET IT:

Who wrote it: a variety of authors: David, Ethan, Heman, Asaph, the Sons of Korah, Solomon, Moses, and others

When it was written: about 1410 B.C.–430 B.C.

Why it was written: to save the songs that the people used in worshiping God and to show the wide variety of feelings people had during this time

LIVE IT:

We can share any emotion with God and He'll listen to us.

FIND IT:

The Glory of the Lord in Creation	*Psalm 8*
The Perfect Revelation of the Lord	*Psalm 19*
The Lord: The Shepherd of His People	*Psalm 23*
The Joy of Forgiveness	*Psalm 32*
Joy in the Fellowship of God	*Psalm 63*
A Song of Praise	*Psalm 100*
Let All Things Praise the Lord	*Psalm 150*

BOOK ONE

Psalms 1–41

PSALM 1

The Way of the Righteous and the End of the Ungodly

1 Blessed *is* the man
Who walks not in the counsel of the ungodly,
Nor stands in the path of sinners,
Nor sits in the seat of the scornful;
2 But his delight *is* in the law of the LORD,
And in His law he meditates day and night.
3 He shall be like a tree
Planted by the rivers of water,
That brings forth its fruit in its season,
Whose leaf also shall not wither;
And whatever he does shall prosper.

4 The ungodly *are* not so,
But *are* like the chaff which the wind drives away.
5 Therefore the ungodly shall not stand in the judgment,
Nor sinners in the congregation of the righteous.

6 For the LORD knows the way of the righteous,
But the way of the ungodly shall perish.

PSALM 2

The Messiah's Triumph and Kingdom

1 Why do the nations rage,
And the people plot a vain thing?
2 The kings of the earth set themselves,
And the rulers take counsel together,
Against the LORD and against His Anointed, *saying,*
3 "Let us break Their bonds in pieces
And cast away Their cords from us."

4 He who sits in the heavens shall laugh;
The Lord shall hold them in derision.
5 Then He shall speak to them in His wrath,
And distress them in His deep displeasure:
6 "Yet I have set My King
On My holy hill of Zion."

7 "I will declare the decree:
The LORD has said to Me,
'You *are* My Son,
Today I have begotten You.
8 Ask of Me, and I will give *You*
The nations *for* Your inheritance,
And the ends of the earth *for* Your possession.
9 You shall break[a] them with a rod of iron;
You shall dash them to pieces like a potter's vessel.'"

10 Now therefore, be wise, O kings;
Be instructed, you judges of the earth.
11 Serve the LORD with fear,
And rejoice with trembling.
12 Kiss the Son,[a] lest He[b] be angry,
And you perish *in* the way,
When His wrath is kindled but a little.
Blessed *are* all those who put their trust in Him.

2:9 [a] Following Masoretic Text and Targum; Septuagint, Syriac, and Vulgate read *rule* (compare Revelation 2:27).
2:12 [a] Septuagint and Vulgate read *Embrace discipline;* Targum reads *Receive instruction.* [b] Septuagint reads *the LORD.*

PSALM 3

The LORD Helps His Troubled People

A Psalm of David when he fled
from Absalom his son.

1 LORD, how they have increased who
trouble me!
Many *are* they who rise up against me.
2 Many *are* they who say of me,
"*There is* no help for him in God." *Selah*

3 But You, O LORD, *are* a shield for me,
My glory and the One who lifts up my
head.
4 I cried to the LORD with my voice,
And He heard me from His holy hill.
Selah

5 I lay down and slept;
I awoke, for the LORD sustained me.
6 I will not be afraid of ten thousands of
people
Who have set *themselves* against me all
around.

7 Arise, O LORD;
Save me, O my God!
For You have struck all my enemies on
the cheekbone;
You have broken the teeth of the
ungodly.

8 Salvation *belongs* to the LORD.
Your blessing *is* upon Your people. *Selah*

PSALM 4

The Safety of the Faithful

To the Chief Musician. With stringed
instruments. A Psalm of David.

1 Hear me when I call, O God of my
righteousness!
You have relieved me in *my* distress;
Have mercy on me, and hear my prayer.

2 How long, O you sons of men,
Will you turn my glory to shame?
How long will you love worthlessness
And seek falsehood? *Selah*
3 But know that the LORD has set apart[a]
for Himself him who is godly;
The LORD will hear when I call to Him.

4 Be angry, and do not sin.
Meditate within your heart on your bed,
and be still. *Selah*
5 Offer the sacrifices of righteousness,
And put your trust in the LORD.

6 *There are* many who say,

4:3 [a] Many Hebrew manuscripts, Septuagint, Targum, and Vulgate read *made wonderful*.

Epic Ideas

2:12 PUT YOUR TRUST IN THE SON OF GOD

In this wonderful psalm David tells about the coming Son of God. When David writes, "The LORD has said to Me, 'You are My Son'" (Psalm 2:7), he is referring to Jesus, who will be born a thousand years later.

Then David tells how God the Father promises to give the nations of the world to His great Son. Finally, David says we should put our trust in the Son of God.

To trust Jesus means to depend on Him for everything. You stop counting on others or yourself to save you from all the bad effects of sin. To trust in Jesus means to start a whole new life with Him as your Friend and Savior. Whoever believes in Him will not perish but have everlasting life (John 3:16). "Everlasting life" is the life that Jesus gives you right now as you trust Him with your whole being. That life will be spent with Him now and forever.

7 So the congregation of the peoples shall surround You;
For their sakes, therefore, return on high.
8 The LORD shall judge the peoples;
Judge me, O LORD, according to my righteousness,
And according to my integrity within me.

9 Oh, let the wickedness of the wicked come to an end,
But establish the just;
For the righteous God tests the hearts and minds.
10 My defense *is* of God,
Who saves the upright in heart.

11 God *is* a just judge,
And God is angry *with the wicked* every day.
12 If he does not turn back,
He will sharpen His sword;
He bends His bow and makes it ready.
13 He also prepares for Himself instruments of death;
He makes His arrows into fiery shafts.

14 Behold, *the wicked* brings forth iniquity;
Yes, he conceives trouble and brings forth falsehood.
15 He made a pit and dug it out,
And has fallen into the ditch *which* he made.
16 His trouble shall return upon his own head,
And his violent dealing shall come down on his own crown.

17 I will praise the LORD according to His righteousness,
And will sing praise to the name of the LORD Most High.

PSALM 8

The Glory of the LORD in Creation

To the Chief Musician. On the instrument of Gath.[a] A Psalm of David.

1 O LORD, our Lord,
How excellent *is* Your name in all the earth,
Who have set Your glory above the heavens!

2 Out of the mouth of babes and nursing infants
You have ordained strength,
Because of Your enemies,
That You may silence the enemy and the avenger.

3 When I consider Your heavens, the work of Your fingers,
The moon and the stars, which You have ordained,
4 What is man that You are mindful of him,
And the son of man that You visit him?
5 For You have made him a little lower than the angels,[a]
And You have crowned him with glory and honor.

6 You have made him to have dominion over the works of Your hands;
You have put all *things* under his feet,
7 All sheep and oxen—
Even the beasts of the field,
8 The birds of the air,
And the fish of the sea
That pass through the paths of the seas.

9 O LORD, our Lord,
How excellent *is* Your name in all the earth!

PSALM 9

Prayer and Thanksgiving for the LORD's Righteous Judgments

To the Chief Musician. To *the tune of* "Death of the Son."[a] A Psalm of David.

1 I will praise *You,* O LORD, with my whole heart;
I will tell of all Your marvelous works.
2 I will be glad and rejoice in You;
I will sing praise to Your name, O Most High.

3 When my enemies turn back,
They shall fall and perish at Your presence.
4 For You have maintained my right and my cause;
You sat on the throne judging in righteousness.
5 You have rebuked the nations,
You have destroyed the wicked;

8:title [a] Hebrew *Al Gittith* **8:5** [a] Hebrew *Elohim, God;* Septuagint, Syriac, Targum, and Jewish tradition translate as *angels.* **9:title** [a] Hebrew *Muth Labben*

You have blotted out their name forever
and ever.

6 O enemy, destructions are finished
forever!
And you have destroyed cities;
Even their memory has perished.
7 But the LORD shall endure forever;
He has prepared His throne for
judgment.
8 He shall judge the world in
righteousness,
And He shall administer judgment for
the peoples in uprightness.

9 The LORD also will be a refuge for the
oppressed,
A refuge in times of trouble.
10 And those who know Your name will
put their trust in You;
For You, LORD, have not forsaken those
who seek You.

11 Sing praises to the LORD, who dwells in
Zion!
Declare His deeds among the people.
12 When He avenges blood, He
remembers them;
He does not forget the cry of the
humble.

13 Have mercy on me, O LORD!
Consider my trouble from those who
hate me,
You who lift me up from the gates of
death,
14 That I may tell of all Your praise
In the gates of the daughter of Zion.
I will rejoice in Your salvation.

15 The nations have sunk down in the pit
which they made;
In the net which they hid, their own foot
is caught.
16 The LORD is known *by* the judgment He
executes;
The wicked is snared in the work of his
own hands.
Meditation.[a] *Selah*

17 The wicked shall be turned into hell,
And all the nations that forget God.
18 For the needy shall not always be
forgotten;
The expectation of the poor shall *not*
perish forever.

19 Arise, O LORD,
Do not let man prevail;
Let the nations be judged in Your sight.
20 Put them in fear, O LORD,
That the nations may know themselves
to be but men. *Selah*

PSALM 10

A Song of Confidence in God's Triumph over Evil

1 Why do You stand afar off, O LORD?
Why do You hide in times of trouble?
2 The wicked in *his* pride persecutes the
poor;

9:16 [a] Hebrew *Higgaion*

Action! WORSHIP

READ IT: PSALM 9:1, 2

Sometimes our worship is puny and ho-hum, but sometimes it's big and awesome. That has nothing to do with the size of the worship experience or the volume or feeling. Big and awesome worship is a choice—it's worshiping God with our whole hearts, not just a little bit.

When you acknowledge God's greatness with your whole life, not holding back parts for your own control, you worship with your whole heart. And that's the best kind of worship, whether you're alone or with other people.

5 "For the oppression of the poor, for the sighing of the needy,
Now I will arise," says the LORD;
"I will set *him* in the safety for which he yearns."

6 The words of the LORD *are* pure words,
Like silver tried in a furnace of earth,
Purified seven times.
7 You shall keep them, O LORD,
You shall preserve them from this generation forever.

8 The wicked prowl on every side,
When vileness is exalted among the sons of men.

PSALM 13

Trust in the Salvation of the LORD

To the Chief Musician. A Psalm of David.

1 How long, O LORD? Will You forget me forever?
How long will You hide Your face from me?
2 How long shall I take counsel in my soul,
Having sorrow in my heart daily?
How long will my enemy be exalted over me?

3 Consider *and* hear me, O LORD my God;
Enlighten my eyes,
Lest I sleep the *sleep of* death;
4 Lest my enemy say,
"I have prevailed against him";
Lest those who trouble me rejoice when I am moved.

5 But I have trusted in Your mercy;
My heart shall rejoice in Your salvation.
6 I will sing to the LORD,
Because He has dealt bountifully with me.

PSALM 14

Folly of the Godless, and God's Final Triumph

To the Chief Musician. *A Psalm* of David.

1 The fool has said in his heart,
"*There is* no God."
They are corrupt,
They have done abominable works,
There is none who does good.

2 The LORD looks down from heaven upon the children of men,
To see if there are any who understand, who seek God.
3 They have all turned aside,
They have together become corrupt;
There is none who does good,
No, not one.

4 Have all the workers of iniquity no knowledge,
Who eat up my people *as* they eat bread,
And do not call on the LORD?
5 There they are in great fear,
For God *is* with the generation of the righteous.
6 You shame the counsel of the poor,
But the LORD *is* his refuge.

7 Oh, that the salvation of Israel *would come* out of Zion!
When the LORD brings back the captivity of His people,
Let Jacob rejoice *and* Israel be glad.

PSALM 15

The Character of Those Who May Dwell with the LORD

A Psalm of David.

1 LORD, who may abide in Your tabernacle?
Who may dwell in Your holy hill?

2 He who walks uprightly,
And works righteousness,
And speaks the truth in his heart;
3 He *who* does not backbite with his tongue,
Nor does evil to his neighbor,
Nor does he take up a reproach against his friend;
4 In whose eyes a vile person is despised,
But he honors those who fear the LORD;
He *who* swears to his own hurt and does not change;
5 He *who* does not put out his money at usury,
Nor does he take a bribe against the innocent.

He who does these *things* shall never be moved.

PSALM 16

The Hope of the Faithful, and the Messiah's Victory

A Michtam of David.

1 Preserve me, O God, for in You I put my
trust.

2 *O my soul,* you have said to the LORD,
"You *are* my Lord,
My goodness is nothing apart from
You."
3 As for the saints who *are* on the earth,
"They are the excellent ones, in whom is
all my delight."

4 Their sorrows shall be multiplied who
hasten *after* another *god;*
Their drink offerings of blood I will not
offer,
Nor take up their names on my lips.

5 O LORD, *You are* the portion of my
inheritance and my cup;
You maintain my lot.
6 The lines have fallen to me in pleasant
places;
Yes, I have a good inheritance.

7 I will bless the LORD who has given me
counsel;
My heart also instructs me in the night
seasons.

8 I have set the LORD always before me;
Because *He is* at my right hand I shall
not be moved.

9 Therefore my heart is glad, and my
glory rejoices;
My flesh also will rest in hope.
10 For You will not leave my soul in Sheol,
Nor will You allow Your Holy One to see
corruption.
11 You will show me the path of life;
In Your presence *is* fullness of joy;
At Your right hand *are* pleasures
forevermore.

PSALM 17

Prayer with Confidence in Final Salvation

A Prayer of David.

1 Hear a just cause, O LORD,
Attend to my cry;
Give ear to my prayer *which is* not from
deceitful lips.
2 Let my vindication come from Your
presence;
Let Your eyes look on the things that are
upright.

3 You have tested my heart;
You have visited *me* in the night;

17:15 WHEN WE WAKE UP IN HEAVEN

What is it like for a Christian to die? It's like going to sleep in the arms of Jesus. He has said to us, "I will never leave you," and He certainly will not leave us in the hour of death. Death is not the enemy of the Christian. We know that we will wake up and Jesus will be there. That will be heaven for us. Isn't it wonderful that David knew this, too? He said, "I will see Your face."

Some people are afraid to die because they don't know Jesus as their Savior. To be honest, we're all at least a little bit afraid of what we don't understand. God knows we don't understand all about dying. He just asks us to trust Him. If we have learned that Jesus never fails us in the other things of life, then we know we can also trust Him when we die.

You have tried me and have found
nothing;
I have purposed that my mouth shall
not transgress.
4 Concerning the works of men,
By the word of Your lips,
I have kept away from the paths of the
destroyer.
5 Uphold my steps in Your paths,
That my footsteps may not slip.

6 I have called upon You, for You will hear
me, O God;
Incline Your ear to me, *and* hear my
speech.
7 Show Your marvelous lovingkindness
by Your right hand,
O You who save those who trust *in You*
From those who rise up *against them.*
8 Keep me as the apple of Your eye;
Hide me under the shadow of Your
wings,
9 From the wicked who oppress me,
From my deadly enemies who
surround me.

10 They have closed up their fat *hearts;*
With their mouths they speak proudly.
11 They have now surrounded us in our
steps;
They have set their eyes, crouching
down to the earth,
12 As a lion is eager to tear his prey,
And like a young lion lurking in secret
places.

13 Arise, O LORD,
Confront him, cast him down;
Deliver my life from the wicked with
Your sword,
14 With Your hand from men, O LORD,
From men of the world *who have* their
portion in *this* life,
And whose belly You fill with Your
hidden treasure.
They are satisfied with children,
And leave the rest of their *possession* for
their babes.

15 As for me, I will see Your face in
righteousness;
I shall be satisfied when I awake in Your
likeness.

PSALM 18

God the Sovereign Savior

To the Chief Musician. *A Psalm* of David the servant of the LORD, who spoke to the LORD the words of this song on the day that the LORD delivered him from the hand of all his enemies and from the hand of Saul. And he said:

1 I will love You, O LORD, my strength.
2 The LORD is my rock and my fortress
and my deliverer;
My God, my strength, in whom I will
trust;
My shield and the horn of my salvation,
my stronghold.
3 I will call upon the LORD, *who is worthy*
to be praised;
So shall I be saved from my enemies.

4 The pangs of death surrounded me,
And the floods of ungodliness made me
afraid.
5 The sorrows of Sheol surrounded me;
The snares of death confronted me.
6 In my distress I called upon the LORD,
And cried out to my God;
He heard my voice from His temple,
And my cry came before Him, *even* to
His ears.

7 Then the earth shook and trembled;
The foundations of the hills also quaked
and were shaken,
Because He was angry.
8 Smoke went up from His nostrils,
And devouring fire from His mouth;
Coals were kindled by it.
9 He bowed the heavens also, and came
down
With darkness under His feet.
10 And He rode upon a cherub, and flew;
He flew upon the wings of the wind.
11 He made darkness His secret place;
His canopy around Him *was* dark
waters
And thick clouds of the skies.
12 From the brightness before Him,
His thick clouds passed with hailstones
and coals of fire.

13 The LORD thundered from heaven,
And the Most High uttered His voice,
Hailstones and coals of fire.[a]

18:13 [a] Following Masoretic Text, Targum, and Vulgate; a few Hebrew manuscripts and Septuagint omit *Hailstones and coals of fire.*

14 He sent out His arrows and scattered
the foe,
Lightnings in abundance, and He
vanquished them.
15 Then the channels of the sea were seen,
The foundations of the world were
uncovered
At Your rebuke, O LORD,
At the blast of the breath of Your
nostrils.

16 He sent from above, He took me;
He drew me out of many waters.
17 He delivered me from my strong enemy,
From those who hated me,
For they were too strong for me.
18 They confronted me in the day of my
calamity,
But the LORD was my support.
19 He also brought me out into a broad
place;
He delivered me because He delighted
in me.

20 The LORD rewarded me according to my
righteousness;
According to the cleanness of my hands
He has recompensed me.
21 For I have kept the ways of the LORD,
And have not wickedly departed from
my God.
22 For all His judgments *were* before me,
And I did not put away His statutes
from me.
23 I was also blameless before Him,
And I kept myself from my iniquity.
24 Therefore the LORD has recompensed
me according to my righteousness,
According to the cleanness of my hands
in His sight.

25 With the merciful You will show
Yourself merciful;
With a blameless man You will show
Yourself blameless;
26 With the pure You will show Yourself
pure;
And with the devious You will show
Yourself shrewd.
27 For You will save the humble people,
But will bring down haughty looks.

28 For You will light my lamp;
The LORD my God will enlighten my
darkness.
29 For by You I can run against a troop,
By my God I can leap over a wall.
30 *As for* God, His way *is* perfect;
The word of the LORD is proven;
He *is* a shield to all who trust in Him.

31 For who *is* God, except the LORD?
And who *is* a rock, except our God?
32 *It is* God who arms me with strength,
And makes my way perfect.
33 He makes my feet like the *feet of* deer,
And sets me on my high places.
34 He teaches my hands to make war,
So that my arms can bend a bow of
bronze.

35 You have also given me the shield of
Your salvation;
Your right hand has held me up,
Your gentleness has made me great.
36 You enlarged my path under me,
So my feet did not slip.

37 I have pursued my enemies and
overtaken them;
Neither did I turn back again till they
were destroyed.
38 I have wounded them,
So that they could not rise;
They have fallen under my feet.
39 For You have armed me with strength
for the battle;
You have subdued under me those who
rose up against me.
40 You have also given me the necks of my
enemies,
So that I destroyed those who hated me.
41 They cried out, but *there was* none to
save;
Even to the LORD, but He did not answer
them.
42 Then I beat them as fine as the dust
before the wind;
I cast them out like dirt in the streets.

43 You have delivered me from the
strivings of the people;
You have made me the head of the
nations;
A people I have not known shall
serve me.
44 As soon as they hear of me they obey
me;
The foreigners submit to me.
45 The foreigners fade away,
And come frightened from their
hideouts.

46 The LORD lives!
Blessed *be* my Rock!
Let the God of my salvation be exalted.
47 *It is* God who avenges me,

And subdues the peoples under me;
48 He delivers me from my enemies.
You also lift me up above those who rise against me;
You have delivered me from the violent man.
49 Therefore I will give thanks to You, O LORD, among the Gentiles,
And sing praises to Your name.

50 Great deliverance He gives to His king,
And shows mercy to His anointed,
To David and his descendants forevermore.

PSALM 19

The Perfect Revelation of the LORD

To the Chief Musician. A Psalm of David.

1 The heavens declare the glory of God;
And the firmament shows His handiwork.
2 Day unto day utters speech,
And night unto night reveals knowledge.
3 *There is* no speech nor language
Where their voice is not heard.
4 Their line[a] has gone out through all the earth,
And their words to the end of the world.

In them He has set a tabernacle for the sun,
5 Which *is* like a bridegroom coming out of his chamber,
And rejoices like a strong man to run its race.
6 Its rising *is* from one end of heaven,
And its circuit to the other end;
And there is nothing hidden from its heat.

7 The law of the LORD *is* perfect, converting the soul;
The testimony of the LORD *is* sure, making wise the simple;
8 The statutes of the LORD *are* right, rejoicing the heart;
The commandment of the LORD *is* pure, enlightening the eyes;
9 The fear of the LORD *is* clean, enduring forever;
The judgments of the LORD *are* true *and* righteous altogether.
10 More to be desired *are they* than gold,
Yea, than much fine gold;
Sweeter also than honey and the honeycomb.
11 Moreover by them Your servant is warned,
And in keeping them *there is* great reward.

12 Who can understand *his* errors?
Cleanse me from secret *faults*.

19:4 [a] Septuagint, Syriac, and Vulgate read *sound;* Targum reads *business.*

COMMUNICATION

READ IT: PSALM 19:14

"Think before you speak!" How many times have you heard that? In this psalm, the author expresses his hope that not only the words he speaks but even the meditation of his heart will be pleasing to God.

There's always a voice in our head, and sometimes it isn't very nice. Even though nobody may ever hear our thoughts, God knows them. Make it a point to spend some time paying attention to what your internal voice says. Set aside some time to listen to it. What kinds of thoughts come to mind? Write them down. Ask God to help the words you say (and the ones you don't) to be pleasing to Him.

13 Keep back Your servant also from
presumptuous *sins;*
Let them not have dominion over me.
Then I shall be blameless,
And I shall be innocent of great
transgression.

14 Let the words of my mouth and the
meditation of my heart
Be acceptable in Your sight,
O LORD, my strength and my Redeemer.

PSALM 20

The Assurance of God's Saving Work

To the Chief Musician. A Psalm of David.

1 May the LORD answer you in the day of
trouble;
May the name of the God of Jacob
defend you;
2 May He send you help from the
sanctuary,
And strengthen you out of Zion;
3 May He remember all your offerings,
And accept your burnt sacrifice. *Selah*

4 May He grant you according to your
heart's *desire,*
And fulfill all your purpose.
5 We will rejoice in your salvation,
And in the name of our God we will set
up *our* banners!
May the LORD fulfill all your petitions.

6 Now I know that the LORD saves His
anointed;
He will answer him from His holy
heaven
With the saving strength of His right
hand.

7 Some *trust* in chariots, and some in
horses;
But we will remember the name of the
LORD our God.
8 They have bowed down and fallen;
But we have risen and stand upright.

9 Save, LORD!
May the King answer us when we call.

PSALM 21

Joy in the Salvation of the LORD

To the Chief Musician. A Psalm of David.

1 The king shall have joy in Your
strength, O LORD;
And in Your salvation how greatly shall
he rejoice!
2 You have given him his heart's desire,
And have not withheld the request of
his lips. *Selah*

3 For You meet him with the blessings of
goodness;
You set a crown of pure gold upon his
head.
4 He asked life from You, *and* You gave *it*
to him—
Length of days forever and ever.
5 His glory *is* great in Your salvation;
Honor and majesty You have placed
upon him.
6 For You have made him most blessed
forever;
You have made him exceedingly glad
with Your presence.
7 For the king trusts in the LORD,
And through the mercy of the Most
High he shall not be moved.

8 Your hand will find all Your enemies;
Your right hand will find those who
hate You.
9 You shall make them as a fiery oven in
the time of Your anger;
The LORD shall swallow them up in His
wrath,
And the fire shall devour them.
10 Their offspring You shall destroy from
the earth,
And their descendants from among the
sons of men.
11 For they intended evil against You;
They devised a plot *which* they are not
able *to perform.*
12 Therefore You will make them turn
their back;
You will make ready *Your arrows* on
Your string toward their faces.

13 Be exalted, O LORD, in Your own
strength!
We will sing and praise Your power.

PSALM 22

The Suffering, Praise, and Posterity of the Messiah

To the Chief Musician. Set to "The Deer of
the Dawn."[a] A Psalm of David.

1 My God, My God, why have You
forsaken Me?

22:title [a] Hebrew *Aijeleth Hashahar*

Why are You so far from helping Me,
And from the words of My groaning?
2 O My God, I cry in the daytime, but You
do not hear;
And in the night season, and am not
silent.

3 But You *are* holy,
Enthroned in the praises of Israel.
4 Our fathers trusted in You;
They trusted, and You delivered them.
5 They cried to You, and were delivered;
They trusted in You, and were not
ashamed.

6 But I *am* a worm, and no man;
A reproach of men, and despised by the
people.
7 All those who see Me ridicule Me;
They shoot out the lip, they shake the
head, *saying,*
8 "He trusted[a] in the LORD, let Him rescue
Him;
Let Him deliver Him, since He delights
in Him!"

9 But You *are* He who took Me out of the
womb;
You made Me trust *while* on My
mother's breasts.
10 I was cast upon You from birth.
From My mother's womb
You *have been* My God.
11 Be not far from Me,
For trouble *is* near;
For *there is* none to help.

12 Many bulls have surrounded Me;
Strong *bulls* of Bashan have
encircled Me.
13 They gape at Me *with* their mouths,
Like a raging and roaring lion.

14 I am poured out like water,
And all My bones are out of joint;
My heart is like wax;
It has melted within Me.
15 My strength is dried up like a potsherd,
And My tongue clings to My jaws;
You have brought Me to the dust of
death.

16 For dogs have surrounded Me;
The congregation of the wicked has
enclosed Me.
They pierced[a] My hands and My feet;
17 I can count all My bones.
They look *and* stare at Me.
18 They divide My garments among them,
And for My clothing they cast lots.

19 But You, O LORD, do not be far from Me;
O My Strength, hasten to help Me!
20 Deliver Me from the sword,
My precious *life* from the power of the
dog.
21 Save Me from the lion's mouth
And from the horns of the wild oxen!

You have answered Me.

22 I will declare Your name to My
brethren;
In the midst of the assembly I will
praise You.
23 You who fear the LORD, praise Him!
All you descendants of Jacob, glorify
Him,
And fear Him, all you offspring of
Israel!
24 For He has not despised nor abhorred
the affliction of the afflicted;
Nor has He hidden His face from Him;
But when He cried to Him, He heard.

25 My praise *shall be* of You in the great
assembly;
I will pay My vows before those who fear
Him.
26 The poor shall eat and be satisfied;
Those who seek Him will praise the
LORD.
Let your heart live forever!

27 All the ends of the world
Shall remember and turn to the LORD,
And all the families of the nations
Shall worship before You.[a]
28 For the kingdom *is* the LORD's,
And He rules over the nations.

29 All the prosperous of the earth
Shall eat and worship;
All those who go down to the dust
Shall bow before Him,
Even he who cannot keep himself alive.

30 A posterity shall serve Him.
It will be recounted of the Lord to the
next generation,

22:8 [a] Septuagint, Syriac, and Vulgate read *hoped;* Targum reads *praised.* **22:16** [a] Following some Hebrew manuscripts, Septuagint, Syriac, Vulgate; Masoretic Text reads *Like a lion.* **22:27** [a] Following Masoretic Text, Septuagint, and Targum; Arabic, Syriac, and Vulgate read *Him.*

31 They will come and declare His
righteousness to a people who will be
born,
That He has done *this*.

PSALM 23

The LORD the Shepherd of His People

A Psalm of David.

1 The LORD *is* my shepherd;
I shall not want.
2 He makes me to lie down in green
pastures;
He leads me beside the still waters.
3 He restores my soul;
He leads me in the paths of
righteousness
For His name's sake.

4 Yea, though I walk through the valley of
the shadow of death,
I will fear no evil;
For You *are* with me;
Your rod and Your staff, they
comfort me.

5 You prepare a table before me in the
presence of my enemies;
You anoint my head with oil;
My cup runs over.
6 Surely goodness and mercy shall follow
me
All the days of my life;
And I will dwell[a] in the house of the
LORD
Forever.

PSALM 24

The King of Glory and His Kingdom

A Psalm of David.

1 The earth *is* the LORD's, and all its
fullness,

23:6 [a] Following Septuagint, Syriac, Targum, and Vulgate; Masoretic Text reads *return*.

Spotlight

THE LORD IS MY SHEPHERD

READ IT: PSALM 23:1–6

GET IT:

King David wrote this song. He had been a shepherd when he was a boy, so he knew all about sheep and protecting them. He was now a king, the shepherd of God's people. In this psalm he's talking about God as both his Shepherd and his King.

LIVE IT:

This psalm is a famous one that is great to memorize. If you don't already know it by heart, work on memorizing it. It will comfort you and help you throughout your life. While you read it, think about what kind of experiences you have had that are like those of David: how God has provided for you so you do not need anything (I shall not want); or how He has given you a calm and peaceful place to live (green pastures, still waters); or how He has helped you during the low points in life (valleys). Think about how God cares for you and protects you. That exercise will make this psalm more meaningful to you right now.

The world and those who dwell therein.
2 For He has founded it upon the seas,
And established it upon the waters.

3 Who may ascend into the hill of the LORD?
Or who may stand in His holy place?
4 He who has clean hands and a pure heart,
Who has not lifted up his soul to an idol,
Nor sworn deceitfully.
5 He shall receive blessing from the LORD,
And righteousness from the God of his salvation.
6 This *is* Jacob, the generation of those who seek Him,
Who seek Your face. *Selah*

7 Lift up your heads, O you gates!
And be lifted up, you everlasting doors!
And the King of glory shall come in.
8 Who *is* this King of glory?
The LORD strong and mighty,
The LORD mighty in battle.
9 Lift up your heads, O you gates!
Lift up, you everlasting doors!
And the King of glory shall come in.
10 Who is this King of glory?
The LORD of hosts,
He *is* the King of glory. *Selah*

PSALM 25

A Plea for Deliverance and Forgiveness

A *Psalm* of David.

1 To You, O LORD, I lift up my soul.
2 O my God, I trust in You;
Let me not be ashamed;
Let not my enemies triumph over me.
3 Indeed, let no one who waits on You be ashamed;
Let those be ashamed who deal treacherously without cause.

4 Show me Your ways, O LORD;
Teach me Your paths.
5 Lead me in Your truth and teach me,
For You *are* the God of my salvation;
On You I wait all the day.

6 Remember, O LORD, Your tender mercies and Your lovingkindnesses,
For they *are* from of old.
7 Do not remember the sins of my youth, nor my transgressions;
According to Your mercy remember me,
For Your goodness' sake, O LORD.

8 Good and upright *is* the LORD;
Therefore He teaches sinners in the way.
9 The humble He guides in justice,
And the humble He teaches His way.
10 All the paths of the LORD *are* mercy and truth,
To such as keep His covenant and His testimonies.
11 For Your name's sake, O LORD,
Pardon my iniquity, for it *is* great.

12 Who *is* the man that fears the LORD?
Him shall He[a] teach in the way He[b] chooses.
13 He himself shall dwell in prosperity,
And his descendants shall inherit the earth.
14 The secret of the LORD *is* with those who fear Him,
And He will show them His covenant.
15 My eyes *are* ever toward the LORD,
For He shall pluck my feet out of the net.

16 Turn Yourself to me, and have mercy on me,
For I *am* desolate and afflicted.
17 The troubles of my heart have enlarged;
Bring me out of my distresses!
18 Look on my affliction and my pain,
And forgive all my sins.
19 Consider my enemies, for they are many;
And they hate me with cruel hatred.
20 Keep my soul, and deliver me;
Let me not be ashamed, for I put my trust in You.
21 Let integrity and uprightness preserve me,
For I wait for You.

22 Redeem Israel, O God,
Out of all their troubles!

PSALM 26

A Prayer for Divine Scrutiny and Redemption

A *Psalm* of David.

1 Vindicate me, O LORD,
For I have walked in my integrity.

25:12 [a] Or *he* [b] Or *he*

I have also trusted in the LORD;
I shall not slip.
2 Examine me, O LORD, and prove me;
Try my mind and my heart.
3 For Your lovingkindness *is* before my eyes,
And I have walked in Your truth.
4 I have not sat with idolatrous mortals,
Nor will I go in with hypocrites.
5 I have hated the assembly of evildoers,
And will not sit with the wicked.

6 I will wash my hands in innocence;
So I will go about Your altar, O LORD,
7 That I may proclaim with the voice of thanksgiving,
And tell of all Your wondrous works.
8 LORD, I have loved the habitation of Your house,
And the place where Your glory dwells.

9 Do not gather my soul with sinners,
Nor my life with bloodthirsty men,
10 In whose hands *is* a sinister scheme,
And whose right hand is full of bribes.

11 But as for me, I will walk in my integrity;
Redeem me and be merciful to me.
12 My foot stands in an even place;
In the congregations I will bless the LORD.

PSALM 27

An Exuberant Declaration of Faith

A *Psalm* of David.

1 The LORD *is* my light and my salvation;
Whom shall I fear?
The LORD *is* the strength of my life;
Of whom shall I be afraid?
2 When the wicked came against me
To eat up my flesh,
My enemies and foes,
They stumbled and fell.
3 Though an army may encamp against me,
My heart shall not fear;
Though war may rise against me,
In this I *will be* confident.

4 One *thing* I have desired of the LORD,
That will I seek:
That I may dwell in the house of the LORD
All the days of my life,
To behold the beauty of the LORD,
And to inquire in His temple.
5 For in the time of trouble
He shall hide me in His pavilion;
In the secret place of His tabernacle
He shall hide me;
He shall set me high upon a rock.

6 And now my head shall be lifted up above my enemies all around me;

Epic Ideas

27:1 GOD MAKES US UNAFRAID

Fear can be a friend as well as an enemy. We ought to be afraid to drive a hundred miles an hour on the highway, and we ought to fear going near a rattlesnake. But many of our fears aren't necessary.

Some people are afraid of being in a room alone. Others are afraid of the darkness. Many people are afraid of unseen enemies. Most people are afraid to die.

God never planned that we should live in fear of the world around us. He also doesn't want us to be afraid of dying. The Bible says, "The wages of sin is death" (Romans 6:23). But that text goes on to say, "But the gift of God is eternal life in Christ Jesus our Lord." If we have eternal life with Jesus, we don't need to be afraid anymore. "The LORD is the strength of my life; of whom shall I be afraid?" (Psalm 27:1).

Therefore I will offer sacrifices of joy in
His tabernacle;
I will sing, yes, I will sing praises to the
LORD.

7 Hear, O LORD, *when* I cry with my voice!
Have mercy also upon me, and
answer me.
8 *When You said,* "Seek My face,"
My heart said to You, "Your face, LORD,
I will seek."
9 Do not hide Your face from me;
Do not turn Your servant away in anger;
You have been my help;
Do not leave me nor forsake me,
O God of my salvation.
10 When my father and my mother forsake
me,
Then the LORD will take care of me.

11 Teach me Your way, O LORD,
And lead me in a smooth path, because
of my enemies.
12 Do not deliver me to the will of my
adversaries;
For false witnesses have risen against
me,
And such as breathe out violence.
13 *I would have lost heart,* unless I had
believed
That I would see the goodness of the
LORD
In the land of the living.

14 Wait on the LORD;
Be of good courage,
And He shall strengthen your heart;
Wait, I say, on the LORD!

PSALM 28

Rejoicing in Answered Prayer

A Psalm of David.

1 To You I will cry, O LORD my Rock:
Do not be silent to me,
Lest, if You *are* silent to me,
I become like those who go down to the
pit.
2 Hear the voice of my supplications
When I cry to You,
When I lift up my hands toward Your
holy sanctuary.

3 Do not take me away with the wicked
And with the workers of iniquity,
Who speak peace to their neighbors,
But evil *is* in their hearts.
4 Give them according to their deeds,
And according to the wickedness of
their endeavors;
Give them according to the work of their
hands;
Render to them what they deserve.
5 Because they do not regard the works of
the LORD,
Nor the operation of His hands,
He shall destroy them
And not build them up.

6 Blessed *be* the LORD,
Because He has heard the voice of my
supplications!
7 The LORD *is* my strength and my shield;
My heart trusted in Him, and I am
helped;
Therefore my heart greatly rejoices,
And with my song I will praise Him.

8 The LORD *is* their strength,[a]
And He *is* the saving refuge of His
anointed.
9 Save Your people,
And bless Your inheritance;
Shepherd them also,
And bear them up forever.

PSALM 29

Praise to God in His Holiness and Majesty

A Psalm of David.

1 Give unto the LORD, O you mighty ones,
Give unto the LORD glory and strength.
2 Give unto the LORD the glory due to His
name;
Worship the LORD in the beauty of
holiness.

3 The voice of the LORD *is* over the waters;
The God of glory thunders;
The LORD *is* over many waters.
4 The voice of the LORD *is* powerful;
The voice of the LORD *is* full of majesty.

5 The voice of the LORD breaks the cedars,
Yes, the LORD splinters the cedars of
Lebanon.
6 He makes them also skip like a calf,
Lebanon and Sirion like a young
wild ox.
7 The voice of the LORD divides the
flames of fire.

28:8 [a] Following Masoretic Text and Targum; Septuagint, Syriac, and Vulgate read *the strength of His people.*

8 The voice of the LORD shakes the wilderness;
The LORD shakes the Wilderness of Kadesh.
9 The voice of the LORD makes the deer give birth,
And strips the forests bare;
And in His temple everyone says, "Glory!"

10 The LORD sat *enthroned* at the Flood,
And the LORD sits as King forever.
11 The LORD will give strength to His people;
The LORD will bless His people with peace.

PSALM 30

The Blessedness of Answered Prayer

A Psalm. A Song at the dedication of the house of David.

1 I will extol You, O LORD, for You have lifted me up,
And have not let my foes rejoice over me.
2 O LORD my God, I cried out to You,
And You healed me.
3 O LORD, You brought my soul up from the grave;
You have kept me alive, that I should not go down to the pit.[a]

4 Sing praise to the LORD, you saints of His,
And give thanks at the remembrance of His holy name.[a]
5 For His anger *is but for* a moment,
His favor *is for* life;
Weeping may endure for a night,
But joy *comes* in the morning.

6 Now in my prosperity I said,
"I shall never be moved."
7 LORD, by Your favor You have made my mountain stand strong;
You hid Your face, *and* I was troubled.

8 I cried out to You, O LORD;

30:3 [a] Following Qere and Targum; Kethib, Septuagint, Syriac, and Vulgate read *from those who descend to the pit.*
30:4 [a] Or *His holiness*

A SONG FOR THE TEMPLE

READ IT: PSALM 30:1–12

GET IT:

At the grand opening of God's temple, the people celebrated and sang songs. This was one of the songs they sang. We don't have the music from long ago, but these are the words that they sang. They remembered the past and all the things that God had done for them. It was a time to celebrate and thank God for everything He had done for His people.

LIVE IT:

This psalm has been around for thousands of years. Lots of people have read it to praise God, to pray to Him, and to thank Him for what He has done for them. What are you thankful for? This psalm can help you remember what you should thank God for. Were you sick and got better? Did your sadness turn to happiness? Maybe you want to repeat verse 10 to ask God to help you.

And to the LORD I made supplication:
9 "What profit *is there* in my blood,
When I go down to the pit?
Will the dust praise You?
Will it declare Your truth?
10 Hear, O LORD, and have mercy on me;
LORD, be my helper!"

11 You have turned for me my mourning
into dancing;
You have put off my sackcloth and
clothed me with gladness,
12 To the end that *my* glory may sing praise
to You and not be silent.
O LORD my God, I will give thanks to
You forever.

PSALM 31

The LORD a Fortress in Adversity

To the Chief Musician. A Psalm of David.

1 In You, O LORD, I put my trust;
Let me never be ashamed;
Deliver me in Your righteousness.
2 Bow down Your ear to me,
Deliver me speedily;
Be my rock of refuge,
A fortress of defense to save me.

3 For You *are* my rock and my fortress;
Therefore, for Your name's sake,
Lead me and guide me.
4 Pull me out of the net which they have
secretly laid for me,
For You *are* my strength.
5 Into Your hand I commit my spirit;
You have redeemed me, O LORD God of
truth.

6 I have hated those who regard useless
idols;
But I trust in the LORD.
7 I will be glad and rejoice in Your mercy,
For You have considered my trouble;
You have known my soul in adversities,
8 And have not shut me up into the hand
of the enemy;
You have set my feet in a wide place.

9 Have mercy on me, O LORD, for I am in
trouble;
My eye wastes away with grief,
Yes, my soul and my body!
10 For my life is spent with grief,
And my years with sighing;
My strength fails because of my
iniquity,
And my bones waste away.
11 I am a reproach among all my enemies,
But especially among my neighbors,
And *am* repulsive to my acquaintances;
Those who see me outside flee from me.
12 I am forgotten like a dead man, out of
mind;
I am like a broken vessel.
13 For I hear the slander of many;
Fear *is* on every side;
While they take counsel together
against me,
They scheme to take away my life.

GRIEF

READ IT: PSALM 30:4, 5

Imagine the longest winter you've ever experienced. It's cold and icy. You can hardly stand to go outside. The clouds never seem to disappear.

Grief can be a lot like a long season. It seems to never have an end. However, every year winter turns to spring, and spring becomes summer. Slowly—day by day—we get closer to a new season.

There is an end to grief. It may be far in the distance, but the sun will shine again. There will be joy. You will make it through the night.

14 But as for me, I trust in You, O LORD;
I say, "You *are* my God."
15 My times *are* in Your hand;
Deliver me from the hand of my enemies,
And from those who persecute me.
16 Make Your face shine upon Your servant;
Save me for Your mercies' sake.
17 Do not let me be ashamed, O LORD, for I have called upon You;
Let the wicked be ashamed;
Let them be silent in the grave.
18 Let the lying lips be put to silence,
Which speak insolent things proudly and contemptuously against the righteous.

19 Oh, how great *is* Your goodness,
Which You have laid up for those who fear You,
Which You have prepared for those who trust in You
In the presence of the sons of men!
20 You shall hide them in the secret place of Your presence
From the plots of man;
You shall keep them secretly in a pavilion
From the strife of tongues.

21 Blessed *be* the LORD,
For He has shown me His marvelous kindness in a strong city!
22 For I said in my haste,
"I am cut off from before Your eyes";
Nevertheless You heard the voice of my supplications
When I cried out to You.

23 Oh, love the LORD, all you His saints!
For the LORD preserves the faithful,
And fully repays the proud person.
24 Be of good courage,
And He shall strengthen your heart,
All you who hope in the LORD.

PSALM 32

The Joy of Forgiveness

A *Psalm* of David. A Contemplation.[a]

1 Blessed *is he whose* transgression *is forgiven,*
Whose sin *is* covered.
2 Blessed *is* the man to whom the LORD does not impute iniquity,
And in whose spirit *there is* no deceit.
3 When I kept silent, my bones grew old
Through my groaning all the day long.
4 For day and night Your hand was heavy upon me;
My vitality was turned into the drought of summer. *Selah*
5 I acknowledged my sin to You,
And my iniquity I have not hidden.
I said, "I will confess my transgressions to the LORD,"
And You forgave the iniquity of my sin. *Selah*

6 For this cause everyone who is godly shall pray to You
In a time when You may be found;
Surely in a flood of great waters
They shall not come near him.
7 You *are* my hiding place;
You shall preserve me from trouble;
You shall surround me with songs of deliverance. *Selah*

8 I will instruct you and teach you in the way you should go;
I will guide you with My eye.
9 Do not be like the horse *or* like the mule,
Which have no understanding,
Which must be harnessed with bit and bridle,
Else they will not come near you.

10 Many sorrows *shall be* to the wicked;
But he who trusts in the LORD, mercy shall surround him.
11 Be glad in the LORD and rejoice, you righteous;
And shout for joy, all *you* upright in heart!

PSALM 33

The Sovereignty of the LORD in Creation and History

1 Rejoice in the LORD, O you righteous!
For praise from the upright is beautiful.
2 Praise the LORD with the harp;
Make melody to Him with an instrument of ten strings.
3 Sing to Him a new song;
Play skillfully with a shout of joy.

4 For the word of the LORD *is* right,
And all His work *is done* in truth.

32:title [a] Hebrew *Maschil*

5 He loves righteousness and justice;
The earth is full of the goodness of the LORD.

6 By the word of the LORD the heavens were made,
And all the host of them by the breath of His mouth.
7 He gathers the waters of the sea together as a heap;[a]
He lays up the deep in storehouses.

8 Let all the earth fear the LORD;
Let all the inhabitants of the world stand in awe of Him.
9 For He spoke, and it was *done;*
He commanded, and it stood fast.

10 The LORD brings the counsel of the nations to nothing;
He makes the plans of the peoples of no effect.
11 The counsel of the LORD stands forever,
The plans of His heart to all generations.
12 Blessed *is* the nation whose God *is* the LORD,
The people He has chosen as His own inheritance.

In Focus

31:23 Saints People who are set apart by God. The word comes from a Hebrew word meaning "holy" or "godly."

13 The LORD looks from heaven;
He sees all the sons of men.
14 From the place of His dwelling He looks
On all the inhabitants of the earth;
15 He fashions their hearts individually;
He considers all their works.

16 No king *is* saved by the multitude of an army;
A mighty man is not delivered by great strength.
17 A horse *is* a vain hope for safety;
Neither shall it deliver *any* by its great strength.

33:7 [a] Septuagint, Targum, and Vulgate read *in a vessel.*

Action!

PRAISE GOD FOR HIS WONDERFUL WORD

READ IT: PSALM 33:6

Some people don't know who God is, so they can't praise Him. You feel like praising God when you know Him and know how much He has done for you.

God says He supports all things "by the word of His power" (Hebrews 1:3). It's hard to imagine anyone making something happen just by speaking. But did you know there are machines today that work when someone speaks to them? So it isn't strange that God "spoke, and it was done" (Psalm 33:9).

God's words are not just noises or sounds. God's words make things happen. The Bible says we are "born again . . . through the word of God which lives and abides forever" (1 Peter 1:23). God's everlasting Word is the power by which He saves you from sin and makes you a new person. Then you can praise Him.

18 Behold, the eye of the LORD *is* on those
who fear Him,
On those who hope in His mercy,
19 To deliver their soul from death,
And to keep them alive in famine.

20 Our soul waits for the LORD;
He *is* our help and our shield.
21 For our heart shall rejoice in Him,
Because we have trusted in His holy
name.
22 Let Your mercy, O LORD, be upon us,
Just as we hope in You.

PSALM 34

The Happiness of Those Who Trust in God

A Psalm of David when he pretended madness before Abimelech, who drove him away, and he departed.

1 I will bless the LORD at all times;
His praise *shall* continually *be* in my
mouth.
2 My soul shall make its boast in the
LORD;
The humble shall hear *of it* and be glad.
3 Oh, magnify the LORD with me,
And let us exalt His name together.

4 I sought the LORD, and He heard me,
And delivered me from all my fears.
5 They looked to Him and were radiant,
And their faces were not ashamed.
6 This poor man cried out, and the LORD
heard *him,*
And saved him out of all his troubles.
7 The angel[a] of the LORD encamps all
around those who fear Him,
And delivers them.

8 Oh, taste and see that the LORD *is* good;
Blessed *is* the man *who* trusts in Him!
9 Oh, fear the LORD, you His saints!
There is no want to those who fear Him.
10 The young lions lack and suffer hunger;
But those who seek the LORD shall not
lack any good *thing.*

11 Come, you children, listen to me;
I will teach you the fear of the LORD.
12 Who *is* the man *who* desires life,
And loves *many* days, that he may see
good?
13 Keep your tongue from evil,
And your lips from speaking deceit.
14 Depart from evil and do good;
Seek peace and pursue it.

15 The eyes of the LORD *are* on the
righteous,
And His ears *are open* to their cry.
16 The face of the LORD *is* against those
who do evil,
To cut off the remembrance of them
from the earth.

17 *The righteous* cry out, and the LORD
hears,
And delivers them out of all their
troubles.
18 The LORD *is* near to those who have a
broken heart,
And saves such as have a contrite spirit.

34:7 [a] Or *Angel*

HONESTY

READ IT: PSALM 34:13

When this verse says to keep our tongues from evil and lips from deceit, it's suggesting that we have a choice when it comes to the words coming out of our mouths. Lying is a sin, and sin is evil. Before the words even touch our lips, before we form the words with our tongues, we have the power to choose what we'll say next.

19 Many *are* the afflictions of the righteous,
But the LORD delivers him out of them all.
20 He guards all his bones;
Not one of them is broken.
21 Evil shall slay the wicked,
And those who hate the righteous shall be condemned.
22 The LORD redeems the soul of His servants,
And none of those who trust in Him shall be condemned.

PSALM 35

The LORD the Avenger of His People

A Psalm of David.

1 Plead *my cause,* O LORD, with those who strive with me;
Fight against those who fight against me.
2 Take hold of shield and buckler,
And stand up for my help.
3 Also draw out the spear,
And stop those who pursue me.
Say to my soul,
"I *am* your salvation."

4 Let those be put to shame and brought to dishonor
Who seek after my life;
Let those be turned back and brought to confusion
Who plot my hurt.
5 Let them be like chaff before the wind,
And let the angel[a] of the LORD chase *them.*
6 Let their way be dark and slippery,
And let the angel of the LORD pursue them.
7 For without cause they have hidden their net for me *in* a pit,
Which they have dug without cause for my life.
8 Let destruction come upon him unexpectedly,
And let his net that he has hidden catch himself;
Into that very destruction let him fall.

9 And my soul shall be joyful in the LORD;
It shall rejoice in His salvation.
10 All my bones shall say,
"LORD, who *is* like You,
Delivering the poor from him who is too strong for him,
Yes, the poor and the needy from him who plunders him?"

11 Fierce witnesses rise up;
They ask me *things* that I do not know.
12 They reward me evil for good,
To the sorrow of my soul.
13 But as for me, when they were sick,
My clothing *was* sackcloth;
I humbled myself with fasting;
And my prayer would return to my own heart.
14 I paced about as though *he were* my friend *or* brother;
I bowed down heavily, as one who mourns *for his* mother.

15 But in my adversity they rejoiced
And gathered together;
Attackers gathered against me,
And I did not know *it;*
They tore *at me* and did not cease;
16 With ungodly mockers at feasts
They gnashed at me with their teeth.

17 Lord, how long will You look on?
Rescue me from their destructions,
My precious *life* from the lions.
18 I will give You thanks in the great assembly;
I will praise You among many people.

19 Let them not rejoice over me who are wrongfully my enemies;
Nor let them wink with the eye who hate me without a cause.
20 For they do not speak peace,
But they devise deceitful matters
Against *the* quiet ones in the land.
21 They also opened their mouth wide against me,
And said, "Aha, aha!
Our eyes have seen *it.*"

22 *This* You have seen, O LORD;
Do not keep silence.
O Lord, do not be far from me.
23 Stir up Yourself, and awake to my vindication,
To my cause, my God and my Lord.
24 Vindicate me, O LORD my God, according to Your righteousness;
And let them not rejoice over me.
25 Let them not say in their hearts, "Ah, so we would have it!"
Let them not say, "We have swallowed him up."

35:5 [a] Or *Angel*

26 Let them be ashamed and brought to mutual confusion
Who rejoice at my hurt;
Let them be clothed with shame and dishonor
Who exalt themselves against me.

27 Let them shout for joy and be glad,
Who favor my righteous cause;
And let them say continually,
"Let the LORD be magnified,
Who has pleasure in the prosperity of His servant."
28 And my tongue shall speak of Your righteousness
And of Your praise all the day long.

PSALM 36

Man's Wickedness and God's Perfections

To the Chief Musician. *A Psalm* of David the servant of the LORD.

1 An oracle within my heart concerning the transgression of the wicked:
There is no fear of God before his eyes.
2 For he flatters himself in his own eyes,
When he finds out his iniquity *and* when he hates.
3 The words of his mouth *are* wickedness and deceit;
He has ceased to be wise *and* to do good.
4 He devises wickedness on his bed;
He sets himself in a way *that is* not good;
He does not abhor evil.

5 Your mercy, O LORD, *is* in the heavens;
Your faithfulness *reaches* to the clouds.
6 Your righteousness *is* like the great mountains;
Your judgments *are* a great deep;
O LORD, You preserve man and beast.

7 How precious *is* Your lovingkindness, O God!
Therefore the children of men put their trust under the shadow of Your wings.
8 They are abundantly satisfied with the fullness of Your house,
And You give them drink from the river of Your pleasures.
9 For with You *is* the fountain of life;
In Your light we see light.

10 Oh, continue Your lovingkindness to those who know You,
And Your righteousness to the upright in heart.
11 Let not the foot of pride come against me,
And let not the hand of the wicked drive me away.

Epic Ideas

36:9 GOD IS THE AUTHOR OF LIFE

Life didn't begin when you were born. Life didn't even begin when God created the heavens and the earth. God had life in Himself forever and ever, before He made anything.

The life you have is a gift from God. When you know God is the Author of your life, then you are more careful about yourself. You should ask yourself questions like, "What does God want me to do with my life?" And, "How should I think about other people?" God gave them life, too.

But God is not only the Author of human life; He is also the Author of all life. God has placed us in charge of the world around us so that all life can be better. Are you a good caretaker of God's world?

God is also the Author of eternal life. We receive the gift of *eternal life* from Jesus who said, "I have come that they may have life" (John 10:10).

12 There the workers of iniquity have fallen;
They have been cast down and are not able to rise.

PSALM 37

The Heritage of the Righteous and the Calamity of the Wicked

A Psalm of David.

1 Do not fret because of evildoers,
Nor be envious of the workers of iniquity.
2 For they shall soon be cut down like the grass,
And wither as the green herb.

3 Trust in the LORD, and do good;
Dwell in the land, and feed on His faithfulness.
4 Delight yourself also in the LORD,
And He shall give you the desires of your heart.

5 Commit your way to the LORD,
Trust also in Him,
And He shall bring *it* to pass.
6 He shall bring forth your righteousness as the light,
And your justice as the noonday.

7 Rest in the LORD, and wait patiently for Him;
Do not fret because of him who prospers in his way,
Because of the man who brings wicked schemes to pass.
8 Cease from anger, and forsake wrath;
Do not fret—*it* only *causes* harm.

9 For evildoers shall be cut off;
But those who wait on the LORD,
They shall inherit the earth.
10 For yet a little while and the wicked *shall be* no *more;*
Indeed, you will look carefully for his place,
But it *shall be* no *more.*
11 But the meek shall inherit the earth,
And shall delight themselves in the abundance of peace.

12 The wicked plots against the just,
And gnashes at him with his teeth.
13 The Lord laughs at him,
For He sees that his day is coming.
14 The wicked have drawn the sword
And have bent their bow,
To cast down the poor and needy,
To slay those who are of upright conduct.
15 Their sword shall enter their own heart,
And their bows shall be broken.

16 A little that a righteous man has
Is better than the riches of many wicked.
17 For the arms of the wicked shall be broken,
But the LORD upholds the righteous.

LIFE'S NOT FAIR

READ IT: PSALM 37:7–13

Sometimes the people making the wrong choices seem to be the ones getting ahead. But sitting around keeping score can drive a person crazy. It starts out innocently enough—you can't help noticing when the guy who is always getting in trouble made the team and you didn't. But it can drag you into a dark place.

- *Don't get angry.* It's not worth your energy.
- *Let it go.* You can't waste your life keeping score.
- *Trust God.* He has promised to bring justice one day—He will!

18 The LORD knows the days of the
upright,
And their inheritance shall be forever.
19 They shall not be ashamed in the evil
time,
And in the days of famine they shall be
satisfied.
20 But the wicked shall perish;
And the enemies of the LORD,
Like the splendor of the meadows, shall
vanish.
Into smoke they shall vanish away.

21 The wicked borrows and does not repay,
But the righteous shows mercy and
gives.
22 For *those* blessed by Him shall inherit
the earth,
But *those* cursed by Him shall be cut off.

23 The steps of a *good* man are ordered by
the LORD,
And He delights in his way.
24 Though he fall, he shall not be utterly
cast down;
For the LORD upholds *him with* His
hand.

25 I have been young, and *now* am old;
Yet I have not seen the righteous
forsaken,
Nor his descendants begging bread.
26 *He is* ever merciful, and lends;
And his descendants *are* blessed.

27 Depart from evil, and do good;
And dwell forevermore.
28 For the LORD loves justice,
And does not forsake His saints;
They are preserved forever,
But the descendants of the wicked shall
be cut off.
29 The righteous shall inherit the land,
And dwell in it forever.

30 The mouth of the righteous speaks
wisdom,
And his tongue talks of justice.
31 The law of his God *is* in his heart;
None of his steps shall slide.

32 The wicked watches the righteous,
And seeks to slay him.
33 The LORD will not leave him in his
hand,
Nor condemn him when he is judged.

34 Wait on the LORD,
And keep His way,
And He shall exalt you to inherit the
land;
When the wicked are cut off, you shall
see *it*.
35 I have seen the wicked in great power,
And spreading himself like a native
green tree.
36 Yet he passed away,[a] and behold, he *was*
no *more;*

37:36 [a] Following Masoretic Text, Septuagint, and Targum; Syriac and Vulgate read *I passed by.*

LONELINESS

READ IT: PSALM 38:9–15

Have you ever felt so alone that you felt desperate? In times like that, it seems as if nobody understands what you're going through, and you feel so separated from the world you can't even speak. Life just doesn't make sense anymore.

You're not the first one to feel this way. The author of this psalm was going through a tough time when he wrote this passage. Feeling alone is a part of life we have to go through. However, those feelings will end. They did for the psalmist. If you keep reading, you'll soon find him celebrating and rejoicing!

Indeed I sought him, but he could not
be found.

37 Mark the blameless *man*, and observe
the upright;
For the future of *that* man *is* peace.
38 But the transgressors shall be destroyed
together;
The future of the wicked shall be cut
off.

39 But the salvation of the righteous *is*
from the LORD;
He is their strength in the time of
trouble.
40 And the LORD shall help them and
deliver them;
He shall deliver them from the wicked,
And save them,
Because they trust in Him.

PSALM 38

Prayer in Time of Chastening

A Psalm of David. To bring to remembrance.

1 O LORD, do not rebuke me in Your
wrath,
Nor chasten me in Your hot displeasure!
2 For Your arrows pierce me deeply,
And Your hand presses me down.

3 *There is* no soundness in my flesh
Because of Your anger,
Nor *any* health in my bones
Because of my sin.
4 For my iniquities have gone over my
head;
Like a heavy burden they are too heavy
for me.
5 My wounds are foul *and* festering
Because of my foolishness.

6 I am troubled, I am bowed down
greatly;
I go mourning all the day long.
7 For my loins are full of inflammation,
And *there is* no soundness in my flesh.
8 I am feeble and severely broken;
I groan because of the turmoil of my
heart.

9 Lord, all my desire *is* before You;
And my sighing is not hidden from You.
10 My heart pants, my strength fails me;
As for the light of my eyes, it also has
gone from me.
11 My loved ones and my friends stand
aloof from my plague,
And my relatives stand afar off.
12 Those also who seek my life lay snares
for me;
Those who seek my hurt speak of
destruction,
And plan deception all the day long.

13 But I, like a deaf *man*, do not hear;
And *I am* like a mute *who* does not open
his mouth.
14 Thus I am like a man who does not hear,
And in whose mouth *is* no response.

15 For in You, O LORD, I hope;
You will hear, O Lord my God.
16 For I said, "*Hear me,* lest they rejoice
over me,
Lest, when my foot slips, they exalt
themselves against me."

17 For I *am* ready to fall,
And my sorrow *is* continually before me.
18 For I will declare my iniquity;
I will be in anguish over my sin.
19 But my enemies *are* vigorous, *and* they
are strong;
And those who hate me wrongfully have
multiplied.
20 Those also who render evil for good,
They are my adversaries, because I
follow *what is* good.

21 Do not forsake me, O LORD;
O my God, be not far from me!
22 Make haste to help me,
O Lord, my salvation!

PSALM 39

Prayer for Wisdom and Forgiveness

To the Chief Musician. To
Jeduthun. A Psalm of David.

1 I said, "I will guard my ways,
Lest I sin with my tongue;
I will restrain my mouth with a muzzle,
While the wicked are before me."
2 I was mute with silence,
I held my peace *even* from good;
And my sorrow was stirred up.
3 My heart was hot within me;
While I was musing, the fire burned.
Then I spoke with my tongue:

4 "LORD, make me to know my end,
And what *is* the measure of my days,

That I may know how frail I *am*.
5 Indeed, You have made my days *as* handbreadths,
And my age *is* as nothing before You;
Certainly every man at his best state *is* but vapor. *Selah*
6 Surely every man walks about like a shadow;
Surely they busy themselves in vain;
He heaps up *riches*,
And does not know who will gather them.

7 "And now, Lord, what do I wait for?
My hope *is* in You.
8 Deliver me from all my transgressions;
Do not make me the reproach of the foolish.
9 I was mute, I did not open my mouth,
Because it was You who did *it*.
10 Remove Your plague from me;
I am consumed by the blow of Your hand.
11 When with rebukes You correct man for iniquity,
You make his beauty melt away like a moth;
Surely every man *is* vapor. *Selah*

12 "Hear my prayer, O LORD,
And give ear to my cry;
Do not be silent at my tears;
For I *am* a stranger with You,
A sojourner, as all my fathers *were*.
13 Remove Your gaze from me, that I may regain strength,
Before I go away and am no more."

PSALM 40

Faith Persevering in Trial

To the Chief Musician. A Psalm of David.

1 I waited patiently for the LORD;
And He inclined to me,
And heard my cry.
2 He also brought me up out of a horrible pit,
Out of the miry clay,
And set my feet upon a rock,
And established my steps.
3 He has put a new song in my mouth—
Praise to our God;
Many will see *it* and fear,
And will trust in the LORD.
4 Blessed *is* that man who makes the LORD his trust,
And does not respect the proud, nor such as turn aside to lies.
5 Many, O LORD my God, *are* Your wonderful works
Which You have done;
And Your thoughts toward us
Cannot be recounted to You in order;
If I would declare and speak *of them*,
They are more than can be numbered.

6 Sacrifice and offering You did not desire;
My ears You have opened.
Burnt offering and sin offering You did not require.
7 Then I said, "Behold, I come;
In the scroll of the book *it is* written of me.
8 I delight to do Your will, O my God,
And Your law *is* within my heart."

9 I have proclaimed the good news of righteousness
In the great assembly;
Indeed, I do not restrain my lips,
O LORD, You Yourself know.
10 I have not hidden Your righteousness within my heart;
I have declared Your faithfulness and Your salvation;
I have not concealed Your lovingkindness and Your truth
From the great assembly.

11 Do not withhold Your tender mercies from me, O LORD;
Let Your lovingkindness and Your truth continually preserve me.
12 For innumerable evils have surrounded me;
My iniquities have overtaken me, so that I am not able to look up;
They are more than the hairs of my head;
Therefore my heart fails me.

13 Be pleased, O LORD, to deliver me;
O LORD, make haste to help me!
14 Let them be ashamed and brought to mutual confusion
Who seek to destroy my life;
Let them be driven backward and brought to dishonor
Who wish me evil.

15 Let them be confounded because of their shame,
Who say to me, "Aha, aha!"

16 Let all those who seek You rejoice and be glad in You;
Let such as love Your salvation say continually,
"The LORD be magnified!"
17 But I *am* poor and needy;
Yet the LORD thinks upon me.
You *are* my help and my deliverer;
Do not delay, O my God.

PSALM 41

The Blessing and Suffering of the Godly

To the Chief Musician. A Psalm of David.

1 Blessed *is* he who considers the poor;
The LORD will deliver him in time of trouble.
2 The LORD will preserve him and keep him alive,
And he will be blessed on the earth;
You will not deliver him to the will of his enemies.
3 The LORD will strengthen him on his bed of illness;
You will sustain him on his sickbed.

4 I said, "LORD, be merciful to me;
Heal my soul, for I have sinned against You."
5 My enemies speak evil of me:
"When will he die, and his name perish?"
6 And if he comes to see *me*, he speaks lies;
His heart gathers iniquity to itself;
When he goes out, he tells *it*.

7 All who hate me whisper together against me;
Against me they devise my hurt.
8 "An evil disease," *they say*, "clings to him.
And *now* that he lies down, he will rise up no more."
9 Even my own familiar friend in whom I trusted,
Who ate my bread,
Has lifted up *his* heel against me.

10 But You, O LORD, be merciful to me, and raise me up,
That I may repay them.
11 By this I know that You are well pleased with me,
Because my enemy does not triumph over me.
12 As for me, You uphold me in my integrity,
And set me before Your face forever.

13 Blessed *be* the LORD God of Israel
From everlasting to everlasting!
Amen and Amen.

BOOK TWO

Psalms 42–72

PSALM 42

Yearning for God in the Midst of Distresses

To the Chief Musician. A Contemplation[a] of the sons of Korah.

1 As the deer pants for the water brooks,
So pants my soul for You, O God.
2 My soul thirsts for God, for the living God.
When shall I come and appear before God?[a]
3 My tears have been my food day and night,
While they continually say to me,
"Where *is* your God?"

4 When I remember these *things*,
I pour out my soul within me.
For I used to go with the multitude;
I went with them to the house of God,
With the voice of joy and praise,
With a multitude that kept a pilgrim feast.

5 Why are you cast down, O my soul?
And *why* are you disquieted within me?
Hope in God, for I shall yet praise Him
For the help of His countenance.[a]

6 O my God,[a] my soul is cast down within me;
Therefore I will remember You from the land of the Jordan,
And from the heights of Hermon,
From the Hill Mizar.
7 Deep calls unto deep at the noise of Your waterfalls;

42:title [a] Hebrew *Maschil* **42:2** [a] Following Masoretic Text and Vulgate; some Hebrew manuscripts, Septuagint, Syriac, and Targum read *I see the face of God*. **42:5** [a] Following Masoretic Text and Targum; a few Hebrew manuscripts, Septuagint, Syriac, and Vulgate read *The help of my countenance, my God*. **42:6** [a] Following Masoretic Text and Targum; a few Hebrew manuscripts, Septuagint, Syriac, and Vulgate put *my God* at the end of verse 5.

All Your waves and billows have gone
over me.
8 The LORD will command His
lovingkindness in the daytime,
And in the night His song *shall be* with
me—
A prayer to the God of my life.

9 I will say to God my Rock,
"Why have You forgotten me?
Why do I go mourning because of the
oppression of the enemy?"
10 *As* with a breaking of my bones,
My enemies reproach me,
While they say to me all day long,
"Where *is* your God?"

11 Why are you cast down, O my soul?
And why are you disquieted within me?
Hope in God;
For I shall yet praise Him,
The help of my countenance and my
God.

PSALM 43

Prayer to God in Time of Trouble

1 Vindicate me, O God,
And plead my cause against an ungodly
nation;
Oh, deliver me from the deceitful and
unjust man!
2 For You *are* the God of my strength;
Why do You cast me off?
Why do I go mourning because of the
oppression of the enemy?

3 Oh, send out Your light and Your truth!
Let them lead me;
Let them bring me to Your holy hill
And to Your tabernacle.
4 Then I will go to the altar of God,
To God my exceeding joy;
And on the harp I will praise You,
O God, my God.

5 Why are you cast down, O my soul?
And why are you disquieted within me?
Hope in God;
For I shall yet praise Him,
The help of my countenance and my
God.

PSALM 44

Redemption Remembered in Present Dishonor

To the Chief Musician. A
Contemplation[a] of the sons of Korah.

1 We have heard with our ears, O God,
Our fathers have told us,
The deeds You did in their days,

44:title [a] Hebrew *Maschil*

DEPRESSION

READ IT: PSALM 42:1–11

Have you ever felt like something was gnawing at you from the inside? Making it hard to function, to smile, to sing? The writer of this psalm knew depression too, but he did three things that helped. You can, too.

- Go to church, even if you don't feel like it.
- Make a list of God's blessings in your life.
- Put your hope in God. Keep looking up.

Lean on Him, especially at night, when depression can be worse. Put a little HOPE sign on your bedside table as a reminder that God's there for you.

In days of old:
2 You drove out the nations with Your hand,
But them You planted;
You afflicted the peoples, and cast them out.
3 For they did not gain possession of the land by their own sword,
Nor did their own arm save them;
But it was Your right hand, Your arm, and the light of Your countenance,
Because You favored them.

4 You are my King, O God;[a]
Command[b] victories for Jacob.
5 Through You we will push down our enemies;
Through Your name we will trample those who rise up against us.
6 For I will not trust in my bow,
Nor shall my sword save me.
7 But You have saved us from our enemies,
And have put to shame those who hated us.
8 In God we boast all day long,
And praise Your name forever. *Selah*

9 But You have cast *us* off and put us to shame,
And You do not go out with our armies.
10 You make us turn back from the enemy,
And those who hate us have taken spoil for themselves.
11 You have given us up like sheep *intended* for food,
And have scattered us among the nations.
12 You sell Your people for *next to* nothing,
And are not enriched by selling them.

13 You make us a reproach to our neighbors,
A scorn and a derision to those all around us.
14 You make us a byword among the nations,
A shaking of the head among the peoples.
15 My dishonor *is* continually before me,
And the shame of my face has covered me,
16 Because of the voice of him who reproaches and reviles,
Because of the enemy and the avenger.

17 All this has come upon us;
But we have not forgotten You,
Nor have we dealt falsely with Your covenant.
18 Our heart has not turned back,
Nor have our steps departed from Your way;
19 But You have severely broken us in the place of jackals,
And covered us with the shadow of death.

20 If we had forgotten the name of our God,
Or stretched out our hands to a foreign god,
21 Would not God search this out?
For He knows the secrets of the heart.
22 Yet for Your sake we are killed all day long;
We are accounted as sheep for the slaughter.

23 Awake! Why do You sleep, O Lord?
Arise! Do not cast *us* off forever.
24 Why do You hide Your face,
And forget our affliction and our oppression?
25 For our soul is bowed down to the dust;
Our body clings to the ground.
26 Arise for our help,
And redeem us for Your mercies' sake.

PSALM 45

The Glories of the Messiah and His Bride

To the Chief Musician. Set to "The Lilies."[a] A Contemplation[b] of the sons of Korah. A Song of Love.

1 My heart is overflowing with a good theme;
I recite my composition concerning the King;
My tongue *is* the pen of a ready writer.

2 You are fairer than the sons of men;
Grace is poured upon Your lips;
Therefore God has blessed You forever.
3 Gird Your sword upon *Your* thigh, O Mighty One,
With Your glory and Your majesty.

44:4 [a] Following Masoretic Text and Targum; Septuagint and Vulgate read *and my God.* [b] Following Masoretic Text and Targum; Septuagint, Syriac, and Vulgate read *Who commands.* **45:title** [a] Hebrew *Shoshannim* [b] Hebrew *Maschil*

4 And in Your majesty ride prosperously
because of truth, humility, *and*
righteousness;
And Your right hand shall teach You
awesome things.
5 Your arrows *are* sharp in the heart of the
King's enemies;
The peoples fall under You.

6 Your throne, O God, *is* forever and ever;
A scepter of righteousness *is* the scepter
of Your kingdom.
7 You love righteousness and hate
wickedness;
Therefore God, Your God, has anointed
You
With the oil of gladness more than Your
companions.
8 All Your garments *are scented* with
myrrh and aloes *and* cassia,
Out of the ivory palaces, by which they
have made You glad.
9 Kings' daughters *are* among Your
honorable women;
At Your right hand stands the queen in
gold from Ophir.

10 Listen, O daughter,
Consider and incline your ear;
Forget your own people also, and your
father's house;
11 So the King will greatly desire your
beauty;
Because He *is* your Lord, worship Him.
12 And the daughter of Tyre *will come* with
a gift;
The rich among the people will seek
your favor.

13 The royal daughter *is* all glorious within
the palace;
Her clothing *is* woven with gold.
14 She shall be brought to the King in
robes of many colors;
The virgins, her companions who follow
her, shall be brought to You.
15 With gladness and rejoicing they shall
be brought;
They shall enter the King's palace.

16 Instead of Your fathers shall be Your sons,
Whom You shall make princes in all the
earth.
17 I will make Your name to be
remembered in all generations;
Therefore the people shall praise You
forever and ever.

PSALM 46

God the Refuge of His People and Conqueror of the Nations

To the Chief Musician. *A Psalm* of the
sons of Korah. A Song for Alamoth.

1 God *is* our refuge and strength,
A very present help in trouble.

Epic Ideas

45:6 GOD IS FOREVER AND EVER

Have you thought about *eternity?* Eternity means forever and ever—no beginning and no ending. You had a beginning, and someday your life in this world will end. Even the world itself will come to an end. In fact, we're so used to everything we know having a beginning and an end, we can hardly think of anything that doesn't end.

God is forever and ever. He is different from everything He made because He never had a beginning and He will never end. He has eternal life in Himself. Then He shares His life with the people He made in His image. So, even if we die in this world, we will go on living somewhere. God wants you to share eternal life with Him. You can live with Him forever if you give your life to Him now. Later may be too late.

2 Therefore we will not fear,
Even though the earth be removed,
And though the mountains be carried
into the midst of the sea;
3 *Though* its waters roar *and* be troubled,
Though the mountains shake with its
swelling. *Selah*

4 *There is* a river whose streams shall
make glad the city of God,
The holy *place* of the tabernacle of the
Most High.
5 God *is* in the midst of her, she shall not
be moved;
God shall help her, just at the break of
dawn.
6 The nations raged, the kingdoms were
moved;
He uttered His voice, the earth melted.

7 The LORD of hosts *is* with us;
The God of Jacob *is* our refuge. *Selah*

8 Come, behold the works of the LORD,
Who has made desolations in the earth.
9 He makes wars cease to the end of the
earth;
He breaks the bow and cuts the spear
in two;
He burns the chariot in the fire.

10 Be still, and know that I *am* God;
I will be exalted among the nations,
I will be exalted in the earth!

11 The LORD of hosts *is* with us;
The God of Jacob *is* our refuge. *Selah*

PSALM 47

Praise to God, the Ruler of the Earth

To the Chief Musician. A Psalm
of the sons of Korah.

1 Oh, clap your hands, all you peoples!
Shout to God with the voice of triumph!
2 For the LORD Most High *is* awesome;
He is a great King over all the earth.
3 He will subdue the peoples under us,
And the nations under our feet.
4 He will choose our inheritance for us,
The excellence of Jacob whom He loves.
Selah

5 God has gone up with a shout,
The LORD with the sound of a trumpet.
6 Sing praises to God, sing praises!
Sing praises to our King, sing praises!
7 For God *is* the King of all the earth;
Sing praises with understanding.

8 God reigns over the nations;
God sits on His holy throne.
9 The princes of the people have gathered
together,
The people of the God of Abraham.

47:8 GOD RULES THE NATIONS

Nearly every day the news reporters tell us about trouble in the world—war and hunger and murder. You may not see much trouble like this in your community, but because we hear and read about it so much, we often wonder how it will all end.

But you don't need to be afraid. God is in charge of the nations. He is leading us all to His final judgment. One day He will call all nations before Him and judge them. In the end, His perfect and everlasting kingdom will come, and the power of this world will pass away.

Have you made sure of your place in God's kingdom? Jesus said, "Come to Me, all you who labor and are heavy laden, and I will give you rest" (Matthew 11:28).

For the shields of the earth *belong* to
God;
He is greatly exalted.

PSALM 48

The Glory of God in Zion

A Song. A Psalm of the sons of Korah.

1 Great *is* the LORD, and greatly to be
praised
In the city of our God,
In His holy mountain.
2 Beautiful in elevation,
The joy of the whole earth,
Is Mount Zion *on* the sides of the north,
The city of the great King.
3 God *is* in her palaces;
He is known as her refuge.

4 For behold, the kings assembled,
They passed by together.
5 They saw *it, and* so they marveled;
They were troubled, they hastened away.
6 Fear took hold of them there,
And pain, as of a woman in birth pangs,
7 *As when* You break the ships of Tarshish
With an east wind.

8 As we have heard,
So we have seen
In the city of the LORD of hosts,
In the city of our God:
God will establish it forever. *Selah*

9 We have thought, O God, on Your
lovingkindness,
In the midst of Your temple.
10 According to Your name, O God,
So *is* Your praise to the ends of the
earth;
Your right hand is full of righteousness.
11 Let Mount Zion rejoice,
Let the daughters of Judah be glad,
Because of Your judgments.

12 Walk about Zion,
And go all around her.
Count her towers;
13 Mark well her bulwarks;
Consider her palaces;
That you may tell *it* to the generation
following.
14 For this *is* God,
Our God forever and ever;
He will be our guide
Even to death.[a]

PSALM 49

The Confidence of the Foolish

To the Chief Musician. A Psalm of
the sons of Korah.

1 Hear this, all peoples;
Give ear, all inhabitants of the world,
2 Both low and high,
Rich and poor together.
3 My mouth shall speak wisdom,
And the meditation of my heart *shall
give* understanding.
4 I will incline my ear to a proverb;
I will disclose my dark saying on the
harp.

5 Why should I fear in the days of evil,
When the iniquity at my heels
surrounds me?
6 Those who trust in their wealth
And boast in the multitude of their
riches,
7 None *of them* can by any means redeem
his brother,
Nor give to God a ransom for him—
8 For the redemption of their souls *is*
costly,
And it shall cease forever—
9 That he should continue to live
eternally,
And not see the Pit.

10 For he sees wise men die;
Likewise the fool and the senseless
person perish,
And leave their wealth to others.
11 Their inner thought *is that* their houses
will last forever,[a]
Their dwelling places to all generations;
They call *their* lands after their own
names.
12 Nevertheless man, *though* in honor,
does not remain;[a]
He is like the beasts *that* perish.

13 This is the way of those who *are* foolish,
And of their posterity who approve their
sayings. *Selah*
14 Like sheep they are laid in the grave;
Death shall feed on them;

48:14 [a] Following Masoretic Text and Syriac; Septuagint and Vulgate read *Forever.* **49:11** [a] Septuagint, Syriac, Targum, and Vulgate read *Their graves shall be their houses forever.* **49:12** [a] Following Masoretic Text and Targum; Septuagint, Syriac, and Vulgate read *understand* (compare verse 20).

The upright shall have dominion over them in the morning;
And their beauty shall be consumed in the grave, far from their dwelling.
15 But God will redeem my soul from the power of the grave,
For He shall receive me. *Selah*

16 Do not be afraid when one becomes rich,
When the glory of his house is increased;
17 For when he dies he shall carry nothing away;
His glory shall not descend after him.
18 Though while he lives he blesses himself
(For *men* will praise you when you do well for yourself),
19 He shall go to the generation of his fathers;
They shall never see light.
20 A man *who is* in honor, yet does not understand,
Is like the beasts *that* perish.

PSALM 50

God the Righteous Judge

A Psalm of Asaph.

1 The Mighty One, God the LORD,
Has spoken and called the earth
From the rising of the sun to its going down.
2 Out of Zion, the perfection of beauty,
God will shine forth.
3 Our God shall come, and shall not keep silent;
A fire shall devour before Him,
And it shall be very tempestuous all around Him.

4 He shall call to the heavens from above,
And to the earth, that He may judge His people:
5 "Gather My saints together to Me,
Those who have made a covenant with Me by sacrifice."
6 Let the heavens declare His righteousness,
For God Himself *is* Judge. *Selah*

7 "Hear, O My people, and I will speak,
O Israel, and I will testify against you;
I *am* God, your God!
8 I will not rebuke you for your sacrifices
Or your burnt offerings,
Which are continually before Me.
9 I will not take a bull from your house,
Nor goats out of your folds.
10 For every beast of the forest *is* Mine,
And the cattle on a thousand hills.
11 I know all the birds of the mountains,
And the wild beasts of the field *are* Mine.

12 "If I were hungry, I would not tell you;
For the world *is* Mine, and all its fullness.
13 Will I eat the flesh of bulls,
Or drink the blood of goats?
14 Offer to God thanksgiving,
And pay your vows to the Most High.
15 Call upon Me in the day of trouble;
I will deliver you, and you shall glorify Me."

16 But to the wicked God says:
"What *right* have you to declare My statutes,
Or take My covenant in your mouth,
17 Seeing you hate instruction
And cast My words behind you?
18 When you saw a thief, you consented[a] with him,
And have been a partaker with adulterers.
19 You give your mouth to evil,
And your tongue frames deceit.
20 You sit *and* speak against your brother;
You slander your own mother's son.
21 These *things* you have done, and I kept silent;
You thought that I was altogether like you;
But I will rebuke you,
And set *them* in order before your eyes.

22 "Now consider this, you who forget God,
Lest I tear *you* in pieces,
And *there be* none to deliver:
23 Whoever offers praise glorifies Me;
And to him who orders *his* conduct *aright*
I will show the salvation of God."

PSALM 51

A Prayer of Repentance

To the Chief Musician. A Psalm of David when Nathan the prophet went to him, after he had gone in to Bathsheba.

1 Have mercy upon me, O God,
According to Your lovingkindness;

50:18 [a] Septuagint, Syriac, Targum, and Vulgate read *ran.*

According to the multitude of Your
tender mercies,
Blot out my transgressions.
2 Wash me thoroughly from my iniquity,
And cleanse me from my sin.

3 For I acknowledge my transgressions,
And my sin *is* always before me.
4 Against You, You only, have I sinned,
And done *this* evil in Your sight—
That You may be found just when You
speak,[a]
And blameless when You judge.

5 Behold, I was brought forth in iniquity,
And in sin my mother conceived me.
6 Behold, You desire truth in the inward
parts,
And in the hidden *part* You will make
me to know wisdom.

7 Purge me with hyssop, and I shall be
clean;
Wash me, and I shall be whiter than
snow.
8 Make me hear joy and gladness,
That the bones You have broken may
rejoice.
9 Hide Your face from my sins,
And blot out all my iniquities.

10 Create in me a clean heart, O God,
And renew a steadfast spirit within me.
11 Do not cast me away from Your
presence,

51:4 [a] Septuagint, Targum, and Vulgate read *in Your words.*

Epic Ideas

SIN HEART CLEANING

READ IT: PSALM 51:1–18

GET IT:

When King David wrote this psalm he was drowning in guilt. He had done some really bad things that hurt a lot of people. But he knew he served a God big enough to forgive him and make him new again. He knew that what God wanted from him was not a big show, but a quiet act of repentance. God wanted a humble heart ready for some holy healing.

David's words make a perfect prayer. Offer them to God when you know your actions have hurt Him. David knew God needed to scrub his sins off his conscience and his heart to prevent them from leaving deep scars. He needed God to make him clean again. So David asked God for mercy and a new heart.

LIVE IT:

If you've messed up, you need healing like King David did. You need God to clean you up again. Tell God about your sin. It's hard to take this first step, but it's an important part of healing.

Ask God to scrub the sin, the shame, and the guilt from your heart and your mind. Ask God to give you a clean spirit that is ready to serve Him. Finally, thank God for His mercy. He forgave David, and He will forgive you, too—no matter what you've done.

And do not take Your Holy Spirit
from me.

12 Restore to me the joy of Your salvation,
And uphold me *by Your* generous Spirit.
13 *Then* I will teach transgressors Your
ways,
And sinners shall be converted to You.

14 Deliver me from the guilt of bloodshed,
O God,
The God of my salvation,
And my tongue shall sing aloud of Your
righteousness.
15 O Lord, open my lips,
And my mouth shall show forth Your
praise.
16 For You do not desire sacrifice, or else I
would give *it;*
You do not delight in burnt offering.
17 The sacrifices of God *are* a broken spirit,
A broken and a contrite heart—
These, O God, You will not despise.

18 Do good in Your good pleasure to Zion;
Build the walls of Jerusalem.
19 Then You shall be pleased with the
sacrifices of righteousness,
With burnt offering and whole burnt
offering;
Then they shall offer bulls on Your altar.

PSALM 52

The End of the Wicked and the Peace of the Godly

To the Chief Musician. A Contemplation[a] of David when Doeg the Edomite went and told Saul, and said to him, "David has gone to the house of Ahimelech."

1 Why do you boast in evil, O mighty
man?
The goodness of God *endures*
continually.
2 Your tongue devises destruction,
Like a sharp razor, working deceitfully.
3 You love evil more than good,
Lying rather than speaking
righteousness. *Selah*
4 You love all devouring words,
You deceitful tongue.

5 God shall likewise destroy you forever;
He shall take you away, and pluck you
out of *your* dwelling place,
And uproot you from the land of the
living. *Selah*

6 The righteous also shall see and fear,
And shall laugh at him, *saying,*
7 "Here is the man *who* did not make God
his strength,
But trusted in the abundance of his
riches,
And strengthened himself in his
wickedness."

8 But I *am* like a green olive tree in the
house of God;
I trust in the mercy of God forever and
ever.
9 I will praise You forever,
Because You have done *it;*
And in the presence of Your saints
I will wait on Your name, for *it is* good.

PSALM 53

Folly of the Godless, and the Restoration of Israel

To the Chief Musician. Set to "Mahalath." A Contemplation[a] of David.

1 The fool has said in his heart,
"*There is* no God."
They are corrupt, and have done
abominable iniquity;
There is none who does good.

2 God looks down from heaven upon the
children of men,
To see if there are *any* who understand,
who seek God.
3 Every one of them has turned aside;
They have together become corrupt;
There is none who does good,
No, not one.

4 Have the workers of iniquity no
knowledge,
Who eat up my people *as* they eat bread,
And do not call upon God?
5 There they are in great fear
Where no fear was,
For God has scattered the bones of him
who encamps against you;
You have put *them* to shame,
Because God has despised them.

6 Oh, that the salvation of Israel would
come out of Zion!
When God brings back the captivity of
His people,
Let Jacob rejoice *and* Israel be glad.

52:title [a] Hebrew *Maschil* **53:title** [a] Hebrew *Maschil*

PSALM 54

Answered Prayer for Deliverance from Adversaries

To the Chief Musician. With stringed instruments.[a] A Contemplation[b] of David when the Ziphites went and said to Saul, "Is David not hiding with us?"

1 Save me, O God, by Your name,
And vindicate me by Your strength.
2 Hear my prayer, O God;
Give ear to the words of my mouth.
3 For strangers have risen up against me,
And oppressors have sought after my life;
They have not set God before them. *Selah*

4 Behold, God *is* my helper;
The Lord *is* with those who uphold my life.
5 He will repay my enemies for their evil.
Cut them off in Your truth.

6 I will freely sacrifice to You;
I will praise Your name, O LORD, for *it is* good.
7 For He has delivered me out of all trouble;
And my eye has seen *its desire* upon my enemies.

PSALM 55

Trust in God Concerning the Treachery of Friends

To the Chief Musician. With stringed instruments.[a] A Contemplation[b] of David.

1 Give ear to my prayer, O God,
And do not hide Yourself from my supplication.
2 Attend to me, and hear me;
I am restless in my complaint, and moan noisily,
3 Because of the voice of the enemy,
Because of the oppression of the wicked;
For they bring down trouble upon me,
And in wrath they hate me.

4 My heart is severely pained within me,
And the terrors of death have fallen upon me.
5 *Fearfulness and trembling* have come upon me,
And horror has overwhelmed me.
6 So I said, "Oh, that I had wings like a dove!
I would fly away and be at rest.
7 Indeed, I would wander far off,
And remain in the wilderness. *Selah*
8 I would hasten my escape
From the windy storm *and* tempest."

9 Destroy, O Lord, *and* divide their tongues,
For I have seen violence and strife in the city.
10 Day and night they go around it on its walls;
Iniquity and trouble *are* also in the midst of it.
11 Destruction *is* in its midst;
Oppression and deceit do not depart from its streets.

12 For *it is* not an enemy *who* reproaches me;
Then I could bear *it*.
Nor *is it* one *who* hates me who has exalted *himself* against me;
Then I could hide from him.
13 But *it was* you, a man my equal,
My companion and my acquaintance.
14 We took sweet counsel together,
And walked to the house of God in the throng.

15 Let death seize them;
Let them go down alive into hell,
For wickedness *is* in their dwellings *and* among them.

16 As for me, I will call upon God,
And the LORD shall save me.
17 Evening and morning and at noon
I will pray, and cry aloud,
And He shall hear my voice.
18 He has redeemed my soul in peace from the battle *that was* against me,
For there were many against me.
19 God will hear, and afflict them,
Even He who abides from of old. *Selah*
Because they do not change,
Therefore they do not fear God.

20 He has put forth his hands against those who were at peace with him;
He has broken his covenant.
21 *The words* of his mouth were smoother than butter,
But war *was* in his heart;

54:title [a] Hebrew *neginoth* [b] Hebrew *Maschil*
55:title [a] Hebrew *neginoth* [b] Hebrew *Maschil*

His words were softer than oil,
Yet they *were* drawn swords.

22 Cast your burden on the LORD,
And He shall sustain you;
He shall never permit the righteous to be moved.

23 But You, O God, shall bring them down to the pit of destruction;
Bloodthirsty and deceitful men shall not live out half their days;
But I will trust in You.

PSALM 56

Prayer for Relief from Tormentors

To the Chief Musician. Set to "The Silent Dove in Distant Lands."[a] A Michtam of David when the Philistines captured him in Gath.

1 Be merciful to me, O God, for man would swallow me up;
Fighting all day he oppresses me.
2 My enemies would hound *me* all day,
For *there are* many who fight against me, O Most High.

3 Whenever I am afraid,
I will trust in You.
4 In God (I will praise His word),
In God I have put my trust;
I will not fear.
What can flesh do to me?

5 All day they twist my words;
All their thoughts *are* against me for evil.
6 They gather together,
They hide, they mark my steps,
When they lie in wait for my life.
7 Shall they escape by iniquity?
In anger cast down the peoples, O God!

8 You number my wanderings;
Put my tears into Your bottle;
Are they not in Your book?
9 When I cry out *to You,*
Then my enemies will turn back;
This I know, because God *is* for me.
10 In God (I will praise *His* word),
In the LORD (I will praise *His* word),
11 In God I have put my trust;
I will not be afraid.
What can man do to me?

12 Vows *made* to You *are binding* upon me, O God;
I will render praises to You,
13 For You have delivered my soul from death.
Have You not *kept* my feet from falling,
That I may walk before God
In the light of the living?

PSALM 57

Prayer for Safety from Enemies

To the Chief Musician. Set to "Do Not Destroy."[a] A Michtam of David when he fled from Saul into the cave.

1 Be merciful to me, O God, be merciful to me!
For my soul trusts in You;

56:title [a] Hebrew *Jonath Elem Rechokim* **57:title** [a] Hebrew *Al Tashcheth*

COURAGE

READ IT: PSALM 56:3–11

People can be mean. In the news we learn about everything there is to be afraid of. Nothing is certain in our world, and that can be scary. When we're afraid, we should trust in God. He always has our best interest in mind and knows exactly what we're up against. When everything else seems to fall apart, God is the One we can always count on!

And in the shadow of Your wings I will make my refuge,
Until *these* calamities have passed by.

2 I will cry out to God Most High,
To God who performs *all things* for me.
3 He shall send from heaven and save me;
He reproaches the one who would swallow me up. *Selah*
God shall send forth His mercy and His truth.

4 My soul *is* among lions;
I lie *among* the sons of men
Who are set on fire,
Whose teeth *are* spears and arrows,
And their tongue a sharp sword.
5 Be exalted, O God, above the heavens;
Let Your glory *be* above all the earth.

6 They have prepared a net for my steps;
My soul is bowed down;
They have dug a pit before me;
Into the midst of it they *themselves* have fallen. *Selah*

7 My heart is steadfast, O God, my heart is steadfast;
I will sing and give praise.
8 Awake, my glory!
Awake, lute and harp!
I will awaken the dawn.

9 I will praise You, O Lord, among the peoples;
I will sing to You among the nations.
10 For Your mercy reaches unto the heavens,
And Your truth unto the clouds.

11 Be exalted, O God, above the heavens;
Let Your glory *be* above all the earth.

PSALM 58

The Just Judgment of the Wicked

To the Chief Musician. Set to "Do Not Destroy."[a] A Michtam of David.

1 Do you indeed speak righteousness, you silent ones?
Do you judge uprightly, you sons of men?
2 No, in heart you work wickedness;
You weigh out the violence of your hands in the earth.

3 The wicked are estranged from the womb;
They go astray as soon as they are born, speaking lies.
4 Their poison *is* like the poison of a serpent;
They are like the deaf cobra *that* stops its ear,
5 Which will not heed the voice of charmers,
Charming ever so skillfully.

6 Break their teeth in their mouth, O God!
Break out the fangs of the young lions, O LORD!
7 Let them flow away as waters *which* run continually;
When he bends *his bow,*
Let his arrows be as if cut in pieces.
8 *Let them be* like a snail which melts away as it goes,
Like a stillborn child of a woman, that they may not see the sun.

9 Before your pots can feel *the burning* thorns,
He shall take them away as with a whirlwind,
As in His living and burning wrath.
10 The righteous shall rejoice when he sees the vengeance;
He shall wash his feet in the blood of the wicked,
11 So that men will say,
"Surely *there is* a reward for the righteous;
Surely He is God who judges in the earth."

PSALM 59

The Assured Judgment of the Wicked

To the Chief Musician. Set to "Do Not Destroy."[a] A Michtam of David when Saul sent men, and they watched the house in order to kill him.

1 Deliver me from my enemies, O my God;
Defend me from those who rise up against me.
2 Deliver me from the workers of iniquity,
And save me from bloodthirsty men.

3 For look, they lie in wait for my life;
The mighty gather against me,

58:title [a] Hebrew *Al Taschcheth* **59:title** [a] Hebrew *Al Taschcheth*

Not *for* my transgression nor *for* my sin,
O LORD.
4 They run and prepare themselves
through no fault *of mine.*

Awake to help me, and behold!
5 You therefore, O LORD God of hosts, the
God of Israel,
Awake to punish all the nations;
Do not be merciful to any wicked
transgressors. *Selah*

6 At evening they return,
They growl like a dog,
And go all around the city.
7 Indeed, they belch with their mouth;
Swords *are* in their lips;
For *they say,* "Who hears?"

8 But You, O LORD, shall laugh at them;
You shall have all the nations in
derision.
9 I will wait for You, O You his Strength;[a]
For God *is* my defense.
10 My God of mercy[a] shall come to meet
me;
God shall let me see *my desire* on my
enemies.

11 Do not slay them, lest my people forget;
Scatter them by Your power,
And bring them down,
O Lord our shield.
12 *For* the sin of their mouth *and* the words
of their lips,
Let them even be taken in their pride,
And for the cursing and lying *which*
they speak.
13 Consume *them* in wrath, consume
them,
That they *may* not *be;*
And let them know that God rules in
Jacob
To the ends of the earth. *Selah*

14 And at evening they return,
They growl like a dog,
And go all around the city.
15 They wander up and down for food,
And howl[a] if they are not satisfied.

16 But I will sing of Your power;
Yes, I will sing aloud of Your mercy in
the morning;
For You have been my defense
And refuge in the day of my trouble.
17 To You, O my Strength, I will sing
praises;
For God *is* my defense,
My God of mercy.

PSALM 60

Urgent Prayer for the Restored Favor of God

To the Chief Musician. Set to "Lily of the Testimony."[a] A Michtam of David. For teaching. When he fought against Mesopotamia and Syria of Zobah, and Joab returned and killed twelve thousand Edomites in the Valley of Salt.

1 O God, You have cast us off;
You have broken us down;
You have been displeased;
Oh, restore us again!
2 You have made the earth tremble;
You have broken it;
Heal its breaches, for it is shaking.
3 You have shown Your people hard
things;
You have made us drink the wine of
confusion.

4 You have given a banner to those who
fear You,
That it may be displayed because of the
truth. *Selah*
5 That Your beloved may be delivered,
Save *with* Your right hand, and hear me.

6 God has spoken in His holiness:
"I will rejoice;
I will divide Shechem
And measure out the Valley of Succoth.
7 Gilead *is* Mine, and Manasseh *is* Mine;
Ephraim also *is* the helmet for My head;
Judah *is* My lawgiver.
8 Moab *is* My washpot;
Over Edom I will cast My shoe;
Philistia, shout in triumph because of
Me."

9 Who will bring me *to* the strong city?
Who will lead me to Edom?
10 *Is it* not You, O God, *who* cast us off?
And You, O God, *who* did not go out
with our armies?

59:9 [a] Following Masoretic Text and Syriac; some Hebrew manuscripts, Septuagint, Targum, and Vulgate read *my Strength.* **59:10** [a] Following Qere; some Hebrew manuscripts, Septuagint, and Vulgate read *My God, His mercy;* Kethib, some Hebrew manuscripts and Targum read *O God, my mercy;* Syriac reads *O God, Your mercy.* **59:15** [a] Following Septuagint and Vulgate; Masoretic Text, Syriac, and Targum read *spend the night.* **60:title** [a] Hebrew *Shushan Eduth*

11 Give us help from trouble,
For the help of man *is* useless.
12 Through God we will do valiantly,
For *it is* He *who* shall tread down our enemies.[a]

PSALM 61

Assurance of God's Eternal Protection

To the Chief Musician. On a stringed instrument.[a] *A Psalm* of David.

1 Hear my cry, O God;
Attend to my prayer.
2 From the end of the earth I will cry to You,
When my heart is overwhelmed;
Lead me to the rock that is higher than I.

3 For You have been a shelter for me,
A strong tower from the enemy.
4 I will abide in Your tabernacle forever;
I will trust in the shelter of Your wings. *Selah*

5 For You, O God, have heard my vows;
You have given *me* the heritage of those who fear Your name.
6 You will prolong the king's life,
His years as many generations.
7 He shall abide before God forever.
Oh, prepare mercy and truth, *which* may preserve him!

8 So I will sing praise to Your name forever,
That I may daily perform my vows.

PSALM 62

A Calm Resolve to Wait for the Salvation of God

To the Chief Musician. To Jeduthun. A Psalm of David.

1 Truly my soul silently *waits* for God;
From Him *comes* my salvation.
2 He only *is* my rock and my salvation;
He is my defense;
I shall not be greatly moved.

3 How long will you attack a man?
You shall be slain, all of you,
Like a leaning wall and a tottering fence.
4 They only consult to cast *him* down from his high position;
They delight in lies;
They bless with their mouth,

60:12 [a] Compare verses 5–12 with 108:6–13
61:title [a] Hebrew *neginah*

63:1 ARE YOU THIRSTY FOR GOD?

Have you ever been so thirsty you thought you couldn't go another minute without a drink of water? Of course you have. That's the way God wants you to feel about Him. Life is weary and dry without God to be with you and lead you.

Not all people know how much they need God. That's very sad, because they really need Him even if they don't know they do. God wants you to desire Him more than everything else in life. After all, knowing God is worth more than anything you can ever own.

It's nice to have a home and friends and possessions. But without God, nothing in this world is worth living for. With God, life is exciting, and *you will always be* satisfied. He knows your needs better than you do. But God must come first in everything. He is always nearby, waiting for the invitation to come into your life.

But they curse inwardly. *Selah*

5 My soul, wait silently for God alone,
For my expectation *is* from Him.
6 He only *is* my rock and my salvation;
He is my defense;
I shall not be moved.
7 In God *is* my salvation and my glory;
The rock of my strength,
And my refuge, *is* in God.

8 Trust in Him at all times, you people;
Pour out your heart before Him;
God *is* a refuge for us. *Selah*

9 Surely men of low degree *are* a vapor,
Men of high degree *are* a lie;
If they are weighed on the scales,
They *are* altogether *lighter* than vapor.
10 Do not trust in oppression,
Nor vainly hope in robbery;
If riches increase,
Do not set *your* heart *on them.*

11 God has spoken once,
Twice I have heard this:
That power *belongs* to God.
12 Also to You, O Lord, *belongs* mercy;
For You render to each one according to
his work.

PSALM 63

Joy in the Fellowship of God

A Psalm of David when he was
in the wilderness of Judah.

1 O God, You *are* my God;
Early will I seek You;
My soul thirsts for You;
My flesh longs for You
In a dry and thirsty land
Where there is no water.
2 So I have looked for You in the
sanctuary,
To see Your power and Your glory.

3 Because Your lovingkindness *is* better
than life,
My lips shall praise You.
4 Thus I will bless You while I live;
I will lift up my hands in Your name.
5 My soul shall be satisfied as with
marrow and fatness,
And my mouth shall praise *You* with
joyful lips.

6 When I remember You on my bed,
I meditate on You in the *night* watches.
7 Because You have been my help,
Therefore in the shadow of Your wings I
will rejoice.
8 My soul follows close behind You;
Your right hand upholds me.

9 But those *who* seek my life, to destroy *it,*
Shall go into the lower parts of the
earth.
10 They shall fall by the sword;
They shall be a portion for jackals.

11 But the king shall rejoice in God;
Everyone who swears by Him shall
glory;
But the mouth of those who speak lies
shall be stopped.

PSALM 64

Oppressed by the Wicked but Rejoicing in the LORD

To the Chief Musician. A Psalm of David.

1 Hear my voice, O God, in my
meditation;
Preserve my life from fear of the enemy.
2 Hide me from the secret plots of the
wicked,
From the rebellion of the workers of
iniquity,
3 Who sharpen their tongue like a sword,
And bend *their bows to shoot* their
arrows—bitter words,
4 That they may shoot in secret at the
blameless;
Suddenly they shoot at him and do not
fear.

5 They encourage themselves *in* an evil
matter;
They talk of laying snares secretly;
They say, "Who will see them?"
6 They devise iniquities:
"We have perfected a shrewd scheme."
Both the inward thought and the heart
of man are deep.

7 But God shall shoot at them *with* an
arrow;
Suddenly they shall be wounded.
8 So He will make them stumble over
their own tongue;
All who see them shall flee away.
9 All men shall fear,
And shall declare the work of God;

For they shall wisely consider His doing.
10 The righteous shall be glad in the LORD, and trust in Him.
And all the upright in heart shall glory.

PSALM 65

Praise to God for His Salvation and Providence

To the Chief Musician. A Psalm of David. A Song.

1 Praise is awaiting You, O God, in Zion;
And to You the vow shall be performed.
2 O You who hear prayer,
To You all flesh will come.
3 Iniquities prevail against me;
As for our transgressions,
You will provide atonement for them.

4 Blessed *is the man* You choose,
And cause to approach *You,*
That he may dwell in Your courts.
We shall be satisfied with the goodness of Your house,
Of Your holy temple.

5 *By* awesome deeds in righteousness You will answer us,
O God of our salvation,
You who are the confidence of all the ends of the earth,
And of the far-off seas;
6 Who established the mountains by His strength,
Being clothed with power;
7 You who still the noise of the seas,
The noise of their waves,
And the tumult of the peoples.
8 They also who dwell in the farthest parts are afraid of Your signs;
You make the outgoings of the morning and evening rejoice.

9 You visit the earth and water it,
You greatly enrich it;
The river of God is full of water;
You provide their grain,
For so You have prepared it.
10 You water its ridges abundantly,
You settle its furrows;
You make it soft with showers,
You bless its growth.

11 You crown the year with Your goodness,
And Your paths drip *with* abundance.
12 They drop *on* the pastures of the wilderness,
And the little hills rejoice on every side.
13 The pastures are clothed with flocks;
The valleys also are covered with grain;
They shout for joy, they also sing.

PSALM 66

Praise to God for His Awesome Works

To the Chief Musician. A Song. A Psalm.

1 Make a joyful shout to God, all the earth!
2 Sing out the honor of His name;
Make His praise glorious.
3 Say to God,
"How awesome are Your works!
Through the greatness of Your power
Your enemies shall submit themselves to You.
4 All the earth shall worship You
And sing praises to You;
They shall sing praises *to* Your name."
Selah

5 Come and see the works of God;
He is awesome *in His* doing toward the sons of men.
6 He turned the sea into dry *land;*
They went through the river on foot.
There we will rejoice in Him.
7 He rules by His power forever;
His eyes observe the nations;
Do not let the rebellious exalt themselves. *Selah*

8 Oh, bless our God, you peoples!
And make the voice of His praise to be heard,
9 Who keeps our soul among the living,
And does not allow our feet to be moved.
10 For You, O God, have tested us;
You have refined us as silver is refined.
11 You brought us into the net;
You laid affliction on our backs.
12 You have caused men to ride over our heads;
We went through fire and through water;
But You brought us out to rich *fulfillment.*

13 I will go into Your house with burnt offerings;

I will pay You my vows,
14 Which my lips have uttered
And my mouth has spoken when I was in trouble.
15 I will offer You burnt sacrifices of fat animals,
With the sweet aroma of rams;
I will offer bulls with goats. *Selah*

16 Come *and* hear, all you who fear God,
And I will declare what He has done for my soul.
17 I cried to Him with my mouth,
And He was extolled with my tongue.
18 If I regard iniquity in my heart,
The Lord will not hear.
19 *But* certainly God has heard *me;*
He has attended to the voice of my prayer.

20 Blessed *be* God,
Who has not turned away my prayer,
Nor His mercy from me!

PSALM 67

An Invocation and a Doxology

To the Chief Musician. On stringed instruments.[a] A Psalm. A Song.

1 God be merciful to us and bless us,
And cause His face to shine upon us, *Selah*

2 That Your way may be known on earth,
Your salvation among all nations.

3 Let the peoples praise You, O God;
Let all the peoples praise You.
4 Oh, let the nations be glad and sing for joy!
For You shall judge the people righteously,
And govern the nations on earth. *Selah*

5 Let the peoples praise You, O God;
Let all the peoples praise You.
6 *Then* the earth shall yield her increase;
God, our own God, shall bless us.
7 God shall bless us,
And all the ends of the earth shall fear Him.

PSALM 68

The Glory of God in His Goodness to Israel

To the Chief Musician. A Psalm of David. A Song.

1 Let God arise,
Let His enemies be scattered;
Let those also who hate Him flee before Him.
2 As smoke is driven away,
So drive *them* away;
As wax melts before the fire,
So let the wicked perish at the presence of God.
3 But let the righteous be glad;
Let them rejoice before God;
Yes, let them rejoice exceedingly.

4 Sing to God, sing praises to His name;
Extol Him who rides on the clouds,[a]
By His name YAH,
And rejoice before Him.

5 A father of the fatherless, a defender of widows,
Is God in His holy habitation.
6 God sets the solitary in families;
He brings out those who are bound into prosperity;
But the rebellious dwell in a dry *land.*

7 O God, when You went out before Your people,
When You marched through the wilderness, *Selah*
8 The earth shook;
The heavens also dropped *rain* at the presence of God;
Sinai itself *was moved* at the presence of God, the God of Israel.
9 You, O God, sent a plentiful rain,
Whereby You confirmed Your inheritance,
When it was weary.
10 Your congregation dwelt in it;
You, O God, provided from Your goodness for the poor.

11 The Lord gave the word;
Great *was* the company of those who proclaimed *it:*
12 "Kings of armies flee, they flee,
And she who remains at home divides the spoil.
13 Though you lie down among the sheepfolds,
You will be like the wings of a dove covered with silver,
And her feathers with yellow gold."

67:title [a] Hebrew *neginoth* 68:4 [a] Masoretic Text reads *deserts;* Targum reads *heavens* (compare verse 34 and Isaiah 19:1).

14 When the Almighty scattered kings in it,
It was *white* as snow in Zalmon.

15 A mountain of God *is* the mountain of Bashan;
A mountain *of many* peaks *is* the mountain of Bashan.
16 Why do you fume with envy, you mountains of *many* peaks?
This is the mountain *which* God desires to dwell in;
Yes, the LORD will dwell *in it* forever.

17 The chariots of God *are* twenty thousand,
Even thousands of thousands;
The Lord is among them *as in* Sinai, in the Holy *Place*.
18 You have ascended on high,
You have led captivity captive;
You have received gifts among men,
Even *from* the rebellious,
That the LORD God might dwell *there*.

19 Blessed *be* the Lord,
Who daily loads us *with benefits*,
The God of our salvation! *Selah*
20 Our God *is* the God of salvation;
And to GOD the Lord *belong* escapes from death.

21 But God will wound the head of His enemies,
The hairy scalp of the one who still goes on in his trespasses.
22 The Lord said, "I will bring back from Bashan,
I will bring *them* back from the depths of the sea,

In Focus

68:19 Salvation Pronounced *sal-VAY-shun*. A work of saving someone from danger or death. In the New Testament, salvation is Christ's work of dying to save us from sin and hell.

23 That your foot may crush *them*[a] in blood,
And the tongues of your dogs *may have* their portion from *your* enemies."

24 They have seen Your procession, O God,
The procession of my God, my King, into the sanctuary.
25 The singers went before, the players on instruments *followed* after;
Among *them were* the maidens playing timbrels.
26 Bless God in the congregations,
The Lord, from the fountain of Israel.
27 There *is* little Benjamin, their leader,
The princes of Judah *and* their company,
The princes of Zebulun *and* the princes of Naphtali.

68:23 [a] Septuagint, Syriac, Targum, and Vulgate read *you may dip your foot*.

Action!

LONELINESS

READ IT: PSALM 68:5, 6

Who are some of the loneliest people in the world today? Children who are missing their families? Someone whose husband or wife has died? God intended for the family to be a safe place so that we would always have someone in our lives. But this doesn't always happen. Sadly, children are left alone and people die. But God sees this and fills in the gaps.

28 Your God has commanded[a] your
strength;
Strengthen, O God, what You have done
for us.
29 Because of Your temple at Jerusalem,
Kings will bring presents to You.
30 Rebuke the beasts of the reeds,
The herd of bulls with the calves of the
peoples,
Till everyone submits himself with
pieces of silver.
Scatter the peoples *who* delight in war.
31 Envoys will come out of Egypt;
Ethiopia will quickly stretch out her
hands to God.

32 Sing to God, you kingdoms of the
earth;
Oh, sing praises to the Lord, *Selah*
33 To Him who rides on the heaven of
heavens, *which were* of old!
Indeed, He sends out His voice, a
mighty voice.
34 Ascribe strength to God;
His excellence *is* over Israel,
And His strength *is* in the clouds.
35 O God, *You are* more awesome than
Your holy places.
The God of Israel *is* He who gives
strength and power to *His* people.

Blessed *be* God!

PSALM 69

An Urgent Plea for Help in Trouble

To the Chief Musician. Set to
"The Lilies."[a] A *Psalm* of David.

1 Save me, O God!
For the waters have come up to
my neck.
2 I sink in deep mire,
Where *there is* no standing;
I have come into deep waters,
Where the floods overflow me.
3 I am weary with my crying;
My throat is dry;
My eyes fail while I wait for my God.

4 Those who hate me without a cause
Are more than the hairs of my head;
They are mighty who would destroy me,
Being my enemies wrongfully;
Though I have stolen nothing,
I *still* must restore *it*.
5 O God, You know my foolishness;
And my sins are not hidden from You.
6 Let not those who wait for You, O Lord
God of hosts, be ashamed because of
me;
Let not those who seek You be
confounded because of me, O God
of Israel.
7 Because for Your sake I have borne
reproach;
Shame has covered my face.
8 I have become a stranger to my
brothers,
And an alien to my mother's children;
9 Because zeal for Your house has eaten
me up,
And the reproaches of those who
reproach You have fallen on me.
10 When I wept *and chastened* my soul with
fasting,
That became my reproach.
11 I also made sackcloth my garment;
I became a byword to them.
12 Those who sit in the gate speak against
me,
And I *am* the song of the drunkards.

13 But as for me, my prayer *is* to You,
O Lord, *in* the acceptable time;
O God, in the multitude of Your
mercy,
Hear me in the truth of Your salvation.
14 Deliver me out of the mire,
And let me not sink;
Let me be delivered from those who
hate me,
And out of the deep waters.
15 Let not the floodwater overflow me,
Nor let the deep swallow me up;
And let not the pit shut its mouth
on me.

16 Hear me, O Lord, for Your
lovingkindness *is* good;
Turn to me according to the multitude
of Your tender mercies.
17 And do not hide Your face from Your
servant,
For I am in trouble;
Hear me speedily.
18 Draw near to my soul, *and* redeem it;
Deliver me because of my enemies.

68:28 [a] Septuagint, Syriac, Targum, and Vulgate read *Command, O God.* **69:title** [a] Hebrew *Shoshannim*

19 You know my reproach, my shame, and
my dishonor;
My adversaries *are* all before You.
20 Reproach has broken my heart,
And I am full of heaviness;
I looked *for someone* to take pity, but
there was none;
And for comforters, but I found none.
21 They also gave me gall for my food,
And for my thirst they gave me vinegar
to drink.

22 Let their table become a snare before
them,
And their well-being a trap.
23 Let their eyes be darkened, so that they
do not see;
And make their loins shake continually.
24 Pour out Your indignation upon them,
And let Your wrathful anger take hold
of them.
25 Let their dwelling place be desolate;
Let no one live in their tents.
26 For they persecute the *ones* You have
struck,
And talk of the grief of those You have
wounded.
27 Add iniquity to their iniquity,
And let them not come into Your
righteousness.
28 Let them be blotted out of the book of
the living,
And not be written with the righteous.

29 But I *am* poor and sorrowful;
Let Your salvation, O God, set me up
on high.
30 I will praise the name of God with a
song,
And will magnify Him with
thanksgiving.
31 *This* also shall please the LORD better
than an ox *or* bull,
Which has horns and hooves.
32 The humble shall see *this and* be glad;
And you who seek God, your hearts
shall live.
33 For the LORD hears the poor,
And does not despise His prisoners.

34 Let heaven and earth praise Him,
The seas and everything that moves in
them.
35 For God will save Zion
And build the cities of Judah,
That they may dwell there and
possess it.

69:17 GOD CARES WHEN YOU ARE IN TROUBLE

Do you sometimes feel all alone with troubles you can't help or understand? You may have no human person you can talk to, but there is a divine Person who cares very much about you. His name is Jesus, which means "Savior." A savior is someone who rescues from danger. Jesus is the great Savior who is always ready to rescue you from the things that trouble you most.

If you have a broken bicycle, you take it to someone who knows all about bicycles to repair it. Jesus knows all about you, and He wants you to come with all the broken pieces of your life and ask Him to mend them. Jesus can do that.

First, however, you must ask Jesus to help you. Go to a place alone and *tell Him all about your trouble.* He will show you the way out of it. He will lead you to somebody you can trust. Jesus knows you and cares about you more than you know.

36 Also, the descendants of His servants
shall inherit it,
And those who love His name shall
dwell in it.

PSALM 70

Prayer for Relief from Adversaries

To the Chief Musician. *A Psalm* of David.
To bring to remembrance.

1 *Make haste,* O God, to deliver me!
Make haste to help me, O LORD!

2 Let them be ashamed and confounded
Who seek my life;
Let them be turned back[a] and confused
Who desire my hurt.
3 Let them be turned back because of
their shame,
Who say, "Aha, aha!"

4 Let all those who seek You rejoice and
be glad in You;
And let those who love Your salvation
say continually,
"Let God be magnified!"

5 But I *am* poor and needy;
Make haste to me, O God!
You *are* my help and my deliverer;
O LORD, do not delay.

PSALM 71

God the Rock of Salvation

1 In You, O LORD, I put my trust;
Let me never be put to shame.
2 Deliver me in Your righteousness, and
cause me to escape;
Incline Your ear to me, and save me.
3 Be my strong refuge,
To which I may resort continually;
You have given the commandment to
save me,
For You *are* my rock and my fortress.

4 Deliver me, O my God, out of the hand
of the wicked,
Out of the hand of the unrighteous and
cruel man.
5 For You are my hope, O Lord GOD;
You are my trust from my youth.
6 By You I have been upheld from birth;
You are He who took me out of my
mother's womb.
My praise *shall be* continually of You.

7 I have become as a wonder to many,
But You *are* my strong refuge.
8 Let my mouth be filled *with* Your praise
And with Your glory all the day.

9 Do not cast me off in the time of old
age;
Do not forsake me when my strength
fails.
10 For my enemies speak against me;
And those who lie in wait for my life
take counsel together,
11 Saying, "God has forsaken him;

70:2 [a] Following Masoretic Text, Septuagint, Targum, and Vulgate; some Hebrew manuscripts and Syriac read *be appalled* (compare 40:15).

HOPE

READ IT: PSALM 71:14

David wrote this when he was struggling with his enemies. He called upon the Lord for help. David told God that he would continue to have hope and would praise God in spite of his troubles. In your life, when things aren't going the way you want them to and it feels like all hope is gone, have hope anyway. God is always faithful.

Pursue and take him, for *there is* none to deliver *him*."

12 O God, do not be far from me;
O my God, make haste to help me!
13 Let them be confounded *and* consumed
Who are adversaries of my life;
Let them be covered *with* reproach and dishonor
Who seek my hurt.

14 But I will hope continually,
And will praise You yet more and more.
15 My mouth shall tell of Your righteousness
And Your salvation all the day,
For I do not know *their* limits.
16 I will go in the strength of the Lord GOD;
I will make mention of Your righteousness, of Yours only.

17 O God, You have taught me from my youth;
And to this *day* I declare Your wondrous works.
18 Now also when *I am* old and grayheaded,
O God, do not forsake me,
Until I declare Your strength to *this* generation,
Your power to everyone *who* is to come.

19 Also Your righteousness, O God, *is* very high,
You who have done great things;
O God, who *is* like You?
20 *You*, who have shown me great and severe troubles,
Shall revive me again,
And bring me up again from the depths of the earth.
21 You shall increase my greatness,
And comfort me on every side.

22 Also with the lute I will praise You—
And Your faithfulness, O my God!
To You I will sing with the harp,
O Holy One of Israel.
23 My lips shall greatly rejoice when I sing to You,
And my soul, which You have redeemed.
24 My tongue also shall talk of Your righteousness all the day long;
For they are confounded,
For they are brought to shame
Who seek my hurt.

72:8 JESUS SHALL REIGN OVER EVERYTHING

Jesus was the kind Savior who grew up in a small town in Palestine. He went about doing good, healing the sick, and even raising the dead. He also had power over nature, as when He made the stormy sea calm. Then He was crucified and died. But on the third day, Jesus rose again, saying that He has the keys of death and hell (Revelation 1:18).

Right now we don't see Jesus anymore, and the world is ruled by human governments. But Jesus said, "I will come again." Someday He truly will come back, and He will rule over the whole world. Everyone will confess that He is Lord.

Life will be changed when Jesus is Ruler of all. There will be no more war or sickness or sin or death. Jesus will make everything beautiful. Are you looking for Jesus to come back?

PSALM 72

Glory and Universality of the Messiah's Reign

A Psalm of Solomon.

1 Give the king Your judgments, O God,
And Your righteousness to the king's Son.
2 He will judge Your people with righteousness,
And Your poor with justice.
3 The mountains will bring peace to the people,
And the little hills, by righteousness.
4 He will bring justice to the poor of the people;
He will save the children of the needy,
And will break in pieces the oppressor.

5 They shall fear You[a]
As long as the sun and moon endure,
Throughout all generations.
6 He shall come down like rain upon the grass before mowing,
Like showers *that* water the earth.
7 In His days the righteous shall flourish,
And abundance of peace,
Until the moon is no more.

8 He shall have dominion also from sea to sea,
And from the River to the ends of the earth.
9 Those who dwell in the wilderness will bow before Him,
And His enemies will lick the dust.
10 The kings of Tarshish and of the isles
Will bring presents;
The kings of Sheba and Seba
Will offer gifts.
11 Yes, all kings shall fall down before Him;
All nations shall serve Him.

12 For He will deliver the needy when he cries,
The poor also, and *him* who has no helper.
13 He will spare the poor and needy,
And will save the souls of the needy.
14 He will redeem their life from oppression and violence;
And precious shall be their blood in His sight.

15 And He shall live;
And the gold of Sheba will be given to Him;
Prayer also will be made for Him continually,
And daily He shall be praised.

16 There will be an abundance of grain in the earth,
On the top of the mountains;
Its fruit shall wave like Lebanon;
And *those* of the city shall flourish like grass of the earth.

17 His name shall endure forever;
His name shall continue as long as the sun.
And *men* shall be blessed in Him;
All nations shall call Him blessed.

18 Blessed *be* the LORD God, the God of Israel,
Who only does wondrous things!
19 And blessed *be* His glorious name forever!
And let the whole earth be filled *with* His glory.
Amen and Amen.

20 The prayers of David the son of Jesse are ended.

BOOK THREE

Psalms 73–89

PSALM 73

The Tragedy of the Wicked, and the Blessedness of Trust in God

A Psalm of Asaph.

1 Truly God *is* good to Israel,
To such as are pure in heart.
2 But as for me, my feet had almost stumbled;
My steps had nearly slipped.
3 For I *was* envious of the boastful,
When I saw the prosperity of the wicked.

4 For *there are* no pangs in their death,
But their strength *is* firm.
5 They *are* not in trouble *as other* men,
Nor are they plagued like *other* men.

72:5 [a] Following Masoretic Text and Targum; Septuagint and Vulgate read *They shall continue.*

6 Therefore pride serves as their necklace;
Violence covers them *like* a garment.
7 Their eyes bulge[a] with abundance;
They have more than heart could wish.
8 They scoff and speak wickedly
concerning oppression;
They speak loftily.
9 They set their mouth against the
heavens,
And their tongue walks through the
earth.

10 Therefore his people return here,
And waters of a full *cup* are drained by
them.
11 And they say, "How does God know?
And is there knowledge in the Most
High?"
12 Behold, these *are* the ungodly,
Who are always at ease;
They increase *in* riches.
13 Surely I have cleansed my heart *in* vain,
And washed my hands in innocence.
14 For all day long I have been plagued,
And chastened every morning.

15 If I had said, "I will speak thus,"
Behold, I would have been untrue to the
generation of Your children.
16 When I thought *how* to understand this,
It *was* too painful for me—
17 Until I went into the sanctuary of God;
Then I understood their end.

18 Surely You set them in slippery places;
You cast them down to destruction.
19 Oh, how they are *brought* to desolation,
as in a moment!
They are utterly consumed with terrors.
20 As a dream when *one* awakes,
So, Lord, when You awake,
You shall despise their image.

21 Thus my heart was grieved,
And I was vexed in my mind.
22 I *was* so foolish and ignorant;
I was *like* a beast before You.
23 Nevertheless I *am* continually with You;
You hold *me* by my right hand.
24 You will guide me with Your counsel,
And afterward receive me *to* glory.

25 Whom have I in heaven *but You?*
And *there is* none upon earth *that* I
desire besides You.
26 My flesh and my heart fail;
But God *is* the strength of my heart and
my portion forever.

27 For indeed, those who are far from You
shall perish;
You have destroyed all those who desert
You for harlotry.
28 But *it is* good for me to draw near to God;
I have put my trust in the Lord GOD,
That I may declare all Your works.

PSALM 74

A Plea for Relief from Oppressors

A Contemplation[a] of Asaph.

1 O God, why have You cast *us* off forever?
Why does Your anger smoke against the
sheep of Your pasture?

73:7 [a] Targum reads *face bulges;* Septuagint, Syriac, and Vulgate read *iniquity bulges.* 74:title [a] Hebrew *Maschil*

GRIEF

READ IT: PSALM 73:24–26

When we're grieving, we often feel alone. Grief is an emotion that is felt so deeply that not many people can truly understand what's going on in our hearts. Even though grief is an emotion, it can make us feel like we're wasting away physically. The psalmist cried out to God in a moment of deep pain. There was nobody on earth who could save him but God. During our weakest times, God gives us strength to make it through.

2 Remember Your congregation, *which* You have purchased of old,
The tribe of Your inheritance, *which* You have redeemed—
This Mount Zion where You have dwelt.
3 Lift up Your feet to the perpetual desolations.
The enemy has damaged everything in the sanctuary.
4 Your enemies roar in the midst of Your meeting place;
They set up their banners *for* signs.
5 They seem like men who lift up
Axes among the thick trees.
6 And now they break down its carved work, all at once,
With axes and hammers.
7 They have set fire to Your sanctuary;
They have defiled the dwelling place of Your name to the ground.
8 They said in their hearts,
"Let us destroy them altogether."
They have burned up all the meeting places of God in the land.

9 We do not see our signs;
There is no longer any prophet;
Nor *is there* any among us who knows how long.

10 O God, how long will the adversary reproach?
Will the enemy blaspheme Your name forever?
11 Why do You withdraw Your hand, even Your right hand?
Take it out of Your bosom and destroy *them*.
12 For God *is* my King from of old,
Working salvation in the midst of the earth.
13 You divided the sea by Your strength;
You broke the heads of the sea serpents in the waters.
14 You broke the heads of Leviathan in pieces,
And gave him *as* food to the people inhabiting the wilderness.
15 You broke open the fountain and the flood;
You dried up mighty rivers.
16 The day *is* Yours, the night also *is* Yours;
You have prepared the light and the sun.
17 You have set all the borders of the earth;
You have made summer and winter.

18 Remember this, *that* the enemy has reproached, O LORD,
And *that* a foolish people has blasphemed Your name.

ALWAYS GIVE THANKS TO GOD

READ IT: PSALM 75:1

Why should you give thanks to God? You should always be thankful when anyone is kind to you. But who has been nearly as kind as God? He provides your home and a free country to live in. He supplies your daily food and clothing. You may think you get these things by your own work or by the work of others, but God provides the opportunity to enjoy all these good things and many, many more. He even provides the air to breathe and give life moment by moment.

It is only right that you should be thankful to your parents and all who do good things for you, but being thankful to God, the One who gave you your parents and all the good things you enjoy, makes even more sense. If you aren't thankful, your life will grow bitter and hateful. Then you will be your own worst enemy.

19 Oh, do not deliver the life of Your turtledove to the wild beast!
Do not forget the life of Your poor forever.
20 Have respect to the covenant;
For the dark places of the earth are full of the haunts of cruelty.
21 Oh, do not let the oppressed return ashamed!
Let the poor and needy praise Your name.

22 Arise, O God, plead Your own cause;
Remember how the foolish man reproaches You daily.
23 Do not forget the voice of Your enemies;
The tumult of those who rise up against You increases continually.

PSALM 75

Thanksgiving for God's Righteous Judgment

To the Chief Musician. Set to "Do Not Destroy."[a] A Psalm of Asaph. A Song.

1 We give thanks to You, O God, we give thanks!
For Your wondrous works declare *that* Your name is near.

2 "When I choose the proper time,
I will judge uprightly.
3 The earth and all its inhabitants are dissolved;
I set up its pillars firmly. *Selah*

4 "I said to the boastful, 'Do not deal boastfully,'
And to the wicked, 'Do not lift up the horn.
5 Do not lift up your horn on high;
Do *not* speak with a stiff neck.'"

6 For exaltation *comes* neither from the east
Nor from the west nor from the south.
7 But God *is* the Judge:
He puts down one,
And exalts another.
8 For in the hand of the LORD *there is* a cup,
And the wine is red;
It is fully mixed, and He pours it out;
Surely its dregs shall all the wicked of the earth
Drain *and* drink down.

9 But I will declare forever,
I will sing praises to the God of Jacob.

10 "All the horns of the wicked I will also cut off,
But the horns of the righteous shall be exalted."

PSALM 76

The Majesty of God in Judgment

To the Chief Musician. On stringed instruments.[a] A Psalm of Asaph. A Song.

1 In Judah God *is* known;
His name *is* great in Israel.
2 In Salem[a] also is His tabernacle,
And His dwelling place in Zion.
3 There He broke the arrows of the bow,
The shield and sword of battle. *Selah*

4 You *are* more glorious and excellent
Than the mountains of prey.
5 The stouthearted were plundered;
They have sunk into their sleep;
And none of the mighty men have found the use of their hands.
6 At Your rebuke, O God of Jacob,
Both the chariot and horse were cast into a dead sleep.

7 You, Yourself, *are* to be feared;
And who may stand in Your presence
When once You are angry?
8 You caused judgment to be heard from heaven;
The earth feared and was still,
9 When God arose to judgment,
To deliver all the oppressed of the earth. *Selah*

10 Surely the wrath of man shall praise You;
With the remainder of wrath You shall gird Yourself.

11 Make vows to the LORD your God, and pay *them;*
Let all who are around Him bring presents to Him who ought to be feared.
12 He shall cut off the spirit of princes;
He is awesome to the kings of the earth.

PSALM 77

The Consoling Memory of God's Redemptive Works

To the Chief Musician. To Jeduthun. A Psalm of Asaph.

1 I cried out to God with my voice—

75:title [a] Hebrew *Al Tashcheth* 76:title [a] Hebrew *neginoth*
76:2 [a] That is, Jerusalem

To God with my voice;
And He gave ear to me.
2 In the day of my trouble I sought the Lord;
My hand was stretched out in the night without ceasing;
My soul refused to be comforted.
3 I remembered God, and was troubled;
I complained, and my spirit was overwhelmed. *Selah*

4 You hold my eyelids *open;*
I am so troubled that I cannot speak.
5 I have considered the days of old,
The years of ancient times.
6 I call to remembrance my song in the night;
I meditate within my heart,
And my spirit makes diligent search.

7 Will the Lord cast off forever?
And will He be favorable no more?
8 Has His mercy ceased forever?
Has *His* promise failed forevermore?
9 Has God forgotten to be gracious?
Has He in anger shut up His tender mercies? *Selah*

10 And I said, "This *is* my anguish;
But I will remember the years of the right hand of the Most High."
11 I will remember the works of the LORD;
Surely I will remember Your wonders of old.
12 I will also meditate on all Your work,
And talk of Your deeds.
13 Your way, O God, *is* in the sanctuary;
Who *is* so great a God as *our* God?
14 You *are* the God who does wonders;
You have declared Your strength among the peoples.
15 You have with *Your* arm redeemed Your people,
The sons of Jacob and Joseph. *Selah*

16 The waters saw You, O God;
The waters saw You, they were afraid;
The depths also trembled.
17 The clouds poured out water;
The skies sent out a sound;
Your arrows also flashed about.
18 The voice of Your thunder *was* in the whirlwind;
The lightnings lit up the world;
The earth trembled and shook.
19 Your way *was* in the sea,
Your path in the great waters,
And Your footsteps were not known.
20 You led Your people like a flock
By the hand of Moses and Aaron.

PSALM 78

God's Kindness to Rebellious Israel

A Contemplation[a] of Asaph.

1 Give ear, O my people, *to* my law;
Incline your ears to the words of my mouth.
2 I will open my mouth in a parable;
I will utter dark sayings of old,
3 Which we have heard and known,
And our fathers have told us.
4 We will not hide *them* from their children,
Telling to the generation to come the praises of the LORD,
And His strength and His wonderful works that He has done.

5 For He established a testimony in Jacob,
And appointed a law in Israel,
Which He commanded our fathers,
That they should make them known to their children;
6 That the generation to come might know *them,*
The children *who* would be born,
That they may arise and declare *them* to their children,
7 That they may set their hope in God,
And not forget the works of God,
But keep His commandments;
8 And may not be like their fathers,
A stubborn and rebellious generation,
A generation *that* did not set its heart aright,
And whose spirit was not faithful to God.

9 The children of Ephraim, *being* armed *and* carrying bows,
Turned back in the day of battle.
10 They did not keep the covenant of God;
They refused to walk in His law,
11 And forgot His works
And His wonders that He had shown them.

12 Marvelous things He did in the sight of their fathers,

78:title [a] Hebrew *Maschil*

In the land of Egypt, *in* the field of
Zoan.
13 He divided the sea and caused them to
pass through;
And He made the waters stand up like
a heap.
14 In the daytime also He led them with
the cloud,
And all the night with a light of fire.
15 He split the rocks in the wilderness,
And gave *them* drink in abundance like
the depths.
16 He also brought streams out of the rock,
And caused waters to run down like
rivers.

17 But they sinned even more against Him
By rebelling against the Most High in
the wilderness.
18 And they tested God in their heart
By asking for the food of their fancy.
19 Yes, they spoke against God:
They said, "Can God prepare a table in
the wilderness?
20 Behold, He struck the rock,
So that the waters gushed out,
And the streams overflowed.
Can He give bread also?
Can He provide meat for His people?"

21 Therefore the LORD heard *this* and was
furious;
So a fire was kindled against Jacob,
And anger also came up against Israel,
22 Because they did not believe in God,
And did not trust in His salvation.
23 Yet He had commanded the clouds
above,
And opened the doors of heaven,
24 Had rained down manna on them to
eat,
And given them of the bread of heaven.
25 Men ate angels' food;
He sent them food to the full.

26 He caused an east wind to blow in the
heavens;
And by His power He brought in the
south wind.
27 He also rained meat on them like the
dust,
Feathered fowl like the sand of the seas;
28 And He let *them* fall in the midst of
their camp,
All around their dwellings.
29 So they ate and were well filled,
For He gave them their own desire.
30 They were not deprived of their craving;
But while their food *was* still in their
mouths,
31 The wrath of God came against them,
And slew the stoutest of them,
And struck down the choice *men* of
Israel.

32 In spite of this they still sinned,
And did not believe in His wondrous
works.
33 Therefore their days He consumed in
futility,
And their years in fear.

34 When He slew them, then they sought
Him;
And they returned and sought earnestly
for God.
35 Then they remembered that God *was*
their rock,
And the Most High God their
Redeemer.
36 Nevertheless they flattered Him with
their mouth,
And they lied to Him with their tongue;
37 For their heart was not steadfast with
Him,
Nor were they faithful in His covenant.
38 But He, *being* full of compassion,
forgave *their* iniquity,
And did not destroy *them*.
Yes, many a time He turned His anger
away,
And did not stir up all His wrath;
39 For He remembered that they *were but*
flesh,
A breath that passes away and does not
come again.

40 How often they provoked Him in the
wilderness,
And grieved Him in the desert!
41 Yes, again and again they tempted God,
And limited the Holy One of Israel.
42 They did not remember His power:
The day when He redeemed them from
the enemy,
43 When He worked His signs in Egypt,
And His wonders in the field of Zoan;
44 Turned their rivers into blood,
And their streams, that they could not
drink.
45 He sent swarms of flies among them,
which devoured them,

And frogs, which destroyed them.
46 He also gave their crops to the caterpillar,
And their labor to the locust.
47 He destroyed their vines with hail,
And their sycamore trees with frost.
48 He also gave up their cattle to the hail,
And their flocks to fiery lightning.
49 He cast on them the fierceness of His anger,
Wrath, indignation, and trouble,
By sending angels of destruction *among them.*
50 He made a path for His anger;
He did not spare their soul from death,
But gave their life over to the plague,
51 And destroyed all the firstborn in Egypt,
The first of *their* strength in the tents of Ham.
52 But He made His own people go forth like sheep,
And guided them in the wilderness like a flock;
53 And He led them on safely, so that they did not fear;
But the sea overwhelmed their enemies.
54 And He brought them to His holy border,
This mountain *which* His right hand had acquired.
55 He also drove out the nations before them,
Allotted them an inheritance by survey,
And made the tribes of Israel dwell in their tents.

56 Yet they tested and provoked the Most High God,
And did not keep His testimonies,
57 But turned back and acted unfaithfully like their fathers;
They were turned aside like a deceitful bow.
58 For they provoked Him to anger with their high places,
And moved Him to jealousy with their carved images.
59 When God heard *this,* He was furious,
And greatly abhorred Israel,
60 So that He forsook the tabernacle of Shiloh,
The tent He had placed among men,
61 And delivered His strength into captivity,
And His glory into the enemy's hand.
62 He also gave His people over to the sword,
And was furious with His inheritance.
63 The fire consumed their young men,
And their maidens were not given in marriage.
64 Their priests fell by the sword,
And their widows made no lamentation.

65 Then the Lord awoke as *from* sleep,
Like a mighty man who shouts because of wine.
66 And He beat back His enemies;
He put them to a perpetual reproach.

67 Moreover He rejected the tent of Joseph,
And did not choose the tribe of Ephraim,
68 But chose the tribe of Judah,
Mount Zion which He loved.
69 And He built His sanctuary like the heights,
Like the earth which He has established forever.
70 He also chose David His servant,
And took him from the sheepfolds;
71 From following the ewes that had young He brought him,
To shepherd Jacob His people,
And Israel His inheritance.
72 So he shepherded them according to the integrity of his heart,
And guided them by the skillfulness of his hands.

PSALM 79

A Dirge and a Prayer for Israel, Destroyed by Enemies

A Psalm of Asaph.

1 O God, the nations have come into Your inheritance;
Your holy temple they have defiled;
They have laid Jerusalem in heaps.
2 The dead bodies of Your servants
They have given *as* food for the birds of the heavens,
The flesh of Your saints to the beasts of the earth.
3 Their blood they have shed like water all around Jerusalem,
And *there was* no one to bury *them.*

4 We have become a reproach to our neighbors,
A scorn and derision to those who are around us.

5 How long, LORD?
Will You be angry forever?
Will Your jealousy burn like fire?
6 Pour out Your wrath on the nations that do not know You,
And on the kingdoms that do not call on Your name.
7 For they have devoured Jacob,
And laid waste his dwelling place.

8 Oh, do not remember former iniquities against us!
Let Your tender mercies come speedily to meet us,
For we have been brought very low.
9 Help us, O God of our salvation,
For the glory of Your name;
And deliver us, and provide atonement for our sins,
For Your name's sake!
10 Why should the nations say,
"Where *is* their God?"
Let there be known among the nations in our sight
The avenging of the blood of Your servants *which has been* shed.

11 Let the groaning of the prisoner come before You;
According to the greatness of Your power
Preserve those who are appointed to die;
12 And return to our neighbors sevenfold into their bosom
Their reproach with which they have reproached You, O Lord.

13 So we, Your people and sheep of Your pasture,
Will give You thanks forever;
We will show forth Your praise to all generations.

PSALM 80

Prayer for Israel's Restoration

To the Chief Musician. Set to "The Lilies."[a] A Testimony[b] of Asaph. A Psalm.

1 Give ear, O Shepherd of Israel,
You who lead Joseph like a flock;
You who dwell *between* the cherubim, shine forth!
2 Before Ephraim, Benjamin, and Manasseh,
Stir up Your strength,
And come *and* save us!

3 Restore us, O God;
Cause Your face to shine,
And we shall be saved!

4 O LORD God of hosts,
How long will You be angry
Against the prayer of Your people?
5 You have fed them with the bread of tears,
And given them tears to drink in great measure.
6 You have made us a strife to our neighbors,
And our enemies laugh among themselves.

7 Restore us, O God of hosts;
Cause Your face to shine,
And we shall be saved!

8 You have brought a vine out of Egypt;
You have cast out the nations, and planted it.
9 You prepared *room* for it,
And caused it to take deep root,
And it filled the land.
10 The hills were covered with its shadow,
And the mighty cedars with its boughs.
11 She sent out her boughs to the Sea,[a]
And her branches to the River.[b]

12 Why have You broken down her hedges,
So that all who pass by the way pluck her *fruit*?
13 The boar out of the woods uproots it,
And the wild beast of the field devours it.

14 Return, we beseech You, O God of hosts;
Look down from heaven and see,
And visit this vine
15 And the vineyard which Your right hand has planted,
And the branch *that* You made strong for Yourself.
16 *It is* burned with fire, it is cut down;

80:title [a] Hebrew *Shoshannim* [b] Hebrew *Eduth*
80:11 [a] That is, the Mediterranean [b] That is, the Euphrates

They perish at the rebuke of Your
countenance.
17 Let Your hand be upon the man of Your
right hand,
Upon the son of man *whom* You made
strong for Yourself.
18 Then we will not turn back from You;
Revive us, and we will call upon Your
name.

19 Restore us, O LORD God of hosts;
Cause Your face to shine,
And we shall be saved!

PSALM 81

An Appeal for Israel's Repentance

To the Chief Musician. On an instrument
of Gath.[a] *A Psalm* of Asaph.

1 Sing aloud to God our strength;
Make a joyful shout to the God of
Jacob.
2 Raise a song and strike the timbrel,
The pleasant harp with the lute.

3 Blow the trumpet at the time of the New
Moon,
At the full moon, on our solemn feast
day.
4 For this *is* a statute for Israel,
A law of the God of Jacob.
5 This He established in Joseph *as* a
testimony,
When He went throughout the land of
Egypt,
Where I heard a language I did not
understand.

6 "I removed his shoulder from the
burden;
His hands were freed from the
baskets.
7 You called in trouble, and I delivered
you;
I answered you in the secret place of
thunder;
I tested you at the waters of Meribah.
Selah

8 "Hear, O My people, and I will admonish
you!
O Israel, if you will listen to Me!
9 There shall be no foreign god among
you;
Nor shall you worship any foreign
god.
10 I *am* the LORD your God,
Who brought you out of the land of
Egypt;
Open your mouth wide, and I will
fill it.

11 "But My people would not heed My
voice,
And Israel would *have* none of Me.
12 So I gave them over to their own
stubborn heart,
To walk in their own counsels.

13 "Oh, that My people would listen
to Me,
That Israel would walk in My ways!
14 I would soon subdue their enemies,
And turn My hand against their
adversaries.
15 The haters of the LORD would pretend
submission to Him,
But their fate would endure forever.
16 He would have fed them also with the
finest of wheat;
And with honey from the rock I would
have satisfied you."

PSALM 82

A Plea for Justice

A Psalm of Asaph.

1 God stands in the congregation of the
mighty;
He judges among the gods.[a]
2 How long will you judge unjustly,
And show partiality to the wicked? *Selah*
3 Defend the poor and fatherless;
Do justice to the afflicted and needy.
4 Deliver the poor and needy;
Free *them* from the hand of the wicked.

5 They do not know, nor do they
understand;
They walk about in darkness;
All the foundations of the earth are
unstable.

6 I said, "You *are* gods,[a]
And all of you *are* children of the Most
High.
7 But you shall die like men,
And fall like one of the princes."

81:title [a] Hebrew *Al Gittith* **82:1** [a] Hebrew *elohim, mighty ones;* that is, the judges **82:6** [a] Hebrew *elohim, mighty ones;* that is, the judges

8 Arise, O God, judge the earth;
For You shall inherit all nations.

PSALM 83

Prayer to Frustrate Conspiracy Against Israel

A Song. A Psalm of Asaph.

1 Do not keep silent, O God!
Do not hold Your peace,
And do not be still, O God!
2 For behold, Your enemies make a tumult;
And those who hate You have lifted up their head.
3 They have taken crafty counsel against Your people,
And consulted together against Your sheltered ones.
4 They have said, "Come, and let us cut them off from *being* a nation,
That the name of Israel may be remembered no more."

5 For they have consulted together with one consent;
They form a confederacy against You:
6 The tents of Edom and the Ishmaelites;
Moab and the Hagrites;
7 Gebal, Ammon, and Amalek;
Philistia with the inhabitants of Tyre;
8 Assyria also has joined with them;
They have helped the children of Lot.
Selah

9 Deal with them as *with* Midian,
As *with* Sisera,
As *with* Jabin at the Brook Kishon,
10 Who perished at En Dor,
Who became *as* refuse on the earth.
11 Make their nobles like Oreb and like Zeeb,
Yes, all their princes like Zebah and Zalmunna,
12 Who said, "Let us take for ourselves
The pastures of God for a possession."

13 O my God, make them like the whirling dust,
Like the chaff before the wind!
14 As the fire burns the woods,
And as the flame sets the mountains on fire,
15 So pursue them with Your tempest,
And frighten them with Your storm.
16 Fill their faces with shame,
That they may seek Your name, O LORD.
17 Let them be confounded and dismayed forever;
Yes, let them be put to shame and perish,
18 That they may know that You, whose name alone *is* the LORD,
Are the Most High over all the earth.

ARE YOU A CHILD OF GOD?

READ IT: PSALM 82:6

Everyone is somebody's child. You are the child of your parents. But if you ran away from home and refused to belong to your parents, you might not feel you were their child anymore. In the same way, everybody belongs to God because He is their Creator. But not everybody wants God to be their Father. They don't want to belong to Him.

You can only be a true child of God when you come to Him and say, "I want You to be my Father; I want to be Your child." Then God accepts you as a member of His family. Then Jesus is not only your Savior from sin, but He is also your older Brother.

Unlike humans, God can never die. He wants to be your Father always. Then Jesus will always be your Brother. Jesus said, "I will never leave you" (Hebrews 13:5).

PSALM 84

The Blessedness of Dwelling in the House of God

To the Chief Musician. On an instrument of Gath.[a] A Psalm of the sons of Korah.

1 How lovely *is* Your tabernacle,
O LORD of hosts!
2 My soul longs, yes, even faints
For the courts of the LORD;
My heart and my flesh cry out for the
living God.

3 Even the sparrow has found a home,
And the swallow a nest for herself,
Where she may lay her young—
Even Your altars, O LORD of hosts,
My King and my God.
4 Blessed *are* those who dwell in Your
house;
They will still be praising You. *Selah*

5 Blessed *is* the man whose strength *is* in
You,
Whose heart *is* set on pilgrimage.
6 *As they* pass through the Valley of Baca,
They make it a spring;
The rain also covers it with pools.
7 They go from strength to strength;
Each one appears before God in Zion.[a]

8 O LORD God of hosts, hear my prayer;
Give ear, O God of Jacob! *Selah*
9 O God, behold our shield,
And look upon the face of Your
anointed.

10 For a day in Your courts *is* better than a
thousand.
I would rather be a doorkeeper in the
house of my God
Than dwell in the tents of wickedness.
11 For the LORD God *is* a sun and shield;
The LORD will give grace and glory;
No good *thing* will He withhold
From those who walk uprightly.

12 O LORD of hosts,
Blessed is the man who trusts in You!

PSALM 85

Prayer that the LORD Will Restore Favor to the Land

To the Chief Musician. A Psalm of the sons of Korah.

1 LORD, You have been favorable to Your
land;
You have brought back the captivity of
Jacob.
2 You have forgiven the iniquity of Your
people;
You have covered all their sin. *Selah*
3 You have taken away all Your wrath;
You have turned from the fierceness of
Your anger.

4 Restore us, O God of our salvation,
And cause Your anger toward us to
cease.
5 Will You be angry with us forever?
Will You prolong Your anger to all
generations?
6 Will You not revive us again,
That Your people may rejoice in You?
7 Show us Your mercy, LORD,
And grant us Your salvation.

8 I will hear what God the LORD will
speak,
For He will speak peace
To His people and to His saints;
But let them not turn back to folly.
9 Surely His salvation *is* near to those who
fear Him,
That glory may dwell in our land.

10 Mercy and truth have met together;
Righteousness and peace have kissed.
11 Truth shall spring out of the earth,
And righteousness shall look down
from heaven.
12 Yes, the LORD will give *what is* good;
And our land will yield its increase.
13 Righteousness will go before Him,
And shall make His footsteps *our*
pathway.

PSALM 86

Prayer for Mercy, with Meditation on the Excellencies of the LORD

A Prayer of David.

1 Bow down Your ear, O LORD, hear me;
For I *am* poor and needy.
2 Preserve my life, for I *am* holy;
You are my God;
Save Your servant who trusts in You!
3 Be merciful to me, O Lord,
For I cry to You all day long.
4 Rejoice the soul of Your servant,
For to You, O Lord, I lift up my soul.

84:title [a] Hebrew *Al Gittith* **84:7** [a] Septuagint, Syriac, and Vulgate read *The God of gods shall be seen.*

5 For You, Lord, *are* good, and ready to forgive,
And abundant in mercy to all those who call upon You.

6 Give ear, O LORD, to my prayer;
And attend to the voice of my supplications.
7 In the day of my trouble I will call upon You,
For You will answer me.

8 Among the gods *there is* none like You, O Lord;
Nor *are there any works* like Your works.
9 All nations whom You have made
Shall come and worship before You, O Lord,
And shall glorify Your name.
10 For You *are* great, and do wondrous things;
You alone *are* God.

11 Teach me Your way, O LORD;
I will walk in Your truth;
Unite my heart to fear Your name.
12 I will praise You, O Lord my God, with all my heart,
And I will glorify Your name forevermore.
13 For great *is* Your mercy toward me,
And You have delivered my soul from the depths of Sheol.

14 O God, the proud have risen against me,
And a mob of violent *men* have sought my life,
And have not set You before them.
15 But You, O Lord, *are* a God full of compassion, and gracious,
Longsuffering and abundant in mercy and truth.

16 Oh, turn to me, and have mercy on me!
Give Your strength to Your servant,
And save the son of Your maidservant.
17 Show me a sign for good,
That those who hate me may see *it* and be ashamed,
Because You, LORD, have helped me and comforted me.

PSALM 87

The Glories of the City of God

A Psalm of the sons of Korah. A Song.

1 His foundation *is* in the holy mountains.
2 The LORD loves the gates of Zion
More than all the dwellings of Jacob.
3 Glorious things are spoken of you,
O city of God! *Selah*

4 "I will make mention of Rahab and Babylon to those who know Me;
Behold, O Philistia and Tyre, with Ethiopia:
'This *one* was born there.'"

5 And of Zion it will be said,
"This *one* and that *one* were born in her;
And the Most High Himself shall establish her."
6 The LORD will record,
When He registers the peoples:
"This *one* was born there." *Selah*

7 Both the singers and the players on instruments *say,*
"All my springs *are* in you."

PSALM 88

A Prayer for Help in Despondency

A Song. A Psalm of the sons of Korah. To the Chief Musician. Set to "Mahalath Leannoth." A Contemplation[a] of Heman the Ezrahite.

1 O LORD, God of my salvation,
I have cried out day and night before You.
2 Let my prayer come before You;
Incline Your ear to my cry.

3 For my soul is full of troubles,
And my life draws near to the grave.
4 I am counted with those who go down to the pit;
I am like a man *who has* no strength,
5 Adrift among the dead,
Like the slain who lie in the grave,
Whom You remember no more,
And who are cut off from Your hand.

6 You have laid me in the lowest pit,
In darkness, in the depths.
7 Your wrath lies heavy upon me,
And You have afflicted *me* with all Your waves. *Selah*
8 You have put away my acquaintances far from me;
You have made me an abomination to them;
I am shut up, and I cannot get out;

88:title [a] Hebrew *Maschil*

9 My eye wastes away because of
affliction.

LORD, I have called daily upon You;
I have stretched out my hands to You.
10 Will You work wonders for the dead?
Shall the dead arise *and* praise You?
Selah
11 Shall Your lovingkindness be declared
in the grave?
Or Your faithfulness in the place of
destruction?
12 Shall Your wonders be known in the
dark?
And Your righteousness in the land of
forgetfulness?

13 But to You I have cried out, O LORD,
And in the morning my prayer comes
before You.
14 LORD, why do You cast off my soul?
Why do You hide Your face from me?
15 I *have been* afflicted and ready to die
from *my* youth;
I suffer Your terrors;
I am distraught.
16 Your fierce wrath has gone over me;
Your terrors have cut me off.
17 They came around me all day long like
water;
They engulfed me altogether.
18 Loved one and friend You have put far
from me,
And my acquaintances into darkness.

PSALM 89

Remembering the Covenant with David, and Sorrow for Lost Blessings

A Contemplation[a] of Ethan the Ezrahite.

1 I will sing of the mercies of the LORD
forever;
With my mouth will I make known
Your faithfulness to all generations.
2 For I have said, "Mercy shall be built up
forever;
Your faithfulness You shall establish in
the very heavens."

3 "I have made a covenant with My chosen,
I have sworn to My servant David:
4 'Your seed I will establish forever,
And build up your throne to all
generations.'" *Selah*

5 And the heavens will praise Your
wonders, O LORD;
Your faithfulness also in the assembly
of the saints.
6 For who in the heavens can be
compared to the LORD?
Who among the sons of the mighty can
be likened to the LORD?
7 God is greatly to be feared in the
assembly of the saints,
And to be held in reverence by all *those*
around Him.
8 O LORD God of hosts,
Who *is* mighty like You, O LORD?
Your faithfulness also surrounds You.
9 You rule the raging of the sea;
When its waves rise, You still them.
10 You have broken Rahab in pieces, as one
who is slain;
You have scattered Your enemies with
Your mighty arm.

11 The heavens *are* Yours, the earth also *is*
Yours;
The world and all its fullness, You have
founded them.
12 The north and the south, You have
created them;
Tabor and Hermon rejoice in Your
name.
13 You have a mighty arm;
Strong is Your hand, *and* high is Your
right hand.
14 Righteousness and justice *are* the
foundation of Your throne;
Mercy and truth go before Your face.
15 Blessed *are* the people who know the
joyful sound!
They walk, O LORD, in the light of Your
countenance.
16 In Your name they rejoice all day long,
And in Your righteousness they are
exalted.
17 For You *are* the glory of their strength,
And in Your favor our horn is exalted.
18 For our shield *belongs* to the LORD,
And our king to the Holy One of Israel.

19 Then You spoke in a vision to Your holy
one,[a]
And said: "I have given help to *one who*
is mighty;
I have exalted one chosen from the
people.
20 I have found My servant David;

89:title [a] Hebrew *Maschil* 89:19 [a] Following many Hebrew manuscripts; Masoretic Text, Septuagint, Targum, and Vulgate read *holy ones*.

With My holy oil I have anointed him,
21 With whom My hand shall be established;
Also My arm shall strengthen him.
22 The enemy shall not outwit him,
Nor the son of wickedness afflict him.
23 I will beat down his foes before his face,
And plague those who hate him.

24 "But My faithfulness and My mercy *shall be* with him,
And in My name his horn shall be exalted.
25 Also I will set his hand over the sea,
And his right hand over the rivers.
26 He shall cry to Me, 'You *are* my Father,
My God, and the rock of my salvation.'
27 Also I will make him *My* firstborn,
The highest of the kings of the earth.
28 My mercy I will keep for him forever,
And My covenant shall stand firm with him.
29 His seed also I will make *to endure* forever,
And his throne as the days of heaven.

30 "If his sons forsake My law
And do not walk in My judgments,
31 If they break My statutes
And do not keep My commandments,
32 Then I will punish their transgression with the rod,
And their iniquity with stripes.
33 Nevertheless My lovingkindness I will not utterly take from him,
Nor allow My faithfulness to fail.
34 My covenant I will not break,
Nor alter the word that has gone out of My lips.
35 Once I have sworn by My holiness;
I will not lie to David:
36 His seed shall endure forever,
And his throne as the sun before Me;
37 It shall be established forever like the moon,
Even *like* the faithful witness in the sky." *Selah*

38 But You have cast off and abhorred,
You have been furious with Your anointed.
39 You have renounced the covenant of Your servant;
You have profaned his crown *by casting it* to the ground.
40 You have broken down all his hedges;
You have brought his strongholds to ruin.
41 All who pass by the way plunder him;
He is a reproach to his neighbors.
42 You have exalted the right hand of his adversaries;
You have made all his enemies rejoice.
43 You have also turned back the edge of his sword,
And have not sustained him in the battle.
44 You have made his glory cease,
And cast his throne down to the ground.
45 The days of his youth You have shortened;
You have covered him with shame. *Selah*

46 How long, LORD?
Will You hide Yourself forever?
Will Your wrath burn like fire?
47 Remember how short my time is;
For what futility have You created all the children of men?
48 What man can live and not see death?
Can he deliver his life from the power of the grave? *Selah*

49 Lord, where *are* Your former lovingkindnesses,
Which You swore to David in Your truth?
50 Remember, Lord, the reproach of Your servants—
How I bear in my bosom *the reproach of* all the many peoples,
51 With which Your enemies have reproached, O LORD,
With which they have reproached the footsteps of Your anointed.

52 Blessed *be* the LORD forevermore!
Amen and Amen.

BOOK FOUR

Psalms 90–106

PSALM 90

The Eternity of God, and Man's Frailty

A Prayer of Moses the man of God.

1 Lord, You have been our dwelling place[a] in all generations.
2 Before the mountains were brought forth,

90:1 [a] Septuagint, Targum, and Vulgate read *refuge*.

Or ever You had formed the earth and
the world,
Even from everlasting to everlasting,
You *are* God.

3 You turn man to destruction,
And say, "Return, O children of men."
4 For a thousand years in Your sight
Are like yesterday when it is past,
And *like* a watch in the night.
5 You carry them away *like* a flood;
They are like a sleep.
In the morning they are like grass *which*
grows up:
6 In the morning it flourishes and grows
up;
In the evening it is cut down and
withers.

7 For we have been consumed by Your
anger,
And by Your wrath we are terrified.
8 You have set our iniquities before You,
Our secret *sins* in the light of Your
countenance.
9 For all our days have passed away in
Your wrath;
We finish our years like a sigh.
10 The days of our lives *are* seventy years;
And if by reason of strength *they are*
eighty years,
Yet their boast *is* only labor and sorrow;
For it is soon cut off, and we fly away.
11 Who knows the power of Your anger?
For as the fear of You, *so is* Your wrath.
12 So teach *us* to number our days,
That we may gain a heart of wisdom.

13 Return, O LORD!
How long?
And have compassion on Your servants.
14 Oh, satisfy us early with Your mercy,
That we may rejoice and be glad all our
days!

MOSES SINGS A SONG TO GOD

READ IT: PSALM 90:1–17

GET IT:

Like most people, you probably didn't know that Moses' song is in the book of Psalms. Well, the book of Psalms is a collection of poems from Israel's history. Many of them record great moments in the lives of God's people. Wandering in the desert was a huge event in their history. Moses was one of their greatest leaders. He wrote this psalm to talk about what God is like and what time is to God and us, and to praise Him.

LIVE IT:

We have a hard time thinking about God. He existed before He created time. He was here before there was earth and sky. He has always been and always will be. God is very different from us, and yet He loves us. He created us because He wanted to, and He made us "in His image." He watches over us all the time and works everything out for our good (even the ugly stuff). He gets angry when we don't follow His instructions ('cause His rules are the best way for us to be happy), but He doesn't stay angry long. He is amazing and wonderful. He is more than worthy of our praise, honor, and worship.

15 Make us glad according to the days *in which* You have afflicted us,
The years *in which* we have seen evil.
16 Let Your work appear to Your servants,
And Your glory to their children.
17 And let the beauty of the LORD our God be upon us,
And establish the work of our hands for us;
Yes, establish the work of our hands.

PSALM 91

Safety of Abiding in the Presence of God

1 He who dwells in the secret place of the Most High
Shall abide under the shadow of the Almighty.
2 I will say of the LORD, "*He is* my refuge and my fortress;
My God, in Him I will trust."

3 Surely He shall deliver you from the snare of the fowler[a]
And from the perilous pestilence.
4 He shall cover you with His feathers,
And under His wings you shall take refuge;
His truth *shall be your* shield and buckler.
5 You shall not be afraid of the terror by night,
Nor of the arrow *that* flies by day,
6 *Nor* of the pestilence *that* walks in darkness,
Nor of the destruction *that* lays waste at noonday.

7 A thousand may fall at your side,
And ten thousand at your right hand;
But it shall not come near you.
8 Only with your eyes shall you look,
And see the reward of the wicked.

9 Because you have made the LORD, *who is* my refuge,
Even the Most High, your dwelling place,
10 No evil shall befall you,
Nor shall any plague come near your dwelling;
11 For He shall give His angels charge over you,
To keep you in all your ways.
12 In *their* hands they shall bear you up,
Lest you dash your foot against a stone.
13 You shall tread upon the lion and the cobra,
The young lion and the serpent you shall trample underfoot.

14 "Because he has set his love upon Me, therefore I will deliver him;
I will set him on high, because he has known My name.
15 He shall call upon Me, and I will answer him;
I *will be* with him in trouble;
I will deliver him and honor him.
16 With long life I will satisfy him,
And show him My salvation."

PSALM 92

Praise to the LORD for His Love and Faithfulness

A Psalm. A Song for the Sabbath day.

1 *It is* good to give thanks to the LORD,
And to sing praises to Your name, O Most High;

91:3 [a] That is, one who catches birds in a trap or snare

ANGELS

READ IT: PSALM 91:11–13

There is great comfort in knowing we are not alone. When you feel like *everything and everyone* is against you, or if you are just having a really, really bad day, remember that you are not alone. God's angels will guard you and keep you strong.

2 To declare Your lovingkindness in the morning,
And Your faithfulness every night,
3 On an instrument of ten strings,
On the lute,
And on the harp,
With harmonious sound.
4 For You, LORD, have made me glad through Your work;
I will triumph in the works of Your hands.

5 O LORD, how great are Your works!
Your thoughts are very deep.
6 A senseless man does not know,
Nor does a fool understand this.
7 When the wicked spring up like grass,
And when all the workers of iniquity flourish,
It is that they may be destroyed forever.

8 But You, LORD, *are* on high forevermore.
9 For behold, Your enemies, O LORD,
For behold, Your enemies shall perish;
All the workers of iniquity shall be scattered.

10 But my horn You have exalted like a wild ox;
I have been anointed with fresh oil.
11 My eye also has seen *my desire* on my enemies;
My ears hear *my desire* on the wicked
Who rise up against me.

12 The righteous shall flourish like a palm tree,
He shall grow like a cedar in Lebanon.
13 Those who are planted in the house of the LORD
Shall flourish in the courts of our God.
14 They shall still bear fruit in old age;
They shall be fresh and flourishing,
15 To declare that the LORD is upright;
He is my rock, and *there is* no unrighteousness in Him.

PSALM 93

The Eternal Reign of the LORD

1 The LORD reigns, He is clothed with majesty;
The LORD is clothed,
He has girded Himself with strength.
Surely the world is established, so that it cannot be moved.
2 Your throne *is* established from of old;
You *are* from everlasting.

3 The floods have lifted up, O LORD,
The floods have lifted up their voice;
The floods lift up their waves.
4 The LORD on high *is* mightier
Than the noise of many waters,
Than the mighty waves of the sea.

5 Your testimonies are very sure;
Holiness adorns Your house,
O LORD, forever.

PSALM 94

God the Refuge of the Righteous

1 O LORD God, to whom vengeance belongs—
O God, to whom vengeance belongs, shine forth!
2 Rise up, O Judge of the earth;
Render punishment to the proud.
3 LORD, how long will the wicked,
How long will the wicked triumph?

4 They utter speech, *and* speak insolent things;
All the workers of iniquity boast in themselves.
5 They break in pieces Your people, O LORD,
And afflict Your heritage.
6 They slay the widow and the stranger,
And murder the fatherless.
7 Yet they say, "The LORD does not see,
Nor does the God of Jacob understand."

8 Understand, you senseless among the people;
And *you* fools, when will you be wise?
9 He who planted the ear, shall He not hear?
He who formed the eye, shall He not see?
10 He who instructs the nations, shall He not correct,
He who teaches man knowledge?
11 The LORD knows the thoughts of man,
That they *are* futile.

12 Blessed *is* the man whom You instruct, O LORD,
And teach out of Your law,
13 That You may give him rest from the days of adversity,
Until the pit is dug for the wicked.

14 For the LORD will not cast off His people,
Nor will He forsake His inheritance.
15 But judgment will return to righteousness,
And all the upright in heart will follow it.

16 Who will rise up for me against the evildoers?
Who will stand up for me against the workers of iniquity?
17 Unless the LORD *had been* my help,
My soul would soon have settled in silence.
18 If I say, "My foot slips,"
Your mercy, O LORD, will hold me up.
19 In the multitude of my anxieties within me,
Your comforts delight my soul.

20 Shall the throne of iniquity, which devises evil by law,
Have fellowship with You?
21 They gather together against the life of the righteous,
And condemn innocent blood.
22 But the LORD has been my defense,
And my God the rock of my refuge.
23 He has brought on them their own iniquity,
And shall cut them off in their own wickedness;
The LORD our God shall cut them off.

PSALM 95

A Call to Worship and Obedience

1 Oh come, let us sing to the LORD!
Let us shout joyfully to the Rock of our salvation.
2 Let us come before His presence with thanksgiving;
Let us shout joyfully to Him with psalms.
3 For the LORD *is* the great God,
And the great King above all gods.
4 In His hand *are* the deep places of the earth;
The heights of the hills *are* His also.
5 The sea *is* His, for He made it;
And His hands formed the dry *land*.

6 Oh come, let us worship and bow down;
Let us kneel before the LORD our Maker.
7 For He *is* our God,
And we *are* the people of His pasture,
And the sheep of His hand.

Today, if you will hear His voice:
8 "Do not harden your hearts, as in the rebellion,[a]
As *in* the day of trial[b] in the wilderness,
9 When your fathers tested Me;
They tried Me, though they saw My work.
10 For forty years I was grieved with *that* generation,
And said, 'It *is* a people who go astray in their hearts,
And they do not know My ways.'
11 So I swore in My wrath,
'They shall not enter My rest.'"

PSALM 96

A Song of Praise to God Coming in Judgment

1 Oh, sing to the LORD a new song!
Sing to the LORD, all the earth.
2 Sing to the LORD, bless His name;
Proclaim the good news of His salvation from day to day.
3 Declare His glory among the nations,
His wonders among all peoples.

4 For the LORD *is* great and greatly to be praised;
He *is* to be feared above all gods.
5 For all the gods of the peoples *are* idols,
But the LORD made the heavens.
6 Honor and majesty *are* before Him;
Strength and beauty *are* in His sanctuary.

7 Give to the LORD, O families of the peoples,
Give to the LORD glory and strength.
8 Give to the LORD the glory *due* His name;
Bring an offering, and come into His courts.
9 Oh, worship the LORD in the beauty of holiness!
Tremble before Him, all the earth.

10 Say among the nations, "The LORD reigns;
The world also is firmly established,
It shall not be moved;
He shall judge the peoples righteously."

95:8 [a] Or *Meribah* [b] Or *Massah*

11 Let the heavens rejoice, and let the earth be glad;
Let the sea roar, and all its fullness;
12 Let the field be joyful, and all that *is* in it.
Then all the trees of the woods will rejoice
13 before the LORD.
For He is coming, for He is coming to judge the earth.
He shall judge the world with righteousness,
And the peoples with His truth.

PSALM 97

A Song of Praise to the Sovereign LORD

1 The LORD reigns;
Let the earth rejoice;
Let the multitude of isles be glad!

2 Clouds and darkness surround Him;
Righteousness and justice *are* the foundation of His throne.
3 A fire goes before Him,
And burns up His enemies round about.
4 His lightnings light the world;
The earth sees and trembles.
5 The mountains melt like wax at the presence of the LORD,
At the presence of the Lord of the whole earth.
6 The heavens declare His righteousness,
And all the peoples see His glory.

7 Let all be put to shame who serve carved images,
Who boast of idols.
Worship Him, all *you* gods.
8 Zion hears and is glad,
And the daughters of Judah rejoice
Because of Your judgments, O LORD.
9 For You, LORD, *are* most high above all the earth;
You are exalted far above all gods.

10 You who love the LORD, hate evil!
He preserves the souls of His saints;
He delivers them out of the hand of the wicked.
11 Light is sown for the righteous,
And gladness for the upright in heart.
12 Rejoice in the LORD, you righteous,
And give thanks at the remembrance of His holy name.[a]

PSALM 98

A Song of Praise to the LORD for His Salvation and Judgment

A Psalm.

1 Oh, sing to the LORD a new song!
For He has done marvelous things;
His right hand and His holy arm have gained Him the victory.

97:12 [a] Or *His holiness*

WORSHIP

READ IT: PSALM 95:6, 7

You can worship God at any moment of any day. You can worship God when you're alone or when you're with a bunch of other people. And you can worship God standing up, kneeling down, or lying in your bed.

But there's something about our physical posture that can help us in worship. When we bow our heads or kneel down or even lie down, we're using our whole bodies to acknowledge God's power and greatness. Try it. Kneel or bow or lie facedown on the floor when you pray sometime. Notice how it makes you feel about your relationship to God.

2 The Lord has made known His salvation;
His righteousness He has revealed in the sight of the nations.
3 He has remembered His mercy and His faithfulness to the house of Israel;
All the ends of the earth have seen the salvation of our God.

4 Shout joyfully to the Lord, all the earth;
Break forth in song, rejoice, and sing praises.
5 Sing to the Lord with the harp,
With the harp and the sound of a psalm,
6 With trumpets and the sound of a horn;
Shout joyfully before the Lord, the King.

7 Let the sea roar, and all its fullness,
The world and those who dwell in it;
8 Let the rivers clap *their* hands;
Let the hills be joyful together
9 before the Lord,
For He is coming to judge the earth.
With righteousness He shall judge the world,
And the peoples with equity.

PSALM 99

Praise to the Lord for His Holiness

1 The Lord reigns;
Let the peoples tremble!
He dwells *between* the cherubim;
Let the earth be moved!
2 The Lord *is* great in Zion,
And He *is* high above all the peoples.
3 Let them praise Your great and awesome name—
He *is* holy.

Epic Ideas

IDENTITY MADE BY GOD

READ IT: PSALM 100

GET IT:

Some people say they're "self-made." It means they've worked hard to get where they are in life. The implication, of course, is that they didn't have help. But that's not true. God was involved in making everyone's identity. Talents, intelligence, sense of humor, athleticism—all these gifts come in unique blends to each of us. Of course, we decide what we'll do with them—if we'll play the flute, study a second language, or practice at the batting cages. But these abilities are gifts from God. He made us this way.

Sometimes it takes awhile to recognize your gifts. And sometimes what you want to be good at doesn't always line up with what you're actually good at. That matchup may take time. While you wait, be grateful for how God made you. It will give you the confidence and motivation to do amazing things with your gifts when the time is right.

LIVE IT:

Have you ever given someone a gift and then hoped you'd catch them using it to know they liked it? Using a gift is one way to show the giver how thankful we are. It also gives joy to the giver. God made us the way we are, and He's delighted when we use the unique gifts He gave us.

4 The King's strength also loves justice;
You have established equity;
You have executed justice and
righteousness in Jacob.
5 Exalt the LORD our God,
And worship at His footstool—
He *is* holy.

6 Moses and Aaron were among His
priests,
And Samuel was among those who
called upon His name;
They called upon the LORD, and He
answered them.
7 He spoke to them in the cloudy pillar;
They kept His testimonies and the
ordinance He gave them.

8 You answered them, O LORD our God;
You were to them God-Who-Forgives,
Though You took vengeance on their
deeds.
9 Exalt the LORD our God,
And worship at His holy hill;
For the LORD our God *is* holy.

PSALM 100

A Song of Praise for the LORD's Faithfulness to His People

A Psalm of Thanksgiving.

1 Make a joyful shout to the LORD, all you
lands!
2 Serve the LORD with gladness;
Come before His presence with singing.
3 Know that the LORD, He *is* God;
It is He *who* has made us, and not we
ourselves;[a]
We are His people and the sheep of His
pasture.

4 Enter into His gates with thanksgiving,
And into His courts with praise.
Be thankful to Him, *and* bless His
name.
5 For the LORD *is* good;
His mercy *is* everlasting,
And His truth endures to all generations.

PSALM 101

Promised Faithfulness to the LORD

A Psalm of David.

1 I will sing of mercy and justice;
To You, O LORD, I will sing praises.

In Focus

Psalm 99:3 Holy You often hear the word *holy*. What does it mean? The word means, first of all, that the holy person or object is "separate." God is separate from us because He is our eternal Creator. God is also perfect in righteousness and love. We also can be holy as we become like God.

2 I will behave wisely in a perfect way.
Oh, when will You come to me?
I will walk within my house with a
perfect heart.

3 I will set nothing wicked before my
eyes;
I hate the work of those who fall away;
It shall not cling to me.
4 A perverse heart shall depart from me;
I will not know wickedness.

5 Whoever secretly slanders his neighbor,
Him I will destroy;
The one who has a haughty look and a
proud heart,
Him I will not endure.

6 My eyes *shall be* on the faithful of the
land,
That they may dwell with me;
He who walks in a perfect way,
He shall serve me.
7 He who works deceit shall not dwell
within my house;
He who tells lies shall not continue in
my presence.
8 Early I will destroy all the wicked of the
land,
That I may cut off all the evildoers from
the city of the LORD.

PSALM 102

The LORD's Eternal Love

A Prayer of the afflicted, when he is overwhelmed and pours out his complaint before the LORD.

1 Hear my prayer, O LORD,
And let my cry come to You.

100:3 [a] Following Kethib, Septuagint, and Vulgate; Qere, many Hebrew manuscripts, and Targum read *we are His*.

2 Do not hide Your face from me in the day of my trouble;
Incline Your ear to me;
In the day that I call, answer me speedily.

3 For my days are consumed like smoke,
And my bones are burned like a hearth.
4 My heart is stricken and withered like grass,
So that I forget to eat my bread.
5 Because of the sound of my groaning
My bones cling to my skin.
6 I am like a pelican of the wilderness;
I am like an owl of the desert.
7 I lie awake,
And am like a sparrow alone on the housetop.

8 My enemies reproach me all day long;
Those who deride me swear an oath against me.
9 For I have eaten ashes like bread,
And mingled my drink with weeping,
10 Because of Your indignation and Your wrath;
For You have lifted me up and cast me away.
11 My days *are* like a shadow that lengthens,
And I wither away like grass.

12 But You, O LORD, shall endure forever,
And the remembrance of Your name to all generations.
13 You will arise *and* have mercy on Zion;
For the time to favor her,
Yes, the set time, has come.
14 For Your servants take pleasure in her stones,
And show favor to her dust.
15 So the nations shall fear the name of the LORD,
And all the kings of the earth Your glory.
16 For the LORD shall build up Zion;
He shall appear in His glory.
17 He shall regard the prayer of the destitute,
And shall not despise their prayer.

18 This will be written for the generation *to come*,
That a people yet to be created may praise the LORD.
19 For He looked down from the height of His sanctuary;
From heaven the LORD viewed the earth,
20 To hear the groaning of the prisoner,
To release those appointed to death,
21 To declare the name of the LORD in Zion,
And His praise in Jerusalem,
22 When the peoples are gathered together,
And the kingdoms, to serve the LORD.

23 He weakened my strength in the way;
He shortened my days.
24 I said, "O my God,
Do not take me away in the midst of my days;
Your years *are* throughout all generations.
25 Of old You laid the foundation of the earth,
And the heavens *are* the work of Your hands.
26 They will perish, but You will endure;
Yes, they will all grow old like a garment;
Like a cloak You will change them,
And they will be changed.
27 But You *are* the same,
And Your years will have no end.
28 The children of Your servants will continue,
And their descendants will be established before You."

PSALM 103

Praise for the LORD's Mercies

A Psalm of David.

1 Bless the LORD, O my soul;
And all that is within me, *bless* His holy name!
2 Bless the LORD, O my soul,
And forget not all His benefits:
3 Who forgives all your iniquities,
Who heals all your diseases,
4 Who redeems your life from destruction,
Who crowns you with lovingkindness and tender mercies,
5 Who satisfies your mouth with good *things*,
So that your youth is renewed like the eagle's.

6 The LORD executes righteousness
And justice for all who are oppressed.
7 He made known His ways to Moses,
His acts to the children of Israel.

8 The LORD *is* merciful and gracious,
Slow to anger, and abounding in mercy.
9 He will not always strive *with us,*
Nor will He keep *His anger* forever.
10 He has not dealt with us according to our sins,
Nor punished us according to our iniquities.

11 For as the heavens are high above the earth,
So great is His mercy toward those who fear Him;
12 As far as the east is from the west,
So far has He removed our transgressions from us.
13 As a father pities *his* children,
So the LORD pities those who fear Him.
14 For He knows our frame;
He remembers that we *are* dust.

15 *As for* man, his days *are* like grass;
As a flower of the field, so he flourishes.
16 For the wind passes over it, and it is gone,
And its place remembers it no more.[a]
17 But the mercy of the LORD *is* from everlasting to everlasting
On those who fear Him,
And His righteousness to children's children,
18 To such as keep His covenant,
And to those who remember His commandments to do them.

19 The LORD has established His throne in heaven,
And His kingdom rules over all.

20 Bless the LORD, you His angels,
Who excel in strength, who do His word,
Heeding the voice of His word.
21 Bless the LORD, all *you* His hosts,
You ministers of His, who do His pleasure.
22 Bless the LORD, all His works,
In all places of His dominion.

Bless the LORD, O my soul!

PSALM 104

Praise to the Sovereign LORD for His Creation and Providence

1 Bless the LORD, O my soul!

O LORD my God, You are very great:
You are clothed with honor and majesty,
2 Who cover *Yourself* with light as *with* a garment,
Who stretch out the heavens like a curtain.

3 He lays the beams of His upper chambers in the waters,
Who makes the clouds His chariot,
Who walks on the wings of the wind,
4 Who makes His angels spirits,
His ministers a flame of fire.

5 *You who* laid the foundations of the earth,
So *that* it should not be moved forever,
6 You covered it with the deep as *with* a garment;
The waters stood above the mountains.
7 At Your rebuke they fled;

103:16 [a] Compare Job 7:10

COMPASSION

READ IT: PSALM 103:8

Do you know someone with a short temper? One small problem is all it takes for some people to fly off the handle. God isn't like that at all. The psalmist writes that God is slow to anger and merciful. He understands our weaknesses and gives us grace and mercy.

At the voice of Your thunder they
hastened away.
8 They went up over the mountains;
They went down into the valleys,
To the place which You founded for
them.
9 You have set a boundary that they may
not pass over,
That they may not return to cover the
earth.

10 He sends the springs into the valleys;
They flow among the hills.
11 They give drink to every beast of the
field;
The wild donkeys quench their thirst.
12 By them the birds of the heavens have
their home;
They sing among the branches.
13 He waters the hills from His upper
chambers;
The earth is satisfied with the fruit of
Your works.

14 He causes the grass to grow for the
cattle,
And vegetation for the service of man,
That he may bring forth food from the
earth,
15 And wine *that* makes glad the heart of
man,
Oil to make *his* face shine,
And bread *which* strengthens man's
heart.
16 The trees of the LORD are full *of sap,*
The cedars of Lebanon which He
planted,
17 Where the birds make their nests;
The stork has her home in the fir trees.
18 The high hills *are* for the wild goats;
The cliffs are a refuge for the rock
badgers.[a]

19 He appointed the moon for seasons;
The sun knows its going down.
20 You make darkness, and it is night,
In which all the beasts of the forest
creep about.
21 The young lions roar after their prey,
And seek their food from God.
22 *When* the sun rises, they gather together
And lie down in their dens.
23 Man goes out to his work
And to his labor until the evening.

24 O LORD, how manifold are Your works!
In wisdom You have made them all.
The earth is full of Your possessions—
25 This great and wide sea,
In which *are* innumerable teeming
things,
Living things both small and great.
26 There the ships sail about;
There is that Leviathan
Which You have made to play there.

27 These all wait for You,
That You may give *them* their food in
due season.
28 *What* You give them they gather in;
You open Your hand, they are filled with
good.
29 You hide Your face, they are troubled;
You take away their breath, they die and
return to their dust.
30 You send forth Your Spirit, they are
created;
And You renew the face of the earth.

31 May the glory of the LORD endure
forever;
May the LORD rejoice in His works.
32 He looks on the earth, and it trembles;
He touches the hills, and they smoke.

33 I will sing to the LORD as long as I live;
I will sing praise to my God while I have
my being.
34 May my meditation be sweet to Him;
I will be glad in the LORD.
35 May sinners be consumed from the
earth,
And the wicked be no more.

Bless the LORD, O my soul!
Praise the LORD!

PSALM 105

The Eternal Faithfulness of the LORD

1 Oh, give thanks to the LORD!
Call upon His name;
Make known His deeds among the
peoples!
2 Sing to Him, sing psalms to Him;
Talk of all His wondrous works!
3 Glory in His holy name;
Let the hearts of those rejoice who seek
the LORD!
4 Seek the LORD and His strength;
Seek His face evermore!

104:18 [a] Or *rock hyrax* (compare Leviticus 11:5)

5 Remember His marvelous works which
He has done,
His wonders, and the judgments of His
mouth,
6 O seed of Abraham His servant,
You children of Jacob, His chosen ones!

7 He *is* the LORD our God;
His judgments *are* in all the earth.
8 He remembers His covenant forever,
The word *which* He commanded, for a
thousand generations,
9 *The covenant* which He made with
Abraham,
And His oath to Isaac,
10 And confirmed it to Jacob for a statute,
To Israel *as* an everlasting covenant,
11 Saying, "To you I will give the land of
Canaan
As the allotment of your inheritance,"
12 When they were few in number,
Indeed very few, and strangers in it.

13 When they went from one nation to
another,
From *one* kingdom to another people,
14 He permitted no one to do them wrong;
Yes, He rebuked kings for their sakes,
15 *Saying*, "Do not touch My anointed
ones,
And do My prophets no harm."

16 Moreover He called for a famine in the
land;
He destroyed all the provision of bread.
17 He sent a man before them—
Joseph—*who* was sold as a slave.
18 They hurt his feet with fetters,
He was laid in irons.
19 Until the time that his word came to
pass,
The word of the LORD tested him.
20 The king sent and released him,
The ruler of the people let him go free.
21 He made him lord of his house,
And ruler of all his possessions,
22 To bind his princes at his pleasure,
And teach his elders wisdom.

23 Israel also came into Egypt,
And Jacob dwelt in the land of Ham.
24 He increased His people greatly,
And made them stronger than their
enemies.
25 He turned their heart to hate His
people,
To deal craftily with His servants.

26 He sent Moses His servant,
And Aaron whom He had chosen.
27 They performed His signs among
them,
And wonders in the land of Ham.
28 He sent darkness, and made *it* dark;
And they did not rebel against His word.
29 He turned their waters into blood,
And killed their fish.
30 Their land abounded with frogs,
Even in the chambers of their kings.
31 He spoke, and there came swarms of
flies,
And lice in all their territory.
32 He gave them hail for rain,
And flaming fire in their land.
33 He struck their vines also, and their fig
trees,
And splintered the trees of their
territory.
34 He spoke, and locusts came,
Young locusts without number,
35 And ate up all the vegetation in their
land,
And devoured the fruit of their ground.
36 He also destroyed all the firstborn in
their land,
The first of all their strength.

37 He also brought them out with silver
and gold,
And *there was* none feeble among His
tribes.
38 Egypt was glad when they departed,
For the fear of them had fallen upon
them.
39 He spread a cloud for a covering,
And fire to give light in the night.
40 *The people* asked, and He brought quail,
And satisfied them with the bread of
heaven.
41 He opened the rock, and water gushed
out;
It ran in the dry places *like* a river.

42 For He remembered His holy promise,
And Abraham His servant.
43 He brought out His people with joy,
His chosen ones with gladness.
44 He gave them the lands of the Gentiles,
And they inherited the labor of the
nations,
45 That they might observe His statutes
And keep His laws.

Praise the LORD!

PSALM 106

Joy in Forgiveness of Israel's Sins

1 Praise the LORD!

Oh, give thanks to the LORD, for *He is* good!
For His mercy *endures* forever.

2 Who can utter the mighty acts of the LORD?
Who can declare all His praise?
3 Blessed *are* those who keep justice,
And he who does[a] righteousness at all times!

4 Remember me, O LORD, with the favor *You have toward* Your people.
Oh, visit me with Your salvation,
5 That I may see the benefit of Your chosen ones,
That I may rejoice in the gladness of Your nation,
That I may glory with Your inheritance.

6 We have sinned with our fathers,
We have committed iniquity,
We have done wickedly.
7 Our fathers in Egypt did not understand Your wonders;
They did not remember the multitude of Your mercies,
But rebelled by the sea—the Red Sea.

8 Nevertheless He saved them for His name's sake,
That He might make His mighty power known.
9 He rebuked the Red Sea also, and it dried up;
So He led them through the depths,
As through the wilderness.
10 He saved them from the hand of him who hated *them*,
And redeemed them from the hand of the enemy.
11 The waters covered their enemies;
There was not one of them left.
12 Then they believed His words;
They sang His praise.

13 They soon forgot His works;
They did not wait for His counsel,
14 *But lusted exceedingly* in the wilderness,
And tested God in the desert.
15 And He gave them their request,
But sent leanness into their soul.

16 When they envied Moses in the camp,
And Aaron the saint of the LORD,
17 The earth opened up and swallowed Dathan,
And covered the faction of Abiram.
18 A fire was kindled in their company;
The flame burned up the wicked.

19 They made a calf in Horeb,
And worshiped the molded image.
20 Thus they changed their glory
Into the image of an ox that eats grass.
21 They forgot God their Savior,
Who had done great things in Egypt,
22 Wondrous works in the land of Ham,
Awesome things by the Red Sea.
23 Therefore He said that He would destroy them,
Had not Moses His chosen one stood before Him in the breach,
To turn away His wrath, lest He destroy *them*.

24 Then they despised the pleasant land;
They did not believe His word,
25 But complained in their tents,
And did not heed the voice of the LORD.
26 Therefore He raised His hand *in an oath* against them,
To overthrow them in the wilderness,
27 To overthrow their descendants among the nations,
And to scatter them in the lands.

28 They joined themselves also to Baal of Peor,
And ate sacrifices made to the dead.
29 Thus they provoked *Him* to anger with their deeds,
And the plague broke out among them.
30 Then Phinehas stood up and intervened,
And the plague was stopped.
31 And that was accounted to him for righteousness
To all generations forevermore.

32 They angered *Him* also at the waters of strife,[a]
So that it went ill with Moses on account of them;
33 Because they rebelled against His Spirit,
So that he spoke rashly with his lips.

34 They did not destroy the peoples,

106:3 [a] Septuagint, Syriac, Targum, and Vulgate read *those who do.* **106:32** [a] Or *Meribah*

Concerning whom the LORD had
commanded them,
35 But they mingled with the Gentiles
And learned their works;
36 They served their idols,
Which became a snare to them.
37 They even sacrificed their sons
And their daughters to demons,
38 And shed innocent blood,
The blood of their sons and daughters,
Whom they sacrificed to the idols of
Canaan;
And the land was polluted with blood.
39 Thus they were defiled by their own
works,
And played the harlot by their own
deeds.

40 Therefore the wrath of the LORD was
kindled against His people,
So that He abhorred His own
inheritance.
41 And He gave them into the hand of the
Gentiles,
And those who hated them ruled over
them.
42 Their enemies also oppressed them,
And they were brought into subjection
under their hand.
43 Many times He delivered them;
But they rebelled in their counsel,
And were brought low for their iniquity.

44 Nevertheless He regarded their
affliction,
When He heard their cry;
45 And for their sake He remembered His
covenant,
And relented according to the multitude
of His mercies.
46 He also made them to be pitied
By all those who carried them away
captive.

47 Save us, O LORD our God,
And gather us from among the
Gentiles,
To give thanks to Your holy name,
To triumph in Your praise.

48 Blessed *be* the LORD God of Israel
From everlasting to everlasting!
And let all the people say, "Amen!"

Praise the LORD!

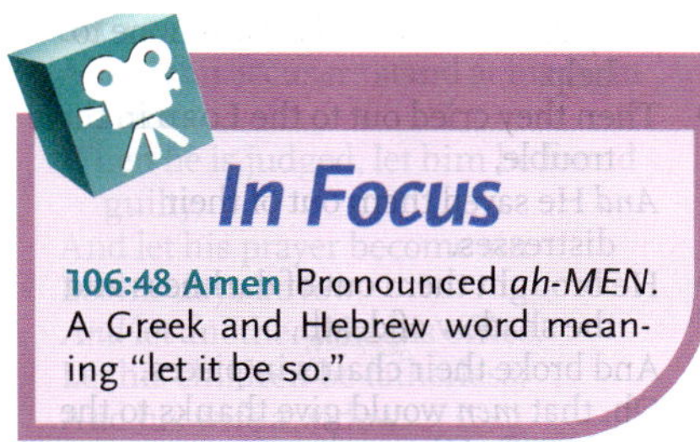

106:48 Amen Pronounced *ah-MEN*. A Greek and Hebrew word meaning "let it be so."

BOOK FIVE

Psalms 107–150

PSALM 107

Thanksgiving to the LORD for His Great Works of Deliverance

1 Oh, give thanks to the LORD, for *He is*
good!
For His mercy *endures* forever.
2 Let the redeemed of the LORD say *so,*
Whom He has redeemed from the hand
of the enemy,
3 And gathered out of the lands,
From the east and from the west,
From the north and from the south.

4 They wandered in the wilderness in a
desolate way;
They found no city to dwell in.
5 Hungry and thirsty,
Their soul fainted in them.
6 Then they cried out to the LORD in their
trouble,
And He delivered them out of their
distresses.
7 And He led them forth by the right way,
That they might go to a city for a
dwelling place.
8 Oh, that *men* would give thanks to the
LORD *for* His goodness,
And *for* His wonderful works to the
children of men!
9 For He satisfies the longing soul,
And fills the hungry soul with
goodness.

10 Those who sat in darkness and in the
shadow of death,
Bound in affliction and irons—
11 Because they rebelled against the words
of God,
And despised the counsel of the Most
High,
12 Therefore He brought down their heart
with labor;

And to those who speak evil against my person.

21 But You, O GOD the Lord,
Deal with me for Your name's sake;
Because Your mercy *is* good, deliver me.
22 For I *am* poor and needy,
And my heart is wounded within me.
23 I am gone like a shadow when it lengthens;
I am shaken off like a locust.
24 My knees are weak through fasting,
And my flesh is feeble from lack of fatness.
25 I also have become a reproach to them;
When they look at me, they shake their heads.

26 Help me, O LORD my God!
Oh, save me according to Your mercy,
27 That they may know that this *is* Your hand—
That You, LORD, have done it!
28 Let them curse, but You bless;
When they arise, let them be ashamed,
But let Your servant rejoice.
29 Let my accusers be clothed with shame,
And let them cover themselves with their own disgrace as with a mantle.

30 I will greatly praise the LORD with my mouth;
Yes, I will praise Him among the multitude.
31 For He shall stand at the right hand of the poor,
To save *him* from those who condemn him.

PSALM 110

Announcement of the Messiah's Reign

A Psalm of David.

1 The LORD said to my Lord,
"Sit at My right hand,
Till I make Your enemies Your footstool."
2 The LORD shall send the rod of Your strength out of Zion.
Rule in the midst of Your enemies!

3 Your people *shall be* volunteers
In the day of Your power;
In the beauties of holiness, from the womb of the morning,
You have the dew of Your youth.
4 The LORD has sworn
And will not relent,
"You *are* a priest forever
According to the order of Melchizedek."

5 The Lord *is* at Your right hand;
He shall execute kings in the day of His wrath.
6 He shall judge among the nations,
He shall fill *the places* with dead bodies,
He shall execute the heads of many countries.
7 He shall drink of the brook by the wayside;
Therefore He shall lift up the head.

PSALM 111

Praise to God for His Faithfulness and Justice

1 Praise the LORD!

I will praise the LORD with *my* whole heart,
In the assembly of the upright and *in* the congregation.

2 The works of the LORD *are* great,
Studied by all who have pleasure in them.
3 His work *is* honorable and glorious,
And His righteousness endures forever.
4 He has made His wonderful works to be remembered;
The LORD *is* gracious and full of compassion.
5 He has given food to those who fear Him;
He will ever be mindful of His covenant.
6 He has declared to His people the power of His works,
In giving them the heritage of the nations.

7 The works of His hands *are* verity and justice;
All His precepts *are* sure.
8 They stand fast forever and ever,
And are done in truth and uprightness.
9 He has sent redemption to His people;
He has commanded His covenant forever:
Holy and awesome *is* His name.

10 The fear of the LORD *is* the beginning of wisdom;

A good understanding have all those
who do *His commandments.*
His praise endures forever.

PSALM 112

The Blessed State of the Righteous

1 Praise the LORD!

Blessed *is* the man *who* fears the LORD,
Who delights greatly in His
commandments.

2 His descendants will be mighty on earth;
The generation of the upright will be
blessed.
3 Wealth and riches *will be* in his house,
And his righteousness endures forever.
4 Unto the upright there arises light in
the darkness;
He is gracious, and full of compassion,
and righteous.
5 A good man deals graciously and lends;
He will guide his affairs with discretion.
6 Surely he will never be shaken;
The righteous will be in everlasting
remembrance.
7 He will not be afraid of evil tidings;
His heart is steadfast, trusting in the
LORD.
8 His heart *is* established;
He will not be afraid,
Until he sees *his desire* upon his
enemies.

9 He has dispersed abroad,
He has given to the poor;
His righteousness endures forever;
His horn will be exalted with honor.
10 The wicked will see *it* and be grieved;
He will gnash his teeth and melt away;
The desire of the wicked shall perish.

PSALM 113

The Majesty and Condescension of God

1 *Praise the LORD!*

Praise, O servants of the LORD,
Praise the name of the LORD!
2 Blessed be the name of the LORD
From this time forth and forevermore!
3 From the rising of the sun to its going
down
The LORD's name *is* to be praised.

4 The LORD *is* high above all nations,
His glory above the heavens.
5 Who *is* like the LORD our God,
Who dwells on high,
6 Who humbles Himself to behold
The things that are in the heavens and in
the earth?

7 He raises the poor out of the dust,
And lifts the needy out of the ash heap,
8 That He may seat *him* with princes—
With the princes of His people.
9 He grants the barren woman a home,
Like a joyful mother of children.

Praise the LORD!

PSALM 114

The Power of God in His Deliverance of Israel

1 When Israel went out of Egypt,
The house of Jacob from a people of
strange language,
2 Judah became His sanctuary,
And Israel His dominion.

3 The sea saw *it* and fled;
Jordan turned back.
4 The mountains skipped like rams,
The little hills like lambs.
5 What ails you, O sea, that you fled?
O Jordan, *that* you turned back?
6 O mountains, *that* you skipped like
rams?
O little hills, like lambs?

7 Tremble, O earth, at the presence of the
Lord,
At the presence of the God of Jacob,
8 Who turned the rock *into* a pool of
water,
The flint into a fountain of waters.

PSALM 115

The Futility of Idols and the Trustworthiness of God

1 Not unto us, O LORD, not unto us,
But to Your name give glory,
Because of Your mercy,
Because of Your truth.
2 Why should the Gentiles say,
"So where *is* their God?"

3 But our God *is* in heaven;
He does whatever He pleases.
4 Their idols *are* silver and gold,
The work of men's hands.

5 They have mouths, but they do not speak;
Eyes they have, but they do not see;
6 They have ears, but they do not hear;
Noses they have, but they do not smell;
7 They have hands, but they do not handle;
Feet they have, but they do not walk;
Nor do they mutter through their throat.
8 Those who make them are like them;
So is everyone who trusts in them.

9 O Israel, trust in the LORD;
He *is* their help and their shield.
10 O house of Aaron, trust in the LORD;
He *is* their help and their shield.
11 You who fear the LORD, trust in the LORD;
He *is* their help and their shield.

12 The LORD has been mindful of *us;*
He will bless us;
He will bless the house of Israel;
He will bless the house of Aaron.
13 He will bless those who fear the LORD,
Both small and great.

14 May the LORD give you increase more and more,
You and your children.
15 *May* you *be* blessed by the LORD,
Who made heaven and earth.

16 The heaven, *even* the heavens, *are* the LORD's;
But the earth He has given to the children of men.
17 The dead do not praise the LORD,
Nor any who go down into silence.
18 But we will bless the LORD
From this time forth and forevermore.

Praise the LORD!

PSALM 116

Thanksgiving for Deliverance from Death

1 I love the LORD, because He has heard
My voice *and* my supplications.
2 Because He has inclined His ear to me,
Therefore I will call *upon Him* as long as I live.

3 The pains of death surrounded me,
And the pangs of Sheol laid hold of me;
I found trouble and sorrow.
4 Then I called upon the name of the LORD:
"O LORD, I implore You, deliver my soul!"

5 Gracious *is* the LORD, and righteous;
Yes, our God *is* merciful.
6 The LORD preserves the simple;
I was brought low, and He saved me.
7 Return to your rest, O my soul,
For the LORD has dealt bountifully with you.

8 For You have delivered my soul from death,
My eyes from tears,
And my feet from falling.
9 I will walk before the LORD
In the land of the living.
10 I believed, therefore I spoke,
"I am greatly afflicted."
11 I said in my haste,
"All men *are* liars."

Action!

CREATION CARE

READ IT: PSALM 115:16

God has given humanity an amazing gift: the earth. Like a new puppy with a bow on Christmas morning, the earth has proven to be unpredictable, challenging, and full of impressive tricks. (If you've ever seen a *rainbow after a rainstorm*, you know it's true.) But just like a puppy, the earth comes with big responsibilities. We don't always treat it the way we should, but the more we see it as a gift, the easier that will be.

12 What shall I render to the LORD
For all His benefits toward me?
13 I will take up the cup of salvation,
And call upon the name of the LORD.
14 I will pay my vows to the LORD
Now in the presence of all His people.

15 Precious in the sight of the LORD
Is the death of His saints.

16 O LORD, truly I *am* Your servant;
I *am* Your servant, the son of Your
maidservant;
You have loosed my bonds.
17 I will offer to You the sacrifice of
thanksgiving,
And will call upon the name of the
LORD.

18 I will pay my vows to the LORD
Now in the presence of all His people,
19 In the courts of the LORD's house,
In the midst of you, O Jerusalem.

Praise the LORD!

PSALM 117

Let All Peoples Praise the LORD

1 Praise the LORD, all you Gentiles!
Laud Him, all you peoples!
2 For His merciful kindness is great
toward us,
And the truth of the LORD *endures*
forever.

Praise the LORD!

PSALM 118

Praise to God for His Everlasting Mercy

1 Oh, give thanks to the LORD, for *He is*
good!
For His mercy *endures* forever.

2 Let Israel now say,
"His mercy *endures* forever."
3 Let the house of Aaron now say,
"His mercy *endures* forever."
4 Let those who fear the LORD now say,

JESUS AND HIS DISCIPLES SING A HYMN

READ IT: PSALM 118:1–29

GET IT:

At the end of the Passover meal the Jews sang a song. Psalm 118 was one of the many songs that were traditionally sung after the celebration. Usually an entire group of psalms (Psalms 115–118) were sung all at the same time. Jesus and His disciples probably sang this psalm after their dinner together. After singing, they went to the Garden of Gethsemane on the Mount of Olives to pray.

LIVE IT:

Singing a praise song is a wonderful way of closing a time of fellowship. This psalm opens and closes with "Oh, give thanks to the LORD, for He is good! For His mercy endures forever" (vv. 1, 29). Think about putting those words to music, either something you made up or a song that fits with the words. Try singing it with family or friends after you finish eating together or after a special time of fellowship.

"His mercy *endures* forever."

5 I called on the LORD in distress;
The LORD answered me *and set me* in a broad place.
6 The LORD *is* on my side;
I will not fear.
What can man do to me?
7 The LORD is for me among those who help me;
Therefore I shall see *my desire* on those who hate me.
8 *It is* better to trust in the LORD
Than to put confidence in man.
9 *It is* better to trust in the LORD
Than to put confidence in princes.

10 All nations surrounded me,
But in the name of the LORD I will destroy them.
11 They surrounded me,
Yes, they surrounded me;
But in the name of the LORD I will destroy them.
12 They surrounded me like bees;
They were quenched like a fire of thorns;
For in the name of the LORD I will destroy them.
13 You pushed me violently, that I might fall,
But the LORD helped me.
14 The LORD *is* my strength and song,
And He has become my salvation.[a]

15 The voice of rejoicing and salvation
Is in the tents of the righteous;
The right hand of the LORD does valiantly.
16 The right hand of the LORD is exalted;
The right hand of the LORD does valiantly.
17 I shall not die, but live,
And declare the works of the LORD.
18 The LORD has chastened me severely,
But He has not given me over to death.

19 Open to me the gates of righteousness;
I will go through them,
And I will praise the LORD.
20 This is the gate of the LORD,
Through which the righteous shall enter.

21 I will praise You,
For You have answered me,
And have become my salvation.

22 The stone *which* the builders rejected
Has become the chief cornerstone.
23 This was the LORD's doing;
It *is* marvelous in our eyes.
24 This *is* the day the LORD has made;
We will rejoice and be glad in it.

25 Save now, I pray, O LORD;
O LORD, I pray, send now prosperity.
26 Blessed *is* he who comes in the name of the LORD!
We have blessed you from the house of the LORD.
27 God *is* the LORD,
And He has given us light;

118:14 [a] Compare Exodus 15:2

IDOL AND HERO WORSHIP

READ IT: PSALM 118:8, 9

To trust someone is to hand over control to that person. That's why it's really hard to completely trust other people—we like holding on to control. It's a mistake to give your trust to someone who's not worthy of it because that's how you get hurt. If there were a contest for your trust between God and another person, who would win? When you think of it like that, it's pretty obvious who deserves your trust.

Bind the sacrifice with cords to the
horns of the altar.
28 You *are* my God, and I will praise You;
You are my God, I will exalt You.

29 Oh, give thanks to the LORD, for *He is*
good!
For His mercy *endures* forever.

PSALM 119

Meditations on the Excellencies of the Word of God

א ALEPH

1 Blessed *are* the undefiled in the way,
Who walk in the law of the LORD!
2 Blessed *are* those who keep His
testimonies,
Who seek Him with the whole heart!
3 They also do no iniquity;
They walk in His ways.
4 You have commanded *us*
To keep Your precepts diligently.
5 Oh, that my ways were directed
To keep Your statutes!
6 Then I would not be ashamed,
When I look into all Your
commandments.
7 I will praise You with uprightness of
heart,
When I learn Your righteous
judgments.
8 I will keep Your statutes;
Oh, do not forsake me utterly!

ב BETH

9 How can a young man cleanse his way?
By taking heed according to Your word.
10 With my whole heart I have sought You;
Oh, let me not wander from Your
commandments!
11 Your word I have hidden in my heart,
That I might not sin against You.
12 Blessed *are* You, O LORD!
Teach me Your statutes.
13 With my lips I have declared
All the judgments of Your mouth.
14 I have rejoiced in the way of Your
testimonies,
As *much as* in all riches.
15 I will meditate on Your precepts,
And contemplate Your ways.
16 I will delight myself in Your statutes;
I will not forget Your word.

In Focus

119:11 Word (God's Word) God speaking in the Scriptures of the Old and New Testaments. In the New Testament, Jesus also is called "the Word" (John 1:1) because He is God's personal Word.

ג GIMEL

17 Deal bountifully with Your servant,
That I may live and keep Your word.
18 Open my eyes, that I may see
Wondrous things from Your law.
19 I *am* a stranger in the earth;
Do not hide Your commandments
from me.
20 My soul breaks with longing
For Your judgments at all times.
21 You rebuke the proud—the cursed,
Who stray from Your commandments.
22 Remove from me reproach and
contempt,
For I have kept Your testimonies.
23 Princes also sit *and* speak against me,
But Your servant meditates on Your
statutes.
24 Your testimonies also *are* my delight
And my counselors.

ד DALETH

25 My soul clings to the dust;
Revive me according to Your word.
26 I have declared my ways, and You
answered me;
Teach me Your statutes.
27 Make me understand the way of Your
precepts;
So shall I meditate on Your wonderful
works.
28 My soul melts from heaviness;
Strengthen me according to Your word.
29 Remove from me the way of lying,
And grant me Your law graciously.
30 I have chosen the way of truth;
Your judgments I have laid *before me.*
31 I cling to Your testimonies;
O LORD, do not put me to shame!

32 I will run the course of Your
commandments,
For You shall enlarge my heart.

ה HE

33 Teach me, O LORD, the way of Your
statutes,
And I shall keep it *to* the end.
34 Give me understanding, and I shall
keep Your law;
Indeed, I shall observe it with *my* whole
heart.
35 Make me walk in the path of Your
commandments,
For I delight in it.
36 Incline my heart to Your testimonies,
And not to covetousness.
37 Turn away my eyes from looking at
worthless things,
And revive me in Your way.[a]
38 Establish Your word to Your servant,
Who *is devoted* to fearing You.
39 Turn away my reproach which I dread,
For Your judgments *are* good.
40 Behold, I long for Your precepts;
Revive me in Your righteousness.

ו WAW

41 Let Your mercies come also to me,
O LORD—
Your salvation according to Your word.
42 So shall I have an answer for him who
reproaches me,
For I trust in Your word.
43 And take not the word of truth utterly
out of my mouth,
For I have hoped in Your ordinances.
44 So shall I keep Your law continually,
Forever and ever.
45 And I will walk at liberty,
For I seek Your precepts.
46 I will speak of Your testimonies also
before kings,
And will not be ashamed.
47 And I will delight myself in Your
commandments,
Which I love.
48 My hands also I will lift up to Your
commandments,
Which I love,
And I will meditate on Your statutes.

ז ZAYIN

49 Remember the word to Your servant,
Upon which You have caused me to
hope.
50 This *is* my comfort in my affliction,
For Your word has given me life.
51 The proud have me in great derision,
Yet I do not turn aside from Your law.
52 I remembered Your judgments of old,
O LORD,
And have comforted myself.
53 Indignation has taken hold of me
Because of the wicked, who forsake
Your law.
54 Your statutes have been my songs
In the house of my pilgrimage.
55 I remember Your name in the night,
O LORD,
And I keep Your law.
56 This has become mine,
Because I kept Your precepts.

ח HETH

57 *You are* my portion, O LORD;
I have said that I would keep Your
words.
58 I entreated Your favor with *my* whole
heart;
Be merciful to me according to Your
word.
59 I thought about my ways,
And turned my feet to Your testimonies.
60 I made haste, and did not delay
To keep Your commandments.
61 The cords of the wicked have bound me,
But I have not forgotten Your law.
62 At midnight I will rise to give thanks to
You,
Because of Your righteous judgments.
63 I *am* a companion of all who fear You,
And of those who keep Your precepts.
64 The earth, O LORD, is full of Your
mercy;
Teach me Your statutes.

ט TETH

65 You have dealt well with Your servant,
O LORD, according to Your word.
66 Teach me good judgment and
knowledge,
For I believe Your commandments.

119:37 [a] Following Masoretic Text, Septuagint, and Vulgate; Targum reads *Your words.*

67 Before I was afflicted I went astray,
But now I keep Your word.
68 You *are* good, and do good;
Teach me Your statutes.
69 The proud have forged a lie against me,
But I will keep Your precepts with *my* whole heart.
70 Their heart is as fat as grease,
But I delight in Your law.
71 *It is* good for me that I have been afflicted,
That I may learn Your statutes.
72 The law of Your mouth *is* better to me
Than thousands of *coins of* gold and silver.

י YOD

73 Your hands have made me and fashioned me;
Give me understanding, that I may learn Your commandments.
74 Those who fear You will be glad when they see me,
Because I have hoped in Your word.
75 I know, O LORD, that Your judgments *are* right,
And *that* in faithfulness You have afflicted me.
76 Let, I pray, Your merciful kindness be for my comfort,
According to Your word to Your servant.
77 Let Your tender mercies come to me, that I may live;
For Your law *is* my delight.
78 Let the proud be ashamed,
For they treated me wrongfully with falsehood;
But I will meditate on Your precepts.
79 Let those who fear You turn to me,
Those who know Your testimonies.
80 Let my heart be blameless regarding Your statutes,
That I may not be ashamed.

כ KAPH

81 My soul faints for Your salvation,
But I hope in Your word.
82 My eyes fail *from searching* Your word,
Saying, "When will You comfort me?"
83 For I have become like a wineskin in smoke,
Yet I do not forget Your statutes.
84 How many *are* the days of Your servant?
When will You execute judgment on those who persecute me?
85 The proud have dug pits for me,
Which *is* not according to Your law.
86 All Your commandments *are* faithful;
They persecute me wrongfully;
Help me!
87 They almost made an end of me on earth,
But I did not forsake Your precepts.
88 Revive me according to Your lovingkindness,
So that I may keep the testimony of Your mouth.

ל LAMED

89 Forever, O LORD,
Your word is settled in heaven.
90 Your faithfulness *endures* to all generations;
You established the earth, and it abides.
91 They continue this day according to Your ordinances,
For all *are* Your servants.
92 Unless Your law *had been* my delight,
I would then have perished in my affliction.
93 I will never forget Your precepts,
For by them You have given me life.
94 I *am* Yours, save me;
For I have sought Your precepts.
95 The wicked wait for me to destroy me,
But I will consider Your testimonies.
96 I have seen the consummation of all perfection,
But Your commandment *is* exceedingly broad.

מ MEM

97 Oh, how I love Your law!
It *is* my meditation all the day.
98 You, through Your commandments, make me wiser than my enemies;
For they *are* ever with me.
99 I have more understanding than all my teachers,
For Your testimonies *are* my meditation.
100 I understand more than the ancients,
Because I keep Your precepts.
101 I have restrained my feet from every evil way,
That I may keep Your word.
102 I have not departed from Your judgments,

For You Yourself have taught me.
103 How sweet are Your words to my taste,
Sweeter than honey to my mouth!
104 Through Your precepts I get understanding;
Therefore I hate every false way.

נ NUN

105 Your word *is* a lamp to my feet
And a light to my path.
106 I have sworn and confirmed
That I will keep Your righteous judgments.
107 I am afflicted very much;
Revive me, O LORD, according to Your word.
108 Accept, I pray, the freewill offerings of my mouth, O LORD,
And teach me Your judgments.
109 My life *is* continually in my hand,
Yet I do not forget Your law.
110 The wicked have laid a snare for me,
Yet I have not strayed from Your precepts.
111 Your testimonies I have taken as a heritage forever,
For they *are* the rejoicing of my heart.

Epic Ideas

THE BIBLE IS THE TRUTH
AGELESS TRUTH

READ IT: PSALM 119:89–96

GET IT:

The truth of God's Word is older than old. In fact, it's forever. That means it's as old as God Himself (who has always existed). The Bible itself—the different books and stories and chapters—do have an age. Real people wrote them down at specific times, in specific places. But the truth that exists within those books and stories and chapters are timeless because they come from God Himself.

These particular verses in Psalm 119 were written in the ancient world, long before Jesus was born. But the truth they tell us—that God can always be trusted, that God made the earth, that God's plan and design for life is the very best—will never be outdated, old-fashioned, or untrue. Even if some things in the stories have changed (like clothes and customs and names and ways of talking), the truth behind the stories never changes.

LIVE IT:

Don't expect to flip open your Bible and find quick and easy answers to things like "What should I have for lunch?" or "What kind of phone should I get?" The Bible isn't a collection of FYIs or Q-and-As. It's the book of life, the source of truth, the heart of God. So pay careful attention to *what it's saying.* Look beyond the things that have changed over time and find the things that are true today. Those are the things that will tell you how to live life as God planned it.

112 I have inclined my heart to perform
Your statutes
Forever, to the very end.

ס SAMEK

113 I hate the double-minded,
But I love Your law.
114 You *are* my hiding place and my shield;
I hope in Your word.
115 Depart from me, you evildoers,
For I will keep the commandments of
my God!
116 Uphold me according to Your word, that
I may live;
And do not let me be ashamed of my
hope.
117 Hold me up, and I shall be safe,
And I shall observe Your statutes
continually.
118 You reject all those who stray from Your
statutes,
For their deceit *is* falsehood.
119 You put away all the wicked of the earth
like dross;
Therefore I love Your testimonies.
120 My flesh trembles for fear of You,
And I am afraid of Your judgments.

ע AYIN

121 I have done justice and righteousness;
Do not leave me to my oppressors.
122 Be surety for Your servant for good;
Do not let the proud oppress me.
123 My eyes fail *from seeking* Your salvation
And Your righteous word.
124 Deal with Your servant according to
Your mercy,
And teach me Your statutes.
125 I *am* Your servant;
Give me understanding,
That I may know Your testimonies.
126 *It is* time for *You* to act, O LORD,
For they have regarded Your law as void.
127 Therefore I love Your commandments
More than gold, yes, than fine gold!
128 Therefore all *Your* precepts *concerning*
all *things*
I consider *to be* right;
I hate every false way.

פ PE

129 Your testimonies are wonderful;
Therefore my soul keeps them.
130 The entrance of Your words gives light;
It gives understanding to the simple.
131 I opened my mouth and panted,
For I longed for Your commandments.
132 Look upon me and be merciful to me,
As Your custom *is* toward those who
love Your name.
133 Direct my steps by Your word,
And let no iniquity have dominion
over me.
134 Redeem me from the oppression of
man,
That I may keep Your precepts.
135 Make Your face shine upon Your
servant,
And teach me Your statutes.
136 Rivers of water run down from my eyes,
Because *men* do not keep Your law.

צ TSADDE

137 Righteous *are* You, O LORD,
And upright *are* Your judgments.
138 Your testimonies, *which* You have
commanded,
Are righteous and very faithful.
139 My zeal has consumed me,
Because my enemies have forgotten
Your words.
140 Your word *is* very pure;
Therefore Your servant loves it.
141 I *am* small and despised,
Yet I do not forget Your precepts.
142 Your righteousness *is* an everlasting
righteousness,
And Your law *is* truth.
143 Trouble and anguish have overtaken
me,
Yet Your commandments *are* my
delights.
144 The righteousness of Your testimonies
is everlasting;
Give me understanding, and I shall live.

ק QOPH

145 I cry out with *my* whole heart;
Hear me, O LORD!
I will keep Your statutes.
146 I cry out to You;
Save me, and I will keep Your
testimonies.
147 I rise before the dawning of the
morning,
And cry for help;
I hope in Your word.

148 My eyes are awake through the *night* watches,
That I may meditate on Your word.
149 Hear my voice according to Your lovingkindness;
O LORD, revive me according to Your justice.
150 They draw near who follow after wickedness;
They are far from Your law.
151 You *are* near, O LORD,
And all Your commandments *are* truth.
152 Concerning Your testimonies,
I have known of old that You have founded them forever.

ר RESH

153 Consider my affliction and deliver me,
For I do not forget Your law.
154 Plead my cause and redeem me;
Revive me according to Your word.
155 Salvation *is* far from the wicked,
For they do not seek Your statutes.
156 Great *are* Your tender mercies, O LORD;
Revive me according to Your judgments.
157 Many *are* my persecutors and my enemies,
Yet I do not turn from Your testimonies.
158 I see the treacherous, and am disgusted,
Because they do not keep Your word.
159 Consider how I love Your precepts;
Revive me, O LORD, according to Your lovingkindness.
160 The entirety of Your word *is* truth,
And every one of Your righteous judgments *endures* forever.

ש SHIN

161 Princes persecute me without a cause,
But my heart stands in awe of Your word.
162 I rejoice at Your word
As one who finds great treasure.
163 I hate and abhor lying,
But I love Your law.
164 Seven times a day I praise You,
Because of Your righteous judgments.
165 Great peace have those who love Your law,
And nothing causes them to stumble.
166 LORD, I hope for Your salvation,
And I do Your commandments.
167 My soul keeps Your testimonies,
And I love them exceedingly.
168 I keep Your precepts and Your testimonies,
For all my ways *are* before You.

ת TAU

169 Let my cry come before You, O LORD;
Give me understanding according to Your word.
170 Let my supplication come before You;
Deliver me according to Your word.
171 My lips shall utter praise,
For You teach me Your statutes.
172 My tongue shall speak of Your word,
For all Your commandments *are* righteousness.
173 Let Your hand become my help,
For I have chosen Your precepts.
174 I long for Your salvation, O LORD,
And Your law *is* my delight.
175 Let my soul live, and it shall praise You;
And let Your judgments help me.
176 I have gone astray like a lost sheep;
Seek Your servant,
For I do not forget Your commandments.

PSALM 120

Plea for Relief from Bitter Foes

A Song of Ascents.

1 In my distress I cried to the LORD,
And He heard me.
2 Deliver my soul, O LORD, from lying lips
And from a deceitful tongue.

3 What shall be given to you,
Or what shall be done to you,
You false tongue?
4 Sharp arrows of the warrior,
With coals of the broom tree!

5 Woe is me, that I dwell in Meshech,
That I dwell among the tents of Kedar!
6 My soul has dwelt too long
With one who hates peace.
7 I *am for* peace;
But when I speak, they *are* for war.

PSALM 121

God the Help of Those Who Seek Him

A Song of Ascents.

1 I will lift up my eyes to the hills—
From whence comes my help?
2 My help *comes* from the LORD,
Who made heaven and earth.

3 He will not allow your foot to be moved;
He who keeps you will not slumber.
4 Behold, He who keeps Israel
Shall neither slumber nor sleep.

5 The LORD *is* your keeper;
The LORD *is* your shade at your right
hand.
6 The sun shall not strike you by day,
Nor the moon by night.

7 The LORD shall preserve you from all evil;
He shall preserve your soul.
8 The LORD shall preserve your going out
and your coming in
From this time forth, and even
forevermore.

PSALM 122

The Joy of Going to the House of the LORD

A Song of Ascents. Of David.

1 I was glad when they said to me,
"Let us go into the house of the LORD."
2 Our feet have been standing
Within your gates, O Jerusalem!

3 Jerusalem is built
As a city that is compact together,
4 Where the tribes go up,
The tribes of the LORD,
To the Testimony of Israel,
To give thanks to the name of
the LORD.
5 For thrones are set there for
judgment,
The thrones of the house of David.

6 Pray for the peace of Jerusalem:
"May they prosper who love you.
7 Peace be within your walls,
Prosperity within your palaces."
8 For the sake of my brethren and
companions,
I will now say, "Peace *be* within you."
9 Because of the house of the LORD our
God
I will seek your good.

GOD WATCHES OVER YOU

READ IT: PSALM 121:1–8

GET IT:

This psalm was a song that the Israelites sang on their journey to the city of Jerusalem to worship God in the temple. The people came from all over the country to Jerusalem to worship God on special holidays. Sometimes they traveled for days to get there. As they came closer to the city, they could see the holy city and God's holy temple on the hill in the distance. They knew that they got their strength from God who was in His temple. They sang this song to declare their trust in God, who never sleeps but watches over His people all the time.

LIVE IT:

The people of Israel used this psalm to share what they believed about God. Make up a poem or a song that tells what you believe about God. You can use some of the things mentioned in this psalm or come up with your own ways of explaining what God means to you.

PSALM 123

Prayer for Relief from Contempt

A Song of Ascents.

1 Unto You I lift up my eyes,
O You who dwell in the heavens.
2 Behold, as the eyes of servants *look* to
the hand of their masters,
As the eyes of a maid to the hand of her
mistress,
So our eyes *look* to the LORD our God,
Until He has mercy on us.

3 Have mercy on us, O LORD, have mercy
on us!
For we are exceedingly filled with
contempt.
4 Our soul is exceedingly filled
With the scorn of those who are
at ease,
With the contempt of the proud.

PSALM 124

The LORD the Defense of His People

A Song of Ascents. Of David.

1 "If it had not been the LORD who was on
our side,"
Let Israel now say—
2 "If it had not been the LORD who was on
our side,
When men rose up against us,
3 Then they would have swallowed us
alive,
When their wrath was kindled against
us;
4 Then the waters would have
overwhelmed us,
The stream would have gone over our
soul;
5 Then the swollen waters
Would have gone over our soul."

6 Blessed *be* the LORD,
Who has not given us *as* prey to their
teeth.
7 Our soul has escaped as a bird from the
snare of the fowlers;[a]
The snare is broken, and we have
escaped.
8 Our help *is* in the name of the LORD,
Who made heaven and earth.

PSALM 125

The LORD the Strength of His People

A Song of Ascents.

1 Those who trust in the LORD
Are like Mount Zion,
Which cannot be moved, *but* abides
forever.
2 As the mountains surround
Jerusalem,
So the LORD surrounds His people
From this time forth and forever.

3 For the scepter of wickedness shall not
rest
On the land allotted to the righteous,
Lest the righteous reach out their hands
to iniquity.

124:7 [a] That is, persons who catch birds in a trap or snare

JOY

READ IT: PSALM 126:2, 3

God's people experienced a dreamlike gladness when they remembered all that the Lord had done for them. Remembering triggered more joy. We can experience joy just like this when we remember what the Lord has done for us. Think about something God has done for you, big or small, and let it fill you with joy.

4 Do good, O LORD, to *those who are* good,
And to *those who are* upright in their hearts.

5 As for such as turn aside to their crooked ways,
The LORD shall lead them away
With the workers of iniquity.

Peace *be* upon Israel!

PSALM 126

A Joyful Return to Zion

A Song of Ascents.

1 When the LORD brought back the captivity of Zion,
We were like those who dream.
2 Then our mouth was filled with laughter,
And our tongue with singing.
Then they said among the nations,
"The LORD has done great things for them."
3 The LORD has done great things for us,
And we are glad.

4 Bring back our captivity, O LORD,
As the streams in the South.

5 Those who sow in tears
Shall reap in joy.
6 He who continually goes forth weeping,
Bearing seed for sowing,
Shall doubtless come again with rejoicing,
Bringing his sheaves *with him.*

PSALM 127

Laboring and Prospering with the LORD

A Song of Ascents. Of Solomon.

1 Unless the LORD builds the house,
They labor in vain who build it;
Unless the LORD guards the city,
The watchman stays awake in vain.
2 *It is* vain for you to rise up early,
To sit up late,
To eat the bread of sorrows;
For so He gives His beloved sleep.

3 Behold, children *are* a heritage from the LORD,
The fruit of the womb *is* a reward.
4 Like arrows in the hand of a warrior,
So *are* the children of one's youth.
5 Happy *is* the man who has his quiver full of them;
They shall not be ashamed,
But shall speak with their enemies in the gate.

PSALM 128

Blessings of Those Who Fear the LORD

A Song of Ascents.

1 Blessed *is* every one who fears the LORD,
Who walks in His ways.

2 When you eat the labor of your hands,

FAMILY

READ IT: PSALM 128:1–6

This psalm is a beautiful image of what a healthy family can be like. It's a picture of what can happen when a family chooses to fear God—to respect Him—and then live out that fear by obeying Him. But this psalm is not a formula for a "perfect family" because that kind of family doesn't exist on this earth. In John 16:33, Jesus reminds us that in the world, everyone will have troubles to face. So use the words of this psalm to remind you that God wants to bring blessing on your family, and He wants you to follow Him.

You *shall be* happy, and *it shall be* well
with you.
3 Your wife *shall be* like a fruitful vine
In the very heart of your house,
Your children like olive plants
All around your table.
4 Behold, thus shall the man be blessed
Who fears the LORD.

5 The LORD bless you out of Zion,
And may you see the good of Jerusalem
All the days of your life.
6 Yes, may you see your children's
children.

Peace *be* upon Israel!

PSALM 129

Song of Victory over Zion's Enemies

A Song of Ascents.

1 "Many a time they have afflicted me
from my youth,"
Let Israel now say—
2 "Many a time they have afflicted me
from my youth;
Yet they have not prevailed against me.
3 The plowers plowed on my back;
They made their furrows long."
4 The LORD *is* righteous;
He has cut in pieces the cords of the
wicked.

5 Let all those who hate Zion
Be put to shame and turned back.
6 Let them be as the grass *on* the
housetops,
Which withers before it grows up,
7 With which the reaper does not fill his
hand,
Nor he who binds sheaves, his arms.
8 Neither let those who pass by them say,
"The blessing of the LORD *be* upon you;
We bless you in the name of the LORD!"

PSALM 130

Waiting for the Redemption of the LORD

A Song of Ascents.

1 Out of the depths I have cried to You,
O LORD;
2 Lord, hear my voice!
Let Your ears be attentive
To the voice of my supplications.

3 If You, LORD, should mark iniquities,
O Lord, who could stand?
4 But *there is* forgiveness with You,
That You may be feared.

5 I wait for the LORD, my soul waits,
And in His word I do hope.
6 My soul *waits* for the Lord
More than those who watch for the
morning—
Yes, more than those who watch for the
morning.

7 O Israel, hope in the LORD;
For with the LORD *there is* mercy,
And with Him *is* abundant redemption.

FORGIVENESS

READ IT: PSALM 130:3, 4

When Jesus died on the cross, your sins died with Him. He doesn't sit up in heaven counting each time you do something that you're not supposed to do. There's no tally board comparing your sin with someone else's. So when someone sins against you down here on earth, are you keeping count? Think about what it would be like to free that person today just as Christ has freed you.

8 And He shall redeem Israel
From all his iniquities.

PSALM 131

Simple Trust in the Lord

A Song of Ascents. Of David.

1 Lord, my heart is not haughty,
Nor my eyes lofty.
Neither do I concern myself with great matters,
Nor with things too profound for me.

2 Surely I have calmed and quieted my soul,
Like a weaned child with his mother;
Like a weaned child *is* my soul within me.

3 O Israel, hope in the Lord
From this time forth and forever.

PSALM 132

The Eternal Dwelling of God in Zion

A Song of Ascents.

1 Lord, remember David
And all his afflictions;
2 How he swore to the Lord,
And vowed to the Mighty One of Jacob:
3 "Surely I will not go into the chamber of my house,
Or go up to the comfort of my bed;
4 I will not give sleep to my eyes
Or slumber to my eyelids,
5 Until I find a place for the Lord,
A dwelling place for the Mighty One of Jacob."

6 Behold, we heard of it in Ephrathah;
We found it in the fields of the woods.[a]
7 Let us go into His tabernacle;
Let us worship at His footstool.
8 Arise, O Lord, to Your resting place,
You and the ark of Your strength.
9 Let Your priests be clothed with righteousness,
And let Your saints shout for joy.

10 For Your servant David's sake,
Do not turn away the face of Your Anointed.

11 The Lord has sworn *in* truth to David;
He will not turn from it:
"I will set upon your throne the fruit of your body.

132:6 [a] Hebrew *Jaar*

132:3–5 MAKE YOUR HEART GOD'S HOME

We have said a lot about how great God is. But have you ever thought that God can also make Himself small? The great and eternal Son of God made Himself very little when He was born as a baby in Bethlehem. Then He lived for more than thirty years in a human body like yours. The Son of God became Jesus.

Some people think they can only find God in big places—like the Grand Canyon, or Mount Everest, or a huge cathedral like Notre Dame. Although these places seem large to us, to God they're very small.

It's just as easy for God to live in you as it is for Him to live in a huge building. In fact, God told the prophet Isaiah (pronounced *eye-ZAY-uh*) that no one could build a place big enough for Him. But God also said He would live in ordinary people like us (see Isaiah 66:1, 2). God wants to live in you.

12 If your sons will keep My covenant
And My testimony which I shall teach them,
Their sons also shall sit upon your throne forevermore."

13 For the LORD has chosen Zion;
He has desired *it* for His dwelling place:
14 "This *is* My resting place forever;
Here I will dwell, for I have desired it.
15 I will abundantly bless her provision;
I will satisfy her poor with bread.
16 I will also clothe her priests with salvation,
And her saints shall shout aloud for joy.
17 There I will make the horn of David grow;
I will prepare a lamp for My Anointed.
18 His enemies I will clothe with shame,
But upon Himself His crown shall flourish."

PSALM 133

Blessed Unity of the People of God

A Song of Ascents. Of David.

1 Behold, how good and how pleasant *it is*
For brethren to dwell together in unity!

2 *It is* like the precious oil upon the head,
Running down on the beard,
The beard of Aaron,
Running down on the edge of his garments.
3 *It is* like the dew of Hermon,
Descending upon the mountains of Zion;
For there the LORD commanded the blessing—
Life forevermore.

PSALM 134

Praising the LORD in His House at Night

A Song of Ascents.

1 Behold, bless the LORD,
All *you* servants of the LORD,
Who by night stand in the house of the LORD!
2 Lift up your hands *in* the sanctuary,
And bless the LORD.

3 The LORD who made heaven and earth
Bless you from Zion!

PSALM 135

Praise to God in Creation and Redemption

1 Praise the LORD!

Praise the name of the LORD;
Praise *Him,* O you servants of the LORD!
2 You who stand in the house of the LORD,
In the courts of the house of our God,
3 Praise the LORD, for the LORD *is* good;
Sing praises to His name, for *it is* pleasant.
4 For the LORD has chosen Jacob for Himself,
Israel for His special treasure.

5 For I know that the LORD *is* great,
And our Lord *is* above all gods.
6 Whatever the LORD pleases He does,
In heaven and in earth,
In the seas and in all deep places.
7 He causes the vapors to ascend from the ends of the earth;
He makes lightning for the rain;
He brings the wind out of His treasuries.

8 He destroyed the firstborn of Egypt,
Both of man and beast.
9 He sent signs and wonders into the midst of you, O Egypt,
Upon Pharaoh and all his servants.
10 He defeated many nations
And slew mighty kings—
11 Sihon king of the Amorites,
Og king of Bashan,
And all the kingdoms of Canaan—
12 And gave their land *as* a heritage,
A heritage to Israel His people.

13 Your name, O LORD, *endures* forever,
Your fame, O LORD, throughout all generations.
14 For the LORD will judge His people,
And He will have compassion on His servants.

15 The idols of the nations *are* silver and gold,
The work of men's hands.
16 They have mouths, but they do not speak;
Eyes they have, but they do not see;
17 They have ears, but they do not hear;
Nor is there *any* breath in their mouths.
18 Those who make them are like them;
So is everyone who trusts in them.

19 Bless the LORD, O house of Israel!
Bless the LORD, O house of Aaron!
20 Bless the LORD, O house of Levi!
You who fear the LORD, bless the LORD!
21 Blessed be the LORD out of Zion,
Who dwells in Jerusalem!

Praise the LORD!

PSALM 136

Thanksgiving to God for His Enduring Mercy

1 Oh, give thanks to the LORD, for *He is* good!
For His mercy *endures* forever.
2 Oh, give thanks to the God of gods!
For His mercy *endures* forever.
3 Oh, give thanks to the Lord of lords!
For His mercy *endures* forever:

4 To Him who alone does great wonders,
For His mercy *endures* forever;
5 To Him who by wisdom made the heavens,
For His mercy *endures* forever;
6 To Him who laid out the earth above the waters,
For His mercy *endures* forever;
7 To Him who made great lights,
For His mercy *endures* forever—
8 The sun to rule by day,
For His mercy *endures* forever;
9 The moon and stars to rule by night,
For His mercy *endures* forever.

10 To Him who struck Egypt in their firstborn,
For His mercy *endures* forever;
11 And brought out Israel from among them,
For His mercy *endures* forever;
12 With a strong hand, and with an outstretched arm,
For His mercy *endures* forever;
13 To Him who divided the Red Sea in two,
For His mercy *endures* forever;
14 And made Israel pass through the midst of it,
For His mercy *endures* forever;
15 But overthrew Pharaoh and his army in the Red Sea,
For His mercy *endures* forever;
16 To Him who led His people through the wilderness,
For His mercy *endures* forever;
17 To Him who struck down great kings,
For His mercy *endures* forever;
18 And slew famous kings,
For His mercy *endures* forever—
19 Sihon king of the Amorites,
For His mercy *endures* forever;
20 And Og king of Bashan,
For His mercy *endures* forever—
21 And gave their land as a heritage,
For His mercy *endures* forever;
22 A heritage to Israel His servant,
For His mercy *endures* forever.

23 Who remembered us in our lowly state,
For His mercy *endures* forever;
24 And rescued us from our enemies,
For His mercy *endures* forever;
25 Who gives food to all flesh,
For His mercy *endures* forever.

COMMUNITY

READ IT: PSALM 133:1–3

There are so many denominations and beliefs in Christianity that sometimes we find ourselves in holy wars (maybe not physical battles, but ugly battles still). Instead of worshiping and praising our God, we fight over the details of small matters. But it's so good and pleasant when we find ourselves bonded together by unity and love. We don't have to agree on every detail, but we do have to learn to get along.

26 Oh, give thanks to the God of heaven!
For His mercy *endures* forever.

PSALM 137

Longing for Zion in a Foreign Land

1 By the rivers of Babylon,
There we sat down, yea, we wept
When we remembered Zion.
2 We hung our harps
Upon the willows in the midst of it.
3 For there those who carried us away captive asked of us a song,
And those who plundered us *requested* mirth,
Saying, "Sing us *one* of the songs of Zion!"

4 How shall we sing the LORD's song
In a foreign land?
5 If I forget you, O Jerusalem,
Let my right hand forget *its skill!*
6 If I do not remember you,
Let my tongue cling to the roof of my mouth—
If I do not exalt Jerusalem
Above my chief joy.

7 Remember, O LORD, against the sons of Edom
The day of Jerusalem,
Who said, "Raze *it,* raze *it,*
To its very foundation!"

8 O daughter of Babylon, who are to be destroyed,
Happy the one who repays you as you have served us!
9 Happy the one who takes and dashes
Your little ones against the rock!

PSALM 138

The LORD's Goodness to the Faithful

A Psalm of David.

1 I will praise You with my whole heart;
Before the gods I will sing praises to You.
2 I will worship toward Your holy temple,
And praise Your name
For Your lovingkindness and Your truth;
For You have magnified Your word above all Your name.
3 In the day when I cried out, You answered me,
And made me bold *with* strength in my soul.

4 All the kings of the earth shall praise You, O LORD,
When they hear the words of Your mouth.
5 Yes, they shall sing of the ways of the LORD,
For great *is* the glory of the LORD.
6 Though the LORD *is* on high,
Yet He regards the lowly;
But the proud He knows from afar.

7 Though I walk in the midst of trouble, You will revive me;
You will stretch out Your hand
Against the wrath of my enemies,
And Your right hand will save me.
8 The LORD will perfect *that which* concerns me;

PRIDE

READ IT: PSALM 138:6

No one has ever been or will ever be more powerful than God. So when we live with arrogance, we ignore the reality of how much *less than* God *we are. This passage* tells us something wonderful and something a little scary. If you're a proud and arrogant person, God will be more distant. But if you're humble, God will be very, very close.

Your mercy, O LORD, *endures* forever;
Do not forsake the works of Your hands.

PSALM 139

God's Perfect Knowledge of Man

For the Chief Musician. A Psalm of David.

1 O LORD, You have searched me and known *me*.
2 You know my sitting down and my rising up;
You understand my thought afar off.
3 You comprehend my path and my lying down,
And are acquainted with all my ways.
4 For *there is* not a word on my tongue,
But behold, O LORD, You know it altogether.
5 You have hedged me behind and before,
And laid Your hand upon me.
6 *Such* knowledge *is* too wonderful for me;
It is high, I cannot *attain* it.

7 Where can I go from Your Spirit?
Or where can I flee from Your presence?
8 If I ascend into heaven, You *are* there;
If I make my bed in hell, behold, You *are there.*
9 *If* I take the wings of the morning,
And dwell in the uttermost parts of the sea,
10 Even there Your hand shall lead me,
And Your right hand shall hold me.
11 If I say, "Surely the darkness shall fall[a] on me,"

In Focus

139:8 Hell A place of endless misery where ungodly people go when they die. It is translated from a word for the burning dumping ground outside Jerusalem in Jesus' time.

Even the night shall be light about me;
12 Indeed, the darkness shall not hide from You,
But the night shines as the day;
The darkness and the light *are* both alike *to You*.

13 For You formed my inward parts;
You covered me in my mother's womb.
14 I will praise You, for I am fearfully *and* wonderfully made;[a]
Marvelous are Your works,
And *that* my soul knows very well.
15 My frame was not hidden from You,
When I was made in secret,
And skillfully wrought in the lowest parts of the earth.
16 Your eyes saw my substance, being yet unformed.
And in Your book they all were written,

139:11 [a] Vulgate and Symmachus read *cover.* 139:14 [a] Following Masoretic Text and Targum; Septuagint, Syriac, and Vulgate read *You are fearfully wonderful.*

Action!

KNOWING AND FINDING GOD

READ IT: PSALM 139:7–10

God isn't just a superhero who is faster, stronger, smarter, bigger, and more powerful than people. He's something else entirely. He's everywhere, all the time. He doesn't have to race from place to place to see what's going on or to hear each of our prayers. No matter where you are, what you are doing, what you are going through, what you are feeling, or what you need, God knows. He is there. He is listening. He is with you.

The days fashioned for me,
When *as yet there were* none of them.

17 How precious also are Your thoughts to me, O God!
How great is the sum of them!
18 *If* I should count them, they would be more in number than the sand;
When I awake, I am still with You.

19 Oh, that You would slay the wicked, O God!
Depart from me, therefore, you bloodthirsty men.
20 For they speak against You wickedly;
Your enemies take *Your name* in vain.[a]
21 Do I not hate them, O LORD, who hate You?
And do I not loathe those who rise up against You?
22 I hate them with perfect hatred;
I count them my enemies.

23 Search me, O God, and know my heart;
Try me, and know my anxieties;
24 And see if *there is any* wicked way in me,
And lead me in the way everlasting.

139:20 [a] Septuagint and Vulgate read *They take Your cities in vain.*

IDENTITY
WONDERFULLY MADE

READ IT: PSALM 139:13, 14

GET IT:

King David wrote this psalm to explain how incredible it is that the Creator of life knows him. You might think all this familiarity is special because he was David—the famous shepherd boy, the giant-killer, the king of Israel. But it's not just about him. God knows you just as well. David was a person like the rest of us, full of flaws and sins—some pretty big ones too! Still, he was created by God and known by God, and you are, too. From the time you were just a tiny bunch of cells, He has known you—known when your heart would beat for the first time, when you would take your first breath, and when you would walk your first steps.

It's kind of mind-blowing, especially when you don't feel very significant and even your friends or your parents barely notice you. But God is so aware of you—every little thing about you. He's literally been watching your fingernails grow since before anyone knew you had fingernails.

LIVE IT:

Even if you feel like your very existence is a fluke, a mistake, it's not. You've never been an "accident" to God. Maybe your parents didn't plan you or you were born with health problems—that doesn't make you a mistake. God didn't fall asleep or look away as all the cells were taking shape to make you into you. The Creator of life created you, and He has never missed a heartbeat or a breath since.

PSALM 140

Prayer for Deliverance from Evil Men

To the Chief Musician. A Psalm of David.

1 Deliver me, O LORD, from evil men;
Preserve me from violent men,
2 Who plan evil things in *their* hearts;
They continually gather together *for* war.
3 They sharpen their tongues like a serpent;
The poison of asps *is* under their lips. *Selah*

4 Keep me, O LORD, from the hands of the wicked;
Preserve me from violent men,
Who have purposed to make my steps stumble.
5 The proud have hidden a snare for me, and cords;
They have spread a net by the wayside;
They have set traps for me. *Selah*

6 I said to the LORD: "You *are* my God;
Hear the voice of my supplications, O LORD.
7 O GOD the Lord, the strength of my salvation,
You have covered my head in the day of battle.
8 Do not grant, O LORD, the desires of the wicked;
Do not further his *wicked* scheme,
Lest they be exalted. *Selah*

9 "*As for* the head of those who surround me,
Let the evil of their lips cover them;
10 Let burning coals fall upon them;
Let them be cast into the fire,
Into deep pits, that they rise not up again.
11 Let not a slanderer be established in the earth;
Let evil hunt the violent man to overthrow *him*."

12 I know that the LORD will maintain
The cause of the afflicted,
And justice for the poor.
13 Surely the righteous shall give thanks to Your name;
The upright shall dwell in Your presence.

PSALM 141

Prayer for Safekeeping from Wickedness

A Psalm of David.

1 LORD, I cry out to You;
Make haste to me!
Give ear to my voice when I cry out to You.
2 Let my prayer be set before You *as* incense,
The lifting up of my hands *as* the evening sacrifice.

3 Set a guard, O LORD, over my mouth;
Keep watch over the door of my lips.
4 Do not incline my heart to any evil thing,
To practice wicked works
With men who work iniquity;
And do not let me eat of their delicacies.

5 Let the righteous strike me;
It shall be a kindness.
And let him rebuke me;
It shall be as excellent oil;
Let my head not refuse it.

For still my prayer *is* against the deeds of the wicked.
6 Their judges are overthrown by the sides of the cliff,
And they hear my words, for they are sweet.
7 Our bones are scattered at the mouth of the grave,
As when one plows and breaks up the earth.

8 But my eyes *are* upon You, O GOD the Lord;
In You I take refuge;
Do not leave my soul destitute.
9 Keep me from the snares they have laid for me,
And from the traps of the workers of iniquity.
10 Let the wicked fall into their own nets,
While I escape safely.

PSALM 142

A Plea for Relief from Persecutors

A Contemplation[a] of David. A Prayer when he was in the cave.

1 I cry out to the LORD with my voice;
With my voice to the LORD I make my supplication.
2 I pour out my complaint before Him;
I declare before Him my trouble.

3 When my spirit was overwhelmed within me,
Then You knew my path.
In the way in which I walk
They have secretly set a snare for me.
4 Look on *my* right hand and see,
For *there is* no one who acknowledges me;
Refuge has failed me;
No one cares for my soul.

5 I cried out to You, O LORD:
I said, "You *are* my refuge,
My portion in the land of the living.
6 Attend to my cry,
For I am brought very low;
Deliver me from my persecutors,
For they are stronger than I.
7 Bring my soul out of prison,
That I may praise Your name;
The righteous shall surround me,
For You shall deal bountifully with me."

PSALM 143

An Earnest Appeal for Guidance and Deliverance

A Psalm of David.

1 Hear my prayer, O LORD,
Give ear to my supplications!
In Your faithfulness answer me,
And in Your righteousness.
2 Do not enter into judgment with Your servant,
For in Your sight no one living is righteous.

3 For the enemy has persecuted my soul;
He has crushed my life to the ground;
He has made me dwell in darkness,
Like those who have long been dead.
4 Therefore my spirit is overwhelmed within me;
My heart within me is distressed.

5 I remember the days of old;
I meditate on all Your works;
I muse on the work of Your hands.
6 I spread out my hands to You;
My soul *longs* for You like a thirsty land. *Selah*

7 Answer me speedily, O LORD;
My spirit fails!
Do not hide Your face from me,
Lest I be like those who go down into the pit.
8 Cause me to hear Your lovingkindness in the morning,
For in You do I trust;
Cause me to know the way in which I should walk,
For I lift up my soul to You.

9 Deliver me, O LORD, from my enemies;
In You I take shelter.[a]
10 Teach me to do Your will,
For You *are* my God;
Your Spirit *is* good.

142:title [a] Hebrew *Maschil* 143:9 [a] Septuagint and Vulgate read *To You I flee.*

LONELINESS

READ IT: PSALM 142:1–4

David was in a cave when he wrote this. That's pretty isolated. His enemies were out to get him, and he pleaded for the Lord to have his back. He knew from experience that even though there were traps set for him, God would never fail him. Next time you feel trapped in your loneliness, reach out to God and ask Him to show you the way out.

Lead me in the land of uprightness.

11 Revive me, O LORD, for Your name's sake!
For Your righteousness' sake bring my soul out of trouble.

12 In Your mercy cut off my enemies,
And destroy all those who afflict my soul;
For I *am* Your servant.

PSALM 144

A Song to the LORD Who Preserves and Prospers His People

A Psalm of David.

1 Blessed *be* the LORD my Rock,
Who trains my hands for war,
And my fingers for battle—

2 My lovingkindness and my fortress,
My high tower and my deliverer,
My shield and *the One* in whom I take refuge,
Who subdues my people[a] under me.

3 LORD, what *is* man, that You take knowledge of him?
Or the son of man, that You are mindful of him?

4 Man is like a breath;
His days *are* like a passing shadow.

5 Bow down Your heavens, O LORD, and come down;
Touch the mountains, and they shall smoke.

6 Flash forth lightning and scatter them;
Shoot out Your arrows and destroy them.

7 Stretch out Your hand from above;
Rescue me and deliver me out of great waters,
From the hand of foreigners,

8 Whose mouth speaks lying words,
And whose right hand *is* a right hand of falsehood.

9 I will sing a new song to You, O God;
On a harp of ten strings I will sing praises to You,

10 *The One* who gives salvation to kings,
Who delivers David His servant
From the deadly sword.

11 Rescue me and deliver me from the hand of foreigners,
Whose mouth speaks lying words,
And whose right hand *is* a right hand of falsehood—

12 That our sons *may be* as plants grown up in their youth;
That our daughters *may be* as pillars,
Sculptured in palace style;

144:2 [a] Following Masoretic Text, Septuagint, and Vulgate; Syriac and Targum read *the peoples* (compare 18:47).

Epic Ideas

143:8 GOD WILL GUIDE YOU

A compass is the most valuable tool you can have when you're lost in a forest. Also, when you're at sea and can't see any land, you need a compass to lead you to a safe harbor.

Many people in the world are like sailors at sea without a compass. They have no guide to show them how to live, and they are soon led into danger by evil men.

You need a guide to show you how to live in happiness in the world. Some people would like you to think sin will make you happy. That is never true. Sin only makes people miserable after they're trapped in it.

God guides you in the way of wisdom, joy, and peace. His Spirit is like a living compass that always tells you when you're going the wrong way. Ask God to lead you "in the way everlasting" (Psalm 139:24).

13 *That* our barns *may be* full,
Supplying all kinds of produce;
That our sheep may bring forth
thousands
And ten thousands in our fields;
14 *That* our oxen *may be* well laden;
That there be no breaking in or going out;
That there be no outcry in our streets.
15 Happy *are* the people who are in such a
state;
Happy *are* the people whose God *is* the
LORD!

PSALM 145

A Song of God's Majesty and Love

A Praise of David.

1 I will extol You, my God, O King;
And I will bless Your name forever and
ever.
2 Every day I will bless You,
And I will praise Your name forever and
ever.
3 Great *is* the LORD, and greatly to be
praised;
And His greatness *is* unsearchable.

4 One generation shall praise Your works
to another,
And shall declare Your mighty acts.
5 I[a] will meditate on the glorious splendor
of Your majesty,
And on Your wondrous works.[b]
6 *Men* shall speak of the might of Your
awesome acts,
And I will declare Your greatness.
7 They shall utter the memory of Your
great goodness,
And shall sing of Your righteousness.

8 The LORD *is* gracious and full of
compassion,
Slow to anger and great in mercy.
9 The LORD *is* good to all,
And His tender mercies *are* over all His
works.

10 All Your works shall praise You,
O LORD,
And Your saints shall bless You.
11 They shall speak of the glory of Your
kingdom,
And talk of Your power,
12 To make known to the sons of men His
mighty acts,
And the glorious majesty of His
kingdom.
13 Your kingdom *is* an everlasting
kingdom,
And Your dominion *endures* throughout
all generations.[a]

14 The LORD upholds all who fall,
And raises up all *who are* bowed down.
15 The eyes of all look expectantly to You,
And You give them their food in due
season.
16 You open Your hand
And satisfy the desire of every living
thing.

17 The LORD *is* righteous in all His ways,
Gracious in all His works.
18 The LORD *is* near to all who call upon
Him,
To all who call upon Him in truth.
19 He will fulfill the desire of those who
fear Him;
He also will hear their cry and save
them.
20 The LORD preserves all who love Him,
But all the wicked He will destroy.
21 My mouth shall speak the praise of the
LORD,
And all flesh shall bless His holy name
Forever and ever.

PSALM 146

The Happiness of Those Whose Help Is the LORD

1 Praise the LORD!

Praise the LORD, O my soul!
2 While I live I will praise the LORD;
I will sing praises to my God while I
have my being.

3 Do not put your trust in princes,
Nor in a son of man, in whom *there is*
no help.
4 His spirit departs, he returns to his
earth;
In that very day his plans perish.

145:5 [a] Following Masoretic Text and Targum; Dead Sea Scrolls, Septuagint, Syriac, and Vulgate read *They.* [b] Literally *on the words of Your wondrous works*
145:13 [a] Following Masoretic Text and Targum; Dead Sea Scrolls, Septuagint, Syriac, and Vulgate add *The LORD is faithful in all His words, And holy in all His works.*

5 Happy *is he* who *has* the God of Jacob for his help,
Whose hope *is* in the LORD his God,
6 Who made heaven and earth,
The sea, and all that *is* in them;
Who keeps truth forever,
7 Who executes justice for the oppressed,
Who gives food to the hungry.
The LORD gives freedom to the prisoners.

8 The LORD opens *the eyes of* the blind;
The LORD raises those who are bowed down;
The LORD loves the righteous.
9 The LORD watches over the strangers;
He relieves the fatherless and widow;
But the way of the wicked He turns upside down.

10 The LORD shall reign forever—
Your God, O Zion, to all generations.

Praise the LORD!

PSALM 147

Praise to God for His Word and Providence

1 Praise the LORD!
For *it is* good to sing praises to our God;
For *it is* pleasant, *and* praise is beautiful.

2 The LORD builds up Jerusalem;
He gathers together the outcasts of Israel.
3 He heals the brokenhearted
And binds up their wounds.
4 He counts the number of the stars;
He calls them all by name.
5 Great *is* our Lord, and mighty in power;
His understanding *is* infinite.
6 The LORD lifts up the humble;
He casts the wicked down to the ground.

7 Sing to the LORD with thanksgiving;
Sing praises on the harp to our God,
8 Who covers the heavens with clouds,
Who prepares rain for the earth,
Who makes grass to grow on the mountains.
9 He gives to the beast its food,
And to the young ravens that cry.

10 He does not delight in the strength of the horse;
He takes no pleasure in the legs of a man.

Epic Ideas

147:3 GOD HEALS BROKEN HEARTS

Sometimes you hear about people who have heart attacks. That isn't the same as a broken heart. A "broken heart" describes people who have lost the desire to go on living. We say they have "lost hope."

There are many brokenhearted people in the world. God cares about brokenhearted people. We ought to tell them that God wants to mend their broken hearts.

The reason many people are brokenhearted is that they don't know God as He truly is. All their lives they have been living as though they didn't need God. They may even become rich and important. Then one day they lose everything.

All the things they lived for are gone—their money, their importance, and their friends. Such people sometimes kill themselves. But many others tell how God rescued them when they were brokenhearted. They prayed to Him and He saved them.

11 The LORD takes pleasure in those who fear Him,
In those who hope in His mercy.

12 Praise the LORD, O Jerusalem!
Praise your God, O Zion!
13 For He has strengthened the bars of your gates;
He has blessed your children within you.
14 He makes peace *in* your borders,
And fills you with the finest wheat.

15 He sends out His command *to the* earth;
His word runs very swiftly.
16 He gives snow like wool;
He scatters the frost like ashes;
17 He casts out His hail like morsels;
Who can stand before His cold?
18 He sends out His word and melts them;
He causes His wind to blow, *and* the waters flow.

19 He declares His word to Jacob,
His statutes and His judgments to Israel.
20 He has not dealt thus with any nation;
And *as for His* judgments, they have not known them.

Praise the LORD!

PSALM 148

Praise to the LORD from Creation

1 Praise the LORD!

Praise the LORD from the heavens;
Praise Him in the heights!
2 Praise Him, all His angels;
Praise Him, all His hosts!
3 Praise Him, sun and moon;
Praise Him, all you stars of light!
4 Praise Him, you heavens of heavens,
And you waters above the heavens!

5 Let them praise the name of the LORD,
For He commanded and they were created.
6 He also established them forever and ever;
He made a decree which shall not pass away.

7 Praise the LORD from the earth,
You great sea creatures and all the depths;
8 Fire and hail, snow and clouds;
Stormy wind, fulfilling His word;
9 Mountains and all hills;
Fruitful trees and all cedars;
10 Beasts and all cattle;
Creeping things and flying fowl;

CHRISTIANS HAVE A NEW SONG

READ IT: PSALM 149:1

What is this new song? David talks about it in Psalm 40:3: "He has put a new song in my mouth—praise to our God." We learn lots of songs in this world. Some of them are great songs, like the national anthem. Other songs tell of the evil that lives in men's hearts. Hard rock music is often like that.

The Christian's "new song" is praise to God. Until God shows Himself to us, we can't praise Him because we don't know Him. Then we see what a great thing He did for us when He saved us from sin, and we can't help praising Him. In Revelation 14:3, we see the saved people of Israel singing this "new song."

Wouldn't it be wonderful if everybody could sing the new song of salvation? We hope you can sing it, too, because God loves you.

11 Kings of the earth and all peoples;
Princes and all judges of the earth;
12 Both young men and maidens;
Old men and children.

13 Let them praise the name of the LORD,
For His name alone is exalted;
His glory *is* above the earth and heaven.
14 And He has exalted the horn of His people,
The praise of all His saints—
Of the children of Israel,
A people near to Him.

Praise the LORD!

PSALM 149

Praise to God for His Salvation and Judgment

1 Praise the LORD!

Sing to the LORD a new song,
And His praise in the assembly of saints.

2 Let Israel rejoice in their Maker;
Let the children of Zion be joyful in their King.
3 Let them praise His name with the dance;
Let them sing praises to Him with the timbrel and harp.
4 For the LORD takes pleasure in His people;
He will beautify the humble with salvation.

5 Let the saints be joyful in glory;
Let them sing aloud on their beds.
6 *Let* the high praises of God *be* in their mouth,
And a two-edged sword in their hand,
7 To execute vengeance on the nations,
And punishments on the peoples;
8 To bind their kings with chains,
And their nobles with fetters of iron;
9 To execute on them the written judgment—
This honor have all His saints.

Praise the LORD!

PSALM 150

Let All Things Praise the LORD

1 Praise the LORD!

Praise God in His sanctuary;
Praise Him in His mighty firmament!

2 Praise Him for His mighty acts;
Praise Him according to His excellent greatness!

3 Praise Him with the sound of the trumpet;
Praise Him with the lute and harp!
4 Praise Him with the timbrel and dance;
Praise Him with stringed instruments and flutes!
5 Praise Him with loud cymbals;
Praise Him with clashing cymbals!

6 Let everything that has breath praise the LORD.

Praise the LORD!

The BOOK of

PROVERBS

950 B.C.–700 B.C.

Behind the Scenes

READ IT:

The book of Proverbs is a collection of good advice and wise sayings from long ago. But proverbs are still useful to us today. A proverb says that "the fear of the LORD is the beginning of knowledge" (1:7).

The first four chapters discuss the importance of wisdom. Then there's a collection of short and powerful two-line sayings that are easy to read and understand. These proverbs cover many different subjects including marriage, social behavior, friendship, justice, poverty, wealth, family, love, and even laziness.

GET IT:

Who wrote it: King Solomon wrote most of the proverbs. Agur and King Lemuel also wrote some.

When it was written: 950 B.C.–700 B.C.

Why it was written: to teach us the wisdom of Solomon, who was the wisest man in the world.

LIVE IT:

God is the source of true wisdom.

A wise person makes good, practical decisions that please God.

FIND IT:

The Beginning of Knowledge	*Proverbs 1*
The Value of Wisdom	*Proverbs 2–3*
The Value of Hard Work	*Proverbs 6:6–11*
Wise Advice	*Proverbs 12*
Wise Words from a Mother	*Proverbs 31*

The Beginning of Knowledge

1 The proverbs of Solomon the son of David, king of Israel:

2 To know wisdom and instruction,
To perceive the words of understanding,
3 To receive the instruction of wisdom,
Justice, judgment, and equity;
4 To give prudence to the simple,
To the young man knowledge and discretion—
5 A wise *man* will hear and increase learning,
And a man of understanding will attain wise counsel,
6 To understand a proverb and an enigma,
The words of the wise and their riddles.

7 The fear of the LORD *is* the beginning of knowledge,
But fools despise wisdom and instruction.

Shun Evil Counsel

8 My son, hear the instruction of your father,
And do not forsake the law of your mother;
9 For they *will be* a graceful ornament on your head,
And chains about your neck.

10 My son, if sinners entice you,
Do not consent.
11 If they say, "Come with us,
Let us lie in wait to *shed* blood;
Let us lurk secretly for the innocent without cause;
12 Let us swallow them alive like Sheol,[a]
And whole, like those who go down to the Pit;
13 We shall find all *kinds* of precious possessions,
We shall fill our houses with spoil;
14 Cast in your lot among us,
Let us all have one purse"—
15 My son, do not walk in the way with them,
Keep your foot from their path;
16 For their feet run to evil,
And they make haste to shed blood.
17 Surely, in vain the net is spread
In the sight of any bird;
18 But they lie in wait for their *own* blood,
They lurk secretly for their *own* lives.
19 So *are* the ways of everyone who is greedy for gain;
It takes away the life of its owners.

The Call of Wisdom

20 Wisdom calls aloud outside;
She raises her voice in the open squares.
21 She cries out in the chief concourses,[a]
At the openings of the gates in the city
She speaks her words:
22 "How long, you simple ones, will you love simplicity?
For scorners delight in their scorning,
And fools hate knowledge.
23 Turn at my rebuke;
Surely I will pour out my spirit on you;
I will make my words known to you.
24 Because I have called and you refused,
I have stretched out my hand and no one regarded,
25 Because you disdained all my counsel,
And would have none of my rebuke,
26 I also will laugh at your calamity;
I will mock when your terror comes,

1:12 [a] Or *the grave* 1:21 [a] Septuagint, Syriac, and Targum read *top of the walls;* Vulgate reads *the head of multitudes.*

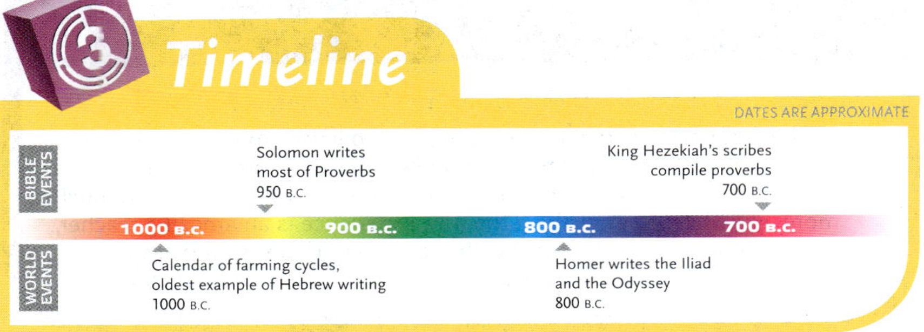

27 When your terror comes like a storm,
And your destruction comes like a whirlwind,
When distress and anguish come upon you.

28 "Then they will call on me, but I will not answer;
They will seek me diligently, but they will not find me.
29 Because they hated knowledge
And did not choose the fear of the LORD,
30 They would have none of my counsel
And despised my every rebuke.
31 Therefore they shall eat the fruit of their own way,
And be filled to the full with their own fancies.
32 For the turning away of the simple will slay them,
And the complacency of fools will destroy them;
33 But whoever listens to me will dwell safely,
And will be secure, without fear of evil."

The Value of Wisdom

2 My son, if you receive my words,
And treasure my commands within you,
2 So that you incline your ear to wisdom,
And apply your heart to understanding;
3 Yes, if you cry out for discernment,
And lift up your voice for understanding,
4 If you seek her as silver,
And search for her as *for* hidden treasures;
5 Then you will understand the fear of the LORD,
And find the knowledge of God.
6 For the LORD gives wisdom;
From His mouth *come* knowledge and understanding;
7 He stores up sound wisdom for the upright;
He is a shield to those who walk uprightly;
8 He guards the paths of justice,
And preserves the way of His saints.
9 Then you will understand righteousness and justice,
Equity *and* every good path.

10 When wisdom enters your heart,
And knowledge is pleasant to your soul,
11 Discretion will preserve you;
Understanding will keep you,
12 To deliver you from the way of evil,
From the man who speaks perverse things,
13 From those who leave the paths of uprightness
To walk in the ways of darkness;
14 Who rejoice in doing evil,
And delight in the perversity of the wicked;
15 Whose ways *are* crooked,
And *who are* devious in their paths;
16 To deliver you from the immoral woman,
From the seductress *who* flatters with her words,

DISCIPLINE

READ IT: PROVERBS 1:1–7

The first part of listening is learning *how* to listen. You can consult a map or the GPS in your parent's car to get where you are going, but if you ask someone who has been where you want to go, you can find out much more, like where to stop along the way. Experience is an amazing teacher, and we should listen to people with experience. That's what these first verses in Proverbs are like—wisdom from someone with experience.

17 Who forsakes the companion of her
youth,
And forgets the covenant of her God.
18 For her house leads down to death,
And her paths to the dead;
19 None who go to her return,
Nor do they regain the paths of life—
20 So you may walk in the way of
goodness,
And keep *to* the paths of righteousness.
21 For the upright will dwell in the land,
And the blameless will remain in it;
22 But the wicked will be cut off from the
earth,
And the unfaithful will be uprooted
from it.

Guidance for the Young

3 My son, do not forget my law,
But let your heart keep my
commands;
2 For length of days and long life
And peace they will add to you.

3 Let not mercy and truth forsake you;
Bind them around your neck,
Write them on the tablet of your heart,
4 *And* so find favor and high esteem
In the sight of God and man.

5 Trust in the LORD with all your heart,
And lean not on your own
understanding;
6 In all your ways acknowledge Him,
And He shall direct[a] your paths.

7 Do not be wise in your own eyes;
Fear the LORD and depart from evil.
8 It will be health to your flesh,[a]
And strength[b] to your bones.

9 Honor the LORD with your possessions,
And with the firstfruits of all your
increase;
10 So your barns will be filled with plenty,
And your vats will overflow with new
wine.

11 My son, do not despise the chastening
of the LORD,
Nor detest His correction;
12 For whom the LORD loves He corrects,
Just as a father the son *in whom* he
delights.

13 Happy *is* the man *who* finds wisdom,
And the man *who* gains understanding;
14 For her proceeds *are* better than the
profits of silver,
And her gain than fine gold.
15 She *is* more precious than rubies,
And all the things you may desire
cannot compare with her.
16 Length of days *is* in her right hand,
In her left hand riches and honor.
17 Her ways *are* ways of pleasantness,
And all her paths *are* peace.
18 She *is* a tree of life to those who take
hold of her,
And happy *are all* who retain her.

19 The LORD by wisdom founded the earth;
By understanding He established the
heavens;
20 By His knowledge the depths were
broken up,
And clouds drop down the dew.

21 My son, let them not depart from your
eyes—
Keep sound wisdom and discretion;
22 So they will be life to your soul
And grace to your neck.
23 Then you will walk safely in your way,
And your foot will not stumble.
24 When you lie down, you will not be
afraid;
Yes, you will lie down and your sleep
will be sweet.
25 Do not be afraid of sudden terror,
Nor of trouble from the wicked when it
comes;
26 For the LORD will be your confidence,
And will keep your foot from being
caught.

27 Do not withhold good from those to
whom it is due,
When it is in the power of your hand to
do *so.*
28 Do not say to your neighbor,
"Go, and come back,
And tomorrow I will give *it,*"
When you have it with you.
29 Do not devise evil against your
neighbor,
For he dwells by you for safety's sake.
30 Do not strive with a man without cause,
If he has done you no harm.

31 Do not envy the oppressor,
And choose none of his ways;

3:6 [a] Or *make smooth* or *straight* **3:8** [a] Literally *navel,* figurative of the body [b] Literally *drink* or *refreshment*

32 For the perverse *person is* an
abomination to the LORD,
But His secret counsel *is* with the
upright.
33 The curse of the LORD *is* on the house of
the wicked,
But He blesses the home of the just.
34 Surely He scorns the scornful,
But gives grace to the humble.
35 The wise shall inherit glory,
But shame shall be the legacy of fools.

Security in Wisdom

4 Hear, *my* children, the instruction of
a father,
And give attention to know
understanding;
2 For I give you good doctrine:
Do not forsake my law.
3 When I was my father's son,
Tender and the only one in the sight of
my mother,
4 He also taught me, and said to me:
"Let your heart retain my words;
Keep my commands, and live.
5 Get wisdom! Get understanding!
Do not forget, nor turn away from the
words of my mouth.
6 Do not forsake her, and she will
preserve you;
Love her, and she will keep you.
7 Wisdom *is* the principal thing;
Therefore get wisdom.
And in all your getting, get
understanding.
8 Exalt her, and she will promote you;
She will bring you honor, when you
embrace her.
9 She will place on your head an
ornament of grace;
A crown of glory she will deliver to you."

10 Hear, my son, and receive my sayings,
And the years of your life will be many.
11 I have taught you in the way of wisdom;
I have led you in right paths.

TRUST IN THE LORD

READ IT: PROVERBS 3:1–35

GET IT:

During Solomon's lifetime he accomplished a lot of things. He built cities and great buildings. He made peace with the nations all around Israel's territory so everything was calm. The people lived well and had enough food and water. He was powerful and respected by other rulers. He was wise, and he continued to think about how to live. Thanks to God, who inspired Solomon to write down some of his advice, we can benefit from Solomon's wisdom today.

LIVE IT:

The best part of this chapter consists of verses 5 and 6. You should memorize those verses so you can remember them and use them as a guide for your life. You might also want to talk with your parents or your *youth leader* about some of the other advice given in this chapter. Some of the words are difficult. Look them up to find the right meaning, or ask someone to help you understand how this advice applies to you.

12 When you walk, your steps will not be hindered,
And when you run, you will not stumble.
13 Take firm hold of instruction, do not let go;
Keep her, for she *is* your life.

14 Do not enter the path of the wicked,
And do not walk in the way of evil.
15 Avoid it, do not travel on it;
Turn away from it and pass on.
16 For they do not sleep unless they have done evil;
And their sleep is taken away unless they make *someone* fall.
17 For they eat the bread of wickedness,
And drink the wine of violence.

18 But the path of the just *is* like the shining sun,[a]
That shines ever brighter unto the perfect day.
19 The way of the wicked *is* like darkness;
They do not know what makes them stumble.

20 My son, give attention to my words;
Incline your ear to my sayings.
21 Do not let them depart from your eyes;
Keep them in the midst of your heart;
22 For they *are* life to those who find them,
And health to all their flesh.
23 Keep your heart with all diligence,
For out of it *spring* the issues of life.
24 Put away from you a deceitful mouth,
And put perverse lips far from you.
25 Let your eyes look straight ahead,
And your eyelids look right before you.
26 Ponder the path of your feet,
And let all your ways be established.
27 Do not turn to the right or the left;
Remove your foot from evil.

The Peril of Adultery

5 My son, pay attention to my wisdom;
Lend your ear to my understanding,
2 That you may preserve discretion,
And your lips may keep knowledge.
3 For the lips of an immoral woman drip honey,
And her mouth *is* smoother than oil;
4 But in the end she is bitter as wormwood,
Sharp as a two-edged sword.
5 Her feet go down to death,
Her steps lay hold of hell.[a]
6 Lest you ponder *her* path of life—
Her ways are unstable;
You do not know *them*.

7 Therefore hear me now, *my* children,
And do not depart from the words of my mouth.
8 Remove your way far from her,
And do not go near the door of her house,
9 Lest you give your honor to others,
And your years to the cruel *one;*
10 Lest aliens be filled with your wealth,
And your labors *go* to the house of a foreigner;
11 And you mourn at last,
When your flesh and your body are consumed,
12 And say:
"How I have hated instruction,
And my heart despised correction!
13 I have not obeyed the voice of my teachers,
Nor inclined my ear to those who instructed me!
14 I was on the verge of total ruin,
In the midst of the assembly and congregation."

15 Drink water from your own cistern,
And running water from your own well.
16 Should your fountains be dispersed abroad,
Streams of water in the streets?
17 Let them be only your own,
And not for strangers with you.
18 Let your fountain be blessed,
And rejoice with the wife of your youth.
19 *As a* loving deer and a graceful doe,
Let her breasts satisfy you at all times;
And always be enraptured with her love.
20 For why should you, my son, be enraptured by an immoral woman,
And be embraced in the arms of a seductress?

21 For the ways of man *are* before the eyes of the LORD,
And He ponders all his paths.
22 His own iniquities entrap the wicked *man*,
And he is caught in the cords of his sin.
23 He shall die for lack of instruction,

4:18 [a] Literally *light* 5:5 [a] Or *Sheol*

And in the greatness of his folly he shall
go astray.

Dangerous Promises

6 My son, if you become surety for your
friend,
If you have shaken hands in pledge for
a stranger,
2 You are snared by the words of your
mouth;
You are taken by the words of your
mouth.
3 So do this, my son, and deliver yourself;
For you have come into the hand of your
friend:
Go and humble yourself;
Plead with your friend.
4 Give no sleep to your eyes,
Nor slumber to your eyelids.
5 Deliver yourself like a gazelle from the
hand *of the hunter,*
And like a bird from the hand of the
fowler.[a]

The Folly of Indolence

6 Go to the ant, you sluggard!
Consider her ways and be wise,
7 Which, having no captain,
Overseer or ruler,
8 Provides her supplies in the summer,
And gathers her food in the harvest.
9 How long will you slumber, O sluggard?
When will you rise from your sleep?
10 A little sleep, a little slumber,
A little folding of the hands to sleep—
11 So shall your poverty come on you like a
prowler,
And your need like an armed man.

The Wicked Man

12 A worthless person, a wicked man,
Walks with a perverse mouth;
13 He winks with his eyes,
He shuffles his feet,
He points with his fingers;
14 Perversity *is* in his heart,
He devises evil continually,
He sows discord.
15 Therefore his calamity shall come
suddenly;
Suddenly he shall be broken without
remedy.

16 These six *things* the LORD hates,
Yes, seven *are* an abomination to Him:
17 A proud look,
A lying tongue,
Hands that shed innocent blood,

6:5 [a] That is, one who catches birds in a trap or snare

LAZINESS LEADS TO POVERTY

READ IT: PROVERBS 6:9–11

Not all people are poor because they're lazy. But a lazy person will nearly always be poor. God expects us to pray, but He also expects us to work.

You may think fun is pleasant and work is unpleasant. That's a false idea. Whatever work God gives you to do in life should also be fun. If your work isn't exciting, then that work may not be for you.

There are many kinds of work that God gives His people to do. All work that is helpful is good work in God's eyes. Start early to find out the work God wants to give you. School days will soon come to an end. Then comes a lifetime of work.

Life is God's gift and must not be wasted. Make up your mind to work in a way that pleases God, blesses others, and provides for your needs.

18 A heart that devises wicked plans,
Feet that are swift in running to evil,
19 A false witness *who* speaks lies,
And one who sows discord among brethren.

Beware of Adultery

20 My son, keep your father's command,
And do not forsake the law of your mother.
21 Bind them continually upon your heart;
Tie them around your neck.
22 When you roam, they[a] will lead you;
When you sleep, they will keep you;
And *when* you awake, they will speak with you.
23 For the commandment *is* a lamp,
And the law a light;
Reproofs of instruction *are* the way of life,
24 To keep you from the evil woman,
From the flattering tongue of a seductress.
25 Do not lust after her beauty in your heart,
Nor let her allure you with her eyelids.
26 For by means of a harlot
A man is reduced to a crust of bread;
And an adulteress[a] will prey upon his precious life.
27 Can a man take fire to his bosom,
And his clothes not be burned?
28 Can one walk on hot coals,
And his feet not be seared?
29 So *is* he who goes in to his neighbor's wife;
Whoever touches her shall not be innocent.

30 *People* do not despise a thief
If he steals to satisfy himself when he is starving.
31 Yet *when* he is found, he must restore sevenfold;
He may have to give up all the substance of his house.
32 Whoever commits adultery with a woman lacks understanding;
He *who* does so destroys his own soul.
33 Wounds and dishonor he will get,
And his reproach will not be wiped away.
34 For jealousy *is* a husband's fury;
Therefore he will not spare in the day of vengeance.
35 He will accept no recompense,
Nor will he be appeased though you give many gifts.

7 My son, keep my words,
And treasure my commands within you.
2 Keep my commands and live,
And my law as the apple of your eye.
3 Bind them on your fingers;
Write them on the tablet of your heart.
4 Say to wisdom, "You *are* my sister,"
And call understanding *your* nearest kin,
5 That they may keep you from the immoral woman,
From the seductress *who* flatters with her words.

The Crafty Harlot

6 For at the window of my house
I looked through my lattice,
7 And saw among the simple,
I perceived among the youths,
A young man devoid of understanding,
8 Passing along the street near her corner;
And he took the path to her house
9 In the twilight, in the evening,
In the black and dark night.

10 And there a woman met him,
With the attire of a harlot, and a crafty heart.
11 She *was* loud and rebellious,
Her feet would not stay at home.
12 At times *she was* outside, at times in the open square,
Lurking at every corner.
13 So she caught him and kissed him;
With an impudent face she said to him:
14 "*I have* peace offerings with me;
Today I have paid my vows.
15 So I came out to meet you,
Diligently to seek your face,
And I have found you.
16 I have spread my bed with tapestry,
Colored coverings of Egyptian linen.
17 I have perfumed my bed
With myrrh, aloes, and cinnamon.
18 Come, let us take our fill of love until morning;
Let us delight ourselves with love.
19 For my husband *is* not at home;
He has gone on a long journey;

6:22 [a] Literally *it* 6:26 [a] Literally *a man's wife*, that is, of another

20 He has taken a bag of money with him,
And will come home on the appointed day."

21 With her enticing speech she caused him to yield,
With her flattering lips she seduced him.
22 Immediately he went after her, as an ox goes to the slaughter,
Or as a fool to the correction of the stocks,[a]
23 Till an arrow struck his liver.
As a bird hastens to the snare,
He did not know it *would cost* his life.

24 Now therefore, listen to me, *my* children;
Pay attention to the words of my mouth:
25 Do not let your heart turn aside to her ways,
Do not stray into her paths;
26 For she has cast down many wounded,
And all who were slain by her were strong *men*.
27 Her house *is* the way to hell,[a]
Descending to the chambers of death.

The Excellence of Wisdom

8 Does not wisdom cry out,
And understanding lift up her voice?
2 She takes her stand on the top of the high hill,
Beside the way, where the paths meet.
3 She cries out by the gates, at the entry of the city,
At the entrance of the doors:
4 "To you, O men, I call,
And my voice *is* to the sons of men.
5 O you simple ones, understand prudence,
And you fools, be of an understanding heart.
6 Listen, for I will speak of excellent things,
And from the opening of my lips *will come* right things;
7 For my mouth will speak truth;
Wickedness *is* an abomination to my lips.
8 All the words of my mouth *are* with righteousness;
Nothing crooked or perverse is in them.
9 They *are* all plain to him who understands,
And right to those who find knowledge.
10 Receive my instruction, and not silver,
And knowledge rather than choice gold;
11 For wisdom *is* better than rubies,
And all the things one may desire cannot be compared with her.

12 "I, wisdom, dwell with prudence,
And find out knowledge *and* discretion.
13 The fear of the LORD *is* to hate evil;
Pride and arrogance and the evil way
And the perverse mouth I hate.
14 Counsel *is* mine, and sound wisdom;
I *am* understanding, I have strength.
15 By me kings reign,
And rulers decree justice.
16 By me princes rule, and nobles,
All the judges of the earth.[a]
17 I love those who love me,
And those who seek me diligently will find me.
18 Riches and honor *are* with me,
Enduring riches and righteousness.
19 My fruit *is* better than gold, yes, than fine gold,
And my revenue than choice silver.
20 I traverse the way of righteousness,
In the midst of the paths of justice,
21 That I may cause those who love me to inherit wealth,
That I may fill their treasuries.

22 "The LORD possessed me at the beginning of His way,
Before His works of old.
23 I have been established from everlasting,
From the beginning, before there was ever an earth.
24 When *there were* no depths I was brought forth,
When *there were* no fountains abounding with water.
25 Before the mountains were settled,
Before the hills, I was brought forth;
26 While as yet He had not made the earth or the fields,
Or the primal dust of the world.
27 When He prepared the heavens, I *was* there,
When He drew a circle on the face of the deep,
28 When He established the clouds above,

7:22 [a] Septuagint, Syriac, and Targum read *as a dog to bonds;* Vulgate reads *as a lamb . . . to bonds.* 7:27 [a] Or *Sheol* 8:16 [a] Masoretic Text, Syriac, Targum, and Vulgate read *righteousness;* Septuagint, Bomberg, and some manuscripts and editions read *earth.*

When He strengthened the fountains of
the deep,
29 When He assigned to the sea its limit,
So that the waters would not transgress
His command,
When He marked out the foundations
of the earth,
30 Then I was beside Him *as* a master
craftsman;[a]
And I was daily *His* delight,
Rejoicing always before Him,
31 Rejoicing in His inhabited world,
And my delight *was* with the sons of
men.

32 "Now therefore, listen to me, *my*
children,
For blessed *are those who* keep my ways.
33 Hear instruction and be wise,
And do not disdain *it*.
34 Blessed is the man who listens to me,
Watching daily at my gates,
Waiting at the posts of my doors.
35 For whoever finds me finds life,
And obtains favor from the LORD;
36 But he who sins against me wrongs his
own soul;
All those who hate me love death."

The Way of Wisdom

9 Wisdom has built her house,
She has hewn out her seven pillars;
2 She has slaughtered her meat,
She has mixed her wine,
She has also furnished her table.
3 She has sent out her maidens,
She cries out from the highest places of
the city,
4 "Whoever *is* simple, let him turn in
here!"
As for him who lacks understanding,
she says to him,
5 "Come, eat of my bread
And drink of the wine I have mixed.
6 Forsake foolishness and live,
And go in the way of understanding.

7 "He who corrects a scoffer gets shame for
himself,
And he who rebukes a wicked *man only*
harms himself.
8 Do not correct a scoffer, lest he hate you;
Rebuke a wise *man*, and he will love
you.
9 Give *instruction* to a wise *man*, and he
will be still wiser;

8:30 [a] A Jewish tradition reads *one brought up*.

Epic Ideas

8:22–29 GOD CREATED THE WORLD BY WISDOM

Wisdom is not mere thoughts. God's wisdom is thoughts that *work*. God thought about the universe He was going to make, and then He put His "thoughts" to work. We have said before that God *spoke* and the worlds came into being.

These verses in Proverbs 8 could refer to the Lord Jesus Christ Himself as the Wisdom of God. In his Gospel, John says that Jesus is "the Word" of God (John 1:1).

Of course, Jesus isn't a word like the printing on a page. He is the *living* Word. Jesus is also the *Wisdom* of God. God's Son Jesus is the Wisdom that God spoke when He caused the worlds to appear. (See Colossians 1:16.) God's wisdom can also help you do wonderful things that please Him. God's wisdom is powerful thinking in action.

Teach a just *man,* and he will increase in learning.

10 "The fear of the LORD *is* the beginning of wisdom,
And the knowledge of the Holy One *is* understanding.
11 For by me your days will be multiplied,
And years of life will be added to you.
12 If you are wise, you are wise for yourself,
And *if* you scoff, you will bear *it* alone."

The Way of Folly

13 A foolish woman is clamorous;
She is simple, and knows nothing.
14 For she sits at the door of her house,
On a seat *by* the highest places of the city,
15 To call to those who pass by,
Who go straight on their way:
16 "Whoever *is* simple, let him turn in here";
And *as for* him who lacks understanding, she says to him,
17 "Stolen water is sweet,
And bread *eaten* in secret is pleasant."
18 But he does not know that the dead *are* there,
That her guests *are* in the depths of hell.[a]

Wise Sayings of Solomon

10 The proverbs of Solomon:

A wise son makes a glad father,
But a foolish son *is* the grief of his mother.

2 Treasures of wickedness profit nothing,
But righteousness delivers from death.
3 The LORD will not allow the righteous soul to famish,
But He casts away the desire of the wicked.

4 He who has a slack hand becomes poor,
But the hand of the diligent makes rich.
5 He who gathers in summer *is* a wise son;
He who sleeps in harvest *is* a son who causes shame.

6 Blessings *are* on the head of the righteous,
But violence covers the mouth of the wicked.
7 The memory of the righteous *is* blessed,
But the name of the wicked will rot.

8 The wise in heart will receive commands,
But a prating fool will fall.

9 He who walks with integrity walks securely,
But he who perverts his ways will become known.

10 He who winks with the eye causes trouble,
But a prating fool will fall.

11 The mouth of the righteous *is* a well of life,
But violence covers the mouth of the wicked.

12 Hatred stirs up strife,
But love covers all sins.

13 Wisdom is found on the lips of him who has understanding,
But a rod *is* for the back of him who is devoid of understanding.

14 Wise *people* store up knowledge,
But the mouth of the foolish *is* near destruction.

15 The rich man's wealth *is* his strong city;
The destruction of the poor *is* their poverty.

16 The labor of the righteous *leads* to life,
The wages of the wicked to sin.

17 He who keeps instruction *is in* the way of life,
But he who refuses correction goes astray.

18 Whoever hides hatred *has* lying lips,
And whoever spreads slander *is* a fool.

19 In the multitude of words sin is not lacking,
But he who restrains his lips *is* wise.
20 The tongue of the righteous *is* choice silver;
The heart of the wicked *is worth* little.
21 The lips of the righteous feed many,
But fools die for lack of wisdom.[a]

22 The blessing of the LORD makes *one* rich,
And He adds no sorrow with it.

9:18 [a] Or *Sheol* 10:21 [a] Literally *heart*

23 To do evil *is* like sport to a fool,
But a man of understanding has wisdom.
24 The fear of the wicked will come upon him,
And the desire of the righteous will be granted.
25 When the whirlwind passes by, the wicked *is* no *more,*
But the righteous *has* an everlasting foundation.

26 As vinegar to the teeth and smoke to the eyes,
So *is* the lazy *man* to those who send him.

27 The fear of the LORD prolongs days,
But the years of the wicked will be shortened.
28 The hope of the righteous *will be* gladness,
But the expectation of the wicked will perish.
29 The way of the LORD *is* strength for the upright,
But destruction *will come* to the workers of iniquity.

30 The righteous will never be removed,
But the wicked will not inhabit the earth.

31 The mouth of the righteous brings forth wisdom,
But the perverse tongue will be cut out.
32 The lips of the righteous know what is acceptable,
But the mouth of the wicked *what is* perverse.

11 Dishonest scales *are* an abomination to the LORD,
But a just weight *is* His delight.

2 When pride comes, then comes shame;
But with the humble *is* wisdom.

3 The integrity of the upright will guide them,
But the perversity of the unfaithful will destroy them.
4 Riches do not profit in the day of wrath,
But righteousness delivers from death.
5 The righteousness of the blameless will direct[a] his way aright,
But the wicked will fall by his own wickedness.
6 The righteousness of the upright will deliver them,
But the unfaithful will be caught by *their* lust.

11:5 [a] Or *make smooth* or *straight*

Epic Ideas

11:1 GOD LOVES HONESTY

Jesus said, "I am . . . the truth" (John 14:6). A compass always points north. God is Truth and always points to the truth. It is impossible for God not to tell the truth or to be dishonest. So God loves honesty in you because you are made in His image.

It isn't always easy to be honest. We're tempted to lie when we know that telling the truth is going to make us look bad to others. But if you love God sincerely, you will also love the truth. This will mean that you will be fair and honest in your dealings with others.

Someone without God has no reason to tell the truth. God is not in his thoughts. So he also cheats in business. Some time ago a lot of banks in the United States were found guilty of cheating. This caused millions of people to suffer. When honesty fails, the nation fails.

7 When a wicked man dies, *his* expectation will perish,
And the hope of the unjust perishes.
8 The righteous is delivered from trouble,
And it comes to the wicked instead.
9 The hypocrite with *his* mouth destroys his neighbor,
But through knowledge the righteous will be delivered.
10 When it goes well with the righteous, the city rejoices;
And when the wicked perish, *there is* jubilation.
11 By the blessing of the upright the city is exalted,
But it is overthrown by the mouth of the wicked.

12 He who is devoid of wisdom despises his neighbor,
But a man of understanding holds his peace.

13 A talebearer reveals secrets,
But he who is of a faithful spirit conceals a matter.

14 Where *there is* no counsel, the people fall;
But in the multitude of counselors *there is* safety.

15 He who is surety for a stranger will suffer,
But one who hates being surety is secure.

16 A gracious woman retains honor,
But ruthless *men* retain riches.
17 The merciful man does good for his own soul,
But *he who is* cruel troubles his own flesh.
18 The wicked *man* does deceptive work,
But he who sows righteousness *will have* a sure reward.
19 As righteousness *leads* to life,
So he who pursues evil *pursues it* to his own death.
20 Those who are of a perverse heart *are* an abomination to the LORD,
But *the* blameless in their ways *are* His delight.
21 *Though they join* forces,[a] the wicked will not go unpunished;
But the posterity of the righteous will be delivered.

22 *As* a ring of gold in a swine's snout,
So is a lovely woman who lacks discretion.

23 The desire of the righteous *is* only good,
But the expectation of the wicked *is* wrath.

24 There is *one* who scatters, yet increases more;
And there is *one* who withholds more than is right,
But it *leads* to poverty.
25 The generous soul will be made rich,
And he who waters will also be watered himself.
26 The people will curse him who withholds grain,
But blessing *will be* on the head of him who sells *it*.

27 He who earnestly seeks good finds favor,
But trouble will come to him who seeks *evil*.

28 He who trusts in his riches will fall,
But the righteous will flourish like foliage.

29 He who troubles his own house will inherit the wind,
And the fool *will be* servant to the wise of heart.

30 The fruit of the righteous *is a* tree of life,
And he who wins souls *is* wise.

31 If the righteous will be recompensed on the earth,
How much more the ungodly and the sinner.

12 Whoever loves instruction loves knowledge,
But he who hates correction *is* stupid.

2 A good *man* obtains favor from the LORD,
But a man of wicked intentions He will condemn.

3 A man is not established by wickedness,
But the root of the righteous cannot be moved.

4 An excellent[a] wife is the crown of her husband,

11:21 [a] Literally *hand to hand* 12:4 [a] Literally *A wife of valor*

But she who causes shame *is* like
rottenness in his bones.

5 The thoughts of the righteous *are*
right,
But the counsels of the wicked *are*
deceitful.
6 The words of the wicked *are,* "Lie in wait
for blood,"
But the mouth of the upright will
deliver them.

7 The wicked are overthrown and *are* no
more,
But the house of the righteous will
stand.

8 A man will be commended according to
his wisdom,
But he who is of a perverse heart will be
despised.

9 Better *is the one* who is slighted but has
a servant,
Than he who honors himself but lacks
bread.

10 A righteous *man* regards the life of his
animal,
But the tender mercies of the wicked
are cruel.

11 He who tills his land will be satisfied
with bread,
But he who follows frivolity *is* devoid of
understanding.[a]

12 The wicked covet the catch of evil
men,
But the root of the righteous yields
fruit.
13 The wicked is ensnared by the
transgression of *his* lips,
But the righteous will come through
trouble.
14 A man will be satisfied with good by the
fruit of *his* mouth,
And the recompense of a man's hands
will be rendered to him.

15 The way of a fool *is* right in his own
eyes,
But he who heeds counsel *is* wise.
16 A fool's wrath is known at once,
But a prudent *man* covers shame.

17 He *who* speaks truth declares
righteousness,
But a false witness, deceit.

18 There is one who speaks like the
piercings of a sword,
But the tongue of the wise *promotes*
health.
19 The truthful lip shall be established
forever,
But a lying tongue *is* but for a
moment.
20 Deceit is in the heart of those who
devise evil,
But counselors of peace have joy.
21 No grave trouble will overtake the
righteous,
But the wicked shall be filled with evil.
22 Lying lips *are* an abomination to the
LORD,
But those who deal truthfully *are* His
delight.

23 A prudent man conceals knowledge,
But the heart of fools proclaims
foolishness.

24 The hand of the diligent will rule,
But the lazy *man* will be put to forced
labor.

25 Anxiety in the heart of man causes
depression,
But a good word makes it glad.

26 The righteous should choose his friends
carefully,
For the way of the wicked leads them
astray.

27 The lazy *man* does not roast what he
took in hunting,
But diligence *is* man's precious
possession.

28 In the way of righteousness *is* life,
And in *its* pathway *there is* no death.

13 A wise son *heeds* his father's
instruction,
But a scoffer does not listen to rebuke.

2 A man shall eat well by the fruit of *his*
mouth,
But the soul of the unfaithful feeds on
violence.
3 He who guards his mouth preserves his
life,

12:11 [a] Literally *heart*

But he who opens wide his lips shall have destruction.

4 The soul of a lazy *man* desires, and *has* nothing;
But the soul of the diligent shall be made rich.

5 A righteous *man* hates lying,
But a wicked *man* is loathsome and comes to shame.

6 Righteousness guards *him whose* way is blameless,
But wickedness overthrows the sinner.

7 There is one who makes himself rich, yet *has* nothing;
And one who makes himself poor, yet *has* great riches.

8 The ransom of a man's life *is* his riches,
But the poor does not hear rebuke.

9 The light of the righteous rejoices,
But the lamp of the wicked will be put out.

10 By pride comes nothing but strife,
But with the well-advised *is* wisdom.

11 Wealth *gained by* dishonesty will be diminished,
But he who gathers by labor will increase.

12 Hope deferred makes the heart sick,
But *when* the desire comes, *it is* a tree of life.

13 He who despises the word will be destroyed,
But he who fears the commandment will be rewarded.

14 The law of the wise *is* a fountain of life,
To turn *one* away from the snares of death.

15 Good understanding gains favor,
But the way of the unfaithful *is* hard.

16 Every prudent *man* acts with knowledge,
But a fool lays open *his* folly.

17 A wicked messenger falls into trouble,
But a faithful ambassador *brings* health.

18 Poverty and shame *will come* to him who disdains correction,
But he who regards a rebuke will be honored.

19 A desire accomplished is sweet to the soul,
But *it is* an abomination to fools to depart from evil.

20 He who walks with wise *men* will be wise,

WORRY CAN KILL YOU

READ IT: PROVERBS 12:25

Everybody who lives in this world has problems. There is a good way and a bad way to deal with your problems. Maybe you failed an exam, or maybe you are in trouble with somebody. What can you do? The first thing some people do when a problem comes is to worry. Not only that, but they *keep on worrying*. They hardly ever do anything to solve their problems.

The first thing to do when you have trouble is to ask God for wisdom and guidance. Then do whatever it takes to get rid of that problem. Study harder for the next exam. If you've done wrong to others, go and tell them the truth. God will stand by you. You will find that God's way of dealing with problems always works in the end. But lots of people get sick and even die because they made a lifelong habit of worrying.

But the companion of fools will be destroyed.

21 Evil pursues sinners,
But to the righteous, good shall be repaid.

22 A good *man* leaves an inheritance to his children's children,
But the wealth of the sinner is stored up for the righteous.

23 Much food *is in* the fallow *ground* of the poor,
And for lack of justice there is waste.[a]

24 He who spares his rod hates his son,
But he who loves him disciplines him promptly.

25 The righteous eats to the satisfying of his soul,
But the stomach of the wicked shall be in want.

14 The wise woman builds her house,
But the foolish pulls it down with her hands.

2 He who walks in his uprightness fears the LORD,
But *he who is* perverse in his ways despises Him.

3 In the mouth of a fool *is* a rod of pride,
But the lips of the wise will preserve them.

4 Where no oxen *are,* the trough *is* clean;
But much increase *comes* by the strength of an ox.

5 A faithful witness does not lie,
But a false witness will utter lies.

6 A scoffer seeks wisdom and does not *find it,*
But knowledge *is* easy to him who understands.

7 Go from the presence of a foolish man,
When you do not perceive *in him* the lips of knowledge.

8 The wisdom of the prudent *is* to understand his way,
But the folly of fools *is* deceit.

9 Fools mock at sin,
But among the upright *there is* favor.

10 The heart knows its own bitterness,
And a stranger does not share its joy.

11 The house of the wicked will be overthrown,
But the tent of the upright will flourish.

12 There is a way *that seems* right to a man,
But its end *is* the way of death.

13:23 [a] Literally *what is swept away*

GROWING UP GOD'S WAY

READ IT: PROVERBS 13:1

You have begun to live in the world. Soon you'll be grown up. Right now you should pray for wisdom to grow up God's way.

Perhaps you've heard, "As the twig is bent, so the tree grows." Ever see a crooked tree? It's almost impossible to make a crooked tree straight. But if the tree had been straightened when it was young, it would never have grown crooked. Right now your mind and body are forming. You need help from older people to be sure you get off to a good start.

Wise teaching will help you make the right choices now. A lot of young people are making choices that will destroy their lives. They will never grow up well because they have chosen habits that will kill them or will ruin them for life. Give yourself a chance—grow up God's way and live!

13 Even in laughter the heart may sorrow,
And the end of mirth *may be* grief.

14 The backslider in heart will be filled with his own ways,
But a good man *will be satisfied* from above.[a]

15 The simple believes every word,
But the prudent considers well his steps.
16 A wise *man* fears and departs from evil,
But a fool rages and is self-confident.
17 A quick-tempered *man* acts foolishly,
And a man of wicked intentions is hated.
18 The simple inherit folly,
But the prudent are crowned with knowledge.
19 The evil will bow before the good,
And the wicked at the gates of the righteous.

20 The poor *man* is hated even by his own neighbor,
But the rich *has* many friends.
21 He who despises his neighbor sins;
But he who has mercy on the poor, happy *is* he.

22 Do they not go astray who devise evil?
But mercy and truth *belong* to those who devise good.

23 In all labor there is profit,
But idle chatter[a] *leads* only to poverty.

24 The crown of the wise is their riches,
But the foolishness of fools *is* folly.

25 A true witness delivers souls,
But a deceitful *witness* speaks lies.

26 In the fear of the LORD *there is* strong confidence,
And His children will have a place of refuge.
27 The fear of the LORD *is* a fountain of life,
To turn *one* away from the snares of death.

28 In a multitude of people *is* a king's honor,
But in the lack of people *is* the downfall of a prince.

29 *He who is* slow to wrath has great understanding,
But *he who is* impulsive[a] exalts folly.

30 A sound heart *is* life to the body,
But envy *is* rottenness to the bones.

31 He who oppresses the poor reproaches his Maker,
But he who honors Him has mercy on the needy.

32 The wicked is banished in his wickedness,
But the righteous has a refuge in his death.

33 Wisdom rests in the heart of him who has understanding,
But *what is* in the heart of fools is made known.

34 Righteousness exalts a nation,
But sin *is* a reproach to *any* people.

14:14 [a] Literally *from above himself* 14:23 [a] Literally *talk of the lips* 14:29 [a] Literally *short of spirit*

KINDNESS

READ IT: PROVERBS 14:21

It doesn't always feel good to do the right thing. It can be painful if we're giving up something—our popularity, our savings, our valuable time. But at the end of the day, there's satisfaction in being kind. That's the sort of happiness King Solomon is talking about. There's joy—deep, heart-level joy—in being kind and merciful to others. And that little stab of gloom you feel about giving up a movie in order to help your grandma will eventually go away.

35 The king's favor *is* toward a wise
servant,
But his wrath *is against* him who causes
shame.

15 A soft answer turns away wrath,
But a harsh word stirs up anger.

2 The tongue of the wise uses knowledge
rightly,
But the mouth of fools pours forth
foolishness.

3 The eyes of the LORD *are* in every place,
Keeping watch on the evil and the good.

4 A wholesome tongue *is* a tree of life,
But perverseness in it breaks the spirit.

5 A fool despises his father's instruction,
But he who receives correction is
prudent.

6 *In* the house of the righteous *there is*
much treasure,
But in the revenue of the wicked is
trouble.

7 The lips of the wise disperse knowledge,
But the heart of the fool *does* not *do* so.

8 The sacrifice of the wicked *is* an
abomination to the LORD,
But the prayer of the upright *is* His
delight.

9 The way of the wicked *is* an
abomination to the LORD,
But He loves him who follows
righteousness.

10 Harsh discipline *is* for him who forsakes
the way,
And he who hates correction will die.

11 Hell[a] and Destruction[b] *are* before the
LORD;
So how much more the hearts of the
sons of men.

12 A scoffer does not love one who corrects
him,
Nor will he go to the wise.

13 A merry heart makes a cheerful
countenance,
But by sorrow of the heart the spirit is
broken.

14 The heart of him who has
understanding seeks knowledge,
But the mouth of fools feeds on
foolishness.

15:11 [a] Or *Sheol* [b] Hebrew *Abaddon*

LEARN SELF-CONTROL

READ IT: PROVERBS 15:1

You will meet people who disagree with you. Sometimes you are right and sometimes you are wrong. Your goal must be to learn the truth, not to win an argument. The desire to win an argument is selfish. The sad thing is that *the truth* nearly always loses in an argument.

When someone disagrees with you, the first thing to do is to listen carefully to what that person says. As you take time to listen, your own feelings will calm down. Then you'll be more concerned about learning the truth than about winning a fight.

As a Christian, you should be against false ideas. But in loving truth, you must first show your self-control. The real battle is not you against someone else. The real struggle is between the Lord, the God of truth, and Satan, the god of lies. People are more often led to the truth by a calm spirit than by anger.

15 All the days of the afflicted *are* evil,
But he who is of a merry heart *has* a continual feast.

16 Better *is* a little with the fear of the LORD,
Than great treasure with trouble.
17 Better *is* a dinner of herbs[a] where love is,
Than a fatted calf with hatred.

18 A wrathful man stirs up strife,
But *he who is* slow to anger allays contention.

19 The way of the lazy *man is* like a hedge of thorns,
But the way of the upright *is* a highway.

20 A wise son makes a father glad,
But a foolish man despises his mother.

21 Folly *is* joy *to him who is* destitute of discernment,
But a man of understanding walks uprightly.

22 Without counsel, plans go awry,
But in the multitude of counselors they are established.

23 A man has joy by the answer of his mouth,
And a word *spoken* in due season, how good *it is!*

24 The way of life *winds* upward for the wise,
That he may turn away from hell[a] below.

25 The LORD will destroy the house of the proud,
But He will establish the boundary of the widow.

26 The thoughts of the wicked *are* an abomination to the LORD,
But the words of the pure *are* pleasant.

27 He who is greedy for gain troubles his own house,
But he who hates bribes will live.

28 The heart of the righteous studies how to answer,
But the mouth of the wicked pours forth evil.

29 The LORD *is* far from the wicked,
But He hears the prayer of the righteous.

30 The light of the eyes rejoices the heart,
And a good report makes the bones healthy.[a]

31 The ear that hears the rebukes of life
Will abide among the wise.
32 He who disdains instruction despises his own soul,
But he who heeds rebuke gets understanding.
33 The fear of the LORD *is* the instruction of wisdom,
And before honor *is* humility.

16 The preparations of the heart *belong* to man,
But the answer of the tongue *is* from the LORD.

2 All the ways of a man *are* pure in his own eyes,
But the LORD weighs the spirits.

3 Commit your works to the LORD,
And your thoughts will be established.

4 The LORD has made all for Himself,
Yes, even the wicked for the day of doom.

5 Everyone proud in heart *is* an abomination to the LORD;
Though they join forces,[a] none will go unpunished.

6 In mercy and truth
Atonement is provided for iniquity;
And by the fear of the LORD *one* departs from evil.

7 When a man's ways please the LORD,
He makes even his enemies to be at peace with him.

8 Better *is* a little with righteousness,
Than vast revenues without justice.

9 A man's heart plans his way,
But the LORD directs his steps.

10 Divination *is* on the lips of the king;
His mouth must not transgress in judgment.
11 Honest weights and scales *are* the LORD's;
All the weights in the bag *are* His work.
12 *It is* an abomination for kings to commit wickedness,

15:17 [a] Or *vegetables* **15:24** [a] Or *Sheol* **15:30** [a] Literally *fat* **16:5** [a] Literally *hand to hand*

For a throne is established by
righteousness.
13 Righteous lips *are* the delight of kings,
And they love him who speaks *what is*
right.
14 As messengers of death *is* the king's
wrath,
But a wise man will appease it.
15 In the light of the king's face *is* life,
And his favor *is* like a cloud of the latter
rain.

16 How much better to get wisdom than
gold!
And to get understanding is to be
chosen rather than silver.

17 The highway of the upright *is* to depart
from evil;
He who keeps his way preserves his
soul.

18 Pride *goes* before destruction,
And a haughty spirit before a fall.
19 Better *to be* of a humble spirit with the
lowly,
Than to divide the spoil with the proud.

20 He who heeds the word wisely will find
good,
And whoever trusts in the LORD, happy
is he.

21 The wise in heart will be called prudent,
And sweetness of the lips increases
learning.

22 Understanding *is* a wellspring of life to
him who has it.
But the correction of fools *is* folly.

23 The heart of the wise teaches his
mouth,
And adds learning to his lips.

24 Pleasant words *are like* a honeycomb,
Sweetness to the soul and health to the
bones.

25 There is a way *that seems* right to a man,
But its end *is* the way of death.

26 The person who labors, labors for
himself,
For his *hungry* mouth drives him *on*.

27 An ungodly man digs up evil,
And *it is* on his lips like a burning fire.
28 A perverse man sows strife,
And a whisperer separates the best of
friends.
29 A violent man entices his neighbor,
And leads him in a way *that is* not good.
30 He winks his eye to devise perverse
things;
He purses his lips *and* brings about evil.

16:2 GOD CAN GIVE YOU A RIGHT ATTITUDE

A bad attitude is a self-righteous attitude: "I am right, and everybody else is wrong." That is the worst attitude of all.

God can change our opinion that we're good enough as we are. But "if we say that we have no sin, we deceive ourselves, and the truth is not in us" (1 John 1:8). So God needs to change our attitudes and help us to see our sins. Then we will be kinder to others who fall into sin.

Think about Jesus dying on the Cross for your sins. He was perfect in every way. Although He never sinned, He let Himself be put to death like a sinner to pay for your sins and mine.

That really puts us in our place, doesn't it? We never deserve to be called "good." Only Jesus is good, and His Father loves us because Jesus died for us.

31 The silver-haired head *is* a crown of glory,
If it is found in the way of righteousness.

32 *He who is* slow to anger *is* better than the mighty,
And he who rules his spirit than he who takes a city.

33 The lot is cast into the lap,
But its every decision *is* from the LORD.

17 Better *is* a dry morsel with quietness,
Than a house full of feasting[a] *with* strife.

2 A wise servant will rule over a son who causes shame,
And will share an inheritance among the brothers.

3 The refining pot *is* for silver and the furnace for gold,
But the LORD tests the hearts.

4 An evildoer gives heed to false lips;
A liar listens eagerly to a spiteful tongue.

5 He who mocks the poor reproaches his Maker;
He who is glad at calamity will not go unpunished.

6 Children's children *are* the crown of old men,
And the glory of children *is* their father.

7 Excellent speech is not becoming to a fool,
Much less lying lips to a prince.

8 A present *is* a precious stone in the eyes of its possessor;
Wherever he turns, he prospers.

9 He who covers a transgression seeks love,
But he who repeats a matter separates friends.

10 Rebuke is more effective for a wise *man*
Than a hundred blows on a fool.

11 An evil *man* seeks only rebellion;
Therefore a cruel messenger will be sent against him.

12 Let a man meet a bear robbed of her cubs,
Rather than a fool in his folly.

13 Whoever rewards evil for good,
Evil will not depart from his house.

14 The beginning of strife *is like* releasing water;
Therefore stop contention before a quarrel starts.

15 He who justifies the wicked, and he who condemns the just,
Both of them alike *are* an abomination to the LORD.

16 Why *is there* in the hand of a fool the purchase price of wisdom,

17:1 [a] Or *sacrificial meals*

FRIENDSHIP

READ IT: PROVERBS 17:9, 17

You've heard the phrase *forgive and forget*, right? Sounds like a great idea until you try to put it into practice. It can be tough to do! But the Bible is clear—being a true friend means you're willing to forgive someone who hurt you and not bring it up again and again. That kind of grace can take friendship to a whole new level. Another friendship step comes when you choose to be a loyal friend. Are you someone who can be counted on not only when friendship is easy but also when it's challenging?

Since *he has* no heart *for it?*

17 A friend loves at all times,
And a brother is born for adversity.

18 A man devoid of understanding shakes hands in a pledge,
And becomes surety for his friend.

19 He who loves transgression loves strife,
And he who exalts his gate seeks destruction.

20 He who has a deceitful heart finds no good,
And he who has a perverse tongue falls into evil.

21 He who begets a scoffer *does so* to his sorrow,
And the father of a fool has no joy.

22 A merry heart does good, *like* medicine,[a]
But a broken spirit dries the bones.

23 A wicked *man* accepts a bribe behind the back[a]
To pervert the ways of justice.

24 Wisdom *is* in the sight of him who has understanding,
But the eyes of a fool *are* on the ends of the earth.

25 A foolish son *is* a grief to his father,
And bitterness to her who bore him.

26 Also, to punish the righteous *is* not good,
Nor to strike princes for *their* uprightness.

27 He who has knowledge spares his words,
And a man of understanding is of a calm spirit.

28 Even a fool is counted wise when he holds his peace;
When he shuts his lips, *he is considered* perceptive.

18 A man who isolates himself seeks his own desire;
He rages against all wise judgment.

2 A fool has no delight in understanding,
But in expressing his own heart.

3 When the wicked comes, contempt comes also;
And with dishonor *comes* reproach.

4 The words of a man's mouth *are* deep waters;
The wellspring of wisdom *is* a flowing brook.

5 *It is* not good to show partiality to the wicked,
Or to overthrow the righteous in judgment.

6 A fool's lips enter into contention,
And his mouth calls for blows.

7 A fool's mouth *is* his destruction,
And his lips *are* the snare of his soul.

8 The words of a talebearer *are* like tasty trifles,[a]

17:22 [a] Or *makes medicine even better* 17:23 [a] Literally *from the bosom* 18:8 [a] A Jewish tradition reads *wounds.*

SELFISHNESS

READ IT: PROVERBS 18:1

Did you know that being a loner can be a form of selfishness? Some people are loners because no one befriends them or welcomes them. But some people choose to be loners because they're not interested in getting to know others, working on friendships, or making the sacrifices that are required in good relationships. If that's you, it's time to move outside of your circle of one. It will take time and effort, but it's the best way to live.

And they go down into the inmost body.

9 He who is slothful in his work
Is a brother to him who is a great destroyer.

10 The name of the LORD *is* a strong tower;
The righteous run to it and are safe.
11 The rich man's wealth *is* his strong city,
And like a high wall in his own esteem.

12 Before destruction the heart of a man is haughty,
And before honor *is* humility.

13 He who answers a matter before he hears *it,*
It *is* folly and shame to him.

14 The spirit of a man will sustain him in sickness,
But who can bear a broken spirit?

15 The heart of the prudent acquires knowledge,
And the ear of the wise seeks knowledge.

16 A man's gift makes room for him,
And brings him before great men.

17 The first *one* to plead his cause *seems* right,
Until his neighbor comes and examines him.

18 Casting lots causes contentions to cease,
And keeps the mighty apart.

19 A brother offended *is harder to win* than a strong city,
And contentions *are* like the bars of a castle.

20 A man's stomach shall be satisfied from the fruit of his mouth;
From the produce of his lips he shall be filled.

21 Death and life *are* in the power of the tongue,
And those who love it will eat its fruit.

22 *He who* finds a wife finds a good *thing,*
And obtains favor from the LORD.

23 The poor *man* uses entreaties,
But the rich answers roughly.

24 A man *who has* friends must himself be friendly,[a]
But there is a friend *who* sticks closer than a brother.

19 Better *is* the poor who walks in his integrity

18:24 [a] Following Greek manuscripts, Syriac, Targum, and Vulgate; Masoretic Text reads *may come to ruin.*

BE A FRIEND

READ IT: PROVERBS 18:24

Some people complain because they have no friends, but to have friends, you must be a friend. Jesus went about doing good, so He had a great many friends. He had some important enemies, of course, but He also had a lot of friends. "The common people heard Him gladly" (Mark 12:37).

The most important thing for a Christian is to *be a friend*. This is what "love your neighbor" really means. Do you know someone who is poor and sick? Go and visit that person, and ask God to go with you. He will.

You need to know one thing: you always have a Friend. That Friend is Jesus, and He sticks closer than a brother. But you must be His friend, too. Then you and He will be together always, wherever you go.

Than *one who is* perverse in his lips, and
is a fool.

2 Also it is not good *for* a soul *to be*
without knowledge,
And he sins who hastens with *his* feet.

3 The foolishness of a man twists his way,
And his heart frets against the LORD.

4 Wealth makes many friends,
But the poor is separated from his
friend.

5 A false witness will not go unpunished,
And *he who* speaks lies will not escape.

6 Many entreat the favor of the nobility,
And every man *is* a friend to one who
gives gifts.

7 All the brothers of the poor hate him;
How much more do his friends go far
from him!
He may pursue *them with* words, *yet*
they abandon *him.*

8 He who gets wisdom loves his own soul;
He who keeps understanding will find
good.

9 A false witness will not go unpunished,
And *he who* speaks lies shall perish.

10 Luxury is not fitting for a fool,
Much less for a servant to rule over
princes.

11 The discretion of a man makes him
slow to anger,
And his glory *is* to overlook a
transgression.

12 The king's wrath *is* like the roaring of a
lion,
But his favor *is* like dew on the grass.

13 A foolish son *is* the ruin of his father,
And the contentions of a wife *are* a
continual dripping.

14 Houses and riches *are* an inheritance
from fathers,
But a prudent wife *is* from the LORD.

15 Laziness casts *one* into a deep sleep,
And an idle person will suffer hunger.

16 He who keeps the commandment keeps
his soul,
But he who is careless[a] of his ways will
die.

17 He who has pity on the poor lends to the
LORD,
And He will pay back what he has given.

18 Chasten your son while there is hope,
And do not set your heart on his
destruction.[a]

19 *A man of* great wrath will suffer
punishment;
For if you rescue *him,* you will have to
do it again.

20 Listen to counsel and receive
instruction,
That you may be wise in your latter
days.

21 There are many plans in a man's heart,
Nevertheless the LORD's counsel—that
will stand.

22 What is desired in a man is kindness,
And a poor man is better than a liar.

23 The fear of the LORD *leads* to life,
And *he who has it* will abide in
satisfaction;
He will not be visited with evil.

24 A lazy *man* buries his hand in the bowl,[a]
And will not so much as bring it to his
mouth again.

25 Strike a scoffer, and the simple will
become wary;
Rebuke one who has understanding,
and he will discern knowledge.

26 He who mistreats *his* father *and* chases
away *his* mother
Is a son who causes shame and brings
reproach.

27 Cease listening to instruction, my son,
And you will stray from the words of
knowledge.

28 A disreputable witness scorns justice,
And the mouth of the wicked devours
iniquity.

29 Judgments are prepared for scoffers,
And beatings for the backs of fools.

20 Wine *is* a mocker,
Strong drink *is* a brawler,

19:16 [a] Literally *despises,* figurative of recklessness or carelessness 19:18 [a] Literally *to put him to death;* a Jewish tradition reads *on his crying.* 19:24 [a] Septuagint and Syriac read *bosom;* Targum and Vulgate read *armpit.*

And whoever is led astray by it is not
wise.

2 The wrath[a] of a king *is* like the roaring
of a lion;
Whoever provokes him to anger sins
against his own life.

3 *It is* honorable for a man to stop striving,
Since any fool can start a quarrel.

4 The lazy *man* will not plow because of
winter;
He will beg during harvest and *have*
nothing.

5 Counsel in the heart of man *is like* deep
water,
But a man of understanding will draw
it out.

6 Most men will proclaim each his own
goodness,
But who can find a faithful man?

7 The righteous *man* walks in his
integrity;
His children *are* blessed after him.

8 A king who sits on the throne of
judgment
Scatters all evil with his eyes.

9 Who can say, "I have made my heart
clean,
I am pure from my sin"?

10 Diverse weights *and* diverse measures,
They *are* both alike, an abomination to
the LORD.

11 Even a child is known by his deeds,
Whether what he does *is* pure and right.

12 The hearing ear and the seeing eye,
The LORD has made them both.

13 Do not love sleep, lest you come to
poverty;
Open your eyes, *and* you will be
satisfied with bread.

14 "*It is* good for nothing,"[a] cries the buyer;
But when he has gone his way, then he
boasts.

15 There is gold and a multitude of rubies,
But the lips of knowledge *are* a precious
jewel.

16 Take the garment of one who is surety
for a stranger,

20:2 [a] Literally *fear* or *terror* which is produced by the king's wrath **20:14** [a] Literally *evil, evil*

ONLY GOD CAN MAKE US PURE

READ IT: PROVERBS 20:9

Some people try very hard not to sin. They don't like to steal, lie, or swear, or commit other sins, and they try not to. But ever since Adam and Eve brought sin into the world, it has been our nature to sin. We can't just make ourselves be good. Without God's help, we will keep falling back into our old ways of sin.

God can change your life. He will give you a new desire to please Him in all your ways. When you truly love God, you leave your sins behind. Sometimes you will fail, because no one is perfect but God. Just remember that God will help you and will give you a heart that sincerely loves the things He loves.

You begin to please God when you honestly tell Him you know you're a sinner. Then ask Him to forgive you and make you able to please Him. God will answer your prayer. "Blessed are the pure in heart, for they shall see God" (Matthew 5:8).

And hold it as a pledge *when it* is for a seductress.

17 Bread gained by deceit *is* sweet to a man,
But afterward his mouth will be filled with gravel.

18 Plans are established by counsel;
By wise counsel wage war.

19 He who goes about *as* a talebearer reveals secrets;
Therefore do not associate with one who flatters with his lips.

20 Whoever curses his father or his mother,
His lamp will be put out in deep darkness.

21 An inheritance gained hastily at the beginning
Will not be blessed at the end.

22 Do not say, "I will recompense evil";
Wait for the LORD, and He will save you.

23 Diverse weights *are* an abomination to the LORD,
And dishonest scales *are* not good.

24 A man's steps *are* of the LORD;
How then can a man understand his own way?

25 *It is* a snare for a man to devote rashly *something as* holy,
And afterward to reconsider *his* vows.

26 A wise king sifts out the wicked,
And brings the threshing wheel over them.

27 The spirit of a man *is* the lamp of the LORD,
Searching all the inner depths of his heart.[a]

28 Mercy and truth preserve the king,
And by lovingkindness he upholds his throne.

29 *The glory of young men is* their strength,
And the splendor of old men *is* their gray head.

30 Blows that hurt cleanse away evil,
As *do* stripes the inner depths of the heart.[a]

21 The king's heart *is* in the hand of the LORD,
Like the rivers of water;
He turns it wherever He wishes.

2 Every way of a man *is* right in his own eyes,
But the LORD weighs the hearts.

3 To do righteousness and justice
Is more acceptable to the LORD than sacrifice.

4 A haughty look, a proud heart,
And the plowing[a] of the wicked *are* sin.

5 The plans of the diligent *lead* surely to plenty,
But *those of* everyone *who is* hasty, surely to poverty.

6 Getting treasures by a lying tongue
Is the fleeting fantasy of those who seek death.[a]

7 The violence of the wicked will destroy them,[a]
Because they refuse to do justice.

8 The way of a guilty man *is* perverse;[a]
But *as for* the pure, his work *is* right.

9 Better to dwell in a corner of a housetop,
Than in a house shared with a contentious woman.

10 The soul of the wicked desires evil;
His neighbor finds no favor in his eyes.

11 When the scoffer is punished, the simple is made wise;
But when the wise is instructed, he receives knowledge.

12 The righteous *God* wisely considers the house of the wicked,
Overthrowing the wicked for *their* wickedness.

13 Whoever shuts his ears to the cry of the poor
Will also cry himself and not be heard.

14 A gift in secret pacifies anger,
And a bribe behind the back,[a] strong wrath.

20:27 [a] Literally *the rooms of the belly* **20:30** [a] Literally *the rooms of the belly* **21:4** [a] Or *lamp* **21:6** [a] Septuagint reads *Pursue vanity on the snares of death;* Vulgate reads *Is vain and foolish, and shall stumble on the snares of death;* Targum reads *They shall be destroyed, and they shall fall who seek death.* **21:7** [a] Literally *drag them away* **21:8** [a] Or *The way of a man is perverse and strange* **21:14** [a] Literally *in the bosom*

15 *It is* a joy for the just to do justice,
But destruction *will come* to the workers of iniquity.

16 A man who wanders from the way of understanding
Will rest in the assembly of the dead.

17 He who loves pleasure *will be* a poor man;
He who loves wine and oil will not be rich.

18 The wicked *shall be* a ransom for the righteous,
And the unfaithful for the upright.

19 Better to dwell in the wilderness,
Than with a contentious and angry woman.

20 *There is* desirable treasure,
And oil in the dwelling of the wise,
But a foolish man squanders it.

21 He who follows righteousness and mercy
Finds life, righteousness, and honor.

22 A wise *man* scales the city of the mighty,
And brings down the trusted stronghold.

23 Whoever guards his mouth and tongue
Keeps his soul from troubles.

24 A proud *and* haughty *man*—"Scoffer" *is* his name;
He acts with arrogant pride.

25 The desire of the lazy *man* kills him,
For his hands refuse to labor.
26 He covets greedily all day long,
But the righteous gives and does not spare.

27 The sacrifice of the wicked *is* an abomination;
How much more *when* he brings it with wicked intent!

28 A false witness shall perish,
But the man who hears *him* will speak endlessly.

29 A wicked man hardens his face,
But *as for* the upright, he establishes[a] his way.

30 *There is* no wisdom or understanding
Or counsel against the LORD.

31 The horse *is* prepared for the day of battle,
But deliverance *is* of the LORD.

22 A *good* name is to be chosen rather than great riches,
Loving favor rather than silver and gold.

2 The rich and the poor have this in common,
The LORD *is* the maker of them all.

3 A prudent *man* foresees evil and hides himself,
But the simple pass on and are punished.

4 By humility *and* the fear of the LORD
Are riches and honor and life.

5 Thorns *and* snares *are* in the way of the perverse;
He who guards his soul will be far from them.

6 Train up a child in the way he should go,
And when he is old he will not depart from it.

7 The rich rules over the poor,
And the borrower *is* servant to the lender.

8 He who sows iniquity will reap sorrow,
And the rod of his anger will fail.

9 He who has a generous eye will be blessed,
For he gives of his bread to the poor.

10 Cast out the scoffer, and contention will leave;
Yes, strife and reproach will cease.

11 He who loves purity of heart
And has grace on his lips,
The king *will be* his friend.

12 The eyes of the LORD preserve knowledge,
But He overthrows the words of the faithless.

13 The lazy *man* says, "*There is* a lion outside!
I shall be slain in the streets!"

14 The mouth of an immoral woman *is* a deep pit;

21:29 [a] Qere and Septuagint read *understands*.

He who is abhorred by the LORD will
fall there.

15 Foolishness *is* bound up in the heart of a
child;
The rod of correction will drive it far
from him.

16 He who oppresses the poor to increase
his *riches,*
And he who gives to the rich, *will* surely
come to poverty.

Sayings of the Wise

17 Incline your ear and hear the words of
the wise,
And apply your heart to my knowledge;
18 For *it is* a pleasant thing if you keep
them within you;
Let them all be fixed upon your lips,
19 So that your trust may be in the LORD;
I have instructed you today, even you.
20 Have I not written to you excellent
things
Of counsels and knowledge,
21 That I may make you know the certainty
of the words of truth,
That you may answer words of truth
To those who send to you?

22 Do not rob the poor because he *is* poor,
Nor oppress the afflicted at the gate;
23 For the LORD will plead their cause,
And plunder the soul of those who
plunder them.

24 Make no friendship with an angry man,
And with a furious man do not go,
25 Lest you learn his ways
And set a snare for your soul.

26 Do not be one of those who shakes
hands in a pledge,
One of those who is surety for debts;
27 If you have nothing *with which* to pay,
Why should he take away your bed from
under you?

28 Do not remove the ancient landmark
Which your fathers have set.

29 Do you see a man *who* excels in his
work?
He will stand before kings;
He will not stand before unknown *men.*

23 When you sit down to eat with a
ruler,
Consider carefully what *is* before you;
2 And put a knife to your throat
If you *are* a man given to appetite.
3 Do not desire his delicacies,

BE KNOWN AS AN HONEST PERSON

READ IT: PROVERBS 22:1

Do you go to church and Sunday school? Do you claim to be a Christian? Then you must also be known as an honest person. Someone who goes to church on Sunday and cheats his neighbor on other days is the worst kind of Christian. In fact, he probably isn't a real Christian at all!

It's a terrible thing to say you're a Christian and not *act* like one. Soon people will say, "That girl lied to me," or, "He steals from people." That's what you call a bad reputation.

What is even worse, you give Jesus a bad reputation, too. Sometimes people who tell the world they're Christians act so badly that everybody laughs at them. At the same time, the world begins to say, "Jesus can't be a real Savior. Look at the dishonest people who follow Him!"

For they *are* deceptive food.

4 Do not overwork to be rich;
Because of your own understanding, cease!
5 Will you set your eyes on that which is not?
For *riches* certainly make themselves wings;
They fly away like an eagle *toward* heaven.

6 Do not eat the bread of a miser,[a]
Nor desire his delicacies;
7 For as he thinks in his heart, so *is* he.
"Eat and drink!" he says to you,
But his heart is not with you.
8 The morsel you have eaten, you will vomit up,
And waste your pleasant words.

9 Do not speak in the hearing of a fool,
For he will despise the wisdom of your words.

10 Do not remove the ancient landmark,
Nor enter the fields of the fatherless;
11 For their Redeemer *is* mighty;
He will plead their cause against you.

12 Apply your heart to instruction,
And your ears to words of knowledge.

13 Do not withhold correction from a child,
For *if* you beat him with a rod, he will not die.
14 You shall beat him with a rod,
And deliver his soul from hell.[a]

15 My son, if your heart is wise,
My heart will rejoice—indeed, I myself;
16 Yes, my inmost being will rejoice
When your lips speak right things.

17 Do not let your heart envy sinners,
But *be zealous* for the fear of the LORD all the day;
18 For surely there is a hereafter,
And your hope will not be cut off.

19 Hear, my son, and be wise;
And guide your heart in the way.
20 Do not mix with winebibbers,
Or with gluttonous eaters of meat;
21 For the drunkard and the glutton will come to poverty,
And drowsiness will clothe *a man* with rags.

22 Listen to your father who begot you,
And do not despise your mother when she is old.

23 Buy the truth, and do not sell *it*,
Also wisdom and instruction and understanding.

24 The father of the righteous will greatly rejoice,
And he who begets a wise *child* will delight in him.
25 Let your father and your mother be glad,
And let her who bore you rejoice.

26 My son, give me your heart,
And let your eyes observe my ways.
27 For a harlot *is* a deep pit,
And a seductress *is* a narrow well.
28 She also lies in wait as *for* a victim,
And increases the unfaithful among men.

29 Who has woe?
Who has sorrow?
Who has contentions?
Who has complaints?
Who has wounds without cause?
Who has redness of eyes?
30 Those who linger long at the wine,
Those who go in search of mixed wine.
31 Do not look on the wine when it is red,
When it sparkles in the cup,
When it swirls around smoothly;
32 At the last it bites like a serpent,
And stings like a viper.
33 Your eyes will see strange things,
And your heart will utter perverse things.
34 Yes, you will be like one who lies down in the midst of the sea,
Or like one who lies at the top of the mast, *saying:*
35 "They have struck me, *but* I was not hurt;
They have beaten me, but I did not feel *it*.
When shall I awake, that I may seek another *drink?*"

24

Do not be envious of evil men,
Nor desire to be with them;
2 For their heart devises violence,
And their lips talk of troublemaking.

3 Through wisdom a house is built,
And by understanding it is established;
4 By knowledge the rooms are filled

23:6 [a] Literally *one who has an evil eye* 23:14 [a] Or *Sheol*

With all precious and pleasant riches.

5 A wise man *is* strong,
Yes, a man of knowledge increases strength;
6 For by wise counsel you will wage your own war,
And in a multitude of counselors *there is* safety.

7 Wisdom *is* too lofty for a fool;
He does not open his mouth in the gate.

8 He who plots to do evil
Will be called a schemer.
9 The devising of foolishness *is* sin,
And the scoffer *is* an abomination to men.

10 *If* you faint in the day of adversity,
Your strength *is* small.

11 Deliver *those who* are drawn toward death,
And hold back *those* stumbling to the slaughter.
12 If you say, "Surely we did not know this,"
Does not He who weighs the hearts consider *it?*
He who keeps your soul, does He *not* know *it?*
And will He *not* render to *each* man according to his deeds?

13 My son, eat honey because *it is* good,
And the honeycomb *which is* sweet to your taste;
14 So *shall* the knowledge of wisdom *be* to your soul;
If you have found *it,* there is a prospect,
And your hope will not be cut off.

15 Do not lie in wait, O wicked *man,* against the dwelling of the righteous;
Do not plunder his resting place;
16 For a righteous *man* may fall seven times
And rise again,
But the wicked shall fall by calamity.

17 Do not rejoice when your enemy falls,
And do not let your heart be glad when he stumbles;
18 Lest the LORD see *it,* and it displease Him,
And He turn away His wrath from him.

19 Do not fret because of evildoers,
Nor be envious of the wicked;
20 For there will be no prospect for the evil *man;*
The lamp of the wicked will be put out.

CHOOSE GOOD ROLE MODELS

READ IT: PROVERBS 24:1

Since you will become like the people you admire, you should pick out people you want to be like. Maybe you have a favorite schoolteacher or scout leader, and you're saying to yourself, "I'd like to be like that person when I'm grown up."

It's always best if your role models (or examples) are your own parents. Let's pray that your parents will be the kind of folks you can look up to and say, "I want to be like you when I grow up, Dad," or "Mother, when I'm older, I'd like to be as kind as you."

But remember, earthly role models will sometimes disappoint you. You must pray to forgive the failures of those you admire. They're human, too. But it's good to know that Jesus never fails. He is the same yesterday, today, and forever (see Hebrews 13:8). What a great role model He is!

21 My son, fear the LORD and the king;
Do not associate with those given to change;
22 For their calamity will rise suddenly,
And who knows the ruin those two can bring?

Further Sayings of the Wise

23 These *things* also *belong* to the wise:

It is not good to show partiality in judgment.
24 He who says to the wicked, "You *are* righteous,"
Him the people will curse;
Nations will abhor him.
25 But those who rebuke *the wicked* will have delight,
And a good blessing will come upon them.

26 He who gives a right answer kisses the lips.

27 Prepare your outside work,
Make it fit for yourself in the field;
And afterward build your house.

28 Do not be a witness against your neighbor without cause,
For would you deceive[a] with your lips?
29 Do not say, "I will do to him just as he has done to me;
I will render to the man according to his work."

30 I went by the field of the lazy *man*,
And by the vineyard of the man devoid of understanding;
31 And there it was, all overgrown with thorns;
Its surface was covered with nettles;
Its stone wall was broken down.
32 When I saw *it*, I considered *it* well;
I looked on *it and* received instruction:
33 A little sleep, a little slumber,
A little folding of the hands to rest;
34 So shall your poverty come *like* a prowler,
And your need like an armed man.

Further Wise Sayings of Solomon

25 These also *are* proverbs of Solomon which the men of Hezekiah king of Judah copied:

2 *It is* the glory of God to conceal a matter,
But the glory of kings *is* to search out a matter.
3 *As* the heavens for height and the earth for depth,
So the heart of kings *is* unsearchable.

4 Take away the dross from silver,
And it will go to the silversmith *for* jewelry.
5 Take away the wicked from before the king,
And his throne will be established in righteousness.

6 Do not exalt yourself in the presence of the king,
And do not stand in the place of the great;
7 For *it is* better that he say to you,
"Come up here,"
Than that you should be put lower in the presence of the prince,
Whom your eyes have seen.

8 Do not go hastily to court;
For what will you do in the end,
When your neighbor has put you to shame?
9 Debate your case with your neighbor,
And do not disclose the secret to another;
10 Lest he who hears *it* expose your shame,
And your reputation be ruined.

11 A word fitly spoken *is like* apples of gold
In settings of silver.
12 *Like* an earring of gold and an ornament of fine gold
Is a wise rebuker to an obedient ear.

13 Like the cold of snow in time of harvest
Is a faithful messenger to those who send him,
For he refreshes the soul of his masters.

14 Whoever falsely boasts of giving
Is like clouds and wind without rain.

15 By long forbearance a ruler is persuaded,
And a gentle tongue breaks a bone.

16 Have you found honey?
Eat only as much as you need,
Lest you be filled with it and vomit.

17 Seldom set foot in your neighbor's house,
Lest he become weary of you and hate you.

24:28 [a] Septuagint and Vulgate read *Do not deceive*.

18 A man who bears false witness against
his neighbor
Is like a club, a sword, and a sharp arrow.

19 Confidence in an unfaithful *man* in
time of trouble
Is like a bad tooth and a foot out of joint.

20 *Like* one who takes away a garment in
cold weather,
And like vinegar on soda,
Is one who sings songs to a heavy heart.

21 If your enemy is hungry, give him bread
to eat;
And if he is thirsty, give him water to
drink;
22 For *so* you will heap coals of fire on his
head,
And the LORD will reward you.

23 The north wind brings forth rain,
And a backbiting tongue an angry
countenance.

24 *It is* better to dwell in a corner of a
housetop,
Than in a house shared with a
contentious woman.

25 *As* cold water to a weary soul,
So *is* good news from a far country.

26 A righteous *man* who falters before the
wicked
Is like a murky spring and a polluted
well.

27 *It is* not good to eat much honey;
So to seek one's own glory *is not* glory.

28 Whoever *has* no rule over his own spirit
Is like a city broken down, without walls.

26 As snow in summer and rain in
harvest,
So honor is not fitting for a fool.

2 Like a flitting sparrow, like a flying
swallow,
So a curse without cause shall not
alight.

3 A whip for the horse,
A bridle for the donkey,
And a rod for the fool's back.
4 Do not answer a fool according to his
folly,
Lest you also be like him.
5 Answer a fool according to his folly,
Lest he be wise in his own eyes.
6 He who sends a message by the hand of
a fool
Cuts off *his own* feet *and* drinks
violence.
7 *Like* the legs of the lame that hang limp
Is a proverb in the mouth of fools.
8 Like one who binds a stone in a sling
Is he who gives honor to a fool.
9 *Like* a thorn *that* goes into the hand of a
drunkard
Is a proverb in the mouth of fools.
10 The great *God* who formed everything
Gives the fool *his* hire and the
transgressor *his* wages.[a]

26:10 [a] The Hebrew is difficult; ancient and modern translators differ greatly.

REVENGE

READ IT: PROVERBS 25:21, 22

If you saw a hungry person, would you want to give him food? What if that hungry person was your greatest enemy? Would you still be excited about helping him? There might be a part of you that would want to let the person stay hungry. He probably deserves it, doesn't he?

God's radical idea is this: don't treat your enemies the way they deserve to be treated. Instead, treat them the way God treats you—with love.

11 As a dog returns to his own vomit,
So a fool repeats his folly.
12 Do you see a man wise in his own eyes?
There is more hope for a fool than for him.

13 The lazy *man* says, "*There is* a lion in the road!
A fierce lion *is* in the streets!"
14 *As* a door turns on its hinges,
So *does* the lazy *man* on his bed.
15 The lazy *man* buries his hand in the bowl;[a]
It wearies him to bring it back to his mouth.
16 The lazy *man is* wiser in his own eyes
Than seven men who can answer sensibly.

17 He who passes by *and* meddles in a quarrel not his own
Is like one who takes a dog by the ears.

18 Like a madman who throws firebrands, arrows, and death,
19 *Is* the man *who* deceives his neighbor,
And says, "I was only joking!"

20 Where *there is* no wood, the fire goes out;
And where *there is* no talebearer, strife ceases.
21 *As* charcoal *is* to burning coals, and wood to fire,
So *is* a contentious man to kindle strife.
22 The words of a talebearer *are* like tasty trifles,
And they go down into the inmost body.

23 Fervent lips with a wicked heart
Are like earthenware covered with silver dross.

24 He who hates, disguises *it* with his lips,
And lays up deceit within himself;
25 When he speaks kindly, do not believe him,
For *there are* seven abominations in his heart;
26 *Though his* hatred is covered by deceit,
His wickedness will be revealed before the assembly.

27 Whoever digs a pit will fall into it,
And he who rolls a stone will have it roll back on him.

28 A lying tongue hates *those who are* crushed by it,
And a flattering mouth works ruin.

27 Do not boast about tomorrow,
For you do not know what a day may bring forth.

2 Let another man praise you, and not your own mouth;
A stranger, and not your own lips.

26:15 [a] Compare 19:24

Epic Ideas

27:1 TRUST GOD FOR TOMORROW

We all make plans for tomorrow, and we hope to carry out our plans. But we really don't know for sure what will happen tomorrow. *Tomorrow is God's time.*

Perhaps you're planning a trip or a party with your friends. Most often your plans turn out OK. But sometimes things happen that cause you to change your plans.

Put your plans in God's hands. He is the One who is making your way. "A man's heart plans his way, but the LORD directs his steps" (Proverbs 16:9). *It is best to ask God to guide your plans each day.* You can trust Him to lead you in the right paths. His way is always better than your way because He is wiser than we are.

3 A stone *is* heavy and sand *is* weighty,
But a fool's wrath *is* heavier than both of them.

4 Wrath *is* cruel and anger a torrent,
But who *is* able to stand before jealousy?

5 Open rebuke *is* better
Than love carefully concealed.

6 Faithful *are* the wounds of a friend,
But the kisses of an enemy *are* deceitful.

7 A satisfied soul loathes the honeycomb,
But to a hungry soul every bitter thing *is* sweet.

8 Like a bird that wanders from its nest
Is a man who wanders from his place.

9 Ointment and perfume delight the heart,
And the sweetness of a man's friend *gives delight* by hearty counsel.

10 Do not forsake your own friend or your father's friend,
Nor go to your brother's house in the day of your calamity;
Better *is* a neighbor nearby than a brother far away.

11 My son, be wise, and make my heart glad,
That I may answer him who reproaches me.

12 A prudent *man* foresees evil *and* hides himself;
The simple pass on *and* are punished.

13 Take the garment of him who is surety for a stranger,
And hold it in pledge *when* he is surety for a seductress.

14 He who blesses his friend with a loud voice, rising early in the morning,
It will be counted a curse to him.

15 A continual dripping on a very rainy day
And a contentious woman are alike;
16 Whoever restrains her restrains the *wind*,
And grasps oil with his right hand.

17 *As* iron sharpens iron,
So a man sharpens the countenance of his friend.

18 Whoever keeps the fig tree will eat its fruit;
So he who waits on his master will be honored.

19 As in water face *reflects* face,
So a man's heart *reveals* the man.

20 Hell[a] and Destruction[b] are never full;
So the eyes of man are never satisfied.

21 The refining pot *is* for silver and the furnace for gold,
And a man *is valued* by what others say of him.

22 Though you grind a fool in a mortar with a pestle along with crushed grain,
Yet his foolishness will not depart from him.

23 Be diligent to know the state of your flocks,
And attend to your herds;
24 For riches *are* not forever,
Nor does a crown *endure* to all generations.
25 *When* the hay is removed, and the tender grass shows itself,
And the herbs of the mountains are gathered in,
26 The lambs *will provide* your clothing,
And the goats the price of a field;
27 *You shall have* enough goats' milk for your food,
For the food of your household,
And the nourishment of your maidservants.

28 The wicked flee when no one pursues,
But the righteous are bold as a lion.

2 Because of the transgression of a land, many *are* its princes;
But by a man of understanding *and* knowledge
Right will be prolonged.

3 A poor man who oppresses the poor
Is like a driving rain which leaves no food.

4 Those who forsake the law praise the wicked,
But such as keep the law contend with them.

5 Evil men do not understand justice,
But those who seek the LORD understand all.

27:20 [a] Or *Sheol* [b] Hebrew *Abaddon*

6 Better *is* the poor who walks in his integrity
Than one perverse *in his* ways, though he *be* rich.

7 Whoever keeps the law *is* a discerning son,
But a companion of gluttons shames his father.

8 One who increases his possessions by usury and extortion
Gathers it for him who will pity the poor.

9 One who turns away his ear from hearing the law,
Even his prayer *is* an abomination.

10 Whoever causes the upright to go astray in an evil way,
He himself will fall into his own pit;
But the blameless will inherit good.

11 The rich man *is* wise in his own eyes,
But the poor who has understanding searches him out.

12 When the righteous rejoice, *there is* great glory;
But when the wicked arise, men hide themselves.

13 He who covers his sins will not prosper,
But whoever confesses and forsakes *them* will have mercy.

14 Happy *is* the man who is always reverent,
But he who hardens his heart will fall into calamity.

15 *Like* a roaring lion and a charging bear
Is a wicked ruler over poor people.

16 A ruler who lacks understanding *is* a great oppressor,
But he who hates covetousness will prolong *his* days.

17 A man burdened with bloodshed will flee into a pit;
Let no one help him.

18 Whoever walks blamelessly will be saved,
But *he who is* perverse *in his* ways will suddenly fall.

19 He who tills his land will have plenty of bread,
But he who follows frivolity will have poverty enough!

In Focus

28:16 Covetousness Pronounced *KUV-ih-tuss-ness.* Envy or the extreme and wrong desire to own what belongs to someone else.

20 A faithful man will abound with blessings,
But he who hastens to be rich will not go unpunished.

21 To show partiality *is* not good,
Because for a piece of bread a man will transgress.

22 A man with an evil eye hastens after riches,
And does not consider that poverty will come upon him.

23 He who rebukes a man will find more favor afterward
Than he who flatters with the tongue.

24 Whoever robs his father or his mother,
And says, "*It is* no transgression,"
The same *is* companion to a destroyer.

25 He who is of a proud heart stirs up strife,
But he who trusts in the LORD will be prospered.

26 He who trusts in his own heart is a fool,
But whoever walks wisely will be delivered.

27 He who gives to the poor will not lack,
But he who hides his eyes will have many curses.

28 When the wicked arise, men hide themselves;
But when they perish, the righteous increase.

29 He who is often rebuked, *and* hardens *his* neck,
Will suddenly be destroyed, and that without remedy.

2 When the righteous are in authority, the people rejoice;
But when a wicked *man* rules, the people groan.

3 Whoever loves wisdom makes his father rejoice,
But a companion of harlots wastes *his* wealth.

4 The king establishes the land by justice,
But he who receives bribes overthrows it.

5 A man who flatters his neighbor
Spreads a net for his feet.

6 By transgression an evil man is snared,
But the righteous sings and rejoices.

7 The righteous considers the cause of the poor,
But the wicked does not understand *such* knowledge.

8 Scoffers set a city aflame,
But wise *men* turn away wrath.

9 *If* a wise man contends with a foolish man,
Whether *the fool* rages or laughs, *there is* no peace.

10 The bloodthirsty hate the blameless,
But the upright seek his well-being.[a]

11 A fool vents all his feelings,[a]
But a wise *man* holds them back.

12 If a ruler pays attention to lies,
All his servants *become* wicked.

13 The poor *man* and the oppressor have this in common:
The LORD gives light to the eyes of both.

14 The king who judges the poor with truth,
His throne will be established forever.

15 The rod and rebuke give wisdom,
But a child left *to himself* brings shame to his mother.

16 When the wicked are multiplied, transgression increases;
But the righteous will see their fall.

17 Correct your son, and he will give you rest;
Yes, he will give delight to your soul.

18 Where *there is* no revelation,[a] the people cast off restraint;
But happy *is* he who keeps the law.

19 A servant will not be corrected by mere words;
For though he understands, he will not respond.

20 Do you see a man hasty in his words?
There is more hope for a fool than for him.

29:10 [a] Literally *soul* 29:11 [a] Literally *spirit* 29:18 [a] Or *prophetic vision*

ANGER

READ IT: PROVERBS 29:11, 22

Letting off steam feels good—briefly. Then we have to live with the consequences of our actions, and the good feeling disappears. After that, all we really want is a time machine to go back and stop ourselves from losing it. But God has given us what we need to control our anger, and it's not a time machine.

- Pray: Ask God to lift burdensome anger from you.
- Turn that intensity into positive action: Exercise. Clean. Create.
- Practice peace: Spend time thanking God for every good gift He's given you.

21 He who pampers his servant from
childhood
Will have him as a son in the end.

22 An angry man stirs up strife,
And a furious man abounds in
transgression.

23 A man's pride will bring him low,
But the humble in spirit will retain
honor.

24 Whoever is a partner with a thief hates
his own life;
He swears to tell the truth,[a] but reveals
nothing.

25 The fear of man brings a snare,
But whoever trusts in the LORD shall
be safe.

26 Many seek the ruler's favor,
But justice for man *comes* from the LORD.

27 An unjust man *is* an abomination to the
righteous,
And *he who is* upright in the way *is* an
abomination to the wicked.

The Wisdom of Agur

30 The words of Agur the son of Jakeh, *his* utterance. This man declared to Ithiel—to Ithiel and Ucal:

2 Surely I *am* more stupid than *any* man,
And do not have the understanding of
a man.
3 I neither learned wisdom
Nor have knowledge of the Holy One.

4 Who has ascended into heaven, or
descended?
Who has gathered the wind in His fists?
Who has bound the waters in a
garment?
Who has established all the ends of the
earth?
What *is* His name, and what *is* His Son's
name,
If you know?

5 Every word of God *is* pure;
He *is* a shield to those who put their
trust in Him.
6 Do not add to His words,
Lest He rebuke you, and you be found
a liar.

7 Two *things* I request of You
(Deprive me not before I die):
8 Remove falsehood and lies far from me;
Give me neither poverty nor riches—
Feed me with the food allotted to me;
9 Lest I be full and deny *You*,
And say, "Who *is* the LORD?"
Or lest I be poor and steal,
And profane the name of my God.

10 Do not malign a servant to his master,
Lest he curse you, and you be found
guilty.

11 *There is* a generation *that* curses its
father,
And does not bless its mother.
12 *There is* a generation *that is* pure in its
own eyes,
Yet is not washed from its filthiness.
13 *There is* a generation—oh, how lofty are
their eyes!

29:24 [a] Literally *hears the adjuration*

GREED

READ IT: PROVERBS 30:8, 9

We should pray to have what we need, not more and not less. That's how Jesus taught us to pray. He showed us this when He said, "Give us this day our daily bread" (Matthew 6:11). He didn't say we should ask for a week's worth or even some dessert on the side. He said we should ask for what we need at the time. God will always provide for you. Trust Him to give you what you need today.

And their eyelids are lifted up.
14 *There is* a generation whose teeth *are like* swords,
And whose fangs *are like* knives,
To devour the poor from off the earth,
And the needy from *among* men.

15 The leech has two daughters—
Give *and* Give!

There are three *things that* are never satisfied,
Four never say, "Enough!":
16 The grave,[a]
The barren womb,
The earth *that* is not satisfied with water—
And the fire never says, "Enough!"

17 The eye *that* mocks *his* father,
And scorns obedience to *his* mother,
The ravens of the valley will pick it out,
And the young eagles will eat it.

18 There are three *things which* are too wonderful for me,
Yes, four *which* I do not understand:
19 The way of an eagle in the air,
The way of a serpent on a rock,
The way of a ship in the midst of the sea,
And the way of a man with a virgin.

20 This *is* the way of an adulterous woman:
She eats and wipes her mouth,
And says, "I have done no wickedness."

21 For three *things* the earth is perturbed,
Yes, for four it cannot bear up:
22 For a servant when he reigns,
A fool when he is filled with food,
23 A hateful *woman* when she is married,
And a maidservant who succeeds her mistress.

24 There are four *things which* are little on the earth,
But they *are* exceedingly wise:
25 The ants *are* a people not strong,
Yet they prepare their food in the summer;
26 The rock badgers[a] are a feeble folk,
Yet they make their homes in the crags;
27 The locusts have no king,
Yet they all advance in ranks;
28 The spider[a] skillfully grasps with its hands,
And it is in kings' palaces.

29 There are three *things which* are majestic in pace,
Yes, four *which* are stately in walk:
30 A lion, *which is* mighty among beasts
And does not turn away from any;
31 A greyhound,[a]
A male goat also,
And a king *whose* troops *are* with him.[b]

32 If you have been foolish in exalting yourself,
Or if you have devised evil, *put your* hand on *your* mouth.
33 For *as* the churning of milk produces butter,
And wringing the nose produces blood,
So the forcing of wrath produces strife.

The Words of King Lemuel's Mother

31 The words of King Lemuel, the utterance which his mother taught him:

2 What, my son?
And what, son of my womb?
And what, son of my vows?
3 Do not give your strength to women,
Nor your ways to that which destroys kings.

4 *It is* not for kings, O Lemuel,
It is not for kings to drink wine,
Nor for princes intoxicating drink;
5 Lest they drink and forget the law,
And pervert the justice of all the afflicted.
6 Give strong drink to him who is perishing,
And wine to those who are bitter of heart.
7 Let him drink and forget his poverty,
And remember his misery no more.

8 Open your mouth for the speechless,
In the cause of all *who are* appointed to die.[a]
9 Open your mouth, judge righteously,
And plead the cause of the poor and needy.

The Virtuous Wife

10 Who[a] can find a virtuous[b] wife?
For her worth *is* far above rubies.
11 The heart of her husband safely trusts her;
So he will have no lack of gain.
12 She does him good and not evil
All the days of her life.

30:16 [a] Or *Sheol* **30:26** [a] Or *hyraxes* **30:28** [a] Or *lizard* **30:31** [a] Exact identity unknown [b] A Jewish tradition reads *a king against whom there is no uprising.* **31:8** [a] Literally *sons of passing away* **31:10** [a] Verses 10 through 31 are an alphabetic acrostic in Hebrew (compare Psalm 119). [b] Literally *a wife of valor,* in the sense of all forms of excellence

13 She seeks wool and flax,
And willingly works with her hands.
14 She is like the merchant ships,
She brings her food from afar.
15 She also rises while it is yet night,
And provides food for her household,
And a portion for her maidservants.
16 She considers a field and buys it;
From her profits she plants a vineyard.
17 She girds herself with strength,
And strengthens her arms.
18 She perceives that her merchandise *is* good,
And her lamp does not go out by night.
19 She stretches out her hands to the distaff,
And her hand holds the spindle.
20 She extends her hand to the poor,
Yes, she reaches out her hands to the needy.
21 She is not afraid of snow for her household,
For all her household *is* clothed with scarlet.
22 She makes tapestry for herself;
Her clothing *is* fine linen and purple.
23 Her husband is known in the gates,
When he sits among the elders of the land.
24 She makes linen garments and sells *them,*
And supplies sashes for the merchants.
25 Strength and honor *are* her clothing;
She shall rejoice in time to come.
26 She opens her mouth with wisdom,
And on her tongue *is* the law of kindness.
27 She watches over the ways of her household,
And does not eat the bread of idleness.
28 Her children rise up and call her blessed;
Her husband *also,* and he praises her:
29 "Many daughters have done well,
But you excel them all."
30 Charm *is* deceitful and beauty *is* passing,
But a woman *who* fears the LORD, she shall be praised.
31 Give her of the fruit of her hands,
And let her own works praise her in the gates.

Starring Roles

The husband of A GREAT WOMAN OF GOD honored her by writing the words in Proverbs 31:10–31. They have remained as God's idea of the kind of wife God honors.

This woman tried to live a life of virtue. Therefore, her husband valued her more than all of his friends and possessions. He trusted her in all of his business matters.

Sometimes this great woman of God was up late or rose early in the morning to be sure her children had enough clothing.

She was not afraid to try new things. She even learned how to buy and sell land. The poor were never turned away hungry from her door.

This great woman may not have been the most beautiful woman in the world, but with God's help, she was a good wife and mother. Her children grew up to praise her. They thanked God for the wisdom she taught them while they were young.

The BOOK of ECCLESIASTES

935 B.C.

Behind the Scenes

READ IT:

The book of Ecclesiastes talks about the meaning of life. Everything in life has some value and is useful. But nothing we have or do has lasting value unless God is at the center of our lives. Respect for God and a real desire to serve God are the most important things to make our lives have meaning.

GET IT:

Who wrote it: King Solomon

When it was written: 935 B.C.

Why it was written: to save Solomon's wisdom so that generations of people could learn from it.

LIVE IT:

Life will have meaning if you have God as your focus.

FIND IT:

The Search for Life's Meaning	*Ecclesiastes 1*
Pleasure and Success Can't Make You Happy	*Ecclesiastes 2*
Everything Has Its Time	*Ecclesiastes 3*
Money and Power Can't Make You Happy	*Ecclesiastes 5–6*

The Vanity of Life

1 The words of the Preacher, the son of David, king in Jerusalem.

2 "Vanity[a] of vanities," says the Preacher;
"Vanity of vanities, all *is* vanity."

3 What profit has a man from all his labor
In which he toils under the sun?
4 *One* generation passes away, and *another* generation comes;
But the earth abides forever.
5 The sun also rises, and the sun goes down,
And hastens to the place where it arose.
6 The wind goes toward the south,
And turns around to the north;
The wind whirls about continually,
And comes again on its circuit.
7 All the rivers run into the sea,
Yet the sea *is* not full;
To the place from which the rivers come,
There they return again.
8 All things *are* full of labor;
Man cannot express *it*.
The eye is not satisfied with seeing,
Nor the ear filled with hearing.

9 That which has been *is* what will be,
That which *is* done is what will be done,
And *there is* nothing new under the sun.
10 Is there anything of which it may be said,
"See, this *is* new"?
It has already been in ancient times before us.
11 *There is* no remembrance of former *things*,
Nor will there be any remembrance of *things* that are to come
By *those* who will come after.

The Grief of Wisdom

12I, the Preacher, was king over Israel in
Jerusalem. 13And I set my heart to seek and
search out by wisdom concerning all that is
done under heaven; this burdensome task
God has given to the sons of man, by which
they may be exercised. 14I have seen all the
works that are done under the sun; and indeed, all *is* vanity and grasping for the wind.

15 *What is* crooked cannot be made straight,
And what is lacking cannot be numbered.

16I communed with my heart, saying,
"Look, I have attained greatness, and have
gained more wisdom than all who were before me in Jerusalem. My heart has understood great wisdom and knowledge." 17And
I set my heart to know wisdom and to know
madness and folly. I perceived that this also
is grasping for the wind.

18 For in much wisdom *is* much grief,
And he who increases knowledge increases sorrow.

1:2 [a] Or *Absurdity, Frustration, Futility, Nonsense;* and so throughout this book

SELFISHNESS

READ IT: ECCLESIASTES 2:10, 11

There's a cost to living a selfish life. In the short-term, it might mean getting everything you want and doing all the things that you think will make you happy. But in the long-term, it means feeling sad and lonely and unsatisfied. If your desires are only focused on yourself, they won't last, and you'll be left saying, "What was it all for, anyway?" You will only find satisfaction if your heart's desires are focused on God and other people.

The Vanity of Pleasure

2 I said in my heart, "Come now, I will
test you with mirth; therefore enjoy
pleasure"; but surely, this also *was* vanity. 2I
said of laughter—"Madness!"; and of mirth,
"What does it accomplish?" 3I searched in
my heart *how* to gratify my flesh with wine,
while guiding my heart with wisdom, and
how to lay hold on folly, till I might see what
was good for the sons of men to do under
heaven all the days of their lives.

4I made my works great, I built myself
houses, and planted myself vineyards. 5I
made myself gardens and orchards, and
I planted all *kinds* of fruit trees in them.
6I made myself water pools from which to
water the growing trees of the grove. 7I acquired male and female servants, and had
servants born in my house. Yes, I had greater possessions of herds and flocks than all
who were in Jerusalem before me. 8I also
gathered for myself silver and gold and the
special treasures of kings and of the provinces. I acquired male and female singers,
the delights of the sons of men, *and* musical
instruments[a] of all kinds.

9So I became great and excelled more
than all who were before me in Jerusalem.
Also my wisdom remained with me.

10 Whatever my eyes desired I did not keep
from them.
I did not withhold my heart from any
pleasure,
For my heart rejoiced in all my labor;
And this was my reward from all my
labor.
11 Then I looked on all the works that my
hands had done
And on the labor in which I had toiled;
And indeed all *was* vanity and grasping
for the wind.
There was no profit under the sun.

The End of the Wise and the Fool

12 Then I turned myself to consider
wisdom and madness and folly;
For what *can* the man *do* who succeeds
the king?—
Only what he has already done.
13 Then I saw that wisdom excels folly
As light excels darkness.
14 The wise man's eyes *are* in his head,
But the fool walks in darkness.
Yet I myself perceived
That the same event happens to them
all.

15 So I said in my heart,
"As it happens to the fool,
It also happens to me,
And why was I then more wise?"
Then I said in my heart,
"This also *is* vanity."
16 For *there is* no more remembrance of the
wise than of the fool forever,
Since all that now *is* will be forgotten in
the days to come.
And how does a wise *man* die?
As the fool!

17Therefore I hated life because the work
that was done under the sun *was* distressing
to me, for all *is* vanity and grasping for the
wind.

18Then I hated all my labor in which I had
toiled under the sun, because I must leave it
to the man who will come after me. 19And
who knows whether he will be wise or a fool?
Yet he will rule over all my labor in which
I toiled and in which I have shown myself
wise under the sun. This also *is* vanity.
20Therefore I turned my heart and despaired
of all the labor in which I had toiled under
the sun. 21For there is a man whose labor *is*
with wisdom, knowledge, and skill; yet he
must leave his heritage to a man who has not
labored for it. This also *is* vanity and a great
evil. 22For what has man for all his labor, and
for the striving of his heart with which he
has toiled under the sun? 23For all his days
are sorrowful, and his work burdensome;
even in the night his heart takes no rest.
This also is vanity.

24Nothing *is* better for a man *than* that
he should eat and drink, and *that* his soul
should enjoy good in his labor. This also, I
saw, was from the hand of God. 25For who
can eat, or who can have enjoyment, more
than I?[a] 26For *God* gives wisdom and knowledge and joy to a man who *is* good in His
sight; but to the sinner He gives the work of
gathering and collecting, that he may give
to *him who is* good before God. This also *is*
vanity and grasping for the wind.

2:8 [a] Exact meaning unknown 2:25 [a] Following Masoretic Text, Targum, and Vulgate; some Hebrew manuscripts, Septuagint, and Syriac read *without Him.*

Everything Has Its Time

3 To everything *there is* a season,
A time for every purpose under heaven:

2 A time to be born,
And a time to die;
A time to plant,
And a time to pluck *what is* planted;
3 A time to kill,
And a time to heal;
A time to break down,
And a time to build up;
4 A time to weep,
And a time to laugh;
A time to mourn,
And a time to dance;
5 A time to cast away stones,
And a time to gather stones;
A time to embrace,
And a time to refrain from embracing;
6 A time to gain,
And a time to lose;
A time to keep,
And a time to throw away;
7 A time to tear,
And a time to sew;
A time to keep silence,
And a time to speak;
8 A time to love,
And a time to hate;
A time of war,
And a time of peace.

The God-Given Task

9 What profit has the worker from that in
which he labors? 10 I have seen the God-given
task with which the sons of men are to be occupied. 11 He has made everything beautiful
in its time. Also He has put eternity in their
hearts, except that no one can find out the
work that God does from beginning to end.
12 I know that nothing *is* better for them
than to rejoice, and to do good in their lives,

A TIME FOR EVERYTHING

READ IT: ECCLESIASTES 3:1–15

GET IT:

Solomon was an author who wrote poems, songs, and words of advice. He also was a deep thinker and thought about the meaning of life. The book of Ecclesiastes includes some of the things he thought about and the conclusions he came to. The first part of this chapter is the most famous passage of this book.

LIVE IT:

Have you ever heard an older person say, "This too shall pass"? Well, this is what Solomon is telling us in this chapter. Everything happens in its time. Good times come and go; so do bad times. Seasons change and return again. We don't control any of it. God does. Think about that for a minute. Try to remember what was bothering you a year ago. You *might* remember if it was a really big problem and it still hurts. But you probably don't even remember the problem if it went away. The same is true for whatever is bothering you now. In time it will change, go away, or be less hurtful. God's got everything under control. We have nothing to fear.

13and also that every man should eat and
drink and enjoy the good of all his labor—it
is the gift of God.

14 I know that whatever God does,
It shall be forever.
Nothing can be added to it,
And nothing taken from it.
God does *it,* that men should fear before
Him.
15 That which is has already been,
And what is to be has already been;
And God requires an account of what
is past.

Injustice Seems to Prevail

16Moreover I saw under the sun:

In the place of judgment,
Wickedness *was* there;
And *in* the place of righteousness,
Iniquity *was* there.

17I said in my heart,

"God shall judge the righteous and the
wicked,
For *there is* a time there for every
purpose and for every work."

18I said in my heart, "Concerning the condition of the sons of men, God tests them,
that they may see that they themselves are
like animals." 19For what happens to the sons
of men also happens to animals; one thing
befalls them: as one dies, so dies the other.
Surely, they all have one breath; man has no
advantage over animals, for all *is* vanity. 20All
go to one place: all are from the dust, and
all return to dust. 21Who knows the spirit of
the sons of men, which goes upward, and
the spirit of the animal, which goes down
to the earth?[a] 22So I perceived that nothing
is better than that a man should rejoice in
his own works, for that *is* his heritage. For
who can bring him to see what will happen
after him?

4 Then I returned and considered all the
oppression that is done under the sun:

And look! The tears of the oppressed,
But they have no comforter—
On the side of their oppressors *there is*
power,
But they have no comforter.
2 Therefore I praised the dead who were
already dead,
More than the living who are still alive.
3 Yet, better than both *is he* who has never
existed,
Who has not seen the evil work that is
done under the sun.

The Vanity of Selfish Toil

4Again, I saw that for all toil and every
skillful work a man is envied by his neighbor. This also *is* vanity and grasping for the
wind.

5 The fool folds his hands
And consumes his own flesh.
6 Better a handful *with* quietness

3:21 [a] Septuagint, Syriac, Targum, and Vulgate read *Who knows whether the spirit . . . goes upward, and whether . . . goes downward to the earth?*

JOY

READ IT: ECCLESIASTES 3:4

You've probably faced some sad times, times that hurt you or brought tears to your eyes. But you can be sure that there will also be times for laughter so strong that it makes your stomach hurt, and wildly wonderful experiences that leave your eyes wet with happy tears. Whether you're crying or laughing, remember there is time for both. Find a friend and laugh your head off. It's good for you, and it's good for your soul.

Than both hands full, *together with* toil
and grasping for the wind.

7 Then I returned, and I saw vanity under
the sun:

8 There is one alone, without companion:
He has neither son nor brother.
Yet *there is* no end to all his labors,
Nor is his eye satisfied with riches.
But he never asks,
"For whom do I toil and deprive myself
of good?"
This also *is* vanity and a grave
misfortune.

The Value of a Friend

9 Two *are* better than one,
Because they have a good reward for
their labor.
10 For if they fall, one will lift up his
companion.
But woe to him *who is* alone when he
falls,
For *he has* no one to help him up.
11 Again, if two lie down together, they
will keep warm;
But how can one be warm *alone?*
12 Though one may be overpowered by
another, two can withstand him.
And a threefold cord is not quickly
broken.

Popularity Passes Away

13 Better a poor and wise youth
Than an old and foolish king who will
be admonished no more.
14 For he comes out of prison to be king,
Although he was born poor in his
kingdom.
15 I saw all the living who walk under the
sun;
They were with the second youth who
stands in his place.
16 *There was* no end of all the people over
whom he was made king;
Yet those who come afterward will not
rejoice in him.
Surely this also *is* vanity and grasping
for the wind.

Fear God, Keep Your Vows

5 Walk prudently when you go to the
house of God; and draw near to hear
rather than to give the sacrifice of fools, for
they do not know that they do evil.

2 Do not be rash with your mouth,
And let not your heart utter anything
hastily before God.
For God *is* in heaven, and you on earth;
Therefore let your words be few.
3 For a dream comes through much
activity,
And a fool's voice *is known* by *his* many
words.

4 When you make a vow to God, do not
delay to pay it;
For *He has* no pleasure in fools.
Pay what you have vowed—
5 Better not to vow than to vow and not pay.

FRIENDSHIP

READ IT: ECCLESIASTES 4:9–12

God designed us to live in community and relationships. At the start of creation, God created Eve to be a companion for Adam so he wouldn't be alone. It can sometimes feel easier to live life on your own because you think you can protect your heart from pain and avoid the risk of being disappointed. But you also miss out on the awesome benefits of friendship. And when it's the right kind of friendship, there is blessing for you and for your friend. Two are definitely better than one!

6 Do not let your mouth cause your flesh to
sin, nor say before the messenger *of God* that
it *was* an error. Why should God be angry at
your excuse[a] and destroy the work of your
hands? 7 For in the multitude of dreams and
many words *there is* also vanity. But fear God.

The Vanity of Gain and Honor

8 If you see the oppression of the poor,
and the violent perversion of justice and
righteousness in a province, do not marvel
at the matter; for high official watches over
high official, and higher officials are over
them.

9 Moreover the profit of the land is for all;
even the king is served from the field.

10 He who loves silver will not be satisfied
with silver;
Nor he who loves abundance, with
increase.
This also *is* vanity.

11 When goods increase,
They increase who eat them;
So what profit have the owners
Except to see *them* with their eyes?

12 The sleep of a laboring man *is* sweet,
Whether he eats little or much;
But the abundance of the rich will not
permit him to sleep.

13 There is a severe evil *which* I have seen
under the sun:
Riches kept for their owner to his hurt.
14 But those riches perish through
misfortune;
When he begets a son, *there is* nothing
in his hand.
15 As he came from his mother's womb,
naked shall he return,
To go as he came;
And he shall take nothing from his
labor
Which he may carry away in his hand.

16 And this also *is* a severe evil—
Just exactly as he came, so shall he go.
And what profit has he who has labored
for the wind?
17 All his days he also eats in darkness,
And *he has* much sorrow and sickness
and anger.

18 Here is what I have seen: *It is* good
and fitting *for one* to eat and drink, and to
enjoy the good of all his labor in which he
toils under the sun all the days of his life
which God gives him; for it *is* his heritage.
19 As for every man to whom God has given
riches and wealth, and given him power to
eat of it, to receive his heritage and rejoice
in his labor—this *is* the gift of God. 20 For he
will not dwell unduly on the days of his life,
because God keeps *him* busy with the joy of
his heart.

6 There is an evil which I have seen under the sun, and it *is* common among
men: 2 A man to whom God has given riches
and wealth and honor, so that he lacks nothing for himself of all he desires; yet God does
not give him power to eat of it, but a foreigner consumes it. This *is* vanity, and it *is* an
evil affliction.

3 If a man begets a hundred *children* and
lives many years, so that the days of his years
are many, but his soul is not satisfied with
goodness, or indeed he has no burial, I say
that a stillborn child *is* better than he— 4 for it
comes in vanity and departs in darkness, and
its name is covered with darkness. 5 Though it
has not seen the sun or known *anything,* this
has more rest than that man, 6 even if he lives
a thousand years twice—but has not seen
goodness. Do not all go to one place?

7 All the labor of man *is* for his mouth,
And yet the soul is not satisfied.
8 For what more has the wise *man* than
the fool?
What does the poor man have,
Who knows *how* to walk before the
living?
9 Better *is* the sight of the eyes than the
wandering of desire.
This also *is* vanity and grasping for the
wind.

10 Whatever one is, he has been named
already,
For it is known that he *is* man;
And he cannot contend with Him who
is mightier than he.
11 Since there are many things that
increase vanity,
How *is* man the better?

12 For who knows what *is* good for man
in life, all the days of his vain life which he
passes like a shadow? Who can tell a man
what will happen after him under the sun?

5:6 [a] Literally *voice*

The Value of Practical Wisdom

7 A good name *is* better than precious ointment,
And the day of death than the day of one's birth;
2 Better to go to the house of mourning
Than to go to the house of feasting,
For that *is* the end of all men;
And the living will take *it* to heart.
3 Sorrow *is* better than laughter,
For by a sad countenance the heart is made better.
4 The heart of the wise *is* in the house of mourning,
But the heart of fools *is* in the house of mirth.

5 *It is* better to hear the rebuke of the wise
Than for a man to hear the song of fools.
6 For like the crackling of thorns under a pot,
So *is* the laughter of the fool.
This also is vanity.
7 Surely oppression destroys a wise *man's* reason,
And a bribe debases the heart.

8 The end of a thing *is* better than its beginning;
The patient in spirit *is* better than the proud in spirit.
9 Do not hasten in your spirit to be angry,
For anger rests in the bosom of fools.
10 Do not say,
"Why were the former days better than these?"
For you do not inquire wisely concerning this.

11 Wisdom *is* good with an inheritance,
And profitable to those who see the sun.
12 For wisdom *is* a defense *as* money *is* a defense,
But the excellence of knowledge *is that* wisdom gives life to those who have it.

13 Consider the work of God;
For who can make straight what He has made crooked?
14 In the day of prosperity be joyful,
But in the day of adversity consider:
Surely God has appointed the one as well as the other,
So that man can find out nothing *that will come* after him.

15 I have seen everything in my days of vanity:

There is a just *man* who perishes in his righteousness,
And there is a wicked *man* who prolongs *life* in his wickedness.

16 Do not be overly righteous,
Nor be overly wise:
Why should you destroy yourself?
17 Do not be overly wicked,
Nor be foolish:
Why should you die before your time?
18 *It is* good that you grasp this,
And also not remove your hand from the other;
For he who fears God will escape them all.

19 Wisdom strengthens the wise
More than ten rulers of the city.

20 For *there is* not a just man on earth who does good
And does not sin.

21 Also do not take to heart everything people say,
Lest you hear your servant cursing you.
22 For many times, also, your own heart has known
That even you have cursed others.

23 All this I have proved by wisdom.
I said, "I will be wise";
But it *was* far from me.
24 As for that which is far off and exceedingly deep,
Who can find it out?
25 I applied my heart to know,
To search and seek out wisdom and the reason *of things*,
To know the wickedness of folly,
Even of foolishness *and* madness.
26 And I find more bitter than death
The woman whose heart *is* snares and nets,
Whose hands *are* fetters.
He who pleases God shall escape from her,
But the sinner shall be trapped by her.

27 "Here is what I have found," says the Preacher,
"*Adding* one thing to the other to find out the reason,
28 Which my soul still seeks but I cannot find:

One man among a thousand I have found,
But a woman among all these I have not found.
29 Truly, this only I have found:
That God made man upright,
But they have sought out many schemes."

8 Who *is* like a wise *man?*
And who knows the interpretation of a thing?
A man's wisdom makes his face shine,
And the sternness of his face is changed.

Obey Authorities for God's Sake

2I *say,* "Keep the king's commandment for the sake of your oath to God. 3Do not be hasty to go from his presence. Do not take your stand for an evil thing, for he does whatever pleases him."

4 Where the word of a king *is, there is* power;
And who may say to him, "What are you doing?"
5 He who keeps his command will experience nothing harmful;
And a wise man's heart discerns both time and judgment,
6 Because for every matter there is a time and judgment,
Though the misery of man increases greatly.
7 For he does not know what will happen;
So who can tell him when it will occur?
8 No one has power over the spirit to retain the spirit,
And no one has power in the day of death.
There is no release from that war,
And wickedness will not deliver those who are given to it.

9All this I have seen, and applied my heart to every work that is done under the sun: *There is* a time in which one man rules over another to his own hurt.

Death Comes to All

10Then I saw the wicked buried, who had come and gone from the place of holiness, and they were forgotten[a] in the city where they had so done. This also *is* vanity.

8:10 [a] Some Hebrew manuscripts, Septuagint, and Vulgate read *praised.*

OBEY YOUR COUNTRY'S LAWS

READ IT: ECCLESIASTES 8:2

God has set up human governments to make laws for guiding our conduct. To disobey your country's laws is to disobey what God commanded. "Keep the king's commandment for the sake of your oath to God."

If you have promised your life to God, you must also obey the state. Then people will respect you as a law-abiding person. If you break your country's laws, then you will not be a useful witness for Jesus either.

Sometimes kings and nations have punished people for being Christians. The apostle Paul and nearly all of the other apostles were put to death for their faith. The emperor of Rome wanted to be worshiped as a god, and Christians who refused were killed. When anyone orders you to do something that is against God's law, then you must disobey that order. God is the Author of true law, and we must put His laws before any of man's laws.

11 Because the sentence against an evil work
is not executed speedily, therefore the heart
of the sons of men is fully set in them to do
evil. 12 Though a sinner does evil a hundred
times, and his *days* are prolonged, yet I surely
know that it will be well with those who fear
God, who fear before Him. 13 But it will not be
well with the wicked; nor will he prolong *his*
days, *which are* as a shadow, because he does
not fear before God.

14 There is a vanity which occurs on earth,
that there are just *men* to whom it happens
according to the work of the wicked; again,
there are wicked *men* to whom it happens
according to the work of the righteous. I said
that this also *is* vanity.

15 So I commended enjoyment, because a
man has nothing better under the sun than
to eat, drink, and be merry; for this will remain
with him in his labor *all* the days of
his life which God gives him under the sun.

16 When I applied my heart to know wisdom
and to see the business that is done on
earth, even though one sees no sleep day or
night, 17 then I saw all the work of God, that
a man cannot find out the work that is done
under the sun. For though a man labors to
discover *it,* yet he will not find *it;* moreover,
though a wise *man* attempts to know *it,* he
will not be able to find *it.*

9 For I considered all this in my heart,
so that I could declare it all: that the
righteous and the wise and their works *are*
in the hand of God. People know neither love
nor hatred *by* anything *they see* before them.
2 All things *come* alike to all:

One event *happens* to the righteous and
the wicked;
To the good,[a] the clean, and the
unclean;
To him who sacrifices and him who
does not sacrifice.
As is the good, so *is* the sinner;

9:2 [a] Septuagint, Syriac, and Vulgate read *good and bad.*

SUCCESS

READ IT: ECCLESIASTES 9:10

- Live it!
- Sing.
- Dance.
- Eat ice cream.
- Swim in the ocean.
- Jump from the high dive.
- Roll down the windows.
- Stand in the rain.

See those two words at the top of this list? That should be what you do with life every day.

LIVE IT:

God loves you so much, and He knows that the very best life—the successful life—is a life that's fully lived, with passion and purpose. Don't "half live." Don't be a zombie. Live life God's way—fully!

He who takes an oath as *he* who fears
an oath.

3This *is* an evil in all that is done under the
sun: that one thing *happens* to all. Truly the
hearts of the sons of men are full of evil;
madness *is* in their hearts while they live,
and after that *they go* to the dead. 4But for
him who is joined to all the living there is
hope, for a living dog is better than a dead
lion.

5 For the living know that they will die;
But the dead know nothing,
And they have no more reward,
For the memory of them is forgotten.
6 Also their love, their hatred, and their
envy have now perished;
Nevermore will they have a share
In anything done under the sun.

7 Go, eat your bread with joy,
And drink your wine with a merry
heart;
For God has already accepted your
works.
8 Let your garments always be white,
And let your head lack no oil.

9Live joyfully with the wife whom you
love all the days of your vain life which He
has given you under the sun, all your days of
vanity; for that *is* your portion in life, and in
the labor which you perform under the sun.
10Whatever your hand finds to do, do *it*
with your might; for *there is* no work or device or knowledge or wisdom in the grave
where you are going.
11I returned and saw under the sun that—

The race *is* not to the swift,
Nor the battle to the strong,
Nor bread to the wise,
Nor riches to men of understanding,
Nor favor to men of skill;
But time and chance happen to them
all.
12 For man also does not know his time:
Like fish taken in a cruel net,
Like birds caught in a snare,
So the sons of men *are* snared in an evil
time,
When it falls suddenly upon them.

Wisdom Superior to Folly

13This wisdom I have also seen under the
sun, and it *seemed* great to me: 14*There was* a
little city with few men in it; and a great king
came against it, besieged it, and built great
snares[a] around it. 15Now there was found in
it a poor wise man, and he by his wisdom
delivered the city. Yet no one remembered
that same poor man.
16Then I said:

"Wisdom *is* better than strength.
Nevertheless the poor man's wisdom *is*
despised,
And his words are not heard.
17 Words of the wise, *spoken* quietly, *should
be* heard
Rather than the shout of a ruler of fools.
18 Wisdom *is* better than weapons of war;
But one sinner destroys much good."

10 Dead flies putrefy[a] the perfumer's
ointment,
And cause it to give off a foul odor;
So does a little folly to one respected for
wisdom *and* honor.
2 A wise man's heart *is* at his right hand,
But a fool's heart at his left.
3 Even when a fool walks along the way,
He lacks wisdom,
And he shows everyone *that* he *is* a fool.
4 If the spirit of the ruler rises against
you,
Do not leave your post;
For conciliation pacifies great offenses.

5 There is an evil I have seen under the
sun,
As an error proceeding from the ruler:
6 Folly is set in great dignity,
While the rich sit in a lowly place.
7 I have seen servants on horses,
While princes walk on the ground like
servants.

8 He who digs a pit will fall into it,
And whoever breaks through a wall will
be bitten by a serpent.
9 He who quarries stones may be hurt by
them,
And he who splits wood may be
endangered by it.
10 If the ax is dull,
And one does not sharpen the edge,
Then he must use more strength;
But wisdom brings success.

11 A serpent may bite when *it is* not
charmed;

9:14 [a] Septuagint, Syriac, and Vulgate read *bulwarks.*
10:1 [a] Targum and Vulgate omit *putrefy.*

The babbler is no different.
12 The words of a wise man's mouth *are* gracious,
But the lips of a fool shall swallow him up;
13 The words of his mouth begin with foolishness,
And the end of his talk *is* raving madness.
14 A fool also multiplies words.
No man knows what is to be;
Who can tell him what will be after him?
15 The labor of fools wearies them,
For they do not even know how to go to the city!

16 Woe to you, O land, when your king *is* a child,
And your princes feast in the morning!
17 Blessed *are* you, O land, when your king *is* the son of nobles,
And your princes feast at the proper time—
For strength and not for drunkenness!
18 Because of laziness the building decays,
And through idleness of hands the house leaks.
19 A feast is made for laughter,
And wine makes merry;
But money answers everything.

20 Do not curse the king, even in your thought;
Do not curse the rich, even in your bedroom;
For a bird of the air may carry your voice,
And a bird in flight may tell the matter.

The Value of Diligence

11 Cast your bread upon the waters,
For you will find it after many days.
2 Give a serving to seven, and also to eight,
For you do not know what evil will be on the earth.

3 If the clouds are full of rain,
They empty *themselves* upon the earth;
And if a tree falls to the south or the north,
In the place where the tree falls, there it shall lie.
4 He who observes the wind will not sow,
And he who regards the clouds will not reap.

5 As you do not know what *is* the way of the wind,[a]
Or how the bones *grow* in the womb of her who is with child,
So you do not know the works of God who makes everything.
6 In the morning sow your seed,
And in the evening do not withhold your hand;
For you do not know which will prosper,
Either this or that,
Or whether both alike *will be* good.

11:5 [a] Or *spirit*

SHARPEN YOUR AX

READ IT: ECCLESIASTES 10:10

- Never bowl overhand.
- Don't run with your eyes closed.
- It's better not to swallow your food before chewing it.
- A dull ax isn't up to doing the job an ax is made for.

A wise life is a successful life. Without wisdom, you're just living ineffectively. Ask Him to come into your life today.

7 Truly the light is sweet,
And *it is* pleasant for the eyes to behold the sun;
8 But if a man lives many years
And rejoices in them all,
Yet let him remember the days of darkness,
For they will be many.
All that is coming *is* vanity.

Seek God in Early Life

9 Rejoice, O young man, in your youth,
And let your heart cheer you in the days of your youth;
Walk in the ways of your heart,
And in the sight of your eyes;
But know that for all these
God will bring you into judgment.
10 Therefore remove sorrow from your heart,
And put away evil from your flesh,
For childhood and youth *are* vanity.

12 Remember now your Creator in the days of your youth,
Before the difficult days come,
And the years draw near when you say,
"I have no pleasure in them":
2 While the sun and the light,
The moon and the stars,
Are not darkened,
And the clouds do not return after the rain;
3 In the day when the keepers of the house tremble,
And the strong men bow down;
When the grinders cease because they are few,
And those that look through the windows grow dim;
4 When the doors are shut in the streets,
And the sound of grinding is low;
When one rises up at the sound of a bird,
And all the daughters of music are brought low.
5 Also they are afraid of height,
And of terrors in the way;
When the almond tree blossoms,
The grasshopper is a burden,
And desire fails.
For man goes to his eternal home,
And the mourners go about the streets.

6 *Remember your Creator* before the silver cord is loosed,[a]

12:6 [a] Following Qere and Targum; Kethib reads *removed;* Septuagint and Vulgate read *broken.*

SHARE WITH OTHERS

READ IT: ECCLESIASTES 11:1

Solomon had ships that sailed to distant ports and brought back wealth—"Cast your bread [meaning, shiploads of grain] upon the waters, for you will find it after many days."

Solomon also saw a lesson for living in his shipping business: By sharing your good things with others, you will receive good things in return. If you bless others with your abilities, then others will bless you also. If you're musical and share your music with others, then you will enjoy your music even more.

Sharing is one of the greatest joys of living. The bonus of sharing with others is that others will then share their gifts with you. Most of all, God will be pleased with your life. The greatest gift you can share with others is the gift of eternal life as you tell them about your living Savior, Jesus.

Or the golden bowl is broken,
Or the pitcher shattered at the fountain,
Or the wheel broken at the well.
7 Then the dust will return to the earth as it was,
And the spirit will return to God who gave it.

8 "Vanity of vanities," says the Preacher,
"All *is* vanity."

The Whole Duty of Man

9And moreover, because the Preacher
was wise, he still taught the people knowledge; yes, he pondered and sought out *and*
set in order many proverbs. 10The Preacher
sought to find acceptable words; and *what*
was written *was* upright—words of truth.
11The words of the wise are like goads, and
the words of scholars[a] are like well-driven
nails, given by one Shepherd. 12And further,
my son, be admonished by these. Of making
many books *there is* no end, and much study
is wearisome to the flesh.

13Let us hear the conclusion of the whole matter:

Fear God and keep His commandments,
For this is man's all.
14 For God will bring every work into judgment,
Including every secret thing,
Whether good or evil.

12:11 [a] Literally *masters of the assemblies*

SEEK GOD WHEN YOU ARE YOUNG

READ IT: ECCLESIASTES 12:1

"Older" may not mean "wiser." The older you get, the harder it is to change your mind and learn new things. Sad to say, some people can't come to Christ because they have been without God for so long they don't know how to search for Him. They can't think anything new anymore.

But your mind is still young. Learning about God and God's ways is the most valuable thing you can do at this time of life. Seek Him now while you're still able.

Start by reading Genesis and learn in chapter 3 how we got lost from God. Then read in the Gospel of John how Jesus, the living Word of God, became a Man. See how He revealed His glory in the great works of healing and raising the dead. Then learn how He died to pay for your sins and how He rose again. Now He is alive forever, and He waits to live in you. Ask Him to come into your life today.

The SONG of SOLOMON

965 B.C.

Behind the Scenes

READ IT:

The book of Song of Solomon is a collection of love poems between a lover and his beloved. It is a beautiful picture of ideal human love and marriage.

GET IT:

Who wrote it: King Solomon

When it was written: 965 B.C.

Why it was written: to show that love and sex are beautiful gifts from God that are at their best saved for marriage.

LIVE IT:

Physical love and sex are gifts from God. They are best saved for marriage.

FIND IT:

Love Is Beautiful *Song of Solomon 2*

1 The song of songs, which *is* Solomon's.

The Banquet

The Shulamite[a]

2 Let him kiss me with the kisses of his mouth—
For your[b] love *is* better than wine.
3 Because of the fragrance of your good ointments,
Your name *is* ointment poured forth;
Therefore the virgins love you.
4 Draw me away!

The Daughters of Jerusalem

We will run after you.[a]

The Shulamite

The king has brought me into his chambers.

The Daughters of Jerusalem

We will be glad and rejoice in you.[b]

We will remember your[c] love more than wine.

The Shulamite

Rightly do they love you.[d]

5 I *am* dark, but lovely,
O daughters of Jerusalem,
Like the tents of Kedar,
Like the curtains of Solomon.
6 Do not look upon me, because I *am* dark,
Because the sun has tanned me.
My mother's sons were angry with me;
They made me the keeper of the vineyards,
But my own vineyard I have not kept.

(To Her Beloved)

7 Tell me, O you whom I love,
Where you feed *your flock,*
Where you make *it* rest at noon.
For why should I be as one who veils herself[a]
By the flocks of your companions?

The Beloved

8 If you do not know, O fairest among women,
Follow in the footsteps of the flock,
And feed your little goats
Beside the shepherds' tents.
9 I have compared you, my love,
To my filly among Pharaoh's chariots.
10 Your cheeks are lovely with ornaments,
Your neck with chains *of gold.*

1:2 [a] A young woman from the town of Shulam or Shunem (compare 6:13). The speaker and audience are identified according to the number, gender, and person of the Hebrew words. Occasionally the identity is not certain. [b] Masculine singular, that is, the Beloved 1:4 [a] Masculine singular, that is, the Beloved [b] Feminine singular, that is, the Shulamite [c] Masculine singular, that is, the Beloved [d] Masculine singular, that is, the Beloved
1:7 [a] Septuagint, Syriac, and Vulgate read *wanders.*

Starring Roles

Solomon was the husband of THE GIRL FROM SHULAM, and he loved her very much. Because he loved her, she also loved him.

A boy should begin early to love and respect his mother. Then he will know how to love and honor that special girl God gives him when he marries. Look for kind things you can do for your mother—like helping with the chores around home.

Then, as you get older, you will begin to notice girls more. You will be building a happy life if you treat all girls with respect—just as you expect your father to treat your mother.

"Respect" means to appreciate the real value of a person. Love happens when you seek the best for that person.

The Daughters of Jerusalem

11 We will make you[a] ornaments of gold
With studs of silver.

The Shulamite

12 While the king *is* at his table,
My spikenard sends forth its fragrance.
13 A bundle of myrrh *is* my beloved to me,
That lies all night between my breasts.
14 My beloved *is* to me a cluster of henna
blooms
In the vineyards of En Gedi.

The Beloved

15 Behold, you *are* fair, my love!
Behold, you *are* fair!
You *have* dove's eyes.

The Shulamite

16 Behold, you *are* handsome, my beloved!
Yes, pleasant!
Also our bed *is* green.
17 The beams of our houses *are* cedar,
And our rafters of fir.

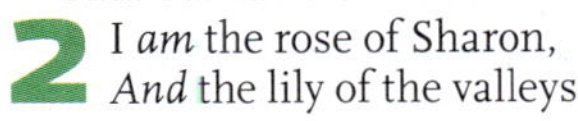

2 I *am* the rose of Sharon,
And the lily of the valleys.

The Beloved

2 Like a lily among thorns,
So is my love among the daughters.

The Shulamite

3 Like an apple tree among the trees of
the woods,
So *is* my beloved among the sons.
I sat down in his shade with great
delight,
And his fruit *was* sweet to my taste.

The Shulamite to the Daughters of Jerusalem

4 He brought me to the banqueting
house,
And his banner over me *was* love.
5 Sustain me with cakes of raisins,
Refresh me with apples,
For I *am* lovesick.

6 His left hand *is* under my head,
And his right hand embraces me.
7 I charge you, O daughters of Jerusalem,
By the gazelles or by the does of the
field,
Do not stir up nor awaken love
Until it pleases.

The Beloved's Request

The Shulamite

8 The voice of my beloved!
Behold, he comes
Leaping upon the mountains,
Skipping upon the hills.
9 My beloved is like a gazelle or a young
stag.
Behold, he stands behind our wall;
He is looking through the windows,
Gazing through the lattice.

10 My beloved spoke, and said to me:
"Rise up, my love, my fair one,
And come away.
11 For lo, the winter is past,
The rain is over *and* gone.
12 The flowers appear on the earth;
The time of singing has come,
And the voice of the turtledove
Is heard in our land.
13 The fig tree puts forth her green figs,
And the vines *with* the tender grapes
Give a *good* smell.
Rise up, my love, my fair one,
And come away!

14 "O my dove, in the clefts of the rock,
In the secret *places* of the cliff,
Let me see your face,
Let me hear your voice;
For your voice *is* sweet,
And your face *is* lovely."

Her Brothers

15 Catch us the foxes,
The little foxes that spoil the vines,
For our vines *have* tender grapes.

The Shulamite

16 My beloved *is* mine, and I *am* his.
He feeds *his flock* among the lilies.

(To Her Beloved)

17 Until the day breaks
And the shadows flee away,
Turn, my beloved,
And be like a gazelle
Or a young stag
Upon the mountains of Bether.[a]

A Troubled Night

The Shulamite

3 By night on my bed I sought the one
I love;

1:11 [a] Feminine singular, that is, the Shulamite
2:17 [a] Literally *Separation*

The Daughters of Jerusalem

6 Where has your beloved gone,
O fairest among women?
Where has your beloved turned aside,
That we may seek him with you?

The Shulamite

2 My beloved has gone to his garden,
To the beds of spices,
To feed *his flock* in the gardens,
And to gather lilies.
3 I *am* my beloved's,
And my beloved *is* mine.
He feeds *his flock* among the lilies.

Praise of the Shulamite's Beauty

The Beloved

4 O my love, you *are as* beautiful as
Tirzah,
Lovely as Jerusalem,
Awesome as *an army* with banners!
5 Turn your eyes away from me,
For they have overcome me.
Your hair *is* like a flock of goats
Going down from Gilead.
6 Your teeth *are* like a flock of sheep
Which have come up from the washing;
Every one bears twins,
And none *is* barren among them.
7 Like a piece of pomegranate
Are your temples behind your veil.

8 There are sixty queens
And eighty concubines,
And virgins without number.
9 My dove, my perfect one,
Is the only one,
The only one of her mother,
The favorite of the one who bore her.
The daughters saw her
And called her blessed,
The queens and the concubines,
And they praised her.

10 Who is she who looks forth as the
morning,
Fair as the moon,
Clear as the sun,
Awesome as *an army* with banners?

The Shulamite

11 I went down to the garden of nuts
To see the verdure of the valley,
To see whether the vine had budded
And the pomegranates had bloomed.
12 Before I was even aware,
My soul had made me
As the chariots of my noble people.[a]

The Beloved and His Friends

13 Return, return, O Shulamite;
Return, return, that we may look upon
you!

The Shulamite

What would you see in the Shulamite—
As it were, the dance of the two camps?[a]

Expressions of Praise

The Beloved

7 How beautiful are your feet in sandals,
O prince's daughter!
The curves of your thighs *are* like
jewels,
The work of the hands of a skillful
workman.
2 Your navel *is* a rounded goblet;
It lacks no blended beverage.
Your waist *is* a heap of wheat
Set about with lilies.
3 Your two breasts *are* like two fawns,
Twins of a gazelle.
4 Your neck *is* like an ivory tower,
Your eyes *like* the pools in Heshbon
By the gate of Bath Rabbim.
Your nose *is* like the tower of Lebanon
Which looks toward Damascus.
5 Your head *crowns* you like *Mount*
Carmel,
And the hair of your head *is* like purple;
A king *is* held captive by *your* tresses.

6 How fair and how pleasant you are,
O love, with your delights!
7 This stature of yours is like a palm tree,
And your breasts *like* its clusters.
8 I said, "I will go up to the palm tree,
I will take hold of its branches."
Let now your breasts be like clusters of
the vine,
The fragrance of your breath like apples,
9 And the roof of your mouth like the best
wine.

The Shulamite

The wine goes *down* smoothly for my
beloved,
Moving gently the lips of sleepers.[a]
10 I *am* my beloved's,

6:12 [a] Hebrew *Ammi Nadib* 6:13 [a] Hebrew *Mahanaim*
7:9 [a] Septuagint, Syriac, and Vulgate read *lips and teeth*.

And his desire *is* toward me.

11 Come, my beloved,
Let us go forth to the field;
Let us lodge in the villages.
12 Let us get up early to the vineyards;
Let us see if the vine has budded,
Whether the grape blossoms are open,
And the pomegranates are in bloom.
There I will give you my love.
13 The mandrakes give off a fragrance,
And at our gates *are* pleasant *fruits,*
All manner, new and old,
Which I have laid up for you, my
beloved.

8 Oh, that you were like my brother,
Who nursed at my mother's breasts!
If I should find you outside,
I would kiss you;
I would not be despised.
2 I would lead you *and* bring you
Into the house of my mother,
She *who* used to instruct me.
I would cause you to drink of spiced
wine,
Of the juice of my pomegranate.

(To the Daughters of Jerusalem)

3 His left hand *is* under my head,
And his right hand embraces me.
4 I charge you, O daughters of Jerusalem,
Do not stir up nor awaken love
Until it pleases.

Love Renewed in Lebanon

A Relative

5 Who *is* this coming up from the
wilderness,
Leaning upon her beloved?

I awakened you under the apple tree.
There your mother brought you forth;
There she *who* bore you brought *you*
forth.

The Shulamite to Her Beloved

6 Set me as a seal upon your heart,
As a seal upon your arm;
For love *is as* strong as death,
Jealousy *as* cruel as the grave;[a]
Its flames *are* flames of fire,
A most vehement flame.[b]

7 Many waters cannot quench love,
Nor can the floods drown it.
If a man would give for love
All the wealth of his house,
It would be utterly despised.

The Shulamite's Brothers

8 We have a little sister,
And she has no breasts.
What shall we do for our sister
In the day when she is spoken for?
9 If she *is* a wall,

8:6 [a] Or *Sheol* [b] Literally *A flame of* YAH (a poetic form of *YHWH, the* LORD)

Epic Ideas

8:14 WHY SOLOMON WROTE HIS SONG

The Song of Solomon, also called the Song of Songs, is a long love poem. The poem is written to show that God blesses true love between a man and a woman. Solomon writes about his love for a beautiful girl. But the young woman's heart remains faithful to her peasant lover who is a young farmer. "Love is as strong as death" (Song of Solomon 8:6).

But there is another great teaching in the Song of Solomon. The Song speaks of the love of Jesus for His people. Jesus proved that love is as strong as death by dying for those He loved. Then He rose again so that His beloved people would be His bride forever. Jesus will love you forever also, if you surrender your life to Him.

We will build upon her
A battlement of silver;
And if she *is* a door,
We will enclose her
With boards of cedar.

The Shulamite

10 I *am* a wall,
And my breasts like towers;
Then I became in his eyes
As one who found peace.
11 Solomon had a vineyard at Baal Hamon;
He leased the vineyard to keepers;
Everyone was to bring for its fruit
A thousand silver *coins*.

(To Solomon)

12 My own vineyard *is* before me.
You, O Solomon, *may have* a thousand,
And those who tend its fruit two
hundred.

The Beloved

13 You who dwell in the gardens,
The companions listen for your voice—
Let me hear it!

The Shulamite

14 Make haste, my beloved,
And be like a gazelle
Or a young stag
On the mountains of spices.

The BOOK of

ISAIAH

740 B.C.–680 B.C.

READ IT:

The book of Isaiah records all that the prophet Isaiah said to God's people. Isaiah warned them that Jerusalem and Judah would be judged because of the people's wickedness. In chapter 39 he predicted that the people would be carried off to Babylon. But he also shared the hope that the kingdom would exist again.

GET IT:

Who wrote it: The prophet Isaiah

When it was written: 740 B.C.–680 B.C.

Why it was written: to warn the people that God would punish them if they didn't change their ways, but that after the punishment, God would heal and save them.

LIVE IT:

You can't live a double life. You can't say you believe in God and then act like you don't.

God keeps His promises, and all the promises made in this book have come true.

FIND IT:

The Wickedness of Judah	*Isaiah 1*
Isaiah Called to Be a Prophet	*Isaiah 6*
The Government of the Promised Son	*Isaiah 9*
The Reign of Jesse's Offspring	*Isaiah 11*
God's People Are Comforted	*Isaiah 40*
There Is No Other God	*Isaiah 44*
The Sin-Bearing Servant	*Isaiah 52–53*
The Glorious New Creation	*Isaiah 65*

1 The vision of Isaiah the son of Amoz, which he saw concerning Judah and Jerusalem in the days of Uzziah, Jotham, Ahaz, *and* Hezekiah, kings of Judah.

The Wickedness of Judah

2 Hear, O heavens, and give ear, O earth!
For the LORD has spoken:
"I have nourished and brought up children,
And they have rebelled against Me;
3 The ox knows its owner
And the donkey its master's crib;
But Israel does not know,
My people do not consider."

4 Alas, sinful nation,
A people laden with iniquity,
A brood of evildoers,
Children who are corrupters!
They have forsaken the LORD,
They have provoked to anger
The Holy One of Israel,
They have turned away backward.

5 Why should you be stricken again?
You will revolt more and more.
The whole head is sick,
And the whole heart faints.
6 From the sole of the foot even to the head,
There is no soundness in it,
But wounds and bruises and putrefying sores;
They have not been closed or bound up,
Or soothed with ointment.

7 Your country *is* desolate,
Your cities *are* burned with fire;
Strangers devour your land in your presence;
And *it is* desolate, as overthrown by strangers.
8 So the daughter of Zion is left as a booth in a vineyard,
As a hut in a garden of cucumbers,
As a besieged city.
9 Unless the LORD of hosts
Had left to us a very small remnant,
We would have become like Sodom,
We would have been made like Gomorrah.

10 Hear the word of the LORD,
You rulers of Sodom;
Give ear to the law of our God,
You people of Gomorrah:
11 "To what purpose *is* the multitude of your sacrifices to Me?"
Says the LORD.
"I have had enough of burnt offerings of rams
And the fat of fed cattle.
I do not delight in the blood of bulls,
Or of lambs or goats.

12 "When you come to appear before Me,
Who has required this from your hand,
To trample My courts?
13 Bring no more futile sacrifices;
Incense is an abomination to Me.
The New Moons, the Sabbaths, and the calling of assemblies—
I cannot endure iniquity and the sacred meeting.
14 Your New Moons and your appointed feasts
My soul hates;

DATES ARE APPROXIMATE

BIBLE EVENTS

- God selects Isaiah to become a prophet 740 B.C.
- Assyria destroys northern Jewish nation of Israel 722 B.C.
- Hezekiah revolts against Assyria 705 B.C.
- Assyria seizes Judah but can't capture Jerusalem 701 B.C.
- Babylon destroys Jerusalem 586 B.C.
- Jewish exiles return to Jerusalem 538 B.C.

800 B.C. 750 B.C. 700 B.C. 650 B.C. 600 B.C. 550 B.C. 500 B.C.

WORLD EVENTS

- First *recorded* Olympic games in Greece 776 B.C.
- Chinese history confirms solar eclipse 775 B.C.
- King Romulus founds Rome 753 B.C.
- Assyrians choose Nineveh as capital and start rebuilding it 705 B.C.
- Cyrus Cylinder confirms return of exiled Jews 539 B.C.

They are a trouble to Me,
I am weary of bearing *them*.
15 When you spread out your hands,
I will hide My eyes from you;
Even though you make many prayers,
I will not hear.
Your hands are full of blood.

16 "Wash yourselves, make yourselves clean;
Put away the evil of your doings from before My eyes.
Cease to do evil,
17 Learn to do good;
Seek justice,
Rebuke the oppressor;[a]
Defend the fatherless,
Plead for the widow.

18 "Come now, and let us reason together,"
Says the LORD,
"Though your sins are like scarlet,
They shall be as white as snow;
Though they are red like crimson,
They shall be as wool.
19 If you are willing and obedient,
You shall eat the good of the land;
20 But if you refuse and rebel,
You shall be devoured by the sword";
For the mouth of the LORD has spoken.

The Degenerate City

21 How the faithful city has become a harlot!
It was full of justice;
Righteousness lodged in it,
But now murderers.
22 Your silver has become dross,
Your wine mixed with water.
23 Your princes *are* rebellious,
And companions of thieves;
Everyone loves bribes,
And follows after rewards.
They do not defend the fatherless,
Nor does the cause of the widow come before them.

24 Therefore the Lord says,
The LORD of hosts, the Mighty One of Israel,
"Ah, I will rid Myself of My adversaries,
And take vengeance on My enemies.
25 I will turn My hand against you,
And thoroughly purge away your dross,
And take away all your alloy.
26 I will restore your judges as at the first,
And your counselors as at the beginning.
Afterward you shall be called the city of righteousness, the faithful city."

27 Zion shall be redeemed with justice,
And her penitents with righteousness.
28 The destruction of transgressors and of sinners *shall be* together,

1:17 [a] Some ancient versions read *the oppressed*.

Starring Roles

ISAIAH was the first of the four major prophets. They were called the major prophets because their books are longer than those of the 12 minor prophets. Isaiah's name is pronounced *eye-ZAY-uh* and means "The Lord Has Saved." He was a relative of the kings of Judah.

Sometimes people call Isaiah the gospel-preaching prophet because he spoke more about the coming of Jesus and salvation than any of the other prophets did. He lived over seven hundred years before Jesus came and died for our sins.

Isaiah's book of 66 chapters is divided into two parts. In the first section, chapters 1–39, Isaiah warns his people about the coming judgment of God. In chapters 40–66, God inspired him to comfort His people with His promises of salvation. The best-loved part of Isaiah's book is chapter 53, where he tells how Jesus would be crucified for our sins.

And those who forsake the LORD shall
be consumed.
29 For they[a] shall be ashamed of the
terebinth trees
Which you have desired;
And you shall be embarrassed because
of the gardens
Which you have chosen.
30 For you shall be as a terebinth whose
leaf fades,
And as a garden that has no water.
31 The strong shall be as tinder,
And the work of it as a spark;
Both will burn together,
And no one shall quench *them*.

The Future House of God

2 The word that Isaiah the son of Amoz saw concerning Judah and Jerusalem.

2 Now it shall come to pass in the latter
days
That the mountain of the LORD's house
Shall be established on the top of the
mountains,
And shall be exalted above the hills;
And all nations shall flow to it.
3 Many people shall come and say,
"Come, and let us go up to the mountain
of the LORD,
To the house of the God of Jacob;
He will teach us His ways,
And we shall walk in His paths."
For out of Zion shall go forth the law,
And the word of the LORD from
Jerusalem.
4 He shall judge between the nations,
And rebuke many people;
They shall beat their swords into
plowshares,
And their spears into pruning hooks;
Nation shall not lift up sword against
nation,
Neither shall they learn war anymore.

The Day of the LORD

5 O house of Jacob, come and let us walk
In the light of the LORD.

6 For You have forsaken Your people, the
house of Jacob,
Because they are filled with eastern
ways;
They *are* soothsayers like the
Philistines,
And they are pleased with the children
of foreigners.
7 Their land is also full of silver and gold,
And there is no end to their treasures;
Their land is also full of horses,
And there is no end to their chariots.
8 Their land is also full of idols;
They worship the work of their own
hands,
That which their own fingers have
made.
9 People bow down,
And each man humbles himself;
Therefore do not forgive them.

10 Enter into the rock, and hide in the dust,
From the terror of the LORD
And the glory of His majesty.
11 The lofty looks of man shall be
humbled,
The haughtiness of men shall be bowed
down,
And the LORD alone shall be exalted in
that day.

12 For the day of the LORD of hosts
Shall come upon everything proud and
lofty,
Upon everything lifted up—
And it shall be brought low—
13 Upon all the cedars of Lebanon *that are*
high and lifted up,
And upon all the oaks of Bashan;
14 Upon all the high mountains,
And upon all the hills *that are* lifted up;
15 Upon every high tower,
And upon every fortified wall;
16 Upon all the ships of Tarshish,
And upon all the beautiful sloops.
17 The loftiness of man shall be bowed
down,
And the haughtiness of men shall be
brought low;
The LORD alone will be exalted in that
day,
18 But the idols He shall utterly abolish.

19 They shall go into the holes of the rocks,
And into the caves of the earth,
From the terror of the LORD
And the glory of His majesty,
When He arises to shake the earth
mightily.

20 In that day a man will cast away his
idols of silver
And his idols of gold,

1:29 [a] Following Masoretic Text, Septuagint, and Vulgate; some Hebrew manuscripts and Targum read *you*.

Which they made, *each* for himself to
worship,
To the moles and bats,
21 To go into the clefts of the rocks,
And into the crags of the rugged rocks,
From the terror of the LORD
And the glory of His majesty,
When He arises to shake the earth
mightily.

22 Sever yourselves from such a man,
Whose breath *is* in his nostrils;
For of what account is he?

Judgment on Judah and Jerusalem

3 For behold, the Lord, the LORD of
hosts,
Takes away from Jerusalem and from
Judah
The stock and the store,
The whole supply of bread and the
whole supply of water;
2 The mighty man and the man of war,
The judge and the prophet,
And the diviner and the elder;
3 The captain of fifty and the honorable
man,
The counselor and the skillful artisan,
And the expert enchanter.

4 "I will give children *to be* their princes,
And babes shall rule over them.
5 The people will be oppressed,
Every one by another and every one by
his neighbor;
The child will be insolent toward the
elder,
And the base toward the honorable."

6 When a man takes hold of his brother
In the house of his father, *saying*,
"You have clothing;
You be our ruler,
And *let* these ruins *be* under your
power,"[a]
7 In that day he will protest, saying,
"I cannot cure *your* ills,
For in my house *is* neither food nor
clothing;
Do not make me a ruler of the people."

8 For Jerusalem stumbled,
And Judah is fallen,
Because their tongue and their doings
Are against the LORD,
To provoke the eyes of His glory.
9 The look on their countenance
witnesses against them,
And they declare their sin as Sodom;
They do not hide *it*.
Woe to their soul!
For they have brought evil upon
themselves.

10 "Say to the righteous that *it shall be* well
with them,
For they shall eat the fruit of their
doings.
11 Woe to the wicked! *It shall be* ill *with
him*,
For the reward of his hands shall be
given him.
12 *As for* My people, children *are* their
oppressors,
And women rule over them.
O My people! Those who lead you cause
you to err,
And destroy the way of your paths."

Oppression and Luxury Condemned

13 The LORD stands up to plead,
And stands to judge the people.
14 The LORD will enter into judgment
With the elders of His people
And His princes:
"For you have eaten up the vineyard;
The plunder of the poor *is* in your
houses.
15 What do you mean by crushing My
people
And grinding the faces of the poor?"
Says the Lord GOD of hosts.

16 Moreover the LORD says:

"Because the daughters of Zion are
haughty,
And walk with outstretched necks
And wanton eyes,
Walking and mincing *as* they go,
Making a jingling with their feet,
17 Therefore the Lord will strike with a
scab
The crown of the head of the daughters
of Zion,
And the LORD will uncover their secret
parts."

18 In that day the Lord will take away the
finery:
The jingling anklets, the scarves, and
the crescents;

3:6 [a] Literally *hand*

19 The pendants, the bracelets, and the
veils;
20 The headdresses, the leg ornaments,
and the headbands;
The perfume boxes, the charms,
21 and the rings;
The nose jewels,
22 the festal apparel, and the mantles;
The outer garments, the purses,
23 and the mirrors;
The fine linen, the turbans, and the
robes.

24And so it shall be:

Instead of a sweet smell there will be a
stench;
Instead of a sash, a rope;
Instead of well-set hair, baldness;
Instead of a rich robe, a girding of
sackcloth;
And branding instead of beauty.
25 Your men shall fall by the sword,
And your mighty in the war.

26 Her gates shall lament and mourn,
And she *being* desolate shall sit on the
ground.

4 And in that day seven women shall
take hold of one man, saying,
"We will eat our own food and wear our
own apparel;
Only let us be called by your name,
To take away our reproach."

The Renewal of Zion

2 In that day the Branch of the LORD shall
be beautiful and glorious;
And the fruit of the earth *shall be*
excellent and appealing
For those of Israel who have escaped.

3And it shall come to pass that *he who is*
left in Zion and remains in Jerusalem will
be called holy—everyone who is recorded among the living in Jerusalem. 4When
the Lord has washed away the filth of the
daughters of Zion, and purged the blood of
Jerusalem from her midst, by the spirit of
judgment and by the spirit of burning, 5then
the LORD will create above every dwelling
place of Mount Zion, and above her assemblies, a cloud and smoke by day and the shining of a flaming fire by night. For over all
the glory there *will be* a covering. 6And there
will be a tabernacle for shade in the daytime
from the heat, for a place of refuge, and for a
shelter from storm and rain.

In Focus

4:2 Branch of the LORD Used several times in the Old Testament as a title of the coming Messiah, or Christ. Christ was a Branch coming from the family of King David who lived a thousand years earlier.

God's Disappointing Vineyard

5 Now let me sing to my Well-beloved
A song of my Beloved regarding His
vineyard:

My Well-beloved has a vineyard
On a very fruitful hill.
2 He dug it up and cleared out its stones,
And planted it with the choicest vine.
He built a tower in its midst,
And also made a winepress in it;
So He expected *it* to bring forth *good*
grapes,
But it brought forth wild grapes.

3 "And now, O inhabitants of Jerusalem
and men of Judah,
Judge, please, between Me and My
vineyard.
4 What more could have been done to My
vineyard
That I have not done in it?
Why then, when I expected *it* to bring
forth *good* grapes,
Did it bring forth wild grapes?
5 And now, please let Me tell you what I
will do to My vineyard:
I will take away its hedge, and it shall be
burned;
And break down its wall, and it shall be
trampled down.
6 I will lay it waste;
It shall not be pruned or dug,
But there shall come up briers and
thorns.
I will also command the clouds
That they rain no rain on it."

7 For the vineyard of the LORD of hosts *is*
the house of Israel,

And the men of Judah are His pleasant
plant.
He looked for justice, but behold,
oppression;
For righteousness, but behold, a cry *for*
help.

Impending Judgment on Excesses

8 Woe to those who join house to house;
They add field to field,
Till *there is* no place
Where they may dwell alone in the
midst of the land!
9 In my hearing the LORD of hosts *said,*
"Truly, many houses shall be desolate,
Great and beautiful ones, without
inhabitant.
10 For ten acres of vineyard shall yield one
bath,
And a homer of seed shall yield one
ephah."

11 Woe to those who rise early in the
morning,
That they may follow intoxicating drink;
Who continue until night, *till* wine
inflames them!
12 The harp and the strings,
The tambourine and flute,
And wine are in their feasts;
But they do not regard the work of the
LORD,
Nor consider the operation of His
hands.

13 Therefore my people have gone into
captivity,
Because *they have* no knowledge;
Their honorable men *are* famished,
And their multitude dried up with
thirst.
14 Therefore Sheol has enlarged itself
And opened its mouth beyond measure;
Their glory and their multitude and
their pomp,
And he who is jubilant, shall descend
into it.
15 People shall be brought down,
Each man shall be humbled,
And the eyes of the lofty shall be
humbled.
16 But the LORD of hosts shall be exalted in
judgment,
And God who is holy shall be hallowed
in righteousness.

17 Then the lambs shall feed in their
pasture,
And in the waste places of the fat ones
strangers shall eat.

18 Woe to those who draw iniquity with
cords of vanity,
And sin as if with a cart rope;
19 That say, "Let Him make speed *and*
hasten His work,
That we may see *it;*
And let the counsel of the Holy One of
Israel draw near and come,
That we may know *it.*"

20 Woe to those who call evil good, and
good evil;
Who put darkness for light, and light for
darkness;
Who put bitter for sweet, and sweet for
bitter!

21 Woe to *those who are* wise in their own
eyes,
And prudent in their own sight!

22 Woe to men mighty at drinking wine,
Woe to men valiant for mixing
intoxicating drink,
23 Who justify the wicked for a bribe,
And take away justice from the
righteous man!

24 Therefore, as the fire devours the
stubble,
And the flame consumes the chaff,
So their root will be as rottenness,
And their blossom will ascend like dust;
Because they have rejected the law of
the LORD of hosts,
And despised the word of the Holy One
of Israel.
25 Therefore the anger of the LORD is
aroused against His people;
He has stretched out His hand against
them
And stricken them,
And the hills trembled.
Their carcasses *were* as refuse in the
midst of the streets.

For all this His anger is not turned
away,
But His hand *is* stretched out still.

26 He will lift up a banner to the nations
from afar,
And will whistle to them from the end
of the earth;

Surely they shall come with speed,
swiftly.
27 No one will be weary or stumble among
them,
No one will slumber or sleep;
Nor will the belt on their loins be
loosed,
Nor the strap of their sandals be broken;
28 Whose arrows *are* sharp,
And all their bows bent;
Their horses' hooves will seem like
flint,
And their wheels like a whirlwind.
29 Their roaring *will be* like a lion,
They will roar like young lions;
Yes, they will roar
And lay hold of the prey;
They will carry *it* away safely,
And no one will deliver.
30 In that day they will roar against them
Like the roaring of the sea.
And if *one* looks to the land,
Behold, darkness *and* sorrow;
And the light is darkened by the clouds.

GOD CALLS THE PROPHET ISAIAH

READ IT: ISAIAH 6:1–13

GET IT:

The Northern Kingdom, Israel, was gone, but the Southern Kingdom, Judah, was still around. Those people were sinful, too. So God sent the prophet Isaiah to warn the people that they would end up like Israel (a destroyed nation) if they didn't change. (Here we go again.)

God spoke to Isaiah through a vision. Isaiah volunteered when God asked, "Whom shall I send[?]" (v. 8). This was a huge assignment and a big challenge. Isaiah had to talk to people who didn't want to listen and didn't want to see what was happening. Right away God told Isaiah what was going to happen. It sounded a bit like a riddle, but God said that the cities would be destroyed, with the people gone, the houses empty, and the land left to grow weeds. And then He gave some hope—what remained (a stump) would still be alive to grow again.

LIVE IT:

Have you ever gotten bad news—really, really bad news, like someone died, your mother or dad lost their job, or you had to move? Our first reaction to bad news is panic and hopelessness: "Now what?" It feels like the world has come to an end and nothing will ever be the same.

Isaiah delivered some really bad news: a warning that the Babylonians would destroy Jerusalem and the land of Judah. But God wanted to give the people hope. So He promised that good times would return. It took time, but it did happen.

When you hear bad news, remember that with God there is hope. Things will change, but the future will be brighter and better than ever.

Isaiah Called to Be a Prophet

6 In the year that King Uzziah died, I
saw the Lord sitting on a throne, high
and lifted up, and the train of His *robe* filled
the temple. 2Above it stood seraphim; each
one had six wings: with two he covered his
face, with two he covered his feet, and with
two he flew. 3And one cried to another and
said:

"Holy, holy, holy *is* the LORD of hosts;
The whole earth *is* full of His glory!"

4And the posts of the door were shaken
by the voice of him who cried out, and the
house was filled with smoke.
5So I said:

"Woe *is* me, for I am undone!
Because I *am* a man of unclean lips,
And I dwell in the midst of a people of
unclean lips;
For my eyes have seen the King,
The LORD of hosts."

6Then one of the seraphim flew to me,

MAKING YOUR FAITH YOUR OWN

I'M HERE, GOD!

READ IT: ISAIAH 6:1–13

GET IT:

In Isaiah's day, God's people were struggling in all kinds of ways. Their country was divided. They were at war with a nearby nation. Many people had abandoned their belief in God. Some had even started worshiping false gods. In the middle of all that, it would have been easy for Isaiah to walk away from his faith and to give up on God. He could have said, "Forget it. I'll live life on my own."

But he didn't. He kept believing and following and trusting God—even though he was surrounded by troubles, even though he was no longer a child whose parents made him believe, even though there were plenty of "logical" reasons to take control of his own life.

Isaiah didn't have faith in God because of this amazing vision or because of God's voice. He was already trusting and following God. He had already made his faith his own. He had already decided to be a man of God. That's why when God called to Isaiah, he was ready to say, "Here am I! Send me" (v. 8).

LIVE IT:

At some point, all people need to decide whether they believe, trust, love, and want to follow God, no matter what happens and no matter what He calls them to do with their lives. How about you? Do you believe, trust, love, and want to follow God? This is the most important question you will ever answer, so think it over. Write down why you believe, trust, love, and want to follow God, what your faith means to you, and how you are going to live for God.

having in his hand a live coal *which* he had
taken with the tongs from the altar. 7And he
touched my mouth *with it,* and said:

"Behold, this has touched your lips;
Your iniquity is taken away,
And your sin purged."

8Also I heard the voice of the Lord,
saying:

"Whom shall I send,
And who will go for Us?"

Then I said, "Here *am* I! Send me."
9And He said, "Go, and tell this people:

'Keep on hearing, but do not
understand;
Keep on seeing, but do not perceive.'

10 "Make the heart of this people dull,
And their ears heavy,
And shut their eyes;
Lest they see with their eyes,
And hear with their ears,
And understand with their heart,
And return and be healed."

11Then I said, "Lord, how long?"
And He answered:

"Until the cities are laid waste and
without inhabitant,
The houses are without a man,
The land is utterly desolate,
12 The LORD has removed men far away,
And the forsaken places *are* many in the
midst of the land.
13 But yet a tenth *will be* in it,
And will return and be for consuming,
As a terebinth tree or as an oak,
Whose stump *remains* when it is cut
down.
So the holy seed *shall be* its stump."

Isaiah Sent to King Ahaz

7 Now it came to pass in the days of Ahaz
the son of Jotham, the son of Uzziah,
king of Judah, *that* Rezin king of Syria and
Pekah the son of Remaliah, king of Israel,
went up to Jerusalem to *make* war against it,
but could not prevail against it. 2And it was
told to the house of David, saying, "Syria's
forces are deployed in Ephraim." So his heart
and the heart of his people were moved as
the trees of the woods are moved with the
wind.
3Then the LORD said to Isaiah, "Go out

In Focus

7:14 Immanuel A Hebrew name meaning "God With Us." The name refers to the coming Messiah, or Christ, in the New Testament. Jesus truly was and is "God With Us."

now to meet Ahaz, you and Shear-Jashub[a]
your son, at the end of the aqueduct from
the upper pool, on the highway to the Fuller's Field, 4and say to him: 'Take heed, and
be quiet; do not fear or be fainthearted for
these two stubs of smoking firebrands, for
the fierce anger of Rezin and Syria, and the
son of Remaliah. 5Because Syria, Ephraim,
and the son of Remaliah have plotted evil
against you, saying, 6"Let us go up against
Judah and trouble it, and let us make a gap
in its wall for ourselves, and set a king over
them, the son of Tabel"— 7thus says the Lord
GOD:

"It shall not stand,
Nor shall it come to pass.
8 For the head of Syria *is* Damascus,
And the head of Damascus *is* Rezin.
Within sixty-five years Ephraim will be
broken,
So that it will not *be* a people.
9 The head of Ephraim *is* Samaria,
And the head of Samaria *is* Remaliah's
son.
If you will not believe,
Surely you shall not be established."'"

The Immanuel Prophecy

10Moreover the LORD spoke again to
Ahaz, saying, 11"Ask a sign for yourself from
the LORD your God; ask it either in the depth
or in the height above."
12But Ahaz said, "I will not ask, nor will I
test the LORD!"
13Then he said, "Hear now, O house of
David! *Is it* a small thing for you to weary men, but will you weary my God also?
14Therefore the Lord Himself will give you
a sign: Behold, the virgin shall conceive
and bear a Son, and shall call His name

7:3 [a] Literally *A Remnant Shall Return*

Immanuel.[a] 15Curds and honey He shall
eat, that He may know to refuse the evil and
choose the good. 16For before the Child shall
know to refuse the evil and choose the good,
the land that you dread will be forsaken by
both her kings. 17The LORD will bring the
king of Assyria upon you and your people
and your father's house—days that have not
come since the day that Ephraim departed
from Judah."

18 And it shall come to pass in that day
That the LORD will whistle for the fly
That *is* in the farthest part of the rivers of Egypt,
And for the bee that *is* in the land of Assyria.
19 They will come, and all of them will rest
In the desolate valleys and in the clefts of the rocks,
And on all thorns and in all pastures.

20 In the same day the Lord will shave with a hired razor,
With those from beyond the River,[a] with the king of Assyria,
The head and the hair of the legs,
And will also remove the beard.

21 It shall be in that day
That a man will keep alive a young cow and two sheep;
22 So it shall be, from the abundance of milk they give,
That he will eat curds;
For curds and honey everyone will eat who is left in the land.

23 It shall happen in that day,
That wherever there could be a thousand vines
Worth a thousand *shekels* of silver,
It will be for briers and thorns.
24 With arrows and bows *men* will come there,
Because all the land will become briers and thorns.

25 *And to any* hill which could be dug with the hoe,
You will not go there for fear of briers and thorns;
But it will become a range for oxen
And a place for sheep to roam.

Assyria Will Invade the Land

8 Moreover the LORD said to me, "Take
a large scroll, and write on it with a
man's pen concerning Maher-Shalal-Hash-
Baz.[a] 2And I will take for Myself faithful
witnesses to record, Uriah the priest and
Zechariah the son of Jeberechiah."

3Then I went to the prophetess, and she
conceived and bore a son. Then the LORD
said to me, "Call his name Maher-Shalal-
Hash-Baz; 4for before the child shall have
knowledge to cry 'My father' and 'My mother,' the riches of Damascus and the spoil of
Samaria will be taken away before the king
of Assyria."

5The LORD also spoke to me again,
saying:

6 "Inasmuch as these people refused
The waters of Shiloah that flow softly,
And rejoice in Rezin and in Remaliah's son;
7 Now therefore, behold, the Lord brings up over them
The waters of the River,[a] strong and mighty—
The king of Assyria and all his glory;
He will go up over all his channels
And go over all his banks.
8 He will pass through Judah,
He will overflow and pass over,
He will reach up to the neck;
And the stretching out of his wings
Will fill the breadth of Your land,
O Immanuel.[a]

9 "Be shattered, O you peoples, and be broken in pieces!
Give ear, all you from far countries.
Gird yourselves, but be broken in pieces;
Gird yourselves, but be broken in pieces.
10 Take counsel together, but it will come to nothing;
Speak the word, but it will not stand,
For God *is* with us."[a]

Fear God, Heed His Word

11For the LORD spoke thus to me with a
strong hand, and instructed me that I should
not walk in the way of this people, saying:

12 "Do not say, 'A conspiracy,'
Concerning all that this people call a conspiracy,
Nor be afraid of their threats, nor be troubled.

7:14 [a] Literally *God-With-Us* 7:20 [a] That is, the Euphrates 8:1 [a] Literally *Speed the Spoil, Hasten the Booty*
8:7 [a] That is, the Euphrates 8:8 [a] Literally *God-With-Us*
8:10 [a] Hebrew *Immanuel*

13 The LORD of hosts, Him you shall
hallow;
Let Him *be* your fear,
And *let* Him *be* your dread.
14 He will be as a sanctuary,
But a stone of stumbling and a rock of
offense
To both the houses of Israel,
As a trap and a snare to the inhabitants
of Jerusalem.
15 And many among them shall stumble;
They shall fall and be broken,
Be snared and taken."

16 Bind up the testimony,
Seal the law among my disciples.
17 And I will wait on the LORD,
Who hides His face from the house of
Jacob;
And I will hope in Him.
18 Here am I and the children whom the
LORD has given me!
We are for signs and wonders in Israel
From the LORD of hosts,
Who dwells in Mount Zion.

19 And when they say to you, "Seek those
who are mediums and wizards, who whisper
and mutter," should not a people seek their
God? *Should they seek* the dead on behalf of
the living? 20 To the law and to the testimony!
If they do not speak according to this word, *it*
is because *there is* no light in them.

21 They will pass through it hard-pressed
and hungry; and it shall happen, when they
are hungry, that they will be enraged and
curse their king and their God, and look upward. 22 Then they will look to the earth, and
see trouble and darkness, gloom of anguish;
and *they will be* driven into darkness.

The Government of the Promised Son

9 Nevertheless the gloom *will* not *be*
upon her who *is* distressed,
As when at first He lightly esteemed
The land of Zebulun and the land of
Naphtali,
And afterward more heavily oppressed
her,
By the way of the sea, beyond the
Jordan,
In Galilee of the Gentiles.
2 The people who walked in darkness
Have seen a great light;
Those who dwelt in the land of the
shadow of death,
Upon them a light has shined.

3 You have multiplied the nation
And increased its joy;[a]
They rejoice before You
According to the joy of harvest,
As *men* rejoice when they divide the
spoil.
4 For You have broken the yoke of his
burden
And the staff of his shoulder,
The rod of his oppressor,
As in the day of Midian.
5 For every warrior's sandal from the
noisy battle,
And garments rolled in blood,
Will be used for burning *and* fuel of
fire.

6 For unto us a Child is born,
Unto us a Son is given;
And the government will be upon His
shoulder.
And His name will be called
Wonderful, Counselor, Mighty God,
Everlasting Father, Prince of Peace.
7 Of the increase of *His* government and
peace
There will be no end,
Upon the throne of David and over His
kingdom,
To order it and establish it with
judgment and justice
From that time forward, even forever.
The zeal of the LORD of hosts will
perform this.

The Punishment of Samaria

8 The Lord sent a word against Jacob,
And it has fallen on Israel.
9 All the people will know—
Ephraim and the inhabitant of
Samaria—
Who say in pride and arrogance of
heart:
10 "The bricks have fallen down,
But we will rebuild with hewn stones;
The sycamores are cut down,
But we will replace *them* with cedars."
11 Therefore the LORD shall set up
The adversaries of Rezin against him,
And spur his enemies on,

9:3 [a] Following Qere and Targum; Kethib and Vulgate read *not increased joy;* Septuagint reads *Most of the people You brought down in Your joy.*

12 The Syrians before and the Philistines behind;
And they shall devour Israel with an open mouth.

For all this His anger is not turned away,
But His hand *is* stretched out still.

13 For the people do not turn to Him who strikes them,
Nor do they seek the LORD of hosts.
14 Therefore the LORD will cut off head and tail from Israel,
Palm branch and bulrush in one day.
15 The elder and honorable, he *is* the head;
The prophet who teaches lies, he *is* the tail.
16 For the leaders of this people cause *them* to err,
And *those who are* led by them are destroyed.
17 Therefore the Lord will have no joy in their young men,
Nor have mercy on their fatherless and widows;
For everyone *is* a hypocrite and an evildoer,
And every mouth speaks folly.

For all this His anger is not turned away,
But His hand *is* stretched out still.

18 For wickedness burns as the fire;
It shall devour the briers and thorns,
And kindle in the thickets of the forest;
They shall mount up *like* rising smoke.
19 Through the wrath of the LORD of hosts
The land is burned up,
And the people shall be as fuel for the fire;
No man shall spare his brother.
20 And he shall snatch on the right hand

GOD PROMISES HIS PEOPLE HOPE

READ IT: ISAIAH 9:6, 7

GET IT:

A long, long time before Jesus was born, prophets gave hints (called prophecies) about a special child who would be a king. The people didn't always understand what the prophet was talking about, and they had no idea how long it would take for a prophecy to come true, but the news gave them a lot of hope. For a long, long time they hoped that someday soon this king would come. They believed what God's prophets said, so they kept waiting and hoping for it to happen. God had a plan for it all to come true, but it would happen at some perfect time in the future.

LIVE IT:

What kind of news would give you hope? That you'd pass your history test? Earn a good grade on your science project? Get invited to a friend's party? Those might be some things that would happen really soon in your life. Do you ever think about the future, years from now? What do you hope will happen when you're an adult? God loves you, and He has a super plan for your future. Just as He gave the people of Israel hope for the future, He gives you hope for your future, too.

And be hungry;
He shall devour on the left hand
And not be satisfied;
Every man shall eat the flesh of his own arm.
21 Manasseh *shall devour* Ephraim, and Ephraim Manasseh;
Together they *shall be* against Judah.

For all this His anger is not turned away,
But His hand *is* stretched out still.

10 "Woe to those who decree unrighteous decrees,
Who write misfortune,
Which they have prescribed
2 To rob the needy of justice,
And to take what is right from the poor of My people,
That widows may be their prey,
And *that* they may rob the fatherless.
3 What will you do in the day of punishment,
And in the desolation *which* will come from afar?
To whom will you flee for help?
And where will you leave your glory?
4 Without Me they shall bow down among the prisoners,
And they shall fall among the slain."

For all this His anger is not turned away,
But His hand *is* stretched out still.

Arrogant Assyria Also Judged

5 "Woe to Assyria, the rod of My anger
And the staff in whose hand is My indignation.
6 I will send him against an ungodly nation,
And against the people of My wrath
I will give him charge,
To seize the spoil, to take the prey,
And to tread them down like the mire of the streets.
7 Yet he does not mean so,
Nor does his heart think so;
But *it is* in his heart to destroy,
And cut off not a few nations.
8 For he says,
'*Are* not my princes altogether kings?
9 *Is* not Calno like Carchemish?
Is not Hamath like Arpad?
Is not Samaria like Damascus?
10 As my hand has found the kingdoms of the idols,
Whose carved images excelled those of Jerusalem and Samaria,
11 As I have done to Samaria and her idols,
Shall I not do also to Jerusalem and her idols?'"

12 Therefore it shall come to pass, when
the Lord has performed all His work on
Mount Zion and on Jerusalem, *that He will*
say, "I will punish the fruit of the arrogant
heart of the king of Assyria, and the glory of
his haughty looks."

13 For he says:

"By the strength of my hand I have done *it,*
And by my wisdom, for I am prudent;
Also I have removed the boundaries of the people,
And have robbed their treasuries;
So I have put down the inhabitants like a valiant *man.*
14 My hand has found like a nest the riches of the people,
And as one gathers eggs *that are* left,
I have gathered all the earth;
And there was no one who moved *his* wing,
Nor opened *his* mouth with even a peep."

15 Shall the ax boast itself against him who chops with it?
Or shall the saw exalt itself against him who saws with it?
As if a rod could wield *itself* against those who lift it up,
Or as if a staff could lift up, *as if it were* not wood!
16 Therefore the Lord, the Lord[a] of hosts,
Will send leanness among his fat ones;
And under his glory
He will kindle a burning
Like the burning of a fire.
17 So the Light of Israel will be for a fire,
And his Holy One for a flame;
It will burn and devour
His thorns and his briers in one day.
18 And it will consume the glory of his forest and of his fruitful field,
Both soul and body;

10:16 [a] Following Bomberg; Masoretic Text and Dead Sea Scrolls read *YHWH* (*the* LORD).

And they will be as when a sick man
wastes away.
19 Then the rest of the trees of his forest
Will be so few in number
That a child may write them.

The Returning Remnant of Israel

20 And it shall come to pass in that day
That the remnant of Israel,
And such as have escaped of the house
of Jacob,
Will never again depend on him who
defeated them,
But will depend on the LORD, the Holy
One of Israel, in truth.
21 The remnant will return, the remnant
of Jacob,
To the Mighty God.
22 For though your people, O Israel, be as
the sand of the sea,
A remnant of them will return;
The destruction decreed shall overflow
with righteousness.
23 For the Lord GOD of hosts
Will make a determined end
In the midst of all the land.

24Therefore thus says the Lord GOD of
hosts: "O My people, who dwell in Zion, do
not be afraid of the Assyrian. He shall strike
you with a rod and lift up his staff against
you, in the manner of Egypt. 25For yet a very
little while and the indignation will cease,
as will My anger in their destruction." 26And
the LORD of hosts will stir up a scourge for
him like the slaughter of Midian at the rock
of Oreb; *as* His rod was on the sea, so will He
lift it up in the manner of Egypt.

27 It shall come to pass in that day
That his burden will be taken away from
your shoulder,
And his yoke from your neck,
And the yoke will be destroyed because
of the anointing oil.

28 He has come to Aiath,
He has passed *Migron;*
At Michmash he has attended to his
equipment.
29 They have gone along the ridge,
They have taken up lodging at Geba.
Ramah is afraid,
Gibeah of Saul has fled.
30 Lift up your voice,
O daughter of Gallim!
Cause it to be heard as far as Laish—
O poor Anathoth![a]
31 Madmenah has fled,
The inhabitants of Gebim seek refuge.
32 As yet he will remain at Nob that day;
He will shake his fist at the mount of
the daughter of Zion,
The hill of Jerusalem.

33 Behold, the Lord,
The LORD of hosts,
Will lop off the bough with terror;
Those of high stature *will be* hewn
down,
And the haughty will be humbled.
34 He will cut down the thickets of the
forest with iron,
And Lebanon will fall by the Mighty
One.

The Reign of Jesse's Offspring

11 There shall come forth a Rod from
the stem of Jesse,
And a Branch shall grow out of his
roots.
2 The Spirit of the LORD shall rest upon
Him,
The Spirit of wisdom and
understanding,
The Spirit of counsel and might,
The Spirit of knowledge and of the fear
of the LORD.

3 His delight *is* in the fear of the LORD,
And He shall not judge by the sight of
His eyes,
Nor decide by the hearing of His ears;
4 But with righteousness He shall judge
the poor,
And decide with equity for the meek of
the earth;
He shall strike the earth with the rod of
His mouth,
And with the breath of His lips He shall
slay the wicked.
5 Righteousness shall be the belt of His
loins,
And faithfulness the belt of His waist.

6 "The wolf also shall dwell with the lamb,
The leopard shall lie down with the
young goat,
The calf and the young lion and the
fatling together;

10:30 [a] Following Masoretic Text, Targum, and Vulgate; Septuagint and Syriac read *Listen to her, O Anathoth.*

And a little child shall lead them.
7 The cow and the bear shall graze;
Their young ones shall lie down together;
And the lion shall eat straw like the ox.
8 The nursing child shall play by the cobra's hole,
And the weaned child shall put his hand in the viper's den.
9 They shall not hurt nor destroy in all My holy mountain,
For the earth shall be full of the knowledge of the LORD
As the waters cover the sea.

10 "And in that day there shall be a Root of Jesse,
Who shall stand as a banner to the people;
For the Gentiles shall seek Him,
And His resting place shall be glorious."

11 It shall come to pass in that day
That the Lord shall set His hand again the second time
To recover the remnant of His people who are left,
From Assyria and Egypt,
From Pathros and Cush,
From Elam and Shinar,
From Hamath and the islands of the sea.

12 He will set up a banner for the nations,
And will assemble the outcasts of Israel,
And gather together the dispersed of Judah
From the four corners of the earth.
13 Also the envy of Ephraim shall depart,
And the adversaries of Judah shall be cut off;
Ephraim shall not envy Judah,
And Judah shall not harass Ephraim.
14 But they shall fly down upon the shoulder of the Philistines toward the west;
Together they shall plunder the people of the East;
They shall lay their hand on Edom and Moab;
And the people of Ammon shall obey them.
15 The LORD will utterly destroy[a] the tongue of the Sea of Egypt;
With His mighty wind He will shake His fist over the River,[b]
And strike it in the seven streams,
And make *men* cross over dry-shod.
16 There will be a highway for the remnant of His people
Who will be left from Assyria,
As it was for Israel
In the day that he came up from the land of Egypt.

A Hymn of Praise

12 And in that day you will say:

"O LORD, I will praise You;
Though You were angry with me,
Your anger is turned away, and You comfort me.
2 Behold, God *is* my salvation,
I will trust and not be afraid;
'For YAH, the LORD, *is* my strength and song;
He also has become my salvation.'"[a]

3 Therefore with joy you will draw water
From the wells of salvation.

4 And in that day you will say:

"Praise the LORD, call upon His name;
Declare His deeds among the peoples,
Make mention that His name is exalted.
5 Sing to the LORD,
For He has done excellent things;
This *is* known in all the earth.
6 Cry out and shout, O inhabitant of Zion,
For great *is* the Holy One of Israel in your midst!"

Proclamation Against Babylon

13 The burden against Babylon which Isaiah the son of Amoz saw.

2 "Lift up a banner on the high mountain,
Raise your voice to them;
Wave your hand, that they may enter the gates of the nobles.
3 I have commanded My sanctified ones;
I have also called My mighty ones for My anger—
Those who rejoice in My exaltation."

4 The noise of a multitude in the mountains,
Like that of many people!

11:15 [a] Following Masoretic Text and Vulgate; Septuagint, Syriac, and Targum read *dry up* [b] That is, the Euphrates
12:2 [a] Exodus 15:2

A tumultuous noise of the kingdoms of
nations gathered together!
The LORD of hosts musters
The army for battle.
5 They come from a far country,
From the end of heaven—
The LORD and His weapons of
indignation,
To destroy the whole land.

6 Wail, for the day of the LORD *is* at hand!
It will come as destruction from the
Almighty.
7 Therefore all hands will be limp,
Every man's heart will melt,
8 And they will be afraid.
Pangs and sorrows will take hold of
them;
They will be in pain as a woman in
childbirth;
They will be amazed at one another;
Their faces *will be like* flames.

9 Behold, the day of the LORD comes,
Cruel, with both wrath and fierce anger,
To lay the land desolate;
And He will destroy its sinners from it.
10 For the stars of heaven and their
constellations
Will not give their light;
The sun will be darkened in its going
forth,
And the moon will not cause its light to
shine.

11 "I will punish the world for *its* evil,
And the wicked for their iniquity;
I will halt the arrogance of the proud,
And will lay low the haughtiness of the
terrible.
12 I will make a mortal more rare than fine
gold,
A man more than the golden wedge of
Ophir.
13 Therefore I will shake the heavens,
And the earth will move out of her
place,
In the wrath of the LORD of hosts
And in the day of His fierce anger.
14 It shall be as the hunted gazelle,
And as a sheep that no man takes up;
Every man will turn to his own people,
And everyone will flee to his own land.
15 Everyone who is found will be thrust
through,
And everyone who is captured will fall
by the sword.
16 Their children also will be dashed to
pieces before their eyes;
Their houses will be plundered
And their wives ravished.

17 "Behold, I will stir up the Medes against
them,
Who will not regard silver;
And *as for* gold, they will not delight
in it.
18 Also *their* bows will dash the young
men to pieces,
And they will have no pity on the fruit
of the womb;
Their eye will not spare children.
19 And Babylon, the glory of kingdoms,
The beauty of the Chaldeans' pride,
Will be as when God overthrew Sodom
and Gomorrah.
20 It will never be inhabited,
Nor will it be settled from generation to
generation;
Nor will the Arabian pitch tents there,
Nor will the shepherds make their
sheepfolds there.
21 But wild beasts of the desert will lie
there,
And their houses will be full of owls;
Ostriches will dwell there,
And wild goats will caper there.
22 The hyenas will howl in their citadels,
And jackals in their pleasant palaces.
Her time *is* near to come,
And her days will not be prolonged."

Mercy on Jacob

14 For the LORD will have mercy on Jacob, and will still choose Israel, and
settle them in their own land. The strangers
will be joined with them, and they will cling
to the house of Jacob. 2 Then people will take
them and bring them to their place, and the
house of Israel will possess them for servants and maids in the land of the LORD;
they will take them captive whose captives
they were, and rule over their oppressors.

Fall of the King of Babylon

3 It shall come to pass in the day the LORD
gives you rest from your sorrow, and from
your fear and the hard bondage in which
you were made to serve, 4 that you will take
up this proverb against the king of Babylon,
and say:

"How the oppressor has ceased,
The golden[a] city ceased!
5 The LORD has broken the staff of the wicked,
The scepter of the rulers;
6 He who struck the people in wrath with a continual stroke,
He who ruled the nations in anger,
Is persecuted *and* no one hinders.
7 The whole earth is at rest *and* quiet;
They break forth into singing.
8 Indeed the cypress trees rejoice over you,
And the cedars of Lebanon,
Saying, 'Since you were cut down,
No woodsman has come up against us.'

9 "Hell from beneath is excited about you,
To meet *you* at your coming;
It stirs up the dead for you,
All the chief ones of the earth;
It has raised up from their thrones
All the kings of the nations.
10 They all shall speak and say to you:
'Have you also become as weak as we?
Have you become like us?
11 Your pomp is brought down to Sheol,
And the sound of your stringed instruments;
The maggot is spread under you,
And worms cover you.'

The Fall of Lucifer

12 "How you are fallen from heaven,
O Lucifer,[a] son of the morning!
How you are cut down to the ground,
You who weakened the nations!
13 For you have said in your heart:
'I will ascend into heaven,
I will exalt my throne above the stars of God;
I will also sit on the mount of the congregation
On the farthest sides of the north;
14 I will ascend above the heights of the clouds,
I will be like the Most High.'
15 Yet you shall be brought down to Sheol,
To the lowest depths of the Pit.

16 "Those who see you will gaze at you,
And consider you, *saying:*
'*Is* this the man who made the earth tremble,
Who shook kingdoms,
17 Who made the world as a wilderness
And destroyed its cities,
Who did not open the house of his prisoners?'

18 "All the kings of the nations,
All of them, sleep in glory,
Everyone in his own house;
19 But you are cast out of your grave
Like an abominable branch,
Like the garment of those who are slain,
Thrust through with a sword,
Who go down to the stones of the pit,
Like a corpse trodden underfoot.
20 You will not be joined with them in burial,
Because you have destroyed your land
And slain your people.
The brood of evildoers shall never be named.
21 Prepare slaughter for his children
Because of the iniquity of their fathers,
Lest they rise up and possess the land,
And fill the face of the world with cities."

Babylon Destroyed

22 "For I will rise up against them," says the LORD of hosts,
"And cut off from Babylon the name and remnant,
And offspring and posterity," says the LORD.
23 "I will also make it a possession for the porcupine,
And marshes of muddy water;
I will sweep it with the broom of destruction," says the LORD of hosts.

Assyria Destroyed

24 The LORD of hosts has sworn, saying,
"Surely, as I have thought, so it shall come to pass,
And as I have purposed, *so* it shall stand:
25 That I will break the Assyrian in My land,
And on My mountains tread him underfoot.
Then his yoke shall be removed from them,

14:4 [a] Or *insolent* 14:12 [a] Literally *Day Star*

And his burden removed from their
shoulders.
26 This *is* the purpose that is purposed
against the whole earth,
And this *is* the hand that is stretched out
over all the nations.
27 For the LORD of hosts has purposed,
And who will annul *it*?
His hand *is* stretched out,
And who will turn it back?"

Philistia Destroyed

28 This is the burden which came in the
year that King Ahaz died.

29 "Do not rejoice, all you of Philistia,
Because the rod that struck you is
broken;
For out of the serpent's roots will come
forth a viper,
And its offspring *will be* a fiery flying
serpent.
30 The firstborn of the poor will feed,
And the needy will lie down in safety;
I will kill your roots with famine,
And it will slay your remnant.
31 Wail, O gate! Cry, O city!
All you of Philistia *are* dissolved;
For smoke will come from the north,
And no one *will be* alone in his
appointed times."

32 What will they answer the messengers
of the nation?
That the LORD has founded Zion,
And the poor of His people shall take
refuge in it.

Proclamation Against Moab

15 The burden against Moab.

Because in the night Ar of Moab is laid
waste
And destroyed,
Because in the night Kir of Moab is laid
waste
And destroyed,
2 He has gone up to the temple[a] and
Dibon,
To the high places to weep.
Moab will wail over Nebo and over
Medeba;
On all their heads *will be* baldness,
And every beard cut off.
3 In their streets they will clothe
themselves with sackcloth;
On the tops of their houses
And in their streets
Everyone will wail, weeping bitterly.
4 Heshbon and Elealeh will cry out,
Their voice shall be heard as far as
Jahaz;
Therefore the armed soldiers[a] of Moab
will cry out;
His life will be burdensome to him.

5 "My heart will cry out for Moab;
His fugitives *shall flee* to Zoar,
Like a three-year-old heifer.[a]
For by the Ascent of Luhith
They will go up with weeping;
For in the way of Horonaim
They will raise up a cry of destruction,
6 For the waters of Nimrim will be
desolate,
For the green grass has withered away;
The grass fails, there is nothing green.
7 Therefore the abundance they have
gained,
And what they have laid up,
They will carry away to the Brook of the
Willows.
8 For the cry has gone all around the
borders of Moab,
Its wailing to Eglaim
And its wailing to Beer Elim.
9 For the waters of Dimon[a] will be full of
blood;
Because I will bring more upon
Dimon,[b]
Lions upon him who escapes from
Moab,
And on the remnant of the land."

Moab Destroyed

16 Send the lamb to the ruler of the
land,
From Sela to the wilderness,
To the mount of the daughter of Zion.
2 For it shall be as a wandering bird
thrown out of the nest;

15:2 [a] Hebrew *bayith,* literally *house* 15:4 [a] Following Masoretic Text, Targum, and Vulgate; Septuagint and Syriac read *loins.* 15:5 [a] Or *The Third Eglath,* an unknown city (compare Jeremiah 48:34) 15:9 [a] Following Masoretic Text and Targum; Dead Sea Scrolls and Vulgate read *Dibon;* Septuagint reads *Rimon.* [b] Following Masoretic Text and Targum; Dead Sea Scrolls and Vulgate read *Dibon;* Septuagint reads *Rimon.*

So shall be the daughters of Moab at the
fords of the Arnon.

3 "Take counsel, execute judgment;
Make your shadow like the night in the
middle of the day;
Hide the outcasts,
Do not betray him who escapes.
4 Let My outcasts dwell with you, O Moab;
Be a shelter to them from the face of the
spoiler.
For the extortioner is at an end,
Devastation ceases,
The oppressors are consumed out of the
land.
5 In mercy the throne will be established;
And One will sit on it in truth, in the
tabernacle of David,
Judging and seeking justice and
hastening righteousness."

6 We have heard of the pride of Moab—
He is very proud—
Of his haughtiness and his pride and
his wrath;
But his lies *shall* not *be* so.
7 Therefore Moab shall wail for Moab;
Everyone shall wail.
For the foundations of Kir Hareseth you
shall mourn;
Surely *they are* stricken.

8 For the fields of Heshbon languish,
And the vine of Sibmah;
The lords of the nations have broken
down its choice plants,
Which have reached to Jazer
And wandered through the wilderness.
Her branches are stretched out,
They are gone over the sea.
9 Therefore I will bewail the vine of
Sibmah,
With the weeping of Jazer;
I will drench you with my tears,
O Heshbon and Elealeh;
For battle cries have fallen
Over your summer fruits and your
harvest.

10 Gladness is taken away,
And joy from the plentiful field;
In the vineyards there will be no
singing,
Nor will there be shouting;
No treaders will tread out wine in the
presses;
I have made their shouting cease.

11 Therefore my heart shall resound like a
harp for Moab,
And my inner being for Kir Heres.

12 And it shall come to pass,
When it is seen that Moab is weary on
the high place,
That he will come to his sanctuary to
pray;
But he will not prevail.

13 This *is* the word which the LORD has
spoken concerning Moab since that time.
14 But now the LORD has spoken, saying,
"Within three years, as the years of a hired
man, the glory of Moab will be despised with
all that great multitude, and the remnant *will
be* very small *and* feeble."

Proclamation Against Syria and Israel

17 The burden against Damascus.

"Behold, Damascus will cease from *being*
a city,
And it will be a ruinous heap.
2 The cities of Aroer *are* forsaken;[a]
They will be for flocks
Which lie down, and no one will make
them afraid.
3 The fortress also will cease from
Ephraim,
The kingdom from Damascus,
And the remnant of Syria;
They will be as the glory of the children
of Israel,"
Says the LORD of hosts.

4 "In that day it shall come to pass
That the glory of Jacob will wane,
And the fatness of his flesh grow lean.
5 It shall be as when the harvester gathers
the grain,
And reaps the heads with his arm;
It shall be as he who gathers heads of
grain
In the Valley of Rephaim.
6 Yet gleaning grapes will be left in it,
Like the shaking of an olive tree,
Two *or* three olives at the top of the
uppermost bough,
Four *or* five in its most fruitful
branches,"
Says the LORD God of Israel.

17:2 [a] Following Masoretic Text and Vulgate; Septuagint reads *It shall be forsaken forever;* Targum reads *Its cities shall be forsaken and desolate.*

7 In that day a man will look to his Maker,
And his eyes will have respect for the
Holy One of Israel.
8 He will not look to the altars,
The work of his hands;
He will not respect what his fingers
have made,
Nor the wooden images[a] nor the
incense altars.

9 In that day his strong cities will be as a
forsaken bough[a]
And an uppermost branch,[b]
Which they left because of the children
of Israel;
And there will be desolation.

10 Because you have forgotten the God of
your salvation,
And have not been mindful of the Rock
of your stronghold,
Therefore you will plant pleasant plants
And set out foreign seedlings;
11 In the day you will make your plant to
grow,
And in the morning you will make your
seed to flourish;
But the harvest *will be* a heap of ruins
In the day of grief and desperate sorrow.

12 Woe to the multitude of many people
Who make a noise like the roar of the
seas,
And to the rushing of nations
That make a rushing like the rushing of
mighty waters!
13 The nations will rush like the rushing
of many waters;
But *God* will rebuke them and they will
flee far away,
And be chased like the chaff of the
mountains before the wind,
Like a rolling thing before the
whirlwind.
14 Then behold, at eventide, trouble!
And before the morning, he *is* no more.
This *is* the portion of those who plunder
us,
And the lot of those who rob us.

Proclamation Against Ethiopia

18 Woe to the land shadowed with
buzzing wings,
Which *is* beyond the rivers of Ethiopia,
2 Which sends ambassadors by sea,
Even in vessels of reed on the waters,
saying,
"Go, swift messengers, to a nation tall
and smooth *of skin,*
To a people terrible from their
beginning onward,
A nation powerful and treading down,
Whose land the rivers divide."

3 All inhabitants of the world and
dwellers on the earth:
When he lifts up a banner on the
mountains, you see *it;*
And when he blows a trumpet, you
hear *it.*
4 For so the LORD said to me,
"I will take My rest,
And I will look from My dwelling place
Like clear heat in sunshine,
Like a cloud of dew in the heat of
harvest."
5 For before the harvest, when the bud is
perfect
And the sour grape is ripening in the
flower,
He will both cut off the sprigs with
pruning hooks
And take away *and* cut down the
branches.
6 They will be left together for the
mountain birds of prey
And for the beasts of the earth;
The birds of prey will summer on them,
And all the beasts of the earth will
winter on them.

7 In that time a present will be brought to
the LORD of hosts
From[a] a people tall and smooth *of skin,*
And from a people terrible from their
beginning onward,
A nation powerful and treading down,
Whose land the rivers divide—
To the place of the name of the LORD of
hosts,
To Mount Zion.

Proclamation Against Egypt

19 The burden against Egypt.

Behold, the LORD rides on a swift cloud,
And will come into Egypt;

17:8 [a] Hebrew *Asherim,* Canaanite deities 17:9 [a] Septuagint reads *Hivites;* Targum reads *laid waste;* Vulgate reads *as the plows.* [b] Septuagint reads *Amorites;* Targum reads *in ruins;* Vulgate reads *corn.* 18:7 [a] Following Dead Sea Scrolls, Septuagint, and Vulgate; Masoretic Text omits *From;* Targum reads *To.*

The idols of Egypt will totter at His presence,
And the heart of Egypt will melt in its midst.

2 "I will set Egyptians against Egyptians;
Everyone will fight against his brother,
And everyone against his neighbor,
City against city, kingdom against kingdom.
3 The spirit of Egypt will fail in its midst;
I will destroy their counsel,
And they will consult the idols and the charmers,
The mediums and the sorcerers.
4 And the Egyptians I will give
Into the hand of a cruel master,
And a fierce king will rule over them,"
Says the Lord, the LORD of hosts.

5 The waters will fail from the sea,
And the river will be wasted and dried up.
6 The rivers will turn foul;
The brooks of defense will be emptied and dried up;
The reeds and rushes will wither.
7 The papyrus reeds by the River,[a] by the mouth of the River,
And everything sown by the River,
Will wither, be driven away, and be no more.
8 The fishermen also will mourn;
All those will lament who cast hooks into the River,
And they will languish who spread nets on the waters.
9 Moreover those who work in fine flax
And those who weave fine fabric will be ashamed;
10 And its foundations will be broken.
All who make wages *will be* troubled of soul.

11 Surely the princes of Zoan *are* fools;
Pharaoh's wise counselors give foolish counsel.
How do you say to Pharaoh, "I *am* the son of the wise,
The son of ancient kings?"
12 Where *are* they?
Where are your wise men?
Let them tell you now,
And let them know what the LORD of hosts has purposed against Egypt.
13 The princes of Zoan have become fools;
The princes of Noph[a] are deceived;
They have also deluded Egypt,
Those who are the mainstay of its tribes.
14 The LORD has mingled a perverse spirit in her midst;
And they have caused Egypt to err in all her work,
As a drunken man staggers in his vomit.
15 Neither will there be *any* work for Egypt,
Which the head or tail,
Palm branch or bulrush, may do.[a]

16In that day Egypt will be like women,
and will be afraid and fear because of the
waving of the hand of the LORD of hosts,
which He waves over it. 17And the land of Judah will be a terror to Egypt; everyone who
makes mention of it will be afraid in himself, because of the counsel of the LORD of
hosts which He has determined against it.

Egypt, Assyria, and Israel Blessed

18In that day five cities in the land of
Egypt will speak the language of Canaan
and swear by the LORD of hosts; one will be
called the City of Destruction.[a]
19In that day there will be an altar to the
LORD in the midst of the land of Egypt, and
a pillar to the LORD at its border. 20And it will
be for a sign and for a witness to the LORD
of hosts in the land of Egypt; for they will
cry to the LORD because of the oppressors,
and He will send them a Savior and a Mighty
One, and He will deliver them. 21Then the
LORD will be known to Egypt, and the Egyptians will know the LORD in that day, and
will make sacrifice and offering; yes, they
will make a vow to the LORD and perform
it. 22And the LORD will strike Egypt, He will
strike and heal *it;* they will return to the
LORD, and He will be entreated by them and
heal them.
23In that day there will be a highway
from Egypt to Assyria, and the Assyrian will
come into Egypt and the Egyptian into Assyria, and the Egyptians will serve with the
Assyrians.
24In that day Israel will be one of three
with Egypt and Assyria—a blessing in the

19:7 [a] That is, the Nile 19:13 [a] That is, ancient Memphis
19:15 [a] Compare Isaiah 9:14–16 19:18 [a] Some Hebrew manuscripts, Arabic, Dead Sea Scrolls, Targum, and Vulgate read *Sun;* Septuagint reads *Asedek* (literally *Righteousness*).

midst of the land, 25whom the LORD of hosts
shall bless, saying, "Blessed *is* Egypt My people, and Assyria the work of My hands, and Israel My inheritance."

The Sign Against Egypt and Ethiopia

20 In the year that Tartan[a] came to
Ashdod, when Sargon the king of Assyria sent him, and he fought against Ashdod and took it,
2at the same time the LORD spoke by Isaiah the son of Amoz, saying, "Go, and remove the sackcloth from your body, and take your sandals off your feet." And he did so, walking naked and barefoot.
3Then the LORD said, "Just as My servant Isaiah has walked naked and barefoot three years *for* a sign and a wonder against Egypt and Ethiopia,
4so shall the king of Assyria lead away the Egyptians as prisoners and the Ethiopians as captives, young and old, naked and barefoot, with their buttocks uncovered, to the shame of Egypt.
5Then they shall be afraid and ashamed of Ethiopia their expectation and Egypt their glory.
6And the inhabitant of this territory will say in that day, 'Surely such *is* our expectation, wherever we flee for help to be delivered from the king of Assyria; and how shall we escape?'"

The Fall of Babylon Proclaimed

21 The burden against the Wilderness of the Sea.

As whirlwinds in the South pass through,
So it comes from the desert, from a terrible land.
2 A distressing vision is declared to me;
The treacherous dealer deals treacherously,
And the plunderer plunders.
Go up, O Elam!
Besiege, O Media!
All its sighing I have made to cease.

3 Therefore my loins are filled with pain;
Pangs have taken hold of me, like the pangs of a woman in labor.
I was distressed when *I* heard *it;*
I was dismayed when *I* saw *it.*
4 My heart wavered, fearfulness frightened me;
The night for which I longed He turned into fear for me.
5 Prepare the table,
Set a watchman in the tower,
Eat and drink.
Arise, you princes,
Anoint the shield!

6 For thus has the Lord said to me:
"Go, set a watchman,
Let him declare what he sees."
7 And he saw a chariot *with* a pair of horsemen,
A chariot of donkeys, *and* a chariot of camels,
And he listened earnestly with great care.
8 Then he cried, "A lion,[a] my Lord!
I stand continually on the watchtower in the daytime;
I have sat at my post every night.
9 And look, here comes a chariot of men *with* a pair of horsemen!"
Then he answered and said,
"Babylon is fallen, is fallen!
And all the carved images of her gods
He has broken to the ground."

10 Oh, my threshing and the grain of my floor!
That which I have heard from the LORD of hosts,
The God of Israel,
I have declared to you.

Proclamation Against Edom

11The burden against Dumah.

He calls to me out of Seir,
"Watchman, what of the night?
Watchman, what of the night?"
12 The watchman said,
"The morning comes, and also the night.
If you will inquire, inquire;
Return! Come back!"

Proclamation Against Arabia

13The burden against Arabia.

In the forest in Arabia you will lodge,
O you traveling companies of Dedanites.
14 O inhabitants of the land of Tema,
Bring water to him who is thirsty;
With their bread they met him who fled.
15 For they fled from the swords, from the drawn sword,

20:1 [a] Or *the Commander in Chief* 21:8 [a] Dead Sea Scrolls read *Then the observer cried.*

From the bent bow, and from the
distress of war.

16For thus the LORD has said to me:
"Within a year, according to the year of a
hired man, all the glory of Kedar will fail;
17and the remainder of the number of archers, the mighty men of the people of Kedar, will be diminished; for the LORD God of
Israel has spoken *it*."

Proclamation Against Jerusalem

22 The burden against the Valley of
Vision.

What ails you now, that you have all
gone up to the housetops,
2 You who are full of noise,
A tumultuous city, a joyous city?
Your slain *men are* not slain with the
sword,
Nor dead in battle.
3 All your rulers have fled together;
They are captured by the archers.
All who are found in you are bound
together;
They have fled from afar.
4 Therefore I said, "Look away from me,
I will weep bitterly;
Do not labor to comfort me
Because of the plundering of the
daughter of my people."

5 For *it is* a day of trouble and treading
down and perplexity
By the Lord GOD of hosts
In the Valley of Vision—
Breaking down the walls
And of crying to the mountain.
6 Elam bore the quiver
With chariots of men *and* horsemen,
And Kir uncovered the shield.
7 It shall come to pass *that* your choicest
valleys
Shall be full of chariots,
And the horsemen shall set themselves
in array at the gate.

8 He removed the protection of Judah.
You looked in that day to the armor of
the House of the Forest;
9 You also saw the damage to the city of
David,
That it was great;
And you gathered together the waters of
the lower pool.
10 You numbered the houses of Jerusalem,
And the houses you broke down
To fortify the wall.
11 You also made a reservoir between the
two walls
For the water of the old pool.
But you did not look to its Maker,
Nor did you have respect for Him who
fashioned it long ago.

12 And in that day the Lord GOD of hosts
Called for weeping and for mourning,
For baldness and for girding with
sackcloth.
13 But instead, joy and gladness,
Slaying oxen and killing sheep,
Eating meat and drinking wine:
"Let us eat and drink, for tomorrow we
die!"

14 Then it was revealed in my hearing by
the LORD of hosts,
"Surely for this iniquity there will be no
atonement for you,
Even to your death," says the Lord GOD
of hosts.

The Judgment on Shebna

15Thus says the Lord GOD of hosts:

"Go, proceed to this steward,
To Shebna, who *is* over the house, *and
say:*
16 'What have you here, and whom have
you here,
That you have hewn a sepulcher here,
As he who hews himself a sepulcher on
high,
Who carves a tomb for himself in a rock?
17 Indeed, the LORD will throw you away
violently,
O mighty man,
And will surely seize you.
18 He will surely turn violently and toss
you like a ball
Into a large country;
There you shall die, and there your
glorious chariots
Shall be the shame of your master's
house.
19 So I will drive you out of your office,
And from your position he will pull you
down.[a]

22:19 [a] Septuagint omits *he will pull you down;* Syriac, Targum, and Vulgate read *I will pull you down.*

20 'Then it shall be in that day,
That I will call My servant Eliakim the son of Hilkiah;
21 I will clothe him with your robe
And strengthen him with your belt;
I will commit your responsibility into his hand.
He shall be a father to the inhabitants of Jerusalem
And to the house of Judah.
22 The key of the house of David
I will lay on his shoulder;
So he shall open, and no one shall shut;
And he shall shut, and no one shall open.
23 I will fasten him *as* a peg in a secure place,
And he will become a glorious throne to his father's house.

24'They will hang on him all the glory of
his father's house, the offspring and the posterity, all vessels of small quantity, from the
cups to all the pitchers. 25In that day,' says
the LORD of hosts, 'the peg that is fastened in
the secure place will be removed and be cut
down and fall, and the burden that *was* on
it will be cut off; for the LORD has spoken.'"

Proclamation Against Tyre

23 The burden against Tyre.

Wail, you ships of Tarshish!
For it is laid waste,
So that there is no house, no harbor;
From the land of Cyprus[a] it is revealed to them.

2 Be still, you inhabitants of the coastland,
You merchants of Sidon,
Whom those who cross the sea have filled.[a]
3 And on great waters the grain of Shihor,
The harvest of the River,[a] *is* her revenue;
And she is a marketplace for the nations.

4 Be ashamed, O Sidon;
For the sea has spoken,
The strength of the sea, saying,
"I do not labor, nor bring forth children;
Neither do I rear young men,
Nor bring up virgins."
5 When the report *reaches* Egypt,
They also will be in agony at the report of Tyre.

6 Cross over to Tarshish;
Wail, you inhabitants of the coastland!
7 *Is* this your joyous *city*,
Whose antiquity *is* from ancient days,
Whose feet carried her far off to dwell?
8 Who has taken this counsel against Tyre, the crowning *city*,
Whose merchants *are* princes,
Whose traders *are* the honorable of the earth?
9 The LORD of hosts has purposed it,
To bring to dishonor the pride of all glory,
To bring into contempt all the honorable of the earth.

10 Overflow through your land like the River,[a]
O daughter of Tarshish;
There is no more strength.
11 He stretched out His hand over the sea,
He shook the kingdoms;
The LORD has given a commandment against Canaan
To destroy its strongholds.
12 And He said, "You will rejoice no more,
O you oppressed virgin daughter of Sidon.
Arise, cross over to Cyprus;
There also you will have no rest."

13 Behold, the land of the Chaldeans,
This people *which* was not;
Assyria founded it for wild beasts of the desert.
They set up its towers,
They raised up its palaces,
And brought it to ruin.

14 Wail, you ships of Tarshish!
For your strength is laid waste.

15Now it shall come to pass in that day
that Tyre will be forgotten seventy years, according to the days of one king. At the end of
seventy years it will happen to Tyre as in the
song of the harlot:

16 "Take a harp, go about the city,
You forgotten harlot;

23:1 [a] Hebrew *Kittim*, western lands, especially Cyprus
23:2 [a] Following Masoretic Text and Vulgate; Septuagint and Targum read *Passing over the water;* Dead Sea Scrolls read *Your messengers passing over the sea.* 23:3 [a] That is, the Nile 23:10 [a] That is, the Nile

Make sweet melody, sing many songs,
That you may be remembered."

17And it shall be, at the end of seventy
years, that the LORD will deal with Tyre. She
will return to her hire, and commit fornication with all the kingdoms of the world on
the face of the earth. 18Her gain and her pay
will be set apart for the LORD; it will not be
treasured nor laid up, for her gain will be for
those who dwell before the LORD, to eat suf-
ficiently, and for fine clothing.

Impending Judgment on the Earth

24 Behold, the LORD makes the earth
empty and makes it waste,
Distorts its surface
And scatters abroad its inhabitants.
2 And it shall be:
As with the people, so with the priest;
As with the servant, so with his master;
As with the maid, so with her mistress;
As with the buyer, so with the seller;
As with the lender, so with the
borrower;
As with the creditor, so with the debtor.
3 The land shall be entirely emptied and
utterly plundered,
For the LORD has spoken this word.

4 The earth mourns *and* fades away,
The world languishes *and* fades away;
The haughty people of the earth
languish.
5 The earth is also defiled under its
inhabitants,
Because they have transgressed the
laws,
Changed the ordinance,
Broken the everlasting covenant.
6 Therefore the curse has devoured the
earth,
And those who dwell in it are desolate.
Therefore the inhabitants of the earth
are burned,
And few men *are* left.

7 The new wine fails, the vine languishes,
All the merry-hearted sigh.
8 The mirth of the tambourine ceases,
The noise of the jubilant ends,
The joy of the harp ceases.
9 They shall not drink wine with a song;
Strong drink is bitter to those who
drink it.
10 The city of confusion is broken down;
Every house is shut up, so that none
may go in.
11 *There is* a cry for wine in the streets,
All joy is darkened,
The mirth of the land is gone.
12 In the city desolation is left,
And the gate is stricken with
destruction.
13 When it shall be thus in the midst of the
land among the people,
It shall be like the shaking of an olive
tree,
Like the gleaning of grapes when the
vintage is done.

14 They shall lift up their voice, they shall
sing;
For the majesty of the LORD
They shall cry aloud from the sea.
15 Therefore glorify the LORD in the
dawning light,
The name of the LORD God of Israel in
the coastlands of the sea.
16 From the ends of the earth we have
heard songs:
"Glory to the righteous!"
But I said, "I am ruined, ruined!
Woe to me!
The treacherous dealers have dealt
treacherously,
Indeed, the treacherous dealers have
dealt very treacherously."

17 Fear and the pit and the snare
Are upon you, O inhabitant of the earth.
18 And it shall be
That he who flees from the noise of the
fear
Shall fall into the pit,
And he who comes up from the midst
of the pit
Shall be caught in the snare;
For the windows from on high are open,
And the foundations of the earth are
shaken.

19 The earth is violently broken,
The earth is split open,
The earth is shaken exceedingly.
20 The earth shall reel to and fro like a
drunkard,
And shall totter like a hut;
Its transgression shall be heavy upon it,
And it will fall, and not rise again.

21 It shall come to pass in that day

That the LORD will punish on high the
host of exalted ones,
And on the earth the kings of the earth.
22 They will be gathered together,
As prisoners are gathered in the pit,
And will be shut up in the prison;
After many days they will be punished.
23 Then the moon will be disgraced
And the sun ashamed;
For the LORD of hosts will reign
On Mount Zion and in Jerusalem
And before His elders, gloriously.

Praise to God

25 O LORD, You *are* my God.
I will exalt You,
I will praise Your name,
For You have done wonderful *things;*
Your counsels of old *are* faithfulness *and*
truth.
2 For You have made a city a ruin,
A fortified city a ruin,
A palace of foreigners to be a city no
more;
It will never be rebuilt.
3 Therefore the strong people will glorify
You;
The city of the terrible nations will fear
You.
4 For You have been a strength to the
poor,
A strength to the needy in his distress,
A refuge from the storm,
A shade from the heat;
For the blast of the terrible ones *is* as a
storm *against* the wall.
5 You will reduce the noise of aliens,
As heat in a dry place;
As heat in the shadow of a cloud,
The song of the terrible ones will be
diminished.

6 And in this mountain
The LORD of hosts will make for all
people
A feast of choice pieces,
A feast of wines on the lees,
Of fat things full of marrow,
Of well-refined wines on the lees.
7 And He will destroy on this mountain
The surface of the covering cast over all
people,
And the veil that is spread over all
nations.
8 He will swallow up death forever,
And the Lord GOD will wipe away tears
from all faces;
The rebuke of His people
He will take away from all the earth;
For the LORD has spoken.

9 And it will be said in that day:
"Behold, this *is* our God;
We have waited for Him, and He will
save us.
This *is* the LORD;
We have waited for Him;
We will be glad and rejoice in His
salvation."

10 For on this mountain the hand of the
LORD will rest,
And Moab shall be trampled down
under Him,
As straw is trampled down for the
refuse heap.
11 And He will spread out His hands in
their midst
As a swimmer reaches out to swim,
And He will bring down their pride
Together with the trickery of their
hands.
12 The fortress of the high fort of your
walls
He will bring down, lay low,
And bring to the ground, down to the
dust.

A Song of Salvation

26 In that day this song will be sung
in the land of Judah:

"We have a strong city;
God will appoint salvation *for* walls and
bulwarks.
2 Open the gates,
That the righteous nation which keeps
the truth may enter in.
3 You will keep *him* in perfect peace,
Whose mind *is* stayed *on You,*
Because he trusts in You.
4 Trust in the LORD forever,
For in YAH, the LORD, *is* everlasting
strength.[a]
5 For He brings down those who dwell on
high,
The lofty city;
He lays it low,
He lays it low to the ground,

26:4 [a] Or *Rock of Ages*

He brings it down to the dust.
6 The foot shall tread it down—
The feet of the poor
And the steps of the needy."

7 The way of the just *is* uprightness;
O Most Upright,
You weigh the path of the just.
8 Yes, in the way of Your judgments,
O LORD, we have waited for You;
The desire of *our* soul *is* for Your name
And for the remembrance of You.
9 With my soul I have desired You in the night,
Yes, by my spirit within me I will seek You early;
For when Your judgments *are* in the earth,
The inhabitants of the world will learn righteousness.

10 Let grace be shown to the wicked,
Yet he will not learn righteousness;
In the land of uprightness he will deal unjustly,
And will not behold the majesty of the LORD.
11 LORD, *when* Your hand is lifted up, they will not see.
But they will see and be ashamed
For *their* envy of people;
Yes, the fire of Your enemies shall devour them.

12 LORD, You will establish peace for us,
For You have also done all our works in us.
13 O LORD our God, masters besides You
Have had dominion over us;
But by You only we make mention of Your name.
14 *They are* dead, they will not live;
They are deceased, they will not rise.
Therefore You have punished and destroyed them,
And made all their memory to perish.
15 You have increased the nation, O LORD,
You have increased the nation;
You are glorified;
You have expanded all the borders of the land.

16 LORD, in trouble they have visited You,
They poured out a prayer *when* Your chastening *was* upon them.
17 As a woman with child
Is in pain and cries out in her pangs,
When she draws near the time of her delivery,
So have we been in Your sight, O LORD.
18 We have been with child, we have been in pain;
We have, as it were, brought forth wind;
We have not accomplished any deliverance in the earth,
Nor have the inhabitants of the world fallen.

19 Your dead shall live;
Together with my dead body[a] they shall arise.
Awake and sing, you who dwell in dust;
For your dew *is like* the dew of herbs,
And the earth shall cast out the dead.

Take Refuge from the Coming Judgment

20 Come, my people, enter your chambers,
And shut your doors behind you;
Hide yourself, as it were, for a little moment,
Until the indignation is past.
21 For behold, the LORD comes out of His place
To punish the inhabitants of the earth for their iniquity;
The earth will also disclose her blood,
And will no more cover her slain.

27 In that day the LORD with His severe sword, great and strong,
Will punish Leviathan the fleeing serpent,
Leviathan that twisted serpent;
And He will slay the reptile that *is* in the sea.

The Restoration of Israel

2 In that day sing to her,
"A vineyard of red wine![a]
3 I, the LORD, keep it,
I water it every moment;
Lest any hurt it,
I keep it night and day.
4 Fury *is* not in Me.
Who would set briers *and* thorns
Against Me in battle?

26:19 [a] Following Masoretic Text and Vulgate; Syriac and Targum read *their dead bodies;* Septuagint reads *those in the tombs.* 27:2 [a] Following Masoretic Text (Kittel's *Biblia Hebraica*), Bomberg, and Vulgate; Masoretic Text (*Biblia Hebraica Stuttgartensia*), some Hebrew manuscripts, and Septuagint read *delight;* Targum reads *choice vineyard.*

I would go through them,
I would burn them together.
5 Or let him take hold of My strength,
That he may make peace with Me;
And he shall make peace with Me."

6 Those who come He shall cause to take root in Jacob;
Israel shall blossom and bud,
And fill the face of the world with fruit.

7 Has He struck Israel as He struck those who struck him?
Or has He been slain according to the slaughter of those who were slain by Him?
8 In measure, by sending it away,
You contended with it.
He removes *it* by His rough wind
In the day of the east wind.
9 Therefore by this the iniquity of Jacob will be covered;
And this *is* all the fruit of taking away his sin:
When he makes all the stones of the altar
Like chalkstones that are beaten to dust,
Wooden images[a] and incense altars shall not stand.

10 Yet the fortified city *will be* desolate,
The habitation forsaken and left like a wilderness;
There the calf will feed, and there it will lie down
And consume its branches.
11 When its boughs are withered, they will be broken off;
The women come *and* set them on fire.
For it *is* a people of no understanding;
Therefore He who made them will not have mercy on them,
And He who formed them will show them no favor.

12 And it shall come to pass in that day
That the LORD will thresh,
From the channel of the River[a] to the Brook of Egypt;
And you will be gathered one by one,
O you children of Israel.

13 So it shall be in that day:
The great trumpet will be blown;
They will come, who are about to perish in the land of Assyria,
And they who are outcasts in the land of Egypt,
And shall worship the LORD in the holy mount at Jerusalem.

Woe to Ephraim and Jerusalem

28 Woe to the crown of pride, to the drunkards of Ephraim,
Whose glorious beauty *is* a fading flower
Which *is* at the head of the verdant valleys,
To those who are overcome with wine!
2 Behold, the Lord has a mighty and strong one,
Like a tempest of hail and a destroying storm,
Like a flood of mighty waters overflowing,
Who will bring *them* down to the earth with *His* hand.
3 The crown of pride, the drunkards of Ephraim,
Will be trampled underfoot;
4 And the glorious beauty is a fading flower
Which *is* at the head of the verdant valley,
Like the first fruit before the summer,
Which an observer sees;
He eats it up while it is still in his hand.

5 In that day the LORD of hosts will be
For a crown of glory and a diadem of beauty
To the remnant of His people,
6 For a spirit of justice to him who sits in judgment,
And for strength to those who turn back the battle at the gate.

7 But they also have erred through wine,
And through intoxicating drink are out of the way;
The priest and the prophet have erred through intoxicating drink,
They are swallowed up by wine,
They are out of the way through intoxicating drink;
They err in vision, they stumble *in* judgment.
8 For all tables are full of vomit *and* filth;
No place *is clean*.

9 "Whom will he teach knowledge?
And whom will he make to understand the message?

27:9 [a] Hebrew *Asherim*, Canaanite deities 27:12 [a] That is, the Euphrates

Those *just* weaned from milk?
Those *just* drawn from the breasts?
10 For precept *must be* upon precept,
precept upon precept,
Line upon line, line upon line,
Here a little, there a little."

11 For with stammering lips and another
tongue
He will speak to this people,
12 To whom He said, "This *is* the rest *with
which*
You may cause the weary to rest,"
And, "This *is* the refreshing";
Yet they would not hear.
13 But the word of the LORD was to them,
"Precept upon precept, precept upon
precept,
Line upon line, line upon line,
Here a little, there a little,"
That they might go and fall backward,
and be broken
And snared and caught.

14 Therefore hear the word of the LORD,
you scornful men,
Who rule this people who *are* in
Jerusalem,
15 Because you have said, "We have made a
covenant with death,
And with Sheol we are in agreement.
When the overflowing scourge passes
through,
It will not come to us,
For we have made lies our refuge,
And under falsehood we have hidden
ourselves."

A Cornerstone in Zion

16 Therefore thus says the Lord GOD:

"Behold, I lay in Zion a stone for a
foundation,
A tried stone, a precious cornerstone, a
sure foundation;
Whoever believes will not act hastily.
17 Also I will make justice the measuring
line,
And righteousness the plummet;
The hail will sweep away the refuge of
lies,
And the waters will overflow the hiding
place.
18 Your covenant with death will be
annulled,
And your agreement with Sheol will not
stand;
When the overflowing scourge passes
through,
Then you will be trampled down by it.
19 As often as it goes out it will take you;
For morning by morning it will pass
over,
And by day and by night;
It will be a terror just to understand the
report."

20 For the bed is too short to stretch out *on*,
And the covering so narrow that one
cannot wrap himself *in it*.
21 For the LORD will rise up as *at* Mount
Perazim,
He will be angry as in the Valley of
Gibeon—
That He may do His work, His awesome
work,
And bring to pass His act, His unusual
act.
22 Now therefore, do not be mockers,
Lest your bonds be made strong;
For I have heard from the Lord GOD of
hosts,
A destruction determined even upon
the whole earth.

Listen to the Teaching of God

23 Give ear and hear my voice,
Listen and hear my speech.
24 Does the plowman keep plowing all day
to sow?
Does he keep turning his soil and
breaking the clods?
25 When he has leveled its surface,
Does he not sow the black cummin
And scatter the cummin,
Plant the wheat in rows,
The barley in the appointed place,
And the spelt in its place?
26 For He instructs him in right judgment,
His God teaches him.

27 For the black cummin is not threshed
with a threshing sledge,
Nor is a cartwheel rolled over the
cummin;
But the black cummin is beaten out
with a stick,
And the cummin with a rod.
28 Bread *flour* must be ground;
Therefore he does not thresh it forever,
Break *it with* his cartwheel,
Or crush it *with* his horsemen.

29 This also comes from the LORD of hosts,
Who is wonderful in counsel *and* excellent in guidance.

Woe to Jerusalem

29 "Woe to Ariel,[a] to Ariel, the city *where* David dwelt!
Add year to year;
Let feasts come around.
2 Yet I will distress Ariel;
There shall be heaviness and sorrow,
And it shall be to Me as Ariel.
3 I will encamp against you all around,
I will lay siege against you with a mound,
And I will raise siegeworks against you.
4 You shall be brought down,
You shall speak out of the ground;
Your speech shall be low, out of the dust;
Your voice shall be like a medium's, out of the ground;
And your speech shall whisper out of the dust.

5 "Moreover the multitude of your foes
Shall be like fine dust,
And the multitude of the terrible ones
Like chaff that passes away;
Yes, it shall be in an instant, suddenly.
6 You will be punished by the LORD of hosts
With thunder and earthquake and great noise,
With storm and tempest
And the flame of devouring fire.
7 The multitude of all the nations who fight against Ariel,
Even all who fight against her and her fortress,
And distress her,
Shall be as a dream of a night vision.
8 It shall even be as when a hungry man dreams,
And look—he eats;
But he awakes, and his soul is still empty;
Or as when a thirsty man dreams,
And look—he drinks;
But he awakes, and indeed *he is* faint,
And his soul still craves:
So the multitude of all the nations shall be,
Who fight against Mount Zion."

The Blindness of Disobedience

9 Pause and wonder!
Blind yourselves and be blind!
They are drunk, but not with wine;
They stagger, but not with intoxicating drink.
10 For the LORD has poured out on you
The spirit of deep sleep,
And has closed your eyes, namely, the prophets;
And He has covered your heads, *namely,* the seers.

11 The whole vision has become to you like
the words of a book that is sealed, which *men*
deliver to one who is literate, saying, "Read
this, please."
And he says, "I cannot, for it *is* sealed."
12 Then the book is delivered to one who is
illiterate, saying, "Read this, please."
And he says, "I am not literate."
13 Therefore the Lord said:

"Inasmuch as these people draw near with their mouths
And honor Me with their lips,
But have removed their hearts far from Me,
And their fear toward Me is taught by the commandment of men,
14 Therefore, behold, I will again do a marvelous work
Among this people,
A marvelous work and a wonder;
For the wisdom of their wise *men* shall perish,
And the understanding of their prudent *men* shall be hidden."

15 Woe to those who seek deep to hide their counsel far from the LORD,
And their works are in the dark;
They say, "Who sees us?" and, "Who knows us?"
16 Surely you have things turned around!
Shall the potter be esteemed as the clay;
For shall the thing made say of him who made it,
"He did not make me"?
Or shall the thing formed say of him who formed it,
"He has no understanding"?

29:1 [a] That is, Jerusalem

Future Recovery of Wisdom

17 *Is* it not yet a very little while
Till Lebanon shall be turned into a fruitful field,
And the fruitful field be esteemed as a forest?
18 In that day the deaf shall hear the words of the book,
And the eyes of the blind shall see out of obscurity and out of darkness.
19 The humble also shall increase *their* joy in the LORD,
And the poor among men shall rejoice
In the Holy One of Israel.
20 For the terrible one is brought to nothing,
The scornful one is consumed,
And all who watch for iniquity are cut off—
21 Who make a man an offender by a word,
And lay a snare for him who reproves in the gate,
And turn aside the just by empty words.

22 Therefore thus says the LORD, who redeemed Abraham, concerning the house of
Jacob:

"Jacob shall not now be ashamed,
Nor shall his face now grow pale;
23 But when he sees his children,
The work of My hands, in his midst,
They will hallow My name,
And hallow the Holy One of Jacob,
And fear the God of Israel.
24 These also who erred in spirit will come to understanding,
And those who complained will learn doctrine."

Futile Confidence in Egypt

30 "Woe to the rebellious children," says the LORD,
"Who take counsel, but not of Me,
And who devise plans, but not of My Spirit,
That they may add sin to sin;
2 Who walk to go down to Egypt,
And have not asked My advice,
To strengthen themselves in the strength of Pharaoh,
And to trust in the shadow of Egypt!
3 Therefore the strength of Pharaoh
Shall be your shame,
And trust in the shadow of Egypt
Shall be *your* humiliation.
4 For his princes were at Zoan,
And his ambassadors came to Hanes.
5 They were all ashamed of a people *who* could not benefit them,
Or be help or benefit,
But a shame and also a reproach."

6 The burden against the beasts of the
South.

Through a land of trouble and anguish,
From which *came* the lioness and lion,
The viper and fiery flying serpent,
They will carry their riches on the backs of young donkeys,
And their treasures on the humps of camels,
To a people *who* shall not profit;
7 For the Egyptians shall help in vain and to no purpose.
Therefore I have called her
Rahab-Hem-Shebeth.[a]

A Rebellious People

8 Now go, write it before them on a tablet,
And note it on a scroll,
That it may be for time to come,
Forever and ever:
9 That this *is* a rebellious people,
Lying children,
Children *who* will not hear the law of the LORD;
10 Who say to the seers, "Do not see,"
And to the prophets, "Do not prophesy to us right things;
Speak to us smooth things, prophesy deceits.
11 Get out of the way,
Turn aside from the path,
Cause the Holy One of Israel
To cease from before us."

12 Therefore thus says the Holy One of
Israel:

"Because you despise this word,
And trust in oppression and perversity,
And rely on them,
13 Therefore this iniquity shall be to you
Like a breach ready to fall,
A bulge in a high wall,
Whose breaking comes suddenly, in an instant.
14 And He shall break it like the breaking of the potter's vessel,

30:7 [a] Literally *Rahab Sits Idle*

Which is broken in pieces;
He shall not spare.
So there shall not be found among its fragments
A shard to take fire from the hearth,
Or to take water from the cistern."

15 For thus says the Lord GOD, the Holy One of Israel:

"In returning and rest you shall be saved;
In quietness and confidence shall be your strength."
But you would not,
16 And you said, "No, for we will flee on horses"—
Therefore you shall flee!
And, "We will ride on swift *horses*"—
Therefore those who pursue you shall be swift!

17 One thousand *shall flee* at the threat of one,
At the threat of five you shall flee,
Till you are left as a pole on top of a mountain
And as a banner on a hill.

God Will Be Gracious

18 Therefore the LORD will wait, that He may be gracious to you;
And therefore He will be exalted, that He may have mercy on you.
For the LORD *is* a God of justice;
Blessed *are* all those who wait for Him.

19 For the people shall dwell in Zion at Jerusalem;
You shall weep no more.
He will be very gracious to you at the sound of your cry;
When He hears it, He will answer you.
20 And *though* the Lord gives you
The bread of adversity and the water of affliction,
Yet your teachers will not be moved into a corner anymore,
But your eyes shall see your teachers.
21 Your ears shall hear a word behind you, saying,
"This *is* the way, walk in it,"
Whenever you turn to the right hand
Or whenever you turn to the left.
22 You will also defile the covering of your images of silver,
And the ornament of your molded images of gold.
You will throw them away as an unclean thing;
You will say to them, "Get away!"

23 Then He will give the rain for your seed
With which you sow the ground,
And bread of the increase of the earth;
It will be fat and plentiful.
In that day your cattle will feed
In large pastures.
24 Likewise the oxen and the young donkeys that work the ground
Will eat cured fodder,
Which has been winnowed with the shovel and fan.
25 There will be on every high mountain
And on every high hill
Rivers *and* streams of waters,
In the day of the great slaughter,
When the towers fall.
26 Moreover the light of the moon will be as the light of the sun,
And the light of the sun will be sevenfold,
As the light of seven days,
In the day that the LORD binds up the bruise of His people
And heals the stroke of their wound.

Judgment on Assyria

27 Behold, the name of the LORD comes from afar,
Burning *with* His anger,
And *His* burden *is* heavy;
His lips are full of indignation,
And His tongue like a devouring fire.
28 His breath is like an overflowing stream,
Which reaches up to the neck,
To sift the nations with the sieve of futility;
And *there shall be* a bridle in the jaws of the people,
Causing *them* to err.

29 You shall have a song
As in the night *when* a holy festival is kept,
And gladness of heart as when one goes with a flute,
To come into the mountain of the LORD,
To the Mighty One of Israel.
30 The LORD will cause His glorious voice to be heard,
And show the descent of His arm,
With the indignation of *His* anger

And the flame of a devouring fire,
With scattering, tempest, and hailstones.
31 For through the voice of the LORD
Assyria will be beaten down,
As He strikes with the rod.
32 And *in* every place where the staff of punishment passes,
Which the LORD lays on him,
It will be with tambourines and harps;
And in battles of brandishing He will fight with it.
33 For Tophet *was* established of old,
Yes, for the king it is prepared.
He has made *it* deep and large;
Its pyre *is* fire with much wood;
The breath of the LORD, like a stream of brimstone,
Kindles it.

The Folly of Not Trusting God

31 Woe to those who go down to Egypt for help,
And rely on horses,
Who trust in chariots because *they are* many,
And in horsemen because they are very strong,
But who do not look to the Holy One of Israel,
Nor seek the LORD!
2 Yet He also *is* wise and will bring disaster,
And will not call back His words,
But will arise against the house of evildoers,
And against the help of those who work iniquity.
3 Now the Egyptians *are* men, and not God;
And their horses are flesh, and not spirit.
When the LORD stretches out His hand,
Both he who helps will fall,
And he who is helped will fall down;
They all will perish together.

God Will Deliver Jerusalem

4For thus the LORD has spoken to me:

"As a lion roars,
And a young lion over his prey
(When a multitude of shepherds is summoned against him,
He will not be afraid of their voice
Nor be disturbed by their noise),
So the LORD of hosts will come down
To fight for Mount Zion and for its hill.
5 Like birds flying about,
So will the LORD of hosts defend Jerusalem.
Defending, He will also deliver *it;*
Passing over, He will preserve *it.*"

6Return *to Him* against whom the children of Israel have deeply revolted. 7For in
that day every man shall throw away his idols
of silver and his idols of gold—sin, which
your own hands have made for yourselves.

8 "Then Assyria shall fall by a sword not of man,
And a sword not of mankind shall devour him.
But he shall flee from the sword,
And his young men shall become forced labor.
9 He shall cross over to his stronghold for fear,
And his princes shall be afraid of the banner,"
Says the LORD,
Whose fire *is* in Zion
And whose furnace *is* in Jerusalem.

A Reign of Righteousness

32 Behold, a king will reign in righteousness,
And princes will rule with justice.
2 A man will be as a hiding place from the wind,
And a cover from the tempest,
As rivers of water in a dry place,
As the shadow of a great rock in a weary land.
3 The eyes of those who see will not be dim,
And the ears of those who hear will listen.
4 Also the heart of the rash will understand knowledge,
And the tongue of the stammerers will be ready to speak plainly.

5 The foolish person will no longer be called generous,
Nor the miser said *to be* bountiful;
6 For the foolish person will speak foolishness,
And his heart will work iniquity:
To practice ungodliness,
To utter error against the LORD,
To keep the hungry unsatisfied,

And he will cause the drink of the thirsty to fail.
7 Also the schemes of the schemer *are* evil;
He devises wicked plans
To destroy the poor with lying words,
Even when the needy speaks justice.
8 But a generous man devises generous things,
And by generosity he shall stand.

Consequences of Complacency

9 Rise up, you women who are at ease,
Hear my voice;
You complacent daughters,
Give ear to my speech.
10 In a year and *some* days
You will be troubled, you complacent women;
For the vintage will fail,
The gathering will not come.
11 Tremble, you *women* who are at ease;
Be troubled, you complacent ones;
Strip yourselves, make yourselves bare,
And gird *sackcloth* on *your* waists.

12 People shall mourn upon their breasts
For the pleasant fields, for the fruitful vine.
13 On the land of my people will come up thorns *and* briers,
Yes, on all the happy homes *in* the joyous city;
14 Because the palaces will be forsaken,
The bustling city will be deserted.
The forts and towers will become lairs forever,
A joy of wild donkeys, a pasture of flocks—
15 Until the Spirit is poured upon us from on high,
And the wilderness becomes a fruitful field,
And the fruitful field is counted as a forest.

The Peace of God's Reign

16 Then justice will dwell in the wilderness,
And righteousness remain in the fruitful field.
17 The work of righteousness will be peace,
And the effect of righteousness, quietness and assurance forever.
18 My people will dwell in a peaceful habitation,
In secure dwellings, and in quiet resting places,
19 Though hail comes down on the forest,
And the city is brought low in humiliation.

20 Blessed *are* you who sow beside all waters,
Who send out freely the feet of the ox and the donkey.

A Prayer in Deep Distress

33 Woe to you who plunder, though you *have* not *been* plundered;
And you who deal treacherously, though they have not dealt treacherously with you!
When you cease plundering,
You will be plundered;
When you make an end of dealing treacherously,
They will deal treacherously with you.

2 O LORD, be gracious to us;
We have waited for You.
Be their[a] arm every morning,
Our salvation also in the time of trouble.
3 At the noise of the tumult the people shall flee;
When You lift Yourself up, the nations shall be scattered;
4 And Your plunder shall be gathered
Like the gathering of the caterpillar;
As the running to and fro of locusts,
He shall run upon them.

5 The LORD is exalted, for He dwells on high;
He has filled Zion with justice and righteousness.
6 Wisdom and knowledge will be the stability of your times,
And the strength of salvation;
The fear of the LORD *is* His treasure.

7 Surely their valiant ones shall cry outside,
The ambassadors of peace shall weep bitterly.
8 The highways lie waste,
The traveling man ceases.
He has broken the covenant,

33:2 [a] Septuagint omits *their;* Syriac, Targum, and Vulgate read *our.*

He has despised the cities,[a]
He regards no man.
9 The earth mourns *and* languishes,
Lebanon is shamed *and* shriveled;
Sharon is like a wilderness,
And Bashan and Carmel shake off *their* fruits.

Impending Judgment on Zion

10 "Now I will rise," says the LORD;
"Now I will be exalted,
Now I will lift Myself up.
11 You shall conceive chaff,
You shall bring forth stubble;
Your breath, *as* fire, shall devour you.
12 And the people shall be *like* the burnings of lime;
Like thorns cut up they shall be burned in the fire.
13 Hear, you *who are* afar off, what I have done;
And you *who are* near, acknowledge My might."

14 The sinners in Zion are afraid;
Fearfulness has seized the hypocrites:
"Who among us shall dwell with the devouring fire?
Who among us shall dwell with everlasting burnings?"
15 He who walks righteously and speaks uprightly,
He who despises the gain of oppressions,
Who gestures with his hands, refusing bribes,
Who stops his ears from hearing of bloodshed,
And shuts his eyes from seeing evil:
16 He will dwell on high;
His place of defense *will be* the fortress of rocks;
Bread will be given him,
His water *will be* sure.

The Land of the Majestic King

17 Your eyes will see the King in His beauty;
They will see the land that is very far off.
18 Your heart will meditate on terror:
"Where *is* the scribe?
Where *is* he who weighs?
Where *is* he who counts the towers?"
19 You will not see a fierce people,
A people of obscure speech, beyond perception,
Of a stammering tongue *that you* cannot understand.

20 Look upon Zion, the city of our appointed feasts;
Your eyes will see Jerusalem, a quiet home,
A tabernacle *that* will not be taken down;
Not one of its stakes will ever be removed,
Nor will any of its cords be broken.
21 But there the majestic LORD *will be* for us
A place of broad rivers *and* streams,
In which no galley with oars will sail,
Nor majestic ships pass by
22 (For the LORD *is* our Judge,
The LORD *is* our Lawgiver,
The LORD *is* our King;
He will save us);
23 Your tackle is loosed,
They could not strengthen their mast,
They could not spread the sail.

Then the prey of great plunder is divided;
The lame take the prey.
24 And the inhabitant will not say, "I am sick";
The people who dwell in it *will be* forgiven *their* iniquity.

Judgment on the Nations

34 Come near, you nations, to hear;
And heed, you people!
Let the earth hear, and all that is in it,
The world and all things that come forth from it.
2 For the indignation of the LORD *is* against all nations,
And *His* fury against all their armies;
He has utterly destroyed them,
He has given them over to the slaughter.
3 Also their slain shall be thrown out;
Their stench shall rise from their corpses,
And the mountains shall be melted with their blood.
4 All the host of heaven shall be dissolved,

33:8 [a] Following Masoretic Text and Vulgate; Dead Sea Scrolls read *witnesses;* Septuagint omits *cities;* Targum reads *They have been removed from their cities.*

And the heavens shall be rolled up like
a scroll;
All their host shall fall down
As the leaf falls from the vine,
And as *fruit* falling from a fig tree.

5 "For My sword shall be bathed in heaven;
Indeed it shall come down on Edom,
And on the people of My curse, for
judgment.
6 The sword of the LORD is filled with
blood,
It is made overflowing with fatness,
With the blood of lambs and goats,
With the fat of the kidneys of rams.
For the LORD has a sacrifice in Bozrah,
And a great slaughter in the land of
Edom.
7 The wild oxen shall come down with
them,
And the young bulls with the mighty
bulls;
Their land shall be soaked with blood,
And their dust saturated with fatness."

8 For *it is* the day of the LORD's vengeance,
The year of recompense for the cause
of Zion.
9 Its streams shall be turned into pitch,
And its dust into brimstone;
Its land shall become burning pitch.
10 It shall not be quenched night or day;
Its smoke shall ascend forever.
From generation to generation it shall
lie waste;
No one shall pass through it forever and
ever.
11 But the pelican and the porcupine shall
possess it,
Also the owl and the raven shall dwell
in it.
And He shall stretch out over it
The line of confusion and the stones of
emptiness.
12 They shall call its nobles to the
kingdom,
But none *shall be* there, and all its
princes shall be nothing.

13 And thorns shall come up in its palaces,
Nettles and brambles in its fortresses;
It shall be a habitation of jackals,
A courtyard for ostriches.
14 The wild beasts of the desert shall also
meet with the jackals,
And the wild goat shall bleat to its
companion;
Also the night creature shall rest there,
And find for herself a place of rest.
15 There the arrow snake shall make her
nest and lay *eggs*
And hatch, and gather *them* under her
shadow;
There also shall the hawks be gathered,
Every one with her mate.

16 "Search from the book of the LORD, and
read:
Not one of these shall fail;
Not one shall lack her mate.
For My mouth has commanded it, and
His Spirit has gathered them.
17 He has cast the lot for them,
And His hand has divided it among
them with a measuring line.
They shall possess it forever;
From generation to generation they
shall dwell in it."

The Future Glory of Zion

35 The wilderness and the wasteland
shall be glad for them,
And the desert shall rejoice and blossom
as the rose;
2 It shall blossom abundantly and rejoice,
Even with joy and singing.
The glory of Lebanon shall be given to it,
The excellence of Carmel and Sharon.
They shall see the glory of the LORD,
The excellency of our God.

3 Strengthen the weak hands,
And make firm the feeble knees.
4 Say to those *who are* fearful-hearted,
"Be strong, do not fear!
Behold, your God will come *with*
vengeance,
With the recompense of God;
He will come and save you."

5 Then the eyes of the blind shall be
opened,
And the ears of the deaf shall be
unstopped.
6 Then the lame shall leap like a deer,
And the tongue of the dumb sing.
For waters shall burst forth in the
wilderness,
And streams in the desert.
7 The parched ground shall become a
pool,
And the thirsty land springs of water;

In the habitation of jackals, where each
lay,
There shall be grass with reeds and
rushes.

8 A highway shall be there, and a road,
And it shall be called the Highway of
Holiness.
The unclean shall not pass over it,
But it *shall be* for others.
Whoever walks the road, although a
fool,
Shall not go astray.
9 No lion shall be there,
Nor shall *any* ravenous beast go up on it;
It shall not be found there.
But the redeemed shall walk *there,*
10 And the ransomed of the LORD shall
return,
And come to Zion with singing,
With everlasting joy on their heads.
They shall obtain joy and gladness,
And sorrow and sighing shall flee away.

Sennacherib Boasts Against the LORD

36 Now it came to pass in the fourteenth year of King Hezekiah
that Sennacherib king of Assyria came up
against all the fortified cities of Judah and
took them. 2Then the king of Assyria sent
the Rabshakeh[a] with a great army from Lachish to King Hezekiah at Jerusalem. And
he stood by the aqueduct from the upper
pool, on the highway to the Fuller's Field.
3And Eliakim the son of Hilkiah, who was
over the household, Shebna the scribe, and
Joah the son of Asaph, the recorder, came
out to him.

4Then *the* Rabshakeh said to them, "Say
now to Hezekiah, 'Thus says the great king,
the king of Assyria: "What confidence is
this in which you trust? 5I say you speak of
having plans and power for war; but *they are*
mere words. Now in whom do you trust, that
you rebel against me? 6Look! You are trusting in the staff of this broken reed, Egypt, on
which if a man leans, it will go into his hand
and pierce it. So *is* Pharaoh king of Egypt to
all who trust in him.

7"But if you say to me, 'We trust in the
LORD our God,' *is it not* He whose high
places and whose altars Hezekiah has tak-
en away, and said to Judah and Jerusalem,
'You shall worship before this altar'?"' 8Now
therefore, I urge you, give a pledge to my
master the king of Assyria, and I will give
you two thousand horses—if you are able
on your part to put riders on them! 9How
then will you repel one captain of the least
of my master's servants, and put your trust
in Egypt for chariots and horsemen? 10Have
I now come up without the LORD against this
land to destroy it? The LORD said to me, 'Go
up against this land, and destroy it.'"

11Then Eliakim, Shebna, and Joah said
to *the* Rabshakeh, "Please speak to your servants in Aramaic, for we understand *it;* and
do not speak to us in Hebrew[a] in the hearing
of the people who *are* on the wall."

12But *the* Rabshakeh said, "Has my master sent me to your master and to you to
speak these words, and not to the men who
sit on the wall, who will eat and drink their
own waste with you?"

13Then *the* Rabshakeh stood and called
out with a loud voice in Hebrew, and said,
"Hear the words of the great king, the king
of Assyria! 14Thus says the king: 'Do not let
Hezekiah deceive you, for he will not be able
to deliver you; 15nor let Hezekiah make you
trust in the LORD, saying, "The LORD will
surely deliver us; this city will not be given
into the hand of the king of Assyria."' 16Do
not listen to Hezekiah; for thus says the king
of Assyria: 'Make *peace* with me *by a* present
and come out to me; and every one of you
eat from his own vine and every one from
his own fig tree, and every one of you drink
the waters of his own cistern; 17until I come
and take you away to a land like your own
land, a land of grain and new wine, a land of
bread and vineyards. 18*Beware* lest Hezekiah
persuade you, saying, "The LORD will deliver
us." Has any one of the gods of the nations
delivered its land from the hand of the king
of Assyria? 19Where *are* the gods of Hamath
and Arpad? Where *are* the gods of Sepharvaim? Indeed, have they delivered Samaria
from my hand? 20Who among all the gods
of these lands have delivered their countries
from my hand, that the LORD should deliver
Jerusalem from my hand?'"

21But they held their peace and answered
him not a word; for the king's command-
ment was, "Do not answer him." 22Then
Eliakim the son of Hilkiah, who *was* over the

36:2 [a] A title, probably *Chief of Staff* or *Governor*
36:11 [a] Literally *Judean*

household, Shebna the scribe, and Joah the
son of Asaph, the recorder, came to Hezekiah with *their* clothes torn, and told him the
words of *the* Rabshakeh.

Isaiah Assures Deliverance

37 And so it was, when King Hezekiah heard *it,* that he tore his clothes,
covered himself with sackcloth, and went
into the house of the LORD. 2Then he sent
Eliakim, who *was* over the household, Shebna the scribe, and the elders of the priests,
covered with sackcloth, to Isaiah the prophet, the son of Amoz. 3And they said to him,
"Thus says Hezekiah: 'This day *is* a day of
trouble and rebuke and blasphemy; for the
children have come to birth, but *there is* no
strength to bring them forth. 4It may be that
the LORD your God will hear the words of
the Rabshakeh, whom his master the king of
Assyria has sent to reproach the living God,
and will rebuke the words which the LORD
your God has heard. Therefore lift up *your*
prayer for the remnant that is left.'"
5So the servants of King Hezekiah came
to Isaiah. 6And Isaiah said to them, "Thus
you shall say to your master, 'Thus says the
LORD: "Do not be afraid of the words which
you have heard, with which the servants of
the king of Assyria have blasphemed Me.
7Surely I will send a spirit upon him, and
he shall hear a rumor and return to his
own land; and I will cause him to fall by the
sword in his own land."'"

Sennacherib's Threat and Hezekiah's Prayer

8Then *the* Rabshakeh returned, and
found the king of Assyria warring against
Libnah, for he heard that he had departed
from Lachish. 9And the king heard concerning Tirhakah king of Ethiopia, "He has
come out to make war with you." So when
he heard *it,* he sent messengers to Hezekiah,
saying, 10"Thus you shall speak to Hezekiah
king of Judah, saying: 'Do not let your God
in whom you trust deceive you, saying, "Jerusalem shall not be given into the hand of
the king of Assyria." 11Look! You have heard
what the kings of Assyria have done to all
lands by utterly destroying them; and shall
you be delivered? 12Have the gods of the nations delivered those whom my fathers have
destroyed, Gozan and Haran and Rezeph,
and the people of Eden who *were* in Telassar?
13Where *is* the king of Hamath, the king of
Arpad, and the king of the city of Sepharvaim, Hena, and Ivah?'"
14And Hezekiah received the letter from
the hand of the messengers, and read it;
and Hezekiah went up to the house of the
LORD, and spread it before the LORD. 15Then
Hezekiah prayed to the LORD, saying: 16"O
LORD of hosts, God of Israel, *the One* who
dwells *between* the cherubim, You *are* God,
You alone, of all the kingdoms of the earth.
You have made heaven and earth. 17Incline
Your ear, O LORD, and hear; open Your eyes,
O LORD, and see; and hear all the words of
Sennacherib, which he has sent to reproach
the living God. 18Truly, LORD, the kings of
Assyria have laid waste all the nations and
their lands, 19and have cast their gods into
the fire; for they *were* not gods, but the work
of men's hands—wood and stone. Therefore
they destroyed them. 20Now therefore, O
LORD our God, save us from his hand, that
all the kingdoms of the earth may know that
You *are* the LORD, You alone."

The Word of the LORD Concerning Sennacherib

21Then Isaiah the son of Amoz sent to
Hezekiah, saying, "Thus says the LORD God
of Israel, 'Because you have prayed to Me
against Sennacherib king of Assyria, 22this
is the word which the LORD has spoken concerning him:

"The virgin, the daughter of Zion,
Has despised you, laughed you to scorn;
The daughter of Jerusalem
Has shaken *her* head behind your back!

23 "Whom have you reproached and
blasphemed?
Against whom have you raised *your*
voice,
And lifted up your eyes on high?
Against the Holy One of Israel.
24 By your servants you have reproached
the Lord,
And said, 'By the multitude of my
chariots
I have come up to the height of the
mountains,
To the limits of Lebanon;
I will cut down its tall cedars
And its choice cypress trees;
I will enter its farthest height,
To its fruitful forest.

25 I have dug and drunk water,
And with the soles of my feet I have dried up
All the brooks of defense.'

26 "Did you not hear long ago
How I made it,
From ancient times that I formed it?
Now I have brought it to pass,
That you should be
For crushing fortified cities *into* heaps of ruins.
27 Therefore their inhabitants *had* little power;
They were dismayed and confounded;
They were *as* the grass of the field
And the green herb,
As the grass on the housetops
And *grain* blighted before it is grown.

28 "But I know your dwelling place,
Your going out and your coming in,
And your rage against Me.
29 Because your rage against Me and your tumult
Have come up to My ears,
Therefore I will put My hook in your nose
And My bridle in your lips,
And I will turn you back
By the way which you came."'

30 "This *shall be* a sign to you:

You shall eat this year such as grows of itself,
And the second year what springs from the same;
Also in the third year sow and reap,
Plant vineyards and eat the fruit of them.
31 And the remnant who have escaped of the house of Judah
Shall again take root downward,
And bear fruit upward.
32 For out of Jerusalem shall go a remnant,
And those who escape from Mount Zion.
The zeal of the LORD of hosts will do this.

33 "Therefore thus says the LORD concerning the king of Assyria:

'He shall not come into this city,
Nor shoot an arrow there,
Nor come before it with shield,
Nor build a siege mound against it.
34 By the way that he came,
By the same shall he return;
And he shall not come into this city,'
Says the LORD.
35 'For I will defend this city, to save it
For My own sake and for My servant David's sake.'"

Sennacherib's Defeat and Death

36 Then the angel[a] of the LORD went out,
and killed in the camp of the Assyrians
one hundred and eighty-five thousand;
and when *people* arose early in the morning, there were the corpses—all dead. 37 So
Sennacherib king of Assyria departed and
went away, returned *home,* and remained at
Nineveh. 38 Now it came to pass, as he was
worshiping in the house of Nisroch his god,
that his sons Adrammelech and Sharezer
struck him down with the sword; and they
escaped into the land of Ararat. Then Esarhaddon his son reigned in his place.

Hezekiah's Life Extended

38 In those days Hezekiah was sick
and near death. And Isaiah the
prophet, the son of Amoz, went to him and
said to him, "Thus says the LORD: 'Set your
house in order, for you shall die and not
live.'"

2 Then Hezekiah turned his face toward
the wall, and prayed to the LORD, 3 and said,
"Remember now, O LORD, I pray, how I have
walked before You in truth and with a loyal
heart, and have done *what is* good in Your
sight." And Hezekiah wept bitterly.

4 And the word of the LORD came to Isaiah, saying, 5 "Go and tell Hezekiah, 'Thus
says the LORD, the God of David your father:
"I have heard your prayer, I have seen your
tears; surely I will add to your days fifteen
years. 6 I will deliver you and this city from
the hand of the king of Assyria, and I will
defend this city."' 7 And this *is* the sign to you
from the LORD, that the LORD will do this
thing which He has spoken: 8 Behold, I will
bring the shadow on the sundial, which has
gone down with the sun on the sundial of
Ahaz, ten degrees backward." So the sun
returned ten degrees on the dial by which it
had gone down.

9 This is the writing of Hezekiah king of

37:36 [a] Or *Angel*

Judah, when he had been sick and had recovered from his sickness:

10 I said,
"In the prime of my life
I shall go to the gates of Sheol;
I am deprived of the remainder of my
years."
11 I said,
"I shall not see YAH,
The LORD[a] in the land of the living;
I shall observe man no more among the
inhabitants of the world.[b]
12 My life span is gone,
Taken from me like a shepherd's tent;
I have cut off my life like a weaver.
He cuts me off from the loom;
From day until night You make an end
of me.
13 I have considered until morning—
Like a lion,
So He breaks all my bones;
From day until night You make an end
of me.
14 Like a crane *or* a swallow, so I chattered;
I mourned like a dove;
My eyes fail *from looking* upward.
O LORD,[a] I am oppressed;
Undertake for me!

15 "What shall I say?
He has both spoken to me,[a]
And He Himself has done *it*.
I shall walk carefully all my years
In the bitterness of my soul.
16 O Lord, by these *things men* live;
And in all these *things is* the life of my
spirit;
So You will restore me and make me
live.
17 Indeed *it was* for *my own* peace
That I had great bitterness;
But You have lovingly *delivered* my soul
from the pit of corruption,
For You have cast all my sins behind
Your back.
18 For Sheol cannot thank You,
Death cannot praise You;
Those who go down to the pit cannot
hope for Your truth.
19 The living, the living man, he shall
praise You,
As I *do* this day;
The father shall make known Your
truth to the children.

20 "The LORD *was ready* to save me;
Therefore we will sing my songs with
stringed instruments
All the days of our life, in the house of
the LORD."

21 Now Isaiah had said, "Let them take a
lump of figs, and apply *it* as a poultice on the
boil, and he shall recover."
22 And Hezekiah had said, "What *is* the
sign that I shall go up to the house of the
LORD?"

The Babylonian Envoys

39 At that time Merodach-Baladan[a]
the son of Baladan, king of Bab-
ylon, sent letters and a present to Hezekiah,
for he heard that he had been sick and had
recovered. 2 And Hezekiah was pleased with
them, and showed them the house of his
treasures—the silver and gold, the spices
and precious ointment, and all his armory—
all that was found among his treasures.
There was nothing in his house or in all his
dominion that Hezekiah did not show them.
3 Then Isaiah the prophet went to King
Hezekiah, and said to him, "What did these
men say, and from where did they come to
you?"
So Hezekiah said, "They came to me
from a far country, from Babylon."
4 And he said, "What have they seen in
your house?"
So Hezekiah answered, "They have seen
all that *is* in my house; there is nothing
among my treasures that I have not shown
them."
5 Then Isaiah said to Hezekiah, "Hear the
word of the LORD of hosts: 6 'Behold, the days
are coming when all that *is* in your house,
and what your fathers have accumulated
until this day, shall be carried to Babylon;
nothing shall be left,' says the LORD. 7 'And
they shall take away *some* of your sons who
will descend from you, whom you will beget;
and they shall be eunuchs in the palace of
the king of Babylon.'"
8 So Hezekiah said to Isaiah, "The word
of the LORD which you have spoken *is* good!"

38:11 [a] Hebrew *YAH, YAH* [b] Following some Hebrew manuscripts; Masoretic Text and Vulgate read *rest;* Septuagint omits *among the inhabitants of the world;* Targum reads *land.* **38:14** [a] Following Bomberg; Masoretic Text and Dead Sea Scrolls read *Lord.* **38:15** [a] Following Masoretic Text and Vulgate; Dead Sea Scrolls and Targum read *And shall I say to Him;* Septuagint omits first half of this verse. **39:1** [a] Spelled *Berodach-Baladan* in 2 Kings 20:12

For he said, "At least there will be peace and truth in my days."

God's People Are Comforted

40 "Comfort, yes, comfort My people!"
Says your God.
2 "Speak comfort to Jerusalem, and cry out to her,
That her warfare is ended,
That her iniquity is pardoned;
For she has received from the LORD's hand
Double for all her sins."

3 The voice of one crying in the wilderness:
"Prepare the way of the LORD;
Make straight in the desert[a]
A highway for our God.
4 Every valley shall be exalted
And every mountain and hill brought low;
The crooked places shall be made straight
And the rough places smooth;
5 The glory of the LORD shall be revealed,
And all flesh shall see *it* together;
For the mouth of the LORD has spoken."

40:3 [a] Following Masoretic Text, Targum, and Vulgate; Septuagint omits *in the desert.*

Epic Ideas

WHO IS GOD? THE SOURCE OF GOOD

READ IT: ISAIAH 40:25–31

GET IT:

Think of a time when you were completely and utterly worn out. Tired and exhausted, you wanted sleep, or a chance to do nothing. Your energy-meter was flashing "running on reserve power."

Now think of what the spiritual equivalent of that feeling would be. Maybe you worked on a big service project with your family or church, and you're weary of caring for other people's needs. Maybe you've been trying to be nice to someone who treats you horribly. You know it's good and honoring God; but you're tired, and you just want a little "me time."

Every human who shows kindness, lives honestly, and serves others can relate to this passage. Everyone who "does good" eventually gets tired of doing good because we don't have enough power in us to keep going. That's why the verse says, "Even the youths shall faint and be weary, and the young men shall utterly fall" (v. 30). That's you!

But God, our loving and endlessly powerful Creator, Father, and Friend, is the power source for everything that is good. That's who God is—the source of all good.

LIVE IT:

God wants to give you the power to be good (which is, by the way, the best life). Get to know God's goodness, and ask Him to transform you, fueling you up with overflowing kindness and love.

6 The voice said, "Cry out!"
And he[a] said, "What shall I cry?"

"All flesh *is* grass,
And all its loveliness *is* like the flower of the field.
7 The grass withers, the flower fades,
Because the breath of the LORD blows upon it;
Surely the people *are* grass.
8 The grass withers, the flower fades,
But the word of our God stands forever."

9 O Zion,
You who bring good tidings,
Get up into the high mountain;
O Jerusalem,
You who bring good tidings,
Lift up your voice with strength,
Lift *it* up, be not afraid;
Say to the cities of Judah, "Behold your God!"

10 Behold, the Lord GOD shall come with a strong *hand,*
And His arm shall rule for Him;
Behold, His reward *is* with Him,
And His work before Him.
11 He will feed His flock like a shepherd;
He will gather the lambs with His arm,
And carry *them* in His bosom,
And gently lead those who are with young.

12 Who has measured the waters[a] in the hollow of His hand,
Measured heaven with a span
And calculated the dust of the earth in a measure?
Weighed the mountains in scales
And the hills in a balance?
13 Who has directed the Spirit of the LORD,
Or *as* His counselor has taught Him?
14 With whom did He take counsel, and *who* instructed Him,
And taught Him in the path of justice?
Who taught Him knowledge,
And showed Him the way of understanding?

15 Behold, the nations *are* as a drop in a bucket,
And are counted as the small dust on the scales;
Look, He lifts up the isles as a very little thing.
16 And Lebanon *is* not sufficient to burn,
Nor its beasts sufficient for a burnt offering.
17 All nations before Him *are* as nothing,
And they are counted by Him less than nothing and worthless.

40:6 [a] Following Masoretic Text and Targum; Dead Sea Scrolls, Septuagint, and Vulgate read *I*. **40:12** [a] Following Masoretic Text, Septuagint, and Vulgate; Dead Sea Scrolls read *waters of the sea;* Targum reads *waters of the world*.

YOU CAN BE STRONG

READ IT: ISAIAH 40:31

Not everybody can be built like a lineman on a football team, but everyone can be strong in spirit.

There is only one way to be strong spiritually: "Wait on the Lord." Does that sound strange? How do you wait on the Lord? Isn't God everywhere?

Yes, God is everywhere at the same time because He is infinite. But He doesn't act the same everywhere at the same time. What the Lord is saying in this text is, "I want to change your life. So wait for me in prayer and trust. Ask me to come into your life." Then you will become strong like an eagle. You will run and never be tired of working for God. Serving Him will be the greatest happiness of your life!

18 To whom then will you liken God?
Or what likeness will you compare to Him?
19 The workman molds an image,
The goldsmith overspreads it with gold,
And the silversmith casts silver chains.
20 Whoever *is* too impoverished for *such* a contribution
Chooses a tree *that* will not rot;
He seeks for himself a skillful workman
To prepare a carved image *that* will not totter.

21 Have you not known?
Have you not heard?
Has it not been told you from the beginning?
Have you not understood from the foundations of the earth?
22 *It is* He who sits above the circle of the earth,
And its inhabitants *are* like grasshoppers,
Who stretches out the heavens like a curtain,
And spreads them out like a tent to dwell in.
23 He brings the princes to nothing;
He makes the judges of the earth useless.

24 Scarcely shall they be planted,
Scarcely shall they be sown,
Scarcely shall their stock take root in the earth,
When He will also blow on them,
And they will wither,
And the whirlwind will take them away like stubble.

25 "To whom then will you liken Me,
Or *to whom* shall I be equal?" says the Holy One.
26 Lift up your eyes on high,
And see who has created these *things*,
Who brings out their host by number;
He calls them all by name,
By the greatness of His might
And the strength of *His* power;
Not one is missing.

27 Why do you say, O Jacob,
And speak, O Israel:
"My way is hidden from the LORD,
And my just claim is passed over by my God"?
28 Have you not known?
Have you not heard?
The everlasting God, the LORD,
The Creator of the ends of the earth,
Neither faints nor is weary.
His understanding is unsearchable.
29 He gives power to the weak,
And to *those who have* no might He increases strength.
30 Even the youths shall faint and be weary,
And the young men shall utterly fall,
31 But those who wait on the LORD
Shall renew *their* strength;
They shall mount up with wings like eagles,
They shall run and not be weary,
They shall walk and not faint.

DEPRESSION

READ IT: ISAIAH 41:10

Depression can feel like a heavy, wet blanket weighing you down, but it doesn't have to. First, don't focus on your fear. Remember you aren't alone in this—the God of the universe is with you. Second, don't focus on your sadness. This doesn't mean you ignore it or pretend it isn't there—*that won't help*. It means you keep asking God to heal the hurt. He has promised He will not abandon you. When you need reminders of this, reach out to a trusted adult and let him or her know you're struggling.

Israel Assured of God's Help

41 "Keep silence before Me,
O coastlands,
And let the people renew *their* strength!
Let them come near, then let them
speak;
Let us come near together for judgment.

2 "Who raised up one from the east?
Who in righteousness called him to His
feet?
Who gave the nations before him,
And made *him* rule over kings?
Who gave *them* as the dust *to* his sword,
As driven stubble to his bow?
3 Who pursued them, *and* passed safely
By the way *that* he had not gone with
his feet?
4 Who has performed and done *it*,
Calling the generations from the
beginning?
'I, the LORD, am the first;
And with the last I *am* He.'"

5 The coastlands saw *it* and feared,
The ends of the earth were afraid;
They drew near and came.
6 Everyone helped his neighbor,
And said to his brother,
"Be of good courage!"
7 So the craftsman encouraged the
goldsmith;
He who smooths *with* the hammer
inspired him who strikes the anvil,
Saying, "It *is* ready for the soldering";
Then he fastened it with pegs,
That it might not totter.

8 "But you, Israel, *are* My servant,
Jacob whom I have chosen,
The descendants of Abraham My friend.
9 *You* whom I have taken from the ends of
the earth,
And called from its farthest regions,
And said to you,
'You *are* My servant,
I have chosen you and have not cast you
away:
10 Fear not, for I *am* with you;
Be not dismayed, for I *am* your God.
I will strengthen you,
Yes, I will help you,
I will uphold you with My righteous
right hand.'

11 "Behold, all those who were incensed
against you
Shall be ashamed and disgraced;
They shall be as nothing,
And those who strive with you shall
perish.
12 You shall seek them and not find
them—
Those who contended with you.
Those who war against you

Action!

COURAGE

READ IT: ISAIAH 41:10

Here's a true story: Three friends were riding their bicycles across the country to help raise money for a charity. As they began cycling up a mountain, one of them began to lose strength. If he didn't make it up and over, the trip would have to end. He was afraid of disappointing his friends and the charity, but he had to stop and ask for help. His friends came along beside him, and each one placed one arm behind his back. Together, their strength helped carry him over the mountain.

In the same way, when we're struggling, weak, and afraid, God is our strength. He is with us and will hold us up with His very own hand. Although we may not be able to feel it, we know it's there.

Shall be as nothing,
As a nonexistent thing.
13 For I, the LORD your God, will hold your right hand,
Saying to you, 'Fear not, I will help you.'

14 "Fear not, you worm Jacob,
You men of Israel!
I will help you," says the LORD
And your Redeemer, the Holy One of Israel.
15 "Behold, I will make you into a new threshing sledge with sharp teeth;
You shall thresh the mountains and beat *them* small,
And make the hills like chaff.
16 You shall winnow them, the wind shall carry them away,
And the whirlwind shall scatter them;
You shall rejoice in the LORD,
And glory in the Holy One of Israel.

17 "The poor and needy seek water, but *there is* none,
Their tongues fail for thirst.
I, the LORD, will hear them;
I, the God of Israel, will not forsake them.
18 I will open rivers in desolate heights,
And fountains in the midst of the valleys;
I will make the wilderness a pool of water,
And the dry land springs of water.
19 I will plant in the wilderness the cedar and the acacia tree,
The myrtle and the oil tree;
I will set in the desert the cypress tree *and* the pine
And the box tree together,
20 That they may see and know,
And consider and understand together,
That the hand of the LORD has done this,
And the Holy One of Israel has created it.

The Futility of Idols

21 "Present your case," says the LORD.
"Bring forth your strong *reasons,*" says the King of Jacob.
22 "Let them bring forth and show us what will happen;
Let them show the former things, what they *were,*
That we may consider them,
And know the latter end of them;
Or declare to us things to come.
23 Show the things that are to come hereafter,
That we may know that you *are* gods;
Yes, do good or do evil,
That we may be dismayed and see *it* together.
24 Indeed you *are* nothing,
And your work *is* nothing;
He who chooses you *is* an abomination.

25 "I have raised up one from the north,
And he shall come;
From the rising of the sun he shall call on My name;
And he shall come against princes as *though* mortar,
As the potter treads clay.
26 Who has declared from the beginning, that we may know?
And former times, that we may say, '*He is* righteous'?
Surely *there is* no one who shows,
Surely *there is* no one who declares,
Surely *there is* no one who hears your words.
27 The first time *I said* to Zion,
'Look, there they are!'
And I will give to Jerusalem one who brings good tidings.
28 For I looked, and *there was* no man;
I looked among them, but *there was* no counselor,
Who, when I asked of them, could answer a word.
29 Indeed they *are* all worthless;[a]
Their works *are* nothing;
Their molded images *are* wind and confusion.

The Servant of the LORD

42 "Behold! My Servant whom I uphold,
My Elect One *in whom* My soul delights!
I have put My Spirit upon Him;
He will bring forth justice to the Gentiles.
2 He will not cry out, nor raise *His voice,*
Nor cause His voice to be heard in the street.

41:29 [a] Following Masoretic Text and Vulgate; Dead Sea Scrolls, Syriac, and Targum read *nothing;* Septuagint omits the first line.

3 A bruised reed He will not break,
And smoking flax He will not quench;
He will bring forth justice for truth.
4 He will not fail nor be discouraged,
Till He has established justice in the earth;
And the coastlands shall wait for His law."

5 Thus says God the LORD,
Who created the heavens and stretched them out,
Who spread forth the earth and that which comes from it,
Who gives breath to the people on it,
And spirit to those who walk on it:
6 "I, the LORD, have called You in righteousness,
And will hold Your hand;
I will keep You and give You as a covenant to the people,
As a light to the Gentiles,
7 To open blind eyes,
To bring out prisoners from the prison,
Those who sit in darkness from the prison house.
8 I *am* the LORD, that *is* My name;
And My glory I will not give to another,
Nor My praise to carved images.
9 Behold, the former things have come to pass,
And new things I declare;
Before they spring forth I tell you of them."

Praise to the LORD

10 Sing to the LORD a new song,
And His praise from the ends of the earth,
You who go down to the sea, and all that is in it,
You coastlands and you inhabitants of them!
11 Let the wilderness and its cities lift up *their voice,*
The villages *that* Kedar inhabits.
Let the inhabitants of Sela sing,
Let them shout from the top of the mountains.
12 Let them give glory to the LORD,
And declare His praise in the coastlands.
13 The LORD shall go forth like a mighty man;
He shall stir up *His* zeal like a man of war.
He shall cry out, yes, shout aloud;
He shall prevail against His enemies.

Promise of the LORD's Help

14 "I have held My peace a long time,
I have been still and restrained Myself.
Now I will cry like a woman in labor,
I will pant and gasp at once.
15 I will lay waste the mountains and hills,
And dry up all their vegetation;
I will make the rivers coastlands,
And I will dry up the pools.
16 I will bring the blind by a way they did not know;
I will lead them in paths they have not known.
I will make darkness light before them,
And crooked places straight.
These things I will do for them,
And not forsake them.
17 They shall be turned back,
They shall be greatly ashamed,
Who trust in carved images,
Who say to the molded images,
'You *are* our gods.'

18 "Hear, you deaf;
And look, you blind, that you may see.
19 Who *is* blind but My servant,
Or deaf as My messenger *whom* I send?
Who *is* blind as *he who is* perfect,
And blind as the LORD's servant?
20 Seeing many things, but you do not observe;
Opening the ears, but he does not hear."

Israel's Obstinate Disobedience

21 The LORD is well pleased for His righteousness' sake;
He will exalt the law and make *it* honorable.
22 But this *is* a people robbed and plundered;
All of them are snared in holes,
And they are hidden in prison houses;
They are for prey, and no one delivers;
For plunder, and no one says, "Restore!"

23 Who among you will give ear to this?
Who will listen and hear for the time to come?
24 Who gave Jacob for plunder, and Israel to the robbers?
Was it not the LORD,

He against whom we have sinned?
For they would not walk in His ways,
Nor were they obedient to His law.
25 Therefore He has poured on him the fury of His anger
And the strength of battle;
It has set him on fire all around,
Yet he did not know;
And it burned him,
Yet he did not take *it* to heart.

The Redeemer of Israel

43 But now, thus says the LORD, who created you, O Jacob,
And He who formed you, O Israel:
"Fear not, for I have redeemed you;
I have called *you* by your name;
You *are* Mine.
2 When you pass through the waters, I *will be* with you;
And through the rivers, they shall not overflow you.
When you walk through the fire, you shall not be burned,
Nor shall the flame scorch you.
3 For I *am* the LORD your God,
The Holy One of Israel, your Savior;
I gave Egypt for your ransom,
Ethiopia and Seba in your place.
4 Since you were precious in My sight,
You have been honored,
And I have loved you;
Therefore I will give men for you,
And people for your life.
5 Fear not, for I *am* with you;
I will bring your descendants from the east,
And gather you from the west;
6 I will say to the north, 'Give them up!'
And to the south, 'Do not keep them back!'
Bring My sons from afar,
And My daughters from the ends of the earth—
7 Everyone who is called by My name,
Whom I have created for My glory;
I have formed him, yes, I have made him."

8 Bring out the blind people who have eyes,
And the deaf who have ears.
9 Let all the nations be gathered together,
And let the people be assembled.
Who among them can declare this,
And show us former things?
Let them bring out their witnesses, that they may be justified;
Or let them hear and say, "*It is* truth."
10 "You *are* My witnesses," says the LORD,
"And My servant whom I have chosen,
That you may know and believe Me,
And understand that I *am* He.
Before Me there was no God formed,
Nor shall there be after Me.

PAIN AND SUFFERING

READ IT: ISAIAH 43:1–3

Life will be hard at times. Bad things will happen to good people, but God has made promises to His children:

- Don't be afraid. You're not alone. God's with you, no matter how difficult life gets.
- Don't give up. You're strong enough to survive. The beautiful language of these verses offers hope. Bad things happen, but they don't have to leave you wounded.
- Trust God. God has cared for His people time and again, and He's cared for you. Trust His promises.

11 I, *even* I, *am* the LORD,
And besides Me *there is* no savior.
12 I have declared and saved,
I have proclaimed,
And *there was* no foreign *god* among
you;
Therefore you *are* My witnesses,"
Says the LORD, "that I *am* God.
13 Indeed before the day *was,* I *am* He;
And *there is* no one who can deliver out
of My hand;
I work, and who will reverse it?"

14 Thus says the LORD, your Redeemer,
The Holy One of Israel:
"For your sake I will send to Babylon,
And bring them all down as fugitives—
The Chaldeans, who rejoice in their
ships.
15 I *am* the LORD, your Holy One,
The Creator of Israel, your King."

16 Thus says the LORD, who makes a way
in the sea
And a path through the mighty waters,
17 Who brings forth the chariot and horse,
The army and the power
(They shall lie down together, they shall
not rise;
They are extinguished, they are
quenched like a wick):
18 "Do not remember the former things,
Nor consider the things of old.
19 Behold, I will do a new thing,
Now it shall spring forth;
Shall you not know it?
I will even make a road in the
wilderness
And rivers in the desert.
20 The beast of the field will honor Me,
The jackals and the ostriches,
Because I give waters in the wilderness
And rivers in the desert,
To give drink to My people, My chosen.
21 This people I have formed for Myself;
They shall declare My praise.

Pleading with Unfaithful Israel

22 "But you have not called upon Me,
O Jacob;
And you have been weary of Me,
O Israel.
23 You have not brought Me the sheep for
your burnt offerings,
Nor have you honored Me with your
sacrifices.
I have not caused you to serve with
grain offerings,
Nor wearied you with incense.
24 You have bought Me no sweet cane with
money,
Nor have you satisfied Me with the fat of
your sacrifices;

Epic Ideas

43:7 WHY GOD CREATED YOU

Sometimes you may be disappointed because you aren't all you'd like to be. Maybe you aren't great at sports, or maybe you don't get the highest grades. But you can still be great because your life glorifies God. A person who can't walk or see can bring honor to God in ways that other people can't. Some have wonderful stories of how Jesus saved them and put a beautiful song in their hearts. The world is blessed by people like that.

Christians should be different because they have eternal life, not because they're VIPs. Such a Christian glorifies God because his or her life proves that Christ makes a difference. Such people make others want to be Christians, too. That's why God created you—to bring that kind of honor to Him.

But you have burdened Me with your sins,
You have wearied Me with your iniquities.

25 "I, *even* I, *am* He who blots out your transgressions for My own sake;
And I will not remember your sins.
26 Put Me in remembrance;
Let us contend together;
State your *case,* that you may be acquitted.
27 Your first father sinned,
And your mediators have transgressed against Me.
28 Therefore I will profane the princes of the sanctuary;
I will give Jacob to the curse,
And Israel to reproaches.

God's Blessing on Israel

44 "Yet hear now, O Jacob My servant,
And Israel whom I have chosen.
2 Thus says the LORD who made you
And formed you from the womb, *who* will help you:
'Fear not, O Jacob My servant;
And you, Jeshurun, whom I have chosen.
3 For I will pour water on him who is thirsty,
And floods on the dry ground;
I will pour My Spirit on your descendants,
And My blessing on your offspring;
4 They will spring up among the grass
Like willows by the watercourses.'

In Focus

44:1 My Servant Refers here to Israel, but in Isaiah 49:6, the term refers to the coming Messiah, or Christ, in the New Testament.

5 One will say, 'I *am* the LORD's';
Another will call *himself* by the name of Jacob;
Another will write *with* his hand, 'The LORD's,'
And name *himself* by the name of Israel.

There Is No Other God

6 "Thus says the LORD, the King of Israel,
And his Redeemer, the LORD of hosts:
'I *am* the First and I *am* the Last;
Besides Me *there is* no God.
7 And who can proclaim as I do?
Then let him declare it and set it in order for Me,
Since I appointed the ancient people.
And the things that are coming and shall come,
Let them show these to them.
8 Do not fear, nor be afraid;
Have I not told you from that time, and declared *it?*
You *are* My witnesses.
Is there a God besides Me?
Indeed *there is* no other Rock;
I know not *one.*'"

Action!

GUILT

READ IT: ISAIAH 43:25

It's hard to believe that God can forget our sins. After all, when someone does something wrong to us, we seem to always remember. However, this verse is all the promise we need. God says He won't remember our sins. How great is that?

Idolatry Is Foolishness

9 Those who make an image, all of them
are useless,
And their precious things shall not
profit;
They *are* their own witnesses;
They neither see nor know, that they
may be ashamed.
10 Who would form a god or mold an
image
That profits him nothing?
11 Surely all his companions would be
ashamed;
And the workmen, they *are* mere men.
Let them all be gathered together,
Let them stand up;
Yet they shall fear,
They shall be ashamed together.

12 The blacksmith with the tongs works
one in the coals,
Fashions it with hammers,
And works it with the strength of his
arms.
Even so, he is hungry, and his strength
fails;
He drinks no water and is faint.

13 The craftsman stretches out *his* rule,
He marks one out with chalk;
He fashions it with a plane,
He marks it out with the compass,
And makes it like the figure of a man,
According to the beauty of a man, that it
may remain in the house.
14 He cuts down cedars for himself,
And takes the cypress and the oak;
He secures *it* for himself among the
trees of the forest.
He plants a pine, and the rain
nourishes *it*.

15 Then it shall be for a man to burn,
For he will take some of it and warm
himself;
Yes, he kindles *it* and bakes bread;
Indeed he makes a god and worships *it;*
He makes it a carved image, and falls
down to it.
16 He burns half of it in the fire;
With this half he eats meat;
He roasts a roast, and is satisfied.
He even warms *himself* and says,
"Ah! I am warm,
I have seen the fire."
17 And the rest of it he makes into a god,
His carved image.
He falls down before it and worships *it,*
Prays to it and says,
"Deliver me, for you *are* my god!"

Epic Ideas

44:6 WHO IS GOD?

God says, "I am the First and I am the Last." So God is the One we have to begin with when we start thinking about anything. If God didn't create all the things in the world, then all you see around you may be only your imagination.

You heard long ago that 2 + 2 = 4. Who decided that? Not just your schoolteacher! God made 2 + 2 = 4 because He created a world where numbers make sense. Right and wrong exist because God gives His Law to live by.

If you take God away, you can never be sure that 2 + 2 = 4 or that good is better than evil. Who would decide for us? What would be the use of learning? The apostle Paul says that people without God can never know the truth (see 2 Timothy 3:7). *But God created all the things in the universe and He is Truth.*

18 They do not know nor understand;
For He has shut their eyes, so that they cannot see,
And their hearts, so that they cannot understand.
19 And no one considers in his heart,
Nor *is there* knowledge nor understanding to say,
"I have burned half of it in the fire,
Yes, I have also baked bread on its coals;
I have roasted meat and eaten *it;*
And shall I make the rest of it an abomination?
Shall I fall down before a block of wood?"
20 He feeds on ashes;
A deceived heart has turned him aside;
And he cannot deliver his soul,
Nor say, "*Is there* not a lie in my right hand?"

Israel Is Not Forgotten

21 "Remember these, O Jacob,
And Israel, for you *are* My servant;
I have formed you, you *are* My servant;
O Israel, you will not be forgotten by Me!
22 I have blotted out, like a thick cloud, your transgressions,
And like a cloud, your sins.
Return to Me, for I have redeemed you."

23 Sing, O heavens, for the LORD has done *it!*
Shout, you lower parts of the earth;
Break forth into singing, you mountains,
O forest, and every tree in it!
For the LORD has redeemed Jacob,
And glorified Himself in Israel.

Judah Will Be Restored

24 Thus says the LORD, your Redeemer,
And He who formed you from the womb:
"I *am* the LORD, who makes all *things,*
Who stretches out the heavens all alone,
Who spreads abroad the earth by Myself;
25 Who frustrates the signs of the babblers,
And drives diviners *mad;*
Who turns wise men backward,
And makes their knowledge foolishness;
26 Who confirms the word of His servant,

In Focus

45:15 Savior Someone who saves our lives. Jesus is our Savior from heaven who died on the Cross to save our souls from sin and hell.

And performs the counsel of His messengers;
Who says to Jerusalem, 'You shall be inhabited,'
To the cities of Judah, 'You shall be built,'
And I will raise up her waste places;
27 Who says to the deep, 'Be dry!
And I will dry up your rivers';
28 Who says of Cyrus, '*He is* My shepherd,
And he shall perform all My pleasure,
Saying to Jerusalem, "You shall be built,"
And to the temple, "Your foundation shall be laid."'

Cyrus, God's Instrument

45 "Thus says the LORD to His anointed,
To Cyrus, whose right hand I have held—
To subdue nations before him
And loose the armor of kings,
To open before him the double doors,
So that the gates will not be shut:
2 'I will go before you
And make the crooked places[a] straight;
I will break in pieces the gates of bronze
And cut the bars of iron.
3 I will give you the treasures of darkness
And hidden riches of secret places,
That you may know that I, the LORD,
Who call *you* by your name,
Am the God of Israel.
4 For Jacob My servant's sake,
And Israel My elect,
I have even called you by your name;
I have named you, though you have not known Me.

45:2 [a] Dead Sea Scrolls and Septuagint read *mountains;* Targum reads *I will trample down the walls;* Vulgate reads *I will humble the great ones of the earth.*

5 I *am* the LORD, and *there is* no other;
There is no God besides Me.
I will gird you, though you have not known Me,
6 That they may know from the rising of the sun to its setting
That *there is* none besides Me.
I *am* the LORD, and *there is* no other;
7 I form the light and create darkness,
I make peace and create calamity;
I, the LORD, do all these *things*.'

8 "Rain down, you heavens, from above,
And let the skies pour down righteousness;
Let the earth open, let them bring forth salvation,
And let righteousness spring up together.
I, the LORD, have created it.

9 "Woe to him who strives with his Maker!
Let the potsherd *strive* with the potsherds of the earth!
Shall the clay say to him who forms it, 'What are you making?'
Or shall your handiwork *say*, 'He has no hands'?
10 Woe to him who says to *his* father, 'What are you begetting?'
Or to the woman, 'What have you brought forth?'"

11 Thus says the LORD,
The Holy One of Israel, and his Maker:
"Ask Me of things to come concerning My sons;
And concerning the work of My hands, you command Me.
12 I have made the earth,
And created man on it.
I—My hands—stretched out the heavens,
And all their host I have commanded.
13 I have raised him up in righteousness,
And I will direct all his ways;
He shall build My city
And let My exiles go free,
Not for price nor reward,"
Says the LORD of hosts.

The LORD, the Only Savior

14 Thus says the LORD:

"The labor of Egypt and merchandise of Cush
And of the Sabeans, men of stature,
Shall come over to you, and they shall be yours;
They shall walk behind you,
They shall come over in chains;
And they shall bow down to you.
They will make supplication to you, *saying*, 'Surely God *is* in you,
And *there is* no other;
There is no other God.'"

15 Truly You *are* God, who hide Yourself,
O God of Israel, the Savior!
16 They shall be ashamed
And also disgraced, all of them;
They shall go in confusion together,
Who are makers of idols.
17 *But* Israel shall be saved by the LORD
With an everlasting salvation;
You shall not be ashamed or disgraced
Forever and ever.

18 For thus says the LORD,
Who created the heavens,
Who is God,
Who formed the earth and made it,
Who has established it,
Who did not create it in vain,
Who formed it to be inhabited:
"I *am* the LORD, and *there is* no other.
19 I have not spoken in secret,
In a dark place of the earth;
I did not say to the seed of Jacob,
'Seek Me in vain';
I, the LORD, speak righteousness,
I declare things that are right.

20 "Assemble yourselves and come;
Draw near together,
You *who have* escaped from the nations.
They have no knowledge,
Who carry the wood of their carved image,
And pray to a god *that* cannot save.
21 Tell and bring forth *your case;*
Yes, let them take counsel together.
Who has declared this from ancient time?
Who has told it from that time?
Have not I, the LORD?
And *there is* no other God besides Me,
A just God and a Savior;
There is none besides Me.

22 "Look to Me, and be saved,
All you ends of the earth!
For I *am* God, and *there is* no other.

23 I have sworn by Myself;
The word has gone out of My mouth *in* righteousness,
And shall not return,
That to Me every knee shall bow,
Every tongue shall take an oath.
24 He shall say,
'Surely in the LORD I have righteousness and strength.
To Him *men* shall come,
And all shall be ashamed
Who are incensed against Him.
25 In the LORD all the descendants of Israel
Shall be justified, and shall glory.'"

Dead Idols and the Living God

46 Bel bows down, Nebo stoops;
Their idols were on the beasts and on the cattle.
Your carriages *were* heavily loaded,
A burden to the weary *beast.*
2 They stoop, they bow down together;
They could not deliver the burden,
But have themselves gone into captivity.

3 "Listen to Me, O house of Jacob,
And all the remnant of the house of Israel,
Who have been upheld *by Me* from birth,
Who have been carried from the womb:
4 Even to *your* old age, I *am* He,
And *even* to gray hairs I will carry *you!*
I have made, and I will bear;
Even I will carry, and will deliver *you.*

5 "To whom will you liken Me, and make *Me* equal
And compare Me, that we should be alike?
6 They lavish gold out of the bag,
And weigh silver on the scales;
They hire a goldsmith, and he makes it a god;
They prostrate themselves, yes, they worship.
7 They bear it on the shoulder, they carry it
And set it in its place, and it stands;
From its place it shall not move.
Though *one* cries out to it, yet it cannot answer
Nor save him out of his trouble.

8 "Remember this, and show yourselves men;
Recall to mind, O you transgressors.
9 Remember the former things of old,
For I *am* God, and *there is* no other;
I am God, and *there is* none like Me,
10 Declaring the end from the beginning,
And from ancient times *things* that are not *yet* done,
Saying, 'My counsel shall stand,
And I will do all My pleasure,'
11 Calling a bird of prey from the east,
The man who executes My counsel, from a far country.
Indeed I have spoken *it;*
I will also bring it to pass.
I have purposed *it;*
I will also do it.

12 "Listen to Me, you stubborn-hearted,
Who *are* far from righteousness:
13 I bring My righteousness near, it shall not be far off;
My salvation shall not linger.
And I will place salvation in Zion,
For Israel My glory.

The Humiliation of Babylon

47 "Come down and sit in the dust,
O virgin daughter of Babylon;
Sit on the ground without a throne,
O daughter of the Chaldeans!
For you shall no more be called
Tender and delicate.
2 Take the millstones and grind meal.
Remove your veil,
Take off the skirt,
Uncover the thigh,
Pass through the rivers.
3 Your nakedness shall be uncovered,
Yes, your shame will be seen;
I will take vengeance,
And I will not arbitrate with a man."

4 *As for* our Redeemer, the LORD of hosts *is* His name,
The Holy One of Israel.

5 "Sit in silence, and go into darkness,
O daughter of the Chaldeans;
For you shall no longer be called
The Lady of Kingdoms.
6 I was angry with My people;
I have profaned My inheritance,
And given them into your hand.
You showed them no mercy;
On the elderly you laid your yoke very heavily.
7 And you said, 'I shall be a lady forever,'

So that you did not take these *things* to
heart,
Nor remember the latter end of them.

8 "Therefore hear this now, *you who are*
given to pleasures,
Who dwell securely,
Who say in your heart, 'I *am,* and *there is*
no one else besides me;
I shall not sit *as* a widow,
Nor shall I know the loss of children';
9 But these two *things* shall come to you
In a moment, in one day:
The loss of children, and widowhood.
They shall come upon you in their
fullness
Because of the multitude of your
sorceries,
For the great abundance of your
enchantments.

10 "For you have trusted in your
wickedness;
You have said, 'No one sees me';
Your wisdom and your knowledge have
warped you;
And you have said in your heart,
'I *am,* and *there is* no one else besides
me.'
11 Therefore evil shall come upon you;
You shall not know from where it arises.
And trouble shall fall upon you;
You will not be able to put it off.
And desolation shall come upon you
suddenly,
Which you shall not know.

12 "Stand now with your enchantments
And the multitude of your sorceries,
In which you have labored from your
youth—
Perhaps you will be able to profit,
Perhaps you will prevail.
13 You are wearied in the multitude of your
counsels;
Let now the astrologers, the stargazers,
And the monthly prognosticators
Stand up and save you
From what shall come upon you.
14 Behold, they shall be as stubble,
The fire shall burn them;
They shall not deliver themselves
From the power of the flame;
It shall not *be* a coal to be warmed by,
Nor a fire to sit before!
15 Thus shall they be to you
With whom you have labored,
Your merchants from your youth;
They shall wander each one to his
quarter.
No one shall save you.

Israel Refined for God's Glory

48 "Hear this, O house of Jacob,
Who are called by the name of
Israel,
And have come forth from the
wellsprings of Judah;
Who swear by the name of the LORD,
And make mention of the God of Israel,
But not in truth or in righteousness;
2 For they call themselves after the holy
city,
And lean on the God of Israel;
The LORD of hosts *is* His name:

3 "I have declared the former things from
the beginning;
They went forth from My mouth, and I
caused them to hear it.
Suddenly I did *them,* and they came to
pass.
4 Because I knew that you *were* obstinate,
And your neck *was* an iron sinew,
And your brow bronze,
5 Even from the beginning I have
declared *it* to you;
Before it came to pass I proclaimed *it*
to you,
Lest you should say, 'My idol has done
them,
And my carved image and my molded
image
Have commanded them.'

6 "You have heard;
See all this.
And will you not declare *it?*
I have made you hear new things from
this time,
Even hidden things, and you did not
know them.
7 They are created now and not from the
beginning;
And before this day you have not heard
them,
Lest you should say, 'Of course I knew
them.'
8 Surely you did not hear,
Surely you did not know;
Surely from long ago your ear was not
opened.

For I knew that you would deal very
treacherously,
And were called a transgressor from the
womb.

9 "For My name's sake I will defer My
anger,
And *for* My praise I will restrain it from
you,
So that I do not cut you off.
10 Behold, I have refined you, but not as
silver;
I have tested you in the furnace of
affliction.
11 For My own sake, for My own sake, I
will do *it;*
For how should *My name* be profaned?
And I will not give My glory to another.

God's Ancient Plan to Redeem Israel

12 "Listen to Me, O Jacob,
And Israel, My called:
I *am* He, I *am* the First,
I *am* also the Last.
13 Indeed My hand has laid the foundation
of the earth,
And My right hand has stretched out
the heavens;
When I call to them,
They stand up together.

14 "All of you, assemble yourselves, and
hear!
Who among them has declared these
things?
The LORD loves him;
He shall do His pleasure on Babylon,
And His arm *shall be against* the
Chaldeans.
15 I, *even* I, have spoken;
Yes, I have called him,
I have brought him, and his way will
prosper.

16 "Come near to Me, hear this:
I have not spoken in secret from the
beginning;
From the time that it was, I *was* there.
And now the Lord GOD and His Spirit
Have[a] sent Me."

17 Thus says the LORD, your Redeemer,
The Holy One of Israel:
"I *am* the LORD your God,
Who teaches you to profit,
Who leads you by the way you should go.
18 Oh, that you had heeded My
commandments!
Then your peace would have been like
a river,
And your righteousness like the waves
of the sea.
19 Your descendants also would have been
like the sand,
And the offspring of your body like the
grains of sand;
His name would not have been cut off
Nor destroyed from before Me."

20 Go forth from Babylon!
Flee from the Chaldeans!
With a voice of singing,
Declare, proclaim this,
Utter it to the end of the earth;
Say, "The LORD has redeemed
His servant Jacob!"
21 And they did not thirst
When He led them through the deserts;
He caused the waters to flow from the
rock for them;
He also split the rock, and the waters
gushed out.

22 "*There is* no peace," says the LORD, "for
the wicked."

The Servant, the Light to the Gentiles

49 "Listen, O coastlands, to Me,
And take heed, you peoples
from afar!
The LORD has called Me from the womb;
From the matrix of My mother He has
made mention of My name.
2 And He has made My mouth like a
sharp sword;
In the shadow of His hand He has
hidden Me,
And made Me a polished shaft;
In His quiver He has hidden Me."

3 "And He said to me,
'You *are* My servant, O Israel,
In whom I will be glorified.'
4 Then I said, 'I have labored in vain,
I have spent my strength for nothing
and in vain;
Yet surely my just reward *is* with the
LORD,
And my work with my God.'"

48:16 [a] The Hebrew verb is singular.

5 "And now the LORD says,
Who formed Me from the womb *to be*
His Servant,
To bring Jacob back to Him,
So that Israel is gathered to Him[a]
(For I shall be glorious in the eyes of the
LORD,
And My God shall be My strength),
6 Indeed He says,
'It is too small a thing that You should
be My Servant
To raise up the tribes of Jacob,
And to restore the preserved ones of
Israel;
I will also give You as a light to the
Gentiles,
That You should be My salvation to the
ends of the earth.'"

7 Thus says the LORD,
The Redeemer of Israel, their Holy One,
To Him whom man despises,
To Him whom the nation abhors,
To the Servant of rulers:
"Kings shall see and arise,
Princes also shall worship,
Because of the LORD who is faithful,
The Holy One of Israel;
And He has chosen You."

8 Thus says the LORD:

"In an acceptable time I have heard You,
And in the day of salvation I have helped
You;
I will preserve You and give You
As a covenant to the people,
To restore the earth,
To cause them to inherit the desolate
heritages;
9 That You may say to the prisoners, 'Go
forth,'
To those who *are* in darkness, 'Show
yourselves.'

"They shall feed along the roads,
And their pastures *shall be* on all
desolate heights.
10 They shall neither hunger nor thirst,
Neither heat nor sun shall strike them;
For He who has mercy on them will lead
them,
Even by the springs of water He will
guide them.
11 I will make each of My mountains a
road,
And My highways shall be elevated.
12 Surely these shall come from afar;
Look! Those from the north and the
west,
And these from the land of Sinim."

13 Sing, O heavens!
Be joyful, O earth!
And break out in singing, O mountains!
For the LORD has comforted His people,
And will have mercy on His afflicted.

God Will Remember Zion

14 But Zion said, "The LORD has forsaken
me,
And my Lord has forgotten me."

15 "Can a woman forget her nursing child,
And not have compassion on the son of
her womb?
Surely they may forget,
Yet I will not forget you.
16 See, I have inscribed you on the palms
of My hands;
Your walls *are* continually before Me.
17 Your sons[a] shall make haste;
Your destroyers and those who laid you
waste
Shall go away from you.
18 Lift up your eyes, look around and see;
All these gather together *and* come to
you.
As I live," says the LORD,
"You shall surely clothe yourselves with
them all as an ornament,
And bind them *on you* as a bride *does.*

19 "For your waste and desolate places,
And the land of your destruction,
Will even now be too small for the
inhabitants;
And those who swallowed you up will
be far away.
20 The children you will have,
After you have lost the others,
Will say again in your ears,
'The place *is* too small for me;
Give me a place where I may dwell.'
21 Then you will say in your heart,
'Who has begotten these for me,
Since I have lost my children and am
desolate,

49:5 [a] Qere, Dead Sea Scrolls, and Septuagint read *is gathered to Him;* Kethib reads *is not gathered.* **49:17** [a] Dead Sea Scrolls, Septuagint, Targum, and Vulgate read *builders.*

A captive, and wandering to and fro?
And who has brought these up?
There I was, left alone;
But these, where *were* they?'"

22 Thus says the Lord GOD:

"Behold, I will lift My hand in an oath to the nations,
And set up My standard for the peoples;
They shall bring your sons in *their* arms,
And your daughters shall be carried on *their* shoulders;
23 Kings shall be your foster fathers,
And their queens your nursing mothers;
They shall bow down to you with *their* faces to the earth,
And lick up the dust of your feet.
Then you will know that I *am* the LORD,
For they shall not be ashamed who wait for Me."

24 Shall the prey be taken from the mighty,
Or the captives of the righteous[a] be delivered?

25 But thus says the LORD:

"Even the captives of the mighty shall be taken away,
And the prey of the terrible be delivered;
For I will contend with him who contends with you,
And I will save your children.
26 I will feed those who oppress you with their own flesh,
And they shall be drunk with their own blood as with sweet wine.
All flesh shall know
That I, the LORD, *am* your Savior,
And your Redeemer, the Mighty One of Jacob."

The Servant, Israel's Hope

50 Thus says the LORD:

"Where *is* the certificate of your mother's divorce,
Whom I have put away?
Or which of My creditors *is it* to whom I have sold you?
For your iniquities you have sold yourselves,
And for your transgressions your mother has been put away.
2 Why, when I came, *was there* no man?
Why, when I called, *was there* none to answer?
Is My hand shortened at all that it cannot redeem?
Or have I no power to deliver?
Indeed with My rebuke I dry up the sea,
I make the rivers a wilderness;
Their fish stink because *there is* no water,
And die of thirst.
3 I clothe the heavens with blackness,
And I make sackcloth their covering."

4 "The Lord GOD has given Me
The tongue of the learned,

49:24 [a] Following Masoretic Text and Targum; Dead Sea Scrolls, Syriac, and Vulgate read *the mighty;* Septuagint reads *unjustly.*

COURAGE

READ IT: ISAIAH 50:7–10

Bring it on. One of the scariest things we can face is thinking we're alone. Friends can turn their backs and start rumors, or we can be treated unfairly. In our fear, it's easy to seek revenge and plead our innocence. This passage reminds us that God is our ultimate defender. He hears every word spoken against us, and because we're His children, we can trust Him to let truth win.

That I should know how to speak
A word in season to *him who is* weary.
He awakens Me morning by morning,
He awakens My ear
To hear as the learned.
5 The Lord GOD has opened My ear;
And I was not rebellious,
Nor did I turn away.
6 I gave My back to those who struck *Me,*
And My cheeks to those who plucked out the beard;
I did not hide My face from shame and spitting.

7 "For the Lord GOD will help Me;
Therefore I will not be disgraced;
Therefore I have set My face like a flint,
And I know that I will not be ashamed.
8 *He is* near who justifies Me;
Who will contend with Me?
Let us stand together.
Who *is* My adversary?
Let him come near Me.
9 Surely the Lord GOD will help Me;
Who *is* he *who* will condemn Me?
Indeed they will all grow old like a garment;
The moth will eat them up.

10 "Who among you fears the LORD?
Who obeys the voice of His Servant?
Who walks in darkness
And has no light?
Let him trust in the name of the LORD
And rely upon his God.
11 Look, all you who kindle a fire,
Who encircle *yourselves* with sparks:
Walk in the light of your fire and in the sparks you have kindled—
This you shall have from My hand:
You shall lie down in torment.

The LORD Comforts Zion

51 "Listen to Me, you who follow after righteousness,
You who seek the LORD:
Look to the rock *from which* you were hewn,
And to the hole of the pit *from which* you were dug.
2 Look to Abraham your father,
And to Sarah *who* bore you;
For I called him alone,
And blessed him and increased him."

3 For the LORD will comfort Zion,
He will comfort all her waste places;
He will make her wilderness like Eden,
And her desert like the garden of the LORD;
Joy and gladness will be found in it,
Thanksgiving and the voice of melody.

4 "Listen to Me, My people;
And give ear to Me, O My nation:
For law will proceed from Me,
And I will make My justice rest
As a light of the peoples.
5 My righteousness *is* near,
My salvation has gone forth,
And My arms will judge the peoples;
The coastlands will wait upon Me,
And on My arm they will trust.
6 Lift up your eyes to the heavens,
And look on the earth beneath.
For the heavens will vanish away like smoke,
The earth will grow old like a garment,
And those who dwell in it will die in like manner;
But My salvation will be forever,
And My righteousness will not be abolished.

7 "Listen to Me, you who know righteousness,
You people in whose heart *is* My law:
Do not fear the reproach of men,
Nor be afraid of their insults.
8 For the moth will eat them up like a garment,
And the worm will eat them like wool;
But My righteousness will be forever,
And My salvation from generation to generation."

9 Awake, awake, put on strength,
O arm of the LORD!
Awake as in the ancient days,
In the generations of old.
Are You not *the arm* that cut Rahab apart,
And wounded the serpent?
10 *Are* You not *the One* who dried up the sea,
The waters of the great deep;
That made the depths of the sea a road
For the redeemed to cross over?
11 So the ransomed of the LORD shall return,
And come to Zion with singing,
With everlasting joy on their heads.

They shall obtain joy and gladness;
Sorrow and sighing shall flee away.

12 "I, *even* I, *am* He who comforts you.
Who *are* you that you should be afraid
Of a man *who* will die,
And of the son of a man *who* will be made like grass?
13 And you forget the LORD your Maker,
Who stretched out the heavens
And laid the foundations of the earth;
You have feared continually every day
Because of the fury of the oppressor,
When *he has* prepared to destroy.
And where *is* the fury of the oppressor?
14 The captive exile hastens, that he may be loosed,
That he should not die in the pit,
And that his bread should not fail.
15 But I *am* the LORD your God,
Who divided the sea whose waves roared—
The LORD of hosts *is* His name.
16 And I have put My words in your mouth;
I have covered you with the shadow of My hand,
That I may plant the heavens,
Lay the foundations of the earth,
And say to Zion, 'You *are* My people.'"

God's Fury Removed

17 Awake, awake!
Stand up, O Jerusalem,
You who have drunk at the hand of the LORD
The cup of His fury;
You have drunk the dregs of the cup of trembling,
And drained *it* out.
18 *There is* no one to guide her
Among all the sons she has brought forth;
Nor *is there any* who takes her by the hand
Among all the sons she has brought up.
19 These two *things* have come to you;
Who will be sorry for you?—
Desolation and destruction, famine and sword—
By whom will I *comfort you?*
20 Your sons have fainted,
They lie at the head of all the streets,
Like an antelope in a net;
They are full of the fury of the LORD,
The rebuke of your God.

21 Therefore please hear this, you afflicted,
And drunk but not with wine.
22 Thus says your Lord,
The LORD and your God,
Who pleads the cause of His people:
"See, I have taken out of your hand
The cup of trembling,
The dregs of the cup of My fury;
You shall no longer drink it.
23 But I will put it into the hand of those who afflict you,
Who have said to you,[a]
'Lie down, that we may walk over you.'
And you have laid your body like the ground,
And as the street, for those who walk over."

God Redeems Jerusalem

52 Awake, awake!
Put on your strength, O Zion;
Put on your beautiful garments,
O Jerusalem, the holy city!
For the uncircumcised and the unclean
Shall no longer come to you.
2 Shake yourself from the dust, arise;
Sit down, O Jerusalem!
Loose yourself from the bonds of your neck,
O captive daughter of Zion!

3 For thus says the LORD:

"You have sold yourselves for nothing,
And you shall be redeemed without money."

4 For thus says the Lord GOD:

"My people went down at first
Into Egypt to dwell there;
Then the Assyrian oppressed them without cause.
5 Now therefore, what have I here," says the LORD,
"That My people are taken away for nothing?
Those who rule over them
Make them wail,"[a] says the LORD,
"And My name *is* blasphemed
continually every day.
6 Therefore My people shall know My name;

51:23 [a] Literally *your soul* 52:5 [a] Dead Sea Scrolls read *Mock;* Septuagint reads *Marvel and wail;* Targum reads *Boast themselves;* Vulgate reads *Treat them unjustly.*

Therefore *they shall know* in that day
That I *am* He who speaks:
'Behold, *it is* I.'"

7 How beautiful upon the mountains
Are the feet of him who brings good news,
Who proclaims peace,
Who brings glad tidings of good *things*,
Who proclaims salvation,
Who says to Zion,
"Your God reigns!"
8 Your watchmen shall lift up *their* voices,
With their voices they shall sing
together;
For they shall see eye to eye
When the LORD brings back Zion.
9 Break forth into joy, sing together,
You waste places of Jerusalem!
For the LORD has comforted His people,
He has redeemed Jerusalem.
10 The LORD has made bare His holy arm
In the eyes of all the nations;
And all the ends of the earth shall see
The salvation of our God.

11 Depart! Depart! Go out from there,
Touch no unclean *thing;*
Go out from the midst of her,
Be clean,
You who bear the vessels of the LORD.
12 For you shall not go out with haste,
Nor go by flight;
For the LORD will go before you,
And the God of Israel *will be* your rear
guard.

The Sin-Bearing Servant

13 Behold, My Servant shall deal
prudently;
He shall be exalted and extolled and be
very high.
14 Just as many were astonished at you,
So His visage was marred more than
any man,
And His form more than the sons of
men;
15 So shall He sprinkle[a] many nations.
Kings shall shut their mouths at Him;
For what had not been told them they
shall see,
And what they had not heard they shall
consider.

53 Who has believed our report?
And to whom has the arm of the
LORD been revealed?
2 For He shall grow up before Him as a
tender plant,
And as a root out of dry ground.
He has no form or comeliness;
And when we see Him,
There is no beauty that we should desire
Him.
3 He is despised and rejected by men,
A Man of sorrows and acquainted with
grief.
And we hid, as it were, *our* faces from
Him;

52:15 [a] Or *startle*

LIFE'S NOT FAIR

READ IT: ISAIAH 53:1–12

When life's unfair, it's good to get perspective—to see things from a different angle. One thing that helps is to remember you're not the only one who's gone through things you didn't deserve. Jesus has been there.

Though it was written long before He was born, this chapter is about Jesus and the suffering He'd one day endure. He knew rejection, sadness, and what it was to be punished when He'd done nothing wrong. Jesus went through all the frustrating emotions we experience, plus more. There is nothing you're feeling He doesn't understand.

He was despised, and we did not esteem
Him.

4 Surely He has borne our griefs
And carried our sorrows;
Yet we esteemed Him stricken,
Smitten by God, and afflicted.
5 But He *was* wounded for our
transgressions,
He was bruised for our iniquities;
The chastisement for our peace *was*
upon Him,
And by His stripes we are healed.
6 All we like sheep have gone astray;
We have turned, every one, to his own
way;
And the LORD has laid on Him the
iniquity of us all.

7 He was oppressed and He was afflicted,
Yet He opened not His mouth;
He was led as a lamb to the slaughter,
And as a sheep before its shearers is
silent,
So He opened not His mouth.
8 He was taken from prison and from
judgment,
And who will declare His generation?
For He was cut off from the land of the
living;
For the transgressions of My people He
was stricken.
9 And they[a] made His grave with the
wicked—
But with the rich at His death,
Because He had done no violence,
Nor *was any* deceit in His mouth.

10 Yet it pleased the LORD to bruise Him;
He has put *Him* to grief.
When You make His soul an offering
for sin,
He shall see *His* seed, He shall prolong
His days,
And the pleasure of the LORD shall
prosper in His hand.

In Focus

53:11 My Righteous Servant Sometimes refers to Israel (see Isaiah 44:1). Here, the term refers to Christ, our sin-bearing Servant.

53:9 [a] Literally *he* or *He*

Epic Ideas

53:6 JESUS CARRIED OUR SINS

You have heard many times that Jesus paid for your sins by dying on the Cross at Calvary. What is so amazing is that Jesus died because of a great plan that God had in mind for a long time. Jesus didn't die just because He made some Jews angry in Palestine two thousand years ago. That's why Isaiah (pronounced *eye-ZAY-uh*) could tell you all about the suffering and death of Jesus over seven hundred years before Jesus was born.

But the prophet told not only about Jesus' death, he also told about the reason for it—"All we like sheep have gone astray; we have turned, every one, to his own way; and the LORD has laid on Him the iniquity of *us all.*" God would lay your sins on His beloved Son. Then the Lord would pronounce you "innocent" of all sin because His Son died in your place. Wasn't that a most amazing plan?

11 He shall see the labor of His soul,[a] *and*
be satisfied.
By His knowledge My righteous Servant
shall justify many,
For He shall bear their iniquities.
12 Therefore I will divide Him a portion
with the great,
And He shall divide the spoil with the
strong,
Because He poured out His soul unto
death,
And He was numbered with the
transgressors,
And He bore the sin of many,
And made intercession for the
transgressors.

A Perpetual Covenant of Peace

54 "Sing, O barren,
You *who* have not borne!
Break forth into singing, and cry aloud,
You *who* have not labored with child!
For more *are* the children of the desolate
Than the children of the married
woman," says the LORD.
2 "Enlarge the place of your tent,
And let them stretch out the curtains of
your dwellings;
Do not spare;
Lengthen your cords,
And strengthen your stakes.
3 For you shall expand to the right and to
the left,
And your descendants will inherit the
nations,
And make the desolate cities inhabited.

4 "Do not fear, for you will not be ashamed;
Neither be disgraced, for you will not be
put to shame;
For you will forget the shame of your
youth,
And will not remember the reproach of
your widowhood anymore.
5 For your Maker *is* your husband,
The LORD of hosts *is* His name;
And your Redeemer *is* the Holy One of
Israel;
He is called the God of the whole earth.
6 For the LORD has called you
Like a woman forsaken and grieved in
spirit,
Like a youthful wife when you were
refused,"
Says your God.
7 "For a mere moment I have forsaken you,
But with great mercies I will gather you.
8 With a little wrath I hid My face from
you for a moment;
But with everlasting kindness I will
have mercy on you,"
Says the LORD, your Redeemer.

9 "For this *is* like the waters of Noah to Me;
For as I have sworn
That the waters of Noah would no
longer cover the earth,
So have I sworn
That I would not be angry with you, nor
rebuke you.
10 For the mountains shall depart
And the hills be removed,
But My kindness shall not depart from
you,
Nor shall My covenant of peace be
removed,"
Says the LORD, who has mercy on you.

11 "O you afflicted one,
Tossed with tempest, *and* not
comforted,
Behold, I will lay your stones with
colorful gems,
And lay your foundations with
sapphires.
12 I will make your pinnacles of rubies,
Your gates of crystal,
And all your walls of precious stones.
13 All your children *shall be* taught by the
LORD,
And great *shall be* the peace of your
children.
14 In righteousness you shall be
established;
You shall be far from oppression, for
you shall not fear;
And from terror, for it shall not come
near you.
15 Indeed they shall surely assemble, *but*
not because of Me.
Whoever assembles against you shall
fall for your sake.

16 "Behold, I have created the blacksmith
Who blows the coals in the fire,
Who brings forth an instrument for his
work;
And I have created the spoiler to destroy.

53:11 [a] Following Masoretic Text, Targum, and Vulgate; Dead Sea Scrolls and Septuagint read *From the labor of His soul He shall see light.*

17 No weapon formed against you shall
prosper,
And every tongue *which* rises against
you in judgment
You shall condemn.
This *is* the heritage of the servants of
the LORD,
And their righteousness *is* from Me,"
Says the LORD.

An Invitation to Abundant Life

55 "Ho! Everyone who thirsts,
Come to the waters;
And you who have no money,
Come, buy and eat.
Yes, come, buy wine and milk
Without money and without price.
2 Why do you spend money for *what is* not
bread,
And your wages for *what* does not
satisfy?
Listen carefully to Me, and eat *what is*
good,
And let your soul delight itself in
abundance.
3 Incline your ear, and come to Me.
Hear, and your soul shall live;
And I will make an everlasting covenant
with you—
The sure mercies of David.
4 Indeed I have given him *as* a witness to
the people,
A leader and commander for the people.
5 Surely you shall call a nation you do not
know,
And nations *who* do not know you shall
run to you,
Because of the LORD your God,
And the Holy One of Israel;
For He has glorified you."

6 Seek the LORD while He may be found,
Call upon Him while He is near.
7 Let the wicked forsake his way,
And the unrighteous man his thoughts;
Let him return to the LORD,
And He will have mercy on him;
And to our God,
For He will abundantly pardon.

8 "For My thoughts *are* not your thoughts,
Nor *are* your ways My ways," says the
LORD.
9 "For *as* the heavens are higher than the
earth,
So are My ways higher than your ways,
And My thoughts than your thoughts.

10 "For as the rain comes down, and the
snow from heaven,
And do not return there,
But water the earth,

55:1 ARE YOU THIRSTY?

Of course you're thirsty sometimes. At those times, a cold soda or a glass of ice water is the greatest thing in the world. There's another kind of thirst that a cool can of soda can't quench. That's the thirst of the soul. Everybody's soul is thirsty sometimes, too.

Those are the times when nothing will satisfy you but God. Jesus said, "He who believes in Me shall never thirst" (John 6:35). Truly you can't drink from Jesus the way you drink water. But the way He satisfies you is *like* a river of living water (see John 7:38).

Imagine Jesus to be *like* a deep well of cool, pure spring water. As you drink from Him, you become filled with His life. Then you find that the life He fills you with overflows and satisfies those around you, too. Ask to be filled with that living water that only Jesus can give.

And make it bring forth and bud,
That it may give seed to the sower
And bread to the eater,
11 So shall My word be that goes forth from My mouth;
It shall not return to Me void,
But it shall accomplish what I please,
And it shall prosper *in the thing* for which I sent it.

12 "For you shall go out with joy,
And be led out with peace;
The mountains and the hills
Shall break forth into singing before you,
And all the trees of the field shall clap *their* hands.
13 Instead of the thorn shall come up the cypress tree,
And instead of the brier shall come up the myrtle tree;
And it shall be to the LORD for a name,
For an everlasting sign *that* shall not be cut off."

Salvation for the Gentiles

56 Thus says the LORD:

"Keep justice, and do righteousness,
For My salvation *is* about to come,
And My righteousness to be revealed.
2 Blessed *is* the man *who* does this,
And the son of man *who* lays hold on it;
Who keeps from defiling the Sabbath,
And keeps his hand from doing any evil."

3 Do not let the son of the foreigner
Who has joined himself to the LORD
Speak, saying,
"The LORD has utterly separated me from His people";
Nor let the eunuch say,
"Here I am, a dry tree."
4 For thus says the LORD:
"To the eunuchs who keep My Sabbaths,
And choose what pleases Me,
And hold fast My covenant,
5 Even to them I will give in My house
And within My walls a place and a name
Better than that of sons and daughters;
I will give them[a] an everlasting name
That shall not be cut off.

6 "Also the sons of the foreigner
Who join themselves to the LORD, to serve Him,
And to love the name of the LORD, to be His servants—
Everyone who keeps from defiling the Sabbath,
And holds fast My covenant—
7 Even them I will bring to My holy mountain,
And make them joyful in My house of prayer.
Their burnt offerings and their sacrifices
Will be accepted on My altar;
For My house shall be called a house of prayer for all nations."

56:5 [a] Literally *him*

KNOWING AND FINDING GOD

READ IT: ISAIAH 55:6, 7

God hates wickedness. When people hurt others, when they act in unloving ways, or when they ignore God's design for creation and life, God gets angry. But He never hates or gives up on a person who does wicked things (and we all do wicked things). It says right here that if a wicked person returns to God, He will welcome and pardon that person. That's good news for all of us!

8 The Lord GOD, who gathers the outcasts of Israel, says,
"Yet I will gather to him
Others besides those who are gathered to him."

Israel's Irresponsible Leaders

9 All you beasts of the field, come to devour,
All you beasts in the forest.
10 His watchmen *are* blind,
They are all ignorant;
They *are* all dumb dogs,
They cannot bark;
Sleeping, lying down, loving to slumber.
11 Yes, *they are* greedy dogs
Which never have enough.
And they *are* shepherds
Who cannot understand;
They all look to their own way,
Every one for his own gain,
From his *own* territory.
12 "Come," *one says,* "I will bring wine,
And we will fill ourselves with intoxicating drink;
Tomorrow will be as today,
And much more abundant."

Israel's Futile Idolatry

57 The righteous perishes,
And no man takes *it* to heart;
Merciful men *are* taken away,
While no one considers
That the righteous is taken away from evil.
2 He shall enter into peace;
They shall rest in their beds,
Each one walking *in* his uprightness.

3 "But come here,
You sons of the sorceress,
You offspring of the adulterer and the harlot!
4 Whom do you ridicule?
Against whom do you make a wide mouth
And stick out the tongue?
Are you not children of transgression,
Offspring of falsehood,
5 Inflaming yourselves with gods under every green tree,
Slaying the children in the valleys,
Under the clefts of the rocks?
6 Among the smooth *stones* of the stream
Is your portion;
They, they, *are* your lot!
Even to them you have poured a drink offering,
You have offered a grain offering.
Should I receive comfort in these?

7 "On a lofty and high mountain
You have set your bed;
Even there you went up
To offer sacrifice.
8 Also behind the doors and their posts
You have set up your remembrance;
For you have uncovered yourself *to those other* than Me,
And have gone up to them;
You have enlarged your bed
And made *a covenant* with them;
You have loved their bed,
Where you saw *their* nudity.[a]
9 You went to the king with ointment,
And increased your perfumes;
You sent your messengers far off,
And *even* descended to Sheol.
10 You are wearied in the length of your way;
Yet you did not say, 'There is no hope.'
You have found the life of your hand;
Therefore you were not grieved.

11 "And of whom have you been afraid, or feared,
That you have lied
And not remembered Me,
Nor taken *it* to your heart?
Is it not because I have held My peace from of old
That you do not fear Me?
12 I will declare your righteousness
And your works,
For they will not profit you.
13 When you cry out,
Let your collection *of idols* deliver you.
But the wind will carry them all away,
A breath will take *them.*
But he who puts his trust in Me shall possess the land,
And shall inherit My holy mountain."

Healing for the Backslider

14 And one shall say,
"Heap it up! Heap it up!
Prepare the way,

57:8 [a] Literally *hand,* a euphemism

Take the stumbling block out of the way
of My people."

15 For thus says the High and Lofty One
Who inhabits eternity, whose name *is*
Holy:
"I dwell in the high and holy *place*,
With him *who* has a contrite and
humble spirit,
To revive the spirit of the humble,
And to revive the heart of the contrite
ones.
16 For I will not contend forever,
Nor will I always be angry;
For the spirit would fail before Me,
And the souls *which* I have made.
17 For the iniquity of his covetousness
I was angry and struck him;
I hid and was angry,
And he went on backsliding in the way
of his heart.
18 I have seen his ways, and will heal him;
I will also lead him,
And restore comforts to him
And to his mourners.

19 "I create the fruit of the lips:
Peace, peace to *him who is* far off and to
him who is near,"
Says the LORD,
"And I will heal him."
20 But the wicked *are* like the troubled sea,
When it cannot rest,
Whose waters cast up mire and dirt.

21 "*There is* no peace,"
Says my God, "for the wicked."

Fasting that Pleases God

58 "Cry aloud, spare not;
Lift up your voice like a trumpet;
Tell My people their transgression,
And the house of Jacob their sins.
2 Yet they seek Me daily,
And delight to know My ways,
As a nation that did righteousness,
And did not forsake the ordinance of
their God.
They ask of Me the ordinances of
justice;
They take delight in approaching God.
3 'Why have we fasted,' *they say*, 'and You
have not seen?
Why have we afflicted our souls, and
You take no notice?'

"In fact, in the day of your fast you find
pleasure,
And exploit all your laborers.
4 Indeed you fast for strife and debate,
And to strike with the fist of
wickedness.
You will not fast as *you do* this day,
To make your voice heard on high.
5 Is it a fast that I have chosen,
A day for a man to afflict his soul?
Is it to bow down his head like a
bulrush,
And to spread out sackcloth and ashes?
Would you call this a fast,
And an acceptable day to the LORD?

6 "*Is* this not the fast that I have chosen:
To loose the bonds of wickedness,
To undo the heavy burdens,
To let the oppressed go free,
And that you break every yoke?
7 *Is it* not to share your bread with the
hungry,
And that you bring to your house the
poor who are cast out;
When you see the naked, that you cover
him,
And not hide yourself from your own
flesh?
8 Then your light shall break forth like
the morning,
Your healing shall spring forth speedily,
And your righteousness shall go before
you;
The glory of the LORD shall be your rear
guard.
9 Then you shall call, and the LORD will
answer;
You shall cry, and He will say, 'Here I
am.'

"If you take away the yoke from your
midst,
The pointing of the finger, and
speaking wickedness,
10 *If* you extend your soul to the hungry
And satisfy the afflicted soul,
Then your light shall dawn in the
darkness,
And your darkness shall *be* as the
noonday.
11 The LORD will guide you continually,
And satisfy your soul in drought,
And strengthen your bones;
You shall be like a watered garden,

And like a spring of water, whose waters
do not fail.
12 Those from among you
Shall build the old waste places;
You shall raise up the foundations of
many generations;
And you shall be called the Repairer of
the Breach,
The Restorer of Streets to Dwell In.

13 "If you turn away your foot from the
Sabbath,
From doing your pleasure on My holy
day,
And call the Sabbath a delight,
The holy *day* of the LORD honorable,
And shall honor Him, not doing your
own ways,
Nor finding your own pleasure,
Nor speaking *your own* words,
14 Then you shall delight yourself in the
LORD;
And I will cause you to ride on the high
hills of the earth,
And feed you with the heritage of Jacob
your father.
The mouth of the LORD has spoken."

Separated from God

59 Behold, the LORD's hand is not
shortened,
That it cannot save;
Nor His ear heavy,
That it cannot hear.
2 But your iniquities have separated you
from your God;
And your sins have hidden *His* face
from you,
So that He will not hear.
3 For your hands are defiled with blood,
And your fingers with iniquity;
Your lips have spoken lies,
Your tongue has muttered perversity.

4 No one calls for justice,
Nor does *any* plead for truth.
They trust in empty words and speak
lies;
They conceive evil and bring forth
iniquity.
5 They hatch vipers' eggs and weave the
spider's web;
He who eats of their eggs dies,
And *from* that which is crushed a viper
breaks out.
6 Their webs will not become garments,
Nor will they cover themselves with
their works;
Their works *are* works of iniquity,
And the act of violence *is* in their hands.
7 Their feet run to evil,
And they make haste to shed innocent
blood;
Their thoughts *are* thoughts of iniquity;
Wasting and destruction *are* in their
paths.
8 The way of peace they have not known,
And *there is* no justice in their ways;
They have made themselves crooked
paths;
Whoever takes that way shall not know
peace.

Sin Confessed

9 Therefore justice is far from us,
Nor does righteousness overtake us;
We look for light, but there is darkness!
For brightness, *but* we walk in
blackness!
10 We grope for the wall like the blind,
And we grope as if *we had* no eyes;
We stumble at noonday as at twilight;
We are as dead *men* in desolate places.
11 We all growl like bears,
And moan sadly like doves;
We look for justice, but *there is* none;
For salvation, *but* it is far from us.
12 For our transgressions are multiplied
before You,
And our sins testify against us;
For our transgressions *are* with us,
And *as for* our iniquities, we know them:
13 In transgressing and lying against the
LORD,
And departing from our God,
Speaking oppression and revolt,
Conceiving and uttering from the heart
words of falsehood.
14 Justice is turned back,
And righteousness stands afar off;
For truth is fallen in the street,
And equity cannot enter.
15 So truth fails,
And he *who* departs from evil makes
himself a prey.

The Redeemer of Zion

Then the LORD saw *it,* and it displeased
Him
That *there was* no justice.

16 He saw that *there was* no man,
And wondered that *there was* no intercessor;
Therefore His own arm brought salvation for Him;
And His own righteousness, it sustained Him.
17 For He put on righteousness as a breastplate,
And a helmet of salvation on His head;
He put on the garments of vengeance for clothing,
And was clad with zeal as a cloak.
18 According to *their* deeds, accordingly He will repay,
Fury to His adversaries,
Recompense to His enemies;
The coastlands He will fully repay.
19 So shall they fear
The name of the LORD from the west,
And His glory from the rising of the sun;
When the enemy comes in like a flood,
The Spirit of the LORD will lift up a standard against him.

20 "The Redeemer will come to Zion,
And to those who turn from transgression in Jacob,"
Says the LORD.

21"As for Me," says the LORD, "this *is* My
covenant with them: My Spirit who *is* upon
you, and My words which I have put in your
mouth, shall not depart from your mouth,
nor from the mouth of your descendants,
nor from the mouth of your descendants'
descendants," says the LORD, "from this time
and forevermore."

The Gentiles Bless Zion

60 Arise, shine;
For your light has come!
And the glory of the LORD is risen upon you.
2 *For behold, the* darkness shall cover the earth,
And deep darkness the people;
But the LORD will arise over you,
And His glory will be seen upon you.
3 The Gentiles shall come to your light,
And kings to the brightness of your rising.

4 "Lift up your eyes all around, and see:
They all gather together, they come to you;
Your sons shall come from afar,
And your daughters shall be nursed at *your* side.
5 Then you shall see and become radiant,
And your heart shall swell with joy;
Because the abundance of the sea shall be turned to you,
The wealth of the Gentiles shall come to you.
6 The multitude of camels shall cover your *land,*
The dromedaries of Midian and Ephah;
All those from Sheba shall come;
They shall bring gold and incense,
And they shall proclaim the praises of the LORD.
7 All the flocks of Kedar shall be gathered together to you,
The rams of Nebaioth shall minister to you;
They shall ascend with acceptance on My altar,
And I will glorify the house of My glory.

8 "Who *are* these *who* fly like a cloud,
And like doves to their roosts?
9 Surely the coastlands shall wait for Me;
And the ships of Tarshish *will come* first,
To bring your sons from afar,
Their silver and their gold with them,
To the name of the LORD your God,
And to the Holy One of Israel,
Because He has glorified you.

10 "The sons of foreigners shall build up your walls,
And their kings shall minister to you;
For in My wrath I struck you,
But in My favor I have had mercy on you.
11 Therefore your gates shall be open continually;
They shall not be shut day or night,
That *men* may bring to you the wealth of the Gentiles,
And their kings in procession.
12 For the nation and kingdom which will not serve you shall perish,
And *those* nations shall be utterly ruined.

13 "The glory of Lebanon shall come to you,
The cypress, the pine, and the box tree together,

To beautify the place of My sanctuary;
And I will make the place of My feet
glorious.
14 Also the sons of those who afflicted you
Shall come bowing to you,
And all those who despised you shall
fall prostrate at the soles of your feet;
And they shall call you The City of the
LORD,
Zion of the Holy One of Israel.

15 "Whereas you have been forsaken and
hated,
So that no one went through *you,*
I will make you an eternal excellence,
A joy of many generations.
16 You shall drink the milk of the Gentiles,
And milk the breast of kings;
You shall know that I, the LORD, *am*
your Savior
And your Redeemer, the Mighty One
of Jacob.

17 "Instead of bronze I will bring gold,
Instead of iron I will bring silver,
Instead of wood, bronze,
And instead of stones, iron.
I will also make your officers peace,
And your magistrates righteousness.
18 Violence shall no longer be heard in
your land,
Neither wasting nor destruction within
your borders;
But you shall call your walls Salvation,
And your gates Praise.

God the Glory of His People

19 "The sun shall no longer be your light by
day,
Nor for brightness shall the moon give
light to you;
But the LORD will be to you an
everlasting light,
And your God your glory.
20 Your sun shall no longer go down,
Nor shall your moon withdraw itself;
For the LORD will be your everlasting
light,
And the days of your mourning shall be
ended.
21 Also your people *shall* all *be* righteous;
They shall inherit the land forever,
The branch of My planting,
The work of My hands,
That I may be glorified.
22 A little one shall become a thousand,

In Focus

61:3 Glorified Pronounced *GLORY-fyed*. God's beauty shines through all the good things Jesus does for needy people.

And a small one a strong nation.
I, the LORD, will hasten it in its time."

The Good News of Salvation

61 "The Spirit of the Lord GOD *is*
upon Me,
Because the LORD has anointed Me
To preach good tidings to the poor;
He has sent Me to heal the
brokenhearted,
To proclaim liberty to the captives,
And the opening of the prison to *those
who are* bound;
2 To proclaim the acceptable year of the
LORD,
And the day of vengeance of our God;
To comfort all who mourn,
3 To console those who mourn in Zion,
To give them beauty for ashes,
The oil of joy for mourning,
The garment of praise for the spirit of
heaviness;
That they may be called trees of
righteousness,
The planting of the LORD, that He may
be glorified."

4 And they shall rebuild the old ruins,
They shall raise up the former
desolations,
And they shall repair the ruined cities,
The desolations of many generations.
5 Strangers shall stand and feed your
flocks,
And the sons of the foreigner
Shall be your plowmen and your
vinedressers.
6 But you shall be named the priests of
the LORD,
They shall call you the servants of our
God.
You shall eat the riches of the Gentiles,
And in their glory you shall boast.

7 Instead of your shame *you shall have* double *honor,*
And *instead of* confusion they shall rejoice in their portion.
Therefore in their land they shall possess double;
Everlasting joy shall be theirs.

8 "For I, the LORD, love justice;
I hate robbery for burnt offering;
I will direct their work in truth,
And will make with them an everlasting covenant.
9 Their descendants shall be known among the Gentiles,
And their offspring among the people.
All who see them shall acknowledge them,
That they *are* the posterity *whom* the LORD has blessed."

10 I will greatly rejoice in the LORD,
My soul shall be joyful in my God;
For He has clothed me with the garments of salvation,
He has covered me with the robe of righteousness,
As a bridegroom decks *himself* with ornaments,
And as a bride adorns *herself* with her jewels.
11 For as the earth brings forth its bud,
As the garden causes the things that are sown in it to spring forth,
So the Lord GOD will cause righteousness and praise to spring forth before all the nations.

Assurance of Zion's Salvation

62 For Zion's sake I will not hold My peace,
And for Jerusalem's sake I will not rest,
Until her righteousness goes forth as brightness,
And her salvation as a lamp *that* burns.
2 The Gentiles shall see your righteousness,
And all kings your glory.
You shall be called by a new name,
Which the mouth of the LORD will name.
3 You shall also be a crown of glory
In the hand of the LORD,
And a royal diadem
In the hand of your God.
4 You shall no longer be termed Forsaken,
Nor shall your land any more be termed Desolate;
But you shall be called Hephzibah,[a] and your land Beulah;[b]
For the LORD delights in you,
And your land shall be married.
5 For *as* a young man marries a virgin,
So shall your sons marry you;
And *as* the bridegroom rejoices over the bride,
So shall your God rejoice over you.

6 I have set watchmen on your walls, O Jerusalem;
They shall never hold their peace day or night.
You who make mention of the LORD, do not keep silent,
7 And give Him no rest till He establishes
And till He makes Jerusalem a praise in the earth.

8 The LORD has sworn by His right hand
And by the arm of His strength:
"Surely I will no longer give your grain
As food for your enemies;
And the sons of the foreigner shall not drink your new wine,
For which you have labored.
9 But those who have gathered it shall eat it,
And praise the LORD;
Those who have brought it together shall drink it in My holy courts."

10 Go through,
Go through the gates!
Prepare the way for the people;
Build up,
Build up the highway!
Take out the stones,
Lift up a banner for the peoples!

11 Indeed the LORD has proclaimed
To the end of the world:
"Say to the daughter of Zion,
'Surely your salvation is coming;
Behold, His reward is with Him,
And His work before Him.'"
12 And they shall call them The Holy People,
The Redeemed of the LORD;
And you shall be called Sought Out,
A City Not Forsaken.

62:4 [a] Literally *My Delight Is in Her* [b] Literally *Married*

The LORD in Judgment and Salvation

63 Who *is* this who comes from Edom,
With dyed garments from Bozrah,
This *One who is* glorious in His apparel,
Traveling in the greatness of His strength?—

"I who speak in righteousness, mighty to save."

2 Why *is* Your apparel red,
And Your garments like one who treads in the winepress?

3 "I have trodden the winepress alone,
And from the peoples no one *was* with Me.
For I have trodden them in My anger,
And trampled them in My fury;
Their blood is sprinkled upon My garments,
And I have stained all My robes.
4 For the day of vengeance *is* in My heart,
And the year of My redeemed has come.
5 I looked, but *there was* no one to help,
And I wondered
That *there was* no one to uphold;
Therefore My own arm brought salvation for Me;
And My own fury, it sustained Me.
6 I have trodden down the peoples in My anger,
Made them drunk in My fury,
And brought down their strength to the earth."

God's Mercy Remembered

7 I will mention the lovingkindnesses of the LORD
And the praises of the LORD,
According to all that the LORD has bestowed on us,
And the great goodness toward the house of Israel,
Which He has bestowed on them according to His mercies,
According to the multitude of His lovingkindnesses.
8 For He said, "Surely they *are* My people,
Children *who* will not lie."
So He became their Savior.
9 In all their affliction He was afflicted,
And the Angel of His Presence saved them;
In His love and in His pity He redeemed them;
And He bore them and carried them
All the days of old.
10 But they rebelled and grieved His Holy Spirit;
So He turned Himself against them as an enemy,
And He fought against them.

11 Then he remembered the days of old,
Moses *and* his people, *saying:*
"Where *is* He who brought them up out of the sea
With the shepherd of His flock?
Where *is* He who put His Holy Spirit within them,
12 Who led *them* by the right hand of Moses,
With His glorious arm,
Dividing the water before them
To make for Himself an everlasting name,
13 Who led them through the deep,
As a horse in the wilderness,
That they might not stumble?"

14 As a beast goes down into the valley,
And the Spirit of the LORD causes him to rest,
So You lead Your people,
To make Yourself a glorious name.

A Prayer of Penitence

15 Look down from heaven,
And see from Your habitation, holy and glorious.
Where *are* Your zeal and Your strength,
The yearning of Your heart and Your mercies toward me?
Are they restrained?
16 Doubtless You *are* our Father,
Though Abraham was ignorant of us,
And Israel does not acknowledge us.
You, O LORD, *are* our Father;
Our Redeemer from Everlasting *is* Your name.
17 O LORD, why have You made us stray from Your ways,
And hardened our heart from Your fear?
Return for Your servants' sake,
The tribes of Your inheritance.
18 Your holy people have possessed *it* but a little while;
Our adversaries have trodden down Your sanctuary.

19 We have become *like* those of old, over
whom You never ruled,
Those who were never called by Your
name.

64 Oh, that You would rend the
heavens!
That You would come down!
That the mountains might shake at
Your presence—
2 As fire burns brushwood,
As fire causes water to boil—
To make Your name known to Your
adversaries,
That the nations may tremble at Your
presence!
3 When You did awesome things *for which*
we did not look,
You came down,
The mountains shook at Your presence.
4 For since the beginning of the world
Men have not heard nor perceived by
the ear,
Nor has the eye seen any God besides
You,
Who acts for the one who waits for Him.
5 You meet him who rejoices and does
righteousness,
Who remembers You in Your ways.
You are indeed angry, for we have
sinned—
In these ways we continue;
And we need to be saved.

6 But we are all like an unclean *thing,*
And all our righteousnesses *are* like
filthy rags;
We all fade as a leaf,
And our iniquities, like the wind,
Have taken us away.
7 And *there is* no one who calls on Your
name,
Who stirs himself up to take hold of
You;
For You have hidden Your face from us,
And have consumed us because of our
iniquities.

8 But now, O LORD,
You *are* our Father;
We *are* the clay, and You our potter;
And all we *are* the work of Your hand.
9 Do not be furious, O LORD,
Nor remember iniquity forever;
Indeed, please look—we all *are* Your
people!
10 Your holy cities are a wilderness,
Zion is a wilderness,
Jerusalem a desolation.
11 Our holy and beautiful temple,
Where our fathers praised You,
Is burned up with fire;
And all our pleasant things are laid
waste.
12 Will You restrain Yourself because of
these *things,* O LORD?
Will You hold Your peace, and afflict us
very severely?

The Righteousness of God's Judgment

65 "I was sought by *those who* did not
ask *for Me;*
I was found by *those who* did not
seek Me.
I said, 'Here I am, here I am,'
To a nation *that* was not called by My
name.
2 I have stretched out My hands all day
long to a rebellious people,
Who walk in a way *that is* not good,
According to their own thoughts;
3 A people who provoke Me to anger
continually to My face;
Who sacrifice in gardens,
And burn incense on altars of brick;
4 Who sit among the graves,
And spend the night in the tombs;
Who eat swine's flesh,
And the broth of abominable things is
in their vessels;
5 Who say, 'Keep to yourself,
Do not come near me,
For I am holier than you!'
These *are* smoke in My nostrils,
A fire that burns all the day.

6 "Behold, *it is* written before Me:
I will not keep silence, but will repay—
Even repay into their bosom—
7 Your iniquities and the iniquities of
your fathers together,"
Says the LORD,
"Who have burned incense on the
mountains
And blasphemed Me on the hills;
Therefore I will measure their former
work into their bosom."

8 Thus says the LORD:

"As the new wine is found in the cluster,
And *one* says, 'Do not destroy it,

For a blessing *is* in it,'
So will I do for My servants' sake,
That I may not destroy them all.
9 I will bring forth descendants from Jacob,
And from Judah an heir of My mountains;
My elect shall inherit it,
And My servants shall dwell there.
10 Sharon shall be a fold of flocks,
And the Valley of Achor a place for herds to lie down,
For My people who have sought Me.

11 "But you *are* those who forsake the LORD,
Who forget My holy mountain,
Who prepare a table for Gad,[a]
And who furnish a drink offering for Meni.[b]
12 Therefore I will number you for the sword,
And you shall all bow down to the slaughter;
Because, when I called, you did not answer;
When I spoke, you did not hear,
But did evil before My eyes,
And chose *that* in which I do not delight."

13 Therefore thus says the Lord GOD:

"Behold, My servants shall eat,
But you shall be hungry;
Behold, My servants shall drink,
But you shall be thirsty;
Behold, My servants shall rejoice,
But you shall be ashamed;
14 Behold, My servants shall sing for joy of heart,
But you shall cry for sorrow of heart,
And wail for grief of spirit.
15 You shall leave your name as a curse to My chosen;
For the Lord GOD will slay you,
And call His servants by another name;
16 So that he who blesses himself in the earth
Shall bless himself in the God of truth;
And he who swears in the earth
Shall swear by the God of truth;
Because the former troubles are forgotten,
And because they are hidden from My eyes.

The Glorious New Creation

17 "For behold, I create new heavens and a new earth;
And the former shall not be remembered or come to mind.
18 But be glad and rejoice forever in what I create;
For behold, I create Jerusalem *as* a rejoicing,
And her people a joy.
19 I will rejoice in Jerusalem,
And joy in My people;
The voice of weeping shall no longer be heard in her,
Nor the voice of crying.

20 "No more shall an infant from there *live but a few* days,
Nor an old man who has not fulfilled his days;
For the child shall die one hundred years old,
But the sinner *being* one hundred years old shall be accursed.
21 They shall build houses and inhabit *them;*
They shall plant vineyards and eat their fruit.
22 They shall not build and another inhabit;
They shall not plant and another eat;
For as the days of a tree, *so shall be* the days of My people,
And My elect shall long enjoy the work of their hands.
23 They shall not labor in vain,
Nor bring forth children for trouble;
For they *shall be* the descendants of the blessed of the LORD,
And their offspring with them.

24 "It shall come to pass
That before they call, I will answer;
And while they are still speaking, I will hear.
25 The wolf and the lamb shall feed together,
The lion shall eat straw like the ox,
And dust *shall be* the serpent's food.
They shall not hurt nor destroy in all My holy mountain,"
Says the LORD.

65:11 [a] Literally *Troop* or *Fortune*, a pagan deity [b] Literally *Number* or *Destiny*, a pagan deity

True Worship and False

66 Thus says the LORD:

"Heaven *is* My throne,
And earth *is* My footstool.
Where *is* the house that you will build Me?
And where *is* the place of My rest?
2 For all those *things* My hand has made,
And all those *things* exist,"
Says the LORD.
"But on this *one* will I look:
On *him who is* poor and of a contrite spirit,
And who trembles at My word.

3 "He who kills a bull *is as if* he slays a man;
He who sacrifices a lamb, *as if* he breaks a dog's neck;
He who offers a grain offering, *as if he offers* swine's blood;
He who burns incense, *as if* he blesses an idol.
Just as they have chosen their own ways,
And their soul delights in their abominations,
4 So will I choose their delusions,
And bring their fears on them;
Because, when I called, no one answered,
When I spoke they did not hear;
But they did evil before My eyes,
And chose *that* in which I do not delight."

The LORD Vindicates Zion

5 Hear the word of the LORD,
You who tremble at His word:
"Your brethren who hated you,
Who cast you out for My name's sake, said,
'Let the LORD be glorified,
That we may see your joy.'
But they shall be ashamed."

6 *The sound of noise from* the city!
A voice from the temple!
The voice of the LORD,
Who fully repays His enemies!

7 "Before she was in labor, she gave birth;
Before her pain came,
She delivered a male child.
8 Who has heard such a thing?
Who has seen such things?
Shall the earth be made to give birth in one day?
Or shall a nation be born at once?
For as soon as Zion was in labor,
She gave birth to her children.
9 Shall I bring to the time of birth, and not cause delivery?" says the LORD.
"Shall I who cause delivery shut up *the womb?*" says your God.
10 "Rejoice with Jerusalem,
And be glad with her, all you who love her;
Rejoice for joy with her, all you who mourn for her;
11 That you may feed and be satisfied
With the consolation of her bosom,
That you may drink deeply and be delighted
With the abundance of her glory."

12 For thus says the LORD:

"Behold, I will extend peace to her like a river,
And the glory of the Gentiles like a flowing stream.
Then you shall feed;
On *her* sides shall you be carried,
And be dandled on *her* knees.
13 As one whom his mother comforts,
So I will comfort you;
And you shall be comforted in Jerusalem."

The Reign and Indignation of God

14 When you see *this,* your heart shall rejoice,
And your bones shall flourish like grass;
The hand of the LORD shall be known to His servants,
And *His* indignation to His enemies.
15 For behold, the LORD will come with fire
And with His chariots, like a whirlwind,
To render His anger with fury,
And His rebuke with flames of fire.
16 For by fire and by His sword
The LORD will judge all flesh;
And the slain of the LORD shall be many.

17 "Those who sanctify themselves and purify themselves,
To go to the gardens
After an *idol* in the midst,

Eating swine's flesh and the
abomination and the mouse,
Shall be consumed together," says the
LORD.

18"For I *know* their works and their
thoughts. It shall be that I will gather all
nations and tongues; and they shall come
and see My glory. 19I will set a sign among
them; and those among them who escape I
will send to the nations: *to* Tarshish and Pul[a]
and Lud, who draw the bow, and Tubal and
Javan, *to* the coastlands afar off who have not
heard My fame nor seen My glory. And they
shall declare My glory among the Gentiles.
20Then they shall bring all your brethren for
an offering to the LORD out of all nations,
on horses and in chariots and in litters, on
mules and on camels, to My holy mountain
Jerusalem," says the LORD, "as the children
of Israel bring an offering in a clean vessel
into the house of the LORD. 21And I will also
take some of them for priests *and* Levites,"
says the LORD.

22 "For as the new heavens and the new earth
Which I will make shall remain before
Me," says the LORD,
"So shall your descendants and your
name remain.
23 And it shall come to pass
That from one New Moon to another,
And from one Sabbath to another,
All flesh shall come to worship before
Me," says the LORD.

24 "And they shall go forth and look
Upon the corpses of the men
Who have transgressed against Me.
For their worm does not die,
And their fire is not quenched.
They shall be an abhorrence to all flesh."

66:19 [a] Following Masoretic Text and Targum; Septuagint reads *Put* (compare Jeremiah 46:9).

66:22 A NEW WORLD COMING

If you think about it for a while, you have to admit that the world we live in is a pretty sad place. There is constant war, crime, sickness, starvation, and death. Our world population doubles and triples, while energy supplies get scarcer and scarcer. Everywhere the earth is polluted. This isn't what God had in mind for those who love Him.

God has in mind new heavens and a new earth, where all the pain and suffering will be no more. He promises it in Isaiah's words, "The new heavens and the new earth which I will make shall remain" (Isaiah 66:22). That means that the old heavens and our present dying world will be gone.

So let's look forward to the new and better things God has in mind—a happy world where death and disease and violence are not present. Ask God to bring in His new world soon, and to make you a citizen of that eternal country.

The BOOK of

JEREMIAH

626 B.C.–586 B.C.

Behind the Scenes

READ IT:

The book of Jeremiah is the story of the prophet Jeremiah and his contact with the people and kings of Judah. God told him to warn Judah about its wickedness. For twenty years Jeremiah tried to bring the people of Judah back to God. Nobody listened.

GET IT:

Who wrote it: The prophet Jeremiah

When it was written: 626 B.C.–586 B.C.

Why it was written: to warn the people of their punishment and to give them hope for the future.

LIVE IT:

Even if we sin, God never stops loving us.

God has a great plan for our lives.

FIND IT:

The Prophet Jeremiah Is Called	*Jeremiah 1*
Idols and the True God	*Jeremiah 10*
Symbol of the Linen Sash	*Jeremiah 13*
Jeremiah's Lifestyle	*Jeremiah 16*
God's Love for Israel	*Jeremiah 31*
Jeremiah Buys a Field	*Jeremiah 32*
Jeremiah's Scroll	*Jeremiah 36*
Jeremiah in the Dungeon	*Jeremiah 38*
Jeremiah Goes Free	*Jeremiah 39–40*

1 The words of Jeremiah the son of Hilkiah, of the priests who *were* in Anathoth
in the land of Benjamin, [2]to whom the word
of the LORD came in the days of Josiah the
son of Amon, king of Judah, in the thirteenth year of his reign. [3]It came also in the
days of Jehoiakim the son of Josiah, king of
Judah, until the end of the eleventh year of
Zedekiah the son of Josiah, king of Judah,
until the carrying away of Jerusalem captive
in the fifth month.

The Prophet Is Called

[4]Then the word of the LORD came to me,
saying:

5 "Before I formed you in the womb I
knew you;
Before you were born I sanctified you;
I ordained you a prophet to the nations."

[6]Then said I:

"Ah, Lord GOD!
Behold, I cannot speak, for I *am* a
youth."

[7]But the LORD said to me:

"Do not say, 'I *am* a youth,'
For you shall go to all to whom I send
you,
And whatever I command you, you shall
speak.
8 Do not be afraid of their faces,
For I *am* with you to deliver you," says
the LORD.

[9]Then the LORD put forth His hand and
touched my mouth, and the LORD said to me:

"Behold, I have put My words in your
mouth.
10 See, I have this day set you over the
nations and over the kingdoms,
To root out and to pull down,
To destroy and to throw down,
To build and to plant."

[11]Moreover the word of the LORD came to
me, saying, "Jeremiah, what do you see?"
And I said, "I see a branch of an almond
tree."
[12]Then the LORD said to me, "You have
seen well, for I am ready to perform My
word."
[13]And the word of the LORD came to me
the second time, saying, "What do you see?"
And I said, "I see a boiling pot, and it is
facing away from the north."
[14]Then the LORD said to me:

"Out of the north calamity shall break
forth
On all the inhabitants of the land.
15 For behold, I am calling
All the families of the kingdoms of the
north," says the LORD;
"They shall come and each one set his
throne
At the entrance of the gates of
Jerusalem,
Against all its walls all around,
And against all the cities of Judah.
16 I will utter My judgments
Against them concerning all their
wickedness,
Because they have forsaken Me,
Burned incense to other gods,
And worshiped the works of their own
hands.

17 "Therefore prepare yourself and arise,

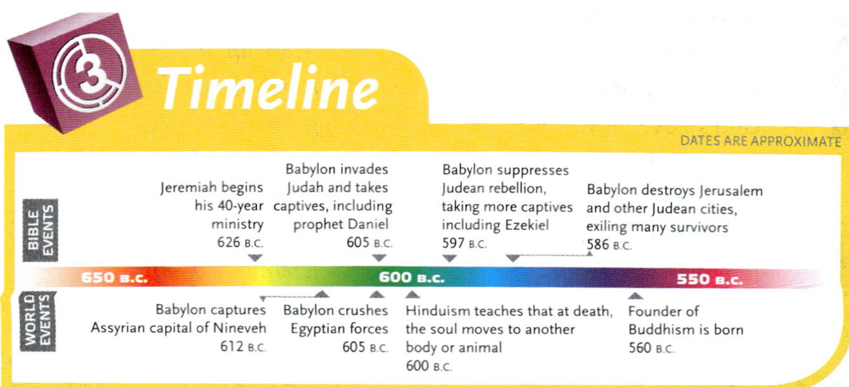

And speak to them all that I command
you.
Do not be dismayed before their faces,
Lest I dismay you before them.
18 For behold, I have made you this day
A fortified city and an iron pillar,
And bronze walls against the whole
land—
Against the kings of Judah,
Against its princes,
Against its priests,
And against the people of the land.
19 They will fight against you,
But they shall not prevail against you.
For I *am* with you," says the LORD, "to
deliver you."

God's Case Against Israel

2 Moreover the word of the LORD came
to me, saying, 2"Go and cry in the
hearing of Jerusalem, saying, 'Thus says the
LORD:

"I remember you,
The kindness of your youth,
The love of your betrothal,
When you went after Me in the
wilderness,
In a land not sown.
3 Israel *was* holiness to the LORD,
The firstfruits of His increase.
All that devour him will offend;
Disaster will come upon them," says the
LORD.'"

4Hear the word of the LORD, O house of
Jacob and all the families of the house of Israel. 5Thus says the LORD:

"What injustice have your fathers found
in Me,
That they have gone far from Me,
Have followed idols,
And have become idolaters?
6 Neither did they say, 'Where *is* the LORD,
Who brought us up out of the land of
Egypt,
Who led us through the wilderness,
Through a land of deserts and pits,
Through a land of drought and the
shadow of death,
Through a land that no one crossed
And where no one dwelt?'
7 I brought you into a bountiful country,
To eat its fruit and its goodness.
But when you entered, you defiled My
land
And made My heritage an abomination.
8 The priests did not say, 'Where *is* the
LORD?'
And those who handle the law did not
know Me;

Starring Roles

JEREMIAH'S name is pronounced *jer-uh-MY-uh* and means "The Lord Lifts Up." Sometimes people call Jeremiah "the weeping prophet" because of the sadness he felt for his people Israel.

Jeremiah's people didn't believe him when he warned them about the suffering that was to come. The armies of Babylon (pronounced *BAB-ih-lon*) would come from the East and burn the city of Jerusalem. The people of Israel would be taken as prisoners to Babylon, and their last king, Zedekiah, would be killed. The king's name is pronounced *zed-uh-KIGH-uh* and means "The Lord My Righteousness," but Zedekiah was not very righteous.

The people of Israel believed Jeremiah was a traitor because he said their enemies would destroy them. But he was only God's spokesman to warn them to turn away from their sins.

In the end, Israel's beloved city was burned and their nation ceased to exist for that time. Jeremiah was kidnapped and taken to Egypt, where he died in his sorrow for Israel.

The rulers also transgressed against
Me;
The prophets prophesied by Baal,
And walked after *things that* do not
profit.

9 "Therefore I will yet bring charges
against you," says the LORD,
"And against your children's children I
will bring charges.
10 For pass beyond the coasts of Cyprus[a]
and see,
Send to Kedar[b] and consider diligently,
And see if there has been such *a thing*.
11 Has a nation changed *its* gods,
Which *are* not gods?
But My people have changed their Glory
For *what* does not profit.
12 Be astonished, O heavens, at this,
And be horribly afraid;
Be very desolate," says the LORD.
13 "For My people have committed two
evils:
They have forsaken Me, the fountain of
living waters,
And hewn themselves cisterns—broken
cisterns that can hold no water.

14 "*Is* Israel a servant?
Is he a homeborn *slave*?
Why is he plundered?
15 The young lions roared at him, *and*
growled;
They made his land waste;
His cities are burned, without
inhabitant.

2:10 [a] Hebrew *Kittim*, western lands, especially Cyprus [b] In the northern Arabian desert, representative of the eastern cultures

On Location

Babylonian Empire 560 B.C.

Jeremiah delivers his prophecies in Jerusalem, capital of Judah. When Babylonian invaders conquer the land, they deport much of the population to Babylon, a city near what is now Baghdad. Jeremiah and a group of survivors who remain in Judah later escape to Egypt.

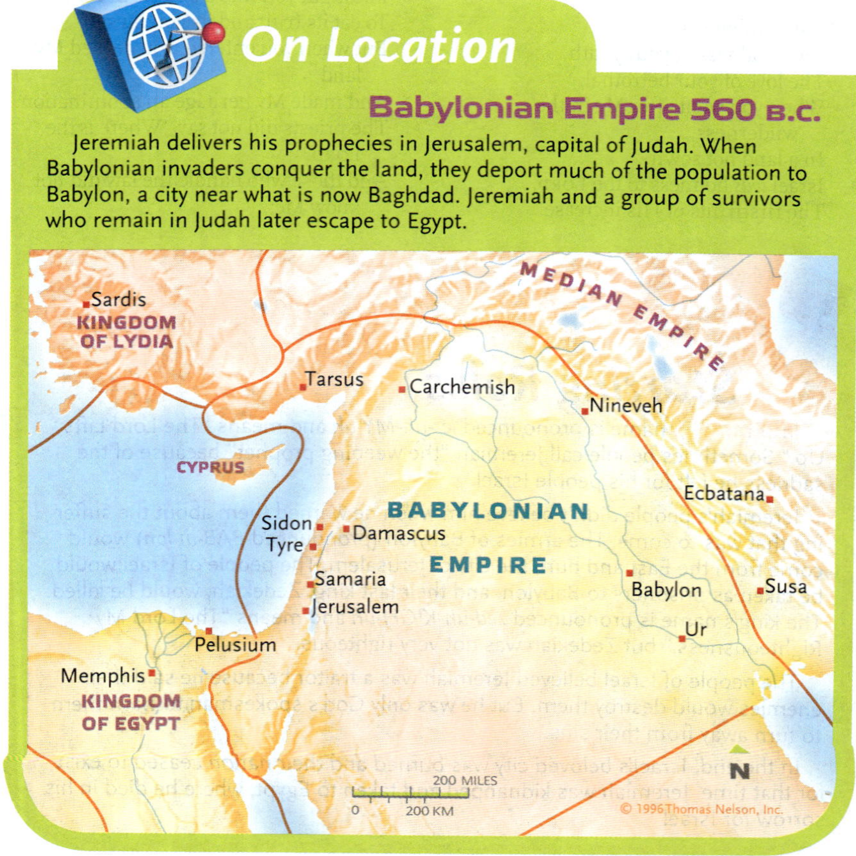

16 Also the people of Noph[a] and
Tahpanhes
Have broken the crown of your head.
17 Have you not brought this on yourself,
In that you have forsaken the LORD your
God
When He led you in the way?
18 And now why take the road to Egypt,
To drink the waters of Sihor?
Or why take the road to Assyria,
To drink the waters of the River?[a]
19 Your own wickedness will correct you,
And your backslidings will rebuke you.
Know therefore and see that *it is* an evil
and bitter *thing*
That you have forsaken the LORD your
God,
And the fear of Me *is* not in you,"
Says the Lord GOD of hosts.

20 "For of old I have broken your yoke *and*
burst your bonds;
And you said, 'I will not transgress,'
When on every high hill and under
every green tree
You lay down, playing the harlot.
21 Yet I had planted you a noble vine, a
seed of highest quality.
How then have you turned before Me
Into the degenerate plant of an alien
vine?
22 For though you wash yourself with lye,
and use much soap,
Yet your iniquity is marked before Me,"
says the Lord GOD.

23 "How can you say, 'I am not polluted,
I have not gone after the Baals'?
See your way in the valley;
Know what you have done:
You are a swift dromedary breaking
loose in her ways,
24 A wild donkey used to the wilderness,
That sniffs at the wind in her desire;
In her time of mating, who can turn her
away?
All those who seek her will not weary
themselves;
In her month they will find her.
25 Withhold your foot from being unshod,
and your throat from thirst.
But you said, 'There is no hope.
No! For I have loved aliens, and after
them I will go.'

26 "As the thief is ashamed when he is
found out,
So is the house of Israel ashamed;
They and their kings and their princes,
and their priests and their prophets,
27 Saying to a tree, 'You *are* my father,'
And to a stone, 'You gave birth to me.'
For they have turned *their* back to Me,
and not *their* face.
But in the time of their trouble
They will say, 'Arise and save us.'
28 But where *are* your gods that you have
made for yourselves?
Let them arise,
If they can save you in the time of your
trouble;
For *according to* the number of your
cities
Are your gods, O Judah.

29 "Why will you plead with Me?
You all have transgressed against Me,"
says the LORD.
30 "In vain I have chastened your children;
They received no correction.
Your sword has devoured your prophets
Like a destroying lion.

31 "O generation, see the word of the LORD!
Have I been a wilderness to Israel,
Or a land of darkness?
Why do My people say, 'We are lords;
We will come no more to You'?
32 Can a virgin forget her ornaments,
Or a bride her attire?
Yet My people have forgotten Me days
without number.

33 "Why do you beautify your way to seek
love?
Therefore you have also taught
The wicked women your ways.
34 Also on your skirts is found
The blood of the lives of the poor
innocents.
I have not found it by secret search,
But plainly on all these things.
35 Yet you say, 'Because I am innocent,
Surely His anger shall turn from me.'
Behold, I will plead My case against you,
Because you say, 'I have not sinned.'
36 Why do you gad about so much to
change your way?

2:16 [a] That is, Memphis in ancient Egypt **2:18** [a] That is, the Euphrates

Also you shall be ashamed of Egypt as
you were ashamed of Assyria.
37 Indeed you will go forth from him
With your hands on your head;
For the LORD has rejected your trusted
allies,
And you will not prosper by them.

Israel Is Shameless

3 "They say, 'If a man divorces his wife,
And she goes from him
And becomes another man's,
May he return to her again?'
Would not that land be greatly polluted?
But you have played the harlot with
many lovers;
Yet return to Me," says the LORD.

2 "Lift up your eyes to the desolate heights
and see:
Where have you not lain *with men?*
By the road you have sat for them
Like an Arabian in the wilderness;
And you have polluted the land
With your harlotries and your
wickedness.
3 Therefore the showers have been
withheld,
And there has been no latter rain.
You have had a harlot's forehead;
You refuse to be ashamed.
4 Will you not from this time cry to Me,
'My Father, You *are* the guide of my
youth?
5 Will He remain angry forever?
Will He keep it to the end?'
Behold, you have spoken and done evil
things,
As you were able."

A Call to Repentance

6 The LORD said also to me in the days of
Josiah the king: "Have you seen what backsliding Israel has done? She has gone up on
every high mountain and under every green
tree, and there played the harlot. 7 And I said,
after she had done all these *things,* 'Return to
Me.' But she did not return. And her treacherous sister Judah saw it. 8 Then I saw that
for all the causes for which backsliding Israel had committed adultery, I had put her
away and given her a certificate of divorce;
yet her treacherous sister Judah did not fear,
but went and played the harlot also. 9 So it
came to pass, through her casual harlotry,
that she defiled the land and committed
adultery with stones and trees. 10 And yet for
all this her treacherous sister Judah has not
turned to Me with her whole heart, but in
pretense," says the LORD.
11 Then the LORD said to me, "Backsliding Israel has shown herself more righteous
than treacherous Judah. 12 Go and proclaim
these words toward the north, and say:

'Return, backsliding Israel,' says the
LORD;
'I will not cause My anger to fall on you.
For I *am* merciful,' says the LORD;
'I will not remain angry forever.
13 Only acknowledge your iniquity,
That you have transgressed against the
LORD your God,
And have scattered your charms
To alien deities under every green tree,
And you have not obeyed My voice,' says
the LORD.

14 "Return, O backsliding children," says
the LORD; "for I am married to you. I will
take you, one from a city and two from a
family, and I will bring you to Zion. 15 And
I will give you shepherds according to My
heart, who will feed you with knowledge and
understanding.
16 "Then it shall come to pass, when you
are multiplied and increased in the land in
those days," says the LORD, "that they will
say no more, 'The ark of the covenant of the
LORD.' It shall not come to mind, nor shall
they remember it, nor shall they visit *it,* nor
shall it be made anymore.
17 "At that time Jerusalem shall be called
The Throne of the LORD, and all the nations
shall be gathered to it, to the name of the
LORD, to Jerusalem. No more shall they follow the dictates of their evil hearts.
18 "In those days the house of Judah shall
walk with the house of Israel, and they shall
come together out of the land of the north to
the land that I have given as an inheritance
to your fathers.
19 "But I said:

'How can I put you among the children
And give you a pleasant land,
A beautiful heritage of the hosts of
nations?'

"And I said:

'You shall call Me, "My Father,"

And not turn away from Me.'
20 Surely, *as* a wife treacherously departs
from her husband,
So have you dealt treacherously with
Me,
O house of Israel," says the LORD.

21 A voice was heard on the desolate
heights,
Weeping *and* supplications of the
children of Israel.
For they have perverted their way;
They have forgotten the LORD their God.

22 "Return, you backsliding children,
And I will heal your backslidings."

"Indeed we do come to You,
For You are the LORD our God.
23 Truly, in vain *is salvation hoped for* from
the hills,
And from the multitude of mountains;
Truly, in the LORD our God
Is the salvation of Israel.
24 For shame has devoured
The labor of our fathers from our
youth—
Their flocks and their herds,
Their sons and their daughters.
25 We lie down in our shame,
And our reproach covers us.
For we have sinned against the LORD
our God,
We and our fathers,
From our youth even to this day,
And have not obeyed the voice of the
LORD our God."

4 "If you will return, O Israel," says the
LORD,
"Return to Me;
And if you will put away your
abominations out of My sight,
Then you shall not be moved.
2 And you shall swear, 'The LORD lives,'
In truth, in judgment, and in
righteousness;
The nations shall bless themselves in
Him,
And in Him they shall glory."

3For thus says the LORD to the men of Judah and Jerusalem:

"Break up your fallow ground,
And do not sow among thorns.
4 Circumcise yourselves to the LORD,
And take away the foreskins of your
hearts,
You men of Judah and inhabitants of
Jerusalem,
Lest My fury come forth like fire,
And burn so that no one can quench *it*,
Because of the evil of your doings."

An Imminent Invasion

5Declare in Judah and proclaim in Jerusalem, and say:

"Blow the trumpet in the land;
Cry, 'Gather together,'
And say, 'Assemble yourselves,
And let us go into the fortified cities.'
6 Set up the standard toward Zion.
Take refuge! Do not delay!
For I will bring disaster from the north,
And great destruction."

7 The lion has come up from his thicket,
And the destroyer of nations is on his
way.
He has gone forth from his place
To make your land desolate.
Your cities will be laid waste,
Without inhabitant.
8 For this, clothe yourself with sackcloth,
Lament and wail.
For the fierce anger of the LORD
Has not turned back from us.

9 "And it shall come to pass in that day,"
says the LORD,
"*That* the heart of the king shall perish,
And the heart of the princes;
The priests shall be astonished,
And the prophets shall wonder."

10 Then I said, "Ah, Lord GOD!
Surely You have greatly deceived this
people and Jerusalem,
Saying, 'You shall have peace,'
Whereas the sword reaches to the
heart."

11 At that time it will be said
To this people and to Jerusalem,
"A dry wind of the desolate heights *blows*
in the wilderness
Toward the daughter of My people—
Not to fan or to cleanse—
12 A wind too strong for these will come
for Me;
Now I will also speak judgment against
them."

13 "Behold, he shall come up like clouds,
And his chariots like a whirlwind.
His horses are swifter than eagles.
Woe to us, for we are plundered!"

14 O Jerusalem, wash your heart from wickedness,
That you may be saved.
How long shall your evil thoughts lodge within you?
15 For a voice declares from Dan
And proclaims affliction from Mount Ephraim:
16 "Make mention to the nations,
Yes, proclaim against Jerusalem,
That watchers come from a far country
And raise their voice against the cities of Judah.
17 Like keepers of a field they are against her all around,
Because she has been rebellious against Me," says the LORD.
18 "Your ways and your doings
Have procured these *things* for you.
This *is* your wickedness,
Because it is bitter,
Because it reaches to your heart."

Sorrow for the Doomed Nation

19 O my soul, my soul!
I am pained in my very heart!
My heart makes a noise in me;
I cannot hold my peace,
Because you have heard, O my soul,
The sound of the trumpet,
The alarm of war.
20 Destruction upon destruction is cried,
For the whole land is plundered.
Suddenly my tents are plundered,
And my curtains in a moment.
21 How long will I see the standard,
And hear the sound of the trumpet?

22 "For My people *are* foolish,
They have not known Me.
They *are* silly children,
And they have no understanding.
They *are* wise to do evil,
But to do good they have no knowledge."

23 I beheld the earth, and indeed *it was* without form, and void;
And the heavens, they *had* no light.
24 I beheld the mountains, and indeed they trembled,
And all the hills moved back and forth.
25 I beheld, and indeed *there was* no man,
And all the birds of the heavens had fled.
26 I beheld, and indeed the fruitful land *was* a wilderness,
And all its cities were broken down
At the presence of the LORD,
By His fierce anger.

27 For thus says the LORD:

"The whole land shall be desolate;
Yet I will not make a full end.
28 For this shall the earth mourn,
And the heavens above be black,
Because I have spoken.
I have purposed and will not relent,
Nor will I turn back from it.
29 The whole city shall flee from the noise of the horsemen and bowmen.
They shall go into thickets and climb up on the rocks.
Every city *shall be* forsaken,
And not a man shall dwell in it.

30 "And *when* you *are* plundered,
What will you do?
Though you clothe yourself with crimson,
Though you adorn *yourself* with ornaments of gold,
Though you enlarge your eyes with paint,
In vain you will make yourself fair;
Your lovers will despise you;
They will seek your life.

31 "For I have heard a voice as of a woman in labor,
The anguish as of her who brings forth her first child,
The voice of the daughter of Zion bewailing herself;
She spreads her hands, *saying*,
'Woe *is* me now, for my soul is weary
Because of murderers!'

The Justice of God's Judgment

5 "Run to and fro through the streets of Jerusalem;
See now and know;
And seek in her open places
If you can find a man,
If there is *anyone* who executes judgment,
Who seeks the truth,
And I will pardon her.

2 Though they say, '*As* the LORD lives,'
Surely they swear falsely."

3 O LORD, *are* not Your eyes on the truth?
You have stricken them,
But they have not grieved;
You have consumed them,
But they have refused to receive
correction.
They have made their faces harder than
rock;
They have refused to return.

4 Therefore I said, "Surely these *are* poor.
They are foolish;
For they do not know the way of the
LORD,
The judgment of their God.
5 I will go to the great men and speak to
them,
For they have known the way of the
LORD,
The judgment of their God."

But these have altogether broken the
yoke
And burst the bonds.
6 Therefore a lion from the forest shall
slay them,
A wolf of the deserts shall destroy them;
A leopard will watch over their cities.
Everyone who goes out from there shall
be torn in pieces,
Because their transgressions are many;
Their backslidings have increased.

7 "How shall I pardon you for this?
Your children have forsaken Me
And sworn by *those that are* not gods.
When I had fed them to the full,
Then they committed adultery
And assembled themselves by troops in
the harlots' houses.
8 They were *like* well-fed lusty stallions;
Every one neighed after his neighbor's
wife.
9 Shall I not punish *them* for these
things?" says the LORD.
"And shall I not avenge Myself on such a
nation as this?

10 "Go up on her walls and destroy,
But do not make a complete end.
Take away her branches,
For they *are* not the LORD's.
11 For the house of Israel and the house of
Judah
Have dealt very treacherously with Me,"
says the LORD.

12 They have lied about the LORD,
And said, "*It is* not He.
Neither will evil come upon us,
Nor shall we see sword or famine.
13 And the prophets become wind,
For the word *is* not in them.
Thus shall it be done to them."

14 Therefore thus says the LORD God of
hosts:

"Because you speak this word,
Behold, I will make My words in your
mouth fire,
And this people wood,
And it shall devour them.
15 Behold, I will bring a nation against you
from afar,
O house of Israel," says the LORD.
"It *is* a mighty nation,
It *is* an ancient nation,
A nation whose language you do not
know,
Nor can you understand what they say.
16 Their quiver *is* like an open tomb;
They *are* all mighty men.
17 And they shall eat up your harvest and
your bread,
Which your sons and daughters should
eat.
They shall eat up your flocks and your
herds;
They shall eat up your vines and your
fig trees;
They shall destroy your fortified cities,
In which you trust, with the sword.

18 "Nevertheless in those days," says the
LORD, "I will not make a complete end of
you. 19 And it will be when you say, 'Why
does the LORD our God do all these *things* to
us?' then you shall answer them, 'Just as you
have forsaken Me and served foreign gods in
your land, so you shall serve aliens in a land
that is not yours.'

20 "Declare this in the house of Jacob
And proclaim it in Judah, saying,
21 'Hear this now, O foolish people,
Without understanding,
Who have eyes and see not,
And who have ears and hear not:
22 Do you not fear Me?' says the LORD.
'Will you not tremble at My presence,

Who have placed the sand as the bound of the sea,
By a perpetual decree, that it cannot pass beyond it?
And though its waves toss to and fro,
Yet they cannot prevail;
Though they roar, yet they cannot pass over it.
23 But this people has a defiant and rebellious heart;
They have revolted and departed.
24 They do not say in their heart,
"Let us now fear the LORD our God,
Who gives rain, both the former and the latter, in its season.
He reserves for us the appointed weeks of the harvest."
25 Your iniquities have turned these *things* away,
And your sins have withheld good from you.

26 'For among My people are found wicked *men;*
They lie in wait as one who sets snares;
They set a trap;
They catch men.
27 As a cage is full of birds,
So their houses *are* full of deceit.
Therefore they have become great and grown rich.
28 They have grown fat, they are sleek;
Yes, they surpass the deeds of the wicked;
They do not plead the cause,
The cause of the fatherless;
Yet they prosper,
And the right of the needy they do not defend.
29 Shall I not punish *them* for these *things?*' says the LORD.
'Shall I not avenge Myself on such a nation as this?'

30 "An astonishing and horrible thing
Has been committed in the land:
31 The prophets prophesy falsely,
And the priests rule by their *own* power;
And My people love *to have it* so.
But what will you do in the end?

Impending Destruction from the North

6 "O you children of Benjamin,
Gather yourselves to flee from the midst of Jerusalem!
Blow the trumpet in Tekoa,
And set up a signal-fire in Beth Haccerem;
For disaster appears out of the north,
And great destruction.
2 I have likened the daughter of Zion
To a lovely and delicate woman.
3 The shepherds with their flocks shall come to her.
They shall pitch *their* tents against her all around.
Each one shall pasture in his own place."

4 "Prepare war against her;
Arise, and let us go up at noon.
Woe to us, for the day goes away,
For the shadows of the evening are lengthening.
5 Arise, and let us go by night,
And let us destroy her palaces."

6 For thus has the LORD of hosts said:

"Cut down trees,
And build a mound against Jerusalem.
This *is* the city to be punished.
She *is* full of oppression in her midst.
7 As a fountain wells up with water,
So she wells up with her wickedness.
Violence and plundering are heard in her.
Before Me continually *are* grief and wounds.
8 Be instructed, O Jerusalem,
Lest My soul depart from you;
Lest I make you desolate,
A land not inhabited."

9 Thus says the LORD of hosts:

"They shall thoroughly glean as a vine the remnant of Israel;
As a grape-gatherer, put your hand back into the branches."

10 To whom shall I speak and give warning,
That they may hear?
Indeed their ear *is* uncircumcised,
And they cannot give heed.
Behold, the word of the LORD is a reproach to them;
They have no delight in it.
11 Therefore I am full of the fury of the LORD.
I am weary of holding *it* in.
"I will pour it out on the children outside,

And on the assembly of young men
together;
For even the husband shall be taken
with the wife,
The aged with *him who is* full of days.
12 And their houses shall be turned over to
others,
Fields and wives together;
For I will stretch out My hand
Against the inhabitants of the land,"
says the LORD.
13 "Because from the least of them even to
the greatest of them,
Everyone *is* given to covetousness;
And from the prophet even to the priest,
Everyone deals falsely.
14 They have also healed the hurt of My
people slightly,
Saying, 'Peace, peace!'
When *there is* no peace.
15 Were they ashamed when they had
committed abomination?
No! They were not at all ashamed;
Nor did they know how to blush.
Therefore they shall fall among those
who fall;
At the time I punish them,
They shall be cast down," says the LORD.

16 Thus says the LORD:

"Stand in the ways and see,
And ask for the old paths, where the
good way *is,*
And walk in it;
Then you will find rest for your souls.
But they said, 'We will not walk *in it.*'
17 Also, I set watchmen over you, *saying,*
'Listen to the sound of the trumpet!'
But they said, 'We will not listen.'
18 Therefore hear, you nations,
And know, O congregation, what *is*
among them.
19 Hear, O earth!
Behold, I will certainly bring calamity
on this people—
The fruit of their thoughts,
Because they have not heeded My words
Nor My law, but rejected it.
20 For what purpose to Me
Comes frankincense from Sheba,
And sweet cane from a far country?
Your burnt offerings *are* not acceptable,
Nor your sacrifices sweet to Me."

21 Therefore thus says the LORD:

"Behold, I will lay stumbling blocks
before this people,
And the fathers and the sons together
shall fall on them.
The neighbor and his friend shall
perish."

22 Thus says the LORD:

"Behold, a people comes from the north
country,
And a great nation will be raised from
the farthest parts of the earth.
23 They will lay hold on bow and spear;
They *are* cruel and have no mercy;
Their voice roars like the sea;
And they ride on horses,
As men of war set in array against you,
O daughter of Zion."

24 We have heard the report of it;
Our hands grow feeble.
Anguish has taken hold of us,
Pain as of a woman in labor.
25 Do not go out into the field,
Nor walk by the way.
Because of the sword of the enemy,
Fear *is* on every side.
26 O daughter of my people,
Dress in sackcloth
And roll about in ashes!
Make mourning *as for* an only son, most
bitter lamentation;
For the plunderer will suddenly come
upon us.

27 "I have set you *as* an assayer *and* a
fortress among My people,
That you may know and test their way.
28 They *are* all stubborn rebels, walking as
slanderers.
They are bronze and iron,
They *are* all corrupters;
29 The bellows blow fiercely,
The lead is consumed by the fire;
The smelter refines in vain,
For the wicked are not drawn off.
30 *People* will call them rejected silver,
Because the LORD has rejected them."

Trusting in Lying Words

7 The word that came to Jeremiah from
the LORD, saying, 2 "Stand in the gate of
the LORD's house, and proclaim there this
word, and say, 'Hear the word of the LORD,
all *you of* Judah who enter in at these gates to
worship the LORD!'" 3 Thus says the LORD of

hosts, the God of Israel: "Amend your ways
and your doings, and I will cause you to
dwell in this place. 4Do not trust in these lying words, saying, 'The temple of the LORD,
the temple of the LORD, the temple of the
LORD *are* these.'
5"For if you thoroughly amend your ways
and your doings, if you thoroughly execute
judgment between a man and his neighbor, 6*if* you do not oppress the stranger, the
fatherless, and the widow, and do not shed
innocent blood in this place, or walk after
other gods to your hurt, 7then I will cause
you to dwell in this place, in the land that I
gave to your fathers forever and ever.
8"Behold, you trust in lying words that
cannot profit. 9Will you steal, murder, commit adultery, swear falsely, burn incense to
Baal, and walk after other gods whom you
do not know, 10and *then* come and stand
before Me in this house which is called by
My name, and say, 'We are delivered to do
all these abominations'? 11Has this house,
which is called by My name, become a den of
thieves in your eyes? Behold, I, even I, have
seen *it*," says the LORD.
12"But go now to My place which *was* in
Shiloh, where I set My name at the first, and
see what I did to it because of the wickedness
of My people Israel. 13And now, because you
have done all these works," says the LORD,
"and I spoke to you, rising up early and
speaking, but you did not hear, and I called
you, but you did not answer, 14therefore I will
do to the house which is called by My name,
in which you trust, and to this place which I
gave to you and your fathers, as I have done
to Shiloh. 15And I will cast you out of My
sight, as I have cast out all your brethren—
the whole posterity of Ephraim.
16"Therefore do not pray for this people,
nor lift up a cry or prayer for them, nor make
intercession to Me; for I will not hear you.
17Do you not see what they do in the cities of
Judah and in the streets of Jerusalem? 18The
children gather wood, the fathers kindle the
fire, and the women knead dough, to make
cakes for the queen of heaven; and *they* pour
out drink offerings to other gods, that they
may provoke Me to anger. 19Do they provoke
Me to anger?" says the LORD. "*Do they* not
provoke themselves, to the shame of their
own faces?"
20Therefore thus says the Lord GOD:
"Behold, My anger and My fury will be
poured out on this place—on man and on
beast, on the trees of the field and on the
fruit of the ground. And it will burn and not
be quenched."
21Thus says the LORD of hosts, the God
of Israel: "Add your burnt offerings to your
sacrifices and eat meat. 22For I did not speak
to your fathers, or command them in the
day that I brought them out of the land of
Egypt, concerning burnt offerings or sacrifices. 23But this is what I commanded them,
saying, 'Obey My voice, and I will be your
God, and you shall be My people. And walk
in all the ways that I have commanded you,
that it may be well with you.' 24Yet they did
not obey or incline their ear, but followed
the counsels *and* the dictates of their evil

OBEDIENCE

READ IT: JEREMIAH 7:23

God's story involves a special group of people. The nation of Israel was very important to God. God kept asking the people of Israel to obey. Sometimes they obeyed (and things always went better for them when they did). But many times they struggled to obey God. Do you ever struggle to obey God? Think about the encouragement that God offered Israel. God told them that if they would obey, it would go well with them and He would be their God.

hearts, and went backward and not forward.
25Since the day that your fathers came out of
the land of Egypt until this day, I have even
sent to you all My servants the prophets,
daily rising up early and sending *them.* 26Yet
they did not obey Me or incline their ear, but
stiffened their neck. They did worse than
their fathers.

27"Therefore you shall speak all these
words to them, but they will not obey you.
You shall also call to them, but they will not
answer you.

Judgment on Obscene Religion

28"So you shall say to them, 'This *is* a nation that does not obey the voice of the LORD
their God nor receive correction. Truth has
perished and has been cut off from their
mouth. 29Cut off your hair and cast *it* away,
and take up a lamentation on the desolate
heights; for the LORD has rejected and forsaken the generation of His wrath.' 30For
the children of Judah have done evil in My
sight," says the LORD. "They have set their
abominations in the house which is called
by My name, to pollute it. 31And they have
built the high places of Tophet, which *is* in
the Valley of the Son of Hinnom, to burn
their sons and their daughters in the fire,
which I did not command, nor did it come
into My heart.

32"Therefore behold, the days are coming," says the LORD, "when it will no more
be called Tophet, or the Valley of the Son
of Hinnom, but the Valley of Slaughter; for
they will bury in Tophet until there is no
room. 33The corpses of this people will be
food for the birds of the heaven and for the
beasts of the earth. And no one will frighten
them away. 34Then I will cause to cease from
the cities of Judah and from the streets of
Jerusalem the voice of mirth and the voice
of gladness, the voice of the bridegroom and
the voice of the bride. For the land shall be
desolate.

8 "At that time," says the LORD, "they
shall bring out the bones of the kings
of Judah, and the bones of its princes, and
the bones of the priests, and the bones of the
prophets, and the bones of the inhabitants
of Jerusalem, out of their graves. 2They shall
spread them before the sun and the moon
and all the host of heaven, which they have
loved and which they have served and after
which they have walked, which they have
sought and which they have worshiped.
They shall not be gathered nor buried; they
shall be like refuse on the face of the earth.
3Then death shall be chosen rather than life
by all the residue of those who remain of
this evil family, who remain in all the places
where I have driven them," says the LORD of
hosts.

The Peril of False Teaching

4"Moreover you shall say to them, 'Thus
says the LORD:

"Will they fall and not rise?
Will one turn away and not return?
5 Why has this people slidden back,
Jerusalem, in a perpetual backsliding?
They hold fast to deceit,
They refuse to return.
6 I listened and heard,
But they do not speak aright.
No man repented of his wickedness,
Saying, 'What have I done?'
Everyone turned to his own course,
As the horse rushes into the battle.

7 "Even the stork in the heavens
Knows her appointed times;
And the turtledove, the swift, and the
swallow
Observe the time of their coming.
But My people do not know the
judgment of the LORD.

8 "How can you say, 'We *are* wise,
And the law of the LORD *is* with us'?
Look, the false pen of the scribe
certainly works falsehood.
9 The wise men are ashamed,
They are dismayed and taken.
Behold, they have rejected the word of
the LORD;
So what wisdom do they have?
10 Therefore I will give their wives to
others,
And their fields to those who will
inherit *them;*
Because from the least even to the
greatest
Everyone is given to covetousness;
From the prophet even to the priest
Everyone deals falsely.
11 For they have healed the hurt of the
daughter of My people slightly,
Saying, 'Peace, peace!'
When *there is* no peace.

12 Were they ashamed when they had committed abomination?
No! They were not at all ashamed,
Nor did they know how to blush.
Therefore they shall fall among those who fall;
In the time of their punishment
They shall be cast down," says the LORD.

13 "I will surely consume them," says the LORD.
"No grapes *shall be* on the vine,
Nor figs on the fig tree,
And the leaf shall fade;
And *the things* I have given them shall pass away from them." ' "

14 "Why do we sit still?
Assemble yourselves,
And let us enter the fortified cities,
And let us be silent there.
For the LORD our God has put us to silence
And given us water of gall to drink,
Because we have sinned against the LORD.

15 "*We* looked for peace, but no good *came;*
And for a time of health, and there was trouble!
16 The snorting of His horses was heard from Dan.
The whole land trembled at the sound of the neighing of His strong ones;
For they have come and devoured the land and all that is in it,
The city and those who dwell in it."

17 "For behold, I will send serpents among you,
Vipers which cannot be charmed,
And they shall bite you," says the LORD.

The Prophet Mourns for the People

18 I would comfort myself in sorrow;
My heart *is* faint in me.
19 Listen! The voice,
The cry of the daughter of my people
From a far country:
"*Is* not the LORD in Zion?
Is not her King in her?"

"Why have they provoked Me to anger
With their carved images—
With foreign idols?"

20 "The harvest is past,
The summer is ended,
And we are not saved!"

21 For the hurt of the daughter of my people I am hurt.
I am mourning;
Astonishment has taken hold of me.
22 *Is there* no balm in Gilead,
Is there no physician there?
Why then is there no recovery
For the health of the daughter of my people?

9 Oh, that my head were waters,
And my eyes a fountain of tears,
That I might weep day and night
For the slain of the daughter of my people!
2 Oh, that I had in the wilderness
A lodging place for travelers;
That I might leave my people,
And go from them!
For they *are* all adulterers,
An assembly of treacherous men.

3 "And *like* their bow they have bent their tongues *for* lies.
They are not valiant for the truth on the earth.
For they proceed from evil to evil,
And they do not know Me," says the LORD.
4 "Everyone take heed to his neighbor,
And do not trust any brother;
For every brother will utterly supplant,
And every neighbor will walk with slanderers.
5 Everyone will deceive his neighbor,
And will not speak the truth;
They have taught their tongue to speak lies;
They weary themselves to commit iniquity.
6 Your dwelling place *is* in the midst of deceit;
Through deceit they refuse to know Me," says the LORD.

7 Therefore thus says the LORD of hosts:

"Behold, I will refine them and try them;
For how shall I deal with the daughter of My people?
8 Their tongue *is* an arrow shot out;
It speaks deceit;
One speaks peaceably to his neighbor with his mouth,
But in his heart he lies in wait.

9 Shall I not punish them for these *things?*" says the LORD.
"Shall I not avenge Myself on such a nation as this?"

10 I will take up a weeping and wailing for the mountains,
And for the dwelling places of the wilderness a lamentation,
Because they are burned up,
So that no one can pass through;
Nor can *men* hear the voice of the cattle.
Both the birds of the heavens and the beasts have fled;
They are gone.

11 "I will make Jerusalem a heap of ruins, a den of jackals.
I will make the cities of Judah desolate, without an inhabitant."

12 Who is the wise man who may understand this? And *who is he* to whom the
mouth of the LORD has spoken, that he may
declare it? Why does the land perish *and*
burn up like a wilderness, so that no one can
pass through?
13 And the LORD said, "Because they have
forsaken My law which I set before them,
and have not obeyed My voice, nor walked
according to it, 14 but they have walked according to the dictates of their own hearts and
after the Baals, which their fathers taught
them," 15 therefore thus says the LORD of
hosts, the God of Israel: "Behold, I will feed
them, this people, with wormwood, and give
them water of gall to drink. 16 I will scatter
them also among the Gentiles, whom neither they nor their fathers have known. And
I will send a sword after them until I have
consumed them."

The People Mourn in Judgment

17 Thus says the LORD of hosts:

"Consider and call for the mourning women,
That they may come;
And send for skillful *wailing* women,
That they may come.
18 Let them make haste
And take up a wailing for us,
That our eyes may run with tears,
And our eyelids gush with water.
19 For a voice of wailing is heard from Zion:
'How we are plundered!
We are greatly ashamed,
Because we have forsaken the land,
Because we have been cast out of our dwellings.'"

20 Yet hear the word of the LORD, O women,
And let your ear receive the word of His mouth;
Teach your daughters wailing,
And everyone her neighbor a lamentation.
21 For death has come through our windows,
Has entered our palaces,
To kill off the children—*no longer to be* outside!
And the young men—*no longer* on the streets!

22 Speak, "Thus says the LORD:

'Even the carcasses of men shall fall as refuse on the open field,
Like cuttings after the harvester,
And no one shall gather *them.*'"

23 Thus says the LORD:

"Let not the wise *man* glory in his wisdom,
Let not the mighty *man* glory in his might,
Nor let the rich *man* glory in his riches;
24 But let him who glories glory in this,
That he understands and knows Me,
That I *am* the LORD, exercising lovingkindness, judgment, and righteousness in the earth.
For in these I delight," says the LORD.

25 "Behold, the days are coming," says the
LORD, "that I will punish all *who are* circumcised with the uncircumcised— 26 Egypt,
Judah, Edom, the people of Ammon, Moab,
and all *who are* in the farthest corners, who
dwell in the wilderness. For all *these* nations
are uncircumcised, and all the house of Israel *are* uncircumcised in the heart."

Idols and the True God

10 Hear the word which the LORD speaks to you, O house of Israel.
2 Thus says the LORD:

"Do not learn the way of the Gentiles;
Do not be dismayed at the signs of heaven,
For the Gentiles are dismayed at them.

3 For the customs of the peoples *are* futile;
For *one* cuts a tree from the forest,
The work of the hands of the workman, with the ax.
4 They decorate it with silver and gold;
They fasten it with nails and hammers
So that it will not topple.
5 They *are* upright, like a palm tree,
And they cannot speak;
They must be carried,
Because they cannot go *by themselves*.
Do not be afraid of them,
For they cannot do evil,
Nor can they do any good."

6 Inasmuch as *there is* none like You, O LORD
(You *are* great, and Your name *is* great in might),
7 Who would not fear You, O King of the nations?
For this is Your rightful due.
For among all the wise *men* of the nations,
And in all their kingdoms,
There is none like You.
8 But they are altogether dull-hearted and foolish;
A wooden idol *is* a worthless doctrine.
9 Silver is beaten into plates;
It is brought from Tarshish,
And gold from Uphaz,
The work of the craftsman
And of the hands of the metalsmith;

Epic Ideas

WHO IS GOD? IDLE IDOLS

READ IT: JEREMIAH 10:1–16

GET IT:

In the ancient world, idols were common. People actually worshiped them. They believed that if they did and said all the right things, made and kept all the right promises, and got lucky enough, the idol would reward them with a long, successful, and healthy life. Even though idols are powerless—they're just manmade things, after all—they can still have a powerful effect on people, causing them to do and say crazy things. That's what makes them so dangerous.

Jeremiah reminds us that idols don't create, aren't wise, and can't love. Instead, they are dull-hearted (uncaring), foolish (unknowing), and lifeless (dead). But God—the only true God—is alive, powerful, personal, caring, wise, and loving. He's everything that idols aren't. He's the only One worth living for.

LIVE IT:

Is there something or someone in your life that you "worship" by giving it your time and attention, hoping that it will fill you, comfort you, and give you meaning and purpose? If so, you've idolized it. God—not your smart phone, not your music, not your extracurricular activities, not your clothes, not even your friends—is the only one who deserves your time, worship, and adoration. Reprioritize your life so that God, not some idol, is at the center.

Blue and purple *are* their clothing;
They *are* all the work of skillful *men.*
10 But the LORD *is* the true God;
He *is* the living God and the everlasting King.
At His wrath the earth will tremble,
And the nations will not be able to endure His indignation.

11 Thus you shall say to them: "The gods
that have not made the heavens and the
earth shall perish from the earth and from
under these heavens."

12 He has made the earth by His power,
He has established the world by His wisdom,
And has stretched out the heavens at His discretion.
13 When He utters His voice,
There is a multitude of waters in the heavens:
"And He causes the vapors to ascend from the ends of the earth.
He makes lightning for the rain,
He brings the wind out of His treasuries."[a]
14 Everyone is dull-hearted, without knowledge;
Every metalsmith is put to shame by an image;
For his molded image *is* falsehood,
And *there is* no breath in them.
15 They *are* futile, a work of errors;
In the time of their punishment they shall perish.
16 The Portion of Jacob *is* not like them,
For He *is* the Maker of all *things,*
And Israel *is* the tribe of His inheritance;
The LORD of hosts *is* His name.

The Coming Captivity of Judah

17 Gather up your wares from the land,
O inhabitant of the fortress!

18 For thus says the LORD:

"Behold, I will throw out at this time
The inhabitants of the land,
And will distress them,
That they may find *it so.*"

19 Woe is me for my hurt!
My wound is severe.
But I say, "Truly this *is* an infirmity,
And I must bear it."
20 My tent is plundered,
And all my cords are broken;
My children have gone from me,
And they *are* no more.
There is no one to pitch my tent anymore,
Or set up my curtains.

21 For the shepherds have become dull-hearted,
And have not sought the LORD;
Therefore they shall not prosper,
And all their flocks shall be scattered.
22 Behold, the noise of the report has come,
And a great commotion out of the north country,
To make the cities of Judah desolate, a den of jackals.

23 O LORD, I know the way of man *is* not in himself;
It is not in man who walks to direct his own steps.
24 O LORD, correct me, but with justice;
Not in Your anger, lest You bring me to nothing.
25 Pour out Your fury on the Gentiles, who do not know You,
And on the families who do not call on Your name;
For they have eaten up Jacob,
Devoured him and consumed him,
And made his dwelling place desolate.

The Broken Covenant

11 The word that came to Jeremiah
from the LORD, saying, 2 "Hear the
words of this covenant, and speak to the
men of Judah and to the inhabitants of Jerusalem; 3 and say to them, 'Thus says the LORD
God of Israel: "Cursed *is* the man who does
not obey the words of this covenant 4 which
I commanded your fathers in the day I
brought them out of the land of Egypt, from
the iron furnace, saying, 'Obey My voice, and
do according to all that I command you; so
shall you be My people, and I will be your
God,' 5 that I may establish the oath which I
have sworn to your fathers, to give them 'a
land flowing with milk and honey,'[a] as *it is*
this day."'"

And I answered and said, "So be it,
LORD."

6 Then the LORD said to me, "Proclaim

10:13 [a] Psalm 135:7 11:5 [a] Exodus 3:8

all these words in the cities of Judah and in
the streets of Jerusalem, saying: 'Hear the
words of this covenant and do them. 7For I
earnestly exhorted your fathers in the day I
brought them up out of the land of Egypt,
until this day, rising early and exhorting,
saying, "Obey My voice." 8Yet they did not
obey or incline their ear, but everyone followed the dictates of his evil heart; therefore
I will bring upon them all the words of this
covenant, which I commanded *them* to do,
but *which* they have not done.' "

9And the LORD said to me, "A conspiracy has been found among the men of Judah
and among the inhabitants of Jerusalem.
10They have turned back to the iniquities
of their forefathers who refused to hear My
words, and they have gone after other gods
to serve them; the house of Israel and the
house of Judah have broken My covenant
which I made with their fathers."

11Therefore thus says the LORD: "Behold,
I will surely bring calamity on them which
they will not be able to escape; and though
they cry out to Me, I will not listen to them.
12Then the cities of Judah and the inhabitants of Jerusalem will go and cry out to the
gods to whom they offer incense, but they
will not save them at all in the time of their
trouble. 13For *according to* the number of your
cities were your gods, O Judah; and *according to* the number of the streets of Jerusalem
you have set up altars to *that* shameful thing,
altars to burn incense to Baal.

14"So do not pray for this people, or lift up
a cry or prayer for them; for I will not hear
them in the time that they cry out to Me because of their trouble.

15 "What has My beloved to do in My house,
Having done lewd deeds with many?
And the holy flesh has passed from you.
When you do evil, then you rejoice.
16 The LORD called your name,
Green Olive Tree, Lovely *and* of Good
Fruit.
With the noise of a great tumult
He has kindled fire on it,
And its branches are broken.

17"For the LORD of hosts, who planted
you, has pronounced doom against you
for the evil of the house of Israel and of
the house of Judah, which they have done
against themselves to provoke Me to anger
in offering incense to Baal."

Jeremiah's Life Threatened

18Now the LORD gave me knowledge *of it,*
and I know *it;* for You showed me their doings. 19But I *was* like a docile lamb brought
to the slaughter; and I did not know that
they had devised schemes against me, *saying,* "Let us destroy the tree with its fruit,
and let us cut him off from the land of the
living, that his name may be remembered
no more."

20 But, O LORD of hosts,
You who judge righteously,
Testing the mind and the heart,
Let me see Your vengeance on them,
For to You I have revealed my cause.

21"Therefore thus says the LORD concerning the men of Anathoth who seek your life,
saying, 'Do not prophesy in the name of the
LORD, lest you die by our hand'— 22therefore
thus says the LORD of hosts: 'Behold, I will
punish them. The young men shall die by
the sword, their sons and their daughters
shall die by famine; 23and there shall be no
remnant of them, for I will bring catastrophe on the men of Anathoth, *even* the year of
their punishment.' "

Jeremiah's Question

12 Righteous *are* You, O LORD, when I
plead with You;
Yet let me talk with You about *Your*
judgments.
Why does the way of the wicked
prosper?
Why are those happy who deal so
treacherously?
2 You have planted them, yes, they have
taken root;
They grow, yes, they bear fruit.
You *are* near in their mouth
But far from their mind.

3 But You, O LORD, know me;
You have seen me,
And You have tested my heart toward
You.
Pull them out like sheep for the
slaughter,
And prepare them for the day of
slaughter.
4 How long will the land mourn,

And the herbs of every field wither?
The beasts and birds are consumed,
For the wickedness of those who dwell there,
Because they said, "He will not see our final end."

The Lord Answers Jeremiah

5 "If you have run with the footmen, and they have wearied you,
Then how can you contend with horses?
And *if* in the land of peace,
In which you trusted, *they wearied you,*
Then how will you do in the floodplain[a] of the Jordan?
6 For even your brothers, the house of your father,
Even they have dealt treacherously with you;
Yes, they have called a multitude after you.
Do not believe them,
Even though they speak smooth words to you.

7 "I have forsaken My house, I have left My heritage;
I have given the dearly beloved of My soul into the hand of her enemies.
8 My heritage is to Me like a lion in the forest;
It cries out against Me;
Therefore I have hated it.
9 My heritage *is* to Me *like* a speckled vulture;
The vultures all around *are* against her.
Come, assemble all the beasts of the field,
Bring them to devour!

10 "Many rulers[a] have destroyed My vineyard,
They have trodden My portion underfoot;
They have made My pleasant portion a desolate wilderness.
11 They have made it desolate;
Desolate, it mourns to Me;
The whole land is made desolate,
Because no one takes *it* to heart.
12 The plunderers have come
On all the desolate heights in the wilderness,
For the sword of the Lord shall devour
From *one* end of the land to the *other* end of the land;
No flesh shall have peace.
13 They have sown wheat but reaped thorns;
They have put themselves to pain *but* do not profit.
But be ashamed of your harvest
Because of the fierce anger of the Lord."

14Thus says the Lord: "Against all My
evil neighbors who touch the inheritance
which I have caused My people Israel to
inherit—behold, I will pluck them out of
their land and pluck out the house of Judah
from among them. 15Then it shall be, after I
have plucked them out, that I will return and
have compassion on them and bring them
back, everyone to his heritage and everyone
to his land. 16And it shall be, if they will learn
carefully the ways of My people, to swear by
My name, 'As the Lord lives,' as they taught
My people to swear by Baal, then they shall
be established in the midst of My people.
17But if they do not obey, I will utterly pluck
up and destroy that nation," says the Lord.

Symbol of the Linen Sash

13 Thus the Lord said to me: "Go and
get yourself a linen sash, and put it
around your waist, but do not put it in water."
2So I got a sash according to the word of
the Lord, and put *it* around my waist.

3And the word of the Lord came to me
the second time, saying, 4"Take the sash
that you acquired, which *is* around your
waist, and arise, go to the Euphrates,[a] and
hide it there in a hole in the rock." 5So I went
and hid it by the Euphrates, as the Lord
commanded me.

6Now it came to pass after many days that
the Lord said to me, "Arise, go to the Euphrates,
and take from there the sash which
I commanded you to hide there." 7Then I
went to the Euphrates and dug, and I took
the sash from the place where I had hidden
it; and there was the sash, ruined. It was
profitable for nothing.

8Then the word of the Lord came to me,
saying, 9"Thus says the Lord: 'In this manner
I will ruin the pride of Judah and the

12:5 [a] Or *thicket* 12:10 [a] Literally *shepherds* or *pastors*
13:4 [a] Hebrew *Perath*

great pride of Jerusalem. 10This evil people,
who refuse to hear My words, who follow the
dictates of their hearts, and walk after other
gods to serve them and worship them, shall
be just like this sash which is profitable for
nothing. 11For as the sash clings to the waist
of a man, so I have caused the whole house
of Israel and the whole house of Judah to
cling to Me,' says the LORD, 'that they may
become My people, for renown, for praise,
and for glory; but they would not hear.'

Symbol of the Wine Bottles

12"Therefore you shall speak to them this
word: 'Thus says the LORD God of Israel:
"Every bottle shall be filled with wine."'

"And they will say to you, 'Do we not certainly know that every bottle will be filled with wine?'

13"Then you shall say to them, 'Thus says
the LORD: "Behold, I will fill all the inhabitants of this land—even the kings who sit
on David's throne, the priests, the prophets,
and all the inhabitants of Jerusalem—with
drunkenness! 14And I will dash them one
against another, even the fathers and the
sons together," says the LORD. "I will not pity
nor spare nor have mercy, but will destroy
them."'"

Pride Precedes Captivity

15 Hear and give ear:
Do not be proud,
For the LORD has spoken.
16 Give glory to the LORD your God
Before He causes darkness,
And before your feet stumble
On the dark mountains,
And while you are looking for light,
He turns it into the shadow of death
And makes *it* dense darkness.
17 But if you will not hear it,
My soul will weep in secret for *your* pride;
My eyes will weep bitterly
And run down with tears,
Because the LORD's flock has been taken captive.

18 Say to the king and to the queen mother,
"*Humble yourselves;*
Sit down,
For your rule shall collapse, the crown of your glory."
19 The cities of the South shall be shut up,
And no one shall open *them;*
Judah shall be carried away captive, all of it;
It shall be wholly carried away captive.

20 Lift up your eyes and see
Those who come from the north.
Where *is* the flock *that* was given to you,
Your beautiful sheep?
21 What will you say when He punishes you?
For you have taught them
To be chieftains, to be head over you.
Will not pangs seize you,
Like a woman in labor?
22 And if you say in your heart,
"Why have these things come upon me?"
For the greatness of your iniquity
Your skirts have been uncovered,
Your heels made bare.
23 Can the Ethiopian change his skin or the leopard its spots?
Then may you also do good who are accustomed to do evil.

24 "Therefore I will scatter them like stubble
That passes away by the wind of the wilderness.
25 This is your lot,
The portion of your measures from Me," says the LORD,
"Because you have forgotten Me
And trusted in falsehood.
26 Therefore I will uncover your skirts over your face,
That your shame may appear.
27 I have seen your adulteries
And your *lustful* neighings,
The lewdness of your harlotry,
Your abominations on the hills in the fields.
Woe to you, O Jerusalem!
Will you still not be made clean?"

Sword, Famine, and Pestilence

14 The word of the LORD that came to Jeremiah concerning the droughts.

2 "Judah mourns,
And her gates languish;
They mourn for the land,
And the cry of Jerusalem has gone up.
3 Their nobles have sent their lads for water;

They went to the cisterns *and* found no
water.
They returned with their vessels empty;
They were ashamed and confounded
And covered their heads.
4 Because the ground is parched,
For there was no rain in the land,
The plowmen were ashamed;
They covered their heads.
5 Yes, the deer also gave birth in the field,
But left because there was no grass.
6 And the wild donkeys stood in the
desolate heights;
They sniffed at the wind like jackals;
Their eyes failed because *there was* no
grass."

7 O LORD, though our iniquities testify
against us,
Do it for Your name's sake;
For our backslidings are many,
We have sinned against You.
8 O the Hope of Israel, his Savior in time
of trouble,
Why should You be like a stranger in
the land,
And like a traveler *who* turns aside to
tarry for a night?
9 Why should You be like a man
astonished,
Like a mighty one *who* cannot save?
Yet You, O LORD, *are* in our midst,
And we are called by Your name;
Do not leave us!

10 Thus says the LORD to this people:

"Thus they have loved to wander;
They have not restrained their feet.
Therefore the LORD does not accept them;
He will remember their iniquity now,
And punish their sins."

11 Then the LORD said to me, "Do not
pray for this people, for *their* good. 12 When
they fast, I will not hear their cry; and when
they offer burnt offering and grain offering,
I will not accept them. But I will consume
them by the sword, by the famine, and by
the pestilence."
13 Then I said, "Ah, Lord GOD! Behold, the
prophets say to them, 'You shall not see the
sword, nor shall you have famine, but I will
give you assured peace in this place.'"
14 And the LORD said to me, "The prophets prophesy lies in My name. I have not
sent them, commanded them, nor spoken
to them; they prophesy to you a false vision,
divination, a worthless thing, and the deceit of their heart. 15 Therefore thus says the
LORD concerning the prophets who prophesy
in My name, whom I did not send, and who
say, 'Sword and famine shall not be in this
land'—'By sword and famine those prophets shall be consumed! 16 And the people to
whom they prophesy shall be cast out in the
streets of Jerusalem because of the famine
and the sword; they will have no one to bury
them—them nor their wives, their sons nor
their daughters—for I will pour their wickedness on them.'
17 "Therefore you shall say this word to
them:

'Let my eyes flow with tears night and
day,
And let them not cease;
For the virgin daughter of my people
Has been broken with a mighty stroke,
with a very severe blow.
18 If I go out to the field,
Then behold, those slain with the
sword!
And if I enter the city,
Then behold, those sick from famine!
Yes, both prophet and priest go about in
a land they do not know.'"

The People Plead for Mercy

19 Have You utterly rejected Judah?
Has Your soul loathed Zion?
Why have You stricken us so that *there is*
no healing for us?
We looked for peace, but *there was* no
good;
And for the time of healing, and there
was trouble.
20 We acknowledge, O LORD, our
wickedness
And the iniquity of our fathers,
For we have sinned against You.
21 Do not abhor *us,* for Your name's sake;
Do not disgrace the throne of Your
glory.
Remember, do not break Your covenant
with us.
22 Are there any among the idols of the
nations that can cause rain?
Or can the heavens give showers?
Are You not He, O LORD our God?
Therefore we will wait for You,
Since You have made all these.

The LORD Will Not Relent

15 Then the LORD said to me, "*Even* if Moses and Samuel stood before Me, My mind *would* not *be* favorable toward this people. Cast *them* out of My sight, and let them go forth.
2 And it shall be, if they say to you, 'Where should we go?' then you shall tell them, 'Thus says the LORD:

"Such as *are* for death, to death;
And such as *are* for the sword, to the sword;
And such as *are* for the famine, to the famine;
And such as *are* for the captivity, to the captivity."'

3 "And I will appoint over them four forms *of destruction,*" says the LORD: "the sword to slay, the dogs to drag, the birds of the heavens and the beasts of the earth to devour and destroy.
4 I will hand them over to trouble, to all kingdoms of the earth, because of Manasseh the son of Hezekiah, king of Judah, for what he did in Jerusalem.

5 "For who will have pity on you, O Jerusalem?
Or who will bemoan you?
Or who will turn aside to ask how you are doing?
6 You have forsaken Me," says the LORD,
"You have gone backward.
Therefore I will stretch out My hand against you and destroy you;
I am weary of relenting!
7 And I will winnow them with a winnowing fan in the gates of the land;
I will bereave *them* of children;
I will destroy My people,
Since they do not return from their ways.
8 Their widows will be increased to Me more than the sand of the seas;
I will bring against them,
Against the mother of the young men,
A plunderer at noonday;
I will cause anguish and terror to fall on them suddenly.

9 "*She languishes* who has borne seven;
She has breathed her last;
Her sun has gone down
While *it was* yet day;
She has been ashamed and confounded.
And the remnant of them I will deliver to the sword
Before their enemies," says the LORD.

Jeremiah's Dejection

10 Woe is me, my mother,
That you have borne me,
A man of strife and a man of contention to the whole earth!
I have neither lent for interest,
Nor have men lent to me for interest.
Every one of them curses me.

11 The LORD said:

"Surely it will be well with your remnant;
Surely I will cause the enemy to intercede with you
In the time of adversity and in the time of affliction.
12 Can anyone break iron,
The northern iron and the bronze?
13 Your wealth and your treasures
I will give as plunder without price,
Because of all your sins,
Throughout your territories.
14 And I will make *you* cross over with[a] your enemies
Into a land *which* you do not know;
For a fire is kindled in My anger,
Which shall burn upon you."

15 O LORD, You know;
Remember me and visit me,
And take vengeance for me on my persecutors.
In Your enduring patience, do not take me away.
Know that for Your sake I have suffered rebuke.
16 Your words were found, and I ate them,
And Your word was to me the joy and rejoicing of my heart;
For I am called by Your name,
O LORD God of hosts.
17 I did not sit in the assembly of the mockers,
Nor did I rejoice;
I sat alone because of Your hand,
For You have filled me with indignation.
18 Why is my pain perpetual
And my wound incurable,
Which refuses to be healed?

15:14 [a] Following Masoretic Text and Vulgate; Septuagint, Syriac, and Targum read *cause you to serve* (compare 17:4).

Will You surely be to me like an
unreliable stream,
As waters *that* fail?

The LORD Reassures Jeremiah

19 Therefore thus says the LORD:

“If you return,
Then I will bring you back;
You shall stand before Me;
If you take out the precious from the
vile,
You shall be as My mouth.
Let them return to you,
But you must not return to them.
20 And I will make you to this people a
fortified bronze wall;
And they will fight against you,
But they shall not prevail against you;
For I *am* with you to save you
And deliver you,” says the LORD.
21 “I will deliver you from the hand of the
wicked,
And I will redeem you from the grip of
the terrible.”

Jeremiah's Lifestyle and Message

16 The word of the LORD also came to
me, saying, 2“You shall not take a
wife, nor shall you have sons or daughters in
this place.” 3For thus says the LORD concerning the sons and daughters who are born in
this place, and concerning their mothers
who bore them and their fathers who begot
them in this land: 4“They shall die gruesome
deaths; they shall not be lamented nor shall
they be buried, *but* they shall be like refuse
on the face of the earth. They shall be consumed by the sword and by famine, and
their corpses shall be meat for the birds of
heaven and for the beasts of the earth.”
5For thus says the LORD: “Do not enter
the house of mourning, nor go to lament
or bemoan them; for I have taken away My
peace from this people,” says the LORD,
“lovingkindness and mercies. 6Both the
great and the small shall die in this land.
They shall not be buried; neither shall men
lament for them, cut themselves, nor make
themselves bald for them. 7Nor shall *men*
break *bread* in mourning for them, to comfort them for the dead; nor shall *men* give
them the cup of consolation to drink for
their father or their mother. 8Also you shall
not go into the house of feasting to sit with
them, to eat and drink.”
9For thus says the LORD of hosts, the God
of Israel: “Behold, I will cause to cease from
this place, before your eyes and in your days,
the voice of mirth and the voice of gladness,
the voice of the bridegroom and the voice of
the bride.
10“And it shall be, when you show this
people all these words, and they say to you,
‘Why has the LORD pronounced all this great
disaster against us? Or what *is* our iniquity?
Or what *is* our sin that we have committed
against the LORD our God?’ 11then you shall
say to them, ‘Because your fathers have forsaken Me,’ says the LORD; ‘they have walked
after other gods and have served them and
worshiped them, and have forsaken Me and
not kept My law. 12And you have done worse
than your fathers, for behold, each one follows the dictates of his own evil heart, so
that no one listens to Me. 13Therefore I will
cast you out of this land into a land that you
do not know, neither you nor your fathers;
and there you shall serve other gods day and
night, where I will not show you favor.’

God Will Restore Israel

14“Therefore behold, the days are coming,” says the LORD, “that it shall no more
be said, ‘The LORD lives who brought up the
children of Israel from the land of Egypt,’
15but, ‘The LORD lives who brought up the
children of Israel from the land of the north
and from all the lands where He had driven
them.’ For I will bring them back into their
land which I gave to their fathers.
16“Behold, I will send for many fishermen,” says the LORD, “and they shall fish
them; and afterward I will send for many
hunters, and they shall hunt them from every mountain and every hill, and out of the
holes of the rocks. 17For My eyes *are* on all
their ways; they are not hidden from My face,
nor is their iniquity hidden from My eyes.
18And first I will repay double for their iniquity and their sin, because they have defiled
My land; they have filled My inheritance
with the carcasses of their detestable and
abominable idols.”

19 O LORD, my strength and my fortress,
My refuge in the day of affliction,
The Gentiles shall come to You
From the ends of the earth and say,

"Surely our fathers have inherited lies,
Worthlessness and unprofitable *things*."
20 Will a man make gods for himself,
Which *are* not gods?

21 "Therefore behold, I will this once cause them to know,
I will cause them to know
My hand and My might;
And they shall know that My name *is* the LORD.

Judah's Sin and Punishment

17 "The sin of Judah *is* written with a pen of iron;
With the point of a diamond *it is* engraved
On the tablet of their heart,
And on the horns of your altars,
2 While their children remember
Their altars and their wooden images[a]
By the green trees on the high hills.
3 O My mountain in the field,
I will give as plunder your wealth, all your treasures,
And your high places of sin within all your borders.
4 And you, even yourself,
Shall let go of your heritage which I gave you;
And I will cause you to serve your enemies
In the land which you do not know;
For you have kindled a fire in My anger *which* shall burn forever."

5 Thus says the LORD:

"Cursed *is* the man who trusts in man
And makes flesh his strength,
Whose heart departs from the LORD.
6 For he shall be like a shrub in the desert,
And shall not see when good comes,
But shall inhabit the parched places in the wilderness,
In a salt land *which is* not inhabited.

7 "Blessed *is* the man who trusts in the LORD,
And whose hope is the LORD.
8 For he shall be like a tree planted by the waters,
Which spreads out its roots by the river,
And will not fear[a] when heat comes;
But its leaf will be green,
And will not be anxious in the year of drought,
Nor will cease from yielding fruit.

9 "The heart *is* deceitful above all *things*,
And desperately wicked;
Who can know it?
10 I, the LORD, search the heart,
I test the mind,
Even to give every man according to his ways,
According to the fruit of his doings.

11 "*As* a partridge that broods but does not hatch,
So is he who gets riches, but not by right;
It will leave him in the midst of his days,
And at his end he will be a fool."

12 A glorious high throne from the beginning
Is the place of our sanctuary.
13 O LORD, the hope of Israel,
All who forsake You shall be ashamed.

"Those who depart from Me
Shall be written in the earth,
Because they have forsaken the LORD,
The fountain of living waters."

Jeremiah Prays for Deliverance

14 Heal me, O LORD, and I shall be healed;
Save me, and I shall be saved,
For You *are* my praise.
15 Indeed they say to me,
"Where *is* the word of the LORD?
Let it come now!"
16 As for me, I have not hurried away from *being* a shepherd *who* follows You,
Nor have I desired the woeful day;
You know what came out of my lips;
It was right there before You.
17 Do not be a terror to me;
You *are* my hope in the day of doom.
18 Let them be ashamed who persecute me,
But do not let me be put to shame;
Let them be dismayed,
But do not let me be dismayed.
Bring on them the day of doom,
And destroy them with double destruction!

17:2 [a] Hebrew *Asherim,* Canaanite deities 17:8 [a] Qere and Targum read *see.*

Hallow the Sabbath Day

19 Thus the LORD said to me: "Go and
stand in the gate of the children of the people, by which the kings of Judah come in and
by which they go out, and in all the gates
of Jerusalem; 20 and say to them, 'Hear the
word of the LORD, you kings of Judah, and
all Judah, and all the inhabitants of Jerusalem, who enter by these gates. 21 Thus says
the LORD: "Take heed to yourselves, and bear
no burden on the Sabbath day, nor bring *it*
in by the gates of Jerusalem; 22 nor carry a
burden out of your houses on the Sabbath
day, nor do any work, but hallow the Sabbath
day, as I commanded your fathers. 23 But they
did not obey nor incline their ear, but made
their neck stiff, that they might not hear nor
receive instruction.

24 "And it shall be, if you heed Me carefully," says the LORD, "to bring no burden
through the gates of this city on the Sabbath
day, but hallow the Sabbath day, to do no
work in it, 25 then shall enter the gates of this
city kings and princes sitting on the throne
of David, riding in chariots and on horses,
they and their princes, accompanied by the
men of Judah and the inhabitants of Jerusalem; and this city shall remain forever.
26 And they shall come from the cities of Judah and from the places around Jerusalem,
from the land of Benjamin and from the
lowland, from the mountains and from the
South, bringing burnt offerings and sacrifices, grain offerings and incense, bringing
sacrifices of praise to the house of the LORD.

27 "But if you will not heed Me to hallow
the Sabbath day, such as not carrying a burden when entering the gates of Jerusalem on
the Sabbath day, then I will kindle a fire in
its gates, and it shall devour the palaces of
Jerusalem, and it shall not be quenched." ' "

The Potter and the Clay

18 The word which came to Jeremiah
from the LORD, saying: 2 "Arise and
go down to the potter's house, and there I
will cause you to hear My words." 3 Then I
went down to the potter's house, and there
he was, making something at the wheel.
4 And the vessel that he made of clay was
marred in the hand of the potter; so he made
it again into another vessel, as it seemed
good to the potter to make.

5 Then the word of the LORD came to me,
saying: 6 "O house of Israel, can I not do with
you as this potter?" says the LORD. "Look, as
the clay *is* in the potter's hand, so *are* you in
My hand, O house of Israel! 7 The instant I
speak concerning a nation and concerning
a kingdom, to pluck up, to pull down, and
to destroy *it*, 8 if that nation against whom I
have spoken turns from its evil, I will relent
of the disaster that I thought to bring upon
it. 9 And the instant I speak concerning a
nation and concerning a kingdom, to build
and to plant *it*, 10 if it does evil in My sight
so that it does not obey My voice, then I will
relent concerning the good with which I said
I would benefit it.

11 "Now therefore, speak to the men of
Judah and to the inhabitants of Jerusalem,
saying, 'Thus says the LORD: "Behold, I am
fashioning a disaster and devising a plan
against you. Return now every one from his
evil way, and make your ways and your doings good." ' "

God's Warning Rejected

12 And they said, "That is hopeless! So we
will walk according to our own plans, and
we will every one obey the dictates of his evil
heart."

13 Therefore thus says the LORD:

"Ask now among the Gentiles,
Who has heard such things?
The virgin of Israel has done a very
horrible thing.
14 Will *a man* leave the snow water of
Lebanon,
Which comes from the rock of the field?
Will the cold flowing waters be forsaken
for strange waters?

15 "Because My people have forgotten Me,
They have burned incense to worthless
idols.
And they have caused themselves to
stumble in their ways,
From the ancient paths,
To walk in pathways and not on a
highway,
16 To make their land desolate *and* a
perpetual hissing;
Everyone who passes by it will be
astonished
And shake his head.
17 I will scatter them as with an east wind
before the enemy;

I will show them[a] the back and not the
face
In the day of their calamity."

Jeremiah Persecuted

18Then they said, "Come and let us devise
plans against Jeremiah; for the law shall not
perish from the priest, nor counsel from the
wise, nor the word from the prophet. Come
and let us attack him with the tongue, and
let us not give heed to any of his words."

19 Give heed to me, O LORD,
And listen to the voice of those who
contend with me!
20 Shall evil be repaid for good?
For they have dug a pit for my life.
Remember that I stood before You
To speak good for them,
To turn away Your wrath from them.
21 Therefore deliver up their children to
the famine,
And pour out their *blood*
By the force of the sword;
Let their wives *become* widows
And bereaved of their children.
Let their men be put to death,
Their young men *be* slain
By the sword in battle.
22 Let a cry be heard from their houses,
When You bring a troop suddenly upon
them;
For they have dug a pit to take me,
And hidden snares for my feet.
23 Yet, LORD, You know all their counsel
Which is against me, to slay *me*.
Provide no atonement for their iniquity,
Nor blot out their sin from Your sight;
But let them be overthrown before You.
Deal *thus* with them
In the time of Your anger.

The Sign of the Broken Flask

19 Thus says the LORD: "Go and get
a potter's earthen flask, and *take*
some of the elders of the people and some
of the elders of the priests. 2And go out to
the Valley of the Son of Hinnom, which *is* by
the entry of the Potsherd Gate; and proclaim
there the words that I will tell you, 3and say,
'Hear the word of the LORD, O kings of Judah
and inhabitants of Jerusalem. Thus says the
LORD of hosts, the God of Israel: "Behold,
I will bring such a catastrophe on this place,
that whoever hears of it, his ears will tingle.
4"Because they have forsaken Me and
made this an alien place, because they have
burned incense in it to other gods whom
neither they, their fathers, nor the kings of
Judah have known, and have filled this place
with the blood of the innocents 5(they have
also built the high places of Baal, to burn
their sons with fire *for* burnt offerings to
Baal, which I did not command or speak,
nor did it come into My mind), 6therefore
behold, the days are coming," says the LORD,
"that this place shall no more be called Tophet or the Valley of the Son of Hinnom, but
the Valley of Slaughter. 7And I will make
void the counsel of Judah and Jerusalem in
this place, and I will cause them to fall by the
sword before their enemies and by the hands
of those who seek their lives; their corpses I
will give as meat for the birds of the heaven
and for the beasts of the earth. 8I will make
this city desolate and a hissing; everyone
who passes by it will be astonished and hiss
because of all its plagues. 9And I will cause
them to eat the flesh of their sons and the
flesh of their daughters, and everyone shall
eat the flesh of his friend in the siege and
in the desperation with which their enemies
and those who seek their lives shall drive
them to despair."'
10"Then you shall break the flask in the
sight of the men who go with you, 11and say
to them, 'Thus says the LORD of hosts: "Even
so I will break this people and this city, as
one breaks a potter's vessel, which cannot be
made whole again; and they shall bury *them*
in Tophet till *there is* no place to bury. 12Thus
I will do to this place," says the LORD, "and
to its inhabitants, and make this city like
Tophet. 13And the houses of Jerusalem and
the houses of the kings of Judah shall be defiled like the place of Tophet, because of all
the houses on whose roofs they have burned
incense to all the host of heaven, and poured
out drink offerings to other gods."'"
14Then Jeremiah came from Tophet,
where the LORD had sent him to prophesy;
and he stood in the court of the LORD's house
and said to all the people, 15"Thus says the
LORD of hosts, the God of Israel: 'Behold, I
will bring on this city and on all her towns
all the doom that I have pronounced against

18:17 [a] Following Septuagint, Syriac, Targum, and Vulgate; Masoretic Text reads *look them in*.

it, because they have stiffened their necks that they might not hear My words.'"

The Word of God to Pashhur

20 Now Pashhur the son of Immer, the priest who *was* also chief governor in the house of the LORD, heard that Jeremiah prophesied these things.
2Then
Pashhur struck Jeremiah the prophet, and put him in the stocks that *were* in the high gate of Benjamin, which *was* by the house of the LORD.
3And it happened on the next day that Pashhur brought Jeremiah out of the stocks. Then Jeremiah said to him, "The LORD has not called your name Pashhur, but Magor-Missabib.[a]
4For thus says the LORD: 'Behold, I will make you a terror to yourself and to all your friends; and they shall fall by the sword of their enemies, and your eyes shall see *it*. I will give all Judah into the hand of the king of Babylon, and he shall carry them captive to Babylon and slay them with the sword.
5Moreover I will deliver all the wealth of this city, all its produce, and all its precious things; all the treasures of the kings of Judah I will give into the hand of their enemies, who will plunder them, seize them, and carry them to Babylon.
6And you, Pashhur, and all who dwell in your house, shall go into captivity. You shall go to Babylon, and there you shall die, and be buried there, you and all your friends, to whom you have prophesied lies.'"

Jeremiah's Unpopular Ministry

7 O LORD, You induced me, and I was persuaded;
You are stronger than I, and have prevailed.
I am in derision daily;
Everyone mocks me.
8 For when I spoke, I cried out;
I shouted, "Violence and plunder!"
Because the word of the LORD was made to me
A reproach and a derision daily.
9 Then I said, "I will not make mention of Him,
Nor speak anymore in His name."
But *His word* was in my heart like a burning fire
Shut up in my bones;
I was weary of holding *it* back,
And I could not.

10 For I heard many mocking:
"Fear on every side!"
"Report," *they say*, "and we will report it!"
All my acquaintances watched for my stumbling, *saying*,
"Perhaps he can be induced;
Then we will prevail against him,
And we will take our revenge on him."

11 But the LORD *is* with me as a mighty, awesome One.
Therefore my persecutors will stumble, and will not prevail.
They will be greatly ashamed, for they will not prosper.
Their everlasting confusion will never be forgotten.
12 But, O LORD of hosts,
You who test the righteous,
And see the mind and heart,
Let me see Your vengeance on them;
For I have pleaded my cause before You.

13 Sing to the LORD! Praise the LORD!
For He has delivered the life of the poor
From the hand of evildoers.

14 Cursed *be* the day in which I was born!
Let the day not be blessed in which my mother bore me!
15 Let the man *be* cursed
Who brought news to my father, saying,
"A male child has been born to you!"
Making him very glad.
16 And let that man be like the cities
Which the LORD overthrew, and did not relent;
Let him hear the cry in the morning
And the shouting at noon,
17 Because he did not kill me from the womb,
That my mother might have been my grave,
And her womb always enlarged *with me*.
18 Why did I come forth from the womb to see labor and sorrow,
That my days should be consumed with shame?

Jerusalem's Doom Is Sealed

21 The word which came to Jeremiah from the LORD when King Zedekiah sent to him Pashhur the son of Melchiah, and Zephaniah the son of Maaseiah, the

---

20:3 [a] Literally *Fear on Every Side*

priest, saying, 2“Please inquire of the LORD
for us, for Nebuchadnezzar[a] king of Babylon
makes war against us. Perhaps the LORD will
deal with us according to all His wonderful
works, that *the king* may go away from us.”

3Then Jeremiah said to them, “Thus you
shall say to Zedekiah, 4‘Thus says the LORD
God of Israel: “Behold, I will turn back the
weapons of war that *are* in your hands, with
which you fight against the king of Babylon
and the Chaldeans[a] who besiege you outside
the walls; and I will assemble them in the
midst of this city. 5I Myself will fight against
you with an outstretched hand and with a
strong arm, even in anger and fury and great
wrath. 6I will strike the inhabitants of this
city, both man and beast; they shall die of
a great pestilence. 7And afterward,” says the
LORD, “I will deliver Zedekiah king of Judah,
his servants and the people, and such as are
left in this city from the pestilence and the
sword and the famine, into the hand of Nebuchadnezzar king of Babylon, into the hand
of their enemies, and into the hand of those
who seek their life; and he shall strike them
with the edge of the sword. He shall not
spare them, or have pity or mercy.”’

8“Now you shall say to this people, ‘Thus
says the LORD: “Behold, I set before you the
way of life and the way of death. 9He who
remains in this city shall die by the sword,
by famine, and by pestilence; but he who
goes out and defects to the Chaldeans who
besiege you, he shall live, and his life shall
be as a prize to him. 10For I have set My face
against this city for adversity and not for
good,” says the LORD. “It shall be given into
the hand of the king of Babylon, and he shall
burn it with fire.”’

Message to the House of David

11“And concerning the house of the king
of Judah, *say,* ‘Hear the word of the LORD, 12O
house of David! Thus says the LORD:

“Execute judgment in the morning;
And deliver *him who is* plundered
Out of the hand of the oppressor,
Lest My fury go forth like fire
And burn so that no one can quench *it,*
Because of the evil of your doings.

13 “Behold, I *am* against you, O inhabitant of the valley,
And rock of the plain,” says the LORD,
“Who say, ‘Who shall come down against us?
Or who shall enter our dwellings?’
14 But I will punish you according to the fruit of your doings,” says the LORD;
“I will kindle a fire in its forest,
And it shall devour all things around it.”’”

22 Thus says the LORD: “Go down
to the house of the king of Judah,
and there speak this word, 2and say, ‘Hear
the word of the LORD, O king of Judah, you
who sit on the throne of David, you and
your servants and your people who enter
these gates! 3Thus says the LORD: “Execute
judgment and righteousness, and deliver
the plundered out of the hand of the oppressor. Do no wrong and do no violence to the
stranger, the fatherless, or the widow, nor
shed innocent blood in this place. 4For if you
indeed do this thing, then shall enter the
gates of this house, riding on horses and in
chariots, accompanied by servants and people, kings who sit on the throne of David.
5But if you will not hear these words, I swear
by Myself,” says the LORD, “that this house
shall become a desolation.”’”

6For thus says the LORD to the house of
the king of Judah:

“You *are* Gilead to Me,
The head of Lebanon;
Yet I surely will make you a wilderness,
Cities *which* are not inhabited.
7 I will prepare destroyers against you,
Everyone with his weapons;
They shall cut down your choice cedars
And cast *them* into the fire.

8And many nations will pass by this city; and
everyone will say to his neighbor, ‘Why has
the LORD done so to this great city?’ 9Then
they will answer, ‘Because they have forsak-
en the covenant of the LORD their God, and
worshiped other gods and served them.’”

10 Weep not for the dead, nor bemoan him;
Weep bitterly for him who goes away,
For he shall return no more,
Nor see his native country.

Message to the Sons of Josiah

11For thus says the LORD concerning
Shallum[a] the son of Josiah, king of Judah,

21:2 [a] Hebrew *Nebuchadrezzar,* and so elsewhere
21:4 [a] Or *Babylonians* **22:11** [a] Also called *Jehoahaz*

who reigned instead of Josiah his father, who went from this place: "He shall not return here anymore, 12but he shall die in the place where they have led him captive, and shall see this land no more.

13 "Woe to him who builds his house by unrighteousness
And his chambers by injustice,
Who uses his neighbor's service without wages
And gives him nothing for his work,
14 Who says, 'I will build myself a wide house with spacious chambers,
And cut out windows for it,
Paneling *it* with cedar
And painting *it* with vermilion.'

15 "Shall you reign because you enclose *yourself* in cedar?
Did not your father eat and drink,
And do justice and righteousness?
Then *it was* well with him.
16 He judged the cause of the poor and needy;
Then *it was* well.
Was not this knowing Me?" says the LORD.
17 "Yet your eyes and your heart *are* for nothing but your covetousness,
For shedding innocent blood,
And practicing oppression and violence."

18Therefore thus says the LORD concerning Jehoiakim the son of Josiah, king of Judah:

"They shall not lament for him,
Saying, 'Alas, my brother!' or 'Alas, my sister!'

"They shall not lament for him,
Saying, 'Alas, master!' or 'Alas, his glory!'
19 He shall be buried with the burial of a donkey,
Dragged and cast out beyond the gates of Jerusalem.

20 "Go up to Lebanon, and cry out,
And lift up your voice in Bashan;
Cry from Abarim,
For all your lovers are destroyed.
21 I spoke to you in your prosperity,
But you said, 'I will not hear.'
This *has been* your manner from your youth,
That you did not obey My voice.
22 The wind shall eat up all your rulers,
And your lovers shall go into captivity;
Surely then you will be ashamed and humiliated
For all your wickedness.
23 O inhabitant of Lebanon,
Making your nest in the cedars,
How gracious will you be when pangs come upon you,
Like the pain of a woman in labor?

Message to Coniah

24"*As* I live," says the LORD, "though
Coniah[a] the son of Jehoiakim, king of Judah, were the signet on My right hand, yet
I would pluck you off; 25and I will give you
into the hand of those who seek your life,
and into the hand *of those* whose face you
fear—the hand of Nebuchadnezzar king
of Babylon and the hand of the Chaldeans.
26So I will cast you out, and your mother who
bore you, into another country where you
were not born; and there you shall die. 27But
to the land to which they desire to return,
there they shall not return.

28 "Is this man Coniah a despised, broken idol—
A vessel in which *is* no pleasure?
Why are they cast out, he and his descendants,
And cast into a land which they do not know?
29 O earth, earth, earth,
Hear the word of the LORD!
30 Thus says the LORD:
'Write this man down as childless,
A man *who* shall not prosper in his days;
For none of his descendants shall prosper,
Sitting on the throne of David,
And ruling anymore in Judah.'"

The Branch of Righteousness

23 "Woe to the shepherds who destroy and scatter the sheep of My
pasture!" says the LORD. 2Therefore thus
says the LORD God of Israel against the
shepherds who feed My people: "You have
scattered My flock, driven them away, and
not attended to them. Behold, I will attend
to you for the evil of your doings," says the
LORD. 3"But I will gather the remnant of

22:24 [a] Also called *Jeconiah* and *Jehoiachin*

My flock out of all countries where I have driven them, and bring them back to their folds; and they shall be fruitful and increase.
4 I will set up shepherds over them who will feed them; and they shall fear no more, nor be dismayed, nor shall they be lacking," says the LORD.

5 "Behold, *the* days are coming," says the LORD,
"That I will raise to David a Branch of righteousness;
A King shall reign and prosper,
And execute judgment and righteousness in the earth.
6 In His days Judah will be saved,
And Israel will dwell safely;
Now this *is* His name by which He will be called:

THE LORD OUR RIGHTEOUSNESS.[a]

7 "Therefore, behold, *the* days are coming," says the LORD, "that they shall no longer say, 'As the LORD lives who brought up the children of Israel from the land of Egypt,'
8 but, 'As the LORD lives who brought up and led the descendants of the house of Israel from the north country and from all the countries where I had driven them.' And they shall dwell in their own land."

False Prophets and Empty Oracles

9 My heart within me is broken
Because of the prophets;
All my bones shake.
I am like a drunken man,
And like a man whom wine has overcome,
Because of the LORD,
And because of His holy words.
10 For the land is full of adulterers;
For because of a curse the land mourns.
The pleasant places of the wilderness are dried up.
Their course of life is evil,
And their might *is* not right.

11 "For both prophet and priest are profane;
Yes, in My house I have found their wickedness," says the LORD.
12 "Therefore their way shall be to them
Like slippery *ways;*
In the darkness they shall be driven on
And fall in them;
For I will bring disaster on them,
The year of their punishment," says the LORD.
13 "And I have seen folly in the prophets of Samaria:

23:6 [a] Hebrew *YHWH Tsidkenu*

23:6 THE LORD OUR RIGHTEOUSNESS

"Righteousness" (pronounced *RIGH-chuss-ness*) usually means something we possess because we do everything "right." But you and I know that we *never* do anything completely right as God measures it. The Bible says that all our righteousness is like "filthy rags" (see Isaiah 64:6). So there goes any idea that we can be righteous all by ourselves.

God doesn't cause us to be actually perfect, and He knows we are sinners. But He said, "*I* will be your righteousness. If you will just accept Jesus as payment for your sins, I will treat you just as if you are as righteous as My own Son." That's amazing! God doesn't see you anymore *just as you are;* God sees you *just as if you were His very own Son!*

Wouldn't you say that's the greatest love you've ever heard of? Doesn't it make you want to leave your sins behind and be His son or daughter forever?

They prophesied by Baal
And caused My people Israel to err.
14 Also I have seen a horrible thing in the prophets of Jerusalem:
They commit adultery and walk in lies;
They also strengthen the hands of evildoers,
So that no one turns back from his wickedness.
All of them are like Sodom to Me,
And her inhabitants like Gomorrah.

15"Therefore thus says the LORD of hosts concerning the prophets:

'Behold, I will feed them with wormwood,
And make them drink the water of gall;
For from the prophets of Jerusalem
Profaneness has gone out into all the land.'"

16Thus says the LORD of hosts:

"Do not listen to the words of the prophets who prophesy to you.
They make you worthless;
They speak a vision of their own heart,
Not from the mouth of the LORD.
17 They continually say to those who despise Me,
'The LORD has said, "You shall have peace"';
And *to* everyone who walks according to the dictates of his own heart, they say,
'No evil shall come upon you.'"

18 For who has stood in the counsel of the LORD,
And has perceived and heard His word?
Who has marked His word and heard *it*?
19 Behold, a whirlwind of the LORD has gone forth in fury—
A violent whirlwind!
It will fall violently on the head of the wicked.
20 The anger of the LORD will not turn back
Until He has executed and performed the thoughts of His heart.
In the latter days you will understand it perfectly.

21 "I have not sent these prophets, yet they ran.
I have not spoken to them, yet they prophesied.
22 But if they had stood in My counsel,
And had caused My people to hear My words,
Then they would have turned them from their evil way
And from the evil of their doings.

23 "*Am* I a God near at hand," says the LORD,
"And not a God afar off?
24 Can anyone hide himself in secret places,
So I shall not see him?" says the LORD;
"Do I not fill heaven and earth?" says the LORD.

25"I have heard what the prophets have
said who prophesy lies in My name, saying,
'I have dreamed, I have dreamed!' 26How
long will *this* be in the heart of the prophets
who prophesy lies? Indeed *they are* prophets
of the deceit of their own heart, 27who try to
make My people forget My name by their
dreams which everyone tells his neighbor,
as their fathers forgot My name for Baal.

28 "The prophet who has a dream, let him tell a dream;
And he who has My word, let him speak My word faithfully.
What *is* the chaff to the wheat?" says the LORD.
29 "*Is* not My word like a fire?" says the LORD,
"And like a hammer *that* breaks the rock in pieces?

30"Therefore behold, I *am* against the
prophets," says the LORD, "who steal My
words every one from his neighbor. 31Behold,
I *am* against the prophets," says the LORD,
"who use their tongues and say, 'He says.'
32Behold, I *am* against those who prophesy false dreams," says the LORD, "and tell
them, and cause My people to err by their
lies and by their recklessness. Yet I did not
send them or command them; therefore
they shall not profit this people at all," says
the LORD.

33"So when these people or the prophet or
the priest ask you, saying, 'What is the oracle of the LORD?' you shall then say to them,
'What oracle?'[a] I will even forsake you," says
the LORD. 34"And *as for* the prophet and the

23:33 [a] Septuagint, Targum, and Vulgate read *'You are the burden.'*

priest and the people who say, 'The oracle of
the LORD!' I will even punish that man and
his house. 35Thus every one of you shall say
to his neighbor, and every one to his brother,
'What has the LORD answered?' and, 'What
has the LORD spoken?' 36And the oracle of
the LORD you shall mention no more. For
every man's word will be his oracle, for you
have perverted the words of the living God,
the LORD of hosts, our God. 37Thus you shall
say to the prophet, 'What has the LORD answered you?' and, 'What has the LORD spoken?' 38But since you say, 'The oracle of the
LORD!' therefore thus says the LORD: 'Because you say this word, "The oracle of the
LORD!" and I have sent to you, saying, "Do
not say, 'The oracle of the LORD!'" 39there-
fore behold, I, even I, will utterly forget you
and forsake you, and the city that I gave you
and your fathers, and *will cast you* out of My
presence. 40And I will bring an everlasting
reproach upon you, and a perpetual shame,
which shall not be forgotten.'"

The Sign of Two Baskets of Figs

24 The LORD showed me, and there
were two baskets of figs set before
the temple of the LORD, after Nebuchadnezzar king of Babylon had carried away
captive Jeconiah the son of Jehoiakim, king
of Judah, and the princes of Judah with the
craftsmen and smiths, from Jerusalem, and
had brought them to Babylon. 2One basket
had very good figs, like the figs *that are* first
ripe; and the other basket *had* very bad figs
which could not be eaten, they were so bad.
3Then the LORD said to me, "What do you
see, Jeremiah?"

And I said, "Figs, the good figs, very
good; and the bad, very bad, which cannot
be eaten, they are so bad."

4Again the word of the LORD came to
me, saying, 5"Thus says the LORD, the God
of Israel: 'Like these good figs, so will I acknowledge those who are carried away captive from Judah, whom I have sent out of
this place for *their own* good, into the land
of the Chaldeans. 6For I will set My eyes on
them for good, and I will bring them back
to this land; I will build them and not pull
them down, and I will plant them and not
pluck *them* up. 7Then I will give them a heart
to know Me, that I *am* the LORD; and they
shall be My people, and I will be their God,
for they shall return to Me with their whole
heart.

8'And as the bad figs which cannot be
eaten, they are so bad'—surely thus says the
LORD—'so will I give up Zedekiah the king
of Judah, his princes, the residue of Jerusalem who remain in this land, and those
who dwell in the land of Egypt. 9I will deliver them to trouble into all the kingdoms
of the earth, for *their* harm, *to be* a reproach
and a byword, a taunt and a curse, in all
places where I shall drive them. 10And I will
send the sword, the famine, and the pestilence among them, till they are consumed
from the land that I gave to them and their
fathers.'"

Seventy Years of Desolation

25 The word that came to Jeremiah
concerning all the people of Judah,
in the fourth year of Jehoiakim the son of Josiah, king of Judah (which *was* the first year
of Nebuchadnezzar king of Babylon), 2which
Jeremiah the prophet spoke to all the people
of Judah and to all the inhabitants of Jerusalem, saying: 3"From the thirteenth year of
Josiah the son of Amon, king of Judah, even
to this day, this *is* the twenty-third year in
which the word of the LORD has come to me;
and I have spoken to you, rising early and
speaking, but you have not listened. 4And
the LORD has sent to you all His servants the
prophets, rising early and sending *them*, but
you have not listened nor inclined your ear
to hear. 5They said, 'Repent now everyone of
his evil way and his evil doings, and dwell
in the land that the LORD has given to you
and your fathers forever and ever. 6Do not go
after other gods to serve them and worship
them, and do not provoke Me to anger with
the works of your hands; and I will not harm
you.' 7Yet you have not listened to Me," says
the LORD, "that you might provoke Me to
anger with the works of your hands to your
own hurt.

8"Therefore thus says the LORD of hosts:
'Because you have not heard My words, 9be-
hold, I will send and take all the families of
the north,' says the LORD, 'and Nebuchadnezzar the king of Babylon, My servant, and
will bring them against this land, against
its inhabitants, and against these nations all
around, and will utterly destroy them, and
make them an astonishment, a hissing, and
perpetual desolations. 10Moreover I will take

from them the voice of mirth and the voice
of gladness, the voice of the bridegroom
and the voice of the bride, the sound of the
millstones and the light of the lamp. 11And
this whole land shall be a desolation *and* an
astonishment, and these nations shall serve
the king of Babylon seventy years.
12'Then it will come to pass, when seventy
years are completed, *that* I will punish the
king of Babylon and that nation, the land of
the Chaldeans, for their iniquity,' says the
LORD; 'and I will make it a perpetual desolation. 13So I will bring on that land all My
words which I have pronounced against it,
all that is written in this book, which Jeremiah has prophesied concerning all the nations. 14(For many nations and great kings
shall be served by them also; and I will repay
them according to their deeds and according
to the works of their own hands.)'"

Judgment on the Nations

15For thus says the LORD God of Israel
to me: "Take this wine cup of fury from My
hand, and cause all the nations, to whom I
send you, to drink it. 16And they will drink
and stagger and go mad because of the
sword that I will send among them."
17Then I took the cup from the LORD's
hand, and made all the nations drink, to
whom the LORD had sent me: 18Jerusalem
and the cities of Judah, its kings and its
princes, to make them a desolation, an astonishment, a hissing, and a curse, as *it is*
this day; 19Pharaoh king of Egypt, his servants, his princes, and all his people; 20all
the mixed multitude, all the kings of the
land of Uz, all the kings of the land of the
Philistines (namely, Ashkelon, Gaza, Ekron,
and the remnant of Ashdod); 21Edom, Moab,
and the people of Ammon; 22all the kings of
Tyre, all the kings of Sidon, and the kings
of the coastlands which *are* across the sea;
23Dedan, Tema, Buz, and all *who are* in the
farthest corners; 24all the kings of Arabia and
all the kings of the mixed multitude who
dwell in the desert; 25all the kings of Zimri,
all the kings of Elam, and all the kings of
the Medes; 26all the kings of the north, far
and near, one with another; and all the kingdoms of the world which *are* on the face of
the earth. Also the king of Sheshach[a] shall
drink after them.
27"Therefore you shall say to them, 'Thus
says the LORD of hosts, the God of Israel:

In Focus

25:34 Dispersion Pronounced *dis-PUR-zhun*. The Jews were scattered among the other nations several times because of the invasions of foreign armies throughout Jewish history.

"Drink, be drunk, and vomit! Fall and rise
no more, because of the sword which I will
send among you."' 28And it shall be, if they
refuse to take the cup from your hand to
drink, then you shall say to them, 'Thus
says the LORD of hosts: "You shall certainly
drink! 29For behold, I begin to bring calamity
on the city which is called by My name, and
should you be utterly unpunished? You shall
not be unpunished, for I will call for a sword
on all the inhabitants of the earth," says the
LORD of hosts.'
30"Therefore prophesy against them all
these words, and say to them:

'The LORD will roar from on high,
And utter His voice from His holy
habitation;
He will roar mightily against His fold.
He will give a shout, as those who tread
the grapes,
Against all the inhabitants of the earth.
31 A noise will come to the ends of the
earth—
For the LORD has a controversy with the
nations;
He will plead His case with all flesh.
He will give those *who are* wicked to the
sword,' says the LORD."

32Thus says the LORD of hosts:

"Behold, disaster shall go forth
From nation to nation,
And a great whirlwind shall be raised up
From the farthest parts of the earth.

33And at that day the slain of the LORD shall
be from *one* end of the earth even to the *other*
end of the earth. They shall not be lamented,

25:26 [a] A code word for Babylon (compare 51:41)

or gathered, or buried; they shall become refuse on the ground.

34 "Wail, shepherds, and cry!
Roll about *in the ashes,*
You leaders of the flock!
For the days of your slaughter and your
dispersions are fulfilled;
You shall fall like a precious vessel.
35 And the shepherds will have no way to
flee,
Nor the leaders of the flock to escape.
36 A voice of the cry of the shepherds,
And a wailing of the leaders to the flock
will be heard.
For the LORD has plundered their
pasture,
37 And the peaceful dwellings are cut
down
Because of the fierce anger of the LORD.
38 He has left His lair like the lion;
For their land is desolate
Because of the fierceness of the
Oppressor,
And because of His fierce anger."

Jeremiah Saved from Death

26 In the beginning of the reign of
Jehoiakim the son of Josiah, king
of Judah, this word came from the LORD,
saying, 2"Thus says the LORD: 'Stand in the
court of the LORD's house, and speak to all
the cities of Judah, which come to worship
in the LORD's house, all the words that I
command you to speak to them. Do not diminish a word. 3Perhaps everyone will listen
and turn from his evil way, that I may relent
concerning the calamity which I purpose to
bring on them because of the evil of their
doings.' 4And you shall say to them, 'Thus
says the LORD: "If you will not listen to Me,
to walk in My law which I have set before
you, 5to heed the words of My servants the
prophets whom I sent to you, both rising up
early and sending *them* (but you have not
heeded), 6then I will make this house like
Shiloh, and will make this city a curse to all
the nations of the earth." ' "

7So the priests and the prophets and all
the people heard Jeremiah speaking these
words in the house of the LORD. 8Now it happened, when Jeremiah had made an end of
speaking all that the LORD had commanded
him to speak to all the people, that the priests
and the prophets and all the people seized
him, saying, "You will surely die! 9Why have
you prophesied in the name of the LORD,
saying, 'This house shall be like Shiloh, and
this city shall be desolate, without an inhabitant'?" And all the people were gathered
against Jeremiah in the house of the LORD.

10When the princes of Judah heard these
things, they came up from the king's house
to the house of the LORD and sat down in the
entry of the New Gate of the LORD's *house.*
11And the priests and the prophets spoke to
the princes and all the people, saying, "This
man deserves to die! For he has prophesied
against this city, as you have heard with your
ears."

12Then Jeremiah spoke to all the princes and all the people, saying: "The LORD
sent me to prophesy against this house and
against this city with all the words that you
have heard. 13Now therefore, amend your
ways and your doings, and obey the voice
of the LORD your God; then the LORD will
relent concerning the doom that He has pronounced against you. 14As for me, here I am,
in your hand; do with me as seems good and
proper to you. 15But know for certain that if
you put me to death, you will surely bring
innocent blood on yourselves, on this city,
and on its inhabitants; for truly the LORD
has sent me to you to speak all these words
in your hearing."

16So the princes and all the people said
to the priests and the prophets, "This man
does not deserve to die. For he has spoken to
us in the name of the LORD our God."

17Then certain of the elders of the land
rose up and spoke to all the assembly of
the people, saying: 18"Micah of Moresheth
prophesied in the days of Hezekiah king of
Judah, and spoke to all the people of Judah,
saying, 'Thus says the LORD of hosts:

"Zion shall be plowed *like* a field,
Jerusalem shall become heaps of ruins,
And the mountain of the temple[a]
Like the bare hills of the forest." '[b]

19Did Hezekiah king of Judah and all Judah
ever put him to death? Did he not fear the
LORD and seek the LORD's favor? And the
LORD relented concerning the doom which
He had pronounced against them. But we
are doing great evil against ourselves."

26:18 [a] Literally *house* [b] Compare Micah 3:12

20Now there was also a man who prophesied in the name of the LORD, Urijah the son of Shemaiah of Kirjath Jearim, who prophesied against this city and against this land according to all the words of Jeremiah. 21And when Jehoiakim the king, with all his mighty men and all the princes, heard his words, the king sought to put him to death; but when Urijah heard *it,* he was afraid and fled, and went to Egypt. 22Then Jehoiakim the king sent men to Egypt: Elnathan the son of Achbor, and *other* men *who went* with him to Egypt. 23And they brought Urijah from Egypt and brought him to Jehoiakim the king, who killed him with the sword and cast his dead body into the graves of the common people.

24Nevertheless the hand of Ahikam the son of Shaphan was with Jeremiah, so that they should not give him into the hand of the people to put him to death.

Symbol of the Bonds and Yokes

27 In the beginning of the reign of Jehoiakim[a] the son of Josiah, king of Judah, this word came to Jeremiah from the LORD, saying,[b] 2"Thus says the LORD to me: 'Make for yourselves bonds and yokes, and put them on your neck, 3and send them to the king of Edom, the king of Moab, the king of the Ammonites, the king of Tyre, and the king of Sidon, by the hand of the messengers who come to Jerusalem to Zedekiah king of Judah. 4And command them to say to their masters, "Thus says the LORD of hosts, the God of Israel—thus you shall say to your masters: 5'I have made the earth, the man and the beast that *are* on the ground, by My great power and by My outstretched arm, and have given it to whom it seemed proper to Me. 6And now I have given all these lands into the hand of Nebuchadnezzar the king of Babylon, My servant; and the beasts of the field I have also given him to serve him. 7So all nations shall serve him *and his son and his son's* son, until the time of his land comes; and then many nations and great kings shall make him serve them. 8And it shall be, *that* the nation and kingdom which will not serve Nebuchadnezzar the king of Babylon, and which will not put its neck under the yoke of the king of Babylon, that nation I will punish,' says the LORD, 'with the sword, the famine, and the pestilence, until I have consumed them by his hand. 9Therefore do not listen to your prophets, your diviners, your dreamers, your soothsayers, or your sorcerers, who speak to you, saying, "You shall not serve the king of Babylon." 10For they prophesy a lie to you, to remove you far from your land; and I will drive you out, and you will perish. 11But the nations that bring their necks under the yoke of the king of Babylon and serve him, I will let them remain in their own land,' says the LORD, 'and they shall till it and dwell in it.'"'"

12I also spoke to Zedekiah king of Judah according to all these words, saying, "Bring your necks under the yoke of the king of Babylon, and serve him and his people, and live! 13Why will you die, you and your people, by the sword, by the famine, and by the pestilence, as the LORD has spoken against the nation that will not serve the king of Babylon? 14Therefore do not listen to the words of the prophets who speak to you, saying, 'You shall not serve the king of Babylon,' for they prophesy a lie to you; 15for I have not sent them," says the LORD, "yet they prophesy a lie in My name, that I may drive you out, and that you may perish, you and the prophets who prophesy to you."

16Also I spoke to the priests and to all this people, saying, "Thus says the LORD: 'Do not listen to the words of your prophets who prophesy to you, saying, "Behold, the vessels of the LORD's house will now shortly be brought back from Babylon"; for they prophesy a lie to you. 17Do not listen to them; serve the king of Babylon, and live! Why should this city be laid waste? 18But if they *are* prophets, and if the word of the LORD is with them, let them now make intercession to the LORD of hosts, that the vessels which are left in the house of the LORD, *in* the house of the king of Judah, and at Jerusalem, do not go to Babylon.'

19"For thus says the LORD of hosts concerning the pillars, concerning the Sea, concerning the carts, and concerning the remainder of the vessels that remain in this city, 20which Nebuchadnezzar king of Babylon did not take, when he carried away captive Jeconiah the son of Jehoiakim, king of Judah, from Jerusalem to Babylon, and all the nobles of Judah and Jerusalem— 21yes,

27:1 [a] Following Masoretic Text, Targum, and Vulgate; some Hebrew manuscripts, Arabic, and Syriac read *Zedekiah* (compare 27:3, 12; 28:1). [b] Septuagint omits verse 1.

thus says the LORD of hosts, the God of Israel, concerning the vessels that remain in
the house of the LORD, and in the house of
the king of Judah and of Jerusalem: 22'They
shall be carried to Babylon, and there they
shall be until the day that I visit them,' says
the LORD. 'Then I will bring them up and
restore them to this place.'"

Hananiah's Falsehood and Doom

28 And it happened in the same year,
at the beginning of the reign of
Zedekiah king of Judah, in the fourth year
and in the fifth month, *that* Hananiah the
son of Azur the prophet, who *was* from
Gibeon, spoke to me in the house of the
LORD in the presence of the priests and of
all the people, saying, 2"Thus speaks the
LORD of hosts, the God of Israel, saying: 'I
have broken the yoke of the king of Babylon.
3Within two full years I will bring back to
this place all the vessels of the LORD's house,
that Nebuchadnezzar king of Babylon took
away from this place and carried to Babylon.
4And I will bring back to this place Jeconiah
the son of Jehoiakim, king of Judah, with all
the captives of Judah who went to Babylon,'
says the LORD, 'for I will break the yoke of
the king of Babylon.'"

5Then the prophet Jeremiah spoke to
the prophet Hananiah in the presence of
the priests and in the presence of all the
people who stood in the house of the LORD,
6and the prophet Jeremiah said, "Amen! The
LORD do so; the LORD perform your words
which you have prophesied, to bring back
the vessels of the LORD's house and all who
were carried away captive, from Babylon
to this place. 7Nevertheless hear now this
word that I speak in your hearing and in
the hearing of all the people: 8The prophets
who have been before me and before you of
old prophesied against many countries and
great kingdoms—of war and disaster and
pestilence. 9As for the prophet who prophesies of peace, when the word of the prophet
comes to pass, the prophet will be known *as*
one whom the LORD has truly sent."

10Then Hananiah the prophet took the
yoke off the prophet Jeremiah's neck and
broke it. 11And Hananiah spoke in the presence of all the people, saying, "Thus says
the LORD: 'Even so I will break the yoke of
Nebuchadnezzar king of Babylon from the
neck of all nations within the space of two
full years.'" And the prophet Jeremiah went
his way.

12Now the word of the LORD came to Jeremiah, after Hananiah the prophet had broken the yoke from the neck of the prophet
Jeremiah, saying, 13"Go and tell Hananiah,
saying, 'Thus says the LORD: "You have broken the yokes of wood, but you have made
in their place yokes of iron." 14For thus says
the LORD of hosts, the God of Israel: "I have
put a yoke of iron on the neck of all these nations, that they may serve Nebuchadnezzar
king of Babylon; and they shall serve him. I
have given him the beasts of the field also."'"

15Then the prophet Jeremiah said to
Hananiah the prophet, "Hear now, Hananiah, the LORD has not sent you, but you make
this people trust in a lie. 16Therefore thus
says the LORD: 'Behold, I will cast you from
the face of the earth. This year you shall die,
because you have taught rebellion against
the LORD.'"

17So Hananiah the prophet died the same
year in the seventh month.

Jeremiah's Letter to the Captives

29 Now these *are* the words of the
letter that Jeremiah the prophet
sent from Jerusalem to the remainder of the
elders who were carried away captive—to
the priests, the prophets, and all the people whom Nebuchadnezzar had carried
away captive from Jerusalem to Babylon.
2(This happened after Jeconiah the king, the
queen mother, the eunuchs, the princes of
Judah and Jerusalem, the craftsmen, and
the smiths had departed from Jerusalem.)
3*The letter was sent* by the hand of Elasah the
son of Shaphan, and Gemariah the son of
Hilkiah, whom Zedekiah king of Judah sent
to Babylon, to Nebuchadnezzar king of Babylon, saying,

4 Thus says the LORD of hosts, the God of
Israel, to all who were carried away captive, whom I have caused to be carried
away from Jerusalem to Babylon:

5 Build houses and dwell *in them;* plant
gardens and eat their fruit. 6Take wives
and beget sons and daughters; and
take wives for your sons and give your
daughters to husbands, so that they may
bear sons and daughters—that you may
be increased there, and not diminished.

7And seek the peace of the city where I
have caused you to be carried away captive, and pray to the LORD for it; for in its
peace you will have peace. 8For thus says
the LORD of hosts, the God of Israel: Do
not let your prophets and your diviners
who are in your midst deceive you, nor
listen to your dreams which you cause
to be dreamed. 9For they prophesy falsely to you in My name; I have not sent
them, says the LORD.

10 For thus says the LORD: After seventy
years are completed at Babylon, I will
visit you and perform My good word
toward you, and cause you to return to
this place. 11For I know the thoughts
that I think toward you, says the LORD,
thoughts of peace and not of evil, to give
you a future and a hope. 12Then you will
call upon Me and go and pray to Me,
and I will listen to you. 13And you will
seek Me and find *Me,* when you search
for Me with all your heart. 14I will be
found by you, says the LORD, and I will
bring you back from your captivity; I
will gather you from all the nations and
from all the places where I have driven
you, says the LORD, and I will bring you

FINDING YOUR PURPOSE IN LIFE
THERE'S HOPE!

READ IT: JEREMIAH 29:11

GET IT:

Loneliness and hopelessness are feelings we often face. When things don't go right it seems like there's no plan for our lives. Maybe we feel like we don't measure up. What's the point of life?

We often read stories about people in the Bible who were discouraged and felt forgotten. God asked the prophet Jeremiah to write a letter to the elders and teachers who were taken from their homes in Jerusalem and sent off to Babylon. Their lives changed in a moment and against their will, even though they were obeying God. What was God's purpose for them now?

God tells them to create peace in their new land. He tells them to pray for it. He tells them He hasn't forgotten them, and He promises to rescue them in His time. He assures them that although this may seem like a mistake, He knows what He's doing. In the same way, we can take comfort in knowing God loves us. He intends for us to have a purpose and a future hope regardless of our circumstances.

LIVE IT:

Think of something in your life that isn't going the way you expected or hoped. Maybe it's a friendship or something at school. Can you take God's words from this passage and apply them to your situation? God has a purpose and hope for you, and He won't let you down.

to the place from which I cause you to
be carried away captive.

15 Because you have said, "The LORD has
raised up prophets for us in Babylon"—
16therefore thus says the LORD concerning the king who sits on the throne of
David, concerning all the people who
dwell in this city, and concerning your
brethren who have not gone out with
you into captivity— 17thus says the
LORD of hosts: Behold, I will send on
them the sword, the famine, and the
pestilence, and will make them like
rotten figs that cannot be eaten, they
are so bad. 18And I will pursue them
with the sword, with famine, and with
pestilence; and I will deliver them to
trouble among all the kingdoms of the
earth—to be a curse, an astonishment,
a hissing, and a reproach among all the
nations where I have driven them, 19be-
cause they have not heeded My words,
says the LORD, which I sent to them by
My servants the prophets, rising up early and sending *them;* neither would you
heed, says the LORD. 20Therefore hear
the word of the LORD, all you of the captivity, whom I have sent from Jerusalem
to Babylon.

21 Thus says the LORD of hosts, the God
of Israel, concerning Ahab the son of
Kolaiah, and Zedekiah the son of Maaseiah, who prophesy a lie to you in My
name: Behold, I will deliver them into
the hand of Nebuchadnezzar king of
Babylon, and he shall slay them before
your eyes. 22And because of them a
curse shall be taken up by all the captivity of Judah who *are* in Babylon, saying,
"The LORD make you like Zedekiah and
Ahab, whom the king of Babylon roasted in the fire"; 23because they have done
disgraceful things in Israel, have committed adultery with their neighbors'
wives, and have spoken lying words in
My name, which I have not commanded
them. Indeed I know, and *am* a witness,
says the LORD.

24 You shall also speak to Shemaiah the
Nehelamite, saying, 25Thus speaks the
LORD of hosts, the God of Israel, saying:
You have sent letters in your name to
all the people who *are* at Jerusalem, to
Zephaniah the son of Maaseiah the
priest, and to all the priests, saying,
26"The LORD has made you priest instead of Jehoiada the priest, so that there
should be officers *in* the house of the
LORD over every man *who* is demented
and considers himself a prophet, that
you should put him in prison and in the
stocks. 27Now therefore, why have you
not rebuked Jeremiah of Anathoth who
makes himself a prophet to you? 28For
he has sent to us *in* Babylon, saying,
'This *captivity is* long; build houses and
dwell *in them,* and plant gardens and eat
their fruit.'"

29Now Zephaniah the priest read this letter
in the hearing of Jeremiah the prophet. 30Then
the word of the LORD came to Jeremiah, saying: 31Send to all those in captivity, saying,
Thus says the LORD concerning Shemaiah the
Nehelamite: Because Shemaiah has prophesied to you, and I have not sent him, and he
has caused you to trust in a lie— 32therefore
thus says the LORD: Behold, I will punish Shemaiah the Nehelamite and his family: he shall
not have anyone to dwell among this people,
nor shall he see the good that I will do for My
people, says the LORD, because he has taught
rebellion against the LORD.

Restoration of Israel and Judah

30 The word that came to Jeremiah
from the LORD, saying, 2"Thus
speaks the LORD God of Israel, saying:
'Write in a book for yourself all the words
that I have spoken to you. 3For behold, the
days are coming,' says the LORD, 'that I will
bring back from captivity My people Israel
and Judah,' says the LORD. 'And I will cause
them to return to the land that I gave to their
fathers, and they shall possess it.'"

4Now these *are* the words that the LORD
spoke concerning Israel and Judah.

5"For thus says the LORD:

'We have heard a voice of trembling,
Of fear, and not of peace.
6 Ask now, and see,
Whether a man is ever in labor with
child?
So why do I see every man with his
hands on his loins
Like a woman in labor,
And all faces turned pale?
7 Alas! For that day *is* great,

So that none *is* like it;
And it *is* the time of Jacob's trouble,
But he shall be saved out of it.

8 'For it shall come to pass in that day,'
Says the LORD of hosts,
'*That* I will break his yoke from your neck,
And will burst your bonds;
Foreigners shall no more enslave them.
9 But they shall serve the LORD their God,
And David their king,
Whom I will raise up for them.

10 'Therefore do not fear, O My servant Jacob,' says the LORD,
'Nor be dismayed, O Israel;
For behold, I will save you from afar,
And your seed from the land of their captivity.
Jacob shall return, have rest and be quiet,
And no one shall make *him* afraid.
11 For I *am* with you,' says the LORD, 'to save you;
Though I make a full end of all nations where I have scattered you,
Yet I will not make a complete end of you.
But I will correct you in justice,
And will not let you go altogether unpunished.'

12 "For thus says the LORD:

'Your affliction *is* incurable,
Your wound *is* severe.
13 *There is* no one to plead your cause,
That you may be bound up;
You have no healing medicines.
14 All your lovers have forgotten you;
They do not seek you;
For I have wounded you with the wound of an enemy,
With the chastisement of a cruel one,
For the multitude of your iniquities,
Because your sins have increased.
15 Why do you cry about your affliction?
Your sorrow *is* incurable.
Because of the multitude of your iniquities,
Because your sins have increased,
I have done these things to you.

16 'Therefore all those who devour you shall be devoured;
And all your adversaries, every one of them, shall go into captivity;
Those who plunder you shall become plunder,
And all who prey upon you I will make a prey.
17 For I will restore health to you
And heal you of your wounds,' says the LORD,
'Because they called you an outcast *saying:*
"This *is* Zion;
No one seeks her." '

18 "Thus says the LORD:

'Behold, I will bring back the captivity of Jacob's tents,
And have mercy on his dwelling places;
The city shall be built upon its own mound,
And the palace shall remain according to its own plan.
19 Then out of them shall proceed thanksgiving
And the voice of those who make merry;
I will multiply them, and they shall not diminish;
I will also glorify them, and they shall not be small.
20 Their children also shall be as before,
And their congregation shall be established before Me;
And I will punish all who oppress them.
21 Their nobles shall be from among them,
And their governor shall come from their midst;
Then I will cause him to draw near,
And he shall approach Me;
For who *is* this who pledged his heart to approach Me?' says the LORD.
22 'You shall be My people,
And I will be your God.' "

23 Behold, the whirlwind of the LORD
Goes forth with fury,
A continuing whirlwind;
It will fall violently on the head of the wicked.
24 The fierce anger of the LORD will not return until He has done it,
And until He has performed the intents of His heart.

In the latter days you will consider it.

The Remnant of Israel Saved

31 "At the same time," says the LORD, "I will be the God of all the families of Israel, and they shall be My people."

2 Thus says the LORD:

"The people who survived the sword
Found grace in the wilderness—
Israel, when I went to give him rest."

3 The LORD has appeared of old to me, *saying:*
"Yes, I have loved you with an everlasting love;
Therefore with lovingkindness I have drawn you.
4 Again I will build you, and you shall be rebuilt,
O virgin of Israel!
You shall again be adorned with your tambourines,
And shall go forth in the dances of those who rejoice.
5 You shall yet plant vines on the mountains of Samaria;
The planters shall plant and eat *them* as ordinary food.
6 For there shall be a day
When the watchmen will cry on Mount Ephraim,
'Arise, and let us go up *to* Zion,
To the LORD our God.'"

7 For thus says the LORD:

"Sing with gladness for Jacob,
And shout among the chief of the nations;
Proclaim, give praise, and say,
'O LORD, save Your people,
The remnant of Israel!'
8 Behold, I will bring them from the north country,
And gather them from the ends of the earth,
Among them the blind and the lame,
The woman with child
And the one who labors with child, together;
A great throng shall return there.
9 They shall come with weeping,
And with supplications I will lead them.
I will cause them to walk by the rivers of waters,
In a straight way in which they shall not stumble;
For I am a Father to Israel,
And Ephraim *is* My firstborn.

10 "Hear the word of the LORD, O nations,
And declare *it* in the isles afar off, and say,
'He who scattered Israel will gather him,
And keep him as a shepherd *does* his flock.'
11 For the LORD has redeemed Jacob,
And ransomed him from the hand of one stronger than he.
12 Therefore they shall come and sing in the height of Zion,
Streaming to the goodness of the LORD—
For wheat and new wine and oil,
For the young of the flock and the herd;
Their souls shall be like a well-watered garden,
And they shall sorrow no more at all.

13 "Then shall the virgin rejoice in the dance,
And the young men and the old, together;
For I will turn their mourning to joy,
Will comfort them,
And make them rejoice rather than sorrow.
14 I will satiate the soul of the priests with abundance,
And My people shall be satisfied with My goodness, says the LORD."

Mercy on Ephraim

15 Thus says the LORD:

"A voice was heard in Ramah,
Lamentation *and* bitter weeping,
Rachel weeping for her children,
Refusing to be comforted for her children,
Because they *are* no more."

16 Thus says the LORD:

"Refrain your voice from weeping,
And your eyes from tears;
For your work shall be rewarded, says the LORD,
And they shall come back from the land of the enemy.
17 There is hope in your future, says the LORD,
That *your* children shall come back to their own border.

18 "I have surely heard Ephraim bemoaning himself:

'You have chastised me, and I was
chastised,
Like an untrained bull;
Restore me, and I will return,
For You *are* the LORD my God.
19 Surely, after my turning, I repented;
And after I was instructed, I struck
myself on the thigh;
I was ashamed, yes, even humiliated,
Because I bore the reproach of my
youth.'
20 *Is* Ephraim My dear son?
Is he a pleasant child?
For though I spoke against him,
I earnestly remember him still;
Therefore My heart yearns for him;
I will surely have mercy on him, says
the LORD.

21 "Set up signposts,
Make landmarks;
Set your heart toward the highway,
The way in *which* you went.
Turn back, O virgin of Israel,
Turn back to these your cities.
22 How long will you gad about,
O you backsliding daughter?
For the LORD has created a new thing in
the earth—
A woman shall encompass a man."

Future Prosperity of Judah

23 Thus says the LORD of hosts, the God
of Israel: "They shall again use this speech
in the land of Judah and in its cities, when I
bring back their captivity: 'The LORD bless
you, O home of justice, *and* mountain of
holiness!' 24 And there shall dwell in Judah
itself, and in all its cities together, farmers
and those going out with flocks. 25 For I have
satiated the weary soul, and I have replen-
ished every sorrowful soul."

26 After this I awoke and looked around,
and my sleep was sweet to me.

27 "Behold, the days are coming, says the
LORD, that I will sow the house of Israel and
the house of Judah with the seed of man and
the seed of beast. 28 And it shall come to pass,
that as I have watched over them to pluck
up, to break down, to throw down, to destroy,
and to afflict, so I will watch over them to
build and to plant, says the LORD. 29 In those
days they shall say no more:

'The fathers have eaten sour grapes,
And the children's teeth are set on edge.'

30 But every one shall die for his own iniquity; every man who eats the sour grapes, his
teeth shall be set on edge.

A New Covenant

31 "Behold, the days are coming, says the
LORD, when I will make a new covenant with
the house of Israel and with the house of Judah— 32 not according to the covenant that
I made with their fathers in the day *that* I
took them by the hand to lead them out of
the land of Egypt, My covenant which they

RELATIONSHIPS

READ IT: JEREMIAH 31:31–34

God loved His people. Even when they broke their promises to always love and serve Him, He still loved them. Because He cared about Israel, He punished them for their disobedience by sending them away to a foreign land. But God didn't forget about His people or leave them far away from home forever. He brought them back home and made a new covenant with them. Their relationship would be better than ever before. It would be such a close relationship that God would be "in their minds" and "on their hearts" (v. 33). That is the same close relationship you have with God when you have Jesus living in your heart.

broke, though I was a husband to them,[a]
says the LORD. 33But this *is* the covenant that
I will make with the house of Israel after
those days, says the LORD: I will put My law
in their minds, and write it on their hearts;
and I will be their God, and they shall be My
people. 34No more shall every man teach his
neighbor, and every man his brother, saying, 'Know the LORD,' for they all shall know
Me, from the least of them to the greatest of
them, says the LORD. For I will forgive their
iniquity, and their sin I will remember no
more."

35 Thus says the LORD,
Who gives the sun for a light by day,
The ordinances of the moon and the
stars for a light by night,
Who disturbs the sea,
And its waves roar
(The LORD of hosts *is* His name):

36 "If those ordinances depart
From before Me, says the LORD,
Then the seed of Israel shall also cease
From being a nation before Me forever."

37Thus says the LORD:

"If heaven above can be measured,
And the foundations of the earth
searched out beneath,
I will also cast off all the seed of Israel
For all that they have done, says the
LORD.

38"Behold, the days are coming, says
the LORD, that the city shall be built for the
LORD from the Tower of Hananel to the Corner Gate. 39The surveyor's line shall again
extend straight forward over the hill Gareb;
then it shall turn toward Goath. 40And the
whole valley of the dead bodies and of the
ashes, and all the fields as far as the Brook
Kidron, to the corner of the Horse Gate toward the east, *shall be* holy to the LORD. It
shall not be plucked up or thrown down anymore forever."

Jeremiah Buys a Field

32 The word that came to Jeremiah
from the LORD in the tenth year of
Zedekiah king of Judah, which was the eighteenth year of Nebuchadnezzar. 2For then
the king of Babylon's army besieged Jerusalem, and Jeremiah the prophet was shut up
in the court of the prison, which *was in* the
king of Judah's house. 3For Zedekiah king
of Judah had shut him up, saying, "Why do
you prophesy and say, 'Thus says the LORD:
"Behold, I will give this city into the hand of
the king of Babylon, and he shall take it; 4and
Zedekiah king of Judah shall not escape
from the hand of the Chaldeans, but shall
surely be delivered into the hand of the king
of Babylon, and shall speak with him face to
face,[a] and see him eye to eye; 5then he shall
lead Zedekiah to Babylon, and there he shall
be until I visit him," says the LORD; "though
you fight with the Chaldeans, you shall not
succeed"'?"

6And Jeremiah said, "The word of the
LORD came to me, saying, 7'Behold, Hanamel the son of Shallum your uncle will
come to you, saying, "Buy my field which *is*
in Anathoth, for the right of redemption *is*
yours to buy *it*."' 8Then Hanamel my uncle's
son came to me in the court of the prison
according to the word of the LORD, and said
to me, 'Please buy my field that *is* in Anathoth, which *is* in the country of Benjamin;
for the right of inheritance *is* yours, and the
redemption yours; buy *it* for yourself.' Then I
knew that this was the word of the LORD. 9So
I bought the field from Hanamel, the son of
my uncle who *was* in Anathoth, and weighed
out to him the money—seventeen shekels of
silver. 10And I signed the deed and sealed
it, took witnesses, and weighed the money
on the scales. 11So I took the purchase deed,
both that which was sealed *according* to the
law and custom, and that which was open;
12and I gave the purchase deed to Baruch
the son of Neriah, son of Mahseiah, in the
presence of Hanamel my uncle's *son*, and in
the presence of the witnesses who signed the
purchase deed, before all the Jews who sat in
the court of the prison.

13"Then I charged Baruch before them,
saying, 14'Thus says the LORD of hosts, the
God of Israel: "Take these deeds, both this
purchase deed which is sealed and this deed
which is open, and put them in an earthen
vessel, that they may last many days." 15For
thus says the LORD of hosts, the God of Israel: "Houses and fields and vineyards shall
be possessed again in this land."'

Jeremiah Prays for Understanding

16"Now when I had delivered the purchase

31:32 [a] Following Masoretic Text, Targum, and Vulgate; Septuagint and Syriac read *and I turned away from them.*
32:4 [a] Literally *mouth to mouth*

deed to Baruch the son of Neriah, I prayed
to the LORD, saying: 17'Ah, Lord GOD! Behold,
You have made the heavens and the earth
by Your great power and outstretched arm.
There is nothing too hard for You. 18 *You* show
lovingkindness to thousands, and repay the
iniquity of the fathers into the bosom of their
children after them—the Great, the Mighty
God, whose name *is* the LORD of hosts. 19 *You
are* great in counsel and mighty in work,
for Your eyes *are* open to all the ways of the
sons of men, to give everyone according to
his ways and according to the fruit of his
doings. 20 You have set signs and wonders in
the land of Egypt, to this day, and in Israel
and among *other* men; and You have made
Yourself a name, as it is this day. 21 You have
brought Your people Israel out of the land
of Egypt with signs and wonders, with a
strong hand and an outstretched arm, and
with great terror; 22 You have given them this
land, of which You swore to their fathers to
give them—"a land flowing with milk and
honey."[a] 23 And they came in and took possession of it, but they have not obeyed Your
voice or walked in Your law. They have done

32:22 [a] Exodus 3:8

GOD'S PROPHET'S PROMISE OF RETURN

READ IT: JEREMIAH 32:26–44

GET IT:

God told Jeremiah exactly what was going to happen to Judah and Jerusalem years before it happened. The king of Judah, of course, didn't like this information and put Jeremiah in prison to keep him from sharing his news. Once again God repeated the story to Jeremiah. But this time He added something. This time God told him what would happen afterward—after the destruction, after the famine, after the killing, after the stay in a foreign country. The good news starts in verse 37. God's anger would end, and He would bring His people back to their land. They would live there safely. God would make a covenant with His people that would last forever. He would live in their hearts so they would never leave Him again. What a great promise! What a comfort when things were going downhill. It sounded too good to be true, but that's what really happened.

LIVE IT:

When you're having a bad day, you think it will never end. A bad week is even worse. *Facing hard times in your family or with your friends seems* almost impossible. Back in Jeremiah's day, the situation seemed impossible. Things were at their very worst for the people of God. But God still loved His people, so He made a promise to do what seemed impossible. He promised to bring the people back to their land where they would live happily ever after. God always gives you hope—your future will be better than anything you've ever experienced.

nothing of all that You commanded them to do; therefore You have caused all this calamity to come upon them.

24 'Look, the siege mounds! They have come to the city to take it; and the city has been given into the hand of the Chaldeans who fight against it, because of the sword and famine and pestilence. What You have spoken has happened; there You see *it!* 25 And You have said to me, O Lord GOD, "Buy the field for money, and take witnesses"!—yet the city has been given into the hand of the Chaldeans.'"

God's Assurance of the People's Return

26 Then the word of the LORD came to Jeremiah, saying, 27 "Behold, I *am* the LORD, the God of all flesh. Is there anything too hard for Me? 28 Therefore thus says the LORD: 'Behold, I will give this city into the hand of the Chaldeans, into the hand of Nebuchadnezzar king of Babylon, and he shall take it. 29 And the Chaldeans who fight against this city shall come and set fire to this city and burn it, with the houses on whose roofs they have offered incense to Baal and poured out drink offerings to other gods, to provoke Me to anger; 30 because the children of Israel and the children of Judah have done only evil before Me from their youth. For the children of Israel have provoked Me only to anger with the work of their hands,' says the LORD. 31 'For this city has been to Me *a provocation of* My anger and My fury from the day that they built it, even to this day; so I will remove it from before My face 32 because of all the evil of the children of Israel and the children of Judah, which they have done to provoke Me to anger—they, their kings, their princes, their priests, their prophets, the men of Judah, and the inhabitants of Jerusalem. 33 And they have turned to Me the back, and not the face; though I taught them, rising up early and teaching *them,* yet they have not listened to receive instruction. 34 But they set their abominations in the house which is called by My name, to defile it. 35 And they built the high places of Baal which *are* in the Valley of the Son of Hinnom, to cause their sons and their daughters to pass through *the fire* to Molech, which I did not command them, nor did it come into My mind that they should do this abomination, to cause Judah to sin.'

36 "Now therefore, thus says the LORD, the God of Israel, concerning this city of which you say, 'It shall be delivered into the hand of the king of Babylon by the sword, by the famine, and by the pestilence: 37 Behold, I will gather them out of all countries where I have driven them in My anger, in My fury, and in great wrath; I will bring them back to this place, and I will cause them to dwell safely. 38 They shall be My people, and I will be their God; 39 then I will give them one heart and one way, that they may fear Me forever, for the good of them and their children after them. 40 And I will make an everlasting covenant with them, that I will not turn away from doing them good; but I will put My fear in their hearts so that they will not depart from Me. 41 Yes, I will rejoice over them to do them good, and I will assuredly

HOPE

READ IT: JEREMIAH 32:27

The God of the entire universe, of every fiber and fragment, has got your back. Is there anything in this world that He can't handle? No. So have hope. Always have hope, even when your situation looks hopeless. Hope doesn't disappoint, and you'll receive an overflow of joy and peace when hope endures.

plant them in this land, with all My heart
and with all My soul.'
42"For thus says the LORD: 'Just as I have
brought all this great calamity on this people, so I will bring on them all the good that
I have promised them. 43And fields will be
bought in this land of which you say, *"It is*
desolate, without man or beast; it has been
given into the hand of the Chaldeans." 44Men
will buy fields for money, sign deeds and
seal *them,* and take witnesses, in the land
of Benjamin, in the places around Jerusalem, in the cities of Judah, in the cities of
the mountains, in the cities of the lowland,
and in the cities of the South; for I will cause
their captives to return,' says the LORD."

Excellence of the Restored Nation

33 Moreover the word of the LORD
came to Jeremiah a second time,
while he was still shut up in the court of the
prison, saying, 2"Thus says the LORD who
made it, the LORD who formed it to establish
it (the LORD *is* His name): 3'Call to Me, and
I will answer you, and show you great and
mighty things, which you do not know.'
4"For thus says the LORD, the God of Israel, concerning the houses of this city and
the houses of the kings of Judah, which
have been pulled down *to fortify*[a] against
the siege mounds and the sword: 5'They
come to fight with the Chaldeans, but *only*
to fill their places[a] with the dead bodies of
men whom I will slay in My anger and My
fury, all for whose wickedness I have hidden
My face from this city. 6Behold, I will bring
it health and healing; I will heal them and
reveal to them the abundance of peace and
truth. 7And I will cause the captives of Judah and the captives of Israel to return, and
will rebuild those places as at the first. 8I
will cleanse them from all their iniquity by
which they have sinned against Me, and I
will pardon all their iniquities by which they
have sinned and by which they have transgressed against Me. 9Then it shall be to Me
a name of joy, a praise, and an honor before
all nations of the earth, who shall hear all
the good that I do to them; they shall fear
and tremble for all the goodness and all the
prosperity that I provide for it.'
10"Thus says the LORD: 'Again there shall
be heard in this place—of which you say,
"It *is* desolate, without man and without
beast"—in the cities of Judah, in the streets
of Jerusalem that are desolate, without man
and without inhabitant and without beast,
11the voice of joy and the voice of gladness,
the voice of the bridegroom and the voice of
the bride, the voice of those who will say:

33:4 [a] Compare Isaiah 22:10 33:5 [a] Compare 2 Kings 23:14

DOUBT AND ASKING QUESTIONS

READ IT: JEREMIAH 33:3

A prophet was someone God appointed to be His messenger. But being a prophet wasn't an easy job, partly because Old Testament prophets shared messages that God's people didn't want to hear. At times, God told one of His prophets to do something that seemed unreasonable—like asking Jeremiah to buy property that was owned by his enemy. It takes real trust to do what God asks, especially when it doesn't seem to make sense. But God honored Jeremiah's obedience and ultimately restored Jerusalem. When you call out to God, He will show you great and mighty things, too.

“Praise the LORD of hosts,
For the LORD *is* good,
For His mercy *endures* forever”—

and of those *who will* bring the sacrifice of praise into the house of the LORD. For I will cause the captives of the land to return as at the first,’ says the LORD.

12“Thus says the LORD of hosts: ‘In this place which is desolate, without man and without beast, and in all its cities, there shall again be a dwelling place of shepherds causing *their* flocks to lie down. 13In the cities of the mountains, in the cities of the lowland, in the cities of the South, in the land of Benjamin, in the places around Jerusalem, and in the cities of Judah, the flocks shall again pass under the hands of him who counts *them*,’ says the LORD.

14‘Behold, the days are coming,’ says the LORD, ‘that I will perform that good thing which I have promised to the house of Israel and to the house of Judah:

15 ‘In those days and at that time
I will cause to grow up to David
A Branch of righteousness;
He shall execute judgment and
righteousness in the earth.
16 In those days Judah will be saved,
And Jerusalem will dwell safely.
And this *is the name* by which she will
be called:

THE LORD OUR RIGHTEOUSNESS.’[a]

17“For thus says the LORD: ‘David shall never lack a man to sit on the throne of the house of Israel; 18nor shall the priests, the Levites, lack a man to offer burnt offerings before Me, to kindle grain offerings, and to sacrifice continually.’ ”

The Permanence of God’s Covenant

19And the word of the LORD came to Jeremiah, saying, 20“Thus says the LORD: ‘If you can break My covenant with the day and My covenant with the night, so that there will not be day and night in their season, 21then My covenant may also be broken with David My servant, so that he shall not have a son to reign on his throne, and with the Levites, the priests, My ministers. 22As the host of heaven cannot be numbered, nor the sand of the sea measured, so will I multiply the descendants of David My servant and the Levites who minister to Me.’ ”

23Moreover the word of the LORD came to Jeremiah, saying, 24“Have you not considered what these people have spoken, saying, ‘The two families which the LORD has chosen, He has also cast them off’? Thus they have despised My people, as if they should no more be a nation before them.

25“Thus says the LORD: ‘If My covenant *is* not with day and night, *and if* I have not appointed the ordinances of heaven and earth, 26then I will cast away the descendants of Jacob and David My servant, *so* that I will not take *any* of his descendants *to be* rulers over the descendants of Abraham, Isaac, and Jacob. For I will cause their captives to return, and will have mercy on them.’ ”

Zedekiah Warned by God

34 The word which came to Jeremiah from the LORD, when Nebuchadnezzar king of Babylon and all his army, all the kingdoms of the earth under his dominion, and all the people, fought against Jerusalem and all its cities, saying, 2“Thus says the LORD, the God of Israel: ‘Go and speak to Zedekiah king of Judah and tell him, “Thus says the LORD: ‘Behold, I will give this city into the hand of the king of Babylon, and he shall burn it with fire. 3And you shall not escape from his hand, but shall surely be taken and delivered into his hand; your eyes shall see the eyes of the king of Babylon, he shall speak with you face to face,[a] and you shall go to Babylon.’ ” ’ 4Yet hear the word of the LORD, O Zedekiah king of Judah! Thus says the LORD concerning you: ‘You shall not die by the sword. 5You shall die in peace; as in the ceremonies of your fathers, the former kings who were before you, so they shall burn *incense* for you and lament for you, *saying*, “Alas, lord!” For I have pronounced the word, says the LORD.’ ”

6Then Jeremiah the prophet spoke all these words to Zedekiah king of Judah in Jerusalem, 7when the king of Babylon’s army fought against Jerusalem and all the cities of Judah that were left, against Lachish and Azekah; for *only* these fortified cities remained of the cities of Judah.

Treacherous Treatment of Slaves

8*This is* the word that came to Jeremiah from the LORD, after King Zedekiah had made a covenant with all the people who *were*

33:16 [a] Compare 23:5, 6 34:3 [a] Literally *mouth to mouth*

at Jerusalem to proclaim liberty to them: 9that
every man should set free his male and female
slave—a Hebrew man or woman—that no
one should keep a Jewish brother in bondage.
10Now when all the princes and all the people,
who had entered into the covenant, heard that
everyone should set free his male and female
slaves, that no one should keep them in
bondage anymore, they obeyed and let *them*
go. 11But afterward they changed their minds
and made the male and female slaves return,
whom they had set free, and brought them
into subjection as male and female slaves.

12Therefore the word of the LORD came
to Jeremiah from the LORD, saying, 13"Thus
says the LORD, the God of Israel: 'I made a
covenant with your fathers in the day that I
brought them out of the land of Egypt, out of
the house of bondage, saying, 14"At the end
of seven years let every man set free his Hebrew brother, who has been sold to him; and
when he has served you six years, you shall
let him go free from you." But your fathers
did not obey Me nor incline their ear. 15Then
you recently turned and did what was right
in My sight—every man proclaiming liberty
to his neighbor; and you made a covenant
before Me in the house which is called by
My name. 16Then you turned around and
profaned My name, and every one of you
brought back his male and female slaves,
whom you had set at liberty, at their pleasure, and brought them back into subjection, to be your male and female slaves.'

17"Therefore thus says the LORD: 'You
have not obeyed Me in proclaiming liberty,
every one to his brother and every one to
his neighbor. Behold, I proclaim liberty to
you,' says the LORD—'to the sword, to pestilence, and to famine! And I will deliver you
to trouble among all the kingdoms of the
earth. 18And I will give the men who have
transgressed My covenant, who have not
performed the words of the covenant which
they made before Me, when they cut the calf
in two and passed between the parts of it—
19the princes of Judah, the princes of Jerusalem, the eunuchs, the priests, and all the
people of the land who passed between the
parts of the calf— 20I will give them into the
hand of their enemies and into the hand of
those who seek their life. Their dead bodies
shall be for meat for the birds of the heaven
and the beasts of the earth. 21And I will give
Zedekiah king of Judah and his princes into
the hand of their enemies, into the hand of
those who seek their life, and into the hand
of the king of Babylon's army which has
gone back from you. 22Behold, I will command,' says the LORD, 'and cause them to
return to this city. They will fight against it
and take it and burn it with fire; and I will
make the cities of Judah a desolation without
inhabitant.'"

The Obedient Rechabites

35 The word which came to Jeremiah
from the LORD in the days of Jehoiakim the son of Josiah, king of Judah,
saying, 2"Go to the house of the Rechabites,
speak to them, and bring them into the
house of the LORD, into one of the chambers,
and give them wine to drink."

3Then I took Jaazaniah the son of Jeremiah, the son of Habazziniah, his brothers
and all his sons, and the whole house of the
Rechabites, 4and I brought them into the
house of the LORD, into the chamber of the
sons of Hanan the son of Igdaliah, a man
of God, which *was* by the chamber of the
princes, above the chamber of Maaseiah
the son of Shallum, the keeper of the door.
5Then I set before the sons of the house of
the Rechabites bowls full of wine, and cups;
and I said to them, "Drink wine."

6But they said, "We will drink no wine,
for Jonadab the son of Rechab, our father,
commanded us, saying, 'You shall drink no
wine, you nor your sons, forever. 7You shall
not build a house, sow seed, plant a vineyard,
nor have *any of these;* but all your days you
shall dwell in tents, that you may live many
days in the land where you are sojourners.'
8Thus we have obeyed the voice of Jonadab
the son of Rechab, our father, in all that he
charged us, to drink no wine all our days,
we, our wives, our sons, or our daughters,
9nor to build ourselves houses to dwell in;
nor do we have vineyard, field, or seed. 10But
we have dwelt in tents, and have obeyed and
done according to all that Jonadab our father
commanded us. 11But it came to pass, when
Nebuchadnezzar king of Babylon came up
into the land, that we said, 'Come, let us go
to Jerusalem for fear of the army of the Chaldeans and for fear of the army of the Syrians.' So we dwell at Jerusalem."

12Then came the word of the LORD to
Jeremiah, saying, 13"Thus says the LORD of

hosts, the God of Israel: 'Go and tell the men of Judah and the inhabitants of Jerusalem, "Will you not receive instruction to obey My words?" says the LORD. 14"The words of Jonadab the son of Rechab, which he commanded his sons, not to drink wine, are performed; for to this day they drink none, and obey their father's commandment. But although I have spoken to you, rising early and speaking, you did not obey Me. 15I have also sent to you all My servants the prophets, rising up early and sending *them,* saying, 'Turn now everyone from his evil way, amend your doings, and do not go after other gods to serve them; then you will dwell in the land which I have given you and your fathers.' But you have not inclined your ear, nor obeyed Me. 16Surely the sons of Jonadab the son of Rechab have performed the commandment of their father, which he commanded them, but this people has not obeyed Me."'

17"Therefore thus says the LORD God of hosts, the God of Israel: 'Behold, I will bring on Judah and on all the inhabitants of Jerusalem all the doom that I have pronounced against them; because I have spoken to them but they have not heard, and I have called to them but they have not answered.'"

18And Jeremiah said to the house of the Rechabites, "Thus says the LORD of hosts, the God of Israel: 'Because you have obeyed the commandment of Jonadab your father, and kept all his precepts and done according to all that he commanded you, 19therefore thus says the LORD of hosts, the God of Israel: "Jonadab the son of Rechab shall not lack a man to stand before Me forever."'"

The Scroll Read in the Temple

36 Now it came to pass in the fourth year of Jehoiakim the son of Josiah, king of Judah, *that* this word came to Jeremiah from the LORD, saying: 2"Take a scroll of a book and write on it all the words that I have spoken to you against Israel, against Judah, and against all the nations, from the day I spoke to you, from the days of Josiah even to this day. 3It may be that the house of Judah will hear all the adversities which I purpose to bring upon them, that everyone may turn from his evil way, that I may forgive their iniquity and their sin."

4Then Jeremiah called Baruch the son of Neriah; and Baruch wrote on a scroll of a book, at the instruction of Jeremiah,[a] all the words of the LORD which He had spoken to him. 5And Jeremiah commanded Baruch, saying, "I *am* confined, I cannot go into the house of the LORD. 6You go, therefore, and read from the scroll which you have written at my instruction,[a] the words of the LORD, in the hearing of the people in the LORD's house on the day of fasting. And you shall also read them in the hearing of all Judah who come from their cities. 7It may be that they will present their supplication before the LORD, and everyone will turn from his evil way. For great *is* the anger and the fury that the LORD has pronounced against this people." 8And Baruch the son of Neriah did according to all that Jeremiah the prophet commanded him, reading from the book the words of the LORD in the LORD's house.

9Now it came to pass in the fifth year of Jehoiakim the son of Josiah, king of Judah, in the ninth month, *that* they proclaimed a fast before the LORD to all the people in Jerusalem, and to all the people who came from the cities of Judah to Jerusalem. 10Then Baruch read from the book the words of Jeremiah in the house of the LORD, in the chamber of Gemariah the son of Shaphan the scribe, in the upper court at the entry of the New Gate of the LORD's house, in the hearing of all the people.

The Scroll Read in the Palace

11When Michaiah the son of Gemariah, the son of Shaphan, heard all the words of the LORD from the book, 12he then went down to the king's house, into the scribe's chamber; and there all the princes were sitting—Elishama the scribe, Delaiah the son of Shemaiah, Elnathan the son of Achbor, Gemariah the son of Shaphan, Zedekiah the son of Hananiah, and all the princes. 13Then Michaiah declared to them all the words that he had heard when Baruch read the book in the hearing of the people. 14Therefore all the princes sent Jehudi the son of Nethaniah, the son of Shelemiah, the son of Cushi, to Baruch, saying, "Take in your hand the scroll from which you have read in the hearing of the people, and come." So Baruch the son of Neriah took the scroll in his hand and came to them. 15And they

---

36:4 [a] Literally *from Jeremiah's mouth* 36:6 [a] Literally *from my mouth*

said to him, "Sit down now, and read it in our
hearing." So Baruch read *it* in their hearing.
16Now it happened, when they had heard
all the words, that they looked in fear from
one to another, and said to Baruch, "We will
surely tell the king of all these words." 17And
they asked Baruch, saying, "Tell us now,
how did you write all these words—at his
instruction?"[a]
18So Baruch answered them, "He proclaimed with his mouth all these words to
me, and I wrote *them* with ink in the book."
19Then the princes said to Baruch, "Go
and hide, you and Jeremiah; and let no one
know where you are."

The King Destroys Jeremiah's Scroll

20And they went to the king, into the
court; but they stored the scroll in the chamber of Elishama the scribe, and told all the
words in the hearing of the king. 21So the
king sent Jehudi to bring the scroll, and he
took it from Elishama the scribe's chamber.
And Jehudi read it in the hearing of the

36:17 [a] Literally *with his mouth*

THE KING BURNS THE SCROLL

READ IT: JEREMIAH 36:1–32

GET IT:

While Ezekiel did God's work in Babylon, Jeremiah was doing His work in Jerusalem. Like Ezekiel, Jeremiah warned the people and the king about what was going to happen. Jeremiah wrote down everything God had told him on a long roll of paper ("a scroll of a book" [v. 4]). It took a year to write everything down. Then Jeremiah's assistant, Baruch, read the book in the temple so all the people could hear what God had to say. When the royal princes heard what was in the book, they knew they had to tell the king about it. They also knew that because it was bad news, the king would not be happy. So Jeremiah and Baruch went into hiding.

Sure enough, the king wasn't pleased with what he heard, so he cut the scroll into pieces and threw it in the fire (as if he could stop the events from happening!). Of course, his idea didn't work. God told Jeremiah to write another scroll. And he did.

LIVE IT:

Jeremiah wrote down all the words God had spoken to him, just as God told him to. Then King Jehoiakim tried to destroy God's words by *burning* Jeremiah's scroll. He thought that if he got rid of the evidence, it would be as if God had never said anything. He was wrong! Jeremiah didn't let the king's bad behavior stop him from obeying God's command. When God told Jeremiah to redo all his work, he and Baruch rewrote the entire scroll. Wow! That was dedication. That was obedience. Jeremiah didn't complain or give up when he faced opposition. The next time someone tries to stop you when you're doing what God wants you to do, remember Jeremiah's strength and stand firm.

king and in the hearing of all the princes
who stood beside the king. 22Now the king
was sitting in the winter house in the ninth
month, with *a fire* burning on the hearth
before him. 23And it happened, when Jehudi
had read three or four columns, *that the king*
cut it with the scribe's knife and cast *it* into
the fire that *was* on the hearth, until all the
scroll was consumed in the fire that *was* on
the hearth. 24Yet they were not afraid, nor did
they tear their garments, the king nor any
of his servants who heard all these words.
25Nevertheless Elnathan, Delaiah, and
Gemariah implored the king not to burn the
scroll; but he would not listen to them. 26And
the king commanded Jerahmeel the king's[a]
son, Seraiah the son of Azriel, and Shelemiah the son of Abdeel, to seize Baruch the
scribe and Jeremiah the prophet, but the
LORD hid them.

Jeremiah Rewrites the Scroll

27Now after the king had burned the
scroll with the words which Baruch had
written at the instruction of Jeremiah,[a] the
word of the LORD came to Jeremiah, saying:
28"Take yet another scroll, and write on it
all the former words that were in the first
scroll which Jehoiakim the king of Judah
has burned. 29And you shall say to Jehoiakim
king of Judah, 'Thus says the LORD: "You
have burned this scroll, saying, 'Why have
you written in it that the king of Babylon will
certainly come and destroy this land, and
cause man and beast to cease from here?' "
30Therefore thus says the LORD concerning
Jehoiakim king of Judah: "He shall have no
one to sit on the throne of David, and his
dead body shall be cast out to the heat of the
day and the frost of the night. 31I will punish
him, his family, and his servants for their
iniquity; and I will bring on them, on the
inhabitants of Jerusalem, and on the men of
Judah all the doom that I have pronounced
against them; but they did not heed." ' "

32Then Jeremiah took another scroll and
gave it to Baruch the scribe, the son of Neriah, who wrote on it at the instruction of
Jeremiah[a] all the words of the book which
Jehoiakim king of Judah had burned in the
fire. And besides, there were added to them
many similar words.

Zedekiah's Vain Hope

37 Now King Zedekiah the son of Josiah reigned instead of Coniah the
son of Jehoiakim, whom Nebuchadnezzar
king of Babylon made king in the land of
Judah. 2But neither he nor his servants nor
the people of the land gave heed to the words
of the LORD which He spoke by the prophet
Jeremiah.

3And Zedekiah the king sent Jehucal
the son of Shelemiah, and Zephaniah the
son of Maaseiah, the priest, to the prophet
Jeremiah, saying, "Pray now to the LORD
our God for us." 4Now Jeremiah was coming
and going among the people, for they had
not *yet* put him in prison. 5Then Pharaoh's
army came up from Egypt; and when the
Chaldeans who were besieging Jerusalem
heard news of them, they departed from
Jerusalem.

6Then the word of the LORD came to the
prophet Jeremiah, saying, 7"Thus says the
LORD, the God of Israel, 'Thus you shall say
to the king of Judah, who sent you to Me
to inquire of Me: "Behold, Pharaoh's army
which has come up to help you will return
to Egypt, to their own land. 8And the Chaldeans shall come back and fight against this
city, and take it and burn it with fire." ' 9Thus
says the LORD: 'Do not deceive yourselves,
saying, "The Chaldeans will surely depart
from us," for they will not depart. 10For
though you had defeated the whole army of
the Chaldeans who fight against you, and
there remained *only* wounded men among
them, they would rise up, every man in his
tent, and burn the city with fire.' "

Jeremiah Imprisoned

11And it happened, when the army of the
Chaldeans left *the siege* of Jerusalem for fear
of Pharaoh's army, 12that Jeremiah went out
of Jerusalem to go into the land of Benjamin
to claim his property there among the people. 13And when he was in the Gate of Benjamin, a captain of the guard *was* there whose
name *was* Irijah the son of Shelemiah, the
son of Hananiah; and he seized Jeremiah
the prophet, saying, "You are defecting to
the Chaldeans!"

14Then Jeremiah said, "False! I am not
defecting to the Chaldeans." But he did not
listen to him.

So Irijah seized Jeremiah and brought
him to the princes. 15Therefore the princes
were angry with Jeremiah, and they struck

36:26 [a] Hebrew *Hammelech* 36:27 [a] Literally *from Jeremiah's mouth* 36:32 [a] Literally *from Jeremiah's mouth*

him and put him in prison in the house of
Jonathan the scribe. For they had made that
the prison.

16When Jeremiah entered the dungeon
and the cells, and Jeremiah had remained
there many days, 17then Zedekiah the king
sent and took him *out*. The king asked him
secretly in his house, and said, "Is there *any*
word from the LORD?"

And Jeremiah said, "There is." Then he
said, "You shall be delivered into the hand of
the king of Babylon!"

18Moreover Jeremiah said to King Zedekiah, "What offense have I committed
against you, against your servants, or against
this people, that you have put me in prison?
19Where now *are* your prophets who prophesied to you, saying, 'The king of Babylon will
not come against you or against this land'?
20Therefore please hear now, O my lord the
king. Please, let my petition be accepted
before you, and do not make me return to
the house of Jonathan the scribe, lest I die
there."

21Then Zedekiah the king commanded
that they should commit Jeremiah to the
court of the prison, and that they should
give him daily a piece of bread from the bakers' street, until all the bread in the city was
gone. Thus Jeremiah remained in the court
of the prison.

Jeremiah in the Dungeon

38 Now Shephatiah the son of Mattan, Gedaliah the son of Pashhur,
Jucal[a] the son of Shelemiah, and Pashhur
the son of Malchiah heard the words that
Jeremiah had spoken to all the people, saying, 2"Thus says the LORD: 'He who remains
in this city shall die by the sword, by famine,
and by pestilence; but he who goes over to
the Chaldeans shall live; his life shall be as a
prize to him, and he shall live.'[a] 3Thus says
the LORD: 'This city shall surely be given
into the hand of the king of Babylon's army,
which shall take it.'"

4Therefore the princes said to the king,
"Please, let this man be put to death, for thus
he weakens the hands of the men of war who
remain in this city, and the hands of all the
people, by speaking such words to them. For
this man does not seek the welfare of this
people, but their harm."

5Then Zedekiah the king said, "Look, he
is in your hand. For the king can *do* nothing
against you." 6So they took Jeremiah and
cast him into the dungeon of Malchiah the
king's[a] son, which *was* in the court of the
prison, and they let Jeremiah down with
ropes. And in the dungeon *there was* no water, but mire. So Jeremiah sank in the mire.

7Now Ebed-Melech the Ethiopian, one of
the eunuchs, who was in the king's house,
heard that they had put Jeremiah in the dungeon. When the king was sitting at the Gate
of Benjamin, 8Ebed-Melech went out of the
king's house and spoke to the king, saying:
9"My lord the king, these men have done
evil in all that they have done to Jeremiah
the prophet, whom they have cast into the
dungeon, and he is likely to die from hunger in the place where he is. For *there is* no
more bread in the city." 10Then the king commanded Ebed-Melech the Ethiopian, saying,
"Take from here thirty men with you, and
lift Jeremiah the prophet out of the dungeon
before he dies." 11So Ebed-Melech took the
men with him and went into the house of
the king under the treasury, and took from
there old clothes and old rags, and let them
down by ropes into the dungeon to Jeremiah.
12Then Ebed-Melech the Ethiopian said to
Jeremiah, "Please put these old clothes and
rags under your armpits, under the ropes."
And Jeremiah did so. 13So they pulled Jeremiah up with ropes and lifted him out of the
dungeon. And Jeremiah remained in the
court of the prison.

Zedekiah's Fears and Jeremiah's Advice

14Then Zedekiah the king sent and had
Jeremiah the prophet brought to him at the
third entrance of the house of the LORD. And
the king said to Jeremiah, "I will ask you
something. Hide nothing from me."

15Jeremiah said to Zedekiah, "If I declare
it to you, will you not surely put me to death?
And if I give you advice, you will not listen
to me."

16So Zedekiah the king swore secretly to
Jeremiah, saying, "*As* the LORD lives, who
made our very souls, I will not put you to
death, nor will I give you into the hand of
these men who seek your life."

17Then Jeremiah said to Zedekiah, "Thus

38:1 [a] Same as *Jehucal* (compare 37:3) 38:2 [a] Compare 21:9
38:6 [a] Hebrew *Hammelech*

says the LORD, the God of hosts, the God of
Israel: 'If you surely surrender to the king of
Babylon's princes, then your soul shall live;
this city shall not be burned with fire, and
you and your house shall live. 18But if you do
not surrender to the king of Babylon's princes, then this city shall be given into the hand
of the Chaldeans; they shall burn it with fire,
and you shall not escape from their hand.'"

19And Zedekiah the king said to Jeremiah, "I am afraid of the Jews who have defected to the Chaldeans, lest they deliver me
into their hand, and they abuse me."

20But Jeremiah said, "They shall not deliver *you*. Please, obey the voice of the LORD
which I speak to you. So it shall be well with
you, and your soul shall live. 21But if you refuse to surrender, this *is* the word that the
LORD has shown me: 22'Now behold, all the
women who are left in the king of Judah's
house *shall be* surrendered to the king of
Babylon's princes, and those *women* shall say:

"Your close friends have set upon you
And prevailed against you;
Your feet have sunk in the mire,
And they have turned away again."

23'So they shall surrender all your wives
and children to the Chaldeans. You shall not
escape from their hand, but shall be taken
by the hand of the king of Babylon. And you
shall cause this city to be burned with fire.'"

24Then Zedekiah said to Jeremiah, "Let
no one know of these words, and you shall
not die. 25But if the princes hear that I have
talked with you, and they come to you and
say to you, 'Declare to us now what you have

JEREMIAH IS STUCK IN A DUNGEON

READ IT: JEREMIAH 38:1–28

GET IT:

Jeremiah continued to speak for God in Jerusalem. When the Babylonian army was outside the city, Jeremiah advised the people to do something strange. He told them to surrender to the enemy if they wanted to live. If they stayed in the city, they would die. His advice wasn't popular. In fact, the princes wanted to kill Jeremiah so they threw him in a dungeon full of mud. They expected Jeremiah to sink down so far that he would suffocate or starve to death. But God wasn't going to let that happen. Ebed-Melech came to Jeremiah's rescue and got him out of the dungeon. Jeremiah spoke to King Zedekiah again and told him what was going to happen to Jerusalem. This time Zedekiah listened, but he still didn't do what Jeremiah (and God) said.

LIVE IT:

Giving somebody bad news is hard. Telling someone to do something completely opposite from what seems logical or normal is really hard. If someone asked you to do something completely different from what you thought was logical or normal, what would you do? Would you listen to that person? What would it take to convince you?

said to the king, and also what the king said
to you; do not hide *it* from us, and we will
not put you to death,' 26then you shall say to
them, 'I presented my request before the
king, that he would not make me return to
Jonathan's house to die there.'"
27Then all the princes came to Jeremiah and asked him. And he told them
according to all these words that the king
had commanded. So they stopped speaking with him, for the conversation had not
been heard. 28Now Jeremiah remained in
the court of the prison until the day that Jerusalem was taken. And he was *there* when
Jerusalem was taken.

The Fall of Jerusalem

39 In the ninth year of Zedekiah
king of Judah, in the tenth month,
Nebuchadnezzar king of Babylon and all
his army came against Jerusalem, and besieged it. 2In the eleventh year of Zedekiah,
in the fourth month, on the ninth *day* of the
month, the city was penetrated.
3Then all the princes of the king of Babylon came in and sat in the Middle Gate:
Nergal-Sharezer, Samgar-Nebo, Sarsechim,
Rabsaris,[a] Nergal-Sarezer, Rabmag,[b] with
the rest of the princes of the king of Babylon.
4So it was, when Zedekiah the king of
Judah and all the men of war saw them, that
they fled and went out of the city by night, by
way of the king's garden, by the gate between
the two walls. And he went out by way of the
plain.[a] 5But the Chaldean army pursued
them and overtook Zedekiah in the plains
of Jericho. And when they had captured
him, they brought him up to Nebuchadnezzar king of Babylon, to Riblah in the land of
Hamath, where he pronounced judgment on
him. 6Then the king of Babylon killed the
sons of Zedekiah before his eyes in Riblah;
the king of Babylon also killed all the nobles
of Judah. 7Moreover he put out Zedekiah's
eyes, and bound him with bronze fetters
to carry him off to Babylon. 8And the Chaldeans burned the king's house and the houses of the people with fire, and broke down
the walls of Jerusalem. 9Then Nebuzaradan
the captain of the guard carried away captive
to Babylon the remnant of the people who
remained in the city and those who defected to him, with the rest of the people who
remained. 10But Nebuzaradan the captain of
the guard left in the land of Judah the poor
people, who had nothing, and gave them
vineyards and fields at the same time.

Jeremiah Goes Free

11Now Nebuchadnezzar king of Babylon
gave charge concerning Jeremiah to Nebuzaradan the captain of the guard, saying,
12"Take him and look after him, and do him
no harm; but do to him just as he says to
you." 13So Nebuzaradan the captain of the
guard sent Nebushasban, Rabsaris, Nergal-
Sharezer, Rabmag, and all the king of Babylon's chief officers; 14then they sent *someone*
to take Jeremiah from the court of the prison, and committed him to Gedaliah the
son of Ahikam, the son of Shaphan, that he
should take him home. So he dwelt among
the people.
15Meanwhile the word of the LORD had
come to Jeremiah while he was shut up in
the court of the prison, saying, 16"Go and
speak to Ebed-Melech the Ethiopian, saying,
'Thus says the LORD of hosts, the God of Israel: "Behold, I will bring My words upon
this city for adversity and not for good, and
they shall be *performed* in that day before
you. 17But I will deliver you in that day," says
the LORD, "and you shall not be given into
the hand of the men of whom you *are* afraid.
18For I will surely deliver you, and you shall
not fall by the sword; but your life shall be
as a prize to you, because you have put your
trust in Me," says the LORD.'"

Jeremiah with Gedaliah the Governor

40 The word that came to Jeremiah
from the LORD after Nebuzaradan
the captain of the guard had let him go from
Ramah, when he had taken him bound in
chains among all who were carried away
captive from Jerusalem and Judah, who were
carried away captive to Babylon.
2And the captain of the guard took Jeremiah and said to him: "The LORD your God
has pronounced this doom on this place.
3Now the LORD has brought *it,* and has done
just as He said. Because you people have
sinned against the LORD, and not obeyed
His voice, therefore this thing has come
upon you. 4And now look, I free you this
day from the chains that *were* on your hand.

39:3 [a] A title, probably *Chief Officer;* also verse 13 [b] A title, probably *Troop Commander;* also verse 13 39:4 [a] Or *the Arabah,* that is, the Jordan Valley

If it seems good to you to come with me to
Babylon, come, and I will look after you. But
if it seems wrong for you to come with me
to Babylon, remain here. See, all the land *is*
before you; wherever it seems good and convenient for you to go, go there."

5 Now while Jeremiah had not yet gone
back, *Nebuzaradan said,* "Go back to Gedaliah the son of Ahikam, the son of Shaphan,
whom the king of Babylon has made governor over the cities of Judah, and dwell with
him among the people. Or go wherever
it seems convenient for you to go." So the
captain of the guard gave him rations and a
gift and let him go. 6 Then Jeremiah went to
Gedaliah the son of Ahikam, to Mizpah, and
dwelt with him among the people who were
left in the land.

7 And when all the captains of the armies
who *were* in the fields, they and their men,
heard that the king of Babylon had made
Gedaliah the son of Ahikam governor in
the land, and had committed to him men,
women, children, and the poorest of the
land who had not been carried away captive
to Babylon, 8 then they came to Gedaliah at
Mizpah—Ishmael the son of Nethaniah,
Johanan and Jonathan the sons of Kareah,
Seraiah the son of Tanhumeth, the sons of
Ephai the Netophathite, and Jezaniah[a] the
son of a Maachathite, they and their men.
9 And Gedaliah the son of Ahikam, the son
of Shaphan, took an oath before them and
their men, saying, "Do not be afraid to serve
the Chaldeans. Dwell in the land and serve
the king of Babylon, and it shall be well with
you. 10 As for me, I will indeed dwell at Mizpah and serve the Chaldeans who come to
us. But you, gather wine and summer fruit
and oil, put *them* in your vessels, and dwell
in your cities that you have taken." 11 Likewise, when all the Jews who *were* in Moab,
among the Ammonites, in Edom, and who
were in all the countries, heard that the king
of Babylon had left a remnant of Judah, and
that he had set over them Gedaliah the son
of Ahikam, the son of Shaphan, 12 then all the
Jews returned out of all places where they
had been driven, and came to the land of
Judah, to Gedaliah at Mizpah, and gathered
wine and summer fruit in abundance.

13 Moreover Johanan the son of Kareah
and all the captains of the forces that *were*
in the fields came to Gedaliah at Mizpah,
14 and said to him, "Do you certainly know
that Baalis the king of the Ammonites has
sent Ishmael the son of Nethaniah to murder you?" But Gedaliah the son of Ahikam
did not believe them.

15 Then Johanan the son of Kareah spoke
secretly to Gedaliah in Mizpah, saying, "Let
me go, please, and I will kill Ishmael the son
of Nethaniah, and no one will know *it.* Why
should he murder you, so that all the Jews
who are gathered to you would be scattered,
and the remnant in Judah perish?"

16 But Gedaliah the son of Ahikam said to
Johanan the son of Kareah, "You shall not do
this thing, for you speak falsely concerning
Ishmael."

Insurrection Against Gedaliah

41 Now it came to pass in the seventh month *that* Ishmael the son
of Nethaniah, the son of Elishama, of the
royal family and of the officers of the king,
came with ten men to Gedaliah the son
of Ahikam, at Mizpah. And there they ate
bread together in Mizpah. 2 Then Ishmael
the son of Nethaniah, and the ten men who
were with him, arose and struck Gedaliah
the son of Ahikam, the son of Shaphan,
with the sword, and killed him whom the
king of Babylon had made governor over the
land. 3 Ishmael also struck down all the Jews
who were with him, *that is,* with Gedaliah at
Mizpah, and the Chaldeans who were found
there, the men of war.

4 And it happened, on the second day after he had killed Gedaliah, when as yet no
one knew *it,* 5 that certain men came from
Shechem, from Shiloh, and from Samaria,
eighty men with their beards shaved and
their clothes torn, having cut themselves,
with offerings and incense in their hand, to
bring *them* to the house of the LORD. 6 Now
Ishmael the son of Nethaniah went out from
Mizpah to meet them, weeping as he went
along; and it happened as he met them that
he said to them, "Come to Gedaliah the son
of Ahikam!" 7 So it was, when they came into
the midst of the city, that Ishmael the son of
Nethaniah killed them *and cast them* into the
midst of a pit, he and the men who were with
him. 8 But ten men were found among them
who said to Ishmael, "Do not kill us, for

40:8 [a] Spelled *Jaazaniah* in 2 Kings 25:23

we have treasures of wheat, barley, oil, and
honey in the field." So he desisted and did
not kill them among their brethren. 9Now
the pit into which Ishmael had cast all the
dead bodies of the men whom he had slain,
because of Gedaliah, *was* the same one Asa
the king had made for fear of Baasha king of
Israel. Ishmael the son of Nethaniah filled
it with *the* slain. 10Then Ishmael carried
away captive all the rest of the people who
were in Mizpah, the king's daughters and all
the people who remained in Mizpah, whom
Nebuzaradan the captain of the guard had
committed to Gedaliah the son of Ahikam.
And Ishmael the son of Nethaniah carried
them away captive and departed to go over
to the Ammonites.

11But when Johanan the son of Kareah
and all the captains of the forces that *were*
with him heard of all the evil that Ishmael
the son of Nethaniah had done, 12they took
all the men and went to fight with Ishmael
the son of Nethaniah; and they found him by
the great pool that *is* in Gibeon. 13So it was,
when all the people who *were* with Ishmael
saw Johanan the son of Kareah, and all the
captains of the forces who *were* with him,
that they were glad. 14Then all the people
whom Ishmael had carried away captive
from Mizpah turned around and came back,
and went to Johanan the son of Kareah. 15But
Ishmael the son of Nethaniah escaped from
Johanan with eight men and went to the
Ammonites.

16Then Johanan the son of Kareah, and
all the captains of the forces that were with
him, took from Mizpah all the rest of the
people whom he had recovered from Ishmael the son of Nethaniah after he had murdered Gedaliah the son of Ahikam—the
mighty men of war and the women and the
children and the eunuchs, whom he had
brought back from Gibeon. 17And they departed and dwelt in the habitation of Chimham, which is near Bethlehem, as they went
on their way to Egypt, 18because of the Chaldeans; for they were afraid of them, because
Ishmael the son of Nethaniah had murdered
Gedaliah the son of Ahikam, whom the king
of Babylon had made governor in the land.

The Flight to Egypt Forbidden

42 Now all the captains of the forces,
Johanan the son of Kareah, Jeza-
niah the son of Hoshaiah, and all the people,
from the least to the greatest, came near 2and
said to Jeremiah the prophet, "Please, let our
petition be acceptable to you, and pray for us
to the LORD your God, for all this remnant
(since we are left *but* a few of many, as you
can see), 3that the LORD your God may show
us the way in which we should walk and the
thing we should do."

4Then Jeremiah the prophet said to
them, "I have heard. Indeed, I will pray to
the LORD your God according to your words,
and it shall be, *that* whatever the LORD answers you, I will declare *it* to you. I will keep
nothing back from you."

5So they said to Jeremiah, "Let the LORD
be a true and faithful witness between us, if
we do not do according to everything which
the LORD your God sends us by you. 6Wheth-
er *it is* pleasing or displeasing, we will obey
the voice of the LORD our God to whom we
send you, that it may be well with us when
we obey the voice of the LORD our God."

7And it happened after ten days that the
word of the LORD came to Jeremiah. 8Then
he called Johanan the son of Kareah, all the
captains of the forces which *were* with him,
and all the people from the least even to the
greatest, 9and said to them, "Thus says the
LORD, the God of Israel, to whom you sent
me to present your petition before Him: 10'If
you will still remain in this land, then I will
build you and not pull *you* down, and I will
plant you and not pluck *you* up. For I relent
concerning the disaster that I have brought
upon you. 11Do not be afraid of the king of
Babylon, of whom you are afraid; do not
be afraid of him,' says the LORD, 'for I *am*
with you, to save you and deliver you from
his hand. 12And I will show you mercy, that
he may have mercy on you and cause you to
return to your own land.'

13"But if you say, 'We will not dwell in this
land,' disobeying the voice of the LORD your
God, 14saying, 'No, but we will go to the land
of Egypt where we shall see no war, nor hear
the sound of the trumpet, nor be hungry
for bread, and there we will dwell'— 15Then
hear now the word of the LORD, O remnant
of Judah! Thus says the LORD of hosts, the
God of Israel: 'If you wholly set your faces
to enter Egypt, and go to dwell there, 16then
it shall be *that* the sword which you feared
shall overtake you there in the land of Egypt;
the famine of which you were afraid shall
follow close after you there *in* Egypt; and

there you shall die. 17So shall it be with all
the men who set their faces to go to Egypt to
dwell there. They shall die by the sword, by
famine, and by pestilence. And none of them
shall remain or escape from the disaster that
I will bring upon them.'

18"For thus says the LORD of hosts, the
God of Israel: 'As My anger and My fury
have been poured out on the inhabitants of
Jerusalem, so will My fury be poured out on
you when you enter Egypt. And you shall be
an oath, an astonishment, a curse, and a reproach; and you shall see this place no more.'

19"The LORD has said concerning you,
O remnant of Judah, 'Do not go to Egypt!'
Know certainly that I have admonished you
this day. 20For you were hypocrites in your
hearts when you sent me to the LORD your
God, saying, 'Pray for us to the LORD our
God, and according to all that the LORD your
God says, so declare to us and we will do *it*.'
21And I have this day declared *it* to you, but
you have not obeyed the voice of the LORD
your God, or anything which He has sent
you by me. 22Now therefore, know certainly
that you shall die by the sword, by famine,
and by pestilence in the place where you desire to go to dwell."

Jeremiah Taken to Egypt

43 Now it happened, when Jeremiah
had stopped speaking to all the
people all the words of the LORD their God,
for which the LORD their God had sent him
to them, all these words, 2that Azariah the
son of Hoshaiah, Johanan the son of Kareah,
and all the proud men spoke, saying to Jeremiah, "You speak falsely! The LORD our God
has not sent you to say, 'Do not go to Egypt to
dwell there.' 3But Baruch the son of Neriah
has set you against us, to deliver us into the
hand of the Chaldeans, that they may put us
to death or carry us away captive to Babylon."
4So Johanan the son of Kareah, all the captains of the forces, and all the people would
not obey the voice of the LORD, to remain in
the land of Judah. 5But Johanan the son of
Kareah and all the captains of the forces took
all the remnant of Judah who had returned
to dwell in the land of Judah, from all nations where they had been driven— 6men,
women, children, the king's daughters,
and every person whom Nebuzaradan the
captain of the guard had left with Gedaliah
the son of Ahikam, the son of Shaphan, and
Jeremiah the prophet and Baruch the son of
Neriah. 7So they went to the land of Egypt,
for they did not obey the voice of the LORD.
And they went as far as Tahpanhes.

8Then the word of the LORD came to
Jeremiah in Tahpanhes, saying, 9"Take large
stones in your hand, and hide them in the
sight of the men of Judah, in the clay in the
brick courtyard which *is* at the entrance
to Pharaoh's house in Tahpanhes; 10and
say to them, 'Thus says the LORD of hosts,
the God of Israel: "Behold, I will send and
bring Nebuchadnezzar the king of Babylon,
My servant, and will set his throne above
these stones that I have hidden. And he will
spread his royal pavilion over them. 11When
he comes, he shall strike the land of Egypt
and deliver to death *those appointed* for death,
and to captivity *those appointed* for captivity, and to the sword *those appointed* for the
sword. 12I[a] will kindle a fire in the houses of
the gods of Egypt, and he shall burn them
and carry them away captive. And he shall
array himself with the land of Egypt, as a
shepherd puts on his garment, and he shall
go out from there in peace. 13He shall also
break the *sacred* pillars of Beth Shemesh[a]
that *are* in the land of Egypt; and the houses
of the gods of the Egyptians he shall burn
with fire."'"

Israelites Will Be Punished in Egypt

44 The word that came to Jeremiah
concerning all the Jews who dwell
in the land of Egypt, who dwell at Migdol,
at Tahpanhes, at Noph,[a] and in the country
of Pathros, saying, 2"Thus says the LORD of
hosts, the God of Israel: 'You have seen all
the calamity that I have brought on Jerusalem and on all the cities of Judah; and behold, this day they *are* a desolation, and no
one dwells in them, 3because of their wickedness which they have committed to provoke Me to anger, in that they went to burn
incense *and* to serve other gods whom they
did not know, they nor you nor your fathers.
4However I have sent to you all My servants
the prophets, rising early and sending *them*,
saying, "Oh, do not do this abominable thing
that I hate!" 5But they did not listen or incline
their ear to turn from their wickedness, to

43:12 [a] Following Masoretic Text and Targum; Septuagint, Syriac, and Vulgate read *He.* 43:13 [a] Literally *House of the Sun*, ancient On; later called Heliopolis 44:1 [a] That is, ancient Memphis

burn no incense to other gods. 6So My fury
and My anger were poured out and kindled
in the cities of Judah and in the streets of
Jerusalem; and they are wasted *and* desolate,
as it is this day.'
7"Now therefore, thus says the LORD, the
God of hosts, the God of Israel: 'Why do you
commit *this* great evil against yourselves, to
cut off from you man and woman, child and
infant, out of Judah, leaving none to remain,
8in that you provoke Me to wrath with the
works of your hands, burning incense to other gods in the land of Egypt where you have
gone to dwell, that you may cut yourselves
off and be a curse and a reproach among all
the nations of the earth? 9Have you forgotten
the wickedness of your fathers, the wickedness of the kings of Judah, the wickedness
of their wives, your own wickedness, and
the wickedness of your wives, which they
committed in the land of Judah and in the
streets of Jerusalem? 10They have not been
humbled, to this day, nor have they feared;
they have not walked in My law or in My statutes that I set before you and your fathers.'
11"Therefore thus says the LORD of hosts,
the God of Israel: 'Behold, I will set My face
against you for catastrophe and for cutting
off all Judah. 12And I will take the remnant
of Judah who have set their faces to go into
the land of Egypt to dwell there, and they
shall all be consumed *and* fall in the land of
Egypt. They shall be consumed by the sword
and by famine. They shall die, from the least
to the greatest, by the sword and by famine;
and they shall be an oath, an astonishment,
a curse and a reproach! 13For I will punish
those who dwell in the land of Egypt, as I
have punished Jerusalem, by the sword, by
famine, and by pestilence, 14so that none of
the remnant of Judah who have gone into the
land of Egypt to dwell there shall escape or
survive, lest they return to the land of Judah,
to which they desire to return and dwell. For
none shall return except those who escape.'"
15Then all the men who knew that their
wives had burned incense *to other gods,*
with all the women who stood by, a great
multitude, and all the people who dwelt in
the land of Egypt, in Pathros, answered Jeremiah, saying: 16"*As for* the word that you have
spoken to us in the name of the LORD, we
will not listen to you! 17But we will certainly
do whatever has gone out of our own mouth,
to burn incense to the queen of heaven and
pour out drink offerings to her, as we have
done, we and our fathers, our kings and our
princes, in the cities of Judah and in the
streets of Jerusalem. For *then* we had plenty
of food, were well-off, and saw no trouble.
18But since we stopped burning incense to
the queen of heaven and pouring out drink
offerings to her, we have lacked everything
and have been consumed by the sword and
by famine."
19*The women also said,* "And when we
burned incense to the queen of heaven and
poured out drink offerings to her, did we
make cakes for her, to worship her, and pour
out drink offerings to her without our husbands' *permission?*"
20Then Jeremiah spoke to all the
people—the men, the women, and all the
people who had given him *that* answer—
saying: 21"The incense that you burned in
the cities of Judah and in the streets of Jerusalem, you and your fathers, your kings and
your princes, and the people of the land, did
not the LORD remember them, and did it *not*
come into His mind? 22So the LORD could no
longer bear *it,* because of the evil of your doings *and* because of the abominations which
you committed. Therefore your land is a desolation, an astonishment, a curse, and without an inhabitant, as *it is* this day. 23Because
you have burned incense and because you
have sinned against the LORD, and have not
obeyed the voice of the LORD or walked in
His law, in His statutes or in His testimonies, therefore this calamity has happened
to you, as *at* this day."
24Moreover Jeremiah said to all the people and to all the women, "Hear the word
of the LORD, all Judah who *are* in the land
of Egypt! 25Thus says the LORD of hosts, the
God of Israel, saying: 'You and your wives
have spoken with your mouths and fulfilled
with your hands, saying, "We will surely
keep our vows that we have made, to burn
incense to the queen of heaven and pour
out drink offerings to her." You will surely
keep your vows and perform your vows!'
26Therefore hear the word of the LORD, all
Judah who dwell in the land of Egypt: 'Behold, I have sworn by My great name,' says
the LORD, 'that My name shall no more be
named in the mouth of any man of Judah in
all the land of Egypt, saying, "The Lord GOD
lives." 27Behold, I will watch over them for
adversity and not for good. And all the men

of Judah who *are* in the land of Egypt shall be
consumed by the sword and by famine, until
there is an end to them. 28 Yet a small number who escape the sword shall return from
the land of Egypt to the land of Judah; and
all the remnant of Judah, who have gone to
the land of Egypt to dwell there, shall know
whose words will stand, Mine or theirs.
29 And this *shall be* a sign to you,' says the
LORD, 'that I will punish you in this place,
that you may know that My words will surely
stand against you for adversity.'

30 "Thus says the LORD: 'Behold, I will
give Pharaoh Hophra king of Egypt into
the hand of his enemies and into the hand
of those who seek his life, as I gave Zedekiah king of Judah into the hand of Nebuchadnezzar king of Babylon, his enemy who
sought his life.' "

Assurance to Baruch

45 The word that Jeremiah the prophet spoke to Baruch the son of Neriah, when he had written these words in a
book at the instruction of Jeremiah,[a] in the
fourth year of Jehoiakim the son of Josiah,
king of Judah, saying, 2 "Thus says the LORD,
the God of Israel, to you, O Baruch: 3 'You
said, "Woe is me now! For the LORD has added grief to my sorrow. I fainted in my sighing, and I find no rest." '

4 "Thus you shall say to him, 'Thus says
the LORD: "Behold, what I have built I will
break down, and what I have planted I will
pluck up, that is, this whole land. 5 And do
you seek great things for yourself? Do not
seek *them;* for behold, I will bring adversity
on all flesh," says the LORD. "But I will give
your life to you as a prize in all places, wherever you go." ' "

Judgment on Egypt

46 The word of the LORD which came
to Jeremiah the prophet against
the nations. 2 Against Egypt.

Concerning the army of Pharaoh Necho,
king of Egypt, which was by the River Euphrates in Carchemish, and which Nebuchadnezzar king of Babylon defeated in the
fourth year of Jehoiakim the son of Josiah,
king of Judah:

3 "Order the buckler and shield,
And draw near to battle!
4 Harness the horses,
And mount up, you horsemen!
Stand forth with *your* helmets,
Polish the spears,
Put on the armor!
5 Why have I seen them dismayed *and* turned back?
Their mighty ones are beaten down;
They have speedily fled,
And did not look back,
For fear *was* all around," says the LORD.
6 "Do not let the swift flee away,
Nor the mighty man escape;
They will stumble and fall
Toward the north, by the River Euphrates.

7 "Who *is* this coming up like a flood,
Whose waters move like the rivers?
8 Egypt rises up like a flood,
And *its* waters move like the rivers;
And he says, 'I will go up *and* cover the earth,
I will destroy the city and its inhabitants.'
9 Come up, O horses, and rage,
O chariots!
And let the mighty men come forth:
The Ethiopians and the Libyans who handle the shield,
And the Lydians who handle *and* bend the bow.
10 For this *is* the day of the Lord GOD of hosts,
A day of vengeance,
That He may avenge Himself on His adversaries.
The sword shall devour;
It shall be satiated and made drunk with their blood;
For the Lord GOD of hosts has a sacrifice
In the north country by the River Euphrates.

11 "Go up to Gilead and take balm,
O virgin, the daughter of Egypt;
In vain you will use many medicines;
You shall not be cured.
12 The nations have heard of your shame,
And your cry has filled the land;
For the mighty man has stumbled against the mighty;
They both have fallen together."

45:1 [a] Literally *from Jeremiah's mouth*

Babylonia Will Strike Egypt

13The word that the LORD spoke to Jeremiah the prophet, how Nebuchadnezzar
king of Babylon would come *and* strike the
land of Egypt.

14 "Declare in Egypt, and proclaim in Migdol;
Proclaim in Noph[a] and in Tahpanhes;
Say, 'Stand fast and prepare yourselves,
For the sword devours all around you.'
15 Why are your valiant *men* swept away?
They did not stand
Because the LORD drove them away.
16 He made many fall;
Yes, one fell upon another.
And they said, 'Arise!
Let us go back to our own people
And to the land of our nativity
From the oppressing sword.'
17 They cried there,
'Pharaoh, king of Egypt, *is but* a noise.
He has passed by the appointed time!'

18 "As I live," says the King,
Whose name *is* the LORD of hosts,
"Surely as Tabor *is* among the mountains
And as Carmel by the sea, *so* he shall
come.
19 O you daughter dwelling in Egypt,
Prepare yourself to go into captivity!
For Noph[a] shall be waste and desolate,
without inhabitant.

20 "Egypt *is* a very pretty heifer,
But destruction comes, it comes from
the north.
21 Also her mercenaries are in her midst
like fat bulls,
For they also are turned back,
They have fled away together.
They did not stand,
For the day of their calamity had come
upon them,
The time of their punishment.
22 Her noise shall go like a serpent,
For they shall march with an army
And come against her with axes,
Like those who chop wood.

23 "They shall cut down her forest," says the
LORD,
"Though it cannot be searched,
Because they *are* innumerable,
And more numerous than grasshoppers.
24 The daughter of Egypt shall be ashamed;
She shall be delivered into the hand
Of the people of the north."

25The LORD of hosts, the God of Israel,
says: "Behold, I will bring punishment on
Amon[a] of No,[b] and Pharaoh and Egypt, with
their gods and their kings—Pharaoh and
those who trust in him. 26And I will deliver
them into the hand of those who seek their
lives, into the hand of Nebuchadnezzar king
of Babylon and the hand of his servants. Afterward it shall be inhabited as in the days of
old," says the LORD.

God Will Preserve Israel

27 "But do not fear, O My servant Jacob,
And do not be dismayed, O Israel!
For behold, I will save you from afar,
And your offspring from the land of
their captivity;
Jacob shall return, have rest and be at
ease;
No one shall make *him* afraid.
28 Do not fear, O Jacob My servant," says
the LORD,
"For I *am* with you;
For I will make a complete end of all the
nations
To which I have driven you,
But I will not make a complete end of
you.
I will rightly correct you,
For I will not leave you wholly
unpunished."

Judgment on Philistia

47 The word of the LORD that came to
Jeremiah the prophet against the
Philistines, before Pharaoh attacked Gaza.
2Thus says the LORD:

"Behold, waters rise out of the north,
And shall be an overflowing flood;
They shall overflow the land and all that
is in it,
The city and those who dwell within;
Then the men shall cry,
And all the inhabitants of the land shall
wail.
3 At the noise of the stamping hooves of
his strong horses,
At the rushing of his chariots,
At the rumbling of his wheels,
The fathers will not look back for *their*
children,

46:14 [a] That is, ancient Memphis **46:19** [a] That is, ancient
Memphis **46:25** [a] A sun god [b] That is, ancient Thebes

Lacking courage,
4 Because of the day that comes to
plunder all the Philistines,
To cut off from Tyre and Sidon every
helper who remains;
For the LORD shall plunder the
Philistines,
The remnant of the country of Caphtor.
5 Baldness has come upon Gaza,
Ashkelon is cut off
With the remnant of their valley.
How long will you cut yourself?

6 "O you sword of the LORD,
How long until you are quiet?
Put yourself up into your scabbard,
Rest and be still!
7 How can it be quiet,
Seeing the LORD has given it a charge
Against Ashkelon and against the
seashore?
There He has appointed it."

Judgment on Moab

48 Against Moab.
Thus says the LORD of hosts, the
God of Israel:

"Woe to Nebo!
For it is plundered,
Kirjathaim is shamed *and* taken;
The high stronghold[a] is shamed and
dismayed—
2 No more praise of Moab.
In Heshbon they have devised evil
against her:
'Come, and let us cut her off as a nation.'
You also shall be cut down, O Madmen![a]
The sword shall pursue you;
3 A voice of crying *shall be* from
Horonaim:
'Plundering and great destruction!'

4 "Moab is destroyed;
Her little ones have caused a cry to be
heard;[a]
5 For in the Ascent of Luhith they ascend
with continual weeping;
For in the descent of Horonaim
the enemies have heard a cry of
destruction.

6 "Flee, save your lives!
And be like the juniper[a] in the
wilderness.
7 For because you have trusted in your
works and your treasures,
You also shall be taken.
And Chemosh shall go forth into
captivity,
His priests and his princes together.

8 And the plunderer shall come against
every city;
No one shall escape.
The valley also shall perish,
And the plain shall be destroyed,
As the LORD has spoken.

9 "Give wings to Moab,
That she may flee and get away;
For her cities shall be desolate,
Without any to dwell in them.
10 Cursed *is* he who does the work of the
LORD deceitfully,
And cursed *is* he who keeps back his
sword from blood.

11 "Moab has been at ease from his[a] youth;
He has settled on his dregs,
And has not been emptied from vessel
to vessel,
Nor has he gone into captivity.
Therefore his taste remained in him,
And his scent has not changed.

12 "Therefore behold, the days are coming,"
says the LORD,
"That I shall send him wine-workers
Who will tip him over
And empty his vessels
And break the bottles.
13 Moab shall be ashamed of Chemosh,
As the house of Israel was ashamed of
Bethel, their confidence.

14 "How can you say, 'We *are* mighty
And strong men for the war'?
15 Moab is plundered and gone up *from* her
cities;
Her chosen young men have gone down
to the slaughter," says the King,
Whose name *is* the LORD of hosts.

16 "The calamity of Moab *is* near at hand,
And his affliction comes quickly.
17 Bemoan him, all you who are around
him;
And all you who know his name,
Say, 'How the strong staff is broken,
The beautiful rod!'

18 "O daughter inhabiting Dibon,
Come down from *your* glory,
And sit in thirst;

48:1 [a] Hebrew *Misgab* **48:2** [a] A city of Moab **48:4** [a] Following Masoretic Text, Targum, and Vulgate; Septuagint reads *Proclaim it in Zoar.* **48:6** [a] Or *Aroer,* a city of Moab **48:11** [a] The Hebrew uses masculine and feminine pronouns interchangeably in this chapter.

For the plunderer of Moab has come
against you,
He has destroyed your strongholds.
19 O inhabitant of Aroer,
Stand by the way and watch;
Ask him who flees
And her who escapes;
Say, 'What has happened?'
20 Moab is shamed, for he is broken down.
Wail and cry!
Tell it in Arnon, that Moab is plundered.

21 "And judgment has come on the plain
country:
On Holon and Jahzah and Mephaath,
22 On Dibon and Nebo and Beth
Diblathaim,
23 On Kirjathaim and Beth Gamul and
Beth Meon,
24 On Kerioth and Bozrah,
On all the cities of the land of Moab,
Far or near.
25 The horn of Moab is cut off,
And his arm is broken," says the LORD.

26 "Make him drunk,
Because he exalted *himself* against the
LORD.
Moab shall wallow in his vomit,
And he shall also be in derision.
27 For was not Israel a derision to you?
Was he found among thieves?
For whenever you speak of him,
You shake *your head in scorn*.
28 You who dwell in Moab,
Leave the cities and dwell in the rock,
And be like the dove *which* makes her
nest
In the sides of the cave's mouth.

29 "We have heard the pride of Moab
(He *is* exceedingly proud),
Of his loftiness and arrogance and
pride,
And of the haughtiness of his heart."

30 "I know his wrath," says the LORD,
"But it *is* not right;
His lies have made nothing right.
31 Therefore I will wail for Moab,
And I will cry out for all Moab;
I[a] will mourn for the men of Kir Heres.
32 O vine of Sibmah! I will weep for you
with the weeping of Jazer.
Your plants have gone over the sea,
They reach to the sea of Jazer.
The plunderer has fallen on your
summer fruit and your vintage.
33 Joy and gladness are taken
From the plentiful field
And from the land of Moab;
I have caused wine to fail from the
winepresses;
No one will tread with joyous
shouting—
Not joyous shouting!

34 "From the cry of Heshbon to Elealeh and
to Jahaz
They have uttered their voice,
From Zoar to Horonaim,
Like a three-year-old heifer;[a]
For the waters of Nimrim also shall be
desolate.

35 "Moreover," says the LORD,
"I will cause to cease in Moab
The one who offers *sacrifices* in the high
places
And burns incense to his gods.
36 Therefore My heart shall wail like flutes
for Moab,
And like flutes My heart shall wail
For the men of Kir Heres.
Therefore the riches they have acquired
have perished.

37 "For every head *shall be* bald, and every
beard clipped;
On all the hands *shall be* cuts, and on
the loins sackcloth—
38 A general lamentation
On all the housetops of Moab,
And in its streets;
For I have broken Moab like a vessel in
which *is* no pleasure," says the LORD.
39 "They shall wail:
'How she is broken down!
How Moab has turned her back with
shame!'
So Moab shall be a derision
And a dismay to all those about her."

40 For thus says the LORD:

"Behold, one shall fly like an eagle,
And spread his wings over Moab.
41 Kerioth is taken,
And the strongholds are surprised;

48:31 [a] Following Dead Sea Scrolls, Septuagint, and Vulgate; Masoretic Text reads *He*. **48:34** [a] Or *The Third Eglath*, an unknown city (compare Isaiah 15:5)

The mighty men's hearts in Moab on that day shall be
Like the heart of a woman in birth pangs.
42 And Moab shall be destroyed as a people,
Because he exalted *himself* against the LORD.
43 Fear and the pit and the snare *shall be* upon you,
O inhabitant of Moab," says the LORD.
44 "He who flees from the fear shall fall into the pit,
And he who gets out of the pit shall be caught in the snare.
For upon Moab, upon it I will bring
The year of their punishment," says the LORD.

45 "Those who fled stood under the shadow of Heshbon
Because of exhaustion.
But a fire shall come out of Heshbon,
A flame from the midst of Sihon,
And shall devour the brow of Moab,
The crown of the head of the sons of tumult.
46 Woe to you, O Moab!
The people of Chemosh perish;
For your sons have been taken captive,
And your daughters captive.

47 "Yet I will bring back the captives of Moab
In the latter days," says the LORD.

Thus far *is* the judgment of Moab.

Judgment on Ammon

49 Against the Ammonites.
Thus says the LORD:

"Has Israel no sons?
Has he no heir?
Why *then* does Milcom[a] inherit Gad,
And his people dwell in its cities?
2 Therefore behold, the days are coming," says the LORD,
"That I will cause to be heard an alarm of war
In Rabbah of the Ammonites;
It shall be a desolate mound,
And her villages shall be burned with fire.
Then Israel shall take possession of his inheritance," says the LORD.

3 "Wail, O Heshbon, for Ai is plundered!
Cry, you daughters of Rabbah,
Gird yourselves with sackcloth!
Lament and run to and fro by the walls;
For Milcom shall go into captivity
With his priests and his princes together.
4 Why do you boast in the valleys,
Your flowing valley, O backsliding daughter?
Who trusted in her treasures, *saying,*
'Who will come against me?'
5 Behold, I will bring fear upon you,"
Says the Lord GOD of hosts,
"From all those who are around you;
You shall be driven out, everyone headlong,
And no one will gather those who wander off.
6 But afterward I will bring back
The captives of the people of Ammon," says the LORD.

Judgment on Edom

7 Against Edom.
Thus says the LORD of hosts:

"*Is* wisdom no more in Teman?
Has counsel perished from the prudent?
Has their wisdom vanished?
8 Flee, turn back, dwell in the depths,
O inhabitants of Dedan!
For I will bring the calamity of Esau upon him,
The time *that* I will punish him.
9 If grape-gatherers came to you,
Would they not leave *some* gleaning grapes?
If thieves by night,
Would they not destroy until they have enough?
10 But I have made Esau bare;
I have uncovered his secret places,[a]
And he shall not be able to hide himself.
His descendants are plundered,
His brethren and his neighbors,
And he *is* no more.
11 Leave your fatherless children,
I will preserve *them* alive;
And let your widows trust in Me."

12 For thus says the LORD: "Behold, those
whose judgment *was* not to drink of the cup
have assuredly drunk. And *are* you the one

49:1 [a] Hebrew *Malcam,* literally *their king,* a god of the Ammonites; also called *Molech* (compare verse 3)
49:10 [a] Compare Obadiah 5, 6

who will altogether go unpunished? You
shall not go unpunished, but you shall surely drink *of it.* 13For I have sworn by Myself,"
says the LORD, "that Bozrah shall become a
desolation, a reproach, a waste, and a curse.
And all its cities shall be perpetual wastes."

14 I have heard a message from the LORD,
And an ambassador has been sent to the nations:
"Gather together, come against her,
And rise up to battle!

15 "For indeed, I will make you small among nations,
Despised among men.
16 Your fierceness has deceived you,
The pride of your heart,
O you who dwell in the clefts of the rock,
Who hold the height of the hill!
Though you make your nest as high as the eagle,
I will bring you down from there," says the LORD.[a]

17 "Edom also shall be an astonishment;
Everyone who goes by it will be astonished
And will hiss at all its plagues.
18 As in the overthrow of Sodom and Gomorrah
And their neighbors," says the LORD,
"No one shall remain there,
Nor shall a son of man dwell in it.

19 "Behold, he shall come up like a lion from the floodplain[a] of the Jordan
Against the dwelling place of the strong;
But I will suddenly make him run away from her.
And who *is* a chosen *man that* I may appoint over her?
For who *is* like Me?
Who will arraign Me?
And who *is* that shepherd
Who will withstand Me?"

20 Therefore hear the counsel of the LORD that He has taken against Edom,
And His purposes that He has proposed against the inhabitants of Teman:
Surely the least of the flock shall draw them out;
Surely He shall make their dwelling places desolate with them.
21 The earth shakes at the noise of their fall;
At the cry its noise is heard at the Red Sea.
22 Behold, He shall come up and fly like the eagle,
And spread His wings over Bozrah;
The heart of the mighty men of Edom in that day shall be
Like the heart of a woman in birth pangs.

Judgment on Damascus

23Against Damascus.

"Hamath and Arpad are shamed,
For they have heard bad news.
They are fainthearted;
There is trouble on the sea;
It cannot be quiet.
24 Damascus has grown feeble;
She turns to flee,
And fear has seized *her.*
Anguish and sorrows have taken her like a woman in labor.
25 Why is the city of praise not deserted, the city of My joy?
26 Therefore her young men shall fall in her streets,
And all the men of war shall be cut off in that day," says the LORD of hosts.
27 "I will kindle a fire in the wall of Damascus,
And it shall consume the palaces of Ben-Hadad."[a]

Judgment on Kedar and Hazor

28Against Kedar and against the kingdoms of Hazor, which Nebuchadnezzar king
of Babylon shall strike.
Thus says the LORD:

"Arise, go up to Kedar,
And devastate the men of the East!
29 Their tents and their flocks they shall take away.
They shall take for themselves their curtains,
All their vessels and their camels;
And they shall cry out to them,
'Fear *is* on every side!'

30 "Flee, get far away! Dwell in the depths,
O inhabitants of Hazor!" says the LORD.
"For Nebuchadnezzar king of Babylon has taken counsel against you,

---

49:16 [a] Compare Obadiah 3, 4 **49:19** [a] Or *thicket*
49:27 [a] Compare Amos 1:4

And has conceived a plan against you.

31 "Arise, go up to the wealthy nation that dwells securely," says the LORD,
"Which has neither gates nor bars,
Dwelling alone.
32 Their camels shall be for booty,
And the multitude of their cattle for plunder.
I will scatter to all winds those in the farthest corners,
And I will bring their calamity from all its sides," says the LORD.
33 "Hazor shall be a dwelling for jackals, a desolation forever;
No one shall reside there,
Nor son of man dwell in it."

Judgment on Elam

34 The word of the LORD that came to
Jeremiah the prophet against Elam, in the
beginning of the reign of Zedekiah king
of Judah, saying, 35 "Thus says the LORD of
hosts:

'Behold, I will break the bow of Elam,
The foremost of their might.
36 Against Elam I will bring the four winds
From the four quarters of heaven,
And scatter them toward all those winds;
There shall be no nations where the outcasts of Elam will not go.
37 For I will cause Elam to be dismayed before their enemies
And before those who seek their life.
I will bring disaster upon them,
My fierce anger,' says the LORD;
'And I will send the sword after them
Until I have consumed them.
38 I will set My throne in Elam,
And will destroy from there the king and the princes,' says the LORD.

39 'But it shall come to pass in the latter days:
I will bring back the captives of Elam,' says the LORD."

Judgment on Babylon and Babylonia

50 The word that the LORD spoke against Babylon *and* against the land of the Chaldeans by Jeremiah the prophet.

2 "Declare among the nations,
Proclaim, and set up a standard;
Proclaim—do not conceal *it*—
Say, 'Babylon is taken, Bel is shamed.
Merodach[a] is broken in pieces;
Her idols are humiliated,
Her images are broken in pieces.'
3 For out of the north a nation comes up against her,
Which shall make her land desolate,
And no one shall dwell therein.
They shall move, they shall depart,
Both man and beast.

4 "In those days and in that time," says the LORD,
"The children of Israel shall come,
They and the children of Judah together;
With continual weeping they shall come,
And seek the LORD their God.
5 They shall ask the way to Zion,
With their faces toward it, *saying,*
'Come and let us join ourselves to the LORD
In a perpetual covenant
That will not be forgotten.'

6 "My people have been lost sheep.
Their shepherds have led them astray;
They have turned them away *on* the mountains.
They have gone from mountain to hill;
They have forgotten their resting place.
7 All who found them have devoured them;
And their adversaries said, 'We have not offended,
Because they have sinned against the LORD, the habitation of justice,
The LORD, the hope of their fathers.'

8 "Move from the midst of Babylon,
Go out of the land of the Chaldeans;
And be like the rams before the flocks.
9 For behold, I will raise and cause to come up against Babylon
An assembly of great nations from the north country,
And they shall array themselves against her;
From there she shall be captured.
Their arrows *shall be* like *those* of an expert warrior;[a]
None shall return in vain.

50:2 [a] A Babylonian god; sometimes spelled *Marduk*
50:9 [a] Following some Hebrew manuscripts, Septuagint, and Syriac; Masoretic Text, Targum, and Vulgate read *a warrior who makes childless.*

10 And Chaldea shall become plunder;
All who plunder her shall be satisfied,"
says the LORD.

11 "Because you were glad, because you
rejoiced,
You destroyers of My heritage,
Because you have grown fat like a heifer
threshing grain,
And you bellow like bulls,
12 Your mother shall be deeply ashamed;
She who bore you shall be ashamed.
Behold, the least of the nations *shall be* a
wilderness,
A dry land and a desert.
13 Because of the wrath of the LORD
She shall not be inhabited,
But she shall be wholly desolate.
Everyone who goes by Babylon shall be
horrified
And hiss at all her plagues.

14 "Put yourselves in array against Babylon
all around,
All you who bend the bow;
Shoot at her, spare no arrows,
For she has sinned against the LORD.
15 Shout against her all around;
She has given her hand,
Her foundations have fallen,
Her walls are thrown down;
For it *is* the vengeance of the LORD.
Take vengeance on her.
As she has done, so do to her.
16 Cut off the sower from Babylon,
And him who handles the sickle at
harvest time.
For fear of the oppressing sword
Everyone shall turn to his own people,
And everyone shall flee to his own land.

17 "Israel *is* like scattered sheep;
The lions have driven *him* away.
First the king of Assyria devoured him;
Now at last this Nebuchadnezzar king
of Babylon has broken his bones."

18 Therefore thus says the LORD of hosts,
the God of Israel:

"Behold, I will punish the king of Babylon
and his land,
As I have punished the king of Assyria.
19 But I will bring back Israel to his home,
And he shall feed on Carmel and
Bashan;
His soul shall be satisfied on Mount
Ephraim and Gilead.
20 In those days and in that time," says the
LORD,
"The iniquity of Israel shall be sought,
but *there shall be* none;
And the sins of Judah, but they shall not
be found;
For I will pardon those whom I
preserve.

21 "Go up against the land of Merathaim,
against it,
And against the inhabitants of Pekod.
Waste and utterly destroy them," says
the LORD,
"And do according to all that I have
commanded you.
22 A sound of battle *is* in the land,
And of great destruction.
23 How the hammer of the whole earth has
been cut apart and broken!
How Babylon has become a desolation
among the nations!
24 I have laid a snare for you;
You have indeed been trapped,
O Babylon,
And you were not aware;
You have been found and also caught,
Because you have contended against the
LORD.
25 The LORD has opened His armory,
And has brought out the weapons of His
indignation;
For this *is* the work of the Lord GOD of
hosts
In the land of the Chaldeans.
26 Come against her from the farthest
border;
Open her storehouses;
Cast her up as heaps of ruins,
And destroy her utterly;
Let nothing of her be left.
27 Slay all her bulls,
Let them go down to the slaughter.
Woe to them!
For their day has come, the time of their
punishment.
28 The voice of those who flee and escape
from the land of Babylon
Declares in Zion the vengeance of the
LORD our God,
The vengeance of His temple.

29 "Call together the archers against
Babylon.
All you who bend the bow, encamp
against it all around;

Let none of them escape.[a]
Repay her according to her work;
According to all she has done, do to her;
For she has been proud against the
LORD,
Against the Holy One of Israel.
30 Therefore her young men shall fall in
the streets,
And all her men of war shall be cut off
in that day," says the LORD.
31 "Behold, I *am* against you,
O most haughty one!" says the Lord
GOD of hosts;
"For your day has come,
The time *that* I will punish you.[a]
32 The most proud shall stumble and fall,
And no one will raise him up;
I will kindle a fire in his cities,
And it will devour all around him."

33 Thus says the LORD of hosts:

"The children of Israel *were* oppressed,
Along with the children of Judah;
All who took them captive have held
them fast;
They have refused to let them go.
34 Their Redeemer *is* strong;
The LORD of hosts *is* His name.
He will thoroughly plead their case,
That He may give rest to the land,
And disquiet the inhabitants of Babylon.

35 "A sword *is* against the Chaldeans," says
the LORD,
"Against the inhabitants of Babylon,
And against her princes and her wise
men.
36 A sword *is* against the soothsayers, and
they will be fools.
A sword *is* against her mighty men, and
they will be dismayed.
37 A sword *is* against their horses,
Against their chariots,
And against all the mixed peoples who
are in her midst;
And they will become like women.
A sword *is* against her treasures, and
they will be robbed.
38 A drought[a] *is* against her waters, and
they will be dried up.
For it *is* the land of carved images,
And they are insane with *their* idols.

39 "Therefore the wild desert beasts shall
dwell *there* with the jackals,
And the ostriches shall dwell in it.
It shall be inhabited no more forever,
Nor shall it be dwelt in from generation
to generation.
40 As God overthrew Sodom and
Gomorrah
And their neighbors," says the LORD,
"*So* no one shall reside there,
Nor son of man dwell in it.

41 "Behold, a people shall come from the
north,
And a great nation and many kings
Shall be raised up from the ends of the
earth.
42 They shall hold the bow and the lance;
They *are* cruel and shall not show
mercy.
Their voice shall roar like the sea;
They shall ride on horses,
Set in array, like a man for the battle,
Against you, O daughter of Babylon.

43 "The king of Babylon has heard the
report about them,
And his hands grow feeble;
Anguish has taken hold of him,
Pangs as of a woman in childbirth.

44 "Behold, he shall come up like a lion
from the floodplain[a] of the Jordan
Against the dwelling place of the strong;
But I will make them suddenly run
away from her.
And who *is* a chosen *man that* I may
appoint over her?
For who *is* like Me?
Who will arraign Me?
And who *is* that shepherd
Who will withstand Me?"

45 Therefore hear the counsel of the LORD
that He has taken against Babylon,
And His purposes that He has proposed
against the land of the Chaldeans:
Surely the least of the flock shall draw
them out;
Surely He will make their dwelling
place desolate with them.
46 At the noise of the taking of Babylon
The earth trembles,
And the cry is heard among the nations.

50:29 [a] Qere, some Hebrew manuscripts, Septuagint, and Targum add *to her.* **50:31** [a] Following Masoretic Text and Targum; Septuagint and Vulgate read *The time of your punishment.* **50:38** [a] Following Masoretic Text, Targum, and Vulgate; Syriac reads *sword;* Septuagint omits *A drought is.* **50:44** [a] Or *thicket*

The Utter Destruction of Babylon

51 Thus says the LORD:

"Behold, I will raise up against Babylon,
Against those who dwell in Leb Kamai,[a]
A destroying wind.
2 And I will send winnowers to Babylon,
Who shall winnow her and empty her
land.
For in the day of doom
They shall be against her all around.
3 Against *her* let the archer bend his bow,
And lift himself up against *her* in his
armor.
Do not spare her young men;
Utterly destroy all her army.
4 Thus the slain shall fall in the land of
the Chaldeans,
And *those* thrust through in her streets.
5 For Israel is not forsaken, nor Judah,
By his God, the LORD of hosts,
Though their land was filled with sin
against the Holy One of Israel."

6 Flee from the midst of Babylon,
And every one save his life!
Do not be cut off in her iniquity,
For this *is* the time of the LORD's
vengeance;
He shall recompense her.
7 Babylon *was* a golden cup in the LORD's
hand,
That made all the earth drunk.
The nations drank her wine;
Therefore the nations are deranged.
8 Babylon has suddenly fallen and been
destroyed.
Wail for her!
Take balm for her pain;
Perhaps she may be healed.

9 We would have healed Babylon,
But she is not healed.
Forsake her, and let us go everyone to
his own country;
For her judgment reaches to heaven and
is lifted up to the skies.
10 The LORD has revealed our
righteousness.
Come and let us declare in Zion the
work of the LORD our God.

11 Make the arrows bright!
Gather the shields!
The LORD has raised up the spirit of the
kings of the Medes.

In Focus

51:8 Balm is a kind of substance taken from trees by cutting the bark. It was used as a perfume and was considered effective as a medicine (Jeremiah 51:8). Although Gilead is mentioned together with balm (see Jeremiah 8:22; 46:11), it was not produced in Gilead. It may have been transported through Gilead or sold there.

For His plan *is* against Babylon to
destroy it,
Because it *is* the vengeance of the LORD,
The vengeance for His temple.
12 Set up the standard on the walls of
Babylon;
Make the guard strong,
Set up the watchmen,
Prepare the ambushes.
For the LORD has both devised and done
What He spoke against the inhabitants
of Babylon.
13 O you who dwell by many waters,
Abundant in treasures,
Your end has come,
The measure of your covetousness.
14 The LORD of hosts has sworn by
Himself:
"Surely I will fill you with men, as with
locusts,
And they shall lift up a shout against
you."

15 He has made the earth by His power;
He has established the world by His
wisdom,
And stretched out the heaven by His
understanding.
16 When He utters *His* voice—
There is a multitude of waters in the
heavens:
"He causes the vapors to ascend from the
ends of the earth;
He makes lightnings for the rain;

51:1 [a] A code word for Chaldea (Babylonia); may be translated *The Midst of Those Who Rise Up Against Me*

He brings the wind out of His
treasuries."[a]

17 Everyone is dull-hearted, without
knowledge;
Every metalsmith is put to shame by the
carved image;
For his molded image *is* falsehood,
And *there is* no breath in them.
18 They *are* futile, a work of errors;
In the time of their punishment they
shall perish.
19 The Portion of Jacob *is* not like them,
For He *is* the Maker of all things;
And *Israel is* the tribe of His
inheritance.
The LORD of hosts *is* His name.

20 "You *are* My battle-ax *and* weapons of
war:
For with you I will break the nation in
pieces;
With you I will destroy kingdoms;
21 With you I will break in pieces the horse
and its rider;
With you I will break in pieces the
chariot and its rider;
22 With you also I will break in pieces man
and woman;
With you I will break in pieces old and
young;
With you I will break in pieces the
young man and the maiden;
23 With you also I will break in pieces the
shepherd and his flock;
With you I will break in pieces the
farmer and his yoke of oxen;
And with you I will break in pieces
governors and rulers.

24 "And I will repay Babylon
And all the inhabitants of Chaldea
For all the evil they have done
In Zion in your sight," says the LORD.

25 "Behold, I *am* against you, O destroying
mountain,
Who destroys all the earth," says the
LORD.
"And I will stretch out My hand against
you,
Roll *you down from the rocks,*
And make you a burnt mountain.
26 They shall not take from you a stone for
a corner
Nor a stone for a foundation,
But you shall be desolate forever," says
the LORD.

27 Set up a banner in the land,
Blow the trumpet among the nations!
Prepare the nations against her,
Call the kingdoms together against her:
Ararat, Minni, and Ashkenaz.
Appoint a general against her;
Cause the horses to come up like the
bristling locusts.
28 Prepare against her the nations,
With the kings of the Medes,
Its governors and all its rulers,
All the land of his dominion.
29 And the land will tremble and sorrow;
For every purpose of the LORD shall be
performed against Babylon,
To make the land of Babylon a
desolation without inhabitant.
30 The mighty men of Babylon have ceased
fighting,
They have remained in their
strongholds;
Their might has failed,
They became *like* women;
They have burned her dwelling places,
The bars of her *gate* are broken.
31 One runner will run to meet another,
And one messenger to meet another,
To show the king of Babylon that his city
is taken on *all* sides;
32 The passages are blocked,
The reeds they have burned with fire,
And the men of war are terrified.

33 For thus says the LORD of hosts, the God
of Israel:

"The daughter of Babylon *is* like a
threshing floor
When it is time to thresh her;
Yet a little while
And the time of her harvest will come."

34 "Nebuchadnezzar the king of Babylon
Has devoured me, he has crushed me;
He has made me an empty vessel,
He has swallowed me up like a monster;
He has filled his stomach with my
delicacies,
He has spit me out.
35 Let the violence *done* to me and my flesh
be upon Babylon,"

51:16 [a] Psalm 135:7

The inhabitant of Zion will say;
"And my blood be upon the inhabitants of Chaldea!"
Jerusalem will say.

36 Therefore thus says the LORD:

"Behold, I will plead your case and take vengeance for you.
I will dry up her sea and make her springs dry.
37 Babylon shall become a heap,
A dwelling place for jackals,
An astonishment and a hissing,
Without an inhabitant.
38 They shall roar together like lions,
They shall growl like lions' whelps.
39 In their excitement I will prepare their feasts;
I will make them drunk,
That they may rejoice,
And sleep a perpetual sleep
And not awake," says the LORD.
40 "I will bring them down
Like lambs to the slaughter,
Like rams with male goats.

41 "Oh, how Sheshach[a] is taken!
Oh, how the praise of the whole earth is seized!
How Babylon has become desolate among the nations!
42 The sea has come up over Babylon;
She is covered with the multitude of its waves.
43 Her cities are a desolation,
A dry land and a wilderness,
A land where no one dwells,
Through which no son of man passes.
44 I will punish Bel in Babylon,
And I will bring out of his mouth what he has swallowed;
And the nations shall not stream to him anymore.
Yes, the wall of Babylon shall fall.

45 "My people, go out of the midst of her!
And let everyone deliver himself from the fierce anger of the LORD.
46 And lest your heart faint,
And you fear for the rumor that *will be* heard in the land
(A rumor will come *one* year,
And after that, in *another* year
A rumor *will come,*
And violence in the land,
Ruler against ruler),
47 Therefore behold, the days are coming
That I will bring judgment on the carved images of Babylon;
Her whole land shall be ashamed,
And all her slain shall fall in her midst.
48 Then the heavens and the earth and all that *is* in them
Shall sing joyously over Babylon;
For the plunderers shall come to her from the north," says the LORD.

49 As Babylon *has caused* the slain of Israel to fall,
So at Babylon the slain of all the earth shall fall.
50 You who have escaped the sword,
Get away! Do not stand still!
Remember the LORD afar off,
And let Jerusalem come to your mind.

51 We are ashamed because we have heard reproach.
Shame has covered our faces,
For strangers have come into the sanctuaries of the LORD's house.

52 "Therefore behold, the days are coming," says the LORD,
"That I will bring judgment on her carved images,
And throughout all her land the wounded shall groan.
53 Though Babylon were to mount up to heaven,
And though she were to fortify the height of her strength,
Yet from Me plunderers would come to her," says the LORD.

54 The sound of a cry *comes* from Babylon,
And great destruction from the land of the Chaldeans,
55 Because the LORD is plundering Babylon
And silencing her loud voice,
Though her waves roar like great waters,
And the noise of their voice is uttered,
56 Because the plunderer comes against her, against Babylon,
And her mighty men are taken.
Every one of their bows is broken;
For the LORD *is* the God of recompense,
He will surely repay.

57 "And I will make drunk

51:41 [a] A code word for Babylon (compare Jeremiah 25:26)

Her princes and wise men,
Her governors, her deputies, and her
mighty men.
And they shall sleep a perpetual sleep
And not awake," says the King,
Whose name *is* the LORD of hosts.

58 Thus says the LORD of hosts:

"The broad walls of Babylon shall be
utterly broken,
And her high gates shall be burned with
fire;
The people will labor in vain,
And the nations, because of the fire;
And they shall be weary."

Jeremiah's Command to Seraiah

59 The word which Jeremiah the prophet commanded Seraiah the son of Neriah, the son of Mahseiah, when he went with Zedekiah the king of Judah to Babylon in the fourth year of his reign. And Seraiah *was* the quartermaster. 60 So Jeremiah wrote in a book all the evil that would come upon Babylon, all these words that are written against Babylon. 61 And Jeremiah said to Seraiah, "When you arrive in Babylon and see it, and read all these words, 62 then you shall say, 'O LORD, You have spoken against this place to cut it off, so that none shall remain in it, neither man nor beast, but it shall be desolate forever.' 63 Now it shall be, when you have finished reading this book, *that* you shall tie a stone to it and throw it out into the Euphrates. 64 Then you shall say, 'Thus Babylon shall sink and not rise from the catastrophe that I will bring upon her. And they shall be weary.'"

Thus far *are* the words of Jeremiah.

The Fall of Jerusalem Reviewed

52 Zedekiah *was* twenty-one years old when he became king, and he reigned eleven years in Jerusalem. His mother's name *was* Hamutal the daughter of Jeremiah of Libnah. 2 He also did evil in the sight of the LORD, according to all that Jehoiakim had done. 3 For because of the anger of the LORD *this* happened in Jerusalem and Judah, till He finally cast them out from His presence. Then Zedekiah rebelled against the king of Babylon.

4 Now it came to pass in the ninth year of his reign, in the tenth month, on the tenth *day* of the month, *that* Nebuchadnezzar king of Babylon and all his army came against Jerusalem and encamped against it; and *they* built a siege wall against it all around. 5 So the city was besieged until the eleventh year of King Zedekiah. 6 By the fourth month, on the ninth day of the month, the famine had become so severe in the city that there was no food for the people of the land. 7 Then the city *wall* was broken through, and all the men of war fled and went out of the city at night by way of the gate between the two walls, which *was* by the king's garden, even though the Chaldeans *were* near the city all around. And they went by way of the plain.[a]

8 But the army of the Chaldeans pursued the king, and they overtook Zedekiah in the plains of Jericho. All his army was scattered from him. 9 So they took the king and brought him up to the king of Babylon at Riblah in the land of Hamath, and he pronounced judgment on him. 10 Then the king of Babylon killed the sons of Zedekiah before his eyes. And he killed all the princes of Judah in Riblah. 11 He also put out the eyes of Zedekiah; and the king of Babylon bound him in bronze fetters, took him to Babylon, and put him in prison till the day of his death.

The Temple and City Plundered and Burned

12 Now in the fifth month, on the tenth *day* of the month (which *was* the nineteenth year of King Nebuchadnezzar king of Babylon), Nebuzaradan, the captain of the guard, *who* served the king of Babylon, came to Jerusalem. 13 He burned the house of the LORD and the king's house; all the houses of Jerusalem, that is, all the houses of the great, he burned with fire. 14 And all the army of the Chaldeans who *were* with the captain of the guard broke down all the walls of Jerusalem all around. 15 Then Nebuzaradan the captain of the guard carried away captive *some* of the poor people, the rest of the people who remained in the city, the defectors who had deserted to the king of Babylon, and the rest of the craftsmen. 16 But Nebuzaradan the captain of the guard left *some* of the poor of the land as vinedressers and farmers.

17 The bronze pillars that *were* in the house of the LORD, and the carts and the bronze Sea that *were* in the house of the LORD, the Chaldeans broke in pieces, and

---

52:7 [a] Or *the Arabah*, that is, the Jordan Valley

carried all their bronze to Babylon. [18]They
also took away the pots, the shovels, the
trimmers, the bowls, the spoons, and all the
bronze utensils with which the *priests* ministered. [19]The basins, the firepans, the bowls,
the pots, the lampstands, the spoons, and
the cups, whatever *was* solid gold and whatever *was* solid silver, the captain of the guard
took away. [20]The two pillars, one Sea, the
twelve bronze bulls which *were* under *it, and*
the carts, which King Solomon had made
for the house of the LORD—the bronze of all
these articles was beyond measure. [21]Now
concerning the pillars: the height of one pillar *was* eighteen cubits, a measuring line of
twelve cubits could measure its circumference, and its thickness *was* four fingers; *it
was* hollow. [22]A capital of bronze *was* on it;
and the height of one capital *was* five cubits,
with a network and pomegranates all around
the capital, all of bronze. The second pillar,
with pomegranates was the same. [23]There
were ninety-six pomegranates on the sides;
all the pomegranates, all around on the network, *were* one hundred.

The People Taken Captive to Babylonia

[24]The captain of the guard took Seraiah
the chief priest, Zephaniah the second
priest, and the three doorkeepers. [25]He also
took out of the city an officer who had charge
of the men of war, seven men of the king's
close associates who were found in the city,
the principal scribe of the army who mustered the people of the land, and sixty men
of the people of the land who were found in
the midst of the city. [26]And Nebuzaradan the
captain of the guard took these and brought
them to the king of Babylon at Riblah.
[27]Then the king of Babylon struck them and
put them to death at Riblah in the land of
Hamath. Thus Judah was carried away captive from its own land.

[28]These *are* the people whom Nebuchadnezzar carried away captive: in the seventh
year, three thousand and twenty-three Jews;
[29]in the eighteenth year of Nebuchadnezzar he carried away captive from Jerusalem
eight hundred and thirty-two persons; [30]in
the twenty-third year of Nebuchadnezzar,
Nebuzaradan the captain of the guard carried away captive of the Jews seven hundred
and forty-five persons. All the persons *were*
four thousand six hundred.

Jehoiachin Released from Prison

[31]Now it came to pass in the thirty-
seventh year of the captivity of Jehoiachin
king of Judah, in the twelfth month, on
the twenty-fifth *day* of the month, *that* Evil-
Merodach[a] king of Babylon, in the *first* year
of his reign, lifted up the head of Jehoiachin
king of Judah and brought him out of prison.
[32]And he spoke kindly to him and gave him a
more prominent seat than those of the kings
who *were* with him in Babylon. [33]So Jehoiachin changed from his prison garments, and
he ate bread regularly before the *king* all the
days of his life. [34]And as for his provisions,
there was a regular ration given him by the
king of Babylon, a portion for each day until
the day of his death, all the days of his life.

52:31 [a] Or *Awil-Marduk*

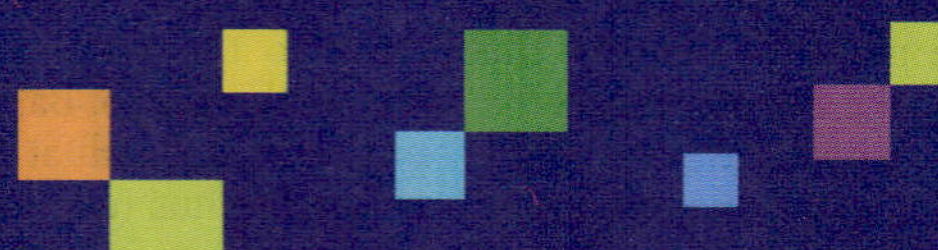

The BOOK of LAMENTATIONS

586 B.C.–584 B.C.

Behind the Scenes

READ IT:

The book of Lamentations is a collection of sad songs. Jeremiah wrote them as he thought about the total destruction of Jerusalem and God's temple. But he also recognized that this was the judgment of a righteous God. Because he knew God was merciful, he prayed to God.

GET IT:

Who wrote it: The prophet Jeremiah

When it was written: 586 B.C.–584 B.C.

Why it was written: to share the feelings of war and the destruction of God's holy city.

LIVE IT:

Sin causes great sorrow and pain.

FIND IT:

The Lament for the Destroyed Jerusalem	*Lamentations 1*
Jeremiah's Anguish and Hope	*Lamentations 3*

Jerusalem in Affliction

1 How lonely sits the city
That was full of people!
How like a widow is she,
Who *was* great among the nations!
The princess among the provinces
Has become a slave!

2 She weeps bitterly in the night,
Her tears *are* on her cheeks;
Among all her lovers
She has none to comfort *her.*
All her friends have dealt treacherously with her;
They have become her enemies.

3 Judah has gone into captivity,
Under affliction and hard servitude;
She dwells among the nations,
She finds no rest;
All her persecutors overtake her in dire straits.

4 The roads to Zion mourn
Because no one comes to the set feasts.
All her gates are desolate;
Her priests sigh,
Her virgins are afflicted,
And she *is* in bitterness.

5 Her adversaries have become the master,
Her enemies prosper;
For the LORD has afflicted her
Because of the multitude of her transgressions.
Her children have gone into captivity before the enemy.

6 And from the daughter of Zion
All her splendor has departed.
Her princes have become like deer
That find no pasture,
That flee without strength
Before the pursuer.

7 In the days of her affliction and roaming,
Jerusalem remembers all her pleasant things
That she had in the days of old.
When her people fell into the hand of the enemy,
With no one to help her,
The adversaries saw her
And mocked at her downfall.[a]

8 Jerusalem has sinned gravely,
Therefore she has become vile.[a]
All who honored her despise her
Because they have seen her nakedness;
Yes, she sighs and turns away.

9 Her uncleanness *is* in her skirts;
She did not consider her destiny;
Therefore her collapse was awesome;
She had no comforter.
"O LORD, behold my affliction,
For *the* enemy is exalted!"

10 The adversary has spread his hand
Over all her pleasant things;
For she has seen the nations enter her sanctuary,
Those whom You commanded
Not to enter Your assembly.

11 All her people sigh,
They seek bread;
They have given their valuables for food to restore life.
"See, O LORD, and consider,
For I am scorned."

12 "*Is it* nothing to you, all you who pass by?
Behold and see
If there is any sorrow like my sorrow,
Which has been brought on me,
Which the LORD has inflicted
In the day of His fierce anger.

13 "From above He has sent fire into my bones,
And it overpowered them;
He has spread a net for my feet
And turned me back;
He has made me desolate
And faint all the day.

14 "The yoke of my transgressions was bound;[a]
They were woven together by His hands,
And thrust upon my neck.
He made my strength fail;
The Lord delivered me into the hands of *those whom* I am not able to withstand.

15 "The Lord has trampled underfoot all my mighty *men* in my midst;
He has called an assembly against me
To crush my young men;

1:7 [a] Vulgate reads *her Sabbaths.* 1:8 [a] Septuagint and Vulgate read *moved* or *removed.* 1:14 [a] Following Masoretic Text and Targum; Septuagint, Syriac, and Vulgate read *watched over.*

The Lord trampled *as* in a winepress
The virgin daughter of Judah.

16 "For these *things* I weep;
My eye, my eye overflows with water;
Because the comforter, who should restore my life,
Is far from me.
My children are desolate
Because the enemy prevailed."

17 Zion spreads out her hands,
But no one comforts her;
The LORD has commanded concerning Jacob
That those around him *become* his adversaries;
Jerusalem has become an unclean thing among them.

18 "The LORD is righteous,
For I rebelled against His commandment.
Hear now, all peoples,
And behold my sorrow;
My virgins and my young men
Have gone into captivity.

19 "I called for my lovers,
But they deceived me;
My priests and my elders
Breathed their last in the city,
While they sought food
To restore their life.

20 "See, O LORD, that I *am* in distress;
My soul is troubled;
My heart is overturned within me,
For I have been very rebellious.
Outside the sword bereaves,
At home *it is* like death.

21 "They have heard that I sigh,
But no one comforts me.
All my enemies have heard of my trouble;
They are glad that You have done *it*.
Bring on the day You have announced,
That they may become like me.

22 "Let all their wickedness come before You,
And do to them as You have done to me
For all my transgressions;
For my sighs *are* many,
And my heart *is* faint."

God's Anger with Jerusalem

2 How the Lord has covered the daughter of Zion
With a cloud in His anger!
He cast down from heaven to the earth
The beauty of Israel,
And did not remember His footstool
In the day of His anger.

2 The Lord has swallowed up and has not pitied
All the dwelling places of Jacob.
He has thrown down in His wrath
The strongholds of the daughter of Judah;
He has brought *them* down to the ground;
He has profaned the kingdom and its princes.

3 He has cut off in fierce anger
Every horn of Israel;
He has drawn back His right hand
From before the enemy.
He has blazed against Jacob like a flaming fire
Devouring all around.

4 Standing like an enemy, He has bent His bow;
With His right hand, like an adversary,
He has slain all *who were* pleasing to His eye;
On the tent of the daughter of Zion,
He has poured out His fury like fire.

5 The Lord was like an enemy.
He has swallowed up Israel,
He has swallowed up all her palaces;
He has destroyed her strongholds,
And has increased mourning and lamentation
In the daughter of Judah.

6 He has done violence to His tabernacle,
As if it were a garden;
He has destroyed His place of assembly;
The LORD has caused
The appointed feasts and Sabbaths to be forgotten in Zion.
In His burning indignation He has spurned the king and the priest.

7 The Lord has spurned His altar,
He has abandoned His sanctuary;
He has given up the walls of her palaces
Into the hand of the enemy.
They have made a noise in the house of the LORD
As on the day of a set feast.

8 The LORD has purposed to destroy
The wall of the daughter of Zion.

He has stretched out a line;
He has not withdrawn His hand from destroying;
Therefore He has caused the rampart and wall to lament;
They languished together.

9 Her gates have sunk into the ground;
He has destroyed and broken her bars.
Her king and her princes *are* among the nations;
The Law *is* no *more,*
And her prophets find no vision from the LORD.

10 The elders of the daughter of Zion
Sit on the ground *and* keep silence;
They throw dust on their heads
And gird themselves with sackcloth.
The virgins of Jerusalem
Bow their heads to the ground.

11 My eyes fail with tears,
My heart is troubled;
My bile is poured on the ground
Because of the destruction of the daughter of my people,
Because the children and the infants
Faint in the streets of the city.

12 They say to their mothers,
"Where *is* grain and wine?"
As they swoon like the wounded
In the streets of the city,
As their life is poured out
In their mothers' bosom.

13 How shall I console you?
To what shall I liken you,
O daughter of Jerusalem?
What shall I compare with you, that I may comfort you,
O virgin daughter of Zion?
For your ruin *is* spread wide as the sea;
Who can heal you?

14 Your prophets have seen for you
False and deceptive visions;
They have not uncovered your iniquity,
To bring back your captives,
But have envisioned for you false prophecies and delusions.

15 All who pass by clap *their* hands at you;
They hiss and shake their heads
At the daughter of Jerusalem:
"*Is* this the city that is called
'The perfection of beauty,
The joy of the whole earth'?"

16 All your enemies have opened their mouth against you;
They hiss and gnash *their* teeth.
They say, "We have swallowed *her* up!
Surely this *is* the day we have waited for;
We have found *it,* we have seen *it!*"

17 The LORD has done what He purposed;
He has fulfilled His word
Which He commanded in days of old.
He has thrown down and has not pitied,
And He has caused an enemy to rejoice over you;
He has exalted the horn of your adversaries.

18 Their heart cried out to the Lord,
"O wall of the daughter of Zion,
Let tears run down like a river day and night;
Give yourself no relief;
Give your eyes no rest.

19 "Arise, cry out in the night,
At the beginning of the watches;
Pour out your heart like water before the face of the Lord.
Lift your hands toward Him
For the life of your young children,
Who faint from hunger at the head of every street."

20 "See, O LORD, and consider!
To whom have You done this?
Should the women eat their offspring,
The children they have cuddled?[a]
Should the priest and prophet be slain
In the sanctuary of the Lord?

21 "Young and old lie
On the ground in the streets;
My virgins and my young men
Have fallen by the sword;
You have slain *them* in the day of Your anger,
You have slaughtered *and* not pitied.

22 "You have invited as to a feast day
The terrors that surround me.
In the day of the LORD's anger
There was no refugee or survivor.
Those whom I have borne and brought up
My enemies have destroyed."

The Prophet's Anguish and Hope

3 I *am* the man *who* has seen affliction by the rod of His wrath.
2 He has led me and made *me* walk
In darkness and not *in* light.

2:20 [a] Vulgate reads *a span long.*

3 Surely He has turned His hand against me
Time and time again throughout the day.

4 He has aged my flesh and my skin,
And broken my bones.
5 He has besieged me
And surrounded *me* with bitterness and woe.
6 He has set me in dark places
Like the dead of long ago.

7 He has hedged me in so that I cannot get out;
He has made my chain heavy.
8 Even when I cry and shout,
He shuts out my prayer.
9 He has blocked my ways with hewn stone;
He has made my paths crooked.

10 He *has been* to me a bear lying in wait,
Like a lion in ambush.
11 He has turned aside my ways and torn me in pieces;
He has made me desolate.
12 He has bent His bow
And set me up as a target for the arrow.

13 He has caused the arrows of His quiver
To pierce my loins.[a]
14 I have become the ridicule of all my people—
Their taunting song all the day.
15 He has filled me with bitterness,
He has made me drink wormwood.

16 He has also broken my teeth with gravel,
And covered me with ashes.
17 You have moved my soul far from peace;
I have forgotten prosperity.
18 And I said, "My strength and my hope
Have perished from the LORD."

19 Remember my affliction and roaming,
The wormwood and the gall.
20 My soul still remembers
And sinks within me.
21 This I recall to my mind,
Therefore I have hope.

22 *Through* the LORD's mercies we are not consumed,
Because His compassions fail not.
23 *They are* new every morning;
Great *is* Your faithfulness.
24 "The LORD *is* my portion," says my soul,
"Therefore I hope in Him!"

25 The LORD *is* good to those who wait for Him,
To the soul *who* seeks Him.
26 *It is* good that *one* should hope and wait quietly
For the salvation of the LORD.
27 *It is* good for a man to bear
The yoke in his youth.

28 Let him sit alone and keep silent,
Because *God* has laid *it* on him;
29 Let him put his mouth in the dust—
There may yet be hope.
30 Let him give *his* cheek to the one who strikes him,
And be full of reproach.

3:13 [a] Literally *kidneys*

COMPASSION

READ IT: LAMENTATIONS 3:22

Have you ever had a day when you were totally exhausted? When all of your energy—emotional, physical, and spiritual—was completely drained? When we're worn out like that, we need grace to fill in the empty spaces. At these times we can trust God's mercy. The Bible promises that His compassion will never fail.

31 For the Lord will not cast off forever.
32 Though He causes grief,
Yet He will show compassion
According to the multitude of His
mercies.
33 For He does not afflict willingly,
Nor grieve the children of men.

34 To crush under one's feet
All the prisoners of the earth,
35 To turn aside the justice *due* a man
Before the face of the Most High,
36 Or subvert a man in his cause—
The Lord does not approve.

37 Who *is* he *who* speaks and it comes to
pass,
When the Lord has not commanded *it?*
38 *Is it* not from the mouth of the Most
High
That woe and well-being proceed?
39 Why should a living man complain,
A man for the punishment of his sins?

40 Let us search out and examine our ways,
And turn back to the LORD;
41 Let us lift our hearts and hands
To God in heaven.
42 We have transgressed and rebelled;
You have not pardoned.

43 You have covered *Yourself* with anger
And pursued us;
You have slain *and* not pitied.
44 You have covered Yourself with a cloud,
That prayer should not pass through.
45 You have made us an offscouring and
refuse
In the midst of the peoples.

46 All our enemies
Have opened their mouths against us.
47 Fear and a snare have come upon us,
Desolation and destruction.
48 My eyes overflow with rivers of water
For the destruction of the daughter of
my people.

49 My eyes flow and do not cease,
Without interruption,
50 Till the LORD from heaven
Looks down and sees.
51 My eyes bring suffering to my soul
Because of all the daughters of my city.

52 My enemies without cause
Hunted me down like a bird.
53 They silenced[a] my life in the pit
And threw stones at me.
54 The waters flowed over my head;
I said, "I am cut off!"

55 I called on Your name, O LORD,
From the lowest pit.
56 You have heard my voice:
"Do not hide Your ear
From my sighing, from my cry for
help."
57 You drew near on the day I called on
You,
And said, "Do not fear!"

58 O Lord, You have pleaded the case for
my soul;
You have redeemed my life.
59 O LORD, You have seen *how* I am
wronged;
Judge my case.
60 You have seen all their vengeance,
All their schemes against me.

61 You have heard their reproach, O LORD,
All their schemes against me,
62 The lips of my enemies
And their whispering against me all
the day.
63 Look at their sitting down and their
rising up;
I *am* their taunting song.

64 Repay them, O LORD,
According to the work of their hands.
65 Give them a veiled[a] heart;
Your curse *be* upon them!
66 In Your anger,
Pursue and destroy them
From under the heavens of the LORD.

The Degradation of Zion

4 How the gold has become dim!
How changed the fine gold!
The stones of the sanctuary are
scattered
At the head of every street.

2 The precious sons of Zion,
Valuable as fine gold,
How they are regarded as clay pots,
The work of the hands of the potter!

3 Even the jackals present their breasts
To nurse their young;
But the daughter of my people *is* cruel,
Like ostriches in the wilderness.

3:53 [a] Septuagint reads *put to death.* 3:65 [a] A Jewish tradition reads *sorrow of.*

4 The tongue of the infant clings
To the roof of its mouth for thirst;
The young children ask for bread,
But no one breaks *it* for them.

5 Those who ate delicacies
Are desolate in the streets;
Those who were brought up in scarlet
Embrace ash heaps.

6 The punishment of the iniquity of the daughter of my people
Is greater than the punishment of the sin of Sodom,
Which was overthrown in a moment,
With no hand to help her!

7 Her Nazirites[a] were brighter than snow
And whiter than milk;
They were more ruddy in body than rubies,
Like sapphire in their appearance.

8 *Now* their appearance is blacker than soot;
They go unrecognized in the streets;
Their skin clings to their bones,
It has become as dry as wood.

9 *Those* slain by the sword are better off
Than *those* who die of hunger;
For these pine away,
Stricken *for lack* of the fruits of the field.

10 The hands of the compassionate women
Have cooked their own children;
They became food for them
In the destruction of the daughter of my people.

11 The LORD has fulfilled His fury,
He has poured out His fierce anger.
He kindled a fire in Zion,
And it has devoured its foundations.

12 The kings of the earth,
And all inhabitants of the world,
Would not have believed
That the adversary and the enemy
Could enter the gates of Jerusalem—

13 Because of the sins of her prophets
And the iniquities of her priests,
Who shed in her midst
The blood of the just.

14 They wandered blind *in the streets;*
They have defiled themselves with blood,
So that no one would touch their garments.

15 They cried out to them,
"Go away, unclean!
Go away, go away,
Do not touch us!"
When they fled and wandered,
Those among the nations said,
"They shall no longer dwell *here.*"

16 The face[a] of the LORD scattered them;
He no longer regards them.
The people do not respect the priests
Nor show favor to the elders.

17 Still our eyes failed us,
Watching vainly for our help;
In our watching we watched
For a nation *that* could not save *us.*

18 They tracked our steps
So that we could not walk in our streets.
Our end was near;
Our days were over,
For our end had come.

19 Our pursuers were swifter
Than the eagles of the heavens.
They pursued us on the mountains
And lay in wait for us in the wilderness.

20 The breath of our nostrils, the anointed of the LORD,
Was caught in their pits,
Of whom we said, "Under his shadow
We shall live among the nations."

21 Rejoice and be glad, O daughter of Edom,
You who dwell in the land of Uz!
The cup shall also pass over to you
And you shall become drunk and make yourself naked.

22 *The punishment of* your iniquity is accomplished,
O daughter of Zion;
He will no longer send you into captivity.
He will punish your iniquity,
O daughter of Edom;
He will uncover your sins!

Prayer for Restoration

5 Remember, O LORD, what has come upon us;
Look, and behold our reproach!
2 Our inheritance has been turned over to aliens,

4:7 [a] Or *nobles* 4:16 [a] Targum reads *anger.*

Ezekiel's Vision of God

1 Now it came to pass in the thirtieth
year, in the fourth *month,* on the fifth
day of the month, as I *was* among the captives by the River Chebar, *that* the heavens
were opened and I saw visions[a] of God. 2On
the fifth *day* of the month, which *was* in the
fifth year of King Jehoiachin's captivity, 3the
word of the LORD came expressly to Ezekiel
the priest the son of Buzi, in the land of the
Chaldeans[a] by the River Chebar; and the
hand of the LORD was upon him there.

4Then I looked, and behold, a whirlwind
was coming out of the north, a great cloud
with raging fire engulfing itself; and brightness *was* all around it and radiating out of
its midst like the color of amber, out of the
midst of the fire. 5Also from within it *came*
the likeness of four living creatures. And
this *was* their appearance: they had the likeness of a man. 6Each one had four faces, and
each one had four wings. 7Their legs *were*
straight, and the soles of their feet *were* like
the soles of calves' feet. They sparkled like
the color of burnished bronze. 8The hands of
a man *were* under their wings on their four
sides; and each of the four had faces and
wings. 9Their wings touched one another.
The creatures did not turn when they went,
but each one went straight forward.

10As for the likeness of their faces, *each*
had the face of a man; each of the four had
the face of a lion on the right side, each of
the four had the face of an ox on the left
side, and each of the four had the face of an
eagle. 11Thus *were* their faces. Their wings
stretched upward; two *wings* of each one
touched one another, and two covered their
bodies. 12And each one went straight forward; they went wherever the spirit wanted
to go, and they did not turn when they went.

13As for the likeness of the living creatures, their appearance *was* like burning
coals of fire, like the appearance of torches
going back and forth among the living creatures. The fire was bright, and out of the fire
went lightning. 14And the living creatures
ran back and forth, in appearance like a
flash of lightning.

15Now as I looked at the living creatures,
behold, a wheel *was* on the earth beside each
living creature with its four faces. 16The
appearance of the wheels and their workings *was* like the color of beryl, and all four
had the same likeness. The appearance of
their workings *was,* as it were, a wheel in
the middle of a wheel. 17When they moved,
they went toward any one of four directions;
they did not turn aside when they went. 18As
for their rims, they were so high they were
awesome; and their rims *were* full of eyes,
all around the four of them. 19When the living creatures went, the wheels went beside
them; and when the living creatures were
lifted up from the earth, the wheels were
lifted up. 20Wherever the spirit wanted to go,
they went, *because* there the spirit went; and
the wheels were lifted together with them,

1:1 [a] Following Masoretic Text, Septuagint, and Vulgate; Syriac and Targum read *a vision.* **1:3** [a] Or *Babylonians,* and so elsewhere in this book

Starring Roles

EZEKIEL'S name is pronounced *ee-ZEEK-yell* and means "God Will Strengthen." He was one of the Hebrew captives in Babylon 11 years before they destroyed Jerusalem and 597 years before Jesus came to earth.

Five years after Ezekiel arrived in Babylon, God called him to be a prophet. He was about 25 years old and was already a priest. After becoming a prophet, Ezekiel was very thankful for the amazing visions God gave him of His glory. You can read about those wonderful visions in chapters 1 and 10 of Ezekiel's book. Those visions show God's greatness, His power, and how He knows all things.

for the spirit of the living creatures[a] *was* in
the wheels. 21 When those went, *these* went;
when those stood, *these* stood; and when
those were lifted up from the earth, the
wheels were lifted up together with them,
for the spirit of the living creatures[a] *was* in
the wheels.

22 The likeness of the firmament above the
heads of the living creatures[a] *was* like the col-
or of an awesome crystal, stretched out over
their heads. 23 And under the firmament their
wings *spread out* straight, one toward another. Each one had two which covered one side,
and each one had two which covered the
other side of the body. 24 When they went, I
heard the noise of their wings, like the noise
of many waters, like the voice of the Almighty, a tumult like the noise of an army;
and when they stood still, they let down their
wings. 25 A voice came from above the firmament that *was* over their heads; whenever
they stood, they let down their wings.

1:20 [a] Literally *living creature;* Septuagint and Vulgate read *spirit of life;* Targum reads *creatures.* 1:21 [a] Literally *living creature;* Septuagint and Vulgate read *spirit of life;* Targum reads *creatures.* 1:22 [a] Following Septuagint, Targum, and Vulgate; Masoretic Text reads *living creature.*

GOD SENDS EZEKIEL A VISION

READ IT: EZEKIEL 1:1–28

GET IT:

Ezekiel was a prophet who was hauled off to Babylon with the second group of people who were captured. God called him to be a prophet to His people who were with him in Babylon. Ezekiel told the people what would happen back in Jerusalem. He also had some spectacular visions from God.

Ezekiel's first vision from God was super special but a little weird, the way dreams can be. The combination of colors, light, wind, fire, lightning, wild creatures, and wheels showed him what God's glory was like. This was how God called Ezekiel to be a prophet. God told Ezekiel to speak to the people of Israel. God warned him that the people might not listen, but it was his job to speak for God anyway. God also told him over and over again to not be afraid.

LIVE IT:

You know how dreams are—kind of scattered and jumpy. First, you're in one place and then in another. Sometimes people flash by who are strangers, but you recognize some of them. Sometimes you know what's going on, but sometimes it's just crazy stuff. Our dreams can mean something, but usually not. In ancient times God spoke to people in visions and dreams. It was a regular kind of thing.

What if you had a dream like this and heard God talk to you? What *would you do? Would* you find it easier to talk to God this way? Or would it be too scary? Do you prefer the calmer approach—where God speaks to us through the Bible?

16Moreover He said to me, “Son of man,
surely I will cut off the supply of bread in
Jerusalem; they shall eat bread by weight
and with anxiety, and shall drink water by
measure and with dread, 17that they may lack
bread and water, and be dismayed with one
another, and waste away because of their
iniquity.

A Sword Against Jerusalem

5 “And you, son of man, take a sharp
sword, take it as a barber’s razor, and
pass *it* over your head and your beard; then
take scales to weigh and divide the *hair*. 2You
shall burn with fire one-third in the midst
of the city, when the days of the siege are
finished; then you shall take one-third and
strike around *it* with the sword, and one-
third you shall scatter in the wind: I will
draw out a sword after them. 3You shall also
take a small number of them and bind them
in the edge of your *garment*. 4Then take
some of them again and throw them into
the midst of the fire, and burn them in the
fire. From there a fire will go out into all the
house of Israel.

5“Thus says the Lord GOD: ‘This *is* Jerusalem; I have set her in the midst of the nations and the countries all around her. 6She
has rebelled against My judgments by doing wickedness more than the nations, and
against My statutes more than the countries
that *are* all around her; for they have refused
My judgments, and they have not walked in
My statutes.’ 7Therefore thus says the Lord
GOD: ‘Because you have multiplied *disobedience* more than the nations that *are* all
around you, have not walked in My statutes
nor kept My judgments, nor even done[a] according to the judgments of the nations that
are all around you’— 8therefore thus says the
Lord GOD: ‘Indeed I, even I, *am* against you
and will execute judgments in your midst
in the sight of the nations. 9And I will do
among you what I have never done, and the
like of which I will never do again, because
of all your abominations. 10Therefore fathers
shall eat *their* sons in your midst, and sons
shall eat their fathers; and I will execute
judgments among you, and all of you who
remain I will scatter to all the winds.

11‘Therefore, *as* I live,’ says the Lord GOD,
‘surely, because you have defiled My sanctuary with all your detestable things and with
all your abominations, therefore I will also
diminish *you;* My eye will not spare, nor will
I have any pity. 12One-third of you shall die
of the pestilence, and be consumed with
famine in your midst; and one-third shall
fall by the sword all around you; and I will
scatter another third to all the winds, and I
will draw out a sword after them.

13‘Thus shall My anger be spent, and I will
cause My fury to rest upon them, and I
will be avenged; and they shall know that
I, the LORD, have spoken *it* in My zeal, when
I have spent My fury upon them. 14More-
over I will make you a waste and a reproach
among the nations that *are* all around you, in
the sight of all who pass by.

15‘So it[a] shall be a reproach, a taunt, a
lesson, and an astonishment to the nations
that *are* all around you, when I execute judgments among you in anger and in fury and
in furious rebukes. I, the LORD, have spoken.
16When I send against them the terrible arrows of famine which shall be for destruction, which I will send to destroy you, I will
increase the famine upon you and cut off
your supply of bread. 17So I will send against
you famine and wild beasts, and they will
bereave you. Pestilence and blood shall pass
through you, and I will bring the sword
against you. I, the LORD, have spoken.’ ”

Judgment on Idolatrous Israel

6 Now the word of the LORD came to me,
saying: 2“Son of man, set your face toward the mountains of Israel, and prophesy
against them, 3and say, ‘O mountains of Israel, hear the word of the Lord GOD! Thus
says the Lord GOD to the mountains, to the
hills, to the ravines, and to the valleys: “Indeed I, *even* I, will bring a sword against you,
and I will destroy your high places. 4Then
your altars shall be desolate, your incense
altars shall be broken, and I will cast down
your slain *men* before your idols. 5And I will
lay the corpses of the children of Israel before their idols, and I will scatter your bones
all around your altars. 6In all your dwelling
places the cities shall be laid waste, and the
high places shall be desolate, so that your altars may be laid waste and made desolate,
your idols may be broken and made to cease,
your incense altars may be cut down, and

5:7 [a] Following Masoretic Text, Septuagint, Targum, and Vulgate; many Hebrew manuscripts and Syriac read *but have done* (compare 11:12). 5:15 [a] Septuagint, Syriac, Targum, and Vulgate read *you*.

your works may be abolished. 7The slain
shall fall in your midst, and you shall know
that I *am* the LORD.
8"Yet I will leave a remnant, so that you
may have *some* who escape the sword among
the nations, when you are scattered through
the countries. 9Then those of you who escape will remember Me among the nations
where they are carried captive, because I was
crushed by their adulterous heart which has
departed from Me, and by their eyes which
play the harlot after their idols; they will
loathe themselves for the evils which they
committed in all their abominations. 10And
they shall know that I *am* the LORD; I have
not said in vain that I would bring this calamity upon them."
11'Thus says the Lord GOD: "Pound your
fists and stamp your feet, and say, 'Alas, for
all the evil abominations of the house of Israel! For they shall fall by the sword, by famine, and by pestilence. 12He who is far off
shall die by the pestilence, he who is near
shall fall by the sword, and he who remains
and is besieged shall die by the famine. Thus
will I spend My fury upon them. 13Then you
shall know that I *am* the LORD, when their
slain are among their idols all around their
altars, on every high hill, on all the mountaintops, under every green tree, and under
every thick oak, wherever they offered sweet
incense to all their idols. 14So I will stretch
out My hand against them and make the
land desolate, yes, more desolate than the
wilderness toward Diblah, in all their dwelling places. Then they shall know that I *am*
the LORD.'"'"

Judgment on Israel Is Near

7 Moreover the word of the LORD came
to me, saying, 2"And you, son of man,
thus says the Lord GOD to the land of Israel:

'An end! The end has come upon the
four corners of the land.
3 Now the end *has come* upon you,
And I will send My anger against you;
I will judge you according to your ways,
And I will repay you for all your
abominations.
4 My eye will not spare you,
Nor will I have pity;
But I will repay your ways,
And your abominations will be in your
midst;
Then you shall know that I *am* the
LORD!'

5"Thus says the Lord GOD:

'A disaster, a singular disaster;
Behold, it has come!
6 An end has come,
The end has come;
It has dawned for you;
Behold, it has come!
7 Doom has come to you, you who dwell
in the land;
The time has come,
A day of trouble *is* near,
And not of rejoicing in the mountains.
8 Now upon you I will soon pour out My
fury,
And spend My anger upon you;
I will judge you according to your ways,
And I will repay you for all your
abominations.

9 'My eye will not spare,
Nor will I have pity;
I will repay you according to your ways,
And your abominations will be in your
midst.
Then you shall know that I *am* the LORD
who strikes.

10 'Behold, the day!
Behold, it has come!
Doom has gone out;
The rod has blossomed,
Pride has budded.
11 Violence has risen up into a rod of
wickedness;
None of them *shall remain,*
None of their multitude,
None of them;
Nor *shall there be* wailing for them.
12 The time has come,
The day draws near.

'Let not the buyer rejoice,
Nor the seller mourn,
For wrath *is* on their whole multitude.
13 For the seller shall not return to what
has been sold,
Though he may still be alive;
For the vision concerns the whole
multitude,
And it shall not turn back;
No one will strengthen himself
Who lives in iniquity.

14 'They have blown the trumpet and made
everyone ready,

But no one goes to battle;
For My wrath *is* on all their multitude.
15 The sword *is* outside,
And the pestilence and famine within.
Whoever *is* in the field
Will die by the sword;
And whoever *is* in the city,
Famine and pestilence will devour him.

16 'Those who survive will escape and be
on the mountains
Like doves of the valleys,
All of them mourning,
Each for his iniquity.
17 Every hand will be feeble,
And every knee will be *as* weak *as* water.
18 They will also be girded with sackcloth;
Horror will cover them;
Shame *will be* on every face,
Baldness on all their heads.

19 'They will throw their silver into the
streets,
And their gold will be like refuse;
Their silver and their gold will not be
able to deliver them
In the day of the wrath of the LORD;
They will not satisfy their souls,
Nor fill their stomachs,
Because it became their stumbling
block of iniquity.

20 'As for the beauty of his ornaments,
He set it in majesty;
But they made from it
The images of their abominations—
Their detestable things;
Therefore I have made it
Like refuse to them.
21 I will give it as plunder
Into the hands of strangers,
And to the wicked of the earth as spoil;
And they shall defile it.
22 I will turn My face from them,
And they will defile My secret place;
For robbers shall enter it and defile it.

23 'Make a chain,
For the land is filled with crimes of
blood,
And the city is full of violence.
24 Therefore I will bring the worst of the
Gentiles,
And they will possess their houses;
I will cause the pomp of the strong to
cease,
And their holy places shall be defiled.
25 Destruction comes;
They will seek peace, but *there shall be*
none.
26 Disaster will come upon disaster,
And rumor will be upon rumor.
Then they will seek a vision from a
prophet;
But the law will perish from the priest,
And counsel from the elders.

27 'The king will mourn,
The prince will be clothed with
desolation,
And the hands of the common people
will tremble.
I will do to them according to their way,
And according to what they deserve I
will judge them;
Then they shall know that I *am* the
LORD!' "

Abominations in the Temple

8 And it came to pass in the sixth year, in
the sixth *month,* on the fifth *day* of the
month, as I sat in my house with the elders
of Judah sitting before me, that the hand of
the Lord GOD fell upon me there. 2Then I
looked, and there was a likeness, like the
appearance of fire—from the appearance
of His waist and downward, fire; and from
His waist and upward, like the appearance
of brightness, like the color of amber. 3He
stretched out the form of a hand, and took
me by a lock of my hair; and the Spirit lifted me up between earth and heaven, and
brought me in visions of God to Jerusalem,
to the door of the north gate of the inner
court, where the seat of the image of jealousy
was, which provokes to jealousy. 4And behold, the glory of the God of Israel *was* there,
like the vision that I saw in the plain.
5Then He said to me, "Son of man, lift
your eyes now toward the north." So I lifted
my eyes toward the north, and there, north
of the altar gate, was this image of jealousy
in the entrance.
6Furthermore He said to me, "Son of
man, do you see what they are doing, the
great abominations that the house of Israel
commits here, to make Me go far away from
My sanctuary? Now turn again, you will see
greater abominations." 7So He brought me
to the door of the court; and when I looked,
there was a hole in the wall. 8Then He said
to me, "Son of man, dig into the wall"; and
when I dug into the wall, there was a door.

9And He said to me, "Go in, and see the wicked abominations which they are doing there." 10So I went in and saw, and there—every sort of creeping thing, abominable beasts, and all the idols of the house of Israel, portrayed all around on the walls. 11And there stood before them seventy men of the elders of the house of Israel, and in their midst stood Jaazaniah the son of Shaphan. Each man had a censer in his hand, and a thick cloud of incense went up. 12Then He said to me, "Son of man, have you seen what the elders of the house of Israel do in the dark, every man in the room of his idols? For they say, 'The LORD does not see us, the LORD has forsaken the land.'"

13And He said to me, "Turn again, *and* you will see greater abominations that they are doing." 14So He brought me to the door of the north gate of the LORD's house; and to my dismay, women were sitting there weeping for Tammuz.

15Then He said to me, "Have you seen *this,* O son of man? Turn again, you will see greater abominations than these." 16So He brought me into the inner court of the LORD's house; and there, at the door of the temple of the LORD, between the porch and the altar, *were* about twenty-five men with their backs toward the temple of the LORD and their faces toward the east, and they were worshiping the sun toward the east.

17And He said to me, "Have you seen *this,* O son of man? Is it a trivial thing to the house of Judah to commit the abominations which they commit here? For they have filled the land with violence; then they have returned to provoke Me to anger. Indeed they put the branch to their nose. 18Therefore I also will act in fury. My eye will not spare nor will I have pity; and though they cry in My ears with a loud voice, I will not hear them."

The Wicked Are Slain

9 Then He called out in my hearing with a loud voice, saying, "Let those who have charge over the city draw near, each *with* a deadly weapon in his hand." 2And suddenly six men came from the direction of the upper gate, which faces north, each with *his* battle-ax *in* his hand. One man among them *was* clothed with linen and had a writer's inkhorn at his side. They went in and stood beside the bronze altar.

3Now the glory of the God of Israel had gone up from the cherub, where it had been, to the threshold of the temple.[a] And He called to the man clothed with linen, who *had* the writer's inkhorn at his side; 4and the LORD said to him, "Go through the midst of the city, through the midst of Jerusalem, and put a mark on the foreheads of the men who sigh and cry over all the abominations that are done within it."

5To the others He said in my hearing, "Go after him through the city and kill; do not let your eye spare, nor have any pity. 6Utterly slay old *and* young men, maidens and little children and women; but do not come near anyone on whom *is* the mark; and begin at My sanctuary." So they began with the elders who *were* before the temple. 7Then He said to them, "Defile the temple, and fill the courts with the slain. Go out!" And they went out and killed in the city.

8So it was, that while they were killing them, I was left *alone;* and I fell on my face and cried out, and said, "Ah, Lord GOD! Will You destroy all the remnant of Israel in pouring out Your fury on Jerusalem?"

9Then He said to me, "The iniquity of the house of Israel and Judah *is* exceedingly great, and the land is full of bloodshed, and the city full of perversity; for they say, 'The LORD has forsaken the land, and the LORD does not see!' 10And as for Me also, My eye will neither spare, nor will I have pity, *but* I will recompense their deeds on their own head."

11Just then, the man clothed with linen, who *had* the inkhorn at his side, reported back and said, "I have done as You commanded me."

The Glory Departs from the Temple

10 And I looked, and there in the firmament that was above the head of the cherubim, there appeared something like a sapphire stone, having the appearance of the likeness of a throne. 2Then He spoke to the man clothed with linen, and said, "Go in among the wheels, under the cherub, fill your hands with coals of fire from among the cherubim, and scatter *them* over the city." And he went in as I watched.

3Now the cherubim were standing on the south side of the temple[a] when the man went in, and the cloud filled the inner court.

9:3 [a] Literally *house* 10:3 [a] Literally *house,* also in verses 4 and 18

4Then the glory of the LORD went up from
the cherub, *and paused* over the threshold of
the temple; and the house was filled with the
cloud, and the court was full of the brightness of the LORD's glory. 5And the sound of
the wings of the cherubim was heard *even*
in the outer court, like the voice of Almighty
God when He speaks.

6Then it happened, when He commanded the man clothed in linen, saying, "Take
fire from among the wheels, from among
the cherubim," that he went in and stood beside the wheels. 7And the cherub stretched
out his hand from among the cherubim to
the fire that *was* among the cherubim, and
took *some of it* and put *it* into the hands of
the *man* clothed with linen, who took *it* and
went out. 8The cherubim appeared to have
the form of a man's hand under their wings.

9And when I looked, there were four
wheels by the cherubim, one wheel by one
cherub and another wheel by each other
cherub; the wheels appeared *to have* the color
of a beryl stone. 10*As for* their appearance, all
four looked alike—as it were, a wheel in the
middle of a wheel. 11When they went, they
went toward *any of* their four directions; they
did not turn aside when they went, but followed in the direction the head was facing.
They did not turn aside when they went.
12And their whole body, with their back, their
hands, their wings, and the wheels that the
four had, *were* full of eyes all around. 13As for
the wheels, they were called in my hearing,
"Wheel."

14Each one had four faces: the first face
was the face of a cherub, the second face the
face of a man, the third the face of a lion,
and the fourth the face of an eagle. 15And the
cherubim were lifted up. This *was* the living
creature I saw by the River Chebar. 16When
the cherubim went, the wheels went beside
them; and when the cherubim lifted their
wings to mount up from the earth, the same
wheels also did not turn from beside them.
17When *the cherubim*[a] stood still, *the wheels*
stood still, and when *one*[b] was lifted up, *the*
other[c] lifted itself up, for the spirit of the living creature *was* in them.

18Then the glory of the LORD departed
from the threshold of the temple and stood
over the cherubim. 19And the cherubim lifted their wings and mounted up from the
earth in my sight. When they went out, the
wheels *were* beside them; and they stood at
the door of the east gate of the LORD's house,
and the glory of the God of Israel *was* above
them.

20This *is* the living creature I saw under
the God of Israel by the River Chebar, and
I knew they *were* cherubim. 21Each one had
four faces and each one four wings, and the
likeness of the hands of a man *was* under
their wings. 22And the likeness of their faces *was* the same *as* the faces which I had
seen by the River Chebar, their appearance
and their persons. They each went straight
forward.

Judgment on Wicked Counselors

11 Then the Spirit lifted me up and
brought me to the East Gate of the
LORD's house, which faces eastward; and
there at the door of the gate were twenty-five
men, among whom I saw Jaazaniah the son
of Azzur, and Pelatiah the son of Benaiah,
princes of the people. 2And He said to me:
"Son of man, these *are* the men who devise
iniquity and give wicked counsel in this city,
3who say, '*The time is* not near to build houses; this *city is* the caldron, and we *are* the
meat.' 4Therefore prophesy against them,
prophesy, O son of man!"

5Then the Spirit of the LORD fell upon
me, and said to me, "Speak! 'Thus says the
LORD: "Thus you have said, O house of Israel; for I know the things that come into
your mind. 6You have multiplied your slain
in this city, and you have filled its streets
with the slain." 7Therefore thus says the
Lord GOD: "Your slain whom you have laid
in its midst, they *are* the meat, and this *city*
is the caldron; but I shall bring you out of the
midst of it. 8You have feared the sword; and
I will bring a sword upon you," says the Lord
GOD. 9"And I will bring you out of its midst,
and deliver you into the hands of strangers,
and execute judgments on you. 10You shall
fall by the sword. I will judge you at the border of Israel. Then you shall know that I *am*
the LORD. 11This *city* shall not be your caldron, nor shall you be the meat in its midst.
I will judge you at the border of Israel. 12And
you shall know that I *am* the LORD; for you
have not walked in My statutes nor executed My judgments, but have done according
to the customs of the Gentiles which *are* all
around you."'"

13Now it happened, while I was prophesying, that Pelatiah the son of Benaiah
died. Then I fell on my face and cried with

10:17 [a] Literally *they* [b] Literally *they* [c] Literally *they*

a loud voice, and said, "Ah, Lord GOD! Will
You make a complete end of the remnant of
Israel?"

God Will Restore Israel

[14]Again the word of the LORD came to
me, saying, [15]"Son of man, your brethren,
your relatives, your countrymen, and all
the house of Israel in its entirety, *are* those
about whom the inhabitants of Jerusalem
have said, 'Get far away from the LORD; this
land has been given to us as a possession.'
[16]Therefore say, 'Thus says the Lord GOD:
"Although I have cast them far off among
the Gentiles, and although I have scattered
them among the countries, yet I shall be a
little sanctuary for them in the countries
where they have gone."' [17]Therefore say,
'Thus says the Lord GOD: "I will gather you
from the peoples, assemble you from the
countries where you have been scattered,
and I will give you the land of Israel."' [18]And
they will go there, and they will take away
all its detestable things and all its abominations from there. [19]Then I will give them
one heart, and I will put a new spirit within
them,[a] and take the stony heart out of their
flesh, and give them a heart of flesh, [20]that
they may walk in My statutes and keep My
judgments and do them; and they shall be
My people, and I will be their God. [21]But *as
for those* whose hearts follow the desire for
their detestable things and their abominations, I will recompense their deeds on their
own heads," says the Lord GOD.

[22]So the cherubim lifted up their wings,
with the wheels beside them, and the glory
of the God of Israel *was* high above them.
[23]And the glory of the LORD went up from the
midst of the city and stood on the mountain,
which *is* on the east side of the city.

[24]Then the Spirit took me up and brought
me in a vision by the Spirit of God into Chaldea,[a] to those in captivity. And the vision that
I had seen went up from me. [25]So I spoke to
those in captivity of all the things the LORD
had shown me.

Judah's Captivity Portrayed

12 Now the word of the LORD came to
me, saying: [2]"Son of man, you dwell
in the midst of a rebellious house, which has
eyes to see but does not see, and ears to hear
but does not hear; for they *are* a rebellious
house.

[3]"Therefore, son of man, prepare your
belongings for captivity, and go into captivity by day in their sight. You shall go from
your place into captivity to another place in
their sight. It may be that they will consider,
though they *are* a rebellious house. [4]By day
you shall bring out your belongings in their
sight, as though going into captivity; and at
evening you shall go in their sight, like those
who go into captivity. [5]Dig through the wall
in their sight, and carry *your belongings* out
through it. [6]In their sight you shall bear *them*
on *your* shoulders *and* carry *them* out at twilight; you shall cover your face, so that you
cannot see the ground, for I have made you
a sign to the house of Israel."

[7]So I did as I was commanded. I brought
out my belongings by day, as though going
into captivity, and at evening I dug through
the wall with my hand. I brought *them* out
at twilight, *and* I bore *them* on *my* shoulder
in their sight.

[8]And in the morning the word of the
LORD came to me, saying, [9]"Son of man, has
not the house of Israel, the rebellious house,
said to you, 'What are you doing?' [10]Say to
them, 'Thus says the Lord GOD: "This burden *concerns* the prince in Jerusalem and all
the house of Israel who are among them."'
[11]Say, 'I *am* a sign to you. As I have done, so
shall it be done to them; they shall be carried away into captivity.' [12]And the prince
who *is* among them shall bear *his belongings*
on *his* shoulder at twilight and go out. They
shall dig through the wall to carry *them* out
through it. He shall cover his face, so that he
cannot see the ground with *his* eyes. [13]I will
also spread My net over him, and he shall
be caught in My snare. I will bring him to
Babylon, *to* the land of the Chaldeans; yet he
shall not see it, though he shall die there. [14]I
will scatter to every wind all who *are* around
him to help him, and all his troops; and I
will draw out the sword after them.

[15]"Then they shall know that I *am* the
LORD, when I scatter them among the nations and disperse them throughout the
countries. [16]But I will spare a few of their
men from the sword, from famine, and from
pestilence, that they may declare all their
abominations among the Gentiles wherever

11:19 [a] Literally *you* **11:24** [a] Or *Babylon,* and so elsewhere in this book

they go. Then they shall know that I *am* the
LORD."

Judgment Not Postponed

17 Moreover the word of the LORD came
to me, saying, 18 "Son of man, eat your bread
with quaking, and drink your water with
trembling and anxiety. 19 And say to the people of the land, 'Thus says the Lord GOD to
the inhabitants of Jerusalem *and* to the land
of Israel: "They shall eat their bread with
anxiety, and drink their water with dread,
so that her land may be emptied of all who
are in it, because of the violence of all those
who dwell in it. 20 Then the cities that are
inhabited shall be laid waste, and the land
shall become desolate; and you shall know
that I *am* the LORD."'"

21 And the word of the LORD came to me,
saying, 22 "Son of man, what *is* this proverb
that you *people* have about the land of Israel,
which says, 'The days are prolonged, and every vision fails'? 23 Tell them therefore, 'Thus
says the Lord GOD: "I will lay this proverb
to rest, and they shall no more use it as a
proverb in Israel."' But say to them, '"The
days are at hand, and the fulfillment of every vision. 24 For no more shall there be any
false vision or flattering divination within
the house of Israel. 25 For I *am* the LORD. I

GOD'S WARNING OF EXILE IN BABYLON

READ IT: EZEKIEL 12:1–16

GET IT:

God told Ezekiel to act out some of the events going on back in Jerusalem (about eight hundred miles away). He did these little plays because the Israelites (called "a rebellious house" in verses 2, 3, and 9) didn't really want to listen to him. They probably hoped to hear good news—that everything was fine back in Judah and that the people there were the lucky ones. But that's not what was happening. Nebuchadnezzar was ready to attack and destroy Jerusalem. He would capture the rest of the people and bring them to Babylon just like the first group. It wasn't good news, that's for sure. And it wasn't what they wanted to hear, but it was Ezekiel's job to tell them what was going on back home.

LIVE IT:

We live in a time of instant and constant news. Check the Internet and you know right away what's going on in Hollywood, New York, Africa, China, or Afghanistan. That's not how it was in Bible times. The captured people in Babylon had no Internet, no TV, and no radio to find out what was happening to the people still in Judah. They had only one "newscaster," Ezekiel, and they really didn't like listening to him. But they couldn't change the channel or check another Internet site. Ezekiel's source was solid—his story came straight from God. Who's your source of information and guidance? Do you listen to people of God as much as you listen to others?

speak, and the word which I speak will come to pass; it will no more be postponed; for in your days, O rebellious house, I will say the word and perform it," says the Lord GOD.'"

26 Again the word of the LORD came to me, saying, 27 "Son of man, look, the house of Israel is saying, 'The vision that he sees *is* for many days *from now,* and he prophesies of times far off.' 28 Therefore say to them, 'Thus says the Lord GOD: "None of My words will be postponed any more, but the word which I speak will be done," says the Lord GOD.'"

Woe to Foolish Prophets

13 And the word of the LORD came to me, saying, 2 "Son of man, prophesy against the prophets of Israel who prophesy, and say to those who prophesy out of their own heart, 'Hear the word of the LORD!'"

3 Thus says the Lord GOD: "Woe to the foolish prophets, who follow their own spirit and have seen nothing! 4 O Israel, your prophets are like foxes in the deserts. 5 You have not gone up into the gaps to build a wall for the house of Israel to stand in battle on the day of the LORD. 6 They have envisioned futility and false divination, saying, 'Thus says the LORD!' But the LORD has not sent them; yet they hope that the word may be confirmed. 7 Have you not seen a futile vision, and have you not spoken false divination? You say, 'The LORD says,' but I have not spoken."

8 Therefore thus says the Lord GOD: "Because you have spoken nonsense and envisioned lies, therefore I *am* indeed against you," says the Lord GOD. 9 "My hand will be against the prophets who envision futility and who divine lies; they shall not be in the assembly of My people, nor be written in the record of the house of Israel, nor shall they enter into the land of Israel. Then you shall know that I *am* the Lord GOD.

10 "Because, indeed, because they have seduced My people, saying, 'Peace!' when *there is* no peace—and one builds a wall, and they plaster it with untempered *mortar*— 11 say to those who plaster *it* with untempered *mortar,* that it will fall. There will be flooding rain, and you, O great hailstones, shall fall; and a stormy wind shall tear *it* down. 12 Surely, when the wall has fallen, will it not be said to you, 'Where *is* the mortar with which you plastered *it?*'"

13 Therefore thus says the Lord GOD: "I will cause a stormy wind to break forth in My fury; and there shall be a flooding rain in My anger, and great hailstones in fury to consume *it.* 14 So I will break down the wall you have plastered with untempered *mortar,* and bring it down to the ground, so that its foundation will be uncovered; it will fall, and you shall be consumed in the midst of it. Then you shall know that I *am* the LORD.

15 "Thus will I accomplish My wrath on the wall and on those who have plastered it with untempered *mortar;* and I will say to you, 'The wall *is* no *more,* nor those who plastered it, 16 *that is,* the prophets of Israel who prophesy concerning Jerusalem, and who see visions of peace for her when *there is* no peace,'" says the Lord GOD.

17 "Likewise, son of man, set your face against the daughters of your people, who prophesy out of their own heart; prophesy against them, 18 and say, 'Thus says the Lord GOD: "Woe to the *women* who sew *magic* charms on their sleeves[a] and make veils for the heads of people of every height to hunt souls! Will you hunt the souls of My people, and keep yourselves alive? 19 And will you profane Me among My people for handfuls of barley and for pieces of bread, killing people who should not die, and keeping people alive who should not live, by your lying to My people who listen to lies?"

20 'Therefore thus says the Lord GOD: "Behold, I *am* against your *magic* charms by which you hunt souls there like birds. I will tear them from your arms, and let the souls go, the souls you hunt like birds. 21 I will also tear off your veils and deliver My people out of your hand, and they shall no longer be as prey in your hand. Then you shall know that I *am* the LORD.

22 "Because with lies you have made the heart of the righteous sad, whom I have not made sad; and you have strengthened the hands of the wicked, so that he does not turn from his wicked way to save his life. 23 Therefore you shall no longer envision futility nor practice divination; for I will deliver My people out of your hand, and you shall know that I *am* the LORD."'"

Idolatry Will Be Punished

14 Now some of the elders of Israel came to me and sat before me. 2 And the word of the LORD came to me, saying, 3 "Son of man, these men have set up their

13:18 [a] Literally *over all the joints of My hands;* Vulgate reads *under every elbow;* Septuagint and Targum read *on all elbows of the hands.*

idols in their hearts, and put before them
that which causes them to stumble into iniquity. Should I let Myself be inquired of at
all by them?
4"Therefore speak to them, and say to
them, 'Thus says the Lord GOD: "Everyone
of the house of Israel who sets up his idols
in his heart, and puts before him what causes him to stumble into iniquity, and then
comes to the prophet, I the LORD will answer
him who comes, according to the multitude
of his idols, 5that I may seize the house of
Israel by their heart, because they are all estranged from Me by their idols." '
6"Therefore say to the house of Israel,
'Thus says the Lord GOD: "Repent, turn
away from your idols, and turn your faces
away from all your abominations. 7For anyone of the house of Israel, or of the strangers
who dwell in Israel, who separates himself
from Me and sets up his idols in his heart
and puts before him what causes him to
stumble into iniquity, then comes to a
prophet to inquire of him concerning Me, I
the LORD will answer him by Myself. 8I will
set My face against that man and make him
a sign and a proverb, and I will cut him off
from the midst of My people. Then you shall
know that I *am* the LORD.
9"And if the prophet is induced to speak
anything, I the LORD have induced that
prophet, and I will stretch out My hand
against him and destroy him from among
My people Israel. 10And they shall bear their
iniquity; the punishment of the prophet
shall be the same as the punishment of the
one who inquired, 11that the house of Israel
may no longer stray from Me, nor be profaned anymore with all their transgressions,
but that they may be My people and I may be
their God," says the Lord GOD.' "

Judgment on Persistent Unfaithfulness

12The word of the LORD came again to
me, saying: 13"Son of man, when a land sins
against Me by persistent unfaithfulness, I
will stretch out My hand against it; I will cut
off its supply of bread, send famine on it, and
cut off man and beast from it. 14Even *if* these
three men, Noah, Daniel, and Job, were in it,
they would deliver *only* themselves by their
righteousness," says the Lord GOD.
15"If I cause wild beasts to pass through
the land, and they empty it, and make it so
desolate that no man may pass through because of the beasts, 16*even though* these three
men *were* in it, *as* I live," says the Lord GOD,
"they would deliver neither sons nor daughters; only they would be delivered, and the
land would be desolate.
17"Or *if* I bring a sword on that land, and
say, 'Sword, go through the land,' and I cut
off man and beast from it, 18even *though*
these three men *were* in it, *as* I live," says the
Lord GOD, "they would deliver neither sons
nor daughters, but only they themselves
would be delivered.
19"Or *if* I send a pestilence into that land
and pour out My fury on it in blood, and
cut off from it man and beast, 20even *though*
Noah, Daniel, and Job *were* in it, *as* I live,"
says the Lord GOD, "they would deliver neither son nor daughter; they would deliver
only themselves by their righteousness."
21For thus says the Lord GOD: "How much
more it shall be when I send My four severe
judgments on Jerusalem—the sword and
famine and wild beasts and pestilence—to
cut off man and beast from it? 22Yet behold,
there shall be left in it a remnant who will be
brought out, *both* sons and daughters; surely
they will come out to you, and you will see
their ways and their doings. Then you will
be comforted concerning the disaster that I
have brought upon Jerusalem, all that I have
brought upon it. 23And they will comfort you,
when you see their ways and their doings;
and you shall know that I have done nothing
without cause that I have done in it," says
the Lord GOD.

The Outcast Vine

15 Then the word of the LORD came
to me, saying: 2"Son of man, how is
the wood of the vine *better* than any other
wood, the vine branch which is among the
trees of the forest? 3Is wood taken from it to
make any object? Or can *men* make a peg
from it to hang any vessel on? 4Instead, it is
thrown into the fire for fuel; the fire devours
both ends of it, and its middle is burned.
Is it useful for *any* work? 5Indeed, when it
was whole, no object could be made from
it. How much less will it be useful for *any*
work when the fire has devoured it, and it
is burned?
6"Therefore thus says the Lord GOD:
'Like the wood of the vine among the trees
of the forest, which I have given to the fire

for fuel, so I will give up the inhabitants of
Jerusalem; 7and I will set My face against
them. They will go out from *one* fire, but
another fire shall devour them. Then you
shall know that I *am* the LORD, when I set
My face against them. 8Thus I will make the
land desolate, because they have persisted in
unfaithfulness,' says the Lord GOD."

God's Love for Jerusalem

16 Again the word of the LORD came
to me, saying, 2"Son of man, cause
Jerusalem to know her abominations, 3and
say, 'Thus says the Lord GOD to Jerusalem:
"Your birth and your nativity *are* from the
land of Canaan; your father *was* an Amorite
and your mother a Hittite. 4*As for* your nativity, on the day you were born your navel
cord was not cut, nor were you washed in
water to cleanse *you;* you were not rubbed
with salt nor wrapped in swaddling cloths.
5No eye pitied you, to do any of these things
for you, to have compassion on you; but you
were thrown out into the open field, when
you yourself were loathed on the day you
were born.

6"And when I passed by you and saw
you struggling in your own blood, I said to
you in your blood, 'Live!' Yes, I said to you
in your blood, 'Live!' 7I made you thrive like
a plant in the field; and you grew, matured,
and became very beautiful. *Your* breasts
were formed, your hair grew, but you *were*
naked and bare.

8"When I passed by you again and looked
upon you, indeed your time *was* the time of
love; so I spread My wing over you and covered your nakedness. Yes, I swore an oath to
you and entered into a covenant with you,
and you became Mine," says the Lord GOD.

9"Then I washed you in water; yes, I thoroughly washed off your blood, and I anointed
you with oil. 10I clothed you in embroidered
cloth and gave you sandals of badger skin; I
clothed you with fine linen and covered you
with silk. 11I adorned you with ornaments,
put bracelets on your wrists, and a chain on
your neck. 12And I put a jewel in your nose,
earrings in your ears, and a beautiful crown
on your head. 13Thus you were adorned with
gold and silver, and your clothing *was of* fine
linen, silk, and embroidered cloth. You ate
pastry of fine flour, honey, and oil. You were
exceedingly beautiful, and succeeded to royalty. 14Your fame went out among the nations
because of your beauty, for it *was* perfect
through My splendor which I had bestowed
on you," says the Lord GOD.

In Focus

16:4 Swaddling Cloths Cloths, like bandages, to wrap newborn babies. In Jesus' time, swaddling cloths were used to keep a baby's limbs straight.

Jerusalem's Harlotry

15"But you trusted in your own beauty,
played the harlot because of your fame, and
poured out your harlotry on everyone passing by who *would have* it. 16You took some
of your garments and adorned multicolored
high places for yourself, and played the harlot on them. *Such* things should not happen,
nor be. 17You have also taken your beautiful
jewelry from My gold and My silver, which I
had given you, and made for yourself male
images and played the harlot with them.
18You took your embroidered garments and
covered them, and you set My oil and My incense before them. 19Also My food which I
gave you—the pastry of fine flour, oil, and
honey *which* I fed you—you set it before
them as sweet incense; and *so* it was," says
the Lord GOD.

20"Moreover you took your sons and your
daughters, whom you bore to Me, and these
you sacrificed to them to be devoured. *Were*
your *acts* of harlotry a small matter, 21that
you have slain My children and offered them
up to them by causing them to pass through
the fire? 22And in all your abominations and
acts of harlotry you did not remember the
days of your youth, when you were naked
and bare, struggling in your blood.

23"Then it was so, after all your
wickedness—'Woe, woe to you!' says the
Lord GOD— 24*that* you also built for yourself
a shrine, and made a high place for yourself
in every street. 25You built your high places at the head of every road, and made your
beauty to be abhorred. You offered yourself
to everyone who passed by, and multiplied
your acts of harlotry. 26You also committed harlotry with the Egyptians, your very

fleshly neighbors, and increased your acts
of harlotry to provoke Me to anger.

27"Behold, therefore, I stretched out My
hand against you, diminished your allotment, and gave you up to the will of those
who hate you, the daughters of the Philistines, who were ashamed of your lewd
behavior. 28You also played the harlot with
the Assyrians, because you were insatiable;
indeed you played the harlot with them and
still were not satisfied. 29Moreover you multiplied your acts of harlotry as far as the land
of the trader, Chaldea; and even then you
were not satisfied.

30"How degenerate is your heart!" says
the Lord God, "seeing you do all these *things,*
the deeds of a brazen harlot.

Jerusalem's Adultery

31"You erected your shrine at the head of
every road, and built your high place in every
street. Yet you were not like a harlot, because
you scorned payment. 32*You are* an adulterous wife, *who* takes strangers instead of her
husband. 33Men make payment to all harlots,
but you made your payments to all your lovers, and hired them to come to you from all
around for your harlotry. 34You are the opposite of *other* women in your harlotry, because
no one solicited you to be a harlot. In that
you gave payment but no payment was given
you, therefore you are the opposite."

Jerusalem's Lovers Will Abuse Her

35'Now then, O harlot, hear the word of
the Lord! 36Thus says the Lord God: "Because your filthiness was poured out and
your nakedness uncovered in your harlotry
with your lovers, and with all your abominable idols, and because of the blood of your
children which you gave to them, 37surely,
therefore, I will gather all your lovers with
whom you took pleasure, all those you loved,
and all those you hated; I will gather them
from all around against you and will uncover
your nakedness to them, that they may see
all your nakedness. 38And I will judge you
as women who break wedlock or shed blood
are judged; I will bring blood upon you in
fury and jealousy. 39I will also give you into
their hand, and they shall throw down your
shrines and break down your high places.
They shall also strip you of your clothes, take
your beautiful jewelry, and leave you naked
and bare.

40"They shall also bring up an assembly
against you, and they shall stone you with
stones and thrust you through with their
swords. 41They shall burn your houses with
fire, and execute judgments on you in the
sight of many women; and I will make you
cease playing the harlot, and you shall no
longer hire lovers. 42So I will lay to rest My
fury toward you, and My jealousy shall depart from you. I will be quiet, and be angry
no more. 43Because you did not remember
the days of your youth, but agitated Me[a] with
all these *things,* surely I will also recompense
your deeds on *your own* head," says the Lord
God. "And you shall not commit lewdness in
addition to all your abominations.

More Wicked than Samaria and Sodom

44"Indeed everyone who quotes proverbs
will use *this* proverb against you: 'Like mother, like daughter!' 45You *are* your mother's
daughter, loathing husband and children;
and you *are* the sister of your sisters, who
loathed their husbands and children; your
mother *was* a Hittite and your father an
Amorite.

46"Your elder sister *is* Samaria, who
dwells with her daughters to the north of
you; and your younger sister, who dwells to
the south of you, *is* Sodom and her daughters. 47You did not walk in their ways nor act
according to their abominations; but, as *if*
that were too little, you became more corrupt
than they in all your ways.

48"*As* I live," says the Lord God, "neither
your sister Sodom nor her daughters have
done as you and your daughters have done.
49Look, this was the iniquity of your sister
Sodom: She and her daughter had pride,
fullness of food, and abundance of idleness;
neither did she strengthen the hand of the
poor and needy. 50And they were haughty
and committed abomination before Me;
therefore I took them away as I saw *fit.*[a]

51"Samaria did not commit half of your
sins; but you have multiplied your abominations more than they, and have justified your
sisters by all the abominations which you
have done. 52You who judged your sisters,

16:43 [a] Following Septuagint, Syriac, Targum, and Vulgate; Masoretic Text reads *were agitated with Me.* **16:50** [a] Vulgate reads *you saw;* Septuagint reads *he saw;* Targum reads *as was revealed to Me.*

bear your own shame also, because the sins
which you committed were more abominable than theirs; they are more righteous
than you. Yes, be disgraced also, and bear
your own shame, because you justified your
sisters.
53"When I bring back their captives, the
captives of Sodom and her daughters, and
the captives of Samaria and her daughters,
then *I will also bring back* the captives of your
captivity among them, 54that you may bear
your own shame and be disgraced by all that
you did when you comforted them. 55When
your sisters, Sodom and her daughters, return to their former state, and Samaria and
her daughters return to their former state,
then you and your daughters will return
to your former state. 56For your sister Sodom was not a byword in your mouth in the
days of your pride, 57before your wickedness
was uncovered. It was like the time of the
reproach of the daughters of Syria[a] and all
those around her, and of the daughters of the
Philistines, who despise you everywhere.
58You have paid for your lewdness and your
abominations," says the LORD. 59For thus
says the Lord GOD: "I will deal with you as
you have done, who despised the oath by
breaking the covenant.

An Everlasting Covenant

60"Nevertheless I will remember My covenant with you in the days of your youth,
and I will establish an everlasting covenant
with you. 61Then you will remember your
ways and be ashamed, when you receive
your older and your younger sisters; for I
will give them to you for daughters, but not
because of My covenant with you. 62And I
will establish My covenant with you. Then
you shall know that I *am* the LORD, 63that you
may remember and be ashamed, and never
open your mouth anymore because of your
shame, when I provide you an atonement for
all you have done," says the Lord GOD.'"

The Eagles and the Vine

17 And the word of the LORD came to
me, saying, 2"Son of man, pose a
riddle, and speak a parable to the house of
Israel, 3and say, 'Thus says the Lord GOD:

"A great eagle with large wings and long
pinions,
Full of feathers of various colors,
Came to Lebanon
And took from the cedar the highest
branch.
4 He cropped off its topmost young twig
And carried it to a land of trade;
He set it in a city of merchants.
5 Then he took some of the seed of the
land
And planted it in a fertile field;
He placed *it* by abundant waters
And set it like a willow tree.
6 And it grew and became a spreading
vine of low stature;
Its branches turned toward him,
But its roots were under it.
So it became a vine,
Brought forth branches,
And put forth shoots.

7 "But there was another[a] great eagle with
large wings and many feathers;
And behold, this vine bent its roots
toward him,
And stretched its branches toward him,
From the garden terrace where it had
been planted,
That he might water it.
8 It was planted in good soil by many
waters,
To bring forth branches, bear fruit,
And become a majestic vine."'

9"Say, 'Thus says the Lord GOD:

"Will it thrive?
Will he not pull up its roots,
Cut off its fruit,
And leave it to wither?
All of its spring leaves will wither,
And no great power or many people
Will be needed to pluck it up by its
roots.
10 Behold, *it is* planted,
Will it thrive?
Will it not utterly wither when the east
wind touches it?
It will wither in the garden terrace
where it grew."'"

11Moreover the word of the LORD came
to me, saying, 12"Say now to the rebellious
house: 'Do you not know what these *things*

16:57 [a] Following Masoretic Text, Septuagint, Targum, and Vulgate; many Hebrew manuscripts and Syriac read *Edom*.
17:7 [a] Following Septuagint, Syriac, and Vulgate; Masoretic Text and Targum read *one*.

mean?' Tell *them,* 'Indeed the king of Babylon went to Jerusalem and took its king and
princes, and led them with him to Babylon.
13And he took the king's offspring, made a
covenant with him, and put him under oath.
He also took away the mighty of the land,
14that the kingdom might be brought low
and not lift itself up, *but* that by keeping his
covenant it might stand. 15But he rebelled
against him by sending his ambassadors to
Egypt, that they might give him horses and
many people. Will he prosper? Will he who
does such *things* escape? Can he break a covenant and still be delivered?

16'*As* I live,' says the Lord GOD, 'surely in the place *where* the king *dwells* who
made him king, whose oath he despised
and whose covenant he broke—with him
in the midst of Babylon he shall die. 17Nor
will Pharaoh with *his* mighty army and great
company do anything in the war, when they
heap up a siege mound and build a wall to
cut off many persons. 18Since he despised the
oath by breaking the covenant, and in fact
gave his hand and still did all these *things,*
he shall not escape.'"

19Therefore thus says the Lord GOD: "*As* I
live, surely My oath which he despised, and
My covenant which he broke, I will recompense on his own head. 20I will spread My
net over him, and he shall be taken in My
snare. I will bring him to Babylon and try
him there for the treason which he committed against Me. 21All his fugitives[a] with all
his troops shall fall by the sword, and those
who remain shall be scattered to every wind;
and you shall know that I, the LORD, have
spoken."

Israel Exalted at Last

22Thus says the Lord GOD: "I will take
also *one* of the highest branches of the high
cedar and set *it* out. I will crop off from the
topmost of its young twigs a tender one, and
will plant *it* on a high and prominent mountain. 23On the mountain height of Israel I
will plant it; and it will bring forth boughs,
and bear fruit, and be a majestic cedar. Under it will dwell birds of every sort; in the
shadow of its branches they will dwell. 24And
all the trees of the field shall know that I, the
LORD, have brought down the high tree and
exalted the low tree, dried up the green tree
and made the dry tree flourish; I, the LORD,
have spoken and have done *it.*"

A False Proverb Refuted

18 The word of the LORD came to me
again, saying, 2"What do you mean

17:21 [a] Following Masoretic Text and Vulgate; many Hebrew manuscripts and Syriac read *choice men;* Targum reads *mighty men;* Septuagint omits *All his fugitives.*

Action!

IT'S UP TO YOU

READ IT: EZEKIEL 18:1–21

Some people try to blame all their problems on someone else. And we sometimes do go wrong because of someone else's actions. But, in the end, what you do with your life is up to you.

In this passage, Israel was reading God's commandment that says the parents' sins affect their children (Exodus 20:4, 5). So they thought all their suffering could be blamed on the sins of their parents. Read how Ezekiel showed the people they were wrong about that.

If you aren't careful, you may make the same mistake Israel made. In fact some people today say young people from unhappy homes can't help the sins they commit later in life. That's false! Are you going God's way—or your own way? It's up to you.

when you use this proverb concerning the land of Israel, saying:

'The fathers have eaten sour grapes,
And the children's teeth are set on edge'?

3"*As* I live," says the Lord GOD, "you shall no longer use this proverb in Israel.

4 "Behold, all souls are Mine;
The soul of the father
As well as the soul of the son is Mine;
The soul who sins shall die.
5 But if a man is just
And does what is lawful and right;
6 If he has not eaten on the mountains,
Nor lifted up his eyes to the idols of the house of Israel,
Nor defiled his neighbor's wife,
Nor approached a woman during her impurity;
7 If he has not oppressed anyone,
But has restored to the debtor his pledge;
Has robbed no one by violence,
But has given his bread to the hungry
And covered the naked with clothing;
8 If he has not exacted usury
Nor taken any increase,
But has withdrawn his hand from iniquity
And executed true judgment between man and man;
9 *If* he has walked in My statutes
And kept My judgments faithfully—
He *is* just;
He shall surely live!"
Says the Lord GOD.

10 "If he begets a son *who is* a robber
Or a shedder of blood,
Who does any of these *things*
11 And does none of those *duties,*
But has eaten on the mountains
Or defiled his neighbor's wife;
12 If he has oppressed the poor and needy,
Robbed by violence,
Not restored the pledge,
Lifted his eyes to the idols,
Or committed abomination;
13 If he has exacted usury
Or taken increase—
Shall he then live?
He shall not live!
If he has done any of these abominations,
He shall surely die;
His blood shall be upon him.

14 "*If,* however, he begets a son
Who sees all the sins which his father has done,
And considers but does not do likewise;
15 *Who* has not eaten on the mountains,
Nor lifted his eyes to the idols of the house of Israel,
Nor defiled his neighbor's wife;
16 Has not oppressed anyone,
Nor withheld a pledge,
Nor robbed by violence,
But has given his bread to the hungry
And covered the naked with clothing;
17 *Who* has withdrawn his hand from the poor[a]
And not received usury or increase,
But has executed My judgments
And walked in My statutes—
He shall not die for the iniquity of his father;
He shall surely live!

18 "*As for* his father,
Because he cruelly oppressed,
Robbed his brother by violence,
And did what *is* not good among his people,
Behold, he shall die for his iniquity.

Turn and Live

19"Yet you say, 'Why should the son not
bear the guilt of the father?' Because the son
has done what is lawful and right, and has
kept all My statutes and observed them, he
shall surely live. 20The soul who sins shall
die. The son shall not bear the guilt of the father, nor the father bear the guilt of the son.
The righteousness of the righteous shall be
upon himself, and the wickedness of the
wicked shall be upon himself.

21"But if a wicked man turns from all his
sins which he has committed, keeps all My
statutes, and does what is lawful and right,
he shall surely live; he shall not die. 22None of
the transgressions which he has committed
shall be remembered against him; because
of the righteousness which he has done, he
shall live. 23Do I have any pleasure at all that
the wicked should die?" says the Lord GOD,
"*and* not that he should turn from his ways
and live?

18:17 [a] Following Masoretic Text, Targum, and Vulgate; Septuagint reads *iniquity* (compare verse 8).

24"But when a righteous man turns away
from his righteousness and commits iniquity, and does according to all the abominations that the wicked *man* does, shall he
live? All the righteousness which he has
done shall not be remembered; because of
the unfaithfulness of which he is guilty and
the sin which he has committed, because of
them he shall die.

25"Yet you say, 'The way of the Lord is not
fair.' Hear now, O house of Israel, is it not
My way which is fair, and your ways which
are not fair? 26When a righteous *man* turns
away from his righteousness, commits iniquity, and dies in it, it is because of the iniquity which he has done that he dies. 27Again,
when a wicked *man* turns away from the
wickedness which he committed, and does
what is lawful and right, he preserves himself alive. 28Because he considers and turns
away from all the transgressions which he
committed, he shall surely live; he shall not
die. 29Yet the house of Israel says, 'The way
of the Lord is not fair.' O house of Israel, is
it not My ways which are fair, and your ways
which are not fair?

30"Therefore I will judge you, O house
of Israel, every one according to his ways,"
says the Lord GOD. "Repent, and turn from
all your transgressions, so that iniquity will
not be your ruin. 31Cast away from you all the
transgressions which you have committed,
and get yourselves a new heart and a new
spirit. For why should you die, O house of
Israel? 32For I have no pleasure in the death
of one who dies," says the Lord GOD. "Therefore turn and live!"

Israel Degraded

19 "Moreover take up a lamentation for
the princes of Israel, 2and say:

'What *is* your mother? A lioness:
She lay down among the lions;
Among the young lions she nourished
her cubs.
3 She brought up one of her cubs,
And he became a young lion;
He learned to catch prey,
And he devoured men.
4 The nations also heard of him;
He was trapped in their pit,
And they brought him with chains to
the land of Egypt.

5 'When she saw that she waited, *that* her
hope was lost,
She took another of her cubs *and* made
him a young lion.
6 He roved among the lions,
And became a young lion;
He learned to catch prey;
He devoured men.
7 He knew their desolate places,[a]
And laid waste their cities;
The land with its fullness was desolated
By the noise of his roaring.
8 Then the nations set against him from
the provinces on every side,
And spread their net over him;
He was trapped in their pit.
9 They put him in a cage with chains,
And brought him to the king of
Babylon;
They brought him in nets,
That his voice should no longer be heard
on the mountains of Israel.

10 'Your mother *was* like a vine in your
bloodline,[a]
Planted by the waters,
Fruitful and full of branches
Because of many waters.
11 She had strong branches for scepters of
rulers.
She towered in stature above the thick
branches,
And was seen in her height amid the
dense foliage.
12 But she was plucked up in fury,
She was cast down to the ground,
And the east wind dried her fruit.
Her strong branches were broken and
withered;
The fire consumed them.
13 And now she *is* planted in the
wilderness,
In a dry and thirsty land.
14 Fire has come out from a rod of her
branches
And devoured her fruit,
So that she has no strong branch—a
scepter for ruling.'"

This *is* a lamentation, and has become a
lamentation.

19:7 [a] Septuagint reads *He stood in insolence;* Targum reads *He destroyed its palaces;* Vulgate reads *He learned to make widows.* 19:10 [a] Literally *blood,* following Masoretic Text, Syriac, and Vulgate; Septuagint reads *like a flower on a pomegranate tree;* Targum reads *in your likeness.*

The Rebellions of Israel

20 It came to pass in the seventh year, in the fifth *month,* on the tenth *day* of the month, *that* certain of the elders of Israel came to inquire of the LORD, and sat before me. 2 Then the word of the LORD came to me, saying, 3 "Son of man, speak to the elders of Israel, and say to them, 'Thus says the Lord GOD: "Have you come to inquire of Me? *As* I live," says the Lord GOD, "I will not be inquired of by you."' 4 Will you judge them, son of man, will you judge *them?* Then make known to them the abominations of their fathers.

5 "Say to them, 'Thus says the Lord GOD: "On the day when I chose Israel and raised My hand in an oath to the descendants of the house of Jacob, and made Myself known to them in the land of Egypt, I raised My hand in an oath to them, saying, 'I *am* the LORD your God.' 6 On that day I raised My hand in an oath to them, to bring them out of the land of Egypt into a land that I had searched out for them, 'flowing with milk and honey,'[a] the glory of all lands. 7 Then I said to them, 'Each of you, throw away the abominations which are before his eyes, and do not defile yourselves with the idols of Egypt. I *am* the LORD your God.' 8 But they rebelled against Me and would not obey Me. They did not all cast away the abominations which were before their eyes, nor did they forsake the idols of Egypt. Then I said, 'I will pour out My fury on them and fulfill My anger against them in the midst of the land of Egypt.' 9 But I acted for My name's sake, that it should not be profaned before the Gentiles among whom they *were,* in whose sight I had made Myself known to them, to bring them out of the land of Egypt.

10 "Therefore I made them go out of the land of Egypt and brought them into the wilderness. 11 And I gave them My statutes and showed them My judgments, 'which, *if* a man does, he shall live by them.'[a] 12 Moreover I also gave them My Sabbaths, to be a sign between them and Me, that they might know that I *am* the LORD who sanctifies them. 13 Yet the house of Israel rebelled against Me in the wilderness; they did not walk in *My statutes; they* despised My judgments, 'which, *if* a man does, he shall live by them';[a] and they greatly defiled My Sabbaths. Then I said I would pour out My fury on them in the wilderness, to consume them. 14 But I acted for My name's sake, that it should not be profaned before the Gentiles, in whose sight I had brought them out. 15 So I also raised My hand in an oath to them in the wilderness, that I would not bring them into the land which I had given *them,* 'flowing with milk and honey,'[a] the glory of all lands, 16 because they despised My judgments and did not walk in My statutes, but profaned My Sabbaths; for their heart went after their idols. 17 Nevertheless My eye spared them from destruction. I did not make an end of them in the wilderness.

18 "But I said to their children in the wilderness, 'Do not walk in the statutes of your fathers, nor observe their judgments, nor defile yourselves with their idols. 19 I *am* the LORD your God: Walk in My statutes, keep My judgments, and do them; 20 hallow My Sabbaths, and they will be a sign between Me and you, that you may know that I *am* the LORD your God.'

21 "Notwithstanding, the children rebelled against Me; they did not walk in My statutes, and were not careful to observe My judgments, 'which, *if* a man does, he shall live by them';[a] but they profaned My Sabbaths. Then I said I would pour out My fury on them and fulfill My anger against them in the wilderness. 22 Nevertheless I withdrew My hand and acted for My name's sake, that it should not be profaned in the sight of the Gentiles, in whose sight I had brought them out. 23 Also I raised My hand in an oath to those in the wilderness, that I would scatter them among the Gentiles and disperse them throughout the countries, 24 because they had not executed My judgments, but had despised My statutes, profaned My Sabbaths, and their eyes were fixed on their fathers' idols.

25 "Therefore I also gave them up to statutes *that were* not good, and judgments by which they could not live; 26 and I pronounced them unclean because of their ritual gifts, in that they caused all their firstborn to pass through *the fire,* that I might make them desolate and that they might know that I am the LORD."'

27 "Therefore, son of man, speak to the house of Israel, and say to them, 'Thus says

---

20:6 [a] Exodus 3:8 **20:11** [a] Leviticus 18:5
20:13 [a] Leviticus 18:5 **20:15** [a] Exodus 3:8
20:21 [a] Leviticus 18:5

the Lord GOD: "In this too your fathers have
blasphemed Me, by being unfaithful to Me.
28 When I brought them into the land *concerning* which I had raised My hand in an
oath to give them, and they saw all the high
hills and all the thick trees, there they offered their sacrifices and provoked Me with
their offerings. There they also sent up their
sweet aroma and poured out their drink offerings. 29 Then I said to them, 'What *is* this
high place to which you go?' So its name is
called Bamah[a] to this day."' 30 Therefore say
to the house of Israel, 'Thus says the Lord
GOD: "Are you defiling yourselves in the
manner of your fathers, and committing
harlotry according to their abominations?
31 For when you offer your gifts and make
your sons pass through the fire, you defile
yourselves with all your idols, even to this
day. So shall I be inquired of by you, O house
of Israel? *As* I live," says the Lord GOD, "I will
not be inquired of by you. 32 What you have in
your mind shall never be, when you say, 'We
will be like the Gentiles, like the families in
other countries, serving wood and stone.'

God Will Restore Israel

33 "*As* I live," says the Lord GOD, "surely
with a mighty hand, with an outstretched
arm, and with fury poured out, I will rule
over you. 34 I will bring you out from the
peoples and gather you out of the countries
where you are scattered, with a mighty hand,
with an outstretched arm, and with fury
poured out. 35 And I will bring you into the
wilderness of the peoples, and there I will
plead My case with you face to face. 36 Just as I
pleaded My case with your fathers in the wilderness of the land of Egypt, so I will plead
My case with you," says the Lord GOD.

37 "I will make you pass under the rod,
and I will bring you into the bond of the covenant; 38 I will purge the rebels from among
you, and those who transgress against Me;
I will bring them out of the country where
they dwell, but they shall not enter the land
of Israel. Then you will know that I *am* the
LORD.

39 "As for you, O house of Israel," thus says
the Lord GOD: "Go, serve every one of you his
idols—and hereafter—if you will not obey
Me; but profane My holy name no more with
your gifts and your idols. 40 For on My holy
mountain, on the mountain height of Israel," says the Lord GOD, "there all the house

In Focus

20:49 Parable Pronounced *PAIR-uh-bull*. A story that teaches a lesson. The story may or may not be based on an actual event. Jesus used parables to teach spiritual truths.

of Israel, all of them in the land, shall serve
Me; there I will accept them, and there I will
require your offerings and the firstfruits of
your sacrifices, together with all your holy
things. 41 I will accept you as a sweet aroma
when I bring you out from the peoples and
gather you out of the countries where you
have been scattered; and I will be hallowed
in you before the Gentiles. 42 Then you shall
know that I *am* the LORD, when I bring you
into the land of Israel, into the country *for*
which I raised My hand in an oath to give
to your fathers. 43 And there you shall remember your ways and all your doings with
which you were defiled; and you shall loathe
yourselves in your own sight because of all
the evils that you have committed. 44 Then
you shall know that I *am* the LORD, when I
have dealt with you for My name's sake, not
according to your wicked ways nor according
to your corrupt doings, O house of Israel,"
says the Lord GOD.'"

Fire in the Forest

45 Furthermore the word of the LORD
came to me, saying, 46 "Son of man, set your
face toward the south; preach against the
south and prophesy against the forest land,
the South,[a] 47 and say to the forest of the
South, 'Hear the word of the LORD! Thus
says the Lord GOD: "Behold, I will kindle a
fire in you, and it shall devour every green
tree and every dry tree in you; the blazing
flame shall not be quenched, and all faces
from the south to the north shall be scorched
by it. 48 All flesh shall see that I, the LORD,
have kindled it; it shall not be quenched."'"

49 Then I said, "Ah, Lord GOD! They say of
me, 'Does he not speak parables?'"

20:29 [a] Literally *High Place* **20:46** [a] Hebrew *Negev*

Babylon, the Sword of God

21 And the word of the LORD came to
me, saying, 2“Son of man, set your
face toward Jerusalem, preach against the
holy places, and prophesy against the land
of Israel; 3and say to the land of Israel, ‘Thus
says the LORD: “Behold, I *am* against you,
and I will draw My sword out of its sheath
and cut off both righteous and wicked from
you. 4Because I will cut off both righteous
and wicked from you, therefore My sword
shall go out of its sheath against all flesh
from south *to* north, 5that all flesh may know
that I, the LORD, have drawn My sword out
of its sheath; it shall not return anymore.”’
6Sigh therefore, son of man, with a breaking
heart, and sigh with bitterness before their
eyes. 7And it shall be when they say to you,
‘Why are you sighing?’ that you shall answer, ‘Because of the news; when it comes,
every heart will melt, all hands will be feeble, every spirit will faint, and all knees will
be weak *as* water. Behold, it is coming and
shall be brought to pass,’ says the Lord GOD.”
8Again the word of the LORD came to
me, saying, 9“Son of man, prophesy and say,
‘Thus says the LORD!’ Say:

‘A sword, a sword is sharpened
And also polished!
10 Sharpened to make a dreadful
slaughter,
Polished to flash like lightning!
Should we then make mirth?
It despises the scepter of My son,
As it does all wood.
11 And He has given it to be polished,
That it may be handled;
This sword is sharpened, and it is
polished
To be given into the hand of the slayer.’

12 “Cry and wail, son of man;
For it will be against My people,
Against all the princes of Israel.
Terrors including the sword will be
against My people;
Therefore strike *your* thigh.

13 “Because *it is* a testing,
And what if *the sword* despises even the
scepter?
The scepter shall be no *more,*”

says the Lord GOD.

14 “You therefore, son of man, prophesy,
And strike *your* hands together.
The third time let the sword do double
damage.
It *is* the sword *that* slays,
The sword that slays the great *men,*
That enters their private chambers.
15 I have set the point of the sword against
all their gates,
That the heart may melt and many may
stumble.
Ah! *It is* made bright;
It is grasped for slaughter:

16 “Swords at the ready!
Thrust right!
Set your blade!
Thrust left—
Wherever your edge is ordered!

17 “I also will beat My fists together,
And I will cause My fury to rest;
I, the LORD, have spoken.”

18The word of the LORD came to me
again, saying: 19“And son of man, appoint for
yourself two ways for the sword of the king
of Babylon to go; both of them shall go from
the same land. Make a sign; put *it* at the head
of the road to the city. 20Appoint a road for
the sword to go to Rabbah of the Ammonites, and to Judah, into fortified Jerusalem.
21For the king of Babylon stands at the parting of the road, at the fork of the two roads,
to use divination: he shakes the arrows, he
consults the images, he looks at the liver. 22In
his right hand is the divination for Jerusalem: to set up battering rams, to call for a
slaughter, to lift the voice with shouting, to
set battering rams against the gates, to heap
up a *siege* mound, and to build a wall. 23And
it will be to them like a false divination in
the eyes of those who have sworn oaths with
them; but he will bring their iniquity to remembrance, that they may be taken.
24“Therefore thus says the Lord GOD:
‘Because you have made your iniquity to be
remembered, in that your transgressions
are uncovered, so that in all your doings
your sins appear—because you have come
to remembrance, you shall be taken in hand.
25‘Now to you, O profane, wicked prince
of Israel, whose day has come, whose iniquity *shall* end, 26thus says the Lord GOD:

“Remove the turban, and take off the
crown;
Nothing *shall remain* the same.
Exalt the humble, and humble the
exalted.
27 Overthrown, overthrown,

I will make it overthrown!
It shall be no *longer,*
Until He comes whose right it is,
And I will give it *to Him*."'

A Sword Against the Ammonites

28"And you, son of man, prophesy and
say, 'Thus says the Lord GOD concerning the
Ammonites and concerning their reproach,'
and say:

'A sword, a sword *is* drawn,
Polished for slaughter,
For consuming, for flashing—
29 While they see false visions for you,
While they divine a lie to you,
To bring you on the necks of the wicked,
the slain
Whose day has come,
Whose iniquity *shall* end.

30 'Return *it* to its sheath.
I will judge you
In the place where you were created,
In the land of your nativity.
31 I will pour out My indignation on you;
I will blow against you with the fire of
My wrath,
And deliver you into the hands of brutal
men *who are* skillful to destroy.
32 You shall be fuel for the fire;
Your blood shall be in the midst of the
land.
You shall not be remembered,
For I the LORD have spoken.'"

Sins of Jerusalem

22 Moreover the word of the LORD
came to me, saying, 2"Now, son
of man, will you judge, will you judge the
bloody city? Yes, show her all her abominations! 3Then say, 'Thus says the Lord GOD:
"The city sheds blood in her own midst, that
her time may come; and she makes idols
within herself to defile herself. 4You have
become guilty by the blood which you have
shed, and have defiled yourself with the
idols which you have made. You have caused
your days to draw near, and have come to *the
end of* your years; therefore I have made you
a reproach to the nations, and a mockery to
all countries. 5*Those* near and *those* far from
you will mock you as infamous *and* full of
tumult.
6"Look, the princes of Israel: each one
has used his power to shed blood in you.
7In you they have made light of father and
mother; in your midst they have oppressed
the stranger; in you they have mistreated
the fatherless and the widow. 8You have despised My holy things and profaned My Sabbaths. 9In you are men who slander to cause
bloodshed; in you are those who eat on the
mountains; in your midst they commit lewdness. 10In you men uncover their fathers' nakedness; in you they violate women who are
set apart during their impurity. 11One commits abomination with his neighbor's wife;
another lewdly defiles his daughter-in-law;
and another in you violates his sister, his
father's daughter. 12In you they take bribes
to shed blood; you take usury and increase;
you have made profit from your neighbors
by extortion, and have forgotten Me," says
the Lord GOD.
13"Behold, therefore, I beat My fists at the
dishonest profit which you have made, and at
the bloodshed which has been in your midst.
14Can your heart endure, or can your hands
remain strong, in the days when I shall deal
with you? I, the LORD, have spoken, and will
do *it*. 15I will scatter you among the nations,
disperse you throughout the countries, and
remove your filthiness completely from you.
16You shall defile yourself in the sight of the
nations; then you shall know that I *am* the
LORD."'"

Israel in the Furnace

17The word of the LORD came to me, saying, 18"Son of man, the house of Israel has
become dross to Me; they *are* all bronze, tin,
iron, and lead, in the midst of a furnace; they
have become dross from silver. 19Therefore
thus says the Lord GOD: 'Because you have
all become dross, therefore behold, I will
gather you into the midst of Jerusalem. 20*As
men* gather silver, bronze, iron, lead, and tin
into the midst of a furnace, to blow fire on
it, to melt *it;* so I will gather *you* in My anger and in My fury, and I will leave *you there*
and melt you. 21Yes, I will gather you and
blow on you with the fire of My wrath, and
you shall be melted in its midst. 22As silver
is melted in the midst of a furnace, so shall
you be melted in its midst; then you shall
know that I, the LORD, have poured out My
fury on you.'"

Israel's Wicked Leaders

23And the word of the LORD came to me,

saying, 24"Son of man, say to her: 'You *are* a
land that is not cleansed[a] or rained on in the
day of indignation.' 25The conspiracy of her
prophets[a] in her midst is like a roaring lion
tearing the prey; they have devoured people; they have taken treasure and precious
things; they have made many widows in her
midst. 26Her priests have violated My law
and profaned My holy things; they have not
distinguished between the holy and unholy,
nor have they made known *the difference* between the unclean and the clean; and they
have hidden their eyes from My Sabbaths, so
that I am profaned among them. 27Her princes in her midst *are* like wolves tearing the
prey, to shed blood, to destroy people, and to
get dishonest gain. 28Her prophets plastered
them with untempered *mortar,* seeing false
visions, and divining lies for them, saying,
'Thus says the Lord GOD,' when the LORD
had not spoken. 29The people of the land
have used oppressions, committed robbery,
and mistreated the poor and needy; and
they wrongfully oppress the stranger. 30So I
sought for a man among them who would
make a wall, and stand in the gap before
Me on behalf of the land, that I should not
destroy it; but I found no one. 31Therefore I
have poured out My indignation on them;
I have consumed them with the fire of My
wrath; and I have recompensed their deeds
on their own heads," says the Lord GOD.

Two Harlot Sisters

23 The word of the LORD came again to me, saying:

2 "Son of man, there were two women,
The daughters of one mother.
3 They committed harlotry in Egypt,
They committed harlotry in their youth;
Their breasts were there embraced,
Their virgin bosom was there pressed.
4 Their names: Oholah[a] the elder and
Oholibah[b] her sister;
They were Mine,
And they bore sons and daughters.
As for their names,
Samaria *is* Oholah, and Jerusalem *is*
Oholibah.

The Older Sister, Samaria

5 "Oholah played the harlot even though
she was Mine;
And she lusted for her lovers, the
neighboring Assyrians,
6 *Who were* clothed in purple,
Captains and rulers,
All of them desirable young men,
Horsemen riding on horses.
7 Thus she committed her harlotry with
them,
All of them choice men of Assyria;
And with all for whom she lusted,
With all their idols, she defiled herself.
8 She has never given up her harlotry
brought from Egypt,
For in her youth they had lain with her,
Pressed her virgin bosom,
And poured out their immorality upon
her.

9 "Therefore I have delivered her
Into the hand of her lovers,
Into the hand of the Assyrians,
For whom she lusted.
10 They uncovered her nakedness,
Took away her sons and daughters,
And slew her with the sword;
She became a byword among women,
For they had executed judgment on her.

The Younger Sister, Jerusalem

11"Now although her sister Oholibah saw
this, she became more corrupt in her lust
than she, and in her harlotry more corrupt
than her sister's harlotry.

12 "She lusted for the neighboring
Assyrians,
Captains and rulers,
Clothed most gorgeously,
Horsemen riding on horses,
All of them desirable young men.
13 Then I saw that she was defiled;
Both *took* the same way.
14 But she increased her harlotry;
She looked at men portrayed on the
wall,
Images of Chaldeans portrayed in
vermilion,
15 Girded with belts around their waists,
Flowing turbans on their heads,
All of them looking like captains,

22:24 [a] Following Masoretic Text, Syriac, and Vulgate; Septuagint reads *showered upon.* 22:25 [a] Following Masoretic Text and Vulgate; Septuagint reads *princes;* Targum reads *scribes.* 23:4 [a] Literally *Her Own Tabernacle* [b] Literally *My Tabernacle Is in Her*

In the manner of the Babylonians of
Chaldea,
The land of their nativity.
16 As soon as her eyes saw them,
She lusted for them
And sent messengers to them in
Chaldea.

17 "Then the Babylonians came to her, into
the bed of love,
And they defiled her with their
immorality;
So she was defiled by them, and
alienated herself from them.
18 She revealed her harlotry and uncovered
her nakedness.
Then I alienated Myself from her,
As I had alienated Myself from her
sister.

19 "Yet she multiplied her harlotry
In calling to remembrance the days of
her youth,
When she had played the harlot in the
land of Egypt.
20 For she lusted for her paramours,
Whose flesh *is like* the flesh of donkeys,
And whose issue *is like* the issue of
horses.
21 Thus you called to remembrance the
lewdness of your youth,
When the Egyptians pressed your
bosom
Because of your youthful breasts.

Judgment on Jerusalem

22 "Therefore, Oholibah, thus says the
Lord GOD:

'Behold, I will stir up your lovers against
you,
From whom you have alienated yourself,
And I will bring them against you from
every side:
23 The Babylonians,
All the Chaldeans,
Pekod, Shoa, Koa,
All the Assyrians with them,
All of them desirable young men,
Governors and rulers,
Captains and men of renown,
All of them riding on horses.
24 And they shall come against you
With chariots, wagons, and war-horses,
With a horde of people.
They shall array against you
Buckler, shield, and helmet all around.

'I will delegate judgment to them,
And they shall judge you according to
their judgments.
25 I will set My jealousy against you,
And they shall deal furiously with you;
They shall remove your nose and your
ears,
And your remnant shall fall by the
sword;
They shall take your sons and your
daughters,
And your remnant shall be devoured
by fire.
26 They shall also strip you of your clothes
And take away your beautiful jewelry.

27 'Thus I will make you cease your
lewdness and your harlotry
Brought from the land of Egypt,
So that you will not lift your eyes to
them,
Nor remember Egypt anymore.'

28 "For thus says the Lord GOD: 'Surely I
will deliver you into the hand of those you
hate, into the hand *of those* from whom you
alienated yourself. 29 They will deal hatefully
with you, take away all you have worked for,
and leave you naked and bare. The nakedness of your harlotry shall be uncovered,
both your lewdness and your harlotry. 30 I
will do these *things* to you because you have
gone as a harlot after the Gentiles, because
you have become defiled by their idols. 31 You
have walked in the way of your sister; therefore I will put her cup in your hand.'

32 "Thus says the Lord GOD:

'You shall drink of your sister's cup,
The deep and wide one;
You shall be laughed to scorn
And held in derision;
It contains much.
33 You will be filled with drunkenness and
sorrow,
The cup of horror and desolation,
The cup of your sister Samaria.
34 You shall drink and drain it,
You shall break its shards,
And tear at your own breasts;
For I have spoken,'
Says the Lord GOD.

35 "Therefore thus says the Lord GOD:

'Because you have forgotten Me and cast
Me behind your back,
Therefore you shall bear the *penalty*
Of your lewdness and your harlotry.'"

Both Sisters Judged

36 The LORD also said to me: "Son of man,
will you judge Oholah and Oholibah? Then
declare to them their abominations. 37 For
they have committed adultery, and blood *is*
on their hands. They have committed adultery with their idols, and even *sacrificed* their
sons whom they bore to Me, passing them
through *the fire,* to devour *them.* 38 Moreover
they have done this to Me: They have defiled
My sanctuary on the same day and profaned
My Sabbaths. 39 For after they had slain their
children for their idols, on the same day they
came into My sanctuary to profane it; and
indeed thus they have done in the midst of
My house.

40 "Furthermore you sent for men to
come from afar, to whom a messenger *was*
sent; and there they came. And you washed
yourself for them, painted your eyes, and
adorned yourself with ornaments. 41 You
sat on a stately couch, with a table prepared
before it, on which you had set My incense
and My oil. 42 The sound of a carefree multitude *was* with her, and Sabeans *were* brought
from the wilderness with men of the common sort, who put bracelets on their wrists
and beautiful crowns on their heads. 43 Then
I said concerning *her who had grown* old in
adulteries, 'Will they commit harlotry with
her now, and she *with them?*' 44 Yet they went
in to her, as men go in to a woman who plays
the harlot; thus they went in to Oholah and
Oholibah, the lewd women. 45 But righteous
men will judge them after the manner of
adulteresses, and after the manner of wom-
en who shed blood, because they *are* adulteresses, and blood *is* on their hands.

46 "For thus says the Lord GOD: 'Bring up
an assembly against them, give them up to
trouble and plunder. 47 The assembly shall
stone them with stones and execute them
with their swords; they shall slay their sons
and their daughters, and burn their houses
with fire. 48 Thus I will cause lewdness to
cease from the land, that all women may be
taught not to practice your lewdness. 49 They
shall repay you for your lewdness, and you
shall pay for your idolatrous sins. Then you
shall know that I *am* the Lord GOD.'"

Symbol of the Cooking Pot

24 Again, in the ninth year, in the
tenth month, on the tenth *day* of
the month, the word of the LORD came to
me, saying, 2 "Son of man, write down the
name of the day, this very day—the king of
Babylon started his siege against Jerusalem
this very day. 3 And utter a parable to the rebellious house, and say to them, 'Thus says
the Lord GOD:

"Put on a pot, set *it* on,
And also pour water into it.
4 Gather pieces *of meat* in it,
Every good piece,
The thigh and the shoulder.
Fill *it* with choice cuts;
5 Take the choice of the flock.
Also pile *fuel* bones under it,
Make it boil well,
And let the cuts simmer in it."

6 'Therefore thus says the Lord GOD:

"Woe to the bloody city,
To the pot whose scum *is* in it,
And whose scum is not gone from it!
Bring it out piece by piece,
On which no lot has fallen.
7 For her blood is in her midst;
She set it on top of a rock;
She did not pour it on the ground,
To cover it with dust.
8 That it may raise up fury and take
vengeance,
I have set her blood on top of a rock,
That it may not be covered."

9 'Therefore thus says the Lord GOD:

"Woe to the bloody city!
I too will make the pyre great.
10 Heap on the wood,
Kindle the fire;
Cook the meat well,
Mix in the spices,
And let the cuts be burned up.

11 "Then set the pot empty on the coals,
That it may become hot and its bronze
may burn,
That its filthiness may be melted in it,
That its scum may be consumed.
12 She has grown weary with lies,
And her great scum has not gone from
her.
Let her scum *be* in the fire!
13 In your filthiness *is* lewdness.

Because I have cleansed you, and you
were not cleansed,
You will not be cleansed of your
filthiness anymore,
Till I have caused My fury to rest upon
you.
14 I, the LORD, have spoken *it;*
It shall come to pass, and I will do *it;*
I will not hold back,
Nor will I spare,
Nor will I relent;
According to your ways
And according to your deeds
They[a] will judge you,"
Says the Lord GOD.'"

The Prophet's Wife Dies

[15]Also the word of the LORD came to me,
saying, [16]"Son of man, behold, I take away
from you the desire of your eyes with one
stroke; yet you shall neither mourn nor
weep, nor shall your tears run down. [17]Sigh
in silence, make no mourning for the dead;
bind your turban on your head, and put your
sandals on your feet; do not cover *your* lips,
and do not eat man's bread *of sorrow.*"

[18]So I spoke to the people in the morning,
and at evening my wife died; and the next
morning I did as I was commanded.

[19]And the people said to me, "Will you
not tell us what these *things signify* to us, that
you behave so?"

[20]Then I answered them, "The word of
the LORD came to me, saying, [21]'Speak to
the house of Israel, "Thus says the Lord
GOD: 'Behold, I will profane My sanctuary,
your arrogant boast, the desire of your eyes,
the delight of your soul; and your sons and
daughters whom you left behind shall fall
by the sword. [22]And you shall do as I have
done; you shall not cover *your* lips nor eat
man's bread *of sorrow.* [23]Your turbans shall
be on your heads and your sandals on your
feet; you shall neither mourn nor weep, but
you shall pine away in your iniquities and
mourn with one another. [24]Thus Ezekiel is a
sign to you; according to all that he has done
you shall do; and when this comes, you shall
know that I *am* the Lord GOD.'"

[25]'And you, son of man—*will it* not *be* in
the day when I take from them their stronghold, their joy and their glory, the desire of
their eyes, and that on which they set their
minds, their sons and their daughters: [26]*that*
on that day one who escapes will come to you
to let *you* hear *it* with *your* ears? [27]On that day
your mouth will be opened to him who has
escaped; you shall speak and no longer be
mute. Thus you will be a sign to them, and
they shall know that I *am* the LORD.'"

Proclamation Against Ammon

25 The word of the LORD came to
me, saying, [2]"Son of man, set your
face against the Ammonites, and prophesy
against them. [3]Say to the Ammonites, 'Hear
the word of the Lord GOD! Thus says the
Lord GOD: "Because you said, 'Aha!' against
My sanctuary when it was profaned, and
against the land of Israel when it was desolate, and against the house of Judah when
they went into captivity, [4]indeed, therefore, I
will deliver you as a possession to the men
of the East, and they shall set their encamp-
ments among you and make their dwellings
among you; they shall eat your fruit, and
they shall drink your milk. [5]And I will make
Rabbah a stable for camels and Ammon a
resting place for flocks. Then you shall know
that I *am* the LORD."

[6]'For thus says the Lord GOD: "Because
you clapped *your* hands, stamped your feet,
and rejoiced in heart with all your disdain
for the land of Israel, [7]indeed, therefore, I
will stretch out My hand against you, and
give you as plunder to the nations; I will cut
you off from the peoples, and I will cause
you to perish from the countries; I will destroy you, and you shall know that I *am* the
LORD."

Proclamation Against Moab

[8]'Thus says the Lord GOD: "Because
Moab and Seir say, 'Look! The house of
Judah *is* like all the nations,' [9]therefore, behold, I will clear the territory of Moab of
cities, of the cities on its frontier, the glory
of the country, Beth Jeshimoth, Baal Meon,
and Kirjathaim. [10]To the men of the East I
will give it as a possession, together with the
Ammonites, that the Ammonites may not
be remembered among the nations. [11]And I
will execute judgments upon Moab, and they
shall know that I *am* the LORD."

Proclamation Against Edom

[12]'Thus says the Lord GOD: "Because of
what Edom did against the house of Judah

24:14 [a] Septuagint, Syriac, Targum, and Vulgate read *I.*

by taking vengeance, and has greatly offended by avenging itself on them," 13therefore thus says the Lord God: "I will also stretch out My hand against Edom, cut off man and beast from it, and make it desolate from Teman; Dedan shall fall by the sword. 14I will lay My vengeance on Edom by the hand of My people Israel, that they may do in Edom according to My anger and according to My fury; and they shall know My vengeance," says the Lord God.

Proclamation Against Philistia

15'Thus says the Lord God: "Because the Philistines dealt vengefully and took vengeance with a spiteful heart, to destroy because of the old hatred," 16therefore thus says the Lord God: "I will stretch out My hand against the Philistines, and I will cut off the Cherethites and destroy the remnant of the seacoast. 17I will execute great vengeance on them with furious rebukes; and they shall know that I *am* the Lord, when I lay My vengeance upon them." ' "

Proclamation Against Tyre

26 And it came to pass in the eleventh year, on the first *day* of the month, *that* the word of the Lord came to me, saying, 2"Son of man, because Tyre has said against Jerusalem, 'Aha! She is broken who *was* the gateway of the peoples; now she is turned over to me; I shall be filled; she is laid waste.'

3"Therefore thus says the Lord God: 'Behold, I *am* against you, O Tyre, and will cause many nations to come up against you, as the sea causes its waves to come up. 4And they shall destroy the walls of Tyre and break down her towers; I will also scrape her dust from her, and make her like the top of a rock. 5It shall be *a place for* spreading nets in the midst of the sea, for I have spoken,' says the Lord God; 'it shall become plunder for the nations. 6Also her daughter *villages* which *are* in the fields shall be slain by the sword. Then they shall know that I am the Lord.'

7"For thus says the Lord God: 'Behold, I will bring against Tyre from the north Nebuchadnezzar[a] king of Babylon, king of kings, with horses, with chariots, and with *horsemen, and an army* with many people. 8He will slay with the sword your daughter *villages* in the fields; he will heap up a siege mound against you, build a wall against you, and raise a defense against you. 9He will direct his battering rams against your walls, and with his axes he will break down your towers. 10Because of the abundance of his horses, their dust will cover you; your walls will shake at the noise of the horsemen, the wagons, and the chariots, when he enters your gates, as men enter a city that has been breached. 11With the hooves of his horses he will trample all your streets; he will slay your people by the sword, and your strong pillars will fall to the ground. 12They will plunder your riches and pillage your merchandise; they will break down your walls and destroy your pleasant houses; they will lay your stones, your timber, and your soil in the midst of the water. 13I will put an end to the sound of your songs, and the sound of your harps shall be heard no more. 14I will make you like the top of a rock; you shall be *a place for* spreading nets, and you shall never be rebuilt, for I the Lord have spoken,' says the Lord God.

15"Thus says the Lord God to Tyre: 'Will the coastlands not shake at the sound of your fall, when the wounded cry, when slaughter is made in the midst of you? 16Then all the princes of the sea will come down from their thrones, lay aside their robes, and take off their embroidered garments; they will clothe themselves with trembling; they will sit on the ground, tremble *every* moment, and be astonished at you. 17And they will take up a lamentation for you, and say to you:

"How you have perished,
O one inhabited by seafaring men,
O renowned city,
Who was strong at sea,
She and her inhabitants,
Who caused their terror *to be* on all her
inhabitants!
18 Now the coastlands tremble on the day
of your fall;
Yes, the coastlands by the sea are
troubled at your departure." '

19"For thus says the Lord God: 'When I make you a desolate city, like cities that are not inhabited, when I bring the deep upon you, and great waters cover you, 20then I will bring you down with those who descend into the Pit, to the people of old, and I will make you dwell in the lowest part of the earth, in

---

26:7 [a] Hebrew *Nebuchadrezzar,* and so elsewhere in this book

places desolate from antiquity, with those
who go down to the Pit, so that you may never be inhabited; and I shall establish glory in
the land of the living. 21I will make you a terror, and you *shall be* no *more;* though you are
sought for, you will never be found again,'
says the Lord GOD."

Lamentation for Tyre

27 The word of the LORD came again
to me, saying, 2"Now, son of man,
take up a lamentation for Tyre, 3and say to
Tyre, 'You who are situated at the entrance
of the sea, merchant of the peoples on many
coastlands, thus says the Lord GOD:

"O Tyre, you have said,
'I *am* perfect in beauty.'
4 Your borders *are* in the midst of the seas.
Your builders have perfected your beauty.
5 They made all *your* planks of fir trees from Senir;
They took a cedar from Lebanon to make you a mast.
6 *Of* oaks from Bashan they made your oars;
The company of Ashurites have inlaid your planks
With ivory from the coasts of Cyprus.[a]
7 Fine embroidered linen from Egypt was what you spread for your sail;
Blue and purple from the coasts of Elishah was what covered you.

8 "Inhabitants of Sidon and Arvad were your oarsmen;
Your wise men, O Tyre, were in you;
They became your pilots.
9 Elders of Gebal and its wise men
Were in you to caulk your seams;
All the ships of the sea
And their oarsmen were in you
To market your merchandise.

10 "Those from Persia, Lydia,[a] and Libya[b]
Were in your army as men of war;
They hung shield and helmet in you;
They gave splendor to you.
11 Men of Arvad with your army *were* on your walls *all* around,
And the men of Gammad were in your towers;
They hung their shields on your walls *all* around;
They made your beauty perfect.

12"Tarshish *was* your merchant because
of your many luxury goods. They gave you
silver, iron, tin, and lead for your goods. 13Ja-
van, Tubal, and Meshech *were* your traders.
They bartered human lives and vessels of
bronze for your merchandise. 14Those from
the house of Togarmah traded for your wares
with horses, steeds, and mules. 15The men
of Dedan *were* your traders; many isles *were*
the market of your hand. They brought you
ivory tusks and ebony as payment. 16Syria
was your merchant because of the abundance of goods you made. They gave you
for your wares emeralds, purple, embroidery, fine linen, corals, and rubies. 17Judah
and the land of Israel *were* your traders.
They traded for your merchandise wheat of
Minnith, millet, honey, oil, and balm. 18Da-
mascus *was* your merchant because of the
abundance of goods you made, because of
your many luxury items, with the wine of
Helbon and with white wool. 19Dan and Javan paid for your wares, traversing back and
forth. Wrought iron, cassia, and cane were
among your merchandise. 20Dedan *was* your
merchant in saddlecloths for riding. 21Ara-
bia and all the princes of Kedar *were* your
regular merchants. They traded with you
in lambs, rams, and goats. 22The merchants
of Sheba and Raamah *were* your merchants.
They traded for your wares the choicest spices, all kinds of precious stones, and gold.
23Haran, Canneh, Eden, the merchants
of Sheba, Assyria, *and* Chilmad *were* your
merchants. 24These *were* your merchants in
choice items—in purple clothes, in embroidered garments, in chests of multicolored
apparel, in sturdy woven cords, which were
in your marketplace.

25 "The ships of Tarshish were carriers of your merchandise.
You were filled and very glorious in the midst of the seas.
26 Your oarsmen brought you into many waters,
But the east wind broke you in the midst of the seas.

27 "Your riches, wares, and merchandise,
Your mariners and pilots,
Your caulkers and merchandisers,
All your men of war who *are* in you,

27:6 [a] Hebrew *Kittim,* western lands, especially Cyprus
27:10 [a] Hebrew *Lud* [b] Hebrew *Put*

And the entire company which *is* in
your midst,
Will fall into the midst of the seas on
the day of your ruin.
28 The common-land will shake at the
sound of the cry of your pilots.

29 "All who handle the oar,
The mariners,
All the pilots of the sea
Will come down from their ships *and*
stand on the shore.
30 They will make their voice heard
because of you;
They will cry bitterly and cast dust on
their heads;
They will roll about in ashes;
31 They will shave themselves completely
bald because of you,
Gird themselves with sackcloth,
And weep for you
With bitterness of heart *and* bitter
wailing.
32 In their wailing for you
They will take up a lamentation,
And lament for you:
'What *city is* like Tyre,
Destroyed in the midst of the sea?

33 'When your wares went out by sea,
You satisfied many people;
You enriched the kings of the earth
With your many luxury goods and your
merchandise.
34 But you are broken by the seas in the
depths of the waters;
Your merchandise and the entire
company will fall in your midst.
35 All the inhabitants of the isles will be
astonished at you;
Their kings will be greatly afraid,
And *their* countenance will be troubled.
36 The merchants among the peoples will
hiss at you;
You will become a horror, and *be* no
more forever.'" ' "

Proclamation Against the King of Tyre

28 The word of the LORD came to me
again, saying, 2"Son of man, say to
the prince of Tyre, 'Thus says the Lord GOD:

"Because your heart *is* lifted up,
And you say, 'I *am* a god,
I sit *in* the seat of gods,
In the midst of the seas,'
Yet you *are* a man, and not a god,
Though you set your heart as the heart
of a god
3 (Behold, you *are* wiser than Daniel!
There is no secret that can be hidden
from you!
4 With your wisdom and your
understanding
You have gained riches for yourself,
And gathered gold and silver into your
treasuries;
5 By your great wisdom in trade you have
increased your riches,
And your heart is lifted up because of
your riches),"

6'Therefore thus says the Lord GOD:

"Because you have set your heart as the
heart of a god,
7 Behold, therefore, I will bring strangers
against you,
The most terrible of the nations;
And they shall draw their swords
against the beauty of your wisdom,
And defile your splendor.
8 They shall throw you down into the Pit,
And you shall die the death of the slain
In the midst of the seas.

9 "Will you still say before him who slays
you,
'I *am* a god'?
But you *shall be* a man, and not a god,
In the hand of him who slays you.
10 You shall die the death of the
uncircumcised
By the hand of aliens;
For I have spoken," says the Lord GOD.'"

Lamentation for the King of Tyre

11Moreover the word of the LORD came to
me, saying, 12"Son of man, take up a lamentation for the king of Tyre, and say to him,
'Thus says the Lord GOD:

"You *were* the seal of perfection,
Full of wisdom and perfect in beauty.
13 You were in Eden, the garden of God;
Every precious stone *was* your covering:
The sardius, topaz, and diamond,
Beryl, onyx, and jasper,
Sapphire, turquoise, and emerald with
gold.
The workmanship of your timbrels and
pipes

Was prepared for you on the day you
were created.

14 "You *were* the anointed cherub who
covers;
I established you;
You were on the holy mountain of God;
You walked back and forth in the midst
of fiery stones.
15 You *were* perfect in your ways from the
day you were created,
Till iniquity was found in you.

16 "By the abundance of your trading
You became filled with violence within,
And you sinned;
Therefore I cast you as a profane thing
Out of the mountain of God;
And I destroyed you, O covering cherub,
From the midst of the fiery stones.

17 "Your heart was lifted up because of your
beauty;
You corrupted your wisdom for the sake
of your splendor;
I cast you to the ground,
I laid you before kings,
That they might gaze at you.

18 "You defiled your sanctuaries
By the multitude of your iniquities,
By the iniquity of your trading;
Therefore I brought fire from your
midst;
It devoured you,
And I turned you to ashes upon the
earth
In the sight of all who saw you.
19 All who knew you among the peoples
are astonished at you;
You have become a horror,
And *shall be* no more forever."'"

Proclamation Against Sidon

20Then the word of the LORD came to me,
saying, 21"Son of man, set your face toward
Sidon, and prophesy against her, 22and say,
'Thus says the Lord GOD:

"Behold, I *am* against you, O Sidon;
I will be glorified in your midst;
And they shall know that I *am* the LORD,
When I execute judgments in her and
am hallowed in her.
23 For I will send pestilence upon her,
And blood in her streets;
The wounded shall be judged in her
midst
By the sword against her on every side;
Then they shall know that I *am* the
LORD.

24"And there shall no longer be a pricking
brier or a painful thorn for the house of Israel from among all *who are* around them,
who despise them. Then they shall know
that I *am* the Lord GOD."

Israel's Future Blessing

25'Thus says the Lord GOD: "When I have
gathered the house of Israel from the peoples among whom they are scattered, and
am hallowed in them in the sight of the Gentiles, then they will dwell in their own land
which I gave to My servant Jacob. 26And they
will dwell safely there, build houses, and
plant vineyards; yes, they will dwell securely, when I execute judgments on all those
around them who despise them. Then they
shall know that I *am* the LORD their God."'"

Proclamation Against Egypt

29 In the tenth year, in the tenth
month, on the twelfth *day* of the
month, the word of the LORD came to me,
saying, 2"Son of man, set your face against
Pharaoh king of Egypt, and prophesy against
him, and against all Egypt. 3Speak, and say,
'Thus says the Lord GOD:

"Behold, I *am* against you,
O Pharaoh king of Egypt,
O great monster who lies in the midst of
his rivers,
Who has said, 'My River[a] *is* my own;
I have made *it* for myself.'
4 But I will put hooks in your jaws,
And cause the fish of your rivers to stick
to your scales;
I will bring you up out of the midst of
your rivers,
And all the fish in your rivers will stick
to your scales.
5 I will leave you in the wilderness,
You and all the fish of your rivers;
You shall fall on the open field;
You shall not be picked up or gathered.[a]
I have given you as food
To the beasts of the field
And to the birds of the heavens.

29:3 [a] That is, the Nile 29:5 [a] Following Masoretic Text, Septuagint, and Vulgate; some Hebrew manuscripts and Targum read *buried.*

6 "Then all the inhabitants of Egypt
Shall know that I *am* the LORD,
Because they have been a staff of reed to
the house of Israel.
7 When they took hold of you with the
hand,
You broke and tore all their shoulders;[a]
When they leaned on you,
You broke and made all their backs
quiver."

8'Therefore thus says the Lord GOD:
"Surely I will bring a sword upon you and
cut off from you man and beast. 9And the
land of Egypt shall become desolate and
waste; then they will know that I *am* the
LORD, because he said, 'The River *is* mine,
and I have made *it*.' 10Indeed, therefore, I
am against you and against your rivers, and
I will make the land of Egypt utterly waste
and desolate, from Migdol[a] *to* Syene, as far
as the border of Ethiopia. 11Neither foot of
man shall pass through it nor foot of beast
pass through it, and it shall be uninhabited
forty years. 12I will make the land of Egypt
desolate in the midst of the countries *that are*
desolate; and among the cities *that are* laid
waste, her cities shall be desolate forty years;
and I will scatter the Egyptians among the
nations and disperse them throughout the
countries."

13'Yet, thus says the Lord GOD: "At the
end of forty years I will gather the Egyptians
from the peoples among whom they were
scattered. 14I will bring back the captives of
Egypt and cause them to return to the land
of Pathros, to the land of their origin, and
there they shall be a lowly kingdom. 15It shall
be the lowliest of kingdoms; it shall never
again exalt itself above the nations, for I will
diminish them so that they will not rule over
the nations anymore. 16No longer shall it be
the confidence of the house of Israel, but
will remind them of *their* iniquity when they
turned to follow them. Then they shall know
that I *am* the Lord GOD."'"

Babylonia Will Plunder Egypt

17And it came to pass in the twenty-
seventh year, in the first *month*, on the first
day of the month, *that* the word of the LORD
came to me, saying, 18"Son of man, Nebuchadnezzar king of Babylon caused his army
to labor strenuously against Tyre; every head
was made bald, and every shoulder rubbed
raw; yet neither he nor his army received
wages from Tyre, for the labor which they ex-
pended on it. 19Therefore thus says the Lord
GOD: 'Surely I will give the land of Egypt to
Nebuchadnezzar king of Babylon; he shall
take away her wealth, carry off her spoil, and
remove her pillage; and that will be the wages for his army. 20I have given him the land of
Egypt *for* his labor, because they worked for
Me,' says the Lord GOD.

21'In that day I will cause the horn of the
house of Israel to spring forth, and I will
open your mouth to speak in their midst.
Then they shall know that I *am* the LORD.'"

Egypt and Her Allies Will Fall

30 The word of the LORD came to
me again, saying, 2"Son of man,
prophesy and say, 'Thus says the Lord GOD:

"Wail, 'Woe to the day!'
3 For the day *is* near,
Even the day of the LORD *is* near;
It will be a day of clouds, the time of the
Gentiles.
4 The sword shall come upon Egypt,
And great anguish shall be in Ethiopia,
When the slain fall in Egypt,
And they take away her wealth,
And her foundations are broken down.

5"Ethiopia, Libya,[a] Lydia,[b] all the mingled
people, Chub, and the men of the lands who
are allied, shall fall with them by the sword."
6'Thus says the LORD:

"Those who uphold Egypt shall fall,
And the pride of her power shall come
down.
From Migdol *to* Syene
Those within her shall fall by the
sword,"
Says the Lord GOD.

7 "They shall be desolate in the midst of
the desolate countries,
And her cities shall be in the midst of
the cities *that are* laid waste.
8 Then they will know that I *am* the LORD,
When I have set a fire in Egypt
And all her helpers are destroyed.
9 On that day messengers shall go forth
from Me in ships

29:7 [a] Following Masoretic Text and Vulgate; Septuagint and Syriac read *hand*. 29:10 [a] Or *tower* 30:5 [a] Hebrew *Put* [b] Hebrew *Lud*

To make the careless Ethiopians afraid,
And great anguish shall come upon them,
As on the day of Egypt;
For indeed it is coming!"

10"Thus says the Lord GOD:

"I will also make a multitude of Egypt to cease
By the hand of Nebuchadnezzar king of Babylon.
11 He and his people with him, the most terrible of the nations,
Shall be brought to destroy the land;
They shall draw their swords against Egypt,
And fill the land with the slain.
12 I will make the rivers dry,
And sell the land into the hand of the wicked;
I will make the land waste, and all that is in it,
By the hand of aliens.
I, the LORD, have spoken."

13"Thus says the Lord GOD:

"I will also destroy the idols,
And cause the images to cease from Noph;[a]
There shall no longer be princes from the land of Egypt;
I will put fear in the land of Egypt.
14 I will make Pathros desolate,
Set fire to Zoan,
And execute judgments in No.[a]
15 I will pour My fury on Sin,[a] the strength of Egypt;
I will cut off the multitude of No,
16 And set a fire in Egypt;
Sin shall have great pain,
No shall be split open,
And Noph *shall be in* distress daily.
17 The young men of Aven[a] and Pi Beseth shall fall by the sword,
And these *cities* shall go into captivity.
18 At Tehaphnehes[a] the day shall also be darkened,[b]
When I break the yokes of Egypt there.
And her arrogant strength shall cease in her;
As for her, a cloud shall cover her,
And her daughters shall go into captivity.
19 Thus I will execute judgments on Egypt,
Then they shall know that I *am* the LORD."'"

Proclamation Against Pharaoh

20And it came to pass in the eleventh year,
in the first *month,* on the seventh *day* of the
month, *that* the word of the LORD came to
me, saying, 21"Son of man, I have broken the
arm of Pharaoh king of Egypt; and see, it has
not been bandaged for healing, nor a splint
put on to bind it, to make it strong enough to
hold a sword. 22Therefore thus says the Lord
GOD: 'Surely I *am* against Pharaoh king of
Egypt, and will break his arms, both the
strong one and the one that was broken; and
I will make the sword fall out of his hand.
23I will scatter the Egyptians among the nations, and disperse them throughout the
countries. 24I will strengthen the arms of
the king of Babylon and put My sword in his
hand; but I will break Pharaoh's arms, and
he will groan before him with the groanings
of a mortally wounded *man.* 25Thus I will
strengthen the arms of the king of Babylon,
but the arms of Pharaoh shall fall down;
they shall know that I *am* the LORD, when
I put My sword into the hand of the king
of Babylon and he stretches it out against
the land of Egypt. 26I will scatter the Egyptians among the nations and disperse them
throughout the countries. Then they shall
know that I *am* the LORD.'"

Egypt Cut Down Like a Great Tree

31 Now it came to pass in the eleventh
year, in the third *month,* on the first
day of the month, *that* the word of the LORD
came to me, saying, 2"Son of man, say to
Pharaoh king of Egypt and to his multitude:

'Whom are you like in your greatness?
3 Indeed Assyria *was* a cedar in Lebanon,
With fine branches that shaded the forest,
And of high stature;
And its top was among the thick boughs.
4 The waters made it grow;

30:13 [a] That is, ancient Memphis 30:14 [a] That is, ancient Thebes 30:15 [a] That is, ancient Pelusium 30:17 [a] That is, ancient On (Heliopolis) 30:18 [a] Spelled *Tahpanhes* in Jeremiah 43:7 and elsewhere [b] Following many Hebrew manuscripts, Bomberg, Septuagint, Syriac, Targum, and Vulgate; Masoretic Text reads *refrained.*

Underground waters gave it height,
With their rivers running around the place where it was planted,
And sent out rivulets to all the trees of the field.

5 'Therefore its height was exalted above all the trees of the field;
Its boughs were multiplied,
And its branches became long because of the abundance of water,
As it sent them out.
6 All the birds of the heavens made their nests in its boughs;
Under its branches all the beasts of the field brought forth their young;
And in its shadow all great nations made their home.

7 'Thus it was beautiful in greatness and in the length of its branches,
Because its roots reached to abundant waters.
8 The cedars in the garden of God could not hide it;
The fir trees were not like its boughs,
And the chestnut[a] trees were not like its branches;
No tree in the garden of God was like it in beauty.
9 I made it beautiful with a multitude of branches,
So that all the trees of Eden envied it,
That *were* in the garden of God.'

10"Therefore thus says the Lord GOD: 'Because you have increased in height, and it set
its top among the thick boughs, and its heart
was lifted up in its height, 11therefore I will
deliver it into the hand of the mighty one of
the nations, and he shall surely deal with it;
I have driven it out for its wickedness. 12And
aliens, the most terrible of the nations, have
cut it down and left it; its branches have fall-
en on the mountains and in all the valleys;
its boughs lie broken by all the rivers of the
land; and all the peoples of the earth have
gone from under its shadow and left it.

13 'On its ruin will remain all the birds of the heavens,
And all the beasts of the field will come to its branches—

14So that no trees by the waters may ever
again exalt themselves for their height, nor
set their tops among the thick boughs, that
no tree which drinks water may ever be high
enough to reach up to them.

'For they have all been delivered to death,
To the depths of the earth,
Among the children of men who go down to the Pit.'

15"Thus says the Lord GOD: 'In the day
when it went down to hell, I caused mourning. I covered the deep because of it. I restrained its rivers, and the great waters were
held back. I caused Lebanon to mourn for it,
and all the trees of the field wilted because
of it. 16I made the nations shake at the sound
of its fall, when I cast it down to hell together with those who descend into the Pit; and
all the trees of Eden, the choice and best of
Lebanon, all that drink water, were comforted in the depths of the earth. 17They also
went down to hell with it, with those slain
by the sword; and *those who were* its *strong*
arm dwelt in its shadows among the nations.
18'To which of the trees in Eden will you
then be likened in glory and greatness? Yet
you shall be brought down with the trees of
Eden to the depths of the earth; you shall
lie in the midst of the uncircumcised, with
those slain by the sword. This *is* Pharaoh and
all his multitude,' says the Lord GOD."

Lamentation for Pharaoh and Egypt

32 And it came to pass in the twelfth
year, in the twelfth *month,* on the
first *day* of the month, *that* the word of the
LORD came to me, saying, 2"Son of man, take
up a lamentation for Pharaoh king of Egypt,
and say to him:

'You are like a young lion among the nations,
And you *are* like a monster in the seas,
Bursting forth in your rivers,
Troubling the waters with your feet,
And fouling their rivers.

3'Thus says the Lord GOD:

"I will therefore spread My net over you with a company of many people,
And they will draw you up in My net.
4 Then I will leave you on the land;
I will cast you out on the open fields,
And cause to settle on you all the birds of the heavens.

31:8 [a] Hebrew *armon*

And with you I will fill the beasts of the
whole earth.
5 I will lay your flesh on the mountains,
And fill the valleys with your carcass.

6 "I will also water the land with the flow
of your blood,
Even to the mountains;
And the riverbeds will be full of you.
7 When *I* put out your light,
I will cover the heavens, and make its
stars dark;
I will cover the sun with a cloud,
And the moon shall not give her light.
8 All the bright lights of the heavens I will
make dark over you,
And bring darkness upon your land,"
Says the Lord GOD.

9'I will also trouble the hearts of many
peoples, when I bring your destruction
among the nations, into the countries which
you have not known. 10 Yes, I will make many
peoples astonished at you, and their kings
shall be horribly afraid of you when I bran-
dish My sword before them; and they shall
tremble *every* moment, every man for his
own life, in the day of your fall.

11"For thus says the Lord GOD: 'The sword
of the king of Babylon shall come upon you.
12By the swords of the mighty warriors, all of
them the most terrible of the nations, I will
cause your multitude to fall.

'They shall plunder the pomp of Egypt,
And all its multitude shall be destroyed.
13 Also I will destroy all its animals
From beside its great waters;
The foot of man shall muddy them no
more,
Nor shall the hooves of animals muddy
them.
14 Then I will make their waters clear,
And make their rivers run like oil,'
Says the Lord GOD.

15 'When I make the land of Egypt desolate,
*And the country is destitute of all that
once filled it,*
When I strike all who dwell in it,
Then they shall know that I *am* the
LORD.

16 'This *is* the lamentation
With which they shall lament her;
The daughters of the nations shall
lament her;
They shall lament for her, for Egypt,
And for all her multitude,'
Says the Lord GOD."

Egypt and Others Consigned to the Pit

17It came to pass also in the twelfth year,
on the fifteenth *day* of the month, *that* the
word of the LORD came to me, saying:

18 "Son of man, wail over the multitude of
Egypt,
And cast them down to the depths of
the earth,
Her and the daughters of the famous
nations,
With those who go down to the Pit:
19 'Whom do you surpass in beauty?
Go down, be placed with the
uncircumcised.'

20 "They shall fall in the midst of *those* slain
by the sword;
She is delivered to the sword,
Drawing her and all her multitudes.
21 The strong among the mighty
Shall speak to him out of the midst of
hell
With those who help him:
'They have gone down,
They lie with the uncircumcised, slain
by the sword.'

22 "Assyria *is* there, and all her company,
With their graves all around her,
All of them slain, fallen by the sword.
23 Her graves are set in the recesses of the
Pit,
And her company is all around her
grave,
All of them slain, fallen by the sword,
Who caused terror in the land of the
living.

24 "There *is* Elam and all her multitude,
All around her grave,
All of them slain, fallen by the sword,
Who have gone down uncircumcised to
the lower parts of the earth,
Who caused their terror in the land of
the living;
Now they bear their shame with those
who go down to the Pit.
25 They have set her bed in the midst of
the slain,
With all her multitude,
With her graves all around it,

All of them uncircumcised, slain by the sword;
Though their terror was caused
In the land of the living,
Yet they bear their shame
With those who go down to the Pit;
It was put in the midst of the slain.

26 "There *are* Meshech and Tubal and all their multitudes,
With all their graves around it,
All of them uncircumcised, slain by the sword,
Though they caused their terror in the land of the living.
27 They do not lie with the mighty
Who are fallen of the uncircumcised,
Who have gone down to hell with their weapons of war;
They have laid their swords under their heads,
But their iniquities will be on their bones,
Because of the terror of the mighty in the land of the living.
28 Yes, you shall be broken in the midst of the uncircumcised,
And lie with *those* slain by the sword.

29 "There *is* Edom,
Her kings and all her princes,
Who despite their might
Are laid beside *those* slain by the sword;
They shall lie with the uncircumcised,
And with those who go down to the Pit.
30 There *are* the princes of the north,
All of them, and all the Sidonians,
Who have gone down with the slain
In shame at the terror which they caused by their might;
They lie uncircumcised with *those* slain by the sword,
And bear their shame with those who go down to the Pit.

31 "Pharaoh will see them
And be comforted over all his multitude,
Pharaoh and all his army,
Slain by the sword,"
Says the Lord GOD.

32 "*For I have caused My* terror in the land of the living;
And he shall be placed in the midst of the uncircumcised
With *those* slain by the sword,
Pharaoh and all his multitude,"
Says the Lord GOD.

The Watchman and His Message

33 Again the word of the LORD came
to me, saying, 2"Son of man, speak
to the children of your people, and say to
them: 'When I bring the sword upon a land,
and the people of the land take a man from
their territory and make him their watchman, 3when he sees the sword coming upon
the land, if he blows the trumpet and warns
the people, 4then whoever hears the sound
of the trumpet and does not take warning,
if the sword comes and takes him away, his
blood shall be on his *own* head. 5He heard
the sound of the trumpet, but did not take
warning; his blood shall be upon himself.
But he who takes warning will save his life.
6But if the watchman sees the sword coming and does not blow the trumpet, and the
people are not warned, and the sword comes
and takes *any* person from among them, he
is taken away in his iniquity; but his blood I
will require at the watchman's hand.'
7"So you, son of man: I have made you a
watchman for the house of Israel; therefore
you shall hear a word from My mouth and
warn them for Me. 8When I say to the wicked, 'O wicked *man,* you shall surely die!' and
you do not speak to warn the wicked from
his way, that wicked *man* shall die in his
iniquity; but his blood I will require at your
hand. 9Nevertheless if you warn the wicked
to turn from his way, and he does not turn
from his way, he shall die in his iniquity; but
you have delivered your soul.
10"Therefore you, O son of man, say to the
house of Israel: 'Thus you say, "If our transgressions and our sins *lie* upon us, and we
pine away in them, how can we then live?"'
11Say to them: '*As* I live,' says the Lord GOD, 'I
have no pleasure in the death of the wicked,
but that the wicked turn from his way and
live. Turn, turn from your evil ways! For why
should you die, O house of Israel?'

The Fairness of God's Judgment

12"Therefore you, O son of man, say to the
children of your people: 'The righteousness
of the righteous man shall not deliver him
in the day of his transgression; as for the
wickedness of the wicked, he shall not fall
because of it in the day that he turns from
his wickedness; nor shall the righteous be

able to live because of *his righteousness* in the
day that he sins.' 13When I say to the righteous *that* he shall surely live, but he trusts
in his own righteousness and commits iniquity, none of his righteous works shall be
remembered; but because of the iniquity
that he has committed, he shall die. 14Again,
when I say to the wicked, 'You shall surely
die,' if he turns from his sin and does what is
lawful and right, 15*if* the wicked restores the
pledge, gives back what he has stolen, and
walks in the statutes of life without committing iniquity, he shall surely live; he shall not
die. 16None of his sins which he has committed shall be remembered against him; he
has done what is lawful and right; he shall
surely live.

17"Yet the children of your people say,
'The way of the Lord is not fair.' But it is their
way which is not fair! 18When the righteous
turns from his righteousness and commits
iniquity, he shall die because of it. 19But
when the wicked turns from his wickedness
and does what is lawful and right, he shall
live because of it. 20Yet you say, 'The way of
the Lord is not fair.' O house of Israel, I will
judge every one of you according to his own
ways."

The Fall of Jerusalem

21And it came to pass in the twelfth year
of our captivity, in the tenth *month,* on the
fifth *day* of the month, *that* one who had escaped from Jerusalem came to me and said,
"The city has been captured!"

22Now the hand of the LORD had been
upon me the evening before the man came
who had escaped. And He had opened my
mouth; so when he came to me in the morning, my mouth was opened, and I was no
longer mute.

The Cause of Judah's Ruin

23Then the word of the LORD came to
me, saying: 24"Son of man, they who inhabit
those ruins in the land of Israel are saying,
'*Abraham was only one,* and he inherited the
land. But we *are* many; the land has been giv-
en to us as a possession.'

25"Therefore say to them, 'Thus says the
Lord GOD: "You eat *meat* with blood, you lift
up your eyes toward your idols, and shed
blood. Should you then possess the land?
26You rely on your sword, you commit abominations, and you defile one another's wives.
Should you then possess the land?"'

27"Say thus to them, 'Thus says the Lord
GOD: "*As* I live, surely those who *are* in the
ruins shall fall by the sword, and the one
who *is* in the open field I will give to the
beasts to be devoured, and those who *are* in
the strongholds and caves shall die of the
pestilence. 28For I will make the land most
desolate, her arrogant strength shall cease,
and the mountains of Israel shall be so desolate that no one will pass through. 29Then
they shall know that I *am* the LORD, when I
have made the land most desolate because
of all their abominations which they have
committed."'

Hearing and Not Doing

30"As for you, son of man, the children
of your people are talking about you beside
the walls and in the doors of the houses; and
they speak to one another, everyone saying
to his brother, 'Please come and hear what
the word is that comes from the LORD.' 31So
they come to you as people do, they sit before you *as* My people, and they hear your
words, but they do not do them; for with
their mouth they show much love, *but* their
hearts pursue their *own* gain. 32Indeed you
are to them as a very lovely song of one who
has a pleasant voice and can play well on an
instrument; for they hear your words, but
they do not do them. 33And when this comes
to pass—surely it will come—then they will
know that a prophet has been among them."

Irresponsible Shepherds

34 And the word of the LORD came to
me, saying, 2"Son of man, prophe-
sy against the shepherds of Israel, prophesy
and say to them, 'Thus says the Lord GOD
to the shepherds: "Woe to the shepherds of
Israel who feed themselves! Should not the
shepherds feed the flocks? 3You eat the fat
and clothe yourselves with the wool; you
slaughter the fatlings, *but* you do not feed
the flock. 4The weak you have not strengthened, nor have you healed those who were
sick, nor bound up the broken, nor brought
back what was driven away, nor sought what
was lost; but with force and cruelty you have
ruled them. 5So they were scattered because
there was no shepherd; and they became food
for all the beasts of the field when they were
scattered. 6My sheep wandered through all
the mountains, and on every high hill; yes,
My flock was scattered over the whole face of

the earth, and no one was seeking or searching *for them*."
7'Therefore, you shepherds, hear the word
of the LORD: 8"*As* I live," says the Lord GOD,
"surely because My flock became a prey, and
My flock became food for every beast of the
field, because *there was* no shepherd, nor did
My shepherds search for My flock, but the
shepherds fed themselves and did not feed
My flock"— 9therefore, O shepherds, hear
the word of the LORD! 10Thus says the Lord
GOD: "Behold, I *am* against the shepherds,
and I will require My flock at their hand; I
will cause them to cease feeding the sheep,
and the shepherds shall feed themselves no
more; for I will deliver My flock from their
mouths, that they may no longer be food for
them."

God, the True Shepherd

11'For thus says the Lord GOD: "Indeed
I Myself will search for My sheep and seek
them out. 12As a shepherd seeks out his flock
on the day he is among his scattered sheep,
so will I seek out My sheep and deliver them
from all the places where they were scattered on a cloudy and dark day. 13And I will
bring them out from the peoples and gather them from the countries, and will bring
them to their own land; I will feed them on
the mountains of Israel, in the valleys and
in all the inhabited places of the country. 14I
will feed them in good pasture, and their
fold shall be on the high mountains of Israel. There they shall lie down in a good fold
and feed in rich pasture on the mountains
of Israel. 15I will feed My flock, and I will
make them lie down," says the Lord GOD.
16"I will seek what was lost and bring back
what was driven away, bind up the broken
and strengthen what was sick; but I will destroy the fat and the strong, and feed them
in judgment."
17'And *as for* you, O My flock, thus says
the Lord GOD: "Behold, I shall judge between sheep and sheep, between rams and
goats. 18*Is it* too little for you to have eaten up
the good pasture, that you must tread down
with your feet the residue of your pasture—
and to have drunk of the clear waters, that
you must foul the residue with your feet?
19And *as for* My flock, they eat what you have
trampled with your feet, and they drink what
you have fouled with your feet."
20'Therefore thus says the Lord GOD to
them: "Behold, I Myself will judge between
the fat and the lean sheep. 21Because you
have pushed with side and shoulder, butt-
ed all the weak ones with your horns, and
scattered them abroad, 22therefore I will save
My flock, and they shall no longer be a prey;
and I will judge between sheep and sheep.
23I will establish one shepherd over them,
and he shall feed them—My servant David.
He shall feed them and be their shepherd.
24And I, the LORD, will be their God, and My
servant David a prince among them; I, the
LORD, have spoken.
25"I will make a covenant of peace with
them, and cause wild beasts to cease from
the land; and they will dwell safely in the
wilderness and sleep in the woods. 26I will
make them and the places all around My hill
a blessing; and I will cause showers to come
down in their season; there shall be showers
of blessing. 27Then the trees of the field shall
yield their fruit, and the earth shall yield her
increase. They shall be safe in their land;
and they shall know that I *am* the LORD,
when I have broken the bands of their yoke
and delivered them from the hand of those
who enslaved them. 28And they shall no longer be a prey for the nations, nor shall beasts
of the land devour them; but they shall dwell
safely, and no one shall make *them* afraid. 29I
will raise up for them a garden of renown,
and they shall no longer be consumed with
hunger in the land, nor bear the shame of
the Gentiles anymore. 30Thus they shall
know that I, the LORD their God, *am* with
them, and they, the house of Israel, *are* My
people," says the Lord GOD.'
31"You are My flock, the flock of My pasture; you *are* men, *and* I *am* your God," says
the Lord GOD.

Judgment on Mount Seir

35 Moreover the word of the LORD
came to me, saying, 2"Son of man,
set your face against Mount Seir and prophesy against it, 3and say to it, 'Thus says the
Lord GOD:

"Behold, O Mount Seir, I *am* against you;
I will stretch out My hand against you,
And make you most desolate;
4 I shall lay your cities waste,
And you shall be desolate.
Then you shall know that I *am* the
LORD.

5"Because you have had an ancient hatred, and have shed *the blood of* the children
of Israel by the power of the sword at the
time of their calamity, when their iniquity
came to an end, 6therefore, *as* I live," says the
Lord God, "I will prepare you for blood, and
blood shall pursue you; since you have not
hated blood, therefore blood shall pursue
you. 7Thus I will make Mount Seir most desolate, and cut off from it the one who leaves
and the one who returns. 8And I will fill its
mountains with the slain; on your hills and
in your valleys and in all your ravines those
who are slain by the sword shall fall. 9I will
make you perpetually desolate, and your
cities shall be uninhabited; then you shall
know that I *am* the LORD.

10"Because you have said, 'These two nations and these two countries shall be mine,
and we will possess them,' although the
LORD was there, 11therefore, *as* I live," says
the Lord God, "I will do according to your
anger and according to the envy which you
showed in your hatred against them; and I
will make Myself known among them when
I judge you. 12Then you shall know that I *am*
the LORD. I have heard all your blasphemies
which you have spoken against the mountains of Israel, saying, 'They are desolate;
they are given to us to consume.' 13Thus
with your mouth you have boasted against
Me and multiplied your words against Me; I
have heard *them*."

14'Thus says the Lord God: "The whole
earth will rejoice when I make you desolate.
15As you rejoiced because the inheritance of
the house of Israel was desolate, so I will do
to you; you shall be desolate, O Mount Seir,
as well as all of Edom—all of it! Then they
shall know that I *am* the LORD."'

Blessing on Israel

36 "And you, son of man, prophesy
to the mountains of Israel, and
say, 'O mountains of Israel, hear the word
of the LORD! 2Thus says the Lord God: "Because the enemy has said of you, 'Aha! The
ancient heights have become our possession,'"' 3therefore prophesy, and say, 'Thus
says the Lord God: "Because they made *you*
desolate and swallowed you up on every
side, so that you became the possession of
the rest of the nations, and you are taken up
by the lips of talkers and slandered by the
people"— 4therefore, O mountains of Israel,
hear the word of the Lord God! Thus says
the Lord God to the mountains, the hills, the
rivers, the valleys, the desolate wastes, and
the cities that have been forsaken, which
became plunder and mockery to the rest
of the nations all around— 5therefore thus
says the Lord God: "Surely I have spoken
in My burning jealousy against the rest of
the nations and against all Edom, who gave
My land to themselves as a possession, with
wholehearted joy *and* spiteful minds, in order to plunder its open country."'

6"Therefore prophesy concerning the
land of Israel, and say to the mountains, the
hills, the rivers, and the valleys, 'Thus says
the Lord God: "Behold, I have spoken in
My jealousy and My fury, because you have
borne the shame of the nations." 7Therefore
thus says the Lord God: "I have raised My
hand in an oath that surely the nations that
are around you shall bear their own shame.
8But you, O mountains of Israel, you shall
shoot forth your branches and yield your
fruit to My people Israel, for they are about
to come. 9For indeed I *am* for you, and I will
turn to you, and you shall be tilled and sown.
10I will multiply men upon you, all the house
of Israel, all of it; and the cities shall be inhabited and the ruins rebuilt. 11I will multiply upon you man and beast; and they shall
increase and bear young; I will make you inhabited as in former times, and do better *for
you* than at your beginnings. Then you shall
know that I *am* the LORD. 12Yes, I will cause
men to walk on you, My people Israel; they
shall take possession of you, and you shall be
their inheritance; no more shall you bereave
them *of children*."

13'Thus says the Lord God: "Because they
say to you, 'You devour men and bereave
your nation *of children*,' 14therefore you shall
devour men no more, nor bereave your nation anymore," says the Lord God. 15"Nor will
I let you hear the taunts of the nations anymore, nor bear the reproach of the peoples
anymore, nor shall you cause your nation to
stumble anymore," says the Lord God.'"

The Renewal of Israel

16Moreover the word of the LORD came to
me, saying: 17"Son of man, when the house
of Israel dwelt in their own land, they defiled
it by their own ways and deeds; to Me their
way was like the uncleanness of a woman
in her customary impurity. 18Therefore I

poured out My fury on them for the blood
they had shed on the land, and for their
idols *with which* they had defiled it. 19So I
scattered them among the nations, and they
were dispersed throughout the countries;
I judged them according to their ways and
their deeds. 20When they came to the nations, wherever they went, they profaned My
holy name—when they said of them, 'These
are the people of the LORD, *and* yet they have
gone out of His land.' 21But I had concern for
My holy name, which the house of Israel had
profaned among the nations wherever they
went.

22"Therefore say to the house of Israel,
'Thus says the Lord GOD: "I do not do *this*
for your sake, O house of Israel, but for My
holy name's sake, which you have profaned
among the nations wherever you went. 23And
I will sanctify My great name, which has
been profaned among the nations, which
you have profaned in their midst; and the
nations shall know that I *am* the LORD," says
the Lord GOD, "when I am hallowed in you
before their eyes. 24For I will take you from
among the nations, gather you out of all
countries, and bring you into your own land.
25Then I will sprinkle clean water on you,
and you shall be clean; I will cleanse you
from all your filthiness and from all your
idols. 26I will give you a new heart and put a
new spirit within you; I will take the heart of
stone out of your flesh and give you a heart
of flesh. 27I will put My Spirit within you and
cause you to walk in My statutes, and you
will keep My judgments and do *them.* 28Then
you shall dwell in the land that I gave to your
fathers; you shall be My people, and I will be
your God. 29I will deliver you from all your
uncleannesses. I will call for the grain and
multiply it, and bring no famine upon you.
30And I will multiply the fruit of your trees
and the increase of your fields, so that you
need never again bear the reproach of famine among the nations. 31Then you will remember your evil ways and your deeds that
were not good; and you will loathe yourselves
in your own sight, for your iniquities and
your abominations. 32Not for your sake do I
do *this,*" says the Lord GOD, "let it be known
to you. Be ashamed and confounded for your
own ways, O house of Israel!"

33'Thus says the Lord GOD: "On the day
that I cleanse you from all your iniquities,
I will also enable *you* to dwell in the cities,
and the ruins shall be rebuilt. 34The desolate
land shall be tilled instead of lying desolate
in the sight of all who pass by. 35So they will
say, 'This land that was desolate has become
like the garden of Eden; and the wasted, desolate, and ruined cities *are now* fortified *and*
inhabited.' 36Then the nations which are left
all around you shall know that I, the LORD,
have rebuilt the ruined places *and* planted
what was desolate. I, the LORD, have spoken
it, and I will do *it.*"

37'Thus says the Lord GOD: "I will also
let the house of Israel inquire of Me to do
this for them: I will increase their men like
a flock. 38Like a flock *offered as* holy *sacrifices,*
like the flock at Jerusalem on its feast days,
so shall the ruined cities be filled with flocks
of men. Then they shall know that I *am* the
LORD."'"

The Dry Bones Live

37 The hand of the LORD came upon
me and brought me out in the Spir-
it of the LORD, and set me down in the midst
of the valley; and it *was* full of bones. 2Then
He caused me to pass by them all around,
and behold, *there were* very many in the open
valley; and indeed *they were* very dry. 3And
He said to me, "Son of man, can these bones
live?"

So I answered, "O Lord GOD, You know."

4Again He said to me, "Prophesy to these
bones, and say to them, 'O dry bones, hear
the word of the LORD! 5Thus says the Lord
GOD to these bones: "Surely I will cause
breath to enter into you, and you shall live. 6I
will put sinews on you and bring flesh upon
you, cover you with skin and put breath in
you; and you shall live. Then you shall know
that I *am* the LORD."'"

7So I prophesied as I was commanded;
and as I prophesied, there was a noise, and
suddenly a rattling; and the bones came together, bone to bone. 8Indeed, as I looked,
the sinews and the flesh came upon them,
and the skin covered them over; but *there was*
no breath in them.

9Also He said to me, "Prophesy to the
breath, prophesy, son of man, and say to the
breath, 'Thus says the Lord GOD: "Come
from the four winds, O breath, and breathe
on these slain, that they may live."'" 10So I
prophesied as He commanded me, and
breath came into them, and they lived, and
stood upon their feet, an exceedingly great
army.

[11]Then He said to me, "Son of man, these
bones are the whole house of Israel. They
indeed say, 'Our bones are dry, our hope is
lost, and we ourselves are cut off!' [12]There-
fore prophesy and say to them, 'Thus says
the Lord GOD: "Behold, O My people, I will
open your graves and cause you to come up
from your graves, and bring you into the
land of Israel. [13]Then you shall know that
I *am* the LORD, when I have opened your
graves, O My people, and brought you up
from your graves. [14]I will put My Spirit in
you, and you shall live, and I will place you
in your own land. Then you shall know that
I, the LORD, have spoken *it* and performed
it," says the LORD.'"

One Kingdom, One King

[15]Again the word of the LORD came to
me, saying, [16]"As for you, son of man, take
a stick for yourself and write on it: 'For Judah and for the children of Israel, his companions.' Then take another stick and write
on it, 'For Joseph, the stick of Ephraim, and
for all the house of Israel, his companions.'
[17]Then join them one to another for yourself
into one stick, and they will become one in
your hand.

[18]"And when the children of your people
speak to you, saying, 'Will you not show us
what you *mean* by these?'— [19]say to them,
'Thus says the Lord GOD: "Surely I will take
the stick of Joseph, which *is* in the hand of
Ephraim, and the tribes of Israel, his companions; and I will join them with it, with
the stick of Judah, and make them one stick,
and they will be one in My hand."' [20]And the
sticks on which you write will be in your
hand before their eyes.

GOD MAKES BONES COME ALIVE

READ IT: EZEKIEL 37:1–14

GET IT:

The people of Israel lived in Babylon for seventy years. Ezekiel was their connection to God during their time away from home. God sent Ezekiel another vision. In this vision Ezekiel saw a valley full of dried out, dead, old bones. These bones represented the people of Israel. Some of them had died, and some were alive but had lost hope or the desire to live. Through the vision God explained how He was about to change all that. He told Ezekiel exactly what He had in mind: the bones would join together and come back to life. God would breathe new breath into them, wake them up, and fill them with new hope and new life.

LIVE IT:

The people of Israel were alive in another country, but they felt dead and hopeless inside. Maybe you've felt that way when you were sick or tired or discouraged because nothing was going right. Ezekiel's vision of long ago can give us hope, too. God never leaves us in our "dead" state. We won't always feel lonely, discouraged, or just plain rotten. God promises to make us come alive again. He wants to bring us back to full health and restore our happiness.

21“Then say to them, ‘Thus says the Lord
God: “Surely I will take the children of Israel
from among the nations, wherever they have
gone, and will gather them from every side
and bring them into their own land; 22and I
will make them one nation in the land, on
the mountains of Israel; and one king shall
be king over them all; they shall no longer
be two nations, nor shall they ever be divided into two kingdoms again. 23They shall
not defile themselves anymore with their
idols, nor with their detestable things, nor
with any of their transgressions; but I will
deliver them from all their dwelling places
in which they have sinned, and will cleanse
them. Then they shall be My people, and I
will be their God.

24“David My servant *shall be* king over
them, and they shall all have one shepherd;
they shall also walk in My judgments and observe My statutes, and do them. 25Then they
shall dwell in the land that I have given to
Jacob My servant, where your fathers dwelt;
and they shall dwell there, they, their children, and their children's children, forever;
and My servant David *shall be* their prince
forever. 26Moreover I will make a covenant
of peace with them, and it shall be an everlasting covenant with them; I will establish
them and multiply them, and I will set My
sanctuary in their midst forevermore. 27My
tabernacle also shall be with them; indeed I
will be their God, and they shall be My people. 28The nations also will know that I, the
Lord, sanctify Israel, when My sanctuary is
in their midst forevermore.”’”

Gog and Allies Attack Israel

38 Now the word of the Lord came
to me, saying, 2“Son of man, set
your face against Gog, of the land of Magog,
the prince of Rosh,[a] Meshech, and Tubal,
and prophesy against him, 3and say, ‘Thus
says the Lord God: “Behold, I *am* against
you, O Gog, the prince of Rosh, Meshech,
and Tubal. 4I will turn you around, put hooks
into your jaws, and lead you out, with all
your army, horses, and horsemen, all splen-
didly clothed, a great company *with* bucklers
and shields, all of them handling swords.
5Persia, Ethiopia,[a] and Libya[b] are with them,
all of them *with* shield and helmet; 6Gomer
and all its troops; the house of Togarmah

In Focus

38:2, 3 Gog and Magog See Revelation 20:8. Gog is the future leader of an army against Israel. Magog is his country to the far north of Israel.

from the far north and all its troops—many
people *are* with you.

7“Prepare yourself and be ready, you and
all your companies that are gathered about
you; and be a guard for them. 8After many
days you will be visited. In the latter years
you will come into the land of those brought
back from the sword *and* gathered from
many people on the mountains of Israel,
which had long been desolate; they were
brought out of the nations, and now all of
them dwell safely. 9You will ascend, coming
like a storm, covering the land like a cloud,
you and all your troops and many peoples
with you.”

10‘Thus says the Lord God: “On that day it
shall come to pass *that* thoughts will arise in
your mind, and you will make an evil plan:
11You will say, ‘I will go up against a land of
unwalled villages; I will go to a peaceful people, who dwell safely, all of them dwelling
without walls, and having neither bars nor
gates’— 12to take plunder and to take booty,
to stretch out your hand against the waste
places *that are again* inhabited, and against a
people gathered from the nations, who have
acquired livestock and goods, who dwell in
the midst of the land. 13Sheba, Dedan, the
merchants of Tarshish, and all their young
lions will say to you, ‘Have you come to take
plunder? Have you gathered your army to
take booty, to carry away silver and gold, to
take away livestock and goods, to take great
plunder?’”’

14“Therefore, son of man, prophesy and
say to Gog, ‘Thus says the Lord God: “On
that day when My people Israel dwell safely,
will you not know *it*? 15Then you will come
from your place out of the far north, you and

38:2 [a] Targum, Vulgate, and Aquila read *chief prince of* (also verse 3). **38:5** [a] Hebrew *Cush* [b] Hebrew *Put*

many peoples with you, all of them riding on horses, a great company and a mighty army. 16 You will come up against My people Israel like a cloud, to cover the land. It will be in the latter days that I will bring you against My land so that the nations may know Me, when I am hallowed in you, O Gog, before their eyes." 17 Thus says the Lord GOD: "Are *you* he of whom I have spoken in former days by My servants the prophets of Israel, who prophesied for years in those days that I would bring you against them?

Judgment on Gog

18 "And it will come to pass at the same time, when Gog comes against the land of Israel," says the Lord GOD, "*that* My fury will show in My face. 19 For in My jealousy *and* in the fire of My wrath I have spoken: 'Surely in that day there shall be a great earthquake in the land of Israel, 20 so that the fish of the sea, the birds of the heavens, the beasts of the field, all creeping things that creep on the earth, and all men who *are* on the face of the earth shall shake at My presence. The mountains shall be thrown down, the steep places shall fall, and every wall shall fall to the ground.' 21 I will call for a sword against Gog throughout all My mountains," says the Lord GOD. "Every man's sword will be against his brother. 22 And I will bring him to judgment with pestilence and bloodshed; I will rain down on him, on his troops, and on the many peoples who *are* with him, flooding rain, great hailstones, fire, and brimstone. 23 Thus I will magnify Myself and sanctify Myself, and I will be known in the eyes of many nations. Then they shall know that I *am* the LORD."'

Gog's Armies Destroyed

39 "And you, son of man, prophesy against Gog, and say, 'Thus says the Lord GOD: "Behold, I *am* against you, O Gog, the prince of Rosh,[a] Meshech, and Tubal; 2 and I will turn you around and lead you on, bringing you up from the far north, and bring you against the mountains of Israel. 3 Then I will knock the bow out of your left hand, and cause the arrows to fall out of your right hand. 4 You shall fall upon the mountains of Israel, you and all your troops and the peoples who *are* with you; I will give you to birds of prey of every sort and *to* the beasts of the field to be devoured. 5 You shall fall on the open field; for I have spoken," says the Lord GOD. 6 "And I will send fire on Magog and on those who live in security in the coastlands. Then they shall know that I *am* the LORD. 7 So I will make My holy name known in the midst of My people Israel, and I will not *let them* profane My holy name anymore. Then the nations shall know that *I am* the LORD, the Holy One in Israel. 8 Surely it is coming, and it shall be done," says the Lord GOD. "This *is* the day of which I have spoken.

9 "Then those who dwell in the cities of Israel will go out and set on fire and burn the weapons, both the shields and bucklers, the bows and arrows, the javelins and spears; and they will make fires with them for seven years. 10 They will not take wood from the field nor cut down *any* from the forests, because they will make fires with the weapons; and they will plunder those who plundered them, and pillage those who pillaged them," says the Lord GOD.

The Burial of Gog

11 "It will come to pass in that day *that* I will give Gog a burial place there in Israel, the valley of those who pass by east of the sea; and it will obstruct travelers, because there they will bury Gog and all his multitude. Therefore they will call *it* the Valley of Hamon Gog.[a] 12 For seven months the house of Israel will be burying them, in order to cleanse the land. 13 Indeed all the people of the land will be burying, and they will gain renown for it on the day that I am glorified," says the Lord GOD. 14 "They will set apart men regularly employed, with the help of a search party,[a] to pass through the land and bury those bodies remaining on the ground, in order to cleanse it. At the end of seven months they will make a search. 15 The search party will pass through the land; and *when anyone* sees a man's bone, he shall set up a marker by it, till the buriers have buried it in the Valley of Hamon Gog. 16 *The* name of *the* city *will* also *be* Hamonah. Thus they shall cleanse the land."'

A Triumphant Festival

17 "And as for you, son of man, thus says

39:1 [a] Targum, Vulgate and Aquila read *chief prince of.*
39:11 [a] Literally *The Multitude of Gog* **39:14** [a] Literally *those who pass through*

the Lord GOD, 'Speak to every sort of bird
and to every beast of the field:

"Assemble yourselves and come;
Gather together from all sides to My
sacrificial meal
Which I am sacrificing for you,
A great sacrificial meal on the
mountains of Israel,
That you may eat flesh and drink blood.
18 You shall eat the flesh of the mighty,
Drink the blood of the princes of the
earth,
Of rams and lambs,
Of goats and bulls,
All of them fatlings of Bashan.
19 You shall eat fat till you are full,
And drink blood till you are drunk,
At My sacrificial meal
Which I am sacrificing for you.
20 You shall be filled at My table
With horses and riders,
With mighty men
And with all the men of war," says the
Lord GOD.

Israel Restored to the Land

21"I will set My glory among the nations;
all the nations shall see My judgment which
I have executed, and My hand which I have
laid on them. 22So the house of Israel shall
know that I *am* the LORD their God from that
day forward. 23The Gentiles shall know that
the house of Israel went into captivity for
their iniquity; because they were unfaithful
to Me, therefore I hid My face from them. I
gave them into the hand of their enemies,
and they all fell by the sword. 24According
to their uncleanness and according to their
transgressions I have dealt with them, and
hidden My face from them."'

25"Therefore thus says the Lord GOD:
'Now I will bring back the captives of Jacob,
and have mercy on the whole house of Israel;
and I will be jealous for My holy name—
26after they have borne their shame, and
all their unfaithfulness in which they were
unfaithful to Me, when they dwelt safely in
their *own* land and no one made *them* afraid.
27When I have brought them back from the
peoples and gathered them out of their enemies' lands, and I am hallowed in them in
the sight of many nations, 28then they shall
know that I *am* the LORD their God, who sent
them into captivity among the nations, but
also brought them back to their land, and
left none of them captive any longer. 29And
I will not hide My face from them anymore;
for I shall have poured out My Spirit on the
house of Israel,' says the Lord GOD."

A New City, a New Temple

40 In the twenty-fifth year of our
captivity, at the beginning of the
year, on the tenth *day* of the month, in the
fourteenth year after the city was captured,
on the very same day the hand of the LORD
was upon me; and He took me there. 2In the
visions of God He took me into the land of
Israel and set me on a very high mountain;
on it toward the south *was* something like
the structure of a city. 3He took me there,
and behold, *there was* a man whose appearance *was* like the appearance of bronze. He
had a line of flax and a measuring rod in his
hand, and he stood in the gateway.

4And the man said to me, "Son of man,
look with your eyes and hear with your ears,
and fix your mind on everything I show you;
for you *were* brought here so that I might show
them to you. Declare to the house of Israel
everything you see." 5Now there was a wall
all around the outside of the temple.[a] In the
man's hand was a measuring rod six cubits
long, each being a cubit and a handbreadth;
and he measured the width of the wall structure, one rod; and the height, one rod.

The Eastern Gateway of the Temple

6Then he went to the gateway which
faced east; and he went up its stairs and measured the threshold of the gateway, *which*
was one rod wide, and the other threshold
was one rod wide. 7Each gate chamber *was*
one rod long and one rod wide; between the
gate chambers *was a space of* five cubits; and
the threshold of the gateway by the vestibule
of the inside gate *was* one rod. 8He also measured the vestibule of the inside gate, one
rod. 9Then he measured the vestibule of the
gateway, eight cubits; and the gateposts, two
cubits. The vestibule of the gate *was* on the
inside. 10In the eastern gateway *were* three
gate chambers on one side and three on the
other; the three *were* all the same size; also
the gateposts were of the same size on this
side and that side.

40:5 [a] Literally *house*, and so elsewhere in this book

11 He measured the width of the entrance
to the gateway, ten cubits; *and* the length of
the gate, thirteen cubits. 12 *There was* a space
in front of the gate chambers, one cubit *on
this side* and one cubit on that side; the gate
chambers *were* six cubits on this side and six
cubits on that side. 13 Then he measured the
gateway from the roof of *one* gate chamber to
the roof of the other; the width *was* twenty-
five cubits, as door faces door. 14 He measured the gateposts, sixty cubits high, and
the court all around the gateway *extended* to
the gatepost. 15 *From* the front of the entrance
gate to the front of the vestibule of the inner gate *was* fifty cubits. 16 *There were* beveled
window *frames* in the gate chambers and in
their intervening archways on the inside of
the gateway all around, and likewise in the
vestibules. *There were* windows all around on
the inside. And on each gatepost *were* palm
trees.

The Outer Court

17 Then he brought me into the outer
court; and *there were* chambers and a pavement made all around the court; thirty
chambers faced the pavement. 18 The pavement was by the side of the gateways, corresponding to the length of the gateways;
this was the lower pavement. 19 Then he measured the width from the front of the lower
gateway to the front of the inner court exte-
rior, one hundred cubits toward the east and
the north.

The Northern Gateway

20 On the outer court was also a gateway
facing north, and he measured its length
and its width. 21 Its gate chambers, three on
this side and three on that side, its gateposts
and its archways, had the same measurements as the first gate; its length *was* fifty
cubits and its width twenty-five cubits. 22 Its
windows and those of its archways, and also
its palm trees, *had* the same measurements
as the gateway facing east; it was ascended
by seven steps, and its archway *was* in front
of it. 23 A gate of the inner court was opposite the northern gateway, just as the eastern
gateway; and he measured from gateway to
gateway, one hundred cubits.

The Southern Gateway

24 After that he brought me toward the
south, and there a gateway was facing south;
and he measured its gateposts and archways
according to these same measurements.
25 *There were* windows in it and in its archways all around like those windows; its
length *was* fifty cubits and its width twenty-
five cubits. 26 Seven steps led up to it, and
its archway *was* in front of them; and it had
palm trees on its gateposts, one on this side
and one on that side. 27 *There was* also a gateway on the inner court, facing south; and he
measured from gateway to gateway toward
the south, one hundred cubits.

Gateways of the Inner Court

28 Then he brought me to the inner court
through the southern gateway; he measured
the southern gateway according to these
same measurements. 29 Also its gate chambers, its gateposts, and its archways *were* according to these same measurements; *there
were* windows in it and in its archways all
around; *it was* fifty cubits long and twenty-
five cubits wide. 30 *There were* archways all
around, twenty-five cubits long and five
cubits wide. 31 Its archways faced the outer
court, palm trees *were* on its gateposts, and
going up to it *were* eight steps.

32 And he brought me into the inner court
facing east; he measured the gateway according to these same measurements. 33 Also its
gate chambers, its gateposts, and its archways *were* according to these same measurements; and *there were* windows in it and in its
archways all around; *it was* fifty cubits long
and twenty-five cubits wide. 34 Its archways
faced the outer court, and palm trees *were*
on its gateposts on this side and on that side;
and going up to it *were* eight steps.

35 Then he brought me to the north gateway and measured *it* according to these
same measurements— 36 also its gate chambers, its gateposts, and its archways. It had
windows all around; its length *was* fifty
cubits and its width twenty-five cubits. 37 Its
gateposts faced the outer court, palm trees
were on its gateposts on this side and on that
side, and going up to it *were* eight steps.

Where Sacrifices Were Prepared

38 *There was* a chamber and its entrance
by the gateposts of the gateway, where they
washed the burnt offering. 39 In the vestibule
of the gateway *were* two tables on this side
and two tables on that side, on which to slay
the burnt offering, the sin offering, and the

trespass offering. 40At the outer side of the
vestibule, as one goes up to the entrance of
the northern gateway, *were* two tables; and
on the other side of the vestibule of the gateway *were* two tables. 41Four tables *were* on
this side and four tables on that side, by the
side of the gateway, eight tables on which
they slaughtered *the sacrifices.* 42*There were*
also four tables of hewn stone for the burnt
offering, one cubit and a half long, one cubit and a half wide, and one cubit high; on
these they laid the instruments with which
they slaughtered the burnt offering and the
sacrifice. 43Inside *were* hooks, a handbreadth
wide, fastened all around; and the flesh of
the sacrifices *was* on the tables.

Chambers for Singers and Priests

44Outside the inner gate *were* the chambers for the singers in the inner court, one
facing south at the side of the northern gateway, and the other facing north at the side of
the southern[a] gateway. 45Then he said to me,
"This chamber which faces south *is* for the
priests who have charge of the temple. 46The
chamber which faces north *is* for the priests
who have charge of the altar; these *are* the
sons of Zadok, from the sons of Levi, who
come near the LORD to minister to Him."

Dimensions of the Inner Court and Vestibule

47And he measured the court, one hundred cubits long and one hundred cubits
wide, foursquare. The altar *was* in front of
the temple. 48Then he brought me to the vestibule of the temple and measured the doorposts of the vestibule, five cubits on this side
and five cubits on that side; and the width of
the gateway was three cubits on this side and
three cubits on that side. 49The length of the
vestibule *was* twenty cubits, and the width
eleven cubits; and by the steps which led up
to it *there were* pillars by the doorposts, one
on this side and another on that side.

Dimensions of the Sanctuary

41 Then he brought me into the sanctuary[a] and measured the doorposts, six cubits wide on one side and six
cubits wide on the other side—the width of
the tabernacle. 2The width of the entryway
was ten cubits, and the side walls of the entrance *were* five cubits on this side and five
cubits on the other side; and he measured
its length, forty cubits, and its width, twenty
cubits.

3Also he went inside and measured the
doorposts, two cubits; and the entrance, six
cubits *high;* and the width of the entrance,
seven cubits. 4He measured the length,
twenty cubits; and the width, twenty cubits,
beyond the sanctuary; and he said to me,
"This *is* the Most Holy *Place.*"

The Side Chambers on the Wall

5Next, he measured the wall of the temple, six cubits. The width of each side chamber all around the temple *was* four cubits on
every side. 6The side chambers *were* in three
stories, one above the other, thirty chambers
in each story; they rested on ledges which
were for the side chambers all around, that
they might be supported, but not fastened to
the wall of the temple. 7As one went up from
story to story, the side chambers became
wider all around, because their supporting
ledges in the wall of the temple ascended
like steps; therefore the width of the structure increased as one went up *from* the lowest *story* to the highest by way of the middle
one. 8I also saw an elevation all around the
temple; it was the foundation of the side
chambers, a full rod, *that is,* six cubits *high.*
9The thickness of the outer wall of the side
chambers *was* five cubits, and so also the
remaining terrace by the place of the side
chambers of the temple. 10And between *it*
and the *wall* chambers was a width of twenty cubits all around the temple on every side.
11The doors of the side chambers opened on
the terrace, one door toward the north and
another toward the south; and the width of
the terrace *was* five cubits all around.

The Building at the Western End

12The building that faced the separating
courtyard at its western end *was* seventy cubits wide; the wall of the building *was* five
cubits thick all around, and its length ninety
cubits.

Dimensions and Design of the Temple Area

13So he measured the temple, one
hundred cubits long; and the separating

40:44 [a] Following Septuagint; Masoretic Text and Vulgate read *eastern.* 41:1 [a] Hebrew *heykal,* here the main room of the temple, sometimes called the *holy place* (compare Exodus 26:33)

courtyard with the building and its walls
was one hundred cubits long; 14also the width
of the eastern face of the temple, including
the separating courtyard, *was* one hundred
cubits. 15He measured the length of the
building behind it, facing the separating
courtyard, with its galleries on the one side
and on the other side, one hundred cubits, as
well as the inner temple and the porches of
the court, 16their doorposts and the beveled
window frames. And the galleries all around
their three stories opposite the threshold
were paneled with wood from the ground to
the windows—the windows were covered—
17from the space above the door, even to the
inner room,[a] as well as outside, and on every wall all around, inside and outside, by
measure.

18And *it was* made with cherubim and
palm trees, a palm tree between cherub and
cherub. *Each* cherub had two faces, 19so that
the face of a man *was* toward a palm tree
on one side, and the face of a young lion toward a palm tree on the other side; thus *it*
was made throughout the temple all around.
20From the floor to the space above the door,
and on the wall of the sanctuary, cherubim
and palm trees *were* carved.

21The doorposts of the temple *were*
square, *as was* the front of the sanctuary;
their appearance was similar. 22The altar *was*
of wood, three cubits high, and its length
two cubits. Its corners, its length, and its
sides *were* of wood; and he said to me, "This
is the table that *is* before the LORD."

23The temple and the sanctuary had two
doors. 24The doors had two panels *apiece,*
two folding panels: two *panels* for one door
and two panels for the other *door.* 25Cher-
ubim and palm trees *were* carved on the
doors of the temple just as they *were* carved
on the walls. A wooden canopy *was* on the
front of the vestibule outside. 26*There were*
beveled window *frames* and palm trees on
one side and on the other, on the sides of the
vestibule—also on the side chambers of the
temple and on the canopies.

The Chambers for the Priests

42 Then he brought me out into the
outer court, by the way toward the
north; and he brought me into the chamber
which *was* opposite the separating courtyard, and which *was* opposite the building
toward the north. 2Facing the length, *which*
was one hundred cubits (the width was fifty
cubits), was the north door. 3Opposite the
inner court of twenty *cubits,* and opposite
the pavement of the outer court, *was* gallery
against gallery in three *stories.* 4In front of
the chambers, toward the inside, *was* a walk
ten cubits wide, at a distance of one cubit;
and their doors faced north. 5Now the upper
chambers *were* shorter, because the galleries
took away *space* from them more than from
the lower and middle stories of the building. 6For they *were* in three *stories* and did
not have pillars like the pillars of the courts;
therefore *the upper level* was shortened more
than the lower and middle levels from the
ground up. 7And a wall which *was* outside
ran parallel to the chambers, at the front of
the chambers, toward the outer court; its
length *was* fifty cubits. 8The length of the
chambers toward the outer court *was* fifty
cubits, whereas that facing the temple *was*
one hundred cubits. 9At the lower chambers
was the entrance on the east side, as one goes
into them from the outer court.

10Also *there were* chambers in the thickness of the wall of the court toward the east,
opposite the separating courtyard and opposite the building. 11*There was* a walk in front
of them also, and their appearance *was* like
the chambers which *were* toward the north;
they *were* as long and as wide as the others,
and all their exits and entrances *were* according to plan. 12And corresponding to the doors
of the chambers that *were* facing south, as
one enters them, *there was* a door in front of
the walk, the way directly in front of the wall
toward the east.

13Then he said to me, "The north chambers *and* the south chambers, which *are* opposite the separating courtyard, *are* the holy
chambers where the priests who approach the
LORD shall eat the most holy offerings. There
they shall lay the most holy offerings—the
grain offering, the sin offering, and the trespass offering—for the place *is* holy. 14When
the priests enter them, they shall not go out
of the holy *chamber* into the outer court; but
there they shall leave their garments in which
they minister, for they *are* holy. They shall put
on other garments; then they may approach
that which *is* for the people."

Outer Dimensions of the Temple

15Now when he had finished measuring
the inner temple, he brought me out through

41:17 [a] Literally *house,* here *the Most Holy Place*

the gateway that faces toward the east, and
measured it all around. 16He measured the
east side with the measuring rod,[a] five hundred rods by the measuring rod all around.
17He measured the north side, five hundred
rods by the measuring rod all around. 18He
measured the south side, five hundred rods
by the measuring rod. 19He came around to
the west side *and* measured five hundred
rods by the measuring rod. 20He measured
it on the four sides; it had a wall all around,
five hundred *cubits* long and five hundred
wide, to separate the holy areas from the
common.

The Temple, the LORD's Dwelling Place

43 Afterward he brought me to the
gate, the gate that faces toward the
east. 2And behold, the glory of the God of Israel came from the way of the east. His voice
was like the sound of many waters; and the
earth shone with His glory. 3*It was* like the
appearance of the vision which I saw—like
the vision which I saw when I[a] came to destroy the city. The visions *were* like the vision
which I saw by the River Chebar; and I fell
on my face. 4And the glory of the LORD came
into the temple by way of the gate which faces toward the east. 5The Spirit lifted me up
and brought me into the inner court; and behold, the glory of the LORD filled the temple.
6Then I heard *Him* speaking to me from
the temple, while a man stood beside me.
7And He said to me, "Son of man, *this is* the
place of My throne and the place of the soles
of My feet, where I will dwell in the midst of
the children of Israel forever. No more shall
the house of Israel defile My holy name, they
nor their kings, by their harlotry or with the
carcasses of their kings on their high places.
8When they set their threshold by My threshold, and their doorpost by My doorpost, with
a wall between them and Me, they defiled
My holy name by the abominations which
they committed; therefore I have consumed
them in My anger. 9Now let them put their
harlotry and the carcasses of their kings far
away from Me, and I will dwell in their midst
forever.

10"Son of man, describe the temple to the
house of Israel, that they may be ashamed
of their iniquities; and let them measure the
pattern. 11And if they are ashamed of all that
they have done, make known to them the
design of the temple and its arrangement,
its exits and its entrances, its entire design
and all its ordinances, all its forms and all
its laws. Write *it* down in their sight, so that
they may keep its whole design and all its
ordinances, and perform them. 12This *is* the
law of the temple: The whole area surrounding the mountaintop *is* most holy. Behold,
this *is* the law of the temple.

Dimensions of the Altar

13"These are the measurements of the
altar in cubits (the cubit *is* one cubit and a
handbreadth): the base one cubit high and
one cubit wide, with a rim all around its
edge of one span. This *is* the height of the
altar: 14from the base on the ground to the
lower ledge, two cubits; the width of the
ledge, one cubit; from the smaller ledge to
the larger ledge, four cubits; and the width
of the ledge, *one* cubit. 15The altar hearth *is*
four cubits high, with four horns extending
upward from the hearth. 16The altar hearth *is*
twelve *cubits* long, twelve wide, square at its
four corners; 17the ledge, fourteen *cubits* long
and fourteen wide on its four sides, with a
rim of half a cubit around it; its base, one
cubit all around; and its steps face toward
the east."

Consecrating the Altar

18And He said to me, "Son of man, thus
says the Lord GOD: 'These *are* the ordinances for the altar on the day when it is made,
for sacrificing burnt offerings on it, and for
sprinkling blood on it. 19You shall give a
young bull for a sin offering to the priests,
the Levites, who are of the seed of Zadok,
who approach Me to minister to Me,' says
the Lord GOD. 20'You shall take some of its
blood and put *it* on the four horns of the altar, on the four corners of the ledge, and on
the rim around it; thus you shall cleanse it
and make atonement for it. 21Then you shall
also take the bull of the sin offering, and
burn it in the appointed place of the temple, outside the sanctuary. 22On the second
day you shall offer a kid of the goats without
blemish for a sin offering; and they shall
cleanse the altar, as they cleansed *it* with the
bull. 23When you have finished cleansing *it*,
you shall offer a young bull without blemish,
and a ram from the flock without blemish.

42:16 [a] Compare 40:5 **43:3** [a] Some Hebrew manuscripts and Vulgate read *He*.

24 When you offer them before the LORD, the
priests shall throw salt on them, and they
will offer them up *as* a burnt offering to the
LORD. 25 Every day for seven days you shall
prepare a goat *for* a sin offering; they shall
also prepare a young bull and a ram from
the flock, both without blemish. 26 Seven
days they shall make atonement for the altar
and purify it, and so consecrate *it*. 27 When
these days are over it shall be, on the eighth
day and thereafter, that the priests shall offer
your burnt offerings and your peace offerings on the altar; and I will accept you,' says
the Lord GOD."

The East Gate and the Prince

44 Then He brought me back to the
outer gate of the sanctuary which
faces toward the east, but it *was* shut. 2 And
the LORD said to me, "This gate shall be shut;
it shall not be opened, and no man shall enter by it, because the LORD God of Israel has
entered by it; therefore it shall be shut. 3 *As for*
the prince, *because* he *is* the prince, he may
sit in it to eat bread before the LORD; he shall
enter by way of the vestibule of the gateway,
and go out the same way."

Those Admitted to the Temple

4 Also He brought me by way of the north
gate to the front of the temple; so I looked,
and behold, the glory of the LORD filled the
house of the LORD; and I fell on my face.
5 And the LORD said to me, "Son of man,
mark well, see with your eyes and hear with
your ears, all that I say to you concerning all
the ordinances of the house of the LORD and
all its laws. Mark well who may enter the
house and all who go out from the sanctuary.

6 "Now say to the rebellious, to the house
of Israel, 'Thus says the Lord GOD: "O house
of Israel, let Us have no more of all your
abominations. 7 When you brought in foreigners, uncircumcised in heart and uncircumcised in flesh, to be in My sanctuary to
defile it—My house—and when you offered
My food the fat and the blood, then they
broke My covenant because of all your abominations. 8 And you have not kept charge of
My holy things, but you have set *others* to
keep charge of My sanctuary for you." 9 Thus
says the Lord GOD: "No foreigner, uncircumcised in heart or uncircumcised in flesh,
shall enter My sanctuary, including any foreigner who is among the children of Israel.

Laws Governing Priests

10 "And the Levites who went far from Me,
when Israel went astray, who strayed away
from Me after their idols, they shall bear
their iniquity. 11 Yet they shall be ministers
in My sanctuary, *as* gatekeepers of the house
and ministers of the house; they shall slay
the burnt offering and the sacrifice for the
people, and they shall stand before them to
minister to them. 12 Because they ministered
to them before their idols and caused the
house of Israel to fall into iniquity, therefore
I have raised My hand in an oath against
them," says the Lord GOD, "that they shall
bear their iniquity. 13 And they shall not come
near Me to minister to Me as priest, nor
come near any of My holy things, nor into
the Most Holy *Place;* but they shall bear their
shame and their abominations which they
have committed. 14 Nevertheless I will make
them keep charge of the temple, for all its
work, and for all that has to be done in it.

15 "But the priests, the Levites, the sons
of Zadok, who kept charge of My sanctuary
when the children of Israel went astray from
Me, they shall come near Me to minister to
Me; and they shall stand before Me to offer
to Me the fat and the blood," says the Lord
GOD. 16 "They shall enter My sanctuary, and
they shall come near My table to minister to
Me, and they shall keep My charge. 17 And it
shall be, whenever they enter the gates of the
inner court, that they shall put on linen garments; no wool shall come upon them while
they minister within the gates of the inner
court or within the house. 18 They shall have
linen turbans on their heads and linen trousers on their bodies; they shall not clothe
themselves with *anything that causes* sweat.
19 When they go out to the outer court, to the
outer court to the people, they shall take off
their garments in which they have ministered, leave them in the holy chambers, and
put on other garments; and in their holy garments they shall not sanctify the people.

20 "They shall neither shave their heads
nor let their hair grow long, but they shall
keep their hair well trimmed. 21 No priest
shall drink wine when he enters the inner
court. 22 They shall not take as wife a widow
or a divorced woman, but take virgins of the
descendants of the house of Israel, or widows of priests.

23 "And they shall teach My people *the difference* between the holy and the unholy, and

cause them to discern between the unclean
and the clean. 24In controversy they shall
stand as judges, *and* judge it according to My
judgments. They shall keep My laws and My
statutes in all My appointed meetings, and
they shall hallow My Sabbaths.

25"They shall not defile *themselves* by
coming near a dead person. Only for father
or mother, for son or daughter, for brother
or unmarried sister may they defile themselves. 26After he is cleansed, they shall
count seven days for him. 27And on the day
that he goes to the sanctuary to minister in
the sanctuary, he must offer his sin offering
in the inner court," says the Lord GOD.

28"It shall be, in regard to their inheritance, *that* I *am* their inheritance. You shall
give them no possession in Israel, for I *am*
their possession. 29They shall eat the grain
offering, the sin offering, and the trespass
offering; every dedicated thing in Israel shall
be theirs. 30The best of all firstfruits of any
kind, and every sacrifice of any kind from
all your sacrifices, shall be the priest's; also
you shall give to the priest the first of your
ground meal, to cause a blessing to rest on
your house. 31The priests shall not eat anything, bird or beast, that died naturally or
was torn *by wild beasts.*

The Holy District

45 "Moreover, when you divide the
land by lot into inheritance, you
shall set apart a district for the LORD, a holy
section of the land; its length *shall be* twenty-
five thousand *cubits,* and the width ten thousand. It *shall be* holy throughout its territory
all around. 2Of this there shall be a square
plot for the sanctuary, five hundred by five
hundred *rods,* with fifty cubits around it for
an open space. 3So this is the district you
shall measure: twenty-five thousand *cubits*
long and ten thousand wide; in it shall be
the sanctuary, the Most Holy *Place.* 4It shall
be a holy *section* of the land, belonging to
the priests, the ministers of the sanctuary,
who come near to minister to the LORD; it
shall be a place for their houses and a holy
place for the sanctuary. 5*An area* twenty-five
thousand *cubits* long and ten thousand wide
shall belong to the Levites, the ministers of
the temple; they shall have twenty chambers
as a possession.[a]

Properties of the City and the Prince

6"You shall appoint as the property of the
city *an area* five thousand *cubits* wide and
twenty-five thousand long, adjacent to the
district of the holy *section;* it shall belong to
the whole house of Israel.

7"The prince shall have *a section* on one
side and the other of the holy district and the
city's property; and bordering on the holy
district and the city's property, extending
westward on the west side and eastward on
the east side, the length *shall be* side by side
with one of the *tribal* portions, from the west
border to the east border. 8The land shall be
his possession in Israel; and My princes
shall no more oppress My people, but they
shall give *the rest of* the land to the house of
Israel, according to their tribes."

Laws Governing the Prince

9'Thus says the Lord GOD: "Enough, O
princes of Israel! Remove violence and plundering, execute justice and righteousness,
and stop dispossessing My people," says the
Lord GOD. 10"You shall have honest scales,
an honest ephah, and an honest bath. 11The
ephah and the bath shall be of the same
measure, so that the bath contains one-tenth
of a homer, and the ephah one-tenth of a homer; their measure shall be according to the
homer. 12The shekel *shall be* twenty gerahs;
twenty shekels, twenty-five shekels, *and* fifteen shekels shall be your mina.

13"This *is* the offering which you shall
offer: you shall give one-sixth of an ephah
from a homer of wheat, and one-sixth of an
ephah from a homer of barley. 14The ordinance concerning oil, the bath of oil, *is* one-
tenth of a bath from a kor. *A kor is* a homer
or ten baths, for ten baths *are* a homer. 15And
one lamb shall be given from a flock of two
hundred, from the rich pastures of Israel.
These shall be for grain offerings, burnt offerings, and peace offerings, to make atonement for them," says the Lord GOD. 16"All the
people of the land shall give this offering for
the prince in Israel. 17Then it shall be the
prince's part *to give* burnt offerings, grain
offerings, and drink offerings, at the feasts,
the New Moons, the Sabbaths, and at all the
appointed seasons of the house of Israel.
He shall prepare the sin offering, the grain
offering, the burnt offering, and the peace
offerings to make atonement for the house
of Israel."

45:5 [a] Following Masoretic Text, Targum, and Vulgate; Septuagint reads *a possession, cities of dwelling.*

Keeping the Feasts

18 'Thus says the Lord GOD: "In the first
month, on the first *day* of the month, you
shall take a young bull without blemish and
cleanse the sanctuary. 19 The priest shall take
some of the blood of the sin offering and put
it on the doorposts of the temple, on the
four corners of the ledge of the altar, and on
the gateposts of the gate of the inner court.
20 And so you shall do on the seventh *day* of
the month for everyone who has sinned unintentionally or in ignorance. Thus you shall
make atonement for the temple.

21 "In the first *month,* on the fourteenth
day of the month, you shall observe the Passover, a feast of seven days; unleavened bread
shall be eaten. 22 And on that day the prince
shall prepare for himself and for all the people of the land a bull *for* a sin offering. 23 On
the seven days of the feast he shall prepare
a burnt offering to the LORD, seven bulls
and seven rams without blemish, daily for
seven days, and a kid of the goats daily *for* a
sin offering. 24 And he shall prepare a grain
offering of one ephah for each bull and one
ephah for each ram, together with a hin of
oil for each ephah.

25 "In the seventh *month,* on the fifteenth
day of the month, at the feast, he shall do
likewise for seven days, according to the sin
offering, the burnt offering, the grain offering, and the oil."

The Manner of Worship

46 'Thus says the Lord GOD: "The
gateway of the inner court that
faces toward the east shall be shut the six
working days; but on the Sabbath it shall be
opened, and on the day of the New Moon
it shall be opened. 2 The prince shall enter
by way of the vestibule of the gateway from
the outside, and stand by the gatepost. The
priests shall prepare his burnt offering and
his peace offerings. He shall worship at the
threshold of the gate. Then he shall go out,
but the gate shall not be shut until evening.
3 Likewise the people of the land shall worship at the entrance to this gateway before
the LORD on the Sabbaths and the New
Moons. 4 The burnt offering that the prince
offers to the LORD on the Sabbath day *shall be*
six lambs without blemish, and a ram without blemish; 5 and the grain offering *shall be*
one ephah for a ram, and the grain offering
for the lambs, as much as he wants to give,
as well as a hin of oil with every ephah. 6 On
the day of the New Moon *it shall be* a young
bull without blemish, six lambs, and a ram;
they shall be without blemish. 7 He shall prepare a grain offering of an ephah for a bull,
an ephah for a ram, as much as he wants to
give for the lambs, and a hin of oil with every
ephah. 8 When the prince enters, he shall go
in by way of the vestibule of the gateway, and
go out the same way.

9 "But when the people of the land come
before the LORD on the appointed feast days,
whoever enters by way of the north gate to
worship shall go out by way of the south
gate; and whoever enters by way of the south
gate shall go out by way of the north gate. He
shall not return by way of the gate through
which he came, but shall go out through the
opposite gate. 10 The prince shall then be in
their midst. When they go in, he shall go in;
and when they go out, he shall go out. 11 At
the festivals and the appointed feast days the
grain offering shall be an ephah for a bull,
an ephah for a ram, as much as he wants
to give for the lambs, and a hin of oil with
every ephah.

12 "Now when the prince makes a voluntary burnt offering or voluntary peace offering to the LORD, the gate that faces toward
the east shall then be opened for him; and
he shall prepare his burnt offering and his
peace offerings as he did on the Sabbath day.
Then he shall go out, and after he goes out
the gate shall be shut.

13 "You shall daily make a burnt offering
to the LORD *of* a lamb of the first year without
blemish; you shall prepare it every morning.
14 And you shall prepare a grain offering with
it every morning, a sixth of an ephah, and a
third of a hin of oil to moisten the fine flour.
This grain offering is a perpetual ordinance,
to be made regularly to the LORD. 15 Thus
they shall prepare the lamb, the grain offering, and the oil, *as* a regular burnt offering
every morning."

The Prince and Inheritance Laws

16 'Thus says the Lord GOD: "If the prince
gives a gift *of some* of his inheritance to any
of his sons, it shall belong to his sons; it is
their possession by inheritance. 17 But if he
gives a gift of some of his inheritance to one
of his servants, it shall be his until the year
of liberty, after which it shall return to the
prince. But his inheritance shall belong to

his sons; it shall become theirs. 18Moreover
the prince shall not take any of the people's
inheritance by evicting them from their
property; he shall provide an inheritance
for his sons from his own property, so that
none of My people may be scattered from his
property."'"

How the Offerings Were Prepared

19Now he brought me through the entrance, which *was* at the side of the gate, into
the holy chambers of the priests which face
toward the north; and there a place *was* situated at their extreme western end. 20And
he said to me, "This *is* the place where the
priests shall boil the trespass offering and
the sin offering, *and* where they shall bake
the grain offering, so that they do not bring
them out into the outer court to sanctify the
people."

21Then he brought me out into the outer
court and caused me to pass by the four corners of the court; and in fact, in every corner of the court *there was another* court. 22In
the four corners of the court *were* enclosed
courts, forty *cubits* long and thirty wide; all
four corners *were* the same size. 23 *There was*
a row *of building stones* all around in them,
all around the four of them; and cooking
hearths were made under the rows of stones
all around. 24And he said to me, "These *are*
the kitchens where the ministers of the temple shall boil the sacrifices of the people."

The Healing Waters and Trees

47 Then he brought me back to the
door of the temple; and there was
water, flowing from under the threshold of
the temple toward the east, for the front of
the temple faced east; the water was flowing from under the right side of the temple,
south of the altar. 2He brought me out by
way of the north gate, and led me around on
the outside to the outer gateway that faces
east; and there was water, running out on
the right side.

3And when the man went out to the
east with the line in his hand, he measured
one thousand cubits, and he brought me
through the waters; the water *came up to my*
ankles. 4Again he measured one thousand
and brought me through the waters; the water *came up to my* knees. Again he measured
one thousand and brought me through;
the water *came up to my* waist. 5Again he
measured one thousand, *and it was* a river
that I could not cross; for the water was too
deep, water in which one must swim, a river that could not be crossed. 6He said to me,
"Son of man, have you seen *this?*" Then he
brought me and returned me to the bank of
the river.

7When I returned, there, along the bank
of the river, *were* very many trees on one
side and the other. 8Then he said to me:
"This water flows toward the eastern region, goes down into the valley, and enters
the sea. *When it* reaches the sea, *its* waters
are healed. 9And it shall be *that* every living
thing that moves, wherever the rivers go,
will live. There will be a very great multitude of fish, because these waters go there;
for they will be healed, and everything will
live wherever the river goes. 10It shall be *that*
fishermen will stand by it from En Gedi to
En Eglaim; they will be *places* for spreading
their nets. Their fish will be of the same
kinds as the fish of the Great Sea, exceedingly many. 11But its swamps and marshes will
not be healed; they will be given over to salt.
12Along the bank of the river, on this side
and that, will grow all *kinds of* trees used for
food; their leaves will not wither, and their
fruit will not fail. They will bear fruit every
month, because their water flows from the
sanctuary. Their fruit will be for food, and
their leaves for medicine."

Borders of the Land

13Thus says the Lord GOD: "These *are* the
borders by which you shall divide the land
as an inheritance among the twelve tribes of
Israel. Joseph *shall have two* portions. 14You
shall inherit it equally with one another; for
I raised My hand in an oath to give it to your
fathers, and this land shall fall to you as your
inheritance.

15"This *shall be* the border of the land on
the north: from the Great Sea, *by* the road
to Hethlon, as one goes to Zedad, 16Hamath,
Berothah, Sibraim (which *is* between the
border of Damascus and the border of Hamath), to Hazar Hatticon (which *is* on the
border of Hauran). 17Thus the boundary
shall be from the Sea to Hazar Enan, the
border of Damascus; and as for the north,
northward, it is the border of Hamath. *This*
is the north side.

18"On the east side you shall mark out
the border from between Hauran and

Damascus, and between Gilead and the land
of Israel, along the Jordan, and along the
eastern side of the sea. *This is* the east side.
19“The south side, toward the South,[a]
shall be from Tamar to the waters of Meribah by Kadesh, along the brook to the Great
Sea. *This is* the south side, toward the South.
20“The west side *shall be* the Great Sea,
from the *southern* boundary until one comes
to a point opposite Hamath. This *is* the west
side.
21“Thus you shall divide this land among
yourselves according to the tribes of Israel.
22It shall be that you will divide it by lot as
an inheritance for yourselves, and for the
strangers who dwell among you and who
bear children among you. They shall be to
you as native-born among the children of Israel; they shall have an inheritance with you
among the tribes of Israel. 23And it shall be
that in whatever tribe the stranger dwells,
there you shall give *him* his inheritance,”
says the Lord GOD.

Division of the Land

48 “Now these *are* the names of the
tribes: From the northern border
along the road to Hethlon at the entrance of
Hamath, to Hazar Enan, the border of Damascus northward, in the direction of Hamath, *there shall be* one *section for* Dan from
its east to its west side; 2by the border of Dan,
from the east side to the west, one *section for*
Asher; 3by the border of Asher, from the east
side to the west, one *section for* Naphtali; 4by
the border of Naphtali, from the east side to
the west, one *section for* Manasseh; 5by the
border of Manasseh, from the east side to the
west, one *section for* Ephraim; 6by the border
of Ephraim, from the east side to the west,
one *section for* Reuben; 7by the border of
Reuben, from the east side to the west, one
section for Judah; 8by the border of Judah,
from the east side to the west, shall be the
district which you shall set apart, twenty-five
thousand cubits in width, *and in* length the
same as one of the *other* portions, from the
east side to the west, with the sanctuary in
the center.
9“The district that you shall set apart for
the LORD *shall be* twenty-five thousand *cubits* in length and ten thousand in width. 10To
these—to the priests—the holy district shall
belong: on the north twenty-five thousand
cubits in length, on the west ten thousand in
width, on the east ten thousand in width,
and on the south twenty-five thousand in
length. The sanctuary of the LORD shall be
in the center. 11*It shall be* for the priests of the
sons of Zadok, who are sanctified, who have
kept My charge, who did not go astray when
the children of Israel went astray, as the Levites went astray. 12And *this* district of land
that is set apart shall be to them a thing most
holy by the border of the Levites.
13“Opposite the border of the priests, the
Levites *shall have an area* twenty-five thousand *cubits* in length and ten thousand in
width; its entire length *shall be* twenty-five
thousand and its width ten thousand. 14And
they shall not sell or exchange any of it; they
may not alienate this best *part* of the land,
for *it is* holy to the LORD.
15“The five thousand *cubits* in width that
remain, along the edge of the twenty-five
thousand, shall be for general use by the
city, for dwellings and common-land; and
the city shall be in the center. 16These *shall be*
its measurements: the north side four thousand five hundred *cubits,* the south side four
thousand five hundred, the east side four
thousand five hundred, and the west side
four thousand five hundred. 17The common-
land of the city shall be: to the north two
hundred and fifty *cubits,* to the south two
hundred and fifty, to the east two hundred
and fifty, and to the west two hundred and
fifty. 18The rest of the length, alongside the
district of the holy *section, shall be* ten thousand *cubits* to the east and ten thousand to
the west. It shall be adjacent to the district
of the holy *section,* and its produce shall be
food for the workers of the city. 19The workers of the city, from all the tribes of Israel,
shall cultivate it. 20The entire district *shall be*
twenty-five thousand *cubits* by twenty-five
thousand *cubits,* foursquare. You shall set
apart the holy district with the property of
the city.
21“The rest *shall belong* to the prince, on
one side and on the other of the holy district
and of the city's property, next to the twenty-
five thousand *cubits* of the *holy* district as far
as the eastern border, and westward next to
the twenty-five thousand as far as the western border, adjacent to the *tribal* portions;
it shall belong to the prince. It shall be the

47:19 [a] Hebrew *Negev*

holy district, and the sanctuary of the temple *shall be* in the center. 22 Moreover, apart from the possession of the Levites and the possession of the city *which are* in the midst of what *belongs* to the prince, *the area* between the border of Judah and the border of Benjamin shall belong to the prince.

23 "As for the rest of the tribes, from the east side to the west, Benjamin *shall have* one *section;* 24 by the border of Benjamin, from the east side to the west, Simeon *shall have* one *section;* 25 by the border of Simeon, from the east side to the west, Issachar *shall have* one *section;* 26 by the border of Issachar, from the east side to the west, Zebulun *shall have* one *section;* 27 by the border of Zebulun, from the east side to the west, Gad *shall have* one *section;* 28 by the border of Gad, on the south side, toward the South,[a] the border shall be from Tamar *to* the waters of Meribah *by* Kadesh, along the brook to the Great Sea. 29 This *is* the land which you shall divide by lot as an inheritance among the tribes of Israel, and these *are* their portions," says the Lord GOD.

The Gates of the City and Its Name

30 "These *are* the exits of the city. On the north side, measuring four thousand five hundred *cubits* 31 (the gates of the city *shall be* named after the tribes of Israel), the three gates northward: one gate for Reuben, one gate for Judah, and one gate for Levi; 32 on the east side, four thousand five hundred *cubits,* three gates: one gate for Joseph, one gate for Benjamin, and one gate for Dan; 33 on the south side, measuring four thousand five hundred *cubits,* three gates: one gate for Simeon, one gate for Issachar, and one gate for Zebulun; 34 on the west side, four thousand five hundred *cubits* with their three gates: one gate for Gad, one gate for Asher, and one gate for Naphtali. 35 All the way around *shall be* eighteen thousand *cubits;* and the name of the city from *that* day *shall be:* THE LORD *IS* THERE."[a]

48:28 [a] Hebrew *Negev* **48:35** [a] Hebrew *YHWH Shammah*

48:35 THE NAME OF THE NEW CITY

What makes heaven really heaven? Is it because the streets are all gold? They are. But that isn't why heaven is heaven. Is it because you'll meet loved ones there who left you long ago? Yes, you will see all those dear ones. You may have watched them die, and you know they went to the Father's house that Jesus describes in John 14:2. And won't it be wonderful to talk to the apostle Paul and the prophet Isaiah? All of these joys wait for you in heaven. But being able to see all those you love isn't what makes heaven, either.

Heaven is really heaven because the Lord is there. We will actually be able to see the Lord Jesus and talk with Him. Jesus will be our eternal Brother, and His Father will be our eternal Father *forever.*

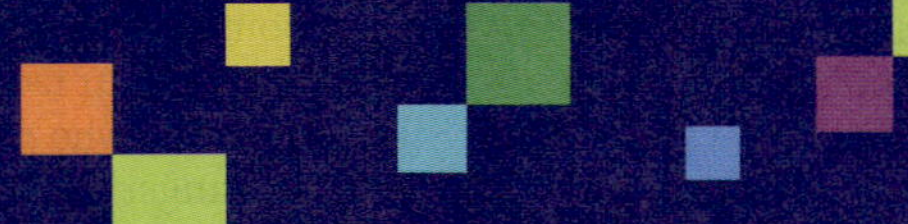

The BOOK of

DANIEL

605 B.C.–530 B.C.

Behind the Scenes

READ IT:

The book of Daniel includes the experiences of Daniel and his friends while they lived in enemy territory—Babylon. It also contains Daniel's dreams and visions that predicted the future.

GET IT:

Who wrote it: The prophet Daniel

When it was written: 605 B.C.–530 B.C.

Why it was written: to encourage God's people (and us) to trust God. He controls rulers, nations, and history.

LIVE IT:

God controls the present and the future of every nation.

We must obey God above any king or ruler.

FIND IT:

Daniel and His Friends Obey God	*Daniel 1*
Nebuchadnezzar's Dream	*Daniel 2*
Daniel's Friends Survive a Fiery Furnace	*Daniel 3*
The Writing on the Wall	*Daniel 5*
Daniel in the Lions' Den	*Daniel 6*

Daniel and His Friends Obey God

1 In the third year of the reign of Jehoiakim king of Judah, Nebuchadnezzar king of Babylon came to Jerusalem and
besieged it. 2And the Lord gave Jehoiakim
king of Judah into his hand, with some of
the articles of the house of God, which he
carried into the land of Shinar to the house
of his god; and he brought the articles into
the treasure house of his god.
3Then the king instructed Ashpenaz,
the master of his eunuchs, to bring some
of the children of Israel and some of the
king's descendants and some of the nobles,
4young men in whom *there was* no blemish,
but good-looking, gifted in all wisdom, possessing knowledge and quick to understand,
who *had* ability to serve in the king's palace,
and whom they might teach the language
and literature of the Chaldeans. 5And the
king appointed for them a daily provision of
the king's delicacies and of the wine which
he drank, and three years of training for
them, so that at the end of *that time* they
might serve before the king. 6Now from
among those of the sons of Judah were Daniel, Hananiah, Mishael, and Azariah. 7To
them the chief of the eunuchs gave names:
he gave Daniel *the name* Belteshazzar; to
Hananiah, Shadrach; to Mishael, Meshach;
and to Azariah, Abed-Nego.
8But Daniel purposed in his heart that
he would not defile himself with the portion
of the king's delicacies, nor with the wine
which he drank; therefore he requested of
the chief of the eunuchs that he might not
defile himself. 9Now God had brought Daniel into the favor and goodwill of the chief of
the eunuchs. 10And the chief of the eunuchs
said to Daniel, "I fear my lord the king, who
has appointed your food and drink. For why
should he see your faces looking worse than
the young men who *are* your age? Then you
would endanger my head before the king."
11So Daniel said to the steward[a] whom
the chief of the eunuchs had set over Daniel,
Hananiah, Mishael, and Azariah, 12"Please
test your servants for ten days, and let them
give us vegetables to eat and water to drink.
13Then let our appearance be examined before you, and the appearance of the young
men who eat the portion of the king's delicacies; and as you see fit, *so* deal with your
servants." 14So he consented with them in
this matter, and tested them ten days.
15And at the end of ten days their features
appeared better and fatter in flesh than all
the young men who ate the portion of the
king's delicacies. 16Thus the steward took
away their portion of delicacies and the
wine that they were to drink, and gave them
vegetables.
17As for these four young men, God gave
them knowledge and skill in all literature
and wisdom; and Daniel had understanding
in all visions and dreams.
18Now at the end of the days, when the
king had said that they should be brought
in, the chief of the eunuchs brought them in
before Nebuchadnezzar. 19Then the king in-
terviewed[a] them, and among them all none
was found like Daniel, Hananiah, Mishael,
and Azariah; therefore they served before
the king. 20And in all matters of wisdom *and*

1:11 [a] Hebrew *Melzar,* also in verse 16 1:19 [a] Literally *talked with them*

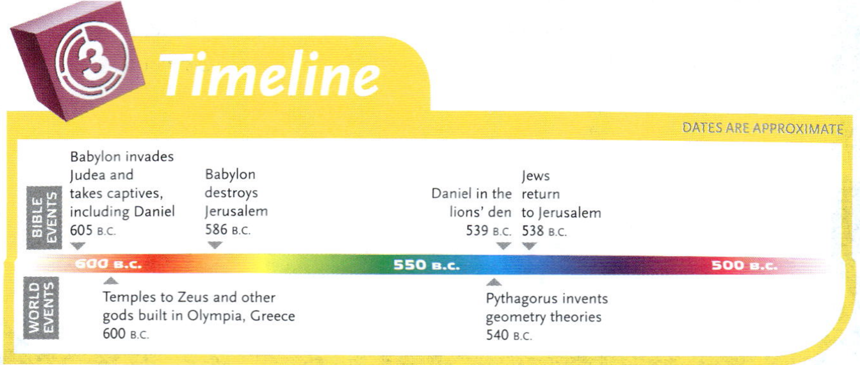

understanding about which the king examined them, he found them ten times better
than all the magicians *and* astrologers who
were in all his realm. 21 Thus Daniel continued until the first year of King Cyrus.

Nebuchadnezzar's Dream

2 Now in the second year of Nebuchadnezzar's reign, Nebuchadnezzar had
dreams; and his spirit was *so* troubled that
his sleep left him. 2 Then the king gave the
command to call the magicians, the astrologers, the sorcerers, and the Chaldeans to tell
the king his dreams. So they came and stood
before the king. 3 And the king said to them,
"I have had a dream, and my spirit is anxious
to know the dream."
4 Then the Chaldeans spoke to the king
in Aramaic,[a] "O king, live forever! Tell your
servants the dream, and we will give the
interpretation."
5 The king answered and said to the
Chaldeans, "My decision is firm: if you do
not make known the dream to me, and its
interpretation, you shall be cut in pieces,
and your houses shall be made an ash heap.
6 However, if you tell the dream and its interpretation, you shall receive from me gifts,
rewards, and great honor. Therefore tell me
the dream and its interpretation."
7 They answered again and said, "Let the
king tell his servants the dream, and we will
give its interpretation."
8 The king answered and said, "I know for
certain that you would gain time, because
you see that my decision is firm: 9 if you do
not make known the dream to me, *there is*
only one decree for you! For you have agreed
to speak lying and corrupt words before me
till the time has changed. Therefore tell me
the dream, and I shall know that you can
give me its interpretation."
10 The Chaldeans answered the king, and
said, "There is not a man on earth who can
tell the king's matter; therefore no king,
lord, or ruler has *ever* asked such things of
any magician, astrologer, or Chaldean. 11 *It is*
a difficult thing that the king requests, and
there is no other who can tell it to the king
except the gods, whose dwelling is not with
flesh."
12 For this reason the king was angry and
very furious, and gave the command to destroy all the wise *men* of Babylon. 13 So the
decree went out, and they began killing the
wise *men;* and they sought Daniel and his
companions, to kill *them.*

God Reveals Nebuchadnezzar's Dream

14 Then with counsel and wisdom Daniel
answered Arioch, the captain of the king's
guard, who had gone out to kill the wise *men*
of Babylon; 15 he answered and said to Arioch
the king's captain, "Why is the decree from

2:4 [a] The original language of Daniel 2:4b through 7:28 is Aramaic.

BEING YOURSELF

READ IT: DANIEL 1:1–17

Daniel was a young man who listened to God and knew what God wanted. He and his friends were in a strange country with different ways of doing things. But Daniel knew who he was. He didn't want to change just because he was in a strange place with nobody around to know what he was doing. He stuck by the rules that he grew up with. He did what he knew God would want him to do. Daniel was confident about his choice to eat vegetables and drink water. And he was right. The test worked. The king noticed, and God gave Daniel and his friends great knowledge.

the king so urgent?" Then Arioch made the
decision known to Daniel.

16So Daniel went in and asked the king
to give him time, that he might tell the king
the interpretation. 17Then Daniel went to
his house, and made the decision known to
Hananiah, Mishael, and Azariah, his companions, 18that they might seek mercies from
the God of heaven concerning this secret, so
that Daniel and his companions might not
perish with the rest of the wise *men* of Babylon. 19Then the secret was revealed to Daniel in a night vision. So Daniel blessed the
God of heaven.

20Daniel answered and said:

"Blessed be the name of God forever and
ever,
For wisdom and might are His.
21 And He changes the times and the
seasons;
He removes kings and raises up kings;
He gives wisdom to the wise
And knowledge to those who have
understanding.
22 He reveals deep and secret things;
He knows what *is* in the darkness,
And light dwells with Him.

23 "I thank You and praise You,
O God of my fathers;
You have given me wisdom and might,

DANIEL GOES TO BABYLON

READ IT: DANIEL 1:1–21

GET IT:

After Josiah died, the kings of Judah did a bad job. They were evil and didn't follow God. So King Nebuchadnezzar of Babylon swept through Judah and snatched up all the smart people and the young princes. Then he hauled them back to his country. Judah was still a nation, but some of its best leaders were gone.

Daniel and his friends were in this first group of people to be captured. When they got to Babylon, they had to decide whether they were going to stick with how they were brought up back home or dump the old ways and follow what the others were doing. Daniel chose to follow God's rules, not the rules of Nebuchadnezzar. He wanted only water and vegetables, not the rich food from the king's kitchen. God rewarded Daniel and his friends for their obedience and gave them knowledge and understanding.

LIVE IT:

When you leave home, do you act completely different from when someone you know is watching? Daniel was far from home with a few of his friends. Nobody in his family was watching. Nobody would know if he ate the king's food. But he remembered his upbringing and knew he was not allowed to eat certain foods. He stuck to what he believed, and God rewarded him. Keep Daniel in mind the next time you're tempted to do something your parents wouldn't approve of when you're on your own. Daniel and his friends did the right thing. You can, too.

And have now made known to me what
we asked of You,
For You have made known to us the
king's demand."

Daniel Explains the Dream

24 Therefore Daniel went to Arioch, whom the king had appointed to destroy the wise *men* of Babylon. He went and said thus to him: "Do not destroy the wise *men* of Babylon; take me before the king, and I will tell the king the interpretation."

25 Then Arioch quickly brought Daniel before the king, and said thus to him, "I have found a man of the captives[a] of Judah, who will make known to the king the interpretation."

26 The king answered and said to Daniel, whose name *was* Belteshazzar, "Are you able to make known to me the dream which I have seen, and its interpretation?"

27 Daniel answered in the presence of the king, and said, "The secret which the king has demanded, the wise *men,* the astrologers, the magicians, and the soothsayers cannot declare to the king. 28 But there is a God in heaven who reveals secrets, and He has made known to King Nebuchadnezzar what will be in the latter days. Your dream, and the visions of your head upon your bed, were these: 29 As for you, O king, thoughts came *to* your *mind while* on your bed, *about* what would come to pass after this; and He who reveals secrets has made known to you what will be. 30 But as for me, this secret has not been revealed to me because I have more wisdom than anyone living, but for *our* sakes who make known the interpretation to the king, and that you may know the thoughts of your heart.

31 "You, O king, were watching; and behold, a great image! This great image, whose splendor *was* excellent, stood before you; and its form *was* awesome. 32 This image's head *was* of fine gold, its chest and arms of silver, its belly and thighs[a] of bronze, 33 its legs of iron, its feet partly of iron and partly of clay.[a] 34 You watched while a stone was cut out without hands, which struck the image on its feet of iron and clay, and broke them in pieces. 35 Then the iron, the clay, the bronze, the silver, and the gold were crushed together, and became like chaff from the summer threshing floors; the wind carried them away so that no trace of them was found. And the stone that struck the image became a great mountain and filled the whole earth.

36 "This *is* the dream. Now we will tell the interpretation of it before the king. 37 You, O king, *are* a king of kings. For the God of heaven has given you a kingdom, power, strength, and glory; 38 and wherever the children of men dwell, or the beasts of the field and the birds of the heaven, He has given *them* into your hand, and has made you ruler over them all—you *are* this head of gold. 39 But after you shall arise another kingdom inferior to yours; then another, a third kingdom of bronze, which shall rule over all the earth. 40 And the fourth kingdom shall be as strong as iron, inasmuch as iron breaks

2:25 [a] Literally *of the sons of the captivity* 2:32 [a] Or *sides*
2:33 [a] Or *baked clay,* and so in verses 34, 35, and 42

HEARING GOD'S VOICE

READ IT: DANIEL 2:21

Daniel prayed (and asked his friends to pray) for God to help him understand the king's mysterious dream. He was wise to ask for understanding. Because of his desire to know, God trusted him with more knowledge. If you're looking for wisdom and keep talking to God, He will show you the deep and hidden things. Light will shine over the dark areas of your life, helping you see.

in pieces and shatters everything; and like
iron that crushes, *that kingdom* will break in
pieces and crush all the others. 41 Whereas
you saw the feet and toes, partly of potter's
clay and partly of iron, the kingdom shall be
divided; yet the strength of the iron shall be
in it, just as you saw the iron mixed with ceramic clay. 42 And *as* the toes of the feet *were*
partly of iron and partly of clay, *so* the kingdom shall be partly strong and partly fragile.
43 As you saw iron mixed with ceramic clay,
they will mingle with the seed of men; but
they will not adhere to one another, just as
iron does not mix with clay. 44 And in the days
of these kings the God of heaven will set up
a kingdom which shall never be destroyed;
and the kingdom shall not be left to other
people; it shall break in pieces and consume
all these kingdoms, and it shall stand forever. 45 Inasmuch as you saw that the stone was
cut out of the mountain without hands, and
that it broke in pieces the iron, the bronze,
the clay, the silver, and the gold—the great
God has made known to the king what will
come to pass after this. The dream is certain,
and its interpretation is sure."

Daniel and His Friends Promoted

46 Then King Nebuchadnezzar fell on his
face, prostrate before Daniel, and commanded that they should present an offering and
incense to him. 47 The king answered Daniel, and said, "Truly your God *is* the God of
gods, the Lord of kings, and a revealer of
secrets, since you could reveal this secret."
48 Then the king promoted Daniel and gave
him many great gifts; and he made him ruler over the whole province of Babylon, and
chief administrator over all the wise *men* of
Babylon. 49 Also Daniel petitioned the king,
and he set Shadrach, Meshach, and Abed-
Nego over the affairs of the province of Babylon; but Daniel *sat* in the gate[a] of the king.

The Image of Gold

3 Nebuchadnezzar the king made an
image of gold, whose height *was* sixty cubits *and* its width six cubits. He set it
up in the plain of Dura, in the province of
Babylon. 2 And King Nebuchadnezzar sent
word to gather together the satraps, the administrators, the governors, the counselors,
the treasurers, the judges, the magistrates,
and all the officials of the provinces, to come
to the dedication of the image which King
Nebuchadnezzar had set up. 3 So the satraps,
the administrators, the governors, the counselors, the treasurers, the judges, the magistrates, and all the officials of the provinces
gathered together for the dedication of the
image that King Nebuchadnezzar had set
up; and they stood before the image that
Nebuchadnezzar had set up. 4 Then a her-
ald cried aloud: "To you it is commanded, O
peoples, nations, and languages, 5 *that* at the

2:49 [a] That is, the king's court

FRIENDSHIP

READ IT: DANIEL 3:1–30

Not only did Shadrach, Meshach, and Abed-Nego have crazy names (to our ears), they also shared a great friendship and a strong love for God. But their friendship faced the ultimate challenge when they refused to bow to the king's idol. Would they remain united and courageous in the face of Nebuchadnezzar's rage, or would their friendship be crushed as they confronted death? These friends chose to use their relationship with each other to strengthen their trust in God even in a situation that seemed impossible. And together they watched God show up in a miraculous way!

time you hear the sound of the horn, flute,
harp, lyre, *and* psaltery, in symphony with
all kinds of music, you shall fall down and
worship the gold image that King Nebuchadnezzar has set up; 6and whoever does not fall
down and worship shall be cast immediately
into the midst of a burning fiery furnace."

7So at that time, when all the people
heard the sound of the horn, flute, harp, *and*
lyre, in symphony with all kinds of music, all
the people, nations, and languages fell down
and worshiped the gold image which King
Nebuchadnezzar had set up.

Daniel's Friends Disobey the King

8Therefore at that time certain Chaldeans
came forward and accused the Jews. 9They
spoke and said to King Nebuchadnezzar, "O
king, live forever! 10You, O king, have made
a decree that everyone who hears the sound
of the horn, flute, harp, lyre, *and* psaltery, in
symphony with all kinds of music, shall fall
down and worship the gold image; 11and whoever does not fall down and worship shall be
cast into the midst of a burning fiery furnace.
12There are certain Jews whom you have set
over the affairs of the province of Babylon:
Shadrach, Meshach, and Abed-Nego; these
men, O king, have not paid due regard to you.
They do not serve your gods or worship the
gold image which you have set up."

13Then Nebuchadnezzar, in rage and
fury, gave the command to bring Shadrach,
Meshach, and Abed-Nego. So they brought
these men before the king. 14Nebuchad-
nezzar spoke, saying to them, "*Is it* true,
Shadrach, Meshach, and Abed-Nego, *that*
you do not serve my gods or worship the gold
image which I have set up? 15Now if you are
ready at the time you hear the sound of the
horn, flute, harp, lyre, *and* psaltery, in symphony with all kinds of music, and you fall
down and worship the image which I have
made, *good!* But if you do not worship, you
shall be cast immediately into the midst of
a burning fiery furnace. And who *is* the god
who will deliver you from my hands?"

16Shadrach, Meshach, and Abed-Nego
answered and said to the king, "O Nebuchadnezzar, we have no need to answer you
in this matter. 17If that *is the case,* our God
whom we serve is able to deliver us from the
burning fiery furnace, and He will deliver
us from your hand, O king. 18But if not, let
it be known to you, O king, that we do not
serve your gods, nor will we worship the gold
image which you have set up."

Saved in Fiery Trial

19Then Nebuchadnezzar was full of fury,
and the expression on his face changed toward Shadrach, Meshach, and Abed-Nego.
He spoke and commanded that they heat the
furnace seven times more than it was usually heated. 20And he commanded certain
mighty men of valor who *were* in his army
to bind Shadrach, Meshach, and Abed-Nego,
and cast *them* into the burning fiery furnace.
21Then these men were bound in their coats,
their trousers, their turbans, and their *other*
garments, and were cast into the midst of
the burning fiery furnace. 22Therefore, because the king's command was urgent, and
the furnace exceedingly hot, the flame of the
fire killed those men who took up Shadrach,
Meshach, and Abed-Nego. 23And these three
men, Shadrach, Meshach, and Abed-Nego,
fell down bound into the midst of the burning fiery furnace.

24Then King Nebuchadnezzar was astonished; and he rose in haste *and* spoke, saying to his counselors, "Did we not cast three
men bound into the midst of the fire?"

They answered and said to the king,
"True, O king."

25"Look!" he answered, "I see four men
loose, walking in the midst of the fire; and
they are not hurt, and the form of the fourth
is like the Son of God."[a]

Nebuchadnezzar Praises God

26Then Nebuchadnezzar went near the
mouth of the burning fiery furnace *and*
spoke, saying, "Shadrach, Meshach, and
Abed-Nego, servants of the Most High God,
come out, and come *here.*" Then Shadrach,
Meshach, and Abed-Nego came from the
midst of the fire. 27And the satraps, administrators, governors, and the king's counselors
gathered together, and they saw these men
on whose bodies the fire had no power; the
hair of their head was not singed nor were
their garments affected, and the smell of fire
was not on them.

28Nebuchadnezzar spoke, saying,
"Blessed be the God of Shadrach, Meshach,
and Abed-Nego, who sent His Angel[a] and
delivered His servants who trusted in Him,

3:25 [a] Or *a son of the gods* 3:28 [a] Or *angel*

and they have frustrated the king's word,
and yielded their bodies, that they should
not serve nor worship any god except their
own God! 29 Therefore I make a decree that
any people, nation, or language which
speaks anything amiss against the God of
Shadrach, Meshach, and Abed-Nego shall be
cut in pieces, and their houses shall be made
an ash heap; because there is no other God
who can deliver like this."

30 Then the king promoted Shadrach,
Meshach, and Abed-Nego in the province of
Babylon.

Nebuchadnezzar's Second Dream

4 Nebuchadnezzar the king,

To all peoples, nations, and languages
that dwell in all the earth:

Peace be multiplied to you.

PRIDE

BEASTLY PROUD

READ IT: DANIEL 4:1–37

GET IT:

We know this chapter is long, but it's a wild story, and we hope you read it. King Nebuchadnezzar (say *neb-uh-cud-NEZZ-er*) had a major pride problem. And pride is a tricky thing.

It's good to experience pride sometimes, right? If your losing soccer team works really hard and finally wins a game, some pride is good and normal. If you aced the test at school, feeling a sense of accomplishment (which could be called pride) makes total sense.

So when does pride become bad? When does pride become a sin? A look at Nebuchadnezzar's story can help us with that.

Nebuchadnezzar had a large, beautiful kingdom. But he had concluded that it was so large and so beautiful because he was absolutely amazing. It was all about him. Nebuchadnezzar's pride was completely tainted by arrogance. And that was his downfall. For a long stretch of time this once-powerful king roamed around like a madman.

Pride and humility don't have to be opposites. If you can, think of a sort of pride that's "completely corrupted" by humility. It's possible to feel pride about your win while realizing that your soccer team is still very capable of more losses. Or you're very aware that you're far from perfect, but still feel pride about your win. It's possible to celebrate your aced school test while still remaining humble.

LIVE IT:

What's something you're proud of about yourself? Something about your character, or maybe an accomplishment? Think about that pride for a minute. Is it pride mixed with arrogance or pride mixed with humility?

2 I thought it good to declare the signs
and wonders that the Most High God
has worked for me.

3 How great *are* His signs,
And how mighty His wonders!
His kingdom *is* an everlasting kingdom,
And His dominion *is* from generation to
generation.

4 I, Nebuchadnezzar, was at rest in my
house, and flourishing in my palace. 5 I
saw a dream which made me afraid, and
the thoughts on my bed and the visions
of my head troubled me. 6 Therefore I
issued a decree to bring in all the wise
men of Babylon before me, that they
might make known to me the interpretation of the dream. 7 Then the magicians, the astrologers, the Chaldeans,
and the soothsayers came in, and I told
them the dream; but they did not make
known to me its interpretation. 8 But at
last Daniel came before me (his name *is*
Belteshazzar, according to the name of
my god; in him *is* the Spirit of the Holy
God), and I told the dream before him,
saying: 9 "Belteshazzar, chief of the magicians, because I know that the Spirit
of the Holy God *is* in you, and no secret
troubles you, explain to me the visions
of my dream that I have seen, and its
interpretation.

10 "These *were* the visions of my head *while*
on my bed:

I was looking, and behold,
A tree in the midst of the earth,
And its height was great.
11 The tree grew and became strong;
Its height reached to the heavens,
And it could be seen to the ends of all
the earth.
12 Its leaves *were* lovely,
Its fruit abundant,
And in it *was* food for all.
The beasts of the field found shade
under it,
The birds of the heavens dwelt in its
branches,
And all flesh was fed from it.

13 "I saw in the visions of my head *while* on
my bed, and there was a watcher, a holy
one, coming down from heaven. 14 He
cried aloud and said thus:

'Chop down the tree and cut off its
branches,
Strip off its leaves and scatter its fruit.
Let the beasts get out from under it,
And the birds from its branches.
15 Nevertheless leave the stump and roots
in the earth,
Bound with a band of iron and bronze,
In the tender grass of the field.
Let it be wet with the dew of heaven,
And *let* him graze with the beasts
On the grass of the earth.
16 Let his heart be changed from *that of* a
man,
Let him be given the heart of a beast,
And let seven times[a] pass over him.

17 'This decision *is* by the decree of the
watchers,
And the sentence by the word of the
holy ones,
In order that the living may know
That the Most High rules in the
kingdom of men,
Gives it to whomever He will,
And sets over it the lowest of men.'

18 "This dream I, King Nebuchadnezzar, have seen. Now you, Belteshazzar,
declare its interpretation, since all the
wise *men* of my kingdom are not able to
make known to me the interpretation;
but you *are* able, for the Spirit of the
Holy God *is* in you."

Daniel Explains the Second Dream

19 Then Daniel, whose name *was* Belteshazzar, was astonished for a time, and
his thoughts troubled him. *So* the king
spoke, and said, "Belteshazzar, do not
let the dream or its interpretation trouble you."

Belteshazzar answered and said,
"My lord, *may* the dream concern those
who hate you, and its interpretation concern your enemies!

20 "The tree that you saw, which grew and
became strong, whose height reached
to the heavens and which *could be*
seen by all the earth, 21 whose leaves
were lovely and its fruit abundant, in
which *was* food for all, under which the
beasts of the field dwelt, and in whose
branches the birds of the heaven had

4:16 [a] Possibly *seven years,* and so in verses 23, 25, and 32

their home— 22it *is* you, O king, who
have grown and become strong; for your
greatness has grown and reaches to the
heavens, and your dominion to the end
of the earth.
23 "And inasmuch as the king saw a
watcher, a holy one, coming down from
heaven and saying, 'Chop down the tree
and destroy it, but leave its stump and
roots in the earth, *bound* with a band
of iron and bronze in the tender grass
of the field; let it be wet with the dew
of heaven, and let him graze with the
beasts of the field, till seven times pass
over him'; 24this is the interpretation, O
king, and this is the decree of the Most
High, which has come upon my lord the
king: 25They shall drive you from men,
your dwelling shall be with the beasts
of the field, and they shall make you
eat grass like oxen. They shall wet you
with the dew of heaven, and seven times
shall pass over you, till you know that
the Most High rules in the kingdom
of men, and gives it to whomever He
chooses.
26 "And inasmuch as they gave the command to leave the stump *and* roots of
the tree, your kingdom shall be assured
to you, after you come to know that
Heaven rules. 27Therefore, O king, let
my advice be acceptable to you; break off
your sins by *being* righteous, and your
iniquities by showing mercy to *the* poor.
Perhaps there may be a lengthening of
your prosperity."

Nebuchadnezzar's Humiliation

28 All *this* came upon King Nebuchadnezzar. 29At the end of the twelve
months he was walking about the royal
palace of Babylon. 30The king spoke,
saying, "Is not this great Babylon, that
I have built for a royal dwelling by my
mighty power and for the honor of my
majesty?"
31 While the word *was still* in the king's
mouth, a voice fell from heaven: "King
Nebuchadnezzar, to you it is spoken: the
kingdom has departed from you! 32And
they shall drive you from men, and your
dwelling *shall be* with the beasts of the
field. They shall make you eat grass like
oxen; and seven times shall pass over
you, until you know that the Most High
rules in the kingdom of men, and gives
it to whomever He chooses."
33 That very hour the word was fulfilled
concerning Nebuchadnezzar; he was
driven from men and ate grass like
oxen; his body was wet with the dew
of heaven till his hair had grown like
eagles' *feathers* and his nails like birds'
claws.

Nebuchadnezzar Praises God

34 And at the end of the time[a] I, Nebuchadnezzar, lifted my eyes to heaven, and my
understanding returned to me; and I
blessed the Most High and praised and
honored Him who lives forever:

For His dominion *is* an everlasting
dominion,
And His kingdom *is* from generation to
generation.
35 All the inhabitants of the earth *are*
reputed as nothing;
He does according to His will in the
army of heaven
And *among* the inhabitants
of the earth.
No one can restrain His hand
Or say to Him, "What have You done?"

36 At the same time my reason returned
to me, and for the glory of my kingdom,
my honor and splendor returned to
me. My counselors and nobles resorted
to me, I was restored to my kingdom,
and excellent majesty was added to me.
37Now I, Nebuchadnezzar, praise and
extol and honor the King of heaven, all
of whose works *are* truth, and His ways
justice. And those who walk in pride He
is able to put down.

Belshazzar's Feast

5 Belshazzar the king made a great
feast for a thousand of his lords, and
drank wine in the presence of the thousand.
2While he tasted the wine, Belshazzar gave
the command to bring the gold and silver
vessels which his father Nebuchadnezzar
had taken from the temple which *had been*
in Jerusalem, that the king and his lords, his
wives, and his concubines might drink from
them. 3Then they brought the gold vessels
that had been taken from the temple of the

4:34 [a] Literally *days*

house of God which *had been* in Jerusalem;
and the king and his lords, his wives, and his
concubines drank from them. 4 They drank
wine, and praised the gods of gold and silver,
bronze and iron, wood and stone.
5 In the same hour the fingers of a man's
hand appeared and wrote opposite the lampstand on the plaster of the wall of the king's
palace; and the king saw the part of the hand
that wrote. 6 Then the king's countenance
changed, and his thoughts troubled him, so
that the joints of his hips were loosened and
his knees knocked against each other. 7 The
king cried aloud to bring in the astrologers,
the Chaldeans, and the soothsayers. The
king spoke, saying to the wise *men* of Babylon, "Whoever reads this writing, and tells
me its interpretation, shall be clothed with
purple and *have* a chain of gold around his
neck; and he shall be the third ruler in the
kingdom." 8 Now all the king's wise *men*
came, but they could not read the writing, or
make known to the king its interpretation.
9 Then King Belshazzar was greatly troubled,
his countenance was changed, and his lords
were astonished.
10 The queen, because of the words of the
king and his lords, came to the banquet hall.

GOD CONTROLS THE NATIONS

READ IT: DANIEL 5:1–30

GET IT:

Daniel had been in Babylon for many years. Several rulers had come and gone since Nebuchadnezzar. Now his grandson, Belshazzar, was king. One night at a huge banquet, a mysterious hand appeared and wrote some strange words on the wall of the palace dining room. None of the wise men in the kingdom had a clue what it meant. But the queen remembered that Daniel had great wisdom and could interpret dreams. So they called Daniel to the banquet room. He knew immediately that this was a message from God. God was angry with Belshazzar because he did not acknowledge the Most High God and had even dared to use the holy wine goblets from God's temple. Belshazzar had never accepted the fact that God was greater than he was and that God ruled the nations. That same night, the next great empire (the Persian Empire) conquered the Babylonians.

LIVE IT:

Who are a few of the most powerful people you know? Do they think they are big stuff? Are they super proud about their position and popularity, or are they cool about it? Their attitude about their importance—humble or proud—might determine what you think about them. God made one thing clear to Belshazzar, and He makes it clear to us: "Pride goes before destruction" (Proverbs 16:18). Destruction happened to one of the greatest empires in world history. It can happen to us, too. God is in control of everything and everyone. Any type of power, position, or popularity comes from Him.

The queen spoke, saying, "O king, live forever! Do not let your thoughts trouble you,
nor let your countenance change. 11 There
is a man in your kingdom in whom *is* the
Spirit of the Holy God. And in the days of
your father, light and understanding and
wisdom, like the wisdom of the gods, were
found in him; and King Nebuchadnezzar
your father—your father the king—made
him chief of the magicians, astrologers,
Chaldeans, *and* soothsayers. 12 Inasmuch as
an excellent spirit, knowledge, understanding, interpreting dreams, solving riddles,
and explaining enigmas[a] were found in this
Daniel, whom the king named Belteshazzar,
now let Daniel be called, and he will give the
interpretation."

The Writing on the Wall Explained

13 Then Daniel was brought in before
the king. The king spoke, and said to Daniel, "*Are* you that Daniel who is one of the
captives[a] from Judah, whom my father the
king brought from Judah? 14 I have heard of
you, that the Spirit of God *is* in you, and *that*
light and understanding and excellent wisdom are found in you. 15 Now the wise *men,*
the astrologers, have been brought in before
me, that they should read this writing and
make known to me its interpretation, but
they could not give the interpretation of the
thing. 16 And I have heard of you, that you can
give interpretations and explain enigmas.
Now if you can read the writing and make
known to me its interpretation, you shall be
clothed with purple and *have* a chain of gold
around your neck, and shall be the third ruler in the kingdom."

17 Then Daniel answered, and said before
the king, "Let your gifts be for yourself, and
give your rewards to another; yet I will read
the writing to the king, and make known to
him the interpretation. 18 O king, the Most
High God gave Nebuchadnezzar your father
a kingdom and majesty, glory and honor.
19 And because of the majesty that He gave
him, all peoples, nations, and languages
trembled and feared before him. Whomever he wished, he executed; whomever he
wished, he kept alive; whomever he wished,
he set up; and whomever he wished, he put
down. 20 But when his heart was lifted up,
and his spirit was hardened in pride, he
was deposed from his kingly throne, and
they took his glory from him. 21 Then he was
driven from the sons of men, his heart was
made like the beasts, and his dwelling *was*
with the wild donkeys. They fed him with
grass like oxen, and his body was wet with
the dew of heaven, till he knew that the Most
High God rules in the kingdom of men, and
appoints over it whomever He chooses.

22 "But you his son, Belshazzar, have not
humbled your heart, although you knew all
this. 23 And you have lifted yourself up against
the Lord of heaven. They have brought the
vessels of His house before you, and you and
your lords, your wives and your concubines,
have drunk wine from them. And you have
praised the gods of silver and gold, bronze
and iron, wood and stone, which do not see
or hear or know; and the God who *holds* your
breath in His hand and owns all your ways,
you have not glorified. 24 Then the fingers[a]
of the hand were sent from Him, and this
writing was written.

25 "And this is the inscription that was
written:

MENE,[a] MENE, TEKEL,[b] UPHARSIN.[c]

26 This *is* the interpretation of *each* word.
MENE: God has numbered your kingdom,
and finished it; 27 TEKEL: You have been
weighed in the balances, and found wanting; 28 PERES: Your kingdom has been divided, and given to the Medes and Persians."[a]
29 Then Belshazzar gave the command, and
they clothed Daniel with purple and *put* a
chain of gold around his neck, and made a
proclamation concerning him that he should
be the third ruler in the kingdom.

Belshazzar's Fall

30 That very night Belshazzar, king of
the Chaldeans, was slain. 31 And Darius the
Mede received the kingdom, *being* about
sixty-two years old.

The Plot Against Daniel

6 It pleased Darius to set over the kingdom one hundred and twenty satraps,
to be over the whole kingdom; 2 and over
these, three governors, of whom Daniel *was*
one, that the satraps might give account to

5:12 [a] Literally *untying knots,* and so in verse 16
5:13 [a] Literally *of the sons of the captivity* **5:24** [a] Literally *palm* **5:25** [a] Literally *a mina* (50 shekels) from the verb "to number" [b] Literally *a shekel* from the verb "to weigh" [c] Literally *and half-shekels* from the verb "to divide" **5:28** [a] Aramaic *Paras,* consonant with *Peres*

them, so that the king would suffer no loss.
3Then this Daniel distinguished himself
above the governors and satraps, because an
excellent spirit *was* in him; and the king gave
thought to setting him over the whole realm.
4So the governors and satraps sought to find
some charge against Daniel concerning the
kingdom; but they could find no charge or
fault, because he *was* faithful; nor was there
any error or fault found in him. 5Then these
men said, "We shall not find any charge
against this Daniel unless we find *it* against
him concerning the law of his God."

6So these governors and satraps thronged
before the king, and said thus to him: "King
Darius, live forever! 7All the governors of the
kingdom, the administrators and satraps,
the counselors and advisors, have consulted
together to establish a royal statute and to
make a firm decree, that whoever petitions

DISCIPLINE

PRAYING IN THE FACE OF DEATH

READ IT: DANIEL 6:1–28

GET IT:

Sometimes people watch an athlete at the top of his or her game and think, *I could do that.* Really? Are they willing to get up at the crack of dawn and exercise? Are they willing to put in the training? Are they willing to practice? The same principle applies to scoring high on tests. Yes, you might think you can do it, but are you willing to put in the work? Daniel worked at his relationship with God in the same way a long distance runner works chasing a gold medal. Daniel opened his windows toward Jerusalem. He kneeled before God and prayed three times a day. Eventually this discipline became part of who Daniel was. Daniel's closeness to God was at the center of who he was, and God rewarded him.

Those who didn't have Daniel's discipline tried to bring him down. Call these people naysayers or dream stealers, but they will be around your entire life. Every school and every job has them. Daniel relied on God to get him through these moments.

We can rely on God just as Daniel did. The lions cannot swallow our souls. Imagine a clear picture of your goal. Be willing to work for it, and nothing will stand in your way.

LIVE IT:

Think about prayer. What is praying? Is it something you do before a meal? Or when you need help on a test? What does prayer mean in your life? Daniel opened the windows of his home and faced toward Jerusalem three times a day, every day. What if you learned that praying was punishable by death? Would you still pray? What part of your faith do you feel is so important that you would be willing to die for it?

any god or man for thirty days, except you,
O king, shall be cast into the den of lions.
8Now, O king, establish the decree and sign
the writing, so that it cannot be changed,
according to the law of the Medes and Persians, which does not alter." 9Therefore King
Darius signed the written decree.

Daniel in the Lions' Den

10Now when Daniel knew that the writing
was signed, he went home. And in his upper
room, with his windows open toward Jerusalem, he knelt down on his knees three times
that day, and prayed and gave thanks before
his God, as was his custom since early days.
11Then these men assembled and found
Daniel praying and making supplication
before his God. 12And they went before the
king, and spoke concerning the king's decree: "Have you not signed a decree that
every man who petitions any god or man

DANIEL IN THE LIONS' DEN

READ IT: DANIEL 6:1–28

GET IT:

More time passed. Daniel was now an old, old man. The Persian ruler, Darius, was in charge of the empire. Like many kings of that time, he kept lions in captivity to use as a form of torture and execution on his enemies. Daniel was a major governor over a huge area of the kingdom. Others in the empire were jealous of Daniel's power and wanted to get rid of him. So they made a law that everyone had to pray only to the king, and they got the king to sign it. The jealous men thought they had trapped Daniel. When Daniel prayed to God as usual, he was arrested and thrown to the lions, but God stopped the lions from eating him. The king, who respected Daniel, was thrilled that Daniel was still alive in the morning. He got Daniel out of the den and commanded that Daniel's enemies be thrown in the den. Then he let everyone in the kingdom know how great the God of Daniel was.

LIVE IT:

Daniel is a great example for us. He was committed to God. Even when he faced the threat of punishment, Daniel did not stop loving, worshiping, and praying to God. He was sure he was doing the right thing, even though it was against the law. He knew people were jealous of his position in the government and his popularity and were "out to get him." Even the threat of dying a horrible death did not make him change his commitment to talking with God three times a day. He didn't hide either; he prayed in front of an open widow so people could see that he remained committed. Are you committed to serving God? How strong is that commitment? Are you willing to be teased or thought odd because of that commitment? Would you stay true to Him even if it caused you discomfort? Being thrown in jail? Death?

within thirty days, except you, O king, shall
be cast into the den of lions?"
The king answered and said, "The thing
is true, according to the law of the Medes and
Persians, which does not alter."
13So they answered and said before the
king, "That Daniel, who is one of the captives[a] from Judah, does not show due regard
for you, O king, or for the decree that you
have signed, but makes his petition three
times a day."
14And the king, when he heard *these*
words, was greatly displeased with himself, and set *his* heart on Daniel to deliver
him; and he labored till the going down of
the sun to deliver him. 15Then these men
approached the king, and said to the king,
"Know, O king, that *it is* the law of the Medes
and Persians that no decree or statute which
the king establishes may be changed."
16So the king gave the command, and
they brought Daniel and cast *him* into the
den of lions. *But* the king spoke, saying to
Daniel, "Your God, whom you serve continually, He will deliver you." 17Then a stone
was brought and laid on the mouth of the
den, and the king sealed it with his own signet ring and with the signets of his lords,
that the purpose concerning Daniel might
not be changed.

Daniel Saved from the Lions

18Now the king went to his palace and
spent the night fasting; and no musicians[a]
were brought before him. Also his sleep
went from him. 19Then the king arose very
early in the morning and went in haste to
the den of lions. 20And when he came to the
den, he cried out with a lamenting voice to
Daniel. The king spoke, saying to Daniel,
"Daniel, servant of the living God, has your
God, whom you serve continually, been able
to deliver you from the lions?"
21Then Daniel said to the king, "O king,
live forever! 22My God sent His angel and
shut the lions' mouths, so that they have not
hurt me, because I was found innocent before Him; and also, O king, I have done no
wrong before you."
23Now the king was exceedingly glad for
him, and commanded that they should take
Daniel up out of the den. So Daniel was tak-
en up out of the den, and no injury whatever
was found on him, because he believed in
his God.

Darius Honors God

24And the king gave the command, and
they brought those men who had accused
Daniel, and they cast *them* into the den of
lions—them, their children, and their wives;
and the lions overpowered them, and broke
all their bones in pieces before they ever
came to the bottom of the den.
25Then King Darius wrote:

To all peoples, nations, and languages
that dwell in all the earth:

Peace be multiplied to you.

26 I make a decree that in every dominion
of my kingdom *men must* tremble and
fear before the God of Daniel.

For He *is* the living God,
And steadfast forever;
His kingdom *is the one* which shall not
be destroyed,
And His dominion *shall endure* to the end.
27 He delivers and rescues,
And He works signs and wonders
In heaven and on earth,
Who has delivered Daniel from the
power of the lions.

28So this Daniel prospered in the reign of
Darius and in the reign of Cyrus the Persian.

Vision of the Four Beasts

7 In the first year of Belshazzar king
of Babylon, Daniel had a dream and
visions of his head *while* on his bed. Then
he wrote down the dream, telling the main
facts.[a]
2Daniel spoke, saying, "I saw in my
vision by night, and behold, the four winds
of heaven were stirring up the Great Sea.
3And four great beasts came up from the sea,
each different from the other. 4The first *was*
like a lion, and had eagle's wings. I watched
till its wings were plucked off; and it was lifted up from the earth and made to stand on
two feet like a man, and a man's heart was
given to it.
5"And suddenly another beast, a second,
like a bear. It was raised up on one side, and
had three ribs in its mouth between its teeth.
And they said thus to it: 'Arise, devour much
flesh!'

6:13 [a] Literally *of the sons of the captivity* 6:18 [a] Exact meaning unknown 7:1 [a] Literally *the head* (or *chief*) *of the words*

6“After this I looked, and there was another, like a leopard, which had on its back
four wings of a bird. The beast also had four
heads, and dominion was given to it.

7“After this I saw in the night visions, and
behold, a fourth beast, dreadful and terrible,
exceedingly strong. It had huge iron teeth;
it was devouring, breaking in pieces, and
trampling the residue with its feet. It *was* different from all the beasts that *were* before it,
and it had ten horns. 8I was considering the
horns, and there was another horn, a little
one, coming up among them, before whom
three of the first horns were plucked out by
the roots. And there, in this horn, *were* eyes
like the eyes of a man, and a mouth speaking
pompous words.

Vision of the Ancient of Days

9 “I watched till thrones were put in place,
And the Ancient of Days was seated;
His garment *was* white as snow,
And the hair of His head *was* like pure
wool.
His throne *was* a fiery flame,
Its wheels a burning fire;
10 A fiery stream issued
And came forth from before Him.
A thousand thousands ministered to
Him;
Ten thousand times ten thousand stood
before Him.
The court[a] was seated,
And the books were opened.

11“I watched then because of the sound
of the pompous words which the horn was
speaking; I watched till the beast was slain,
and its body destroyed and given to the burning flame. 12As for the rest of the beasts, they
had their dominion taken away, yet their
lives were prolonged for a season and a time.

13 “I was watching in the night visions,
And behold, *One* like the Son of Man,
Coming with the clouds of heaven!
He came to the Ancient of Days,
And they brought Him near before
Him.
14 Then to Him was given dominion and
glory and a kingdom,
That all peoples, nations, and languages
should serve Him.
His dominion *is* an everlasting
dominion,
Which shall not pass away,
And His kingdom *the one*
Which shall not be destroyed.

Daniel’s Visions Interpreted

15“I, Daniel, was grieved in my spirit
within *my* body, and the visions of my head
troubled me. 16I came near to one of those
who stood by, and asked him the truth of all
this. So he told me and made known to me
the interpretation of these things: 17‘Those
great beasts, which are four, *are* four kings[a]
which arise out of the earth. 18But the saints
of the Most High shall receive the kingdom,
and possess the kingdom forever, even forever and ever.’

19“Then I wished to know the truth about
the fourth beast, which was different from
all the others, exceedingly dreadful, *with* its
teeth of iron and its nails of bronze, *which*
devoured, broke in pieces, and trampled the
residue with its feet; 20and the ten horns that
were on its head, and the other *horn* which
came up, before which three fell, namely, that horn which had eyes and a mouth
which spoke pompous words, whose appearance *was* greater than his fellows.

21“I was watching; and the same horn was
making war against the saints, and prevail-
ing against them, 22until the Ancient of Days
came, and a judgment was made *in favor* of
the saints of the Most High, and the time
came for the saints to possess the kingdom.

23“Thus he said:

‘The fourth beast shall be
A fourth kingdom on earth,
Which shall be different from all *other*
kingdoms,
And shall devour the whole earth,
Trample it and break it in pieces.
24 The ten horns *are* ten kings
Who shall arise from this kingdom.
And another shall rise after them;
He shall be different from the first *ones*,
And shall subdue three kings.
25 He shall speak *pompous* words against
the Most High,
Shall persecute[a] the saints of the Most
High,
And shall intend to change times and law.
Then *the saints* shall be given into his
hand
For a time and times and half a time.

7:10 [a] Or *judgment* 7:17 [a] Representing their kingdoms (compare verse 23) 7:25 [a] Literally *wear out*

26 'But the court shall be seated,
And they shall take away his dominion,
To consume and destroy *it* forever.
27 Then the kingdom and dominion,
And the greatness of the kingdoms
under the whole heaven,
Shall be given to the people, the saints
of the Most High.
His kingdom *is* an everlasting kingdom,
And all dominions shall serve and obey
Him.'

28"This *is* the end of the account.[a] As for
me, Daniel, my thoughts greatly troubled
me, and my countenance changed; but I kept
the matter in my heart."

Vision of a Ram and a Goat

8 In the third year of the reign of King
Belshazzar a vision appeared *to* me—
to me, Daniel—after the one that appeared
to me the first time. 2I saw in the vision, and
it so happened while I was looking, that I
was in Shushan, the citadel, which *is* in the
province of Elam; and I saw in the vision that
I was by the River Ulai. 3Then I lifted my
eyes and saw, and there, standing beside the
river, was a ram which had two horns, and
the two horns *were* high; but one *was* higher than the other, and the higher *one* came
up last. 4I saw the ram pushing westward,
northward, and southward, so that no animal could withstand him; nor *was there any*
that could deliver from his hand, but he did
according to his will and became great.

5And as I was considering, suddenly a
male goat came from the west, across the
surface of the whole earth, without touching
the ground; and the goat *had* a notable horn
between his eyes. 6Then he came to the ram
that had two horns, which I had seen standing beside the river, and ran at him with furious power. 7And I saw him confronting the
ram; he was moved with rage against him,
attacked the ram, and broke his two horns.
There was no power in the ram to withstand
him, but he cast him down to the ground
and trampled him; and there was no one that
could deliver the ram from his hand.

8Therefore the male goat grew very great;
but when he became strong, the large horn
was broken, and in place of it four notable
ones came up toward the four winds of heav-
en. 9And out of one of them came a little
horn which grew exceedingly great toward
the south, toward the east, and toward the
Glorious *Land.* 10And it grew up to the host of
heaven; and it cast down *some* of the host and
some of the stars to the ground, and trampled them. 11He even exalted *himself* as high
as the Prince of the host; and by him the daily *sacrifices* were taken away, and the place
of His sanctuary was cast down. 12Because
of transgression, an army was given over *to
the horn* to oppose the daily *sacrifices;* and he
cast truth down to the ground. He did *all this*
and prospered.

13Then I heard a holy one speaking; and
another holy one said to that certain *one* who
was speaking, "How long *will* the vision *be,
concerning* the daily *sacrifices* and the transgression of desolation, the giving of both
the sanctuary and the host to be trampled
underfoot?"

14And he said to me, "For two thousand
three hundred days;[a] then the sanctuary
shall be cleansed."

Gabriel Interprets the Vision

15Then it happened, when I, Daniel, had
seen the vision and was seeking the meaning, that suddenly there stood before me
one having the appearance of a man. 16And I
heard a man's voice between *the banks of* the
Ulai, who called, and said, "Gabriel, make
this *man* understand the vision." 17So he
came near where I stood, and when he came
I was afraid and fell on my face; but he said
to me, "Understand, son of man, that the vision *refers* to the time of the end."

18Now, as he was speaking with me, I was
in a deep sleep with my face to the ground;
but he touched me, and stood me upright.
19And he said, "Look, I am making known
to you what shall happen in the latter time
of the indignation; for at the appointed time
the end *shall be.* 20The ram which you saw,
having the two horns—*they are* the kings of
Media and Persia. 21And the male goat *is* the
kingdom[a] of Greece. The large horn that *is*
between its eyes *is* the first king. 22As for the
broken *horn* and the four that stood up in its
place, four kingdoms shall arise out of that
nation, but not with its power.

23 "And in the latter time of their kingdom,
When the transgressors have reached
their fullness,

7:28 [a] Literally *the word* 8:14 [a] Literally *evening-mornings*
8:21 [a] Literally *king,* representing his kingdom (compare 7:17, 23)

A king shall arise,
Having fierce features,
Who understands sinister schemes.
24 His power shall be mighty, but not by
his own power;
He shall destroy fearfully,
And shall prosper and thrive;
He shall destroy the mighty, and *also*
the holy people.

25 "Through his cunning
He shall cause deceit to prosper under
his rule;[a]
And he shall exalt *himself* in his heart.
He shall destroy many in *their*
prosperity.
He shall even rise against the Prince of
princes;
But he shall be broken without *human*
means.[b]

26 "And the vision of the evenings and
mornings
Which was told is true;
Therefore seal up the vision,
For *it refers* to many days *in the*
future."

27And I, Daniel, fainted and was sick for
days; afterward I arose and went about the
king's business. I was astonished by the
vision, but no one understood it.

Daniel's Prayer for the People

9 In the first year of Darius the son
of Ahasuerus, of the lineage of the
Medes, who was made king over the realm
of the Chaldeans— 2in the first year of his
reign I, Daniel, understood by the books the
number of the years *specified* by the word of
the LORD through Jeremiah the prophet, that
He would accomplish seventy years in the
desolations of Jerusalem.

3Then I set my face toward the Lord
God to make request by prayer and supplications, with fasting, sackcloth, and ashes.
4And I prayed to the LORD my God, and
made confession, and said, "O Lord, great
and awesome God, who keeps His covenant
and mercy with those who love Him, and
with those who keep His commandments,
5we have sinned and committed iniquity,
we have done wickedly and rebelled, even
by departing from Your precepts and Your
judgments. 6Neither have we heeded Your
servants the prophets, who spoke in Your
name to our kings and our princes, to our
fathers and all the people of the land. 7O
Lord, righteousness *belongs* to You, but to us
shame of face, as *it is* this day—to the men
of Judah, to the inhabitants of Jerusalem
and all Israel, those near and those far off
in all the countries to which You have driven
them, because of the unfaithfulness which
they have committed against You.

8"O Lord, to us *belongs* shame of face,
to our kings, our princes, and our fathers,

8:25 [a] Literally *hand* [b] Literally *hand*

REBELLION

READ IT: DANIEL 9:9

Daniel interpreted dreams. He knew the message God had sent the original king, and now Daniel was serving that king's son. The time of joy and prosperity was coming to an end because of the constant rebellion of the people (including the king) against the ways of God.

Daniel prayed hard. He prayed that God would have mercy on the *people despite their rebellion.* God heard Daniel's prayer and graciously spared them, forgiving all the people even though they had rebelled.

God wants to forgive you for your rebellion if you want His mercy.

because we have sinned against You. 9To the
Lord our God *belong* mercy and forgiveness,
though we have rebelled against Him. 10We
have not obeyed the voice of the LORD our
God, to walk in His laws, which He set before us by His servants the prophets. 11Yes,
all Israel has transgressed Your law, and has
departed so as not to obey Your voice; therefore the curse and the oath written in the
Law of Moses the servant of God have been
poured out on us, because we have sinned
against Him. 12And He has confirmed His
words, which He spoke against us and
against our judges who judged us, by bringing upon us a great disaster; for under the
whole heaven such has never been done as
what has been done to Jerusalem.

13"As *it is* written in the Law of Moses,
all this disaster has come upon us; yet we
have not made our prayer before the LORD
our God, that we might turn from our iniquities and understand Your truth. 14There-
fore the LORD has kept the disaster in mind,
and brought it upon us; for the LORD our
God *is* righteous in all the works which He
does, though we have not obeyed His voice.
15And now, O Lord our God, who brought
Your people out of the land of Egypt with a
mighty hand, and made Yourself a name, as
it is this day—we have sinned, we have done
wickedly!

16"O Lord, according to all Your righteousness, I pray, let Your anger and Your fury be
turned away from Your city Jerusalem, Your
holy mountain; because for our sins, and for
the iniquities of our fathers, Jerusalem and
Your people *are* a reproach to all *those* around
us. 17Now therefore, our God, hear the prayer
of Your servant, and his supplications, and
for the Lord's sake cause Your face to shine
on Your sanctuary, which is desolate. 18O
my God, incline Your ear and hear; open
Your eyes and see our desolations, and the
city which is called by Your name; for we do
not present our supplications before You be-
cause of our righteous deeds, but because of
Your great mercies. 19O Lord, hear! O Lord,
forgive! O Lord, listen and act! Do not delay
for Your own sake, my God, for Your city and
Your people are called by Your name."

The Seventy-Weeks Prophecy

20Now while I *was* speaking, praying, and
confessing my sin and the sin of my people Israel, and presenting my supplication

In Focus

9:25, 26 Messiah Pronounced *muh-SIGH-uh*. A Hebrew word meaning "Anointed One." Christos (pronounced *KRISS-tos*) is a Greek word from which we get the word "Christ" and means the same as "Messiah."

before the LORD my God for the holy mountain of my God, 21yes, while I *was* speaking
in prayer, the man Gabriel, whom I had seen
in the vision at the beginning, being caused
to fly swiftly, reached me about the time of
the evening offering. 22And he informed *me,*
and talked with me, and said, "O Daniel,
I have now come forth to give you skill to
understand. 23At the beginning of your supplications the command went out, and I have
come to tell *you,* for you *are* greatly beloved;
therefore consider the matter, and understand the vision:

24 "Seventy weeks[a] are determined
For your people and for your holy city,
To finish the transgression,
To make an end of[b] sins,
To make reconciliation for iniquity,
To bring in everlasting righteousness,
To seal up vision and prophecy,
And to anoint the Most Holy.

25 "Know therefore and understand,
That from the going forth of the
command
To restore and build Jerusalem
Until Messiah the Prince,
There shall be seven weeks and sixty-two
weeks;
The street[a] shall be built again, and the
wall,[b]
Even in troublesome times.

26 "And after the sixty-two weeks
Messiah shall be cut off, but not for
Himself;

9:24 [a] Literally *sevens,* and so throughout the chapter [b] Following Qere, Septuagint, Syriac, and Vulgate; Kethib and Theodotion read *To seal up.* 9:25 [a] Or *open square* [b] Or *moat*

And the people of the prince who is to
come
Shall destroy the city and the sanctuary.
The end of it *shall be* with a flood,
And till the end of the war desolations
are determined.
27 Then he shall confirm a covenant with
many for one week;
But in the middle of the week
He shall bring an end to sacrifice and
offering.
And on the wing of abominations shall
be one who makes desolate,
Even until the consummation, which is
determined,
Is poured out on the desolate."

Vision of the Glorious Man

10 In the third year of Cyrus king of
Persia a message was revealed to
Daniel, whose name was called Belteshazzar. The message *was* true, but the appointed time *was* long;[a] and he understood the
message, and had understanding of the vision. 2 In those days I, Daniel, was mourning
three full weeks. 3 I ate no pleasant food, no
meat or wine came into my mouth, nor did
I anoint myself at all, till three whole weeks
were fulfilled.

4 Now on the twenty-fourth day of the first
month, as I was by the side of the great river, that *is,* the Tigris,[a] 5 I lifted my eyes and
looked, and behold, a certain man clothed
in linen, whose waist *was* girded with gold of
Uphaz! 6 His body *was* like beryl, his face like
the appearance of lightning, his eyes like
torches of fire, his arms and feet like burnished bronze in color, and the sound of his
words like the voice of a multitude.

7 And I, Daniel, alone saw the vision, for
the men who were with me did not see the
vision; but a great terror fell upon them, so
that they fled to hide themselves. 8 Therefore
I was left alone when I saw this great vision,
and no strength remained in me; for my vig-
or was turned to frailty in me, and I retained
no strength. 9 Yet I heard the sound of his
words; and while I heard the sound of his
words I was in a deep sleep on my face, with
my face to the ground.

Prophecies Concerning Persia and Greece

10 Suddenly, a hand touched me, which
made me tremble on my knees and *on* the
palms of my hands. 11 And he said to me, "O
Daniel, man greatly beloved, understand
the words that I speak to you, and stand
upright, for I have now been sent to you."
While he was speaking this word to me, I
stood trembling.

12 Then he said to me, "Do not fear, Daniel, for from the first day that you set your
heart to understand, and to humble yourself
before your God, your words were heard; and
I have come because of your words. 13 But the
prince of the kingdom of Persia withstood
me twenty-one days; and behold, Michael,
one of the chief princes, came to help me,
for I had been left alone there with the kings
of Persia. 14 Now I have come to make you
understand what will happen to your people
in the latter days, for the vision *refers* to *many*
days yet *to come.*"

15 When he had spoken such words to me,
I turned my face toward the ground and became speechless. 16 And suddenly, *one* having
the likeness of the sons[a] of men touched my
lips; then I opened my mouth and spoke,
saying to him who stood before me, "My
lord, because of the vision my sorrows have
overwhelmed me, and I have retained no
strength. 17 For how can this servant of my
lord talk with you, my lord? As for me, no
strength remains in me now, nor is any
breath left in me."

18 Then again, *the one* having the likeness
of a man touched me and strengthened
me. 19 And he said, "O man greatly beloved,
fear not! Peace *be* to you; be strong, yes, be
strong!"

So when he spoke to me I was strengthened, and said, "Let my lord speak, for you
have strengthened me."

20 Then he said, "Do you know why I have
come to you? And now I must return to fight
with the prince of Persia; and when I have
gone forth, indeed the prince of Greece will
come. 21 But I will tell you what is noted in
the Scripture of Truth. (No one upholds me
against these, except Michael your prince.

11 "Also in the first year of Darius the
Mede, I, *even* I, stood up to confirm
and strengthen him.) 2 And now I will tell
you the truth: Behold, three more kings will

10:1 [a] Or *and of great conflict* 10:4 [a] Hebrew *Hiddekel*
10:16 [a] Theodotion and Vulgate read *the son;* Septuagint reads *a hand.*

arise in Persia, and the fourth shall be far
richer than *them* all; by his strength, through
his riches, he shall stir up all against the
realm of Greece. 3Then a mighty king shall
arise, who shall rule with great dominion,
and do according to his will. 4And when he
has arisen, his kingdom shall be broken up
and divided toward the four winds of heaven,
but not among his posterity nor according to
his dominion with which he ruled; for his
kingdom shall be uprooted, even for others
besides these.

Warring Kings of North and South

5"Also the king of the South shall become
strong, as well as *one* of his princes; and he
shall gain power over him and have dominion. His dominion *shall be* a great dominion.
6And at the end of *some* years they shall join
forces, for the daughter of the king of the
South shall go to the king of the North to
make an agreement; but she shall not retain
the power of her authority,[a] and neither he
nor his authority[b] shall stand; but she shall
be given up, with those who brought her,
and with him who begot her, and with him
who strengthened her in *those* times. 7But
from a branch of her roots *one* shall arise in
his place, who shall come with an army, enter the fortress of the king of the North, and
deal with them and prevail. 8And he shall
also carry their gods captive to Egypt, with
their princes[a] *and* their precious articles of
silver and gold; and he shall continue *more*
years than the king of the North.

9"Also *the king of the North* shall come to
the kingdom of the king of the South, but
shall return to his own land. 10However his
sons shall stir up strife, and assemble a multitude of great forces; and *one* shall certainly come and overwhelm and pass through;
then he shall return to his fortress and stir
up strife.

11"And the king of the South shall be
moved with rage, and go out and fight with
him, with the king of the North, who shall
muster a great multitude; but the multitude
shall be given into the hand of his *enemy*.
12When he has taken away the multitude,
his heart will be lifted up; and he will cast
down tens of thousands, but he will not prevail. 13For the king of the North will return
and muster a multitude greater than the
former, and shall certainly come at the end
of some years with a great army and much
equipment.

14"Now in those times many shall rise up
against the king of the South. Also, violent
men[a] of your people shall exalt themselves
in fulfillment of the vision, but they shall
fall. 15So the king of the North shall come
and build a siege mound, and take a fortified city; and the forces[a] of the South shall
not withstand *him*. Even his choice troops
shall have no strength to resist. 16But he who
comes against him shall do according to his
own will, and no one shall stand against
him. He shall stand in the Glorious Land
with destruction in his power.[a]

17"He shall also set his face to enter with
the strength of his whole kingdom, and upright ones[a] with him; thus shall he do. And
he shall give him the daughter of women to
destroy it; but she shall not stand *with him,*
or be for him. 18After this he shall turn his
face to the coastlands, and shall take many.
But a ruler shall bring the reproach against
them to an end; and with the reproach removed, he shall turn back on him. 19Then
he shall turn his face toward the fortress of
his own land; but he shall stumble and fall,
and not be found.

20"There shall arise in his place one who
imposes taxes *on* the glorious kingdom; but
within a few days he shall be destroyed, but
not in anger or in battle. 21And in his place
shall arise a vile person, to whom they will
not give the honor of royalty; but he shall
come in peaceably, and seize the kingdom
by intrigue. 22With the force[a] of a flood they
shall be swept away from before him and be
broken, and also the prince of the covenant.
23And after the league *is made* with him he
shall act deceitfully, for he shall come up and
become strong with a small *number of* people. 24He shall enter peaceably, even into the
richest places of the province; and he shall
do *what* his fathers have not done, nor his
forefathers: he shall disperse among them
the plunder, spoil, and riches; and he shall
devise his plans against the strongholds, but
only for a time.

25"He shall stir up his power and his
courage against the king of the South with a

11:6 [a] Literally *arm* [b] Literally *arm* **11:8** [a] Or *molded images* **11:14** [a] Or *robbers,* literally *sons of breakage* **11:15** [a] Literally *arms* **11:16** [a] Literally *hand* **11:17** [a] Or *bring equitable terms* **11:22** [a] Literally *arms*

great army. And the king of the South shall
be stirred up to battle with a very great and
mighty army; but he shall not stand, for they
shall devise plans against him. 26 Yes, those
who eat of the portion of his delicacies shall
destroy him; his army shall be swept away,
and many shall fall down slain. 27 Both these
kings' hearts *shall be* bent on evil, and they
shall speak lies at the same table; but it shall
not prosper, for the end *will* still *be* at the appointed time. 28 While returning to his land
with great riches, his heart shall be *moved*
against the holy covenant; so he shall do
damage and return to his own land.

The Northern King's Blasphemies

29 "At the appointed time he shall return
and go toward the south; but it shall not
be like the former or the latter. 30 For ships
from Cyprus[a] shall come against him; therefore he shall be grieved, and return in rage
against the holy covenant, and do *damage*.

"So he shall return and show regard for
those who forsake the holy covenant. 31 And
forces[a] shall be mustered by him, and they
shall defile the sanctuary fortress; then they
shall take away the daily *sacrifices*, and place
there the abomination of desolation. 32 Those
who do wickedly against the covenant he
shall corrupt with flattery; but the people
who know their God shall be strong, and
carry out *great exploits*. 33 And those of the
people who understand shall instruct many;
yet *for many* days they shall fall by sword and
flame, by captivity and plundering. 34 Now
when they fall, they shall be aided with a little help; but many shall join with them by intrigue. 35 And *some* of those of understanding
shall fall, to refine them, purify *them*, and
make *them* white, *until* the time of the end;
because *it is* still for the appointed time.

36 "Then the king shall do according to his
own will: he shall exalt and magnify himself
above every god, shall speak blasphemies
against the God of gods, and shall prosper
till the wrath has been accomplished; for
what has been determined shall be done.
37 He shall regard neither the God[a] of his fathers nor the desire of women, nor regard
any god; for he shall exalt himself above
them all. 38 But in their place he shall hon-
or a god of fortresses; and a god which his
fathers did not know he shall honor with
gold and silver, with precious stones and
pleasant things. 39 Thus he shall act against
the strongest fortresses with a foreign god,
which he shall acknowledge, *and* advance *its*
glory; and he shall cause them to rule over
many, and divide the land for gain.

The Northern King's Conquests

40 "At the time of the end the king of the
South shall attack him; and the king of the
North shall come against him like a whirlwind, with chariots, horsemen, and with
many ships; and he shall enter the countries,
overwhelm *them*, and pass through. 41 He
shall also enter the Glorious Land, and many
countries shall be overthrown; but these shall
escape from his hand: Edom, Moab, and the
prominent people of Ammon. 42 He shall
stretch out his hand against the countries,
and the land of Egypt shall not escape. 43 He
shall have power over the treasures of gold
and silver, and over all the precious things of
Egypt; also the Libyans and Ethiopians *shall
follow* at his heels. 44 But news from the east
and the north shall trouble him; therefore he
shall go out with great fury to destroy and
annihilate many. 45 And he shall plant the
tents of his palace between the seas and the
glorious holy mountain; yet he shall come to
his end, and no one will help him.

Prophecy of the End Time

12 "At that time Michael shall stand up,
The great prince who stands *watch*
over the sons of your people;
And there shall be a time of trouble,
Such as never was since there was a
nation,
Even to that time.
And at that time your people shall be
delivered,
Every one who is found written in the
book.
2 And many of those who sleep in the
dust of the earth shall awake,
Some to everlasting life,
Some to shame *and* everlasting
contempt.
3 Those who are wise shall shine
Like the brightness of the firmament,
And those who turn many to
righteousness
Like the stars forever and ever.

4 "But you, Daniel, shut up the words,

11:30 [a] Hebrew *Kittim*, western lands, especially Cyprus
11:31 [a] Literally *arms* 11:37 [a] Or *gods*

and seal the book until the time of the end;
many shall run to and fro, and knowledge
shall increase."
5Then I, Daniel, looked; and there stood
two others, one on this riverbank and the
other on that riverbank. 6And *one* said to the
man clothed in linen, who *was* above the waters of the river, "How long shall the fulfillment of these wonders *be?*"
7Then I heard the man clothed in linen,
who *was* above the waters of the river, when
he held up his right hand and his left hand to
heaven, and swore by Him who lives forever,
that *it shall be* for a time, times, and half *a*
time; and when the power of the holy people has been completely shattered, all these
things shall be finished.
8Although I heard, I did not understand.
Then I said, "My lord, what *shall be* the end
of these *things?*"
9And he said, "Go *your way,* Daniel, for
the words *are* closed up and sealed till the
time of the end. 10Many shall be purified,
made white, and refined, but the wicked
shall do wickedly; and none of the wicked shall understand, but the wise shall
understand.
11"And from the time *that* the daily *sac-*
rifice is taken away, and the abomination of
desolation is set up, *there shall be* one thousand two hundred and ninety days. 12Blessed
is he who waits, and comes to the one thousand three hundred and thirty-five days.
13"But you, go *your way* till the end; for
you shall rest, and will arise to your inheritance at the end of the days."

The BOOK of HOSEA

750 B.C.–720 B.C.

Behind the Scenes

READ IT:

The book of Hosea tells the story of the prophet Hosea and his unusual family. Hosea's home situation was an example of how the people of Israel were treating God. Hosea told the people that God would not tolerate their unfair, unjust, and wicked lifestyle.

GET IT:

Who wrote it: The prophet Hosea

When it was written: 750 B.C.–720 B.C.

Why it was written: to remind Israel that God continues to be faithful to them even when they are unfaithful to God.

LIVE IT:

We must be faithful to God.

God is faithful to us even when we are unfaithful to Him.

FIND IT:

The Family of Hosea	*Hosea 1*
Judgment on Israel and Judah	*Hosea 5*
A Call to Repentance	*Hosea 6*
God's Continuing Love for Israel	*Hosea 11*
Israel Restored at Last	*Hosea 14*

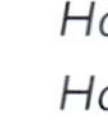

1 The word of the LORD that came to
Hosea the son of Beeri, in the days
of Uzziah, Jotham, Ahaz, *and* Hezekiah,
kings of Judah, and in the days of Jeroboam
the son of Joash, king of Israel.

The Family of Hosea

2 When the LORD began to speak by Hosea, the LORD said to Hosea:

"Go, take yourself a wife of harlotry
And children of harlotry,
For the land has committed great
harlotry
By departing from the LORD."

3 So he went and took Gomer the daughter of
Diblaim, and she conceived and bore him a
son. 4 Then the LORD said to him:

"Call his name Jezreel,
For in a little *while*
I will avenge the bloodshed of Jezreel on
the house of Jehu,
And bring an end to the kingdom of the
house of Israel.
5 It shall come to pass in that day
That I will break the bow of Israel in the
Valley of Jezreel."

6 And she conceived again and bore a
daughter. Then *God* said to him:

"Call her name Lo-Ruhamah,[a]
For I will no longer have mercy on the
house of Israel,
But I will utterly take them away.[b]
7 Yet I will have mercy on the house of
Judah,
Will save them by the LORD their God,
And will not save them by bow,
Nor by sword or battle,
By horses or horsemen."

8 Now when she had weaned Lo-
Ruhamah, she conceived and bore a son.
9 Then *God* said:

"Call his name Lo-Ammi,[a]
For you *are* not My people,
And I will not be your *God.*

The Restoration of Israel

10 "Yet the number of the children of Israel
Shall be as the sand of the sea,
Which cannot be measured or
numbered.
And it shall come to pass
In the place where it was said to them,
'You *are* not My people,'[a]
There it shall be said to them,
'*You are* sons of the living God.'
11 Then the children of Judah and the
children of Israel
Shall be gathered together,
And appoint for themselves one head;
And they shall come up out of the land,
For great *will be* the day of Jezreel!

1:6 [a] Literally *No-Mercy* [b] Or *That I may forgive them at all*
1:9 [a] Literally *Not-My-People* 1:10 [a] Hebrew *lo-ammi* (compare verse 9)

Starring Roles

HOSEA'S name is pronounced *ho-ZAY-uh* and means "Deliverance." His work as a prophet took place during the time that Isaiah lived. You will notice that the same kings were reigning in Judah when Hosea and Isaiah were prophets (see Isaiah 1:1). Isaiah was a great preacher in the Southern Kingdom of Judah; Hosea preached in the Northern Kingdom of Israel just before the army of Assyria conquered them 722 years before the coming of Jesus.

People have often been puzzled about Hosea because he married a young woman who had been a great sinner. But God forgave her and Hosea loved her. God loves you that way, too. He forgives your sins because Jesus died for you.

Hosea knew the hardships that Israel would soon experience when the army of Assyria came. But Hosea also was thankful for God's promise that He would bring back their nation one day.

2 Say to your brethren, 'My people,'[a]
And to your sisters, 'Mercy[b] *is shown*.'

God's Unfaithful People

2 "Bring charges against your mother, bring charges;
For she *is* not My wife, nor *am* I her Husband!
Let her put away her harlotries from her sight,
And her adulteries from between her breasts;
3 Lest I strip her naked
And expose her, as in the day she was born,
And make her like a wilderness,
And set her like a dry land,
And slay her with thirst.

4 "I will not have mercy on her children,
For they *are* the children of harlotry.
5 For their mother has played the harlot;
She who conceived them has behaved shamefully.
For she said, 'I will go after my lovers,
Who give *me* my bread and my water,
My wool and my linen,
My oil and my drink.'

6 "Therefore, behold,
I will hedge up your way with thorns,
And wall her in,
So that she cannot find her paths.
7 She will chase her lovers,
But not overtake them;
Yes, she will seek them, but not find *them*.
Then she will say,
'I will go and return to my first husband,
For then *it was* better for me than now.'
8 For she did not know
That I gave her grain, new wine, and oil,
And multiplied her silver and gold—
Which they prepared for Baal.

9 "Therefore I will return and take away
My grain in its time
And My new wine in its season,
And will take back My wool and My linen,
Given to cover her nakedness.
10 Now I will uncover her lewdness in the sight of her lovers,
And no one shall deliver her from My hand.
11 I will also cause all her mirth to cease,
Her feast days,

In Focus

2:19 Betroth Pronounced *be-TROTH*. Like being engaged to be married, but to be betrothed in Bible times was more serious and legally binding than being engaged today.

Her New Moons,
Her Sabbaths—
All her appointed feasts.

12 "And I will destroy her vines and her fig trees,
Of which she has said,
'These *are* my wages that my lovers have given me.'
So I will make them a forest,
And the beasts of the field shall eat them.
13 I will punish her
For the days of the Baals to which she burned incense.
She decked herself with her earrings and jewelry,
And went after her lovers;
But Me she forgot," says the LORD.

God's Mercy on His People

14 "Therefore, behold, I will allure her,
Will bring her into the wilderness,
And speak comfort to her.
15 I will give her her vineyards from there,
And the Valley of Achor as a door of hope;
She shall sing there,
As in the days of her youth,
As in the day when she came up from the land of Egypt.

16 "And it shall be, in that day,"
Says the LORD,
"*That* you will call Me 'My Husband,'[a]
And no longer call Me 'My Master,'[b]
17 For I will take from her mouth the names of the Baals,
And they shall be remembered by their name no more.
18 In that day I will make a covenant for them

2:1 [a] Hebrew *Ammi* (compare 1:9, 10) [b] Hebrew *Ruhamah* (compare 1:6) 2:16 [a] Hebrew *Ishi* [b] Hebrew *Baali*

With the beasts of the field,
With the birds of the air,
And *with* the creeping things of the ground.
Bow and sword of battle I will shatter from the earth,
To make them lie down safely.

19 "I will betroth you to Me forever;
Yes, I will betroth you to Me
In righteousness and justice,
In lovingkindness and mercy;
20 I will betroth you to Me in faithfulness,
And you shall know the LORD.

21 "It shall come to pass in that day
That I will answer," says the LORD;
"I will answer the heavens,
And they shall answer the earth.
22 The earth shall answer
With grain,
With new wine,
And with oil;
They shall answer Jezreel.[a]
23 Then I will sow her for Myself in the earth,
And I will have mercy on *her who had* not obtained mercy;[a]
Then I will say to *those who were* not My people,[b]
'You *are* My people!'
And they shall say, *'You are* my God!' "

Israel Will Return to God

3 Then the LORD said to me, "Go again,
love a woman *who is* loved by a lover[a]
and is committing adultery, just like the love
of the LORD for the children of Israel, who
look to other gods and love *the* raisin cakes
of the pagans."
2So I bought her for myself for fifteen
shekels of silver, and one and one-half homers of barley. 3And I said to her, "You shall
stay with me many days; you shall not play
the harlot, nor shall you have a man—so,
too, *will* I *be* toward you."
4For the children of Israel shall abide
many days without king or prince, without
sacrifice or *sacred* pillar, without ephod or
teraphim. 5Afterward the children of Israel
shall return and seek the LORD their God
and David their king. They shall fear the
LORD and His goodness in the latter days.

God's Charge Against Israel

4 Hear the word of the LORD,
You children of Israel,
For the LORD *brings* a charge against the inhabitants of the land:

"There is no truth or mercy
Or knowledge of God in the land.
2 *By* swearing and lying,
Killing and stealing and committing adultery,
They break all restraint,
With bloodshed upon bloodshed.
3 Therefore the land will mourn;
And everyone who dwells there will waste away
With the beasts of the field
And the birds of the air;
Even the fish of the sea will be taken away.

4 "Now let no man contend, or rebuke another;
For your people *are* like those who contend with the priest.
5 Therefore you shall stumble in the day;
The prophet also shall stumble with you in the night;
And I will destroy your mother.
6 My people are destroyed for lack of knowledge.
Because you have rejected knowledge,
I also will reject you from being priest for Me;
Because you have forgotten the law of your God,
I also will forget your children.

7 "The more they increased,
The more they sinned against Me;
I will change[a] their glory[b] into shame.
8 They eat up the sin of My people;
They set their heart on their iniquity.
9 And it shall be: like people, like priest.
So I will punish them for their ways,
And reward them for their deeds.
10 For they shall eat, but not have enough;
They shall commit harlotry, but not increase;
Because they have ceased obeying the LORD.

The Idolatry of Israel

11 "Harlotry, wine, and new wine enslave the heart.

2:22 [a] Literally *God Will Sow* 2:23 [a] Hebrew *lo-ruhamah* [b] Hebrew *lo-ammi* 3:1 [a] Literally *friend* or *husband* 4:7 [a] Following Masoretic Text, Septuagint, and Vulgate; scribal tradition, Syriac, and Targum read *They will change.* [b] Following Masoretic Text, Septuagint, Syriac, Targum, and Vulgate; scribal tradition reads *My glory.*

12 My people ask counsel from their
wooden *idols,*
And their staff informs them.
For the spirit of harlotry has caused
them to stray,
And they have played the harlot against
their God.
13 They offer sacrifices on the
mountaintops,
And burn incense on the hills,
Under oaks, poplars, and terebinths,
Because their shade *is* good.
Therefore your daughters commit
harlotry,
And your brides commit adultery.

14 "I will not punish your daughters when
they commit harlotry,
Nor your brides when they commit
adultery;
For *the men* themselves go apart with
harlots,
And offer sacrifices with a ritual harlot.[a]
Therefore people *who* do not understand
will be trampled.

15 "Though you, Israel, play the harlot,
Let not Judah offend.
Do not come up to Gilgal,
Nor go up to Beth Aven,
Nor swear an oath, *saying,* 'As the LORD
lives'—

16 "For Israel is stubborn
Like a stubborn calf;
Now the LORD will let them forage
Like a lamb in open country.

17 "Ephraim *is* joined to idols,
Let him alone.
18 Their drink is rebellion,
They commit harlotry continually.
Her rulers dearly[a] love dishonor.
19 The wind has wrapped her up in its
wings,
And they shall be ashamed because of
their sacrifices.

Impending Judgment on Israel and Judah

5 "Hear this, O priests!
Take heed, O house of Israel!
Give ear, O house of the king!
For yours *is* the judgment,
Because you have been a snare to
Mizpah
And a net spread on Tabor.
2 The revolters are deeply involved in
slaughter,
Though I rebuke them all.
3 I know Ephraim,
And Israel is not hidden from Me;
For now, O Ephraim, you commit
harlotry;
Israel is defiled.

4 "They do not direct their deeds
Toward turning to their God,
For the spirit of harlotry is in their
midst,
And they do not know the LORD.
5 The pride of Israel testifies to his face;
Therefore Israel and Ephraim stumble
in their iniquity;
Judah also stumbles with them.

6 "With their flocks and herds
They shall go to seek the LORD,
But they will not find *Him;*
He has withdrawn Himself from them.
7 They have dealt treacherously with the
LORD,
For they have begotten pagan children.
Now a New Moon shall devour them
and their heritage.

8 "Blow the ram's horn in Gibeah,
The trumpet in Ramah!
Cry aloud *at* Beth Aven,
'*Look* behind you, O Benjamin!'
9 Ephraim shall be desolate in the day of
rebuke;
Among the tribes of Israel I make
known what is sure.

10 "The princes of Judah are like those who
remove a landmark;
I will pour out My wrath on them like
water.
11 Ephraim is oppressed *and* broken in
judgment,
Because he willingly walked by *human*
precept.
12 Therefore I *will be* to Ephraim like a
moth,
And to the house of Judah like
rottenness.

13 "When Ephraim saw his sickness,
And Judah *saw* his wound,
Then Ephraim went to Assyria
And sent to King Jareb;

4:14 [a] Compare Deuteronomy 23:18 4:18 [a] Hebrew is difficult; a Jewish tradition reads *Her rulers shamefully love, 'Give!'*

Yet he cannot cure you,
Nor heal you of your wound.
14 For I *will be* like a lion to Ephraim,
And like a young lion to the house of Judah.
I, *even* I, will tear *them* and go away;
I will take *them* away, and no one shall rescue.
15 I will return again to My place
Till they acknowledge their offense.
Then they will seek My face;
In their affliction they will earnestly seek Me."

A Call to Repentance

6 Come, and let us return to the LORD;
For He has torn, but He will heal us;
He has stricken, but He will bind us up.
2 After two days He will revive us;
On the third day He will raise us up,
That we may live in His sight.
3 Let us know,
Let us pursue the knowledge of the LORD.
His going forth is established as the morning;
He will come to us like the rain,
Like the latter *and* former rain to the earth.

Impenitence of Israel and Judah

4 "O Ephraim, what shall I do to you?
O Judah, what shall I do to you?
For your faithfulness is like a morning cloud,
And like the early dew it goes away.
5 Therefore I have hewn *them* by the prophets,
I have slain them by the words of My mouth;
And your judgments *are like* light *that* goes forth.
6 For I desire mercy and not sacrifice,
And the knowledge of God more than burnt offerings.

7 "But like men[a] they transgressed the covenant;
There they dealt treacherously with Me.
8 Gilead *is* a city of evildoers
And defiled with blood.
9 As bands of robbers lie in wait for a man,
So the company of priests murder on the way to Shechem;
Surely they commit lewdness.
10 I have seen a horrible thing in the house of Israel:
There *is* the harlotry of Ephraim;
Israel is defiled.
11 Also, O Judah, a harvest is appointed for you,
When I return the captives of My people.

7 "When I would have healed Israel,
Then the iniquity of Ephraim was uncovered,
And the wickedness of Samaria.
For they have committed fraud;
A thief comes in;
A band of robbers takes spoil outside.
2 They do not consider in their hearts
That I remember all their wickedness;
Now their own deeds have surrounded them;
They are before My face.
3 They make a king glad with their wickedness,
And princes with their lies.

4 "They *are* all adulterers.
Like an oven heated by a baker—
He ceases stirring *the fire* after kneading the dough,
Until it is leavened.
5 In the day of our king
Princes have made *him* sick, inflamed with wine;
He stretched out his hand with scoffers.
6 They prepare their heart like an oven,
While they lie in wait;
Their baker[a] sleeps all night;
In the morning it burns like a flaming fire.
7 They are all hot, like an oven,
And have devoured their judges;
All their kings have fallen.
None among them calls upon Me.

8 "Ephraim has mixed himself among the peoples;
Ephraim is a cake unturned.
9 Aliens have devoured his strength,
But he does not know *it;*
Yes, gray hairs are here and there on him,
Yet he does not know *it*.

6:7 [a] Or *like Adam* 7:6 [a] Following Masoretic Text and Vulgate; Syriac and Targum read *Their anger;* Septuagint reads *Ephraim*.

10 And the pride of Israel testifies to his face,
But they do not return to the LORD their God,
Nor seek Him for all this.

Futile Reliance on the Nations

11 "Ephraim also is like a silly dove, without sense—
They call to Egypt,
They go to Assyria.
12 Wherever they go, I will spread My net on them;
I will bring them down like birds of the air;
I will chastise them
According to what their congregation has heard.

13 "Woe to them, for they have fled from Me!
Destruction to them,
Because they have transgressed against Me!
Though I redeemed them,
Yet they have spoken lies against Me.
14 They did not cry out to Me with their heart
When they wailed upon their beds.

"They assemble together for[a] grain and new wine,
They rebel against Me;[b]
15 Though I disciplined *and* strengthened their arms,
Yet they devise evil against Me;
16 They return, *but* not to the Most High;[a]
They are like a treacherous bow.
Their princes shall fall by the sword
For the cursings of their tongue.
This *shall be* their derision in the land of Egypt.

The Apostasy of Israel

8 "*Set* the trumpet[a] to your mouth!
He shall come like an eagle against the house of the LORD,
Because they have transgressed My covenant
And rebelled against My law.
2 Israel will cry to Me,
'My God, we know You!'
3 Israel has rejected the good;
The enemy will pursue him.

4 "They set up kings, but not by Me;
They made princes, but I did not acknowledge *them*.
From their silver and gold
They made idols for themselves—
That they might be cut off.
5 Your calf is rejected, O Samaria!
My anger is aroused against them—
How long until they attain to innocence?
6 For from Israel *is* even this:
A workman made it, and it *is* not God;
But the calf of Samaria shall be broken to pieces.

7 "They sow the wind,
And reap the whirlwind.
The stalk has no bud;
It shall never produce meal.
If it should produce,
Aliens would swallow it up.
8 Israel is swallowed up;
Now they are among the Gentiles
Like a vessel in which *is* no pleasure.
9 For they have gone up to Assyria,
Like a wild donkey alone by itself;
Ephraim has hired lovers.
10 Yes, though they have hired among the nations,
Now I will gather them;
And they shall sorrow a little,[a]
Because of the burden[b] of the king of princes.

11 "Because Ephraim has made many altars for sin,
They have become for him altars for sinning.
12 I have written for him the great things of My law,
But they were considered a strange thing.
13 *For* the sacrifices of My offerings they sacrifice flesh and eat *it*,
But the LORD does not accept them.
Now He will remember their iniquity and punish their sins.
They shall return to Egypt.

14 "For Israel has forgotten his Maker,
And has built temples;[a]

7:14 [a] Following Masoretic Text and Targum; Vulgate reads *thought upon;* Septuagint reads *slashed themselves for* (compare 1 Kings 18:28). [b] Following Masoretic Text, Syriac, and Targum; Septuagint omits *They rebel against Me;* Vulgate reads *They departed from Me.* 7:16 [a] Or *upward* 8:1 [a] Hebrew *shophar,* ram's horn 8:10 [a] Or *begin to diminish* [b] Or *oracle* 8:14 [a] Or *palaces*

Judah also has multiplied fortified
cities;
But I will send fire upon his cities,
And it shall devour his palaces."

Judgment of Israel's Sin

9 Do not rejoice, O Israel, with joy like
other peoples,
For you have played the harlot against
your God.
You have made love *for* hire on every
threshing floor.
2 The threshing floor and the winepress
Shall not feed them,
And the new wine shall fail in her.

3 They shall not dwell in the LORD's land,
But Ephraim shall return to Egypt,
And shall eat unclean *things* in Assyria.
4 They shall not offer wine *offerings* to the
LORD,
Nor shall their sacrifices be pleasing to
Him.
It shall be like bread of mourners to
them
All who eat it shall be defiled.
For their bread *shall be* for their *own* life;
It shall not come into the house of the
LORD.

5 What will you do in the appointed day,
And in the day of the feast of the LORD?
6 For indeed they are gone because of
destruction.
Egypt shall gather them up;
Memphis shall bury them.
Nettles shall possess their valuables of
silver;
Thorns *shall be* in their tents.

7 The days of punishment have come;
The days of recompense have come.
Israel knows!
The prophet *is* a fool,
The spiritual man *is* insane,
Because of the greatness of your
iniquity and great enmity.
8 The watchman of Ephraim *is* with my
God
But the prophet *is* a fowler's[a] snare in all
his ways—
Enmity in the house of his God.
9 They are deeply corrupted,
As in the days of Gibeah.
He will remember their iniquity;
He will punish their sins.

10 "I found Israel
Like grapes in the wilderness;
I saw your fathers
As the firstfruits on the fig tree in its
first season.
But they went to Baal Peor,
And separated themselves *to that*
shame;
They became an abomination like the
thing they loved.
11 *As for* Ephraim, their glory shall fly
away like a bird—
No birth, no pregnancy, and no
conception!
12 Though they bring up their children,
Yet I will bereave them to the last man.
Yes, woe to them when I depart from
them!
13 Just as I saw Ephraim like Tyre, planted
in a pleasant place,
So Ephraim will bring out his children
to the murderer."

14 Give them, O LORD—
What will You give?
Give them a miscarrying womb
And dry breasts!

15 "All their wickedness *is* in Gilgal,
For there I hated them.
Because of the evil of their deeds
I will drive them from My house;
I will love them no more.
All their princes *are* rebellious.
16 Ephraim is stricken,
Their root is dried up;
They shall bear no fruit.
Yes, were they to bear children,
I would kill the darlings of their womb."

17 My God will cast them away,
Because they did not obey Him;
And they shall be wanderers among the
nations.

Israel's Sin and Captivity

10 Israel empties *his* vine;
He brings forth fruit for himself.
According to the multitude of his fruit
He has increased the altars;
According to the bounty of his land
They have embellished *his sacred* pillars.
2 Their heart is divided;
Now they are held guilty.
He will break down their altars;
He will ruin their *sacred* pillars.

9:8 [a] That is, one who catches birds in a trap or snare

3 For now they say,
"We have no king,
Because we did not fear the LORD.
And as for a king, what would he do for us?"
4 They have spoken words,
Swearing falsely in making a covenant.
Thus judgment springs up like hemlock in the furrows of the field.

5 The inhabitants of Samaria fear
Because of the calf[a] of Beth Aven.
For its people mourn for it,
And its priests shriek for it—
Because its glory has departed from it.
6 *The idol* also shall be carried to Assyria
As a present for King Jareb.
Ephraim shall receive shame,
And Israel shall be ashamed of his own counsel.

7 *As for* Samaria, her king is cut off
Like a twig on the water.
8 Also the high places of Aven, the sin of Israel,
Shall be destroyed.
The thorn and thistle shall grow on their altars;
They shall say to the mountains, "Cover us!"
And to the hills, "Fall on us!"

9 "O Israel, you have sinned from the days of Gibeah;
There they stood.
The battle in Gibeah against the children of iniquity[a]
Did not overtake them.
10 When *it is* My desire, I will chasten them.
Peoples shall be gathered against them
When I bind them for their two transgressions.[a]
11 Ephraim *is* a trained heifer
That loves to thresh *grain;*
But I harnessed her fair neck,
I will make Ephraim pull *a plow.*
Judah shall plow;
Jacob shall break his clods."

12 Sow for yourselves righteousness;
Reap in mercy;
Break up your fallow ground,
For *it is* time to seek the LORD,
Till He comes and rains righteousness on you.
13 You have plowed wickedness;
You have reaped iniquity.
You have eaten the fruit of lies,
Because you trusted in your own way,
In the multitude of your mighty men.
14 Therefore tumult shall arise among your people,
And all your fortresses shall be plundered
As Shalman plundered Beth Arbel in the day of battle—
A mother dashed in pieces upon *her* children.
15 Thus it shall be done to you, O Bethel,
Because of your great wickedness.
At dawn the king of Israel
Shall be cut off utterly.

God's Continuing Love for Israel

11 "When Israel *was* a child, I loved him,
And out of Egypt I called My son.
2 *As* they called them,[a]
So they went from them;[b]
They sacrificed to the Baals,
And burned incense to carved images.

3 "I taught Ephraim to walk,
Taking them by their arms;[a]
But they did not know that I healed them.
4 I drew them with gentle cords,[a]
With bands of love,
And I was to them as those who take the yoke from their neck.[b]
I stooped *and* fed them.

5 "He shall not return to the land of Egypt;
But the Assyrian shall be his king,
Because they refused to repent.
6 And the sword shall slash in his cities,
Devour his districts,
And consume *them,*
Because of their own counsels.
7 My people are bent on backsliding from Me.
Though they call to the Most High,[a]
None at all exalt *Him.*

10:5 [a] Literally *calves* 10:9 [a] So read many Hebrew manuscripts, Septuagint, and Vulgate; Masoretic Text reads *unruliness.* 10:10 [a] Or *in their two habitations* 11:2 [a] Following Masoretic Text and Vulgate; Septuagint reads *Just as I called them;* Targum interprets as *I sent prophets to a thousand of them.* [b] Following Masoretic Text, Targum, and Vulgate; Septuagint reads *from My face.* 11:3 [a] Some Hebrew manuscripts, Septuagint, Syriac, and Vulgate read *My arms.* 11:4 [a] Literally *cords of a man* [b] Literally *jaws* 11:7 [a] Or *upward*

8 "How can I give you up, Ephraim?
How can I hand you over, Israel?
How can I make you like Admah?
How can I set you like Zeboiim?
My heart churns within Me;
My sympathy is stirred.
9 I will not execute the fierceness of My anger;
I will not again destroy Ephraim.
For I *am* God, and not man,
The Holy One in your midst;
And I will not come with terror.[a]

10 "They shall walk after the LORD.
He will roar like a lion.
When He roars,
Then His sons shall come trembling from the west;
11 They shall come trembling like a bird from Egypt,
Like a dove from the land of Assyria.
And I will let them dwell in their houses,"
Says the LORD.

God's Charge Against Ephraim

12 "Ephraim has encircled Me with lies,
And the house of Israel with deceit;
But Judah still walks with God,
Even with the Holy One[a] *who is* faithful.

12 "Ephraim feeds on the wind,
And pursues the east wind;
He daily increases lies and desolation.
Also they make a covenant with the Assyrians,
And oil is carried to Egypt.

2 "The LORD also *brings* a charge against Judah,
And will punish Jacob according to his ways;
According to his deeds He will recompense him.
3 He took his brother by the heel in the womb,
And in his strength he struggled with God.[a]
4 Yes, he struggled with the Angel and prevailed;
He wept, and sought favor from Him.
He found Him *in* Bethel,
And there He spoke to us—
5 That is, the LORD God of hosts.
The LORD *is* His memorable name.
6 So you, by *the help of* your God, return;
Observe mercy and justice,
And wait on your God continually.

11:9 [a] Or *I will not enter a city* 11:12 [a] Or *holy ones*
12:3 [a] Compare Genesis 32:28

Epic Ideas

11:1–4 GOD'S LOVE FOR ISRAEL

The prophet Hosea's unhappy life with his wife, Gomer, also shows God's unhappy experience with His people Israel. Gomer was unfaithful to Hosea, and Israel was unfaithful to the Lord. Hosea still loved Gomer, and God still loved Israel.

In this book God reminds Israel how He loved them when they were slaves in Egypt. The Lord led them out of their slavery. But for hundreds of years, Israel kept turning away from God. So Israel was always a rebel against God.

Now the Lord continues to love His disobedient people. He has been trying to win them back to Himself all these long centuries. Someday they will return to serve Him.

The book of Hosea also describes how much God loves *you*. He will plead with you till you turn to Him.

7 "A cunning Canaanite!
Deceitful scales *are* in his hand;
He loves to oppress.
8 And Ephraim said,
'Surely I have become rich,
I have found wealth for myself;
In all my labors
They shall find in me no iniquity that *is* sin.'

9 "But I *am* the LORD your God,
Ever since the land of Egypt;
I will again make you dwell in tents,
As in the days of the appointed feast.
10 I have also spoken by the prophets,
And have multiplied visions;
I have given symbols through the witness of the prophets."

11 Though Gilead *has* idols—
Surely they are vanity—
Though they sacrifice bulls in Gilgal,
Indeed their altars *shall be* heaps in the furrows of the field.

12 Jacob fled to the country of Syria;
Israel served for a spouse,
And for a wife he tended *sheep*.
13 By a prophet the LORD brought Israel out of Egypt,
And by a prophet he was preserved.
14 Ephraim provoked *Him* to anger most bitterly;
Therefore his Lord will leave the guilt of his bloodshed upon him,
And return his reproach upon him.

Relentless Judgment on Israel

13 When Ephraim spoke, trembling,
He exalted *himself* in Israel;
But when he offended through Baal *worship*, he died.
2 Now they sin more and more,
And have made for themselves molded images,
Idols of their silver, according to their skill;
All of it *is* the work of craftsmen.
They say of them,
"Let the men who sacrifice[a] kiss the calves!"
3 Therefore they shall be like the morning cloud
And like the early dew that passes away,
Like chaff blown off from a threshing floor
And like smoke from a chimney.

4 "Yet I *am* the LORD your God
Ever since the land of Egypt,
And you shall know no God but Me;
For *there is* no savior besides Me.
5 I knew you in the wilderness,
In the land of great drought.
6 When they had pasture, they were filled;
They were filled and their heart was exalted;
Therefore they forgot Me.

7 "So I will be to them like a lion;
Like a leopard by the road I will lurk;
8 I will meet them like a bear deprived *of her cubs;*
I will tear open their rib cage,
And there I will devour them like a lion.
The wild beast shall tear them.

9 "O Israel, you are destroyed,[a]
But your help[b] *is* from Me.
10 I will be your King;[a]
Where *is any other,*
That he may save you in all your cities?
And your judges to whom you said,
'Give me a king and princes'?
11 I gave you a king in My anger,
And took *him* away in My wrath.

12 "The iniquity of Ephraim *is* bound up;
His sin *is* stored up.
13 The sorrows of a woman in childbirth shall come upon him.
He *is* an unwise son,
For he should not stay long where children are born.

14 "I will ransom them from the power of the grave;[a]
I will redeem them from death.
O Death, I will be your plagues![b]
O Grave,[c] I will be your destruction![d]
Pity is hidden from My eyes."

15 Though he is fruitful among *his* brethren,
An east wind shall come;
The wind of the LORD shall come up from the wilderness.
Then his spring shall become dry,

13:2 [a] Or *those who offer human sacrifice* 13:9 [a] Literally *it or he destroyed you* [b] Literally *in your help* 13:10 [a] Septuagint, Syriac, Targum, and Vulgate read *Where is your king?* 13:14 [a] Or *Sheol* [b] Septuagint reads *where is your punishment?* [c] Or *Sheol* [d] Septuagint reads *where is your sting?*

And his fountain shall be dried up.
He shall plunder the treasury of every desirable prize.
16 Samaria is held guilty,[a]
For she has rebelled against her God.
They shall fall by the sword,
Their infants shall be dashed in pieces,
And their women with child ripped open.

Israel Restored at Last

14 O Israel, return to the LORD your God,
For you have stumbled because of your iniquity;
2 Take words with you,
And return to the LORD.
Say to Him,
"Take away all iniquity;
Receive *us* graciously,
For we will offer the sacrifices[a] of our lips.
3 Assyria shall not save us,
We will not ride on horses,
Nor will we say anymore to the work of our hands, '*You are* our gods.'
For in You the fatherless finds mercy."

4 "I will heal their backsliding,
I will love them freely,
For My anger has turned away from him.
5 I will be like the dew to Israel;
He shall grow like the lily,
And lengthen his roots like Lebanon.
6 His branches shall spread;
His beauty shall be like an olive tree,
And his fragrance like Lebanon.
7 Those who dwell under his shadow shall return;
They shall be revived *like* grain,
And grow like a vine.
Their scent[a] *shall be* like the wine of Lebanon.

8 "Ephraim *shall say*, 'What have I to do anymore with idols?'
I have heard and observed him.
I *am* like a green cypress tree;
Your fruit is found in Me."

9 Who *is* wise?
Let him understand these things.
Who is prudent?
Let him know them.
For the ways of the LORD *are* right;
The righteous walk in them,
But transgressors stumble in them.

13:16 [a] Septuagint reads *shall be disfigured* **14:2** [a] Literally *bull calves;* Septuagint reads *fruit.* **14:7** [a] Literally *remembrance*

REBELLION

READ IT: HOSEA 14:9

This verse is quite a bit simpler than it might sound. It's saying that if you're wise, walking with God and living for Him isn't that difficult. With God's strength and guidance, right living will come naturally to you. But if you're committed to wrong living—selfishness, greed, rebellion—you'll always stumble on the path of life. In short: rebels trip.

The BOOK of

JOEL

835 B.C.–805 B.C.

Behind the Scenes

READ IT:

The book of Joel tells the story of a horrible locust plague that occurred in Palestine. In this event Joel saw a sign for the final judgment and warned the people to turn back to God. Joel announced that the "day of the LORD" was coming. It would be a time of judgment.

GET IT:

Who wrote it: The prophet Joel

When it was written: 835 B.C.–805 B.C.

Why it was written: to warn us of the coming day of judgment: the day of the Lord.

LIVE IT:

The day of judgment is real. God will judge everyone.

If we say we're sorry for what we've done wrong and accept Jesus as Savior, we'll be okay.

FIND IT:

The Land Laid Waste by Locusts	*Joel 1*
The Day of the Lord	*Joel 2:1*
God's Spirit Poured Out	*Joel 2:28*
God Judges the Nations	*Joel 3*

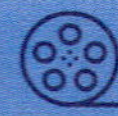

1 The word of the LORD that came to Joel
the son of Pethuel.

The Land Laid Waste

2 Hear this, you elders,
And give ear, all you inhabitants of the
land!
Has *anything like* this happened in your
days,
Or even in the days of your fathers?
3 Tell your children about it,
Let your children *tell* their children,
And their children another generation.

4 What the chewing locust[a] left, the
swarming locust has eaten;
What the swarming locust left, the
crawling locust has eaten;
And what the crawling locust left, the
consuming locust has eaten.

5 Awake, you drunkards, and weep;
And wail, all you drinkers of wine,
Because of the new wine,
For it has been cut off from your mouth.
6 For a nation has come up against My
land,
Strong, and without number;
His teeth *are* the teeth of a lion,
And he has the fangs of a fierce lion.
7 He has laid waste My vine,
And ruined My fig tree;
He has stripped it bare and thrown *it*
away;
Its branches are made white.

8 Lament like a virgin girded with
sackcloth
For the husband of her youth.
9 The grain offering and the drink
offering
Have been cut off from the house of the
LORD;
The priests mourn, who minister to the
LORD.
10 The field is wasted,
The land mourns;
For the grain is ruined,
The new wine is dried up,
The oil fails.

11 Be ashamed, you farmers,
Wail, you vinedressers,
For the wheat and the barley;
Because the harvest of the field has
perished.
12 The vine has dried up,
And the fig tree has withered;
The pomegranate tree,
The palm tree also,
And the apple tree—
All the trees of the field are withered;
Surely joy has withered away from the
sons of men.

Mourning for the Land

13 Gird yourselves and lament, you priests;
Wail, you who minister before the altar;

1:4 [a] Exact identity of these locusts is unknown.

Starring Roles

JOEL'S name is pronounced *JO-el* and means "The Lord Is God." People remember him because he told about the coming of the Holy Spirit hundreds of years later. You can read about this great happening in Acts 2 in the New Testament.

Joel's book also describes God's future judgment, which he calls "the day of the LORD." We should always be expecting that great "Day" when God will bring all nations before Him for judgment. He is going to judge everyone, according to what they have done. See Revelation 20:12 in the New Testament.

You can escape God's judgment if you learn to be sorry for your sin and turn to Jesus. Even though Jesus is not talked about by name in the Old Testament, He was their Savior, too.

Come, lie all night in sackcloth,
You who minister to my God;
For the grain offering and the drink
offering
Are withheld from the house of your
God.
14 Consecrate a fast,
Call a sacred assembly;
Gather the elders
And all the inhabitants of the land
Into the house of the LORD your God,
And cry out to the LORD.

15 Alas for the day!
For the day of the LORD *is* at hand;
It shall come as destruction from the
Almighty.
16 Is not the food cut off before our eyes,
Joy and gladness from the house of our
God?
17 The seed shrivels under the clods,
Storehouses are in shambles;
Barns are broken down,
For the grain has withered.
18 How the animals groan!
The herds of cattle are restless,
Because they have no pasture;
Even the flocks of sheep suffer
punishment.[a]

19 O LORD, to You I cry out;
For fire has devoured the open pastures,
And a flame has burned all the trees of
the field.
20 The beasts of the field also cry out to You,
For the water brooks are dried up,
And fire has devoured the open
pastures.

The Day of the LORD

2 Blow the trumpet in Zion,
And sound an alarm in My holy
mountain!
Let all the inhabitants of the land
tremble;
For the day of the LORD is coming,
For it is at hand:
2 A day of darkness and gloominess,
A day of clouds and thick darkness,
Like the morning *clouds* spread over the
mountains.
A *people come,* great and strong,
The like of whom has never been;
Nor will there ever be any *such* after
them,
Even for many successive generations.

3 A fire devours before them,
And behind them a flame burns;
The land *is* like the Garden of Eden
before them,
And behind them a desolate wilderness;
Surely nothing shall escape them.
4 Their appearance is like the appearance
of horses;
And like swift steeds, so they run.
5 With a noise like chariots
Over mountaintops they leap,
Like the noise of a flaming fire that
devours the stubble,
Like a strong people set in battle array.

6 Before them the people writhe in pain;
All faces are drained of color.[a]
7 They run like mighty men,
They climb the wall like men of war;
Every one marches in formation,
And they do not break ranks.
8 They do not push one another;
Every one marches in his own column.[a]
Though they lunge between the weapons,
They are not cut down.[b]
9 They run to and fro in the city,
They run on the wall;
They climb into the houses,
They enter at the windows like a thief.

10 The earth quakes before them,
The heavens tremble;
The sun and moon grow dark,
And the stars diminish their brightness.
11 The LORD gives voice before His army,
For His camp is very great;
For strong *is the One* who executes His
word.
For the day of the LORD *is* great and very
terrible;
Who can endure it?

A Call to Repentance

12 "Now, therefore," says the LORD,
"Turn to Me with all your heart,
With fasting, with weeping, and with
mourning."
13 So rend your heart, and not your
garments;
Return to the LORD your God,
For He *is* gracious and merciful,

1:18 [a] Septuagint and Vulgate read *are made desolate.*
2:6 [a] Septuagint, Targum, and Vulgate read *gather blackness.* 2:8 [a] Literally *his own highway* [b] That is, they are not halted by losses

Slow to anger, and of great kindness;
And He relents from doing harm.
14 Who knows *if* He will turn and relent,
And leave a blessing behind Him—
A grain offering and a drink offering
For the LORD your God?

15 Blow the trumpet in Zion,
Consecrate a fast,
Call a sacred assembly;
16 Gather the people,
Sanctify the congregation,
Assemble the elders,
Gather the children and nursing babes;
Let the bridegroom go out from his chamber,
And the bride from her dressing room.
17 Let the priests, who minister to the LORD,
Weep between the porch and the altar;
Let them say, "Spare Your people, O LORD,
And do not give Your heritage to reproach,
That the nations should rule over them.
Why should they say among the peoples,
'Where is their God?' "

The Land Refreshed

18 Then the LORD will be zealous for His land,
And pity His people.
19 The LORD will answer and say to His people,
"Behold, I will send you grain and new wine and oil,
And you will be satisfied by them;
I will no longer make you a reproach among the nations.

20 "But I will remove far from you the northern *army*,
And will drive him away into a barren and desolate land,
With his face toward the eastern sea
And his back toward the western sea;
His stench will come up,
And his foul odor will rise,
Because he has done monstrous things."

21 Fear not, O land;
Be glad and rejoice,
For the LORD has done marvelous things!
22 Do not be afraid, you beasts of the field;
For the open pastures are springing up,
And the tree bears its fruit;
The fig tree and the vine yield their strength.
23 Be glad then, you children of Zion,
And rejoice in the LORD your God;
For He has given you the former rain faithfully,[a]
And He will cause the rain to come down for you—
The former rain,
And the latter rain in the first *month*.
24 The threshing floors shall be full of wheat,
And the vats shall overflow with new wine and oil.

25 "So I will restore to you the years that the swarming locust has eaten,
The crawling locust,
The consuming locust,
And the chewing locust,[a]
My great army which I sent among you.
26 You shall eat in plenty and be satisfied,
And praise the name of the LORD your God,
Who has dealt wondrously with you;
And My people shall never be put to shame.
27 Then you shall know that I *am* in the midst of Israel:
I *am* the LORD your God
And there is no other.
My people shall never be put to shame.

God's Spirit Poured Out

28 "And it shall come to pass afterward
That I will pour out My Spirit on all flesh;
Your sons and your daughters shall prophesy,
Your old men shall dream dreams,
Your young men shall see visions.
29 And also on *My* menservants and on *My* maidservants
I will pour out My Spirit in those days.

30 "And I will show wonders in the heavens and in the earth:
Blood and fire and pillars of smoke.
31 The sun shall be turned into darkness,
And the moon into blood,
Before the coming of the great and awesome day of the LORD.
32 And it shall come to pass

2:23 [a] Or *the teacher of righteousness* 2:25 [a] Compare 1:4

That whoever calls on the name of the
LORD
Shall be saved.
For in Mount Zion and in Jerusalem
there shall be deliverance,
As the LORD has said,
Among the remnant whom the LORD calls.

God Judges the Nations

3 "For behold, in those days and at that
time,
When I bring back the captives of Judah
and Jerusalem,
2 I will also gather all nations,
And bring them down to the Valley of
Jehoshaphat;
And I will enter into judgment with
them there
On account of My people, My heritage
Israel,
Whom they have scattered among the
nations;
They have also divided up My land.
3 They have cast lots for My people,
Have given a boy *as payment* for a harlot,
And sold a girl for wine, that they may
drink.

4 "Indeed, what have you to do with Me,
O Tyre and Sidon, and all the coasts of
Philistia?
Will you retaliate against Me?
But if you retaliate against Me,
Swiftly and speedily I will return your
retaliation upon your own head;
5 Because you have taken My silver and
My gold,
And have carried into your temples My
prized possessions.
6 Also the people of Judah and the people
of Jerusalem
You have sold to the Greeks,
That you may remove them far from
their borders.

7 "Behold, I will raise them
Out of the place to which you have sold
them,
And will return your retaliation upon
your own head.
8 I will sell your sons and your daughters
Into the hand of the people of Judah,
And they will sell them to the Sabeans,[a]
To a people far off;
For the LORD has spoken."

9 Proclaim this among the nations:
"Prepare for war!
Wake up the mighty men,

3:8 [a] Literally *Shebaites* (compare Isaiah 60:6 and Ezekiel 27:22)

2:28, 29 GOD HAS SENT HIS SPIRIT

There are *three Persons* in the *one God*. They are the Father, the Son, and the Holy Spirit. The Holy Spirit helped at Creation (see Genesis 1:2), and He spoke through the prophets of the Old Testament.

But in the New Testament, the Holy Spirit came in greater power to believers than He did in the Old Testament. The Holy Spirit came in that greater power after Jesus rose from the dead and went back to heaven.

In Acts 2:16–21, you can read how Joel's promise of the Holy Spirit was fulfilled in the New Testament. The Holy Spirit not only spoke through the apostles in the New Testament, but He also came to live in all believers. Jesus called the Holy Spirit the "Helper" (see John 14:16). If you are a Christian, you have the Holy Spirit living in you. The Holy Spirit helps you know you are God's child, and He helps you understand God's Word.

Let all the men of war draw near,
Let them come up.
10 Beat your plowshares into swords
And your pruning hooks into spears;
Let the weak say, 'I *am* strong.'"
11 Assemble and come, all you nations,
And gather together all around.
Cause Your mighty ones to go down
there, O LORD.

12 "Let the nations be wakened, and come
up to the Valley of Jehoshaphat;
For there I will sit to judge all the
surrounding nations.
13 Put in the sickle, for the harvest is ripe.
Come, go down;
For the winepress is full,
The vats overflow—
For their wickedness *is* great."

14 Multitudes, multitudes in the valley of
decision!
For the day of the LORD *is* near in the
valley of decision.
15 The sun and moon will grow dark,
And the stars will diminish their
brightness.
16 The LORD also will roar from Zion,
And utter His voice from Jerusalem;
The heavens and earth will shake;
But the LORD will be a shelter for His
people,
And the strength of the children of Israel.

17 "So you shall know that I *am* the LORD
your God,
Dwelling in Zion My holy mountain.
Then Jerusalem shall be holy,
And no aliens shall ever pass through
her again."

God Blesses His People

18 And it will come to pass in that day
That the mountains shall drip with new
wine,
The hills shall flow with milk,
And all the brooks of Judah shall be
flooded with water;
A fountain shall flow from the house of
the LORD
And water the Valley of Acacias.

19 "Egypt shall be a desolation,
And Edom a desolate wilderness,
Because of violence *against* the people
of Judah,
For they have shed innocent blood in
their land.
20 But Judah shall abide forever,
And Jerusalem from generation to
generation.
21 For I will acquit them of the guilt of
bloodshed, whom I had not acquitted;
For the LORD dwells in Zion."

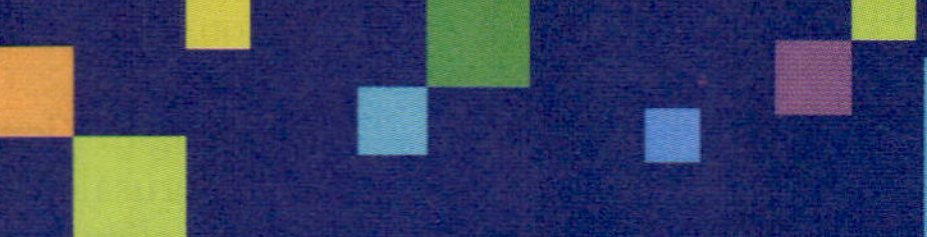

The BOOK of AMOS

760 B.C.

Behind the Scenes

READ IT:

The book of Amos contains the announcements and five visions of the prophet Amos. He announced that God would judge the people because they forgot about God, were cruel to the poor, and were selfish. He told the people to get ready to meet God. For those who loved God, however, Amos had some hope. The day was coming when David's kingdom would come back again and God's people would live in safety.

GET IT:

Who wrote it: The prophet Amos

When it was written: 760 B.C.

Why it was written: to warn us that if we forget about God our society will suffer.

LIVE IT:

God will judge us for how we treat others.

We must show God's mercy and justice to others.

FIND IT:

God Will Judge the Nations	*Amos 1*
Punishment for Israel	*Amos 3*
A Call to Repentance	*Amos 5*

1 The words of Amos, who was among the sheepbreeders[a] of Tekoa, which he saw concerning Israel in the days of Uzziah king of Judah, and in the days of Jeroboam the son of Joash, king of Israel, two years before the earthquake.

2 And he said:

"The LORD roars from Zion,
And utters His voice from Jerusalem;
The pastures of the shepherds mourn,
And the top of Carmel withers."

Judgment on the Nations

3 Thus says the LORD:

"For three transgressions of Damascus, and for four,
I will not turn away its *punishment*,
Because they have threshed Gilead with implements of iron.
4 But I will send a fire into the house of Hazael,
Which shall devour the palaces of Ben-Hadad.
5 I will also break the *gate* bar of Damascus,
And cut off the inhabitant from the Valley of Aven,
And the one who holds the scepter from Beth Eden.
The people of Syria shall go captive to Kir,"
Says the LORD.

6 Thus says the LORD:

"For three transgressions of Gaza, and for four,
I will not turn away its *punishment*,
Because they took captive the whole captivity
To deliver *them* up to Edom.
7 But I will send a fire upon the wall of Gaza,
Which shall devour its palaces.
8 I will cut off the inhabitant from Ashdod,
And the one who holds the scepter from Ashkelon;
I will turn My hand against Ekron,
And the remnant of the Philistines shall perish,"
Says the Lord GOD.

9 Thus says the LORD:

"For three transgressions of Tyre, and for four,
I will not turn away its *punishment*,
Because they delivered up the whole captivity to Edom,
And did not remember the covenant of brotherhood.
10 But I will send a fire upon the wall of Tyre,
Which shall devour its palaces."

11 Thus says the LORD:

"For three transgressions of Edom, and for four,

1:1 [a] Compare 2 Kings 3:4

Starring Roles

Strange to say, AMOS (pronounced *AY-mos*) was not always a prophet, and none of his family were prophets. He was a farmer. Just the same, God called Amos from his home in the Southern Kingdom of Judah to be a prophet to the *Northern Kingdom of Israel*.

They didn't like Amos much in Israel. He warned the rich people that they were making God angry by cheating the poor with heavy taxes. Some of the religious leaders complained about his tough words, but Amos had to be a good "Burden Bearer," which is the meaning of his name. He had to carry the burden of God's message.

When the people didn't listen, the army of Assyria came and conquered the Northern Kingdom.

I will not turn away its *punishment,*
Because he pursued his brother with
the sword,
And cast off all pity;
His anger tore perpetually,
And he kept his wrath forever.
12 But I will send a fire upon Teman,
Which shall devour the palaces of
Bozrah."

13 Thus says the LORD:

"For three transgressions of the people of
Ammon, and for four,
I will not turn away its *punishment,*
Because they ripped open the women
with child in Gilead,
That they might enlarge their territory.
14 But I will kindle a fire in the wall of
Rabbah,
And it shall devour its palaces,
Amid shouting in the day of battle,
And a tempest in the day of the
whirlwind.
15 Their king shall go into captivity,
He and his princes together,"
Says the LORD.

2 Thus says the LORD:

"For three transgressions of Moab, and
for four,
I will not turn away its *punishment,*
Because he burned the bones of the
king of Edom to lime.
2 But I will send a fire upon Moab,
And it shall devour the palaces of
Kerioth;
Moab shall die with tumult,
With shouting *and* trumpet sound.
3 And I will cut off the judge from its
midst,
And slay all its princes with him,"
Says the LORD.

Judgment on Judah

4 Thus says the LORD:

"For three transgressions of Judah, and
for four,
I will not turn away its *punishment,*
Because they have despised the law of
the LORD,
And have not kept His commandments.
Their lies lead them astray,
Lies which their fathers followed.
5 But I will send a fire upon Judah,
And it shall devour the palaces of
Jerusalem."

Judgment on Israel

6 Thus says the LORD:

"For three transgressions of Israel, and
for four,
I will not turn away its *punishment,*
Because they sell the righteous for
silver,
And the poor for a pair of sandals.
7 They pant after[a] the dust of the earth
which is on the head of the poor,
And pervert the way of the humble.
A man and his father go in to the *same*
girl,
To defile My holy name.
8 They lie down by every altar on clothes
taken in pledge,
And drink the wine of the condemned
in the house of their god.

9 "Yet *it was* I *who* destroyed the Amorite
before them,
Whose height *was* like the height of the
cedars,
And he *was as* strong as the oaks;
Yet I destroyed his fruit above
And his roots beneath.
10 Also *it was* I *who* brought you up from
the land of Egypt,
And led you forty years through the
wilderness,
To possess the land of the Amorite.
11 I raised up some of your sons as
prophets,
And some of your young men as
Nazirites.
Is it not so, O you children of Israel?"
Says the LORD.
12 "But you gave the Nazirites wine to
drink,
And commanded the prophets saying,
'Do not prophesy!'

13 "Behold, I am weighed down by you,
As a cart full of sheaves is weighed
down.
14 Therefore flight shall perish from the
swift,
The strong shall not strengthen his
power,
Nor shall the mighty deliver himself;

2:7 [a] Or *trample on*

15 He shall not stand who handles the bow,
The swift of foot shall not escape,
Nor shall he who rides a horse deliver
himself.
16 The most courageous men of might
Shall flee naked in that day,"
Says the LORD.

Authority of the Prophet's Message

3 Hear this word that the LORD has spoken against you, O children of Israel, against the whole family which I brought up from the land of Egypt, saying:

2 "You only have I known of all the
families of the earth;
Therefore I will punish you for all your
iniquities."

3 Can two walk together, unless they are
agreed?
4 Will a lion roar in the forest, when he
has no prey?
Will a young lion cry out of his den, if
he has caught nothing?
5 Will a bird fall into a snare on the earth,
where there is no trap for it?
Will a snare spring up from the earth, if
it has caught nothing at all?
6 If a trumpet is blown in a city, will not
the people be afraid?
If there is calamity in a city, will not the
LORD have done *it*?

7 Surely the Lord GOD does nothing,
Unless He reveals His secret to His
servants the prophets.
8 A lion has roared!
Who will not fear?
The Lord GOD has spoken!
Who can but prophesy?

Punishment of Israel's Sins

9 "Proclaim in the palaces at Ashdod,[a]
And in the palaces in the land of Egypt,
and say:
'Assemble on the mountains of Samaria;
See great tumults in her midst,
And the oppressed within her.
10 For they do not know to do right,'
Says the LORD,
'Who store up violence and robbery in
their palaces.'"

11 Therefore thus says the Lord GOD:

"An adversary *shall be* all around the
land;
He shall sap your strength from you,
And your palaces shall be plundered."

12 Thus says the LORD:

"As a shepherd takes from the mouth of
a lion
Two legs or a piece of an ear,
So shall the children of Israel be taken
out
Who dwell in Samaria—
In the corner of a bed and on the edge[a]
of a couch!
13 Hear and testify against the house of
Jacob,"
Says the Lord GOD, the God of hosts,
14 "That in the day I punish Israel for their
transgressions,
I will also visit *destruction* on the altars
of Bethel;
And the horns of the altar shall be cut
off
And fall to the ground.
15 I will destroy the winter house along
with the summer house;
The houses of ivory shall perish,
And the great houses shall have an end,"
Says the LORD.

4 Hear this word, you cows of Bashan,
who *are* on the mountain of Samaria,
Who oppress the poor,
Who crush the needy,
Who say to your husbands,[a] "Bring
wine, let us drink!"
2 The Lord GOD has sworn by His
holiness:
"Behold, the days shall come upon you
When He will take you away with
fishhooks,
And your posterity with fishhooks.
3 You will go out *through* broken *walls,*
Each one straight ahead of her,
And you will be cast into Harmon,"
Says the LORD.

4 "Come to Bethel and transgress,
At Gilgal multiply transgression;
Bring your sacrifices every morning,
Your tithes every three days.[a]
5 Offer a sacrifice of thanksgiving with
leaven,

3:9 [a] Following Masoretic Text; Septuagint reads *Assyria.* 3:12 [a] The Hebrew is uncertain. 4:1 [a] Literally *their lords* or *their masters* 4:4 [a] Or *years* (compare Deuteronomy 14:28)

Proclaim *and* announce the freewill
offerings;
For this you love,
You children of Israel!"
Says the Lord GOD.

Israel Did Not Accept Correction

6 "Also I gave you cleanness of teeth in all
your cities,
And lack of bread in all your places;
Yet you have not returned to Me,"
Says the LORD.

7 "I also withheld rain from you,
When *there were* still three months to
the harvest.
I made it rain on one city,
I withheld rain from another city.
One part was rained upon,
And where it did not rain the part
withered.
8 So two *or* three cities wandered to
another city to drink water,
But they were not satisfied;
Yet you have not returned to Me,"
Says the LORD.

9 "I blasted you with blight and mildew.
When your gardens increased,
Your vineyards,
Your fig trees,
And your olive trees,
The locust devoured *them;*
Yet you have not returned to Me,"
Says the LORD.

10 "I sent among you a plague after the
manner of Egypt;
Your young men I killed with a sword,
Along with your captive horses;
I made the stench of your camps come
up into your nostrils;
Yet you have not returned to Me,"
Says the LORD.

11 "I overthrew *some* of you,
As God overthrew Sodom and
Gomorrah,
And you were like a firebrand plucked
from the burning;
Yet you have not returned to Me,"
Says the LORD.

12 "Therefore thus will I do to you, O Israel;
Because I will do this to you,
Prepare to meet your God, O Israel!"

13 For behold,
He who forms mountains,
And creates the wind,
Who declares to man what his[a] thought *is,*
And makes the morning darkness,
Who treads the high places of the
earth—
The LORD God of hosts *is* His name.

A Lament for Israel

5 Hear this word which I take up against
you, a lamentation, O house of Israel:

2 The virgin of Israel has fallen;
She will rise no more.
She lies forsaken on her land;
There is no one to raise her up.

3 For thus says the Lord GOD:

"The city that goes out by a thousand
Shall have a hundred left,
And that which goes out by a hundred
Shall have ten left to the house of
Israel."

A Call to Repentance

4 For thus says the LORD to the house of
Israel:

"Seek Me and live;
5 But do not seek Bethel,
Nor enter Gilgal,
Nor pass over to Beersheba;
For Gilgal shall surely go into captivity,
And Bethel shall come to nothing.
6 Seek the LORD and live,
Lest He break out like fire *in* the house
of Joseph,
And devour *it,*
With no one to quench *it* in Bethel—
7 You who turn justice to wormwood,
And lay righteousness to rest in the
earth!"

8 He made the Pleiades and Orion;
He turns the shadow of death into
morning
And makes the day dark as night;
He calls for the waters of the sea
And pours them out on the face of the
earth;
The LORD *is* His name.
9 He rains ruin upon the strong,
So that fury comes upon the fortress.

10 They hate the one who rebukes in the
gate,

4:13 [a] Or *His*

And they abhor the one who speaks
uprightly.
11 Therefore, because you tread down the
poor
And take grain taxes from him,
Though you have built houses of hewn
stone,
Yet you shall not dwell in them;
You have planted pleasant vineyards,
But you shall not drink wine from them.
12 For I know your manifold
transgressions
And your mighty sins:
Afflicting the just *and* taking bribes;
Diverting the poor *from justice* at the
gate.
13 Therefore the prudent keep silent at that
time,
For it *is* an evil time.

14 Seek good and not evil,
That you may live;
So the LORD God of hosts will be with
you,
As you have spoken.
15 Hate evil, love good;
Establish justice in the gate.
It may be that the LORD God of hosts
Will be gracious to the remnant of
Joseph.

The Day of the LORD

16 Therefore the LORD God of hosts, the
Lord, says this:

"*There shall be* wailing in all streets,
And they shall say in all the highways,
'Alas! Alas!'
They shall call the farmer to mourning,
And skillful lamenters to wailing.
17 In all vineyards *there shall be* wailing,
For I will pass through you,"
Says the LORD.

18 Woe to you who desire the day of the
LORD!
For what good *is* the day of the LORD to
you?
It *will be* darkness, and not light.
19 It *will be* as though a man fled from a
lion,
And a bear met him!
Or *as though* he went into the house,
Leaned his hand on the wall,
And a serpent bit him!
20 *Is* not the day of the LORD darkness, and
not light?
Is it not very dark, with no brightness
in it?

21 "I hate, I despise your feast days,
And I do not savor your sacred
assemblies.
22 Though you offer Me burnt offerings
and your grain offerings,
I will not accept *them*,
Nor will I regard your fattened peace
offerings.
23 Take away from Me the noise of your
songs,
For I will not hear the melody of your
stringed instruments.
24 But let justice run down like water,

GOD'S JUSTICE

READ IT: AMOS 5:14, 15, 24

Things weren't going well. People were claiming to worship God, but their actions said otherwise. They were overtaxing the poor and taking things in the name of God. Amos sent out a wise warning: go after good things, not evil. When people take advantage of the poor or take what isn't fair for their own benefit, God gets angry and will fight for those in need. When we seek good and not evil, we are on God's side in that fight.

And righteousness like a mighty
stream.

25 "Did you offer Me sacrifices and
offerings
In the wilderness forty years, O house
of Israel?
26 You also carried Sikkuth[a] your king[b]
And Chiun,[c] your idols,
The star of your gods,
Which you made for yourselves.
27 Therefore I will send you into captivity
beyond Damascus,"
Says the LORD, whose name *is* the God
of hosts.

Warnings to Zion and Samaria

6 Woe to you *who are* at ease in Zion,
And trust in Mount Samaria,
Notable persons in the chief nation,
To whom the house of Israel comes!
2 Go over to Calneh and see;
And from there go to Hamath the great;
Then go down to Gath of the Philistines.
Are you better than these kingdoms?
Or is their territory greater than your
territory?

3 *Woe to* you who put far off the day of
doom,
Who cause the seat of violence to come
near;
4 Who lie on beds of ivory,
Stretch out on your couches,
Eat lambs from the flock
And calves from the midst of the stall;
5 Who sing idly to the sound of stringed
instruments,
And invent for yourselves musical
instruments like David;
6 Who drink wine from bowls,
And anoint yourselves with the best
ointments,
But are not grieved for the affliction of
Joseph.
7 Therefore they shall now go captive as
the first of the captives,
And those who recline at banquets shall
be removed.

8 The Lord GOD has sworn by Himself,
The LORD God of hosts says:
"I abhor the pride of Jacob,
And hate his palaces;
Therefore I will deliver up *the* city
And all that is in it."

9 Then it shall come to pass, that if
ten men remain in one house, they shall
die. 10 And when a relative *of the dead,* with
one who will burn *the bodies,* picks up the
bodies[a] to take them out of the house, he will
say to one inside the house, *"Are there* any
more with you?"

Then someone will say, "None."

And he will say, "Hold your tongue! For
we dare not mention the name of the LORD."

11 For behold, the LORD gives a command:
He will break the great house into bits,
And the little house into pieces.

12 Do horses run on rocks?
Does *one* plow *there* with oxen?
Yet you have turned justice into gall,
And the fruit of righteousness into
wormwood,
13 You who rejoice over Lo Debar,[a]
Who say, "Have we not taken Karnaim[b]
for ourselves
By our own strength?"

14 "But, behold, I will raise up a nation
against you,
O house of Israel,"
Says the LORD God of hosts;
"And they will afflict you from the
entrance of Hamath
To the Valley of the Arabah."

Vision of the Locusts

7 Thus the Lord GOD showed me: Behold, He formed locust swarms at the
beginning of the late crop; indeed *it was* the
late crop after the king's mowings. 2 And so it
was, when they had finished eating the grass
of the land, that I said:

"O Lord GOD, forgive, I pray!
Oh, that Jacob may stand,
For he *is* small!"
3 *So* the LORD relented concerning this.
"It shall not be," said the LORD.

Vision of the Fire

4 Thus the Lord GOD showed me: Behold,
the Lord GOD called for conflict by fire, and
it consumed the great deep and devoured the
territory. 5 Then I said:

5:26 [a] A pagan deity [b] Septuagint and Vulgate read *tabernacle of Moloch.* [c] A pagan deity **6:10** [a] Literally *bones*
6:13 [a] Literally *Nothing* [b] Literally *Horns,* symbol of strength

"O Lord GOD, cease, I pray!
Oh, that Jacob may stand,
For he *is* small!"
6 *So* the LORD relented concerning this.
"This also shall not be," said the Lord GOD.

Vision of the Plumb Line

7Thus He showed me: Behold, the Lord
stood on a wall *made* with a plumb line, with
a plumb line in His hand. 8And the LORD
said to me, "Amos, what do you see?"

And I said, "A plumb line."
Then the Lord said:

"Behold, I am setting a plumb line
In the midst of My people Israel;
I will not pass by them anymore.
9 The high places of Isaac shall be desolate,
And the sanctuaries of Israel shall be laid waste.
I will rise with the sword against the house of Jeroboam."

Amaziah's Complaint

10Then Amaziah the priest of Bethel sent
to Jeroboam king of Israel, saying, "Amos
has conspired against you in the midst of
the house of Israel. The land is not able to
bear all his words. 11For thus Amos has said:

'Jeroboam shall die by the sword,
And Israel shall surely be led away captive
From their own land.'"

12Then Amaziah said to Amos:

"Go, you seer!
Flee to the land of Judah.
There eat bread,
And there prophesy.
13 But never again prophesy at Bethel,
For it *is* the king's sanctuary,
And it *is* the royal residence."

14Then Amos answered, and said to Amaziah:

"I *was* no prophet,
Nor *was* I a son of a prophet,
But I *was* a sheepbreeder[a]
And a tender of sycamore fruit.
15 Then the LORD took me as I followed the flock,
And the LORD said to me,
'Go, prophesy to My people Israel.'
16 Now therefore, hear the word of the LORD:
You say, 'Do not prophesy against Israel,
And do not spout against the house of Isaac.'

17"Therefore thus says the LORD:

'Your wife shall be a harlot in the city;
Your sons and daughters shall fall by the sword;
Your land shall be divided by *survey* line;
You shall die in a defiled land;
And Israel shall surely be led away captive
From his own land.'"

Vision of the Summer Fruit

8 Thus the Lord GOD showed me: Behold, a basket of summer fruit. 2And
He said, "Amos, what do you see?"

So I said, "A basket of summer fruit."
Then the LORD said to me:

"The end has come upon My people Israel;
I will not pass by them anymore.
3 And the songs of the temple
Shall be wailing in that day,"
Says the Lord GOD—
"Many dead bodies everywhere,
They shall be thrown out in silence."

4 Hear this, you who swallow up[a] the needy,
And make the poor of the land fail,

5Saying:

"When will the New Moon be past,
That we may sell grain?
And the Sabbath,
That we may trade wheat?
Making the ephah small and the shekel large,
Falsifying the scales by deceit,
6 That we may buy the poor for silver,
And the needy for a pair of sandals—
Even sell the bad wheat?"

7 The LORD has sworn by the pride of Jacob:
"Surely I will never forget any of their works.
8 Shall the land not tremble for this,
And everyone mourn who dwells in it?
All of it shall swell like the River,[a]

7:14 [a] Compare 2 Kings 3:4 **8:4** [a] Or *trample on* (compare 2:7) **8:8** [a] That is, the Nile; some Hebrew manuscripts, Septuagint, Syriac, Targum, and Vulgate read *River;* Masoretic Text reads *the light.*

Heave and subside
Like the River of Egypt.

9 "And it shall come to pass in that day,"
says the Lord GOD,
"That I will make the sun go down at noon,
And I will darken the earth in broad
daylight;
10 I will turn your feasts into mourning,
And all your songs into lamentation;
I will bring sackcloth on every waist,
And baldness on every head;
I will make it like mourning for an only
son,
And its end like a bitter day.

11 "Behold, the days are coming," says the
Lord GOD,
"That I will send a famine on the land,
Not a famine of bread,
Nor a thirst for water,
But of hearing the words of the LORD.
12 They shall wander from sea to sea,
And from north to east;
They shall run to and fro, seeking the
word of the LORD,
But shall not find *it.*

13 "In that day the fair virgins
And strong young men
Shall faint from thirst.
14 Those who swear by the sin[a] of Samaria,
Who say,
'As your god lives, O Dan!'
And, 'As the way of Beersheba lives!'
They shall fall and never rise again."

The Destruction of Israel

9 I saw the Lord standing by the altar,
and He said:

"Strike the doorposts, that the thresholds
may shake,
And break them on the heads of them all.
I will slay the last of them with the sword.
He who flees from them shall not get away,
And he who escapes from them shall
not be delivered.

2 "Though they dig into hell,[a]
From there My hand shall take them;
Though they climb up to heaven,
From there I will bring them down;
3 And though they hide themselves on
top of Carmel,
From there I will search and take them;
Though they hide from My sight at the
bottom of the sea,

8:14 [a] Or *Ashima,* a Syrian goddess 9:2 [a] Or *Sheol*

TREASURE GOD'S WORD

READ IT: AMOS 8:11–13

The prophet Amos warns you that a time is coming when young people will search for the Word of God and not be able to find it anymore.

Perhaps you don't open your Bible very often. You have to go to school every day and do all the things your teacher tells you. Then you have sports and parties to go to. You may find less and less time for reading God's Word.

These are days when your memory is sharp and strong. Now is the time to store the Scriptures in your mind. "Your word I have hidden in my heart, that I might not sin against You" (Psalm 119:11). If you are going to know God as He really is, and love Him as He wants you to, the Bible must be your best-loved Book. Make a habit of reading God's Word at the same time every day.

From there I will command the serpent,
And it shall bite them;
4 Though they go into captivity before their enemies,
From there I will command the sword,
And it shall slay them.
I will set My eyes on them for harm and not for good."

5 The Lord GOD of hosts,
He who touches the earth and it melts,
And all who dwell there mourn;
All of it shall swell like the River,[a]
And subside like the River of Egypt.
6 He who builds His layers in the sky,
And has founded His strata in the earth;
Who calls for the waters of the sea,
And pours them out on the face of the earth—
The LORD *is* His name.

9:5 [a] That is, the Nile

GOD'S PROPHET TALKS ABOUT THE FUTURE

READ IT: AMOS 9:5–15

GET IT:

God was mad! He was super angry. He sent prophets—Elijah, Elisha, Jonah, Hosea, and Amos—to warn the people of Israel that they had to change. They had to stop worshiping idols and stop ignoring God. God sent warning after warning after warning. But nobody listened. God couldn't put up with the bad behavior anymore, so He was going to punish the people of Israel. Their enemies, the Assyrians, would destroy their nation and carry the people away or kill them. But God wouldn't forget His people. He still cared about them, so instead of giving up on them, He punished them. Then He promised to forgive them and restore their nation. He promised to "raise up its ruins, and rebuild it" (v. 11). God would bring them back to their land and give them a new start.

LIVE IT:

You know how it goes with rules. If you do something wrong, you get a warning. Do it again and something happens—being sent to the principal's office at school, no computer at home. There are consequences for bad behavior and breaking rules. That's what was happening in Israel, only a hundred times worse.

You probably don't like the thought of limits or punishment. But ultimately the right kind of punishment means that someone cares about you and loves you. We don't live in a perfect world, so sometimes punishment is unfair or too harsh. But in the best situation, punishment comes from someone who doesn't want to see you mess up your life. You might scream at your parents, "You're mean" or "You hate me" when they punish you. But because they love you and care about you, they correct you and make sure you're going in the right direction.

7 "*Are* you not like the people of Ethiopia to
Me,
O children of Israel?" says the LORD.
"Did I not bring up Israel from the land
of Egypt,
The Philistines from Caphtor,
And the Syrians from Kir?

8 "Behold, the eyes of the Lord GOD *are* on
the sinful kingdom,
And I will destroy it from the face of the
earth;
Yet I will not utterly destroy the house
of Jacob,"
Says the LORD.

9 "For surely I will command,
And will sift the house of Israel among
all nations,
As *grain* is sifted in a sieve;
Yet not the smallest grain shall fall to
the ground.
10 All the sinners of My people shall die by
the sword,
Who say, 'The calamity shall not
overtake nor confront us.'

Israel Will Be Restored

11 "On that day I will raise up
The tabernacle[a] of David, which has
fallen down,
And repair its damages;
I will raise up its ruins,
And rebuild it as in the days of old;
12 That they may possess the remnant of
Edom,[a]
And all the Gentiles who are called by
My name,"
Says the LORD who does this thing.

In Focus

9:12 Gentiles All peoples and nations who are not of the Hebrew race. God promised that the Jews would be a blessing to the Gentiles. Jesus fulfilled that promise.

13 "Behold, the days are coming," says the
LORD,
"When the plowman shall overtake the
reaper,
And the treader of grapes him who sows
seed;
The mountains shall drip with sweet wine,
And all the hills shall flow *with it*.
14 I will bring back the captives of My
people Israel;
They shall build the waste cities and
inhabit *them;*
They shall plant vineyards and drink
wine from them;
They shall also make gardens and eat
fruit from them.
15 I will plant them in their land,
And no longer shall they be pulled up
From the land I have given them,"
Says the LORD your God.

9:11 [a] Literally *booth*, figure of a deposed dynasty
9:12 [a] Septuagint reads *mankind*.

The BOOK of

OBADIAH

586 B.C.

Behind the Scenes

READ IT:

The book of Obadiah is a book of prophecy against the nation of Edom. This country invaded and damaged Jerusalem at least four times. Now it was time for God to punish the people of Edom for what they had done.

GET IT:

Who wrote it: The prophet Obadiah

When it was written: 586 B.C.

Why it was written: to tell God's people that they weren't the only ones being punished for disobeying God.

LIVE IT:

God will judge proud and arrogant nations and people.

FIND IT:

The Judgment on Edom *Obadiah 1*

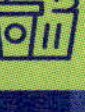

The Coming Judgment on Edom

The vision of Obadiah.

Thus says the Lord GOD concerning
Edom
(We have heard a report from the LORD,
And a messenger has been sent among
the nations, *saying,*
"Arise, and let us rise up against her for
battle"):

2 "Behold, I will make you small among
the nations;
You shall be greatly despised.
3 The pride of your heart has deceived
you,
You who dwell in the clefts of the rock,
Whose habitation is high;
You who say in your heart, 'Who will
bring me down to the ground?'
4 Though you ascend *as* high as the eagle,
And though you set your nest among
the stars,
From there I will bring you down," says
the LORD.

5 "If thieves had come to you,
If robbers by night—
Oh, how you will be cut off!—
Would they not have stolen till they had
enough?
If grape-gatherers had come to you,
Would they not have left *some*
gleanings?

6 "Oh, how Esau shall be searched out!
How his hidden treasures shall be
sought after!
7 All the men in your confederacy
Shall force you to the border;
The men at peace with you
Shall deceive you *and* prevail against you.
Those who eat your bread shall lay a trap[a]
for you.
No one is aware of it.

8 "Will I not in that day," says the LORD,
"Even destroy the wise *men* from Edom,
And understanding from the
mountains of Esau?
9 Then your mighty men, O Teman, shall
be dismayed,
To the end that everyone from the
mountains of Esau
May be cut off by slaughter.

Edom Mistreated His Brother

10 "For violence against your brother Jacob,
Shame shall cover you,
And you shall be cut off forever.
11 In the day that you stood on the other
side—
In the day that strangers carried captive
his forces,
When foreigners entered his gates
And cast lots for Jerusalem—
Even you *were* as one of them.

12 "But you should not have gazed on the
day of your brother
In the day of his captivity;[a]

7 [a] Or *wound*, or *plot* 12 [a] Literally *On the day he became a foreigner*

Starring Roles

OBADIAH'S book is the shortest one in the Old Testament. His name is pronounced *oh-buh-DIE-uh* and means "Servant of the Lord."

In Genesis 27, you can read how Jacob and Esau became enemies. When God chose Jacob to be the father of Israel, Esau went to live in a land south of Israel that became know as Edom (pronounced *EE-dom*), another name for Esau.

Obadiah's prophecy is against the people of Edom because they persecuted Israel. In his prophecy, he told the people of Edom that God would destroy them, even though they felt safe in their mountain fortress. History books tell us that the people of Edom were forced to leave their high place in the mountains because the traders didn't bring food to their city anymore.

Nor should you have rejoiced over the
children of Judah
In the day of their destruction;
Nor should you have spoken proudly
In the day of distress.
13 You should not have entered the gate of
My people
In the day of their calamity.
Indeed, you should not have gazed on
their affliction
In the day of their calamity,
Nor laid *hands* on their substance
In the day of their calamity.
14 You should not have stood at the
crossroads
To cut off those among them who
escaped;
Nor should you have delivered up those
among them who remained
In the day of distress.

15 "For the day of the LORD upon all the
nations *is* near;
As you have done, it shall be done to
you;
Your reprisal shall return upon your
own head.
16 For as you drank on My holy mountain,
So shall all the nations drink
continually;
Yes, they shall drink, and swallow,
And they shall be as though they had
never been.

Israel's Final Triumph

17 "But on Mount Zion there shall be
deliverance,
And there shall be holiness;
The house of Jacob shall possess their
possessions.
18 The house of Jacob shall be a fire,
And the house of Joseph a flame;
But the house of Esau *shall be* stubble;
They shall kindle them and devour
them,
And no survivor shall *remain* of the
house of Esau,"
For the LORD has spoken.

19 The South[a] shall possess the mountains
of Esau,
And the Lowland shall possess Philistia.
They shall possess the fields of Ephraim
And the fields of Samaria.
Benjamin *shall possess* Gilead.
20 And the captives of this host of the
children of Israel
Shall possess the land of the Canaanites
As far as Zarephath.
The captives of Jerusalem who are in
Sepharad
Shall possess the cities of the South.[a]
21 Then saviors[a] shall come to Mount Zion
To judge the mountains of Esau,
And the kingdom shall be the LORD's.

19 [a] Hebrew *Negev* 20 [a] Hebrew *Negev* 21 [a] Or *deliverers*

PRIDE

READ IT: OBADIAH 3, 4

Think of a time when you got deceived. Someone lied to you and you believed it. Or something you bought failed to deliver on its promises. It's a horrible feeling to realize you were lied to.

Pride does that all the time. Pride loves to tell you, "You're amazing! You are the only one able to do this! You are better than other people." But pride is a liar. Don't be deceived by something as lame as pride.

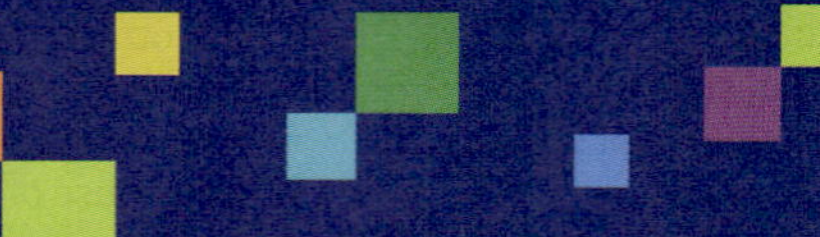

The BOOK of JONAH

750 B.C.

Behind the Scenes

READ IT:

The book of Jonah contains the adventures of the prophet Jonah. God told Jonah to go to the wicked city of Nineveh and tell them about the true God. Jonah disobeyed God and tried to run away. Later Jonah went to Nineveh and preached. He got angry when the people said they were sorry for sinning, but he learned that God forgives even wicked, horrible people.

GET IT:

Who wrote it: The prophet Jonah

When it was written: 750 B.C.

Why it was written: to teach us that God will forgive even the worst people if they are sorry for their sins.

LIVE IT:

If God is compassionate to us, we should be compassionate to others.

FIND IT:

Jonah's Disobedience	*Jonah 1*
Jonah Preaches at Nineveh	*Jonah 3*
Jonah's Anger and God's Kindness	*Jonah 4*

Jonah's Disobedience

1 Now the word of the LORD came to Jonah the son of Amittai, saying, 2 "Arise,
go to Nineveh, that great city, and cry out
against it; for their wickedness has come
up before Me." 3 But Jonah arose to flee to
Tarshish from the presence of the LORD. He
went down to Joppa, and found a ship going
to Tarshish; so he paid the fare, and went
down into it, to go with them to Tarshish
from the presence of the LORD.

The Storm at Sea

4 But the LORD sent out a great wind on
the sea, and there was a mighty tempest
on the sea, so that the ship was about to be
broken up

5 Then the mariners were afraid; and
every man cried out to his god, and threw
the cargo that *was* in the ship into the sea, to
lighten the load.[a] But Jonah had gone down
into the lowest parts of the ship, had lain
down, and was fast asleep.

6 So the captain came to him, and said to
him, "What do you mean, sleeper? Arise,
call on your God; perhaps your God will consider us, so that we may not perish."

7 And they said to one another, "Come,
let us cast lots, that we may know for whose
cause this trouble *has come* upon us." So they
cast lots, and the lot fell on Jonah. 8 Then

1:5 [a] Literally *from upon them*

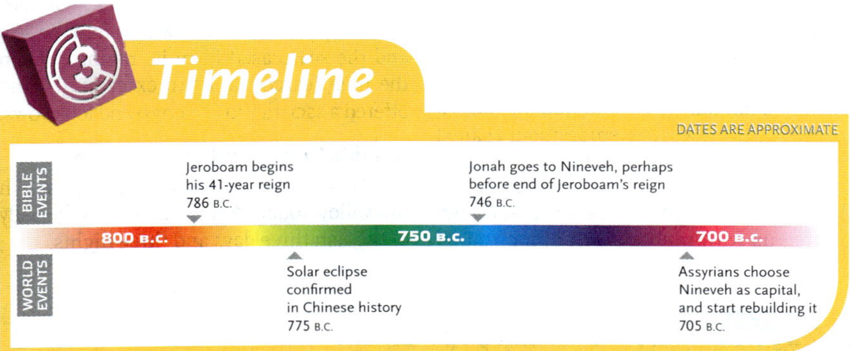

Starring Roles

JONAH was that amazing prophet who was swallowed alive by a very big fish—and lived to tell the story! But God had a far more important reason for putting Jonah's book in the Bible. One day He commanded Jonah to go and warn the wicked citizens of Nineveh (pronounced *NIN-uh-vuh*) that their city was going to be destroyed.

At first Jonah didn't want to go warn the people, and he tried to run away. He got on a boat that was sailing away from Nineveh.

But the Lord sent a powerful storm on the sea, and the ship nearly sank. You can read in chapter 1 of Jonah's book of all the terrifying things that changed his mind about obeying God. Jonah finally decided to go preach to the people in Nineveh.

To his surprise the people gave up their sins and accepted the Lord as their God. Therefore, the Lord didn't destroy Nineveh after all.

they said to him, "Please tell us! For whose
cause *is* this trouble upon us? What is your
occupation? And where do you come from?
What is your country? And of what people
are you?"
9 So he said to them, "I *am* a Hebrew;
and I fear the LORD, the God of heaven, who
made the sea and the dry *land*."

Jonah Thrown into the Sea

10 Then the men were exceedingly afraid,
and said to him, "Why have you done this?"
For the men knew that he fled from the presence of the LORD, because he had told them.
11 Then they said to him, "What shall we do
to you that the sea may be calm for us?"—for
the sea was growing more tempestuous.
12 And he said to them, "Pick me up and
throw me into the sea; then the sea will become calm for you. For I know that this great
tempest *is* because of me."
13 Nevertheless the men rowed hard to return to land, but they could not, for the sea
continued to grow more tempestuous against
them. 14 Therefore they cried out to the LORD
and said, "We pray, O LORD, please do not
let us perish for this man's life, and do not
charge us with innocent blood; for You, O
LORD, have done as it pleased You." 15 So they
picked up Jonah and threw him into the sea,
and the sea ceased from its raging. 16 Then
the men feared the LORD exceedingly, and
offered a sacrifice to the LORD and took vows.

Jonah's Prayer and Deliverance

17 Now the LORD had prepared a great fish
to swallow Jonah. And Jonah was in the belly
of the fish three days and three nights.

In Focus

1:7 Casting Lots The way people in ancient times often made difficult choices—by closing their eyes and picking marked "lots" (like dice) out of a jar. See also Acts 1:26.

2:2 Sheol Sometimes means "grave." Also a place where souls live after death if they reject God's offer of salvation during their earthly lives.

On Location

The Travels of Jonah

The story begins in Israel, continues somewhere aboard a ship in the Mediterranean Sea, then inside a fish. It ends in Nineveh, an Assyrian city in what is now northern Iraq.

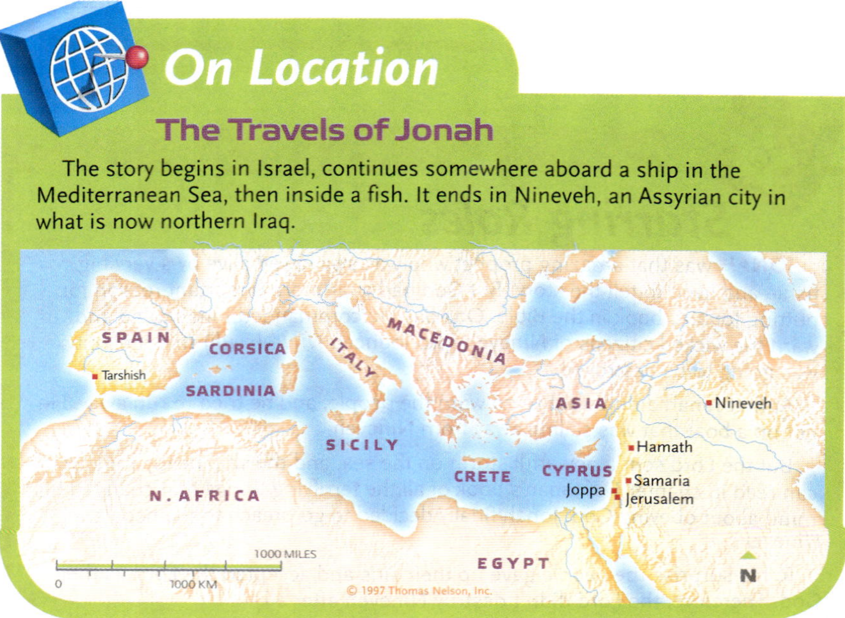

2 Then Jonah prayed to the LORD his God from the fish's belly. 2And he said:

"I cried out to the LORD because of my affliction,
And He answered me.

"Out of the belly of Sheol I cried,
And You heard my voice.
3 For You cast me into the deep,
Into the heart of the seas,
And the floods surrounded me;
All Your billows and Your waves passed over me.
4 Then I said, 'I have been cast out of Your sight;
Yet I will look again toward Your holy temple.'
5 The waters surrounded me, *even* to my soul;
The deep closed around me;
Weeds were wrapped around my head.
6 I went down to the moorings of the mountains;
The earth with its bars *closed* behind me forever;

GOD SAVES JONAH

READ IT: JONAH 1:1—2:10

GET IT:

Everybody knows the story about Jonah—the man who got swallowed by a whale (really a very large fish) and lived to tell about it. But there's more to the story of Jonah than just that. Jonah was a prophet in the kingdom of Israel. Other prophets, like Amos, talked to the people of Israel about God. But Jonah had a different kind of challenge. God asked him to talk to Israel's enemy, the Assyrians, in their capital city of Nineveh. Jonah didn't like this idea one bit. He thought God was being totally unreasonable. Why would God want to show love to these wicked folks? Jonah didn't want any part of it, so he ran away. But God didn't let him get away with it. After God saved Jonah, He told him again to go to Nineveh and preach. This time Jonah obeyed.

God loves everybody. He wanted and wants everyone to know about Him and have the chance to experience the life He made for them in the best way possible. He loves and saves us because He wants to, not because of who we are or what we do.

LIVE IT:

Jonah didn't want to do what God wanted. He had decided long ago that the Assyrians in Nineveh didn't deserve God's mercy; after all, they were a horrible enemy of Israel. They were wicked people who were known for their terrible practices in war. The problem was that only God gets to judge other people. Only God gets to decide whom He will have mercy on and whom He will punish. Not Jonah, not us. All people are God's creation, made in His image. Their future lies in God's hands, not ours. God never assigned us to judge others. Instead, He asked Jonah and He asks us to bring everyone the good news of salvation.

Yet You have brought up my life from
the pit,
O LORD, my God.

7 "When my soul fainted within me,
I remembered the LORD;
And my prayer went *up* to You,
Into Your holy temple.

8 "Those who regard worthless idols
Forsake their own Mercy.

9 But I will sacrifice to You
With the voice of thanksgiving;
I will pay what I have vowed.
Salvation *is* of the LORD."

10 So the LORD spoke to the fish, and it
vomited Jonah onto dry *land*.

Jonah Preaches at Nineveh

3 Now the word of the LORD came to Jonah the second time, saying, 2 "Arise,

LEARNING

HOORAY FOR SECOND CHANCES

READ IT: JONAH 3:1–10

GET IT:

Second chances are one of the best things ever—*if* we choose to act on what we learned from the first go-around. Jonah botched things up the first time God told him to go preach in Nineveh, so he ended up spending three days inside a fish. But Jonah got another shot at it. He could have run again. He could have hid (as if hiding from God works). He could have tried to make excuses. He could have begged God to choose someone else.

But Jonah had learned his lesson—the hard way! And the second time God called to him, Jonah jumped into action.

It's great when we get things right the first time. Life is easy when we say the right thing, make the best choice, avoid the things that will hurt us, and live like Jesus. But it doesn't take a whole lot of honesty to admit that we don't always get things right the first time. Sometimes that's because we choose sin. And other times it's because we just make a silly, uninformed choice.

Even lousy choices can be turned around into opportunities to learn. The worst decisions can shape your next decision, which, hopefully, will be a better one.

LIVE IT:

Are you a learner? We're not talking about how well you do in school. Being a learner is an attitude, and it applies to every stage of life. Being a learner is a choice, and no one else can make that choice for you.

What's something you have learned already today? How will that impact the rest of your week?

go to Nineveh, that great city, and preach to it the message that I tell you." 3 So Jonah arose and went to Nineveh, according to the word of the LORD. Now Nineveh was an exceedingly great city, a three-day journey[a] *in extent.* 4 And Jonah began to enter the city on the first day's walk. Then he cried out and said, "Yet forty days, and Nineveh shall be overthrown!"

The People of Nineveh Believe

5 So the people of Nineveh believed God, proclaimed a fast, and put on sackcloth, from the greatest to the least of them. 6 Then word came to the king of Nineveh; and he arose from his throne and laid aside his robe, covered *himself* with sackcloth and sat in ashes. 7 And he caused *it* to be proclaimed and published throughout Nineveh by the decree of the king and his nobles, saying,

> Let neither man nor beast, herd nor flock, taste anything; do not let them eat, or drink water. 8 But let man and beast be covered with sackcloth, and cry mightily to God; yes, let every one turn from his evil way and from the violence that is in his hands. 9 Who can tell *if* God will turn and relent, and turn away from His fierce anger, so that we may not perish?

10 Then God saw their works, that they turned from their evil way; and God relented from the disaster that He had said He would bring upon them, and He did not do it.

Jonah's Anger and God's Kindness

4 But it displeased Jonah exceedingly, and he became angry. 2 So he prayed to the LORD, and said, "Ah, LORD, was not this what I said when I was still in my country? Therefore I fled previously to Tarshish; for I know that You *are* a gracious and merciful God, slow to anger and abundant in lovingkindness, One who relents from doing harm. 3 Therefore now, O LORD, please take my life from me, for *it is* better for me to die than to live!"

4 Then the LORD said, "*Is it* right for you to be angry?"

5 So Jonah went out of the city and sat on the east side of the city. There he made himself a shelter and sat under it in the shade, till he might see what would become of the city. 6 And the LORD God prepared a plant[a] and

3:3 [a] Exact meaning unknown 4:6 [a] Hebrew *kikayon,* exact identity unknown

Epic Ideas

3:2 NINEVEH

Nineveh, the capital of ancient Assyria, was one of the largest and oldest cities of the world in Jonah's day. It had been founded by Nimrod, a great-grandson of Noah (see Genesis 10:8–11).

Surrounding nations destroyed Nineveh in 612 B.C. For hundreds of years no one knew exactly where the city was located. But about 150 years ago Sir Austen Layard discovered and dug up its ruins. So now we know a great deal about Nineveh.

You can read about King Sennacherib (pronounced *Sen-AK-er-ib*) in Isaiah 36 and 37. He built a wall fifty feet high surrounding inner Nineveh. Scholars have also discovered there the beautiful palaces of King Sennacherib and King Ashurbanipal, as well as a huge library.

In 763 B.C. Jonah warned the people of Nineveh that the city would be destroyed because of their wickedness. But the Ninevites repented of their sins, and the city was spared for nearly two hundred years more.

made it come up over Jonah, that it might
be shade for his head to deliver him from
his misery. So Jonah was very grateful for
the plant. 7But as morning dawned the next
day God prepared a worm, and it *so* damaged
the plant that it withered. 8And it happened,
when the sun arose, that God prepared a
vehement east wind; and the sun beat on
Jonah's head, so that he grew faint. Then he
wished death for himself, and said, "*It is* better for me to die than to live."

9Then God said to Jonah, "*Is it* right for
you to be angry about the plant?"

And he said, "*It is* right for me to be angry, even to death!"

10But the LORD said, "You have had pity
on the plant for which you have not labored,
nor made it grow, which came up in a night
and perished in a night. 11And should I not
pity Nineveh, that great city, in which are
more than one hundred and twenty thousand persons who cannot discern between their right hand and their left—and much livestock?"

ANGER

READ IT: JONAH 4

God wanted to give the people of Nineveh another chance to repent, but Jonah didn't think they deserved it. Jonah didn't think God was being fair. He didn't like God's plan—it wasn't what he expected. And showing mercy to Nineveh wasn't what he expected God to require of him. Jonah said he'd rather die than see God do something unfair. Maybe you've been that angry over what you perceived as God's unfairness, too. But ultimately Jonah did something worthwhile with that anger. He gave it to God—even in his despair.

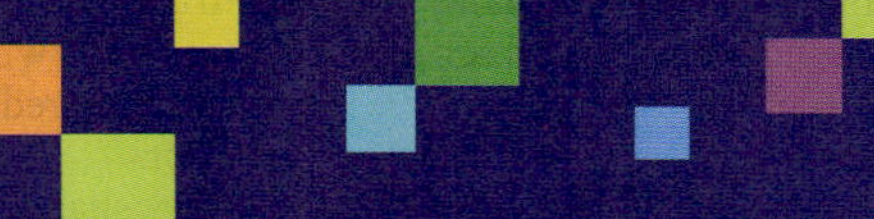

The BOOK of MICAH

730 B.C.

Behind the Scenes

READ IT:

The book of Micah contains the prophecies of the prophet Micah. He told the people of Jerusalem and Samaria that God would judge them because they and their rulers, prophets, and priests were so sinful. Their lives and actions didn't show that they belonged to a holy God.

GET IT:

Who wrote it: The prophet Micah

When it was written: 730 B.C.

Why it was written: to tell us that how we act and treat others must be acceptable to God.

LIVE IT:

We must show God's mercy and justice to others.

FIND IT:

The Coming Judgment	*Micah 1–4*
The Lord's Reign in Zion	*Micah 4*

1 The word of the LORD that came to Micah of Moresheth in the days of Jotham, Ahaz, *and* Hezekiah, kings of Judah, which he saw concerning Samaria and Jerusalem.

The Coming Judgment on Israel

2 Hear, all you peoples!
Listen, O earth, and all that is in it!
Let the Lord GOD be a witness against you,
The Lord from His holy temple.

3 For behold, the LORD is coming out of His place;
He will come down
And tread on the high places of the earth.
4 The mountains will melt under Him,
And the valleys will split
Like wax before the fire,
Like waters poured down a steep place.
5 All this is for the transgression of Jacob
And for the sins of the house of Israel.
What *is* the transgression of Jacob?
Is it not Samaria?
And what *are* the high places of Judah?
Are they not Jerusalem?

6 "Therefore I will make Samaria a heap of ruins in the field,
Places for planting a vineyard;
I will pour down her stones into the valley,
And I will uncover her foundations.
7 All her carved images shall be beaten to pieces,
And all her pay as a harlot shall be burned with the fire;
All her idols I will lay desolate,
For she gathered *it* from the pay of a harlot,
And they shall return to the pay of a harlot."

Mourning for Israel and Judah

8 Therefore I will wail and howl,
I will go stripped and naked;
I will make a wailing like the jackals
And a mourning like the ostriches,
9 For her wounds *are* incurable.
For it has come to Judah;
It has come to the gate of My people—
To Jerusalem.

10 Tell *it* not in Gath,
Weep not at all;
In Beth Aphrah[a]
Roll yourself in the dust.
11 Pass by in naked shame, you inhabitant of Shaphir;
The inhabitant of Zaanan[a] does not go out.
Beth Ezel mourns;
Its place to stand is taken away from you.

12 For the inhabitant of Maroth pined[a] for good,
But disaster came down from the LORD
To the gate of Jerusalem.

1:10 [a] Literally *House of Dust* 1:11 [a] Literally *Going Out*
1:12 [a] Literally *was sick*

Starring Roles

MICAH'S name is pronounced *MY-ka* and means "Who Is Like the Lord?" Most people remember Micah because, like Isaiah, he told about the birth of Jesus, who was born over seven hundred years later. See Micah 5:2, then look at Isaiah 9:6.

And like Amos, who was a prophet to the Northern Kingdom, Micah warned the rich about their actions in the Southern Kingdom. God wanted everyone in Israel to live on the land without paying rent, but rich landowners were cruel to people whose land had been stolen from them. Also, some of the merchants *were cheating the people* and bribing the leaders.

But Micah was glad he could promise his people that God would someday take away all their sins.

13 O inhabitant of Lachish,
Harness the chariot to the swift steeds
(She *was* the beginning of sin to the
daughter of Zion),
For the transgressions of Israel were
found in you.

14 Therefore you shall give presents to
Moresheth Gath;[a]
The houses of Achzib[b] *shall be* a lie to
the kings of Israel.
15 I will yet bring an heir to you,
O inhabitant of Mareshah;[a]
The glory of Israel shall come to
Adullam.
16 Make yourself bald and cut off your
hair,
Because of your precious children;
Enlarge your baldness like an eagle,
For they shall go from you into captivity.

Woe to Evildoers

2 Woe to those who devise iniquity,
And work out evil on their beds!
At morning light they practice it,
Because it is in the power of their hand.
2 They covet fields and take *them* by
violence,
Also houses, and seize *them*.
So they oppress a man and his house,
A man and his inheritance.

3 Therefore thus says the LORD:

"Behold, against this family I am
devising disaster,
From which you cannot remove your
necks;
Nor shall you walk haughtily,
For this *is* an evil time.
4 In that day *one* shall take up a proverb
against you,
And lament with a bitter lamentation,
saying:
'We are utterly destroyed!
He has changed the heritage of my
people;
How He has removed *it* from me!
To a turncoat He has divided our
fields.' "

5 Therefore you will have no one to
determine boundaries[a] by lot
In the assembly of the LORD.

Lying Prophets

6 "Do not prattle," *you say to those* who
prophesy.
So they shall not prophesy to you;[a]
They shall not return insult for insult.[b]
7 *You who are* named the house of Jacob:
"Is the Spirit of the LORD restricted?
Are these His doings?
Do not My words do good
To him who walks uprightly?

8 "Lately My people have risen up as an
enemy—
You pull off the robe with the garment
From those who trust *you*, as they pass
by,
Like men returned from war.
9 The women of My people you cast out
From their pleasant houses;
From their children
You have taken away My glory forever.

10 "Arise and depart,
For this *is* not *your* rest;
Because it is defiled, it shall destroy,
Yes, with utter destruction.
11 If a man should walk in a false spirit
And speak a lie, *saying,*
'I will prophesy to you of wine and
drink,'
Even he would be the prattler of this
people.

Israel Restored

12 "I will surely assemble all of you,
O Jacob,
I will surely gather the remnant of
Israel;
I will put them together like sheep of
the fold,[a]
Like a flock in the midst of their
pasture;
They shall make a loud noise because of
so many people.
13 The one who breaks open will come up
before them;
They will break out,
Pass through the gate,
And go out by it;
Their king will pass before them,
With the LORD at their head."

Wicked Rulers and Prophets

3 And I said:

"Hear now, O heads of Jacob,

1:14 [a] Literally *Possession of Gath* [b] Literally *Lie*
1:15 [a] Literally *Inheritance* 2:5 [a] Literally *one casting a surveyor's line* 2:6 [a] Literally *to these* [b] Vulgate reads *He shall not take shame.* 2:12 [a] Hebrew *Bozrah*

And you rulers of the house of Israel:
Is it not for you to know justice?
2 You who hate good and love evil;
Who strip the skin from My people,[a]
And the flesh from their bones;
3 Who also eat the flesh of My people,
Flay their skin from them,
Break their bones,
And chop *them* in pieces
Like *meat* for the pot,
Like flesh in the caldron."

4 Then they will cry to the LORD,
But He will not hear them;
He will even hide His face from them at that time,
Because they have been evil in their deeds.

5 Thus says the LORD concerning the prophets
Who make my people stray;
Who chant "Peace"
While they chew with their teeth,
But who prepare war against him
Who puts nothing into their mouths:
6 "Therefore you shall have night without vision,
And you shall have darkness without divination;
The sun shall go down on the prophets,
And the day shall be dark for them.
7 So the seers shall be ashamed,
And the diviners abashed;
Indeed they shall all cover their lips;
For *there is* no answer from God."

8 But truly I am full of power by the Spirit of the LORD,
And of justice and might,
To declare to Jacob his transgression
And to Israel his sin.
9 Now hear this,
You heads of the house of Jacob
And rulers of the house of Israel,
Who abhor justice
And pervert all equity,
10 Who build up Zion with bloodshed
And Jerusalem with iniquity:
11 Her heads judge for a bribe,
Her priests teach for pay,
And her prophets divine for money.
Yet they lean on the LORD, and say,
"Is not the LORD among us?
No harm can come upon us."
12 Therefore because of you
Zion shall be plowed *like* a field,
Jerusalem shall become heaps of ruins,
And the mountain of the temple[a]
Like the bare hills of the forest.

The LORD's Reign in Zion

4 Now it shall come to pass in the latter days
That the mountain of the LORD's house
Shall be established on the top of the mountains,
And shall be exalted above the hills;
And peoples shall flow to it.
2 Many nations shall come and say,
"Come, and let us go up to the mountain of the LORD,
To the house of the God of Jacob;
He will teach us His ways,
And we shall walk in His paths."
For out of Zion the law shall go forth,
And the word of the LORD from Jerusalem.
3 He shall judge between many peoples,
And rebuke strong nations afar off;
They shall beat their swords into plowshares,
And their spears into pruning hooks;
Nation shall not lift up sword against nation,
Neither shall they learn war anymore.[a]

4 But everyone shall sit under his vine and under his fig tree,
And no one shall make *them* afraid;
For the mouth of the LORD of hosts has spoken.
5 For all people walk each in the name of his god,
But we will walk in the name of the LORD our God
Forever and ever.

Zion's Future Triumph

6 "In that day," says the LORD,
"I will assemble the lame,
I will gather the outcast
And those whom I have afflicted;
7 I will make the lame a remnant,
And the outcast a strong nation;
So the LORD will reign over them in Mount Zion
From now on, even forever.
8 And you, O tower of the flock,

3:2 [a] Literally *them* 3:12 [a] Literally *house* 4:3 [a] Compare Isaiah 2:2–4

The stronghold of the daughter of Zion,
To you shall it come,
Even the former dominion shall come,
The kingdom of the daughter of
Jerusalem."

9 Now why do you cry aloud?
Is there no king in your midst?
Has your counselor perished?
For pangs have seized you like a woman
in labor.
10 Be in pain, and labor to bring forth,
O daughter of Zion,
Like a woman in birth pangs.
For now you shall go forth from the city,
You shall dwell in the field,
And to Babylon you shall go.
There you shall be delivered;
There the LORD will redeem you
From the hand of your enemies.

11 Now also many nations have gathered
against you,
Who say, "Let her be defiled,
And let our eye look upon Zion."
12 But they do not know the thoughts of
the LORD,
Nor do they understand His counsel;
For He will gather them like sheaves to
the threshing floor.

13 "Arise and thresh, O daughter of Zion;
For I will make your horn iron,
And I will make your hooves bronze;
You shall beat in pieces many peoples;
I will consecrate their gain to the LORD,
And their substance to the Lord of the
whole earth."

5 Now gather yourself in troops,
O daughter of troops;
He has laid siege against us;
They will strike the judge of Israel with
a rod on the cheek.

The Coming Messiah

2 "But you, Bethlehem Ephrathah,
Though you are little among the
thousands of Judah,
Yet out of you shall come forth to Me
The One to be Ruler in Israel,
Whose goings forth *are* from of old,
From everlasting."

3 Therefore He shall give them up,
Until the time *that* she who is in labor
has given birth;
Then the remnant of His brethren
Shall return to the children of Israel.
4 And He shall stand and feed *His flock*
In the strength of the LORD,
In the majesty of the name of the LORD
His God;

5:2 JESUS WILL BE BORN IN BETHLEHEM

Did you know that the Christmas story is also told in the Old Testament? Isaiah 7:14 and Micah 5:2 tell about the birth of Jesus, the coming Messiah—over seven hundred years before He was born!

Micah even tells where Jesus would be born—in Bethlehem. This city of Israel has a long history. Bethlehem became famous first in the book of Ruth. Ruth was the great-grandmother of David, who called Bethlehem "the city of David." A thousand years later, Mary and Joseph came from the family of David. At that time, the Roman government made a law that everyone had to go back to his hometown to sign his name in a government book. Therefore, Mary and Joseph had to go to Bethlehem (see Luke 2:3, 4).

Bethlehem means "House of Bread." The city truly was a house of bread, because Jesus, "the Bread of Life," came from Bethlehem (see John 6:35).

And they shall abide,
For now He shall be great
To the ends of the earth;
5 And this *One* shall be peace.

Judgment on Israel's Enemies

When the Assyrian comes into our land,
And when he treads in our palaces,
Then we will raise against him
Seven shepherds and eight princely
men.
6 They shall waste with the sword the
land of Assyria,
And the land of Nimrod at its entrances;
Thus He shall deliver *us* from the
Assyrian,
When he comes into our land
And when he treads within our borders.

7 Then the remnant of Jacob
Shall be in the midst of many peoples,
Like dew from the LORD,
Like showers on the grass,
That tarry for no man
Nor wait for the sons of men.
8 And the remnant of Jacob
Shall be among the Gentiles,
In the midst of many peoples,
Like a lion among the beasts of the
forest,
Like a young lion among flocks of
sheep,
Who, if he passes through,
Both treads down and tears in pieces,
And none can deliver.
9 Your hand shall be lifted against your
adversaries,
And all your enemies shall be cut off.
10 "And it shall be in that day," says the
LORD,
"That I will cut off your horses from your
midst
And destroy your chariots.
11 I will cut off the cities of your land
And throw down all your strongholds.
12 I will cut off sorceries from your hand,
And you shall have no soothsayers.
13 Your carved images I will also cut off,
And your *sacred* pillars from your midst;
You shall no more worship the work of
your hands;
14 I will pluck your wooden images[a] from
your midst;
Thus I will destroy your cities.
15 And I will execute vengeance in anger
and fury
On the nations that have not heard."[a]

God Pleads with Israel

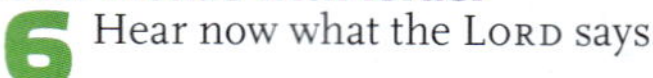

6 Hear now what the LORD says:

"Arise, plead your case before the
mountains,
And let the hills hear your voice.
2 Hear, O you mountains, the LORD's
complaint,
And you strong foundations of the
earth;
For the LORD has a complaint against
His people,

5:14 [a] Hebrew *Asherim,* Canaanite deities
5:15 [a] Or *obeyed*

GOD'S JUSTICE

READ IT: MICAH 6:8

Sometimes keeping it simple is the best way to get back to what's real in life. With so many things demanding our attention, it can be tough to know what God's saying to us. How will we know what to do if we're not sure what He's asking? This verse is a good starting point for when you start feeling overwhelmed. What does God require? Do justly, love mercy, and walk humbly with God. How can you do those things today?

And He will contend with Israel.

3 "O My people, what have I done to you?
And how have I wearied you?
Testify against Me.
4 For I brought you up from the land of Egypt,
I redeemed you from the house of bondage;
And I sent before you Moses, Aaron, and Miriam.
5 O My people, remember now
What Balak king of Moab counseled,
And what Balaam the son of Beor answered him,
From Acacia Grove[a] to Gilgal,
That you may know the righteousness of the LORD."

6 With what shall I come before the LORD,
And bow myself before the High God?
Shall I come before Him with burnt offerings,
With calves a year old?
7 Will the LORD be pleased with thousands of rams,
Ten thousand rivers of oil?
Shall I give my firstborn *for* my transgression,
The fruit of my body *for* the sin of my soul?

8 He has shown you, O man, what *is* good;
And what does the LORD require of you
But to do justly,
To love mercy,
And to walk humbly with your God?

Punishment of Israel's Injustice

9 The LORD's voice cries to the city—
Wisdom shall see Your name:

"Hear the rod!
Who has appointed it?
10 Are there yet the treasures of wickedness
In the house of the wicked,
And the short measure *that is* an abomination?
11 Shall I count pure *those* with the wicked scales,
And with the bag of deceitful weights?
12 For her rich men are full of violence,
Her inhabitants have spoken lies,
And their tongue is deceitful in their mouth.

13 "Therefore I will also make *you* sick by striking you,
By making *you* desolate because of your sins.
14 You shall eat, but not be satisfied;
Hunger[a] *shall be* in your midst.
You may carry *some* away,[b] but shall not save *them;*
And what you do rescue I will give over to the sword.

15 "You shall sow, but not reap;
You shall tread the olives, but not anoint yourselves with oil;
And *make* sweet wine, but not drink wine.
16 For the statutes of Omri are kept;
All the works of Ahab's house *are done;*
And you walk in their counsels,
That I may make you a desolation,
And your inhabitants a hissing.
Therefore you shall bear the reproach of My people."[a]

Sorrow for Israel's Sins

7 Woe is me!
For I am like those who gather summer fruits,
Like those who glean vintage grapes;
There is no cluster to eat
Of the first-ripe fruit *which* my soul desires.
2 The faithful *man* has perished from the earth,
And *there is* no one upright among men.
They all lie in wait for blood;
Every man hunts his brother with a net.

3 That they may successfully do evil with both hands—
The prince asks *for gifts,*
The judge *seeks* a bribe,
And the great *man* utters his evil desire;
So they scheme together.
4 The best of them *is* like a brier;
The most upright *is sharper* than a thorn hedge;
The day of your watchman and your punishment comes;
Now shall be their perplexity.

6:5 [a] Hebrew *Shittim* (compare Numbers 25:1; Joshua 2:1; 3:1) 6:14 [a] Or *Emptiness* or *Humiliation* [b] Targum and Vulgate read *You shall take hold.* 6:16 [a] Following Masoretic Text, Targum, and Vulgate; Septuagint reads *of nations.*

5 Do not trust in a friend;
Do not put your confidence in a companion;
Guard the doors of your mouth
From her who lies in your bosom.
6 For son dishonors father,
Daughter rises against her mother,
Daughter-in-law against her mother-in-law;
A man's enemies *are* the men of his own household.
7 Therefore I will look to the LORD;
I will wait for the God of my salvation;
My God will hear me.

Israel's Confession and Comfort

8 Do not rejoice over me, my enemy;
When I fall, I will arise;
When I sit in darkness,
The LORD *will be* a light to me.
9 I will bear the indignation of the LORD,
Because I have sinned against Him,
Until He pleads my case
And executes justice for me.
He will bring me forth to the light;
I will see His righteousness.
10 Then *she who is* my enemy will see,
And shame will cover her who said to me,
"Where is the LORD your God?"
My eyes will see her;
Now she will be trampled down
Like mud in the streets.

11 *In* the day when your walls are to be built,
In that day the decree shall go far and wide.[a]
12 *In* that day they[a] shall come to you
From Assyria and the fortified cities,[b]
From the fortress[c] to the River,[d]
From sea to sea,
And mountain *to* mountain.
13 Yet the land shall be desolate
Because of those who dwell in it,
And for the fruit of their deeds.

God Will Forgive Israel

14 Shepherd Your people with Your staff,
The flock of Your heritage,
Who dwell solitarily *in* a woodland,
In the midst of Carmel;
Let them feed *in* Bashan and Gilead,
As in days of old.

15 "As in the days when you came out of the land of Egypt,
I will show them[a] wonders."

16 The nations shall see and be ashamed of all their might;

7:11 [a] Or *the boundary shall be extended* 7:12 [a] Literally *he,* collective of the captives [b] Hebrew *arey mazor,* possibly *cities of Egypt* [c] Hebrew *mazor,* possibly *Egypt* [d] That is, the Euphrates 7:15 [a] Literally *him,* collective for the captives

Action!

GUILT

READ IT: MICAH 7:18, 19

When we mess up, it hurts God. He never intended sin to be in the world, but it is. Sins that aren't confessed get in the way of our relationship with God. There may even be consequences. But God promises that when we confess our sins, He has mercy on us. He takes our sins and throws them "into the depths of the sea" (v. 19).

After we confess our sins, it's easy to still feel guilty about them. Imagine your sins at the bottom of the ocean. There's no way you can see to the bottom. God doesn't remember your sins anymore. Ask for help in releasing your own sins. If you live near a lake or ocean, write your sins on a rock and throw it as far as you can to symbolize letting go.

They shall put *their* hand over *their* mouth
Their ears shall be deaf.
17 They shall lick the dust like a serpent;
They shall crawl from their holes like snakes of the earth.
They shall be afraid of the LORD our God,
And shall fear because of You.
18 Who *is* a God like You,
Pardoning iniquity
And passing over the transgression of the remnant of His heritage?
He does not retain His anger forever,
Because He delights *in* mercy.
19 He will again have compassion on us,
And will subdue our iniquities.

You will cast all our[a] sins
Into the depths of the sea.
20 You will give truth to Jacob
And mercy to Abraham,
Which You have sworn to our fathers
From days of old.

7:19 [a] Literally *their*

The BOOK of NAHUM

620 B.C.

Behind the Scenes

READ IT:

The book of Nahum contains the prophecy against Nineveh, the capital of Assyria. The prophet Nahum described how cruel the Assyrians were as they conquered nation after nation. He predicted that the capital city of Nineveh would be destroyed and the Assyrian Empire would end.

GET IT:

Who wrote it: The prophet Nahum

When it was written: 620 B.C.

Why it was written: to show us that God is in charge. He judges the nations.

LIVE IT:

God will judge everyone and every nation. If we believe in Jesus, God will save us from that judgment.

FIND IT:

God's Wrath on His Enemies	*Nahum 1*
The Destruction of Nineveh	*Nahum 2–3*

1 The burden[a] against Nineveh. The book of the vision of Nahum the Elkoshite.

God's Wrath on His Enemies

2 God *is* jealous, and the LORD avenges;
The LORD avenges and *is* furious.
The LORD will take vengeance on His adversaries,
And He reserves *wrath* for His enemies;
3 The LORD *is* slow to anger and great in power,
And will not at all acquit *the wicked*.

The LORD has His way
In the whirlwind and in the storm,
And the clouds *are* the dust of His feet.
4 He rebukes the sea and makes it dry,
And dries up all the rivers.
Bashan and Carmel wither,
And the flower of Lebanon wilts.
5 The mountains quake before Him,
The hills melt,
And the earth heaves[a] at His presence,
Yes, the world and all who dwell in it.

6 Who can stand before His indignation?
And who can endure the fierceness of His anger?
His fury is poured out like fire,
And the rocks are thrown down by Him.

7 The LORD *is* good,
A stronghold in the day of trouble;
And He knows those who trust in Him.
8 But with an overflowing flood
He will make an utter end of its place,
And darkness will pursue His enemies.

9 What do you conspire against the LORD?
He will make an utter end *of it*.
Affliction will not rise up a second time.
10 For while tangled *like* thorns,
And while drunken *like* drunkards,
They shall be devoured like stubble fully dried.
11 From you comes forth *one*
Who plots evil against the LORD,
A wicked counselor.

12 Thus says the LORD:

"Though *they are* safe, and likewise many,
Yet in this manner they will be cut down
When he passes through.
Though I have afflicted you,
I will afflict you no more;
13 For now I will break off his yoke from you,
And burst your bonds apart."

14 The LORD has given a command concerning you:

1:1 [a] Or *oracle* 1:5 [a] Targum reads *burns*.

Starring Roles

NAHUM'S name is pronounced *NAY-hum* and means "Compassionate." His little book should be read along with Jonah's prophecy, because both books are about the city of Nineveh.

Jonah was sent to preach the gospel to Nineveh about 760 years before Christ, and to Jonah's surprise the people believed him and repented. Because the people turned to God, Nineveh was not destroyed at that time.

Years later, Nahum again warned that Nineveh was going to be destroyed, but the people didn't listen to him. So his book describes how Nineveh was destroyed in a terrible street battle. You can almost hear the clatter of the horses' hooves, see the flash of the spears, and smell the smoke of the burning city!

Over one hundred years before, the army of Assyria had conquered the Northern Kingdom of Israel. But now Nineveh, the capital of Assyria itself, was destroyed.

"Your name shall be perpetuated no longer.
Out of the house of your gods
I will cut off the carved image and the molded image.
I will dig your grave,
For you are vile."

15 Behold, on the mountains
The feet of him who brings good tidings,
Who proclaims peace!
O Judah, keep your appointed feasts,
Perform your vows.
For the wicked one shall no more pass through you;
He is utterly cut off.

The Destruction of Nineveh

2 He who scatters[a] has come up before your face.
Man the fort!
Watch the road!
Strengthen *your* flanks!
Fortify *your* power mightily.

2 For the LORD will restore the excellence of Jacob
Like the excellence of Israel,
For the emptiers have emptied them out
And ruined their vine branches.

3 The shields of his mighty men *are* made red,
The valiant men *are* in scarlet.
The chariots *come* with flaming torches
In the day of his preparation,
And the spears are brandished.[a]
4 The chariots rage in the streets,
They jostle one another in the broad roads;
They seem like torches,
They run like lightning.

5 He remembers his nobles;
They stumble in their walk;
They make haste to her walls,
And the defense is prepared.
6 The gates of the rivers are opened,
And the palace is dissolved.
7 It is decreed:[a]
She shall be led away captive,
She shall be brought up;
And her maidservants shall lead *her* as with the voice of doves,
Beating their breasts.

8 Though Nineveh of old *was* like a pool of water,
Now they flee away.
"Halt! Halt!" *they cry;*
But no one turns back.
9 Take spoil of silver!
Take spoil of gold!

2:1 [a] Vulgate reads *He who destroys.* 2:3 [a] Literally *the cypresses are shaken;* Septuagint and Syriac read *the horses rush about;* Vulgate reads *the drivers are stupefied.*
2:7 [a] Hebrew *Huzzab*

ANXIETY

READ IT: NAHUM 1:7

Sometimes our worry stems from a desire for control. We don't like being helpless, but the kind of power we desire is God's alone. That's why we have to cling to Him like a stronghold—a fortress of safety—when anxiety sets in. Remember:

- God knows you. Trust Him with your worries.
- God is good. He wants what's best for you.
- God is almighty. You can rely on Him to comfort you and not give you anything you can't handle.

There is no end of treasure,
Or wealth of every desirable prize.
10 She is empty, desolate, and waste!
The heart melts, and the knees shake;
Much pain *is* in every side,
And all their faces are drained of color.[a]

11 Where *is* the dwelling of the lions,
And the feeding place of the young lions,
Where the lion walked, the lioness *and* lion's cub,
And no one made *them* afraid?
12 The lion tore in pieces enough for his cubs,
Killed for his lionesses,
Filled his caves with prey,
And his dens with flesh.

13"Behold, I *am* against you," says the
LORD of hosts, "I will burn your[a] chariots
in smoke, and the sword shall devour your
young lions; I will cut off your prey from the
earth, and the voice of your messengers shall
be heard no more."

The Woe of Nineveh

3 Woe to the bloody city!
It *is* all full of lies *and* robbery.
Its victim never departs.
2 The noise of a whip
And the noise of rattling wheels,
Of galloping horses,
Of clattering chariots!
3 Horsemen charge with bright sword and glittering spear.
There is a multitude of slain,
A great number of bodies,
Countless corpses—
They stumble over the corpses—
4 Because of the multitude of harlotries of the seductive harlot,
The mistress of sorceries,
Who sells nations through her harlotries,
And families through her sorceries.

5 "Behold, I *am* against you," says the LORD of hosts;
"I will lift your skirts over your face,
I will show the nations your nakedness,
And the kingdoms your shame.
6 I will cast abominable filth upon you,
Make you vile,
And make you a spectacle.
7 It shall come to pass *that* all who look upon you
Will flee from you, and say,
'Nineveh is laid waste!
Who will bemoan her?'
Where shall I seek comforters for you?"

8 Are you better than No Amon[a]
That was situated by the River,[b]
That had the waters around her,
Whose rampart *was* the sea,
Whose wall *was* the sea?
9 Ethiopia and Egypt *were* her strength,
And *it was* boundless;
Put and Lubim were your[a] helpers.
10 Yet she *was* carried away,
She went into captivity;
Her young children also were dashed to pieces
At the head of every street;
They cast lots for her honorable men,
And all her great men were bound in chains.
11 You also will be drunk;
You will be hidden;
You also will seek refuge from the enemy.

12 All your strongholds *are* fig trees with ripened figs:
If they are shaken,
They fall into the mouth of the eater.
13 Surely, your people in your midst *are* women!
The gates of your land are wide open for your enemies;
Fire shall devour the bars of your *gates*.

14 Draw your water for the siege!
Fortify your strongholds!
Go into the clay and tread the mortar!
Make strong the brick kiln!
15 There the fire will devour you,
The sword will cut you off;
It will eat you up like a locust.

Make yourself many—like the locust!
Make yourself many—like the *swarming* locusts!
16 You have multiplied your merchants more than the stars of heaven.
The locust plunders and flies away.
17 Your commanders *are* like *swarming* locusts,
And your generals like great grasshoppers,
Which camp in the hedges on a cold day;
When the sun rises they flee away,

2:10 [a] Compare Joel 2:6 2:13 [a] Literally *her* 3:8 [a] That is, ancient Thebes; Targum and Vulgate read *populous Alexandria*. [b] Literally *rivers*, that is, the Nile and the surrounding canals 3:9 [a] Septuagint reads *her*.

And the place where they *are* is not
known.

18 Your shepherds slumber, O king of
Assyria;
Your nobles rest *in the dust.*
Your people are scattered on the
mountains,
And no one gathers them.
19 Your injury *has* no healing,
Your wound is severe.
All who hear news of you
Will clap *their* hands over you,
For upon whom has not your
wickedness passed continually?

Behind the Scenes

The BOOK of HABAKKUK

612 B.C.

READ IT:

The book of Habakkuk contains Habakkuk's conversation with God. Habakkuk saw that the leaders in Judah were mistreating the poor, so he asked God why He allowed those wicked people to do so well in life. After he asked more questions and got God's answer, Habakkuk praised God.

GET IT:

Who wrote it: The prophet Habakkuk

When it was written: 612 B.C.

Why it was written: to assure us that God knows what's going on. Wicked people don't really succeed.

LIVE IT:

When things get tough in life, believe that God is in control. He will never fail you.

FIND IT:

Habakkuk's Questions, the Lord's Reply — *Habakkuk 1–2*

Habakkuk's Prayer — *Habakkuk 3*

1 The burden[a] which the prophet Habakkuk saw.

The Prophet's Question

2 O LORD, how long shall I cry,
And You will not hear?
Even cry out to You, "Violence!"
And You will not save.
3 Why do You show me iniquity,
And cause *me* to see trouble?
For plundering and violence *are* before me;
There is strife, and contention arises.
4 Therefore the law is powerless,
And justice never goes forth.
For the wicked surround the righteous;
Therefore perverse judgment proceeds.

The LORD's Reply

5 "Look among the nations and watch—
Be utterly astounded!
For *I will* work a work in your days
Which you would not believe, though it were told *you*.
6 For indeed I am raising up the Chaldeans,
A bitter and hasty nation
Which marches through the breadth of the earth,
To possess dwelling places *that are* not theirs.
7 They are terrible and dreadful;
Their judgment and their dignity proceed from themselves.
8 Their horses also are swifter than leopards,
And more fierce than evening wolves.
Their chargers charge ahead;
Their cavalry comes from afar;
They fly as the eagle *that* hastens to eat.

9 "They all come for violence;
Their faces are set *like* the east wind.
They gather captives like sand.
10 They scoff at kings,
And princes are scorned by them.
They deride every stronghold,
For they heap up earthen *mounds* and seize it.
11 Then *his* mind[a] changes, and he transgresses;
He commits offense,
Ascribing this power to his god."

The Prophet's Second Question

12 Are You not from everlasting,
O LORD my God, my Holy One?
We shall not die.
O LORD, You have appointed them for judgment;
O Rock, You have marked them for correction.

1:1 [a] Or *oracle* 1:11 [a] Literally *spirit* or *wind*

Starring Roles

HABAKKUK wrote his book to tell you how he waited until God answered his hard questions. His name is pronounced *huh-BACK-kuk* and means "Embraced by God."

Habakkuk wanted the Lord to tell him why He was allowing so much crime in his land. You may sometimes hear your parents ask the same question about your own country.

But God told Habakkuk that He was only giving the people time to change their ways. If they didn't, He would send their enemies against them. Habakkuk was sad because he couldn't believe the Lord would destroy their cities. So he waited for the Lord's answer, like a man watching on a tower.

God proved that Habakkuk could trust Him to always do what is right. He did punish the people as they deserved, but later He helped them build their cities again. So Habakkuk learned to sing for joy to God his Savior.

13 *You are* of purer eyes than to behold evil,
And cannot look on wickedness.
Why do You look on those who deal treacherously,
And hold Your tongue when the wicked devours
A *person* more righteous than he?
14 *Why* do You make men like fish of the sea,
Like creeping things *that have* no ruler over them?

15 They take up all of them with a hook,
They catch them in their net,
And gather them in their dragnet.
Therefore they rejoice and are glad.
16 Therefore they sacrifice to their net,
And burn incense to their dragnet;
Because by them their share *is* sumptuous
And their food plentiful.
17 Shall they therefore empty their net,
And continue to slay nations without pity?

2 I will stand my watch
And set myself on the rampart,
And watch to see what He will say to me,
And what I will answer when I am corrected.

The Just Live by Faith

2 Then the LORD answered me and said:
"Write the vision
And make *it* plain on tablets,
That he may run who reads it.
3 For the vision *is* yet for an appointed time;
But at the end it will speak, and it will not lie.
Though it tarries, wait for it;
Because it will surely come,
It will not tarry.

4 "Behold the proud,
His soul is not upright in him;
But the just shall live by his faith.

Woe to the Wicked

5 "Indeed, because he transgresses by wine,
He is a proud man,
And he does not stay at home.
Because he enlarges his desire as hell,[a]
And he *is* like death, and cannot be satisfied,
He gathers to himself all nations
And heaps up for himself all peoples.

6 "Will not all these take up a proverb against him,
And a taunting riddle against him, and say,
'Woe to him who increases
What is not his—how long?

2:5 [a] Or *Sheol*

LIFE'S NOT FAIR

READ IT: HABAKKUK 1:2–4

When life's hard, it can seem like God isn't paying attention. And it's hard not to get angry when it seems like He's not coming to rescue us when we think He should. Just remember:

- *Take a deep breath.* Things aren't always as bad as they seem.
- *Hang in there.* Life has ups and downs. We have to get through the hard stuff in order to get to the good stuff.
- *Keep praying.* God hasn't stopped listening, no matter how quiet He seems.

And to him who loads himself with
many pledges'?[a]
7 Will not your creditors[a] rise up
suddenly?
Will they not awaken who oppress you?
And you will become their booty.
8 Because you have plundered many
nations,
All the remnant of the people shall
plunder you,
Because of men's blood
And the violence of the land *and* the city,
And of all who dwell in it.

9 "Woe to him who covets evil gain for his
house,
That he may set his nest on high,
That he may be delivered from the
power of disaster!
10 You give shameful counsel to your
house,
Cutting off many peoples,
And sin *against* your soul.
11 For the stone will cry out from the wall,
And the beam from the timbers will
answer it.

12 "Woe to him who builds a town with
bloodshed,
Who establishes a city by iniquity!
13 Behold, *is it* not of the LORD of hosts
That the peoples labor to feed the fire,[a]
And nations weary themselves in vain?
14 For the earth will be filled
With the knowledge of the glory of the
LORD,
As the waters cover the sea.

15 "Woe to him who gives drink to his
neighbor,
Pressing[a] *him to* your bottle,
Even to make *him* drunk,
That you may look on his nakedness!
16 You are filled with shame instead of
glory.
You also—drink!
And be exposed as uncircumcised![a]
The cup of the LORD's right hand *will be*
turned against you,
And utter shame will be on your glory.
17 For the violence *done to* Lebanon will
cover you,
And the plunder of beasts *which* made
them afraid,
Because of men's blood
And the violence of the land *and* the city,
And of all who dwell in it.

18 "What profit is the image, that its maker
should carve it,
The molded image, a teacher of lies,
That the maker of its mold should trust
in it,
To make mute idols?
19 Woe to him who says to wood, 'Awake!'
To silent stone, 'Arise! It shall teach!'
Behold, it is overlaid with gold and
silver,
Yet in it there is no breath at all.

20 "But the LORD is in His holy temple.
Let all the earth keep silence before
Him."

The Prophet's Prayer

3 A prayer of Habakkuk the prophet, on
Shigionoth.[a]

2 O LORD, I have heard Your speech *and*
was afraid;
O LORD, revive Your work in the midst
of the years!
In the midst of the years make *it* known;
In wrath remember mercy.

3 God came from Teman,
The Holy One from Mount Paran. *Selah*

His glory covered the heavens,
And the earth was full of His praise.
4 *His* brightness was like the light;
He had rays *flashing* from His hand,
And there His power *was* hidden.
5 Before Him went pestilence,
And fever followed at His feet.

6 He stood and measured the earth;
He looked and startled the nations.
And the everlasting mountains were
scattered,
The perpetual hills bowed.
His ways *are* everlasting.
7 I saw the tents of Cushan in affliction;
The curtains of the land of Midian
trembled.

8 O LORD, were *You* displeased with the
rivers,
Was Your anger against the rivers,
Was Your wrath against the sea,

2:6 [a] Syriac and Vulgate read *thick clay.* 2:7 [a] Literally *those who bite you* 2:13 [a] Literally *for what satisfies fire,* that is, for what is of no lasting value 2:15 [a] Literally *Attaching* or *Joining* 2:16 [a] Dead Sea Scrolls and Septuagint read *And reel!;* Syriac and Vulgate read *And fall fast asleep!* 3:1 [a] Exact meaning unknown

That You rode on Your horses,
Your chariots of salvation?
9 Your bow was made quite ready;
Oaths were sworn over *Your* arrows.[a]
Selah

You divided the earth with rivers.
10 The mountains saw You *and* trembled;
The overflowing of the water passed by.
The deep uttered its voice,
And lifted its hands on high.
11 The sun and moon stood still in their habitation;
At the light of Your arrows they went,
At the shining of Your glittering spear.

12 You marched through the land in indignation;
You trampled the nations in anger.
13 You went forth for the salvation of Your people,
For salvation with Your Anointed.
You struck the head from the house of the wicked,
By laying bare from foundation to neck.
Selah

14 You thrust through with his own arrows
The head of his villages.
They came out like a whirlwind to scatter me;
Their rejoicing was like feasting on the poor in secret.
15 You walked through the sea with Your horses,
Through the heap of great waters.

16 When I heard, my body trembled;
My lips quivered at *the* voice;
Rottenness entered my bones;
And I trembled in myself,
That I might rest in the day of trouble.
When he comes up to the people,
He will invade them with his troops.

A Hymn of Faith

17 Though the fig tree may not blossom,
Nor fruit be on the vines;
Though the labor of the olive may fail,
And the fields yield no food;
Though the flock may be cut off from the fold,
And there be no herd in the stalls—
18 Yet I will rejoice in the LORD,
I will joy in the God of my salvation.

19 The LORD God[a] is my strength;
He will make my feet like deer's *feet,*
And He will make me walk on my high hills.

To the Chief Musician. With my stringed instruments.

3:9 [a] Literally *rods* or *tribes* (compare verse 14) 3:19 [a] Hebrew *YHWH Adonai*

HOPE

READ IT: HABAKKUK 3:17, 18

Nothing going right? Have hope anyway. This passage is a song of praise during the storms of life. The author was struggling just to make it through but still praised God and had hope. It's easy to have hope when things are going smoothly, but to have hope when things are bad is an exercise in faith. Stretch your muscles!

The BOOK of

ZEPHANIAH

607 B.C.

Behind the Scenes

READ IT:

The book of Zephaniah includes the warnings of the prophet Zephaniah to God's people. Zephaniah encouraged the people to go back to worshiping God. He warned them that the day of the Lord would bring judgment on Judah and Jerusalem. Zephaniah predicted that other nations would be destroyed, too. Then he gave them hope for a far-off time in the future.

GET IT:

Who wrote it: The prophet Zephaniah

When it was written: 607 B.C.

Why it was written: to show that God will punish His people to discipline them, but His love for them continues forever.

LIVE IT:

If we have a relationship with God we will have a true and rich life.

FIND IT:

The Great Day of the Lord	*Zephaniah 1*
Seek the Lord	*Zephaniah 2*
Joy in God's Faithfulness	*Zephaniah 3*

1 The word of the LORD which came to Zephaniah the son of Cushi, the son of Gedaliah, the son of Amariah, the son of Hezekiah, in the days of Josiah the son of Amon, king of Judah.

The Great Day of the LORD

2 "I will utterly consume everything
From the face of the land,"
Says the LORD;
3 "I will consume man and beast;
I will consume the birds of the heavens,
The fish of the sea,
And the stumbling blocks[a] along with the wicked.
I will cut off man from the face of the land,"
Says the LORD.

4 "I will stretch out My hand against Judah,
And against all the inhabitants of Jerusalem.
I will cut off every trace of Baal from this place,
The names of the idolatrous priests[a] with the *pagan* priests—
5 Those who worship the host of heaven on the housetops;
Those who worship and swear *oaths* by the LORD,
But who *also* swear by Milcom;[a]
6 Those who have turned back from *following* the LORD,
And have not sought the LORD, nor inquired of Him."

7 Be silent in the presence of the Lord GOD;
For the day of the LORD *is* at hand,
For the LORD has prepared a sacrifice;
He has invited[a] His guests.

8 "And it shall be,
In the day of the LORD's sacrifice,
That I will punish the princes and the king's children,
And all such as are clothed with foreign apparel.
9 In the same day I will punish
All those who leap over the threshold,[a]
Who fill their masters' houses with violence and deceit.

10 "And there shall be on that day," says the LORD,
"The sound of a mournful cry from the Fish Gate,
A wailing from the Second Quarter,
And a loud crashing from the hills.
11 Wail, you inhabitants of Maktesh![a]
For all the merchant people are cut down;
All those who handle money are cut off.

1:3 [a] Figurative of idols 1:4 [a] Hebrew *chemarim* 1:5 [a] Or *Malcam*, an Ammonite god, also called *Molech* (compare Leviticus 18:21) 1:7 [a] Literally *set apart, consecrated* 1:9 [a] Compare 1 Samuel 5:5 1:11 [a] Literally *Mortar*, a market district of Jerusalem

Starring Roles

ZEPHANIAH'S name is pronounced *zef-uh-NIGH-uh* and means "The Lord Has Hidden." God does hide some things from us until we are ready to understand them. Zephaniah spoke his message to his people during the reign of good King Josiah about 640 years before Jesus was born. The great Jeremiah was also a prophet during Zephaniah's time.

Zephaniah spoke very sternly to his people, using strong words to describe God's coming judgment on them and their neighbors. The "great day of the LORD" would be dark and gloomy. Zephaniah described the Lord as searching Jerusalem with lamps to discover their sins.

But in the end he told his people to sing and shout for joy because God would forgive their sins, and after they had been captives for a while in a foreign country, the Lord would bring them back to their own land.

12 "And it shall come to pass at that time
That I will search Jerusalem with lamps,
And punish the men
Who are settled in complacency,[a]
Who say in their heart,
'The LORD will not do good,
Nor will He do evil.'
13 Therefore their goods shall become booty,
And their houses a desolation;
They shall build houses, but not inhabit *them;*
They shall plant vineyards, but not drink their wine."

14 The great day of the LORD *is* near;
It is near and hastens quickly.
The noise of the day of the LORD is bitter;
There the mighty men shall cry out.
15 That day *is* a day of wrath,
A day of trouble and distress,
A day of devastation and desolation,
A day of darkness and gloominess,
A day of clouds and thick darkness,
16 A day of trumpet and alarm
Against the fortified cities
And against the high towers.

17 "I will bring distress upon men,
And they shall walk like blind men,
Because they have sinned against the LORD;
Their blood shall be poured out like dust,
And their flesh like refuse."

18 Neither their silver nor their gold
Shall be able to deliver them
In the day of the LORD's wrath;
But the whole land shall be devoured
By the fire of His jealousy,
For He will make speedy riddance
Of all those who dwell in the land.

A Call to Repentance

2 Gather yourselves together, yes, gather together,
O undesirable[a] nation,
2 Before the decree is issued,
Or the day passes like chaff,
Before the LORD's fierce anger comes upon you,
Before the day of the LORD's anger comes upon you!
3 Seek the LORD, all you meek of the earth,
Who have upheld His justice.
Seek righteousness, seek humility.
It may be that you will be hidden
In the day of the LORD's anger.

Judgment on Nations

4 For Gaza shall be forsaken,
And Ashkelon desolate;
They shall drive out Ashdod at noonday,
And Ekron shall be uprooted.
5 Woe to the inhabitants of the seacoast,
The nation of the Cherethites!
The word of the LORD *is* against you,
O Canaan, land of the Philistines:
"I will destroy you;
So there shall be no inhabitant."

6 The seacoast shall be pastures,
With shelters[a] for shepherds and folds for flocks.
7 The coast shall be for the remnant of the house of Judah;

1:12 [a] Literally *on their lees,* that is, settled like the dregs of wine 2:1 [a] Or *shameless* 2:6 [a] Literally *excavations,* either underground huts or cisterns

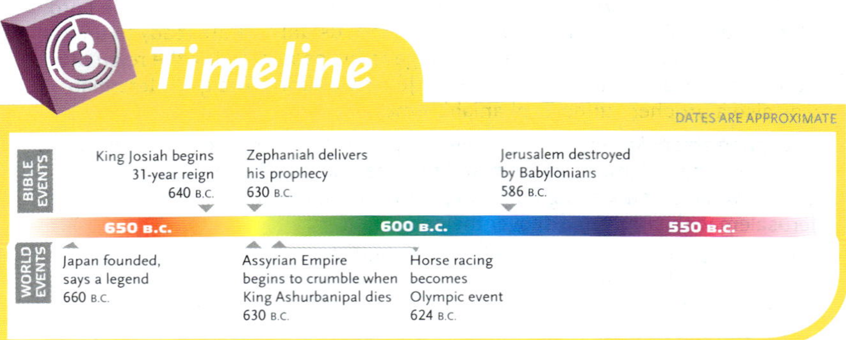

They shall feed *their* flocks there;
In the houses of Ashkelon they shall lie down at evening.
For the LORD their God will intervene for them,
And return their captives.

8 "I have heard the reproach of Moab,
And the insults of the people of Ammon,
With which they have reproached My people,
And made arrogant threats against their borders.
9 Therefore, as I live,"
Says the LORD of hosts, the God of Israel,
"Surely Moab shall be like Sodom,
And the people of Ammon like Gomorrah—
Overrun with weeds and saltpits,
And a perpetual desolation.
The residue of My people shall plunder them,
And the remnant of My people shall possess them."

10 This they shall have for their pride,
Because they have reproached and made arrogant threats
Against the people of the LORD of hosts.
11 The LORD *will be* awesome to them,
For He will reduce to nothing all the gods of the earth;
People shall worship Him,
Each one from his place,
Indeed all the shores of the nations.

12 "You Ethiopians also,
You shall be slain by My sword."

13 And He will stretch out His hand against the north,
Destroy Assyria,
And make Nineveh a desolation,
As dry as the wilderness.
14 The herds shall lie down in her midst,
Every beast of the nation.
Both the pelican and the bittern
Shall lodge on the capitals *of* her *pillars;*
Their voice shall sing in the windows;
Desolation *shall be* at the threshold;
For He will lay bare the cedar work.
15 This is the rejoicing city
That dwelt securely,
That said in her heart,
"I *am it,* and *there is* none besides me."
How has she become a desolation,
A place for beasts to lie down!
Everyone who passes by her
Shall hiss and shake his fist.

The Wickedness of Jerusalem

3 Woe to her who is rebellious and polluted,
To the oppressing city!
2 She has not obeyed *His* voice,
She has not received correction;
She has not trusted in the LORD,
She has not drawn near to her God.

3 Her princes in her midst *are* roaring lions;
Her judges *are* evening wolves
That leave not a bone till morning.
4 Her prophets are insolent, treacherous people;
Her priests have polluted the sanctuary,
They have done violence to the law.
5 The LORD *is* righteous in her midst,
He will do no unrighteousness.
Every morning He brings His justice to light;
He never fails,
But the unjust knows no shame.

6 "I have cut off nations,
Their fortresses are devastated;
I have made their streets desolate,
With none passing by.
Their cities are destroyed;
There is no one, no inhabitant.
7 I said, 'Surely you will fear Me,
You will receive instruction'—
So that her dwelling would not be cut off,
Despite everything for which I punished her.
But they rose early and corrupted all their deeds.

A Faithful Remnant

8 "Therefore wait for Me," says the LORD,
"Until the day I rise up for plunder;[a]
My determination *is* to gather the nations
To My assembly of kingdoms,
To pour on them My indignation,
All My fierce anger;
All the earth shall be devoured
With the fire of My jealousy.

9 "For then I will restore to the peoples a pure language,
That they all may call on the name of the LORD,

3:8 [a] Septuagint and Syriac read *for witness;* Targum reads *for the day of My revelation for judgment;* Vulgate reads *for the day of My resurrection that is to come.*

To serve Him with one accord.
10 From beyond the rivers of Ethiopia
My worshipers,
The daughter of My dispersed ones,
Shall bring My offering.
11 In that day you shall not be shamed for
any of your deeds
In which you transgress against Me;
For then I will take away from your
midst
Those who rejoice in your pride,
And you shall no longer be haughty
In My holy mountain.
12 I will leave in your midst
A meek and humble people,
And they shall trust in the name of the
LORD.
13 The remnant of Israel shall do no
unrighteousness
And speak no lies,
Nor shall a deceitful tongue be found in
their mouth;
For they shall feed *their* flocks and lie down,
And no one shall make *them* afraid."

Joy in God's Faithfulness

14 Sing, O daughter of Zion!
Shout, O Israel!
Be glad and rejoice with all *your* heart,
O daughter of Jerusalem!

GOD LOVES YOU
GOD DELIGHTS IN US

READ IT: ZEPHANIAH 3:17

GET IT:

When God loves His children, the prophet Zephaniah says, He rejoices in them. What exactly does that mean?

If you've ever scored a game-winning point, got a good grade on a test, volunteered to help someone, or gone on a mission trip, someone who loves you might have said how proud he or she was of you. Have you ever been to a celebration like a birthday party or maybe your grandparents' fiftieth wedding anniversary? Those types of encouragement and celebrations are a small example of how God rejoices over us!

Zephaniah says God is with us and rejoices over us with gladness and singing. God's love is a love that never stops. Zephaniah writes that even in tough times, God will save us. God will quiet us—or calm us—with His love as He rejoices.

LIVE IT:

God isn't disappointed when bad times come. Those are the times He wants us to ask Him to help us and lean on Him for guidance. He is our Savior! Next time you face a difficulty, ask God for help and thank Him for singing over you with His love. He always delights in you! When you turn to Him during hard times, He rejoices even more because of your strong faith in Him.

15 The LORD has taken away your judgments,
He has cast out your enemy.
The King of Israel, the LORD, *is* in your midst;
You shall see[a] disaster no more.

16 In that day it shall be said to Jerusalem:
"Do not fear;
Zion, let not your hands be weak.
17 The LORD your God in your midst,
The Mighty One, will save;
He will rejoice over you with gladness,
He will quiet *you* with His love,
He will rejoice over you with singing."

18 "I will gather those who sorrow over the appointed assembly,
Who are among you,
To whom its reproach *is* a burden.
19 Behold, at that time
I will deal with all who afflict you;
I will save the lame,
And gather those who were driven out;
I will appoint them for praise and fame
In every land where they were put to shame.
20 At that time I will bring you back,
Even at the time I gather you;
For I will give you fame and praise
Among all the peoples of the earth,
When I return your captives before your eyes,"
Says the LORD.

3:15 [a] Some Hebrew manuscripts, Septuagint, and Bomberg read *see;* Masoretic Text and Vulgate read *fear.*

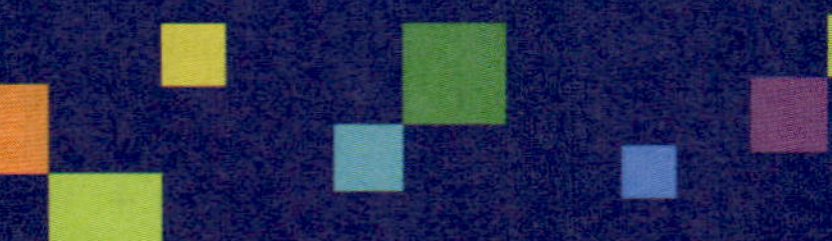

The BOOK of

HAGGAI

520 B.C.

Behind the Scenes

READ IT:

The book of Haggai contains the prophet Haggai's message to the Jews who returned to Jerusalem after living in Babylon. He announced that it was time to build God's house. With Haggai's encouragement, the people rebuilt the temple. Haggai told the people that this new temple would be better than the old one because God would fill this house with His glory.

GET IT:

Who wrote it: The prophet Haggai

When it was written: 520 B.C.

Why it was written: to encourage the people to stop thinking about themselves and rebuild God's temple.

LIVE IT:

Keep your priorities straight—God comes first in everything we do and say.

FIND IT:

The Command to Build God's House

1 In the second year of King Darius, in
the sixth month, on the first day of the
month, the word of the LORD came by Haggai the prophet to Zerubbabel the son of
Shealtiel, governor of Judah, and to Joshua
the son of Jehozadak, the high priest, saying, 2"Thus speaks the LORD of hosts, saying: 'This people says, "The time has not
come, the time that the LORD's house should
be built."' "

3Then the word of the LORD came by
Haggai the prophet, saying, 4"*Is it* time for
you yourselves to dwell in your paneled
houses, and this temple[a] *to lie* in ruins?"
5Now therefore, thus says the LORD of hosts:
"Consider your ways!

6 "You have sown much, and bring in
little;
You eat, but do not have enough;
You drink, but you are not filled with
drink;
You clothe yourselves, but no one is
warm;
And he who earns wages,
Earns wages *to put* into a bag with
holes."

7Thus says the LORD of hosts: "Consider your ways! 8Go up to the mountains and
bring wood and build the temple, that I may
take pleasure in it and be glorified," says the
LORD. 9"*You* looked for much, but indeed *it*
came to little; and when you brought it home,
I blew it away. Why?" says the LORD of hosts.
"Because of My house that *is in* ruins, while
every one of you runs to his own house.
10Therefore the heavens above you withhold
the dew, and the earth withholds its fruit.
11For I called for a drought on the land and
the mountains, on the grain and the new
wine and the oil, on whatever the ground
brings forth, on men and livestock, and on
all the labor of *your* hands."

The People's Obedience

12Then Zerubbabel the son of Shealtiel,
and Joshua the son of Jehozadak, the high
priest, with all the remnant of the people,
obeyed the voice of the LORD their God,
and the words of Haggai the prophet, as the
LORD their God had sent him; and the people feared the presence of the LORD. 13Then
Haggai, the LORD's messenger, spoke the
LORD's message to the people, saying, "I

In Focus

2:7 The Desire of All Nations A reference to the coming Messiah, or Christ, in the New Testament. There are several names for Christ in the Old Testament.

am with you, says the LORD." 14So the LORD
stirred up the spirit of Zerubbabel the son
of Shealtiel, governor of Judah, and the spirit of Joshua the son of Jehozadak, the high
priest, and the spirit of all the remnant of
the people; and they came and worked on the
house of the LORD of hosts, their God, 15on
the twenty-fourth day of the sixth month, in
the second year of King Darius.

The Coming Glory of God's House

2 In the seventh *month,* on the twenty-
first of the month, the word of the
LORD came by Haggai the prophet, saying:
2"Speak now to Zerubbabel the son of Shealtiel, governor of Judah, and to Joshua the
son of Jehozadak, the high priest, and to the
remnant of the people, saying: 3'Who is left
among you who saw this temple[a] in its former glory? And how do you see it now? In
comparison with it, *is this* not in your eyes as
nothing? 4Yet now be strong, Zerubbabel,'
says the LORD; 'and be strong, Joshua, son of
Jehozadak, the high priest; and be strong, all
you people of the land,' says the LORD, 'and
work; for I *am* with you,' says the LORD of
hosts. 5'*According to* the word that I covenanted with you when you came out of Egypt, so
My Spirit remains among you; do not fear!'

6"For thus says the LORD of hosts: 'Once
more (it *is* a little while) I will shake heaven
and earth, the sea and dry land; 7and I will
shake all nations, and they shall come to the
Desire of All Nations,[a] and I will fill this
temple with glory,' says the LORD of hosts.
8'The silver *is* Mine, and the gold *is* Mine,'
says the LORD of hosts. 9'The glory of this latter temple shall be greater than the former,'
says the LORD of hosts. 'And in this place I
will give peace,' says the LORD of hosts."

1:4 [a] Literally *house,* and so in verse 8 **2:3** [a] Literally *house,* and so in verses 7 and 9 **2:7** [a] Or *the desire of all nations*

The People Are Defiled

10 On the twenty-fourth *day* of the ninth
month, in the second year of Darius, the
word of the LORD came by Haggai the prophet, saying, 11 "Thus says the LORD of hosts:
'Now, ask the priests *concerning the* law, saying, 12 "If one carries holy meat in the fold of
his garment, and with the edge he touches
bread or stew, wine or oil, or any food, will it
become holy?" ' "

Then the priests answered and said, "No."

13 And Haggai said, "If *one who is* unclean
because of a dead body touches any of these,
will it be unclean?"

So the priests answered and said, "It shall be unclean."

14 Then Haggai answered and said, " 'So is
this people, and so is this nation before Me,'
says the LORD, 'and so is every work of their
hands; and what they offer there is unclean.

Promised Blessing

15 'And now, carefully consider from this
day forward: from before stone was laid upon
stone in the temple of the LORD— 16 since
those *days,* when *one* came to a heap of twenty ephahs, there were *but* ten; when *one* came
to the wine vat to draw out fifty baths from
the press, there were *but* twenty. 17 I struck
you with blight and mildew and hail in all
the labors of your hands; yet you did not *turn*
to Me,' says the LORD. 18 'Consider now from
this day forward, from the twenty-fourth day
of the ninth month, from the day that the
foundation of the LORD's temple was laid—
consider it: 19 Is the seed still in the barn? As
yet the vine, the fig tree, the pomegranate,
and the olive tree have not yielded *fruit. But*
from this day I will bless *you.*' "

Zerubbabel Chosen as a Signet

20 And again the word of the LORD came
to Haggai on the twenty-fourth day of the
month, saying, 21 "Speak to Zerubbabel, governor of Judah, saying:

'I will shake heaven and earth.
22 I will overthrow the throne of kingdoms;
I will destroy the strength of the Gentile kingdoms.
I will overthrow the chariots
And those who ride in them;
The horses and their riders shall come down,
Every one by the sword of his brother.

23 'In that day,' says the LORD of hosts, 'I
will take you, Zerubbabel My servant, the
son of Shealtiel,' says the LORD, 'and will
make you like a signet *ring;* for I have chosen
you,' says the LORD of hosts."

2:9 THE BEAUTY OF GOD'S HOUSE

Just like Israel in the days of Zerubbabel (pronounced *zeh-RUB-uh-bell*), we often think the beauty of God's house must be something you can see with your eyes. We look at the sunset, and we say, "How beautiful!" And this is true. Many church buildings also are truly beautiful works of art. Solomon's temple was very beautiful. It was so beautiful that, when the Jews later built a new temple, they were disappointed in it. But when Jesus came into the temple, His presence there made the temple beautiful. (See John 2:13–22.)

Can we, too, find the beauty of Jesus? We find His beauty whenever we *come into His presence* to pray. His beauty is the beauty of the holy God you can't see with your eyes; you see Him with your heart.

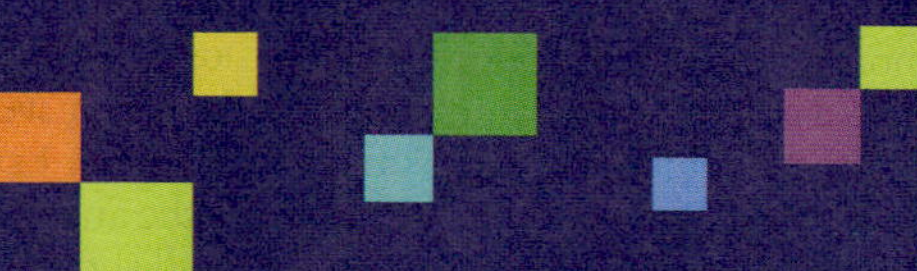

The BOOK of

ZECHARIAH

515 B.C.

READ IT:

The book of Zechariah contains the words and visions of the prophet Zechariah. He told the Jews to stay close to God so He would not have to judge and punish them again. Zechariah's visions encouraged the temple builders who were ready to give up. Zechariah comforted them by telling them God had a long-range plan for Israel.

GET IT:

Who wrote it: The prophet Zechariah

When it was written: 515 B.C.

Why it was written: to encourage God's people and give them hope for the future.

LIVE IT:

We should not be discouraged when we face difficult projects.

FIND IT:

Eight Mysterious Visions	*Zechariah 1–6*
The Importance of Obedience	*Zechariah 7*
The Coming King	*Zechariah 9:9, 10*
The Shepherd Savior	*Zechariah 13:7*

A Call to Repentance

1 In the eighth month of the second year
of Darius, the word of the LORD came
to Zechariah the son of Berechiah, the son
of Iddo the prophet, saying, 2“The LORD has
been very angry with your fathers. 3There-
fore say to them, ‘Thus says the LORD of
hosts: “Return to Me,” says the LORD of
hosts, “and I will return to you,” says the
LORD of hosts. 4“Do not be like your fathers,
to whom the former prophets preached, saying, ‘Thus says the LORD of hosts: “Turn now
from your evil ways and your evil deeds.” ’
But they did not hear nor heed Me,” says the
LORD.

5 “Your fathers, where *are* they?
And the prophets, do they live forever?
6 Yet surely My words and My statutes,
Which I commanded My servants the
prophets,
Did they not overtake your fathers?

“So they returned and said:

‘Just as the LORD of hosts determined to
do to us,
According to our ways and according to
our deeds,
So He has dealt with us.’ ” ’ ”

Vision of the Horses

7On the twenty-fourth day of the eleventh
month, which is the month Shebat, in the
second year of Darius, the word of the LORD
came to Zechariah the son of Berechiah, the
son of Iddo the prophet: 8I saw by night, and
behold, a man riding on a red horse, and it
stood among the myrtle trees in the hollow;
and behind him *were* horses: red, sorrel,
and white. 9Then I said, “My lord, what *are*
these?” So the angel who talked with me said
to me, “I will show you what they *are*.”

10And the man who stood among the
myrtle trees answered and said, “These *are*
the ones whom the LORD has sent to walk to
and fro throughout the earth.”

11So they answered the Angel of the LORD,
who stood among the myrtle trees, and said,
“We have walked to and fro throughout the
earth, and behold, all the earth is resting
quietly.”

The LORD Will Comfort Zion

12Then the Angel of the LORD answered
and said, “O LORD of hosts, how long will
You not have mercy on Jerusalem and on the
cities of Judah, against which You were angry these seventy years?”

13And the LORD answered the angel who
talked to me, *with* good *and* comforting
words. 14So the angel who spoke with me
said to me, “Proclaim, saying, ‘Thus says
the LORD of hosts:

“I am zealous for Jerusalem
And for Zion with great zeal.
15 I am exceedingly angry with the nations
at ease;
For I was a little angry,
And they helped—*but* with evil *intent*.”

16‘Therefore thus says the LORD:

Starring Roles

ZECHARIAH served as a prophet in Judah along with Haggai when his people came back from being prisoners in Babylon. His name is pronounced *zek-uh-RIGH-uh* and means “The Lord Remembers.” The Lord really did remember His promises to His people when He took them back home to their own land over five hundred years before Jesus came.

Zechariah spoke of Jesus eight times in his book. In Zechariah 9:9, he told how Jesus would enter Jerusalem like a humble Man, riding on a donkey. You can read how this really happened in Matthew 21:5 of the New Testament.

In Zechariah 12:10, you can also read how Zechariah’s people would someday be sorry because they crucified their Messiah, the Lord Jesus Christ.

"I am returning to Jerusalem with mercy;
My house shall be built in it," says the LORD of hosts,
"And a *surveyor's* line shall be stretched out over Jerusalem."'

17"Again proclaim, saying, 'Thus says the
LORD of hosts:

"My cities shall again spread out through prosperity;
The LORD will again comfort Zion,
And will again choose Jerusalem."'"

Vision of the Horns

18Then I raised my eyes and looked, and
there *were* four horns. 19And I said to the angel who talked with me, "What *are* these?"
So he answered me, "These *are* the
horns that have scattered Judah, Israel, and
Jerusalem."
20Then the LORD showed me four craftsmen. 21And I said, "What are these coming
to do?"
So he said, "These *are* the horns that
scattered Judah, so that no one could lift
up his head; but the craftsmen[a] are coming
to terrify them, to cast out the horns of the
nations that lifted up *their* horn against the
land of Judah to scatter it."

Vision of the Measuring Line

2 Then I raised my eyes and looked,
and behold, a man with a measuring
line in his hand. 2So I said, "Where are you
going?"
And he said to me, "To measure Jerusalem, to see what *is* its width and what *is* its
length."
3And there *was* the angel who talked
with me, going out; and another angel was
coming out to meet him, 4who said to him,
"Run, speak to this young man, saying: 'Jerusalem shall be inhabited *as* towns without
walls, because of the multitude of men and
livestock in it. 5For I,' says the LORD, 'will be
a wall of fire all around her, and I will be the
glory in her midst.'"

Future Joy of Zion and Many Nations

6"Up, up! Flee from the land of the
north," says the LORD; "for I have spread you
abroad like the four winds of heaven," says
the LORD. 7"Up, Zion! Escape, you who dwell
with the daughter of Babylon."
8For thus says the LORD of hosts: "He sent
Me after glory, to the nations which plunder
you; for he who touches you touches the apple of His eye. 9For surely I will shake My
hand against them, and they shall become
spoil for their servants. Then you will know
that the LORD of hosts has sent Me.
10"Sing and rejoice, O daughter of Zion!
For behold, I am coming and I will dwell in
your midst," says the LORD. 11"Many nations
shall be joined to the LORD in that day, and
they shall become My people. And I will
dwell in your midst. Then you will know that
the LORD of hosts has sent Me to you. 12And
the LORD will take possession of Judah as
His inheritance in the Holy Land, and will
again choose Jerusalem. 13Be silent, all flesh,
before the LORD, for He is aroused from His
holy habitation!"

Vision of the High Priest

3 Then he showed me Joshua the high
priest standing before the Angel of the
LORD, and Satan standing at his right hand
to oppose him. 2And the LORD said to Satan,
"The LORD rebuke you, Satan! The LORD
who has chosen Jerusalem rebuke you! *Is*
this not a brand plucked from the fire?"
3Now Joshua was clothed with filthy garments, and was standing before the Angel.
4Then He answered and spoke to those
who stood before Him, saying, "Take away
the filthy garments from him." And to him
He said, "See, I have removed your iniquity from you, and I will clothe you with rich
robes."
5And I said, "Let them put a clean turban
on his head."
So they put a clean turban on his head,
and they put the clothes on him. And the
Angel of the LORD stood by.

The Coming Branch

6Then the Angel of the LORD admonished Joshua, saying, 7"Thus says the LORD
of hosts:

'If you will walk in My ways,
And if you will keep My command,
Then you shall also judge My house,
And likewise have charge of My courts;
I will give you places to walk
Among these who stand here.

1:21 [a] Literally *these*

8 'Hear, O Joshua, the high priest,
You and your companions who sit before you,
For they are a wondrous sign;
For behold, I am bringing forth My Servant the BRANCH.
9 For behold, the stone
That I have laid before Joshua:
Upon the stone *are* seven eyes.
Behold, I will engrave its inscription,'
Says the LORD of hosts,
'And I will remove the iniquity of that land in one day.
10 In that day,' says the LORD of hosts,
'Everyone will invite his neighbor
Under his vine and under his fig tree.'"

Vision of the Lampstand and Olive Trees

4 Now the angel who talked with me
came back and wakened me, as a man
who is wakened out of his sleep. 2And he
said to me, "What do you see?"
So I said, "I am looking, and there *is* a
lampstand of solid gold with a bowl on top of
it, and on the *stand* seven lamps with seven
pipes to the seven lamps. 3Two olive trees *are*
by it, one at the right of the bowl and the other at its left." 4So I answered and spoke to the
angel who talked with me, saying, "What *are*
these, my lord?"
5Then the angel who talked with me answered and said to me, "Do you not know
what these are?"
And I said, "No, my lord."
6So he answered and said to me:

"This *is* the word of the LORD to Zerubbabel:
'Not by might nor by power, but by My Spirit,'
Says the LORD of hosts.
7 'Who *are* you, O great mountain?
Before Zerubbabel *you shall become* a plain!
And he shall bring forth the capstone
With shouts of "Grace, grace to it!"'"

8Moreover the word of the LORD came to
me, saying:

9 "The hands of Zerubbabel
Have laid the foundation of this temple;[a]
His hands shall also finish *it*.
Then you will know
That the LORD of hosts has sent Me to you.
10 For who has despised the day of small things?
For these seven rejoice to see
The plumb line in the hand of Zerubbabel.
They are the eyes of the LORD,
Which scan to and fro throughout the whole earth."

11Then I answered and said to him,
"What *are* these two olive trees—at the right
of the lampstand and at its left?" 12And I further answered and said to him, "What *are*
these two olive branches that *drip* into the re-
ceptacles[a] of the two gold pipes from which
the golden *oil* drains?"
13Then he answered me and said, "Do
you not know what these *are*?"
And I said, "No, my lord."
14So he said, "These *are* the two anointed
ones, who stand beside the Lord of the whole
earth."

Vision of the Flying Scroll

5 Then I turned and raised my eyes, and
saw there a flying scroll.
2And he said to me, "What do you see?"
So I answered, "I see a flying scroll. Its
length *is* twenty cubits and its width ten
cubits."
3Then he said to me, "This *is* the curse
that goes out over the face of the whole earth:
'Every thief shall be expelled,' according *to*
this side of *the scroll;* and, 'Every perjurer
shall be expelled,' according *to* that side of it."

4 "I will send out *the curse*," says the LORD of hosts;
"It shall enter the house of the thief
And the house of the one who swears falsely by My name.
It shall remain in the midst of his house
And consume it, with its timber and stones."

Vision of the Woman in a Basket

5Then the angel who talked with me
came out and said to me, "Lift your eyes now,
and see what this *is* that goes forth."
6So I asked, "What *is* it?" And he said, "It
is a basket[a] that is going forth."

4:9 [a] Literally *house* 4:12 [a] Literally *into the hands of*
5:6 [a] Hebrew *ephah*, a measuring container, and so elsewhere

He also said, "This *is* their resemblance
throughout the earth: 7 Here *is* a lead disc lifted up, and this *is* a woman sitting inside the
basket"; 8 then he said, "This *is* Wickedness!"
And he thrust her down into the basket, and
threw the lead cover[a] over its mouth. 9 Then
I raised my eyes and looked, and there *were*
two women, coming with the wind in their
wings; for they had wings like the wings of a
stork, and they lifted up the basket between
earth and heaven.

10 So I said to the angel who talked with
me, "Where are they carrying the basket?"

11 And he said to me, "To build a house for
it in the land of Shinar;[a] when it is ready, *the*
basket will be set there on its base."

Vision of the Four Chariots

6 Then I turned and raised my eyes and
looked, and behold, four chariots *were*
coming from between two mountains, and
the mountains *were* mountains of bronze.
2 With the first chariot *were* red horses,
with the second chariot black horses, 3 with
the third chariot white horses, and with
the fourth chariot dappled horses—strong
steeds. 4 Then I answered and said to the angel who talked with me, "What *are* these, my
lord?"

5 And the angel answered and said to
me, "These *are* four spirits of heaven, who
go out from *their* station before the Lord of
all the earth. 6 The one with the black horses
is going to the north country, the white are
going after them, and the dappled are going
toward the south country." 7 Then the strong
steeds went out, eager to go, that they might
walk to and fro throughout the earth. And
He said, "Go, walk to and fro throughout the
earth." So they walked to and fro throughout
the earth. 8 And He called to me, and spoke
to me, saying, "See, those who go toward the
north country have given rest to My Spirit in
the north country."

The Command to Crown Joshua

9 Then the word of the LORD came to me,
saying: 10 "Receive *the gift* from the captives—
from Heldai, Tobijah, and Jedaiah, who have
come from Babylon—and go the same day
and enter the house of Josiah the son of
Zephaniah. 11 Take the silver and gold, make
an elaborate crown, and set *it* on the head of
Joshua the son of Jehozadak, the high priest.
12 Then speak to him, saying, 'Thus says the
LORD of hosts, saying:

"Behold, the Man whose name *is* the
BRANCH!
From His place He shall branch out,
And He shall build the temple of the
LORD;
13 Yes, He shall build the temple of the
LORD.
He shall bear the glory,
And shall sit and rule on His throne;
So He shall be a priest on His
throne,
And the counsel of peace shall be
between them both."'

14 "Now the elaborate crown shall be for
a memorial in the temple of the LORD for
Helem,[a] Tobijah, Jedaiah, and Hen the son
of Zephaniah. 15 Even those from afar shall
come and build the temple of the LORD.
Then you shall know that the LORD of hosts
has sent Me to you. And *this* shall come to
pass if you diligently obey the voice of the
LORD your God."

Obedience Better than Fasting

7 Now in the fourth year of King Darius it came to pass *that* the word of the
LORD came to Zechariah, on the fourth *day*
of the ninth month, Chislev, 2 when *the peo-*
ple[a] sent Sherezer,[b] with Regem-Melech and
his men, *to* the house of God,[c] to pray before
the LORD, 3 *and* to ask the priests who *were*
in the house of the LORD of hosts, and the
prophets, saying, "Should I weep in the fifth
month and fast as I have done for so many
years?"

4 Then the word of the LORD of hosts
came to me, saying, 5 "Say to all the people
of the land, and to the priests: 'When you
fasted and mourned in the fifth and seventh *months* during those seventy years,
did you really fast for Me—for Me? 6 When
you eat and when you drink, do you not eat
and drink *for yourselves*? 7 *Should you* not
have obeyed the words which the LORD proclaimed through the former prophets when
Jerusalem and the cities around it were

5:8 [a] Literally *stone* **5:11** [a] That is, Babylon **6:14** [a] Following Masoretic Text, Targum, and Vulgate; Syriac reads *for Heldai* (compare verse 10); Septuagint reads *for the patient ones.* **7:2** [a] Literally *they* (compare verse 5) [b] Or *Sar-Ezer* [c] Hebrew *Bethel*

inhabited and prosperous, and the South[a]
and the Lowland were inhabited?' "

Disobedience Resulted in Captivity

8 Then the word of the LORD came to
Zechariah, saying, 9 "Thus says the LORD of
hosts:

'Execute true justice,
Show mercy and compassion
Everyone to his brother.
10 Do not oppress the widow or the
fatherless,
The alien or the poor.
Let none of you plan evil in his
heart
Against his brother.'

11 "But they refused to heed, shrugged
their shoulders, and stopped their ears so
that they could not hear. 12 Yes, they made
their hearts like flint, refusing to hear the
law and the words which the LORD of hosts
had sent by His Spirit through the former
prophets. Thus great wrath came from the
LORD of hosts. 13 Therefore it happened,
that just as He proclaimed and they would
not hear, so they called out and I would not
listen," says the LORD of hosts. 14 "But I scattered them with a whirlwind among all the
nations which they had not known. Thus
the land became desolate after them, so that
no one passed through or returned; for they
made the pleasant land desolate."

Jerusalem, Holy City of the Future

8 Again the word of the LORD of hosts
came, saying, 2 "Thus says the LORD of
hosts:

'I am zealous for Zion with great zeal;
With great fervor I am zealous for her.'

3 "Thus says the LORD:

'I will return to Zion,
And dwell in the midst of Jerusalem.
Jerusalem shall be called the City of
Truth,
The Mountain of the LORD of hosts,
The Holy Mountain.'

4 "Thus says the LORD of hosts:

'Old men and old women shall again sit
In the streets of Jerusalem,
Each one with his staff in his hand
Because of great age.
5 The streets of the city
Shall be full of boys and girls
Playing in its streets.'

6 "Thus says the LORD of hosts:

'If it is marvelous in the eyes of the
remnant of this people in these days,
Will it also be marvelous in My eyes?'
Says the LORD of hosts.

7 "Thus says the LORD of hosts:

7:7 [a] Hebrew *Negev*

GOD'S JUSTICE

READ IT: ZECHARIAH 7:9, 10

People who don't have resources or other people to help them are often left vulnerable. Think of a widow or a single parent who may need help. Or think of children who don't have access to food. This doesn't happen only in Third World countries; it happens in our own backyards.

Ask someone in your family or your church if he or she knows of any places you would be able to help someone who's vulnerable. What about having a friend over who has a tough life at home, helping a widow with yard work like raking leaves or pulling weeds, or asking your parents if you can all volunteer at a soup kitchen?

'Behold, I will save My people from the land of the east
And from the land of the west;
8 I will bring them *back,*
And they shall dwell in the midst of Jerusalem.
They shall be My people
And I will be their God,
In truth and righteousness.'

9"Thus says the LORD of hosts:

'Let your hands be strong,
You who have been hearing in these days
These words by the mouth of the prophets,
Who *spoke* in the day the foundation was laid
For the house of the LORD of hosts,
That the temple might be built.
10 For before these days
There were no wages for man nor any hire for beast;
There was no peace from the enemy for whoever went out or came in;
For I set all men, everyone, against his neighbor.

11But now I *will* not *treat* the remnant of this
people as in the former days,' says the LORD
of hosts.

12 'For the seed *shall be* prosperous,
The vine shall give its fruit,
The ground shall give her increase,
And the heavens shall give their dew—
I will cause the remnant of this people
To possess all these.
13 And it shall come to pass
That just as you were a curse among the nations,
O house of Judah and house of Israel,
So I will save you, and you shall be a blessing.
Do not fear,
Let your hands be strong.'

14"For thus says the LORD of hosts:

'Just as I determined to punish you
When your fathers provoked Me to wrath,'
Says the LORD of hosts,
'And I would not relent,
15 So again in these days
I am determined to do good
To Jerusalem and to the house of Judah.
Do not fear.
16 These *are* the things you shall do:
Speak each man the truth to his neighbor;
Give judgment in your gates for truth, justice, and peace;
17 Let none of you think evil in your[a] heart against your neighbor;
And do not love a false oath.
For all these *are things* that I hate,'
Says the LORD."

18Then the word of the LORD of hosts
came to me, saying, 19"Thus says the LORD
of hosts:

'The fast of the fourth *month,*
The fast of the fifth,
The fast of the seventh,
And the fast of the tenth,

8:17 [a] Literally *his*

HONESTY

READ IT: ZECHARIAH 8:16, 17

These verses are all about what we should do and how God's blessing will flow on us when we obey Him. Love what the Lord loves, and hate what the Lord hates. The Lord hates lies and loves truth. So we are to hate lies and love truth as well. Keep it honest, and you will be blessed.

Shall be joy and gladness and cheerful
feasts
For the house of Judah.
Therefore love truth and peace.'

20"Thus says the LORD of hosts:

'Peoples shall yet come,
Inhabitants of many cities;
21 The inhabitants of one *city* shall go to
another, saying,
"Let us continue to go and pray before
the LORD,
And seek the LORD of hosts.
I myself will go also."
22 Yes, many peoples and strong nations
Shall come to seek the LORD of hosts in
Jerusalem,
And to pray before the LORD.'

23"Thus says the LORD of hosts: 'In those
days ten men from every language of the nations shall grasp the sleeve of a Jewish man,
saying, "Let us go with you, for we have
heard *that* God *is* with you."'"

Israel Defended Against Enemies

9 The burden[a] of the word of the LORD
Against the land of Hadrach,
And Damascus its resting place
(For the eyes of men
And all the tribes of Israel
Are on the LORD);
2 Also *against* Hamath, *which* borders on it,
And *against* Tyre and Sidon, though
they are very wise.

3 For Tyre built herself a tower,
Heaped up silver like the dust,
And gold like the mire of the streets.
4 Behold, the Lord will cast her out;
He will destroy her power in the sea,
And she will be devoured by fire.

5 Ashkelon shall see *it* and fear;
Gaza also shall be very sorrowful;
And Ekron, for He dried up her
expectation.
The king shall perish from Gaza,
And Ashkelon shall not be inhabited.

6 "A mixed race shall settle in Ashdod,
And I will cut off the pride of the
Philistines.
7 I will take away the blood from his
mouth,
And the abominations from between
his teeth.
But he who remains, even he *shall be* for
our God,
And shall be like a leader in Judah,
And Ekron like a Jebusite.
8 I will camp around My house
Because of the army,
Because of him who passes by and him
who returns.
No more shall an oppressor pass
through them,
For now I have seen with My eyes.

The Coming King

9 "Rejoice greatly, O daughter of Zion!
Shout, O daughter of Jerusalem!
Behold, your King is coming to you;
He *is* just and having salvation,
Lowly and riding on a donkey,
A colt, the foal of a donkey.
10 I will cut off the chariot from Ephraim
And the horse from Jerusalem;
The battle bow shall be cut off.
He shall speak peace to the nations;
His dominion *shall be* 'from sea to sea,
And from the River to the ends of the
earth.'[a]

God Will Save His People

11 "As for you also,
Because of the blood of your covenant,
I will set your prisoners free from the
waterless pit.
12 Return to the stronghold,
You prisoners of hope.
Even today I declare
That I will restore double to you.
13 For I have bent Judah, My *bow,*
Fitted the bow with Ephraim,
And raised up your sons, O Zion,
Against your sons, O Greece,
And made you like the sword of a
mighty man."

14 Then the LORD will be seen over them,
And His arrow will go forth like
lightning.
The Lord GOD will blow the trumpet,
And go with whirlwinds from the south.
15 The LORD of hosts will defend them;
They shall devour and subdue with
slingstones.
They shall drink *and* roar as if with
wine;

9:1 [a] Or *oracle* 9:10 [a] Psalm 72:8

They shall be filled *with blood* like
basins,
Like the corners of the altar.
16 The LORD their God will save them in
that day,
As the flock of His people.
For they *shall be like* the jewels of a
crown,
Lifted like a banner over His land—
17 For how great is its[a] goodness
And how great its[b] beauty!
Grain shall make the young men thrive,
And new wine the young women.

Restoration of Judah and Israel

10 Ask the LORD for rain
In the time of the latter rain.[a]
The LORD will make flashing clouds;
He will give them showers of rain,
Grass in the field for everyone.

2 For the idols[a] speak delusion;
The diviners envision lies,
And tell false dreams;
They comfort in vain.
Therefore *the people* wend their way like
sheep;
They are in trouble because *there is* no
shepherd.

3 "My anger is kindled against the
shepherds,
And I will punish the goatherds.
For the LORD of hosts will visit His
flock,
The house of Judah,
And will make them as His royal horse
in the battle.
4 From him comes the cornerstone,
From him the tent peg,
From him the battle bow,
From him every ruler[a] together.
5 They shall be like mighty men,
Who tread down *their enemies*
In the mire of the streets in the battle.
They shall fight because the LORD is
with them,
And the riders on horses shall be put to
shame.

6 "I will strengthen the house of Judah,
And I will save the house of Joseph.
I will bring them back,
Because I have mercy on them.
They shall be as though I had not cast
them aside;
For I am the LORD their God,
And I will hear them.
7 *Those of* Ephraim shall be like a mighty
man,
And their heart shall rejoice as if with
wine.
Yes, their children shall see *it* and be
glad;
Their heart shall rejoice in the LORD.
8 I will whistle for them and gather them,
For I will redeem them;
And they shall increase as they once
increased.

9 "I will sow them among the peoples,
And they shall remember Me in far
countries;
They shall live, together with their
children,
And they shall return.
10 I will also bring them back from the
land of Egypt,
And gather them from Assyria.
I will bring them into the land of Gilead
and Lebanon,
Until no *more room* is found for them.
11 He shall pass through the sea with
affliction,
And strike the waves of the sea:
All the depths of the River[a] shall dry up.
Then the pride of Assyria shall be
brought down,
And the scepter of Egypt shall depart.

12 "So I will strengthen them in the LORD,
And they shall walk up and down in His
name,"
Says the LORD.

Desolation of Israel

11 Open your doors, O Lebanon,
That fire may devour your cedars.
2 Wail, O cypress, for the cedar has fallen,
Because the mighty *trees* are ruined.
Wail, O oaks of Bashan,
For the thick forest has come down.
3 *There is* the sound of wailing shepherds!
For their glory is in ruins.
There is the sound of roaring lions!
For the pride[a] of the Jordan is in ruins.

Prophecy of the Shepherds

4 Thus says the LORD my God, "Feed the

9:17 [a] Or *His* [b] Or *His* **10:1** [a] That is, spring rain **10:2** [a] Hebrew *teraphim* **10:4** [a] Or *despot* **10:11** [a] That is, the Nile **11:3** [a] Or *floodplain, thicket*

flock for slaughter, 5whose owners slaughter them and feel no guilt; those who sell
them say, 'Blessed be the LORD, for I am
rich'; and their shepherds do not pity them.
6For I will no longer pity the inhabitants of
the land," says the LORD. "But indeed I will
give everyone into his neighbor's hand and
into the hand of his king. They shall attack
the land, and I will not deliver *them* from
their hand."

7So I fed the flock for slaughter, in particular the poor of the flock.[a] I took for
myself two staffs: the one I called Beauty,[b]
and the other I called Bonds;[c] and I fed the
flock. 8I dismissed the three shepherds in
one month. My soul loathed them, and their
soul also abhorred me. 9Then I said, "I will
not feed you. Let what is dying die, and what
is perishing perish. Let those that are left
eat each other's flesh." 10And I took my staff,
Beauty, and cut it in two, that I might break
the covenant which I had made with all the
peoples. 11So it was broken on that day. Thus
the poor[a] of the flock, who were watching
me, knew that it *was* the word of the LORD.
12Then I said to them, "If it is agreeable to
you, give *me* my wages; and if not, refrain."
So they weighed out for my wages thirty
pieces of silver.

13And the LORD said to me, "Throw it to
the potter"—that princely price they set on
me. So I took the thirty *pieces* of silver and
threw them into the house of the LORD for
the potter. 14Then I cut in two my other staff,
Bonds, that I might break the brotherhood
between Judah and Israel.

15And the LORD said to me, "Next, take for
yourself the implements of a foolish shepherd. 16For indeed I will raise up a shepherd
in the land *who* will not care for those who
are cut off, nor seek the young, nor heal
those that are broken, nor feed those that
still stand. But he will eat the flesh of the fat
and tear their hooves in pieces.

17 "Woe to the worthless shepherd,
Who leaves the flock!
A sword *shall be* against his arm
And against his right eye;
His arm shall completely wither,
And his right eye shall be totally
blinded."

The Coming Deliverance of Judah

12 The burden[a] of the word of the
LORD against Israel. Thus says the
LORD, who stretches out the heavens, lays
the foundation of the earth, and forms the
spirit of man within him: 2"Behold, I will
make Jerusalem a cup of drunkenness to
all the surrounding peoples, when they lay
siege against Judah and Jerusalem. 3And it
shall happen in that day that I will make Jerusalem a very heavy stone for all peoples;
all who would heave it away will surely be
cut in pieces, though all nations of the earth
are gathered against it. 4In that day," says the
LORD, "I will strike every horse with confusion, and its rider with madness; I will
open My eyes on the house of Judah, and
will strike every horse of the peoples with
blindness. 5And the governors of Judah shall
say in their heart, 'The inhabitants of Jerusalem *are* my strength in the LORD of hosts,
their God.' 6In that day I will make the governors of Judah like a firepan in the woodpile,
and like a fiery torch in the sheaves; they
shall devour all the surrounding peoples
on the right hand and on the left, but Jerusalem shall be inhabited again in her own
place—Jerusalem.

7"The LORD will save the tents of Judah
first, so that the glory of the house of David
and the glory of the inhabitants of Jerusalem
shall not become greater than that of Judah.
8In that day the LORD will defend the inhabitants of Jerusalem; the one who is feeble
among them in that day shall be like David,
and the house of David *shall be* like God, like
the Angel of the LORD before them. 9It shall
be in that day *that* I will seek to destroy all
the nations that come against Jerusalem.

Mourning for the Pierced One

10"And I will pour on the house of David
and on the inhabitants of Jerusalem the
Spirit of grace and supplication; then they
will look on Me whom they pierced. Yes,
they will mourn for Him as one mourns
for *his* only *son*, and grieve for Him as one
grieves for a firstborn. 11In that day there
shall be a great mourning in Jerusalem,
like the mourning at Hadad Rimmon in
the plain of Megiddo.[a] 12And the land shall
mourn, every family by itself: the family of
the house of David by itself, and their wives

11:7 [a] Following Masoretic Text, Targum, and Vulgate; Septuagint reads *for the Canaanites.* [b] Or *Grace,* and so in verse 10 [c] Or *Unity,* and so in verse 14 **11:11** [a] Following Masoretic Text, Targum, and Vulgate; Septuagint reads *the Canaanites.* **12:1** [a] Or *oracle* **12:11** [a] Hebrew *Megiddon*

by themselves; the family of the house of
Nathan by itself, and their wives by themselves; 13the family of the house of Levi by
itself, and their wives by themselves; the
family of Shimei by itself, and their wives
by themselves; 14all the families that remain,
every family by itself, and their wives by
themselves.

Idolatry Cut Off

13 "In that day a fountain shall be
opened for the house of David and
for the inhabitants of Jerusalem, for sin and
for uncleanness.
2"It shall be in that day," says the LORD
of hosts, "*that* I will cut off the names of the
idols from the land, and they shall no longer
be remembered. I will also cause the prophets and the unclean spirit to depart from the
land. 3It shall come to pass *that* if anyone still
prophesies, then his father and mother who
begot him will say to him, 'You shall not live,
because you have spoken lies in the name of
the LORD.' And his father and mother who
begot him shall thrust him through when
he prophesies.
4"And it shall be in that day *that* every
prophet will be ashamed of his vision when
he prophesies; they will not wear a robe of
coarse hair to deceive. 5But he will say, 'I *am*
no prophet, I *am* a farmer; for a man taught
me to keep cattle from my youth.' 6And *one*
will say to him, 'What are these wounds between your arms?'[a] Then he will answer,
'*Those* with which I was wounded in the
house of my friends.'

The Shepherd Savior

7 "Awake, O sword, against My Shepherd,
Against the Man who is My
Companion,"
Says the LORD of hosts.
"Strike the Shepherd,
And the sheep will be scattered;
Then I will turn My hand against the
little ones.
8 And it shall come to pass in all the
land,"
Says the LORD,
"*That* two-thirds in it shall be cut off *and*
die,
But *one*-third shall be left in it:
9 I will bring the *one*-third through the
fire,
Will refine them as silver is refined,
And test them as gold is tested.
They will call on My name,
And I will answer them.
I will say, 'This *is* My people';
And each one will say, 'The LORD *is* my
God.'"

The Day of the LORD

14 Behold, the day of the LORD is
coming,
And your spoil will be divided in your
midst.
2 For I will gather all the nations to battle
against Jerusalem;
The city shall be taken,
The houses rifled,
And the women ravished.
Half of the city shall go into captivity,
But the remnant of the people shall not
be cut off from the city.

3 Then the LORD will go forth
And fight against those nations,
As He fights in the day of battle.
4 And in that day His feet will stand on
the Mount of Olives,
Which faces Jerusalem on the east.
And the Mount of Olives shall be split
in two,
From east to west,
Making a very large valley;
Half of the mountain shall move toward
the north
And half of it toward the south.

5 Then you shall flee *through* My
mountain valley,
For the mountain valley shall reach to
Azal.
Yes, you shall flee
As you fled from the earthquake
In the days of Uzziah king of Judah.

Thus the LORD my God will come,
And all the saints with You.[a]

6 It shall come to pass in that day
That there will be no light;
The lights will diminish.
7 It shall be one day
Which is known to the LORD—
Neither day nor night.
But at evening time it shall happen
That it will be light.

13:6 [a] Or *hands* 14:5 [a] Or *you;* Septuagint, Targum, and Vulgate read *Him.*

8 And in that day it shall be
That living waters shall flow from Jerusalem,
Half of them toward the eastern sea
And half of them toward the western sea;
In both summer and winter it shall occur.
9 And the LORD shall be King over all the earth.
In that day it shall be—
"The LORD *is* one,"[a]
And His name one.

10All the land shall be turned into a plain
from Geba to Rimmon south of Jerusalem.
Jerusalem[a] shall be raised up and inhabited
in her place from Benjamin's Gate to the
place of the First Gate and the Corner Gate,
and *from* the Tower of Hananel to the king's
winepresses.

11 *The people* shall dwell in it;
And no longer shall there be utter destruction,
But Jerusalem shall be safely inhabited.

12And this shall be the plague with which
the LORD will strike all the people who
fought against Jerusalem:

Their flesh shall dissolve while they stand on their feet,
Their eyes shall dissolve in their sockets,
And their tongues shall dissolve in their mouths.

13 It shall come to pass in that day
That a great panic from the LORD will be among them.
Everyone will seize the hand of his neighbor,
And raise his hand against his neighbor's hand;
14 Judah also will fight at Jerusalem.
And the wealth of all the surrounding nations
Shall be gathered together:
Gold, silver, and apparel in great abundance.

15 Such also shall be the plague
On the horse *and* the mule,
On the camel and the donkey,
And on all the cattle that will be in those camps.
So *shall* this plague *be*.

The Nations Worship the King

16And it shall come to pass *that* everyone
who is left of all the nations which came
against Jerusalem shall go up from year to
year to worship the King, the LORD of hosts,
and to keep the Feast of Tabernacles. 17And it
shall be *that* whichever of the families of the
earth do not come up to Jerusalem to worship the King, the LORD of hosts, on them
there will be no rain. 18If the family of Egypt
will not come up and enter in, they *shall*
have no *rain;* they shall receive the plague
with which the LORD strikes the nations
who do not come up to keep the Feast of
Tabernacles. 19This shall be the punishment
of Egypt and the punishment of all the nations that do not come up to keep the Feast
of Tabernacles.

20In that day "HOLINESS TO THE
LORD" shall be *engraved* on the bells of the
horses. The pots in the LORD's house shall
be like the bowls before the altar. 21Yes, every
pot in Jerusalem and Judah shall be holiness
to the LORD of hosts.[a] Everyone who sacrifices shall come and take them and cook in
them. In that day there shall no longer be a
Canaanite in the house of the LORD of hosts.

14:9 [a] Compare Deuteronomy 6:4 **14:10** [a] Literally *She*
14:21 [a] Or *on every pot . . . shall be (engraved) "HOLINESS TO THE LORD OF HOSTS"*

The BOOK of

MALACHI

430 B.C.

Behind the Scenes

READ IT:

The book of Malachi contains the words of the prophet Malachi. He preached to the people after they returned from Babylon. The Jews' religious life was not good. The men had married foreign women. They didn't honor God and they failed to do what God asked. Malachi told them that God would judge them. But he also said that people who obeyed God didn't have to worry. Their names were listed in God's book and they would be saved.

GET IT:

Who wrote it: The prophet Malachi

When it was written: 430 B.C.

Why it was written: to encourage the people to worship God or they would be punished.

LIVE IT:

We must love and honor God even when life is difficult.

FIND IT:

The Coming Messenger	*Malachi 3:1–7*
A Book of Remembrance	*Malachi 3:16–18*
The Great Day of the Lord	*Malachi 4*

1 The burden[a] of the word of the LORD to
Israel by Malachi.

Israel Beloved of God

2 "I have loved you," says the LORD.
"Yet you say, 'In what way have You loved
us?'
Was not Esau Jacob's brother?"
Says the LORD.
"Yet Jacob I have loved;
3 But Esau I have hated,
And laid waste his mountains and his
heritage
For the jackals of the wilderness."

4 Even though Edom has said,
"We have been impoverished,
But we will return and build the
desolate places,"

Thus says the LORD of hosts:

"They may build, but I will throw down;
They shall be called the Territory of
Wickedness,
And the people against whom the LORD
will have indignation forever.
5 Your eyes shall see,
And you shall say,
'The LORD is magnified beyond the
border of Israel.'

Polluted Offerings

6 "A son honors *his* father,
And a servant *his* master.
If then I am the Father,
Where *is* My honor?
And if I *am* a Master,
Where *is* My reverence?
Says the LORD of hosts
To you priests who despise My name.
Yet you say, 'In what way have we
despised Your name?'

7 "You offer defiled food on My altar,
But say,
'In what way have we defiled You?'
By saying,
'The table of the LORD is contemptible.'
8 And when you offer the blind as a
sacrifice,
Is it not evil?
And when you offer the lame and sick,
Is it not evil?
Offer it then to your governor!
Would he be pleased with you?
Would he accept you favorably?"
Says the LORD of hosts.

9 "But now entreat God's favor,
That He may be gracious to us.
While this is being *done* by your hands,
Will He accept you favorably?"
Says the LORD of hosts.
10 "Who *is there* even among you who would
shut the doors,

1:1 [a] Or *oracle*

Starring Roles

MALACHI had the honor of being the prophet who brought the Old Testament to a close. His name is pronounced *MAL-uh-kigh* and means "My Messenger."

After Malachi's prophecy, God did not speak to His people again until John the Baptist baptized Jesus in the Jordan River (see Matthew 3) four hundred years later.

Malachi warned his people about robbing God. This means they were not supporting God's house with their tithes. A "tithe" is a tenth of the money you earn. This tenth belongs to the Lord to help in His great work of the gospel.

Most of all, Malachi had the great joy of promising his people the coming Jesus. Malachi called Him the "Sun of Righteousness," who would rise and heal all their sins.

So that you would not kindle fire *on* My
altar in vain?
I have no pleasure in you,"
Says the LORD of hosts,
"Nor will I accept an offering from your
hands.
11 For from the rising of the sun, even to
its going down,
My name *shall be* great among the
Gentiles;
In every place incense *shall be* offered to
My name,
And a pure offering;
For My name shall be great among the
nations,"
Says the LORD of hosts.

12 "But you profane it,
In that you say,
'The table of the LORD[a] is defiled;
And its fruit, its food, *is* contemptible.'
13 You also say,
'Oh, what a weariness!'
And you sneer at it,"
Says the LORD of hosts.
"And you bring the stolen, the lame, and
the sick;
Thus you bring an offering!
Should I accept this from your hand?"
Says the LORD.
14 "But cursed *be* the deceiver
Who has in his flock a male,
And takes a vow,
But sacrifices to the Lord what is
blemished—
For I *am* a great King,"
Says the LORD of hosts,
"And My name *is to be* feared among the
nations.

Corrupt Priests

2 "And now, O priests, this
commandment is for you.
2 If you will not hear,
And if you will not take *it* to heart,
To give glory to My name,"
Says the LORD of hosts,
"I will send a curse upon you,
And I will curse your blessings.
Yes, I have cursed them already,
Because you do not take *it* to heart.

3 "Behold, I will rebuke your descendants
And spread refuse on your faces,
The refuse of your solemn feasts;
And *one* will take you away with it.
4 Then you shall know that I have sent
this commandment to you,
That My covenant with Levi may
continue,"
Says the LORD of hosts.
5 "My covenant was with him, *one* of life
and peace,
And I gave them to him *that he might*
fear *Me*;
So he feared Me
And was reverent before My name.
6 The law of truth[a] was in his mouth,
And injustice was not found on his lips.
He walked with Me in peace and equity,
And turned many away from iniquity.

7 "For the lips of a priest should keep
knowledge,
And *people* should seek the law from his
mouth;
For he is the messenger of the LORD of
hosts.

1:12 [a] Following Bomberg; Masoretic Text reads *Lord*. 2:6 [a] Or *true instruction*

8 But you have departed from the way;
You have caused many to stumble at
the law.
You have corrupted the covenant of
Levi,"
Says the LORD of hosts.
9 "Therefore I also have made you
contemptible and base
Before all the people,
Because you have not kept My ways
But have shown partiality in the
law."

Treachery of Infidelity

10 Have we not all one Father?
Has not one God created us?
Why do we deal treacherously with one
another
By profaning the covenant of the
fathers?
11 Judah has dealt treacherously,
And an abomination has been
committed in Israel and in
Jerusalem,
For Judah has profaned
The LORD's holy *institution* which He
loves:
He has married the daughter of a
foreign god.
12 May the LORD cut off from the tents of
Jacob
The man who does this, being awake
and aware,[a]
Yet who brings an offering to the LORD
of hosts!

13 And this is the second thing you do:
You cover the altar of the LORD with tears,
With weeping and crying;
So He does not regard the offering
anymore,
Nor receive *it* with goodwill from your
hands.
14 Yet you say, "For what reason?"
Because the LORD has been witness
Between you and the wife of your youth,
With whom you have dealt
treacherously;
Yet she is your companion
And your wife by covenant.
15 But did He not make *them* one,
Having a remnant of the Spirit?
And why one?
He seeks godly offspring.
Therefore take heed to your spirit,
And let none deal treacherously with the
wife of his youth.

16 "For the LORD God of Israel says
That He hates divorce,
For it covers one's garment with
violence,"
Says the LORD of hosts.
"Therefore take heed to your spirit,
That you do not deal treacherously."

17 You have wearied the LORD with your
words;
Yet you say,
"In what way have we wearied *Him?*"
In that you say,
"Everyone who does evil
Is good in the sight of the LORD,
And He delights in them,"
Or, "Where *is* the God of justice?"

On Location

The Prophets of Israel

The prophet Malachi is one of several who addressed Jews in Jerusalem.

2:12 [a] Talmud and Vulgate read *teacher and student.*

The Coming Messenger

3 "Behold, I send My messenger,
And he will prepare the way
before Me.
And the Lord, whom you seek,
Will suddenly come to His temple,
Even the Messenger of the covenant,
In whom you delight.
Behold, He is coming,"
Says the LORD of hosts.

2 "But who can endure the day of His
coming?
And who can stand when He appears?
For He *is* like a refiner's fire
And like launderers' soap.
3 He will sit as a refiner and a purifier of
silver;
He will purify the sons of Levi,
And purge them as gold and silver,
That they may offer to the LORD
An offering in righteousness.

4 "Then the offering of Judah and
Jerusalem
Will be pleasant to the LORD,
As in the days of old,
As in former years.
5 And I will come near you for judgment;
I will be a swift witness
Against sorcerers,
Against adulterers,
Against perjurers,
Against those who exploit wage earners
and widows and orphans,
And against those who turn away an
alien—
Because they do not fear Me,"
Says the LORD of hosts.

6 "For I *am* the LORD, I do not change;
Therefore you are not consumed,
O sons of Jacob.
7 Yet from the days of your fathers
You have gone away from My
ordinances
And have not kept *them*.
Return to Me, and I will return to you,"
Says the LORD of hosts.
"But you said,
'In what way shall we return?'

Do Not Rob God

8 "Will a man rob God?
Yet you have robbed Me!
But you say,
'In what way have we robbed You?'
In tithes and offerings.
9 You are cursed with a curse,
For you have robbed Me,

Epic Ideas

3:1 JESUS COMES TO THE TEMPLE

You should read how Jesus came and drove the merchants out of the temple (see John 2:13–22). Over four hundred years before Jesus was born, the prophet Malachi described Jesus coming "suddenly" to the temple.

Usually we think of Jesus as being a quiet, mild Man, but Matthew, Mark, Luke, and John all describe Jesus' violent actions when He drove out the people who were doing business in the temple. Jesus said His Father's house should be a place of prayer. You need to help others remember this, too. God's house and God's work are not places where we make ourselves rich. It is where we serve God and preach His Word.

Jesus also comes wherever we worship and serve Him. Let us be sure that all we do brings honor to Him wherever we are—at church or in the streets.

Even this whole nation.
10 Bring all the tithes into the storehouse,
That there may be food in My house,
And try Me now in this,"
Says the LORD of hosts,
"If I will not open for you the windows of heaven
And pour out for you *such* blessing
That *there will* not *be room* enough *to receive it*.

11 "And I will rebuke the devourer for your sakes,
So that he will not destroy the fruit of your ground,
Nor shall the vine fail to bear fruit for you in the field,"
Says the LORD of hosts;
12 "And all nations will call you blessed,
For you will be a delightful land,"
Says the LORD of hosts.

The People Complain Harshly

13 "Your words have been harsh against Me,"
Says the LORD,
"Yet you say,
'What have we spoken against You?'
14 You have said,
'It is useless to serve God;
What profit *is it* that we have kept His ordinance,
And that we have walked as mourners
Before the LORD of hosts?
15 So now we call the proud blessed,
For those who do wickedness are raised up;
They even tempt God and go free.'"

A Book of Remembrance

16 Then those who feared the LORD spoke to one another,
And the LORD listened and heard *them;*
So a book of remembrance was written before Him
For those who fear the LORD
And who meditate on His name.

17 "They shall be Mine," says the LORD of hosts,
"On the day that I make them My jewels.[a]
And I will spare them
As a man spares his own son who serves him."
18 Then you shall again discern
Between the righteous and the wicked,
Between one who serves God
And one who does not serve Him.

The Great Day of God

4 "For behold, the day is coming,
Burning like an oven,
And all the proud, yes, all who do wickedly will be stubble.
And the day which is coming shall burn them up,"
Says the LORD of hosts,
"That will leave them neither root nor branch.
2 But to you who fear My name
The Sun of Righteousness shall arise
With healing in His wings;
And you shall go out

3:17 [a] Literally *special treasure*

Action!

HEARING GOD'S VOICE

READ IT: MALACHI 3:18

Wisdom is more than having a good vocabulary. God can give you the ability to choose well, to decide between right and wrong, to know the difference between good and evil people. Let God lead you in your friendships and other relationships. He'll reveal what you need to know every step of the way.

New Testament

The GOSPEL ACCORDING to

MATTHEW

A.D. 50–A.D. 65

Behind the Scenes

READ IT:

The book of Matthew tells the stories about Jesus' life from His birth in 4 B.C. to His death in A.D. 30. It shares the good news that the long-awaited Messiah had come to save people—both Jews and Gentiles. The author includes many of Jesus' teachings and sermons.

GET IT:

Who wrote it: Matthew, a disciple of Jesus

When it was written: A.D. 50– A.D. 65

Why it was written: to tell the Jews about Jesus' life and teachings, and to prove to them that Jesus was the Messiah they had been waiting for.

LIVE IT:

We can look at Jesus' words and actions to know how we should live today.

FIND IT:

Wise Men from the East	*Matthew 2*
The Beatitudes	*Matthew 5*
The Lord's Prayer	*Matthew 6*
Jesus Feeds the Five Thousand	*Matthew 14*
The Parable of the Lost Sheep	*Matthew 18*
Jesus Institutes the Lord's Supper	*Matthew 26*
Jesus' Trial and Death	*Matthew 27*
Jesus' Resurrection	*Matthew 28*

The Genealogy of Jesus Christ

1 The book of the genealogy of Jesus
Christ, the Son of David, the Son of
Abraham:
2Abraham begot Isaac, Isaac begot Jacob,
and Jacob begot Judah and his brothers.
3Judah begot Perez and Zerah by Tamar, Perez begot Hezron, and Hezron begot Ram.
4Ram begot Amminadab, Amminadab begot Nahshon, and Nahshon begot Salmon.
5Salmon begot Boaz by Rahab, Boaz begot
Obed by Ruth, Obed begot Jesse, 6and Jesse
begot David the king.

David the king begot Solomon by her *who
had been the wife*[a] of Uriah. 7Solomon begot
Rehoboam, Rehoboam begot Abijah, and
Abijah begot Asa.[a] 8Asa begot Jehoshaphat,
Jehoshaphat begot Joram, and Joram begot
Uzziah. 9Uzziah begot Jotham, Jotham begot
Ahaz, and Ahaz begot Hezekiah. 10Hezekiah
begot Manasseh, Manasseh begot Amon,[a]
and Amon begot Josiah. 11Josiah begot Jeconiah and his brothers about the time they
were carried away to Babylon.

12And after they were brought to Babylon,
Jeconiah begot Shealtiel, and Shealtiel begot
Zerubbabel. 13Zerubbabel begot Abiud, Abi-
ud begot Eliakim, and Eliakim begot Azor.
14Azor begot Zadok, Zadok begot Achim, and
Achim begot Eliud. 15Eliud begot Eleazar,
Eleazar begot Matthan, and Matthan begot
Jacob. 16And Jacob begot Joseph the husband
of Mary, of whom was born Jesus who is
called Christ.

17So all the generations from Abraham
to David *are* fourteen generations, from
David until the captivity in Babylon *are*
fourteen generations, and from the captivity in Babylon until the Christ *are* fourteen
generations.

In Focus

1:1 Genealogy The history of a family listing the most famous ancestors from the beginning. This genealogy of Jesus begins with Abraham and ends with Joseph, husband of Mary.

1:16 Christ The divine title of the Man Jesus. The word means "the Anointed" (by the Holy Spirit). *Christos* is a Greek word translated from the Hebrew *Messiah*.

1:6 [a] Words in italic type have been added for clarity. They are not found in the original Greek. **1:7** [a] NU-Text reads *Asaph*. **1:10** [a] NU-Text reads *Amos*.

Starring Roles

MATTHEW'S name is pronounced *MATH-you* and means "The Gift of the Lord." Some people were surprised when Jesus called him to be one of His 12 disciples.

Matthew was a tax collector. Everybody hated tax collectors because they took their people's money and gave it to their Roman enemies. Even the Romans themselves treated the tax collectors with hatred because they didn't care about their own people.

Jesus was different, though. He didn't hate Matthew, and He was the first Person who ever made him feel wanted. One day Jesus went to the shop where Matthew collected taxes. Jesus just looked into his eyes and said two words: "Follow Me!"

Matthew never knew such love as Jesus showed him that day, and he became one of Jesus' disciples from then on. A disciple is a learner, and you can be a disciple, too.

Christ Born of Mary

18Now the birth of Jesus Christ was as follows: After His mother Mary was betrothed
to Joseph, before they came together, she
was found with child of the Holy Spirit.
19Then Joseph her husband, being a just
man, and not wanting to make her a public
example, was minded to put her away secretly. 20But while he thought about these things,
behold, an angel of the Lord appeared to him
in a dream, saying, "Joseph, son of David, do
not be afraid to take to you Mary your wife,
for that which is conceived in her is of the
Holy Spirit. 21And she will bring forth a Son,
and you shall call His name JESUS, for He
will save His people from their sins."
22So all this was done that it might be fulfilled which was spoken by the Lord through
the prophet, saying: 23"Behold, the virgin
shall be with child, and bear a Son, and they
shall call His name Immanuel,"[a] which is
translated, "God with us."
24Then Joseph, being aroused from sleep,
did as the angel of the Lord commanded him
and took to him his wife, 25and did not know
her till she had brought forth her firstborn
Son.[a] And he called His name JESUS.

Wise Men from the East

2 Now after Jesus was born in Bethlehem of Judea in the days of Herod the
king, behold, wise men from the East came
to Jerusalem, 2saying, "Where is He who
has been born King of the Jews? For we have
seen His star in the East and have come to
worship Him."
3When Herod the king heard *this,* he was
troubled, and all Jerusalem with him. 4And
when he had gathered all the chief priests and
scribes of the people together, he inquired of
them where the Christ was to be born.

On Location

Jesus' Ministry Beyond Galilee

The story of Jesus unfolds in what is now Israel, beginning in His hometown region of Galilee, and continuing southward through Samaria and into Judea, where He dies and is resurrected in the city of Jerusalem.

1:23 [a] Isaiah 7:14 1:25 [a] NU-Text reads *a Son.*

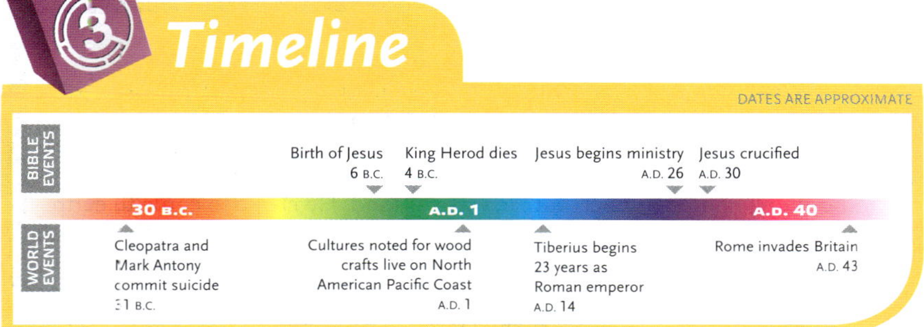

5So they said to him, "In Bethlehem of
Judea, for thus it is written by the prophet:

6 'But you, Bethlehem, *in* the land of
Judah,
Are not the least among the rulers of
Judah;
For out of you shall come a Ruler
Who will shepherd My people Israel.' "[a]

7Then Herod, when he had secretly
called the wise men, determined from them
what time the star appeared. 8And he sent
them to Bethlehem and said, "Go and search
carefully for the young Child, and when you
have found *Him,* bring back word to me, that
I may come and worship Him also."
9When they heard the king, they departed; and behold, the star which they had
seen in the East went before them, till it
came and stood over where the young Child
was. 10When they saw the star, they rejoiced
with exceedingly great joy. 11And when they
had come into the house, they saw the young
Child with Mary His mother, and fell down
and worshiped Him. And when they had
opened their treasures, they presented gifts
to Him: gold, frankincense, and myrrh.
12Then, being divinely warned in a dream
that they should not return to Herod, they
departed for their own country another way.

The Flight into Egypt

13Now when they had departed, behold,
an angel of the Lord appeared to Joseph in a
dream, saying, "Arise, take the young Child
and His mother, flee to Egypt, and stay there
until I bring you word; for Herod will seek
the young Child to destroy Him."
14When he arose, he took the young Child
and His mother by night and departed for
Egypt, 15and was there until the death of
Herod, that it might be fulfilled which was
spoken by the Lord through the prophet, saying, "Out of Egypt I called My Son."[a]

Massacre of the Innocents

16Then Herod, when he saw that he was
deceived by the wise men, was exceedingly
angry; and he sent forth and put to death all
the male children who were in Bethlehem
and in all its districts, from two years old and
under, according to the time which he had
determined from the wise men. 17Then was
fulfilled what was spoken by Jeremiah the
prophet, saying:

18 "A voice was heard in Ramah,
Lamentation, weeping, and great
mourning,
Rachel weeping *for* her children,
Refusing to be comforted,
Because they are no more."[a]

The Home in Nazareth

19Now when Herod was dead, behold,
an angel of the Lord appeared in a dream
to Joseph in Egypt, 20saying, "Arise, take
the young Child and His mother, and go to
the land of Israel, for those who sought the
young Child's life are dead." 21Then he arose,

2:6 [a] Micah 5:2 2:15 [a] Hosea 11:1 2:18 [a] Jeremiah 31:15

RELATIONSHIPS

READ IT: MATTHEW 1:18–25

Immanuel! You may sing it in songs at Christmastime or hear the word at church, but what does it really mean? *Immanuel* means "God with us"! Immanuel was the name that Isaiah prophesied regarding Jesus in the Old Testament (Isaiah 7:14); it was a sign of what was coming. Jesus was born of a human mother, but He was still God. He chose to come to earth to join us, to be with us, to help us understand what it meant to have a relationship with Him. He modeled how to live out faith. His Holy Spirit continues to guide and direct us today.

took the young Child and His mother, and
came into the land of Israel.

22But when he heard that Archelaus was
reigning over Judea instead of his father
Herod, he was afraid to go there. And being
warned by God in a dream, he turned aside
into the region of Galilee. 23And he came and
dwelt in a city called Nazareth, that it might
be fulfilled which was spoken by the prophets, "He shall be called a Nazarene."

John the Baptist Prepares the Way

3 In those days John the Baptist came
preaching in the wilderness of Judea,
2and saying, "Repent, for the kingdom of
heaven is at hand!" 3For this is he who was
spoken of by the prophet Isaiah, saying:

> "The voice of one crying in the
> wilderness:
> 'Prepare the way of the LORD;
> Make His paths straight.' "[a]

4Now John himself was clothed in cam-
el's hair, with a leather belt around his waist;
and his food was locusts and wild honey.
5Then Jerusalem, all Judea, and all the region around the Jordan went out to him 6and
were baptized by him in the Jordan, confessing their sins.

7But when he saw many of the Pharisees
and Sadducees coming to his baptism, he
said to them, "Brood of vipers! Who warned
you to flee from the wrath to come? 8There-
fore bear fruits worthy of repentance, 9and
do not think to say to yourselves, 'We have
Abraham as *our* father.' For I say to you that
God is able to raise up children to Abraham
from these stones. 10And even now the ax is
laid to the root of the trees. Therefore every
tree which does not bear good fruit is cut
down and thrown into the fire. 11I indeed

3:3 [a] Isaiah 40:3

THE WISE MEN WORSHIP JESUS

READ IT: MATTHEW 2:1–12

GET IT:

Around the time Jesus was born, a magnificent star showed up in the sky. Astrologers (wise men) far away from Bethlehem studied this special star and concluded that it announced the birth of a king. Wanting to meet the latest king to arrive on earth, the wise men traveled from their homeland (maybe India) toward Judea. It took them a long time to follow the star and track down where Jesus lived with Mary and Joseph. The wise men showed up many months after Jesus was born. He was no longer a baby but a child.

LIVE IT:

It's wonderful that we can think of Jesus as our closest companion and friend. But the wise men remind us that Jesus is also a king who is worthy of our respect, our honor, and our worship. He is the King of kings and Lord of lords. He is the Son of God. There never was as grand or glorious a king as Jesus in the world, and there never will be. Take time to worship and honor Jesus this week. How will knowing that Jesus is the King of the universe affect how you come into His presence and talk to Him?

baptize you with water unto repentance, but
He who is coming after me is mightier than
I, whose sandals I am not worthy to carry.
He will baptize you with the Holy Spirit and fire.[a] 12His winnowing fan *is* in His
hand, and He will thoroughly clean out His
threshing floor, and gather His wheat into
the barn; but He will burn up the chaff with
unquenchable fire."

John Baptizes Jesus

13Then Jesus came from Galilee to John
at the Jordan to be baptized by him. 14And
John *tried to* prevent Him, saying, "I need
to be baptized by You, and are You coming
to me?"
15But Jesus answered and said to him,
"Permit *it to be so* now, for thus it is fitting
for us to fulfill all righteousness." Then he
allowed Him.
16When He had been baptized, Jesus
came up immediately from the water; and
behold, the heavens were opened to Him,
and He[a] saw the Spirit of God descending
like a dove and alighting upon Him. 17And
suddenly a voice *came* from heaven, saying,
"This is My beloved Son, in whom I am well
pleased."

Satan Tempts Jesus

4 Then Jesus was led up by the Spirit
into the wilderness to be tempted by

3:11 [a] M-Text omits *and fire*. 3:16 [a] Or *he*

JESUS' MINISTRY BEGINS

READ IT: MATTHEW 3:1–17

GET IT:

Jesus was thirty years old when He started publicly teaching, speaking, and healing. Up until that time He lived a pretty ordinary life in Nazareth, probably as a carpenter. Now it was time for Him to show who He really was and why He really was on earth. John the Baptist had been telling people about Jesus. Now Jesus went to John the Baptist to be baptized like the other people were doing. When Jesus was baptized, a dove came down from heaven and the voice of God said, "This is My Son" (v. 17). Wow, what an introduction! All the people who were gathered at the Jordan River heard and saw this amazing sight. Jesus was ready now to preach the good news, to perform miracles, and to save people from their sins.

LIVE IT:

Thirty years sounds like a really long time to wait around to do something important in life. Most of us want to be somebody or do something right now, before we get old—like thirty. But sometimes we have to be patient and wait for God's timing, just like Jesus did. When the time was right, Jesus stepped out on the stage of life and made His entrance. It was all in God's timing and in God's plan. Whenever you feel impatient about getting on with your life and doing something big, remember that God's timing and plan are perfect.

the devil. [2]And when He had fasted forty
days and forty nights, afterward He was
hungry. [3]Now when the tempter came to
Him, he said, "If You are the Son of God,
command that these stones become bread."
[4]But He answered and said, "It is written, 'Man shall not live by bread alone, but
by every word that proceeds from the mouth
of God.'"[a]
[5]Then the devil took Him up into the
holy city, set Him on the pinnacle of the temple, [6]and said to Him, "If You are the Son of
God, throw Yourself down. For it is written:

'He shall give His angels charge over
you,'

and,

'In *their* hands they shall bear you up,
Lest you dash your foot against a
stone.'"[a]

[7]Jesus said to him, "It is written again,
'You shall not tempt the LORD your God.'"[a]
[8]Again, the devil took Him up on an exceedingly high mountain, and showed Him
all the kingdoms of the world and their glory. [9]And he said to Him, "All these things I
will give You if You will fall down and worship me."
[10]Then Jesus said to him, "Away with
you,[a] Satan! For it is written, 'You shall worship the LORD your God, and Him only you
shall serve.'"[b]
[11]Then the devil left Him, and behold,
angels came and ministered to Him.

Jesus Begins His Galilean Ministry

[12]Now when Jesus heard that John had
been put in prison, He departed to Galilee.
[13]And leaving Nazareth, He came and dwelt
in Capernaum, which is by the sea, in the
regions of Zebulun and Naphtali, [14]that it
might be fulfilled which was spoken by Isaiah the prophet, saying:

15 "The land of Zebulun and the land of
Naphtali,
By the way of the sea, beyond the
Jordan,
Galilee of the Gentiles:
16 The people who sat in darkness have
seen a great light,
And upon those who sat in the region
and shadow of death
Light has dawned."[a]

In Focus

4:1 The Devil The title of the angel who rebelled against God's authority. The word means "liar," "slanderer," or "accuser." Satan, meaning "Enemy," is his personal name.

4:23 Gospel Means "good news." The word is taken from the early English word *godspel*. In the New Testament, it is the Good News about Jesus Christ.

4:24 Demon-Possessed A person controlled by one or more demons living in him. A demon is an invisible spirit-being who serves Satan.

[17]From that time Jesus began to preach
and to say, "Repent, for the kingdom of heav-
en is at hand."

Four Fishermen Called as Disciples

[18]And Jesus, walking by the Sea of Galilee, saw two brothers, Simon called Peter,
and Andrew his brother, casting a net into
the sea; for they were fishermen. [19]Then He
said to them, "Follow Me, and I will make
you fishers of men." [20]They immediately left
their nets and followed Him.
[21]Going on from there, He saw two other brothers, James *the son* of Zebedee, and
John his brother, in the boat with Zebedee
their father, mending their nets. He called
them, [22]and immediately they left the boat
and their father, and followed Him.

Jesus Heals a Great Multitude

[23]And Jesus went about all Galilee, teaching in their synagogues, preaching the gospel of the kingdom, and healing all kinds
of sickness and all kinds of disease among
the people. [24]Then His fame went throughout all Syria; and they brought to Him all
sick people who were afflicted with various
diseases and torments, and those who were

4:4 [a] Deuteronomy 8:3 **4:6** [a] Psalm 91:11, 12
4:7 [a] Deuteronomy 6:16 **4:10** [a] M-Text reads *Get behind Me.*
[b] Deuteronomy 6:13 **4:16** [a] Isaiah 9:1, 2

demon-possessed, epileptics, and paralyt-
ics; and He healed them. 25 Great multitudes
followed Him—from Galilee, and *from* Decapolis, Jerusalem, Judea, and beyond the
Jordan.

The Beatitudes

5 And seeing the multitudes, He went
up on a mountain, and when He was
seated His disciples came to Him. 2 Then He
opened His mouth and taught them, saying:

3 "Blessed *are* the poor in spirit,
For theirs is the kingdom of heaven.
4 Blessed *are* those who mourn,
For they shall be comforted.
5 Blessed *are* the meek,
For they shall inherit the earth.
6 Blessed *are* those who hunger and thirst
for righteousness,
For they shall be filled.
7 Blessed *are* the merciful,
For they shall obtain mercy.
8 Blessed *are* the pure in heart,
For they shall see God.
9 Blessed *are* the peacemakers,
For they shall be called sons of God.
10 Blessed *are* those who are persecuted for
righteousness' sake,
For theirs is the kingdom of heaven.

11 Blessed are you when they revile and persecute you, and say all kinds of evil against
you falsely for My sake. 12 Rejoice and be exceedingly glad, for great *is* your reward in
heaven, for so they persecuted the prophets
who were before you.

Believers Are Salt and Light

13 "You are the salt of the earth; but if the
salt loses its flavor, how shall it be seasoned?
It is then good for nothing but to be thrown
out and trampled underfoot by men.

14 "You are the light of the world. A city
that is set on a hill cannot be hidden. 15 Nor
do they light a lamp and put it under a basket, but on a lampstand, and it gives light
to all *who are* in the house. 16 Let your light
so shine before men, that they may see
your good works and glorify your Father in
heaven.

Christ Fulfills the Law

17 "Do not think that I came to destroy
the Law or the Prophets. I did not come to

In Focus

5:24 Reconciled Pronounced *RECK-un-cyld*. To be at peace with someone. God is at peace with us because Christ died for our sins. So now we should put our faith in Jesus' death for us and be at peace with God.

destroy but to fulfill. 18 For assuredly, I say
to you, till heaven and earth pass away, one
jot or one tittle will by no means pass from
the law till all is fulfilled. 19 Whoever therefore breaks one of the least of these commandments, and teaches men so, shall be
called least in the kingdom of heaven; but
whoever does and teaches *them*, he shall be
called great in the kingdom of heaven. 20 For
I say to you, that unless your righteousness
exceeds *the righteousness* of the scribes and
Pharisees, you will by no means enter the
kingdom of heaven.

Murder Begins in the Heart

21 "You have heard that it was said to those
of old, 'You shall not murder,[a] and whoever
murders will be in danger of the judgment.'
22 But I say to you that whoever is angry with
his brother without a cause[a] shall be in danger of the judgment. And whoever says to
his brother, 'Raca!' shall be in danger of the
council. But whoever says, 'You fool!' shall
be in danger of hell fire. 23 Therefore if you
bring your gift to the altar, and there remember that your brother has something against
you, 24 leave your gift there before the altar,
and go your way. First be reconciled to your
brother, and then come and offer your gift.
25 Agree with your adversary quickly, while
you are on the way with him, lest your adversary deliver you to the judge, the judge hand
you over to the officer, and you be thrown
into prison. 26 Assuredly, I say to you, you will
by no means get out of there till you have
paid the last penny.

5:21 [a] Exodus 20:13; Deuteronomy 5:17 **5:22** [a] NU-Text omits *without a cause*.

Adultery in the Heart

27 “You have heard that it was said to those
of old,[a] ‘You shall not commit adultery.’ [b]
28 But I say to you that whoever looks at a
woman to lust for her has already committed
adultery with her in his heart. 29 If your right
eye causes you to sin, pluck it out and cast
it from you; for it is more profitable for you
that one of your members perish, than for
your whole body to be cast into hell. 30 And if
your right hand causes you to sin, cut it off
and cast *it* from you; for it is more profitable
for you that one of your members perish,
than for your whole body to be cast into hell.

Marriage Is Sacred and Binding

31 “Furthermore it has been said, ‘Whoever divorces his wife, let him give her a
certificate of divorce.’ 32 But I say to you that
whoever divorces his wife for any reason except sexual immorality[a] causes her to commit adultery; and whoever marries a woman
who is divorced commits adultery.

Jesus Forbids Oaths

33 “Again you have heard that it was said to
those of old, ‘You shall not swear falsely, but
shall perform your oaths to the Lord.’ 34 But
I say to you, do not swear at all: neither by
heaven, for it is God’s throne; 35 nor by the
earth, for it is His footstool; nor by Jerusalem, for it is the city of the great King. 36 Nor
shall you swear by your head, because you

5:27 [a] NU-Text and M-Text omit *to those of old.* [b] Exodus 20:14; Deuteronomy 5:18 **5:32** [a] Or *fornication*

LOVE
LOVE YOUR ENEMIES

READ IT: MATTHEW 5:43, 44

GET IT:

When someone hurts you, it’s easy to want revenge or to drop them from your life. It’s easy to love those we’re close to and hate those who are against us. But Jesus challenges the way we think.

Jesus doesn’t just say, “Love your enemy” and leave it at that. He tells us to do things that aren’t easy to do for someone we consider an enemy.

What about those who curse us? (I need to defend myself!) Jesus says to bless them.

Well, what about those who hate us? (What did I do? Why do I have to like them?) Jesus says like them, and do good to them!

But not the people who use me, right? (It’s not fair!) Jesus says to pray for them.

Jesus’ kind of love is revolutionary. It doesn’t make sense. It challenges the status quo. And it shows people that Christians are different.

LIVE IT:

Love is tough stuff! Think of ways you can bless your enemies and do good to them. Not only will they see your love, others will too, and that will ultimately bring glory to God.

cannot make one hair white or black. 37But
let your 'Yes' be 'Yes,' and your 'No,' 'No.'
For whatever is more than these is from the
evil one.

Go the Second Mile

38"You have heard that it was said, 'An eye
for an eye and a tooth for a tooth.'[a] 39But I tell
you not to resist an evil person. But whoever slaps you on your right cheek, turn the
other to him also. 40If anyone wants to sue
you and take away your tunic, let him have
your cloak also. 41And whoever compels you
to go one mile, go with him two. 42Give to
him who asks you, and from him who wants
to borrow from you do not turn away.

Love Your Enemies

43"You have heard that it was said, 'You
shall love your neighbor[a] and hate your enemy.' 44But I say to you, love your enemies,
bless those who curse you, do good to those
who hate you, and pray for those who spitefully use you and persecute you,[a] 45that you
may be sons of your Father in heaven; for
He makes His sun rise on the evil and on
the good, and sends rain on the just and on
the unjust. 46For if you love those who love
you, what reward have you? Do not even the
tax collectors do the same? 47And if you greet
your brethren[a] only, what do you do more
than others? Do not even the tax collectors[b]
do so? 48Therefore you shall be perfect, just
as your Father in heaven is perfect.

Do Good to Please God

6 "Take heed that you do not do your
charitable deeds before men, to be
seen by them. Otherwise you have no reward
from your Father in heaven. 2Therefore,
when you do a charitable deed, do not sound
a trumpet before you as the hypocrites do in
the synagogues and in the streets, that they
may have glory from men. Assuredly, I say to
you, they have their reward. 3But when you
do a charitable deed, do not let your left hand
know what your right hand is doing, 4that
your charitable deed may be in secret; and
your Father who sees in secret will Himself
reward you openly.[a]

The Model Prayer

5"And when you pray, you shall not be like
the hypocrites. For they love to pray standing
in the synagogues and on the corners of the
streets, that they may be seen by men. Assuredly, I say to you, they have their reward.
6But you, when you pray, go into your room,
and when you have shut your door, pray to
your Father who *is* in the secret *place;* and
your Father who sees in secret will reward
you openly.[a] 7And when you pray, do not use

5:38 [a] Exodus 21:24; Leviticus 24:20; Deuteronomy 19:21
5:43 [a] Compare Leviticus 19:18 5:44 [a] NU-Text omits three clauses from this verse, leaving, *"But I say to you, love your enemies and pray for those who persecute you."*
5:47 [a] M-Text reads *friends.* [b] NU-Text reads *Gentiles.*
6:4 [a] NU-Text omits *openly.* 6:6 [a] NU-Text omits *openly.*

PRAYER

READ IT: MATTHEW 6:5–13

Did you know how we pray matters? Remember:

- It's not a show. If you're praying to impress people around you, don't bother. God would rather have you pray silently by yourself. (He really would!)
- Talk straight when you're talking to God. It's not about big words—just say what you mean.
- Praise God when you pray—don't just present Him with a wish list. Thank Him for who He is and everything good you enjoy—from your friendly dog to your comfy bed.

vain repetitions as the heathen *do*. For they
think that they will be heard for their many
words.

8“Therefore do not be like them. For your
Father knows the things you have need of
before you ask Him. 9In this manner, therefore, pray:

Our Father in heaven,
Hallowed be Your name.
10 Your kingdom come.
Your will be done
On earth as *it is* in heaven.
11 Give us this day our daily bread.
12 And forgive us our debts,
As we forgive our debtors.
13 And do not lead us into temptation,
But deliver us from the evil one.
For Yours is the kingdom and the power
and the glory forever. Amen.[a]

14“For if you forgive men their trespasses,
your heavenly Father will also forgive you.
15But if you do not forgive men their trespasses, neither will your Father forgive your
trespasses.

Fasting to Be Seen Only by God

16“Moreover, when you fast, do not be like
the hypocrites, with a sad countenance. For
they disfigure their faces that they may appear to men to be fasting. Assuredly, I say to
you, they have their reward. 17But you, when
you fast, anoint your head and wash your
face, 18so that you do not appear to men to be
fasting, but to your Father who *is* in the secret *place;* and your Father who sees in secret
will reward you openly.[a]

Lay Up Treasures in Heaven

19“Do not lay up for yourselves treasures
on earth where moth and rust destroy and
where thieves break in and steal; 20but lay up
for yourselves treasures in heaven, where
neither moth nor rust destroys and where
thieves do not break in and steal. 21For where
your treasure is, there your heart will be also.

The Lamp of the Body

22“The lamp of the body is the eye. If
therefore your eye is good, your whole body
will be full of light. 23But if your eye is bad,
your whole body will be full of darkness. If
therefore the light that is in you is darkness,
how great *is* that darkness!

You Cannot Serve God and Riches

24“No one can serve two masters; for

6:24 Mammon Money, wealth, or material goods that are treated as more important than God. To serve mammon is to worship money instead of God.

either he will hate the one and love the other, or else he will be loyal to the one and despise the other. You cannot serve God and
mammon.

Do Not Worry

25“Therefore I say to you, do not worry
about your life, what you will eat or what you
will drink; nor about your body, what you
will put on. Is not life more than food and
the body more than clothing? 26Look at the
birds of the air, for they neither sow nor reap
nor gather into barns; yet your heavenly Father feeds them. Are you not of more value
than they? 27Which of you by worrying can
add one cubit to his stature?

28“So why do you worry about clothing?
Consider the lilies of the field, how they
grow: they neither toil nor spin; 29and yet I
say to you that even Solomon in all his glory
was not arrayed like one of these. 30Now if
God so clothes the grass of the field, which
today is, and tomorrow is thrown into the
oven, *will He* not much more *clothe* you, O
you of little faith?

31“Therefore do not worry, saying, ‘What
shall we eat?’ or ‘What shall we drink?’ or
‘What shall we wear?’ 32For after all these
things the Gentiles seek. For your heavenly
Father knows that you need all these things.
33But seek first the kingdom of God and His
righteousness, and all these things shall be
added to you. 34Therefore do not worry about
tomorrow, for tomorrow will worry about its
own things. Sufficient for the day *is* its own
trouble.

Do Not Judge

7 “Judge not, that you be not judged. 2For
with what judgment you judge, you will

6:13 [a] NU-Text omits *For Yours* through *Amen.* 6:18 [a] NU-Text and M-Text omit *openly.*

be judged; and with the measure you use, it
will be measured back to you. 3And why do
you look at the speck in your brother's eye,
but do not consider the plank in your own
eye? 4Or how can you say to your brother,
'Let me remove the speck from your eye';
and look, a plank *is* in your own eye? 5Hypo-
crite! First remove the plank from your own
eye, and then you will see clearly to remove
the speck from your brother's eye.
6"Do not give what is holy to the dogs; nor
cast your pearls before swine, lest they trample them under their feet, and turn and tear
you in pieces.

Keep Asking, Seeking, Knocking

7"Ask, and it will be given to you; seek,
and you will find; knock, and it will be
opened to you. 8For everyone who asks receives, and he who seeks finds, and to him
who knocks it will be opened. 9Or what man
is there among you who, if his son asks for
bread, will give him a stone? 10Or if he asks
for a fish, will he give him a serpent? 11If you
then, being evil, know how to give good gifts
to your children, how much more will your
Father who is in heaven give good things to
those who ask Him! 12Therefore, whatever
you want men to do to you, do also to them,
for this is the Law and the Prophets.

The Narrow Way

13"Enter by the narrow gate; for wide *is* the
gate and broad *is* the way that leads to destruction, and there are many who go in by
it. 14Because[a] narrow *is* the gate and difficult
is the way which leads to life, and there are
few who find it.

You Will Know Them by Their Fruits

15"Beware of false prophets, who come to
you in sheep's clothing, but inwardly they
are ravenous wolves. 16You will know them
by their fruits. Do men gather grapes from
thornbushes or figs from thistles? 17Even so,
every good tree bears good fruit, but a bad
tree bears bad fruit. 18A good tree cannot bear
bad fruit, nor *can* a bad tree bear good fruit.
19Every tree that does not bear good fruit is
cut down and thrown into the fire. 20There-
fore by their fruits you will know them.

I Never Knew You

21"Not everyone who says to Me, 'Lord,
Lord,' shall enter the kingdom of heaven, but
he who does the will of My Father in heaven.
22Many will say to Me in that day, 'Lord, Lord,
have we not prophesied in Your name, cast
out demons in Your name, and done many
wonders in Your name?' 23And then I will
declare to them, 'I never knew you; depart
from Me, you who practice lawlessness!'

Build on the Rock

24"Therefore whoever hears these sayings
of Mine, and does them, I will liken him to
a wise man who built his house on the rock:
25and the rain descended, the floods came, and
the winds blew and beat on that house; and it
did not fall, for it was founded on the rock.

7:14 [a] NU-Text and M-Text read *How . . . !*

JUDGING OTHERS

READ IT: MATTHEW 7:1–5

Have you ever participated in a service project with your family or church group? How long did it take before you started noticing who wasn't pulling his or her own weight? It's really easy to keep track of who is not working as hard as you are, but almost nobody keeps track of who's *working harder*. Jesus calls us to be honest with ourselves. Should you really be passing judgment when you're not perfect yourself? Can you really sit in the shade and tell someone else to go back to work?

26"But everyone who hears these sayings
of Mine, and does not do them, will be like a
foolish man who built his house on the sand:
27and the rain descended, the floods came,
and the winds blew and beat on that house;
and it fell. And great was its fall."

28And so it was, when Jesus had ended
these sayings, that the people were astonished at His teaching, 29for He taught them as
one having authority, and not as the scribes.

Jesus Cleanses a Leper

8 When He had come down from the
mountain, great multitudes followed
Him. 2And behold, a leper came and worshiped Him, saying, "Lord, if You are willing, You can make me clean."

3Then Jesus put out *His* hand and
touched him, saying, "I am willing; be
cleansed." Immediately his leprosy was
cleansed.

4And Jesus said to him, "See that you
tell no one; but go your way, show yourself
to the priest, and offer the gift that Moses
commanded, as a testimony to them."

Jesus Heals a Centurion's Servant

5Now when Jesus had entered Capernaum, a centurion came to Him, pleading
with Him, 6saying, "Lord, my servant is lying
at home paralyzed, dreadfully tormented."

7And Jesus said to him, "I will come and
heal him."

8The centurion answered and said,
"Lord, I am not worthy that You should come
under my roof. But only speak a word, and
my servant will be healed. 9For I also am a
man under authority, having soldiers under
me. And I say to this *one,* 'Go,' and he goes;
and to another, 'Come,' and he comes; and to
my servant, 'Do this,' and he does *it.*"

10When Jesus heard *it,* He marveled,
and said to those who followed, "Assuredly, I say to you, I have not found such great
faith, not even in Israel! 11And I say to you
that many will come from east and west, and
sit down with Abraham, Isaac, and Jacob in
the kingdom of heaven. 12But the sons of the
kingdom will be cast out into outer darkness. There will be weeping and gnashing
of teeth." 13Then Jesus said to the centurion,
"Go your way; and as you have believed, *so*
let it be done for you." And his servant was
healed that same hour.

Peter's Mother-in-Law Healed

14Now when Jesus had come into Peter's
house, He saw his wife's mother lying sick
with a fever. 15So He touched her hand, and
the fever left her. And she arose and served
them.[a]

Many Healed in the Evening

16When evening had come, they brought
to Him many who were demon-possessed.
And He cast out the spirits with a word, and
healed all who were sick, 17that it might be
fulfilled which was spoken by Isaiah the
prophet, saying:

8:15 [a] NU-Text and M-Text read *Him.*

BULLYING

READ IT: MATTHEW 7:12

Sometimes people who've been bullied become bullies themselves, which kind of makes sense. They're just treating others the way they've been treated. They're just getting even. They're just making things fair. But the Bible says we should live differently than that. It says we should treat others the way we *want* to be treated, not necessarily the way we *have* been treated. That's the Golden Rule.

"He Himself took our infirmities
And bore *our* sicknesses." [a]

The Cost of Discipleship

18And when Jesus saw great multitudes about Him, He gave a command to depart to the other side. 19Then a certain scribe came and said to Him, "Teacher, I will follow You wherever You go."

20And Jesus said to him, "Foxes have holes and birds of the air *have* nests, but the Son of Man has nowhere to lay *His* head."

21Then another of His disciples said to Him, "Lord, let me first go and bury my father."

22But Jesus said to him, "Follow Me, and let the dead bury their own dead."

Wind and Wave Obey Jesus

23Now when He got into a boat, His disciples followed Him. 24And suddenly a great tempest arose on the sea, so that the boat was covered with the waves. But He was asleep. 25Then His disciples came to *Him* and awoke Him, saying, "Lord, save us! We are perishing!"

26But He said to them, "Why are you fearful, O you of little faith?" Then He arose and rebuked the winds and the sea, and there was a great calm. 27So the men marveled, saying, "Who can this be, that even the winds and the sea obey Him?"

Two Demon-Possessed Men Healed

28When He had come to the other side, to the country of the Gergesenes,[a] there met Him two demon-possessed *men,* coming out of the tombs, exceedingly fierce, so that no one could pass that way. 29And suddenly they cried out, saying, "What have we to do with You, Jesus, You Son of God? Have You come here to torment us before the time?"

30Now a good way off from them there was a herd of many swine feeding. 31So the demons begged Him, saying, "If You cast us out, permit us to go away[a] into the herd of swine."

32And He said to them, "Go." So when they had come out, they went into the herd of swine. And suddenly the whole herd of swine ran violently down the steep place into the sea, and perished in the water.

33Then those who kept *them* fled; and they went away into the city and told everything, including what *had happened* to the demon-possessed *men.* 34And behold, the whole city came out to meet Jesus. And when they saw Him, they begged *Him* to depart from their region.

Jesus Forgives and Heals a Paralytic

9 So He got into a boat, crossed over, and came to His own city. 2Then behold, they brought to Him a paralytic lying on a bed. When Jesus saw their faith, He said to the paralytic, "Son, be of good cheer; your sins are forgiven you."

3And at once some of the scribes said within themselves, "This Man blasphemes!"

4But Jesus, knowing their thoughts, said, "Why do you think evil in your hearts? 5For which is easier, to say, '*Your* sins are forgiven you,' or to say, 'Arise and walk'? 6But that you may know that the Son of Man has power on earth to forgive sins"—then He said to the paralytic, "Arise, take up your bed, and go to your house." 7And he arose and departed to his house.

8Now when the multitudes saw *it,* they marveled[a] and glorified God, who had given such power to men.

Matthew the Tax Collector

9As Jesus passed on from there, He saw a man named Matthew sitting at the tax office. And He said to him, "Follow Me." So he arose and followed Him.

10Now it happened, as Jesus sat at the table in the house, *that* behold, many tax collectors and sinners came and sat down with Him and His disciples. 11And when the Pharisees saw *it,* they said to His disciples, "Why does your Teacher eat with tax collectors and sinners?"

12When Jesus heard *that,* He said to them, "Those who are well have no need of a physician, but those who are sick. 13But go and learn what *this* means: 'I desire mercy and not sacrifice.' [a] For I did not come to call the righteous, but sinners, to repentance." [b]

Jesus Is Questioned About Fasting

14Then the disciples of John came to Him, saying, "Why do we and the Pharisees fast often,[a] but Your disciples do not fast?"

8:17 [a] Isaiah 53:4 **8:28** [a] NU-Text reads *Gadarenes.* **8:31** [a] NU-Text reads *send us.* **9:8** [a] NU-Text reads *were afraid.* **9:13** [a] Hosea 6:6 [b] NU-Text omits *to repentance.* **9:14** [a] NU-Text brackets *often* as disputed.

15 And Jesus said to them, "Can the
friends of the bridegroom mourn as long
as the bridegroom is with them? But the
days will come when the bridegroom will
be taken away from them, and then they
will fast. 16 No one puts a piece of unshrunk
cloth on an old garment; for the patch pulls
away from the garment, and the tear is made
worse. 17 Nor do they put new wine into old
wineskins, or else the wineskins break, the
wine is spilled, and the wineskins are ruined. But they put new wine into new wineskins, and both are preserved."

A Girl Restored to Life and a Woman Healed

18 While He spoke these things to them,
behold, a ruler came and worshiped Him,
saying, "My daughter has just died, but
come and lay Your hand on her and she will
live." 19 So Jesus arose and followed him, and
so *did* His disciples.
20 And suddenly, a woman who had a flow
of blood for twelve years came from behind
and touched the hem of His garment. 21 For
she said to herself, "If only I may touch His
garment, I shall be made well." 22 But Jesus
turned around, and when He saw her He
said, "Be of good cheer, daughter; your faith
has made you well." And the woman was
made well from that hour.
23 When Jesus came into the ruler's house,
and saw the flute players and the noisy crowd
wailing, 24 He said to them, "Make room, for
the girl is not dead, but sleeping." And they
ridiculed Him. 25 But when the crowd was
put outside, He went in and took her by the
hand, and the girl arose. 26 And the report of
this went out into all that land.

Two Blind Men Healed

27 When Jesus departed from there, two
blind men followed Him, crying out and saying, "Son of David, have mercy on us!"
28 And when He had come into the house,
the blind men came to Him. And Jesus said
to them, "Do you believe that I am able to
do this?"
They said to Him, "Yes, Lord."
29 Then He touched their eyes, saying,
"According to your faith let it be to you."
30 And their eyes were opened. And Jesus
sternly warned them, saying, "See *that* no
one knows *it*." 31 But when they had departed,

In Focus

9:33 Demon An invisible spirit-being who is a servant of Satan. Demons can live in people and hurt them. Demons also cause people to curse God and His people.

they spread the news about Him in all that
country.

A Mute Man Speaks

32 As they went out, behold, they brought
to Him a man, mute and demon-possessed.
33 And when the demon was cast out, the
mute spoke. And the multitudes marveled,
saying, "It was never seen like this in Israel!"
34 But the Pharisees said, "He casts out
demons by the ruler of the demons."

The Compassion of Jesus

35 Then Jesus went about all the cities
and villages, teaching in their synagogues,
preaching the gospel of the kingdom, and
healing every sickness and every disease
among the people.[a] 36 But when He saw the
multitudes, He was moved with compassion
for them, because they were weary[a] and scattered, like sheep having no shepherd. 37 Then
He said to His disciples, "The harvest truly
is plentiful, but the laborers *are* few. 38 Therefore pray the Lord of the harvest to send out
laborers into His harvest."

The Twelve Apostles

10 And when He had called His twelve
disciples to *Him,* He gave them
power *over* unclean spirits, to cast them out,
and to heal all kinds of sickness and all kinds
of disease. 2 Now the names of the twelve
apostles are these: first, Simon, who is called
Peter, and Andrew his brother; James the *son*
of Zebedee, and John his brother; 3 Philip and
Bartholomew; Thomas and Matthew the tax
collector; James the *son* of Alphaeus, and
Lebbaeus, whose surname was[a] Thaddaeus;

9:35 [a] NU-Text omits *among the people.* 9:36 [a] NU-Text and M-Text read *harassed.* 10:3 [a] NU-Text omits *Lebbaeus, whose surname was.*

4 Simon the Cananite,[a] and Judas Iscariot, who also betrayed Him.

Sending Out the Twelve

5 These twelve Jesus sent out and commanded them, saying: "Do not go into the way of the Gentiles, and do not enter a city of the Samaritans. 6 But go rather to the lost sheep of the house of Israel. 7 And as you go, preach, saying, 'The kingdom of heaven is at hand.' 8 Heal the sick, cleanse the lepers, raise the dead,[a] cast out demons. Freely you have received, freely give. 9 Provide neither gold nor silver nor copper in your money belts, 10 nor bag for *your* journey, nor two tunics, nor sandals, nor staffs; for a worker is worthy of his food.

11 "Now whatever city or town you enter, inquire who in it is worthy, and stay there till you go out. 12 And when you go into a household, greet it. 13 If the household is worthy, let your peace come upon it. But if it is not worthy, let your peace return to you. 14 And whoever will not receive you nor hear your words, when you depart from that house or city, shake off the dust from your feet. 15 Assuredly, I say to you, it will be more tolerable for the land of Sodom and Gomorrah in the day of judgment than for that city!

Persecutions Are Coming

16 "Behold, I send you out as sheep in the midst of wolves. Therefore be wise as serpents and harmless as doves. 17 But beware of men, for they will deliver you up to councils and scourge you in their synagogues. 18 You will be brought before governors and kings for My sake, as a testimony to them and to the Gentiles. 19 But when they deliver you up, do not worry about how or what you should speak. For it will be given to you in that hour what you should speak; 20 for it is not you who speak, but the Spirit of your Father who speaks in you.

21 "Now brother will deliver up brother to death, and a father *his* child; and children will rise up against parents and cause them to be put to death. 22 And you will be hated by all for My name's sake. But he who endures to the end will be saved. 23 When they persecute you in this city, flee to another. For assuredly, I say to you, you will not have gone through the cities of Israel before the Son of Man comes.

In Focus

10:2 Apostle Pronounced *uh-POSS-ul.* One of the men Jesus sent to preach the Good News of salvation. The word comes from a Greek word meaning "sent."

10:24 Disciple Pronounced *dih-SIGH-pul.* A learner or pupil. A Christian is a pupil of Jesus. The Holy Spirit teaches us to become like Jesus, as we are shown in the Bible.

24 "A disciple is not above *his* teacher, nor a servant above his master. 25 It is enough for a disciple that he be like his teacher, and a servant like his master. If they have called the master of the house Beelzebub,[a] how much more *will they call* those of his household! 26 Therefore do not fear them. For there is nothing covered that will not be revealed, and hidden that will not be known.

Jesus Teaches the Fear of God

27 "Whatever I tell you in the dark, speak in the light; and what you hear in the ear, preach on the housetops. 28 And do not fear those who kill the body but cannot kill the soul. But rather fear Him who is able to destroy both soul and body in hell. 29 Are not two sparrows sold for a copper coin? And not one of them falls to the ground apart from your Father's will. 30 But the very hairs of your head are all numbered. 31 Do not fear therefore; you are of more value than many sparrows.

Confess Christ Before Men

32 "Therefore whoever confesses Me before men, him I will also confess before My Father who is in heaven. 33 But whoever denies Me before men, him I will also deny before My Father who is in heaven.

Christ Brings Division

34 "Do not think that I came to bring peace

10:4 [a] NU-Text reads *Cananaean.* **10:8** [a] NU-Text reads *raise the dead, cleanse the lepers;* M-Text omits *raise the dead.* **10:25** [a] NU-Text and M-Text read *Beelzebul.*

on earth. I did not come to bring peace but a sword. 35For I have come to 'set a man against his father, a daughter against her mother, and a daughter-in-law against her mother-in-law'; 36and 'a man's enemies *will be* those of his *own* household.'[a] 37He who loves father or mother more than Me is not worthy of Me. And he who loves son or daughter more than Me is not worthy of Me. 38And he who does not take his cross and follow after Me is not worthy of Me. 39He who finds his life will lose it, and he who loses his life for My sake will find it.

A Cup of Cold Water

40"He who receives you receives Me, and he who receives Me receives Him who sent Me. 41He who receives a prophet in the name of a prophet shall receive a prophet's reward. And he who receives a righteous man in the name of a righteous man shall receive a righteous man's reward. 42And whoever gives one of these little ones only a cup of cold *water* in the name of a disciple, assuredly, I say to you, he shall by no means lose his reward."

John the Baptist Sends Messengers to Jesus

11 Now it came to pass, when Jesus finished commanding His twelve disciples, that He departed from there to teach and to preach in their cities.

2And when John had heard in prison about the works of Christ, he sent two of[a] his disciples 3and said to Him, "Are You the Coming One, or do we look for another?"

4Jesus answered and said to them, "Go and tell John the things which you hear and see: 5*The* blind see and *the* lame walk; *the* lepers are cleansed and *the* deaf hear; *the* dead are raised up and *the* poor have the gospel preached to them. 6And blessed is he who is not offended because of Me."

7As they departed, Jesus began to say to the multitudes concerning John: "What did you go out into the wilderness to see? A reed shaken by the wind? 8But what did you go out to see? A man clothed in soft garments? Indeed, those who wear soft *clothing* are in kings' houses. 9But what did you go out to see? A prophet? Yes, I say to you, and more than a prophet. 10For this is *he* of whom it is written:

'Behold, I send My messenger before
Your face,
Who will prepare Your way before
You.'[a]

11"Assuredly, I say to you, among those born of women there has not risen one greater than John the Baptist; but he who is least in the kingdom of heaven is greater than he. 12And from the days of John the Baptist until now the kingdom of heaven suffers violence, and the violent take it by force. 13For all the prophets and the law prophesied until John. 14And if you are willing to receive *it*, he is Elijah who is to come. 15He who has ears to hear, let him hear!

16"But to what shall I liken this generation? It is like children sitting in the marketplaces and calling to their companions, 17and saying:

'We played the flute for you,
And you did not dance;
We mourned to you,
And you did not lament.'

18For John came neither eating nor drinking, and they say, 'He has a demon.' 19The Son of Man came eating and drinking, and they say, 'Look, a glutton and a winebibber, a friend of tax collectors and sinners!' But wisdom is justified by her children."[a]

Woe to the Impenitent Cities

20Then He began to rebuke the cities in which most of His mighty works had been done, because they did not repent: 21"Woe to you, Chorazin! Woe to you, Bethsaida! For if the mighty works which were done in you had been done in Tyre and Sidon, they would have repented long ago in sackcloth and ashes. 22But I say to you, it will be more tolerable for Tyre and Sidon in the day of judgment than for you. 23And you, Capernaum, who are exalted to heaven, will be[a] brought down to Hades; for if the mighty works which were done in you had been done in Sodom, it would have remained until this day. 24But I say to you that it shall be more tolerable for the land of Sodom in the day of judgment than for you."

10:36 [a] Micah 7:6 **11:2** [a] NU-Text reads *by* for *two of*. **11:10** [a] Malachi 3:1 **11:19** [a] NU-Text reads *works*. **11:23** [a] NU-Text reads *will you be exalted to heaven? No, you will be.*

Jesus Gives True Rest

25At that time Jesus answered and said, "I
thank You, Father, Lord of heaven and earth,
that You have hidden these things from *the*
wise and prudent and have revealed them
to babes. 26Even so, Father, for so it seemed
good in Your sight. 27All things have been
delivered to Me by My Father, and no one
knows the Son except the Father. Nor does
anyone know the Father except the Son,
and *the one* to whom the Son wills to reveal
Him. 28Come to Me, all *you* who labor and are
heavy laden, and I will give you rest. 29Take
My yoke upon you and learn from Me, for I
am gentle and lowly in heart, and you will
find rest for your souls. 30For My yoke *is* easy
and My burden is light."

Jesus Is Lord of the Sabbath

12 At that time Jesus went through
the grainfields on the Sabbath.
And His disciples were hungry, and began
to pluck heads of grain and to eat. 2And
when the Pharisees saw *it,* they said to Him,
"Look, Your disciples are doing what is not
lawful to do on the Sabbath!"

3But He said to them, "Have you not
read what David did when he was hungry,
he and those who were with him: 4how he
entered the house of God and ate the showbread which was not lawful for him to eat,
nor for those who were with him, but only
for the priests? 5Or have you not read in the
law that on the Sabbath the priests in the
temple profane the Sabbath, and are blameless? 6Yet I say to you that in this place there
is *One* greater than the temple. 7But if you
had known what *this* means, 'I desire mercy
and not sacrifice,'[a] you would not have condemned the guiltless. 8For the Son of Man is
Lord even[a] of the Sabbath."

Healing on the Sabbath

9Now when He had departed from there,
He went into their synagogue. 10And behold,
there was a man who had a withered hand.
And they asked Him, saying, "Is it lawful
to heal on the Sabbath?"—that they might
accuse Him.

11Then He said to them, "What man is
there among you who has one sheep, and if
it falls into a pit on the Sabbath, will not lay
hold of it and lift *it* out? 12Of how much more
value then is a man than a sheep? Therefore it is lawful to do good on the Sabbath."

In Focus

12:9 Synagogue Pronounced *SIN-uh-gog.* From a Greek word meaning "gather together." The Jews have worshiped at buildings called synagogues ever since they lived in countries where they could no longer go to the temple.

13Then He said to the man, "Stretch out your
hand." And he stretched *it* out, and it was
restored as whole as the other. 14Then the
Pharisees went out and plotted against Him,
how they might destroy Him.

Behold, My Servant

15But when Jesus knew *it,* He withdrew
from there. And great multitudes[a] followed Him, and He healed them all. 16Yet
He warned them not to make Him known,
17that it might be fulfilled which was spoken
by Isaiah the prophet, saying:

18 "Behold! My Servant whom I have chosen,
My Beloved in whom My soul is well pleased!
I will put My Spirit upon Him,
And He will declare justice to the Gentiles.
19 He will not quarrel nor cry out,
Nor will anyone hear His voice in the streets.
20 A bruised reed He will not break,
And smoking flax He will not quench,
Till He sends forth justice to victory;
21 And in His name Gentiles will trust."[a]

A House Divided Cannot Stand

22Then one was brought to Him who was
demon-possessed, blind and mute; and He
healed him, so that the blind and[a] mute man
both spoke and saw. 23And all the multitudes
were amazed and said, "Could this be the
Son of David?"

24Now when the Pharisees heard it they

12:7 [a] Hosea 6:6 12:8 [a] NU-Text and M-Text omit *even.*
12:15 [a] NU-Text brackets *multitudes* as disputed.
12:21 [a] Isaiah 42:1–4 12:22 [a] NU-Text omits *blind and.*

said, "This *fellow* does not cast out demons
except by Beelzebub,[a] the ruler of the
demons."

25But Jesus knew their thoughts, and said
to them: "Every kingdom divided against itself is brought to desolation, and every city
or house divided against itself will not stand.
26If Satan casts out Satan, he is divided
against himself. How then will his kingdom
stand? 27And if I cast out demons by Beelzebub, by whom do your sons cast *them* out?
Therefore they shall be your judges. 28But if
I cast out demons by the Spirit of God, surely the kingdom of God has come upon you.
29Or how can one enter a strong man's house
and plunder his goods, unless he first binds
the strong man? And then he will plunder
his house. 30He who is not with Me is against
Me, and he who does not gather with Me
scatters abroad.

The Unpardonable Sin

31"Therefore I say to you, every sin and
blasphemy will be forgiven men, but the
blasphemy *against* the Spirit will not be
forgiven men. 32Anyone who speaks a word
against the Son of Man, it will be forgiven
him; but whoever speaks against the Holy
Spirit, it will not be forgiven him, either in
this age or in the *age* to come.

A Tree Known by Its Fruit

33"Either make the tree good and its fruit
good, or else make the tree bad and its fruit
bad; for a tree is known by *its* fruit. 34Brood
of vipers! How can you, being evil, speak
good things? For out of the abundance of
the heart the mouth speaks. 35A good man
out of the good treasure of his heart[a] brings
forth good things, and an evil man out of the
evil treasure brings forth evil things. 36But I
say to you that for every idle word men may
speak, they will give account of it in the day
of judgment. 37For by your words you will
be justified, and by your words you will be
condemned."

The Scribes and Pharisees Ask for a Sign

38Then some of the scribes and Pharisees
answered, saying, "Teacher, we want to see a
sign from You."

39But He answered and said to them, "An
evil and adulterous generation seeks after a
sign, and no sign will be given to it except
the sign of the prophet Jonah. 40For as Jonah
was three days and three nights in the belly
of the great fish, so will the Son of Man be
three days and three nights in the heart of
the earth. 41The men of Nineveh will rise up
in the judgment with this generation and
condemn it, because they repented at the
preaching of Jonah; and indeed a greater
than Jonah *is* here. 42The queen of the South
will rise up in the judgment with this generation and condemn it, for she came from the
ends of the earth to hear the wisdom of Solomon; and indeed a greater than Solomon
is here.

An Unclean Spirit Returns

43"When an unclean spirit goes out of a
man, he goes through dry places, seeking
rest, and finds none. 44Then he says, 'I will
return to my house from which I came.' And
when he comes, he finds *it* empty, swept,
and put in order. 45Then he goes and takes
with him seven other spirits more wicked
than himself, and they enter and dwell there;
and the last *state* of that man is worse than
the first. So shall it also be with this wicked
generation."

Jesus' Mother and Brothers Send for Him

46While He was still talking to the multitudes, behold, His mother and brothers
stood outside, seeking to speak with Him.
47Then one said to Him, "Look, Your mother and Your brothers are standing outside,
seeking to speak with You."

48But He answered and said to the one
who told Him, "Who is My mother and
who are My brothers?" 49And He stretched
out His hand toward His disciples and said,
"Here are My mother and My brothers! 50For
whoever does the will of My Father in heav-
en is My brother and sister and mother."

The Parable of the Sower

13 On the same day Jesus went out of
the house and sat by the sea. 2And
great multitudes were gathered together to
Him, so that He got into a boat and sat; and
the whole multitude stood on the shore.

3Then He spoke many things to them
in parables, saying: "Behold, a sower went
out to sow. 4And as he sowed, some *seed*
fell by the wayside; and the birds came and

12:24 [a] NU-Text and M-Text read *Beelzebul.* 12:35 [a] NU-Text and M-Text omit *of his heart.*

devoured them. 5Some fell on stony places,
where they did not have much earth; and
they immediately sprang up because they
had no depth of earth. 6But when the sun
was up they were scorched, and because they
had no root they withered away. 7And some
fell among thorns, and the thorns sprang up
and choked them. 8But others fell on good
ground and yielded a crop: some a hundredfold, some sixty, some thirty. 9He who has
ears to hear, let him hear!"

The Purpose of Parables

10And the disciples came and said to Him,
"Why do You speak to them in parables?"
11He answered and said to them, "Because it has been given to you to know the
mysteries of the kingdom of heaven, but to
them it has not been given. 12For whoever
has, to him more will be given, and he will
have abundance; but whoever does not have,
even what he has will be taken away from
him. 13Therefore I speak to them in parables,
because seeing they do not see, and hearing
they do not hear, nor do they understand.
14And in them the prophecy of Isaiah is fulfilled, which says:

'Hearing you will hear and shall not
understand,
And seeing you will see and not
perceive;
15 For the hearts of this people have grown
dull.
Their ears are hard of hearing,
And their eyes they have closed,
Lest they should see with *their* eyes and
hear with *their* ears,
Lest they should understand with *their*
hearts and turn,
So that I should[a] heal them.'[b]

16But blessed *are* your eyes for they see, and
your ears for they hear; 17for assuredly, I say
to you that many prophets and righteous
men desired to see what you see, and did not
see *it*, and to hear what you hear, and did not
hear *it*.

The Parable of the Sower Explained

18"Therefore hear the parable of the sower: 19When anyone hears the word of the
kingdom, and does not understand *it*, then
the wicked *one* comes and snatches away
what was sown in his heart. This is he who
received seed by the wayside. 20But he who
received the seed on stony places, this is he
who hears the word and immediately receives it with joy; 21yet he has no root in himself, but endures only for a while. For when
tribulation or persecution arises because of
the word, immediately he stumbles. 22Now

13:15 [a] NU-Text and M-Text read *would*. [b] Isaiah 6:9, 10

13:3–9 FOUR KINDS OF SOIL

Telling others about Jesus is like planting wheat. In order to have a good crop, you have to scatter seed everywhere in the field. Some of the seed falls on bad ground and never grows, but the farmer expects that much of his seed will come up and multiply.

Jesus says that spreading the gospel is like that. Some people are like the hard ground. They're too hard-hearted to listen to the Good News of Jesus. Others aren't very serious about being Christians. They're like shallow, stony ground. Still others are more concerned about making money than pleasing God. They're like the seed choked by thorny weeds.

Are you like the good kind of soil? If so, you will grow up and multiply yourself many times by leading many others to know the Savior.

he who received seed among the thorns is
he who hears the word, and the cares of this
world and the deceitfulness of riches choke
the word, and he becomes unfruitful. 23But
he who received seed on the good ground is
he who hears the word and understands *it,*
who indeed bears fruit and produces: some a
hundredfold, some sixty, some thirty."

The Parable of the Wheat and the Tares

24Another parable He put forth to them,
saying: "The kingdom of heaven is like a
man who sowed good seed in his field; 25but
while men slept, his enemy came and sowed
tares among the wheat and went his way.
26But when the grain had sprouted and produced a crop, then the tares also appeared.
27So the servants of the owner came and said
to him, 'Sir, did you not sow good seed in
your field? How then does it have tares?'
28He said to them, 'An enemy has done this.'
The servants said to him, 'Do you want us
then to go and gather them up?' 29But he
said, 'No, lest while you gather up the tares
you also uproot the wheat with them. 30Let
both grow together until the harvest, and at
the time of harvest I will say to the reapers,
"First gather together the tares and bind
them in bundles to burn them, but gather
the wheat into my barn." ' "

The Parable of the Mustard Seed

31Another parable He put forth to them,
saying: "The kingdom of heaven is like a
mustard seed, which a man took and sowed
in his field, 32which indeed is the least of all
the seeds; but when it is grown it is greater
than the herbs and becomes a tree, so that
the birds of the air come and nest in its
branches."

The Parable of the Leaven

33Another parable He spoke to them:
"The kingdom of heaven is like leaven,
which a woman took and hid in three measures[a] of meal till it was all leavened."

Prophecy and the Parables

34All these things Jesus spoke to the multitude in parables; and without a parable
He did not speak to them, 35that it might be
fulfilled which was spoken by the prophet,
saying:

"I will open My mouth in parables;
I will utter things kept secret from the
foundation of the world." [a]

The Parable of the Tares Explained

36Then Jesus sent the multitude away
and went into the house. And His disciples
came to Him, saying, "Explain to us the parable of the tares of the field."
37He answered and said to them: "He
who sows the good seed is the Son of Man.
38The field is the world, the good seeds are
the sons of the kingdom, but the tares are
the sons of the wicked *one.* 39The enemy
who sowed them is the devil, the harvest is
the end of the age, and the reapers are the
angels. 40Therefore as the tares are gathered
and burned in the fire, so it will be at the
end of this age. 41The Son of Man will send
out His angels, and they will gather out of
His kingdom all things that offend, and
those who practice lawlessness, 42and will
cast them into the furnace of fire. There will
be wailing and gnashing of teeth. 43Then the
righteous will shine forth as the sun in the
kingdom of their Father. He who has ears to
hear, let him hear!

The Parable of the Hidden Treasure

44"Again, the kingdom of heaven is like
treasure hidden in a field, which a man
found and hid; and for joy over it he goes
and sells all that he has and buys that field.

The Parable of the Pearl of Great Price

45"Again, the kingdom of heaven is like
a merchant seeking beautiful pearls, 46who,
when he had found one pearl of great price,
went and sold all that he had and bought it.

The Parable of the Dragnet

47"Again, the kingdom of heaven is like
a dragnet that was cast into the sea and
gathered some of every kind, 48which, when
it was full, they drew to shore; and they sat
down and gathered the good into vessels, but
threw the bad away. 49So it will be at the end
of the age. The angels will come forth, separate the wicked from among the just, 50and
cast them into the furnace of fire. There will
be wailing and gnashing of teeth."

13:33 [a] Greek *sata,* approximately two pecks in all
13:35 [a] Psalm 78:2

51Jesus said to them,[a] "Have you understood all these things?"
They said to Him, "Yes, Lord."[b]
52Then He said to them, "Therefore every
scribe instructed concerning[a] the kingdom
of heaven is like a householder who brings
out of his treasure *things* new and old."

Jesus Rejected at Nazareth

53Now it came to pass, when Jesus had
finished these parables, that He departed
from there. 54When He had come to His
own country, He taught them in their synagogue, so that they were astonished and
said, "Where did this *Man* get this wisdom
and *these* mighty works? 55Is this not the carpenter's son? Is not His mother called Mary?
And His brothers James, Joses,[a] Simon, and
Judas? 56And His sisters, are they not all with
us? Where then did this *Man* get all these
things?" 57So they were offended at Him.
But Jesus said to them, "A prophet is not
without honor except in his own country
and in his own house." 58Now He did not do
many mighty works there because of their
unbelief.

John the Baptist Beheaded

14 At that time Herod the tetrarch
heard the report about Jesus 2and
said to his servants, "This is John the Baptist; he is risen from the dead, and therefore
these powers are at work in him." 3For Herod
had laid hold of John and bound him, and
put *him* in prison for the sake of Herodias,
his brother Philip's wife. 4Because John had
said to him, "It is not lawful for you to have
her." 5And although he wanted to put him to
death, he feared the multitude, because they
counted him as a prophet.
6But when Herod's birthday was celebrated, the daughter of Herodias danced before
them and pleased Herod. 7Therefore he
promised with an oath to give her whatever
she might ask.
8So she, having been prompted by her
mother, said, "Give me John the Baptist's
head here on a platter."
9And the king was sorry; nevertheless,
because of the oaths and because of those
who sat with him, he commanded *it* to
be given to *her*. 10So he sent and had John
beheaded in prison. 11And his head was
brought on a platter and given to the girl,
and she brought *it* to her mother. 12Then his
disciples came and took away the body and
buried it, and went and told Jesus.

Feeding the Five Thousand

13When Jesus heard *it*, He departed from
there by boat to a deserted place by Himself.
But when the multitudes heard it, they followed Him on foot from the cities. 14And
when Jesus went out He saw a great multitude; and He was moved with compassion
for them, and healed their sick. 15When it
was evening, His disciples came to Him,
saying, "This is a deserted place, and the
hour is already late. Send the multitudes
away, that they may go into the villages and
buy themselves food."
16But Jesus said to them, "They do not
need to go away. You give them something
to eat."
17And they said to Him, "We have here
only five loaves and two fish."
18He said, "Bring them here to Me."
19Then He commanded the multitudes to
sit down on the grass. And He took the five
loaves and the two fish, and looking up to
heaven, He blessed and broke and gave the
loaves to the disciples; and the disciples gave
to the multitudes. 20So they all ate and were
filled, and they took up twelve baskets full
of the fragments that remained. 21Now those
who had eaten were about five thousand
men, besides women and children.

Jesus Walks on the Sea

22Immediately Jesus made His disciples
get into the boat and go before Him to the
other side, while He sent the multitudes
away. 23And when He had sent the multitudes away, He went up on the mountain by
Himself to pray. Now when evening came,
He was alone there. 24But the boat was now
in the middle of the sea,[a] tossed by the
waves, for the wind was contrary.
25Now in the fourth watch of the night
Jesus went to them, walking on the sea.
26And when the disciples saw Him walking
on the sea, they were troubled, saying, "It is
a ghost!" And they cried out for fear.
27But immediately Jesus spoke to them,
saying, "Be of good cheer! It is I; do not be
afraid."

13:51 [a] NU-Text omits *Jesus said to them*. [b] NU-Text omits *Lord*. 13:52 [a] Or *for* 13:55 [a] NU-Text reads *Joseph*.
14:24 [a] NU-Text reads *many furlongs away from the land*.

28And Peter answered Him and said,
"Lord, if it is You, command me to come to
You on the water."
29So He said, "Come." And when Peter
had come down out of the boat, he walked
on the water to go to Jesus. 30But when he
saw that the wind *was* boisterous,[a] he was
afraid; and beginning to sink he cried out,
saying, "Lord, save me!"
31And immediately Jesus stretched out
His hand and caught him, and said to him,
"O you of little faith, why did you doubt?"
32And when they got into the boat, the wind
ceased.
33Then those who were in the boat came
and[a] worshiped Him, saying, "Truly You are
the Son of God."

Many Touch Him and Are Made Well

34When they had crossed over, they came
to the land of[a] Gennesaret. 35And when the
men of that place recognized Him, they sent
out into all that surrounding region, brought
to Him all who were sick, 36and begged Him
that they might only touch the hem of His
garment. And as many as touched *it* were
made perfectly well.

Defilement Comes from Within

15 Then the scribes and Pharisees who
were from Jerusalem came to Jesus,
saying, 2"Why do Your disciples transgress
the tradition of the elders? For they do not
wash their hands when they eat bread."
3He answered and said to them, "Why
do you also transgress the commandment
of God because of your tradition? 4For God
commanded, saying, 'Honor your father and
your mother';[a] and, 'He who curses father
or mother, let him be put to death.'[b] 5But you
say, 'Whoever says to his father or mother,
"Whatever profit you might have received
from me *is* a gift *to God*"— 6then he need
not honor his father or mother.'[a] Thus you
have made the commandment[b] of God of no
effect by your tradition. 7Hypocrites! Well
did Isaiah prophesy about you, saying:

8 'These people draw near to Me with
their mouth,
And[a] honor Me with *their* lips,
But their heart is far from Me.
9 And in vain they worship Me,
Teaching *as* doctrines the
commandments of men.' "[a]

10When He had called the multitude to
Himself, He said to them, "Hear and understand: 11Not what goes into the mouth defiles

14:30 [a] NU-Text brackets *that* and *boisterous* as disputed. **14:33** [a] NU-Text omits *came and.* **14:34** [a] NU-Text reads *came to land at.* **15:4** [a] Exodus 20:12; Deuteronomy 5:16 [b] Exodus 21:17 **15:6** [a] NU-Text omits *or mother.* [b] NU-Text reads *word.* **15:8** [a] NU-Text omits *draw near to Me with their mouth, And.* **15:9** [a] Isaiah 29:13

DOUBT AND ASKING QUESTIONS

READ IT: MATTHEW 14:22–36

Jesus' disciples experienced doubt, so surely He isn't surprised when we have doubts of our own. Look at this famous story of Peter walking on the water. Even though he knew Jesus and loved Him, Peter still bounced between courage and uncertainty—between belief and doubt. Jumping over the side of the boat strengthened Peter's faith and the faith of the other disciples. The same is true today. If you're willing to be honest with Jesus in all your emotions—including fear and doubt—He'll be there to catch you.

a man; but what comes out of the mouth,
this defiles a man."
12 Then His disciples came and said to
Him, "Do You know that the Pharisees were
offended when they heard this saying?"
13 But He answered and said, "Every plant
which My heavenly Father has not planted
will be uprooted. 14 Let them alone. They are
blind leaders of the blind. And if the blind
leads the blind, both will fall into a ditch."
15 Then Peter answered and said to Him,
"Explain this parable to us."
16 So Jesus said, "Are you also still without
understanding? 17 Do you not yet understand
that whatever enters the mouth goes into
the stomach and is eliminated? 18 But those
things which proceed out of the mouth
come from the heart, and they defile a man.
19 For out of the heart proceed evil thoughts,
murders, adulteries, fornications, thefts,
false witness, blasphemies. 20 These are *the
things* which defile a man, but to eat with unwashed hands does not defile a man."

A Gentile Shows Her Faith

21 Then Jesus went out from there and departed to the region of Tyre and Sidon. 22 And
behold, a woman of Canaan came from that
region and cried out to Him, saying, "Have
mercy on me, O Lord, Son of David! My
daughter is severely demon-possessed."
23 But He answered her not a word.
And His disciples came and urged Him,
saying, "Send her away, for she cries out after us."
24 But He answered and said, "I was not
sent except to the lost sheep of the house of
Israel."
25 Then she came and worshiped Him,
saying, "Lord, help me!"
26 But He answered and said, "It is not
good to take the children's bread and throw
it to the little dogs."
27 And she said, "Yes, Lord, yet even the
little dogs eat the crumbs which fall from
their masters' table."
28 Then Jesus answered and said to her,
"O woman, great *is* your faith! Let it be to you
as you desire." And her daughter was healed
from that very hour.

Jesus Heals Great Multitudes

29 Jesus departed from there, skirted the
Sea of Galilee, and went up on the mountain
and sat down there. 30 Then great multitudes
came to Him, having with them *the* lame,

15:32–38 JESUS FEEDS MORE THAN FOUR THOUSAND PEOPLE

Jesus actually fed four thousand men, besides women and children. So the number of people Jesus fed was several times more than four thousand.

The disciples had only seven loaves of bread and a few fish. Yet Jesus fed everybody! You and I are the disciples of Jesus, and we don't have very much to offer Him. But He will take the little we have and multiply it many times over.

Like the disciples long ago, you must be willing to give Jesus what you have. As you give to Him your little gift, He surprises you by making it big. Then many people are blessed.

When the offering plate is passed at church on Sunday, don't say, "My *little bit won't do any good. I'm only one person.*" Say instead, "I don't have much, Jesus. But You can have it. Please use it to bless many." Then you will see how very much He can do with your little bit.

blind, mute, maimed, and many others;
and they laid them down at Jesus' feet, and
He healed them. 31So the multitude marveled when they saw *the* mute speaking, *the*
maimed made whole, *the* lame walking, and
the blind seeing; and they glorified the God
of Israel.

Feeding the Four Thousand

32Now Jesus called His disciples to *Him-*
self and said, "I have compassion on the multitude, because they have now continued
with Me three days and have nothing to eat.
And I do not want to send them away hungry, lest they faint on the way."
33Then His disciples said to Him, "Where
could we get enough bread in the wilderness
to fill such a great multitude?"
34Jesus said to them, "How many loaves
do you have?"

And they said, "Seven, and a few little
fish."
35So He commanded the multitude to sit
down on the ground. 36And He took the sev-
en loaves and the fish and gave thanks, broke
them and gave *them* to His disciples; and the
disciples *gave* to the multitude. 37So they all
ate and were filled, and they took up seven
large baskets full of the fragments that were
left. 38Now those who ate were four thousand
men, besides women and children. 39And He
sent away the multitude, got into the boat,
and came to the region of Magdala.[a]

The Pharisees and Sadducees Seek a Sign

16 Then the Pharisees and Sadducees
came, and testing Him asked that
He would show them a sign from heaven.
2He answered and said to them, "When it is
evening you say, '*It will be* fair weather, for
the sky is red'; 3and in the morning, '*It will*
be foul weather today, for the sky is red and
threatening.' Hypocrites![a] You know how to
discern the face of the sky, but you cannot
discern the signs of the times. 4A wicked and
adulterous generation seeks after a sign, and
no sign shall be given to it except the sign of
the prophet[a] Jonah." And He left them and
departed.

The Leaven of the Pharisees and Sadducees

5Now when His disciples had come to the
other side, they had forgotten to take bread.
6Then Jesus said to them, "Take heed and
beware of the leaven of the Pharisees and the
Sadducees."
7And they reasoned among themselves,
saying, "*It is* because we have taken no
bread."
8But Jesus, being aware of *it,* said to them,
"O you of little faith, why do you reason
among yourselves because you have brought
no bread?[a] 9Do you not yet understand, or remember the five loaves of the five thousand
and how many baskets you took up? 10Nor the
seven loaves of the four thousand and how
many large baskets you took up? 11How is it
you do not understand that I did not speak
to you concerning bread?—*but* to beware of
the leaven of the Pharisees and Sadducees."
12Then they understood that He did not tell
them to beware of the leaven of bread, but of
the doctrine of the Pharisees and Sadducees.

Peter Confesses Jesus as the Christ

13When Jesus came into the region of
Caesarea Philippi, He asked His disciples,
saying, "Who do men say that I, the Son of
Man, am?"
14So they said, "Some *say* John the Baptist, some Elijah, and others Jeremiah or one
of the prophets."
15He said to them, "But who do you say
that I am?"
16Simon Peter answered and said, "You
are the Christ, the Son of the living God."
17Jesus answered and said to him,
"Blessed are you, Simon Bar-Jonah, for flesh
and blood has not revealed *this* to you, but
My Father who is in heaven. 18And I also say
to you that you are Peter, and on this rock I
will build My church, and the gates of Hades
shall not prevail against it. 19And I will give
you the keys of the kingdom of heaven, and
whatever you bind on earth will be bound in
heaven, and whatever you loose on earth will
be loosed[a] in heaven."
20Then He commanded His disciples
that they should tell no one that He was
Jesus the Christ.

Jesus Predicts His Death and Resurrection

21From that time Jesus began to show to
His disciples that He must go to Jerusalem,

15:39 [a] NU-Text reads *Magadan.* **16:3** [a] NU-Text omits *Hypocrites.* **16:4** [a] NU-Text omits *the prophet.* **16:8** [a] NU-Text reads *you have no bread.* **16:19** [a] Or *will have been bound . . . will have been loosed*

and suffer many things from the elders and
chief priests and scribes, and be killed, and
be raised the third day.
22 Then Peter took Him aside and began
to rebuke Him, saying, "Far be it from You,
Lord; this shall not happen to You!"
23 But He turned and said to Peter, "Get
behind Me, Satan! You are an offense to Me,
for you are not mindful of the things of God,
but the things of men."

Take Up the Cross and Follow Him

24 Then Jesus said to His disciples, "If
anyone desires to come after Me, let him
deny himself, and take up his cross, and
follow Me. 25 For whoever desires to save his
life will lose it, but whoever loses his life for
My sake will find it. 26 For what profit is it to
a man if he gains the whole world, and loses his own soul? Or what will a man give in
exchange for his soul? 27 For the Son of Man
will come in the glory of His Father with
His angels, and then He will reward each
according to his works. 28 Assuredly, I say to
you, there are some standing here who shall
not taste death till they see the Son of Man
coming in His kingdom."

Jesus Transfigured on the Mount

17 Now after six days Jesus took Peter,
James, and John his brother, led
them up on a high mountain by themselves;
2 and He was transfigured before them. His
face shone like the sun, and His clothes
became as white as the light. 3 And behold,
Moses and Elijah appeared to them, talking
with Him. 4 Then Peter answered and said
to Jesus, "Lord, it is good for us to be here;
if You wish, let us[a] make here three tabernacles: one for You, one for Moses, and one
for Elijah."
5 While he was still speaking, behold, a
bright cloud overshadowed them; and suddenly a voice came out of the cloud, saying,
"This is My beloved Son, in whom I am well
pleased. Hear Him!" 6 And when the disciples heard *it,* they fell on their faces and were
greatly afraid. 7 But Jesus came and touched
them and said, "Arise, and do not be afraid."
8 When they had lifted up their eyes, they saw
no one but Jesus only.
9 Now as they came down from the mountain, Jesus commanded them, saying, "Tell
the vision to no one until the Son of Man is
risen from the dead."
10 And His disciples asked Him, saying,
"Why then do the scribes say that Elijah
must come first?"
11 Jesus answered and said to them, "Indeed, Elijah is coming first[a] and will restore
all things. 12 But I say to you that Elijah has
come already, and they did not know him but
did to him whatever they wished. Likewise
the Son of Man is also about to suffer at their
hands." 13 Then the disciples understood that
He spoke to them of John the Baptist.

A Boy Is Healed

14 And when they had come to the multitude, a man came to Him, kneeling down
to Him and saying, 15 "Lord, have mercy on
my son, for he is an epileptic[a] and suffers
severely; for he often falls into the fire and
often into the water. 16 So I brought him to
Your disciples, but they could not cure him."
17 Then Jesus answered and said, "O faithless and perverse generation, how long shall
I be with you? How long shall I bear with
you? Bring him here to Me." 18 And Jesus rebuked the demon, and it came out of him;
and the child was cured from that very hour.
19 Then the disciples came to Jesus privately and said, "Why could we not cast it
out?"
20 So Jesus said to them, "Because of your
unbelief;[a] for assuredly, I say to you, if you
have faith as a mustard seed, you will say to
this mountain, 'Move from here to there,'
and it will move; and nothing will be impossible for you. 21 However, this kind does not
go out except by prayer and fasting."[a]

Jesus Again Predicts His Death and Resurrection

22 Now while they were staying[a] in Galilee, Jesus said to them, "The Son of Man is
about to be betrayed into the hands of men,
23 and they will kill Him, and the third day
He will be raised up." And they were exceedingly sorrowful.

Peter and His Master Pay Their Taxes

24 When they had come to Capernaum,[a]

17:4 [a] NU-Text reads *I will.* 17:11 [a] NU-Text omits *first.* 17:15 [a] Literally *moonstruck* 17:20 [a] NU-Text reads *little faith.* 17:21 [a] NU-Text omits this verse. 17:22 [a] NU-Text reads *gathering together.* 17:24 [a] NU-Text reads *Capharnaum* (here and elsewhere).

those who received the *temple* tax came to
Peter and said, "Does your Teacher not pay
the *temple* tax?"
25He said, "Yes."
And when he had come into the house,
Jesus anticipated him, saying, "What do you
think, Simon? From whom do the kings of
the earth take customs or taxes, from their
sons or from strangers?"
26Peter said to Him, "From strangers."
Jesus said to him, "Then the sons are
free. 27Nevertheless, lest we offend them,
go to the sea, cast in a hook, and take the
fish that comes up first. And when you have
opened its mouth, you will find a piece of
money;[a] take that and give it to them for Me
and you."

Who Is the Greatest?

18 At that time the disciples came to
Jesus, saying, "Who then is greatest
in the kingdom of heaven?"
2Then Jesus called a little child to Him,
set him in the midst of them, 3and said, "Assuredly,
I say to you, unless you are converted
and become as little children, you will
by no means enter the kingdom of heaven.
4Therefore whoever humbles himself as this
little child is the greatest in the kingdom of
heaven. 5Whoever receives one little child
like this in My name receives Me.

Jesus Warns of Offenses

6"But whoever causes one of these little
ones who believe in Me to sin, it would be better
for him if a millstone were hung around
his neck, and he were drowned in the depth
of the sea. 7Woe to the world because of offenses!
For offenses must come, but woe to
that man by whom the offense comes!
8"If your hand or foot causes you to sin,
cut it off and cast *it* from you. It is better for
you to enter into life lame or maimed, rather
than having two hands or two feet, to be
cast into the everlasting fire. 9And if your
eye causes you to sin, pluck it out and cast *it*
from you. It is better for you to enter into life
with one eye, rather than having two eyes, to
be cast into hell fire.

The Parable of the Lost Sheep

10"Take heed that you do not despise one
of these little ones, for I say to you that in
heaven their angels always see the face of
My Father who is in heaven. 11For the Son of
Man has come to save that which was lost.[a]

17:27 [a] Greek *stater,* the exact amount to pay the temple tax (didrachma) for two 18:11 [a] NU-Text omits this verse.

Epic Ideas

17:22, 23 JESUS CAME TO DIE FOR OUR SINS

Some people think you can cure sin by just teaching people what is good and right. But Jesus knew His teaching would do no good unless He died on the Cross to destroy our sins. Sin is not just the bad things we do. Sin is deep inside us, in our wills. Only God can change our deep rebellion against Him and His ways.

You can see your temperature rise with a thermometer, but you can't see the disease that causes you to feel hot and uncomfortable. In the same way, you can feel the unhappiness that sin causes, but you can't see the sin deep inside.

Jesus is the great Doctor who cures sin. The medicine is His blood poured out on the Cross. Tell Jesus you want Him to heal the deep sin of your heart and be your Friend forever.

12"What do you think? If a man has a hundred sheep, and one of them goes astray, does he not leave the ninety-nine and go to the mountains to seek the one that is straying? 13And if he should find it, assuredly, I say to you, he rejoices more over that *sheep* than over the ninety-nine that did not go astray. 14Even so it is not the will of your Father who is in heaven that one of these little ones should perish.

Dealing with a Sinning Brother

15"Moreover if your brother sins against you, go and tell him his fault between you and him alone. If he hears you, you have gained your brother. 16But if he will not hear, take with you one or two more, that 'by the mouth of two or three witnesses every word may be established.'[a] 17And if he refuses to hear them, tell *it* to the church. But if he refuses even to hear the church, let him be to you like a heathen and a tax collector.

18"Assuredly, I say to you, whatever you bind on earth will be bound in heaven, and whatever you loose on earth will be loosed in heaven.

19"Again I say[a] to you that if two of you agree on earth concerning anything that they ask, it will be done for them by My Father in heaven. 20For where two or three are gathered together in My name, I am there in the midst of them."

The Parable of the Unforgiving Servant

21Then Peter came to Him and said, "Lord, how often shall my brother sin against me, and I forgive him? Up to seven times?"

22Jesus said to him, "I do not say to you, up to seven times, but up to seventy times seven. 23Therefore the kingdom of heaven is like a certain king who wanted to settle accounts with his servants. 24And when he had begun to settle accounts, one was brought to him who owed him ten thousand talents. 25But as he was not able to pay, his master commanded that he be sold, with his wife and children and all that he had, and that payment be made. 26The servant therefore fell down before him, saying, 'Master, have patience with me, and I will pay you all.' 27Then the master of that servant was moved with compassion, released him, and forgave him the debt.

28"But that servant went out and found one of his fellow servants who owed him a hundred denarii; and he laid hands on him and took *him* by the throat, saying, 'Pay me what you owe!' 29So his fellow servant fell down at his feet[a] and begged him, saying, 'Have patience with me, and I will pay you all.'[b] 30And he would not, but went and threw him into prison till he should pay the debt. 31So when his fellow servants saw what had been done, they were very grieved, and came and told their master all that had been done. 32Then his master, after he had called him, said to him, 'You wicked servant! I forgave you all that debt because you begged me. 33Should you not also have had compassion on your fellow servant, just as I had pity on you?' 34And his master was angry, and delivered him to the torturers until he should pay all that was due to him.

35"So My heavenly Father also will do to you if each of you, from his heart, does not forgive his brother his trespasses."[a]

Marriage and Divorce

19 Now it came to pass, when Jesus had finished these sayings, *that* He departed from Galilee and came to the region of Judea beyond the Jordan. 2And great multitudes followed Him, and He healed them there.

3The Pharisees also came to Him, testing Him, and saying to Him, "Is it lawful for a man to divorce his wife for *just* any reason?"

4And He answered and said to them, "Have you not read that He who made[a] *them* at the beginning 'made them male and female,'[b] 5and said, 'For this reason a man shall leave his father and mother and be joined to his wife, and the two shall become one flesh'?[a] 6So then, they are no longer two but one flesh. Therefore what God has joined together, let not man separate."

7They said to Him, "Why then did Moses command to give a certificate of divorce, and to put her away?"

8He said to them, "Moses, because of the hardness of your hearts, permitted you to divorce your wives, but from the beginning it was not so. 9And I say to you, whoever

---

18:16 [a] Deuteronomy 19:15 **18:19** [a] NU-Text and M-Text read *Again, assuredly, I say.* **18:29** [a] NU-Text omits *at his feet.* [b] NU-Text and M-Text omit *all.* **18:35** [a] NU-Text omits *his trespasses.* **19:4** [a] NU-Text reads *created.* [b] Genesis 1:27; 5:2 **19:5** [a] Genesis 2:24

divorces his wife, except for sexual immorality,[a] and marries another, commits adultery;
and whoever marries her who is divorced
commits adultery."
10 His disciples said to Him, "If such is
the case of the man with *his* wife, it is better
not to marry."

Jesus Teaches on Celibacy

11 But He said to them, "All cannot accept this saying, but only *those* to whom it
has been given: 12 For there are eunuchs who
were born thus from *their* mother's womb,
and there are eunuchs who were made eunuchs by men, and there are eunuchs who
have made themselves eunuchs for the kingdom of heaven's sake. He who is able to accept *it,* let him accept *it.*"

Jesus Blesses Little Children

13 Then little children were brought to
Him that He might put *His* hands on them
and pray, but the disciples rebuked them.
14 But Jesus said, "Let the little children come
to Me, and do not forbid them; for of such is
the kingdom of heaven." 15 And He laid *His*
hands on them and departed from there.

Jesus Counsels the Rich Young Ruler

16 Now behold, one came and said to Him,
"Good[a] Teacher, what good thing shall I do
that I may have eternal life?"
17 So He said to him, "Why do you call Me
good?[a] No one *is* good but One, *that is,* God.[b]
But if you want to enter into life, keep the
commandments."
18 He said to Him, "Which ones?"
Jesus said, "'You shall not murder,' 'You
shall not commit adultery,' 'You shall not
steal,' 'You shall not bear false witness,'
19 'Honor your father and *your* mother,' [a] and,
'You shall love your neighbor as yourself.' "[b]
20 The young man said to Him, "All these
things I have kept from my youth.[a] What do
I still lack?"
21 Jesus said to him, "If you want to be perfect, go, sell what you have and give to the
poor, and you will have treasure in heaven;
and come, follow Me."
22 But when the young man heard that
saying, he went away sorrowful, for he had
great possessions.

With God All Things Are Possible

23 Then Jesus said to His disciples, "Assuredly, I say to you that it is hard for a rich
man to enter the kingdom of heaven. 24 And
again I say to you, it is easier for a camel to
go through the eye of a needle than for a rich
man to enter the kingdom of God."
25 When His disciples heard *it,* they were
greatly astonished, saying, "Who then can
be saved?"
26 But Jesus looked at *them* and said to
them, "With men this is impossible, but
with God all things are possible."
27 Then Peter answered and said to Him,
"See, we have left all and followed You.
Therefore what shall we have?"

19:9 [a] Or *fornication* **19:16** [a] NU-Text omits *Good.* **19:17** [a] NU-Text reads *Why do you ask Me about what is good?* [b] NU-Text reads *There is One who is good.* **19:19** [a] Exodus 20:12–16; Deuteronomy 5:16–20 [b] Leviticus 19:18 **19:20** [a] NU-Text omits *from my youth.*

FORGIVENESS

READ IT: MATTHEW 18:21, 22

Sometimes forgiveness is an ongoing process. Think about a sin in your life that you just can't seem to shake. Jesus doesn't hesitate to forgive you each and every time you do it. So when someone has hurt you and it seems too hard to forgive, go ahead and forgive him or her anyway—not just seven times, like Peter assumed, but again and again until the hurt is gone.

28So Jesus said to them, "Assuredly I say
to you, that in the regeneration, when the
Son of Man sits on the throne of His glory,
you who have followed Me will also sit on
twelve thrones, judging the twelve tribes of
Israel. 29And everyone who has left houses
or brothers or sisters or father or mother or
wife[a] or children or lands, for My name's
sake, shall receive a hundredfold, and inherit
eternal life. 30But many *who are* first will be
last, and the last first.

In Focus

19:28 Regeneration Pronounced *re-jen-uh-RAY-shun*. A word meaning to "create all over again." Regeneration is what God does for us when we are "born again" (see definition at John 3:3).

The Parable of the Workers in the Vineyard

20 "For the kingdom of heaven is
like a landowner who went out
early in the morning to hire laborers for his
vineyard. 2Now when he had agreed with the
laborers for a denarius a day, he sent them
into his vineyard. 3And he went out about the
third hour and saw others standing idle in
the marketplace, 4and said to them, 'You also
go into the vineyard, and whatever is right I
will give you.' So they went. 5Again he went
out about the sixth and the ninth hour, and
did likewise. 6And about the eleventh hour
he went out and found others standing idle,[a]
and said to them, 'Why have you been standing here idle all day?' 7They said to him,
'Because no one hired us.' He said to them,
'You also go into the vineyard, and whatever
is right you will receive.'[a]

8"So when evening had come, the owner of the vineyard said to his steward, 'Call
the laborers and give them *their* wages,
beginning with the last to the first.' 9And
when those came who *were hired* about the
eleventh hour, they each received a denarius. 10But when the first came, they supposed
that they would receive more; and they likewise received each a denarius. 11And when
they had received *it*, they complained against
the landowner, 12saying, 'These last *men*
have worked *only* one hour, and you made
them equal to us who have borne the burden
and the heat of the day.' 13But he answered
one of them and said, 'Friend, I am doing
you no wrong. Did you not agree with me for
a denarius? 14Take *what is* yours and go your
way. I wish to give to this last man *the same*
as to you. 15Is it not lawful for me to do what
I wish with my own things? Or is your eye
evil because I am good?' 16So the last will be
first, and the first last. For many are called,
but few chosen."[a]

19:29 [a] NU-Text omits *or wife*. **20:6** [a] NU-Text omits *idle*.
20:7 [a] NU-Text omits the last clause of this verse.
20:16 [a] NU-Text omits the last sentence of this verse.

Action!

SELFISHNESS

READ IT: MATTHEW 20:20–28

Even after spending several years as two of Jesus' closest friends—traveling with Him, serving with Him, and listening to Him teach—James and John didn't get it. They wanted Jesus to promise them a place of importance, power, and prestige. When He didn't, they were mad. Then *Jesus' other* friends heard what James and John wanted, and they were mad. That's what a selfish, self-centered attitude does—it leads to anger, then jealousy, then other hurtful things.

Jesus a Third Time Predicts His Death and Resurrection

17Now Jesus, going up to Jerusalem, took
the twelve disciples aside on the road and
said to them, 18"Behold, we are going up to
Jerusalem, and the Son of Man will be betrayed to the chief priests and to the scribes;
and they will condemn Him to death, 19and
deliver Him to the Gentiles to mock and to
scourge and to crucify. And the third day He
will rise again."

Greatness Is Serving

20Then the mother of Zebedee's sons
came to Him with her sons, kneeling down
and asking something from Him.
21And He said to her, "What do you
wish?"
She said to Him, "Grant that these two
sons of mine may sit, one on Your right hand
and the other on the left, in Your kingdom."
22But Jesus answered and said, "You do
not know what you ask. Are you able to drink
the cup that I am about to drink, and be baptized with the baptism that I am baptized
with?"[a]
They said to Him, "We are able."
23So He said to them, "You will indeed
drink My cup, and be baptized with the
baptism that I am baptized with;[a] but to sit
on My right hand and on My left is not Mine
to give, but *it is for those* for whom it is prepared by My Father."
24And when the ten heard *it,* they were
greatly displeased with the two brothers.
25But Jesus called them to *Himself* and said,
"You know that the rulers of the Gentiles
lord it over them, and those who are great
exercise authority over them. 26Yet it shall
not be so among you; but whoever desires
to become great among you, let him be your
servant. 27And whoever desires to be first
among you, let him be your slave— 28just as
the Son of Man did not come to be served,
but to serve, and to give His life a ransom
for many."

Two Blind Men Receive Their Sight

29Now as they went out of Jericho, a great
multitude followed Him. 30And behold, two
blind men sitting by the road, when they
heard that Jesus was passing by, cried out,
saying, "Have mercy on us, O Lord, Son of
David!"

20:22 [a] NU-Text omits *and be baptized with the baptism that I am baptized with.* 20:23 [a] NU-Text omits *and be baptized with the baptism that I am baptized with.*

Epic Ideas

20:20–28 WHO WILL BE NUMBER ONE?

Have you been watching any football games? Sometimes you'll see a fast fullback outrun his tacklers and speed across the goal line. Then he spikes the ball on the ground and runs around waving his finger in the air. He's saying to the crowd, *"I'm Number One!"*

Being "Number One" in sports is great. And you should be the very best you can be in all the contests of life. But remember, God has a reason for your being "Number One." That's so you can be of more use to others in a needy world.

Some of Jesus' followers wanted to be "Number One" just so they could look important. People like that are selfish. Jesus made it clear to His disciples that He came into the world to serve, not to be served by others. Have you heard about Mother Teresa, the famous missionary to India? She gave her life for others. She's a really good example of how to be a "Number One."

31 Then the multitude warned them that
they should be quiet; but they cried out all
the more, saying, "Have mercy on us, O
Lord, Son of David!"

32 So Jesus stood still and called them,
and said, "What do you want Me to do for
you?"

33 They said to Him, "Lord, that our eyes
may be opened." 34 So Jesus had compassion
and touched their eyes. And immediately
their eyes received sight, and they followed
Him.

The Triumphal Entry

21 Now when they drew near Jerusalem, and came to Bethphage,[a] at
the Mount of Olives, then Jesus sent two
disciples, 2 saying to them, "Go into the village opposite you, and immediately you will
find a donkey tied, and a colt with her. Loose
them and bring *them* to Me. 3 And if anyone
says anything to you, you shall say, 'The Lord
has need of them,' and immediately he will
send them."

4 All[a] this was done that it might be fulfilled which was spoken by the prophet,
saying:

5 "Tell the daughter of Zion,
'Behold, your King is coming to you,
Lowly, and sitting on a donkey,
A colt, the foal of a donkey.' "[a]

6 So the disciples went and did as Jesus
commanded them. 7 They brought the donkey and the colt, laid their clothes on them,
and set *Him*[a] on them. 8 And a very great
multitude spread their clothes on the road;
others cut down branches from the trees and
spread *them* on the road. 9 Then the multitudes who went before and those who followed cried out, saying:

"Hosanna to the Son of David!
'Blessed *is* He who comes in the name of
the LORD!'[a]
Hosanna in the highest!"

10 And when He had come into Jerusalem, all the city was moved, saying, "Who
is this?"

11 So the multitudes said, "This is Jesus,
the prophet from Nazareth of Galilee."

Jesus Cleanses the Temple

12 Then Jesus went into the temple of
God[a] and drove out all those who bought and
sold in the temple, and overturned the tables
of the money changers and the seats of those
who sold doves. 13 And He said to them, "It is
written, 'My house shall be called a house
of prayer,'[a] but you have made it a 'den of
thieves.' "[b]

14 Then *the* blind and *the* lame came to
Him in the temple, and He healed them.
15 But when the chief priests and scribes saw
the wonderful things that He did, and the
children crying out in the temple and saying, "Hosanna to the Son of David!" they
were indignant 16 and said to Him, "Do You
hear what these are saying?"

And Jesus said to them, "Yes. Have you
never read,

'Out of the mouth of babes and nursing
infants
You have perfected praise'?"[a]

17 Then He left them and went out of the
city to Bethany, and He lodged there.

The Fig Tree Withered

18 Now in the morning, as He returned to
the city, He was hungry. 19 And seeing a fig
tree by the road, He came to it and found
nothing on it but leaves, and said to it, "Let
no fruit grow on you ever again." Immediately the fig tree withered away.

The Lesson of the Withered Fig Tree

20 And when the disciples saw *it,* they
marveled, saying, "How did the fig tree
wither away so soon?"

21 So Jesus answered and said to them,
"Assuredly, I say to you, if you have faith
and do not doubt, you will not only do what
was done to the fig tree, but also if you say
to this mountain, 'Be removed and be cast
into the sea,' it will be done. 22 And whatever
things you ask in prayer, believing, you will
receive."

Jesus' Authority Questioned

23 Now when He came into the temple,
the chief priests and the elders of the people
confronted Him as He was teaching, and
said, "By what authority are You doing these
things? And who gave You this authority?"

24 But Jesus answered and said to them,

21:1 [a] M-Text reads *Bethsphage.* **21:4** [a] NU-Text omits *All.*
21:5 [a] Zechariah 9:9 **21:7** [a] NU-Text reads *and He sat.*
21:9 [a] Psalm 118:26 **21:12** [a] NU-Text omits *of God.*
21:13 [a] Isaiah 56:7 [b] Jeremiah 7:11 **21:16** [a] Psalm 8:2

"I also will ask you one thing, which if you
tell Me, I likewise will tell you by what authority I do these things: 25The baptism of
John—where was it from? From heaven or
from men?"

And they reasoned among themselves,
saying, "If we say, 'From heaven,' He will say
to us, 'Why then did you not believe him?'
26But if we say, 'From men,' we fear the multitude, for all count John as a prophet." 27So
they answered Jesus and said, "We do not
know."

And He said to them, "Neither will I tell
you by what authority I do these things.

The Parable of the Two Sons

28"But what do you think? A man had two
sons, and he came to the first and said, 'Son,
go, work today in my vineyard.' 29He answered and said, 'I will not,' but afterward he
regretted it and went. 30Then he came to the
second and said likewise. And he answered
and said, 'I *go,* sir,' but he did not go. 31Which
of the two did the will of *his* father?"

They said to Him, "The first."

Jesus said to them, "Assuredly, I say to
you that tax collectors and harlots enter the
kingdom of God before you. 32For John came
to you in the way of righteousness, and you
did not believe him; but tax collectors and
harlots believed him; and when you saw *it,*
you did not afterward relent and believe him.

The Parable of the Wicked Vinedressers

33"Hear another parable: There was a
certain landowner who planted a vineyard
and set a hedge around it, dug a winepress
in it and built a tower. And he leased it to
vinedressers and went into a far country.
34Now when vintage-time drew near, he sent
his servants to the vinedressers, that they
might receive its fruit. 35And the vinedressers took his servants, beat one, killed one,
and stoned another. 36Again he sent other
servants, more than the first, and they did
likewise to them. 37Then last of all he sent
his son to them, saying, 'They will respect
my son.' 38But when the vinedressers saw
the son, they said among themselves, 'This
is the heir. Come, let us kill him and seize
his inheritance.' 39So they took him and cast
him out of the vineyard and killed *him.*

40"Therefore, when the owner of the

In Focus

21:12 Money Changers Bankers who exchanged temple money for the money of another nation. Some money changers in the temple charged a large fee.

vineyard comes, what will he do to those
vinedressers?"

41They said to Him, "He will destroy
those wicked men miserably, and lease *his*
vineyard to other vinedressers who will render to him the fruits in their seasons."

42Jesus said to them, "Have you never
read in the Scriptures:

'The stone which the builders rejected
Has become the chief cornerstone.
This was the LORD's doing,
And it is marvelous in our eyes'?[a]

43"Therefore I say to you, the kingdom of
God will be taken from you and given to a
nation bearing the fruits of it. 44And whoever falls on this stone will be broken; but
on whomever it falls, it will grind him to
powder."

45Now when the chief priests and Pharisees heard His parables, they perceived that
He was speaking of them. 46But when they
sought to lay hands on Him, they feared
the multitudes, because they took Him for
a prophet.

The Parable of the Wedding Feast

22 And Jesus answered and spoke to
them again by parables and said:
2"The kingdom of heaven is like a certain
king who arranged a marriage for his son,
3and sent out his servants to call those who
were invited to the wedding; and they were
not willing to come. 4Again, he sent out
other servants, saying, 'Tell those who are
invited, "See, I have prepared my dinner;
my oxen and fatted cattle *are* killed, and all
things *are* ready. Come to the wedding."'
5But they made light of it and went their
ways, one to his own farm, another to his

21:42 [a] Psalm 118:22, 23

business. 6And the rest seized his servants, treated *them* spitefully, and killed *them.* 7But when the king heard *about it,* he was furious. And he sent out his armies, destroyed those murderers, and burned up their city. 8Then he said to his servants, 'The wedding is ready, but those who were invited were not worthy. 9Therefore go into the highways, and as many as you find, invite to the wedding.' 10So those servants went out into the highways and gathered together all whom they found, both bad and good. And the wedding *hall* was filled with guests.

11"But when the king came in to see the guests, he saw a man there who did not have on a wedding garment. 12So he said to him, 'Friend, how did you come in here without a wedding garment?' And he was speechless. 13Then the king said to the servants, 'Bind him hand and foot, take him away, and[a] cast *him* into outer darkness; there will be weeping and gnashing of teeth.'

14"For many are called, but few *are* chosen."

The Pharisees: Is It Lawful to Pay Taxes to Caesar?

15Then the Pharisees went and plotted how they might entangle Him in *His* talk. 16And they sent to Him their disciples with the Herodians, saying, "Teacher, we know that You are true, and teach the way of God in truth; nor do You care about anyone, for You do not regard the person of men. 17Tell us, therefore, what do You think? Is it lawful to pay taxes to Caesar, or not?"

18But Jesus perceived their wickedness, and said, "Why do you test Me, *you* hypocrites? 19Show Me the tax money."

So they brought Him a denarius.

20And He said to them, "Whose image and inscription *is* this?"

21They said to Him, "Caesar's."

And He said to them, "Render therefore to Caesar the things that are Caesar's, and to God the things that are God's." 22When they had heard *these words,* they marveled, and left Him and went their way.

The Sadducees: What About the Resurrection?

23The same day the Sadducees, who say there is no resurrection, came to Him and asked Him, 24saying: "Teacher, Moses said that if a man dies, having no children, his brother shall marry his wife and raise up offspring for his brother. 25Now there were with us seven brothers. The first died after he had married, and having no offspring, left his wife to his brother. 26Likewise the second also, and the third, even to the seventh. 27Last of all the woman died also. 28Therefore, in the resurrection, whose wife of the seven will she be? For they all had her."

In Focus

22:16 Herodians Pronounced *huh-ROH-dih-uns.* A group of Jews in Jesus' time who supported the Herod kings and the rule of Rome. They also wanted to bring Greek pagan customs into Jewish life.

29Jesus answered and said to them, "You are mistaken, not knowing the Scriptures nor the power of God. 30For in the resurrection they neither marry nor are given in marriage, but are like angels of God[a] in heaven. 31But concerning the resurrection of the dead, have you not read what was spoken to you by God, saying, 32'I am the God of Abraham, the God of Isaac, and the God of Jacob'?[a] God is not the God of the dead, but of the living." 33And when the multitudes heard *this,* they were astonished at His teaching.

The Scribes: Which Is the First Commandment of All?

34But when the Pharisees heard that He had silenced the Sadducees, they gathered together. 35Then one of them, a lawyer, asked Him *a question,* testing Him, and saying, 36"Teacher, which *is* the great commandment in the law?"

37Jesus said to him, "'You shall love the LORD your God with all your heart, with all your soul, and with all your mind.'[a] 38This is *the* first and great commandment. 39And *the* second *is* like it: 'You shall love your neighbor as yourself.'[a] 40On these two commandments hang all the Law and the Prophets."

22:13 [a] NU-Text omits *take him away, and.* 22:30 [a] NU-Text omits *of God.* 22:32 [a] Exodus 3:6, 15 22:37 [a] Deuteronomy 6:5 22:39 [a] Leviticus 19:18

Jesus: How Can David Call His Descendant "Lord"?

41 While the Pharisees were gathered together, Jesus asked them, 42 saying, "What
do you think about the Christ? Whose Son
is He?"

They said to Him, "*The Son* of David."
43 He said to them, "How then does David
in the Spirit call Him 'Lord,' saying:

44 'The LORD said to my Lord,
"Sit at My right hand,
Till I make Your enemies Your
footstool"'?[a]

45 If David then calls Him 'Lord,' how is He
his Son?" 46 And no one was able to answer
Him a word, nor from that day on did anyone dare question Him anymore.

Woe to the Scribes and Pharisees

23 Then Jesus spoke to the multitudes and to His disciples, 2 saying: "The scribes and the Pharisees sit in
Moses' seat. 3 Therefore whatever they tell
you to observe,[a] *that* observe and do, but do
not do according to their works; for they say,
and do not do. 4 For they bind heavy burdens,
hard to bear, and lay *them* on men's shoulders; but they *themselves* will not move them
with one of their fingers. 5 But all their works
they do to be seen by men. They make their
phylacteries broad and enlarge the borders
of their garments. 6 They love the best places
at feasts, the best seats in the synagogues,
7 greetings in the marketplaces, and to be
called by men, 'Rabbi, Rabbi.' 8 But you, do
not be called 'Rabbi'; for One is your Teacher,
the Christ,[a] and you are all brethren. 9 Do not
call anyone on earth your father; for One is
your Father, He who is in heaven. 10 And do
not be called teachers; for One is your Teacher, the Christ. 11 But he who is greatest among
you shall be your servant. 12 And whoever exalts himself will be humbled, and he who
humbles himself will be exalted.

13 "But woe to you, scribes and Pharisees,
hypocrites! For you shut up the kingdom of
heaven against men; for you neither go in
yourselves, nor do you allow those who are
entering to go in. 14 Woe to you, scribes and
Pharisees, hypocrites! For you devour widows' houses, and for a pretense make long
prayers. Therefore you will receive greater
condemnation.[a]

15 "Woe to you, scribes and Pharisees,
hypocrites! For you travel land and sea to
win one proselyte, and when he is won, you

22:44 [a] Psalm 110:1 23:3 [a] NU-Text omits *to observe.* 23:8 [a] NU-Text omits *the Christ.* 23:14 [a] NU-Text omits this verse.

22:37 THE GREAT COMMANDMENT

Some people say we should love others, but they don't think loving God is important. They say you can't see God, but you can see people, so you should just love people.

What if your parents took a trip and left you in charge of your little brother and sister? Which would you love most—your parents, or your brother and sister? The fact is, you would still care most about your father and mother even though you could not see them. You would care for your brother and sister just because they were your parents' children.

That's why we care about other people, too—they are our heavenly Father's children. And we love Him too much to neglect those in the world He commanded us to love. The whole world belongs to our Father, and we love Him first because He is Lord of the world He created.

make him twice as much a son of hell as yourselves.

16“Woe to you, blind guides, who say, ‘Whoever swears by the temple, it is nothing; but whoever swears by the gold of the temple, he is obliged *to perform it.*’ 17Fools and blind! For which is greater, the gold or the temple that sanctifies[a] the gold? 18And, ‘Whoever swears by the altar, it is nothing; but whoever swears by the gift that is on it, he is obliged *to perform it.*’ 19Fools and blind! For which is greater, the gift or the altar that sanctifies the gift? 20Therefore he who swears by the altar, swears by it and by all things on it. 21He who swears by the temple, swears by it and by Him who dwells[a] in it. 22And he who swears by heaven, swears by the throne of God and by Him who sits on it.

23“Woe to you, scribes and Pharisees, hypocrites! For you pay tithe of mint and anise and cummin, and have neglected the weightier *matters* of the law: justice and mercy and faith. These you ought to have done, without leaving the others undone. 24Blind guides, who strain out a gnat and swallow a camel!

25“Woe to you, scribes and Pharisees, hypocrites! For you cleanse the outside of the cup and dish, but inside they are full of extortion and self-indulgence.[a] 26Blind Pharisee, first cleanse the inside of the cup and dish, that the outside of them may be clean also.

27“Woe to you, scribes and Pharisees, hypocrites! For you are like whitewashed tombs which indeed appear beautiful outwardly, but inside are full of dead *men's* bones and all uncleanness. 28Even so you also outwardly appear righteous to men, but inside you are full of hypocrisy and lawlessness.

29“Woe to you, scribes and Pharisees, hypocrites! Because you build the tombs of the prophets and adorn the monuments of the righteous, 30and say, ‘If we had lived in the days of our fathers, we would not have been partakers with them in the blood of the prophets.’

31“Therefore you are witnesses against yourselves that you are sons of those who murdered the prophets. 32Fill up, then, the *measure of your fathers' guilt.* 33Serpents, brood of vipers! How can you escape the condemnation of hell? 34Therefore, indeed, I send you prophets, wise men, and scribes: *some* of them you will kill and crucify, and *some* of them you will scourge in your synagogues and persecute from city to city, 35that on you may come all the righteous blood shed on the earth, from the blood of righteous Abel to the blood of Zechariah, son of Berechiah, whom you murdered between the temple and the altar. 36Assuredly, I say to you, all these things will come upon this generation.

Jesus Laments over Jerusalem

37“O Jerusalem, Jerusalem, the one who kills the prophets and stones those who are sent to her! How often I wanted to gather your children together, as a hen gathers her chicks under *her* wings, but you were not willing! 38See! Your house is left to you desolate; 39for I say to you, you shall see Me no more till you say, ‘Blessed *is* He who comes in the name of the LORD!’ ”[a]

Jesus Predicts the Destruction of the Temple

24 Then Jesus went out and departed from the temple, and His disciples came up to show Him the buildings of the temple. 2And Jesus said to them, “Do you not see all these things? Assuredly, I say to you, not *one* stone shall be left here upon another, that shall not be thrown down.”

The Signs of the Times and the End of the Age

3Now as He sat on the Mount of Olives, the disciples came to Him privately, saying, “Tell us, when will these things be? And what *will be* the sign of Your coming, and of the end of the age?”

4And Jesus answered and said to them: “Take heed that no one deceives you. 5For many will come in My name, saying, ‘I am the Christ,’ and will deceive many. 6And you will hear of wars and rumors of wars. See that you are not troubled; for all[a] *these things* must come to pass, but the end is not yet. 7For nation will rise against nation, and kingdom against kingdom. And there will be famines, pestilences,[a] and earthquakes in various places. 8All these *are* the beginning of sorrows.

23:17 [a] NU-Text reads *sanctified.* 23:21 [a] M-Text reads *dwelt.* 23:25 [a] M-Text reads *unrighteousness.* 23:39 [a] Psalm 118:26 24:6 [a] NU-Text omits *all.* 24:7 [a] NU-Text omits *pestilences.*

9“Then they will deliver you up to tribulation and kill you, and you will be hated by
all nations for My name’s sake. 10And then
many will be offended, will betray one another, and will hate one another. 11Then many
false prophets will rise up and deceive many.
12And because lawlessness will abound, the
love of many will grow cold. 13But he who endures to the end shall be saved. 14And this
gospel of the kingdom will be preached in all
the world as a witness to all the nations, and
then the end will come.

The Great Tribulation

15“Therefore when you see the ‘abomination of desolation,’[a] spoken of by Daniel
the prophet, standing in the holy place”
(whoever reads, let him understand), 16“then
let those who are in Judea flee to the mountains. 17Let him who is on the housetop not
go down to take anything out of his house.
18And let him who is in the field not go back
to get his clothes. 19But woe to those who are
pregnant and to those who are nursing babies in those days! 20And pray that your flight
may not be in winter or on the Sabbath. 21For
then there will be great tribulation, such
as has not been since the beginning of the
world until this time, no, nor ever shall be.
22And unless those days were shortened, no
flesh would be saved; but for the elect’s sake
those days will be shortened.

23“Then if anyone says to you, ‘Look, here
is the Christ!’ or ‘There!’ do not believe *it.*
24For false christs and false prophets will
rise and show great signs and wonders to
deceive, if possible, even the elect. 25See, I
have told you beforehand.

26“Therefore if they say to you, ‘Look, He
is in the desert!’ do not go out; *or* ‘Look, *He is*
in the inner rooms!’ do not believe *it.* 27For as
the lightning comes from the east and flashes to the west, so also will the coming of the
Son of Man be. 28For wherever the carcass
is, there the eagles will be gathered together.

The Coming of the Son of Man

29“Immediately after the tribulation of
those days the sun will be darkened, and the
moon will not give its light; the stars will fall
from heaven, and the powers of the heavens
will be shaken. 30Then the sign of the Son of
Man will appear in heaven, and then all the
tribes of the earth will mourn, and they will
see the Son of Man coming on the clouds of
heaven with power and great glory. 31And He
will send His angels with a great sound of a
trumpet, and they will gather together His
elect from the four winds, from one end of
heaven to the other.

The Parable of the Fig Tree

32“Now learn this parable from the fig
tree: When its branch has already become
tender and puts forth leaves, you know that
summer *is* near. 33So you also, when you see
all these things, know that it[a] is near—at the
doors! 34Assuredly, I say to you, this generation will by no means pass away till all these
things take place. 35Heaven and earth will
pass away, but My words will by no means
pass away.

No One Knows the Day or Hour

36“But of that day and hour no one knows,
not even the angels of heaven,[a] but My Father only. 37But as the days of Noah *were,* so
also will the coming of the Son of Man be.
38For as in the days before the flood, they
were eating and drinking, marrying and
giving in marriage, until the day that Noah
entered the ark, 39and did not know until
the flood came and took them all away, so
also will the coming of the Son of Man be.
40Then two *men* will be in the field: one
will be taken and the other left. 41Two *wom-
en will be* grinding at the mill: one will be
taken and the other left. 42Watch therefore,
for you do not know what hour[a] your Lord is
coming. 43But know this, that if the master
of the house had known what hour the thief
would come, he would have watched and not
allowed his house to be broken into. 44There-
fore you also be ready, for the Son of Man is
coming at an hour you do not expect.

The Faithful Servant and the Evil Servant

45“Who then is a faithful and wise servant, whom his master made ruler over
his household, to give them food in due
season? 46Blessed *is* that servant whom his
master, when he comes, will find so doing.
47Assuredly, I say to you that he will make
him ruler over all his goods. 48But if that evil
servant says in his heart, ‘My master is delaying his coming,’[a] 49and begins to beat *his*

24:15 [a] Daniel 11:31; 12:11 **24:33** [a] Or *He* **24:36** [a] NU-Text adds *nor the Son.* **24:42** [a] NU-Text reads *day.* **24:48** [a] NU-Text omits *his coming.*

fellow servants, and to eat and drink with
the drunkards, 50 the master of that servant
will come on a day when he is not looking
for *him* and at an hour that he is not aware
of, 51 and will cut him in two and appoint *him*
his portion with the hypocrites. There shall
be weeping and gnashing of teeth.

The Parable of the Wise and Foolish Virgins

25 "Then the kingdom of heaven
shall be likened to ten virgins who
took their lamps and went out to meet the
bridegroom. 2 Now five of them were wise,
and five *were* foolish. 3 Those who *were* foolish took their lamps and took no oil with
them, 4 but the wise took oil in their vessels
with their lamps. 5 But while the bridegroom
was delayed, they all slumbered and slept.

6 "And at midnight a cry was *heard:* 'Behold, the bridegroom is coming;[a] go out to
meet him!' 7 Then all those virgins arose
and trimmed their lamps. 8 And the foolish
said to the wise, 'Give us *some* of your oil, for
our lamps are going out.' 9 But the wise answered, saying, '*No,* lest there should not be
enough for us and you; but go rather to those
who sell, and buy for yourselves.' 10 And while
they went to buy, the bridegroom came, and
those who were ready went in with him to
the wedding; and the door was shut.

11 "Afterward the other virgins came also,
saying, 'Lord, Lord, open to us!' 12 But he answered and said, 'Assuredly, I say to you, I do
not know you.'

13 "Watch therefore, for you know neither
the day nor the hour[a] in which the Son of
Man is coming.

The Parable of the Talents

14 "For *the kingdom of heaven is* like a man
traveling to a far country, *who* called his own
servants and delivered his goods to them.
15 And to one he gave five talents, to another
two, and to another one, to each according to
his own ability; and immediately he went on
a journey. 16 Then he who had received the
five talents went and traded with them, and
made another five talents. 17 And likewise he
who *had received* two gained two more also.
18 But he who had received one went and dug

25:6 [a] NU-Text omits *is coming.* 25:13 [a] NU-Text omits the rest of this verse.

24:44 JESUS IS COMING BACK AGAIN

When you study your history lessons, you may wonder where the world is heading. The books can't tell you, because they can only describe what has happened in the past.

It's a wonderful thing to learn that God is in charge of all of history. The more you read and study your Bible, the more you will realize that what happens in our world is not pointless. Everything that happens has a purpose in God's plan.

God keeps history going to give people the chance to obey Him. We notice in the Old Testament that God gave Israel many chances—for many hundreds of years—to follow His commandments. Only then God's severe punishment came.

God is now giving our world a chance to return to Him and His laws. One day, though, the Lord will come and judge His world "at an hour you do not expect." Are you ready to meet God when He comes? Have you surrendered your life to Him?

in the ground, and hid his lord's money.
[19]After a long time the lord of those servants
came and settled accounts with them.

[20]"So he who had received five talents
came and brought five other talents, saying,
'Lord, you delivered to me five talents; look, I
have gained five more talents besides them.'
[21]His lord said to him, 'Well *done,* good and
faithful servant; you were faithful over a
few things, I will make you ruler over many
things. Enter into the joy of your lord.' [22]He
also who had received two talents came and
said, 'Lord, you delivered to me two talents;
look, I have gained two more talents besides
them.' [23]His lord said to him, 'Well *done,*
good and faithful servant; you have been
faithful over a few things, I will make you
ruler over many things. Enter into the joy of
your lord.

[24]"Then he who had received the one talent came and said, 'Lord, I knew you to be a
hard man, reaping where you have not sown,
and gathering where you have not scattered
seed. [25]And I was afraid, and went and hid
your talent in the ground. Look, *there* you
have *what is* yours.'

[26]"But his lord answered and said to him,
'You wicked and lazy servant, you knew that
I reap where I have not sown, and gather
where I have not scattered seed. [27]So you
ought to have deposited my money with the
bankers, and at my coming I would have received back my own with interest. [28]So take
the talent from him, and give *it* to him who
has ten talents.

[29]'For to everyone who has, more will be
given, and he will have abundance; but from
him who does not have, even what he has
will be taken away. [30]And cast the unprofitable servant into the outer darkness. There
will be weeping and gnashing of teeth.'

The Son of Man Will Judge the Nations

[31]"When the Son of Man comes in His
glory, and all the holy[a] angels with Him,
then He will sit on the throne of His glory. [32]All the nations will be gathered before
Him, and He will separate them one from
another, as a shepherd divides *his* sheep
from the goats. [33]And He will set the sheep
on His right hand, but the goats on the left.
[34]Then the King will say to those on His
right hand, 'Come, you blessed of My Father,
inherit the kingdom prepared for you from
the foundation of the world: [35]for I was hungry and you gave Me food; I was thirsty and
you gave Me drink; I was a stranger and you
took Me in; [36]I *was* naked and you clothed
Me; I was sick and you visited Me; I was in
prison and you came to Me.'

[37]"Then the righteous will answer Him,
saying, 'Lord, when did we see You hungry
and feed *You,* or thirsty and give *You* drink?
[38]When did we see You a stranger and take
You in, or naked and clothe *You?* [39]Or when
did we see You sick, or in prison, and come
to You?' [40]And the King will answer and say

25:31 [a] NU-Text omits *holy.*

Action!

GOD'S JUSTICE

READ IT: MATTHEW 25:31–46

Does God really care how we treat others, especially those in need? In this passage, Jesus tells us what will happen if we neglect the poor. He says people who see those in need and help them will be given their reward. Those who neglect people in need will be separated from Him forever. He says something profound in this story: "As you did not do it to one of the least of these, you did not do it to Me" (v. 45). Jesus says when we ignore those in need, we ignore Him.

to them, 'Assuredly, I say to you, inasmuch as you did *it* to one of the least of these My brethren, you did *it* to Me.'

41"Then He will also say to those on the left hand, 'Depart from Me, you cursed, into the everlasting fire prepared for the devil and his angels: 42for I was hungry and you gave Me no food; I was thirsty and you gave Me no drink; 43I was a stranger and you did not take Me in, naked and you did not clothe Me, sick and in prison and you did not visit Me.'

44"Then they also will answer Him,[a] saying, 'Lord, when did we see You hungry or thirsty or a stranger or naked or sick or in prison, and did not minister to You?' 45Then He will answer them, saying, 'Assuredly, I say to you, inasmuch as you did not do *it* to one of the least of these, you did not do *it* to Me.' 46And these will go away into everlasting punishment, but the righteous into eternal life."

In Focus

25:46 Eternal Life The endless life of God. God gives His eternal life to people who trust in Jesus as their Savior. God Himself comes to live in them.

The Plot to Kill Jesus

26 Now it came to pass, when Jesus had finished all these sayings, *that* He said to His disciples, 2"You know that after two days is the Passover, and the Son of Man will be delivered up to be crucified."

3Then the chief priests, the scribes,[a] and the elders of the people assembled at the palace of the high priest, who was called Caiaphas, 4and plotted to take Jesus by trickery and kill *Him.* 5But they said, "Not during the feast, lest there be an uproar among the people."

The Anointing at Bethany

6And when Jesus was in Bethany at the house of Simon the leper, 7a woman came to Him having an alabaster flask of very costly fragrant oil, and she poured *it* on His head as He sat *at the table.* 8But when His disciples saw *it,* they were indignant, saying, "Why this waste? 9For this fragrant oil might have been sold for much and given to *the* poor."

10But when Jesus was aware of *it,* He said to them, "Why do you trouble the woman? For she has done a good work for Me. 11For you have the poor with you always, but Me you do not have always. 12For in pouring this fragrant oil on My body, she did *it* for My burial. 13Assuredly, I say to you, wherever this gospel is preached in the whole world, what this woman has done will also be told as a memorial to her."

25:44 [a] NU-Text and M-Text omit *Him.* 26:3 [a] NU-Text omits *the scribes.*

Action!

KINDNESS

READ IT: MATTHEW 25:34–40

Some of the kind deeds in these verses might seem overwhelming to you. After all, maybe you haven't had any opportunities to visit a person in prison. But the idea is that when we care for people who are struggling, we're caring for Jesus. That's how God sees it. And people are struggling all around us. So help the boy who spills his backpack, or give that girl a tissue. Start each day by praying, *Lord, help me notice the people who need me today, and give me courage to be kind.*

Judas Agrees to Betray Jesus

14 Then one of the twelve, called Judas Iscariot, went to the chief priests 15 and said,
"What are you willing to give me if I deliver
Him to you?" And they counted out to him
thirty pieces of silver. 16 So from that time he
sought opportunity to betray Him.

Jesus Celebrates Passover with His Disciples

17 Now on the first *day of the Feast* of the
Unleavened Bread the disciples came to
Jesus, saying to Him, "Where do You want
us to prepare for You to eat the Passover?"
18 And He said, "Go into the city to a certain man, and say to him, 'The Teacher says,
"My time is at hand; I will keep the Passover
at your house with My disciples."'"
19 So the disciples did as Jesus had directed them; and they prepared the Passover.
20 When evening had come, He sat down
with the twelve. 21 Now as they were eating,
He said, "Assuredly, I say to you, one of you
will betray Me."
22 And they were exceedingly sorrowful, and each of them began to say to Him,
"Lord, is it I?"
23 He answered and said, "He who dipped
his hand with Me in the dish will betray
Me. 24 The Son of Man indeed goes just as
it is written of Him, but woe to that man by
whom the Son of Man is betrayed! It would
have been good for that man if he had not
been born."
25 Then Judas, who was betraying Him,
answered and said, "Rabbi, is it I?"
He said to him, "You have said it."

Jesus Institutes the Lord's Supper

26 And as they were eating, Jesus took
bread, blessed[a] and broke *it*, and gave *it* to
the disciples and said, "Take, eat; this is My
body."
27 Then He took the cup, and gave thanks,
and gave *it* to them, saying, "Drink from it,
all of you. 28 For this is My blood of the new[a]
covenant, which is shed for many for the re-
mission of sins. 29 But I say to you, I will not
drink of this fruit of the vine from now on
until that day when I drink it new with you
in My Father's kingdom."
30 And when they had sung a hymn, they
went out to the Mount of Olives.

Jesus Predicts Peter's Denial

31 Then Jesus said to them, "All of you
will be made to stumble because of Me this
night, for it is written:

'I will strike the Shepherd,
And the sheep of the flock will be
scattered.'[a]

32 But after I have been raised, I will go before
you to Galilee."
33 Peter answered and said to Him, "Even
if all are made to stumble because of You, I
will never be made to stumble."
34 Jesus said to him, "Assuredly, I say to
you that this night, before the rooster crows,
you will deny Me three times."
35 Peter said to Him, "Even if I have to die
with You, I will not deny You!"
And so said all the disciples.

The Prayer in the Garden

36 Then Jesus came with them to a place
called Gethsemane, and said to the disciples,
"Sit here while I go and pray over there."
37 And He took with Him Peter and the two
sons of Zebedee, and He began to be sorrowful and deeply distressed. 38 Then He said to
them, "My soul is exceedingly sorrowful,
even to death. Stay here and watch with Me."
39 He went a little farther and fell on His
face, and prayed, saying, "O My Father, if it
is possible, let this cup pass from Me; nevertheless, not as I will, but as You *will*."
40 Then He came to the disciples and
found them sleeping, and said to Peter,
"What! Could you not watch with Me one
hour? 41 Watch and pray, lest you enter into
temptation. The spirit indeed *is* willing, but
the flesh *is* weak."
42 Again, a second time, He went away
and prayed, saying, "O My Father, if this cup
cannot pass away from Me unless[a] I drink it,
Your will be done." 43 And He came and found
them asleep again, for their eyes were heavy.
44 So He left them, went away again,
and prayed the third time, saying the same
words. 45 Then He came to His disciples and
said to them, "Are *you* still sleeping and resting? Behold, the hour is at hand, and the Son
of Man is being betrayed into the hands of
sinners. 46 Rise, let us be going. See, My betrayer is at hand."

Betrayal and Arrest in Gethsemane

47 And while He was still speaking, behold,

26:26 [a] M-Text reads *gave thanks for*. 26:28 [a] NU-Text omits *new*. 26:31 [a] Zechariah 13:7 26:42 [a] NU-Text reads *if this may not pass away unless*.

Judas, one of the twelve, with a great multitude with swords and clubs, came from the
chief priests and elders of the people.
48Now His betrayer had given them a
sign, saying, "Whomever I kiss, He is the
One; seize Him." 49Immediately he went up
to Jesus and said, "Greetings, Rabbi!" and
kissed Him.
50But Jesus said to him, "Friend, why
have you come?"
Then they came and laid hands on Jesus
and took Him. 51And suddenly, one of those
who were with Jesus stretched out *his* hand
and drew his sword, struck the servant of the
high priest, and cut off his ear.
52But Jesus said to him, "Put your sword
in its place, for all who take the sword will
perish[a] by the sword. 53Or do you think that
I cannot now pray to My Father, and He will
provide Me with more than twelve legions of
angels? 54How then could the Scriptures be
fulfilled, that it must happen thus?"
55In that hour Jesus said to the multitudes, "Have you come out, as against a robber, with swords and clubs to take Me? I sat
daily with you, teaching in the temple, and
you did not seize Me. 56But all this was done
that the Scriptures of the prophets might be
fulfilled."
Then all the disciples forsook Him and
fled.

Jesus Faces the Sanhedrin

57And those who had laid hold of Jesus
led *Him* away to Caiaphas the high priest,
where the scribes and the elders were assembled. 58But Peter followed Him at a distance
to the high priest's courtyard. And he went
in and sat with the servants to see the end.
59Now the chief priests, the elders,[a] and
all the council sought false testimony against
Jesus to put Him to death, 60but found none.
Even though many false witnesses came forward, they found none.[a] But at last two false
witnesses[b] came forward 61and said, "This
fellow said, 'I am able to destroy the temple
of God and to build it in three days.'"
62And the high priest arose and said to
Him, "Do You answer nothing? What *is it*
these men testify against You?" 63But Jesus
kept silent. And the high priest answered
and said to Him, "I put You under oath by
the living God: Tell us if You are the Christ,
the Son of God!"
64Jesus said to him, "*It is as* you said. Nevertheless, I say to you, hereafter you will see
the Son of Man sitting at the right hand of the
Power, and coming on the clouds of heaven."

26:52 [a] M-Text reads *die.* **26:59** [a] NU-Text omits *the elders.* **26:60** [a] NU-Text puts a comma after *but found none,* does not capitalize *Even,* and omits *they found none.* [b] NU-Text omits *false witnesses.*

26:36–46 JESUS PRAYS IN THE GARDEN

Jesus planned to die, but He didn't want to die! You may wonder how death could hurt Jesus, the Son of God! Remember, Jesus was also a Man, and dying was a horrible thought for this special Man who was still so young.

It's hard to think about. But try to imagine yourself having nails driven through your hands and feet. Then imagine hanging on a cross for hours before death comes. It's horrible, isn't it?

But that isn't all there was to it. No, Jesus, the very Son of God, would carry all of the sins of the whole world on the Cross. And that was the suffering He feared most. Even His own Father would have to leave Him alone during those long hours. Jesus was judged for your sins so you wouldn't have to be judged.

65Then the high priest tore his clothes,
saying, "He has spoken blasphemy! What
further need do we have of witnesses? Look,
now you have heard His blasphemy! 66What
do you think?"
They answered and said, "He is deserving of death."
67Then they spat in His face and beat
Him; and others struck *Him* with the palms
of their hands, 68saying, "Prophesy to us,
Christ! Who is the one who struck You?"

Peter Denies Jesus, and Weeps Bitterly

69Now Peter sat outside in the courtyard.
And a servant girl came to him, saying, "You
also were with Jesus of Galilee."
70But he denied it before *them* all, saying,
"I do not know what you are saying."
71And when he had gone out to the gateway, another *girl* saw him and said to those
who were there, "This *fellow* also was with
Jesus of Nazareth."
72But again he denied with an oath, "I do
not know the Man!"
73And a little later those who stood by
came up and said to Peter, "Surely you also
are *one* of them, for your speech betrays you."
74Then he began to curse and swear, *saying,* "I do not know the Man!"
Immediately a rooster crowed. 75And Peter remembered the word of Jesus who had
said to him, "Before the rooster crows, you
will deny Me three times." So he went out
and wept bitterly.

Jesus Handed Over to Pontius Pilate

27 When morning came, all the chief
priests and elders of the people
plotted against Jesus to put Him to death.
2And when they had bound Him, they led
Him away and delivered Him to Pontius[a]
Pilate the governor.

Judas Hangs Himself

3Then Judas, His betrayer, seeing that
He had been condemned, was remorseful
and brought back the thirty pieces of silver
to the chief priests and elders, 4saying, "I
have sinned by betraying innocent blood."
And they said, "What *is that* to us? You
see *to it!*"
5Then he threw down the pieces of silver
in the temple and departed, and went and
hanged himself.
6But the chief priests took the silver pieces and said, "It is not lawful to put them into
the treasury, because they are the price of
blood." 7And they consulted together and
bought with them the potter's field, to bury
strangers in. 8Therefore that field has been
called the Field of Blood to this day.
9Then was fulfilled what was spoken
by Jeremiah the prophet, saying, "And they
took the thirty pieces of silver, the value of
Him who was priced, whom they of the children of Israel priced, 10and gave them for the
potter's field, as the LORD directed me."[a]

Jesus Faces Pilate

11Now Jesus stood before the governor.
And the governor asked Him, saying, "Are
You the King of the Jews?"
Jesus said to him, "*It is as* you say." 12And
while He was being accused by the chief
priests and elders, He answered nothing.
13Then Pilate said to Him, "Do You not
hear how many things they testify against
You?" 14But He answered him not one word,
so that the governor marveled greatly.

Taking the Place of Barabbas

15Now at the feast the governor was accustomed to releasing to the multitude one prisoner whom they wished. 16And at that time
they had a notorious prisoner called Barabbas.[a] 17Therefore, when they had gathered
together, Pilate said to them, "Whom do you
want me to release to you? Barabbas, or Jesus
who is called Christ?" 18For he knew that they
had handed Him over because of envy.
19While he was sitting on the judgment
seat, his wife sent to him, saying, "Have
nothing to do with that just Man, for I have
suffered many things today in a dream because of Him."
20But the chief priests and elders persuaded the multitudes that they should ask
for Barabbas and destroy Jesus. 21The governor answered and said to them, "Which of
the two do you want me to release to you?"
They said, "Barabbas!"
22Pilate said to them, "What then shall I
do with Jesus who is called Christ?"
They all said to him, "Let Him be
crucified!"

27:2 [a] NU-Text omits *Pontius.* 27:10 [a] Jeremiah 32:6–9
27:16 [a] NU-Text reads *Jesus Barabbas.*

23Then the governor said, "Why, what
evil has He done?"

But they cried out all the more, saying,
"Let Him be crucified!"

24When Pilate saw that he could not prevail at all, but rather *that* a tumult was rising,
he took water and washed *his* hands before
the multitude, saying, "I am innocent of the
blood of this just Person.[a] You see *to it*."

25And all the people answered and said,
"His blood *be* on us and on our children."

26Then he released Barabbas to them;
and when he had scourged Jesus, he delivered *Him* to be crucified.

The Soldiers Mock Jesus

27Then the soldiers of the governor took
Jesus into the Praetorium and gathered the
whole garrison around Him. 28And they
stripped Him and put a scarlet robe on Him.
29When they had twisted a crown of thorns,
they put *it* on His head, and a reed in His
right hand. And they bowed the knee before
Him and mocked Him, saying, "Hail, King
of the Jews!" 30Then they spat on Him, and
took the reed and struck Him on the head.
31And when they had mocked Him, they
took the robe off Him, put His *own* clothes
on Him, and led Him away to be crucified.

The King on a Cross

32Now as they came out, they found a
man of Cyrene, Simon by name. Him they
compelled to bear His cross. 33And when
they had come to a place called Golgotha,
that is to say, Place of a Skull, 34they gave
Him sour[a] wine mingled with gall to drink.
But when He had tasted *it*, He would not
drink.

35Then they crucified Him, and divided
His garments, casting lots,[a] that it might be
fulfilled which was spoken by the prophet:

"They divided My garments among
them,
And for My clothing they cast lots."[b]

36Sitting down, they kept watch over Him
there. 37And they put up over His head the
accusation written against Him:

THIS IS JESUS THE KING
OF THE JEWS.

38Then two robbers were crucified with
Him, one on the right and another on the
left.

39And those who passed by blasphemed
Him, wagging their heads 40and saying,
"You who destroy the temple and build *it* in
three days, save Yourself! If You are the Son
of God, come down from the cross."

41Likewise the chief priests also, mock-
ing with the scribes and elders,[a] said, 42"He
saved others; Himself He cannot save. If
He is the King of Israel,[a] let Him now come
down from the cross, and we will believe
Him.[b] 43He trusted in God; let Him deliver
Him now if He will have Him; for He said,
'I am the Son of God.'"

44Even the robbers who were crucified
with Him reviled Him with the same thing.

27:24 [a] NU-Text omits *just*. 27:34 [a] NU-Text omits *sour*. 27:35 [a] NU-Text and M-Text omit the rest of this verse. [b] Psalm 22:18 27:41 [a] M-Text reads *with the scribes, the Pharisees, and the elders*. 27:42 [a] NU-Text reads *He is the King of Israel!* [b] NU-Text and M-Text read *we will believe in Him*.

BULLYING

READ IT: MATTHEW 27:27–31

Jesus knows what it feels like to be bullied, both verbally and physically. He was stripped, spit on, injured, and mocked in front of a crowd of people who did nothing to stop it. He didn't deserve it. It was totally unfair. If you've ever been bullied in any way, you can talk to Jesus about what's going on, confident that He understands, listens, and cares.

Jesus Dies on the Cross

45 Now from the sixth hour until the ninth
hour there was darkness over all the land.
46 And about the ninth hour Jesus cried out
with a loud voice, saying, "Eli, Eli, lama sabachthani?" that is, "My God, My God, why
have You forsaken Me?"[a]

47 Some of those who stood there, when
they heard *that,* said, "This Man is calling
for Elijah!" 48 Immediately one of them ran
and took a sponge, filled *it* with sour wine
and put *it* on a reed, and offered it to Him
to drink.

49 The rest said, "Let Him alone; let us see
if Elijah will come to save Him."

50 And Jesus cried out again with a loud
voice, and yielded up His spirit.

51 Then, behold, the veil of the temple
was torn in two from top to bottom; and the
earth quaked, and the rocks were split, 52 and
the graves were opened; and many bodies of
the saints who had fallen asleep were raised;
53 and coming out of the graves after His resurrection, they went into the holy city and
appeared to many.

54 So when the centurion and those with
him, who were guarding Jesus, saw the
earthquake and the things that had happened, they feared greatly, saying, "Truly
this was the Son of God!"

55 And many women who followed Jesus
from Galilee, ministering to Him, were
there looking on from afar, 56 among whom
were Mary Magdalene, Mary the mother of
James and Joses,[a] and the mother of Zebedee's sons.

Jesus Buried in Joseph's Tomb

57 Now when evening had come, there
came a rich man from Arimathea, named
Joseph, who himself had also become a disciple of Jesus. 58 This man went to Pilate and
asked for the body of Jesus. Then Pilate commanded the body to be given to him. 59 When
Joseph had taken the body, he wrapped it in
a clean linen cloth, 60 and laid it in his new
tomb which he had hewn out of the rock;
and he rolled a large stone against the door
of the tomb, and departed. 61 And Mary Magdalene was there, and the other Mary, sitting
opposite the tomb.

Pilate Sets a Guard

62 On the next day, which followed the
Day of Preparation, the chief priests and
Pharisees gathered together to Pilate, 63 saying, "Sir, we remember, while He was still
alive, how that deceiver said, 'After three
days I will rise.' 64 Therefore command that
the tomb be made secure until the third day,
lest His disciples come by night[a] and steal
Him *away,* and say to the people, 'He has ris-
en from the dead.' So the last deception will
be worse than the first."

65 Pilate said to them, "You have a guard;
go your way, make *it* as secure as you know
how." 66 So they went and made the tomb secure, sealing the stone and setting the guard.

He Is Risen

28 Now after the Sabbath, as the first
day of the week began to dawn,
Mary Magdalene and the other Mary came to
see the tomb. 2 And behold, there was a great
earthquake; for an angel of the Lord descended from heaven, and came and rolled back the
stone from the door,[a] and sat on it. 3 His countenance was like lightning, and his clothing
as white as snow. 4 And the guards shook for
fear of him, and became like dead *men.*

5 But the angel answered and said to the
women, "Do not be afraid, for I know that
you seek Jesus who was crucified. 6 He is not
here; for He is risen, as He said. Come, see
the place where the Lord lay. 7 And go quickly
and tell His disciples that He is risen from
the dead, and indeed He is going before you
into Galilee; there you will see Him. Behold,
I have told you."

8 So they went out quickly from the tomb
with fear and great joy, and ran to bring His
disciples word.

The Women Worship the Risen Lord

9 And as they went to tell His disciples,[a]
behold, Jesus met them, saying, "Rejoice!"
So they came and held Him by the feet and
worshiped Him. 10 Then Jesus said to them,
"Do not be afraid. Go *and* tell My brethren
to go to Galilee, and there they will see Me."

The Soldiers Are Bribed

11 Now while they were going, behold,
some of the guard came into the city and reported to the chief priests all the things that

---

27:46 [a] Psalm 22:1 **27:56** [a] NU-Text reads *Joseph.* **27:64** [a] NU-Text omits *by night.* **28:2** [a] NU-Text omits *from the door.* **28:9** [a] NU-Text omits the first clause of this verse.

had happened. 12 When they had assembled
with the elders and consulted together, they
gave a large sum of money to the soldiers,
13 saying, "Tell them, 'His disciples came at
night and stole Him *away* while we slept.'
14 And if this comes to the governor's ears, we
will appease him and make you secure." 15 So
they took the money and did as they were
instructed; and this saying is commonly reported among the Jews until this day.

The Great Commission

16 Then the eleven disciples went away
into Galilee, to the mountain which Jesus
had appointed for them. 17 When they saw
Him, they worshiped Him; but some
doubted.

18 And Jesus came and spoke to them,
saying, "All authority has been given to Me
in heaven and on earth. 19 Go therefore[a] and
make disciples of all the nations, baptizing
them in the name of the Father and of the
Son and of the Holy Spirit, 20 teaching them
to observe all things that I have commanded
you; and lo, I am with you always, *even* to the
end of the age." Amen.[a]

28:19 [a] M-Text omits *therefore*. 28:20 [a] NU-Text omits *Amen*.

JESUS' RESURRECTION AND APPEARANCES

READ IT: MATTHEW 28:1–20

GET IT:

After Jesus died, He was buried in a tomb owned by a man named Joseph from Arimathea. This disciple quickly prepared the body for burial and put it in the tomb. Mary Magdalene and Jesus' mother, Mary, watched so they knew where the tomb was. The next day was the Sabbath, so everyone rested. On the first day of the week, the women came back to Jesus' tomb to put spices on His body. They were terribly sad, but when they were close to the tomb, an angel told them that Jesus was alive. Immediately their sadness turned to joy. What a surprise! It was too good to be true! The impossible had happened! The soldiers had killed Jesus, but He didn't stay dead. He was risen!

LIVE IT:

Most of us don't like to be sad. Sadness makes us feel miserable and tired. We'd much rather be happy and laugh. Can you think of a time when you got great news that made you really happy? Maybe you got a gift that you didn't expect for your birthday. Maybe you heard the news that someone was getting better after being really sick. Every time we hear the Easter story we should be excited about the news that Jesus came back to life. This is the most exciting news we will ever get because it means that death for us isn't the end. Jesus proved that death doesn't get the final say. His body came alive again. Ours will too someday.

The GOSPEL ACCORDING to

MARK

A.D. 60s

Behind the Scenes

READ IT:

The book of Mark includes the facts and actions of Jesus' life. It is the most exciting account of the life of Jesus among the four Gospels (Matthew, Mark, Luke, and John). Although it is the shortest of the four books, it often gives the most details of what happened. Mark starts his book with the stories of Jesus' ministry (not Jesus' birth) and includes a lot of His miracles.

GET IT:

Who wrote it: Mark, a Christian associate of Peter

When it was written: A.D. 60s

Why it was written: to tell the non-Jews (the Gentiles) the story of Jesus and that He died to save everyone.

LIVE IT:

We must be servants to others as Jesus was. We must love, care for, and be kind to other people.

FIND IT:

Preparation for Ministry	*Mark 1*
Jesus Teaches Through Parables	*Mark 4*
A Demon-Possessed Man Healed	*Mark 5*
Jesus Transfigured on the Mount	*Mark 9*
The Anointing at Bethany	*Mark 14*
Jesus' Trial and Death	*Mark 15*
He Is Risen	*Mark 16*

John the Baptist Prepares the Way

1 The beginning of the gospel of Jesus
Christ, the Son of God. 2As it is written
in the Prophets:[a]

"Behold, I send My messenger before
Your face,
Who will prepare Your way before
You." [b]
3 "The voice of one crying in the
wilderness:
'Prepare the way of the LORD;
Make His paths straight.' " [a]

4John came baptizing in the wilderness
and preaching a baptism of repentance for
the remission of sins. 5Then all the land of
Judea, and those from Jerusalem, went out
to him and were all baptized by him in the
Jordan River, confessing their sins.

6Now John was clothed with camel's hair
and with a leather belt around his waist,
and he ate locusts and wild honey. 7And he
preached, saying, "There comes One after
me who is mightier than I, whose sandal
strap I am not worthy to stoop down and
loose. 8I indeed baptized you with water, but
He will baptize you with the Holy Spirit."

John Baptizes Jesus

9It came to pass in those days *that* Jesus
came from Nazareth of Galilee, and was baptized by John in the Jordan. 10And immediately, coming up from[a] the water, He saw the
heavens parting and the Spirit descending
upon Him like a dove. 11Then a voice came
from heaven, "You are My beloved Son, in
whom I am well pleased."

Satan Tempts Jesus

12Immediately the Spirit drove Him into
the wilderness. 13And He was there in the
wilderness forty days, tempted by Satan,
and was with the wild beasts; and the angels
ministered to Him.

Jesus Begins His Galilean Ministry

14Now after John was put in prison, Jesus
came to Galilee, preaching the gospel of the
kingdom[a] of God, 15and saying, "The time is
fulfilled, and the kingdom of God is at hand.
Repent, and believe in the gospel."

Four Fishermen Called as Disciples

16And as He walked by the Sea of Galilee, He saw Simon and Andrew his brother
casting a net into the sea; for they were fishermen. 17Then Jesus said to them, "Follow
Me, and I will make you become fishers of
men." 18They immediately left their nets and
followed Him.

19When He had gone a little farther from
there, He saw James the *son* of Zebedee, and
John his brother, who also *were* in the boat
mending their nets. 20And immediately He
called them, and they left their father Zebedee in the boat with the hired servants, and
went after Him.

1:2 [a] NU-Text reads *Isaiah the prophet.* [b] Malachi 3:1
1:3 [a] Isaiah 40:3 1:10 [a] NU-Text reads *out of.* 1:14 [a] NU-Text omits *of the kingdom.*

Starring Roles

MARK was the youngest of Jesus' disciples. In fact, he was too young to understand a lot of the things Jesus said when he listened to Him, but he couldn't stay away from Him. Jesus seemed like a great older Brother to Mark. When He was crucified, Mark was afraid. Like most of the others, he ran away from Calvary where they killed the best Brother Mark had ever known.

When Mark grew up, he became a useful helper to the apostles Paul and Peter. An apostle was someone "sent" by God with the gospel. While Mark was living in Rome, Peter helped him to write this earliest Gospel about the life and work of Jesus on earth.

Mark's Gospel is the shortest of the four. He wrote it so the Roman people would be able to know and love his great Brother who is now in heaven.

Jesus Casts Out an Unclean Spirit

21Then they went into Capernaum, and
immediately on the Sabbath He entered
the synagogue and taught. 22And they were
astonished at His teaching, for He taught
them as one having authority, and not as the
scribes.

23Now there was a man in their synagogue with an unclean spirit. And he cried
out, 24saying, "Let *us* alone! What have we
to do with You, Jesus of Nazareth? Did You
come to destroy us? I know who You are—
the Holy One of God!"

25But Jesus rebuked him, saying, "Be
quiet, and come out of him!" 26And when
the unclean spirit had convulsed him and
cried out with a loud voice, he came out of
him. 27Then they were all amazed, so that
they questioned among themselves, saying,
"What is this? What new doctrine *is* this?
For with authority[a] He commands even the
unclean spirits, and they obey Him." 28And
immediately His fame spread throughout all
the region around Galilee.

Peter's Mother-in-Law Healed

29Now as soon as they had come out of
the synagogue, they entered the house of
Simon and Andrew, with James and John.
30But Simon's wife's mother lay sick with a
fever, and they told Him about her at once.
31So He came and took her by the hand and
lifted her up, and immediately the fever left
her. And she served them.

Many Healed After Sabbath Sunset

32At evening, when the sun had set,
they brought to Him all who were sick and
those who were demon-possessed. 33And the
whole city was gathered together at the door.
34Then He healed many who were sick with
various diseases, and cast out many demons;
and He did not allow the demons to speak,
because they knew Him.

Preaching in Galilee

35Now in the morning, having risen a
long while before daylight, He went out
and departed to a solitary place; and there
He prayed. 36And Simon and those *who were*
with Him searched for Him. 37When they
found Him, they said to Him, "Everyone is
looking for You."

38But He said to them, "Let us go into the
next towns, that I may preach there also, because for this purpose I have come forth."

39And He was preaching in their synagogues throughout all Galilee, and casting
out demons.

Jesus Cleanses a Leper

40Now a leper came to Him, imploring

1:27 [a] NU-Text reads *What is this? A new doctrine with authority.*

Starring Roles

God sent His Son Jesus from heaven so that everybody could see what God is like, but nobody has ever seen the **HOLY SPIRIT**. He is like the wind that blows. You feel His presence, but you can't see Him. The word *spirit* comes from a Bible word meaning "wind." The Holy Spirit is the "Wind" of God, but He is also a Person just as much as Jesus and His Father are Persons. He has *always been a part of* God, just as the Father and the Son are part of God.

The Holy Spirit's work is to make God's plans happen in the world. At the very beginning of time, He was the One who made the Creation happen when God spoke the command: "Let there be light." (See Genesis 1:2, 3.)

The Holy Spirit is also the One who took the place of Jesus in the world, and He keeps on doing His great works. He wants to live in you so Jesus can do His works through you.

Him, kneeling down to Him and saying to
Him, "If You are willing, You can make me
clean."

41 Then Jesus, moved with compassion,
stretched out *His* hand and touched him,
and said to him, "I am willing; be cleansed."
42 As soon as He had spoken, immediately
the leprosy left him, and he was cleansed.
43 And He strictly warned him and sent him
away at once, 44 and said to him, "See that
you say nothing to anyone; but go your way,
show yourself to the priest, and offer for your
cleansing those things which Moses commanded, as a testimony to them."

45 However, he went out and began to proclaim *it* freely, and to spread the matter, so
that Jesus could no longer openly enter the
city, but was outside in deserted places; and
they came to Him from every direction.

Jesus Forgives and Heals a Paralytic

2 And again He entered Capernaum after *some* days, and it was heard that He
was in the house. 2 Immediately[a] many gathered together, so that there was no longer
room to receive *them,* not even near the door.
And He preached the word to them. 3 Then
they came to Him, bringing a paralytic who
was carried by four *men.* 4 And when they
could not come near Him because of the
crowd, they uncovered the roof where He
was. So when they had broken through, they
let down the bed on which the paralytic was
lying.

5 When Jesus saw their faith, He said to
the paralytic, "Son, your sins are forgiven
you."

6 And some of the scribes were sitting
there and reasoning in their hearts, 7 "Why
does this *Man* speak blasphemies like this?
Who can forgive sins but God alone?"

8 But immediately, when Jesus perceived
in His spirit that they reasoned thus within
themselves, He said to them, "Why do you
reason about these things in your hearts?
9 Which is easier, to say to the paralytic,
'*Your* sins are forgiven you,' or to say, 'Arise,
take up your bed and walk'? 10 But that you
may know that the Son of Man has power
on earth to forgive sins"—He said to the
paralytic, 11 "I say to you, arise, take up your
bed, and go to your house." 12 Immediately he
arose, took up the bed, and went out in the
presence of them all, so that all were amazed

2:2 [a] NU-Text omits *Immediately.*

REPENT AND BELIEVE IN THE GOSPEL

READ IT: MARK 1:15

The New Testament was first written in Greek, and the word *repent* comes from a Greek word meaning "to turn around," or change your mind. So repentance doesn't mean simply being sorry for your sins. Being sorry alone doesn't change anything. Repenting means changing your mind about how you're going to live. You used to live for yourself. Now you'll live for Jesus.

To "believe in the gospel" simply means trusting Jesus. Trusting Jesus is something like learning to swim. As long as you keep fighting the water, you'll sink. But just as soon as you let yourself relax in the water, you'll float. In the same way, trusting Jesus is relaxing in what Jesus has promised. Then you will find out that everything He has promised will come true for you.

and glorified God, saying, "We never saw
anything like this!"

Matthew the Tax Collector

13Then He went out again by the sea;
and all the multitude came to Him, and He
taught them. 14As He passed by, He saw Levi
the *son* of Alphaeus sitting at the tax office.
And He said to him, "Follow Me." So he
arose and followed Him.

15Now it happened, as He was dining in
Levi's house, that many tax collectors and
sinners also sat together with Jesus and
His disciples; for there were many, and they
followed Him. 16And when the scribes and[a]
Pharisees saw Him eating with the tax collectors and sinners, they said to His disciples, "How *is it* that He eats and drinks with
tax collectors and sinners?"

17When Jesus heard *it,* He said to them,
"Those who are well have no need of a physician, but those who are sick. I did not
come to call *the* righteous, but sinners, to
repentance."[a]

Jesus Is Questioned About Fasting

18The disciples of John and of the Pharisees were fasting. Then they came and said
to Him, "Why do the disciples of John and
of the Pharisees fast, but Your disciples do
not fast?"

19And Jesus said to them, "Can the
friends of the bridegroom fast while the
bridegroom is with them? As long as they
have the bridegroom with them they cannot
fast. 20But the days will come when the bridegroom will be taken away from them, and
then they will fast in those days. 21No one
sews a piece of unshrunk cloth on an old
garment; or else the new piece pulls away
from the old, and the tear is made worse.
22And no one puts new wine into old wineskins; or else the new wine bursts the wineskins, the wine is spilled, and the wineskins
are ruined. But new wine must be put into
new wineskins."

Jesus Is Lord of the Sabbath

23Now it happened that He went through
the grainfields on the Sabbath; and as they
went His disciples began to pluck the heads
of grain. 24And the Pharisees said to Him,
"Look, why do they do what is not lawful on
the Sabbath?"

25But He said to them, "Have you never

In Focus

2:17 Repentance Pronounced *re-PEN-tunce.* Turning away from sin to obey God. You repent when you leave your sins to receive Christ as your Savior and Master of your life.

2:26 Showbread A symbol of God's presence and supply. In the temple every Sabbath, 12 loaves of bread were arranged on a table about 36 inches long by 18 inches wide by 27 inches high.

read what David did when he was in need
and hungry, he and those with him: 26how
he went into the house of God *in the days* of
Abiathar the high priest, and ate the showbread, which is not lawful to eat except for
the priests, and also gave some to those who
were with him?"

27And He said to them, "The Sabbath was
made for man, and not man for the Sabbath.
28Therefore the Son of Man is also Lord of
the Sabbath."

Healing on the Sabbath

3 And He entered the synagogue again,
and a man was there who had a withered hand. 2So they watched Him closely,
whether He would heal him on the Sabbath,
so that they might accuse Him. 3And He
said to the man who had the withered hand,
"Step forward." 4Then He said to them, "Is
it lawful on the Sabbath to do good or to do
evil, to save life or to kill?" But they kept silent. 5And when He had looked around at
them with anger, being grieved by the hardness of their hearts, He said to the man,
"Stretch out your hand." And he stretched
it out, and his hand was restored as whole
as the other.[a] 6Then the Pharisees went out
and immediately plotted with the Herodians
against Him, how they might destroy Him.

A Great Multitude Follows Jesus

7But Jesus withdrew with His disciples

2:16 [a] NU-Text reads *of the.* 2:17 [a] NU-Text omits *to repentance.* 3:5 [a] NU-Text omits *as whole as the other.*

to the sea. And a great multitude from Galilee followed Him, and from Judea 8and Jerusalem and Idumea and beyond the Jordan; and those from Tyre and Sidon, a great multitude, when they heard how many things He was doing, came to Him. 9So He told His disciples that a small boat should be kept ready for Him because of the multitude, lest they should crush Him. 10For He healed many, so that as many as had afflictions pressed about Him to touch Him. 11And the unclean spirits, whenever they saw Him, fell down before Him and cried out, saying, "You are the Son of God." 12But He sternly warned them that they should not make Him known.

The Twelve Apostles

13And He went up on the mountain and called to *Him* those He Himself wanted. And they came to Him. 14Then He appointed twelve,[a] that they might be with Him and that He might send them out to preach, 15and to have power to heal sicknesses and[a] to cast out demons: 16Simon,[a] to whom He gave the name Peter; 17James the *son* of Zebedee and John the brother of James, to whom He gave the name Boanerges, that is, "Sons of Thunder"; 18Andrew, Philip, Bartholomew, Matthew, Thomas, James the *son* of Alphaeus, Thaddaeus, Simon the Cananite; 19and Judas Iscariot, who also betrayed Him. And they went into a house.

A House Divided Cannot Stand

20Then the multitude came together again, so that they could not so much as eat bread. 21But when His own people heard *about this,* they went out to lay hold of Him, for they said, "He is out of His mind."

22And the scribes who came down from Jerusalem said, "He has Beelzebub," and, "By the ruler of the demons He casts out demons."

23So He called them to *Himself* and said to them in parables: "How can Satan cast out Satan? 24If a kingdom is divided against itself, that kingdom cannot stand. 25And if a house is divided against itself, that house cannot stand. 26And if Satan has risen up against himself, and is divided, he cannot stand, but has an end. 27No one can enter a strong man's house and plunder his goods, unless he first binds the strong man. And then he will plunder his house.

The Unpardonable Sin

28"Assuredly, I say to you, all sins will be forgiven the sons of men, and whatever blasphemies they may utter; 29but he who blasphemes against the Holy Spirit never has forgiveness, but is subject to eternal condemnation"— 30because they said, "He has an unclean spirit."

Jesus' Mother and Brothers Send for Him

31Then His brothers and His mother came, and standing outside they sent to Him, calling Him. 32And a multitude was sitting around Him; and they said to Him, "Look, Your mother and Your brothers[a] are outside seeking You."

33But He answered them, saying, "Who is My mother, or My brothers?" 34And He looked around in a circle at those who sat about Him, and said, "Here are My mother and My brothers! 35For whoever does the will of God is My brother and My sister and mother."

The Parable of the Sower

4 And again He began to teach by the sea. And a great multitude was gathered to Him, so that He got into a boat and sat *in it* on the sea; and the whole multitude was on the land facing the sea. 2Then He taught them many things by parables, and said to them in His teaching:

3"Listen! Behold, a sower went out to sow. 4And it happened, as he sowed, *that* some *seed* fell by the wayside; and the birds of the air[a] came and devoured it. 5Some fell on stony ground, where it did not have much earth; and immediately it sprang up because it had no depth of earth. 6But when the sun was up it was scorched, and because it had no root it withered away. 7And some *seed* fell among thorns; and the thorns grew up and choked it, and it yielded no crop. 8But other *seed* fell on good ground and yielded a crop that sprang up, increased and produced: some thirtyfold, some sixty, and some a hundred."

9And He said to them,[a] "He who has ears to hear, let him hear!"

3:14 [a] NU-Text adds *whom He also named apostles.*
3:15 [a] NU-Text omits *to heal sicknesses and.* 3:16 [a] NU-Text reads *and He appointed the twelve: Simon . . . .* 3:32 [a] NU-Text and M-Text add *and Your sisters.* 4:4 [a] NU-Text and M-Text omit *of the air.* 4:9 [a] NU-Text and M-Text omit *to them.*

The Purpose of Parables

[10]But when He was alone, those around
Him with the twelve asked Him about the
parable. [11]And He said to them, "To you it has
been given to know the mystery of the kingdom of God; but to those who are outside, all
things come in parables, [12]so that

'Seeing they may see and not perceive,
And hearing they may hear and not
understand;
Lest they should turn,
And *their* sins be forgiven them.' "[a]

The Parable of the Sower Explained

[13]And He said to them, "Do you not
understand this parable? How then will you
understand all the parables? [14]The sower
sows the word. [15]And these are the ones by
the wayside where the word is sown. When
they hear, Satan comes immediately and
takes away the word that was sown in their
hearts. [16]These likewise are the ones sown
on stony ground who, when they hear the
word, immediately receive it with gladness;
[17]and they have no root in themselves, and so
endure only for a time. Afterward, when tribulation or persecution arises for the word's
sake, immediately they stumble. [18]Now these
are the ones sown among thorns; *they are*
the ones who hear the word, [19]and the cares
of this world, the deceitfulness of riches,
and the desires for other things entering
in choke the word, and it becomes unfruitful. [20]But these are the ones sown on good
ground, those who hear the word, accept *it,*
and bear fruit: some thirtyfold, some sixty,
and some a hundred."

Light Under a Basket

[21]Also He said to them, "Is a lamp brought
to be put under a basket or under a bed? Is it
not to be set on a lampstand? [22]For there is
nothing hidden which will not be revealed,
nor has anything been kept secret but that it
should come to light. [23]If anyone has ears to
hear, let him hear."

[24]*Then He said to them,* "Take heed what
you hear. With the same measure you use,
it will be measured to you; and to you who
hear, more will be given. [25]For whoever has,
to him more will be given; but whoever does
not have, even what he has will be taken
away from him."

The Parable of the Growing Seed

[26]And He said, "The kingdom of God
is as if a man should scatter seed on the
ground, [27]and should sleep by night and rise
by day, and the seed should sprout and grow,
he himself does not know how. [28]For the
earth yields crops by itself: first the blade,
then the head, after that the full grain in the
head. [29]But when the grain ripens, immediately he puts in the sickle, because the harvest has come."

The Parable of the Mustard Seed

[30]Then He said, "To what shall we liken
the kingdom of God? Or with what para-
ble shall we picture it? [31]*It is* like a mustard
seed which, when it is sown on the ground,
is smaller than all the seeds on earth; [32]but
when it is sown, it grows up and becomes
greater than all herbs, and shoots out large
branches, so that the birds of the air may
nest under its shade."

Jesus' Use of Parables

[33]And with many such parables He spoke
the word to them as they were able to hear
it. [34]But without a parable He did not speak
to them. And when they were alone, He explained all things to His disciples.

Wind and Wave Obey Jesus

[35]On the same day, when evening had
come, He said to them, "Let us cross over to
the other side." [36]Now when they had left the
multitude, they took Him along in the boat
as He was. And other little boats were also
with Him. [37]And a great windstorm arose,
and the waves beat into the boat, so that it
was already filling. [38]But He was in the stern,
asleep on a pillow. And they awoke Him and
said to Him, "Teacher, do You not care that
we are perishing?"

[39]Then He arose and rebuked the wind,
and said to the sea, "Peace, be still!" And
the wind ceased and there was a great calm.
[40]But He said to them, "Why are you so fearful? How *is it* that you have no faith?"[a] [41]And
they feared exceedingly, and said to one another, "Who can this be, that even the wind
and the sea obey Him!"

A Demon-Possessed Man Healed

5 Then they came to the other side of the
sea, to the country of the Gadarenes.[a]
[2]And when He had come out of the boat,

4:12 [a] Isaiah 6:9, 10 4:40 [a] NU-Text reads *Have you still no faith?* 5:1 [a] NU-Text reads *Gerasenes.*

immediately there met Him out of the
tombs a man with an unclean spirit, 3who
had *his* dwelling among the tombs; and no
one could bind him,[a] not even with chains,
4because he had often been bound with
shackles and chains. And the chains had
been pulled apart by him, and the shackles
broken in pieces; neither could anyone tame
him. 5And always, night and day, he was in
the mountains and in the tombs, crying out
and cutting himself with stones.

6When he saw Jesus from afar, he ran
and worshiped Him. 7And he cried out with
a loud voice and said, "What have I to do
with You, Jesus, Son of the Most High God?
I implore You by God that You do not torment me."

8For He said to him, "Come out of the
man, unclean spirit!" 9Then He asked him,
"What *is* your name?"

And he answered, saying, "My name *is*
Legion; for we are many." 10Also he begged
Him earnestly that He would not send them
out of the country.

11Now a large herd of swine was feeding there near the mountains. 12So all the
demons begged Him, saying, "Send us to
the swine, that we may enter them." 13And
at once Jesus[a] gave them permission. Then
the unclean spirits went out and entered the
swine (there were about two thousand); and
the herd ran violently down the steep place
into the sea, and drowned in the sea.

14So those who fed the swine fled, and
they told *it* in the city and in the country. And
they went out to see what it was that had happened. 15Then they came to Jesus, and saw
the one *who had been* demon-possessed and
had the legion, sitting and clothed and in
his right mind. And they were afraid. 16And
those who saw it told them how it happened
to him *who had been* demon-possessed, and
about the swine. 17Then they began to plead
with Him to depart from their region.

18And when He got into the boat, he who
had been demon-possessed begged Him
that he might be with Him. 19However,
Jesus did not permit him, but said to him,
"Go home to your friends, and tell them
what great things the Lord has done for you,
and how He has had compassion on you."
20And he departed and began to proclaim in
Decapolis all that Jesus had done for him;
and all marveled.

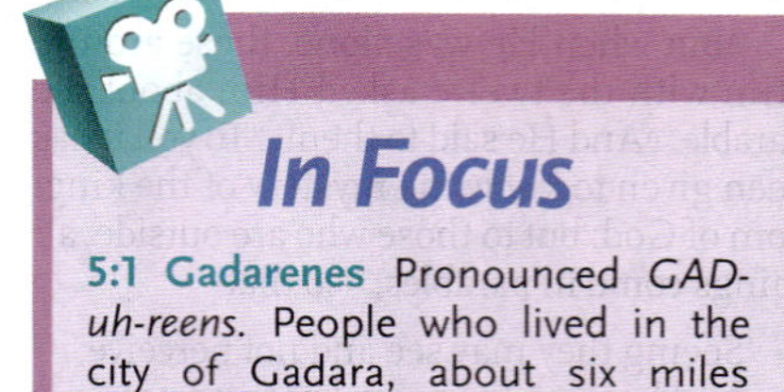

5:1 Gadarenes Pronounced *GAD-uh-reens.* People who lived in the city of Gadara, about six miles southeast of the Sea of Galilee. Gadara was one of the group called "Ten Cities."

A Girl Restored to Life and a Woman Healed

21Now when Jesus had crossed over again
by boat to the other side, a great multitude
gathered to Him; and He was by the sea.
22And behold, one of the rulers of the synagogue came, Jairus by name. And when
he saw Him, he fell at His feet 23and begged
Him earnestly, saying, "My little daughter
lies at the point of death. Come and lay Your
hands on her, that she may be healed, and
she will live." 24So *Jesus* went with him, and a
great multitude followed Him and thronged
Him.

25Now a certain woman had a flow of
blood for twelve years, 26and had suffered
many things from many physicians. She had
spent all that she had and was no better, but
rather grew worse. 27When she heard about
Jesus, she came behind *Him* in the crowd
and touched His garment. 28For she said, "If
only I may touch His clothes, I shall be made
well."

29Immediately the fountain of her blood
was dried up, and she felt in *her* body that
she was healed of the affliction. 30And Jesus,
immediately knowing in Himself that power
had gone out of Him, turned around in the
crowd and said, "Who touched My clothes?"

31But His disciples said to Him, "You see
the multitude thronging You, and You say,
'Who touched Me?' "

32And He looked around to see her who
had done this thing. 33But the woman, fearing and trembling, knowing what had happened to her, came and fell down before
Him and told Him the whole truth. 34And
He said to her, "Daughter, your faith has

5:3 [a] NU-Text adds *anymore.* 5:13 [a] NU-Text reads *And He gave.*

made you well. Go in peace, and be healed of
your affliction."
35 While He was still speaking, *some* came
from the ruler of the synagogue's *house* who
said, "Your daughter is dead. Why trouble
the Teacher any further?"
36 As soon as Jesus heard the word that
was spoken, He said to the ruler of the synagogue, "Do not be afraid; only believe." 37 And
He permitted no one to follow Him except
Peter, James, and John the brother of James.
38 Then He came to the house of the ruler of
the synagogue, and saw a tumult and those
who wept and wailed loudly. 39 When He
came in, He said to them, "Why make this
commotion and weep? The child is not dead,
but sleeping."
40 And they ridiculed Him. But when He
had put them all outside, He took the father and the mother of the child, and those
who were with Him, and entered where the
child was lying. 41 Then He took the child by
the hand, and said to her, "Talitha, cumi,"
which is translated, "Little girl, I say to you,
arise." 42 Immediately the girl arose and
walked, for she was twelve years *of age*. And
they were overcome with great amazement.
43 But He commanded them strictly that no
one should know it, and said that *something*
should be given her to eat.

Jesus Rejected at Nazareth

6 Then He went out from there and
came to His own country, and His disciples followed Him. 2 And when the Sabbath
had come, He began to teach in the synagogue. And many hearing *Him* were astonished, saying, "Where *did* this Man *get* these
things? And what wisdom *is* this which is
given to Him, that such mighty works are
performed by His hands! 3 Is this not the
carpenter, the Son of Mary, and brother of

JESUS RAISES A GIRL FROM THE DEAD

READ IT: MARK 5:21–24, 35–43

GET IT:

The father of this twelve-year-old girl was an important leader in the synagogue who handled the maintenance of the building and led in worship. He knew that Jesus' touch could heal his daughter. But when his daughter died, he was very upset, and he had no idea that Jesus was able to raise someone from the dead. In fact, even the disciples were surprised when it happened. This had never happened before. It was the first time Jesus performed such a miracle.

LIVE IT:

Jairus knew he could ask Jesus to heal his daughter, but he didn't have a clue to later ask Him to make her come alive again. That seemed like an impossible thing to ask for. But Jesus can do anything. He is God. He can do more than we can ask or imagine (Ephesians 3:20). All things are possible for Him (Matthew 19:26). What are you facing that seems impossible, that you aren't even sure God can do something about? Hand your problem over to God. Trust Him to handle it. Then watch what He does.

James, Joses, Judas, and Simon? And are not His sisters here with us?" So they were offended at Him.

4But Jesus said to them, "A prophet is not without honor except in his own country, among his own relatives, and in his own house." 5Now He could do no mighty work there, except that He laid His hands on a few sick people and healed *them.* 6And He marveled because of their unbelief. Then He went about the villages in a circuit, teaching.

Sending Out the Twelve

7And He called the twelve to *Himself,* and began to send them out two *by* two, and gave them power over unclean spirits. 8He commanded them to take nothing for the journey except a staff—no bag, no bread, no copper in *their* money belts— 9but to wear sandals, and not to put on two tunics.

10Also He said to them, "In whatever place you enter a house, stay there till you depart from that place. 11And whoever[a] will not receive you nor hear you, when you depart from there, shake off the dust under your feet as a testimony against them.[b] Assuredly, I say to you, it will be more tolerable for Sodom and Gomorrah in the day of judgment than for that city!"

12So they went out and preached that *people* should repent. 13And they cast out many demons, and anointed with oil many who were sick, and healed *them.*

John the Baptist Beheaded

14Now King Herod heard *of Him,* for His name had become well known. And he said, "John the Baptist is risen from the dead, and therefore these powers are at work in him."

15Others said, "It is Elijah."

And others said, "It is the Prophet, or[a] like one of the prophets."

16But when Herod heard, he said, "This is John, whom I beheaded; he has been raised from the dead!" 17For Herod himself had sent and laid hold of John, and bound him in prison for the sake of Herodias, his brother Philip's wife; for he had married her. 18Because John had said to Herod, "It is not lawful for you to have your brother's wife."

19Therefore Herodias held it against him and wanted to kill him, but she could not; 20for Herod feared John, knowing that he *was* a just and holy man, and he protected him. And when he heard him, he did many things, and heard him gladly.

21Then an opportune day came when Herod on his birthday gave a feast for his nobles, the high officers, and the chief *men* of Galilee. 22And when Herodias' daughter herself came in and danced, and pleased Herod and those who sat with him, the king said to the girl, "Ask me whatever you want, and I will give *it* to you." 23He also swore to her, "Whatever you ask me, I will give you, up to half my kingdom."

24So she went out and said to her mother, "What shall I ask?"

And she said, "The head of John the Baptist!"

25Immediately she came in with haste to the king and asked, saying, "I want you to give me at once the head of John the Baptist on a platter."

26And the king was exceedingly sorry; *yet,* because of the oaths and because of those who sat with him, he did not want to refuse her. 27Immediately the king sent an executioner and commanded his head to be brought. And he went and beheaded him in prison, 28brought his head on a platter, and gave it to the girl; and the girl gave it to her mother. 29When his disciples heard *of it,* they came and took away his corpse and laid it in a tomb.

Feeding the Five Thousand

30Then the apostles gathered to Jesus and told Him all things, both what they had done and what they had taught. 31And He said to them, "Come aside by yourselves to a deserted place and rest a while." For there were many coming and going, and they did not even have time to eat. 32So they departed to a deserted place in the boat by themselves.

33But the multitudes[a] saw them departing, and many knew Him and ran there on foot from all the cities. They arrived before them and came together to Him. 34And Jesus, when He came out, saw a great multitude and was moved with compassion for them, because they were like sheep not having a shepherd. So He began to teach them many things. 35When the day was now far

---

6:11 [a] NU-Text reads *whatever place.* [b] NU-Text omits the rest of this verse. 6:15 [a] NU-Text and M-Text omit *or.* 6:33 [a] NU-Text and M-Text read *they.*

spent, His disciples came to Him and said,
"This is a deserted place, and already the
hour *is* late. 36Send them away, that they may
go into the surrounding country and villages and buy themselves bread;[a] for they have
nothing to eat.'
37But He answered and said to them,
"You give them something to eat."

And they said to Him, "Shall we go and
buy two hundred denarii worth of bread and
give them *something* to eat?"
38But He said to them, "How many loaves
do you have? Go and see."

6:36 [a] NU-Text reads *something to eat* and omits the rest of this verse.

Action!

COMPASSION

MULTIPLYING COMPASSION

READ IT: MARK 6:30–44

GET IT:

The apostles had just finished a busy season of hard work. They'd been preaching, teaching, praying, healing—you name it. They went back to Jesus to report on what they'd been doing. Knowing how hard they had been working, Jesus showed them compassion. He basically told them to go on vacation.

The disciples got on a boat and sailed away. But people in the town figured out where the disciples were headed, took a shortcut, and got there before the disciples. The disciples' vacation was suddenly interrupted.

Jesus saw what happened and had compassion on the people who had traveled to meet them. Late in the day the disciples suggested that Jesus send the people away to get food. Jesus' reply? *You* feed them.

The disciples were confused. There were thousands of people. Were they supposed to go to the market and somehow buy enough food for everyone? That would be impossible. But Jesus did the impossible. He took a kid's lunch and multiplied it into food for everyone.

Jesus' heart of compassion shines in this story. He had compassion on the disciples and told them to rest. He taught the crowd even though everyone was exhausted. And He performed a miracle so both the disciples' need for rest and the people's need for food were met.

LIVE IT:

Our God is compassionate. He often brings relief in unexpected ways. In the same way, because Jesus lives in us, we are equipped to show compassion. If you know of people in your life who are having a difficult time, how can you show them compassion? How can you help them find rest? Could you volunteer your time by helping out at church, helping an elderly neighbor, or helping your mom or dad?

And when they found out they said, "Five, and two fish."

39 Then He commanded them to make them all sit down in groups on the green grass. 40 So they sat down in ranks, in hundreds and in fifties. 41 And when He had taken the five loaves and the two fish, He looked up to heaven, blessed and broke the loaves, and gave *them* to His disciples to set before them; and the two fish He divided among *them* all. 42 So they all ate and were filled. 43 And they took up twelve baskets full of fragments and of the fish. 44 Now those who had eaten the loaves were about[a] five thousand men.

Jesus Walks on the Sea

45 Immediately He made His disciples get into the boat and go before Him to the other side, to Bethsaida, while He sent the multitude away. 46 And when He had sent them away, He departed to the mountain to pray. 47 Now when evening came, the boat was in the middle of the sea; and He *was* alone on the land. 48 Then He saw them straining at rowing, for the wind was against them. Now about the fourth watch of the night He came to them, walking on the sea, and would have passed them by. 49 And when they saw Him walking on the sea, they supposed it was a ghost, and cried out; 50 for they all saw Him and were troubled. But immediately He talked with them and said to them, "Be of good cheer! It is I; do not be afraid." 51 Then He went up into the boat to them, and the wind ceased. And they were greatly amazed in themselves beyond measure, and marveled. 52 For they had not understood about the loaves, because their heart was hardened.

Many Touch Him and Are Made Well

53 When they had crossed over, they came to the land of Gennesaret and anchored there. 54 And when they came out of the boat, immediately the people recognized Him, 55 ran through that whole surrounding region, and began to carry about on beds those who were sick to wherever they heard He was. 56 Wherever He entered, into villages, cities, or the country, they laid the sick in the marketplaces, and begged Him that they might just touch the hem of His garment. And as many as touched Him were made well.

Defilement Comes from Within

7 Then the Pharisees and some of the scribes came together to Him, having come from Jerusalem. 2 Now when[a] they saw some of His disciples eat bread with defiled, that is, with unwashed hands, they found fault. 3 For the Pharisees and all the Jews do not eat unless they wash *their* hands in a special way, holding the tradition of the elders. 4 *When they come* from the marketplace, they do not eat unless they wash. And there are many other things which they have received and hold, *like* the washing of cups, pitchers, copper vessels, and couches.

5 Then the Pharisees and scribes asked Him, "Why do Your disciples not walk according to the tradition of the elders, but eat bread with unwashed hands?"

6 He answered and said to them, "Well did Isaiah prophesy of you hypocrites, as it is written:

'This people honors Me with *their* lips,
But their heart is far from Me.
7 And in vain they worship Me,
Teaching *as* doctrines the
commandments of men.'[a]

8 For laying aside the commandment of God, you hold the tradition of men[a]—the washing of pitchers and cups, and many other such things you do."

9 He said to them, "*All too* well you reject the commandment of God, that you may keep your tradition. 10 For Moses said, 'Honor your father and your mother';[a] and, 'He who curses father or mother, let him be put to death.'[b] 11 But you say, 'If a man says to his father or mother, "Whatever profit you might have received from me *is* Corban"—' (that is, a gift *to God*), 12 then you no longer let him do anything for his father or his mother, 13 making the word of God of no effect through your tradition which you have handed down. And many such things you do."

14 When He had called all the multitude to *Himself,* He said to them, "Hear Me, everyone, and understand: 15 There is nothing that enters a man from outside which can defile him; but the things which come out of him, those are the things that defile a man. 16 If anyone has ears to hear, let him hear!"[a]

6:44 [a] NU-Text and M-Text omit *about.* **7:2** [a] NU-Text omits *when* and *they found fault.* **7:7** [a] Isaiah 29:13 **7:8** [a] NU-Text omits the rest of this verse. **7:10** [a] Exodus 20:12; Deuteronomy 5:16 [b] Exodus 21:17 **7:16** [a] NU-Text omits this verse.

17When He had entered a house away
from the crowd, His disciples asked Him
concerning the parable. 18So He said to
them, "Are you thus without understanding
also? Do you not perceive that whatever enters a man from outside cannot defile him,
19because it does not enter his heart but his
stomach, and is eliminated, *thus* purifying
all foods?"[a] 20And He said, "What comes
out of a man, that defiles a man. 21For from
within, out of the heart of men, proceed evil
thoughts, adulteries, fornications, murders,
22thefts, covetousness, wickedness, deceit,
lewdness, an evil eye, blasphemy, pride, foolishness. 23All these evil things come from
within and defile a man."

A Gentile Shows Her Faith

24From there He arose and went to the
region of Tyre and Sidon.[a] And He entered
a house and wanted no one to know *it,* but
He could not be hidden. 25For a woman
whose young daughter had an unclean spirit heard about Him, and she came and fell at
His feet. 26The woman was a Greek, a Syro-
Phoenician by birth, and she kept asking
Him to cast the demon out of her daughter.
27But Jesus said to her, "Let the children be
filled first, for it is not good to take the children's bread and throw *it* to the little dogs."

28And she answered and said to Him,
"Yes, Lord, yet even the little dogs under the
table eat from the children's crumbs."

29Then He said to her, "For this saying
go your way; the demon has gone out of your
daughter."

30And when she had come to her house,
she found the demon gone out, and her
daughter lying on the bed.

Jesus Heals a Deaf-Mute

31Again, departing from the region of
Tyre and Sidon, He came through the midst
of the region of Decapolis to the Sea of Galilee. 32Then they brought to Him one who
was deaf and had an impediment in his
speech, and they begged Him to put His
hand on him. 33And He took him aside from
the multitude, and put His fingers in his
ears, and He spat and touched his tongue.
34Then, looking up to heaven, He sighed,
and said to him, "Ephphatha," that is, "Be
opened."

35Immediately his ears were opened, and
the impediment of his tongue was loosed,
and he spoke plainly. 36Then He commanded them that they should tell no one; but
the more He commanded them, the more
widely they proclaimed *it.* 37And they were
astonished beyond measure, saying, "He has
done all things well. He makes both the deaf
to hear and the mute to speak."

Feeding the Four Thousand

8 In those days, the multitude being
very great and having nothing to eat,
Jesus called His disciples *to Him* and said to
them, 2"I have compassion on the multitude,
because they have now continued with Me
three days and have nothing to eat. 3And if I
send them away hungry to their own houses,
they will faint on the way; for some of them
have come from afar."

4Then His disciples answered Him,
"How can one satisfy these people with
bread here in the wilderness?"

5He asked them, "How many loaves do
you have?"

And they said, "Seven."

6So He commanded the multitude to sit
down on the ground. And He took the seven
loaves and gave thanks, broke *them* and gave
them to His disciples to set before *them;* and
they set *them* before the multitude. 7They
also had a few small fish; and having blessed
them, He said to set them also before *them.*
8So they ate and were filled, and they took
up seven large baskets of leftover fragments.
9Now those who had eaten were about four
thousand. And He sent them away, 10imme-
diately got into the boat with His disciples,
and came to the region of Dalmanutha.

The Pharisees Seek a Sign

11Then the Pharisees came out and began
to dispute with Him, seeking from Him a
sign from heaven, testing Him. 12But He
sighed deeply in His spirit, and said, "Why
does this generation seek a sign? Assuredly,
I say to you, no sign shall be given to this
generation."

Beware of the Leaven of the Pharisees and Herod

13And He left them, and getting into the
boat again, departed to the other side. 14Now

7:19 [a] NU-Text ends quotation with *eliminated,* setting off the final clause as Mark's comment that Jesus has declared all foods clean. 7:24 [a] NU-Text omits *and Sidon.*

the disciples[a] had forgotten to take bread,
and they did not have more than one loaf
with them in the boat. 15 Then He charged
them, saying, "Take heed, beware of the leav-
en of the Pharisees and the leaven of Herod."
16 And they reasoned among themselves,
saying, "*It is* because we have no bread."
17 But Jesus, being aware of *it,* said to
them, "Why do you reason because you have
no bread? Do you not yet perceive nor understand? Is your heart still[a] hardened? 18 Having eyes, do you not see? And having ears,
do you not hear? And do you not remember?
19 When I broke the five loaves for the five
thousand, how many baskets full of fragments did you take up?"
They said to Him, "Twelve."
20 "Also, when I broke the seven for the
four thousand, how many large baskets full
of fragments did you take up?"
And they said, "Seven."
21 So He said to them, "How *is it* you do
not understand?"

A Blind Man Healed at Bethsaida

22 Then He came to Bethsaida; and they
brought a blind man to Him, and begged
Him to touch him. 23 So He took the blind
man by the hand and led him out of the
town. And when He had spit on his eyes and
put His hands on him, He asked him if he
saw anything.
24 And he looked up and said, "I see men
like trees, walking."
25 Then He put *His* hands on his eyes
again and made him look up. And he was
restored and saw everyone clearly. 26 Then
He sent him away to his house, saying, "Neither go into the town, nor tell anyone in the
town."[a]

Peter Confesses Jesus as the Christ

27 Now Jesus and His disciples went out to
the towns of Caesarea Philippi; and on the
road He asked His disciples, saying to them,
"Who do men say that I am?"
28 So they answered, "John the Baptist;
but some *say,* Elijah; and others, one of the
prophets."
29 He said to them, "But who do you say
that I am?"
Peter answered and said to Him, "You
are the Christ."
30 Then He strictly warned them that they
should tell no one about Him.

Jesus Predicts His Death and Resurrection

31 And He began to teach them that the
Son of Man must suffer many things, and
be rejected by the elders and chief priests
and scribes, and be killed, and after three
days rise again. 32 He spoke this word openly. Then Peter took Him aside and began
to rebuke Him. 33 But when He had turned
around and looked at His disciples, He rebuked Peter, saying, "Get behind Me, Satan!
For you are not mindful of the things of
God, but the things of men."

Take Up the Cross and Follow Him

34 When He had called the people to *Himself,* with His disciples also, He said to them,
"Whoever desires to come after Me, let him
deny himself, and take up his cross, and
follow Me. 35 For whoever desires to save his
life will lose it, but whoever loses his life for
My sake and the gospel's will save it. 36 For
what will it profit a man if he gains the whole
world, and loses his own soul? 37 Or what will
a man give in exchange for his soul? 38 For
whoever is ashamed of Me and My words
in this adulterous and sinful generation, of
him the Son of Man also will be ashamed
when He comes in the glory of His Father
with the holy angels."

9 And He said to them, "Assuredly, I say
to you that there are some standing
here who will not taste death till they see the
kingdom of God present with power."

Jesus Transfigured on the Mount

2 Now after six days Jesus took Peter,
James, and John, and led them up on a high
mountain apart by themselves; and He was
transfigured before them. 3 His clothes became shining, exceedingly white, like snow,
such as no launderer on earth can whiten
them. 4 And Elijah appeared to them with
Moses, and they were talking with Jesus.
5 Then Peter answered and said to Jesus,
"Rabbi, it is good for us to be here; and let
us make three tabernacles: one for You, one
for Moses, and one for Elijah"— 6 because
he did not know what to say, for they were
greatly afraid.
7 And a cloud came and overshadowed

8:14 [a] NU-Text and M-Text read *they.* **8:17** [a] NU-Text omits *still.* **8:26** [a] NU-Text reads *"Do not even go into the town."*

them; and a voice came out of the cloud, saying, "This is My beloved Son. Hear Him!"
8Suddenly, when they had looked around,
they saw no one anymore, but only Jesus
with themselves.
9Now as they came down from the mountain, He commanded them that they should
tell no one the things they had seen, till the
Son of Man had risen from the dead. 10So
they kept this word to themselves, questioning what the rising from the dead meant.
11And they asked Him, saying, "Why do
the scribes say that Elijah must come first?"
12Then He answered and told them, "Indeed, Elijah is coming first and restores all
things. And how is it written concerning
the Son of Man, that He must suffer many
things and be treated with contempt? 13But
I say to you that Elijah has also come, and
they did to him whatever they wished, as it
is written of him."

A Boy Is Healed

14And when He came to the disciples,
He saw a great multitude around them, and
scribes disputing with them. 15Immediate-
ly, when they saw Him, all the people were
greatly amazed, and running to *Him,* greeted Him. 16And He asked the scribes, "What
are you discussing with them?"
17Then one of the crowd answered and
said, "Teacher, I brought You my son, who
has a mute spirit. 18And wherever it seizes
him, it throws him down; he foams at the
mouth, gnashes his teeth, and becomes
rigid. So I spoke to Your disciples, that they
should cast it out, but they could not."
19He answered him and said, "O faithless
generation, how long shall I be with you?
How long shall I bear with you? Bring him to
Me." 20Then they brought him to Him. And
when he saw Him, immediately the spirit
convulsed him, and he fell on the ground
and wallowed, foaming at the mouth.
21So He asked his father, "How long has
this been happening to him?"
And he said, "From childhood. 22And
often he has thrown him both into the fire
and into the water to destroy him. But if You
can do anything, have compassion on us and
help us."
23Jesus said to him, "If you can believe,[a]
all things *are* possible to him who believes."
24Immediately the father of the child
cried out and said with tears, "Lord, I believe; help my unbelief!"
25When Jesus saw that the people came
running together, He rebuked the unclean
spirit, saying to it, "Deaf and dumb spirit,
I command you, come out of him and enter
him no more!" 26Then *the spirit* cried out,
convulsed him greatly, and came out of him.
And he became as one dead, so that many
said, "He is dead." 27But Jesus took him by
the hand and lifted him up, and he arose.
28And when He had come into the house,
His disciples asked Him privately, "Why
could we not cast it out?"
29So He said to them, "This kind can
come out by nothing but prayer and
fasting."[a]

Jesus Again Predicts His Death and Resurrection

30Then they departed from there and
passed through Galilee, and He did not want
anyone to know *it.* 31For He taught His disciples and said to them, "The Son of Man is
being betrayed into the hands of men, and
they will kill Him. And after He is killed,
He will rise the third day." 32But they did not
understand this saying, and were afraid to
ask Him.

Who Is the Greatest?

33Then He came to Capernaum. And
when He was in the house He asked them,
"What was it you disputed among yourselves
on the road?" 34But they kept silent, for on
the road they had disputed among themselves who *would be the* greatest. 35And He
sat down, called the twelve, and said to them,
"If anyone desires to be first, he shall be last
of all and servant of all." 36Then He took a
little child and set him in the midst of them.
And when He had taken him in His arms,
He said to them, 37"Whoever receives one
of these little children in My name receives
Me; and whoever receives Me, receives not
Me but Him who sent Me."

Jesus Forbids Sectarianism

38Now John answered Him, saying,
"Teacher, we saw someone who does not follow us casting out demons in Your name,

9:23 [a] NU-Text reads *"'If You can!' All things . . . ."*
9:29 [a] NU-Text omits *and fasting.*

and we forbade him because he does not follow us."

39 But Jesus said, "Do not forbid him, for no one who works a miracle in My name can soon afterward speak evil of Me. 40 For he who is not against us is on our[a] side. 41 For whoever gives you a cup of water to drink in My name, because you belong to Christ, assuredly, I say to you, he will by no means lose his reward.

Jesus Warns of Offenses

42 "But whoever causes one of these little ones who believe in Me to stumble, it would be better for him if a millstone were hung around his neck, and he were thrown into the sea. 43 If your hand causes you to sin, cut it off. It is better for you to enter into life maimed, rather than having two hands, to go to hell, into the fire that shall never be quenched— 44 where

'Their worm does not die,
And the fire is not quenched.' [a]

45 And if your foot causes you to sin, cut it off. It is better for you to enter life lame, rather than having two feet, to be cast into hell, into the fire that shall never be quenched— 46 where

'Their worm does not die
And the fire is not quenched.' [a]

47 And if your eye causes you to sin, pluck it out. It is better for you to enter the kingdom of God with one eye, rather than having two eyes, to be cast into hell fire— 48 where

'Their worm does not die,
And the fire is not quenched.' [a]

Tasteless Salt Is Worthless

49 "For everyone will be seasoned with fire,[a] and every sacrifice will be seasoned with salt. 50 Salt *is* good, but if the salt loses its flavor, how will you season it? Have salt in yourselves, and have peace with one another."

Marriage and Divorce

10 Then He arose from there and came to the region of Judea by the other side of the Jordan. And multitudes gathered to Him again, and as He was accustomed, He taught them again.

2 The Pharisees came and asked Him, "Is it lawful for a man to divorce *his* wife?" testing Him.

3 And He answered and said to them, "What did Moses command you?"

4 They said, "Moses permitted *a man* to write a certificate of divorce, and to dismiss *her.*"

5 And Jesus answered and said to them, "Because of the hardness of your heart he wrote you this precept. 6 But from the beginning of the creation, God 'made them male and female.' [a] 7 'For this reason a man shall leave his father and mother and be joined to his wife, 8 and the two shall become one flesh';[a] so then they are no longer two, but one flesh. 9 Therefore what God has joined together, let not man separate."

10 In the house His disciples also asked Him again about the same *matter.* 11 So He said to them, "Whoever divorces his wife and marries another commits adultery against her. 12 And if a woman divorces her husband and marries another, she commits adultery."

Jesus Blesses Little Children

13 Then they brought little children to Him, that He might touch them; but the disciples rebuked those who brought *them.* 14 But when Jesus saw *it,* He was greatly displeased and said to them, "Let the little children come to Me, and do not forbid them; for of such is the kingdom of God. 15 Assuredly, I say to you, whoever does not receive the kingdom of God as a little child will by no means enter it." 16 And He took them up in His arms, laid *His* hands on them, and blessed them.

Jesus Counsels the Rich Young Ruler

17 Now as He was going out on the road, one came running, knelt before Him, and asked Him, "Good Teacher, what shall I do that I may inherit eternal life?"

18 So Jesus said to him, "Why do you call Me good? No one *is* good but One, *that is,* God. 19 You know the commandments: 'Do not commit adultery,' 'Do not murder,' 'Do not steal,' 'Do not bear false witness,' 'Do not defraud,' 'Honor your father and your mother.' "[a]

9:40 [a] M-Text reads *against you is on your side.* **9:44** [a] NU-Text omits this verse. **9:46** [a] NU-Text omits the last clause of verse 45 and all of verse 46. **9:48** [a] Isaiah 66:24 **9:49** [a] NU-Text omits the rest of this verse. **10:6** [a] Genesis 1:27; 5:2 **10:8** [a] Genesis 2:24 **10:19** [a] Exodus 20:12–16; Deuteronomy 5:16–20

20And he answered and said to Him,
"Teacher, all these things I have kept from
my youth."
21Then Jesus, looking at him, loved him,
and said to him, "One thing you lack: Go
your way, sell whatever you have and give to
the poor, and you will have treasure in heav-
en; and come, take up the cross, and follow
Me."
22But he was sad at this word, and went
away sorrowful, for he had great possessions.

With God All Things Are Possible

23Then Jesus looked around and said to
His disciples, "How hard it is for those who
have riches to enter the kingdom of God!"
24And the disciples were astonished at His
words. But Jesus answered again and said
to them, "Children, how hard it is for those
who trust in riches[a] to enter the kingdom of
God! 25It is easier for a camel to go through
the eye of a needle than for a rich man to
enter the kingdom of God."
26And they were greatly astonished, saying among themselves, "Who then can be
saved?"
27But Jesus looked at them and said,

10:24 [a] NU-Text omits *for those who trust in riches.*

GOD LOVES YOU JESUS LOVES THE LITTLE CHILDREN

READ IT: MARK 10:13–16

GET IT:

Have you ever heard the song "Jesus Loves the Little Children"? It's a Sunday school song, and the lyrics are simple but true.

Jesus loves the little children,
All the children of the world.
Red and yellow, black and white,
They are precious in His sight.
Jesus loves the little children of the world.

In this passage, we're introduced to how much Jesus loves children. It shows us how much Jesus opens His arms to children . . . and everyone. Sometimes toddlers can be annoying. They can barely walk, they can't really say much, they're needy, and they get dirty really fast. Now think of Jesus. Here we have the King of kings—God in human form. When Jesus was teaching, many of the people started bringing Him their children. The disciples tried to stop them, saying that Jesus was too busy to spend time with the kids. But Jesus wasn't happy with the disciples. Instead, He said, "Let the little children come to Me" (v. 14).

LIVE IT:

Write down the words to the song on a piece of paper and place it somewhere you'll see it. Let it remind you how much Jesus loves you.

"With men *it is* impossible, but not with
God; for with God all things are possible."
28 Then Peter began to say to Him, "See,
we have left all and followed You."
29 So Jesus answered and said, "Assuredly, I say to you, there is no one who has left
house or brothers or sisters or father or
mother or wife[a] or children or lands, for My
sake and the gospel's, 30 who shall not receive
a hundredfold now in this time—houses
and brothers and sisters and mothers and
children and lands, with persecutions—and
in the age to come, eternal life. 31 But many
who are first will be last, and the last first."

Jesus a Third Time Predicts His Death and Resurrection

32 Now they were on the road, going up
to Jerusalem, and Jesus was going before
them; and they were amazed. And as they

10:29 [a] NU-Text omits *or wife.*

MONEY

POCKETS FULL OF CASH

READ IT: MARK 10:17–31

GET IT:

The story of the rich young ruler is packed with goodies. The young man came running up and threw himself at Jesus' feet. Jesus knew what the man was about to ask before the man opened his mouth. "What shall I do that I may inherit eternal life?" (v. 17). Jesus saw into this man and felt love for him.

Jesus listed six commandments, all having to do with loving others. But when the rich guy said he had kept all those commandments, Jesus threw him a curve ball. Jesus told him to go and sell everything. This wasn't an instruction to the crowd. Jesus was not preaching here. This was a message directly for this one rich person. Jesus met the man exactly where he lived. Jesus didn't question the man's love for God or God's laws. He questioned how the man treated others.

Do you want a fulfilling life? You have to think of others before you think of yourself. The rich young ruler walked away, unwilling. Notice that Jesus didn't send the man away. The man turned away on his own. Jesus had nothing but love for him.

LIVE IT:

Jesus meets us where we are. We cannot hide anything from Him. Jesus knows our true selves before we even open our mouths to say, "What must I do?"

We know what God wants of us: love God and love others. Why is this so hard sometimes? Even if we're not wealthy like the man in this story, we all have a tendency to hang on to our stuff. Jesus knows we can never live the best life if we hold on tightly to money and the things it buys.

followed they were afraid. Then He took the twelve aside again and began to tell them the things that would happen to Him: 33"Behold, we are going up to Jerusalem, and the Son of Man will be betrayed to the chief priests and to the scribes; and they will condemn Him to death and deliver Him to the Gentiles; 34and they will mock Him, and scourge Him, and spit on Him, and kill Him. And the third day He will rise again."

Greatness Is Serving

35Then James and John, the sons of Zebedee, came to Him, saying, "Teacher, we want You to do for us whatever we ask."

36And He said to them, "What do you want Me to do for you?"

37They said to Him, "Grant us that we may sit, one on Your right hand and the other on Your left, in Your glory."

38But Jesus said to them, "You do not know what you ask. Are you able to drink the cup that I drink, and be baptized with the baptism that I am baptized with?"

39They said to Him, "We are able."

So Jesus said to them, "You will indeed drink the cup that I drink, and with the baptism I am baptized with you will be baptized; 40but to sit on My right hand and on My left is not Mine to give, but *it is for those* for whom it is prepared."

41And when the ten heard *it,* they began to be greatly displeased with James and John. 42But Jesus called them to *Himself* and said to them, "You know that those who are considered rulers over the Gentiles lord it over them, and their great ones exercise authority over them. 43Yet it shall not be so among you; but whoever desires to become great among you shall be your servant. 44And whoever of you desires to be first shall be slave of all. 45For even the Son of Man did not come to be served, but to serve, and to give His life a ransom for many."

Jesus Heals Blind Bartimaeus

46Now they came to Jericho. As He went out of Jericho with His disciples and a great multitude, blind Bartimaeus, the son of Timaeus, sat by the road begging. 47And when he heard that it was Jesus of Nazareth, he began to cry out and say, "Jesus, Son of David, have mercy on me!"

48Then many warned him to be quiet; but he cried out all the more, "Son of David, have mercy on me!"

49So Jesus stood still and commanded him to be called.

Then they called the blind man, saying to him, "Be of good cheer. Rise, He is calling you."

50And throwing aside his garment, he rose and came to Jesus.

51So Jesus answered and said to him, "What do you want Me to do for you?"

The blind man said to Him, "Rabboni, that I may receive my sight."

52Then Jesus said to him, "Go your way; your faith has made you well." And immediately he received his sight and followed Jesus on the road.

The Triumphal Entry

11 Now when they drew near Jerusalem, to Bethphage[a] and Bethany, at the Mount of Olives, He sent two of His disciples; 2and He said to them, "Go into the village opposite you; and as soon as you have entered it you will find a colt tied, on which no one has sat. Loose it and bring *it.* 3And if anyone says to you, 'Why are you doing this?' say, 'The Lord has need of it,' and immediately he will send it here."

4So they went their way, and found the[a] colt tied by the door outside on the street, and they loosed it. 5But some of those who stood there said to them, "What are you doing, loosing the colt?"

6And they spoke to them just as Jesus had commanded. So they let them go. 7Then they brought the colt to Jesus and threw their clothes on it, and He sat on it. 8And many spread their clothes on the road, and others cut down leafy branches from the trees and spread *them* on the road. 9Then those who went before and those who followed cried out, saying:

"Hosanna!
'Blessed *is* He who comes in the name of
the LORD!'[a]
10 Blessed *is* the kingdom of our father
David
That comes in the name of the Lord![a]
Hosanna in the highest!"

11And Jesus went into Jerusalem and into the temple. So when He had looked around at all

11:1 [a] M-Text reads *Bethsphage.* 11:4 [a] NU-Text and M-Text read *a.* 11:9 [a] Psalm 118:26 11:10 [a] NU-Text omits *in the name of the Lord.*

things, as the hour was already late, He went
out to Bethany with the twelve.

The Fig Tree Withered

12 Now the next day, when they had come
out from Bethany, He was hungry. 13 And
seeing from afar a fig tree having leaves, He
went to see if perhaps He would find something on it. When He came to it, He found
nothing but leaves, for it was not the season
for figs. 14 In response Jesus said to it, "Let no
one eat fruit from you ever again."
And His disciples heard *it*.

Jesus Cleanses the Temple

15 So they came to Jerusalem. Then Jesus
went into the temple and began to drive out
those who bought and sold in the temple,
and overturned the tables of the money
changers and the seats of those who sold
doves. 16 And He would not allow anyone to
carry wares through the temple. 17 Then He
taught, saying to them, "Is it not written,
'My house shall be called a house of prayer
for all nations'?[a] But you have made it a 'den
of thieves.' "[b]
18 And the scribes and chief priests heard
it and sought how they might destroy Him;
for they feared Him, because all the people
were astonished at His teaching. 19 When evening had come, He went out of the city.

The Lesson of the Withered Fig Tree

20 Now in the morning, as they passed by,
they saw the fig tree dried up from the roots.
21 And Peter, remembering, said to Him,
"Rabbi, look! The fig tree which You cursed
has withered away."
22 So Jesus answered and said to them,
"Have faith in God. 23 For assuredly, I say
to you, whoever says to this mountain, 'Be
removed and be cast into the sea,' and does
not doubt in his heart, but believes that
those things he says will be done, he will
have whatever he says. 24 Therefore I say to
you, whatever things you ask when you pray,
believe that you receive *them*, and you will
have *them*.

Forgiveness and Prayer

25 "And whenever you stand praying, if
you have anything against anyone, forgive
him, that your Father in heaven may also
forgive you your trespasses. 26 But if you do
not forgive, neither will your Father in heav-
en forgive your trespasses."[a]

Jesus' Authority Questioned

27 Then they came again to Jerusalem.

11:17 [a] Isaiah 56:7 [b] Jeremiah 7:11 **11:26** [a] NU-Text omits this verse.

11:7–10 JESUS RODE ON A DONKEY

What a strange thing! Jesus was the King of Glory. Yet He rode on a donkey as He entered God's beloved city of Jerusalem. Why didn't He find the most handsome white horse and enter the city in a great show of power? He easily could have, you know.

In a way, it seems funny to us that Jesus rode a donkey instead of a horse. He was saying to everybody, "I don't need to show off My power." Jesus didn't need to make a big hit with people. He was already "the Greatest!"

Jesus also showed you and me what is important. You don't have to act important if you're a son or daughter of the great King of heaven. You're *already important to the God who created* you and saved you at the cost of the royal blood of Jesus. It sure takes a lot of foolish strain out of life when you stop needing to be important.

And as He was walking in the temple, the
chief priests, the scribes, and the elders
came to Him. 28And they said to Him, "By
what authority are You doing these things?
And who gave You this authority to do these
things?"

29But Jesus answered and said to them, "I
also will ask you one question; then answer
Me, and I will tell you by what authority I do
these things: 30The baptism of John—was it
from heaven or from men? Answer Me."

31And they reasoned among themselves,
saying, "If we say, 'From heaven,' He will
say, 'Why then did you not believe him?'
32But if we say, 'From men'"—they feared the
people, for all counted John to have been a
prophet indeed. 33So they answered and said
to Jesus, "We do not know."

And Jesus answered and said to them,
"Neither will I tell you by what authority I
do these things."

The Parable of the Wicked Vinedressers

12 Then He began to speak to them in
parables: "A man planted a vineyard
and set a hedge around *it,* dug *a place for* the
wine vat and built a tower. And he leased it
to vinedressers and went into a far country.
2Now at vintage-time he sent a servant to the
vinedressers, that he might receive some of
the fruit of the vineyard from the vinedressers. 3And they took *him* and beat him and
sent *him* away empty-handed. 4Again he sent
them another servant, and at him they threw
stones,[a] wounded *him* in the head, and sent
him away shamefully treated. 5And again he
sent another, and him they killed; and many
others, beating some and killing some.
6Therefore still having one son, his beloved,
he also sent him to them last, saying, 'They
will respect my son.' 7But those vinedressers
said among themselves, 'This is the heir.
Come, let us kill him, and the inheritance
will be ours.' 8So they took him and killed
him and cast *him* out of the vineyard.

9"Therefore what will the owner of the
vineyard do? He will come and destroy the
vinedressers, and give the vineyard to others. 10Have you not even read this Scripture:

> 'The stone which the builders rejected
> Has become the chief cornerstone.
> 11 This was the LORD's doing,
> And it is marvelous in our eyes'?"[a]

12And they sought to lay hands on Him, but
feared the multitude, for they knew He had
spoken the parable against them. So they left
Him and went away.

The Pharisees: Is It Lawful to Pay Taxes to Caesar?

13Then they sent to Him some of the Pharisees and the Herodians, to catch Him in *His*
words. 14When they had come, they said to
Him, "Teacher, we know that You are true,
and care about no one; for You do not regard
the person of men, but teach the way of God
in truth. Is it lawful to pay taxes to Caesar, or
not? 15Shall we pay, or shall we not pay?"

12:4 [a] NU-Text omits *and at him they threw stones.*
12:11 [a] Psalm 118:22, 23

FORGIVENESS

READ IT: MARK 11:25

When we pray, it's easy to tell God about how much someone has hurt us and how we want Him to do something about it. But how easily could the conversation turn back to us and our own sins? None of us is innocent. In this passage, the Lord is reminding us that when we pray, we should start by forgiving others before we go to Him for forgiveness for ourselves.

But He, knowing their hypocrisy, said to
them, "Why do you test Me? Bring Me a denarius that I may see *it*." 16 So they brought *it*.
And He said to them, "Whose image
and inscription *is* this?" They said to Him,
"Caesar's."
17 And Jesus answered and said to them,
"Render to Caesar the things that are Caesar's, and to God the things that are God's."
And they marveled at Him.

The Sadducees: What About the Resurrection?

18 Then *some* Sadducees, who say there
is no resurrection, came to Him; and they
asked Him, saying: 19 "Teacher, Moses wrote
to us that if a man's brother dies, and leaves
his wife behind, and leaves no children, his
brother should take his wife and raise up
offspring for his brother. 20 Now there were
seven brothers. The first took a wife; and dying, he left no offspring. 21 And the second
took her, and he died; nor did he leave any
offspring. And the third likewise. 22 So the
seven had her and left no offspring. Last of
all the woman died also. 23 Therefore, in the
resurrection, when they rise, whose wife will
she be? For all seven had her as wife."
24 Jesus answered and said to them, "Are
you not therefore mistaken, because you
do not know the Scriptures nor the power
of God? 25 For when they rise from the dead,
they neither marry nor are given in marriage, but are like angels in heaven. 26 But
concerning the dead, that they rise, have you
not read in the book of Moses, in the *burning*
bush *passage,* how God spoke to him, saying,
'I *am* the God of Abraham, the God of Isaac,
and the God of Jacob'?[a] 27 He is not the God of
the dead, but the God of the living. You are
therefore greatly mistaken."

The Scribes: Which Is the First Commandment of All?

28 Then one of the scribes came, and having
heard them reasoning together, perceiving[a]
that He had answered them well, asked Him,
"Which is the first commandment of all?"
29 Jesus answered him, "The first of all
the commandments *is:* 'Hear, O Israel, the
LORD our God, the LORD is one. 30 And you
shall love the LORD your God with all your
heart, with all your soul, with all your mind,
and with all your strength.'[a] This *is* the first
commandment.[b] 31 And the second, like *it, is*
this: 'You shall love your neighbor as yourself.'[a] There is no other commandment
greater than these."
32 So the scribe said to Him, "Well *said,*
Teacher. You have spoken the truth, for there
is one God, and there is no other but He.
33 And to love Him with all the heart, with
all the understanding, with all the soul,[a] and
with all the strength, and to love one's neighbor as oneself, is more than all the whole
burnt offerings and sacrifices."
34 Now when Jesus saw that he answered
wisely, He said to him, "You are not far from
the kingdom of God."
But after that no one dared question
Him.

Jesus: How Can David Call His Descendant "Lord"?

35 Then Jesus answered and said, while
He taught in the temple, "How *is it* that the
scribes say that the Christ is the Son of David? 36 For David himself said by the Holy
Spirit:

'The LORD said to my Lord,
"Sit at My right hand,
Till I make Your enemies Your
footstool."'[a]

37 Therefore David himself calls Him 'Lord';
how is He *then* his Son?"
And the common people heard Him
gladly.

Beware of the Scribes

38 Then He said to them in His teaching,
"Beware of the scribes, who desire to go
around in long robes, *love* greetings in the
marketplaces, 39 the best seats in the synagogues, and the best places at feasts, 40 who
devour widows' houses, and for a pretense
make long prayers. These will receive greater condemnation."

The Widow's Two Mites

41 Now Jesus sat opposite the treasury and
saw how the people put money into the treasury. And many *who were* rich put in much.
42 Then one poor widow came and threw in
two mites,[a] which make a quadrans. 43 So
He called His disciples to *Himself* and said

12:26 [a] Exodus 3:6, 15 **12:28** [a] NU-Text reads *seeing.* **12:30** [a] Deuteronomy 6:4, 5 [b] NU-Text omits this sentence. **12:31** [a] Leviticus 19:18 **12:33** [a] NU-Text omits *with all the soul.* **12:36** [a] Psalm 110:1 **12:42** [a] Greek *lepta,* very small copper coins worth a fraction of a penny

to them, "Assuredly, I say to you that this
poor widow has put in more than all those
who have given to the treasury; 44for they all
put in out of their abundance, but she out of
her poverty put in all that she had, her whole
livelihood."

Jesus Predicts the Destruction of the Temple

13 Then as He went out of the temple,
one of His disciples said to Him,
"Teacher, see what manner of stones and
what buildings *are here!*"
2And Jesus answered and said to him,
"Do you see these great buildings? Not *one*
stone shall be left upon another, that shall
not be thrown down."

The Signs of the Times and the End of the Age

3Now as He sat on the Mount of Olives
opposite the temple, Peter, James, John, and
Andrew asked Him privately, 4"Tell us, when
will these things be? And what *will be* the
sign when all these things will be fulfilled?"
5And Jesus, answering them, began to
say: "Take heed that no one deceives you.
6For many will come in My name, saying, 'I
am *He,*' and will deceive many. 7But when
you hear of wars and rumors of wars, do
not be troubled; for *such things* must happen, but the end *is* not yet. 8For nation will
rise against nation, and kingdom against
kingdom. And there will be earthquakes
in various places, and there will be famines
and troubles.[a] These *are* the beginnings of
sorrows.
9"But watch out for yourselves, for they
will deliver you up to councils, and you
will be beaten in the synagogues. You will
be brought[a] before rulers and kings for My
sake, for a testimony to them. 10And the gospel must first be preached to all the nations.
11But when they arrest *you* and deliver you
up, do not worry beforehand, or premeditate[a] what you will speak. But whatever
is given you in that hour, speak that; for it
is not you who speak, but the Holy Spirit.
12Now brother will betray brother to death,
and a father *his* child; and children will rise
up against parents and cause them to be put
to death. 13And you will be hated by all for My
name's sake. But he who endures to the end
shall be saved.

The Great Tribulation

14"So when you see the 'abomination
of desolation,'[a] spoken of by Daniel the
prophet,[b] standing where it ought not" (let
the reader understand), "then let those who
are in Judea flee to the mountains. 15Let him
who is on the housetop not go down into the
house, nor enter to take anything out of his
house. 16And let him who is in the field not
go back to get his clothes. 17But woe to those
who are pregnant and to those who are nursing babies in those days! 18And pray that your
flight may not be in winter. 19For *in* those
days there will be tribulation, such as has
not been since the beginning of the creation
which God created until this time, nor ever
shall be. 20And unless the Lord had shortened those days, no flesh would be saved;
but for the elect's sake, whom He chose, He
shortened the days.
21"Then if anyone says to you, 'Look, here
is the Christ!' or, 'Look, *He is* there!' do not
believe it. 22For false christs and false prophets will rise and show signs and wonders
to deceive, if possible, even the elect. 23But
take heed; see, I have told you all things
beforehand.

The Coming of the Son of Man

24"But in those days, after that tribulation,
the sun will be darkened, and the moon will
not give its light; 25the stars of heaven will
fall, and the powers in the heavens will be
shaken. 26Then they will see the Son of Man
coming in the clouds with great power and
glory. 27And then He will send His angels,
and gather together His elect from the four
winds, from the farthest part of earth to the
farthest part of heaven.

The Parable of the Fig Tree

28"Now learn this parable from the fig
tree: When its branch has already become
tender, and puts forth leaves, you know that
summer is near. 29So you also, when you
see these things happening, know that it[a] is
near—at the doors! 30Assuredly, I say to you,
this generation will by no means pass away
till all these things take place. 31Heaven and
earth will pass away, but My words will by no
means pass away.

13:8 [a] NU-Text omits *and troubles.* **13:9** [a] NU-Text and M-Text read *will stand.* **13:11** [a] NU-Text omits *or premeditate.* **13:14** [a] Daniel 11:31; 12:11 [b] NU-Text omits *spoken of by Daniel the prophet.* **13:29** [a] Or *He*

No One Knows the Day or Hour

32“But of that day and hour no one knows,
not even the angels in heaven, nor the Son,
but only the Father. 33Take heed, watch and
pray; for you do not know when the time is.
34*It is* like a man going to a far country, who
left his house and gave authority to his servants, and to each his work, and commanded
the doorkeeper to watch. 35Watch therefore,
for you do not know when the master of the
house is coming—in the evening, at midnight, at the crowing of the rooster, or in the
morning— 36lest, coming suddenly, he find
you sleeping. 37And what I say to you, I say
to all: Watch!”

The Plot to Kill Jesus

14 After two days it was the Passover and *the Feast* of Unleavened
Bread. And the chief priests and the scribes
sought how they might take Him by trickery
and put *Him* to death. 2But they said, “Not
during the feast, lest there be an uproar of
the people.”

The Anointing at Bethany

3And being in Bethany at the house
of Simon the leper, as He sat at the table,
a woman came having an alabaster flask
of very costly oil of spikenard. Then she
broke the flask and poured *it* on His head.
4But there were some who were indignant
among themselves, and said, “Why was this
fragrant oil wasted? 5For it might have been
sold for more than three hundred denarii
and given to the poor.” And they criticized
her sharply.

6But Jesus said, “Let her alone. Why do
you trouble her? She has done a good work
for Me. 7For you have the poor with you always, and whenever you wish you may do
them good; but Me you do not have always.
8She has done what she could. She has come
beforehand to anoint My body for burial.
9Assuredly, I say to you, wherever this gospel is preached in the whole world, what this
woman has done will also be told as a memorial to her.”

Judas Agrees to Betray Jesus

10Then Judas Iscariot, one of the twelve,
went to the chief priests to betray Him to
them. 11And when they heard *it,* they were
glad, and promised to give him money. So
he sought how he might conveniently betray
Him.

WATCH FOR THE COMING OF JESUS

READ IT: MARK 13:24–37

This present world will come to an end. Even modern science tells us so. Then Jesus will come and set up His government over a new world that will never pass away.

God has a better plan for the ages than the disease, destruction, and death we see around us every day. Now you can see around the world in an instant on the television or the internet, but what do you see? There is misery everywhere.

So it makes a lot of sense that Jesus, who came and died and rose again, will come back to bring His beautiful life into a grand new world. Jesus commands one thing—“*Watch!*” This means making sure you are getting ready to meet Him. He wants you to have a part in His new world.

Jesus Celebrates the Passover with His Disciples

[12]Now on the first day of Unleavened
Bread, when they killed the Passover *lamb,*
His disciples said to Him, "Where do You
want us to go and prepare, that You may eat
the Passover?"

[13]And He sent out two of His disciples
and said to them, "Go into the city, and a
man will meet you carrying a pitcher of water; follow him. [14]Wherever he goes in, say to
the master of the house, 'The Teacher says,
"Where is the guest room in which I may eat
the Passover with My disciples?"' [15]Then he
will show you a large upper room, furnished
and prepared; there make ready for us."

[16]So His disciples went out, and came
into the city, and found it just as He had said
to them; and they prepared the Passover.

[17]In the evening He came with the twelve.
[18]Now as they sat and ate, Jesus said, "Assuredly, I say to you, one of you who eats
with Me will betray Me."

[19]And they began to be sorrowful, and to
say to Him one by one, "*Is* it I?" And another
said, "*Is* it I?"[a]

14:19 [a] NU-Text omits this sentence.

JESUS CELEBRATES PASSOVER WITH HIS DISCIPLES

READ IT: MARK 14:12–26

GET IT:

The Jewish festival of Passover was the biggest holiday in the year for the Jews. This was the feast that helped the people remember that God had freed them from slavery in Egypt long ago. Jesus celebrated the Passover with His disciples. But what was supposed to be a happy celebration turned into a sad time as Jesus announced that someone would turn Him over to His enemies. Then at the end of the feast, Jesus started a new tradition—a way of remembering His suffering and death. This is the celebration that we have come to know as the Lord's Supper.

LIVE IT:

You probably already know what the Lord's Supper (in your church it might be called *communion* or *Eucharist*) is all about. But how much do you know about Passover? Jesus and His disciples celebrated this feast together on the last night Jesus was alive. To better understand what that feast is all about, ask your parents to help you do some research online on Passover. If you know someone who is Jewish, ask for his or her help. Or ask for help from your pastor, religion teacher, or youth leader. Find out what the feast is all about and what the people ate, drank, and said. Review the story in Exodus 12. Then get a group together to observe this special feast as Jesus and His disciples did. And next time you take communion at church, think about Jesus and His disciples starting this practice just before Jesus went to the cross.

20He answered and said to them, "*It is*
one of the twelve, who dips with Me in the
dish. 21The Son of Man indeed goes just as
it is written of Him, but woe to that man by
whom the Son of Man is betrayed! It would
have been good for that man if he had never
been born."

Jesus Institutes the Lord's Supper

22And as they were eating, Jesus took
bread, blessed and broke *it,* and gave *it* to
them and said, "Take, eat;[a] this is My body."
23Then He took the cup, and when He
had given thanks He gave *it* to them, and
they all drank from it. 24And He said to them,
"This is My blood of the new[a] covenant,
which is shed for many. 25Assuredly, I say to
you, I will no longer drink of the fruit of the
vine until that day when I drink it new in the
kingdom of God."
26And when they had sung a hymn, they
went out to the Mount of Olives.

Jesus Predicts Peter's Denial

27Then Jesus said to them, "All of you
will be made to stumble because of Me this
night,[a] for it is written:

'I will strike the Shepherd,
And the sheep will be scattered.'[b]

28"But after I have been raised, I will go
before you to Galilee."
29Peter said to Him, "Even if all are made
to stumble, yet I *will* not *be*."
30Jesus said to him, "Assuredly, I say to
you that today, *even* this night, before the
rooster crows twice, you will deny Me three
times."
31But he spoke more vehemently, "If I
have to die with You, I will not deny You!"
And they all said likewise.

The Prayer in the Garden

32Then they came to a place which was
named Gethsemane; and He said to His disciples, "Sit here while I pray." 33And He took
Peter, James, and John with Him, and He
began to be troubled and deeply distressed.
34Then He said to them, "My soul is exceedingly sorrowful, *even* to death. Stay here and
watch."
35He went a little farther, and fell on the
ground, and prayed that if it were possible,
the hour might pass from Him. 36And He
said, "Abba, Father, all things *are* possible for
You. Take this cup away from Me; nevertheless, not what I will, but what You *will*."
37Then He came and found them sleeping, and said to Peter, "Simon, are you sleeping? Could you not watch one hour? 38Watch
and pray, lest you enter into temptation.
The spirit indeed *is* willing, but the flesh *is*
weak."
39Again He went away and prayed, and
spoke the same words. 40And when He returned, He found them asleep again, for
their eyes were heavy; and they did not know
what to answer Him.
41Then He came the third time and said
to them, "Are you still sleeping and resting?
It is enough! The hour has come; behold, the
Son of Man is being betrayed into the hands
of sinners. 42Rise, let us be going. See, My
betrayer is at hand."

Betrayal and Arrest in Gethsemane

43And immediately, while He was still
speaking, Judas, one of the twelve, with a
great multitude with swords and clubs, came
from the chief priests and the scribes and the
elders. 44Now His betrayer had given them a
signal, saying, "Whomever I kiss, He is the
One; seize Him and lead *Him* away safely."
45As soon as he had come, immediately
he went up to Him and said to Him, "Rabbi,
Rabbi!" and kissed Him.
46Then they laid their hands on Him and
took Him. 47And one of those who stood by
drew his sword and struck the servant of the
high priest, and cut off his ear.
48Then Jesus answered and said to them,
"Have you come out, as against a robber,
with swords and clubs to take Me? 49I was
daily with you in the temple teaching, and
you did not seize Me. But the Scriptures
must be fulfilled."
50Then they all forsook Him and fled.

A Young Man Flees Naked

51Now a certain young man followed
Him, having a linen cloth thrown around
his naked *body*. And the young men laid hold
of him, 52and he left the linen cloth and fled
from them naked.

Jesus Faces the Sanhedrin

53And they led Jesus away to the high

14:22 [a] NU-Text omits *eat.* 14:24 [a] NU-Text omits *new.* 14:27 [a] NU-Text omits *because of Me this night.* [b] Zechariah 13:7

priest; and with him were assembled all the
chief priests, the elders, and the scribes.
54But Peter followed Him at a distance, right
into the courtyard of the high priest. And he
sat with the servants and warmed himself
at the fire.
55Now the chief priests and all the council
sought testimony against Jesus to put Him
to death, but found none. 56For many bore
false witness against Him, but their testimonies did not agree.
57Then some rose up and bore false witness against Him, saying, 58"We heard Him
say, 'I will destroy this temple made with
hands, and within three days I will build another made without hands.'" 59But not even
then did their testimony agree.
60And the high priest stood up in the
midst and asked Jesus, saying, "Do You answer nothing? What *is it* these men testify

In Focus

14:36 Abba A word for father from the ancient Aramaic language (pronounced *air-uh-MAY-ik*). The word is like our words *daddy* and *papa*.

against You?" 61But He kept silent and answered nothing.
Again the high priest asked Him, saying
to Him, "Are You the Christ, the Son of the
Blessed?"
62Jesus said, "I am. And you will see
the Son of Man sitting at the right hand of
the Power, and coming with the clouds of
heaven."

Spotlight

JESUS PRAYS IN THE GARDEN

READ IT: MARK 14:32–72

GET IT:

After Jesus and His disciples sang their song, they walked outside the city to a garden. The Garden of Gethsemane was a quiet place where Jesus often went to pray. It was late at night, and the disciples were tired. When Jesus went off by Himself to pray, the disciples fell asleep. In His prayer, Jesus begged God to somehow get Him out of what was going to happen. Because He was human, He didn't want to suffer the pain. He didn't want to die. But in the end He was willing to do what God had asked Him to do. He was willing to face cruel words, torture, pain, and death.

LIVE IT:

Have you ever pleaded with God for something to happen or not to happen? Jesus prayed that God would spare Him from death and all the pain and find some other way to get the results. But God said no. It had to happen. Once Jesus realized that things couldn't change, He gave Himself over to God's will. When God's answer to our prayer is *no* or *not yet*, we have to be willing to accept His will. We have to believe that He has a greater plan for us.

[63]Then the high priest tore his clothes
and said, "What further need do we have of
witnesses? [64]You have heard the blasphemy!
What do you think?"

And they all condemned Him to be deserving of death.

[65]Then some began to spit on Him, and
to blindfold Him, and to beat Him, and to
say to Him, "Prophesy!" And the officers
struck Him with the palms of their hands.[a]

Peter Denies Jesus, and Weeps

[66]Now as Peter was below in the courtyard, one of the servant girls of the high
priest came. [67]And when she saw Peter
warming himself, she looked at him and
said, "You also were with Jesus of Nazareth."
[68]But he denied it, saying, "I neither
know nor understand what you are saying."

14:65 [a] NU-Text reads *received Him with slaps.*

THE VALUE OF WORDS

POWERFUL WORDS

READ IT: MARK 14:66–72

GET IT:

Have you ever had a friend talk about you behind your back? Peter was one of Jesus' disciples—one of His closest friends. He was always in the middle of the action when Jesus and the disciples were performing miracles or preaching. But that didn't stop him from denying Jesus when he was afraid.

The night before Jesus' crucifixion, a servant girl saw Peter and recognized him. She called him out, saying, "You also were with Jesus of Nazareth" (v. 67). Since Jesus had just been sentenced to die, it makes sense that Peter would be frightened to admit that he was a disciple of Jesus. He said he had no idea what the girl was talking about. After he finished, a rooster crowed.

But Peter didn't just deny Jesus once. Later the girl saw him again and told everyone around her that Peter was one of Jesus' disciples. He denied it a second time. The people didn't let up. "Surely you are one of them," they said (v. 70). The Bible says that Peter began to curse and swear, denying Jesus a third time. A rooster crowed again.

This wasn't a surprise to Jesus. He actually told Peter ahead of time that he was going to deny Him three times before a rooster crowed twice. When Peter heard the rooster crow the second time, he realized the huge mistake he had made and began to cry.

LIVE IT:

Words are powerful. Some have the power to encourage, and some hurt others. Sometimes we use words to protect ourselves, even if they're not true. Can you think of a time when you wanted to lie about your faith in order to save face?

And he went out on the porch, and a rooster
crowed.
69 And the servant girl saw him again, and
began to say to those who stood by, "This is
one of them." 70 But he denied it again.
And a little later those who stood by said
to Peter again, "Surely you are *one* of them;
for you are a Galilean, and your speech
shows *it*."[a]
71 Then he began to curse and swear, "I
do not know this Man of whom you speak!"
72 A second time *the* rooster crowed. Then
Peter called to mind the word that Jesus had
said to him, "Before the rooster crows twice,
you will deny Me three times." And when he
thought about it, he wept.

Jesus Faces Pilate

15 Immediately, in the morning, the
chief priests held a consultation
with the elders and scribes and the whole
council; and they bound Jesus, led *Him* away,

14:70 [a] NU-Text omits *and your speech shows it.*

JESUS DIES ON THE CROSS

READ IT: MARK 15:1–47

GET IT:

The Jewish religious leaders arrested Jesus in the Garden of Gethsemane. They took Jesus back into the city, where He faced various authorities throughout the night. Jesus' trial in front of these people was unfair. He was innocent of all the charges against Him. And yet He was willing to take the blame—to suffer and even die—for us. On Friday morning He faced the governor, Pontius Pilate. Jesus had done nothing wrong. He had told the truth and preached wisely, but the people just didn't believe what He said. Then He was mocked, bullied by the soldiers, and beaten up. And His death by crucifixion was the worst way to die. It was cruel, humiliating, painful, and terribly slow—sometimes a person hung on a cross for days before dying of suffocation. But Jesus willingly did this for us. Through this horrible death, He saved us from the punishment we deserve because of our sins.

LIVE IT:

What's the worst pain you've ever faced? The worst humiliation? The worst misery and hurt? Have you ever felt alone, rejected by everyone? We usually do whatever we can right away to make the pain stop. Would you be willing to go through that all over again for somebody else? It's not surprising if you said, "No way!" Nobody wants to be uncomfortable or in pain. While nothing we experience can really compare to what Jesus went through, we need to try to understand what He did for us. Jesus felt all those human feelings and pain rolled together a thousand times more than what we've ever felt. He didn't have to do this for us. His suffering and death were a free gift to us so that we can live.

and delivered *Him* to Pilate. 2Then Pilate
asked Him, "Are You the King of the Jews?"
He answered and said to him, "*It is as* you
say."
3And the chief priests accused Him of
many things, but He answered nothing.
4Then Pilate asked Him again, saying, "Do
You answer nothing? See how many things
they testify against You!"[a] 5But Jesus still
answered nothing, so that Pilate marveled.

Taking the Place of Barabbas

6Now at the feast he was accustomed to
releasing one prisoner to them, whomever
they requested. 7And there was one named
Barabbas, *who was* chained with his fellow
rebels; they had committed murder in the rebellion. 8Then the multitude, crying aloud,[a]
began to ask *him to do* just as he had always
done for them. 9But Pilate answered them,
saying, "Do you want me to release to you
the King of the Jews?" 10For he knew that the
chief priests had handed Him over because
of envy.
11But the chief priests stirred up the
crowd, so that he should rather release
Barabbas to them. 12Pilate answered and said
to them again, "What then do you want me
to do *with Him* whom you call the King of
the Jews?"
13So they cried out again, "Crucify Him!"
14Then Pilate said to them, "Why, what
evil has He done?"
But they cried out all the more, "Crucify
Him!"
15So Pilate, wanting to gratify the crowd,
released Barabbas to them; and he delivered
Jesus, after he had scourged *Him,* to be
crucified.

The Soldiers Mock Jesus

16Then the soldiers led Him away into
the hall called Praetorium, and they called
together the whole garrison. 17And they
clothed Him with purple; and they twisted a
crown of thorns, put it on His *head,* 18and began to salute Him, "Hail, King of the Jews!"
19Then they struck Him on the head with a
reed and spat on Him; and bowing the knee,
they worshiped Him. 20And when they had
mocked Him, they took the purple off Him,
put His own clothes on Him, and led Him
out to crucify Him.

The King on a Cross

21Then they compelled a certain man,

In Focus

15:16 Praetorium Pronounced *prih-TOE-rih-um.* The headquarters of the Roman governor of Judea. This was located at Antonia Castle, where Pilate questioned Jesus.

Simon a Cyrenian, the father of Alexander
and Rufus, as he was coming out of the
country and passing by, to bear His cross.
22And they brought Him to the place Golgotha, which is translated, Place of a Skull.
23Then they gave Him wine mingled with
myrrh to drink, but He did not take *it.* 24And
when they crucified Him, they divided His
garments, casting lots for them *to determine*
what every man should take.
25Now it was the third hour, and they
crucified Him. 26And the inscription of His
accusation was written above:

THE KING OF THE JEWS.

27With Him they also crucified two robbers, one on His right and the other on His
left. 28So the Scripture was fulfilled[a] which
says, "And He was numbered with the
transgressors."[b]
29And those who passed by blasphemed
Him, wagging their heads and saying, "Aha!
You who destroy the temple and build *it* in
three days, 30save Yourself, and come down
from the cross!"
31Likewise the chief priests also, mocking
among themselves with the scribes, said,
"He saved others; Himself He cannot save.
32Let the Christ, the King of Israel, descend
now from the cross, that we may see and
believe."[a]
Even those who were crucified with Him
reviled Him.

Jesus Dies on the Cross

33Now when the sixth hour had come,
there was darkness over the whole land until the ninth hour. 34And at the ninth hour
Jesus cried out with a loud voice, saying,

15:4 [a] NU-Text reads *of which they accuse You.* 15:8 [a] NU-Text reads *going up.* 15:28 [a] Isaiah 53:12 [b] NU-Text omits this verse. 15:32 [a] M-Text reads *believe Him.*

"Eloi, Eloi, lama sabachthani?" which is
translated, "My God, My God, why have You
forsaken Me?"[a]
35Some of those who stood by, when
they heard *that,* said, "Look, He is calling
for Elijah!" 36Then someone ran and filled
a sponge full of sour wine, put *it* on a reed,
and offered *it* to Him to drink, saying, "Let
Him alone; let us see if Elijah will come to
take Him down."
37And Jesus cried out with a loud voice,
and breathed His last.
38Then the veil of the temple was torn in
two from top to bottom. 39So when the centurion, who stood opposite Him, saw that He
cried out like this and breathed His last,[a] he
said, "Truly this Man was the Son of God!"
40There were also women looking on
from afar, among whom were Mary Magdalene, Mary the mother of James the Less
and of Joses, and Salome, 41who also followed
Him and ministered to Him when He was
in Galilee, and many other women who
came up with Him to Jerusalem.

Jesus Buried in Joseph's Tomb

42Now when evening had come, because
it was the Preparation Day, that is, the day
before the Sabbath, 43Joseph of Arimathea,
a prominent council member, who was
himself waiting for the kingdom of God,

15:34 [a] Psalm 22:1 15:39 [a] NU-Text reads *that He thus breathed His last.*

FINDING YOUR PURPOSE IN LIFE
DON'T JUST STAND THERE . . . GO!

READ IT: MARK 16:14–18

GET IT:

Jesus was crucified and buried. Then He rose from the dead. He appeared to two of His disciples who ran and told the others. But they refused to believe the news. "Really? You saw Jesus alive again?"

Later Jesus met with His disciples over dinner. Can you imagine how shocked the disciples must have been? After He called them out for their unbelief, Jesus gave them the greatest mission known to humans: "Go into all the world and preach the gospel to every creature" (v. 15).

The disciples had no excuse now. There was no room left for doubt. Jesus was the Savior who was promised to them. Through His death and resurrection, He proved it. When Jesus laid out the command to "go into all the world," He was also giving us, His disciples more than two thousand years later, the same command. When we believe that Jesus Christ is Lord we are to share this good news with the world around us.

LIVE IT:

There are many ways we can be obedient to this calling. Even though our backgrounds and surroundings are different, we all share this one purpose in life: to preach the gospel. Pray for God to show you ways that you can tell others about Him.

coming and taking courage, went in to Pilate and asked for the body of Jesus. 44Pilate marveled that He was already dead; and summoning the centurion, he asked him if He had been dead for some time. 45So when he found out from the centurion, he granted the body to Joseph. 46Then he bought fine linen, took Him down, and wrapped Him in the linen. And he laid Him in a tomb which had been hewn out of the rock, and rolled a stone against the door of the tomb. 47And Mary Magdalene and Mary *the mother* of Joses observed where He was laid.

He Is Risen

16 Now when the Sabbath was past, Mary Magdalene, Mary *the mother* of James, and Salome bought spices, that they might come and anoint Him. 2Very early in the morning, on the first *day* of the week, they came to the tomb when the sun had risen. 3And they said among themselves, "Who will roll away the stone from the door of the tomb for us?" 4But when they looked up, they saw that the stone had been rolled away—for it was very large. 5And entering the tomb, they saw a young man clothed in a long white robe sitting on the right side; and they were alarmed.

6But he said to them, "Do not be alarmed. You seek Jesus of Nazareth, who was crucified. He is risen! He is not here. See the place where they laid Him. 7But go, tell His disciples—and Peter—that He is going before you into Galilee; there you will see Him, as He said to you."

8So they went out quickly[a] and fled from the tomb, for they trembled and were amazed. And they said nothing to anyone, for they were afraid.

Mary Magdalene Sees the Risen Lord

9Now when *He* rose early on the first *day* of the week, He appeared first to Mary Magdalene, out of whom He had cast seven demons. 10She went and told those who had been with Him, as they mourned and wept. 11And when they heard that He was alive and had been seen by her, they did not believe.

Jesus Appears to Two Disciples

12After that, He appeared in another form to two of them as they walked and went into the country. 13And they went and told *it* to the rest, *but* they did not believe them either.

The Great Commission

14Later He appeared to the eleven as they sat at the table; and He rebuked their unbelief and hardness of heart, because they did not believe those who had seen Him after He had risen. 15And He said to them, "Go into all the world and preach the gospel to every creature. 16He who believes and is baptized will be saved; but he who does not believe will be condemned. 17And these signs will follow those who believe: In My name they will cast out demons; they will speak with new tongues; 18they[a] will take up serpents; and if they drink anything deadly, it will by no means hurt them; they will lay hands on the sick, and they will recover."

Christ Ascends to God's Right Hand

19So then, after the Lord had spoken to them, He was received up into heaven, and sat down at the right hand of God. 20And they went out and preached everywhere, the Lord working with *them* and confirming the word through the accompanying signs. Amen.[a]

16:8 [a] NU-Text and M-Text omit *quickly.* **16:18** [a] NU-Text reads *and in their hands they will.* **16:20** [a] Verses 9–20 are bracketed in NU-Text as not original. They are lacking in Codex Sinaiticus and Codex Vaticanus, although nearly all other manuscripts of Mark contain them.

Behind the Scenes

The GOSPEL ACCORDING *to*

LUKE

A.D. 60–A.D. 65

READ IT:

The book of Luke tells the stories of Jesus' birth, ministry, death, and resurrection. It focuses on the fact that Jesus loved all kinds of people. Luke, the author, wrote about and identified by name the women Jesus met and spoke to. He also mentioned children more than any other Gospel writer. And in many of the parables, he wrote about the poor and outsiders.

GET IT:

Who wrote it: Luke, a physician who traveled with Paul

When it was written: A.D. 60–A.D. 65

Why it was written: to collect all the stories about Jesus and give us a complete and accurate description of Jesus' life.

LIVE IT:

We must be kind and compassionate to everyone, even to people who aren't accepted or approved by others. We need to do this because Jesus did.

FIND IT:

Jesus' Coming and Birth	*Luke 1–2*
The Beatitudes	*Luke 6*
The Parable of the Good Samaritan	*Luke 10*
The Parables of Lost Sheep, Coin, Son	*Luke 15*
Ten Lepers Cleansed	*Luke 17*
The Pharisee and the Tax Collector	*Luke 18*
Jesus Comes to Zacchaeus' House	*Luke 19*
Jesus Appears to the Disciples	*Luke 24*

Dedication to Theophilus

1 Inasmuch as many have taken in hand
to set in order a narrative of those things
which have been fulfilled[a] among us, 2just as
those who from the beginning were eyewitnesses and ministers of the word delivered
them to us, 3it seemed good to me also, having had perfect understanding of all things
from the very first, to write to you an orderly
account, most excellent Theophilus, 4that
you may know the certainty of those things
in which you were instructed.

John's Birth Announced to Zacharias

5There was in the days of Herod, the king
of Judea, a certain priest named Zacharias,
of the division of Abijah. His wife *was* of the
daughters of Aaron, and her name *was* Elizabeth. 6And they were both righteous before
God, walking in all the commandments and
ordinances of the Lord blameless. 7But they
had no child, because Elizabeth was barren,
and they were both well advanced in years.

8So it was, that while he was serving as
priest before God in the order of his division,
9according to the custom of the priesthood,
his lot fell to burn incense when he went
into the temple of the Lord. 10And the whole
multitude of the people was praying outside
at the hour of incense. 11Then an angel of
the Lord appeared to him, standing on the
right side of the altar of incense. 12And when
Zacharias saw *him,* he was troubled, and fear
fell upon him.

13But the angel said to him, "Do not be
afraid, Zacharias, for your prayer is heard;
and your wife Elizabeth will bear you a son,
and you shall call his name John. 14And you
will have joy and gladness, and many will
rejoice at his birth. 15For he will be great in
the sight of the Lord, and shall drink neither
wine nor strong drink. He will also be filled
with the Holy Spirit, even from his mother's
womb. 16And he will turn many of the children of Israel to the Lord their God. 17He will
also go before Him in the spirit and power
of Elijah, 'to turn the hearts of the fathers
to the children,'[a] and the disobedient to the
wisdom of the just, to make ready a people
prepared for the Lord."

18And Zacharias said to the angel, "How
shall I know this? For I am an old man, and
my wife is well advanced in years."

19And the angel answered and said to
him, "I am Gabriel, who stands in the presence of God, and was sent to speak to you
and bring you these glad tidings. 20But behold, you will be mute and not able to speak
until the day these things take place, because you did not believe my words which
will be fulfilled in their own time."

1:1 [a] Or *are most surely believed* 1:17 [a] Malachi 4:5, 6

Starring Roles

LUKE felt unworthy to write about Jesus because he hadn't known Him well, but God guided him to do just that.

Luke was Greek by birth. As a medical doctor, the birth of Jesus was important to him. First, he talked to Mary the mother of Jesus and to Joseph, her husband. Then he got more facts from the parents of John the Baptizer.

Luke even went out to meet the shepherds in the hills of Bethlehem. They had been visited by the angels who sent them to a stable where they found the Baby Jesus.

Luke came to believe that Jesus truly was the Son of God, and he trusted in Him.

Later, Luke also wrote the book of Acts. In that book, he tells about the work of Jesus' apostles after He went back to heaven. You should read the book of Acts after you read the Gospel of Luke.

21 And the people waited for Zacharias,
and marveled that he lingered so long in the
temple. 22 But when he came out, he could
not speak to them; and they perceived that
he had seen a vision in the temple, for he
beckoned to them and remained speechless.
23 So it was, as soon as the days of his service were completed, that he departed to his
own house. 24 Now after those days his wife
Elizabeth conceived; and she hid herself five
months, saying, 25 "Thus the Lord has dealt
with me, in the days when He looked on *me,*
to take away my reproach among people."

Christ's Birth Announced to Mary

26 Now in the sixth month the angel Gabriel was sent by God to a city of Galilee
named Nazareth, 27 to a virgin betrothed to a
man whose name was Joseph, of the house
of David. The virgin's name *was* Mary. 28 And
having come in, the angel said to her, "Rejoice, highly favored *one,* the Lord *is* with
you; blessed *are* you among women!"[a]
29 But when she saw *him,*[a] she was troubled at his saying, and considered what manner of greeting this was. 30 Then the angel
said to her, "Do not be afraid, Mary, for you
have found favor with God. 31 And behold,
you will conceive in your womb and bring
forth a Son, and shall call His name JESUS.
32 He will be great, and will be called the Son
of the Highest; and the Lord God will give
Him the throne of His father David. 33 And
He will reign over the house of Jacob forever,
and of His kingdom there will be no end."
34 Then Mary said to the angel, "How can
this be, since I do not know a man?"
35 And the angel answered and said to
her, "*The* Holy Spirit will come upon you,
and the power of the Highest will overshadow you; therefore, also, that Holy One
who is to be born will be called the Son of
God. 36 Now indeed, Elizabeth your relative
has also conceived a son in her old age; and
this is now the sixth month for her who was
called barren. 37 For with God nothing will be
impossible."
38 Then Mary said, "Behold the maidservant of the Lord! Let it be to me according to
your word." And the angel departed from her.

Mary Visits Elizabeth

39 Now Mary arose in those days and went
into the hill country with haste, to a city of
Judah, 40 and entered the house of Zacharias
and greeted Elizabeth. 41 And it happened,
when Elizabeth heard the greeting of Mary,
that the babe leaped in her womb; and Elizabeth was filled with the Holy Spirit. 42 Then
she spoke out with a loud voice and said,
"Blessed *are* you among women, and blessed
is the fruit of your womb! 43 But why *is* this
granted to me, that the mother of my Lord
should come to me? 44 For indeed, as soon
as the voice of your greeting sounded in my
ears, the babe leaped in my womb for joy.
45 Blessed *is* she who believed, for there will
be a fulfillment of those things which were
told her from the Lord."

The Song of Mary

46 And Mary said:

"My soul magnifies the Lord,

1:28 [a] NU-Text omits *blessed are you among women.*
1:29 [a] NU-Text omits *when she saw him.*

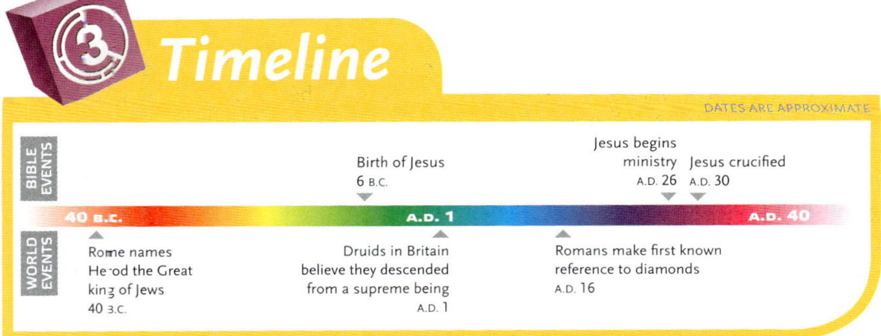

47 And my spirit has rejoiced in God my
Savior.
48 For He has regarded the lowly state of
His maidservant;
For behold, henceforth all generations
will call me blessed.
49 For He who is mighty has done great
things for me,
And holy *is* His name.
50 And His mercy *is* on those who fear
Him
From generation to generation.
51 He has shown strength with His arm;
He has scattered *the* proud in the
imagination of their hearts.
52 He has put down the mighty from *their*
thrones,
And exalted *the* lowly.
53 He has filled *the* hungry with good
things,
And *the* rich He has sent away empty.
54 He has helped His servant Israel,
In remembrance of *His* mercy,
55 As He spoke to our fathers,
To Abraham and to his seed forever."

56And Mary remained with her about
three months, and returned to her house.

Birth of John the Baptist

57Now Elizabeth's full time came for her
to be delivered, and she brought forth a son.
58When her neighbors and relatives heard
how the Lord had shown great mercy to her,
they rejoiced with her.

Circumcision of John the Baptist

59So it was, on the eighth day, that they
came to circumcise the child; and they
would have called him by the name of his father, Zacharias. 60His mother answered and
said, "No; he shall be called John."
61But they said to her, "There is no one
among your relatives who is called by this
name." 62So they made signs to his father—
what he would have him called.
63And he asked for a writing tablet, and
wrote, saying, "His name is John." So they
all marveled. 64Immediately his mouth was
opened and his tongue *loosed,* and he spoke,
praising God. 65Then fear came on all who
dwelt around them; and all these sayings
were discussed throughout all the hill country of Judea. 66And all those who heard *them*
kept *them* in their hearts, saying, "What kind
of child will this be?" And the hand of the
Lord was with him.

Zacharias' Prophecy

67Now his father Zacharias was filled
with the Holy Spirit, and prophesied, saying:

68 "Blessed *is* the Lord God of Israel,
For He has visited and redeemed His
people,
69 And has raised up a horn of salvation for us

Starring Roles

MARY was an ordinary young woman living in Nazareth, a town in the Roman province of Galilee. One day she was surprised by a visit from Gabriel, a man from heaven. He was an angel whose name is pronounced *GAY-brih-ell* and means "My God Is Great."

Gabriel told Mary that she was going to be the mother of the Son of God! She didn't know what to say, so she just said, "Let it be to me according to your word." Then she sang the beautiful song you can read in this chapter.

At first, Joseph, the man Mary was going to marry, was very upset, but he understood later. Their Savior from heaven was going to be born, just as the ancient prophets had said (see Isaiah 7:14).

As Mary's Son grew up, she realized He could never really belong to her. He was the Son of God. Sorrow would come to her because one day He would be crucified.

In the house of His servant David,
70 As He spoke by the mouth of His holy prophets,
Who *have been* since the world began,
71 That we should be saved from our enemies
And from the hand of all who hate us,
72 To perform the mercy *promised* to our fathers
And to remember His holy covenant,
73 The oath which He swore to our father Abraham:
74 To grant us that we,
Being delivered from the hand of our enemies,
Might serve Him without fear,
75 In holiness and righteousness before Him all the days of our life.

76 "And you, child, will be called the prophet of the Highest;
For you will go before the face of the Lord to prepare His ways,
77 To give knowledge of salvation to His people
By the remission of their sins,
78 Through the tender mercy of our God,
With which the Dayspring from on high has visited[a] us;

1:78 [a] NU-Text reads *shall visit.*

Spotlight

A BIRTH FORETOLD

READ IT: LUKE 1:26–56

GET IT:

Mary and Joseph had agreed to get married (that's what *betrothed* means). Their agreement was serious and legal and almost impossible to break. But then Mary had a big surprise—a visit from an angel who said she would become pregnant by the Holy Spirit. This was a miracle and a mystery, but it really messed up their plans. What would people think? But Joseph believed that God had planned it this way (Matthew 1:18–25) so he quietly married Mary right away. Mary was really excited that God had chosen her to be the mother of Jesus. She knew how important it would be when people realized that her son was the Son of God.

LIVE IT:

Everybody talks. And the people in Mary's town had lots to talk about—it was scandalous that a young girl like Mary was pregnant without being married! The stories must have been flying! Have you ever been the one everybody was talking about? Have you ever had to face rumors? What helped you get through that difficult time? Mary knew she had nothing to be ashamed about. She knew she was doing the right thing. She was obeying God, doing what she was asked to do. We don't know exactly how she faced the people in her small hometown, but with the help and support of her relative Elizabeth, she had the courage to deal with the gossip. Perhaps she replied to prying questions with the same simple answer she had given the angel: "I'm the Lord's servant." Handling rumors is difficult, but the best option may be that from the Bible: "A soft answer turns away wrath" (Proverbs 15:1).

spirit,[a] filled with wisdom; and the grace of
God was upon Him.

The Boy Jesus Amazes the Scholars

41His parents went to Jerusalem every
year at the Feast of the Passover. 42And when
He was twelve years old, they went up to Jerusalem according to the custom of the feast.
43When they had finished the days, as they
returned, the Boy Jesus lingered behind in
Jerusalem. And Joseph and His mother[a]
did not know *it;* 44but supposing Him to
have been in the company, they went a day's
journey, and sought Him among *their* relatives and acquaintances. 45So when they did
not find Him, they returned to Jerusalem,
seeking Him. 46Now so it was *that* after three
days they found Him in the temple, sitting
in the midst of the teachers, both listening
to them and asking them questions. 47And
all who heard Him were astonished at His
understanding and answers. 48So when they
saw Him, they were amazed; and His mother said to Him, "Son, why have You done this
to us? Look, Your father and I have sought
You anxiously."

49And He said to them, "Why did you
seek Me? Did you not know that I must be
about My Father's business?" 50But they did
not understand the statement which He
spoke to them.

2:40 [a] NU-Text omits *in spirit.* **2:43** [a] NU-Text reads *And His parents.*

WHO IS GOD? THREE-IN-ONE

READ IT: LUKE 3:21–23

GET IT:

Jesus was a human being. He did things that normal people do. He ate, slept, worked, had friends, went to weddings, fished, took long walks, cried, and got tired. Because He was God in flesh, He was perfect. Sinless. He didn't need to confess or repent or get baptized (a public display of being part of God's family). Jesus was part of God's family long before He was born, even before time began. So why did He get baptized?

Jesus' baptism shows that He was one of us, a person, fully human. But His baptism was different than ours because all three persons of God showed up together: Father, Son, and Holy Spirit, the Trinity. And the Father announced that Jesus is His Son.

This idea of three-in-one isn't easy to understand. The one true God has three different forms: the heavenly Father, the earthly Son, and the Spirit who lives in the hearts of believers. All three are important. All three are God. All three are part of our lives.

LIVE IT:

It's important to know about the three persons of the Trinity. Read about God in Psalms 135–150. Read about Jesus in Matthew, Mark, Luke, or John. And find out about the Holy Spirit in Romans 8.

Jesus Advances in Wisdom and Favor

51Then He went down with them and
came to Nazareth, and was subject to them,
but His mother kept all these things in her
heart. 52And Jesus increased in wisdom and
stature, and in favor with God and men.

John the Baptist Prepares the Way

3 Now in the fifteenth year of the reign
of Tiberius Caesar, Pontius Pilate being governor of Judea, Herod being tetrarch
of Galilee, his brother Philip tetrarch of
Iturea and the region of Trachonitis, and
Lysanias tetrarch of Abilene, 2while Annas
and Caiaphas were high priests,[a] the word
of God came to John the son of Zacharias in
the wilderness. 3And he went into all the region around the Jordan, preaching a baptism
of repentance for the remission of sins, 4as it
is written in the book of the words of Isaiah
the prophet, saying:

"The voice of one crying in the
wilderness:
'Prepare the way of the LORD;
Make His paths straight.
5 Every valley shall be filled
And every mountain and hill brought
low;
The crooked places shall be made
straight
And the rough ways smooth;
6 And all flesh shall see the salvation of
God.' "[a]

John Preaches to the People

7Then he said to the multitudes that
came out to be baptized by him, "Brood of
vipers! Who warned you to flee from the
wrath to come? 8Therefore bear fruits worthy of repentance, and do not begin to say
to yourselves, 'We have Abraham as *our* father.' For I say to you that God is able to raise
up children to Abraham from these stones.
9And even now the ax is laid to the root of the
trees. Therefore every tree which does not
bear good fruit is cut down and thrown into
the fire."

10So the people asked him, saying, "What
shall we do then?"

11He answered and said to them, "He
who has two tunics, let him give to him who
has none; and he who has food, let him do
likewise."

12Then tax collectors also came to be
baptized, and said to him, "Teacher, what
shall we do?"

13And he said to them, "Collect no more
than what is appointed for you."

14Likewise the soldiers asked him, saying,
"And what shall we do?"

So he said to them, "Do not intimidate
anyone or accuse falsely, and be content with
your wages."

15Now as the people were in expectation,
and all reasoned in their hearts about John,
whether he was the Christ *or* not, 16John
answered, saying to all, "I indeed baptize
you with water; but One mightier than I is
coming, whose sandal strap I am not worthy
to loose. He will baptize you with the Holy
Spirit and fire. 17His winnowing fan *is* in His
hand, and He will thoroughly clean out His
threshing floor, and gather the wheat into
His barn; but the chaff He will burn with
unquenchable fire."

18And with many other exhortations
he preached to the people. 19But Herod the
tetrarch, being rebuked by him concerning
Herodias, his brother Philip's wife,[a] and for
all the evils which Herod had done, 20also
added this, above all, that he shut John up
in prison.

John Baptizes Jesus

21When all the people were baptized,
it came to pass that Jesus also was baptized; and while He prayed, the heaven was
opened. 22And the Holy Spirit descended in
bodily form like a dove upon Him, and a
voice came from heaven which said, "You are
My beloved Son; in You I am well pleased."

In Focus

3:23 Son of . . . (Genealogy) The history of a family showing the family members of each generation from the beginning. This genealogy of Jesus traces His ancestors all the way back to Adam, whose Father was God.

3:2 [a] NU-Text and M-Text read *in the high priesthood of Annas and Caiaphas.* 3:6 [a] Isaiah 40:3–5 3:19 [a] NU-Text reads *his brother's wife.*

The Genealogy of Jesus Christ

23 Now Jesus Himself began *His ministry*
at about thirty years of age, being (as was
supposed) *the* son of Joseph, *the son* of Heli,
24 *the son* of Matthat,[a] *the son* of Levi, *the son*
of Melchi, *the son* of Janna, *the son* of Joseph,
25 *the son* of Mattathiah, *the son* of Amos, *the*
son of Nahum, *the son* of Esli, *the son* of Nag-
gai, 26 *the son* of Maath, *the son* of Mattathiah,
the son of Semei, *the son* of Joseph, *the son* of
Judah, 27 *the son* of Joannas, *the son* of Rhesa,
the son of Zerubbabel, *the son* of Shealtiel,
the son of Neri, 28 *the son* of Melchi, *the son*
of Addi, *the son* of Cosam, *the son* of Elmo-
dam, *the son* of Er, 29 *the son* of Jose, *the son* of
Eliezer, *the son* of Jorim, *the son* of Matthat,
the son of Levi, 30 *the son* of Simeon, *the son*
of Judah, *the son* of Joseph, *the son* of Jonan,
the son of Eliakim, 31 *the son* of Melea, *the son*
of Menan, *the son* of Mattathah, *the son* of
Nathan, *the son* of David, 32 *the son* of Jesse,
the son of Obed, *the son* of Boaz, *the son* of
Salmon, *the son* of Nahshon, 33 *the son* of Amminadab, *the son* of Ram, *the son* of Hezron,
the son of Perez, *the son* of Judah, 34 *the son* of
Jacob, *the son* of Isaac, *the son* of Abraham,
the son of Terah, *the son* of Nahor, 35 *the son*
of Serug, *the son* of Reu, *the son* of Peleg, *the*
son of Eber, *the son* of Shelah, 36 *the son* of Cainan, *the son* of Arphaxad, *the son* of Shem,
the son of Noah, *the son* of Lamech, 37 *the son*
of Methuselah, *the son* of Enoch, *the son* of
Jared, *the son* of Mahalalel, *the son* of Cainan,
38 *the son* of Enosh, *the son* of Seth, *the son* of
Adam, *the son* of God.

Satan Tempts Jesus

4 Then Jesus, being filled with the Holy
Spirit, returned from the Jordan and
was led by the Spirit into[a] the wilderness,
2 being tempted for forty days by the devil.
And in those days He ate nothing, and afterward, when they had ended, He was hungry.

3 And the devil said to Him, "If You are
the Son of God, command this stone to become bread."

4 But Jesus answered him, saying,[a] "It is
written, 'Man shall not live by bread alone,
but by every word of God.' "[b]

5 Then the devil, taking Him up on a high
mountain, showed Him[a] all the kingdoms
of the world in a moment of time. 6 And the
devil said to Him, "All this authority I will
give You, and their glory; for *this* has been
delivered to me, and I give it to whomever I
wish. 7 Therefore, if You will worship before
me, all will be Yours."

8 And Jesus answered and said to him,
"Get behind Me, Satan![a] For[b] it is written,
'You shall worship the LORD your God, and
Him only you shall serve.' "[c]

9 Then he brought Him to Jerusalem, set
Him on the pinnacle of the temple, and said
to Him, "If You are the Son of God, throw
Yourself down from here. 10 For it is written:

'He shall give His angels charge over you,
To keep you,'

11 and,

'In *their* hands they shall bear you up,
Lest you dash your foot against a
stone.' "[a]

12 And Jesus answered and said to him, "It
has been said, 'You shall not tempt the LORD
your God.' "[a]

13 Now when the devil had ended every
temptation, he departed from Him until an
opportune time.

Jesus Begins His Galilean Ministry

14 Then Jesus returned in the power of the
Spirit to Galilee, and news of Him went out
through all the surrounding region. 15 And
He taught in their synagogues, being glorified by all.

Jesus Rejected at Nazareth

16 So He came to Nazareth, where He had
been brought up. And as His custom was,
He went into the synagogue on the Sabbath
day, and stood up to read. 17 And He was
handed the book of the prophet Isaiah. And
when He had opened the book, He found the
place where it was written:

18 "The Spirit of the LORD *is* upon Me,
Because He has anointed Me
To preach the gospel to *the* poor;
He has sent Me to heal the
brokenhearted,[a]

3:24 [a] This and several other names in the genealogy are spelled somewhat differently in the NU-Text. Since the New King James Version uses the Old Testament spelling for persons mentioned in the New Testament, these variations, which come from the Greek, have not been footnoted. **4:1** [a] NU-Text reads *in.* **4:4** [a] Deuteronomy 8:3 [b] NU-Text omits *but by every word of God.* **4:5** [a] NU-Text reads *And taking Him up, he showed Him.* **4:8** [a] NU-Text omits *Get behind Me, Satan.* [b] NU-Text and M-Text omit *For.* [c] Deuteronomy 6:13 **4:11** [a] Psalm 91:11, 12 **4:12** [a] Deuteronomy 6:16 **4:18** [a] NU-Text omits *to heal the brokenhearted.*

To proclaim liberty to *the* captives
And recovery of sight to *the* blind,
To set at liberty those who are
oppressed;
19 To proclaim the acceptable year of the
LORD."[a]

20 Then He closed the book, and gave *it* back
to the attendant and sat down. And the eyes
of all who were in the synagogue were fixed
on Him. 21 And He began to say to them,
"Today this Scripture is fulfilled in your
hearing." 22 So all bore witness to Him, and
marveled at the gracious words which proceeded out of His mouth. And they said, "Is
this not Joseph's son?"
23 He said to them, "You will surely say
this proverb to Me, 'Physician, heal yourself! Whatever we have heard done in Capernaum,[a] do also here in Your country.'"
24 Then He said, "Assuredly, I say to you,
no prophet is accepted in his own country.
25 But I tell you truly, many widows were in
Israel in the days of Elijah, when the heaven
was shut up three years and six months, and
there was a great famine throughout all the
land; 26 but to none of them was Elijah sent
except to Zarephath,[a] *in the region* of Sidon,
to a woman *who was* a widow. 27 And many
lepers were in Israel in the time of Elisha
the prophet, and none of them was cleansed
except Naaman the Syrian."
28 So all those in the synagogue, when
they heard these things, were filled with
wrath, 29 and rose up and thrust Him out
of the city; and they led Him to the brow of
the hill on which their city was built, that
they might throw Him down over the cliff.
30 Then passing through the midst of them,
He went His way.

Jesus Casts Out an Unclean Spirit

31 Then He went down to Capernaum, a
city of Galilee, and was teaching them on the
Sabbaths. 32 And they were astonished at His
teaching, for His word was with authority.
33 Now in the synagogue there was a man
who had a spirit of an unclean demon. And
he cried out with a loud voice, 34 saying, "Let
us alone! What have we to do with You, Jesus
of Nazareth? Did You come to destroy us? I
know who You are—the Holy One of God!"
35 But Jesus rebuked him, saying, "Be quiet, and come out of him!" And when the demon had thrown him in *their* midst, it came
out of him and did not hurt him. 36 Then they
were all amazed and spoke among themselves, saying, "What a word this *is!* For with
authority and power He commands the unclean spirits, and they come out." 37 And the
report about Him went out into every place
in the surrounding region.

Peter's Mother-in-Law Healed

38 Now He arose from the synagogue and
entered Simon's house. But Simon's wife's
mother was sick with a high fever, and they
made request of Him concerning her. 39 So
He stood over her and rebuked the fever, and
it left her. And immediately she arose and
served them.

Many Healed After Sabbath Sunset

40 When the sun was setting, all those
who had any that were sick with various
diseases brought them to Him; and He laid
His hands on every one of them and healed
them. 41 And demons also came out of many,
crying out and saying, "You are the Christ,[a]
the Son of God!"
And He, rebuking *them,* did not allow
them to speak, for they knew that He was
the Christ.

Jesus Preaches in Galilee

42 Now when it was day, He departed and
went into a deserted place. And the crowd
sought Him and came to Him, and tried to
keep Him from leaving them; 43 but He said
to them, "I must preach the kingdom of God
to the other cities also, because for this purpose I have been sent." 44 And He was preaching in the synagogues of Galilee.[a]

Four Fishermen Called as Disciples

5 So it was, as the multitude pressed
about Him to hear the word of God,
that He stood by the Lake of Gennesaret,
2 and saw two boats standing by the lake; but
the fishermen had gone from them and were
washing *their* nets. 3 Then He got into one
of the boats, which was Simon's, and asked
him to put out a little from the land. And
He sat down and taught the multitudes from
the boat.

4:19 [a] Isaiah 61:1, 2 **4:23** [a] Here and elsewhere the NU-Text spelling is *Capharnaum.* **4:26** [a] Greek *Sarepta* **4:41** [a] NU-Text omits *the Christ.* **4:44** [a] NU-Text reads *Judea.*

4When He had stopped speaking, He
said to Simon, "Launch out into the deep
and let down your nets for a catch."

5But Simon answered and said to Him,
"Master, we have toiled all night and caught
nothing; nevertheless at Your word I will let
down the net." 6And when they had done
this, they caught a great number of fish, and
their net was breaking. 7So they signaled to
their partners in the other boat to come and
help them. And they came and filled both
the boats, so that they began to sink. 8When
Simon Peter saw *it,* he fell down at Jesus'
knees, saying, "Depart from me, for I am a
sinful man, O Lord!"

9For he and all who were with him were
astonished at the catch of fish which they
had taken; 10and so also *were* James and John,
the sons of Zebedee, who were partners with
Simon. And Jesus said to Simon, "Do not be
afraid. From now on you will catch men."
11So when they had brought their boats to
land, they forsook all and followed Him.

Jesus Cleanses a Leper

12And it happened when He was in a certain city, that behold, a man who was full of
leprosy saw Jesus; and he fell on *his* face and
implored Him, saying, "Lord, if You are willing, You can make me clean."

13Then He put out *His* hand and touched
him, saying, "I am willing; be cleansed."
Immediately the leprosy left him. 14And He
charged him to tell no one, "But go and show
yourself to the priest, and make an offering
for your cleansing, as a testimony to them,
just as Moses commanded."

15However, the report went around concerning Him all the more; and great multitudes came together to hear, and to be
healed by Him of their infirmities. 16So He
Himself *often* withdrew into the wilderness
and prayed.

Jesus Forgives and Heals a Paralytic

17Now it happened on a certain day, as He
was teaching, that there were Pharisees and
teachers of the law sitting by, who had come
out of every town of Galilee, Judea, and Jerusalem. And the power of the Lord was *present*
to heal them.[a] 18Then behold, men brought
on a bed a man who was paralyzed, whom
they sought to bring in and lay before Him.
19And when they could not find how they
might bring him in, because of the crowd,
they went up on the housetop and let him

5:17 [a] NU-Text reads *present with Him to heal.*

5:28 WHO WERE THE TAX COLLECTORS?

The Roman government, which ruled the Jews in Jesus' day, required several kinds of taxes, including a land tax and a personal tax.

The Jewish tax collectors were despised because they worked for the hated Romans. Besides, some tax collectors kept tax money for themselves. So these men were treated as "sinners" by the rest of the people. John the Baptist warned the tax collectors to be honest in their work (see Luke 3:12, 13).

It may seem strange that Jesus befriended tax collectors. He even asked Matthew, a tax collector, to be one of His disciples! Matthew is the disciple who wrote the first Gospel of the New Testament.

Jesus loved men and women that most people hated! Doesn't that make you stop and think?

26 Woe to you[a] when all[b] men speak well of
you,
For so did their fathers to the false
prophets.

Love Your Enemies

27"But I say to you who hear: Love your enemies, do good to those who hate you, 28bless those who curse you, and pray for those who spitefully use you. 29To him who strikes you on the *one* cheek, offer the other also. And from him who takes away your cloak, do not withhold *your* tunic either. 30Give to everyone who asks of you. And from him who takes away your goods do not ask *them* back. 31And just as you want men to do to you, you also do to them likewise.

32"But if you love those who love you, what credit is that to you? For even sinners love those who love them. 33And if you do good to those who do good to you, what credit is that to you? For even sinners do the same. 34And if you lend *to those* from whom you hope to receive back, what credit is that to you? For even sinners lend to sinners to receive as much back. 35But love your enemies, do good, and lend, hoping for nothing in return; and your reward will be great, and you will be sons of the Most High. For He is kind to the unthankful and evil. 36Therefore be merciful, just as your Father also is merciful.

Do Not Judge

37"Judge not, and you shall not be judged. Condemn not, and you shall not be condemned. Forgive, and you will be forgiven. 38Give, and it will be given to you: good measure, pressed down, shaken together, and running over will be put into your bosom. For with the same measure that you use, it will be measured back to you."

39And He spoke a parable to them: "Can the blind lead the blind? Will they not both fall into the ditch? 40A disciple is not above his teacher, but everyone who is perfectly trained will be like his teacher. 41And why do you look at the speck in your brother's eye, but do not perceive the plank in your own eye? 42Or how can you say to your brother, 'Brother, let me remove the speck that *is* in your eye,' when you yourself do not see the plank that *is* in your own eye? Hypocrite! First remove the plank from your own eye, and then you will see clearly to remove the speck that is in your brother's eye.

A Tree Is Known by Its Fruit

43"For a good tree does not bear bad fruit, nor does a bad tree bear good fruit. 44For every tree is known by its own fruit. For *men* do not gather figs from thorns, nor do they gather grapes from a bramble bush. 45A good man out of the good treasure of his heart brings forth good; and an evil man out of the evil treasure of his heart[a] brings forth evil. For out of the abundance of the heart his mouth speaks.

Build on the Rock

46"But why do you call Me 'Lord, Lord,' and not do the things which I say? 47Whoever comes to Me, and hears My sayings and does them, I will show you whom he is like: 48He is like a man building a house, who dug deep and laid the foundation on the rock. And when the flood arose, the stream beat vehemently against that house, and could not shake it, for it was founded on the rock.[a] 49But he who heard and did nothing is like a man who built a house on the earth without a foundation, against which the stream beat vehemently; and immediately it fell.[a] And the ruin of that house was great."

Jesus Heals a Centurion's Servant

7 Now when He concluded all His sayings in the hearing of the people, He entered Capernaum. 2And a certain centurion's servant, who was dear to him, was sick and ready to die. 3So when he heard about Jesus, he sent elders of the Jews to Him, pleading with Him to come and heal his servant. 4And when they came to Jesus, they begged Him earnestly, saying that the one for whom He should do this was deserving, 5"for he loves our nation, and has built us a synagogue."

6Then Jesus went with them. And when He was already not far from the house, the centurion sent friends to Him, saying to Him, "Lord, do not trouble Yourself, for I am not worthy that You should enter under my roof. 7Therefore I did not even think myself worthy to come to You. But say the word, and my servant will be healed. 8For I also am a

6:26 [a] NU-Text and M-Text omit *to you.* [b] M-Text omits *all.* **6:45** [a] NU-Text omits *treasure of his heart.* **6:48** [a] NU-Text reads *for it was well built.* **6:49** [a] NU-Text reads *collapsed.*

man placed under authority, having soldiers
under me. And I say to one, 'Go,' and he
goes; and to another, 'Come,' and he comes;
and to my servant, 'Do this,' and he does *it*."
9 When Jesus heard these things, He
marveled at him, and turned around and
said to the crowd that followed Him, "I say
to you, I have not found such great faith, not
even in Israel!" 10 And those who were sent,
returning to the house, found the servant
well who had been sick.[a]

Jesus Raises the Son of the Widow of Nain

11 Now it happened, the day after, *that*
He went into a city called Nain; and many
of His disciples went with Him, and a large
crowd. 12 And when He came near the gate
of the city, behold, a dead man was being
carried out, the only son of his mother; and
she was a widow. And a large crowd from the
city was with her. 13 When the Lord saw her,
He had compassion on her and said to her,
"Do not weep." 14 Then He came and touched
the open coffin, and those who carried *him*
stood still. And He said, "Young man, I say
to you, arise." 15 So he who was dead sat up
and began to speak. And He presented him
to his mother.
16 Then fear came upon all, and they glorified God, saying, "A great prophet has ris-
en up among us"; and, "God has visited His
people." 17 And this report about Him went
throughout all Judea and all the surrounding region.

John the Baptist Sends Messengers to Jesus

18 Then the disciples of John reported to
him concerning all these things. 19 And John,
calling two of his disciples to *him*, sent *them*
to Jesus,[a] saying, "Are You the Coming One,
or do we look for another?"
20 When the men had come to Him, they
said, "John the Baptist has sent us to You,
saying, 'Are You the Coming One, or do we
look for another?'" 21 And that very hour He
cured many of infirmities, afflictions, and
evil spirits; and to many blind He gave sight.
22 Jesus answered and said to them, "Go
and tell John the things you have seen and
heard: that *the* blind see, *the* lame walk, *the*
lepers are cleansed, *the* deaf hear, *the* dead
are raised, *the* poor have the gospel preached
to them. 23 And blessed is *he* who is not offended because of Me."
24 When the messengers of John had departed, He began to speak to the multitudes
concerning John: "What did you go out into
the wilderness to see? A reed shaken by the
wind? 25 But what did you go out to see? A
man clothed in soft garments? Indeed those
who are gorgeously appareled and live in
luxury are in kings' courts. 26 But what did
you go out to see? A prophet? Yes, I say to
you, and more than a prophet. 27 This is *he* of
whom it is written:

> 'Behold, I send My messenger before
> Your face,
> Who will prepare Your way before
> You.'[a]

28 For I say to you, among those born of wom-
en there is not a greater prophet than John
the Baptist;[a] but he who is least in the kingdom of God is greater than he."
29 And when all the people heard *Him,*
even the tax collectors justified God, having been baptized with the baptism of John.
30 But the Pharisees and lawyers rejected the
will of God for themselves, not having been
baptized by him.
31 And the Lord said,[a] "To what then shall
I liken the men of this generation, and what
are they like? 32 They are like children sitting
in the marketplace and calling to one another, saying:

> 'We played the flute for you,
> And you did not dance;
> We mourned to you,
> And you did not weep.'

33 For John the Baptist came neither eating
bread nor drinking wine, and you say, 'He
has a demon.' 34 The Son of Man has come
eating and drinking, and you say, 'Look, a
glutton and a winebibber, a friend of tax collectors and sinners!' 35 But wisdom is justified by all her children."

A Sinful Woman Forgiven

36 Then one of the Pharisees asked Him
to eat with him. And He went to the Pharisee's house, and sat down to eat. 37 And behold, a woman in the city who was a sinner,

---

7:10 [a] NU-Text omits *who had been sick.* **7:19** [a] NU-Text reads *the Lord.* **7:27** [a] Malachi 3:1 **7:28** [a] NU-Text reads *there is none greater than John.* **7:31** [a] NU-Text and M-Text omit *And the Lord said.*

when she knew that *Jesus* sat at the table in
the Pharisee's house, brought an alabaster
flask of fragrant oil, [38]and stood at His feet
behind *Him* weeping; and she began to wash
His feet with her tears, and wiped *them* with
the hair of her head; and she kissed His feet
and anointed *them* with the fragrant oil.
[39]Now when the Pharisee who had invited
Him saw *this,* he spoke to himself, saying,
"This Man, if He were a prophet, would

JUDGING OTHERS

THE UNDERWATER BEACH BALL

READ IT: LUKE 7:36–50

GET IT:

In the original language of the New Testament—Greek—Jesus doesn't just say, "She has washed My feet with her tears" (v. 44). He says, "She has rained her tears on My feet." This wasn't just a single teardrop dripping off the woman's cheek. Her tears flooded over Jesus' feet like rain. She was at a point in her life where she couldn't bear to think of who she had become. People judged her so harshly she couldn't take it anymore. She walked into a stranger's home uninvited and threw herself at the feet of the man she truly believed to be God's Son. She cried enough tears to wash His feet. And then Jesus said to her, "Your sins are forgiven" (v. 48).

LIVE IT:

We bury things:

- The thing she said that one time
- The moment when the person you trusted turned out to be untrustworthy
- The time when it seemed like the whole world suddenly knew about your secret
- The time when you knew better but thought it couldn't hurt to try something once

We bury these moments down deep inside us. We think they're gone, but they come to the surface, like a beach ball that you try to hold under water. When everything you've tried to bury comes out, here's what you should do:

- Pray.
- Admit that you need help.
- Talk to your minister or another trusted adult.
- Ask your parents to help you find a support group.
- Forgive yourself.

That's when healing can begin.

know who and what manner of woman *this*
is who is touching Him, for she is a sinner."
40 And Jesus answered and said to him,
"Simon, I have something to say to you."
So he said, "Teacher, say it."
41 "There was a certain creditor who had
two debtors. One owed five hundred denarii,
and the other fifty. 42 And when they had
nothing with which to repay, he freely forgave them both. Tell Me, therefore, which of
them will love him more?"
43 Simon answered and said, "I suppose
the *one* whom he forgave more."
And He said to him, "You have rightly
judged." 44 Then He turned to the woman
and said to Simon, "Do you see this woman?
I entered your house; you gave Me no water for My feet, but she has washed My feet
with her tears and wiped *them* with the hair
of her head. 45 You gave Me no kiss, but this
woman has not ceased to kiss My feet since
the time I came in. 46 You did not anoint My
head with oil, but this woman has anointed
My feet with fragrant oil. 47 Therefore I say to
you, her sins, which *are* many, are forgiven,
for she loved much. But to whom little is forgiven, *the same* loves little."
48 Then He said to her, "Your sins are
forgiven."

In Focus

8:10 Mysteries Things that are not known. Paul spoke about "the mysteries of God." These were things that weren't known until Jesus came and revealed the gospel.

49 And those who sat at the table with Him
began to say to themselves, "Who is this who
even forgives sins?"
50 Then He said to the woman, "Your
faith has saved you. Go in peace."

Many Women Minister to Jesus

8 Now it came to pass, afterward, that
He went through every city and village, preaching and bringing the glad tidings of the kingdom of God. And the twelve
were with Him, 2 and certain women who had
been healed of evil spirits and infirmities—
Mary called Magdalene, out of whom had
come seven demons, 3 and Joanna the wife of
Chuza, Herod's steward, and Susanna, and

Action!

LET YOUR LIGHT SHINE

READ IT: LUKE 8:16–18

What good is a light if it doesn't help you see in the dark? What would you think if your parents went around covering all the lamps in your home? Wouldn't that be foolish!

Jesus commands you to *let your light shine*. What light? Let the light of Jesus shine in your life. Your actions must show that Jesus lives in you. People look for a light when it is dark. They need the light of Jesus to show them the way through a dark and frightening world.

Some Christians hide their light. They seem afraid to let others know how much Jesus means to them. If people can see how much Jesus has done for you, then they, too, will come to Jesus. Jesus is this dark world's true light (see John 9:5). He is the only One who can light our way to heaven.

many others who provided for Him[a] from
their substance.

The Parable of the Sower

4 And when a great multitude had gathered, and they had come to Him from every
city, He spoke by a parable: 5 "A sower went
out to sow his seed. And as he sowed, some
fell by the wayside; and it was trampled
down, and the birds of the air devoured it.
6 Some fell on rock; and as soon as it sprang
up, it withered away because it lacked moisture. 7 And some fell among thorns, and the
thorns sprang up with it and choked it. 8 But
others fell on good ground, sprang up, and
yielded a crop a hundredfold." When He had
said these things He cried, "He who has ears
to hear, let him hear!"

The Purpose of Parables

9 Then His disciples asked Him, saying,
"What does this parable mean?"
10 And He said, "To you it has been giv-
en to know the mysteries of the kingdom of
God, but to the rest *it is given* in parables,
that

'Seeing they may not see,
And hearing they may not understand.'[a]

The Parable of the Sower Explained

11 "Now the parable is this: The seed is the
word of God. 12 Those by the wayside are the
ones who hear; then the devil comes and
takes away the word out of their hearts, lest
they should believe and be saved. 13 But the
ones on the rock *are those* who, when they
hear, receive the word with joy; and these
have no root, who believe for a while and in
time of temptation fall away. 14 Now the ones
that fell among thorns are those who, when
they have heard, go out and are choked with
cares, riches, and pleasures of life, and bring
no fruit to maturity. 15 But the ones *that* fell
on the good ground are those who, having
heard the word with a noble and good heart,
keep it and bear fruit with patience.

The Parable of the Revealed Light

16 "No one, when he has lit a lamp, covers
it with a vessel or puts *it* under a bed, but
sets *it* on a lampstand, that those who enter
may see the light. 17 For nothing is secret that
will not be revealed, nor *anything* hidden
that will not be known and come to light.
18 Therefore take heed how you hear. For
whoever has, to him *more* will be given; and
whoever does not have, even what he seems
to have will be taken from him."

Jesus' Mother and Brothers Come to Him

19 Then His mother and brothers came to
Him, and could not approach Him because
of the crowd. 20 And it was told Him *by some,*
who said, "Your mother and Your brothers
are standing outside, desiring to see You."
21 But He answered and said to them, "My
mother and My brothers are these who hear
the word of God and do it."

Wind and Wave Obey Jesus

22 Now it happened, on a certain day, that
He got into a boat with His disciples. And
He said to them, "Let us cross over to the
other side of the lake." And they launched
out. 23 But as they sailed He fell asleep. And a
windstorm came down on the lake, and they
were filling *with water,* and were in jeopardy.
24 And they came to Him and awoke Him,
saying, "Master, Master, we are perishing!"
Then He arose and rebuked the wind
and the raging of the water. And they ceased,
and there was a calm. 25 But He said to them,
"Where is your faith?"
And they were afraid, and marveled, saying to one another, "Who can this be? For
He commands even the winds and water,
and they obey Him!"

A Demon-Possessed Man Healed

26 Then they sailed to the country of the
Gadarenes,[a] which is opposite Galilee. 27 And
when He stepped out on the land, there met
Him a certain man from the city who had
demons for a long time. And he wore no
clothes,[a] nor did he live in a house but in the
tombs. 28 When he saw Jesus, he cried out,
fell down before Him, and with a loud voice
said, "What have I to do with You, Jesus, Son
of the Most High God? I beg You, do not
torment me!" 29 For He had commanded the
unclean spirit to come out of the man. For it
had often seized him, and he was kept under
guard, bound with chains and shackles; and
he broke the bonds and was driven by the
demon into the wilderness.

8:3 [a] NU-Text and M-Text read *them.* 8:10 [a] Isaiah 6:9
8:26 [a] NU-Text reads *Gerasenes.* 8:27 [a] NU-Text reads *who had demons and for a long time wore no clothes.*

30 Jesus asked him, saying, "What is your name?"

And he said, "Legion," because many demons had entered him. 31 And they begged Him that He would not command them to go out into the abyss.

32 Now a herd of many swine was feeding there on the mountain. So they begged Him that He would permit them to enter them. And He permitted them. 33 Then the demons went out of the man and entered the swine, and the herd ran violently down the steep place into the lake and drowned.

34 When those who fed *them* saw what had happened, they fled and told *it* in the city and in the country. 35 Then they went out to see what had happened, and came to Jesus, and found the man from whom the demons had departed, sitting at the feet of Jesus, clothed and in his right mind. And they were afraid. 36 They also who had seen *it* told them by what means he who had been demon-possessed was healed. 37 Then the whole multitude of the surrounding region of the Gadarenes[a] asked Him to depart from them, for they were seized with great fear. And He got into the boat and returned.

38 Now the man from whom the demons had departed begged Him that he might be with Him. But Jesus sent him away, saying, 39 "Return to your own house, and tell what great things God has done for you." And he went his way and proclaimed throughout the whole city what great things Jesus had done for him.

A Girl Restored to Life and a Woman Healed

40 So it was, when Jesus returned, that the multitude welcomed Him, for they were all waiting for Him. 41 And behold, there came a man named Jairus, and he was a ruler of the synagogue. And he fell down at Jesus' feet and begged Him to come to his house, 42 for he had an only daughter about twelve years of age, and she was dying.

But as He went, the multitudes thronged Him. 43 Now a woman, having a flow of blood for twelve years, who had spent all her livelihood on physicians and could not be healed by any, 44 came from behind and touched the border of His garment. And immediately her flow of blood stopped.

45 And Jesus said, "Who touched Me?"

When all denied it, Peter and those with him[a] said, "Master, the multitudes throng and press You, and You say, 'Who touched Me?' "[b]

46 But Jesus said, "Somebody touched Me, for I perceived power going out from Me." 47 Now when the woman saw that she was not hidden, she came trembling; and falling down before Him, she declared to Him in the presence of all the people the reason she had touched Him and how she was healed immediately.

48 And He said to her, "Daughter, be of good cheer;[a] your faith has made you well. Go in peace."

49 While He was still speaking, someone came from the ruler of the synagogue's *house*, saying to him, "Your daughter is dead. Do not trouble the Teacher."[a]

50 But when Jesus heard *it*, He answered him, saying, "Do not be afraid; only believe, and she will be made well." 51 When He came into the house, He permitted no one to go in[a] except Peter, James, and John,[b] and the father and mother of the girl. 52 Now all wept and mourned for her; but He said, "Do not weep; she is not dead, but sleeping." 53 And they ridiculed Him, knowing that she was dead.

54 But He put them all outside,[a] took her by the hand and called, saying, "Little girl, arise." 55 Then her spirit returned, and she arose immediately. And He commanded that she be given *something* to eat. 56 And her parents were astonished, but He charged them to tell no one what had happened.

Sending Out the Twelve

9 Then He called His twelve disciples together and gave them power and authority over all demons, and to cure diseases. 2 He sent them to preach the kingdom of God and to heal the sick. 3 And He said to them, "Take nothing for the journey, neither staffs nor bag nor bread nor money; and do not have two tunics apiece.

4 "Whatever house you enter, stay there, and from there depart. 5 And whoever will not receive you, when you go out of that city, shake off the very dust from your feet as a testimony against them."

8:37 [a] NU-Text reads *Gerasenes.* **8:45** [a] NU-Text omits *and those with him.* [b] NU-Text omits *and You say, 'Who touched Me?'* **8:48** [a] NU-Text omits *be of good cheer.* **8:49** [a] NU-Text adds *anymore.* **8:51** [a] NU-Text adds *with Him.* [b] NU-Text and M-Text read *Peter, John, and James.* **8:54** [a] NU-Text omits *put them all outside.*

⁶So they departed and went through the
towns, preaching the gospel and healing
everywhere.

Herod Seeks to See Jesus

⁷Now Herod the tetrarch heard of all that
was done by Him; and he was perplexed, because it was said by some that John had risen
from the dead, ⁸and by some that Elijah had
appeared, and by others that one of the old
prophets had risen again. ⁹Herod said, "John
I have beheaded, but who is this of whom I
hear such things?" So he sought to see Him.

Feeding the Five Thousand

¹⁰And the apostles, when they had returned, told Him all that they had done.
Then He took them and went aside privately
into a deserted place belonging to the city
called Bethsaida. ¹¹But when the multitudes

HOPE

HOPE IN THE HEM

READ IT: LUKE 8:40–48

GET IT:

Think of the last time you were sick. Not just when you had a few sniffles, but when you were so sick you had to stay home from school. Do you remember how miserable you felt? Now imagine feeling that way for twelve years. You're so sick that you can't leave your house. Your family doesn't want to be around you. And doctors can't treat your symptoms or make you feel any better.

Would you have any hope?

That was the life this woman was living. For twelve years she had a condition that caused chronic bleeding. She spent every cent she had on medical care. She became an outcast in her own community. A better life seemed hopeless—until she heard about Jesus and the miraculous healings He was performing in town. Hope sprang out of a hopeless situation.

Could Jesus heal her? She was desperate to find out, and she had hope that He could. She took a chance and went out to where the crowd was forming around Him and pushed her way through, probably crawling on her hands and knees. She made it to Jesus, and when she touched the hem of His robe, she was healed of her suffering.

Without hope, this woman wouldn't have left her house. She wouldn't have believed she could be healed. After all, the doctors who tried to heal her had failed. Without hope, she would have spent the rest of her life in despair and anguish. But hope won.

LIVE IT:

When you are faced with what seems like a hopeless situation, remember that when we reach for Jesus, there is always hope, and hope never fails us.

knew *it,* they followed Him; and He received
them and spoke to them about the kingdom
of God, and healed those who had need of
healing. 12When the day began to wear away,
the twelve came and said to Him, "Send the
multitude away, that they may go into the
surrounding towns and country, and lodge
and get provisions; for we are in a deserted
place here."
13But He said to them, "You give them
something to eat."
And they said, "We have no more than
five loaves and two fish, unless we go and
buy food for all these people." 14For there
were about five thousand men.
Then He said to His disciples, "Make
them sit down in groups of fifty." 15And they
did so, and made them all sit down.
16Then He took the five loaves and the
two fish, and looking up to heaven, He
blessed and broke them, and gave *them* to
the disciples to set before the multitude. 17So
they all ate and were filled, and twelve baskets of the leftover fragments were taken up
by them.

Peter Confesses Jesus as the Christ

18And it happened, as He was alone praying, *that* His disciples joined Him, and He
asked them, saying, "Who do the crowds say
that I am?"
19So they answered and said, "John the
Baptist, but some *say* Elijah; and others *say*
that one of the old prophets has risen again."
20He said to them, "But who do you say
that I am?"
Peter answered and said, "The Christ of
God."

Jesus Predicts His Death and Resurrection

21And He strictly warned and commanded them to tell this to no one, 22saying, "The
Son of Man must suffer many things, and
be rejected by the elders and chief priests
and scribes, and be killed, and be raised the
third day."

Take Up the Cross and Follow Him

23Then He said to *them* all, "If anyone
desires to come after Me, let him deny himself, and take up his cross daily,[a] and follow
Me. 24For whoever desires to save his life will
lose it, but whoever loses his life for My sake
will save it. 25For what profit is it to a man
if he gains the whole world, and is himself
destroyed or lost? 26For whoever is ashamed
of Me and My words, of him the Son of Man
will be ashamed when He comes in His *own*
glory, and *in His* Father's, and of the holy
angels. 27But I tell you truly, there are some
standing here who shall not taste death till
they see the kingdom of God."

Jesus Transfigured on the Mount

28Now it came to pass, about eight days
after these sayings, that He took Peter, John,
and James and went up on the mountain to
pray. 29As He prayed, the appearance of His
face was altered, and His robe *became* white
and glistening. 30And behold, two men talked

9:23 [a] M-Text omits *daily.*

BEING YOURSELF

READ IT: LUKE 9:25

That little voice inside you is your conscience. Often it's the nudge you get from the Holy Spirit when you should (or should not) do something. If you've ever ignored it, you know the strange feeling you get. Even when you're offered something important in the world's eyes, if it's going against what God tells you, it's not worth it.

with Him, who were Moses and Elijah, 31who
appeared in glory and spoke of His decease
which He was about to accomplish at Jerusalem. 32But Peter and those with him were
heavy with sleep; and when they were fully
awake, they saw His glory and the two men
who stood with Him. 33Then it happened, as
they were parting from Him, *that* Peter said
to Jesus, "Master, it is good for us to be here;
and let us make three tabernacles: one for
You, one for Moses, and one for Elijah"—not
knowing what he said.
34While he was saying this, a cloud came
and overshadowed them; and they were fearful as they entered the cloud. 35And a voice
came out of the cloud, saying, "This is My
beloved Son.[a] Hear Him!" 36When the voice
had ceased, Jesus was found alone. But they
kept quiet, and told no one in those days any
of the things they had seen.

A Boy Is Healed

37Now it happened on the next day, when
they had come down from the mountain,
that a great multitude met Him. 38Suddenly
a man from the multitude cried out, saying,
"Teacher, I implore You, look on my son, for
he is my only child. 39And behold, a spirit seizes him, and he suddenly cries out; it
convulses him so that he foams *at the mouth;*
and it departs from him with great difficulty,
bruising him. 40So I implored Your disciples
to cast it out, but they could not."
41Then Jesus answered and said, "O
faithless and perverse generation, how long
shall I be with you and bear with you? Bring
your son here." 42And as he was still coming,
the demon threw him down and convulsed
him. Then Jesus rebuked the unclean spirit,
healed the child, and gave him back to his
father.

Jesus Again Predicts His Death

43And they were all amazed at the majesty of God.
But while everyone marveled at all the
things which Jesus did, He said to His disciples, 44"Let these words sink down into your
ears, for the Son of Man is about to be betrayed into the hands of men." 45But they did
not understand this saying, and it was hidden from them so that they did not perceive
it; and they were afraid to ask Him about this
saying.

Who Is the Greatest?

46Then a dispute arose among them as
to which of them would be greatest. 47And
Jesus, perceiving the thought of their heart,
took a little child and set him by Him, 48and
said to them, "Whoever receives this little
child in My name receives Me; and whoever
receives Me receives Him who sent Me. For
he who is least among you all will be great."

Jesus Forbids Sectarianism

49Now John answered and said, "Master,
we saw someone casting out demons in Your
name, and we forbade him because he does
not follow with us."
50But Jesus said to him, "Do not forbid
him, for he who is not against us[a] is on our[b]
side."

A Samaritan Village Rejects the Savior

51Now it came to pass, when the time had
come for Him to be received up, that He
steadfastly set His face to go to Jerusalem,
52and sent messengers before His face. And
as they went, they entered a village of the
Samaritans, to prepare for Him. 53But they
did not receive Him, because His face was
set for the journey to Jerusalem. 54And when
His disciples James and John saw *this,* they
said, "Lord, do You want us to command fire
to come down from heaven and consume
them, just as Elijah did?"[a]
55But He turned and rebuked them,[a]
and said, "You do not know what manner of
spirit you are of. 56For the Son of Man did
not come to destroy men's lives but to save
them."[a] And they went to another village.

The Cost of Discipleship

57Now it happened as they journeyed on
the road, *that* someone said to Him, "Lord, I
will follow You wherever You go."
58And Jesus said to him, "Foxes have
holes and birds of the air *have* nests, but the
Son of Man has nowhere to lay *His* head."
59Then He said to another, "Follow Me."
But he said, "Lord, let me first go and
bury my father."
60Jesus said to him, "Let the dead bury

9:35 [a] NU-Text reads *This is My Son, the Chosen One.*
9:50 [a] NU-Text reads *you.* [b] NU-Text reads *your.*
9:54 [a] NU-Text omits *just as Elijah did.* 9:55 [a] NU-Text omits the rest of this verse. 9:56 [a] NU-Text omits the first sentence of this verse.

their own dead, but you go and preach the
kingdom of God."
61And another also said, "Lord, I will
follow You, but let me first go *and* bid them
farewell who are at my house."
62But Jesus said to him, "No one, having
put his hand to the plow, and looking back,
is fit for the kingdom of God."

The Seventy Sent Out

10 After these things the Lord appointed seventy others also,[a] and
sent them two by two before His face into
every city and place where He Himself was
about to go. 2Then He said to them, "The
harvest truly *is* great, but the laborers *are*
few; therefore pray the Lord of the harvest
to send out laborers into His harvest. 3Go
your way; behold, I send you out as lambs
among wolves. 4Carry neither money bag,
knapsack, nor sandals; and greet no one
along the road. 5But whatever house you enter, first say, 'Peace to this house.' 6And if a
son of peace is there, your peace will rest on
it; if not, it will return to you. 7And remain
in the same house, eating and drinking such

10:1 [a] NU-Text reads *seventy-two others*.

JESUS DEFINES THE WORD *NEIGHBOR*

READ IT: LUKE 10:25–37

GET IT:

The road from Jerusalem to Jericho was super steep. It wound through the mountains down to the flat land where Jericho was. There were loads of places for bad guys to hide and jump out to attack innocent travelers. The traveler here was probably a Jew. The priest was a Jew who was required to follow lots of rules in order to do his work in God's temple. He didn't help the injured man because if he touched any blood, he wouldn't be allowed to go into the temple. The Levite was a person who helped the priest and helped take care of the temple. He followed the same rules and regulations as the priest, so he wouldn't help the traveler either. The Samaritan was a hated foreigner. The Jews didn't want anything to do with Samaritans. He was the least likely one to help out a Jew, but he did. He cared for the man and even spent money on him. Through this story Jesus made it very clear that our neighbor is anyone who needs our help.

LIVE IT:

How far would you go to help someone in need? Using the hallway of your school as the setting, make up your own version of this story. Who would play each character? How would your story end? Draw pictures, write it, or tell it to your parents. You'll get a better understanding of what Jesus was talking about when you put this story in your own words with people you encounter every day. How will knowing this story change how you act toward others?

things as they give, for the laborer is worthy
of his wages. Do not go from house to house.
8Whatever city you enter, and they receive
you, eat such things as are set before you.
9And heal the sick there, and say to them,
'The kingdom of God has come near to you.'
10But whatever city you enter, and they do not
receive you, go out into its streets and say,
11'The very dust of your city which clings to
us[a] we wipe off against you. Nevertheless
know this, that the kingdom of God has
come near you.' 12But[a] I say to you that it will
be more tolerable in that Day for Sodom than
for that city.

Woe to the Impenitent Cities

13"Woe to you, Chorazin! Woe to you,
Bethsaida! For if the mighty works which
were done in you had been done in Tyre and
Sidon, they would have repented long ago,
sitting in sackcloth and ashes. 14But it will be
more tolerable for Tyre and Sidon at the judgment than for you. 15And you, Capernaum,
who are exalted to heaven, will be brought
down to Hades.[a] 16He who hears you hears
Me, he who rejects you rejects Me, and he
who rejects Me rejects Him who sent Me."

The Seventy Return with Joy

17Then the seventy[a] returned with joy,
saying, "Lord, even the demons are subject
to us in Your name."

18And He said to them, "I saw Satan fall
like lightning from heaven. 19Behold, I give
you the authority to trample on serpents and
scorpions, and over all the power of the enemy, and nothing shall by any means hurt
you. 20Nevertheless do not rejoice in this,
that the spirits are subject to you, but rather[a] rejoice because your names are written
in heaven."

Jesus Rejoices in the Spirit

21In that hour Jesus rejoiced in the Spirit
and said, "I thank You, Father, Lord of heav-
en and earth, that You have hidden these
things from *the* wise and prudent and revealed them to babes. Even so, Father, for so
it seemed good in Your sight. 22All[a] things
have been delivered to Me by My Father, and
no one knows who the Son is except the Father, and who the Father is except the Son,
and *the one* to whom the Son wills to reveal
Him."

23Then He turned to *His* disciples and
said privately, "Blessed *are* the eyes which
see the things you see; 24for I tell you that
many prophets and kings have desired to see
what you see, and have not seen *it*, and to
hear what you hear, and have not heard *it*."

In Focus

10:33 Samaritan Pronounced *suh-MARE-ih-tun*. A person who lived in Samaria (pronounced *suh-MARE-ee-ah*), a district north of Judea. Jews hated Samaritans, partly because they were a mixed race.

The Parable of the Good Samaritan

25And behold, a certain lawyer stood up
and tested Him, saying, "Teacher, what shall
I do to inherit eternal life?"

26He said to him, "What is written in the
law? What is your reading *of it*?"

27So he answered and said, "'You shall
love the LORD your God with all your heart,
with all your soul, with all your strength,
and with all your mind,'[a] and 'your neighbor as yourself.'"[b]

28And He said to him, "You have answered rightly; do this and you will live."

29But he, wanting to justify himself, said
to Jesus, "And who is my neighbor?"

30Then Jesus answered and said: "A
certain *man* went down from Jerusalem
to Jericho, and fell among thieves, who
stripped him of his clothing, wounded *him*,
and departed, leaving *him* half dead. 31Now
by chance a certain priest came down that
road. And when he saw him, he passed by
on the other side. 32Likewise a Levite, when
he arrived at the place, came and looked, and
passed by on the other side. 33But a certain
Samaritan, as he journeyed, came where he
was. And when he saw him, he had compassion. 34So he went to *him* and bandaged his
wounds, pouring on oil and wine; and he
set him on his own animal, brought him to

10:11 [a] NU-Text reads *our feet*. **10:12** [a] NU-Text and M-Text omit *But*. **10:15** [a] NU-Text reads *will you be exalted to heaven? You will be thrust down to Hades!* **10:17** [a] NU-Text reads *seventy-two*. **10:20** [a] NU-Text and M-Text omit *rather*. **10:22** [a] M-Text reads *And turning to the disciples He said, "All . . . .* **10:27** [a] Deuteronomy 6:5 [b] Leviticus 19:18

an inn, and took care of him. [35]On the next
day, when he departed,[a] he took out two denarii, gave *them* to the innkeeper, and said to
him, 'Take care of him; and whatever more
you spend, when I come again, I will repay
you.' [36]So which of these three do you think
was neighbor to him who fell among the
thieves?"
[37]And he said, "He who showed mercy on
him."

Then Jesus said to him, "Go and do likewise."

Mary and Martha Worship and Serve

[38]Now it happened as they went that He
entered a certain village; and a certain woman named Martha welcomed Him into her
house. [39]And she had a sister called Mary,

10:35 [a] NU-Text omits *when he departed.*

ANXIETY

THE BIG PICTURE

READ IT: LUKE 10:38–42

GET IT:

Have you ever been so caught up in the details that you couldn't see the big picture? That's what happened to Martha, and those details were stressing her out. She was anxious about the work she thought was important and frustrated with her sister for not helping. But it turns out Martha was worrying about things that didn't really matter. It wasn't wrong that she wanted to serve the people in her home, but she was focusing on the wrong things that day. Martha was seeing a list of chores and the burden of doing them alone, but what really mattered was learning from Jesus. That was the big picture on that special day, and that's what Mary saw that Martha didn't.

LIVE IT:

When worry gets the better of you, it can make you feel like you're tied up in knots inside. You snap at your friends and talk back to your parents, all because little details are gnawing at you. But are you seeing the big picture?

- Sometimes today's worries are quickly forgotten tomorrow. Don't let them get the better of you.
- It's easy to take out our stress on the people around us, but it will only make things worse. Control your tongue when you feel stressed out.
- Keep your perspective. Remember what's important to God, and make that what matters to you.
- Give God your concerns. Pray and hand them over. God wants to carry them for you.

who also sat at Jesus'[a] feet and heard His
word. 40But Martha was distracted with
much serving, and she approached Him and
said, "Lord, do You not care that my sister
has left me to serve alone? Therefore tell her
to help me."

41And Jesus[a] answered and said to her,
"Martha, Martha, you are worried and troubled about many things. 42But one thing is
needed, and Mary has chosen that good part,
which will not be taken away from her."

The Model Prayer

11 Now it came to pass, as He was
praying in a certain place, when He
ceased, *that* one of His disciples said to Him,
"Lord, teach us to pray, as John also taught
his disciples."

2So He said to them, "When you pray,
say:

Our Father in heaven,[a]
Hallowed be Your name.
Your kingdom come.[b]
Your will be done
On earth as *it is* in heaven.
3 Give us day by day our daily bread.
4 And forgive us our sins,
For we also forgive everyone who is
indebted to us.
And do not lead us into temptation,
But deliver us from the evil one."[a]

A Friend Comes at Midnight

5And He said to them, "Which of you
shall have a friend, and go to him at midnight and say to him, 'Friend, lend me three
loaves; 6for a friend of mine has come to me
on his journey, and I have nothing to set before him'; 7and he will answer from within
and say, 'Do not trouble me; the door is now
shut, and my children are with me in bed;
I cannot rise and give to you'? 8I say to you,
though he will not rise and give to him because he is his friend, yet because of his per-
sistence he will rise and give him as many
as he needs.

10:39 [a] NU-Text reads *the Lord's.* **10:41** [a] NU-Text reads *the Lord.* **11:2** [a] NU-Text omits *Our* and *in heaven.* [b] NU-Text omits the rest of this verse. **11:4** [a] NU-Text omits *But deliver us from the evil one.*

ASK, SEEK, KNOCK

READ IT: LUKE 11:9

Maybe you pray to God sometimes, but did you know that He really hears and understands your feelings?

People who think God is far away are called "deists" (pronounced *DEE-ists*). God is then seen as the One who created the universe but has nothing to do with how people get along. Deists think the world is like a machine that just runs on its own.

Another false idea is that everyone and everything is *part of God,* so there is no difference between God and us. That way of thinking is called "pantheism" (pronounced *PAN-thee-ism*).

Jesus tells us that God is *our Father* who is closer to us than breath. When you pray to Him, He hears you. Jesus means that you should keep on knocking at the door of your heavenly Father. He will open the door and answer your needs.

Jesus wants you to seek Him. If you take the time to pray and tell Him what is on your heart, you are following through with what He has invited you to do.

Keep Asking, Seeking, Knocking

9 “So I say to you, ask, and it will be given
to you; seek, and you will find; knock, and
it will be opened to you. 10 For everyone who
asks receives, and he who seeks finds, and to
him who knocks it will be opened. 11 If a son
asks for bread[a] from any father among you,
will he give him a stone? Or if *he asks* for a
fish, will he give him a serpent instead of
a fish? 12 Or if he asks for an egg, will he offer him a scorpion? 13 If you then, being evil,
know how to give good gifts to your children,
how much more will *your* heavenly Father
give the Holy Spirit to those who ask Him!”

A House Divided Cannot Stand

14 And He was casting out a demon, and
it was mute. So it was, when the demon had
gone out, that the mute spoke; and the multitudes marveled. 15 But some of them said,
“He casts out demons by Beelzebub,[a] the
ruler of the demons.”

16 Others, testing *Him,* sought from Him
a sign from heaven. 17 But He, knowing their
thoughts, said to them: “Every kingdom divided against itself is brought to desolation,
and a house *divided* against a house falls. 18 If
Satan also is divided against himself, how
will his kingdom stand? Because you say
I cast out demons by Beelzebub. 19 And if I
cast out demons by Beelzebub, by whom do
your sons cast *them* out? Therefore they will
be your judges. 20 But if I cast out demons
with the finger of God, surely the kingdom of God has come upon you. 21 When a
strong man, fully armed, guards his own
palace, his goods are in peace. 22 But when a
stronger than he comes upon him and overcomes him, he takes from him all his armor
in which he trusted, and divides his spoils.
23 He who is not with Me is against Me, and
he who does not gather with Me scatters.

An Unclean Spirit Returns

24 “When an unclean spirit goes out of a
man, he goes through dry places, seeking
rest; and finding none, he says, ‘I will return
to my house from which I came.’ 25 And when
he comes, he finds *it* swept and put in order.
26 Then he goes and takes with *him* seven
other spirits more wicked than himself, and
they enter and dwell there; and the last *state*
of that man is worse than the first.”

Keeping the Word

27 And it happened, as He spoke these
things, that a certain woman from the crowd
raised her voice and said to Him, “Blessed
is the womb that bore You, and *the* breasts
which nursed You!”

28 But He said, “More than that, blessed *are*
those who hear the word of God and keep it!”

Seeking a Sign

29 And while the crowds were thickly gathered together, He began to say, “This is an
evil generation. It seeks a sign, and no sign
will be given to it except the sign of Jonah
the prophet.[a] 30 For as Jonah became a sign to
the Ninevites, so also the Son of Man will be
to this generation. 31 The queen of the South
will rise up in the judgment with the men of
this generation and condemn them, for she
came from the ends of the earth to hear the
wisdom of Solomon; and indeed a greater
than Solomon *is* here. 32 The men of Nineveh
will rise up in the judgment with this generation and condemn it, for they repented at
the preaching of Jonah; and indeed a greater
than Jonah *is* here.

The Lamp of the Body

33 “No one, when he has lit a lamp, puts
it in a secret place or under a basket, but on
a lampstand, that those who come in may
see the light. 34 The lamp of the body is the
eye. Therefore, when your eye is good, your
whole body also is full of light. But when *your*
eye is bad, your body also *is* full of darkness.
35 Therefore take heed that the light which is
in you is not darkness. 36 If then your whole
body *is* full of light, having no part dark, *the*
whole *body* will be full of light, as when the
bright shining of a lamp gives you light.”

Woe to the Pharisees and Lawyers

37 And as He spoke, a certain Pharisee
asked Him to dine with him. So He went
in and sat down to eat. 38 When the Pharisee
saw *it,* he marveled that He had not first
washed before dinner.

39 Then the Lord said to him, “Now you
Pharisees make the outside of the cup and
dish clean, but your inward part is full of
greed and wickedness. 40 Foolish ones! Did

11:11 [a] NU-Text omits the words from *bread* through *for* in the next sentence. **11:15** [a] NU-Text and M-Text read *Beelzebul.* **11:29** [a] NU-Text omits *the prophet.*

not He who made the outside make the
inside also? 41 But rather give alms of such
things as you have; then indeed all things
are clean to you.
42 "But woe to you Pharisees! For you tithe
mint and rue and all manner of herbs, and
pass by justice and the love of God. These
you ought to have done, without leaving the
others undone. 43 Woe to you Pharisees! For
you love the best seats in the synagogues
and greetings in the marketplaces. 44 Woe to
you, scribes and Pharisees, hypocrites![a] For
you are like graves which are not seen, and
the men who walk over *them* are not aware
of them."
45 Then one of the lawyers answered
and said to Him, "Teacher, by saying these
things You reproach us also."
46 And He said, "Woe to you also, lawyers!
For you load men with burdens hard to bear,
and you yourselves do not touch the burdens
with one of your fingers. 47 Woe to you! For
you build the tombs of the prophets, and
your fathers killed them. 48 In fact, you bear
witness that you approve the deeds of your
fathers; for they indeed killed them, and you
build their tombs. 49 Therefore the wisdom
of God also said, 'I will send them prophets and apostles, and *some* of them they will
kill and persecute,' 50 that the blood of all the
prophets which was shed from the foundation of the world may be required of this generation, 51 from the blood of Abel to the blood
of Zechariah who perished between the altar
and the temple. Yes, I say to you, it shall be
required of this generation.
52 "Woe to you lawyers! For you have taken
away the key of knowledge. You did not enter
in yourselves, and those who were entering
in you hindered."
53 And as He said these things to them,[a]
the scribes and the Pharisees began to assail
Him vehemently, and to cross-examine Him
about many things, 54 lying in wait for Him,
and seeking to catch Him in something He
might say, that they might accuse Him.[a]

Beware of Hypocrisy

12 In the meantime, when an innumerable multitude of people had
gathered together, so that they trampled one
another, He began to say to His disciples
first *of all*, "Beware of the leaven of the Pharisees, which is hypocrisy. 2 For there is nothing covered that will not be revealed, nor
hidden that will not be known. 3 Therefore
whatever you have spoken in the dark will be
heard in the light, and what you have spoken
in the ear in inner rooms will be proclaimed
on the housetops.

Jesus Teaches the Fear of God

4 "And I say to you, My friends, do not be
afraid of those who kill the body, and after
that have no more that they can do. 5 But I
will show you whom you should fear: Fear
Him who, after He has killed, has power to
cast into hell; yes, I say to you, fear Him!
6 "Are not five sparrows sold for two copper coins?[a] And not one of them is forgotten
before God. 7 But the very hairs of your head
are all numbered. Do not fear therefore; you
are of more value than many sparrows.

Confess Christ Before Men

8 "Also I say to you, whoever confesses Me
before men, him the Son of Man also will
confess before the angels of God. 9 But he
who denies Me before men will be denied
before the angels of God.
10 "And anyone who speaks a word against
the Son of Man, it will be forgiven him; but
to him who blasphemes against the Holy
Spirit, it will not be forgiven.
11 "Now when they bring you to the synagogues and magistrates and authorities, do
not worry about how or what you should answer, or what you should say. 12 For the Holy
Spirit will teach you in that very hour what
you ought to say."

The Parable of the Rich Fool

13 Then one from the crowd said to Him,
"Teacher, tell my brother to divide the inheritance with me."
14 But He said to him, "Man, who made
Me a judge or an arbitrator over you?" 15 And
He said to them, "Take heed and beware
of covetousness,[a] for one's life does not
consist in the abundance of the things he
possesses."
16 Then He spoke a parable to them,
saying: "The ground of a certain rich man
yielded plentifully. 17 And he thought within himself, saying, 'What shall I do, since I
have no room to store my crops?' 18 So he said,

11:44 [a] NU-Text omits *scribes and Pharisees, hypocrites.*
11:53 [a] NU-Text reads *And when He left there.* **11:54** [a] NU-Text omits *and seeking* and *that they might accuse Him.*
12:6 [a] Greek *assarion,* a coin of very small value
12:15 [a] NU-Text reads *all covetousness.*

'I will do this: I will pull down my barns and
build greater, and there I will store all my
crops and my goods. 19 And I will say to my
soul, "Soul, you have many goods laid up
for many years; take your ease; eat, drink,
and be merry."' 20 But God said to him, 'Fool!
This night your soul will be required of you;
then whose will those things be which you
have provided?'

21 "So *is* he who lays up treasure for himself, and is not rich toward God."

Do Not Worry

22 Then He said to His disciples, "Therefore I say to you, do not worry about your life,
what you will eat; nor about the body, what
you will put on. 23 Life is more than food, and
the body *is more* than clothing. 24 Consider
the ravens, for they neither sow nor reap,
which have neither storehouse nor barn; and
God feeds them. Of how much more value
are you than the birds? 25 And which of you
by worrying can add one cubit to his stature?
26 If you then are not able to do *the* least, why
are you anxious for the rest? 27 Consider the
lilies, how they grow: they neither toil nor
spin; and yet I say to you, even Solomon
in all his glory was not arrayed like one of
these. 28 If then God so clothes the grass,
which today is in the field and tomorrow is
thrown into the oven, how much more *will*
He clothe you, O *you* of little faith?

29 "And do not seek what you should eat or
what you should drink, nor have an anxious
mind. 30 For all these things the nations of
the world seek after, and your Father knows
that you need these things. 31 But seek the
kingdom of God, and all these things[a] shall
be added to you.

32 "Do not fear, little flock, for it is your
Father's good pleasure to give you the kingdom. 33 Sell what you have and give alms;
provide yourselves money bags which do not
grow old, a treasure in the heavens that does
not fail, where no thief approaches nor moth
destroys. 34 For where your treasure is, there
your heart will be also.

The Faithful Servant and the Evil Servant

35 "Let your waist be girded and *your*
lamps burning; 36 and you yourselves be
like men who wait for their master, when
he will return from the wedding, that when
he comes and knocks they may open to him
immediately. 37 Blessed *are* those servants
whom the master, when he comes, will find
watching. Assuredly, I say to you that he will
gird himself and have them sit down *to eat,*
and will come and serve them. 38 And if he
should come in the second watch, or come
in the third watch, and find *them* so, blessed
are those servants. 39 But know this, that if
the master of the house had known what
hour the thief would come, he would have
watched and[a] not allowed his house to be
broken into. 40 Therefore you also be ready,
for the Son of Man is coming at an hour you
do not expect."

12:31 [a] NU-Text reads *His kingdom, and these things.*
12:39 [a] NU-Text reads *he would not have allowed.*

GREED

READ IT: LUKE 12:13–21

Maybe you've had a chance to make some money or earn an allowance. Maybe you've been taught to give a tithe to the church when you earn money doing chores. God wants us to think of our money as a tool for Him, something to be shared and given freely when God asks. When we become greedy and won't let go of the blessings that God has given us, we rob Him and His kingdom.

41Then Peter said to Him, "Lord, do You
speak this parable *only* to us, or to all *people?*"
42And the Lord said, "Who then is that
faithful and wise steward, whom *his* master
will make ruler over his household, to give
them their portion of food in due season?
43Blessed *is* that servant whom his master
will find so doing when he comes. 44Truly, I
say to you that he will make him ruler over
all that he has. 45But if that servant says in
his heart, 'My master is delaying his coming,' and begins to beat the male and female
servants, and to eat and drink and be drunk,
46the master of that servant will come on
a day when he is not looking for *him,* and
at an hour when he is not aware, and will
cut him in two and appoint *him* his portion
with the unbelievers. 47And that servant who
knew his master's will, and did not prepare
himself or do according to his will, shall be
beaten with many *stripes.* 48But he who did
not know, yet committed things deserving
of stripes, shall be beaten with few. For
everyone to whom much is given, from him
much will be required; and to whom much
has been committed, of him they will ask
the more.

Christ Brings Division

49"I came to send fire on the earth, and
how I wish it were already kindled! 50But I
have a baptism to be baptized with, and
how distressed I am till it is accomplished!
51Do *you* suppose that I came to give peace
on earth? I tell you, not at all, but rather division. 52For from now on five in one house
will be divided: three against two, and
two against three. 53Father will be divided
against son and son against father, mother against daughter and daughter against
mother, mother-in-law against her daughter-
in-law and daughter-in-law against her
mother-in-law."

Discern the Time

54Then He also said to the multitudes,
"Whenever you see a cloud rising out of
the west, immediately you say, 'A shower is
coming'; and so it is. 55And when *you see* the
south wind blow, you say, 'There will be hot
weather'; and there is. 56Hypocrites! You can
discern the face of the sky and of the earth,
but how *is it* you do not discern this time?

Make Peace with Your Adversary

57"Yes, and why, even of yourselves, do
you not judge what is right? 58When you go
with your adversary to the magistrate, make
every effort along the way to settle with him,
lest he drag you to the judge, the judge deliver you to the officer, and the officer throw
you into prison. 59I tell you, you shall not

ANXIETY

READ IT: LUKE 12:22–31

God doesn't want you to be weighed down with worry—even about things you need like shelter and food. It's important to remember that worrying never fixed a problem or provided for anyone. Anxiety and worry have only one outcome: more anxiety and worry.

- Be a person of prayer and action. Do something about your concerns.
- Control your thoughts. When they stray into worry, go do something worthwhile like riding your bike.
- Know when to ask for help. Sometimes anxiety is difficult to shake. If you're having a hard time, talk to a trusted adult.

depart from there till you have paid the very
last mite."

Repent or Perish

13 There were present at that season
some who told Him about the Galileans whose blood Pilate had mingled with
their sacrifices. 2 And Jesus answered and
said to them, "Do you suppose that these
Galileans were worse sinners than all *other* Galileans, because they suffered such
things? 3 I tell you, no; but unless you repent
you will all likewise perish. 4 Or those eighteen on whom the tower in Siloam fell and
killed them, do you think that they were
worse sinners than all *other* men who dwelt
in Jerusalem? 5 I tell you, no; but unless you
repent you will all likewise perish."

The Parable of the Barren Fig Tree

6 He also spoke this parable: "A certain
man had a fig tree planted in his vineyard,
and he came seeking fruit on it and found
none. 7 Then he said to the keeper of his
vineyard, 'Look, for three years I have come
seeking fruit on this fig tree and find none.
Cut it down; why does it use up the ground?'
8 But he answered and said to him, 'Sir, let it
alone this year also, until I dig around it and
fertilize *it*. 9 And if it bears fruit, *well*. But if
not, after that[a] you can cut it down.'"

A Spirit of Infirmity

10 Now He was teaching in one of the
synagogues on the Sabbath. 11 And behold,
there was a woman who had a spirit of infirmity eighteen years, and was bent over and
could in no way raise *herself* up. 12 But when
Jesus saw her, He called *her* to *Him* and said
to her, "Woman, you are loosed from your
infirmity." 13 And He laid *His* hands on her,
and immediately she was made straight, and
glorified God.

14 But the ruler of the synagogue answered with indignation, because Jesus had
healed on the Sabbath; and he said to the
crowd, "There are six days on which men
ought to work; therefore come and be healed
on them, and not on the Sabbath day."

15 The Lord then answered him and said,
"Hypocrite![a] Does not each one of you on
the Sabbath loose his ox or donkey from
the stall, and lead *it* away to water it? 16 So
ought not this woman, being a daughter of

13:9 [a] NU-Text reads *And if it bears fruit after that, well. But if not, you can cut it down.* 13:15 [a] NU-Text and M-Text read *Hypocrites.*

REMEMBER YOUR REPENTANCE

READ IT: LUKE 13:5

Repenting is something you do when you first trust in Jesus for salvation (see Mark 1:15). Your heart is set on God rather than on sin.

Then, as you go through life, perhaps you begin to notice that you aren't perfect. Sometimes you speak roughly to your brother or sister. Maybe you complain if your mother asks you to do your chores. Or you're holding a grudge against a classmate at school. Or some bad habit may be getting a hold on your life.

It's important to stay on the path you entered when you first repented (turned away from sin and toward God). To do this, you are wise to begin every day by asking, "Search me, O God . . . and see if there is any wicked way in me" (Psalm 139:23, 24). So start each day like a new page in your life. Try to walk with God in ways that please Him.

Abraham, whom Satan has bound—think of it—for eighteen years, be loosed from this bond on the Sabbath?" 17And when He said these things, all His adversaries were put to shame; and all the multitude rejoiced for all the glorious things that were done by Him.

The Parable of the Mustard Seed

18Then He said, "What is the kingdom of God like? And to what shall I compare it? 19It is like a mustard seed, which a man took and put in his garden; and it grew and became a large[a] tree, and the birds of the air nested in its branches."

The Parable of the Leaven

20And again He said, "To what shall I liken the kingdom of God? 21It is like leaven, which a woman took and hid in three measures[a] of meal till it was all leavened."

The Narrow Way

22And He went through the cities and villages, teaching, and journeying toward Jerusalem. 23Then one said to Him, "Lord, are there few who are saved?"

And He said to them, 24"Strive to enter through the narrow gate, for many, I say to you, will seek to enter and will not be able. 25When once the Master of the house has risen up and shut the door, and you begin to stand outside and knock at the door, saying, 'Lord, Lord, open for us,' and He will answer and say to you, 'I do not know you, where you are from,' 26then you will begin to say, 'We ate and drank in Your presence, and You taught in our streets.' 27But He will say, 'I tell you I do not know you, where you are from. Depart from Me, all you workers of iniquity.' 28There will be weeping and gnashing of teeth, when you see Abraham and Isaac and Jacob and all the prophets in the kingdom of God, and yourselves thrust out. 29They will come from the east and the west, from the north and the south, and sit down in the kingdom of God. 30And indeed there are last who will be first, and there are first who will be last."

31On that very day[a] some Pharisees came, saying to Him, "Get out and depart from here, for Herod wants to kill You."

32And He said to them, "Go, tell that fox, 'Behold, I cast out demons and perform cures today and tomorrow, and the third *day* I shall be perfected.' 33Nevertheless I must journey today, tomorrow, and the *day* following; for it cannot be that a prophet should perish outside of Jerusalem.

Jesus Laments over Jerusalem

34"O Jerusalem, Jerusalem, the one who kills the prophets and stones those who are sent to her! How often I wanted to gather your children together, as a hen *gathers* her brood under *her* wings, but you were not willing! 35See! Your house is left to you desolate; and assuredly,[a] I say to you, you shall not see Me until *the time* comes when you say, 'Blessed is He who comes in the name of the LORD!' "[b]

A Man with Dropsy Healed on the Sabbath

14 Now it happened, as He went into the house of one of the rulers of the Pharisees to eat bread on the Sabbath, that they watched Him closely. 2And behold, there was a certain man before Him who had dropsy. 3And Jesus, answering, spoke to the lawyers and Pharisees, saying, "Is it lawful to heal on the Sabbath?"[a]

4But they kept silent. And He took *him* and healed him, and let him go. 5Then He answered them, saying, "Which of you, having a donkey[a] or an ox that has fallen into a pit, will not immediately pull him out on the Sabbath day?" 6And they could not answer Him regarding these things.

Take the Lowly Place

7So He told a parable to those who were invited, when He noted how they chose the best places, saying to them: 8"When you are invited by anyone to a wedding feast, do not sit down in the best place, lest one more honorable than you be invited by him; 9and he who invited you and him come and say to you, 'Give place to this man,' and then you begin with shame to take the lowest place. 10But when you are invited, go and sit down in the lowest place, so that when he who invited you comes he may say to you, 'Friend, go up higher.' Then you will have glory in the presence of those who sit at the table with you. 11For whoever exalts himself will

13:19 [a] NU-Text omits *large.* 13:21 [a] Greek *sata,* approximately two pecks in all 13:31 [a] NU-Text reads *In that very hour.* 13:35 [a] NU-Text and M-Text omit *assuredly.* [b] Psalm 118:26 14:3 [a] NU-Text adds *or not.* 14:5 [a] NU-Text and M-Text read *son.*

be humbled, and he who humbles himself
will be exalted."

12 Then He also said to him who invited
Him, "When you give a dinner or a supper,
do not ask your friends, your brothers, your
relatives, nor rich neighbors, lest they also
invite you back, and you be repaid. 13 But
when you give a feast, invite *the* poor, *the*
maimed, *the* lame, *the* blind. 14 And you will
be blessed, because they cannot repay you;
for you shall be repaid at the resurrection of
the just."

The Parable of the Great Supper

15 Now when one of those who sat at the
table with Him heard these things, he said
to Him, "Blessed *is* he who shall eat bread[a]
in the kingdom of God!"

16 Then He said to him, "A certain man
gave a great supper and invited many, 17 and
sent his servant at supper time to say to those
who were invited, 'Come, for all things are
now ready.' 18 But they all with one *accord* began to make excuses. The first said to him,
'I have bought a piece of ground, and I must
go and see it. I ask you to have me excused.'
19 And another said, 'I have bought five yoke
of oxen, and I am going to test them. I ask
you to have me excused.' 20 Still another
said, 'I have married a wife, and therefore
I cannot come.' 21 So that servant came and
reported these things to his master. Then
the master of the house, being angry, said to
his servant, 'Go out quickly into the streets
and lanes of the city, and bring in here *the*
poor and *the* maimed and *the* lame and *the*
blind.' 22 And the servant said, 'Master, it is
done as you commanded, and still there is
room.' 23 Then the master said to the servant, 'Go out into the highways and hedges,
and compel *them* to come in, that my house
may be filled. 24 For I say to you that none of
those men who were invited shall taste my
supper.'"

Leaving All to Follow Christ

25 Now great multitudes went with Him.
And He turned and said to them, 26 "If anyone comes to Me and does not hate his father
and mother, wife and children, brothers and
sisters, yes, and his own life also, he cannot
be My disciple. 27 And whoever does not bear
his cross and come after Me cannot be My
disciple. 28 For which of you, intending to
build a tower, does not sit down first and
count the cost, whether he has *enough* to
finish *it*— 29 lest, after he has laid the foundation, and is not able to finish, all who see *it*
begin to mock him, 30 saying, 'This man began to build and was not able to finish'? 31 Or
what king, going to make war against another king, does not sit down first and consider
whether he is able with ten thousand to meet
him who comes against him with twenty
thousand? 32 Or else, while the other is still a
great way off, he sends a delegation and asks
conditions of peace. 33 So likewise, whoever
of you does not forsake all that he has cannot
be My disciple.

Tasteless Salt Is Worthless

34 "Salt *is* good; but if the salt has lost its
flavor, how shall it be seasoned? 35 It is neither fit for the land nor for the dunghill, *but*
men throw it out. He who has ears to hear,
let him hear!"

The Parable of the Lost Sheep

15 Then all the tax collectors and the
sinners drew near to Him to hear
Him. 2 And the Pharisees and scribes complained, saying, "This Man receives sinners
and eats with them." 3 So He spoke this parable to them, saying:

4 "What man of you, having a hundred
sheep, if he loses one of them, does not leave
the ninety-nine in the wilderness, and go
after the one which is lost until he finds it?
5 And when he has found *it*, he lays *it* on his
shoulders, rejoicing. 6 And when he comes
home, he calls together *his* friends and
neighbors, saying to them, 'Rejoice with me,
for I have found my sheep which was lost!'
7 I say to you that likewise there will be more
joy in heaven over one sinner who repents
than over ninety-nine just persons who need
no repentance.

The Parable of the Lost Coin

8 "Or what woman, having ten silver
coins,[a] if she loses one coin, does not light
a lamp, sweep the house, and search carefully until she finds *it*? 9 And when she has
found *it*, she calls *her* friends and neighbors
together, saying, 'Rejoice with me, for I have
found the piece which I lost!' 10 Likewise, I
say to you, there is joy in the presence of the
angels of God over one sinner who repents."

14:15 [a] M-Text reads *dinner.* 15:8 [a] Greek *drachma,* a valuable coin often worn in a ten-piece garland by married women

The Parable of the Lost Son

11Then He said: "A certain man had two
sons. 12And the younger of them said to *his*
father, 'Father, give me the portion of goods
that falls *to me.*' So he divided to them *his*
livelihood. 13And not many days after, the
younger son gathered all together, journeyed
to a far country, and there wasted his possessions with prodigal living. 14But when he had
spent all, there arose a severe famine in that
land, and he began to be in want. 15Then he
went and joined himself to a citizen of that

PEER PRESSURE

WE LIKE TO CELEBRATE

READ IT: LUKE 15:11–32

GET IT:

Birthdays. Sleepovers. Fiestas. Barbeques. Holidays. Graduations. Weddings. Parties are more than just a lot of fun. They mark milestones in our lives. They shape who we are. They help us find our place in the communities we live in. Parties are the highlights of our lives. But parties can also destroy us.

The prodigal son was drawn in by the glitz and glamour of living the wild party life, free from the watchful eye of his parents. Using his inheritance, he partied as hard as he could, spending his money unwisely and doing foolish things, and he found lots of friends who wanted to join the party. But when the money ran out and the party ended, he felt empty on the inside and ruined on the outside. Sick of sharing a pen with pigs, the prodigal son came to his senses and headed home to beg for his father's forgiveness.

When he arrived home, the prodigal son was greeted not with anger but with compassion and the best party he ever attended. Unlike other parties, this one was fueled not by the chase for fun but by a father's love. It was the kind of party that goes on in heaven every time a person realizes Jesus is the way, the truth, and the life.

LIVE IT:

Being away from home and not following your parents' rules and God's ways may seem like fun in the moment, but in the end it will only cause you pain. Have you been to a party and made some bad decisions and done things you know God isn't happy about? Like watching a TV show you aren't allowed to watch or playing a video game you know your parents don't approve of?

Your heavenly Father is waiting with open arms and forgiveness for your return.

God delights in blessing His children. Celebrate God's blessings.

country, and he sent him into his fields to feed swine. 16And he would gladly have filled his stomach with the pods that the swine ate, and no one gave him *anything*.

17"But when he came to himself, he said, 'How many of my father's hired servants have bread enough and to spare, and I perish with hunger! 18I will arise and go to my father, and will say to him, "Father, I have sinned against heaven and before you, 19and I am no longer worthy to be called your son. Make me like one of your hired servants." '

20"And he arose and came to his father. But when he was still a great way off, his father saw him and had compassion, and ran and fell on his neck and kissed him. 21And the son said to him, 'Father, I have sinned against heaven and in your sight, and am no longer worthy to be called your son.'

22"But the father said to his servants, 'Bring[a] out the best robe and put *it* on him, and put a ring on his hand and sandals on *his* feet. 23And bring the fatted calf here and kill *it*, and let us eat and be merry; 24for this my son was dead and is alive again; he was lost and is found.' And they began to be merry.

25"Now his older son was in the field. And as he came and drew near to the house, he heard music and dancing. 26So he called one of the servants and asked what these things meant. 27And he said to him, 'Your brother has come, and because he has received him safe and sound, your father has killed the fatted calf.'

28"But he was angry and would not go in. Therefore his father came out and pleaded with him. 29So he answered and said to *his* father, 'Lo, these many years I have been serving you; I never transgressed your commandment at any time; and yet you never gave me a young goat, that I might make merry with my friends. 30But as soon as this son of yours came, who has devoured your livelihood with harlots, you killed the fatted calf for him.'

31"And he said to him, 'Son, you are always with me, and all that I have is yours. 32It was right that we should make merry and be glad, for your brother was dead and is alive again, and was lost and is found.' "

The Parable of the Unjust Steward

16 He also said to His disciples: "There was a certain rich man who had a steward, and an accusation was brought to him that this man was wasting his goods. 2So he called him and said to him, 'What is this I hear about you? Give an account of your stewardship, for you can no longer be steward.'

3"Then the steward said within himself, 'What shall I do? For my master is taking the stewardship away from me. I cannot dig; I am ashamed to beg. 4I have resolved what to do, that when I am put out of the stewardship, they may receive me into their houses.'

5"So he called every one of his master's

15:22 [a] NU-Text reads *Quickly bring.*

MONEY

READ IT: LUKE 16:13

The beauty of this verse comes in the word *or*. Jesus says we have a choice. We can serve God *or* we can serve money. Of course, God provides the best stuff of life: happiness and joy and love. So which do you want more: happiness or money? The *or* says you've got to pick one. This *isn't just* a question for adults; you can set your priorities—what you think are the most important things in life—now, and they'll form who you become for the rest of your life.

debtors to *him,* and said to the first, 'How
much do you owe my master?' 6And he said,
'A hundred measures[a] of oil.' So he said to
him, 'Take your bill, and sit down quickly
and write fifty.' 7Then he said to another,
'And how much do you owe?' So he said, 'A
hundred measures[a] of wheat.' And he said
to him, 'Take your bill, and write eighty.' 8So
the master commended the unjust steward
because he had dealt shrewdly. For the sons
of this world are more shrewd in their generation than the sons of light.

9"And I say to you, make friends for yourselves by unrighteous mammon, that when
you fail,[a] they may receive you into an everlasting home. 10He who *is* faithful in *what is*
least is faithful also in much; and he who is
unjust in *what is* least is unjust also in much.
11Therefore if you have not been faithful in
the unrighteous mammon, who will com-
mit to your trust the true *riches?* 12And if you
have not been faithful in what is another
man's, who will give you what is your own?

13"No servant can serve two masters;
for either he will hate the one and love the
other, or else he will be loyal to the one and
despise the other. You cannot serve God and
mammon."

The Law, the Prophets, and the Kingdom

14Now the Pharisees, who were lovers
of money, also heard all these things, and
they derided Him. 15And He said to them,
"You are those who justify yourselves before
men, but God knows your hearts. For what
is highly esteemed among men is an abomination in the sight of God.

16"The law and the prophets *were* until
John. Since that time the kingdom of God
has been preached, and everyone is pressing
into it. 17And it is easier for heaven and earth
to pass away than for one tittle of the law to
fail.

18"Whoever divorces his wife and marries another commits adultery; and whoever
marries her who is divorced from *her* husband commits adultery.

The Rich Man and Lazarus

19"There was a certain rich man who was
clothed in purple and fine linen and fared
sumptuously every day. 20But there was a
certain beggar named Lazarus, full of sores,
who was laid at his gate, 21desiring to be fed
with the crumbs which fell[a] from the rich
man's table. Moreover the dogs came and
licked his sores. 22So it was that the beggar
died, and was carried by the angels to Abraham's bosom. The rich man also died and
was buried. 23And being in torments in Hades, he lifted up his eyes and saw Abraham
afar off, and Lazarus in his bosom.

24"Then he cried and said, 'Father Abraham, have mercy on me, and send Lazarus
that he may dip the tip of his finger in water
and cool my tongue; for I am tormented in
this flame.' 25But Abraham said, 'Son, remember that in your lifetime you received
your good things, and likewise Lazarus evil
things; but now he is comforted and you are
tormented. 26And besides all this, between
us and you there is a great gulf fixed, so that
those who want to pass from here to you cannot, nor can those from there pass to us.'

27"Then he said, 'I beg you therefore,
father, that you would send him to my father's house, 28for I have five brothers, that
he may testify to them, lest they also come
to this place of torment.' 29Abraham said to
him, 'They have Moses and the prophets; let
them hear them.' 30And he said, 'No, father
Abraham; but if one goes to them from the
dead, they will repent.' 31But he said to him,
'If they do not hear Moses and the prophets,
neither will they be persuaded though one
rise from the dead.'"

Jesus Warns of Offenses

17 Then He said to the disciples, "It is
impossible that no offenses should
come, but woe *to him* through whom they
do come! 2It would be better for him if a
millstone were hung around his neck, and
he were thrown into the sea, than that he
should offend one of these little ones. 3Take
heed to yourselves. If your brother sins
against you,[a] rebuke him; and if he repents,
forgive him. 4And if he sins against you sev-
en times in a day, and seven times in a day
returns to you,[a] saying, 'I repent,' you shall
forgive him."

Faith and Duty

5And the apostles said to the Lord, "Increase our faith."

16:6 [a] Greek *batos,* eight or nine gallons each (Old Testament *bath*) **16:7** [a] Greek *koros,* ten or twelve bushels each (Old Testament *kor*) **16:9** [a] NU-Text reads *it fails.* **16:21** [a] NU-Text reads *with what fell.* **17:3** [a] NU-Text omits *against you.* **17:4** [a] M-Text omits *to you.*

6So the Lord said, "If you have faith as a
mustard seed, you can say to this mulberry
tree, 'Be pulled up by the roots and be planted in the sea,' and it would obey you. 7And
which of you, having a servant plowing or
tending sheep, will say to him when he has
come in from the field, 'Come at once and
sit down to eat'? 8But will he not rather say to
him, 'Prepare something for my supper, and
gird yourself and serve me till I have eaten
and drunk, and afterward you will eat and
drink'? 9Does he thank that servant because
he did the things that were commanded
him? I think not.[a] 10So likewise you, when
you have done all those things which you
are commanded, say, 'We are unprofitable
servants. We have done what was our duty
to do.'"

Ten Lepers Cleansed

11Now it happened as He went to Jerusalem that He passed through the midst of
Samaria and Galilee. 12Then as He entered a
certain village, there met Him ten men who
were lepers, who stood afar off. 13And they
lifted up *their* voices and said, "Jesus, Master,
have mercy on us!"

14So when He saw *them,* He said to them,
"Go, show yourselves to the priests." And so
it was that as they went, they were cleansed.
15And one of them, when he saw that he
was healed, returned, and with a loud voice
glorified God, 16and fell down on *his* face at
His feet, giving Him thanks. And he was a
Samaritan.

17So Jesus answered and said, "Were
there not ten cleansed? But where *are* the
nine? 18Were there not any found who returned to give glory to God except this foreigner?" 19And He said to him, "Arise, go
your way. Your faith has made you well."

The Coming of the Kingdom

20Now when He was asked by the Pharisees when the kingdom of God would come,
He answered them and said, "The kingdom
of God does not come with observation; 21nor
will they say, 'See here!' or 'See there!'[a] For
indeed, the kingdom of God is within you."

22Then He said to the disciples, "The
days will come when you will desire to see
one of the days of the Son of Man, and you
will not see *it.* 23And they will say to you,
'Look here!' or 'Look there!'[a] Do not go after
them or follow *them.* 24For as the lightning
that flashes out of one *part* under heaven

17:9 [a] NU-Text ends verse with *commanded;* M-Text omits *him.* **17:21** [a] NU-Text reverses *here* and *there.* **17:23** [a] NU-Text reverses *here* and *there.*

BE HONEST WITH GOD

READ IT: LUKE 18:13

Do you have a clear conscience? Or do you just have a bad memory?

One man in Jesus' story seemed to have a bad memory. He didn't remember any sin he had done. He was very pleased with himself. The other man was a hated tax collector, but he knew he was a sinner, and he knew he needed God's forgiveness.

Let's all pray that we never become like the proud Pharisee. All he could remember were all the good works he thought he had done. But the Pharisee's good works were useless because they weren't works of love. His deeds were done just to show off before a watching world.

Pray, too, that your conscience will always be like the tax collector's. You are closest to God when you realize that you are a sinner wanting His forgiveness.

shines to the other *part* under heaven, so also the Son of Man will be in His day. 25 But first He must suffer many things and be rejected by this generation. 26 And as it was in the days of Noah, so it will be also in the days of the Son of Man: 27 They ate, they drank, they married wives, they were given in marriage, until the day that Noah entered the ark, and the flood came and destroyed them all. 28 Likewise as it was also in the days of Lot: They ate, they drank, they bought, they sold, they planted, they built; 29 but on the day that Lot went out of Sodom it rained fire and brimstone from heaven and destroyed *them* all. 30 Even so will it be in the day when the Son of Man is revealed.

31 "In that day, he who is on the housetop, and his goods *are* in the house, let him not come down to take them away. And likewise the one who is in the field, let him not turn back. 32 Remember Lot's wife. 33 Whoever seeks to save his life will lose it, and whoever loses his life will preserve it. 34 I tell you, in that night there will be two *men* in one bed: the one will be taken and the other will be left. 35 Two *women* will be grinding together: the one will be taken and the other left. 36 Two *men* will be in the field: the one will be taken and the other left."[a]

37 And they answered and said to Him, "Where, Lord?"

So He said to them, "Wherever the body is, there the eagles will be gathered together."

The Parable of the Persistent Widow

18 Then He spoke a parable to them, that men always ought to pray and not lose heart, 2 saying: "There was in a certain city a judge who did not fear God nor regard man. 3 Now there was a widow in that city; and she came to him, saying, 'Get justice for me from my adversary.' 4 And he would not for a while; but afterward he said *within himself, 'Though I do not fear God* nor regard man, 5 yet because this widow troubles me I will avenge her, lest by her continual coming she weary me.'"

6 Then the Lord said, "Hear what the unjust judge said. 7 And shall God not avenge His own elect who cry out day and night to Him, though He bears long with them? 8 I tell you that He will avenge them speedily. Nevertheless, when the Son of Man comes, will He really find faith on the earth?"

The Parable of the Pharisee and the Tax Collector

9 Also He spoke this parable to some who trusted in themselves that they were righteous, and despised others: 10 "Two men went up to the temple to pray, one a Pharisee and the other a tax collector. 11 The Pharisee stood and prayed thus with himself, 'God, I thank You that I am not like other men—extortioners, unjust, adulterers, or even as this tax collector. 12 I fast twice a week; I give tithes of all that I possess.' 13 And the tax collector, standing afar off, would not so much as raise *his* eyes to heaven, but beat his breast, saying, 'God, be merciful to me a sinner!' 14 I tell you, this man went down to his house justified *rather* than the other; for everyone who exalts himself will be humbled, and he who humbles himself will be exalted."

Jesus Blesses Little Children

15 Then they also brought infants to Him that He might touch them; but when the disciples saw *it,* they rebuked them. 16 But Jesus called them to *Him* and said, "Let the little children come to Me, and do not forbid them; for of such is the kingdom of God. 17 Assuredly, I say to you, whoever does not receive the kingdom of God as a little child will by no means enter it."

Jesus Counsels the Rich Young Ruler

18 Now a certain ruler asked Him, saying, "Good Teacher, what shall I do to inherit eternal life?"

19 So Jesus said to him, "Why do you call Me good? No one *is* good but One, *that is,* God. 20 You know the commandments: 'Do not commit adultery,' 'Do not murder,' 'Do not steal,' 'Do not bear false witness,' 'Honor your father and your mother.' "[a]

21 And he said, "All these things I have kept from my youth."

22 So when Jesus heard these things, He said to him, "You still lack one thing. Sell all that you have and distribute to the poor, and

17:36 [a] NU-Text and M-Text omit verse 36. **18:20** [a] Exodus 20:12–16; Deuteronomy 5:16–20

you will have treasure in heaven; and come, follow Me."

23But when he heard this, he became very sorrowful, for he was very rich.

With God All Things Are Possible

24And when Jesus saw that he became very sorrowful, He said, "How hard it is for those who have riches to enter the kingdom of God! 25For it is easier for a camel to go through the eye of a needle than for a rich man to enter the kingdom of God."

26And those who heard it said, "Who then can be saved?"

27But He said, "The things which are impossible with men are possible with God."

28Then Peter said, "See, we have left all[a] and followed You."

29So He said to them, "Assuredly, I say to you, there is no one who has left house or parents or brothers or wife or children, for the sake of the kingdom of God, 30who shall not receive many times more in this present time, and in the age to come eternal life."

Jesus a Third Time Predicts His Death and Resurrection

31Then He took the twelve aside and said to them, "Behold, we are going up to Jerusalem, and all things that are written by the prophets concerning the Son of Man will be accomplished. 32For He will be delivered to the Gentiles and will be mocked and insulted and spit upon. 33They will scourge *Him* and kill Him. And the third day He will rise again."

34But they understood none of these things; this saying was hidden from them, and they did not know the things which were spoken.

A Blind Man Receives His Sight

35Then it happened, as He was coming near Jericho, that a certain blind man sat by the road begging. 36And hearing a multitude passing by, he asked what it meant. 37So they told him that Jesus of Nazareth was passing by. 38And he cried out, saying, "Jesus, Son of David, have mercy on me!"

39Then those who went before warned him that he should be quiet; but he cried out all the more, "Son of David, have mercy on me!"

40So Jesus stood still and commanded him to be brought to Him. And when he had come near, He asked him, 41saying, "What do you want Me to do for you?"

He said, "Lord, that I may receive my sight."

42Then Jesus said to him, "Receive your sight; your faith has made you well." 43And immediately he received his sight, and followed Him, glorifying God. And all the people, when they saw *it,* gave praise to God.

Jesus Comes to Zacchaeus' House

19 Then *Jesus* entered and passed through Jericho. 2Now behold, *there was* a man named Zacchaeus who was a chief tax collector, and he was rich. 3And he sought to see who Jesus was, but could not because of the crowd, for he was of short stature. 4So he ran ahead and climbed up into a sycamore tree to see Him, for He was going to pass that *way.* 5And when Jesus came to the place, He looked up and saw him,[a] and said to him, "Zacchaeus, make haste and come down, for today I must stay at your house." 6So he made haste and came down, and received Him joyfully. 7But when they saw *it,* they all complained, saying, "He has gone to be a guest with a man who is a sinner."

8Then Zacchaeus stood and said to the Lord, "Look, Lord, I give half of my goods to the poor; and if I have taken anything from anyone by false accusation, I restore fourfold."

9And Jesus said to him, "Today salvation has come to this house, because he also is a son of Abraham; 10for the Son of Man has come to seek and to save that which was lost."

The Parable of the Minas

11Now as they heard these things, He spoke another parable, because He was near Jerusalem and because they thought the kingdom of God would appear immediately. 12Therefore He said: "A certain nobleman went into a far country to receive for himself a kingdom and to return. 13So he called ten of his servants, delivered to them ten minas,[a] and said to them, 'Do business till I come.' 14But his citizens hated him, and sent a delegation after him, saying, 'We will not have this *man* to reign over us.'

18:28 [a] NU-Text reads *our own.* 19:5 [a] NU-Text omits *and saw him.* 19:13 [a] The *mina* (Greek *mna,* Hebrew *minah*) was worth about three months' salary.

15“And so it was that when he returned,
having received the kingdom, he then commanded these servants, to whom he had
given the money, to be called to him, that
he might know how much every man had
gained by trading. 16Then came the first,
saying, ‘Master, your mina has earned ten
minas.’ 17And he said to him, ‘Well *done,*
good servant; because you were faithful in
a very little, have authority over ten cities.’
18And the second came, saying, ‘Master, your
mina has earned five minas.’ 19Likewise he
said to him, ‘You also be over five cities.’

20“Then another came, saying, ‘Master,
here is your mina, which I have kept put
away in a handkerchief. 21For I feared you,
because you are an austere man. You collect
what you did not deposit, and reap what you
did not sow.’ 22And he said to him, ‘Out of
your own mouth I will judge you, *you* wicked servant. You knew that I was an austere
man, collecting what I did not deposit and
reaping what I did not sow. 23Why then did
you not put my money in the bank, that at
my coming I might have collected it with
interest?’

24“And he said to those who stood by,
‘Take the mina from him, and give *it* to him
who has ten minas.’ 25(But they said to him,
‘Master, he has ten minas.’) 26‘For I say to
you, that to everyone who has will be given;
and from him who does not have, even what
he has will be taken away from him. 27But
bring here those enemies of mine, who did
not want me to reign over them, and slay
them before me.’ ”

The Triumphal Entry

28When He had said this, He went on
ahead, going up to Jerusalem. 29And it came
to pass, when He drew near to Bethphage[a]
and Bethany, at the mountain called Olivet,
that He sent two of His disciples, 30saying,
“Go into the village opposite *you,* where as
you enter you will find a colt tied, on which
no one has ever sat. Loose it and bring *it here.*
31And if anyone asks you, ‘Why are you loosing *it?*’ thus you shall say to him, ‘Because
the Lord has need of it.’ ”

32So those who were sent went their way
and found *it* just as He had said to them.
33But as they were loosing the colt, the owners of it said to them, “Why are you loosing
the colt?”

34And they said, “The Lord has need of
him.” 35Then they brought him to Jesus. And
they threw their own clothes on the colt, and
they set Jesus on him. 36And as He went,
many spread their clothes on the road.

37Then, as He was now drawing near the
descent of the Mount of Olives, the whole
multitude of the disciples began to rejoice
and praise God with a loud voice for all the
mighty works they had seen, 38saying:

“ ‘Blessed *is* the King who comes in the
name of the LORD!’ [a]
Peace in heaven and glory in the
highest!”

39And some of the Pharisees called to
Him from the crowd, “Teacher, rebuke Your
disciples.”

40But He answered and said to them, “I
tell you that if these should keep silent, the
stones would immediately cry out.”

Jesus Weeps over Jerusalem

41Now as He drew near, He saw the city
and wept over it, 42saying, “If you had known,
even you, especially in this your day, the
things *that make* for your peace! But now
they are hidden from your eyes. 43For days
will come upon you when your enemies
will build an embankment around you, surround you and close you in on every side,
44and level you, and your children within
you, to the ground; and they will not leave in
you one stone upon another, because you did
not know the time of your visitation.”

Jesus Cleanses the Temple

45Then He went into the temple and began to drive out those who bought and sold
in it,[a] 46saying to them, “It is written, ‘My
house is[a] a house of prayer,’ [b] but you have
made it a ‘den of thieves.’ ”[c]

47And He was teaching daily in the temple. But the chief priests, the scribes, and the
leaders of the people sought to destroy Him,
48and were unable to do anything; for all the
people were very attentive to hear Him.

Jesus’ Authority Questioned

20 Now it happened on one of those
days, as He taught the people in
the temple and preached the gospel, *that* the
chief priests and the scribes, together with
the elders, confronted *Him* 2and spoke to

19:29 [a] M-Text reads *Bethsphage.* 19:38 [a] Psalm 118:26
19:45 [a] NU-Text reads *those who were selling.* 19:46 [a] NU-Text reads *shall be.* [b] Isaiah 56:7 [c] Jeremiah 7:11

Him, saying, "Tell us, by what authority are
You doing these things? Or who is he who
gave You this authority?"
3But He answered and said to them, "I
also will ask you one thing, and answer Me:
4The baptism of John—was it from heaven
or from men?"
5And they reasoned among themselves,
saying, "If we say, 'From heaven,' He will
say, 'Why then[a] did you not believe him?'
6But if we say, 'From men,' all the people will
stone us, for they are persuaded that John
was a prophet." 7So they answered that they
did not know where *it was* from.
8And Jesus said to them, "Neither will I
tell you by what authority I do these things."

The Parable of the Wicked Vinedressers

9Then He began to tell the people this
parable: "A certain man planted a vineyard,
leased it to vinedressers, and went into a far
country for a long time. 10Now at vintage-
time he sent a servant to the vinedressers,
that they might give him some of the fruit of
the vineyard. But the vinedressers beat him
and sent *him* away empty-handed. 11Again
he sent another servant; and they beat him
also, treated *him* shamefully, and sent *him*
away empty-handed. 12And again he sent a
third; and they wounded him also and cast
him out.
13"Then the owner of the vineyard said,
'What shall I do? I will send my beloved son.
Probably they will respect *him* when they
see him.' 14But when the vinedressers saw
him, they reasoned among themselves, saying, 'This is the heir. Come, let us kill him,
that the inheritance may be ours.' 15So they
cast him out of the vineyard and killed *him*.
Therefore what will the owner of the vineyard do to them? 16He will come and destroy
those vinedressers and give the vineyard to
others."
And when they heard *it* they said, "Certainly not!"
17Then He looked at them and said,
"What then is this that is written:

'The stone which the builders rejected
Has become the chief cornerstone' ?[a]

18Whoever falls on that stone will be broken;
but on whomever it falls, it will grind him
to powder."
19And the chief priests and the scribes
that very hour sought to lay hands on Him,
but they feared the people[a]—for they knew
He had spoken this parable against them.

The Pharisees: Is It Lawful to Pay Taxes to Caesar?

20So they watched *Him*, and sent spies
who pretended to be righteous, that they
might seize on His words, in order to deliver
Him to the power and the authority of the
governor.
21Then they asked Him, saying, "Teacher, we know that You say and teach rightly,
and You do not show personal favoritism,
but teach the way of God in truth: 22Is it lawful for us to pay taxes to Caesar or not?"
23But He perceived their craftiness, and
said to them, "Why do you test Me?[a] 24Show
Me a denarius. Whose image and inscription does it have?"
They answered and said, "Caesar's."
25And He said to them, "Render therefore
to Caesar the things that are Caesar's, and to
God the things that are God's."
26But they could not catch Him in His
words in the presence of the people. And
they marveled at His answer and kept silent.

The Sadducees: What About the Resurrection?

27Then some of the Sadducees, who deny
that there is a resurrection, came to *Him*
and asked Him, 28saying: "Teacher, Moses
wrote to us *that* if a man's brother dies, having a wife, and he dies without children, his
brother should take his wife and raise up
offspring for his brother. 29Now there were
seven brothers. And the first took a wife,
and died without children. 30And the second[a] took her as wife, and he died childless.
31Then the third took her, and in like manner the seven also; and they left no children,[a]
and died. 32Last of all the woman died also.
33Therefore, in the resurrection, whose wife
does she become? For all seven had her as
wife."
34Jesus answered and said to them, "The
sons of this age marry and are given in marriage. 35But those who are counted worthy to
attain that age, and the resurrection from

20:5 [a] NU-Text and M-Text omit *then*. 20:17 [a] Psalm 118:22 20:19 [a] M-Text reads *but they were afraid*. 20:23 [a] NU-Text omits *Why do you test Me?* 20:30 [a] NU-Text ends verse 30 here. 20:31 [a] NU-Text and M-Text read *the seven also left no children*.

the dead, neither marry nor are given in
marriage; 36nor can they die anymore, for
they are equal to the angels and are sons of
God, being sons of the resurrection. 37But
even Moses showed in the *burning* bush *passage* that the dead are raised, when he called
the Lord 'the God of Abraham, the God of
Isaac, and the God of Jacob.'[a] 38For He is not
the God of the dead but of the living, for all
live to Him."

39Then some of the scribes answered
and said, "Teacher, You have spoken well."
40But after that they dared not question Him
anymore.

Jesus: How Can David Call His Descendant Lord?

41And He said to them, "How can they say
that the Christ is the Son of David? 42Now
David himself said in the Book of Psalms:

'The LORD said to my Lord,
"Sit at My right hand,
43 Till I make Your enemies Your
footstool." '[a]

44Therefore David calls Him 'Lord'; how is
He then his Son?"

Beware of the Scribes

45Then, in the hearing of all the people, He said to His disciples, 46"Beware of
the scribes, who desire to go around in
long robes, love greetings in the marketplaces, the best seats in the synagogues,
and the best places at feasts, 47who devour
widows' houses, and for a pretense make
long prayers. These will receive greater
condemnation."

The Widow's Two Mites

21 And He looked up and saw the rich
putting their gifts into the treasury,
2and He saw also a certain poor widow putting in two mites. 3So He said, "Truly I say
to you that this poor widow has put in more
than all; 4for all these out of their abundance
have put in offerings for God,[a] but she out
of her poverty put in all the livelihood that
she had."

Jesus Predicts the Destruction of the Temple

5Then, as some spoke of the temple, how
it was adorned with beautiful stones and do-
nations, He said, 6"These things which you
see—the days will come in which not *one*
stone shall be left upon another that shall
not be thrown down."

The Signs of the Times and the End of the Age

7So they asked Him, saying, "Teacher,
but when will these things be? And what
sign *will there be* when these things are about
to take place?"

8And He said: "Take heed that you not be
deceived. For many will come in My name,
saying, 'I am *He,*' and, 'The time has drawn
near.' Therefore[a] do not go after them. 9But
when you hear of wars and commotions,
do not be terrified; for these things must
come to pass first, but the end *will* not *come*
immediately."

10Then He said to them, "Nation will rise
against nation, and kingdom against kingdom. 11And there will be great earthquakes
in various places, and famines and pestilences; and there will be fearful sights and great
signs from heaven. 12But before all these
things, they will lay their hands on you and
persecute *you,* delivering *you* up to the synagogues and prisons. You will be brought
before kings and rulers for My name's sake.
13But it will turn out for you as an occasion
for testimony. 14Therefore settle *it* in your
hearts not to meditate beforehand on what
you will answer; 15for I will give you a mouth
and wisdom which all your adversaries will
not be able to contradict or resist. 16You will
be betrayed even by parents and brothers,
relatives and friends; and they will put *some*
of you to death. 17And you will be hated by all
for My name's sake. 18But not a hair of your
head shall be lost. 19By your patience possess
your souls.

The Destruction of Jerusalem

20"But when you see Jerusalem surrounded by armies, then know that its desolation is
near. 21Then let those who are in Judea flee
to the mountains, let those who are in the
midst of her depart, and let not those who
are in the country enter her. 22For these are
the days of vengeance, that all things which
are written may be fulfilled. 23But woe to
those who are pregnant and to those who are
nursing babies in those days! For there will

20:37 [a] Exodus 3:6, 15 **20:43** [a] Psalm 110:1 **21:4** [a] NU-Text omits *for God.* **21:8** [a] NU-Text omits *Therefore.*

be great distress in the land and wrath upon
this people. 24And they will fall by the edge
of the sword, and be led away captive into all
nations. And Jerusalem will be trampled by
Gentiles until the times of the Gentiles are
fulfilled.

The Coming of the Son of Man

25"And there will be signs in the sun, in
the moon, and in the stars; and on the earth
distress of nations, with perplexity, the sea
and the waves roaring; 26men's hearts failing
them from fear and the expectation of those
things which are coming on the earth, for
the powers of the heavens will be shaken.
27Then they will see the Son of Man coming
in a cloud with power and great glory. 28Now
when these things begin to happen, look up
and lift up your heads, because your redemption draws near."

Action!

COMMUNITY

JESUS' BUDDIES

READ IT: LUKE 22:7–23

GET IT:

Imagine what it looked like to be a part of the Passover Supper. It was just Jesus and His best friends around a table, eating a meal that many generations of people before them had eaten. It's a beautiful picture of community and what we should all strive for today.

Even though it became a solemn evening as they talked about Jesus' impending betrayal and death, the disciples were all close. They didn't fully understand what Jesus was talking about, but they trusted Him and knew something big was about to happen. And they were all going to be a part of it.

When Jesus began His ministry at the age of thirty, He went in search of the twelve men who would become His disciples. These were the people Jesus would entrust to spread the gospel to the far ends of the earth. But they meant so much more to Him than that. They were His friends—His community—and He knew He would need them standing beside Him as His death drew near.

God didn't create us to be alone, but to have community. We need people in our lives to stand with us through the good and the bad. Jesus and His disciples were the ultimate example of that.

LIVE IT:

You probably have a group of friends whom you talk to all of the time and with whom you spend the majority of your time. Who are they? Are they friends who are building you up toward growth in your relationship with Christ? If not, you ought to consider who you allow to have influence in your life. The kinds of people you surround yourself with determine the kind of person you will become. Who do you want to be?

The Parable of the Fig Tree

[29]Then He spoke to them a parable: "Look
at the fig tree, and all the trees. [30]When they
are already budding, you see and know for
yourselves that summer is now near. [31]So
you also, when you see these things happening, know that the kingdom of God is near.
[32]Assuredly, I say to you, this generation will
by no means pass away till all things take
place. [33]Heaven and earth will pass away, but
My words will by no means pass away.

The Importance of Watching

[34]"But take heed to yourselves, lest your
hearts be weighed down with carousing,
drunkenness, and cares of this life, and that
Day come on you unexpectedly. [35]For it will
come as a snare on all those who dwell on
the face of the whole earth. [36]Watch therefore, and pray always that you may be counted worthy[a] to escape all these things that
will come to pass, and to stand before the
Son of Man."

[37]And in the daytime He was teaching
in the temple, but at night He went out and
stayed on the mountain called Olivet. [38]Then
early in the morning all the people came to
Him in the temple to hear Him.

The Plot to Kill Jesus

22 Now the Feast of Unleavened
Bread drew near, which is called
Passover. [2]And the chief priests and the
scribes sought how they might kill Him, for
they feared the people.

[3]Then Satan entered Judas, surnamed
Iscariot, who was numbered among the
twelve. [4]So he went his way and conferred
with the chief priests and captains, how
he might betray Him to them. [5]And they
were glad, and agreed to give him money.
[6]So he promised and sought opportunity to
betray Him to them in the absence of the
multitude.

Jesus and His Disciples Prepare the Passover

[7]Then came the Day of Unleavened
Bread, when the Passover must be killed.
[8]And He sent Peter and John, saying, "Go
and prepare the Passover for us, that we may
eat."

[9]So they said to Him, "Where do You
want us to prepare?"

[10]And He said to them, "Behold, when
you have entered the city, a man will meet
you carrying a pitcher of water; follow him
into the house which he enters. [11]Then you
shall say to the master of the house, 'The
Teacher says to you, "Where is the guest
room where I may eat the Passover with My
disciples?"' [12]Then he will show you a large,
furnished upper room; there make ready."

[13]So they went and found it just as He
had said to them, and they prepared the
Passover.

Jesus Institutes the Lord's Supper

[14]When the hour had come, He sat down,
and the twelve[a] apostles with Him. [15]Then
He said to them, "With *fervent* desire I have
desired to eat this Passover with you before I
suffer; [16]for I say to you, I will no longer eat of
it until it is fulfilled in the kingdom of God."

[17]Then He took the cup, and gave thanks,
and said, "Take this and divide *it* among
yourselves; [18]for I say to you,[a] I will not drink
of the fruit of the vine until the kingdom of
God comes."

[19]And He took bread, gave thanks and
broke *it*, and gave *it* to them, saying, "This
is My body which is given for you; do this in
remembrance of Me."

[20]Likewise He also *took* the cup after supper, saying, "This cup *is* the new covenant
in My blood, which is shed for you. [21]But behold, the hand of My betrayer *is* with Me on
the table. [22]And truly the Son of Man goes as

In Focus

22:20 New Covenant A covenant (pronounced *KUV-uh-nunt*) is a legal agreement. Under the Old Covenant (or Old Testament), people sacrificed animals to atone for sins and ask God's forgiveness. Under the New Covenant (or New Testament), Christ made the ultimate sacrifice—His life—so that whoever believes in Him is forever forgiven.

21:36 [a] NU-Text reads *may have strength*. 22:14 [a] NU-Text omits *twelve*. 22:18 [a] NU-Text adds *from now on*.

it has been determined, but woe to that man
by whom He is betrayed!"
23Then they began to question among
themselves, which of them it was who would
do this thing.

The Disciples Argue About Greatness

24Now there was also a dispute among
them, as to which of them should be considered the greatest. 25And He said to them,
"The kings of the Gentiles exercise lordship
over them, and those who exercise authority over them are called 'benefactors.' 26But
not so *among* you; on the contrary, he who is
greatest among you, let him be as the younger, and he who governs as he who serves. 27For
who *is* greater, he who sits at the table, or he
who serves? *Is* it not he who sits at the table?
Yet I am among you as the One who serves.
28"But you are those who have continued
with Me in My trials. 29And I bestow upon
you a kingdom, just as My Father bestowed
one upon Me, 30that you may eat and drink at
My table in My kingdom, and sit on thrones
judging the twelve tribes of Israel."

Jesus Predicts Peter's Denial

31And the Lord said,[a] "Simon, Simon! Indeed, Satan has asked for you, that he may
sift *you* as wheat. 32But I have prayed for you,
that your faith should not fail; and when
you have returned to *Me,* strengthen your
brethren."
33But he said to Him, "Lord, I am ready
to go with You, both to prison and to death."
34Then He said, "I tell you, Peter, the
rooster shall not crow this day before you
will deny three times that you know Me."

Supplies for the Road

35And He said to them, "When I sent you
without money bag, knapsack, and sandals,
did you lack anything?"
So they said, "Nothing."
36Then He said to them, "But now, he
who has a money bag, let him take *it,* and
likewise a knapsack; and he who has no
sword, let him sell his garment and buy one.
37For I say to you that this which is written
must still be accomplished in Me: 'And He
was numbered with the transgressors.' [a] For
the things concerning Me have an end."
38So they said, "Lord, look, here *are* two
swords."
And He said to them, "It is enough."

The Prayer in the Garden

39Coming out, He went to the Mount of
Olives, as He was accustomed, and His disciples also followed Him. 40When He came
to the place, He said to them, "Pray that you
may not enter into temptation."
41And He was withdrawn from them
about a stone's throw, and He knelt down
and prayed, 42saying, "Father, if it is Your
will, take this cup away from Me; nevertheless not My will, but Yours, be done." 43Then
an angel appeared to Him from heaven,
strengthening Him. 44And being in agony,
He prayed more earnestly. Then His sweat
became like great drops of blood falling
down to the ground.[a]
45When He rose up from prayer, and had
come to His disciples, He found them sleeping from sorrow. 46Then He said to them,
"Why do you sleep? Rise and pray, lest you
enter into temptation."

Betrayal and Arrest in Gethsemane

47And while He was still speaking, behold, a multitude; and he who was called
Judas, one of the twelve, went before them
and drew near to Jesus to kiss Him. 48But
Jesus said to him, "Judas, are you betraying
the Son of Man with a kiss?"
49When those around Him saw what was
going to happen, they said to Him, "Lord,
shall we strike with the sword?" 50And one
of them struck the servant of the high priest
and cut off his right ear.
51But Jesus answered and said, "Permit
even this." And He touched his ear and
healed him.
52Then Jesus said to the chief priests,
captains of the temple, and the elders who
had come to Him, "Have you come out, as
against a robber, with swords and clubs?
53When I was with you daily in the temple,
you did not try to seize Me. But this is your
hour, and the power of darkness."

Peter Denies Jesus, and Weeps Bitterly

54Having arrested Him, they led *Him* and
brought Him into the high priest's house.
But Peter followed at a distance. 55Now when
they had kindled a fire in the midst of the

22:31 [a] NU-Text omits *And the Lord said.* **22:37** [a] Isaiah 53:12 **22:44** [a] NU-Text brackets verses 43 and 44 as not in the original text.

courtyard and sat down together, Peter sat
among them. 56 And a certain servant girl,
seeing him as he sat by the fire, looked intently at him and said, "This man was also
with Him."

57 But he denied Him,[a] saying, "Woman, I
do not know Him."

58 And after a little while another saw him
and said, "You also are of them."

But Peter said, "Man, I am not!"

59 Then after about an hour had passed,
another confidently affirmed, saying, "Surely this *fellow* also was with Him, for he is a
Galilean."

60 But Peter said, "Man, I do not know
what you are saying!"

Immediately, while he was still speaking,
the rooster[a] crowed. 61 And the Lord turned
and looked at Peter. Then Peter remembered the word of the Lord, how He had said
to him, "Before the rooster crows,[a] you will
deny Me three times." 62 So Peter went out
and wept bitterly.

Jesus Mocked and Beaten

63 Now the men who held Jesus mocked
Him and beat Him. 64 And having blindfolded
Him, they struck Him on the face and asked
Him,[a] saying, "Prophesy! Who is the one
who struck You?" 65 And many other things
they blasphemously spoke against Him.

Jesus Faces the Sanhedrin

66 As soon as it was day, the elders of the
people, both chief priests and scribes, came
together and led Him into their council, saying, 67 "If You are the Christ, tell us."

But He said to them, "If I tell you, you
will by no means believe. 68 And if I also ask
you, you will by no means answer Me or let
Me go.[a] 69 Hereafter the Son of Man will sit
on the right hand of the power of God."

70 Then they all said, "Are You then the
Son of God?"

So He said to them, "You *rightly* say that
I am."

71 And they said, "What further testimony
do we need? For we have heard it ourselves
from His own mouth."

Jesus Handed Over to Pontius Pilate

23 Then the whole multitude of them
arose and led Him to Pilate. 2 And
they began to accuse Him, saying, "We
found this *fellow* perverting the[a] nation, and
forbidding to pay taxes to Caesar, saying that
He Himself is Christ, a King."

3 Then Pilate asked Him, saying, "Are
You the King of the Jews?"

He answered him and said, "*It is as* you
say."

4 So Pilate said to the chief priests and the
crowd, "I find no fault in this Man."

5 But they were the more fierce, saying,
"He stirs up the people, teaching throughout all Judea, beginning from Galilee to this
place."

Jesus Faces Herod

6 When Pilate heard of Galilee,[a] he asked
if the Man were a Galilean. 7 And as soon as
he knew that He belonged to Herod's juris-
diction, he sent Him to Herod, who was also
in Jerusalem at that time. 8 Now when Herod
saw Jesus, he was exceedingly glad; for he
had desired for a long *time* to see Him, because he had heard many things about Him,
and he hoped to see some miracle done by
Him. 9 Then he questioned Him with many
words, but He answered him nothing. 10 And
the chief priests and scribes stood and vehemently accused Him. 11 Then Herod, with his
men of war, treated Him with contempt and
mocked *Him,* arrayed Him in a gorgeous
robe, and sent Him back to Pilate. 12 That
very day Pilate and Herod became friends
with each other, for previously they had been
at enmity with each other.

Taking the Place of Barabbas

13 Then Pilate, when he had called together
the chief priests, the rulers, and the people,
14 said to them, "You have brought this Man to
me, as one who misleads the people. And indeed, having examined *Him* in your presence,
I have found no fault in this Man concerning
those things of which you accuse Him; 15 no,
neither did Herod, for I sent you back to him;[a]
and indeed nothing deserving of death has
been done by Him. 16 I will therefore chastise
Him and release *Him*" 17 (for it was necessary
for him to release one to them at the feast).[a]

18 And they all cried out at once, saying,
"Away with this *Man,* and release to us

22:57 [a] NU-Text reads *denied it.* **22:60** [a] NU-Text and M-Text read *a rooster.* **22:61** [a] NU-Text adds *today.* **22:64** [a] NU-Text reads *And having blindfolded Him, they asked Him.* **22:68** [a] NU-Text omits *also* and *Me or let Me go.* **23:2** [a] NU-Text reads *our.* **23:6** [a] NU-Text omits *of Galilee.* **23:15** [a] NU-Text reads *for he sent Him back to us.* **23:17** [a] NU-Text omits verse 17.

Barabbas"— 19 who had been thrown into
prison for a certain rebellion made in the
city, and for murder.

20 Pilate, therefore, wishing to release
Jesus, again called out to them. 21 But they
shouted, saying, "Crucify *Him,* crucify
Him!"

22 Then he said to them the third time,
"Why, what evil has He done? I have found
no reason for death in Him. I will therefore
chastise Him and let *Him* go."

23 But they were insistent, demanding
with loud voices that He be crucified. And
the voices of these men and of the chief
priests prevailed.[a] 24 So Pilate gave sentence
that it should be as they requested. 25 And
he released to them[a] the one they requested, who for rebellion and murder had been
thrown into prison; but he delivered Jesus
to their will.

The King on a Cross

26 Now as they led Him away, they laid
hold of a certain man, Simon a Cyrenian,
who was coming from the country, and on
him they laid the cross that he might bear
it after Jesus.

27 And a great multitude of the people followed Him, and women who also mourned
and lamented Him. 28 But Jesus, turning to
them, said, "Daughters of Jerusalem, do not
weep for Me, but weep for yourselves and for
your children. 29 For indeed the days are coming in which they will say, 'Blessed *are* the
barren, wombs that never bore, and breasts
which never nursed!' 30 Then they will begin
'to say to the mountains, "Fall on us!" and to
the hills, "Cover us!"'[a] 31 For if they do these
things in the green wood, what will be done
in the dry?"

32 There were also two others, criminals,
led with Him to be put to death. 33 And when
they had come to the place called Calvary,
there they crucified Him, and the criminals,
one on the right hand and the other on the
left. 34 Then Jesus said, "Father, forgive them,
for they do not know what they do."[a]

And they divided His garments and cast
lots. 35 And the people stood looking on. But
even the rulers with them sneered, saying,
"He saved others; let Him save Himself if
He is the Christ, the chosen of God."

36 The soldiers also mocked Him, coming and offering Him sour wine, 37 and
saying, "If You are the King of the Jews, save
Yourself."

38 And an inscription also was written
over Him in letters of Greek, Latin, and
Hebrew:[a]

THIS IS THE KING OF THE JEWS.

39 Then one of the criminals who were
hanged blasphemed Him, saying, "If You
are the Christ,[a] save Yourself and us."

40 But the other, answering, rebuked him,
saying, "Do you not even fear God, seeing
you are under the same condemnation?
41 And we indeed justly, for we receive the due
reward of our deeds; but this Man has done
nothing wrong." 42 Then he said to Jesus,
"Lord,[a] remember me when You come into
Your kingdom."

43 And Jesus said to him, "Assuredly,
I say to you, today you will be with Me in
Paradise."

Jesus Dies on the Cross

44 Now it was[a] about the sixth hour, and
there was darkness over all the earth until
the ninth hour. 45 Then the sun was darkened,[a] and the veil of the temple was torn
in two. 46 And when Jesus had cried out with
a loud voice, He said, "Father, 'into Your
hands I commit My spirit.'"[a] Having said
this, He breathed His last.

47 So when the centurion saw what had
happened, he glorified God, saying, "Certainly this was a righteous Man!"

48 And the whole crowd who came together to that sight, seeing what had been done,
beat their breasts and returned. 49 But all
His acquaintances, and the women who followed Him from Galilee, stood at a distance,
watching these things.

Jesus Buried in Joseph's Tomb

50 Now behold, *there was* a man named
Joseph, a council member, a good and just
man. 51 He had not consented to their decision and deed. *He was* from Arimathea,
a city of the Jews, who himself was also

23:23 [a] NU-Text omits *and of the chief priests.* **23:25** [a] NU-Text and M-Text omit *to them.* **23:30** [a] Hosea 10:8 **23:34** [a] NU-Text brackets the first sentence as a later addition. **23:38** [a] NU-Text omits *written* and *in letters of Greek, Latin, and Hebrew.* **23:39** [a] NU-Text reads *Are You not the Christ?* **23:42** [a] NU-Text reads *And he said, "Jesus, remember me.* **23:44** [a] NU-Text adds *already.* **23:45** [a] NU-Text reads *obscured.* **23:46** [a] Psalm 31:5

waiting[a] for the kingdom of God. 52This
man went to Pilate and asked for the body
of Jesus. 53Then he took it down, wrapped it
in linen, and laid it in a tomb *that was* hewn
out of the rock, where no one had ever lain
before. 54That day was the Preparation, and
the Sabbath drew near.

55And the women who had come with
Him from Galilee followed after, and they
observed the tomb and how His body was
laid. 56Then they returned and prepared spices and fragrant oils. And they rested on the
Sabbath according to the commandment.

He Is Risen

24 Now on the first *day* of the week,
very early in the morning, they,
and certain *other women* with them,[a] came to
the tomb bringing the spices which they had
prepared. 2But they found the stone rolled
away from the tomb. 3Then they went in
and did not find the body of the Lord Jesus.
4And it happened, as they were greatly[a]
perplexed about this, that behold, two men
stood by them in shining garments. 5Then,
as they were afraid and bowed *their* faces to
the earth, they said to them, "Why do you
seek the living among the dead? 6He is not
here, but is risen! Remember how He spoke
to you when He was still in Galilee, 7saying,
'The Son of Man must be delivered into the
hands of sinful men, and be crucified, and
the third day rise again.'"

8And they remembered His words. 9Then
they returned from the tomb and told all
these things to the eleven and to all the rest.
10It was Mary Magdalene, Joanna, Mary *the
mother* of James, and the other *women* with
them, who told these things to the apostles.
11And their words seemed to them like idle
tales, and they did not believe them. 12But
Peter arose and ran to the tomb; and stoop-
ing down, he saw the linen cloths lying[a] by
themselves; and he departed, marveling to
himself at what had happened.

The Road to Emmaus

13Now behold, two of them were traveling
that same day to a village called Emmaus,
which was seven miles[a] from Jerusalem.
14And they talked together of all these things
which had happened. 15So it was, while they
conversed and reasoned, that Jesus Himself
drew near and went with them. 16But their

In Focus

23:33 Calvary Pronounced *KAL-vuh-ree*. From a Latin word meaning "the skull." It seems to be the place outside Jerusalem where criminals were put to death and where Jesus, also, was crucified.

eyes were restrained, so that they did not
know Him.

17And He said to them, "What kind of
conversation *is* this that you have with one
another as you walk and are sad?"[a]

18Then the one whose name was Cleo-
pas answered and said to Him, "Are You the
only stranger in Jerusalem, and have You not
known the things which happened there in
these days?"

19And He said to them, "What things?"

So they said to Him, "The things concerning Jesus of Nazareth, who was a
Prophet mighty in deed and word before
God and all the people, 20and how the chief
priests and our rulers delivered Him to be
condemned to death, and crucified Him.
21But we were hoping that it was He who was
going to redeem Israel. Indeed, besides all
this, today is the third day since these things
happened. 22Yes, and certain women of our
company, who arrived at the tomb early, astonished us. 23When they did not find His
body, they came saying that they had also
seen a vision of angels who said He was
alive. 24And certain of those *who were* with
us went to the tomb and found *it* just as the
women had said; but Him they did not see."

25Then He said to them, "O foolish ones,
and slow of heart to believe in all that the
prophets have spoken! 26Ought not the
Christ to have suffered these things and to
enter into His glory?" 27And beginning at
Moses and all the Prophets, He expounded
to them in all the Scriptures the things concerning Himself.

23:51 [a] NU-Text reads *who was waiting.* **24:1** [a] NU-Text omits *and certain other women with them.* **24:4** [a] NU-Text omits *greatly.* **24:12** [a] NU-Text omits *lying.* **24:13** [a] Literally *sixty stadia* **24:17** [a] NU-Text reads *as you walk? And they stood still, looking sad.*

The Disciples' Eyes Opened

28 Then they drew near to the village where they were going, and He indicated that He would have gone farther. 29 But they constrained Him, saying, "Abide with us, for it is toward evening, and the day is far spent." And He went in to stay with them.

30 Now it came to pass, as He sat at the table with them, that He took bread, blessed and broke *it,* and gave it to them. 31 Then their eyes were opened and they knew Him; and He vanished from their sight.

32 And they said to one another, "Did not our heart burn within us while He talked with us on the road, and while He opened the Scriptures to us?" 33 So they rose up that very hour and returned to Jerusalem, and found the eleven and those *who were* with them gathered together, 34 saying, "The Lord is risen indeed, and has appeared to Simon!" 35 And they told about the things *that had happened* on the road, and how He was known to them in the breaking of bread.

Jesus Appears to His Disciples

36 Now as they said these things, Jesus Himself stood in the midst of them, and said to them, "Peace to you." 37 But they were terrified and frightened, and supposed they had seen a spirit. 38 And He said to them, "Why are you troubled? And why do doubts arise in your hearts? 39 Behold My hands and My feet, that it is I Myself. Handle Me and see, for a spirit does not have flesh and bones as you see I have."

40 When He had said this, He showed them His hands and His feet.[a] 41 But while they still did not believe for joy, and marveled, He said to them, "Have you any food here?" 42 So they gave Him a piece of a broiled fish and some honeycomb.[a] 43 And He took *it* and ate in their presence.

The Scriptures Opened

44 Then He said to them, "These *are* the words which I spoke to you while I was still with you, that all things must be fulfilled which were written in the Law of Moses and *the* Prophets and *the* Psalms concerning Me." 45 And He opened their understanding, that they might comprehend the Scriptures.

46 Then He said to them, "Thus it is written, and thus it was necessary for the Christ to suffer and to rise[a] from the dead the third day, 47 and that repentance and remission

24:40 [a] Some printed New Testaments omit this verse. It is found in nearly all Greek manuscripts. **24:42** [a] NU-Text omits *and some honeycomb.* **24:46** [a] NU-Text reads *written, that the Christ should suffer and rise.*

24:26 JESUS HAD TO DIE

Do you think Jesus was crucified just because a mob in Jerusalem wanted Him to die? No! God had always planned that Jesus would be crucified for our sins. If Jesus had not died, we all would have been condemned for our sins, just as we deserved.

The Old Testament sacrifice was an example of the sacrifice of Jesus on the Cross. The priests of the Old Testament brought a lamb for sacrifice and killed it. This was a terrible act. But the sacrifice of the lamb on the Old Testament altar is a dreadful picture of the even more awesome cost of sin—the death of God's own Son!

Everything has a price, and sin has its own price. God loved you so much that He was willing to pay with the life of His own Son so you would not have to pay for your sins.

of sins should be preached in His name to all nations, beginning at Jerusalem.
48And you are witnesses of these things.
49Behold, I send the Promise of My Father upon you; but tarry in the city of Jerusalem[a] until you are endued with power from on high."

The Ascension

50And He led them out as far as Bethany, and He lifted up His hands and blessed them.
51Now it came to pass, while He blessed them, that He was parted from them and carried up into heaven.
52And they worshiped Him, and returned to Jerusalem with great joy,
53and were continually in the temple praising and[a] blessing God. Amen.[b]

24:49 [a] NU-Text omits *of Jerusalem.* 24:53 [a] NU-Text omits *praising and.* [b] NU-Text omits *Amen.*

JOY

A BIG REASON FOR JOY

READ IT: LUKE 24:1–53

GET IT:

The disciples had just experienced the biggest letdown of their lives. For three years they had followed Jesus, believing that He would be their hope and new king. When He was brutally killed, hope was lost. It was a painful, low feeling.

But then Jesus returned to them—alive! The grave was empty, and the disciples saw Him whole again. They stared in disbelief, wondering if this was a dream. But it wasn't. He had the scars to prove that it was really Him.

Adrenaline. Excitement. Feelings of happiness returned.

Imagine their surprise. Imagine how they felt to have their Messiah and hope returned to them.

LIVE IT:

What was the lowest moment of your week? Think about how it changed things and affected your mood. Now imagine Jesus walking into your situation, coming to give you hope. What would He say to you? And how would it make you feel?

The GOSPEL ACCORDING *to*

JOHN

A.D. 86–A.D. 92

Behind the Scenes

READ IT:

The book of John tells the stories of Jesus' ministry on earth. It focuses on Jesus' miracles (called signs) to prove that Jesus is God and has supernatural powers. This book contains none of Jesus' parables but talks a lot about Jesus' relationships with individuals. The stories show us that Jesus was very human—He was tired, sad, hungry, and loving.

GET IT:

Who wrote it: John, the disciple of Jesus

When it was written: A.D. 86–A.D. 92

Why it was written: so that "you may believe that Jesus is the Christ, the Son of God, and that believing you may have life in His name" (John 20:31).

LIVE IT:

If we believe in Jesus as our Lord and Savior, we will receive eternal life.

FIND IT:

The Word Becomes Flesh	*John 1*
Water Turned to Wine	*John 2*
The New Birth	*John 3*
Jesus Defends His Self-Witness	*John 8*
The Death of Lazarus	*John 11*
Jesus Washes the Disciples' Feet	*John 13*
Jesus' Instructions and Prayers	*John 14–17*
Jesus' Trial and Death	*John 18–19*
Jesus' Resurrection and Appearances	*John 20–21*

The Eternal Word

1 In the beginning was the Word, and
the Word was with God, and the Word
was God. 2He was in the beginning with
God. 3All things were made through Him,
and without Him nothing was made that
was made. 4In Him was life, and the life
was the light of men. 5And the light shines
in the darkness, and the darkness did not
comprehend[a] it.

John's Witness: The True Light

6There was a man sent from God, whose
name *was* John. 7This man came for a witness, to bear witness of the Light, that all
through him might believe. 8He was not that
Light, but *was sent* to bear witness of that
Light. 9That was the true Light which gives
light to every man coming into the world.[a]

10He was in the world, and the world was
made through Him, and the world did not
know Him. 11He came to His own,[a] and His
own[b] did not receive Him. 12But as many as
received Him, to them He gave the right to
become children of God, to those who believe in His name: 13who were born, not of
blood, nor of the will of the flesh, nor of the
will of man, but of God.

The Word Becomes Flesh

14And the Word became flesh and dwelt
among us, and we beheld His glory, the
glory as of the only begotten of the Father,
full of grace and truth.

15John bore witness of Him and cried out,
saying, "This was He of whom I said, 'He
who comes after me is preferred before me,
for He was before me.'"

16And[a] of His fullness we have all received, and grace for grace. 17For the law was
given through Moses, *but* grace and truth
came through Jesus Christ. 18No one has
seen God at any time. The only begotten
Son,[a] who is in the bosom of the Father, He
has declared *Him*.

A Voice in the Wilderness

19Now this is the testimony of John, when
the Jews sent priests and Levites from Jerusalem to ask him, "Who are you?"

20He confessed, and did not deny, but
confessed, "I am not the Christ."

21And they asked him, "What then? Are
you Elijah?"

He said, "I am not."

"Are you the Prophet?"

And he answered, "No."

22Then they said to him, "Who are you,

1:5 [a] Or *overcome* 1:9 [a] Or *That was the true Light which, coming into the world, gives light to every man.* 1:11 [a] That is, His own things or domain [b] That is, His own people 1:16 [a] NU-Text reads *For.* 1:18 [a] NU-Text reads *only begotten God.*

Starring Roles

Nearly everybody loves **JOHN'S** Gospel because he tells very clearly who Jesus really is. He was not just a wonderful man who became our Savior. He is the Lord from heaven.

John relayed the stories of how Jesus told lonely and needy people that He came to give them a whole new life. Nicodemus and the woman at the well were two such people.

Jesus told His disciples that He was the Bread of Life. He also said that He would be like a spring of Everlasting Water living in people.

One day Jesus' friend Lazarus became sick and died, but Jesus said that those who trust Him never really die. Then Jesus raised Lazarus from death.

The Lord Jesus Himself later arose from the tomb. He now wants you to know Him as the One who can keep you safe for Himself. Whoever believes in Jesus lives with Him forever.

that we may give an answer to those who
sent us? What do you say about yourself?"
23 He said: "I *am*

'The voice of one crying in the
wilderness:
"Make straight the way of the LORD," '[a]

as the prophet Isaiah said."
24 Now those who were sent were from
the Pharisees. 25 And they asked him, saying,
"Why then do you baptize if you are not the
Christ, nor Elijah, nor the Prophet?"
26 John answered them, saying, "I baptize
with water, but there stands One among you
whom you do not know. 27 It is He who, coming after me, is preferred before me, whose
sandal strap I am not worthy to loose."
28 These things were done in Bethabara[a]
beyond the Jordan, where John was
baptizing.

The Lamb of God

29 The next day John saw Jesus coming
toward him, and said, "Behold! The Lamb
of God who takes away the sin of the world!
30 This is He of whom I said, 'After me comes
a Man who is preferred before me, for He
was before me.' 31 I did not know Him; but
that He should be revealed to Israel, therefore I came baptizing with water."
32 And John bore witness, saying, "I saw
the Spirit descending from heaven like a
dove, and He remained upon Him. 33 I did
not know Him, but He who sent me to baptize with water said to me, 'Upon whom you
see the Spirit descending, and remaining on
Him, this is He who baptizes with the Holy
Spirit.' 34 And I have seen and testified that
this is the Son of God."

The First Disciples

35 Again, the next day, John stood with
two of his disciples. 36 And looking at Jesus
as He walked, he said, "Behold the Lamb of
God!"

1:23 [a] Isaiah 40:3 1:28 [a] NU-Text and M-Text read *Bethany*.

JESUS IS GOD

READ IT: JOHN 1:1–18

GET IT:

John, the author of this book, starts the story of Jesus in a completely different way from the other people who wrote about Jesus' life. John repeats the first words of the Bible, "In the beginning" (Genesis 1:1), to help us connect God with Jesus Christ, the Word. He also talks about Jesus as the true Light (v. 9) who gives light to everyone in the world. He wants us to understand the idea that Jesus, the Son of God, came to earth in human form (flesh). The name *John* in verse 6 refers to John the Baptist, the messenger who announced that Jesus was coming soon and that everybody should get ready to listen to Him.

LIVE IT:

This reading is all about Jesus being the Word sent from God. You'll get a better idea of what this reading is all about if you rewrite the first five verses. As you write them out, replace the words *the Word*, *He*, and *Him* with the words *Jesus Christ*. Then reread the passage.

37 The two disciples heard him speak, and
they followed Jesus. 38 Then Jesus turned,
and seeing them following, said to them,
"What do you seek?"
They said to Him, "Rabbi" (which is to
say, when translated, Teacher), "where are
You staying?"
39 He said to them, "Come and see." They
came and saw where He was staying, and remained with Him that day (now it was about
the tenth hour).
40 One of the two who heard John *speak,*
and followed Him, was Andrew, Simon
Peter's brother. 41 He first found his own
brother Simon, and said to him, "We have
found the Messiah" (which is translated, the
Christ). 42 And he brought him to Jesus.
Now when Jesus looked at him, He said,
"You are Simon the son of Jonah.[a] You shall
be called Cephas" (which is translated, A
Stone).

Philip and Nathanael

43 The following day Jesus wanted to go
to Galilee, and He found Philip and said to
him, "Follow Me." 44 Now Philip was from
Bethsaida, the city of Andrew and Peter.
45 Philip found Nathanael and said to him,
"We have found Him of whom Moses in the
law, and also the prophets, wrote—Jesus of
Nazareth, the son of Joseph."
46 And Nathanael said to him, "Can anything good come out of Nazareth?"
Philip said to him, "Come and see."
47 Jesus saw Nathanael coming toward
Him, and said of him, "Behold, an Israelite
indeed, in whom is no deceit!"
48 Nathanael said to Him, "How do You
know me?"
Jesus answered and said to him, "Before
Philip called you, when you were under the
fig tree, I saw you."
49 Nathanael answered and said to Him,
"Rabbi, You are the Son of God! You are the
King of Israel!"
50 Jesus answered and said to him, "Because I said to you, 'I saw you under the fig
tree,' do you believe? You will see greater
things than these." 51 And He said to him,
"Most assuredly, I say to you, hereafter[a] you
shall see heaven open, and the angels of God
ascending and descending upon the Son of
Man."

Water Turned to Wine

2 On the third day there was a wedding
in Cana of Galilee, and the mother of
Jesus was there. 2 Now both Jesus and His
disciples were invited to the wedding. 3 And
when they ran out of wine, the mother of
Jesus said to Him, "They have no wine."
4 Jesus said to her, "Woman, what does
your concern have to do with Me? My hour
has not yet come."

1:42 [a] NU-Text reads *John.* 1:51 [a] NU-Text omits *hereafter.*

Action!

CELEBRATING

READ IT: JOHN 2:1–11

Jesus' first recorded miracle—turning water into wine—happened at a party. Some people try to make Jesus out to be a super-serious, boring, "all work and no play" kind of person, but that wasn't the case. Jesus regularly participated in festivals and celebrations and often met with friends to eat meals with them. Some people even thought that Jesus went to too many parties (see Matthew 11:19). The truth is that parties were an important part of Jesus' ministry because they were important to the culture He ministered in. Jesus celebrated because His ministry meant victory over sin and death for all those who believed in Him. And that's worth celebrating.

5His mother said to the servants, "Whatever He says to you, do *it*."
6Now there were set there six waterpots of
stone, according to the manner of purification of the Jews, containing twenty or thirty
gallons apiece. 7Jesus said to them, "Fill the
waterpots with water." And they filled them
up to the brim. 8And He said to them, "Draw
some out now, and take *it* to the master of
the feast." And they took *it*. 9When the master of the feast had tasted the water that was
made wine, and did not know where it came
from (but the servants who had drawn the
water knew), the master of the feast called
the bridegroom. 10And he said to him, "Every man at the beginning sets out the good
wine, and when the *guests* have well drunk,
then the inferior. You have kept the good
wine until now!"
11This beginning of signs Jesus did in
Cana of Galilee, and manifested His glory;
and His disciples believed in Him.
12After this He went down to Capernaum, He, His mother, His brothers, and
His disciples; and they did not stay there
many days.

Jesus Cleanses the Temple

13Now the Passover of the Jews was at
hand, and Jesus went up to Jerusalem. 14And
He found in the temple those who sold oxen
and sheep and doves, and the money changers doing business. 15When He had made a
whip of cords, He drove them all out of the
temple, with the sheep and the oxen, and
poured out the changers' money and overturned the tables. 16And He said to those
who sold doves, "Take these things away! Do
not make My Father's house a house of merchandise!" 17Then His disciples remembered
that it was written, "Zeal for Your house has
eaten[a] Me up."[b]
18So the Jews answered and said to Him,
"What sign do You show to us, since You do
these things?"
19Jesus answered and said to them, "Destroy this temple, and in three days I will
raise it up."
20Then the Jews said, "It has taken forty-
six years to build this temple, and will You
raise it up in three days?"
21But He was speaking of the temple of
His body. 22Therefore, when He had risen
from the dead, His disciples remembered
that He had said this to them;[a] and they

In Focus

3:3 Born Again When God changes a person to become a Christian. The change is so great that Jesus said it is like being born all over again.

3:16 Believes Accepting what God has said in the Bible and trusting Jesus to save you from your sins. To believe as a Christian is to receive Jesus Christ into your life.

believed the Scripture and the word which
Jesus had said.

The Discerner of Hearts

23Now when He was in Jerusalem at the
Passover, during the feast, many believed in
His name when they saw the signs which
He did. 24But Jesus did not commit Himself
to them, because He knew all *men*, 25and had
no need that anyone should testify of man,
for He knew what was in man.

The New Birth

3 There was a man of the Pharisees
named Nicodemus, a ruler of the Jews.
2This man came to Jesus by night and said to
Him, "Rabbi, we know that You are a teacher come from God; for no one can do these
signs that You do unless God is with him."
3Jesus answered and said to him, "Most
assuredly, I say to you, unless one is born
again, he cannot see the kingdom of God."
4Nicodemus said to Him, "How can a
man be born when he is old? Can he enter
a second time into his mother's womb and
be born?"
5Jesus answered, "Most assuredly, I say
to you, unless one is born of water and the
Spirit, he cannot enter the kingdom of God.
6That which is born of the flesh is flesh, and
that which is born of the Spirit is spirit. 7Do
not marvel that I said to you, 'You must be
born again.' 8The wind blows where it wishes, and you hear the sound of it, but cannot

2:17 [a] NU-Text and M-Text read *will eat*. [b] Psalm 69:9
2:22 [a] NU-Text and M-Text omit *to them*.

tell where it comes from and where it goes.
So is everyone who is born of the Spirit."
9 Nicodemus answered and said to Him,
"How can these things be?"
10 Jesus answered and said to him, "Are
you the teacher of Israel, and do not know
these things? 11 Most assuredly, I say to you,
We speak what We know and testify what
We have seen, and you do not receive Our
witness. 12 If I have told you earthly things
and you do not believe, how will you believe if I tell you heavenly things? 13 No one
has ascended to heaven but He who came
down from heaven, *that is,* the Son of Man
who is in heaven.[a] 14 And as Moses lifted up
the serpent in the wilderness, even so must
the Son of Man be lifted up, 15 that whoever
believes in Him should not perish but[a] have
eternal life. 16 For God so loved the world that
He gave His only begotten Son, that whoever
believes in Him should not perish but have
everlasting life. 17 For God did not send His
Son into the world to condemn the world,
but that the world through Him might be
saved.
18 "He who believes in Him is not condemned; but he who does not believe is condemned already, because he has not believed
in the name of the only begotten Son of God.

3:13 [a] NU-Text omits *who is in heaven.* 3:15 [a] NU-Text omits *not perish but.*

SALVATION NICK AT NIGHT

READ IT: JOHN 3:1–21

GET IT:

People who've never read the Bible have heard of John 3:16. Even guys with rainbow 'fro wigs and wild outfits hold it up on poster boards behind football end zones. In fact, John 3:16 is probably the most famous verse in the whole Bible.

But it wasn't a Bible verse when Nicodemus heard the words. They were the words of Jesus, spoken directly to him. Can you imagine that?

Nicodemus (let's call him Nick) was an important guy. He had power and influence. And seeking out Jesus was a risky move for him, which is why he came to Jesus in the dark, at night. Nick didn't want to be caught, but he had burning questions he just had to ask.

It's important to know that Nick was also a religious leader. In fact, he was doing everything "right." He wasn't a guy anyone would have considered a sinner. But Jesus told him that being religious wasn't enough. Jesus said everyone has to be "born again" (v. 3) in order to gain salvation.

LIVE IT:

If you want to experience the life you were made for, you have to be saved (that's what salvation means) from your own sin. You can't do it alone. Being religious isn't enough. Only Jesus can save you. Believe and ask and He will do it.

19And this is the condemnation, that the
light has come into the world, and men loved
darkness rather than light, because their
deeds were evil. 20For everyone practicing
evil hates the light and does not come to the
light, lest his deeds should be exposed. 21But
he who does the truth comes to the light,
that his deeds may be clearly seen, that they
have been done in God."

John the Baptist Exalts Christ

22After these things Jesus and His disci-
ples came into the land of Judea, and there
He remained with them and baptized. 23Now
John also was baptizing in Aenon near
Salim, because there was much water there.
And they came and were baptized. 24For John
had not yet been thrown into prison.

25Then there arose a dispute between
some of John's disciples and the Jews about
purification. 26And they came to John and
said to him, "Rabbi, He who was with
you beyond the Jordan, to whom you have
testified—behold, He is baptizing, and all
are coming to Him!"

27John answered and said, "A man can
receive nothing unless it has been given to
him from heaven. 28You yourselves bear me
witness, that I said, 'I am not the Christ,' but,
'I have been sent before Him.' 29He who has
the bride is the bridegroom; but the friend of
the bridegroom, who stands and hears him,
rejoices greatly because of the bridegroom's
voice. Therefore this joy of mine is fulfilled.
30He must increase, but I *must* decrease. 31He
who comes from above is above all; he who
is of the earth is earthly and speaks of the
earth. He who comes from heaven is above
all. 32And what He has seen and heard,
that He testifies; and no one receives His

JESUS IS THE WAY
THE WAY TO LIFE

READ IT: JOHN 3:16

GET IT:

God loves us! God's love for you is massive, beyond any love you will ever experience anywhere else. God's love is perfect and never wavers or slips, even when you do something really bad. In fact, God loves us so much that He gave His Son, Jesus, to die for us. That's pretty amazing love!

And, the verse tells us, anyone who believes that Jesus is who He said He was—the Son of God and the only Savior—will experience life forever.

That life starts now—not only someday out there after you die. Eternal life is the gift God offers you, through His Son, Jesus, to start living today.

LIVE IT:

Have you ever acknowledged Jesus as your Savior? Lots of people go to church and do all sorts of religious things (even reading the Bible), but have never made this choice that will impact them for all eternity.

If you've never taken this step, you can do it now! Just thank God for loving you, and tell Him you believe that Jesus' death paid for your sins.

testimony. 33He who has received His testimony has certified that God is true. 34For
He whom God has sent speaks the words
of God, for God does not give the Spirit by
measure. 35The Father loves the Son, and
has given all things into His hand. 36He who
believes in the Son has everlasting life; and
he who does not believe the Son shall not see
life, but the wrath of God abides on him."

A Samaritan Woman Meets Her Messiah

4 Therefore, when the Lord knew that
the Pharisees had heard that Jesus
made and baptized more disciples than
John 2(though Jesus Himself did not baptize, but His disciples), 3He left Judea and
departed again to Galilee. 4But He needed to
go through Samaria.

5So He came to a city of Samaria which
is called Sychar, near the plot of ground that
Jacob gave to his son Joseph. 6Now Jacob's
well was there. Jesus therefore, being wearied from *His* journey, sat thus by the well. It
was about the sixth hour.

7A woman of Samaria came to draw water. Jesus said to her, "Give Me a drink." 8For
His disciples had gone away into the city to
buy food.

9Then the woman of Samaria said to
Him, "How is it that You, being a Jew, ask
a drink from me, a Samaritan woman?" For
Jews have no dealings with Samaritans.

10Jesus answered and said to her, "If you
knew the gift of God, and who it is who says
to you, 'Give Me a drink,' you would have
asked Him, and He would have given you
living water."

11The woman said to Him, "Sir, You have
nothing to draw with, and the well is deep.
Where then do You get that living water?
12Are You greater than our father Jacob, who
gave us the well, and drank from it himself,
as well as his sons and his livestock?"

13Jesus answered and said to her, "Whoever *drinks of this* water *will* thirst again,
14but whoever drinks of the water that I shall
give him will never thirst. But the water that
I shall give him will become in him a fountain of water springing up into everlasting
life."

15The woman said to Him, "Sir, give me
this water, that I may not thirst, nor come
here to draw."

16Jesus said to her, "Go, call your husband, and come here."

17The woman answered and said, "I have
no husband."

Jesus said to her, "You have well said,
'I have no husband,' 18for you have had five
husbands, and the one whom you now have
is not your husband; in that you spoke truly."

19The woman said to Him, "Sir, I perceive that You are a prophet. 20Our fathers
worshiped on this mountain, and you *Jews*
say that in Jerusalem is the place where one
ought to worship."

21Jesus said to her, "Woman, believe Me,
the hour is coming when you will neither on
this mountain, nor in Jerusalem, worship
the Father. 22You worship what you do not
know; we know what we worship, for salvation is of the Jews. 23But the hour is coming,
and now is, when the true worshipers will
worship the Father in spirit and truth; for
the Father is seeking such to worship Him.
24God *is* Spirit, and those who worship Him
must worship in spirit and truth."

25The woman said to Him, "I know that
Messiah is coming" (who is called Christ).
"When He comes, He will tell us all things."

26Jesus said to her, "I who speak to you
am *He*."

The Whitened Harvest

27And at this *point* His disciples came,
and they marveled that He talked with a
woman; yet no one said, "What do You
seek?" or, "Why are You talking with her?"

28The woman then left her waterpot,
went her way into the city, and said to the
men, 29"Come, see a Man who told me all
things that I ever did. Could this be the
Christ?" 30Then they went out of the city and
came to Him.

31In the meantime His disciples urged
Him, saying, "Rabbi, eat."

32But He said to them, "I have food to eat
of which you do not know."

33Therefore the disciples said to one another, "Has anyone brought Him *anything*
to eat?"

34Jesus said to them, "My food is to do the
will of Him who sent Me, and to finish His
work. 35Do you not say, 'There are still four
months and *then* comes the harvest'? Behold, I say to you, lift up your eyes and look
at the fields, for they are already white for
harvest! 36And he who reaps receives wages,

and gathers fruit for eternal life, that both
he who sows and he who reaps may rejoice
together. 37For in this the saying is true: 'One
sows and another reaps.' 38I sent you to reap
that for which you have not labored; others
have labored, and you have entered into their
labors."

The Savior of the World

39And many of the Samaritans of that city
believed in Him because of the word of the
woman who testified, "He told me all that
I *ever* did." 40So when the Samaritans had
come to Him, they urged Him to stay with
them; and He stayed there two days. 41And
many more believed because of His own
word.

42Then they said to the woman, "Now we
believe, not because of what you said, for we
ourselves have heard *Him* and we know that
this is indeed the Christ,[a] the Savior of the
world."

Welcome at Galilee

43Now after the two days He departed
from there and went to Galilee. 44For Jesus
Himself testified that a prophet has no hon-
or in his own country. 45So when He came to
Galilee, the Galileans received Him, having
seen all the things He did in Jerusalem at
the feast; for they also had gone to the feast.

A Nobleman's Son Healed

46So Jesus came again to Cana of Galilee
where He had made the water wine. And
there was a certain nobleman whose son
was sick at Capernaum. 47When he heard
that Jesus had come out of Judea into Galilee, he went to Him and implored Him to
come down and heal his son, for he was at
the point of death. 48Then Jesus said to him,
"Unless you *people* see signs and wonders,
you will by no means believe."

49The nobleman said to Him, "Sir, come
down before my child dies!"

50Jesus said to him, "Go your way; your
son lives." So the man believed the word that
Jesus spoke to him, and he went his way.
51And as he was now going down, his servants met him and told *him,* saying, "Your
son lives!"

52Then he inquired of them the hour
when he got better. And they said to him,
"Yesterday at the seventh hour the fever left
him." 53So the father knew that *it was* at the
same hour in which Jesus said to him, "Your
son lives." And he himself believed, and his
whole household.

54This again *is* the second sign Jesus did
when He had come out of Judea into Galilee.

A Man Healed at the Pool of Bethesda

5 After this there was a feast of the Jews,
and Jesus went up to Jerusalem. 2Now
there is in Jerusalem by the Sheep *Gate* a
pool, which is called in Hebrew, Bethesda,[a]

4:42 [a] NU-Text omits *the Christ.* 5:2 [a] NU-Text reads *Bethzatha.*

WORSHIP

READ IT: JOHN 4:23, 24

Worshiping God in spirit and truth means that we worship God with our whole lives, not only by being religious. John, the author of this book, was writing to Jewish people who were believers in Jesus. They were very comfortable with the practices of worship (which for us would be things like going to church, giving tithes, and singing worship songs).

But John is telling us that, while all those practices are good, God really loves it when His people worship Him with their whole lives.

having five porches. [3]In these lay a great
multitude of sick people, blind, lame, paralyzed, waiting for the moving of the water.
[4]For an angel went down at a certain time
into the pool and stirred up the water; then
whoever stepped in first, after the stirring of
the water, was made well of whatever disease
he had.[a] [5]Now a certain man was there who
had an infirmity thirty-eight years. [6]When
Jesus saw him lying there, and knew that
he already had been *in that condition* a long
time, He said to him, "Do you want to be
made well?"

[7]The sick man answered Him, "Sir, I
have no man to put me into the pool when
the water is stirred up; but while I am coming, another steps down before me."

[8]Jesus said to him, "Rise, take up your
bed and walk." [9]And immediately the man
was made well, took up his bed, and walked.

And that day was the Sabbath. [10]The Jews
therefore said to him who was cured, "It is
the Sabbath; it is not lawful for you to carry
your bed."

[11]He answered them, "He who made
me well said to me, 'Take up your bed and
walk.'"

[12]Then they asked him, "Who is the
Man who said to you, 'Take up your bed and
walk'?" [13]But the one who was healed did not
know who it was, for Jesus had withdrawn,
a multitude being in *that* place. [14]Afterward
Jesus found him in the temple, and said to
him, "See, you have been made well. Sin no
more, lest a worse thing come upon you."

[15]The man departed and told the Jews
that it was Jesus who had made him well.

Honor the Father and the Son

[16]For this reason the Jews persecuted
Jesus, and sought to kill Him,[a] because
He had done these things on the Sabbath.
[17]But Jesus answered them, "My Father has
been working until now, and I have been
working."

[18]Therefore the Jews sought all the more
to kill Him, because He not only broke the
Sabbath, but also said that God was His
Father, making Himself equal with God.
[19]Then Jesus answered and said to them,
"Most assuredly, I say to you, the Son can
do nothing of Himself, but what He sees the
Father do; for whatever He does, the Son also
does in like manner. [20]For the Father loves
the Son, and shows Him all things that He
Himself does; and He will show Him greater
works than these, that you may marvel. [21]For
as the Father raises the dead and gives life to
them, even so the Son gives life to whom He
will. [22]For the Father judges no one, but has
committed all judgment to the Son, [23]that all
should honor the Son just as they honor the
Father. He who does not honor the Son does
not honor the Father who sent Him.

Life and Judgment Are Through the Son

[24]"Most assuredly, I say to you, he who
hears My word and believes in Him who sent
Me has everlasting life, and shall not come
into judgment, but has passed from death
into life. [25]Most assuredly, I say to you, the
hour is coming, and now is, when the dead
will hear the voice of the Son of God; and
those who hear will live. [26]For as the Father
has life in Himself, so He has granted the
Son to have life in Himself, [27]and has given
Him authority to execute judgment also, because He is the Son of Man. [28]Do not marvel at this; for the hour is coming in which
all who are in the graves will hear His voice
[29]and come forth—those who have done
good, to the resurrection of life, and those
who have done evil, to the resurrection of
condemnation. [30]I can of Myself do nothing.
As I hear, I judge; and My judgment is righteous, because I do not seek My own will but
the will of the Father who sent Me.

The Fourfold Witness

[31]"If I bear witness of Myself, My witness
is not true. [32]There is another who bears
witness of Me, and I know that the witness
which He witnesses of Me is true. [33]You have
sent to John, and he has borne witness to the
truth. [34]Yet I do not receive testimony from
man, but I say these things that you may
be saved. [35]He was the burning and shining lamp, and you were willing for a time
to rejoice in his light. [36]But I have a greater
witness than John's; for the works which
the Father has given Me to finish—the very
works that I do—bear witness of Me, that
the Father has sent Me. [37]And the Father
Himself, who sent Me, has testified of Me.
You have neither heard His voice at any time,

5:4 [a] NU-Text omits *waiting for the moving of the water* at the end of verse 3, and all of verse 4. **5:16** [a] NU-Text omits *and sought to kill Him.*

nor seen His form. 38But you do not have His
word abiding in you, because whom He sent,
Him you do not believe. 39You search the
Scriptures, for in them you think you have
eternal life; and these are they which testify
of Me. 40But you are not willing to come to
Me that you may have life.

41"I do not receive honor from men. 42But
I know you, that you do not have the love of
God in you. 43I have come in My Father's
name, and you do not receive Me; if another comes in his own name, him you will
receive. 44How can you believe, who receive
honor from one another, and do not seek the
honor that *comes* from the only God? 45Do
not think that I shall accuse you to the Father; there is *one* who accuses you—Moses,
in whom you trust. 46For if you believed
Moses, you would believe Me; for he wrote
about Me. 47But if you do not believe his writings, how will you believe My words?"

Feeding the Five Thousand

6 After these things Jesus went over the
Sea of Galilee, which is *the Sea* of Tiberias. 2Then a great multitude followed Him,

JESUS FEEDS FIVE THOUSAND PEOPLE

READ IT: JOHN 6:1–14

GET IT:

Jesus and the disciples were out in the countryside, far from towns or villages. Word had spread that Jesus could heal the sick, so a huge crowd of people tracked Him down. It was near suppertime, but all the food the people had brought with them for the day was gone. Jesus cared about the practical aspects of life as well as people's spiritual lives. He was concerned about this hungry crowd, so He asked Philip, who was from the area, where they could buy some food. But He knew that even if food was nearby, eight months' pay wouldn't buy enough to feed everyone. So Jesus worked with what was available—two small fish and five barley rolls—and miraculously fed everyone.

LIVE IT:

The boy with the lunch offered what he had. It certainly wasn't enough to feed five thousand people, but he offered it anyway. This would be like you sharing your two bags of Skittles with the entire congregation in your church. You know it's not enough, but you decide to hand it over anyway. You would be amazed if, after the candy was passed around, there was enough for everyone and some left over. Now take that up a notch. You have a talent, an ability, an interest, but you have no idea how you can use it for God. In fact, you think it's kind of dumb and unimportant. God still wants you to offer it to His service. When you hand over what you have to God, He can do miraculous things with it. No talent, no ability, no interest is ever too small to make a contribution to God's work because it's not about the size or quality of your gift—it's about the power of our God.

because they saw His signs which He performed on those who were diseased. 3And Jesus went up on the mountain, and there He sat with His disciples.

4Now the Passover, a feast of the Jews, was near. 5Then Jesus lifted up *His* eyes, and seeing a great multitude coming toward Him, He said to Philip, "Where shall we buy bread, that these may eat?" 6But this He said to test him, for He Himself knew what He would do.

7Philip answered Him, "Two hundred denarii worth of bread is not sufficient for them, that every one of them may have a little."

8One of His disciples, Andrew, Simon Peter's brother, said to Him, 9"There is a lad here who has five barley loaves and two small fish, but what are they among so many?"

10Then Jesus said, "Make the people sit down." Now there was much grass in the place. So the men sat down, in number about five thousand. 11And Jesus took the loaves, and when He had given thanks He distributed *them* to the disciples, and the disciples[a] to those sitting down; and likewise of the fish, as much as they wanted. 12So when they were filled, He said to His disciples, "Gather up the fragments that remain, so that nothing is lost." 13Therefore they gathered *them* up, and filled twelve baskets with the fragments of the five barley loaves which were left over by those who had eaten. 14Then those men, when they had seen the sign that Jesus did, said, "This is truly the Prophet who is to come into the world."

Jesus Walks on the Sea

15Therefore when Jesus perceived that they were about to come and take Him by force to make Him king, He departed again to the mountain by Himself alone.

16Now when evening came, His disciples went down to the sea, 17got into the boat, and went over the sea toward Capernaum. And it was already dark, and Jesus had not come to them. 18Then the sea arose because a great wind was blowing. 19So when they had rowed about three or four miles,[a] they saw Jesus walking on the sea and drawing near the boat; and they were afraid. 20But He said to them, "It is I; do not be afraid." 21Then they willingly received Him into the boat, and immediately the boat was at the land where they were going.

The Bread from Heaven

22On the following day, when the people who were standing on the other side of the sea saw that there was no other boat there, except that one which His disciples had entered,[a] and that Jesus had not entered the boat with His disciples, but His disciples had gone away alone— 23however, other boats came from Tiberias, near the place where they ate bread after the Lord had given thanks— 24when the people therefore saw that Jesus was not there, nor His disciples, they also got into boats and came to Capernaum, seeking Jesus. 25And when they found Him on the other side of the sea, they said to Him, "Rabbi, when did You come here?"

26Jesus answered them and said, "Most assuredly, I say to you, you seek Me, not because you saw the signs, but because you ate of the loaves and were filled. 27Do not labor for the food which perishes, but for the food which endures to everlasting life, which the Son of Man will give you, because God the Father has set His seal on Him."

28Then they said to Him, "What shall we do, that we may work the works of God?"

29Jesus answered and said to them, "This is the work of God, that you believe in Him whom He sent."

30Therefore they said to Him, "What sign will You perform then, that we may see it and believe You? What work will You do? 31Our fathers ate the manna in the desert; as it is written, 'He gave them bread from heaven to eat.' "[a]

32Then Jesus said to them, "Most assuredly, I say to you, Moses did not give you the bread from heaven, but My Father gives you the true bread from heaven. 33For the bread of God is He who comes down from heaven and gives life to the world."

34Then they said to Him, "Lord, give us *this* bread always."

35And Jesus said to them, "I am the bread of life. He who comes to Me shall never hunger, and he who believes in Me shall never thirst. 36But I said to you that you have seen

---

6:11 [a] NU-Text omits *to the disciples, and the disciples.* **6:19** [a] Literally *twenty-five or thirty stadia* **6:22** [a] NU-Text omits *that* and *which His disciples had entered.* **6:31** [a] Exodus 16:4; Nehemiah 9:15; Psalm 78:24

Me and yet do not believe. 37All that the Father gives Me will come to Me, and the one
who comes to Me I will by no means cast
out. 38For I have come down from heaven,
not to do My own will, but the will of Him
who sent Me. 39This is the will of the Father
who sent Me, that of all He has given Me I
should lose nothing, but should raise it up
at the last day. 40And this is the will of Him
who sent Me, that everyone who sees the Son
and believes in Him may have everlasting
life; and I will raise him up at the last day."

Rejected by His Own

41The Jews then complained about Him,
because He said, "I am the bread which
came down from heaven." 42And they said,
"Is not this Jesus, the son of Joseph, whose
father and mother we know? How is it
then that He says, 'I have come down from
heaven'?"

43Jesus therefore answered and said to
them, "Do not murmur among yourselves.
44No one can come to Me unless the Father
who sent Me draws him; and I will raise
him up at the last day. 45It is written in the
prophets, 'And they shall all be taught by
God.'[a] Therefore everyone who has heard
and learned[b] from the Father comes to Me.
46Not that anyone has seen the Father, except
He who is from God; He has seen the Father. 47Most assuredly, I say to you, he who
believes in Me[a] has everlasting life. 48I am
the bread of life. 49Your fathers ate the manna in the wilderness, and are dead. 50This is
the bread which comes down from heaven,
that one may eat of it and not die. 51I am the
living bread which came down from heaven.
If anyone eats of this bread, he will live forever; and the bread that I shall give is My flesh,
which I shall give for the life of the world."

52The Jews therefore quarreled among
themselves, saying, "How can this Man give
us *His* flesh to eat?"

53Then Jesus said to them, "Most assuredly, I say to you, unless you eat the flesh
of the Son of Man and drink His blood, you
have no life in you. 54Whoever eats My flesh
and drinks My blood has eternal life, and
I will raise him up at the last day. 55For My
flesh is food indeed,[a] and My blood is drink
indeed. 56He who eats My flesh and drinks
My blood abides in Me, and I in him. 57As
the living Father sent Me, and I live because
of the Father, so he who feeds on Me will
live because of Me. 58This is the bread which

6:45 [a] Isaiah 54:13 [b] M-Text reads *hears and has learned.* 6:47 [a] NU-Text omits *in Me.* 6:55 [a] NU-Text reads *true food* and *true drink.*

6:35 HAVE YOU EATEN THE BREAD OF HEAVEN?

Bread is a basic food around the world. It is made from nourishing grain and satisfies hunger. We take bread for granted because we live in a land of plenty. We have lots of meat, fish, poultry, and vegetables. We also enjoy sweet things—candy and cookies and ice cream!

Jesus compared Himself to bread because bread is so basic to life. He said, "I am the bread of life." If we put our faith in Jesus, He promises us we will never hunger again. Of course, we will still need our daily meals. But the bread that Jesus gives us is the bread of heaven. Sometimes we sing the words of the Welsh hymn writer William Williams, "Bread of heaven . . . feed me till I want no more!" So Jesus simply says that He is our source of the greatest kind of life—life that is perfect and never ends.

came down from heaven—not as your fathers ate the manna, and are dead. He who
eats this bread will live forever."

59 These things He said in the synagogue
as He taught in Capernaum.

Many Disciples Turn Away

60 Therefore many of His disciples, when
they heard *this,* said, "This is a hard saying;
who can understand it?"

61 When Jesus knew in Himself that His
disciples complained about this, He said to
them, "Does this offend you? 62 *What* then if
you should see the Son of Man ascend where
He was before? 63 It is the Spirit who gives
life; the flesh profits nothing. The words
that I speak to you are spirit, and *they* are
life. 64 But there are some of you who do not
believe." For Jesus knew from the beginning
who they were who did not believe, and who
would betray Him. 65 And He said, "Therefore I have said to you that no one can come
to Me unless it has been granted to him by
My Father."

66 From that *time* many of His disciples
went back and walked with Him no more.
67 Then Jesus said to the twelve, "Do you also
want to go away?"

68 But Simon Peter answered Him, "Lord,
to whom shall we go? You have the words of
eternal life. 69 Also we have come to believe
and know that You are the Christ, the Son of
the living God."[a]

70 Jesus answered them, "Did I not choose
you, the twelve, and one of you is a devil?"
71 He spoke of Judas Iscariot, *the son* of Simon, for it was he who would betray Him,
being one of the twelve.

Jesus' Brothers Disbelieve

7 After these things Jesus walked in
Galilee; for He did not want to walk in
Judea, because the Jews[a] sought to kill Him.
2 Now the Jews' Feast of Tabernacles was at
hand. 3 His brothers therefore said to Him,
"Depart from here and go into Judea, that
Your disciples also may see the works that
You are doing. 4 For no one does anything in
secret while he himself seeks to be known
openly. If You do these things, show Yourself to the world." 5 For even His brothers did
not believe in Him.

6 Then Jesus said to them, "My time has
not yet come, but your time is always ready.
7 The world cannot hate you, but it hates Me
because I testify of it that its works are evil.
8 You go up to this feast. I am not yet[a] going
up to this feast, for My time has not yet fully
come." 9 When He had said these things to
them, He remained in Galilee.

The Heavenly Scholar

10 But when His brothers had gone up,
then He also went up to the feast, not openly, but as it were in secret. 11 Then the Jews
sought Him at the feast, and said, "Where
is He?" 12 And there was much complaining
among the people concerning Him. Some
said, "He is good"; others said, "No, on the
contrary, He deceives the people." 13 However,
no one spoke openly of Him for fear of the
Jews.

14 Now about the middle of the feast Jesus
went up into the temple and taught. 15 And
the Jews marveled, saying, "How does this
Man know letters, having never studied?"

16 Jesus[a] answered them and said, "My
doctrine is not Mine, but His who sent Me.
17 If anyone wills to do His will, he shall know
concerning the doctrine, whether it is from
God or *whether* I speak on My own *authority.*
18 He who speaks from himself seeks his own
glory; but He who seeks the glory of the One
who sent Him is true, and no unrighteousness is in Him. 19 Did not Moses give you the
law, yet none of you keeps the law? Why do
you seek to kill Me?"

20 The people answered and said, "You
have a demon. Who is seeking to kill You?"

21 Jesus answered and said to them, "I
did one work, and you all marvel. 22 Moses
therefore gave you circumcision (not that it
is from Moses, but from the fathers), and
you circumcise a man on the Sabbath. 23 If a
man receives circumcision on the Sabbath,
so that the law of Moses should not be broken, are you angry with Me because I made
a man completely well on the Sabbath? 24 Do
not judge according to appearance, but judge
with righteous judgment."

Could This Be the Christ?

25 Now some of them from Jerusalem said,
"Is this not He whom they seek to kill? 26 But
look! He speaks boldly, and they say nothing
to Him. Do the rulers know indeed that this

6:69 [a] NU-Text reads *You are the Holy One of God.*
7:1 [a] That is, the ruling authorities **7:8** [a] NU-Text omits *yet.* **7:16** [a] NU-Text and M-Text read *So Jesus.*

is truly[a] the Christ? 27However, we know
where this Man is from; but when the Christ
comes, no one knows where He is from."

28Then Jesus cried out, as He taught in
the temple, saying, "You both know Me, and
you know where I am from; and I have not
come of Myself, but He who sent Me is true,
whom you do not know. 29But[a] I know Him,
for I am from Him, and He sent Me."

30Therefore they sought to take Him;
but no one laid a hand on Him, because His
hour had not yet come. 31And many of the
people believed in Him, and said, "When the
Christ comes, will He do more signs than
these which this *Man* has done?"

Jesus and the Religious Leaders

32The Pharisees heard the crowd mur-
muring these things concerning Him, and
the Pharisees and the chief priests sent officers to take Him. 33Then Jesus said to them,[a]
"I shall be with you a little while longer, and
then I go to Him who sent Me. 34You will
seek Me and not find *Me*, and where I am
you cannot come."

35Then the Jews said among themselves,
"Where does He intend to go that we shall
not find Him? Does He intend to go to the
Dispersion among the Greeks and teach the
Greeks? 36What is this thing that He said,
'You will seek Me and not find Me, and
where I am you cannot come'?"

The Promise of the Holy Spirit

37On the last day, that great *day* of the
feast, Jesus stood and cried out, saying,
"If anyone thirsts, let him come to Me and
drink. 38He who believes in Me, as the Scripture has said, out of his heart will flow rivers
of living water." 39But this He spoke concerning the Spirit, whom those believing[a]
in Him would receive; for the Holy[b] Spirit
was not yet *given*, because Jesus was not yet
glorified.

Who Is He?

40Therefore many[a] from the crowd, when
they heard this saying, said, "Truly this is the
Prophet." 41Others said, "This is the Christ."

But some said, "Will the Christ come out
of Galilee? 42Has not the Scripture said that the
Christ comes from the seed of David and from
the town of Bethlehem, where David was?"
43So there was a division among the people
because of Him. 44Now some of them wanted
to take Him, but no one laid hands on Him.

Rejected by the Authorities

45Then the officers came to the chief
priests and Pharisees, who said to them,
"Why have you not brought Him?"

46The officers answered, "No man ever
spoke like this Man!"

47Then the Pharisees answered them,
"Are you also deceived? 48Have any of the
rulers or the Pharisees believed in Him?
49But this crowd that does not know the law
is accursed."

50Nicodemus (he who came to Jesus by
night,[a] being one of them) said to them,
51"Does our law judge a man before it hears
him and knows what he is doing?"

52They answered and said to him, "Are
you also from Galilee? Search and look, for
no prophet has arisen[a] out of Galilee."

An Adulteress Faces the Light of the World

53And everyone went to his *own* house.[a]

8 But Jesus went to the Mount of Olives.
2Now early[a] in the morning He came
again into the temple, and all the people
came to Him; and He sat down and taught
them. 3Then the scribes and Pharisees
brought to Him a woman caught in adultery. And when they had set her in the midst,
4they said to Him, "Teacher, this woman was
caught[a] in adultery, in the very act. 5Now Moses, in the law, commanded[a] us that such
should be stoned.[b] But what do You say?"[c]
6This they said, testing Him, that they might
have *something* of which to accuse Him. But
Jesus stooped down and wrote on the ground
with *His* finger, as though He did not hear.[a]

7So when they continued asking Him, He
raised Himself up[a] and said to them, "He
who is without sin among you, let him throw
a stone at her first." 8And again He stooped

7:26 [a] NU-Text omits *truly*. 7:29 [a] NU-Text and M-Text omit *But*. 7:33 [a] NU-Text and M-Text omit *to them*. 7:39 [a] NU-Text reads *who believed*. [b] NU-Text omits *Holy*. 7:40 [a] NU-Text reads *some*. 7:50 [a] NU-Text reads *before*. 7:52 [a] NU-Text reads *is to rise*. 7:53 [a] The words *And everyone* through *sin no more* (8:11) are bracketed by NU-Text as not original. They are present in over 900 manuscripts. 8:2 [a] M-Text reads *very early*. 8:4 [a] M-Text reads *we found this woman*. 8:5 [a] M-Text reads *in our law Moses commanded*. [b] NU-Text and M-Text read *to stone such*. [c] M-Text adds *about her*. 8:6 [a] NU-Text and M-Text omit *as though He did not hear*. 8:7 [a] M-Text reads *He looked up*.

down and wrote on the ground. 9Then those
who heard *it,* being convicted by *their* conscience,[a] went out one by one, beginning
with the oldest *even* to the last. And Jesus
was left alone, and the woman standing in
the midst. 10When Jesus had raised Himself
up and saw no one but the woman, He said
to her,[a] "Woman, where are those accusers
of yours?[b] Has no one condemned you?"
11She said, "No one, Lord."
And Jesus said to her, "Neither do I condemn you; go and[a] sin no more."
12Then Jesus spoke to them again, saying, "I am the light of the world. He who
follows Me shall not walk in darkness, but
have the light of life."

Jesus Defends His Self-Witness

13The Pharisees therefore said to Him,
"You bear witness of Yourself; Your witness
is not true."
14Jesus answered and said to them,
"Even if I bear witness of Myself, My witness is true, for I know where I came from
and where I am going; but you do not know
where I come from and where I am going.
15You judge according to the flesh; I judge no
one. 16And yet if I do judge, My judgment is
true; for I am not alone, but I *am* with the Father who sent Me. 17It is also written in your
law that the testimony of two men is true.
18I am One who bears witness of Myself, and
the Father who sent Me bears witness of Me."
19Then they said to Him, "Where is Your
Father?"
Jesus answered, "You know neither Me
nor My Father. If you had known Me, you
would have known My Father also."
20These words Jesus spoke in the treasury, as He taught in the temple; and no one
laid hands on Him, for His hour had not yet
come.

Jesus Predicts His Departure

21Then Jesus said to them again, "I am
going away, and you will seek Me, and will
die in your sin. Where I go you cannot come."
22So the Jews said, "Will He kill Himself,
because He says, 'Where I go you cannot
come'?"
23And He said to them, "You are from
beneath; I am from above. You are of this

8:9 [a] NU-Text and M-Text omit *being convicted by their conscience.* 8:10 [a] NU-Text omits *and saw no one but the woman;* M-Text reads *He saw her and said.* [b] NU-Text and M-Text omit *of yours.* 8:11 [a] NU-Text and M-Text add *from now on.*

Epic Ideas

8:12 HAVE YOU SEEN THE LIGHT OF THE WORLD?

Just like food, light is necessary for life. No one can live very long in darkness. Even plants need light to grow. And without light, we can't see.

God says we are like people who live in darkness if we don't know Him. When Jesus came, the Old Testament prophecy also came true: "The people who walked in darkness have seen a great light" (Isaiah 9:2). That is why Jesus could say, "I am the light of the world."

As you look around you, you will see many people who are walking in darkness. Many are prisoners of dark habits and lifestyles that lead to disappointment, disease, and even death.

Jesus came to be the Light to the dark world around you. Will you carry His light wherever you go? His light can shine in you and lead others to know Him, but you must first ask Jesus to live in you.

world; I am not of this world. 24 Therefore I
said to you that you will die in your sins; for
if you do not believe that I am *He,* you will
die in your sins."

25 Then they said to Him, "Who are You?"
And Jesus said to them, "Just what I have
been saying to you from the beginning. 26 I
have many things to say and to judge concerning you, but He who sent Me is true;
and I speak to the world those things which
I heard from Him."

27 They did not understand that He spoke
to them of the Father.

28 Then Jesus said to them, "When you lift
up the Son of Man, then you will know that
I am *He,* and *that* I do nothing of Myself;
but as My Father taught Me, I speak these
things. 29 And He who sent Me is with Me.
The Father has not left Me alone, for I always
do those things that please Him." 30 As He
spoke these words, many believed in Him.

The Truth Shall Make You Free

31 Then Jesus said to those Jews who believed Him, "If you abide in My word, you
are My disciples indeed. 32 And you shall
know the truth, and the truth shall make
you free."

33 They answered Him, "We are Abraham's descendants, and have never been in
bondage to anyone. How *can* You say, 'You
will be made free'?"

34 Jesus answered them, "Most assuredly, I say to you, whoever commits sin is a
slave of sin. 35 And a slave does not abide in
the house forever, *but* a son abides forever.
36 Therefore if the Son makes you free, you
shall be free indeed.

Abraham's Seed and Satan's

37 "I know that you are Abraham's descendants, but you seek to kill Me, because My
word has no place in you. 38 I speak what I
have seen with My Father, and you do what
you have seen with[a] your father."

39 They answered and said to Him, "Abraham is our father."

Jesus said to them, "If you were Abraham's children, you would do the works of
Abraham. 40 But now you seek to kill Me,
a Man who has told you the truth which I
heard from God. Abraham did not do this.
41 You do the deeds of your father."

Then they said to Him, "We were not born
of fornication; we have one Father—God."

42 Jesus said to them, "If God were your
Father, you would love Me, for I proceeded
forth and came from God; nor have I come
of Myself, but He sent Me. 43 Why do you not
understand My speech? Because you are not
able to listen to My word. 44 You are of *your*
father the devil, and the desires of your father
you want to do. He was a murderer from the
beginning, and does not stand in the truth,
because there is no truth in him. When he
speaks a lie, he speaks from his own *resources,* for he is a liar and the father of it. 45 But because I tell the truth, you do not believe Me.
46 Which of you convicts Me of sin? And if I
tell the truth, why do you not believe Me? 47 He
who is of God hears God's words; therefore
you do not hear, because you are not of God."

Before Abraham Was, I AM

48 Then the Jews answered and said to
Him, "Do we not say rightly that You are a
Samaritan and have a demon?"

49 Jesus answered, "I do not have a demon;
but I honor My Father, and you dishonor Me.
50 And I do not seek My *own* glory; there is
One who seeks and judges. 51 Most assuredly, I say to you, if anyone keeps My word he
shall never see death."

52 Then the Jews said to Him, "Now we
know that You have a demon! Abraham
is dead, and the prophets; and You say, 'If
anyone keeps My word he shall never taste
death.' 53 Are You greater than our father
Abraham, who is dead? And the prophets are
dead. Who do You make Yourself out to be?"

54 Jesus answered, "If I honor Myself, My
honor is nothing. It is My Father who honors
Me, of whom you say that He is your[a] God.
55 Yet you have not known Him, but I know
Him. And if I say, 'I do not know Him,' I shall
be a liar like you; but I do know Him and keep
His word. 56 Your father Abraham rejoiced to
see My day, and he saw *it* and was glad."

57 Then the Jews said to Him, "You are
not yet fifty years old, and have You seen
Abraham?"

58 Jesus said to them, "Most assuredly, I
say to you, before Abraham was, I AM."

59 Then they took up stones to throw at
Him; but Jesus hid Himself and went out
of the temple,[a] going through the midst of
them, and so passed by.

8:38 [a] NU-Text reads *heard from.* 8:54 [a] NU-Text and M-Text read *our.* 8:59 [a] NU-Text omits the rest of this verse.

A Man Born Blind Receives Sight

9 Now as *Jesus* passed by, He saw a man who was blind from birth. 2And His disciples asked Him, saying, "Rabbi, who sinned, this man or his parents, that he was born blind?"

3Jesus answered, "Neither this man nor his parents sinned, but that the works of God should be revealed in him. 4I[a] must work the works of Him who sent Me while it is day; *the* night is coming when no one can work. 5As long as I am in the world, I am the light of the world."

6When He had said these things, He spat on the ground and made clay with the saliva; and He anointed the eyes of the blind man with the clay. 7And He said to him, "Go, wash in the pool of Siloam" (which is translated, Sent). So he went and washed, and came back seeing.

8Therefore the neighbors and those who previously had seen that he was blind[a] said, "Is not this he who sat and begged?"

9Some said, "This is he." Others *said,* "He is like him."[a]

He said, "I am *he.*"

10Therefore they said to him, "How were your eyes opened?"

11He answered and said, "A Man called Jesus made clay and anointed my eyes and said to me, 'Go to the pool of[a] Siloam and wash.' So I went and washed, and I received sight."

12Then they said to him, "Where is He?"

He said, "I do not know."

The Pharisees Excommunicate the Healed Man

13They brought him who formerly was blind to the Pharisees. 14Now it was a Sabbath when Jesus made the clay and opened his eyes. 15Then the Pharisees also asked him again how he had received his sight. He said to them, "He put clay on my eyes, and I washed, and I see."

16Therefore some of the Pharisees said, "This Man is not from God, because He does not keep the Sabbath."

Others said, "How can a man who is a sinner do such signs?" And there was a division among them.

9:4 [a] NU-Text reads *We.* 9:8 [a] NU-Text reads *a beggar.* 9:9 [a] NU-Text reads *"No, but he is like him."* 9:11 [a] NU-Text omits *the pool of.*

8:32 THE TRUTH MAKES YOU FREE

Ignorance is caused by sin. When people don't understand the world around them, they become afraid. Fear comes from not knowing the truth. Such fear often leads to anger and violence as people try to defend themselves against what they fear.

Ignorance exists only where God is not known. But knowing God causes you to understand the meaning of life. When God is first in your life, *then the world is no longer a strange and frightening* place.

A little boy needed a light on at night when his father was away. But when his dad came home, the boy said, "You can turn the light off now. Daddy's home!"

Jesus is living Truth who sets you free from the fear of living in the dark unknown. It is enough that the One who knows all is at home in your heart. Now you, too, can sleep in peace.

17They said to the blind man again,
"What do you say about Him because He
opened your eyes?"
He said, "He is a prophet."
18But the Jews did not believe concerning
him, that he had been blind and received
his sight, until they called the parents of
him who had received his sight. 19And they
asked them, saying, "Is this your son, who
you say was born blind? How then does he
now see?"
20His parents answered them and said,
"We know that this is our son, and that he
was born blind; 21but by what means he now
sees we do not know, or who opened his eyes
we do not know. He is of age; ask him. He
will speak for himself." 22His parents said
these *things* because they feared the Jews,
for the Jews had agreed already that if anyone
confessed *that* He *was* Christ, he would
be put out of the synagogue. 23Therefore his
parents said, "He is of age; ask him."
24So they again called the man who was
blind, and said to him, "Give God the glory!
We know that this Man is a sinner."
25He answered and said, "Whether He is
a sinner *or not* I do not know. One thing I
know: that though I was blind, now I see."
26Then they said to him again, "What did
He do to you? How did He open your eyes?"
27He answered them, "I told you already,
and you did not listen. Why do you want to

JESUS HEALS A BLIND MAN

READ IT: JOHN 9:1–34

GET IT:

In Bible times people believed that blindness or any sickness was punishment for sin. This was a way of thinking that had started long before Jesus. In this miracle Jesus not only gave the man his sight, but He corrected a wrong way of thinking. Then Jesus taught a lot more about who He was and what it meant to believe in Him. The Pharisees who followed the law of Moses struggled to understand and believe. The blind man, although he was grilled by other people, stuck to his story. But the people who didn't like the man's praise of Jesus threw him out of the synagogue. So the man followed Jesus, believed He was the Son of God, and worshiped Him.

LIVE IT:

The Jewish people had a hard time accepting who Jesus was, what He did, and what He said about Himself. They didn't want to change their thinking. They thought only one way about religion—the old, traditional way. Jesus was too radical a change for them. It just didn't make sense. Some things about Jesus don't always make sense. Some things are a mystery because God hasn't explained everything to us. That's where faith comes in. Faith is more than knowing the facts. It's believing that Jesus is the way to God, even if we don't have all the answers to our questions.

hear *it* again? Do you also want to become
His disciples?"
28 Then they reviled him and said, "You
are His disciple, but we are Moses' disciples. 29 We know that God spoke to Moses;
as for this *fellow,* we do not know where He
is from."
30 The man answered and said to them,
"Why, this is a marvelous thing, that you
do not know where He is from; yet He has
opened my eyes! 31 Now we know that God
does not hear sinners; but if anyone is a worshiper of God and does His will, He hears
him. 32 Since the world began it has been un-
heard of that anyone opened the eyes of one
who was born blind. 33 If this Man were not
from God, He could do nothing."
34 They answered and said to him, "You
were completely born in sins, and are you
teaching us?" And they cast him out.

True Vision and True Blindness

35 Jesus heard that they had cast him out;
and when He had found him, He said to
him, "Do you believe in the Son of God?"[a]
36 He answered and said, "Who is He,
Lord, that I may believe in Him?"
37 And Jesus said to him, "You have both
seen Him and it is He who is talking with
you."
38 Then he said, "Lord, I believe!" And he
worshiped Him.
39 And Jesus said, "For judgment I have
come into this world, that those who do not
see may see, and that those who see may be
made blind."
40 Then *some* of the Pharisees who were
with Him heard these words, and said to
Him, "Are we blind also?"
41 Jesus said to them, "If you were blind,
you would have no sin; but now you say, 'We
see.' Therefore your sin remains.

Jesus the True Shepherd

10 "Most assuredly, I say to you, he
who does not enter the sheepfold
by the door, but climbs up some other way,
the same is a thief and a robber. 2 But he
who enters by the door is the shepherd of
the sheep. 3 To him the doorkeeper opens,
and the sheep hear his voice; and he calls
his own sheep by name and leads them out.
4 And when he brings out his own sheep,
he goes before them; and the sheep follow
him, for they know his voice. 5 Yet they will
by no means follow a stranger, but will flee
from him, for they do not know the voice of
strangers." 6 Jesus used this illustration, but
they did not understand the things which
He spoke to them.

Jesus the Good Shepherd

7 Then Jesus said to them again, "Most
assuredly, I say to you, I am the door of the
sheep. 8 All who *ever* came before Me[a] are
thieves and robbers, but the sheep did not
hear them. 9 I am the door. If anyone enters
by Me, he will be saved, and will go in and
out and find pasture. 10 The thief does not
come except to steal, and to kill, and to destroy. I have come that they may have life,
and that they may have *it* more abundantly.
11 "I am the good shepherd. The good
shepherd gives His life for the sheep. 12 But
a hireling, *he who is* not the shepherd, one
who does not own the sheep, sees the wolf
coming and leaves the sheep and flees;
and the wolf catches the sheep and scatters
them. 13 The hireling flees because he is a
hireling and does not care about the sheep.
14 I am the good shepherd; and I know My
sheep, and am known by My own. 15 As the
Father knows Me, even so I know the Father;
and I lay down My life for the sheep. 16 And
other sheep I have which are not of this fold;
them also I must bring, and they will hear
My voice; and there will be one flock *and* one
shepherd.
17 "Therefore My Father loves Me, because
I lay down My life that I may take it again.
18 No one takes it from Me, but I lay it down
of Myself. I have power to lay it down, and I
have power to take it again. This command I
have received from My Father."
19 Therefore there was a division again
among the Jews because of these sayings.
20 And many of them said, "He has a demon
and is mad. Why do you listen to Him?"
21 Others said, "These are not the words
of one who has a demon. Can a demon open
the eyes of the blind?"

The Shepherd Knows His Sheep

22 Now it was the Feast of Dedication in

9:35 [a] NU-Text reads *Son of Man.* 10:8 [a] M-Text omits *before Me.*

Jerusalem, and it was winter. [23]And Jesus
walked in the temple, in Solomon's porch.
[24]Then the Jews surrounded Him and said to
Him, "How long do You keep us in doubt? If
You are the Christ, tell us plainly."
[25]Jesus answered them, "I told you, and
you do not believe. The works that I do in
My Father's name, they bear witness of Me.
[26]But you do not believe, because you are not
of My sheep, as I said to you.[a] [27]My sheep
hear My voice, and I know them, and they
follow Me. [28]And I give them eternal life, and
they shall never perish; neither shall anyone
snatch them out of My hand. [29]My Father,
who has given *them* to Me, is greater than all;
and no one is able to snatch *them* out of My
Father's hand. [30]I and *My* Father are one."

10:26 [a] NU-Text omits *as I said to you.*

GRIEF

JESUS KNOWS SADNESS

READ IT: JOHN 11:1–44

GET IT:

We know that Jesus was God, but He was also human. He experienced emotions just as we do.

Lazarus was a family friend of Jesus. Martha and Mary, Lazarus' sisters, sent word to Jesus: "Lord, behold, he whom You love is sick" (v. 3). Lazarus was not some long-lost, crazy uncle, but a close companion. When Lazarus died, Jesus decided to return to Judea. The disciples were worried. The last time they were in Judea, people had tried to kill Jesus. Now He wanted to go back for a dead friend?

When Jesus arrived, Lazarus had been dead for four days. Both Mary and Martha were distressed, and they both said, "If You had been here, my brother would not have died" (vv. 21, 32). The Bible says Jesus groaned in the spirit. Later, in the shortest verse in the English Bible, we learn that "Jesus wept" (v. 35). And shortly after, we're told for the third time of Jesus' grief as He approached the tomb. Scripture makes it very clear Jesus knows what it feels like to have a friend die.

When Jesus saw Lazarus' body, He commanded Lazarus to rise, and Lazarus returned to life. Because of this miracle, the faith of the disciples who were with Jesus, along with the faith of the people who were at the tomb, was increased. Even though Jesus knew what was going to happen in the end, He still experienced the same pain we feel when someone we love passes away.

LIVE IT:

Next time you lose someone or something you treasure, remember Jesus knows the deep pain you're feeling inside. Talk to Him like you would to a friend, sharing what you feel. He understands.

Renewed Efforts to Stone Jesus

31 Then the Jews took up stones again to stone Him. 32 Jesus answered them, "Many good works I have shown you from My Father. For which of those works do you stone Me?"

33 The Jews answered Him, saying, "For a good work we do not stone You, but for blasphemy, and because You, being a Man, make Yourself God."

34 Jesus answered them, "Is it not written in your law, 'I said, "You are gods" '?[a] 35 If He called them gods, to whom the word of God came (and the Scripture cannot be broken), 36 do you say of Him whom the Father sanctified and sent into the world, 'You are blaspheming,' because I said, 'I am the Son of God'? 37 If I do not do the works of My Father, do not believe Me; 38 but if I do, though you do not believe Me, believe the works, that you may know and believe[a] that the Father *is* in Me, and I in Him." 39 Therefore they sought again to seize Him, but He escaped out of their hand.

The Believers Beyond Jordan

40 And He went away again beyond the Jordan to the place where John was baptizing at first, and there He stayed. 41 Then many came to Him and said, "John performed no sign, but all the things that John spoke about this Man were true." 42 And many believed in Him there.

The Death of Lazarus

11 Now a certain *man* was sick, Lazarus of Bethany, the town of Mary and her sister Martha. 2 It was *that* Mary who anointed the Lord with fragrant oil and wiped His feet with her hair, whose brother Lazarus was sick. 3 Therefore the sisters sent to Him, saying, "Lord, behold, he whom You love is sick."

4 When Jesus heard *that,* He said, "This sickness is not unto death, but for the glory of God, that the Son of God may be glorified through it."

5 Now Jesus loved Martha and her sister and Lazarus. 6 *So, when He heard that he was* sick, He stayed two more days in the place where He was. 7 Then after this He said to *the* disciples, "Let us go to Judea again."

8 *The* disciples said to Him, "Rabbi, lately the Jews sought to stone You, and are You going there again?"

9 Jesus answered, "Are there not twelve hours in the day? If anyone walks in the day, he does not stumble, because he sees the light of this world. 10 But if one walks in the night, he stumbles, because the light is not in him." 11 These things He said, and after that He said to them, "Our friend Lazarus sleeps, but I go that I may wake him up."

12 Then His disciples said, "Lord, if he sleeps he will get well." 13 However, Jesus spoke of his death, but they thought that He was speaking about taking rest in sleep.

14 Then Jesus said to them plainly, "Lazarus is dead. 15 And I am glad for your sakes that I was not there, that you may believe. Nevertheless let us go to him."

16 Then Thomas, who is called the Twin, said to his fellow disciples, "Let us also go, that we may die with Him."

I Am the Resurrection and the Life

17 So when Jesus came, He found that he had already been in the tomb four days. 18 Now Bethany was near Jerusalem, about two miles[a] away. 19 And many of the Jews had joined the women around Martha and Mary, to comfort them concerning their brother.

20 Then Martha, as soon as she heard that Jesus was coming, went and met Him, but Mary was sitting in the house. 21 Now Martha *said to Jesus,* "Lord, if You had been here, my brother would not have died. 22 But even now I know that whatever You ask of God, God will give You."

23 Jesus said to her, "Your brother will rise again."

24 Martha said to Him, "I know that he

In Focus

10:35 Word of God God speaking in the Scriptures of the Old and New Testaments. Jesus also is called "the Word" (John 1:1) because He is God's *personal* Word.

11:25 Resurrection Pronounced *rez-er-RECK-shun.* The rising of Jesus from death. Jesus has promised that those who trust Him will also be raised up as He was.

10:34 [a] Psalm 82:6 **10:38** [a] NU-Text reads *understand.*
11:18 [a] Literally *fifteen stadia*

will rise again in the resurrection at the last
day."
25Jesus said to her, "I am the resurrection
and the life. He who believes in Me, though
he may die, he shall live. 26And whoever lives
and believes in Me shall never die. Do you
believe this?"
27She said to Him, "Yes, Lord, I believe
that You are the Christ, the Son of God, who
is to come into the world."

Jesus and Death, the Last Enemy

28And when she had said these things,
she went her way and secretly called Mary
her sister, saying, "The Teacher has come
and is calling for you." 29As soon as she
heard *that,* she arose quickly and came to
Him. 30Now Jesus had not yet come into the
town, but was[a] in the place where Martha
met Him. 31Then the Jews who were with
her in the house, and comforting her, when
they saw that Mary rose up quickly and went
out, followed her, saying, "She is going to the
tomb to weep there."[a]
32Then, when Mary came where Jesus
was, and saw Him, she fell down at His feet,
saying to Him, "Lord, if You had been here,
my brother would not have died."
33Therefore, when Jesus saw her weeping, and the Jews who came with her
weeping, He groaned in the spirit and was
troubled. 34And He said, "Where have you
laid him?"
They said to Him, "Lord, come and see."
35Jesus wept. 36Then the Jews said, "See
how He loved him!"
37And some of them said, "Could not this
Man, who opened the eyes of the blind, also
have kept this man from dying?"

Lazarus Raised from the Dead

38Then Jesus, again groaning in Himself,
came to the tomb. It was a cave, and a stone
lay against it. 39Jesus said, "Take away the
stone."
Martha, the sister of him who was dead,
said to Him, "Lord, by this time there is a
stench, for he has been *dead* four days."
40Jesus said to her, "Did I not say to you
that if you would believe you would see the
glory of God?" 41Then they took away the
stone *from the place* where the dead man was
lying.[a] And Jesus lifted up *His* eyes and said,
"Father, I thank You that You have heard Me.
42And I know that You always hear Me, but
because of the people who are standing by I
said *this,* that they may believe that You sent
Me." 43Now when He had said these things,
He cried with a loud voice, "Lazarus, come
forth!" 44And he who had died came out
bound hand and foot with graveclothes, and
his face was wrapped with a cloth. Jesus said
to them, "Loose him, and let him go."

The Plot to Kill Jesus

45Then many of the Jews who had come
to Mary, and had seen the things Jesus did,
believed in Him. 46But some of them went
away to the Pharisees and told them the
things Jesus did. 47Then the chief priests
and the Pharisees gathered a council and
said, "What shall we do? For this Man works
many signs. 48If we let Him alone like this,
everyone will believe in Him, and the Romans will come and take away both our
place and nation."
49And one of them, Caiaphas, being high
priest that year, said to them, "You know
nothing at all, 50nor do you consider that it
is expedient for us[a] that one man should die
for the people, and not that the whole nation
should perish." 51Now this he did not say on
his own *authority;* but being high priest that
year he prophesied that Jesus would die for
the nation, 52and not for that nation only,
but also that He would gather together in
one the children of God who were scattered
abroad.
53Then, from that day on, they plotted to
put Him to death. 54Therefore Jesus no longer walked openly among the Jews, but went
from there into the country near the wilderness, to a city called Ephraim, and there remained with His disciples.
55And the Passover of the Jews was
near, and many went from the country up
to Jerusalem before the Passover, to purify
themselves. 56Then they sought Jesus, and
spoke among themselves as they stood in the
temple, "What do you think—that He will
not come to the feast?" 57Now both the chief
priests and the Pharisees had given a command, that if anyone knew where He was, he
should report *it,* that they might seize Him.

11:30 [a] NU-Text adds *still.* **11:31** [a] NU-Text reads *supposing that she was going to the tomb to weep there.* **11:41** [a] NU-Text omits *from the place where the dead man was lying.* **11:50** [a] NU-Text reads *you.*

The Anointing at Bethany

12 Then, six days before the Passover, Jesus came to Bethany, where
Lazarus was who had been dead,[a] whom
He had raised from the dead. 2There they
made Him a supper; and Martha served,
but Lazarus was one of those who sat at the
table with Him. 3Then Mary took a pound of
very costly oil of spikenard, anointed the feet
of Jesus, and wiped His feet with her hair.
And the house was filled with the fragrance
of the oil.
4But one of His disciples, Judas Iscariot, Simon's *son,* who would betray Him,
said, 5"Why was this fragrant oil not sold
for three hundred denarii[a] and given to the
poor?" 6This he said, not that he cared for
the poor, but because he was a thief, and had
the money box; and he used to take what was
put in it.
7But Jesus said, "Let her alone; she has
kept[a] this for the day of My burial. 8For the
poor you have with you always, but Me you
do not have always."

The Plot to Kill Lazarus

9Now a great many of the Jews knew
that He was there; and they came, not for
Jesus' sake only, but that they might also
see Lazarus, whom He had raised from the
dead. 10But the chief priests plotted to put
Lazarus to death also, 11because on account
of him many of the Jews went away and believed in Jesus.

The Triumphal Entry

12The next day a great multitude that had
come to the feast, when they heard that Jesus
was coming to Jerusalem, 13took branches of
palm trees and went out to meet Him, and
cried out:

"Hosanna
'Blessed *is* He who comes in the name of
the LORD!' [a]
The King of Israel!"

14Then Jesus, when He had found a
young donkey, sat on it; as it is written:

15 "Fear not, daughter of Zion;
Behold, your King is coming,
Sitting on a donkey's colt." [a]

16His disciples did not understand these
things at first; but when Jesus was glorified,
then they remembered that these things
were written about Him and *that* they had
done these things to Him.
17Therefore the people, who were with
Him when He called Lazarus out of his
tomb and raised him from the dead, bore
witness. 18For this reason the people also
met Him, because they heard that He had
done this sign. 19The Pharisees therefore
said among themselves, "You see that you
are accomplishing nothing. Look, the world
has gone after Him!"

The Fruitful Grain of Wheat

20Now there were certain Greeks among
those who came up to worship at the feast.
21Then they came to Philip, who was from
Bethsaida of Galilee, and asked him, saying,
"Sir, we wish to see Jesus."
22Philip came and told Andrew, and in
turn Andrew and Philip told Jesus.
23But Jesus answered them, saying, "The
hour has come that the Son of Man should
be glorified. 24Most assuredly, I say to you,
unless a grain of wheat falls into the ground
and dies, it remains alone; but if it dies, it
produces much grain. 25He who loves his life
will lose it, and he who hates his life in this
world will keep it for eternal life. 26If anyone
serves Me, let him follow Me; and where I
am, there My servant will be also. If anyone
serves Me, him *My* Father will honor.

Jesus Predicts His Death on the Cross

27"Now My soul is troubled, and what
shall I say? 'Father, save Me from this hour'?
But for this purpose I came to this hour. 28Fa-
ther, glorify Your name."
Then a voice came from heaven, *saying,*
"I have both glorified *it* and will glorify *it*
again."
29Therefore the people who stood by and
heard *it* said that it had thundered. Others
said, "An angel has spoken to Him."
30Jesus answered and said, "This voice
did not come because of Me, but for your
sake. 31Now is the judgment of this world;
now the ruler of this world will be cast out.
32And I, if I am lifted up from the earth, will
draw all *peoples* to Myself." 33This He said,
signifying by what death He would die.
34The people answered Him, "We have

12:1 [a] NU-Text omits *who had been dead.* **12:5** [a] About one year's wages for a worker **12:7** [a] NU-Text reads *that she may keep.* **12:13** [a] Psalm 118:26 **12:15** [a] Zechariah 9:9

heard from the law that the Christ remains
forever; and how *can* You say, 'The Son of
Man must be lifted up'? Who is this Son of
Man?"

35 Then Jesus said to them, "A little while
longer the light is with you. Walk while you
have the light, lest darkness overtake you; he
who walks in darkness does not know where
he is going. 36 While you have the light, believe in the light, that you may become sons
of light." These things Jesus spoke, and departed, and was hidden from them.

Who Has Believed Our Report?

37 But although He had done so many
signs before them, they did not believe in
Him, 38 that the word of Isaiah the prophet
might be fulfilled, which he spoke:

"Lord, who has believed our report?
And to whom has the arm of the LORD
been revealed?" [a]

39 Therefore they could not believe, because Isaiah said again:

40 "He has blinded their eyes and hardened
their hearts,
Lest they should see with *their* eyes,
Lest they should understand with *their*
hearts and turn,
So that I should heal them." [a]

41 These things Isaiah said when[a] he saw His
glory and spoke of Him.

Walk in the Light

42 Nevertheless even among the rulers
many believed in Him, but because of the
Pharisees they did not confess *Him,* lest they
should be put out of the synagogue; 43 for they
loved the praise of men more than the praise
of God.

44 Then Jesus cried out and said, "He who
believes in Me, believes not in Me but in
Him who sent Me. 45 And he who sees Me
sees Him who sent Me. 46 I have come *as* a
light into the world, that whoever believes
in Me should not abide in darkness. 47 And
if anyone hears My words and does not believe,[a] I do not judge him; for I did not come
to judge the world but to save the world.
48 He who rejects Me, and does not receive
My words, has that which judges him—
the word that I have spoken will judge him
in the last day. 49 For I have not spoken on
My own *authority;* but the Father who sent
Me gave Me a command, what I should say
and what I should speak. 50 And I know that
His command is everlasting life. Therefore,
whatever I speak, just as the Father has told
Me, so I speak."

Jesus Washes the Disciples' Feet

13 Now before the Feast of the Passover, when Jesus knew that His
hour had come that He should depart from
this world to the Father, having loved His
own who were in the world, He loved them
to the end.

12:38 [a] Isaiah 53:1 12:40 [a] Isaiah 6:10 12:41 [a] NU-Text reads *because.* 12:47 [a] NU-Text reads *keep them.*

TREATMENT OF OTHERS

READ IT: JOHN 13:1–12

When people walked on dusty roads in Bible times, their feet got really dirty! So washing people's feet was a normal practice, but it was usually a job for servants. When Jesus washed the disciples' feet, He was showing them a whole different way to live. Serve people. Show them love, even if it makes you uncomfortable.

God expects us to live this way, too. Being a servant to others will truly make a difference in the world and will change your life for the better.

give a piece of bread when I have dipped *it*."
And having dipped the bread, He gave *it* to
Judas Iscariot, *the son* of Simon. 27Now after
the piece of bread, Satan entered him. Then
Jesus said to him, "What you do, do quickly."
28But no one at the table knew for what reason He said this to him. 29For some thought,
because Judas had the money box, that Jesus
had said to him, "Buy *those things* we need
for the feast," or that he should give something to the poor.

30Having received the piece of bread, he
then went out immediately. And it was night.

The New Commandment

31So, when he had gone out, Jesus said,
"Now the Son of Man is glorified, and God
is glorified in Him. 32If God is glorified in
Him, God will also glorify Him in Himself,
and glorify Him immediately. 33Little children, I shall be with you a little while longer. You will seek Me; and as I said to the
Jews, 'Where I am going, you cannot come,'
so now I say to you. 34A new commandment
I give to you, that you love one another; as
I have loved you, that you also love one another. 35By this all will know that you are My
disciples, if you have love for one another."

Jesus Predicts Peter's Denial

36Simon Peter said to Him, "Lord, where
are You going?"

Jesus answered him, "Where I am going
you cannot follow Me now, but you shall follow Me afterward."

37Peter said to Him, "Lord, why can I not
follow You now? I will lay down my life for
Your sake."

38Jesus answered him, "Will you lay
down your life for My sake? Most assuredly,
I say to you, the rooster shall not crow till you
have denied Me three times.

The Way, the Truth, and the Life

14 "Let not your heart be troubled; you
believe in God, believe also in Me.
2In My Father's house are many mansions;[a]
if *it were* not *so,* I would have told you. I go to
prepare a place for you.[b] 3And if I go and prepare a place for you, I will come again and
receive you to Myself; that where I am, *there*
you may be also. 4And where I go you know,
and the way you know."

5Thomas said to Him, "Lord, we do not
know where You are going, and how can we
know the way?"

In Focus

14:16 Helper The Holy Spirit, who is sometimes called "the Comforter." The Holy Spirit lives in you when you receive Jesus. He is your "Helper" in understanding God's Word.

6Jesus said to him, "I am the way, the
truth, and the life. No one comes to the Father except through Me.

The Father Revealed

7"If you had known Me, you would have
known My Father also; and from now on you
know Him and have seen Him."

8Philip said to Him, "Lord, show us the
Father, and it is sufficient for us."

9Jesus said to him, "Have I been with
you so long, and yet you have not known Me,
Philip? He who has seen Me has seen the
Father; so how can you say, 'Show us the Father'? 10Do you not believe that I am in the
Father, and the Father in Me? The words
that I speak to you I do not speak on My own
authority; but the Father who dwells in Me
does the works. 11Believe Me that I *am* in the
Father and the Father in Me, or else believe
Me for the sake of the works themselves.

The Answered Prayer

12"Most assuredly, I say to you, he who
believes in Me, the works that I do he will do
also; and greater *works* than these he will do,
because I go to My Father. 13And whatever
you ask in My name, that I will do, that the
Father may be glorified in the Son. 14If you
ask[a] anything in My name, I will do *it.*

Jesus Promises Another Helper

15"If you love Me, keep[a] My commandments. 16And I will pray the Father, and He
will give you another Helper, that He may
abide with you forever— 17the Spirit of truth,
whom the world cannot receive, because it
neither sees Him nor knows Him; but you

14:2 [a] Literally *dwellings* [b] NU-Text adds a word which would cause the text to read either *if it were not so, would I have told you that I go to prepare a place for you?* or *if it were not so I would have told you; for I go to prepare a place for you.* **14:14** [a] NU-Text adds *Me.* **14:15** [a] NU-Text reads *you will keep.*

know Him, for He dwells with you and will
be in you. 18I will not leave you orphans; I
will come to you.

Indwelling of the Father and the Son

19"A little while longer and the world will
see Me no more, but you will see Me. Because I live, you will live also. 20At that day
you will know that I *am* in My Father, and
you in Me, and I in you. 21He who has My
commandments and keeps them, it is he
who loves Me. And he who loves Me will be
loved by My Father, and I will love him and
manifest Myself to him."

22Judas (not Iscariot) said to Him, "Lord,
how is it that You will manifest Yourself to
us, and not to the world?"

23Jesus answered and said to him, "If
anyone loves Me, he will keep My word;
and My Father will love him, and We will
come to him and make Our home with him.
24He who does not love Me does not keep My
words; and the word which you hear is not
Mine but the Father's who sent Me.

The Gift of His Peace

25"These things I have spoken to you
while being present with you. 26But the
Helper, the Holy Spirit, whom the Father
will send in My name, He will teach you all
things, and bring to your remembrance all
things that I said to you. 27Peace I leave with
you, My peace I give to you; not as the world
gives do I give to you. Let not your heart be
troubled, neither let it be afraid. 28You have
heard Me say to you, 'I am going away and
coming *back* to you.' If you loved Me, you
would rejoice because I said,[a] 'I am going to
the Father,' for My Father is greater than I.

29"And now I have told you before it
comes, that when it does come to pass, you
may believe. 30I will no longer talk much
with you, for the ruler of this world is coming, and he has nothing in Me. 31But that the
world may know that I love the Father, and as
the Father gave Me commandment, so I do.
Arise, let us go from here.

The True Vine

15 "I am the true vine, and My Father
is the vinedresser. 2Every branch in
Me that does not bear fruit He takes away;[a]
and every *branch* that bears fruit He prunes,
that it may bear more fruit. 3You are already
clean because of the word which I have spoken to you. 4Abide in Me, and I in you. As

---

14:28 [a] NU-Text omits *I said.* 15:2 [a] Or *lifts up*

15:1 I AM THE TRUE VINE

This is another I AM of Jesus. Why does Jesus describe himself as a vine?

If you ever see a grapevine, you will notice that it is a mass of many branches. Some of the branches have luscious grapes on them. Other branches just use up the life of the vine by making big leaves, but they never make any grapes! So they have to be cut away to let the good branches produce more grapes.

The many branches in Jesus are the people who say they are Christians. Many people are like the vine branches with big leaves, but they don't live for Jesus and they don't do anything for Him that lasts. They LOOK great—but they have no fruit!

Make up your mind that you're going to find out how Jesus wants to work through you. If His life is in you, you will do things for God that will last forever.

the branch cannot bear fruit of itself, unless
it abides in the vine, neither can you, unless
you abide in Me.
5“I am the vine, you *are* the branches. He
who abides in Me, and I in him, bears much
fruit; for without Me you can do nothing. 6If
anyone does not abide in Me, he is cast out
as a branch and is withered; and they gather them and throw *them* into the fire, and
they are burned. 7If you abide in Me, and My
words abide in you, you will[a] ask what you
desire, and it shall be done for you. 8By this
My Father is glorified, that you bear much
fruit; so you will be My disciples.

Love and Joy Perfected

9“As the Father loved Me, I also have
loved you; abide in My love. 10If you keep My
commandments, you will abide in My love,
just as I have kept My Father's commandments and abide in His love.
11“These things I have spoken to you, that
My joy may remain in you, and *that* your joy
may be full. 12This is My commandment,
that you love one another as I have loved you.
13Greater love has no one than this, than to
lay down one's life for his friends. 14You are
My friends if you do whatever I command
you. 15No longer do I call you servants, for
a servant does not know what his master is
doing; but I have called you friends, for all
things that I heard from My Father I have
made known to you. 16You did not choose
Me, but I chose you and appointed you that
you should go and bear fruit, and *that* your
fruit should remain, that whatever you ask
the Father in My name He may give you.
17These things I command you, that you love
one another.

The World's Hatred

18“If the world hates you, you know that
it hated Me before *it hated* you. 19If you were
of the world, the world would love its own.
Yet because you are not of the world, but
I chose you out of the world, therefore the
world hates you. 20Remember the word that I
said to you, ‘A servant is not greater than his
master.’ If they persecuted Me, they will also
persecute you. If they kept My word, they
will keep yours also. 21But all these things
they will do to you for My name's sake, because they do not know Him who sent Me.
22If I had not come and spoken to them, they
would have no sin, but now they have no excuse for their sin. 23He who hates Me hates
My Father also. 24If I had not done among
them the works which no one else did, they
would have no sin; but now they have seen
and also hated both Me and My Father.
25But *this happened* that the word might be
fulfilled which is written in their law, ‘They
hated Me without a cause.’ [a]

The Coming Rejection

26“But when the Helper comes, whom I

15:7 [a] NU-Text omits *you will.* 15:25 [a] Psalm 69:4

FRIENDSHIP

READ IT: JOHN 15:13–15

What a supreme privilege and gift that Christ would consider you His friend! He demonstrated His friendship to you by sharing God's truth and love with you and dying for you on the cross. And what does He ask in return? That you follow Him and the ways He wants you to live. Scripture is filled with His commands, including how to be a friend to others. You probably will never face the situation of dying in place of a friend, but you can definitely love, encourage, and listen to your friend even when that's really tough to do.

shall send to you from the Father, the Spirit
of truth who proceeds from the Father, He
will testify of Me. 27 And you also will bear
witness, because you have been with Me
from the beginning.

16 "These things I have spoken to
you, that you should not be made to
stumble. 2 They will put you out of the synagogues; yes, the time is coming that whoever
kills you will think that he offers God service. 3 And these things they will do to you[a]
because they have not known the Father nor
Me. 4 But these things I have told you, that
when the[a] time comes, you may remember
that I told you of them.

"And these things I did not say to you at
the beginning, because I was with you.

The Work of the Holy Spirit

5 "But now I go away to Him who sent
Me, and none of you asks Me, 'Where are
You going?' 6 But because I have said these
things to you, sorrow has filled your heart.
7 Nevertheless I tell you the truth. It is to your
advantage that I go away; for if I do not go
away, the Helper will not come to you; but if
I depart, I will send Him to you. 8 And when
He has come, He will convict the world of
sin, and of righteousness, and of judgment:
9 of sin, because they do not believe in Me;
10 of righteousness, because I go to My Father
and you see Me no more; 11 of judgment, because the ruler of this world is judged.

12 "I still have many things to say to you,
but you cannot bear *them* now. 13 However,
when He, the Spirit of truth, has come, He
will guide you into all truth; for He will not
speak on His own *authority,* but whatever
He hears He will speak; and He will tell
you things to come. 14 He will glorify Me, for
He will take of what is Mine and declare *it*
to you. 15 All things that the Father has are
Mine. Therefore I said that He will take of
Mine and declare *it* to you.[a]

Sorrow Will Turn to Joy

16 "A little while, and you will not see Me;
and again a little while, and you will see Me,
because I go to the Father."

17 Then *some* of His disciples said among
themselves, "What is this that He says to
us, 'A little while, and you will not see Me;
and again a little while, and you will see Me';
and, 'because I go to the Father'?" 18 They

16:3 [a] NU-Text and M-Text omit *to you.* 16:4 [a] NU-Text reads *their.* 16:15 [a] NU-Text and M-Text read *He takes of Mine and will declare it to you.*

16:33 DON'T BE AFRAID

Some people are afraid of the dark. Others are afraid of heights. Many people are just afraid of being in a world of so many sights and sounds.

We're sometimes afraid of the things we don't understand. That's one reason Jesus came—so that you could know the truth. Then you would never need to be afraid again.

You aren't God, and you can't know all that God knows. So you have to live in a world you often don't understand. What can you do about that? Of course, you can read a lot and learn more about your world and yourself, but you soon find out that the more you learn, the more there is still to learn.

God knows all, and He will take care of you. You can trust Him with your life and with everything you don't understand. Then you won't be afraid anymore.

said therefore, "What is this that He says,
'A little while'? We do not know what He is
saying."
19 Now Jesus knew that they desired to
ask Him, and He said to them, "Are you in-
quiring among yourselves about what I said,
'A little while, and you will not see Me; and
again a little while, and you will see Me'?
20 Most assuredly, I say to you that you will
weep and lament, but the world will rejoice;
and you will be sorrowful, but your sorrow
will be turned into joy. 21 A woman, when she
is in labor, has sorrow because her hour has
come; but as soon as she has given birth to
the child, she no longer remembers the anguish, for joy that a human being has been
born into the world. 22 Therefore you now
have sorrow; but I will see you again and
your heart will rejoice, and your joy no one
will take from you.
23 "And in that day you will ask Me nothing. Most assuredly, I say to you, whatever
you ask the Father in My name He will give
you. 24 Until now you have asked nothing in
My name. Ask, and you will receive, that
your joy may be full.

Jesus Christ Has Overcome the World

25 "These things I have spoken to you in
figurative language; but the time is coming
when I will no longer speak to you in figurative language, but I will tell you plainly
about the Father. 26 In that day you will ask
in My name, and I do not say to you that I
shall pray the Father for you; 27 for the Father
Himself loves you, because you have loved
Me, and have believed that I came forth from
God. 28 I came forth from the Father and have
come into the world. Again, I leave the world
and go to the Father."
29 His disciples said to Him, "See, now
You are speaking plainly, and using no figure of speech! 30 Now we are sure that You
know all things, and have no need that anyone should question You. By this we believe
that You came forth from God."
31 Jesus answered them, "Do you now believe? 32 Indeed the hour is coming, yes, has
now come, that you will be scattered, each
to his own, and will leave Me alone. And yet
I am not alone, because the Father is with
Me. 33 These things I have spoken to you, that
in Me you may have peace. In the world you
will[a] have tribulation; but be of good cheer, I
have overcome the world."

Jesus Prays for Himself

17 Jesus spoke these words, lifted up
His eyes to heaven, and said: "Father, the hour has come. Glorify Your Son,
that Your Son also may glorify You, 2 as You
have given Him authority over all flesh, that
He should[a] give eternal life to as many as
You have given Him. 3 And this is eternal
life, that they may know You, the only true
God, and Jesus Christ whom You have sent.
4 I have glorified You on the earth. I have finished the work which You have given Me to
do. 5 And now, O Father, glorify Me together
with Yourself, with the glory which I had
with You before the world was.

Jesus Prays for His Disciples

6 "I have manifested Your name to the
men whom You have given Me out of the
world. They were Yours, You gave them to
Me, and they have kept Your word. 7 Now
they have known that all things which You
have given Me are from You. 8 For I have giv-
en to them the words which You have given
Me; and they have received *them,* and have
known surely that I came forth from You;
and they have believed that You sent Me.
9 "I pray for them. I do not pray for the
world but for those whom You have given Me,
for they are Yours. 10 And all Mine are Yours,
and Yours are Mine, and I am glorified in
them. 11 Now I am no longer in the world, but
these are in the world, and I come to You.
Holy Father, keep through Your name those
whom You have given Me,[a] that they may be
one as We *are.* 12 While I was with them in
the world,[a] I kept them in Your name. Those
whom You gave Me I have kept;[b] and none of
them is lost except the son of perdition, that
the Scripture might be fulfilled. 13 But now I
come to You, and these things I speak in the
world, that they may have My joy fulfilled in
themselves. 14 I have given them Your word;
and the world has hated them because they
are not of the world, just as I am not of the
world. 15 I do not pray that You should take
them out of the world, but that You should
keep them from the evil one. 16 They are not
of the world, just as I am not of the world.
17 Sanctify them by Your truth. Your word is

16:33 [a] NU-Text and M-Text omit *will.* **17:2** [a] M-Text reads *shall.* **17:11** [a] NU-Text and M-Text read *keep them through Your name which You have given Me.* **17:12** [a] NU-Text omits *in the world.* [b] NU-Text reads *in Your name which You gave Me. And I guarded them;* (or *it;*).

truth. [18]As You sent Me into the world, I also
have sent them into the world. [19]And for their
sakes I sanctify Myself, that they also may be
sanctified by the truth.

Jesus Prays for All Believers

[20]"I do not pray for these alone, but also
for those who will[a] believe in Me through
their word; [21]that they all may be one, as You,
Father, *are* in Me, and I in You; that they also
may be one in Us, that the world may believe
that You sent Me. [22]And the glory which You
gave Me I have given them, that they may be
one just as We are one: [23]I in them, and You
in Me; that they may be made perfect in one,
and that the world may know that You have
sent Me, and have loved them as You have
loved Me.

[24]"Father, I desire that they also whom
You gave Me may be with Me where I am,
that they may behold My glory which You
have given Me; for You loved Me before the
foundation of the world. [25]O righteous Father! The world has not known You, but I
have known You; and these have known that
You sent Me. [26]And I have declared to them
Your name, and will declare *it*, that the love
with which You loved Me may be in them,
and I in them."

17:20 [a] NU-Text and M-Text omit *will*.

THE BIBLE IS THE TRUTH
FACT OR FICTION?

READ IT: JOHN 17:17

GET IT:

Sometimes we get "facts" and "truth" confused. They're not the same thing. Some of the best works of fiction (nonfactual, made-up stories) are full of truth. The Bible has lots of facts in it—real events, real people, real places. The Bible also has nonfactual things in it—parables, poems, dreams, visions, and songs. All of the nonfactual things in the Bible are full of truth, just as much as the historical events.

The stories about Jesus are factual—they really happened. But they are also true—they have something to teach us about life, God, and ourselves. The letters in the New Testament are factual—they were written and read by real people. But they are also true.

LIVE IT:

When you read the Bible, look for truth. The facts point to something deeper, something more important. Fact: Some of Jesus' closest friends were fisherman. Truth: Anyone—even if they don't have the most glamorous or highest paying job—is invited to be a close friend of Jesus. Fact: David was younger, smaller, and weaker than Goliath. Truth: Regardless of your age, size, or status, God can use you to accomplish amazing things *if you'll let Him.*

So open that Bible. Read. Notice the facts. Then dig for the truth.

Betrayal and Arrest in Gethsemane

18 When Jesus had spoken these
words, He went out with His disciples over the Brook Kidron, where there
was a garden, which He and His disciples
entered. 2 And Judas, who betrayed Him, also
knew the place; for Jesus often met there
with His disciples. 3 Then Judas, having received a detachment *of troops,* and officers
from the chief priests and Pharisees, came
there with lanterns, torches, and weapons.
4 Jesus therefore, knowing all things that
would come upon Him, went forward and
said to them, "Whom are you seeking?"
5 They answered Him, "Jesus of Nazareth."
Jesus said to them, "I am *He.*" And Judas,
who betrayed Him, also stood with them.
6 Now when He said to them, "I am *He,*" they
drew back and fell to the ground.
7 Then He asked them again, "Whom are
you seeking?"
And they said, "Jesus of Nazareth."
8 Jesus answered, "I have told you that I
am *He.* Therefore, if you seek Me, let these
go their way," 9 that the saying might be fulfilled which He spoke, "Of those whom You
gave Me I have lost none."
10 Then Simon Peter, having a sword,
drew it and struck the high priest's servant,
and cut off his right ear. The servant's name
was Malchus.
11 So Jesus said to Peter, "Put your sword
into the sheath. Shall I not drink the cup
which My Father has given Me?"

Before the High Priest

12 Then the detachment *of troops* and the
captain and the officers of the Jews arrested
Jesus and bound Him. 13 And they led Him
away to Annas first, for he was the father-
in-law of Caiaphas who was high priest that
year. 14 Now it was Caiaphas who advised
the Jews that it was expedient that one man
should die for the people.

Peter Denies Jesus

15 And Simon Peter followed Jesus, and
so *did* another[a] disciple. Now that disciple
was known to the high priest, and went with
Jesus into the courtyard of the high priest.
16 But Peter stood at the door outside. Then
the other disciple, who was known to the
high priest, went out and spoke to her who
kept the door, and brought Peter in. 17 Then
the servant girl who kept the door said to
Peter, "You are not also *one* of this Man's disciples, are you?"
He said, "I am not."
18 Now the servants and officers who had
made a fire of coals stood there, for it was
cold, and they warmed themselves. And Peter stood with them and warmed himself.

Jesus Questioned by the High Priest

19 The high priest then asked Jesus about
His disciples and His doctrine.
20 Jesus answered him, "I spoke openly to
the world. I always taught in synagogues and
in the temple, where the Jews always meet,[a]
and in secret I have said nothing. 21 Why do
you ask Me? Ask those who have heard Me
what I said to them. Indeed they know what
I said."
22 And when He had said these things,
one of the officers who stood by struck Jesus
with the palm of his hand, saying, "Do You
answer the high priest like that?"
23 Jesus answered him, "If I have spoken
evil, bear witness of the evil; but if well, why
do you strike Me?"
24 Then Annas sent Him bound to
Caiaphas the high priest.

Peter Denies Twice More

25 Now Simon Peter stood and warmed
himself. Therefore they said to him, "You
are not also *one* of His disciples, are you?"
He denied *it* and said, "I am not!"
26 One of the servants of the high priest, a
relative *of him* whose ear Peter cut off, said,
"Did I not see you in the garden with Him?"
27 Peter then denied again; and immediately
a rooster crowed.

In Pilate's Court

28 Then they led Jesus from Caiaphas to
the Praetorium, and it was early morning.
But they themselves did not go into the Praetorium, lest they should be defiled, but that
they might eat the Passover. 29 Pilate then
went out to them and said, "What accusation
do you bring against this Man?"
30 They answered and said to him, "If He
were not an evildoer, we would not have delivered Him up to you."
31 Then Pilate said to them, "You take
Him and judge Him according to your law."

18:15 [a] M-Text reads *the other.* **18:20** [a] NU-Text reads *where all the Jews meet.*

Therefore the Jews said to him, "It is
not lawful for us to put anyone to death,"
32 that the saying of Jesus might be fulfilled
which He spoke, signifying by what death
He would die.

33 Then Pilate entered the Praetorium
again, called Jesus, and said to Him, "Are
You the King of the Jews?"

34 Jesus answered him, "Are you speaking
for yourself about this, or did others tell you
this concerning Me?"

35 Pilate answered, "Am I a Jew? Your own
nation and the chief priests have delivered
You to me. What have You done?"

36 Jesus answered, "My kingdom is not
of this world. If My kingdom were of this
world, My servants would fight, so that I
should not be delivered to the Jews; but now
My kingdom is not from here."

37 Pilate therefore said to Him, "Are You
a king then?"

Jesus answered, "You say *rightly* that I
am a king. For this cause I was born, and for
this cause I have come into the world, that I
should bear witness to the truth. Everyone
who is of the truth hears My voice."

38 Pilate said to Him, "What is truth?"
And when he had said this, he went out
again to the Jews, and said to them, "I find
no fault in Him at all.

Taking the Place of Barabbas

39 "But you have a custom that I should
release someone to you at the Passover. Do
you therefore want me to release to you the
King of the Jews?"

40 Then they all cried again, saying, "Not
this Man, but Barabbas!" Now Barabbas was
a robber.

The Soldiers Mock Jesus

19 So then Pilate took Jesus and
scourged *Him*. 2 And the soldiers
twisted a crown of thorns and put *it* on His
head, and they put on Him a purple robe.
3 Then they said,[a] "Hail, King of the Jews!"
And they struck Him with their hands.

4 Pilate then went out again, and said to
them, "Behold, I am bringing Him out to
you, that you may know that I find no fault
in Him."

Pilate's Decision

5 Then Jesus came out, wearing the
crown of thorns and the purple robe. And
Pilate said to them, "Behold the Man!"

6 Therefore, when the chief priests and
officers saw Him, they cried out, saying,
"Crucify *Him*, crucify *Him!*"

Pilate said to them, "You take Him and
crucify *Him*, for I find no fault in Him."

7 The Jews answered him, "We have a law,
and according to our[a] law He ought to die,
because He made Himself the Son of God."

8 Therefore, when Pilate heard that
saying, he was the more afraid, 9 and went
again into the Praetorium, and said to Jesus,
"Where are You from?" But Jesus gave him
no answer.

10 Then Pilate said to Him, "Are You not
speaking to me? Do You not know that I
have power to crucify You, and power to release You?"

11 Jesus answered, "You could have no
power at all against Me unless it had been
given you from above. Therefore the one who
delivered Me to you has the greater sin."

12 From then on Pilate sought to release
Him, but the Jews cried out, saying, "If you
let this Man go, you are not Caesar's friend.
Whoever makes himself a king speaks
against Caesar."

13 When Pilate therefore heard that saying, he brought Jesus out and sat down in
the judgment seat in a place that is called
The Pavement, but in Hebrew, Gabbatha.
14 Now it was the Preparation Day of the Passover, and about the sixth hour. And he said
to the Jews, "Behold your King!"

15 But they cried out, "Away with *Him*,
away with *Him!* Crucify Him!"

Pilate said to them, "Shall I crucify your
King?"

The chief priests answered, "We have no
king but Caesar!"

16 Then he delivered Him to them to be
crucified. Then they took Jesus and led *Him*
away.[a]

The King on a Cross

17 And He, bearing His cross, went out
to a place called *the Place* of a Skull, which
is called in Hebrew, Golgotha, 18 where they
crucified Him, and two others with Him,
one on either side, and Jesus in the center.
19 Now Pilate wrote a title and put *it* on the
cross. And the writing was:

19:3 [a] NU-Text reads *And they came up to Him and said.*
19:7 [a] NU-Text reads *the law.* 19:16 [a] NU-Text omits *and led Him away.*

She said to them, "Because they have tak-
en away my Lord, and I do not know where
they have laid Him."
14Now when she had said this, she turned
around and saw Jesus standing *there,* and
did not know that it was Jesus. 15Jesus said to
her, "Woman, why are you weeping? Whom
are you seeking?"
She, supposing Him to be the gardener,
said to Him, "Sir, if You have carried Him
away, tell me where You have laid Him, and
I will take Him away."
16Jesus said to her, "Mary!"
She turned and said to Him,[a] "Rabboni!"
(which is to say, Teacher).
17Jesus said to her, "Do not cling to Me,
for I have not yet ascended to My Father; but
go to My brethren and say to them, 'I am ascending to My Father and your Father, and
to My God and your God.'"
18Mary Magdalene came and told the disciples that she had seen the Lord,[a] and *that*
He had spoken these things to her.

The Apostles Commissioned

19Then, the same day at evening, being
the first *day* of the week, when the doors were
shut where the disciples were assembled,[a] for
fear of the Jews, Jesus came and stood in the
midst, and said to them, "Peace *be* with you."
20When He had said this, He showed them
His hands and His side. Then the disciples
were glad when they saw the Lord.
21So Jesus said to them again, "Peace to
you! As the Father has sent Me, I also send
you." 22And when He had said this, He
breathed on *them,* and said to them, "Receive
the Holy Spirit. 23If you forgive the sins of
any, they are forgiven them; if you retain the
sins of any, they are retained."

Seeing and Believing

24Now Thomas, called the Twin, one of
the twelve, was not with them when Jesus
came. 25The other disciples therefore said to
him, "We have seen the Lord."
So he said to them, "Unless I see in His
hands the print of the nails, and put my finger into the print of the nails, and put my
hand into His side, I will not believe."
26And after eight days His disciples were
again inside, and Thomas with them. Jesus
came, the doors being shut, and stood in the
midst, and said, "Peace to you!" 27Then He
said to Thomas, "Reach your finger here,
and look at My hands; and reach your hand
here, and put *it* into My side. Do not be unbelieving, but believing."
28And Thomas answered and said to
Him, "My Lord and my God!"
29Jesus said to him, "Thomas,[a] because
you have seen Me, you have believed.
Blessed *are* those who have not seen and *yet*
have believed."

That You May Believe

30And truly Jesus did many other signs in
the presence of His disciples, which are not
written in this book; 31but these are written
that you may believe that Jesus is the Christ,
the Son of God, and that believing you may
have life in His name.

Breakfast by the Sea

21 After these things Jesus showed
Himself again to the disciples at the
Sea of Tiberias, and in this way He showed
Himself: 2Simon Peter, Thomas called the
Twin, Nathanael of Cana in Galilee, the *sons*
of Zebedee, and two others of His disciples
were together. 3Simon Peter said to them, "I
am going fishing."
They said to him, "We are going with
you also." They went out and immediately[a]
got into the boat, and that night they caught
nothing. 4But when the morning had now
come, Jesus stood on the shore; yet the disciples did not know that it was Jesus. 5Then
Jesus said to them, "Children, have you any
food?"
They answered Him, "No."
6And He said to them, "Cast the net on
the right side of the boat, and you will find
some." So they cast, and now they were not
able to draw it in because of the multitude
of fish.
7Therefore that disciple whom Jesus
loved said to Peter, "It is the Lord!" Now
when Simon Peter heard that it was the
Lord, he put on *his* outer garment (for he had
removed it), and plunged into the sea. 8But
the other disciples came in the little boat (for
they were not far from land, but about two
hundred cubits), dragging the net with fish.
9Then, as soon as they had come to land,

20:16 [a] NU-Text adds *in Hebrew.* **20:18** [a] NU-Text reads *disciples, "I have seen the Lord," . . .* **20:19** [a] NU-Text omits *assembled.* **20:29** [a] NU-Text and M-Text omit *Thomas.* **21:3** [a] NU-Text omits *immediately.*

they saw a fire of coals there, and fish laid
on it, and bread. 10 Jesus said to them, "Bring
some of the fish which you have just caught."
11 Simon Peter went up and dragged the
net to land, full of large fish, one hundred
and fifty-three; and although there were so
many, the net was not broken. 12 Jesus said
to them, "Come *and* eat breakfast." Yet none
of the disciples dared ask Him, "Who are
You?"—knowing that it was the Lord. 13 Jesus
then came and took the bread and gave it to
them, and likewise the fish.
14 This *is* now the third time Jesus showed
Himself to His disciples after He was raised
from the dead.

Jesus Restores Peter

15 So when they had eaten breakfast, Jesus
said to Simon Peter, "Simon, *son* of Jonah,[a]
do you love Me more than these?"
He said to Him, "Yes, Lord; You know
that I love You."
He said to him, "Feed My lambs."
16 He said to him again a second time,
"Simon, *son* of Jonah,[a] do you love Me?"
He said to Him, "Yes, Lord; You know
that I love You."
He said to him, "Tend My sheep."

21:15 [a] NU-Text reads *John*. 21:16 [a] NU-Text reads *John*.

BREAKFAST ON THE BEACH

READ IT: JOHN 21:1–19

GET IT:

In the weeks after Jesus arose, He appeared to His disciples two times when they were all together in one room. Then one morning, while His disciples were out in their boat fishing, Jesus showed up on the beach. The fishermen had no idea who was shouting at them, but they listened to His instructions and caught a boatload of fish. Then John realized Jesus was the person standing on the edge of the water. After coming to shore, the disciples sat down with Jesus for breakfast. Jesus asked Peter three times, "Do you love Me?" (vv. 15–17). Peter answered, "Yes, Lord; You know that I love You" (vv. 15, 16). Then Jesus gave him instructions to care for His "sheep," the people who would become the new believers in the church.

LIVE IT:

Every once in a while, your mom or dad, a coach, or a teacher may have to ask you more than once to do something. It's bad enough if the person asks twice. But it's really annoying if he or she repeats the same request three times. Jesus asked Peter if he loved Him three times. In reply, Jesus said more than "That's good." He asked Peter to do something. If you love Jesus, you need to go beyond just saying you love Him in a prayer or song. You need to show you love Jesus by loving and caring for others. What can you do this week that will show Jesus your love for Him by showing care and love to others?

Prologue

1 The former account I made, O Theophilus, of all that Jesus began both to do
and teach, 2until the day in which He was
taken up, after He through the Holy Spirit
had given commandments to the apostles
whom He had chosen, 3to whom He also presented Himself alive after His suffering by
many infallible proofs, being seen by them
during forty days and speaking of the things
pertaining to the kingdom of God.

The Holy Spirit Promised

4And being assembled together with
them, He commanded them not to depart
from Jerusalem, but to wait for the Promise
of the Father, "which," *He said,* "you have
heard from Me; 5for John truly baptized
with water, but you shall be baptized with
the Holy Spirit not many days from now."
6Therefore, when they had come together,
they asked Him, saying, "Lord, will You at
this time restore the kingdom to Israel?"
7And He said to them, "It is not for you to
know times or seasons which the Father has
put in His own authority. 8But you shall receive power when the Holy Spirit has come
upon you; and you shall be witnesses to Me[a]
in Jerusalem, and in all Judea and Samaria,
and to the end of the earth."

Jesus Ascends to Heaven

9Now when He had spoken these things,
while they watched, He was taken up, and a
cloud received Him out of their sight. 10And
while they looked steadfastly toward heaven
as He went up, behold, two men stood by
them in white apparel, 11who also said, "Men
of Galilee, why do you stand gazing up into
heaven? This *same* Jesus, who was taken up
from you into heaven, will so come in like
manner as you saw Him go into heaven."

The Upper Room Prayer Meeting

12Then they returned to Jerusalem from
the mount called Olivet, which is near Jerusalem, a Sabbath day's journey. 13And when
they had entered, they went up into the upper room where they were staying: Peter,
James, John, and Andrew; Philip and Thomas; Bartholomew and Matthew; James *the*
son of Alphaeus and Simon the Zealot; and
Judas *the son* of James. 14These all continued
with one accord in prayer and supplication,[a]
with the women and Mary the mother of
Jesus, and with His brothers.

Matthias Chosen

15And in those days Peter stood up in
the midst of the disciples[a] (altogether the
number of names was about a hundred and
twenty), and said, 16"Men *and* brethren, this
Scripture had to be fulfilled, which the Holy
Spirit spoke before by the mouth of David
concerning Judas, who became a guide to
those who arrested Jesus; 17for he was numbered with us and obtained a part in this
ministry."

18(Now this man purchased a field with
the wages of iniquity; and falling headlong,
he burst open in the middle and all his entrails gushed out. 19And it became known to
all those dwelling in Jerusalem; so that field
is called in their own language, Akel Dama,
that is, Field of Blood.)

1:8 [a] NU-Text reads *My witnesses.* 1:14 [a] NU-Text omits *and supplication.* 1:15 [a] NU-Text reads *brethren.*

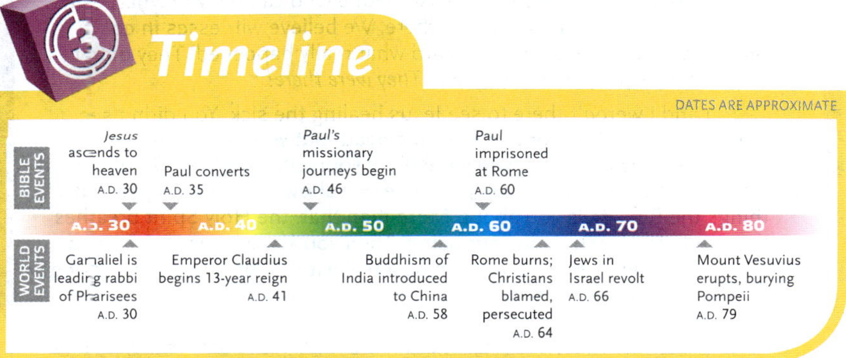

20"For it is written in the Book of Psalms:

'Let his dwelling place be desolate,
And let no one live in it';[a]

and,

'Let [b] another take his office.' [c]

21"Therefore, of these men who have
accompanied us all the time that the Lord
Jesus went in and out among us, 22begin-
ning from the baptism of John to that day
when He was taken up from us, one of
these must become a witness with us of His
resurrection."
23And they proposed two: Joseph called
Barsabas, who was surnamed Justus, and
Matthias. 24And they prayed and said, "You,
O Lord, who know the hearts of all, show
which of these two You have chosen 25to take
part in this ministry and apostleship from
which Judas by transgression fell, that he
might go to his own place." 26And they cast
their lots, and the lot fell on Matthias. And
he was numbered with the eleven apostles.

Coming of the Holy Spirit

2 When the Day of Pentecost had fully
come, they were all with one accord[a]
in one place. 2And suddenly there came a
sound from heaven, as of a rushing mighty
wind, and it filled the whole house where
they were sitting. 3Then there appeared to
them divided tongues, as of fire, and *one* sat
upon each of them. 4And they were all filled
with the Holy Spirit and began to speak
with other tongues, as the Spirit gave them
utterance.

The Crowd's Response

5And there were dwelling in Jerusalem
Jews, devout men, from every nation under
heaven. 6And when this sound occurred,
the multitude came together, and were confused, because everyone heard them speak
in his own language. 7Then they were all
amazed and marveled, saying to one another, "Look, are not all these who speak Galileans? 8And how *is it that* we hear, each in
our own language in which we were born?
9Parthians and Medes and Elamites, those
dwelling in Mesopotamia, Judea and Cappadocia, Pontus and Asia, 10Phrygia and

1:20 [a] Psalm 69:25 [b] Psalm 109:8 [c] Greek *episkopen*, position of overseer 2:1 [a] NU-Text reads *together.*

ARE YOU A WITNESS FOR JESUS?

READ IT: ACTS 1:8

What is a witness? A witness is someone who can tell you what really happened because he or she was there. We believe witnesses in court only when they have seen and heard what really happened. They didn't hear the news from someone else. *They were there!*

You and I weren't there to see Jesus healing the sick. You didn't see Him die on the Cross or rise from the dead. But you can know that He did those things just as if you were there yourself. How? The Spirit of God travels across time and takes you there. He shows your *inner* eyes those things the Bible tells you about. More than that, the Holy Spirit breathes the risen life of Jesus into your being. Then you *know* Jesus is risen and alive and living in you! So you can be a real witness of what He has done to make you a new person.

Pamphylia, Egypt and the parts of Libya
adjoining Cyrene, visitors from Rome, both
Jews and proselytes, 11Cretans and Arabs—
we hear them speaking in our own tongues
the wonderful works of God." 12So they were
all amazed and perplexed, saying to one another, "Whatever could this mean?"
13Others mocking said, "They are full of
new wine."

Peter's Sermon

14But Peter, standing up with the eleven,
raised his voice and said to them, "Men of
Judea and all who dwell in Jerusalem, let this
be known to you, and heed my words. 15For
these are not drunk, as you suppose, since it
is *only* the third hour of the day. 16But this is
what was spoken by the prophet Joel:

In Focus

2:1 Day of Pentecost The day coming fifty days after the Jewish Passover (see definition of Passover at Exodus 12:11). Pentecost (pronounced *PEN-tih-cost*) is also called the Feast of Harvest.

17 'And it shall come to pass in the last
days, says God,
That I will pour out of My Spirit on all
flesh;

On Location

Major Areas in Acts

The story covers the first 30 years of Christian history, beginning in Jerusalem. There, the apostles witness the ascension of Jesus into heaven. Ten days later, when the promised Holy Spirit arrives and fills them with power and boldness, the men immediately start preaching the good news about Jesus. Thousands convert. The church quickly expands beyond Jerusalem into most of the Roman Empire. Within three decades Christians are worshiping in house churches throughout what is now Israel, Syria, Turkey, Greece, and even Rome, some 2,000 miles away.

Your sons and your daughters shall prophesy,
Your young men shall see visions,
Your old men shall dream dreams.
18 And on My menservants and on My maidservants
I will pour out My Spirit in those days;
And they shall prophesy.
19 I will show wonders in heaven above
And signs in the earth beneath:
Blood and fire and vapor of smoke.
20 The sun shall be turned into darkness,
And the moon into blood,
Before the coming of the great and awesome day of the LORD.
21 And it shall come to pass
That whoever calls on the name of the LORD
Shall be saved.' [a]

22 "Men of Israel, hear these words: Jesus of Nazareth, a Man attested by God to you by miracles, wonders, and signs which God did through Him in your midst, as

2:21 [a] Joel 2:28–32

THE HOLY SPIRIT COMES AT PENTECOST

READ IT: ACTS 2:1–47

GET IT:

After His resurrection, Jesus stayed on earth for another forty days. Then one day, while He was with His disciples, Jesus was suddenly taken up into heaven. His ministry on earth was complete. It was now up to the disciples to spread the good news. Jesus had told them to remain in Jerusalem until they were baptized with the Holy Spirit. On the day of Pentecost, when they were all together in one room, the Holy Spirit came with something that sounded like wind and looked like flames. Suddenly the people in the room could speak in all sorts of other languages. The Holy Spirit gave those in the room special abilities to preach, teach, and perform miracles. Now they were fully prepared to share the good news throughout the area and in the world.

LIVE IT:

On Pentecost, everyone knew that God's Spirit had entered the room. There was absolutely no doubt. Throughout the Bible, God made His presence known in different ways at different times. Sometimes He was loud and obvious—like at Mount Sinai (Exodus 19:16–19); sometimes He spoke in a whisper (1 Kings 19:12). So how do we know God's presence today? Sometimes He speaks during a worship service when everyone is singing at the top of their voices. He also speaks through His Word and through the wisdom of others. But most of the time He speaks when we are quiet and thinking about Him. "Be still, and know that I am God" (Psalm 46:10).

you yourselves also know— 23 Him, being
delivered by the determined purpose and
foreknowledge of God, you have taken[a] by
lawless hands, have crucified, and put to
death; 24 whom God raised up, having loosed
the pains of death, because it was not possible that He should be held by it. 25 For David
says concerning Him:

'I foresaw the LORD always before my
face,
For He is at my right hand, that I may
not be shaken.
26 Therefore my heart rejoiced, and my
tongue was glad;
Moreover my flesh also will rest in
hope.
27 For You will not leave my soul in Hades,
Nor will You allow Your Holy One to see
corruption.
28 You have made known to me the ways of
life;
You will make me full of joy in Your
presence.'[a]

29 "Men *and* brethren, let *me* speak freely
to you of the patriarch David, that he is both
dead and buried, and his tomb is with us to
this day. 30 Therefore, being a prophet, and
knowing that God had sworn with an oath
to him that of the fruit of his body, according

2:23 [a] NU-Text omits *have taken*. 2:28 [a] Psalm 16:8–11

Epic Ideas

JESUS IS THE WAY
ONE WAY

READ IT: ACTS 2:14–41

GET IT:

In this passage, Peter points to some really important truth for us. He and the other Jesus followers had just experienced the Holy Spirit coming on them, and many were speaking in languages they didn't know, praising God. Others who spoke those languages were hearing about God, but they were confused about how the people knew those languages. They decided the Jesus followers must be drunk!

Peter explained what was going on. He gave a short overview of who Jesus was and is—the Son of God who came to save the world. All those listening had their own religions and worshiped other gods. But Peter was clear: the God you're hearing about here is the one and only true God. And His Son, Jesus, is the only way to God.

This story could easily happen today. You'll hear lots of people telling you that all religions are equal, or that Jesus is one of many ways to God. But the Bible tells us that Jesus is the only Savior and the only way to God.

LIVE IT:

What do you believe about Jesus? Do you believe, like some, that He was a wise teacher and nothing more than that? Or do you believe, as the Bible says, that Jesus is the one and only Savior, the only One who can help us have a relationship with God?

to the flesh, He would raise up the Christ to
sit on his throne,[a] 31he, foreseeing this, spoke
concerning the resurrection of the Christ,
that His soul was not left in Hades, nor did
His flesh see corruption. 32This Jesus God
has raised up, of which we are all witnesses.
33Therefore being exalted to the right hand
of God, and having received from the Father
the promise of the Holy Spirit, He poured
out this which you now see and hear.
34"For David did not ascend into the heavens, but he says himself:

'The LORD said to my Lord,
"Sit at My right hand,
35 Till I make Your enemies Your footstool."'[a]

36"Therefore let all the house of Israel
know assuredly that God has made this
Jesus, whom you crucified, both Lord and
Christ."
37Now when they heard *this,* they were cut
to the heart, and said to Peter and the rest of
the apostles, "Men *and* brethren, what shall
we do?"
38Then Peter said to them, "Repent, and
let every one of you be baptized in the name
of Jesus Christ for the remission of sins; and
you shall receive the gift of the Holy Spirit.
39For the promise is to you and to your children, and to all who are afar off, as many as
the Lord our God will call."

2:30 [a] NU-Text omits *according to the flesh, He would raise up the Christ* and completes the verse with *He would seat one on his throne.* 2:35 [a] Psalm 110:1

PETER HEALS A CRIPPLED BEGGAR

READ IT: ACTS 3:1–16

GET IT:

After they received the Holy Spirit, the disciples preached in Jerusalem. Every day they went to the temple to tell others the good news. Jesus' disciple Peter was one of the main leaders in the early church. He was outspoken and boldly told the story of Jesus. One day as he came into the temple through one of the gates, he saw a crippled man begging for money. Peter didn't have money, but he had something much better to give the man: the ability to walk for the first time in his entire life. Peter performed his first miracle through the power of Jesus' name. The man who could now walk was jumping around, praising God. He was a living example of what the power of Jesus could do.

LIVE IT:

Peter didn't have any money to give this beggar who couldn't walk. But he offered him what he did have—in the name of Jesus he healed the man. Sometimes you might think that you don't have anything to give to others because you don't have a big enough allowance or you don't have any kind of job. But money isn't the only thing you can give. You need to give what you do have. What can you give right now? What talent or ability do you have that could help someone else and show them God's love?

A Vital Church Grows

40And with many other words he testified
and exhorted them, saying, "Be saved from
this perverse generation." 41Then those who
gladly[a] received his word were baptized; and
that day about three thousand souls were
added *to them.* 42And they continued steadfastly in the apostles' doctrine and fellowship, in the breaking of bread, and in prayers.
43Then fear came upon every soul, and many
wonders and signs were done through the
apostles. 44Now all who believed were together, and had all things in common, 45and sold
their possessions and goods, and divided
them among all, as anyone had need.

46So continuing daily with one accord in
the temple, and breaking bread from house
to house, they ate their food with gladness
and simplicity of heart, 47praising God and
having favor with all the people. And the
Lord added to the church[a] daily those who
were being saved.

A Lame Man Healed

3 Now Peter and John went up together
to the temple at the hour of prayer, the
ninth *hour.* 2And a certain man lame from
his mother's womb was carried, whom they
laid daily at the gate of the temple which
is called Beautiful, to ask alms from those
who entered the temple; 3who, seeing Peter
and John about to go into the temple, asked
for alms. 4And fixing his eyes on him, with
John, Peter said, "Look at us." 5So he gave
them his attention, expecting to receive
something from them. 6Then Peter said,
"Silver and gold I do not have, but what
I do have I give you: In the name of Jesus
Christ of Nazareth, rise up and walk." 7And
he took him by the right hand and lifted
him up, and immediately his feet and ankle
bones received strength. 8So he, leaping up,
stood and walked and entered the temple
with them—walking, leaping, and praising
God. 9And all the people saw him walking
and praising God. 10Then they knew that it
was he who sat begging alms at the Beauti-
ful Gate of the temple; and they were filled
with wonder and amazement at what had
happened to him.

Preaching in Solomon's Portico

11Now as the lame man who was healed
held on to Peter and John, all the people ran
together to them in the porch which is called
Solomon's, greatly amazed. 12So when Peter
saw *it,* he responded to the people: "Men of
Israel, why do you marvel at this? Or why
look so intently at us, as though by our own
power or godliness we had made this man
walk? 13The God of Abraham, Isaac, and
Jacob, the God of our fathers, glorified His
Servant Jesus, whom you delivered up and
denied in the presence of Pilate, when he was
determined to let *Him* go. 14But you denied
the Holy One and the Just, and asked for a
murderer to be granted to you, 15and killed
the Prince of life, whom God raised from the
dead, of which we are witnesses. 16And His
name, through faith in His name, has made
this man strong, whom you see and know.
Yes, the faith which *comes* through Him
has given him this perfect soundness in the
presence of you all.

17"Yet now, brethren, I know that you
did *it* in ignorance, as *did* also your rulers.
18But those things which God foretold by the
mouth of all His prophets, that the Christ
would suffer, He has thus fulfilled. 19Repent
therefore and be converted, that your sins
may be blotted out, so that times of refreshing may come from the presence of the Lord,
20and that He may send Jesus Christ, who
was preached to you before,[a] 21whom heaven
must receive until the times of restoration
of all things, which God has spoken by the
mouth of all His holy prophets since the
world began. 22For Moses truly said to the fathers, 'The LORD your God will raise up for
you a Prophet like me from your brethren.
Him you shall hear in all things, whatever
He says to you. 23And it shall be *that* every
soul who will not hear that Prophet shall be
utterly destroyed from among the people.'[a]
24Yes, and all the prophets, from Samuel and
those who follow, as many as have spoken,
have also foretold[a] these days. 25You are sons
of the prophets, and of the covenant which
God made with our fathers, saying to Abraham, 'And in your seed all the families of the
earth shall be blessed.'[a] 26To you first, God,
having raised up His Servant Jesus, sent
Him to bless you, in turning away every one
of you from your iniquities."

Peter and John Arrested

4 Now as they spoke to the people, the
priests, the captain of the temple, and

2:41 [a] NU-Text omits *gladly.* **2:47** [a] NU-Text omits *to the church.* **3:20** [a] NU-Text and M-Text read *Christ Jesus, who was ordained for you before.* **3:23** [a] Deuteronomy 18:15, 18, 19 **3:24** [a] NU-Text and M-Text read *proclaimed.* **3:25** [a] Genesis 22:18; 26:4; 28:14

the Saddducees came upon them, 2being
greatly disturbed that they taught the people
and preached in Jesus the resurrection from
the dead. 3And they laid hands on them, and
put *them* in custody until the next day, for
it was already evening. 4However, many of
those who heard the word believed; and the
number of the men came to be about five
thousand.

Addressing the Sanhedrin

5And it came to pass, on the next day, that
their rulers, elders, and scribes, 6as well as
Annas the high priest, Caiaphas, John, and
Alexander, and as many as were of the family of the high priest, were gathered together
at Jerusalem. 7And when they had set them
in the midst, they asked, "By what power or
by what name have you done this?"

8Then Peter, filled with the Holy Spirit, said to them, "Rulers of the people and
elders of Israel: 9If we this day are judged
for a good deed *done* to a helpless man, by
what means he has been made well, 10let it
be known to you all, and to all the people
of Israel, that by the name of Jesus Christ
of Nazareth, whom you crucified, whom
God raised from the dead, by Him this man
stands here before you whole. 11This is the
'stone which was rejected by you builders,
which has become the chief cornerstone.'[a]
12Nor is there salvation in any other, for there
is no other name under heaven given among
men by which we must be saved."

The Name of Jesus Forbidden

13Now when they saw the boldness of
Peter and John, and perceived that they
were uneducated and untrained men, they
marveled. And they realized that they had
been with Jesus. 14And seeing the man who
had been healed standing with them, they
could say nothing against it. 15But when they
had commanded them to go aside out of the
council, they conferred among themselves,
16saying, "What shall we do to these men?
For, indeed, that a notable miracle has been
done through them *is* evident to all who
dwell in Jerusalem, and we cannot deny *it.*
17But so that it spreads no further among the
people, let us severely threaten them, that
from now on they speak to no man in this
name."

18So they called them and commanded
them not to speak at all nor teach in the
name of Jesus. 19But Peter and John answered and said to them, "Whether it is right
in the sight of God to listen to you more than
to God, you judge. 20For we cannot but speak
the things which we have seen and heard."
21So when they had further threatened them,
they let them go, finding no way of punishing them, because of the people, since they
all glorified God for what had been done.
22For the man was over forty years old on
whom this miracle of healing had been
performed.

Prayer for Boldness

23And being let go, they went to their
own *companions* and reported all that the
chief priests and elders had said to them.
24So when they heard that, they raised their
voice to God with one accord and said: "Lord,
You *are* God, who made heaven and earth
and the sea, and all that is in them, 25who by
the mouth of Your servant David[a] have said:

'Why did the nations rage,
And the people plot vain things?
26 The kings of the earth took their stand,
And the rulers were gathered together
Against the LORD and against His
Christ.'[a]

27"For truly against Your holy Servant
Jesus, whom You anointed, both Herod and
Pontius Pilate, with the Gentiles and the
people of Israel, were gathered together 28to
do whatever Your hand and Your purpose
determined before to be done. 29Now, Lord,
look on their threats, and grant to Your servants that with all boldness they may speak
Your word, 30by stretching out Your hand to
heal, and that signs and wonders may be
done through the name of Your holy Servant
Jesus."

31And when they had prayed, the place
where they were assembled together was
shaken; and they were all filled with the
Holy Spirit, and they spoke the word of God
with boldness.

Sharing in All Things

32Now the multitude of those who believed were of one heart and one soul; neither did anyone say that any of the things
he possessed was his own, but they had all

4:11 [a] Psalm 118:22 **4:25** [a] NU-Text reads *who through the Holy Spirit, by the mouth of our father, Your servant David.*
4:26 [a] Psalm 2:1, 2

things in common. 33And with great power the apostles gave witness to the resurrection of the Lord Jesus. And great grace
was upon them all. 34Nor was there anyone
among them who lacked; for all who were
possessors of lands or houses sold them, and
brought the proceeds of the things that were
sold, 35and laid *them* at the apostles' feet; and
they distributed to each as anyone had need.
36And Joses,[a] who was also named Barnabas by the apostles (which is translated Son
of Encouragement), a Levite of the country of
Cyprus, 37having land, sold *it,* and brought
the money and laid *it* at the apostles' feet.

Lying to the Holy Spirit

5 But a certain man named Ananias,
with Sapphira his wife, sold a possession. 2And he kept back *part* of the proceeds,
his wife also being aware *of it,* and brought
a certain part and laid *it* at the apostles' feet.
3But Peter said, "Ananias, why has Satan
filled your heart to lie to the Holy Spirit and
keep back *part* of the price of the land for
yourself? 4While it remained, was it not your
own? And after it was sold, was it not in your

4:36 [a] NU-Text reads *Joseph.*

SALVATION ONE WAY

READ IT: ACTS 4:1–12

GET IT:

Peter and John, two of Jesus' disciples, have been arrested by the religious leaders for telling people that Jesus was raised from the dead. Peter affirms that Jesus was murdered on a cross and that God raised Him from the dead. Then Peter tells them some really important things.

First, he calls Jesus the "chief cornerstone" (v. 11). For a building made of stone, a cornerstone is the most important stone, the one that has to be perfect since the rest of the entire building is built out from and rests on that cornerstone. Peter is telling us that Jesus is the only way to experience salvation.

Then Peter says the same thing more clearly, stating that there's no salvation anywhere else. Only Jesus can provide the rescue we all need: from our own sins, from our pain and suffering, and from the evil one. The power of Jesus is the one and only way to be connected with the loving God who made you.

LIVE IT:

Do you ever look for salvation in places other than Jesus? That might be a confusing question, but many people think there are lots of ways to God. In fact, we're often told that all religions basically say the same thing. But this verse is really clear about one thing: only Jesus can save you, and only Jesus can give you true life. How might that change your thoughts about Jesus today?

own control? Why have you conceived this
thing in your heart? You have not lied to
men but to God."

5Then Ananias, hearing these words,
fell down and breathed his last. So great fear
came upon all those who heard these things.
6And the young men arose and wrapped him
up, carried *him* out, and buried *him.*

7Now it was about three hours later when
his wife came in, not knowing what had
happened. 8And Peter answered her, "Tell
me whether you sold the land for so much?"

She said, "Yes, for so much."

9Then Peter said to her, "How is it that
you have agreed together to test the Spirit of
the Lord? Look, the feet of those who have
buried your husband *are* at the door, and they
will carry you out." 10Then immediately she
fell down at his feet and breathed her last.
And the young men came in and found her
dead, and carrying *her* out, buried *her* by her
husband. 11So great fear came upon all the
church and upon all who heard these things.

Continuing Power in the Church

12And through the hands of the apostles many signs and wonders were done
among the people. And they were all with
one accord in Solomon's Porch. 13Yet none
of the rest dared join them, but the people
esteemed them highly. 14And believers were
increasingly added to the Lord, multitudes of
both men and women, 15so that they brought
the sick out into the streets and laid *them* on
beds and couches, that at least the shadow
of Peter passing by might fall on some of
them. 16Also a multitude gathered from the
surrounding cities to Jerusalem, bringing
sick people and those who were tormented
by unclean spirits, and they were all healed.

Imprisoned Apostles Freed

17Then the high priest rose up, and
all those who *were* with him (which is the
sect of the Sadducees), and they were filled
with indignation, 18and laid their hands on
the apostles and put them in the common
prison. 19But at night an angel of the Lord
opened the prison doors and brought them
out, and said, 20"Go, stand in the temple and
speak to the people all the words of this life."

21And when they heard *that,* they entered
the temple early in the morning and taught.
But the high priest and those with him came
and called the council together, with all the
elders of the children of Israel, and sent to
the prison to have them brought.

Apostles on Trial Again

22But when the officers came and did not

PRAYER MAKES YOU BRAVE

READ IT: ACTS 4:31

John and Peter were put in jail for telling people about Jesus. Do you think that's strange? Why should people be arrested just for talking? Yet even today, people can get in trouble with the law for talking about Jesus. If you tell about Jesus in the streets or in public school, you can be in great trouble. This is something new in our country, where people used to be free to preach the gospel anywhere.

When Peter and John were released from jail, they told the other Christians what happened. But the Christians didn't complain to anyone about how they were treated. *They prayed!* Then God made them strong and brave enough to tell about Jesus even more than they had before.

Christians can't expect much help from the world. The place to go when you need help is to God. He gives strength for all things.

find them in the prison, they returned and
reported, [23]saying, "Indeed we found the
prison shut securely, and the guards standing outside[a] before the doors; but when we
opened them, we found no one inside!"
[24]Now when the high priest,[a] the captain of
the temple, and the chief priests heard these
things, they wondered what the outcome
would be. [25]So one came and told them,

5:23 [a] NU-Text and M-Text omit *outside.* 5:24 [a] NU-Text omits *the high priest.*

Action!

SELFISHNESS

WHO, ME?

READ IT: ACTS 5:1–11

GET IT:

Ananias and Sapphira were part of a church that shared everything (see Acts 4:32–37). No one was self-centered; everyone thought of others first.

Except for Ananias and Sapphira. They wanted to be known as generous and caring, like the others, so they sold something and gave what they claimed was all the money to the church leaders. Their selfishness led to all kinds of other problems. First they kept part of the money for themselves (greed), and then they denied it to the church leaders (lying).

Selfishness—thinking more highly of "me" than God or others—is the cause of all sin. Jesus said the greatest command is to love God and love others, but that's pretty difficult if someone is busy loving and looking out for number one, for "me."

Selfishness leads to broken relationships with God, with others, and ultimately with ourselves. We are only truly "me" when we are part of a larger "we" that lives in community—loving and helping and caring for each other while serving God.

LIVE IT:

Make a determined effort to start living a less-of-self, more-of-others life. That means:

- Sharing what you have
- Offering to help out at home
- Paying attention to people who get ignored or overlooked
- Giving part of your money to church
- Not obsessing about being first or best
- Not spending all your time trying to become more popular or build a certain reputation
- Not worrying about how much stuff you own
- Not focusing only on your own desires and wants and wishes

It means putting your priorities in order: first God, then others, then self.

saying,[a] "Look, the men whom you put in
prison are standing in the temple and teaching the people!"

26 Then the captain went with the officers and brought them without violence, for
they feared the people, lest they should be
stoned. 27 And when they had brought them,
they set *them* before the council. And the
high priest asked them, 28 saying, "Did we
not strictly command you not to teach in this
name? And look, you have filled Jerusalem
with your doctrine, and intend to bring this
Man's blood on us!"

29 But Peter and the *other* apostles answered and said: "We ought to obey God
rather than men. 30 The God of our fathers
raised up Jesus whom you murdered by
hanging on a tree. 31 Him God has exalted
to His right hand *to be* Prince and Savior,
to give repentance to Israel and forgiveness
of sins. 32 And we are His witnesses to these
things, and *so* also *is* the Holy Spirit whom
God has given to those who obey Him."

Gamaliel's Advice

33 When they heard *this,* they were furious
and plotted to kill them. 34 Then one in the
council stood up, a Pharisee named Gamaliel, a teacher of the law held in respect by
all the people, and commanded them to put
the apostles outside for a little while. 35 And
he said to them: "Men of Israel, take heed to
yourselves what you intend to do regarding
these men. 36 For some time ago Theudas
rose up, claiming to be somebody. A number of men, about four hundred, joined him.
He was slain, and all who obeyed him were
scattered and came to nothing. 37 After this
man, Judas of Galilee rose up in the days
of the census, and drew away many people
after him. He also perished, and all who
obeyed him were dispersed. 38 And now I say
to you, keep away from these men and let
them alone; for if this plan or this work is of
men, it will come to nothing; 39 but if it is of
God, you cannot overthrow it—lest you even
be found to fight against God."

40 And they agreed with him, and when
they had called for the apostles and beaten
them, they commanded that they should not
speak in the name of Jesus, and let them go.
41 So they departed from the presence of the
council, rejoicing that they were counted
worthy to suffer shame for His[a] name. 42 And
daily in the temple, and in every house, they
did not cease teaching and preaching Jesus
as the Christ.

Seven Chosen to Serve

6 Now in those days, when *the number
of* the disciples was multiplying, there
arose a complaint against the Hebrews by
the Hellenists,[a] because their widows were
neglected in the daily distribution. 2 Then
the twelve summoned the multitude of the
disciples and said, "It is not desirable that
we should leave the word of God and serve
tables. 3 Therefore, brethren, seek out from
among you seven men of *good* reputation,
full of the Holy Spirit and wisdom, whom
we may appoint over this business; 4 but we
will give ourselves continually to prayer and
to the ministry of the word."

5 And the saying pleased the whole multitude. And they chose Stephen, a man full of
faith and the Holy Spirit, and Philip, Proch-
orus, Nicanor, Timon, Parmenas, and Nicolas, a proselyte from Antioch, 6 whom they
set before the apostles; and when they had
prayed, they laid hands on them.

7 Then the word of God spread, and the
number of the disciples multiplied greatly in
Jerusalem, and a great many of the priests
were obedient to the faith.

Stephen Accused of Blasphemy

8 And Stephen, full of faith[a] and power, did great wonders and signs among
the people. 9 Then there arose some from
what is called the Synagogue of the Freed-
men (Cyrenians, Alexandrians, and those
from Cilicia and Asia), disputing with Stephen. 10 And they were not able to resist the
wisdom and the Spirit by which he spoke.
11 Then they secretly induced men to say, "We
have heard him speak blasphemous words
against Moses and God." 12 And they stirred
up the people, the elders, and the scribes;
and they came upon *him,* seized him, and
brought *him* to the council. 13 They also set
up false witnesses who said, "This man
does not cease to speak blasphemous[a] words
against this holy place and the law; 14 for we
have heard him say that this Jesus of Nazareth will destroy this place and change the
customs which Moses delivered to us." 15 And

5:25 [a] NU-Text and M-Text omit *saying.* **5:41** [a] NU-Text reads *the name;* M-Text reads *the name of Jesus.* **6:1** [a] That is, Greek-speaking Jews **6:8** [a] NU-Text reads *grace.* **6:13** [a] NU-Text omits *blasphemous.*

all who sat in the council, looking steadfastly at him, saw his face as the face of an angel.

Stephen's Address: The Call of Abraham

7 Then the high priest said, "Are these things so?"

2And he said, "Brethren and fathers, listen: The God of glory appeared to our father Abraham when he was in Mesopotamia, before he dwelt in Haran, 3and said to him, 'Get out of your country and from your relatives, and come to a land that I will show you.'[a] 4Then he came out of the land of the Chaldeans and dwelt in Haran. And from there, when his father was dead, He moved him to this land in which you now dwell. 5And *God* gave him no inheritance in it, not even *enough* to set his foot on. But even when *Abraham* had no child, He promised to give it to him for a possession, and to his descendants after him. 6But God spoke in this way: that his descendants would dwell in a foreign land, and that they would bring them into bondage and oppress *them* four hundred years. 7'And the nation to whom they will be in bondage I will judge,'[a] said God, 'and after that they shall come out and serve Me in this place.'[b] 8Then He gave him the covenant of circumcision; and so *Abraham* begot Isaac and circumcised him on the eighth day; and Isaac *begot* Jacob, and Jacob *begot* the twelve patriarchs.

In Focus

6:1 Hellenists Pronounced *HELL-ih-nists.* Jews in Jesus' time who spoke Greek and tried to follow the ancient Greek style of living and thinking. That style was called Hellenism.

The Patriarchs in Egypt

9"And the patriarchs, becoming envious, sold Joseph into Egypt. But God was with him 10and delivered him out of all his troubles, and gave him favor and wisdom in the presence of Pharaoh, king of Egypt; and he made him governor over Egypt and all his house. 11Now a famine and great trouble came over all the land of Egypt and Canaan, and our fathers found no sustenance. 12But when Jacob heard that there was grain in Egypt, he sent out our fathers first. 13And the second *time* Joseph was made known to his brothers, and Joseph's family became known to the Pharaoh. 14Then Joseph sent and called his father Jacob and all his relatives to *him*, seventy-five[a] people. 15So Jacob

7:3 [a] Genesis 12:1 **7:7** [a] Genesis 15:14 [b] Exodus 3:12
7:14 [a] Or *seventy* (compare Exodus 1:5)

Starring Roles

STEPHEN (pronounced *STEVE-un*) means "A Crown." He was one of the seven men chosen to serve the needs of the Greek-speaking widows in Jerusalem. Stephen never planned to be a preacher, but God gave him the gift of speaking and debate. That was when his trouble started.

Some of the Jews hated Jesus. Stephen preached that the temple and the old ways of worship were passing away. Jesus had already told them that His own body was the true temple of God.

So they brought Stephen before the council of 101 men that had also condemned Jesus. When they asked him if what they heard about him was true, Stephen told them they had always disobeyed God, and they had killed Jesus, His only Son. Then they threw stones at Stephen until they had killed him.

But Stephen could see Jesus standing at God's right hand. He was calling Stephen home to heaven.

went down to Egypt; and he died, he and our fathers. 16And they were carried back to Shechem and laid in the tomb that Abraham bought for a sum of money from the sons of Hamor, *the father* of Shechem.

God Delivers Israel by Moses

17"But when the time of the promise drew near which God had sworn to Abraham, the people grew and multiplied in Egypt 18till another king arose who did not know Joseph. 19This man dealt treacherously with our people, and oppressed our forefathers, making them expose their babies, so that they might not live. 20At this time Moses was born, and was well pleasing to God; and he was brought up in his father's house for three months. 21But when he was set out, Pharaoh's daughter took him away and brought him up as her own son. 22And Moses was learned in all the wisdom of the Egyptians, and was mighty in words and deeds.

23"Now when he was forty years old, it came into his heart to visit his brethren, the children of Israel. 24And seeing one of *them* suffer wrong, he defended and avenged him who was oppressed, and struck down the Egyptian. 25For he supposed that his brethren would have understood that God would deliver them by his hand, but they did not understand. 26And the next day he appeared to *two of* them as they were fighting, and *tried to* reconcile them, saying, 'Men, you are brethren; why do you wrong one another?' 27But he who did his neighbor wrong pushed him away, saying, 'Who made you a ruler and a judge over us? 28Do you want to kill me as you did the Egyptian yesterday?' [a] 29Then, at this saying, Moses fled and became a dweller in the land of Midian, where he had two sons.

30"And when forty years had passed, an Angel of the Lord[a] appeared to him in a flame of fire in a bush, in the wilderness of Mount Sinai. 31When Moses saw *it,* he marveled at the sight; and as he drew near to observe, the voice of the Lord came to him, 32*saying,* 'I *am* the God of your fathers—the God of Abraham, the God of Isaac, and the God of Jacob.' [a] And Moses trembled and *dared not look.* 33'*Then the* LORD said to him, "Take your sandals off your feet, for the place where you stand is holy ground. 34I have surely seen the oppression of My people who are in Egypt; I have heard their groaning and have come down to deliver them. And now come, I will send you to Egypt." ' [a]

35"This Moses whom they rejected, saying, 'Who made you a ruler and a judge?' [a] is the one God sent *to be* a ruler and a deliverer by the hand of the Angel who appeared to him in the bush. 36He brought them out, after he had shown wonders and signs in the land of Egypt, and in the Red Sea, and in the wilderness forty years.

Israel Rebels Against God

37"This is that Moses who said to the children of Israel,[a] 'The LORD your God will raise up for you a Prophet like me from your brethren. Him you shall hear.' [b]

38"This is he who was in the congregation in the wilderness with the Angel who spoke to him on Mount Sinai, and *with* our fathers, the one who received the living oracles to give to us, 39whom our fathers would not obey, but rejected. And in their hearts they turned back to Egypt, 40saying to Aaron, 'Make us gods to go before us; *as for* this Moses who brought us out of the land of Egypt, we do not know what has become of him.' [a] 41And they made a calf in those days, offered sacrifices to the idol, and rejoiced in the works of their own hands. 42Then God turned and gave them up to worship the host of heaven, as it is written in the book of the Prophets:

'Did you offer Me slaughtered animals
 and sacrifices *during* forty years in
 the wilderness,
O house of Israel?
43 You also took up the tabernacle of
 Moloch,
And the star of your god Remphan,
Images which you made to worship;
And I will carry you away beyond
 Babylon.' [a]

God's True Tabernacle

44"Our fathers had the tabernacle of witness in the wilderness, as He appointed, instructing Moses to make it according to the pattern that he had seen, 45which our fathers, having received it in turn, also brought with Joshua into the land possessed by the

---

7:28 [a] Exodus 2:14 **7:30** [a] NU-Text omits *of the Lord.* **7:32** [a] Exodus 3:6, 15 **7:34** [a] Exodus 3:5, 7, 8, 10 **7:35** [a] Exodus 2:14 **7:37** [a] Deuteronomy 18:15 [b] NU-Text and M-Text omit *Him you shall hear.* **7:40** [a] Exodus 32:1, 23 **7:43** [a] Amos 5:25–27

Gentiles whom God drove out before the
face of our fathers until the days of David,
46who found favor before God and asked to
find a dwelling for the God of Jacob. 47But
Solomon built Him a house.

48"However, the Most High does not
dwell in temples made with hands, as the
prophet says:

49 'Heaven *is* My throne,
And earth *is* My footstool.
What house will you build for Me? says
the LORD,
Or what *is* the place of My rest?
50 Has My hand not made all these
things?' [a]

Israel Resists the Holy Spirit

51"*You* stiff-necked and uncircumcised in
heart and ears! You always resist the Holy
Spirit; as your fathers *did,* so *do* you. 52Which
of the prophets did your fathers not persecute? And they killed those who foretold the
coming of the Just One, of whom you now
have become the betrayers and murderers,
53who have received the law by the direction
of angels and have not kept *it.*"

Stephen the Martyr

54When they heard these things they
were cut to the heart, and they gnashed at
him with *their* teeth. 55But he, being full of
the Holy Spirit, gazed into heaven and saw
the glory of God, and Jesus standing at the
right hand of God, 56and said, "Look! I see
the heavens opened and the Son of Man
standing at the right hand of God!"

57Then they cried out with a loud voice,
stopped their ears, and ran at him with one
accord; 58and they cast *him* out of the city and
stoned *him.* And the witnesses laid down
their clothes at the feet of a young man
named Saul. 59And they stoned Stephen as
he was calling on *God* and saying, "Lord
Jesus, receive my spirit." 60Then he knelt
down and cried out with a loud voice, "Lord,
do not charge them with this sin." And when
he had said this, he fell asleep.

Saul Persecutes the Church

8 Now Saul was consenting to his death.
At that time a great persecution arose
against the church which was at Jerusalem;
and they were all scattered throughout the
regions of Judea and Samaria, except the
apostles. 2And devout men carried Stephen
to his burial, and made great lamentation
over him.

3As for Saul, he made havoc of the
church, entering every house, and dragging

7:50 [a] Isaiah 66:1, 2

7:37 WHAT IS A PROPHET?

The word *prophet* comes from a Hebrew word meaning "mouthpiece." Sometimes you may hear an attorney referred to in slang as a "mouthpiece." An attorney *speaks for* his client in a court of law. In the same way, a prophet speaks for the Lord. The prophet doesn't speak about his own beliefs or thoughts. He tells what God tells him to say.

You have read about a lot of prophets in the Old Testament. Moses, the first great prophet, told the people only what God told him to say. Moses said that someday a greater Prophet would come. He was referring to Jesus, who would come about fifteen hundred years after Moses. Jesus would be the perfect Prophet because He was the Son of God from heaven. You aren't a prophet like Moses, but every Christian can tell people what God says in His Word.

off men and women, committing *them* to prison.

Christ Is Preached in Samaria

4 Therefore those who were scattered went everywhere preaching the word. 5 Then Philip went down to the[a] city of Samaria and preached Christ to them. 6 And the multitudes with one accord heeded the things spoken by Philip, hearing and seeing the miracles which he did. 7 For unclean spirits, crying with a loud voice, came out of many who were possessed; and many who were paralyzed and lame were healed. 8 And there was great joy in that city.

The Sorcerer's Profession of Faith

9 But there was a certain man called Simon, who previously practiced sorcery in the city and astonished the people of Samaria, claiming that he was someone great, 10 to whom they all gave heed, from the least to the greatest, saying, "This man is the great power of God." 11 And they heeded him because he had astonished them with his sorceries for a long time. 12 But when they believed Philip as he preached the things concerning the kingdom of God and the name of Jesus Christ, both men and women were baptized. 13 Then Simon himself also believed; and when he was baptized he continued with Philip, and was amazed, seeing the miracles and signs which were done.

The Sorcerer's Sin

14 Now when the apostles who were at Jerusalem heard that Samaria had received the word of God, they sent Peter and John to them, 15 who, when they had come down, prayed for them that they might receive the Holy Spirit. 16 For as yet He had fallen upon none of them. They had only been baptized in the name of the Lord Jesus. 17 Then they laid hands on them, and they received the Holy Spirit.

18 And when Simon saw that through the laying on of the apostles' hands the Holy Spirit was given, he offered them money, 19 saying, "Give me this power also, that anyone on whom I lay hands may receive the *Holy Spirit.*"

20 But Peter said to him, "Your money perish with you, because you thought that the gift of God could be purchased with money! 21 You have neither part nor portion in this matter, for your heart is not right in the sight of God. 22 Repent therefore of this your wickedness, and pray God if perhaps the thought of your heart may be forgiven you. 23 For I see that you are poisoned by bitterness and bound by iniquity."

In Focus

8:9–13 Sorcery Pronounced *SORE-sah-ree.* The practice of magic, using secret potions and spells to control nature and persons. The Bible forbids sorcery.

24 Then Simon answered and said, "Pray to the Lord for me, that none of the things which you have spoken may come upon me."

25 So when they had testified and preached the word of the Lord, they returned to Jerusalem, preaching the gospel in many villages of the Samaritans.

Christ Is Preached to an Ethiopian

26 Now an angel of the Lord spoke to Philip, saying, "Arise and go toward the south along the road which goes down from Jerusalem to Gaza." This is desert. 27 So he arose and went. And behold, a man of Ethiopia, a eunuch of great authority under Candace the queen of the Ethiopians, who had charge of all her treasury, and had come to Jerusalem to worship, 28 was returning. And sitting in his chariot, he was reading Isaiah the prophet. 29 Then the Spirit said to Philip, "Go near and overtake this chariot."

30 So Philip ran to him, and heard him reading the prophet Isaiah, and said, "Do you understand what you are reading?"

31 And he said, "How can I, unless someone guides me?" And he asked Philip to come up and sit with him. 32 The place in the Scripture which he read was this:

"He was led as a sheep to the slaughter;
And as a lamb before its shearer *is* silent,
So He opened not His mouth.
33 In His humiliation His justice was taken away,

8:5 [a] Or *a*

And who will declare His generation?
For His life is taken from the earth."[a]

34So the eunuch answered Philip and
said, "I ask you, of whom does the prophet
say this, of himself or of some other man?"
35Then Philip opened his mouth, and beginning at this Scripture, preached Jesus to
him. 36Now as they went down the road, they
came to some water. And the eunuch said,
"See, *here is* water. What hinders me from
being baptized?"
37Then Philip said, "If you believe with all
your heart, you may."
And he answered and said, "I believe that
Jesus Christ is the Son of God."[a]
38So he commanded the chariot to stand
still. And both Philip and the eunuch went
down into the water, and he baptized him.
39Now when they came up out of the water,
the Spirit of the Lord caught Philip away,
so that the eunuch saw him no more; and
he went on his way rejoicing. 40But Philip
was found at Azotus. And passing through,
he preached in all the cities till he came to
Caesarea.

The Damascus Road: Saul Converted

9 Then Saul, still breathing threats and
murder against the disciples of the
Lord, went to the high priest 2and asked

8:33 [a] Isaiah 53:7, 8 8:37 [a] NU-Text and M-Text omit this verse. It is found in Western texts, including the Latin tradition.

THE BIBLE IS THE TRUTH
SAY WHAT?

READ IT: ACTS 8:26–40

GET IT:

The Bible is the world's bestselling book, but it's not the most read book. Lots of Bibles sit on shelves, lie in drawers, and hide under beds. They are left unopened and unread. That's too bad because the only way to experience the truth of God's Word is to actually read it.

That's what the Ethiopian was doing—actually reading God's Word. He was a super-important person who worked for a super-powerful foreign queen. He hadn't grown up hearing Bible stories, and he didn't understand it completely. He could have made up excuses about strange names or boring details, but he kept reading and kept working at it. And then along came Philip who knew the Bible, understood it, believed it, and trusted it. Philip was able to help the Ethiopian understand what the Bible said. He explained who Jesus was and how to have new life.

LIVE IT:

The Bible is the best place to learn about God, Jesus, and life. If you don't understand something, ask for help. As you get to know the Bible better, you might have the chance to help someone else understand it, just like Philip did. So . . .

Read it. Learn it. Trust it. Live it. Share it.

letters from him to the synagogues of Damascus, so that if he found any who were of
the Way, whether men or women, he might
bring them bound to Jerusalem.
3As he journeyed he came near Damascus, and suddenly a light shone around him
from heaven. 4Then he fell to the ground,
and heard a voice saying to him, "Saul, Saul,
why are you persecuting Me?"
5And he said, "Who are You, Lord?"
Then the Lord said, "I am Jesus, whom
you are persecuting.[a] It *is* hard for you to
kick against the goads."
6So he, trembling and astonished, said,
"Lord, what do You want me to do?"
Then the Lord *said* to him, "Arise and go
into the city, and you will be told what you
must do."
7And the men who journeyed with him
stood speechless, hearing a voice but seeing
no one. 8Then Saul arose from the ground,
and when his eyes were opened he saw
no one. But they led him by the hand and
brought *him* into Damascus. 9And he was
three days without sight, and neither ate nor
drank.

Ananias Baptizes Saul

10Now there was a certain disciple at Damascus named Ananias; and to him the
Lord said in a vision, "Ananias."
And he said, "Here I am, Lord."
11So the Lord *said* to him, "Arise and go to
the street called Straight, and inquire at the
house of Judas for *one* called Saul of Tarsus,
for behold, he is praying. 12And in a vision
he has seen a man named Ananias coming
in and putting *his* hand on him, so that he
might receive his sight."
13Then Ananias answered, "Lord, I have
heard from many about this man, how much
harm he has done to Your saints in Jerusalem. 14And here he has authority from the
chief priests to bind all who call on Your
name."
15But the Lord said to him, "Go, for he is
a chosen vessel of Mine to bear My name before Gentiles, kings, and the children of Israel. 16For I will show him how many things
he must suffer for My name's sake."
17And Ananias went his way and entered
the house; and laying his hands on him he
said, "Brother Saul, the Lord Jesus,[a] who appeared to you on the road as you came, has
sent me that you may receive your sight and
be filled with the Holy Spirit." 18Immediately
there fell from his eyes *something* like scales,
and he received his sight at once; and he
arose and was baptized.
19So when he had received food, he was
strengthened. Then Saul spent some days
with the disciples at Damascus.

Saul Preaches Christ

20Immediately he preached the Christ[a] in
the synagogues, that He is the Son of God.
21Then all who heard were amazed, and
said, "Is this not he who destroyed those who
called on this name in Jerusalem, and has
come here for that purpose, so that he might
bring them bound to the chief priests?"
22But Saul increased all the more in
strength, and confounded the Jews who
dwelt in Damascus, proving that this *Jesus*
is the Christ.

Saul Escapes Death

23Now after many days were past, the
Jews plotted to kill him. 24But their plot became known to Saul. And they watched the
gates day and night, to kill him. 25Then the
disciples took him by night and let *him* down
through the wall in a large basket.

Saul at Jerusalem

26And when Saul had come to Jerusalem,
he tried to join the disciples; but they were
all afraid of him, and did not believe that he
was a disciple. 27But Barnabas took him and
brought *him* to the apostles. And he declared
to them how he had seen the Lord on the
road, and that He had spoken to him, and
how he had preached boldly at Damascus in
the name of Jesus. 28So he was with them at
Jerusalem, coming in and going out. 29And
he spoke boldly in the name of the Lord
Jesus and disputed against the Hellenists,
but they attempted to kill him. 30When the
brethren found out, they brought him down
to Caesarea and sent him out to Tarsus.

The Church Prospers

31Then the churches[a] throughout all
Judea, Galilee, and Samaria had peace and
were edified. And walking in the fear of the
Lord and in the comfort of the Holy Spirit,
they were multiplied.

9:5 [a] NU-Text and M-Text omit the last sentence of verse 5 and begin verse 6 with *But arise and go.* **9:17** [a] M-Text omits *Jesus.* **9:20** [a] NU-Text reads *Jesus.* **9:31** [a] NU-Text reads *church . . . was edified.*

Aeneas Healed

[32]Now it came to pass, as Peter went
through all *parts of the country,* that he also
came down to the saints who dwelt in Lydda.
[33]There he found a certain man named Aeneas, who had been bedridden eight years
and was paralyzed. [34]And Peter said to him,
"Aeneas, Jesus the Christ heals you. Arise
and make your bed." Then he arose immediately. [35]So all who dwelt at Lydda and Sharon
saw him and turned to the Lord.

Dorcas Restored to Life

[36]At Joppa there was a certain disciple
named Tabitha, which is translated Dorcas.
This woman was full of good works and
charitable deeds which she did. [37]But it happened in those days that she became sick
and died. When they had washed her, they
laid *her* in an upper room. [38]And since Lydda
was near Joppa, and the disciples had heard
that Peter was there, they sent two men to
him, imploring *him* not to delay in coming
to them. [39]Then Peter arose and went with
them. When he had come, they brought *him*
to the upper room. And all the widows stood
by him weeping, showing the tunics and
garments which Dorcas had made while she
was with them. [40]But Peter put them all out,
and knelt down and prayed. And turning to

SAUL'S CONVERSION

READ IT: ACTS 9:1–31

GET IT:

Peter and the other disciples preached about Jesus, and the church grew. But some Jews were furious that their religion and traditions were being challenged. The idea of change scared them. They wanted to follow the Law, not Jesus. They hated the Christians. Saul, a Jew and a leader in the Jewish synagogue, was the biggest Christian-hater of his day. He was out to get anyone who was a Christian. He had believers arrested, thrown in jail, or even killed. Then one day, as Saul was traveling to Damascus to round up the Christians in that city, God interrupted his life. God called out to Saul in a blinding light and a booming voice. Suddenly everything changed for Saul. He changed from a Christian-hater to God's greatest spokesperson. He preached the good news all over the world.

LIVE IT:

Have you ever played with Transformers—toys that change from an ordinary object into a robot action figure? That's kind of like the transformation that happened with Saul. One day he was a persecutor of Christians, and the next day he was a preacher for Christ. God interrupted Saul's life and transformed him. When you committed yourself to Jesus, did you have a major change in your life? Were you transformed? Some people have to make major changes in their lives when they become Christians—others not so much. But all of us need to look at ourselves closely and make sure that our actions, words, and thoughts have been transformed to the way Jesus taught us to live.

the body he said, "Tabitha, arise." And she
opened her eyes, and when she saw Peter she
sat up. 41 Then he gave her *his* hand and lifted
her up; and when he had called the saints
and widows, he presented her alive. 42 And
it became known throughout all Joppa, and
many believed on the Lord. 43 So it was that
he stayed many days in Joppa with Simon,
a tanner.

Cornelius Sends a Delegation

10 There was a certain man in Caesarea called Cornelius, a centurion
of what was called the Italian Regiment, 2 a
devout *man* and one who feared God with all
his household, who gave alms generously to
the people, and prayed to God always. 3 About
the ninth hour of the day he saw clearly in a
vision an angel of God coming in and saying
to him, "Cornelius!"

4 And when he observed him, he was
afraid, and said, "What is it, lord?"

So he said to him, "Your prayers and your
alms have come up for a memorial before
God. 5 Now send men to Joppa, and send for
Simon whose surname is Peter. 6 He is lodging with Simon, a tanner, whose house is by
the sea.[a] He will tell you what you must do."
7 And when the angel who spoke to him had
departed, Cornelius called two of his household servants and a devout soldier from
among those who waited on him continually. 8 So when he had explained all *these* things
to them, he sent them to Joppa.

Peter's Vision

9 The next day, as they went on their journey and drew near the city, Peter went up on
the housetop to pray, about the sixth hour.
10 Then he became very hungry and wanted
to eat; but while they made ready, he fell into
a trance 11 and saw heaven opened and an
object like a great sheet bound at the four
corners, descending to him and let down to
the earth. 12 In it were all kinds of four-footed
animals of the earth, wild beasts, creeping
things, and birds of the air. 13 And a voice
came to him, "Rise, Peter; kill and eat."

14 But Peter said, "Not so, Lord! For I have
never eaten anything common or unclean."

15 And a voice *spoke* to him again the second time, "What God has cleansed you must
not call common." 16 This was done three
times. And the object was taken up into
heaven again.

Summoned to Caesarea

17 Now while Peter wondered within
himself what this vision which he had seen
meant, behold, the men who had been
sent from Cornelius had made inquiry for
Simon's house, and stood before the gate.
18 And they called and asked whether Simon,
whose surname was Peter, was lodging
there.

19 While Peter thought about the vision,
the Spirit said to him, "Behold, three men
are seeking you. 20 Arise therefore, go down
and go with them, doubting nothing; for I
have sent them."

21 Then Peter went down to the men who
had been sent to him from Cornelius,[a] and
said, "Yes, I am he whom you seek. For what
reason have you come?"

22 And they said, "Cornelius *the* centurion, a just man, one who fears God and has a
good reputation among all the nation of the
Jews, was divinely instructed by a holy angel to summon you to his house, and to hear
words from you." 23 Then he invited them in
and lodged *them*.

On the next day Peter went away with
them, and some brethren from Joppa accompanied him.

Peter Meets Cornelius

24 And the following day they entered
Caesarea. Now Cornelius was waiting for
them, and had called together his relatives
and close friends. 25 As Peter was coming
in, Cornelius met him and fell down at his
feet and worshiped *him*. 26 But Peter lifted
him up, saying, "Stand up; I myself am
also a man." 27 And as he talked with him,
he went in and found many who had come
together. 28 Then he said to them, "You know
how unlawful it is for a Jewish man to keep
company with or go to one of another nation.
But God has shown me that I should not call
any man common or unclean. 29 Therefore I
came without objection as soon as I was sent
for. I ask, then, for what reason have you sent
for me?"

30 So Cornelius said, "Four days ago I
was fasting until this hour; and at the ninth
hour[a] I prayed in my house, and behold, a
man stood before me in bright clothing,

10:6 [a] NU-Text and M-Text omit the last sentence of this verse. **10:21** [a] NU-Text and M-Text omit *who had been sent to him from Cornelius.* **10:30** [a] NU-Text reads *Four days ago to this hour, at the ninth hour.*

31and said, 'Cornelius, your prayer has been
heard, and your alms are remembered in the
sight of God. 32Send therefore to Joppa and
call Simon here, whose surname is Peter. He
is lodging in the house of Simon, a tanner,
by the sea.[a] When he comes, he will speak
to you.' 33So I sent to you immediately, and
you have done well to come. Now therefore,
we are all present before God, to hear all the
things commanded you by God."

Preaching to Cornelius' Household

34Then Peter opened *his* mouth and said:
"In truth I perceive that God shows no partiality. 35But in every nation whoever fears
Him and works righteousness is accepted
by Him. 36The word which *God* sent to the
children of Israel, preaching peace through
Jesus Christ—He is Lord of all— 37that word
you know, which was proclaimed throughout all Judea, and began from Galilee after
the baptism which John preached: 38how
God anointed Jesus of Nazareth with the
Holy Spirit and with power, who went about
doing good and healing all who were oppressed by the devil, for God was with Him.
39And we are witnesses of all things which
He did both in the land of the Jews and in
Jerusalem, whom they[a] killed by hanging
on a tree. 40Him God raised up on the third
day, and showed Him openly, 41not to all the
people, but to witnesses chosen before by
God, *even* to us who ate and drank with Him
after He arose from the dead. 42And He commanded us to preach to the people, and to
testify that it is He who was ordained by God
to be Judge of the living and the dead. 43To
Him all the prophets witness that, through
His name, whoever believes in Him will receive remission of sins."

The Holy Spirit Falls on the Gentiles

44While Peter was still speaking these
words, the Holy Spirit fell upon all those
who heard the word. 45And those of the circumcision who believed were astonished, as
many as came with Peter, because the gift of
the Holy Spirit had been poured out on the
Gentiles also. 46For they heard them speak
with tongues and magnify God.

Then Peter answered, 47"Can anyone forbid water, that these should not be baptized
who have received the Holy Spirit just as
we *have*?" 48And he commanded them to be
baptized in the name of the Lord. Then they
asked him to stay a few days.

Peter Defends God's Grace

11 Now the apostles and brethren who
were in Judea heard that the Gentiles had also received the word of God. 2And
when Peter came up to Jerusalem, those of
the circumcision contended with him, 3say-
ing, "You went in to uncircumcised men
and ate with them!"

4But Peter explained *it* to them in order
from the beginning, saying: 5"I was in the
city of Joppa praying; and in a trance I saw
a vision, an object descending like a great
sheet, let down from heaven by four corners; and it came to me. 6When I observed
it intently and considered, I saw four-footed
animals of the earth, wild beasts, creeping
things, and birds of the air. 7And I heard a
voice saying to me, 'Rise, Peter; kill and eat.'
8But I said, 'Not so, Lord! For nothing common or unclean has at any time entered my
mouth.' 9But the voice answered me again
from heaven, 'What God has cleansed you
must not call common.' 10Now this was
done three times, and all were drawn up
again into heaven. 11At that very moment,
three men stood before the house where
I was, having been sent to me from Caesarea. 12Then the Spirit told me to go with
them, doubting nothing. Moreover these six
brethren accompanied me, and we entered
the man's house. 13And he told us how he
had seen an angel standing in his house,
who said to him, 'Send men to Joppa, and
call for Simon whose surname is Peter,
14who will tell you words by which you and
all your household will be saved.' 15And as
I began to speak, the Holy Spirit fell upon
them, as upon us at the beginning. 16Then I
remembered the word of the Lord, how He
said, 'John indeed baptized with water, but
you shall be baptized with the Holy Spirit.'
17If therefore God gave them the same gift
as *He gave* us when we believed on the Lord
Jesus Christ, who was I that I could withstand God?"

18When they heard these things they became silent; and they glorified God, saying,
"Then God has also granted to the Gentiles
repentance to life."

10:32 [a] NU-Text omits the last sentence of this verse.
10:39 [a] NU-Text and M-Text add *also*.

Barnabas and Saul at Antioch

19Now those who were scattered after the
persecution that arose over Stephen traveled
as far as Phoenicia, Cyprus, and Antioch,
preaching the word to no one but the Jews
only. 20But some of them were men from
Cyprus and Cyrene, who, when they had
come to Antioch, spoke to the Hellenists,
preaching the Lord Jesus. 21And the hand of
the Lord was with them, and a great number
believed and turned to the Lord.

22Then news of these things came to the
ears of the church in Jerusalem, and they
sent out Barnabas to go as far as Antioch.
23When he came and had seen the grace of
God, he was glad, and encouraged them
all that with purpose of heart they should
continue with the Lord. 24For he was a good
man, full of the Holy Spirit and of faith. And
a great many people were added to the Lord.

25Then Barnabas departed for Tarsus to
seek Saul. 26And when he had found him,
he brought him to Antioch. So it was that
for a whole year they assembled with the
church and taught a great many people. And
the disciples were first called Christians in
Antioch.

Relief to Judea

27And in these days prophets came from
Jerusalem to Antioch. 28Then one of them,
named Agabus, stood up and showed by
the Spirit that there was going to be a great
famine throughout all the world, which
also happened in the days of Claudius Caesar. 29Then the disciples, each according to
his ability, determined to send relief to the
brethren dwelling in Judea. 30This they also
did, and sent it to the elders by the hands of
Barnabas and Saul.

Herod's Violence to the Church

12 Now about that time Herod the
king stretched out *his* hand to harass some from the church. 2Then he killed
James the brother of John with the sword.
3And because he saw that it pleased the Jews,
he proceeded further to seize Peter also.
Now it was *during* the Days of Unleavened
Bread. 4So when he had arrested him, he
put *him* in prison, and delivered *him* to four
squads of soldiers to keep him, intending to
bring him before the people after Passover.

Peter Freed from Prison

5Peter was therefore kept in prison, but

In Focus

11:26 Christians People who believe in and follow Jesus Christ. People were first called Christians after Jesus rose from death.

constant[a] prayer was offered to God for him
by the church. 6And when Herod was about
to bring him out, that night Peter was sleeping, bound with two chains between two soldiers; and the guards before the door were
keeping the prison. 7Now behold, an angel
of the Lord stood by *him*, and a light shone
in the prison; and he struck Peter on the side
and raised him up, saying, "Arise quickly!"
And his chains fell off *his* hands. 8Then the
angel said to him, "Gird yourself and tie on
your sandals"; and so he did. And he said to
him, "Put on your garment and follow me."
9So he went out and followed him, and did
not know that what was done by the angel
was real, but thought he was seeing a vision.
10When they were past the first and the second guard posts, they came to the iron gate
that leads to the city, which opened to them
of its own accord; and they went out and
went down one street, and immediately the
angel departed from him.

11And when Peter had come to himself,
he said, "Now I know for certain that the
Lord has sent His angel, and has delivered
me from the hand of Herod and *from* all the
expectation of the Jewish people."

12So, when he had considered *this*, he
came to the house of Mary, the mother of
John whose surname was Mark, where
many were gathered together praying. 13And
as Peter knocked at the door of the gate, a
girl named Rhoda came to answer. 14When
she recognized Peter's voice, because of *her*
gladness she did not open the gate, but ran
in and announced that Peter stood before
the gate. 15But they said to her, "You are beside yourself!" Yet she kept insisting that it
was so. So they said, "It is his angel."

16Now Peter continued knocking; and
when they opened *the door* and saw him,
they were astonished. 17But motioning to

12:5 [a] NU-Text reads *constantly* (or *earnestly*).

them with his hand to keep silent, he declared to them how the Lord had brought him out of the prison. And he said, "Go, tell these things to James and to the brethren." And he departed and went to another place.

18 Then, as soon as it was day, there was no small stir among the soldiers about what had become of Peter. 19 But when Herod had searched for him and not found him, he examined the guards and commanded that *they* should be put to death.

And he went down from Judea to Caesarea, and stayed *there*.

Herod's Violent Death

20 Now Herod had been very angry with the people of Tyre and Sidon; but they came to him with one accord, and having made Blastus the king's personal aide their friend, they asked for peace, because their country was supplied with food by the king's *country*.

21 So on a set day Herod, arrayed in royal apparel, sat on his throne and gave an oration to them. 22 And the people kept shouting, "The voice of a god and not of a man!" 23 Then immediately an angel of the Lord struck him, because he did not give glory to God. And he was eaten by worms and died.

24 But the word of God grew and multiplied.

Barnabas and Saul Appointed

25 And Barnabas and Saul returned from[a] Jerusalem when they had fulfilled *their* ministry, and they also took with them John whose surname was Mark.

13 Now in the church that was at Antioch there were certain prophets and teachers: Barnabas, Simeon who was called Niger, Lucius of Cyrene, Manaen who had been brought up with Herod the tetrarch, and Saul. 2 As they ministered to the Lord and fasted, the Holy Spirit said, "Now separate to Me Barnabas and Saul for the work to which I have called them." 3 Then, having fasted and prayed, and laid hands on them, they sent *them* away.

Preaching in Cyprus

4 So, being sent out by the Holy Spirit, they went down to Seleucia, and from there they sailed to Cyprus. 5 And when they arrived in Salamis, they preached the word of God in the synagogues of the Jews. They also had John as *their* assistant.

6 Now when they had gone through the island[a] to Paphos, they found a certain sorcerer, a false prophet, a Jew whose name *was* Bar-Jesus, 7 who was with the proconsul, Sergius Paulus, an intelligent man. This man called for Barnabas and Saul and sought to hear the word of God. 8 But Elymas the sorcerer (for so his name is translated) withstood them, seeking to turn the proconsul away from the faith. 9 Then Saul, who also *is called* Paul, filled with the Holy Spirit, looked intently at him 10 and said, "O full of all deceit and all fraud, *you* son of the devil, *you* enemy of all righteousness, will you not cease perverting the straight ways of the Lord? 11 And now, indeed, the hand of the Lord *is* upon you, and you shall be blind, not seeing the sun for a time."

And immediately a dark mist fell on him, and he went around seeking someone to lead him by the hand. 12 Then the proconsul believed, when he saw what had been done, being astonished at the teaching of the Lord.

At Antioch in Pisidia

13 Now when Paul and his party set sail from Paphos, they came to Perga in Pamphylia; and John, departing from them, returned to Jerusalem. 14 But when they departed from Perga, they came to Antioch in Pisidia, and went into the synagogue on the Sabbath day and sat down. 15 And after the reading of the Law and the Prophets, the rulers of the synagogue sent to them, saying, "Men *and* brethren, if you have any word of exhortation for the people, say on."

16 Then Paul stood up, and motioning with *his* hand said, "Men of Israel, and you who fear God, listen: 17 The God of this people Israel[a] chose our fathers, and exalted the people when they dwelt as strangers in the land of Egypt, and with an uplifted arm He brought them out of it. 18 Now for a time of about forty years He put up with their ways in the wilderness. 19 And when He had destroyed seven nations in the land of Canaan, He distributed their land to them by allotment.

20 "After that He gave *them* judges for about four hundred and fifty years, until Samuel the prophet. 21 And afterward they asked for a king; so God gave them Saul the son of Kish, a man of the tribe of Benjamin, for forty years. 22 And when He had removed him, He raised up for them David as king,

---

12:25 [a] NU-Text and M-Text read *to.* **13:6** [a] NU-Text reads *the whole island.* **13:17** [a] M-Text omits *Israel.*

to whom also He gave testimony and said,
'I have found David[a] the *son* of Jesse, a man
after My *own* heart, who will do all My will.'[b]
23From this man's seed, according to *the*
promise, God raised up for Israel a Savior—
Jesus—[a] 24after John had first preached, before His coming, the baptism of repentance
to all the people of Israel. 25And as John was
finishing his course, he said, 'Who do you
think I am? I am not *He*. But behold, there
comes One after me, the sandals of whose
feet I am not worthy to loose.'
26"Men *and* brethren, sons of the family of Abraham, and those among you who
fear God, to you the word of this salvation
has been sent. 27For those who dwell in Jerusalem, and their rulers, because they did
not know Him, nor even the voices of the
Prophets which are read every Sabbath,

In Focus

13:15 Exhortation Pronounced *egg-zor-TAY-shun*. A speech or writing that is meant to warn or encourage people.

have fulfilled *them* in condemning *Him*.
28And though they found no cause for death
in Him, they asked Pilate that He should be
put to death. 29Now when they had fulfilled
all that was written concerning Him, they

13:22 [a] Psalm 89:20 [b] 1 Samuel 13:14 13:23 [a] M-Text reads *for Israel salvation*.

Spotlight

PAUL PREACHES THE GOSPEL ON HIS FIRST TRIP

READ IT: ACTS 13:4–52

GET IT:

Saul became a great missionary for God. He was first called by his Jewish name, Saul. Later he changed his name to Paul, the Greek translation of Saul. At first he preached in the area around Jerusalem. Then he became a missionary to areas farther away. On his first mission trip he went to the island of Cyprus and to cities in Asia Minor (modern-day Turkey). He preached to the Jews in the synagogues, performed miracles, and amazed everyone. The non-Jews (Gentiles) in Antioch wanted to hear what Paul preached as well. So Paul also preached to them, but the Jews got jealous and ran Paul and his helper Barnabas out of town.

LIVE IT:

God commanded Paul to preach, so when the Jews in Antioch wouldn't listen, he preached to the other people. He had to change his thinking and remember what his primary purpose was—to preach the good news. Sometimes we have big plans and a specific goal. But then we find out that we have to adjust partway through. We shouldn't quit completely; we just need to make an adjustment and move on toward the goal.

took *Him* down from the tree and laid *Him*
in a tomb. 30But God raised Him from the
dead. 31He was seen for many days by those
who came up with Him from Galilee to Jerusalem, who are His witnesses to the people.
32And we declare to you glad tidings—that
promise which was made to the fathers.
33God has fulfilled this for us their children,
in that He has raised up Jesus. As it is also
written in the second Psalm:

'You are My Son,
Today I have begotten You.' [a]

34And that He raised Him from the dead, no
more to return to corruption, He has spoken
thus:

'I will give you the sure mercies of
David.' [a]

35Therefore He also says in another *Psalm:*

'You will not allow Your Holy One to see
corruption.' [a]

36"For David, after he had served his own
generation by the will of God, fell asleep, was
buried with his fathers, and saw corruption;
37but He whom God raised up saw no corruption. 38Therefore let it be known to you,
brethren, that through this Man is preached
to you the forgiveness of sins; 39and by Him
everyone who believes is justified from all
things from which you could not be justified
by the law of Moses. 40Beware therefore, lest
what has been spoken in the prophets come
upon you:

41 'Behold, you despisers,
Marvel and perish!
For I work a work in your days,
A work which you will by no means
believe,
Though one were to declare it to you.' " [a]

Blessing and Conflict at Antioch

42So when the Jews went out of the synagogue,[a] the Gentiles begged that these words
might be preached to them the next Sabbath.
43Now when the congregation had broken
up, many of the Jews and devout proselytes
followed Paul and Barnabas, who, speaking
to them, persuaded them to continue in the
grace of God.

44On the next Sabbath almost the whole
city came together to hear the word of God.
45But when the Jews saw the multitudes, they
were filled with envy; and contradicting and
blaspheming, they opposed the things spoken by Paul. 46Then Paul and Barnabas grew
bold and said, "It was necessary that the
word of God should be spoken to you first;
but since you reject it, and judge yourselves
unworthy of everlasting life, behold, we turn
to the Gentiles. 47For so the Lord has commanded us:

'I have set you as a light to the Gentiles,
That you should be for salvation to the
ends of the earth.' " [a]

48Now when the Gentiles heard this, they
were glad and glorified the word of the Lord.
And as many as had been appointed to eternal life believed.

49And the word of the Lord was being
spread throughout all the region. 50But the
Jews stirred up the devout and prominent
women and the chief men of the city, raised
up persecution against Paul and Barnabas,
and expelled them from their region. 51But
they shook off the dust from their feet
against them, and came to Iconium. 52And
the disciples were filled with joy and with
the Holy Spirit.

At Iconium

14 Now it happened in Iconium that
they went together to the syna-
gogue of the Jews, and so spoke that a great
multitude both of the Jews and of the Greeks
believed. 2But the unbelieving Jews stirred
up the Gentiles and poisoned their minds
against the brethren. 3Therefore they stayed
there a long time, speaking boldly in the
Lord, who was bearing witness to the word
of His grace, granting signs and wonders to
be done by their hands.

4But the multitude of the city was divided: part sided with the Jews, and part with
the apostles. 5And when a violent attempt
was made by both the Gentiles and Jews,
with their rulers, to abuse and stone them,
6they became aware of it and fled to Lystra
and Derbe, cities of Lycaonia, and to the surrounding region. 7And they were preaching
the gospel there.

Idolatry at Lystra

8And in Lystra a certain man without

13:33 [a] Psalm 2:7 13:34 [a] Isaiah 55:3 13:35 [a] Psalm 16:10
13:41 [a] Habakkuk 1:5 13:42 [a] Or *And when they went out of the synagogue of the Jews;* NU-Text reads *And when they went out, they begged.* 13:47 [a] Isaiah 49:6

strength in his feet was sitting, a cripple
from his mother's womb, who had never
walked. 9 *This* man heard Paul speaking.
Paul, observing him intently and seeing
that he had faith to be healed, 10 said with a
loud voice, "Stand up straight on your feet!"
And he leaped and walked. 11 Now when the
people saw what Paul had done, they raised
their voices, saying in the Lycaonian *language,* "The gods have come down to us in
the likeness of men!" 12 And Barnabas they
called Zeus, and Paul, Hermes, because he
was the chief speaker. 13 Then the priest of
Zeus, whose temple was in front of their
city, brought oxen and garlands to the gates,
intending to sacrifice with the multitudes.

14 But when the apostles Barnabas and
Paul heard this, they tore their clothes and
ran in among the multitude, crying out
15 and saying, "Men, why are you doing these
things? We also are men with the same
nature as you, and preach to you that you
should turn from these useless things to the
living God, who made the heaven, the earth,
the sea, and all things that are in them, 16 who
in bygone generations allowed all nations to
walk in their own ways. 17 Nevertheless He
did not leave Himself without witness, in
that He did good, gave us rain from heaven
and fruitful seasons, filling our hearts with
food and gladness." 18 And with these sayings
they could scarcely restrain the multitudes
from sacrificing to them.

Stoning, Escape to Derbe

19 Then Jews from Antioch and Iconium
came there; and having persuaded the multitudes, they stoned Paul *and* dragged *him*
out of the city, supposing him to be dead.
20 However, when the disciples gathered
around him, he rose up and went into the
city. And the next day he departed with Barnabas to Derbe.

Strengthening the Converts

21 And when they had preached the gospel
to that city and made many disciples, they
returned to Lystra, Iconium, and Antioch,
22 strengthening the souls of the disciples,
exhorting *them* to continue in the faith, and
saying, "We must through many tribulations enter the kingdom of God." 23 So when
they had appointed elders in every church,
and prayed with fasting, they commended
them to the Lord in whom they had believed.
24 And after they had passed through Pisidia,
they came to Pamphylia. 25 Now when they
had preached the word in Perga, they went
down to Attalia. 26 From there they sailed to
Antioch, where they had been commended
to the grace of God for the work which they
had completed.

27 Now when they had come and gathered the church together, they reported all
that God had done with them, and that He
had opened the door of faith to the Gentiles.
28 So they stayed there a long time with the
disciples.

Conflict over Circumcision

15 And certain *men* came down from
Judea and taught the brethren,
"Unless you are circumcised according to
the custom of Moses, you cannot be saved."
2 Therefore, when Paul and Barnabas had
no small dissension and dispute with them,
they determined that Paul and Barnabas and
certain others of them should go up to Jerusalem, to the apostles and elders, about this
question.

3 So, being sent on their way by the
church, they passed through Phoenicia and
Samaria, describing the conversion of the
Gentiles; and they caused great joy to all the
brethren. 4 And when they had come to Jerusalem, they were received by the church and
the apostles and the elders; and they reported all things that God had done with them.
5 But some of the sect of the Pharisees who
believed rose up, saying, "It is necessary to
circumcise them, and to command *them* to
keep the law of Moses."

The Jerusalem Council

6 Now the apostles and elders came together to consider this matter. 7 And when there
had been much dispute, Peter rose up *and*
said to them: "Men *and* brethren, you know
that a good while ago God chose among us,
that by my mouth the Gentiles should hear
the word of the gospel and believe. 8 So God,
who knows the heart, acknowledged them
by giving them the Holy Spirit, just as *He
did* to us, 9 and made no distinction between
us and them, purifying their hearts by faith.
10 Now therefore, why do you test God by putting a yoke on the neck of the disciples which
neither our fathers nor we were able to bear?
11 But we believe that through the grace of the

15:11 [a] NU-Text and M-Text omit *Christ.*

Lord Jesus Christ[a] we shall be saved in the
same manner as they."
12 Then all the multitude kept silent and
listened to Barnabas and Paul declaring
how many miracles and wonders God had
worked through them among the Gentiles.
13 And after they had become silent, James
answered, saying, "Men *and* brethren, listen to me: 14 Simon has declared how God at
the first visited the Gentiles to take out of
them a people for His name. 15 And with this
the words of the prophets agree, just as it is
written:

16 'After this I will return
And will rebuild the tabernacle of
David, which has fallen down;
I will rebuild its ruins,
And I will set it up;
17 So that the rest of mankind may seek
the LORD,
Even all the Gentiles who are called by
My name,
Says the LORD who does all these
things.'[a]

18 "Known to God from eternity are all His
works.[a] 19 Therefore I judge that we should
not trouble those from among the Gentiles
who are turning to God, 20 but that we write
to them to abstain from things polluted by
idols, *from* sexual immorality,[a] *from* things
strangled, and *from* blood. 21 For Moses has
had throughout many generations those
who preach him in every city, being read in
the synagogues every Sabbath."

The Jerusalem Decree

22 Then it pleased the apostles and elders,
with the whole church, to send chosen men
of their own company to Antioch with Paul
and Barnabas, *namely,* Judas who was also
named Barsabas,[a] and Silas, leading men
among the brethren.
23 They wrote this *letter* by them:

The apostles, the elders, and the
brethren,

To the brethren who are of the Gentiles
in Antioch, Syria, and Cilicia:

Greetings.

24 Since we have heard that some who
went out from us have troubled you with
words, unsettling your souls, saying,
"*You must* be circumcised and keep
the law"[a]—to whom we gave no *such*
commandment— 25 it seemed good to
us, being assembled with one accord,
to send chosen men to you with our
beloved Barnabas and Paul, 26 men who
have risked their lives for the name
of our Lord Jesus Christ. 27 We have
therefore sent Judas and Silas, who will
also report the same things by word
of mouth. 28 For it seemed good to the
Holy Spirit, and to us, to lay upon you
no greater burden than these necessary
things: 29 that you abstain from things
offered to idols, from blood, from things
strangled, and from sexual immorality.[a]
If you keep yourselves from these, you
will do well.

Farewell.

In Focus

15:3 Conversion Pronounced *kon-VERR-zhun.* Means changing over from one kind of life to another kind. A person is "converted" by being "born again" (see definition at John 3:3).

Continuing Ministry in Syria

30 So when they were sent off, they came
to Antioch; and when they had gathered the
multitude together, they delivered the letter.
31 When they had read it, they rejoiced over
its encouragement. 32 Now Judas and Silas,
themselves being prophets also, exhorted
and strengthened the brethren with many
words. 33 And after they had stayed *there* for
a time, they were sent back with greetings
from the brethren to the apostles.[a]
34 However, it seemed good to Silas to
remain there.[a] 35 Paul and Barnabas also remained in Antioch, teaching and preaching
the word of the Lord, with many others also.

15:17 [a] Amos 9:11, 12 **15:18** [a] NU-Text (combining with verse 17) reads *Says the Lord, who makes these things known from eternity (of old).* **15:20** [a] Or *fornication* **15:22** [a] NU-Text and M-Text read *Barsabbas.* **15:24** [a] NU-Text omits *saying, "You must be circumcised and keep the law."* **15:29** [a] Or *fornication* **15:33** [a] NU-Text reads *to those who had sent them.* **15:34** [a] NU-Text and M-Text omit this verse.

Division over John Mark

36 Then after some days Paul said to
Barnabas, "Let us now go back and visit
our brethren in every city where we have
preached the word of the Lord, *and see* how
they are doing." 37 Now Barnabas was determined to take with them John called Mark.
38 But Paul insisted that they should not take
with them the one who had departed from
them in Pamphylia, and had not gone with
them to the work. 39 Then the contention became so sharp that they parted from one another. And so Barnabas took Mark and sailed
to Cyprus; 40 but Paul chose Silas and departed, being commended by the brethren to
the grace of God. 41 And he went through Syria and Cilicia, strengthening the churches.

Timothy Joins Paul and Silas

16 Then he came to Derbe and Lystra.
And behold, a certain disciple was
there, named Timothy, *the* son of a certain
Jewish woman who believed, but his father
was Greek. 2 He was well spoken of by the
brethren who were at Lystra and Iconium.
3 Paul wanted to have him go on with him.
And he took *him* and circumcised him because of the Jews who were in that region,
for they all knew that his father was Greek.
4 And as they went through the cities, they

PAUL PREACHES IN PHILIPPI ON HIS SECOND TRIP

READ IT: ACTS 16:1–40

GET IT:

After his first trip, Paul went back to Jerusalem for a church meeting. Then he went on a second mission trip. He first stopped in some cities in Asia Minor (Derbe and Lystra), where a man named Timothy joined the church as a preacher. Then one night Paul had a vision telling him to go to Macedonia (modern-day northern Greece). He sailed to the seaport Neapolis. Then he walked ten miles up the mountain road to Philippi. There were only a few Jews in this city, so they didn't have a synagogue. Paul preached to a group of women a few miles outside the city by the river. Lydia believed what she heard. Later a jailer also believed. And so a Christian church started in Philippi.

LIVE IT:

Have you ever been invited to a party and then wondered if you should go? Maybe you worried that you'd be disappointed—the food would be gross, you wouldn't know anybody, or the music would be weird. When he showed up someplace, Paul never worried about what he would find. He went all the way to Macedonia because Jesus told him to (v. 10). When he got there, he found only a small group of Jewish women to preach to. Had *he come all this way* just for this? Yes. He was happy to preach to anyone who would listen. We need to follow Paul's example: just go, just do it. It might turn out much, much better than we think.

delivered to them the decrees to keep, which
were determined by the apostles and elders at Jerusalem. 5So the churches were
strengthened in the faith, and increased in
number daily.

The Macedonian Call

6Now when they had gone through
Phrygia and the region of Galatia, they
were forbidden by the Holy Spirit to preach
the word in Asia. 7After they had come to
Mysia, they tried to go into Bithynia, but
the Spirit[a] did not permit them. 8So passing
by Mysia, they came down to Troas. 9And a
vision appeared to Paul in the night. A man
of Macedonia stood and pleaded with him,
saying, "Come over to Macedonia and help
us." 10Now after he had seen the vision, immediately we sought to go to Macedonia,
concluding that the Lord had called us to
preach the gospel to them.

Lydia Baptized at Philippi

11Therefore, sailing from Troas, we ran a
straight course to Samothrace, and the next
day came to Neapolis, 12and from there to
Philippi, which is the foremost city of that
part of Macedonia, a colony. And we were
staying in that city for some days. 13And on
the Sabbath day we went out of the city to
the riverside, where prayer was customari-
ly made; and we sat down and spoke to the
women who met *there.* 14Now a certain woman named Lydia heard *us.* She was a seller of
purple from the city of Thyatira, who worshiped God. The Lord opened her heart to
heed the things spoken by Paul. 15And when
she and her household were baptized, she
begged *us,* saying, "If you have judged me
to be faithful to the Lord, come to my house
and stay." So she persuaded us.

Paul and Silas Imprisoned

16Now it happened, as we went to prayer,
that a certain slave girl possessed with a
spirit of divination met us, who brought
her masters much profit by fortune-telling.
17This girl followed Paul and us, and cried
out, saying, "These men are the servants of
the Most High God, who proclaim to us the
way of salvation." 18And this she did for many
days.

But Paul, greatly annoyed, turned and
said to the spirit, "I command you in the
name of Jesus Christ to come out of her."
And he came out that very hour. 19But when
her masters saw that their hope of profit was
gone, they seized Paul and Silas and dragged
them into the marketplace to the authorities.

20And they brought them to the magistrates, and said, "These men, being Jews, exceedingly trouble our city; 21and they teach
customs which are not lawful for us, being
Romans, to receive or observe." 22Then the
multitude rose up together against them;
and the magistrates tore off their clothes

16:7 [a] NU-Text adds *of Jesus.*

Starring Roles

You should pronounce **LYDIA'S** name *LID-ee-ah.* She was a wealthy business-woman in the city of Philippi (pronounced *FILL-ih-pie*). The city was named for King Philip, the father of Alexander the Great.

Lydia's original home was in Thyatira (pronounced *thigh-uh-TIE-ruh*). Thyatira was in Asia Minor, across the Aegean Sea from Greece. She sold purple cloth that was used to make clothing for royalty and wealthy people.

On the Sabbath day, she always went with Jewish believers to pray by a river outside Philippi. One day the apostle Paul went with his friends—Luke, Silas, and Timothy—and told the people there about Jesus the Savior.

Lydia and her whole family believed in Jesus as their Lord and Savior that day, and they were all baptized.

and commanded *them* to be beaten with rods. 23And when they had laid many stripes on them, they threw *them* into prison, commanding the jailer to keep them securely. 24Having received such a charge, he put them into the inner prison and fastened their feet in the stocks.

The Philippian Jailer Saved

25But at midnight Paul and Silas were praying and singing hymns to God, and the prisoners were listening to them. 26Suddenly there was a great earthquake, so that the foundations of the prison were shaken; and immediately all the doors were opened and everyone's chains were loosed. 27And the keeper of the prison, awaking from sleep and seeing the prison doors open, supposing the prisoners had fled, drew his sword and was about to kill himself. 28But Paul called with a loud voice, saying, "Do yourself no harm, for we are all here."

29Then he called for a light, ran in, and fell down trembling before Paul and Silas. 30And he brought them out and said, "Sirs, what must I do to be saved?"

31So they said, "Believe on the Lord Jesus Christ, and you will be saved, you and your household." 32Then they spoke the word of the Lord to him and to all who were in his house. 33And he took them the same hour of the night and washed *their* stripes. And immediately he and all his *family* were baptized. 34Now when he had brought them into his house, he set food before them; and he rejoiced, having believed in God with all his household.

Paul Refuses to Depart Secretly

35And when it was day, the magistrates sent the officers, saying, "Let those men go."

36So the keeper of the prison reported these words to Paul, saying, "The magistrates have sent to let you go. Now therefore depart, and go in peace."

37But Paul said to them, "They have beaten us openly, uncondemned Romans, *and* have thrown *us* into prison. And now do they put us out secretly? No indeed! Let them come themselves and get us out."

38*And the officers* told these words to the magistrates, and they were afraid when they heard that they were Romans. 39Then they came and pleaded with them and brought *them* out, and asked *them* to depart from the city. 40So they went out of the prison and entered *the house of* Lydia; and when they had seen the brethren, they encouraged them and departed.

Preaching Christ at Thessalonica

17 Now when they had passed through Amphipolis and Apollonia, they came to Thessalonica, where there was a synagogue of the Jews. 2Then Paul, as his custom was, went in to them, and for three Sabbaths reasoned with them from the Scriptures, 3explaining and demonstrating that the Christ had to suffer and rise again from the dead, and *saying,* "This Jesus whom I preach to you is the Christ." 4And some of them were persuaded; and a great multitude of the devout Greeks, and not a few of the leading women, joined Paul and Silas.

Assault on Jason's House

5But the Jews who were not persuaded, becoming envious,[a] took some of the evil men from the marketplace, and gathering a mob, set all the city in an uproar and attacked the house of Jason, and sought to bring them out to the people. 6But when they did not find them, they dragged Jason and some brethren to the rulers of the city, crying out, "These who have turned the world upside down have come here too. 7Jason has harbored them, and these are all acting contrary to the decrees of Caesar, saying there is another king—Jesus." 8And they troubled the crowd and the rulers of the city when they heard these things. 9So when they had taken security from Jason and the rest, they let them go.

Ministering at Berea

10Then the brethren immediately sent Paul and Silas away by night to Berea. When they arrived, they went into the synagogue of the Jews. 11These were more fair-minded than those in Thessalonica, in that they received the word with all readiness, and searched the Scriptures daily *to find out* whether these things were so. 12Therefore many of them believed, and also not a few of the Greeks, prominent women as well as men. 13But when the Jews from Thessalonica learned that the word of God was preached

17:5 [a] NU-Text omits *who were not persuaded;* M-Text omits *becoming envious.*

by Paul at Berea, they came there also and
stirred up the crowds. 14Then immediately
the brethren sent Paul away, to go to the sea;
but both Silas and Timothy remained there.
15So those who conducted Paul brought him
to Athens; and receiving a command for
Silas and Timothy to come to him with all
speed, they departed.

The Philosophers at Athens

16Now while Paul waited for them at
Athens, his spirit was provoked within
him when he saw that the city was given
over to idols. 17Therefore he reasoned in
the synagogue with the Jews and with the
Gentile worshipers, and in the marketplace
daily with those who happened to be there.
18Then[a] certain Epicurean and Stoic philos-
ophers encountered him. And some said,
"What does this babbler want to say?"

Others said, "He seems to be a proclaim-
er of foreign gods," because he preached to
them Jesus and the resurrection.

19And they took him and brought him to
the Areopagus, saying, "May we know what
this new doctrine *is* of which you speak?
20For you are bringing some strange things
to our ears. Therefore we want to know what
these things mean." 21For all the Athenians
and the foreigners who were there spent
their time in nothing else but either to tell
or to hear some new thing.

Addressing the Areopagus

22Then Paul stood in the midst of the Areopagus and said, "Men of Athens, I perceive
that in all things you are very religious; 23for
as I was passing through and considering
the objects of your worship, I even found an
altar with this inscription:

TO THE UNKNOWN GOD.

Therefore, the One whom you worship
without knowing, Him I proclaim to you:
24God, who made the world and everything
in it, since He is Lord of heaven and earth,
does not dwell in temples made with hands.
25Nor is He worshiped with men's hands, as
though He needed anything, since He gives
to all life, breath, and all things. 26And He
has made from one blood[a] every nation of
men to dwell on all the face of the earth, and
has determined their preappointed times
and the boundaries of their dwellings, 27so
that they should seek the Lord, in the hope
that they might grope for Him and find
Him, though He is not far from each one of
us; 28for in Him we live and move and have
our being, as also some of your own poets
have said, 'For we are also His offspring.'
29Therefore, since we are the offspring of
God, we ought not to think that the Divine
Nature is like gold or silver or stone, something shaped by art and man's devising.
30Truly, these times of ignorance God overlooked, but now commands all men everywhere to repent, 31because He has appointed
a day on which He will judge the world in
righteousness by the Man whom He has

17:18 [a] NU-Text and M-Text add *also*. **17:26** [a] NU-Text omits *blood*.

KNOWING AND FINDING GOD

READ IT: ACTS 17:24–28

God wants everyone to seek Him, know Him, love Him, and live with Him. Even though He made everything in heaven and earth, His greatest desire is that each and every person would look for Him. He doesn't make it hard. He doesn't hide in some faraway place. He doesn't send us on a wild goose chase. He's near to each of us because He is everywhere, waiting for us to reach out to Him.

ordained. He has given assurance of this to
all by raising Him from the dead."
32 And when they heard of the resurrection of the dead, some mocked, while others
said, "We will hear you again on this *matter*." 33 So Paul departed from among them.
34 However, some men joined him and believed, among them Dionysius the Areopa-
gite, a woman named Damaris, and others
with them.

Ministering at Corinth

18 After these things Paul departed
from Athens and went to Corinth.
2 And he found a certain Jew named Aquila, born in Pontus, who had recently come
from Italy with his wife Priscilla (because
Claudius had commanded all the Jews to depart from Rome); and he came to them. 3 So,
because he was of the same trade, he stayed
with them and worked; for by occupation
they were tentmakers. 4 And he reasoned in
the synagogue every Sabbath, and persuaded both Jews and Greeks.
5 When Silas and Timothy had come
from Macedonia, Paul was compelled by the
Spirit, and testified to the Jews *that* Jesus
is the Christ. 6 But when they opposed him
and blasphemed, he shook *his* garments
and said to them, "Your blood *be* upon your
own heads; I *am* clean. From now on I will
go to the Gentiles." 7 And he departed from
there and entered the house of a certain
man named Justus,[a] *one* who worshiped
God, whose house was next door to the
synagogue. 8 Then Crispus, the ruler of the
synagogue, believed on the Lord with all his
household. And many of the Corinthians,
hearing, believed and were baptized.

18:7 [a] NU-Text reads *Titius Justus*.

PAUL PREACHES IN CORINTH

READ IT: ACTS 18:1–28

GET IT:

Paul continued his journey in Greece. He preached to the Greeks in Athens, a city that was full of idols. Then he traveled south to the city of Corinth. The city was full of temples for Greek gods and goddesses. Paul stayed in Corinth with Priscilla and Aquila for over a year. He worked as a tentmaker and preached every Sabbath day in the synagogue. After a while he started preaching to the non-Jews and established a church in the city. But the Jews were not happy with Paul. They brought him to court, but the case was dismissed. Paul's preaching led some people to believe in Jesus, but other people made Paul's life difficult.

LIVE IT:

Do people get nasty when you act differently because you are a Christian? Do they make fun of you or call you stupid because you choose to show love, not hate, toward everyone? Paul stood up for what he believed and for what he preached even when the Jews got violent or dragged him into court. It may be hard, but we need to be strong like Paul. We need to do the right thing and show love to others even when the group we hang with does something else.

[9]Now the Lord spoke to Paul in the night
by a vision, "Do not be afraid, but speak, and
do not keep silent; [10]for I am with you, and
no one will attack you to hurt you; for I have
many people in this city." [11]And he continued *there* a year and six months, teaching the
word of God among them.

[12]When Gallio was proconsul of Achaia,
the Jews with one accord rose up against
Paul and brought him to the judgment seat,
[13]saying, "This *fellow* persuades men to worship God contrary to the law."

[14]And when Paul was about to open *his*
mouth, Gallio said to the Jews, "If it were a
matter of wrongdoing or wicked crimes, O
Jews, there would be reason why I should
bear with you. [15]But if it is a question of
words and names and your own law, look *to*
it yourselves; for I do not want to be a judge
of such *matters*." [16]And he drove them from
the judgment seat. [17]Then all the Greeks[a]
took Sosthenes, the ruler of the synagogue,
and beat *him* before the judgment seat. But
Gallio took no notice of these things.

Paul Returns to Antioch

[18]So Paul still remained a good while.
Then he took leave of the brethren and sailed
for Syria, and Priscilla and Aquila *were* with
him. He had *his* hair cut off at Cenchrea, for
he had taken a vow. [19]And he came to Ephesus, and left them there; but he himself entered the synagogue and reasoned with the
Jews. [20]When they asked *him* to stay a longer
time with them, he did not consent, [21]but
took leave of them, saying, "I must by all
means keep this coming feast in Jerusalem;[a]
but I will return again to you, God willing."
And he sailed from Ephesus.

[22]And when he had landed at Caesarea,
and gone up and greeted the church, he
went down to Antioch. [23]After he had spent
some time *there*, he departed and went over
the region of Galatia and Phrygia in order,
strengthening all the disciples.

Ministry of Apollos

[24]Now a certain Jew named Apollos, born
at Alexandria, an eloquent man *and* mighty
in the Scriptures, came to Ephesus. [25]This
man had been instructed in the way of the
Lord; and being fervent in spirit, he spoke
and taught accurately the things of the
Lord, though he knew only the baptism of
John. [26]So he began to speak boldly in the
synagogue. When Aquila and Priscilla heard
him, they took him aside and explained to
him the way of God more accurately. [27]And
when he desired to cross to Achaia, the
brethren wrote, exhorting the disciples to
receive him; and when he arrived, he greatly helped those who had believed through
grace; [28]for he vigorously refuted the Jews
publicly, showing from the Scriptures that
Jesus is the Christ.

Paul at Ephesus

19 And it happened, while Apollos was
at Corinth, that Paul, having passed
through the upper regions, came to Ephesus. And finding some disciples [2]he said to
them, "Did you receive the Holy Spirit when
you believed?"

So they said to him, "We have not so
much as heard whether there is a Holy
Spirit."

[3]And he said to them, "Into what then
were you baptized?"

So they said, "Into John's baptism."

[4]Then Paul said, "John indeed baptized
with a baptism of repentance, saying to the
people that they should believe on Him who
would come after him, that is, on Christ
Jesus."

[5]When they heard *this*, they were baptized in the name of the Lord Jesus. [6]And
when Paul had laid hands on them, the Holy
Spirit came upon them, and they spoke with
tongues and prophesied. [7]Now the men were
about twelve in all.

[8]And he went into the synagogue and
spoke boldly for three months, reasoning
and persuading concerning the things of
the kingdom of God. [9]But when some were
hardened and did not believe, but spoke evil
of the Way before the multitude, he departed
from them and withdrew the disciples, reasoning daily in the school of Tyrannus. [10]And
this continued for two years, so that all who
dwelt in Asia heard the word of the Lord
Jesus, both Jews and Greeks.

Miracles Glorify Christ

[11]Now God worked unusual miracles
by the hands of Paul, [12]so that even hand-
kerchiefs or aprons were brought from his
body to the sick, and the diseases left them

18:17 [a] NU-Text reads *they all.* **18:21** [a] NU-Text omits *I must* through *Jerusalem.*

and the evil spirits went out of them. 13 Then
some of the itinerant Jewish exorcists took
it upon themselves to call the name of the
Lord Jesus over those who had evil spirits,
saying, "We[a] exorcise you by the Jesus whom
Paul preaches." 14 Also there were seven sons
of Sceva, a Jewish chief priest, who did so.
15 And the evil spirit answered and said,
"Jesus I know, and Paul I know; but who are
you?"
16 Then the man in whom the evil spirit
was leaped on them, overpowered[a] them,
and prevailed against them,[b] so that they
fled out of that house naked and wounded. 17 This became known both to all Jews
and Greeks dwelling in Ephesus; and fear
fell on them all, and the name of the Lord
Jesus was magnified. 18 And many who had
believed came confessing and telling their
deeds. 19 Also, many of those who had practiced magic brought their books together
and burned *them* in the sight of all. And they
counted up the value of them, and *it* totaled
fifty thousand *pieces* of silver. 20 So the word
of the Lord grew mightily and prevailed.

The Riot at Ephesus

21 When these things were accomplished,
Paul purposed in the Spirit, when he had
passed through Macedonia and Achaia, to
go to Jerusalem, saying, "After I have been
there, I must also see Rome." 22 So he sent
into Macedonia two of those who ministered
to him, Timothy and Erastus, but he himself
stayed in Asia for a time.
23 And about that time there arose a great
commotion about the Way. 24 For a certain
man named Demetrius, a silversmith, who
made silver shrines of Diana,[a] brought no
small profit to the craftsmen. 25 He called
them together with the workers of similar occupation, and said: "Men, you know
that we have our prosperity by this trade.
26 Moreover you see and hear that not only
at Ephesus, but throughout almost all Asia,
this Paul has persuaded and turned away
many people, saying that they are not gods
which are made with hands. 27 So not only is
this trade of ours in danger of falling into
disrepute, but also the temple of the great
goddess Diana may be despised and her
magnificence destroyed,[a] whom all Asia and
the world worship."
28 Now when they heard *this,* they were
full of wrath and cried out, saying, "Great *is*
Diana of the Ephesians!" 29 So the whole city
was filled with confusion, and rushed into

19:13 [a] NU-Text reads *I.* 19:16 [a] M-Text reads *and they overpowered.* [b] NU-Text reads *both of them.* 19:24 [a] Greek *Artemis* 19:27 [a] NU-Text reads *she be deposed from her magnificence.*

19:28 THE RIOT OVER DIANA

"Diana" was the Roman name for the Greek goddess Artemis (pronounced *ARE-teh-miss*). She was the goddess of the moon, hunting, wild animals, and purity. Diana was the main god at Ephesus (pronounced *EFF-uh-sus*). A great statue of Diana stood at the head of the harbor of Ephesus, and silver workers made a lot of money by selling small silver idols of Diana.

That was how Paul got in trouble. He told the people of Ephesus that anything made by human hands could not be a god. So the silver workers of Ephesus began to lose their business, and they started a riot.

Sometimes you have to expect trouble when you tell people the truth. The truth may even hurt some people—just as it hurt those silversmiths. But we can never be free by living in error and making money by doing so.

the theater with one accord, having seized
Gaius and Aristarchus, Macedonians, Paul's
travel companions. 30And when Paul wanted
to go in to the people, the disciples would
not allow him. 31Then some of the officials
of Asia, who were his friends, sent to him
pleading that he would not venture into the
theater. 32Some therefore cried one thing
and some another, for the assembly was confused, and most of them did not know why
they had come together. 33And they drew Alexander out of the multitude, the Jews putting him forward. And Alexander motioned
with his hand, and wanted to make his defense to the people. 34But when they found
out that he was a Jew, all with one voice cried
out for about two hours, "Great *is* Diana of
the Ephesians!"

35And when the city clerk had quieted
the crowd, he said: "Men of Ephesus, what
man is there who does not know that the
city of the Ephesians is temple guardian of
the great goddess Diana, and of the *image*
which fell down from Zeus? 36Therefore,
since these things cannot be denied, you
ought to be quiet and do nothing rashly. 37For
you have brought these men here who are
neither robbers of temples nor blasphemers
of your[a] goddess. 38Therefore, if Demetrius
and his fellow craftsmen have a case against
anyone, the courts are open and there are
proconsuls. Let them bring charges against
one another. 39But if you have any other inquiry to make, it shall be determined in the
lawful assembly. 40For we are in danger of
being called in question for today's uproar,
there being no reason which we may give to
account for this disorderly gathering." 41And
when he had said these things, he dismissed
the assembly.

Journeys in Greece

20 After the uproar had ceased, Paul
called the disciples to *himself,* embraced *them,* and departed to go to Macedonia. 2Now when he had gone over that region
and encouraged them with many words, he
came to Greece 3and stayed three months.
And when the Jews plotted against him as
he was about to sail to Syria, he decided to
return through Macedonia. 4And Sopater of
Berea accompanied him to Asia—also Aristarchus and Secundus of the Thessalonians,
and Gaius of Derbe, and Timothy, and Tychicus and Trophimus of Asia. 5These men,
going ahead, waited for us at Troas. 6But we
sailed away from Philippi after the Days of
Unleavened Bread, and in five days joined
them at Troas, where we stayed seven days.

Ministering at Troas

7Now on the first *day* of the week, when
the disciples came together to break bread,
Paul, ready to depart the next day, spoke to
them and continued his message until midnight. 8There were many lamps in the upper
room where they[a] were gathered together.
9And in a window sat a certain young man
named Eutychus, who was sinking into a
deep sleep. He was overcome by sleep; and
as Paul continued speaking, he fell down
from the third story and was taken up dead.
10But Paul went down, fell on him, and embracing *him* said, "Do not trouble yourselves,
for his life is in him." 11Now when he had
come up, had broken bread and eaten, and
talked a long while, even till daybreak, he departed. 12And they brought the young man in
alive, and they were not a little comforted.

From Troas to Miletus

13Then we went ahead to the ship and
sailed to Assos, there intending to take Paul
on board; for so he had given orders, intending himself to go on foot. 14And when he met
us at Assos, we took him on board and came
to Mitylene. 15We sailed from there, and the
next *day* came opposite Chios. The following
day we arrived at Samos and stayed at Tro-
gyllium. The next *day* we came to Miletus.
16For Paul had decided to sail past Ephesus,
so that he would not have to spend time in
Asia; for he was hurrying to be at Jerusalem,
if possible, on the Day of Pentecost.

The Ephesian Elders Exhorted

17From Miletus he sent to Ephesus and
called for the elders of the church. 18And
when they had come to him, he said to
them: "You know, from the first day that I
came to Asia, in what manner I always lived
among you, 19serving the Lord with all humility, with many tears and trials which
happened to me by the plotting of the Jews;
20how I kept back nothing that was helpful,
but proclaimed it to you, and taught you publicly and from house to house, 21testifying to
Jews, and also to Greeks, repentance toward

19:37 [a] NU-Text reads *our.* 20:8 [a] NU-Text and M-Text read *we.*

God and faith toward our Lord Jesus Christ.
22And see, now I go bound in the spirit to
Jerusalem, not knowing the things that will
happen to me there, 23except that the Holy
Spirit testifies in every city, saying that
chains and tribulations await me. 24But none
of these things move me; nor do I count my
life dear to myself,[a] so that I may finish my
race with joy, and the ministry which I received from the Lord Jesus, to testify to the
gospel of the grace of God.

25"And indeed, now I know that you all,
among whom I have gone preaching the
kingdom of God, will see my face no more.
26Therefore I testify to you this day that I
am innocent of the blood of all *men.* 27For
I have not shunned to declare to you the
whole counsel of God. 28Therefore take heed
to yourselves and to all the flock, among
which the Holy Spirit has made you overseers, to shepherd the church of God[a] which
He purchased with His own blood. 29For I
know this, that after my departure savage
wolves will come in among you, not sparing the flock. 30Also from among yourselves
men will rise up, speaking perverse things,
to draw away the disciples after themselves.
31Therefore watch, and remember that for
three years I did not cease to warn everyone
night and day with tears.

32"So now, brethren, I commend you to
God and to the word of His grace, which is
able to build you up and give you an inheritance among all those who are sanctified.
33I have coveted no one's silver or gold or apparel. 34Yes,[a] you yourselves know that these
hands have provided for my necessities, and
for those who were with me. 35I have shown
you in every way, by laboring like this, that
you must support the weak. And remember
the words of the Lord Jesus, that He said, 'It
is more blessed to give than to receive.'"

36And when he had said these things, he
knelt down and prayed with them all. 37Then
they all wept freely, and fell on Paul's neck
and kissed him, 38sorrowing most of all for
the words which he spoke, that they would
see his face no more. And they accompanied
him to the ship.

Warnings on the Journey to Jerusalem

21 Now it came to pass, that when we
had departed from them and set
sail, running a straight course we came to
Cos, the following *day* to Rhodes, and from
there to Patara. 2And finding a ship sailing over to Phoenicia, we went aboard and
set sail. 3When we had sighted Cyprus, we
passed it on the left, sailed to Syria, and landed at Tyre; for there the ship was to unload
her cargo. 4And finding disciples,[a] we stayed
there seven days. They told Paul through the
Spirit not to go up to Jerusalem. 5When we
had come to the end of those days, we departed and went on our way; and they all accompanied us, with wives and children, till
we were out of the city. And we knelt down
on the shore and prayed. 6When we had tak-
en our leave of one another, we boarded the
ship, and they returned home.

7And when we had finished *our* voyage
from Tyre, we came to Ptolemais, greeted
the brethren, and stayed with them one day.
8On the next *day* we who were Paul's companions[a] departed and came to Caesarea,
and entered the house of Philip the evangelist, who was *one* of the seven, and stayed
with him. 9Now this man had four virgin
daughters who prophesied. 10And as we
stayed many days, a certain prophet named
Agabus came down from Judea. 11When he
had come to us, he took Paul's belt, bound
his *own* hands and feet, and said, "Thus says
the Holy Spirit, 'So shall the Jews at Jerusalem bind the man who owns this belt, and
deliver *him* into the hands of the Gentiles.'"

12Now when we heard these things, both
we and those from that place pleaded with
him not to go up to Jerusalem. 13Then Paul
answered, "What do you mean by weeping
and breaking my heart? For I am ready not

In Focus

21:8 Evangelist Pronounced *ih-VAN-juh-list.* A person who preaches the Good News of salvation through Jesus Christ. The word comes from a Greek word meaning "preach the gospel."

20:24 [a] NU-Text reads *But I do not count my life of any value or dear to myself.* **20:28** [a] M-Text reads *of the Lord and God.* **20:34** [a] NU-Text and M-Text omit *Yes.* **21:4** [a] NU-Text reads *the disciples.* **21:8** [a] NU-Text omits *who were Paul's companions.*

only to be bound, but also to die at Jerusalem for the name of the Lord Jesus."

14 So when he would not be persuaded, we ceased, saying, "The will of the Lord be done."

Paul Urged to Make Peace

15 And after those days we packed and went up to Jerusalem. 16 Also some of the disciples from Caesarea went with us and brought with them a certain Mnason of Cyprus, an early disciple, with whom we were to lodge.

17 And when we had come to Jerusalem, the brethren received us gladly. 18 On the following *day* Paul went in with us to James, and all the elders were present. 19 When he had greeted them, he told in detail those things which God had done among the Gentiles through his ministry. 20 And when they heard *it*, they glorified the Lord. And they said to him, "You see, brother, how many myriads of Jews there are who have believed, and they are all zealous for the law; 21 but they have been informed about you that you teach all the Jews who are among the Gentiles to forsake Moses, saying that they ought not to circumcise *their* children nor to walk according to the customs. 22 What then? The assembly must certainly meet, for they will[a] hear that you have come. 23 Therefore do what we tell you: We have four men who have taken a vow. 24 Take them and be purified with them, and pay their expenses so that they may shave *their* heads, and that all may know that those things of which they were informed concerning you are nothing, but *that* you yourself also walk orderly and keep the law. 25 But concerning the Gentiles who believe, we have written *and* decided that they should observe no such thing, except[a] that they should keep themselves from *things* offered to idols, from blood, from things strangled, and from sexual immorality."

Arrested in the Temple

26 Then Paul took the men, and the next day, having been purified with them, entered the temple to announce the expiration of the days of purification, at which time an offering should be made for each one of them.

27 Now when the seven days were almost ended, the Jews from Asia, seeing him in the temple, stirred up the whole crowd and laid hands on him, 28 crying out, "Men of Israel, help! This is the man who teaches all *men* everywhere against the people, the law, and this place; and furthermore he also brought Greeks into the temple and has defiled this holy place." 29 (For they had previously[a] seen Trophimus the Ephesian with him in the city, whom they supposed that Paul had brought into the temple.)

30 And all the city was disturbed; and the people ran together, seized Paul, and dragged him out of the temple; and immediately the doors were shut. 31 Now as they were seeking to kill him, news came to the commander of the garrison that all Jerusalem was in an uproar. 32 He immediately took soldiers and centurions, and ran down to them. And when they saw the commander and the soldiers, they stopped beating Paul. 33 Then the commander came near and took him, and commanded *him* to be bound with two chains; and he asked who he was and what he had done. 34 And some among the multitude cried one thing and some another.

So when he could not ascertain the truth because of the tumult, he commanded him to be taken into the barracks. 35 When he reached the stairs, he had to be carried by the soldiers because of the violence of the mob. 36 For the multitude of the people followed after, crying out, "Away with him!"

Addressing the Jerusalem Mob

37 Then as Paul was about to be led into the barracks, he said to the commander, "May I speak to you?"

He replied, "Can you speak Greek? 38 Are you not the Egyptian who some time ago stirred up a rebellion and led the four thousand assassins out into the wilderness?"

39 But Paul said, "I am a Jew from Tarsus, in Cilicia, a citizen of no mean city; and I implore you, permit me to speak to the people."

40 So when he had given him permission, Paul stood on the stairs and motioned with his hand to the people. And when there was a great silence, he spoke to *them* in the Hebrew language, saying,

22 "Brethren and fathers, hear my defense before you now." 2 And when

21:22 [a] NU-Text reads *What then is to be done? They will certainly.* 21:25 [a] NU-Text omits *that they should observe no such thing, except.* 21:29 [a] M-Text omits *previously.*

they heard that he spoke to them in the Hebrew language, they kept all the more silent.
Then he said: 3"I am indeed a Jew, born
in Tarsus of Cilicia, but brought up in this
city at the feet of Gamaliel, taught according
to the strictness of our fathers' law, and was
zealous toward God as you all are today. 4I
persecuted this Way to the death, binding
and delivering into prisons both men and
women, 5as also the high priest bears me
witness, and all the council of the elders,
from whom I also received letters to the
brethren, and went to Damascus to bring in
chains even those who were there to Jerusalem to be punished.
6"Now it happened, as I journeyed and
came near Damascus at about noon, suddenly a great light from heaven shone around
me. 7And I fell to the ground and heard a
voice saying to me, 'Saul, Saul, why are you

BEING YOURSELF

DID HE REALLY CHANGE?

READ IT: ACTS 22:1–29

GET IT:

Paul wasn't always a hero of faith. Before he became a Christian, he was out to harm and even kill Christians. However, after his radical transformation on the road to Damascus (Acts 9), he went from persecuting the gospel to preaching it.

It's not surprising that a lot of people doubted Paul because of his past. Wouldn't you have trouble believing someone could do a complete 180-degree turnaround? But people's doubts didn't stop Paul from preaching and didn't shake his faith in how Jesus had transformed him.

In Acts 22, Paul tells the story of his transformation. The crowd that has brought him to the Roman officials is angry because he's preaching that Jesus is for everyone, not just the Jews. Paul begins by first acknowledging that he too is a Jew. He takes responsibility for his past. Both of these things help him gain some credibility. However, when he brings up the idea that Christ died for people of every nation, the people want him arrested. They shout, "He is not fit to live!" (v. 22). Fortunately, Paul has more to share: he is also a Roman citizen. This means the Romans cannot harm him, and they release him.

LIVE IT:

Do you ever worry about your past affecting your ability to share the gospel? Remember Paul's testimony. Because he was willing to accept both his past mistakes and God's work in his life, he was able to demonstrate God's power to a very suspicious crowd. Ask God to give you the courage to share your story. Think about how Christ has worked in your heart and what it means for you to be a Christian.

persecuting Me?' 8 So I answered, 'Who are
You, Lord?' And He said to me, 'I am Jesus
of Nazareth, whom you are persecuting.'
9 "And those who were with me indeed
saw the light and were afraid,[a] but they did
not hear the voice of Him who spoke to me.
10 So I said, 'What shall I do, Lord?' And the
Lord said to me, 'Arise and go into Damascus, and there you will be told all things
which are appointed for you to do.' 11 And
since I could not see for the glory of that
light, being led by the hand of those who
were with me, I came into Damascus.
12 "Then a certain Ananias, a devout man
according to the law, having a good testimony with all the Jews who dwelt *there*, 13 came
to me; and he stood and said to me, 'Brother
Saul, receive your sight.' And at that same
hour I looked up at him. 14 Then he said, 'The
God of our fathers has chosen you that you
should know His will, and see the Just One,
and hear the voice of His mouth. 15 For you will
be His witness to all men of what you have
seen and heard. 16 And now why are you waiting? Arise and be baptized, and wash away
your sins, calling on the name of the Lord.'
17 "Now it happened, when I returned to
Jerusalem and was praying in the temple,
that I was in a trance 18 and saw Him saying
to me, 'Make haste and get out of Jerusalem
quickly, for they will not receive your testimony concerning Me.' 19 So I said, 'Lord, they
know that in every synagogue I imprisoned
and beat those who believe on You. 20 And
when the blood of Your martyr Stephen was
shed, I also was standing by consenting to
his death,[a] and guarding the clothes of those
who were killing him.' 21 Then He said to me,
'Depart, for I will send you far from here to
the Gentiles.'"

Paul's Roman Citizenship

22 And they listened to him until this
word, and *then* they raised their voices and
said, "Away with such a *fellow* from the
earth, for he is not fit to live!" 23 Then, as
they cried out and tore off *their* clothes and
threw dust into the air, 24 the commander ordered him to be brought into the barracks,
and said that he should be examined under
scourging, so that he might know why they
shouted so against him. 25 And as they bound
him with thongs, Paul said to the centurion
who stood by, "Is it lawful for you to scourge
a man who is a Roman, and uncondemned?"

In Focus

22:20 Martyr Pronounced *MAR-ter*. A person who is put to death for being a Christian. The word comes from a Greek word meaning "witness."

26 When the centurion heard *that*, he went
and told the commander, saying, "Take care
what you do, for this man is a Roman."
27 Then the commander came and said to
him, "Tell me, are you a Roman?"
He said, "Yes."
28 The commander answered, "With a
large sum I obtained this citizenship."
And Paul said, "But I was born *a citizen*."
29 Then immediately those who were
about to examine him withdrew from him;
and the commander was also afraid after he
found out that he was a Roman, and because
he had bound him.

The Sanhedrin Divided

30 The next day, because he wanted to
know for certain why he was accused by the
Jews, he released him from *his* bonds, and
commanded the chief priests and all their
council to appear, and brought Paul down
and set him before them.
23 Then Paul, looking earnestly at
the council, said, "Men *and* brethren, I have lived in all good conscience before God until this day." 2 And the high priest
Ananias commanded those who stood by
him to strike him on the mouth. 3 Then Paul
said to him, "God will strike you, *you* whitewashed wall! For you sit to judge me according to the law, and do you command me to
be struck contrary to the law?"
4 And those who stood by said, "Do you
revile God's high priest?"
5 Then Paul said, "I did not know, brethren, that he was the high priest; for it is written, 'You shall not speak evil of a ruler of
your people.'"[a]
6 But when Paul perceived that one part
were Sadducees and the other Pharisees, he

22:9 [a] NU-Text omits *and were afraid*. **22:20** [a] NU-Text omits *to his death*. **23:5** [a] Exodus 22:28

cried out in the council, "Men *and* brethren,
I am a Pharisee, the son of a Pharisee; concerning the hope and resurrection of the
dead I am being judged!"

7And when he had said this, a dissension arose between the Pharisees and the
Sadducees; and the assembly was divided. 8For Sadducees say that there is no
resurrection—and no angel or spirit; but
the Pharisees confess both. 9Then there
arose a loud outcry. And the scribes of the
Pharisees' party arose and protested, saying,
"We find no evil in this man; but if a spirit or
an angel has spoken to him, let us not fight
against God."[a]

10Now when there arose a great dissension, the commander, fearing lest Paul
might be pulled to pieces by them, commanded the soldiers to go down and take
him by force from among them, and bring
him into the barracks.

The Plot Against Paul

11But the following night the Lord stood
by him and said, "Be of good cheer, Paul; for
as you have testified for Me in Jerusalem, so
you must also bear witness at Rome."

12And when it was day, some of the Jews
banded together and bound themselves under an oath, saying that they would neither
eat nor drink till they had killed Paul. 13Now
there were more than forty who had formed
this conspiracy. 14They came to the chief
priests and elders, and said, "We have bound
ourselves under a great oath that we will eat
nothing until we have killed Paul. 15Now you,
therefore, together with the council, suggest
to the commander that he be brought down
to you tomorrow,[a] as though you were going
to make further inquiries concerning him;
but we are ready to kill him before he comes
near."

16So when Paul's sister's son heard of
their ambush, he went and entered the barracks and told Paul. 17Then Paul called one
of the centurions to *him* and said, "Take this
young man to the commander, for he has
something to tell him." 18So he took him and
brought *him* to the commander and said,
"Paul the prisoner called me to *him* and
asked *me* to bring this young man to you.
He has something to say to you."

19Then the commander took him by the
hand, went aside, and asked privately, "What
is it that you have to tell me?"

20And he said, "The Jews have agreed to
ask that you bring Paul down to the council tomorrow, as though they were going to
inquire more fully about him. 21But do not
yield to them, for more than forty of them
lie in wait for him, men who have bound
themselves by an oath that they will neither
eat nor drink till they have killed him; and
now they are ready, waiting for the promise
from you."

22So the commander let the young man
depart, and commanded *him*, "Tell no one
that you have revealed these things to me."

Sent to Felix

23And he called for two centurions, saying, "Prepare two hundred soldiers, seventy
horsemen, and two hundred spearmen to go
to Caesarea at the third hour of the night;
24and provide mounts to set Paul on, and
bring *him* safely to Felix the governor." 25He
wrote a letter in the following manner:

26 Claudius Lysias,

To the most excellent governor Felix:

Greetings.

27 This man was seized by the Jews and
was about to be killed by them. Coming
with the troops I rescued him, having
learned that he was a Roman. 28And
when I wanted to know the reason they
accused him, I brought him before
their council. 29I found out that he was
accused concerning questions of their
law, but had nothing charged against
him deserving of death or chains. 30And
when it was told me that the Jews lay in
wait for the man,[a] I sent him immediately to you, and also commanded his
accusers to state before you the charges
against him.

Farewell.

31Then the soldiers, as they were commanded, took Paul and brought *him* by
night to Antipatris. 32The next day they left
the horsemen to go on with him, and returned to the barracks. 33When they came
to Caesarea and had delivered the letter to
the governor, they also presented Paul to
him. 34And when the governor had read *it*,
he asked what province he was from. And

23:9 [a] NU-Text omits last clause and reads *what if a spirit or an angel has spoken to him?* 23:15 [a] NU-Text omits *tomorrow.* 23:30 [a] NU-Text reads *there would be a plot against the man.*

when he understood that *he was* from Cilicia,
35he said, "I will hear you when your accusers
also have come." And he commanded him to
be kept in Herod's Praetorium.

Accused of Sedition

24 Now after five days Ananias the
high priest came down with the
elders and a certain orator *named* Tertullus.
These gave evidence to the governor against
Paul.

2And when he was called upon, Tertullus
began his accusation, saying: "Seeing that
through you we enjoy great peace, and prosperity is being brought to this nation by your
foresight, 3we accept *it* always and in all places, most noble Felix, with all thankfulness.
4Nevertheless, not to be tedious to you any
further, I beg you to hear, by your courtesy,
a few words from us. 5For we have found
this man a plague, a creator of dissension
among all the Jews throughout the world,
and a ringleader of the sect of the Nazarenes.
6He even tried to profane the temple, and
we seized him,[a] and wanted to judge him
according to our law. 7But the commander
Lysias came by and with great violence took
him out of our hands, 8commanding his accusers to come to you. By examining him
yourself you may ascertain all these things
of which we accuse him." 9And the Jews also
assented,[a] maintaining that these things
were so.

The Defense Before Felix

10Then Paul, after the governor had nod-
ded to him to speak, answered: "Inasmuch
as I know that you have been for many
years a judge of this nation, I do the more
cheerfully answer for myself, 11because you
may ascertain that it is no more than twelve
days since I went up to Jerusalem to worship. 12And they neither found me in the
temple disputing with anyone nor inciting
the crowd, either in the synagogues or in
the city. 13Nor can they prove the things of
which they now accuse me. 14But this I confess to you, that according to the Way which
they call a sect, so I worship the God of my
fathers, believing all things which are written in the Law and in the Prophets. 15I have
hope in God, which they themselves also
accept, that there will be a resurrection of
the dead,[a] both of *the* just and *the* unjust.
16This *being* so, I myself always strive to have
a conscience without offense toward God
and men.

17"Now after many years I came to bring
alms and offerings to my nation, 18in the
midst of which some Jews from Asia found
me purified in the temple, neither with a
mob nor with tumult. 19They ought to have
been here before you to object if they had
anything against me. 20Or else let those who
are *here* themselves say if they found any
wrongdoing[a] in me while I stood before the
council, 21unless *it is* for this one statement
which I cried out, standing among them,

24:6 [a] NU-Text ends the sentence here and omits the rest of verse 6, all of verse 7, and the first clause of verse 8.
24:9 [a] NU-Text and M-Text read *joined the attack*.
24:15 [a] NU-Text omits *of the dead*.
24:20 [a] NU-Text and M-Text read *say what wrongdoing they found*.

HONESTY

READ IT: ACTS 24:15, 16

There are few things that feel better than having a clear conscience. When our hearts and minds are filled with lies and deceit, it's hard to keep things straight. Soon we don't know where one lie ends and the next begins. When our conscience is clear, we're able to hear God better because there's less competing for our attention.

'Concerning the resurrection of the dead I am being judged by you this day.'"

Felix Procrastinates

22But when Felix heard these things, having more accurate knowledge of *the* Way, he adjourned the proceedings and said, "When Lysias the commander comes down, I will make a decision on your case." 23So he commanded the centurion to keep Paul and to let *him* have liberty, and told him not to forbid any of his friends to provide for or visit him.

24And after some days, when Felix came with his wife Drusilla, who was Jewish, he sent for Paul and heard him concerning the faith in Christ. 25Now as he reasoned about righteousness, self-control, and the judgment to come, Felix was afraid and answered, "Go away for now; when I have a convenient time I will call for you." 26Meanwhile he also hoped that money would be given him by Paul, that he might release him.[a] Therefore he sent for him more often and conversed with him.

27But after two years Porcius Festus succeeded Felix; and Felix, wanting to do the Jews a favor, left Paul bound.

Paul Appeals to Caesar

25 Now when Festus had come to the province, after three days he went up from Caesarea to Jerusalem. 2Then the high priest[a] and the chief men of the Jews informed him against Paul; and they petitioned him, 3asking a favor against him, that he would summon him to Jerusalem—while *they* lay in ambush along the road to kill him. 4But Festus answered that Paul should be kept at Caesarea, and that he himself was going *there* shortly. 5"Therefore," he said, "let those who have authority among you go down with *me* and accuse this man, to see if there is any fault in him."

6And when he had remained among them more than ten days, he went down to Caesarea. And the next day, sitting on the judgment seat, he commanded Paul to be brought. 7When he had come, the Jews who had come down from Jerusalem stood about and laid many serious complaints against Paul, which they could not prove, 8while he *answered for himself,* "Neither against the law of the Jews, nor against the temple, nor against Caesar have I offended in anything at all."

9But Festus, wanting to do the Jews a favor, answered Paul and said, "Are you willing to go up to Jerusalem and there be judged before me concerning these things?"

10So Paul said, "I stand at Caesar's judgment seat, where I ought to be judged. To the Jews I have done no wrong, as you very well know. 11For if I am an offender, or have committed anything deserving of death, I do not object to dying; but if there is nothing in these things of which these men accuse me, no one can deliver me to them. I appeal to Caesar."

12Then Festus, when he had conferred with the council, answered, "You have appealed to Caesar? To Caesar you shall go!"

Paul Before Agrippa

13And after some days King Agrippa and Bernice came to Caesarea to greet Festus. 14When they had been there many days, Festus laid Paul's case before the king, saying: "There is a certain man left a prisoner by Felix, 15about whom the chief priests and the elders of the Jews informed *me,* when I was in Jerusalem, asking for a judgment against him. 16To them I answered, 'It is not the custom of the Romans to deliver any man to destruction[a] before the accused meets the accusers face to face, and has opportunity to answer for himself concerning the charge against him.' 17Therefore when they had come together, without any delay, the next day I sat on the judgment seat and commanded the man to be brought in. 18When the accusers stood up, they brought no accusation against him of such things as I supposed, 19but had some questions against him about their own religion and about a certain Jesus, who had died, whom Paul affirmed to be alive. 20And because I was uncertain of such questions, I asked whether he was willing to go to Jerusalem and there be judged concerning these matters. 21But when Paul appealed to be reserved for the decision of Augustus, I commanded him to be kept till I could send him to Caesar."

22Then Agrippa said to Festus, "I also would like to hear the man myself."

"Tomorrow," he said, "you shall hear him."

23So the next day, when Agrippa and Bernice had come with great pomp, and

---

24:26 [a] NU-Text omits *that he might release him.*
25:2 [a] NU-Text reads *chief priests.* 25:16 [a] NU-Text omits *to destruction,* although it is implied.

had entered the auditorium with the commanders and the prominent men of the city,
at Festus' command Paul was brought in.
24And Festus said: "King Agrippa and all the
men who are here present with us, you see
this man about whom the whole assembly
of the Jews petitioned me, both at Jerusalem
and here, crying out that he was not fit to live
any longer. 25But when I found that he had
committed nothing deserving of death, and
that he himself had appealed to Augustus, I
decided to send him. 26I have nothing certain
to write to my lord concerning him. Therefore I have brought him out before you, and
especially before you, King Agrippa, so that
after the examination has taken place I may
have something to write. 27For it seems to me
unreasonable to send a prisoner and not to
specify the charges against him."

Paul's Early Life

26 Then Agrippa said to Paul,
"You are permitted to speak for
yourself."

So Paul stretched out his hand and answered for himself: 2"I think myself happy,
King Agrippa, because today I shall answer
for myself before you concerning all the
things of which I am accused by the Jews,
3especially because you are expert in all customs and questions which have to do with
the Jews. Therefore I beg you to hear me
patiently.

4"My manner of life from my youth,
which was spent from the beginning among
my own nation at Jerusalem, all the Jews
know. 5They knew me from the first, if they
were willing to testify, that according to the
strictest sect of our religion I lived a Pharisee. 6And now I stand and am judged for
the hope of the promise made by God to our
fathers. 7To this *promise* our twelve tribes,
earnestly serving *God* night and day, hope to
attain. For this hope's sake, King Agrippa, I
am accused by the Jews. 8Why should it be
thought incredible by you that God raises
the dead?

9"Indeed, I myself thought I must do
many things contrary to the name of Jesus of
Nazareth. 10This I also did in Jerusalem, and
many of the saints I shut up in prison, having received authority from the chief priests;
and when they were put to death, I cast my
vote against *them.* 11And I punished them
often in every synagogue and compelled
them to blaspheme; and being exceedingly
enraged against them, I persecuted *them*
even to foreign cities.

Paul Recounts His Conversion

12"While thus occupied, as I journeyed to
Damascus with authority and commission
from the chief priests, 13at midday, O king,
along the road I saw a light from heaven,
brighter than the sun, shining around me
and those who journeyed with me. 14And
when we all had fallen to the ground, I
heard a voice speaking to me and saying in
the Hebrew language, 'Saul, Saul, why are
you persecuting Me? *It is* hard for you to kick
against the goads.' 15So I said, 'Who are You,
Lord?' And He said, 'I am Jesus, whom you
are persecuting. 16But rise and stand on your
feet; for I have appeared to you for this purpose, to make you a minister and a witness
both of the things which you have seen and
of the things which I will yet reveal to you.
17I will deliver you from the *Jewish* people, as
well as *from* the Gentiles, to whom I now[a]
send you, 18to open their eyes, *in order* to
turn *them* from darkness to light, and *from*
the power of Satan to God, that they may receive forgiveness of sins and an inheritance
among those who are sanctified by faith in
Me.'

Paul's Post-Conversion Life

19"Therefore, King Agrippa, I was not
disobedient to the heavenly vision, 20but
declared first to those in Damascus and in
Jerusalem, and throughout all the region
of Judea, and *then* to the Gentiles, that they
should repent, turn to God, and do works
befitting repentance. 21For these reasons the
Jews seized me in the temple and tried to kill
me. 22Therefore, having obtained help from
God, to this day I stand, witnessing both to
small and great, saying no other things than
those which the prophets and Moses said
would come— 23that the Christ would suffer,
that He would be the first to rise from the
dead, and would proclaim light to the *Jewish*
people and to the Gentiles."

Agrippa Parries Paul's Challenge

24Now as he thus made his defense, Festus said with a loud voice, "Paul, you are beside yourself! Much learning is driving you
mad!"

25But he said, "I am not mad, most noble

26:17 [a] NU-Text and M-Text omit *now.*

Festus, but speak the words of truth and
reason. 26 For the king, before whom I also
speak freely, knows these things; for I am
convinced that none of these things escapes
his attention, since this thing was not done
in a corner. 27 King Agrippa, do you believe
the prophets? I know that you do believe."
28 Then Agrippa said to Paul, "You almost
persuade me to become a Christian."
29 And Paul said, "I would to God that not
only you, but also all who hear me today,
might become both almost and altogether
such as I am, except for these chains."
30 When he had said these things, the
king stood up, as well as the governor and
Bernice and those who sat with them; 31 and
when they had gone aside, they talked
among themselves, saying, "This man is
doing nothing deserving of death or chains."
32 Then Agrippa said to Festus, "This
man might have been set free if he had not
appealed to Caesar."

The Voyage to Rome Begins

27 And when it was decided that we
should sail to Italy, they delivered
Paul and some other prisoners to *one* named
Julius, a centurion of the Augustan Regiment. 2 So, entering a ship of Adramyttium,
we put to sea, meaning to sail along the
coasts of Asia. Aristarchus, a Macedonian
of Thessalonica, was with us. 3 And the next

SHIPWRECK AND ROME

READ IT: ACTS 27:1–44

GET IT:

After Paul had preached in other countries, he returned to Jerusalem. The priests and the Jewish leaders hated Paul for preaching about Jesus and saying the Jewish way was wrong. They tried to kill him, and they had him arrested. Paul went to various courts and appeared before big-name leaders. Finally he said he wanted to talk to Caesar in Rome. Paul wanted more than anything to take the message of Jesus to Rome. This had been his goal for a long time, but it wasn't an easy trip. Almost everything that could go wrong did. He was under arrest, it was the wrong time of year to go out to sea (storm season), and then a storm wrecked the ship and left everyone stranded on an island. But eventually Paul arrived safely in Rome.

LIVE IT:

The journey to Rome wasn't working out as planned. In fact, everyone thought they would die during the storm. Paul was a prisoner with a guard named Julius, who was assigned to watch him constantly. Julius got to know Paul and respected him, gave him a bit of freedom on the ship, and later spared his life (v. 43). He was with Paul through the most terrifying times in his life. If someone was assigned to watch you 24/7 *under normal circumstances*, what would they witness? What would your words, actions, and even your silence tell them about you and about what you believe?

day we landed at Sidon. And Julius treated
Paul kindly and gave *him* liberty to go to his
friends and receive care. 4When we had put
to sea from there, we sailed under *the shelter*
of Cyprus because the winds were contrary.
5And when we had sailed over the sea which
is off Cilicia and Pamphylia, we came to
Myra, *a city* of Lycia. 6There the centurion
found an Alexandrian ship sailing to Italy,
and he put us on board.

7When we had sailed slowly many days,
and arrived with difficulty off Cnidus, the
wind not permitting us to proceed, we sailed
under *the shelter of* Crete off Salmone. 8Pass-
ing it with difficulty, we came to a place
called Fair Havens, near the city *of* Lasea.

Paul's Warning Ignored

9Now when much time had been spent,
and sailing was now dangerous because the
Fast was already over, Paul advised them,
10saying, "Men, I perceive that this voyage
will end with disaster and much loss, not
only of the cargo and ship, but also our
lives." 11Nevertheless the centurion was
more persuaded by the helmsman and the
owner of the ship than by the things spoken
by Paul. 12And because the harbor was not
suitable to winter in, the majority advised
to set sail from there also, if by any means
they could reach Phoenix, a harbor of Crete
opening toward the southwest and north-
west, and winter *there*.

In the Tempest

13When the south wind blew softly, supposing that they had obtained *their* desire,
putting out to sea, they sailed close by Crete.
14But not long after, a tempestuous head
wind arose, called Euroclydon.[a] 15So when
the ship was caught, and could not head into
the wind, we let *her* drive. 16And running
under *the shelter of* an island called Clauda,[a]
we secured the skiff with difficulty. 17When
they had taken it on board, they used cables
to undergird the ship; and fearing lest they
should run aground on the Syrtis[a] *Sands,*
they struck sail and so were driven. 18And because we were exceedingly tempest-tossed,
the next *day* they lightened the ship. 19On
the third *day* we threw the ship's tackle overboard with our own hands. 20Now when neither sun nor stars appeared for many days,
and no small tempest beat on *us,* all hope
that we would be saved was finally given up.
21But after long abstinence from food,

In Focus

27:14 Euroclydon Pronounced *you-ROCK-lah-din.* A powerful wind that often blows in the eastern Mediterranean Sea in the springtime. The word means "east wind" because it comes from the northeast.

27:14 [a] NU-Text reads *Euraquilon.* 27:16 [a] NU-Text reads *Cauda.* 27:17 [a] M-Text reads *Syrtes.*

Action!

ANGELS

READ IT: ACTS 27:23, 24

Everybody around Paul was scared out of their pants. Paul said, "I talked to an angel. Everything will be okay." Notice how in this case, Paul was the messenger. Paul told them, "Don't be afraid." The task in front of them wasn't easy (in fact, the ship was demolished!), but not one sailor lost even a single hair on his head. This is how God works. Is it easy? Of course not! But God is beside us all the way.

then Paul stood in the midst of them and
said, "Men, you should have listened to me,
and not have sailed from Crete and incurred
this disaster and loss. 22And now I urge you
to take heart, for there will be no loss of life
among you, but only of the ship. 23For there
stood by me this night an angel of the God to
whom I belong and whom I serve, 24saying,
'Do not be afraid, Paul; you must be brought
before Caesar; and indeed God has granted
you all those who sail with you.' 25Therefore
take heart, men, for I believe God that it will
be just as it was told me. 26However, we must
run aground on a certain island."

27Now when the fourteenth night had
come, as we were driven up and down in

ENTERTAINMENT

SURPRISE GUESTS

READ IT: ACTS 28:1–10

GET IT:

Paul and the 275 other people who had been on his ship found themselves floating in the ocean. Their ship had been destroyed. They finally drifted onto the shore of an island called Malta. Paul was exhausted, but he gathered sticks for a fire to keep everyone warm. While he was throwing the sticks on the fire, a snake bit him. God miraculously spared Paul's life and kept the snakebite from injuring him.

While on Malta, a man named Publius helped Paul and the crew from the ship. Publius owned a large estate close to where they were stranded. Publius generously hosted this large crowd of people for three days and entertained them. This gave Paul the opportunity to minister to the people on the island by healing the sick.

Publius was willing to entertain his surprise guests, and that created an opportunity for Paul to do ministry. This is a great reminder to be on the lookout for surprise guests in your life. God just might cross your path with someone in need that you can "entertain" for His glory.

LIVE IT:

Do you want to entertain the surprise guests you encounter in your life? Here's how you can do it!

- Pray and ask God for the opportunity to help someone in need.
- Trust that God will lead you to someone you can help.
- Keep your eyes wide open for people around you in need.
- When you find a need, meet that need as best you can.
- When you see someone hurting, pray with the person and *ask God to help him or her.*
- Thank God for the opportunity to entertain the surprise guests in your life.

the Adriatic *Sea,* about midnight the sailors
sensed that they were drawing near some
land. 28And they took soundings and found
it to be twenty fathoms; and when they had
gone a little farther, they took soundings
again and found *it* to be fifteen fathoms.
29Then, fearing lest we should run aground
on the rocks, they dropped four anchors
from the stern, and prayed for day to come.
30And as the sailors were seeking to escape
from the ship, when they had let down the
skiff into the sea, under pretense of putting
out anchors from the prow, 31Paul said to the
centurion and the soldiers, "Unless these
men stay in the ship, you cannot be saved."
32Then the soldiers cut away the ropes of the
skiff and let it fall off.

33And as day was about to dawn, Paul implored *them* all to take food, saying, "Today
is the fourteenth day you have waited and
continued without food, and eaten nothing.
34Therefore I urge you to take nourishment,
for this is for your survival, since not a hair
will fall from the head of any of you." 35And
when he had said these things, he took bread
and gave thanks to God in the presence of
them all; and when he had broken *it* he began to eat. 36Then they were all encouraged,
and also took food themselves. 37And in all
we were two hundred and seventy-six persons on the ship. 38So when they had eaten
enough, they lightened the ship and threw
out the wheat into the sea.

Shipwrecked on Malta

39When it was day, they did not recognize the land; but they observed a bay with
a beach, onto which they planned to run the
ship if possible. 40And they let go the anchors
and left *them* in the sea, meanwhile loosing
the rudder ropes; and they hoisted the main-
sail to the wind and made for shore. 41But
striking a place where two seas met, they ran
the ship aground; and the prow stuck fast
and remained immovable, but the stern was
being broken up by the violence of the waves.

42And the soldiers' plan was to kill the
prisoners, lest any of them should swim
away and escape. 43But the centurion, wanting to save Paul, kept them from *their* purpose, and commanded that those who could
swim should jump *overboard* first and get
to land, 44and the rest, some on boards and
some on *parts* of the ship. And so it was that
they all escaped safely to land.

Paul's Ministry on Malta

28 Now when they had escaped, they
then found out that the island was
called Malta. 2And the natives showed us unusual kindness; for they kindled a fire and
made us all welcome, because of the rain
that was falling and because of the cold. 3But
when Paul had gathered a bundle of sticks
and laid *them* on the fire, a viper came out
because of the heat, and fastened on his
hand. 4So when the natives saw the creature
hanging from his hand, they said to one
another, "No doubt this man is a murderer,
whom, though he has escaped the sea, yet
justice does not allow to live." 5But he shook
off the creature into the fire and suffered no
harm. 6However, they were expecting that he
would swell up or suddenly fall down dead.
But after they had looked for a long time and
saw no harm come to him, they changed
their minds and said that he was a god.

7In that region there was an estate of the
leading citizen of the island, whose name
was Publius, who received us and entertained us courteously for three days. 8And
it happened that the father of Publius lay
sick of a fever and dysentery. Paul went in
to him and prayed, and he laid his hands
on him and healed him. 9So when this was
done, the rest of those on the island who had
diseases also came and were healed. 10They
also honored us in many ways; and when we
departed, they provided such things as were
necessary.

Arrival at Rome

11After three months we sailed in an Alexandrian ship whose figurehead was the
Twin Brothers, which had wintered at the
island. 12And landing at Syracuse, we stayed
three days. 13From there we circled round
and reached Rhegium. And after one day the
south wind blew; and the next day we came
to Puteoli, 14where we found brethren, and
were invited to stay with them seven days.
And so we went toward Rome. 15And from
there, when the brethren heard about us,
they came to meet us as far as Appii Forum
and Three Inns. When Paul saw them, he
thanked God and took courage.

16Now when we came to Rome, the centurion delivered the prisoners to the captain of the
guard; but Paul was permitted to dwell by himself with the soldier who guarded him.

Paul's Ministry at Rome

17And it came to pass after three days that
Paul called the leaders of the Jews together.
So when they had come together, he said to
them: "Men *and* brethren, though I have done
nothing against our people or the customs of
our fathers, yet I was delivered as a prisoner
from Jerusalem into the hands of the Romans,
18who, when they had examined me, wanted to
let *me* go, because there was no cause for putting me to death. 19But when the Jews[a] spoke
against *it,* I was compelled to appeal to Caesar, not that I had anything of which to accuse
my nation. 20For this reason therefore I have
called for you, to see *you* and speak with *you,*
because for the hope of Israel I am bound with
this chain."

21Then they said to him, "We neither received letters from Judea concerning you, nor
have any of the brethren who came reported
or spoken any evil of you. 22But we desire to
hear from you what you think; for concerning
this sect, we know that it is spoken against
everywhere."

23So when they had appointed him a day,
many came to him at *his* lodging, to whom he
explained and solemnly testified of the kingdom of God, persuading them concerning
Jesus from both the Law of Moses and the
Prophets, from morning till evening. 24And
some were persuaded by the things which
were spoken, and some disbelieved. 25So when
they did not agree among themselves, they departed after Paul had said one word: "The Holy
Spirit spoke rightly through Isaiah the prophet
to our[a] fathers, 26saying,

'Go to this people and say:
"Hearing you will hear, and shall not
understand;
And seeing you will see, and not perceive;
27 For the hearts of this people have grown
dull.
Their ears are hard of hearing,
And their eyes they have closed,
Lest they should see with *their* eyes and
hear with *their* ears,
Lest they should understand with *their*
hearts and turn,
So that I should heal them."'[a]

28"Therefore let it be known to you that the
salvation of God has been sent to the Gentiles,
and they will hear it!" 29And when he had said
these words, the Jews departed and had a great
dispute among themselves.[a]

30Then Paul dwelt two whole years in his
own rented house, and received all who came
to him, 31preaching the kingdom of God and
teaching the things which concern the Lord
Jesus Christ with all confidence, no one forbidding him.

28:19 [a] That is, the ruling authorities **28:25** [a] NU-Text reads *your.* **28:27** [a] Isaiah 6:9, 10 **28:29** [a] NU-Text omits this verse.

28:16 PAUL AT ROME

God had worked everything out in a wonderful way for Paul. Paul had used his right to be tried at Rome. There Paul was allowed to rent his own house where a Roman soldier guarded him. Of course, the Roman government found no fault with Paul. They didn't care what the Jews said about him, because Paul hadn't broken any Roman laws. Later, we read in Paul's letters how he was able to win many to Christ at Rome—even people who lived at the emperor's palace!

After two years, Paul was set free. After that, we think he was able to go as far as Spain and preach the gospel. Later, Paul was arrested again and accused of treason. Like many other Christians, he refused to worship Emperor Nero. So the great apostle was beheaded at the Mamartine prison. (See Paul's second letter to Timothy.)

The EPISTLE of PAUL the APOSTLE to the

ROMANS

A.D. 57

Behind the Scenes

READ IT:

The book of Romans simply and clearly presents the basics of the Christian faith: sin, salvation, and service. Paul explains that we are all sinful. Jesus came to earth to save us. Salvation is God's free gift to us; we can't work for it or earn it. We love and serve Him because we are thankful for what He did.

GET IT:

Who wrote it: Paul

When it was written: A.D. 57

Why it was written: to tell the good news to the Christians in Rome and prepare them for Paul's visit.

LIVE IT:

We should live Christian lives that are holy and pleasing to God.

FIND IT:

Everyone Is Sinful	*Romans 3*
God Justifies Through Faith	*Romans 4*
Christ Died for Us	*Romans 5*
Dead to Sin, Alive to God	*Romans 6*
The Spirit of Life in Christ	*Romans 8*
Living Sacrifices to God	*Romans 12*
Living for Christ	*Romans 13–14*

Greeting

1 Paul, a bondservant of Jesus Christ, called *to be* an apostle, separated to the gospel of God 2which He promised before through His prophets in the Holy Scriptures, 3concerning His Son Jesus Christ our Lord, who was born of the seed of David according to the flesh, 4*and* declared *to be* the Son of God with power according to the Spirit of holiness, by the resurrection from the dead. 5Through Him we have received grace and apostleship for obedience to the faith among all nations for His name, 6among whom you also are the called of Jesus Christ;

7To all who are in Rome, beloved of God, called *to be* saints:

Grace to you and peace from God our Father and the Lord Jesus Christ.

Desire to Visit Rome

8First, I thank my God through Jesus Christ for you all, that your faith is spoken of throughout the whole world. 9For God is my witness, whom I serve with my spirit in the gospel of His Son, that without ceasing I make mention of you always in my prayers, 10making request if, by some means, now at last I may find a way in the will of God to come to you. 11For I long to see you, that I may impart to you some spiritual gift, so that you may be established— 12that is, that I may be encouraged together with you by the mutual faith both of you and me.

13Now I do not want you to be unaware, brethren, that I often planned to come to you (but was hindered until now), that I might have some fruit among you also, just as among the other Gentiles. 14I am a debtor both to Greeks and to barbarians, both to wise and to unwise. 15So, as much as is in me, *I am* ready to preach the gospel to you who are in Rome also.

The Just Live by Faith

16For I am not ashamed of the gospel of Christ,[a] for it is the power of God to salvation for everyone who believes, for the Jew first and also for the Greek. 17For in it the righteousness of God is revealed from faith to faith; as it is written, "The just shall live by faith." [a]

God's Wrath on Unrighteousness

18For the wrath of God is revealed from heaven against all ungodliness and unrighteousness of men, who suppress the truth in unrighteousness, 19because what may be known of God is manifest in them, for God has shown *it* to them. 20For since the creation of the world His invisible *attributes* are clearly seen, being understood by the things that are made, *even* His eternal power and Godhead, so that they are without excuse, 21because, although they knew God, they did not glorify *Him* as God, nor were thankful, but became futile in their thoughts, and their foolish hearts were darkened. 22Professing to be wise, they became fools, 23and changed the glory of the incorruptible God into an image made like corruptible man—and birds and four-footed animals and creeping things.

24Therefore God also gave them up to uncleanness, in the lusts of their hearts, to dishonor their bodies among themselves,

1:16 [a] NU-Text omits *of Christ*. 1:17 [a] Habakkuk 2:4

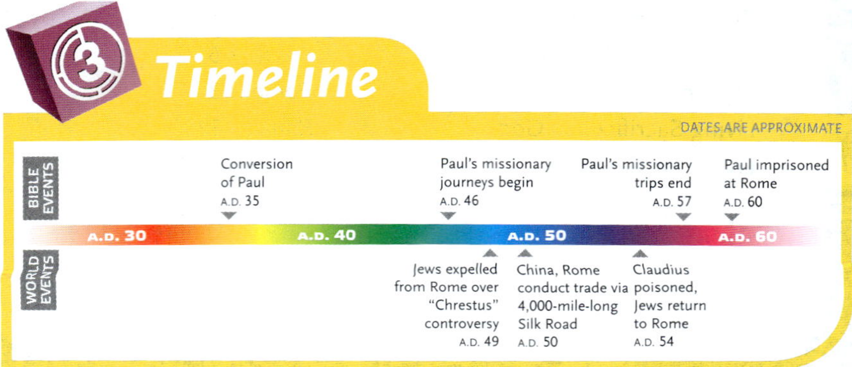

[25]who exchanged the truth of God for the lie,
and worshiped and served the creature rather than the Creator, who is blessed forever.
Amen.

[26]For this reason God gave them up to
vile passions. For even their women exchanged the natural use for what is against
nature. [27]Likewise also the men, leaving the
natural use of the woman, burned in their
lust for one another, men with men committing what is shameful, and receiving in
themselves the penalty of their error which
was due.

[28]And even as they did not like to retain
God in *their* knowledge, God gave them over
to a debased mind, to do those things which
are not fitting; [29]being filled with all unrighteousness, sexual immorality,[a] wickedness,
covetousness, maliciousness; full of envy,
murder, strife, deceit, evil-mindedness; *they
are* whisperers, [30]backbiters, haters of God,
violent, proud, boasters, inventors of evil
things, disobedient to parents, [31]undiscern-
ing, untrustworthy, unloving, unforgiving,[a]
unmerciful; [32]who, knowing the righteous
judgment of God, that those who practice
such things are deserving of death, not only
do the same but also approve of those who
practice them.

God's Righteous Judgment

2 Therefore you are inexcusable, O man,
whoever you are who judge, for in
whatever you judge another you condemn
yourself; for you who judge practice the
same things. [2]But we know that the judgment of God is according to truth against
those who practice such things. [3]And do
you think this, O man, you who judge those
practicing such things, and doing the same,
that you will escape the judgment of God?
[4]Or do you despise the riches of His goodness, forbearance, and longsuffering, not
knowing that the goodness of God leads you
to repentance? [5]But in accordance with your
hardness and your impenitent heart you
are treasuring up for yourself wrath in the
day of wrath and revelation of the righteous
judgment of God, [6]who "will render to each
one according to his deeds":[a] [7]eternal life to
those who by patient continuance in doing

In Focus

2:7 Immortality Pronounced *im-or-TAL-ih-tee*. Life that never ends. Paul uses it to describe our everlasting life with God.

1:29 [a] NU-Text omits *sexual immorality.* **1:31** [a] NU-Text omits *unforgiving.* **2:6** [a] Psalm 62:12; Proverbs 24:12

Starring Roles

PAUL didn't deserve to be an apostle for Jesus. He tried to destroy God's people who made up the church. He even gave permission to the mob that stoned poor Stephen to death (see Acts 7), but later he was comforted to know that young man in heaven.

Paul realized that by doing those evil things, he was really doing them to *Jesus Himself.* One day the risen Savior met Paul (once called Saul) on a lonely road to Damascus (pronounced *duh-MASK-us*) where he was going to punish the Christians. Jesus was as bright as the sun shining in his eyes, and Paul was blinded. Soon after that he, too, became a Christian, and he served God faithfully after that.

Paul wrote most of the letters to people in the New Testament. Paul knew that Jesus is the only One who can save us and that He died on the Cross to pay for our sins.

good seek for glory, honor, and immortality;
[8]but to those who are self-seeking and do not
obey the truth, but obey unrighteousness—
indignation and wrath, [9]tribulation and anguish, on every soul of man who does evil, of
the Jew first and also of the Greek; [10]but glory, honor, and peace to everyone who works
what is good, to the Jew first and also to the
Greek. [11]For there is no partiality with God.

[12]For as many as have sinned without law
will also perish without law, and as many as
have sinned in the law will be judged by the
law [13](for not the hearers of the law *are* just
in the sight of God, but the doers of the law
will be justified; [14]for when Gentiles, who do
not have the law, by nature do the things in
the law, these, although not having the law,
are a law to themselves, [15]who show the work
of the law written in their hearts, their conscience also bearing witness, and between
themselves *their* thoughts accusing or else
excusing *them*) [16]in the day when God will
judge the secrets of men by Jesus Christ, according to my gospel.

The Jews Guilty as the Gentiles

[17]Indeed[a] you are called a Jew, and rest on
the law, and make your boast in God, [18]and
know *His* will, and approve the things that
are excellent, being instructed out of the
law, [19]and are confident that you yourself are
a guide to the blind, a light to those who are
in darkness, [20]an instructor of the foolish, a
teacher of babes, having the form of knowledge and truth in the law. [21]You, therefore,
who teach another, do you not teach yourself? You who preach that a man should not
steal, do you steal? [22]You who say, "Do not
commit adultery," do you commit adultery?
You who abhor idols, do you rob temples?
[23]You who make your boast in the law, do
you dishonor God through breaking the
law? [24]For "the name of God is blasphemed
among the Gentiles because of you," [a] as it
is written.

Circumcision of No Avail

[25]For circumcision is indeed profitable if
you keep the law; but if you are a breaker of
the law, your circumcision has become uncircumcision. [26]Therefore, if an uncircumcised man keeps the righteous requirements
of the law, will not his uncircumcision be
counted as circumcision? [27]And will not the
physically uncircumcised, if he fulfills the

2:17 [a] NU-Text reads *But if.* 2:24 [a] Isaiah 52:5; Ezekiel 36:22

PAUL AND THE GOSPEL

READ IT: ROMANS 1:16

By now you know that the word *gospel* means "good news." The Good News from God is that His Son Jesus has died in your place so you can also be a son or daughter of God.

Paul had been a very religious man. He had been a Pharisee—a Jewish scholar who tried to please God by keeping the Jewish law. But one day Jesus appeared to Paul. Then he realized that his sins were too great to fight all by himself. He needed Jesus to change him so he would love to please God in all things.

Jesus changed Paul and gave him a new nature. Then Paul loved God and others in a way he never could before. Now he wanted to share that *Good News with everybody.*

Has Jesus come into your life? He wants to make you a new person who loves God and others as Paul did.

law, judge you who, *even* with *your* written *code* and circumcision, *are* a transgressor of the law? 28For he is not a Jew who *is one* outwardly, nor *is* circumcision that which *is* outward in the flesh; 29but *he is* a Jew who *is one* inwardly; and circumcision *is that* of the heart, in the Spirit, not in the letter; whose praise *is* not from men but from God.

God's Judgment Defended

3 What advantage then has the Jew, or what *is* the profit of circumcision? 2Much in every way! Chiefly because to them were committed the oracles of God. 3For what if some did not believe? Will their unbelief make the faithfulness of God without effect? 4Certainly not! Indeed, let God be true but every man a liar. As it is written:

"That You may be justified in Your
words,
And may overcome when You are
judged."[a]

5But if our unrighteousness demonstrates the righteousness of God, what shall we say? Is God unjust who inflicts wrath? (I speak as a man.) 6Certainly not! For then how will God judge the world?

7For if the truth of God has increased through my lie to His glory, why am I also still judged as a sinner? 8And *why* not *say,* "Let us do evil that good may come"?—as we are slanderously reported and as some affirm that we say. Their condemnation is just.

All Have Sinned

9What then? Are we better *than they*? Not at all. For we have previously charged both Jews and Greeks that they are all under sin.

10As it is written:

"There is none righteous, no, not one;
11 There is none who understands;
There is none who seeks after God.
12 They have all turned aside;
They have together become
unprofitable;
There is none who does good, no, not
one."[a]
13 "Their throat *is* an open tomb;
With their tongues they have practiced
deceit";[a]
"The poison of asps *is* under their lips";[b]
14 "Whose mouth *is* full of cursing and
bitterness."[a]
15 "Their feet *are* swift to shed blood;

In Focus

3:25 Propitiation Pronounced *pro-pish-ee-AY-shun.* The work of Jesus on the Cross. By dying for us, Jesus paid the penalty we owed God for breaking His laws.

16 Destruction and misery *are* in their
ways;
17 And the way of peace they have not
known."[a]
18 "There is no fear of God before their
eyes."[a]

19Now we know that whatever the law says, it says to those who are under the law, that every mouth may be stopped, and all the world may become guilty before God. 20Therefore by the deeds of the law no flesh will be justified in His sight, for by the law *is* the knowledge of sin.

God's Righteousness Through Faith

21But now the righteousness of God apart from the law is revealed, being witnessed by the Law and the Prophets, 22even the righteousness of God, through faith in Jesus Christ, to all and on all[a] who believe. For there is no difference; 23for all have sinned and fall short of the glory of God, 24being justified freely by His grace through the redemption that is in Christ Jesus, 25whom God set forth *as* a propitiation by His blood, through faith, to demonstrate His righteousness, because in His forbearance God had passed over the sins that were previously committed, 26to demonstrate at the present time His righteousness, that He might be just and the justifier of the one who has faith in Jesus.

Boasting Excluded

27Where *is* boasting then? It is excluded. By what law? Of works? No, but by the law of faith. 28Therefore we conclude that a man is justified by faith apart from the deeds of

3:4 [a] Psalm 51:4 **3:12** [a] Psalms 14:1–3; 53:1–3; Ecclesiastes 7:20 **3:13** [a] Psalm 5:9 [b] Psalm 140:3 **3:14** [a] Psalm 10:7 **3:17** [a] Isaiah 59:7, 8 **3:18** [a] Psalm 36:1 **3:22** [a] NU-Text omits *and on all.*

the law. 29Or *is He* the God of the Jews only?
Is He not also the God of the Gentiles? Yes,
of the Gentiles also, 30since *there is* one God
who will justify the circumcised by faith
and the uncircumcised through faith. 31Do
we then make void the law through faith?
Certainly not! On the contrary, we establish
the law.

Abraham Justified by Faith

4 What then shall we say that Abraham
our father has found according to the
flesh?[a] 2For if Abraham was justified by
works, he has *something* to boast about, but
not before God. 3For what does the Scripture
say? "Abraham believed God, and it was accounted to him for righteousness." [a] 4Now to
him who works, the wages are not counted
as grace but as debt.

David Celebrates the Same Truth

5But to him who does not work but believes on Him who justifies the ungodly, his
faith is accounted for righteousness, 6just as
David also describes the blessedness of the
man to whom God imputes righteousness
apart from works:

7 "Blessed *are those* whose lawless deeds
are forgiven,
And whose sins are covered;
8 Blessed *is the* man to whom the LORD
shall not impute sin." [a]

Abraham Justified Before Circumcision

9*Does* this blessedness then *come* upon

4:1 [a] Or *Abraham our (fore)father according to the flesh has found?* 4:3 [a] Genesis 15:6 4:8 [a] Psalm 32:1, 2

SIN FALLING SHORT

READ IT: ROMANS 3:21–26

GET IT:

You know that feeling you get in your stomach when you realize you've done something terribly wrong? Maybe you can't look yourself in the mirror or you want to cry. It's okay to feel that way—it's you being fully human. It's you living with the reality that you aren't ever going to be perfect. But it's still difficult to face your feelings at that moment. It's especially uncomfortable when you want to do what's right, but you slide so easily into doing what's wrong.

Every one of us has been there. Every human who ever lived has sinned. The only person who didn't sin was Jesus. The rest of us have to deal with our sins. Some of us try to clean up the mess on our own. Some just completely give up the fight to do anything good. But if you give up, you'll end up being alone with your sinful self and distant from God. There's another option. We can go to Jesus and cling to His grace. He will cancel our sin and keep us in His arms.

LIVE IT:

Ask Jesus to free you from your sinfulness—it's what He came to do. Then God will work in your life to make you more like Jesus. Your struggle against sin will get easier as you practice doing what's right again and again.

the circumcised *only,* or upon the uncircumcised also? For we say that faith was accounted to Abraham for righteousness. 10How
then was it accounted? While he was circumcised, or uncircumcised? Not while circumcised, but while uncircumcised. 11And he
received the sign of circumcision, a seal of
the righteousness of the faith which *he had
while still* uncircumcised, that he might be
the father of all those who believe, though
they are uncircumcised, that righteousness
might be imputed to them also, 12and the father of circumcision to those who not only
are of the circumcision, but who also walk in
the steps of the faith which our father Abraham *had while still* uncircumcised.

The Promise Granted Through Faith

13For the promise that he would be the
heir of the world *was* not to Abraham or to
his seed through the law, but through the
righteousness of faith. 14For if those who are
of the law *are* heirs, faith is made void and
the promise made of no effect, 15because the
law brings about wrath; for where there is no
law *there is* no transgression.

16Therefore *it is* of faith that *it might be* according to grace, so that the promise might
be sure to all the seed, not only to those who
are of the law, but also to those who are of the
faith of Abraham, who is the father of us all
17(as it is written, "I have made you a father
of many nations" [a]) in the presence of Him
whom he believed—God, who gives life to
the dead and calls those things which do not
exist as though they did; 18who, contrary to
hope, in hope believed, so that he became
the father of many nations, according to
what was spoken, "So shall your descendants be." [a] 19And not being weak in faith, he
did not consider his own body, already dead
(since he was about a hundred years old),
and the deadness of Sarah's womb. 20He did
not waver at the promise of God through unbelief, but was strengthened in faith, giving
glory to God, 21and being fully convinced
that what He had promised He was also able
to perform. 22And therefore "it was accounted to him for righteousness." [a]

23Now it was not written for his sake
alone that it was imputed to him, 24but also
for us. It shall be imputed to us who believe
in Him who raised up Jesus our Lord from
the dead, 25who was delivered up because of
our offenses, and was raised because of our
justification.

Faith Triumphs in Trouble

5 Therefore, having been justified by
faith, we have[a] peace with God through
our Lord Jesus Christ, 2through whom also
we have access by faith into this grace in
which we stand, and rejoice in hope of the
glory of God. 3And not only *that,* but we also
glory in tribulations, knowing that tribulation produces perseverance; 4and perseverance, character; and character, hope. 5Now
hope does not disappoint, because the love
of God has been poured out in our hearts by
the Holy Spirit who was given to us.

Christ in Our Place

6For when we were still without strength,
in due time Christ died for the ungodly. 7For
scarcely for a righteous man will one die;
yet perhaps for a good man someone would
even dare to die. 8But God demonstrates His
own love toward us, in that while we were
still sinners, Christ died for us. 9Much more
then, having now been justified by His
blood, we shall be saved from wrath through
Him. 10For if when we were enemies we were
reconciled to God through the death of His
Son, much more, having been reconciled,
we shall be saved by His life. 11And not only
that, but we also rejoice in God through our
Lord Jesus Christ, through whom we have
now received the reconciliation.

Death in Adam, Life in Christ

12Therefore, just as through one man sin
entered the world, and death through sin,
and thus death spread to all men, because
all sinned— 13(For until the law sin was
in the world, but sin is not imputed when
there is no law. 14Nevertheless death reigned
from Adam to Moses, even over those who
had not sinned according to the likeness of
the transgression of Adam, who is a type of
Him who was to come. 15But the free gift *is*
not like the offense. For if by the one man's
offense many died, much more the grace of
God and the gift by the grace of the one Man,
Jesus Christ, abounded to many. 16And the
gift *is* not like *that which came* through the
one who sinned. For the judgment *which*

4:17 [a] Genesis 17:5 **4:18** [a] Genesis 15:5 **4:22** [a] Genesis 15:6 **5:1** [a] Another ancient reading is, *let us have peace.*

came from one *offense resulted* in condemnation, but the free gift *which came* from
many offenses *resulted* in justification. 17For
if by the one man's offense death reigned
through the one, much more those who receive abundance of grace and of the gift of
righteousness will reign in life through the
One, Jesus Christ.)

18Therefore, as through one man's offense *judgment came* to all men, resulting in
condemnation, even so through one Man's
righteous act *the free gift came* to all men, resulting in justification of life. 19For as by one
man's disobedience many were made sinners, so also by one Man's obedience many
will be made righteous.

20Moreover the law entered that the offense might abound. But where sin abounded, grace abounded much more, 21so that as
sin reigned in death, even so grace might
reign through righteousness to eternal life
through Jesus Christ our Lord.

Dead to Sin, Alive to God

6 What shall we say then? Shall we continue in sin that grace may abound?
2Certainly not! How shall we who died
to sin live any longer in it? 3Or do you not
know that as many of us as were baptized
into Christ Jesus were baptized into His
death? 4Therefore we were buried with Him
through baptism into death, that just as
Christ was raised from the dead by the glory
of the Father, even so we also should walk in
newness of life.

5For if we have been united together in
the likeness of His death, certainly we also
shall be *in the likeness* of *His* resurrection,
6knowing this, that our old man was crucified with *Him,* that the body of sin might be
done away with, that we should no longer
be slaves of sin. 7For he who has died has
been freed from sin. 8Now if we died with
Christ, we believe that we shall also live with
Him, 9knowing that Christ, having been
raised from the dead, dies no more. Death
no longer has dominion over Him. 10For *the*
death that He died, He died to sin once for
all; but *the life* that He lives, He lives to God.
11Likewise you also, reckon yourselves to be
dead indeed to sin, but alive to God in Christ
Jesus our Lord.

TRUSTING JESUS BRINGS PEACE

READ IT: ROMANS 5:1

As you get a little older you may hear more about being "justified by faith." This means that God accepts you as His son or daughter. He does this when you confess your sins and trust that Jesus has taken them away by dying on the Cross. When you're trusting Jesus to save you from your sins, you also receive peace from God.

Right now you may be having a lot of trouble. Maybe you've lost a friend. Perhaps someone special to you has died. Possibly you've done something really wrong. We do sometimes, no matter how hard we try to be good. What are you going to do to fix it?

Whatever happens, God can give you peace in the world. First of all, get alone with Jesus in prayer. Tell Him all that troubles you. Jesus will *show you how* to make everything right, and you will have God's peace. Whether you are sick or hurt or even have to go to prison, God will be right there with you always.

12 Therefore do not let sin reign in your
mortal body, that you should obey it in its
lusts. 13 And do not present your members
as instruments of unrighteousness to sin,
but present yourselves to God as being alive
from the dead, and your members *as* instruments of righteousness to God. 14 For sin
shall not have dominion over you, for you
are not under law but under grace.

From Slaves of Sin to Slaves of God

15 What then? Shall we sin because we
are not under law but under grace? Certainly not! 16 Do you not know that to whom you
present yourselves slaves to obey, you are
that one's slaves whom you obey, whether
of sin *leading* to death, or of obedience *lead-*
ing to righteousness? 17 But God be thanked
that *though* you were slaves of sin, yet you
obeyed from the heart that form of doctrine
to which you were delivered. 18 And having
been set free from sin, you became slaves of
righteousness. 19 I speak in human *terms* because of the weakness of your flesh. For just
as you presented your members *as* slaves of
uncleanness, and of lawlessness *leading* to
more lawlessness, so now present your members *as* slaves *of* righteousness for holiness.

20 For when you were slaves of sin, you
were free in regard to righteousness. 21 What
fruit did you have then in the things of
which you are now ashamed? For the end of
those things *is* death. 22 But now having been
set free from sin, and having become slaves
of God, you have your fruit to holiness, and
the end, everlasting life. 23 For the wages of
sin *is* death, but the gift of God *is* eternal life
in Christ Jesus our Lord.

Freed from the Law

7 Or do you not know, brethren (for I
speak to those who know the law), that

GOD LOVES YOU
DYING FOR THE UNGODLY

READ IT: ROMANS 5:5–8

GET IT:

It's hard to understand why someone would want to die for someone else. Paul writes that rarely would anyone die for a righteous or holy person, let alone a good person. What about the really bad people?

Without Jesus Christ, we are all ungodly. Because of sin, we were separated from God. Paul even goes as far to say we were "enemies" of God. When Jesus died on the cross, He took all of our sin, and when we accept Him as Lord of our lives, we no longer have to face a life apart from God. In fact, Paul says we get to celebrate this!

LIVE IT:

Next time you think you're not worthy of God's love, remember this Scripture reading. God doesn't love you because you've been good or bad. He loves you because He sees you through the filter of the cross. If you're feeling unlovable, know that God loves you. In fact, Paul says God's love has been poured into you!

the law has dominion over a man as long as
he lives? 2For the woman who has a husband
is bound by the law to *her* husband as long
as he lives. But if the husband dies, she is released from the law of *her* husband. 3So then
if, while *her* husband lives, she marries another man, she will be called an adulteress; but
if her husband dies, she is free from that law,
so that she is no adulteress, though she has
married another man. 4Therefore, my brethren, you also have become dead to the law
through the body of Christ, that you may be
married to another—to Him who was raised
from the dead, that we should bear fruit to
God. 5For when we were in the flesh, the sinful passions which were aroused by the law
were at work in our members to bear fruit to
death. 6But now we have been delivered from
the law, having died to what we were held by,
so that we should serve in the newness of the
Spirit and not *in* the oldness of the letter.

Sin's Advantage in the Law

7What shall we say then? *Is* the law sin?
Certainly not! On the contrary, I would not
have known sin except through the law. For
I would not have known covetousness unless
the law had said, "You shall not covet." [a] 8But
sin, taking opportunity by the commandment, produced in me all *manner of evil*
desire. For apart from the law sin *was* dead.
9I was alive once without the law, but when
the commandment came, sin revived and I
died. 10And the commandment, which *was*
to *bring* life, I found to *bring* death. 11For sin,
taking occasion by the commandment, deceived me, and by it killed *me*. 12Therefore
the law *is* holy, and the commandment holy
and just and good.

Law Cannot Save from Sin

13Has then what is good become death
to me? Certainly not! But sin, that it might
appear sin, was producing death in me
through what is good, so that sin through
the commandment might become exceedingly sinful. 14For we know that the law is
spiritual, but I am carnal, sold under sin.
15For what I am doing, I do not understand.
For what I will to do, that I do not practice;
but what I hate, that I do. 16If, then, I do what
I will not to do, I agree with the law that *it is*
good. 17But now, *it is* no longer I who do it,
but sin that dwells in me. 18For I know that
in me (that is, in my flesh) nothing good
dwells; for to will is present with me, but *how*
to perform what is good I do not find. 19For
the good that I will *to do,* I do not do; but the

7:7 [a] Exodus 20:17; Deuteronomy 5:21

THE GREATEST GIFT

READ IT: ROMANS 6:23

Everyone can think of something they want more than anything. What would you like? A million dollars? A new bike? A trip to Disneyworld?

God wants to give you a gift so great that you can't even imagine it. If you knew what that gift was, you would never trade it for anything. It's called *eternal life*!

We know that everybody's soul is going to live forever somewhere. For many people, that will mean everlasting misery because God won't be there. But listen! That isn't the same as "eternal life." Eternal life is a special kind of life that God has, and He can give that life to you. Eternal life means enjoying God's special kind of life forever and ever. That life can start right now for you. Just tell God you're sorry for your sins, and ask Him to give you His gift of eternal life.

evil I will not *to do,* that I practice. [20]Now if I
do what I will not *to do,* it is no longer I who
do it, but sin that dwells in me.

[21]I find then a law, that evil is present
with me, the one who wills to do good.
[22]For I delight in the law of God according
to the inward man. [23]But I see another law
in my members, warring against the law of
my mind, and bringing me into captivity to
the law of sin which is in my members. [24]O
wretched man that I am! Who will deliver
me from this body of death? [25]I thank God—
through Jesus Christ our Lord!

So then, with the mind I myself serve the
law of God, but with the flesh the law of sin.

Free from Indwelling Sin

8 *There is* therefore now no condemnation to those who are in Christ Jesus,[a]
who do not walk according to the flesh, but
according to the Spirit. [2]For the law of the
Spirit of life in Christ Jesus has made me free
from the law of sin and death. [3]For what the
law could not do in that it was weak through
the flesh, God *did* by sending His own Son
in the likeness of sinful flesh, on account of
sin: He condemned sin in the flesh, [4]that the
righteous requirement of the law might be
fulfilled in us who do not walk according
to the flesh but according to the Spirit. [5]For
those who live according to the flesh set their
minds on the things of the flesh, but those
who live according to the Spirit, the things
of the Spirit. [6]For to be carnally minded *is*
death, but to be spiritually minded *is* life and
peace. [7]Because the carnal mind *is* enmity
against God; for it is not subject to the law of
God, nor indeed can be. [8]So then, those who
are in the flesh cannot please God.

In Focus

8:15 Adoption Pronounced *uh-DOP-shun.* God's work of making us His sons and daughters. When we believe in Jesus for salvation, God sends His Spirit to live in us. The Spirit of God teaches us that we are God's children.

8:1 [a] NU-Text omits the rest of this verse.

Action!

SONS AND DAUGHTERS OF GOD

READ IT: ROMANS 8:16

When you believe in Jesus as your Savior, then the Holy Spirit of God Himself comes to live in you. As the Holy Spirit lives in you, He makes you know that you're God's very own child. This means that God has *adopted* you. So the Bible also calls the Holy Spirit the "Spirit of Adoption," because He reminds us that God has taken us to be His own sons and daughters.

Remember, having the Holy Spirit is the same as having the Spirit of Jesus Himself living in you.

When you know you're an adopted son or daughter of God, then you know Jesus died for your sins. You also have a deep desire to be like Jesus in every way. Sons and daughters are like their parents. So sons and daughters of God are like God.

9 But you are not in the flesh but in the
Spirit, if indeed the Spirit of God dwells in
you. Now if anyone does not have the Spirit of
Christ, he is not His. 10 And if Christ *is* in you,
the body *is* dead because of sin, but the Spirit
is life because of righteousness. 11 But if the
Spirit of Him who raised Jesus from the dead
dwells in you, He who raised Christ from the
dead will also give life to your mortal bodies
through His Spirit who dwells in you.

Sonship Through the Spirit

12 Therefore, brethren, we are debtors—
not to the flesh, to live according to the flesh.
13 For if you live according to the flesh you will
die; but if by the Spirit you put to death the
deeds of the body, you will live. 14 For as many
as are led by the Spirit of God, these are sons
of God. 15 For you did not receive the spirit
of bondage again to fear, but you received
the Spirit of adoption by whom we cry out,
"Abba, Father." 16 The Spirit Himself bears
witness with our spirit that we are children
of God, 17 and if children, then heirs—heirs
of God and joint heirs with Christ, if indeed
we suffer with *Him,* that we may also be glorified together.

From Suffering to Glory

18 For I consider that the sufferings of this
present time are not worthy *to be compared*
with the glory which shall be revealed in us.

FINDING YOUR PURPOSE IN LIFE

NOT JUST SOME THINGS—ALL THINGS

READ IT: ROMANS 8:28

GET IT:

"Everything happens for a reason." Most of us have heard that sentiment at some time. That's not so hard to take. But the Bible takes it further, saying things happen for our good. How can that be? What about the really bad stuff? How can cancer or death or divorce turn out for good?

There's tension between bad things that happen in life and the promise that everything works out for good. The good part may not immediately be obvious, and sometimes it can be extremely painful.

To work things for good means that God's purpose is clear and powerful. Even as you try to figure out what your purpose in life might be, God is already at work, making things good for you. And because God's love for us is so deep, nothing—not even the bad things in life—can separate us from His love. God's love for us is the ultimate form of goodness.

LIVE IT:

Let's face it, at times things are going to go wrong in your life. It's hard to believe that God has a purpose for the bad things. But instead of giving up, ask God to help you see how you can be more like Jesus while you're hurting. Ask Him to show you how the good and the bad things are working together to make you holier.

[19]For the earnest expectation of the creation
eagerly waits for the revealing of the sons of
God. [20]For the creation was subjected to futility, not willingly, but because of Him who
subjected *it* in hope; [21]because the creation
itself also will be delivered from the bondage of corruption into the glorious liberty of
the children of God. [22]For we know that the
whole creation groans and labors with birth
pangs together until now. [23]Not only *that,*
but we also who have the firstfruits of the
Spirit, even we ourselves groan within ourselves, eagerly waiting for the adoption, the
redemption of our body. [24]For we were saved
in this hope, but hope that is seen is not
hope; for why does one still hope for what
he sees? [25]But if we hope for what we do not
see, we eagerly wait for *it* with perseverance.

[26]Likewise the Spirit also helps in our
weaknesses. For we do not know what we
should pray for as we ought, but the Spirit Himself makes intercession for us[a] with
groanings which cannot be uttered. [27]Now
He who searches the hearts knows what the
mind of the Spirit *is,* because He makes intercession for the saints according to *the will*
of God.

[28]And we know that all things work together for good to those who love God, to those
who are the called according to *His* purpose.
[29]For whom He foreknew, He also predestined *to be* conformed to the image of His Son,
that He might be the firstborn among many

In Focus

8:29 Foreknew Means "knew beforehand." Because God is all-knowing, He foreknows the people who will become believers. This also means that He loved them before they knew Him.

8:26 [a] NU-Text omits *for us.*

Spotlight

NOTHING CAN SEPARATE US FROM GOD

READ IT: ROMANS 8:18–39

GET IT:

Paul wrote to the church in Rome long before he arrived there. The Christians in Rome were being persecuted by the emperor because they believed in Jesus. Paul's letter described the gospel of salvation—Jesus died for sinners. Chapter 8 told them that the Holy Spirit lived in them if they believed. It encouraged the Christians to stay strong in their faith because nothing could separate them from God's love.

LIVE IT:

Everybody feels all alone sometimes. This Scripture passage is good to read when you feel alone or afraid. It will reassure you that absolutely, positively nothing is able to separate us from God's love. God loves us and always will. At any time, in any place, God's love tops everything.

brethren. 30Moreover whom He predestined,
these He also called; whom He called, these
He also justified; and whom He justified,
these He also glorified.

God's Everlasting Love

31What then shall we say to these things?
If God *is* for us, who *can be* against us? 32He
who did not spare His own Son, but delivered Him up for us all, how shall He not
with Him also freely give us all things?
33Who shall bring a charge against God's
elect? *It is* God who justifies. 34Who *is* he
who condemns? *It is* Christ who died, and
furthermore is also risen, who is even at
the right hand of God, who also makes
intercession for us. 35Who shall separate us
from the love of Christ? *Shall* tribulation, or
distress, or persecution, or famine, or nakedness, or peril, or sword? 36As it is written:

> "For Your sake we are killed all day long;
> We are accounted as sheep for the slaughter." [a]

37Yet in all these things we are more than
conquerors through Him who loved us.
38For I am persuaded that neither death nor
life, nor angels nor principalities nor powers, nor things present nor things to come,

8:36 [a] Psalm 44:22

GOD LOVES YOU
NOTHING CAN SEPARATE US

READ IT: ROMANS 8:35–39

GET IT:

Sometimes God seems far away. Paul lets us know in this passage of Scripture that there's no person or thing that can separate us from God's love. Not war, famine, or hard times. Nothing! Instead, the Bible says we are more than conquerors through Christ's power—we can defeat anything that might try to get in the way of our relationship with God. Why is this? Because the love of God is in Jesus Christ, so when we have a relationship with Him, that love is also in us.

What's interesting in these verses is that Paul repeats himself. In verse 35, Paul first asks what can separate us from God, implying that nothing can. In verse 39, he tells us again there isn't a thing that separates us from the love of God. If he says it twice, it must be twice as important to remember!

LIVE IT:

Make a list of things you feel separate you from God's love. Are there any people who make you feel bad or situations that get in the way of your relationship with Jesus? Ask yourself if those things can truly separate you from God's love. Compare the list to these verses. How does your list stack up? By the time you're done, you'll be able to see that not a single thing can separate you from God's love.

39 nor height nor depth, nor any other created thing, shall be able to separate us from the love of God which is in Christ Jesus our Lord.

Israel's Rejection of Christ

9 I tell the truth in Christ, I am not lying, my conscience also bearing me witness in the Holy Spirit, 2 that I have great sorrow and continual grief in my heart. 3 For I could wish that I myself were accursed from Christ for my brethren, my countrymen[a] according to the flesh, 4 who are Israelites, to whom *pertain* the adoption, the glory, the covenants, the giving of the law, the service *of God,* and the promises; 5 of whom *are* the fathers and from whom, according to the flesh, Christ *came,* who is over all, *the* eternally blessed God. Amen.

Israel's Rejection and God's Purpose

6 But it is not that the word of God has taken no effect. For they *are* not all Israel who *are* of Israel, 7 nor *are they* all children because they are the seed of Abraham; but, "In Isaac your seed shall be called." [a] 8 That is, those who *are* the children of the flesh, these *are* not the children of God; but the children of the promise are counted as the seed. 9 For this *is* the word of promise: "At this time I will come and Sarah shall have a son." [a]

10 And not only *this,* but when Rebecca also had conceived by one man, *even* by our father Isaac 11 (for *the children* not yet being born, nor having done any good or evil, that the purpose of God according to election might stand, not of works but of Him who calls), 12 it was said to her, "The older shall serve the younger." [a] 13 As it is written, "Jacob I have loved, but Esau I have hated." [a]

Israel's Rejection and God's Justice

14 What shall we say then? *Is there* unrighteousness with God? Certainly not! 15 For He says to Moses, "I will have mercy on whomever I will have mercy, and I will have compassion on whomever I will have compassion." [a] 16 So then *it is* not of him who wills, nor of him who runs, but of God who shows mercy. 17 For the Scripture says to the Pharaoh, "For this very purpose I have raised you up, that I may show My power in you, and that My name may be declared in all the earth." [a] 18 Therefore He has mercy

In Focus

8:30 Predestined Pronounced *pre-DESS-tend.* All that God decided before time existed. Everything that ever happens has always been part of God's never-changing, forever plan.

8:30 Called The way God draws people to Himself. He calls them when they hear the gospel. By calling people, God gives them the desire to come to Him.

on whom He wills, and whom He wills He hardens.

19 You will say to me then, "Why does He still find fault? For who has resisted His will?" 20 But indeed, O man, who are you to reply against God? Will the thing formed say to him who formed *it,* "Why have you made me like this?" 21 Does not the potter have power over the clay, from the same lump to make one vessel for honor and another for dishonor?

22 *What* if God, wanting to show *His* wrath and to make His power known, endured with much longsuffering the vessels of wrath prepared for destruction, 23 and that He might make known the riches of His glory on the vessels of mercy, which He had prepared beforehand for glory, 24 even us whom He called, not of the Jews only, but also of the Gentiles?

25 As He says also in Hosea:

"I will call them My people, who were not
  My people,
And her beloved, who was not
  beloved." [a]

26 "And it shall come to pass in the place
  where it was said to them,
'*You are* not My people,'
There they shall be called sons of the
  living God." [a]

9:3 [a] Or *relatives* **9:7** [a] Genesis 21:12 **9:9** [a] Genesis 18:10, 14 **9:12** [a] Genesis 25:23 **9:13** [a] Malachi 1:2, 3 **9:15** [a] Exodus 33:19 **9:17** [a] Exodus 9:16 **9:25** [a] Hosea 2:23 **9:26** [a] Hosea 1:10

[27]Isaiah also cries out concerning Israel:[a]

"Though the number of the children of
Israel be as the sand of the sea,
The remnant will be saved.
28 For He will finish the work and cut *it*
short in righteousness,
Because the LORD will make a short
work upon the earth." [a]

[29]And as Isaiah said before:

"Unless the LORD of Sabaoth [a] had left us
a seed,
We would have become like Sodom,
And we would have been made like
Gomorrah." [b]

Present Condition of Israel

[30]What shall we say then? That Gentiles,
who did not pursue righteousness, have attained to righteousness, even the righteousness of faith; [31]but Israel, pursuing the law
of righteousness, has not attained to the
law of righteousness.[a] [32]Why? Because *they*
did not *seek it* by faith, but as it were, by the
works of the law.[a] For they stumbled at that
stumbling stone. [33]As it is written:

"Behold, I lay in Zion a stumbling stone
and rock of offense,
And whoever believes on Him will not
be put to shame." [a]

9:27 [a] Isaiah 10:22, 23 9:28 [a] NU-Text reads *For the LORD will finish the work and cut it short upon the earth.* 9:29 [a] Literally, in Hebrew, *Hosts* [b] Isaiah 1:9 9:31 [a] NU-Text omits *of righteousness.* 9:32 [a] NU-Text reads *by works.* 9:33 [a] Isaiah 8:14; 28:16

SALVATION IN THE CLUB

READ IT: ROMANS 10:9–13

GET IT:

Have you ever started a club with your friends? Maybe it was just you and one other friend, but you gave the club an awesome name and made a sign or drew a special logo for the club.

One of the complaints some people have about Christianity is that it seems like an exclusive club. In some ways, that's true: Christianity is a club of people who have received salvation through Jesus. And in these verses, Paul clearly lays out the rules for who can be in the club and how someone joins. But the "rules" are a bit surprising and wonderfully simple. Paul uses the word *whoever* a couple times. That means anyone can be a part of this club! Anyone who acknowledges that Jesus is who He said He was—the Son of God, who died for our sins and whom God raised from the dead—can be in the club. Anyone who believes in Him. Anyone who calls out to Him in His name. Salvation is generously offered to anyone who believes in Jesus!

LIVE IT:

It makes sense, then, to ask yourself: What do I believe about Jesus? Spend a few minutes thinking about that question. Pray your thoughts, telling God what you believe to be true. Then thank Jesus for welcoming you into His club!

Israel Needs the Gospel

10 Brethren, my heart's desire and
prayer to God for Israel[a] is that they
may be saved. 2For I bear them witness that
they have a zeal for God, but not according
to knowledge. 3For they being ignorant of
God's righteousness, and seeking to establish their own righteousness, have not
submitted to the righteousness of God. 4For
Christ *is* the end of the law for righteousness
to everyone who believes.

5For Moses writes about the righteousness which is of the law, "The man who does
those things shall live by them." [a] 6But the
righteousness of faith speaks in this way,
"Do not say in your heart, 'Who will ascend
into heaven?' " [a] (that is, to bring Christ
down *from above*) 7or, " 'Who will descend
into the abyss?' " [a] (that is, to bring Christ up
from the dead). 8But what does it say? "The
word is near you, in your mouth and in your
heart" [a] (that is, the word of faith which we
preach): 9that if you confess with your mouth
the Lord Jesus and believe in your heart that
God has raised Him from the dead, you will
be saved. 10For with the heart one believes
unto righteousness, and with the mouth
confession is made unto salvation. 11For the
Scripture says, "Whoever believes on Him
will not be put to shame." [a] 12For there is no
distinction between Jew and Greek, for the
same Lord over all is rich to all who call upon
Him. 13For "whoever calls on the name of the
LORD shall be saved." [a]

Israel Rejects the Gospel

14How then shall they call on Him in
whom they have not believed? And how shall
they believe in Him of whom they have not
heard? And how shall they hear without a
preacher? 15And how shall they preach unless they are sent? As it is written:

"How beautiful are the feet of those who
preach the gospel of peace,[a]
Who bring glad tidings of good things!" [b]

16But they have not all obeyed the gospel. For
Isaiah says, "LORD, who has believed our report?" [a] 17So then faith *comes* by hearing, and
hearing by the word of God.

18But I say, have they not heard? Yes
indeed:

"Their sound has gone out to all the earth,
And their words to the ends of the world." [a]

19But I say, did Israel not know? First Moses says:

"I will provoke you to jealousy by *those
who are* not a nation,
I will move you to anger by a foolish
nation." [a]

20But Isaiah is very bold and says:

"I was found by those who did not seek
Me;
I was made manifest to those who did
not ask for Me." [a]

21But to Israel he says:

"All day long I have stretched out My
hands
To a disobedient and contrary people." [a]

Israel's Rejection Not Total

11 I say then, has God cast away His
people? Certainly not! For I also am
an Israelite, of the seed of Abraham, *of* the
tribe of Benjamin. 2God has not cast away
His people whom He foreknew. Or do you
not know what the Scripture says of Elijah,
how he pleads with God against Israel, saying, 3"LORD, they have killed Your prophets
and torn down Your altars, and I alone am
left, and they seek my life" ?[a] 4But what does
the divine response say to him? "I have reserved for Myself seven thousand men who
have not bowed the knee to Baal." [a] 5Even so
then, at this present time there is a remnant
according to the election of grace. 6And if by
grace, then *it is* no longer of works; otherwise grace is no longer grace.[a] But if *it is* of
works, it is no longer grace; otherwise work
is no longer work.

7What then? Israel has not obtained what
it seeks; but the elect have obtained it, and
the rest were blinded. 8Just as it is written:

"God has given them a spirit of stupor,
Eyes that they should not see
And ears that they should not hear,
To this very day." [a]

10:1 [a] NU-Text reads *them*. **10:5** [a] Leviticus 18:5
10:6 [a] Deuteronomy 30:12 **10:7** [a] Deuteronomy 30:13
10:8 [a] Deuteronomy 30:14 **10:11** [a] Isaiah 28:16
10:13 [a] Joel 2:32 **10:15** [a] NU-Text omits *preach the gospel of peace, Who.* [b] Isaiah 52:7; Nahum 1:15 **10:16** [a] Isaiah 53:1 **10:18** [a] Psalm 19:4 **10:19** [a] Deuteronomy 32:21
10:20 [a] Isaiah 65:1 **10:21** [a] Isaiah 65:2 **11:3** [a] 1 Kings 19:10, 14 **11:4** [a] 1 Kings 19:18 **11:6** [a] NU-Text omits the rest of this verse. **11:8** [a] Deuteronomy 29:4; Isaiah 29:10

9 And David says:

"Let their table become a snare and a
trap,
A stumbling block and a recompense
to them.
10 Let their eyes be darkened, so that they
do not see,
And bow down their back always."[a]

Israel's Rejection Not Final

11 I say then, have they stumbled that they
should fall? Certainly not! But through their
fall, to provoke them to jealousy, salvation
has come to the Gentiles. 12 Now if their fall
is riches for the world, and their failure riches for the Gentiles, how much more their
fullness!

13 For I speak to you Gentiles; inasmuch
as I am an apostle to the Gentiles, I magnify
my ministry, 14 if by any means I may provoke
to jealousy *those who are* my flesh and save
some of them. 15 For if their being cast away
is the reconciling of the world, what *will* their
acceptance *be* but life from the dead?

16 For if the firstfruit *is* holy, the lump *is*
also *holy;* and if the root *is* holy, so *are* the
branches. 17 And if some of the branches were
broken off, and you, being a wild olive tree,
were grafted in among them, and with them
became a partaker of the root and fatness
of the olive tree, 18 do not boast against the
branches. But if you do boast, *remember that*
you do not support the root, but the root *supports* you.

19 You will say then, "Branches were broken off that I might be grafted in." 20 Well
said. Because of unbelief they were broken
off, and you stand by faith. Do not be haughty, but fear. 21 For if God did not spare the
natural branches, He may not spare you either. 22 Therefore consider the goodness and
severity of God: on those who fell, severity;
but toward you, goodness,[a] if you continue
in *His* goodness. Otherwise you also will be
cut off. 23 And they also, if they do not continue in unbelief, will be grafted in, for God
is able to graft them in again. 24 For if you
were cut out of the olive tree which is wild by
nature, and were grafted contrary to nature
into a cultivated olive tree, how much more
will these, who *are* natural *branches,* be grafted into their own olive tree?

25 For I do not desire, brethren, that you
should be ignorant of this mystery, lest you
should be wise in your own opinion, that
blindness in part has happened to Israel
until the fullness of the Gentiles has come
in. 26 And so all Israel will be saved,[a] as it is
written:

11:10 [a] Psalm 69:22, 23 11:22 [a] NU-Text adds *of God.* 11:26 [a] Or *delivered*

GIVE YOURSELF TO GOD

READ IT: ROMANS 12:1

If you wanted to give God a present, what do you think He would like? Some of your money? Some of your talents? Some of your time? God can use all these things, but He only wants them on one condition—these gifts must come with the gift of your whole self.

God is looking for your undivided loyalty. That kind of giving yourself is the simplest way after all. Then you don't have to worry about how much of *you* is *being given to God, and how much you're* keeping. Just give it all! Then wherever you are, all your hours and days will be spent doing the things God enjoys seeing you do. Jesus DIED for you. Will you LIVE for Him?

"The Deliverer will come out of Zion,
And He will turn away ungodliness
from Jacob;
27 For this *is* My covenant with them,
When I take away their sins." [a]

28 Concerning the gospel *they are* enemies
for your sake, but concerning the election
they are beloved for the sake of the fathers.
29 For the gifts and the calling of God *are*
irrevocable. 30 For as you were once disobedient to God, yet have now obtained mercy through their disobedience, 31 even so
these also have now been disobedient, that
through the mercy shown you they also
may obtain mercy. 32 For God has committed
them all to disobedience, that He might have
mercy on all.

33 Oh, the depth of the riches both of the
wisdom and knowledge of God! How unsearchable *are* His judgments and His ways
past finding out!

34 "For who has known the mind of the LORD?
Or who has become His counselor?" [a]
35 "Or who has first given to Him
And it shall be repaid to him?" [a]

36 For of Him and through Him and to
Him *are* all things, to whom *be* glory forever.
Amen.

Living Sacrifices to God

12 I beseech you therefore, brethren,
by the mercies of God, that you
present your bodies a living sacrifice, holy,
acceptable to God, *which is* your reasonable
service. 2 And do not be conformed to this
world, but be transformed by the renewing
of your mind, that you may prove what *is* that
good and acceptable and perfect will of God.

Serve God with Spiritual Gifts

3 For I say, through the grace given to
me, to everyone who is among you, not to
think *of himself* more highly than he ought
to think, but to think soberly, as God has
dealt to each one a measure of faith. 4 For as
we have many members in one body, but all
the members do not have the same function,
5 so we, *being* many, are one body in Christ,
and individually members of one another.
6 Having then gifts differing according to
the grace that is given to us, *let us use them:* if
prophecy, *let us prophesy* in proportion to our
faith; 7 or ministry, *let us use it* in *our* ministering; he who teaches, in teaching; 8 he who
exhorts, in exhortation; he who gives, with

11:27 [a] Isaiah 59:20, 21 11:34 [a] Isaiah 40:13; Jeremiah 23:18 11:35 [a] Job 41:11

GET ALONG WITH PEOPLE

READ IT: ROMANS 12:18

If you're a Christian, you will often find yourself disagreeing with a lot of opinions you hear. And sometimes you *should* disagree! But that doesn't mean you should quarrel with people—even people you know are wrong.

God knows all about the evil and false opinions in the world. When you have the chance, you may try to help people who are mistaken. But very often you will drive people farther away from Jesus by arguing with them. Instead of being their friend, you become their enemy.

So, as much as possible, get along with people. After all, your best argument is a cheerful attitude and a kind deed. Then people will be less afraid to talk to you about Jesus. But remember, you can't please everybody. The devil will see to that.

liberality; he who leads, with diligence; he
who shows mercy, with cheerfulness.

Behave Like a Christian

9*Let* love *be* without hypocrisy. Abhor
what is evil. Cling to what is good. 10*Be* kindly affectionate to one another with brotherly
love, in honor giving preference to one another; 11not lagging in diligence, fervent in
spirit, serving the Lord; 12rejoicing in hope,
patient in tribulation, continuing steadfastly
in prayer; 13distributing to the needs of the
saints, given to hospitality.

14Bless those who persecute you; bless
and do not curse. 15Rejoice with those who
rejoice, and weep with those who weep. 16Be
of the same mind toward one another. Do
not set your mind on high things, but associate with the humble. Do not be wise in your
own opinion.

17Repay no one evil for evil. Have regard
for good things in the sight of all men. 18If
it is possible, as much as depends on you,
live peaceably with all men. 19Beloved, do not
avenge yourselves, but *rather* give place to
wrath; for it is written, "Vengeance *is* Mine,
I will repay," [a] says the Lord. 20Therefore

"If your enemy is hungry, feed him;
If he is thirsty, give him a drink;
For in so doing you will heap coals of
fire on his head." [a]

21Do not be overcome by evil, but overcome
evil with good.

Submit to Government

13 Let every soul be subject to the governing authorities. For there is no
authority except from God, and the authorities that exist are appointed by God. 2There-
fore whoever resists the authority resists the
ordinance of God, and those who resist will
bring judgment on themselves. 3For rulers
are not a terror to good works, but to evil.
Do you want to be unafraid of the authority?
Do what is good, and you will have praise
from the same. 4For he is God's minister to
you for good. But if you do evil, be afraid; for
he does not bear the sword in vain; for he is
God's minister, an avenger to *execute* wrath
on him who practices evil. 5Therefore *you*
must be subject, not only because of wrath
but also for conscience' sake. 6For because
of this you also pay taxes, for they are God's
ministers attending continually to this very
thing. 7Render therefore to all their due: taxes to whom taxes *are due,* customs to whom
customs, fear to whom fear, honor to whom
honor.

Love Your Neighbor

8Owe no one anything except to love

12:19 [a] Deuteronomy 32:35 12:20 [a] Proverbs 25:21, 22

AUTHORITY

READ IT: ROMANS 13:1–7

Here are some suggestions to live by:

- Follow those who follow God.
- If you break the laws made in God's name, it's not just the police who will be angry with you.
- Don't keep quiet just because the sign says Quiet Please. Do so out of respect for the authority of the people who placed the sign.
- Everybody contributes and everybody benefits.

one another, for he who loves another has
fulfilled the law. 9 For the commandments,
"You shall not commit adultery," "You shall
not murder," "You shall not steal," "You shall
not bear false witness,"[a] "You shall not covet,"[b] and if *there is* any other commandment,
are *all* summed up in this saying, namely,
"You shall love your neighbor as yourself."[c]
10 Love does no harm to a neighbor; therefore
love *is* the fulfillment of the law.

Put on Christ

11 And *do* this, knowing the time, that now
it is high time to awake out of sleep; for now
our salvation *is* nearer than when we *first*
believed. 12 The night is far spent, the day is
at hand. Therefore let us cast off the works
of darkness, and let us put on the armor of
light. 13 Let us walk properly, as in the day, not
in revelry and drunkenness, not in lewdness
and lust, not in strife and envy. 14 But put on
the Lord Jesus Christ, and make no provision for the flesh, to *fulfill its* lusts.

The Law of Liberty

14 Receive one who is weak in the
faith, *but* not to disputes over
doubtful things. 2 For one believes he may
eat all things, but he who is weak eats *only*
vegetables. 3 Let not him who eats despise
him who does not eat, and let not him who
does not eat judge him who eats; for God has
received him. 4 Who are you to judge another's servant? To his own master he stands or
falls. Indeed, he will be made to stand, for
God is able to make him stand.

5 One person esteems *one* day above another; another esteems every day *alike*. Let
each be fully convinced in his own mind.
6 He who observes the day, observes *it* to
the Lord;[a] and he who does not observe the
day, to the Lord he does not observe *it*. He
who eats, eats to the Lord, for he gives God
thanks; and he who does not eat, to the Lord
he does not eat, and gives God thanks. 7 For
none of us lives to himself, and no one dies
to himself. 8 For if we live, we live to the Lord;
and if we die, we die to the Lord. Therefore,
whether we live or die, we are the Lord's. 9 For
to this end Christ died and rose[a] and lived
again, that He might be Lord of both the
dead and the living. 10 But why do you judge
your brother? Or why do you show contempt

13:9 [a] NU-Text omits *"You shall not bear false witness."* [b] Exodus 20:13–15, 17; Deuteronomy 5:17–19, 21 [c] Leviticus 19:18 **14:6** [a] NU-Text omits the rest of this sentence. **14:9** [a] NU-Text omits *and rose.*

WHAT REALLY PLEASES GOD?

READ IT: ROMAN 13:8

Some people think that if you go around with a long face or pray a lot or go to church, you're pleasing God.

Christians love to go to church and to pray, but if they are miserable doing those things, they aren't pleasing God. "God loves a cheerful giver" (*2 Corinthians* 9:7). That includes the time you give to praying and going to church.

What really counts with God is *love*. That means caring about others. If we aren't loving people, we're probably only wasting time by going to church. At church we hear God's Word. But God's Word should change our lives so that we bring some sunshine into the lives of others. "He who loves another has fulfilled the law" (v. 8). That's what pleases God.

for your brother? For we shall all stand before the judgment seat of Christ.[a] 11 For it is written:

> "*As* I live, says the LORD,
> Every knee shall bow to Me,
> And every tongue shall confess to
> God." [a]

12 So then each of us shall give account of himself to God. 13 Therefore let us not judge one another anymore, but rather resolve this, not to put a stumbling block or a cause to fall in *our* brother's way.

The Law of Love

14 I know and am convinced by the Lord Jesus that *there is* nothing unclean of itself; but to him who considers anything to be unclean, to him *it is* unclean. 15 Yet if your brother is grieved because of *your* food, you are no longer walking in love. Do not destroy with your food the one for whom Christ died. 16 Therefore do not let your good be spoken of as evil; 17 for the kingdom of God is not eating and drinking, but righteousness and peace and joy in the Holy Spirit. 18 For he who serves Christ in these things[a] *is* acceptable to God and approved by men.

19 Therefore let us pursue the things *which make* for peace and the things by which one may edify another. 20 Do not destroy the work of God for the sake of food. All things indeed *are* pure, but *it is* evil for the man who eats with offense. 21 *It is* good neither to eat meat nor drink wine nor *do anything* by which your brother stumbles or is offended or is made weak.[a] 22 Do you have faith? Have[a] *it* to yourself before God. Happy *is* he who does not condemn himself in what he approves. 23 But he who doubts is condemned if he eats, because *he does* not *eat* from faith; for whatever *is* not from faith is sin.[a]

Bearing Others' Burdens

15 We then who are strong ought to bear with the scruples of the weak, and not to please ourselves. 2 Let each of us please *his* neighbor for *his* good, leading to edification. 3 For even Christ did not please Himself; but as it is written, "The

---

14:10 [a] NU-Text reads *of God.* **14:11** [a] Isaiah 45:23 **14:18** [a] NU-Text reads *this.* **14:21** [a] NU-Text omits *or is offended or is made weak.* **14:22** [a] NU-Text reads *The faith which you have—have.* **14:23** [a] M-Text puts Romans 16:25–27 here.

DO YOUR BEST TO PLEASE OTHER PEOPLE

READ IT: ROMANS 15:1

Everybody likes to be pleased. Mostly we like to please ourselves. So why in the world does Paul tell us to please others? Did Paul know something we don't know? Yes, he did.

Believe it or not, a sure way to become unhappy is always to be pleasing yourself. When you live only to please yourself, you get very lonely because you've been *thinking only about yourself.* Suddenly you find you really are all alone, and you have no friends.

You see, God wants us to be a *family.* In a real family, everybody cares for the happiness of others. That means doing things that bring happiness to others. Have you tried to be a friend to a lonely boy or girl at school? Have you visited a sick friend lately? Try to think of ways to make life bright for people around you.

reproaches of those who reproached You fell
on Me." [a] 4For whatever things were written
before were written for our learning, that
we through the patience and comfort of the
Scriptures might have hope. 5Now may the
God of patience and comfort grant you to be
like-minded toward one another, according
to Christ Jesus, 6that you may with one mind
and one mouth glorify the God and Father of
our Lord Jesus Christ.

Glorify God Together

7Therefore receive one another, just as
Christ also received us,[a] to the glory of God.
8Now I say that Jesus Christ has become a
servant to the circumcision for the truth of
God, to confirm the promises *made* to the
fathers, 9and that the Gentiles might glorify
God for *His* mercy, as it is written:

"For this reason I will confess to You
among the Gentiles,
And sing to Your name." [a]

10And again he says:

"Rejoice, O Gentiles, with His people!" [a]

11And again:

"Praise the LORD, all you Gentiles!
Laud Him, all you peoples!" [a]

12And again, Isaiah says:

"There shall be a root of Jesse;
And He who shall rise to reign over the
Gentiles,
In Him the Gentiles shall hope." [a]

13Now may the God of hope fill you with
all joy and peace in believing, that you may
abound in hope by the power of the Holy
Spirit.

From Jerusalem to Illyricum

14Now I myself am confident concerning
you, my brethren, that you also are full of
goodness, filled with all knowledge, able
also to admonish one another.[a] 15Neverthe-
less, brethren, I have written more boldly
to you on *some* points, as reminding you,
because of the grace given to me by God,
16that I might be a minister of Jesus Christ
to the Gentiles, ministering the gospel of
God, that the offering of the Gentiles might
be acceptable, sanctified by the Holy Spirit.
17Therefore I have reason to glory in Christ
Jesus in the things *which pertain* to God.
18For I will not dare to speak of any of those
things which Christ has not accomplished
through me, in word and deed, to make the
Gentiles obedient— 19in mighty signs and
wonders, by the power of the Spirit of God,
so that from Jerusalem and round about to
Illyricum I have fully preached the gospel
of Christ. 20And so I have made it my aim
to preach the gospel, not where Christ was
named, lest I should build on another man's
foundation, 21but as it is written:

"To whom He was not announced, they
shall see;
And those who have not heard shall
understand." [a]

15:3 [a] Psalm 69:9 **15:7** [a] NU-Text and M-Text read *you.* **15:9** [a] 2 Samuel 22:50; Psalm 18:49 **15:10** [a] Deuteronomy 32:43 **15:11** [a] Psalm 117:1 **15:12** [a] Isaiah 11:10 **15:14** [a] M-Text reads *others.* **15:21** [a] Isaiah 52:15

Action!

HOPE

READ IT: ROMANS 15:13

Hope is defined as "a feeling of expectation and desire for a certain thing to happen." When the woman with the bleeding problem (Luke 8:40–48) was on her way to see Jesus, do you think she felt joy through the hope she had that Jesus could heal her? Joy and peace come when our hope is in Jesus and His Spirit is our guide.

Plan to Visit Rome

22For this reason I also have been much
hindered from coming to you. 23But now no
longer having a place in these parts, and having a great desire these many years to come
to you, 24whenever I journey to Spain, I shall
come to you.[a] For I hope to see you on my
journey, and to be helped on my way there
by you, if first I may enjoy your *company* for
a while. 25But now I am going to Jerusalem
to minister to the saints. 26For it pleased
those from Macedonia and Achaia to make
a certain contribution for the poor among
the saints who are in Jerusalem. 27It pleased
them indeed, and they are their debtors. For
if the Gentiles have been partakers of their
spiritual things, their duty is also to minister to them in material things. 28Therefore,
when I have performed this and have sealed
to them this fruit, I shall go by way of you to
Spain. 29But I know that when I come to you,
I shall come in the fullness of the blessing of
the gospel[a] of Christ.

30Now I beg you, brethren, through the
Lord Jesus Christ, and through the love of
the Spirit, that you strive together with me in
prayers to God for me, 31that I may be delivered from those in Judea who do not believe,
and that my service for Jerusalem may be
acceptable to the saints, 32that I may come to
you with joy by the will of God, and may be
refreshed together with you. 33Now the God
of peace *be* with you all. Amen.

Sister Phoebe Commended

16 I commend to you Phoebe our sister, who is a servant of the church
in Cenchrea, 2that you may receive her in the
Lord in a manner worthy of the saints, and
assist her in whatever business she has need
of you; for indeed she has been a helper of
many and of myself also.

Greeting Roman Saints

3Greet Priscilla and Aquila, my fellow
workers in Christ Jesus, 4who risked their
own necks for my life, to whom not only I
give thanks, but also all the churches of the
Gentiles. 5Likewise *greet* the church that is
in their house.

Greet my beloved Epaenetus, who is the
firstfruits of Achaia[a] to Christ. 6Greet Mary,
who labored much for us. 7Greet Andronicus
and Junia, my countrymen and my fellow

15:24 [a] NU-Text omits *I shall come to you* (and joins *Spain* with the next sentence). 15:29 [a] NU-Text omits *of the gospel.* 16:5 [a] NU-Text reads *Asia.*

TAKE A PRESENT TO GOD

READ IT: ROMANS 15:16

Paul gave a present to God. This is what he means by his words "the offering of the Gentiles." The Gentiles were the non-Jews, the Greeks and the Romans of Paul's time. And Paul had brought many of these people to God as "an offering"—a gift to God. That's a nice way to say it, isn't it? Whenever you lead another person to know Jesus, you are bringing that person as "an offering" or gift to God.

Have you brought any offerings like that to God? Maybe you go to church on Sunday, and you put an offering in the collection plate. God appreciates offerings like that, but the best offering you can make is *someone you bring to Jesus.* Has Jesus come into your heart? Then why not share Him with someone else, too? That is the greatest present you can give to God.

prisoners, who are of note among the apostles, who also were in Christ before me.

8 Greet Amplias, my beloved in the Lord. 9 Greet Urbanus, our fellow worker in Christ, and Stachys, my beloved. 10 Greet Apelles, approved in Christ. Greet those who are of the *household* of Aristobulus. 11 Greet Herodion, my countryman.[a] Greet those who are of the *household* of Narcissus who are in the Lord.

12 Greet Tryphena and Tryphosa, who have labored in the Lord. Greet the beloved Persis, who labored much in the Lord. 13 Greet Rufus, chosen in the Lord, and his mother and mine. 14 Greet Asyncritus, Phlegon, Hermas, Patrobas, Hermes, and the brethren who are with them. 15 Greet Philologus and Julia, Nereus and his sister, and Olympas, and all the saints who are with them.

16 Greet one another with a holy kiss. The[a] churches of Christ greet you.

Avoid Divisive Persons

17 Now I urge you, brethren, note those who cause divisions and offenses, contrary to the doctrine which you learned, and avoid them. 18 For those who are such do not serve our Lord Jesus[a] Christ, but their own belly, and by smooth words and flattering speech deceive the hearts of the simple. 19 For your obedience has become known to all. Therefore I am glad on your behalf; but I want you to be wise in what is good, and simple concerning evil. 20 And the God of peace will crush Satan under your feet shortly.

The grace of our Lord Jesus Christ *be* with you. Amen.

Greetings from Paul's Friends

21 Timothy, my fellow worker, and Lucius, Jason, and Sosipater, my countrymen, greet you.

22 I, Tertius, who wrote *this* epistle, greet you in the Lord.

23 Gaius, my host and *the host* of the whole church, greets you. Erastus, the treasurer of the city, greets you, and Quartus, a brother. 24 The grace of our Lord Jesus Christ *be* with you all. Amen.[a]

Benediction

25 Now to Him who is able to establish you according to my gospel and the preaching of Jesus Christ, according to the revelation of the mystery kept secret since the world began 26 but now made manifest, and by the prophetic Scriptures made known to all nations, according to the commandment of the everlasting God, for obedience to the faith— 27 to God, alone wise, *be* glory through Jesus Christ forever. Amen.[a]

16:11 [a] Or *relative* **16:16** [a] NU-Text reads *All the churches.* **16:18** [a] NU-Text and M-Text omit *Jesus.* **16:24** [a] NU-Text omits this verse. **16:27** [a] M-Text puts Romans 16:25–27 after Romans 14:23.

Starring Roles

PRISCILLA and her husband, **AQUILA**, had to leave Italy when Emperor Claudius (pronounced *CLAW-dee-us*) commanded all Jews to leave Rome. So they went to live at Corinth where they met Paul.

Paul, Priscilla, and Aquila were all tentmakers, and sometimes they also made sails for boats.

Later they met Apollos, a fine young preacher. But there were some things Apollos had to learn, so they took him aside and taught him more about the Good News of Jesus the Savior. After that, many people believed in Jesus when they heard Apollos preach.

Priscilla and Aquila's meetings with Paul from time to time were special treats. When he passed through Corinth, he would stay at their home. Once Paul stayed with them for 18 months. They were glad to have a place for Paul, because he had no home or wife. Paul's whole Christian life was spent for his Lord.

The FIRST EPISTLE of PAUL the APOSTLE to the

CORINTHIANS

A.D. 56

Behind the Scenes

READ IT:

The book of 1 Corinthians is a letter from Paul to the church in Corinth, Greece. These Christians were having some problems, so Paul gave them instructions and advice on how to keep unity, love, and order in their new church.

GET IT:

Who wrote it: Paul

When it was written: in the spring of A.D. 56

Why it was written: to teach the new Christians in Corinth practical lessons about the Christian life so they would know right from wrong.

LIVE IT:

We all are given gifts to share with others in the church. One gift is not better than others. Every gift is important to support Christ's work.

FIND IT:

Glorify God in Body and Spirit	*1 Corinthians 6*
Instructions on the Lord's Supper	*1 Corinthians 11*
Spiritual Gifts: Unity in Diversity	*1 Corinthians 12*
Love—the Greatest Gift	*1 Corinthians 13*
The Risen Christ	*1 Corinthians 15*

you *are* strong! You *are* distinguished, but
we *are* dishonored! 11 To the present hour we
both hunger and thirst, and we are poorly
clothed, and beaten, and homeless. 12 And
we labor, working with our own hands. Being reviled, we bless; being persecuted, we
endure; 13 being defamed, we entreat. We
have been made as the filth of the world, the
offscouring of all things until now.

Paul's Paternal Care

14 I do not write these things to shame
you, but as my beloved children I warn *you.*
15 For though you might have ten thousand
instructors in Christ, yet *you do* not *have*
many fathers; for in Christ Jesus I have begotten you through the gospel. 16 Therefore I
urge you, imitate me. 17 For this reason I have
sent Timothy to you, who is my beloved and

On Location

Paul's Second Missionary Journey

Paul's letter is addressed to Christians in a young church he started a few years earlier, during his second missionary journey (shown on the map), at Corinth, perhaps the busiest city in ancient Greece. Located south of Athens, Corinth is near a four-mile-wide land bridge separating the Aegean Sea in the east and the Adriatic Sea in the west.

Eastern trade ships carrying products destined for Rome and other western cities would often stop in Corinth. If the ship were small enough, it could be hauled up onto a huge wagon, wheeled across the isthmus, then launched into the Adriatic. This saved merchants a 200-mile trip around the tip of Greece, sparing them from storms and pirates. Larger ships unloaded their cargo and had it hauled to other ships waiting at the Adriatic port. Nero started a canal in A.D. 66, but the project was stopped after engineers doubted it could be done and Corinthians complained that a canal would keep travelers from stopping in the city. The project was completed in 1893 and is still used.

faithful son in the Lord, who will remind
you of my ways in Christ, as I teach everywhere in every church.

18 Now some are puffed up, as though I
were not coming to you. 19 But I will come to
you shortly, if the Lord wills, and I will know,
not the word of those who are puffed up, but
the power. 20 For the kingdom of God *is* not
in word but in power. 21 What do you want?
Shall I come to you with a rod, or in love and
a spirit of gentleness?

Immorality Defiles the Church

5 It is actually reported *that there is* sexual immorality among you, and such
sexual immorality as is not even named[a]
among the Gentiles—that a man has his father's wife! 2 And you are puffed up, and have
not rather mourned, that he who has done
this deed might be taken away from among
you. 3 For I indeed, as absent in body but present in spirit, have already judged (as though
I were present) him who has so done this
deed. 4 In the name of our Lord Jesus Christ,
when you are gathered together, along with
my spirit, with the power of our Lord Jesus
Christ, 5 deliver such a one to Satan for the
destruction of the flesh, that his spirit may
be saved in the day of the Lord Jesus.[a]

6 Your glorying *is* not good. Do you not
know that a little leaven leavens the whole
lump? 7 Therefore purge out the old leaven,
that you may be a new lump, since you truly are unleavened. For indeed Christ, our
Passover, was sacrificed for us.[a] 8 Therefore
let us keep the feast, not with old leaven, nor
with the leaven of malice and wickedness,
but with the unleavened *bread* of sincerity
and truth.

Immorality Must Be Judged

9 I wrote to you in my epistle not to keep
company with sexually immoral people. 10 Yet
I certainly *did* not *mean* with the sexually immoral people of this world, or with the covetous, or extortioners, or idolaters, since then
you would need to go out of the world. 11 But
now I have written to you not to keep company with anyone named a brother, who is sexually immoral, or covetous, or an idolater, or
a reviler, or a drunkard, or an extortioner—
not even to eat with such a person.

12 For what *have* I *to do* with judging those
also who are outside? Do you not judge those
who are inside? 13 But those who are outside

5:1 [a] NU-Text omits *named.* 5:5 [a] NU-Text omits *Jesus.*
5:7 [a] NU-Text omits *for us.*

CAN YOU DO AS YOU PLEASE?

READ IT: 1 CORINTHIANS 6:12

Some people say, "I can do anything I please." And so they *can*. But what happens when they *do?*

What happens if you ride your bicycle over a cliff? You know the answer to that. What happens if you go swimming in the middle of the ocean with nobody around to help you if you go under? That story has a bad ending, too. How about jumping out of an airplane at thirty thousand feet—without a parachute? That would be your last day on earth.

So you can do anything you please, but a lot of things are not very good for you. In fact, they really hurt you. You can spend your life just playing games, or even doing nothing at all. But then you've lost a lifetime that you can never replace. "Only one life; 'twill soon be past. Only what's done for Christ will last."

God judges. Therefore "put away from yourselves the evil person." [a]

Do Not Sue the Brethren

6 Dare any of you, having a matter against another, go to law before the unrighteous, and not before the saints? [2]Do you not know that the saints will judge the world? And if the world will be judged by you, are you unworthy to judge the smallest matters? [3]Do you not know that we shall judge angels? How much more, things that pertain to this life? [4]If then you have judgments concerning things pertaining to this life, do you appoint those who are least esteemed by the church to judge? [5]I say this to your shame. Is it so, that there is not a wise man among you, not even one, who will be able to judge between his brethren? [6]But brother goes to law against brother, and that before unbelievers!

[7]Now therefore, it is already an utter failure for you that you go to law against one another. Why do you not rather accept wrong? Why do you not rather *let yourselves* be cheated? [8]No, you yourselves do wrong and cheat, and *you do* these things *to your* brethren! [9]Do you not know that the unrighteous will not inherit the kingdom of God? Do not be deceived. Neither fornicators, nor idolaters, nor adulterers, nor homosexuals,[a] nor sodomites, [10]nor thieves, nor covetous, nor drunkards, nor revilers, nor extortioners will inherit the kingdom of God. [11]And such were some of you. But you were washed, but you were sanctified, but you were justified in the name of the Lord Jesus and by the Spirit of our God.

Glorify God in Body and Spirit

[12]All things are lawful for me, but all things are not helpful. All things are lawful for me, but I will not be brought under the power of any. [13]Foods for the stomach and the stomach for foods, but God will destroy both it and them. Now the body *is* not for sexual immorality but for the Lord, and the Lord for the body. [14]And God both raised up the Lord and will also raise us up by His power.

[15]Do you not know that your bodies are members of Christ? Shall I then take the members of Christ and make *them* members of a harlot? Certainly not! [16]Or do you not know that he who is joined to a harlot is one body *with her*? For "the two," He says, "shall become one flesh." [a] [17]But he who is joined to the Lord is one spirit *with Him*.

[18]Flee sexual immorality. Every sin that a man does is outside the body, but he who commits sexual immorality sins against his own body. [19]Or do you not know that your body is the temple of the Holy Spirit *who is* in you, whom you have from God, and you are not your own? [20]For you were bought at a price; therefore glorify God in your body[a] and in your spirit, which are God's.

Principles of Marriage

7 Now concerning the things of which you wrote to me:

It is good for a man not to touch a woman. [2]Nevertheless, because of sexual immorality, let each man have his own wife, and let each woman have her own husband. [3]Let the husband render to his wife the affection due her, and likewise also the wife to her husband. [4]The wife does not have authority over her own body, but the husband *does*. And likewise the husband does not have authority over his own body, but the wife *does*. [5]Do not deprive one another except with consent for a time, that you may give yourselves to fasting and prayer; and come together again so that Satan does not tempt you because of your lack of self-control. [6]But I say this as a concession, not as a commandment. [7]For I wish that all men were even as I myself. But each one has his own gift from God, one in this manner and another in that.

[8]But I say to the unmarried and to the widows: It is good for them if they remain even as I am; [9]but if they cannot exercise self-control, let them marry. For it is better to marry than to burn *with passion*.

Keep Your Marriage Vows

[10]Now to the married I command, *yet* not I but the Lord: A wife is not to depart from *her* husband. [11]But even if she does depart, let her remain unmarried or be reconciled to *her* husband. And a husband is not to divorce *his* wife.

[12]But to the rest I, not the Lord, say: If any brother has a wife who does not believe,

---

5:13 [a] Deuteronomy 17:7; 19:19; 22:21, 24; 24:7 **6:9** [a] That is, catamites **6:16** [a] Genesis 2:24 **6:20** [a] NU-Text ends the verse at *body*.

and she is willing to live with him, let him
not divorce her. 13And a woman who has a
husband who does not believe, if he is willing to live with her, let her not divorce him.
14For the unbelieving husband is sanctified
by the wife, and the unbelieving wife is
sanctified by the husband; otherwise your
children would be unclean, but now they
are holy. 15But if the unbeliever departs, let
him depart; a brother or a sister is not under
bondage in such *cases*. But God has called
us to peace. 16For how do you know, O wife,
whether you will save *your* husband? Or how
do you know, O husband, whether you will
save *your* wife?

Live as You Are Called

17But as God has distributed to each one,
as the Lord has called each one, so let him
walk. And so I ordain in all the churches.
18Was anyone called while circumcised?
Let him not become uncircumcised. Was
anyone called while uncircumcised? Let
him not be circumcised. 19Circumcision is
nothing and uncircumcision is nothing, but
keeping the commandments of God *is what*
matters. 20Let each one remain in the same
calling in which he was called. 21Were you
called *while* a slave? Do not be concerned
about it; but if you can be made free, rather use *it*. 22For he who is called in the Lord
while a slave is the Lord's freedman. Likewise he who is called *while* free is Christ's
slave. 23You were bought at a price; do not
become slaves of men. 24Brethren, let each
one remain with God in that *state* in which
he was called.

To the Unmarried and Widows

25Now concerning virgins: I have no commandment from the Lord; yet I give judgment as one whom the Lord in His mercy
has made trustworthy. 26I suppose therefore that this is good because of the present
distress—that *it is* good for a man to remain
as he is: 27Are you bound to a wife? Do not
seek to be loosed. Are you loosed from a
wife? Do not seek a wife. 28But even if you do
marry, you have not sinned; and if a virgin
marries, she has not sinned. Nevertheless
such will have trouble in the flesh, but I
would spare you.

29But this I say, brethren, the time *is*
short, so that from now on even those who
have wives should be as though they had
none, 30those who weep as though they did
not weep, those who rejoice as though they
did not rejoice, those who buy as though
they did not possess, 31and those who use
this world as not misusing *it*. For the form
of this world is passing away.

32But I want you to be without care. He
who is unmarried cares for the things of the
Lord—how he may please the Lord. 33But he
who is married cares about the things of the
world—how he may please *his* wife. 34There
is[a] a difference between a wife and a virgin.
The unmarried woman cares about the
things of the Lord, that she may be holy both
in body and in spirit. But she who is married cares about the things of the world—
how she may please *her* husband. 35And this

7:34 [a] M-Text adds *also*.

MARRIAGE AND DIVORCE

READ IT: 1 CORINTHIANS 7:10,11

No matter what the world says or believes, God wants marriages to work and to be an example of His love. When marriages don't seem to be working (for so many reasons), God says, "Don't give up quickly; you *should try to help each other, and I will help you!*" God never gives up on us, and we should have the same kind of commitment to each other and to our relationships.

I say for your own profit, not that I may put a
leash on you, but for what is proper, and that
you may serve the Lord without distraction.
36But if any man thinks he is behaving
improperly toward his virgin, if she is past
the flower of youth, and thus it must be, let
him do what he wishes. He does not sin; let
them marry. 37Nevertheless he who stands
steadfast in his heart, having no necessity,
but has power over his own will, and has so
determined in his heart that he will keep his
virgin,[a] does well. 38So then he who gives
her[a] in marriage does well, but he who does
not give *her* in marriage does better.
39A wife is bound by law as long as her
husband lives; but if her husband dies, she is
at liberty to be married to whom she wishes,
only in the Lord. 40But she is happier if she remains as she is, according to my judgment—
and I think I also have the Spirit of God.

Be Sensitive to Conscience

8 Now concerning things offered to
idols: We know that we all have knowledge. Knowledge puffs up, but love edifies.
2And if anyone thinks that he knows anything, he knows nothing yet as he ought to
know. 3But if anyone loves God, this one is
known by Him.
4Therefore concerning the eating of
things offered to idols, we know that an
idol *is* nothing in the world, and that *there*
is no other God but one. 5For even if there
are so-called gods, whether in heaven or on
earth (as there are many gods and many
lords), 6yet for us *there is* one God, the Father,
of whom *are* all things, and we for Him; and
one Lord Jesus Christ, through whom *are* all
things, and through whom we *live.*
7However, *there is* not in everyone that
knowledge; for some, with consciousness of
the idol, until now eat *it* as a thing offered to
an idol; and their conscience, being weak, is
defiled. 8But food does not commend us to
God; for neither if we eat are we the better,
nor if we do not eat are we the worse.
9But beware lest somehow this liberty
of yours become a stumbling block to those
who are weak. 10For if anyone sees you who
have knowledge eating in an idol's temple,
will not the conscience of him who is weak
be emboldened to eat those things offered to
idols? 11And because of your knowledge shall
the weak brother perish, for whom Christ
died? 12But when you thus sin against the
brethren, and wound their weak conscience,
you sin against Christ. 13Therefore, if food
makes my brother stumble, I will never again
eat meat, lest I make my brother stumble.

A Pattern of Self-Denial

9 Am I not an apostle? Am I not free?
Have I not seen Jesus Christ our Lord?

7:37 [a] Or *virgin daughter* 7:38 [a] NU-Text reads *his own virgin.*

WE HAVE A LOT TO LEARN

READ IT: 1 CORINTHIANS 8:2

No wonder someone has said God will laugh at us (see Psalm 2:4). We think we know so much. Right now you may be very excited about science. We have learned a lot from science. But as you get older, you may begin to notice that many of the things scientists believe today will be debunked later.

We must keep on trying to learn all we can. But when we have learned as much as we can, we're not much closer to knowing everything than we were before. The universe keeps getting older and older, and even scientists tell us it will die one day. But God will live forever. Knowing Him is what matters when everything else is passing away.

Are you not my work in the Lord? 2If I am
not an apostle to others, yet doubtless I am
to you. For you are the seal of my apostleship
in the Lord.

3My defense to those who examine me is
this: 4Do we have no right to eat and drink?
5Do we have no right to take along a believing wife, as *do* also the other apostles, the
brothers of the Lord, and Cephas? 6Or *is it*
only Barnabas and I *who* have no right to refrain from working? 7Who ever goes to war
at his own expense? Who plants a vineyard
and does not eat of its fruit? Or who tends a
flock and does not drink of the milk of the
flock?

8Do I say these things as a *mere* man? Or
does not the law say the same also? 9For it is
written in the law of Moses, "You shall not
muzzle an ox while it treads out the grain."[a]
Is it oxen God is concerned about? 10Or does
He say *it* altogether for our sakes? For our
sakes, no doubt, *this* is written, that he who
plows should plow in hope, and he who
threshes in hope should be partaker of his
hope. 11If we have sown spiritual things for
you, *is it* a great thing if we reap your material things? 12If others are partakers of *this*
right over you, *are* we not even more?

In Focus

9:27 Discipline Pronounced *DIS-ih-plin*. Comes from the same word as "disciple." To discipline means to "train" or "teach."

Nevertheless we have not used this right,
but endure all things lest we hinder the gospel of Christ. 13Do you not know that those
who minister the holy things eat *of the things*
of the temple, and those who serve at the altar partake of *the offerings of* the altar? 14Even
so the Lord has commanded that those
who preach the gospel should live from the
gospel.

15But I have used none of these things,
nor have I written these things that it should
be done so to me; for it *would be* better for
me to die than that anyone should make my
boasting void. 16For if I preach the gospel, I
have nothing to boast of, for necessity is laid

9:9 [a] Deuteronomy 25:4

Action!

LEARN TO BE A SERVANT

READ IT: 1 CORINTHIANS 9:19

Everybody wants to be the boss. Nobody wants to be a servant. But can you believe that God's way UP is DOWN? Jesus was the Son of the Highest, but He made Himself a servant. That was a long way down for Jesus. Why did He do that?

There were two reasons. First, Jesus had to be a servant to die for our sins. Jesus was greater than Pilate and greater than the emperor of Rome, but He made Himself the Servant of all. He let Himself be nailed to a cross by the Jews and the Romans. He was the Highest, but He let Himself be treated like the lowest of men.

The second reason was that Jesus wanted to show you what true greatness is like. Real greatness is being a successful servant of people. You may be the president or you may be the janitor. But God calls you to be His servant in both places.

upon me; yes, woe is me if I do not preach
the gospel! 17For if I do this willingly, I have
a reward; but if against my will, I have been
entrusted with a stewardship. 18What is my
reward then? That when I preach the gospel,
I may present the gospel of Christ[a] without
charge, that I may not abuse my authority in
the gospel.

Serving All Men

19For though I am free from all *men,*
I have made myself a servant to all, that I
might win the more; 20and to the Jews I
became as a Jew, that I might win Jews; to
those *who are* under the law, as under the
law,[a] that I might win those *who are* under
the law; 21to those *who are* without law, as
without law (not being without law toward
God,[a] but under law toward Christ[b]), that
I might win those *who are* without law; 22to
the weak I became as[a] weak, that I might
win the weak. I have become all things to all
men, that I might by all means save some.
23Now this I do for the gospel's sake, that I
may be partaker of it with *you.*

Striving for a Crown

24Do you not know that those who run
in a race all run, but one receives the prize?
Run in such a way that you may obtain *it.*
25And everyone who competes *for the prize*
is temperate in all things. Now they *do it*
to obtain a perishable crown, but we *for* an
imperishable *crown.* 26Therefore I run thus:
not with uncertainty. Thus I fight: not as *one*
who beats the air. 27But I discipline my body
and bring *it* into subjection, lest, when I have
preached to others, I myself should become
disqualified.

Old Testament Examples

10 Moreover, brethren, I do not want
you to be unaware that all our fathers were under the cloud, all passed
through the sea, 2all were baptized into Moses in the cloud and in the sea, 3all ate the
same spiritual food, 4and all drank the same
spiritual drink. For they drank of that spiritual Rock that followed them, and that Rock
was Christ. 5But with most of them God was
not well pleased, for *their bodies* were scattered in the wilderness.

6Now these things became our examples, to the intent that we should not lust
after evil things as they also lusted. 7And do
not become idolaters as *were* some of them.
As it is written, "The people sat down to eat
and drink, and rose up to play." [a] 8Nor let us
commit sexual immorality, as some of them
did, and in one day twenty-three thousand
fell; 9nor let us tempt Christ, as some of
them also tempted, and were destroyed by
serpents; 10nor complain, as some of them
also complained, and were destroyed by the
destroyer. 11Now all[a] these things happened
to them as examples, and they were written
for our admonition, upon whom the ends of
the ages have come.

12Therefore let him who thinks he stands
take heed lest he fall. 13No temptation has
overtaken you except such as is common to
man; but God *is* faithful, who will not allow
you to be tempted beyond what you are able,
but with the temptation will also make the
way of escape, that you may be able to bear *it.*

Flee from Idolatry

14Therefore, my beloved, flee from idolatry. 15I speak as to wise men; judge for
yourselves what I say. 16The cup of blessing
which we bless, is it not the communion of
the blood of Christ? The bread which we
break, is it not the communion of the body of
Christ? 17For we, *though* many, are one bread
and one body; for we all partake of that one
bread.

18Observe Israel after the flesh: Are not
those who eat of the sacrifices partakers of
the altar? 19What am I saying then? That an
idol is anything, or what is offered to idols
is anything? 20Rather, that the things which
the Gentiles sacrifice they sacrifice to demons and not to God, and I do not want you
to have fellowship with demons. 21You cannot drink the cup of the Lord and the cup
of demons; you cannot partake of the Lord's
table and of the table of demons. 22Or do we
provoke the Lord to jealousy? Are we stronger than He?

All to the Glory of God

23All things are lawful for me,[a] but not
all things are helpful; all things are lawful
for me,[b] but not all things edify. 24Let no
one seek his own, but each one the other's
well-being.

9:18 [a] NU-Text omits *of Christ.* **9:20** [a] NU-Text adds *though not being myself under the law.* **9:21** [a] NU-Text reads *God's law.* [b] NU-Text reads *Christ's law.* **9:22** [a] NU-Text omits *as.* **10:7** [a] Exodus 32:6 **10:11** [a] NU-Text omits *all.* **10:23** [a] NU-Text omits *for me.* [b] NU-Text omits *for me.*

25 Eat whatever is sold in the meat market, asking no questions for conscience' sake; 26 for "the earth *is* the LORD's, and all its fullness." [a]

27 If any of those who do not believe invites you *to dinner,* and you desire to go, eat whatever is set before you, asking no question for conscience' sake. 28 But if anyone says to you, "This was offered to idols," do not eat it for the sake of the one who told you, and for conscience' sake;[a] for "the earth *is* the LORD's, and all its fullness." [b] 29 "Conscience," I say, not your own, but that of the other. For why is my liberty judged by another *man's* conscience? 30 But if I partake with thanks, why am I evil spoken of for *the food* over which I give thanks?

31 Therefore, whether you eat or drink, or whatever you do, do all to the glory of God. 32 Give no offense, either to the Jews or to the Greeks or to the church of God, 33 just as I also please all *men* in all *things,* not seeking my own profit, but the *profit* of many, that they may be saved.

11 Imitate me, just as I also *imitate* Christ.

Head Coverings

2 Now I praise you, brethren, that you remember me in all things and keep the traditions just as I delivered *them* to you. 3 But I want you to know that the head of every man is Christ, the head of woman *is* man, and the head of Christ *is* God. 4 Every man praying or prophesying, having *his* head covered, dishonors his head. 5 But every woman who prays or prophesies with *her* head uncovered dishonors her head, for that is one and the same as if her head were shaved. 6 For if a woman is not covered, let her also be shorn. But if it is shameful for a woman to be shorn or shaved, let her be covered. 7 For a man indeed ought not to cover *his* head, since he is the image and glory of God; but woman is the glory of man. 8 For man is not from woman, but woman from man. 9 Nor was man created for the woman, but woman for the man. 10 For this reason the woman ought to have *a symbol of* authority on *her* head, because of the angels. 11 Nevertheless, neither *is* man independent of woman, nor woman independent of man, in the Lord. 12 For as woman *came* from man, even so man also *comes* through woman; but all things are from God.

13 Judge among yourselves. Is it proper for a woman to pray to God with her head uncovered? 14 Does not even nature itself teach you that if a man has long hair, it is a dishonor to him? 15 But if a woman has long hair, it is a glory to her; for *her* hair is given to her[a] for a covering. 16 But if anyone seems to be contentious, we have no such custom, nor *do* the churches of God.

Conduct at the Lord's Supper

17 Now in giving these instructions I do not praise *you,* since you come together not

10:26 [a] Psalm 24:1 10:28 [a] NU-Text omits the rest of this verse. [b] Psalm 24:1 11:15 [a] M-Text omits *to her.*

PEER PRESSURE

READ IT: 1 CORINTHIANS 10:13

This verse confirms that you will face temptation—the opportunity or desire to do something you know is wrong—in your life. That probably doesn't surprise you, but how do you handle temptation when you face it? *When temptation walks through the door* of your life, God opens a window to help you escape. He promises to create a way for you to avoid temptation. God creates an escape route, and it's your job to take it!

for the better but for the worse. 18For first of
all, when you come together as a church,
I hear that there are divisions among you,
and in part I believe it. 19For there must also
be factions among you, that those who are
approved may be recognized among you.
20Therefore when you come together in
one place, it is not to eat the Lord's Supper.
21For in eating, each one takes his own supper ahead of *others;* and one is hungry and
another is drunk. 22What! Do you not have
houses to eat and drink in? Or do you despise the church of God and shame those
who have nothing? What shall I say to you?
Shall I praise you in this? I do not praise *you.*

Institution of the Lord's Supper

23For I received from the Lord that which
I also delivered to you: that the Lord Jesus
on the *same* night in which He was betrayed
took bread; 24and when He had given thanks,
He broke *it* and said, "Take, eat;[a] this is My
body which is broken[b] for you; do this in remembrance of Me." 25In the same manner
He also *took* the cup after supper, saying,
"This cup is the new covenant in My blood.
This do, as often as you drink *it,* in remembrance of Me."

26For as often as you eat this bread and
drink this cup, you proclaim the Lord's
death till He comes.

Examine Yourself

27Therefore whoever eats this bread or

In Focus

12:1 Spiritual Gifts The abilities God gives to all believers for serving Him in different ways. Every Christian has one or more spiritual gifts as described by Paul.

drinks *this* cup of the Lord in an unworthy
manner will be guilty of the body and blood[a]
of the Lord. 28But let a man examine himself,
and so let him eat of the bread and drink of
the cup. 29For he who eats and drinks in an
unworthy manner[a] eats and drinks judgment to himself, not discerning the Lord's[b]
body. 30For this reason many *are* weak and
sick among you, and many sleep. 31For if
we would judge ourselves, we would not be
judged. 32But when we are judged, we are
chastened by the Lord, that we may not be
condemned with the world.

33Therefore, my brethren, when you
come together to eat, wait for one another. 34But if anyone is hungry, let him eat at

11:24 [a] NU-Text omits *Take, eat.* [b] NU-Text omits *broken.* 11:27 [a] NU-Text and M-Text read *the blood.* 11:29 [a] NU-Text omits *in an unworthy manner.* [b] NU-Text omits *Lord's.*

Action!

ENTERTAINMENT

READ IT: 1 CORINTHIANS 10:23–33

Ever hear one Christian state a belief and then hear another say something that's totally opposite? In Corinth (where the Corinthians lived), meat was sacrificed to idols and then sold in the markets or served at a dinner. Many Christians believed it wasn't right to eat the meat from those sacrifices. Others thought it was no big deal. Paul taught the people how to deal with something that some people thought was wrong and others thought was right. Honor God first and not other people. When in doubt, please God rather than people. But respect other people's opinions, and don't offend them.

home, lest you come together for judgment.
And the rest I will set in order when I come.

Spiritual Gifts: Unity in Diversity

12 Now concerning spiritual *gifts,*
brethren, I do not want you to be ignorant: 2 You know that[a] you were Gentiles,
carried away to these dumb idols, however
you were led. 3 Therefore I make known to
you that no one speaking by the Spirit of
God calls Jesus accursed, and no one can say
that Jesus is Lord except by the Holy Spirit.
4 There are diversities of gifts, but the
same Spirit. 5 There are differences of min-
istries, but the same Lord. 6 And there are
diversities of activities, but it is the same
God who works all in all. 7 But the manifestation of the Spirit is given to each one for the
profit *of all:* 8 for to one is given the word of
wisdom through the Spirit, to another the
word of knowledge through the same Spirit,
9 to another faith by the same Spirit, to another gifts of healings by the same[a] Spirit, 10 to
another the working of miracles, to another
prophecy, to another discerning of spirits, to
another *different* kinds of tongues, to another
the interpretation of tongues. 11 But one and

12:2 [a] NU-Text and M-Text add *when.* 12:9 [a] NU-Text reads *one.*

Epic Ideas

IDENTITY
EARS, FEET, AND HANDS

READ IT: 1 CORINTHIANS 12:12–27

GET IT:

We sometimes create a false pecking order in the Church. We put the really famous Christian preachers at the top, then our pastors, missionaries, Sunday school teachers, and so on. By the time we're finished we've put ourselves at the bottom. Why? Because we have a hard time imagining that we matter all that much, especially when we're young.

But all believers are part of the body—the body of Christ, the Church with a capital *C*—and no part is less important than any other. The Bible gives us this amazing word picture of body parts because it makes sense. Could you really say that your ears are more valuable to you than your fingers? Or that your stomach is more important than your kidneys? Ultimately every body part matters and has a specific role to play in keeping us alive and healthy—it's the same for the Church.

LIVE IT:

It takes all kinds of people who love all kinds of things to keep us all going in general. So why do we have a hard time accepting that we don't all have to be the same in the Church?

Your personality and your gifts will help you determine what part you play in the body of Christ. Don't put off finding what you can contribute until you get older. Your gifts may change over the years, but you have a contribution to make right now, just as you are.

the same Spirit works all these things, dis-
tributing to each one individually as He wills.

Unity and Diversity in One Body

12For as the body is one and has many
members but all the members of that one
body, being many, are one body, so also *is*
Christ. 13For by one Spirit we were all baptized into one body—whether Jews or
Greeks, whether slaves or free—and have all
been made to drink into[a] one Spirit. 14For in
fact the body is not one member but many.
15If the foot should say, "Because I am not
a hand, I am not of the body," is it therefore
not of the body? 16And if the ear should say,
"Because I am not an eye, I am not of the
body," is it therefore not of the body? 17If the
whole body *were* an eye, where *would be* the
hearing? If the whole *were* hearing, where
would be the smelling? 18But now God has set
the members, each one of them, in the body
just as He pleased. 19And if they were all one
member, where *would* the body *be?*
20But now indeed *there are* many members, yet one body. 21And the eye cannot say
to the hand, "I have no need of you"; nor
again the head to the feet, "I have no need of
you." 22No, much rather, those members of
the body which seem to be weaker are necessary. 23And those *members* of the body which
we think to be less honorable, on these we
bestow greater honor; and our unpresentable
parts have greater modesty, 24but our present-
able *parts* have no need. But God composed
the body, having given greater honor to that
part which lacks it, 25that there should be no
schism in the body, but *that* the members
should have the same care for one another.
26And if one member suffers, all the members suffer with *it;* or if one member is honored, all the members rejoice with *it.*
27Now you are the body of Christ, and
members individually. 28And God has appointed these in the church: first apostles,
second prophets, third teachers, after that

12:13 [a] NU-Text omits *into.*

CHRISTIAN LOVE

READ IT: 1 CORINTHIANS 13:1–13

GET IT:

Paul wrote a long letter to the church that he had established in Corinth. In his letter he talked about three very important characteristics: faith, hope, and love. He focused on how important love is for being a Christian. He clearly stated some ways that we should show love to one another as Christian brothers and sisters. Love is at the foundation of Christian living because Jesus was all about showing love to others.

LIVE IT:

Getting back at others who do you wrong isn't an option if you love Jesus. Jesus said to His followers, "Love your enemies, do good" (Luke 6:35), and "Love one another; as I have loved you" (John 13:34). In this chapter in Corinthians, Paul explains how we need to love one another. Think about the things you can do to follow each of these guidelines. How will you show love to someone tomorrow?

miracles, then gifts of healings, helps, ad-
ministrations, varieties of tongues. 29*Are* all
apostles? *Are* all prophets? *Are* all teachers?
Are all workers of miracles? 30Do all have
gifts of healings? Do all speak with tongues?
Do all interpret? 31But earnestly desire the
best[a] gifts. And yet I show you a more excellent way.

The Greatest Gift

13 Though I speak with the tongues
of men and of angels, but have
not love, I have become sounding brass or
a clanging cymbal. 2And though I have *the
gift of* prophecy, and understand all mysteries and all knowledge, and though I have all
faith, so that I could remove mountains, but
have not love, I am nothing. 3And though
I bestow all my goods to feed *the poor,* and
though I give my body to be burned,[a] but
have not love, it profits me nothing.
4Love suffers long *and* is kind; love does
not envy; love does not parade itself, is not
puffed up; 5does not behave rudely, does
not seek its own, is not provoked, thinks no
evil; 6does not rejoice in iniquity, but rejoices in the truth; 7bears all things, believes all
things, hopes all things, endures all things.

12:31 [a] NU-Text reads *greater.* 13:3 [a] NU-Text reads *so I may boast.*

Epic Ideas

LOVE WHAT IS LOVE?

READ IT: 1 CORINTHIANS 13:4–8

GET IT:

Let's take a closer look at these characteristics of love in words of today:

- Love is patient and caring (v. 4).
- Love isn't jealous (v. 4).
- Love doesn't need to boast; it's humble (v. 4).
- Love treats others well (v. 5).
- Love is unselfish, isn't angry, and thinks good things (v. 5).
- When bad things happen, even to our enemies, if we love we won't be happy. Love celebrates when honesty wins (v. 6).
- Love carries the weight of everything. It trusts, it believes the best about any person and any situation, and it stands the test of time (v. 7).
- Love will always come through (v. 8).

LIVE IT:

Love is genuine and comes from the heart. It doesn't always come easily or naturally. But when we take our knowledge of love and combine it with action, love will shine through our lives. When you wonder how to act in a situation, think back on this verse and decide on the most loving way to act.

[8]Love never fails. But whether *there are*
prophecies, they will fail; whether *there are*
tongues, they will cease; whether *there is*
knowledge, it will vanish away. [9]For we know
in part and we prophesy in part. [10]But when
that which is perfect has come, then that
which is in part will be done away.

[11]When I was a child, I spoke as a child,
I understood as a child, I thought as a child;
but when I became a man, I put away childish things. [12]For now we see in a mirror,
dimly, but then face to face. Now I know in
part, but then I shall know just as I also am
known.

[13]And now abide faith, hope, love, these
three; but the greatest of these *is* love.

Prophecy and Tongues

14 Pursue love, and desire spiritual
gifts, but especially that you may
prophesy. [2]For he who speaks in a tongue
does not speak to men but to God, for no
one understands *him;* however, in the spirit
he speaks mysteries. [3]But he who prophesies speaks edification and exhortation and
comfort to men. [4]He who speaks in a tongue
edifies himself, but he who prophesies
edifies the church. [5]I wish you all spoke with
tongues, but even more that you prophesied;
for[a] he who prophesies *is* greater than he
who speaks with tongues, unless indeed
he interprets, that the church may receive
edification.

Tongues Must Be Interpreted

[6]But now, brethren, if I come to you
speaking with tongues, what shall I profit
you unless I speak to you either by revelation,
by knowledge, by prophesying, or by teaching? [7]Even things without life, whether flute
or harp, when they make a sound, unless
they make a distinction in the sounds, how
will it be known what is piped or played? [8]For
if the trumpet makes an uncertain sound,
who will prepare for battle? [9]So likewise you,
unless you utter by the tongue words easy
to understand, how will it be known what
is spoken? For you will be speaking into the
air. [10]There are, it may be, so many kinds of
languages in the world, and none of them *is*
without significance. [11]Therefore, if I do not

14:5 [a] NU-Text reads *and.*

Action!

YOUR GREATEST GIFT FROM GOD

READ IT: 1 CORINTHIANS 13:13

Some people would like to have great faith. Then they could do great miracles and surprise everybody with their power. Such people could put on a show and make millions of dollars. Other people would like to have great hope. Then nothing could ever make them afraid. But remember, there probably has never been a Christian who was not sad or afraid sometimes.

But Paul says the greatest gift from God is love. What is love? Paul tells us what love is like in 1 Corinthians 13. Love is different from just *liking* somebody. We *like* people who please us by their appearance or actions, but we truly *love* people when we care about them even when they aren't nice. That's like the love of Jesus for us. He loved us when we were ugly with sin. Love is what really proves we're Christians. That kind of love is God's greatest gift to you.

know the meaning of the language, I shall
be a foreigner to him who speaks, and he
who speaks *will be* a foreigner to me. 12 Even
so you, since you are zealous for spiritual
gifts, let it be for the edification of the church
that you seek to excel.

13 Therefore let him who speaks in a
tongue pray that he may interpret. 14 For if
I pray in a tongue, my spirit prays, but my
understanding is unfruitful. 15 What is *the*
conclusion then? I will pray with the spirit,
and I will also pray with the understanding.
I will sing with the spirit, and I will also sing
with the understanding. 16 Otherwise, if you
bless with the spirit, how will he who occu-
pies the place of the uninformed say "Amen"
at your giving of thanks, since he does not
understand what you say? 17 For you indeed
give thanks well, but the other is not edified.

18 I thank my God I speak with tongues
more than you all; 19 yet in the church I would
rather speak five words with my understanding, that I may teach others also, than ten
thousand words in a tongue.

Tongues a Sign to Unbelievers

20 Brethren, do not be children in understanding; however, in malice be babes, but in
understanding be mature.

21 In the law it is written:

"With *men of* other tongues and other
lips
I will speak to this people;
And yet, for all that, they will not hear
Me,"[a]

says the Lord.

22 Therefore tongues are for a sign, not
to those who believe but to unbelievers; but
prophesying is not for unbelievers but for
those who believe. 23 Therefore if the whole
church comes together in one place, and all
speak with tongues, and there come in *those*
who are uninformed or unbelievers, will they
not say that you are out of your mind? 24 But if
all prophesy, and an unbeliever or an uninformed person comes in, he is convinced by
all, he is convicted by all. 25 And thus[a] the secrets of his heart are revealed; and so, falling
down on *his* face, he will worship God and
report that God is truly among you.

14:21 [a] Isaiah 28:11, 12 **14:25** [a] NU-Text omits *And thus.*

THE GREATEST TRUTH OF ALL

READ IT: 1 CORINTHIANS 15:20

What is the most amazing thing you've ever heard? For many people living today, the greatest discovery was splitting the atom, resulting in nuclear energy. And can you imagine what people said when they saw the first television picture? "Amazing!"

Then think of what the people of Jesus' day said when they saw His miracles. Yet changing water to wine, multiplying the loaves and fish, and healing a withered hand were easy for Jesus.

The hardest thing for Jesus was letting Himself be led to a cross and having nails driven through His hands and feet. He was the sinless Son of God, and He didn't deserve to be crucified.

But the greatest truth of all is that Jesus conquered sin and death when He rose up on that first Easter. Without the resurrection of Jesus, no other truth in the world could ever matter. We would all be slaves of death. Jesus' rising from the dead is a promise that many would rise after Him.

Order in Church Meetings

26How is it then, brethren? Whenever you come together, each of you has a psalm, has a teaching, has a tongue, has a revelation, has an interpretation. Let all things be done for edification. 27If anyone speaks in a tongue, *let there be* two or at the most three, *each* in turn, and let one interpret. 28But if there is no interpreter, let him keep silent in church, and let him speak to himself and to God. 29Let two or three prophets speak, and let the others judge. 30But if *anything* is revealed to another who sits by, let the first keep silent. 31For you can all prophesy one by one, that all may learn and all may be encouraged. 32And the spirits of the prophets are subject to the prophets. 33For God is not *the author* of confusion but of peace, as in all the churches of the saints.

34Let your[a] women keep silent in the churches, for they are not permitted to speak; but *they are* to be submissive, as the law also says. 35And if they want to learn something, let them ask their own husbands at home; for it is shameful for women to speak in church.

36Or did the word of God come *originally* from you? Or *was it* you only that it reached? 37If anyone thinks himself to be a prophet or spiritual, let him acknowledge that the things which I write to you are the commandments of the Lord. 38But if anyone is ignorant, let him be ignorant.[a]

39Therefore, brethren, desire earnestly to prophesy, and do not forbid to speak with tongues. 40Let all things be done decently and in order.

The Risen Christ, Faith's Reality

15 Moreover, brethren, I declare to you the gospel which I preached to you, which also you received and in which you stand, 2by which also you are saved, if you hold fast that word which I preached to you—unless you believed in vain.

3For I delivered to you first of all that which I also received: that Christ died for our sins according to the Scriptures, 4and that He was buried, and that He rose again the third day according to the Scriptures, 5and that He was seen by Cephas, then by the twelve. 6After that He was seen by over five hundred brethren at once, of whom the greater part remain to the present, but some have fallen asleep. 7After that He was seen by James, then by all the apostles. 8Then last of all He was seen by me also, as by one born out of due time.

9For I am the least of the apostles, who am not worthy to be called an apostle, because I persecuted the church of God. 10But by the grace of God I am what I am, and His grace toward me was not in vain; but I labored more abundantly than they all, yet not I, but the grace of God *which was* with me. 11Therefore, whether *it was* I or they, so we preach and so you believed.

The Risen Christ, Our Hope

12Now if Christ is preached that He has been raised from the dead, how do some among you say that there is no resurrection of the dead? 13But if there is no resurrection of the dead, then Christ is not risen. 14And if Christ is not risen, then our preaching *is* empty and your faith *is* also empty. 15Yes, and we are found false witnesses of God, because we have testified of God that He raised up Christ, whom He did not raise up—if in fact the dead do not rise. 16For if *the* dead do not rise, then Christ is not risen. 17And if Christ is not risen, your faith *is* futile; you are still in your sins! 18Then also those who have fallen asleep in Christ have perished. 19If in this life only we have hope in Christ, we are of all men the most pitiable.

The Last Enemy Destroyed

20But now Christ is risen from the dead, *and* has become the firstfruits of those who have fallen asleep. 21For since by man *came* death, by Man also *came* the resurrection of the dead. 22For as in Adam all die, even so in Christ all shall be made alive. 23But each one in his own order: Christ the firstfruits, afterward those *who are* Christ's at His coming. 24Then *comes* the end, when He delivers the kingdom to God the Father, when He puts an end to all rule and all authority and power. 25For He must reign till He has put all enemies under His feet. 26The last enemy *that* will be destroyed *is* death. 27For "He has put all things under His feet."[a] But when He says "all things are put under *Him*," *it is* evident that He who put all things under Him

---

14:34 [a] NU-Text omits *your.* **14:38** [a] NU-Text reads *if anyone does not recognize this, he is not recognized.*
15:27 [a] Psalm 8:6

is excepted. 28Now when all things are made
subject to Him, then the Son Himself will
also be subject to Him who put all things
under Him, that God may be all in all.

Effects of Denying the Resurrection

29Otherwise, what will they do who are
baptized for the dead, if the dead do not
rise at all? Why then are they baptized for
the dead? 30And why do we stand in jeopardy every hour? 31I affirm, by the boasting in
you which I have in Christ Jesus our Lord, I
die daily. 32If, in the manner of men, I have
fought with beasts at Ephesus, what advantage *is it* to me? If *the* dead do not rise, "Let us
eat and drink, for tomorrow we die!" [a]

33Do not be deceived: "Evil company cor-
rupts good habits." 34Awake to righteousness, and do not sin; for some do not have
the knowledge of God. I speak *this* to your
shame.

A Glorious Body

35But someone will say, "How are the
dead raised up? And with what body do they
come?" 36Foolish one, what you sow is not
made alive unless it dies. 37And what you
sow, you do not sow that body that shall be,
but mere grain—perhaps wheat or some
other *grain*. 38But God gives it a body as He
pleases, and to each seed its own body.

39All flesh *is* not the same flesh, but *there
is* one *kind of* flesh[a] of men, another flesh
of animals, another of fish, *and* another of
birds.

40*There are* also celestial bodies and terrestrial bodies; but the glory of the celestial
is one, and the *glory* of the terrestrial *is* another. 41*There is* one glory of the sun, another
glory of the moon, and another glory of the
stars; for *one* star differs from *another* star
in glory.

42So also *is* the resurrection of the dead.
The body is sown in corruption, it is raised
in incorruption. 43It is sown in dishonor, it is
raised in glory. It is sown in weakness, it is
raised in power. 44It is sown a natural body, it
is raised a spiritual body. There is a natural
body, and there is a spiritual body. 45And so
it is written, "The first man Adam became a
living being." [a] The last Adam *became* a life-
giving spirit.

46However, the spiritual is not first,
but the natural, and afterward the spiritual. 47The first man *was* of the earth, *made*
of dust; the second Man *is* the Lord[a] from
heaven. 48As *was* the *man* of dust, so also
are those *who are made* of dust; and as *is*
the heavenly *Man*, so also *are* those *who are*
heavenly. 49And as we have borne the image
of the *man* of dust, we shall also bear[a] the
image of the heavenly *Man*.

Our Final Victory

50Now this I say, brethren, that flesh and
blood cannot inherit the kingdom of God;
nor does corruption inherit incorruption.
51Behold, I tell you a mystery: We shall not
all sleep, but we shall all be changed— 52in
a moment, in the twinkling of an eye, at the
last trumpet. For the trumpet will sound,
and the dead will be raised incorruptible,
and we shall be changed. 53For this corruptible must put on incorruption, and this mortal *must* put on immortality. 54So when this
corruptible has put on incorruption, and this
mortal has put on immortality, then shall be
brought to pass the saying that is written:
"Death is swallowed up in victory." [a]

55 "O Death, where *is* your sting?[a]
O Hades, where *is* your victory?" [b]

56The sting of death *is* sin, and the strength
of sin *is* the law. 57But thanks *be* to God, who
gives us the victory through our Lord Jesus
Christ.

58Therefore, my beloved brethren, be
steadfast, immovable, always abounding in
the work of the Lord, knowing that your labor is not in vain in the Lord.

Collection for the Saints

16 Now concerning the collection for
the saints, as I have given orders
to the churches of Galatia, so you must do
also: 2On the first *day* of the week let each
one of you lay something aside, storing up as
he may prosper, that there be no collections
when I come. 3And when I come, whomever
you approve by *your* letters I will send to bear
your gift to Jerusalem. 4But if it is fitting that
I go also, they will go with me.

Personal Plans

5Now I will come to you when I pass

15:32 [a] Isaiah 22:13 **15:39** [a] NU-Text and M-Text omit *of flesh*. **15:45** [a] Genesis 2:7 **15:47** [a] NU-Text omits *the Lord*. **15:49** [a] M-Text reads *let us also bear*. **15:54** [a] Isaiah 25:8 **15:55** [a] Hosea 13:14 [b] NU-Text reads *O Death, where is your victory? O Death, where is your sting?*

through Macedonia (for I am passing
through Macedonia). [6]And it may be that I
will remain, or even spend the winter with
you, that you may send me on my journey,
wherever I go. [7]For I do not wish to see you
now on the way; but I hope to stay a while
with you, if the Lord permits.

[8]But I will tarry in Ephesus until Pentecost. [9]For a great and effective door
has opened to me, and *there are* many
adversaries.

[10]And if Timothy comes, see that he may
be with you without fear; for he does the
work of the Lord, as I also *do*. [11]Therefore let
no one despise him. But send him on his
journey in peace, that he may come to me;
for I am waiting for him with the brethren.

[12]Now concerning *our* brother Apollos,
I strongly urged him to come to you with
the brethren, but he was quite unwilling
to come at this time; however, he will come
when he has a convenient time.

Final Exhortations

[13]Watch, stand fast in the faith, be brave,
be strong. [14]Let all *that* you *do* be done with
love.

[15]I urge you, brethren—you know the
household of Stephanas, that it is the firstfruits of Achaia, and *that* they have devoted
themselves to the ministry of the saints—
[16]that you also submit to such, and to everyone who works and labors with *us*.

[17]I am glad about the coming of
Stephanas, Fortunatus, and Achaicus, for
what was lacking on your part they supplied.
[18]For they refreshed my spirit and yours.
Therefore acknowledge such men.

Greetings and a Solemn Farewell

[19]The churches of Asia greet you. Aquila
and Priscilla greet you heartily in the Lord,
with the church that is in their house. [20]All
the brethren greet you.

Greet one another with a holy kiss.

[21]The salutation with my own
hand—Paul's.

[22]If anyone does not love the Lord Jesus
Christ, let him be accursed.[a] O Lord, come![b]

[23]The grace of our Lord Jesus Christ *be*
with you. [24]My love *be* with you all in Christ
Jesus. Amen.

16:22 [a] Greek *anathema* [b] Aramaic *Maranatha*

The SECOND EPISTLE of PAUL the APOSTLE to the

CORINTHIANS

A.D. 56

Behind the Scenes

READ IT:

After Paul heard that the church in Corinth had fixed their problems, he wrote them another letter. He comforted them because they were suffering, and he shared with them what he had experienced. Then he defended himself against the people who were saying untrue things about him. He explained that he was a true apostle of Jesus.

GET IT:

Who wrote it: Paul

When it was written: in the fall of A.D. 56

Why it was written: to comfort the Corinthians, to instruct them in church issues, and to defend Paul's position of leader and apostle.

LIVE IT:

If we accept Jesus, we're a "new creation" (5:17).

As Christians, we're totally new and different, and our lives should show it.

FIND IT:

Comfort in Suffering	*2 Corinthians 1*
Forgive the Offender	*2 Corinthians 2*
Marks of the Ministry	*2 Corinthians 6*
The Cheerful Giver	*2 Corinthians 9*
Strength in Weakness	*2 Corinthians 12*

Greeting

1 Paul an apostle of Jesus Christ by the
will of God, and Timothy *our* brother,

To the church of God which is at Corinth,
with all the saints who are in all Achaia:

2Grace to you and peace from God our
Father and the Lord Jesus Christ.

Comfort in Suffering

3Blessed *be* the God and Father of our
Lord Jesus Christ, the Father of mercies
and God of all comfort, 4who comforts us
in all our tribulation, that we may be able
to comfort those who are in any trouble,
with the comfort with which we ourselves
are comforted by God. 5For as the sufferings
of Christ abound in us, so our consolation
also abounds through Christ. 6Now if we are
afflicted, *it is* for your consolation and salvation, which is effective for enduring the
same sufferings which we also suffer. Or if
we are comforted, *it is* for your consolation
and salvation. 7And our hope for you *is* steadfast, because we know that as you are partakers of the sufferings, so also *you will partake*
of the consolation.

Delivered from Suffering

8For we do not want you to be ignorant,
brethren, of our trouble which came to us
in Asia: that we were burdened beyond measure, above strength, so that we despaired
even of life. 9Yes, we had the sentence of
death in ourselves, that we should not trust
in ourselves but in God who raises the dead,
10who delivered us from so great a death, and
does[a] deliver us; in whom we trust that He
will still deliver *us,* 11you also helping together in prayer for us, that thanks may be given
by many persons on our[a] behalf for the gift
granted to us through many.

Paul's Sincerity

12For our boasting is this: the testimony
of our conscience that we conducted ourselves in the world in simplicity and godly
sincerity, not with fleshly wisdom but by
the grace of God, and more abundantly toward you. 13For we are not writing any other
things to you than what you read or understand. Now I trust you will understand, even
to the end 14(as also you have understood us
in part), that we are your boast as you also *are*
ours, in the day of the Lord Jesus.

Sparing the Church

15And in this confidence I intended to
come to you before, that you might have a
second benefit— 16to pass by way of you to
Macedonia, to come again from Macedonia
to you, and be helped by you on my way to
Judea. 17Therefore, when I was planning
this, did I do it lightly? Or the things I plan,
do I plan according to the flesh, that with
me there should be Yes, Yes, and No, No?
18But *as* God *is* faithful, our word to you was
not Yes and No. 19For the Son of God, Jesus
Christ, who was preached among you by
us—by me, Silvanus, and Timothy—was
not Yes and No, but in Him was Yes. 20For
all the promises of God in Him *are* Yes, and
in Him Amen, to the glory of God through
us. 21Now He who establishes us with you in
Christ and has anointed us *is* God, 22who also
has sealed us and given us the Spirit in our
hearts as a guarantee.

23Moreover I call God as witness against
my soul, that to spare you I came no more to
Corinth. 24Not that we have dominion over
your faith, but are fellow workers for your
joy; for by faith you stand.

2 But I determined this within myself,
that I would not come again to you in
sorrow. 2For if I make you sorrowful, then
who is he who makes me glad but the one
who is made sorrowful by me?

Forgive the Offender

3And I wrote this very thing to you, lest,
when I came, I should have sorrow over
those from whom I ought to have joy, having
confidence in you all that my joy is *the joy*
of you all. 4For out of much affliction and
anguish of heart I wrote to you, with many
tears, not that you should be grieved, but
that you might know the love which I have
so abundantly for you.

5But if anyone has caused grief, he
has not grieved me, but all of you to some
extent—not to be too severe. 6This punishment which *was inflicted* by the majority *is*
sufficient for such a man, 7so that, on the
contrary, you *ought* rather to forgive and
comfort *him,* lest perhaps such a one be
swallowed up with too much sorrow. 8There-
fore I urge you to reaffirm *your* love to him.
9For to this end I also wrote, that I might

1:10 [a] NU-Text reads *shall.* **1:11** [a] M-Text reads *your behalf.*

put you to the test, whether you are obedient in all things. 10Now whom you forgive
anything, I also *forgive.* For if indeed I have
forgiven anything, I have forgiven that one[a]
for your sakes in the presence of Christ, 11lest
Satan should take advantage of us; for we are
not ignorant of his devices.

Triumph in Christ

12Furthermore, when I came to Troas
to *preach* Christ's gospel, and a door was
opened to me by the Lord, 13I had no rest in
my spirit, because I did not find Titus my
brother; but taking my leave of them, I departed for Macedonia.

14Now thanks *be* to God who always leads
us in triumph in Christ, and through us dif-
fuses the fragrance of His knowledge in every place. 15For we are to God the fragrance of
Christ among those who are being saved and
among those who are perishing. 16To the one
we are the aroma of death *leading* to death,
and to the other the aroma of life *leading* to
life. And who *is* sufficient for these things?
17For we are not, as so many,[a] peddling the
word of God; but as of sincerity, but as from
God, we speak in the sight of God in Christ.

Christ's Epistle

3 Do we begin again to commend ourselves? Or do we need, as some *others,*
epistles of commendation to you or *letters* of
commendation from you? 2You are our epistle written in our hearts, known and read by
all men; 3clearly you are an epistle of Christ,
ministered by us, written not with ink but
by the Spirit of the living God, not on tablets
of stone but on tablets of flesh, *that is,* of the
heart.

The Spirit, Not the Letter

4And we have such trust through Christ
toward God. 5Not that we are sufficient of
ourselves to think of anything as *being* from
ourselves, but our sufficiency *is* from God,
6who also made us sufficient as ministers
of the new covenant, not of the letter but of
the Spirit;[a] for the letter kills, but the Spirit
gives life.

Glory of the New Covenant

7But if the ministry of death, written *and*
engraved on stones, was glorious, so that the
children of Israel could not look steadily at
the face of Moses because of the glory of his
countenance, which *glory* was passing away,
8how will the ministry of the Spirit not be
more glorious? 9For if the ministry of condemnation *had* glory, the ministry of righteousness exceeds much more in glory. 10For
even what was made glorious had no glory in
this respect, because of the glory that excels.
11For if what is passing away *was* glorious,
what remains *is* much more glorious.

12Therefore, since we have such hope,
we use great boldness of speech— 13unlike
Moses, *who* put a veil over his face so that
the children of Israel could not look steadily
at the end of what was passing away. 14But
their minds were blinded. For until this day
the same veil remains unlifted in the reading of the Old Testament, because the *veil*
is taken away in Christ. 15But even to this
day, when Moses is read, a veil lies on their
heart. 16Nevertheless when one turns to the
Lord, the veil is taken away. 17Now the Lord
is the Spirit; and where the Spirit of the Lord
is, there *is* liberty. 18But we all, with unveiled
face, beholding as in a mirror the glory of the
Lord, are being transformed into the same
image from glory to glory, just as by the Spirit of the Lord.

The Light of Christ's Gospel

4 Therefore, since we have this ministry, as we have received mercy, we do
not lose heart. 2But we have renounced the
hidden things of shame, not walking in
craftiness nor handling the word of God deceitfully, but by manifestation of the truth
commending ourselves to every man's conscience in the sight of God. 3But even if our
gospel is veiled, it is veiled to those who are
perishing, 4whose minds the god of this age
has blinded, who do not believe, lest the light
of the gospel of the glory of Christ, who is
the image of God, should shine on them.
5For we do not preach ourselves, but Christ
Jesus the Lord, and ourselves your bondservants for Jesus' sake. 6For it is the God who
commanded light to shine out of darkness,
who has shone in our hearts to *give* the light
of the knowledge of the glory of God in the
face of Jesus Christ.

Cast Down but Unconquered

7But we have this treasure in earthen vessels, that the excellence of the power may be

---

2:10 [a] NU-Text reads *For indeed, what I have forgiven, if I have forgiven anything, I did it.* 2:17 [a] M-Text reads *the rest.* 3:6 [a] Or *spirit*

of God and not of us. 8 *We are* hard-pressed on
every side, yet not crushed; *we are* perplexed,
but not in despair; 9persecuted, but not forsaken; struck down, but not destroyed—
10always carrying about in the body the dying
of the Lord Jesus, that the life of Jesus also
may be manifested in our body. 11For we who
live are always delivered to death for Jesus'
sake, that the life of Jesus also may be manifested in our mortal flesh. 12So then death is
working in us, but life in you.

13And since we have the same spirit of
faith, according to what is written, "I believed and therefore I spoke," [a] we also believe and therefore speak, 14knowing that He
who raised up the Lord Jesus will also raise
us up with Jesus, and will present *us* with
you. 15For all things *are* for your sakes, that
grace, having spread through the many, may
cause thanksgiving to abound to the glory
of God.

Seeing the Invisible

16Therefore we do not lose heart. Even
though our outward man is perishing, yet
the inward *man* is being renewed day by day.
17For our light affliction, which is but for a
moment, is working for us a far more exceeding *and* eternal weight of glory, 18while
we do not look at the things which are seen,
but at the things which are not seen. For the
things which are seen *are* temporary, but the
things which are not seen *are* eternal.

Assurance of the Resurrection

5 For we know that if our earthly house,
this tent, is destroyed, we have a building from God, a house not made with hands,
eternal in the heavens. 2For in this we groan,
earnestly desiring to be clothed with our
habitation which is from heaven, 3if indeed,
having been clothed, we shall not be found
naked. 4For we who are in *this* tent groan,
being burdened, not because we want to be
unclothed, but further clothed, that mortality may be swallowed up by life. 5Now He
who has prepared us for this very thing *is*
God, who also has given us the Spirit as a
guarantee.

6So *we are* always confident, knowing
that while we are at home in the body we are
absent from the Lord. 7For we walk by faith,
not by sight. 8We are confident, yes, well
pleased rather to be absent from the body
and to be present with the Lord.

The Judgment Seat of Christ

9Therefore we make it our aim, whether

4:13 [a] Psalm 116:10

BE A WALKING BIBLE

READ IT: 2 CORINTHIANS 3:2

It's hard to get everybody to read the Bible. But in a real way, you can be a walking Bible that everyone can read.

God doesn't want the thoughts in the Bible to stay between the covers of that great Book. He wants those words to leap out of the pages and into your life. As the words of God pass through your eyes and ears, they are something like vitamins. The words of God give you the strength of Jesus inside. After a while you begin to be a walking Bible. Even more than that, you begin to live and speak and think the way Jesus would. Jesus said, "The words that I speak . . . are life" (John 6:63).

That's a thrilling idea, isn't it? You can actually become like Jesus in the world. And the more you become like Jesus, the more your life will change people around you—just the way Jesus' life did.

present or absent, to be well pleasing to Him.
10 For we must all appear before the judgment
seat of Christ, that each one may receive the
things *done* in the body, according to what
he has done, whether good or bad. 11 Knowing, therefore, the terror of the Lord, we
persuade men; but we are well known to
God, and I also trust are well known in your
consciences.

Be Reconciled to God

12 For we do not commend ourselves again
to you, but give you opportunity to boast on
our behalf, that you may have *an answer* for
those who boast in appearance and not in
heart. 13 For if we are beside ourselves, *it is* for
God; or if we are of sound mind, *it is* for you.
14 For the love of Christ compels us, because
we judge thus: that if One died for all, then
all died; 15 and He died for all, that those who
live should live no longer for themselves, but
for Him who died for them and rose again.

16 Therefore, from now on, we regard no
one according to the flesh. Even though
we have known Christ according to the
flesh, yet now we know *Him thus* no longer.
17 Therefore, if anyone *is* in Christ, *he is* a new
creation; old things have passed away; behold, all things have become new. 18 Now all

SIN **THE SINLESS ONE**

READ IT: 2 CORINTHIANS 5:20, 21

GET IT:

Jesus was completely pure—no selfishness, no dishonesty, no greed, no dark side. It's hard for us to imagine, but the Bible tells us it's true. Jesus was fully human, but He was also fully God, which made Him sinless. He knew every part of being a person. He was hungry. He was sad. He had sore muscles. But He never once sinned.

Jesus' pain and death on the cross is even more significant to us when we realize that He didn't deserve to die. He went through the humiliation and torture of a common criminal even though He never had a sinful thought. He took the full punishment of sin—our sin—despite the fact that He was sinless. Why would He do that? Because He loves us. He did it to pay the price of sin on our behalf.

LIVE IT:

After Jesus took the punishment for sin at His crucifixion, He rose again. He came back to life, giving Him victory over sin and death. This means that through Him we have that victory, too.

If you haven't accepted Jesus' offer to forgive your sins, accept it now. Just say, "Thank You, Jesus, for dying for my sins. I need the forgiveness only You can give me."

Ask God to make Jesus' righteousness stronger in your life than the power of sin. Say, "Please help me, God, to turn away from the sin in my life. Help me to be more like Jesus every day."

things *are* of God, who has reconciled us to
Himself through Jesus Christ, and has giv-
en us the ministry of reconciliation, 19that is,
that God was in Christ reconciling the world
to Himself, not imputing their trespasses to
them, and has committed to us the word of
reconciliation.

20Now then, we are ambassadors for
Christ, as though God were pleading
through us: we implore *you* on Christ's behalf, be reconciled to God. 21For He made
Him who knew no sin *to be* sin for us, that
we might become the righteousness of God
in Him.

Marks of the Ministry

6 We then, *as* workers together *with Him*
also plead with *you* not to receive the
grace of God in vain. 2For He says:

> "In an acceptable time I have heard you,
> And in the day of salvation I have helped
> you." [a]

Behold, now *is* the accepted time; behold,
now *is* the day of salvation.

3We give no offense in anything, that
our ministry may not be blamed. 4But in all
things we commend ourselves as ministers
of God: in much patience, in tribulations, in
needs, in distresses, 5in stripes, in impris-
onments, in tumults, in labors, in sleeplessness, in fastings; 6by purity, by knowledge,
by longsuffering, by kindness, by the Holy
Spirit, by sincere love, 7by the word of truth,
by the power of God, by the armor of righteousness on the right hand and on the left,
8by honor and dishonor, by evil report and
good report; as deceivers, and *yet* true; 9as
unknown, and *yet* well known; as dying,
and behold we live; as chastened, and *yet* not
killed; 10as sorrowful, yet always rejoicing; as
poor, yet making many rich; as having nothing, and *yet* possessing all things.

Be Holy

11O Corinthians! We have spoken openly to you, our heart is wide open. 12You are
not restricted by us, but you are restricted
by your *own* affections. 13Now in return for
the same (I speak as to children), you also
be open.

14Do not be unequally yoked together
with unbelievers. For what fellowship has
righteousness with lawlessness? And what

6:2 [a] Isaiah 49:8

MAKE GOD'S FRIENDS YOUR FRIENDS

READ IT: 2 CORINTHIANS 6:14

You become like your friends, and your friends become like you. If your friends are interested in sports, you will likely be someone who likes sports, too. If your friends are into drugs, you also are in danger of becoming a drug user. So it matters a lot who your friends are since we like to be with people who enjoy what we enjoy.

Christians mostly enjoy God. In fact, Christians know their greatest reason for living is to honor God in their lives and to *enjoy* Him forever. Making friends with people who enjoy God's friends is a pretty good idea. After all, these are the people you're going to be in heaven with forever. If you don't enjoy the friendship of other Christians, it may be a sign that you don't enjoy God's friendship either. People who enjoy God enjoy one another also.

communion has light with darkness? 15And
what accord has Christ with Belial? Or what
part has a believer with an unbeliever? 16And
what agreement has the temple of God with
idols? For you[a] are the temple of the living
God. As God has said:

"I will dwell in them
And walk among *them*.
I will be their God,
And they shall be My people." [b]

17Therefore

"Come out from among them
And be separate, says the Lord.
Do not touch what is unclean,
And I will receive you." [a]
18 "I will be a Father to you,
And you shall be My sons and
daughters,
Says the LORD Almighty." [a]

7 Therefore, having these promises, beloved, let us cleanse ourselves from all
filthiness of the flesh and spirit, perfecting
holiness in the fear of God.

The Corinthians' Repentance

2Open *your hearts* to us. We have wronged
no one, we have corrupted no one, we have
cheated no one. 3I do not say *this* to condemn; for I have said before that you are in
our hearts, to die together and to live together. 4Great *is* my boldness of speech toward
you, great *is* my boasting on your behalf. I
am filled with comfort. I am exceedingly joyful in all our tribulation.

5For indeed, when we came to Macedonia, our bodies had no rest, but we were troubled on every side. Outside *were* conflicts,
inside *were* fears. 6Nevertheless God, who
comforts the downcast, comforted us by the
coming of Titus, 7and not only by his coming, but also by the consolation with which
he was comforted in you, when he told us
of your earnest desire, your mourning, your
zeal for me, so that I rejoiced even more.

8For even if I made you sorry with my
letter, I do not regret it; though I did regret
it. For I perceive that the same epistle made
you sorry, though only for a while. 9Now I
rejoice, not that you were made sorry, but
that your sorrow led to repentance. For you
were made sorry in a godly manner, that you
might suffer loss from us in nothing. 10For
godly sorrow produces repentance *leading* to
salvation, not to be regretted; but the sorrow
of the world produces death. 11For observe
this very thing, that you sorrowed in a godly
manner: What diligence it produced in you,
what clearing *of yourselves, what* indignation,
what fear, *what* vehement desire, *what* zeal,
what vindication! In all *things* you proved
yourselves to be clear in this matter. 12There-
fore, although I wrote to you, *I did* not *do it*

6:16 [a] NU-Text reads *we*. [b] Leviticus 26:12; Jeremiah 32:38; Ezekiel 37:27 **6:17** [a] Isaiah 52:11; Ezekiel 20:34, 41 **6:18** [a] 2 Samuel 7:14

RELATIONSHIPS

READ IT: 2 CORINTHIANS 6:16

Paul's second letter to the people of the church in Corinth is an urgent cry for them to cling to God's grace and not be lured away from their faith by things that are not of God. He pleads with them to remember the truth of the Scriptures: God wants them to be His loyal people. God wants their faith, trust, and love. He's not a distant God—He wants to be in deep *relationship with His people*, whom He loves. Paul's words are true for us today as well. God longs for you to be truly His. Is there anything you need to adjust to give your heart fully to Him?

for the sake of him who had done the wrong, nor for the sake of him who suffered wrong, but that our care for you in the sight of God might appear to you.

The Joy of Titus

[13]Therefore we have been comforted in your comfort. And we rejoiced exceedingly more for the joy of Titus, because his spirit has been refreshed by you all. [14]For if in anything I have boasted to him about you, I am not ashamed. But as we spoke all things to you in truth, even so our boasting to Titus was found true. [15]And his affections are greater for you as he remembers the obedience of you all, how with fear and trembling you received him. [16]Therefore I rejoice that I have confidence in you in everything.

Excel in Giving

8 Moreover, brethren, we make known to you the grace of God bestowed on the churches of Macedonia: [2]that in a great trial of affliction the abundance of their joy and their deep poverty abounded in the riches of their liberality. [3]For I bear witness that according to *their* ability, yes, and beyond *their* ability, *they were* freely willing, [4]imploring us with much urgency that we would receive[a] the gift and the fellowship of the ministering to the saints. [5]And not *only* as we had hoped, but they first gave themselves to the Lord, and *then* to us by the will of God. [6]So we urged Titus, that as he had begun, so he would also complete this grace in you as well. [7]But as you abound in everything—in faith, in speech, in knowledge, in all diligence, and in your love for us—*see* that you abound in this grace also.

Christ Our Pattern

[8]I speak not by commandment, but I am testing the sincerity of your love by the diligence of others. [9]For you know the grace of our Lord Jesus Christ, that though He was rich, yet for your sakes He became poor, that you through His poverty might become rich.

[10]And in this I give advice: It is to your advantage not only to be doing what you began and were desiring to do a year ago; [11]but now you also must complete the doing *of it;* that as *there was* a readiness to desire *it,* so *there* also *may be* a completion out of what *you* have. [12]For if there is first a willing mind, *it is* accepted according to what one has, *and* not according to what he does not have.

[13]For *I do* not *mean* that others should be eased and you burdened; [14]but by an equality, *that* now at this time your abundance *may supply* their lack, that their abundance also may *supply* your lack—that there may be equality. [15]As it is written, "He who *gathered* much had nothing left over, and he who *gathered* little had no lack."[a]

Collection for the Judean Saints

[16]But thanks *be* to God who puts[a] the same earnest care for you into the heart of Titus. [17]For he not only accepted the exhortation, but being more diligent, he went to you of his own accord. [18]And we have sent with him the brother whose praise *is* in the gospel throughout all the churches, [19]and not only *that,* but who was also chosen by the churches to travel with us with this gift, which is administered by us to the glory of the Lord Himself and *to show* your ready mind, [20]avoiding this: that anyone should blame us in this lavish gift which is administered by us— [21]providing honorable things, not only in the sight of the Lord, but also in the sight of men.

[22]And we have sent with them our brother whom we have often proved diligent in many things, but now much more diligent, because of the great confidence which *we have* in you. [23]If *anyone inquires* about Titus, *he is* my partner and fellow worker concerning you. Or if our brethren *are inquired about, they are* messengers of the churches, the glory of Christ. [24]Therefore show to them, and[a] before the churches, the proof of your love and of our boasting on your behalf.

Administering the Gift

9 Now concerning the ministering to the saints, it is superfluous for me to write to you; [2]for I know your willingness, about which I boast of you to the Macedonians, that Achaia was ready a year ago; and your zeal has stirred up the majority. [3]Yet I have sent the brethren, lest our boasting of you should be in vain in this respect, that, as I said, you may be ready; [4]lest if *some* Macedonians come with me and find you unprepared, we (not to mention you!) should be ashamed of this confident boasting.[a]

8:4 [a] NU-Text and M-Text omit *that we would receive,* thus changing text to *urgency for the favor and fellowship . . . .*
8:15 [a] Exodus 16:18 8:16 [a] NU-Text reads *has put.*
8:24 [a] NU-Text and M-Text omit *and.* 9:4 [a] NU-Text reads *this confidence.*

5 Therefore I thought it necessary to exhort
the brethren to go to you ahead of time,
and prepare your generous gift beforehand,
which *you had* previously promised, that it
may be ready as *a matter of* generosity and
not as a grudging obligation.

The Cheerful Giver

6 But this *I say:* He who sows sparingly
will also reap sparingly, and he who sows
bountifully will also reap bountifully. 7 *So let*
each one *give* as he purposes in his heart,
not grudgingly or of necessity; for God loves
a cheerful giver. 8 And God *is* able to make all
grace abound toward you, that you, always
having all sufficiency in all *things,* may have
an abundance for every good work. 9 As it is
written:

> "He has dispersed abroad,
> He has given to the poor;
> His righteousness endures forever." [a]

10 Now may[a] He who supplies seed to the
sower, and bread for food, supply and multiply the seed you have *sown* and increase
the fruits of your righteousness, 11 while *you
are* enriched in everything for all liberality,
which causes thanksgiving through us to
God. 12 For the administration of this service
not only supplies the needs of the saints, but
also is abounding through many thanksgivings to God, 13 while, through the proof
of this ministry, they glorify God for the
obedience of your confession to the gospel
of Christ, and for *your* liberal sharing with
them and all *men,* 14 and by their prayer for
you, who long for you because of the exceeding grace of God in you. 15 Thanks *be* to God
for His indescribable gift!

The Spiritual War

10 Now I, Paul, myself am pleading
with you by the meekness and gentleness of Christ—who in presence *am* lowly
among you, but being absent am bold toward
you. 2 But I beg *you* that when I am present
I may not be bold with that confidence by
which I intend to be bold against some, who
think of us as if we walked according to the
flesh. 3 For though we walk in the flesh, we
do not war according to the flesh. 4 For the
weapons of our warfare *are* not carnal but
mighty in God for pulling down strongholds, 5 casting down arguments and every high thing that exalts itself against the

9:9 [a] Psalm 112:9 9:10 [a] NU-Text reads *Now He who supplies . . . will supply . . . .*

BE A CHEERFUL GIVER

READ IT: 2 CORINTHIANS 9:7

What do you think to yourself when you give a gift to someone? Do you think, *I wish that gift hadn't cost so much,* or, *I wish I had the money back that I spent on that gift*? Nobody wants to receive a gift from someone who thinks like that. Most of all, God doesn't want gifts that come from a grudging heart. God loves a cheerful giver.

But how can you be cheerful when giving to others takes away your money? That question has a mistake in it. It isn't "your" money! "Your" money comes from God. Everything you have comes from Him. There's a little hymn that goes like this: "We give You what You gave. . . . All that we have is Yours alone, a gift, O Lord, from You."

You can't beat God in your giving. The more you give to God, the more He gives back to you. Just try giving with a thankful heart. You'll see how generous God can be.

knowledge of God, bringing every thought
into captivity to the obedience of Christ, 6and
being ready to punish all disobedience when
your obedience is fulfilled.

Reality of Paul's Authority

7Do you look at things according to the
outward appearance? If anyone is convinced
in himself that he is Christ's, let him again
consider this in himself, that just as he *is*
Christ's, even so we *are* Christ's.[a] 8For even
if I should boast somewhat more about our
authority, which the Lord gave us[a] for edification and not for your destruction, I shall
not be ashamed— 9lest I seem to terrify you
by letters. 10"For *his* letters," they say, "*are*
weighty and powerful, but *his* bodily presence *is* weak, and *his* speech contemptible."
11Let such a person consider this, that what
we are in word by letters when we are absent, such *we will* also *be* in deed when we
are present.

Limits of Paul's Authority

12For we dare not class ourselves or compare ourselves with those who commend
themselves. But they, measuring themselves
by themselves, and comparing themselves
among themselves, are not wise. 13We, however, will not boast beyond measure, but
within the limits of the sphere which God
appointed us—a sphere which especially
includes you. 14For we are not overextend-
ing ourselves (as though *our authority* did
not extend to you), for it was to you that
we came with the gospel of Christ; 15not
boasting of things beyond measure, *that
is*, in other men's labors, but having hope,
that as your faith is increased, we shall be
greatly enlarged by you in our sphere, 16to
preach the gospel in the *regions* beyond you,
and not to boast in another man's sphere of
accomplishment.
17But "he who glories, let him glory in the
LORD."[a] 18For not he who commends himself
is approved, but whom the Lord commends.

Concern for Their Faithfulness

11 Oh, that you would bear with me in
a little folly—and indeed you do bear
with me. 2For I am jealous for you with godly jealousy. For I have betrothed you to one
husband, that I may present *you as* a chaste
virgin to Christ. 3But I fear, lest somehow, as
the serpent deceived Eve by his craftiness, so
your minds may be corrupted from the simplicity[a] that is in Christ. 4For if he who comes
preaches another Jesus whom we have not
preached, or *if* you receive a different spirit
which you have not received, or a different
gospel which you have not accepted—you
may well put up with it!

Paul and False Apostles

5For I consider that I am not at all inferior
to the most eminent apostles. 6Even though
I am untrained in speech, yet *I am* not in
knowledge. But we have been thoroughly
manifested[a] among you in all things.
7Did I commit sin in humbling myself that you might be exalted, because I
preached the gospel of God to you free of
charge? 8I robbed other churches, taking
wages *from them* to minister to you. 9And
when I was present with you, and in need, I
was a burden to no one, for what I lacked the
brethren who came from Macedonia supplied. And in everything I kept myself from
being burdensome to you, and so I will keep
myself. 10As the truth of Christ is in me, no
one shall stop me from this boasting in the
regions of Achaia. 11Why? Because I do not
love you? God knows!
12But what I do, I will also continue to do,
that I may cut off the opportunity from those
who desire an opportunity to be regarded
just as we are in the things of which they
boast. 13For such *are* false apostles, deceitful
workers, transforming themselves into apostles of Christ. 14And no wonder! For Satan
himself transforms himself into an angel of
light. 15Therefore *it is* no great thing if his
ministers also transform themselves into
ministers of righteousness, whose end will
be according to their works.

Reluctant Boasting

16I say again, let no one think me a fool. If
otherwise, at least receive me as a fool, that I
also may boast a little. 17What I speak, I speak
not according to the Lord, but as it were, foolishly, in this confidence of boasting. 18Seeing
that many boast according to the flesh, I also
will boast. 19For you put up with fools gladly,
since you *yourselves* are wise! 20For you put
up with it if one brings you into bondage, if
one devours *you*, if one takes *from you*, if one
exalts himself, if one strikes you on the face.
21To *our* shame I say that we were too weak

10:7 [a] NU-Text reads *even as we are*. 10:8 [a] NU-Text omits *us*. 10:17 [a] Jeremiah 9:24 11:3 [a] NU-Text adds *and purity*. 11:6 [a] NU-Text omits *been*.

for that! But in whatever anyone is bold—I
speak foolishly—I am bold also.

Suffering for Christ

22Are they Hebrews? So *am* I. Are they
Israelites? So *am* I. Are they the seed of
Abraham? So *am* I. 23Are they ministers of
Christ?—I speak as a fool—I *am* more: in
labors more abundant, in stripes above measure, in prisons more frequently, in deaths
often. 24From the Jews five times I received
forty *stripes* minus one. 25Three times I was
beaten with rods; once I was stoned; three
times I was shipwrecked; a night and a day
I have been in the deep; 26*in* journeys often,
in perils of waters, *in* perils of robbers, *in*
perils of *my own* countrymen, *in* perils of
the Gentiles, *in* perils in the city, *in* perils
in the wilderness, *in* perils in the sea, *in*
perils among false brethren; 27in weariness
and toil, in sleeplessness often, in hunger
and thirst, in fastings often, in cold and nakedness— 28besides the other things, what
comes upon me daily: my deep concern for
all the churches. 29Who is weak, and I am
not weak? Who is made to stumble, and I do
not burn *with indignation?*

30If I must boast, I will boast in the
things which concern my infirmity. 31The
God and Father of our Lord Jesus Christ,
who is blessed forever, knows that I am not
lying. 32In Damascus the governor, under
Aretas the king, was guarding the city of
the Damascenes with a garrison, desiring to
arrest me; 33but I was let down in a basket
through a window in the wall, and escaped
from his hands.

The Vision of Paradise

12 It is doubtless[a] not profitable for
me to boast. I will come to visions
and revelations of the Lord: 2I know a man
in Christ who fourteen years ago—whether
in the body I do not know, or whether out of
the body I do not know, God knows—such a
one was caught up to the third heaven. 3And
I know such a man—whether in the body or
out of the body I do not know, God knows—
4how he was caught up into Paradise and
heard inexpressible words, which it is not
lawful for a man to utter. 5Of such a one I
will boast; yet of myself I will not boast, except in my infirmities. 6For though I might
desire to boast, I will not be a fool; for I will
speak the truth. But I refrain, lest anyone

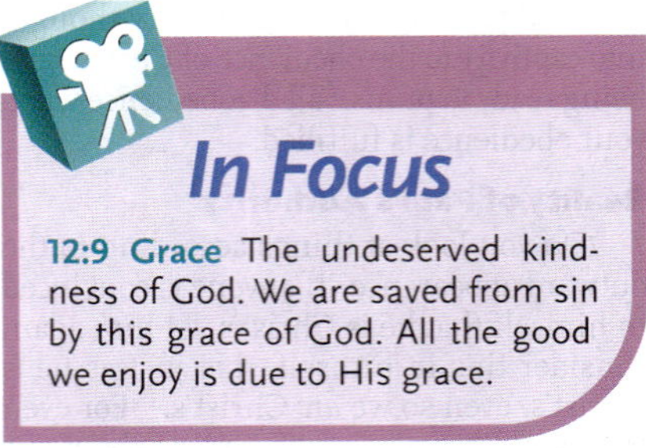

should think of me above what he sees me *to
be* or hears from me.

The Thorn in the Flesh

7And lest I should be exalted above measure by the abundance of the revelations, a
thorn in the flesh was given to me, a messenger of Satan to buffet me, lest I be exalted above measure. 8Concerning this thing
I pleaded with the Lord three times that
it might depart from me. 9And He said to
me, "My grace is sufficient for you, for My
strength is made perfect in weakness."
Therefore most gladly I will rather boast in
my infirmities, that the power of Christ may
rest upon me. 10Therefore I take pleasure in
infirmities, in reproaches, in needs, in persecutions, in distresses, for Christ's sake.
For when I am weak, then I am strong.

Signs of an Apostle

11I have become a fool in boasting;[a] you
have compelled me. For I ought to have been
commended by you; for in nothing was I behind the most eminent apostles, though I
am nothing. 12Truly the signs of an apostle
were accomplished among you with all perseverance, in signs and wonders and mighty
deeds. 13For what is it in which you were inferior to other churches, except that I myself
was not burdensome to you? Forgive me this
wrong!

Love for the Church

14Now *for* the third time I am ready to
come to you. And I will not be burdensome
to you; for I do not seek yours, but you. For
the children ought not to lay up for the parents, but the parents for the children. 15And
I will very gladly spend and be spent for your

12:1 [a] NU-Text reads *necessary, though not profitable, to boast.* 12:11 [a] NU-Text omits *in boasting.*

souls; though the more abundantly I love
you, the less I am loved.
16But be that *as it may,* I did not burden
you. Nevertheless, being crafty, I caught you
by cunning! 17Did I take advantage of you by
any of those whom I sent to you? 18I urged
Titus, and sent our brother with *him.* Did Titus take advantage of you? Did we not walk
in the same spirit? Did *we* not *walk* in the
same steps?
19Again, do you think[a] that we excuse
ourselves to you? We speak before God in
Christ. But *we do* all things, beloved, for
your edification. 20For I fear lest, when I
come, I shall not find you such as I wish,
and *that* I shall be found by you such as you
do not wish; lest *there be* contentions, jealousies, outbursts of wrath, selfish ambitions,
backbitings, whisperings, conceits, tumults;
21lest, when I come again, my God will humble me among you, and I shall mourn for
many who have sinned before and have not
repented of the uncleanness, fornication,
and lewdness which they have practiced.

Coming with Authority

13 This *will be* the third *time* I am
coming to you. "By the mouth of
two or three witnesses every word shall be
established."[a] 2I have told you before, and
foretell as if I were present the second time,
and now being absent I write[a] to those who
have sinned before, and to all the rest, that
if I come again I will not spare— 3since you
seek a proof of Christ speaking in me, who
is not weak toward you, but mighty in you.
4For though He was crucified in weakness,
yet He lives by the power of God. For we also
are weak in Him, but we shall live with Him
by the power of God toward you.
5Examine yourselves *as to* whether you
are in the faith. Test yourselves. Do you
not know yourselves, that Jesus Christ is in
you?—unless indeed you are disqualified.
6But I trust that you will know that we are
not disqualified.

Paul Prefers Gentleness

7Now I[a] pray to God that you do no evil,
not that we should appear approved, but that
you should do what is honorable, though
we may seem disqualified. 8For we can do
nothing against the truth, but for the truth.
9For we are glad when we are weak and you
are strong. And this also we pray, that you
may be made complete. 10Therefore I write
these things being absent, lest being present I should use sharpness, according to the
authority which the Lord has given me for
edification and not for destruction.

Greetings and Benediction

11Finally, brethren, farewell. Become
complete. Be of good comfort, be of one
mind, live in peace; and the God of love and
peace will be with you.
12Greet one another with a holy kiss.
13All the saints greet you.
14The grace of the Lord Jesus Christ, and
the love of God, and the communion of the
Holy Spirit *be* with you all. Amen.

12:19 [a] NU-Text reads *You have been thinking for a long time . . . .* **13:1** [a] Deuteronomy 19:15 **13:2** [a] NU-Text omits *I write.* **13:7** [a] NU-Text reads *we.*

The EPISTLE *of* PAUL *the* APOSTLE *to the*

GALATIANS

A.D. 48

Behind the Scenes

READ IT:

The book of Galatians is a letter from Paul to the churches in the area called Galatia. False teachers were confusing the Christians in what they believed. Paul wrote to them to straighten things out and to remind them they were saved by God's grace through faith in Jesus, not by what they did or whether they kept all the rules of the Jewish law.

GET IT:

Who wrote it: Paul

When it was written: A.D. 48

Why it was written: to explain to the Christians that they were saved by God's grace, not by keeping the law.

LIVE IT:

We are saved by God's free gift of grace through our faith in Jesus. Nothing we *do* can save us.

FIND IT:

Paul's Life Story	*Galatians 1*
Paul Defends the Gospel	*Galatians 2*
Justification by Faith	*Galatians 3*
Christian Liberty	*Galatians 5*
Instructions for Living	*Galatians 6*

Greeting

1 Paul, an apostle (not from men nor
through man, but through Jesus Christ
and God the Father who raised Him from the
dead), 2and all the brethren who are with me,

To the churches of Galatia:

3Grace to you and peace from God the
Father and our Lord Jesus Christ, 4who gave
Himself for our sins, that He might deliver
us from this present evil age, according to
the will of our God and Father, 5to whom *be*
glory forever and ever. Amen.

Only One Gospel

6I marvel that you are turning away so
soon from Him who called you in the grace
of Christ, to a different gospel, 7which is not
another; but there are some who trouble you
and want to pervert the gospel of Christ. 8But
even if we, or an angel from heaven, preach
any other gospel to you than what we have
preached to you, let him be accursed. 9As we
have said before, so now I say again, if anyone preaches any other gospel to you than
what you have received, let him be accursed.

10For do I now persuade men, or God? Or
do I seek to please men? For if I still pleased
men, I would not be a bondservant of Christ.

Call to Apostleship

11But I make known to you, brethren, that
the gospel which was preached by me is not
according to man. 12For I neither received it
from man, nor was I taught *it,* but *it came*
through the revelation of Jesus Christ.

13For you have heard of my former conduct in Judaism, how I persecuted the
church of God beyond measure and *tried to*
destroy it. 14And I advanced in Judaism beyond many of my contemporaries in my own
nation, being more exceedingly zealous for
the traditions of my fathers.

15But when it pleased God, who separated me from my mother's womb and called
me through His grace, 16to reveal His Son
in me, that I might preach Him among the
Gentiles, I did not immediately confer with
flesh and blood, 17nor did I go up to Jerusalem to those *who were* apostles before me;
but I went to Arabia, and returned again to
Damascus.

Contacts at Jerusalem

18Then after three years I went up to Jerusalem to see Peter,[a] and remained with him
fifteen days. 19But I saw none of the other
apostles except James, the Lord's brother.
20(Now *concerning* the things which I write
to you, indeed, before God, I do not lie.)

In Focus

1:12 Revelation Pronounced *rev-uh-LAY-shun.* What God has revealed or shown about His plan for all time. This revelation is the gospel or Good News the whole Bible tells about.

1:18 [a] NU-Text reads *Cephas.*

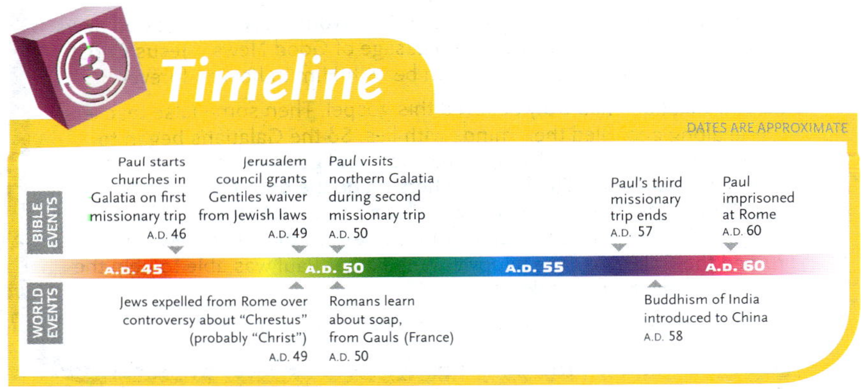

[21]Afterward I went into the regions of
Syria and Cilicia. [22]And I was unknown by
face to the churches of Judea which *were* in
Christ. [23]But they were hearing only, "He
who formerly persecuted us now preaches
the faith which he once *tried to* destroy."
[24]And they glorified God in me.

Defending the Gospel

2 Then after fourteen years I went up
again to Jerusalem with Barnabas, and
also took Titus with *me*. [2]And I went up by
revelation, and communicated to them that
gospel which I preach among the Gentiles,
but privately to those who were of reputation,
lest by any means I might run, or had run,
in vain. [3]Yet not even Titus who *was* with
me, being a Greek, was compelled to be
circumcised. [4]And *this occurred* because of
false brethren secretly brought in (who came
in by stealth to spy out our liberty which we
have in Christ Jesus, that they might bring
us into bondage), [5]to whom we did not yield
submission even for an hour, that the truth
of the gospel might continue with you.

[6]But from those who seemed to be
something—whatever they were, it makes
no difference to me; God shows personal favoritism to no man—for those who seemed
to be something added nothing to me. [7]But on
the contrary, when they saw that the gospel
for the uncircumcised had been committed
to me, as *the gospel* for the circumcised *was*
to Peter [8](for He who worked effectively in
Peter for the apostleship to the circumcised
also worked effectively in me toward the
Gentiles), [9]and when James, Cephas, and
John, who seemed to be pillars, perceived
the grace that had been given to me, they
gave me and Barnabas the right hand of
fellowship, that we *should go* to the Gentiles
and they to the circumcised. [10]*They desired*
only that we should remember the poor, the
very thing which I also was eager to do.

No Return to the Law

[11]Now when Peter[a] had come to Antioch,
I withstood him to his face, because he was
to be blamed; [12]for before certain men came
from James, he would eat with the Gentiles;
but when they came, he withdrew and separated himself, fearing those who were of
the circumcision. [13]And the rest of the Jews
also played the hypocrite with him, so that
even Barnabas was carried away with their
hypocrisy.

2:11 [a] NU-Text reads *Cephas*.

THERE IS ONLY ONE GOSPEL

READ IT: GALATIANS 1:6

The word *gospel* means "good news." Everyone likes to hear good news of all kinds. But God has just one message of Good News—Jesus Christ died to take away our sins so we can be with Him in heaven forever.

The Galatians had truly believed this gospel. Then some false teachers came along and filled their minds with lies. So the Galatians began to believe another so-called gospel that was not "good news" at all. In fact, it was very *bad news*. The false teachers made the poor Galatians believe they had to obey a lot of manmade rules to go to heaven. Actually, nobody could ever perfectly keep all those rules. So that "bad news" nearly ruined the Galatians. The happy ending is that Paul was able to help the Galatians see their mistake.

Jesus is your only way to heaven. He paid your way completely.

14But when I saw that they were not
straightforward about the truth of the gospel, I said to Peter before *them* all, "If you,
being a Jew, live in the manner of Gentiles
and not as the Jews, why do you[a] compel
Gentiles to live as Jews?[b] 15We *who are* Jews
by nature, and not sinners of the Gentiles,
16knowing that a man is not justified by the
works of the law but by faith in Jesus Christ,
even we have believed in Christ Jesus, that
we might be justified by faith in Christ and
not by the works of the law; for by the works
of the law no flesh shall be justified.
17"But if, while we seek to be justified
by Christ, we ourselves also are found sinners, *is* Christ therefore a minister of sin?
Certainly not! 18For if I build again those

2:14 [a] NU-Text reads *how can you.* [b] Some interpreters stop the quotation here.

IDOL AND HERO WORSHIP

READ IT: GALATIANS 2:6

In the eyes of God, all people are created equal. It's important to remember that no matter how famous, rich, or successful someone becomes, he or she will never be greater than God. In this letter, Paul reminds the Galatians that they should not be overly impressed with other people. They should only be impressed with God.

JESUS LIVES IN YOU

READ IT: GALATIANS 2:20

Jesus lives in you if you have trusted Him with your life. Have you put your life in the hands of Jesus? If so, then Jesus lives in you, and He now gives you the power to live for Him.

Paul said, "I have been crucified with Christ." That's a big statement. It means that the old Paul (the one who lived before he trusted in Jesus) is *dead. Now a new* Paul is living. The new Paul is the Paul that lives by the power of Jesus who lives in him.

Jesus wants to live in you, too. He wants you to leave behind the old person you used to be. Then that old person is dead. Now the new person is living because *Jesus lives in you*.

Jesus won a new life for you when He rose from the dead after He was crucified. He gives you that new life by coming to live in your body.

things which I destroyed, I make myself a
transgressor. 19For I through the law died to
the law that I might live to God. 20I have been
crucified with Christ; it is no longer I who
live, but Christ lives in me; and the *life* which
I now live in the flesh I live by faith in the
Son of God, who loved me and gave Himself
for me. 21I do not set aside the grace of God;
for if righteousness *comes* through the law,
then Christ died in vain."

Justification by Faith

3 O foolish Galatians! Who has be-
witched you that you should not obey
the truth,[a] before whose eyes Jesus Christ
was clearly portrayed among you[b] as crucified? 2This only I want to learn from you:
Did you receive the Spirit by the works of the
law, or by the hearing of faith? 3Are you so
foolish? Having begun in the Spirit, are you
now being made perfect by the flesh? 4Have
you suffered so many things in vain—if indeed *it was* in vain?

5Therefore He who supplies the Spirit to
you and works miracles among you, *does He*
do it by the works of the law, or by the hearing of faith?— 6just as Abraham "believed
God, and it was accounted to him for righteousness." [a] 7Therefore know that *only* those
who are of faith are sons of Abraham. 8And
the Scripture, foreseeing that God would
justify the Gentiles by faith, preached the
gospel to Abraham beforehand, *saying,* "In
you all the nations shall be blessed." [a] 9So
then those who *are* of faith are blessed with
believing Abraham.

The Law Brings a Curse

10For as many as are of the works of the
law are under the curse; for it is written,
"Cursed *is* everyone who does not continue
in all things which are written in the book
of the law, to do them." [a] 11But that no one is
justified by the law in the sight of God *is* evident, for "the just shall live by faith." [a] 12Yet
the law is not of faith, but "the man who
does them shall live by them." [a]

13Christ has redeemed us from the curse
of the law, having become a curse for us (for
it is written, "Cursed *is* everyone who hangs
on a tree" [a]), 14that the blessing of Abraham
might come upon the Gentiles in Christ
Jesus, that we might receive the promise of
the Spirit through faith.

The Changeless Promise

15Brethren, I speak in the manner of
men: Though *it is* only a man's covenant,
yet *if it is* confirmed, no one annuls or adds
to it. 16Now to Abraham and his Seed were
the promises made. He does not say, "And
to seeds," as of many, but as of one, "And
to your Seed," [a] who is Christ. 17And this I
say, *that* the law, which was four hundred
and thirty years later, cannot annul the covenant that was confirmed before by God in
Christ,[a] that it should make the promise of
no effect. 18For if the inheritance *is* of the law,
it is no longer of promise; but God gave *it* to
Abraham by promise.

Purpose of the Law

19What purpose then *does* the law *serve?* It
was added because of transgressions, till the
Seed should come to whom the promise was
made; *and it was* appointed through angels
by the hand of a mediator. 20Now a mediator
does not *mediate* for one *only,* but God is one.

21*Is* the law then against the promises of
God? Certainly not! For if there had been a
law given which could have given life, truly
righteousness would have been by the law.
22But the Scripture has confined all under
sin, that the promise by faith in Jesus Christ
might be given to those who believe. 23But
before faith came, we were kept under guard
by the law, kept for the faith which would
afterward be revealed. 24Therefore the law
was our tutor *to bring us* to Christ, that we
might be justified by faith. 25But after faith
has come, we are no longer under a tutor.

Sons and Heirs

26For you are all sons of God through
faith in Christ Jesus. 27For as many of you
as were baptized into Christ have put on
Christ. 28There is neither Jew nor Greek,
there is neither slave nor free, there is neither male nor female; for you are all one in
Christ Jesus. 29And if you *are* Christ's, then
you are Abraham's seed, and heirs according
to the promise.

3:1 [a] NU-Text omits *that you should not obey the truth.* [b] NU-Text omits *among you.* **3:6** [a] Genesis 15:6 **3:8** [a] Genesis 12:3; 18:18; 22:18; 26:4; 28:14 **3:10** [a] Deuteronomy 27:26 **3:11** [a] Habakkuk 2:4 **3:12** [a] Leviticus 18:5 **3:13** [a] Deuteronomy 21:23 **3:16** [a] Genesis 12:7; 13:15; 24:7 **3:17** [a] NU-Text omits *in Christ.*

4 Now I say *that* the heir, as long as he
is a child, does not differ at all from a
slave, though he is master of all, 2but is under guardians and stewards until the time
appointed by the father. 3Even so we, when
we were children, were in bondage under
the elements of the world. 4But when the
fullness of the time had come, God sent
forth His Son, born[a] of a woman, born
under the law, 5to redeem those who were
under the law, that we might receive the
adoption as sons.
6And because you are sons, God has sent
forth the Spirit of His Son into your hearts,
crying out, "Abba, Father!" 7Therefore you
are no longer a slave but a son, and if a son,
then an heir of[a] God through Christ.

Fears for the Church

8But then, indeed, when you did not
know God, you served those which by nature
are not gods. 9But now after you have known
God, or rather are known by God, how *is it*
that you turn again to the weak and beggar-
ly elements, to which you desire again to be
in bondage? 10You observe days and months
and seasons and years. 11I am afraid for you,
lest I have labored for you in vain.
12Brethren, I urge you to become like
me, for I *became* like you. You have not injured me at all. 13You know that because of
physical infirmity I preached the gospel to
you at the first. 14And my trial which was in
my flesh you did not despise or reject, but
you received me as an angel of God, *even* as
Christ Jesus. 15What[a] then was the blessing
you *enjoyed?* For I bear you witness that, if
possible, you would have plucked out your
own eyes and given them to me. 16Have I
therefore become your enemy because I tell
you the truth?
17They zealously court you, *but* for no
good; yes, they want to exclude you, that you
may be zealous for them. 18But it is good to
be zealous in a good thing always, and not
only when I am present with you. 19My little
children, for whom I labor in birth again until Christ is formed in you, 20I would like to
be present with you now and to change my
tone; for I have doubts about you.

Two Covenants

21Tell me, you who desire to be under
the law, do you not hear the law? 22For it is
written that Abraham had two sons: the
one by a bondwoman, the other by a freewoman. 23But he *who was* of the bondwoman
was born according to the flesh, and he of
the freewoman through promise, 24which
things are symbolic. For these are the[a] two
covenants: the one from Mount Sinai which
gives birth to bondage, which is Hagar—
25for this Hagar is Mount Sinai in Arabia,
and corresponds to Jerusalem which now is,
and is in bondage with her children— 26but
the Jerusalem above is free, which is the
mother of us all. 27For it is written:

"Rejoice, O barren,
You who do not bear!
Break forth and shout,
You who are not in labor!
For the desolate has many more
children
Than she who has a husband." [a]

28Now we, brethren, as Isaac *was,* are children of promise. 29But, as he who was born
according to the flesh then persecuted him
who was born according to the Spirit, even so
it is now. 30Nevertheless what does the Scripture say? "Cast out the bondwoman and her
son, for the son of the bondwoman shall not
be heir with the son of the freewoman." [a]
31So then, brethren, we are not children of
the bondwoman but of the free.

Christian Liberty

5 Stand fast therefore in the liberty by
which Christ has made us free,[a] and do
not be entangled again with a yoke of bondage. 2Indeed I, Paul, say to you that if you
become circumcised, Christ will profit you
nothing. 3And I testify again to every man
who becomes circumcised that he is a debtor
to keep the whole law. 4You have become estranged from Christ, you who *attempt to* be
justified by law; you have fallen from grace.
5For we through the Spirit eagerly wait for
the hope of righteousness by faith. 6For in
Christ Jesus neither circumcision nor uncircumcision avails anything, but faith working through love.

4:4 [a] Or *made* **4:7** [a] NU-Text reads *through God* and omits *through Christ.* **4:15** [a] NU-Text reads *Where.* **4:24** [a] NU-Text and M-Text omit *the.* **4:27** [a] Isaiah 54:1 **4:30** [a] Genesis 21:10 **5:1** [a] NU-Text reads *For freedom Christ has made us free; stand fast therefore.*

Love Fulfills the Law

7 You ran well. Who hindered you from obeying the truth? 8 This persuasion does not *come* from Him who calls you. 9 A little leaven leavens the whole lump. 10 I have confidence in you, in the Lord, that you will have no other mind; but he who troubles you shall bear his judgment, whoever he is.

11 And I, brethren, if I still preach circumcision, why do I still suffer persecution? Then the offense of the cross has ceased. 12 I could wish that those who trouble you would even cut themselves off!

13 For you, brethren, have been called to liberty; only do not *use* liberty as an opportunity for the flesh, but through love serve one another. 14 For all the law is fulfilled in one word, *even* in this: "You shall love your neighbor as yourself."[a] 15 But if you bite and devour one another, beware lest you be consumed by one another!

Walking in the Spirit

16 I say then: Walk in the Spirit, and you shall not fulfill the lust of the flesh. 17 For the flesh lusts against the Spirit, and the Spirit against the flesh; and these are contrary to one another, so that you do not do the things that you wish. 18 But if you are led by the Spirit, you are not under the law.

19 Now the works of the flesh are evident, which are: adultery,[a] fornication, uncleanness, lewdness, 20 idolatry, sorcery, hatred, contentions, jealousies, outbursts of wrath, selfish ambitions, dissensions, heresies, 21 envy, murders,[a] drunkenness, revelries, and the like; of which I tell you beforehand, just as I also told *you* in time past, that those who practice such things will not inherit the kingdom of God.

22 But the fruit of the Spirit is love, joy, peace, longsuffering, kindness, goodness, faithfulness, 23 gentleness, self-control. Against such there is no law. 24 And those *who are* Christ's have crucified the flesh with its passions and desires. 25 If we live in the Spirit, let us also walk in the Spirit. 26 Let us not become conceited, provoking one another, envying one another.

Bear and Share Burdens

6 Brethren, if a man is overtaken in any trespass, you who *are* spiritual restore

5:14 [a] Leviticus 19:18 5:19 [a] NU-Text omits *adultery.*
5:21 [a] NU-Text omits *murders.*

JESUS CHRIST MAKES YOU FREE

READ IT: GALATIANS 5:1

Democracy stands for freedom. But even though we have democracy, we aren't free as long as we are slaves to sin.

Jesus is the One who can make you free from the sins that make you a slave. A slave is the property of someone else. And people without God are slaves to sin. When a slave is made free, he can go and do what he wishes. When Jesus makes you free, then your whole wish is to please Him who made you free.

Serving someone we love is not slavery. So serving Jesus is the greatest joy of our lives because He has made us free citizens of the kingdom of heaven. A citizen isn't a slave anymore. You aren't a slave either if you give your life to Jesus.

such a one in a spirit of gentleness, considering yourself lest you also be tempted. 2 Bear
one another's burdens, and so fulfill the law
of Christ. 3 For if anyone thinks himself to be
something, when he is nothing, he deceives
himself. 4 But let each one examine his own
work, and then he will have rejoicing in himself alone, and not in another. 5 For each one
shall bear his own load.

Be Generous and Do Good

6 Let him who is taught the word share in
all good things with him who teaches.
7 Do not be deceived, God is not mocked;
for whatever a man sows, that he will also
reap. 8 For he who sows to his flesh will of
the flesh reap corruption, but he who sows
to the Spirit will of the Spirit reap everlasting
life. 9 And let us not grow weary while doing
good, for in due season we shall reap if we
do not lose heart. 10 Therefore, as we have opportunity, let us do good to all, especially to
those who are of the household of faith.

Glory Only in the Cross

11 See with what large letters I have written to you with my own hand! 12 As many as
desire to make a good showing in the flesh,
these *would* compel you to be circumcised,
only that they may not suffer persecution for
the cross of Christ. 13 For not even those who
are circumcised keep the law, but they desire
to have you circumcised that they may boast
in your flesh. 14 But God forbid that I should
boast except in the cross of our Lord Jesus
Christ, by whom[a] the world has been crucified to me, and I to the world. 15 For in Christ
Jesus neither circumcision nor uncircumcision avails anything, but a new creation.

Blessing and a Plea

16 And as many as walk according to this
rule, peace and mercy *be* upon them, and
upon the Israel of God.
17 From now on let no one trouble me, for I
bear in my body the marks of the Lord Jesus.
18 Brethren, the grace of our Lord Jesus
Christ *be* with your spirit. Amen.

6:14 [a] Or *by which* (the cross)

In Focus

5:20 Heresies Pronounced *HAIR-uh-sees*. False teachings. Any teaching or cult that contradicts the Word of God is a heresy.

TREATMENT OF OTHERS

READ IT: GALATIANS 6:1–10

Bearing one another's burdens means helping others in their pain and troubles.

Do you ever get tired of doing good things? Would it be easier to just stop? How can you find the strength to keep doing good even when stopping would be easier?

There's a special instruction in these verses to do good things for people in your church. What could you do this week to help someone in need?

The EPISTLE *of* PAUL *the* APOSTLE *to the*

EPHESIANS

A.D. 60

Behind the Scenes

READ IT:

The book of Ephesians is a letter from Paul to the churches in and near the city of Ephesus. Paul encouraged the people to change their old lives of idol worship, casual sex, and foolish thinking and to live new lives as believers in Jesus. They were Christians now with a whole new identity. Paul also gave them some practical ways to live in unity with God and others.

GET IT:

Who wrote it: Paul

When it was written: A.D. 60

Why it was written: to encourage the believers by reminding them of their spiritual blessings and instructing them to live holy lives.

LIVE IT:

Our identity is in Jesus.

We have a new life, a new way of thinking that will give us a purpose for living.

FIND IT:

Redemption in Christ	*Ephesians 1*
Salvation by Grace Through Faith	*Ephesians 2–3*
Instructions for Living	*Ephesians 4–5*
The Whole Armor of God	*Ephesians 6*

Greeting

1 Paul, an apostle of Jesus Christ by the
will of God,

To the saints who are in Ephesus, and
faithful in Christ Jesus:

2Grace to you and peace from God our
Father and the Lord Jesus Christ.

Redemption in Christ

3Blessed *be* the God and Father of our
Lord Jesus Christ, who has blessed us with
every spiritual blessing in the heavenly *places* in Christ, 4just as He chose us in Him
before the foundation of the world, that we
should be holy and without blame before
Him in love, 5having predestined us to adoption as sons by Jesus Christ to Himself, according to the good pleasure of His will, 6to
the praise of the glory of His grace, by which
He made us accepted in the Beloved.

7In Him we have redemption through
His blood, the forgiveness of sins, according
to the riches of His grace 8which He made
to abound toward us in all wisdom and
prudence, 9having made known to us the
mystery of His will, according to His good
pleasure which He purposed in Himself,
10that in the dispensation of the fullness
of the times He might gather together in
one all things in Christ, both[a] which are in
heaven and which are on earth—in Him.
11In Him also we have obtained an inheritance, being predestined according to the
purpose of Him who works all things according to the counsel of His will, 12that we
who first trusted in Christ should be to the
praise of His glory.

13In Him you also *trusted,* after you heard
the word of truth, the gospel of your salvation; in whom also, having believed, you
were sealed with the Holy Spirit of promise,
14who[a] is the guarantee of our inheritance
until the redemption of the purchased possession, to the praise of His glory.

Prayer for Spiritual Wisdom

15Therefore I also, after I heard of your
faith in the Lord Jesus and your love for all
the saints, 16do not cease to give thanks for
you, making mention of you in my prayers:
17that the God of our Lord Jesus Christ, the
Father of glory, may give to you the spirit of
wisdom and revelation in the knowledge of
Him, 18the eyes of your understanding[a] being enlightened; that you may know what is
the hope of His calling, what are the riches
of the glory of His inheritance in the saints,
19and what *is* the exceeding greatness of His

1:10 [a] NU-Text and M-Text omit *both.* 1:14 [a] NU-Text reads *which.* 1:18 [a] NU-Text and M-Text read *hearts.*

LIVING IN HEAVENLY PLACES

READ IT: EPHESIANS 1:3

You don't have to die to be in heaven. Heaven is where Jesus is. If you know Jesus as your Friend, you have some of heaven right now.

Often this world is not a very happy place. There is a lot of anger and hatred and violence. But you can live in this unhappy world and carry some of heaven around with you just the same.

What happens when you turn on a light in a dark room? The room is filled with light, and *the darkness can't stop the light.* That's what happens when you carry Jesus around in your life. You bring the light of heaven to people living in misery. Do you have some unhappy friends from unhappy homes? You can bring some of heaven into their lives by showing Jesus to them in all the things you do and say. Then they will want to know Him, too.

power toward us who believe, according to
the working of His mighty power 20which He
worked in Christ when He raised Him from
the dead and seated *Him* at His right hand in
the heavenly *places,* 21far above all principality and power and might and dominion, and
every name that is named, not only in this
age but also in that which is to come.

22And He put all *things* under His feet,
and gave Him *to be* head over all *things* to the
church, 23which is His body, the fullness of
Him who fills all in all.

By Grace Through Faith

2 And you *He made alive,* who were dead
in trespasses and sins, 2in which you
once walked according to the course of this
world, according to the prince of the power
of the air, the spirit who now works in the
sons of disobedience, 3among whom also we
all once conducted ourselves in the lusts of
our flesh, fulfilling the desires of the flesh
and of the mind, and were by nature children of wrath, just as the others.

4But God, who is rich in mercy, because
of His great love with which He loved us,
5even when we were dead in trespasses,
made us alive together with Christ (by grace
you have been saved), 6and raised *us* up together, and made *us* sit together in the heavenly *places* in Christ Jesus, 7that in the ages
to come He might show the exceeding riches
of His grace in *His* kindness toward us in
Christ Jesus. 8For by grace you have been

Epic Ideas

THE BIBLE IS THE TRUTH
GOOD NEWS!

READ IT: EPHESIANS 1:13, 14

GET IT:

Some people think the Bible is useful only for the holidays, for when they're feeling seriously sad and depressed, or for weddings and funerals. The Bible is good for all those events, but the main purpose of the Bible is to tell us about God's relationship to people. In His desire to relate to us, He created us in His image. He loves humans so much that even after the first two messed things up, He didn't stop loving us. In fact, He loved us enough to come to earth as Jesus and die for our sins even though we didn't deserve it. He loves us and wants us to be saved and to live a new life with Him.

The saving He does for us is called "salvation." The good news about the saving is called the "gospel." Ephesians 1:13 calls the good news of how God came to save us the "gospel of your salvation." That is really what the Bible is all about. Even the Old Testament stories point to Jesus and the good news of salvation.

LIVE IT:

Don't let your Bible be a holiday/special occasion/pick-me-up book. *Open your Bible expecting to read* good news about how God saves us and gives us new life. And then be sure to tell others about it, just like Philip did with the Ethiopian in Acts 8:26–40.

saved through faith, and that not of yourselves; *it is* the gift of God, 9 not of works, lest
anyone should boast. 10 For we are His workmanship, created in Christ Jesus for good
works, which God prepared beforehand that
we should walk in them.

Brought Near by His Blood

11 Therefore remember that you, once
Gentiles in the flesh—who are called Uncircumcision by what is called the Circumcision made in the flesh by hands— 12 that
at that time you were without Christ, being
aliens from the commonwealth of Israel
and strangers from the covenants of promise, having no hope and without God in the
world. 13 But now in Christ Jesus you who
once were far off have been brought near by
the blood of Christ.

Christ Our Peace

14 For He Himself is our peace, who has
made both one, and has broken down the
middle wall of separation, 15 having abolished
in His flesh the enmity, *that is,* the law of
commandments *contained* in ordinances, so
as to create in Himself one new man *from*
the two, *thus* making peace, 16 and that He

SALVATION
THE BEST GIFT EVER

READ IT: EPHESIANS 2:8, 9

GET IT:

What was the best gift you ever received? A bike, a gaming system, a computer? What made that gift so special? Was it because it was something you really, really wanted? Or was there something more to it? The very best gifts—the ones that deserve the word *gift*—are those that someone gives freely, without any expectation of behavior or payment or good work.

Jesus gives us that type of good gift. We don't deserve salvation. We didn't earn our rescue. And while there are certainly good things about you—lots of them—they'll never be enough to pay Jesus back for salvation.

That's what grace is all about: getting something we don't deserve—and not getting what we do deserve! God gives with grace because God gives freely, without expecting anything in return. Salvation then is the very best gift you could ever, ever receive!

LIVE IT:

Jesus offers you salvation *completely free of charge*. It's a gift. Think about that: Are you receiving it as a gift of grace? Or have you been trying to earn it, thinking you're good enough so Jesus would obviously offer you salvation?

How might you live differently now that you know salvation is a gift? What response might you have in your day-to-day life?

might reconcile them both to God in one body through the cross, thereby putting to death the enmity.
17And He came and preached peace to you who were afar off and to those who were near.
18For through Him we both have access by one Spirit to the Father.

Christ Our Cornerstone

19Now, therefore, you are no longer strangers and foreigners, but fellow citizens with the saints and members of the household of God,
20having been built on the foundation of the apostles and prophets, Jesus Christ Himself being the chief corner*stone*,
21in whom the whole building, being fitted together, grows into a holy temple in the Lord,
22in whom you also are being built together for a dwelling place of God in the Spirit.

The Mystery Revealed

3 For this reason I, Paul, the prisoner of Christ Jesus for you Gentiles—
2if indeed you have heard of the dispensation of the grace of God which was given to me for you,
3how that by revelation He made known to me the mystery (as I have briefly written already,
4by which, when you read, you may understand my knowledge in the mystery of Christ),
5which in other ages was not made known to the sons of men, as it has now been revealed by the Spirit to His holy apostles and prophets:
6that the Gentiles should be fellow heirs, of the same body, and partakers of His promise in Christ through the gospel,
7of which I became a minister according to the gift of the grace of God given to me by the effective working of His power.

Purpose of the Mystery

8To me, who am less than the least of all the saints, this grace was given, that I should preach among the Gentiles the unsearchable riches of Christ,
9and to make all see what *is* the fellowship[a] of the mystery, which from the beginning of the ages has been hidden in God who created all things through Jesus Christ;[b]
10to the intent that now the manifold wisdom of God might be made known by the church to the principalities and powers in the heavenly *places,*
11according to the eternal purpose which He accomplished in Christ Jesus our Lord,
12in whom we have boldness

3:9 [a] NU-Text and M-Text read *stewardship* (dispensation). [b] NU-Text omits *through Jesus Christ.*

BE YOUR NEW SELF

READ IT: EPHESIANS 4:24

Paul says, "Put on the new man." Are you a Christian? Have you trusted Jesus with your life? Then take off the *old* clothes of your old life without Christ, and put on the *new* clothes of your new life with Christ.

Jesus lives in you now. So your "inside" life has been made new. Now all you have to do is throw away all those old habits and actions that aren't part of your new life. Then your "inside" life will be happy with your "outside" life.

Do you have a habit of lying? Throw away that habit. Do you use bad words or profanity? You can put an end to that now. Are you bad-tempered? Just "take off" your bad temper and trash it. Who needs those things anymore? Let your "outside" life show to everyone what you're like inside—where Jesus now lives.

and access with confidence through faith in
Him. [13]Therefore I ask that you do not lose
heart at my tribulations for you, which is
your glory.

Appreciation of the Mystery

[14]For this reason I bow my knees to the
Father of our Lord Jesus Christ,[a] [15]from
whom the whole family in heaven and earth
is named, [16]that He would grant you, according
to the riches of His glory, to be strengthened
with might through His Spirit in the
inner man, [17]that Christ may dwell in your
hearts through faith; that you, being rooted
and grounded in love, [18]may be able to comprehend
with all the saints what *is* the width
and length and depth and height— [19]to
know the love of Christ which passes knowledge;
that you may be filled with all the fullness
of God.

[20]Now to Him who is able to do exceedingly
abundantly above all that we ask or
think, according to the power that works in
us, [21]to Him *be* glory in the church by Christ
Jesus to all generations, forever and ever.
Amen.

Walk in Unity

4 I therefore, the prisoner of the Lord,
beseech you to walk worthy of the
calling with which you were called, [2]with
all lowliness and gentleness, with longsuffering,
bearing with one another in love,
[3]endeavoring to keep the unity of the Spirit
in the bond of peace. [4]*There is* one body
and one Spirit, just as you were called in one
hope of your calling; [5]one Lord, one faith,
one baptism; [6]one God and Father of all, who
is above all, and through all, and in you[a] all.

Spiritual Gifts

[7]But to each one of us grace was given
according to the measure of Christ's gift.
[8]Therefore He says:

"When He ascended on high,
He led captivity captive,
And gave gifts to men." [a]

[9](Now this, "He ascended"—what does it
mean but that He also first[a] descended into
the lower parts of the earth? [10]He who descended
is also the One who ascended far
above all the heavens, that He might fill all
things.)

[11]And He Himself gave some *to be* apostles,
some prophets, some evangelists, and
some pastors and teachers, [12]for the equipping
of the saints for the work of ministry,
for the edifying of the body of Christ, [13]till
we all come to the unity of the faith and of
the knowledge of the Son of God, to a perfect
man, to the measure of the stature of the

3:14 [a] NU-Text omits *of our Lord Jesus Christ.* 4:6 [a] NU-Text omits *you;* M-Text reads *us.* 4:8 [a] Psalm 68:18
4:9 [a] NU-Text omits *first.*

Action!

ANGER

READ IT: EPHESIANS 4:26, 27

If you expect to be able to live without anger just because you follow Christ, you probably won't last past Tuesday. Anger in the face of life's frustrations is as natural as tears.

But anger can lead to sin and can easily become a voice inside your head that drowns out other important voices, like happiness. Anger can get so loud that you can't even hear God whispering words of comfort and calm, and that's dangerous. You don't need to pretend anger never speaks, but you do need to know how to turn it down so peace and forgiveness can be heard loud and clear.

fullness of Christ; 14that we should no longer be children, tossed to and fro and carried
about with every wind of doctrine, by the
trickery of men, in the cunning craftiness of
deceitful plotting, 15but, speaking the truth
in love, may grow up in all things into Him
who is the head—Christ— 16from whom
the whole body, joined and knit together by
what every joint supplies, according to the
effective working by which every part does
its share, causes growth of the body for the
edifying of itself in love.

The New Man

17This I say, therefore, and testify in the
Lord, that you should no longer walk as the
rest of[a] the Gentiles walk, in the futility of
their mind, 18having their understanding
darkened, being alienated from the life
of God, because of the ignorance that is
in them, because of the blindness of their
heart; 19who, being past feeling, have given
themselves over to lewdness, to work all uncleanness with greediness.

20But you have not so learned Christ, 21if
indeed you have heard Him and have been
taught by Him, as the truth is in Jesus:
22that you put off, concerning your former
conduct, the old man which grows corrupt
according to the deceitful lusts, 23and be renewed in the spirit of your mind, 24and that
you put on the new man which was created
according to God, in true righteousness and
holiness.

Do Not Grieve the Spirit

25Therefore, putting away lying, "*Let* each
one *of you* speak truth with his neighbor," [a]
for we are members of one another. 26"Be angry, and do not sin" :[a] do not let the sun go
down on your wrath, 27nor give place to the
devil. 28Let him who stole steal no longer, but
rather let him labor, working with *his* hands
what is good, that he may have something
to give him who has need. 29Let no corrupt
word proceed out of your mouth, but what
is good for necessary edification, that it
may impart grace to the hearers. 30And do
not grieve the Holy Spirit of God, by whom
you were sealed for the day of redemption.
31Let all bitterness, wrath, anger, clamor, and
evil speaking be put away from you, with all
malice. 32And be kind to one another, tenderhearted, forgiving one another, even as God
in Christ forgave you.

Walk in Love

5 Therefore be imitators of God as dear
children. 2And walk in love, as Christ
also has loved us and given Himself for
us, an offering and a sacrifice to God for a
sweet-smelling aroma.

3But fornication and all uncleanness
or covetousness, let it not even be named
among you, as is fitting for saints; 4neither

4:17 [a] NU-Text omits *the rest of.* 4:25 [a] Zechariah 8:16
4:26 [a] Psalm 4:4

COMMUNICATION

READ IT: EPHESIANS 5:1–7

In this passage Paul asks followers of Jesus to be "imitators of God" (v. 1). That's a pretty big task! But Paul gives us a few ideas about how we can start, including how we speak. He advises us that empty words, mean-spirited joking, and filthy talk don't please God. Instead, we're to offer thanks and show love through our words.

Next time you find *yourself in a conversation* that's headed in the *wrong direction*, you can step up to turn it around. If people are being negative, find something positive to say or change the subject.

filthiness, nor foolish talking, nor coarse
jesting, which are not fitting, but rather
giving of thanks. 5For this you know,[a] that
no fornicator, unclean person, nor covetous
man, who is an idolater, has any inheritance in the kingdom of Christ and God.
6Let no one deceive you with empty words,
for because of these things the wrath of
God comes upon the sons of disobedience.
7Therefore do not be partakers with them.

Walk in Light

8For you were once darkness, but now
you are light in the Lord. Walk as children
of light 9(for the fruit of the Spirit[a] *is* in all
goodness, righteousness, and truth), 10find-
ing out what is acceptable to the Lord. 11And
have no fellowship with the unfruitful works
of darkness, but rather expose *them.* 12For it
is shameful even to speak of those things
which are done by them in secret. 13But all
things that are exposed are made manifest
by the light, for whatever makes manifest is
light. 14Therefore He says:

"Awake, you who sleep,
Arise from the dead,
And Christ will give you light."

Walk in Wisdom

15See then that you walk circumspectly,
not as fools but as wise, 16redeeming the
time, because the days are evil.

17Therefore do not be unwise, but understand what the will of the Lord *is.* 18And do
not be drunk with wine, in which is dissipation; but be filled with the Spirit, 19speaking
to one another in psalms and hymns and
spiritual songs, singing and making melody in your heart to the Lord, 20giving thanks
always for all things to God the Father in the
name of our Lord Jesus Christ, 21submitting
to one another in the fear of God.[a]

Marriage—Christ and the Church

22Wives, submit to your own husbands,

5:5 [a] NU-Text reads *For know this.* 5:9 [a] NU-Text reads *light.* 5:21 [a] NU-Text reads *Christ.*

LIVING WISELY

READ IT: EPHESIANS 5:1–21

GET IT:

On one of his mission trips, Paul spent time preaching in the city of Ephesus. Later he wrote this letter to the Christian church there. He wanted to help them understand how to live for God as Christians. The Ephesian Christians lived in a city that had a huge temple for the Greek goddess Diana. Everybody worshiped this goddess. Paul told the Christians to live differently from the way everyone else was living. This chapter told them exactly what to do. It was written a very long time ago, but the message is clear for us today, too.

LIVE IT:

Take Paul's challenge to live differently from others who are not Christians. Study these phrases. What do they mean for you today? Think of some specific, real-life examples of what Paul says to do and not do. How will you make them happen in your life?

as to the Lord. 23For the husband is head of
the wife, as also Christ is head of the church;
and He is the Savior of the body. 24There-
fore, just as the church is subject to Christ,
so *let* the wives *be* to their own husbands in
everything.

25Husbands, love your wives, just as
Christ also loved the church and gave Himself for her, 26that He might sanctify and
cleanse her with the washing of water by the
word, 27that He might present her to Himself
a glorious church, not having spot or wrin-
kle or any such thing, but that she should
be holy and without blemish. 28So husbands
ought to love their own wives as their own
bodies; he who loves his wife loves himself.
29For no one ever hated his own flesh, but
nourishes and cherishes it, just as the Lord
does the church. 30For we are members of
His body,[a] of His flesh and of His bones.
31"For this reason a man shall leave his father
and mother and be joined to his wife, and
the two shall become one flesh." [a] 32This is a
great mystery, but I speak concerning Christ
and the church. 33Nevertheless let each one
of you in particular so love his own wife as
himself, and let the wife *see* that she respects
her husband.

Children and Parents

6 Children, obey your parents in the
Lord, for this is right. 2"Honor your

In Focus

6:6 Eyeservice Living in a way that looks good to people but doesn't please God. We may deceive others, but we can't deceive God.

father and mother," which is the first commandment with promise: 3"that it may be
well with you and you may live long on the
earth." [a]

4And you, fathers, do not provoke your
children to wrath, but bring them up in the
training and admonition of the Lord.

Bondservants and Masters

5Bondservants, be obedient to those who
are your masters according to the flesh,
with fear and trembling, in sincerity of
heart, as to Christ; 6not with eyeservice, as
men-pleasers, but as bondservants of Christ,
doing the will of God from the heart, 7with
goodwill doing service, as to the Lord, and
not to men, 8knowing that whatever good

5:30 [a] NU-Text omits the rest of this verse. **5:31** [a] Genesis 2:24 **6:3** [a] Deuteronomy 5:16

Action!

FAMILY

READ IT: EPHESIANS 6:1–4

Ephesians is Paul's letter to the Jesus-followers living in Ephesus. Paul was encouraging God's people and reminding them how to live out their faith. These verses describe how God intended for children and parents to relate with each other.

When we read Scripture, it's sometimes easy to focus on what other people are supposed to do. Parents like to point out to kids what the Bible says to them; husbands like to remind their wives about the directions *they should follow. But when you* read verses like this, focus on the sections that are written to you! Your parents won't always get things right—no one can—but God is still telling you to obey and honor them.

anyone does, he will receive the same from
the Lord, whether *he is* a slave or free.

9And you, masters, do the same things
to them, giving up threatening, knowing
that your own Master also[a] is in heaven, and
there is no partiality with Him.

The Whole Armor of God

10Finally, my brethren, be strong in the
Lord and in the power of His might. 11Put
on the whole armor of God, that you may be
able to stand against the wiles of the devil.
12For we do not wrestle against flesh and
blood, but against principalities, against
powers, against the rulers of the darkness of
this age,[a] against spiritual *hosts* of wickedness in the heavenly *places*. 13Therefore take
up the whole armor of God, that you may be
able to withstand in the evil day, and having
done all, to stand.

14Stand therefore, having girded your
waist with truth, having put on the breastplate of righteousness, 15and having shod
your feet with the preparation of the gospel
of peace; 16above all, taking the shield of faith
with which you will be able to quench all the
fiery darts of the wicked one. 17And take the
helmet of salvation, and the sword of the
Spirit, which is the word of God; 18praying
always with all prayer and supplication in
the Spirit, being watchful to this end with
all perseverance and supplication for all the
saints— 19and for me, that utterance may be
given to me, that I may open my mouth boldly to make known the mystery of the gospel,
20for which I am an ambassador in chains;
that in it I may speak boldly, as I ought to
speak.

A Gracious Greeting

21But that you also may know my affairs
and how I am doing, Tychicus, a beloved
brother and faithful minister in the Lord,
will make all things known to you; 22whom
I have sent to you for this very purpose, that
you may know our affairs, and *that* he may
comfort your hearts.

23Peace to the brethren, and love with
faith, from God the Father and the Lord
Jesus Christ. 24Grace *be* with all those who
love our Lord Jesus Christ in sincerity.
Amen.

6:9 [a] NU-Text reads *He who is both their Master and yours.*
6:12 [a] NU-Text reads *rulers of this darkness.*

WISDOM

READ IT: EPHESIANS 6:10–20

The armor of God, described in this passage, is a great summary of the way a wise person lives. Living the way God wants you to, having peace and faith, being confident in your salvation, and studying the Bible—that's what it looks like to live a life of wisdom. You don't have to be an adult to live this way. Think about each piece of that armor (read them from the passage), and imagine putting them on today.

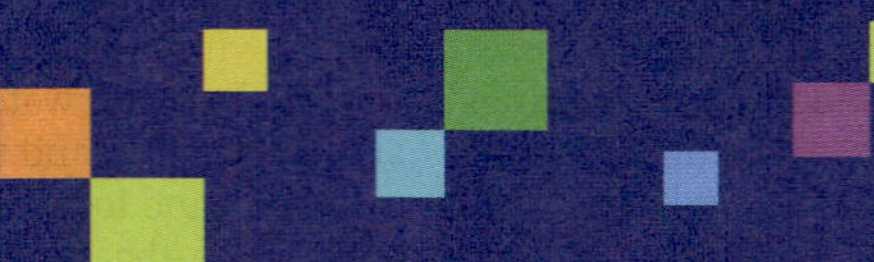

The EPISTLE *of* PAUL *the* APOSTLE *to the*

PHILIPPIANS

A.D. 61

Behind the Scenes

READ IT:

Philippians is a book containing Paul's letter to the church in the city of Philippi, Greece. Paul thanked the Philippians for their love and support while he was in prison. Even though Paul was writing from prison, his letter was full of joy. The words *joy* or *rejoice* are used fourteen times. Paul told the people to watch out for false teachers, to live in harmony with others, and to obey God.

GET IT:

Who wrote it: Paul

When it was written: A.D. 61

Why it was written: to thank the church in Philippi for their support and to tell them how to live as Christians.

LIVE IT:

We should do everything without complaining and without anxiety.

We should imitate Jesus in everything we do—He is perfect.

We should get our minds out of the trash and think about things that are noble, right, pure, lovely, excellent, admirable, and praiseworthy.

FIND IT:

Paul's Views on Life	*Philippians 1*
Christ's Humility: An Example for Us	*Philippians 2*
Instructions and Words of Encouragement	*Philippians 3–4*

Greeting

1 Paul and Timothy, bondservants of
Jesus Christ,

To all the saints in Christ Jesus who are
in Philippi, with the bishops[a] and deacons:

2Grace to you and peace from God our
Father and the Lord Jesus Christ.

Thankfulness and Prayer

3I thank my God upon every remembrance of you, 4always in every prayer of
mine making request for you all with joy, 5for
your fellowship in the gospel from the first
day until now, 6being confident of this very
thing, that He who has begun a good work
in you will complete *it* until the day of Jesus
Christ; 7just as it is right for me to think this
of you all, because I have you in my heart,
inasmuch as both in my chains and in the
defense and confirmation of the gospel, you
all are partakers with me of grace. 8For God
is my witness, how greatly I long for you all
with the affection of Jesus Christ.

9And this I pray, that your love may
abound still more and more in knowledge
and all discernment, 10that you may approve
the things that are excellent, that you may
be sincere and without offense till the day of
Christ, 11being filled with the fruits of righteousness which *are* by Jesus Christ, to the
glory and praise of God.

Christ Is Preached

12But I want you to know, brethren, that
the things *which happened* to me have actually turned out for the furtherance of the
gospel, 13so that it has become evident to the
whole palace guard, and to all the rest, that
my chains are in Christ; 14and most of the
brethren in the Lord, having become confident by my chains, are much more bold to
speak the word without fear.

15Some indeed preach Christ even from
envy and strife, and some also from goodwill: 16The former[a] preach Christ from selfish ambition, not sincerely, supposing to add
affliction to my chains; 17but the latter out
of love, knowing that I am appointed for the
defense of the gospel. 18What then? Only *that*
in every way, whether in pretense or in truth,
Christ is preached; and in this I rejoice, yes,
and will rejoice.

To Live Is Christ

19For I know that this will turn out for
my deliverance through your prayer and the

In Focus

1:1 Deacons Pronounced *DEE-kuns.* From a Greek word meaning "servants." Sometimes deacons are ministers, and sometimes they are not. *Minister* also means "servant."

1:1 [a] Literally *overseers* 1:16 [a] NU-Text reverses the contents of verses 16 and 17.

HEARING GOD'S VOICE

READ IT: PHILIPPIANS 1:9–11

It's God's plan for us to grow in love and for us to experience more knowledge of Him. But why does it matter so much? So you can decide what's best. So you can be pure. And so you can be blameless.

When you understand more about God and know Him better and better, you'll love Him and others more. You'll know the right thing to do. If you understand God better, you'll find it's a lot easier to hear His voice.

supply of the Spirit of Jesus Christ, 20according-
ing to my earnest expectation and hope that
in nothing I shall be ashamed, but with all
boldness, as always, so now also Christ will
be magnified in my body, whether by life or
by death. 21For to me, to live *is* Christ, and
to die *is* gain. 22But if *I* live on in the flesh,
this *will mean* fruit from *my* labor; yet what
I shall choose I cannot tell. 23For[a] I am hard-
pressed between the two, having a desire to
depart and be with Christ, *which is* far better. 24Nevertheless to remain in the flesh *is*
more needful for you. 25And being confident
of this, I know that I shall remain and continue with you all for your progress and joy
of faith, 26that your rejoicing for me may be
more abundant in Jesus Christ by my coming to you again.

Striving and Suffering for Christ

27Only let your conduct be worthy of the
gospel of Christ, so that whether I come and
see you or am absent, I may hear of your affairs, that you stand fast in one spirit, with
one mind striving together for the faith of
the gospel, 28and not in any way terrified by
your adversaries, which is to them a proof of
perdition, but to you of salvation,[a] and that
from God. 29For to you it has been granted on
behalf of Christ, not only to believe in Him,
but also to suffer for His sake, 30having the
same conflict which you saw in me and now
hear *is* in me.

Unity Through Humility

2 Therefore if *there is* any consolation in
Christ, if any comfort of love, if any
fellowship of the Spirit, if any affection and
mercy, 2fulfill my joy by being like-minded,
having the same love, *being* of one accord,
of one mind. 3*Let* nothing *be done* through
selfish ambition or conceit, but in lowliness
of mind let each esteem others better than
himself. 4Let each of you look out not only for
his own interests, but also for the interests
of others.

The Humbled and Exalted Christ

5Let this mind be in you which was also
in Christ Jesus, 6who, being in the form of
God, did not consider it robbery to be equal
with God, 7but made Himself of no reputation, taking the form of a bondservant, *and*
coming in the likeness of men. 8And being

1:23 [a] NU-Text and M-Text read *But.* 1:28 [a] NU-Text reads *of your salvation.*

LET CHRIST LIVE IN YOU

READ IT: PHILIPPIANS 1:21

Becoming a Christian is a little like learning a new language. At first the language is hard for you, but as time goes by, you can speak the new language without even thinking about how to say the words. The language becomes part of you.

You may spend a lot of time reading the Bible and learning how God wants you to live. At first it seems very puzzling. But then one day you realize what it really means to be a Christian—Christ Himself must take over your life until He is everything and you are nothing. Then you live as a Christian because Jesus lives in you and *through* you. You no longer live by a set of rules. Living, loving, and speaking as Jesus did becomes *part of you.*

Yes, you do go on living, but in a real way your new life is Jesus living in you.

found in appearance as a man, He humbled
Himself and became obedient to *the point of*
death, even the death of the cross. 9There-
fore God also has highly exalted Him and
given Him the name which is above every
name, 10that at the name of Jesus every knee
should bow, of those in heaven, and of those
on earth, and of those under the earth, 11and
that every tongue should confess that Jesus
Christ *is* Lord, to the glory of God the Father.

Light Bearers

12Therefore, my beloved, as you have always obeyed, not as in my presence only, but
now much more in my absence, work out
your own salvation with fear and trembling;
13for it is God who works in you both to will
and to do for *His* good pleasure.

14Do all things without complaining and
disputing, 15that you may become blameless
and harmless, children of God without fault
in the midst of a crooked and perverse generation, among whom you shine as lights in
the world, 16holding fast the word of life, so
that I may rejoice in the day of Christ that I
have not run in vain or labored in vain.

17Yes, and if I am being poured out *as a*
drink offering on the sacrifice and service of
your faith, I am glad and rejoice with you all.
18For the same reason you also be glad and
rejoice with me.

Timothy Commended

19But I trust in the Lord Jesus to send
Timothy to you shortly, that I also may be
encouraged when I know your state. 20For I
have no one like-minded, who will sincerely
care for your state. 21For all seek their own,
not the things which are of Christ Jesus.
22But you know his proven character, that as
a son with *his* father he served with me in
the gospel. 23Therefore I hope to send him at
once, as soon as I see how it goes with me.
24But I trust in the Lord that I myself shall
also come shortly.

Epaphroditus Praised

25Yet I considered it necessary to send to
you Epaphroditus, my brother, fellow worker, and fellow soldier, but your messenger
and the one who ministered to my need;
26since he was longing for you all, and was
distressed because you had heard that he
was sick. 27For indeed he was sick almost
unto death; but God had mercy on him, and
not only on him but on me also, lest I should
have sorrow upon sorrow. 28Therefore I sent
him the more eagerly, that when you see him
again you may rejoice, and I may be less sorrowful. 29Receive him therefore in the Lord
with all gladness, and hold such men in
esteem; 30because for the work of Christ he
came close to death, not regarding his life,
to supply what was lacking in your service
toward me.

All for Christ

3 Finally, my brethren, rejoice in the
Lord. For me to write the same things
to you *is* not tedious, but for you *it is* safe.

2Beware of dogs, beware of evil workers, beware of the mutilation! 3For we are
the circumcision, who worship God in the
Spirit,[a] rejoice in Christ Jesus, and have no
confidence in the flesh, 4though I also might
have confidence in the flesh. If anyone else
thinks he may have confidence in the flesh, I
more so: 5circumcised the eighth day, of the
stock of Israel, *of* the tribe of Benjamin, a
Hebrew of the Hebrews; concerning the law,
a Pharisee; 6concerning zeal, persecuting
the church; concerning the righteousness
which is in the law, blameless.

7But what things were gain to me, these
I have counted loss for Christ. 8Yet indeed I
also count all things loss for the excellence of
the knowledge of Christ Jesus my Lord, for
whom I have suffered the loss of all things,
and count them as rubbish, that I may gain
Christ 9and be found in Him, not having my
own righteousness, which *is* from the law,
but that which *is* through faith in Christ, the
righteousness which is from God by faith;
10that I may know Him and the power of His
resurrection, and the fellowship of His sufferings, being conformed to His death, 11if,
by any means, I may attain to the resurrection from the dead.

Pressing Toward the Goal

12Not that I have already attained, or am
already perfected; but I press on, that I may
lay hold of that for which Christ Jesus has
also laid hold of me. 13Brethren, I do not
count myself to have apprehended; but one

3:3 [a] NU-Text and M-Text read *who worship in the Spirit of God.*

thing *I do,* forgetting those things which are
behind and reaching forward to those things
which are ahead, 14I press toward the goal for
the prize of the upward call of God in Christ
Jesus.

15Therefore let us, as many as are mature,
have this mind; and if in anything you think
otherwise, God will reveal even this to you.
16Nevertheless, to *the degree* that we have already attained, let us walk by the same rule,[a]
let us be of the same mind.

Our Citizenship in Heaven

17Brethren, join in following my example,
and note those who so walk, as you have us
for a pattern. 18For many walk, of whom I
have told you often, and now tell you even
weeping, *that they are* the enemies of the
cross of Christ: 19whose end *is* destruction,
whose god *is their* belly, and *whose* glory *is*

3:16 [a] NU-Text omits *rule* and the rest of the verse.

TRADE EVERYTHING FOR JESUS

READ IT: PHILIPPIANS 3:8

You may ask yourself, *What do I want more than anything in the world?* What is the answer? A trip around the world? To be president of your country? To be the richest person you know?

The trouble with all these things—and a lot more—is that they don't last. Anything you might want more than everything else is something that comes to an end all too soon. Where are all the millionaires of the year 1900? What do you do after a trip around the world? What do you know about the man who was president in 1893?

All these things and many more are soon gone, but the friendship of Jesus Christ is "the same yesterday, today, and forever" (Hebrews 13:8). So you would be wise to trade all your dreams for the friendship of Jesus.

PERSEVERANCE

READ IT: PHILIPPIANS 3:13, 14

Our past cannot be a barrier to the future. That's why Paul makes a point of saying that he doesn't look back. Paul is thinking about his past as someone who persecuted Christians. But now Paul's commitment *can't be questioned*. He changed his course and stayed with it. He writes with total confidence that—no matter what he did in the past—he will be called to the winner's stand and be waving at the crowds.

in their shame—who set their mind on
earthly things. 20For our citizenship is in
heaven, from which we also eagerly wait
for the Savior, the Lord Jesus Christ, 21who
will transform our lowly body that it may be
conformed to His glorious body, according
to the working by which He is able even to
subdue all things to Himself.

4 Therefore, my beloved and longed-for
brethren, my joy and crown, so stand
fast in the Lord, beloved.

Be United, Joyful, and in Prayer

2I implore Euodia and I implore Syntyche
to be of the same mind in the Lord. 3And[a]
I urge you also, true companion, help these
women who labored with me in the gospel,
with Clement also, and the rest of my fellow
workers, whose names *are* in the Book of Life.

4Rejoice in the Lord always. Again I will
say, rejoice!

5Let your gentleness be known to all
men. The Lord *is* at hand.

6Be anxious for nothing, but in everything by prayer and supplication, with
thanksgiving, let your requests be made
known to God; 7and the peace of God, which
surpasses all understanding, will guard
your hearts and minds through Christ Jesus.

Meditate on These Things

8Finally, brethren, whatever things are
true, whatever things *are* noble, whatever
things *are* just, whatever things *are* pure,
whatever things *are* lovely, whatever things
are of good report, if *there is* any virtue and if
there is anything praiseworthy—meditate on

In Focus

4:3 Book of Life The book containing the names of all of God's people saved by faith in Christ.

these things. 9The things which you learned
and received and heard and saw in me, these
do, and the God of peace will be with you.

Philippian Generosity

10But I rejoiced in the Lord greatly that
now at last your care for me has flourished
again; though you surely did care, but you
lacked opportunity. 11Not that I speak in regard to need, for I have learned in whatever
state I am, to be content: 12I know how to be
abased, and I know how to abound. Everywhere and in all things I have learned both
to be full and to be hungry, both to abound
and to suffer need. 13I can do all things
through Christ[a] who strengthens me.

14Nevertheless you have done well that
you shared in my distress. 15Now you Philippians know also that in the beginning of
the gospel, when I departed from Macedonia, no church shared with me concerning
giving and receiving but you only. 16For even
in Thessalonica you sent *aid* once and again

4:3 [a] NU-Text and M-Text read *Yes.* 4:13 [a] NU-Text reads *Him who.*

Action!

ENTERTAINMENT

READ IT: PHILIPPIANS 4:8, 9

To meditate on something means to think about it so much that you really begin to understand it. What do you spend the most time thinking about? How are your thoughts influenced by what you watch, hear, and read? Guarding what you take in will inspire your mind to think the right kinds of thoughts.

for my necessities. 17 Not that I seek the gift,
but I seek the fruit that abounds to your account. 18 Indeed I have all and abound. I am
full, having received from Epaphroditus
the things *sent* from you, a sweet-smelling
aroma, an acceptable sacrifice, well pleasing to God. 19 And my God shall supply all
your need according to His riches in glory by
Christ Jesus. 20 Now to our God and Father *be*
glory forever and ever. Amen.

Greeting and Blessing

21 Greet every saint in Christ Jesus. The
brethren who are with me greet you. 22 All
the saints greet you, but especially those
who are of Caesar's household.

23 The grace of our Lord Jesus Christ be
with you all.[a] Amen.

4:23 [a] NU-Text reads *your spirit.*

CONFIDENCE

READ IT: PHILIPPIANS 4:13

In this passage Paul is sharing with the Philippians about contentment. He has been on both sides of the coin: with plenty and in need. He thanks the people in Philippi for their care when he has been in need, and he expresses confidence that God will care for him no matter what he is facing. Paul knows God will give him strength to walk the road he's been put on.

The EPISTLE of PAUL the APOSTLE to the

COLOSSIANS

A.D. 60

Behind the Scenes

READ IT:

The book of Colossians contains the letter of Paul to the church in Colosse. The people there were confused. False teachers were telling them to worship angels and to follow special rules and ceremonies. Paul wrote this letter from prison to tell them again the basics of Christianity and that Christ is superior in position and power to everything.

GET IT:

Who wrote it: Paul

When it was written: A.D. 60

Why it was written: to explain that Christ is superior to every ruler, power, or authority in heaven or earth, and that He completely saves us.

LIVE IT:

We must practice our faith every day in what we do.

Our attitudes and actions should reflect what Jesus would do.

FIND IT:

The Preeminence of Christ	*Colossians 1–2*
Instructions for Christian Living	*Colossians 3–4*

Greeting

1 Paul, an apostle of Jesus Christ by the
will of God, and Timothy our brother,

2 To the saints and faithful brethren in
Christ *who are* in Colosse:

Grace to you and peace from God our Father and the Lord Jesus Christ.[a]

Their Faith in Christ

3 We give thanks to the God and Father
of our Lord Jesus Christ, praying always for
you, 4 since we heard of your faith in Christ
Jesus and of your love for all the saints; 5 because of the hope which is laid up for you
in heaven, of which you heard before in the
word of the truth of the gospel, 6 which has
come to you, as *it has* also in all the world,
and is bringing forth fruit,[a] as *it is* also
among you since the day you heard and
knew the grace of God in truth; 7 as you also
learned from Epaphras, our dear fellow servant, who is a faithful minister of Christ on
your behalf, 8 who also declared to us your
love in the Spirit.

Preeminence of Christ

9 For this reason we also, since the day we
heard it, do not cease to pray for you, and to
ask that you may be filled with the knowledge of His will in all wisdom and spiritual
understanding; 10 that you may walk worthy
of the Lord, fully pleasing *Him,* being fruitful in every good work and increasing in
the knowledge of God; 11 strengthened with
all might, according to His glorious power,
for all patience and longsuffering with joy;
12 giving thanks to the Father who has qualified us to be partakers of the inheritance of
the saints in the light. 13 He has delivered us
from the power of darkness and conveyed
us into the kingdom of the Son of His love,
14 in whom we have redemption through His
blood,[a] the forgiveness of sins.
15 He is the image of the invisible God,
the firstborn over all creation. 16 For by Him

1:2 [a] NU-Text omits *and the Lord Jesus Christ.* **1:6** [a] NU-Text and M-Text add *and growing.* **1:14** [a] NU-Text and M-Text omit *through His blood.*

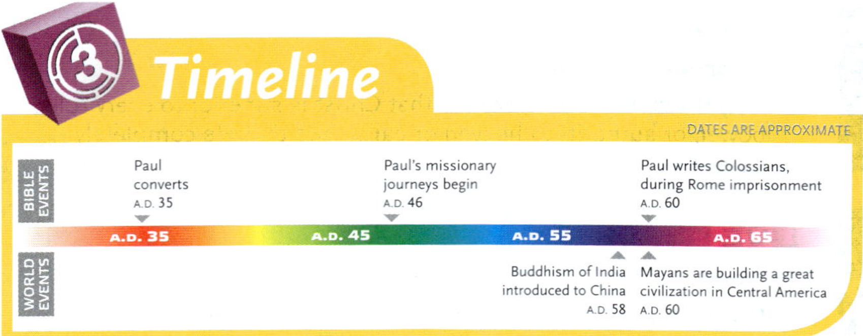

ANGELS

READ IT: COLOSSIANS 1:16

These special beings show up throughout Scripture. Sometimes we think that angels are like small, naked babies with harps and wings flitting about God's head like gnats. The truth is, angels are God's awesome warriors who usually show up in full armor with flaming swords.

all things were created that are in heaven
and that are on earth, visible and invisible,
whether thrones or dominions or principalities or powers. All things were created
through Him and for Him. 17And He is before all things, and in Him all things consist.
18And He is the head of the body, the church,
who is the beginning, the firstborn from
the dead, that in all things He may have the
preeminence.

Reconciled in Christ

19For it pleased *the Father that* in Him
all the fullness should dwell, 20and by Him
to reconcile all things to Himself, by Him,
whether things on earth or things in heav-
en, having made peace through the blood of
His cross.

21And you, who once were alienated and
enemies in your mind by wicked works, yet
now He has reconciled 22in the body of His
flesh through death, to present you holy,
and blameless, and above reproach in His
sight— 23if indeed you continue in the faith,
grounded and steadfast, and are not moved
away from the hope of the gospel which you
heard, which was preached to every creature
under heaven, of which I, Paul, became a
minister.

Sacrificial Service for Christ

24I now rejoice in my sufferings for you,
and fill up in my flesh what is lacking in the
afflictions of Christ, for the sake of His body,
which is the church, 25of which I became a
minister according to the stewardship from
God which was given to me for you, to fulfill the word of God, 26the mystery which
has been hidden from ages and from generations, but now has been revealed to His
saints. 27To them God willed to make known
what are the riches of the glory of this mystery among the Gentiles: which[a] is Christ
in you, the hope of glory. 28Him we preach,
warning every man and teaching every man
in all wisdom, that we may present every
man perfect in Christ Jesus. 29To this *end* I
also labor, striving according to His working
which works in me mightily.

Not Philosophy but Christ

2 For I want you to know what a great
conflict I have for you and those in Laodicea, and *for* as many as have not seen my
face in the flesh, 2that their hearts may be
encouraged, being knit together in love, and
attaining to all riches of the full assurance
of understanding, to the knowledge of the
mystery of God, both of the Father and[a] of
Christ, 3in whom are hidden all the treasures
of wisdom and knowledge.

4Now this I say lest anyone should deceive you with persuasive words. 5For though
I am absent in the flesh, yet I am with you
in spirit, rejoicing to see your *good* order and
the steadfastness of your faith in Christ.

6As you therefore have received Christ
Jesus the Lord, so walk in Him, 7rooted and

1:27 [a] M-Text reads *who.* 2:2 [a] NU-Text omits *both of the Father and.*

PEER PRESSURE

READ IT: COLOSSIANS 2:8

Paul wrote this letter to the church in the city of Colosse. The people in that church felt peer pressure from new teachers who taught them the wrong things. These teachers tried to create their own religion and convince the Colossians to follow it. Paul encouraged the people reading his letter to refuse to believe false teachers. Paul asked them to trust the teaching that they believed when they followed Christ and to reject what was different.

built up in Him and established in the faith,
as you have been taught, abounding in it[a]
with thanksgiving.
8Beware lest anyone cheat you through
philosophy and empty deceit, according to
the tradition of men, according to the basic
principles of the world, and not according to
Christ. 9For in Him dwells all the fullness of
the Godhead bodily; 10and you are complete
in Him, who is the head of all principality
and power.

Not Legalism but Christ

11In Him you were also circumcised with
the circumcision made without hands, by
putting off the body of the sins[a] of the flesh,
by the circumcision of Christ, 12buried with
Him in baptism, in which you also were
raised with *Him* through faith in the working of God, who raised Him from the dead.
13And you, being dead in your trespasses and
the uncircumcision of your flesh, He has
made alive together with Him, having forgiven you all trespasses, 14having wiped out
the handwriting of requirements that was
against us, which was contrary to us. And
He has taken it out of the way, having nailed
it to the cross. 15Having disarmed principalities and powers, He made a public spectacle
of them, triumphing over them in it.
16So let no one judge you in food or in
drink, or regarding a festival or a new moon
or sabbaths, 17which are a shadow of things

2:7 [a] NU-Text omits *in it*. 2:11 [a] NU-Text omits *of the sins*.

WHO IS GOD? GOD IN A BOD

READ IT: COLOSSIANS 2:9

GET IT:

Lots of people say Jesus was a good man, a great teacher, a good example, and gentle, kind, and loving. Those people are right, but they don't know the whole Jesus. He was so much more! And if you miss the so-much-more, you've missed Jesus entirely. And if you miss Jesus, you miss God because the Bible tells us that Jesus is God Himself. All of God's character, power, goodness, and love exist in Jesus.

Jesus (in some miraculous, amazing way) was God with skin on. That means Jesus' words, Jesus' actions, Jesus' teachings, Jesus' whole life show us the heart of God. If you get to know Jesus, you'll find that God is neither as soft nor as hard as most people think He is. That is, God neither tells us, "You're super, don't change a thing," nor "You're so bad there's no hope for you." God cares more about us than either of those options. Jesus' life proves it.

LIVE IT:

If we look at Jesus, we can know and understand enough about God to believe Him, love Him, and follow Him. Read about Jesus in the book of *Mark* and pay attention to what He says and does. Notice who He spends time with, what advice He gives, and what stories He tells. What do these things tell you about God?

to come, but the substance is of Christ. 18Let
no one cheat you of your reward, taking delight in *false* humility and worship of angels,
intruding into those things which he has
not[a] seen, vainly puffed up by his fleshly
mind, 19and not holding fast to the Head,
from whom all the body, nourished and knit
together by joints and ligaments, grows with
the increase *that is* from God.

20Therefore,[a] if you died with Christ
from the basic principles of the world, why,
as *though* living in the world, do you subject yourselves to regulations— 21"Do not
touch, do not taste, do not handle," 22which
all concern things which perish with the
using—according to the commandments
and doctrines of men? 23These things indeed have an appearance of wisdom in self-
imposed religion, *false* humility, and neglect
of the body, *but are* of no value against the
indulgence of the flesh.

Not Carnality but Christ

3 If then you were raised with Christ,
seek those things which are above,
where Christ is, sitting at the right hand of
God. 2Set your mind on things above, not on
things on the earth. 3For you died, and your
life is hidden with Christ in God. 4When
Christ *who is* our life appears, then you also
will appear with Him in glory.

5Therefore put to death your members
which are on the earth: fornication, uncleanness, passion, evil desire, and covetousness,
which is idolatry. 6Because of these things
the wrath of God is coming upon the sons of
disobedience, 7in which you yourselves once
walked when you lived in them.

In Focus

2:8 Philosophy Pronounced *fih-LOS-uh-fee*. A word meaning "love of wisdom." Many ancient Greeks worshiped human wisdom. They believed they could solve all problems by thinking. True wisdom comes from God's Word in the Bible.

8But now you yourselves are to put off
all these: anger, wrath, malice, blasphemy,
filthy language out of your mouth. 9Do not
lie to one another, since you have put off the
old man with his deeds, 10and have put on
the new *man* who is renewed in knowledge
according to the image of Him who created
him, 11where there is neither Greek nor Jew,
circumcised nor uncircumcised, barbarian,
Scythian, slave *nor* free, but Christ *is* all and
in all.

Character of the New Man

12Therefore, as *the* elect of God, holy and
beloved, put on tender mercies, kindness,
humility, meekness, longsuffering; 13bear-
ing with one another, and forgiving one
another, if anyone has a complaint against
another; even as Christ forgave you, so you
also *must do*. 14But above all these things

2:18 [a] NU-Text omits *not*. 2:20 [a] NU-Text and M-Text omit *Therefore*.

Action!

ENTERTAINMENT

READ IT: COLOSSIANS 3:2

It's amazing how little we think about what we're thinking! Paul taught the Colossians that they had control over their thoughts. Paul told them to not waste their thoughts on meaningless things. Paul understood that thinking about God is the first step toward pleasing God.

Action!

BULLYING

READ IT: COLOSSIANS 3:8

Everyone knows that words can hurt as much as sticks and stones, no matter what the nursery rhyme says. Our feelings can affect our words. If we're angry, frustrated, irritated, or disappointed, we have to watch what we say so that our words don't bully others with our anger, frustration, irritation, and disappointment. Hurting other people doesn't stop our own hurt.

Epic Ideas

LOVE
LOVE LOOKS GOOD ON YOU!

READ IT: COLOSSIANS 3:12–14

GET IT:

It's the first day of school. You want to look your best. You carefully go through your clothes and pick out your best jeans, a great shirt, and those awesome new shoes. You spend a little extra time on your hair and make sure there's nothing stuck between your teeth before you walk out the door.

Did you know you can also "wear" love? Paul is writing a letter to the Colossians listing some of the same characteristics he mentioned in the Love Passage (1 Corinthians 13). We should offer tender mercy, kindness, humility, meekness, longsuffering, and forgiveness to each other as Christ did to us. God knows this is tough for us. And that's why Paul offers this advice: "But above all these things put on love" (v. 14).

When we wear love, we're covered in it. You wouldn't go out in public without wearing clothes, right? In the same way, when we forget to put on love, we're heading out into the world unprepared.

LIVE IT:

Where do you get ready in the morning? Whether it's at your mirror or in your bedroom closet, make a note card with verse 14 on it. Then you can remind yourself to "put on love" as you prepare for your day. It's the best accessory to any outfit!

put on love, which is the bond of perfection. 15And let the peace of God rule in your
hearts, to which also you were called in
one body; and be thankful. 16Let the word
of Christ dwell in you richly in all wisdom,
teaching and admonishing one another in
psalms and hymns and spiritual songs,
singing with grace in your hearts to the
Lord. 17And whatever you do in word or deed,
do all in the name of the Lord Jesus, giving
thanks to God the Father through Him.

The Christian Home

18Wives, submit to your own husbands,
as is fitting in the Lord.

19Husbands, love your wives and do not
be bitter toward them.

20Children, obey your parents in all
things, for this is well pleasing to the Lord.

21Fathers, do not provoke your children,
lest they become discouraged.

22Bondservants, obey in all things your
masters according to the flesh, not with
eyeservice, as men-pleasers, but in sincerity
of heart, fearing God. 23And whatever you
do, do it heartily, as to the Lord and not to
men, 24knowing that from the Lord you will
receive the reward of the inheritance; for[a]
you serve the Lord Christ. 25But he who does
wrong will be repaid for what he has done,
and there is no partiality.

4 Masters, give your bondservants what
is just and fair, knowing that you also
have a Master in heaven.

Christian Graces

2Continue earnestly in prayer, being vigilant in it with thanksgiving; 3meanwhile
praying also for us, that God would open to
us a door for the word, to speak the mystery
of Christ, for which I am also in chains, 4that
I may make it manifest, as I ought to speak.

5Walk in wisdom toward those *who
are* outside, redeeming the time. 6*Let* your
speech always *be* with grace, seasoned with
salt, that you may know how you ought to
answer each one.

Final Greetings

7Tychicus, a beloved brother, faithful
minister, and fellow servant in the Lord, will
tell you all the news about me. 8I am sending him to you for this very purpose, that he[a]
may know your circumstances and comfort
your hearts, 9with Onesimus, a faithful and

3:24 [a] NU-Text omits *for*. 4:8 [a] NU-Text reads *you may know our circumstances and he may.*

Action!

WHAT YOU DO WILL COME BACK TO YOU

READ IT: COLOSSIANS 3:25

Can you remember a mean thing you once said or did to somebody? Maybe you think it's all past and forgotten. But don't count on it!

Better go to that person and make right what you did. If you don't, someday that mean thing will come back to you. When you remember the mean thing you did, you'll feel so bad you could almost wish to die. By that time it may be too late to say you're sorry. The person you hurt may even be dead. Then all you can do is ask God to forgive you because Jesus died for you. You can also ask Him to help you never do anything like that again.

But the best policy is to learn to do kind things to people every chance you get. Then you'll always have good memories.

beloved brother, who is *one* of you. They will
make known to you all things which *are happening* here.

10Aristarchus my fellow prisoner greets
you, with Mark the cousin of Barnabas
(about whom you received instructions: if
he comes to you, welcome him), 11and Jesus
who is called Justus. These *are my* only fellow workers for the kingdom of God who are
of the circumcision; they have proved to be
a comfort to me.

12Epaphras, who is *one* of you, a bondservant of Christ, greets you, always laboring fervently for you in prayers, that you may stand
perfect and complete[a] in all the will of God.
13For I bear him witness that he has a great
zeal[a] for you, and those who are in Laodicea,
and those in Hierapolis. 14Luke the beloved
physician and Demas greet you. 15Greet the
brethren who are in Laodicea, and Nymphas
and the church that *is* in his[a] house.

Closing Exhortations and Blessing

16Now when this epistle is read among
you, see that it is read also in the church of
the Laodiceans, and that you likewise read
the *epistle* from Laodicea. 17And say to Ar-
chippus, "Take heed to the ministry which
you have received in the Lord, that you may
fulfill it."

18This salutation by my own hand—Paul.
Remember my chains. Grace *be* with you.
Amen.

4:12 [a] NU-Text reads *fully assured.* 4:13 [a] NU-Text reads *concern.* 4:15 [a] NU-Text reads *Nympha . . . her house.*

BE CAREFUL WHAT YOU SAY

READ IT: COLOSSIANS 4:6

There are too many words in the world. That's another way of saying people often talk too much. If you talk too much, sooner or later you're likely to say something you shouldn't say.

How can we solve this problem of too much talking? The answer is simple, but doing it may not be easy: think more than you talk, and always think before you speak.

Just imagine that you carry a "talk meter" around with you. The talk meter flashes "great" when you say something good. But every time you speak before you think, your talk meter flashes "you goofed"!

When you think more than you talk, then you'll usually have something worth saying. Also, people will listen to you more. But if you just babble on and on, nobody will listen to you.

All of us need to ask God to help us control our talking at all times.

The FIRST EPISTLE of PAUL the APOSTLE to the

THESSALONIANS

A.D. 51

Behind the Scenes

READ IT:

The book of 1 Thessalonians is a letter from Paul to the church in Thessalonica, Greece. He praised them for growing their faith. He encouraged them to live by the instructions he gave them for holy living. And he told them the exciting news that Jesus would return to earth someday. Finally he reminded them, "Rejoice always" (5:16).

GET IT:

Who wrote it: Paul

When it was written: A.D. 51

Why it was written: to instruct the Thessalonian Christians on how to live in a way that pleased God and to tell them that Jesus was coming again.

LIVE IT:

We should ask ourselves, "Does God approve of what I'm doing? If Jesus comes to earth tomorrow, am I ready to face Him?"

FIND IT:

The Thessalonians' Good Example	*1 Thessalonians 1–3*
Plea for Purity and Christ's Coming	*1 Thessalonians 4–5*

Greeting

1 Paul, Silvanus, and Timothy,

To the church of the Thessalonians in
God the Father and the Lord Jesus Christ:

Grace to you and peace from God our Father and the Lord Jesus Christ.[a]

Their Good Example

2We give thanks to God always for you
all, making mention of you in our prayers,
3remembering without ceasing your work
of faith, labor of love, and patience of hope
in our Lord Jesus Christ in the sight of our
God and Father, 4knowing, beloved brethren, your election by God. 5For our gospel
did not come to you in word only, but also in
power, and in the Holy Spirit and in much
assurance, as you know what kind of men we
were among you for your sake.

6And you became followers of us and of
the Lord, having received the word in much
affliction, with joy of the Holy Spirit, 7so that
you became examples to all in Macedonia
and Achaia who believe. 8For from you the
word of the Lord has sounded forth, not only
in Macedonia and Achaia, but also in every
place. Your faith toward God has gone out,
so that we do not need to say anything. 9For
they themselves declare concerning us what
manner of entry we had to you, and how you
turned to God from idols to serve the living
and true God, 10and to wait for His Son from
heaven, whom He raised from the dead, *even*
Jesus who delivers us from the wrath to come.

Paul's Conduct

2 For you yourselves know, brethren,
that our coming to you was not in vain.
2But even[a] after we had suffered before and
were spitefully treated at Philippi, as you
know, we were bold in our God to speak to
you the gospel of God in much conflict. 3For
our exhortation *did* not *come* from error or
uncleanness, nor *was it* in deceit.

4But as we have been approved by God
to be entrusted with the gospel, even so we
speak, not as pleasing men, but God who
tests our hearts. 5For neither at any time did
we use flattering words, as you know, nor a
cloak for covetousness—God *is* witness. 6Nor
did we seek glory from men, either from you
or from others, when we might have made
demands as apostles of Christ. 7But we were
gentle among you, just as a nursing *mother*

1:1 [a] NU-Text omits *from God our Father and the Lord Jesus Christ.* 2:2 [a] NU-Text and M-Text omit *even.*

BELIEVING WHAT GOD SAYS

READ IT: 1 THESSALONIANS 2:13

God speaks in the Bible, which is His Word. When the Spirit of God (also called the Spirit of Christ) lives in you, then He tells you that the Bible is the Word of God, and you believe and obey what God says.

There are a lot of voices in the world. Some voices make good sense and others don't, but God's Word is the gauge by which you measure the truth of what people say.

God's Word also must be the gauge by which you measure the truth of what *you* say. If you're always guessing at the truth, or if you're just lying, then you have broken God's Word. The Bible says, "You shall not bear false witness [tell lies]" (Matthew 19:18).

But believing what God says is the key to obeying what God says. When you believe that God has spoken in the Bible, then you know you must obey because God Himself has spoken to you.

cherishes her own children. 8So, affection-
ately longing for you, we were well pleased
to impart to you not only the gospel of God,
but also our own lives, because you had become dear to us. 9For you remember, brethren, our labor and toil; for laboring night and
day, that we might not be a burden to any of
you, we preached to you the gospel of God.
10You *are* witnesses, and God *also,* how
devoutly and justly and blamelessly we behaved ourselves among you who believe; 11as
you know how we exhorted, and comforted,
and charged[a] every one of you, as a father
does his own children, 12that you would walk
worthy of God who calls you into His own
kingdom and glory.

Their Conversion

13For this reason we also thank God without ceasing, because when you received the
word of God which you heard from us, you
welcomed *it* not *as* the word of men, but as
it is in truth, the word of God, which also effectively works in you who believe. 14For you,
brethren, became imitators of the churches
of God which are in Judea in Christ Jesus.
For you also suffered the same things from
your own countrymen, just as they *did* from
the Judeans, 15who killed both the Lord Jesus
and their own prophets, and have persecuted us; and they do not please God and are
contrary to all men, 16forbidding us to speak
to the Gentiles that they may be saved, so as
always to fill up *the measure of* their sins; but
wrath has come upon them to the uttermost.

Longing to See Them

17But we, brethren, having been taken
away from you for a short time in presence,
not in heart, endeavored more eagerly to see
your face with great desire. 18Therefore we
wanted to come to you—even I, Paul, time
and again—but Satan hindered us. 19For
what *is* our hope, or joy, or crown of rejoicing? *Is it* not even you in the presence of our
Lord Jesus Christ at His coming? 20For you
are our glory and joy.

Concern for Their Faith

3 Therefore, when we could no longer
endure it, we thought it good to be
left in Athens alone, 2and sent Timothy, our
brother and minister of God, and our fellow
laborer in the gospel of Christ, to establish
you and encourage you concerning your
faith, 3that no one should be shaken by these
afflictions; for you yourselves know that we
are appointed to this. 4For, in fact, we told
you before when we were with you that we
would suffer tribulation, just as it happened,
and you know. 5For this reason, when I could
no longer endure it, I sent to know your
faith, lest by some means the tempter had
tempted you, and our labor might be in vain.

Encouraged by Timothy

6But now that Timothy has come to us
from you, and brought us good news of your
faith and love, and that you always have good
remembrance of us, greatly desiring to see
us, as we also *to see* you— 7therefore, brethren, in all our affliction and distress we were
comforted concerning you by your faith. 8For
now we live, if you stand fast in the Lord.
9For what thanks can we render to God
for you, for all the joy with which we rejoice
for your sake before our God, 10night and day
praying exceedingly that we may see your
face and perfect what is lacking in your faith?

Prayer for the Church

11Now may our God and Father Himself,
and our Lord Jesus Christ, direct our way to
you. 12And may the Lord make you increase
and abound in love to one another and to all,
just as we *do* to you, 13so that He may establish your hearts blameless in holiness before
our God and Father at the coming of our
Lord Jesus Christ with all His saints.

Plea for Purity

4 Finally then, brethren, we urge and exhort in the Lord Jesus that you should
abound more and more, just as you received
from us how you ought to walk and to please
God; 2for you know what commandments
we gave you through the Lord Jesus.
3For this is the will of God, your sanctification: that you should abstain from sexual
immorality; 4that each of you should know
how to possess his own vessel in sanctification and honor, 5not in passion of lust, like
the Gentiles who do not know God; 6that no
one should take advantage of and defraud his
brother in this matter, because the Lord *is* the
avenger of all such, as we also forewarned
you and testified. 7For God did not call us
to uncleanness, but in holiness. 8Therefore
he who rejects *this* does not reject man, but
God, who has also given[a] us His Holy Spirit.

2:11 [a] NU-Text and M-Text read *implored.* **4:8** [a] NU-Text reads *who also gives.*

A Brotherly and Orderly Life

9But concerning brotherly love you have
no need that I should write to you, for you
yourselves are taught by God to love one another; 10and indeed you do so toward all the
brethren who are in all Macedonia. But we
urge you, brethren, that you increase more
and more; 11that you also aspire to lead a quiet life, to mind your own business, and to
work with your own hands, as we commanded you, 12that you may walk properly toward
those who are outside, and *that* you may lack
nothing.

The Comfort of Christ's Coming

13But I do not want you to be ignorant,
brethren, concerning those who have fallen
asleep, lest you sorrow as others who have no
hope. 14For if we believe that Jesus died and
rose again, even so God will bring with Him
those who sleep in Jesus.[a]

15For this we say to you by the word of the
Lord, that we who are alive *and* remain until
the coming of the Lord will by no means pre-
cede those who are asleep. 16For the Lord Himself will descend from heaven with a shout,
with the voice of an archangel, and with the
trumpet of God. And the dead in Christ will
rise first. 17Then we who are alive *and* remain
shall be caught up together with them in the
clouds to meet the Lord in the air. And thus
we shall always be with the Lord. 18Therefore
comfort one another with these words.

The Day of the Lord

5 But concerning the times and the seasons, brethren, you have no need that
I should write to you. 2For you yourselves
know perfectly that the day of the Lord so
comes as a thief in the night. 3For when they
say, "Peace and safety!" then sudden destruction comes upon them, as labor pains
upon a pregnant woman. And they shall not
escape. 4But you, brethren, are not in darkness, so that this Day should overtake you as
a thief. 5You are all sons of light and sons of
the day. We are not of the night nor of darkness. 6Therefore let us not sleep, as others
do, but let us watch and be sober. 7For those
who sleep, sleep at night, and those who get
drunk are drunk at night. 8But let us who are
of the day be sober, putting on the breastplate of faith and love, and *as* a helmet the
hope of salvation. 9For God did not appoint
us to wrath, but to obtain salvation through
our Lord Jesus Christ, 10who died for us, that
whether we wake or sleep, we should live together with Him.

4:14 [a] Or *those who through Jesus sleep*

WE WILL LIVE FOREVER WITH JESUS

READ IT: 1 THESSALONIANS 4:14

Jesus didn't die and rise again from death just to prove He could do it. Jesus was no "show-off." He had a great purpose in what He did. He died to take away your sins. But He rose again so that death would never have real power over you. He rose again so that you could have the kind of life that He brought back from the dead. That is life that lasts forever. That is the life of God Himself.

So if you have trusted your life to Jesus, then you have the very life of Jesus within you. Some people will *exist* forever, but they won't have the life of God. To exist without God is worse than death. We call that kind of existence "hell." So being saved from sin and hell means having the life of Christ Himself. We call that kind of life "eternal life."

[11]Therefore comfort each other and edify
one another, just as you also are doing.

Various Exhortations

[12]And we urge you, brethren, to recognize
those who labor among you, and are over
you in the Lord and admonish you, [13]and
to esteem them very highly in love for their
work's sake. Be at peace among yourselves.
[14]Now we exhort you, brethren, warn
those who are unruly, comfort the fainthearted, uphold the weak, be patient with
all. [15]See that no one renders evil for evil to
anyone, but always pursue what is good both
for yourselves and for all.
[16]Rejoice always, [17]pray without ceasing,
[18]in everything give thanks; for this is the
will of God in Christ Jesus for you.
[19]Do not quench the Spirit. [20]Do not despise
prophecies. [21]Test all things; hold fast what is
good. [22]Abstain from every form of evil.

Blessing and Admonition

[23]Now may the God of peace Himself
sanctify you completely; and may your whole
spirit, soul, and body be preserved blameless
at the coming of our Lord Jesus Christ. [24]He
who calls you *is* faithful, who also will do *it*.
[25]Brethren, pray for us.
[26]Greet all the brethren with a holy kiss.
[27]I charge you by the Lord that this epistle
be read to all the holy[a] brethren.
[28]The grace of our Lord Jesus Christ *be*
with you. Amen.

5:27 [a] NU-Text omits *holy*.

REVENGE

READ IT: 1 THESSALONIANS 5:12–15

God says you shouldn't return evil with more evil. That sounds good, but what are you supposed to do instead? How do you respond when you feel like evil has been done to you? If you return evil with evil, you create more evil. God wants you to stop creating evil and pursue what is good. So return evil with good. That's a great plan for your life!

PRAYER

READ IT: 1 THESSALONIANS 5:17

Prayer isn't just for meals and church. It should be an ongoing conversation. God wants to be part of that little back and forth you do in your head throughout the day: *Should I eat a banana or potato chips*? Talk to God about it—that's how close He wants to be to you!

Put this verse as a reminder in places you don't usually pray—for example, stick it on your bathroom mirror—and practice talking to God throughout your day.

The SECOND EPISTLE *of* PAUL *the* APOSTLE *to the*

THESSALONIANS

A.D. 51

Behind the Scenes

READ IT:

This book is Paul's second letter to the Thessalonians. The people there misunderstood what Paul said in the first letter. They thought Jesus was coming in the next week or so. Paul wrote to correct that thinking. He encouraged them to live disciplined lives, to work hard, and to focus on the hope for eternity.

GET IT:

Who wrote it: Paul

When it was written: A.D. 51

Why it was written: to encourage the Christians to work hard while they waited for Jesus to come again.

LIVE IT:

We should work hard and use our time wisely.

We need to stay strong in our faith and not be swayed by other ideas.

FIND IT:

God's Judgment and Glory	*2 Thessalonians 1–2*
Warning Against Idleness	*2 Thessalonians 3*

Greeting

1 Paul, Silvanus, and Timothy,

To the church of the Thessalonians in
God our Father and the Lord Jesus Christ:

2Grace to you and peace from God our
Father and the Lord Jesus Christ.

God's Final Judgment and Glory

3We are bound to thank God always for
you, brethren, as it is fitting, because your
faith grows exceedingly, and the love of every one of you all abounds toward each other,
4so that we ourselves boast of you among the
churches of God for your patience and faith
in all your persecutions and tribulations that
you endure, 5*which is* manifest evidence of
the righteous judgment of God, that you
may be counted worthy of the kingdom of
God, for which you also suffer; 6since *it is*
a righteous thing with God to repay with
tribulation those who trouble you, 7and to
give you who are troubled rest with us when
the Lord Jesus is revealed from heaven with
His mighty angels, 8in flaming fire taking
vengeance on those who do not know God,
and on those who do not obey the gospel of
our Lord Jesus Christ. 9These shall be punished with everlasting destruction from the
presence of the Lord and from the glory of
His power, 10when He comes, in that Day, to
be glorified in His saints and to be admired
among all those who believe,[a] because our
testimony among you was believed.

11Therefore we also pray always for you
that our God would count you worthy of
this calling, and fulfill all the good pleasure
of *His* goodness and the work of faith with
power, 12that the name of our Lord Jesus
Christ may be glorified in you, and you in
Him, according to the grace of our God and
the Lord Jesus Christ.

The Great Apostasy

2 Now, brethren, concerning the coming
of our Lord Jesus Christ and our gathering together to Him, we ask you, 2not to
be soon shaken in mind or troubled, either
by spirit or by word or by letter, as if from
us, as though the day of Christ[a] had come.
3Let no one deceive you by any means; for

1:10 [a] NU-Text and M-Text read *have believed*. 2:2 [a] NU-Text reads *the Lord*.

LET YOUR FAITH GROW

READ IT: 2 THESSALONIANS 1:3

Anything that lives also grows. If you have living faith, you also have growing faith. Your faith is growing if you are living more and more in friendship with Jesus.

Your body lives and grows by breathing, drinking, eating, resting, and exercise. Your faith is breathing if you receive the Holy Spirit every moment. Do you know the hymn, "Breathe on Me, Breath of God"? Your faith also grows by eating and drinking the life of Jesus Himself: "He who comes to Me shall never hunger, and he who believes in Me shall never thirst" (John 6:35). Find this life of Jesus in His words in the Bible. Jesus also says, "Come to Me . . . and I will give you rest" (Matthew 11:28). That means trusting Jesus so you don't have to be afraid of anything in the world.

Finally, your growing faith needs exercise in doing all the things Jesus commands you. By works of love and mercy, show and tell others what Jesus is like. Then you will have a living and growing faith.

that Day will not come unless the falling away
comes first, and the man of sin[a] is revealed,
the son of perdition, 4who opposes and exalts
himself above all that is called God or that is
worshiped, so that he sits as God[a] in the temple of God, showing himself that he is God.
5Do you not remember that when I was
still with you I told you these things? 6And
now you know what is restraining, that he
may be revealed in his own time. 7For the
mystery of lawlessness is already at work;
only He[a] who now restrains *will do so* until
He[b] is taken out of the way. 8And then the
lawless one will be revealed, whom the Lord
will consume with the breath of His mouth
and destroy with the brightness of His
coming. 9The coming of the *lawless one* is
according to the working of Satan, with all
power, signs, and lying wonders, 10and with
all unrighteous deception among those who
perish, because they did not receive the love
of the truth, that they might be saved. 11And
for this reason God will send them strong
delusion, that they should believe the lie,
12that they all may be condemned who did
not believe the truth but had pleasure in
unrighteousness.

Stand Fast

13But we are bound to give thanks to God
always for you, brethren beloved by the Lord,
because God from the beginning chose you
for salvation through sanctification by the
Spirit and belief in the truth, 14to which He
called you by our gospel, for the obtaining of
the glory of our Lord Jesus Christ. 15There-
fore, brethren, stand fast and hold the
traditions which you were taught, whether
by word or our epistle.
16Now may our Lord Jesus Christ Himself, and our God and Father, who has loved
us and given *us* everlasting consolation and
good hope by grace, 17comfort your hearts and
establish you in every good word and work.

Pray for Us

3 Finally, brethren, pray for us, that the
word of the Lord may run *swiftly* and
be glorified, just as *it is* with you, 2and that
we may be delivered from unreasonable and
wicked men; for not all have faith.
3But the Lord is faithful, who will establish you and guard *you* from the evil one.
4And we have confidence in the Lord concerning you, both that you do and will do
the things we command you.
5Now may the Lord direct your hearts into
the love of God and into the patience of Christ.

Warning Against Idleness

6But we command you, brethren, in the
name of our Lord Jesus Christ, that you
withdraw from every brother who walks
disorderly and not according to the tradition
which he[a] received from us. 7For you yourselves know how you ought to follow us, for
we were not disorderly among you; 8nor did
we eat anyone's bread free of charge, but
worked with labor and toil night and day,
that we might not be a burden to any of you,
9not because we do not have authority, but

2:3 [a] NU-Text reads *lawlessness.* 2:4 [a] NU-Text omits *as God.*
2:7 [a] Or *he* [b] Or *he* 3:6 [a] NU-Text and M-Text read *they.*

CONFIDENCE

READ IT: 2 THESSALONIANS 3:1–3

Paul wrote this letter to the Thessalonians, asking for prayer. He knew that there would always be bad people because not everyone has faith in Jesus. However, he shared his confidence that God would be faithful and would protect His people.

God will always protect us from the evil one. God will protect you.

to make ourselves an example of how you
should follow us.
10For even when we were with you, we
commanded you this: If anyone will not
work, neither shall he eat. 11For we hear that
there are some who walk among you in a
disorderly manner, not working at all, but
are busybodies. 12Now those who are such
we command and exhort through our Lord
Jesus Christ that they work in quietness and
eat their own bread.
13But *as for* you, brethren, do not grow
weary *in* doing good. 14And if anyone does not
obey our word in this epistle, note that person and do not keep company with him, that
he may be ashamed. 15Yet do not count *him*
as an enemy, but admonish *him* as a brother.

Benediction

16Now may the Lord of peace Himself
give you peace always in every way. The Lord
be with you all.
17The salutation of Paul with my own
hand, which is a sign in every epistle; so I
write.
18The grace of our Lord Jesus Christ *be*
with you all. Amen.

In Focus

3:11 Busybodies People who mind other people's business. Paul said that some Christians were not doing their own work but were meddling in other people's affairs.

Action!

CHOOSE YOUR FRIENDS

READ IT: 2 THESSALONIANS 3:6

When you read about the life of Jesus in Matthew, Mark, Luke, and John, you notice that Jesus mixed with many kinds of people. But He always kept His place as the Son of God, and He witnessed to everybody.

Jesus chose His friends carefully. He said, "You are My friends if you do whatever I command you" (John 15:14). Your friends must also be Jesus' friends. You cannot become close friends with young people who swear, lie, steal, use drugs, or don't believe in Jesus. If you do, chances are you will become like them. They will not become like you.

Remember, this doesn't mean you should hate young people who are not friends of Jesus, but you must make up your mind not to do the things they do. If you do, you can get into real trouble with God—and with people, too.

The FIRST EPISTLE of PAUL the APOSTLE to

TIMOTHY

A.D. 62

Behind the Scenes

READ IT:

First Timothy contains Paul's letter to the young pastor Timothy. Paul wrote this very personal letter to Timothy to give him advice on how to run the church. He warned him about false teachers whose teachings were the opposite of what God said. This letter also includes the qualifications and duties of pastors.

GET IT:

Who wrote it: Paul

When it was written: in the fall of A.D. 62

Why it was written: to encourage Timothy and tell him how to do his ministry work.

LIVE IT:

Even if you're young you can set an example for others in what you say and how you act.

Don't hope for or love money and stuff. Put your hope in God instead.

Do good. Be generous. Be willing to share.

FIND IT:

There Is No Other Doctrine	*1 Timothy 1*
Instructions for the Church	*1 Timothy 2–5*
Personal Advice	*1 Timothy 6*

Greeting

1 Paul, an apostle of Jesus Christ, by the
commandment of God our Savior and
the Lord Jesus Christ, our hope,

2To Timothy, a true son in the faith:

Grace, mercy, *and* peace from God our
Father and Jesus Christ our Lord.

No Other Doctrine

3As I urged you when I went into
Macedonia—remain in Ephesus that you
may charge some that they teach no other
doctrine, 4nor give heed to fables and endless genealogies, which cause disputes rather than godly edification which is in faith.
5Now the purpose of the commandment
is love from a pure heart, *from* a good conscience, and *from* sincere faith, 6from which
some, having strayed, have turned aside to
idle talk, 7desiring to be teachers of the law,
understanding neither what they say nor the
things which they affirm.
8But we know that the law *is* good if one
uses it lawfully, 9knowing this: that the law is
not made for a righteous person, but for *the*
lawless and insubordinate, for *the* ungodly
and for sinners, for *the* unholy and profane,
for murderers of fathers and murderers of
mothers, for manslayers, 10for fornicators,
for sodomites, for kidnappers, for liars, for
perjurers, and if there is any other thing that
is contrary to sound doctrine, 11according to

Starring Roles

TIMOTHY grew up in Lystra (pronounced *LISS-trah*) where his Hebrew mother and grandmother taught him the Old Testament Scriptures. His father was Greek. His name means "Honored by God." Timothy also had the honor of being the apostle Paul's friend. Paul even referred to him as his "beloved and faithful son in the Lord" (1 Corinthians 4:17).

After meeting Paul during his second preaching trip, Timothy traveled with him. Paul had to leave Thessalonica when they accused him of treason against the emperor of Rome. So Timothy went to that city and helped to strengthen the Christians. He also helped Paul in his hard ministry at Corinth.

During Paul's first time as a prisoner at Rome, Timothy was able to stand by and help him. But the second time, Paul was sent to jail for treason against the cruel Emperor Nero, and they put him to death. Before he was killed, he wrote another wonderful letter to Timothy.

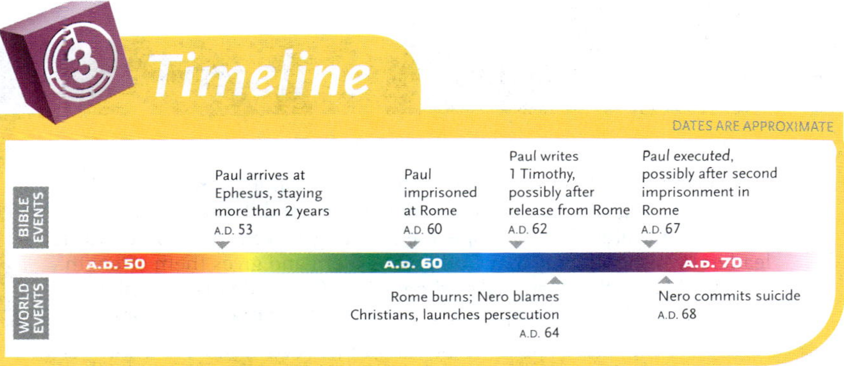

the glorious gospel of the blessed God which
was committed to my trust.

Glory to God for His Grace

12And I thank Christ Jesus our Lord who
has enabled me, because He counted me
faithful, putting *me* into the ministry, 13al-
though I was formerly a blasphemer, a persecutor, and an insolent man; but I obtained
mercy because I did *it* ignorantly in unbelief.
14And the grace of our Lord was exceedingly
abundant, with faith and love which are in
Christ Jesus. 15This *is* a faithful saying and
worthy of all acceptance, that Christ Jesus
came into the world to save sinners, of whom
I am chief. 16However, for this reason I obtained mercy, that in me first Jesus Christ
might show all longsuffering, as a pattern
to those who are going to believe on Him
for everlasting life. 17Now to the King eternal, immortal, invisible, to God who alone
is wise,[a] *be* honor and glory forever and ever.
Amen.

Fight the Good Fight

18This charge I commit to you, son Timothy, according to the prophecies previously made concerning you, that by them you
may wage the good warfare, 19having faith
and a good conscience, which some having
rejected, concerning the faith have suffered
shipwreck, 20of whom are Hymenaeus and
Alexander, whom I delivered to Satan that
they may learn not to blaspheme.

Pray for All Men

2 Therefore I exhort first of all that supplications, prayers, intercessions, *and*
giving of thanks be made for all men, 2for
kings and all who are in authority, that we
may lead a quiet and peaceable life in all godliness and reverence. 3For this *is* good and
acceptable in the sight of God our Savior,
4who desires all men to be saved and to come
to the knowledge of the truth. 5For *there is*
one God and one Mediator between God and
men, *the* Man Christ Jesus, 6who gave Himself a ransom for all, to be testified in due
time, 7for which I was appointed a preacher
and an apostle—I am speaking the truth in
Christ[a] *and* not lying—a teacher of the Gentiles in faith and truth.

Men and Women in the Church

8I desire therefore that the men pray
everywhere, lifting up holy hands, without
wrath and doubting; 9in like manner also,
that the women adorn themselves in modest
apparel, with propriety and moderation, not
with braided hair or gold or pearls or costly
clothing, 10but, which is proper for women
professing godliness, with good works. 11Let
a woman learn in silence with all submission. 12And I do not permit a woman to teach
or to have authority over a man, but to be in
silence. 13For Adam was formed first, then
Eve. 14And Adam was not deceived, but the
woman being deceived, fell into transgression. 15Nevertheless she will be saved in
childbearing if they continue in faith, love,
and holiness, with self-control.

1:17 [a] NU-Text reads *to the only God.* 2:7 [a] NU-Text omits *in Christ.*

AUTHORITY

READ IT: 1 TIMOTHY 2:1–3

Leadership is about trust. There's a certain amount of responsibility that goes along with the job. Whether you are fire drill captain or president of the United States, people are counting on you. We should pray for leaders. We should pray that God guides them and gives them strength. We should pray that God makes them wise. We should pray that they will decide what's best for the people they serve. These prayers honor God.

Qualifications of Overseers

3 This *is* a faithful saying: If a man desires the position of a bishop,[a] he desires a good work. 2A bishop then must be
blameless, the husband of one wife, temperate, sober-minded, of good behavior, hospitable, able to teach; 3not given to wine, not
violent, not greedy for money,[a] but gentle,
not quarrelsome, not covetous; 4one who
rules his own house well, having *his* children in submission with all reverence 5(for
if a man does not know how to rule his own
house, how will he take care of the church
of God?); 6not a novice, lest being puffed up
with pride he fall into the *same* condemnation as the devil. 7Moreover he must have a
good testimony among those who are outside, lest he fall into reproach and the snare
of the devil.

Qualifications of Deacons

8Likewise deacons *must be* reverent, not
double-tongued, not given to much wine,
not greedy for money, 9holding the mystery
of the faith with a pure conscience. 10But
let these also first be tested; then let them
serve as deacons, being *found* blameless.
11Likewise, *their* wives *must be* reverent, not
slanderers, temperate, faithful in all things.

In Focus

2:5 Mediator Pronounced *MEE-dee-ay-tor.* Someone who brings two groups or individuals to agreement. Jesus is the Mediator who brings God and people to agreement by His death on the Cross.

12Let deacons be the husbands of one wife,
ruling *their* children and their own houses
well. 13For those who have served well as deacons obtain for themselves a good standing
and great boldness in the faith which is in
Christ Jesus.

The Great Mystery

14These things I write to you, though I
hope to come to you shortly; 15but if I am
delayed, *I write* so that you may know how
you ought to conduct yourself in the house of

3:1 [a] Literally *overseer* 3:3 [a] NU-Text omits *not greedy for money.*

Action!

JESUS BECAME YOUR RANSOM

READ IT: 1 TIMOTHY 2:6

Ransom is a word you may have seen from time to time. A ransom is the price that people have to pay to get back their loved ones who have been kidnapped. A ransom is usually a lot of money.

But the Bible uses the word *ransom* to explain what Jesus did when He died for your sins. You were, in a real way, kidnapped by Satan, who planned to keep you as his prisoner. Then Jesus came and said, "I will *pay the ransom price to* set My loved ones free." And you know what that ransom price was—it was the very blood of Jesus Himself. He gave His life and even suffered the punishment of hell to buy back your soul from Satan's power.

Now you belong to Jesus—unless you want to be Satan's prisoner! Jesus has broken down the door of Satan's prison, and you can come out a free person. Jesus paid for your freedom.

God, which is the church of the living God,
the pillar and ground of the truth. 16And
without controversy great is the mystery of
godliness:

God[a] was manifested in the flesh,
Justified in the Spirit,
Seen by angels,
Preached among the Gentiles,
Believed on in the world,
Received up in glory.

The Great Apostasy

4 Now the Spirit expressly says that in
latter times some will depart from the
faith, giving heed to deceiving spirits and
doctrines of demons, 2speaking lies in hypocrisy, having their own conscience seared
with a hot iron, 3forbidding to marry, *and
commanding* to abstain from foods which
God created to be received with thanksgiving by those who believe and know the
truth. 4For every creature of God *is* good, and
nothing is to be refused if it is received with
thanksgiving; 5for it is sanctified by the word
of God and prayer.

A Good Servant of Jesus Christ

6If you instruct the brethren in these
things, you will be a good minister of Jesus
Christ, nourished in the words of faith and
of the good doctrine which you have carefully followed. 7But reject profane and old
wives' fables, and exercise yourself toward
godliness. 8For bodily exercise profits a little, but godliness is profitable for all things,
having promise of the life that now is and
of that which is to come. 9This *is* a faithful
saying and worthy of all acceptance. 10For to
this *end* we both labor and suffer reproach,[a]
because we trust in the living God, who is
the Savior of all men, especially of those who
believe. 11These things command and teach.

Take Heed to Your Ministry

12Let no one despise your youth, but
be an example to the believers in word, in
conduct, in love, in spirit,[a] in faith, in purity. 13Till I come, give attention to reading,
to exhortation, to doctrine. 14Do not neglect
the gift that is in you, which was given to
you by prophecy with the laying on of the
hands of the eldership. 15Meditate on these
things; give yourself entirely to them, that
your progress may be evident to all. 16Take
heed to yourself and to the doctrine. Continue in them, for in doing this you will save
both yourself and those who hear you.

Treatment of Church Members

5 Do not rebuke an older man, but exhort *him* as a father, younger men as
brothers, 2older women as mothers, younger
women as sisters, with all purity.

Honor True Widows

3Honor widows who are really widows.
4But if any widow has children or grandchildren, let them first learn to show piety at
home and to repay their parents; for this is
good and[a] acceptable before God. 5Now she
who is really a widow, and left alone, trusts
in God and continues in supplications and

3:16 [a] NU-Text reads *Who.* 4:10 [a] NU-Text reads *we labor and strive.* 4:12 [a] NU-Text omits *in spirit.* 5:4 [a] NU-Text and M-Text omit *good and.*

MATURITY

READ IT: 1 TIMOTHY 4:12

Maturity isn't just about age. There's not a magic birthday when—ta da!—all of a sudden, maturity happens. Maturity does have something *to do with life experience*, but it has even more to do with attitude toward all of life. Anyone, no matter his or her age, can demonstrate maturity by speaking and acting in ways that are loving, faithful, and pure.

prayers night and day. 6But she who lives in
pleasure is dead while she lives. 7And these
things command, that they may be blameless. 8But if anyone does not provide for his
own, and especially for those of his household, he has denied the faith and is worse
than an unbeliever.

9Do not let a widow under sixty years old
be taken into the number, *and not unless* she
has been the wife of one man, 10well reported
for good works: if she has brought up children, if she has lodged strangers, if she has
washed the saints' feet, if she has relieved
the afflicted, if she has diligently followed
every good work.

11But refuse *the* younger widows; for
when they have begun to grow wanton
against Christ, they desire to marry, 12hav-
ing condemnation because they have cast
off their first faith. 13And besides they learn
to be idle, wandering about from house to
house, and not only idle but also gossips and
busybodies, saying things which they ought
not. 14Therefore I desire that *the* younger
widows marry, bear children, manage the
house, give no opportunity to the adversary
to speak reproachfully. 15For some have already turned aside after Satan. 16If any believing man or[a] woman has widows, let
them relieve them, and do not let the church
be burdened, that it may relieve those who
are really widows.

Honor the Elders

17Let the elders who rule well be counted

In Focus

4:14 Eldership The council of men who governed God's people in Old Testament and New Testament times. Sometimes these "elders" were teachers and preachers.

5:16 [a] NU-Text omits *man or.*

Action!

HONOR YOUR ELDERS

READ IT: 1 TIMOTHY 5:1, 2

It's sad that many young people snub older folks. When young people do this, they miss out on all that the older people could have taught them. Older people can save you a lot of grief by sharing what they have learned about living in the world.

There's another side to honoring older folks, too. God's plan for a happy and prosperous society says that we should respect our elders. If we refuse to follow God's plan, He will let us get into lots of trouble. An ancient king of Judah refused to listen to his senior advisors, so he lost most of his kingdom (see 1 Kings 12:8–24).

"Honor your father and your mother" also means that you should have respect for everyone who has authority. You may not always agree with your elders, but you should always consider that God expects you to treat them with respect.

A special way of showing respect for elders is the way you care for them when they are too old to care for themselves. Blessed are the merciful, for they shall receive mercy.

worthy of double honor, especially those
who labor in the word and doctrine. 18For
the Scripture says, "You shall not muzzle an
ox while it treads out the grain,"[a] and, "The
laborer *is* worthy of his wages."[b] 19Do not receive an accusation against an elder except
from two or three witnesses. 20Those who
are sinning rebuke in the presence of all,
that the rest also may fear.

21I charge *you* before God and the Lord
Jesus Christ and the elect angels that you observe these things without prejudice, doing
nothing with partiality. 22Do not lay hands
on anyone hastily, nor share in other people's sins; keep yourself pure.

23No longer drink only water, but use a
little wine for your stomach's sake and your
frequent infirmities.

24Some men's sins are clearly evident,
preceding *them* to judgment, but those of
some *men* follow later. 25Likewise, the good
works *of some* are clearly evident, and those
that are otherwise cannot be hidden.

Honor Masters

6 Let as many bondservants as are under
the yoke count their own masters worthy of all honor, so that the name of God and
His doctrine may not be blasphemed. 2And
those who have believing masters, let them
not despise *them* because they are brethren,
but rather serve *them* because those who are
benefited are believers and beloved. Teach
and exhort these things.

Error and Greed

3If anyone teaches otherwise and does
not consent to wholesome words, *even* the
words of our Lord Jesus Christ, and to the
doctrine which accords with godliness, 4he
is proud, knowing nothing, but is obsessed
with disputes and arguments over words,
from which come envy, strife, reviling, evil
suspicions, 5useless wranglings[a] of men of
corrupt minds and destitute of the truth,
who suppose that godliness is a *means of*
gain. From such withdraw yourself.[b]

6Now godliness with contentment is
great gain. 7For we brought nothing into *this*
world, *and it is* certain[a] we can carry nothing
out. 8And having food and clothing, with
these we shall be content. 9But those who
desire to be rich fall into temptation and
a snare, and *into* many foolish and harmful lusts which drown men in destruction
and perdition. 10For the love of money is a
root of all *kinds of* evil, for which some have
strayed from the faith in their greediness,
and pierced themselves through with many
sorrows.

The Good Confession

11But you, O man of God, flee these
things and pursue righteousness, godliness,
faith, love, patience, gentleness. 12Fight the
good fight of faith, lay hold on eternal life,
to which you were also called and have confessed the good confession in the presence
of many witnesses. 13I urge you in the sight
of God who gives life to all things, and *before*
Christ Jesus who witnessed the good confession before Pontius Pilate, 14that you keep *this*
commandment without spot, blameless until our Lord Jesus Christ's appearing, 15which
He will manifest in His own time, *He who is*
the blessed and only Potentate, the King of
kings and Lord of lords, 16who alone has immortality, dwelling in unapproachable light,
whom no man has seen or can see, to whom
be honor and everlasting power. Amen.

Instructions to the Rich

17Command those who are rich in this
present age not to be haughty, nor to trust in
uncertain riches but in the living God, who
gives us richly all things to enjoy. 18*Let them*
do good, that they be rich in good works,
ready to give, willing to share, 19storing up
for themselves a good foundation for the
time to come, that they may lay hold on eternal life.

Guard the Faith

20O Timothy! Guard what was committed to your trust, avoiding the profane *and*
idle babblings and contradictions of what is
falsely called knowledge— 21by professing it
some have strayed concerning the faith.

Grace *be* with you. Amen.

5:18 [a] Deuteronomy 25:4 [b] Luke 10:7 6:5 [a] NU-Text and M-Text read *constant friction.* [b] NU-Text omits this sentence. 6:7 [a] NU-Text omits *and it is certain.*

The SECOND EPISTLE *of* PAUL *the* APOSTLE *to*

TIMOTHY

A.D. 67

Behind the Scenes

READ IT:

This book is Paul's second letter to Timothy while Paul was in jail. Knowing he didn't have long to live, Paul asked Timothy to come see him. He encouraged Timothy as a minister so he would be ready to continue Paul's missionary work after Paul's death. Paul gave Timothy instructions for leading a church. He also warned him to stay away from false teachers and told him to be faithful to true Christian teachings.

GET IT:

Who wrote it: Paul

When it was written: in the fall of A.D. 67

Why it was written: to tell Timothy to continue Paul's ministry work after Paul's death.

LIVE IT:

We can be strong in our faith because God has given us a spirit of power.

We know the Bible is true because it is inspired by God.

FIND IT:

Don't Be Ashamed of the Gospel *2 Timothy 1*

Work Approved by God *2 Timothy 2*

The Word of God 2 Timothy 3–4

Greeting

1 Paul, an apostle of Jesus Christ[a] by the
will of God, according to the promise of
life which is in Christ Jesus,

2 To Timothy, a beloved son:

Grace, mercy, *and* peace from God the
Father and Christ Jesus our Lord.

Timothy's Faith and Heritage

3 I thank God, whom I serve with a pure
conscience, as *my* forefathers *did,* as without
ceasing I remember you in my prayers night
and day, 4 greatly desiring to see you, being
mindful of your tears, that I may be filled
with joy, 5 when I call to remembrance the
genuine faith that is in you, which dwelt first
in your grandmother Lois and your mother
Eunice, and I am persuaded is in you also.
6 Therefore I remind you to stir up the gift
of God which is in you through the laying
on of my hands. 7 For God has not given us a
spirit of fear, but of power and of love and of
a sound mind.

Not Ashamed of the Gospel

8 Therefore do not be ashamed of the testimony of our Lord, nor of me His prisoner,

1:1 [a] NU-Text and M-Text read *Christ Jesus.*

EUNICE (pronounced *YOU-niss*) was Timothy's mother. Her family met the apostle Paul on one of his travels through the town of Lystra (pronounced *LISS-trah*) in Asia Minor.

At that time Eunice and her Greek husband were very proud of their young son Timothy. His mother and grandmother had been careful to teach him the Scriptures from the time he was a young boy.

When Paul preached in Lystra, Eunice's family accepted Jesus as their Lord and Savior. Timothy wanted to travel with Paul to other countries to help preach the gospel, so they all agreed that he should go with Paul and Luke, the doctor.

Eunice would always prize the two letters the beloved Paul wrote to her son. Timothy eventually became the pastor at Ephesus (pronounced *EFF-uh-sus*).

COURAGE

READ IT: 2 TIMOTHY 1:7

It's late at night, and you can't fall asleep. Thoughts are running through your head uncontrollably. You toss and turn, but there's no relief. This is a perfect time to remember this verse. Instead of counting sheep, *repeat it over and over, and trust* the authority in the verse that says, "For God has not given us a spirit of fear, but of power and of love and of a sound mind."

but share with me in the sufferings for the
gospel according to the power of God, [9]who
has saved us and called *us* with a holy calling, not according to our works, but according to His own purpose and grace which
was given to us in Christ Jesus before time
began, [10]but has now been revealed by the
appearing of our Savior Jesus Christ, *who*
has abolished death and brought life and
immortality to light through the gospel, [11]to
which I was appointed a preacher, an apostle, and a teacher of the Gentiles.[a] [12]For this
reason I also suffer these things; nevertheless I am not ashamed, for I know whom I
have believed and am persuaded that He is
able to keep what I have committed to Him
until that Day.

Be Loyal to the Faith

[13]Hold fast the pattern of sound words
which you have heard from me, in faith and
love which are in Christ Jesus. [14]That good
thing which was committed to you, keep by
the Holy Spirit who dwells in us.

[15]This you know, that all those in Asia
have turned away from me, among whom
are Phygellus and Hermogenes. [16]The Lord
grant mercy to the household of Onesiphorus, for he often refreshed me, and was not
ashamed of my chain; [17]but when he arrived
in Rome, he sought me out very zealously
and found *me*. [18]The Lord grant to him that

1:11 [a] NU-Text omits *of the Gentiles.*

FINDING YOUR PURPOSE IN LIFE
FITTING IN WITH THE CROWD

READ IT: 2 TIMOTHY 1:6–10

GET IT:

The fear of being rejected can be paralyzing. When an opportunity presents itself to share our faith through our words or actions, we might stop right before we dive in and think, *What if I mess this up? What if they make fun of me?*

Everyone wants to fit in. But the desire to fit in can really mess with us in the process of figuring out our purpose in life. In 2 Timothy, Paul reminds Timothy, a younger follower of Jesus, not to be afraid or ashamed of what may happen when he shares the story about Jesus. He reminds us we've been saved and called with a holy calling that has absolutely nothing to do with us and everything to do with Jesus. In fact, Paul says our calling was determined before time even began—God's been planning this for a while!

LIVE IT:

Sometimes people get made fun of for being religious. So we want to hide our faith in order to blend in with everyone else. As a Christian, you need to remember that God has called you to stand out, not to draw attention to yourself, but to draw attention to Jesus. Not everyone will understand, but that's okay. You never know who will need the little bit of hope you offer when you show Christ's love through your words and actions.

he may find mercy from the Lord in that
Day—and you know very well how many
ways he ministered *to me*[a] at Ephesus.

Be Strong in Grace

2 You therefore, my son, be strong in the
grace that is in Christ Jesus. 2And the
things that you have heard from me among
many witnesses, commit these to faithful
men who will be able to teach others also.
3You therefore must endure[a] hardship as
a good soldier of Jesus Christ. 4No one engaged in warfare entangles himself with the
affairs of *this* life, that he may please him
who enlisted him as a soldier. 5And also
if anyone competes in athletics, he is not
crowned unless he competes according to
the rules. 6The hardworking farmer must be
first to partake of the crops. 7Consider what I
say, and may[a] the Lord give you understanding in all things.

8Remember that Jesus Christ, of the seed
of David, was raised from the dead according
to my gospel, 9for which I suffer trouble as
an evildoer, *even* to the point of chains; but
the word of God is not chained. 10Therefore
I endure all things for the sake of the elect,
that they also may obtain the salvation which
is in Christ Jesus with eternal glory.

11 *This is* a faithful saying:

For if we died with *Him,*
We shall also live with *Him.*
12 If we endure,
We shall also reign with *Him.*
If we deny *Him,*
He also will deny us.
13 If we are faithless,
He remains faithful;
He cannot deny Himself.

Approved and Disapproved Workers

14Remind *them* of these things, charging
them before the Lord not to strive about
words to no profit, to the ruin of the hearers.
15Be diligent to present yourself approved
to God, a worker who does not need to be
ashamed, rightly dividing the word of truth.
16But shun profane *and* idle babblings, for
they will increase to more ungodliness.
17And their message will spread like cancer. Hymenaeus and Philetus are of this
sort, 18who have strayed concerning the
truth, saying that the resurrection is already
past; and they overthrow the faith of some.
19Nevertheless the solid foundation of God
stands, having this seal: "The Lord knows
those who are His," and, "Let everyone who
names the name of Christ[a] depart from
iniquity."

20But in a great house there are not only
vessels of gold and silver, but also of wood
and clay, some for honor and some for dishonor. 21Therefore if anyone cleanses himself from the latter, he will be a vessel for
honor, sanctified and useful for the Master,
prepared for every good work. 22Flee also
youthful lusts; but pursue righteousness,
faith, love, peace with those who call on the
Lord out of a pure heart. 23But avoid foolish
and ignorant disputes, knowing that they
generate strife. 24And a servant of the Lord
must not quarrel but be gentle to all, able to
teach, patient, 25in humility correcting those
who are in opposition, if God perhaps will
grant them repentance, so that they may
know the truth, 26and *that* they may come
to their senses *and escape* the snare of the
devil, having been taken captive by him to
do his will.

Perilous Times and Perilous Men

3 But know this, that in the last days perilous times will come: 2For men will
be lovers of themselves, lovers of money,
boasters, proud, blasphemers, disobedient to
parents, unthankful, unholy, 3unloving, unforgiving, slanderers, without self-control,
brutal, despisers of good, 4traitors, head-
strong, haughty, lovers of pleasure rather
than lovers of God, 5having a form of godliness but denying its power. And from such
people turn away! 6For of this sort are those
who creep into households and make captives of gullible women loaded down with
sins, led away by various lusts, 7always learning and never able to come to the knowledge
of the truth. 8Now as Jannes and Jambres
resisted Moses, so do these also resist the
truth: men of corrupt minds, disapproved
concerning the faith; 9but they will progress
no further, for their folly will be manifest to
all, as theirs also was.

The Man of God and the Word of God

10But you have carefully followed my

1:18 [a] *To me* is from the Vulgate and a few Greek manuscripts. 2:3 [a] NU-Text reads *You must share.* 2:7 [a] NU-Text reads *the Lord will give you.* 2:19 [a] NU-Text and M-Text read *the Lord.*

doctrine, manner of life, purpose, faith, longsuffering, love, perseverance, 11persecutions, afflictions, which happened to me at Antioch, at Iconium, at Lystra—what persecutions I endured. And out of *them* all the Lord delivered me. 12Yes, and all who desire to live godly in Christ Jesus will suffer persecution. 13But evil men and impostors will grow worse and worse, deceiving and being deceived. 14But you must continue in the things which you have learned and been assured of, knowing from whom you have learned *them,* 15and that from childhood you have known the Holy Scriptures, which are able to make you wise for salvation through faith which is in Christ Jesus.

16All Scripture *is* given by inspiration of God, and *is* profitable for doctrine, for reproof, for correction, for instruction in righteousness, 17that the man of God may be complete, thoroughly equipped for every good work.

Preach the Word

4 I charge *you* therefore before God and the Lord Jesus Christ, who will judge the living and the dead at[a] His appearing and His kingdom: 2Preach the word! Be ready in season *and* out of season. Convince, rebuke, exhort, with all longsuffering and teaching. 3For the time will come when they will not endure sound doctrine, but according to their own desires, *because* they have itching ears, they will heap up for themselves teachers; 4and they will turn *their* ears away from the truth, and be turned aside to fables. 5But you be watchful in all things, endure afflictions, do the work of an evangelist, fulfill your ministry.

Paul's Valedictory

6For I am already being poured out as a drink offering, and the time of my departure is at hand. 7I have fought the good fight, I have finished the race, I have kept the faith. 8Finally, there is laid up for me the crown of righteousness, which the Lord, the righteous Judge, will give to me on that Day, and not to me only but also to all who have loved His appearing.

The Abandoned Apostle

9Be diligent to come to me quickly; 10for Demas has forsaken me, having loved this present world, and has departed for Thessalonica—Crescens for Galatia, Titus for Dalmatia. 11Only Luke is with me. Get Mark and bring him with you, for he is useful to me for ministry. 12And Tychicus I have sent to Ephesus. 13Bring the cloak that I left with Carpus at Troas when you come—and the books, especially the parchments.

14Alexander the coppersmith did me much harm. May the Lord repay him according to his works. 15You also must beware of him, for he has greatly resisted our words.

4:1 [a] NU-Text omits *therefore* and reads *and by* for *at.*

PERSEVERANCE

READ IT: 2 TIMOTHY 3:10, 11

Paul is writing to Timothy in this passage. He's more than a mentor to Timothy at this point, and he addresses Timothy as if he were his own son. Paul is tired. He knows his own life—his own race—is close to ending. So he tells Timothy to keep working, keep trying, keep praying, and persevere. Paul believes he has paid his dues; for him perseverance is over. But he wants Timothy to experience the feeling that comes from a life of perseverance.

16At my first defense no one stood with
me, but all forsook me. May it not be charged
against them.

The Lord Is Faithful

17But the Lord stood with me and
strengthened me, so that the message might
be preached fully through me, and *that* all
the Gentiles might hear. Also I was delivered
out of the mouth of the lion. 18And the Lord
will deliver me from every evil work and preserve *me* for His heavenly kingdom. To Him
be glory forever and ever. Amen!

Come Before Winter

19Greet Prisca and Aquila, and the household of Onesiphorus. 20Erastus stayed in
Corinth, but Trophimus I have left in Miletus
sick.

21Do your utmost to come before winter.
Eubulus greets you, as well as Pudens,
Linus, Claudia, and all the brethren.

Farewell

22The Lord Jesus Christ[a] be with your
spirit. Grace be with you. Amen.

4:22 [a] NU-Text omits *Jesus Christ.*

Epic Ideas

THE BIBLE IS THE TRUTH
LISTEN UP!

READ IT: 2 TIMOTHY 3:16, 17

GET IT:

The Bible was written by real people over hundreds of years. It's an unbelievable collection of literature that's got everything you could possibly imagine. And behind all of those human writers was a single source of inspiration—God Himself. It says so right here in verse 16. God didn't actually write down the words. But He inspired them. He breathed them into the human writers. All of them. So you can trust, follow, and believe every word you read.

The Bible tells us about God—who He is and what He's done.

The Bible tells us about ourselves—where we've made mistakes and how we should live.

The Bible tells us the good news of salvation and then equips us for living a Christian life.

LIVE IT:

When you read the Bible, be on the lookout for instructions on how to live, an interesting story, an encouraging word, or a helpful how-to. They're all there (though not usually all in the same verse). You may not actually hear God's voice, but you can read words, ideas, and thoughts that He inspired. Carefully listen to (read) what He has to say.

The EPISTLE *of* PAUL *the* APOSTLE *to*

TITUS

A.D. 64

Behind the Scenes

READ IT:

The book of Titus is a letter Paul wrote to Titus, a minister on the island of Crete. The church in Crete was a bit unorganized, so Paul told Titus how to lead the church. The people needed a lot of instruction on how to be Christians, so Paul explained how God's people should behave.

GET IT:

Who wrote it: Paul

When it was written: A.D. 64

Why it was written: to instruct Titus on how to be a good leader and teacher in the church.

LIVE IT:

Because God gives us the gift of salvation, we live self-controlled lives and do the right thing.

FIND IT:

Instructions for Leaders in the Church *Titus 1–3*

Greeting

1 Paul, a bondservant of God and an apostle of Jesus Christ, according to the faith of God's elect and the acknowledgment of the truth which accords with godliness, 2in hope of eternal life which God, who cannot lie, promised before time began, 3but has in due time manifested His word through preaching, which was committed to me according to the commandment of God our Savior;

4To Titus, a true son in *our* common faith:

Grace, mercy, *and* peace from God the Father and the Lord Jesus Christ[a] our Savior.

Qualified Elders

5For this reason I left you in Crete, that you should set in order the things that are lacking, and appoint elders in every city as I commanded you— 6if a man is blameless, the husband of one wife, having faithful children not accused of dissipation or insubordination. 7For a bishop[a] must be blameless, as a steward of God, not self-willed, not quick-tempered, not given to wine, not violent, not greedy for money, 8but hospitable, a lover of what is good, sober-minded, just, holy, self-controlled, 9holding fast the faithful word as he has been taught, that he may be able, by sound doctrine, both to exhort and convict those who contradict.

The Elders' Task

10For there are many insubordinate, both idle talkers and deceivers, especially those of the circumcision, 11whose mouths must be stopped, who subvert whole households, teaching things which they ought not, for the sake of dishonest gain. 12One of them, a prophet of their own, said, "Cretans *are* always liars, evil beasts, lazy gluttons." 13This testimony is true. Therefore rebuke them sharply, that they may be sound in the faith, 14not giving heed to Jewish fables and commandments of men who turn from the truth. 15To the pure all things are pure, but to those who are defiled and unbelieving nothing is pure; but even their mind and conscience are defiled. 16They profess to know God, but in works they deny *Him,* being abominable, disobedient, and disqualified for every good work.

Qualities of a Sound Church

2 But as for you, speak the things which are proper for sound doctrine: 2that the older men be sober, reverent, temperate, sound in faith, in love, in patience; 3the older women likewise, that they be reverent in behavior, not slanderers, not given to much wine, teachers of good things— 4that they admonish the young women to love their husbands, to love their children, 5*to be*

1:4 [a] NU-Text reads *and Christ Jesus.* 1:7 [a] Literally *overseer*

Starring Roles

TITUS' name means "Pleasant" and is pronounced *TIGHT-us.* You don't read about him in the book of Acts, but the apostle Paul thought very highly of him and his ministry.

You first read about Titus in Galatians 2:1–3. He traveled with Paul and Barnabas to Jerusalem. There Paul showed the Jewish Christians that non-Jews don't have to obey the religious customs of the Jews.

When some members of the church at Corinth were in trouble, Paul sent Titus to help them. He solved the problems of quarreling and sinful living there, and Paul was very pleased.

The next big task came for Titus when Paul sent him to be pastor of some churches on the island of Crete. Later he went on a missionary journey to Dalmatia (pronounced *dal-MAY-she-ah*), part of the country we now call Croatia.

discreet, chaste, homemakers, good, obedient to their own husbands, that the word of God may not be blasphemed.
6Likewise, exhort the young men to
be sober-minded, 7in all things showing
yourself *to be* a pattern of good works; in doctrine *showing* integrity, reverence, incorruptibility,[a] 8sound speech that cannot be condemned, that one who is an opponent may be ashamed, having nothing evil to say of you.[a]
9*Exhort* bondservants to be obedient to
their own masters, to be well pleasing in all

2:7 [a] NU-Text omits *incorruptibility*. 2:8 [a] NU-Text and M-Text read *us*.

LISTEN TO GOOD TEACHERS

READ IT: TITUS 1:10, 11

As you live in the world, you will find out that some teachers have strange ideas. Jesus described these teachers as wolves in sheep's clothing (see Matthew 7:15). It's hard to explain why some people get these strange notions. For example, some teachers even deny that Jesus was really the Savior from heaven. They say He was just a good man who was also a good teacher. That sounds great to some people, but it's a lie! Satan, the great liar, puts such lies into people's minds.

The important thing is to know the Scriptures so well that you won't be tricked by the false teachers of the world. Jesus said His people would not follow strangers (see John 10:5). Be sure to attend a gospel-preaching, Bible-teaching church. There you will find teachers who will help you understand the Bible more and more every day.

COMMUNICATION

READ IT: TITUS 2:8

What's in your heart and mind will eventually come out in your words. When people hear what you have to say, your reputation is at stake, and so is the reputation of other Christians. If you speak only loving and positive words, you can have a big impact on others.

For a week, decide to speak only kind words. Make encouraging comments to your friends. Say "please" and "thank you" to strangers. Text your friends to tell them you're praying for them. Notice what happens when you keep a positive attitude at the front of your mind and use only helpful words.

things, not answering back, 10not pilfering, but
showing all good fidelity, that they may adorn
the doctrine of God our Savior in all things.

Trained by Saving Grace

11For the grace of God that brings salvation has appeared to all men, 12teaching
us that, denying ungodliness and worldly
lusts, we should live soberly, righteously,
and godly in the present age, 13looking for
the blessed hope and glorious appearing of
our great God and Savior Jesus Christ, 14who
gave Himself for us, that He might redeem
us from every lawless deed and purify for
Himself *His* own special people, zealous for
good works.

15Speak these things, exhort, and rebuke
with all authority. Let no one despise you.

Graces of the Heirs of Grace

3 Remind them to be subject to rulers
and authorities, to obey, to be ready for
every good work, 2to speak evil of no one, to
be peaceable, gentle, showing all humility
to all men. 3For we ourselves were also once
foolish, disobedient, deceived, serving various lusts and pleasures, living in malice and
envy, hateful and hating one another. 4But
when the kindness and the love of God our
Savior toward man appeared, 5not by works
of righteousness which we have done, but according to His mercy He saved us, through
the washing of regeneration and renewing of
the Holy Spirit, 6whom He poured out on us
abundantly through Jesus Christ our Savior,
7that having been justified by His grace we
should become heirs according to the hope
of eternal life.

8This is a faithful saying, and these
things I want you to affirm constantly, that
those who have believed in God should be
careful to maintain good works. These
things are good and profitable to men.

Avoid Dissension

9But avoid foolish disputes, genealogies,
contentions, and strivings about the law; for
they are unprofitable and useless. 10Reject a
divisive man after the first and second admonition, 11knowing that such a person is
warped and sinning, being self-condemned.

Final Messages

12When I send Artemas to you, or Tychicus, be diligent to come to me at Nicopolis,
for I have decided to spend the winter there.
13Send Zenas the lawyer and Apollos on their
journey with haste, that they may lack nothing. 14And let our *people* also learn to maintain good works, to *meet* urgent needs, that
they may not be unfruitful.

Farewell

15All who *are* with me greet you. Greet
those who love us in the faith.

Grace *be* with you all. Amen.

GOD'S JUSTICE

READ IT: TITUS 3:14

Earthquakes. Tornadoes. Fires. Floods. Death. Sickness. Loss. Sometimes someone needs help immediately. Are you ready to respond? When disasters strike or something urgent happens, we may feel like we can't contribute much. But through God, we can. In these times we can completely rely on His power to help us meet needs around us.

Next time someone needs something right away, ask how you can help. Maybe you can help raise money, contribute food or water, or help someone clean up after a tragedy. Maybe you can pray. There's always a way you can help. Ask God and an adult what's the best way.

The EPISTLE *of* PAUL *the* APOSTLE *to*

PHILEMON

A.D. 60

Behind the Scenes

READ IT:

This very short book is Paul's letter to his friend Philemon in Ephesus. Paul gave this letter to Onesimus, a former slave who had become a Christian. Onesimus was on his way back to his master, Philemon. Paul begged Philemon to forgive Onesimus and to treat him as a brother in Christ instead of a runaway slave.

GET IT:

Who wrote it: Paul

When it was written: A.D. 60

Why it was written: to encourage Philemon to accept his former slave as an equal brother in Christ.

LIVE IT:

We must forgive one another.

FIND IT:

Paul's Appeal to Philemon — *Philemon 4–22*

Greeting

Paul, a prisoner of Christ Jesus, and Timothy *our* brother,

To Philemon our beloved *friend* and fellow laborer, 2to the beloved[a] Apphia, Archip-
pus our fellow soldier, and to the church in
your house:

3Grace to you and peace from God our
Father and the Lord Jesus Christ.

Philemon's Love and Faith

4I thank my God, making mention of you
always in my prayers, 5hearing of your love
and faith which you have toward the Lord
Jesus and toward all the saints, 6that the
sharing of your faith may become effective
by the acknowledgment of every good thing
which is in you[a] in Christ Jesus. 7For we
have[a] great joy[b] and consolation in your love,
because the hearts of the saints have been
refreshed by you, brother.

---

2 [a] NU-Text reads *to our sister Apphia.* 6 [a] NU-Text and M-Text read *us.* 7 [a] NU-Text reads *had.* [b] M-Text reads *thanksgiving.*

Starring Roles

ONESIMUS is pronounced *oh-NESS-ih-muss* and means "Useful." Onesimus was probably the happiest slave in the whole world!

Paul the apostle would occasionally visit Onesimus' master, Philemon (pronounced *fih-LEE-mun*). Philemon loved to hear Paul preach, and Onesimus came to think of him as his own father. So Onesimus later ran away from his master and went to live in Rome where Paul was then a prisoner.

Paul was glad to see Onesimus, and they had good times together. Paul was allowed to live at his own house at that time. There Paul led Onesimus to become a Christian.

But Paul began to realize they were not treating Onesimus' master, Philemon, right by letting Onesimus stay in Rome. They both agreed, then, that Onesimus should go back to Philemon in Colosse (pronounced *ko-LAH-see*), so Paul sent him back to Philemon with this letter about Onesimus. After that, Philemon and Onesimus were true brothers in Christ.

Action!

FORGIVENESS

READ IT: PHILEMON 8–16

Just as Christ carried our sins for us, Paul is asking Philemon to forgive Onesimus. It's as if Paul is saying, "Blame me, not him." Would you do that for someone you love? It's often the ones we love the most who hurt us the most. The next time you're faced with forgiving someone you love, be quick to let him or her off the hook. Someday the shoe might be on the other foot.

The Plea for Onesimus

[8]Therefore, though I might be very bold
in Christ to command you what is fitting,
[9]*yet* for love's sake I rather appeal *to you*—
being such a one as Paul, the aged, and now
also a prisoner of Jesus Christ— [10]I appeal
to you for my son Onesimus, whom I have
begotten *while* in my chains, [11]who once was
unprofitable to you, but now is profitable to
you and to me.

[12]I am sending him back.[a] You therefore
receive him, that is, my own heart, [13]whom
I wished to keep with me, that on your behalf he might minister to me in my chains
for the gospel. [14]But without your consent I
wanted to do nothing, that your good deed
might not be by compulsion, as it were, but
voluntary.

[15]For perhaps he departed for a while for
this *purpose,* that you might receive him forever, [16]no longer as a slave but more than a
slave—a beloved brother, especially to me
but how much more to you, both in the flesh
and in the Lord.

Philemon's Obedience Encouraged

[17]If then you count me as a partner, receive him as *you would* me. [18]But if he has
wronged you or owes anything, put that on
my account. [19]I, Paul, am writing with my
own hand. I will repay—not to mention to
you that you owe me even your own self besides. [20]Yes, brother, let me have joy from
you in the Lord; refresh my heart in the Lord.

[21]Having confidence in your obedience, I
write to you, knowing that you will do even
more than I say. [22]But, meanwhile, also prepare a guest room for me, for I trust that
through your prayers I shall be granted to you.

Farewell

[23]Epaphras, my fellow prisoner in Christ
Jesus, greets you, [24]*as do* Mark, Aristarchus,
Demas, Luke, my fellow laborers.

[25]The grace of our Lord Jesus Christ *be*
with your spirit. Amen.

---

12 [a] NU-Text reads *back to you in person, that is, my own heart.*

BE A SOUL WINNER

READ IT: PHILEMON 10

What is a soul winner? A soul winner is someone who wins people to trust in Jesus. Soul winning calls for three main personal traits: (1) love; (2) gentleness; and (3) wisdom.

Paul had all these personal traits. When the slave Onesimus (pronounced *oh-NESS-ih-muss*) came to him, Paul wasn't angry because the young man had run away. Paul loved Onesimus. Also, Paul was gentle to Onesimus, and led him to know Jesus as Savior and Lord. Then both Paul and Onesimus agreed that Onesimus should go back home and face his master, Philemon (pronounced *fih-LEE-mun*).

After that, Paul and Philemon were probably better friends than ever. Some scholars say Onesimus later became pastor of the church at Ephesus (pronounced *EFF-uh-sus*) in Asia Minor. So you can see that winning just one soul was a great benefit to many people.

Philemon is one of the most beautiful books in the New Testament. Paul wrote it from prison, and it shows how much he loved a slave.

The EPISTLE to the

HEBREWS

BEFORE A.D. 64

Behind the Scenes

READ IT:

The book of Hebrews is a letter written to the Jewish Christians in either Palestine or Rome. These Christians were ready to give up their faith in Jesus and return to the Jewish faith because they were being persecuted. The writer of this letter encouraged the Christians to stay strong in their faith. He presented very good reasons for why Christian faith is better than Old Testament law. The book also includes a great summary of the heroes whose stories are included in the Old Testament.

GET IT:

Who wrote it: No one knows for sure.

When it was written: sometime before A.D. 64

Why it was written: to explain that Christ is superior to angels and that Jesus and faith in Him are greater than the people or laws of the Old Testament.

LIVE IT:

People of the Old Testament lived in faith, hoping for God's promise to come true. We know God kept His promise and sent Jesus as the Messiah. This knowledge will help us to keep on believing in Jesus.

FIND IT:

Christ Is Greater than Angels	*Hebrews 1–2*
Christ Is Greater than Moses and Joshua	*Hebrews 3–4*
Christ as the Great High Priest	*Hebrews 7–8*
The Greatness of Christ's Sacrifice	*Hebrews 9–10*
The Heroes of the Faith	*Hebrews 11*
God's Discipline	*Hebrews 12*

God's Supreme Revelation

1 God, who at various times and in various ways spoke in time past to the
fathers by the prophets, 2has in these last
days spoken to us by *His* Son, whom He has
appointed heir of all things, through whom
also He made the worlds; 3who being the
brightness of *His* glory and the express image of His person, and upholding all things
by the word of His power, when He had by
Himself[a] purged our[b] sins, sat down at the
right hand of the Majesty on high, 4having
become so much better than the angels, as
He has by inheritance obtained a more excellent name than they.

The Son Exalted Above Angels

5For to which of the angels did He ever
say:

"You are My Son,
Today I have begotten You"?[a]

And again:

"I will be to Him a Father,
And He shall be to Me a Son"?[b]

6But when He again brings the firstborn
into the world, He says:

1:3 [a] NU-Text omits *by Himself.* [b] NU-Text omits *our.*
1:5 [a] Psalm 2:7 [b] 2 Samuel 7:14

JESUS IS THE WAY
LIAR, LUNATIC, OR LORD?

READ IT: HEBREWS 1:1–4

GET IT:

Most people today believe that Jesus was a real person. But lots of people stop there: they believe He was a real person who lived and died and said some good things about how we should live.

But this passage in Hebrews says Jesus was much more than that. It says that God created the world through Jesus. It says that when we see Jesus, we see God, because they're one and the same. That tells us that a big part of why God sent Jesus to earth to live as a human was so we could know God.

The passage also tells us that Jesus is the One (and only one) who saves us from our sin. And it says that Jesus is alive today, sitting next to God.

LIVE IT:

Sometimes people say that if you read what Jesus says about Himself, you can only conclude that He was either a liar, a lunatic, or the Lord. This passage implies something similar about the whole Bible.

Unless you cut this passage (and a whole bunch of other passages) out of your Bible, you can only conclude that the Bible is either lying about Jesus, or it's full of inaccurate crazy-talk, or it tells the truth about Jesus being God and our only Savior. Which do you believe?

"Let all the angels of God worship Him." [a]

7And of the angels He says:

"Who makes His angels spirits
And His ministers a flame of fire." [a]

8But to the Son *He says:*

"Your throne, O God, *is* forever and ever;
A scepter of righteousness *is* the scepter
of Your kingdom.
9 You have loved righteousness and hated
lawlessness;
Therefore God, Your God, has anointed
You
With the oil of gladness more than Your
companions." [a]

10And:

"You, LORD, in the beginning laid the
foundation of the earth,
And the heavens are the work of Your
hands.
11 They will perish, but You remain;
And they will all grow old like a
garment;
12 Like a cloak You will fold them up,
And they will be changed.
But You are the same,
And Your years will not fail." [a]

13But to which of the angels has He ever said:

"Sit at My right hand,
Till I make Your enemies Your
footstool"?[a]

14Are they not all ministering spirits sent forth to minister for those who will inherit salvation?

Do Not Neglect Salvation

2 Therefore we must give the more earnest heed to the things we have heard,
lest we drift away. 2For if the word spoken
through angels proved steadfast, and every
transgression and disobedience received a
just reward, 3how shall we escape if we neglect so great a salvation, which at the first
began to be spoken by the Lord, and was confirmed to us by those who heard *Him,* 4God
also bearing witness both with signs and
wonders, with various miracles, and gifts of
the Holy Spirit, according to His own will?

The Son Made Lower than Angels

5For He has not put the world to come, of
which we speak, in subjection to angels. 6But
one testified in a certain place, saying:

"What is man that You are mindful of
him,
Or the son of man that You take care of
him?
7 You have made him a little lower than
the angels;
You have crowned him with glory and
honor,[a]
And set him over the works of Your
hands.
8 You have put all things in subjection
under his feet." [a]

For in that He put all in subjection under him, He left nothing *that is* not put under

---

1:6 [a] Deuteronomy 32:43 (Septuagint, Dead Sea Scrolls); Psalm 97:7 1:7 [a] Psalm 104:4 1:9 [a] Psalm 45:6, 7 1:12 [a] Psalm 102:25–27 1:13 [a] Psalm 110:1 2:7 [a] NU-Text and M-Text omit the rest of verse 7. 2:8 [a] Psalm 8:4–6

ANGELS

READ IT: HEBREWS 1:14

This verse sounds like an embrace. Sometimes things seem so bad we just want to be hugged. We want the safe feeling of someone's arms around us. We ache to be held. Angels are the beings God sends to say, "Shhhh. It's okay now."

him. But now we do not yet see all things
put under him. [9]But we see Jesus, who was
made a little lower than the angels, for the
suffering of death crowned with glory and
honor, that He, by the grace of God, might
taste death for everyone.

Bringing Many Sons to Glory

[10]For it was fitting for Him, for whom
are all things and by whom *are* all things,
in bringing many sons to glory, to make the
captain of their salvation perfect through
sufferings. [11]For both He who sanctifies and
those who are being sanctified *are* all of one,
for which reason He is not ashamed to call
them brethren, [12]saying:

> "I will declare Your name to My
> brethren;
> In the midst of the assembly I will sing
> praise to You." [a]

[13]And again:

> "I will put My trust in Him." [a]

And again:

> "Here am I and the children whom God
> has given Me." [b]

[14]Inasmuch then as the children have
partaken of flesh and blood, He Himself
likewise shared in the same, that through
death He might destroy him who had the
power of death, that is, the devil, [15]and release those who through fear of death were
all their lifetime subject to bondage. [16]For
indeed He does not give aid to angels, but
He does give aid to the seed of Abraham.
[17]Therefore, in all things He had to be made
like *His* brethren, that He might be a merciful and faithful High Priest in things *pertaining* to God, to make propitiation for the
sins of the people. [18]For in that He Himself
has suffered, being tempted, He is able to
aid those who are tempted.

The Son Was Faithful

3 Therefore, holy brethren, partakers
of the heavenly calling, consider the
Apostle and High Priest of our confession,
Christ Jesus, [2]who was faithful to Him who
appointed Him, as Moses also *was faithful*
in all His house. [3]For this One has been

2:12 [a] Psalm 22:22 **2:13** [a] 2 Samuel 22:3; Isaiah 8:17
[b] Isaiah 8:18

THE AUTHOR OF YOUR SALVATION

READ IT: HEBREWS 2:10

You know that "salvation" means that your sins are forgiven, and you belong to God because Jesus died in your place. So salvation is a work that somebody did *for* you because you couldn't do it for yourself.

Imagine that you fall out of a boat into a lake, and you can't swim. You're splashing and floundering in the water, and you're going down for *the last time. Just then* a lifeguard puts his arm under you and pulls you to shore. You've been saved! That's a real kind of salvation.

So the lifeguard is not only your savior from drowning. He is also the *author* of your salvation. He trained a long time for the day when he would have to jump into the water to save you.

Jesus also is the Author of your salvation. You couldn't save yourself. But Jesus carried out His ancient plan to rescue you from your sins.

counted worthy of more glory than Moses, inasmuch as He who built the house
has more honor than the house. 4For every
house is built by someone, but He who built
all things *is* God. 5And Moses indeed *was*
faithful in all His house as a servant, for a
testimony of those things which would be
spoken *afterward,* 6but Christ as a Son over
His own house, whose house we are if we
hold fast the confidence and the rejoicing of
the hope firm to the end.[a]

Be Faithful

7Therefore, as the Holy Spirit says:

"Today, if you will hear His voice,
8 Do not harden your hearts as in the rebellion,
In the day of trial in the wilderness,
9 Where your fathers tested Me, tried Me,
And saw My works forty years.
10 Therefore I was angry with that generation,
And said, 'They always go astray in *their* heart,
And they have not known My ways.'
11 So I swore in My wrath,
'They shall not enter My rest.' "[a]

3:6 [a] NU-Text omits *firm to the end.* 3:11 [a] Psalm 95:7–11

Epic Ideas

THE BIBLE IS THE TRUTH
LET THE BIBLE READ YOU

READ IT: HEBREWS 4:12, 13

GET IT:

We all read books, right? (At least, that's what we're supposed to do.) Same thing with the Bible. We read the Bible (or we should). It's a book, after all. What else could you do with it?

Well, how about letting the Bible read you? The Bible is a very powerful book because it's the Word and truth of God. If you have an open mind, an open heart, and a listening ear when you read the Bible, you'll start to discover that the Bible is reading you, too. It reads you by showing you your real thoughts, by uncovering your real attitudes and intentions, and by exposing your inner motives. Sometimes it can be pretty painful because some of our thoughts, attitudes, intentions, and motives are, well, ugly. That's why the writer of Hebrews says the Bible is sharper than a two-edged sword. It cuts right through all of your masks and excuses and posing to expose the real you.

LIVE IT:

Each time you read your Bible, ask God to make you a good reader of His Word and a good listener. Allow yourself to be read by the Bible. Let God's Word show you what you need to know about yourself—what's really going on in your mind and your heart. Then you can give those thoughts to God and let Him start making you into the person He wants you to be. It might hurt at first, pierce through you even, but the end result will be worth it.

12 Beware, brethren, lest there be in any
of you an evil heart of unbelief in departing
from the living God; 13 but exhort one another daily, while it is called "Today," lest any of
you be hardened through the deceitfulness
of sin. 14 For we have become partakers of
Christ if we hold the beginning of our confidence steadfast to the end, 15 while it is said:

"Today, if you will hear His voice,
Do not harden your hearts as in the
rebellion." [a]

Failure of the Wilderness Wanderers

16 For who, having heard, rebelled? Indeed, *was it* not all who came out of Egypt,
led by Moses? 17 Now with whom was He angry forty years? *Was it* not with those who
sinned, whose corpses fell in the wilderness? 18 And to whom did He swear that they
would not enter His rest, but to those who
did not obey? 19 So we see that they could not
enter in because of unbelief.

The Promise of Rest

4 Therefore, since a promise remains of
entering His rest, let us fear lest any
of you seem to have come short of it. 2 For
indeed the gospel was preached to us as well
as to them; but the word which they heard
did not profit them,[a] not being mixed with
faith in those who heard *it*. 3 For we who have
believed do enter that rest, as He has said:

"So I swore in My wrath,
'They shall not enter My rest,' " [a]

although the works were finished from the
foundation of the world. 4 For He has spoken
in a certain place of the seventh *day* in this
way: "And God rested on the seventh day
from all His works";[a] 5 and again in this
place: "They shall not enter My rest." [a]

6 Since therefore it remains that some
must enter it, and those to whom it was first
preached did not enter because of disobedience, 7 again He designates a certain day,
saying in David, "Today," after such a long
time, as it has been said:

"Today, if you will hear His voice,
Do not harden your hearts." [a]

8 For if Joshua had given them rest, then
He would not afterward have spoken of another day. 9 There remains therefore a rest for
the people of God. 10 For he who has entered
His rest has himself also ceased from his
works as God *did* from His.

The Word Discovers Our Condition

11 Let us therefore be diligent to enter
that rest, lest anyone fall according to the
same example of disobedience. 12 For the
word of God *is* living and powerful, and
sharper than any two-edged sword, piercing
even to the division of soul and spirit, and
of joints and marrow, and is a discerner of
the thoughts and intents of the heart. 13 And
there is no creature hidden from His sight,

3:15 [a] Psalm 95:7, 8 4:2 [a] NU-Text and M-Text read *profit them, since they were not united by faith with those who heeded it.* 4:3 [a] Psalm 95:11 4:4 [a] Genesis 2:2 4:5 [a] Psalm 95:11 4:7 [a] Psalm 95:7, 8

CONFIDENCE

READ IT: HEBREWS 4:14–16

As Christians we have a direct connection with God through Jesus. When Jesus became a human being, He faced the same kinds of temptations that we face. Because of that, we know that God can sympathize with us. He knows what it's like to live in a broken and sinful world. Since God has mercy on us, we can have confidence that we may approach Him boldly. He knows what we need. We just need to ask.

but all things *are* naked and open to the eyes
of Him to whom we *must give* account.

Our Compassionate High Priest

14Seeing then that we have a great High
Priest who has passed through the heavens,
Jesus the Son of God, let us hold fast *our* confession. 15For we do not have a High Priest
who cannot sympathize with our weakness-
es, but was in all *points* tempted as *we are, yet*
without sin. 16Let us therefore come boldly
to the throne of grace, that we may obtain
mercy and find grace to help in time of need.

Qualifications for High Priesthood

5 For every high priest taken from
among men is appointed for men in
things *pertaining* to God, that he may offer
both gifts and sacrifices for sins. 2He can
have compassion on those who are ignorant
and going astray, since he himself is also
subject to weakness. 3Because of this he is
required as for the people, so also for himself, to offer *sacrifices* for sins. 4And no man
takes this honor to himself, but he who is
called by God, just as Aaron *was.*

A Priest Forever

5So also Christ did not glorify Himself to
become High Priest, but *it was* He who said
to Him:

"You are My Son,
Today I have begotten You." [a]

6As *He* also says in another *place:*

"You *are* a priest forever
According to the order of
Melchizedek" ;[a]

7who, in the days of His flesh, when He
had offered up prayers and supplications,
with vehement cries and tears to Him who
was able to save Him from death, and was
heard because of His godly fear, 8though He
was a Son, *yet* He learned obedience by the
things which He suffered. 9And having been
perfected, He became the author of eternal
salvation to all who obey Him, 10called by
God as High Priest "according to the order
of Melchizedek," 11of whom we have much
to say, and hard to explain, since you have
become dull of hearing.

Spiritual Immaturity

12For though by this time you ought to
be teachers, you need *someone* to teach you
again the first principles of the oracles of
God; and you have come to need milk and
not solid food. 13For everyone who partakes
only of milk *is* unskilled in the word of righteousness, for he is a babe. 14But solid food
belongs to those who are of full age, *that is,*
those who by reason of use have their senses
exercised to discern both good and evil.

The Peril of Not Progressing

6 Therefore, leaving the discussion of
the elementary *principles* of Christ, let
us go on to perfection, not laying again the

5:5 [a] Psalm 2:7 5:6 [a] Psalm 110:4

Action!

LEARNING

READ IT: HEBREWS 5:8

Our painful experiences are often the best learning opportunities. It's not that you should wish for painful experiences, of course. But even Jesus learned from His painful experiences.

Jesus learned to obey! His pain taught Him to obey the Father. What have you learned from the things in your life that have been painful? And how can those lessons help you obey God more fully?

foundation of repentance from dead works
and of faith toward God, 2of the doctrine of
baptisms, of laying on of hands, of resurrection of the dead, and of eternal judgment.
3And this we will[a] do if God permits.

4For *it is* impossible for those who were
once enlightened, and have tasted the heavenly gift, and have become partakers of the
Holy Spirit, 5and have tasted the good word
of God and the powers of the age to come, 6if
they fall away,[a] to renew them again to repentance, since they crucify again for themselves the Son of God, and put *Him* to an
open shame.

7For the earth which drinks in the rain
that often comes upon it, and bears herbs
useful for those by whom it is cultivated,
receives blessing from God; 8but if it bears
thorns and briers, *it is* rejected and near to
being cursed, whose end *is* to be burned.

A Better Estimate

9But, beloved, we are confident of better
things concerning you, yes, things that ac-
company salvation, though we speak in this
manner. 10For God *is* not unjust to forget
your work and labor of[a] love which you have
shown toward His name, *in that* you have
ministered to the saints, and do minister.
11And we desire that each one of you show
the same diligence to the full assurance of
hope until the end, 12that you do not become
sluggish, but imitate those who through
faith and patience inherit the promises.

God's Infallible Purpose in Christ

13For when God made a promise to
Abraham, because He could swear by no
one greater, He swore by Himself, 14saying,
"Surely blessing I will bless you, and multiplying I will multiply you." [a] 15And so, after he had patiently endured, he obtained
the promise. 16For men indeed swear by the
greater, and an oath for confirmation *is* for
them an end of all dispute. 17Thus God, determining to show more abundantly to the
heirs of promise the immutability of His
counsel, confirmed *it* by an oath, 18that by
two immutable things, in which it *is* impossible for God to lie, we might[a] have strong

6:18 Immutable Pronounced *im-MYOOT-uh-bull*. Unchanging. God does not change in His character, His truth, or His promises.

6:3 [a] M-Text reads *let us do.* 6:6 [a] Or *and have fallen away*
6:10 [a] NU-Text omits *labor of.* 6:14 [a] Genesis 22:17
6:18 [a] M-Text omits *might.*

MATURITY

READ IT: HEBREWS 6:1

It's very important to know the basics about who God is and what it means to follow Jesus. But it's just as important to move beyond the basics, the elementary principles, toward mature living. No one wants to stay in kindergarten his or her whole life. Or learn the alphabet but never learn how to read. Or learn numbers but never learn how to add. There is so much more to experience and learn and enjoy about God and life than just the basics. But that requires growing and maturing and moving forward.

consolation, who have fled for refuge to lay
hold of the hope set before *us.*
19This *hope* we have as an anchor of the
soul, both sure and steadfast, and which enters the *Presence* behind the veil, 20where the
forerunner has entered for us, *even* Jesus,
having become High Priest forever according to the order of Melchizedek.

The King of Righteousness

7 For this Melchizedek, king of Salem,
priest of the Most High God, who met
Abraham returning from the slaughter of
the kings and blessed him, 2to whom also
Abraham gave a tenth part of all, first being
translated "king of righteousness," and then
also king of Salem, meaning "king of peace,"
3without father, without mother, without genealogy, having neither beginning of days
nor end of life, but made like the Son of God,
remains a priest continually.
4Now consider how great this man *was,*
to whom even the patriarch Abraham gave
a tenth of the spoils. 5And indeed those who
are of the sons of Levi, who receive the priesthood, have a commandment to receive tithes
from the people according to the law, that is,
from their brethren, though they have come
from the loins of Abraham; 6but he whose
genealogy is not derived from them received
tithes from Abraham and blessed him who
had the promises. 7Now beyond all contra-
diction the lesser is blessed by the better.
8Here mortal men receive tithes, but there
he *receives them,* of whom it is witnessed that
he lives. 9Even Levi, who receives tithes, paid
tithes through Abraham, so to speak, 10for
he was still in the loins of his father when
Melchizedek met him.

Need for a New Priesthood

11Therefore, if perfection were through
the Levitical priesthood (for under it the people received the law), what further need *was*
there that another priest should rise according to the order of Melchizedek, and not be
called according to the order of Aaron? 12For
the priesthood being changed, of necessity
there is also a change of the law. 13For He
of whom these things are spoken belongs to
another tribe, from which no man has offi-
ciated at the altar.
14For *it is* evident that our Lord arose
from Judah, of which tribe Moses spoke
nothing concerning priesthood.[a] 15And it
is yet far more evident if, in the likeness of
Melchizedek, there arises another priest
16who has come, not according to the law of a
fleshly commandment, but according to the
power of an endless life. 17For He testifies:[a]

"You *are* a priest forever
According to the order of
Melchizedek."[b]

18For on the one hand there is an annul-
ling of the former commandment because
of its weakness and unprofitableness, 19for
the law made nothing perfect; on the other hand, *there is the* bringing in of a better
hope, through which we draw near to God.

Greatness of the New Priest

20And inasmuch as *He was* not *made*
priest without an oath 21(for they have become priests without an oath, but He with
an oath by Him who said to Him:

"The LORD has sworn
And will not relent,
'You *are* a priest forever[a]
According to the order of
Melchizedek' "),[b]

22by so much more Jesus has become a surety of a better covenant.
23Also there were many priests, because
they were prevented by death from continuing. 24But He, because He continues forever,
has an unchangeable priesthood. 25There-
fore He is also able to save to the uttermost
those who come to God through Him, since
He always lives to make intercession for
them.
26For such a High Priest was fitting for
us, *who is* holy, harmless, undefiled, separate from sinners, and has become higher
than the heavens; 27who does not need daily,
as those high priests, to offer up sacrifices,
first for His own sins and then for the people's, for this He did once for all when He
offered up Himself. 28For the law appoints
as high priests men who have weakness, but
the word of the oath, which came after the
law, *appoints* the Son who has been perfected
forever.

The New Priestly Service

8 Now *this is* the main point of the things
we are saying: We have such a High

7:14 [a] NU-Text reads *priests.* 7:17 [a] NU-Text reads *it is testified.* [b] Psalm 110:4 7:21 [a] NU-Text ends the quotation here. [b] Psalm 110:4

Priest, who is seated at the right hand of the
throne of the Majesty in the heavens, 2a Minister of the sanctuary and of the true tabernacle which the Lord erected, and not man.
3For every high priest is appointed to
offer both gifts and sacrifices. Therefore *it*
is necessary that this One also have something to offer. 4For if He were on earth, He
would not be a priest, since there are priests
who offer the gifts according to the law; 5who
serve the copy and shadow of the heavenly
things, as Moses was divinely instructed
when he was about to make the tabernacle.
For He said, "See *that* you make all things
according to the pattern shown you on the
mountain." [a] 6But now He has obtained a
more excellent ministry, inasmuch as He
is also Mediator of a better covenant, which
was established on better promises.

A New Covenant

7For if that first *covenant* had been faultless, then no place would have been sought
for a second. 8Because finding fault with
them, He says: "Behold, the days are coming, says the LORD, when I will make a new
covenant with the house of Israel and with
the house of Judah— 9not according to the
covenant that I made with their fathers in
the day when I took them by the hand to lead
them out of the land of Egypt; because they
did not continue in My covenant, and I disre-
garded them, says the LORD. 10For this *is* the
covenant that I will make with the house of
Israel after those days, says the LORD: I will
put My laws in their mind and write them
on their hearts; and I will be their God, and
they shall be My people. 11None of them shall
teach his neighbor, and none his brother,
saying, 'Know the LORD,' for all shall know
Me, from the least of them to the greatest
of them. 12For I will be merciful to their unrighteousness, and their sins and their lawless deeds [a] I will remember no more." [b]
13In that He says, "A new *covenant*," He
has made the first obsolete. Now what is becoming obsolete and growing old is ready to
vanish away.

The Earthly Sanctuary

9 Then indeed, even the first *covenant*
had ordinances of divine service and
the earthly sanctuary. 2For a tabernacle was
prepared: the first *part*, in which *was* the
lampstand, the table, and the showbread,

In Focus

9:4 Ark of the Covenant A gold-covered wooden chest about 45 inches long by 27 inches wide by 27 inches high. The chest first contained the Ten Commandments, but later also contained some manna and Aaron's wooden staff.

which is called the sanctuary; 3and behind
the second veil, the part of the tabernacle
which is called the Holiest of All, 4which had
the golden censer and the ark of the covenant
overlaid on all sides with gold, in which *were*
the golden pot that had the manna, Aaron's
rod that budded, and the tablets of the
covenant; 5and above it were the cherubim
of glory overshadowing the mercy seat. Of
these things we cannot now speak in detail.

Limitations of the Earthly Service

6Now when these things had been thus
prepared, the priests always went into the
first part of the tabernacle, performing the
services. 7But into the second part the high
priest *went* alone once a year, not without
blood, which he offered for himself and *for*
the people's sins *committed* in ignorance;
8the Holy Spirit indicating this, that the
way into the Holiest of All was not yet made
manifest while the first tabernacle was still
standing. 9It *was* symbolic for the present
time in which both gifts and sacrifices are
offered which cannot make him who performed the service perfect in regard to the
conscience— 10*concerned* only with foods
and drinks, various washings, and fleshly ordinances imposed until the time of
reformation.

The Heavenly Sanctuary

11But Christ came *as* High Priest of the
good things to come,[a] with the greater and
more perfect tabernacle not made with
hands, that is, not of this creation. 12Not
with the blood of goats and calves, but with

8:5 [a] Exodus 25:40 **8:12** [a] NU-Text omits *and their lawless deeds.* [b] Jeremiah 31:31–34 **9:11** [a] NU-Text reads *that have come.*

His own blood He entered the Most Holy Place once for all, having obtained eternal redemption. [13]For if the blood of bulls and goats and the ashes of a heifer, sprinkling the unclean, sanctifies for the purifying of the flesh, [14]how much more shall the blood of Christ, who through the eternal Spirit offered Himself without spot to God, cleanse your conscience from dead works to serve the living God? [15]And for this reason He is the Mediator of the new covenant, by means of death, for the redemption of the transgressions under the first covenant, that those who are called may receive the promise of the eternal inheritance.

The Mediator's Death Necessary

[16]For where there *is* a testament, there must also of necessity be the death of the testator. [17]For a testament *is* in force after men are dead, since it has no power at all while the testator lives. [18]Therefore not even the first *covenant* was dedicated without blood. [19]For when Moses had spoken every precept to all the people according to the law, he took the blood of calves and goats, with water, scarlet wool, and hyssop, and sprinkled both the book itself and all the people, [20]saying, "This *is* the blood of the covenant which God has commanded you."[a] [21]Then likewise he sprinkled with blood both the tabernacle and all the vessels of the ministry. [22]And according to the law almost all things are purified with blood, and without shedding of blood there is no remission.

Greatness of Christ's Sacrifice

[23]Therefore *it was* necessary that the copies of the things in the heavens should be purified with these, but the heavenly things themselves with better sacrifices than these. [24]For Christ has not entered the holy places made with hands, *which are* copies of the true, but into heaven itself, now to appear in the presence of God for us; [25]not that He should offer Himself often, as the high priest enters the Most Holy Place every year with blood of another— [26]He then would have had to suffer often since the foundation of the world; but now, once at the end of the ages, He has appeared to put away sin by the sacrifice of Himself. [27]And as it is appointed for men to die once, but after this the judgment, [28]so Christ was offered once to bear the sins of many. To those who eagerly wait for Him He will appear a second time, apart from sin, for salvation.

Animal Sacrifices Insufficient

10 For the law, having a shadow of the good things to come, *and* not the very image of the things, can never with these same sacrifices, which they offer continually year by year, make those who approach perfect. [2]For then would they not have ceased to be offered? For the worshipers, once purified, would have had no more consciousness of sins. [3]But in those *sacrifices*

9:20 [a] Exodus 24:8

COMMUNITY

READ IT: HEBREWS 10:19–25

Following the death and resurrection of Jesus, the old temple laws were destroyed, and He became the new law. Because of this, the disciples began meeting together weekly for worship and Bible study in the temple. That's like the church services we participate in today.

Our community of believers often comes through the church, but be open to community found at school, on sports teams or clubs, and or in your neighborhood!

there is a reminder of sins every year. 4For *it is*
not possible that the blood of bulls and goats
could take away sins.

Christ's Death Fulfills God's Will

5Therefore, when He came into the
world, He said:

"Sacrifice and offering You did not
desire,
But a body You have prepared for Me.
6 In burnt offerings and *sacrifices* for sin
You had no pleasure.
7 Then I said, 'Behold, I have come—
In the volume of the book it is written
of Me—
To do Your will, O God.' "[a]

8Previously saying, "Sacrifice and offering,
burnt offerings, and *offerings* for sin You did
not desire, nor had pleasure *in them*" (which
are offered according to the law), 9then He
said, "Behold, I have come to do Your will, O
God."[a] He takes away the first that He may
establish the second. 10By that will we have
been sanctified through the offering of the
body of Jesus Christ once *for all.*

Christ's Death Perfects the Sanctified

11And every priest stands ministering
daily and offering repeatedly the same sacrifices, which can never take away sins. 12But
this Man, after He had offered one sacrifice
for sins forever, sat down at the right hand
of God, 13from that time waiting till His enemies are made His footstool. 14For by one
offering He has perfected forever those who
are being sanctified.

15But the Holy Spirit also witnesses to us;
for after He had said before,

16"This *is* the covenant that I will make
with them after those days, says the LORD:
I will put My laws into their hearts, and in
their minds I will write them,"[a] 17*then He
adds,* "Their sins and their lawless deeds
I will remember no more."[a] 18Now where
there is remission of these, *there is* no longer
an offering for sin.

Hold Fast Your Confession

19Therefore, brethren, having boldness to
enter the Holiest by the blood of Jesus, 20by
a new and living way which He consecrated
for us, through the veil, that is, His flesh,
21and *having* a High Priest over the house
of God, 22let us draw near with a true heart
in full assurance of faith, having our hearts
sprinkled from an evil conscience and our
bodies washed with pure water. 23Let us
hold fast the confession of *our* hope without
wavering, for He who promised *is* faithful.
24And let us consider one another in order to
stir up love and good works, 25not forsaking
the assembling of ourselves together, as *is*
the manner of some, but exhorting *one another,* and so much the more as you see the
Day approaching.

The Just Live by Faith

26For if we sin willfully after we have
received the knowledge of the truth, there
no longer remains a sacrifice for sins, 27but

10:7 [a] Psalm 40:6–8 **10:9** [a] NU-Text and M-Text omit *O God.* **10:16** [a] Jeremiah 31:33 **10:17** [a] Jeremiah 31:34

GUILT

READ IT: HEBREWS 10:22, 23

When we sin, we feel guilty. But once we confess our sins to God, we shouldn't feel ashamed anymore. Because of Jesus, our sins have been washed away. We are made clean and new! God promises He is faithful to forgive our sins and see us as white as snow.

a certain fearful expectation of judgment,
and fiery indignation which will devour
the adversaries. 28 Anyone who has rejected
Moses' law dies without mercy on *the testimony of* two or three witnesses. 29 Of how
much worse punishment, do you suppose,
will he be thought worthy who has trampled
the Son of God underfoot, counted the blood
of the covenant by which he was sanctified
a common thing, and insulted the Spirit of
grace? 30 For we know Him who said, "Vengeance is Mine, I will repay,"[a] says the Lord.[b]
And again, "The LORD will judge His people."[c] 31 It is a fearful thing to fall into the
hands of the living God.

32 But recall the former days in which,
after you were illuminated, you endured a
great struggle with sufferings: 33 partly while
you were made a spectacle both by reproaches and tribulations, and partly while you
became companions of those who were so
treated; 34 for you had compassion on me[a] in
my chains, and joyfully accepted the plundering of your goods, knowing that you
have a better and an enduring possession
for yourselves in heaven.[b] 35 Therefore do not

10:30 [a] Deuteronomy 32:35 [b] NU-Text omits *says the Lord.* [c] Deuteronomy 32:36 10:34 [a] NU-Text reads *the prisoners* instead of *me in my chains.* [b] NU-Text omits *in heaven.*

IDENTITY
EMBRACING CONFIDENCE

READ IT: HEBREWS 10:35

GET IT:

The author of Hebrews wants us to understand that in Christ we have gifts that should change how we see ourselves and how we live. We have salvation, we have faith, we have hope, and if we aren't boldly embracing these gifts and the confidence—the security—they can give us, we're missing out. This confidence can get us through hard times because we can go to the Creator of the universe with our problems. It can help us stay faithful to God because we know eternity with Him is waiting. And this confidence can hold us together as the church, simply because we share it.

LIVE IT:

Would your last shopping trip have gone smoother if you'd had a personal shopper, a no-limit credit card, and a guarantee that everything would fit? Who would turn down a cool experience like that?

But that's kind of what we do when we don't embrace the confidence Christ offers us. We can take the kind of risks that lead to amazing opportunities because we have faith. We're never alone because we have the Lord at our side. We can forgive others because we've been forgiven. Through salvation we have the emotional freedom that is as foreign to others as that dream shopping trip might be to you. You have the confidence and security deep in your heart that all the talent, money, and power in the world can't buy. You have something to celebrate.

cast away your confidence, which has great
reward. 36For you have need of endurance, so
that after you have done the will of God, you
may receive the promise:

37 "For yet a little while,
And He[a] who is coming will come and
will not tarry.
38 Now the[a] just shall live by faith;
But if *anyone* draws back,
My soul has no pleasure in him."[b]

39But we are not of those who draw back to
perdition, but of those who believe to the saving of the soul.

By Faith We Understand

11 Now faith is the substance of things
hoped for, the evidence of things not
seen. 2For by it the elders obtained a *good*
testimony.
3By faith we understand that the worlds
were framed by the word of God, so that
the things which are seen were not made of
things which are visible.

Faith at the Dawn of History

4By faith Abel offered to God a more excellent sacrifice than Cain, through which he obtained witness that he was righteous, God testifying of his gifts; and through it he being dead still speaks.
5By faith Enoch was taken away so that
he did not see death, "and was not found,
because God had taken him";[a] for before
he was taken he had this testimony, that
he pleased God. 6But without faith *it is* impossible to please *Him*, for he who comes to
God must believe that He is, and *that* He is a
rewarder of those who diligently seek Him.
7By faith Noah, being divinely warned of
things not yet seen, moved with godly fear,
prepared an ark for the saving of his household, by which he condemned the world and
became heir of the righteousness which is
according to faith.

10:37 [a] Or *that which* 10:38 [a] NU-Text reads *My just one.* [b] Habakkuk 2:3, 4 11:5 [a] Genesis 5:24

GREAT HEROES OF THE FAITH

READ IT: HEBREWS 11:1–40

GET IT:

This letter was written to the Jews who had joined the Christian church. The Jews were very proud of their history, so the writer of this letter spent time talking to them about how faith worked for their people long before Jesus came to earth. All of the people mentioned here have their stories told somewhere in the Old Testament. They are important characters in God's story of His love for His people. You might want to go back and read some of their stories again to see how these people trusted God.

LIVE IT:

This chapter summarizes the stories of some of the great people in the Old Testament. Do you know a Christian whom you would call a hero of the faith? What has he or she done that you admire and have learned from? What has this person done that helped you better understand what faith in Jesus Christ really means? Perhaps you should tell the person that you admire him or her. Ask this hero to share his or her story of faith with you.

Faithful Abraham

8By faith Abraham obeyed when he was
called to go out to the place which he would
receive as an inheritance. And he went out,
not knowing where he was going. 9By faith
he dwelt in the land of promise as *in* a foreign country, dwelling in tents with Isaac
and Jacob, the heirs with him of the same
promise; 10for he waited for the city which
has foundations, whose builder and maker
is God.

11By faith Sarah herself also received
strength to conceive seed, and she bore a
child[a] when she was past the age, because
she judged Him faithful who had promised.
12Therefore from one man, and him as good
as dead, were born *as many* as the stars of the
sky in multitude—innumerable as the sand
which is by the seashore.

The Heavenly Hope

13These all died in faith, not having received the promises, but having seen them
afar off were assured of them,[a] embraced
them and confessed that they were strangers
and pilgrims on the earth. 14For those who
say such things declare plainly that they
seek a homeland. 15And truly if they had
called to mind that *country* from which they
had come out, they would have had opportunity to return. 16But now they desire a better,
that is, a heavenly *country*. Therefore God is
not ashamed to be called their God, for He
has prepared a city for them.

The Faith of the Patriarchs

17By faith Abraham, when he was tested,
offered up Isaac, and he who had received
the promises offered up his only begotten
son, 18of whom it was said, "In Isaac your
seed shall be called,"[a] 19concluding that God
was able to raise *him* up, even from the dead,
from which he also received him in a figurative sense.

20By faith Isaac blessed Jacob and Esau
concerning things to come.

21By faith Jacob, when he was dying,
blessed each of the sons of Joseph, and worshiped, *leaning* on the top of his staff.

22By faith Joseph, when he was dying,
made mention of the departure of the children of Israel, and gave instructions concerning his bones.

The Faith of Moses

23By faith Moses, when he was born, was
hidden three months by his parents, because
they saw *he was* a beautiful child; and they
were not afraid of the king's command.

24By faith Moses, when he became of age,
refused to be called the son of Pharaoh's
daughter, 25choosing rather to suffer affliction with the people of God than to enjoy the
passing pleasures of sin, 26esteeming the reproach of Christ greater riches than the treasures in[a] Egypt; for he looked to the reward.

11:11 [a] NU-Text omits *she bore a child.* **11:13** [a] NU-Text and M-Text omit *were assured of them.* **11:18** [a] Genesis 21:12 **11:26** [a] NU-Text and M-Text read *of.*

MAKING YOUR FAITH YOUR OWN

READ IT: HEBREWS 11:1–40

This chapter is like a Hall of Fame for people who lived lives of faith. They did incredible things—not by their own power or strength, but through faith in God. They did different things—each of their stories is *unique*. Living a life of faith doesn't mean doing what someone else is doing. It means doing what God calls you to do, with His help and strength. How will your life finish the sentence "By faith . . ."?

27By faith he forsook Egypt, not fearing
the wrath of the king; for he endured as seeing Him who is invisible. 28By faith he kept
the Passover and the sprinkling of blood, lest
he who destroyed the firstborn should touch
them.

29By faith they passed through the Red
Sea as by dry *land, whereas* the Egyptians,
attempting to do so, were drowned.

By Faith They Overcame

30By faith the walls of Jericho fell down
after they were encircled for seven days. 31By
faith the harlot Rahab did not perish with
those who did not believe, when she had received the spies with peace.

32And what more shall I say? For the
time would fail me to tell of Gideon and
Barak and Samson and Jephthah, also *of*
David and Samuel and the prophets: 33who
through faith subdued kingdoms, worked
righteousness, obtained promises, stopped
the mouths of lions, 34quenched the violence
of fire, escaped the edge of the sword, out of
weakness were made strong, became valiant
in battle, turned to flight the armies of the
aliens. 35Women received their dead raised
to life again.

Others were tortured, not accepting deliverance, that they might obtain a better
resurrection. 36Still others had trial of mock-
ings and scourgings, yes, and of chains and
imprisonment. 37They were stoned, they
were sawn in two, were tempted,[a] were
slain with the sword. They wandered about
in sheepskins and goatskins, being destitute, afflicted, tormented— 38of whom the
world was not worthy. They wandered in
deserts and mountains, *in* dens and caves of
the earth.

39And all these, having obtained a good
testimony through faith, did not receive the
promise, 40God having provided something
better for us, that they should not be made
perfect apart from us.

The Race of Faith

12 Therefore we also, since we are surrounded by so great a cloud of witnesses, let us lay aside every weight, and the
sin which so easily ensnares *us,* and let us
run with endurance the race that is set before us, 2looking unto Jesus, the author and
finisher of *our* faith, who for the joy that was

11:37 [a] NU-Text omits *were tempted.*

RUN THE RACE OF FAITH

READ IT: HEBREWS 12:1, 2

Sometimes we describe faith in Jesus as resting in Jesus. This means that the world around you can't frighten you because you trust Jesus for everything. In a way, that's resting.

But faith in Jesus is also like running a race. This means trusting Jesus in a way that makes sure you reach the goal of life that Jesus sets for you. The goal of life is to reach heaven and to be given the prize of doing the work Jesus gives you to do on earth.

The first thing you must do in training to run is to be sure tobacco, alcohol, or drugs don't make you short of breath. Those things also make you unable to run our race for Jesus in the world.

The next thing you think about is getting rid of any extra weight. There are many good things a Christian can enjoy in the world. But even the weight of too many good things leaves no time for serving Jesus.

set before Him endured the cross, despising
the shame, and has sat down at the right
hand of the throne of God.

The Discipline of God

3For consider Him who endured such
hostility from sinners against Himself, lest
you become weary and discouraged in your
souls. 4You have not yet resisted to bloodshed, striving against sin. 5And you have
forgotten the exhortation which speaks to
you as to sons:

“My son, do not despise the chastening
of the LORD,
Nor be discouraged when you are
rebuked by Him;
6 For whom the LORD loves He chastens,
And scourges every son whom He
receives.”[a]

7If[a] you endure chastening, God deals
with you as with sons; for what son is there
whom a father does not chasten? 8But if you
are without chastening, of which all have
become partakers, then you are illegitimate
and not sons. 9Furthermore, we have had human fathers who corrected *us,* and we paid
them respect. Shall we not much more readily be in subjection to the Father of spirits and
live? 10For they indeed for a few days chastened *us* as seemed *best* to them, but He for
our profit, that *we* may be partakers of His
holiness. 11Now no chastening seems to be
joyful for the present, but painful; nevertheless, afterward it yields the peaceable fruit
of righteousness to those who have been
trained by it.

Renew Your Spiritual Vitality

12Therefore strengthen the hands which
hang down, and the feeble knees, 13and make
straight paths for your feet, so that what is lame
may not be dislocated, but rather be healed.

14Pursue peace with all *people,* and holiness, without which no one will see the Lord:
15looking carefully lest anyone fall short of
the grace of God; lest any root of bitterness
springing up cause trouble, and by this
many become defiled; 16lest there *be* any fornicator or profane person like Esau, who for
one morsel of food sold his birthright. 17For
you know that afterward, when he wanted
to inherit the blessing, he was rejected, for
he found no place for repentance, though he
sought it diligently with tears.

The Glorious Company

18For you have not come to the mountain
that[a] may be touched and that burned with
fire, and to blackness and darkness[b] and
tempest, 19and the sound of a trumpet and
the voice of words, so that those who heard *it*

12:6 [a] Proverbs 3:11, 12 12:7 [a] NU-Text and M-Text read *It is for discipline that you endure; God* . . . . 12:18 [a] NU-Text reads *to that which.* [b] NU-Text reads *gloom.*

DISCIPLINE

READ IT: HEBREWS 12:5–7, 9–11

We spend a great deal of time asking, “Why are you doing this to me?” or “Why are you so mean?” If we’re honest, these are common questions in prayer as well. At the time, no discipline is fun. For example, being grounded isn’t as much fun as hanging out with your friends. Having extra chores as a result of getting in trouble isn’t something anyone would ask for. But if a dad smacks the hand of a two-year-old who’s about to put a paper clip in an electrical socket, it doesn’t mean the dad hates his child. When God disciplines you, it’s because He loves you.

Are you willing to accept God’s discipline?

begged that the word should not be spoken
to them anymore. 20(For they could not endure what was commanded: "And if so much
as a beast touches the mountain, it shall be
stoned[a] or shot with an arrow." [b] 21And so terrifying was the sight *that* Moses said, "I am
exceedingly afraid and trembling."[a])

22But you have come to Mount Zion and
to the city of the living God, the heavenly Jerusalem, to an innumerable company of angels, 23to the general assembly and church of
the firstborn *who are* registered in heaven, to
God the Judge of all, to the spirits of just men
made perfect, 24to Jesus the Mediator of the
new covenant, and to the blood of sprinkling
that speaks better things than *that of* Abel.

Hear the Heavenly Voice

25See that you do not refuse Him who
speaks. For if they did not escape who refused Him who spoke on earth, much more
shall we not escape if we turn away from Him
who *speaks* from heaven, 26whose voice then
shook the earth; but now He has promised,
saying, "Yet once more I shake [a] not only the
earth, but also heaven." [b] 27Now this, "Yet
once more," indicates the removal of those
things that are being shaken, as of things
that are made, that the things which cannot
be shaken may remain.

28Therefore, since we are receiving a
kingdom which cannot be shaken, let us
have grace, by which we may[a] serve God ac-
ceptably with reverence and godly fear. 29For
our God *is* a consuming fire.

Concluding Moral Directions

13 Let brotherly love continue. 2Do
not forget to entertain strangers,
for by so *doing* some have unwittingly entertained angels. 3Remember the prisoners
as if chained with them—those who are
mistreated—since you yourselves are in the
body also.

4Marriage *is* honorable among all, and
the bed undefiled; but fornicators and adulterers God will judge.

5*Let your* conduct *be* without covetousness; *be* content with such things as you
have. For He Himself has said, "I will never leave you nor forsake you." [a] 6So we may
boldly say:

"The LORD *is* my helper;
I will not fear.
What can man do to me?" [a]

Concluding Religious Directions

7Remember those who rule over you, who
have spoken the word of God to you, whose
faith follow, considering the outcome of *their*
conduct. 8Jesus Christ *is* the same yesterday,
today, and forever. 9Do not be carried about[a]
with various and strange doctrines. For *it is*
good that the heart be established by grace,

12:20 [a] NU-Text and M-Text omit the rest of this verse. [b] Exodus 19:12, 13 **12:21** [a] Deuteronomy 9:19 **12:26** [a] NU-Text reads *will shake.* [b] Haggai 2:6 **12:28** [a] M-Text omits *may.* **13:5** [a] Deuteronomy 31:6, 8; Joshua 1:5 **13:6** [a] Psalm 118:6 **13:9** [a] NU-Text and M-Text read *away.*

WORSHIP

READ IT: HEBREWS 12:28

What's something you're afraid of? Spiders? Snakes? Bullies? Embarrassment? Those are the things we normally think of when we hear the word *fear.* But when the Bible talks about fearing God, it's not suggesting we be *afraid* of God. Fear, in this sense, means that we know that God is all-powerful, and that we are not! To fear God is an act of worship.

not with foods which have not profited those
who have been occupied with them.
[10]We have an altar from which those
who serve the tabernacle have no right to
eat. [11]For the bodies of those animals, whose
blood is brought into the sanctuary by the
high priest for sin, are burned outside the
camp. [12]Therefore Jesus also, that He might
sanctify the people with His own blood, suffered outside the gate. [13]Therefore let us go
forth to Him, outside the camp, bearing His
reproach. [14]For here we have no continuing
city, but we seek the one to come. [15]Therefore
by Him let us continually offer the sacrifice
of praise to God, that is, the fruit of *our* lips,
giving thanks to His name. [16]But do not forget to do good and to share, for with such
sacrifices God is well pleased.
[17]Obey those who rule over you, and
be submissive, for they watch out for your
souls, as those who must give account. Let
them do so with joy and not with grief, for
that would be unprofitable for you.

Prayer Requested

[18]Pray for us; for we are confident that we
have a good conscience, in all things desiring to live honorably. [19]But I especially urge
you to do this, that I may be restored to you
the sooner.

Benediction, Final Exhortation, Farewell

[20]Now may the God of peace who brought
up our Lord Jesus from the dead, that great
Shepherd of the sheep, through the blood
of the everlasting covenant, [21]make you
complete in every good work to do His will,
working in you[a] what is well pleasing in His
sight, through Jesus Christ, to whom *be* glory forever and ever. Amen.
[22]And I appeal to you, brethren, bear with
the word of exhortation, for I have written
to you in few words. [23]Know that *our* brother Timothy has been set free, with whom I
shall see you if he comes shortly.
[24]Greet all those who rule over you, and
all the saints. Those from Italy greet you.
[25]Grace *be* with you all. Amen.

13:21 [a] NU-Text and M-Text read *us*.

JESUS NEVER LEAVES YOU

READ IT: HEBREWS 13:5

Have you ever been alone? Do you remember what it was like not to know when your parents would come home? It was frightening not to have someone near.

It's nice and comforting to have friends and those who love you, but what if they were all taken away? Would you be alone then?

Jesus has given you perhaps the greatest promise in the Bible—"I will never leave you." If Jesus is always with you, then you really need no one else.

Do you know Jesus as your forever Friend from heaven? You can. All you have to do is ask Him. Right now, say, "Lord Jesus, come into my life and be my Savior from sin and my Friend forever." He'll do it. As you talk to Him every day, you'll find He is a Friend who never leaves you.

The EPISTLE of

JAMES

A.D. 44–A.D. 46

Behind the Scenes

READ IT:

The book of James is a letter to the early Christian church. James, a leader in the Jerusalem church and a brother of Jesus, wrote this letter to teach Christians how to live what they believed. He insisted that if we have real faith, we will show it by acting like Christians. He gave practical advice on things like anger, quarreling, choosing favorites, talking, boasting, patience, and prayer.

GET IT:

Who wrote it: James, the brother of Jesus

When it was written: A.D. 44–A.D. 46

Why it was written: to encourage the early Christians and teach them how to put their Christian faith into action.

LIVE IT:

We should be like Jesus in what we say, blog, tweet, and put on Facebook.

It's wrong to say you're a Christian but act like you're not.

FIND IT:

Loving God Under Trials	*James 1*
Faith Without Works Is Dead	*James 2*
Controlling the Tongue	*James 3*
Fighting Pride and Materialism	*James 4*
Be Patient and Persevere	*James 5*

Greeting to the Twelve Tribes

1 James, a bondservant of God and of the Lord Jesus Christ,

To the twelve tribes which are scattered abroad:

Greetings.

Profiting from Trials

2My brethren, count it all joy when you fall into various trials, 3knowing that the testing of your faith produces patience. 4But let patience have *its* perfect work, that you may be perfect and complete, lacking nothing. 5If any of you lacks wisdom, let him ask of God, who gives to all liberally and without reproach, and it will be given to him. 6But let him ask in faith, with no doubting, for he who doubts is like a wave of the sea driven and tossed by the wind. 7For let not that man suppose that he will receive anything from the Lord; 8*he is* a double-minded man, unstable in all his ways.

The Perspective of Rich and Poor

9Let the lowly brother glory in his exaltation, 10but the rich in his humiliation, because as a flower of the field he will pass away. 11For no sooner has the sun risen with a burning heat than it withers the grass; its flower falls, and its beautiful appearance perishes. So the rich man also will fade away in his pursuits.

Loving God Under Trials

12Blessed *is* the man who endures temptation; for when he has been approved, he will receive the crown of life which the Lord has promised to those who love Him. 13Let no one say when he is tempted, "I am tempted by God"; for God cannot be tempted by evil, nor does He Himself tempt anyone. 14But each one is tempted when he is drawn away by his own desires and enticed. 15Then, when desire has conceived, it gives birth to sin; and sin, when it is full-grown, brings forth death.

16Do not be deceived, my beloved brethren. 17Every good gift and every perfect gift is from above, and comes down from the Father of lights, with whom there is no variation or shadow of turning. 18Of His own will He brought us forth by the word of truth, that we might be a kind of firstfruits of His creatures.

Qualities Needed in Trials

19So then,[a] my beloved brethren, let every man be swift to hear, slow to speak, slow to wrath; 20for the wrath of man does not produce the righteousness of God.

Doers—Not Hearers Only

21Therefore lay aside all filthiness and

1:19 [a] NU-Text reads *Know this* or *This you know.*

Starring Roles

You first meet JAMES in Matthew 13:55 and also in Mark 6:3. He was James, the oldest of Jesus' younger brothers. His mother Mary was also the mother of Jesus, but Jesus' Father was God.

At first James and his brothers didn't believe in Jesus as the Son of God. Later, after Jesus rose from death, James believed in Him as his Savior and Lord. After that, the apostles of Jesus gave James the task of being leader of the Christians in Jerusalem.

You meet James again in Acts 15. Paul and his friends went to Jerusalem to show the Jews why non-Jewish Christians did not need to keep the Jewish religious customs. So they understood that those special customs couldn't help to take away sin.

Jesus, the oldest Brother of James, paid the whole cost of your salvation by His death on the Cross.

overflow of wickedness, and receive with
meekness the implanted word, which is able
to save your souls.
22 But be doers of the word, and not hearers only, deceiving yourselves. 23 For if anyone is a hearer of the word and not a doer, he
is like a man observing his natural face in a
mirror; 24 for he observes himself, goes away,
and immediately forgets what kind of man
he was. 25 But he who looks into the perfect
law of liberty and continues *in it,* and is not a
forgetful hearer but a doer of the work, this
one will be blessed in what he does.
26 If anyone among you[a] thinks he is religious, and does not bridle his tongue but
deceives his own heart, this one's religion *is*
useless. 27 Pure and undefiled religion before
God and the Father is this: to visit orphans
and widows in their trouble, *and* to keep oneself unspotted from the world.

Beware of Personal Favoritism

2 My brethren, do not hold the faith of
our Lord Jesus Christ, *the Lord* of glory, with partiality. 2 For if there should come
into your assembly a man with gold rings,
in fine apparel, and there should also come
in a poor man in filthy clothes, 3 and you pay
attention to the one wearing the fine clothes
and say to him, "You sit here in a good

1:26 [a] NU-Text omits *among you.*

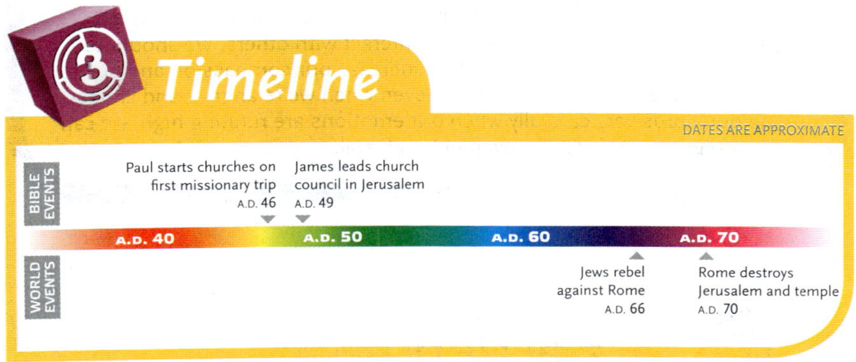

DOUBT AND ASKING QUESTIONS

READ IT: JAMES 1:5–8

Being willing to really search for answers to your doubts is very different from having a wishy-washy faith. When you come to God and ask for His wisdom to answer your questions, He will honor your search. God is generous, and He wants you to understand Him more! But if you're halfhearted about it and don't really believe God will help you, Scripture says you will feel unsettled and unbalanced. If you find yourself in this place, tossed around on the sea of doubt, make the decision to come to God with faith and expectation. He will answer you!

place," and say to the poor man, "You stand
there," or, "Sit here at my footstool," 4have
you not shown partiality among yourselves,
and become judges with evil thoughts?
5Listen, my beloved brethren: Has God
not chosen the poor of this world *to be* rich
in faith and heirs of the kingdom which
He promised to those who love Him? 6But
you have dishonored the poor man. Do not
the rich oppress you and drag you into the

ANGER

READ IT: JAMES 1:19, 20

If life's frustrations don't make you angry sometimes, you may not have a pulse. But anger can take root and crowd out love—the thing we Christians should be known for. That's why James asks us to be smart gardeners of our emotions when we interact with others. We should be watering and feeding behaviors that increase our compassion and our ability to forgive. By listening well—even when we're angry—and choosing our words very carefully when our emotions are running high, we can grow mercy and kindness, even in tough soil.

HEARING IS NOT ENOUGH

READ IT: JAMES 1:22

Too many times we may hear someone talking, but we aren't listening to what that person is saying. Do you sometimes hear your teacher say, "Now pay attention, class"? That's because the teacher can see you're not really listening. The same thing happens when you go to church. You hear the teacher or the pastor talking on and on—but you aren't paying attention.

There's another way of hearing but not listening. That's when you listen to everything someone says, and then go away and forget about it. That's like the story Jesus told in Matthew 13. Some of the farmer's seeds fell on hard ground. They didn't take root, and the birds ate up the seeds. In the same way, sometimes you hear or read God's words, but you don't think about what God says. You don't let His words take root and become *part of your life*. Then you become a hearer, but you're not a doer. That kind of hearing is useless. God is looking for people who will do what He commands.

courts? 7Do they not blaspheme that noble
name by which you are called?

8If you really fulfill *the* royal law according to the Scripture, "You shall love your
neighbor as yourself,"[a] you do well; 9but if
you show partiality, you commit sin, and are
convicted by the law as transgressors. 10For
whoever shall keep the whole law, and yet
stumble in one *point,* he is guilty of all. 11For
He who said, "Do not commit adultery,"[a]
also said, "Do not murder."[b] Now if you do
not commit adultery, but you do murder, you
have become a transgressor of the law. 12So
speak and so do as those who will be judged
by the law of liberty. 13For judgment is without mercy to the one who has shown no mercy. Mercy triumphs over judgment.

Faith Without Works Is Dead

14What *does it* profit, my brethren, if
someone says he has faith but does not have
works? Can faith save him? 15If a brother or
sister is naked and destitute of daily food,
16and one of you says to them, "Depart in
peace, be warmed and filled," but you do not
give them the things which are needed for
the body, what *does it* profit? 17Thus also faith
by itself, if it does not have works, is dead.

18But someone will say, "You have faith,
and I have works." Show me your faith without your[a] works, and I will show you my
faith by my[b] works. 19You believe that there
is one God. You do well. Even the demons
believe—and tremble! 20But do you want
to know, O foolish man, that faith without
works is dead?[a] 21Was not Abraham our father justified by works when he offered Isaac
his son on the altar? 22Do you see that faith
was working together with his works, and
by works faith was made perfect? 23And the
Scripture was fulfilled which says, "Abraham believed God, and it was accounted to
him for righteousness."[a] And he was called
the friend of God. 24You see then that a man
is justified by works, and not by faith only.

25Likewise, was not Rahab the harlot also
justified by works when she received the
messengers and sent *them* out another way?

26For as the body without the spirit is
dead, so faith without works is dead also.

The Untamable Tongue

3 My brethren, let not many of you become teachers, knowing that we shall
receive a stricter judgment. 2For we all stumble in many things. If anyone does not stumble in word, he *is* a perfect man, able also
to bridle the whole body. 3Indeed,[a] we put
bits in horses' mouths that they may obey
us, and we turn their whole body. 4Look also
at ships: although they are so large and are
driven by fierce winds, they are turned by a
very small rudder wherever the pilot desires.

2:8 [a] Leviticus 19:18 2:11 [a] Exodus 20:14; Deuteronomy 5:18 [b] Exodus 20:13; Deuteronomy 5:17 2:18 [a] NU-Text omits *your.* [b] NU-Text omits *my.* 2:20 [a] NU-Text reads *useless.* 2:23 [a] Genesis 15:6 3:3 [a] NU-Text reads *Now if.*

MAKING YOUR FAITH YOUR OWN

READ IT: JAMES 2:18–26

People who really believe in God with genuine faith will show it in the way they live. They will live a loving life. They will obey God. They will care about other people. They will honor God in what they say and do. Living that kind of life doesn't earn God's love or make someone a Christian. Instead, that kind of life is a response to God's love and His gift of salvation and new life.

5 Even so the tongue is a little member and
boasts great things.
See how great a forest a little fire kindles!
6 And the tongue *is* a fire, a world of iniquity.
The tongue is so set among our members that
it defiles the whole body, and sets on fire the
course of nature; and it is set on fire by hell.
7 For every kind of beast and bird, of reptile
and creature of the sea, is tamed and has been
tamed by mankind. 8 But no man can tame the
tongue. *It is* an unruly evil, full of deadly poison. 9 With it we bless our God and Father, and
with it we curse men, who have been made in
the similitude of God. 10 Out of the same mouth
proceed blessing and cursing. My brethren,
these things ought not to be so. 11 Does a spring
send forth fresh *water* and bitter from the same
opening? 12 Can a fig tree, my brethren, bear

COMMUNICATION

READ IT: JAMES 3:1–12

Have you ever tried to train a dog? It takes time and patience. It's just as hard to train our words. James describes it well: the same mouth speaks both blessings and curses. Our speech is a powerful thing. It has the power to bring life or bring darkness depending on how we use it. Ask God to show you how you can bring life to the conversations you have today.

YOUR TONGUE CAN START A FIRE

READ IT: JAMES 3:5

You've probably never thought about that. Fires are started with matches, not tongues! Just the same, God says the tongue starts its own kind of fire.

When you say mean things about someone, you're starting a fire. Just like a fire, your ugly story can travel all around. Pretty soon no one is speaking to the one you hurt with the fiery words of your tongue.

Some people have lost their jobs, and others have taken their own lives, all because of mean stories someone told about them.

A story doesn't have to be a lie to hurt someone. You may hear something true that can do a lot of harm. Make up your mind not to tell anyone else. And ask the person who told you to stop talking about it. Stop the fire from spreading.

olives, or a grapevine bear figs? Thus no spring
yields both salt water and fresh.[a]

Heavenly Versus Demonic Wisdom

13 Who *is* wise and understanding among
you? Let him show by good conduct *that* his
works *are done* in the meekness of wisdom.
14 But if you have bitter envy and self-seeking
in your hearts, do not boast and lie against
the truth. 15 This wisdom does not descend
from above, but *is* earthly, sensual, demonic.
16 For where envy and self-seeking *exist,* confusion and every evil thing *are* there. 17 But
the wisdom that is from above is first pure,
then peaceable, gentle, willing to yield, full
of mercy and good fruits, without partiality and without hypocrisy. 18 Now the fruit of
righteousness is sown in peace by those who
make peace.

Pride Promotes Strife

4 Where do wars and fights *come* from
among you? Do *they* not *come* from
your *desires for* pleasure that war in your
members? 2 You lust and do not have. You
murder and covet and cannot obtain. You
fight and war. Yet[a] you do not have because
you do not ask. 3 You ask and do not receive,
because you ask amiss, that you may spend
it on your pleasures. 4 Adulterers and[a] adulteresses! Do you not know that friendship
with the world is enmity with God? Whoever therefore wants to be a friend of the world
makes himself an enemy of God. 5 Or do you
think that the Scripture says in vain, "The
Spirit who dwells in us yearns jealously"?
6 But He gives more grace. Therefore He
says:

"God resists the proud,
But gives grace to the humble." [a]

Humility Cures Worldliness

7 Therefore submit to God. Resist the
devil and he will flee from you. 8 Draw
near to God and He will draw near to you.
Cleanse *your* hands, *you* sinners; and purify *your* hearts, *you* double-minded. 9 Lament
and mourn and weep! Let your laughter be
turned to mourning and *your* joy to gloom.
10 Humble yourselves in the sight of the Lord,
and He will lift you up.

3:12 [a] NU-Text reads *Neither can a salty spring produce fresh water.* 4:2 [a] NU-Text and M-Text omit *Yet.* 4:4 [a] NU-Text omits *Adulterers and.* 4:6 [a] Proverbs 3:34

SUBMIT TO GOD, RESIST THE DEVIL

READ IT: JAMES 4:7

It's a mistake to think you can ever really be your own boss. Right now you have to obey your parents or your teachers. Someday you might like to be free so you can do what you want to do in the world. But that day will never really come. Even grown-ups have to obey someone else where they work.

You can choose who your great Master is going to be. And you will be very wise if you decide right now that God is going to run your life. When you decide to do that, then you won't be all upset because you have to obey certain people, too.

Making God your Master will also mean that the devil can have his way with you as long as God isn't in your life. But when you put Jesus first, the devil can't lead you into trouble.

Do Not Judge a Brother

11Do not speak evil of one another, brethren. He who speaks evil of a brother and
judges his brother, speaks evil of the law and
judges the law. But if you judge the law, you
are not a doer of the law but a judge. 12There
is one Lawgiver,[a] who is able to save and to
destroy. Who[b] are you to judge another?[c]

Do Not Boast About Tomorrow

13Come now, you who say, "Today or tomorrow we will[a] go to such and such a city,
spend a year there, buy and sell, and make a
profit"; 14whereas you do not know what *will
happen* tomorrow. For what *is* your life? It
is even a vapor that appears for a little time
and then vanishes away. 15Instead you *ought*
to say, "If the Lord wills, we shall live and
do this or that." 16But now you boast in your
arrogance. All such boasting is evil.

17Therefore, to him who knows to do
good and does not do *it,* to him it is sin.

Rich Oppressors Will Be Judged

5 Come now, *you* rich, weep and howl for
your miseries that are coming upon
you! 2Your riches are corrupted, and your
garments are moth-eaten. 3Your gold and
silver are corroded, and their corrosion will
be a witness against you and will eat your
flesh like fire. You have heaped up treasure
in the last days. 4Indeed the wages of the laborers who mowed your fields, which you
kept back by fraud, cry out; and the cries of
the reapers have reached the ears of the Lord
of Sabaoth.[a] 5You have lived on the earth in
pleasure and luxury; you have fattened your
hearts as[a] in a day of slaughter. 6You have
condemned, you have murdered the just; he
does not resist you.

Be Patient and Persevering

7Therefore be patient, brethren, until
the coming of the Lord. See *how* the farmer waits for the precious fruit of the earth,
waiting patiently for it until it receives the
early and latter rain. 8You also be patient.

4:12 [a] NU-Text adds *and Judge.* [b] NU-Text and M-Text read *But who.* [c] NU-Text reads *a neighbor.* 4:13 [a] M-Text reads *let us.* 5:4 [a] Literally, in Hebrew, *Hosts* 5:5 [a] NU-Text omits *as.*

HOW TO LIVE AS A CHRISTIAN

READ IT: JAMES 5:1–20

GET IT:

James was the brother of Jesus and the head of the church council in Jerusalem. He wrote this letter to the early Christians to tell them how to live their faith. James believed that actions showed what Christians believed. He said that their faith had to affect their actions, their talk, their lives. What they believed inside their hearts and their heads had to come out in what they did. Christians can't just say that they believe in God and have Jesus as their Lord. They have to live it.

LIVE IT:

James gives us some very practical advice on behavior, attitudes, and speech. Ask yourself: In an average day, how do I compare to the points that James made? What am I doing that matches up with James' suggestions? What can I do tomorrow to better show that I'm a Christian?

Establish your hearts, for the coming of the
Lord is at hand.
9Do not grumble against one another,
brethren, lest you be condemned.[a] Behold,
the Judge is standing at the door! 10My
brethren, take the prophets, who spoke
in the name of the Lord, as an example of
suffering and patience. 11Indeed we count
them blessed who endure. You have heard
of the perseverance of Job and seen the end

5:9 [a] NU-Text and M-Text read *judged*.

COMPASSION

READ IT: JAMES 5:11

Endurance. To *endure* means to continue on a path or a task despite stress, fear, being tired, or other difficulties. Whether it's mental endurance when you're studying for a test or physical endurance when you're preparing for a race, it's something that takes time and discipline to build.

It can also be really tough to have endurance in your faith. When you feel like you're ready to give up, ask God to show you His compassion. Job suffered for a season, but he persevered, and God came through just as He promised. God can do the same for you.

GOD HEALS THE SICK

READ IT: JAMES 5:15

In the books of Matthew, Mark, Luke, and John, you can read how Jesus had power over sickness and death. He proved He was Lord of both the body and the soul.

But none of the people Jesus healed lived forever. They all finally died from some kind of disease, violence, or old age. Yet Jesus had to show them that He really was Lord over their bodies. When they died, they knew He would give them a new life and a new body like His that could never be sick or destroyed again.

There are also people today who can tell you that Jesus has healed their bodies of some disease. Even now, though Jesus doesn't heal everyone, He does heal some people as a sign that He is Lord over the body.

Someday you may be there when a Christian dies. Then you will know that death is not your greatest enemy. Christians don't really die. They just go to be with Jesus. Jesus said, "Whoever lives and believes in Me shall never die" (John 11:26).

intended by the Lord—that the Lord is very
compassionate and merciful.
12But above all, my brethren, do not swear,
either by heaven or by earth or with any other oath. But let your "Yes" be "Yes," and *your*
"No," "No," lest you fall into judgment.[a]

Meeting Specific Needs

13Is anyone among you suffering? Let
him pray. Is anyone cheerful? Let him sing
psalms. 14Is anyone among you sick? Let him
call for the elders of the church, and let them
pray over him, anointing him with oil in the
name of the Lord. 15And the prayer of faith
will save the sick, and the Lord will raise him
up. And if he has committed sins, he will be
forgiven. 16Confess *your* trespasses[a] to one
another, and pray for one another, that you
may be healed. The effective, fervent prayer
of a righteous man avails much. 17Elijah was
a man with a nature like ours, and he prayed
earnestly that it would not rain; and it did
not rain on the land for three years and six
months. 18And he prayed again, and the heav-
en gave rain, and the earth produced its fruit.

Bring Back the Erring One

19Brethren, if anyone among you wanders from the truth, and someone turns him
back, 20let him know that he who turns a sinner from the error of his way will save a soul[a]
from death and cover a multitude of sins.

5:12 [a] M-Text reads *hypocrisy.* 5:16 [a] NU-Text reads *Therefore confess your sins.* 5:20 [a] NU-Text reads *his soul.*

The FIRST EPISTLE of
PETER

A.D. 64

Behind the Scenes

READ IT:

This book is Peter's first letter to the early Christians in Asia Minor. They were being persecuted for their faith, so Peter told them to remember that Jesus suffered, too. They needed to follow Jesus' example and trust God to take care of them. Peter also told them how to live as Christians in a sinful world and have hope for the future.

GET IT:

Who wrote it: Peter

When it was written: A.D. 64

Why it was written: to encourage the Christians who faced persecution for their faith and instruct them to live holy lives.

LIVE IT:

Difficulties and hard times shouldn't wear us down. We should look at bad times as God's way of making us stronger and getting us ready for the next challenge in life.

FIND IT:

Living in Hope and Holiness	*1 Peter 1*
Living in Society	*1 Peter 2–3*
Serving and Suffering for God	*1 Peter 4*

Greeting to the Elect Pilgrims

1 Peter, an apostle of Jesus Christ,

To the pilgrims of the Dispersion in Pontus, Galatia, Cappadocia, Asia, and Bithynia,
2elect according to the foreknowledge of God
the Father, in sanctification of the Spirit, for
obedience and sprinkling of the blood of
Jesus Christ:

Grace to you and peace be multiplied.

A Heavenly Inheritance

3Blessed *be* the God and Father of our
Lord Jesus Christ, who according to His
abundant mercy has begotten us again to
a living hope through the resurrection of
Jesus Christ from the dead, 4to an inheritance incorruptible and undefiled and that
does not fade away, reserved in heaven for
you, 5who are kept by the power of God
through faith for salvation ready to be revealed in the last time.

6In this you greatly rejoice, though now
for a little while, if need be, you have been
grieved by various trials, 7that the genuine-
ness of your faith, *being* much more precious
than gold that perishes, though it is tested by
fire, may be found to praise, honor, and glory

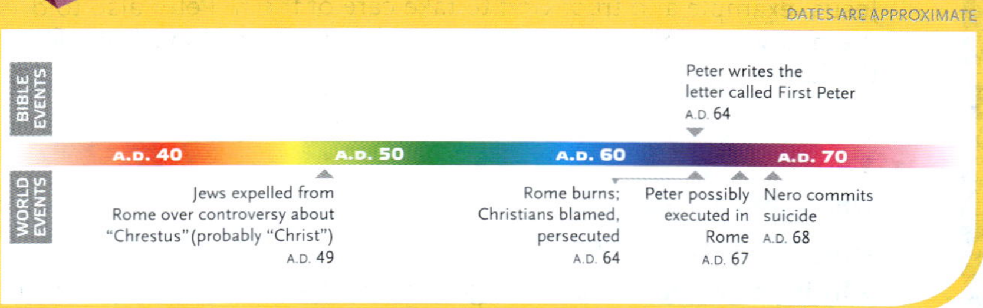

Starring Roles

PETER once thought he loved Jesus so much that he would do anything for Him. He even told Him he would die for Him.

Imagine Peter's shock when the Lord Jesus told him he would be the very one to deny he ever knew Him! That seemed impossible to Peter.

When the Master was arrested, Peter was crushed. How could He let them do that to Him? It seemed to Peter that Jesus had failed as the Messiah, the One God had sent to save them. So Peter was very disappointed. Then he denied that he even knew the Lord. At that very moment, Jesus turned and looked in Peter's eyes, and Peter remembered His warning (Luke 22:59–61). Peter cried because he knew he had failed Him.

Then they crucified Jesus, and all seemed lost to Peter.

But one morning Jesus met His disciples again by the seashore and made breakfast for them. Then He forgave Peter's sins. Jesus was alive again!

at the revelation of Jesus Christ, 8whom having not seen[a] you love. Though now you do
not see *Him*, yet believing, you rejoice with joy
inexpressible and full of glory, 9receiving the
end of your faith—the salvation of *your* souls.
10Of this salvation the prophets have inquired and searched carefully, who prophesied of the grace *that would come* to you,
11searching what, or what manner of time,
the Spirit of Christ who was in them was
indicating when He testified beforehand
the sufferings of Christ and the glories that
would follow. 12To them it was revealed that,
not to themselves, but to us[a] they were ministering the things which now have been
reported to you through those who have
preached the gospel to you by the Holy Spirit sent from heaven—things which angels
desire to look into.

Living Before God Our Father

13Therefore gird up the loins of your
mind, be sober, and rest *your* hope fully
upon the grace that is to be brought to you at
the revelation of Jesus Christ; 14as obedient
children, not conforming yourselves to the
former lusts, *as* in your ignorance; 15but as
He who called you *is* holy, you also be holy in
all *your* conduct, 16because it is written, "Be
holy, for I am holy." [a]
17And if you call on the Father, who
without partiality judges according to each
one's work, conduct yourselves throughout
the time of your stay *here* in fear; 18knowing
that you were not redeemed with corruptible
things, *like* silver or gold, from your aimless
conduct *received* by tradition from your fathers, 19but with the precious blood of Christ,
as of a lamb without blemish and without
spot. 20He indeed was foreordained before
the foundation of the world, but was manifest in these last times for you 21who through
Him believe in God, who raised Him from
the dead and gave Him glory, so that your
faith and hope are in God.

The Enduring Word

22Since you have purified your souls in
obeying the truth through the Spirit[a] in sincere love of the brethren, love one another
fervently with a pure heart, 23having been

1:8 [a] M-Text reads *known*. 1:12 [a] NU-Text and M-Text read *you*. 1:16 [a] Leviticus 11:44, 45; 19:2; 20:7 1:22 [a] NU-Text omits *through the Spirit*.

GOD'S WORD LASTS FOREVER

READ IT: 1 PETER 1:25

Everywhere you look you can see a world that has lasted a very long time, but it won't last forever. Jesus said that the heavens and the earth would pass away, but His words would never pass away (see Matthew 24:35).

What does God mean when He says His Word will last forever? He means that everything He ever promised will happen just as He said. He promised Abraham that his descendants would possess their land forever. So, in the new world that God has promised, the people of Israel will have their own land.

One day God is going to judge the world. People who believe His Word and accept Jesus as Savior and Lord will live with God forever. But people who refuse to accept God's free offer of salvation will be separated from God. Then there will be everlasting crying and sorrow. That's what Jesus called hell (see Matthew 10:28).

born again, not of corruptible seed but incorruptible, through the word of God which lives and abides forever,[a] 24because

"All flesh *is* as grass,
And all the glory of man[a] as the flower of the grass.
The grass withers,
And its flower falls away,
25 But the word of the LORD endures forever."[a]

Now this is the word which by the gospel was preached to you.

2 Therefore, laying aside all malice, all deceit, hypocrisy, envy, and all evil speaking, 2as newborn babes, desire the pure milk of the word, that you may grow thereby,[a] 3if indeed you have tasted that the Lord *is* gracious.

The Chosen Stone and His Chosen People

4Coming to Him *as to* a living stone, rejected indeed by men, but chosen by God *and* precious, 5you also, as living stones, are being built up a spiritual house, a holy priesthood, to offer up spiritual sacrifices acceptable to God through Jesus Christ. 6Therefore it is also contained in the Scripture,

"Behold, I lay in Zion
A chief cornerstone, elect, precious,
And he who believes on Him will by no means be put to shame."[a]

7Therefore, to you who believe, *He is* precious; but to those who are disobedient,[a]

"The stone which the builders rejected
Has become the chief cornerstone,"[b]

8and

"A stone of stumbling
And a rock of offense."[a]

They stumble, being disobedient to the word, to which they also were appointed.

9But you *are* a chosen generation, a royal priesthood, a holy nation, His own special

1:23 [a] NU-Text omits *forever.* 1:24 [a] NU-Text reads *all its glory.* 1:25 [a] Isaiah 40:6–8 2:2 [a] NU-Text adds *up to salvation.* 2:6 [a] Isaiah 28:16 2:7 [a] NU-Text reads *to those who disbelieve.* [b] Psalm 118:22 2:8 [a] Isaiah 8:14

Action!

GOD NEEDS YOU TO BE A LIVING ROCK

READ IT: 1 PETER 2:5

Buildings are often made of rocks or stones, and those buildings last a long time. But God is also building a big house in heaven that can never be destroyed. It's made of *living stones.* Those living stones are people like you. God calls that building His "church." So churches aren't *really* made of wood or stone. Yes, the *building* is made of such materials, but the real church is the *people.* God will dwell in the living building of His people forever.

Every living stone in God's building fits in a special place with all the other stones. That means you have a special place in God's building, the church. He has a special work in the church that only you can do, and that work will last forever!

There are lots of stones in the world, but they are of no use until they become part of a building. You're useful to God when you become part of His building, the church of Jesus Christ.

people, that you may proclaim the praises of
Him who called you out of darkness into His
marvelous light; 10who once *were* not a people but *are* now the people of God, who had
not obtained mercy but now have obtained
mercy.

Living Before the World

11Beloved, I beg *you* as sojourners and pilgrims, abstain from fleshly lusts which war
against the soul, 12having your conduct honorable among the Gentiles, that when they
speak against you as evildoers, they may, by
your good works which they observe, glorify
God in the day of visitation.

Submission to Government

13Therefore submit yourselves to every ordinance of man for the Lord's sake, whether
to the king as supreme, 14or to governors, as
to those who are sent by him for the punishment of evildoers and *for the* praise of those
who do good. 15For this is the will of God,
that by doing good you may put to silence
the ignorance of foolish men— 16as free, yet
not using liberty as a cloak for vice, but as
bondservants of God. 17Honor all *people*. Love
the brotherhood. Fear God. Honor the king.

Submission to Masters

18Servants, *be* submissive to *your* masters
with all fear, not only to the good and gentle,
but also to the harsh. 19For this *is* commendable, if because of conscience toward God
one endures grief, suffering wrongfully.
20For what credit *is it* if, when you are beat-
en for your faults, you take it patiently? But
when you do good and suffer, if you take it
patiently, this *is* commendable before God.
21For to this you were called, because Christ
also suffered for us,[a] leaving us[b] an example,
that you should follow His steps:

22 "Who committed no sin,
Nor was deceit found in His mouth";[a]

23who, when He was reviled, did not revile in
return; when He suffered, He did not threat-
en, but committed *Himself* to Him who judges righteously; 24who Himself bore our sins
in His own body on the tree, that we, having
died to sins, might live for righteousness—
by whose stripes you were healed. 25For you
were like sheep going astray, but have now
returned to the Shepherd and Overseer[a] of
your souls.

Submission to Husbands

3 Wives, likewise, *be* submissive to your
own husbands, that even if some do
not obey the word, they, without a word, may
be won by the conduct of their wives, 2when
they observe your chaste conduct *accompanied* by fear. 3Do not let your adornment be
merely outward—arranging the hair, wearing gold, or putting on *fine* apparel— 4rather

2:21 [a] NU-Text reads *you*. [b] NU-Text and M-Text read *you*.
2:22 [a] Isaiah 53:9 2:25 [a] Greek *Episkopos*

COMPASSION

READ IT: 1 PETER 3:8

Because God has compassion on us, we're able to show compassion to others. When you show someone compassion, you're putting their needs ahead of your own. Kindness like this can be an example that will encourage others.

Showing someone compassion doesn't have to be complicated. Simple things like opening doors, helping someone carry a heavy item, or saying please and thank you are all courteous and simple ways to help make someone else's day a little better.

let it be the hidden person of the heart, with
the incorruptible *beauty* of a gentle and quiet
spirit, which is very precious in the sight of
God. 5For in this manner, in former times,
the holy women who trusted in God also
adorned themselves, being submissive to
their own husbands, 6as Sarah obeyed Abraham, calling him lord, whose daughters you
are if you do good and are not afraid with
any terror.

A Word to Husbands

7Husbands, likewise, dwell with *them*
with understanding, giving honor to the
wife, as to the weaker vessel, and as *being*
heirs together of the grace of life, that your
prayers may not be hindered.

Called to Blessing

8Finally, all *of you be* of one mind, having
compassion for one another; love as brothers, *be* tenderhearted, *be* courteous;[a] 9not returning evil for evil or reviling for reviling,

3:8 [a] NU-Text reads *humble.*

REVENGE

READ IT: 1 PETER 3:8–14

This section of Scripture begins with an encouragement to "be of one mind" (v. 8). That means to live together with other people in peace. Have you ever had a friend or family member that you wish you could get along with better? The way to do it is to take this passage seriously and practice one of its key principles. When the person brings evil to you, return a courteous blessing. Difficult? Yes. Powerful? An even bigger yes.

PAIN AND SUFFERING

READ IT: 1 PETER 3:13–17

If you're being made fun of or bullied because of your faith, you're not alone. It's been going on since time began. Still, that kind of suffering can be painful, so here are some ways you can stay strong:

- Don't be afraid. God sees. He's with you.
- Don't get angry. The person who mocks faith needs it most. Remember you're reflecting Christ.
- Don't pull away from your Christian friends. You need them.
- Don't let it get you down. You'll be blessed for keeping the faith.

but on the contrary blessing, knowing that
you were called to this, that you may inherit
a blessing. 10For

"He who would love life
And see good days,
Let him refrain his tongue from evil,
And his lips from speaking deceit.
11 Let him turn away from evil and do good;
Let him seek peace and pursue it.
12 For the eyes of the LORD *are* on the righteous,
And His ears *are open* to their prayers;
But the face of the LORD *is* against those who do evil."[a]

Suffering for Right and Wrong

13And who *is* he who will harm you if
you become followers of what is good? 14But
even if you should suffer for righteousness'
sake, *you are* blessed. "And do not be afraid
of their threats, nor be troubled."[a] 15But sanctify the Lord God[a] in your hearts, and always
be ready to *give* a defense to everyone who
asks you a reason for the hope that is in you,
with meekness and fear; 16having a good conscience, that when they defame you as evildoers, those who revile your good conduct in
Christ may be ashamed. 17For *it is* better, if it
is the will of God, to suffer for doing good
than for doing evil.

Christ's Suffering and Ours

18For Christ also suffered once for sins,
the just for the unjust, that He might bring
us[a] to God, being put to death in the flesh
but made alive by the Spirit, 19by whom also
He went and preached to the spirits in prison, 20who formerly were disobedient, when
once the Divine longsuffering waited[a] in
the days of Noah, while *the* ark was being
prepared, in which a few, that is, eight souls,
were saved through water. 21There is also an
antitype which now saves us—baptism (not
the removal of the filth of the flesh, but the
answer of a good conscience toward God),
through the resurrection of Jesus Christ,
22who has gone into heaven and is at the right
hand of God, angels and authorities and
powers having been made subject to Him.

4 Therefore, since Christ suffered for
us[a] in the flesh, arm yourselves also
with the same mind, for he who has suffered in the flesh has ceased from sin, 2that
he no longer should live the rest of *his* time
in the flesh for the lusts of men, but for the
will of God. 3For we *have spent* enough of
our past lifetime[a] in doing the will of the
Gentiles—when we walked in lewdness,
lusts, drunkenness, revelries, drinking
parties, and abominable idolatries. 4In regard to these, they think it strange that you
do not run with *them* in the same flood of
dissipation, speaking evil of *you*. 5They will
give an account to Him who is ready to judge

3:12 [a] Psalm 34:12–16 **3:14** [a] Isaiah 8:12 **3:15** [a] NU-Text reads *Christ as Lord.* **3:18** [a] NU-Text and M-Text read *you.* **3:20** [a] NU-Text and M-Text read *when the longsuffering of God waited patiently.* **4:1** [a] NU-Text omits *for us.* **4:3** [a] NU-Text reads *time.*

ATTITUDES

READ IT: 1 PETER 4:1, 2

No one likes pain. In fact, most people do all they can to avoid it. The Bible makes it crystal clear that Jesus withstood pain and suffered for us, and He wants us to be willing to endure pain for Him. If you're following God's will in your life and sorrow or pain comes your way, don't be afraid. Stand strong, and be confident that God will use it to help make you stronger and more like Jesus. Scripture promises that sin will become less tempting, and you'll be more excited to do God's will.

the living and the dead. 6For this reason the
gospel was preached also to those who are
dead, that they might be judged according to
men in the flesh, but live according to God
in the spirit.

Serving for God's Glory

7But the end of all things is at hand;
therefore be serious and watchful in your
prayers. 8And above all things have fervent
love for one another, for "love will cover a
multitude of sins." [a] 9*Be* hospitable to one another without grumbling. 10As each one has
received a gift, minister it to one another, as
good stewards of the manifold grace of God.
11If anyone speaks, *let him speak* as the oracles of God. If anyone ministers, *let him do it*
as with the ability which God supplies, that
in all things God may be glorified through
Jesus Christ, to whom belong the glory and
the dominion forever and ever. Amen.

Suffering for God's Glory

12Beloved, do not think it strange concerning the fiery trial which is to try you,
as though some strange thing happened
to you; 13but rejoice to the extent that you
partake of Christ's sufferings, that when
His glory is revealed, you may also be glad
with exceeding joy. 14If you are reproached
for the name of Christ, blessed *are you,* for
the Spirit of glory and of God rests upon
you.[a] On their part He is blasphemed, but
on your part He is glorified. 15But let none of
you suffer as a murderer, a thief, an evildoer,
or as a busybody in other people's matters.
16Yet if *anyone suffers* as a Christian, let him
not be ashamed, but let him glorify God in
this matter.[a]

17For the time *has come* for judgment to
begin at the house of God; and if *it begins*
with us first, what will *be* the end of those
who do not obey the gospel of God? 18Now

"If the righteous one is scarcely saved,
Where will the ungodly and the sinner
appear?" [a]

19Therefore let those who suffer according to
the will of God commit their souls *to Him* in
doing good, as to a faithful Creator.

Shepherd the Flock

5 The elders who are among you I exhort, I who am a fellow elder and a
witness of the sufferings of Christ, and also
a partaker of the glory that will be revealed:
2Shepherd the flock of God which is among
you, serving as overseers, not by compulsion
but willingly,[a] not for dishonest gain but eagerly; 3nor as being lords over those entrusted to you, but being examples to the flock;
4and when the Chief Shepherd appears, you
will receive the crown of glory that does not
fade away.

4:8 [a] Proverbs 10:12 **4:14** [a] NU-Text omits the rest of this verse. **4:16** [a] NU-Text reads *name.* **4:18** [a] Proverbs 11:31 **5:2** [a] NU-Text adds *according to God.*

FAMILY

READ IT: 1 PETER 4:8

Peter constantly encouraged Christians to live out their faith in every area of their lives—from dealing with personal pain and disappointment to being an example for other people in every situation. But even more importantly, he encouraged them to live out their faith by loving others with a "fervent love"—a love that is intense and enthusiastic. Why? Because when you love someone deeply, you tend to have more grace for that person. Is there someone in your family whom you need to love more intensely and enthusiastically? Above all else, love that person—fervently!

Submit to God, Resist the Devil

[5]Likewise you younger people, submit
yourselves to *your* elders. Yes, all of *you* be
submissive to one another, and be clothed
with humility, for

"God resists the proud,
But gives grace to the humble."[a]

[6]Therefore humble yourselves under the
mighty hand of God, that He may exalt you
in due time, [7]casting all your care upon Him,
for He cares for you.

[8]Be sober, be vigilant; because[a] your adversary the devil walks about like a roaring
lion, seeking whom he may devour. [9]Resist
him, steadfast in the faith, knowing that
the same sufferings are experienced by
your brotherhood in the world. [10]But may[a]
the God of all grace, who called us[b] to His
eternal glory by Christ Jesus, after you have
suffered a while, perfect, establish, strength-
en, and settle *you*. [11]To Him *be* the glory and
the dominion forever and ever. Amen.

Farewell and Peace

[12]By Silvanus, our faithful brother as I
consider him, I have written to you briefly,
exhorting and testifying that this is the true
grace of God in which you stand.

[13]She who is in Babylon, elect together
with *you*, greets you; and *so does* Mark my
son. [14]Greet one another with a kiss of love.

Peace to you all who are in Christ Jesus.
Amen.

5:5 [a] Proverbs 3:34 5:8 [a] NU-Text and M-Text omit *because.* 5:10 [a] NU-Text reads *But the God of all grace . . . will perfect, establish, strengthen, and settle you.* [b] NU-Text and M-Text read *you.*

WHY SHOULD YOU OBEY YOUR ELDERS?

READ IT: 1 PETER 5:5

Not all boys and girls have two living parents. If you do, you're very fortunate. Many young people have only one parent, and some have none at all. But God has placed someone in charge of your life. You will be wise to obey your parents or the elders you live with.

First of all, your elders have to answer to God for how you grow up in the world. Don't make your folks ashamed of you. Remember, too, your elders know a lot more about getting along in the world than you do. They've been in the world longer. So doesn't it make sense to listen to what they have to say?

Sometimes you'll think you know better than your parents or teachers. You won't always feel like obeying them. But someday you'll be glad you did. A lot of young people get into serious trouble because they won't listen.

The SECOND EPISTLE of PETER

A.D. 65

Behind the Scenes

READ IT:

This book is Peter's second letter to the early Christian churches. The Christians were confused by false teachers. Peter told them the best way to not be tricked by false ideas: to know what they believed really well and to practice their faith. He guaranteed them that God would destroy the false teachers. Peter also reminded these Christians to live holy lives because Jesus was coming.

GET IT:

Who wrote it: Peter, a disciple of Jesus

When it was written: A.D. 65

Why it was written: to warn the church about false teachers who were twisting the truth.

LIVE IT:

Know what you believe and grow in that knowledge so you aren't swayed to believe something false.

FIND IT:

Grow in the Faith	*2 Peter 1*
Beware False Teachers	*2 Peter 2*
The Day of the Lord Is Coming	*2 Peter 3*

Greeting the Faithful

1 Simon Peter, a bondservant and apostle
of Jesus Christ,

To those who have obtained like precious
faith with us by the righteousness of our
God and Savior Jesus Christ:

2 Grace and peace be multiplied to you
in the knowledge of God and of Jesus our
Lord, 3 as His divine power has given to us
all things that *pertain* to life and godliness,
through the knowledge of Him who called
us by glory and virtue, 4 by which have been
given to us exceedingly great and precious
promises, that through these you may be
partakers of the divine nature, having escaped the corruption *that is* in the world
through lust.

Fruitful Growth in the Faith

5 But also for this very reason, giving all
diligence, add to your faith virtue, to virtue
knowledge, 6 to knowledge self-control, to
self-control perseverance, to perseverance
godliness, 7 to godliness brotherly kindness,
and to brotherly kindness love. 8 For if these
things are yours and abound, *you* will be neither barren nor unfruitful in the knowledge
of our Lord Jesus Christ. 9 For he who lacks
these things is shortsighted, even to blindness, and has forgotten that he was cleansed
from his old sins.

10 Therefore, brethren, be even more diligent to make your call and election sure,
for if you do these things you will never
stumble; 11 for so an entrance will be supplied
to you abundantly into the everlasting kingdom of our Lord and Savior Jesus Christ.

Peter's Approaching Death

12 For this reason I will not be negligent to
remind you always of these things, though
you know and are established in the present
truth. 13 Yes, I think it is right, as long as I
am in this tent, to stir you up by reminding
you, 14 knowing that shortly I *must* put off my
tent, just as our Lord Jesus Christ showed
me. 15 Moreover I will be careful to ensure
that you always have a reminder of these
things after my decease.

The Trustworthy Prophetic Word

16 For we did not follow cunningly devised
fables when we made known to you the power and coming of our Lord Jesus Christ, but
were eyewitnesses of His majesty. 17 For He
received from God the Father honor and glory when such a voice came to Him from the
Excellent Glory: "This is My beloved Son, in
whom I am well pleased." 18 And we heard
this voice which came from heaven when we
were with Him on the holy mountain.

19 And so we have the prophetic word
confirmed,[a] which you do well to heed as a
light that shines in a dark place, until the day
dawns and the morning star rises in your
hearts; 20 knowing this first, that no prophecy

1:19 [a] Or *We also have the more sure prophetic word.*

PERSEVERANCE

READ IT: 2 PETER 1:5–8

Imagine you've been outside helping your parents in the yard on a hot August day. Your clothing is drenched in sweat. Your hair is stuck to your head, and sweat is running down your face. Then someone hands you an ice-cold glass of your favorite drink. The first few swallows bring you so much pleasure! You feel cooled down and refreshed.

When your faith is filled with the characteristics listed in this passage, your faith is like that cold drink, bringing refreshment to your weary soul.

of Scripture is of any private interpretation,[a]
21 for prophecy never came by the will of man,
but holy men of God[a] spoke *as they were*
moved by the Holy Spirit.

Destructive Doctrines

2 But there were also false prophets
among the people, even as there will
be false teachers among you, who will secretly bring in destructive heresies, even denying the Lord who bought them, *and* bring
on themselves swift destruction. 2 And many
will follow their destructive ways, because of
whom the way of truth will be blasphemed.
3 By covetousness they will exploit you with
deceptive words; for a long time their judgment has not been idle, and their destruction does[a] not slumber.

Doom of False Teachers

4 For if God did not spare the angels who
sinned, but cast *them* down to hell and delivered *them* into chains of darkness, to be
reserved for judgment; 5 and did not spare
the ancient world, but saved Noah, *one of*
eight *people,* a preacher of righteousness,
bringing in the flood on the world of the
ungodly; 6 and turning the cities of Sodom
and Gomorrah into ashes, condemned *them*
to destruction, making *them* an example to
those who afterward would live ungodly;
7 and delivered righteous Lot, *who was* oppressed by the filthy conduct of the wicked
8 (for that righteous man, dwelling among
them, tormented *his* righteous soul from
day to day by seeing and hearing *their* lawless deeds)— 9 *then* the Lord knows how to
deliver the godly out of temptations and to
reserve the unjust under punishment for
the day of judgment, 10 and especially those
who walk according to the flesh in the lust
of uncleanness and despise authority. *They
are* presumptuous, self-willed. They are not
afraid to speak evil of dignitaries, 11 whereas
angels, who are greater in power and might,
do not bring a reviling accusation against
them before the Lord.

Depravity of False Teachers

12 But these, like natural brute beasts
made to be caught and destroyed, speak
evil of the things they do not understand,
and will utterly perish in their own corruption, 13 *and* will receive the wages of unrighteousness, *as* those who count it pleasure
to carouse in the daytime. *They are* spots

1:20 [a] Or *origin* 1:21 [a] NU-Text reads *but men spoke from God.* 2:3 [a] M-Text reads *will not.*

A LIGHT SHINES IN THE DARKNESS

READ IT: 2 PETER 1:19

It's dangerous to be in a strange and dark place without a light to show you the way. That's why a car needs headlights. And the greatest friend of a ship at sea may be a lighthouse along the shore. The lighthouse tells the sailors there are rocks nearby that could destroy the ship's hull.

Peter is also talking about a lighthouse that shines in a dark world. That lighthouse is the Bible. Light brings knowledge. The Bible is a lighthouse that lights your way in a dark, dangerous, and often evil world.

Remember that Jesus said, "I am the light of the world" (John 8:12). He also said, "I am . . . the truth" (John 14:6). There can be no ignorance where the light of truth is shining.

and blemishes, carousing in their own de-
ceptions while they feast with you, 14having
eyes full of adultery and that cannot cease
from sin, enticing unstable souls. They have
a heart trained in covetous practices, *and*
are accursed children. 15They have forsaken
the right way and gone astray, following the
way of Balaam the *son* of Beor, who loved
the wages of unrighteousness; 16but he was
rebuked for his iniquity: a dumb donkey
speaking with a man's voice restrained the
madness of the prophet.
17These are wells without water, clouds[a]
carried by a tempest, for whom is reserved
the blackness of darkness forever.[b]

Deceptions of False Teachers

18For when they speak great swelling
words of emptiness, they allure through the
lusts of the flesh, through lewdness, the
ones who have actually escaped[a] from those
who live in error. 19While they promise them
liberty, they themselves are slaves of corruption; for by whom a person is overcome, by
him also he is brought into bondage. 20For
if, after they have escaped the pollutions
of the world through the knowledge of the
Lord and Savior Jesus Christ, they are again
entangled in them and overcome, the latter
end is worse for them than the beginning.
21For it would have been better for them not
to have known the way of righteousness,
than having known *it*, to turn from the holy
commandment delivered to them. 22But it
has happened to them according to the true
proverb: "A dog returns to his own vomit,"[a]
and, "a sow, having washed, to her wallow-
ing in the mire."

God's Promise Is Not Slack

3 Beloved, I now write to you this second
epistle (in *both of* which I stir up your
pure minds by way of reminder), 2that you
may be mindful of the words which were
spoken before by the holy prophets, and of
the commandment of us,[a] the apostles of
the Lord and Savior, 3knowing this first:
that scoffers will come in the last days, walking according to their own lusts, 4and saying, "Where is the promise of His coming?
For since the fathers fell asleep, all things
continue as *they were* from the beginning
of creation." 5For this they willfully forget:
that by the word of God the heavens were of
old, and the earth standing out of water and
in the water, 6by which the world *that* then
existed perished, being flooded with water.
7But the heavens and the earth *which* are now
preserved by the same word, are reserved for
fire until the day of judgment and perdition
of ungodly men.

2:17 [a] NU-Text reads *and mists.* [b] NU-Text omits *forever.* 2:18 [a] NU-Text reads *are barely escaping.* 2:22 [a] Proverbs 26:11 3:2 [a] NU-Text and M-Text read *commandment of the apostles of your Lord and Savior* or *commandment of your apostles of the Lord and Savior.*

AUTHORITY

READ IT: 2 PETER 2:10

There have always been people who think, *If it feels good, do it.* They don't care how their actions affect others. If the sign says Ten Items or Less, they aren't embarrassed to walk through the checkout line with a full cart.

In baseball you don't run to second base first. When you play a game, you don't roll a three on the dice but then move six spaces just because you feel like it. Rules are in place for a reason. And if you cheat, you're being selfish rather than seeing other people the way God sees them.

8 But, beloved, do not forget this one
thing, that with the Lord one day *is* as a
thousand years, and a thousand years as
one day. 9 The Lord is not slack concerning
His promise, as some count slackness, but
is longsuffering toward us,[a] not willing that
any should perish but that all should come
to repentance.

The Day of the Lord

10 But the day of the Lord will come as
a thief in the night, in which the heavens
will pass away with a great noise, and the
elements will melt with fervent heat; both
the earth and the works that are in it will
be burned up.[a] 11 Therefore, since all these
things will be dissolved, what manner *of*
persons ought you to be in holy conduct and
godliness, 12 looking for and hastening the
coming of the day of God, because of which
the heavens will be dissolved, being on fire,
and the elements will melt with fervent
heat? 13 Nevertheless we, according to His
promise, look for new heavens and a new
earth in which righteousness dwells.

Be Steadfast

14 Therefore, beloved, looking forward to
these things, be diligent to be found by Him
in peace, without spot and blameless; 15 and
consider *that* the longsuffering of our Lord *is*
salvation—as also our beloved brother Paul,
according to the wisdom given to him, has
written to you, 16 as also in all his epistles,
speaking in them of these things, in which
are some things hard to understand, which
untaught and unstable *people* twist to their
own destruction, as *they do* also the rest of
the Scriptures.

17 You therefore, beloved, since you know
this beforehand, beware lest you also fall
from your own steadfastness, being led away
with the error of the wicked; 18 but grow in
the grace and knowledge of our Lord and
Savior Jesus Christ.

To Him *be* the glory both now and forever. Amen.

3:9 [a] NU-Text reads *you.* **3:10** [a] NU-Text reads *laid bare* (literally *found*).

The FIRST EPISTLE *of*

JOHN

A.D. 90

Behind the Scenes

READ IT:

This book is John's first letter to the early Christians. John warned the Christians not to listen to false teachers who were saying Jesus was not the Son of God because He was a man. John corrected this: Jesus Christ was both God and man. John encouraged the Christians to keep their faith strong and to love one another. Christians can know they are God's children if they love one another and obey God's commands.

GET IT:

Who wrote it: John, a disciple of Jesus

When it was written: A.D. 90

Why it was written: to teach Christians how to know the truth, how to stay away from sin, and how to live in love for God and for other people.

LIVE IT:

You are a child of God! Live in love for God and others.

God is love. If you live in love, God lives in you.

FIND IT:

Walk in Truth and Light	*1 John 1*
The Importance of Love	*1 John 3–4*
Obedience by Faith	1 John 5

What Was Heard, Seen, and Touched

1 That which was from the beginning,
which we have heard, which we have
seen with our eyes, which we have looked
upon, and our hands have handled, concerning the Word of life— 2the life was manifested, and we have seen, and bear witness,
and declare to you that eternal life which
was with the Father and was manifested to
us— 3that which we have seen and heard we
declare to you, that you also may have fellowship with us; and truly our fellowship *is* with
the Father and with His Son Jesus Christ.
4And these things we write to you that your[a]
joy may be full.

Fellowship with Him and One Another

5This is the message which we have
heard from Him and declare to you, that
God is light and in Him is no darkness at all.
6If we say that we have fellowship with Him,
and walk in darkness, we lie and do not practice the truth. 7But if we walk in the light as
He is in the light, we have fellowship with
one another, and the blood of Jesus Christ
His Son cleanses us from all sin.

8If we say that we have no sin, we deceive
ourselves, and the truth is not in us. 9If we
confess our sins, He is faithful and just to
forgive us *our* sins and to cleanse us from all
unrighteousness. 10If we say that we have not
sinned, we make Him a liar, and His word
is not in us.

2 My little children, these things I write
to you, so that you may not sin. And
if anyone sins, we have an Advocate with
the Father, Jesus Christ the righteous. 2And
He Himself is the propitiation for our sins,
and not for ours only but also for the whole
world.

The Test of Knowing Him

3Now by this we know that we know
Him, if we keep His commandments. 4He
who says, "I know Him," and does not keep
His commandments, is a liar, and the truth
is not in him. 5But whoever keeps His word,
truly the love of God is perfected in him. By
this we know that we are in Him. 6He who
says he abides in Him ought himself also to
walk just as He walked.

7Brethren,[a] I write no new commandment to you, but an old commandment
which you have had from the beginning.
The old commandment is the word which
you heard from the beginning.[b] 8Again, a
new commandment I write to you, which
thing is true in Him and in you, because the
darkness is passing away, and the true light
is already shining.

9He who says he is in the light, and hates
his brother, is in darkness until now. 10He
who loves his brother abides in the light, and
there is no cause for stumbling in him. 11But
he who hates his brother is in darkness and
walks in darkness, and does not know where
he is going, because the darkness has blinded his eyes.

Their Spiritual State

12 I write to you, little children,
Because your sins are forgiven you for
His name's sake.
13 I write to you, fathers,

1:4 [a] NU-Text and M-Text read *our*. 2:7 [a] NU-Text reads *Beloved*. [b] NU-Text omits *from the beginning*.

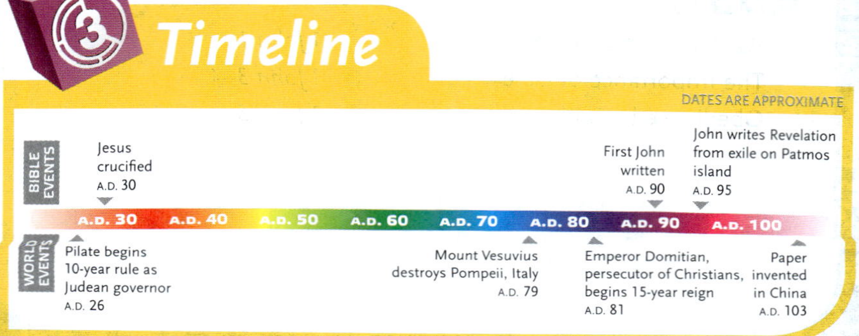

Because you have known Him *who is* from the beginning.
I write to you, young men,
Because you have overcome the wicked one.
I write to you, little children,
Because you have known the Father.
14 I have written to you, fathers,
Because you have known Him *who is* from the beginning.
I have written to you, young men,
Because you are strong, and the word of God abides in you,
And you have overcome the wicked one.

Do Not Love the World

15Do not love the world or the things in
the world. If anyone loves the world, the love
of the Father is not in him. 16For all that *is* in
the world—the lust of the flesh, the lust of
the eyes, and the pride of life—is not of the
Father but is of the world. 17And the world is
passing away, and the lust of it; but he who
does the will of God abides forever.

Deceptions of the Last Hour

18Little children, it is the last hour; and as
you have heard that the[a] Antichrist is coming, even now many antichrists have come,
by which we know that it is the last hour.
19They went out from us, but they were not
of us; for if they had been of us, they would
have continued with us; but *they went out*

In Focus

2:18 Antichrist Pronounced *AN-tih-krist.* A man who will rise up at the end of this age to lead the forces of evil against Christ and His church in the world.

that they might be made manifest, that none
of them were of us.
20But you have an anointing from the
Holy One, and you know all things.[a] 21I have
not written to you because you do not know
the truth, but because you know it, and that
no lie is of the truth.
22Who is a liar but he who denies that
Jesus is the Christ? He is antichrist who
denies the Father and the Son. 23Whoever
denies the Son does not have the Father either; he who acknowledges the Son has the
Father also.

Let Truth Abide in You

24Therefore let that abide in you which
you heard from the beginning. If what you
heard from the beginning abides in you, you
also will abide in the Son and in the Father.

2:18 [a] NU-Text omits *the.* 2:20 [a] NU-Text reads *you all know.*

Starring Roles

JOHN saw and heard with his own eyes and ears what Jesus did and said.

When the Lord Jesus came from heaven to earth two thousand years ago, He came to show us what God is like. So He went about doing good—healing the sick, giving sight to the blind, and even bringing some dead people back to life. He also taught that His Father wants us to love one another, just the way Jesus loves us.

John was there when they nailed Jesus our Savior to the Cross. But that wasn't the end of the story! Three days later He came back to life in a body that could never die again. How did John know this? He was there, and he even touched Jesus with his own hands! Then John saw Him go back to heaven.

John didn't just hear about what Jesus did. *He was there!*

25 And this is the promise that He has promised us—eternal life.
26 These things I have written to you concerning those who *try to* deceive you. 27 But
the anointing which you have received from
Him abides in you, and you do not need that
anyone teach you; but as the same anointing
teaches you concerning all things, and is
true, and is not a lie, and just as it has taught
you, you will[a] abide in Him.

The Children of God

28 And now, little children, abide in Him,
that when[a] He appears, we may have confidence and not be ashamed before Him at His
coming. 29 If you know that He is righteous,
you know that everyone who practices righteousness is born of Him.

3 Behold what manner of love the Father
has bestowed on us, that we should
be called children of God![a] Therefore the
world does not know us,[b] because it did not
know Him. 2 Beloved, now we are children of
God; and it has not yet been revealed what
we shall be, but we know that when He is
revealed, we shall be like Him, for we shall
see Him as He is. 3 And everyone who has
this hope in Him purifies himself, just as
He is pure.

2:27 [a] NU-Text reads *you abide.* 2:28 [a] NU-Text reads *if.*
3:1 [a] NU-Text adds *And we are.* [b] M-Text reads *you.*

Epic Ideas

GOD LOVES YOU
WE ARE CHILDREN OF GOD

READ IT: 1 JOHN 3:1

GET IT:

In the Bible, we're referred to as children of God. God wants the relationship between parents and their children to be one of the most special relationships ever. Children are supposed to look up to and love their parents. Parents need to know their children really well, inside and out, and love them unconditionally. Some people don't have the best parents; maybe these people were abused or neglected, or maybe they never knew their parents. This wasn't what God intended.

God is the perfect example of a parent. He doesn't expect us to be perfect. Sometimes we may feel like little children: awkward, dirty, and with nothing to offer. But this is exactly how Jesus wants us to be when we search for Him. When the children came to Jesus, He took them in His arms and blessed them. That's how much He loved those little children, and that's how much He loves you.

LIVE IT:

Know this: God loves you as His child. Think about the things you would do for your children if you were a parent. How would you show them you love them? Would you tell them every day? Give them what they needed? Now think of ways you know that God loves you. Ask your parents or youth leader to help you find verses in the Bible that show you this and write them down.

Sin and the Child of God

4Whoever commits sin also commits
lawlessness, and sin is lawlessness. 5And you
know that He was manifested to take away
our sins, and in Him there is no sin. 6Who-
ever abides in Him does not sin. Whoever
sins has neither seen Him nor known Him.
7Little children, let no one deceive you.
He who practices righteousness is righteous, just as He is righteous. 8He who sins
is of the devil, for the devil has sinned from
the beginning. For this purpose the Son of
God was manifested, that He might destroy
the works of the devil. 9Whoever has been
born of God does not sin, for His seed remains in him; and he cannot sin, because
he has been born of God.

The Imperative of Love

10In this the children of God and the children of the devil are manifest: Whoever does
not practice righteousness is not of God, nor
is he who does not love his brother. 11For this
is the message that you heard from the beginning, that we should love one another,
12not as Cain *who* was of the wicked one and
murdered his brother. And why did he murder him? Because his works were evil and
his brother's righteous.
13Do not marvel, my brethren, if the
world hates you. 14We know that we have
passed from death to life, because we love
the brethren. He who does not love *his*
brother[a] abides in death. 15Whoever hates
his brother is a murderer, and you know that
no murderer has eternal life abiding in him.

The Outworking of Love

16By this we know love, because He laid
down His life for us. And we also ought to
lay down *our* lives for the brethren. 17But
whoever has this world's goods, and sees his
brother in need, and shuts up his heart from
him, how does the love of God abide in him?
18My little children, let us not love in
word or in tongue, but in deed and in truth.
19And by this we know[a] that we are of the
truth, and shall assure our hearts before
Him. 20For if our heart condemns us, God is
greater than our heart, and knows all things.
21Beloved, if our heart does not condemn
us, we have confidence toward God. 22And
whatever we ask we receive from Him, because we keep His commandments and do
those things that are pleasing in His sight.
23And this is His commandment: that we
should believe on the name of His Son Jesus
Christ and love one another, as He gave us[a]
commandment.

The Spirit of Truth and the Spirit of Error

24Now he who keeps His commandments

3:14 [a] NU-Text omits *his brother.* **3:19** [a] NU-Text reads *we shall know.* **3:23** [a] M-Text omits *us.*

Action!

KINDNESS

READ IT: 1 JOHN 3:17, 18

When God asks us to love, it's not just feelings or words. The expectation is that love will make us kind. Kindness should be something we *practice every day.* Here's how:

- *Be generous.* Share what you can, whether it's a cookie or part of your allowance for a good cause.
- *Speak respectfully to everyone.* Say hi to people, and don't forget your manners.
- *Think up nice things to do for others.* A kind note might brighten an entire week for a friend.

abides in Him, and He in him. And by this we know that He abides in us, by the Spirit whom He has given us.

4 Beloved, do not believe every spirit, but test the spirits, whether they are of God; because many false prophets have gone out into the world. 2By this you know the Spirit of God: Every spirit that confesses that Jesus Christ has come in the flesh is of God, 3and every spirit that does not confess that[a] Jesus Christ has come in the flesh is not of God. And this is the *spirit* of the Antichrist, which you have heard was coming, and is now already in the world.

4You are of God, little children, and have overcome them, because He who is in you is greater than he who is in the world. 5They are of the world. Therefore they speak *as* of the world, and the world hears them. 6We are of God. He who knows God hears us; he who is not of God does not hear us. By this we know the spirit of truth and the spirit of error.

Knowing God Through Love

7Beloved, let us love one another, for love is of God; and everyone who loves is born of God and knows God. 8He who does not love does not know God, for God is love. 9In this the love of God was manifested toward us, that God has sent His only begotten Son into the world, that we might live through Him. 10In this is love, not that we loved God, but that He loved us and sent His Son *to be* the propitiation for our sins. 11Beloved, if God so loved us, we also ought to love one another.

Seeing God Through Love

12No one has seen God at any time. If we love one another, God abides in us, and His love has been perfected in us. 13By this we know that we abide in Him, and He in us, because He has given us of His Spirit. 14And we have seen and testify that the Father has sent the Son *as* Savior of the world. 15Whoever confesses that Jesus is the Son of God, God abides in him, and he in God. 16And we have known and believed the love that God has for us. God is love, and he who abides in love abides in God, and God in him.

The Consummation of Love

17Love has been perfected among us in this: that we may have boldness in the day of judgment; because as He is, so are we in this world. 18There is no fear in love; but perfect love casts out fear, because fear involves torment. But he who fears has not been made perfect in love. 19We love Him[a] because He first loved us.

Obedience by Faith

20If someone says, "I love God," and hates his brother, he is a liar; for he who does not love his brother whom he has seen, how can[a] he love God whom he has not seen? 21And this commandment we have from Him: that he who loves God *must* love his brother also.

4:3 [a] NU-Text omits *that* and *Christ has come in the flesh.*
4:19 [a] NU-Text omits *Him.* **4:20** [a] NU-Text reads *he cannot.*

PEER PRESSURE

READ IT: 1 JOHN 4:4

This letter was written to the followers of Christ to help them with a big problem. Inside of their church they had many new teachers who acted like they knew it all. These false teachers were trying to move Christians away from the teachings of Christ to their own teachings. They were not *trying to help the people* in the church. The great truth given here is that God is stronger than His enemy, Satan, who created the lies these false teachers were teaching.

5 Whoever believes that Jesus is the
Christ is born of God, and everyone
who loves Him who begot also loves him
who is begotten of Him. 2By this we know
that we love the children of God, when we
love God and keep His commandments.
3For this is the love of God, that we keep His
commandments. And His commandments
are not burdensome. 4For whatever is born of
God overcomes the world. And this is the victory that has overcome the world—our[a] faith.
5Who is he who overcomes the world, but he
who believes that Jesus is the Son of God?

The Certainty of God's Witness

6This is He who came by water and
blood—Jesus Christ; not only by water, but
by water and blood. And it is the Spirit who
bears witness, because the Spirit is truth.
7For there are three that bear witness in
heaven: the Father, the Word, and the Holy
Spirit; and these three are one. 8And there
are three that bear witness on earth:[a] the
Spirit, the water, and the blood; and these
three agree as one.

9If we receive the witness of men, the witness of God is greater; for this is the witness
of God which[a] He has testified of His Son.
10He who believes in the Son of God has the
witness in himself; he who does not believe
God has made Him a liar, because he has

5:4 [a] M-Text reads *your*. 5:8 [a] NU-Text and M-Text omit the words from *in heaven* (verse 7) through *on earth* (verse 8). Only four or five very late manuscripts contain these words in Greek. 5:9 [a] NU-Text reads *God, that*.

GOD LOVES YOU GOD IS LOVE

READ IT: 1 JOHN 4:8–10, 16

GET IT:

What does real love look like? Hollywood makes us think of love as a feeling or over-the-top romance. The media makes us believe we can buy love. We use the word *love* very casually when we say, "I love ice cream!" or "I love that game!" How are we supposed to know what real love is?

The Bible says that God is love. He is the source of all things that are good in the world. John tells us that one characteristic of love is sacrifice. God loves us so much He gave His only Son to die in our place so we could live and have a full relationship with God. It's not that *we* love *God*, even though we do! The only reason we can love God is because through Jesus, He loved us first. When we have a relationship with Jesus, the same love that God sacrificially demonstrated to us also lives in us, and we can show that love to those around us.

LIVE IT:

Real love, the kind that God shows us, gives sacrificially. Who are some people in your life whom you love? Maybe they're family members or friends. What are some ways you can sacrifice to show them love? Is there something—time, a gift, an encouraging word—that you can give them? Love isn't always easy. Look for ways to go above and beyond what's normal and stretch yourself.

not believed the testimony that God has giv-
en of His Son. 11And this is the testimony:
that God has given us eternal life, and this
life is in His Son. 12He who has the Son has
life; he who does not have the Son of God
does not have life. 13These things I have written to you who believe in the name of the
Son of God, that you may know that you have
eternal life,[a] and that you may *continue to* believe in the name of the Son of God.

Confidence and Compassion in Prayer

14Now this is the confidence that we have in
Him, that if we ask anything according to His
will, He hears us. 15And if we know that He
hears us, whatever we ask, we know that we
have the petitions that we have asked of Him.
16If anyone sees his brother sinning a sin
which does not *lead* to death, he will ask, and
He will give him life for those who commit
sin not *leading* to death. There is sin *leading*
to death. I do not say that he should pray
about that. 17All unrighteousness is sin, and
there is sin not *leading* to death.

Knowing the True—Rejecting the False

18We know that whoever is born of God
does not sin; but he who has been born of
God keeps himself,[a] and the wicked one
does not touch him.
19We know that we are of God, and the
whole world lies *under the sway of* the wicked
one.
20And we know that the Son of God has
come and has given us an understanding,
that we may know Him who is true; and we
are in Him who is true, in His Son Jesus
Christ. This is the true God and eternal life.
21Little children, keep yourselves from
idols. Amen.

5:13 [a] NU-Text omits the rest of this verse. 5:18 [a] NU-Text reads *him*.

HAVING JESUS IS ETERNAL LIFE

READ IT: 1 JOHN 5:12

There's probably a big bank near where you live. Just imagine you have ten million dollars in that bank. If you live wisely, you'll probably never spend it all. You'll always have enough for all you need every day. You'll never have to work to earn your living because it's all in the bank.

That's what it's like to have Jesus. You never run out of eternal life with Jesus. You can go back to Him every day, and He keeps giving you more and more life. When something bad happens to you, you can go to Jesus.

You have Jesus, and He is all you need now and forever. "He who has the Son has life."

The SECOND EPISTLE of

JOHN

A.D. 90

Behind the Scenes

READ IT:

This little book is John's second letter to the church. He talked about love and how important it was for Christians to love one another and to obey God's commandments. He warned the Christians to watch out for false ideas about Jesus.

GET IT:

Who wrote it: John, a disciple of Jesus

When it was written: A.D. 90

Why it was written: to advise Christians to be alert to false teachers.

LIVE IT:

Be really sure of what you believe. Make sure it shows in how you live.

FIND IT:

Walk in Christ's Commandments	*2 John 4–6*
Beware of Antichrist Deceivers	*2 John 7–11*

Greeting the Elect Lady

The Elder,

To the elect lady and her children, whom
I love in truth, and not only I, but also all
those who have known the truth, 2because
of the truth which abides in us and will be
with us forever:

3Grace, mercy, *and* peace will be with
you[a] from God the Father and from the Lord
Jesus Christ, the Son of the Father, in truth
and love.

Walk in Christ's Commandments

4I rejoiced greatly that I have found *some*
of your children walking in truth, as we received commandment from the Father. 5And
now I plead with you, lady, not as though I
wrote a new commandment to you, but that
which we have had from the beginning: that
we love one another. 6This is love, that we
walk according to His commandments. This
is the commandment, that as you have heard
from the beginning, you should walk in it.

Beware of Antichrist Deceivers

7For many deceivers have gone out into
the world who do not confess Jesus Christ *as*

3 [a] NU-Text and M-Text read *us*.

Epic Ideas

JESUS IS THE WAY
LIAR, LIAR, PANTS ON FIRE

READ IT: 2 JOHN 7

GET IT:

The writer of this Bible book warned his readers to watch out for all the people who said that Jesus didn't really come "in the flesh." He's not suggesting that people were saying a man named Jesus didn't live and die. The liars he's talking about were saying that Jesus wasn't really who He said He was: God. We have the same liars all around us today. They don't think they're lying, of course. But they're telling a story about Jesus that isn't true.

Where does this lie come from? It's not just from the imaginations of people or their lack of faith. This verse tells us that the lie comes from the evil one—from the devil himself. Satan does more than work to make people do really bad things. Satan's greatest triumph, actually, is to get lots of people to believe that Jesus was just a good man and go on with their lives. Satan wins when that happens because people don't get to know the real Jesus. They are kept from knowing the God who loves them.

LIVE IT:

What untruths about Jesus have you heard? Where do you think those opinions and beliefs come from? Why might Satan do a little victory dance every time he hears someone say Jesus was just a man? Read the next verse (v. 8). What does it tell you about how you can stand up to deceits of the evil one?

coming in the flesh. This is a deceiver and
an antichrist. 8 Look to yourselves, that we[a]
do not lose those things we worked for, but
that we[b] may receive a full reward.
9 Whoever transgresses[a] and does not
abide in the doctrine of Christ does not have
God. He who abides in the doctrine of Christ
has both the Father and the Son. 10 If anyone
comes to you and does not bring this doctrine, do not receive him into your house nor
greet him; 11 for he who greets him shares in
his evil deeds.

John's Farewell Greeting

12 Having many things to write to you, I
did not wish *to do so* with paper and ink; but
I hope to come to you and speak face to face,
that our joy may be full.
13 The children of your elect sister greet
you. Amen.

8 [a] NU-Text reads *you.* [b] NU-Text reads *you.* 9 [a] NU-Text reads *goes ahead.*

Action!

THE OLD COMMANDMENT

READ IT: 2 JOHN 6

John isn't teaching anything new. He is only reminding us of what Jesus had said a long time before: "Love one another as I have loved you" (John 13:34).

Love is not that excitement you feel when you see a pretty girl or when you meet a nice boy. The love John is talking about also means caring for everyone in the same way Jesus did.

Love doesn't just happen. You have to decide you're going to love some people even when you don't feel like loving them. That means you're going to make the best things happen for as many people as you can. After a while that kind of love becomes a good habit of life.

The THIRD EPISTLE *of*

JOHN

A.D. 90

Behind the Scenes

READ IT:

This short book is John's third letter to the church. It was a very personal letter to his friend Gaius to praise and thank him for his help. John also scolded Diotrephes for not cooperating.

GET IT:

Who wrote it: John, a disciple of Jesus

When it was written: A.D. 90

Why it was written: to encourage Christians to show hospitality to visitors and strangers.

LIVE IT:

Don't imitate what is evil.

Do what is good.

Those who do evil don't know God.

FIND IT:

Praise of Gaius, Correction of Others	*3 John 5–12*
Farewell Greeting	*3 John 13, 14*

Greeting to Gaius

The Elder,

To the beloved Gaius, whom I love in
truth:

2Beloved, I pray that you may prosper
in all things and be in health, just as your
soul prospers. 3For I rejoiced greatly when
brethren came and testified of the truth *that*
is in you, just as you walk in the truth. 4I have
no greater joy than to hear that my children
walk in truth.[a]

Gaius Commended for Generosity

5Beloved, you do faithfully whatever you
do for the brethren and[a] for strangers, 6who
have borne witness of your love before the
church. *If* you send them forward on their
journey in a manner worthy of God, you
will do well, 7because they went forth for His
name's sake, taking nothing from the Gentiles. 8We therefore ought to receive[a] such,
that we may become fellow workers for the
truth.

Diotrephes and Demetrius

9I wrote to the church, but Diotrephes,

4 [a] NU-Text reads *the truth.* 5 [a] NU-Text adds *especially.* 8 [a] NU-Text reads *support.*

Starring Roles

GAIUS is pronounced *GAY-us*. Some of his friends at the church told the apostle John some kind things about Gaius and Demetrius (pronounced *dih-MEE-tree-us*), so John wrote Gaius this letter.

Gaius was honored to receive such a letter from the Beloved Apostle. John did try to write to his church once before, but one of the church leaders wouldn't let the people read the letter. You will hear more about that bad leader later.

Gaius did sincerely love the Lord Jesus, and he tried to live as Jesus taught.

God doesn't want us to be big in our own eyes. He does want us to obey Him in everyday things He gives us to do. When we can be trusted in the little things, then someday He will give us greater things to do for Him.

Action!

SUCCESS

READ IT: 3 JOHN 2

Notice the word *soul*? The Greek word there is *psuche* (*psoo-khay*). It's a wonderful word that can mean "mind, heart, body, soul, spirit, and breath." It's emotional, physical, and spiritual. John is writing to a very good friend and prays every day that his *psuche* will be prosperous. What if your mind-body-soul-spirit-breath were all functioning together perfectly? What would your everyday life be like?

who loves to have the preeminence among
them, does not receive us. 10 Therefore, if I
come, I will call to mind his deeds which
he does, prating against us with malicious
words. And not content with that, he himself
does not receive the brethren, and forbids
those who wish to, putting *them* out of the
church.

11 Beloved, do not imitate what is evil, but
what is good. He who does good is of God,
but[a] he who does evil has not seen God.

12 Demetrius has a *good* testimony from
all, and from the truth itself. And we also
bear witness, and you know that our testimony is true.

Farewell Greeting

13 I had many things to write, but I do not
wish to write to you with pen and ink; 14 but
I hope to see you shortly, and we shall speak
face to face.

Peace to you. Our friends greet you.
Greet the friends by name.

11 [a] NU-Text and M-Text omit *but.*

THE FIRST SHALL BE LAST

READ IT: 3 JOHN 9

In many places in today's world, you will be first if you can scare somebody else into being second. Being "the greatest" is very important to many people. That leaves no room for everyone else.

If you want to get God's attention, you can't be trying to grab first place. God says, "Come and let Me put you in the place I have chosen for you. That's where you'll be happy." But if you're just trying to be important all the time, you're going to be miserable. You won't win most of the time, but you will wear yourself out by trying.

The man in John's story, Diotrephes (pronounced *die-OT-rah-fees*), wanted to be first, so he ended up being last. But Demetrius (pronounced *dih-MEE-tree-us*) was a good friend to everyone, so he ended up first.

The EPISTLE of

JUDE

A.D. 60–A.D. 64

Behind the Scenes

READ IT:

The book of Jude is a letter from Jude to the early Christian church. He warned the Christians not to listen to false teachers who led the people to do wrong and said that Jesus was not the Son of God. Jude guaranteed that God would punish and destroy the false teachers like He punished sinners in the Old Testament.

GET IT:

Who wrote it: Jude

When it was written: A.D. 60–A.D. 64

Why it was written: to warn Christians about false teachers who were trying to destroy the church.

LIVE IT:

If we grow in our faith, pray, and stay close to God, we can resist evil and false ideas.

FIND IT:

Beware of False Teachers	*Jude 3–23*
Glory to God	*Jude 24, 25*

Greeting to the Called

Jude, a bondservant of Jesus Christ, and
brother of James,

To those who are called, sanctified[a]
by God the Father, and preserved in Jesus
Christ:

2 Mercy, peace, and love be multiplied to
you.

Contend for the Faith

3 Beloved, while I was very diligent to
write to you concerning our common salvation, I found it necessary to write to you
exhorting you to contend earnestly for the
faith which was once for all delivered to the
saints. 4 For certain men have crept in unno-
ticed, who long ago were marked out for this
condemnation, ungodly men, who turn the
grace of our God into lewdness and deny the
only Lord God[a] and our Lord Jesus Christ.

Old and New Apostates

5 But I want to remind you, though you
once knew this, that the Lord, having saved

1 [a] NU-Text reads *beloved*. 4 [a] NU-Text omits *God*.

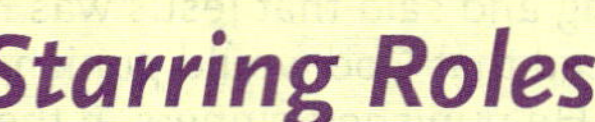

JUDE and his brother James were both younger sons of Mary and Joseph, but only Jesus was the Son of God.

Jude's main reason for writing this letter was because some men were teaching lies to the people in the churches. Followers of Jesus needed to know what these men were saying.

Those false teachers denied that Jesus was the Lord from heaven, and they were not examples of how Christians should live. Such men are complainers and noisy talkers. You should learn to recognize such men as Satan's workers. You may remember that Satan told the first lie to Eve in the Garden of Eden.

Be sure to store up God's Word in your thoughts. Then you may even help false teachers to see their falsehoods.

AUTHORITY

READ IT: JUDE 8

You are part of something bigger than yourself. If you don't respect that, you're more alone than you can imagine. God created the whole earth and has placed people in authority (whether we like it or not). This verse warns us about rejecting authority. And even more, it warns us *against speaking poorly* about those in authority. If you remember that God has placed you in His big creation, you'll also remember that people in authority are part of God's bigger plan.

the people out of the land of Egypt, afterward destroyed those who did not believe.
6And the angels who did not keep their proper domain, but left their own abode, He has
reserved in everlasting chains under darkness for the judgment of the great day; 7as
Sodom and Gomorrah, and the cities around
them in a similar manner to these, having
given themselves over to sexual immorality
and gone after strange flesh, are set forth
as an example, suffering the vengeance of
eternal fire.

8Likewise also these dreamers defile
the flesh, reject authority, and speak evil of
dignitaries. 9Yet Michael the archangel, in
contending with the devil, when he disputed about the body of Moses, dared not bring
against him a reviling accusation, but said,
"The Lord rebuke you!" 10But these speak
evil of whatever they do not know; and whatever they know naturally, like brute beasts,
in these things they corrupt themselves.
11Woe to them! For they have gone in the
way of Cain, have run greedily in the error
of Balaam for profit, and perished in the rebellion of Korah.

Apostates Depraved and Doomed

12These are spots in your love feasts,
while they feast with you without fear, serving *only* themselves. *They are* clouds without
water, carried about[a] by the winds; late autumn trees without fruit, twice dead, pulled
up by the roots; 13raging waves of the sea,
foaming up their own shame; wandering
stars for whom is reserved the blackness of
darkness forever.

14Now Enoch, the seventh from Adam,
prophesied about these men also, saying,
"Behold, the Lord comes with ten thousands
of His saints, 15to execute judgment on all,
to convict all who are ungodly among them
of all their ungodly deeds which they have
committed in an ungodly way, and of all the
harsh things which ungodly sinners have
spoken against Him."

Apostates Predicted

16These are grumblers, complainers,
walking according to their own lusts; and
they mouth great swelling *words*, flattering

12 [a] NU-Text and M-Text read *along*.

GOD CAN KEEP YOU FROM STUMBLING

READ IT: JUDE 24

It's not fatal to stumble if you don't fall and break your neck!

God knows you may stumble over some sin sometimes. You say words that you're ashamed of. You do something in secret that should never be done. You allow hateful thoughts to come into your mind. You stumble in those ways. The important things is to *know when you stumble, then tell it to God.* He will always understand and forgive you if you honestly love Him. He will also prevent you from destroying your life when you stumble.

Some people live their whole lives without putting their faith in Jesus as Savior. They don't just stumble over sin. They fall all the way down to hell. They say, "We don't care about Jesus. We're going our own way." Ask God to help you show people like this that they need to know Jesus.

people to gain advantage. 17 But you, beloved,
remember the words which were spoken before by the apostles of our Lord Jesus Christ:
18 how they told you that there would be
mockers in the last time who would walk according to their own ungodly lusts. 19 These
are sensual persons, who cause divisions,
not having the Spirit.

Maintain Your Life with God

20 But you, beloved, building yourselves
up on your most holy faith, praying in the
Holy Spirit, 21 keep yourselves in the love of
God, looking for the mercy of our Lord Jesus
Christ unto eternal life.

22 And on some have compassion, making
a distinction;[a] 23 but others save with fear,
pulling *them* out of the fire,[a] hating even the
garment defiled by the flesh.

Glory to God

24 Now to Him who is able to keep you[a]
from stumbling,
And to present *you* faultless
Before the presence of His glory with
exceeding joy,
25 To God our Savior,[a]
Who alone is wise,[b]
Be glory and majesty,
Dominion and power,[c]
Both now and forever.
Amen.

---

22 [a] NU-Text reads *who are doubting* (or *making distinctions*). 23 [a] NU-Text adds *and on some have mercy with fear* and omits *with fear* in first clause. 24 [a] M-Text reads *them*. 25 [a] NU-Text reads *To the only God our Savior.* [b] NU-Text omits *Who . . . is wise* and adds *Through Jesus Christ our Lord.* [c] NU-Text adds *Before all time.*

The REVELATION of JESUS CHRIST

A.D. 96

Behind the Scenes

READ IT:

The apostle John wrote the book of Revelation during his time on the island of Patmos. It contains many symbols, beasts, and wild images, but one thing is clear—Jesus Christ is Lord and ruler over everyone and everything. He is in control. Someday He will judge and punish what is evil. Then He will establish His kingdom with a new heaven and a new earth.

GET IT:

Who wrote it: John, a disciple of Jesus

When it was written: A.D. 96

Why it was written: to report John's God-given visions about the conflict between Christ and His enemies, and Christ's ultimate victory.

LIVE IT:

Even when evil seems strong, we can take comfort in knowing that Christ is in control and He will win.

Someday we will be part of a crowd in heaven that praises God forever and ever.

FIND IT:

John's Vision of the Son of Man	*Revelation 1*
The Letters to the Seven Churches	*Revelation 2–3*
The Throne Room of Heaven	*Revelation 4–5*
Seven Seals and Seven Trumpets	*Revelation 6–11*
The War in Heaven	*Revelation 12*
The Seven Bowls	*Revelation 16*
The Thousand Years	*Revelation 20*
The New Jerusalem	*Revelation 21–22*

Introduction and Benediction

1 The Revelation of Jesus Christ, which
God gave Him to show His servants—
things which must shortly take place. And
He sent and signified *it* by His angel to His
servant John, 2who bore witness to the word
of God, and to the testimony of Jesus Christ,
to all things that he saw. 3Blessed *is* he who
reads and those who hear the words of this
prophecy, and keep those things which are
written in it; for the time *is* near.

Greeting the Seven Churches

4John, to the seven churches which are
in Asia:

Grace to you and peace from Him who is
and who was and who is to come, and from
the seven Spirits who are before His throne,
5and from Jesus Christ, the faithful witness,
the firstborn from the dead, and the ruler
over the kings of the earth.

To Him who loved us and washed[a] us
from our sins in His own blood, 6and has
made us kings[a] and priests to His God and
Father, to Him *be* glory and dominion forever and ever. Amen.

7Behold, He is coming with clouds,
and every eye will see Him, even they who
pierced Him. And all the tribes of the earth
will mourn because of Him. Even so, Amen.

8"I am the Alpha and the Omega, *the*
Beginning and *the* End,"[a] says the Lord,[b]
"who is and who was and who is to come,
the Almighty."

Vision of the Son of Man

9I, John, both[a] your brother and companion in the tribulation and kingdom and patience of Jesus Christ, was on the island that
is called Patmos for the word of God and for
the testimony of Jesus Christ. 10I was in the
Spirit on the Lord's Day, and I heard behind
me a loud voice, as of a trumpet, 11saying,
"I am the Alpha and the Omega, the First
and the Last," and,[a] "What you see, write
in a book and send *it* to the seven churches
which are in Asia:[b] to Ephesus, to Smyrna, to
Pergamos, to Thyatira, to Sardis, to Philadelphia, and to Laodicea."

12Then I turned to see the voice that
spoke with me. And having turned I saw
seven golden lampstands, 13and in the midst
of the seven lampstands *One* like the Son of
Man, clothed with a garment down to the

1:5 [a] NU-Text reads *loves us and freed;* M-Text reads *loves us and washed.* 1:6 [a] NU-Text and M-Text read *a kingdom.* 1:8 [a] NU-Text and M-Text omit *the Beginning and the End.* [b] NU-Text and M-Text add *God.* 1:9 [a] NU-Text and M-Text omit *both.* 1:11 [a] NU-Text and M-Text omit *I am* through third *and.* [b] NU-Text and M-Text omit *which are in Asia.*

JESUS IS REVEALED

READ IT: REVELATION 1:1

What do we mean when we say something is "revealed"? We mean that something hidden has now become known.

All through the Bible, God revealed Himself in many ways—as the Angel of the Lord, as a burning torch (Genesis 15), as a wrestler (Genesis 32), as a burning bush (Exodus 3), and in voices and visions given to people throughout the Old Testament. Still, God was mostly hidden from people—like the sun just peeping through the clouds.

Then Jesus came, and John says, "We beheld [saw] His glory" (John 1:14). Finally, in the book of Revelation, we see God in all His majesty (see Revelation 1:13–15; 4:3–5). The Bible is really a book that gradually unfolds or "reveals" the mighty God and His Son, Jesus Christ.

feet and girded about the chest with a gold-
en band. 14His head and hair *were* white like
wool, as white as snow, and His eyes like a
flame of fire; 15His feet *were* like fine brass,
as if refined in a furnace, and His voice as
the sound of many waters; 16He had in His
right hand seven stars, out of His mouth
went a sharp two-edged sword, and His
countenance *was* like the sun shining in its
strength. 17And when I saw Him, I fell at His
feet as dead. But He laid His right hand on
me, saying to me,[a] "Do not be afraid; I am
the First and the Last. 18I *am* He who lives,
and was dead, and behold, I am alive forevermore. Amen. And I have the keys of Hades
and of Death. 19Write[a] the things which you
have seen, and the things which are, and the
things which will take place after this. 20The
mystery of the seven stars which you saw in
My right hand, and the seven golden lampstands: The seven stars are the angels of the
seven churches, and the seven lampstands
which you saw[a] are the seven churches.

The Loveless Church

2 "To the angel of the church of Ephesus
write,
'These things says He who holds the sev-
en stars in His right hand, who walks in the
midst of the seven golden lampstands: 2"I
know your works, your labor, your patience,
and that you cannot bear those who are evil.
And you have tested those who say they are
apostles and are not, and have found them
liars; 3and you have persevered and have patience, and have labored for My name's sake
and have not become weary. 4Nevertheless
I have *this* against you, that you have left
your first love. 5Remember therefore from
where you have fallen; repent and do the
first works, or else I will come to you quickly
and remove your lampstand from its place—
unless you repent. 6But this you have, that
you hate the deeds of the Nicolaitans, which
I also hate.
7"He who has an ear, let him hear what the
Spirit says to the churches. To him who overcomes I will give to eat from the tree of life,
which is in the midst of the Paradise of God."'

The Persecuted Church

8"And to the angel of the church in Smyrna write,
'These things says the First and the Last,

1:17 [a] NU-Text and M-Text omit *to me.* **1:19** [a] NU-Text and M-Text read *Therefore, write.* **1:20** [a] NU-Text and M-Text omit *which you saw.*

In Focus

1:8 The Alpha and the Omega Pronounced *AL-fuh* and *oh-MEG-uh*. The first and last letters of the Greek alphabet. This is one of the names for Christ who is the First and the Last of all things.

2:6 Nicolaitans Pronounced *Nick-oh-LAY-ih-tons*. A group led by a false teacher named Nicolas. This was a group who believed they could be immoral and still be Christians.

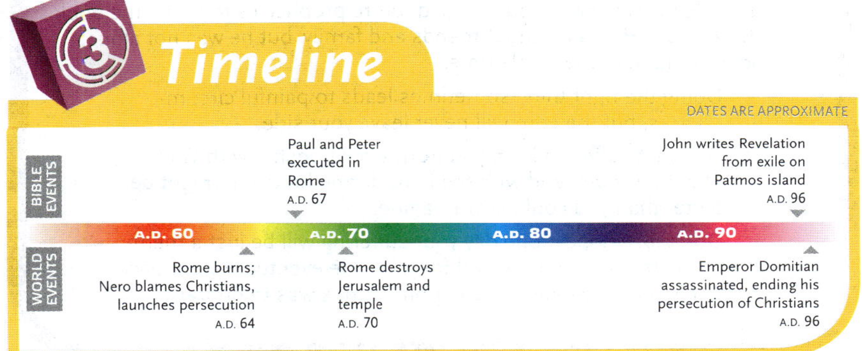

who was dead, and came to life: 9"I know
your works, tribulation, and poverty (but
you are rich); and *I know* the blasphemy of
those who say they are Jews and are not, but
are a synagogue of Satan. 10Do not fear any
of those things which you are about to suffer. Indeed, the devil is about to throw *some*
of you into prison, that you may be tested,
and you will have tribulation ten days. Be
faithful until death, and I will give you the
crown of life.

11"He who has an ear, let him hear what
the Spirit says to the churches. He who overcomes shall not be hurt by the second death." '

PAIN AND SUFFERING

ALONE ON AN ISLAND

READ IT: REVELATION 1:9–16

GET IT:

The writer of Revelation is widely believed to be Jesus' disciple John, the same John who wrote one of the four Gospels. He had been preaching about Jesus in the city of Ephesus, in ancient Greece, when he was arrested for witnessing. The Roman emperor Domitian wanted his people to worship the royal family as gods. He considered other religions to be political competition—a threat to his empire. For this reason, Domitian exiled John to a Greek island called Patmos, where he lived alone, some say in a cave.

It's hard to imagine what that would have been like. Nowadays we see people playing at surviving in nature on reality TV shows, but what if this was real and it wasn't your choice and the Aegean Sea separated you from everyone you loved? What if the only reason you were sent away to suffer loneliness and hunger was because you wanted to tell people about Jesus?

LIVE IT:

We don't know how many years John spent on Patmos, but we know that while he was there God revealed future prophecies to him—the book of Revelation. He was without friends and family, but he was not alone. God was with him the whole time.

- Doing the right thing sometimes leads to painful circumstances, but the Lord will never leave your side.
- Don't let suffering keep you from a relationship with God. The time you spend with the Lord during hardship might be better than you could ever imagine.
- Don't lose hope—one day your suffering will be just a memory. Patmos wasn't the end for John. He eventually went back to his ministry—his suffering on Patmos was temporary.

The Compromising Church

[12]"And to the angel of the church in Pergamos write,
'These things says He who has the sharp
two-edged sword: [13]"I know your works, and
where you dwell, where Satan's throne *is*.
And you hold fast to My name, and did not
deny My faith even in the days in which Antipas *was* My faithful martyr, who was killed
among you, where Satan dwells. [14]But I have
a few things against you, because you have
there those who hold the doctrine of Balaam,
who taught Balak to put a stumbling block
before the children of Israel, to eat things
sacrificed to idols, and to commit sexual
immorality. [15]Thus you also have those who
hold the doctrine of the Nicolaitans, which
thing I hate.[a] [16]Repent, or else I will come to
you quickly and will fight against them with
the sword of My mouth.
[17]"He who has an ear, let him hear what the
Spirit says to the churches. To him who overcomes I will give some of the hidden manna
to eat. And I will give him a white stone, and
on the stone a new name written which no
one knows except him who receives *it*."'

The Corrupt Church

[18]"And to the angel of the church in Thyatira write,
'These things says the Son of God, who
has eyes like a flame of fire, and His feet

2:15 [a] NU-Text and M-Text read *likewise* for *which thing I hate.*

On Location

Churches of Revelation

John writes from fifty miles offshore of western Turkey, on the rocky island of Patmos, about ten miles long and five miles wide. He begins the book with letters addressed to churches in seven cities near the coast of western Turkey. The futuristic visions that John writes about involve the entire planet. He says the last battle between good and evil will take place in the Valley of Armageddon, known today as Megiddo, and that God will make a new Jerusalem. Since the genre of the book is apocalyptic, characterized by extreme symbolism, scholars debate whether John had any of these actual sites in mind.

like fine brass: 19“I know your works, love,
service, faith,[a] and your patience; and *as* for
your works, the last *are* more than the first.
20Nevertheless I have a few things against
you, because you allow[a] that woman[b] Jezebel, who calls herself a prophetess, to teach
and seduce[c] My servants to commit sexual immorality and eat things sacrificed to
idols. 21And I gave her time to repent of her
sexual immorality, and she did not repent.[a]
22Indeed I will cast her into a sickbed, and
those who commit adultery with her into
great tribulation, unless they repent of their[a]
deeds. 23I will kill her children with death,
and all the churches shall know that I am
He who searches the minds and hearts. And
I will give to each one of you according to
your works.

24“Now to you I say, and[a] to the rest in
Thyatira, as many as do not have this doctrine, who have not known the depths of Satan, as they say, I will[b] put on you no other
burden. 25But hold fast what you have till I
come. 26And he who overcomes, and keeps
My works until the end, to him I will give
power over the nations—

27 ‘He shall rule them with a rod of iron;
They shall be dashed to pieces like the
potter’s vessels’ [a]—

as I also have received from My Father; 28and
I will give him the morning star.

29“He who has an ear, let him hear what
the Spirit says to the churches.”’

The Dead Church

3 “And to the angel of the church in
Sardis write,

‘These things says He who has the seven
Spirits of God and the seven stars: “I know
your works, that you have a name that you
are alive, but you are dead. 2Be watchful,
and strengthen the things which remain,
that are ready to die, for I have not found
your works perfect before God.[a] 3Remember
therefore how you have received and heard;
hold fast and repent. Therefore if you will
not watch, I will come upon you as a thief,

2:19 [a] NU-Text and M-Text read *faith, service.* 2:20 [a] NU-Text and M-Text read *I have against you that you tolerate.* [b] M-Text reads *your wife Jezebel.* [c] NU-Text and M-Text read *and teaches and seduces.* 2:21 [a] NU-Text and M-Text read *time to repent, and she does not want to repent of her sexual immorality.* 2:22 [a] NU-Text and M-Text read *her.* 2:24 [a] NU-Text and M-Text omit *and.* [b] NU-Text and M-Text omit *will.* 2:27 [a] Psalm 2:9 3:2 [a] NU-Text and M-Text read *My God.*

Action!

THE SEVEN CHURCHES

READ IT: REVELATION 2:7

In Revelation 2 and 3 you read about “the seven churches of Asia” (called Asia Minor today). These were actual churches. The majestic Christ that John saw sends a letter to each of these churches. To most of the seven churches, Jesus pays a compliment. But He finds some faults in all except two of them—Smyrna and Philadelphia.

As you read about each of these churches, you are reminded of what some Christians are like today. One church has left its “first love.” That means the people don’t love Christ as much as they did in the beginning. Two churches are allowing filthy and indecent behavior by their members. One church is “dead”—they still pretend to be Christians, but they don’t really love Jesus anymore. Another church is “lukewarm”—they are only half-hearted for Jesus. But Jesus says He wishes they were either hot or cold—all or nothing!

Are you like any of these churches?

and you will not know what hour I will come
upon you. 4You[a] have a few names even in
Sardis who have not defiled their garments;
and they shall walk with Me in white, for
they are worthy. 5He who overcomes shall
be clothed in white garments, and I will not
blot out his name from the Book of Life; but
I will confess his name before My Father and
before His angels.
6"He who has an ear, let him hear what
the Spirit says to the churches."'

The Faithful Church

7"And to the angel of the church in Philadelphia write,
'These things says He who is holy, He
who is true, "He who has the key of David,
He who opens and no one shuts, and shuts
and no one opens":[a] 8"I know your works.
See, I have set before you an open door,
and no one can shut it;[a] for you have a little
strength, have kept My word, and have not
denied My name. 9Indeed I will make *those*
of the synagogue of Satan, who say they are
Jews and are not, but lie—indeed I will make
them come and worship before your feet,
and to know that I have loved you. 10Because
you have kept My command to persevere,
I also will keep you from the hour of trial
which shall come upon the whole world, to
test those who dwell on the earth. 11Behold,[a] I
am coming quickly! Hold fast what you have,
that no one may take your crown. 12He who
overcomes, I will make him a pillar in the
temple of My God, and he shall go out no
more. I will write on him the name of My
God and the name of the city of My God, the
New Jerusalem, which comes down out of
heaven from My God. And *I will write on him*
My new name.
13"He who has an ear, let him hear what
the Spirit says to the churches."'

The Lukewarm Church

14"And to the angel of the church of the
Laodiceans[a] write,
'These things says the Amen, the Faithful and True Witness, the Beginning of the
creation of God: 15"I know your works, that
you are neither cold nor hot. I could wish
you were cold or hot. 16So then, because you
are lukewarm, and neither cold nor hot,[a] I
will vomit you out of My mouth. 17Because
you say, 'I am rich, have become wealthy,
and have need of nothing'—and do not
know that you are wretched, miserable,
poor, blind, and naked— 18I counsel you to
buy from Me gold refined in the fire, that
you may be rich; and white garments, that
you may be clothed, *that* the shame of your
nakedness may not be revealed; and anoint

3:4 [a] NU-Text and M-Text read *Nevertheless you have a few names in Sardis.* **3:7** [a] Isaiah 22:22 **3:8** [a] NU-Text and M-Text read *which no one can shut.* **3:11** [a] NU-Text and M-Text omit *Behold.* **3:14** [a] NU-Text and M-Text read *in Laodicea.* **3:16** [a] NU-Text and M-Text read *hot nor cold.*

DISCIPLINE

READ IT: REVELATION 3:19

If you were standing along the road and you saw your best friend in a car riding past you, not noticing the Bridge Out sign, you would do something to get his attention. Maybe you'd even toss a rock and take out the car's windshield. You care about him so much that you would do whatever it takes. God is often shouting, "You're going the wrong way!" But still we step on the gas pedal. We can stop and shake our fist at the sky and say, "Why, God?" Or we can say, "What is it I'm supposed to be learning here?"

your eyes with eye salve, that you may see.
19As many as I love, I rebuke and chasten.
Therefore be zealous and repent. 20Behold, I
stand at the door and knock. If anyone hears
My voice and opens the door, I will come in
to him and dine with him, and he with Me.
21To him who overcomes I will grant to sit
with Me on My throne, as I also overcame
and sat down with My Father on His throne.

22"He who has an ear, let him hear what
the Spirit says to the churches."'"

The Throne Room of Heaven

4 After these things I looked, and behold, a door *standing* open in heaven.
And the first voice which I heard *was* like a
trumpet speaking with me, saying, "Come
up here, and I will show you things which
must take place after this."

2Immediately I was in the Spirit; and behold, a throne set in heaven, and *One* sat on
the throne. 3And He who sat there was[a] like
a jasper and a sardius stone in appearance;
and *there was* a rainbow around the throne,
in appearance like an emerald. 4Around the
throne *were* twenty-four thrones, and on the
thrones I saw twenty-four elders sitting,
clothed in white robes; and they had crowns[a]
of gold on their heads. 5And from the throne
proceeded lightnings, thunderings, and
voices.[a] Seven lamps of fire *were* burning before the throne, which are the[b] seven Spirits
of God.

6Before the throne *there was*[a] a sea of
glass, like crystal. And in the midst of the
throne, and around the throne, *were* four
living creatures full of eyes in front and in
back. 7The first living creature *was* like a
lion, the second living creature like a calf,
the third living creature had a face like a
man, and the fourth living creature *was* like
a flying eagle. 8*The* four living creatures,
each having six wings, were full of eyes
around and within. And they do not rest day
or night, saying:

"Holy, holy, holy,[a]
Lord God Almighty,
Who was and is and is to come!"

9Whenever the living creatures give glory
and honor and thanks to Him who sits on
the throne, who lives forever and ever, 10the
twenty-four elders fall down before Him
who sits on the throne and worship Him

4:3 [a] M-Text omits *And He who sat there was* (which makes the description in verse 3 modify the throne rather than God). 4:4 [a] NU-Text and M-Text read *robes, with crowns.* 4:5 [a] NU-Text and M-Text read *voices, and thunderings.* [b] M-Text omits *the.* 4:6 [a] NU-Text and M-Text add *something like.* 4:8 [a] M-Text has *holy* nine times.

WHAT GOD IS LIKE IN HEAVEN

READ IT: REVELATION 4:2–5

John, the author of this book, could not see everything clearly in heaven. There was a rainbow, like a mist, that surrounded God on His throne. It was hard for John to describe all that he saw. He could see a mixture of the beauty of two precious stones—the jasper stone stands for purity, while the sardius (or sard) is reddish in color. This scene reminds you that God is glorious to behold.

Part of that glory of God is the red blood of Jesus, the Lamb of God who died for your sins. It is good to be reminded that Jesus in heaven is still God's sacrifice for sins. Jesus is the Lamb of God whose red blood is always before God's throne. You can see Jesus the Lamb in Revelation 5:6. You, too, will be allowed to see God like this only because Jesus died for you.

who lives forever and ever, and cast their
crowns before the throne, saying:

11 "You are worthy, O Lord,[a]
To receive glory and honor and power;
For You created all things,
And by Your will they exist[b] and were
created."

The Lamb Takes the Scroll

5 And I saw in the right *hand* of Him
who sat on the throne a scroll written
inside and on the back, sealed with seven
seals. 2Then I saw a strong angel proclaiming with a loud voice, "Who is worthy to
open the scroll and to loose its seals?" 3And
no one in heaven or on the earth or under
the earth was able to open the scroll, or to
look at it.

4So I wept much, because no one was
found worthy to open and read[a] the scroll, or
to look at it. 5But one of the elders said to me,
"Do not weep. Behold, the Lion of the tribe
of Judah, the Root of David, has prevailed to
open the scroll and to loose[a] its seven seals."

6And I looked, and behold,[a] in the midst
of the throne and of the four living creatures,
and in the midst of the elders, stood a Lamb
as though it had been slain, having seven
horns and seven eyes, which are the seven
Spirits of God sent out into all the earth.
7Then He came and took the scroll out of the
right hand of Him who sat on the throne.

Worthy Is the Lamb

8Now when He had taken the scroll, the
four living creatures and the twenty-four
elders fell down before the Lamb, each having a harp, and golden bowls full of incense,
which are the prayers of the saints. 9And
they sang a new song, saying:

"You are worthy to take the scroll,
And to open its seals;
For You were slain,
And have redeemed us to God by Your
blood
Out of every tribe and tongue and
people and nation,
10 And have made us[a] kings[b] and priests to
our God;
And we[c] shall reign on the earth."

11Then I looked, and I heard the voice of
many angels around the throne, the living

4:11 [a] NU-Text and M-Text read *our Lord and God.* [b] NU-Text and M-Text read *existed.* **5:4** [a] NU-Text and M-Text omit *and read.* **5:5** [a] NU-Text and M-Text omit *to loose.* **5:6** [a] NU-Text and M-Text read *I saw in the midst . . . a Lamb standing.* **5:10** [a] NU-Text and M-Text read *them.* [b] NU-Text reads *a kingdom.* [c] NU-Text and M-Text read *they.*

THE BOOK OF THE FUTURE

READ IT: REVELATION 5:1

Lots of people have written books about the past. That's why you can study history in school. But God has written the book about the future. The book (or scroll) John sees in heaven contains God's complete plan for all time. The remaining chapters of the book of Revelation show the main outlines of God's great scheme for the coming time.

One thing you will notice is that no man or angel was able to open God's book. Jesus, the Lamb of God (v. 5), is the only One who can unlock the book of the future for us. When Jesus opens the book you can go on to read about the coming judgments of God on the earth. When Jesus returns to earth, Satan and his people and nations are thrown into hell. But in the end, the Lord brings in His beautiful new heavens and new earth. Then He reigns over all in peace forever and ever.

creatures, and the elders; and the number of
them was ten thousand times ten thousand,
and thousands of thousands, 12saying with
a loud voice:

"Worthy is the Lamb who was slain
To receive power and riches and
wisdom,
And strength and honor and glory and
blessing!"

13And every creature which is in heaven
and on the earth and under the earth and
such as are in the sea, and all that are in
them, I heard saying:

"Blessing and honor and glory and power
Be to Him who sits on the throne,
And to the Lamb, forever and ever!"[a]

14Then the four living creatures said,
"Amen!" And the twenty-four[a] elders fell
down and worshiped Him who lives forever
and ever.[b]

First Seal: The Conqueror

6 Now I saw when the Lamb opened one
of the seals;[a] and I heard one of the
four living creatures saying with a voice like
thunder, "Come and see." 2And I looked, and
behold, a white horse. He who sat on it had a
bow; and a crown was given to him, and he
went out conquering and to conquer.

Second Seal: Conflict on Earth

3When He opened the second seal, I
heard the second living creature saying,
"Come and see."[a] 4Another horse, fiery red,
went out. And it was granted to the one who
sat on it to take peace from the earth, and
that *people* should kill one another; and there
was given to him a great sword.

Third Seal: Scarcity on Earth

5When He opened the third seal, I heard
the third living creature say, "Come and
see." So I looked, and behold, a black horse,
and he who sat on it had a pair of scales in
his hand. 6And I heard a voice in the midst
of the four living creatures saying, "A quart[a]
of wheat for a denarius,[b] and three quarts of
barley for a denarius; and do not harm the
oil and the wine."

Fourth Seal: Widespread Death on Earth

7When He opened the fourth seal, I
heard the voice of the fourth living creature
saying, "Come and see." 8So I looked, and
behold, a pale horse. And the name of him
who sat on it was Death, and Hades followed
with him. And power was given to them over
a fourth of the earth, to kill with sword, with
hunger, with death, and by the beasts of the
earth.

Fifth Seal: The Cry of the Martyrs

9When He opened the fifth seal, I saw
under the altar the souls of those who had
been slain for the word of God and for the
testimony which they held. 10And they cried
with a loud voice, saying, "How long, O Lord,
holy and true, until You judge and avenge
our blood on those who dwell on the earth?"
11Then a white robe was given to each of
them; and it was said to them that they
should rest a little while longer, until both
the number of their fellow servants and their
brethren, who would be killed as they *were,*
was completed.

Sixth Seal: Cosmic Disturbances

12I looked when He opened the sixth seal,
and behold,[a] there was a great earthquake;
and the sun became black as sackcloth of
hair, and the moon[b] became like blood. 13And
the stars of heaven fell to the earth, as a fig
tree drops its late figs when it is shaken by
a mighty wind. 14Then the sky receded as a
scroll when it is rolled up, and every mountain and island was moved out of its place.
15And the kings of the earth, the great men,
the rich men, the commanders,[a] the mighty
men, every slave and every free man, hid
themselves in the caves and in the rocks of
the mountains, 16and said to the mountains
and rocks, "Fall on us and hide us from the
face of Him who sits on the throne and from
the wrath of the Lamb! 17For the great day
of His wrath has come, and who is able to
stand?"

The Sealed of Israel

7 After these things I saw four angels
standing at the four corners of the

5:13 [a] M-Text adds *Amen.* 5:14 [a] NU-Text and M-Text omit *twenty-four.* [b] NU-Text and M-Text omit *Him who lives forever and ever.* 6:1 [a] NU-Text and M-Text read *seven seals.* 6:3 [a] NU-Text and M-Text omit *and see.* 6:6 [a] Greek *choinix;* that is, approximately one quart [b] This was approximately one day's wage for a worker. 6:12 [a] NU-Text and M-Text omit *behold.* [b] NU-Text and M-Text read *the whole moon.* 6:15 [a] NU-Text and M-Text read *the commanders, the rich men.*

earth, holding the four winds of the earth,
that the wind should not blow on the earth,
on the sea, or on any tree. 2Then I saw another angel ascending from the east, having
the seal of the living God. And he cried with
a loud voice to the four angels to whom it
was granted to harm the earth and the sea,
3saying, "Do not harm the earth, the sea, or
the trees till we have sealed the servants of
our God on their foreheads." 4And I heard
the number of those who were sealed. One
hundred *and* forty-four thousand of all the
tribes of the children of Israel *were* sealed:

5 of the tribe of Judah twelve thousand
were sealed;[a]
of the tribe of Reuben twelve thousand
were sealed;
of the tribe of Gad twelve thousand *were*
sealed;
6 of the tribe of Asher twelve thousand
were sealed;
of the tribe of Naphtali twelve thousand
were sealed;
of the tribe of Manasseh twelve
thousand *were* sealed;
7 of the tribe of Simeon twelve thousand
were sealed;

7:5 [a] In NU-Text and M-Text *were sealed* is stated only in verses 5a and 8c; the words are understood in the remainder of the passage.

JOHN'S VISION

READ IT: REVELATION 7:1–17

GET IT:

John was a disciple of Jesus who wrote the Gospel of John, the letters of 1, 2, 3 John, and this book. John was arrested for his Christian beliefs and sent to the island of Patmos. While John was on the island, he received a vision about the future. His visions were full of symbolism of the battle between good and evil and Jesus' final victory. His writings gave hope to the believers in the church who were being persecuted for their faith. Knowing that Jesus would be victorious over all His enemies in heaven and earth gave them strength. The vision of the saints singing in the courts of heaven reassured the believers that the best was coming.

LIVE IT:

Have you ever been to a college or professional sporting event? How does it feel to be in a big crowd cheering on the team? It's super exciting and noisy. It's also fun to sing your school's song at the top of your lungs. Karaoke singing can be fun too, and so can singing a favorite song with a group of friends. Now imagine a huge group singing together to praise God. This huge group of believers you just read about were in heaven in front of God's throne praising God day and night. We don't have to wait until heaven to sing praise to God. We can start right now. Maybe you've already experienced singing God's praises in church. How did it make you feel? Were you excited? Did you feel really pumped? Keep singing. God deserves our praise on earth and in heaven.

of the tribe of Levi twelve thousand *were*
sealed;
of the tribe of Issachar twelve thousand
were sealed;
8 of the tribe of Zebulun twelve thousand
were sealed;
of the tribe of Joseph twelve thousand
were sealed;
of the tribe of Benjamin twelve
thousand *were* sealed.

A Multitude from the Great Tribulation

9 After these things I looked, and behold, a great multitude which no one could
number, of all nations, tribes, peoples, and
tongues, standing before the throne and
before the Lamb, clothed with white robes,
with palm branches in their hands, 10 and
crying out with a loud voice, saying, "Salvation *belongs* to our God who sits on the
throne, and to the Lamb!" 11 All the angels
stood around the throne and the elders and
the four living creatures, and fell on their
faces before the throne and worshiped God,
12 saying:

"Amen! Blessing and glory and wisdom,
Thanksgiving and honor and power and
might,
Be to our God forever and ever.
Amen."

13 Then one of the elders answered, saying to me, "Who are these arrayed in white
robes, and where did they come from?"
14 And I said to him, "Sir,[a] you know."
So he said to me, "These are the ones
who come out of the great tribulation, and
washed their robes and made them white in
the blood of the Lamb. 15 Therefore they are
before the throne of God, and serve Him day
and night in His temple. And He who sits
on the throne will dwell among them. 16 They
shall neither hunger anymore nor thirst
anymore; the sun shall not strike them, nor
any heat; 17 for the Lamb who is in the midst
of the throne will shepherd them and lead
them to living fountains of waters.[a] And God
will wipe away every tear from their eyes."

Seventh Seal: Prelude to the Seven Trumpets

8 When He opened the seventh seal,
there was silence in heaven for about
half an hour. 2 And I saw the seven angels
who stand before God, and to them were
given seven trumpets. 3 Then another angel,
having a golden censer, came and stood at
the altar. He was given much incense, that
he should offer *it* with the prayers of all
the saints upon the golden altar which was
before the throne. 4 And the smoke of the
incense, with the prayers of the saints, ascended before God from the angel's hand.
5 Then the angel took the censer, filled it with
fire from the altar, and threw *it* to the earth.
And there were noises, thunderings, lightnings, and an earthquake.
6 So the seven angels who had the seven
trumpets prepared themselves to sound.

First Trumpet: Vegetation Struck

7 The first angel sounded: And hail and
fire followed, mingled with blood, and they
were thrown to the earth.[a] And a third of the
trees were burned up, and all green grass
was burned up.

Second Trumpet: The Seas Struck

8 Then the second angel sounded: And
something like a great mountain burning
with fire was thrown into the sea, and a third
of the sea became blood. 9 And a third of the
living creatures in the sea died, and a third
of the ships were destroyed.

Third Trumpet: The Waters Struck

10 Then the third angel sounded: And a
great star fell from heaven, burning like a
torch, and it fell on a third of the rivers and
on the springs of water. 11 The name of the
star is Wormwood. A third of the waters became wormwood, and many men died from
the water, because it was made bitter.

Fourth Trumpet: The Heavens Struck

12 Then the fourth angel sounded: And a
third of the sun was struck, a third of the
moon, and a third of the stars, so that a third
of them were darkened. A third of the day
did not shine, and likewise the night.
13 And I looked, and I heard an angel[a]
flying through the midst of heaven, saying
with a loud voice, "Woe, woe, woe to the
inhabitants of the earth, because of the remaining blasts of the trumpet of the three
angels who are about to sound!"

7:14 [a] NU-Text and M-Text read *My lord.* 7:17 [a] NU-Text and M-Text read *to fountains of the waters of life.* 8:7 [a] NU-Text and M-Text add *and a third of the earth was burned up.* 8:13 [a] NU-Text and M-Text read *eagle.*

Fifth Trumpet: The Locusts from the Bottomless Pit

9 Then the fifth angel sounded: And I
saw a star fallen from heaven to the
earth. To him was given the key to the bottomless pit. 2And he opened the bottomless
pit, and smoke arose out of the pit like the
smoke of a great furnace. So the sun and
the air were darkened because of the smoke
of the pit. 3Then out of the smoke locusts
came upon the earth. And to them was giv-
en power, as the scorpions of the earth have
power. 4They were commanded not to harm
the grass of the earth, or any green thing,
or any tree, but only those men who do not
have the seal of God on their foreheads. 5And
they were not given *authority* to kill them,
but to torment them *for* five months. Their
torment *was* like the torment of a scorpion
when it strikes a man. 6In those days men
will seek death and will not find it; they will
desire to die, and death will flee from them.

7The shape of the locusts was like horses prepared for battle. On their heads were
crowns of something like gold, and their faces *were* like the faces of men. 8They had hair
like women's hair, and their teeth were like
lions' *teeth*. 9And they had breastplates like
breastplates of iron, and the sound of their
wings *was* like the sound of chariots with
many horses running into battle. 10They had
tails like scorpions, and there were stings in
their tails. Their power *was* to hurt men five
months. 11And they had as king over them
the angel of the bottomless pit, whose name
in Hebrew *is* Abaddon, but in Greek he has
the name Apollyon.

12One woe is past. Behold, still two more
woes are coming after these things.

Sixth Trumpet: The Angels from the Euphrates

13Then the sixth angel sounded: And I
heard a voice from the four horns of the gold-
en altar which is before God, 14saying to the
sixth angel who had the trumpet, "Release
the four angels who are bound at the great
river Euphrates." 15So the four angels, who
had been prepared for the hour and day and
month and year, were released to kill a third
of mankind. 16Now the number of the army
of the horsemen *was* two hundred million;
I heard the number of them. 17And thus I
saw the horses in the vision: those who sat
on them had breastplates of fiery red, hya-
cinth blue, and sulfur yellow; and the heads
of the horses *were* like the heads of lions; and
out of their mouths came fire, smoke, and
brimstone. 18By these three *plagues* a third
of mankind was killed—by the fire and the
smoke and the brimstone which came out of
their mouths. 19For their power[a] is in their
mouth and in their tails; for their tails *are*
like serpents, having heads; and with them
they do harm.

20But the rest of mankind, who were not
killed by these plagues, did not repent of the
works of their hands, that they should not
worship demons, and idols of gold, silver,
brass, stone, and wood, which can neither
see nor hear nor walk. 21And they did not repent of their murders or their sorceries[a] or
their sexual immorality or their thefts.

The Mighty Angel with the Little Book

10 I saw still another mighty angel
coming down from heaven, clothed
with a cloud. And a rainbow *was* on his head,
his face *was* like the sun, and his feet like
pillars of fire. 2He had a little book open in
his hand. And he set his right foot on the sea
and *his* left *foot* on the land, 3and cried with
a loud voice, as *when* a lion roars. When he
cried out, seven thunders uttered their voices. 4Now when the seven thunders uttered
their voices,[a] I was about to write; but I heard
a voice from heaven saying to me,[b] "Seal up
the things which the seven thunders uttered, and do not write them."

5The angel whom I saw standing on the
sea and on the land raised up his hand[a] to
heaven 6and swore by Him who lives forever
and ever, who created heaven and the things
that are in it, the earth and the things that
are in it, and the sea and the things that are
in it, that there should be delay no longer,
7but in the days of the sounding of the seventh angel, when he is about to sound, the
mystery of God would be finished, as He declared to His servants the prophets.

John Eats the Little Book

8Then the voice which I heard from heav-
en spoke to me again and said, "Go, take

9:19 [a] NU-Text and M-Text read *the power of the horses.*
9:21 [a] NU-Text and M-Text read *drugs.* **10:4** [a] NU-Text and M-Text read *sounded.* [b] NU-Text and M-Text omit *to me.*
10:5 [a] NU-Text and M-Text read *right hand.*

the little book which is open in the hand of
the angel who stands on the sea and on the
earth."
9 So I went to the angel and said to him,
"Give me the little book."
And he said to me, "Take and eat it; and it
will make your stomach bitter, but it will be
as sweet as honey in your mouth."
10 Then I took the little book out of the angel's hand and ate it, and it was as sweet as
honey in my mouth. But when I had eaten it,
my stomach became bitter. 11 And he[a] said to
me, "You must prophesy again about many
peoples, nations, tongues, and kings."

The Two Witnesses

11 Then I was given a reed like a measuring rod. And the angel stood,[a]
saying, "Rise and measure the temple of
God, the altar, and those who worship there.
2 But leave out the court which is outside the
temple, and do not measure it, for it has
been given to the Gentiles. And they will
tread the holy city underfoot *for* forty-two
months. 3 And I will give *power* to my two
witnesses, and they will prophesy one thousand two hundred and sixty days, clothed in
sackcloth."
4 These are the two olive trees and the two
lampstands standing before the God[a] of the
earth. 5 And if anyone wants to harm them,
fire proceeds from their mouth and devours
their enemies. And if anyone wants to harm
them, he must be killed in this manner.
6 These have power to shut heaven, so that
no rain falls in the days of their prophecy;
and they have power over waters to turn
them to blood, and to strike the earth with
all plagues, as often as they desire.

The Witnesses Killed

7 When they finish their testimony, the
beast that ascends out of the bottomless
pit will make war against them, overcome
them, and kill them. 8 And their dead bodies
will lie in the street of the great city which
spiritually is called Sodom and Egypt, where
also our[a] Lord was crucified. 9 Then *those*
from the peoples, tribes, tongues, and na-
tions will see their dead bodies three-and-a-
half days, and not allow[a] their dead bodies to
be put into graves. 10 And those who dwell on
the earth will rejoice over them, make merry, and send gifts to one another, because
these two prophets tormented those who
dwell on the earth.

In Focus

11:4 Olive Tree A small tree characterized by a long life. Its hard wood, which shows a rich grain when finished, was used for ornamental carpentry. Its fruit was pressed for oil, and the oil was used for cooking or as a fuel for lamps. The Mediterranean cultural area is practically the only area where olives are grown.

The Witnesses Resurrected

11 Now after the three-and-a-half days the
breath of life from God entered them, and
they stood on their feet, and great fear fell
on those who saw them. 12 And they[a] heard
a loud voice from heaven saying to them,
"Come up here." And they ascended to
heaven in a cloud, and their enemies saw
them. 13 In the same hour there was a great
earthquake, and a tenth of the city fell. In
the earthquake seven thousand people were
killed, and the rest were afraid and gave glory to the God of heaven.
14 The second woe is past. Behold, the
third woe is coming quickly.

Seventh Trumpet: The Kingdom Proclaimed

15 Then the seventh angel sounded: And
there were loud voices in heaven, saying,
"The kingdoms[a] of this world have become
the kingdoms of our Lord and of His Christ,
and He shall reign forever and ever!" 16 And
the twenty-four elders who sat before God
on their thrones fell on their faces and worshiped God, 17 saying:

"We give You thanks, O Lord God
Almighty,

10:11 [a] NU-Text and M-Text read *they.* **11:1** [a] NU-Text and M-Text omit *And the angel stood.* **11:4** [a] NU-Text and M-Text read *Lord.* **11:8** [a] NU-Text and M-Text read *their.* **11:9** [a] NU-Text and M-Text read *nations see . . . and will not allow.* **11:12** [a] M-Text reads *I.* **11:15** [a] NU-Text and M-Text read *kingdom . . . has become.*

The One who is and who was and who
is to come,[a]
Because You have taken Your great
power and reigned.
18 The nations were angry, and Your wrath
has come,
And the time of the dead, that they
should be judged,
And that You should reward Your
servants the prophets and the saints,
And those who fear Your name, small
and great,
And should destroy those who destroy
the earth."

19 Then the temple of God was opened
in heaven, and the ark of His covenant[a] was
seen in His temple. And there were lightnings, noises, thunderings, an earthquake,
and great hail.

The Woman, the Child, and the Dragon

12 Now a great sign appeared in heav-
en: a woman clothed with the sun,
with the moon under her feet, and on her
head a garland of twelve stars. 2 Then being
with child, she cried out in labor and in pain
to give birth.
3 And another sign appeared in heaven:
behold, a great, fiery red dragon having sev-
en heads and ten horns, and seven diadems
on his heads. 4 His tail drew a third of the
stars of heaven and threw them to the earth.
And the dragon stood before the woman
who was ready to give birth, to devour her
Child as soon as it was born. 5 She bore a
male Child who was to rule all nations with
a rod of iron. And her Child was caught up to
God and His throne. 6 Then the woman fled
into the wilderness, where she has a place
prepared by God, that they should feed her
there one thousand two hundred and sixty
days.

Satan Thrown Out of Heaven

7 And war broke out in heaven: Michael
and his angels fought with the dragon; and
the dragon and his angels fought, 8 but they
did not prevail, nor was a place found for
them[a] in heaven any longer. 9 So the great
dragon was cast out, that serpent of old,
called the Devil and Satan, who deceives the
whole world; he was cast to the earth, and his
angels were cast out with him.

10 Then I heard a loud voice saying in
heaven, "Now salvation, and strength, and
the kingdom of our God, and the power of
His Christ have come, for the accuser of our
brethren, who accused them before our God
day and night, has been cast down. 11 And
they overcame him by the blood of the Lamb
and by the word of their testimony, and they
did not love their lives to the death. 12 Therefore rejoice, O heavens, and you who dwell
in them! Woe to the inhabitants of the earth
and the sea! For the devil has come down to
you, having great wrath, because he knows
that he has a short time."

The Woman Persecuted

13 Now when the dragon saw that he had
been cast to the earth, he persecuted the
woman who gave birth to the male *Child.*
14 But the woman was given two wings of a
great eagle, that she might fly into the wilderness to her place, where she is nourished
for a time and times and half a time, from
the presence of the serpent. 15 So the serpent
spewed water out of his mouth like a flood
after the woman, that he might cause her to
be carried away by the flood. 16 But the earth
helped the woman, and the earth opened its
mouth and swallowed up the flood which
the dragon had spewed out of his mouth.
17 And the dragon was enraged with the woman, and he went to make war with the rest
of her offspring, who keep the commandments of God and have the testimony of
Jesus Christ.[a]

The Beast from the Sea

13 Then I[a] stood on the sand of the
sea. And I saw a beast rising up
out of the sea, having seven heads and ten
horns,[b] and on his horns ten crowns, and on
his heads a blasphemous name. 2 Now the
beast which I saw was like a leopard, his feet
were like *the feet of* a bear, and his mouth like
the mouth of a lion. The dragon gave him
his power, his throne, and great authority.
3 And I saw one of his heads as if it had been
mortally wounded, and his deadly wound
was healed. And all the world marveled and

11:17 [a] NU-Text and M-Text omit *and who is to come.*
11:19 [a] M-Text reads *the covenant of the Lord.* **12:8** [a] M-Text reads *him.* **12:17** [a] NU-Text and M-Text omit *Christ.*
13:1 [a] NU-Text reads *he.* [b] NU-Text and M-Text read *ten horns and seven heads.*

followed the beast. 4So they worshiped the
dragon who gave authority to the beast; and
they worshiped the beast, saying, "Who *is*
like the beast? Who is able to make war with
him?"

5And he was given a mouth speaking
great things and blasphemies, and he was
given authority to continue[a] for forty-two
months. 6Then he opened his mouth in
blasphemy against God, to blaspheme His
name, His tabernacle, and those who dwell
in heaven. 7It was granted to him to make war
with the saints and to overcome them. And
authority was given him over every tribe,[a]
tongue, and nation. 8All who dwell on the
earth will worship him, whose names have
not been written in the Book of Life of the
Lamb slain from the foundation of the world.

9If anyone has an ear, let him hear. 10He
who leads into captivity shall go into captivity; he who kills with the sword must be
killed with the sword. Here is the patience
and the faith of the saints.

The Beast from the Earth

11Then I saw another beast coming up
out of the earth, and he had two horns like
a lamb and spoke like a dragon. 12And he ex-
ercises all the authority of the first beast in
his presence, and causes the earth and those
who dwell in it to worship the first beast,
whose deadly wound was healed. 13He performs great signs, so that he even makes fire
come down from heaven on the earth in the
sight of men. 14And he deceives those[a] who
dwell on the earth by those signs which he
was granted to do in the sight of the beast,
telling those who dwell on the earth to make
an image to the beast who was wounded by
the sword and lived. 15He was granted *power*
to give breath to the image of the beast, that
the image of the beast should both speak
and cause as many as would not worship the
image of the beast to be killed. 16He causes
all, both small and great, rich and poor, free
and slave, to receive a mark on their right
hand or on their foreheads, 17and that no one
may buy or sell except one who has the mark
or[a] the name of the beast, or the number of
his name.

18Here is wisdom. Let him who has understanding calculate the number of the
beast, for it is the number of a man: His
number *is* 666.

The Lamb and the 144,000

14 Then I looked, and behold, a[a] Lamb
standing on Mount Zion, and with
Him one hundred *and* forty-four thousand,
having[b] His Father's name written on their
foreheads. 2And I heard a voice from heav-
en, like the voice of many waters, and like
the voice of loud thunder. And I heard the
sound of harpists playing their harps. 3They
sang as it were a new song before the throne,
before the four living creatures, and the elders; and no one could learn that song except
the hundred *and* forty-four thousand who
were redeemed from the earth. 4These are
the ones who were not defiled with women,
for they are virgins. These are the ones who
follow the Lamb wherever He goes. These
were redeemed[a] from *among* men, *being*
firstfruits to God and to the Lamb. 5And in
their mouth was found no deceit,[a] for they
are without fault before the throne of God.[b]

The Proclamations of Three Angels

6Then I saw another angel flying in the
midst of heaven, having the everlasting
gospel to preach to those who dwell on the
earth—to every nation, tribe, tongue, and
people— 7saying with a loud voice, "Fear
God and give glory to Him, for the hour of
His judgment has come; and worship Him
who made heaven and earth, the sea and
springs of water."

8And another angel followed, saying,
"Babylon[a] is fallen, is fallen, that great city,
because she has made all nations drink of
the wine of the wrath of her fornication."

9Then a third angel followed them, saying with a loud voice, "If anyone worships
the beast and his image, and receives *his*
mark on his forehead or on his hand, 10he
himself shall also drink of the wine of the
wrath of God, which is poured out full
strength into the cup of His indignation. He
shall be tormented with fire and brimstone
in the presence of the holy angels and in the
presence of the Lamb. 11And the smoke of

13:5 [a] M-Text reads *make war.* **13:7** [a] NU-Text and M-Text add *and people.* **13:14** [a] M-Text reads *my own people.* **13:17** [a] NU-Text and M-Text omit *or.* **14:1** [a] NU-Text and M-Text read *the.* [b] NU-Text and M-Text add *His name and.* **14:4** [a] M-Text adds *by Jesus.* **14:5** [a] NU-Text and M-Text read *falsehood.* [b] NU-Text and M-Text omit *before the throne of God.* **14:8** [a] NU-Text reads *Babylon the great is fallen, is fallen, which has made;* M-Text reads *Babylon the great is fallen. She has made.*

their torment ascends forever and ever; and
they have no rest day or night, who worship
the beast and his image, and whoever receives the mark of his name."
12 Here is the patience of the saints; here
are those[a] who keep the commandments of
God and the faith of Jesus.
13 Then I heard a voice from heaven saying to me,[a] "Write: 'Blessed *are* the dead who
die in the Lord from now on.'"
"Yes," says the Spirit, "that they may rest
from their labors, and their works follow them."

Reaping the Earth's Harvest

14 Then I looked, and behold, a white
cloud, and on the cloud sat *One* like the Son
of Man, having on His head a golden crown,
and in His hand a sharp sickle. 15 And another angel came out of the temple, crying with
a loud voice to Him who sat on the cloud,
"Thrust in Your sickle and reap, for the time
has come for You[a] to reap, for the harvest
of the earth is ripe." 16 So He who sat on the
cloud thrust in His sickle on the earth, and
the earth was reaped.

Reaping the Grapes of Wrath

17 Then another angel came out of the
temple which is in heaven, he also having
a sharp sickle.
18 And another angel came out from the
altar, who had power over fire, and he cried
with a loud cry to him who had the sharp
sickle, saying, "Thrust in your sharp sickle and gather the clusters of the vine of the
earth, for her grapes are fully ripe." 19 So the
angel thrust his sickle into the earth and
gathered the vine of the earth, and threw
it into the great winepress of the wrath of
God. 20 And the winepress was trampled
outside the city, and blood came out of the
winepress, up to the horses' bridles, for one
thousand six hundred furlongs.

Prelude to the Bowl Judgments

15 Then I saw another sign in heaven,
great and marvelous: seven angels
having the seven last plagues, for in them
the wrath of God is complete.
2 And I saw *something* like a sea of glass
mingled with fire, and those who have the
victory over the beast, over his image and
over his mark[a] *and* over the number of his
name, standing on the sea of glass, having
harps of God. 3 They sing the song of Moses,
the servant of God, and the song of the
Lamb, saying:

"Great and marvelous *are* Your works,
Lord God Almighty!
Just and true *are* Your ways,
O King of the saints![a]
4 Who shall not fear You, O Lord, and
glorify Your name?
For *You* alone *are* holy.
For all nations shall come and worship
before You,
For Your judgments have been
manifested."

5 After these things I looked, and behold,[a]
the temple of the tabernacle of the testimony in heaven was opened. 6 And out of the
temple came the seven angels having the
seven plagues, clothed in pure bright linen,
and having their chests girded with golden
bands. 7 Then one of the four living creatures
gave to the seven angels seven golden bowls
full of the wrath of God who lives forever
and ever. 8 The temple was filled with smoke
from the glory of God and from His power,
and no one was able to enter the temple till
the seven plagues of the seven angels were
completed.
16 Then I heard a loud voice from the
temple saying to the seven angels,
"Go and pour out the bowls[a] of the wrath of
God on the earth."

First Bowl: Loathsome Sores

2 So the first went and poured out his
bowl upon the earth, and a foul and loathsome sore came upon the men who had the
mark of the beast and those who worshiped
his image.

Second Bowl: The Sea Turns to Blood

3 Then the second angel poured out his
bowl on the sea, and it became blood as of
a dead *man;* and every living creature in the
sea died.

Third Bowl: The Waters Turn to Blood

4 Then the third angel poured out his
bowl on the rivers and springs of water, and

14:12 [a] NU-Text and M-Text omit *here are those.* **14:13** [a] NU-Text and M-Text omit *to me.* **14:15** [a] NU-Text and M-Text omit *for You.* **15:2** [a] NU-Text and M-Text omit *over his mark.* **15:3** [a] NU-Text and M-Text read *nations.* **15:5** [a] NU-Text and M-Text omit *behold.* **16:1** [a] NU-Text and M-Text read *seven bowls.*

they became blood. 5And I heard the angel of
the waters saying:

"You are righteous, O Lord,[a]
The One who is and who was and who
is to be,[b]
Because You have judged these things.
6 For they have shed the blood of saints
and prophets,
And You have given them blood to
drink.
For[a] it is their just due."

7And I heard another from[a] the altar saying, "Even so, Lord God Almighty, true and
righteous *are* Your judgments."

Fourth Bowl: Men Are Scorched

8Then the fourth angel poured out his
bowl on the sun, and power was given to
him to scorch men with fire. 9And men
were scorched with great heat, and they blasphemed the name of God who has power
over these plagues; and they did not repent
and give Him glory.

Fifth Bowl: Darkness and Pain

10Then the fifth angel poured out his
bowl on the throne of the beast, and his
kingdom became full of darkness; and they
gnawed their tongues because of the pain.
11They blasphemed the God of heaven because of their pains and their sores, and did
not repent of their deeds.

Sixth Bowl: Euphrates Dried Up

12Then the sixth angel poured out his
bowl on the great river Euphrates, and its water was dried up, so that the way of the kings
from the east might be prepared. 13And I
saw three unclean spirits like frogs *coming*
out of the mouth of the dragon, out of the
mouth of the beast, and out of the mouth of
the false prophet. 14For they are spirits of demons, performing signs, *which* go out to the
kings of the earth and[a] of the whole world,
to gather them to the battle of that great day
of God Almighty.

15"Behold, I am coming as a thief. Blessed
is he who watches, and keeps his garments,
lest he walk naked and they see his shame."

16*And they gathered them* together to the
place called in Hebrew, Armageddon.[a]

Seventh Bowl: The Earth Utterly Shaken

17Then the seventh angel poured out his

In Focus

16:16 Armageddon Pronounced *are-muh-GED-un.* From two Hebrew words meaning "the hill of Megiddo." It was the place of many ancient battles in northern Palestine.

bowl into the air, and a loud voice came out
of the temple of heaven, from the throne,
saying, "It is done!" 18And there were noises
and thunderings and lightnings; and there
was a great earthquake, such a mighty and
great earthquake as had not occurred since
men were on the earth. 19Now the great city
was divided into three parts, and the cities
of the nations fell. And great Babylon was
remembered before God, to give her the cup
of the wine of the fierceness of His wrath.
20Then every island fled away, and the mountains were not found. 21And great hail from
heaven fell upon men, *each hailstone* about
the weight of a talent. Men blasphemed God
because of the plague of the hail, since that
plague was exceedingly great.

The Scarlet Woman and the Scarlet Beast

17 Then one of the seven angels who
had the seven bowls came and
talked with me, saying to me,[a] "Come, I will
show you the judgment of the great harlot
who sits on many waters, 2with whom the
kings of the earth committed fornication,
and the inhabitants of the earth were made
drunk with the wine of her fornication."

3So he carried me away in the Spirit into
the wilderness. And I saw a woman sitting
on a scarlet beast *which was* full of names
of blasphemy, having seven heads and ten
horns. 4The woman was arrayed in purple
and scarlet, and adorned with gold and precious stones and pearls, having in her hand
a golden cup full of abominations and the

16:5 [a] NU-Text and M-Text omit *O Lord.* [b] NU-Text and M-Text read *who was, the Holy One.* **16:6** [a] NU-Text and M-Text omit *For.* **16:7** [a] NU-Text and M-Text omit *another from.* **16:14** [a] NU-Text and M-Text omit *of the earth and.* **16:16** [a] M-Text reads *Megiddo.* **17:1** [a] NU-Text and M-Text omit *to me.*

filthiness of her fornication.[a] 5 And on her
forehead a name *was* written:

MYSTERY,
BABYLON THE GREAT,
THE MOTHER OF HARLOTS
AND OF THE ABOMINATIONS
OF THE EARTH.

6 I saw the woman, drunk with the blood of
the saints and with the blood of the martyrs
of Jesus. And when I saw her, I marveled
with great amazement.

The Meaning of the Woman and the Beast

7 But the angel said to me, "Why did
you marvel? I will tell you the mystery of
the woman and of the beast that carries
her, which has the seven heads and the ten
horns. 8 The beast that you saw was, and is
not, and will ascend out of the bottomless pit
and go to perdition. And those who dwell on
the earth will marvel, whose names are not
written in the Book of Life from the foundation of the world, when they see the beast
that was, and is not, and yet is.[a]

9 "Here *is* the mind which has wisdom:
The seven heads are seven mountains on
which the woman sits. 10 There are also seven
kings. Five have fallen, one is, *and* the other
has not yet come. And when he comes, he
must continue a short time. 11 The beast that
was, and is not, is himself also the eighth,
and is of the seven, and is going to perdition.

12 "The ten horns which you saw are ten
kings who have received no kingdom as
yet, but they receive authority for one hour
as kings with the beast. 13 These are of one
mind, and they will give their power and
authority to the beast. 14 These will make
war with the Lamb, and the Lamb will overcome them, for He is Lord of lords and King
of kings; and those *who are* with Him *are*
called, chosen, and faithful."

15 Then he said to me, "The waters which
you saw, where the harlot sits, are peoples,
multitudes, nations, and tongues. 16 And the
ten horns which you saw on[a] the beast, these
will hate the harlot, make her desolate and
naked, eat her flesh and burn her with fire.
17 For God has put it into their hearts to fulfill
His purpose, to be of one mind, and to give
their kingdom to the beast, until the words
of God are fulfilled. 18 And the woman whom
you saw is that great city which reigns over
the kings of the earth."

The Fall of Babylon the Great

18 After these things I saw another
angel coming down from heaven,
having great authority, and the earth was illuminated with his glory. 2 And he cried mightily[a] with a loud voice, saying, "Babylon the great
is fallen, is fallen, and has become a dwelling
place of demons, a prison for every foul spirit,
and a cage for every unclean and hated bird!
3 For all the nations have drunk of the wine of
the wrath of her fornication, the kings of the
earth have committed fornication with her,
and the merchants of the earth have become
rich through the abundance of her luxury."

4 And I heard another voice from heaven
saying, "Come out of her, my people, lest you
share in her sins, and lest you receive of her
plagues. 5 For her sins have reached[a] to heaven, and God has remembered her iniquities.
6 Render to her just as she rendered to you,[a]
and repay her double according to her works;
in the cup which she has mixed, mix double
for her. 7 In the measure that she glorified
herself and lived luxuriously, in the same
measure give her torment and sorrow; for
she says in her heart, 'I sit *as* queen, and am
no widow, and will not see sorrow.' 8 Therefore her plagues will come in one day—
death and mourning and famine. And she
will be utterly burned with fire, for strong *is*
the Lord God who judges[a] her.

The World Mourns Babylon's Fall

9 "The kings of the earth who committed
fornication and lived luxuriously with her
will weep and lament for her, when they see
the smoke of her burning, 10 standing at a distance for fear of her torment, saying, 'Alas,
alas, that great city Babylon, that mighty city!
For in one hour your judgment has come.'

11 "And the merchants of the earth will
weep and mourn over her, for no one buys
their merchandise anymore: 12 merchandise
of gold and silver, precious stones and pearls,
fine linen and purple, silk and scarlet, every
kind of citron wood, every kind of object of

17:4 [a] M-Text reads *the filthiness of the fornication of the earth.* 17:8 [a] NU-Text and M-Text read *and shall be present.* 17:16 [a] NU-Text and M-Text read *saw, and the beast.* 18:2 [a] NU-Text and M-Text omit *mightily.* 18:5 [a] NU-Text and M-Text read *have been heaped up.* 18:6 [a] NU-Text and M-Text omit *to you.* 18:8 [a] NU-Text and M-Text read *has judged.*

ivory, every kind of object of most precious
wood, bronze, iron, and marble; 13and cinnamon and incense, fragrant oil and frankincense, wine and oil, fine flour and wheat,
cattle and sheep, horses and chariots, and
bodies and souls of men. 14The fruit that your
soul longed for has gone from you, and all the
things which are rich and splendid have gone
from you,[a] and you shall find them no more
at all. 15The merchants of these things, who
became rich by her, will stand at a distance
for fear of her torment, weeping and wailing,
16and saying, 'Alas, alas, that great city that
was clothed in fine linen, purple, and scarlet,
and adorned with gold and precious stones
and pearls! 17For in one hour such great riches
came to nothing.' Every shipmaster, all who
travel by ship, sailors, and as many as trade
on the sea, stood at a distance 18and cried out
when they saw the smoke of her burning,
saying, 'What *is* like this great city?'

19"They threw dust on their heads and
cried out, weeping and wailing, and saying,
'Alas, alas, that great city, in which all who
had ships on the sea became rich by her
wealth! For in one hour she is made desolate.'

20"Rejoice over her, O heaven, and *you*
holy apostles[a] and prophets, for God has
avenged you on her!"

Finality of Babylon's Fall

21Then a mighty angel took up a stone like
a great millstone and threw *it* into the sea,
saying, "Thus with violence the great city
Babylon shall be thrown down, and shall not
be found anymore. 22The sound of harpists,
musicians, flutists, and trumpeters shall not
be heard in you anymore. No craftsman of
any craft shall be found in you anymore, and
the sound of a millstone shall not be heard
in you anymore. 23The light of a lamp shall
not shine in you anymore, and the voice of
bridegroom and bride shall not be heard in
you anymore. For your merchants were the
great men of the earth, for by your sorcery all
the nations were deceived. 24And in her was
found the blood of prophets and saints, and
of all who were slain on the earth."

Heaven Exults over Babylon

19 After these things I heard[a] a loud
voice of a great multitude in heav-
en, saying, "Alleluia! Salvation and glory
and honor and power *belong* to the Lord[b]
our God! 2For true and righteous *are* His
judgments, because He has judged the great
harlot who corrupted the earth with her
fornication; and He has avenged on her the
blood of His servants *shed* by her." 3Again
they said, "Alleluia! Her smoke rises up forever and ever!" 4And the twenty-four elders
and the four living creatures fell down and
worshiped God who sat on the throne, saying, "Amen! Alleluia!" 5Then a voice came
from the throne, saying, "Praise our God, all
you His servants and those who fear Him,
both[a] small and great!"

6And I heard, as it were, the voice of a
great multitude, as the sound of many waters
and as the sound of mighty thunderings,
saying, "Alleluia! For the[a] Lord God Omnipotent reigns! 7Let us be glad and rejoice and
give Him glory, for the marriage of the Lamb
has come, and His wife has made herself
ready." 8And to her it was granted to be arrayed in fine linen, clean and bright, for the
fine linen is the righteous acts of the saints.

9Then he said to me, "Write: 'Blessed *are*
those who are called to the marriage supper
of the Lamb!'" And he said to me, "These
are the true sayings of God." 10And I fell at
his feet to worship him. But he said to me,
"See *that you do* not *do that!* I am your fellow
servant, and of your brethren who have the
testimony of Jesus. Worship God! For the
testimony of Jesus is the spirit of prophecy."

Christ on a White Horse

11Now I saw heaven opened, and behold,
a white horse. And He who sat on him *was*

In Focus

19:6 Alleluia Pronounced *al-uh-LOO-yah.* From the Hebrew word *Hallelujah* (pronounced *hal-uh-LOO-yah*), meaning "Praise the Lord."

19:6 Omnipotent Pronounced *ahm-NIP-uh-tent.* Almighty or All-powerful.

18:14 [a] NU-Text and M-Text read *been lost to you.*
18:20 [a] NU-Text and M-Text read *saints and apostles.*
19:1 [a] NU-Text and M-Text add *something like.* [b] NU-Text and M-Text omit *the Lord.* **19:5** [a] NU-Text and M-Text omit *both.* **19:6** [a] NU-Text and M-Text read *our.*

called Faithful and True, and in righteousness He judges and makes war. 12His eyes
were like a flame of fire, and on His head
were many crowns. He had[a] a name written that no one knew except Himself. 13He
was clothed with a robe dipped in blood,
and His name is called The Word of God.
14And the armies in heaven, clothed in fine
linen, white and clean,[a] followed Him on
white horses. 15Now out of His mouth goes
a sharp[a] sword, that with it He should strike
the nations. And He Himself will rule them
with a rod of iron. He Himself treads the
winepress of the fierceness and wrath of Almighty God. 16And He has on *His* robe and
on His thigh a name written:

KING OF KINGS AND
LORD OF LORDS.

The Beast and His Armies Defeated

17Then I saw an angel standing in the
sun; and he cried with a loud voice, saying to
all the birds that fly in the midst of heaven,
"Come and gather together for the supper of
the great God,[a] 18that you may eat the flesh
of kings, the flesh of captains, the flesh of
mighty men, the flesh of horses and of those
who sit on them, and the flesh of all *people,*
free[a] and slave, both small and great."
19And I saw the beast, the kings of the
earth, and their armies, gathered together to
make war against Him who sat on the horse
and against His army. 20Then the beast was
captured, and with him the false prophet
who worked signs in his presence, by which
he deceived those who received the mark of
the beast and those who worshiped his image. These two were cast alive into the lake
of fire burning with brimstone. 21And the
rest were killed with the sword which proceeded from the mouth of Him who sat on
the horse. And all the birds were filled with
their flesh.

Satan Bound 1,000 Years

20 Then I saw an angel coming down
from heaven, having the key to the
bottomless pit and a great chain in his hand.
2He laid hold of the dragon, that serpent of
old, who is *the* Devil and Satan, and bound
him for a thousand years; 3and he cast him
into the bottomless pit, and shut him up,
and set a seal on him, so that he should deceive the nations no more till the thousand
years were finished. But after these things
he must be released for a little while.

19:12 [a] M-Text adds *names written, and.* 19:14 [a] NU-Text and M-Text read *pure white linen.* 19:15 [a] M-Text adds *two-edged.* 19:17 [a] NU-Text and M-Text read *the great supper of God.* 19:18 [a] NU-Text and M-Text read *both free.*

YOU CAN BE A KING

READ IT: REVELATION 20:4

A long time ago there were great kings, and small kings ruled under the great kings. The kings of the Herod family of Judea ruled during the time of Jesus and Paul on earth. But the Herods were small kings who ruled under the authority of the great Roman emperors.

You are a king if you are in charge of what God gives you to do. Right now God wants you to take charge of your own life. As you prove you can rule over your own life by living for Him, then God will give you greater work to do. He will be your great King, but you will be a king under Him.

People get in trouble because they believe they can be kings and queens without God. Sad to say, such people usually end up in ruin. God has to be King of your life because He is your Creator. Your life belongs to Him. (See Revelation 3:21.)

The Saints Reign with Christ 1,000 Years

⁴And I saw thrones, and they sat on them,
and judgment was committed to them. Then
I saw the souls of those who had been beheaded for their witness to Jesus and for the
word of God, who had not worshiped the
beast or his image, and had not received *his*
mark on their foreheads or on their hands.
And they lived and reigned with Christ for
a[a] thousand years. ⁵But the rest of the dead
did not live again until the thousand years
were finished. This *is* the first resurrection.
⁶Blessed and holy *is* he who has part in the
first resurrection. Over such the second
death has no power, but they shall be priests
of God and of Christ, and shall reign with
Him a thousand years.

Satanic Rebellion Crushed

⁷Now when the thousand years have expired, Satan will be released from his prison
⁸and will go out to deceive the nations which
are in the four corners of the earth, Gog
and Magog, to gather them together to battle, whose number *is* as the sand of the sea.
⁹They went up on the breadth of the earth
and surrounded the camp of the saints and
the beloved city. And fire came down from
God out of heaven and devoured them. ¹⁰The
devil, who deceived them, was cast into the
lake of fire and brimstone where[a] the beast
and the false prophet *are*. And they will be
tormented day and night forever and ever.

The Great White Throne Judgment

¹¹Then I saw a great white throne and
Him who sat on it, from whose face the
earth and the heaven fled away. And there
was found no place for them. ¹²And I saw
the dead, small and great, standing before
God,[a] and books were opened. And another
book was opened, which is *the Book* of Life.
And the dead were judged according to their
works, by the things which were written in
the books. ¹³The sea gave up the dead who
were in it, and Death and Hades delivered up
the dead who were in them. And they were
judged, each one according to his works.
¹⁴Then Death and Hades were cast into the
lake of fire. This is the second death.[a] ¹⁵And
anyone not found written in the Book of Life
was cast into the lake of fire.

20:4 [a] M-Text reads *the*. **20:10** [a] NU-Text and M-Text add *also*. **20:12** [a] NU-Text and M-Text read *the throne*. **20:14** [a] NU-Text and M-Text add *the lake of fire*.

THE LAST JUDGMENT

READ IT: REVELATION 20:12–15

Quite often you have to take exams at school. The grades you get will help decide what you're going to be later in life. There are many good careers, but your exams will help guide you to the best career for you.

Someday God also is going to give everybody a big exam. Some people will pass—but others will fail the test. You don't have to be clever to pass God's exam. All you have to do is listen to God's Word in the Bible. God's Word tells you that you don't measure up to the way God planned you should. The Bible says "all have sinned and fall short of the glory of God" (Romans 3:23).

So what can you do? You can't go back and fix all your failures. The good news is that *God* can fix them! Jesus took *your* place and died in *your place*. *If you* give yourself to Jesus, you don't need to fear the last judgment of God. Jesus took that final test for you.

All Things Made New

21 Now I saw a new heaven and a new
earth, for the first heaven and the
first earth had passed away. Also there was
no more sea. 2Then I, John,[a] saw the holy city,
New Jerusalem, coming down out of heaven
from God, prepared as a bride adorned for her
husband. 3And I heard a loud voice from heav-
en saying, "Behold, the tabernacle of God *is*
with men, and He will dwell with them, and
they shall be His people. God Himself will be
with them *and be* their God. 4And God will
wipe away every tear from their eyes; there
shall be no more death, nor sorrow, nor crying. There shall be no more pain, for the former things have passed away."
5Then He who sat on the throne said,
"Behold, I make all things new." And He
said to me,[a] "Write, for these words are true
and faithful."
6And He said to me, "It is done![a] I am the
Alpha and the Omega, the Beginning and
the End. I will give of the fountain of the water of life freely to him who thirsts. 7He who
overcomes shall inherit all things,[a] and I will
be his God and he shall be My son. 8But the
cowardly, unbelieving,[a] abominable, murderers, sexually immoral, sorcerers, idolaters, and all liars shall have their part in the
lake which burns with fire and brimstone,
which is the second death."

21:2 [a] NU-Text and M-Text omit *John*. 21:5 [a] NU-Text and M-Text omit *to me*. 21:6 [a] M-Text omits *It is done*. 21:7 [a] M-Text reads *overcomes, I shall give him these things*. 21:8 [a] M-Text adds *and sinners*.

RELATIONSHIPS

READ IT: REVELATION 21:3

If you think you have a pretty good relationship with God now, just wait. At the end of time, when Jesus comes again, there will be a new heaven and a new earth. We will experience the ultimate Immanuel. God will live with us. He will be with us as Jesus was once here on earth thousands of years ago. We will be in a very, very close relationship with Him, better than anything we can imagine.

GRIEF

READ IT: REVELATION 21:4

It's kind of a bummer, but there will always be suffering on earth. There will always be pain and sadness. But in Christ, we can have hope for eternity. We are promised that on the other side of death there is no more death or sorrow or pain. Can you imagine?

The New Jerusalem

9Then one of the seven angels who had
the seven bowls filled with the seven last
plagues came to me[a] and talked with me,
saying, "Come, I will show you the bride, the
Lamb's wife."[b] 10And he carried me away in
the Spirit to a great and high mountain, and
showed me the great city, the holy[a] Jerusalem, descending out of heaven from God,
11having the glory of God. Her light *was* like a
most precious stone, like a jasper stone, clear
as crystal. 12Also she had a great and high
wall with twelve gates, and twelve angels at
the gates, and names written on them, which
are *the names* of the twelve tribes of the children of Israel: 13three gates on the east, three
gates on the north, three gates on the south,
and three gates on the west.

14Now the wall of the city had twelve
foundations, and on them were the names[a]
of the twelve apostles of the Lamb. 15And he
who talked with me had a gold reed to measure the city, its gates, and its wall. 16The city
is laid out as a square; its length is as great
as its breadth. And he measured the city
with the reed: twelve thousand furlongs. Its
length, breadth, and height are equal. 17Then
he measured its wall: one hundred *and*
forty-four cubits, *according* to the measure of
a man, that is, of an angel. 18The construction of its wall was *of* jasper; and the city *was*
pure gold, like clear glass. 19The foundations
of the wall of the city *were* adorned with all
kinds of precious stones: the first foundation *was* jasper, the second sapphire, the
third chalcedony, the fourth emerald, 20the
fifth sardonyx, the sixth sardius, the seventh
chrysolite, the eighth beryl, the ninth topaz,
the tenth chrysoprase, the eleventh jacinth,
and the twelfth amethyst. 21The twelve gates
were twelve pearls: each individual gate was
of one pearl. And the street of the city *was*
pure gold, like transparent glass.

The Glory of the New Jerusalem

22But I saw no temple in it, for the Lord
God Almighty and the Lamb are its temple.
23The city had no need of the sun or of the
moon to shine in it,[a] for the glory[b] of God illuminated it. The Lamb *is* its light. 24And the
nations of those who are saved[a] shall walk

21:9 [a] NU-Text and M-Text omit *to me.* [b] M-Text reads *I will show you the woman, the Lamb's bride.* **21:10** [a] NU-Text and M-Text omit *the great* and read *the holy city, Jerusalem.* **21:14** [a] NU-Text and M-Text read *twelve names.* **21:23** [a] NU-Text and M-Text omit *in it.* [b] M-Text reads *the very glory.* **21:24** [a] NU-Text and M-Text omit *of those who are saved.*

GOD MAKES ALL THINGS NEW

READ IT: REVELATION 21:5

God enjoys creating things. He enjoyed creating the world, even though we later spoiled His world by our sins. Someday He is going to create the world all over again. Sin and the miseries of sin will be gone forever.

In fact, God has already begun His new creation. He is making people new again everywhere in the world. You can be part of God's new creation if you ask Him to give you His new life. Jesus said, "Unless one is born again, he cannot see the kingdom of God" (John 3:3). You become a new creation of God when you are "born again."

Of course, you can't be born again the way you were born the first time, but God can change you inside. What a thrilling idea! A new start! A brand-new life! And God will do it for you in a single moment if you will sincerely ask Him.

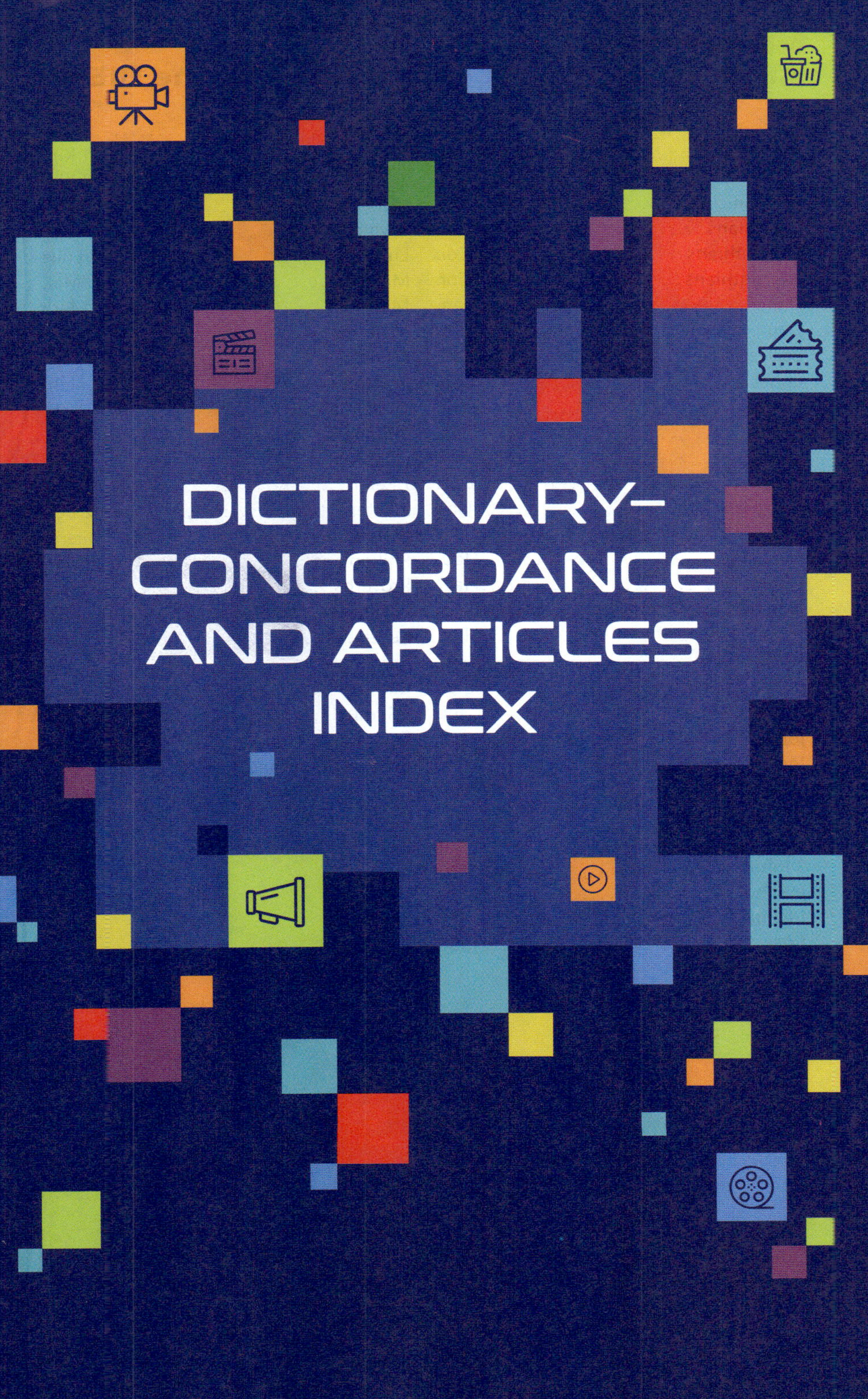
DICTIONARY-
CONCORDANCE
AND ARTICLES
INDEX

ABBREVIATIONS for the BOOKS of the BIBLE

Acts	Acts
Amos	Amos
1 Chronicles	1 Chr.
2 Chronicles	2 Chr.
Colossians	Col.
1 Corinthians	1 Cor.
2 Corinthians	2 Cor.
Daniel	Dan.
Deuteronomy	Deut.
Ecclesiastes	Eccl.
Ephesians	Eph.
Esther	Esth.
Exodus	Ex.
Ezekiel	Ezek.
Ezra	Ezra
Galatians	Gal.
Genesis	Gen.
Habakkuk	Hab.
Haggai	Hag.
Hebrews	Heb.
Hosea	Hos.
Isaiah	Is.
James	James
Jeremiah	Jer.
Job	Job
Joel	Joel
John (Gospel)	John
1 John	1 John
2 John	2 John
3 John	3 John
Jonah	Jon.
Joshua	Josh.
Jude	Jude
Judges	Judg.
1 Kings	1 Kin.
2 Kings	2 Kin.
Lamentations	Lam.
Leviticus	Lev.
Luke	Luke
Malachi	Mal.
Mark	Mark
Matthew	Matt.
Micah	Mic.
Nahum	Nah.
Nehemiah	Neh.
Numbers	Num.
Obadiah	Obad.
1 Peter	1 Pet.
2 Peter	2 Pet.
Philemon	Philem.
Philippians	Phil.
Proverbs	Prov.
Psalms	Ps.
Revelation	Rev.
Romans	Rom.
Ruth	Ruth
1 Samuel	1 Sam.
2 Samuel	2 Sam.
Song of Solomon	Song
1 Thessalonians	1 Thess.
2 Thessalonians	2 Thess.
1 Timothy	1 Tim.
2 Timothy	2 Tim.
Titus	Titus
Zechariah	Zech.
Zephaniah	Zeph.

BOOKS of the BIBLE

Old Testament

Genesis (JEN-ih-sis)
Exodus (EX-oh-dus)
Leviticus (leh-VIT-ih-kus)
Numbers
Deuteronomy (dew-ter-ONN-oh-mee)
Joshua (JOSH-you-uh)
Judges
Ruth
1 and 2 Samuel (SAM-you-ell)
1 and 2 Kings
1 and 2 Chronicles (KRON-ih-kuls)
Ezra (EZ-ruh)
Nehemiah (nee-huh-MY-uh)
Esther (ESS-ter)
Job (JOBE)
Psalms (SALMS)
Proverbs (PRAH-verbs)
Ecclesiastes (ih-klee-zih-ASS-tees)
Song of Solomon
Isaiah (eye-ZAY-uh)
Jeremiah (jer-uh-MY-uh)
Lamentations (lam-men-TAY-shuns)
Ezekiel (ee-ZEEK-yell)
Daniel (DAN-yell)
Hosea (ho-ZAY-uh)
Joel (JO-ell)
Amos (AY-mus)
Obadiah (oh-buh-DIE-uh)
Jonah (JO-nuh)
Micah (MY-kuh)
Nahum (NAY-hum)
Habakkuk (huh-BACK-kuk)
Zephaniah (zef-uh-NIGH-uh)
Haggai (HAG-ay-eye)
Zechariah (zek-uh-RIGH-uh)
Malachi (MAL-uh-kigh)

New Testament

Matthew (MATH-you)
Mark
Luke
John
Acts
Romans (ROW-muns)
1 and 2 Corinthians (ko-RIN-thee-uns)
Galatians (guh-LAY-shuns)
Ephesians (ee-FEE-zhuns)
Philippians (fil-LIP-ih-uns)
Colossians (ko-LOSH-shuns)
1 and 2 Thessalonians (thess-uh-LOW-nih-uns)
1 and 2 Timothy
Titus (TIGHT-us)
Philemon (fih-LEE-mun)
Hebrews (HE-brews)
James
1 and 2 Peter
1, 2, and 3 John
Jude (JEWD)
Revelation (rev-uh-LAY-shun)

DICTIONARY–CONCORDANCE

This dictionary-concordance will help you to find the meanings of words used in the Bible and also to locate key passages in which those words occur.

The more difficult words show pronunciation. The meaning follows the word itself (or the pronunciation) and this is followed by the concordance listing. In the concordance listing only the first letter of the word is used—"l." for "love." The references give you the name of the Bible book, then the chapter, and then the verse or verses. Thus, Luke 24:30–51 would be Luke, chapter 24, verses 30 through 51. See the abbreviations for Bible books listed on page 1536.

A

Aaron (AIR-un) The older brother of Moses (Ex. 6:20; 7:7); the spokesman for Moses (Ex. 7:1); brings on plagues with his rod (Ex. 7:10—8:17); from him are descended the class of priests in Israel (Ex. 29:9); he makes atonement and stops a plague (Num. 16:41–50); his rod buds (Num. 17:1–11); his death (Num. 20:22–29).

Abba (AB-buh) Aramaic for "Father" (Mark 14:36; Rom. 8:15; Gal. 4:6).

Abed-Nego (ah-BED-nee-go) Babylonian name of one of Daniel's companions (Dan. 1:7; 3:16).

Abel (AY-bull) Son of Adam; murdered by his brother Cain (Gen. 4:2ff). He is described as righteous (Matt. 23:35; 1 John 3:12). In Hebrews 11:4 he stands at the head of the heroes of faith.

abhor To despise, hate.
I hate and a. lying Ps. 119:163
Nations will a. him Prov. 24:24
A. what is evil Rom. 12:9

abomination (ah-bom-ih-NAY-shun) Something loathsome.
Wickedness is an a. Prov. 8:7
is an a. in the sight of God Luke 16:15

Abraham; Abram (AY-bruh-ham; AY-brum) Israel's first great patriarch or leader. Through faith in God's promise to make of him a great nation, he is led from Ur to Canaan (Gen. 11:31—15:7). God makes a covenant with him (Gen. 15:7–21); an angel of God promises that Sarah shall give birth to a son (Gen. 18:10); God tests Abraham's faith (Gen. 22:1–19). He stands as the father of all the faithful (Gal. 3:7).

Absalom (AB-suh-lum) Son of David and Maacah; turned the people against his father; was defeated and then slain by Joab, to the great sorrow of David (2 Sam. 3:3; 13:20—19:10).

Adam (ADD-um) The first man, from whom is descended all mankind. Created on the same day as the animals, he is particularly blessed by God (Gen. 1:27, 28). He and Eve were driven from the Garden of Eden because of their disobedience (Gen. 3:1–14).

adultery (ah-DULL-ter-ih) Unchastity; unfaithfulness to one's husband or wife.
You shall not commit a. Ex. 20:14
You shall not commit a. Deut. 5:18
has already committed a. with her Matt. 5:28

advise To tell, inform.
I will a. you what Num. 24:14

advocate One who speaks in defense of another. Christ is so called (1 John 2:1).

affliction Distress; pain; adversity.
God has seen my a. Gen. 31:42

agape (ah-GAH-pe) A Greek word meaning "love." It is also used to denote the "love feasts" of the early Christians (Jude 12).

Agrippa (ah-GRIP-uh) King of Judea before whom Paul appeared to plead his defense (Acts 25:13—26:32).

Ahab (AY-hab) An evil king of the northern kingdom of Israel in the time of Elijah; married Jezebel, a Sidonian princess, which caused religious turmoil; robbed Naboth of his vineyard and then caused his death (1 Kin. 16:29—22:40).

Ahasuerus (ah-haz-you-EAR-us) The name of two kings in the Old Testament. 1. A king of Persia and the husband of the Jewess Esther (Esth. 1:2, 19; 2:16, 17). Through her guardian, Mordecai, Esther was able to save her people, Israel, from an evil plan. 2. A king of the Medes and the father of Darius (Dan. 9:1).

Ahaz (AY-haz) A name which means "he has grasped." 1. A wicked king of Judah who worshiped idols on the "high places" and even offered one of his own sons on an altar (2 Kin. 16:3, 4); refused to listen to the prophet Isaiah when he encouraged the king to call on God instead of seeking foreign aid against the army of Syria (Is. 7:1–16); heard the wonderful announcement of the promised Messiah. Hosea and Micah also prophesied during the reign of Ahaz (Hos. 1:1; Mic. 1:1). 2. A descendant of King Saul, the son of Micah and the father of Jehoaddah (1 Chr. 8:35, 36; 9:42).

alien A foreigner.
give it to the a. Deut. 14:21

Alleluia (al-uh-LOO-yah) Hallelujah; "Praise the Lord" (Rev. 19:1, 3, 4, 6).

Almighty, the God, as being all powerful.
I am A. God Gen. 17:1
as God A. Ex. 6:3
Holy, holy, holy, Lord God A. Rev. 4:8

Alpha and Omega (AL-fuh; oh-MEE-guh) The first and last letters of the Greek alphabet; hence, "the First and the Last." Applied to God (Rev. 1:8, 11; 21:6) and to Christ (Rev. 22:13).

altar Table of sacrifice.
Noah built an a. Gen. 8:20
Moses built an a. Ex. 17:15

Am Exist; be. The reply to Moses' question for the name of the Deity, "I AM WHO I AM" (Ex. 3:14), indicates that the Lord makes Himself present as He wills.

Amen *Verily; so be it (Matt. 6:13; Rev. 3:14).*

Amos (AY-mus) A prophet of Israel; the first to proclaim that God is the ruler of the whole universe; foretold the downfall of the northern kingdom. The OT Book of Amos is the third of the 12 Minor Prophets.

Ananias (ann-uh-NIGH-us) 1. A Christian of Jerusalem who lost his life for lying and attempting to hold back part of the price of property he had sold (Acts 5:1–10). 2. A Christian of Damascus who received Paul into Christian fellowship (Acts 9:10–17; 22:12–16). 3. A Jewish high priest before whom Paul was tried in Jerusalem (Acts 23:2; 24:1).

Ancient of Days The judge in Daniel's vision; probably intended to be God Himself (Dan. 7:9, 13, 22).

Andrew One of the first of the 12 apostles of Jesus; brother of Simon Peter (Matt. 4:18; 10:2–4; Mark 1:16–20, 29; 3:16–19; 13:3; John 1:35–42, 44; 6:8; 12:20–22; 21:15–17; Acts 1:13). He was a former disciple of John the Baptist (John 1:35–40). *See* Simon.

angel A heavenly messenger.
an a. spoke to me 1 Kin. 13:18
a little lower than the a. Ps. 8:5
a. came and ministered Matt. 4:11
the a. Gabriel was sent Luke 1:26
a. of the bottomless pit Rev. 9:11

Angel of the Lord The heavenly messenger whose presence is evidence of God Himself (Gen. 16:7; Ex. 3:2; Num. 22:23; 1 Kin. 19:7; Matt. 28:2; Luke 1:11; 2:9).

anoint To consecrate; to pour oil upon in a ceremony.
a. my head with oil Ps. 23:5
to a. My body Mark 14:8
You did not a. Luke 7:46

answer A reply.
soft a. turns away wrath Prov. 15:1

ant An insect
Go to the a., you sluggard Prov. 6:6

antichrist (AN-tih-krist) Opponent or enemy of Christ.
He is a. who denies 1 John 2:22
deceiver and an a. 2 John 7

Antioch (ANN-tee-ock) 1. In Syria; the name "Christian" was first used here (Acts 11:26). 2. In Pisidia; visited by Paul and Barnabas (Acts 13:14–52).

anxious Worried; careful.
Be a. for nothing Phil. 4:6

Apollos (uh-POLL-us) A well-educated Jew and a follower of John the Baptist; knew the Old Testament well and taught others (Acts 18:24–28); learned of the Holy Spirit from Aquila and Priscilla in

Ephesus; preached in Corinth (1 Cor. 1:12; 3:4–6, 22; 4:6). Some teachers think Apollos wrote the Letter to the Hebrews.

apostle (uh-POSS-ul) One of the 12 disciples chosen by Jesus (Matt. 10:2–4) or certain other early Christian leaders (Acts 14:14; Rom. 16:7; Gal. 1:1).

apple A fruit.
a. of His eye Deut. 32:10; Ps. 17:8

appoint 1. To consecrate, or set apart as for the ministry.
a. elders in every church Acts 14:23
a. elders in every city Titus 1:5
2. To establish.
I will a. a place 1 Chr. 17:9

Aquila (ak-WILL-uh) A Jew who lived in Rome with his wife Priscilla until the emperor ordered all Jewish people to leave; moved to Corinth where he worked as a tentmaker with Paul (Acts 18:1–3); traveled with Paul to Syria (Acts 18:18, 19).

Arabia; Arabians The NW part of the large peninsula in SW Asia; scene of many biblical events. The peoples of the area were nomads.

Arameans (air-uh-ME-uns) A Semitic people, traditionally descendants of Shem, the oldest son of Noah (Gen. 10:1, 22, 23). They were nomads, wandering along the W side of the Syrian desert.

Ararat (AIR-uh-rat) The mountain on which the ark came to rest after the Flood (Gen. 8:4); the land of Ararat is Armenia.

Archangel (ark-AYN-jel) An angel of the highest order.
the voice of an a. 1 Thess. 4:16
Michael the a. Jude 9

ark A floating vessel; ship.
Noah's a. Gen. 6:14—8:19
Noah entered the a. Matt. 24:38

ark of the Testimony The chest which held the two stone tablets on which were inscribed the Ten Commandments (Ex. 25:10–22). Also called the ark of the covenant (1 Kin. 8:6; 2 Chr. 5:2).

Armageddon (are-muh-GED-un) The *name means "mountain* of Megiddo." The large valley of Jezreel or Plain of Esdraelon near the ancient fortified city of Megiddo in northern Israel. According to prophecy, this is the place where the last battle of this age will be fought between the forces of good and evil.

Artaxerxes (are-tack-SURK-sees) The name of two Persian kings: the first, mentioned in Ezra 7 and Nehemiah 2; 13; his grandson, the second, may have been the builder of the palace described in Esth. 1:5, 6.

Ascension (ah-SEN-shun) The return of the risen Christ to heaven (Luke 24:51; Acts 1:9) on the fortieth day after the Resurrection.

Ascents, Song of A title given to each of Psalms 120–134; probably so called because of their use in a procession ascending to the temple or for pilgrims going up to Jerusalem.

Asher (ASH-er) The eighth son of Jacob, the second by Zilpah (Gen. 30:12ff); one of the 12 tribes of Israel.

Asherah (ah-SHE-rah) The wife of the Canaanite god Baal. Asherah often refers to a wooden pole that stood near Canaanite high places of worship ("grove"). Gideon was ordered by the Lord to destroy the wooden image beside the altar (Judg. 6:25).

Asia (AY-zhuh) A Roman province in the western part of what we call Asia Minor (Acts 16:6; 20:18; 1 Pet. 1:1; Rev. 1:4).

ask To request.
A., and it will be given Matt. 7:7
a. in prayer, believing Matt. 21:22
do not know what you a. Mark 10:38

Assyria (ah-SEER-ih-uh) A kingdom between the Tigris and Euphrates Rivers in Mesopotamia; ruled over the ancient world from the 9th to the 7th centuries B.C. (before Christ). After defeating the northern kingdom of Israel in 722 B.C., the Assyrians captured and carried away thousands of Israelites to their country. In 701 B.C., Assyria attacked the southern kingdom of Judah, but did not succeed because a plague from the "Angel of the Lord" struck down the soldiers (2 Kin. 19:35). Thousands died, and Jerusalem, the capital, was saved. (Find out more about Assyria in the Book of Jonah and in Is. 10:5; Ezek. 16:28; and Hos. 8:9).

Athens (ATH-ins) The capital city of the

ancient Greeks as well as the modern capital, located on the southern coast of Attica; center of Greek art, architecture, literature, and politics during the golden age of Grecian history. The world's most famous building—the Parthenon—stands here in ruins. During his second missionary journey, the apostle Paul preached his famous sermon on Areopagus, Mars' Hill (Acts 17:15—18:1).

Atonement, Day of An annual fast day of the Jews. Ordained in the Law as a day of humbling oneself and making amends for sins (Lev. 23:27).

B

Baal (BAYL) One of the fertility gods of Canaan. There were many local Baals. (Elijah met the prophets of Baal in a contest (1 Kin. 18:1–40).

Babel (BAY-bull) Hebrew form of the name "Babylon," capital of Babylonia; site of the Tower of Babel (Gen. 11:1–9).

babes Infants; small children.
Out of the mouth of b. Ps. 8:2; Matt. 21:16

Babylon (BAB-ih-lun) An ancient walled city, once the capital of the Babylonian Empire, located between the Tigris and Euphrates Rivers. In 586 B.C., the leading citizens of Judah were taken captive by King Nebuchadnezzar and brought to Babylon where they stayed for 70 years during the period called the Exile. (You can read about this period of history in the books of Isaiah, Jeremiah, Ezekiel, and Daniel.) Here were the famous hanging gardens and, nearby, the Tower of Babel (Gen. 11:1–9).

baptism A ceremony in which one enters the church family. It is a way of showing that you have been washed free of sin by the death and rising from the dead of *Jesus Christ.*
John's b. of Jesus Matt. 3:13–17
b. by the disciples John 4:1, 2

Barabbas (bar-RAB-bus) A robber held in prison by the Roman authorities at the time of Jesus' trial; Pilate freed him and condemned Jesus to death (Matt. 27:20–26; Mark 15:7–15; Luke 23:18–25; John 18:39, 40).

Barnabas (BARN-nuh-bus) The surname given by the apostles to Joses or Joseph, a Levite of Cyprus, who was sent by them to Antioch to confirm the church there. Accompanied Paul on his first missionary journey (Acts 4:36, 37; 9:27; 11:22, 25, 30; 12:25; 13:1–13, 43–52; 14:12, 14, 20; 15:2ff; 1 Cor. 9:6; Gal. 2:1, 9, 13; Col. 4:10).

Bartholomew (bar-THAHL-uh-mew) One of the 12 apostles of Jesus (Matt. 10:3; Mark 3:18; Luke 6:14; Acts 1:13).

Baruch (bar-OOK) Jeremiah's scribe, or secretary (Jer. 36:4ff).

basket The container for holding a dry measure.
under a b. Matt. 5:15; Mark 4:21; Luke 11:33

bath A liquid measure equal to the dry measure ephah (Ezek. 45:11); about six gallons.
just ephah, and a just b. Ezek. 45:10

Bathsheba (bath-SHE-bah) The wife of Uriah, the Hittite, and King David (2 Sam. 11; 12:24); the woman with whom David sinned. David had her husband, Uriah, killed in battle. Then David married her and she became the mother of Solomon, who ruled after David's death.

beard The growth of hair on the lower part of a man's face. The Hebrews were forbidden to cut the edges of their beards (Lev. 19:27). The shaving off of beards was an indignity (2 Sam. 10:4, 5).

beast Animal (used for all living things other than man, as a general term); in the Book of Revelation the word is used of both "heavenly" beasts and "beasts from the bottomless pit."

Beatitudes (bee-AT-ih-tyoods) The blessings listed by Jesus in the Sermon on the Mount (Matt. 5:3–12; Luke 6:20–23).

Beelzebub (bee-EL-zee-bub) The prince of demons whom Jesus refers to as Satan (Matt. 10:25; 12:26; Mark 3:23; Luke 11:15, 18). The Jews considered this heathen god as the supreme evil spirit.

beginning Outset; start.
In the b. God created Gen. 1:1
In the b. was the Word John 1:1

begotten Having been brought into being.
The only b. Son John 1:18

benediction (ben-ih-DICK-shun) An asking for God's blessing, as by a minister or priest at the conclusion of a church service; a blessing.

Benjamin The youngest son of Jacob. His mother, Rachel, died at his birth (Gen. 35:18). Especially beloved by his father and by Joseph, his only full brother (Gen. 42:4, 36; 43:14–16, 29, 34; 44:12; 45:12, 14, 22). Ancestor of the tribe of Benjamin, the smallest of the 12 tribes of Israel.

Bethany (BETH-un-nee) A small village on the E slope of the Mount of Olives, about one and one-half miles E of Jerusalem. From here Jesus made His triumphal entry into Jerusalem (Mark 11:1–11); the home of Simon the leper (Matt. 26:6; Mark 14:3); home of Lazarus, Mary, and Martha (John 11:1–44); site of Jesus' final parting from His disciples (Luke 24:50, 51).

Bethel (BETH-ul) City 14 miles N of Jerusalem. Near here Abraham built an altar (Gen. 12:8; 13:3, 4); here Jacob's name was changed to Israel (Gen. 35:10–15); the ark of the Testimony rested here (Judg. 20:18–28); Jeroboam made it a place of idolatry (1 Kin. 12:29—13:32), which Josiah destroyed (2 Kin. 23:4–15).

Bethlehem A very old town about six miles SSW of Jerusalem; the birthplace of Jesus (Matt. 2:1–16; Luke 2:4–15; John 7:42); also associated with David (1 Sam. 16:1–13; 17:12, 15; 20:6, 28), Ruth (Ruth 1:1, 2, 19, 22; 2:4; 4:11), and other persons of the OT.

bird A winged creature.
let b. fly above Gen. 1:20
b. of the air Gen. 6:7; Matt. 6:26

birthright Privilege of the firstborn of a family.
Esau despised his b. Gen. 25:34

bishop A high-ranking minister, head of a district or diocese.
A b. then must be blameless 1 Tim. 3:2

blood The life-giving fluid of the body. In the OT it is regarded as the seat of life; but since shed blood signifies death, the word is used of both life and death.
you shall not eat any b. Lev. 7:26; Deut. 12:16
this is My b. Matt. 26:28; Mark 14:24
new covenant in My b. Luke 22:20
eats My flesh and drinks My b. John 6:54
redemption through His b. Eph. 1:7; Col. 1:14
precious b. of Christ 1 Pet. 1:19

Boaz (BOH-az) A wealthy Bethlehemite who married Ruth (Ruth 2:1—4:22).

body The physical human being or animal. The church is called "the body of Christ" as the living spiritual community of which Christ is the head and all believers are members. At the Lord's Supper, Jesus broke bread to represent His body given in sacrifice for sinners.
touches the dead b. Num. 19:11
lamp of the b. is the eye Matt. 6:22
this is My b. Matt. 26:26; Mark 14:22; Luke 22:19; 1 Cor. 11:24
many members in one b. Rom. 12:4
you are the b. of Christ 1 Cor. 12:27

Booths, Feast of *See* Feast of Tabernacles.

bread A food made of a dough of flour or meal and water and baked; sustenance in general. Often used in offerings by OT peoples. In the NT, also used in reference to the coming of the kingdom of God or to Jesus Himself.
not live by b. alone Deut. 8:3
shall eat unleavened b. Deut. 16:8
Cast your b. upon the Eccl. 11:1
not live by b. alone Matt. 4:4
Give us this day our daily b. Matt. 6:11; Luke 11:3
eat b. in the kingdom Luke 14:15
the true b. from heaven John 6:32
I am the b. of life John 6:35

bread, breaking of Since the earliest form of the Lord's Supper involved the "breaking of bread," the term has been used for worship in general (Acts 2:42).

bread from heaven The food miraculously provided by God for the Israelites in their wanderings through the wilderness (Ex. 16:15).

brother A male relative of the same parents; a close associate.
Am I my b.'s keeper Gen. 4:9
b. is born for adversity Prov. 17:17
sticks closer than a b. Prov. 18:24
is My b. and sister and Matt. 12:50

C

Cain Son of Adam; murdered his brother Abel (Gen. 4:2ff); prototype of wicked men (1 John 3:12; Jude 11).

Calvary (KAL-vuh-ree) From the Latin word meaning "skull." A place outside the second wall of Jerusalem where Jesus was crucified (Luke 23:33). Since Jerusalem has been destroyed and rebuilt so many times, no one knows for sure where this event took place, but there are at least two opinions: (1) A spot under the Church of the Holy Sepulcher; (2) "Gordon's Calvary," named for General Charles Gordon, a British soldier and explorer. The Hebrew name for the place where Jesus was crucified is *Golgotha* (Matt. 27:33; Mark 15:22; John 19:17).

camel A large animal of desert areas.
a c. to go through Matt. 19:24
and swallow a c. Matt. 23:24

Canaan; Canaanites (KAY-nun; KAY-nun-nights) 1. The fourth son of Ham and grandson of Noah (Gen. 9:18–27; 10:6, 15). 2. The region along the Mediterranean Sea known as the Promised Land—the land given by God to Abraham and the Children of Israel; known as Israel today; the land bridge between three continents—Africa, Europe, and Asia. Because of its position, this narrow strip of land has always been very important to invading armies as well as to traders.

Capernaum (kuh-PURR-nah-um) A city on the NW shore of the Sea of Galilee. Jesus lived there (Mark 2:1); home of Peter and Andrew (Matt. 8:5, 14); here Jesus healed the man with an unclean spirit (Mark 1:21–28) and the paralytic (Mark 2:1–12) and held discussions about true greatness (Mark 9:33–37) and paying the half-shekel tax (Matt. 17:24–27).

Carmel, Mount (KAR-mel) A mountain range in northern Palestine, Israel; stretches SE from the Mediterranean Sea about thirteen miles. Here Elijah held his famous contest with the Baal priests (1 Kin. 18:19, 20); saw the cloud which marked the end of a long drought (1 Kin. 8:44).

cheek The side of the face.
slaps you on your right c. Matt. 5:39; Luke 6:29

cherubim (CHER-uh-bim) Winged creatures, statues of which were fixed to the mercy seat of the ark of the Testimony. Two cherubim carved from olive wood were placed within the inner room of the temple.
two c. of gold Ex. 25:18
made two c. of olive 1 Kin. 6:23

child A young person of either sex.
a c. is known by his Prov. 20:11
unto us a C. is born Is. 9:6
little c. shall lead Is. 11:6

children Young persons of either sex.
become as little c. Matt. 18:3
Let the little c. come Matt. 19:14

Christians Followers of Christ.
first called C. in Antioch Acts 11:26

Christmas The holiday on December 25 which celebrates the birth of Jesus Christ.

church The people of God; those destined to inherit the kingdom of God. Also, any local group of believers.
I will build My c. Matt. 16:18
Christ is head of the c. Eph. 5:23
head of the body, the c. Col. 1:18
the seven c. Rev. 1:4, 11, 20

clean Free from defilement or dirt. Under the Hebrew law certain animals are declared clean and others unclean (Lev. 11:1–47; Deut. 14:3–21).
c. hands and a pure heart Ps. 24:4
can make me c. Matt. 8:2; Mark 1:40; Luke 5:12
c. the outside of the cup Matt. 23:25; Luke 11:39
all things are c. Luke 11:41

cloud A visible mass of water particles in the air above the earth.
pillar of c. Ex. 13:21; Num. 12:5
c. covered the mountain Ex. 24:15

Colosse; Colossians (ko-LAH-see; ko-LOSH-uns) A city in Asia Minor. Paul wrote an epistle to the Christians of this city.

commandment Any of the Ten Commandments or laws given to Moses by God at Mount Sinai (Ex. 20:1–17; Deut. 5:6–21); other OT laws.

keep the c. Matt. 19:17
which is the great c. Matt. 22:36
you love Me., keep My c. John 14:15

confess To admit to a fault or sin, particularly as a sign of repentance; to acknowledge God's redeeming acts and openly acknowledge that Jesus is the Messiah, Lord, and Son of God (as Peter's great confession in Matt. 16:16; Mark 8:29; Luke 9:20); to offer praise and thanksgiving to God.
c. that he has sinned Lev. 5:5
c. Me before men Matt. 10:32; Luke 12:8
c. their sins Mark 1:5
c. that Jesus Christ is Phil. 2:11
C. your trespasses to one James 5:16

congregation An assembly; gathering.
c. of the righteous Ps. 1:5
God stands in the c. Ps. 82:1
in the c. of saints Ps. 149:1

converted Changed, as one's religion or belief.
unless you are c. Matt. 18:3
Repent . . . and be c. Acts 3:19

Corinth (KOR-inth) Most important trade city of ancient Greece (Acts 18:1; 19:1; 1 Cor. 1:2; 2 Cor 1:1; 2 Tim.. 4:20); situated on the Isthmus of Corinth, a narrow strip of land between the Aegean and Ionian Seas. Today a deep canal saves scores of miles of sea travel. Corinth was a very wealthy and wicked city in Paul's day. He did establish a strong church here to which he wrote letters—1 and 2 Corinthians.

Cornelius (kor-NEEL-yus) A Roman soldier stationed in Caesarea who was the first recorded Gentile convert to Christianity (Acts 10:1–33). Even before his conversion, he was a God-fearing man who believed in the Jewish teaching of one God (monotheism) and opposed the worship of idols. The apostle Peter took part in Cornelius' conversion.

counselor An advisor or teacher. Counselors seem to have been court officials of the Israelite kings (1 Chr. 27:33; Job 3:14; Prov. 11:14). The coming Messiah is so called (Is. 9:6).

courier Messenger.
letters were sent by c. Esth. 3:13
c. who rode on royal horses Esth. 8:14

covenant (KUV-uh-nunt) A binding agreement. The great covenant between God and Israel was made at Sinai (Ex. 24:3–8); the tablets on which the Ten Commandments were engraved were called "the tablets of the covenant" (Deut. 9:11). The chest in which these tablets were placed was called the "ark of the Testimony" (Ex. 25:22). The new covenant came into being through the blood of Christ.
My blood of the new c. Mark 14:24
cup is the new c. 1 Cor. 11:25

creation The act of God in making heaven and earth and bringing forth all life; the whole universe.
the story of c. Gen. 1:1—2:25
c. which God created Mark 13:19
the whole c. groans Rom. 8:22

creator; Creator The maker; originator; hence, **Creator:** God; the Lord.
Remember now your C. Eccl. 12:1
C. of the ends of the Is. 40:28
creature rather than the C. Rom. 1:25

creature Any living thing that God has made.
great sea c. Gen. 1:21
called each living c. Gen. 2:19
every c. of God is good 1 Tim. 4:4

creeping thing Reptile.
every c. that creeps Gen. 1:26
C. and flying fowl Ps. 148:10
wild beasts, c. Acts 10:12

cross An upright post with cross-beam on which victims of execution were nailed; used by the Romans. A symbol of Christianity.
who does not take his c. Matt. 10:38
take up his c. Matt. 16:24; Mark 8:34
come down from the c. Matt. 27:40
Simon . . . to bear His c. Mark 15:21
stood by the c. of Jesus John 19:25

crown A headdress of gold, precious stones, etc.; a wreath encircling the head.
A c. of glory Prov. 4:9; 16:31
excellent wife is the c. Prov. 12:4
c. of thorns Matt. 27:29; Mark 15:17; John 19:2, 5
perishable c. 1 Cor. 9:25

Crucifixion, the (crew-sih-FIX-shun) Jesus' execution on the Cross by the Romans at

the instigation of the Jewish leaders (Matt. 27; Mark 15; Luke 23; John 19).

crucify (CREW-sih-fy) To put to death by fastening to a cross.
scourge and to c. Matt. 20:19
Let Him be c. Matt. 27:22
C. Him Mark 15:13; Luke 23:21; John 19:6

cubit A measure of length of about 18 inches.
add one c. to Matt. 6:27; Luke 12:25

cup A vessel from which to drink.
My c. runs over Ps. 23:5
c. of cold water Matt. 10:42; Mark 9:41
drink the c. Matt. 20:22; Mark 10:39
outside of the c. Matt. 23:25
took the c. Matt. 26:27; Mark 14:23; Luke 22:17; 1 Cor. 11:25
c. pass from Me Matt. 26:39; Mark 14:36; Luke 22:42
c. which My Father John 18:11

curse To call on God to punish.
c. him who curses you Gen. 12:3
Whoever c. his God Lev. 24:15
C. God and die Job 2:9
bless those who c. you Mark 5:44; Luke 6:28
began to c. Matt. 26:74; Mark 14:71
fig tree which You c. Mark 11:21

Cyrus (SIGH-rus) The powerful king of Persia (559–530 B.C.), sometimes called "Cyrus the Great." In 536 B.C., he wrote an edict or law which allowed the Jewish captives in Babylon to return to their homeland in Jerusalem; praised in the OT as God's "shepherd" and "anointed" (Is. 44:28; 45:1); encouraged the rebuilding of the temple. God often uses nonbelievers in working out His plans for His people. (Find out more about Cyrus in Ezra 3:7; 4:3, 5; 5:13, 14, 17; 6:3, 14; Dan. 1:21; 6:28; 10:1.)

Dagon (DAY-gun) The chief god of the Philistines (1 Sam. 5:2–7). When the Philistines defeated Israel, they captured the ark of the covenant and took it to the temple of Dagon in Ashdod. Samson, blinded by his captors, had been brought into the temple and tied between the two pillars which supported the roof. When he called on the Lord to return his strength, he brought down the building with his bare hands and died along with hundreds of Philistines (Judg. 16:23–30).

Damascus (duh-MASK-us) A very ancient city, capital of Syria; in OT times the capital of the Aramean kingdom. Site of Saul's conversion (Acts 9:1–22).

Dan The fifth son of Jacob, born of Bilhah (Gen. 30:1–6); one of the 12 tribes of Israel.

dance To move in rhythm, usually to the sound of music.
mourn, And a time to d. Eccl. 3:4
you did not d. Matt. 11:17; Luke 7:32

Daniel The Jewish prophet at the Babylonian court about whom the OT Book of Daniel is written. Interpreted dreams (Dan. 2:1–45) and the handwriting on the wall (5:17–30); saved by God from the lions (6:16–24).

David The second and greatest king over Israel; youngest son of Jesse (1 Sam. 17:12, 14); slew Goliath (1 Sam. 17:41–50); friend of Jonathan (1 Sam. 19:1—20:42); a fugitive from Saul's wrath (1 Sam 21—27; 30); king of Judah (2 Sam. 1:1—5:5); king of Israel (2 Sam. 3:6—1 Kin. 2:11); brought the ark of the Testimony to Jerusalem (2 Sam. 6:1–17); his great sin in coveting Bathsheba (2 Sam. 11:1–27); rebellion of his son Absalom (2 Sam. 14–18); his psalm of thanksgiving (2 Sam. 22); names Solomon, his son, to succeed him (1 Kin. 1:11—2:12).

day The time between sunrise and sunset; a period of 24 hours.
God called the light D. Gen. 1:5
neither the d. nor Matt. 25:13
D. come on you unexpectedly Luke 21:34

day of the Lord In the OT, the day when God punishes evil (Amos 5:18–20); a day of universal disaster (Is. 2; 13; 24; Zeph. 1:7–18; 2:2, 3; 3:8). In the NT, the day of the Last Judgment and the end of the world (1 Cor. 4:5; 5:5; 1 Thess. 5:2; Rev. 16:14).

deacon A servant or minister; an officer of a local church who assists the minister or priest.
with the bishops and d. Phil. 1:1
d. must be reverent, not 1 Tim. 3:8

Dead Sea The salt lake at the mouth of the Jordan River. Biblical names: "Salt Sea" (Gen. 14:3; Num. 34:3, 12; Deut. 3:17; Josh. 3:16; 12:3; 15:2, 5; 18:19); "eastern sea" (Joel 2:20).

death The condition of being without life; the act of dying. Symobl of the final state of the unsaved (John 8:51; Rom. 6:23; Rev. 20:6), and of the power that rules over man in the age of sin (Rom. 5:14; Rev. 6:8).
valley of the shadow of d. Ps. 23:4
swallow up d. forever Is. 25:8
not taste d. Matt. 16:28; Mark 9:1; Luke 9:27
D., where is your sting 1 Cor. 15:55

Deborah 1. Rebekah's nurse and companion (Gen. 35:8). 2. An early "judge" of Israel; aroused the scattered tribes to opposition to Canaanite oppression; Song of Deborah (Judg. 5:2–31) celebrates her achievement.

debts Obligations; anything owed to another.
forgive us our d. Matt. 6:12

Dedication, Feast of An eight-day festival observing the victories of Judas Maccabaeus and the purification and rededication of the temple (John 10:22). Also called Feast of Lights; Hanukkah; Chanukah.

Delilah (dih-LIE-luh) A woman from the Valley of Sorek; betrayed Samson to the Philistines (Judg. 16:4–22).

deliverer, the In five OT passages (2 Sam. 22:2; Ps. 18:2; 40:17; 70:5; 144:2) God is referred to as "the deliverer"; but even though Christ is the instrument of God's deliverance of mankind from sin, the NT does not use the word except when Paul repeats Isaiah 59:20, using "Deliverer" instead of "Redeemer" (Rom. 11:26).

demon An evil spirit.
sacrifices to d. Lev. 17:7; Deut. 32:17
who were d.-possessed Matt. 4:24; 9:32; 12:22
He has a d. Matt. 11:18; Luke 7:33

den Lair; cave of a wild animal.
into the d. of lions Dan. 6:7
a '*d. of thieves*' Matt. 21:13; Mark 11:17

detestable Abominable; loathsome.
not eat any d. thing Deut. 14:3

Deuteronomy (dew-ter-ONN-oh-mee) The fifth book of the Law in the OT; teaches that God's laws are given for our own good—to help us stay close to Him in attitude and action. The name means "second law" or the second time the Law was given. (Look up Ex. 20:1–17 for the first giving of the Law.)

Devil The chief demon, Satan.
Jesus . . . tempted by the d. Matt. 4:1–11
serpent of old, called the D. Rev. 12:9; 20:2

die Perish; lose life.
you shall surely d. Gen. 2:17
born, And a time to d. Eccl. 3:2
for tomorrow we d. Is. 22:13
in Me shall never d. John 11:26

disciple (dih-SIGH-pul) A learner; a follower, particularly one who follows Jesus Christ.
called His twelve d. Matt. 10:1; Luke 6:13
sent two of his d. Matt. 11:2
d. rebuked them Matt. 19:13
d. were first called Christians Acts 11:26

Dispersion (dis-PURR-zhun) The widespread settlement of Jews outside of Palestine from the time of the Exile through the following centuries.

doctrine Teaching or instruction, particularly that of Jesus or the apostles concerning God's will.
My d. is pure Job 11:4
My d. is not Mine John 7:16
the d. of baptisms Heb. 6:2

door Entrance way.
will pass over the d. Ex. 12:23
and the d. was shut Matt. 25:10
I am the d. John 10:9
d. standing open in heaven Rev. 4:1

doxology A hymn, usually in a set formula, for expressing praise to God. Luke 2:14 ("Glory to God in the highest") has influenced Christian doxologies.

dreadful Awesome; feared; terrible.
d. day of the Lord Mal. 4:5

dust Fine, dry, powdery earth.
God formed man of the d. Gen. 2:7
d. you are, And to d. Gen. 3:19

E

earth The planet on which we live; the soil.
God created the . . . e. Gen. 1:1
the e. is the LORD's Ps. 24:1

meek shall inherit the e. Ps. 37:11
And e. is My footstool Is. 66:1
meek, . . . shall inherit the e. Matt. 5:5
Your will be done On e. Matt. 6:10
on e. peace, goodwill Luke 2:14
new heaven and a new e. Rev. 21:1

Easter A Christian festival celebrating the Resurrection of Jesus; on a Sunday between March 22 and April 25.

eat To consume food.
shall not e. of every Gen. 3:1
e. and drink, for tomorrow Is. 22:13
Take, e.; this is My body Matt. 26:26

Ebal, Mount (EE-bull) A mountain in N Israel opposite Mount Gerizim (Deut. 11:29). It became known as the Mount of Cursing when Joshua read the curses of the Law. People on the mountain cried out with an "Amen!" When he read the blessings, people on nearby Mount Gerizim responded in the same way. These two mountains marked the center of the land of the Samaritans in the OT. *See* Gerizim, Mount.

Eden, Garden of A garden of trees planted by the Lord (Gen. 2:8) in which Adam and Eve first lived; actual site unknown; symbolically identified with Paradise.

Edom; Edomites (EE-dum; EE-duh-mights) A country to the E and S of Israel; its people had a close relationship to the Israelites, being descendants of Esau.

Egypt A land of NE Africa. Temporary home of Abraham (Gen. 12:10–20); Joseph sold "into Egypt" (Gen. 37:28, 36); Joseph as governor (Gen. 41:37—47:26); Israel in bondage (Ex. 1:1—12:36); the Exodus (Ex. 12:37—14:31); Jesus taken there (Matt. 2:13).

Elah, Valley of (EE-luh) A narrow valley surrounded by low hills, SW of Jerusalem, where David killed Goliath (1 Sam. 17:2; 21:9).

Elohim (EL-oh-heem) One of the names of God; another is Yahweh (YAH-way). Elohim appears first in Gen. 1:1 and is plural, meaning to Christians—"Trinity"—not three gods! The abbreviated form, El, is found in many biblical names—Beth*el*, Ezek*iel*, Dan*iel*, *El*izabeth.

elders Seniors; among the Jews, the old and mature men who were civil and religious leaders; in the Christian church, leaders of the local church.
seventy of the e. of Israel Ex. 24:9
tradition of the e. Matt. 15:2; Mark 7:3
appointed e. in every Acts 14:23
the e. who rule well 1 Tim. 5:17
twenty-four e. Rev. 4:4

Eli (EE-lie) The priest of Shiloh to whom the boy Samuel was brought (1 Sam. 1–4).

Elijah (ih-LIE-jah) A prophet from Tishbe to Gilead in the northern kingdom; fed by ravens (1 Kin. 17:6); performs miracles (1 Kin. 17:14–24; 20:30; 2 Kin. 1:10–12; 2:8); taken up by a whirlwind into heaven (2 Kin. 2:11). Malachi prophesies his return before the day of the Lord (Mal. 4:5). In NT times, some thought Jesus to be Elijah (Matt. 16:14; Luke 9:8); others thought John the Baptist to be Elijah (John 1:21). In the early church, John was regarded as the heir to the spirit and power of Elijah (Luke 1:17) or as Elijah reborn (Matt. 11:14; 17:10–13). At the Transfiguration, Elijah appears with Moses (Matt. 17:3, 4; Mark 9:4, 5).

Elisha (ih-LIE-shuh) A prophet; disciple and successor to Elijah; performed many miracles (2 Kin. 2:14–24; 3:16–20; 4:2–7, 32–44; 5:10–14, 27; 6:5–7, 18–20); contact with his bones revives a dead man (2 Kin. 13:20, 21).

Elizabeth Wife of the priest Zacharias, and mother of John the Baptist (Luke 1:5–66).

ephah (EE-fah) A dry measure equal to the liquid measure bath; estimated as three-eighths to two-thirds of a bushel.
balances, a just e. Ezek. 45:10

Emmanuel (em-MAN-you-el) *See* Immanuel.

Emmaus (em-MAY-us) A village in Judea, probably NW of Jerusalem, where Jesus revealed Himself to two disciples on the road after His resurrection from the grave (Luke 24:13–29).

enemies Foes; opponents.
presence of my e. Ps. 23:5
love your e. Matt. 5:44; Luke 6:27, 35

enter To go or come into.
E. into His gates with Ps. 100:4
E. by the narrow gate Matt. 7:13; Luke 13:24

Ephesus; Ephesians (EFF-uh-sus; ee-FEE-zhuns) A seaport in the Roman province of Asia; visited by Paul on his second and third journeys. Paul's NT epistle to the Ephesians seems to be a general letter to the churches of Asia Minor.

Ephraim (EE-frah-im) The younger son of Joseph; adopted by Jacob (Gen. 48:1ff); ancestor of one of the most powerful of the 12 tribes of Israel.

epistle (ee-PIS-ul) Letter; specifically those letters written by the apostles that are included in the NT. **Pastoral Epistles:** The NT books of 1 and 2 Timothy and Titus, which are written in the name of Paul as the chief pastor of the churches. **General (Catholic) Epistles:** The NT books of James, 1 and 2 Peter, 1, 2, and 3 John, and Jude.

Esau (EE-saw) Son of Isaac and Rebekah who traded his birthright to his younger twin brother Jacob for a bowl of pottage (Gen. 25:22–34; 27; 33:1–16).

Essenes A Jewish community in Palestine at the time of Jesus; strict adherents of Jewish law.

Esther A Jewess of Shushan who became Ahasuerus' queen and thwarted a plot to kill all the Jews, later commemorated by the Jewish festival of Purim. The Book of Esther tells the story.

Euphrates (you-FRAY-tees) Means "that which waters." The longest river in W Asia and one of the two major rivers in Mesopotamia; begins in the mountains of Turkey and runs down to the Persian Gulf, almost two thousand miles away. The ruins of many ancient cities, including Babylon, Nippur, and Ur of the Chaldees, are located along this river in Iraq.

Eve The first woman; wife of Adam (Gen. 2:21–25); tempted by the serpent (Gen. 3:1–5).

everlasting Eternal; never ending.
the E. God Gen. 21:33; Is. 40:28
underneath are the e. arms Deut. 33:27
into the e. fire Matt. 18:8; 25:41
inherit e. life Matt. 19:29
have e. life John 3:16, 36; 5:24

evil Wickedness; slanderous or injurious actions.
tree . . . of good and e. Gen. 2:9
I will fear no e. Ps. 23:4
Depart from e. Ps. 37:27
deliver us from the e. Matt. 6:13
what e. has He done Matt. 27:23; Mark 15:14; Luke 23:22
love of money is a root of all kinds of e. 1 Tim. 6:10

Exile, the A period during which most of the people of Judah and Jerusalem were forced to live in Babylonia.

Exodus The going out of Israel from Egypt as recorded in the second book of the OT. It includes the deliverance from slavery, the wandering through the wilderness, the covenant with the Lord at Mount Sinai, and the provision of the tabernacle and ark of the covenant.

eye The organ of sight.
e. of both of them were opened Gen. 3:7
e. for e. Ex. 21:24; Lev. 24:20; Deut. 19:21; Matt. 5:38
lift up my e. to the hills Ps. 121:1
wise in your own e. Prov. 3:7
if your right e. causes you Matt. 5:29; 18:9; Mark 9:47

Ezekiel (ee-ZEEK-yell) A major Jewish prophet; author of the OT Book of Ezekiel; one of the captives of the Babylonian exile. Vision of God (Ezek. 1:4–28); parable of the two eagles and the vine (17:1–24); the fall of Jerusalem (24:1–27); various prophecies about other nations (25–32).

Ezra (EZ-ruh) A priest and scribe; supposed author of the OT Book of Ezra, which details the first return of the Israelites from Babylon and the rebuilding of the temple.

face The front of the head; the surface or top side; frequently used to indicate the presence of God. Among the Hebrews, "seeking the face of God" referred to attendance at public worship (Ps. 27:8).
on the f. of the deep Gen. 1:2
In the sweat of your f. you shall Gen. 3:19
Lord spoke to Moses f. to f. Ex. 33:11
make His f. shine upon you Num. 6:25

Seek My f. Ps. 27:8
f. of the Lord is against Ps. 34:16
the f. of My Father Matt. 18:10
My messenger before Your f. Mark 1:2
but then f. to f. 1 Cor. 13:12

faith Belief or trust in someone or something. Among Christians, belief in the Holy Trinity.
your f. has made you Matt. 9:22; Mark 5:34; 10:52; Luke 8:48; 17:19
f. as a mustard seed Matt. 17:20; Luke 17:6
just shall live by f. Rom. 1:17
man is justified by f. Rom. 3:28, 5:1; Gal. 2:16; 3:24
f. is accounted for righteousness Rom. 4:5
saved through f. Eph. 2:8
one Lord, one f., one Eph. 4:5
f. is the substance of Heb. 11:1
f. without works is dead James 2:20

Fall, the A sinking into sin; the disobedience of Adam and Eve whereby sin entered the world (Gen. 3).

falsehood Lying.
love worthlessness And seek f. Ps. 4:2
destroy those who speak f. Ps. 5:6

fast To go without food.
when you f., do not be Matt. 6:16
Pharisees f. often Matt. 9:14; Mark 2:18

Father The male parent or ancestor. In the OT, use of God as the One who made a covenant with the people of Israel.
be a f. of many nations Gen. 17:4
Honor your f. and Ex. 20:12; Lev. 19:3; Deut. 5:16
who curses his f. Ex. 21:17; Lev. 20:9
David rested with his f. 1 Kin. 2:10
f. of the fatherless, . . . Is God Ps. 68:5
Lord, You are our F. Is. 64:8

Father The First Person of the Holy Trinity.
your F. in heaven Matt. 5:16, 45
Our F. in Matt. 6:9; Luke 11:2
Abba, F. Mark 14:36; Rom. 8:15; Gal. 4:6
baptizing them in the name of the F. Matt. 28:19
about My F.'s business Luke 2:49
who the F. is but the Son Luke 10:22
the Promise of My F. Luke 24:49
the only begotten of the F. John 1:14
one F.—God John 8:41
I and My F. are one John 10:30
comes to the F. except through Me John 14:6
ask the F. in My name John 15:16

fear To dread; to be afraid of; to be anxious.
I will f. no evil Ps. 23:4
Whom shall I f. Ps. 27:1
F. not, for I am Is. 41:10; 43:5

fear of the LORD The term used in the OT for "religion" (Deut. 6:2; 10:20; 28:58; Ps. 111:10; Prov. 1:7; 8:13; Eccl. 12:13). In the NT, "those who fear the Lord" are the faithful (Luke 1:50; 18:4) or converts to Judaism (Acts 10:2; 13:26).

feast A festival; in ancient Israel associated with occasions of religious joy. Those mentioned in the Bible: 1. **Passover and Feast of Unleavened Bread** (Ex. 12:1–30; Lev. 23:4–14; Deut. 16:1–8). 2. **Feast of Weeks** or **Pentecost** (Lev. 23:15–21; Deut. 16:9–12). 3. **Feast of Tabernacles** (Lev. 23:34–36; Deut. 16:13–15). 4. **Purim** (Esth. 9:20–28). 5. **Feast of Dedication** or **Feast of Lights** (John 10:22).

fellowship Companionship; a group of persons with a common interest. Among Christians, the common bond is their faith in Christ, particularly in partaking of the Lord's Supper.
into the f. of His Son 1 Cor. 1:9
the right hand of f. Gal. 2:9
any f. of the Spirit Phil. 2:1
our f. is with the Father 1 John 1:3

fight Struggle against; do battle.
F. the good f. of faith 1 Tim. 6:12

firmament Sky; heavens.
Let there be a f. in Gen. 1:6
f. shows His handiwork Ps. 19:1

first Before all others.
f. will be last Matt. 19:30; Mark 10:31

First and the Last, the A title used by Isaiah (Is. 41:4; 44:6; 48:12) to convey the idea of God's everlasting sovereignty and eternal majesty and power. The same title is used in Revelation (1:11, 17; 2:8; 22:13) implying God's sovereign lordship manifest in Jesus Christ.

firstborn, firstfruits The eldest; the earliest fruits harvested. The consecration of the first of the male children, of animals, and of fruits was an important part of the religion of Israel.
LORD struck all the f. Ex. 12:29

flesh The soft part of the human body; all mankind.
All f. is grass Is. 40:6; 1 Pet. 1:24
but the f. is weak Matt. 26:41; Mark 14:38
the Word became f. John 1:14

Flood, the The covering of the earth with water because of man's wickedness. Noah's family and the animals of the earth are saved in an ark (Gen. 6:1—8:19).

fool A silly or senseless person.
f. despise wisdom Prov. 1:7
f. is right in his own eyes Prov. 12:15
folly of f. is deceit Prov. 14:8
f. for Christ's sake 1 Cor. 4:10

foolish Silly; unwise. Parables of Jesus deal with: foolish and wise virgins (Matt. 25:1–13) and a foolish rich man (Luke 12:16–21).

forgive To pardon; show mercy to.
f. us . . ., As we f. Matt. 6:12; Luke 11:4
F., and you will be Luke 6:37
Father, f. them Luke 23:34

fountain The source, as the spring from which water flows. The Lord is called "the fountain of living waters" (Jer. 2:13; cf. John 4:14) and the "fountain of life" (Ps. 36:9).

frankincense A fragrant incense.
spices . . . and pure f. Ex. 30:34
gold, f., and myrrh Matt. 2:11

friend An associate whom one likes.
the rich has many f. Prov. 14:20
A f. loves at all times Prov. 17:17
a f. who sticks closer Prov. 18:24

G

Gabriel (GAY-brih-el) An angel of high rank (Dan. 8:16; 9:21; Luke 1:19, 26).

Gad The seventh son of Jacob; born of Leah's maid Zilpah (Gen. 30:10, 11), ancestor of the tribe of Gad.

Galatia; Galatians (guh-LAY-she-uh; guh-LAY-shuns) A region and Roman province in Asia Minor. Paul, in the NT epistle to the Galatians, tells of his own conversion.

Galilee (GAL-ih-lee) A region of N Palestine, including the Sea of Galilee on the E side. OT references include: Solomon gives 20 cities of Galilee to Hiram (1 Kin. 9:11); the prophecy of Isaiah (Is. 9:1) concerning "Galilee of the Gentiles" (cf. Matt. 4:13). Called "land of Gennesaret" (Matt. 14:34; Mark 6:53), Jesus' active ministry was almost entirely within its borders.

Galilee, Sea of The larger of the two freshwater lakes on the Jordan River system. Site of miracles: the great catch of fish (Luke 5:1–11); Jesus stills the sea (Matt. 8:23–26; Mark 4:35–39; Luke 8:22–24); Jesus walks on the sea (Matt. 14:25–27; Mark 6:48–51; John 6:19, 20). Also called "Chinnereth" (Num. 34:11; Deut. 3:17; Josh. 13:27); "Chinneroth" (Josh. 12:3); "Gennesaret" (Luke 5:1); and "Tiberias" (John 6:1; 21:1).

Gamaliel (guh-MAY-lih-el) A famous member of the Jewish Sanhedrin and a teacher of the Law; taught Paul in Tarsus (Acts 22:3); advised the Sanhedrin in Jerusalem to treat well the apostles of the young Christian church. His approach was simple: If Jesus was a false prophet, Christianity would soon fail. If the movement was of God, "You cannot overthrow it!" (Acts 5:39).

gate Doorway.
Enter into His g. with Ps. 100:4
Enter by the narrow g. Matt. 7:13

Gaza (GAY-zuh; GAH-zuh) One of the five principal cities of the Philistines, located along the southern Mediterranean coast of Israel, on the great caravan route between Mesopotamia and Egypt. Philip preached to the Ethiopian eunuch on the road to Gaza and baptized him (Acts 8:26–40).

Gehenna (geh-HEN-uh) Or "Valley of Hinnom" in the NT. A deep, narrow, curving valley at the south end of Jerusalem, used as a garbage dump where waste and dead animals were burned; children sacrificed to the god Molech (2 Kin. 23:10); high places of heathen worship destroyed by good King Josiah; "hell" (NKJV).

Gerizim, Mount (geh-RIGH-zim) A mountain in N Israel, close to Mount Ebal in the district of Samaria. The main north-south road through central Palestine ran between these mountains. Jacob's Well, where Jesus talked with the Samaritan woman, is situated at the

foot of Mount Gerizim (John 4:14). *See* Ebal, Mount.

Gethsemane (geth-SEM-uh-neh) A garden on the Mount of Olives where Jesus prayed and where He was betrayed by Judas (Matt. 26:36; Mark 14:32).

Gideon (GID-ee-un) A prophet of Israel especially favored by the Lord with revelations and unusual powers (Judg. 6:11—8:35).

Gilead (GILL-ih-ud) A rugged, mountainous region E of the Jordan. Possibly also a city (Judg. 10:17; Hos. 6:8) and a tribe (Judg. 5:17).

Gilgal (GILL-gal) The name of several places in the OT, one of them a city of the tribe of Benjamin, near Jericho; site of the first encampment of the Israelites after crossing the Jordan (Josh. 3; 4); there Saul was made king (1 Sam. 11:14, 15).

give To bestow; hand over to another.
G. us this day our daily Matt. 6:11
it will be g. to you Matt. 7:7; Luke 6:38; 11:9
more blessed to g. than Acts 20:35

giver One who bestows.
God loves a cheerful g. 2 Cor 9:7

glad tidings Good news; the gospel (used in Luke 1:19; 8:1; Acts 13:32; and Rom. 10:15).

Gloria in Excelsis The proclamation of the heavenly host at the birth of Christ. "Glory to God in the highest" (Luke 2:14).

glory of the Lord The word *glory* is sometimes synonymous with "God" to avoid referring to God in human form (Ex. 33:22). In the OT, used of the fiery presence at Sinai (Ex. 24:16, 17) and of the radiance that filled the tabernacle (Ex. 40:34). In the NT, used of the divine Presence (Mark 8:38; Luke 2:9), of the quality of Jesus' appearance in His transfiguration (Luke 9:29, 31), and of Jesus' Second Coming (Matt. 25:31).

gnat A tiny insect.
strain out a g. and swallow Matt. 23:24

God, kingdom of *See* kingdom of God; heaven, kingdom of.

gods Idols.
have no other g. before Ex. 20:3

Golden Gate The eastern gate of Jerusalem, sometimes called the Gate Beautiful on the Temple Mount, directly across the Kidron Valley from the Garden of Gethsemane where Judas betrayed Jesus. According to prophecy, this gate will be opened when the Messiah, Jesus, returns the second time.

Golden Rule A commandment given by Jesus in the Sermon on the Mount (Matt. 7:12; Luke 6:31).

Golgotha (GOLL-goth-uh) Place where Jesus was crucified (Matt. 27:33, 35; Mark 15:22; John 19:17).

Goliath (go-LIE-uth) A Philistine giant about 9½ to 11 feet tall; from a family of giants called the Anakim, who lived in Gath (Num. 13:33). David, while still a young man, killed Goliath with a stone from his sling (1 Sam. 17:4–51).

Gomer (GO-mer) A prostitute whom God told the prophet Hosea to marry as a lesson to Israel about their relationship to Him. Hosea's forgiveness of his wife symbolized God's forgiving love toward Israel (Hos. 1:2; 14:1–4).

Gomorrah (go-MAR-uh) One of the two cities destroyed by the Lord because of their wickedness (Gen. 19:24–28).

good Virtuous; honorable
g. name . . . rather than great Prov. 22:1
No one is g. but One Matt. 19:17; Luke 18:19

Good Friday The Friday before Easter; the anniversary of the Crucifixion of Jesus.

Goshen (GO-shun) A fertile part of the Nile delta in N Egypt, given to the family of Joseph by Pharaoh because of the famine in Israel (Gen. 45:10–13).

gospel Good news; glad tidings. Hence, the teachings of Jesus and of the apostles. The NT books of Matthew, Mark, Luke, and John are called the Gospels.
g. of the kingdom Matt. 4:23
the g. of Jesus Christ Mark 1:1
and believe in the g. Mark 1:15
preach the g. Luke 4:18
hear the word of the g. Acts 15:7
the g. of Christ Rom. 1:16

grace OT usage: "favor" in the expression "found g. in the eyes of" (Gen. 6:8). In NT usage: "the unmerited and abundant gift of God's love and favor to man," particularly made effective in

Jesus Christ for the Christian. Used by Paul as an opening and farewell greeting (Rom. 16:24; 1 Cor. 1:3).

g. and truth came through Jesus John 1:17
g. of God and the gift by the g. Rom. 5:15
G. to you and 1 Cor. 1:3; Eph. 1:2
by the g. of God I am 1 Cor. 15:10
g. of God in vain 2 Cor 6:1
g. of our Lord Jesus 2 Cor 8:9; 13:14
by g. you have been saved Eph. 2:5

guarantee A pledge.
given us the Spirit as a g. 2 Cor 5:5
who is the g. of our inheritance Eph. 1:14

H

Habakkuk (huh-BACK-kuk) A prophet of Judah; the OT book which bears his name is the eighth of the 12 Minor Prophets.

Hagar (HAY-gar) The Egyptian servant of Sarah, Abraham's wife; mother of Abraham's son, Ishmael (Gen. 16:1–16). When Sarah was very old, God gave her a son Isaac, who became the father of the Jewish nation. Hagar's son Ishmael, his half brother, became the father of the Arab nation. The two nations cannot get along to this day!

Haggai (HAG-ay-eye) A Jewish prophet contemporary with Zechariah; the tenth of the 12 Minor Prophets of the OT.

Hallelujah (hal-luh-LOO-yah) "Praise the Lord" (not used in the NKJV). *See* Alleluia.

hallowed Make sacred; consecrated.
H. be Your name Matt. 6:9

hand The end of the arm.
Into Your h. I commit Ps. 31:5
not let your left h. know Matt. 6:3
if your h. or foot Matt. 18:8; Mark 9:43

hands, laying on of A symbolic ritual: 1. Of divine blessing (Matt. 19:13–15), sometimes accompanied by the gift of the Holy Spirit (Acts 19:6). 2. Of divine healing (Mark 7:32). 3. Of consecration of a man for a specific office (Acts 13:2, 3; 1 Tim. 4:14). 4. Of dedication of an animal as for sacrifice (Lev. 16:21).

Hannah (HAN-uh) The wife of Elkanah the priest and mother of Samuel. For many years, Hannah prayed for a child, promising God that she would dedicate him to the Lord's service. Samuel, who became a great judge, priest, and prophet, was God's answer to her prayers (1 Sam. 1:11–17, 22).

Hanukkah (HAH-nuh-kah) Hebrew word for "dedication." *See* Dedication, Feast of.

Haran (HAY-ran) A city of N Mesopotamia, on one of the main trade routes between Babylon and the Mediterranean Sea; home of Abraham and his father, Terah (Gen. 11:31, 32; 12:4, 5); home of Jacob and his wives, Leah and Rachel (Gen. 28:10; 29:4–6).

harp A stringed musical instrument.
play the h. and flute Gen. 4:21
David would take a h. and 1 Sam. 16:23

haughty Overbearing; proud
h. spirit before a fall Prov. 16:18

Hazael (HAY-zay-el) A Syrian official whom the prophet Elijah anointed king of Syria at God's command (1 Kin. 19:15); sent by Ben-Hadad, king of Syria, to the prophet Elisha to ask whether the king would recover from an illness; assassinated Ben-Hadad and took the throne (2 Kin. 8:7–15); fought against God's people when the Lord's anger "became aroused against Israel" (2 Kin. 13:3).

heart The physical organ thought of as being the seat of the affections.
A broken and contrite h. Ps. 51:17
Blessed are the pure in h. Matt. 5:8
not your h. be troubled John 14:1

heaven A term sometimes used for "God."
I have sinned against h. Luke 15:18
it has been given to him from h. John 3:27

heaven; heavens 1. The sky; the space in which the sun, the moon, and the stars move; the firmament.
God called the firmament H. Gen. 1:8
He adorned the h. Job 26:13
h. declare the glory of God Ps. 19:1
stretch out the h. Ps. 104:2; Is. 40:22
saw h. opened and Acts 10:11

2. The place where God, the risen Christ, the angels, and the saints reside; the future home of the redeemed.
new h. and Is. 65:17; Rev. 21:1
till h. and earth pass Matt. 5:18

Father in h. Matt. 6:9; Luke 11:2
looked . . . toward h. as Acts 1:10
eternal in the h. 2 Cor 5:1

heaven, kingdom of Used throughout the Gospel of Matthew for "kingdom of God." *See* kingdom of God.
the kingdom of h. is at hand Matt. 3:2; 10:7
theirs is the kingdom of h. Matt. 5:3, 10
least in the kingdom of h. Matt. 5:19; 11:11
kingdom of h. is like Matt. 13:24
such is the kingdom of h. Matt. 19:14

heavenly host *See* host, heavenly.

Hebrews (HE-brews) The descendants of Eber (Gen. 10:21); sometimes used interchangeably with "Israelites."

Hebron (HE-brun) An ancient city in the mountains of Judah, 19 miles S of Jerusalem. Here Abraham purchased a cave for a family burial place (Gen. 23:1–20). David's capital city for the first seven and one-half years of his reign (2 Sam 2:1—5:5).

Helper The Holy Spirit; the intercessor promised by Christ to help and guide believers (John 14:26; 15:26; 16:7).

heresy (HAIR-uh-see) False doctrine or teaching which denies the truth about God or Jesus Christ. In the Book of 2 Corinthians, Paul spoke against "false apostles" and "deceitful workers" who claimed to be "apostles of Christ" (2 Cor 11:13); in 1 John, the writer also condemned a group known as the gnostics, who denied that Jesus was the Son of God (1 John 2:22).

Hermon, Mount (HUR-man) "Sacred mountain." The highest mountain in the area (9,232 feet), which marks the N boundary of Canaan; the major source of the Jordan River because of its melting snows and glaciers. Some scholars think Jesus' Transfiguration took place near Caesarea Philippi, at the southern base of Mount Hermon.

Herod (HAIR-ud) 1. Ruler of Jewish Palestine under Rome (37–4 B.C.); sent the wise men to search out the infant Jesus (Matt. 2:1–9). 2. **Herod Antipas:** Tetrarch of Galilee (4 B.C.–A.D. 39); put John the Baptist to death (Matt. 14:1–12; Mark 6:14–29; Luke 3:19, 20; 9:7–9).

Hezekiah (hez-uh-KIGH-uh) The name of four persons in the OT, one of whom was king of Judah (715–687 B.C.; 2 Kin. 18–20; 2 Chr. 29–32; Is. 36–39).

Hinnom, Valley of (HEN-um) *See* "Gehenna," the Greek term for the same location.

Hiram (HIGH-rum) A king of Tyre and friend of both David and Solomon (2 Sam. 5:11; 1 Kin. 10:11, 22; 2 Chr. 8:2, 18); furnished cedar wood from the famous Cedars of Lebanon and workmen to help David build his palace; sent supplies and skilled laborers to help Solomon build the temple in Jerusalem.

Hittites (HIT-tights) A people of the ancient world who lived in Asia Minor between 1900 and 1200 B.C.; spread into N Syria and later into the land promised Abraham; had to be driven out when Israel conquered Canaan under Joshua (Ex. 3:8, 17; Deut. 7:1; Judg. 3:5). The most famous Hittite was Uriah, the husband of Bathsheba. David had Uriah killed in battle so he could marry Bathsheba.

holy of holies The innermost room of the temple or tabernacle in which the ark of the Testimony was kept.

Holy Spirit *See* Spirit, Holy.

Holy Trinity *See* Trinity.

Holy Week The week before Easter.

honor To esteem; to give respect.
H. your father and your mother Ex. 20:12; Matt. 15:4
before h. is humility Prov. 15:33
prophet is not without h. Matt. 13:57
h. to whom h. Rom. 13:7

Horeb, Mount (HOE-reb) A sacred mountain (Ex. 3:1; Deut. 1:2, 6, 19; 4:10; 5:2) which may be the same mountain as Mount Sinai.

Hosea (ho-ZAY-uh) A prophet of Israel; the first of the 12 Minor Prophets of the OT.

host, heavenly 1. The celestial bodies—the sun, moon, and stars.
all the h. of heaven Deut. 4:19; Jer. 8:2
worshiped all the h. of 2 Kin. 17:16
2. The mighty army in God's service, including the angels.
all the h. of them Gen. 2:1
heavens, with all their h. Neh. 9:6
the h. of them by Ps. 33:6

brings out their h. Is. 40:26
worship the h. of heaven Acts 7:42

Hosts, LORD of God, first as leader of the armies of Israel (1 Sam. 17:45), then as leader of the "heavenly host."
LORD of h., He is the King Ps. 24:10
LORD of h. is His name Is. 47:4; 51:15; Jer. 10:16; 31:35
name is the God of h. Amos 5:27

house 1. A dwelling place.
not covet your neighbor's h. Ex. 20:17
Set your h. in order 2 Kin. 20:1
dwell in the h. of the LORD Ps. 23:6
Father's h. are many mansions John 14:2
2. A family group; a nation.
h. divided against itself Matt. 12:25; Luke 11:17

hypocrite (HIP-puh-krit) A person who pretends to be what he or she is not. In the Greek theater of NT times, a hypocrite was an actor who wore a mask and played a part on the stage. **hypocrisy** (hip-POCK-rih-see) Jesus spoke against the hypocrisy of many persons who opposed Him, especially the scribes and Pharisees, who tried to give the appearance of being godly, but were actually blind to the truth of God (Luke 20:19, 20).
for everyone is a h. Is. 9:17
You are full of h. Matt. 23:28
Let love be without h. Rom. 12:9

idol A false god; an image or figure regarded as an object of worship.
Do not turn to i. Lev. 19:4
who regard vain i. Ps. 31:6
gods of the peoples are i. Ps. 96:5
And with foreign i. Jer. 8:19
the i. of the nations Jer. 14:22
keep yourselves from i. 1 John 5:21

image A likeness; an idol.
make man in Our i. Gen. 1:26
not make . . . any carved i. Ex. 20:4

Immanuel (em-MAN-you-el) A Hebrew name meaning "God With Us," used by Isaiah in foretelling the birth of the Messiah.
call His name I. Is. 7:14
of Your land, O I. Is. 8:8
shall call His name I. Matt. 1:23

immediately Right now.
i. he stumbles Matt. 13:21
end will not come i. Luke 21:9

Incarnation (in-car-NAY-shun) The taking by God of human characteristics in the person of Jesus; God's presence on earth.

iniquity (ih-NICK-kwih-tih) Sin; wickedness. *See* sin.
the i. of the fathers Ex. 20:5; Deut. 5:9
Pardon my i. Ps. 25:11
we bear their i. Lam. 5:7

intercession A plea on behalf of another; for example, Christ's prayer for His followers (John 17:6–26).
i. for the transgressors Is. 53:12
the Spirit Himself makes i. Rom. 8:26
He ever lives to make i. Heb. 7:25

Isaac (EYE-zik) The son of Abraham and Sarah, and half brother of Ishmael; by his wife Rebekah he was the father of Jacob and Esau (Gen. 21:1–12; 22:1–19; 24:62–67; 25:9–11, 19, 20; 26:1—28:5; 35:27–29).

Isaiah (eye-ZAY-uh) A prophet of Israel; the first book of the OT Major Prophets.

Ishmael (ISH-may-el) The name of six persons in the OT, one of them Abraham's son by Hagar (Gen. 16; 17:18–26; 21:8–21; 25:12–18).

Israel (IZ-ray-el) The name that Jacob received after his mysterious struggle at Jabbok (Gen. 32:22–30); also the name of the whole people descended from him. After the separation into two kingdoms under Jeroboam, the name was confined to the northern kingdom of the ten tribes.

Israelites (IZ-ray-el-lights) A name applied to Israel (the people); also called "Hebrews," mostly by foreigners, as was the name "Jews"; the latter arose at the time when Judah, after the fall of the northern kingdom, represented the entire people.

Issachar (IZ-uh-kar) The ninth son of Jacob, the fifth by Leah (Gen. 30:17, 18); ancestor of the tribe of Issachar.

Jacob (JAY-kob) Son of Isaac and Rebekah; younger twin brother of Esau; father of the people of Israel. Gained by craft the blessing meant for Esau;

married Leah and Rachel, the daughters of his uncle Laban; received the name Israel; finally found refuge in Egypt with his favorite son, Joseph (Gen. 25:21–34; 27–35; 37:1–3; 47:28—49:33).

Jacob's Well An ancient well near Shechem and Mount Ebal and Mount Gerizim in central Palestine; dug by hand and crude tools; site of a conversation between Jesus and a Samaritan woman, in which He told her how to find "living water" (John 4:5–10).

James The name of several persons in the NT. 1. "The Elder," son of Zebedee and brother of John; one of the 12 apostles; martyred under Herod Agrippa (Matt. 4:21; 10:2; 17:1; 20:20; 26:37; Mark 1:19, 20, 29; 3:17; 5:37; 9:2; 10:35, 41; 13:3; 14:33; Luke 5:10; 6:14; 8:51; 9:28, 54; Acts 1:13; 12:1, 2). 2. The son of Alphaeus, also one of the 12 apostles (Matt. 10:3; Mark 3:18; Luke 6:15; Acts 1:13). 3. One of the sons of Mary; known as "the Less" (Matt. 27:56; Mark 15:40; 16:1; Luke 24:10). Tradition regards James (3) to be the same person as James (2). 4. The father of Judas (Luke 6:16; Acts 1:13). 5. "The brother of the Lord"; a pillar of the church at Jerusalem; called "James the Just"; traditionally the author of the epistle of James (Matt. 13:55; Mark 6:3; Acts 12:17; 15:13; 21:18; 1 Cor. 15:7; Gal. 1:19; 2:9, 12; James 1:1; Jude 1).

jealous Envious; suspicious; full of zeal. When used of God, jealousy describes either His anger against His unfaithful people or His zeal to protect His persecuted people.

a j. God Ex. 20:5; Deut. 4:24

Jehovah (jeh-HOE-vuh) The LORD; God. Used by some Bible translators for the name of the covenant God of Israel (Ex. 6:3; Ps. 83:18; Is. 12:2; 26:4).

Jephthah (JEFF-thah) A warrior of Gilead; sacrificed his daughter in fulfillment of a vow (Judg. 11:1—12:7).

Jeremiah (jer-uh-MY-uh) The name of ten persons in the OT, one of them the prophet Jeremiah (c. 626–580 B.C.). His prophecies, visions, and life story are narrated in the second book of the OT Major Prophets, which bears his name. The almond rod and the boiling pot (1:11–19); the potter's wheel (18:2–10); the good and bad figs (24:1–10); Baruch records Jeremiah's prophecies (36:4–32).

Jericho (JERRY-ko) An ancient city at the S end of the Jordan Valley; the fall of the city is told in Joshua 6:1–25.

Jeroboam (jer-uh-BOW-um) 1. The first king of Israel (c. 922–901 B.C.); son of Nebat (1 Kin. 11:26—14:20; 2 Kin. 17:21, 22; 2 Chr. 10:2–15; 13:1–20). 2. King of Israel (c. 786–747 B.C.); son and successor of Joash (2 Kin. 14:23–29).

Jerusalem (jeh-ROO-suh-lem) The chief city of Palestine; most sacred city of both Jews and Christians; mentioned under one name or another (Shalem; Salem; City of David; Moriah; Jebus; Zion; Ariel) in about 40 of the 66 books of the Bible. David captured the city (2 Sam. 5:6–9; 1 Chr. 11:4–8) and made it his capital; brought the ark of the Testimony to the city (2 Sam. 6:1–17). Solomon built the temple and other buildings there (1 Kin. 5–7). Captured by Nebuchadnezzar (Jer. 39); rebuilt by Ezra and Nehemiah. Several events in the life of Jesus occurred there: His presentation in the temple (Luke 2:22–38); the cleansing of the temple (John 2:13–25); the conversation with Nicodemus (John 2:23; 3:1–21); and the events of the last week of His life (Matt. 21–28; Mark 11–16; Luke 19:28—24:53; John 12:12—21:25).

Jesse (JESS-ih) Son of Obed; grandson of Boaz and Ruth; father of David (1 Sam. 16:1–13; 17:12ff).

Jesus Christ The personal name of the One whose title gave its name to the Christian religion. Since "Jesus" was a fairly common name in the first century, distinguishing phrases were used when referring to Him (Jesus of Nazareth; Jesus, Son of David; Christ Jesus; the Messiah Jesus; and Jesus Christ). The four Gospels detail His life and ministry: birth (Matt. 1:18–25; Luke 2:1–20); baptism (Matt. 3:13–17; Mark 1:9–11; Luke 3:21, 22); makes water into wine (John 2:1–12); the Sermon on the Mount (Matt. 5:1—7:29; Luke 6:20–49); stilling of the storm (Mark 4:35–41; Luke 8:22–25); sending the unclean spirits into the swine (Mark 5:1–20); feeding of the 5,000 (Matt.

14:13–21; Mark 6:30–44; Luke 9:10–17; John 6:1–14); walking on the water (Matt. 14:22–33; Mark 6:45–52; John 6:15–21); feeding of the 4,000 (Matt. 15:32–39; Mark 8:1–10); the Transfiguration (Matt. 17:1–8; Mark 9:2–8; Luke 9:28–36); entry into Jeru-salem (Matt. 21:1–10; Mark 11:1–11; Luke 19:28–44; John 12:12–19); raises Lazarus from the dead (John 11:1–44); the Lord's Supper (Matt. 26:26–29; Mark 14:22–25; Luke 22:15–20); is arrested (Matt. 26:47–56; Mark 14:43–52; Luke 22:47–50; John 18:2–12); trial before Pilate (Matt. 27:11–14; Mark 15:1–5; Luke 23:1–5; John 18:33–38); the Crucifixion and burial (Matt. 27:32–61; Mark 15:21–47; Luke 23:26–56; John 19:17–42); the Resurrection and Ascension (Matt. 28:1–20; Mark 16:1–20; Luke 24:1–53; John 20; 21).

Job (JOBE) Chief character in the OT Book of Job; unknown otherwise.

Joel (JO-ell) The name of several persons in the OT, including the prophet, son of Pethuel, author of the second book of the 12 Minor Prophets.

John The name of five persons in the NT, among them: 1. **John the apostle:** A son of Zebedee, brother of James (Matt. 4:21, 22; Mark 1:19, 20; Luke 5:10); sometimes called "the beloved disciple" and "Saint John"; traditional author of the fourth Gospel, the three epistles of John, and the Book of Revelation. 2. **John the Baptist:** The son of Elizabeth and Zacharias (Luke 1:5–25, 57–66); a prophet, called the forerunner of Jesus (John 1:15–28); baptized Jesus (Matt. 3:13–17; Mark 1:9–11; Luke 3:21, 22; John 1:29–34); imprisoned by Herod and beheaded (Matt. 14:3–12; Mark 6:17–29). 3. **John Mark**: *See* Mark.

Jonah (JO-nuh) The name of two persons of the OT, one of whom was the prophet about whom the fifth book of the 12 Minor Prophets was written. Swallowed by a great fish (Jon. 1:17—2:10).

Jonathan (JOHN-uh-thun) The name of 15 persons in the OT, one of whom was the oldest son of Saul; David's friend (1 Sam. 13:2; 14:1–45; 19:1–7; 20).

Jordan (JOR-dun) The chief river of Palestine, flowing from the slopes of Mount Hermon through Lake Huleh and the Sea of Galilee to the Dead Sea. The waters were miraculously stopped for the Israelites to pass (Josh. 3:14—4:24). Jesus was baptized there (Matt. 3:13; Mark 1:9).

Joseph; Joses (JOE-sef; JOE-sus) The name of 14 persons in the Bible, among them: 1. The son of Jacob and Rachel (Gen. 30:22–24); his coat of many colors (Gen. 37:3); sold into Egypt by his brothers (Gen. 37:18–36); imprisoned on false accusations (Gen. 39:7–23); interpreted Pharaoh's dreams, thus gaining favor (Gen. 41:1–36); as administrator of Egypt (Gen. 41:37—50:26); his brothers come to him for food (Gen. 42–45). 2 The husband of Mary mother of Jesus; resident of Nazareth; descended from David (Matt. 1:16–25; Luke 2:4–7; John 1:45). 3. **Joseph of Arimathea:** A member of the Sanhedrin; buried the body of Jesus on his own property (Matt. 27:57–60; Mark 15:43–46; Luke 23:50–53; John 19:38–42).

Joshua; Jeshua (JOSH-you-ah; JESH-you-ah) The name of several persons in the OT, the most important being Joshua, son of Nun, the central figure of the Book of Joshua. This book tells the story of Moses' successor as leader of the Israelites, the conquest of Canaan, and the division of the country among the 12 tribes. His miraculous crossing of the Jordan (Josh. 3:14—4:24); conquest of Jericho (Josh. 6:1–21).

Josiah (jo-SIGH-uh) One of the few good kings of Judah; son of Amon and grandson of Manasseh (2 Kin. 21:23—23:30); became king at the age of 8; found the Book of the Law while the house of the Lord was being repaired (2 Chr. 34:14); read the Book to the inhabitants of Judah (2 Chr. 34:29–32), resulting in repentance and reform.

Judah (JEW-duh) The fourth son of Jacob by Leah (Gen. 29:31, 35); ancestor of the tribe of Judah.

Judas (JEW-dus) The name of six persons in the NT, including: 1. A brother of Jesus (Matt. 13:55; Mark 6:3). *See* Jude, The General Epistle of. 2. **Judas Iscariot** (iz-CARE-ih-ut): One of the 12 apostles; the betrayer of Jesus (Matt. 26:20–25, 47–50; Mark 14:18–20, 43–46; Luke 22:47, 48; John 13:21–26). 3. The

brother of James; one of the 12 apostles (Luke 6:16; John 14:22; Acts 1:13). *See* Thaddaeus. 4. **Judas Barsabas** (BAR-sab-bus): A Jewish Christian (Acts 15:22, 27, 32).

Jude, The General Epistle of This NT letter designates its author as a "servant of Jesus Christ, and brother of James." *See* Judas (1).

Judea (jew-DEE-uh) An area of SW Palestine; formerly called Judah.

judge To decide; form an opinion.
J. not, that you be not Matt. 7:1

judge One who forms an opinion. In the OT Book of Judges, one chosen by God to save the people from foreign oppressors; a military leader with both legislative and executive authority.
made you . . . a j. over us Ex. 2:14

Judge God; Christ.
J. of all the earth Gen. 18:25
J. of the living and the dead Acts 10:42
to God the J. of all Heb. 12:23

justified (JUS-tih-fyed) The way sinful human beings are made acceptable to a holy God. Christianity is different from all other religions because of its teaching of being justified by grace (Rom. 3:24)—an act of love from God to undeserving sinners. We can have grace and be justified when we believe and have faith that Jesus died on the Cross to save us from our sins (Rom. 3:25–30; 4:3, 5, 9; John 6:28, 29; Phil. 1:29).

K

keeper One who guards or takes care of someone or something.
Am I my brother's k. Gen. 4:9

Kidron Valley (KID-run) A very important valley E of the walls of Jerusalem and extending all the way to the Dead Sea; site of Nehemiah's inspection of the broken-down walls of Jerusalem (Neh. 2:13–15); site of a common burial ground (2 Kin. 23:6); dumping ground for ashes of idols (1 Kin. 15:13; 2 Kin. 23:4; 2 Chr. 29:16; 30:14). Jesus crossed the valley to go to the Garden of Gethsemane to pray just before He was arrested and crucified (John 18:1).

king A chief ruler; among ancient peoples, a religious leader often held to be divine. God and Jesus Christ are called "King."
trees . . . anoint a k. Judg. 9:8
My K. and my God Ps. 5:2; 84:3
the K. of glory shall Ps. 24:7
seen the K., The LORD Is. 6:5
no k. but Caesar John 19:15
K. of kings and Lord 1 Tim. 6:15

kingdom of God The eternal sovereignty or kingly rule of God, manifested in its acceptance by men on earth and the hope for the future; the central theme of Jesus' teaching. The phrase does not occur in the OT, but the idea is present in "Your kingdom," "My kingdom," etc., which are also sometimes used in the NT. "Kingdom of heaven" is used in Matthew's Gospel; "kingdom of the Son of His love" (Col. 1:13); "kingdom of our Lord and Savior Jesus Christ" (2 Pet. 1:11).
Yours is the k., O LORD 1 Chr. 29:11
the scepter of Your k. Ps. 45:6
Your k. come Matt. 6:10; Luke 11:2
seek first the k. of God Matt. 6:33; Luke 12:31
with you in My Father's k. Matt. 26:29
k. of God is at hand Mark 1:15
cannot see the k. of God John 3:3
inherit the k. of God 1 Cor. 6:10; Gal. 5:21

L

Laban (LAY-bun) Brother of Rebekah and father-in-law of Jacob; lived near Haran where Abraham once lived; instrumental in two important marriages—Isaac to Rebekah (Gen. 24) and Jacob to Leah and Rachel (Gen. 29).

ladder A framework of uprights and crosspieces on which one may ascend or descend. Jacob dreams of a ladder (Gen. 28:12).

lamb The young of a sheep, commonly used as the sacrificial animal of the Passover.
God will provide . . . l. Gen. 22:8
a l. to the slaughter Is. 53:7
wolf and the l. shall feed Is. 65:25
Feed My l. John 21:15

Lamb (of God) Christ, whose sacrificial death removed the sins of the world. By extension of "lamb" as the most common

victim of OT sacrifices, particularly the "Passover." Christ, our Passover (1 Cor. 5:7).
Behold! The L. of God John 1:29, 36
a l. without blemish 1 Pet. 1:19
stood a L. as though it had Rev. 5:6
L. slain from the foundation Rev. 13:8
L. will overcome them Rev. 17:14

lamp A device producing light.
spirit of a man is the l. Prov. 20:27
light a l. and put it Matt. 5:15
ten virgins who took their l. Matt. 25:1
light of a l. shall not shine Rev. 18:23

lampstand Particularly the seven-branched lampstand of the tabernacle and the temple, and the symbolic ones of Revelation.
make a l. of pure gold Ex. 25:31
I saw seven golden l. Rev. 1:12

last The final one.
first will be l. Matt. 19:30; Mark 10:31
I am the First and the L. Rev. 1:17

Last Supper The last meal eaten by Jesus with His Apostles, on the night before His crucifixion.

laver (LAY-ver) A basin in which priests washed their hands for purification purposes while serving at the altar of the tabernacle or temple; made by Moses so Aaron and the priests could wash their hands and feet before offering sacrifices (Ex. 30:18–21). Ten bronze lavers, decorated with lions, oxen, and cherubim, were made by Hiram for Solomon's temple (1 Kin. 7:27–39).

law Rules of conduct; particularly rules given by God to Moses by which the Israelites were to live and which were defined in the Pentateuch (the Law of Moses).
l. of the LORD is perfect Ps. 19:7
not . . . to destroy the L. Matt. 5:17
l. was given through Moses John 1:17

Lazarus (LAZ-uh-rus) 1. The beggar in a parable told by Jesus (Luke 16:19–31). 2. A friend of Jesus; brother of Martha and Mary (John 11:1–44; 12:1–11).

Leah (LEE-uh) Elder daughter of Laban; Jacob's first wife to whom were born six of his sons (Gen. 29:16—30:21).

leaven (LEV-in) Yeast or other fermenting agent. It was forbidden to the Israelites in all offerings made with fire (Lev. 2:11; 6:17) and at the Passover (Ex. 12:17–19).
beware of the l. Matt. 16:6
a little l. leavens 1 Cor. 5:6

Lebanon (LEB-uh-nun) A nation just N of Israel (ancient Phoenicia in Bible times); named for the snow-capped range of mountains running the entire length of the country; has been conquered by the Egyptians, Assyrians, Persians, Greeks, Romans, Arabs, and Turks; famous for the Cedars of Lebanon, the wood of which was used in Solomon's temple and palace. Well-known cities include Byblos, from which we get the word "Bible," Sidon, and Tyre (Gen. 10:19; Matt. 15:21–28; Mark 7:24–31).

Lent The 40 weekdays preceding Easter; a period of fasting and repentance in Christian churches.

leopard (LEP-urd) A wild animal of the cat family.
l. shall lie down with the Is. 11:6

let Allow.
l. me first go Matt. 8:21
L. the little children Matt. 19:14; Mark 10:14; Luke 18:16

Levi; Levites (LEE-vigh; LEE-vights) Third son of Jacob and Leah (Gen. 29:31, 34); ancestor of the tribe of Levites, who were charged with the care of the tabernacle and the temple.

Leviticus (leh-VIT-ih-kus) The third book of the OT; it deals mainly with the priests and their duties.

life The union of body and soul. Christ is called the "Prince of life" (Acts 3:15).
The tree of l. was also Gen. 2:9
the resurrection and the l. John 11:25

light Brightness; radiance.
Let there be l. Gen. 1:3
my l. and my salvation Ps. 27:1
the l. of the world Matt. 5:14
I am the l. of the world John 8:12

Lights, Feast of *See* Dedication, Feast of.

lilies Flowering plants that grow from bulbs.
He feeds his flock among the l. Song 6:3
Consider the l. of the Matt. 6:28

lord One who has authority over persons or things; hence, **Lord:** God, as the supreme authority; Jesus, as leader during

His ministry and as the Son of God. When large and small capitals are used for LORD, the original Hebrew reads YHWH.
L. Himself is God Deut. 4:35; 1 Kin. 18:39
the L. is one Deut. 6:4
L. of the whole earth Ps. 97:5
says to Me, L., L. Matt. 7:21
L. of heaven and earth Matt. 11:25
Son of Man is also L. Mark 2:28
My L. and my God John 20:28
both L. and Christ Acts 2:36
crucified the L. of glory 1 Cor. 2:8
is L. of l. and King Rev. 17:14

LORD of Hosts *See* Hosts, LORD of.

Lord's Day Sunday (Rev. 1:10).

Lord's Prayer The prayer, taught by Jesus to His disciples, that begins "Our Father" (Matt. 6:9–13; Luke 11:2–4).

Lord's Supper 1. Holy Communion (1 Cor. 11:20). 2. Last Supper.

lost Mislaid; not to be found.
the l. sheep Matt. 18:12–14; Luke 15:4–7
the l. coin Luke 15:8–10
the l. (prodigal) son Luke 15:11–32

Lot The nephew of Abraham who came with him to Canaan (Gen. 11:27—13:12). Saved from Sodom's destruction (Gen. 19:1–38). His wife was turned into a pillar of salt (Gen. 19:26).

love 1. A deep affection; devotion.
l. covers all sins Prov. 10:12
Greater l. has no one John 15:13
l. of money is a root 1 Tim. 6:10
God is l. 1 John 4:8
2. To have deep affection for someone or something.
l. your neighbor Lev. 19:18; Matt. 22:39; James 2:8
l. the LORD your God Deut. 6:5; Matt. 22:37
l. your enemies Matt. 5:44; Luke 6:27
God so l. the world John 3:16

Luke *Probable author of the Book of Luke* and the Acts of the Apostles; Gentile, the only non-Jewish writer of a NT book; a "fellow laborer" of the apostle Paul, who accompanied him on parts of the second and third missionary journeys and the journey to Rome (2 Tim. 4:11; Philem. 24); a physician by profession (Col. 4:14).

Lydia (LID-ee-uh) A prosperous businesswoman from the city of Thyatira in W Asia Minor (Turkey), a seller of purple cloth; lived in Philippi in N Greece, where she heard Paul preach about Jesus and became the first convert to Christianity in Europe (Acts 16:14, 15, 40).

Lystra (LISS-trah) A city of Lycaonia in central Asia Minor (Turkey); home of Timothy (Acts 16:1, 2). Paul preached and healed here on his first and second missionary journeys; was stoned and left for dead (Acts 14:6–21; 2 Tim. 3:11).

Macedonia (mass-uh-DOH-nee-uh) A mountainous country N of Greece which Paul visited on his missionary journeys after receiving his "Macedonian call" (Acts 16:9); at Philippi, the first European convert to Christianity was Lydia, a businesswoman (Acts 16:14, 15, 40). Philip II of Macedon, father of Alexander the Great, established his capital at Philippi and made Macedon internationally important.

Machpelah (mack-PEA-luh) The name of a field, a cave, and the surrounding land which Abraham bought as a burial place for his wife, Sarah, from Ephron the Hittite. Abraham, Sarah, Isaac, Rebekah, Jacob, and Leah are all buried in this cave (Gen. 49:31; 50:13). The modern city of Hebron was built around this site, now covered by a large Muslim mosque.

Magi (MAY-ji) The wise men who came to worship the infant Jesus (Matt. 2:1–12); because they offered three gifts, it is often assumed that there were three Magi.

maker One who brings into being; creator; hence, **Maker:** God.
more pure than his M. Job 4:17
man will look to his M. Is. 17:7
builder and m. is God Heb. 11:10

Malachi (MAL-uh-kigh) An OT prophet, author of the last book of the OT, one of the 12 Minor Prophets.

man A male human being; the whole human race.
God is not a m. Num. 23:19
m. is born to trouble Job 5:7

M. shall not live by Matt. 4:4
not m. for the Sabbath Mark 2:27

Manasseh (mah-NASS-uh) 1. Joseph's eldest son, born in Egypt (Gen. 41:50, 51). Like his younger brother, Ephraim, Manasseh was half Hebrew and half Egyptian. Both of Joseph's sons were "adopted" by Jacob and became two of the heads of the tribes of Israel. 2. King of Judah (2 Kin. 21:1–18); reigned longer than any of the Israelite kings, but was the most wicked; rebuilt the altars to idols that had been destroyed by King Hezekiah and even sacrificed his own son to the heathen god Molech; deported to Babylon where he repented (2 Chr. 33:11–13); tried to introduce reforms when he returned, but was opposed by his wicked son Amon, who succeeded him.

mark A sign.
set a m. on Cain Gen. 4:15
his m. on his forehead Rev. 14:9

Mark; John Mark Son of Mary of Jerusalem; companion of Paul and other early Christian missionaries; the traditional author of the second Gospel (Acts 12:12, 25; 15:37).

marriage The union of one man and one woman. Explained by Jesus (Mark 10:6–9).
are given in m. Matt. 22:30
M. is honorable among all Heb. 13:4

martyr (MAR-ter) A witness. Because the early Christians often suffered for their faith, the word soon came to mean one who suffered or died because of his witness to Christ. The apostle Paul called Stephen a martyr (Acts 22:20); the Book of Revelation mentions "the martyrs of Jesus" (Rev. 17:6).

Mary The name of seven persons in the NT, among them: 1. The mother of Jesus (Matt. 1:16, 18–25; Luke 2:5–20). 2. **Mary Magdalene:** A Galilean follower of Jesus (Matt. 27:55, 56, 61; 28:1; Mark 15:40, 47; 16:1; Luke 8:2; 24:10; John 19:25; 20:1, 18). 3. The sister of Martha and Lazarus (Luke 10:38–42; John 11:1–45; 12:1–8). 4. The mother of James "the Less" (Matt. 27:55, 56, 61; 28:1–10; Mark 15:40, 41, 47; 16:1–8; Luke 24:1–11). 5. The mother of John Mark (Acts 12:12).

master A male person in authority; one who controls someone or something; owner.
is free from his m. Job 3:19
can serve two m. Matt. 6:24; Luke 16:13
nor a servant above his m. Matt. 10:24

Matthew (MATH-you) One of the 12 apostles; called "Levi the son of Alphaeus" in Mark 2:14; traditional author of the first Gospel.

measure A certain amount; capacity.
have a . . . just m. Deut. 25:15
same m. you use Matt. 7:2; Mark 4:24; Luke 6:38
good m., pressed down Luke 6:38

mediator (MEE-dee-ay-tor) One who acts as a go-between in making an agreement between two parties. Moses is so designated (Gal. 3:19) in making the covenant at Sinai. Christ is called the "one Mediator between God and men" (1 Tim. 2:5).

meditate To study; contemplate.
he m. day and night Ps. 1:2

meek Humble; gentle.
m. shall inherit the earth Ps. 37:11
Blessed are the m. Matt. 5:5

Megiddo (muh-GID-oh) A fortified, walled city at the foot of the Carmel mountain range in N Israel, overlooking the Valley of Jezreel where the last battle between good and evil will be fought (Rev. 16:16); a chariot city for Kings Solomon and Ahab; site of many important OT battles. Megiddo is another name for Armageddon.

Melchizedek (mel-KIZ-uh-dek) A king of Salem (Jerusalem) and priest of the Most High God (Gen. 14:18–20; Ps. 110:4; Heb. 5:6–11; 6:20—7:21); appeared and disappeared somewhat mysteriously in the Book of Genesis; bestowed a blessing on Abraham and praised God for giving him a victory in battle (Gen. 14:18–20). Melchizedek is seen as a type of Christ in both Psalm 110 and the Book of Hebrews.

"Mene, Mene, Tekel, Upharsin" (ME-neh, ME-neh, TEK-ul, you-FAR-sin) Means "numbered, numbered, weighed, and divided." An inscription that appeared on the wall of the palace

of King Belshazzar in Babylon, written by a mysterious hand during a feast (Dan. 5:1–29). The king ordered that the gold vessels taken from the temple of Jerusalem be brought in for the guests to use in eating and drinking. When the words appeared on the wall, Daniel was called in to interpret. Daniel told the king that God had weighed him on the scales of righteousness, and he did not measure up. The kingdom would be divided between his enemies, the Medes and the Persians. That very night, Belshazzar was killed and his kingdom fell.

Mephibosheth (meh-FIB-oh-sheth) A son of Jonathan and grandson of King Saul; only five years old when his father and grandfather were killed on Mount Gilboa in the Battle of Jezreel (2 Sam. 4:4); dropped by his nurse and crippled for the rest of his life (2 Sam. 4:4); treated kindly by King David because of an agreement made between the king and his father, Jonathan (2 Sam. 9:7–13).

merciful Forgiving; unwilling to punish.
LORD God, m. and gracious Ex. 34:6
God be m. to us Ps. 67:1
Blessed are the m. Matt. 5:7
m. to me a sinner Luke 18:13

mercy Forgiveness or kindness, particularly to a wrongdoer.
His m. endures forever Ezra 3:11
they shall obtain m. Matt. 5:7

mercy seat Literally, "covering." The lid of the ark of the Testimony, from above which God spoke to His people (Ex. 25:22).

merry Joyous; happy.
m. heart makes a cheerful Prov. 15:13
m. heart does good Prov. 17:22
eat, drink, and be m. Eccl. 8:15; Luke 12:19

Meshach (ME-shack) The Babylonian name of one of Daniel's friends (Dan. 1:7; 3:12).

Mesopotamia (mess-uh-puh-TAY-mee-uh) "Land between the rivers." A region between the Tigris and Euphrates Rivers in the modern countries of Iraq and Iran; the "cradle of civilization"; traditional site of the Garden of Eden; Ur of the Chaldees is located in the S part of the region (Acts 7:2).

Messiah (muh-SIGH-uh) Literally, "anointed one"; one sent by God to save others. In Hebrew belief, the coming Savior of the Jewish people; in Christianity, Jesus.

Methuselah (meh-THOO-zuh-luh) Noah's grandfather; lived for 969 years, the oldest person mentioned in the Bible (Gen. 5:27).

Micah (MY-kuh) A Judean prophet, contemporary of Isaiah, whose prophecies appear in the OT Book of Micah, the sixth of the 12 Minor Prophets.

mighty Powerful; very strong.
He was a m. hunter Gen. 10:9
a great and m. nation Gen. 18:18
How the m. have fallen 2 Sam. 1:19
m. in deed and word Luke 24:19

ministry God's service.
to the m. of the word Acts 6:4
m. of reconciliation 2 Cor 5:18

miracle An event that exceeds the known laws of nature and science. Usually an act of God done through human agents.

The OT miracles include:
ten plagues of Egypt Ex. 7:14—12:30
parting of the Red Sea Ex. 14:21–31
feeding with bread from heaven Ex. 16:14–35
walls of Jericho fall Josh. 6:1–21
strength of Samson Judg. 14:1—16:30
Elijah taken by a whirlwind 2 Kin. 2:11
Elisha revives dead child 2 Kin. 4:18–37
three men saved from furnace Dan. 3:19–27
Daniel saved from lions Dan. 6:16–23
Jonah saved Jon. 1:10—2:10

The NT miracles of Jesus include:
the leper cured Matt. 8:2, 3; Mark 1:40–42; Luke 5:12, 13
centurion's servant healed Matt. 8:5–13; Luke 7:1–10
the storm stilled Matt. 8:23–26; Mark 4:35–39; Luke 8:22–24
demons entered into swine Matt. 8:28–32; Mark 5:1–13; Luke 8:26–33
dumb demoniac healed Matt. 9:32, 33
feeding the 5,000 Matt. 14:15–21; Mark 6:35–44; Luke 9:10–17; John 6:1–14
Jesus walks on the sea Matt. 14:25–27; Mark 6:48–51; John 6:19–21
feeding the 4,000 Matt. 15:32–38; Mark 8:1–9
ten lepers cleansed Luke 17:11–19
water changed to wine John 2:1–11

Lazarus raised from dead John 11:38–44
Other NT miracles include:
the gift of tongues Acts 2:4–11
Peter restores Tabitha Acts 9:36–41
Peter's release from prison Acts 12:5–10

mite A copper coin of small value.
widow . . . threw in two m. Mark 12:42

money Riches; coins.
the tax m. Matt. 22:19
no copper in their m. belts Mark 6:8
love of m. is a root of all . . . evil 1 Tim. 6:10

money changers Bankers who exchanged one nation's currency for another, often charging too much for this service. Twice, Jesus found them in the temple, made a whip of cords, and drove them out, along with those who sold oxen, sheep, and doves (John 2:13–16; Matt. 21:12, 13). Jesus said, "Do not make My Father's house a house of merchandise!" (John 2:16).

Mordecai (MOR-duh-kigh) The Jewish hero of the OT Book of Esther.

Moses (MO-zez) The great deliverer and lawgiver of Israel; born during the oppression of the Israelites in Egypt (Ex. 1:22—2:2); brought up in Pharaoh's house (Ex. 2:5–10); fled to Midian where he lived 40 years (Ex. 2:15–25); called by God from the burning bush (Ex. 3:2–5) to deliver the Israelites; after performing ten miracles of plagues (Ex. 7:14—12:30) he got Pharaoh's consent to take the Israelites from Egypt; led them 40 years through the wilderness; received the Ten Commandments from God (Ex. 20). The OT books of Exodus, Leviticus, Numbers, and Deuteronomy detail his life and deeds.

Most High, the A name used of God.
When the Most H. divided Deut. 32:8
the Most H. rules in Dan. 4:25
the Most H. does not dwell Acts 7:48

mother Female parent.
Honor . . . your m. Ex. 20:12; Matt. 19:19
Like m., like daughter Ezek. 16:44
disciple, "Behold your m. John 19:27

Mount of Olives A ridge of hills E of Jerusalem, where Jesus was betrayed by Judas on the night before His crucifixion; site of Jesus' triumphal entry into Jerusalem, when He wept over the city because the people would not believe (Luke 19:37–41); traditional location of the tomb of Mary, Jesus' mother; site of Jesus' ascension (Matt. 28:16).

mourn To grieve for.
Blessed are those who m. Matt. 5:4

murder To kill; cause the death of.
You shall not m. Ex. 20:13; Deut. 5:17; Matt. 5:21

myrrh An aromatic, resinous substance used in incense and perfumes.
of liquid m. Ex. 30:23
frankincense, and m. Matt. 2:11
wine mingled with m. Mark 15:23

Naaman (NAY-uh-mun) Commander of the Syrian army, who was "a great and honorable man in the eyes of his master" (Ben-Hadad, king of Syria), but he was a leper (2 Kin. 5:1–27); served by a young Israelite girl who had been captured on one of Syria's frequent raids of Israel; encouraged to see the prophet Elisha, who could heal his leprosy; finally following Elisha's instructions, dipped himself seven times in the Jordan River and was healed; became a worshiper of God.

Nahum (NAY-hum) A prophet, the prophecies of whom are given in the OT Book of Nahum, the seventh of the 12 Minor Prophets.

name The word by which a person, place, or thing is called.
n. of the LORD your God in vain Ex. 20:7
How excellent is Your n. Ps. 8:1
Hallowed be Your n. Matt. 6:9; Luke 11:2
in My n. Matt. 24:5; Mark 13:6; Luke 21:8
My n. is Legion Mark 5:9
ask the Father in My n. John 15:16

Naomi (nay-OH-mee) The mother-in-law of Ruth, the Moabitess. After her husband and two sons died, Naomi returned to Bethlehem with her daughter-in-law Ruth, who insisted on going with her (Ruth 1:16, 17). Ruth became an ancestor of Jesus Christ when she married her kinsman, Boaz (Ruth 4:21, 22; Matt. 1:5).

Naphtali (NAF-tah-ligh) The sixth son of Jacob, the second born of Bilhah (Gen. 30:7, 8); ancestor of one of the 12 tribes of Israel.

narrow Not wide; small in width.
n. is the gate . . . which Matt. 7:14

Nathan (NAY-thun) A prophet during the reign of David and Solomon; told David that he would not be the one to build the temple at Jerusalem (1 Chr. 17:1–15); confronted David after he had Uriah killed in battle so he could marry his wife, Bathsheba (2 Sam. 12:9–15).

nation A group of people under one government or sharing the same history.
make you a great n. Gen. 12:2
n. will rise against n. Matt. 24:7; Mark 13:8

Nazareth (NAZ-uh-reth) The town in Lower Galilee where Jesus was brought up (Luke 2:39, 51).

Nazirite (NAZ-uh-right) A person who took a vow to be separated from the world and completely dedicated to God (Num. 6:1–8). They promised not to touch strong drink, not to shave or cut their hair (Samson), not to touch or go near a dead body, not even to bury a relative (Num. 6:5–12; Prov. 20:1; Eph. 5:17, 18).

Nebuchadnezzar (neb-you-kad-NEZ-zer) King of Babylonia (605–562 B.C.).

Nehemiah (nee-huh-MY-uh) The name of three persons in the OT, one of whom was the rebuilder of Jerusalem after the Babylonian Exile. The Book of Nehemiah tells his story.

neighbor A person who lives near another.
false witness against your n. Ex. 20:16
love your n. as yourself Lev. 19:18; Matt. 19:19

Nicodemus (nick-uh-DEE-mus) A wealthy, well-educated and well-respected Pharisee and member of the Sanhedrin, who probably became a disciple of Jesus; visited Jesus at night to learn more about His teachings (John 3:1–8; 7:50). On this visit Jesus told him he must be "born again" (John 3:7); later gave him the gospel in one verse: John 3:16! Nicodemus defended Jesus before the Sanhedrin; purchased a hundred pounds of spices to be placed between the folds of the cloth in which Jesus was buried (John 19:39).

night The period of darkness between sunset and sunrise.
darkness He called N. Gen. 1:5
Watchman, what of the n. Is. 21:11
the n. is coming when no John 9:4

Nineveh (NIN-uh-vuh) One of the oldest and greatest cities of Mesopotamia; capital of Assyria; destroyed 612 B.C. (Gen. 10:11, 12; 2 Kin. 19:36; Is. 37:37; Jon. 1:2; 4:11; Nah. 1:1; 2:8; 3:7).

Nisan (NIGH-san) The name given, after the captivity lasting 70 years, to the former month of Abib—the first month of the Jewish sacred year (Esth. 3:7).

Noah (NO-uh) The ninth descendant of Adam; the survivor, with his family, of the Flood (Gen. 6–9).

Obadiah (oh-buh-DIE-uh) The name of 11 persons in the OT, none of whom can be assumed to be the author of the Book of Obadiah, the shortest OT book and fourth of the 12 Minor Prophets.

offering Something given in worship. In the OT we find offerings of: 1. **grain:** Consisting of unleavened bread, cakes, wafers, or grain mixed with salt and, except when a sin offering, with olive oil (Lev. 2:1–16; 5:11; 6:14–23; Num. 15:4, 6, 9). Sometimes accepted from the poor as a sin offering in place of the burnt offering (Lev. 5:11–13). 2. **drink:** Consisting of wine and used with the grain and burnt offerings, except in the sin and trespass offerings (Num. 6:17; 15:5, 10). 3. **animals,** or **sacrifice:** Cattle, sheep, and goats that were free from blemish (Lev. 1:3). These were used with: a. The **burnt offering** in which a male lamb, ram, goat, bull, dove, or pigeon was entirely consumed on the altar (Lev. 1; 6:9–13). b. The **sin offering** in which a bull, a male or female goat, a female lamb, a dove, or a pigeon was given (Lev. 4; 5:7; 6:25–30). c. The **trespass offering** in which a ram or lamb was used (Lev. 5:6, 15; 6:6; 7:1–8; 14:12, 21). d. The **peace offering,** including the giving of thanks (Lev. 7:12–15), the payment of a vow (Lev. 7:16–20; Num. 6:13–21), and the voluntary or freewill offering (Lev. 7:16–20); for these any animal without blemish of either sex could

be used, except birds (Lev. 3; 7:11–27). In sacrifices, the term "wave offering" is used of those portions consecrated to the Lord by the rite of "waving" (Lev. 7:30–34; Num. 6:17–20); and the term "heave offering" is used of those portions taken away and set apart for the Lord (Lev. 7:14, 32–34; Num. 18:8–32).

oil Any of several greasy liquids that can be burned.

anoint my head with o. Ps. 23:5

Olives, Mount of; Olivet, mount called A mountain E of Jerusalem (2 Sam. 15:30; Zech. 14:4). Closely associated with the last days in the life of Jesus (in the four Gospels and Acts 1:12).

P

Palestine (PAL-es-tine) The Greek and Roman names for Canaan; modern usage applies the name to the territory alloted to the 12 tribes of Israel.

Palm Sunday The Sunday before Easter; commemorates the triumphal entry of Jesus into Jerusalem (John 12:12, 13).

parable (PAIR-uh-bull) A short story teaching a moral lesson. Among those of the OT are:

Samson's riddle Judg. 14:14
field of the slothful Prov. 24:30–34
two harlots Ezek. 23
healing waters Ezek. 47:1–12

In the NT, parables are only by Jesus, and include:

lamp under a basket Matt. 5:14–16; Mark 4:21–23; Luke 8:16–18
unshrunk cloth on an old garment Matt. 9:16, 17; Mark 2:21, 22; Luke 5:36–39
weeds among wheat Matt. 13:24–30
the mustard seed Matt. 13:31, 32; Mark 4:30–32; Luke 13:18, 19
lost sheep Matt. 18:12–14; Luke 15:4–7
laborers in vineyard Matt. 20:1–16
wise and foolish virgins Matt. 25:1–13
the talents Matt. 25:14–30
two debtors Luke 7:41–50
Good Samaritan Luke 10:30–37
Prodigal Son Luke 15:11–32
Pharisee and tax collector Luke 18:9–14
shepherd and the sheep John 10:1–30

Passover 1. A seven-day Jewish festival held in March or April, commemorating the slaying of the firstborn just before the Israelites were freed from slavery in Egypt (Ex. 12); combined with the Feast of Unleavened Bread which commemorates the actual Exodus flight (Ex. 13:3–16). 2. The sacrificial lamb of the Passover (Ex. 12:11, 21, 27). Paul refers to Christ as the Paschal Lamb.

Christ, our P., was sacrificed 1 Cor. 5:7

Pastoral Epistles The epistles to Timothy and Titus are so called because they deal chiefly with directions about the work of the pastor of a church.

pasture Grassy land where cattle and sheep graze.

me to lie down in green p. Ps. 23:2

Patmos, Island of (PAT-mus) A small, rocky, irregularly shaped island off the western coast of Asia Minor or modern Turkey; used by the Romans to hold exiled criminals, one of whom was the apostle John, who received messages from the Lord, which became the Book of Revelation (Rev. 1:9–11).

Paul As Saul, the son of Hebrew parents, he persecuted the followers of Jesus (Acts 8:3; Gal. 1:13). Miraculously converted (Acts 9:1ff) and name changed to Paul (Acts 13:9), he became the leading missionary of early Christianity. His life is detailed in the NT Book of Acts. He founded many churches in Asia Minor and Greece and carried on extensive correspondence with them.

peace Freedom from turmoil and war.

of war, And a time of p. Eccl. 3:8
is no p. . . . for the wicked Is. 57:21
not come to bring p. but a sword Matt. 10:34
on earth p., goodwill Luke 2:14
P. to you Luke 24:36; John 20:19

peeled Stripped off the bark.

rods which he had p. Gen. 30:38

Pentecost (PEN-tih-cost) A Jewish festival on the fiftieth day after Passover; also called Feast of Weeks (Lev. 23:15, 16). Observed by the Christian church as the day on which the gift of the Holy Spirit was given to the church (Acts 2:1).

perish To die; to be destroyed.

way of the ungodly shall p. Ps. 1:6
believes in Him should not p. John 3:16

Peter; Simon Peter A fisherman on the Sea of Galilee who was called with his brother Andrew by Jesus (Matt. 4:18–20; Mark 1:16–18; Luke 5:1–11; John 1:35–41). He became the "first" of the 12 apostles (Matt. 10:2), and sometimes spoke for all the disciples. Jesus changed his name from Simon to Peter (Matt. 16:18; Mark 3:16; Luke 6:14; John 1:42). His mother-in-law healed by Jesus (Matt. 8:14, 15; Mark 1:30, 31; Luke 4:38, 39; his confession that Jesus is the Christ (Matt. 16:16; Mark 8:29 Luke 9:20); his denial of Jesus (Matt. 26:69–75; Mark 14:66–72; Luke 22:54–62). The traditional author of two NT epistles.

Pharaoh (FAY-row) A title used as a name, or prefixed to a name, of the king of Egypt. Joseph interprets Pharaoh's dream (Gen. 41:1–36); the Pharaoh of the Exodus (Ex. 7–14).

Pharisee (FAIR-uh-see) A member of a strict Jewish sect, holding the Mosaic Law and their own traditions as binding. The parable of the Pharisee and the publican (Luke 18:9–14).

Philemon (fih-LEE-mun) A Christian of Colosse to whom the NT Epistle to Philemon was written by Paul. In the letter Paul asks Philemon to pardon Onesimus, a runaway slave whom Paul has converted.

Philip The name of four persons in the NT, among them: 1. The apostle (Matt. 10:3; Mark 3:18; Luke 6:14; John 1:43–48; 6:5, 7; 12:21, 22; 14:8, 9; Acts 1:13). 2. The evangelist (Acts 6:5; 8:5–40; 21:8).

Philippi; Philippians (FILL-ih-pie; fih-LIP-ih-uns) A city of Macedonia where Paul founded his first Christian congregation in Europe. The NT Epistle to the Philippians was written by Paul to the church there.

Philistines (fih-LIS-teens) The people who lived along the S coast of Palestine; often at war with the Israelites. Goliath was a champion of the Philistines (1 Sam. 17:23–51).

Phoenicia (fe-NISH-she-uh) A country W of the Lebanon range and Galilee on the coast of the Mediterranean Sea (Acts 11:19; 15:3; 21:2); its chief cities were Tyre and Sidon.

physician A medical doctor.
is there no p. there Jer. 8:22
who are well have no need of a p. Matt. 9:12
P., heal yourself Luke 4:23
Luke the beloved p. Col. 4:14

Pilate; Pontius Pilate (PIE-lut; PON-chus) The Roman governor of Judea (A.D. 26–36); the judge in the trial and execution of Jesus (Matt. 27:1–26; Mark 15:1–15; Luke 23:1–25; John 18:28—19:16).

pillar An upright column.
became a p. of salt Gen. 19:26
by day in a p. of cloud Ex. 13:21
by night in a p. of fire Ex. 13:21

plank A log; a piece of timber.
remove the p. Matt. 7:5

plowing
will be neither p. nor harvesting Gen. 45:6
in p. time and in harvest Ex. 34:21

plowshare The cutting blade of a plow.
their swords into p. Is. 2:4
Beat your p. into swords Joel 3:10

poor Needy; having little or no goods or money.
the p. shall not give less Ex. 30:15
Blessed are the p. in spirit Matt. 5:3
have the p. with you always Matt. 26:11; Mark 14:7

prayer Words addressed to God.
house of p. Is. 56:7; Matt. 21:13; Mark 11:17; Luke 19:46
by p. and fasting Matt. 17:21; Mark 9:29
you ask in p. Matt. 21:22

pride Conceit; vanity.
P. goes before destruction Prov. 16:18

priest A minister. Aaron and his sons, of the tribe of Levi, were appointed to the priesthood at Sinai; the office became hereditary and restricted to that family (Ex. 28:1; 40:12–15).
p. of God Most High Gen. 14:18

prince One who has authority or influence; a ruler; hence, **Prince:** the Messiah; Christ.
made you a p. . . . over us Ex. 2:14
Do not put your trust in p. Ps. 146:3
P. of Peace Is. 9:6
the P. of princes Dan. 8:25
killed the P. of life Acts 3:15

prodigal (PROD-ih-gul) Wasteful. The parable of the Prodigal Son is given in Luke 15:11–32.

prophet (PROFF-et) A man called by God to be His spokesman.
I will raise up for them a P. Deut. 18:18
p. is not without honor Matt. 13:57; Mark 6:4; John 4:44
no p. is accepted in his Luke 4:24

propitiation (pro-pish-ee-AY-shun) Expiation; removal of guilt by atonement (Rom. 3:25; 1 John 2:2; 4:10).

proverb (PRAH-verb); **Proverbs, the Book of** A short, meaningful saying about the nature of man and life. Proverbs in the Bible, most of which were written down by Solomon (1 Kin. 4:32), help to explain God's truths for wise and godly living.

psalm; Psalms, the Book of The hymn book of the Bible—a collection of prayers, poems, and hymns that focus the worshiper's thoughts on God in praise; the longest (150 psalms) book in the Bible. The title comes from a Greek word which means "a song sung to the accompaniment of a musical instrument." Subjects include God and His creation, war, worship, wisdom, sin and evil, judgment, justice, and the coming of the Messiah. Psalms are grouped by subject—thanksgiving, repentance, praise, confession, messianic, as well as psalms to be sung by pilgrims as they traveled to Jerusalem.

Purim (PEW-reem) A Jewish festival celebrating the deliverance from massacre (Esth. 9:20–28).

R

Rabbi (RAB-eye) Master; teacher.
They said to Him, "R. John 1:38

Rachel (RAY-chul) The younger daughter of Laban; Jacob's second wife; mother of Joseph and Benjamin (Gen. 29:1—31:35; 35:16–19).

Rebekah (ree-BECK-uh) Wife of Isaac; mother of Esau and Jacob (Gen. 24:10–67; 25:20–26, 28; 26:6–11; 27:5–17).

redeemer One who buys back, rescues (as from sin), or ransoms. Jesus is called, "the Redeemer," through His sacrificial death, although the word does not appear in the NT.
I know that my R. lives Job 19:25
LORD, my strength and my r. Ps. 19:14
R. will come to Zion Is. 59:20

Red Sea; Sea of Reeds The body of water between Arabia and Africa; the miraculous parting of the sea (Ex. 14:21–31) enabled the Israelites to escape the Egyptians.

remember To bring to mind again.
R. the Sabbath day Ex. 20:8
R. Lot's wife Luke 17:32

repent To feel regret; to change one's mind about.
r. in dust and ashes Job 42:6
R., for the kingdom Matt. 3:2
unless you r. you will Luke 13:3
R., and . . . be baptized Acts 2:38
R. therefore and be Acts 3:19

resurrection (rez-er-RECK-shun) A rising from the dead; a return to life; hence, **Resurrection:** The rising of Christ from the dead (Matt. 28; Mark 16; Luke 24; John 20; 1 Cor. 15).
there is no r. Matt. 22:23; Mark 12:18
I am the r. and the life John 11:25
This is the first r. Rev. 20:5

Reuben; Reubenites (ROO-bin; ROO-bin-nights) The firstborn son of Jacob, by Leah (Gen. 29:32); the ancestor of the tribe of Reuben.

revelation (rev-uh-LAY-shun) The making known of something previously concealed.
through the r. of Jesus Christ Gal. 1:12
The R. of Jesus Christ Rev. 1:1

reward To give payment for something done; used particularly of God's blessing upon the obedient and His punishment of the wicked.
r. in heaven Matt. 5:12; Luke 6:23
receive his own r. 1 Cor. 3:8

rich Wealthy; having money or property.
Do not overwork to be r. Prov. 23:4
for he was very r. Luke 18:23

riches Wealth; property; material goods.
r. are not forever Prov. 27:24
deceitfulness of r. Matt. 13:22; Mark 4:19

righteous One who does what is right; a virtuous person.

LORD knows the way of the r. Ps. 1:6
not come to call the r. Matt. 9:13

righteousness Virtue; right action; particularly, conformity to God's will.
in the paths of r. Ps. 23:3
hunger and thirst for r. Matt. 5:6
grace might reign through r. Rom. 5:21

rock A mass of stone; anything hard like a rock.
are my r. and my fortress Ps. 31:3
on this r. I will build Matt. 16:18

Rock The Lord.
Of the R. who begot you Deut. 32:18
The LORD is my r. Ps. 18:2

Rome; Romans The capital of the Roman Empire; Christianity probably came to Rome early in the apostolic age. Paul wrote the NT Epistle to the Romans to the Christian community there.

rooster
before the r. crows Matt. 26:34, 75

Ruth A Moabite woman who became an ancestress of David through her second marriage, to Boaz. Her story of devotion is told in the OT Book of Ruth.

sabbath The day of rest ordained by God. Among Jews, the seventh day (Saturday); among Christians, the first day of the week (Sunday), the day of divine worship (1 Cor. 16:2).
Remember the S. day Ex. 20:8
a s. of solemn rest for you Lev. 16:31
S was made for man Mark 2:27

sacrifice (SACK-rih-fyce) An offering, usually of the life of a person or an animal, made to God.
s. to the LORD Ex. 5:17
love . . . is more than . . . s. Mark 12:33
put away sin by the s. of Heb. 9:26

Sadducees (SAD-you-sees) The aristocratic party of the Jews at the time of Christ. They collaborated with the Romans to maintain their favorable status.

salt A seasoning; a preservative.
became a pillar of s. Gen. 19:26
You are the s. of the earth Matt. 5:13

salvation (sal-VAY-shun) Deliverance from evil, danger, or trouble; God's gift, through Christ, to save men's souls.
the God of my s. Ps. 25:5
to the Rock of our s. Ps. 95:1
shall see the s. of God Luke 3:6
this will turn out for my s. Phil. 1:19
grace of God that brings s. Titus 2:11
the author of their s. Heb. 2:10

Samaria; Samaritans (suh-MARE-ee-ah; suh-MARE-ih-tuns) The capital city of the northern kingdom, Israel. Also the name of the territory near the city. The term "Samaritan" is usually applied to a member of a religious sect living in that area. The parable of the Good Samaritan told by Jesus (Luke 10:30–37).

Samson A hero of the tribe of Dan, noted for his great strength (Judg. 13–16).

Samuel (SAM-you-ell) The last "judge" of Israel; a prophet of the eleventh century B.C. The two OT books of Samuel record his life and deeds and the history of Israel through the reigns of Solomon and David. The Lord calls Samuel (1 Sam. 3); Samuel anoints David (1 Sam. 16:11–13).

sanctify (SANK-tih-fy) To set apart as holy; to consecrate to religious use; to make holy.
seventh day and s. it Gen. 2:3
s. by the Holy Spirit Rom. 15:16

sanctuary (SANK-shoe-air-ih) A building or place set apart for religious worship; in the OT, the tabernacle (Ex. 25:8) or the temple (1 Chr. 22:19).

sandal strap Thong to fasten a sandal.
whose s. I am not worthy John 1:27

Sanhedrin (SAN-hee-drun) A council or assembly, the highest ruling body and court of justice among the Jewish people in the time of Jesus; headed by the high priest of Israel; composed of 71 members, among whom were Joseph of Arimathea (Mark 15:43), Gamaliel, Paul's teacher (Acts 5:34), Nicodemus (John 3:1; 7:50), the high priests, Annas and Caiaphas (Luke 3:2) and Ananias (Acts 23:2); given limited authority over certain religious, civil, and criminal matters involving foreign nations that dominated Israel at various times in its history.

Sarah; Sarai The wife of Abraham; mother of Isaac in accord with divine promise (Gen. 17:15–21; 18:1–15).

Satan (SAY-tun) The devil; the adversary of God and Christ.
S. casts out S. Matt. 12:26; Mark 3:23
forty days, tempted by S. Mark 1:13
lest S. should take advantage 2 Cor 2:11
S. will be released from Rev. 20:7

Saul Son of Kish, of the tribe of Benjamin; first king over Israel. The prophet Samuel anoints him to be king (1 Sam. 10:1); he disobeys the Lord (1 Sam. 15); David enters his service (1 Sam. 16:14–23); he tries to kill David (1 Sam. 19:9, 10); David spares his life (1 Sam. 26:6–24).

Saul of Tarsus *See* Paul.

Savior Literally, "one who saves or delivers"; Christ, as the One who delivers us from the sins of this life and through whom salvation is obtained; God, as the deliverer of the Israelites from oppression and as the redeemer of all peoples.
my refuge; My S. 2 Sam. 22:3
A just God and a S. Is. 45:21
rejoiced in God my S. Luke 1:47
Christ, the S. of the world John 4:42
Christ . . . the S. of the body Eph. 5:23
S., the Lord Jesus Christ Phil. 3:20
God our S., Who alone is wise Jude 25

scripture; Scriptures, the Any writing, particularly that of a sacred nature; hence, the Bible. Also "Scriptures"; "Holy Scripture"; "Holy Scriptures."
Have you not read this S. Mark 12:10
search the S. John 5:39
S. is given by inspiration 2 Tim. 3:16

seek To search for; to try to find.
s., and you will find Matt. 7:7; Luke 11:9
none who s. after God Rom. 3:11

Sermon on the Mount Name given to a talk by Jesus while teaching His disciples in the hill country of Galilee early in His ministry (Matt. 5:3—7:27). It includes a series of blessings, the Beatitudes (5:3–12); the Lord's Prayer (6:9–13); and the Golden Rule (7:12). A similar discourse in Luke 6:17–49 is called the "Sermon on the Plain."

serpent A snake; in biblical usage, many times synonymous with "Satan."
s. was more cunning than Gen. 3:1
will take up s. Mark 16:18
s. deceived Eve 2 Cor 11:3
s. of old, who is the Devil Rev. 20:2

Shadrach (SHAD-rack) The Babylonian name of one of Daniel's companions (Dan. 1:7; 3:12).

Sheba, queen of (SHE-bah) A queen, probably Arabian, who came to test Solomon's wisdom (1 Kin. 10:1–13; 2 Chr. 9:1–12).

Shem The eldest son of Noah who stands as the ancestor of the Semites generally and of the Hebrews specifically (Gen. 5:32; 9:18–27; 10:21–31; Luke 3:36).

shepherd One who herds and takes care of sheep; by extension, the ruler or king of a people. The Lord is the shepherd of Israel; Christ is the Good Shepherd (John 10:7–18).
The LORD is my s. Ps. 23:1
s. . . . keeping watch over Luke 2:8
one flock and one s. John 10:16
Lord Jesus . . . that great S. Heb. 13:20

Silas; Silvanus (SIGH-lus; sil-VAY-nus) One of the earliest of the apostolic missionaries, associated with both Paul (Acts 16:19ff; 1 Thess. 1:1; 2:1, 2) and Peter (1 Pet. 5:12).

Siloam, Pool of (sigh-LOW-um) A storage pool and tunnel that provided a water supply for the residents of Jerusalem, fed by the Gihon Spring; dug through solid rock in the time of King Hezekiah of Judah (2 Chr. 32:30). Water still flows through the tunnel to this day!

Simeon (SIM-ee-un) The name of six persons in the Bible, including: 1. The second son of Jacob, by Leah (Gen. 29:33); ancestor of the tribe of Simeon. 2. A devout man who blessed the infant Jesus when His parents presented Him in the temple (Luke 2:25–35).

Simon (SIGH-mun) The name of nine persons in the NT, including: 1. **Simon Peter:** *See* Peter (Matt. 16:17, 18; John 1:42). 2. **Simon the Zealot:** Also one of the 12 apostles (Luke 6:15). 3. **Simon the Pharisee,** in whose home Jesus was anointed by the sinful woman (Luke 7:36–50). 4. **Simon the leper,** in whose home Jesus was anointed by Mary (Mark 14:3–9; John 12:1–8). 5. **Simon of Cyrene,** who was forced to carry Jesus' cross (Matt. 27:32; Mark 15:21; Luke 23:26). 6. **Simon the sorcerer,** who

offered money to Peter and John for the power of the Holy Spirit (Acts 8:9–24).

sin 1. An offense or revolt against God (as Adam and Eve in the Garden of Eden); deliberate defiance; wickedness; iniquity; ungodliness.
put to death for his own s. Deut. 24:16
our s. testify against us Is. 59:12
power on earth to forgive s. Matt. 9:6
Who can forgive s. Mark 2:7; Luke 5:21
takes away the s. of John 1:29
He who is without s. John 8:7
gave Himself for our s. Gal. 1:4
2. To commit an offense against God; to be wicked.
is no one who does not s. 1 Kin. 8:46
soul who s. shall die Ezek. 18:4
S. no more, lest a John 5:14
cannot s., because he has been born of God 1 John 3:9

Sinai, Mount (SIGH-nigh) The name of a peninsula, a wilderness, and a mountain. 1. The barren, triangular-shaped peninsula stands between Egypt and Israel. 2. In the wilderness, there are no flowing streams or rivers, only wadis (dry stream beds which carry off the occasional rains). 3. The traditional mountain where Moses received the Ten Commandments (Ex. 19:3–20) is in the Sinai range and is called Jebel Musa, the mountain of Moses. When the Israelites camped there, it was called Sinai (Ex. 19:11), or sometimes called Horeb (Ex. 3:1).

sinful Wicked; full of iniquity.
s. nation, A people laden Is. 1:4
in the likeness of s. flesh Rom. 8:3

sinner One who commits an offense against God.
stands in the path of s. Ps. 1:1
Why does your Teacher eat with . . . s. Matt. 9:11; Mark 2:16; Luke 5:30
come to call . . . s., to repentance Matt. 9:14; Mark 2:17; Luke 5:32
over one s. who repents Luke 15:7
be merciful to me a s. Luke 18:13

Sodom (SOD-um) One of the two cities destroyed by the Lord because of their wickedness (Gen. 19:24–28).

Solomon Son of David and Bathsheba; third king of Israel; under his reign the kingdom reached its zenith; noted for his wisdom (1 Kin. 3:16–28) and his gift of expressing himself. The OT books of Proverbs, Ecclesiastes, and Song of Solomon, and Psalms 72 and 127 are attributed to him. He built the temple (1 Kin. 6; 7; 2 Chr. 3); was visited by the queen of Sheba (1 Kin. 10:1–13; 2 Chr. 9:1–12).

son A male child or man as related to his parents; a male descendant.
wise s. makes a glad father Prov. 10:1
Unto us a S. is given Is. 9:6
Is this not the carpenter's s. Matt. 13:55

Son; Son of God The Second Person of the Trinity; Christ.
is My beloved S. Matt. 3:17; 17:5; Mark 1:11; Luke 9:35
S. of the living God Matt. 16:16; John 6:69
this is the S. of God John 1:34
gave His only begotten S. John 3:16

son of man Any human being (Ps. 8:4); the prophet Ezekiel (used throughout the OT Book of Ezekiel); in the Gospels, Jesus uses "Son of Man" as a self-designation, particularly in the passages relating to His Second Coming.

sons of God Angels (Job 1:6; Dan. 3:25); any human beings, as created in God's image (Hos. 1:10); Christians (Rom. 8:14).

soul The life principle of a human being; the immortal element of man; the spirit; the living individual.
obey . . . with all your s. Deut. 30:2
Hear, and your s. shall live Is. 55:3
all s. are Mine Ezek. 18:4
destroy both s. and body Matt. 10:28
loses his own s. Matt. 16:26; Mark 8:36
s. be subject to the governing Rom. 13:1

sow To plant.
s. in tears Shall reap in joy Ps. 126:5
man s., that he will also reap Gal. 6:7

spirit That part of a person's being thought of as the center of life, the will, thinking, feeling; that part of man that survives death.
Into Your hand I commit my s. Ps. 31:5
a haughty s. before Prov. 16:18
yielded up His s. Matt. 27:50; John 19:30
the s. indeed is willing Matt. 26:41; Mark 14:38
to the s. of just men Heb. 12:23

Spirit, Holy The Third Person of the Trinity; that divine Spirit, referred to in

the OT as "Spirit of the LORD"or "Spirit of God," through which men receive power, particularly effective through Jesus Christ in bringing men into fellowship with God. Some Bible translators use "Holy Ghost" rather than "Holy Spirit."
in the name of the . . . Holy S. Matt. 28:19
baptize you with the Holy S. Matt. 3:11; Mark 1:8; Luke 3:16; John 1:33
be filled with the Holy S. Luke 1:15
Holy S. was not yet given John 7:39
Helper, the Holy S. John 14:26
promise of the Holy S. Acts 2:33
witness in the Holy S. Rom. 9:1
except by the Holy S. 1 Cor. 12:3
communion of the Holy S. 2 Cor 13:14

Spirit of the Lord; Spirit of God; Holy Spirit The divine source of all life; a special manifestation of God's divine Presence.
S. of God was hovering Gen. 1:2
S. is poured upon us Is. 32:15
S. of the Lord GOD is Is. 61:1; Luke 4:18
S. descending . . . like a dove Mark 1:10; John 1:32
God is S. John 4:24
not grieve the Holy S. of Eph. 4:30

Stephen The first Christian martyr; one of the seven men chosen by the apostles for the special "service of tables"; his death was the signal for a general persecution of the Christians (Acts 6:1—8:3).

stew A thick soup.
Esau sells birthright for s. Gen. 25:29–34

steward A manager of a household or of property; used of Christians, particularly ministers, as guardians of the affairs of God.
faithful and wise s. Luke 12:42
s. of the mysteries of God 1 Cor. 4:1
s. of the manifold grace of God 1 Pet. 4:10

stone A rock; a hard mineral.
dash your foot against a s. Ps. 91:12; Matt. 4:6; Luke 4:11
not one s. . . . upon another Matt. 24:2; Mark 13:2; Luke 19:44; 21:6
s. to become bread Luke 4:3

sufficient *Enough; ample.*
S. for the day is its own Matt. 6:34

Supper, Last *See* Last Supper.

Supper, Lord's *See* Lord's Supper.

swear To declare under oath.
not s. by My name falsely Lev. 19:12
not s. at all Matt. 5:34

sword A sharp-bladed weapon with a hilt or handle.
beat their s. into plowshares Is. 2:4; Mic. 4:3
Beat your plowshares into s. Joel 3:10
sharper than any two-edged s. Heb. 4:12

synagogue (SIN-uh-gog) A building where Jewish religious services and schools and other meetings are held.
preached the word of God in the s. Acts 13:5

T

tabernacle (TAB-er-nak-kel) Literally, "tent of meeting"; the portable shelter used by the Israelites as a place of worship.
pattern of the t. Ex. 25:9

Tabernacles, Feast of One of the three great joyous festivals of the Jewish year; held in autumn at the end of the harvest; celebrates a renewal of the covenant and recalls the wilderness pilgrimage (Ex. 23:16; Lev. 23:34–36; Deut. 16:13–15). Also called "Feast of Booths" (Lev. 23:42); "the Feast of Ingathering" (Ex. 23:16; 34:22).

tablets Flat stones bearing inscriptions.
two t. of the Testimony Ex. 31:18

talent A unit of money or of weight. Parable of the talents (Matt. 25:14–30).

Tarsus (TAR-sus) The birthplace of Saul, who, after his conversion, was called Paul (Acts 9:11; 22:3); chief city of Cilicia, a province in SW Asia Minor or modern Turkey; located on the banks of the Cydnus River, about ten miles from the Mediterranean Sea; a learning center of the world. "I am a Jew from Tarsus, in Cilicia, a citizen of no mean city," declared Paul (Acts 21:39).

tax collector One who collects taxes.
Matthew the t. Matt. 10:3
a friend of t. and sinners Matt. 11:19
saw a t. named Levi Luke 5:27

Teacher Title, used of Jesus during His ministry.
your T., the Christ Matt. 23:8, 10
trouble the T. Mark 5:35
call Me T. and Lord John 13:13

temple A building for the worship of a deity; hence, the temple at Jerusalem. See 1 Kings 5–8 for description of Solomon's temple.
LORD is in His holy t. Ps. 11:4
destroy the t. of God Matt. 26:61; 27:40; Mark 15:29; John 2:19

temptation An attempt to get someone to do something wrong; a test of character.
not lead us into t. Matt. 6:13; Luke 11:4

temptations of Jesus *See* Matthew 4:1–11; Luke 4:1–13.

Ten Commandments The ten laws given by God to Moses on Mount Sinai (Ex. 20:1–17; Deut. 5:6–21).

tent of meeting *See* tabernacle.

testimony In OT: the divine law, especially the Ten Commandments; in NT: witness.
law and to the t. Is. 8:20
know that his t. is true John 21:24
to the t. of Jesus Christ Rev. 1:2

Thaddaeus (THAD-ee-us) One of the 12 apostles of Jesus (Mark 3:18), also called Lebbaeus (Matt. 10:3) and probably Judas. *See* Judas (3).

Thessalonica; Thessalonians (thess-uh-low-NIGH-kuh; thess-uh-LOW-nih-uns) An important city of Macedonia where Paul and his associates founded an early Christian church. The two NT epistles to the Thessalonians were among the earliest written by Paul.

Thomas One of the 12 apostles; his incredulity of Jesus' resurrection gained him the name "doubting Thomas" (Matt. 10:3; Mark 3:18; Luke 6:15; John 11:16; 14:5; 20:24–29; Acts 1:13).

Timothy A trusted companion and assistant of Paul, from the early part of the latter's second missionary journey. *According to tradition* the two epistles to Timothy were written near the close of Paul's life.

tithe The tenth part of one's income paid to support God's work (Lev. 27:30–32).

Titus (TIGHT-us) A Gentile Christian associate of Paul (2 Cor 7:5–7); according to Titus 1:4, 5, Paul wrote the letter bearing his name in order to encourage him in his work in the churches of Crete.

tomb A place of burial.
like whitewashed t. Matt. 23:27

Torah (TOE-ruh) Guidance or direction from God to His people for living the covenant relationship—a total way of life; in earlier times, a term referring directly to the first five books of Moses, but came to mean both the hearing and doing of the Law (Deut. 32:46). Later, the Hebrew OT included the books of wisdom and prophets, and this entire collection became known as the Torah.

Transfiguration Jesus' glorious and radiant change in appearance; witnessed by three disciples (Matt. 17:1–9; Mark 9:2–10; Luke 9:28–36; 2 Pet. 1:16–18).

transgression A sin; rebellion against God's will.
t. of Adam Rom. 5:14

Trinity The doctrine held by most Christians that there are three divine Persons (Father, Son, and Holy Spirit) united in the one Supreme Divine Being. NT teachings (Matt. 12:32; 28:19; Luke 12:10; Acts 2:33; 1 Cor. 12:4–6; 2 Cor 13:14) support this doctrine.

trust To have or put confidence in someone or something.
T. in the LORD with all Prov. 3:5
those who t. in riches Mark 10:24

truth A proven sincerity, verity, honesty; righteousness.
A God of t. and without Deut. 32:4
t. shall make you free John 8:32
I am the way, the t. John 14:6
He, the Spirit of t., has John 16:13

tunic An outer garment.
made him a t. of many colors Gen. 37:3
do not have two t. Luke 9:3

Tyropoeon Valley (tie-ROW-pih-un) A small valley in the city of Jerusalem, which divides hill Ophel, the original City of David, from the Western Hill, or Upper City.

unleavened bread Bread baked from unfermented dough, or dough without yeast or "leaven" (Gen. 19:3; Josh. 5:11; 1 Sam. 28:24); the flat bread used in the

Passover celebration and the priestly rituals, recalling the Exodus, when the Hebrews left Egypt so quickly that they had no time to wait for the bread to rise (Ex. 12:8, 15–20, 34, 39; 13:6, 7).

Ur An ancient city on the Euphrates, called "Ur of the Chaldees"; home of Abraham (Gen. 11:28).

Uzziah (uh-ZIGH-uh) The name of three persons in the OT, one of them a king of Judah (c. 783–742 B.C.).

vanity Futility; emptiness.
V. of v., all is v. Eccl. 1:2

viper A poisonous snake.
stings like a v. Prov. 23:32

vision Something seen other than by ordinary sight, as in a dream. God's revelations to the prophets were usually by visions.
They err in v. Is. 28:7
revealed to Daniel in a night v. Dan. 2:19
Tell the v. to no one Matt. 17:9

voice A sound uttered through the mouth as in speaking.
a still small v. 1 Kin. 19:12
v. of the turtledove is heard Song 2:12
v. of one crying Is. 40:3; Matt. 3:3; Mark 1:3; Luke 3:4; John 1:23

wadi (WAH-dih) A valley, ravine, or riverbed that usually remains dry except during the rainy season; similar to an arroyo in the western United States; also "brook" (Josh. 15:47; 2 Kin. 23:12) and "torrent" (Judg. 5:21) in the Bible.

wages The payment for services.
be content with your w. Luke 3:14
the w. of sin is death Rom. 6:23

walk To move by stepping.
w. through the valley of Ps. 23:4
saw Him w. on the sea Matt. 14:26
shall not w. in darkness John 8:12

want To lack or need (*not* in the sense of "to desire").
I shall not w. Ps. 23:1

war Fighting with weapons between large groups.
A time of w., And a time Eccl. 3:8
w. and rumors of w. Matt. 24:6; Mark 13:7; Luke 21:9

wash To clean with water or other liquid.
w. His feet with her tears Luke 7:38
w. the disciples' feet John 13:5

water The colorless fluid that falls as rain.
over the face of the w. Gen. 1:2
the flood of w. was on Gen. 7:6
Planted by the rivers of w. Ps. 1:3
me beside the still w. Ps. 23:2
Cast your bread upon the w. Eccl. 11:1
baptized you with w. Mark 1:8; Luke 3:16; John 1:26

way The direction; path; man's mode of living.
the w. of the righteous Ps. 1:6
Train up a child in the w. Prov. 22:6
Prepare the w. of the LORD Is. 40:3; Matt. 3:3; Mark 1:3; Luke 3:4; John 1:23
I am the w., the truth John 14:6

Weeks, Feast of Seven weeks after Passover (Lev. 23:15–21; Deut. 16:9–12). Also called Feast of Harvest (Ex. 23:16). *See* Pentecost.

will Desire; something wished.
Your w. be done Matt. 6:10; Luke 11:2
good w. toward men Luke 2:14

wine The fermented juice of fruits.
W. is a mocker Prov. 20:1
new w. into new wineskins Matt. 9:17; Mark 2:22; Luke 5:37

wise Having good judgment.
tree desirable to make one w. Gen. 3:6
man w. in his own eyes Prov. 26:12
w. men from the East Matt. 2:1

witness Someone or something that bears testimony to the truthfulness of a statement or to the occurrence of a happening.
be a w. between you Gen. 31:44
as a w. to all the nations Matt. 24:14
My w. is true John 8:14
The people . . . bore w. John 12:17
God is my w., whom Rom. 1:9
bore w. to the word Rev. 1:2

word A spoken sound having meaning.
God spoke all these w. Ex. 20:1
w. fitly spoken is like Prov. 25:11

Word; Word of God; word of the LORD God's revealed will; the Holy Scriptures.
the w. is very near Deut. 30:14; Rom. 10:8

By the w. of the LORD Ps. 33:6
hear the w. of the LORD Jer. 29:20
hear the w. of God Luke 8:21
for the w. of God Rev. 1:9

Word; Word of God A title of Christ.
the W. was God John 1:1
concerning the W. of life 1 John 1:1
is called The W. of God Rev. 19:13

work 1. Labor; effort.
God ended His w. Gen. 2:2
the w. of Your fingers Ps. 8:3
2. To labor; to toil.
Father has been w. John 5:17
all things w. together Rom. 8:28
faith w. through love Gal. 5:6

works Deeds; efforts.
according to his w. Matt. 16:27; 2 Tim. 4:14
w. which the Father John 5:36
its w. are evil John 7:7
not of w., lest anyone Eph. 2:9

world The earth; the universe.
the w. is Mine, and all Ps. 50:12
You are the light of the w. Matt. 5:14
gains the whole w. Matt. 16:26
God so loved the w. John 3:16
I am the light of the w. John 8:12
brought nothing into this w. 1 Tim. 6:7

worry Be or become anxious.
by w. can add one cubit Matt. 6:27
do not w. about tomorrow Matt. 6:34
do not w. beforehand Mark 13:11
do not w. about your life Luke 12:22

worship To honor; to show reverence for.
you shall w. no other god Ex. 34:14
w. at His footstool Ps. 99:5
w. the LORD your God Matt. 4:10; Luke 4:8
where one ought to w. John 4:20

wrath Great anger, especially God's punishment of sin.
soft answer turns away w. Prov. 15:1
w. to come Matt. 3:7; Luke 3:7
w. in the day of w. Rom. 2:5
delivers us from the w. 1 Thess. 1:10

Yahweh (YAH-way) The covenant God of Israel, YHWH in the original Hebrew. According to Jewish custom, because of reverence the divine name was not to be spoken, so the Hebrew words for Lord and God were substituted. Whenever the words *LORD* and *GOD* appear in large and small capital letters, the original Hebrew reads YHWH.

Zacchaeus (zack-KEY-us) Chief tax collector of Jericho at the time of one of Jesus' visits (Luke 19:2–8).

Zealot (ZELL-ut) A term used to designate the more radical Jewish rebels against foreign, particularly Roman, rule; one motivated by zeal for the Jewish law.

Zebedee (ZEB-uh-dee) The father of the apostles James and John (Matt. 4:21; Mark 1:19, 20; Luke 5:10; John 21:2).

Zebulum (ZEB-you-lun) The tenth son of Jacob, the sixth by Leah (Gen. 30:19, 20); ancestor of the tribe of Zebulun.

Zechariah; Zecher; Zacharias (zek-uh-RIGH-uh; zek-ur; zack-uh-RIGH-us) The name of 33 persons in the Bible, including: 1. Son of the priest Jehoiada (2 Chr. 24:20, 21). 2. One of the OT minor prophets; contemporary of Haggai; urged the rebuilding of the temple (Ezra 5:1; 6:14; Zech. 1:1, 7; 7:1, 8). 3. The father of John the Baptist (Luke 1:5–67; 3:2).

Zedekiah (zed-uh-KIGH-uh) The name of three persons in the OT, including the last king of Judah (c. 597–587 B.C.). Also called Mattaniah.

Zephaniah (zef-uh-NIGH-uh) The name of four persons in the OT, including a prophet during the time of Josiah; his prophecies appear in the OT Book of Zephaniah, the ninth of the 12 Minor Prophets.

Zion; Sion (ZIGH-un; SIGH-un) Originally the name of the fortified hill of pre-Israelite Jerusalem; poetically extended to refer to the religious capital of Israel.

ARTICLES INDEX

Behind the Scenes

Action!